FAMILY LAW

Cases, Notes and Materials

Fifth Edition

FAMILY LAW

Cases, Notes and Materials

Fifth Edition

by

BEREND HOVIUS

B.A., LL.B., LL.M.
Professor of Law,
University of Western Ontario

CARSWELL
Thomson Professional Publishing

Canadian Cataloguing in Publication Data

Hovius, Berend, 1951-
    Family law: cases, notes and materials

5th ed., student ed.
ISBN 0-459-23935-X

1. Domestic relations - Canada - Cases.
2. Domestic relations - Ontario - Cases.
I. Title

KE539.H68   2000   346.7101'5   C00-931526-8
KF504.H68   2000

CARSWELL
Thomson Professional Publishing

One Corporate Plaza, 2075 Kennedy Road, Scarborough, Ontario M1T 3V4
Customer Service:
Toronto 1-416-609-3800
Elsewhere in Canada/U.S. 1-800-387-5164
Fax 1-416-298-5094

This book is dedicated to
my mother, Wiebrigje (Wilma) Wielsma Hovius Bouwknegt

May 19, 1919 – January 10, 2000

PREFACE

As stated in the prefaces of the previous editions of this book, family law continues to undergo significant change. Since the publication of the fourth edition only four years ago, the Supreme Court of Canada has decided a number of highly important cases such as *M.* v. *H., Francis* v. *Baker, Chartier* v. *Chartier, Best* v. *Best, Bracklow* v. *Bracklow, N.B. (Minister of Health and Community Services)* v. *G. (J.)*, and *Winnipeg Child and Family Services* v. *G. (D.F.)*. There have also been numerous legislative changes, both provincial and federal. Many were dictated by the reasons and result in *M.* v. *H.* As well, *Child Support Guidelines* have come into effect, spawning many issues and cases.

Readers familiar with the first four editions will note that their structure and format have been retained. My principal aim continues to be to provide a teaching and learning tool for a basic course in family law, although it is hoped that the lawyer whose practice includes family law will find the book a useful research and reference aid. The book is designed to accommodate a wide range of academic interests, teaching styles and philosophies. The cases and materials reproduced have been chosen to expose the student to the fundamental concepts embodied in the substantive law, the various methods available to deal with legal problems arising in a family context, and the current issues that should be the subject of critical analysis and debate. Articles and other secondary materials that place the legal issues in a broader social context again feature prominently. The Notes and Questions have been for-mulated so as to stimulate further thought and to facilitate additional reading and research. They are also used to introduce topics and issues not specifically covered by the reproduced cases and materials. Descriptive text has been included mostly to introduce topics and to provide background information.

This book is meant to be used in company with a separate compilation of statutory materials. Few excerpts from legislation have been reproduced. To avoid undue repetition, citations for the following statutes have not been included in the text: the *Child and Family Services Act*, R.S.O. 1990, c. C.11 (the *CFSA*); the *Children's Law Reform Act*, R.S.O. 1990, c. C.12 (the *CLRA*); the *Family Law Act*, R.S.O. 1990, c. F.3 (the *FLA*); the *Marriage Act*, R.S.O. 1990, c. M.3; the *Criminal Code*, R.S.C. 1985, c. C-46; and the *Divorce Act*, R.S.C. 1985 (2nd Supp.), c.3.

The focus of this book has gradually, but significantly, changed since the first edition was published in 1982. Separate chapters are still included on the traditional subjects of family law: marriage, divorce, family property, support obligations, custody and access, domestic contracts, the intervention of the state in the child-parent relationship, and adoption. However, the number of pages devoted to each of these topics has changed significantly since the first edition to reflect their changing importance. In addition, topics of current interest and concern such as the rights and obligations of unmarried cohabitees, including same-sex couples, and violence within the family are now dealt with extensively. Finally, the nature of the material reproduced has changed. The later editions contain more excerpts from secondary sources such as articles, Law Reform Commission reports, and texts. Sometimes this secondary material efficiently summarizes the law on a particular topic. More often, it provides a broader focus by giving background information and raising policy issues.

This book does not purport to deal comprehensively with all the areas of law that arguably fall within the rubric of "family law". Nor, obviously, does it cover all laws which affect the family. For example, such topics as the law of succession, income taxation, fatal accidents legislation, young offenders, immigration, and social security have not been given separate coverage and are only referred to peripherally. This reflects the fact that these topics have, to a large extent, been allocated to other courses in the typical law school curriculum. Undoubtedly, some readers will be disappointed by the limited coverage allocated to these and other topics, but a casebook designed for a basic family law course must be kept within manageable limits. Arguably, this book is already too long.

Also, it is still true that the book focuses on family law in Ontario. Family law in the various provinces is becoming ever more similar, partly due to the unifying influence of the Supreme Court of Canada and federal initiatives such as the *Child Support Guidelines*. Nevertheless, any attempt to provide a detailed analysis of family law in all the jurisdictions in Canada would result in a book of gigantic proportions. On the other hand, a book which dealt with family law issues at such a general level that it would be equally applicable to all jurisdictions in Canada would likely not allow students to learn sufficient substantive law.

It remains to thank those who have helped in this endeavour. Over the years a large number of individuals have assisted in the production of one or more editions and I thank them all, even if I do not mention them by name here. In preparing the fifth edition, student research assistants Mr. W. Cho, Ms Katherine Kirkpatrick, and Ms Christine O'Connor made major contributions. I am indebted to the Ontario Law Foundation and the Faculty of Law at the University of Western Ontario for providing research funds that permitted me to hire them. I would also like to acknowledge my gratitude to all the people at Carswell who made these five editions possible. A special "thank you" goes to Mysty Clayton, who spent many hours proofreading the fifth edition.

Finally, I am grateful to those authors, publishers, and institutions who gave permission for the use of copyrighted materials. A list follows this preface.

Berend Hovius
Professor of Law and Associate
Dean (Administration)
Faculty of Law
University of Western Ontario
May, 2000

ACKNOWLEDGMENTS

Abella, "Procedural Aspects of Arrangements for Children upon Divorce in Canada" (1983), 61 Can. Bar Rev. 443.

Austin and Jaffe, "Annotation" (1995), 10 R.F.L. (4th) 92.

Austin, Jaffe and Hurley, "Incorporating Children's Needs and Views in Alternative Dispute Resolution Approaches" (1992), 8 C.F.L.Q. 69 at 71-72.

Baker, "Thinking About Families: Trends and Policies" in Baker, ed., *Canada's Changing Families: Challenges to Public Policy* (Ottawa: The Vanier Institute of the Family, 1994) 1-9.

Bala, "An Introduction to Child Protection Problems" in Bala *et al.*, eds., *Canadian Child Welfare Law: Children, Families and the State* (Toronto: Thompson Educational Publishing Inc., 1991) 1.

Bala, "Reforming Ontario's *Child and Family Services Act*: Is the Pendulum Swinging Back Too Far?" (1999), 17 C.F.L.Q. 121.

Bala, "Spousal Support Law Transformed — Fairer Treatment for Women" (1994), 11 C.F.L.Q. 13.

Bala and Wildgoose, *Canadian Children's Law: A Coursebook*, Vol. 1 (1985), 371-375.

Canada Law Book, "Headnote" for *Montgomery* v. *Montgomery* (2000), 181 D.L.R. (4th) 181 (N.S. C.A.).

Canada Law Book, "Headnote" for *Van de Perre* v. *Edwards* (2000), 184 D.L.R. (4th) 486 (B.C. C.A.).

Castel, *Canadian Conflict of Laws*, 3rd ed. (Toronto: Butterworths, 1994) para. 226.

Davies, "Native Children and the Child Welfare System in Canada" (1992), 30 Alta. L. Rev. 1200.

Davies, "Racial and Cultural Matters in Custody Disputes" (1993), 10 C.F.L.Q. 1, at 8-13, 14-16, and 21-24.

Davies, "Spousal Support under the *Divorce Act*: From *Moge* to *Bracklow*" (1999) 44 R.F.L. (4th) 61.

Department of Justice, *Evaluation of the Divorce Act: Phase II: Monitoring and Evaluation* (Ottawa: Department of Justice, Bureau of Review, 1990) iv-vi, 1-9, 31-36, 41-42, 72, 74-76, and 94-98.

Department of Justice, *The New Child Support Package* (Ottawa: Government of Canada, March 6, 1996) 11-17, 20-23, and 30-31.

Drakich and Guberman, "Violence in the Family" in Anderson *et al.*, eds., *Family Matters: Sociology and Contemporary Canadian Families* (Toronto: Methuen, 1987) 201, at 206-217 and 220-230.

Fineberg, "Joint Custody of Infants: Breakthrough or Fad?" (1979), 2 Can. J. Fam. L. 417.

Fineman, "Implementing Equality: Ideology, Contradiction and Social Change: A Study of Rhetoric and Results in the Regulation of the Consequences of Divorce" [1983] Wis. L. Rev. 789 (Copyright © by the University of Wisconsin).

Garber, *The Report of the Special Commissioner, Disclosure of Adoption Information* (Toronto: Queen's Printer, 1985).

Hahlo, *Nullity of Marriage in Canada* (Toronto: Butterworths, 1979) 1-5 and 43-44.

Hogg, *Constitutional Law of Canada*, 3rd ed. (Toronto: Carswell, 1992) c. 26.

Hovius, "The Matrimonial Home: An Analysis of Part II of the *Family Law Act, 1986*" (1988), 16 R.F.L. (3d) 1.

Hovius and Youdan, *The Law of Family Property* (Toronto: Carswell, 1991) 241-242, 291-314, 383-389, 449-470, and 580-585.

Huddart and Ensminger, "Hearing the Voice of Children" (1992), 8 C.F.L.Q. 95 at 96 and 99-102.

Law Reform Commission of British Columbia, *Working Paper on Property Rights on Marriage Breakdown* (Vancouver: Ministry of the Attorney General, 1989) 59-60 and 62-65.

Law Reform Commission of Canada, *Maintenance on Divorce: Working Paper 12* (Ottawa: Law Reform Commission of Canada, 1975) 17-19, 23-27 and 35-36.

Law Society of Upper Canada, "Headnote" for *Maddock v. Maddock*, [1958] O.R. 810.

Leonoff, "Joint Custody and Beyond" (1995), 29 The Law Society Gazette 29.

London Family Court Clinic Inc., *Final Report: Wife Assault as a Crime: The Perspectives of Victims and Police Officers on a Charging Policy in London, Ontario from 1980-1990* (London: London Family Court Clinic Inc., 1991) iii-vi, 1-3 and 5-12.

MacLeod, *Battered But Not Beaten. . .Preventing Wife Battering in Canada* (Ottawa: Canadian Advisory Council on the Status of Women, 1987) 38-45.

Manitoba Law Reform Commission, *Report on the Confidentiality of Adoption Records* (1979) 8-11.

McLeod, "Annotation" (1987), 6 R.F.L. (3d) 147 at 148.

McLeod, "Annotation" (1987), 7 R.F.L. (3d) 226 at 232-233.

McLeod, "Annotation" (1988), 10 R.F.L. (3d) 225.

McLeod, "Annotation" (1993), 42 R.F.L. (3d) 350.

McLeod, "Annotation" (1994), 4 R.F.L. (4th) 2.

McLeod, "Annotation" (1997), 29 R.F.L. (4th) 43.

McLeod, "Annotation" (1997), 30 R.F.L. (4th) 108.

McLeod, "Annotation" (1998), 32 R.F.L. (4th) 98.

McLeod, "Annotation" (1998), 40 R.F.L. (4th) 129.

McLeod, "Annotation" (1999), 49 R.F.L. (4th) 163.

McLeod, "Annotation" (2000), 1 R.F.L. (5th) 121.

Mnookin, "Divorce Bargaining: The Limits on Private Ordering" in Eekelaar and Katz, eds., *The Resolution of Family Conflict: Comparative Legal Perspectives* (Toronto: Butterworths, 1984) 366-372 and 375-379.

Ontario Law Reform Commission, *Report on Pensions as Family Property: Valuation and Division* (Toronto: 1995) 8-17, 25-29, 33-45, 59-62, 84-87, and 260-267.

Payne, "Family Conflict Resolution: Dealing with the Consequences of Marriage Breakdown Through Counseling, Negotiation, Mediation and Arbitration" (Paper presented in the Faculty of Law at the University of Saskatchewan, 1997).

Payne, "Family Law in Canada" in Baker, ed., *Canada's Changing Families: Challenges to Public Policy* (Ottawa: The Vanier Institute of the Family, 1994) 13-17 and 22.

Payne, "The Dichotomy Between Family Law and Family Crises on Marriage Breakdown" (1989), 20 R.G.D. 109.

Report of the Special Joint Committee on Child Custody and Access, *For the Sake of the Children* (December, 1998).

Richardson, "Children of Divorce" in Anderson *et al.*, eds., *Family Matters: Sociology and Contemporary Canadian Families* (Toronto: Methuen, 1987) 166-174.

Rogerson, "Spousal Support After *Moge*" (1997), 14 C.F.L.Q. 280, at 303-304 and 385-387.

Rogerson, "The Causal Connection Test in Spousal Support Law" (1989), 8 Can. J. Fam. L. 95, at 95-96 and 106-118.

Ryan, "Joint Custody in Canada: Time for a Second Look" (1986), 49 R.F.L. (2d) 119.

Shaffer and Melamed, "Separation Agreements Post *Moge*, *Willick* and *L.G.* v. *G.B.*" (1999), 1 Can. J. Fam. L. 51.

Silverman, "Conflict of Laws: Some Matrimonial Problems" (1979), 2 Fam. L. Rev. 103.

Singer and Reynolds, "A Dissent on Joint Custody" (1988), 47 Maryland Law Rev. 497.

Sopinka, "The *Divorce Act, 1968*: Collusion Confined" (1969), 47 Can. Bar Rev. 31-39.

Thompson, "Case Comment: *B.(R.)* v. *Children's Aid Society of Metropolitan Toronto*" (1995), 9 R.F.L. (4th) 345.

Thompson, "Rules and Rulelessness in Family Law: Recent Developments, Judicial and Legislative" (Paper prepared for National Judicial Institute, 1999).

Thomson, "Eliminating Role Confusion in the Child's Lawyer: The Ontario Experience" (1983), 4 Can. J. Fam. L. 125.

Tobin, "Enforcement of Support Orders in Ontario" (1998), 15 C.F.L.Q. 317.

Wardell, "*King* v. *Low*: A Case Comment" (1985), 4 Can. J. Fam. L. 514.

Weiss, "The Misuse of Adoption by the Custodial Parent" (1979), 2 Can. J. Fam. L. 141.

Ziff, "Recent Developments in Marriage and Divorce" (1986), 18 Ottawa Law Rev. 121, at 135-137.

TABLE OF CONTENTS

TABLE OF CASES

A case name and a page number in bold face indicates a case that is reproduced in full or in some material part.

1

INTRODUCTION

1.   Changing Canadian Family Forms

BAKER, "THINKING ABOUT FAMILIES: TRENDS AND POLICIES"

Baker, ed., *Canada's Changing Families: Challenges to Public Policy* (Ottawa: The Vanier Institute of the Family, 1994) 1-9 (Endnotes omitted)

INTRODUCTION

Over the past three decades, major changes have occurred in family life, providing new challenges for family members, employers, service providers and policy makers. . . .

Defining Family and Family Policy

Many different definitions of "family" have been used for purposes of research, census-taking, social policy and the delivery of social benefits. Most include single parents and couples sharing a home, regardless of their marital status, but not all definitions include same-sex couples. Most definitions include parents and their children, while some also involve couples who do not have children. Others extend the definition of family to grandparents, aunts, uncles and cousins.

The most prevalent definition used in Canadian research and policy making is Statistics Canada's "census family." This unit includes married couples with or without never-married children (and cohabiting couples who have lived together for longer than one year), or a single parent living together with never-married children. As with any definition, some social scientists and cultural groups feel that this particular definition is too narrow and does not encompass fully the group which most people consider to be their family, either through blood relationships, adoption, legal marriage, or feelings of closeness. Yet a common definition must be agreed upon when taking a census, initiating a social policy or designing any research project.

The Canadian government also uses the term "household" in gathering statistics relating to family and personal life. By household, they are referring to people sharing a dwelling, whether or not they are related by blood, adoption or marriage. For example, a boarder might be part of the household, but not necessarily part of the family.

Although the "census family" will be a prevalent definition in this book, the term "families" in the plural will be used to indicate that there are many family structures and acceptable definitions. . . .

All social and economic policies influence families in some way, but the term "family policy" usually refers specifically to the pursuit and attainment of collective goals and values in addressing problems of families in relation to society. . . . Family policy is often more broadly defined to include aspects of social or economic policies indirectly influencing families, such as educational practices, tax concessions, labour market policies and social services. In this book, family policy is defined in this broader sense, focusing on the implicit and explicit ideas about the government's role in family life inherent in programs related to marriage and divorce, procreation, childbearing and childrearing, education, and the care of dependents.

Families, the State and Society

Social scientists have used the term "state" to refer not only to government departments and their policies, but also to government-funded agencies which implement and enforce these policies. This would encompass the child welfare agencies, social services, the criminal justice system and the public schools. There are many reasons why the state would be interested in people's private lives. Information on marriages, births and deaths needs to be collected in order to plan and provide public services and facilities. Marriages and births are recorded and regulated to ensure that dependents are supported, to help prevent potential birth defects through inbreeding, to assist individuals to preserve private property, to minimize social conflict, and to protect the community. The state monitors childrearing practices and interpersonal relations between family members in order to protect vulnerable members and to maintain social order.

In North America, laws and practices assume that families are responsible for many services which are invaluable to the state. Although adults want children for their own personal reasons, the state needs them to reproduce the taxpayers, consumers and labour force members of the nation. Families help define and enforce at what age a person is allowed to engage in a sexual relationship and with whom, and what degree of closeness is too close for a sexual liaison. The state needs parents to socialize or discipline children to be law-abiding citizens, to fit into educational systems and labour force requirements, to perpetuate the culture, and to establish permanent relationships and reproduce the next generation.

Many critics have argued, however, that state involvement in family life varies for different income and cultural groups, and tends to be more interventionist for visible minorities and for those on social assistance. Furthermore, involvement is not always based on informed policy about how people actually live or why they live this way. Instead, programs and policies are often based on preconceived notions about the preferred structure of families, the role of women in families, the responsibilities of parents toward their children, and the reasons behind the need for social assistance. These ideas permeate our culture but change over time with economic and social trends.

Throughout this century, "the family" has been viewed as the basic unit of economic, physical and emotional support. North American governments have only stepped in to intervene when a child has been neglected or abused or when there are insufficient financial resources. According to current family law both parents are responsible for the care and support of their children, even after divorce, and spouses are expected to assist each other during marriage. Family members are required to register their marriages, births, and deaths; pay their taxes; feed and clothe their children; send their children to school; complete their census forms; and generally be law-abiding and peaceful. As long as these obligations are fulfilled, the state's direct involvement in family life is minimal.

Ideologies Behind Family Policies

Although many changes have occurred in family life throughout the last century, an understanding of these changes has not always been reflected in social policies. In many programs and policies created over the years, the homogeneity or uniform nature of families has been overemphasized, implying that most people live in nuclear family units consisting of breadwinner/father and home-maker/mother, legally married and living with their two or three children. Recent statistics from the Canadian government indicate that this family model is no longer dominant. For example, lone-parent families accounted for 20% of families with children in 1991, and 17% of children live with just one parent . . . .

In addition, most mothers are now employed or looking for paid work. Although lone-parent mothers used to have a higher rate of employment than mothers in two-parent families, this situation is now reversed. In families with children under 16 years old, 64.6% of mothers in two-parent families were employed in 1991, compared to 52.2% of female lone parents . . . . In families with children between 6 and 15 years, 70.3% of mothers in two-parent families were employed compared to 62.2% of lone-parent mothers. This lower rate of employment for lone-parent mothers suggests that many are unemployed but looking for work, studying, or living on welfare. In addition, there appears to be a generational difference in work patterns as younger wives and mothers are more likely to be employed than those who are older.

Another trend away from the 'traditional' single-earner nuclear family is that a growing percentage of couples are not legally married. Twelve percent of all people in couple unions were living common-law in 1990, although this figure reached 82% for 15- to 19-year-olds and 50% for 20- to 24-year-olds . . . . Yet governments and social scientists still talk about "the family" as though there were few variations in structure and as though any variation from the nuclear family model were unusual or "deviant.". . .

Policy makers often bring to their jobs assumptions about the way families live, and these ideas are not always representative of the broad range of lifestyles prevalent in modern society. Also, because their advisors have often come from similar gender, cultural and socioeconomic backgrounds and receive their training in specialized fields such as law or economics, they do not always reflect the thinking of everyday people or even the wider range of the social sciences . . . . These factors help to perpetuate the transmission of biases and myths in policy making. Although it was feminist social scientists who first articulated their concerns about these biases, now most researchers and some policy makers are trying to present a more balanced and realistic portrayal of family life.

Regardless of their view of the world, most researchers and social service workers now agree that families are not "havens from the harsh world" as they were once portrayed. The distinction between the so-called "private world of family" and the "public world of work" is now criticized as inaccurate. There is also a recognition that such a distinction has negative consequences in policy-making. For example, this view has allowed governments to assume that domestic services are provided willingly at home for no pay and that workers leave family responsibilities at home when they enter the workplace. Therefore, employees do not need child care services, flexible hours or special leave for family responsibilities. Until recently, this false dichotomy has also enabled the state and community to turn a blind eye to family violence. In fact, some researchers and activists argue that viewing family life as "private" and outside the realm of government regulation has encouraged social policies which have disadvantaged women and children . . . .

Policymakers can no longer assume that what takes place at home is of no relevance to the community or to governments. As a society and as community members, we are becoming more concerned about the physical and emotional safety of women, children and the elderly in their homes. Educators continue to try to counteract some of the more negative influences of their students' family lives. Similarly, there is an understanding of the important connection between domestic responsibilities and employment status, and that parents with dependent children, especially mothers, require assistance in resolving the inevitable conflicts between employment demands and family life.

The field of family policy is not without controversy. An attempt to create a more explicit and cohesive family policy arises from two separate traditions. One tradition is based on the realization that families are changing, with more two-income and lone-parent families, that parents make an important contribution to society in having children and that they increasingly need social support to combine more effectively family life with earning a living. The other tradition assumes that "the family" is deteriorating and attempts must be made to legislate supports to help the traditional nuclear family maintain its position against the intrusion of alternative lifestyles. In both cases, there has been a new emphasis placed on strengthening families. Yet those who applaud new family forms are suspicious of the call for "a family policy" because they fear that it could represent a conservative agenda opposing greater equality for women, gays, and "families of choice." Creating social policies which bring together these two opposing viewpoints and deal adequately with the multidimensional aspects of family life is indeed a challenge.

Several major trends have influenced family policy in Canada over the past few decades.

Changing Family Trends

Especially since World War Two, the structure of family life has changed in western industrialized countries, including Canada. Before any discussion of family policies, there needs to be an understanding of these trends, as new policies usually are initiated by people lobbying governments to ameliorate what they perceive to be "problems" caused by rapid social change. Several important socioeconomic and demographic changes have taken place which have direct implications for social policies.

1. Birthrates Have Been Declining

Since the late 1800s, birthrates have been falling in most industrialized countries, and Canada is no exception. In the period 1851 to 1861, for example, the crude birthrate in Canada (or the number of births per 1,000 population) was 45. Although there was an increase after the Second World War (the Post-War Baby Boom), the crude birthrate fell to 14.4 by 1987 before rising slightly to 15.2 in 1990 and then falling again to 14.9 in 1991.

There are many reasons why birthrates tend to decline with industrialization. As societies industrialize, manufacturing, office and service jobs are created in towns and cities, and people tend to migrate to these towns in search of work. The cost of housing and food are usually higher in urban compared to rural areas, however, and industrialization also creates the need for new technical skills and literacy, requiring a more educated labour force. Parents need to keep their children in school to better enable them to find work, and compulsory education laws often follow . . . . As such, children become economic liabilities rather than assets. As the cost of living rises and one wage is no longer enough to support a family, both husbands and wives enter the paid work force. Unless other relatives are able to care for the children, child care becomes a problematic and expensive issue.

Having fewer children is often the only way couples can reduce conflicts between earning a living and raising a family. As a result, public demand for birth control tends to increase, contraceptive technology expands, and family planning becomes more widespread and socially acceptable. Ideologies supporting a more public role for women often emerge, and birthrates continue to decline. Although this pattern has been prevalent in many industrialized countries, there are, of course, cultural variations within as well as between countries in the use of contraception, birthrates and the participation of mothers in the paid labour force.

The consequences of declining birthrates are not necessarily the same for women, families and society. From a woman's perspective, fewer children may mean higher quality care for each existing child, more time and opportunity to participate in the labour force or self-development activities, and a higher standard of living . . . . For families, fewer children could mean a higher per capita income, less time over the life course devoted to child care activities, easier residential mobility and, logistically, an easier and less costly divorce. From the state's viewpoint, falling birthrates lead to an aging population, which may increase concerns about how to fund future social programs with a shrinking labour force contributing to the tax base of the nation. In addition, governments may be concerned about the rising cost of medical care which has been disproportionately costly for the "old elderly". Rapidly declining birthrates among cultural minorities could be seen as leading to decreasing power within the entire nation or region. In addition, some economists have warned about declining economic productivity and prosperity with lower birthrates. In other words, declining birthrates have been interpreted differently by various groups . . . .

Crude birthrates are not very accurate measures because they are influenced by the average age as well as the ratio of men to women in the population. In addition, in any one year, the crude birthrate can be affected by high unemployment and a slow economy. The more accurate measure is the total fertility rate, which is the average number of children a woman is likely to have in her lifetime. The same trend is apparent for this measure, however. In 1921, a woman had on average 3.5 children . . . compared to 1.8 in 1990 . . . . Fertility rates are also calculated for different age categories, called "age-specific fertility rates", as they are quite different for older or younger women. Many of today's young women are delaying childbirth until they finish their education, find steady work, and build up some savings. It also appears as though an increasing percentage of couples are not having any children (between 15% and 20%), either through choice or infertility problems, although it is difficult to determine this percentage more accurately until the postwar baby boom generation reaches the end of their childbearing years.

2. *Rising Life Expectancy At Birth*

Throughout this century, life expectancies at birth have gradually increased. For example, in 1931 the average life expectancy of a Canadian male was 60.0 years while it was 62.1 for females. By 1990, this had changed to about 74 for men and 81 for women . . . . There are several reasons for this rise in life expectancy. In the early part of the century, infant mortality rates and maternal death rates declined in response to improved sanitation, diet, housing and health services, including the invention of antibiotics and inoculations for use against contagious diseases. In addition, occupational health and safety regulations have prevented some work-related deaths, and medical breakthroughs have prolonged life for accident victims and people with acute and degenerative illnesses.

Rising life expectancies have led to several other social trends and policy changes. Fewer infant deaths, for example, contribute to a lower birthrate as families no longer need to have more children than they want in order to ensure that some live to adulthood. Rising life expectancy also means the potential for longer marriages, more generations per family, and more grandparents seeing their grandchildren mature. However, longer life expectancy may also result in divorce becoming more prevalent. In the last century, some unhappy marriages continued because of feelings of duty, absence of the concept of "free will", or dissolution of the marriage through early death.

As the average age of Canada's population increases, the greater proportion of elderly people makes it necessary to plan for different kinds of housing, health and social services, and expanded pension costs. Organizations catering to elderly persons will be competing for the same scarce resources as organizations serving children and youth.

3. More People Are Living Together Outside Marriage

In comparison with previous decades, more Canadians are now living together without being legally married. In 1990, Statistics Canada reported that 12% of all couples were in common-law relationships compared to 6% in 1981 . . . . Quebec had the highest percentage of residents aged 15 and over living in common-law relationships (13%), while New Brunswick had the lowest (5%). Given that most common-law partners are relatively young, it is not surprising that the vast majority have never been legally married. From 1984-90, the proportion of Canadians aged 18 to 64 who had ever lived common-law nearly doubled, but among those aged 40 to 49, the proportion almost tripled. More than half the women and 43% of the men who lived common-law in 1986 were younger than age 30. Since 1984 the median age of common-law partners has continued to rise . . . .

Common-law relationships in Canada used to be considered as temporary arrangements that could be seen as trial marriages. Now they are becoming more like legal marriages. Yet statistically, common-law relationships still differ from legal marriage in that their duration is shorter and their fertility rates are lower. Furthermore, marriages that are preceded by cohabitation have slightly higher rate of dissolution . . . . However, the 1991 census has shown that these relationships are becoming more prevalent, especially in Quebec. Furthermore, 42% of these relationships in Canada include children, either born to the common-law partners or brought into the family from other unions. These trends are very similar to many European countries, where the distinction between legal marriage and cohabitation is becoming blurred both legally and socially.

4. More Mothers Are Working For Pay

- In 1941, about 4.5% of married women were working in the labour force
  . . . .

- By 1992, this had risen to 61.4% . . . .

- About three quarters of mothers with children under 12 are now working for pay, compared to 35% of all women aged 45 and over.

- In addition, married women are as likely, or more likely, to be working for pay as separated, divorced or widowed women . . . .

The implications of the participation of married women in the labour force are many. In the last century, when married men and fathers left the home/farm due to industrialization in order to find work, their authority gradually diminished as family "heads". In addition, the patriarchal family or the family in which men have more legal authority than women has further declined now that most wives and mothers are working for pay. When men are no longer sole breadwinners, wives often increase their decision-making power within the marriage. . . . Changes are also taking place in the division of labour within the home as women spend more time at paid employment. Most research still indicates, however, that women continue to spend more time than men at family caregiving and housework, and also retain responsibility for these tasks . . . . Laws and social policies are beginning to change in recognition of these transitions in family and economic roles.

5. The Percentage Of Lone-Parent Families Has Been Rising

From 1961 to 1991, lone-parent families as a percentage of all families with children increased from 11% to 20% . . . . Separation and divorce is the major reason for rising rates of one-parent families, while a second reason is the increase in births outside marriage.

a. Separation and Divorce

Throughout this century, and especially since the late 1960s, rates of separation and divorce have risen in Canada, but also in many industrialized countries. In 1921, for example, the divorce rate per 100,000 population in Canada was 6.4. By 1987, the rate had risen to 355.1 before falling slightly to 308.1 in 1988 and 294 in 1990 . . . .

There are many reasons for rising separation and divorce rates. The growing separation of religion and the state has encouraged people to view marriage as a contract which can be broken under certain circumstances, just like business contracts. In addition, growing individualism, including the idea that people deserve happiness in their personal relationships, has discouraged couples from staying together out of duty or concern for family reputation. Furthermore, the logistics of divorce may be easier with fewer children per family. In addition, now that more women are working for pay and can at least partially support themselves, divorce may be more economically feasible for both men and women in unhappy marriages. Finally, divorce laws were liberalized in Canada in 1968 and 1985, and these reforms eased the process of divorce and thereby further contributed to rising divorce rates.

Most divorced people remarry, and about three-quarters of men and two-thirds of women remarry after divorce . . . . Research indicates, however, that lone parents have higher remarriage rates than those without children. . . . Men are more likely than women to remarry after divorce, but remarriage rates have been declining for both men and women as cohabitation has become more socially acceptable.

Although the personal and family consequences of divorce can be at least temporarily devastating for some while energizing for others, the policy implications of higher rates of separation/divorce and one-parent families are very consequential.

After divorce and support laws in Canada and the United States were reformed, divorce rates increased rapidly and growing numbers of children now live in households with just one parent. On the assumption that most women were at least partially self-supporting, the new laws removed some of the legal protection for the economic support of women and children. . . . Furthermore, even when the court ordered non-custodial parents to pay support to former spouses and to their children, a majority failed to pay. Private enforcement procedures have proven ineffective. Consequently, the numbers of separated and divorced women and their children living on public assistance has grown with rising rates of marriage dissolution. Today, one of the major family policy issues in countries with private child support enforcement procedures is how to retrieve more of this money from non-custodial parents.

b. *Rise in Births Outside Marriage*

In addition to the creation of one-parent families though separation and divorce, a growing percentage of births are occurring outside marriage. In Canada, however, many of these children are born to couples who are living in permanent but non-marital relationships. As an example of the rise in births outside marriage, only 11% of female lone parents and 4% of male lone parents were never-married in 1981 compared to 20% and 8% in 1991 . . . . In Quebec, 33% of all children were born outside of legal marriage in 1988 . . . .

There are several reasons for an increase in births outside marriage. As society has become more secularized, attitudes have changed about the state's right to be involved in personal life. Sexual attitudes and practices have become more liberal since the 1950s, especially within unmarried but "committed" relationships. Legislative changes to protect women and children have made legal marriage and cohabitation, as well as the rights of children born inside and outside of marriage, very similar. These changes were made in response to demands for legal reform, but may have discouraged people from legally marrying before bearing children.

In 1968, about 70% of unmarried mothers in Ontario had their children placed for adoption. By 1977, this figure declined to about 12% . . . . Since that time, the percentage of unmarried mothers across North America who allow their children to be adopted has dwindled (although reliable statistics are not available). More women are able to support themselves and their children financially either through paid employment or improved social welfare benefits. Also, attitudes towards sex and illegitimacy have contributed to a change in the former trend to give up a baby for adoption. In addition, many mothers have made a deliberate choice to reproduce outside marriage and many are involved in permanent but non-marital relationships. . . .

Increasing numbers of one-parent families have meant higher government expenditures to support women and children without adequate incomes. According to Statistics Canada data, 61% of single-parent mothers were living below the poverty line in 1990, with very little support from the non-custodial parent. Consequently, policies relating to child custody after divorce, awarding support and enforcing support have been questioned. Despite the principle of equality enshrined in family law, women who were formerly homemakers often need government assistance in job training, finding work or obtaining higher wages. In addition, there is a growing demand for more generous maternity and parental benefits and public child care services to assist all parents to better combine work and family life.

Changing Trends

In summary, families are changing in Canada along with changes in the structure of the economy, the labour force, laws, and social attitudes. Life expectancies at birth are increasing, especially for women, and birthrates are declining. Both families and households are becoming smaller, and two-income families are now in the majority. Childbearing tends to be completed earlier than several generations ago, although many middle-class women are delaying first births until after their education is completed. In addition, families are becoming less permanent units with rising rates of separation, divorce and re-coupling.

Although the popularity of legal marriage has been declining recently, the percentage living as couples has been relatively stable since 1981 . . . . Most people eventually marry and most who divorce remarry. Furthermore, people are still closely tied to their extended family even when they live far apart.

———————

Many of the trends identified by Professor Baker have continued or intensified in the last few years (sources: Dept. of Justice, *Selected Statistics on Canadian Families and Family Law* (Ottawa: Nov./97); Stats. Canada, *1996 Census: Marital Status, Common-law Unions and Families* (Ottawa:1997); and Stats. Canada, *Report on the Demographic Situation in Canada 1998-1999* (Ottawa:1999). Never has fertility been so low in Canada as in the last half of the 1990s. In 1997, the total fertility rate reached 1.55 per woman, the lowest level ever recorded in Canada. That year also marked the seventh consecutive year in which the total number of births dropped. Meanwhile the number of abortions reached record levels and there was approximately one abortion for every three live births.

The marriage rate has continued to decline. By 1995, it dipped to 541 marriages per 100,000 population, compared to about 900 in the early seventies. The rate in Quebec was considerably lower than in the other provinces. The number of marriages in Canada in 1997 was down 24% from the peak year of 1972. Not since 1966, when Canada's population was much smaller, had there been such a small number of marriages. The average age of first-time brides was up to 27.4, while first-time grooms averaged 29.5 years of age. More than one third of mothers were waiting until after their thirtieth birthday to have their first child.

Not all provinces were equally affected by the drop in the marriage rate, a drop directly attributable to the increased popularity of living "common law". Already in 1976, Quebec's total marriage rate of 640 per 1,000 was lower than that of other provinces. However, Quebec's rate fell by almost half in the next twenty years, while the other provinces' rates fell by about 25%. In the most recent years, however, Quebec's marriage rate has stabilized, while that of the other provinces continues to fall. This leads Statistics Canada to speculate that the phenomenon of common-law unions may be approaching a leveling off point in Quebec and that other provinces will reach a similar saturation point.

In the 1996 Canada Census, 84% of the Canadian population lived in "census families", defined as indicated at the start of the excerpt from Professor Baker's work. Married couples with children represented 45% of all families, 29% were married couples without children, 15% were lone-parent families, 6% were common-law couples with children, and 6% were common-law couples without children. One couple in seven was living common-law, compared to one in nine in 1991. Between 1991 and 1996, the rate of increase in common-law families was about sixteen times greater than that for married couple families. The proportion of couples living together outside of marriage varies considerably by age and province. As noted, common-law couples are by far most frequent in Quebec, where one couple in four lived common-law by 1996. Statistics Canada estimates that 54% of Quebec couples in which the female partner is aged 25 to 29 are living in common-law relationships, as compared to 22% of comparable couples in the other provinces.

The number of divorces, which stabilized at about 80,000 per year at the start of the 1990s, dropped steeply from 1995 to 1997. It stood at 67,400 in 1997. Two factors appear at work. First, much of the drop is simply due to the decrease in marriages several years earlier, thereby reducing the candidates for divorce. Second, there has been a significant increase in the average age at marriage and marriages entered into by older persons tend to last longer.

The changing look of Canada's families was reflected in the 1996 distribution of children living in the three family structures: married couple, common law and lone parent. Between 1991 and 1996, the percentage of all children living in families of married couples fell from 78 to 73. In 1996, about 8% of all children were living in common-law families. For children under the age of 6, this figure was 14% nationally and 31% in Quebec. Almost 20% of all children lived in lone-parent families. Women headed 83% of these families. About 9% of children under the age of 12 were living with a stepparent. The 1995 General Social Survey found that 10% of couple families with children were blended families. Of those, slightly over half consisted of couples who were currently married, while the remainder were common-law couples.

The sharp rise in non-marital cohabitation has raised important concerns about its consequences for the process of family formation and dissolution. In "Dissolution of Premarital Cohabitation in Canada" (1995), 32 Demography 521, Professors Wu and Balakrishnan reported that most unmarried relationships were transitory and short-lived, ending either in marriage or separation. Fewer than half of these relationships last longer than 3 years. Although many cohabitees eventually married their partners, about two-fifths of women and one-fifth of men chose to terminate the relationship. The authors concluded (at 529):

> [A]mple evidence exists to suggest that premarital cohabitation actually leads to less stable marriages. . . . Empirically we know that cohabiting unions are less stable than marital unions. . . . Together these results support the argument that cohabiting unions are fragile and transient, and that they weaken the institution of marriage by undermining "its central foundation of permanence".

See also Ambert, *Divorce: Facts, Figures and Consequences* (Vanier Institute of the Family, 1999) which similarly reports that common-law relationships are less stable than marriage and that there is a higher divorce rate amongst couples who have lived together before marriage. Indeed, premarital cohabitation is associated with lower marital stability, whether the participants marry each other or others. Two explanations have been suggested. First, those who cohabit may have characteristics, such as certain values or attitudes, that are conducive to marital instability. Second, the experience of cohabitation may make persons more likely to divorce by fostering a more casual attitude to marriage.

As part of the Government of Canada's Child Development Initiatives, Human Resources Development Canada has been directing and funding the National Longitudinal Survey of Children and Youth (NLSCY) in partnership with Statistics Canada. Almost 23,000 children, ranging in age from birth to 11 years will be followed into adulthood. In the 1998 report based on this study, *Growing up with*

Mom and Dad? The Intricate Family Life of Canadian Children (Ottawa: Minister of Industry, catalogue no. 89-566-XIE), Nicole Marcil-Gratton reports (at 16) that children in Quebec are the most likely in Canada to live in lone-parent families before the age of ten precisely because their parents are more likely to be living common-law at their birth. In all the NLSCY cohorts (arranged by year of birth), children born to married parents who have not lived in a common-law union before-hand are the least likely (13.6%) to experience family breakdown before the age of 10. About 25% of children whose parents lived in a common-law union and then married after their birth experienced a family breakdown before age 10. The comparable figure for those children whose parents lived common-law and married before their birth was 28.4%. Over 63% of children whose parents lived common-law at their birth and never married watched their parents separate before the age of 10, "confirming the more short-lived nature of these relationships, even when there are children".

2.   Legal Regulation of the Family

(1) NATURE OF FAMILY LAW

Family law may be defined as that area of the law governing the relationships between members of a family. The focal point of this definition is obviously the concept of family. Until fairly recently, the family in Canadian society could be described as the basic social unit normally consisting of a husband and wife and their children, if any. Traditionally, family law has been concerned with the relationships between husband and wife and parent and child.

The main subjects of family law have, therefore, traditionally been marriage, separation and divorce, property rights of spouses during the marriage and on marriage breakdown, support obligations of spouses to one another, the care and custody of children, support obligations of parents to their children, the intervention of the state in the parent-child relationship through child protection legislation, and the establishment of a parent-child relationship through adoption. The law impinges on family relationships at so many different points, however, that it could be claimed, quite legitimately, that family law also encompasses such diverse topics as the law of succession, income taxation, fatal accidents legislation, juvenile delinquency, and social security schemes such as welfare, family benefits, and unemployment insurance. To a large extent, these segments of family law have been allocated to other courses in the typical law school curriculum in order to keep a course on family law within workable limits. A glance at the Table of Contents reveals that these topics are not given separate coverage in this book although they are referred to from time to time.

The traditional definition of family law has to be modified to take into account those laws that now govern non-traditional families. In recent years, more and more individuals have begun to live together without marriage and to perform the tasks generally associated with the family. In a functional sense, these units are clearly families and are frequently indistinguishable from the traditional family except for the fact that there is no marital relationship uniting any of its members. The laws governing the relationship of individuals within these informal families must also be considered part of family law and will be examined whenever appropriate to the subject being covered in a particular chapter of this book.

In the following excerpt, Professor Payne examines the changing nature of Canadian family law.

PAYNE, "FAMILY LAW IN CANADA"

Baker, ed., *Canada's Changing Families: Challenges to Public Policy*
(Ottawa: The Vanier Institute of the Family, 1994) 13-17.

Changing Social and Economic Trends Affecting Canadian Family Law

Canadian family law has been historically linked to the status of marriage. The
formation of marriage, the consequences of marriage, and the annulment or dissolution of marriage have long been regarded as subject to state regulation and outside
the control of the individual. "Marriage" has been judicially defined as "a voluntary
union for life of one man and one woman to the exclusion of all others." Although
this definition has been challenged under section 15 of the *Canadian Charter of
Rights and Freedoms* as contravening the equality rights of same-sex cohabitants,
the outcome of this challenge must await a definitive ruling by the Supreme Court
of Canada. If the challenge is upheld, the implications for the future of Canadian
family law could be immense.

Federal divorce laws reflect the nuclear family. Even the rights and responsibilities of members of the extended family, such as grandparents, aunts and uncles,
receive scant attention. Although provincial legislation deals with more diverse
aspects of family dysfunction, its traditional emphasis on the breakdown of the
nuclear family is still predominant.

Recent years have witnessed changing family structures in Canada. High divorce and remarriage rates, increases in common-law and same-sex relationships,
the two-income family, the changing needs of the labour force, cultural diversity,
and the aging of the population all present new challenges for Canada. Contemporary
family policy issues include the following:

- How can the economic interests of women and children be protected in the
  event of marriage breakdown or divorce?

- How can parental ties be preserved notwithstanding separation and divorce?

- Is a national child care program feasible or desirable?

- How should Canada respond to declining birthrates? Are financial incentives
  for parenthood, such as those adopted in Quebec, a solution? Does the answer
  lie in increased immigration?

- How should Canada address the problem of the ageing of its population?
  What will be its impact on health care, residential care, or family care for the
  aged?

- Should new reproductive technologies be outlawed or regulated?

- How should law and society respond to domestic violence?

- To what extent should Canadian law recognize rights and responsibilities
  between unmarried cohabitants of the opposite sex or of the same sex?

- How should Canadian family law be administered? By traditional courts?
  By Unified Family Courts? By Administrative Tribunals? By Governmental
  or Community Agencies? What do innovative processes, such as mediation
  and arbitration, offer as alternative means of resolving family disputes?
  Should they be subsidized by the state?

- To what extent should Canadians be entitled to regulate the legal consequences of family breakdown by marriage contracts, cohabitation agreements
  or separation agreements?

- How should Canadian law respond to native families with their own cultural
  identity and heritage? Does the answer lie in new substantive laws or in
  delegating decision-making authority to the native communities? Do immigrant families require special recognition?

Many of the above issues fall outside the scope of this analysis, which will
concentrate on separation and divorce. Within these terms of reference, the following
information is important for future policy- and lawmakers:

- The vast majority of Canadians will marry at least once during their lifetime.
  Projections suggest that 28% of all marriages will end in divorce but 75% of
  all divorcees will marry again or form permanent cohabitational relationships.
  Marriages that end in divorce have an average duration of 12.5 years and the
  median is 10.7 years (Canada, Department of Justice, 1990:35 and 41; Vanier
  Institute of the Family, 1992A:9).

- Two-income families are the norm in Canada. The number of married women
  in the Canadian labour force has increased over the last 20 years from 35%
  to over 61% (Vanier Institute of the Family, 1992A:13; Statistics Canada,
  February 1992:8). Separated and divorced women who are incapable of
  achieving economic self-sufficiency in the labour force are likely to live in
  poverty unless they remarry or form a new permanent marriage-like relationship (Canadian Research Institute for Law and the Family, 1989:51-74).

- Three generational families living under the same roof represent approximately 6 percent of all families. With an ever-increasing ageing population,
  this statistic may increase dramatically over the next 20 years (Vanier Institute
  of the Family, 1992C:11).

- Approximately 12% of all adults live in common-law relationships with
  members of the opposite sex. More than 50% of them are between the ages
  of 20 and 35 and have never been married (Vanier Institute of the Family,
  1992A).

- One out of every six children in Canada lives in poverty. Associated with
  poverty are poorer health, lower educational achievements and emotional
  and behavioural problems.

- Single-parent households represent 20% of all Canadian families with children (Lindsay, 1992:9). More than 75% of these households are headed by
  women. Separation and divorce result in single parenthood more frequently
  than death. When children are living with their mother in a single-parent
  household, they are five times more likely to live in poverty than children
  who are living with two parents. It is not true, however, that children in
  poverty are more frequently living in a single-parent household. Two-parent
  families with children represent the largest group of families living in poverty.

- More than one million children have encountered the divorce of their parents
  during the last 25 years. In 74% of all divorce cases, mothers obtain sole
  custody of the children. Approximately one in eight fathers (13%) receive
  sole custody of their children. Some form of joint custody arrangement

exist[s] in 11% of all divorces, and third-party custody arrangements are found in less than 1% of all divorces (Millar, 1991:86).

- More than 50% of the children of divorce will live in a family unit with their custodial parent's new partner. Ten percent of these children will encounter a second family breakdown and will live in two or more reconstituted families.

- The high rate of default in the payment of court-ordered spousal and child support is rarely related to inability to pay. Even when payments are made in full, they generally provide only a standard of living at the poverty level.

- In the 1950s, six out of ten immigrants were European. Today, one out of two immigrants is from Asia, the Caribbean, Africa and Central America. More than 20% of Canadians have a cultural heritage that is neither English nor French (Vanier Institute of the Family, 1992A:11).

Canadian family law faces an uncertain future as it grapples with diverse family structures and cultural norms and the problems of dysfunctional families. Given the above information, it might be thought that the state should assume greater responsibility for ensuring the economic well-being of family members, both old and young, regardless of whether or not the family relationship has broken down. This prospect seems remote in the face of huge federal and provincial deficits. Ironically, as certain advocacy groups call for a state-subsidized national child care program, provincial governments are calling for family members to assume additional responsibilities for the care and support of ageing parents.

The Evolution of Canadian Family Law During the Past Twenty-Five Years

Canadian family law has focused on the pathology of family relationships. It concentrates on the rights and obligations of family members when their relationships become dysfunctional or break down completely.

The primary sources of family law in Canada are found in federal and provincial statutes. Federal legislation regulates divorce whereas provincial legislation regulates the rights and duties of family members independently of divorce. Appreciation of the underlying principles of Canadian family law can probably best be achieved by an overview of major legal developments that have occurred during the last 25 years.

The actual or prospective role of the law in regulating, molding and sustaining family relationships has been a neglected field of research in Canada. Federal and provincial statutory reforms have been piecemeal and have lacked a coherent vision of family policies. The predominant legal trend has been towards the assertion of individual rights and liberties rather than the assertion of any family right. Consequently, the rights of members of the extended family, such as grandparents, aunts, uncles, and ex-in-laws are often ignored as the law focuses on husbands, wives and children. Family law statutes reflect the philosophy that state intervention is an intrusion upon privacy that can only be justified by serious family dysfunction or breakdown.

Since 1968, Canadian family law has undergone radical changes. It began with divorce reform. Before 1968, adultery constituted the sole ground for divorce, except in Nova Scotia where matrimonial cruelty constituted an alternative ground for relief. In Quebec and Newfoundland, divorce was only available by private Act of Parliament prior to the introduction of judicial divorce in 1968. With the enactment of the first comprehensive federal *Divorce Act* in 1968, several no-fault divorce grounds were introduced in addition to an extended list of offence grounds. The *Divorce Act* of 1968 also broke new ground by establishing formal legal equality of support rights and obligations between divorcing men and women. Divorcing husbands became legally entitled to sue their wives for support for the first time in Canadian history. Although the *Divorce Act, 1985* has since amended the law relating to the criteria for divorce, spousal support, child support, custody and access, the radical breakthroughs occurred with the *Divorce Act* of 1968 which laid the groundwork for future federal and provincial statutory changes.

Before 1968, the support of divorcing or divorced spouses was regulated by provincial statutes that imposed a unilateral obligation on a "guilty" husband to maintain his "innocent" wife in the event of a breakdown of their marriage ensuing from his commission of a matrimonial offence. The same principles applied to spousal support claims brought independently of divorce. During the 1970s and 1980s, most provinces enacted legislation eliminating the offence concept as the foundation of spousal support rights and obligations, although spousal misconduct is not always totally excluded from judicial consideration in the determination of the right to, amount or duration of spousal support on marriage breakdown. In addition, following the precedent established by the federal *Divorce Act* of 1968, the right to spousal support on marriage breakdown in the absence of divorce is no longer confined to wives, under provincial legislation; a financially dependent spouse of either gender may look to his or her marital partner for financial support on the breakdown of their marriage. The governing consideration is no longer gender-based but turns upon the reasonable needs of the claimant and the ability of his or her spouse to pay. Each spouse is expected to strive for financial self-sufficiency to the extent that this is practicable. Thus, marriage is no longer perceived as creating an automatic right to lifelong financial support for a dependent spouse in the event of marriage breakdown. The promotion of self-sufficiency by lawyers and the courts is warranted in short-term marriages where transitional spousal support arrangements will permit full reintegration into the labour force. Longer term marriages, where one spouse, almost invariably the wife and mother, has sacrificed her employment potential and future earning capacity for the benefit of her husband and their children, warrant different treatment. Short-term transitional spousal support orders are singularly inappropriate for displaced homemaking spouses of long-standing. Unfortunately, many courts have in the past asserted the notion of self-sufficiency to the prejudice of wives and mothers who sacrificed their economic well-being for the welfare of the family. Whether the recent more enlightened approach of the Supreme Court of Canada in the Moge case will ameliorate the situation is yet to be seen as courts grapple with the contemporary notion of "compensatory support."

These changes in the right to divorce and the right to spousal support on divorce or marriage breakdown were accompanied by equally fundamental changes in provincial statutes governing the division of property on marriage breakdown or divorce. Separated and divorced wives no longer find themselves in the prejudicial position in which Irene Murdoch found herself in the mid-1970s, when the Supreme Court of Canada denied her any interest in a ranch held in her husband's name, notwithstanding that she had worked alongside her husband in the fields. Although the Supreme Court of Canada subsequently abandoned the Murdoch decision in favour of a more enlightened approach, the inequities of the Murdoch case triggered provincial legislation that provides for property sharing on marriage breakdown that is no longer dependent on who owns the property or who purchased it.

A qualified concept of "children's rights" has also evolved. Former legal distinctions drawn between legitimate and illegitimate children have been eliminated. Where the state threatens to remove a child from the family, a court may order that the child be represented by an independent lawyer. Many provincial child protection statutes expressly endorse principles of family autonomy and minimal state intervention consistent with the best interests of the child. Rules of evidence have been relaxed so as to protect the interests of children who appear as witnesses in criminal prosecutions for sexual assault or child abuse. In contested custody proceedings, an independent assessment may be ordered by the court to determine the needs of the children and the respective abilities of the parents to accommodate those needs.

Many new legal procedures have been introduced to facilitate family dispute resolution. Mandatory financial and property statements are now prepared by the spouses to provide information that will expedite the settlement or adjudication of support and property disputes. Pre-trial conferences have been devised to reduce or eliminate contentious issues. The discretionary jurisdiction of the court over the costs of litigation is being exercised so as to promote the consensual resolution of issues. The consolidation of issues in a single court proceeding has been facilitated by statutory changes and by amendments to provincial rules of court. The use of mediation as an alternative or supplement to litigation has been endorsed by the federal *Divorce Act, 1985* and by several provincial statutes. In a few urban centres, Unified Family Courts have been established with comprehensive and exclusive jurisdiction over family law matters and with access to support services that can deflect the need for hostile negotiations or costly litigation. There still remains, however, considerable room for improvement in the development of alternative processes to litigation that will aid in the constructive resolution of family conflict.

Professor Thompson examined the extent to which family law provided for rules and some certainty and predictability in a paper prepared for the National Judicial Institute. He described family law in Canada today as largely characterized by "rulelessness", where, at best, the legislation and cases identified "factors" to be taken into account in the exercise of considerable discretion. He acknowledged that there were some "islands of rules" in the areas of property division and child support. His introduction and conclusion are reproduced below.

THOMPSON "RULES AND RULELESSNESS IN FAMILY LAW:RECENT DEVELOPMENTS, JUDICIAL AND LEGISLATIVE"

(1999)

We — and I mean all of us, courts and lawyers, parents and spouses — find ourselves at an awkward moment in the evolution of family law. Family law is statute law. But the legislators often appear deer-like, frozen in the bright headlights of divided public opinion and gender politics. Those same "political" disputes are then played out, one case at a time, before trial and appeal courts, and even the Supreme Court of Canada. Constitutional challenges are raised to the differential treatment of family forms by government, whether in the distribution of benefits or the imposition of "family" rights and obligations through legislation. No less "political", however, are difficult questions of property division, spousal support, child custody and child protection.

Buried within each case is the larger question for judges, especially appellate judges: in the absence of clear legislative "rules", should the court enunciate a ruling any broader than this individual case? If not, is it possible to maintain the legitimacy of family law in this state of "rulelessness"? . . .

Conclusion: The Homogenization of Canadian Family Law

Thanks to the federal divorce power, the Supreme Court of Canada, and the *Charter*, Canadian family law is becoming homogenized, one law from sea to sea, for better or worse.

The federal divorce power encompasses corollary relief, including custody and access, child support and spousal support. The *Federal Child Support Guidelines* offer a classic example of how the federal government can reform the whole of federal and provincial family law, through its mixture of policy-making resources and spending power. Once "federal" family law has changed, there are strong practical pressures for the provinces to "get into sync", so as not to confuse those parents and spouses who must live under both laws. No doubt the same will hold true once the federal government completes its review of custody and access law. And, sadly, the federal vagueness on spousal support equally infects the interpretation of provincial law, as happened in *Moge* and more pointedly in *Bracklow*.

The Supreme Court uses the national impact of the *Divorce Act* as one of its anchors for "national significance" or "public importance" in giving leave for family law cases. A case like *Gordon* v. *Goertz* then permits the Court to set out relocation law [the law governing mobility of custodial parents] for the whole of Canada, a marvel to an American who must cope with 50 state laws and 50 state courts on the same mobility issue. But the Court is not confined to federal statutes. Thanks to our unitary court structure, the Supreme Court of Canada is also the last court of appeal for the interpretation of provincial statutes, including such areas as child protection, property division and pensions. No field of family law is exempt from Supreme Court review and hence national direction.

Finally, the *Charter of Rights* is forcing both courts and legislatures to reduce disparities in the treatment of different family forms. Section 15 is a driving force for national homogenization. If all Canadian provinces extend support rights to common law spouses, then why not Alberta? If same-sex couples are read in to Ontario's family legislation, then so too in other provinces. Even section 7 is a homogenizing force. What's shocking about the absence of counsel in New Brunswick child protection cases is that every other Canadian province treats such cases as a priority within their legal aid plans. When the Supreme Court does interpret sections 15 or 7, then the *Charter* makes it apply across the whole country, as a minimum content of provincial family laws. All of these changes leave less and less room for experimentation, for the development of provincial family law "rules", whether legislative or judicial.

The Supreme Court appears to prefer "contextualism" and "standards" and "discretion" in family law, the costs of which fall upon lower courts, counsel and parties. In some areas of law, like child custody and spousal support, the Supreme Court — and courts generally — can fall back upon the "rule-less" legislation. But that's only a partial defence, as the courts can still develop intermediate solutions, something more like presumptions or even tighter and shorter lists of factors. In the area of child protection, the legislation is clear, but the Supreme Court and many appellate courts have moved away from rules and towards greater discretion through the interpretive vehicle of "best interests".

(2) CONSTITUTIONAL FRAMEWORK

The distribution of powers over family law and the potential for conflict between laws enacted by the Parliament of Canada and laws enacted by a provincial legislature will be surveyed whenever relevant to the topic covered by a particular chapter in this book. The following excerpt from Professor Hogg's constitutional law text provides a framework for this later analysis.

HOGG, *CONSTITUTIONAL LAW OF CANADA*

3rd ed. (Toronto: Carswell, 1992) c. 26 (Footnotes Omitted)

The Family

26.1 Distribution of powers

In principle, one would expect the bulk of family law to come within provincial power. Family law has little or no effect on trade or transportation or other aspects of the national economy. It rather concerns the ways in which people choose to live their private lives, and may be expected to reflect values which differ from one part of the country to another.

While most family law is within provincial jurisdiction, the Constitution Act, 1867, by s. 91(26), allocates to the federal Parliament the power to make laws in relation to "marriage and divorce". The national interest in marriage and divorce consists in the desirability of nation-wide recognition of marriages and divorces. If marriage and divorce were provincial responsibilities, and if markedly different rules developed among provinces, there would be no assurance that a marriage or divorce performed or obtained in one province would be recognized by the courts of another province. This has been a problem in the United States where marriage and divorce are state responsibilities. Australia has followed the Canadian pattern of allocating marriage and divorce to the federal Parliament.

The Constitution Act, 1867, by s. 92(12), confers on the provincial Legislatures the power to make laws in relation to "the solemnization of marriage in the province". The boundary between this power and the federal power over "marriage" is discussed later in this chapter. Most provincial power over family law is derived from that expansive phrase in s. 92(13), "property and civil rights in the province", which encompasses property and contract law and other private-law relations, including, for example, matrimonial property, succession, support of spouses and children, adoption, guardianship, custody, legitimacy, affiliation and names.

The various federal and provincial powers are discussed in the following sections of this chapter, including the problem of conflict between differing orders of custody or support made under federal and provincial laws. A final section will briefly examine the constitutional problems of the administration of justice in family law matters.

26.2 Crime and delinquency

Juvenile delinquency and criminal charges arising out of family disputes are within the legislative competence of the federal Parliament under the "criminal law"

power (s. 91(27)). The validity of the federal Young Offenders Act (and its predecessor, the Juvenile Delinquent's Act) have been specifically upheld on this basis,
and family-related offences under the federal Criminal Code, such as corrupting
children (s. 172), failing to provide necessaries of life (s. 215), assault (s. 266) and
abduction (s. 281), are clearly valid criminal laws. These elements of family law that
are sustained by the criminal law power will not be further discussed in this chapter.

26.3 Marriage

(a) Formation of marriage

The federal authority in relation to "marriage" — the first branch of s. 91(26)
— has to be read side by side with the provincial authority in relation to "solemnization of marriage in the province" (s. 92(12)). In fact, most of the laws concerning
marriage have been enacted by the provinces, and the courts have tended to construe
the provincial power liberally. The scope of federal power has been left largely
undetermined.

The only federal law ever to come before the courts was one which declared
that every marriage performed in accordance with the laws of the place where it was
performed was to be recognized as a valid marriage everywhere in Canada. In [*Re
Questions concerning Marriage*, [1912] A.C. 880, 7 D.L.R. 629 (P.C.), hereinafter
cited as] the *Marriage Reference*, the Privy Council through Viscount Haldane held
that the law was invalid. According to their lordships, the difficulty with the law
was that it assumed that all rules bearing on the validity of a marriage were within
the federal power over "marriage". But this would relegate the provincial power
over "the solemnization of marriage" to the laying down of merely directory rules,
that is, rules which if broken would not impair the validity of the resulting marriage.
Their lordships rejected this view, holding that the provincial power extended to the
enactment of "conditions as to solemnization which may affect the validity of the
contract". Since the provincial power was subtracted from the federal power, it
followed that the federal Parliament could not legislate with respect to all questions
of validity, and the impugned law was bad.

Following the *Marriage Reference*, it is clear that a province has power to
stipulate pre-ceremonial requirements, such as, the issue of a licence or the publication of banns, and to stipulate the qualifications of the person performing the
ceremony, even if breach of the stipulations renders the marriage a nullity. These
are matters closely associated with the performance of the ceremony — the solemnization. Much less clearly associated with the ceremony is a requirement of parental
consent to the marriage of a minor, but in two cases the Supreme Court of Canada
has held that a province may enact that parental consent is a condition of a valid
marriage. These cases were decided on the dubious ground that parental consent was
a "formality" of marriage rather than a matter governing the capacity of the parties.
Laws governing the capacity of the parties are outside provincial power, for example,
a law prescribing the prohibited degrees of consanguinity and affinity, or a law
prescribing the capacity of divorced people to remarry.

(b) Consequences of marriage

Does the federal power over "marriage" extend to the consequences of marriage, for example, the obligation to support a dependent spouse or children, custody
of children, and the property rights of married people? In fact, until 1968 laws on

these topics had only been enacted by the provinces, and the laws had been held to be valid as matters coming within "property and civil rights in the province" (s. 92(13)). In 1968, the federal Parliament provided for alimony, maintenance and custody in the new Divorce Act, but only as corollary relief in divorce proceedings. These provisions of the Divorce Act have been upheld as an exercise of the "divorce" power, and it has not been necessary to consider whether they could have been enacted by the federal Parliament as measures unrelated to divorce. In Australia, the federal marriage power empowers regulation of the relationship between married persons and their children, and it is arguable that the Canadian power is no less broad.

26.4 Divorce

The federal Parliament's power to make laws in relation to "divorce" — the second branch of s. 91(26) — lay almost dormant until 1968 when for the first time a comprehensive, Canada-wide Divorce Act was enacted. Before that time, the law differed from province to province, depending upon the date when English Law had been received in the province, the terms of pre-confederation laws on the topic, and several federal statutes which did not apply in all provinces. In Newfoundland and Quebec, and in Ontario until 1930, there was no judicial procedure to obtain a divorce, and a federal statute was necessary in every case.

The Divorce Act confers jurisdiction on the superior court in each province to grant divorces, establishes a procedure by way of "application" (formerly "petition") for obtaining decrees of divorce, and stipulates the grounds upon which decrees may be granted. The constitutionality of these primary parts of the Act cannot be doubted. The Act also contains provisions for the award of corollary relief to the parties: alimony, maintenance and the custody of children. The provisions for corollary relief cover matters which before 1968 had been the responsibility of the provinces, and they have been constitutionally controversial. In the next two sections of this chapter, we shall see that all constitutional challenges have been unsuccessful.

26.5 Custody and support of children

(a) Custody of children

In the *Adoption Reference* [*Re Adoption Act*, [1938] S.C.R. 398, 71 C.C.C. 110], the Supreme Court of Canada held that it was competent to the province to enact laws providing for the adoption of children and for the maintenance of children and deserted wives. Duff C.J. for the Court explained that the welfare and education of children and the protection of the poor and distressed were matters of provincial responsibility. He did not explain to which head of legislative power this responsibility was to be attributed, but it has subsequently been generally assumed to be "property and civil rights in the province" (s. 92(13)) rather than "matters of a merely local or private nature in the province" (s. 92(16)).

Since the *Adoption Reference* it has never been doubted that adoption, legitimacy, custody, guardianship, child welfare, affiliation, and maintenance of children are within provincial power, and of course every province has enacted statutes on these and related topics. What has not been so clear is the extent of federal power on these topics by virtue of the federal Parliament's power over "marriage and divorce" (s. 91(26)). The possibility of some federal authority was raised but not decided by Duff C.J. in the *Adoption Reference*, and the question was not presented for decision until after the enactment of the federal Divorce Act in 1968.

The question of the validity of the corollary relief provisions of the Divorce Act had to be decided in *Papp* v. *Papp* [[1970] 1 O.R. 331 (C.A.)], a case in which a custody order had been made under the Divorce Act. Laskin J.A., sitting alone as the Ontario Court of Appeal, upheld the custody provisions of the Divorce Act. He pointed out that the provisions applied only to the children of the marriage whose dissolution was sought, and that no corollary relief could be awarded at trial if the petition failed. The provisions were valid, he held, because there was a "rational, functional connection" between them and the admittedly valid provisions of the Act concerning divorce. In his view, the custody of children was "bound up with the direct consequences of marriage and divorce" and was "complementary" to the divorce itself.

Papp v. *Papp* concerned an "interim" order of custody, that is, an order of custody made after the application for divorce to cover the period up to the trial. But the decision has been consistently followed in subsequent cases challenging other forms of corollary relief. Appellate courts in Manitoba and Alberta have upheld the constitutionality of "permanent" custody orders, that is, orders made on the granting of the divorce. More difficult is the question of the validity of the authority given by the Divorce Act to the court subsequently to vary a custody order made at the time of the divorce. On an application for variation, the divorce is over, and the only issue for decision is the best interests of the child. Is there still a "rational, functional connection" with the divorce? In *Skjonsby* v. *Skjonsby* [[1975] 4 W.W.R. 319 (Alta. C.A.)] the Appellate Division of the Alberta Supreme Court answered yes, upholding the power of variation.

(b) Support of children

The Divorce Act's provisions authorizing the court to order payments of support (formerly called maintenance) in respect of the children of the marriage are as valid as those concerning custody, and for the same reason, namely, their close connection with the divorce. The power to vary support orders, long after the divorce, is also valid. Moreover, the original order for support need not be finally made at the time of granting the divorce. In *Zacks* v. *Zacks* [[1973] S.C.R. 891], a judge of the Supreme Court of British Columbia, on granting a decree nisi for divorce, ordered that the wife and child of the marriage were entitled to support, but directed a reference to the registrar of the Court to recommend the amount. The decree absolute, finalizing the divorce, was entered before the amount was fixed. The Supreme Court of Canada had no difficulty in deciding that both the language of the Divorce Act and the "divorce" power extended to the fixing of quantum after the grant of the divorce. Of course, in that case the application for support had been made in a timely fashion and the trial judge had declared that the respondent wife was entitled to support. The Supreme Court of Canada therefore did not have to decide, and expressly left open, the question whether a divorce court could entertain an application for support which had been made for the first time after the decree absolute had been granted.

26.6 Support of spouse

The previous section of this chapter dealt with the custody and support of children. This section of the chapter is concerned with payments for the support of

a dependent spouse. Such payments used to be called either alimony or maintenance. . . .

It is clear that the provinces have the power to provide for support payments
by one spouse to the other. This was one of the points decided in the *Adoption
Reference*. . . .

The federal Divorce Act includes, as part of the corollary relief available in
divorce proceedings, provisions . . . for the support of a spouse. There is no doubt
as to the validity of these provisions. *Zacks* v. *Zacks*, the decision of the Supreme
Court of Canada which has already been discussed in connection with maintenance
of children, upheld the validity of an order made under the Divorce Act which was
for the support of the wife as well as the child of the marriage. Martland J. for the
Court spoke of "alimony, maintenance and the custody of children" as subjects
which were all "inseparable from [Parliament's] jurisdiction to pass laws governing
the change of status resulting from a dissolution of marriage".

26.7 Division of property

The Divorce Act, by s. 15 [now s.15.2], authorizes the payment of maintenance
for the support of a spouse or children by "lump sum" as well as by periodic sums.
The power to order payment by lump sum has been interpreted as not including the
power to order the transfer of real estate or other specific assets.

It has been suggested that an order for the transfer of specific property would
in any case be outside the constitutional power of the federal Parliament, because it
would be within "property and civil rights in the province" (s. 92(13)). It is of course
true that laws in relation to property, including matrimonial property, are within the
competence of the provinces under their power over property and civil rights. But
that is also true of support and custody. The federal Parliament has the power to
provide for support and custody as corollary relief in divorce proceedings because
of the "rational, functional connection" between laws which provide for the dissolution of a marriage and laws which provide for these forms of corollary relief. It
could surely be argued that a similar connection exists between the dissolution of a
marriage and the disposition of the matrimonial property. Thus, while the federal
Parliament probably could not enact a comprehensive regime of family property,
the cases so far decided under the Divorce Act (all of which have sustained federal
power) suggest that there would be no constitutional impediment to the expansion
of the Divorce Act's corollary relief provisions to permit the court, on the making
of a decree for divorce, to order transfers of specific property from one spouse to the
other.

26.8 Conflict between orders made under federal and provincial law

(a) General principles

There is provincial legislation providing for support and custody, and the
validity of this legislation is not in doubt. Since the introduction in 1968 of the
corollary relief provisions of the federal Divorce Act, there has been the possibility
of conflict between orders made under provincial law and orders made under the
Divorce Act. In my opinion, the existence of conflict and its consequences should
be determined by the relatively well-settled body of constitutional law which resolves
conflicts between federal and provincial laws, that is to say, the doctrine of federal

paramountcy. Instead, the courts have often disregarded the doctrine of paramountcy and have produced a remarkably inconsistent patchwork of decisions.

Some of the difficulty seems to have been caused by confusion with the rules of conflict of laws (or private international law). In *McKee* v. *McKee* [[1951] A.C. 352 (P.C.)], the Privy Council decided that the Supreme Court of Ontario had jurisdiction to make an order for the custody of a child resident in Ontario, despite the existence of an inconsistent custody order made in another jurisdiction (California). Their lordships pointed out that under Ontario law the welfare of the infant was the paramount consideration in questions of custody, and this consideration should prevail over all others, including the existence of a foreign order.

The rule of *McKee* v. *McKee* resolves conflicts as to custody between a province and a foreign jurisdiction, or between two provinces. But where the conflict is between federal and provincial law an issue of constitutional law is presented which cannot be resolved by the rules of the conflict of laws. An order for custody or other corollary relief which is made under the Divorce Act by the superior court of a province is not an order of a "foreign" court in other provinces. On the contrary, s. 20 of the Divorce Act provides (and federal legislative power supports the provision) that the order "has legal effect throughout Canada", and s. 20 further provides that the order may be registered in any province as an order of the superior court of that province and may then be enforced "as an order of that court". Surely any order for corollary relief under the Divorce Act must render inoperative any inconsistent order under provincial law by virtue of the doctrine of paramountcy.

The question then arises: when is an order for corollary relief under the Divorce Act inconsistent with an order under provincial law? Under the "express contradiction" test of inconsistency, which has now been accepted by the Supreme Court of Canada, there can be no doubt about custody orders. An order under the Divorce Act granting the custody of a child to spouse W expressly contradicts an order under provincial law granting the custody of the same child to spouse H. Assuming that W and H are living apart, a child cannot be in the custody of both at the same time. The case of support (whether of spouse or children) is not so clear. An order under the Divorce Act requiring spouse H to pay $500 per month to spouse W does not expressly contradict an order under provincial law requiring spouse H to pay $600 to spouse W. Both orders can be complied with by spouse H paying $1,100 to spouse W! This is absurd because it is obvious that each order was intended to occupy the field, exhaustively defining H's obligation, and by implication excluding any additional obligation. It has been decided that there is an inconsistency between two orders requiring the payment of different amounts of support, and that the provincial order is inoperative. The rest of this chapter will proceed on the realistic assumption that this decision is correct. But it should not be overlooked that a relentless application of the express contradiction test would lead to a finding that two orders requiring the payment of different amounts of support are not inconsistent.

(b) Variation under provincial law of orders under Divorce Act

The first situation to be examined is where a divorce has been granted by the superior court of a province, and the court has also made an order for corollary relief (custody or support) under the Divorce Act. Is it later open to a court (in the same or another province), acting under provincial law, to make an order for custody or [support] which is inconsistent with the pre-existing Divorce Act order?

In *Emerson* v. *Emerson* [[1972] 3 O.R. 5 (H.C.)], a divorce had been granted by the Supreme Court of New Brunswick, and the Court had awarded the wife maintenance for the support of the child of the marriage. The husband lived in New Brunswick, but the wife and child lived in Ontario. The wife wished to vary the amount of maintenance. The Divorce Act includes a power to vary orders for corollary relief, but at that time the Act provided that the power was exercisable only "by the court that made the order". The wife therefore had to go to New Brunswick to take advantage of this provision. Instead, she applied to the Supreme Court of Ontario for maintenance under the provincial Infants Act. Wright J., invoking an earlier decision of his own, applied the conflict of laws rule of *McKee* v. *McKee* to hold that the welfare of the child was the primary consideration and that he was free to order maintenance under the provincial law even in the face of an inconsistent order under the federal Divorce Act.

Wright J.'s decision in *Emerson* v. *Emerson* to grant relief in Ontario where the wife and child lived is certainly understandable. The Divorce Act of 1968 was deficient in only allowing orders to be varied in the province where the divorce was granted. (The current Act, enacted in 1986, permits variation by a court in a province where either former spouse is ordinarily resident, whether or not that court granted the divorce and originally ordered corollary relief [ss. 5 and 18]). But the fact remains that the Divorce Act maintenance order, although made in New Brunswick, had legal force in Ontario, and was enforceable in Ontario, by virtue of a valid federal law. Since the Divorce Act of 1968 gave Wright J. no power directly to vary the order made under the Divorce Act, the result of the decision is to produce two inconsistent orders for maintenance, both enforceable in Ontario. This is precisely the situation which the doctrine of paramountcy is designed to resolve, and it dictates that the order made under the federal Act must prevail. Wright J. should have declined jurisdiction, since his order (made under provincial law) would have to be futile.

The authority of *Emerson* v. *Emerson* has been limited and perhaps destroyed by two decisions of provincial courts of appeal. In *Ramsay* v. *Ramsay* [[1976] 13 O.R. (2d) 85 (C.A.), 23 R.F.L. 147], the Ontario Court of Appeal held that an Ontario court had no authority to vary an order for maintenance of a spouse made under the Divorce Act in Manitoba. Their lordships added, *obiter*, however, that questions of the custody or welfare of children stood on a different footing: in their view the Divorce Act should not be construed as depriving the provincial courts of the ancient *parens patriae* jurisdiction over children within their territorial jurisdiction. Although their lordships did not refer to *Emerson* v. *Emerson*, this dictum could be read as supporting the outcome of that case since the case did involve the welfare of a child.

In *Re Hall and Hall* [[1976] 4 W.W.R. 634 (B.C. C.A.)], the British Columbia Court of Appeal rejected the obiter dictum in *Ramsay* v. *Ramsay* and the decision in *Emerson* v. *Emerson*. The Court held that a British Columbia court had no jurisdiction to vary an order for the custody of a child made under the Divorce Act in Quebec. The Divorce Act of 1968 gave no such jurisdiction, and an order made under provincial law (whether under statute or the *parens patriae* jurisdiction) would simply be inconsistent with the Divorce Act. It seems to me, with respect, that *Re Hall and Hall* is rightly decided and that the obiter dictum in *Ramsay* v. *Ramsay* and the decision in *Emerson* v. *Emerson* (as well as cases which have followed it) are inconsistent with the doctrine of federal paramountcy.

The decisions and dicta which seem to ignore the doctrine of federal paramountcy reflect a concern that an order for corollary relief under the Divorce Act should not preclude forever the making of an inconsistent order under provincial law. It may be possible to construct a sound constitutional basis to avoid that result. It will be recalled that the validity of the corollary relief provisions of the Divorce

Act depends upon their "rational, functional connection" with divorce. It is arguable, therefore, that an order for corollary relief is inherently temporary, expiring naturally as the divorce retreats into the past and its impact on the circumstances of the parties diminishes. On this basis, it would eventually be open to a court to decide that the effects of a divorce had been exhausted, and that an order made under the Divorce Act could be reviewed and replaced by a different order made under provincial law.

(c) Orders under provincial law where no order under Divorce Act

The second situation to be examined is where a divorce has been granted by the superior court of a province, but no order for corollary relief (custody or support) has been made. What is the effect of the divorce decree on an order for custody or support made under provincial law? The order under provincial law might have been made before or after the divorce decree.

Wright J.'s decision in *Emerson* v. *Emerson* would clearly assert the Court's power to act under provincial law. I have already given my reasons for thinking that *Emerson* v. *Emerson* is wrongly decided. However, it seems to me that the Ontario Court of Appeal in *Richards* v. *Richards* [[1972] 2 O.R. 596 (C.A.)] went too far in the other direction when Gale C.J.O. for the Court asserted that the Divorce Act, by occupying the "field" of corollary relief, had rendered ineffective all provincial laws "in that field". This dictum was not necessary for the actual decision in *Richards* v. *Richards*, and it conflicts with recent decisions of the Supreme Court of Canada which have consistently rejected the covering-the-field test of inconsistency between federal and provincial laws, and have insisted upon a more direct conflict ("express contradiction") to trigger the paramountcy doctrine. On the basis of the express contradiction test, as long as no order has in fact been made under the Divorce Act, an order made under provincial law would not be deemed inconsistent with the Divorce Act and would therefore be legally effective. Of course, if and when a valid order is made under the Divorce Act, it will render the competing order inoperative.

(d) Variation under Divorce Act of orders under provincial law

The third and final situation to be examined is where an order has been made for support or custody under provincial law before the commencement of divorce proceedings. In subsequent divorce proceedings in the same or another province, can an order for corollary relief be made which is inconsistent with the pre-existing order?

This was the situation in *Gillespie* v. *Gillespie* [(1972), 13 R.F.L. 344 (N.B. C.A.)] in which the New Brunswick Appellate Division held that the Supreme Court of New Brunswick had jurisdiction, on the granting of a divorce, to make an order for the custody of a child of the marriage, although the child was in Ontario and was the subject of a custody order made under Ontario's Infants Act. The Court held, correctly in my opinion, that the conflict between the two orders was to be resolved by the doctrine of paramountcy, the order made under the federal Divorce Act prevailing over the order made under the provincial Infants Act.

26.9 Jurisdiction of Family Courts

(a) Fragmentation of jurisdiction

In most provinces, matters of family law are adjudicated upon by several different courts. There is now a strong movement to unite the various jurisdictions in a new unified family court. The existing fragmentation of jurisdiction is mainly an accident or series of accidents of history, but part of the explanation, and an impediment to radical reorganization, is the Constitution. Not only does the Constitution divide legislative jurisdiction over family law in the ways already discussed in this chapter, it also imposes restraints on the kinds of courts which can be invested with jurisdiction to determine family disputes.

(b) Federal courts

Section 101 of the Constitution Act, 1867 confers on the federal Parliament the power to establish federal courts. This power has been exercised by the establishment of the Federal Court of Canada, but the Federal Court has not been given any significant jurisdiction in family matters. Section 101 of the Constitution Act, 1867 limits federally established courts to the adjudication of issues governed by federal law. Since much substantive family law is outside federal legislative competence, no federal court could in any event be given an extensive family jurisdiction. Any court exercising comprehensive family jurisdiction would have to be a provincial court.

(c) Provincial courts invested by province

Section 92(14) of the Constitution Act, 1867 confers on the provincial Legislatures the power to make laws in relation to "the administration of justice in the province, including the constitution, maintenance, and organization of provincial courts". Provincial courts established under this provision are not confined to issues governed by provincial law; they may be given jurisdiction to administer federal as well as provincial law. However, s. 96 (and the associated judicature sections) of the Constitution Act, 1867 do impose limits on the power of the provincial Legislatures to invest provincial courts with jurisdiction. It has been decided that s. 96 implicitly stipulates that a province may not vest in an inferior court (that is, a court which is not a superior, district or county court) a jurisdiction analogous to that exercised by a superior, district or county court.

Most of what we now regard as family law has come into existence since confederation, and as the provincial Legislatures have created new bodies of law they have tended to vest adjudicatory power in the inferior courts in the province. In the *Adoption Reference* (1938), the Supreme Court of Canada had to determine the constitutionality of provincial statutes which vested in inferior courts powers to grant adoptions, to award "maintenance" to deserted wives and children, to make affiliation orders and award maintenance for illegitimate children and to make orders for the care of children in need of protection. Duff C.J., for the Court, upheld each of these jurisdictions as "broadly conform[ing] to a type of jurisdiction generally exercisable by courts of summary jurisdiction rather than the jurisdiction exercised by courts within the purview of s. 96". In *Re B.C. Family Relations Act [Ontario (Attorney General)* v. *Canada (Attorney General)*, [1982] 3 W.W.R. 1 (S.C.C.)], the Supreme Court of Canada held that, since a province could confer on an inferior court jurisdiction over adoption, it could also confer jurisdiction over guardianship and custody, which were "lesser rungs" on the ladder of family relationships. These two decisions of the Supreme Court of Canada establish that most family law can be administered by inferior courts. Of course, the powers upheld in the two cases could also be vested in a s. 96 court if a province wished to follow that route. All that the two cases decide is that there is no fetter on the provincial competence to confer those powers.

There are still some matters of family law that, although within provincial legislative competence, must be vested in a s. 96 court. In *Re B.C. Family Relations Act*, the Court, while upholding the jurisdiction over guardianship and custody (as related above), struck down an attempt to confer on the inferior court jurisdiction over occupancy of (and access to) the family residence. That jurisdiction could be conferred only on a s. 96 court, because of its impact on proprietary rights and its similarity to injunctive relief. This decision shows that a unified family court really has to be established at the level of a superior, district or county court (so that it is a s. 96 court).

(d) Provincial courts invested by Dominion

There is no doubt that jurisdiction to grant a divorce decree, and probably relief ancillary to a divorce decree, may be conferred by the provincial Legislatures only on a s. 96 court. But, because the substantive law of divorce is within federal legislative authority, the federal Parliament also has the power to invest courts with divorce jurisdiction. Moreover, s. 96 and the associated sections of the Constitution Act, 1867 do not apply to federal courts and tribunals. Therefore, the federal Parliament could if it chose confer divorce jurisdiction on a federally established court or tribunal which did not satisfy the rules stipulated by ss. 96 to 100. [In a footnote, Professor Hogg indicates that, as a result of the reasons in *McEvoy* v. *New Brunswick (Attorney General)*, [1983] 1 S.C.R. 704, Parliament probably could not confer divorce jurisdiction on a provincially established court or tribunal that did not satisfy ss. 96 to 100.]

The federal Parliament has in fact chosen to confer divorce jurisdiction on the superior court in each province. The action of the federal Parliament has not completely eliminated the s. 96 difficulty, however.

NOTES AND QUESTIONS

1. In *Kunkel* v. *Kunkel* (1994), 2 R.F.L. (4th) 1 (Alta. C.A.), the parties divorced in 1985 and the mother was granted custody of their son. The father was ordered to pay child support under the *Divorce Act*. The mother remarried and her new husband adopted the child. A majority of the Alberta Court of Appeal held that the father's obligation to pay child support ended when the adoption occurred even though there had been no variation of the order. Hetherington J.A. stated (at 9):

> [I]t is an implied term of every order for corollary relief under the *Divorce Act* that it is not final, and that if circumstances change, it may be superseded by an order of any court having jurisdiction, whether under the *Divorce Act*, a provincial statute, or the parens patriae jurisdiction of the court. For example, if a court granted an adoption order or a wardship order under provincial legislation, and that order was inconsistent with a prior order under the *Divorce Act*, the adoption order or wardship order would supersede the order for corollary relief.

If all corollary relief orders under the *Divorce Act* are interpreted in this way (and the Alberta Court of Appeal specifically indicated (at 8) that its reasoning applied to custody and access orders as well as support orders) the constitutional paramountcy issue is effectively finessed whenever a court is asked to make an order under provincial legislation at variance with the divorce order. As long as there has been a change in circumstances, the provincial order will supersede the divorce order. This has not been the predominant approach in the cases, however.

2. In *Lewkoski* v. *Lewkoski* (1998), 40 R.F.L. (4th) 86 (Ont. Gen. Div.), the court confirmed that it had jurisdiction to issue a child support order under the *Divorce Act* even though a final order had been

made under provincial legislation. However, the court added that it had a discretion not to exercise this jurisdiction and would do so only because this would be in the child's best interests. See also *Schaff* v. *Schaff* (1997), 30 R.F.L. (4th) 63 (B.C.C.A.).

The *Canadian Charter of Rights and Freedoms* became part of the Constitution of Canada in 1982. By virtue of s. 52(1) of the *Constitution Act, 1982* any law that is inconsistent with the *Charter* "is to the extent of the inconsistency of no force or effect". Therefore, the *Charter* can be used to challenge a law dealing with family matters on the basis that the law infringes or denies a guaranteed freedom or right. Sections 7 and 15 predictably have been the most commonly used *Charter* provisions in a family law context. Section 7 specifies that "[e]veryone has the right to life, liberty and security of the person and the right not to be deprived thereof except in accordance with the principles of fundamental justice". It could be argued that this section constitutionally guarantees the right to enjoy family life as an aspect of the "liberty and security of the person" (see generally Bala and Cruikshank, "Children and The Charter of Rights" in Landau, ed., *Children's Rights in the Practice of Family Law* (Toronto: Carswell, 1986) c. 2). Section 15 provides that "[e]very individual is equal before and under the law and has the right to the equal protection and equal benefit of the law without discrimination and, in particular, without discrimination based on race, national or ethnic origin, colour, religion, sex, age, or mental or physical handicap".

It should be stressed that not every law that affects or even infringes a guaranteed right or freedom is in conflict with the *Charter*. Section 1 of the *Charter* stipulates that "[t]he Canadian Charter of Rights and Freedoms guarantees the rights and freedoms set out in it subject only to such reasonable limits prescribed by law as can be demonstrably justified in a free and democratic society". A law that meets the test set out in s. 1 is not in conflict with the *Charter* even if a guaranteed right or freedom is curtailed by it. The leading case on the application of s. 1 is still *R*. v. *Oakes*, [1986] 1 S.C.R. 103, 50 C.R. (3d) 1.

In Canada, the potential impact of the *Charter* was dramatically exhibited in *R*. v. *Morgentaler*, [1988] 1 S.C.R. 30, 62 C.R. (3d) 1, where the Supreme Court of Canada, in a five-to-two decision, struck down s. 251 of the *Criminal Code*, which restricted the circumstances in which an abortion could legally be performed. Canadian courts have also begun to apply the *Charter* to the body of law traditionally referred to as family law, most notably in child protection and adoption proceedings. For example, in *M. (N.)* v. *Superintendent of Family & Child Services*, 10 B.C.L.R. (2d) 234, [1987] 3 W.W.R. 176 (S.C.), the court declared that a provincial law that required the consent to adoption of both parents if they were married, but only the mother's consent if the parents were not married, conflicted with s. 15 of the *Charter*. The law unjustifiably discriminated on the basis of marital status and sex.

At first, however, s. 2(c) and s. 7 claims made by parents in child protection hearings were generally denied without much analysis. See Thompson, "A Family Law Hitchhiker's Guide to the Charter Galaxy" (1989), 10 C.F.L.Q. 315; Thompson, "Why Hasn't the Charter Mattered in Child Protection?" (1989) 8 Can. J. Fam. L. 133; and Zylerberg, "Minimum Constitutional Guarantees in Child Protection Cases" (1992) 10 Can. J. Fam. L. 257. More recently, the *Charter* has began to play an increasingly prominent role in this context as a result of *B. (R.)* v. *C.A.S. of Metropolitan Toronto* (1995), 9 R.F.L. (4th) 157 (S.C.C.) (reproduced in Chapter 10), even though the parents' challenge to the procedures used to provide a blood transfusion to their infant failed. Significantly, La Forest J. stated (at p. 206): ". . . I would have thought it plain that the right to nurture a child, to care for its develop-ment, and to make decisions for it in fundamental matters, such as medical care, are part of the liberty interest of a parent." Gonthier, McLachlin, and L'Heureux-Dubé JJ. concurred with this statement, but Lamer C.J.C. disagreed (at p. 176): ". . . [S]ection 7 includes neither the right of parents to choose (or refuse) medical treat-ment for their children nor, more generally, the right to bring up or educate their children without undue influence by the state." Iacobucci and Major JJ. (Cory J. concurring) took a middle ground and concluded (at 250) that while some parental decisions might fall within the interests protected by s. 7, ". . . the right to liberty embedded in s. 7 does not include a parent's right to deny a child medical treatment that has been adjudged necessary by a medical professional". Mr. Justice Sopinka left the issue open, resting his holding that there had been no infringement of s. 7 on the fact that the procedure used accorded with the principles of fundamental justice.

In *B. (R.)*, five justices also concluded that freedom of religion guaranteed by s. 2(a) included the parents' right to raise children according to their religious beliefs. Any state interference with a parental decision to refuse medical treatment for their children because it conflicted with the tenets of the parents' faith had to be justified under s. 1. Four justices determined that a parent's freedom of religion did not include the right to impose religious practices on children that threaten their safety, health, or life.

The division within the S.C.C. over the scope of the liberty interest in s. 7 was avoided in *N.B. (Minister of Health & Community Services)* v. *G. (J.)* (1999), 177 D.L.R. (4th) 124 (S.C.C.) where the court unanimously concluded that the provincial government was under a constitutional duty to provide a mother with legal counsel in a child protection hearing which could lead to her children's placement in the care of the state. The court did not address whether the mother's liberty was engaged, but found that the proceedings affected her "security of the person". The proceedings did not comply with the principles of justice unless the mother, who could not afford a lawyer, had legal counsel. The effects of the proceeding, its complexity, and the mother's limited capabilities indicated that she could not get a fair hearing without counsel.

Also in the last half of the nineties, the courts have generally concluded that the limitation of familial rights and obligations to married persons or to opposite-sex relationships constitutes an unjustified infringement of s. 15. See *Miron* v. *Trudel* (1995), 13 R.F.L. (4th) 1 (S.C.C.); *Egan* v. *Canada* (1995), 12 R.F.L. (4th) 201 (S.C.C.); *Re K.* (1995), 15 R.F.L. (4th) 129 (Ont. Prov. Div.); *Taylor* v. *Rossu* (1998), 39 R.F.L. (4th) 242 (Alta. C.A.); *M.* v. *H.* (1999), 46 R.F.L. (4th) 32 (S.C.C.); and *Walsh* v. *Bona* (April 19, 2000), (unreported), Doc. C.A. 159139 (N.S.). These cases are discussed later in this chapter.

(3) INSTITUTIONAL FRAMEWORK

Historically, matters of family law were adjudicated by several different courts, some with provincially appointed judges and some with federally appointed ones. In "On Unified Family Courts" (1985), 42 R.F.L. (2d) 270, Judge Weisman identified the problems caused by this fragmented court system and advocated the creation of a Unified Family Court with jurisdiction to hear all family law matters. See also Law Reform Commission of Canada, *Family Law Court, Working Paper #1* (To-ronto: Ministry of the Attorney General, 1974) and Ontario Law Reform Commis-sion, *Report on Family Law, Part V: Family Courts* (Toronto: Ministry of the Attorney General, 1974).

Because s. 96 of the *Constitution Act, 1867* implicitly prevents a province from conferring a jurisdiction analogous to that exercised by a superior, district or county court in 1867 upon a provincially appointed judge, any Unified Family Court must be presided over by a federally appointed judge. Therefore, federal and provincial governments must co-operate in order to create a Unified Family Court.

In Ontario, a Unified Family Court was established in the judicial district of Hamilton-Wentworth in 1977. To deal with the problems created by s. 96 of the *Constitution Act, 1867*, judges of the Unified Family Court were appointed by concurrent action of the provincial and federal governments. A set of rules developed to provide for simplified procedures and for conciliation and mediation. Further, the Unified Family Court worked closely with other social agencies of the province. In *Report of the Ontario Courts Inquiry* (Toronto: Ministry of the Attorney General, 1987), the Honourable T.G. Zuber concluded (at 99):

> The Unified Family Court of Hamilton-Wentworth is working well and has worked for the benefit of the people it serves for the past ten years. It is therefore apparent that the concept of the unified family court is not only good in theory; it is good in practice.

Mr. Justice Zuber recommended that there should be a Unified Family Court for the province of Ontario as part of the provincial court system. He acknowledged (at 102) that this would require a constitutional amendment to permit the province to appoint judges with full power to deal with family law matters.

In 1994 the Ontario Legislature amended the *Courts of Justice Act* to create a branch of the Ontario Court (General Division) (now the Superior Court of Justice) known as the Family Court (S.O. 1994, c. 12, s. 8). The Unified Family Court was amalgamated with and continued as part of the Family Court. The Family Court has jurisdiction in the Regional Municipality of Hamilton-Wentworth and in the additional areas named by proclamation of the Lieutenant Governor in Council. In the fall of 1995, Family Courts began to operate in London, Newmarket, Kingston, and Napanee. As a branch of the Superior Court of Justice, the Family Court is a s. 96 court with federally appointed and federally paid judges. The amendments to the *Courts of Justice Act* provided for the establishment of a "community resources committee" to "develop links between the court and social services available in the community, identify needed resources and develop strategies for putting them in place" and also stipulated that an alternative dispute resolution service "may be established, maintained and operated as part of the Family Court".

The utility of the judicial process, featuring the traditional adversarial approach, as a mechanism for dealing with family breakdown is itself being questioned. In the following presentation to students in the Faculty of Law at the University of Saskatchewan, Professor Payne examined alternatives to litigation.

PAYNE, "FAMILY CONFLICT RESOLUTION: DEALING WITH THE CONSEQUENCES OF MARRIAGE BREAKDOWN THROUGH COUNSELING, NEGOTIATION, MEDIATION AND ARBITRATION"

(1997)

1.   Recent Trends in Family Dispute Resolution

Many lawyers and judges have now joined their critics from other disciplines by acknowledging the limitations of the legal system in resolving disputes between separated and divorced spouses. Statutory provisions, regulations and rules of court governing such matters as mandatory financial disclosure, case management, pre-trials, mediation, independent expert assessments, and formal offers to settle, manifest the realization that litigation must be regarded as a last resort in the resolution of family disputes. There is a desperate need for family law to focus much more on processes for dispute resolution. Sections 9 and 10 of the Divorce Act pay lip service to the benefits of counseling, negotiation and mediation as processes for resolving family disputes but do nothing to foster the use of these processes. More far reaching statutory provisions respecting mediation are found in some provincial statutes. Legal aid is sometimes available to meet the costs of mediation. Several provincial law societies have endorsed the practice of family mediation by legal practitioners. These are all signposts for the future.

Although court-connected mediation services are not new to Canada in family dispute resolution, they are likely to play a more substantial role in the future as governments seek to reduce the cost of access to justice. Budgetary restraints will, of course, continue to limit the resources available to promote the consensual resolution of family disputes with the aid of court-connected services. Consequently, there will be a growing demand for private and community services.

2.   The Crises of Marriage Breakdown

For most families, marriage breakdown provokes three crises: an emotional crisis; an economic crisis; and a parenting crisis. Both of the spouses and their children suffer severe emotional upheaval when the unity of the family disintegrates. Furthermore, few families encounter separation or divorce without suffering financial setbacks. The emotional and economic crises resulting from marriage breakdown are compounded by the co-parental divorce when there are dependent children. Bonding between children and their absent parent is inevitably threatened by marriage breakdown.

Constructive resolution of these three crises requires the passage of time and appropriate intervention by professionals who are consulted by the family members. The dynamics of marriage breakdown, which are multi-faceted, cannot be addressed in isolation. In the search for appropriate processes to deal with breakdown, divorcing couples must not lose control over their own lives. Judicial decrees and expert assessments that exclude the family members from the decision making are insufficient. Omniscience is not the prerogative of any profession and the family's right to self-determination should not be lightly ignored.

3.   The Emotional Divorce

When marriage breakdown occurs, a grieving process is experienced by each of the spouses and their children. This grieving process or "emotional divorce" passes through various stages, including denial, hostility and depression, to the ultimate acceptance of the death of the marriage. Working through the spousal emotional divorce rarely takes less than 2 years. In the meantime, permanent and legally binding decisions are often made to regulate the economic and parenting consequences of the marriage breakdown. Separated spouses, lawyers, and mediators must become more aware of the risk of premature settlements negotiated at a time when one or both of the spouses are undergoing the emotional trauma of marriage breakdown. Indeed, when either spouse is going through severe emotional turmoil, a cooling-off period would be desirable during which time any negotiated settlement should focus on the short term, rather than the long term, needs and concerns of the spouses and their children. Spouses, lawyers and mediators should assess the potential for temporary agreements being only the first stage in the resolution of the economic and parenting consequences of the marriage breakdown.

Although divorce is rarely painless, especially when children are involved, the trauma of marriage breakdown can be eased by therapy, counseling and by access to informational and educational programs. In some urban centres, divorcing parents are required to attend programs that examine the impact of their conduct on the children and offer advice to parents that can reduce harmful conduct, such as using children as weapons or pawns in the spousal conflict, fighting over the children, criticizing the other spouse in the presence of the children, or competing for the children's affection. Time may also be spent in dealing with practical matters such as household budgets, reaching fair child support arrangements and providing guidelines or structures for parenting arrangements. Separate courses are sometimes provided for the children of divorcing parents that are designed to help the children deal with their feelings of loss, guilt, fear and grief.

4.   Marriage and Family Counseling

Counseling is readily available to families in crisis who reside in urban centres. Professionals in private practice who have expertise in social work, psychology or psychiatry, offer marriage, family and individual counseling on a fee paying basis. Community agencies may provide counseling services free of charge or assess a fee based on a sliding scale to reflect the ability to pay.

In previous generations, marriage and family counseling focused on reconciliation. A couple contemplating divorce was urged to reconcile. Today, reconciliation is regarded as only one option. Marriage and family counseling is increasingly directed towards helping families understand how they will be affected by separation or divorce and how they can deal with the emotional, economic and parenting consequences of marriage breakdown. Marriage and family counseling is regarded as therapeutic in nature, even if it falls short of providing a sustained program of family therapy. The day-to-day consequences of marriage breakdown are important aspects of family counseling. Family members may be referred to specialized community services, such as safe havens for battered women, alcohol and drug addiction treatment centres, vocational retraining programs, social assistance agencies and housing services. In recent years, community-based Family Service Agencies have provided mediation services to deal with parenting disputes between separated and divorced spouses. They rarely mediate disputes concerning property or spousal support.

5.   Negotiation

Less than 4 percent of divorces involve a trial of contested issues in open court. Divorcing spouses normally settle their disputes by negotiation, often with the benefit of legal representation. Couples caught up in the emotional dynamics of marriage breakdown have difficulty communicating with each other. Their emotions cloud their judgment. One or both may not have worked through the emotional divorce. The interplay between the emotional dynamics of marriage breakdown and regulation of the economic consequences of marriage breakdown may be demonstrated by the following examples. A needy spouse who makes no claim for spousal support may be manifesting a hope for reconciliation or a state of depression. A guilty spouse may seek to expiate guilt by asking for too little or by giving too much. A hostile spouse, who is seeking revenge for rejection, may exact too heavy a price, even at the risk of triggering acrimonious negotiations or protracted litigation. These are all inappropriate responses to dealing with the practical consequences of marriage breakdown. The object of any negotiations is to reach a reasonable settlement that both spouses can live with and that reflects the interests of any children.

Equitable and workable settlements in the emotionally charged atmosphere of marriage breakdown or divorce often necessitate the intervention of lawyers or other third parties, such as mediators, who can bring objectivity to the bargaining table.

(a) The Importance of Negotiation

Negotiation is the most effective way of resolving disputes. It leaves the decision-making authority with the disputants. It is also cost-efficient and time-saving when compared to other means of dispute resolution. Good negotiation skills are a prerequisite to the constructive resolution of family disputes.

(b) Negotiation Techniques

There are three basic approaches to negotiation: (i) hard bargaining; (ii) soft bargaining; and (iii) principled negotiation. These approaches are reviewed by Roger Fisher and William Ury in their best selling book, *Getting to Yes*. At the risk of over simplification, the following summary may shed light on their differences.

Hard bargaining reflects a competitive or adversarial approach to negotiation. The hard bargainer takes a position and is difficult to shift from that position. He or she makes concessions reluctantly but demands liberal concessions from the other side. Hard bargaining does not necessarily involve unethical or improper conduct but does imply that the dispute involves a contest of wills which the hard bargainer is seeking to win.

Soft bargaining signifies an excessive degree of compliance and the avoidance of confrontation. Soft bargainers make too many concessions without demanding a fair return. Soft bargainers are particularly vulnerable when negotiating with hard bargainers.

So-called principled negotiators, unlike hard and soft bargainers, strive to avoid positional bargaining. They perceive themselves as joint problem solvers. Fisher and Ury have identified the following five characteristics of principled negotiation:

1. Separate the people from the problem.
2. Focus on interests, not positions.
3. Generate options that will be advantageous to both parties.
4. Insist that the result be based on objective standards.
5. Know the best alternative to a negotiated settlement (BATNA).

In separating the people from the problem in family disputes, the disputants must avoid the blame game. They should attack the problem, not each other.

Fisher and Ury's insistence that negotiations focus on interests, not positions, implies that behind every demand there is a need, desire or concern. Interests may be material, such as money or property, or they may be psychological, such as the need for recognition or security. Focusing on interests can identify complementary and disparate interests of the disputants and provide opportunities for compromise or trade-offs that lead to agreement.

Generating options for mutual gain fosters successful negotiations. For example, it may be better for both the spouses and the children if the parents share responsibility for raising their children rather than leaving the responsibility to one of the parents and relegating the other parent to the status of a passive bystander. Options that are advantageous to both sides increase the prospect of reaching a mutually acceptable solution.

The use of objective standards to evaluate possible solutions promotes reasonable settlements. Objective criteria relied on by family law practitioners include relevant statutory provisions, case law and, most recently, the proposed federal Child Support Guidelines.

Knowing and keeping in mind the best alternative to a negotiated agreement enables disputants to accept reasonable settlements and reject unreasonable proposals.

The idea that principled negotiation will substitute win/win solutions for the win/lose philosophy of adversarial bargaining is not without its critics. It may, nevertheless, prove attractive to separated and divorced spouses who can ill-afford to engage in hostile legal negotiations or protracted litigation.

6.   Mediation

(a)   Nature of Mediation

The essence of mediation is that the family members are themselves responsible for determining the consequences of their divorce. Self-determination with the aid of an impartial third party is the cornerstone of mediation. The mediator must defuse family conflict to a level where the parties can communicate with each other. They can then look at their options and apply objective standards with a view to negotiating a reasonable settlement. Mediation is not to be confused with family therapy. Divorce mediation is a process that is aimed at facilitating the consensual resolution of the economic and parenting problems that result from marriage breakdown. It is a time-limited process that is intended to produce a formal settlement. Mediators are not marriage counsellors or therapists. They deal with the consequences, not the causes, of marriage breakdown.

(b)   Approaches to Mediation

Mediation is not a monolithic process. Systems and processes vary even though the goal of consensual resolution is constant. Mediators may be engaged in private practice. They may be connected with courts. They may work in community agencies.

Many mediators are either social workers or psychologists. There are a few psychiatrists and lawyers who practise mediation. Mediators without legal qualifications usually, but not always, confine their practice to parenting disputes. Some mediators have no direct link with the established professions and are self-made, and in some cases self-proclaimed. Successful mediation presupposes high professional standards because of the control a mediator exercises over the process and because one or both of the clients are frequently disadvantaged by the trauma of marriage breakdown. Mediation may belong to the parties but a successful outcome is dependent on the expertise of the mediator. Family members who look to private mediation as a means of dispute resolution must undertake careful inquiries to ensure that they have recourse to a competent and experienced mediator.

There are two schools of thought respecting the fundamental nature of the mediation process. Some mediators characterize the process as transformational. They contend that it is a process that empowers disputants to foster their personal growth on their way to resolving the particular disputes that brought them into mediation. Others regard the mediation process as being far less ambitious in scope. They believe that mediation focuses on the resolution of practical problems rather than on transforming the disputants who have recourse to the process. The difference between these two schools of thought may be one of degree rather than kind. It is noteworthy, however, that court-connected mediation services often place a heavy emphasis on rights-based, rather than interest-based negotiation, and positive evaluation of these services is usually premised on the settlement rates achieved.

(c) Reasons for Mediation

The most common responses to conflict are "fight or flight." Often neither is the right response. Mediation provides an alternative when spouses or former spouses cannot negotiate directly with each other but wish to avoid the adversarial postures of the legal process. For many couples, mediation offers greater opportunities for them to retain control over their own lives. Mediation can facilitate tailor-made solutions to individual problems. Family members are often intimidated by the formal complexity and adversarial nature of the legal process. Mediation is less threatening than the legal process and its self-determined agreements may prove more durable and adaptable than court-ordered settlements.

Successful mediation is much cheaper than protracted litigation. However, comparing the costs of successful mediation and litigation is misleading. Not all mediation attempts are successful. Furthermore, the vast majority of divorces involve the negotiation of settlements by lawyers. Very few divorces involve a trial. Assisted negotiation through the mediation process is not necessarily cheaper than assisted negotiation through the legal process.

In parenting disputes, mediation can establish a framework for future communication and an ongoing exchange of information and ideas respecting the upbringing of the children.

(d) Circumstances in which Mediation is Inappropriate

Mediation is not appropriate for everyone. In some cases, inequalities of bargaining power between the spouses may render mediation inappropriate. People with a "winner take all" mentality are not good candidates for mediation which requires an attitude of "give and take" and compromise. Some feminist commentators have suggested that mediation is always disadvantageous to women because of an inherent imbalance of power between the sexes. It is questionable whether legal processes, or any other processes, assure any greater protection to women in the absence of domestic violence. Many mediators contend that mediation is inappropriate when either of the parties is physically violent, addicted to alcohol or drugs, or cannot face the reality of the death of the marriage. Spouses falling within the last category may need counseling or therapy as a prelude to participating in a mediation process.

(e) Role of Mediator; Neutrality of Mediator

Unlike the lawyer, whose role is to represent the interests of his or her client, mediators must preserve a neutral stance; they must also be perceived as non-partisan by the disputants. If a mediator is perceived as taking sides, his or her credibility is destroyed and the parties will lose confidence in the process. The term "neutral" does not mean a mediator must be passive. Mediators can take active roles to facilitate settlement and their training and personal value systems will clearly affect their overall approach to the mediation process. Intervention, though quite legitimate for such purposes as restructuring the lines of communication or identifying new avenues for exploration, must stop short of taking the decision making authority away from the parties.

(f) Redressing Power Imbalances

Mediation can be an empowering process insofar as it fosters respect and cooperation but a successful outcome depends on active participation by both spouses and requires a relatively balanced capacity to negotiate. True equality in the balance of power may be impossible to achieve, but the mediator must prevent an abuse of power by either disputant. Mediators can use a variety of techniques to redress an imbalance of power between the parties. For example, if inequality of bargaining power stems from lack of knowledge, information can be provided. Unequal negotiating skills can sometimes be balanced by insightful intervention and restructuring by the mediator or by the allocation of joint assignments to the parties. Intimidating negotiation patterns can be interrupted and reframed in order to provide support to the disadvantaged party. However, where the imbalance of power is considered to be so great that the mediator cannot intervene without endangering his or her neutrality, the mediator should recommend other means of resolving the dispute.

(g) Professional and Community Responses to Mediation

The future of family mediation will largely depend on its use by professional groups and by Canadian families in crisis. There is a public need for broadly based and ongoing sources of information, whether provided through the mass media, the schools, community agencies, or under professional auspices, such as the Church, Medicine and Law. The professions must themselves become educated.

Information is required to dispel the myths of mediation. Members of the legal community, who view their vested interests as being threatened by the emerging process of mediation, have to be reassured that the legal system is not undermined by mediation. Indeed, the legal system and mediation are complementary, rather than competing or contradictory, processes. Both seek to provide a solution to disputes. Each has its place. Neither is self-sufficient.

(h) The Future of Family Mediation

Mediation, whether court-connected or private, has found a growing place in the resolution of family disputes during the last 15 years. At present, divorce mediation in Canada is largely confined to parenting disputes. This is being done primarily by mediators with training in social work, psychology or psychiatry. On rare occasions, support and property disputes on marriage breakdown are mediated. In these cases, the mediator is much more likely to be a lawyer. This division of function, whereby non-lawyers mediate parenting disputes while lawyers mediate the economics of divorce, is a division of convenience that is currently acceptable to most, but not all, mediators. In the long term, comprehensive or "total package" mediation will become commonplace.

A closer association must be established between lawyers and other professionals engaged in advising and assisting families in crisis. Indeed, the time will come when community centres, staffed by lawyers, doctors, psychologists, social workers and other professionals, as well as by volunteers, will provide a comprehensive approach to the resolution of the multi-faceted crises of marriage breakdown. In the meantime, the various professions and federal, provincial and municipal governmental agencies (including Departments as diverse as Communications, Education, Employment, Housing Finance, Revenue Canada, Health and Welfare, and Justice), which are directly or indirectly involved in the systemic management of the human process of marriage breakdown, must recognize their own limitations and foster effective lines of communication in the search for solutions to the human and socio-economic problems associated with marriage breakdown.

7.   Arbitration

Mediation of family disputes leaves decision making to the parties. If they cannot resolve the issues, an independent arbiter may be called upon to determine their respective rights and obligations. Traditionally, this function has been discharged by courts.

Private arbitration has displaced litigation as a means of resolving labour disputes. To a much lesser extent, arbitration has also been recognized as an effective means of resolving commercial disputes. The use of binding arbitration instead of litigation to resolve spousal disputes respecting property division, spousal and child support, and child custody and access on marriage breakdown or divorce is rare in Canada.

(a)   Advantages of Arbitration

Private arbitration has the following potential advantages over litigation as a family dispute resolution process:

1.   The parties are directly involved in the appointment of the arbitrator. An arbitrator can be selected having regard to the nature of the dispute and the arbitrator's qualifications and expertise. In litigation, the parties are not free to select a particular judge. Furthermore, the judge is not usually a specialist in family law and may have no interest in, or even an aversion to, adjudicating spousal or parental disputes.
2.   Litigants are often intimidated by the formality and adversarial atmosphere of the court. An arbitration hearing can be as formal or informal as the parties wish.
3.   Arbitrators make themselves available to suit the convenience of the disputants.
4.   Arbitration can be procedurally less complex and much speedier than contested litigation.
5.   Arbitrations are conducted in private. Courtrooms are open to the public and the media.
6.   Arbitration is usually cheaper than litigation, even though the disputants pay the arbitrator's fees.
7.   The costs of arbitration are more predictable than those of litigation.

Some disadvantages of arbitration may be:

1. Arbitrators, unlike judges, may not be bound by substantive and procedural laws. The absence of "due process" can lead to arbitrary results.
2. Arbitrators may be inclined to split the difference on substantive matters in dispute without sufficient regard to the merits of the case.
3. Some arbitrators are disinclined to order costs in favour of either party.

(b) Court-Annexed Arbitration

Some form of court-annexed arbitration might ultimately be endorsed in Canada as an alternative process for the resolution of family disputes. Court-annexed arbitration has been introduced in several jurisdictions in the United States to cope with the flood of civil litigation. Court-annexed arbitration differs from private arbitration in several ways. Court-annexed arbitration is usually mandatory rather than voluntary and the arbitrator is assigned by the court and not chosen by the disputants. Most importantly, court-annexed arbitration is usually advisory, rather than binding. If the disputants accept the arbitration award, it is entered as a court judgment and is enforceable as such. If the arbitration award is rejected by either party, the issues go to trial and are adjudicated without reference being made to the arbitration award. Most court-annexed programs impose penalties on a disputant if the trial judgment affords no greater relief than that given under the arbitration award.

(c) Evaluation of Arbitration

Arbitration is a rational alternative to litigation for separated and divorced spouses. They should be entitled to opt for binding private arbitration, with or without a right of appeal, instead of being compelled to resort to overcrowded trial courts. A residual discretionary jurisdiction should be vested in the courts, however, to override an arbitration award when the best interests of a child necessitate judicial intervention.

8.   Med-Arb

Mediation and arbitration need not be exclusive of one another. "Med-Arb" is a process that utilizes both approaches. Typically, a fixed time will be set aside for mediation, with the understanding that if no consensus is reached, the mediator will then act as an arbitrator who will give a final and binding decision. Knowing that unresolved issues will proceed to arbitration may help parties to reach a consensus in the final stages of the mediation process.

9.   Concluding Observations

This paper has focused on counseling, negotiation, mediation, arbitration and med-arb as processes that can be used as alternatives to, or in conjunction with, litigation as means of resolving the emotional, economic and parenting consequences of marriage breakdown. This paper does not canvass or even catalogue all of the processes that can be applied or adapted to family conflict management and dispute resolution. Nor does it recommend the outright rejection of legal processes in favour of other processes. Indeed, separated and divorced spouses will usually find it advantageous to avoid locking themselves into a single process in their attempts to resolve the multi-faceted problems generated by their marriage breakdown. Let me take a few examples of when it is appropriate to utilize more than one process. Negotiations do, and must, continue even after legal proceedings have been instituted. Indeed, the institution of legal proceedings may trigger an early settlement and, even when matters proceed further, eve of trial settlements are common. Divorcing or divorced couples may use different processes to deal with different aspects of their marriage breakdown. Individual or family counseling and therapy may be appropriate as a prelude to mediation. Arbitration may be used to resolve an impasse that has been reached in mediation. Parenting mediation may co-exist with a motion to a court, perhaps on consent, to determine urgent matters relating to interim possession of the family home or the amount of spousal or child support.

Separated and divorced couples must be made aware of the diversity of processes available to foster family conflict management and dispute resolution. Only then can they examine their options in such a way as to reflect their respective interests and those of any children.

NOTES AND QUESTIONS

1. Section 9(2) of the *Divorce Act* requires that the lawyer acting in the divorce proceeding discuss with his or her client "the advisability of negotiating the matters that may be the subject of a support order or a custody order" and inform the client "of the mediation facilities known to him or her that might be able to assist the spouses in negotiating those matters". See also s. 9(3).

Section 31(1) of the Ontario *Children's Law Reform Act* authorizes the court, at the request of the parties, to appoint a person selected by the parties to mediate any aspect of a custody dispute. Mediation conducted pursuant to this section can be either "open" or "closed" at the option of the parties. See ss. 31(4) and (7). In "open" mediation, what goes on and is said during the mediation is revealed if a settlement is not reached. In "closed" mediation, the opposite occurs and everything is confidential. The latter type is prevalent.

Do you think that the legislation should go further and impose mandatory mediation of, at least, custody and access disputes? The Special Joint Committee of the House of Commons and the Senate reported in *For the Sake of the Children* (1999), at 32, that Quebec legislation requires divorcing parents to attend at least one information session about the benefits of mediation. If the parents then decide to use mediation, they are entitled to up to six sessions at public expense. The legislation permits opting out of the process, including the information session, in cases of domestic violence. The committee recommended (at 33) that "divorcing parents be encouraged to attend at least one mediation session to help them develop a parenting plan for their children". It added:

> Where there is a proven history of violence by one parent toward the other or toward the children, alternative forms of dispute resolution should be used only when the safety of the person who has been the victim of the violence is assured and where the risk of violence has passed. The resulting parental plan must focus on parental responsibilities for the children and contain measures to ensure safety and security for parents and children.

2. Even where parties can reach a mediated settlement, independent legal advice may be important. Indeed, most mediators encourage or require the parties to seek such advice prior to mediation so that they can make informed choices during the mediation with knowledge of their legal rights. Furthermore, it is common practice for the parties' lawyers to review a mediated settlement and prepare a formal contract or minutes of settlement.

3. For further reading on mediation, see Ryan, "The Lawyer as Mediator: A New Role for Lawyers in the Practice of Nonadversarial Divorce" (1986-87), 1 C.F.L.Q. 105; Leitch, "The Politics of Compromise: A Feminist Perspective on Mediation" (1987), 14/15 Mediation Q. 163; Shaffer, "Divorce Mediation: A Feminist Perspective" (1988), 46 U. of T. Fac. L. Rev. 162; Bailey, "Unpacking the 'Rational Alternative': A Critical Review of Family Mediation Claims" (1989), 8 Can. J. Fam. L. 61;

Austin, Jaffe, and Hurley, "Incorporating Children's Needs and Views in Alternative Dispute Resolution Approaches" (1992), 8 C.F.L.Q. 69; Hubley, "Mediation — At the Crossroads" (1992), 9 C.F.L.Q. 73; *Court-Connected Family Mediation Programs in Canada* (Edmonton: Alberta Law Reform Institute, 1994); Miller, "Mediation in Divorce" (1994), 18 L. Now 16; Irving and Benjamin, *Family Mediation* (Toronto: Sage Pub., 1995); Phegan, "The Family Mediation System: An Art of Distributions" (1995), 40 McGill L.J. 365; Landau *et al*, *Family Mediation Handbook*, 2nd.ed. (Butterworths, 1997); Goundry *et al*, *Family Mediation in Canada: Implications for Women's Equality* (Status of Women Canada, 1998); Reeve, "The Quandary of Setting Standards for Mediators: Where Are We Headed?" (1998), 23 Queen's L.J. 441; Irving and Benjamin, "Child Custody Disputes, Family Mediation and Proposed Reform of *Divorce Act*" (1999), 16 C.F.L.Q. 413; and Noble, *Family Mediation: A Guide for Lawyers* (Canada Law Book, 1999).

4. To encourage settlement through negotiation, the new *Family Law Rules*, O. Reg. 114/99, envision at least one and possibly two or three conferences before a trial. In every defended case there must be at least one case conference to explore the chances of settlement, identify the issues that are in dispute, provide disclosure, note admissions, and set the next steps in the case. In addition, there can also be a settlement conference and a trial management conference or a combination of both. These rules apply to the Superior Court of Justice (Family Court) and the Court of Justice. The *Rules of Procedure*, R.R.O. 1990, Reg. 194 (as amended), which continue to apply to family cases in the Superior Court of Justice in those parts of the province where a unified Family Court has not yet been established, deal with pre-trials in Rule 50.

(4) CONFLICT OF LAWS

Canadians live in a mobile society. As a result, courts are often called upon to deal with cases in which there is a relevant foreign element. The body of rules and principles that has developed to resolve these cases is called conflict of laws. It is hoped that the following extract will help the student understand the nature of conflict of laws and why this subject is important in family law. Although some conflict of laws issues will be referred to at various times in this book, students who wish to practise in the area of family law are urged to take a specific course dealing with the conflict of laws.

SILVERMAN, "CONFLICT OF LAWS: SOME MATRIMONIAL PROBLEMS"

(1979), 2 Fam. L. Rev. 103

In the realm of conflict of laws, there are three kinds of problems which the courts have to face. First, a court may have to decide whether to apply the law of its own country or of a foreign country in deciding a case. For example, if a person from Ontario makes a business contract with a person from New York, should it be the law of Ontario or of New York which determines whether the contract has been breached? This is called a *choice of law* problem.

Second, a court may have to decide whether to assume jurisdiction in a certain case. For example, if a husband and wife in New York are fighting about who should have custody of their child, and the husband "kidnaps" the child into Ontario, should he be able to bring an action in Ontario for the custody of the child? This is called a *jurisdiction* problem.

Finally, a court may have to decide whether to recognize the judgment of the court of a foreign country. For example, if a Canadian couple goes to Mexico to get a divorce should a Canadian court recognize the Mexican divorce? This is called a *recognition* problem. One special kind of recognition problem is that of *enforcement*. For example, if a wife obtains a maintenance order against her husband in New

York, and then he moves to Ontario, should an Ontario court be able to enforce the maintenance order against him?

Sometimes jurisdiction problems and choice of law problems blend into each other. This is because in some cases the courts feel that they should only assume jurisdiction to hear a case if it is the law of their country which is the proper law to apply. For example, courts may be unwilling to apply the divorce law of other countries, hence they will only assume jurisdiction if the divorce law of their country is the proper law to apply.

As a result, a special body of rules and legal principles has arisen to make some order out of a potentially chaotic situation, and this special body is called Conflict of Laws.

Before a case can be heard in our courts, the first prerequisite is that the court process should be available to the petitioner and that the court has jurisdiction to hear the case, *e.g.* do the parties have status to bring the proceeding in that court, and have all of the prerequisite procedural devices been followed. After that is satisfied, the court has to determine the nature of the case before it, *i.e.* is it one of contract, tort, divorce, or whatever, which is called either classification of the cause of action or characterization of the issue (or question); and then it has to decide which legal system to apply to decide the matter. The foregoing illustration of the stages which a court will follow is really an oversimplification of what may happen, for it should be noted that the questions of jurisdiction and classification are frequently so closely interwoven that they cannot be answered separately and in a step-by-step fashion.

Thus in solving the problems which we have set out above in our various examples, the courts make use of what they call *connecting factors*. For example, in dealing with a choice of law problem in contracts, the court may say that the connecting factor is the place where the contract was made, so that it is the law of that country which should be applied. Or in dealing with a jurisdiction problem in a custody case, the court may decide that the connecting factor is the place where the child ordinarily resides, so that it is the courts of that country which should have jurisdiction. Similarly, in a divorce recognition case, the court may say that the connecting factor is the place where the couple makes their home, so that it will recognize the divorce decree only if it was made by a court of that country. Therefore, one of the most important issues in conflict of laws is determining what connecting factors should be used by the courts in solving conflicts problems.

[For further reading, see Pilcow and Melamed, "A Practitioner's Guide to Conflicts in Family Law" (1988), 3 C.F.L.Q. 227; McLeod, "The Judicial Approach to Matrimonial Property Disputes and the Conflict of Laws" (1993), 9 C.F.L.Q. 203; Welling, "Conflict of Laws Issues Arising from Matrimonial Property Statutes in Canada" (1993), 9 C.F.L.Q. 225; Dicey and Morris, *The Conflict of Laws*, 12th ed. (London: Sweet & Maxwell, 1993); and Castel, *Canadian Conflict of Laws*, 4th ed. (Toronto: Butterworths, 1997).]

(5) LEGAL DEFINITION OF THE FAMILY

While the majority of cohabiting couples in Canada continue to be married to one another, cohabitation without marriage has become much more common. One of the issues confronted by the legislatures and courts in the past few decades is whether this type of familial relationship should be accorded legal recognition. In particular, should the status, rights and responsibilities granted to married spouses be extended to unmarried cohabitees? If so, should same-sex couples be included in this legal regime? In one sense, these questions require the legal system to determine what entity qualifies as a "family". Beginning in the seventies, most provincial legislatures gradually extended some of the family law rules, particularly those relating to support, to some unmarried cohabitees of opposite sex. The provincial legislatures and Parliament also began to treat certain unmarried cohabitees as spouses for tax purposes and for statutory benefits. However, significant differences in the legal treatment of married and common-law couples remained. This gave rise to *Charter* litigation based on s. 15 in the 1990's, as did the legislative differentiation between opposite-sex couples and same-sex couples.

TAYLOR v. ROSSU

(1998), 39 R.F.L. (4th) 242 (Alta. C.A.)

Per curiam: This appeal involves a challenge to the constitutionality of the support provisions of the Alberta *Domestic Relations Act*, R.S.A. 1980, c. D-37 (*DRA*). At trial, the Respondent Taylor successfully argued that her equality rights under s. 15 of the . . . *Charter* . . . were breached because the support provisions of the *DRA* applied only to legally married spouses. Taylor and Rossu lived together for some 29 years. By withholding the benefit of access to support from her, the trial judge held that the legislation discriminated on the basis of marital status. Reliance was placed on *Miron v. Trudel*, [1995] 2 S.C.R. 418, 124 D.L.R. (4th) 693, 13 R.F.L. (4th) 1 (S.C.C.) (cited to R.F.L.) (*Miron*), in which it was held that marital status was analogous to the prohibited grounds of discrimination enumerated in s. 15 of the *Charter*. [In *Miron*, certain benefits under an Ontario Standard Automobile Policy, the terms of which were set by the provincial *Insurance Act*, were available only to "spouses" of the insured motorist. The term was not defined in the legislation, but it was interpreted to include only married persons. In 1990, after the accident giving rise to the constitutional challenge, the definition was amended to include persons who cohabited for three or more years or cohabited in a relationship of some permanence if they were the biological or adoptive parents of a child. This amendment was not retroactive and so did not apply to the accident in question. In a 5-4 decision, the S.C.C. held that the legislation, as it existed prior to the amendment, violated s. 15(1) of the *Charter* because it discriminated on the basis of marital status, a ground analogous to those listed in s. 15(1).]

After finding that the word "spouse" in the *DRA* could not be interpreted as meaning both legally married and common law spouses, the trial judge held that the *Act* breached the respondent's *Charter* rights. His remedy was to read in "common law spouse" to the word "spouse" in the impugned provisions. He then awarded Taylor interim support. No trial has yet been held in this matter. Thus the claim for permanent support, as well as claims for a division of property, including an unjust enrichment action and a *Charter* challenge of the *Matrimonial Property Act*, R.S.A. 1980, c. M-9, remain outstanding. The Appellant Rossu appeals that ruling.

Facts

Taylor and Rossu lived together between 1964 and 1994. For most of that period they resided in a Calgary house that Rossu had purchased prior to the commencement of the relationship. Taylor had a daughter from a previous relationship, and was having difficulties with her finances and with child welfare authorities when she met Rossu. Rossu's concern for the child's welfare played a large role in his decision to allow Taylor and her child to move into his home. He promised the child welfare authorities that he would provide for the child, and he believed it was incumbent upon him to honour this commitment.

During the relationship, Rossu assisted with the child's care and provided funds for her support, including paying for groceries, clothing and other items. The child lived with Rossu and Taylor until she married in her early twenties. Rossu also supported Taylor during the relationship while she assisted him with chores around the house. She worked during part of the relationship and the parties had a joint bank account for a four- or five-year period.

The parties had sexual relations throughout the first 25 years of the relationship, although they maintained separate bedrooms. Rossu's affidavit states that Taylor was repeatedly unfaithful to him. This caused difficulties between the parties, but Taylor allegedly answered Rossu's reproaches with comments to the effect that as she was not married to him, she was free to do whatever she wanted. Rossu states that he ceased having sexual relations with Taylor in 1989 because he was concerned about possible health consequences of her infidelity.

Rossu is now 68 years of age. The trial judge found his current income to be $1,506.00 per month. This income is composed of his pension from the Canadian Pacific Railway (C.P.R.), the Canada Pension Plan (C.P.P.) and Old Age Security (O.A.S.). He also has approximately $50,000.00 in R.R.S.P.'s. He lives alone in the house in which the parties cohabited, which is worth approximately $100,000.00.

Taylor is now 54 years of age. She suffers from bipolar affective disorder. This disorder causes cyclical manic and depressive episodes but can be treated with medication. She lives with her daughter. Her income is $549.00 per month from social assistance. At trial she claimed monthly expenses of $638.48 (including legal fees of $138.48) but at the appeal she quantified those expenses at $500.38 per month.

Taylor may have certain claims to Rossu's income beyond this litigation. She can apply for a division of his C.P.P. credits, which would have the effect of reducing his pension income, and entitling her to a pension at age 60. She has not yet applied for these credits because Rossu has disputed that she was his common law partner. It is unclear whether her pension entitlement is being eroded by this delay. In the event of his death, she would be entitled to a survivor's benefit of $433.00 from the C.P.P. If she predeceases him, she realizes no benefit. There also appears to be a survivor's benefit based on actuarial values under the O.A.S.

The trial of this action includes a constructive trust claim, a claim under the *Matrimonial Property Act*, and a claim for permanent support. The property division and permanent support arguments are accompanied by *Charter* arguments comparable to the argument here. The Queen's Bench order under appeal granted Taylor interim alimony in the amount of $750.00 per month. It also prevented Rossu from dissipating his assets before the trial. . . .

Legislation in other Canadian Jurisdictions

Most Canadian jurisdictions have extended their family legislation to provide for support for common law partners. However, the definition of common law spouse is not consistent among jurisdictions. Some require a two year relationship and application within one year of separation, and others impose five, three or one year qualifying periods. One jurisdiction simply specifies a relationship of "some permanence". Most jurisdictions agree that partners who have had a natural child together constitute common law partners, and some provide that partners who have adopted a child together constitute common law partners.

The extension of rights and obligations to common law partners has been done on a piecemeal basis. For example, those jurisdictions which extend support rights and obligations to cohabitants do not always extend rights and obligations with respect to property division. None make provision for unmarried cohabitants in their intestacy legislation. However, several jurisdictions (British Columbia, Manitoba, New Brunswick, Ontario, P.E.I., Saskatchewan, Northwest Territories and Yukon Territory) provide for unmarried cohabitants in their dependant relief laws.

Alberta is in the minority of Canadian jurisdictions, along with Quebec, Prince Edward Island and the Northwest Territories, which have not extended their support legislation to provide support for nonmarried cohabitants. . . .

Ontario

The support provisions of the Ontario *Family Law Act*, R.S.O. 1990, c. F.3, have been extended in ss. 29 and 30 to a man and a woman who have cohabited continuously for not less than three years, or cohabited in a relationship of some permanence in which they are the natural or adoptive parents of a child. . . .

While cohabitants are protected by statutory support provisions in Ontario, they are excluded from other benefits provided to married couples. For example, the parts of the *Act* dealing with division of property apply only to married couples. Cohabitants must make an unjust enrichment argument for property division (Holland, Professor Winifred H., "Marriage and Cohabitation - Has the Time Come to Bridge the Gap?", *Family Law: Roles, Fairness and Equality* (Special Lectures of the Law Society of Upper Canada, 1993) (*Holland 1993*) at 371). In addition, cohabitants are unable to access Part II of the *FLA*, which deals with occupational and other rights in the matrimonial home. They are not protected by the spousal intestacy provisions in the *Succession Law Reform Act*, R.S.O. 1990, c. S.26. Part V of that *Act* gives them the same status as other, non-spousal dependants (*Holland 1993, supra* at 377).

Professor Holland observes, however, that

> [t]he *Equality Rights Amendment Act, 1986* amended the definition of the term 'spouse' in a number of different statutes to include cohabitees. This statute was passed to bring Ontario statute law into conformity with s. 15(1) of the *Charter*, a fact expressly recognized in the heading to the statute. It must have been assumed by the Ontario government that marital status was an included head within s. 15(1). (*Holland 1993, supra* at 383 (footnotes omitted)). . . .

In 1993, the Ontario Law Reform Commission issued its Report on the Rights and Responsibilities of Cohabitants. It recommended that heterosexual cohabitants should have the same rights and responsibilities as married spouses throughout the *FLA*. Professor Holland states with respect to this Report:

> The Commission also proposes adopting the concept of a 'registered domestic partnership'. This would provide a mechanism for opting into the *Family Law Act*. It would be available to same sex couples, heterosexual couples and indeed any couple (for example two sisters) who wish to avail themselves of the opportunity to register as domestic partners. Appropriate formalities must be observed, the partners must be at least 18 years of age and not be already married or in a registered domestic partnership with another. Failure to comply with such requirements would render the agreement void. Registered domestic partnerships can be revoked unilaterally upon giving notice to the other partner. Presumably this option would be used by heterosexual cohabitants who have not lived together for three years (or whatever period is specified in the legislation) and not the parents of a child. (*Holland 1993, supra* at 398.)

We note that under the Commission's proposals, an individual would lack the capacity to enter a registered domestic partnership if he or she were already married or in a registered and unrevoked domestic partnership with another. There are even greater controls on legal marriage. Not only does a married person lack the capacity to enter a new marriage, but the criminal law prohibits bigamy. There are no comparable rules in place governing common law unions and the informal, unregistered nature of common law unions would make such laws challenging both to draft and to administer. We will return to the topic of capacity in the Remedy section of this judgment. . . .

Domestic Relations Act

Statutory Interpretation [The court concluded that the term "spouse" did not include common law spouses unless the legislation specifically indicated such inclusion.]

The *Charter* Challenge

Taylor argued that the exclusion of support provisions for unmarried cohabitants breached her s. 15(1) equality rights, and that this breach could not be justified under s. 1. She relied primarily on the majority finding in *Miron* that marital status is analogous to the prohibited grounds of discrimination enumerated in s. 15(1).

There are two themes underlying the parties' arguments. Taylor's theme emphasizes dependency. She argues that the legislation is intended to relieve dependency following the breakdown of relationships, and the presence or absence of legal marriage therefore ought not be determinative of support obligations. Rossu's theme centres on freedom of choice, and responsibility for that choice. He argues that many unmarried cohabitants may have deliberately chosen to avoid marriage in order to avoid the legal obligations of marriage. A party to such an unmarried cohabitation ought not to have marital obligations thrust upon him or her against his or her will. On the contrary, both parties chose to enter a relationship other than marriage, and this choice, along with its consequences, should be respected. He argues that where the legislature is faced with two equally valid policy alternatives, in this case protecting choice or protecting dependent partners, the Court should not interfere with the legislative decision.

We note that the majority in *Miron* expressly rejected the argument that marital status is a matter of free choice. They held that, along with the reluctance of one's partner to marry, religious, financial and social reasons can prevent an individual from marrying. We agree that the decision of whether to marry is not made in a vacuum, and the will of one's partner or legal impediments can thwart a plan to marry. Clearly, however, the individual retains the right not to cohabit in that situation. But the result of *Miron* is that the decision to cohabit is respected in the same way as a decision to marry.

We note that the facts in *Miron* were different from the facts here. In that case, the parties made a public declaration that they were committed to each other. They were economically intertwined, and considered themselves a family in every sense of the word. In effect, their relationship could be characterised as a common law marriage in the traditional sense of that word. Although the couple did not undergo a legal marriage ceremony or registration, they did make a public announcement of their union, and made a personal and financial commitment to each other. In other words, the parties voluntarily undertook, and indeed demanded, the rights and obligations of marriage, albeit without a marriage certificate. There was no issue of coercing individuals into marital status against their will.

In this case, it is alleged there was no such declaration. On the contrary, Rossu denies the existence of any form of commitment or obligation between the parties, with the exception of his promise to raise Taylor's daughter, which he fulfilled. This lack of commitment was mutual he contends, as is demonstrated by his evidence that at various times during the relationship, Taylor was unfaithful to him, and explained her actions with comments to the effect that she was free to do as she liked since she was not married to him. Rossu argues that imposing marital obligations upon him in this case would be tantamount to coercive imposition of marital status upon him against his will. A unilateral declaration of a conjugal relationship may well be considerably different from the mutual, joint declaration found in *Miron*. Nevertheless, we accept the Supreme Court's finding that marital status is an analogous ground, and their rejection of the freedom of choice arguments in favour of protecting the dependent partner in common law unions. We must govern ourselves accordingly.

Section 15 Analysis . . .

Miron v. *Trudel*

The facts in *Miron* concerned insurance benefits payable to married but not to unmarried cohabitants. The insurance company based its denial of benefits on the Ontario *Insurance Act*, which at that time did not include common law spouses in its definition of "spouse". Because the *Act* was amended to include common law spouses before the case was decided by the Supreme Court, the Court was essentially backdating the legislative changes for constitutional reasons. It was not making a potentially controversial change to the legislation, as it is alleged we are being asked to do here. Rossu asks that we note this important difference.

Rossu argues that there are a number of additional ways in which *Miron* may be distinguished from this case.

First, he argues that the Supreme Court's finding that marital status is analogous to the prohibited grounds of discrimination enumerated in s. 15 in the context of insurance benefits, does not mean that marital status is always an analogous ground. He emphasizes the difference between rights granted by the government, or another third party, to an unmarried couple, and rights of unmarried partners between themselves. He concedes that in *Miron* unmarried couples were disadvantaged by the denial of benefits available to married couples, but emphasizes that the disadvantage accrued to the couple as a unit. He argues that the denial of support rights would at most disadvantage only 50% of unmarried spouses, since in any relationship one person would be a potential payor, and the other a potential payee. Since the potential payors are actually benefitted by the denial of support rights, it cannot be said that the *DRA* disadvantages or discriminates against unmarried partners. It disadvantages only one of the partners. In his view, since the disadvantaged group consists only of the economically dependent unmarried partners, that is too narrow a group to be recognized under the *Charter*. Such recognition would individualize s. 15 and would be unacceptable given that, according to him, the purpose of s. 15 is to protect groups.

Second, Rossu argues that in *Miron* the partners' public declaration of commitment and economic interdependence may have been important. In *Miron*, there was no doubt that the couple considered themselves a family in every sense of the word and simply lacked a marriage certificate. In those circumstances, McLachlin J.'s comments about the freedom to live life with the mate of one's choice in the fashion of one's choice make sense. However, Rossu asserts that the same might not be true in the facts of this case. Here, not only had Taylor and Rossu not declared their commitment and interdependence, Rossu vehemently denies the existence of any commitment or economic understanding between them. Relying on Taylor's unilateral declaration that they had a spouse-like relationship would result in the coercive imposition of marital rights and obligations upon Rossu without his consent. Indeed, it is possible that Taylor and Rossu deliberately chose to remain unmarried in order to avoid the personal and legal obligations of marriage. There is some evidence that Taylor herself did not consider herself to be committed to Rossu during the relationship. Rossu alleges that Taylor was repeatedly unfaithful to him and would answer his reproaches with comments to the effect that she did not have to be faithful since she was not married to him.

The argument continues that forcing Rossu to assume marital obligations against his will, simply because Taylor now claims corresponding rights, would actually interfere with his freedom of choice. Imposing marital obligations in this situation would be akin to saying, "Yes, you have the right to live life with the mate of your choice in the fashion of your choice, provided that fashion is marriage, since we will impose marital obligations upon you regardless of the form of cohabitational relationship you choose."

Permitting one partner to coerce the other into marital obligations raises the issue of whether a third party such as the government can coerce a member of a common law union into marital obligations against the will of both partners. This situation could arise if an ex-partner to a common law union were receiving welfare, and the government had a subrogated claim to support from his or her ex-partner. Could the parties in that situation successfully argue they had no economic commitment to each other, or could the government impose marital obligations over the protests of both partners? This possibility raises the spectre of governmental inquiries into the intimate details of relationships even where neither party requested such intervention, and indeed where such inquiry may be against the will of both parties.

Defining the Affected Group

The composition of the affected group is also in issue in this case. Rossu argues that since not all unmarried spouses are disadvantaged by the *DRA*, the relevant group is not unmarried spouses, and the ground of distinction is not marital status.

We do not accept Rossu's arguments for several reasons. In our view, these arguments misunderstand the nature of the benefit at issue here. The *DRA* does not confer a right to support since not every applicant for support will receive support. Rather, the *DRA* confers a right to apply for support. It is the right to apply that is the benefit married partners are given, and from which unmarried partners are excluded. Entitlement to support, and the quantum of that support, is determined at a later stage after an examination of the nature of the relationship and the parties' economic positions. It is only at the entitlement stage that the relative economic positions of the parties becomes relevant, and Rossu's argument about dependent versus independent partners arises. It may well be that a law which limits support claims to dependent common law spouses would survive *Charter* scrutiny. We need not address the full dimensions of that issue since it is clear that all unmarried partners have been deprived of the right to even apply for support.

It is not necessary to establish that every individual member of the group would exercise the entitlement to claim support. If it were, it would be akin to finding that a law prohibiting maternity leave is not discrimination on the basis of gender because only pregnant employed women are actually disadvantaged by it.

A better approach would be to examine whether a member of a group has access to a benefit regardless of whether he or she actually intends to claim the benefit, or would be entitled to receive it if he or she did so. In this case, unmarried spouses lack access to the benefit of a legislated right to apply for spousal support. . . .

We see no reason to limit *Charter* scrutiny of distinctions based on marital status only to those situations in which the couple is living together as an intact family unit. To do so would allow couples to pick and choose those rights and responsibilities which they wished to have attached to their common law marriage. Not surprisingly, one could reasonably expect that the couple would be asserting rights to benefits rather than demanding that burdens be imposed on them. More troubling yet, it would potentially allow one member of the relationship to take all the benefits and leave the other with all the burdens. Those legally married do not enjoy this freedom to pick and choose what benefits and burdens will apply to them. We therefore decline to sanction an interpretation which would put those living common law in a better position than those legally married. Having a possible claim to secure support from each other under applicable government legislation is no different than securing access to government funded benefit plans for those who are "married" or for that matter, to those sponsored and paid for by private parties. If the latter two categories might possibly engage "marital status" as a prohibited analogous ground under s. 15 of the *Charter*, so too does the former. The only difference is that in the first example, one member of the common law relationship may be required to pay money to the other; in the last two, the money or benefit may be paid for by the public or the private parties. This distinction does not warrant differential treatment amongst these categories. Indeed, a more compelling case can be made that those living common law should, as between themselves, assume personal responsibility for the outcome of their relationship.

For all these reasons, we have concluded that the support provisions of the *DRA* discriminate against partners living in a common law relationship by depriving them of the benefit of a legislated right to apply for spousal support based on a prohibited analogous ground of discrimination under s. 15 of the *Charter* — marital status.

Section 1 Analysis

The test to be applied under s. 1 was set out in the *Oakes* decision and remains good law. In a s. 1 analysis, the onus is on the defender (usually the government, but in this case a private litigant) to show that the infringement is a reasonable limitation, demonstrably justified in a free and democratic society. In *Miron*, the Court explained the s. 1 test as follows (at 61):

> Determining whether it has been demonstrated that the impugned distinction is 'demonstrably justified in a free and democratic society' involves two inquiries. First, the goal of the legislation is ascertained and examined to see if it is of pressing and substantial importance. Then the court must carry out a proportionality analysis to balance the interests of society with those of individuals and groups. The proportionality analysis comprises three branches. First, the connection between the goal and the discriminatory distinction is examined to ascertain if it is rational. Second, the law must impair the right no more than is reasonably necessary to accomplish the objective.

Finally, if these two conditions are met, the court must weigh whether the effect of the discrimination is proportionate to the benefit thereby achieved. See *R.* v. *Oakes*, [1986] 1 S.C.R. 103.

What is the Goal and Is It A Pressing and Substantial Objective?

The first step in this analysis, therefore, is to determine the goal of the impugned legislation and assess whether it is pressing and substantial. This task is more problematic given the absence of governmental intervention and submissions.

The trial judge found that the purpose of the support provisions of the *DRA* was "to sustain spouses, when the members of the relationship decide to go their separate ways." In other words, he concluded that the relief of dependency, rather than the promotion of legal marriage, was the purpose of the legislation. Although he did not specifically find that the exclusion of common law couples from the legislation was not rationally connected with the purpose of the legislation, we can infer this from his reasons. Since there was no rational connection, it was not necessary for him to look at whether the exclusion met the minimal impairment test or the proportionality test. He remedied the breach by reading in the broader definition of spouse adopted in *Miron* (which included heterosexual couples who have cohabited for three years or more, or who have lived in a permanent relationship with a child or children) to the support provisions of the *DRA*.

Rossu argues that the trial judge erred in that conclusion, and that the purpose of the support provisions of the *DRA* is to promote and protect marriage as a fundamental unit of our society. He argues that the legislature would not have expressly restricted the sections to married spouses if it intended to relieve dependency in any intimate relationship. He concedes that the majority of Canadian jurisdictions have amended their support legislation to include unmarried spouses, but denies that there is any constitutional mandate for such action. . . .

There are three difficulties with this argument. First, it is debatable whether imposing support obligations on separated or divorced spouses promotes the institution of marriage. It could be argued that such obligations actually promote the breakdown of marriages by providing a type of governmental condonation of marital breakdown, while reducing the economic consequences of a break-up on the dependent spouse. That is, while the absence of support obligations benefits the economically powerful spouse at break-up, the presence of support obligations benefits the economically dependent spouse at break-up. Neither can clearly be said to promote the institution of marriage since neither provides an incentive or benefit to both parties to marry or remain married.

Second, and more important, is the fact that however fundamental the state of marriage may be to our society, the statistics show that the prevalence of families based on common law relationships is increasing dramatically . . . .

Third, given the changes in the philosophical and policy underpinnings of Canada's spousal support laws over the last thirty years, it is difficult to conclude that the promotion of marriage is the underlying goal of the *DRA* support provisions. . . . Further, in any event, the *DRA* itself does not contemplate that support will be awarded based solely on status. In fact, we note that on an application for interim support, under s. 16(2), no order shall be made if the applicant has sufficient means of support independent of the defendant. This provision militates heavily in favour of the conclusion that the goal of the support provisions under the *DRA* is to relieve dependency.

We conclude from all this that the *DRA* support provisions have two possible goals: to relieve dependency upon the breakdown of an intimate relationship; and to promote marriage by limiting claims to support to those who are legally married. The first is most assuredly a pressing and substantial objective. Placing the burden of providing for an individual who has suffered economic disadvantage as a result of an intimate relationship upon his or her ex-partner, rather than upon the public purse, certainly falls into this category.

The more difficult question is whether the goal of relieving dependency is exclusive of, or inconsistent with, the goal of promoting marriage. Ensuring that dependency arising from a marriage will be redressed surely promotes those unions in terms of the benefits and obligations arising upon breakdown. But is it marriage itself that is promoted? Or is the goal rather to promote all forms of stable, enduring relationships that form the basis of a healthy social structure? It is argued that the objective of promoting and protecting a single type of relationship to the exclusion of all others, regardless of social changes, may not be a pressing and substantial objective. While marriage may be the most common family basis, statistical evidence shows that an increasing number of Canadian couples have chosen, and are choosing, an alternative. Promoting marriage as the sole form of legally recognized relationship in the face of this statistical evidence thus arguably does not reflect social reality and may not amount to a pressing and substantial objective.

While we recognize the increasing prevalence of common law unions, we concede that the statistical evidence is that many of these unions tend to be precursors to marriage, rather than replacements for marriage. They have been likened to a form of extended courtship. We also recognize the central role legal marriage has played, and continues to play, in our social system. In the end, it is not necessary for us to definitively resolve this controversial issue because other aspects of the s. 1 analysis compel us to conclude that the limitation cannot be justified whatever the goal of the legislation.

Proportionality Test

The second component of the s. 1 analysis is the three-branch proportionality test. The first branch involves an examination of whether the connection between the goal and the discriminatory legislation is rational. The goal of promoting and promulgating marriage fails the rational connection test for two reasons. First, there is no evidence that providing access to support for separated or divorced legal spouses promotes marriage in terms of encouraging both parties to enter or to remain in marriages. The existence of these provisions does not appear to have resulted in increased marriage rates, or reduced separation rates. Nor does it appear that people have been discouraged from entering common law relationships by the existence of this legislation. On the contrary, there is evidence that an increasing number of couples are choosing to cohabit without legal marriage. Moreover, we take judicial notice of the fact that divorce and separation rates amongst married couples have also increased over the last twenty years.

Second, there is no evidence that common law couples must be excluded from access to spousal support in order to promote marriage. There are other reasons and other values that lead individuals to choose legal marriage as a preferred lifestyle choice.

The goal of relieving dependency following the break-down of intimate relationships also fails the rational connection test, because the exclusion of 11.6% of Alberta couples from the right to apply for support is not rationally connected to the relief of dependency. If the government's intention were to relieve dependency, there would be no reason to restrict the application of the legislation to legally married spouses. Rather, the government would have drafted its legislation to capture as many intimate relationships as possible. . . .

Since the legislation cannot pass the rational connection test, it is not necessary to determine whether it could pass the minimal impairment or proportionality tests. That said, we are of the view that this legislation would fail both of those branches of the test in any event. An absolute exclusion of all common law couples from the right to even apply for spousal support is not a minimal impairment of s. 15 equality rights. Similarly, any putative benefits to the institution of marriage are outweighed by the deleterious effects on economically dependent common law partners following the breakdown of the relationship. We fail to see any benefit in terms of relief of dependency that would not in fact be increased by the inclusion of common law couples in the legislation. We conclude that the support provisions of the Alberta *DRA* cannot be saved under s. 1.

Concerns

A number of concerns have been raised about the coercive nature of state imposition of marital obligations upon those who may have deliberately avoided marriage in order to avoid the attached obligations. While some of these concerns are appealing, the counter-arguments about the exploitation of the economically weaker partner for the benefit of the stronger, are, in our view, more meritorious. That reasoning can be applied to the situation in Alberta in which the economically stronger member of an unmarried relationship may enjoy all the benefits of marriage, both emotional and economic, without bearing any of the obligations, such as support and asset division. Where the unmarried relationship mimics a traditional marriage in all ways except a marriage certificate, the argument that they should be treated equally in terms of equal benefit to and of the law is compelling.

However, the parties to unmarried relationships remain unmarried for a myriad of reasons, and govern their affairs in a myriad of ways, some of which bear little resemblance to a traditional marriage. The argument that these relationships should not be treated as marriages is also valid. For example, a "modern" relationship in which both parties intend to be "free spirits", and conduct their affairs accordingly so that neither is disadvantaged by the relationship, would not be likely to attract a support order. We note that a comparable legal marriage would be similarly unlikely to attract a support order. . . .

If the legislature wishes to respect individuals' ability to choose intimate relationships other than traditional marriage while protecting the economically vulnerable in such relationships, support criteria could be revised to emphasize that support will be awarded only where the nature of the relationship was such that the parties could reasonably be said to have undertaken obligations to each other, or where one partner has been economically disadvantaged by the relationship. . . .

Remedy

After finding that s. 15 of the *DRA* breached s. 15 of the *Charter*, and could not be saved under s. 1 of the *Charter*, the trial judge ordered the remedy of reading-in. He read in "common law spouse" to the term "spouse" in s. 15 of the *DRA*. There are a number of difficulties with this remedy. We have the following comments to make about the remedy, and about the issue in general.

First, the support provisions of the *DRA* not only exclude common law spouses from their definition of "spouse", they include preconditions to applications that presume the existence of a legal marriage. . . . Unless these preconditions are struck, or the provisions establishing entitlement to the preconditions are themselves amended to include unmarried cohabitants, merely including the phrase "common law spouse" in the word "spouse" has no practical effect since unmarried spouses cannot meet the existing preconditions.

Second, since there is no universally accepted definition of common law spouse, simply reading in the term without defining it is insufficient. . . .

Third, if support obligations are extended to unmarried cohabitants, the government may choose to revise its support regime. For example, it could implement new guidelines for the award of support, such as permitting trial judges to consider the nature of the relationship and the extent of the commitment between the parties along with the normal considerations in awarding support. This would allow courts to consider the parties' reasons for not entering a legal marriage, and could help assuage concerns about imposing marital obligations on partners who deliberately chose not to marry in order to avoid the legal obligations of marriage. . . .

Fourth, the extension of rights and obligations to common law partners has been done on a piecemeal basis. . . . This *Charter* decision that it is unconstitutional to distinguish between married and unmarried cohabitants with regard to their obligations *inter se* could preclude such piecemeal legislation unless it could be justified under s. 1. The government therefore may also choose to amend other legislation which distinguishes on the basis of marital status. It ought to have the opportunity to design a comprehensive new legislative scheme that conforms with *Charter* requirements, rather than having the Court amend some parts and the legislature other parts, with the result that the whole would be less than unified or ideal.

Fifth, the issue of capacity to enter legally recognized common law relationships must be addressed. Legally married people not only lack the capacity to enter a new marriage, but face criminal sanctions for doing so. There are no comparable bigamy rules in place to govern common law unions, and, as stated elsewhere in this judgment, the informal, unregistered nature of common law unions would make such laws challenging both to draft and to administer. But there are already cases in which a legally married person has been permitted to enter a binding common law union, complete with legal rights and obligations, despite the fact that person would not have had the capacity to enter another legal marriage. Therefore, the legislature may wish to consider whether there should be any impediment to individuals assuming the benefits of multiple common law marriages, as long as they are also required to assume the associated financial responsibilities. . . .

For all of these reasons, we conclude that the correct remedy is to strike the offending legislation, but to suspend the declaration of invalidity [for one year] to allow the government time to draft its own legislation in this complex area. . . .

M. v. H.

(1999), 46 R.F.L. (4th) 32 (S.C.C.)

CORY and IACOBUCCI JJ. (LAMER C.J.C., L'HEUREUX-DUBE, McLACHLIN, and BINNIE JJ. concurring):

I. Introduction and Overview

The principal issue raised in this appeal is whether the definition of "spouse" in s. 29 of the *Family Law Act*, R.S.O. 1990, c. F.3 (''*FLA*'') infringes s. 15(1) of the *Canadian Charter of Rights and Freedoms*, and, if so, whether the legislation is nevertheless saved by s. 1 of the *Charter*. In addition, M. was granted leave to cross-appeal on the issue of the appropriate remedy to be granted and also as to costs.

Our view on this principal issue may be summarized as follows. Section 15(1) of the *Charter* is infringed by the definition of "spouse" in s. 29 of the *FLA*. This definition, which only applies to Part III of the *FLA*, draws a distinction between individuals in conjugal, opposite-sex relationships of a specific degree of duration and individuals in conjugal, same-sex relationships of a specific degree of duration. We emphasize that the definition of "spouse" found in s. 1(1) of the *FLA*, and which applies to other parts of the *FLA*, includes only married persons and is not at issue in this appeal. Essentially, the definition of "spouse" in s. 29 of the *FLA* extends the obligation to provide spousal support, found in Part III of the *FLA*, beyond married persons to include individuals in conjugal opposite-sex relationships of some permanence. Same-sex relationships are capable of being both conjugal and lengthy, but individuals in such relationships are nonetheless denied access to the court-enforced system of support provided by the *FLA*. This differential treatment is on the basis of a personal characteristic, namely sexual orientation, that, in previous jurisprudence, has been found to be analogous to those characteristics specifically enumerated in s.15(1).

The crux of the issue is that this differential treatment discriminates in a substantive sense by violating the human dignity of individuals in same-sex relationships. As *Law* v. *Canada (Minister of Employment & Immigration)* (1999), 60 C.R.R. (2d) 1 (S.C.C.) established, the inquiry into substantive discrimination is to be undertaken in a purposive and contextual manner. In the present appeal, several factors are important to consider. First, individuals in same-sex relationships face significant pre-existing disadvantage and vulnerability, which is exacerbated by the impugned legislation. Second, the legislation at issue fails to take into account the claimant's actual situation. Third, there is no compelling argument that the ameliorative purpose of the legislation does anything to lessen the charge of discrimination in this case. Fourth, the nature of the interest affected is fundamental, namely the ability to meet basic financial needs following the breakdown of a relationship characterized by intimacy and economic dependence. The exclusion of same-sex partners from the benefits of the spousal support scheme implies that they are judged to be incapable of forming intimate relationships of economic interdependence, without regard to their actual circumstances. Taking these factors into account, it is clear that the human dignity of individuals in same-sex relationships is violated by the definition of "spouse" in s. 29 of the *FLA*.

This infringement is not justified under s.1 of the *Charter* because there is no rational connection between the objectives of the spousal support provisions and the means chosen to further this objective. The objectives were accurately identified by Charron, J.A., in the court below, as providing for the equitable resolution of economic disputes when intimate relationships between financially interdependent individuals break down, and alleviating the burden on the public purse to provide for dependent spouses. Neither of these objectives is furthered by the exclusion of individuals in same-sex couples from the spousal support regime. If anything, these goals are undermined by this exclusion.

In this case, the remedy of reading in is inappropriate, as it would unduly recast the legislation, and striking down the *FLA* as a whole is excessive. Therefore the appropriate remedy is to declare s. 29 of no force and effect and to suspend the application of the declaration for a period of six months. . . .

Cory J.: At the outset, it must be stressed that the questions to be answered are narrow and precise in their scope. The *FLA* provides a means whereby designated persons may apply to the court for support from a spouse or, if unmarried, from a man or woman with whom they lived in an opposite-sex conjugal relationship. The Act specifically extends the obligation for support beyond married persons who, as a result of their married status, have additional rights under the Act.

The question to be resolved is whether the extension of the right to seek support to members of unmarried opposite-sex couples infringes s. 15(1) of the *Charter* by failing to provide the same rights to members of same-sex couples.

II. Factual Background

M. and H. are women who met while on vacation in 1980. It is agreed that in 1982 they started living together in a same-sex relationship that continued for at least five years. That relationship may have lasted ten years, but that figure is disputed by H. During that time they occupied a home which H. had owned since 1974. H. paid for the upkeep of the home, but the parties agreed to share living expenses and household responsibilities equally. At the time, H. was employed in an advertising firm and M. ran her own company.

In 1982, M. and H. started their own advertising business. The business enjoyed immediate success and was the main source of income for the couple during the relationship. H.'s contribution to this company was greater than that of M. Epstein J., the trial judge, observed that this disparity was probably due to the fact that M. had no previous experience in advertising, and, as time went on, she was content to devote more of her time to domestic tasks rather than the business. Nevertheless, the parties continued to be equal shareholders in the company.

In 1983, M. and H. purchased a business property together. In 1986, they purchased as joint tenants a vacation property in the country. They later sold the business property and used the proceeds to finance the construction of a home on the country property.

As a result of a dramatic downturn in the advertising business in the late 1980s, the parties' debt increased significantly. H. took a job outside the firm and placed a mortgage on her home to pay for her expenses and those of M. M. also tried to find employment but was unsuccessful. Her company, which she had continued to run on a casual basis throughout the relationship, produced very little income.

By September of 1992, M. and H.'s relationship had deteriorated. H. was concerned about what she perceived to be an unfair disparity in their relative financial contributions. H. presented M. with a draft agreement to settle their affairs. The same day that the agreement was presented, M. took some of her personal belongings and left the common home. Upon M.'s departure, H. changed the locks on the house.

The parties did not divide the personal property or household contents. M. alleged that she encountered serious financial problems after the separation. In October 1992, M. sought an order for partition and sale of the house; a declaration that she was the beneficial owner of certain lands and premises owned by H. and by the companies M. named as defendants; and an accounting of the transactions carried out by the companies. By Notice of Cross-Application, H. and the corporate defendants sought damages for slander of title, partition and sale of property, the repayment of certain loans, and other relief. M. then amended her application to include a claim for support pursuant to the provisions of the *FLA*, and served Notice of a Constitutional Question challenging the validity of the definition of "spouse" in s. 29 of the Act. . . .

In February 1996, Epstein J. released her judgment on the constitutional issues. She held that s. 29 of the *FLA* offends s. 15(1) of the *Charter*, and that it is not saved by s. 1. H. appealed the judgment and was joined in the appeal by the intervenor, the Attorney General of Ontario.

The Ontario Court of Appeal ultimately upheld this decision, but suspended implementation of the declaration of invalidity for one year, to give the Ontario legislature time to amend the *FLA*. Neither of the respondents appealed this decision. Leave to appeal to this Court was ultimately granted to the Attorney General of Ontario on the condition that M.'s costs were to be paid regardless of the outcome. M. was also granted the right to cross-appeal with respect to the Court of Appeal's one-year suspension of the declaration, and the issue of costs.

Shortly before the appeal was heard in this Court, M. and H. concluded a settlement of the financial issues raised in the proceedings. . . .

B. Does s. 29 of the *FLA* Infringe s. 15(1) of the *Charter*?

1. *Approach to Section 15(1)*

In the recent decision of this Court in *Law, supra*, Iacobucci J. summarized some of the main guidelines for analysis under s. 15(1) to be derived from the jurisprudence of this Court. He emphasized that these guidelines do not represent a strict test, but rather should be understood as points of reference for a court that is called upon to decide whether a claimant's right to equality without discrimination under the *Charter* has been infringed: see para. 88.

Iacobucci J. explained that the s. 15(1) equality guarantee is to be interpreted and applied in a purposive and contextual manner, in order to permit the realization of the provision's strong remedial purpose, and to avoid the pitfalls of a formalistic or mechanical approach. Following a review of this Court's jurisprudence regarding the fundamental purpose of s. 15(1), he stated this purpose in the following terms, at para. 88:

> In general terms, the purpose of s. 15(1) is to prevent the violation of essential human dignity and freedom through the imposition of disadvantage, stereotyping, or political or social prejudice, and to promote a society in which all persons enjoy equal recognition at law as human beings or as members of Canadian society, equally capable and equally deserving of concern, respect and consideration.

Iacobucci J. stated that the existence of a conflict between the purpose or effect of an impugned law, on the one hand, and this fundamental purpose of the equality guarantee, on the other, is essential in order to found a discrimination claim.

In *Law*, Iacobucci J. reviewed various articulations of the proper approach to be taken in analyzing a s. 15(1) claim, as expressed in the jurisprudence of this Court. At para. 39, he summarized the basic elements of this Court's approach as involving three broad inquiries, in the following terms:

> In my view, the proper approach to analyzing a claim of discrimination under s. 15(1) of the *Charter* involves a synthesis of these various articulations. Following upon the analysis in *Andrews, supra*, and the two-step framework set out in *Egan, supra*, and *Miron, supra*, among other cases, a court that is called upon to determine a discrimination claim under s. 15(1) should make the following three broad inquiries. First, does the impugned law (a) draw a formal distinction between the claimant and others on the basis of one or more personal characteristics, or (b) fail to take into account the claimant's already disadvantaged position within Canadian society resulting in substantively differential treatment between the claimant and others on the basis of one or more personal characteristics? If so, there is differential treatment for the purpose of s. 15(1). Second, was the claimant subject to differential treatment on the basis of one or more of the enumerated and analogous grounds? And third, does the differential treatment discriminate

in a substantive sense, bringing into play the purpose of s. 15(1) of the *Charter* in remedying such ills as prejudice, stereotyping, and historical disadvantage? [Emphasis in original.]

2. *The Structure of the Family Law Act*

To begin, it may be useful to review briefly the structure of the *FLA* and the rights and obligations it establishes. First and foremost, it is of critical importance to recognize that the *FLA* contains more than one definition of "spouse". The first definition is set out in s. 1(1) and includes only persons who are actually married, or who have entered into a void or voidable marriage in good faith. This definition applies to *all* parts of the Act.

The second definition is found in s. 29, and extends the meaning of "spouse", but only for certain purposes. Specifically, unmarried opposite-sex couples who have cohabited for at least three years, or who are the natural or adoptive parents of a child and have also cohabited in a relationship of "some permanence", bear a mutual obligation of support under Part III of the *FLA*. They also have the right to enter into cohabitation agreements to regulate their relationship under Part IV, and may bring a claim for dependants' relief in tort under Part V.

All these rights and obligations are obviously available to married persons as well. However, married persons have additional rights under the *FLA* that are denied common law cohabitants, even those who meet the requirements of s. 29. Under Part I, a husband or wife may apply for an equal share of the wealth generated during the marriage, and of the matrimonial home. Under Part II, both married spouses have a right to possession of the matrimonial home, regardless of who owns the property. Moreover, the ability of the owner of the matrimonial home to sell or encumber the property without the consent of the other spouse is severely restricted. These mutual rights and obligations are denied *all* unmarried opposite-sex cohabitants.

These observations on the structure of the *FLA* serve to emphasize that this appeal has nothing to do with marriage *per se*. Much of the *FLA* is devoted solely to regulating the relationship that exists between married persons, or persons who intend to be married. They alone are guaranteed certain property rights that are not extended to any unmarried persons. In some specific instances — such as Part III dealing with support obligations — the legislature has seen fit to extend the rights and obligations that arise under the *FLA beyond* married persons to include certain *unmarried* persons as well.

In other words, the *FLA* draws a distinction by specifically according rights to individual members of unmarried cohabiting opposite-sex couples, which by omission it fails to accord to individual members of same-sex couples who are living together. It is this distinction that lies at the heart of the s. 15 analysis. The rights and obligations that exist between married persons play no part in this analysis. The legislature did not extend full marital status, for the purposes of all the rights and obligations under the *FLA*, to those unmarried cohabitants included in s. 29 of the Act. Rather, the definition of "spouse" in s. 29 only applies for certain purposes. Specifically, it allows persons who became financially dependent in the course of a lengthy intimate relationship some relief from financial hardship resulting from the breakdown of that relationship. It follows that this provision was designed to reduce the demands on the public welfare system. This will be discussed more fully in the s. 1 analysis below.

It is true that women in common law relationships often tended to become financially dependent on their male partners because they raised their children and because of their unequal earning power. But the legislature drafted s. 29 to allow either a man *or* a woman to apply for support, thereby recognizing that financial dependence can arise in an intimate relationship in a context entirely unrelated either to child-rearing or to any gender-based discrimination existing in our society. See discussion of s. 1 of the *Charter*, below. Indeed, the special situation of financial dependence potentially created by procreation is specifically addressed in s. 29(*b*). This appeal is concerned only with s. 29(*a*). That section is aimed at remedying situations of dependence in intimate relationships without imposing any limitation relating to the circumstances that may give rise to that dependence.

It is thus apparent that in this appeal there is no need to consider whether same-sex couples can marry, or whether same-sex couples must, for all purposes, be treated in the same manner as unmarried opposite-sex couples. The only determination that must be made is whether, in extending the spousal support obligations set out in Part III of the *FLA* to include unmarried men or women in certain opposite-sex relation-ships, the legislature infringed the equality rights of men or women in similar same-sex relationships, and if so, whether that infringement may be saved by s. 1 of the *Charter*.

3. *The Existence of Differential Treatment*

A consideration of the essence of M.'s claim requires a more detailed review of Part III of the *FLA*. In Part III, ss. 30 to 32 impose an obligation on persons to support themselves and their dependants. A "dependant" can be the spouse, child or parent of the person who must fulfil the support obligation. The definition of "spouse" in s. 29 applies to all of Part III and includes a person who is actually married, and also:

> . . . either of a man and woman who are not married to each other and have cohabited,
>
> (a) continuously for a period of not less than three years, or
>
> (b) in a relationship of some permanence, if they are the natural or adoptive parents of a child.

Section 1(1) defines "cohabit" as "to live together in a conjugal relationship, whether within or outside marriage".

The definition clearly indicates that the legislature decided to extend the obli-gation to provide spousal support *beyond* married persons. Obligations to provide support were no longer dependent upon marriage. The obligation was extended to include those relationships which: (i) exist between a man and a woman; (ii) have a specific degree of permanence; (iii) are conjugal. Only individuals in relationships which meet these minimum criteria may apply for a support order under Part III of the *FLA*.

Same-sex relationships are capable of meeting the last two requirements. Cer-tainly same-sex couples will often form long, lasting, loving and intimate relation-ships. The choices they make in the context of those relationships may give rise to the financial dependence of one partner on the other. Though it might be argued that same-sex couples do not live together in "conjugal" relationships, in the sense that they cannot "hold themselves out" as husband and wife, on this issue I am in agreement with the reasoning and conclusions of the majority of the Court of Appeal.

Molodowich v. *Penttinen* (1980), 17 R.F.L. (2d) 376 (Ont. Dist. Ct.) sets out the generally accepted characteristics of a conjugal relationship. They include shared shelter, sexual and personal behaviour, services, social activities, economic support and children, as well as the societal perception of the couple. However, it was recognized that these elements may be present in varying degrees and not all are necessary for the relationship to be found to be conjugal. While it is true that there may not be any consensus as to the societal perception of same-sex couples, there is agreement that same-sex couples share many other "conjugal" characteristics. In order to come within the definition, neither opposite-sex couples nor same-sex couples are required to fit precisely the traditional marital model to demonstrate that the relationship is "conjugal".

Certainly an opposite-sex couple may, after many years together, be considered to be in a conjugal relationship although they have neither children nor sexual relations. Obviously the weight to be accorded the various elements or factors to be considered in determining whether an opposite-sex couple is in a conjugal relationship will vary widely and almost infinitely. The same must hold true of same-sex couples. Courts have wisely determined that the approach to determining whether a relationship is conjugal must be flexible. This must be so, for the relationships of all couples will vary widely. In these circumstances, the Court of Appeal correctly concluded that there is nothing to suggest that same-sex couples do not meet the legal definition of "conjugal".

Since gay and lesbian individuals are capable of being involved in conjugal relationships, and since their relationships are capable of meeting the *FLA*'s temporal requirements, the distinction of relevance to this appeal is between persons in an opposite-sex, conjugal relationship of some permanence and persons in a same-sex, conjugal relationship of some permanence. In this regard, I must disagree with the dissenting opinion in the court below, which characterized the distinction arising in s. 29 as being between opposite-sex and same-sex *couples*. This conclusion would require that the section be scrutinized for any discriminatory impact it may have on same-sex couples, and not on the individual members of that couple. Section 29 defines "spouse" as "*either* of a man and a woman" who meet the other requirements of the section. It follows that the definition could not have been meant to define a couple. Rather it explicitly refers to the *individual* members of the couple. Thus the distinction of relevance must be between individual persons in a same-sex, conjugal relationship of some permanence and individual persons in an opposite-sex, conjugal relationship of some permanence.

Thus it is apparent that the legislation has drawn a formal distinction between the claimant and others, based on personal characteristics. As stated in *Law, supra*, the first broad inquiry in the s. 15(1) analysis determines whether there is differential treatment imposed by the impugned legislation between the claimant and others. It is clear that there is differential treatment here. Under s. 29 of the *FLA*, members of opposite-sex couples who can meet the requirements of the statute are able to gain access to the court-enforced system of support provided by the *FLA*. It is this system that ensures the provision of support to a dependent spouse. Members of same-sex couples are denied access to this system entirely on the basis of their sexual orientation.

4. *Sexual Orientation is an Analogous Ground*

Not every legislative distinction is discriminatory. Before it can be found that it gives rise to discrimination, it must be shown that an equality right was denied on the basis of an enumerated or analogous ground, and that this differential treatment discriminates "in a substantive sense, bringing into play the *purpose* of s. 15(1) of the *Charter*": *Law, supra*, at para. 39 (emphasis in original).

In *Egan,*[(1995), 12 R.F.L. (4th) 201] this Court unanimously affirmed that sexual orientation is an analogous ground to those enumerated in s. 15(1). Sexual orientation is "a deeply personal characteristic that is either unchangeable or changeable only at unacceptable personal costs" (para. 5). In addition, a majority of this Court explicitly recognized that gays, lesbians and bisexuals, "whether as individuals or couples, form an identifiable minority who have suffered and continue to suffer serious social, political and economic disadvantage" (at para. 175 *per* Cory J.; at para. 89 *per* L'Heureux-Dubé J.).

5. *The Existence of Discrimination in a Purposive Sense*

The determination of whether differential treatment imposed by legislation on an enumerated or analogous ground is discriminatory within the meaning of s. 15(1) of the *Charter* is to be undertaken in a purposive and contextual manner. The relevant inquiry is whether the differential treatment imposes a burden upon or withholds a benefit from the claimant in a manner that reflects the stereotypical application of presumed group or personal characteristics, or which otherwise has the effect of perpetuating or promoting the view that the individual is less capable or worthy of recognition or value as a human being or as a member of Canadian society, equally deserving of concern, respect, and consideration: *Law, supra*, at para. 88.

The respondent H. has argued that the differential treatment imposed by s. 29 of the *FLA* does not deny the respondent M. the equal benefit of the law since same-sex spouses are not being denied an economic benefit, but simply the opportunity to gain access to a court-enforced process. Such an analysis takes too narrow a view of "benefit" under the law. It is a view this Court should not adopt. The type of benefit salient to the s. 15(1) analysis cannot encompass only the conferral of an economic benefit. It must also include access to a process that could confer an economic or other benefit: *Egan, supra*, at paras. 158-59; *Vriend* v. *Alberta*, [1998] 1 S.C.R. 493 (S.C.C.), at para. 87. Further, the spousal support provisions of the *FLA* help protect the economic interests of individuals in intimate relationships. When a relationship breaks down, the support provisions help to ensure that a member of a couple who has contributed to the couple's welfare in intangible ways will not find himself or herself utterly abandoned. This protective aspect of the spousal support provisions is properly considered in relation to s. 15(1). Thus it is appropriate to conclude that s. 29 of the *FLA* creates a distinction that withholds a benefit from the respondent M. The question is whether this denial of a benefit violates the purpose of s. 15(1). . . .

One factor which may demonstrate that legislation that treats the claimant differently has the effect of demeaning the claimant's dignity is the existence of pre-existing disadvantage, stereotyping, prejudice, or vulnerability experienced by the individual or group at issue. . . .

In this case, there is significant pre-existing disadvantage and vulnerability, and these circumstances are exacerbated by the impugned legislation. The legislative provision in question draws a distinction that prevents persons in a same-sex relationship from gaining access to the court-enforced and -protected support system. This system clearly provides a benefit to unmarried heterosexual persons who come within the definition set out in s. 29, and thereby provides a measure of protection for their economic interests. This protection is denied to persons in a same-sex relationship who would otherwise meet the statute's requirements, and as a result, a person in the position of the claimant is denied a benefit regarding an important aspect of life in today's society. Neither common law nor equity provides the remedy of maintenance that is made available by the *FLA*. The denial of that potential benefit, which may impose a financial burden on persons in the position of the claimant, contributes to the general vulnerability experienced by individuals in same-sex relationships.

A second contextual factor that was discussed in *Law* as being potentially relevant to the s. 15(1) inquiry is the correspondence, or the lack of it, between the ground on which a claim is based and the actual need, capacity, or circumstances of the claimant or others: para. 70. Iacobucci J. nonetheless cautioned that the mere fact that the impugned legislation takes into account the claimant's actual situation will not necessarily defeat a s. 15(1) claim, as the focus of the inquiry must always remain upon the central question of whether, viewed from the perspective of the claimant, the differential treatment imposed by the legislation has the effect of violating human dignity. However, the legislation at issue in the current appeal fails to take into account the claimant's actual situation. As I have already discussed, access to the court-enforced spousal support regime provided in the *FLA* is given to individuals in conjugal relationships of a specific degree of permanence. Being in a same-sex relationship does not mean that it is an impermanent or a non-conjugal relationship.

A third contextual factor referred to by Iacobucci J. in *Law, supra*, at para. 72, is the question of whether the impugned legislation has an ameliorative purpose or effect for a group historically disadvantaged in the context of the legislation . . . . In other words, the existence of an ameliorative purpose or effect may help to establish that human dignity is not violated where the person or group that is excluded is more advantaged with respect to the circumstances addressed by the legislation. Gonthier J. argues that the legislation under scrutiny in the present appeal is just such ameliorative legislation — that it is meant to target women in married or opposite-sex relationships. He proceeds to argue that in this legal context, women in same-sex relationships are not similarly disadvantaged. For the reasons expressed elsewhere, we disagree with this characterization of the legislation. Accordingly, we reject the idea that the allegedly ameliorative purpose of this legislation does anything to lessen the charge of discrimination in this case.

A fourth contextual factor specifically adverted to by Iacobucci J. in *Law*, at para. 74, was the nature of the interest affected by the impugned legislation. Drawing upon the reasons of L'Heureux-Dubé J. in *Egan, supra*, Iacobucci J. stated that the discriminatory calibre of differential treatment cannot be fully appreciated without considering whether the distinction in question restricts access to a fundamental social institution, or affects a basic aspect of full membership in Canadian society, or constitutes a complete non-recognition of a particular group. In the present case, the interest protected by s. 29 of the *FLA* is fundamental, namely the ability to meet basic financial needs following the breakdown of a relationship characterized by intimacy and economic dependence. Members of same-sex couples are entirely ignored by the statute, notwithstanding the undeniable importance to them of the benefits accorded by the statute.

The societal significance of the benefit conferred by the statute cannot be overemphasized. The exclusion of same-sex partners from the benefits of s. 29 of the *FLA* promotes the view that M., and individuals in same-sex relationships generally, are less worthy of recognition and protection. It implies that they are judged to be incapable of forming intimate relationships of economic interdependence as compared to opposite-sex couples, without regard to their actual circumstances. As the intervener EGALE submitted, such exclusion perpetuates the disadvantages suffered by individuals in same-sex relationships and contributes to the erasure of their existence.

Therefore I conclude that an examination of the four factors outlined above, in the context of the present appeal, indicate that the human dignity of individuals in same-sex relationships is violated by the impugned legislation. In light of this, I conclude that the definition of spouse in s. 29 of the *FLA* violates s. 15(1).

Iacobucci J.: C. Is Section 29 of the FLA Justified Under Section 1 of the Charter?

1. *Stare Decisis and Egan*

At the outset, I wish to address the appellant's submission that an independent examination of the s. 1 issues is unnecessary in the present case. The appellant asserts that the principle of *stare decisis* binds this Court to the decision in *Egan, supra,* and that the s. 1 analysis in that case ought to apply with equal force to the case at bar. [In *Egan,* the federal *Old Age Security Act* provided an allowance for needy spouses of pensioners once they reached sixty years of age. Five members of the court found that the definition of "spouse", which included opposite-sex individuals involved in a common-law relationship of at least one-year duration, discriminated on the basis of sexual orientation. However, one of these five, Sopinka J., concluded that this infringement of s. 15 could be justified under s. 1. He, therefore, joined the four members who had concluded that there was no discrimination in finding that the legislation did not violate the *Charter.*] Although I recognize the fundamental role of precedent in legal analysis, I cannot accept this submission. Granted, *Egan,* like the case now before this Court, was also concerned with the opposite-sex definition of "spouse" in provincial [*sic*] legislation. However, the similar focus of the two cases is not sufficient to bind the Court to the *Egan* decision. The instant case is based on entirely different legislation with its own unique objectives and legislative context. As a result, it must be evaluated on its own merits.

2. *Approach to Section 1*

. . .Under s. 1, the burden is on the legislature to prove that the infringement of a right is justified. In attempting to discharge this burden, the legislature will have to provide the court with evidence and arguments to support its general claim of justification. Sometimes this will involve demonstrating why the legislature had to make certain policy choices and why it considered these choices to be reasonable in the circumstances. These policy choices may be of the type that the legislature is in a better position than the court to make, as in the case of difficult policy judgments regarding the claims of competing groups or the evaluation of complex and conflicting social science research . . . . Courts must be cautious not to overstep the bounds of their institutional competence in reviewing such decisions. The question of deference, therefore, is intimately tied up with the nature of the particular claim or evidence at issue and not in the general application of the s. 1 test; it can only be discussed in relation to such specific claims or evidence and not at the outset of the analysis. . . .

3. *Pressing and Substantial Objective*

Section 29 of the *FLA* defines "spouse" as being either of a man and woman who are married to each other or cohabiting within the meaning of the Act. Same-sex couples are necessarily excluded from this definition, thereby giving rise to the charge that the legislation is underinclusive. In *Vriend*, at paras. 109-11, this Court found that where a law violates the *Charter* owing to under-inclusion, the first stage of the s. 1 analysis is properly concerned with the object of the legislation as a whole, the impugned provisions of the Act, and the omission itself.

As to the objective of the *FLA* as a whole, I note that the submissions of the appellant do not directly address this issue. Nevertheless, I am of the view, as was Charron J.A. in the court below, that a suitable starting point for determining the purpose of the *FLA* is the preamble of the Act . . . . Although the preamble of the *FLA* provides some insight into the objective of the Act, its utility is limited. For example, the reference to "marriage" is somewhat misleading. As recognized by members of the legislature during debate concerning the *Family Law Reform Act, 1978*, S.O. 1978, c. 2 ("*FLRA*"), this reference does not reflect the full purpose of the amended Act, which accords rights to both married and unmarried couples. Further, it was also noted in debate that the emphasis on encouraging and strengthening the role of the family is inaccurate as the legislation is actually intended to deal with the breakup of the family: *Legislature of Ontario Debates*, October 18, 1977, at p. 904.

It seems to me that a more complete and accurate statement of the objective of the current version of the *FLA* is provided by the Ontario Law Reform Commission ("OLRC") in the following excerpt from the *Report on the Rights and Responsibilities of Cohabitants Under the Family Law Act* (Toronto: Ministry of the Attorney General, 1993), at pp. 43-44:

> The purpose of the *Family Law Act* is to provide for the equitable resolution of economic disputes that arise when intimate relationships between individuals who have been financially interdependent break down (Parts I-IV). As well, it ensures that family members have a means to seek redress when an immediate relative is injured or killed through the negligence of a third party (Part V).

This statement is largely consistent with the preamble but better reflects the design of the current legislation.

Turning to the objective of the impugned provisions, s. 29 of the *FLA* defines the term "spouse" as it appears in the support obligation provisions of Part III of the Act. There is considerable disagreement between the parties as to the underlying purpose of these provisions. The appellant submits that their objective is twofold. First, Part III of the *FLA* is said to have been designed to remedy the systemic inequality associated with opposite-sex relationships, including the economic dependence of women on men resulting from women assuming primary responsibility for child care and from gender-based inequality in earning power. In his reasons in this appeal, Bastarache J. has identified this same inequality as the "mischief and defect" that the Part III provisions were meant to address. Second, Part III is said to reflect a concern for children and the conditions under which they are raised.

Although I do not dispute the claim that economically dependent heterosexual women and children are well served by the spousal support provisions in Part III of the *FLA*, in my view, there is insufficient evidence to demonstrate that the protection of these groups informs the fundamental legislative objectives behind this part of the Act. In fact, with respect to Bastarache J., it seems to me that the legislative history and the terms of the provisions themselves contradict the appellant's assertions.

With respect to the first of the proposed objectives described above, the appellant submits that the government accepted the conclusion of the OLRC in 1974-75 that married women tend to become economically dependent upon their partners owing to the traditional division of labour between husbands and wives. By enacting Part II of the *FLRA* (now Part III of the *FLA*), the government was said to have recognized and addressed the need of such women for spousal support. However, it seems to me that these submissions overlook the import of the changes introduced by the new legislation.

In contrast to predecessor legislation (i.e., the *Deserted Wives' and Children's Maintenance Act*, R.S.O. 1937, c. 211 (as amended by S.O. 1954, c. 22; S.O. 1958, c. 23; R.S.O. 1960, c. 105; R.S.O. 1970, c. 128; S.O. 1971, c. 98; S.O. 1973, c. 133)), the 1978 *FLRA* abandoned a statutory spousal support regime under which only a wife could oblige her husband to pay support in favour of one which imposed mutual support obligations on both men and women. Indeed, the thrust of the OLRC's 1975 remarks which preceded the new legislation emphasize the importance of a gender-neutral scheme. . . .

The inaccuracy of the appellant's submissions with respect to the first of the purported objectives is also reflected in the terms of Part III of the *Act*. For example, the provisions of the *FLA* that establish the right to receive support as well as the obligation to provide it use gender-neutral language. . . .

In addition, s. 33(9), which sets out various factors for the courts to consider in determining the amount and duration of support, is also cast in gender-neutral terms and makes no mention of the position of heterosexual women or their needs. Moreover, s. 33(8) establishes the purposes of an order for the support of a spouse but is silent with respect to the economic vulnerability of heterosexual women, their tendency to take on primary responsibility for parenting, the greater earning capacity of men, and systemic sexual inequality. In the face of this clearly gender-neutral scheme, the fact that a significant majority of the spousal support claimants are women does not, in my view, establish that the goal of Part III of the *FLA* is to address the special needs of women in opposite-sex relationships.

The terms of the spousal support provisions of Part III are also inconsistent with the second of the appellant's proposed objectives, namely, protecting children and ensuring that the conditions under which they are raised are adequate. Although the provisions of Part III that deal exclusively with child support clearly reflect these legitimate legislative concerns (see ss. 31 and 33(7)), it seems to me that the spousal support provisions do not share the same focus. Part III of the *FLA* imposes spousal support obligations on opposite-sex couples irrespective of whether or not they have children. Indeed, as noted by the intervenor EGALE, cohabiting opposite-sex partners who are not the parents of a child are expressly included in the s. 29 definition of "spouse" after three years of cohabitation.

As I see the matter, the objectives of the impugned spousal support provisions were accurately identified by Charron J.A. in the court below. Relying in part on the OLRC description of the goal of the *FLA* set out above, she identified the objectives of the Part III provisions as both a means to provide "for the equitable resolution of economic disputes that arise when intimate relationships between individuals who have been financially interdependent break down" and to "alleviate the burden on the public purse by shifting the obligation to provide support for needy persons to those parents and spouses who have the capacity to provide support to these individuals" (p. 450). I find support for this position in the legislative debates, the terms of the provisions, as well as the jurisprudence of this Court. . . ..

Having discussed the objective of the legislation as a whole and of the impugned provision, I turn to the objective of the omission. As I have already stated, when dealing with underinclusive legislation it is important also to consider the impugned omission when construing the objective. Often legislation does not simply further one goal but rather strikes a balance among several goals, some of which may be in tension. This balancing exercise may only become apparent after asking whether, in the case of underinclusive legislation, there is any objective being furthered by the impugned omission. A consideration of what is omitted from legislation may also lead a court to refine its interpretation of the objectives of the impugned legislation, perhaps reducing its scope. I agree with my colleague, Bastarache J., at para. 329, that if the omission is not taken into account in construing the objective then it is more likely that the omission will cause the impugned legislation to fail the rational connection step of the proportionality analysis.

However, the concerns just outlined do not imply that the court must find that there is a separate objective being furthered by the omission. Even if there is no such objective the omission must still be evaluated as part of the means chosen to further the objective of the specific provision in question, under the proportionality analysis. Otherwise the court risks collapsing the two stages of the *Oakes* test (pressing and substantial objective and proportionality) into a general question regarding the reasonableness of the omission. There may be exceptions to this general approach, such as when there is evidence of a deliberate omission by the legislature that is "on its face the very antithesis of the principles embodied in the legislation as a whole": *Vriend, supra*, at para. 116.

With these concerns in mind, I turn to the present appeal. The appellant does not argue that a separate objective is furthered by the impugned omission. Rather, the argument is that a proper consideration of the exclusion of same-sex couples from the definition of "spouse" in s. 29 of the *FLA* reduces the apparent scope of the objective furthered by that provision. The appellant made two arguments in this regard. First, the appellant argued that the *FLA* is a remedial statute designed to address the power imbalance that continues to exist in many opposite-sex relationships. Thus, it was submitted that the inclusion of same-sex couples in a scheme established to deal with problems that are not typical of their relationships is inappropriate. Further, the appellant asserted that where persons fall outside the rationale for which a benefit was established, the legislature is justified in withholding it from those persons.

With respect, I disagree with these submissions. As I stated above, I do not believe that the purpose of the *FLA* in general, nor Part III in particular, is to remedy the disadvantages suffered by women in opposite-sex relationships.

The second objective for the omission advanced by the appellant is the promotion of opposite-sex relationships to ensure the protection of children. Having found that neither the *FLA* as a whole nor the spousal support provisions in Part III of the Act are primarily concerned with the protection of children, I must also reject the submission that this is part of the objective of s. 29 of the *FLA*.

Finally, I note that Bastarache J. accepts that the rejection of the *Equality Rights Statute Law Amendment Act, 1994* [which would have amended the definition of "spouse" in s. 29 and numerous other statutes to include same-sex partners] by the Ontario legislature can provide evidence regarding the objective of s. 29 of the *FLA*. In particular, he argues, at para. 349: "It can therefore be inferred that the legislature's purpose was also to exclude all types of relationships not typically characterized by the state of economic dependency apparent in traditional family relationships." With respect, I cannot agree that a failed amendment can provide evidence as to the objective of the legislation that was to have been amended. . . .

Therefore I endorse the description of the objectives of the impugned provisions provided by Charron J.A. in the court below. These objectives are consonant with the overall scheme of the *FLA* and are not plausibly reinterpreted through examining the omission of same-sex spouses. Providing for the equitable resolution of economic disputes when intimate relationships between financially interdependent individuals break down, and alleviating the burden on the public purse to provide for dependent spouses, are to my mind pressing and substantial objectives. . . .

4. *Proportionality Analysis*

(a) *Rational Connection*

At the second stage of the s. 1 analysis, the focus shifts from the objective alone to the nexus between the objective of the provisions under attack and the means chosen by the government to implement this objective. . . . I concluded above that the dual objectives put forth by the appellant do not reflect the true purposes of the spousal support provisions in Part III of the *FLA* and relied instead on those set out by the court below. Nevertheless, it seems to me that no rational connection exists irrespective of which of the objectives is relied upon for this analysis.

Even if I were to accept that Part III of the Act is meant to address the systemic sexual inequality associated with opposite-sex relationships, the required nexus between this objective and the chosen measures is absent in this case. In my view, it defies logic to suggest that a gender-neutral support system is rationally connected to the goal of improving the economic circumstances of heterosexual women upon relationship breakdown. In addition, I can find no evidence to demonstrate that the exclusion of same-sex couples from the spousal support regime of the *FLA* in any way furthers the objective of assisting heterosexual women.

Although there is evidence to suggest that same-sex relationships are not typically characterized by the same economic and other inequalities which affect opposite-sex relationships (see, e.g., M.S. Schneider, "The Relationships of Cohabiting Lesbian and Heterosexual Couples: A Comparison", *Psychology of Women Quarterly*, 10 (1986), 234-239, at p. 237, and J.M. Lynch and M.E. Reilly, "Role Relationships: Lesbian Perspectives", *Journal of Homosexuality*, 12(2) (Winter 1985/86), 53-69, at pp. 53-54, 66), this does not, in my mind, explain why the right to apply for support is limited to heterosexuals. As submitted by LEAF, the infrequency with which members of same-sex relationships find themselves in circumstances resembling those of many heterosexual women is no different from heterosexual men who, notwithstanding that they tend to benefit from the gender-based division of labour and inequality of earning power, have as much right to apply for support as their female partners.

Put another way, it is important to recall that the ability to make a claim for spousal support does not automatically translate into a support order. To the extent that *any* relationship is characterized by more or less economic dependence, this will affect the amount and duration, if any, of an award under s. 33(9) of the *FLA*. Thus, it is no answer to say that same-sex couples should not have access to the spousal support scheme because their relationships are typically more egalitarian. In the case at bar, the respondent does not seek a support order, but rather only access to the support structure provided by the Act.

The second of the objectives put forth by the appellant, namely, the protection of children, also fails the rational connection test. The appellant submits that the exclusion of same-sex partners from Part III of the *FLA* is rationally connected to this objective as such couples are far less likely to engage in parenting than opposite-sex couples. I have several comments to make by way of response.

Even if I were to accept that the object of the legislation is the protection of children, I would have to conclude that the spousal support provisions in Part III of the *FLA* are simultaneously underinclusive and overinclusive. They are overinclusive because members of opposite-sex couples are entitled to apply for spousal support irrespective of whether or not they are parents and regardless of their reproductive capabilities or desires. Thus, if the legislation was meant to protect children, it would be incongruous that childless opposite-sex couples were included among those eligible to apply for and to receive the support in question.

The impugned provisions are also underinclusive. An increasing percentage of children are being conceived and raised by lesbian and gay couples as a result of adoption, surrogacy and donor insemination. Although their numbers are still fairly small, it seems to me that the goal of protecting children cannot be but incompletely achieved by denying some children the benefits that flow from a spousal support award merely because their parents were in a same-sex relationship. As Cory J. and I noted in *Egan, supra*, at para. 191, "[i]f there is an intention to ameliorate the position of a group, it cannot be considered entirely rational to assist only a portion of that group".

The same result follows from the objectives identified by Charron J.A. in the court below. No evidence has been supplied to support the notion that the exclusion of same-sex couples from the spousal support regime furthers the objective of providing for the equitable resolution of economic disputes that arise upon the breakdown of financially interdependent relationships. Similarly, it is nonsensical to suggest that the goal of reducing the burden on the public purse is advanced by limiting the right to make private claims for support to heterosexuals. The impugned legislation has the deleterious effect of driving a member of a same-sex couple who is in need of maintenance to the welfare system and it thereby imposes additional costs on the general taxpaying public.

If anything, the goals of the legislation are undermined by the impugned exclusion. Indeed, the *inclusion* of same-sex couples in s. 29 of the *FLA* would better achieve the objectives of the legislation while respecting the *Charter* rights of individuals in same-sex relationships. In these circumstances, I conclude that the exclusion of same-sex couples from s. 29 of the Act is simply not rationally connected to the dual objectives of the spousal support provisions of the legislation.

Given this lack of a rational connection, s. 29 of the *FLA* is not saved by s. 1 of the *Charter*. Although it is therefore not strictly necessary to consider the other two branches of the second stage of the *Oakes* test, I will discuss them briefly in order to clarify some fundamental misunderstandings advanced in this appeal.

(b) *Minimal Impairment*

In the present case, the government has failed to show that it had a reasonable basis for concluding that the rights of same-sex couples were impaired no more than was reasonably necessary to achieve its goals. The exclusion from the s. 29 definition of "spouse", and consequently from the FLA spousal support regime, is absolute. No effort has been made to tailor the limiting measure. I conclude that the appellant's case also fails at the minimal impairment stage of the s. 1 analysis.

(c) *Proportionality Between the Effect of the Measure and the Objective*

In order for the impugned legislation to survive the final stage of the s. 1 analysis, there "must be a proportionality between the deleterious effects of the measures which are responsible for limiting the rights or freedoms in question and the objective, and *there must be a proportionality between the deleterious and the salutary effects of the measures*": *Dagenais* v. *Canadian Broadcasting Corp.*, [1994] 3 S.C.R. 835 (S.C.C.), at p. 889 (emphasis in original). The damaging effects engendered by the exclusion of same-sex couples from s. 29 of the *FLA*, as noted by Cory J., are numerous and severe. Such harms cannot be justified where the statute has not achieved what it set out to do. Where, as here, the impugned measures actually undermine the objectives of the legislation it cannot be said that the deleterious effects of the measures are outweighed by the promotion of any laudable legislative goals, nor by the salutary effects of those measures.

I therefore conclude that the exclusion of same-sex couples from s. 29 of the *FLA* cannot be justified as a reasonable limit on constitutional rights under s. 1 of the *Charter*. Before turning to a discussion of the appropriate remedy, I wish to emphasize, like Cory J., that the sole issue presented by this case is whether the *Charter* mandates that same-sex couples be accorded the right to apply for spousal support under the *FLA*. This appeal does not challenge traditional conceptions of marriage, as s. 29 of the Act expressly applies to *unmarried* opposite-sex couples. That being said, I do not wish to be understood as making any comment on marriage or indeed on related issues.

In addition, despite the contentions of the appellant, the facts of this case do not require me to consider whether financially interdependent individuals who live together in non-conjugal relationships, such as friends or siblings, ought to be constitutionally entitled to apply for support upon the breakdown of their relationships. Any such claims would require an independent constitutional analysis, the outcome of which cannot be predicted in advance. Thus, arguments based on the possible extension of the definition of "spouse" beyond the circumstances of this case are entirely speculative and cannot justify the violation of the constitutional rights of same-sex couples in the case at bar.

VI. Remedy

Having found that the exclusion of same-sex couples from s. 29 of the *FLA* is unconstitutional and cannot be saved under s. 1 of the *Charter*, I must now consider the issue of remedy under s. 52 of the *Constitution Act, 1982*. In the court below, the words "a man and woman" were read out of the definition of "spouse" in s. 29 of the *FLA* and replaced with the words "two persons". The application of the order was suspended for a period of one year. With respect, I am not convinced that that is a suitable remedy in the circumstances of the present case. . . .

In the present case, the defect in the definition of "spouse" can be precisely traced to the use of the phrase "a man and woman", which has the effect of excluding same-sex partners from the spousal support scheme under the *FLA*. I recognize that there is remedial precision in so far as reading down this phrase and reading in the words "two persons" will, without more "remedy the constitutional wrong". However, I am not persuaded that reading in will also "ensure the validity of the legislation".

If the remedy adopted by the court below is allowed to stand, s. 29 of the *FLA* will entitle members of same-sex couples who otherwise qualify under the definition of "spouse" to apply for spousal support. However, any attempt to opt out of this regime by means of a cohabitation agreement provided for in s. 53 or a separation agreement set out in s. 54 would not be recognized under the Act. Both ss. 53 and 54 extend to common-law cohabitants but apply only to agreements entered into between "a man and a woman". Any extension of s. 29 of the Act would have no effect upon these Part IV domestic contract provisions of the *FLA*, which do not rely upon the Part III definition of "spouse". Thus, same-sex partners would find themselves in the anomalous position of having no means of opting out of the default system of support rights. As this option is available to opposite-sex couples, and protects the ability of couples to choose to order their own affairs in a manner reflecting their own expectations, reading in would in effect remedy one constitutional wrong only to create another, and thereby fail to ensure the validity of the legislation.

In addition, reading into the definition of "spouse" in s. 29 of the Act will have the effect of including same-sex couples in Part V of the *FLA* (Dependants' Claim for Damages), as that part of the Act relies upon the definition of "spouse" as it is defined in Part III. In my opinion, where reading in to one part of a statute will have significant repercussions for a separate and distinct scheme under that Act, it is not safe to assume that the legislature would have enacted the statute in its altered form. . . .

On the basis of the foregoing, I conclude that severing s. 29 of the Act such that it alone is declared of no force or effect is the most appropriate remedy in the present case. This remedy should be temporarily suspended for a period of six months. Although we have been advised against the imposition of a suspension by both the appellant and the respondent, for the reasons which follow, I find that a suspension is necessary.

. . . I note that declaring s. 29 of the *FLA* to be of no force or effect may well affect numerous other statutes that rely upon a similar definition of the term "spouse". The legislature may wish to address the validity of these statutes in light of the unconstitutionality of s. 29 of the *FLA*. On this point, I agree with the majority of the Court of Appeal which noted that if left up to the courts, these issues could only be resolved on a case-by-case basis at great cost to private litigants and the public purse. Thus, I believe the legislature ought to be given some latitude in order to address these issues in a more comprehensive fashion.

. . . I would declare s. 29 of no force or effect but temporarily suspend the effect of that declaration for a period of six months.

Gonthier J. (dissenting): I - Introduction

Plainly, this appeal raises elemental social and legal issues. Indeed, it is no exaggeration to observe that it represents something of a watershed. I have had the benefit of reading the reasons of my colleagues Cory and Iacobucci JJ. I gratefully adopt their account of the facts of this appeal. However, I am unable to agree with my colleagues' disposition of this appeal or their underlying reasons for so doing. I believe that the stance adopted by the majority today will have far-reaching effects beyond the present appeal. The majority contends, at para. 135, that it need not consider whether a constitutionally mandated expansion of the definition of "spouse" would open the door to a raft of other claims, because such a concern is "entirely speculative". I cannot agree. The majority's decision makes further claims not only foreseeable, but very likely. . . .

The disagreement in this appeal arises from differing views on the purpose of the legislation. Cory and Iacobucci JJ. ascribe a purpose to s. 29 of the *FLA* that centres on the interdependency of "intimate" relationships which they refer to as "conjugal" relationships of a specific degree of duration. In contrast, Bastarache J. believes that this legislation deals with individuals in "permanent and serious" relationships which cause or enhance economic disparity between the partners. In my opinion, this legislation seeks to recognize the specific social function of opposite-sex couples in society, and to address a *dynamic* of dependence unique to both men and women in opposite-sex couples that flows from three basic realities. First, this dynamic of dependence relates to the biological reality of the opposite-sex relationship and its unique potential for giving birth to children and its being the primary forum for raising them. Second, this dynamic relates to a unique form of dependence that is unrelated to children but is specific to heterosexual relationships. And third, this dynamic of dependence is particularly acute for women in opposite-sex relationships, who suffer from pre-existing economic disadvantage as compared with men. Providing a benefit (and concomitantly imposing a burden) on a group that uniquely possesses this social function, biological reality and economic disadvantage, in my opinion, is not discriminatory. Although the legislature is free to extend this benefit to others who do not possess these characteristics, the Constitution does not impose such a duty on that sovereign body.

These differing views on the purpose of the legislation are determinative in this appeal. Because Cory and Iacobucci JJ. (and Major J. by reference) suggest that the *FLA* targets intimate relationships, they understandably conclude that the legislation is unnecessarily underinclusive. Bastarache J. concludes that the *FLA* targets relationships typically characterized by permanence and economic dependency, and notes that same-sex relationships are not typically characterized by economic dependency. Nonetheless, Bastarache J. sees no reason to exclude individuals in same-sex relationships. In my judgment, the respondent M.'s claim fails because the legislation targets individuals who are in relationships which are fundamentally different from same-sex relationships. The legislation "corresponds" to the actual need, capacity, and circumstances of the claimant and those of the group the legislation targets. As such, I find that there is no "discrimination" within the meaning of that term in s. 15(1) of the *Charter* on the facts of this appeal. Accordingly, I would allow the Attorney General's appeal. . . .

Purpose of s. 29 of the Family Law Act

The primary purpose of the *FLA* is to recognize the social function specific to opposite-sex couples and their position as a fundamental unit in society, and to address the dynamic of dependence unique to men and women in opposite-sex relationships. This dynamic of dependence stems from this specific social function, the roles regularly taken by one member of that relationship, the biological reality of the relationship, and the pre-existing economic disadvantage that is usually, but not exclusively, suffered by women. This purpose is apparent from the text of the provision, the preamble to the legislation, and the legislative history of the provision. . . .

With respect, my colleagues attribute a purpose to the impugned provision, and the *FLA* as a whole, that it does not bear. Rather than analyze the *FLA* itself, Iacobucci J., like the majority of the Court of Appeal below, ascribes to the impugned legislation a purpose that bears little relation to the actual statute, its structure, or its history. It comes as no surprise that, having ascribed to the *FLA* a purpose that its language does not bear, my colleague then strikes down the legislation for failing to fulfil a purpose never intended by the Legislative Assembly. Given that my colleague's analysis depends upon the purpose so chosen, my view is that his failure to determine the true purpose of the *FLA* fatally undermines that analysis. . . .

G.   Does the Differential Treatment Discriminate?

. . . .Having established that the legislation confers a benefit, we must then turn to the question of whether the benefit is withheld "in a manner which reflects the stereotypical application of presumed group or personal characteristics, or which otherwise has the effect of perpetuating or promoting the view that the individual is less capable or worthy of recognition or value as a human being or as a member of Canadian society, equally deserving of concern, respect, and consideration": *Law*, *supra*, at para. 88. As I explain below, the concept of "stereotyping" often is linked to the contextual factor of "correspondence". Where the legislation takes into account the actual need, capacity or circumstances of the claimant and the comparator, then it is unlikely to rest on a stereotype. . . .

The contextual factor of correspondence is critical for determining the central issue in this appeal, whether the analogous ground of sexual orientation nourishes a challenge to the definition of "spouse" and renders the exclusion of gay and lesbian persons from that definition discriminatory under s. 15(1) of the *Charter*. The definition of "spouse", as I have already suggested, is an extension of marriage. To be a spouse is, in essence, to be as if married, whether or not one is actually married. Spousehood [*sic*] is a social and cultural institution, not merely an instrument of economic policy. The concept of "spouse", while a social construct, is one with deep roots in our history. It informs our legal system: the status of "spouse" is defined, recognized, and regulated by the Legislature. Under the *Constitution Act, 1867*, the federal government regulates capacity to marry (s. 91(26)), and the provincial governments regulate solemnization of marriage, that is, matters of form and ceremony (s. 92(12)), along with property and civil rights (s. 92(13)). It is rooted in Western history, in which the concept of "spouse" has always referred to a member of a cohabiting opposite-sex couple. That is what it means to be a spouse: *Andrews* v. *Ontario (Minister of Health)* (1988), 64 O.R. (2d) 258 (Ont. H.C.), at p. 261; *Dean* v. *District of Columbia*, 653 A.2d 307 (U.S. D.C. 1995), at p. 362. That well-recognized definition does not discriminate on the basis of sexual orientation, any more than the status of "child" or "adult" discriminates on the basis of age, or "male" or "female" discriminates on the basis of sex.

Our system of family law is, to a great degree, based upon the legal rights and duties flowing from marriage. The law recognizes marriage as a status voluntarily acquired through contract, and endows that status with both rights and duties. Individuals who do not live within the institution of marriage are, for the most part, not subject to the rights and obligations that attach to it. So, for example, the *FLA*'s sections on family property (Part I) and the matrimonial home (Part II) apply only to married couples, not unmarried, cohabiting opposite-sex couples, or anyone else. In general, unmarried individuals who cohabit outside marriage do not bear the full range of legal responsibilities of a married couple, and neither the benefits nor the burdens of marriage extend to them. As I explained in *Miron, supra* (and as La Forest J. outlined in greater detail in *Egan, supra*), marriage is a fundamental social institution because it is the crucible of human procreation and the usual forum for the raising of children. That is the primary, though not sole, purpose of the institution of marriage: *Layland* v. *Ontario (Minister of Consumer & Commercial Relations)* (1993), 104 D.L.R. (4th) 214 (Ont. Div. Ct.), at pp. 222-23 . . .

Mere appeal to history or tradition, of course, is insufficient to establish the existence of the actual need, capacity, or circumstances of the claimant or others: *Edwards* v. *Canada (Attorney General)* (1929), [1930] A.C. 124 (Canada P.C.), at p. 134. The proper evaluation of an equality claim requires the Court to subject our social practices to critical evaluation. . . . Nonetheless, the recognition that social values change and evolve does not alter the reality that certain biological and social realities endure. . . . The *Charter* requires the Court to subject our social institutions to a critical eye, but it does not mandate that we should sweep them away. Legislative distinctions based on an accurate appreciation of biological and social realities may not amount to discrimination, where the legislation corresponds to the characteristics in a manner that respects the claimant's human dignity.

Legislation such as Part III of the *FLA*, which provides differing economic and legal treatment for married couples and opposite-sex common law couples is premised on certain assumptions about the nature of the economic, social, and legal dynamic of the relationships those individuals have. That economic, social, and legal dynamic, I should emphasize, is a multi-faceted one, and some of its features will be shared by other relationships, including some long-term same-sex relationships. One of the central questions, therefore, is whether those underlying assumptions, embodied in the distinction drawn in s. 29, are based on stereotypes. As La Forest J. recognized in *Egan, supra*, at para. 25, an opposite-sex couple is

> the social unit that uniquely has the *capacity* to procreate children and generally cares for their upbringing, and as such warrants support by Parliament to meet its needs. This is the only unit in society that expends resources to care for children on a routine and sustained basis.... [T]his is the unit in society that fundamentally anchors other social relationships and other aspects of society. [Emphasis in original.]

The spousal support obligation is unquestionably a core feature of the institution of marriage itself. True, that obligation has been extended to unmarried cohabiting opposite-sex couples by legislative action. Yet that should not obscure the fact that the extension was carefully tailored for a specific purpose, and that the nature of the obligation was established in the marriage context before it was ever extended to unmarried cohabiting opposite-sex couples. I thus find Cory J.'s statement that "this appeal has nothing to do with marriage *per se*" (para. 52) entirely unconvincing.

The Legislative Assembly has restricted the meaning of "spouse" in Part III of the *FLA*. However, it is critical to see that the restriction has not been made on the basis of stereotypical assumptions regarding group or personal characteristics, as set out in para. 64 of Iacobucci J.'s reasons in *Law*, and as I have set out above. To the contrary, s. 29's definition of "spouse" corresponds with an accurate account of the actual needs, capacity and circumstances of opposite-sex couples as compared to others, including same-sex couples. Those differences stem, in part, from the biological reality that only opposite-sex couples can bear children. That biological reality means that opposite-sex couples play a unique social role. That social role often leads to the well-established economic vulnerability of women in long-term opposite-sex relationships, often (though not always) stemming from the decision to bear and raise children.

Cohabiting opposite-sex couples are the natural and most likely site for the procreation and raising of children. This is their specific, unique role. Section 29 of the *FLA* is specially structured to meet this reality. This can be seen from the fact that the necessary cohabitation period to come within the scope of the section is reduced where there is a child of the relationship. As well, a child may make a claim under Part III of the *FLA* against his or her parents, regardless of the parents' relationship when the child was conceived, raised, or thereafter (s. 31).

This unique social role of opposite-sex couples has two related features. First, it is notorious, as my colleague Iacobucci J. noted in *Symes* v. *R.*, [1993] 4 S.C.R. 695 (S.C.C.), at p. 762, that "women bear a disproportionate share of the child care burden in Canada", and that this burden is borne both by working mothers and mothers who stay at home with their children. The second feature is that one partner (most often the woman) tends to become economically dependent upon the other.

The evidence is uncontroverted that women in long-term opposite-sex relationships tend to become economically dependent upon their spouses. This dependence arises for several related reasons. First, women as a group are economically disadvantaged by comparison to men. Women, on average, earn less than men do. A woman cohabiting in an opposite-sex relationship is thus likely to earn less than her male partner. This relative economic disadvantage is both the cause and the effect of gender roles. Second, women in long-term opposite-sex relationships commonly — though, I emphasize, not inevitably — waive educational and employment opportunities or prospects for economic advancement in order to bear and raise children and to shoulder a greater share of domestic responsibilities. They are also more likely to choose employment that facilitates temporary exit from and subsequent re-entry into the work force, employment that tends to be more insecure and to pay less.

Of course, not all procreation takes place within marriage. Indeed, recognition of this growing reality was an important impetus to the legislature's decision to extend certain rights and obligations to unmarried common law opposite-sex couples in the 1970s. There is, obviously, no requirement that married couples bear children, or have the capacity to do so. Some married couples are unable to have children. Some choose not to have children. Some married couples adopt children. Conversely, it is possible for same-sex couples to have children, either from previous opposite-sex relationships, through adoption, or through artificial insemination. So too, of course, can some single individuals. These circumstances are, however, as La Forest J. observed in *Egan, supra*, at para. 26, "exceptional". To acknowledge that they exist does not alter the demographic, social, and biological reality that the overwhelming majority of children are born to, and raised by, married or cohabiting couples of the opposite sex, and that they are the only couples capable of procreation. Indeed, by definition, no child can be born of a same-sex union: a third party must be involved.

Even in the absence of children, women in cohabiting opposite-sex relationships often take on increased domestic responsibilities which limit their prospects for outside employment, precisely because their lower average earnings make this an efficient division of labour for the couple. Again, gender roles are both a cause and effect of this division of labour. If the relationship breaks down, the woman is usually left in a worse situation, probably with impaired earning capacity and limited employment opportunities. The economic disadvantages faced by women upon the breakdown of opposite-sex relationships, as indicated by reduced earning capacity, more fragile employment prospects, and underinvestment in education and training, occur for the very reason that the woman did not anticipate that she would have to support herself. She engaged in a division of labour with her former partner in the expectation that such an arrangement would yield a higher joint economic position.

. . . Although in most cases, the woman in an opposite-sex relationship will be the one to suffer from the systemic dynamic of dependence, this will not always be the case. As I discussed above, as women's economic situation improves, more claims will likely be brought by men in the future. However, I emphasize that while women are the *primary* group who suffer from this dynamic of dependence, they are not the *exclusive* group. The evidence before this Court demonstrates that when the female partner is not suffering from this dynamic of dependence, the male partner often is. In 1992, for example, 25.2 percent of all married couples were characterized by the wife being the full-time wage-earner, and the husband either working part-time or not at all: Statistics Canada, *Family Expenditure in Canada 1992*, at p. 160. Studies presented to this Court demonstrate that when men are in such a position, they expect less from their partner in housework: P. Blumstein and P. Schwartz, *American Couples* (1983), at p. 151. In other words, the dynamic of dependence also exists for men in opposite-sex relationships, as a type of "division of labour" is created, where the man will often assume additional duties at home while his partner is at work: M.S. Schneider, "The Relationships of Cohabiting Lesbian and Hetero-sexual Couples: A Comparison", *Psychology of Women Quarterly*, 10 (1986), 234-39, at p. 234. Other evidence submitted to this Court demonstrate other forms of dependency that are similarly unique to individuals in opposite-sex relationships: J.M. Lynch and M.E. Reilly, "Role Relationships: Lesbian Perspectives", *Journal of Homosexuality*, 12(2) (Winter 1985/86), 53-69, at p. 53. Although the dynamic of dependence unique to opposite-sex relationships plays out differently for men, it flows from similar factors: in essence, the dynamic of dependence reduces autonomy and increases attachment in heterosexual relationships: *ibid*, at p. 56.

These realities are captured in the status of "spouse". To my mind, they are realities that the legislature may address by extending some (though not all) of the rights and obligations that attach to marriage to cohabiting opposite-sex couples (again, it must not be forgotten that not all opposite-sex couples are included within the scope of the definition) without transgressing constitutional boundaries on leg-islative action if it does not also extend them to same-sex couples. It is both legitimate and reasonable for the Legislative Assembly to extend special treatment to an im-portant social institution. The position I advance also finds support in foreign juris-prudence, including the recent decision of the Court of Justice of the European Communities in *Grant* v. *South-West Trains Ltd.*, [1998] 1 F.L.R. 839, 1 I.C.R. 449 (European Ct. Just.), at p. 478, paras. 35-36.

It is *this* dynamic of dependence that the legislature has sought to address by way of Part III of the *FLA*. The question before this Court is whether the *Charter* compels the extension of the legislature's efforts to address this problem to long-term same-sex couples. In arguing that the *Charter* does just that, the respondent M. and several of the interveners contend that long-term same-sex relationships manifest many of the features of long-term opposite-sex relationships. This may well be true. But to my mind, this argument is inadequate. It fails to demonstrate that the specific feature of long-term opposite-sex relationships that the legislature has sought to address by way of Part III of the *FLA*, what I have called the dynamic of dependence, is also present in long-term same-sex relationships. Indeed, it is almost certain that it could not be, because the dependency of women in long-term opposite-sex rela-tionships arises precisely because they are opposite-sex relationships. There is simply no evidence that same-sex couples in long-term relationships exhibit this type of dependency in any significant numbers.

Indeed, the evidence before us is to the contrary. That evidence indicates that lesbian relationships are characterized by a more even distribution of labour, a rejection of stereotypical gender roles, and a lower degree of financial interdepend-ence than is prevalent in opposite-sex relationships: Schneider, *supra*, at p. 237. Same-sex couples are much less likely to adopt traditional sex roles than are opposite-sex couples: M. Cardell, S. Finn, and J. Marecek, "Sex-Role Identity, Sex-Role Behavior, and Satisfaction in Heterosexual, Lesbian, and Gay Male Couples", *Psy-chology of Women Quarterly*, 5 (Spring 1981), 488-94, at pp. 492-93. Indeed, "research shows that most lesbians and gay men actively reject traditional hus-band-wife or masculine-feminine roles as a model for enduring relationships": L.A.

Peplau, "Lesbian and Gay Relationships", in J.C. Gonsiorek and J.D. Weinrich, eds., *Homosexuality: Research Implications for Public Policy* (1991), 177, at p. 183.

The evidence before us also indicates that partners in a lesbian couple are more likely to each pursue a career and to work outside the home than are partners in an opposite-sex couple: *ibid.*, at pp. 183-84; N.S. Eldridge and L.A. Gilbert, "Correlates of Relationship Satisfaction in Lesbian Couples", *Psychology of Women Quarterly*, 14 (1990), 43-62, at p. 44. As members of same-sex couples are, obviously, of the same sex, they are more likely than members of opposite-sex couples to earn similar incomes, because no male-female income differential is present. For the same reason, the gendered division of domestic and child-care responsibilities that continues to characterize opposite-sex relationships simply has no purchase in same-sex relationships.

Undoubtedly, in some same-sex relationships, one partner may become financially dependent on the other. This may happen for any number of reasons, including explicit or implicit agreement, differences in age, health, or education, and so on. However, no *pattern* of dependence emerges. Put another way, dependence in same-sex relationships is not systemic: it does not exhibit the gendered dependency characteristic of many cohabiting opposite-sex relationships. Due to the high degree of equality observed in lesbian relationships, very few women were dependent on their same-sex partners for financial support, and even differences in income between same-sex partners did not affect women's perception of their financial dependence on one another in same-sex relationships: Lynch and Reilly, *supra*, at p. 66.

Mere need in an individual case, unrelated to systemic factors, is, in my view, insufficient to render the *FLA*'s scheme constitutionally underinclusive. This is especially true because the scheme involves, in counterpart to an access to support, a restriction on freedom and a burden. Taken as a group, same-sex relationships simply do not resemble opposite-sex relationships on this fundamental point. Consequently, I see no reason why the *Charter* requires the legislature to treat them identically with regard to it. The *FLA* scheme was intended to address need of a particular kind, and does so. There is no evidence that that particular need exists to any significant degree outside of long-term opposite-sex relationships. Consequently, although the distinction drawn by s. 29 of the *FLA* undoubtedly denies a benefit to individuals in same-sex couples, and the distinction may be seen, in its effects, to be drawn on the basis of sexual orientation, no discrimination arises, because no stereotypical assumptions motivate the distinction. On the contrary, the legislation takes into account the claimant's actual need, capacity and circumstances as compared with individuals in opposite-sex couples and by doing so it does not violate human dignity.

Indeed, the then Chair of the Ontario Law Reform Commission, discussing the Commission's 1993 Report, made just such an observation (J.D. McCamus, "Family Law Reform in Ontario" in *Special Lectures of the Law Society of Upper Canada 1993: Family Law: Roles, Fairness and Equality* (1994), 451, at pp. 470-71):

> The provisions of the *Family Law Act* appear to be designed to give effect to the sorts of reasonable expectations and to compensate for the kinds of uncompensated contributions that are likely to occur in marital relationships and in unmarried heterosexual relationships that follow a similar pattern. The kinds of expectations and contributions that arise in these contexts rest, to some extent at least, on gender-based assumptions concerning such questions as the division of labour within the home and the making of decisions concerning career choices and other economic matters.... The general pattern of such relationships, and, moreover, the confusion generated by partial coverage, was sufficient justification, in the Commission's view, to warrant inclusion of unmarried heterosexual couples on an ascriptive basis. It was also the Commission's view,

however, that we have, at the present time, no sound basis for assuming that similar considerations would apply to significant numbers of gay and lesbian couples. It may be that gay and lesbian relationships do not, as a general proposition, correspond to the same model and accordingly, that equality considerations do not demand identical treatment. [Emphasis added.]

My colleague Iacobucci J. concedes this point in stating that "there is evidence to suggest that same-sex relationships are not typically characterized by the same economic and other inequalities which affect opposite-sex relationships" (para. 110). In his view, however, this only goes to show that allowing members of same-sex couples to bring applications under Part III of the *FLA* might not, as a practical matter, result in the award of many support orders, because such individuals would only infrequently exhibit the dependence or need necessary to obtain an award. This leads Iacobucci J. to the conclusion that the mere prediction that few claims by members of same-sex couples would succeed if such claims could be brought cannot be used to support the position that such claims should be barred from the beginning. As I discussed earlier, this same line of thought pervades the reasons of my colleague Bastarache J.

However, this contention also proves too much. Indeed, as Professor (now Dean) Hogg indicates (*Constitutional Law of Canada* (loose-leaf ed.), vol. 2, at s. 52.7(b)), carried to its logical conclusion, few limitations upon the category of individuals eligible to seek a support order under Part III of the *FLA* could withstand constitutional scrutiny. Friends who share an apartment do not typically exhibit a relationship of financial dependence. Yet there may be particular cases in which they do, and if so, according to my colleague's reasoning, at least so long as an enumerated or analogous ground can be located, be it race, age, physical handicap or other, one of them should be able to seek a spousal support order under Part III of the *FLA*, because the legislation would have failed to take into account their already disadvantaged position within Canadian society: *Law*, *supra*, at para. 88. I find this reasoning unattractive. As I indicated in *Thibaudeau* v. *R.*, [1995] 2 S.C.R. 627 (S.C.C.), at para. 143, "legislation must be assessed in terms of the majority of cases to which it applies. The fact that it may create a disadvantage in certain exceptional cases while benefitting a legitimate group as a whole does not justify the conclusion that it is prejudicial." Indeed, such was the case in *Law*, where it was shown that, in the exceptional case, some younger women may be less capable of providing for their own long-term need. In this case, many couples (and indeed, groups) live in relationships not comprehended by s. 29's definition of "spouse". Thus, the distinction drawn by the *FLA* is not between (1) opposite-sex couples and (2) same-sex couples; it is between (1) certain opposite-sex couples and (2) all non-spousal relationships.

I pause to underline that nothing in my reasons should be taken as suggesting that same-sex couples are incapable of forming enduring relationships of love and support, nor do I wish to imply that individuals living in same-sex relationships are less deserving of respect. . . .

It is plain to any observer that same-sex couples may, and do, form relationships which are similar in many ways to those formed by opposite-sex couples. Much of the respondent M.'s argument and evidence sought to demonstrate the similarities between same-sex relationships and opposite-sex relationships. Same-sex couples may exhibit companionship, love, loyalty, and economic intermingling. The under-lying assumption of the respondent M.'s argument is that s. 29 relies on a stereotype in suggesting that only a couple made up of a "man and woman" exhibit these features.

This argument, in my view, misses the mark. The distinction drawn by s. 29 does not discriminate because it does not involve the stereotypical application of presumed group or personal characteristics, and it does not otherwise have the effect of perpetuating or promoting the view that individuals in same-sex relationships are less deserving of concern, respect, and consideration. The evidence bears out the contention that the legislative distinction is drawn on the basis of a true appreciation of the facts. . . .

III — Conclusion

. . . In this appeal, the impugned legislation sought to redress a historical fact that individuals in opposite-sex relationships suffer a *systemic* dynamic of dependence, which manifests in a support obligation that exists not only while the two individuals are in the relationship, but also after the relationship breaks down. Usually, it is the female partner who suffers the greatest burden upon marriage or common-law relationship breakdown: *Moge* v. *Moge, supra.* The legislature has, since 1859, used a variety of legislative tools to alleviate this systemic suffering, which is unique to opposite-sex relationships. The statutory language, the preamble, and the legislative debates reveal that this legislation is one of those tools.

In my view, the s. 15(1) claim in this case fails because s. 29 of the *FLA* seeks to ameliorate a historical and structural disadvantage specific to individuals in certain types of opposite-sex relationships, and in so doing, accurately corresponds with the needs, capacity, and circumstances of the claimant and these opposite-sex couples. Although individuals in same-sex relationships suffer pre-existing disadvantage in many areas of life, it has not been shown that this is one of them. In fact, the contrary has been shown: individuals in same-sex relationships generally exhibit less dependency in the relationship; they do not have a structural wage differential between the partners in the relationship; and they do not exhibit the same gendered division of domestic and child-care responsibilities. Although any of these elements may be present in a same-sex relationship, none will have been created by the structural dynamic of dependence which the legislature has seen fit to address, but rather will be attributable to the individual idiosyncrasies of the claimant.

In this case, the respondent M. claimed that a benefit granted opposite-sex couples has been denied her on a distinction based on the analogous ground of sexual orientation. However, the contextual factors demonstrate that there has been no discrimination and the claimant falls outside the scope of protection accorded by that ground. This distinction does not rest on the stereotypical application of presumed group or individual characteristics; to the contrary, it rests on the correspondence between the ground of distinction and the actual needs, capacity, and circumstances of the claimant and those of the group the legislation targets. The right to equality in s. 15(1) does not guarantee equality in the abstract; it rests on a comparison with others. This requires us to examine whether the claimant group suffers pre-existing disadvantage, stereotyping, prejudice or vulnerability *as compared with* the selected comparison group, and as related to the subject-matter of the legislation. In this case, individuals in same-sex relationships are not disadvantaged in relation to the dynamic of dependence which the legislation seeks to address. As such, the ameliorative purpose of the *FLA* is not underinclusive of a group which is disadvantaged in relation to that purpose. Moreover, although the claimant is affected by her exclusion from the mandatory support regime, this regime both confers a benefit *and* imposes a burden. Mandatory support restricts personal choice and reduces the concomitant financial advantages. The legislation does not render individuals in same-sex relationships "invisible". They are fully entitled to impose support obligations upon themselves, if they so choose. However, the circumstances unique to individuals in opposite-sex relationships which warrant the reduction of that group's autonomy do not similarly exist in same-sex relationships.

By analyzing all of the contextual factors, it is apparent that the claimant's human dignity is not violated by s. 29 of the *FLA*. A reasonable person in the position of the claimant, having taken into account all of the contextual factors relevant to the claim, would not find their human dignity violated by a provision which appropriately takes into account their actual needs, capacity, and circumstances as compared to those of opposite-sex couples subject to the legislation. For these reasons, it is my view that the s. 15(1) claim must fail.

WALSH v. BONA

(April 19, 2000), Doc. C.A. 159139 (N.S. C.A.)

FLINN J.A.(for the court): The appellant, Susan Walsh and the respondent, Wayne Bona, while not married, lived together in a "common law relationship" (as they both described the relationship in their respective affidavits) for approximately ten years. Two children were born out of this relationship, in 1988 and 1990 respectively. The appellant and the respondent separated in 1995.

In January, 1999, the appellant commenced an application under the *Matrimonial Property Act*, R.S.N.S. 1989, c. 275 (*MPA*), seeking an equal division of the parties' assets. In conjunction with that application, the appellant sought a declaration that the *Canadian Charter of Rights and Freedoms* is infringed by the definition of "spouse" in s. 2(g) of the *MPA*. The *MPA* does not apply to the appellant and the respondent because they do not come within the definition of "spouse" in s. 2(g)
. . . .

In her application, the appellant claims that s. 2(g) discriminates against her as a common law spouse in violation of s. 15(1) of the *Charter*; and that such discrimination cannot be justified under s. 1 of the *Charter*. The relief which the appellant seeks is "an order reading into the definition of spouse s. 2(g) of the *MPA*, the definition of common law spouse contained in the *Family Maintenance Act*, R.S.N.S. 1989, c. 160". The definition of "common law spouse" is contained in s. 2(m) of the *Family Maintenance Act* and provides as follows:

> 2 In this Act, ...
>
> (m) "spouse" means a person married to another person and, for the purpose of this Act, includes a man and woman who, not being married to each other, live together as husband and wife for one year.

With respect to her claim for a division of the assets, including real estate, of the respondent, the appellant deposes in her affidavit, inter alia, as follows:

> 12. THAT I am advised by my solicitor, and do verily believe, that the matrimonial property legislation in Nova Scotia does not apply to common-law relationships and as a result I have the legal obligation in any claim against the property of establishing not only that I have a claim, but the extent of that claim.
>
> 13. THAT I am advised by my solicitor, and do verily believe, that if I were married to the Defendant the Matrimonial Property Act would require the Defendant to establish that I was not entitled to an equal division of all assets accumulated prior to and during the marriage.

. . .The Crown concedes, on this appeal, that since the *MPA* applies only to married persons and not to cohabitees living in a conjugal relationship, that there is differential treatment for the purpose of s. 15(1) of the *Charter*. The Crown also concedes that marital status is an analogous ground of discrimination. The Crown submits, however, that the differential treatment which arises, here, is not discrimination under the *Charter*; and, if it is discrimination, then it is saved by s. 1 of the *Charter*.

SECTION 15(1) – ANALYSIS:

In the recent decision of the Supreme Court of Canada in *Law* v. *Canada (Minister of Employment & Immigration)*, [1999] 1 S.C.R. 497, Justice Iacobucci, for the Court, summarizes the Court's approach to the interpretation of s. 15(1) *Charter* issues, and provides a set of guidelines for courts that are called upon to analyze a discrimination claim under the *Charter*. . . at pp. 548-549:

> Accordingly, a court that is called upon to determine a discrimination claim under s. 15(1) should make the following three broad inquiries:
>
> (A) Does the impugned law (a) draw a formal distinction between the claimant and others on the basis of one or more personal characteristics, or (b) fail to take into account the claimant's already disadvantaged position within Canadian society resulting in substantively differential treatment between the claimant and others on the basis of one or more personal characteristics?
>
> (B) Is the claimant subject to differential treatment based on one or more enumerated and analogous grounds? and
>
> (C) Does the differential treatment discriminate, by imposing a burden upon or withholding a benefit from the claimant in a manner which reflects the stereotypical application of presumed group or personal characteristics, or which otherwise has the effect of perpetuating or promoting the view that the individual is less capable or worthy of recognition or value as a human being or as a member of Canadian society, equally deserving of concern, respect, and consideration?

An Overview of the MPA:

In the *Final Report* on *Reform of the Law Dealing with Matrimonial Property in Nova Scotia* (Halifax: Law Reform Commission of Nova Scotia, March 1997) at p. 5, the Commission said the following concerning the adoption, in Nova Scotia, of the *MPA* in 1980:

> The *Matrimonial Property Act* was adopted in Nova Scotia in 1980 as part of a general law reform movement in all the common law provinces which attempted to address dissatisfaction with the existing law regarding division of property on the ending of marriage. Prior to these reforms the law had been based on a concept known as "separate property". This was a concept developed in the late nineteenth century which provided that upon marriage termination, whether by death or divorce, each spouse could retain only that property to which they could show legal title. In other words, there was no such thing as "family property" or "matrimonial assets". This meant that in Nova Scotia until 1980, all property owned by a married couple was considered to belong either to the wife exclusively or to the husband exclusively, unless they had *expressly* obtained legal title together as co-owners of the property.
>
> The Nova Scotia *Matrimonial Property Act* changed the existing law in two main ways:
>
> (1) by creating a "pool" of assets owned by either spouse, known as "matrimonial assets", which could be divided, regardless of legal title, in equal shares between the spouses upon marriage breakdown, divorce or the death of a spouse; and

(2) by giving each spouse an equal right of possession in the matrimonial home, without regard to which spouse has the title in law; and providing that no sale or mortgage of the matrimonial home can occur without the consent of both spouses.

The right to equal division is a *presumption* only, in that the *Act* also allows judges to make an unequal division in some cases, for example where the length of the marriage might indicate that an equal division would result in unfairness. The right to equal division arises only at the *end* of a marriage. Before then, each spouse retains title to whatever property is in their name, and they may freely dispose of it without the consent of the other spouse. The only exceptions to this are the right to equal possession of the matrimonial home, and to veto any sale or mortgage of it. These rights arise at the moment of marriage and continue *during* the marriage.

Does the MPA draw a formal distinction between the appellant and others on the basis of one or more personal characteristics?

As to the first of the three broad inquiries which the Court must make in analyzing a claim for discrimination under s. 15(1) of the *Charter* (see *Law*), the *MPA* denies a person in a common law relationship benefits which are granted to a similar person in a marriage relationship. This denial of equal benefit, on the basis of marital status, a personal characteristic, is therefore established. Counsel for the Crown agrees that there is differential treatment for the purpose of s. 15(1) of the *Charter*.

Is the appellant subject to differential treatment on the basis of one or more of the enumerated and analogous ground?

As to the second broad inquiry, marital status is not one of the enumerated grounds upon which a claim for discrimination under s. 15(1) can be made. Is it an analogous ground? The Crown concedes that it is an analogous ground on the basis of the majority decision in *Miron* v. *Trudel*, [1995] 2 S.C.R. 418. . . .

Does the differential treatment of the appellant by the provisions of the MPA discriminate in the substantive sense intended by s. 15(1) of the Charter? Does it violate the purpose of s. 15(1)?

. . . The appellant has had a long standing relationship with the respondent. They have lived together for approximately 10 years. Two children have been born of this relationship. The appellant and the respondent own their own home. Other assets have been acquired during their relationship. This relationship has all the hallmarks of a marriage, with the exception that the appellant and the respondent have not gone through a formal marriage ceremony.

Upon separation, the appellant has the right, under the provisions of the *Family Maintenance Act*, R.S.N.S. 1989, c. 160 to make application for:1) custody of the children; 2) spousal and child support; and 3) limited rights to "occupation" of the family home. . . .

The appellant is denied, however, the benefits of the *MPA*. Those benefits include the presumption that the married spouse is entitled to an equal division of the assets accumulated during the marriage. The other married spouse has the onus of rebutting that presumption. The appellant, on the other hand, as an unmarried cohabitee, has only available to her the common law remedies of resulting trust and unjust enrichment, about which I will say more later in these reasons. The benefits under the *MPA* also include the ability of the married spouse to apply for exclusive possession of the matrimonial home. The appellant's rights, on the other hand, are, at best, restricted to a limited right of "occupation" of the family home. The only reason the appellant is denied the benefits of the *MPA* is because she is not married.

I recognize that the appellant and the respondent could have entered into a cohabitation agreement under which the appellant, on the termination of the relationship, would receive the same, or similar, benefits as are provided for in the *MPA*. However, a married couple has the ability to do that as well. The problem is that, in each case, it requires the agreement of two persons. Such an agreement is not something over which the appellant, or the married spouse, has sole control. The legislature obviously recognized that fact, in enacting the *MPA*, but only to the extent of making provision for the married spouse.

As an unmarried spouse, the appellant loses the benefit of the presumptions contained in the *MPA* in the event that no cohabitation agreement is reached. If a married couple either does not think about an agreement or thinks an agreement is unnecessary, or is unable to reach a consensus in a pre-nuptial agreement, the *MPA*, as the default position, will apply in the event of a separation. The common law couple on the other hand is denied the benefit of the Act as the default position, if they for whatever reason do not enter into an agreement. . . .

Essentially, the appellant contends that the *MPA* does not recognize the contribution which she has made to the economic survival and growth of her family. That, she claims, is discrimination under s. 15(1) of the *Charter*.

The appellant's claim must be looked at objectively, and from her perspective. Does the denial of the benefit of the provisions of the *MPA* to the appellant violate the purpose of s. 15(1)? In light of the historical, social, political and legal context of the appellant's claim, does the *MPA* have the effect of demeaning the appellant's human dignity, and does it thereby constitute discrimination within the meaning of s. 15(1) of the *Charter*?

Of the contextual factors referred to in *Law* (as points of reference for the Court in determining whether the *MPA* violates the purpose of s. 15(1)), the most relevant factors in this case are pre-existing disadvantage, and the nature of the interest which is affected.

. . . Persons involved in an unmarried relationship constitute a historically disadvantaged group. Justice McLachlin [in *Miron*] says that there is ample evidence that unmarried partners have often suffered social disadvantage and prejudice. Historically, in our society, the unmarried partner has been regarded as less worthy than the married partner. Disadvantages have ranged from social ostracism through denial of status and benefits. In theory, Justice McLachlin says, the individual is free to choose whether to marry or not; however, the reality may be otherwise. She compares discrimination, on the basis of marital status, to discrimination on the ground of religion - to the extent that it finds its roots in moral disapproval of all sexual unions except those sanctioned by the church and state. Justice McLachlin then notes that there is some recognition that distinguishing between cohabiting couples, on the basis of whether they are married or not, fails to accord with current social values or reality. Some benefits have been accorded to unmarried partners who have cohabited in a conjugal relationship (child and spousal support - the right to claim on the basis of unjust enrichment and resulting trust). This, she suggests, is recognition of the fact that it is often wrong to deny equal benefit of the law because a person is not married. I will refer, later in these reasons, to some of the Nova Scotia Statutes which make such provision.

The Crown submits, in this case:

1) the marital spouse is not "entitled" to 50% of the matrimonial assets under the *MPA*. The marital spouse has only a *presumption* of entitlement. It cannot be said to be the denial of an equal benefit under the law simply because the appellant cannot avail herself of a *presumption* that she is entitled to 50% of the assets on the break-up of her relationship with the respondent; and

2) unlike *Miron*, where there was no other avenue open to the unmarried spouse to obtain the insurance benefits which were the subject of that action, the appellant has available to her the common law rights to claim benefits using the concepts of unjust enrichment and constructive trust. Also, unlike *Miron*, the appellant has the ability to contract into a joint property regime (with respect to this latter point, I have already dealt with that issue previously in these reasons); and

3) the presumption of entitlement in the *MPA* does not deal with the merit or worth of the relationship itself (i.e., whether it was long, short, loving or abusive), but with respect to the disposition of property acquired by married persons. That, counsel submits, does not go to human dignity.

With respect to the Crown's first point, as Justice Cory noted in *M. v. H.*, the Crown's analysis takes too narrow a view of "benefit" under the law, and it is a view that the Court should not adopt. . . .

With respect to the second point, the fact that the appellant might be able to avail herself of the equitable remedies of unjust enrichment and resulting trust, can hardly be equated with the presumptive rights that a married person enjoys under the *MPA*. Pursuing such equitable remedies is difficult, time consuming, costly and uncertain (see, for example, *Peter* v. *Beblow*, [1993] 1 S.C.R. 980). If the appellant must resort to these equitable remedies, she has the burden of proof on several issues. She must prove that she made a contribution related to the acquisition of property, the value of that contribution, and that there was a reasonable expectation of receiving compensation. Another difficulty, associated with such equitable remedies, is that it may not be easy to marshal the necessary evidence in the context of a spousal relationship.

As to the third point . . . The affront to the appellant's human dignity which is caused by the *MPA* is the fact that the *MPA* recognizes that a legally married spouse contributes to the marriage relationship, financially, and in other ways (e.g., raising a family). The *MPA* also recognizes that these contributions allow a married couple to accumulate matrimonial assets . . . The appellant enjoys no such recognition. She must resort to the equitable principles of resulting trust and unjust enrichment, and I have already referred to the difficulties associated with those remedies. Further, in a constructive trust action, the factors which are considered by the Court under s. 13 of the *MPA* (in determining whether to make an unequal division of assets) are not, generally, applicable. Further, on this third point, the appellant may have, at best, limited rights to occupation of her family home; whereas the married spouse may apply for exclusive possession of the matrimonial home under the *MPA*. A further benefit to the married spouse, under the *MPA* - which an unmarried spouse does not enjoy - is protection from disposition of the matrimonial home. The appellant's dignity is violated because her relationship with the respondent is considered less worthy of recognition than the relationship of a married couple; and, as a result, she is denied access to the benefits of the *MPA*.

. . . In my opinion, a reasonable person in circumstances similar to those of the appellant would find that the *MPA*, which imposes differential treatment, has the effect of demeaning the appellant's human dignity. As a result, there is a violation of s. 15(1) of the *Charter*.

SECTION 1 ANALYSIS:

Pressing and Substantial Objective:

. . . The Crown tendered no evidence to discharge its onus under s. 1; and, as a result, the Court is left with only the Crown's submissions in its factum and during the course of oral argument in support of justification. Before dealing with the Crown's submissions there are two points which should be noted, with respect to this case on the general subject of justification under s. 1:

> 1) this is not a case where including those in a common law relationship within the provisions of the *MPA* would have a financial impact on government; and

> 2) there is no suggestion that including those in a common law relationship within the provisions of the *MPA* would have any negative impact on married persons.

The Crown submits that the purpose of the *MPA* is to strengthen the role of the family in society; and that the "promotion of marriage" is also a purpose of the legislation.

In considering the objective of the *MPA* as a whole, the preamble is somewhat misleading. The functional objective of the legislation is, clearly, to provide for an orderly and equitable settlement of the economic affairs of married persons on the breakdown of the marriage relationship.

In the sense that the legislation recognizes that the contribution of spouses to a marriage, regardless of their form, are equal - and should be shared equally - it could be said to be an objective of the legislation to strengthen the role of the family in society. However, since the functional purpose of the legislation is to make provision for the resolution of property disputes upon termination of the marriage, it can hardly be said to be an objective of this legislation to promote marriage. However, even if it could be said that the objective of the legislation was to support the institution of marriage over, for example, common law relationships, such an objective has been called into question as a discriminatory objective which could not be justified under s. 1, in light of the decision of the Supreme Court of Canada in *Miron* (see: *Constitution Law of Canada*, Peter W. Hogg, looseleaf edition, vol. 2, s. 52.17).

Nevertheless, as the Law Reform Commission of Nova Scotia noted in its *Final Report*, by deeming contributions to a marriage relationship to be equal, regardless of their form, the legislation effected an important change in the law which had traditionally ignored, or undervalued, unpaid work in the home. Or, as Justice Wilson said in *Clarke*, [[1990] 2 S.C.R. 795] the legislation recognized "the contribution made by women to the economic survival and growth of the family". To that extent, the objective of the legislation is pressing and substantial.

In determining whether the objective of the legislation is pressing and substantial I must also consider the impugned provision and the omission itself; that is, the omission, of those in a common law relationship, from the definition of "spouse". Is there any clear objective of this legislation for which the exclusion of those in a common law relationship is pressing and substantial? What objective of this legislation makes it pressing and substantial that it is to apply for the benefit of those in a marriage relationship (no matter how short the duration of the marriage); and yet it does not apply for the benefit of those in a long standing common law relationship such as that of the appellant and the respondent?

The Crown submits that the two forms of relationship (i.e., marriage on the one hand, and the common law relationship of the appellant and the respondent on the other hand) are clearly different and deserve different treatment. In support of that proposition, the Crown cites C. Davies, "Cohabitation Outside of Marriage: The Path to Reform" in M.E. Hughes, E.D. Pask, eds., *National Themes in Family Law* (Toronto: Carswell, 1988) 195; and C. Davies, "Matrimonial Property Legislation: Justifiably Restrictive or Offensively Narrow?" (National Judicial Institute, Family Law Seminar, February 9-11, 2000) [unpublished]. The thesis of the author is that the distribution provisions of statutes like the *MPA*, should not be extended to people who cohabit outside of marriage. There are, of course, others who take the opposite position (see W.H. Holland, "Intimate relationships in the new millennium: the assimilation of marriage and cohabitation?" Can. J. Fam. L. [forthcoming in 2000] and W. Holland, "Marriage and Cohabitation - Has the Time Come to Bridge the Gap?" (L.S.U.C. Special Lectures in Family Law, 1993). The Ontario Law Reform Commission's *Report on The Rights and Responsibilities of Cohabitants Under the Family Law Act* (Toronto: 1993) strongly recommends the inclusion of those in a common law relationship within the provisions of the Ontario *Family Law Act.* . . .

Similarly, the Law Reform Commission of Nova Scotia recommends such changes. It proposes a new Domestic Property Division Act which defines a "domestic relationship" as meaning a relationship where two adults have cohabited for at least one year in a personal relationship in which one provides personal or financial commitment and support of a domestic nature for the benefit of the other.

Further, in response to the Crown's submission that marriage and common law relationships are different, and, therefore, deserve to be treated differently, there is strong *dicta* from the Supreme Court of Canada on the subject of whether these two relationships are different when considering the division of property and assets. In *Pettkus* v. *Becker*, [1980] 2 S.C.R. 834, the Court considered the applicability of constructive and resulting trusts to a common law relationship. Dickson, J. (as he then was) noted that courts in other jurisdictions have not regarded the absence of a marital bond as any problem in applying the doctrine of unjust enrichment to common law relationships. He said the following at p. 850:

> I see no basis for any distinction, in dividing property and assets, between marital relationships and those more informal relationships which subsist for a lengthy period. This was not an economic partnership nor a mere business relationship, nor a casual encounter. Mr. Pettkus and Miss Becker lived as man and wife for almost twenty years. Their lives and their economic well-being were fully integrated.

More recently, in *Peter* v. *Beblow, (supra)*, one of the issues was whether the provision of domestic services during 12 years of cohabitation in a common law relationship is sufficient to establish the proprietary link which is required before the remedy of constructive trust can be applied to redress the unjust enrichment of one of the parties in the relationship. In the course of referring to the submission of counsel that the British Columbia Legislature had chosen to exclude unmarried couples from the right to claim an interest in the matrimonial assets under the *Family Law Act* of British Columbia, McLachlin, J. (as she then was), referred to that exclusion as an "injustice". She said the following at p. 994:

> Finally, I come to the argument that, because the legislature has chosen to exclude unmarried couples from the right to claim an interest in the matrimonial assets on the basis of contribution to the relationship, the court should not use the equitable doctrine of unjust enrichment to remedy the situation. Again, the argument seems flawed. It is precisely where an injustice arises without a legal remedy that equity finds a role.

The Crown also suggests that marital relationships are more stable than common law relationships, providing another basis which justifies making a distinction between the two relationships. The Crown provides no evidence in support of that submission. However, even assuming marriage relationships to be more stable, stability is hardly justification for providing that only married persons should have the benefits of legislation the functional purpose of which is to provide for an orderly and equitable settlement of the economic affairs of married persons on the breakdown of their marriage. Further, Statistics Canada indicates that substantial changes are taking place in both marriage relationships and common law relationships, and there is a narrowing of the gap between the two.

. .The Crown also submits that any interference with the present distinction which is made between married couples and those in a common law relationship, would interfere with the right to individual autonomy of those who do not wish to marry. In my view, providing those in a common law relationship with the ability to contract out of the *MPA* is of far less consequence than denying all others in a common law relationship the benefits of the *MPA*.

The Legislature of Nova Scotia has seen fit, in some of its legislation, to treat common law relationships in the same way as marriages. Common law spouses under these statutes are allowed to make the same claims, or seek the same benefits, as those who are (or were) married. In some of these statutes common law spouses are included within an expanded definition of spouse (see: *Family Maintenance Act*, R.S.N.S. 1989 as am. by S.N.S. 1997, c. 3, s. 1, and *Pension Benefits Act*, R.S.N.S. 1989, c. 340 as am. by S.N.S. 1992, c. 27; 1993, c. 35). In others there is a separate definition setting out who is a spouse (including a common law spouse), (see: *Workers' Compensation Act*, S.N.S. 1994-95 and *Compensation for Victims of Crime Act*, R.S.N.S. 1989, c. 83). As well, there are statutes that have separate provisions pertaining to those in common law relationships (see: *Fatal Injuries Act*, R.S.N.S. 1989, c. 163).

The Legislature has also provided, in the *Human Rights Act*, R.S. 1989, c. 214, that it is unlawful to discriminate against an individual or class of individuals on account of marital status, in respect of the provision of or access to services or facilities; accommodation; purchase or sale of property; employment; volunteer public service; a publication broadcast or advertisement; and membership in a professional association, business or trade association, employer's organization or employees' organization.

The Crown has not provided any satisfactory explanation as to why it is pressing and substantial to exclude persons in a common law relationship from the provisions of the *MPA* while, at the same time, including them, on the same basis as married persons, in other provincial legislation.

Finally, the Crown submits in its factum:

> . . . an extension of property rights in the face of uncertainty in relationships between persons gives rise to a great deal of uncertainty in the law, particularly with respect to conveyancing and estate matters. An extension of proprietary interests, particularly in the sphere of real estate, to include cohabitants under the Act may well do considerable harm to the interests of outsiders who will be affected and who have no notice of the state of the internal affairs [of] cohabitants.
> . . .

In my view, this is a practical problem which can be overcome by carefully drafted legislation prepared after consultation with members of the legal profession. Further, whatever that practical problem is, it is not so insurmountable as to justify what has been determined in these reasons to be a violation of s .15(1) of the *Charter*. As an aside, whatever the practical problem, it did not prevent the Legislature of the Northwest Territories from providing a regime for both those in a marriage relationship and those in a defined common law relationship to have the same rights with respect to property and assets in its new *Family Law Act*. This Statute was adopted by Nunavut (see *Family Law Act* (Nunavut) S.N.W.T. 1997, c. 18, as duplicated for Nunavut pursuant to the *Nunavut Act*, S.C. 1993, c. 28, s. 29; as am. S.C. 1998, c. 15, s. 4.)

In view of all of the above, the Crown has not demonstrated that the exclusion, from the provisions of the *MPA*, of those in a common law relationship, is "pressing and substantial". That being the case, the Crown has failed to discharge its onus of proving that the discrimination in this case is demonstrably justified in a free and democratic society.

REMEDY:

. . . In my opinion, it is for the Legislature, not the Court, to define with precision common law relationships which are to be included within the provisions of the *MPA* so as to comply with the constitution. Obviously, it is not required that the *MPA* apply to any transitory relationship. However, whether the recommendations of the Law Reform Commission of Nova Scotia (supra), some refinement of those recommendations, or a completely different scheme is adopted, is a matter which is best decided by the Legislature. Likewise, it is the Legislature's role to deal with such other refinements to the *MPA* which are occasioned by the inclusion of parties in a common law relationship, including whatever transitional provisions are deemed necessary.

I would, therefore, allow this appeal. I would declare s. 2(g) of the *MPA* to be of no force or effect. However, I would temporarily suspend the effect of that declaration for a period of twelve (12) months to enable the Legislature to devise new criteria for eligibility under the *MPA*, including whatever transitional provisions may be deemed necessary, and to pass new legislation that meets the constitutional requirements of s. 15(1) of the *Charter*, as set out in these reasons for judgment.

NOTES AND QUESTIONS

1. In response to *Taylor* v. *Rossu*, the Alberta legislature amended the *Domestic Relations Act* to extend support rights and obligations to parties to a "common law relationship". "Common law relationship" was defined to mean:

. . . a relationship between two people of the opposite sex who although not legally married to each other:

i) continuously cohabited in a marriage-like relationship for at least three years, or

ii) if there is a child of the relationship by birth or adoption, cohabited in a relationship of some permanence.

Could someone who becomes economically dependent on another during a childless common law relationship where cohabitation lasted 33 months successfully challenge this legislation?

2. Until recently it would have been generally accepted that one of the basic functions of family law was to "buttress the institution of marriage". Is this now an unconstitutional purpose in light of *Miron* v. *Trudel,Taylor* v. *Rossu,* and *Walsh* v. *Bona*?

3. In *Walsh* v. *Bona*, the Crown provided no evidence to establish that marital relationships are more stable than common-law relationships. As noted earlier in this chapter, there is startling proof of that fact coming out of the National Longitudinal Survey of Children and Youth being conducted by Statistics Canada. Would this proof have made any difference in *Walsh* v. *Bona* ? In light of the Statistics

Canada findings should the state encourage people to marry before they have children? How can it if the objective of supporting "the institution of marriage over, for example, common law relationships . . . has been called into question as a discriminatory objective which could not be justified under s. 1" of the *Charter*?

4. Under s. 91(26) of the *Constitution Act, 1867* the Parliament of Canada has exclusive jurisdiction over "marriage and divorce". Can this fact be used to argue that the constitution recognizes marriage as a valuable, unique institution that can give rise to special rights and responsibilities? Is this point addressed in *Taylor* v. *Rossu* or *Walsh* v. *Bona*? As a result of s. 92(26), Parliament can legislate regarding the rights and obligations of married persons on marriage breakdown. On the other hand, only the provinces can deal with the rights and obligations of unmarried cohabitees. How then can the legislatures or courts ensure that the rights and obligations arising out of a common-law relationship will be the same as those arising out of marriage?

5. In his annotation to *Taylor* v. *Rossu* in the RFLs, Professor McLeod suggested that the Alberta Court of Appeal did not address the following relevant questions: Should a court extend marital rights to people who are prohibited from marrying? Should a court extend marital rights to people who refuse to marry for personal reasons? If a person is willing to cohabit with someone who will not marry and will not agree by contract to extend spousal rights, why should judges grant him or her spousal rights? Are cohabiting relationships so important to society as to justify the state's intervening in a private relationship and imposing rights on the parties that they did not consider or agree to themselves? He concluded:

> The question of whether to extend rights to partners in quasi-spousal relationships involves complex social, political, religious and economic issues. With respect, such issues should be dealt with by the legislators, not the courts. That being said, it is probably too late to stop the inexorable process of judicial rewriting of family law. The legislators' inaction in most provinces forced the judiciary into [the role of] lawmakers to ensure that certain policy ends are achieved. Unfortunately, most judges are hesitant to identify just what social policy is achieved by granting support rights to unmarried spouses. Lots of people are dependent on others for financial or emotional support, but judges and legislators do not impose a legal obligation on one to support the other. Judges decided that unmarried couples resemble married couples and so should have the same or similar rights as married couples and are prepared to use constitutional law to reform family law. If the legislators disagreed with the judges' actions, they could have invoked the "notwithstanding" clause in the Charter to validate their legislation. To date, no level of government has done so.

6. For a general description of the laws governing unmarried cohabitation in Canada, see Holland and Stalbecker-Pountney, eds., *Cohabitation: The Law in Canada* (Toronto: Carswell) (looseleaf).

7. For further analysis of the arguments for and against maintaining a distinction between marriage and unmarried cohabitation, see Deech, "The Case Against Legal Recognition of Cohabitation" (1980), 29 International & Comp. L.Q. 480; Eekelaar and Katz, eds., *Marriage and Cohabitation in Contemporary Societies* (Toronto: Butterworths, 1980); Blumberg, "Cohabitation Without Marriage: A Different Perspective" (1981), 28 U.C.L.A. L. Rev 1125; Davies, "Cohabitation Outside of Marriage: The Path to Reform" in Hughes and Pask, eds., *National Themes in Family Law* (Toronto: Carswell, 1988) 195; and Holland, "Cohabitation and Marriage - A Meeting at the Crossroads? (1990-91), 7 C.F.L.Q. 33.

8. Is it now safe to conclude that any family law statute is invalid insofar as it grants to married partners rights that are withheld from unmarried partners, regardless of sexual orientation?

9. As noted in *Taylor* v. *Rossu*, the Ontario Law Reform Commission recommended in its 1993 *Report on the Rights and Responsibilities of Cohabitants under the Family Law Act*, that the definition of "spouse" in s. 1(1) of the *Family Law Act* (the general definition that applies to all of the *FLA*) be amended to include either of a man or woman who are not married to each other and have cohabited: (i) continuously for a period of not less than 3 years; or (ii) in a relationship of some permanence, if they are the parents of a child. Unmarried cohabitees who satisfied this definition would be accorded the same rights and obligations as married persons.

In the same report the O.L.R.C. recommended against ascribing spousal status under the *Family Law Act* to all same-sex couples who had cohabited for 3 consecutive years. The commission urged the legislature to acquire more information concerning same-sex relationships, including information about the attitudes and expectations within the gay and lesbian community, before taking such action. In the meantime, it suggested that the legislature permit the registration of Registered Domestic Partnerships by any two adults (certain conditions which are not directly relevant to the present analysis were recommended). A Registered Domestic Partner would be entitled to revoke the registration unilaterally, upon giving notice to the other partner. Registered Domestic Partners would have the rights and obligations ascribed to spouses under the *Family Law Act*.

Both of the report's main recommendations would require consequent amendments to key provisions in Part 1 (Family Property) of the *Family Law Act*.

10. The Registered Domestic Partnership proposed by the Ontario Law Reform Commission is somewhat similar to the Danish "Registered Partnership" under which the individuals involved have all the rights and responsibilities of married persons except that they cannot jointly adopt a child or have joint custody of a child: Nielson, "Family Rights and the Registered Partnership in Denmark" (1990), 4 International Journal of Law and the Family 297 and Pederson, "Denmark: Homosexual Marriages and New Rules Regarding Separation and Divorce" (1992-93), 30 Journal of Family Law 289. Several other jurisdictions — varying from the municipal level to the state level — have adopted a version of this registered domestic partnership model. See Henson, "A Comparative Analysis of Same-sex Partnership Protections: Recommendations for American Reform" (1993), 7 International Journal of Law and the Family 282. See also Davies, "The Extension of Marital Rights and Obligations to the Unmarried: Registered Domestic Partnerships and Other Methods" (2000), 17 C.F.L.Q. 247.

11. In 1977, Quebec became the first province to make sexual orientation a prohibited ground of discrimination in its human rights legislation. Most other provinces followed suit in the 1990's and the S.C.C. held in *Vriend* v. *Alberta* (1998), 156 D.L.R. (4th) 385 that failure to do so conflicted with the *Charter*. The *Canadian Human Rights Act* was amended in the spring of 1996 to include sexual orientation as a prohibited ground. This action followed the Ontario Court of Appeal holding in *Haig* v. *Canada* (1992), 9 O.R. (3d) 495 that the failure of the Act to prohibit discrimination on the basis of sexual orientation was a violation of the *Charter*. The court "read in" this prohibition into the legislation, and the federal government did not appeal. Partly as a result of these developments, employment and pension benefits in both the public and private sectors have gradually been extended to same-sex couples in the same way as they have been to unmarried opposite-sex couples.

12. The *M.* v. *H.* decision was announced in the midst of an Ontario election campaign. The leader of the ultimately victorious Progressive Conservatives indicated that, although he personally disagreed with the S.C.C.'s concept of family, appropriate legislation would be forthcoming. Possible options included simply amending the definition of spouse in Part III of the *Family Law Act*. British Columbia had already adopted legislation of this type in 1997. See the *Family Relations Act*, R.S.B.C. 1996, c. 128, as amended. Another possibility was illustrated by Quebec's response to the decision. The Quebec National Assembly approved an omnibus bill amending the definition of spouse in all provincial legislation so that same sex couples were treated in the same manner as unmarried opposite-sex cohabitees: Bill 32, *An Act to Amend Various Legislative Provisions Concerning De Facto Spouses*, 1st Session, 36th Legislature of Quebec, 1999. Another option was the adoption of a system of registered domestic partnerships for all unmarried cohabitees. In late October, the Ontario legislature chose a third option. It passed Bill 5, with the interesting title *Amendments Because of the Supreme Court of Canada Decision in M. v. H. Act, 1999*, S.O. 1999, c. 6. The bill amended the *Family Law Act* and sixty-six other statutes so that they apply to same-sex couples in the same way as they apply to unmarried, opposite-sex couples. This result was achieved, however, not by redefining the term "spouse" but by having separate provisions indicating that the statutes apply to same-sex partners. The term "same-sex partner" is defined as "either of two persons of the same sex who have cohabited : (a) continuously for a period of not less than three years; or (b) in a relationship of some permanence, if they are the natural or adoptive parents of a child". The Attorney General explained: "The bill responds to the Supreme Court of Canada ruling, while preserving the traditional values of the family by protecting the definition of

spouse." Some commentators argued that *M.* v. *H.* was "more about spirit and dignity and human rights than it was about anything financial or material" and that the bill failed to comply with the spirit of the decision. See *National Post*, October 26, 1999, A1.

The Parliament of Canada responded in 2000 to the *M.* v. *H.* decision by passing Bill C-23, *An Act to Modernize the Statutes of Canada in Relation to Benefits and Obligations*. This Bill amended some 67 federal statutes so that the benefits, rights and obligations which apply to married persons or spouses apply in the same way to "common law partners" . The term "common law partnership" is defined as "the relationship between two persons who are cohabiting in a conjugal relationship, having done so for a period of at least one year". Because same-sex partners will be required to combine their incomes to determine eligibility, the Finance Department estimated that 93,000 of an estimated 140,000 same-sex couples would have to forego the approximately $28 million they collectively previously claimed in the goods and services tax credit. On the other hand, it was estimated that the government would lose about $8 million in taxes, mainly because some same-sex partners would be able to claim the equivalent-to-married credit for supporting a dependent. See *National Post*, November 15, 1999, A8. Extending other government benefits to same-sex couples will, obviously, also be costly.

13. Treating unmarried couples, whether gay or straight, in the same way as spouses raises concerns about policing the tax and benefits system because there is no practical way to confirm a claimed relationship or to establish a relationship where it is denied or simply not claimed. The possibility exists that unmarried couples will only claim or acknowledge that status when it is financially beneficial. Any potential for abuse would be reduced through a system of registered domestic partnerships.

14. The Ontario definition of "same-sex partner" indicates that a same-sex couple can be the "natural . . . parents of a child". Many considered this a drafting error because it seemed to refer to a biological impossibility. But the legislature proved to be rather prescient as a few weeks later a Los Angeles court ruled that two British men could be named as the legal parents of twin boys due to be born to an American woman. The men, who had lived together for eleven years, bought donor eggs which were then fertilized using sperm from both of them and implanted in a surrogate mother. The couple spent about $500,000 for the process after their application to adopt was rejected by Essex social services. It was reported that this would be the first time in British history that a male who was neither the biological nor the adoptive father would be registered as a parent on the birth certificate. See *Guardian Weekly*, November 4-10, 1999, 8.

15. The Law Reform Commission of Canada is currently studying the possibility of extending legal rights and obligations to an even broader range of relationships of economic dependency. Professor Macdonald reportedly stated (see *National Post*, July 19, 1999, A12):

For example, why can't two sisters who have always lived with each other be able to designate each other as RRSP, CPP or private pension plan beneficiaries? And why can't two army buddies who move in together be able to share in dental and other contributory plans? And again, why can't a mother and daughter who share a house be able to claim the same tax deduction as a married couple with no children?

16. The "pro-family" political movement supporting laws and policies favouring the "traditional family" appears to be considerably stronger in the United States than in Canada. Nonetheless, there are a few Canadian voices echoing these concerns. See, e.g., Gairdner, *The War Against the Family* (Toronto: Stoddart, 1992) who writes (at 592):

The laws, too, need reconstitution on a family basis. A pro-family society must define marriage as a socially privileged institution for the joining of man and woman in society's procreation project, thus establishing the natural family as the ideal model. All efforts to loosen this definition must be resisted and treated as absurdities proposed by opportunistic individuals attempting to gain advantages they have not earned.

Similarly, David Frum states in "How far do we take gay rights?" Dec. 95/Jan. 96 *Saturday Night* 66, at 70:

It's a bizarre society that would be surprised by the information that children fare best when they live with their mother and father, and that married women live more securely than their single or cohabiting sisters. [This is a reference to the conclusions in McLanahan and Sandefur, *Growing Up with a Single Parent* (Cambridge: Harvard University Press, 1994) and *Mothers and Children: One Decade Later* (Halifax: N.S. Department of Community Services, 1991).] But under ideological pressure, our society has been bent into some pretty bizarre shapes. It is an undeniable fact that Canadians are increasingly substituting a succession of cohabitational relationships for marriage. . . . Today, nearly one-quarter of families are nonmarital, divided about evenly between single-parent families and cohabiting couples.

By almost any definition, this is a social crisis of the first magnitude, but our lawmakers and — especially — judges have chosen to regard it as a mere change in public taste, like the disappearance of the hat, to be accommodated and hurried along.

So employers have been told that the employee benefits they once provided to married spouses as their contribution to sustaining a crucial social institution must now be provided to anyone whom the employee decides to share an apartment with for a year. . . .

In a society that fully valued and celebrated marriage, claims that equal respect should be granted to marriage and to nonmarital relationships would appear almost literally incomprehensible. How could anyone compare the social importance of a lifelong commitment to mutual care and the raising of children to an impermanent sexual attachment? But we do worse than compare the two. We deploy the coercive power of government to punish any employer who insists on noticing the difference. Homosexuals have more than a little justice on their side when they wonder why their cohabitational relationships should not be treated like heterosexual common-law relationships. The only reply is to treat all cohabitations — gay and straight equally — as purely private matters entitled to no subsidy from third parties and sharply distinct from the legal institution of marriage.

. . . The restructuring of the family, the weakening of marital ties, the loosening of standards of sexual morality — these form the subtext of the great debate over gay rights. Advocates of gay rights see these as either welcome in themselves or, at any rate, as the inevitable price of liberation from the stultifying morality of a generation and more ago.

17. Two cases which are reproduced in later chapters of this book involve issues similar to those discussed in this section. In *Layland* v. *Ontario (Minister of Consumer and Commercial Relations)* (1993), 14 O.R. (3d) 658 (Div. Ct.), reproduced in Chapter 2, the court ruled that it was not contrary to the *Charter* to preclude marriages between persons of the same sex. In *Re K.* (1995), 23 O.R. (3d) 679 (reproduced in Chapter 11), Nevins Prov. Div. J. ruled that the Ontario legislation which precluded joint adoption applications by two persons of the same sex conflicted with the *Charter*.

18. For further reading, see Herman, "Are We Family?: Lesbian Rights and Women's Liberation" (1990), 28 Osgoode Hall L.J. 789; Ryder, "Equality Rights and Sexual Orientation: Confronting Heterosexual Family Privilege" (1990), 6 Can. J. Fam. L. 39; Henson, "A Comparative Analysis of Same-Sex Partnership Protections: Recommendations For American Reform" (1993), 7 Int'l J.L & Fam. 282; Woolley, "Excluded by Definition: Same-Sex Couples and the Right to Marry" (1995), 45 U.T.L.J. 471; Stychin, "Novel Concepts: A Comment on *Egan and Nesbit* v. *The Queen*" (1995), 6 Constitutional Forum 101; McAllister, "Egan: A Crucible For Human Rights" (1995), 5 N.J.C.L. 95; Finnis, "Law, Morality and Sexual Orientation" (1995), 9 Notre Dame J.L., Ethics, & Public Policy II; Dupuis, "The Impact of Culture, Society, and History on the Legal Process: An Analysis of the Legal Status of Same-Sex Relationships in the United States and Denmark" (1995), 9 Int'l J.L. & Fam. 86; Celeste, "Gay and Lesbian Issues: Family, Domestic Partnership and Marriage" (1995), 24 Colorado Law 1309; Berg, "Fumbling Towards Equality: Promise and Peril in *Egan*" (1995), 5 N.J.C.L. 263; Boyd, " Best Friends or Spouses?: Privatization and the Recognition of Lesbian Relationships in *M.* v. *H.*" (1996), 13 Can. J. Fam. L. 321; Barclay, "For Richer or for Poorer: A Comparison of Same-sex Support and Benefit Rights in *M.* v. *H.* and *Rosenberg* v. *Canada (Attorney General)*" (1998), 16 C.F.L.Q. 213; and McCarthy and Radbord, " Family Law for Same Sex Couples: Chart(er)ing the Course" (1998), 15 Can. J. Fam. Law 101.

Both Professor Ryder and Professor Herman express some reservations about the type of argument that succeeded in *M.* v. *H.* Ryder observes (at 45-46):

It should be recognized that according the same benefits to same-sex couples as are currently granted to heterosexual couples may further entrench the privilege of coupled (nuclear) family units at the expense of other familial arrangements. Indeed, treating individuals living alone or in groups differently from persons living as couples or in nuclear families when their needs are the same may constitute discrimination on the basis of family status or marital status.

Herman suggests (at 797) that attempts by same sex couples to be treated as "spouses" or "a family" will unnecessarily divide the lesbian community according to their different lifestyles and may give support to "the very institutional structures that create and perpetuate women's oppression". She approvingly quotes (at 797) the following passage from Smart, *The Ties That Bind: Law, Marriage and The Reproduction of Patriarchal Relations* (London: Routledge & Kegan Paul, 1984):

A primary goal must be to jettison the privileged status of the heterosexual married couple, but not in order to create a different hierarchy of unmarried households. The aim is not to extend the legal and social definition of marriage to cover cohabitees or even homosexual couples, it is to abandon the status of marriage altogether and to devise a system of rights, duties and obligations which are not dependent on any form of coupledom or marriage or quasi-marriage.

3.   Violence: The Dark Side of Family Life

DRAKICH AND GUBERMAN, "VIOLENCE IN THE FAMILY"

Anderson et al., eds., *Family Matters: Sociology and Contemporary Canadian Families* (Toronto: Methuen, 1987) 201 at 206-217 and 220-230 (Permission to reproduce this excerpt was granted by Nelson Canada, a Division of International Thomson Publishing, which holds the copyright.)

THE NATURE OF FAMILY VIOLENCE

Wife Assault

Violence against wives is not a new phenomenon in our culture. One author has pointed out that "wife beating is a matter of historical record" (Davidson, 1980:99). Although husbands are no longer legally allowed to chastise wives, the toleration of wife assault is built into patriarchal social attitudes and social arrangements.

In the last 15 years, studies conducted throughout Canada, the United States, and Great Britain have shown that violence against wives is a fact of family life. Despite a lack of uniformity in data collection, it is currently estimated that at least one Canadian woman in ten, living with a man, is assaulted by her partner (MacLeod, 1980). This estimate is considered conservative by many working in the field. The FBI estimates that a woman is severely beaten in the United States every 18 seconds (Sinclair, 1985).

Wife assault is rarely a single, isolated event. Data from the National Crime Survey, conducted by the Bureau of Justice Statistics in the United States, shows a high risk that, once battered, women will be beaten repeatedly (Goalkasian, 1986). A Canadian study showed that women were beaten as many as 35 times before they made contact with the police (Jaffe and Burris, 1982).

A Scottish study by the well-respected team of Dobash and Dobash found that 76 percent of all physical attacks in the family setting were directed at wives by their husbands. Children were victims in 10.7 percent of cases, while assaults by wives against husbands constituted 1.1 percent of incidents (Dobash and Dobash, 1979). . . .

Women are hit in the head and the face, assaulted with weapons such as stove burner coils, broken bottles, knives, and guns. Assaults result in bruises, broken bones, internal injuries, and even death. Statistics from 1982 show that one-fifth of all Canadian homicides derive from wife assault. Over half (60 percent) of all female homicide victims in Canada are killed in a family context: this is more than double the number of male victims killed in similar situations (Statistics Canada, 1982). Twenty percent of visits to emergency medical services are the direct result of wife assault (Stark and Fillitcraft, 1982). Pregnant women are especially vulnerable to violence. Forty percent of wife assaults begin during the woman's first pregnancy (Education Wife Assault Fact Sheet, 1985). This phenomenon is explained by a pregnant woman's more limited access to resources and the greater dependency on her partner that results. (Sinclair, 1985)

Sexual, psychological, and emotional abuse often accompany physical beatings. Sexual abuse may involve forced intercourse after a beating, having pain inflicted during intercourse, or being forced against her will to take part in sex acts like those portrayed in violent pornographic magazines. Nowadays, a man can be charged with abusing his wife sexually, but prior to January 1983 it was not an offense for a husband to rape his wife.

Psychological and emotional abuse can take various forms, such as forcing a woman to do degrading things like breaking her favourite vase or licking the dishes clean, making threats to harm the victim or her loved ones, attacking her personality and belittling her, or terrorizing her by tying a noose around her neck, or driving through red lights. This psychological torture renders a woman in a constant state of fear for her safety (Sinclair, 1985).

Much previous research on wife assault has assumed that violent behaviour arose from the psychopathology of the woman who was beaten, the man who did the beating, or the marriage in which the violence occurred. Wife assault has sometimes been explained as an example of a dysfunctional family, or the woman is blamed for being masochistic, for provoking the violence, and for staying in the violent relationship. Yet both these theories place too much responsibility for the violence on the beaten woman herself.

Why do men assault their wives? Are men who batter mentally ill? Are they economically impoverished? Are they ignorant? Are they violent because they are addicted to drugs or alcohol? Do they batter because there is too much stress in their lives?

The answer to all of these questions is a definite "No." Many people are under great stress, yet don't resort to violent behaviour. While many batterers do abuse alcohol and drugs, many others do not. Research has shown that batterers come from all walks of life. They represent all ages, all education levels, all ethnic and religious groups, and all socio-economic classes, and are found in both urban and rural communities (Walker, 1979; Moore, 1979).

Most obviously, men are violent toward their wives because they are allowed to be. As has been discussed, violence is a cultural style in our society. And it is a cultural style belonging particularly to men (Cole, 1985). Men are socialized to believe that they are superior and that they have a right to dominate and control. They are taught that physical power equals masculinity: ". . . violence used by men against women in the family . . . attempts to establish or maintain a patriarchal social order" (Dobash and Dobash, 77-78:150). This violence is positively reinforced by our social structure.

Moreover, men assault their wives because violence is a highly effective method of controlling behaviour (National Institute of Justice, 1986). To avoid further beatings, a woman will spend a great deal of energy trying to stay out of her husband's way and anticipating his needs and desires. Abusive men often explain their violence by insisting that they have a right to control "their" women. Violent behaviour is a way of coercing their wives to do what they want them to do.

Who is the battered woman? The demographic profile of the assaulted woman looks very similar to that of the man who beats her. She can be any age, comes from all ethnic and cultural backgrounds, from all socio-economic groups; she lives in the city and she lives in rural areas. She very likely holds traditional notions of male and female behaviour: that the family is sacrosanct, that her husband is the head of the household, and that she must be supportive to him, even if it means being beaten. (Moore, 1979). Women who are beaten by their husbands almost always believe that it is their fault, that they deserve to be beaten. . . .

A woman often thinks she has caused the beating because she did something wrong. But the violence has little to do with her behaviour or her personality. Women grow up believing it is their responsibility to make a marriage work and that if it doesn't, somehow it is their fault.

Why do battered women stay in the home? There is no simple answer. They do not stay because they ask for, or deserve, to be beaten. They stay with or return to abusive relationships for many reasons which include economic dependence, ambivalence, hope, fear, disbelief, and low self-esteem. Few women have the financial independence to leave their marriages. Battered women are not always being abused, and their partners are not always violent. Batterers often become kind, loving, and contrite after an attack. They often promise the beatings will never happen again (Walker, 1979). Women want to believe the promises. They want the violence to end, not the marriage. Besides, many battered women stay in abusive relationships out of fear. They are afraid of staying and afraid of leaving. Loneliness, financial devastation, a sense of failure, the possible loss of family and friends, and fear of the unknown are very real. Leaving is "a very drastic and lonely move for her to consider. After all, if the one who loves you treats you like that, what might the rest of the world do to you?" (Moore, 1979:22). . . .When a woman has been beaten repeatedly, her self-esteem and her belief in herself are shattered. The more severe the abuse and the longer it has continued, the poorer self-image she will have (Sinclair, 1985:35). . . .

Domestic violence is not merely an interaction between two people, however. The sheer number of violent relationships in our society indicate that wife assault can no longer be treated as a private or personal dilemma. It is a major public and social concern.

The Sexual Abuse of Children

The sexual abuse of children is a much greater problem within our society than previously thought possible. A national survey conducted in Canada in 1984 reported that one in every two females, or 53.5 percent, had experienced unwanted sexual acts (defined as exposure, threats, touching, and attacks). Slightly fewer than one in three males (30.6 percent) had been a victim. About one in five (22.3 percent) of the female victims reported experiencing two or more sexual offenses, while only about one in 15 males (6.6 percent) had been involved in two or more incidents (Badgley, 1984:179-180).

The study also found that about three out of four people who had been sexually assaulted for the first time as children were females (71.8 percent) and that about one in four (28.2 percent) were male. Many other studies showed that a far greater proportion of girls was abused than of boys — estimates range from three in five to nine in ten. . . .

Our assumption in this society is that most sexual abuse of children is perpetrated by individuals who are strangers to them, persons outside of the family. But this is not necessarily the case. Child sexual abuse is also inflicted by family members and within the family setting. Defining sexual assault as "any type of sexual touching of the child by another person" (Badgley, 1984:195), the Badgley Report found that well over half (55.4 percent) of the incidents occurred in the homes of victims or perpetrators (Badgley, 1984:201). Home is a place we have traditionally considered safe, and which is normally closed to scrutiny by the public. Yet most perpetrators of sexual abuse live under the same roof as their victims. . . .

Social scientists currently doing work in the field of incestuous abuse repeatedly report that between 92 and 95 percent of the victims are female and that 97 to 99 percent of the offenders are male (Berliner, 1977; Burgess et al., 1977; Giaretto, 1976). The fact that the greatest amount of sexual abuse within the family is perpetrated by males, and that the majority of victims are younger females, suggests that we must look at this problem as one of extreme inequality between genders and generations (Russell, 1986:11). The theory that violence occurs between persons at extremes of power within the family holds true in this example.

Children are powerless to protect themselves from unwanted behaviour, to avoid their abusers, or to stop their abuse. Having been taught to obey their parents and to be polite to all adults, children frequently consent to behaviour, sexual or otherwise, when the request or order comes from an adult. In our society, obedience and deference to older family members is generally both expected and rewarded (Russell, 1986:54). Incestuous assault fits into our earlier analysis of the family and the power that the husband or father has within it. It is the abuse of power. It cannot be reduced to an aberrant act out of a "particular configuration of family interaction or personality types," nor does it occur when families become dysfunctional (Butler, 1980). Such an analysis serves to excuse offenders. "To assign each family member a role in causing the incestuous assault is to imply that whatever happens to women and children in [their] homes can be traced back to something that is [the women's] fault" (Butler, 1980:49).

Elder Abuse

Our population is aging, and the percentage of older people in the population is increasing. Less than 10 percent of the population in Canada was elderly in 1976, but it is estimated that, by 2031, 20 percent of the population will be over 65. In the United States, the total population has increased 300 percent since the turn of the century, while the population of people aged 65 years and over has increased almost 800 percent (U.S. Bureau of the Census, 1979, in Pagelow). . . .

In Canada, the majority of single elderly parents are women; first, because they live an average of seven years longer than men; second, because women have tended to marry men older than themselves. In addition, men of 65 who are widowed or divorced remarry at a rate seven times that of women of the same age. American figures show 77 percent of elderly men living with their wives, with only 36 percent of elderly women living with their husbands (U.S. Bureau of the Census, 1979).

Where and how do the majority of these older women live, if 64 percent of them do not live with their husbands? Contrary to popular belief, fewer than five percent of the elderly population live in institutional settings such as nursing homes, though approximately 75 percent of people 65 or older are both physically and financially dependent. Thus about 20 percent of the elderly population live in some kind of family setting with varying degrees of dependency on adult care-providers (C.M. Long, 1981:124). It is these people, the older people who live in some kind of household or family setting, and who depend on a related adult to provide care, who are at the greatest risk of becoming victims of abuse in the family context.

What is elder abuse? Like other forms of abuse in the family, it can take many forms. It may include financial exploitation, where pension cheques or other monies are taken; physical injury including beatings or restraints; threats, ridicule, insults, humiliation, and imposed isolation (both physical and social); or a forced change in living arrangements. Neglect is elder abuse, and so is refusing or failing (whether intentionally or unintentionally) to provide food, health care, or aid. Elder abuse usually follows a chronic or repetitive pattern in which the older parent is malnourished or dehydrated, in which personal hygiene is ignored, or medications are administered or withheld in order to keep the older person "manageable."

The problem of elder abuse in institutional settings was exposed years ago, but the abuse of elderly parents by their adult children is just now coming to public attention. Awareness of the issue is at the stage where awareness of wife assault was, ten years ago. . . .

Documenting the incidence of abuse is difficult, because, first of all, observable signs of physical abuse such as breaks and bruises can easily be attributed to falls and injuries that frequently happen to older people anyway. Second, it is difficult to document elder abuse, because our society stereotypes older people as prone to forgetfulness and confusion; if the aged report their abuse, they leave themselves open to having their credibility questioned. Third, elder abuse is currently reported under the generic heading of "domestic violence." It does not have a category of violence of its own. Last, older people are reluctant to report abuse because they have no other choice for shelter, they are afraid of being placed in nursing homes, they lack support services, they fear retaliation, they want to avoid the humiliation and embarrassment of being abused and of not being able to take care of themselves, or they are ashamed that they raised a child who now abuses them. Elder abuse is bound to become more common in the future (simply because of the increase in the number of elderly people) unless society provides the needed support services for caring for the old and aging. . . .

EXPLANATIONS FOR VIOLENCE IN THE FAMILY

Explanations for violence in the family range from blaming the individual to placing responsibility on the social structure. Four theories are discussed in the following section. The first, Violence as Individual Pathology, deals with the psychopathological model of violence from both the biological and psychological perspectives. The second, Violence as a By-Product, looks at the association of violence and stress and violence and drug or alcohol abuse. The third, Violence as Learned Behaviour, explores how individuals learn violent behaviours, and examines the cycle of family violence. The fourth, Society Constructs Family Violence, pulls the argument together that we have made throughout this chapter: that family violence is best understood in its historical, cultural, and structural context.

Violence as Individual Pathology

Historically, the treatment of violence in the family has been the focus of medical and mental health professionals. The professional training and experience of these practitioners directed their analysis of family violence to biological and psychological anomalies which produce and characterize perpetrators of violence. The medical model, also known as the "pathological model," proposes that individuals who assault members of their family physically or sexually possess distinguishing personality characteristics that reflect some form of mental illness or pathology. . . .

The psychopathological model has been approached from biological and psychological perspectives. These perspectives share the definitions of pathology, but differ in their explanations of the causes. According to the biological perspective, violent behaviour is the effect on a person's physiological makeup as a result of (1) bad genes (Ellis, 1982; Hutchings and Mednick, 1977); (2) hormonal imbalances (Jeffrey, 1980); (3) nutritional factors; or (4) exposure to physiological stress (Humphrey and Palmer, 1982). In the psychological perspective, defective personality structures result in individuals who are impulsive, unable to control their emotions or behaviour, immature, depressed, and insecure. In this view, individuals who are violent toward other family members are seen as incapable of love or of forming empathic attachments or nurturing characteristics (Helfer and Kempe, 1968). However, researchers have not been able to develop a personality profile that identifies abusers or potential abusers. . . .

Violence Viewed as a By-product of Alcohol, Drugs, and Stress

In this view of family violence, the perpetrator remains the primary source of violence, but is considered to have been pushed to it by external factors of stress and alcohol or drug abuse. . . .

The family is a receptacle for both inside and outside stresses. Farrington (1980:113), in his development of a general stress model for family violence, states that "violence occurs so often in the family setting because (1) the family encounters a high amount of stress; (2) it tends to be poorly equipped to handle stress; and (3) there is thus a great potential for frustration within the family." Researchers have indeed found evidence of violence associated with stress. Among some of the stresses related to violence are pregnancy (Gelles, 1975), poverty (Gil, 1971), and failure to achieve economic reward (O'Brien, 1971). That stress exists in the family or that it may precipitate violence cannot be denied; however, attention must extend beyond the precipitating factor of stress to such social factors as implicit norms which allow men to release stress and tension through violence directed toward family members. . . .

Another factor commonly used as an explanation for violence is the abuse of alcohol and/or drugs. Langley and Levy (1977) suggest that alcoholism is present in 49 to 95 percent of cases of wife abuse. Fagan, Stewart, and Hansen (1983) found in their study of 270 wife-assault victims that alcoholism was involved in more than half of the cases and drugs in one-fourth. Okum (1984:57-58) conveniently summarizes the results of a number of studies: "Gelles found alcohol abuse in 48% of his violent couples, Gayford in 52% of his cases, Carlson in 60% of her sample of couples, and Eisenberg and Micklow in 70%. Roy found that 85% of batterers in her sample were also substance abusers." The contribution of alcohol or drugs to incidents of violence cannot be denied; yet it would be illogical to conclude that substance abuse is the cause of violent behaviour. Gingold (1976) suggests that alcohol abuse is a "disavowal technique" which releases the individual from feeling responsibility for violent behaviour. Research shows that people do get drunk and beat up their wives and children (Langley and Levy, 1977; Hilberman and Munson,

1977; Gelles, 1974). Yet they do not abuse because of the alcohol, but drink to supply the abuse with an explanation.

Stress, drugs, and alcohol may facilitate violent behaviour; but these external factors do not address the central questions of why violence is the way to release tension in response to these factors. Later, we will examine why violence is most likely to be used as a response within the family.

Violence Viewed as Learned Behaviour

According to social learning theory, violence is learned in interaction with others. Through observation of violence between parents, or between sisters and brothers, children may learn that violence is useful for achieving one's goals, for gaining power, or for controlling and manipulating others. As victims of violence, children learn that violence goes unpunished as a form of interpersonal behaviour. In other words, it is socially acceptable. Thus, not only are the acts of violence learned, so are the family's attitudes to violence and their acceptance of it. . . .

While the old adage, "Spare the rod and spoil the child," embodies the principle that physical punishment will teach children appropriate behaviour, the use of punishment teaches children other things as well. Straus (1978:45) states that children learn that violence is appropriate with those we love. Moreover, the moral rightness of physical punishment is established by being used to teach acceptable and correct behaviour.

According to social learning theory, physical punishment provides a model of aggressive behaviour which the individual imitates in interaction with others. The propensity to repeat violent behaviour is influenced by success or failure which is, in turn, dependent on the reaction or outcome to the behaviour. If the behaviour is successful, the individual will repeat it; if it proves unsuccessful, it will be discarded (Bandura, 1973).

Straus (1983:229) found that the more violent parents are to their children, the more violent these children are to their siblings; the more violent the husband is toward the wife, the more violent the wife is toward her children. This suggests that victims of violence perpetuate rather than prevent this behaviour. Many argue that victims of childhood abuse recreate the familial context of their upbringing in their own homes. This latter point has been extensively studied, and has come to be known as "the intergenerational transmission of violence." That is, the violence experienced and learned in the family of origin is perpetuated in the family of procreation. Steinmetz (1977) reports on a number of studies which found that a proportion of perpetrators of violence suffered from or observed violence in their families of orientation (Gaylord, 1975; Ownes and Straus, 1975; Silver, Dublin, and Lourie, 1969). In lay terms, "violence breeds violence." Numerous studies support this assumption. Adults who were physically abused as children are more likely to abuse their own children than are adults who were not abused as children (Kalmuss, 1984; Straus et al., 1980; Steinmetz, 1977; Gelles, 1976; Spinetta and Rigler, 1972). Kalmuss (1984) studied the effects on the subsequent generation of being a victim of family violence and observing family violence including marital abuse. She found that observing parental hitting had more of an influence on future violent behaviour toward a spouse than being a victim of parental abuse. The reason she offers for this is that, in addition to learning that violence is acceptable between their mothers and fathers, children generalize that aggression between husbands and wives is acceptable. Children learn that physical strength and power are the appropriate means of controlling behaviour.

Another factor that plays a part in the future use of violence is that the more violence children are exposed to, the greater the chances of their using violence in the future. Yet, although the studies we have referred to indicate that children from violent homes are more likely than children from non-violent homes to be perpetrators of violence as adults, Steinmetz (1977) cautions the reader in the interpretation of the evidence. While there are data supporting the intergenerational transmission of violence for some of the perpetrators of violence, there is also evidence that many victims of abuse do not abuse in adulthood. In fact, in a national study of violence in the United States, Straus, Gelles, and Steinmetz (1979) found that being abused as a child did not directly lead to abusive behaviour, and that not all abusers were abused as children. As in the case of the relationship of mental illness to violence, the connection is possible, rather than inevitable.

We have now looked at the more commonly known explanations for violence in the family, the pathological model, explaining violence in terms of personality dysfunctions, the by-product model, which identifies drugs, alcohol and stress as precursors to violent acts, and the learning model, which indicates that violence is learned behaviour. These perspectives provide explanations of how individuals learn to be violent, and identify factors that facilitate violence, but they do not tell us why individuals are violent in the family. Further, these explanations obscure our understanding of violence by locating the responsibility for abuse with the individual alone, and by emphasizing the pathology of the individual. When the individual is blamed, society and the structure of the family are absolved of any responsibility. However, the pervasiveness of family violence, and the fact that women and children are overwhelmingly the targets of violence, cannot be explained by pathology, substance abuse, or stress, nor by examining an individual's behaviour apart from the setting of the family. The social learning model directs us implicitly to take the social context into account; as suggested earlier, violence is encouraged, supported, and rewarded by the social system. It is learned in interaction with others. The structure of the family, and the relative position of men, women, and children within it, is a most useful focus for an analysis of the occurrence of family violence. The next section summarizes our position that violence in the family is socially constructed and maintained.

SOCIETY CONSTRUCTS VIOLENCE IN THE FAMILY

. . . There are three factors common to all experiences of domestic violence. These include power differentials, social isolation, and psychological abuse.

Power Determines Abuse

Power is common to all forms of violence. The perpetrators of violence and their victims usually occupy differential positions of power. That is, the ones who are stronger or bigger, the ones with greater access to important resources, and the ones who are culturally defined as being dominant are the ones who can impose their wills on others who are smaller, weaker, lacking resources, or culturally defined as subordinate. Finkelhor (1983:17-18) states that the common patterns of violence "are not merely for the more powerful to abuse the less powerful but for the most powerful to abuse the least. This is an interesting commonality: Abuse tends to gravitate to the relationships of greatest power differential." . . .

All family members do not have equal status. Status depends on sex, age, roles, physical strength, financial resources, and access to other resources. Some adult males may be in subordinate, powerless positions compared to others in society as a whole, but within the family unit they often have ultimate power. Thus it is important to consider power differences within the family and society. Studies have shown that the less power the wife has — when she is not in the paid labour force, when she is excluded from family decision-making, and when she has less education than her husband — the more her husband is likely to abuse his greater power (Finkelhor, 1983). On the other hand, as a woman earns a wage or salary of her own and gains some economic independence from her husband, the husband loses some of his power over her (Eichler, 1983:188-189). . . .

A power imbalance is also an important factor in the abuse of an elderly parent. The more self-sufficient and able the elderly parent is, the less likely she is to be abused by her caretakers.

Social Isolation Encourages Abuse

Another recurring factor in family violence is that of social isolation. Evidence shows that the family's condition as a private institution makes it prone to violence (Gelles, 1979). . . .

This isolation is social, not necessarily geographic. It includes isolation caused by poverty, unusual social values, or family disorganization (Finkelhor, 1979). Isolation in this case refers to the insulation of the family from the rules of the larger society. Gelles (1978) also noted that, as privacy increases, the level of social control decreases. It has been found that most father/daughter incest occurs in families which are isolated and dominated by the father in the extreme (Herman and Hirschman, 1980). Family isolation, combined with a social attitude that parents own their children, makes it difficult for any outside prevention or intervention in cases of sexual abuse (MacFarlane and Lieber, 1978:88). The family is not obliged to explain its behaviour inside or outside the home. Studies of wife abuse show that many of the women are isolated in the home, while their husbands have many social contacts and friendship networks outside it (Dobash and Dobash, 1979). This is also the case with abused elderly people, especially when their mobility is restricted and contact with people outside of where they live is limited. When they are unable to get out of the house and maintain their friendship networks, they increasingly come under the control of their caretakers. If they have moved into their child's home, neighbours often don't know they even exist.

Psychological Abuse

A third common factor is that victims of all types of family violence share a sense of humiliation and low self-esteem. The terrible shame and sense of worthlessness that a woman feels when she has been beaten by her husband is also felt by the child who has been sexually molested or by the elderly parent who has been mistreated. Each form of physical abuse is accompanied by psychological abuse . . . .

As we have shown, historical antecedents and other aspects of the social structure support the direction of violence from men to women and children. The family is a hierarchically organized social unit with some of its members having more power, more status, and more privileges than others. The grounds are age and gender, with men in positions of power over women and children and parents in positions of power over their children. To trace this development historically is beyond the scope of this chapter. Suffice it to say that economic and social conditions contributed to the establishment of the patriarchy which permeates the social and structural relationships in the family.

. . . While men's violence toward their wives and children is no longer legally sanctioned, vestiges of this male prerogative in the family remain. This is not surprising, considering the differential status and power of men and women in society and in the family. Practices of socialization and the ideologies of gender still sanction male dominance, female subordination, and men's aggressiveness.

Violence is the overt manifestation of inequalities of gender and power. It is an extension of men's power over women and children or, more generally, an extension of power over the powerless. . . .

Any analysis of violence in the family is complex. We have situated our argument in those historical, cultural, and structural contexts of the family by which relationships of power and ideologies of gender legitimate and perpetuate violence. Through social learning processes we develop the knowledge of and readiness to be violent that can be brought to the surface by drugs, alcohol and stress. In the majority of cases, violence is carried out by normal men who are living up to what they've learned they can do within a male role.

MacLEOD, BATTERED BUT NOT BEATEN . . . PREVENTING WIFE BAT-TERING IN CANADA

(Ottawa: Canadian Advisory Council on the Status of Women, 1987) 38-45 (Footnotes Omitted)

Explaining Why Wife Battering Exists

Although society is still far from understanding why wife battering exists, research studies and field experience have taught us much. It is now widely known that very few batterers conform to the easy-to-accept image of a mentally or physiologically deranged person, although there have been physiological studies showing that many wife batterers do suffer from food allergies and abnormally low blood-sugar levels. Further, it is known that, while alcohol or drug abuse may frequently be associated with wife battering, and that unemployment or poverty, like other life stresses, including the women's pregnancy, can precipitate wife battering by lowering inhibitions against it, there is no conclusive evidence that any of these factors **cause** wife battering.

As a result of the growing acceptance of this knowledge, it has become almost a cliché in writings and public presentations about wife battering to state that we are all potentially battered women or batterers. This statement is an important one to reiterate because it can never be stressed too often that research done over the past ten years has repeatedly shown that battered women and batterers can come from all walks of life. They may be working outside the home or in the home. They may be unemployed or have a steady job. They may be rich or poor, well-educated or illiterate, of any nationality or race, young or old, with or without children.

In fact, it is likely that both the fascination and the horror of wife battering for many Canadians lies in the growing recognition that, based on our expanding knowledge, wife battering can happen to any woman, and that there are no easily identifiable causes that can simply be eradicated or avoided.

Despite the difficulty of understanding wife battering, two major types of explanation have emerged over the last decade which have been widely used to respond to battered women, their children, and the men who batter them. Both of these types of explanation will be summarized briefly in the sections that follow.

Power-Based Theories

Theorists from this school have expanded our awareness that wife battering and violence against women generally are socially created. These theorists explain that violence against women is perpetuated by society's power structure which makes men dominant over women through the creation of separate and unequal roles for each gender. This dominance is also reinforced through institutional rules and structures based on male supremacy. . . .

Power-based theories of wife battering emphasizing sex-based inequality and the patriarchal structure of society originated among feminists and have gained widespread acceptance by policy-makers and service-providers in this field. This explanation for the existence of wife battering appears in most writings on the subject and helps guide intervention techniques in most services for battered women, their partners, and their children.

Research on the power dynamics in battering families also asserts that power is a more highly valued commodity in battering families than in non-battering families. On the surface, this power may not always overtly rest with the man. However, research findings suggest that, in families where the woman is dominant in terms of decision-making or earning power, or where the woman is perceived to be superior in some other way, violence is often used by the man to shift the balance of power. So, for example, Adler found that, while both partners **might** use violence against one another in their relationships, "the use of violence by husbands was strongly associated with their dominance over their wives". In other words, men tend to use violence to reassert their power and authority over their wives. Violence by women tends to be used most often as a means of protection or retaliation. Other researchers have also found that, when the husband had a less prestigious or lower-paying job, or a lower level of education than his wife, he was more likely "to use force and violence on family members than when the husband had the 'resource' of a higher-prestige occupation". Further, many counsellors reported that many men resort to physical violence when they feel their wives are more articulate than they are. These men frequently complain that they can't win an argument with their wives, so they "shut them up" by the use of force.

These reports and the preceding research findings suggest that, in accordance with the tenets of the power-based theories, the acceptance and social reinforcement of violence in the family is a means to establish and to maintain the male in a dominant relationship over his wife. . .

Learning Theories

Learning theorists basically argue that witnessing or suffering violence teaches people to use violence to try to solve problems or deal with stress in their lives. This argument is supported by research and by statements from service-providers which reveal that many batterers come from families where their mothers were battered and/or where they themselves were physically, sexually, or psychologically abused as children. These findings are also corroborated by the statistics collected for this study. Sixty-one per cent of the partners of the women who stayed in transition houses in 1985 had been abused as children. Thirty-nine per cent of the battered women reported being physically abused as children, 24% reported being sexually abused, and 48% reported being emotionally abused as well. It is very noteworthy that, of the women who said they physically abused their own children, 69% said they had themselves been physically abused during their childhood.

Learning theorists also argue that the use of violence as a discipline tool can teach violence. In this vein, researchers report a "strong relationship between parental punishment and aggression" and suggest that

> ... increasing evidence indicates that a high price is paid for maintaining order in the family through violence. The norms that legitimate violence assure a family institution and a society characterized by violence for years to come.

Learning theorists also frequently explain the perpetuation of violence, that is, the factor that turns isolated violent incidents into the **persistent** violence which characterizes wife battering, by stating that victims, friends, and society as a whole unintentionally reinforce the violence.

> Often times their violence at home is inadvertently reinforced by what follows the battering episode. Many of these men have been experiencing mounting pressure and psychological tension. When they become violent, they experience a reduction in that physical tension and that drop in physiological arousal can be a powerful reinforcer. Sometimes there are other reinforcers as well. The victim after the beating, may indeed do as he insists; others may treat him with more respect and often he feels more in control. Even if he feels remorseful or guilty about her injuries he (and sometimes the victim herself) tends to blame the victim for 'causing' him to 'lose control'. He denies responsibility for the negative behaviour. Due to the tacit acceptance of family violence in society and to the lack of clear messages that his violent behaviour must stop, his violence is rarely punished.

Finally, learning theorists also suggest that witnessing violence vicariously, as opposed to the direct witnessing of actual wife battering or the experience of child abuse, can teach some men to use violence in their lives whether within or outside the family. This particular tenet has created considerable concern about pornography as a teaching tool for violence.

> Pornography (especially as it is legitimized in mainstream T.V. shows, ads, movies, fashion layouts, etc.) socializes some men into thinking that the maltreatment of women is erotic, sexually desirable, desired by women and a necessary proof of virility.

· · ·

These two types of explanations, one based on the structure of power in our society, the other on learning theory, have clarified our understanding of wife battering, and have helped to guide intervention efforts. Yet many shelter workers and other service-providers lamented that, while these explanations seemed sufficiently clear in the past, they no longer seem to provide a complete enough explanation to expand our vision of what battered women and their children need and want. More and more service-providers also worried that "these theories that seem so clear to us just don't seem to ring true for too many of the women who come to us". Many service-providers believe that the answers are more complex. They believe that theories are needed which will make room for ambiguity and for the emotional bond between battered women and their partners who batter them.

"The answers" as to why wife battering exists are still far from being known. In order to better grapple with these persistent questions, and to attempt to incorporate some of the ambiguity of wife battering into an understanding of the problem, the perceptions of the battered women will be re-examined. In the next section, accounts of the battered women's understanding of wife battering will be presented. These accounts are not indirect critiques of the theories presented earlier, but are presented to complement these theories and to draw a fuller picture of our understanding of wife battering.

How Do Battered Women Understand The Battering?

Battered women understand the battering partly in terms of power in their families, but they speak of a shifting, ambiguous type of power. They spoke sometimes of feeling powerless against their husbands or partners. They also spoke of their power in the relationship and of the powerlessness of their partners. Many of them believe that, basically, women are more powerful than men in society, as the quote below elucidates:

> I can't quite make sense of what the women here [at the shelter] are saying about the patriarchal structure of society and about power and society making men more powerful and all that. When I was growing up, my mother was for sure stronger than my Dad in every way but physically. She was smarter, could do more, and more people respected her. I think it's the same with my husband and me. There's no way he's stronger than me, except physically, and that's why he hits me, because he feels so low.

Other women elaborated this theme in terms of a mother-son model of relationships between themselves and their partners.

> My husband and all the men I've ever known are like little boys. We're really like their mothers, underneath. Everyone keeps telling me to leave him; they say he'll destroy me. But they don't know how strong I am and how weak he is underneath.

Others spoke of the power they feel in the relationship.

> Sure I feel sorry for him. He says he would have nothing without me and the kids. I know he's pretty rotten sometimes. But he really needs me. I guess that's why I keep going back. He makes me feel important.

Still others spoke of their partners as victims or losers in society.

> You can talk about men being powerful in our society if you want, but you're not talking about my husband. My husband's never had any power in his whole life. He's never had a chance. He was born poor. He was born Indian. He's never felt better than anyone. He's never felt better than me. It's because he's so low that he hits me.

In these women's words, even if they don't represent the experiences of all battered women, is a perception that, although they don't like being hit, the batterers themselves make the women feel important, needed, even powerful within the relationship. In these women's words as well is a realization that many battered women are strong. Many battered women do not feel like powerless victims, and will not respond positively to services which treat them like victims instead of survivors.

These experiences remind us of the complexity of the realization of power in individual relationships. They also remind us that power in our society is not just gender-based; it is also class-, race-, and age-based.

Many battered women also understand battering as a something that "got out of hand", as an extension (at least at the beginning) of a normal part of a normal relationship. Many battered women feel that their relationship started out much like any other relationship and, in fact, some emphasize that they feel they had an unusually loving, intense, and close relationship. In other words, they support the understanding that, over time, wife battering may take on a life of its own and become a pathological syndrome which reinforces or produces certain psychological and behavioural characteristics in both the batterer and the battered woman. However, they argue that, **at first**, wife battering often begins as actions at the extreme end of a continuum of behaviour which occurs in most relationships, particularly in relationships which have a sexual element.

It is important to acknowledge the apparently "normal" context within which most first acts of battering occur to understand why so many women do tolerate battering. This is certainly not to say that wife battering is therefore normal, acceptable, or excusable. . . .

We can understand better what battered women are saying if we consider the nature of intimate relationships in our society. Intimate relationships, by definition, generate a wide range of emotions and responses. The image of romantic love idealized in our society is characterized by highs and lows. Being "in love" is living "on the edge", participating in a kind of emotional aerobics. Our society highly values energy and "living on the edge". The socially accepted use of drugs, the preoccupation with "having it all", with creative stress, the fitness craze, and even our social addiction to soap operas and violent television shows emphasize high energy and intense emotional highs and lows.

For these reasons, wife battering at the outset is often difficult, if not impossible, to prevent, or even to identify, because some violence (rough sexual play and psychological games intended to elicit jealousy) is intertwined with our whole ideal of "being in love" (isolation and possessiveness). In different socio-economic groups, this violence may be more or less psychological, or more or less physical, but the romantic desire to be alone together in a private world and the desire to have constant physical contact with your loved one are simply the "positive" faces of the jealousy and isolation which become part of most wife-battering experiences.

Battered women often talk of the intensity of their love for the batterer. Throughout this study, many battered women made the following kinds of statements: "I've never had better sex with anyone". "I just can't believe he'd hit me. I know he really loves me as much as I love him". "No one's ever loved me the way he does". Battered women also speak of the highs and lows of the relationship:

> *You know, life was a roller-coaster with Bill. In the end, of course, that became unbearable all the tension. But in the beginning, it was just so thrilling. I never wanted to come down.*

Many battered women, like so many people in our society, are guilty of no greater "weakness" than being in love with being in love. It's their attempt to stay in love, to retain an idealized vision of their partner, that often prevents many battered women from realizing that they are being battered until the battering has become a part of life.

Women who are battered do not generally define themselves as battered women the first time they are battered. In fact, because wife battering includes emotional, verbal, and financial battering, as well as physical and sexual battering, it may be very difficult to define when the first incident actually occurred, either for the battered woman, or for an outsider. This ambivalence is evident in the words battered women use to describe their early experiences with the batterer. It is not uncommon for battered women to say:

> *I was flattered by his jealousy at first — I thought it meant he loved me.*

> *He said he would rather stay home, just with me, than go out with friends. I loved the attention and closeness at first. I thought he was the most romantic man in the world.*

Even the first case of physical abuse is not always clear-cut. In many cases, the woman is "just pushed". While pushing can result in very severe injuries, depending on the location of the push — down the stairs, over a chair, into a pot of boiling water on the stove, etc. — the push itself can be easily re-interpreted by the batterer and by the woman who is battered as something very minor. The results of the push (a fall down a set of stairs, a scalding, etc.) can be viewed as an accident, rather than as a direct result of the push. Again, battered women speak of this ambiguity:

> *I was just baffled the first time he hit me. It wasn't really a hit you know, not like a punch or even a slap, he just pushed me really hard. I broke an arm, but it was from falling backward over a chair, not from his push.*

. . .

One real problem is that, in many homes, battering begins with a relatively minor incident, at least in terms of the severity of the violence. Another real problem is that, while violence almost always escalates, it may not do so in many homes for months or even years. The result is that women accept the violence as an unpleasant but bearable part of life, given the good things about the relationships (and most battering relationships do still provide sporadic periods of closeness during the honeymoon phases of the violence, even if these become shorter and less frequent as the violence progresses), until they are so enmeshed in the cycle of violence and so demoralized and trapped by it that they can't "just leave".

Many service-providers, and even women who have been battered, counsel that leaving or calling the police "the first time it happens" is the most effective way to ensure that it won't happen again. However, given that it may be hard to define "that first incident", especially since definitions of intolerable violence are culturally relative and since most women have a lot of emotional and practical investment in their relationships, this advice frequently has an unreal, hollow ring to it.

In many battering relationships, certainly in the early stages of the battering, it is the **persistence** of the violence, not always the objectively definable, evident severity which characterizes the violence as battering and separates it from similar isolated episodes of psychological or physical violence in non-battering relationships.

. . .

There is growing evidence that leaving provides little or no guarantee that the battering will stop and may even escalate the violence. In the present study, 12% of the women were separated or divorced. Anecdotal information suggests that the majority of these women were battered by their ex-husbands, some by new partners. Michael Smith, in his telephone survey of 315 Toronto women, found that, while the rate of abuse for all women interviewed was 18.1%, for women who were separated or divorced, the rate jumped to 42.6%. . . .

The reactions of most battered women, not only at the beginning of the battering, but throughout their battering experiences, are often strong and logical and must be seen and treated this way if we are to reach out to battered women and provide services for them which "ring true", will be helpful, and will be used by a greater number of battered women. It is easy as an outsider providing an alternative to violence to scoff at, or be discouraged by, the astonished response of many women to the suggestion that they leave their violent husbands: "But he's my husband, and the father of my children. . . . I can't just abandon him". It's easy from an outside vantage point which assumes that the batterer, the battered wife, their relationship, or all three are defective, to dismiss as misguided sentiment the woman's heroic attempts to keep her marriage together, to keep her children from knowing about the violence, to insist that she loves her husband. The woman's actions and statements are easy to dismiss as long as we assume that the battered woman, along with her partner and their relationship, are somehow basically different from us and from non-battering relationships, not just in terms of the violence, but in terms of the basic personality of the man and woman and in terms of the initial quality of the relationship.

However, as this study has established repeatedly, research shows that battered women do not fit one psychological or socio-economic mould. Few common characteristics which are not the direct result of the battering have been cited. In fact, in the one study known to the author where the personality traits of battered women **before** the violence were discussed, Lenore Walker found that women who are battered "perceive themselves as more liberal than most" in their relationships with men — a far cry from the stereotype of the battered woman as a traditional woman totally oppressed by, and dependent on, her partner.

It is **after** prolonged battering, as a result of the battering, that battered women begin to display certain similar psychological traits. After prolonged battering, women suffer from low self-esteem and isolation. They are emotionally dependent on the batterer, are compliant, feel guilty, and blame themselves for the violence and yet demonstrate great loyalty to the batterer. Not only do they want the relationship to continue, they state that they are staying for the sake of the family. They believe the batterer's promises to change and they frequently believe that the violence would stop if only their partners would get the one lucky break they've always wanted.

To truly understand the women who are battered and what they want, as well as the batterers and what they want, it is important to erase the assumption that battered women are somehow intrinsically different from non-battered women. To understand the actions and perceptions of battered women, it is important to think of how we all act in relationships, what we want, and the extent to which many of us will go to preserve a relationship. As one shelter worker poignantly said:

> Relationships are hard to come by. Sure we should help women know that they have worth outside their marriages, but a marriage isn't just status and a piece of paper . . . it's warmth, belonging, and a future. Battered women don't always get these good things out of their relationships, but most of them did in the beginning, and they just keep hoping it will come back. People will go to any lengths to feel loved, and love is not just waiting around the next corner for every battered woman who leaves her batterer.

Even the majority of women who report the violence do so out of hope — that, by reporting the violence, she and her partner will be helped to return to their pre-violent state. Of course, she may also hope that she will get attention and be listened to because she is frequently lonely and unnurtured as a result of the isolation most batterers impose on their victims. She may also hope he will be punished or "get his just deserts". But behind it all, she often just wants them to be happy again. The importance of these hopes should not be diminished.

Unfortunately, as will be demonstrated in subsequent chapters, many of the services and initiatives which have been created for battered women and for their partners have been built on the assumption, either consciously or unconsciously, that the relationship is not worth saving and ignore or belittle the woman's hopes to save and rekindle it. The hope of the service-providers is most often to save or protect the woman as an individual or to help or change the batterer as an individual in some way. This well-intentioned, institutional hope often buries the woman's pleas for a different kind of help. It is this very basic discrepancy between the battered woman's hopes and the hopes of the service-providers which renders so many of the initiatives taken inappropriate and frustrating for the women who are battered and which contribute to the burnout and despair of the sincere and hopeful people who try to help the women, their children, and their partners.

LONDON FAMILY COURT CLINIC INC., FINAL REPORT: WIFE ASSAULT AS A CRIME: THE PERSPECTIVES OF VICTIMS AND POLICE OFFICERS ON A CHARGING POLICY IN LONDON, ONTARIO FROM 1980-1990

(London: London Family Court Clinic, Inc., 1991) iii-vi, 1-3 and 5-12

Within the past decade, Canadian society has accepted the reality that "wife assault is a crime". During the 1970's considerable documentation through research and the popular press indicated that women who were assaulted in their own homes were treated as second-class victims of violence (MacLeod, 1987; Jaffe & Burris, 1981). Police officers rarely laid charges except in the most extreme circumstances that involved life-threatening injuries and the use of weapons. However, public awareness, lobby groups and federal/provincial government hearings on family violence in the 1980's concluded that the status quo had to change. Women assaulted by their partners were seen to be victims that had a fundamental right to police protection and personal safety. It was suggested that these victims should not be left to defend themselves, but rather the police forces across the country should lay charges under the *Criminal Code of Canada*. Victims were not to seek individual, civil solutions to the violence, but rather law enforcement professionals were to act on behalf of all citizens to indicate that wife assault would not be tolerated or deemed a lesser offence.

"Wife assault is a crime" has become a national focus with a clear commitment from federal and provincial governments. Various government ministries responsible for the justice system have made major efforts to improve awareness and sensitivity of law enforcement professionals on the plight of abused women. At the cornerstone of these initiatives is the clear directive that police should lay charges in cases of wife assault when they have reasonable and probable grounds to believe that an assault took place. In a similar vein, Crown Attorneys have been directed to prosecute wife assault cases with the same vigour as other criminal proceedings dealing with violence. Parallel initiatives have recently been announced to create greater sensitivity on the part of judges to deal with these complex matters (Schmitz, 1991).

Although there has been widespread agreement that the "wife assault is a crime" trend in the criminal justice system is a commendable shift in attitude, there has been very little research to examine the effectiveness of this policy. Preliminary research in London, Ontario — one of the first police forces in North America to have a formal policy in regard to wife assault — indicates several important findings that call into question several traditional myths in this field. (Burris & Jaffe, 1983; Jaffe, Wolfe, Telford & Austin, 1986).

Myth 1:   Police officers rarely have reasonable and probable grounds that an assault has taken place.

Finding: Police officers had reasonable and probable grounds in over 30 times as many cases as they had been laying charges for before the policy directive.

Myth 2:   Victims will not cooperate with the justice system in testifying against their partner.

Finding: Victims were more likely to follow through on court appearances and court testimony when the police laid charges compared to victims laying a private information (victim laid charge).

Myth 3:   Victim's lack of cooperation will lead to most charges being dismissed or withdrawn.

Finding: Fewer cases were dismissed or withdrawn during court proceedings when police laid charges.

Myth 4:   Laying charges has no impact on violent behaviour.

Finding: Victims reported a significant reduction in violence after police laid charges.

CUNNINGHAM LAUNCHES TWO DOMESTIC VIOLENCE COURTS

(News Release, February 23, 1998)

. . . The two new courts being launched today [in London and Hamilton] are part of the six new domestic violence court projects opening in centres throughout the province. Three of the new projects (Ottawa, Hamilton, London) are based on a model currently in place in downtown Toronto; the others (Durham Region, Brampton and North Bay) are based on the approach being used at the North York court.

The downtown Toronto model, identified as the K Court model, deals with serious domestic assault cases only. It uses specialized investigative and prosecutorial techniques to prosecute crimes of domestic assault more effectively and to reduce pressure on victims who testify in court. The North York model deals with first-time offenders and focuses on prevention and breaking the cycle of abuse while ensuring abusers are held accountable for their crimes. Offenders must agree to plead guilty and to complete a mandatory counselling program. The victim must also agree to this arrangement.

A preliminary evaluation of the two court models indicate that the percentage of guilty pleas in domestic assault cases has increased from 40 to 50 per cent since January 1997 when the downtown Toronto K Court began prosecuting cases. Police, prosecutors and victim/witness staff believe the models are working because fewer victims are withdrawing from the process and evidence collection has improved.

Based on the Toronto K Court model, the domestic violence courts opening today in London and Hamilton will deal with serious domestic assault cases. A dedicated team of police, Crown Attorneys and victim/witness staff, who have been specially trained in domestic assault, work together. In this approach, police routinely collect more evidence than the victim's statement — such as 911 tapes, medical reports and audio/video victim statements. Male Batterer programs help break the cycle of abuse by counselling abusive men to recognize the consequences of their behaviour, and to control and change their abusive behaviour. The counselling programs, averaging 20 weeks in duration, are a mandatory component of each domestic court program.

"Victim support is an extremely important component of prosecuting domestic assault cases," said Attorney General Charles Harnick. "Because of fear or intimidation, victims are often reluctant to testify in court or recant their initial statements to the police. These courts will help solve this problem." While thousands of women are abused and assaulted in their homes, a 1993 Statistics Canada Violence Against Women survey found that only 26 per cent of wife assault incidents were reported to police. Women have been hesitant to report domestic violence because their abusers may threaten their lives or the lives of their children. . . .

DOMESTIC VIOLENCE COURTS PROJECT BACKGROUNDER

How Domestic Violence Courts Work

The purpose of the domestic violence courts is: to provide more support to victims; to prosecute domestic assault cases more effectively; and to intervene early in abusive situations. To be successful, domestic violence courts require co-operation among the police, Crown Attorneys, victim/witness staff, the judiciary and courts' administration. All communities in which the courts are located must also have accredited intervention programs for batterers.

Victim Support

An important aspect of domestic violence courts is the help provided to the victim by victim/witness staff. Early in the proceedings, the victim is asked to come to the court house to meet with Crown Attorneys and victim/witness personnel. During the meetings, the victim is told about the domestic violence court, helped to feel more comfortable with the court process, and provided with information about community services or agencies that can help. In addition, victim/witness staff give the victim much-needed emotional support. One of the results of this type of assistance is that the victim has more input into the case and can make better-informed decisions and choices.

Effective Prosecution

Ontario police are required to lay charges in all domestic abuse cases, when there are reasonable and probable grounds to believe that a criminal offence has occurred. Once these cases move to the Crown Attorney's office, however, the ability to proceed with the prosecution largely depends on the victim — who must testify at trial. Because of fear or intimidation, victims often recant their original statement to the police or refuse to testify altogether. As a result, while the number of assault charges have risen, more cases have been withdrawn or stayed by the prosecution because, without the victim, there is no reasonable prospect of conviction.

Domestic violence courts use a dedicated team to ensure that domestic violence cases are prosecuted more effectively. The team is composed of: police who have been trained in the investigation of domestic assault; Crown Attorneys specially trained in the prosecution of domestic violence; and staff of the Victim/Witness Assistance Program who help victims through the process.

A key tool in prosecuting accused batterers is evidence. That is why, in domestic violence courts, Crown Attorneys routinely ask police to collect much more evidence than the victim's statement. This evidence can include 911-tapes, medical reports, photographs of injuries, interviews with family and neighbours, and audio-and/or video-taped victim statements. Prosecutors try to use this evidence to proceed with the cases, even if victims fail to attend court or recant their original statements to police.

The Batterers' Program

The purpose of the Batterers' Program is to intervene early enough in abusive domestic situations, through intensive counselling, so that the cycle of long-term abuse can be broken. In some domestic violence courts (e.g. North York), Crown Attorneys and victim/witness staff screen domestic assault cases to determine which offenders are appropriate for a batterers' program. To be eligible, the abuser must be a first-time accused and have caused no significant injuries to the victim. The accused must also be willing to take part in the program, and the victim also has to agree to the accused's participation.

In other courts (e.g. Toronto), whether an accused pleads guilty or is found guilty at trial, the Crown Attorney generally requests the judge, during sentencing, to refer the abuser to a batterers' program as a term of probation.

When offenders complete the counselling program satisfactorily, they are given a conditional discharge. If the program isn't completed, or batterers re-offend during its course, a new charge of failing to comply with a court order is laid against them. Batterers' programs are funded partly by the Ministry of the Solicitor General and Correctional Services and partly by the offender (who pays a fee based on ability to pay). They are delivered by a variety of community agencies.

NOTES AND QUESTIONS

1. Professor Johnson proposes in "Patriarchal Terrorism and Common Couple Violence: Two Forms of Violence Against Women" (1995), 57 Journal of Marriage and the Family 283 that the phenomenon of "domestic violence" be broken down into two distinct patterns that he labels patriarchal terrorism and common couple violence. The first label describes violence in which women are highly victimized by husbands who seek control. The second represents occasional violence that is often enacted and initiated equally by men and women during conflicts that get out of hand. He argues that studies of women seeking assistance for wife battering generally include only women who experience patriarchal terrorism and that it is inappropriate to generalize from those studies to all violent couples. On the other hand, representative surveys reach individuals experiencing common couple violence, but under-represent those experiencing extreme forms of violence because both highly violent and highly victimized individuals are unlikely to participate in this type of survey.

Similarly, two California-based mental health professionals, Janet Johnston and Linda Campbell, have developed a differentiated set of "profiles" of relationships involving interspousal abuse: "Parent-Child Relationships in Domestic Violence Families Disputing Custody" (1993) , 31 Fam. & Con. Cts. Rev. 282. They argue that parent-child relationships differ in each of the following situations:

A. On-going or Episodic Male Battering (just less than 20% of their sample): Male physical abuse is on-going or intermittent. The male is possessive, domineering and jealous. The potential for abuse is high and may escalate after separation. Child visitation should be supervised or suspended.

B. Male Controlling Interactive Violence (about 20% of their sample): Here the man attempts to control his partner through an authoritarian or dictatorial style. There tends to be mutual blaming and anger. Once separated, there is a good prognosis for terminating violence. Access should be structured to minimize possibilities of power struggles.

C. Separation-Engendered and Post-Divorce Trauma (about 25% of their sample): Violence is absent during the relationship, but one or more incidents occurs after separation. There is a good chance for a positive parent-child relationship and a violence-free relationship between the parents.

D. Female Initiated Violence (just below 15% of their sample): The woman initiates aggression, usually against a passive, sometimes depressed, male. The father is not a good role model and the children have ambivalent feelings towards their mother.

E. Psychotic and Paranoid Reactions (about 5% of their sample): There are unpredictable attacks by either spouse based on disordered thinking or a drug-induced state. Visitation should be supervised or suspended.

See also Bala, "Spousal Abuse and Children of Divorce: A Differentiated Approach" (1996), 13 Can. J. Fam. L. 215.

2. One of the most complete studies about abuse of women by their partners was the 1994 Statistics Canada report involving a telephone survey of 12,300 women: Rodgers, "Wife Assault: The Findings of a National Survey" (March, 1994), Juristat 14:9. Of those women who were or ever had lived in a married or common law relationship with a man, 29% reported at least one physical or sexual assault from a partner or former partner and one third of these feared for their lives at some point. Forty-eight per cent of all women reported an assault in a prior relationship, suggesting that almost one half of all divorced or separated women had experienced violence. Three per cent of all women indicated that they had been physically assaulted in the previous twelve months, with the highest rates for women who were younger, less educated and with less income. About one third of those women who reported physical abuse indicated more than 10 incidents and a similar proportion stated that there had been only one incident. The most common physical abuse reported was a slap, shove, or a threatened slap or shove (which constitutes assault), but 5% of those reporting violence mentioned the threat or use of a knife or gun. About one third of all the woman reported serious emotional abuse such as verbal denigration.

3. An abused spouse may be able to obtain a court order for exclusive possession of the matrimonial home so as to exclude the batterer. See Chapter 5: **THE MATRIMONIAL HOME**. In such circumstances it may also be prudent to obtain an order under s. 46(1) of the *Family Law Act* that restrains the batterer from molesting, annoying or harassing the victim. Section 46(2) establishes the offence of contravening a restraining order and s. 46(3) deals with police powers to arrest a person suspected of this offence. Regarding restraining orders and their enforcement, see *Maurico* v. *Maurico* (1979), 9 R.F.L. (2d) 243 (Ont. Prov. Ct.); *Layton* v. *Layton* (1982), 37 O.R. (2d) 201 (H.C.); *Scono* v. *Scono* (1984), 41 R.F.L. (2d) 57 (Ont. H.C.); *Wilkins* v. *Wilkins* (1987), 7 R.F.L. (3d) 199 (Ont. Prov. Ct.); *Colley* v. *Colley* (1991), 31 R.F.L. (3d) 281 (Ont. U.F.C.); *Oliver* v. *Oliver* (1996), 20 R.F.L. (4th) 460 (Ont. Gen. Div.); *Hamilton* v. *Hamilton* (1996), 92 O.A.C. 103 (Ont. C.A.); *Chau* v. *Jiang (Guardian of)*(1997), 34 R.F.L. (4th) 249 (Alta. Q.B.); and *Cole* v. *Cole* (1998), 40 R.F.L. (4th) 54 (Ont. Gen. Div.).

Several provinces have recently enacted legislation to provide emergency relief where there is domestic violence. One of the remedies provided is a temporary exclusive possession order of the family residence. Typically, such legislation permits short-term orders without notice to the other party where family violence has occurred and the circumstances are serious or urgent. Police officers may be specifically directed to remove the other party from the residence. See *Protection Against Family Violence Act*, S.A. 1998, c. P-19.2 ; *The Domestic Violence and Stalking Prevention, Protection and Prevention Act*, S.M. 1998, c. 41; *Victims of Family Violence Act*, R.S.P.E.I. 1988, c. V-3.2 (in force 1996); and *The Victims of Domestic Violence Act*, R.S.S. 1994, c. V-6.02. This legislation deals explicitly with a number of issues that are left to be worked out through procedural rules or creative judicial interpretation in Ontario. For example, the *Family Law Act* does not provide expressly for applications without notice but cases such as *Pifer* v. *Pifer* (1986), 3 R.F.L. (3d) 167 (Ont. Dist. Ct.) and *Perrier* v. *Perrier* (1989), 20 R.F.L. (3d) 388 (Ont. H.C.) indicate that they are possible. See also *Family Law Rules*, O. Reg. 114, r. 14(12) - (15).

Court-ordered eviction from one's home without an opportunity to present evidence or argument obviously raises concerns of procedural fairness. See *C.(A.L.G.)* v. *Prince Edward Island* (1998), 157 D.L.R. (4th) 523 (P.E.I.T.D.), where certain aspects of Prince Edward Island's legislation were found to infringe s. 7 of the *Canadian Charter of Rights and Freedoms*. See also *Dolgopol* v. *Dolgopol* (1995), 127 Sask. R. 237 (Q.B.) and *Bella* v. *Bella* (1995), 132 Sask. R. 17 (Q.B.) where the reviewing judges concluded that the justices of the peace had acted without the urgency needed for an *ex parte* order.

A victim of violence may also seek protection by securing a court order under s. 810 of the *Criminal Code*. The informant must prove that she has reasonable grounds to fear that the defendant will cause personal injury or property damage. If this is established, the defendant may be required to enter a recognizance, with or without sureties, to keep the peace and be of good behaviour for a period up to one year. Failure to abide by the terms of this "peace bond" is a summary conviction offence.

Why might these remedies prove ineffective in preventing further abuse?

4. A related provision is s. 264 of the *Criminal Code*. Enacted in 1993 this section makes "criminal harassment" or "stalking", as it is more popularly known, an offence. For cases applying this provision, see *R.* v. *Sousa*, [1995] O.J. No. 1435 (Gen. Div.); *R.* v. *Ryback* (1996), 105 C.C.C. (3d) 140 (B.C.C.A.); *R.* v. *Doodnauth*, [1998] O.J. No. 5973 (Gen. Div.); *R.* v. *Meehan* (1998), 158 Nfld. & P.E.I.R. 217 (Nfld. T.D.); and *R.* v. *M.R.W.*, [1999] B.C.J. No. 2149 (S.C.). See also Way, "The Criminalization of Stalking: An Exercise in Media Manipulation and Political Opportunism" (1994), 39 McGill L.J. 379.

5. It is obviously a criminal offence for anyone to physically abuse another, whether or not the abuse is inflicted in a family setting. It is also a tortious act that could found a civil proceeding leading to a damage award. Until fairly recently it was rare for one family member to sue another for assault and battery. In the last decade or so, however, there have been a large number of cases in which victims have successfully sued for damages as a result of child sexual abuse or wife abuse. See e.g., *Harder* v. *Brown* (1989), 50 C.C.L.T. 85 (B.C.S.C.); *N. (J.L.)* v. *L. (A.M.)* (1988), 47 C.C.L.T. 65 (Man. Q.B.); *B. (K.L.)* v. *B. (K.E.)* (1991), 7 C.C.L.T. (2d) 105 (Man. Q.B.); *P. (B.)* v. *W. (B.)* (1992), 11 O.R. (3d) 161 (Gen. Div.); *Belanger* v. *Belanger* (1995), 14 R.F.L. (4th) 448 (Sask. Q.B.); and *K.(G.)* v. *K.(D.)* (1999), 122 O.A.C. 36 (Ont. C.A.). In *Booth* v. *Booth* (1995), 80 O.A.C. 399 (C.A.), it was held that a claim for assault can be joined with a divorce proceeding under the *Divorce Act*. Similarly, in *Valenti* v. *Valenti* (1996), 21 R.F.L. (4th) 246 (Ont. Gen. Div.), affirmed (1998), 41 R.F.L. (4th) 289 (Ont. C.A.) a wife's and son's claims for damages for assault were joined with a property and support claim under provincial legislation. See generally, Bala, " Tort Remedies and the Family Law Practitioner" (1999), 16 C.F.L.Q. 423.

In *M. (K.)* v. *M. (H.)* (1992), 96 D.L.R. (4th) 289, the Supreme Court of Canada held (1) the limitation period applicable to the tort of assault and battery does not begin to run in an incest case until the victim is reasonably capable of discovering the wrongful nature of the perpetrator's act and her injuries; (2) incest is a breach of a parent's fiduciary duty to protect the infant child's well-being and health; and (3) as it is an equitable claim, an action for compensation for a breach of a fiduciary duty is not governed by the Ontario *Limitations Act*. For an article that anticipated much of the analysis in this case, see Des Rosiers, "Limitation Periods and Civil Remedies for Childhood Sexual Abuse" (1993), 9 C.F.L.Q. 43. See generally Neeb and Harper, *Civil Action for Childhood Sexual Abuse* (Toronto: Butterworths, 1994) and Feldthusen, "The Civil Action for Sexual Battery: Therapeutic Jurisprudence?" (1993), 25 Ottawa L. Rev. 203.

6. The impact on children of witnessing domestic violence will be examined in Chapter 7, **CUSTODY AND ACCESS** and Chapter 10: **CHILD IN NEED OF PROTECTION**, where the topic of child abuse will also be addressed.

7. In "Gender Differences in Patterns of Relationship Violence in Alberta" (1999), 31 Can. J. Beh. Sc. 150, Professors Kwong, Bartholomew and Dutton re-analyzed data from a 1987 representative survey and came to the following conclusions (at 158-59):

> . . . Consistent with research outside of Canada, men and women reported similar rates of violence and victimization. And, while more comprehensive study is needed, it appears that a substantial proportion of women's violence cannot be explained as acts of self-defense. Both genders reported that women do initiate violence and are sometimes the sole perpetrators of aggression in relationships. Also consistent with prior research, the violence reported by respondents generally differed from the prototypical batterer/victim pattern. The majority of respondents in violent relationships reported a pattern of violence that was bidirectional, minor, infrequent, and not physically injurious.

> While the importance of eliminating violence against women is obvious, the need to stop women's violence may be less evident. Our society seems to harbour an implicit acceptance of women's violence as relatively harmless, even amusing. . . .[A]lthough a low level of violence between men and women may not be physically injurious, it is associated with high marital and individual

stress. . . . Furthermore, the failure to acknowledge the possibility of women's violence, in the face of sound research evidence, jeopardizes the credibility of all theory and research directed toward ending violence against women. It also does an injustice to men who are victims of female violence and to women who need help in learning more constructive strategies to deal with the inevitable conflicts and frustrations that arise in intimate relationships.

. . . [F]indings that many men and women are involved in relationships with often low-level, often mutual, violence do not negate the problem of severe relationship violence in which men are likely the primary perpetrators and women the primary victims.

See also chapter 2 of Fekete, *Moral Panic: Biopolitics Rising* (Montreal, Robert Davies Publishing, 1994).

8. Partner abuse is not limited to opposite-sex relationships: Faulkner, "Lesbian Abuse: The Social and Legal Realities" (1991), 16 Queen's L.J. 261.

9. For further reading on domestic violence, see Migus, *Elder Abuse* (Ottawa: Health and Welfare Canada, 1990); Rusen, *Silencing Their Screams: The Legal System's Response to Male Battering of Women* (Ottawa: National Association of Women and the Law, 1992); Schollenberg and Gibbons, "Domestic Violence Protection Orders: A Comparative Review" (1992), 10 Can. J. Fam. L. 191; Thorne-Finch, *Ending the Silence: The Origins and Treatment of Male Violence Against Women* (Toronto: University of Toronto Press, 1992); Freeman and Villancourt (co-chairs), *Final Report of the Canadian Panel on Violence Against Women* (Ottawa: The Panel, 1993); Lakeman, *99 Federal Steps Toward an End to Family Violence against Women* (Toronto: National Action Committee on the Status of Women, 1993); Drumbl, "Civil, Constitutional and Criminal Justice Responses to Female Partner Abuse: Proposals for Reform" (1994), 12 Can. J. Fam. L. 115; Wiegers, "Compensation for Wife Abuse: Empowering Victims?" (1994), 28 U.B.C.L. Rev. 247; Ginn, "Mandatory Reporting of Wife Assault by Health Care Professionals" (1994), 17 Dalhousie L.J. 105; Ginn, "Wife Assault, the Justice System and Professional Responsibility" (1995), 33 Alta. L. Rev. 908; Lenton, "Power Versus Feminist Theories of Wife Abuse" (1995), 37 Can. J. Crim. 305; Lenton, "Feminist Versus Interpersonal Power Theories of Wife Abuse Revisited" (1995), 37 Can. J. Crim. 567; De Keseredy, "Patterns of Family Violence" in Baker, ed. *Families: Changing Trends in Canada* (McGraw-Hill Ryerson, Toronto: 1996); Bala, "Spousal Abuse and Children of Divorce: A Differentiated Approach" (1996), 13 Can. J. Fam. L. 215; De Keseredy and MacLeod, *Woman Abuse: A Sociological Story* (Harcourt Brace, Toronto:1997); Kerr and Jaffe, "Legal and Clinical Issues in Child Custody Disputes Involving Domestic Violence" (1999), 17 C.F.L.Q. 1; and Ferris and Strike, "Mandatory Duty to Report Spousal Assault Victims: Medico-Legal Issues, Women's Health and Physicians" (1999), 19 Health L. Can. 65.

R. v. LAVALLEE

[1990] 1 S.C.R. 852, 55 C.C.C. 97

WILSON J.: [Dickson C.J.C., Lamer, L'Heureux-Dubé, Gonthier and McLachlin JJ. concurred in these reasons. Sopinka J. wrote a brief concurring opinion.] — The narrow issue raised on this appeal is the adequacy of a trial judge's instructions to the jury regarding expert evidence. The broader issue concerns the utility of expert evidence in assisting a jury confronted by a plea of self-defence to a murder charge by a common law wife who had been battered by the deceased.

1. *The facts*

The appellant, who was 22 years old at the time, had been living with Kevin Rust for some three to four years. Their residence was the scene of a boisterous party on August 30, 1986. In the early hours of August 31st, after most of the guests had departed, the appellant and Rust had an argument in the upstairs bedroom which was used by the appellant. Rust was killed by a single shot in the back of the head from a .303 caliber rifle fired by the appellant as he was leaving the room.

The appellant did not testify but her statement made to police on the night of the shooting was put in evidence. Portions of it read as follows:

> Me and Wendy argued as usual and I ran in the house after Kevin pushed me. I was scared, I was really scared. I locked the door. Herb was downstairs with Joanne and I called for Herb but I was crying when I called him. I said, "Herb come up here please." Herb came up to the top of the stairs and I told him that Kevin was going to hit me actually beat on me again. Herb said he knew and that if I was his old lady things would be different, he gave me a hug. OK, we're friends, there's nothing between us. He said "Yeah, I know" and he went outside to talk to Kevin leaving the door unlocked. I went upstairs and hid in my closet from Kevin. I was so scared . . . My window was open and I could hear Kevin asking questions about what I was doing and what I was saying. Next thing I know he was coming up the stairs for me. He came into my bedroom and said "Wench, where are you?" And he turned on my light and he said "Your purse is on the floor" and he kicked it. OK then he turned and he saw me in the closet. He wanted me to come out but I didn't want to come out because I was scared. I was so scared. [The officer who took the statement then testified that the appellant started to cry at this point and stopped after a minute or two.] He grabbed me by the arm right there. There's a bruise on my face also where he slapped me. He didn't slap me right then, first he yelled at me then he pushed me and I pushed him back and he hit me twice on the right hand side of my head. I was scared. All I thought about was all the other times he used to beat me, I was scared, I was shaking as usual. The rest is a blank, all I remember is he gave me the gun and a shot was fired through my screen. This is all so fast. And then the guns were in another room and he loaded it the second shot and gave it to me. And I was going to shoot myself. I pointed it to myself, I was so upset. OK and then he went and I was sitting on the bed and he started going like this with his finger [the appellant made a shaking motion with an index finger] and said something like "You're my old lady and you do as you're told" or something like that. He said "wait until everybody leaves, you'll get it then" and he said something to the effect of "either you kill me or I'll get you" that was what it was. He kind of smiled and then he turned around. I shot him but I aimed out. I thought I aimed above him and a piece of his head went that way.

The relationship between the appellant and Rust was volatile and punctuated by frequent arguments and violence. They would apparently fight for two or three days at a time or several times a week. Considerable evidence was led at trial indicating that the appellant was frequently a victim of physical abuse at the hands of Rust. Between 1983 and 1986, the appellant made several trips to hospital for injuries including severe bruises, a fractured nose, multiple contusions and a black eye. One of the attending physicians, Dr. Dirks, testified that he disbelieved the appellant's explanation on one such occasion that she had sustained her injuries by falling from a horse. . . .

The expert evidence which forms the subject-matter of the appeal came from Dr. Fred Shane, a psychiatrist with extensive professional experience in the treatment of battered wives. At the request of defence counsel Dr. Shane prepared a psychiatric assessment of the appellant. The substance of Dr. Shane's opinion was that the appellant had been terrorized by Rust to the point of feeling trapped, vulnerable, worthless and unable to escape the relationship despite the violence. At the same time, the continuing pattern of abuse put her life in danger. In Dr. Shane's opinion the appellant's shooting of the deceased was a final desperate act by a woman who sincerely believed that she would be killed that night:

> I think she felt, she felt in the final tragic moment that her life was on the line, that unless she defended herself, unless she reacted in a violent way that she would die. I mean he made it very explicit to her, from what she told me and from the information I have from the material that you forwarded to me, that she had, I think, to defend herself against his violence.

. . . The appellant was acquitted by a jury but the verdict was overturned by a majority of the Manitoba Court of Appeal and the case sent back for retrial. . . .

3. Relevant legislation

Criminal Code, R.S.C. 1985, c. C-46:

34(2) Every one who is unlawfully assaulted and who causes death or grievous bodily harm in repelling the assault is justified if

(a) he causes it under reasonable apprehension of death or grievous bodily harm from the violence with which the assault was orginally made or with which the assailant pursues his purposes, and

(b) he believes on reasonable and probable grounds, that he cannot otherwise preserve himself from death or grievous bodily harm.

. . .

5. Analysis

(i) *Admissibility of expert evidence*

. . .Where expert evidence is tendered in such fields as engineering or pathology, the paucity of the lay person's knowledge is uncontentious. The long-standing recognition that psychiatric or psychological testimony also falls within the realm of expert evidence is predicated on the realization that in some circumstances the average person may not have sufficient knowledge of or experience with human behaviour to draw an appropriate inference from the facts before him or her. . . .

The need for expert evidence in these areas can, however, be obfuscated by the belief that judges and juries are thoroughly knowledgeable about "human nature" and that no more is needed. They are, so to speak, their own experts on human behaviour. This, in effect, was the primary submission of the Crown to this court.

The bare facts of this case, which I think are amply supported by the evidence, are that the appellant was repeatedly abused by the deceased but did not leave him (although she twice pointed a gun at him), and ultimately shot him in the back of the head as he was leaving her room. The Crown submits that these facts disclose all the information a jury needs in order to decide whether or not the appellant acted in self-defence. I have no hesitation in rejecting the Crown's submission.

Expert evidence on the psychological effect of battering on wives and common law partners must, it seems to me, be both relevant and necessary in the context of the present case. How can the mental state of the appellant be appreciated without it? The average member of the public (or of the jury) can be forgiven for asking: Why would a woman put up with this kind of treatment? Why should she continue to live with such a man? How could she love a partner who beat her to the point of requiring hospitalization? We would expect the woman to pack her bags and go. Where is her self-respect? Why does she not cut loose and make a new life for herself? Such is the reaction of the average person confronted with the so-called "battered wife syndrome". We need help to understand it and help is available from trained professionals. . . .

Fortunately, there has been a growing awareness in recent years that no man has a right to abuse any woman under any circumstances. Legislative initiatives designed to educate police, judicial officers and the public, as well as more aggressive investigation and charging policies all signal a concerted effort by the criminal justice system to take spousal abuse seriously. However, a woman who comes before a judge or jury with the claim that she has been battered and suggests that this may be a relevant factor in evaluating her subsequent actions still faces the prospect of being condemned by popular mythology about domestic violence. Either she was not as badly beaten as she claims or she would have left the man long ago. Or, if she was battered that severely, she must have stayed out of some masochistic enjoyment of it. . . .

(ii) *The relevance of expert testimony to the elements of self-defence* . . .

A. *Reasonable apprehension of death*

Section 34(2)(a) requires that an accused who intentionally causes death or grievous bodily harm in repelling an assault is justified if he or she does so "under reasonable apprehension of death or grievous bodily harm". In the present case, the assault precipitating the appellant's alleged defensive act was Rust's threat to kill her when everyone else had gone.

It will be observed that s. 34(2)(a) does not actually stipulate that the accused apprehend imminent danger when he or she acts. Case-law has, however, read that requirement into the defence: see *Reilly* v. *The Queen, supra*; *R.* v. *Baxter* (1975), 27 C.C.C. (2d) 96, 33 C.R.N.S. 22 (Ont. C.A.); *R.* v. *Bogue* (1976), 30 C.C.C. (2d) 403, 70 D.L.R. (3d) 603, 13 O.R. (2d) 272 (Ont. C.A.). The sense in which "imminent" is used conjures up the image of "an uplifted knife" or a pointed gun. The rationale for the imminence rule seems obvious. The law of self-defence is designed to ensure that the use of defensive force is really necessary. It justifies the act because the defender reasonably believed that he or she had no alternative but to take the attacker's life. If there is a significant time interval between the original unlawful assault and the accused's response, one tends to suspect that the accused was motivated by revenge rather than self-defence. In the paradigmatic case of a one-time bar-room brawl between two men of equal size and strength, this inference makes sense. How can one feel endangered to the point of firing a gun at an unarmed man who utters a death threat, then turns his back and walks out of the room? One cannot be certain of the gravity of the threat or his capacity to carry it out. Besides, one can always take the opportunity to flee or to call the police. If he comes back and raises his fist, one can respond in kind if need be. These are the tacit assumptions that underlie the imminence rule.

All of these assumptions were brought to bear on the respondent in *R.* v. *Whynot* (1983), 9 C.C.C. 449, 37 C.R. (3d) 198, 61 N.S.R. (2d) 33 (C.A.). The respondent, Jane Stafford, shot her sleeping common law husband as he lay passed out in his truck. The evidence at trial indicated that the deceased "dominated the household and exerted his authority by striking and slapping the various members and from time to time administering beatings to Jane Stafford and the others" (at p. 452). The respondent testified that the deceased threatened to kill all of the members of her family, one by one, if she tried to leave him. On the night in question he threatened to kill her son. After he passed out the respondent got one of the many shotguns kept by her husband and shot him. The Nova Scotia Court of Appeal held that the trial judge erred in leaving s. 37 (preventing assault against oneself or anyone under one's protection) with the jury. . . .

The implication of the court's reasoning is that it is inherently unreasonable to apprehend death or grievous bodily harm unless and until the physical assault is actually in progress, at which point the victim can presumably gauge the requisite amount of force needed to repel the attack and act accordingly. In my view, expert testimony can cast doubt on these assumptions as they are applied in the context of a battered wife's efforts to repel an assault.

The situation of the appellant was not unlike that of Jane Stafford in the sense that she too was routinely beaten over the course of her relationship with the man she ultimately killed. According to the testimony of Dr. Shane these assaults were not entirely random in their occurrence. . . . [D]irect examination elicited a discernible pattern to the abuse . . . .

The cycle described by Dr. Shane conforms to the Walker Cycle Theory of Violence named for clinical psychologist Dr. Lenore Walker, the pioneer researcher in the field of the battered-wife syndrome. Dr. Shane acknowledged his debt to Dr. Walker in the course of establishing his credentials as an expert at trial. Dr. Walker first describes the cycle in the book, *The Battered Woman*, (1979). In her 1984 book, *The Battered Woman Syndrome*, Dr. Walker reports the results of a study involving 400 battered women. Her research was designed to test empirically the theories expounded in her earlier book. At pp. 95-6 of *The Battered Woman Syndrome*, she summarizes the Cycle Theory as follows:

> A second major theory that was tested in this project is the Walker Cycle Theory of Violence (Walker, 1979). This tension reduction theory states that there are three distinct phases associated in a recurring battering cycle: (1) tension building, (2) the acute battering incident, and (3) loving contrition. During the first phase, there is a gradual escalation of tension displayed by discrete acts causing increased friction such as name-calling, other mean intentional behaviors, and/or physical abuse. The batterer expresses dissatisfaction and hostility but not in an extreme or maximally explosive form. The woman attempts to placate the batterer, doing what she thinks might please him, calm him down, or at least, what will not further aggravate him. She tries not to respond to his hostile actions and uses general anger reduction techniques. Often she succeeds for a little while which reinforces her unrealistic belief that she can control this man . . .

> The tension continues to escalate and eventually she is unable to continue controlling his angry response pattern. "Exhausted from the constant stress, she usually withdraws from the batterer, fearing she will inadvertently set off an explosion. He begins to move more oppressively toward her as he observes her withdrawal . . . Tension between the two becomes unbearable" (Walker, 1979, p. 59). The second phase, the acute battering incident, becomes inevitable without intervention. Sometimes, she precipitates the inevitable explosion so as to control where and when it occurs, allowing her to take better precautions to minimize her injuries and pain.

> "Phase two is characterized by the uncontrollable discharge of the tensions that have built up during phase one" (p. 59). The batterer typically unleashes a barrage of verbal and physical aggression that can leave the woman severely shaken and injured. In fact, when injuries do occur it usually happens during this second phase. It is also the time police become involved, if they are called at all. The acute battering phase is concluded when the batterer stops, usually bringing with its cessation a sharp physiological reduction in tension. This in itself is naturally reinforcing. Violence often succeeds because it does work.

> In phase three which follows, the batterer may apologize profusely, try to assist his victim, show kindness and remorse, and shower her with gifts and/or promises. The batterer himself may believe at this point that he will never allow himself to be violent again. The woman wants to believe the batterer and, early in the relationship at least, may renew her hope in his ability to change. This third phase provides the positive reinforcement for remaining in the relationship, for the woman. In fact, our results showed that phase three could also be characterized by an absence of tension or violence, and no observable loving-contrition behaviour, and still be reinforcing for the woman.

. . .Given the relational context in which the violence occurs, the mental state of an accused at the critical moment she pulls the trigger cannot be understood except in terms of the cumulative effect of months or years of brutality. As Dr. Shane explained in his testimony, the deterioration of the relationship between the appellant and Rust in the period immediately preceding the killing led to feelings of escalating terror on the part of the appellant:

> But their relationship some weeks to months before was definitely escalating in terms of tension and in terms of the discordant quality about it. They were sleeping in separate bedrooms. Their intimate relationship was lacking and things were building and building and to a point, I think, where it built to that particular point where she couldn't — she felt so threatened and so over-whelmed that she had to — that she reacted in a violent way because of her fear of survival and also because, I think because of her, I guess, final sense that she was — that she had to defend herself and her own sense of violence towards this man who had really desecrated her and damaged her for so long.

Another aspect of the cyclical nature of the abuse is that it begets a degree of predictability to the violence that is absent in an isolated violent encounter between two strangers. This also means that it may in fact be possible for a battered spouse to accurately predict the onset of violence before the first blow is struck, even if an outsider to the relationship cannot. Indeed, it has been suggested that a battered woman's knowledge of her partner's violence is so heightened that she is able to anticipate the nature and extent (though not the onset) of the violence by his conduct beforehand. In her article "Potential Uses for Expert Testimony: Ideas Toward the Representation of Battered Women Who Kill", 9 *Women's Rights Law Reporter* 227 (1986), psychologist Julie Blackman describes this characteristic at p. 229:

> Repeated instances of violence enable battered women to develop a continuum along which they can "rate" the tolerability or survivability of episodes of their partner's violence. Thus, signs of unusual violence are detected. For battered women, this response to the ongoing violence of their situations is a survival skill. Research shows that battered women who kill experience remarkably severe and frequent violence relative to battered women who do not kill. They know what sorts of danger are familiar and which are novel. They have had myriad opportunities to develop and hone their perceptions of their partner's violence. And, importantly, they can say what made the final episode of violence different from the others: they can name the features of the last battering that enabled them to know that this episode would result in life-threatening action by the abuser.

At p. 236, Dr. Blackman relates the role of expert testimony in cases where a battered woman kills her batterer while he is sleeping (or not actively posing a threat to her) and pleads self-defence:

> Perhaps the single most important idea conveyed by expert testimony in such a case pertains to the notion that a battered woman, because of her extensive experience with her abuser's violence, can detect changes or signs of novelty in the pattern of normal violence that connote increased danger. Support for this assertion must come from the woman herself, in her sponta-neous, self-initiated description of the events that precede her action against the abuser. Only then can testimony from an expert offer scientific support for the idea that such a danger detection process can occur and can be expected to be as accurate as the "reasonable man" standard would imply.

Of course, as Dr. Blackman points out, it is up to the jury to decide whether the distinction drawn between "typical" violence and the particular events the ac-cused perceived as "life threatening" is compelling. According to the appellant's statement to police, Rust actually handed her a shotgun and warned her that if she did not kill him, he would kill her. I note in passing a remarkable observation made by Dr. Walker in her 1984 study, *The Battered Woman Syndrome*. Writing about the fifty battered women she interviewed who had killed their partners, she comments at p. 40:

> Most of the time the women killed the men with a gun; usually one of several that belonged to him. *Many of the men actually dared or demanded the woman use the gun on him first, or else he said he'd kill her with it.* (Emphasis added.)

Where evidence exists that an accused is in a battering relationship, expert testimony can assist the jury in determining whether the accused had a "reasonable" apprehension of death when she acted by explaining the heightened sensitivity of a battered woman to her partner's acts. Without such testimony I am skeptical that the average fact-finder would be capable of appreciating why her subjective fear may have been reasonable in the context of the relationship. After all, the hypothetical "reasonable man" observing only the final incident may have been unlikely to recognize the batterer's threat as potentially lethal. Using the case at bar as an example the "reasonable man" might have thought, as the majority of the Court of Appeal seemed to, that it was unlikely that Rust would make good on his threat to kill the appellant that night because they had guests staying overnight.

The issue is not, however, what an outsider would have reasonably perceived but what the accused reasonably perceived, given her situation and her experience.

Even accepting that a battered woman may be uniquely sensitized to danger from her batterer, it may yet be contended that the law ought to require her to wait until the knife is uplifted, the gun pointed or the fist clenched before her apprehension is deemed reasonable. This would allegedly reduce the risk that the woman is mistaken in her fear, although the law does not require her fear to be correct, only reasonable. In response to this contention, I need only point to the observation made by Huband J.A. that the evidence showed that when the appellant and Rust physically fought, the appellant "invariably got the worst of it". I do not think it is an unwarranted generalization to say that due to their size, strength, socialization and lack of training, women are typically no match for men in hand-to-hand combat. The requirement imposed in *Whynot* that a battered woman wait until the physical assault is "underway" before her apprehensions can be validated in law would, in the words of an American court, be tantamount to sentencing her to "murder by installment": *State* v. *Gallegos*, 719 P.2d 1268 at p. 1271 (1986) (N.M.). I share the view expressed by M.J. Willoughby in "Rendering Each Woman Her Due: Can a Battered Woman Claim Self-Defense When She Kills Her Sleeping Batterer" (1989), 38 *Kan. L. Rev.* 169 at p. 184 (1989), that "society gains nothing, except perhaps the additional risk that the battered woman will herself be killed, because she must wait until her abusive husband instigates another battering episode before she can justifiably act".

B. *Lack of alternatives to self-help*

Section 34(2) requires an accused who pleads self-defence to believe "on reasonable grounds" that it is not possible to otherwise preserve him or herself from death or grievous bodily harm. The obvious question is if the violence was so intolerable, why did the appellant not leave her abuser long ago? This question does not really go to whether she had an alternative to killing the deceased at the critical moment. Rather, it plays on the popular myth already referred to that a woman who says she was battered yet stayed with her batterer was either not as badly beaten as she claimed or else she liked it. Nevertheless, to the extent that her failure to leave the abusive relationship earlier may be used in support of the proposition that she was free to leave at the final moment, expert testimony can provide useful insights.

Dr. Shane attempted to explain in his testimony how and why, in the case at bar, the appellant remained with Rust . . .

Apparently, another manifestation of this victimization is a reluctance to disclose to others the fact or extent of the beatings. For example, the hospital records indicate that on each occasion the appellant attended the emergency department to be treated for various injuries she explained the cause of those injuries as accidental. Both in its address to the jury and in its written submissions before this court the Crown insisted that the appellant's injuries were as consistent with her explanations as with being battered and, therefore, in the words of Crown counsel at trial: "The myth is, in this particular case, that Miss Lavallee was a battered spouse." In his testimony Dr. Shane testified that the appellant admitted to him that she lied to hospital staff and others about the cause of her injuries. In Dr. Shane's opinion this was consistent with her over-all feeling of being trapped and helpless. . . .

The account given by Dr. Shane comports with that documented in the literature. Reference is often made to it as a condition of "learned helplessness", a phrase coined by Dr. Charles Seligman, the psychologist who first developed the theory by experimenting on animals in the manner described by Dr. Shane in his testimony. A related theory used to explain the failure of women to leave battering relationships is described by psychologist and lawyer, Charles Patrick Ewing, in his book, *Battered Women Who Kill*, (1987). Ewing describes a phenomenon labelled "traumatic bonding" that has been observed between hostages and captors, battered children and their parents, concentration camp prisoners and guards, and batterers and their spouses. . . .

This strong "affective bond" may be helpful in explaining not only why some battered women remain with their abusers but why they even profess to love them. Of course, as Dr. Ewing adds, environmental factors may also impair the woman's ability to leave — lack of job skills, the presence of children to care for, fear of retaliation by the man, etc., may each have a role to play in some cases.

This is not to say that in the course of a battering relationship a woman may never attempt to leave her partner or try to defend herself from assault. In *The Battered Woman Syndrome*, Dr. Walker notes at p. 30 that women may sometimes "react to men's violence against them by striking back, but their actions are generally ineffective at hurting or stopping the men. They may be effective in controlling the level of the man's violence against them". . . .

The same psychological factors that account for a woman's inability to leave a battering relationship may also help to explain why she did not attempt to escape at the moment she perceived her life to be in danger. The following extract from Dr. Shane's testimony on direct examination elucidates this point:

> Q. Now, we understand from the evidence that on this night she went — I think you've already described it in your evidence — and hid in the closet?
>
> A. Yes.
>
> Q. Can you tell the jury why she, for instance, would stay in that house if she had this fear? Why wouldn't she so [*sic*] someplace else? Why would she have to hide in the closet in the same house?
>
> A. Well, I think this is a reflection of what I've been talking about, this ongoing psychological process, her own psychology and the relationship, that she felt trapped. There was no out for her, this learned helplessness, if you will, the fact that she felt paralyzed, she felt tyrannized. She felt, although there were obviously no steel fences around, keeping her in, there were steel fences in her mind which created for her an incredible barrier psychologically that prevented her from moving out. Although she had attempted on occasion, she came back in a magnetic sort of a way.

And she felt also that she couldn't expect anything more. Not only this learned helplessness about being beaten, beaten, where her motivation is taken away, but her whole sense of herself. She felt this victim mentality, this concentration camp mentality if you will, where she could not see herself be in any other situation except being tyrannized, punished and crucified physically and psychologically.

I emphasize at this juncture that it is not for the jury to pass judgment on the fact that an accused battered woman stayed in the relationship. Still less is it entitled to conclude that she forfeited her right to self-defence for having done so. I would also point out that traditional self-defence doctrine does not require a person to retreat from her home instead of defending herself: *R. v. Antley*, [1964] 2 C.C.C. 142, [1964] 1 O.R. 545, 42 C.R. 384 (C.A.). A man's home may be his castle but it is also the woman's home even if it seems to her more like a prison in the circumstances.

If, after hearing the evidence (including the expert testimony), the jury is satisfied that the accused had a reasonable apprehension of death or grievous bodily harm and felt incapable of escape, it must ask itself what the "reasonable person" would do in such a situation. The situation of the battered woman as described by Dr. Shane strikes me as somewhat analogous to that of a hostage. If the captor tells her that he will kill her in three days' time, is it potentially reasonable for her to seize an opportunity presented on the first day to kill the captor or must she wait until he makes the attempt on the third day? I think the question the jury must ask itself is whether, given the history, circumstances and perceptions of the appellant, her belief that she could not preserve herself from being killed by Rust that night except by killing him first was reasonable. To the extent that expert evidence can assist the jury in making that determination, I would find such testimony to be both relevant and necessary.

In light of the foregoing discussion I would summarize as follows the principles upon which expert testimony is properly admitted in cases such as this:

1. Expert testimony is admissible to assist the fact-finder in drawing inferences in areas where the expert has relevant knowledge or experience beyond that of the lay person.

2. It is difficult for the lay person to comprehend the battered-wife syndrome. It is commonly thought that battered women are not really beaten as badly as they claim; otherwise they would have left the relationship. Alternatively, some believe that women enjoy being beaten, that they have a masochistic strain in them. Each of these stereotypes may adversely affect consideration of a battered woman's claim to have acted in self-defence in killing her mate.

3. Expert evidence can assist the jury in dispelling these myths.

4. Expert testimony relating to the ability of an accused to perceive danger from her mate may go to the issue of whether she "reasonably apprehended" death or grievous bodily harm on a particular occasion.

5. Expert testimony pertaining to why an accused remained in the battering relationship may be relevant in assessing the nature and extent of the alleged abuse.

6. By providing an explanation as to why an accused did not flee when she perceived her life to be in danger, expert testimony may also assist the jury in assessing the reasonableness of her belief that killing her batterer was the only way to save her own life.

... In my view, the trial judge did not err in admitting Dr. Shane's expert testimony in order to assist the jury in determining whether the appellant had a reasonable apprehension of death or grievous bodily harm and believed on reasonable grounds that she had no alternative but to shoot Kevin Rust on the night in question.

Obviously the fact that the appellant was a battered woman does not entitle her to an acquittal. Battered women may well kill their partners other than in self-defence. The focus is not on who the woman is, but on what she did. In "The Meaning of Equality for Battered Women Who Kill Men in Self-Defense", 8 *Harv. Women's L.J.* 121 at p. 149 (1985), Phyllis Crocker makes the point succinctly:

> The issue in a self-defence trial is not whether the defendant is a battered woman, but whether she justifiably killed her husband. The defendant introduces testimony to offer the jury an explanation of reasonableness that is an alternative to the prosecution's stereotypic explanations. It is not intended to earn her the status of a battered woman, as if that would make her not guilty.

The trial judge, to his credit, articulated the same principle when introducing Dr. Shane's testimony in the course of his instructions to the jury. After referring to "the so-called battered-spouse syndrome", he cautions:

> Let me say at the outset that I think it is better that we try not to attach labels to this. It doesn't matter what we call it. What is important is the evidence itself and how it impacts on the critical areas of the intent of the accused and the issue of self-defence.

Ultimately, it is up to the jury to decide whether, in fact, the accused's perceptions and actions were reasonable. Expert evidence does not and cannot usurp that function of the jury. The jury is not compelled to accept the opinions proffered by the expert about the effects of battering on the mental state of victims generally or on the mental state of the accused in particular. But fairness and the integrity of the trial process demand that the jury have the opportunity to hear them. . . .

NOTES AND QUESTIONS

1. In "The Battered Wife Syndrome and Self-Defence: *Lavallee* v. *R.*" (1990), 9 Can. J. Fam. L. 171, Professor Boyle, while generally applauding the Supreme Court decision, raises the following concerns:

(a) She suggests that it is perhaps time to consider a general obligation to retreat, if possible, even from one's home, provided the feasibility of retreat is examined in a way that is sensitive to the situation of the battered woman. She states (at 176 and 177):

> If there is no duty to leave home rather than use violence, and if a preemptive strike can sometimes be seen as reasonable, this could make it extremely difficult to distinguish between revenge and self-defence. . . .

> The present law seems to be that there is no need for a jury to distinguish between a woman who could safely leave home and a woman who could not. In my view, this issue needs more consideration than that reflected in the passing reference to it in *Lavallee*.

(b) She states (at 177): "A possible danger flowing from the admission of expert evidence on syndromes is that women who do not fit the syndrome will not be able to make their perspective 'reasonable' to fact finders."

(c) The focus on the battered woman syndrome emphasizes victimization and learned helplessness rather than a woman's actions to ensure her survival. She writes (at 177): "*Lavallee* does not address the question of how to understand, on the one hand, a woman's learned helplessness and, on the other, her vigorous action in self-defence."

Do you share these concerns?

2. In the infamous Bernardo case, the Crown called expert testimony characterizing Karla Homolka as a "battered wife" to explain why she aided her husband in the sexual assault and killing of three young women, including Homolka's sister.

3. The battered wife defence has been used in an attempt to explain why a woman remained on welfare without being eligible: "Abused wife defence raised in fraud case", *Globe and Mail*, 3 January, 1996.

4. In *R.* v. *Mallot* (1998), 155 D.L.R. (4th) 526 (S.C.C.), the court unanimously dismissed an appeal of a woman who argued that the trial judge had failed to explain the relevance of expert testimony on battered wives' syndrome to her claim of self-defence in accordance with *Lavallee*. The accused had been convicted of murdering her common law husband and of attempting to murder his new girlfriend. The deceased had abused the accused physically, sexually, and psychologically for many years. A few months before the shooting the deceased separated from the accused, took their son and went to live with his girlfriend. The accused and their daughter continued to live with the deceased's mother. On the day of the shooting, the accused was scheduled to go to a medical centre with the deceased to get prescription drugs for use in the deceased's illegal drug trade. She took a pistol from the deceased's gun cabinet, loaded it and put it in her purse. On the way to the centre, the deceased became angry and grabbed her. The accused went to the centre's door and discovered that it was locked. She testified that she thought the deceased would be very angry because he needed the drugs. The deceased opened the car door as she approached and appeared to be getting out. She testified that she shot him at that time because she thought he would hurt her again. The accused then took a taxi to the girlfriend's house, shot her and stabbed her with a knife. The girlfriend survived to testify at trial. The accused relied primarily on self-defence and led expert testimony to show that she suffered from battered woman syndrome. The jury convicted her on both charges.

5. For further reading, see Walker, *The Battered Woman* (New York: Harper & Row, 1979); Walker, *The Battered Woman Syndrome* (New York: Springer Pub. Co., 1984); Schneider, "Describing and Changing: Women's Self-Defense Work and the Problem of Expert Testimony on Battering" (1986), 9 Women's Rights Law Reporter 195; Mihajlovich, "Does Plight Make Right? The Battered Woman Syndrome, Expert Testimony and the Law of Self-Defense" (1987), 62 Ind. L.J. 1256; Ewing, *Battered Women Who Kill* (Lexington, Mass: Lexington Books, 1987); Willoughby, "Rendering Each Woman Her Due: Can a Battered Woman Claim Self-Defence When She Kills Her Sleeping Batterer?" (1989), 38 Kan. L. Rev. 169; Shaffer, "*R.* v. *Lavallee:* A Review Essay" (1990), 22 Ottawa Law Rev. 607; Comack, *Feminist Engagement with the Law: The Recognition of the Battered Woman Syndrome* (Ottawa: CRIAW, 1993); Rosen, "On Self-Defense, Imminence, and Women Who Kill Their Batterers" (1993), 71 N.C. Law Rev. 371; Dershowitz, *The Abuse Excuse* (New York: Little Brown, 1994); Stubbs and Tolmie, "Race, Gender, and the Battered Woman Syndrome: An Australian Case Study" (1995), 8 C.J.W.L. 122; and Shaffer, "The Battered Woman's Syndrome Revisited: Some Complicating Thoughts Five Years After *R.* v. *Lavallee*" (1997), 47 U.T.L.J. 1.

2

CREATING A VALID MARRIAGE

1. Introduction

In this chapter, the legal requirements for a valid marriage will be analyzed. To the extent that the law attaches certain rights and privileges only to the marriage status, the distinction between a valid marriage and an invalid marriage is of obvious importance. It may also be of significance to the parties if, for some reason, they wish to formally end the relationship.

In the following excerpt Professor Hahlo outlines the distinction between an annulment and a divorce and examines the significance of the distinction.

HAHLO, *NULLITY OF MARRIAGE IN CANADA*

(Toronto: Butterworths, 1979) 1-5 (Footnotes Omitted)

A decree of nullity is not a divorce by another name. Divorce presupposes a valid marriage. It is based on a post-nuptial event, and depending on the legal system, the event may be a serious matrimonial offence, such as adultery, cruelty or desertion; irretrievable marriage breakdown; or simply the will of the spouses or even of only one of them to put an end to the marriage. And it dissolves the marriage *ex nunc* — as from the date of the decree. Nullity results from some defect or disability which exists at the time of the marriage ceremony (*ex causa praecedenti*) and prevents an unassailable marriage from coming into existence. Where the ground of annulment is one which renders the marriage void *ab initio*, the decree of nullity declares that there never was a marriage; where the ground of annulment is one which renders the marriage voidable, the decree of nullity annuls it, at common law, with retroactive effect. . . .

Although divorce and nullity are, in theory, designed to deal with different situations, in practice they have proved — to some extent — complementary. Actions for annulment thrive when divorce is difficult or impossible to obtain. They wither away when divorce is easy. In the Middle Ages, when *divorce a vinculo* was not admitted, spouses desiring to escape from a hateful marriage looked for, and not rarely succeeded, in discovering an impediment on which an action for annulment could be based.

Today, when almost everywhere in the Western world divorce is easy, nullity actions are, statistically speaking, insignificant, and one or two countries, including Sweden, have done away with them. Where, as in modern Swedish law, a divorce can be obtained on demand, with but a short delay if one party objects and there are young children of the marriage, there is no need for annulment actions. The fact remains that, although the same remedy may provide adequate relief in both situations, the distinction between an initially defective marriage and a valid marriage which has broken up is fundamental and exists even if the legislature chooses to call the judicial remedies by the same name.

In most Western countries nullity actions have been retained, but there is a general trend to approximate the effects of a decree of nullity, at least as regards voidable marriages, to those of a decree of divorce. . . .

Not only has there been a tendency to equate the legal consequences of an invalid marriage with those of a valid marriage, but legal developments, both judicial and legislative, in recent years have largely assimilated the legal rights and obligations of those who cohabit in a relatively permanent relationship without ever going through a marriage ceremony with those of husband and wife. See Chapter 1: **INTRODUCTION**.

The law distinguishes between the essential validity of a marriage and the formal validity of a marriage. Essential validity concerns the legal capacity of the parties to marry, while formal validity involves ceremonial or evidentiary requirements imposed by a state as conditions precedent to a marriage. This distinction is important for two reasons. For constitutional purposes the legal capacity of the parties to marry is a federal matter falling within s. 91(26) of the *Constitution Act, 1867*, while formal validity is a provincial matter falling within s. 92(12). The Parliament of Canada, therefore, has exclusive jurisdiction to pass laws in relation to the essential validity of marriage. On the other hand, the provinces have exclusive legislative power to deal with the formal validity of marriage. See *Re Marriage Legislation in Canada*, [1912] A.C. 880 (P.C.); *Kerr* v. *Kerr*, [1934] S.C.R. 72, [1934] 2 D.L.R. 369; *Alberta (Attorney General)* v. *Underwood*, [1934] S.C.R. 635, 4 D.L.R. 167; *Ross* v. *MacQueen*, [1948] 1 W.W.R. 258, [1948] 2 D.L.R. 536 (Alta. S.C.); *Teagle* v. *Teagle*, 6 W.W.R. 327, [1952] 3 D.L.R. 843 (B.C. S.C.); *Gilham* v. *Steele*, [1953] 2 D.L.R. 89 (B.C. C.A.); *Re Schepull*, [1954] O.R. 67, [1954] 2 D.L.R. 5 (H.C.); and *Alspector* v. *Alspector*, [1957] O.R. 454, 9 D.L.R. (2d) 679 (C.A.) for cases dealing with this distinction for constitutional purposes.

The distinction between essential validity and formal validity is also important for conflict of laws problems. The choice of laws rule differs depending on whether the essential validity or formal validity of the marriage is at issue. The formal validity of the marriage is determined by the law of the place where the ceremony occurred. The traditional view is that a person's capacity to marry is governed by the law of the jurisdiction of the pre-marriage domicile. However, the Federal Court of Appeal held in *Canada (Minister of Employment and Immigration)* v. *Narwal* (1990), 26 R.F.L. (3d) 95 that the marriage will also be valid if both parties have the capacity to marry according to the law of the jurisdiction of the intended matrimonial home. The Parliament of Canada has never legislated comprehensive, specific criteria governing essential validity. In 1930, it passed the *Divorce Act (Ontario)*, 1930 which conferred jurisdiction on the Supreme Court of Ontario to hear nullity actions and incorporated by reference the law of England relating to the dissolution and annulment of marriage as that law existed on July 15, 1870. Except for minor modifications, the law of England of July 15, 1870 still governs the essential validity of marriage in Ontario. See, now, the *Annulment of Marriages Act (Ontario)*, R.S.C. 1970, c. A-14.

Shortly after the passage of the *Divorce Act (Ontario)*, *1930*, Ontario passed a complementary statute: the *Marriage Act*, S.O. 1933, c. 29. It incorporated by reference those provisions of the federal statute that were within the province's jurisdiction. In other words, by a two-stage process of incorporation, the law of England of July 15, 1870 governed formal validity of marriage in Ontario except to the extent that it was varied by Ontario legislation. Despite the passage of rather comprehensive Acts dealing with the formal requirements of marriage, this provision remained part of the law of Ontario until it was dropped from the *Matrimonial Causes Act* when that statute was re-enacted as chapter 258 of the Revised Statutes of Ontario, 1980. Now the *Marriage Act*, R.S.O. 1990, c. M-3 (as amended) governs the formal validity of marriages taking place in Ontario.

FURTHER READING

1. On the topic of nullity of marriage generally, see Hahlo, *Nullity of Marriage in Canada* (Toronto; Butterworths, 1979).

2. Regarding conflict of laws and the validity of marriage, see Lysyk, "Jurisdiction and Recognition of Foreign Decrees in Nullity Suits" (1964), 29 Sask. Bar Rev. 143; MacKinnon, "Nullity Jurisdiction and Problems of Domicile" (1966), 1 Ottawa L. Rev. 216; Maddaugh, "Validity of Marriage and the Conflict of Laws: A Critique of the Present Anglo-American Position" (1973), 23 U.T. L.J. 117; Rafferty, "Recognition of Foreign Nullity Decrees" (1982), 46 Sask. L. Rev. 73; and Davie, "The Breaking-up of Essential Validity of Marriage Choice of Law Rules in English Conflict of Laws" (1994), 23 Anglo-American Law Rev. 32 .

3. The possibility that same-sex marriages might soon be valid in some jurisdictions and not in others has resulted in renewed academic interest in the recognition of foreign marriages. See Hovermill, "Conflict of Laws and Morals: The Choice of Law Implications of Hawaii's Recognition of Same-Sex Marriages" (1994), 59 Mod. L. Rev. 450; MacDougall, " Marriage Resolution and Recognition in Canada" (1995), 29 Fam. L.Q. 541; Adams, "Same-Sex Relationships and Anglo-Canadian Choice of Law: An Argument for Universal Validity", [1996] Canadian Y. B. Int'l L. 103; "Note: In Sickness and in Health, in Hawaii and Where Else?: Conflict of Laws and Recognition of Same-Sex Marriages" (1996), 109 Harv. L. Rev. 2038; Paige, "Comment: Wagging the Dog-If the State of Hawaii Accepts Same-Sex Marriage Will Other States Have To? An Examination of Conflict of Laws and Escape Devices" (1997), 47 Am. U.L. Rev. 165; Bailey, "How Will Canada Respond to Same-Sex Marriages?" (1998), 32 Creighton L. Rev.105; and Borchers, "Implications of Interjurisdictional Recognition of Non-Traditional Marriages" (1998), 32 Creighton L. Rev. 147.

4. While this chapter focuses only on the legal grounds for annulment, a spouse may also be concerned with the availability of annulment pursuant to the laws of his or her religion. The grounds for such annulment may differ considerably from those recognized by the civil courts. The Roman Catholic Church has expanded the basis on which an annulment can be obtained from church tribunals. See "Church Adopts Annulment Law", *Globe and Mail* (March 29, 1983); "Church Recognizes Many Grounds for Annulment", *The Montreal Gazette* (July 2, 1983); Riga, "The Catholic View of Marriage in the New Code of Canon Law of 1983 and the Nullity of Marriage in Canon 1095" (1992), 9 J.L. & Relig. 515; and Mendonca, "Consensual Incapacity for Marriage" (1994), The Jurist 477. Of course, an annulment obtained from a church tribunal does not legally end the marriage.

2.   Essential Validity of Marriage

(1) OPPOSITE SEXES

LAYLAND v. ONTARIO (MINISTER OF CONSUMER & COMMERCIAL RELATIONS)

(1993), 14 O.R. (3d) 658, 104 D.L.R. (4th) 214, 17 C.R.R. (2d) 168 (Div. Ct.)

SOUTHEY J. (SIROIS J. concurring): — This is an application under s. 8(4) of the *Marriage Act*, R.S.O. 1990, c. M.3, for judicial review of the refusal of the City Clerk's Office in Ottawa to issue a marriage licence to the applicants on the ground that the marriage of persons of the same sex is illegal in Canada. The applicants are both male. They had cohabited with one another in a homosexual relationship for more than five months before submitting an application for a marriage licence on January 16, 1992. They wished to be married.

The applicants accept that the common law recognizes as valid only marriages between persons of opposite sex, but submit that such restriction is a breach of their equality rights under s. 15 of the *Canadian Charter of Rights and Freedoms*. They submit that such restriction discriminates against them on the ground of their sexual orientation. The applicants are supported by the Intervenor, Metropolitan Community Church of Ottawa/Eglise communautaire métropolitaine d'Ottawa (hereinafter called the "Community Church"). The Community Church takes as well a more fundamental objection to the refusal. The Community Church contends first that there is no restriction of marriage at common law to persons of opposite sex.

The respondent Minister opposes the application on the ground that the applicants lack the capacity at common law to marry one another for the reason given by the City Clerk's Office. The Minister takes no position on the alleged *Charter* violation, because capacity to marry is a matter within the exclusive legislative authority of the Parliament of Canada under Class 26 of s. 91 of the *Constitution Act, 1867*. The Attorney General of Canada (the "Attorney General") opposes the application on the ground that the concept of marriage at common law is limited to persons of opposite sex and denies that such limitation violates s. 15 of the *Charter*.

Capacity to marry at common law

It is common ground that there is no statutory provision that defines marriage in a way that excludes the union of persons of the same sex. The respondent Minister and the Attorney General rely on the decided cases as authority for the proposition that "marriage" at common law consists only of the union of one man and one woman and cannot include a homosexual union.

The Manitoba case of *North* v. *Matheson* (1974), 20 R.F.L. 112, 53 D.L.R. (3d) 280 (Co. Ct.), is on all fours with the case at bar. It was decided before the *Charter* became part of the supreme law of Canada, but it clearly explains the common law definition of marriage. Philp Co. Ct. J., now a member of the Manitoba Court of Appeal, dismissed an application under the *Vital Statistics Act* of Manitoba, R.S.M. 1970, c. V60, for an order requiring the registration of the marriage of the applicants, two men, who had gone through a form of marriage and purported to have complied with the procedural requirements of the *Marriage Act* of Manitoba, R.S.M. 1970, c. M50. Judge Philp held that the ceremony in which the applicants participated was not a ceremony of marriage, and was a nullity, because both parties were of the same sex. His reasons for judgment include the following at pp. 116-17:

> The issue is whether or not, on the facts before me, there was a marriage.
>
> "Marriage" has not been defined in the legislation, either by the Parliament of Canada or by the Legislature of Manitoba. However, marriage has been defined judicially. In *Hyde* v. *Hyde and Woodmansee* (1866), L.R. 1 P. & D. 130, Lord Penzance, the Judge Ordinary, at p. 133 stated:
>
>> "Marriage has been well said to be something more than a contract, either religious or civil — to be an Institution. It creates mutual rights and obligations, as all contracts do, but beyond that it confers a status. The position or status of 'husband' and 'wife' is a recognised one throughout Christendom: the laws of all Christian nations throw about that status a variety of legal incidents during the lives of the parties, and induce definite rights upon their offspring. What, then, is the nature of this institution as understood in Christendom? Its incidents vary in different countries, but what are its essential elements and invariable features? If it be of common acceptance and

existence, it must needs (however varied in different countries in its minor incidents) have some pervading identity and universal basis. *I conceive that marriage, as understood in Christendom, may for this purpose be defined as the voluntary union for life of one man and one woman, to the exclusion of all others.*" (The italics are mine.)

And in *Corbett* v. *Corbett (Ashley) (No. 2)*, [1970] 2 All E.R. 33, Ormrod J. at p. 48 stated:

"The fundamental purpose of law is the regulation of the relations between persons, and between persons and the State or community. For the limited purposes of this case, legal relations can be classified into those in which the sex of the individuals concerned is either irrelevant, relevant or an essential determinant of the nature of the relationship . . . *sex is clearly an essential determinant of the relationship called marriage, because it is and always has been recognised as the union of man and woman.* It is the institution on which the family is built, and in which the capacity for natural heterosexual intercourse is an essential element. It has, of course, many other characteristics, of which companionship and mutual support is an important one, but *the characteristics which distinguish it from all other relationships can only be met by two persons of opposite sex.*" (The italics are mine.)

It is of equal importance in the determination of the issue before me that the meaning of marriage is universally accepted by society in the same sense. "Marriage" is defined in Webster's Third New International Dictionary (1961), as: "the state of being united to a person of the opposite sex as husband or wife; the mutual relation of husband and wife; wedlock; the institution whereby men and women are joined in a special kind of social and legal dependence for the purpose of founding and maintaining a family". In Encyclopedia Americana (1964), under the topic "Marriage", it is stated:

"In the natural history sense, marriage may be defined as a more or less durable union between one or more husbands and one or more wives, sanctioned by society and lasting until after the birth and rearing of offspring. In the legal sense, marriage is a contract between one or more males and one or more females for the establishment of a family."

And in Encylopedia Britannica (1955), under the topic "Marriage", it is stated:

"Human beings, like all higher animals, multiply by the union of the two sexes. But neither conjugation nor even the production of offspring is as a rule sufficient for the maintenance of the species. The further advanced the animal in the order of evolution, the longer the immaturity and the helplessness of the young and the greater the need for prolonged parental care and training. It is thus the combination of mating with parenthood which constitutes marriage in the higher animals, including man. Even in its biological aspect, marriage is rooted in the family rather than the family in marriage (Westermarck)".

I view it as self-evidence that the ceremony performed on 11th February 1974 was not a ceremony of marriage, it was nullity.

   . . .

The Attorney General filed in the case at bar the affidavit of Dr. Charles Hobart, a professor of Sociology at the University of Alberta in Edmonton. One of Professor Hobart's main interests throughout his career has been the sociology of sexual behaviour, marriage and courtship. Professor Hobart's affidavit concluded with the following:

5. As a general proposition, it is my opinion that there is no recorded tradition of recognizing homosexual relationships as equivalent to marriage or recognizing homosexual "marriage" in Western society. As the report attached as Exhibit "B" indicates, the only two recorded instances of homosexual marriages per se were in ancient China and during the last period of the Roman Empire.

6. It is quite clear that the concept of marriage both in Western and other societies, including both modern and ancient societies for which there are records, is a concept which is consistently confined to heterosexual relationships. The only exceptions are the Roman and Chinese traditions,

which I have previously mentioned, and the situation in certain native North American cultures where an individual who is male took on the role of the female, the "berdach".

I find that under the common law of Canada applicable to Ontario a valid marriage can take place only between a man and a woman, and that persons of the same sex do not have the capacity to marry one another.

Section 15 of the Charter

The next question is whether the foregoing definition of marriage, in so far as it excludes homosexual unions, constitutes a violation of the equality rights of the applicants under s. 15(1) of the *Charter* by discriminating against them on the basis of sexual orientation.

. . .

In the case at bar, the disadvantage to the applicants arises directly from the legal distinction being challenged. It does not exist apart from nor is it independent of such distinction. Also, in considering the larger context, the court must keep in mind the nature and purpose of marriage as defined at common law and as accepted by society.

On the other hand, professed homosexuals, in my view, make up a discrete and insular minority. The possible benefit to them from expanding the legal definition of marriage to include same-sex unions is summarized as follows at the conclusion of a report of Dr. Rosemary A. Barnes, a psychologist at Women's College Hospital in Toronto, filed on behalf of the applicants:

> Legally recognized marriage would contribute substantially to the well being of lesbians, gay men, their families of origin and their children. The opportunity for marriage would reduce the stigmatization of all lesbians and gay men, enhance the stability of the relationships of lesbians and gay men who do choose to marry and provide a socially and legally recognized structure for the functioning of lesbian and gay partners at times of family transitions or crises such as childbirth, illness, disability, and death. The provision of full legal recognition and authority to lesbian and gay relationships would enhance the integration of lesbians and gay men into the mainstream of society, improve the psychological well being of individual lesbians and gay men and provide less stigmatized and more consistent parenting arrangements for the children of lesbians and gay men.

Section 15(1) is directed not only against discrimination on the grounds enumerated in the section, but also against discrimination on grounds analogous to those enumerated. The Court of Appeal had recently held in *Haig* v. *Canada* (1992), 9 O.R. (3d) 495, 10 C.R.R. (2d) 287, that sexual orientation is an analogous ground of discrimination under s. 15 of the *Charter*.

. . .

The personal difference involved in the case at bar is homosexuality, which is a matter of capacity. That characteristic is not irrelevant to the restriction of marriage at common law to unions of persons of opposite sex. One of the principal purposes of the institution of marriage is the founding and maintaining of families in which children will be produced and cared for, a procedure which is necessary for the continuance of the species (see the authorities in the passage from *North* v. *Matheson* quoted above).

That principal purpose of marriage cannot, as a general rule, be achieved in a homosexual union because of the biological limitations of such a union. It is this reality that is recognized in the limitation of marriage to persons of opposite sex.

It is true that some married couples are unable or unwilling to have children, and that the incapacity or unwillingness to procreate is not a bar to marriage or a ground for divorce. Despite these circumstances in which a marriage will be child-less, the institution of marriage is intended by the states, by religions and by society to encourage the procreation of children.

The law does not prohibit marriage by homosexuals provided it takes place between persons of the opposite sex. Some homosexuals do marry. The fact that many homosexuals do not choose to marry, because they do not want unions with persons of the opposite sex, is the result of their own preferences, not a requirement of the law. Unions of persons of the same sex are not "marriages", because of the definition of marriage. The applicants are, in effect, seeking to use s. 15 of the *Charter* to bring about a change in the definition of marriage. I do not think the *Charter* has that effect.

In my judgment, the common law limitation of marriage to persons of opposite sex does not constitute discrimination against the applicants contrary to s. 15 of the *Charter*.

Whether parties to homosexual unions should receive the same benefits as parties to a marriage, without discrimination because of the nature of their unions, is another question.

The application is dismissed. It is not an appropriate case for costs.

GREER J. (dissenting):— I have had the opportunity of reading the reasons of Southey and Sirois JJ., and with respect, I cannot agree with their reasoning and conclusions regarding the applicants' application for judicial review of the refusal by an employee of the Ottawa City Clerk's Office to grant them a marriage licence.

. . .

I am of the view that restricting marriages to heterosexual couples infringes and violates the applicants' s. 15(1) *Charter* rights and that such violation cannot be justified under s. 1 of the *Charter*. I also agree with the position of the Church that there is no common law prohibition against same-sex marriages in Canada.

1. The facts

. . .

Many same-sex religious commitment ceremonies are taking place in Canada and the United States today but do not have the sanctity of being a marriage recognized by the state. Such ceremonies are performed by the Metropolitan Community Church of Ottawa and in other Canadian cities where the Church has branches. The parties participating in the ceremony receive a "Certificate of Holy Union" issued by the Church which states that the parties "were joined together in the Rite of Holy Union according to the Scriptural practice of the Church of Jesus, the Christ". Reverend Virginia Reinecker, the pastor of the Church in Ottawa, states in her Affidavit sworn May 19, 1992 in support of the applicants' position, that these commitment ceremonies are analogous to marriages for lesbian and gay couples. It is her belief that there is no "qualitative difference between heterosexual and homosexual commitments which would warrant restricting the right to marry to heterosexuals".

. . .

4. *The Charter*

. . . The *Charter* cases show that our courts have found that "choice" is a benefit of the law. In the case at bar, the applicants have been denied their right to choose whom they wish to marry. In my view, the right to choose is a fundamental right and applies to the context of marriage in our society.

It is a basic theory in our society that the state will respect choices made by individuals and the state will avoid subordinating these choices to any one conception: see *R. v. Morgentaler*, [1988] 1 S.C.R. 30, 31 C.R.R. 1. An individual's s. 15 guarantees are designed to protect the individual's right to choose. Our courts and the state have always attempted to redress historic prejudice and bigotry through the application of the law. In my view, this is what the *Charter* was intended to do.

The Attorney General argued that the law is not one which is directly discriminatory. He took the position that the proper question for the court to determine is whether the *Charter* requires the courts to extend the common law definition of marriage to gays and lesbians. Is the law discriminatory and does it require the common law to be expanded? I think it does and it has.

. . . I adopt the reasoning of the court in *Haig*. In my view, the impact of the denial of the granting of a marriage certificate to the applicants, is discriminatory. It is burdensome on the applicants and others who wish to marry persons of the same sex. The message they receive must surely give them the perception that they are inferior persons in our society.

The same type of discriminatory impact was seen in *Leshner v. Ontario*, unreported, Ontario Human Rights Board of Inquiry, August 31, 1992. There the Board held at p. 2 of its decision that:

> . . . marriage and the "traditional family" are sustaining institutions of society, but that they should not be used as a means to impose discrimination and disadvantage on others. Support for the traditional family or for the institution of marriage should not entail the exclusion and disadvantaging of other family forms.

. . . Having met the test in s. 15(1) of the *Charter*, the burden then shifts from the applicants to the Attorney General who is seeking to uphold the Ministry's denial to issue the marriage licence. The Attorney General argued that the denial satisfies s. 1 of the *Charter* and that such denial is demonstrably justified in a free and democratic society . . . In the case at bar, it is surely in the interest of the state to foster all family relationships, be they heterosexual or same-sex relationships. It is clear from an analysis of recent Supreme Court of Canada decisions on *Charter* issues, that gay and lesbian persons do have rights which our courts have protected. To say that the state must preserve only traditional heterosexual families is discriminatory and contrary to the equal benefits and guarantees they are entitled to at law. A rule with a discriminatory purpose may not be justified under s. 1. Further, any such justification would fail the proportionality limb of the *Oakes* test. To exclude gays and lesbians from marriage will not prevent heterosexuals from marrying. Therefore, heterosexuals will not be circumscribed or in any way limited by extending to gays and lesbians the right to marry.

Further, I agree with counsel for the applicants that there is no rational connection between supporting heterosexual families and denying homosexuals the right to marry. It is illogical and has no beneficial impact on the goal. To deny them the right to marry is a complete denial of their relationship and a denial of their constitutional rights.

The Attorney General further argued that the case at bar does not fit neatly into the tests as set out in *Oakes* and in *R. v. Swain*, [1991] 1 S.C.R. 933, 3 C.R.R. (2d) 1, whereby the court found that the common law rule did violate the *Charter*. Even though the Attorney General was urging the court to uphold the law as it was set out in pre-*Charter* cases involving a definition of marriage, and urging the court to consider the dictionary meanings of the word, he then took the position that a common law prohibition against same-sex marriages was not judge-made law. He was of the view that if it creates discrimination, it is not direct discrimination and therefore is saved by s. 1 of the *Charter*. Further, the Attorney General argued that the *Charter* does not guarantee the right of a man to marry another man but if the court holds that it does, the court must reformulate the institution of marriage because marriage involves the granting or receiving of certain benefits when one becomes a "spouse".

I have noted that much of the legislation regarding benefits to spouses has already been found to be in breach of the *Charter* and same-sex partners have been found to have the right to the same benefits, be it pension legislation or visiting rights for prisoners. In my view, the interests of gays and lesbians cannot be fully accommodated without the incidents of marriage or its legislative equivalent.

As I have pointed out, there is no statutory prohibition against same-sex marriages. If the legislature intended one to exist it would have put it in the legislation. Therefore, if such a prohibition exists, it must be a common law one. I am of the view that denial of the applicants' s. 15(1) rights is not saved by s. 1 of the *Charter*.

5. *The common law*

In the opening paragraphs of these reasons, I have noted that the common law must grow to meet society's expanding needs. It is clear from the supporting materials submitted by the applicants and the intervenor Church, that gays and lesbians have been, for many decades, entering into permanent relationships which are sanctified by their Church. Other jurisdictions have recognized these partnerships through legislation.

It was the Church's position that the Attorney General was taking an "anti-change" attitude in its position. The Church's position is that there is no common law prohibition against same-sex marriages. It argues that the definition of marriage in *Hyde* is outdated and not applicable. The *Hyde* case uses the words "for life", with respect to marriages, which is clearly not applicable in today's society of multiple marriages. In my view, none of the cases presented by the Attorney General really analyzes what the common law position is regarding marriage. A case-by-case analysis seems to indicate that the courts, in expanding rights and equalities by applying the *Charter* to read out words of legislation which offend the rights of gays and lesbians as protected by the *Charter*, are providing them piece by piece with benefits which would all be granted to them under the umbrella of "marriage", if marriage certificates were issued to them.

The report prepared by Dr. Hobart on behalf of the Attorney General really did not assist me in determining what the common law position is regarding same-sex marriages. Nowhere in either parts of his report is there any data which sets out the views of North American society in the 20th century respecting same sex marriages. The Church, on the other hand, has been performing its holy union services since 1968 and presented data in its materials that it has performed approximately 10,000 such services in same-sex unions. In a recent survey made by the Church, it has received data which indicates that the Church has in recent times performed 242 acts of holy union in Canada, 4,192 in the United States, 468 in other countries. In many cases, records have not been kept by the Church and one can assume that other such services of union have been performed by other affiliations in North America and elsewhere.

Counsel for the applicants argued that the granting of marriage licences for same-sex unions would be a substantial step towards alleviating the stigma associated with homosexual orientation and would help strengthen their ties to each other, their families and our society at large. This is a compelling argument. In some homosexual families, there are children of former marriages. Any stigma created for these children by their parent's homosexual union would be lessened if the relationship was one of marriage sanctified by the state.

. . .

The Attorney General takes the position that the only jurisdiction in the world which has set up a legislative system parallel to marriage for the benefit of same-sex partners is Denmark, and that it allows them to enter into a "registered partnership". Two recent articles set out how these partnerships operate: see Nielson, Linda, "Family Rights and the Registered Partnership in Denmark" (1990), 4 *International Journal of Law and the Family* 297, and Pederson, Marianne, "Denmark: Homosexual Marriages and New Rules regarding Separation and Divorce" (1991-92), 30 *Journal of Family Law* 289. It is pointed out by Nielson at p. 298 of her article that two of the objectives of the legislation in Denmark are as follows:

> A formal recognition through express legislation will improve the chances of long-lasting and steady relationships developing between persons of the same sex. A hostile social response may impede such a development.

> A legal institution is the precondition for securing for two persons of the same sex who live in a permanent partnership the same legal rights as married couples, such as rights regarding housing, pensions, immigration and entitlement to work.

Nielson further points out at p. 301 that in Denmark, those persons who have registered as partnerships have the identical support obligations and the same property regimes as married people.

Pedersen, in her article, points out at p. 290 that:

> As a starting point, the legal effects of registered partnership are the same as those of marriage. This applies not only to the family law legislation regarding mutual obligations of maintenance, financial circumstances and the like, but also to all other Danish legislation, including that regarding compensation and insurance. However, the parties in a registered partnership cannot adopt a child and cannot have custody of a child jointly.

It therefore can be seen that societies in other jurisdictions have an evolving concept of marriage, and have adopted legislation to meet those needs.

. . .

NOTES AND QUESTIONS

1. The plaintiffs in *Layland* launched an appeal but later abandoned it on the basis that it would be better to first pursue equal treatment with unmarried opposite-sex cohabitees than have an early loss on the issue of marriage. It was suggested that "you don't build the penthouse until you have constructed the first 19 floors." See the discussion of the case in McCarthy and Radford, "Family Law for Same Sex Couples: Chart(er)ing the Course" (1998), 15 Can. J. Fam. L. 101.

2. Can the majority's reasons in *Layland* be reconciled with *M.* v. *H.* (1999), 171 D.L.R. (4th) 577 (S.C.C.) (reproduced in Chapter 1)? In light of *M.* v. *H.* can the result in *Layland* stand?

Following the decision in *M.* v. *H.*, the House of Commons passed a resolution by a 216-55 vote affirming that "marriage is and should remain the union of one man and one woman to the exclusion of all others". The Minister of Justice, Anne McLellan, stated that the government supported the motion introduced by a Reform Party member because this definition was "already clear in law" and "the government had no intention of changing the definition of marriage or of legislating same sex marriages". Peter McKay, a Progressive Conservative MP, stated during the debate that *M.* v. *H.* "had nothing to do with marriage" and that the Reform Party's fear that it indicated a likely acceptance by the courts of same-sex marriages was unwarranted. Do you agree? After studying Bill C-23, *An Act to Modernize the Statutes of Canada in Relation to Benefits and Obligations*, the Standing Committee on Justice and Human Rights suggested, with the government's support, on March 23, 2000 that a new section 1.1 be added. It reads: "For greater certainty, the amendments made by this Act do not affect the meaning of the word 'marriage', that is, the lawful union of one man and one woman to the exclusion of all others." What effect, if any, will these developments have when the courts deal with the next *Charter* challenge to the definition of marriage?

3. Until recently, the American case law took the same view as the majority in *Layland*. In *Singer* v. *Hara*, 522 P.2d 1187 (Wash. App., 1974), the court commented as follows on the opposite sex rule:

> It is based upon the State's recognition that our society as a whole views marriage as the appropriate and desirable forum for procreation and the rearing of children. This is true even though married couples are not required to become parents and even though some couples are incapable of becoming parents and even though not all couples who produce children are married. These, however, are exceptional situations. The fact remains that marriage exists as a protected legal institution primarily because of societal values associated with the propagation of the human race. Further, it is apparent that no same sex couple offers the possibility of the birth of children by their union. Thus, the refusal of the state to authorize same-sex marriage results from such impossibility of reproduction rather than from an invidious discrimination 'on account of sex'.

The court viewed marriage as "so clearly related to the public interest in affording a favourable environment for the growth of children that we are unable to say that there is not a rational basis upon which the state may limit the protection of its marriage laws to the legal union of one man and one woman".

Similarly, in *Adams and Sullivan* v. *Howerton*, 486 Fed. Supp. 1119 (U.S. Dist. Ct., 1980), Irving Hill, Chief Judge reasoned:

> . . . [T]he main justification in this age for societal recognition and protection of the institution of marriage is procreation, perpetuation of the race. Plaintiffs argue that some persons are allowed to marry and their union is given full recognition and constitutional protection even though the above stated justification — procreation — is not possible. They point to marriages being sanctioned between couples who are sterile because of age or physical infirmity, and between couples who make clear that they have chosen not to have children. Plaintiffs go on to claim that sanctioning such unions within the protection of legal marriage, while excluding their union, constitutes an illegal discrimination against them. In my view, if the classification of the group who may validly marry is overinclusive, it does not affect the validity of the classification. In traditional equal protection terminology, it seems beyond dispute that the state has a compelling interest in encouraging and fostering procreation of the race and providing status and stability to the environment in which children are raised. This has always been one of society's paramount goals. There is no real alternative to some overbreadth in achieving this goal. The state has chosen to allow legal marriage as between all couples of opposite sex. The alternative would be to inquire of each couple, before issuing a marriage license, as to their plans for children and to give sterility tests to all applicants, refusing licenses to those found sterile or unwilling to raise a family. Such tests and inquiries would themselves raise serious constitutional questions.

More recently some American courts have begun to reconsider. Hawaii's Supreme Court, in a 3-1 decision, ruled in 1993 that marriage laws which require partners to be of different sexes presumptively violated Hawaii's Equal Rights Amendment, which bars discrimination on the basis of sex: *Baehr* v. *Lewin*, 852 P.2d 44 (Haw. 1993). The court found that the laws could only be upheld on remand if the state could establish a compelling state interest. While these subsequent proceedings were pending, the state legislature voted to affirm that marriages must have opposite-sex partners: N.Y. Times, April 27, 1994, p. A18. Similar action was taken in about twenty-six states. Also in response, Congress enacted the *Defense of Marriage Act* (DOMA), Pub.L. 104-199, 110 Stat. 2419. It specifies that only opposite-sex couples can qualify for spousal benefits under federal legislation and programs. It also allows states to refuse to recognize same-sex marriages performed in other states. For critical commentary, see Donovan, "DOMA: An Unconstitutional Establishment of Fundamentalist Christianity" (1997), 4 Mich. Gender & L. 335 and Koppelman, "Dumb and DOMA: Why the Defense of Marriage Act is Unconstitutional" (1997), 83 Iowa Law Rev. 1. On remand of the Hawaiian case, the Circuit Court found that the state failed to justify the refusal of a marriage license: *Baehr* v. *Miike,* 910 P. 2d 112 (1996). The ruling was stayed pending appeal. In the meantime, the state's voters overwhelmingly endorsed an amendment to the State's constitution stating that the legislature had the power to reserve marriage for opposite-sex couples. See *Hawaii Constitution*, art. I, para. 23. As an attempted compromise, the state legislature granted some of the rights and obligations associated with marriage to registered domestic partnerships, which can include same-sex couples. In Alaska, an amendment to the state constitution also followed a lower court decision in favour of same-sex marriage: *Alaska Constitution*, art. I, para. 25. A challenge of an official's refusal to issue a marriage licence to two men in New York recently failed: *Storrs* v. *Holcomb*, 645 NYS 2d 286 (1997). However, the Vermont Supreme Court ruled in *Baker* v. *State of Vermont* (Dec. 20/99) that the state was required by the *Vermont Constitution*'s Common Benefits Clause "to extend to same-sex couples the common benefits and protections that flow from marriage under Vermont law". It added: "Whether this ultimately takes the form of inclusion within the marriage laws themselves or a parallel 'domestic partnership' system or some other equivalent statutory alternative rests with the Legislature." The court rejected the state's argument that limiting the benefits and obligations to opposite-sex couples was justified by the state's strong interest in promoting a permanent commitment between couples who have children to ensure that their offspring receive ongoing parental guidance and support. It noted that a small, but significant, number of same-sex couples were raising children and concluded: "The laudable governmental goal of promoting a commitment between married persons to promote the security of their children and the community as a whole provides no reasonable basis for denying the legal benefits and protections of marriage to same-sex couples, who are no differently situated with respect to this goal than their opposite-sex counterparts". Finally, the court left for another day and another case the question whether, "notwithstanding equal benefits and protections under Vermont law, the denial of a marriage licence operated *per se* to deny constitutionally protected rights".

4. Within the gay and lesbian community there is controversy about the extension of the concept of marriage to their relationships. Professor Didi Herman commented in "Are We Family? Lesbian Rights and Women's Liberation" (1990), 28 Osgoode Hall L.J. 789, at 797:

> Our [lesbian and gay] relationships simply cannot be family, because family necessitates the productive, reproductive, and sexual exploitation of women by men. Our ceremonies of commitment cannot be marriages because marriage is the legal tie binding women to family. And the word 'spouse' cannot include us because its meaning must be derived from the legal relationship that has historically defined women's subordination within family, which is marriage.

> . . . By appropriating familial ideology, lesbians and gay men may be supporting the very institutional structures that create and perpetuate women's oppression. Our reliance on the language of monogamy, cohabitation, life-long commitment, and other essentials of *bona fide* heterosexual coupledom may divide us, not only from other lesbians and gays who do not live in this fashion, but from all people defined as 'single' by virtue of their exclusion from the model.

5. As noted in *Baker,* an alternative to the recognition of same-sex marriages might be registered domestic partnerships whereby same-sex couples who formally register their relationships are treated as legally equivalent to married couples for specified (perhaps all) legal purposes. Madame Justice Greer noted in *Layland* that Denmark adopted such a scheme. The Netherlands, Norway, Sweden, Hungary, Iceland and Spain have similar regimes. These registered domestic partnerships create most of the consequences of marriage regarding property and support. Still, many of the regimes restrict adoption to opposite sex couples. Recall that the Ontario Law Reform Commission recommended in its *Report on The Rights and Responsibilities of Cohabitants under the Family Law Act* (1993) the enactment of legislation to allow two individuals to become "Registered Domestic Partners" and assume all the rights and responsibilities of "spouses" under the *Family Law Act*. To avoid requiring individuals to "reveal intimate details" about their lives, the Commission recommended (at 53) that any two individuals such as "two sisters or friends" be able to register to acquire this status.

6. In *Corbett* v. *Corbett (Ashley) (No. 2)*, [1970] 2 All E.R. 33 (P.D. & A. Div.), a marriage between a man and another person who had been registered as a male at birth but had undergone a sex change operation was held to be void. However, the court in *T. (M.)* v. *T. (J.)* 355 A.2d 204 (N.J. Super. A.D., 1976) refused to follow this case and concluded that "if the anatomical or genital features of a genuine transsexual are made to conform to the person's gender, psyche or psychological sex, then identity by sex must be governed by the congruence of these standards." The approach taken in *T. (M.)* is generally supported in the academic literature. See Smith, "Comment: Transsexualism, Sex Reassignment Surgery and the Law" (1970-71), 56 Cornell L.R. 963; Green, "Transsexualism and Marriage" (1970), 120 New Law Journal 210; Parschin-Rybkin, "Annotation" (1972), 5 Ottawa L. Rev. 583; and Lupton, "The Validity of Post-Operative Transsexual Marriages" (1976), 93 S.A.L.J. 385. See also Brent, "Some Legal Problems of the Postoperative Transsexual" (1972), 12 J. Fam. L. 405; Kennedy, "Transsexual and the Single Sex Marriage" (1973), 2 Anglo-Am. L.R. 112; Hawley, "The Legal Problems of Sex Determination" (1977), 15 Alta. L. Rev. 122; Finlay, "Sexual Identity and the Law of Nullity" (1980), 54 Aust. L.J. 115; Sharpe, "The Transexual and Marriage: Law's Contradictory Desires" (1997), 7 Australasian Gay & Lesbian L.J. 1; and Ong, "The Test for Sex for Marriage in Singapore" (1998), 12 Int'l J. L., Policy & Fam. 161.

In *B.* v. *A.* (1990), 1 O.R. (3d) 569, 29 R.F.L. (3d) 258 (Master), the determination of the sex of one of the parties arose in a different context. B. had bilateral mastectomies, a hysterectomy, hormonal treatment and gender therapy. She began to live socially as a man. However, her genitalia remained those of a female. She subsequently entered into a relationship with A., a female. They cohabited for 20 years. At the end of the relationship B. applied for support under the *Family Law Act*. Master Cork concluded that B. continued to be a female for legal purposes despite an amendment of her birth registration under the *Vital Statistics Act*. As a result, A. and B. were a same-sex couple who did not qualify as spouses under Part III of the *Family Law Act*. For a critical comment, see Majury, "Annotation" (1991), 29 R.F.L. (2d) 258. *B.* v. *A.* was followed in the context of the determination of the validity of a marriage in *C. (L.)* v. *C. (C.)* (1992), 10 O.R. (3d) 254 (Gen. Div.).

7. For further reading, see Zimmer, "Family, Marriage, and the Same-Sex Couple" (1990), 12 Cordoza L. Rev. 681; Pederson, "Denmark: Homosexual Marriages and New Rules Regarding Separation and Divorce" (1992-93), 30 Journal of Family Law 289; Friedman, "Same-Sex Marriage and the Right to Privacy: Abandoning Scriptural, Canonical, and Natural Law Based Definitions of Marriage" (1992), 35 Howard L.J. 173; Henson, "A Comparative Analysis of Same-Sex Partnership Protections: Recommendations for American Reform" (1993), 7 International Journal of Law and the Family 282; Woolley, "Excluded by Definition: Same-Sex Couples and the Right to Marry" (1995), 45 U.T.L.J. 471; Mohr, "The Case for Gay Marriage" (1995), 9 Notre Dame J. L. Ethics & Pub. Pol'y 215; Keane, "Aloha, Marriage? Constitutional and Choice of Law Arguments for Recognition of Same-Sex Marriages" (1995), 47 Stanford L. Rev. 499; Dupuis, "The Impact of Culture, Society and History on the Legal Process: An Analysis of the Legal Status of Same-Sex Relationships in the United States and Denmark" (1995), 9 Int'l J.L. & Fam. 86; Celeste, "Gay and Lesbian Issues: Family, Domestic Partnership and Marriage" (1995), 24 Colorado Law 1309; Chambers, "What if? The Legal Consequences of Marriage and the Legal Needs of Lesbian and Gay Male Couples'" (1996), 95 Mich. L. Rev. 447; Kohn, "The Homosexual 'Union': Should Gay and Lesbian Partnerships be Granted the Same Status as Marriage?" (1996), 22 J. Contemp. L. 51; Kendall, "Principles and Prejudice: Lesbian and Gay Civil Marriage and the Realization of Equality" (1996), 22 J. Contemp. L. 81; Roth, "The Norwegian Act on Registered Partnership for Homosexual Couples" (1997), 35 J. Fam. L. 467; McCarthy and Radbord, "Family Law for Same Sex Couples: Chart(er)ing the Course" (1998), 15 Can. J. Fam. L. 101; Christensen, "If not Marriage? On Securing Gay and Lesbian Family Values by a 'Simulacrum of Marriage'" (1998), 56 Fordham Law Rev. 1699; and Davies, " The Extension of Marital Rights and Obligations to the Unmarried : Registered Domestic Partnerships and Other Methods" (2000), 17 C.F.L.Q. 247.

(2) ABILITY TO CONSUMMATE

GAJAMUGAN v. GAJAMUGAN

(1979), 10 R.F.L. (2d) 280 (Ont. H.C.)

CARRUTHERS J.: — This is an action for annulment. The parties went through a civil form of marriage on 23rd June 1978, followed by a religious ceremony on 24th June 1978. Following the religious ceremony on 24th June, in the evening, the parties retired to a room in a hotel and there slept together for the first time.

The plaintiff's evidence and the defendant's evidence consisted, in part, of an extremely detailed account of their respective memories of what occurred during the evening and night that they first slept together. The effect of the plaintiff's evidence is that he attempted to have sexual intercourse with the defendant but as soon as he touched her face with his hand he had a mental revulsion to the marks on her face. The effect of this reaction, so far as sexual intercourse is concerned, according to the plaintiff, was that his penis, which had become erect, became flaccid. He said that this occurred within a minute. There never was any penetration. Thereafter, the parties slept in the same bed, but, as the plaintiff said, "apart". This abortive attempt at sexual intercourse occurred about 10:30 or 11:00 p.m. on the evening of 24th June 1978. No further attempts were made over the course of that evening. The parties slept together again on the evening of 25th June 1978 and a further attempt was made at sexual intercourse and, according to the plaintiff, "the same thing happened". He was not able to proceed with intercourse. There was no penetration. He said in evidence that when he kissed and touched the defendant's face he "lost his erection". They again slept together, that is, in the same bed, but, as the plaintiff said, "apart". There were no further attempts made at sexual intercourse while the parties were together in Malaysia where they were married.

As planned the plaintiff left Malaysia to return to Canada on 27th June. The defendant was unable to accompany him because of difficulty with her visa. She arrived in Woodstock on 3rd January 1979. On the night of her arrival, the parties again attempted sexual intercourse. The plaintiff said again that he lost his erection because of "the same mind", due to a revulsion because of the marks on the defendant's face. He described it as being a repeat of what had happened on the previous attempts at intercourse. He said it was "in my mind" and it was caused by "touching". That night the plaintiff slept in a separate room. They never slept together again and no further attempts at sexual intercourse have ever been made.

The plaintiff said in evidence that he tried to overcome the problem by simply trying to forget it. He said he could not. The plaintiff denies that he had any problem of impotence, having had a child by his first marriage and, from his description, a reasonably active sexual life during the course of that marriage and on occasions thereafter, prior to his marriage to the defendant. He had no idea before this marriage to the defendant that he would have the problem he now describes as having had on the occasions when he attempted sexual intercourse with the defendant. His first knowledge was in the hotel where they first slept together on the evening of 24th June 1978.

The defendant remained with the plaintiff in his house in Woodstock for nine days after her arrival. He said that during that time he could not look at her face. He could not talk with the defendant and after three days he did not want to come home. He could not eat what she cooked.

He said that on no occasion was his problem due to the consumption of alcohol or a drug. On 12th January 1979 the plaintiff advised the defendant that, "This marriage isn't going to work out". He bought her a ticket to go home. He felt that it was best for her to go home because she had a sister there "to console her". He bought her a one-way ticket on Air France. He took her to the airport in Toronto and left her at security.

The defendant did not return home in January 1979. Apparently she passed out at the airport and eventually she was returned to Woodstock. The incident at the airport followed by five days an incident which occurred at the home in Woodstock when she drank a quantity of liquid bleach upon learning that the plaintiff was sending her back to Malaysia. She indicated that in Malaysia, girls can only marry once. She could not, if she returned to Malaysia, face people and, therefore, wished to remain in Woodstock, married to the plaintiff.

In her evidence she confirmed the evidence of the plaintiff as to the nights upon which they had slept together following their marriage. She denied, however, that the plaintiff had any other difficulty other than being "impatient" and his refusal to "push hard enough" in order to bring about penetration. Specifically she said that at no time was she aware of any problem that the plaintiff was having in maintaining an erection. She said that he never mentioned anything about the marks on her face. At the time of her first attempt to have intercourse with the plaintiff she was a virgin, never having had sexual intercourse previous to that date.

For the purposes of my decision, I am prepared to adopt an overview of the essential ingredients to be proved in an action of nullity because of impotence as outlined in an article by J. David Fine, "Annulment of Marriage for Impotence in the Common Law of Canada" (1973), 8 R.F.L. 129. It reads as follows [p. 129]:

> A good overview of the essential ingredients to be proved in an action for nullity because of impotence was provided by Laidlaw J.A. in the Ontario Court of Appeal in 1944: *Rae* v. *Rae*, [1944] O.R. 266, [1944] 2 D.L.R. 604; summarized in *Hardick (Fox)* v. *Fox* (1970), 3 R.F.L. 153 (Ont.); (1) Impotence must exist at the time of the marriage: *Napier* v. *Napier*, [1915] P.184 at 190; (2) the incapacity pleaded must be such as to render intercourse impractical: *D.* v. *A.* (1845), 1 Rob. Ecc. 279, 163 E.R. 1039; (3) the incapacity may stem from 'a physical or mental or moral disability': *H.* v. *P.(H)* (1873), L.R. 3 P. & D. 126; and (4) the impotence must be incurable: *Welde (Aston)* v. *Welde* (1731), 2 Lee 580, 161 E.R. 446.

I am prepared to accept the evidence of the plaintiff, particularly where it conflicts with that of the defendant. When I consider her evidence in the light of her demeanour and attitude seen while she was in the witness-box, I conclude that what she had to say was influenced by her personal concern of having to return home not married.

I must confess that the decision I have reached in this matter was not reached without anxious consideration. My prime concern stems from the requirement that the disability, mental in this case, must be found to be incurable. No evidence was led specifically to deal with this point. Counsel for the plaintiff asks that the court infer, because the condition existed on two nights in June 1978 and again in January 1979, that it be deemed incurable, particularly when it is such a subjective matter and something about which medical evidence would be of little value in assisting the court to come to a conclusion. I am prepared to accept that position.

There will, therefore, be a declaration that the marriage in question is void. . .

NORMAN v. NORMAN

(1979), 9 R.F.L. (2d) 345 (Ont. U.F.C.)

STEINBERG U.F.C.J.: — This is an application for an order declaring the marriage between the parties null and void due to the respondent husband's inability to consummate the marriage. The parties were married on 13th April 1978 at Hamilton, at which time Mrs. Norman, who is now 64 years of age, was a widow and Mr. Norman, who is now 65 years of age, was a widower. I am satisfied that during the ensuing cohabitation the respondent was unable to achieve an erection, and that the parties never engaged in sexual intercourse with each other. They ceased to reside together on 25th August 1978, following an argument.

In response to some questions directed to the applicant by myself (the application being unopposed) her evidence was as follows:

Q. How long a courtship did you have with Mr. Norman? A. It was the end of October of 1977.

Q. I see, and between . . . and during your courtship did you and he engage in sexual relations of any kind? A. No, your Honour, we never.

Q. I see. Did you discuss with him the possibility of sexual relations? A. Not at that time, he just told me that he hadn't had it for two years before with his first wife.

Q. I see. Were the two of you looking forward to having sexual relations? A. Well, not really, we wanted more of a companionship.

Q. And what caused the two of you to break up? A. Well he just had a wild temper and we never fought, never argued until the day he was tailoring a suit for my daughter-in-law and he got so mad at something and I just let him have it, so an hour after he said we would part, and I agreed.

Q. Well, were sexual relations an important part from your point of view? A. Not really.

Q. I see. Would you have stayed with him notwithstanding the fact that you had no sexual life together? A. I would have, yes sir.

I am satisfied that the parties separated because of a quarrel and not because of the lack of sexual contact. The applicant's prime motive for the marriage was, as she said, companionship.

Aylesworth J.A. in *Miller* v. *Miller*, [1947] O.R. 213 at 221, [1947] 3 D.L.R. 354 (C.A.), stated:

> On the question of the sincerity of the complaint in an action for annulment of marriage, the law is well settled that the sincerity to be shown is that the Court must be satisfied that impotency is the real reason for bringing the action: *G.* v. *M.* (1885), 10 App. Cas. 171 (H.L.).

I am of the clear view that the respondent's impotency was not the real reason for the institution of this action. It is not open to the applicant, having entered into what might be termed a platonic marriage, to complain of the absence of sexual intercourse.

The application is therefore dismissed without costs.

AISAICAN v. KAHNAPACE

(1996), 24 R.F.L.(4th) 143 (Sask. Q.B.)

GUNN J.: — The applicant seeks to annul her marriage to the respondent on the basis that he is impotent and cannot consummate the marriage. The only evidence presented to support the petitioner's claim is her own affidavit in which she says: ". . .b) The Respondent, Sheldon Troy Kahnapace, was *insofar as the depondent knows*, unable to have sexual intercourse. The depondent and the Respondent did not engage in sexual intercourse whatsoever after the date of the marriage. (c) The

Respondent was, two weeks prior to the marriage, shot by persons unknown and as such, is a quadriplegic and is incapable of having intercourse." [emphasis added]

The evidence is clear that the parties did not engage in sexual intercourse following the marriage, but what is not so clear is the incapacity of the respondent to do so. The petitioner's claim is qualified by the phrase "insofar as the deponent knows". Further there is no medical evidence before me to suggest that either the respondent in particular or quadriplegics in general are incapable of having intercourse.

A further question to be addressed would be the knowledge of the applicant at the time of the marriage, assuming the respondent's incapacity is established.

Cowan C.J.T.D. addressed this issue in *R. v. R.* (1976), 28 R.F.L. 283 (N.S. T.D.), at 287 and 288:

> The position of an impotent spouse, who seeks a declaration of nullity on the ground of his own impotence, was exhaustively considered by the Court of Appeal in *Harthan* v. *Harthan*, [1949] P. 115, [1948] 2 All E.R. 639. In that case, it was decided that, provided that there are no circumstances which bar him or her, e.g. knowledge of the defect at the time of the marriage, an impotent spouse is entitled to petition for a decree of nullity, and the right to do so is not conditional on the repudiation of the marriage by the other spouse. As I understand the decision of Lord Merriman P. in that case, knowledge on the part of the petitioning spouse of his or her impotence is only one reason for denying the remedy of nullity to the impotent spouse.

Arguably, this bar to a decree of nullity should work both ways. Therefore, if the petitioner knew of the respondent's incapacity prior to the marriage and married him despite that knowledge, she too ought to be denied a decree of nullity. In *G.* v. *M.* (1885), 10 App. Cas. 171 (H.L.), at 186 for example, the court discussed the doctrine of sincerity and held that if an applicant approbated the marriage with knowledge of the circumstances set forth as grounds for the annulment, the decree would not be granted.

> . . . [T]here may be conduct on the part of the person seeking this remedy which ought to estop that person from having it; as, for instance, any act from which the inference ought to be drawn that during the antecedent time the party has, with a knowledge of the facts and of the law, approbated the marriage which he or she afterwards seeks to get rid of. . .

More recently, in *Norman* v. *Norman* (1979), 9 R.F.L. (2d) 345 at 349 (Ont. U.F.C.), the court held that where the parties have married for companionship and separate because of a quarrel rather than for the lack of sexual contact, it is not open to the applicant, who knowingly entered into a platonic marriage, to complain of the absence of sexual intercourse.

Finally, if the applicant is not entitled to a decree of nullity for the evidentiary reasons previously identified, the mere fact the respondent has not opposed the application is irrelevant. In *W.* v. *W.* (1987), 5 R.F.L. (3d) 323 (P.E.I. S.C.), at 325, McQuaid J. stated that "[i]f the facts and the law warrant its granting, then she [the petitioner] is entitled to the relief sought; if the facts and the law do not warrant it, the husband's consent alone will not further her cause."

I decline to grant the order on two grounds:

1. The evidence adduced to establish the claim is insufficient.

2. The physical condition of the respondent, if established, pre-dates the marriage. If the petitioner entered into the marriage with knowledge of this condition, she would be barred from successfully prosecuting an action to annul the marriage on that basis.

I decline to grant a declaration of nullity.

NOTES AND QUESTIONS

1. In determining whether an inability to consummate exists, the courts have attempted to apply the principle laid down by Dr. Lushington in *D-E* v. *A-G (Falsely calling herself D-E)* (1845), 1 Rob. Eccl. 279 at 298, 163 E.R. 1039: "Sexual intercourse, in the proper meaning of the term, is ordinary and complete intercourse; it does not mean partial and imperfect intercourse." On the question of what constitutes complete intercourse, see also *Hale* v. *Hale*, [1927] 2 W.W.R. 366, 22 Alta. L.R. 565, [1927] 3 D.L.R. 481 (C.A.); *Miller* v. *Miller*, [1947] O.R. 213, [1947] 3 D.L.R. 354 (C.A.); *Baxter* v. *Baxter*, [1948] A.C. 274, [1947] 2 All E.R. 886 (H.L.); and *S.* v. *S. (Otherwise W.)*, [1963] P. 162, [1962] 2 All E.R. 816 (C.A).

2. In *S.* v. *S. (No. 2)*, [1962] 3 All E.R. 55 (C.A.), the wife had a malformed vagina too short to admit full penetration but according to medical evidence capable of being enlarged by an operation. The operation would involve removal of the soft tissues where the normal vagina would be in order to create a passage that would be lined by skin from the thigh. The absence of the natural membrane and its special sensory quality and of normal secretions would affect the degree of sexual satisfaction obtained from intercourse by the wife but not materially that of the husband. The passage would end in a cul-de-sac and there could be no conception of children as the wife would have no uterus. The court, on a petition for a decree of nullity by the husband, held that the wife's incapacity was curable and that the decree had to be refused. Would the incapacity have been incurable if the wife refused to have the operation? See *Dashevsky* v. *Dashevsky* (1973), 13 R.F.L. 1 (Ont. H.C.).

3. The Canadian and English cases on the inability to consummate due to psychological repugnance or aversion to the sexual act were reviewed in *W.* v. *W.* (1987), 5 R.F.L. (3d) 323 (P.E.I. S.C.). McQuaid J. made the following comment on the *Gajamugan* decision (at 331): "With all respect to the learned trial judge, however, I am unable to agree that one might 'infer' incurability in the absence of medical evidence, on the experience of the parties on only three nights." The wife's petition was dismissed in *W.* v. *W.* because, although she could establish that a psychological condition inhibited her from consummating the marriage with the respondent, she could not prove that this was caused by an "invincible repugnance or aversion to the sexual act with the respondent".

See also *Juretic* v. *Ruiz* (1999), 49 R.F.L. (4th) 299 (B.C. C.A.) where the wife indicated on two occasions that she did not want her husband to embrace her, but that he could have sex with her as long as "he did not touch her". The husband considered that a sexual act under these circumstances was tantamount to rape and he made no further attempts to have sexual relations with his wife. The trial judge's conclusion that the husband had not established an "invincible aversion" was upheld by the appellate court which noted (at 303): "Put another way, it could be said that Mr. Juretic's situation fell short of an 'unconquerable repugnance' ".

4. In *M.* v. *M. (A.)* (1984), 42 R.F.L. (2d) 55 (P.E.I. S.C.), the parties cohabited after marriage and enjoyed "what appeared to the plaintiff to be a normal sexual relationship". However, the wife was a latent transsexual and she eventually began living as a male and indicated an intention to undergo a sex-change operation. The husband's application for a declaration of nullity was successful. McQuaid J. reasoned (at 59-60):

> If my understanding of the transsexual personality is correct, although the physical capacity for normal heterosexual intercourse may exist, there also exist psychological factors, inherent in the personality, which preclude or otherwise inhibit the actual exercise of such physical capacity. These psychological factors may be initially patent, in which case there is simply no capacity to exercise the function, or they may be latent or suppressed, in which case the capacity to exercise the function does exist, and may indeed be exercised, but the exercise thereof simply makes patent what was earlier latent and the act of heterosexual intercourse thereby becomes abhorrent to the point where it becomes, in effect, a continuing incapacity. The incapacitating condition was present in the marriage from its outset; it was merely triggered into transition from the state of latent potentiality into the state of patent actuality by the circumstances of the intimacy arising out of the married relationship, which, being heterosexual in nature, was incompatible with the inherent nature of the respondent.I find, therefore, that there existed at the outset of this marriage, a latent physical incapacity for natural heterosexual intercourse, which incapacity became patent

only subsequent to the solemnization of the marriage, of such consequence as would render the said marriage voidable and by reason thereof I now declare the said marriage be, and the same is, annulled.

Is this extension of the grounds for annulment justified?

5. Inability to consummate renders a marriage voidable, not void: *Jones* v. *Jones*, [1948] O.R. 22 (C.A.). Accordingly, the marriage continues to exist until terminated by a declaration of nullity or by divorce.

6. The *Divorce Act*, R.S.C. 1970, c. D-8, s. 4(1)(d) permitted a spouse to petition for divorce on the basis that the marriage had not been consummated, and the respondent, for a period of not less than one year, had been unable by reason of illness or disability to consummate it or had refused to consummate it. What differences were there between this ground for divorce and inability to consummate as a basis for a nullity action? The grounds for divorce set out in s. 4(1)(d) of the old *Divorce Act* were not retained in the 1985 *Divorce Act*.

7. Is any useful purpose served by retaining inability to consummate as a basis for a nullity action in light of the liberal grounds for divorce in the *Divorce Act*?

(3) OUTSIDE PROHIBITED DEGREES OF CONSANGUINITY AND AFFINITY

In order for two persons to marry, they must not fall within the prohibited degrees of consanguinity (relationship by blood) and affinity (relationship by marriage). By virtue of the *Annulment of Marriages Act (Ontario)*, R.S.C. 1970, c. A-14, the law of England of 15 July, 1870 applies in Ontario to determine the prohibited degrees, except to the extent that this law has been altered by legislation of the Parliament of Canada. The prohibited degrees established by the law of England of 15 July, 1870 were those listed in Archbishop Parker's Table of 1563, which was reproduced in the Church of England's *Book of Common Prayer*. This list contained the following degrees for women (and the corresponding ones for men): grandfather, grandmother's husband, husband's grandfather, uncle, husband's uncle, father, step-father, husband's father, son, husband's son, daughter's husband, brother, grandson, granddaughter's husband, husband's grandson, nephew, husband's nephew, niece's husband, and husband's brother. The law stipulating the prohibited degrees was altered by the *Marriage Act (Canada)*, R.S.C. 1970, c. M-5. It was originally enacted in 1882 and effectively removed wife's sister, wife's niece, husband's brother and husband's nephew from the list of prohibited degrees. In 1990, Parliament enacted the *Marriage (Prohibited Degrees) Act*, S.C. 1990, c. 46, which came into force in 1991. By virtue of s. 4, this legislation contains "all of the prohibitions in law in Canada against marriage by reason of the parties being related". Under this Act, two persons are within the prohibited degrees only if (i) they are related lineally by consanguinity or adoption; (ii) they are brother and sister by consanguinity, whether by the whole blood or the half blood; or (iii) they are brother and sister by adoption. The background to this legislation is outlined in the following article.

ZIFF, "RECENT DEVELOPMENTS IN MARRIAGE AND DIVORCE"

(1986), 18 Ottawa Law Rev. 121 at 135-137 (Footnotes Omitted)

In 1984, just prior to the federal election of that year, a Senate Bill was introduced which was designed to reduce and rationalize the law in this area. After receiving second reading, the Bill died on the order paper; but under the Conservative government a similar Bill has been tabled. In its original form, the Bill provided that a marriage would be void if entered into by two persons related lineally by consanguinity, or as brother or sister by the whole or half-blood. These were intended to be the only marriage prohibitions based on the proximity of relationships. Following deliberations, the Standing Committee on Legal and Constitutional Affairs recommended that the prohibitions be extended to include lineal and sibling relationships arising from adoption.

The traditional policies behind affinal restrictions, put succinctly, are the insulation of the nuclear or extended family from sexual meddling, the promotion of marriage outside of the family and the preservation of perceived societal norms or Judeo-Christian religious beliefs. Restrictions based on consanguinity have been supported on these grounds, but there is, as well, the additional concern that genetic and even eugenic defects are more common in the offspring of close blood relations. The amendments reflect an abandonment of the first cluster of reasons, presumably either because they no longer reflect public policy, or because marriage prohibitions are seen as ineffective vehicles with which to pursue these goals. A reduction in the restrictions based on consanguinity seems in accord with current scientific opinion that the physical dangers are not as significant as once thought, particularly where the blood relationship between the parents is not close.

It is with respect to the relevance of adoption that the major debate under the Bill has festered. The policy issues centred on whether or not adopted children should be treated in exactly the same way as natural children for these purposes. . . .

In considering the appropriate policy, one must look beyond the question of whether or not the reasons supporting the remaining marriage prohibitions under the Bill apply to adopted children. Insofar as these reasons relate to matters of eugenics or genetics, clearly they would not be relevant. But the policy underlying adoption law demand attention too. Adoption creates a legal fiction and is designed to facilitate the adopted child's assimilation and integration into the new home. Holding such a child to the prohibitions attached to natural children promotes the integrative process. Admittedly, these concerns are weakened when one remembers that it is only when the adopted child becomes an adult that the practical issue will have to be addressed. In any event, this entire issue will be far less acute under the proposed legislation as the ambit of the prohibitions would be drastically reduced.

For a history of Canadian legislation on prohibited degrees, see Stevenson, "Federal Marriage Legislation in Canada" (1997), 9 J. Church L. Assoc. Can. 149.

(4) NO PRIOR EXISTING MARRIAGE

A marriage is void if one of the parties is, at the time of the marriage, already a party to a prior existing marriage. Therefore, a declaration of invalidity is not required to end the marriage. However, often a party will seek to have this state of affairs affirmed by a court. Invariably, the issue in such cases is whether the prior marriage was terminated as a result of death or divorce.

MESZAROS v. MESZAROS

[1969] 2 O.R. 336, 5 D.L.R. (3d) 294 (H.C.)

PARKER J.: — This is an action for dissolution of marriage based on the ground of cruelty.

The petitioner was married on February 23, 1953, to Theodor Hamaida at the Town of Paris, in the Province of Ontario. She and Mr. Hamaida lived together until about the month of December, 1956, when he deserted her. Shortly before the desertion he advised her that he had a wife in Russia but she was unable to verify this information.

On June 20, 1966, she secured an order under s. 11(1) of the *Marriage Act*, R.S.O 1950, c. 228, declaring that Theodor Hamaida was dead. The supporting affidavit executed by her at that time was filed as an exhibit in the present action. The petitioner deposed that she had not heard from her husband since the separation, that he had been continually absent for seven years, that to the best of her knowledge and belief no other person or persons had heard from her husband, that she had made inquiries among their friends and relatives to ascertain whether they had heard from or of her husband from the time of the separation up to the time she deposed to and she was informed and verily believed that they had not heard from him nor of him and by reason thereof she had no reason to believe that her husband was living.

On April 23, 1966, the petitioner married the respondent Leslie Meszaros and lived with him until the month of May, 1968, when he forcibly ejected her from the matrimonial home. The evidence indicated that during their cohabitation the petitioner was subjected to considerable mental and physical cruelty. At the conclusion of the evidence I found that the cruelty was sufficient to come within s. 3(d) of the *Divorce Act*, 1967-68 (Can.), c. 24, but reserved judgment to consider the validity of the marriage.

Dealing first with the marriage between the petitioner and the respondent there is a strong presumption that the parties who have lived together and held themselves out as man and wife are validly married: *Beattie* v. *Beattie*, [1945] O.R. 129, [1945] 1 D.L.R. 574. This is a presumption that can only be overcome by the most cogent evidence but may be rebutted by evidence of a prior marriage. The certificate of the Hamaida marriage having been filed is probably sufficient to rebut this presumption. I think the same initial presumption of validity would apply to the petitioner's marriage to Mr. Hamaida. . . .

I doubt that the hearsay evidence that Mr. Hamaida had a wife in Russia is sufficient to rebut this presumption of validity.

If Mr. Hamaida was still alive at the time of the petitioner's second marriage, then her second marriage is a nullity. However, there was no evidence before me to suggest that he was alive at that time. On the contrary, the evidence in her affidavit raises a presumption of death. The rule with respect to presumption of death is set out in *Re Phene's Trusts* (1870), L.R. 5 Ch. 139 [headnote]:

> If a person has not been heard of for seven years, there is a presumption of law that he is dead; but at what time within that period he died is not a matter of presumption, but of evidence, and the *onus* of proving that the death took place at any particular time within the seven years lies upon the person who claims a right to the establishment of which that fact is essential.

. . .

If Mr. Hamaida may be presumed to be dead then the petitioner was a widow at the time of her second marriage and this marriage may once again be presumed to be valid. What was the effect of the order under the *Marriage Act*, s. 11(3) [s. 9 of the current Ontario *Marriage Act*.]?

. . .

Since marriage and divorce are under Dominion jurisdiction by reason of s. 91(26) of the *B.N.A. Act, 1867*, and solemnization of marriage is reserved to the

Provinces under s. 92(12) one must presume that s. 11 of the *Marriage Act* intended to deal only with the formality of securing a licence without regard to the status of the applicant. The order permitted the petitioner to apply for a marriage licence. The second union may therefore be presumed to be valid unless and until it is shown that the person presumed dead was not in fact dead at the time of the solemnization of the second marriage. Until that event occurs the petitioner is entitled to petition for a divorce.

Having previously decided that the respondent treated the petitioner with physical and mental cruelty of such a kind as to render intolerable the continued cohabitation of the spouses, judgment *nisi* is granted with costs against the respondent.

BATE v. BATE

(1978), 1 R.F.L. (2d) 298 (Ont. H.C.)

BOLAND J.: — This matter concerns a petition for divorce on the grounds of adultery and three years' separation. The wife is also seeking maintenance and costs. The husband opposes the action on the grounds that the alleged marriage between the petitioner and the respondent on 19th May 1969 in Las Vegas, Nevada, was *void ab initio* by reason of a valid marriage subsisting at the time between the petitioner and her first husband, David Whitfield Simser.

The issue to be determined by this court is whether the parties are presently married under the laws of this jurisdiction. This will depend on whether this court recognizes the 1957 Nevada divorce purporting to dissolve the marriage between the petitioner and her first husband, David Whitfield Simser, as a valid and effective divorce in Ontario.

The petitioner has been married three times. Her first marriage was to David Whitfield Simser on 10th December 1950, in the town of Keswick, Ontario. There were two children of this marriage and the husband has never remarried. This marriage was purportedly dissolved by a decree of divorce granted on 23rd May 1957 in the Eighth Judicial District Court of the state of Nevada. The second marriage was to John Arne Smedstam on 19th August 1958, in the state of Indiana. This marriage was dissolved by a judgment of the Falu South Judicial District Court, Sweden, on 1st February 1963. Her third marriage was to the respondent on 19th May 1969, in Las Vegas Nevada. At the time of the marriage ceremony, both parties were Canadian citizens and were residing in Toronto, Ontario, where they returned shortly after the alleged marriage and where they have continued to reside. There were no children with respect to the second and third marriages. It is the first divorce, granted on 23rd May 1957 in the state of Nevada, which purported to dissolve the marriage between the petitioner and David Whitfield Simser that is under attack in this action. Hence, only that divorce concerns us and will be discussed here.

Submissions were made at trial concerning certain presumptions and raising the question of who has the onus of proof in a case of this type. Before dealing with the issue of recognition of a foreign divorce, I think it advisable to settle this issue. On the authority of *Powell* v. *Cockburn*, [1977] 2 S.C.R. 218, 22 R.F.L. 155, 68 D.L.R. (3d) 700, 8 N.R. 215, counsel for the petitioner submitted that there are certain presumptions in favour of his client which shift the burden of proof to the respondent. That is, once the petitioner adduces evidence that a marriage ceremony took place between the petitioner and the respondent, which has been done by the filing of the marriage certificate, then there is a presumption of the validity of that marriage. Similarly, once evidence is presented in support of the foreign divorce, which was done by filing the decree of divorce, then there is a presumption of the validity of the foreign divorce decree. The burden then shifts to the respondent to prove his allegations of the invalidity of the marriage and the foreign divorce on the balance of probabilities. The relevant passage from *Powell* v. *Cockburn*, supra, dealing with this question can be found at p. 161:

> The factums in this case make frequent reference to 'presumptions', each side seeking to throw the burden of adducing evidence upon the other. There would seem to be some confusion as to the legal effect of presumptions. In the case before us, there are three presumptions which may be relevant: (i) the presumption of validity of marriage . . .(ii) the presumption of validity of a foreign divorce decree . . . and (iii) the presumption in favour of the domicile of origin. Strictly speaking, they do not conflict nor cancel each other out, nor do they give added probative value.

> Their only effect is to impose a duty on the party against whom they operate to adduce some evidence: see 9 Wigmore on Evidence, p. 281, s. 2487. They may, as in the present case, impose an alternating duty to produce evidence which shifts from one party to the other, a process which Wigmore describes as 'successive presumptions': p. 292, s. 2493. At the outset the appellant Powell faced a presumption of validity with regard to his marriage to the wife. He satisfied this presumption by leading evidence to show the existence of her prior marriage. With regard to this marriage, too, there was a presumption of validity, but the two presumptions did not conflict. Rather, the wife had to lead evidence to show that the previous marriage had been terminated. This she did by evidence of the foreign divorce. Evidence having been led on each issue the presumptions disappeared. It fell then to the trier of fact to decide the issues upon all of the evidence adduced. In this case if the trier of fact was not satisfied on a balance of probabilities that Powell had proved his case (that the Powell-Cockburn marriage was a nullity), then Powell must fail. The ultimate burden of proof, the risk of non-persuasion of the trier of fact, rested on Powell throughout.

It is clear from the above that the presumptions in question do not provide any probative conclusiveness. Rather, they merely require from the party against whom they operate a rebuttal, the test of which is the adducing of "some evidence". Thus, at the outset, the respondent was faced with the presumption of validity with regard to his marriage to the petitioner. He satisfied this presumption by giving evidence in the form of a marriage certificate to show the existence of her prior marriage to David Whitfield Simser. This first marriage also carried with it a presumption of validity imposing on the petitioner a duty to produce "some evidence" to show that the previous marriage had been terminated. This she did by filing the Nevada decree of divorce. The foreign divorce decree also carried with it a presumption of validity imposing a duty on the respondent to submit some evidence establishing its invalidity. This he did by presenting some evidence concerning the intentions of the petitioner in travelling to Las Vegas, Nevada, in 1957, which will be discussed in more detail. Some evidence having been led on all issues, the presumptions of validity disappeared. It is now up to this court to decide the issues upon all of the evidence adduced. There is no question that the ultimate burden of proof, the risk of non-persuasion, on a balance of probabilities rests with the respondent.

[Madame Justice Boland found that the Las Vegas divorce could not be recognized in Ontario and that the petitioner was still validly married to David Whitfield Simser thus rendering her marriage to the respondent null and void. The petition was dismissed.]

NOTES AND QUESTIONS

1. According to *Meszaros*, what is the effect of an order under s. 9 of the Ontario *Marriage Act*? See also *Re Larsen* (1980), 18 R.F.L. (2d) 14 (B.C. S.C.) where Mr. Larsen re-appeared some 17 years after Mrs. Larsen obtained an order under the *Survivor and Presumption of Death Act* specifying that

her husband was presumed dead. Mrs. Larsen had married twice in the interim. Today, someone in the same position as Mrs. Meszaros found herself in 1966 could obtain a divorce under s. 8(2)(a) of the *Divorce Act.*

2. In the United States, a presumption of validity operates in favour of a second marriage to the extent that the party attacking the validity of the marriage must prove a valid prior marriage that has not been dissolved by divorce or ended by death. See Hahlo, *Nullity of Marriage in Canada* (Toronto: Butterworths, 1979) at 14. However, in *Stevenson* v. *Stevenson* (May 8, 1997), Doc. Nelson 6547 (B.C.S.C.) McEwan J. (para. 15) held that once a man seeking a declaration of invalidity established that he was married prior to going through a marriage ceremony with the defendant, the burden of showing that the first marriage ended before the impugned marriage took place shifted to the defendant. Is this similar to the position taken in *Meszaros* and *Bate*? How do the various presumptions relate to the ultimate burden of proof?

3. For further reading, see Bates, "Presumption of Marriage in Canada: Its Past, Present, and Future" (1979), 17 U.W.O.L. Rev. 169.

(5) CONSENT

(a) Capacity to Understand

BANTON v. BANTON

(1998), 164 D.L.R. (4th) 176 (Ont. Gen. Div.)

CULLITY J.:— **Background:** The issues to be tried in this case were defined in an order for directions of Sheard J., dated June 6, 1996. Before I address them, the following bare chronological outline of facts that are, for the most part, not materially in dispute will indicate the background and the context in which the issues arose.

1.   George Banton was born in England on June 13, 1906. He emigrated to Canada and for the greater part of his life he lived in Toronto where he was employed by a chemical company for over 60 years. For most of that time he was a sales representative.

2.   George Banton married three times. He and his first wife, Kathleen, had five children, Victor, George (George Jr.), Joan, Patricia and Sheila, each of whom is a respondent to this application. There are 18 grandchildren. Kathleen died in 1970. In 1971 George Banton married her sister Lily.

3.   In the 1980's Lily became increasingly afflicted with Alzheimer's disease. By the end of that period, George Banton's physical deterioration was also evident. In 1990 he was diagnosed as having cancer of the prostate. He underwent surgery in 1991, 1992 and 1993. After the second operation his family was told that his life expectancy was two or three years. In the third operation, in November 1993, his testicles were removed in an attempt to retard the spread of the disease.

4.   George Banton was also severely afflicted with deafness. He had a number of different hearing aids but by the early 1990's, and perhaps even earlier, this problem was so acute that, in order to carry on any serious discussion, he was accustomed to use headphones and a microphone that would be placed between him and the person with whom he was conversing. His mobility also became affected and, by 1994, he required a frame to enable him to move about. He had several falls and was incontinent.

5. By the time of his operation in 1991 it was evident to George Banton's family that he was no longer able to care for Lily and, in July, she was placed in a retirement or nursing establishment ("Meadowcroft") that had facilities for the care of individuals suffering from Alzheimer's disease.

6. On January 30, 1991, George Banton executed a will in which he directed that $25,000 be set aside for the care and maintenance of Lily if and after her own funds were exhausted. Subject to that provision, his estate was to be divided equally among his five children with substitutional gifts to the legitimate children of any children who predeceased him.

7. George Banton continued to live by himself in his house at 22 Coral Cove Crescent, North York, until July 1993 when a decision was made for him to move into a retirement home ("Lifestyles").. . . .

8. Lily died in June 1994. By at least the end of the following month — and probably earlier — George Banton had formed a friendship, which quickly developed into a close attachment, with the Applicant, Muna Yassin ("Muna"), a waitress in the restaurant at Lifestyles. Muna was 31 years of age. . . .

10. During the last three months of 1994, George Banton's children became increasingly disturbed about his relationship with Muna. At the beginning of November, Joan made an appointment for George Banton with Dr. Janice Lessard, the Director of Geriatrics at Scarborough General Hospital, where his third operation in November had been performed. Dr. Lessard saw him on two occasions. Patricia was present each time, and Joan, also, was there on the second occasion. As a result of these meetings, Dr. Lessard expressed the opinion that George Banton was financially incompetent and issued a Certificate of Incompetence under the *Mental Health Act* on November 14. She notified the Public Guardian and Trustee and, two days later, she issued a Notice of Continuance of Certificate of Incompetence to Manage One's Own Estate pursuant to the statute. Dr. Lessard was not called as a witness and her opinion is not relied upon by the Respondents for the purpose of these proceedings. I mention it, and it is admissible, only for the purpose of explaining subsequent conduct of the parties and events that occurred in the remaining months of George Banton's life.

11. On hearing that George Banton had been certified under the *Mental Health Act* and after receiving reports from officials at the bank that George Banton, accompanied by Muna, had withdrawn $10,000 from his account and that he had been trying to cash further cheques, George Jr. and Victor, became concerned to protect his assets which at this time consisted of term deposits and bank accounts in excess of $470,000.. . .

12. Unknown to any of his children, on December 14, 1994, George Banton and Muna had obtained a licence to marry. . . .

14. On Saturday, December 17, 1994, George Banton and Muna were married at her apartment by the Reverend Jack Allen who had a license to perform marriages. No one else was present except the minister's wife, who had to be fetched from Brampton to act as a witness, and another person who had been approached in the foyer of the apartment building for that purpose. George Banton's children were not aware that the marriage was taking place.

15. George Banton stayed at Muna's apartment on the night of December 17 and returned to Lifestyles on the following day. In the meantime, the staff

at Lifestyles had become aware of his absence and had contacted the family as he had not signed out or informed anyone that he would be leaving the premises.

16. George Banton's family were concerned and contacted the police. Victor, Joan and Victor's wife were present at Lifestyles on Sunday, December 18, when George Banton and Muna entered the building. Although the details are disputed, it is clear that some sort of argument or altercation occurred. It was alleged by Muna, and denied by Victor and Joan, that Victor pushed his father into a door causing bruises to one of his arms. Victor testified that he put his hand on George's wrist or his arm and guided him through the door into his room.

17. The next day, Monday, December 19, George Banton and Muna attended at the offices of the law firm, Devry, Smith & Frank in Don Mills and met with Wayne Wolfe, a solicitor experienced in drawing wills. Mr. Wolfe was informed that George Banton and Muna were married, and that George Banton wished to make a new will and to give Muna a power of attorney. At that first meeting, Mr. Wolfe asked them for a copy of their marriage certificate. They left and returned with this the next day, Tuesday, December 20, 1994. On that day, Mr. Wolfe was instructed that in George Banton's new will his entire estate would be left to Muna with a gift over to the Salvation Army in the event of her prior death. Mr. Wolfe prepared the will and his secretary, Carol Davis, prepared the power of attorney and these documents were signed by George Banton on Wednesday, December 21, 1994. Mr. Wolfe and Ms. Davis signed as witnesses to each of the documents.

18. In January 1995, the family were informed that George Banton had retained Devry, Smith & Frank to challenge Dr. Lessard's finding of incompetence. On April 10, 1995, an application was made on his behalf to the Consent and Capacity Review Board for this purpose. On May 1, George Banton's solicitors were informed that the application had been dismissed for want of jurisdiction.

19. On April 13, 1995, George Banton left Lifestyles and moved into Muna's apartment.

20. On May 4, George Banton and Muna attended again at the offices of Devry, Smith & Frank where George Banton executed a will and power of attorney identical to those dated December 21, 1994.

21. On May 11, 1995, Dr. Michel Silberfeld of Baycrest Geriatric Centre conducted an assessment of George Banton at the request of his solicitors. Dr. Silberfeld reported on May 17, 1995, that, in his opinion, George Banton had capacity to manage his property and to give a power of attorney.

22. On May 27, 1995, the Public Guardian and Trustee brought an application to be appointed statutory guardian of George Banton's property, and an order was made for an assessment of his capacity. This assessment was made by Dr. Chin Kwan Chung, a newly-appointed designated capacity assessor under the *Substitute Decisions Act*. On June 19, 1995, Dr. Chung provided his opinion that George Banton was incapable of managing property but had capacity to give a power of attorney and capacity for personal care "under the present circumstances and support structure".

23. The application of the Public Guardian and Trustee was opposed by George Banton and he and Muna swore affidavits deposing to his capacity. Muna

also brought an application to be appointed his statutory guardian in the event that the Court made a finding of incapacity.

24. On October 27, 1995, George Banton was [admitted] to Sunnybrook Hospital severely ill and confused. He had further surgery.

25. On November 16, 1995, Muna was cross-examined on her affidavit in the guardianship proceedings.

26. On December 22, 1995, George Banton was discharged from Sunnybrook Hospital to the Village Park Nursing Home.

27. On February 5, 1996, George Banton was admitted to Women's College Hospital where he died on February 14, 1996. . . .

No expert medical evidence was given with respect to capacity to marry or testamentary capacity and, on the issue of capacity to manage property, the medical experts were not in agreement. They agreed only that George Banton had capacity to give a power of attorney over property. While there is no reason to doubt the appropriateness of having different tests for different capacities, the task of reaching conclusions — even on the balance of probabilities — on the basis of rather fine distinctions when the issues relate to the deteriorating mental state at a particular time of an elderly person now deceased, is not easy. The difficulty is exacerbated where, as here, there are significant discrepancies between the testimony of the applicant and the respondents.

The law with respect to the burden of proof of capacity to marry, testamentary capacity and undue influence is also reasonably settled. In the first case, the burden is on a person attacking the validity of the marriage. . . .

It is hardly necessary to say that the principle of freedom of testamentary disposition is in the background to the issues relating to the validity of the wills of December 21, 1994 and May 4, 1995. If George Banton had capacity and was not subject to undue influence at the time of the execution of one of those wills, its validity and effect are not open to challenge on the ground that he thereby disinherited his children. In this jurisdiction, unlike others in Canada and elsewhere, unless the children are dependants, a capable parent, acting voluntarily, is entitled to do this however mean and ungrateful it may seem, or how selfish the motive; hence the focus in this case, as in so many others, on testamentary capacity and undue influence.

[Cullity J. concluded that the wills of 1994 and 1995 were invalid because Banton lacked testamentary capacity and Muna had subjected him to undue influence. She was a strong-willed person out to get the property of a lonely, depressed, terminally-ill, severely disabled and cognitively impaired old man. To determine whether the will of 1991 had been revoked by the deceased's third marriage in accordance with the *Wills Act*, it was necessary to enquire into the validity of this marriage.]

The marriage of George Banton and Muna was solemnized at her apartment by the Reverend Jack Allen on December 17, 1994. George and Muna had completed the application for a licence to marry on December 14. Mr Allen had been contacted by Muna through a company in the business of arranging marriage services. No one else had been informed of the pending ceremony and, after arriving at Muna's apartment and finding that there were no witnesses, Mr Allen returned to Brampton to fetch his wife. Muna asked a person she found in the foyer of the apartment building to act as the second witness.

Mr. Allen testified that he was aware of the prohibition in the *Marriage Act* of marriages of persons who are "mentally ill". He stated that he had no concerns at all about George Banton's mental condition. He said he remembered George as being "quite a good conversationalist" and that there was nothing to indicate that he did not understand the purpose and nature of the ceremony. Mr. Allen also saw no signs of depression and nothing to suggest that George was afraid of, or being manipulated or controlled by, Muna. On the contrary, George's mood was convivial, he seemed affectionate towards Muna and, after the marriage was performed, he responded to the invitation to kiss her. Mr. Allen testified that he left immediately after the ceremony and did not participate in any reception or party. He did not see a walking frame or canes and he made no mention of any hearing disability or of hearing aids. His conclusion about George Banton's mental capacity appears to have been formed on the basis of George's general demeanour and his answers to the questions in the service rather than from any questions asked specifically for the purpose.

The formal validity of George Banton's marriage to Muna has not been challenged. It was submitted by Mr Shaw that it was void on the ground of undue influence and lack of capacity.

Marriage is, of course, a legal contract and, to some extent, it is governed by the laws applicable to contracts in general. I am satisfied, however, that it is not subject to the operation or application of the presumptions and principles which determine whether contracts may be avoided on the ground of undue influence. Fraud, of course, is another matter but the evidence in this case does not support such a finding . . . .

A marriage can be set aside on the ground of duress or coercion of a degree sufficient to negative consent. Although I am in respectful agreement with Mendes da Costa J. in *S. (A.)* v. *S. (A.)* (1988), 15 R.F.L. (3d) 443 (Ont. U.F.C.) at pp. 453-6 that fear need not be proven, the evidence does not warrant a conclusion that there was duress in this case with respect to George Banton's participation in the marriage.

In late September and early October 1994 George Banton had tried to resist Muna's attempts to seduce him into marriage but, in November, he capitulated and consented to it. Although I have also found that marriage was part of Muna's carefully planned and tenaciously implemented scheme to obtain control and, ultimately, the ownership of his property, as far as the marriage was concerned he was, at the end, a willing victim. Shortly thereafter he told Victor that he had wanted "one last fling".

In view of my finding that George Banton consented to the marriage, it is unnecessary to deal with the questions whether duress makes a marriage void or voidable and, if the consequence is that the marriage is voidable, whether it can be set aside by anyone other than the parties. I express no opinion on these issues. . . .

George Banton wanted to marry Muna and the evidence of Ms. Yolanda Miranda, referred to below, indicates that he never regretted this. She may have misled him as to her motives but he was, as I have said, a willing victim who consented to the marriage. In these circumstances, I do not believe the marriage can be set aside if George Banton had the requisite capacity and, particularly, not by persons other than the parties to the marriage. My finding that there was undue influence sufficient to invalidate his testamentary dispositions does not require a similar conclusion with respect to the marriage from which he obtained benefits of care and companionship.

Consent, in the sense in which I have used the term is an act of will. In this sense it must be distinguished from capacity to marry. Although a lack of mental capacity may be said to vitiate or negative consent, they are obviously different concepts. A lack of consent does not presuppose, or entail, an absence of mental capacity.

A finding of a lack of testamentary capacity does not necessarily determine whether an individual has the mental capacity to marry; nor is testamentary capacity at the time of marriage required before the marriage will revoke a will: *McElroy, Re*

(1978), 22 O.R. (2d) 381 (Ont. Surr. Ct.); *Park Estate, Re*, [1953] 2 All E.R. 1411 (Eng. C.A.).

It is well established that an individual will not have capacity to marry unless he or she is capable of understanding the nature of the relationship and the obligations and responsibilities it involves. The burden of proof on this question is on those attacking the validity of the marriage and, in my judgment, it has not been discharged in this case. There is virtually nothing in the evidence to suggest that George Banton's mental deterioration had progressed to the extent that he was no longer able to pass this not particularly rigorous test. The medical evidence indicates his acceptance of the marriage and even in the last months of his life when he was at Village Park, he spoke of his wish to return to his wife — albeit along with his then caregiver and companion, Ms. Yolanda Miranda.

The only matter that raises any doubt in my mind with respect to George Banton's understanding of the responsibilities of marriage are the fact that he permitted Muna to return him to Lifestyles the day after the marriage, and that he remained there until the beginning of April 1995 when he moved to Muna's apartment. I do not believe I would be justified in concluding from this that he did not appreciate that the duty to cohabit is inherent in the marriage relationship. I believe it is far more likely that he would have preferred to cohabit with Muna but that this was not part of her plan until the commencement of the guardianship proceedings made it desirable, from her point of view, that he be continuously under her control, and not accessible to his family. We do not know what reason Muna gave him for returning him to Lifestyles on December 18 but, as I have already indicated, I am satisfied that he was, by then, completely under her domination and quite incapable of insisting on his right to cohabit with her.

George Banton had been married twice before his marriage to Muna and I find that, despite his weakened mental condition, he had sufficient memory and understanding to continue to appreciate the nature and the responsibilities of the relationship to satisfy what I have described as the first requirement of the test of mental capacity to marry.

In the Canadian cases to which I have been referred, no other requirement for mental capacity has been considered: *Milson* v. *Hough*, [1951] O.W.N. 450 (Ont. H.C.); *Capon* v. *McLay*, [1965] 2 O.R. 83 (Ont. C.A.); *McElroy, Re* (1979), 22 O.R. (2d) 381 (Ont. Surr. Ct.). An additional requirement is, however, recognized in the English authorities that have been cited with approval in our courts. The decision to which its source is attributed is that of Sir John Nicholl in *Browning* v. *Reane* (1812), 161 E.R. 1080 (Eng. Ecc.) where it was stated:

> If the capacity be such . . . that the party is incapable of understanding the nature of the contract itself, and incapable, from mental imbecility, to take care of his or her own person and property, such an individual cannot dispose of his or her person and property by the matrimonial contract, any more than by any other contract.[at pp. 70-1].

The principle that a lack of ability to manage oneself and one's property will negative capacity to marry was accepted and, possibly extended, by Willmer J. in *Spier* v. *Bengen*, [1947] W.N. 46 (Eng. P.D.A.). . .

While I believe that it may well be the case that a person who is incapable both with respect to personal care and with respect to property may be incapable of contracting marriage, I do not believe that incapacity of the latter kind should, by itself, have this effect. Marriage does, of course, have an effect on property rights and obligations, but to treat the ability to manage property as essential to the relationship would, I believe, be to attribute inordinate weight to the proprietary aspects of marriage and would be unfortunate. Elderly married couples whose property is administered for them under a continuing power of attorney, or by a statutory guardian, may continue to live comfortably together. They may have capacity to make wills and give powers of attorney. I see no reason why this state of affairs should be confined to those who married before incapacity to manage property supervened.

George Banton was found by Dr. Chung to have capacity as far as personal care was concerned. Moreover, despite his physical problems, his weakened mental condition and his loss of memory, he was able to carry on more or less normal discourse on simple everyday matters. Strangers, like Carol Davis and Mr Allen, who met him briefly did not notice anything abnormal about his mental state. On the basis of a one-hour examination Dr. Silberfeld concluded that he had capacity to manage his property. Obviously he was still capable of presenting a brave face to the world. The more thorough examination by Dr. Chung revealed what those close to him already knew: that his judgment was severely impaired and his contact with reality tenuous. Despite these problems, I have no doubt that, with care and attention and avoidance of stress, he was capable of coping with the more mundane problems of everyday living and I do not see why the right to marry should be withheld from persons in his position.

Accordingly, on the basis of *Browning* v. *Reane* and in the absence of binding authority to the contrary, I find that, notwithstanding George Banton's incapacity to manage property on December 17, 1994, he had capacity to marry and that his marriage to Muna was valid. In consequence, his will of January 30, 1991, was revoked and, in view of my other findings, he died intestate.

NOTES AND QUESTIONS

1. In *Webb* v. *Webb* (1968), 3 R.F.L. 129, 3 D.L.R. (3d) 100 (N.S. T.D.), Cowan C.J.T.D. quoted Sir James Hannen P.'s statement in *Durham* v. *Durham* (1885), 10 P.D. 80 (at 81-82) that "it appears to me that the contract of marriage is a very simple one, which does not require a high degree of intelligence to comprehend. It is an engagement between a man and woman to live together, and love one another as husband and wife, to the exclusion of all others".

2. Regarding the question whether a marriage is void or voidable as a result of incapacity to understand, Professor Hahlo suggests in *Nullity of Marriage in Canada* (Toronto: Butterworths, 1979) at 26: "As the essential ingredient is lacking, a marriage contracted by an insane person should, on principle, be treated as void, and this is also the prevailing judicial opinion in Canada. And certain it is that either party, the sane as well as the insane, is entitled to have the marriage annulled. However, there is much to be said for the view that the marriage becomes unassailable if the parties continue to cohabit as man and wife after the insane partner has recovered his reason." He therefore categorizes a marriage contracted while one of the parties is insane as "void but capable of ratification by continued cohabitation after recovery".

3. Note ss. 7 and 35(2) of the Ontario *Marriage Act*.

4. It has been suggested that restrictions on the marriage of mentally disabled persons are "straightforward violations of the section 15 [of the *Charter*] guarantees of equality under the law without discrimination because of mental . . . disability": Day, "The Charter and Family Law" in Sloss, ed., *Family Law in Canada: New Directions* (Ottawa: Canadian Advisory Council on the Status of Women, 1985). Do you agree? See also Thompson, "A Consideration of the Mental Capacity Provisions of the Marriage Act in View of the Charter of Rights and Freedoms and Webb v. Webb" (1986), 9 Can. Community L.J. 101. For further reading, see Wright, "Marriage for Mentally Retarded Persons in Canada" (1976), 26 Mental Retardation 15 and Mecredy-Williams, "Marriage Law and the Mentally Retarded" (1979), 2 Can. J. Fam. L. 63.

(b) Duress

S. (A.) v. S. (A.)

(1988), 15 R.F.L. (3d) 443 (Ont. U.F.C.)

MENDES DA COSTA U.F.C.J.: — In this case, the applicant is A.S. and the respondent is A.S. The applicant seeks the annulment of her marriage to the respondent or, in the alternative, a divorce. The respondent did not file an answer or appear at the hearing. The applicant's testimony was the only evidence adduced to the court.

1. *The facts*

The applicant was born on 9th April 1969. On 28th February 1986 she went through a form of marriage with the respondent, who had recently arrived in Canada. The marriage was celebrated at the city hall, Hamilton, and the certificate of marriage was filed as Ex. 2. At this date, the applicant was 16 years of age. Her parents had separated, and she was living with her mother and her stepfather. The consent of the mother to the marriage was contained in a certificate of consent filed as Ex. 3.

Paragraph 8 of the application contains the grounds for relief and comprises subparas. (a) to (e). Subparagraphs (b), (c) and (d) read as follows:

> (b) The applicant married the respondent after considerable pressure being applied against her by her natural mother and step-father. The applicant did not know the respondent but was told that he would be ordered to leave Canada unless he married a Canadian citizen.
>
> (c) The applicant's mother and step-father were to receive $500.00 for arranging to have the applicant marry the respondent. This was the motive for their participation. The applicant was particularly sensitive to the pressure because there was a history of sexual abuse by the step-father toward her. In fact, the applicant was removed from the home for a period of three years by the Children's Aid Society in Calgary Alberta because of this abuse.
>
> (d) The applicant never lived with the Respondent and she has never had sexual intercourse with him.

The applicant stated that she was first approached by her mother and her stepfather, who applied pressure to her to marry the respondent. The applicant was told that the respondent wished to marry because he wanted to live in Canada. She testified that her mother and stepfather told her that there was $2,000 involved and that they said that "we can have all this nice stuff that we didn't have before with all this money." The applicant said that she told her mother that she did not want to marry the respondent, that her mother "was talking to my step-father and then there was more pressure." The applicant further testified that she did not want to marry the respondent, that she did not live with him after the ceremony, that the parties never engaged in sexual intercourse, and that the respondent subsequently left Canada. The applicant, in her evidence, stated that a few years ago she had been made a ward of the Children's Aid Society in Alberta because she had been sexually abused by her stepfather, and that she had remained in care until she turned 16 years.

I was impressed with the demeanor of the applicant. In my opinion, she gave her evidence in a forthright fashion and I consider her a credible witness. However, during the submissions of Mr. Rogers, counsel for the applicant, I expressed doubt as to whether the applicant was entitled to the relief of annulment. Mr. Rogers requested an opportunity to file written submissions. He stated that he had canvassed with his client the effects and the meaning of divorce and annulment, and that she had expressed a preference for annulment. Accordingly, the matter was adjourned for the filing of written submissions. In my deliberations, I have had the benefit of the submissions.

[The judge concluded that the fact that the respondent entered into the marriage so as to facilitate residence in Canada did not affect the validity of the marriage. He next considered the issue of parental consent. Mr. Rogers submitted that the consent given by the mother was invalid because it was motivated by improper considerations. Mendes da Costa U.F.C.J. concluded (at 453) that the *Marriage Act* of Ontario "does not render the quality of consent a justiciable issue, and the court is not empowered to determine whether consent was given too readily, or, indeed, for an improper motive." Further, the judge held that lack of parental consent did not affect the validity of the marriage under the Act.]

4. *Duress*

It was submitted by Mr. Rogers that the applicant was pressured into marrying the respondent by her mother and stepfather and that, given the surrounding circumstances, she was not able to withstand that pressure. During argument, I questioned this submission.

The applicant made no allegation of the use of physical force, nor did she allege that the use of physical force had been threatened. Moreover, the conduct alleged as duress did not emanate from the respondent. The conduct contended by Mr. Rogers to constitute duress was pressure of a non-physical nature, which was directed at the applicant by the mother and stepfather, who sought to obtain financial benefit from the proposed marriage, be it $500, as stated in para. 8(b) of the application, or $2,000 as related by the applicant during her evidence.

There are relatively few reported cases dealing with annulment of marriage induced by duress, and the applicable principles seem to have emerged in a series of older decisions: *Field's Marriage Annulling Bill* (1848), 2 H.L. Cas. 48, 9 E.R. 1010, where there is a reference to early cases; *Scott* v. *Sebright* (1886), 12 P.D. 21; *Cooper* v. *Crane*, [1891] P. 369. In *Scott* v. *Sebright*, Butt J., at pp. 23-24, in an oft-cited passage, stated:

> The Courts of law have always refused to recognize as binding contracts to which the consent of either party has been obtained by fraud or duress, and the validity of a contract of marriage must be tested and determined in precisely the same manner as that of any other contract. True it is that in contracts of marriage there is an interest involved above and beyond that of the immediate parties. Public policy requires that marriages should not be lightly set aside, and there is in some cases the strongest temptation to the parties more immediately interested to act in collusion in obtaining a dissolution of the marriage tie. These reasons necessitate great care and circumspection on the part of the tribunal, but they in no wise [*sic*] alter the principle or the grounds on which this, like any other contract, may be avoided. It has sometimes been said that in order to avoid a contract entered into through fear, the fear must be such as would impel a person of ordinary courage and resolution to yield to it. I do not think that is an accurate statement of the law. Whenever from natural weakness of intellect or from fear — whether reasonably entertained or not — either party is actually in a state of mental incompetence to resist pressure improperly brought to bear, there is no more consent than in the case of a person of stronger intellect and more robust courage yielding to a more serious danger. The difficulty consists not in any uncertainty of the law on the subject, but in its application to the facts of each individual case.

The principles expounded by Butt J. seem as sound today as they were when they were uttered in 1886. Public policy still requires that marriages "should not be lightly set aside". No doubt, also, there is in some cases the "strongest temptation to the parties more immediately interested to act in collusion". A court is, indeed, required to exercise care and circumspection to ensure that the ground alleged as duress has been established. However, since 1886 there has been a considerable change in the availability of divorce. Under the Divorce Act, 1985, S.C. 1986, c. 4, the ground for divorce is breakdown of marriage. Leaving aside adultery and cruelty, relief is available where, in general terms, the spouses have lived separate and apart for at least one year. As a more or less parallel development, the status of illegitimacy has been eradicated from the law of the province and, to some extent, "spouse" has received an expanded definition in the Family Law Act, 1986, S.C. 1986, c. 4. At this point in time there seems no need for parties to turn to the law of nullity simply to obtain relief denied them by divorce law. I believe, therefore, that the courts should approach a proceeding for nullity in a manner no different from that of any other matrimonial cause.

The above passage from *Scott* v. *Sebright* was referred to in *Thompson* v. *Thompson*, 4 R.F.L. 376, [1971] 4 W.W.R. 383, 19 D.L.R. (3d) 608 (Sask. Q.B.). In this case, the plaintiff sought the annulment of her marriage to the defendant. The court found that the plaintiff had agreed to marry the defendant as a result of his persistent urging, at a time when her resistance was reduced by her state of depression arising from her rejection by another man. Once the wedding plans were underway, the plaintiff was not able to muster sufficient courage to cancel them, because of the social consequences insofar as her family was concerned. She believed that, if she did cancel the marriage plans, there would be a rift between herself and her family. The plaintiff's mother, the court concluded, had exerted influence on the plaintiff to continue with the plans. The marriage was consummated, albeit reluctantly on the part of the plaintiff. The court held that the plaintiff had not established a case that would fall within the principles enunciated in the authorities and dismissed the action. Annulment has also been refused in the following cases: *Singh* v. *Kaur* (1959), 29 W.W.R. 95 (B.C. S.C.); *Parihar* v. *Bhatti* (1980), 17 R.F.L. (2d) 289 (B.C. S.C.); *K.* v. *K.*, [1921] 1 W.W.R. 1072, 57 D.L.R. 746 (sub nom. *Korulak* v. *Korulak*) (Sask. K.B.); *Kawaluk* v. *Kawaluk*, [1927] 3 D.L.R. 493 (Sask. K.B.); *Kecskemethy* v. *Magyar*, [1961] 2 F.L.R. 437 (N.S.W. S.C.); *Williams* v. *Williams*, [1966] V.R. 60 (S.C.).

In *Pascuzzi* v. *Pascuzzi*, [1955] O.W.N. 853 (H.C.), the plaintiff sought an annulment of her marriage. The claim was unopposed. At the time of the marriage she was 15 years of age and the defendant was 19 years of age. Prior to the marriage, during a visit to Toronto, the parties engaged in sexual intercourse. The plaintiff being a juvenile, complaints were made to the police and both the plaintiff and the defendant were taken into custody, the plaintiff being detained on a charge of juvenile delinquency and the defendant being faced with a criminal charge. According to the evidence, it was intimated to the plaintiff that if she and the defendant were married no criminal charges would be laid. It was necessary to secure the consent of the plaintiff's mother to the marriage and, at first, she refused but finally, after she had been called upon by a solicitor representing the defendant, she gave her consent. The plaintiff was not only reluctant to go through a form of marriage but, on more than one occasion, protested that she would not do so. As stated by Aylen J. at p. 854:

> No doubt with the best intentions in the world, those to whom the plaintiff turned for advice all urged her so strongly to marry the defendant that it became practically an impossibility for a child of her age to continue to refuse, especially as her only home at the time was with the defendant's parents.

The ceremony was performed on 27th February 1954, and the plaintiff left the defendant on or about 31st December 1954. The court considered the delay in the plaintiff leaving the defendant understandable in the circumstances. After a reference to the law of duress, the court held that the marriage between the plaintiff and the defendant should be declared a nullity. Annulment has also been granted in the following cases: *H.* v. *H.*, [1954] P. 258, [1953] 3 W.L.R. 849, [1953] 2 All E.R. 1229; *Buckland* v. *Buckland*, [1968] P. 296, [1967] 2 W.L.R. 1506, [1967] 2 All E.R. 300. The last decision I will mention is *Marriage of S.* (1980), 42 F.L.R. 94 (Aust. Fam. Ct.). In this case, the court pointed out that the emphasis on terror or fear in some judgments seemed unnecessarily limiting. In granting a decree of nullity, Watson J., at p. 102, stated that it was "the effect of the oppression on his mind that should be the operative factor, not the form of such oppression." I turn now to state my understanding of the authorities.

A valid marriage is grounded upon the consent of each party. Oppression may vitiate consent and, if there is no consent, there is no valid marriage. Different people may respond to oppression in different ways, and conduct that may overmaster the mind of one person may not have this impact upon the mind of another. It matters not, therefore, whether the will of a person of reasonable fortitude would — or would not — have been overborne; the issue is, rather, the state of mind of the applicant. To constitute duress, it must be established that the applicant's mind was so overcome by oppression that there was an absence of free choice. The point that falls for decision is whether the consent given at the time of the ceremony was a real, understanding and voluntary consent. Oppression can take various forms; it may be generated by fear, or by persuasion or pressure. Essentially, the matter is one of degree, and this raises a question of fact for the court. The determination involves a consideration of all relevant circumstances, including the age of the applicant, the maturity of the applicant, the applicant's emotional state and vulnerability, the lapse of time between the conduct alleged as duress and the marriage ceremony, whether the marriage was consummated, whether the parties resided together as man and wife and the lapse of time between the marriage ceremony and the institution of the annulment proceeding. As long as the oppression affects the mind of the applicant in the fashion stated, physical force is not required and, no more so, is the threat of such force a necessary ingredient. Nor is the source of the conduct material. Where duress is alleged, the onus of proof is upon the party seeking annulment, and it is an onus that is not lightly discharged.

The principles of law relating to duress seem to be relatively clear and certain. However, as pointed out by Butt J. in *Scott* v. *Sebright*, the difficulty consists in the application of the law to the facts of each individual case. I have given this matter my most anxious consideration and, upon reflection, I am satisfied that the applicant has discharged the onus of proof and is entitled to a declaration of nullity. It appears to have been the view that lack of consent rendered a marriage void. Curiously, however, it seems also to have been considered that a marriage, void for lack of consent, could be subsequently ratified when oppression was withdrawn. I prefer, however, to adopt the view of Taylor J., in the *Kawaluk* case, that consent obtained by duress renders a marriage voidable on the application of the aggrieved party. . . .

For reasons I have stated, a decree of annulment is granted.

NOTES AND QUESTIONS

1. In *Buckland* v. *Buckland*, [1968] P. 296, [1967] 2 All E.R. 300, Scarman J. held that the coerced party had to establish: first, that a sufficient degree of fear was present to vitiate consent; second, that the fear was reasonably entertained; and third, that the fear arose from external circumstances for which the coerced party was not responsible. Did the judge in *S.* v. *S.* apply this test?

2. Arranged marriages may be the focus of inter-generational conflict in South Asian and other minority communities in western societies. From one perspective, the arranged marriage "is an essential part of the gigantic and oppressive framework of the joint family which has for so many generations kept women in subjugation" (Wilson, *Finding a Voice* (London: Virago, 1978), at 117). However, Ballard and others have cautioned against the dangers of ethnocentricity in evaluating the institution. He argues for the appreciation of arranged marriages in the context of joint and extended families, with economic and social ties emphasizing family loyalty rather than individualism and self-interest. See V.S. Khan, ed., *Minority Families in Britain* (London: MacMillan, 1979) c. 7. For further reading, see Bradney, "Duress, Family Law and the Coherent Legal System" (1994), 57 Mod. Law Rev. 963 and Parkinson, "Taking Multiculturalism Seriously: Marriage Law and the Rights of Minorities" (1994), 16 Sydney L. Rev. 473.

In *Parihar* v. *Bhatti* (1980), 17 R.F.L. (2d) 289 (B.C. S.C.), the bride's family arranged a marriage with someone she hardly knew. Although she protested several times before the wedding date, she participated in the ceremony. MacKinnon L.J.S.C. stated (at 291 and 292):

> I accept as a fact that great pressure from her family was brought upon the plaintiff to marry the defendant. The freedom of choice to marry — or not to marry — a person of one's choice, enjoyed by most people in our country, is not shared by all societies. The plaintiff was clearly caught in such a dilemma.
>
> Had she wanted to alienate herself completely from her family, probably necessitating leaving home, she could have refused to go through with the marriage. . . .
>
> There are many situations where families, or others, bring great persuasion upon a person to enter into marriage. However, the cases indicate that the duress sufficient to set aside the marriage must be of such a nature that her powers of volition were so affected that it really was no consent. . . .
>
> In my opinion, the evidence here does not satisfy me the marriage ought to be declared null and void. There was no corroboration at all of the plaintiff's allegations of fear. It may be that the alternative to her going through with the marriage would be most unpleasant for her but I do not consider that the facts presented to me justify the relief requested.

Several Commonwealth decisions suggest, however, that the duress threshold may be lowering in the context of arranged marriages. In *Hirani* v. *Hirani* (1983), 4 F.L.R. 232 (C.A.) a young Hindu woman was faced with the choice of marrying a man chosen by her parents or leaving home on her own. It appears she had no alternative accommodation or means of support. She was held to have married under such duress as to destroy consent. For a discussion of this case, see Bradley, "Duress and Arranged Marriages" (1983), 46 Mod. Law Rev. 499. In *Marriage of S.* (1980), 42 F.L.R. 94 (Aust. Fam. Ct.) a young Egyptian woman participated in an arranged marriage solely out of love and respect for her parents and to avoid any prejudice to the future marital opportunities of her younger sisters. There were no other tangible or intangible repercussions that would have flowed from a refusal to marry. Watson S.J., emphasizing the need to view the situation from the subjective vantage point of the unwilling bride, held that duress vitiating consent should be broad enough to encompass non-violent but controlling parental coercion. The marriage was annulled. See also *Mahmood* v. *Mahmood*, [1993] S.L.T. 589 and *Mahmud* v. *Mahmud*, [1994] S.L.T. 599.

(c) Limited purpose marriages, fraud, and mistake

IANTSIS v. PAPATHEODOROU

(1970), 3 R.F.L. 158, [1971] 1 O.R. 245 (C.A.)

SCHROEDER J.A.: — This matter comes before this Court under an order of reference made by Hughes J. on the 11th May 1970 pursuant to s. 32(1) of The Judicature Act, R.S.O. 1960, c. 197, on the ground that he deemed a decision previously given by Stewart J. in *Johnson (Smith)* v. *Smith*, [1968] 2 O.R. 699, 70 D.L.R. (2d) 374, to be wrong and of sufficient importance to be considered in a higher court. . . .

The plaintiff pleaded the following material facts in her statement of claim:

(a) That the parties went through a form of marriage at Windsor, Ontario, the plaintiff then being 20 years of age.

(b) That the parties never cohabited.

(c) That the defendant fraudulently tricked the plaintiff into marriage in order that he might obtain a status which would enable him to remain in Canada.

(d) That the defendant who was born in Samos, Greece, did not at the time of the marriage have the appropriate status to apply for permanent citizenship in Canada.

(e) That three days after the marriage ceremony the defendant, vested with his new status, applied for permanent admission to Canada. It is not alleged that his application was granted but, presumably, it was.

(f) That after 15th September 1969 the defendant refused to have anything to do with the plaintiff.

The plaintiff asked for a declaration that the purported marriage was void.

The defendant admitted all the allegations contained in the statement of claim except the allegation of trickery to achieve the ends imputed to him. He further pleaded that the plaintiff was fully aware of his status in Canada; that she appreciated the nature and quality of the ceremony; and that he did not refuse to have anything to do with her, but, on the contrary, was at all times ready, willing, and able to discharge his marriage obligations.

Attached to the order of reference herein is a certificate of the Deputy Registrar General of Ontario certifying that the marriage between the parties was solemnized by Zuber Co. Ct. J. of the County Court of the County of Essex on 12th September 1969.

At the commencement of the trial the learned Judge expressed a substantial doubt as to whether the statement of claim disclosed a cause of action. It was urged by counsel for the plaintiff that the facts were identical with those in *Johnson (Smith)* v. *Smith*, supra, in which Stewart J. granted relief to the plaintiff similar to the relief claimed herein. The learned Judge expressed grave doubts as to the correctness of that decision and proceeded to state the reasons for his dissenting view. In the circumstances he considered it in the best interests of all concerned that the present action should be referred to this Court.

I am bound to state, and I do so with the utmost deference, that in my opinion the doubts entertained by Hughes J., as stated in his reasons, are well founded. A reading of the reasons of Stewart J. readily suggests that he was more greatly influenced in determining the law, as laid down and applied by him, by an obiter dictum of Learned Hand J. an eminent American jurist, in *United States* v. *Rubenstein* (1945), 151 F. (2d) 915, than by English and Canadian authorities, to some of which I shall hereafter refer. He quoted the following passage from the judgment of Learned Hand J. at pp. 918-9 of the above report:

> But, that aside, Spitz and Sandler were never married at all. Mutual consent is necessary to every contract; and no matter what forms or ceremonies the parties may go through indicating the contrary, they do not contract if they do not in fact assent, which may always be proved . . . Marriage is no exception to this rule: a marriage in jest is not a marriage at all . . . It is quite true that a marriage without subsequent consummation will be valid; but if the spouses agree to a marriage only for the sake of representing it as such to the outside world and with the understanding that they will put an end to it as soon as it has served its purpose to deceive, they have never really agreed to be married at all. They must assent to enter into the relation as it is ordinarily understood, and it is not ordinarily understood as merely a pretence, or cover, to deceive others.

The *Rubenstein* case was an appeal from a conviction on a charge of conspiracy to obtain the entry of a person into the United States by false representations and by wilful concealment of material facts. A foreign woman married an American citizen to enable her to remain in the United States. She had paid the groom $200 and they had agreed that a divorce should take place in six months after the marriage. Learned Hand J. found that the suppression of these facts by both parties constituted a fraud upon the immigration authorities, even though the marriage was valid.

The dictum of Learned Hand J. above quoted relates to a case where both parties had agreed to enter into marriage of convenience, and the learned Jurist would appear to have put a marriage and an ordinary civil contract on the same footing. Marriage is something more than a contract. It creates mutual rights and obligations as all contracts do, but beyond that it confers a status. In its essence it may be defined as the voluntary union, for life, of one man and one woman to the exclusion of all others: *Hyde* v. *Hyde and Woodmansee* (1866), L.R. 1 P.&.D. 130; *Robb* v. *Robb* (1891), 20 O.R. 591.

In *Swift* v. *Kelly* (1835), 3 Knapp. 257 at 293, 12 E.R. 648, the Judicial Committee of the Privy Council expressed the following opinion as to the effect of fraud and deception upon the validity of a marriage:

> It should seem, indeed, to be the general law of all countries, as it certainly is of England, that unless there be some positive provision of statute law, requiring certain things to be done in a specified manner, no marriage shall be held void merely upon proof that it had been contracted upon false representations, and that but for such contrivances, consent never would have been obtained. Unless the party imposed upon has been deceived as to the person, and thus has given no consent at all, there is no degree of deception which can avail to set aside a contract of marriage knowingly made.

[The court referred to a number of English authorities and concluded (at 162) that they "consistently lay down the rule that neither a fraudulent nor an innocent misrepresentation will of itself affect the validity of a marriage unless, of course, the misrepresentation induces an operative mistake, e.g. as to the nature of the ceremony, or deception as to the identity of one of the persons to the marriage, as when A is induced to marry B, believing that she is marrying C".]

In the result, since we are of the opinion that *Johnson (Smith)* v. *Smith*, supra, was wrongly decide, judgement should issue dismissing the action with costs.

TRUONG (MALIA) v. MALI

(1975), 25 R.F.L. 256 (Ont. H.C.)

O'LEARY J.: — The plaintiff, since January 1973, has had landed immigrant status in Canada. She returned to Vietnam and took a teaching position at the University of Hue. As the total collapse of the South Vietnamese government approached, she was evacuated to Saigon in March 1975 but was not allowed to leave the country and could only avoid being trapped in Vietnam, with grave risks to life, safety and freedom by fleeing the country, by first becoming on paper the wife of an American citizen. She went through a form of marriage, for the purpose of escape, with an American citizen, the defendant herein, who obliged her in that regard to facilitate her escape. They were not lovers, nor did they have any intention to cohabit, nor have sexual relations occurred between them.

The plaintiff came immediately to Canada via Guam and has been in Ottawa since April 1975. She intends to make Ontario her permanent home.

I am satisfied that there was no intention to marry but only to bring into existence a marriage document and that in the circumstances the plaintiff cannot be criticized for the trick she used to avoid the desperate situation in which she found herself.

Judgment declaring null and void the form of marriage entered into between the plaintiff and the defendant on 19th April 1975 at Phu Nhuan Village, South Vietnam, by reason of lack of intention to marry on the part of both parties. No order as to costs.

NOTES AND QUESTIONS

1. The Ontario Court of Appeal has reaffirmed that an "immigration marriage" is valid: *Leonotion* v. *Leonotion* (1977), 4 R.F.L. (2d) 94 and *Laroia* v. *Laroia* (1986), 54 O.R. (2d) 224. See also *Ciresi (Ahmad)* v. *Ahmad*, 31 R.F.L. (2d) 326, [1983] 1 W.W.R. 710 (Alta. Q.B.); *Fernandez (Alarcio)* v. *Fernandez*, 34 R.F.L. (2d) 249, [1983] 4 W.W.R. 755 (Man. Q.B.); *Singla* v. *Singla* (1985), 46 R.F.L. (2d) 235, 69 N.S.R. (2d) 60 (N.S. T.D.); and *S. (A.)* v. *S. (A.)* (1988), 15 R.F.L. (3d) 443 (Ont. U.F.C.). In the latter case, Mendes da Costa U.F.C.J. stated (at 448):

> The mere fact, therefore, that parties go through a form of marriage for a "limited" or "extraneous" purpose will not, of itself, render the marriage invalid. In this respect, no heed is paid to their mental reservations. Indeed, their motive would seem to support a finding of validity. Where parties seek, by marriage, to confer upon a respondent a right to reside in Canada, it would seem to follow that they do only what they intend: enter into a marriage relationship as the means of achieving the desired result.

Compare *Asser* v. *Peermohamed* (1984), 40 R.F.L. (2d) 299, 46 O.R. (2d) 664 (H.C.) where such a marriage was held void. It should be noted that this case was decided by the same judge whose decision in *Laroia* was subsequently overturned on appeal.

In contrast to the view of the Ontario Court of Appeal, the courts of France and Scotland, as well as Judge Learned Hand in *U.S.* v. *Rubenstein*, 151 F.2d 915 (1945), have held such marriages to be nullities on the ground of lack of consent. See Hahlo, *Nullity of Marriage in Canada* (Toronto: Butterworths, 1979) at 32. Which approach do you prefer?

2. Even if the "immigration marriage" is valid, the immigrant's desire to obtain status to enter into or remain in Canada may be frustrated. Under the *Immigration Act*, R.S.C. 1985, c. I-2 and the Regulations a person can sponsor an application for landed immigrant's status by his or her spouse. However, this is not permitted if the applicant spouse "entered into the marriage primarily for the purpose of gaining admission to Canada as a member of the family class and not with the intention of residing permanently with the other spouse" (*Immigration Regulations, 1978*, SOR/78 - 172, s. 4(3) [added by SOR/84-140; 92-101; 93-44]). In *Johnson* v. *Ahmad* (1981), 22 R.F.L. (2d) 141 (Alta. Q.B.), the husband had been ordered deported and in *Fernandez (Alarcio)* v. *Fernandez*, above, one of the spouses had already been deported.

3. In light of *Iantsis*, *Leonotion*, and *Laroia*, is the result in *Truong (Malia)* v. *Malia* supportable? On what basis?

4. A and B go through a marriage ceremony. At the time A thinks B is pregnant with his child. B is, in fact, pregnant by C. Is the marriage valid? See *Moss* v. *Moss*, [1897] P. 263.

5. In order to win a bet with friends who "dare" them to do so, Bob and Sue go through a marriage ceremony before a Justice of the Peace after obtaining a licence. They have no intention of living as husband and wife and, indeed, never do so. Are they validly married? See *Brooks-Bischoffberger* v. *Brooks-Bischoffberger* (1930), 149 A. 606, 129 Me. 52 and *Parker* v. *Parker* (1757), 2 Lee 382, 161 E.R. 377.

6. Mistakes as to the nature of the ceremony occasionally occur. See *Sobush* v. *Sobush*, [1931] 2 W.W.R. 900 (Sask. Q.B.) and *Jiwani (Samji)* v. *Samji* (1979), 11 R.F.L. (2d) 188 (B.C. S.C.).

7. Whether an essential mistake regarding the identity of the party one is marrying or the nature of the ceremony renders a marriage void or only voidable is not settled. Professor Hahlo concludes in *Nullity of Marriage in Canada* (Toronto: Butterworths, 1979) (at 30):

> Seeing that essential mistake nullifies consent, one should think, on principle, that it renders the marriage null and void, not only voidable. However, it would appear that only the mistaken party can attack the validity of the marriage, and that the marriage becomes unassailable if he or she approbates or acquiesces in it after the discovery of the mistake. If this is so, the marriage is voidable rather than void.

(6) AGE

The age at which a person has the capacity to marry is a matter within federal legislative competence under s. 91(26) of the *Constitution Act, 1867*. The *Annulment of Marriages Act (Ontario)*, R.S.C. 1970, c. A-14 simply incorporates, by reference, the law of England relating to the annulment of marriage, as that law was on July 15, 1870. The law of England governing the age at which a person could validly marry at that time was common law. The British Columbia Supreme Court, in *Legebokoff* v. *Legebokoff* (1982), 28 R.F.L. (2d) 212 at 215, held that the following rules applied:

> [T]he marriage of a child of less than seven is void. The marriage of a male older than seven years but younger than 14 years, or a female older than seven but younger than 12 years is voidable at the instance of the infant upon his or her attaining the requisite minimum age. Further, a marriage where either or both parties were under age becomes validated if they continue to cohabit as husband and wife after reaching the age of capacity.

(See also Hahlo, *Nullity of Marriage in Canada* (Toronto: Butterworths, 1979) at 21 and Ontario Law Reform Commission, *Report on Family Law, Part II: Marriage* (Toronto: Ministry of the Attorney General, 1970) at 36-38).

Regarding the minimum age at which a person should have capacity to marry, the Ontario Law Reform Commission concluded (at 38):

> [C]ontinued reliance upon the rules provided by the common law is completely unjustified in a nation which is otherwise as advanced as Canada. A legislative correction of this situation would be recommended were the matter one within provincial jurisdiction. The Commission strongly feels that the ages defining capacity to marry should be revised upward but can go no further than to say that the power to enact the necessary corrective legislation is clearly within the powers assigned to the Parliament of Canada by the British North America Act.

Notwithstanding the constitutional problem, the provinces have attempted to fill the gap caused by federal inaction in this area (see the Ontario *Marriage Act*). The effect of these provisions on the validity of a marriage contracted by minors and their constitutionality will be explored in the next section of the casebook.

3.   Formal Validity of Marriage

As noted in the introduction to this chapter, a province has the power under s. 92(12) of the *Constitution Act, 1867* to legislate regarding the formalities to be followed by those intending to marry. It may make the creation of a valid marriage conditional upon the observance of these formalities.

Unlike the federal level, the provinces have enacted recent, comprehensive legislation concerning marriage. In Ontario, the *Marriage Act* deals with such preliminary formalities as the need for a licence or banns, who can officiate, the form of the ceremony, and registration of the marriage. All of these provisions clearly relate to the formal validity of marriage and the province has the constitutional power to legislate that any marriage that does not comply is invalid.

Much of the Ontario *Marriage Act* is directed at the person who issues the licence or publishes the banns or officiates at the marriage. These persons are obligated to determine whether or not they are entitled to issue a licence, publish banns or officiate at the marriage of the two individuals involved. Many of the grounds on which they are obligated to refuse to issue a licence, publish banns, or officiate would appear to relate to the capacity of the individuals to marry: mental capacity, prohibited degrees of consanguinity and affinity, and age.

The structure and wording of the *Marriage Act* raises several legal issues that are examined in the cases and Notes and Questions that follow:

1. Are any of the provisions of the *Marriage Act* preconditions to a valid marriage?

2. What is the effect of s. 31? How is it interpreted and applied?

3. Can the province, as a constitutional matter, attach the sanction of invalidity to marriages performed in breach of a section of the *Marriage Act* that appears to relate to capacity? Can the province, as a constitutional matter, prevent the issuance of a licence on grounds that relate to capacity?

ALSPECTOR v. ALSPECTOR

[1957] O.R. 454, 9 D.L.R. (2d) 679 (C.A.)

[Mr. Alspector, an elderly widower, married Mrs. Noodleman, an elderly widow, in a marriage ceremony performed at the home of a cantor with all the requirements of the Jewish faith. The parties had neglected to obtain a marriage licence. The evidence indicated that Mr. Alspector had been informed by a friend and by the cantor that he should obtain a licence. Mr. Alspector believed that they did not need a licence as they intended to live in Israel after the marriage.

The couple lived together for some seven years. During this time each held out the other as spouse. After Mr. Alspector suffered a stroke, his family challenged the validity of the marriage. Mrs. Alspector brought an action for a declaration that the marriage was valid. Mr. Alspector died before trial.

The trial judge took the view that both parties intended to be married in accordance with both Jewish law and Ontario law and that s. 33 of the *Marriage Act* (now s. 31)] applied. Mr. Alspector's daughter appealed.]

ROACH J.A.: — . . . I turn now to a consideration of the provisions in The Marriage Act concerning a marriage licence.

It must now be taken as established beyond legal controversy that it is within the legislative competence of a Provincial Legislature to enact conditions as to solemnization of marriage in the Province which may affect the validity of the contract: *Re Marriage Legislation in Canada*, [1912] A.C. 880, 11 E.L.R. 255, 7 D.L.R. 629. In *Kerr* v. *Kerr*, [1934] S.C.R. 72, [1934] 2 D.L.R. 369, Duff C.J. at p. 75 put it thus: —

> The authority of the provinces, therefore, extends not only to prescribing such formalities as properly fall within the matters designated by 'Solemnization of Marriage': they have the power to enforce the rules laid down by penalty, by attaching the consequence of invalidity, and by attaching such consequences absolutely or conditionally.

The issuance of a licence or special permit and the publication of banns as preceremonial requirements, are formalities falling within the matters designated by "Solemnization of Marriage". The legislature has sought to enforce compliance with those requirements by the imposition of a penalty on the official who solemnizes a marriage without one of those three alternative requirements having been complied with. The question is, has the legislature also enacted the consequence of invalidity either absolutely or conditionally for non-compliance therewith? In my opinion it has enacted it conditionally. Section 4(1) and s. 33 must be read together in order to ascertain the legislature's intention in that regard. For convenience I set out those sections: —

> 4(1). No minister, clergyman or other person shall solemnize any marriage unless duly authorized so to do by licence under the hand and seal of the Lieutenant-Governor or of his deputy, or by certificate under this Act, unless the intention of the persons to intermarry has been published as provided by subsection 2.

Subsection 2 deals with the publication of banns.

> 33. Every marriage solemnized in good faith and intended to be in compliance with this Act between persons not under a legal disqualification to contract such marriage shall be deemed a valid marriage so far as respects the civil rights in Ontario of the parties or their issue and in respect of all matters within the jurisdiction of this Legislature, notwithstanding that the clergyman, minister or other person who solemnized the marriage was not duly authorized to solemnize marriage, and notwithstanding any irregularity or insufficiency in the proclamation of intention to intermarry or in the issue of the licence or certificate or notwithstanding the entire absence of both; provided that the parties, after such solemnization, lived together and cohabited as man and wife.

In considering s. 33 it becomes necessary, in the circumstances of this case, to determine only the scope and meaning of the words "intended to be in compliance with this Act." It should be held that the legislature did not assume, believe or expect that every couple who should intermarry in the Province would be familiar with *this* Act. It would be the rare case, indeed, in which either of them would know of the existence of The Marriage Act. All that they would know is that there would be some law in effect in the Province respecting the solemnization of marriages. The phrase should therefore be interpreted as meaning, — intended to be in compliance with that law. The next question is, — intended by whom? Must it be so intended by both of the parties or if it is so intended by one of the parties is that sufficient?

I cannot conceive a case in which if *both* of the parties acted in good faith *one* of them could be held not to have intended the marriage ceremony to be in compliance with the law of the Province, and therefore, a nullity. If, for example, the groom knew of the non-compliance with some essential requirement to the solemnization and went through the ceremony intending that the result would be a nullity then he would not be acting in good faith. Moreover, if knowing of such non-compliance, he intended the ceremony to be a nullity, the law will not permit him in a subsequent action to plead his own fraud upon the bride in order to have the ceremony declared a nullity. The law would not permit him thus to bastardize the offspring of the union and the fact that there may be none does not alter the policy of the law.

Turning now to the evidence: —

Even if the cantor's evidence be accepted that he told Mr. Alspector that because no licence had been issued the marriage would not be a civil marriage there is no evidence that that opinion was conveyed to the plaintiff. The evidence is confused as to whether or not the plaintiff knew that a licence had not been issued. In a number of places in her evidence she states that she did not know it: in other passages she says that she heard the cantor and Mr. Alspector discussing it as a fact. Even if it should be held that she knew as a fact that a licence had not been issued, I think it fair to conclude on her evidence that she did not know that the absence of a licence in the circumstances of this case could affect the validity of her marriage, and that she intended that the marriage be in compliance with the law of the Province. As for Mr. Alspector, it is not unreasonable to conclude that although he knew that a licence had not been issued he proceeded in good faith believing that a licence was not necessary because of his intention shortly thereafter to go with the plaintiff to reside in Israel.

The appeal should be dismissed with costs.

McKENZIE v. SINGH

[1972] 5 W.W.R. 387, 29 D.L.R. (3d) 380 (B.C. S.C.)

DRYER J.: — . . . In October 1970 the plaintiff, then 18 years of age, as a result of some difference with her mother, left her parents' home and went to live with a woman friend. She was unable to find work and became short of money. A female acquaintance told her that she could arrange for her to be paid $200 if she would marry someone "in name only", i.e., on the understanding that after the ceremony she would never have to see the man she married again and that in three months the marriage would be "wiped out" and there would be no record of it. The plaintiff agreed and on 13th November 1970 the female acquaintance introduced her to a man whom I will hereafter call "the broker". At the same time she met the defendant. The four of them then drove to Abbotsford.

At Abbotsford she and the defendant sat in the car while the broker went into the office of a marriage commissioner, one A.K. Paul, and returned with a form which was apparently intended to take the place of the notice of marriage (Form M3) and the statutory declaration (Form M2) referred to in s. 19 of the Marriage Act, R.S.B.C. 1960, c. 232, before its repeal in 1971 [1971, c. 32, s. 4]. The defendant signed that form while in the car and a copy of it as signed is now Ex. 8 in these proceedings. Later the plaintiff, the defendant, the broker and the female acquaintance went into the marriage commissioner's office and the plaintiff and defendant went through a marriage ceremony before him with the two others as witnesses.

The date "November 9th, 1970" on Ex. 8 is therefore false; and it is apparent on the evidence that notice was not given to the marriage commissioner three days before the day of the marriage as required by s. 19 of the Marriage Act.

Following the ceremony the broker gave the plaintiff $100 and the four drove back to Vancouver. The plaintiff and defendant then separated and she did not see him again until around 1st December 1970, when she accompanied him to the Immigration Offices and there declared herself to be married to him. She then parted from him again. On this occasion the broker gave her another $100, the balance of her fee. The marriage was never consummated and she has never at any time cohabited with the defendant.

She now asks for a declaration that she is not married to the defendant.

I reject the contention of plaintiff's counsel that the plaintiff went through the ceremony of marriage because of fear and that there was therefore no real consent on her part. She did consent to the marriage and went through with it and the subsequent visit to the Immigration Office in complete disregard of principle simply to obtain money. She is not entitled to sympathetic consideration by the Court. However, the matter not being discretionary or equitable, if no valid marriage was effected, the Court should, on application, so declare: see *Pertreis* v. *Tondear (Pertreis)* (1790), 1 Hag. Con. 136 at 138, 161 E.R. 502. It is clear that s. 19 (and consequently s. 20 [rep. 1971, c. 32, s. 4]) of the Act were not complied with.

In *Gilham* v. *Steele*, 8 W.W.R. (N.S.) 62, [1953] 2 D.L.R. 89 at 96 (B.C. C.A.), Bird J.A. (as he then was) referred to:

> . . . the principle expressed by Dr. Lushington in *Catterall* v. *Sweetman (Catterall)* (1845), 1 Rob. Ecc. 304, 163 E.R. 1047, applied by the Court of Appeal, Saskatchewan, in *Wylie (Patton)* v. *Patton*, 24 Sask. L.R. 285, [1930] 1 W.W.R. 216, [1930] 1 D.L.R. 747, i.e., that although a statute prohibits a solemnization of marriage without observance of requirements, therein described as prerequisite, failure to observe any such requirement does not render a marriage void, nor is nullity to be implied in consequence unless the statute so provides either expressly or by clear necessary intendment.

Here, as in that case, counsel for the plaintiff does not question the soundness of that principle but submits that "the provisions of ss. 19, 20 and 21 of the Marriage Act, by necessary intendment, enact the consequence of invalidity for non-compliance with ss. 19 and 20 if the condition of good faith is not present". In November 1970 the Marriage Act, s. 21 [rep. 1971, c. 32, s. 4] read as follows:

> 21. No irregularity in the compliance with sections 19 and 20 invalidates a marriage solemnized in pursuance of these sections if the marriage is entered into in good faith.

Ordinarily, a claim of lack of good faith is made by someone against someone else. Here the plaintiff was herself guilty of lack of good faith. So, of course, was the defendant. However, guilt on the part of the plaintiff cannot convert the marriage ceremony in question in these proceedings into "a marriage. . . entered into in good faith".

Section 21 does not say directly that if the marriage is not entered into in good faith it will be invalid if the provisions of ss. 19 and 20 are not complied with, but I think it does so by "clear necessary intendment" since, if the legislature did not so intend, I can see no reason for saying in s. 21 that if the marriage were entered into in good faith it would not be invalid. In contrast, s. 31 reads as follows:

> 31. Nothing in section 29 or 30 contained invalidates any marriage.

Sections 29 [am. 1971, c. 32, ss. 10, 12, 13] and 30 relate to the marriage of minors. . . .

[Declaration granted.]

NOTES AND QUESTIONS

1. If the parties go through a marriage ceremony and then cohabit, it is presumed that they complied with the necessary formalities. The person who is claiming that there was a formal defect has the onus

of proving it. See *Friedman* v. *Smookler* (1963), 43 D.L.R. (2d) 210 (Ont. H.C.); *Re Lin* (1992), 44 R.F.L. (3d) 60 (Alta. Q.B.); and *Lehoux* v. *Woolward* (1994), 2 R.F.L. (4th) 382 (B.C. S.C.). In an annotation to the latter case, Professor McLeod commented:

> The presumption arose when marriage records were not organized or kept in a central location, and the onus was very important. Now that records are systematized, the presumption can be easily rebutted.

2. A number of cases hold that marriages entered into in conformity with aboriginal custom will be recognized in some circumstances: *Connally* v. *Woolrich* (1867), 11 L.C. Jur. 197, 17 R.J.R.Q. 75, 1 C.N.L.C. 70 (Que. S.C.); *The Queen* v. *Nan-E-Quis-A-Ka* (1889), 2 C.N.L.C. 368, 1 Terr. L.R. 211 (S.C.); *R.* v. *Bear's Shin Bone* (1899), 4 Terr. L.R. 173 (S.C.); *R.* v. *Williams*, (1921), 30 B.C.R. 303 (S.C.); and *Re Noah Estate* (1961), 32 D.L.R. (2d) 185, 36 W.W.R. 577 (N.W.T.S.C.). See also *Casimel* v. *Insurance Corp. of British Columbia* (1993), 106 D.L.R. (4th) 720 (B.C. C.A.) where these cases are examined, and Zlotkin, "Judicial Recognition of Aboriginal Customary Law in Canada: Selected Marriage and Adoption Cases" [1984] 4 C.N.L.R. 1.

3. The conflict of laws rule governing the formal validity of marriage stipulates that a marriage is formally valid if it is celebrated in accordance with a form required or recognized by the law of the place where the marriage was celebrated (the *lex loci celebrationis*). However, a marriage which fails to comply with the *lex loci celebrationis* has historically been recognized as valid if it conforms with the requirements of the common law and took place in a country where the use of the local form is impossible or in a country where the parties have not submitted to the local law. See Davies, *Family Law in Canada* (Toronto: Carswell, 1984) at 17; Hall, "Common Law Marriage" (1987), 46 Camb. L.J. 106; and *Keddie* v. *Currie* (1991), 85 D.L.R. (4th) 342 (B.C. C.A.). These "common law marriages" must, of course, be distinguished from cohabitation outside marriage altogether even though the latter may be described as a common law relationship in common parlance.

4. In *Christians (Wiltshire)* v. *Hill* (1981), 22 R.F.L. (2d) 199, the Alberta Court of Queen's Bench held that a province could not withhold a marriage licence where a woman wished to marry her divorced husband's brother since this relationship did not fall within the federally-established prohibited degrees.

5. Examine ss. 5 and 6 of the *Marriage Act*. The courts have held that the provinces may require parental consent as a formal requirement of the marriage ceremony and may stipulate that a marriage without the consent is void: *Kerr* v. *Kerr*, [1934] S.C.R. 72 and *Alberta (Attorney General)* v. *Underwood*, [1934] S.C.R. 635. What is the status of a marriage entered into in Ontario by a 16-year-old without parental consent or a court order dispensing with the requirement of parental consent? In *S.* v. *S.* (1988), 15 R.F.L. (3d) 443 (Ont. U.F.C.), Mendes da Costa U.F.C.J. concluded (at 452) "that there is nothing in the legislation of 1980 that shows an intention on the part of legislature to make parental consent a condition precedent to the validity of a marriage".

Section 5(2) directs licence issuers to refuse to issue licences to anyone under 16. Has the province overstepped its constitutional powers? Is a marriage entered into in Ontario between two persons aged 15 valid if the parties somehow manage to obtain a licence and persuade an authorized person to officiate? Does this make any difference to the constitutional issue?

The requirements of s. 5 may also be subject to a constitutional challenge on the ground that they discriminate on the basis of age and therefore violate s. 15 of the *Canadian Charter of Rights and Freedoms*. Do you think such a challenge would be successful? In *Moe* v. *Dinkins*, 533 F. Supp. 623 (S.D.N.Y., Aug. 17, 1981) the U.S. District Court of New York held that the requirement of parental consent for a marriage by a minor was constitutional as it was "rationally related to the State's legitimate interest in mature decision-making with respect to marriage by minors and preventing unstable marriages".

6. Which defects are cured by s. 31 of the *Marriage Act*? Some formal defects, such as a failure to have two witnesses as specified in s. 25 or a failure to solemnize the marriage in the presence of the parties as required by s. 25, may not be covered by s. 31. Does this mean that such defects are of no effect or that they result in invalidity that cannot be cured?

7. What are the requirements that must be met for s. 31 to apply? In particular, what is meant by "intended to be in compliance with this Act"? Do both parties have to act in good faith? Is evidence of sexual relations necessary to prove the parties cohabited as husband and wife? See *Friedman* v. *Smookler*, [1964] 1 O.R. 577, 43 D.L.R. (2d) 210 (H.C.).

8. Under the *Family Law Act*, "spouse" includes parties to a void or voidable marriage entered "in good faith on the part of the person asserting a right under this Act". In *Reaney* v. *Reaney* (1990), 28 R.F.L. (3d) 52, the Ontario High Court held that a man who knew he was already married when he went through a second wedding ceremony did not enter the marriage in good faith and could not claim under Part I of the Act. In *Debora* v. *Debora* (1998), 43 R.F.L. (4th) 179 (Ont. C.A.), the parties were married in a religious ceremony that did not comply with the *Marriage Act*. The man advised the woman that he wished to continue receiving a widower's pension and, therefore, their marriage should not be registered with the authorities for some time. Seven years later, the couple married in a civil ceremony. The Ontario Court of Appeal held that the woman only became a "spouse" for the purposes of Part I of the *FLA* after the second ceremony. It stated (at 184) that a person who participated in a marriage ceremony knowing that it did not comply with the provincial law could not claim to be acting "in good faith" even if he or she believed the ceremony created a marriage. For a critical comment, see McLeod, "Annotation" (1998), 43 R.F.L. (4th) 179.

Provision is made in s. 6 of the Ontario *Marriage Act* for a judicial order dispensing with the need for parental consent. The following case dealt with an application for such an order under previous Ontario legislation.

RE FOX

[1973] 1 O.R. 146 (Co. Ct.)

LAZIER, Co. Ct. J. (orally) : — This is an application brought under the *Marriage Act*, R.S.O. 1970, c. 261, by Catherine May Fox who is 16 years of age. The application arises because of the provisions of s. 7 of the Act which states in part that:

7(1) No person shall,

(*a*) issue a licence . . . to;

any person under the age of eighteen years unless the consent in writing of the father is obtained.

The father, Alfred Fox, would not consent in writing to the obtaining of the marriage licence.

There is then provision in s. 9(1) of the Act which, in effect, states that where the father "unreasonably or arbitrarily withholds his consent or is by his actions not interested in the maintenance or well-being of" the applicant, the person who needs the consent may apply to a Judge without the intervention of a next friend for an order under s. 9.

Subsection (2) of s. 9 provides that:

(2) The judge shall hear the application in a summary manner and may make an order dispensing with the consent.

I would like to make it clear that this is not an application for an order directing that a marriage take place. The effect of dispensing with the father's consent would make the way clearer to the licence being obtainable and nothing more.

The Saskatchewan cases (*Dickson* v. *Dickson et ux.* (1960), 32 W.W.R. 317, and *Glass* v. *Glass et ux.* (1959), 32 W.W.R. 321) that counsel cited to me in argument can be distinguished as in both of those decisions the Court took a more direct approach to the matters there in question and went into much detail about the chances of success of the marriages the respective applicants were seeking to enter into. Under the relevant Ontario legislation such an approach is not appropriate.

As it is the father whose consent has not been given, it is to his evidence that I must look. I have nothing but the greatest sympathy for parents of a young son or daughter who wants to get married. That is not a legal approach to the matter. The question is, has the consent been unreasonably or arbitrarily withheld.

Considering the testimony of Alfred Fox who gave it in a very frank and forthright manner, as did all the witnesses, there is no doubt that he is extremely concerned at the prospect of his daughter getting married. I think the concern is based on the fact that she is only 16 years of age and is not older. In other words, he feels that she is too young, as I understand his evidence.

There is certainly nothing wrong with the girl's behaviour or the prospective bridegroom.

The prospective bridegroom who is 18 years of age, appears to be independent and able to look after his own affairs, certainly better than most people his age. It is seldom that you would find one as young as he is in the process of purchasing a home. That shows quite some degree of stability. He has been employed for over three years at the same place and has had a recent increase in pay. I took it from his evidence that his job could be regarded as permanent.

I repeat that I have the greatest of sympathy with parents who are concerned about young people getting married. However, the Legislature recognizes that people under 18 years of age do get married or it would not have provided that marriage licences for them may be issued in certain circumstances without parental consent.

If there is some reason, valid at law, for not dispensing with consent in this case, I have not heard it.

In fact, on the father's testimony he stated: "If she wants to go ahead, she can do what she likes."

The mother of the applicant testified that while she would not consent, she would not oppose the marriage.

I can only come to the conclusion on the evidence that the consent is being unreasonably and arbitrarily withheld and I have no alternative than to make an order dispensing with the consent of the father in this case and I will make such an order.

4.   The Effect of Invalidity

(1)   THE VOID/VOIDABLE DISTINCTION

Reproduced below is a table identifying different defects and their conse-quences. It should be noted that, with regards to insanity, essential mistake, and non-age, Professor Hahlo takes the view that the marriage might be void but capable of ratification. He explains this apparent contradiction (*Nullity of Marriage in Canada* (Toronto: Butterworths, 1979) at 42-43):

> [I]t is generally recognized by now that the stark differentiation between void and voidable juridical acts is an over-simplification, and that there are cases which fall somewhere between these two categories. A marriage contracted without the required consent may well be one of those cases. If, to take an example, a person goes through a form of marriage, while insane, the essential consent is lacking, with the result that on principle, the marriage ought to be regarded as null and void *ab initio*. But assuming the parties live together for years after the erstwhile lunatic has recovered his mental health, is there a court in the world which would, perhaps decades

later, perhaps after the death of one of the spouses, annul the marriage on the ground that at the time of the solemnization of the marriage one of the parties was insane? Either the marriage was voidable only, which goes against the principle that lack of consent renders a juridical act void; or this is one of the cases where a void act, contrary to norm, is capable of ratification.

HAHLO, *NULLITY OF MARRIAGE IN CANADA*

(Toronto: Butterworths, 1979) 43-44

Table Of Impediments and Defects

Impediment or Defect Effect on the Marriage

Identity of Sex — not true in Ont.	Marriage void (non-marriage)
Prior Existing Marriage	Marriage void
Relationship within the Prohibited Degrees	Marriage void . . .
Informal Marriage	Marriage void (non-marriage)
Failure to comply with specific statutory formalities	Marriage valid, except where the applicable Marriage Act, expressly or by necessary intendment, decrees nullity
Non-age: either party below the marriageable age of the common law (boys 14 years, girls 12 years)	Marriage void (except, possibly, where the applicable Marriage Act otherwise decrees) but capable of ratification by continued cohabitation after attainment of age
Non-age: marriage contracted by a minor of marriageable age but below the age of marriage majority without the required consent of parent or guardian	Marriage valid unless the applicable Marriage Act, expressly or by necessary intendment, decrees nullity
Insanity	Marriage void but capable of ratification by continued cohabitation after recovery
Drunkenness or drug intoxication depriving party of reason and volition	Marriage void but capable of ratification by continued cohabitation after sobering-up
Force, fear, duress	Marriage voidable at instance of coerced party
Mistake as to the nature of the ceremony or the identity of the other party	Arguable whether marriage void or voidable. Better view: voidable at instance of the party in error. If void, capable of ratification by mistaken party.
Mistake as to qualities or attributes of the other party	Marriage valid
Fraud	Marriage valid, unless fraud induced a material mistake, *i.e.*, a mistake as to the nature of the ceremony or the identity of the other party

Formally correct marriage contracted without the intention to establish a true marriage relationship (limited or extraneous purpose marriage, such as an "immigration marriage")	Marriage valid (controversial)
Impotence	Marriage voidable at the instance of either spouse.

(2) THE EFFECTS OF THE VOID/VOIDABLE DISTINCTION

(a) The general rule

Lord Greene M. R. succinctly expressed the distinction between a void and voidable marriage in *De Reneville* v. *De Reneville*, [1948] P. 100 at 111, [1948] 1 All E.R. 56 (C.A.):

> [A] void marriage is one that will be regarded by every court in any case in which the existence of the marriage is in issue as never having taken place and can be so treated by both parties to it without the necessity of any decree annulling it; a voidable marriage is one that will be regarded by every court as a valid subsisting marriage until a decree annulling it has been pronounced by a court of competent jurisdiction .

The parties to a voidable marriage can obtain a divorce, but no divorce can be granted if the marriage is void.

(b) The right of third parties to question the validity of the marriage

In proceedings to determine the right of a third party, a court may hold that a particular marriage is void whenever the validity of the marriage is relevant to the third party's rights. The validity of a voidable marriage can only be questioned in proceedings brought by one of the parties to the marriage. A voidable marriage can, therefore, never be challenged after the marriage is ended by the death of one of the parties.

(c) Property rights under the *Family Law Act*

For the purposes of the *Family Law Act*, a "spouse" is defined as either of a man and woman who (i) are married to one another or (ii) have entered into a marriage that is void or voidable, in good faith on the part of the person asserting a right under the Act (see s. 1(1)). If the parties to a void or voidable marriage satisfy this definition, they qualify for the property rights set out in Parts I and II of the Act. See the discussion of *Reaney* and *Debora* in the previous section.

The date the marriage is declared a nullity may serve as a "valuation date" for the purpose of Part I (see s. 4(1)) and it triggers the entitlement under s. 5(1) of the *Family Law Act*. The significance of this will become apparent when Chapter 4 is studied.

(d) Support obligations

Part III of the *Family Law Act* imposes obligations on "spouses" to support themselves and each other. The general definition of "spouse" set out in s. 1(1) again applies. For the purposes of Part III only, "spouse" also includes "either of a man and woman who are not married to each other and have cohabited (a) continuously for a period of not less than three years, or (b) in a relationship of some permanence, if they are the natural or adoptive parents of a child": s. 29. This latter provision may apply where the parties to a void or voidable marriage fail to meet the good faith requirement of s. 1(1).

(e) Children

There is a general duty on a parent to support his or her child: s. 31, *Family Law Act.* No distinction is drawn in the Act between children born in a void, voidable, or valid marriage. Indeed, no distinction is drawn between children born within or outside marriage. This follows from the general abolition of the status of illegitimacy by the *Children's Law Reform Act.*

3

DIVORCE

1. Introduction

(1) HISTORY OF CANADIAN DIVORCE LAW

Prior to 1968, the divorce law varied from province to province. In Newfoundland and Quebec, there was no judicial divorce. Persons domiciled in these provinces had to procure the passage of a private Act of Parliament to dissolve their marriages. Judicial divorce was introduced in Ontario in 1930 by the *Divorce Act (Ontario)*, S.C. 1930, c. 14. This Act, which governed the dissolution of marriage in Ontario until 1968, incorporated by reference the law of England of July 15, 1870 regarding the dissolution of marriage insofar as that law had not been modified or repealed by federal legislation. In substance, therefore, the grounds for divorce in Ontario were those specified in the *English Matrimonial Causes Act, 1857*, (20-21 Vict., c. 85), as modified by the *Divorce Act*, S.C. 1925, c. 41.

The *Divorce Act (Ontario)* brought the divorce laws applicable to persons domiciled in Ontario into line with those that already prevailed in Alberta, British Columbia, Manitoba, the Northwest Territories, Saskatchewan, and the Yukon Territory. The basis for the divorce laws in these jurisdictions was the *Matrimonial Causes Act, 1857*. It permitted a husband to obtain a divorce on the ground of his wife's adultery. Under this Act, a wife could not obtain a divorce unless she proved that her husband had been guilty of incestuous adultery, rape, sodomy, bestiality, bigamy, adultery coupled with cruelty, or adultery coupled with desertion for at least two years. The *Divorce Act* of 1925 removed this double standard and permitted a wife to petition on the grounds of adultery alone. In 1967, therefore, judicial divorce could be obtained in Alberta, British Columbia, Manitoba, the Northwest Territories, Ontario, Saskatchewan, and the Yukon Territory on the following grounds. A husband could obtain a divorce only by proving his wife's adultery. A wife could petition on the grounds of adultery, rape, sodomy, bestiality, or bigamy.

Unlike the other provinces, New Brunswick, Nova Scotia and Prince Edward Island each enacted a divorce law prior to Confederation. By s. 129 of the *B.N.A. Act* (now the *Constitution Act, 1867*), these laws continued in effect until the Parliament of Canada enacted the *Divorce Act* of 1968. In all of these provinces, adultery was a ground for divorce. In New Brunswick and Prince Edward Island, frigidity or impotence was also a ground. Divorce on the basis of cruelty was available only in Nova Scotia.

Section 23 of the *Divorce Act* of 1968 repealed all prior divorce laws. This statute provided, for the first time, a Canada-wide law of divorce.

As outlined above, only matrimonial offences were grounds for divorce in Canada prior to 1968. The 1968 *Divorce Act* introduced the concept of permanent marriage breakdown as a ground for divorce. Section 4 of the Act provided that where a husband and wife were living separate and apart a petition could be brought on the ground that there had been a permanent breakdown of marriage by reason of one of the circumstances listed in s. 4(1). It should be emphasized that it was only by establishing one of the circumstances listed that a petitioner could rely on the permanent marriage breakdown ground. It was not sufficient to convince the court that the marriage relationship was at an end.

The circumstances listed in sections 4(1)(a) through (e) of the 1968 *Divorce Act* included: imprisonment, alcohol and narcotic addiction, whereabouts of spouse unknown, non-consummation, separation, and petitioner's desertion.

Section 4(1)(a) — Imprisonment: The respondent must have been imprisoned for an aggregate period of at least three years during the five year period immediately preceding the petition. If the sentence was a death sentence or for a term of ten years or more, then a petition could be presented to the court after two years of imprisonment.

Section 4(1)(b) — Alcohol or Narcotic Addiction: The Act required that the respondent be "grossly addicted to alcohol or a narcotic", without reasonable expectation of rehabilitation within a foreseeable period.

Section 4(1)(c) — Whereabouts of Spouse Unknown: If, for a period of not less than three years, the petitioner had no knowledge or information as to the whereabouts of the respondent it was considered that the whereabouts of the spouse were unknown.

Section 4(1)(d) — Non-consummation: The marriage must not have been consummated and, for a period of not less than one year, the respondent must have been unable to consummate the marriage by reason of illness or disability or refused to consummate it.

Section 4(1)(e) — Separation and Desertion: The spouses must have been living separate and apart for a period of not less than three years immediately preceding the petition. If the petitioner were the deserting spouse, then he or she had to wait a period of at least five years before a petition could be presented. Desertion involved abandonment of marital obligations without agreement between the spouses.

Section 3 retained the matrimonial offence basis for divorce. The offences under s. 3, which included adultery, sodomy, bestiality, rape, homosexual act(s), form of marriage with another, and physical or mental cruelty, were considered to strike at the very root of the pledge that the spouses remain faithful and devoted to each other.

The Law Reform Commission of Canada urged substantial reforms of the divorce law in 1976 (see *Report on Family Law* (Ottawa: Canada Law Reform Commission, 1976)). It proposed that "marriage breakdown", conclusively established whenever a spouse claimed that it had occurred, be the only basis for divorce. A husband and wife would not be required to separate or live apart as a condition of participating in the dissolution process, but there would be a minimum waiting period of six months following the filing by a spouse or both spouses of the "notice of intent to seek dissolution" before the marriage was actually dissolved by a court.

In January, 1984 the Liberal government tabled Bill C-10, *An Act to Amend the Divorce Act*, which provided for divorce solely on the basis of one year of separation. Due to the dissolution of Parliament in the summer of 1984, this Bill died on the Order Paper. In May, 1985 the Progressive Conservative government introduced Bill C-47, which ultimately received royal assent on February 13, 1986 and came into force as the *Divorce Act, 1985* on June 1, 1986. The excerpts from the Department of Justice study that follow explain the background to and leading features of this legislation.

DEPARTMENT OF JUSTICE, *EVALUATION OF THE DIVORCE ACT: PHASE II: MONITORING AND EVALUATION*

(Ottawa: Department of Justice, Bureau of Review, 1990) 1-9 (Footnotes Omitted) (Reproduced with the permission of the Minister of Supply and Services Canada, 1991)

[This study relied on research conducted in two phases. In the first phase in 1985, data were collected from the court files of 1,310 divorce cases in St. John's, Montreal, Ottawa and Saskatoon. In addition, 617 interviews were conducted with divorced persons whose files had been reviewed. The second phase was essentially a replication of the first. During 1988, 1,478 divorce files in the four cities were reviewed and 599 persons were interviewed. In addition, the study drew on data from the Central Divorce Registry, comments by family law lawyers, and reported cases.]

On June 1, 1986, the *Divorce Act* came into force. The Act represents an attempt to modernize the law pertaining to divorce. The stated objectives at the time of Bill C-47 were:

    (a) to make the divorce process less adversarial while increasing chances for the reconciliation of the spouses;

    (b) to provide a more humane and fairer resolution of the consequences of divorce;

    (c) to recognize provincial responsibilities and provide for a process of divorce which will operate with as few complications or duplications as possible.

The *Divorce Act* is, in many ways, a response to a number of criticisms of the 1968 *Divorce Act*. Almost from its inception, that Act was seen as a compromise piece of legislation, one which, even at the time, did not reflect the realities of marriage breakdown. Indeed, as early as 1973, Julien Payne, in preparing his massive background report on unified family courts, could already draw upon an impressive body of literature critical of family law and its administration. And, over the rest of that decade, the Law Reform Commission prepared a number of focused working papers which documented what were then perceived to be the main problems and inadequacies of existing legislation and procedures in the area of family law in Canada.

Underlying many of these criticisms was a perception of family law as in many ways unique in that it falls somewhere between civil and criminal law. While containing elements of both, it was argued that it has neither the "legal rationality" of pure civil litigation or, for the most part, the retributive and moral elements inherent in criminal proceedings. As one commentator observed, family litigation is distinguished from other civil actions in that it involves a greater human and emotional element. Dissolution of marriage, requires, then, "a procedure different from the one that suffices for recovery of damages for breach of a commercial contract or reparation for forcible aggression upon person or property."

The general conclusion reached by the Law Reform Commission and echoed by many other critics was that the adversarial approach and the related notion of fault are inappropriate in the context of marriage dissolution. In particular, the adversarial approach was seen not only as inappropriate but as also intensifying and exacerbating pain and suffering and impeding the likelihood of an amicable settlement. Thus, the Commission depicted the adversary system as "one of Canada's great self-inflicted wounds" and as an approach "inherently inconsistent with the harmonious resolution of family disputes". In the Commission's view, it is an approach which should not be available "as an extension of the destructive capacity of spouses who disagree over their personal relationship."

Also under attack was the fault orientation of the existing legislation. Fault, and therefore the notion of a guilty party, was seen as seldom relevant in marriage breakdown since the *grounds* for divorce and the *reasons* for divorce are usually quite far apart. The Commission argued that the fault principle merely reflects the futile effort of the state to attempt, through legislation, to uphold the sanctity of the traditional family by reducing the incidence of marriage breakdown. As the Law Reform Commission concluded, restrictive divorce laws simply force those committed to obtaining a divorce to find or fabricate grounds. Those who can do neither are left in the position of living apart, neither married nor unmarried. For similar reasons, the Commission was equally critical of the present three- or five-year waiting period or any designated waiting period for that matter. Rather, where both spouses are agreed that their marriage has broken down, the waiting period was seen as too long and as creating unnecessary hardships and delays in the process of reorganization.

In the period between the Law Reform Commission's studies and the 1983 proposal for reform of the divorce legislation, many changes had occurred in family law. All provinces and territories had, by then, enacted legislation concerning division of matrimonial property, child custody and child and spousal support. Usually, these reforms replaced the plethora of antiquated and sexist acts pertaining to various aspects of family relations and conflicts with new legislation gender neutral in its language and premised on an assumption of sexual equality in marriage. The "best interests of the child" principle became the sole basis for awarding custody, thereby undermining the earlier notion of paternal rights and the later maternal preference when children are in "their tender years".

It is apparent, too, that through less formal means, many of the problems identified by the Law Reform Commission were being addressed. In terms of attitudes and practices, family law was no longer the same as the Law Reform Commission had depicted it in the 1970's. For example, alternatives to the adversarial approach, such as divorce mediation, seen, in the 1970's as novel and controversial had, by the mid-1980's, become institutionalized in many parts of Canada. And, while there no doubt remain some extremely litigious lawyers in the area of family law, there is reason to believe that most family law practitioners were coming to believe that when custody and access are at issue, a better settlement results from negotiation than from litigation. Moreover, there now seemed to be few family court judges who believed that, in the matter of custody, the adversarial approach will "reveal the truth" of who is the better parent. Many were coming to rely much more — sometimes invariably — on custody assessments or investigations or they were referring the disputing spouses to mediation.

It is evident that the proposed divorce reform was, in many respects, an effort to catch up with the provincial legislation and the changing climate in family law. The proposed divorce reform drew heavily upon the Law Reform Commission reports and, depending on point of view, addressed many of the concerns and recommendations of the Commission. However, in retrospect, these can be seen as concerns of the 1970's. Many of them emerged from or were influenced by the radical critiques of the family and the generally positive conception of divorce as often a constructive rather than a destructive process — a solution rather than a problem. Family and marriage — went this argument — oppresses everyone, but particularly women, and it was not the role of the state to stand in the way of individual fulfilment or to buttress failed marriages.

When new divorce legislation was being proposed in the 1980's, the climate had shifted and new issues and concerns had surfaced. First, in a more conservative era, the traditional nuclear family was under less attack than in the two previous decades. Indeed, new and voluble groups had emerged to oppose legislation and programmes which, in their view, undermine the sanctity of the traditional male breadwinner nuclear family. Second, the rather short-lived period during the early 1970s when divorce was seen as a creative process had given way to a more dismal image as more was learned about the social, psychological and economic consequences of marriage breakdown, particularly for women. The American experience had suggested that family law reform though based on assumptions of sexual equality is actually premised on an "illusion of sexual equality". Many of the innovations and assumptions, initially welcomed by feminists, were being shown to produce unanticipated and negative consequences for women and children in divorce. Third, fathers' rights groups also were beginning to see sexual equality in family law as largely illusory since in terms of support and custody, the courts are alleged by them to be biased in favour of women.

Thus, by the time Bill C-47 reached the Committee stage, many women's groups and religious groups of long-standing existence and newly formed fathers' rights groups were anxious to make their concerns known and to press for amendments to the proposed legislation. The criticism by religious and fundamentalist groups was diffuse and aimed, ultimately, at making divorce more difficult to obtain on the premise that more liberal divorce laws threaten the sanctity of the family. Predictably, the concerns of fathers' rights groups were more focused. Their demand was for a presumption of joint legal custody.

Women's groups represented a far larger constituency than the fathers' rights groups, but were also focused in their concerns. First, much of their effort went to opposing a presumption of joint legal custody. Second, they wished to broaden the grounds for variation of support orders in order to soften the possible impact of time fixed orders. Here, the concern was that the principle of self-sufficiency, if taken too literally, would be unfair to older women who had not worked outside the home during the marriage. This was opposed by various lawyers' groups who wanted legislation which would allow for finality and greater certainty in advice given to their clients. As well, the recently formed association, Family Mediation Canada, wished there to be a provision requiring a mandatory visit to divorce mediation where child custody is being contested. Finally, there were some who urged that the language of "custody" and "access" be abandoned in favour of terms such as "primary caregiver" and "secondary caregiver."

By the time Bill C-47 was ready for passage, four major issues had emerged: a presumption of joint custody; mandatory mediation; factors and objectives of spousal support, especially potential abuse of the objective of self-sufficiency; and variations of support orders. As in 1968, the legislation was again an attempt by the government to find compromises which would meet these sometimes conflicting demands. As we describe in the next section, the various groups were only partially successful in their efforts to include amendments which would address their particular concerns. . . .

The *Divorce Act*

Grounds

For those undergoing divorce, an important change, one which affects virtually all divorces, is the adoption of "marriage breakdown" as the sole ground for divorce and, in particular, the reduction of the separation period from three or five years to one year. The previous legislation contained 15 different fault grounds and ways of demonstrating marriage breakdown. Of these, the vast majority of divorcing couples relied on separation (to demonstrate marriage breakdown) and adultery and physical or mental cruelty (as methods of demonstrating fault). Adultery and mental and physical cruelty are retained but they are now viewed, along with one-year separation as methods of demonstrating marriage breakdown. In principle, use of these former fault grounds would allow for "immediate" divorce. In practice, since it is possible to file for divorce before having actually lived separate and apart for one year, it is debatable whether there would be much time advantage in choosing one of these methods over another.

Reconciliation and Mediation

The provision in the 1968 *Divorce Act*, requiring lawyers to inquire as to the possibility of reconciliation and to advise clients of marriage counselling services in the community, is retained in the new legislation. Lawyers are now under the additional legal obligation to advise their clients about the advantages of negotiation and of the divorce mediation services available in their community. There is not, however, any obligation on the part of lawyers actively to refer clients with disputes to mediation though, of course, they are free to do so if they so desire.

As well, the provision that spouses may resume cohabitation for purposes of reconciliation for 90 days during the separation period has been retained. Now, however, it is possible for couples to make several attempts at such cohabitation as long as the total time does not exceed 90 days.

Spousal and Child Support

In making an order for support, the *Divorce Act* specifies that the court shall *not* take into consideration fault or misconduct of the spouse in relation to the marriage. Courts are required to take into account not only the "conditions, means, needs and other circumstances of each spouse" but also "the length of time the spouses cohabited and the functions performed by each spouse during cohabitation". It was made clear, at the time the legislation was announced, that this provision was intended to take into account the plight of older women coming out of a long-term traditional single income family.

Courts are also directed to take into account four objectives of support:

(a) to recognize any economic advantages or disadvantages to the spouses arising from the marriage or its breakdown;

(b) to apportion between the spouses any financial consequences arising from the care of any child of the marriage over and above the obligation apportioned between the spouses pursuant to subsection (7);

(c) to relieve any economic hardship of the spouses arising from the breakdown of the marriage; and

(d) insofar as practicable, to promote the economic self-sufficiency of each spouse within a reasonable period of time.

Courts are, therefore, empowered to make orders of fixed duration when the goal of self-sufficiency can and should be achieved and, conversely, to make permanent orders when there is no likelihood of self-sufficiency and there is evidence of economic hardship.

Variation of Support Orders

Before a variation [of an order of fixed duration] will be considered, it must be demonstrated that present economic hardship is directly related to the marriage and the changed circumstances would have resulted in a different original order had they existed at the time of the original order. We note, however, that this provision does not include variations downward.

Child Custody and Access

The sole criteria for the making of an order of custody and access is "the best interests of the child of the marriage as determined by reference to the conditions, means, needs and other circumstances of the child". Subject to the criteria of best interests of the child is what is known as the principle of "maximum contact". A child should have as much contact with each parent as is consistent with his or her best interests and, for that purpose, courts shall consider the willingness of any person seeking custody to facilitate such contact.

Two other significant additions were made to the custody section. First, the Act seeks to eliminate the consideration of past conduct by allowing the court to consider only conduct relevant to the ability of that person to act as a parent of a child. Secondly, the legislation recognizes joint custody by permitting courts to grant custody or access to any *one or more persons*. In the marginal note is stated "joint custody or access".

The additional provisions favour non-custodial parents. First, she or he may now make inquiries and is to be given information concerning the health, education and welfare of the child. Second, the court may include a term giving the right to receive a minimum 30 day advance notice of any change in residence and the address of the new residence.

Procedures

The *Divorce Act* introduces the possibility of two new procedures both of which are intended to simplify the divorce process and to make it less adversarial. The first of these, which is built into the Act, is that parties to the divorce may now petition jointly when, presumably, no matters are in dispute. The second is that the necessity, under the previous legislation, of a trial has now been eliminated. Provinces are now permitted to make rules by which, if no matters are to be litigated, divorce may be granted by a judge without an oral hearing.

NOTES AND QUESTIONS

1. In explaining the retention of fault grounds in s. 8(2), The Hon. J.C. Crosbie, Minister of Justice, told the Ontario Branch of the Canadian Bar Association:

Many Canadians for moral or religious reasons feel that it is immoral to withhold a divorce for one year where adultery or cruelty can be shown. Others are concerned about the well-being of an abused spouse. Immediate divorce might remove the spouse from the dangerous situation. Furthermore, adultery and cruelty have long been considered proof of marriage breakdown. (Feb. 6, 1986, as quoted in Ziff, "Recent Developments in Canadian Law: Marriage and Divorce" (1986), 18 Ottawa L. Rev. 121, at 141).

2. To some extent the grounds for divorce are symbolic, signaling societal attitudes about the institution of marriage. In *Elgaard* v. *Elgaard* (1986), 1 R.F.L. (3d) 256, at 261 (B.C. S.C.), Southin J. made the following observation regarding the new *Divorce Act*:

Social attitudes have so changed since the early 1960s that Parliament . . . has embodied in legislation the concept that marriage is a trivial social custom unworthy of judicial attention. When the Act is proclaimed, a marriage will more easily be put asunder than a contract of purchase of realty.

As you study the new Act, consider whether this comment captures its essence.

3. Under the 1968 *Divorce Act*, an innocent spouse had considerable bargaining power if the other spouse wished an immediate divorce because the latter would have to wait five years before petitioning. Because this bargaining power is lost under a liberal divorce law, Doris Anderson, President of the National Action Committee on the Status of Women, described the Liberal government's reform proposals in 1984 as "bad for women" (*Calgary Herald* (January 21, 1984)). In *The Divorce Revolution: The Unexpected Social and Economic Consequences for Women and Children in America* (New York: Free Press, 1985), Lenore Weitzman also emphasized the bargaining power of innocent spouses under fault divorce. She concluded, however, (at 383): "The solution, at least for California today, is not to reintroduce fault and its penalties, but rather to strengthen the economic provisions of the new laws to assure adequate protection for wives and children." See also Ellman, "The Misguided Movement to Revive Fault Divorce, and Why Reformers Should Look Instead to the American Law Institute" (1997), 11 Int. J. Law & Fam. 216.

4. In its 1990 study of the operation of the 1985 *Divorce Act*, the Justice Department found that 82.8% of all divorce proceedings in Canada in 1987-1988 were based on the separation ground. However, in Quebec and Alberta the percentages were only 56.2 and 62.6 respectively. The study indicated (at 40) that the reason for this variation among provinces was unknown.

5. By the time a divorce proceeding instituted on the basis of either cruelty or adultery is determined by the court, the parties may have been living separate and apart for over a year. The allegations of fault are then irrelevant to the granting of the divorce. The court may decline to determine if the adultery or cruelty is proved and simply use the separate and apart ground. See *Ondik* v. *Ondik* (1994) 1 R.F.L. (4th) 376 (Sask. Q.B.) and *Liedtke* v. *Liedtke*, [1997] B.C.J. No. 1868 (S.C.).

6. Even if a divorce is based on non-fault grounds, cruelty may be relevant to other issues such as possession of the matrimonial home, spousal support, and custody and access. See Chapter 5, **THE MATRIMONIAL HOME**, Chapter 6, **SPOUSAL SUPPORT** and Chapter 7, **CUSTODY AND ACCESS**. Also, spousal abuse may be a basis for a tort action. Although Canadian family lawyers have traditionally been reluctant to make tort claims in the context of separation or divorce, more recently spousal tort actions have been joined with matrimonial claims or been litigated simultaneously with such claims. See, e.g., *Booth* v. *Booth* (1995), 80 O.A.C. 399 (C.A.); *Maher* v. *Maher*, [1995] O.J. 1497 (Gen. Div.); and *Valenti* v. *Valenti* (1996), 21 R.F.L. (4th) 246 (Ont. Gen. Div.), affirmed (1998), 41 R.F.L. (4th) 289 (Ont. C.A.). See generally, Spector, "Marital Torts: Actions for Tortious Conduct Occurring During Marriage" (1991), 5 Am. J. Fam. L. 71; Case, "Turning Marital Misery into Financial Fortune" (1994-95), 33 J. Fam. L. 10; Krause, "On the Danger of Allowing Marital Fault to Re-Emerge in the Guise of Torts" (1998), 73 Notre Dame L. Rev. 1355; and Bala, "Tort Remedies & the Family Law Practitioner" (1998-99), 16 C.F.L.Q. 423.

7. Section 9(1)(a) of the 1968 *Divorce Act* stipulated that a divorce decree could only be granted "after a trial which shall be by a judge, without jury". Section 7 of the 1985 *Divorce Act* specifies that the jurisdiction to grant a divorce "shall be exercised only by a judge of the court without a jury". There

is no longer a requirement that a formal trial be held. Section 25 of the Act gives wide power to provincial rule-making bodies to make rules governing divorce practice and procedure including the manner in which the divorce comes before the court. Further, the rule-making bodies may make rules providing for the disposition of a divorce proceeding without an oral hearing. The intent is to permit the provincial rule-making bodies to limit trials to those cases where they are absolutely necessary to deal with contested issues. Most divorces in Canada to-day are uncontested and are granted without a personal appearance in court by either party. Only in Newfoundland must a petitioner appear before a judge, even in an uncontested divorce, in what is known as a "forthwith divorce". Uncontested divorces without a hearing are referred to as "affidavit divorces" in New Brunswick, Prince Edward Island, Ontario and Manitoba; "paper divorces" in Nova Scotia and Saskatchewan; and "desk divorces" in Alberta, British Columbia and the territories. A trial will still occur where the parties contest the divorce or, more typically, issues such as support. Virtually all the divorces in the Department of Justice's Saskatoon and Ottawa samples proceeded without a formal hearing. See Department of Justice, *Evaluation of the Divorce Act: Phase II: Monitoring and Evaluation* (Ottawa: Department of Justice, Bureau of Review, 1990) (at 44-45).

8. Where the divorce is uncontested but collateral issues such as property or support remain in dispute, a court has jurisdiction to sever the issues and grant a divorce prior to the trial of the remaining issues. For cases examining whether this should be done, see *Darling* v. *Darling* (1987), 21 C.P.C. (2d) 80 (Ont. H.C.); *Heon* v. *Heon* (1988), 17 R.F.L. (3d) 417 (Ont. C.A.); *Marinovic* v. *Marinovic* (1989), 20 R.F.L. (3d) 404 (Ont. H.C.); *Zimmerman* v. *Zimmerman* (1992), 41 R.F.L. (3d) 291 (Alta. Q.B.); *McIntosh* v. *McIntosh* (1993), 49 R.F.L. (3d) 20 (Ont. Gen. Div.); *Desjardins* v. *Desjardins* (1993), 89 Man. L.R. (2d) 140 (Q.B.); *Buwalda* v. *Buwalda* (1996), 22 R.F.L. (4th) 61 (Alta. Q.B.); *Cochran* v. *Cochran* (1996), 22 R.F.L. (4th) 170 (Ont. Gen. Div.); *Friesen* v. *Friesen* (1996), 24 R.F.L. (4th) 186 (Man. C.A.); *Wong* v. *Wong* (1997), 30 R.F.L. (4th) 382 (B.C.S.C.); *Bhullar* v. *Bhullar* (1997), 33 R.F.L. (4th) 163 (B.C.S.C.); *Jones* v. *Jones* (1998), 40 R.F.L. (4th) 292 (Sask. Q.B.); and *Potter* v. *Potter* (1999), 48 R.F.L. (4th) 450 (Alta. C.A.).

9. Under the *Divorce Act*, it is possible for spouses to petition or apply jointly for a divorce on the basis of a separation for the requisite period. The Department of Justice found that slightly less than 5% of divorcing couples used this procedure: *Evaluation of the Divorce Act: Phase II: Monitoring and Evaluation* (Ottawa: Department of Justice, Bureau of Review, 1990) (at 37).

10. In 1990, the *Divorce Act* was amended to specify that the court can dismiss an application filed under the Act or strike out any other pleadings filed under the Act if the spouse has failed to remove any barriers to the remarriage of the other spouse within the latter's religion. This power might be exercised, for example, where a husband petitioning for divorce unreasonably refused to grant a gett — a divorce recognized by Jewish law — to his wife. Since Jewish law does not permit a wife to grant a gett (she only has authority to refuse to accept one), a wife who is anxious to remarry within the Jewish faith is vulnerable to undue pressure to agree to unfavourable settlement terms in exchange for a divorce recognized by her faith. The amendments are an attempt to prevent spouses from using the gett as a bargaining chip. See also ss. 2(4), (5), (6) and 56(5) of the *Family Law Act*. See generally, "Solution Sought to Problems of Jewish Divorce", *Globe and Mail* (June 15, 1985); "Ontario Measure Should Remove Simmering Jewish Divorce Issue", *Globe and Mail* (December 14, 1985); Syrtash, "Removing Barriers to Religious Remarriage in Ontario: Rights and Remedies" (1986-87) 1 C.F.L.Q. 309; "The Ties that Continue to Bind", *Globe and Mail* (January 28, 1989); "Religious Laws to be Removed as 'Bargaining Chip' in Divorces", *Globe and Mail* (December 21, 1989); and Colman, "Gett Law Must be Used Cautiously by Lawyers" *Lawyers Weekly* (July, 1997).

(2) THE SOCIAL CONTEXT OF DIVORCE

DEPARTMENT OF JUSTICE, *EVALUATION OF THE DIVORCE ACT: PHASE II: MONITORING AND EVALUATION*

(Ottawa: Department of Justice, Bureau of Review, 1990) 31-36, 41-42, IV-VI and 94-98 (Footnotes Omitted) (Reproduced with the permission of the Minister of Supply and Services Canada, 1991)

Divorce Rates in Canada

While from a demographic perspective, a number of family trends have changed rather dramatically in the past two decades, the one which has received the most attention is the marked increase in the divorce rate between 1968 and the present. There was a particularly large jump following the first uniform Canadian divorce legislation which came into force in 1968. In the year preceding this legislation, the rate was 54.8 per 100,000 people. In the year following the legislation, the rate jumped to 124.2 per 100,000 people and, contrary to expectations at the time, there has only been one three year period since 1968 when the divorce rate has fallen: 1982 to 1985. It is interesting to note that this period coincides with the end of the recession and the beginning of a period of unprecedented economic growth in Canada. . . . [I]t peaked at 285.9 per 100,000 in 1982 and, by 1985, had fallen to 244.4 per 100,000. . . .

But, since 1986, when the *Divorce Act* came into force, there has, again, been a sharp increase (308.8 and 339.5 per 100,000 population in 1986 and 1987, respectively). Because couples wishing to demonstrate marriage breakdown by separation now need be separated for one rather than three years, this increase was anticipated but was expected to be a short term phenomenon. It is, at this point premature to reach conclusions as to whether the increase can be attributed mainly to the change in legislation or represents an actual increase in marriage breakdown and divorce.

To put these rates into what are, perhaps, more understandable terms, a divorce rate of 339.5 per 100,000 population means that, in 1987, approximately 87,000 Canadian marriages were ended by divorce. Statistics Canada demographers estimate that should age-specific divorce rates remain as they have been in the 1980's, 28 to 30 percent of all Canadian marriages will end in divorce. Obviously, should the divorce rate continue to rise, this percentage will also increase. What makes divorce a public rather than a private issue is that one in two divorces, involve dependent children. Since the average number of children is 1.8 (for couples with children), this has meant that during the 1980's, annually, from 55 to 65 thousand children in Canada became "children of divorce" a figure which climbed to approximately 74,000 in 1987.

The divorce rate does not fully capture the actual rate of *marital dissolution* in Canada and elsewhere. For religious, economic or other reasons, an unknown number of couples separate through a private arrangement or provincial legislation and do not subsequently obtain a divorce; unless one wishes to remarry, there is no legal reason to do so. Since these separations are not shown in the federal divorce statistics, reliance on these, alone, provides us with only a partial picture. McVey and Robinson using census data, estimate that when separation and divorce rates are combined, the marital dissolution rate in the early 1980's was about one and a half times higher than indicated by the divorce rate. However, a limitation of their analysis is that we do not know what proportion of the divorce rate of subsequent years consists of marriages which had ended in separation at some earlier period. . . .

Divorce Reform and Marriage Breakdown

Most Canadians welcomed the reforms contained in the 1985 legislation. But, for those who believe in the sanctity of the traditional nuclear family, any movement towards liberalization of divorce laws and procedures represents an undermining of the family and are changes which should be opposed. The assumption is that the easier it is to divorce, the more likely divorce will occur. In one sense, this is of course true: if divorce is forbidden in a society, the divorce rate will be zero. But, the historical record shows that where State and/or Church have attempted to do just this, people found other ways to circumvent the law and have, generally, shown great resilience to such attempts to intervene into family matters. Thus, as our own history shows, prior to the introduction of uniform legislation in Canada, couples separated and men often deserted their wives. Simply, the divorce rate and the rate of marriage breakdown may be quite separate matters; actually seeking a divorce may often be to formalize, legally, what for some time was a *fait accompli*.

It is, in any event, extraordinarily difficult to show empirically, that there is a relationship between divorce reform and changes in the divorce rate let alone the marital dissolution rate. Present statistics seem, at first glance, to provide empirical support for those opposed to divorce reform. But, contained in the present upswing in the Canadian divorce rate is an unknown proportion of divorces which, under the previous requirement of a three year period of separation, would have entered the process in later years and been part of subsequent rather than present statistics. Further, innovations in the legislation, such as a divorce without a formal hearing and the possibility of a joint petition, may mean that divorce is now more attractive to some who would previously have sought relief through provincial legislation or have lived for a long time with a separation agreement.

More generally, it is to broader structural and cultural factors than legislative reform that we must look for explanations of what is undoubtedly a real and not just an apparent increase in marriage breakdown in recent decades. Structural factors include the greater participation rate of women in the labour force which makes divorce a more feasible alternative to an unhappy marriage. Cultural factors include the growing secularization of most Western societies, the growing emphasis on individualism, what is popularly known as the "me generation" and the general de-institutionalization of the family such that there are fewer constraints on family-type behaviour and greater tolerance for alternative family forms. These are tides of change which, in our view, cannot either be dammed through more repressive legislation or accelerated through liberal reform. . . .

Economic Consequences

In our Phase I and II samples of clients, women's average income following divorce was found to be 64 percent and 69 percent, respectively, of men's income. The difference in this ratio is due to a larger proportion of women in the Phase II than in the Phase I sample having paid employment rather than to an increase in support quantum. In Phase I, 58 percent of women had total incomes below the poverty lines for various family sizes. In our Phase II sample, some 46 percent of women who were interviewed reported total incomes below these poverty lines. In contrast, after paying support, the proportion of men with incomes below the poverty line for a one-person household was found to be 11 percent and 13 percent respectively, in the two time periods.

Despite these obvious economic inequalities between divorced men and women, a separate spousal support award is rarely requested and even more rarely incorporated as a separate award in the divorce judgement. . . .

There is an amount for child support incorporated into the final judgement in 65 and 68 percent of the divorce files reviewed in Phase I and II, respectively. Ninety percent of the women interviewed with custody of their children had requested child support compared to 21 percent of men who had been awarded sole custody. Some 93 percent of women and 61 percent of men who had made this request were granted child support. There is little change in these percentages between Phase I and II. . . .

Divorce and Impoverishment

A variety of studies, both American and Canadian, have examined the impact on men's and women's income after divorce assuming that the support is actually paid. While the percentages vary from study to study, depending on the assumptions made and methods used, the overall picture is consistent: it is mainly women and children who suffer economically from divorce. . . . Divorce, in other words, is increasingly depicted as a leading cause of feminization of poverty.

In light of these findings, considerable attention was devoted in Phase I to undertaking similar analyses of the 1986 database. The conclusion was highly similar to the previous studies and equally dismal. Some 10 percent of men were found to be below the poverty line after paying support and average income was still $13,500.00 above the poverty line for one person households. About 58 percent of women had total incomes, including employment, support and other sources of income, below these various poverty lines. Were women to depend solely on support, 97 percent of those with custody would be well below the poverty lines for various family sizes. Without these support payments, some 73 percent would be living in poverty. These statistics, then, merely confirmed, for a larger Canadian sample, that, generally, support awards are inadequate and have only marginal impact on reducing the impoverishment of women and children following divorce. . . .

NOTES

1. The number of divorces in Canada has dropped significantly since peaking at 96,200 in 1987. Statistics Canada reported on May 18, 1999 (www.statcan.ca/Daily) that 67,408 couples divorced in 1997, the lowest number since 1985. Some 39,204 divorces in 1997 involved a child custody order. The divorce rate (number of divorces per 100,000 population) fell to 222.6 in 1997. Based on 1997 rates, the percentage of marriages expected to end in divorce within 30 years of marriage declined to 34.8%. Statistics Canada speculated that a key factor in the decline in divorces was the drop in the number of marriages, from 190,640 in 1989 to 156,691 in 1996. Separations following either marriage or cohabitation without marriage are not reflected in the divorce statistics. However, there was some indication of increased marriage stability as, on average, marriages ending in divorce were lasting longer. The average duration increased from 12.3 years in 1993 to 13.3 years in 1997. In its *Report on the Demographic Situation in Canada 1998-1999* (Ministry of Industry, 1999), Statistics Canada concluded (at 41):

> There is every indication that a new downward trend in divorce has recently begun in Canada. . . . This decline in divorce could be due to a natural selection effect associated with the increase in common-law unions (there is a growing tendency for unions most likely to end in a breakdown

not to be legalized), and also to the increase in the average age at marriage [which increases the chances of stability]. Nevertheless, it is hard to predict when this downward trend will end and at what level a new stage of stability will be reached.

2. In *Selected Statistics on Canadian Families and Family Law* (November, 1997), the Department of Justice drew on various demographic studies to provide the following picture: 15% of all "census families" in 1996 were lone-parent families, 22% of all families with children were lone-parent families, 83% of lone-parent families were headed by females, and 17% of all children or 1.8 million children lived in lone-parent families. The number of families with an income below the Statistics Canada low income cut-offs (a frequently used, but controversial, basis for determining poverty levels) was 1,187,000 in 1995. Most of these families (33.2%) were two-parent families with children under 18, but 323,000 or 27.2% were headed by divorced, separated or never-married mothers. The latter family type had by far the highest poverty rate. See also National Council of Welfare, *Women and Poverty Revisited* (Ottawa: Minister of Supply and Services, 1990) and National Council of Welfare, *Poverty Profile 1995* (Spring, 1997).

3. The adverse economic effect of separation or divorce is typically greater for women than men. Focusing on married persons with children who separated between 1987 and 1993, a study entitled *Family Income After Separation* conducted by Diane Galarneau and Jim Sturrock for Statistics Canada (1997) found that one year after separation women experienced a 23% loss in family income adjusted for the number of family members. This loss (32%) was greatest for women who had not formed new relationships. At the same time, men registered a 10% gain in adjusted income. Two factors were cited to explain the gap. First, married women generally earn less than married men and so lose a major source of financial support on separation. Second, women almost always have custody of the children. See also Finnie, "Women, Men, and the Economic Consequences of Divorce: Evidence from Canadian Longitudinal Data" (1993), 30 Can. Rev. of Sociology and Anthropology 205.

RICHARDSON, "CHILDREN OF DIVORCE"

Anderson *et al.*, eds., *Family Matters: Sociology and Contemporary Canadian Families* (Toronto: Methuen, 1987) 166-174 (Footnotes Omitted) (Permission to reproduce these excerpts was granted by Nelson Canada, a division of International Thomson Publishing, which holds the copyright.)

. . . More than anyone else, small children live their lives in the circumscribed world of the family. Intuitively, therefore, we expect changes in family patterns or structure to have a momentous impact on children and children's lives. Marriage breakdown obviously begins a process of major restructuring of the family and a bewildering array of alternatives. There is, first of all, the transition from living in a nuclear family with two parents to living in a single-parent family, often with a substantial reduction in standard of living. For some children there will also be a sense of abandonment when one parent — usually the father — becomes absent. Others must learn to cope with the tension and awkwardness of now having a "weekend" father. A minority will go through the as yet little-known experience of alternating between two homes and two diverging lifestyles as a result of a joint custody arrangement. And for many children there is the likelihood that they will acquire one or more stepparents as their parents make the shift from divorce back into marriage. . . .

But, just as there are many types of marriage, so there are many types of divorce. Some couples, on their own or with the help of professionals, may end their marriage rather amicably and continue to co-operate in matters affecting their children. Others will continue to be hostile to one another long after the divorce is granted, and may use the children to wound and attack one another. Moreover, the breakdown of a marriage in an impoverished family will have quite different economic consequences and entail quite different stresses than in families better able to handle legal costs and setting up new households.

There is also the question of whether, when we talk about the effects of divorce on children, we are concerned with such short-term effects as regression, return to bed-wetting, discipline problems, truancy, and juvenile delinquency, or with long-term effects on their later adult personality and interpersonal behaviour and skills such as, for example, an inability to form close relationships, lower self-esteem, or the greater likelihood that they, too, will become divorced.

RESEARCH INTO THE EFFECTS OF DIVORCE ON CHILDREN

Understandably, given the complexity of the problems facing children and the variety of ways couples go about ending a marriage, researchers have put considerable effort into assessing the impact on children of divorce and separation. With some simplification, we can say that this research falls into several related categories or areas of inquiry. First, a sizeable body of research has sought, but quite unsuccessfully, to demonstrate that divorce is a direct cause of a number of emotional, cognitive, and behavioural problems in children. These include such things as retarded emotional development, poor school performance, delinquency, and discipline problems. A second and closely related body of research is what has come to be called the "father absent" literature. That is, since most separated or divorced families are headed by females, there has been considerable effort devoted to determining the consequences for children of growing up without a father or alternative male figure.

Another body of research has been concerned with the more easily measured and obvious economic consequences that follow from marriage breakdown, and the impact these have on the subsequent life chances of children. Finally, much of the more recent research has attempted to describe children's experience and their feelings about divorce, and to assess the various factors associated with this important change in a child's life.

Despite our intuitive sense that the breakup of the parents' marriage should have momentous and easily observable consequences for children, it turns out to be extremely difficult to generalize about the aftermath of divorce and separation. . . .

[T]he major problem in determining the effects of divorce on children is that it is extraordinarily difficult to sort out what is an effect of divorce per se and what is the result of other factors. In particular, we can expect that prior to actual separation there will usually have been considerable marital discord. Although it seems that the children are sometimes not aware of this, or of the magnitude of the conflict between their parents, there nevertheless remains the question of whether it is the experience of having lived in an unhappy family or the breakup of their parents' marriage which is the crucial factor. . . .

As with other research in this area, the results of father-absence research are inconclusive. While some studies have found negative effects for children where the father is absent, many have not; and some have even reported positive effects for children of having their father absent from the family. What is apparent is that father absence is related to poverty and, in turn, poverty is related to a variety of behavioural and psychological problems.

. . .

CHILDREN'S EXPERIENCE OF MARITAL BREAKDOWN

The inconclusive nature of research on divorce outcomes and father absence should not be taken to mean that the breakup of the parents' marriage does not have emotional impact on children. Indeed, as more and more studies have been done which rely on the accounts of children themselves, we are learning that parents may often seriously underestimate or be unaware of how extremely difficult a time it is for children and what feelings of anger, bitterness, confusion, and guilt are engendered. Much of this, particularly guilt, may be inexplicable to adults. . .

Most studies of children in divorce have been able to take only one measure, and have had to rely mainly on parents' and children's memories of feelings at the time of the separation. That is, there have been few longitudinal studies designed to follow children from the point of separation to several years after. The much-cited exception is the ambitious study by Judith Wallerstein and Joan Kelly, *Surviving the Breakup*. The authors studied 60 California families (with 131 children) from the point of separation through a five-year follow-up. In addition, one of the authors (Wallerstein) is carrying out a ten-year follow-up study of these same families.

Surviving the Breakup is a rich and complex study, not easy to summarize in a few paragraphs. However, in general, it shows that for all of the children the breakup of their parents' marriage was a highly stressful and disruptive experience, and that the effects of the divorce persist long after the actual separation. At the time of the separation, the breakup of the family evoked in these children "shock, intense fears and grieving." While all lived in Marin County, California, notorious for its high rate of marital instability, the ordinariness of marriage breakdown was irrelevant to their level of distress and fear about what the future would hold. Nor did it seem to matter what level of conflict had preceded the parents' decision to separate.

The research suggests also that divorce has different kinds of impact and evokes different responses in children of different ages. Pre-school children were often very confused about the meaning of the separation, and blamed themselves. Their response was to regress in terms of toilet training and speech. Older children generally understood what was happening but manifested their concerns through anger and depression. At the 18-month follow-up, things had not improved very much, and some children were found to be actually worse off than when initially interviewed. Even at the five-year point, some 37 percent of the children were still "moderately to severely depressed." This finding, and the fact that many of the children had not come to terms with their parents' divorce, lead the authors to conclude that divorce is a process which takes place over a much more extended period than had previously been assumed.

The findings from the Wallerstein and Kelly study present a rather bleak picture of the effects of divorce on children. However, we should be cautious about generalizing their findings as being necessarily true of all children of divorce. As noted earlier, the respondents in this study were ones who had been seen as in need of counselling and came from families perhaps more distressed than the normal population of divorcing families. . . . As the authors acknowledge, by the five-year follow-up, many other factors besides the divorce of their parents had also been at work. Finally, the children of the study were not compared with a group of children from intact families. . . .

Despite these qualifications, *Surviving the Breakup* is an important study. Its real contribution is made, not in showing that children are upset and distressed when their parents separate — we would expect that — but in its ability to identify what helps or hinders children to adjust to their new situation. Two key factors emerge as helpful: 1) easy access and an ongoing relationship with a non-custodial parent, and 2) a post-divorce mother-father relationship in which conflict is kept to a minimum. . . .[T] these two findings bolster the case for joint custody and shared parenting and the need for separation and divorce counselling and mediation.

REPORT OF THE SPECIAL JOINT COMMITTEE ON CHILD CUSTODY AND ACCESS, *FOR THE SAKE OF THE CHILDREN* (December, 1998) (pp. 7-15).

[In 1997, the federal government introduced legislation adopting child support guidelines and ending the tax regime whereby child support was a deduction from the payor's income and an inclusion in the recipient's income. To assuage critics and gain the support of conservative Senators, the government agreed to establish a joint committee of the Senate and the House of Commons to study custody and access. The controversial hearings that followed often featured fathers' groups presenting their grievances to a generally sympathetic committee. The committee's recommendations and the government's response will be examined in Chapter 7, **Custody and Access.**]

The Committee was given a mandate to assess the need for a more child-centred approach to family law policies that would emphasize joint parental responsibilities and child-focused parenting arrangements based on children's needs and best interests. . . .

The Committee heard directly from children about how divorce had affected their lives. These children, who presented as individuals and in groups, told the Committee about the pain and upset that their parents' divorce had caused them. They spoke about their worries and fears, their sense of loss, and their feelings of exclusion from a legal process that had such a direct impact on their lives. These children wanted changes in the ways their parents and the courts made decisions that affected them. In particular, the children and young adults who testified about the impact of their parents' divorce stressed the need for more formal and informal mechanisms for child participation in decisions about parenting arrangements. Children who reported a positive experience to the Committee generally described post-separation arrangements in which their relationship with both parents was unrestricted and a good deal of control over schedules was in their own hands.

A. Statistics About Children and Divorce

The high divorce rate meant that in 1994 and 1995, more than 47,000 children were the subjects of custody orders under the *Divorce Act*. As a result, more children - and younger children - are experiencing rearrangements in their households. Their parents' remarriages or other new relationships following divorce compound the complexity of these children's lives. Some 75% of divorced men and women re-marry, so that children from first marriages have to develop relationships with step-parents. In 1992, 13% of divorces were of second marriages. Professor James Richardson of the University of New Brunswick, who testified during a meeting in Fredericton, has looked at some of the reasons for the increased divorce rate and concluded that our attitudes about marriage have changed significantly in recent years. First, people no longer believe they should marry or stay married or have children to conform with community expectations. Second, people "take it for granted that they will marry for love and emotional gratification rather than for economic or other instrumental reasons." Third, "more people now than in the past can afford to base marriage on emotional rather than purely economical considerations."[1]

Although the divorce rate is increasing, Richardson reports that most divorces are concluded without extensive conflict over parenting arrangements. Referring to a 1990 Department of Justice study, Richardson reports that in Canada,

> well over 90% of divorces are now granted without a formal court hearing. As only non-contested divorces can be processed in this way, it is evident that, contrary to popular and media images of divorce, most divorces do not involve bitter and protracted battles over custody and property. Indeed, the evidence from the evaluations is that less than 5% of divorces are contested to the extent that matters must be settled in court. The central issues in these are more often spousal and child support, and division of property, than child custody.[2]

Finally, Richardson comments on custody arrangements after divorce:

> The evidence, then, shows that there is no great revolution with respect to child custody. Apparently, most divorcing spouses believe that children are better off with the mother, and the matter is not formally contested. While fathers' rights groups have been able to point to the exceptions, the reality is that most fathers are not interested in custody and day-to-day care of the children (or are advised by their lawyers that their chances of success are probably slim).[3]

Richardson's assertions were contested by many of the witnesses who testified before this Committee.

B.   Attitudes Toward Divorce

Most Canadians consider divorce to be a right. Adults are free to marry whom they wish, and if one of the partners finds the relationship unsatisfactory, unhealthy, or unsafe, he or she is free to end the relationship through divorce. The 1985 changes to the *Divorce Act* removed most of the blame from divorce proceedings, and since then Canada has had, in effect, no-fault divorce.

When Canada joined other countries and moved toward less constraining divorce law in the 1960s, '70s, and '80s, the prevalent assumption held by mental health professionals was that it was better for children to grow up in a divorced family than to grow up in a family where at least one of the parents was unhappy with the relationship. While acknowledging that divorce is a difficult and painful experience for all family members, the prevailing belief was that divorce did not cause long-term harm to children. Clinical literature from that era focused on the need for preventive counselling for children. It was assumed that if children were given the opportunity to talk about their feelings, long-term emotional complications could be avoided.

For example, Dr. Richard Gardner, known more recently for his ideas about parental alienation syndrome, wrote in his 1970 book, *The Boys and Girls Book about Divorce*, "the child living with unhappily married parents more often gets into psychiatric difficulties than the one whose mismatched parents have been healthy and strong enough to sever their troubled relationship."

---

1 Richardson, "Divorce and Remarriage" in *Families: Changing Trends in Canada* (Toronto: McGraw-Hill Ryerson, 1996) at 233.

2 *Ibid*, at 231.

3 *Ibid*, at 234.

The assumption that children would be better off in a divorced family than in a stressed or difficult intact family resulted in a significant shift in professional thinking about divorce. Until the 1970s, divorce often carried a social stigma, but since then it has become more acceptable in Canadian society. Many articles in the professional literature commented on the relative harmlessness of divorce. Although divorce was recognized as stressful, it was not thought to present any serious emotional dangers for those who experienced it. Happy parents, even if they lived apart, were thought to be able to provide the best environment for their children.

In fact, divorce was seen by many as an opportunity to leave behind a flawed relationship and try again. A 1975 report of the Law Reform Commission of Canada suggested that "divorce is not necessarily destructive to family life." The Commission argued that since many divorced people remarry, "divorce may sometimes offer a constructive solution to marital conflict through the provision of new and more viable homes for spouses and children."

The Committee heard several witnesses testify that most divorces in Canada are "low-conflict" divorces. These witnesses claimed that up to 90% of divorcing parents do so with only minimal conflict. Such parents are apparently able to dissolve their marriages and make good plans for the children without having to go to court. Since mental health research shows that children are harmed by exposure to continuing conflict between parents, it might seem to follow that low-conflict divorces would not be permanently damaging to children.

All witnesses agreed, however, that high-conflict divorces are very damaging to the children and the adults involved. No one could give an accurate number for these situations, but the often quoted 10% figure means that, based on the 1994-95 statistics, approximately 4,700 children each year are exposed to ongoing tension, fighting, and even violence between their parents.

C. The Impact of Divorce on Children

In hearings across Canada, the Committee heard moving evidence about the negative impact of divorce on children. Very few witnesses supported the assertion that decisions made on the basis of the parents' right to personal happiness were automatically in the children's best interests. Witnesses' evidence of the detrimental effects of divorce on their children is supported to a great extent by more recent mental health literature on this subject.

> Divorce is seen from an individual's as opposed to societal perspective. The *Divorce Act* gives legal status to an individual's decision to terminate his or her marriage, thus recognizing, for legal purposes, an individual's right to marry and to end a marriage. The fact that this individual right, if realized, may impact on the rights of others is not recognized in our laws. Accordingly, the balance of rights, which characterizes most social legislation, is absent from divorce and family law legislation. (Alexandra Raphael, Meeting #13, Toronto)

A few witnesses even suggested that the current no-fault divorce law should be repealed and parents should be required to stay together for the sake of their children. This thinking is apparently behind recent changes in divorce law in the state of Louisiana, which have made it more difficult for parents with children to have access to a quick no-fault divorce. In effect since August 1997, the Louisiana *Covenant Marriage Act* obliges couples to have premarital counseling and to seek marriage counseling if problems arise. The act also reintroduces the concept of conduct into applications for divorce.

In 1989 Judith Wallerstein and Sandra Blakeslee published *Second Chances: Men, Women and Children a Decade after Divorce.* This groundbreaking study, cited by a number of witnesses, followed 161 children from 60 families for 10 years after a divorce. The study provoked a great deal of reaction from mental health professionals, because the findings challenged the idea that most children are unharmed by divorce. Contrary to Wallerstein's own expectations, most of the children in her study showed severe difficulties in school and in personal and social relationships. There was a noticeable increase in drug and alcohol use and a higher rate of delinquency. The children of divorce showed high rates of depression, aggression and social withdrawal. The study also challenged the idea that helping children express their feelings in therapy at the time of divorce would have long-term preventive benefits. Many were experiencing serious difficulties in their adult relationships.

The professional reaction to this work was highly skeptical. Critics argued that Wallerstein's sample was too small and questioned her research methodology. However, almost ten years later, at the 1998 Annual Conference of the Association of Family and Conciliation Courts in Washington, D.C. - which was attended by a group of Members of this Committee - a panel of sociologists and psychologists argued that Wallerstein's findings were correct, because larger research studies in the United States and Great Britain had subsequently supported them.

Lamb, Sternberg and Thompson wrote about the negative impact of divorce on children in 1997:

> Most children of divorce experience dramatic declines in their economic circumstances, abandonment (or the fear of abandonment) by one or both parents, the diminished capacity of both parents to attend meaningfully and constructively to their children's needs (because they are preoccupied with their own psychological, social and economic distress as well as stresses related to the legal divorce), and diminished contact with many familiar or potential sources of psychosocial support (friends, neighbours, teachers, schoolmates, etc.) as well as familiar living settings. As a consequence, the experience of divorce is a psychosocial stressor and significant life transition for most children, with long-term repercussions for many. Some children from divorced homes show long-term behaviour problems, depression, poor school performance, acting out, low self-esteem, and (in adolescence and young adulthood) difficulties with intimate heterosexual relationships.[4]

Amato and Keith analyzed 37 divorce studies, involving 81,000 individuals, that investigated the long-term consequences of parental divorce for adult well-being. This analysis showed a significant pattern of problematic after-effects for adults and children. The authors concluded:

> The data show that parental divorce has broad negative consequences for quality of life in adulthood. These include depression, low life satisfaction, low marital quality and divorce, low educational attainment, income, and occupational prestige, and physical health problems. These results lead to a pessimistic conclusion: the argument that parental divorce presents few problems for children's long-term development is simply inconsistent with the literature on this topic.[5]

In 1997, Hope, Power and Rodgers reported on a research project that used as its base a national longitudinal study of 11,407 men and women born in Britain in

---

4 "The Effects of Divorce and Custody Arrangements on Children's Behaviour, Development and Adjustment" (1997-98), 35 Family and Reconciliation Courts Review 395-96.
5 "Parental Divorce and Adult Well-being: A Meta-analysis" (1991), 53 Journal of Marriage and the Family 54.

1958.[6] This study showed that by the age of 33, the adult children of divorced parents were much more likely to engage in problem drinking than adults whose parents had not divorced.

Finally, Wallerstein's research showed that ways had not yet been found to prepare children adequately for the stress of divorce. Therapy and counseling may be helpful at the time, but they do not seem to have long-term preventive effects.

Recent studies on children's attachment patterns also indicate that divorce can cause serious emotional difficulties for younger children (0 to 48 months). . . . Dr. Pamela Ludolph and Dr. Michelle Viro reported in 1998 that even the normal upset and disorganization caused by a so-called friendly divorce caused young children to slip from secure feelings of attachment to insecure attachment behaviour. In high-conflict cases, secure children were observed to slip to disorganized and disoriented states of attachment with their parents.[7]

Both the mental health literature and the testimony of witnesses, especially the young people, have convinced this Committee that the impact of divorce on children is significant and potentially harmful. Parents and their advisers must be made aware of the potential repercussions of their decisions on their children and work to minimize any damage. Certainly a number of mitigating factors, many of which are within the control of parents, can ameliorate the post-separation scenario for children. The Committee was impressed by the creative solutions adopted by some parents and encouraged by the handful of very positive stories we heard about successful parenting arrangements. By expanding our understanding of the consequences of divorce for children and investigating all potential aids to parents and children dealing with divorce, this Committee and the others who continue with this work can contribute to improving outcomes for children whose parents divorce.

A number of issues were brought to the Committee by groups and individuals representing the interests of the adult members of divorcing families. Many women presented the Committee with ideas and concerns about parenting arrangements for children after divorce. Some witnesses were mothers who told of their personal experiences. Others represented local and national women's groups. Others spoke of their experiences working in social service agencies and women's shelters. These witnesses identified three main areas of concern.

First, they testified that violence is a major problem for many women during their marriages and that the risk of violence for women and children escalates around the time of separation. Many individual women, as well as researchers and representatives from women's groups, community social service agencies, and women's shelters, testified about domestic violence. These witnesses often referred to statistics documenting the prevalence of violence against women, including Statistics Canada's *Violence Against Women Survey*. That 1993 survey, which documented the experiences of 12,000 women, indicated that 29% of Canadian women reported experiencing violence in their married or common-law relationships. . . .

Second, they told the Committee that in most families women are still the primary caregivers for children and questioned why this arrangement should change dramatically after divorce. Advocates for women insisted that, in the majority of cases, women are the primary caregivers of children before separation and should

---

6 "The Relationship between Parental Separation in Childhood and Problem Drinking in Adulthood" (1998), 93 Addiction 505.

7 "Attachment Theory and Research: Implications for Professionals Assisting Families of High Conflict Divorce" (Paper Given at 35th Annual Conference of the Association of Family and Conciliation Courts, Washington, D.C., May, 1998).

therefore continue in that role after separation and divorce. These witnesses stated that most women today would prefer that their husbands play a more prominent role in child care, but they referred to studies showing that women continue to have primary responsibility for the day-to-day care of children. Women's advocates argued that many men ask for shared parenting after divorce in order to continue to exercise control over decision making by their former wives or to avoid having to pay as much financial support for their children, not out of a genuine desire to share parenting responsibilities. . . .

Finally, these witnesses reported that problems with shared parenting arrangements are not a question of denial of parenting time: they testified that it is often difficult to keep fathers involved with children after divorce.

Although many fathers testified about the problem of denial of access, many women argued that the problem for them was the opposite: fathers who do not make use of the access they have been given by agreement or in a court order. Mothers and women's groups testified that, in these types of situations, it is the mothers who have to deal with their children's disappointment, sadness and anger when their fathers do not appear when expected. . . .

As has been widely reported by the media, many fathers from across Canada testified before the Committee. Some began preparing their presentations and alerting others to the Committee's existence before public hearings were officially announced. Whether testifying as individuals or as representatives of fathers' groups, these men shared their profound unhappiness about difficult separations and divorces that culminate all too often in a minimal or non-existent relationship with their children. Most of these witnesses emphasized the importance of strong father-child relationships after divorce.

The main grievances brought to the Committee by these witnesses related to obstacles to maintaining fathers' relationships with their children, such as gender bias in the courts, unethical practices by lawyers, flaws in the legal system, false allegations of abuse, parental alienation, and inadequate enforcement of access orders and agreements. . . .

D. Child-Parent Relationships Must Survive Divorce

The Committee heard a great deal of moving and sincere testimony from parents, grandparents and professionals about the harm done to children when their relationship with one parent is interfered with by the other parent. Non-residential parents, often fathers, testified not only about their own pain when parenting time is denied, but also about the harm that such denial does to their children.

A great deal of the professional literature about children and divorce concludes that it is in the child's best interests to have continuing contact with both parents after divorce. The exception to this general rule arises when the child experiences violence by one parent toward the child or the other parent. In these cases, most experts believe that the abusive parent's parenting time should be restricted or supervised. . . .

Edward Kruk, a professor of social work at the University of British Columbia, has studied children and divorce for 20 years. He testified about a U.S. study showing that over 50% of children lose contact with their non-custodial fathers. Using 1994 Canadian data showing that there were 47,667 children about whom there was a custody decision, 33,164 of whom were placed in sole custody arrangements with their mother, Professor Kruk concluded that 16,582 of these children would eventually lose all contact with their fathers.

Those who work in the area of grief and loss say that there is nothing worse than the loss of a child, no matter how that loss came about, but there is something far worse; for a child, the loss of a parent who's been a constant, loving presence in one's life, the loss of a parent who is part of who one is, an integral part of one's identity. (Edward Kruk, Meeting #27, Vancouver)

PAYNE, "THE DICHOTOMY BETWEEN FAMILY LAW AND FAMILY CRISES ON MARRIAGE BREAKDOWN"

(1989), 20 R.G.D. 109

I. THE THREE CRISES OF MARRIAGE BREAKDOWN

For most families, marriage breakdown provokes three crises: an emotional crisis; an economic crisis; and a parenting crisis. Both spouses and their children suffer severe emotional upheaval when the unity of the family disintegrates. Failure in the most basic of life's commitments is not lightly shrugged off by its victims. Marriage breakdown, whether or not accompanied by divorce, is a painful experience. Furthermore, relatively few families weather the storm of spousal separation or divorce without encountering serious financial hardship. The emotional and economic crises resulting from marriage breakdown are compounded by the co-parental divorce when there are dependent children. Bonding between children and their absent parent is inevitably threatened by spousal separation and divorce.

Paul Bohannan identified six "stations" in the highly complex human process of marriage breakdown: (i) the emotional divorce; (ii) the legal divorce; (iii) the economic divorce; (iv) the co-parental divorce; (v) the community divorce; and (vi) the psychic divorce. Each of these stations of divorce involves an evolutionary process and there is substantial interaction between them. The dynamics of marriage breakdown, which are multi-faceted, cannot be addressed in isolation. History demonstrates a predisposition to seek the solution to the crises of marriage breakdown in external systems. During the past one hundred and fifty years, the Church, Law and Medicine have each been called upon to face the crises of marriage breakdown. Understandably, each system has been found wanting in its search for solutions. People are naturally averse to losing control over their own lives. Decrees and "expert" rulings that exclude the affected parties from the decision-making process do not pass unchallenged. Omniscience is not the prerogative of any profession. Nor should the family's right to self-determination be lightly ignored. Let us, therefore, address the three crises of marriage breakdown in that light.

II. THE EMOTIONAL CRISIS

For many people, there are two criteria of self-fulfilment. One is satisfaction on the job. The other, and more important one, is satisfaction in the marital or familial environment. When marriage breakdown occurs, there is a fundamental sense of loss and isolation, if not desolation, that is experienced by each of the spouses. Separated spouses find themselves living alone in a couples-oriented society. The concept of the "swinging single" was belied by reality long before the AIDS crisis. The devastating effect of marriage breakdown is particularly evident with the displaced long-term homemaking spouse whose united family has crumbled and who is ill-equipped, both psychologically and otherwise, to convert homemaking skills into significant gainful employment.

In Canada, eighty-five per cent of divorces are uncontested and only a relatively small proportion of initally contested cases result in protracted litigation. Issues relating to the economic and parenting consequences of marriage breakdown are typically resolved by negotiation between the spouses, who are usually represented by independent lawyers. Because the overwhelming majority of all divorces are uncontested, it might be assumed that the legal system works well in resolving the economic and parenting consequences of marriage breakdown. That assumption, however, cannot pass unchallenged.

In the typical divorce scenario, the spouses negotiate a settlement at a time when one or both are undergoing the emotional trauma of marriage breakdown. Psychiatrists and psychologists agree that the "emotional divorce" passes through a variety of states, including denial, hostility and depression, to the ultimate acceptance of the reality of the death of the marriage. A constructive resolution of the spousal emotional divorce requires the passage of time, which varies according to the circumstances but is rarely less, and not infrequently more, than twelve months. In the interim, decisions, often of a permanent and legally binding nature, are made to regulate the economic and parenting consequences of the marriage breakdown. From the lawyer's perspective, the economic and parenting consequences of marriage breakdown are interdependent. Decisions respecting any continued occupation of the matrimonial home, the amount of child support, and the amount of spousal support, if any, are conditioned on the arrangements made for the future upbringing of the children. The perceived legal interdependence of property rights, support rights and parental rights after divorce naturally affords opportunities for abuse by lawyers and their clients. The lawyer who has been imbued with "the will to win" from the outset of his or her career, coupled with the client who negotiates a settlement when his or her emotional divorce is unresolved, can wreak future havoc on the spouses and on the children, the innocent victims of the broken marriage. All too often, when settlements are negotiated, the children become pawns or weapons in the hands of game-playing or warring adults and the battles do not cease with the judicial dissolution of the marriage.

The interplay between the emotional dynamics of marriage breakdown and regulation of the economic consequences of marriage breakdown may be demonstrated in a meaningful way to lawyers by reference to the following examples. A *needy* spouse who insists that no claim for spousal support should be pursued may well be manifesting a hope for reconciliation, a sense of guilt respecting the marriage breakdown, or a state of depression. A spouse who insists that his or her marital partner be "nailed to the wall" is obviously manifesting hostility. And a spouse who proffers an unduly generous financial settlement may be expiating guilt or temporarily calming the potentially troubled waters of a new "meaningful relationship". Guilt, depression and hostility are all typical manifestations of the emotional divorce. Like most emotional states, however, they will change with the passage of time. Practicing lawyers, who ignore the human dynamics of marriage breakdown, should not be unduly surprised if returning clients take no solace from the "finality doctrine" espoused by the Supreme Court of Canada in *Pelech*, *Richardson* and *Caron*. Lawyers, like mediators, should always be aware of the dangers of premature settlements. Indeed, the notion of a "cooling-off" period, though unsuccessful as a means of divorce avoidance in jurisdictions in which it was implemented, might have significant attractions in the context of negotiated spousal settlements on marriage breakdown. Certainly, lawyers should more frequently assess the strategic potential of interim agreements as a possible "stage" in a longer-term divorce adjustment and negotiation process.

Lawyers must not only be alert to the fact that the legal divorce and the emotional divorce are not coincidental in point of time. They must also be alert to the fact that the emotional divorce is not usually contemporaneous for the respective spouses. Lawyers frequently encounter situations where one spouse regards the marriage as over but the other spouse is unable or unwilling to accept that reality. In circumstances where one of the spouses is adamantly opposed to cutting the marital umbilical cord, embittered negotiations or contested litigation over custody or access, support or property division often reflect the unresolved emotional divorce. Spouses who have not worked their way through the emotional divorce "displace" what is essentially a non-litigable issue relating to the preservation or dissolution of the marriage by fighting over one or more of these litigable issues. Not surprisingly, therefore, the judicial divorce often fails to terminate the spousal hostilities arising from the emotional trauma of marriage breakdown. And when the legal battles over support and property have been finally adjudicated by the courts, the most effective means of continuing the spousal conflict is through the children. . . .

III. THE ECONOMIC CRISIS

. . .

For the vast majority of Canadian families, spousal property entitlements on marriage breakdown cannot provide long-term economic security for the future. Where one spouse is a high income earner, constructive implementation of the new statutory criteria for spousal support can mitigate the economic crises that so frequently face the displaced long-term homemaker on divorce. Only a small minority of Canadian families, however, will benefit over the long-term in consequence of federal and provincial legislative responses to capital and income redistribution on divorce or marriage breakdown through the mechanisms of property sharing and spousal and child support orders.

Equal property sharing regimes, the formulation of sound policy objectives respecting spousal support, and more effective enforcement processes, which were recently implemented by the joint cooperation of the federal and provincial governments to ensure the discharge of support obligations, will not significantly reduce the economic deprivation sustained by dependent spouses and their children on marriage breakdown. There is ample empirical evidence to demonstrate that, even if all support orders were paid in full and on time, the vast majority of recipients would be destined to live at or near the poverty level. In an age of sequential marriages, solutions to the financial crises of marriage breakdown must be sought not simply within the parameters of Family Law, but in social and economic policies that promote the financial viability of all persons in need, including the victims of marriage breakdown. The war on the feminization of poverty must be won by innovative and coherent socio-economic policies that effectively promote equal pay and equal opportunities for men and women in the labour force and that guarantee a basic income for all financially disadvantaged Canadians. The opportunities for paid employment in the home, rather than the office or factory, the development of well-defined policies for job sharing, and the feasibility of establishing child care or nursery facilities in the schools or in places of employment must be more fully explored. The relationship between support payments, social assistance and earned income must also be rationalized if a reasonable level of income security is to be guaranteed to the economic victims of marriage breakdown. Otherwise, faced with the projection that 40 per cent of all married Canadians will divorce at least once and the fact that the average duration of dissolved marriages is between 10 and 12 years, it is probable that the private law system of spousal and child support will ultimately break down under the strain of sequentially dissolved marriages. At or before that time, the State will be required to intervene to guarantee basic income security for all Canadians, including the increasing number of economic victims of marriage breakdown. Indeed, by the 21st century, it is likely that the private law system of Family Law as we know it today will be the exclusive preserve of the wealthy classes. Administrative systems of income redistribution, will, in all probability, regulate the economic consequences of marriage breakdown or divorce for the vast majority of Canadian families. . . .

While there is little doubt that the mediation process can more adequately respond to the emotional trauma of marriage breakdown than any formal and relatively rigid legal process, it must be realized that neither process will resolve the economic crises of divorce. Both lawyers and mediators, nevertheless, have a role to play in addressing potential solutions to these crises. Most lawyers are generally aware of the income tax implications of support payments and spousal property redistribution on marriage breakdown. But how many lawyers or mediators are familiar with existing social welfare schemes that provide some minimal income security for the financial disadvantaged or with the potential for subsidized housing or with training programmes for entry or re-entry into the labour force? There is a lesson to be learned from the following extra-judicial observations of Madam Justice Bertha Wilson of the Supreme Court of Canada:

> Where the parties were living close to the poverty line prior to the breakdown of the marriage so that there simply is not enough money to support them both in separate establishments, then the court must look beyond the parties' own resources and make an award which is fair, having regard to any welfare entitlement either may have. [. . .] It is fair to say, on the basis of very sparse Canadian authority, that we are beginning to think about the relationship between family law as administered by the courts and welfare as administered by the state. We are groping for the right principles and the right policies. We are, however, a long way from the level of sophistication in England and other common law jurisdictions, where the welfare implications of various levels of awards are put before the courts in the same way as the tax implications are now being put before the courts here. . . .

IV. THE PARENTING CRISIS

. . .

The notion that fighting over children, whether in or out of court, can provide a therapeutic catharsis for all or any members of the family is generally condemned by professionals in all disciplines. Embittered negotiations or protracted litigation between warring spouses, championed by aggressive legal gladiators, cannot heal the inevitable wounds of marriage breakdown. Indeed, they re-open the wounds and allow them to fester long after the legal conflict has been terminated. The infection usually spreads to the children and impairs the prospect of meaningful child bonds being preserved with the absent parent after the marriage breakdown.

It must be conceded that custody litigation is rare. The same is not true of access disputes that arise after the marriage breakdown. This is clearly demonstrated by the pre-Christmas blitz of access applications before the courts. The potential for post-dissolution counselling in this context has been described in the following words by Florence Bienenfeld, a Senior Family Counselor on the staff of the Conciliation Court, Superior Court, Los Angeles County, California:

> Post-dissolution visitation counseling in court settings is still very new. I consider it one of our most valuable services to the community. If help is not given in time to help these parents develop a cooperative post-dissolution parental relationship, great harm can result not only to their children, but their children's children. I believe that this post-dissolution visitation counseling

service has the potential of being able to break this vicious cycle and help parents move forward, away from the hostility of the marriage. This helps the parents to become more helpful, effective and responsive to the needs of their children.

This service to couples already divorced grew out of the court's ongoing concern for the best interests of the children. The success of this service cannot be measured only in terms of the number of amicable agreements reached. Either way, parents still take important things away from the counselling experience. At times, the parties that were unable to reach an agreement contact the Conciliation Court at a later date, willing to continue to work on unresolved problems.

This service provides the opportunity for parents to leave the dark past and to take themselves and their children into the light once again.

Too much emphasis may be placed, however, on court-connected counselling or conciliation services. Indeed, most behavioural scientist [sic] acknowledge that therapeutic counselling in family conflict situations must not be confined to circumstances in which litigation is imminent. If we are to avoid the dangers of "too little, too late", the need for community-based mediation and counselling services must be acknowledged.

The inherent limitations of the law and the legal process in resolving the parenting crises of marriage breakdown may be exemplified by the following scenarios. Relatively recently, courts have retreated from their former aversion to impose the sanctions of imprisonment or fine on the custodial parent who persistently denies court-ordered access privileges to the non-custodial parent. Such sanctions do not, of course, re-establish harmony between the warring parents. Nor are they likely to cement any bond between the children and their non-custodial parent. Committal for contempt, to use the legal terminology, provides a punitive response to disrespect for the administration of justice. Imprisonment or fines may be inappropriate, however, if viewed from the child's perspective. Nor does the civil remedy of an order for a change of custody resolve the problem. A custodial parent, who alienates a child from his or her non-custodial parent, may evoke trenchant criticism but that is hardly a sufficient basis in itself for ordering a change in the parenting arrangements. Indeed, the more successful the alienation, the greater the reason for denying a change of custody, unless a counselling bridge can re-construct the lost bonding between the absent parent and the child. Cases involving parental child abduction pose similar problems. Judicial application of the legal maxim that a person should not benefit from his or her own wrongdoing has little, or no, place in determining the appropriate environment for the child. Penal sanctions may be imposed for parental child abduction pursuant to the provisions of the *Criminal Code*, but concepts of guilt and punishment should not be paramount in civil proceedings wherein the "best interests of the child" is the determinative criterion.

It is obvious that we must look beyond legal solutions. The focus must be on prevention, not punitive sanctions. There is no doubt that the law has come a long way during the past decade in shifting the focus away from the adversarial legal process as a means of resolving the parenting crises of marriage breakdown. In 1982, the voluntary mediation of parenting disputes was legislatively endorsed in Ontario by section 31 of the *Children's Law Reform Amendment Act*. In addition, section 30 of the *Act* empowered the courts to order a mandatory independent assessment in custody and access disputes, even if neither parent consented. The federal *Divorce Act, 1985* imposed a duty on lawyers to advise their clients of the advisability of resolving custody, access and support disputes by negotiation or mediation. These legislative provisions clearly acknowledge the limitations of the adversarial legal process.

NOTES

1. In *Young* v. *Young*, 49 R.F.L. (3d) 117, [1993] 4 S.C.R. 3, Justice L'Heureux-Dubé described (at R.F.L. 208-211) several influential studies of the effects of divorce on children:

> I acknowledge at the outset the limits in applying such research to the wider population, as the studies to date have tended to focus on groups within a particular social class or locale. Furthermore, the conclusions of some studies, for example, those by Judith S. Wallerstein and Joan Berlin Kelly, *Surviving the Breakup: How Children and Parents Cope with Divorce* (New York: Basic Books, 1980), have been used to support a number of different propositions concerning the best intersts of the child on divorce. (See M. Fineman, *The Illusion of Equality*, [(Chicago: University of Chicago Press: 1991)] at p. 118.) In addition, notions concerning the optimum child-rearing conditions on the breakdown of the marriage are subject to a degree of difference and controversy between professionals working in the field. This is illustrated, for example, in the contrasting conclusions reached by Goldstein, Freud, and Solnit [*Beyond the Best Interests of the Child* (New York: Free Press, 1979)], and those of Wallerstein and Kelly.
>
> Nonetheless, a number of conclusions about the effects of divorce on children emerge with remarkable consistency in all of the major studies and psychological literature on children after divorce. One of the most important of these is the role of conflict in the welfare of the child. Along with the quality of the relationship with the custodial parent and the ability to maintain contact with the non-custodial parent, there is substantial evidence that continuing conflict is the most important factor affecting the ability of children to readjust to the new family situation after divorce (Weisman, ["On Access After Parental Separation" (1992), 36 R.F.L. (3d) 35,] at pp. 47-48). It appears that, above and beyond the disruption caused by divorce or separation itself, it is the discord and disharmony within the family which are most damaging to children in the aftermath of divorce.
>
> Two of the major studies on divorce and the effects of conflict on the emotional and psychological well-being of children forcefully make the point that the ability to reduce conflict is crucial to the welfare of children. The study of Wallerstein and Kelly, although limited to white middle class families in California without previous clinical histories who volunteered to participate in the study, is the most comprehensive long-term study on the effects of divorce on children. A ten-year follow-up of the same subjects is reported in Judith S. Wallerstein and Sandra Blakeslee, *Second Chances: Men, Women, and Children a Decade after Divorce* (New York: Ticknor & Fields, 1989). Among the most significant findings of these two reports is that separation or divorce cannot be regarded as a discrete event to be dealt with once and for all, but is most often the beginning in a continuum of disruptive events in the life of the child. The stress resulting from changing family structures and reduced financial support following divorce in many cases continues to be experienced by children long after the divorce is final. While many children do adjust in such situations, the notion that children automatically can and do "get used to" new family situations in a relatively short period of time is not borne out by the results of the study. By all such indicators as success at educational endeavours and the later ability to establish stable personal and professional lives, children of divorce appear in general to be subject to more stresses than their counterparts in intact families. While the authors found considerable evidence that divorce was beneficial to the parents, there was no comparable evidence regarding children. The majority of such children neither experienced relief at the time of the divorce nor felt it had resulted in an improvement in their lives five years later. Moreover, Wallerstein and Blakeslee reported in the later study that problems and conflicts in some children resulting from divorce did not manifest themselves until much later, particularly in the case of girls, who, in the earlier study, had generally appeared to cope better with divorce than boys. Rather, it appears that the long-term effects of divorce cannot always be predicted from the reactions of children at the outset. (See Wallerstein and Blakeslee, at p. 15.)
>
> At the five-year point, Wallerstein and Kelly concluded that, while no factor could in every case be associated with a good outcome, the extent to which conflict between the parents had been

resolved was the single most important factor in the well-being of the child. Following interviews ten years after their initial contact with the subjects, Wallerstein and Blakeslee again identified prolonged hostility between the parents as the single most destructive outcome for the children on divorce. Children subject to fierce legal battles between parents appear to be the most vulnerable group, and ongoing litigation is consistently identified as detrimental to the welfare of children (*Second Chances*, at p. 196). Wallerstein and Kelly also determined, as have other researchers, that children generally fare best when they are able to maintain a continuing relationship with both parents. However, an equally important corollary to this conclusion is often ignored. That is, continued contact may only be in the best interests of the child where parents are not adversarial and where interaction between the child and the access parent is not beset by conflict. Where conflict cannot be resolved or minimized, the detriment of continued contact may outweigh the benefit, as forced co-operation between hostile parents may lead to further litigation and conflict, which itself extends and increases the difficulties faced by children. . . .

These findings are largely corroborated in another U.S. study of the impact of divorce on children. Hetherington, Cox, and Cox in "Effects of Divorce on Parents and Children," in Michael E. Lamb, ed., *Nontraditional Families: Parenting and Child Development* (Hillsdale, N.J.: L. Erlbaum & Associates, 1982), in a study of white middle class preschool children in the custody of their mothers, focused on the effects of conflict on children by comparing its effects in both divorced and intact families. The role of conflict in the welfare of children is highly visible in this study, as the authors determined that two years after divorce, children in low conflict divorced families actually fared better than those in high conflict intact families. Other studies which have come to similar conclusions about the role of conflict in the adjustment of the child after divorce include: Edythe S. Ellison, "Issues Concerning Parental Harmony and Children's Psychosocial Adjustment" (1983), 53 Am. J. Orthopsychiatry 73; R.E. Emery, "Interparental Conflict and the Children of Discord and Divorce" (1982), 92 Psych. Bull. 310; M. Rutter, "Protective Factors in Children's Responses to Stress and Disadvantage," in Martha Whalen Kent and Jon E. Rolf, eds., *Primary Prevention of Psychopathology: Social Competence in Children*, Vol. 3, p. 49; J.R. Johnston, M. Kline, and J.M. Tschann, "Ongoing Postdivorce Conflict: Effects on Children of Joint Custody and Frequent Access" (1989) 59 Am. J. Orthopsychiatry 576.

Thus, while most research discloses that continued contact with both parents after divorce is normally in the best interests of the child, that finding cannot be separated from a consideration of the degree of conflict to which the child will be subject (Weisman). Ironically, unrestricted access may, in some circumstances, cause the continuation of the very stresses from which the parties sought relief when they divorced, and the desire to maintain the pre-existing roles of each parent may in fact result in no ending at all.

   2. In *Growing Up with a Single Parent: What Hurts, What Helps* (Harvard U. Press, Cambridge: 1994), Professors McLanahan and Sandfur set out their conclusion in the first two pages:

We have been studying this question for ten years, and in our opinion the evidence is quite clear: **Children who grow up in a household with only one biological parent are worse off, on average, than children who grow up in a household with both of their biological parents, regardless of their parents' race or educational background, regardless of whether the parents are married when the child is born, and regardless of whether the resident parent remarries.** Compared with teenagers of similar background who grow up with both parents at home, adolescents who have lived apart from one of their parents during some period of childhood are twice as likely to drop out of high school, twice as likely to have a child before twenty, and one and a half times as likely to be "idle" — out of school and out of work — in their late teens and early twenties. [Emphasis in the original.]

At p. 3 they state:

Low income — and the sudden drop in income that is often associated with divorce — is the most important factor in children's lower achievement in single-parent homes, accounting for about half of the disadvantage. Inadequate parental guidance and attention and the lack of ties to community resources account for most of the remaining disadvantage.

They also suggest (at 7) that studies such as Furstenberg, Morgan, and Allison, "Paternal Participation and Children's Well-Being" (1987), 52 American Sociological Review 52 and King, "Nonresident Father Involvement and Child Well-Being: Can Dads Make a Difference?" (1994), 1 Journal of Family Issues 78 have found little evidence that high levels of contact with both biological parents can reduce or eliminate the negative consequences associated with family breakdown.

3. The complexity of the subject of the impact of divorce on children and the increasing sophistication of the research is evident in Kelly, "Current Research on Children's Postdivorce Adjustment: No Simple Answers" (1993), 31 Family and Conciliation Courts Review 29. The author reports that the research demonstrates that significantly more adjustment problems face children, especially boys, of divorced parents than those in families with two biological parents. However, when assessed years later, these children generally are functioning within normal limits. Ms. Kelly also states (at 34-35):

> Recent studies suggest that the relationship between child adjustment and conflict is neither universal, simple, nor particularly straightforward. . . .

> It appears that, rather than discord per se, it is the **manner** in which parental conflict is expressed that may affect children's adjustment. . . .

> These studies indicate that children can escape the negative consequences of parental conflict when they are not caught in it by their parents or when their parents avoid direct, aggressive expressions of their conflict in front of the child or use compromise styles of conflict resolution.

In addition, she reports (at 37) that findings are increasingly mixed or inconclusive regarding the role of the non-custodial parent in children's adjustment after divorce. She concludes as follows (at 45):

> Overall, the evidence suggests that when children begin the divorce experience in good psychological shape, with close or loving relationships with both parents, their adjustment will be maintained by continuing their relationship with both parents on a meaningful basis. There will be gender and age differences within this framework. Parents will maintain their childrens' positive adjustment by reducing their conflict or working their disputed issues out in a mediative or counseling forum and avoid placing their children in the middle of their struggles.

> When children are compromised by a highly conflicted marriage, compromised parent-child relationship, and a history of adjustment problems, there is no specific formula that will produce better adjustment for these youngsters after separation. Some will need counseling or other support systems and the collective resources of two struggling parents. Others will need relief from an abusive, critical or rejecting parent or from the anxiety and fear of violence between parents, thus enabling these children to benefit from the changes in their lives.

2.   Conflict of Laws

(1) JURISDICTION

HINTER v. HINTER

(1996), 24 R.F.L. (4th) 401 (Ont. Gen. Div.)

Epstein J.: – This case involves questions of jurisdiction. The petitioner (wife) has commenced three separate proceedings against the husband. They are as follows:

(a) On 11 December 1995, action No. 95-28131 in Miami, Florida, against the husband for an injunction against domestic violence.

(b) On 28 December 1995, action No. 95-29645 in Miami, Florida, against the husband for support unconnected with divorce, and against R.C. Consulting Corporation and Jody-Jen Investments Limited, restraining the disposition of certain property.

(c) On 22 March 1996, a divorce petition against the husband in Ontario claiming a divorce, relief under the *Family Law Act*, R.S.O. 1990, c. F.3, and corollary relief under the *Divorce Act*, R.S.C. 1985, c.3 (2nd Supp.).

The husband disputes the jurisdiction of the Ontario Court and moves for an order dismissing the petition in this action on the basis of this court's lack of jurisdiction, and for an order staying all claims on the grounds of duplication with the Florida proceedings.

The thrust of the husband's jurisdictional argument is that the wife was not ordinarily resident in Ontario for the 12 months prior to when the petition was issued in March of 1996. In fact, she was a resident of Miami, Florida. Secondly, the support claim ought not to proceed in two jurisdictions and the convenient forum for this claim is Florida. . . .

The Facts

For the past two and a half years, the husband has been spending most of his time living and working in Amsterdam. He has come to Ontario periodically. When he did so, at least until November 1995, he stayed with the wife in their home in Toronto.

During this period of time, the wife alternated staying in Toronto and in a condominium in Miami, Florida. This condominium is in the name of a company that is owned by both parties. The key issue centres on the wife's connection with Florida. I find the facts relevant to this issue to be as follows:

(a) In mid-1994, the wife began to consider separation seriously;

(b) Some time that year, the wife started an intimate relationship with a man who resides in Florida. In fact, the wife from time to time works with this man in his business;

(c) The wife had at least reduced contact with her family doctor from October 1994 to September 1995;

(d) In November 1995, the wife told the husband that she did not want him in the Florida condominium at Christmas. Apparently, she spent Christmas 1995 in Florida with her new partner;

(e) On December 11, 1995, the wife started her first Florida action, in which she swore that she "lived" in Florida;

(f) On December 28, 1995, in her second Florida action, the wife swore two statements that the Florida condominium was "where she currently resides" and that she "is presently residing apart from the husband, in the state of Florida."

(g) An order has issued on consent out of the Florida court granting the wife exclusive use and occupancy of the matrimonial home;

(h) The wife's 1995 tax return is filed on the basis that she is a resident of Ontario;

(i) The wife is in Florida now. Virtually all of her affidavits in these various proceedings have been sworn there;

(j) Her house in Toronto has been according to her "stripped bare of all its contents"; yet, she has stayed in Florida rather than come here to investigate and deal with the situation;

(k) She has provided no evidence as to when she plans to return to Toronto. All she says is that she plans to "return to Toronto shortly."

It is also of note that in this divorce petition the wife states that both parties have lived in Ontario since 1980. However, she lists her husband's address as "unknown." Further, in this proceeding she has sworn an affidavit that she "is not a permanent resident of Florida.". . .

Finally, to address one additional factual issue relevant to jurisdiction, I find that the husband is not ordinarily resident in Ontario. There is no evidence before me to the contrary and, in fact, the wife states in her Notice of Motion that the husband has been working and living in Amsterdam for the past 18 months.

The question is: does the evidence placed before the court by the husband support the dismissal of the petition or the staying of all claims for corollary relief and all claims under the *Family Law Act*, based on the failure of the parties to meet the residency requirement under the *Divorce Act*, and based on *forum conveniens*?

The Law

Section 3(1) of the *Divorce Act* reads as follows:

> A court in a province has jurisdiction to hear and determine a divorce proceeding if either spouse has been ordinarily resident in the province for at least one year immediately proceeding the commencement of the proceeding.

Numerous cases have dealt with the proper interpretation to be given to the phrase "ordinarily resident". One of the earliest of these is *Thomson* v. *Minister of National Revenue*, [1946] S.C.R. 209, which dealt with the meaning of the phrase in question as used in the *Income War Tax Act*, R.S.C. 1927, c.97. In the course of his reasons, Rand J. stated at page 224:

> The expression "ordinarily resident" carries a restricted signification, and although the first impression seems to be that of preponderance in time, the decisions on the English Act reject that view. It is held to mean residence in the course of the customary mode of life of the person concerned, and it is contrasted with special or occasional or casual residence. The general mode of life is, therefore, relevant to a question of its application.

In a separate concurring judgment, Estey J. stated at page 231:

> A reference to the dictionary and judicial comments upon the meaning of these terms indicates that one is "ordinarily resident" in the place where in the settled routine of his life he regularly, normally or customarily lives. One "sojourns" at a place where he unusually, casually or inter-mittently visits or stays. In the former the element of permanence; in the latter that of the temporary predominates. The difference cannot be stated in precise and definite terms, but each case must be determined after all of the relevant factors are taken into consideration, but the foregoing indicates in a general way the essential difference. It is not the length of the visit or stay that determines the question.

In *Hardy* v. *Hardy*, [1969] 2 O.R. 875 (H.C.), the petitioner was born in Ontario and resided there until he joined the army. He returned to his parents' home in Ontario while he was on leave. In arriving at the conclusion that the petitioner was "ordinarily resident" in Ontario, Houlden J. stated the test as follows at page 877:

Where did the petitioner regularly, normally or customarily live in the year preceding the filing of the petition? Or using the test of Karminski, J., "Where was his real home in that period?"

The Ontario Court of Appeal has also dealt with this issue in *MacPherson* v. *MacPherson* (1976), 28 R.F.L. 106. In that case, the petitioner was born in Ontario and resided there until her marriage in 1968. The respondent husband was born in Glace Bay, Nova Scotia, where he resided until he came to Ontario in search of employment in 1965. The parties were married in Glace Bay and resided there until 1969, when they moved to Ontario. In 1973, the parties moved back to Glace Bay, where they established a home. Apart from a three-week long visit by the wife to Ontario, the family lived in Glace Bay until 1974, when the wife returned to Ontario. The wife stated that she never intended to establish a permanent residence in Glace Bay, while the husband maintained the opposite.

In concluding that the petitioner had not fulfilled the "ordinarily resident" requirement, Evans J.A. stated at page 112:

> In my opinion, the arrival of a person in a new locality with the intention of making a home in that locality for an indefinite period makes that person ordinarily resident in that community. In the present matter, while the husband and wife expressed opposing views as to their intention with respect to the establishment of a permanent residence in Nova Scotia, I do not believe that that intention alone can determine the issue of ordinary residence. Mrs. MacPherson left Ontario to reside with her husband and family with the intention of residing in Nova Scotia for an indefinite period of time. Her stated intention of returning to live in Ontario does not detract from the fact that she was ordinarily resident in Nova Scotia for that period which continued until she moved and established her residence in Ontario. The fact that Mr. MacPherson returned to Ontario in search of employment, leaving his wife and children in Nova Scotia, does not destroy the intimate community ties which Mrs. MacPherson had established in that province.

> In the view which I take of the matter, the petitioner wife has not complied with the jurisdictional requirement that she be ordinarily resident in Ontario for a period of at least one year immediately preceding the presentation of her petition. Accordingly the trial judge had no jurisdiction to grant a judgment nisi.

Interestingly, Evans J.A. referred in his reasons to the following comments of Somervell L.J. in *Macrae* v. *Macrae*, [1949] P. 397, [1949] 2 All E.R. 34 (C.A.):

> Ordinary residence is a thing which can be changed in a day. A man is ordinarily resident in one place up till a particular day. He then cuts the connection he has with that place — in this case he left his wife; in another case he might have disposed of his house — and makes arrangements to have his home somewhere else. Where there are indications that the place to which he moves is the place which he intends to make his home for, at any rate, an indefinite period, as from that date he is ordinarily resident at that place.

In *Wrixon* v. *Wrixon* (1982), 30 R.F.L. (2d) 107 (Alta. Q.B.), the petitioner, who had resided in Alberta for more than 20 years, filed a petition for divorce in that province only two months after returning from an 18-month stay in Hawaii. During at least part of her stay in Hawaii, the petitioner was gainfully employed. Her furniture was stored in Alberta for the eighteen-month period. Purvis J. found that, in the circumstances, the petitioner was not ordinarily resident in Alberta "for a period of at least one year immediately preceding the presentation of the petition" as required by section 5(1) [now 3(1)] of the *Divorce Act*, R.S.C. 1970, c. D-8. His Lordship stated at pages 108-109:

> She [the petitioner] testified that her stay in Hawaii was "an extended vacation". While she did not maintain living accommodation in Alberta to be immediately available for occupancy upon her return, she did put her furniture in storage in the province. It appears that while she was in

Hawaii, she acquired fixed addresses at several locations, and was gainfully employed for at least part of the time. This is inconsistent with her suggestion that her sojourn of a year and a half in Hawaii was merely an extended vacation. . . .

In my view, in the circumstances of this case the period of one year within which the petitioner must have been ordinarily resident in Alberta must be calculated from 1st May 1982. It cannot be said that in the 12 months immediately preceding presentation of the petition, the petitioner in the settled routine of her life regularly, normally or customarily lived in Alberta, which the phrase "ordinarily resident" connotes: *Thomson* v. *M.N.R.*, [1946] S.C.R. 209 at 232, [1946] C.T.C. 51, [1946] 1 D.L.R. 689. [Text within brackets mine.]

In *MacLean* v. *MacLean*, [1990] B.C.J. No. 50 (B.C. S.C.), Drost L.J.S.C. made the following comments:

In the case at bar (assuming that the respondent was ordinarily resident in this province while living with his parents between September 1977 and February 1988) in order that this court have jurisdiction it must be established that between February 1987 and September 1987, the respondent was ordinarily resident in British Columbia, notwithstanding that during a substantial part of that period he was living and working in Seattle, Washington.

In my view, that finding depends on whether or not, when he and the petitioner moved to Seattle, they did so with the intention of making that city their home for an indefinite period. In her affidavit of October 23, 1989, the petitioner states that whenever they resided outside British Columbia it was in furtherance of the respondent's career, that such periods of residence were intended to be of short duration only and that their goal was to return to Vancouver. She says that even when they resided elsewhere they maintained bank accounts, real estate, automobiles and various social memberships in British Columbia and that they rented storage space in Vancouver where they stored personal belongings. . . .

On the authority of *MacPherson v. MacPherson* and the subsequent cases such as *Mahar v. Mahar* (supra) that have followed that decision, in order to refute the claim of jurisdiction the respondent need only establish that when he and the petitioner moved to Seattle, Washington, they did so with the intention of making that city their home for an indefinite period.

I am satisfied that was the case. The decision to move to Seattle was a joint decision. It was made, in part at least, for the purpose of advancing the respondent's career. It was a voluntary move and there is no suggestion that they fixed any time limit for their stay in Seattle.

I am mindful of the fact that an application to stay or dismiss a divorce proceeding should only be granted "in a clear and obvious case": see *Fareed* v. *Latif* (1991), 31 R.F.L. (3d) 354 (Man. Q.B.). Based on the governing case law as set out above and on the particular circumstances of this case, it is "clear and obvious" that this court does not have jurisdiction to entertain the petitioner's claim for a divorce.

The wife has lived in Florida since she left the matrimonial home in November of 1995. In fact, she has spent a good part of her time in Florida over the last two years. The wife has not fixed any time limit for her stay in Florida. She has failed to provide the court with any date on which she plans to leave Florida and return to Ontario. In my view, when the wife left for Florida in November of 1995, she did so with the intention of making her home there for an indefinite period.

The wife has exclusive possession of the condominium in Florida. She has established a personal relationship with a gentleman there, and has worked in his business. As well, even though the matrimonial home in Toronto "has been stripped of most of the household contents", and the locks have been changed, the wife has not seen fit to return to Toronto to deal with this matter herself, preferring instead to send a friend. The wife, herself, gave two separate sworn statements in December of 1995 in which she referred to herself as a "resident" of Florida.

The overwhelming preponderance of the evidence is that the wife is ordinarily resident in Florida, and has been since early December, 1995. The wife "regularly, normally or customarily lives" in Florida. Consequently, the wife has not been ordinarily resident in Ontario for "at least one year immediately preceding the commencement of the proceeding" on March 22, 1996, as required by section 3(1) of the *Divorce Act*. This court therefore does not have jurisdiction to hear and determine the petition.

[Nevertheless, the judge denied the husband's request for an order staying the support and property claims brought pursuant to the *Family Law Act*.]

NOTES AND QUESTIONS

1. In *Byrn* v. *Mackin* (1983), 32 R.F.L. (2d) 207 (Que. S.C.) the petitioner's husband administered a company's business in Montreal, living in apartments leased by the company. The wife and children continued to reside in the matrimonial home in British Columbia. After approximately one year, during which the husband returned frequently to his family in British Columbia, he announced that the marriage was over. He took his personal effects to Montreal and petitioned for divorce in Quebec. The court held that the husband had been ordinarily resident in British Columbia prior to his decision to end the marriage relationship.

2. In *Molson* v. *Molson* (1998), 38 R.F.L. (4th) 385, the Alberta Court of Queen's Bench followed *Hinter* and the cases referred to in it and concluded that Mrs. Molson had become ordinarily resident in Alberta when she moved her furniture there and moved in with a friend, intending to stay in the province indefinitely.

3. Section 5(1) of the 1968 *Divorce Act* referred to a period of ordinary residence of at least one year "immediately preceding the presentation of the petition". The courts held that a petition was presented for the purpose of s. 5(1) when it was filed with the Registrar of the Court: *Khalifa* v. *Khalifa* (1971), 4 N.S.R. (2d) 576, 19 D.L.R. (3d) 460 (T.D.); *Weston* v. *Weston*, 5 R.F.L. 244, [1972] 2 W.W.R. 402 (B.C. S.C.); *Stapleton* v. *Stapleton* (1977), 1 R.F.L. (2d) 190, 80 D.L.R. (3d) 562 (Man. C.A.); and *Jablonowski* v. *Jablonowski*, 8 R.F.L. 36, [1972] 3 O.R. 410 (H.C.). Section 3 of the 1985 *Divorce Act* refers to "the commencement of the proceeding" rather than the "presentation of the petition". This change in wording does not alter the previous law. A proceeding should not be considered to have commenced for the purpose of s. 3 until the document that begins the proceeding is filed with the court. Under *Family Law Rules*, Ontario Reg. 114/99, r. 36, this document is an "application" if the proceedings are brought in the Family Court of the Ontario Superior Court of Justice. In those areas in Ontario where the Family Court has not yet been established as a special branch of the Ontario Superior Court, this document is still a "petition for divorce". See Rules of Civil Procedure, R.R.O. 1990, Reg. 194, r. 69.03(1).

4. By virtue of s. 6(1) of the *Divorce Act* where a divorce proceeding involves an application for a custody or access order that is opposed and the child concerned is most substantially connected with another province, the court having original jurisdiction may, on application by a spouse or on its own motion, transfer the divorce proceeding to a court in that other province. Subsections 6(2) and (3) govern transfers of corollary relief and variation proceedings in similar circumstances. The court to which the proceeding is transferred will then be vested with exclusive jurisdiction: s. 6(4). Cases dealing with applications for a transfer pursuant to s. 6 include: *Chenkie* v. *Chenkie* (1987), 6 R.F.L. (3d) 371 (Alta. Q.B.); *Astle* v. *Walton* (1987), 10 R.F.L. (3d) 199 (Alta. Q.B.); *Kern* v. *Kern* (1989), 19 R.F.L. (3d) 350 (B.C. S.C.); *D. (T.W.)* v. *D. (Y.M.)* (1989), 20 R.F.L. (3d) 183 (N.S. T.D.); *Cormier* v. *Cormier* (1990), 26 R.F.L. (3d) 169 (N.B. Q.B.); *Mohrbutter* v. *Mohrbutter* (1991), 34 R.F.L. (3d) 357 (Sask. Q.B.); *Ellet* v. *Ellet* (1994), 4 R.F.L. (4th) 358 (Alta. Q.B.); *Bell* v. *Nelson* (1997), 35 R.F.L. (4th) 9 (Sask. Q.B.); and *Johnson* v. *Lennert* (1998), 41 R.F.L. (4th) 442 (Nfld. C.A.). See also Black, "Section 6 of the Divorce Act: What May be Transferred?" (1992), 37 R.F.L. (3d) 307.

5. A husband and wife are ordinarily resident in Ontario until January 2 when the husband leaves to take up a new job in Newfoundland. The wife, who refuses to accompany her husband to Newfound-

land, moves to Alberta on the same day. Each has severed all connections with Ontario and intends to live in Newfoundland and Alberta respectively for the foreseeable future. Assuming that each has grounds for divorce, when and where can each commence proceedings?

If the husband commences divorce proceedings in Newfoundland on February 2nd of the following year and the wife commences divorce proceedings in Alberta on February 3rd, which court has jurisdiction? If both commence such proceedings on February 2nd, which court has jurisdiction?

6. A husband begins divorce proceedings in a non-Canadian court and the wife then brings proceedings in Ontario. If both courts have jurisdiction, how should the Ontario court determine whether to stay proceedings? See *Nicholas* v. *Nicholas* (1996), 24 R.F.L. (4th) 358 (Ont. C.A.).

(2) RECOGNITION OF FOREIGN DECREES

CASTEL, *CANADIAN CONFLICT OF LAWS*

3rd ed. (Toronto: Butterworths, 1994) para. 226.

In the common law provinces and territories of Canada, the question of the recognition to be accorded to a foreign decree of divorce has arisen in nullity suits, alimony actions, prosecutions for bigamy or for neglecting to provide necessaries for a wife, cases involving the right to custody of children or the right to obtain a marriage licence, or a share in the estate of the deceased spouse and in many other instances. . . .

Sub-section (1) of s. 22 applies to foreign decrees granted after June 1, 1986, the date of the coming into force of the Act. Decrees granted before June 1, 1986 continue to be subject to the old rules as to recognition. The important change involves the adoption of the test of ordinary residence of either spouse in the foreign country for at least one year immediately preceding the commencement of the proceeding for the divorce. In other words, if either spouse was ordinarily resident in the granting country for at least one year immediately preceding the institution of the proceeding, the decree will be recognized in Canada even if the foreign court took jurisdiction on a different ground.

Sub-section (2) of s. 22 preserves the statutory ground for recognition of foreign divorces adopted by sub-s. (2) of s. 6 of the 1968 Divorce Act, namely the independent domicile of the wife in the country where the divorce was granted.

Since the existing rules for recognition for foreign divorces in Canada are retained by sub-s. (3) of s. 22, the old common law rules as to recognition are still in force. It is unlikely that they will be used extensively to recognize divorces granted after June 1, 1986.

In determining the conditions for recognition of foreign divorces in Canada, the courts of the common law provinces and territories have followed the common law rules developed by English courts.

In Canada, the basic common law jurisdictional rule of recognition was the domicile of both spouses in the foreign jurisdiction at the commencement of the proceeding combined with the now obsolete common law rule that upon marriage the wife acquires the husband's domicile.

In determining whether the husband's domicile was in the foreign jurisdiction, Canadian courts apply the *lex fori*. Thus, Canadian courts held that a foreign divorce decree rendered by the court of the husband's domicile will be recognized as valid in Canada[28] provided proper notice was given to the respondent[29] and the divorce was not obtained by fraud.[30]

Consent or submission of one or both spouses cannot cure a defect of jurisdiction.[31]

As a matter of policy, Canadian courts do not recognize the retroactive legislation of a foreign state purporting to validate a divorce even though the spouse who obtained the divorce was domiciled in that state at the time of the original proceedings.[32]

Canadian courts give recognition to a foreign decree of divorce, wherever pronounced, if it would be recognized by the domicile of the spouses at the time it was pronounced[33] or immediately thereafter.[34] The justification for this rule is that if the status of the spouses is changed or recognized as having been changed in the country of their domicile, the change of status must be recognized in Canada.

Canadian courts have also recognized foreign divorce decrees, where in roughly comparable circumstances they would have exercised jurisdiction by virtue of Canadian domestic law, as it would be contrary to principle and inconsistent with comity if Canadian courts were to refuse to recognize a jurisdiction which *mutatis mutandis* they claim for themselves.[35] In other words, this rule applies regardless of the basis upon which the foreign court assumed jurisdiction.

In recent years, Canadian courts have been committed to the view that they will recognize foreign decrees of divorce where there existed some real and substantial connection between the petitioner or the respondent and the granting jurisdiction at the time of the commencement of the proceedings.[36] The purpose of the rule is to avoid limping marriages. A divorce should also be recognized when it would be recognized by the courts of the country with which the petitioner had a real and substantial connection at the relevant time, though she or he had no such connection with the country where it was granted.[37]

Whether there exists a real and substantial connection between the granting jurisdiction and either the petitioner or the respondent must be determined by the court upon an analysis of all the relevant facts.[38]

Although ordinary residence is a sufficient real and substantial connection at common law, one would anticipate that it might be slightly more difficult to have a foreign decree recognized in Canada on the basis of ordinary residence of less than a year since at common law no particular length of ordinary residence is necessary, whereas the Divorce Act requires a period of one year immediately preceding the commencement of the proceeding in the foreign country.

---

28 Based on *Le Mesurier* v. *Le Mesurier*, [1895] A.C. 517, 11 T.L.R. 481 (P.C.); *Hill* v. *Hill* (1981), 10 Sask. R. 276 (Q.B.) (Mexican divorce not recognized); *Re Jones* (1974), 6 O.R. (2d) 11, 51 D.L.R. (3d) 655 (H.C.J.).

29 *Infra*, para. 228. Additional grounds on which a foreign divorce may be refused recognition.

30 *Ibid.*

31 *Stephens* v. *Falchi*, [1938] S.C.R. 354; *Foggo* v. *Foggo* (1952), 5 W.W.R. (N.S.) 40, [1952] 2 D.L.R. 701 (B.C.C.A.); *MacGuigan* v. *MacGuigan*, [1954] O.R. 318, [1954] 3 D.L.R. 127; affd. [1954] O.W.N. 861, [1955] 1 D.L.R. 92 (C.A.); *Cody* v. *Cody*, [1927] 3 D.L.R. 349 (Sask.).

32 *Ambrose* v. *Ambrose* (1959), 30 W.W.R. 49, 21 D.L.R. (2d) 722; affd. (1960), 32 W.W.R. 433, 25 D.L.R. (2d) 1 (B.C.C.A.).

33 Based on *Armitage* v. *A.G.*, [1906] P. 135, 75 L.J.P. 42, 22 T.L.R. 306; *Walker* v. *Walker*, [1950] 2 W.W.R. 411, [1950] 4 D.L.R. 253 (B.C.C.A.); *Wyllie* v. *Martin*, [1931] 3 W.W.R. 465 (B.C.S.C.); *McCormack* v. *McCormack*, [1920] 2 W.W.R. 714, 55 D.L.R. 386 (Alta. C.A.); *Burnfiel* v. *Burnfiel*, [1926] 1 W.W.R. 657, 20 Sask. L.R. 407, [1926] 2 D.L.R. 129 (C.A.); *Chatenay* v. *Chatenay*, [1938] 1 W.W.R. 885, 53 B.C.R. 13, [1938] 3 D.L.R. 379; *Yeger and Duder* v. *Registrar General of Vital*

Statistics (1958), 26 W.W.R. 651 (Alta.); *Plummer* v. *Plummer* (1962), 38 W.W.R. 193, 31 D.L.R. (2d) 723 (B.C.S.C.); *Viccari* v. *Viccari*, [1972] 3 O.R. 706, 7 R.F.L. 241, 29 D.L.R. (3d) 297; *Lyon* v. *Lyon*, [1959] O.R. 305, [1959] O.W.N. 170, 18 D.L.R. (2d) 753 (C.A.); *Pledge* v. *Walter* (1961), 36 W.W.R. 95 (Alta.); *Re Jones: Royal Trust Co.* v. *Jones* (1961), 25 D.L.R. (2d) 595 (B.C.); revd. 34 W.W.R. 540, 28 D.L.R. (2d) 767; revd. [1962] S.C.R. 132, 37 W.W.R. 1, 31 D.L.R. (2d) 292. *Cf. Holmes* v. *Holmes*, [1927] 2 W.W.R. 253, [1927] 2 D.L.R. 979 (Alta.).

34 *Schwebel* v. *Ungar* (1964), 42 D.L.R. (2d) 622, at 633 (Ont. C.A.); affd. [1965] S.C.R. 148, 48 D.L.R. (2d) 644; for the decision of the High Court see 37 D.L.R. (2d) 467 (Ont.); for a note on this case see Lysyk, (1965), 43 Can. Bar Rev. 363; Hartley (1965), 4 West. Ont. L. Rev. 99; Webb (1965), 14 Int. & Comp. L.Q. 659.

35 Based on *Travers* v. *Holley*, [1953] P. 246, [1953] 2 All E.R. 794 (C.A.) and *Robinson-Scott* v. *Robinson-Scott*, [1958] P. 71, [1957] 3 W.L.R. 842, [1957] 3 All E.R. 473; *Januszkiewicz* v. *Janusz-kiewicz* (1966), 55 W.W.R. 73, 55 D.L.R. (2d) 727, at 735 (Man. Q.B.); *Allarie* v. *Director of Vital Statistics* (1963), 44 W.W.R. 568, 41 D.L.R. (2d) 553 (Alta); *B. and B.* v. *Deputy Registrar General of Vital Statistics* (1960), 31 W.W.R. 40, 24 D.L.R. (2d) 238 (Alta.); *Pledge* v. *Walter, supra*, note 33; *Yeger and Duder* v. *Registrar General of Vital Statistics, supra*, note 33; *Re Capon; Capon* v. *McLay*, [1965] 2 O.R. 83, 49 D.L.R. (2d) 675 (C.A.) (nullity decree); for a note on this case see Castel, (1965), 43 Can. Bar Rev. 647; also *Needham* v. *Needham*, [1964] 1 O.R. 645, 43 D.L.R. (2d) 405 (H.C.J.); *Travers* v. *Holley* was not followed in *La Pierre* v. *Walter* (1960), 31 W.W.R. 26, 24 D.L.R. (2d) 483 (Alta.). It seems to be possible to combine *Travers* v. *Holley, supra*, with *Armitage* v. *A.G., supra*, note 33; *Mountbatten* v. *Mountbatten*; [1959] 1 All E.R. 99.

36 *Indyka* v. *Indyka*, [1969] 1 A.C. 33, [1967] 3 W.L.R. 510, [1967] 2 All E.R. 689 (H.L.); *Powell* v. *Cockburn*, [1973] 2 O.R. 188, 11 R.F.L. 248, 33 D.L.R. (3d) 284 (C.A.); revd. on other grounds, [1977] 2 S.C.R. 218, 22 R.F.L. 155, 8 N.R. 215, 68 D.L.R. (3d) 700; *Re Hassan* (1976), 12 O.R. (2d) 432, 28 R.F.L. 121 (*sub nom. Hassan* v. *Hassan*), 69 D.L.R. (3d) 224 (H.C.J.); *Kish* v. *Director of Vital Statistics*, [1973] 2 W.W.R. 678, 10 R.F.L. 71, 35 D.L.R. (3d) 530 (Alta. S.C.), noted Bloom, (1973), 11 Can. Y.B. Int. L. 193; *Rowland* v. *Rowland* (1973), 2 O.R. (2d) 161, 13 R.F.L. 311, 42 D.L.R. (3d) 205, *obiter, MacNeill* v. *MacNeill* (1974), 6 O.R. (2d) 598, 17 R.F.L. 163, 53 D.L.R. (3d) 486; *Abbruscato* v. *Abbruscato* (1973), 12 R.F.L. 257 (Ont.); *Jani* v. *Jani* (1976), 20 R.F.L. 361 (Ont.); *Holub* v. *Holub*, [1976] 5 W.W.R. 527, 26 R.F.L. 263, 71 D.L.R. (3d) 698 (Man. C.A.); *Wood* v. *Wood*, [1974] 5 W.W.R. 18, 15 R.F.L. 197 (Alta.); *La Carte* v. *La Carte* (1975), 23 R.F.L. 112, 60 D.L.R. (3d) 507 (B.C.S.C.); *Bevington (Hewitson)* v. *Hewitson* (1974), 4 O.R. (2d) 226, 16 R.F.L. 44, 47 D.L.R. (3d) 510; *Siebert* v. *Siebert* (1978), 3 R.F.L. (2d) 338, 82 D.L.R. (3d) 70 (B.C.S.C.); *Re Karnenas* (1978), 3 R.F.L. (2d) 213 (Ont. Surr. Ct.); *Keresztessy* v. *Keresztessy* (1976), 14 O.R. (2d) 255, 30 R.F.L. 194, 73 D.L.R. 347 (H.C.J.); *Goldin* v. *Goldin* (1979), 25 O.R. (2d) 629, 104 D.L.R. (3d) 76 (H.C.J.); *Szabo* v. *Szabo* (1980), 15 R.F.L. (2d) 13 (Ont. U.F.C.); *Re Casterton* (1978), 23 O.R. (2d) 24, 94 D.L.R. (3d) 290 (H.C.J.); *Clarkson* v. *Clarkson* (1978), 86 D.L.R. (3d) 694 (Man. Q.B.); *Haut* v. *Haut* (1978), 20 O.R. (2d) 126, 3 R.F.L. (2d) 239, 86 D.L.R. (3d) 757 (H.C.J.); *Kapur* v. *Can. (Min. of Employment & Immigration)* (1987), 2 Imm. L.R. (2d) 292 (Imm. Ap. Bd.); *Re Edward and Edward* (1987), 57 Sask. R. 67, 39 D.L.R. (4th) 654, 8 R.F.L. (3d) 370 (Sask. C.A.) noted Glenn, (1989), 34 McGill L.J. 186; *Singh* v. *Mohammed* (1986), 41 Man. R. (2d) 235 (Q.B.).

37 Combining *Indyka* v. *Indyka, ibid.*, with *Armitrage* v. *A.G., supra*, note 33; *Mather* v. *Mahoney*, [1968] 1 W.L.R. 1773, [1968] 3 All E.R. 223; *Messina* v. *Smith*, [1971] P. 322, [1971] 2 All E.R. 1046.

38 *Kish* v. *Director of Vital Statistics, supra*, note 36; *Rowland* v. *Rowland* (1973), 2 O.R. (2d) 161, 13 R.F.L. 311, 42 D.L.R. (3d) 205, at 212 (H.C.J.); *Keresztessy* v. *Keresztessy, supra*, note 36; *Siebert* v. *Siebert, supra*, note 36, *El-Sohemy* v. *El-Sohemy* (1978), 21 O.R. (2d) 35, 3 R.F.L. (2d) 184, 89 D.L.R. (3d) 145 (H.C.J.); *Re Casterton, supra*, note 36; *Bate* v. *Bate* (1978), 1 R.F.L. (2d) 298 (Ont. H.C.J.); *Clarkson* v. *Clarkson* (1978), 86 D.L.R. (3d) 694.

NOTES AND QUESTIONS

1. The concept of domicile is an important connecting factor in the conflict of laws. Every person has a domicile. At birth, an individual is fixed with a domicile of origin. At common law, a legitimate

child took as his or her domicile of origin the domicile of the father at the time of birth, while an illegitimate child's domicile of origin was that of the mother at the time of birth. Section 67 of the *Family Law Act* establishes statutory rules for determining the domicile of a minor (these rules first appeared in slightly different form in s. 68 of the *Family Law Reform Act, 1978*). In light of the abolition of the legal concept of illegitimacy by s. 1 of the *Children's Law Reform Act*, it would appear that s. 67 is intended to alter both the rules governing determination of a person's domicile of origin and those governing the minor's domicile of dependency.

A domicile of choice can be acquired by a person who has capacity to acquire an independent domicile. It is the jurisdiction, other than a person's domicile of origin, in which a person resides with the intention to remain there permanently. A domicile of choice can be changed by an actual change of residence coupled with an intention to remain in the new place of residence. If a person abandons his or her domicile of choice without acquiring a new one, that person's domicile is once again his or her domicile of origin.

At common law, married women, minors and mental incompetents did not have the capacity to acquire an independent domicile. A married woman's domicile was that of her husband. She, therefore, had a domicile of dependency. The common law rule that a married woman had the same domicile as her husband was abolished for purposes of recognition of divorce decrees by the *Divorce Act* of 1968 (see now s. 22(2) of *Divorce Act*). Section 65 of the *Family Law Reform Act, 1978* abolished the remaining vestiges of the concept of unity of legal personality of husband and wife (see now s. 64 of *Family Law Act*). This concept formed the basis for the common law rule that a married woman had the same domicile as her husband.

For a more complete analysis of the concept of domicile, see Mendes da Costa, "Some Comments on the Conflict of Laws Provisions of the Divorce Act, 1968" (1968), 46 Can. Bar Rev. 252 and Castel, *Canadian Conflict of Laws*, 4th ed. (Toronto: Butterworths, 1997) 38.

2. In *Messina* v. *Smith*, [1971] P. 322, [1971] 2 All E.R. 1046, Omrod J. stated (at (P.) 336): "All through the history of the recognition rules in this country there can be traced, in different shapes and guises, two fundamental *desiderata*. The first is the need to avoid creating 'limping' or 'unilateral marriages' or 'the scandal which arises when a man and a woman are held to be man and wife in one country and strangers in another'. . . . The second is the wish to protect the standards of marriage in this country against the laxer standards believed to obtain in other countries." Does the adoption of the real and substantial connection test ensure the proper balancing of these two policy considerations?

3. The fact that a foreign divorce has been held invalid or non-recognizable according to the conflict of laws rules of the forum does not mean that the foreign divorce has no effect in the forum. Certainly, the status of the parties in such a case continues to be that of married persons and neither has the capacity to remarry. However, by virtue of the doctrine of preclusion, a party who has obtained an invalid foreign divorce decree or voluntarily acquiesced in the proceedings may be prevented from denying the validity of the decree in certain collateral proceedings brought in the forum. The issue of preclusion has arisen most frequently in cases where inheritance or support was involved. See especially, *Downton* v. *Royal Trust Co.*, [1973] S.C.R. 437, 3 Nfld. & P.E.I.R. 576.

4. Section 13 of the *Divorce Act* provides that a divorce granted under the Act has legal effect throughout Canada. Accordingly, a divorce granted under the Act must be accepted as validly terminating the marriage regardless of which province is the forum.

3. Grounds

(1) LIVING SEPARATE AND APART

(a) Definition

Under the *Divorce Act* of 1968, a petitioner could establish permanent break-down of the marriage by proving that the spouses had lived separate and apart for a period of three years prior to the presentation of the petition. If the petitioner had deserted the respondent, the requisite period was five years. There were numerous cases under the Act explaining the meaning of the concept of living separate and apart. These cases continue to guide the courts in the application of s. 8(2)(a) of the 1985 *Divorce Act*. See, e.g., *Thorogood* v. *Thorogood* (1987), 11 R.F.L. (3d) 82 (Ont. U.F.C.) and *Ginter* v. *Ginter* (1988), 15 R.F.L. (3d) 203 (Sask. Q.B.).

RUSHTON v. RUSHTON

(1968), 66 W.W.R. 764, 2 D.L.R. (3d) 25 (B.C. S.C.)

MCINTYRE J.: — The parties were married in 1936. By 1960 they had come upon difficulties and had begun to live separate lives, although they continued to reside in the same suite in an apartment building. In February 1965, and probably from an earlier date, sexual intercourse ceased entirely. The petitioner lived in one room of the suite, the respondent in another, there was almost no contact between them. The wife performed no domestic services for the husband. She shopped and cooked only for herself. He bought his own food, did his own cooking, his own laundry and received no services from his wife. He paid her a sum monthly for maintenance. While it is true that they lived in the same suite of rooms, they followed separate and individual lives.

The petitioner continued to live in the suite because she and her husband were the joint caretakers of the apartment building in which the suite was situate, and to keep the position it was necessary to be, or to appear to be, husband and wife and to reside in the caretaker's suite.

In August 1968, they became responsible for another apartment building where no such requirement exists. They now maintain separate suites in the same building. . . .

I am of the opinion that in the case at bar the parties have been living separate and apart for three years within the meaning of s. 4(1)(e)(i) of the Divorce Act. The words "separate and apart" are disjunctive. They mean, in my view, that there must be a withdrawal from the matrimonial obligation with the intent of destroying the matrimonial consortium, as well as physical separation. The two conditions must be met. I hold that they are met here. The mere fact that the parties are under one roof does not mean that they are not living separate and apart within the meaning of the Act. There can be, and I hold that here there has been, a physical separation within the one suite of rooms. To hold otherwise would be to deprive the petitioner here of any remedy under the new Divorce Act simply because she is precluded, or was for a period of time precluded, by economic circumstances from acquiring a different suite in which to live. There will be a decree nisi. . . .

DUPERE v. DUPERE

(1974), 19 R.F.L. 270, 9 N.B.R. (2d) 554 (Q.B.)

STEVENSON J.: — . . . In any case where the parties continue to live under the same roof the court must carefully consider the evidence in determining whether the spouses have been "living separate and apart" resulting in "a permanent breakdown of their marriage" within the meaning of those expressions in s. 4(1) of the Divorce Act, R.S.C. 1970,c. D-8. Particular care is called for where, as here, both spouses seek a divorce on that ground alone.

The parties were married on 27th February 1960. The petitioner was 26 and the respondent 18. She had borne a child, Randle, of which the petitioner was the father, on 13th July 1958. There are two other children of the marriage — Heather, born 30th November 1960, and Jacqueline, born 9th February 1965.

Difficulties between the parties apparently developed in 1965 and they separated in 1966. A written separation agreement (Ex. R-1) was entered into on 12th July 1966. The respondent was to have custody of the children and the petitioner assumed financial obligations which were not clearly defined. The respondent took an apartment. When she was unable to pay the rent she rented a small house without toilet facilities for $30 per month. She and her two daughters resided there. Randle stayed with his maternal grandmother. The petitioner provided some financial support on a rather irregular basis.

In the fall of 1968, the petitioner moved in with the respondent and normal marital relations were resumed for about a month. However in December of that year the parties began to occupy separate bedrooms and both testify there has been no sexual intercourse between them since that time. They subsequently moved twice and had lived together at 72 Pauline Street in East Saint John from March 1970 until a week before the trial when the respondent moved to another address, taking the children with her.

The petitioner says he and the respondent stayed in the same house "for the sake of the kids". While I suspect the respondent may have stayed as a matter of economic necessity the evidence does not justify such a finding. The petitioner has supported the home, has clothed his wife and family and has given the respondent a $20 weekly allowance. The respondent says she was just a maid. It is not a situation where there was no communication between the parties and apparently where the children were concerned there was often mutual discussion and agreement. For instance the parties were able to jointly decide on how much should be spent on the children at Christmas and they "always made a big thing of Christmas". As between the parties discord continued and on only two occasions in the past five years did they go out together. The respondent has been friendly with another man with the knowledge and at least tacit consent of the petitioner.

The situation is not unlike that described by Holland J. in *Cooper* v. *Cooper* (1972), 10 R.F.L. 184 (Ont.) [at 186]:

> The parties obviously cannot get along and clearly there is considerable bad feeling between them. At the same time there is clearly good feeling towards the children, the children are being well looked after and are receiving all necessary care and attention from their parents, in spite of the fact that the attitude of the parents toward each other must be upsetting for each of them.

I have read most, if not all, of the decisions reported since the advent of the Divorce Act dealing with cases where marriage breakdown is alleged on the grounds of separation even though the spouses continue to live under the same roof. . . .

I think the following general statements can be extracted as representing the weight of judicial opinion:

(1) Great care must be exercised in considering the evidence and each case determined on its own circumstances.

(2) There can be a physical separation within a single dwelling unit.

(3) A case is not taken out of the statute just because a spouse remains in the same house for reasons of economic necessity.

(4) To meet the statute there must be both (a) physical separation and (b) a withdrawal by one or both spouses from the matrimonial obligation with the intent of destroying the matrimonial consortium.

(5) Cessation of sexual intercourse is not conclusive but is only one factor to be considered in determining the issue.

(6) There may be an atmosphere of severe incompatibility but remain one household and one home — a distinction may be drawn between an unhappy household and a separated one. . . .

In *Cooper* v. *Cooper, supra,* Holland J. pointed out that generally a finding that spouses were living separate and apart was made where the following circumstances were present [p. 187]:

(i) Spouses occupying separate bedrooms.

(ii) Absence of sexual relations.

(iii) Little, if any, communication between spouses.

(iv) Wife providing no domestic services for her husband.

(v) Eating meals separately.

(vi) No social activities together.

It is probably not necessary to establish all six elements in each case and each case must stand or fall on its own merits. I refrain from commenting on the wisdom of incompatible spouses remaining together "for the sake of the children" but I do not think it was the intention of Parliament that a spouse who does so, under circumstances in this case, can at his or her option at any time after such circumstances have continued for three years or more elect to opt out of the marriage and claim a divorce on the ground of permanent marriage breakdown. A mutual opting out in such circumstances would be little more than divorce by consent, something Parliament has not yet provided for.

The evidence does not satisfy me that for three years or more prior to presentation of the petition in this action the parties were living separate and apart within the meaning of the Act or that there was an intention on the part of either spouse to destroy the matrimonial consortium. Accordingly both the petition and the counter-petition will be dismissed.

[This result was affirmed on appeal: (1975), 10 N.B.R. (2d) 148 (C.A.). Limerick J. A., who wrote separate, concurring reasons, stated at 154-155:

I am in accord that husband and wife live separate and apart even though they live under the same roof where the six circumstances exist as set out in the judgment of Holland, J. in *Cooper* v. *Cooper*. . . .

I would however qualify somewhat circumstance (4), where the husband and wife enter into a contract for economic reasons and the husband pays the wife an agreed amount for preparing his meals for him I would consider them living separate and apart if the other five circumstances applied. In such case the service of the wife would not arise out of or be referable to a matrimonial relationship but would be a matter of separate and independent contract. I would add a further condition; viz., they do not share living room and recreational facilities, such as television, together.

The living conditions of the parties in this action do not comply with the above circumstance. I therefore concur with the judgment of my brother Ryan and dismiss the appeal.]

DORCHESTER v. DORCHESTER

3 R.F.L. 396, [1971] 2 W.W.R. 634 (B.C. S.C.)

MACFARLANE J.: — The bare facts are that the petitioner took his wife to the Riverview Hospital for treatment of a mental illness on February 17, 1967, and she has been since that date a patient. The parties have not cohabited since the admission of the wife to the said hospital.

The date of the presentation of the petition was June 11, 1970.

The following evidence was given by the petitioner in cross-examination by counsel for the Public Trustee:

> Q Who took your wife to hospital when she was admitted in February, 1967?
>
> A I did.
>
> Q Why did you take her?
>
> A Or did they take her with the ambulance? I can't remember.
>
> Q Why did you take —
>
> A On the doctor's recommendation.
>
> Q You were living with her up to the time that she was admitted to the hospital, is that correct?
>
> A Yes.
>
> Q Then when did you decide to destroy, or shall we say, forget about the marriage entirely? When did you make up your mind that the marriage was broken up and decided to leave your wife for good?
>
> A Well, it was about the time I came in here and filed for a divorce for the simple reason that my property is tied up. Nobody will listen to me. I can't do anything. Nobody listens to me.
>
> Q You made up your mind about the time you filed your divorce papers?
>
> A Yes.
>
> Q Mr. Dorchester, your petition for divorce is dated June 11th, 1970. In other words according to what you just said you decided to leave your wife for good and forget about the marriage, so to speak, as of June 11th, 1970?
>
> A Yes.

The physical separation of husband and wife is one of the factors which must be taken into consideration in cases of this kind, but there may be physical separation of the parties without there being a finding that the parties are living "separate and apart". For instance, a serviceman may be posted overseas and be away from his wife for over three years without the parties living "separate and apart" within the meaning of the Act.

The evidence in any given case must be examined to determine upon what date the parties were not only living apart but also on what date did the matrimonial relationship cease to exist.

In this case the matrimonial relationship was subsisting when the wife was admitted to the hospital. The only evidence I have from the petitioner with regard to the cessation of the matrimonial relationship was that this occurred just prior to the presentation of his petition on June 11, 1970. On that evidence I am unable to find that the spouses had been living separate and apart for a period of not less than three years immediately preceding the presentation of the petition.

The petition therefore must be dismissed, without costs.

NOTES AND QUESTIONS

1. Which of the factors listed in *Cooper* v. *Cooper* (1972), 10 R.F.L. 184 (Ont. H.C.) should be given the greatest weight in determining whether spouses residing under the same roof are living separate

and apart for the purposes of the *Divorce Act*? Does the seventh circumstance suggested by Limerick J.A. in *Dupere* add anything to the *Cooper* test? To what extent should the court be influenced by the reason why the spouses are still residing under the same roof?

2. For other cases determining whether or not spouses who live under the same roof are living separate and apart for the purposes of the *Divorce Act*, see *Galbraith* v. *Galbraith* (1969), 69 W.W.R. 390, 5 D.L.R. (3d) 543 (Man. C.A.); *Seminuk* v. *Seminuk* (1970), 72 W.W.R. 304, 10 D.L.R. (3d) 590 (Sask. C.A.); *Rousell* v. *Rousell* (1969), 69 W.W.R. 568, 6 D.L.R. (3d) 639 (Sask. Q.B.); *Cherewick* v. *Cherewick* (1969), 1 R.F.L. 225, 69 W.W.R. 235 (Man. Q.B.); *Reid* v. *Reid* (1969), 1 R.F.L. 229, 71 W.W.R. 375 (B.C. S.C.); *Pybus* v. *Pybus* (1969), 1 R.F.L. 234, 72 W.W.R. 315 (B.C. S.C.); *Smith* v. *Smith* (1970), 2 R.F.L. 214, 74 W.W.R. 462 (B.C. S.C.); *Newman* v. *Newman* (1970), 2 R.F.L. 219 (Ont. C.A.); *Mayberry* v. *Mayberry*, 3 R.F.L. 395, [1971] 2 O.R. 378 (C.A.); *Dick* v. *Dick*, 2 R.F.L. 225, [1971] 2 W.W.R. 138 (B.C. S.C.); *Burt* v. *Burt* (1972), 7 R.F.L. 155, 24 D.L.R. (3d) 497 (N.S. T.D.); *Kobayashi* v. *Kobayashi*, 6 R.F.L. 358, [1972] 3 W.W.R. 221 (Man. Q.B.); *Cridge* v. *Cridge* (1973), 12 R.F.L. 348 (B.C. S.C.); *McKenna* v. *McKenna* (1974), 19 R.F.L. 357, 10 N.S.R. (2d) 268 (C.A.); *Boulos* v. *Boulos* (1980), 14 R.F.L. (2d) 206, 24 Nfld. & P.E.I.R. 370 (Nfld. T.D.); *Smith* v. *Smith* (1980), 28 Nfld. & P.E.I.R. 99, 4 Fam. L. Rev. 1 (P.E.I. S.C.); *Wood* v. *Wood* (1980), 6 Man. R. (2d) 36 (Q.B.); *Lauzon* v. *Lauzon* (1982), 27 R.F.L. (2d) 259 (B.C. S.C.); *Follett* v. *Follett* (1984), 49 Nfld. & P.E.I.R. 58 (Nfld. U.F.C.); *Thorogood* v. *Thorogood* (1987), 11 R.F.L. (3d) 82 (Ont. U.F.C.); *Ginter* v. *Ginter* (1988), 15 R.F.L. (3d) 203 (Sask. Q.B.); *Woolgar* v. *Woolgar* (1995), 10 R.F.L. (4th) 309 (Nfld. U.F.C.); and *Gannon* v. *Gannon* (1996), 149 N.S.R. (2d) 211 (N.S. S.C.).

3. As *Dorchester* illustrates and as is made clear by s. 8(3)(a) of the *Divorce Act*, physical separation alone does not mean that the spouses are living separate and apart for purposes of divorce. For other cases involving long-term hospitalization, see *Hills* v. *Hills* (1969), 1 R.F.L. 236 (N.S. T.D.); *Rowland* v. *Rowland* (1969), 1 R.F.L. 221 (Ont. H.C.); *Herman* v. *Herman* (1969), 1 R.F.L. 41 (N.S. T.D.); and *Norman* v. *Norman* (1974), 12 R.F.L. 252 (N.S. C.A.). See also *Compton* v. *Compton* (1970), 1 R.F.L. 244 (N.S. T.D.), where there was an indefinite separation on the advice of the petitioner's doctors; *Singh* v. *Singh* (1975), 23 R.F.L. 379 (Ont. H.C.), where the husband immigrated to Canada intending that his wife would follow later; and *Dowd* v. *Dowd* (1975), 25 R.F.L. 80 (Man. Q.B.), where the husband was imprisoned. Where the parties are physically separated for reasons such as these, what evidence would the court rely on to determine if and when the period of living separate and apart had begun?

4. Under the *Divorce Act* of 1968, the parties had to be living separate and apart for the requisite three or five years prior to the presentation of the petition. Under the 1985 *Divorce Act*, the one-year period of separation need not immediately precede the commencement of the divorce proceeding, merely its determination. The parties must, however, be living separate and apart at the commencement of the proceedings. It is now possible for spouses to separate and for one or both of them to apply for divorce on the ground of separation a day after the separation. Might divorce proceedings be resorted to prematurely under this provision?

5. Section 8(1) of the *Divorce Act* contemplates that a divorce judgment may be granted to both spouses. The spouses may jointly apply or petition for divorce where the grounds for divorce are separation for the requisite period and there is no contested claim for other relief. See ss. 8(1) and (2) of the *Divorce Act*, Family Law Rules, O. Reg. 114/99, r. 36(2), and Rules of Civil Procedure, R.R.O. 1990, Reg. 194, r. 69.03(5) and (6).

6. As indicated in the cases reproduced and noted in this section, separation has both a physical and mental element. In *Calvert (Litigation Guardian of)* v. *Calvert* (1997), 27 R.F.L. (4th) 394 (Ont. Gen. Div.), the court concluded that a wife who was in the early stages of Alzheimer's disease had the capacity to separate. The Ontario Court of Appeal affirmed this conclusion, (1998), 36 R.F.L. (4th) 169, and also held that it was irrelevant whether the wife still had this capacity when divorce proceedings began. As the wife had the capacity to separate when the parties first began to live apart and as she did not waver from her wish to remain separate and apart as long as she had capacity, the period of separation continued uninterrupted by virtue of s. 8(3)(b)(i) of the *Divorce Act*.

7. For further reading regarding the definition of "living separate and apart", see Hubbard, "Calculating the Period of Living Separate and Apart Under S. 4(1)(e) of the Divorce Act" (1983), 13 Man. L.J. 53.

8. The determination of the date of separation may be significant in determining property issues under Part I of the Ontario *Family Law Act* or the matrimonial property regimes in other provinces. See, e.g., *Winegarden* v. *Winegarden* (1988), 15 R.F.L. (3d) 284 (Ont. Dist. Ct.); *Vogel* v. *Vogel* (1989), 18 R.F.L. (3d) 445 (Ont. H.C.); *Oswell* v. *Oswell* (1990), 28 R.F.L. (3d) 10 (Ont. H.C.); *De Acetis* v. *De Acetis* (1991), 33 R.F.L. (3d) 372 (Ont. Gen. Div.); *Newton* v. *Newton* (1995), 11 R.F.L. (4th) 251 (Ont. U.F.C.); *Memisoglu* v. *Memiche* (1995), 170 N.B.R. (2d) 285 (C.A.); *Arvelin* v. *Arvelin* (1996), 20 R.F.L. (4th) 87 (Ont. Gen. Div.); *Pelchat* v. *Pelchat* (1996), 13 O.T.C. (Gen. Div.); and *Raymond* v. *Raymond* (1997), 34 R.F.L. (4th) 234 (N.B.Q.B.). Property issues are dealt with in the next chapter.

(b) Reconciliation and resumption of cohabitation

ROGLER v. ROGLER

(1977), 1 R.F.L. (2d) 398 (Ont. H.C.)

FANJOY L.J.S.C.: — This is an undefended petition for divorce founded on s. 4(1)(*e*) of the Divorce Act, R.S.C. 1970, c. D-8. At the conclusion of the evidence I reserved judgment and I have had the benefit of thorough and succinct written argument by Mr. Staats, counsel for the petitioner.

The husband and wife separated in September 1973 and the divorce proceedings commenced on 28th December 1976. In or about the fall of 1974 the petitioner and the respondent had sexual intercourse and the only issue is whether this sexual intercourse interrupted the period of living separate and apart. At the outset I would say that I accept fully the evidence of the petitioner and find her to be a most credible witness. The only evidence before me with respect to these acts of sexual intercourse is her evidence. She stated that her husband would now and again come to her house around 2:00 a.m. in the morning and would leave at approximately 4:00 a.m. They would have sex and her stated reason was that she felt that it was the right thing to do "in the sight of God" since they were married. Other than that, they did not live together. He did not eat at the house; she performed no services for him. His presence in the house was only during these nightly hours "once in a while".

In *Foote* v. *Foote*, [1971] 1 O.R. 338, 2 R.F.L. 221, 15 D.L.R. (3d) 292, Donnelly J. held that the period of "living separate and apart" was interrupted by an act of sexual intercourse between the petitioner and the respondent and dismissed the petition.

However, the Ontario Court of Appeal in *Deslippe* v. *Deslippe* (1974), 4 O.R. (2d) 35, 16 R.F.L. 38, 47 D.L.R. (3d) 30, since the decision in *Foote* v. *Foote* reviewed the law fully and came to a different conclusion on the facts before them. In that case the husband insisted on going with the wife to a party and during the evening the husband became intoxicated and "pushy"; to avoid difficulty with him, the wife stayed with him at her girlfriend's home and had sexual intercourse with him. It was found, as a fact, that the wife did not intend, by this act, to reconcile with her husband. In the case before me I make the same findings with respect to the intention to reconcile.

Following the reasoning set out in the *Deslippe* case I am of the view that the issue of whether the couple were living together must be determined on all the facts. Sexual intercourse is only one of the concomitants of marriage. While more recent trends in society have, to some extent, changed the services normally performed by a wife in marriage, I am still of the view that they generally include the preparation of meals, the washing and ironing of clothes and many other services too numerous to mention. They also, of course, include the many mutual, physical, mental and moral supports, including those with respect to the children.

In the case at bar the only element which existed was that of sexual intercourse which was somewhat in the nature of an "affair", even though the two parties were married. I cannot distinguish in this case between one act of sexual intercourse and a number of acts under the same conditions.

I therefore find that the acts of sexual intercourse did not interrupt the period of "living separate and apart". There will therefore be a decree nisi [of divorce].

NOTES AND QUESTIONS

1. In *McGeachy* v. *McGeachy* (1980), 15 R.F.L. (2d) 274 (Ont. H.C.), the spouses, after separation, had frequent contact with each other and on several occasions took vacations together. On some of these occasions sexual intercourse occurred. Applying *Deslippe* and *Rogler*, McCart L.J.S.C. held that there had been no resumption of cohabitation or interruption of the period of living separate and apart. See also *Spinney* v. *Spinney* (1981), 33 Nfld. & P.E.I.R. 61 (P.E.I.C.A.).

2. Section 9(3)(b) of the *Divorce Act* of 1968 specified that a period during which a husband and wife were living separate and apart was not considered to have been interrupted or terminated "by reason only that there has been a resumption of cohabitation by the spouse during a single period of not more than ninety days with reconciliation as its primary purpose". There was conflicting case-law on whether more than one period of cohabitation was permitted. *Crawford* v. *Crawford*, 24 R.F.L. 172, [1976] 3 W.W.R. 767 (Man. C.A.) and *Ross* v. *Ross* (1979), 12 R.F.L. (2d) 360 (B.C. S.C.) held that more than one period of cohabitation did not interrupt the period during which the spouses were living separate and apart provided the spouses did not cohabit for any single period of more than 90 days. *Nolan* v. *Nolan* (1977), 1 R.F.L. (2d) 280, 15 O.R. (2d) 358 (H.C.) and *McLellan* v. *McLellan* (1983), 36 R.F.L. (2d) 113, 50 N.B.R. (2d) 432 (C.A.) held that s. 9(3)(b) permitted only one period of resumption of cohabitation. How does s. 8(3)(b) of the 1985 *Divorce Act* deal with this problem?

3. Section 8(3)(b)(ii) is only one of the provisions of the *Divorce Act* designed to encourage attempts at reconciliation. See **Reconciliation and Conciliation**, below.

(2) ADULTERY

(a) Nature of adultery

In the following two cases, it was alleged that artificial insemination of a married woman by a donor who was not her husband constituted adultery. This argument forced the courts to examine, in some detail, the legal definition of adultery.

ORFORD v. ORFORD

(1921), 49 O.L.R. 15, 58 D.L.R. 251 (H.C.)

[This was an action by the wife for alimony. The husband alleged that the wife had committed adultery and was therefore not entitled to alimony. The wife admitted that she had given birth to a child some two years after the marriage and that the husband was not the father. She denied the allegation of adultery, claiming that the child had been conceived as a result of artificial insemination. Mr. Justice Orde indicated that he did not believe her story, but went on to discuss the legal issue raised if it were believed.]

MR. JUSTICE ORDE: — . . . The plaintiff contends . . . that it is not adultery for a woman to become "artificially inseminated" or "artificially impregnated" by means of a man other than her husband and without her husband's knowledge, and to bear a child in consequence thereof; . . .

Mr. White argues that to constitute adultery there must be actual sexual intercourse in the ordinary natural way, and he cites many definitions of the word "adultery" from legal dictionaries and text-books in support thereof. He lays stress upon the distinction between the act of adultery and the consequences of it, contending that insemination or pregnancy is merely the result of the act of adultery, and that as a matter of law adultery is confined to the act of sexual intercourse in the ordinary acceptance of that term. . . .

Mr. White contended that the essential element of adultery rested in the moral turpitude of the act of sexual intercourse as ordinarily understood. With this I cannot agree. The sin or offence of adultery, as affecting the marriage-tie, may, without going farther back, be traced from the Mosaic law down through the canon or ecclesiastical law to present date. . . .

In its essence, adultery was always regarded as an invasion of the marital rights of the husband or the wife. When the incontinence was that of the wife, the offence which she had committed rested upon deeper and more vital ground than that she had merely committed an act of moral turpitude, or had even seen fit to give to another man something to which her husband alone was entitled. The marriage-tie had for its primary object the perpetuation of the human race. For example, the Church of England marriage-service, which in this respect may well serve as the voice of the Ecclesiastical Courts of England, gives as the first of "the causes for which matrimony was ordained" that of "the procreation of children."

That no authority can be found declaring, directly or indirectly, that "artificial insemination" would constitute adultery is not to be wondered at. This is probably the first time in history that such a suggestion has been put forward in a Court of justice. But can any one read the Mosaic law against those sins which, whether of adultery or otherwise, in any way affect the sanctity of the reproductive functions of the people of Israel, without being convinced that, had such a thing as "artificial insemination" entered the mind of the lawgiver, it would have been regarded with the utmost horror and detestation as an invasion of the most sacred of the marital rights of husband and wife, and have been the subject of the severest penalties?

In my judgment, the essence of the offence of adultery consists, not in the moral turpitude of the act of sexual intercourse, but in the voluntary surrender to another person of the reproductive powers or faculties of the guilty person; and any submission of those powers to the service or enjoyment of any person other than the husband or the wife comes within the definition of "adultery."

The fact that it has been held that anything short of actual sexual intercourse, no matter how indecent or improper the act may be, does not constitute adultery, really tends to strengthen my view that it is not the moral turpitude that is involved, but the invasion of the reproductive function. So long as nothing takes place which can by any possibility affect that function, there can be no adultery; so that, unless and until there is actual sexual intercourse, there can be no adultery. But to argue, from that, that adultery necessarily begins and ends there is utterly fallacious. Sexual intercourse is adulterous because in the case of the woman it involves the possibility of introducing into the family of the husband a false strain of blood. Any act on the part of the wife which does that would, therefore, be adulterous. That such a thing could be accomplished in any other than the natural manner probably never entered the heads of those who considered the question before. Assuming the plaintiff's story to be true, what took place here was the introduction into her body by unusual means of the seed of a man other than her husband. If it were necessary to do so, I would hold that that in itself was "sexual intercourse." It is conceivable that such an act performed upon a woman against her will might constitute rape.

Mr. White was driven, as a result of his argument, to contend that it would not be adultery for a woman living with her husband to produce by artificial insemination a child of which some man other than her husband was the father! A monstrous conclusion surely. If such a thing has never before been declared to be adultery, then, on grounds of public policy, the Court should now declare it so. . . .

MACLENNAN v. MACLENNAN

[1958] Sess. Cas. 105 (Scott. Ct. of Session)

LORD WHEATLEY'S OPINION: — The pursuer seeks decree of divorce from the defender on the ground of her adultery, and *prima facie* his case is essentially simple. The parties were married on 25th August 1952, and it is a matter of agreement that they have not lived together or had marital relations since 31st May 1954. On 10th July 1955 the defender admittedly gave birth to a female child in Brooklyn, New York, and on that historical narrative of events the pursuer asks the Court to find proven facts, circumstances and qualifications from which an inference of the defender's adultery can be drawn. In the uncomplicated days before science began to innovate on the natural processes of procreation, the lapse of time between the last act of marital intercourse and the birth of the child would have led to the inevitable inference that the defender had been guilty of an adulterous act with another man by means of the normal and natural physiological mechanism, as a result of which the child was conceived. The defender, however, has tendered an explanation by way of defence, which is unique in the annals of our law, and which seeks to establish that she conceived the child not as a result of sexual intercourse with another man, as that phrase is commonly understood, but as a result of artificial insemination from a donor. She does not aver, however, that the pursuer was a consenting party to such an artificial process of conception, and the pursuer maintains that he never agreed to the defender adopting it, if in fact it ever took place. The defender submits that artificial insemination by a donor, even without the consent of the husband, is not adultery as the law understands and has interpreted that term, and that proof of conception by such means would rebut the inference which would otherwise be raised from the fourteen months' period of non-access followed by the birth of a child.

The issue comes before me as a matter of relevancy, since the pursuer has submitted that such a general defence is irrelevant, on the ground that artificial insemination by a donor without the consent of the husband is adultery in the eyes of the law, and I am accordingly obliged to accept the defender's averments *pro veritate* at this stage. It should be noted, however, for the purposes of the record, that, while the defender does not aver that the artificial insemination by a donor was without the consent of her husband, the whole argument proceeded on the basis that there was no such consent. . . .

There are manifestly grave moral, ethical, social, and personal considerations involved in the practice of artificial insemination in its various forms which will no doubt be fully developed elsewhere. It is almost trite to say that a married woman who, without the consent of her husband, has the seed of a male donor injected into her person by mechanical means, in order to procreate a child who would not be a child of the marriage, has committed a grave and heinous breach of the contract of marriage. The question for my determination, however, is not the moral culpability of such an act, but is whether such an act constitutes adultery in its legal meaning. A wife or a husband could commit an act of gross indecency with a member of the opposite sex which would be a complete violation of the marital relationship, but which could not be classified as adultery. It would indeed be easy according to one's personal viewpoint to allow oneself to be influenced by the moral, ethical, social, and personal considerations to which I have referred and to reach a conclusion based on these considerations, but this problem which I am called upon to solve must be decided by the objective standard of legal principles as these have been developed and must be confined to the narrow issue of whether this form of insemination constitutes adultery in the eyes of the law. If it is not adultery, although a grave breach of the marriage contract, that is a matter for the Legislature if it be thought that a separate legal remedy should be provided.

[Lord Wheatley concluded that the following propositions emerged from English and Scottish case law:]

1. For adultery to be committed there must be two parties physically present and engaging in the sexual act at the same time. 2. To constitute the sexual act there must be an act of union involving some degree of penetration of the female organ by the male organ. 3. It is not a necessary concomitant of adultery that male seed should be deposited in the female's ovum. 4. The placing of the male seed in the female ovum need not necessarily result from the sexual act, and if it does not, but is placed there by some other means, there is no sexual intercourse. . . .

If artificial insemination by a donor without the husband's consent is to be deemed adultery, the first question which seems to call for a decision is whether the donor whose seed has been used has himself been guilty of adultery. If the answer is in the affirmative, the further question arises, at what point of time has he done so? If it be at the point when the seed is extracted from his body, certain interesting considerations would arise. I gather that seed so obtained can be retained for a considerable time before being used, and in some cases it may not be used at all. If the donor's seed is taken merely to lie *in retentis* it surely cannot be adultery if that seed is never used. Thus, if his adultery is to be deemed to take place at the time of the parting with the seed, it can only be an adultery subject to defeasance in the event of the seed not being used. Such a statement need only be stated for its absurdity to be manifested. If, on the other hand, his adultery is deemed to take place when the seed is injected into the woman's ovum, this latter act may take place after his death, and in that case the woman's conduct would constitute not only adultery but necrophilism. Such a proposition seems to me to be equally absurd. The third alternative is that the whole process should be regarded as an act of adultery, but as this might in certain cases result in the act covering a period of say two years, and be committed partly during the lifetime and partly after the death of the donor, I cannot distinguish between the absurdity of such a proposition and the absurdity of the other alternatives. Senior counsel for the pursuer appreciated the illogicality and absurdity of these consequences of the proposition that the donor had committed adultery, and accepted that he had not. This then forced him to argue that the wife could commit adultery by herself. One need not consider the interesting point whether the administrator could be said to commit adultery, because the administrator might be a woman or the seed might be self-injected by the wife herself operating the syringe. The idea that a woman is committing adultery when alone in the privacy of her bedroom she injects into her ovum by means of a syringe the seed of a man she does not know and has never seen is one which I am afraid I cannot accept. Unilateral adultery is possible, as in the case of a married man who ravishes a woman not his wife, but self-adultery is a conception as yet unknown to the law. The argument of pursuers' counsel was that adultery meant the introduction of a foreign element into the marital relationship. That, however, seems to me to beg the question, because what has still to be determined is what is the foreign element? For the reasons which I have already explained, that foreign element is the physical contact with an alien and unlawful sexual organ, and without that element there cannot be what the law regards as adultery. The introduction of a spurious element into the family, with all its consequences, may be the result of such conduct, but it not a necessary result, and it is by the means and not by the result that this issue is to be judged. If artificial insemination by a donor were to be regarded as adultery, then I opine the view that it would be adultery whether the seed germinated or not, and yet in the latter case there would be no resultant adulteration of the strain. At the root of the argument for the pursuer was the proposition that impregnation is at the basis of adultery, and it was argued that the view of the English Judges that there must be penetration indicated that there must be the possibility of insemination. Whatever the moral and ethical aspects of that argument may be, the Courts have now accepted that adultery can take place when the possibility of insemination has been excluded either by natural causes or artificial expedients, and so that argument must fail.

It accordingly follows, in my opinion, that artificial insemination by a donor does not constitute adultery according to our law. . . .

NOTES AND QUESTIONS

1. For further discussion of the issue raised in the two cases reproduced above, see Tallin, "Artificial Insemination" (1956), 34 Can. Bar Rev. 1; Hubbard, "Artificial Insemination: A Reply to Dean Tallin" (1956), 34 Can. Bar Rev. 425; Payne, "Artificial Insemination Heterologous and the Matrimonial Offence of Adultery" (1961), 40 N.C.L.R. 111; Lang, "Does Artificial Insemination Constitute Adultery?" (1966), 2 Man. L.J. 87; and Fullerton, "Artificial Insemination" (1979), 2 Fam. L. Rev. 31.

2. Artificial insemination raises other complex legal issues, as well as religious and moral ones. Generally, see Fullerton, "Artificial Insemination" (1979), 2 Fam. L. Rev. 31; Ontario Law Reform Commission, *Report on Human Artificial Reproduction and Related Matters* (Toronto: Ministry of the Attorney General, 1985); Royal Commission on New Reproductive Technologies, *Proceed with Care: Final Report of the Royal Commission on New Reproductive Technologies* (Ottawa: Minister of Government Services, 1993); and Arnup, "Finding Fathers: Artificial Insemination, Lesbians and the Law" (1994), 7 C.J.W.L. 97.

3. Consent is a necessary ingredient of adultery. When a woman is sexually assaulted she does not commit adultery: *Redpath* v. *Redpath*, [1950] 1 All E.R. 600 (C.A.) and *Barnett* v. *Barnett*, [1957] P. 78 at 82, [1957] 1 All E.R. 388. See also: *T. v. T.*, 1 R.F.L. 23, [1970] 2 O.R. 139, 10 D.L.R. (3d) 125 at 128 (H.C.). A woman may also be so drunk that she will be held not to have consented to the sexual intercourse: *Cunningham* v. *Cunningham* (1966), 11 F.L.R. 399 (Qld. S.C.).

4. When Monica Lewinsky performed oral sex on President Clinton, did he have "sexual intercourse with that woman"? Did the President commit adultery?

5. Is sexual intercourse between a married, but separated, person and a third party adultery? See *Horvath* v. *Fraess* (1997), 36 R.F.L. (4th) 32 (Sask. Q.B.).

(b) Proof of adultery

(i) *Standard and Nature of Proof*

SHAW v. SHAW

(1971), 4 R.F.L. 392, 7 N.S.R. (2d) 77 (T.D.)

DUBINSKY J.: — At the conclusion of the hearing in this case I granted a decree nisi in the divorce petition by Mrs. Shaw on the ground of cruelty. I reserved my decision on the counter-petition by Mr. Shaw on the ground of adultery.

Harold Bellefontaine, the co-respondent named in the counter-petition, denied that he had committed adultery with Mrs. Shaw, the respondent by the counter-petition.

I am on safe ground in saying that there is no *direct* evidence of any adulterous relationship between Mrs. Shaw and Mr. Bellefontaine. It follows, therefore, that if adultery is to be found herein on the part of the respondent (the respondent by the counter-petition), it must be inferred from the proven facts.

Power on Divorce, 2nd ed., 1964, p. 425 states as follows:

> Since it is almost never possible to adduce direct evidence of the act of adultery its commission is permitted to be proven by evidence of acts or a course of conduct which convinces the court that it should infer that it did occur.
>
> The inference can be drawn although both parties deny their guilt. The drawing of the inference must always be with caution and evidence that creates only a suspicion of adultery is insufficient.
>
> It is now settled that the standard of proof required in a divorce action wherein no question of legitimacy arises is not that applicable to criminal cases where the prosecution must prove guilt beyond a reasonable doubt, but is the standard required in civil actions where the preponderance of probabilities determines the issues. . . . Where, as is usually the case, the evidence is circumstantial, it is not necessary that the facts should be inconsistent with any other rational conclusion than that the defendant is guilty. In such a case, and speaking generally of the standard of proof in an action for divorce, it is sufficient if the circumstances are such as would lead the guarded discretion of a reasonable or just man to that conclusion. . . .
>
> It is impossible to lay down any general rule defining the circumstances which are sufficient in an action for divorce to justify a finding of adultery, except that the circumstances must be such as lead by fair and reasonable inference to that conclusion. Each case depends on its own particular facts. Evidence of familiarities between the parties and of facts showing opportunity for the commission of adultery raise a *prima facie* case that adultery has been committed, but the inference should always be drawn with extreme caution and it has been held should not be drawn unless there is proof of an inclination to commit adultery.

It would, in my opinion, be a reasonable and guarded inference from the facts that Mrs. Shaw and Mr. Bellefontaine, a married man with two children, were seeing so much of each other that the *opportunities* for her to commit adultery were present. However, Lord Atkin in *Ross* v. *Ellison (Ross)*, [1930] A.C. 1 at 23, points out:

> That there were opportunities for committing adultery is nothing; *there must be circumstances amounting to proof that the opportunities would be used.* (The italics are mine.)

. . . I would regard it as a sorry day if a married person could not have and enjoy the warm friendship of one of the opposite sex, without being stamped with the stigma of impropriety.

In two fairly recent cases, where the same sort of situation existed, I did draw the inference that adultery had been committed. In each of these cases there was something which led me to find as I did. In the first case there was evidence that on one occasion the respondent and co-respondent, who were both present at a party, were found lying fully clothed on the bed of a darkened bedroom. This uncontradicted piece of evidence led me to conclude that they were there for an amorous purpose. This incident, coupled with other evidence, led me to infer that adultery had taken place between the respondent and co-respondent.

In the other case there was introduced a letter which had been written by the respondent to the co-respondent and which referred to the great love that existed between them, as well as to other things. That letter, when added to other evidence which had been given, led me to infer that adultery had been committed.

In each of these two cases I had in mind what Lord Buckmaster said in *Ross v. Ellison (Ross)*, supra, at p. 7:

> Adultery is essentially an act which can rarely be proved by direct evidence. It is a matter of inference and circumstance. It is easy to suggest conditions which can leave no doubt that adultery has been committed, but the mere fact that people are thrown together in an environment which lends itself to the commission of the offence is not enough unless it can be shown by *documents, e.g., letters and diaries, or antecedent conduct that the association of the parties was so intimate and their mutual passion so clear that adultery might reasonably be assumed as the result of an opportunity for its occurrence.* (The italics are mine.)

. . .

In short, keeping in mind the authorities quoted above and reviewing all the evidence given in the present case touching upon the allegation of adultery, I am not led to the conclusion that adultery was committed by Mrs. Shaw and Mr. Bellefontaine. Accordingly, I dismiss the counter-petition.

NOTES AND QUESTIONS

1. It is now established that a civil standard of proof applies to determine if adultery has been established. Nevertheless, the gravity of the consequences of a finding of adultery must be considered in applying that standard. Some older cases therefore appear to require proof beyond a reasonable doubt where the result of a finding of adultery would render a child illegitimate: *Hiuser v. Hiuser*, [1962] O.W.N. 220 (C.A.) and *Loewen v. Loewen* (1969), 2 R.F.L. 230, 68 W.W.R. 767 (B.C. S.C.). Note that the concept of illegitimacy has been abolished in Ontario by s. 1 of the *Children's Law Reform Act*.

Are the effects of a finding of adultery in today's society so benign that the standard of proof should not be a very onerous one? See *Dewer v. Dewer* (1968), 12 F.L.R. 319 (Vic. Sup. Ct.) where McInerney J. suggested (at 325) that comments made in older cases regarding the standard of proof required for a finding of adultery should no longer be mechanically applied "at the present time when the fabric of marriage is noticeably weaker and the general attitude of society towards what have come to be known as '*de facto* relationships' noticeably more complaisant".

2. Direct evidence of adultery is obviously rare. In contested cases, the finding that the respondent has committed adultery is usually an inference drawn from circumstantial evidence. In *Burbage v. Burbage* (1985), 46 R.F.L. (2d) 33 (Ont. H.C.), Stortini L.J.S.C. stated (at 37): "In my view, once opportunity and intimacy are established on a balance of probabilities, there is a burden on the alleged adulterers to call evidence in rebuttal sufficient to dislodge the preponderant evidence."

3. Under the applicable Ontario rules, proof of adultery can be established in uncontested cases by affidavit evidence of the applicant or petitioner, the respondent spouse, or the third party involved. It should also be noted that it is no longer necessary to name the third party in an application or petition based on adultery. See *Family Law Rules*, O. Reg. 114/99, r. 36(3) and *Rules of Civil Procedure*, R.R.O. 194, r. 69.03(4). In *d'Entremount v. d'Entremount* (1992), 44 R.F.L. (3d) 224 (N.S.C.A.), the affidavit of the respondent husband acknowledging uncondoned adultery with an unnamed person was sufficient evidence to prove adultery.

(ii) *Section 10 of the Ontario Evidence Act*

Section 23(1) of the *Divorce Act* incorporates by reference the provincial laws of evidence. Accordingly, the *Evidence Act*, R.S.O. 1990, c. E.23 applies to divorce proceedings in Ontario. By virtue of s. 8, parties to an action and their spouses are competent and compellable witnesses. However, s. 11 provides that persons cannot be compelled to disclose any communication between themselves and their spouses during the marriage. Moreover, s. 10 stipulates:

> The parties to a proceeding instituted in consequence of adultery and the husbands and wives of such parties are competent to give evidence in such proceedings, but no witness in any such proceeding, whether a party to the suit or not, is liable to be asked or bound to answer any question tending to show that he or she is guilty of adultery, unless such witness has already given evidence in the same proceeding in disproof of his or her alleged adultery.

Section 10 applies wherever a divorce petition or counter-petition relies on s. 8(2)(b)(i) of the *Divorce Act* as a ground for divorce: *Hunter* v. *Hunter*, 11 R.F.L. 94, [1973] 1 O.R. 162 (H.C.) and *Tapson* v. *Tapson*, 2 R.F.L. 232, [1970] 1 O.R. 696 (Master). Whether or not other grounds are also pleaded is irrelevant. See *Boylen* v. *Boylen* (1974), 20 R.F.L. 69, 6 O.R. (2d) 81 (H.C.). The section may apply in divorce proceedings even if s. 8(2)(b)(i) is not one of the grounds relied upon by either party. In *Burt* v. *Burt* (1979), 11 R.F.L. (2d) 143, 27 O.R. (2d) 163 (H.C.) the court held that the privilege arose where the wife's petition was based solely on cruelty, but one of the allegations was that the husband had treated the wife cruelly in that he had so associated himself with a woman that any reasonable person would believe he was committing adultery. See also *Anderson* v. *Anderson* (1974), 17 R.F.L. 394 (Ont. H.C.). But see *Rayner* v. *Rayner*, 7 R.F.L. 103, [1972] 2 O.R. 588 (C.A.), which was effectively distinguished in *Burt*.

The protection given by s. 10 can obviously be waived by a witness. Where an oral hearing occurs, it is advisable for counsel to inform the witness of the protection granted by s. 10 before the witness is sworn. After the witness is sworn it is prudent to establish that the witness is aware of the protection and has expressly waived it before asking the relevant questions. See *Elliott* v. *Elliott*, [1933] O.R. 206, [1933] 2 D.L.R. 40 (H.C.) and *Welstead* v. *Brown*, [1952] 1 S.C.R. 3 at 23, 102 C.C.C. 46. In most jurisdictions, it is now possible to establish adultery by affidavit evidence alone in certain cases. Rule 69.19(3) of the *Rules of Civil Procedure*, R.R.O. 1990, Reg. 194 specifies that where the respondent's affidavit acknowledges the adultery, it has to stipulate that the respondent is aware that there is no obligation to give evidence of the adultery and that the evidence is willingly provided. There are similar provisions regarding third party affidavits admitting adultery: *Rules of Civil Procedure*, R.R.O. 1990, Reg. 194, r. 69, 19(5). Similar rules existed in the old *Family Court Rules* (R.R.O. 1990, Reg. 202, r. 82(4) and r. 82(6)). The new *Family Law Rules*, O. Reg. 114/99 have not retained these requirements.

NOTES AND QUESTIONS

1. Despite the statutory protection, the court may consider a party's failure to present evidence in disproof of adultery in deciding if the adultery has been established: *Poyser* v. *Poyser*, [1952] 2 All E.R. 949 (C.A.); *Chung* v. *Chung* (1966), 60 D.L.R. (2d) 526 (N.S. C.A.); *Furlong* v. *Furlong* (1963), 49 M.P.R. 377 at 389, 44 D.L.R. (2d) 594 (N.B. C.A.); *Lemenson* v. *Lemenson* (1969), 1 R.F.L. 206, 70 W.W.R. 749 (Man. Q.B.); and *Fogel* v. *Fogel* (1976), 24 R.F.L. 18 (Ont. H.C.), affirmed (1979), 9 R.F.L. (2d) 55 (Ont. C.A.). Does this tend to defeat the legislative policy behind the legislation?

2. The effect of s. 10 is to prevent a party from commencing a proceeding on the ground of adultery unless the adultery can be proved by independent testimony or unless one of the adulterers consents to give evidence. Is s. 10 an outdated anomaly that should be repealed? The rule against self-incrimination in adultery cases has been repealed in England and several provinces. The Ontario Law Reform Commission has urged its repeal. See *Report on the Law of Evidence* (Ottawa: Ministry of the Attorney General, 1976) at 105-112.

3. For further reading, see Rosen, "The Privilege Against Incrimination as to Adultery. Should it be Abolished?" (1960), 23 M.L.R. 275.

(3) CRUELTY

KNOLL v. KNOLL

1 R.F.L. 141, [1970] 2 O.R. 169 (C.A.)

[The wife appealed a judgment dismissing a petition based on s. 3(d) and s. 4(1)(b) of the 1968 *Divorce Act*. Evidence at trial indicated that the husband drank heavily and that the wife left the matrimonial home because of the husband's abusive conduct towards her after he drank. Corroborated evidence indicated that the husband assaulted his wife on a number of occasions and once shoved her forcibly against a chimney, causing her physical injury. When the husband was inebriated, he treated the wife very coarsely, rudely and disrespectfully, applying vile epithets to her. The wife's doctor testified at trial that the marital situation had ruined the wife's nerves. She had high blood pressure, was completely run-down, and had lost 19 lbs. before she left the home. Medication had been prescribed. The court's reasons regarding s. 3(d) are reproduced below. The wording of s. 3(d) was virtually identical to that in s. 8(2)(b)(ii) of the 1985 *Divorce Act*.]

SCHROEDER J.A.: — . . . It is evident that the learned Judge held and gave effect to the view that cruelty within the meaning of s. 3(*d*) of the Divorce Act was legal cruelty as defined in *Russell* v. *Russell*, [1897] A.C. 395 at 467, and in Ontario in *Bagshaw* v. *Bagshaw* (1920), 48 O.L.R. 52, 52 D.L.R. 634, and in many English and Canadian cases in which the principle there enunciated has been consistently followed and applied, a rule which required proof of conduct of such a character as to cause danger to life, limb or health (bodily or mental), or as to give rise to a reasonable apprehension of such danger. He must have concluded that the concept of cruelty as laid down in those cases was unaffected by the provisions of s. 3 of the Divorce Act. . . .

In enacting the Divorce Act of 1968, Parliament has expressed the public will to soften the rigours of the marriage bonds as recognized in English canon law and founded upon the thesis that the general happiness of married life was secured by the indissolubility of the marriage bond, even though in individual cases its principles operated with great severity. Unhappy spouses were required to sleep in their beds as they had made them except in those extreme cases as outlined in Lord Stowell's judgment in *Evans* v. *Evans* (1790), 1 Hag. Con. 35, 161 E.R. 466.

Over the years the courts have steadfastly refrained from attempting to formulate a general definition of cruelty. As used in ordinary parlance "cruelty" signifies a disposition to inflict suffering; to delight in or exhibit indifference to the pain or misery of others; mercilessness or hard-heartedness as exhibited in action. If in the marriage relationship one spouse by his conduct causes wanton, malicious or unnecessary infliction of pain or suffering upon the body, the feelings or emotions of the other, his conduct may well constitute cruelty which will entitle a petitioner to dissolution of the marriage if, in the court's opinion, it amounts to physical or mental cruelty "of such a kind as to render intolerable the continued cohabitation of the spouses". That is the standard which the courts are to apply, and in the context of s. 3(*d*) of the Act that standard is expressed in language which must be taken to exclude the qualifications laid down in *Russell* v. *Russell, supra*, and in the numerous other cases which have followed and applied the ancient ecclesiastical rule in matrimonial disputes. . . .

Care must be exercised in applying the standard set forth in s. 3(*d*) that conduct relied upon to establish cruelty is not a trivial act, but one of a "grave and weighty" nature, and not merely conduct which can be characterized as little more than a manifestation of incompatibility of temperament between the spouses. The whole matrimonial relations must be considered, especially if the cruelty consists of re-proaches, complaints, accusations, or constant carping criticisms. A question most relevant for consideration is the effect of the conduct complained of upon the mind of the affected spouse. The determination of what constitutes cruelty in a given case must, in the final analysis, depend upon the circumstances of the particular case, having due regard to the physical and mental condition of the parties, their character and their attitudes towards the marriage relationship.

In the present case it is the cumulative effect of the acts of the defendant upon the petitioner which must be considered and given proper weight. The wife's return to her home after a day's work only to find her husband in an inebriated state, given to quarrelsomeness and abuse, heaping insult upon insult and indignity upon indig-nity, was clearly conduct amounting to mental cruelty of such a kind as to render intolerable the continued cohabitation of the spouses. I cannot be convinced that our community standards require a wife to tolerate such an intolerable situation. . . .

GILBERT v. GILBERT

(1980), 18 R.F.L. (2d) 240, 39 N.S.R. (2d) 241 (T.D.)

[In 1978, the combined effect of working, looking after her young daughter and maintaining a home became too much for Mrs. Gilbert. She suffered from loss of sleep; she lost weight and she was eventually admitted to hospital suffering from heart palpitations. After her discharge, she began to see a psychologist regularly. On 27th October, 1979, Mrs. Gilbert left the family home with her daughter, stating that life with Mr. Gilbert had become intolerable. Mrs. Gilbert petitioned for divorce on the ground of mental cruelty. Mr. Gilbert opposed the petition. The petitioner's principal complaint was that the respondent had a domineering personality and often criticized her.]

HALLETT J.: — . . .I formed the impression from the evidence and from my observation of the respondent that the worst that can be said about the respondent is that he is a very smug and self-satisfied person, and I accept the petitioner's evidence that she found it intolerable to continue living with him as far as she was concerned, but I do not think that the acts of which she complains constituted mental cruelty. The acts complained of were not grave and weighty but merely reflected a concern he had for the family's financial affairs and concern he had to see that his wife and child developed their personalities. It has been said many times that in the test as to whether the actions of a spouse constitute cruelty one must look at what effect the spouse's actions have had on the petitioner, not what effect they might have on a person of a different temperament. I accept that as a proper principle, but the conduct must be grave and weighty, and there is nothing in the evidence that measures up to this test of cruelty. I can understand that the petitioner was unhappy and that her husband's personality contributed to her unhappiness, but I do not feel his conduct amounted to mental cruelty of such a kind as to render intolerable the continued cohabitation of the parties. . . .

The practice of the court in granting divorces on flimsy evidence in uncontested cases involving mental cruelty has, in my view, led petitioners and their counsel to overlook the fact that a petitioner must prove both that the conduct of the respondent was *cruel* and that it rendered cohabitation *intolerable: Luther* v. *Luther* (1978), 26 N.S.R. (2d) 232, 5 R.F.L. (2d) 285, 40 A.P.R. 232 (C.A.).

The acts of cruelty must be grave and weighty. The petitioner has testified that she could not stand living with the respondent and left. However, I am not satisfied that the evidence supports her allegations that he treated her with *mental cruelty* in that there was nothing in the evidence to show acts of a *grave and weighty nature* as necessary to establish this ground for divorce. The evidence shows the parties were of very different personalities, the petitioner somewhat shy and reserved and the respondent self-confident and self-satisfied. Such personality clashes cannot be elevated to form the basis for a decree to be granted on the ground of mental cruelty, notwithstanding the fact that one must look at the acts of the respondent in such a way as to ascertain what effect those acts had on *this* petitioner. I am not satisfied that the difficulties the petitioner had over the last year of their marriage can be attributed to conduct of the respondent that constituted mental cruelty. I am satisfied that pressures were present over which the respondent had little or no control. These pressures had an effect on the petitioner and she found she could not continue living with him and left.

The petition is dismissed. . . .

DELANEY v. DELANEY

5 R.F.L. 44, [1972] 1 O.R. 34 (C.A.)

SCHROEDER J.A. (orally): — . . . The parties were married on 10th May 1969 and lived together until 13th July 1970, when the appellant deserted the respondent under the circumstances hereinafter mentioned.

It is alleged by the appellant that she and her husband had intercourse only four or five times within the first eight weeks of the marriage, but that, since that time, no further acts of intercourse took place; that the husband had persistently refused to gratify her wishes, although she requested him to have intercourse with her on numerous occasions during the remainder of the period of their life together. She suggested that he seek medical advice or other professional counselling, but he refused to do so.

In this case the marriage has admittedly been consummated, since there were four or five acts of sexual intercourse between the parties in the first and second month of the marriage. It would appear, and, indeed, there is nothing in the evidence to suggest the contrary, that this young woman had the normal sex drive, and the husband's abnormal reaction to her repeated invitations could have no other effect upon a normal healthy young woman of 21 years of age than to convince her that she was a total failure, wholly inadequate, perhaps a hopeless case. The erosion of her self-esteem, the feelings of despair and frustration, which would be thus engendered in her, could well, and, in this case, did have unwholesome consequences upon the petitioner's mental and physical health. Her father, who gave evidence, stated that she had become in his opinion a "nervous wreck". She lost a great deal of weight and her general physical health was impaired. The wife was brought face to face, therefore, with the alternative of having to live out her years under these intolerable conditions in a marriage state filled with mental anguish and despair, or to seek to put an end to it by divorce proceedings without further delay.

. . . The conduct on the part of the husband was clearly calculated to render intolerable the continued cohabitation of the spouses within the meaning of s. 3(d) of the Divorce Act. . . .

BARRON v. BULL

(1987), 5 R.F.L. (3d) 427 (Alta. Q.B.)

BRACCO J.: — . . . The petitioner seeks to divorce the respondent on the grounds of "a breakdown of the marriage by Section 8 subsection 2(b)(ii)". In his petition, he states that there is no possibility of reconciliation, stating: "We talked but efforts failed." In his affidavit of 12th November 1986, the petitioner is more forthcoming in setting out the details of their problems. He attests as follows:

4. That my grounds for Divorce are Marital Breakdown with Mental Cruelty.

(a) The Respondent threatened several times over the past 9 months to leave me; holding all debts.

(b) The Respondent demanded a family of her own: a child would make our marriage work.

(c) She is jealous of material items that others have that she doesn't have, whether she needs them or not i.e.

(1) a "new" car

(2) new furniture

(3) a dog

(4) to travel — like her friends

(d) She was continually discussing our marital problems with family, friends and co-workers.

i.e. She complained to her mother approximately 6 months ago that we never have time to ourselves. Shortly after, she was continually inviting family and friends to our home or volunteering to babysit nephews. She suggested to my Sister-In-Law that I may be seeing someone else due to our lack of sex. At that time and to this date she has been on fertility drugs. At that time I told her to seek professional help because of her continual lying.

(e) The Motorcycle and car were sold to help pay off bills as well as cashing in my personal life insurance.

(f) EIGHT HUNDRED DOLLARS was given to her for the first month's rent and damage deposit.

In response to Chief Justice Moore's request for clarification, Barron filed his supplementary affidavit in which he attested as follows:

2. This is a further explanation to Paragraph 4(b).

She believed that if we were to start a family then all our marital problems would have been resolved. I felt that a child would only add to our problems, since our financial situation require (sic) that we have two incomes to make ends meet. I still believe that having a child would only be a temporary status symbol to her. The baby and her would be the centre of attention for a few months. When the glamour and hype of a new born baby wore off, things could only get worse as time went by.

This is the reason that I did not wish to have children. I fell (sic) that two people should not have to have and use children to make a marriage work. It would not be fair to the children.

To put the petitioner's concern about debts in perspective, I note that both the petitioner and respondent are employees of the city of Calgary and their annual declared earnings for 1985 were $32,832 and $20,917 respectively.

Their total current debt to three merchants and three credit card companies is $8,333.81 on which they pay $498 monthly. There are no arrears. . . .

The cruelty subsection of the Divorce Act, 1985 is essentially the same as the cruelty subsection in the preceding Divorce Act.

At p. 36 of Payne's Commentaries on The Divorce Act, 1985 the relevance of cases defining cruelty under the old Act is considered:

> Because the express language of paragraph 3(d) of the *Divorce Act*, R.S.C. 1970, c. D-8 has been incorporated in the current provisions of paragraph 8(2)(b)(ii) of the *Divorce Act*, 1985, it is apparent that the jurisprudence that has evolved under paragraph 3(d) will furnish significant guidelines respecting the principles implicit in paragraph 8(2)(b)(ii), notwithstanding that each case is to be determined in the final analysis on its own facts . . .

I have not been able to find any reported cases in which cruelty was considered following the proclamation of the Divorce Act, 1985. There are, however, a number of decisions which discuss cruelty under the previous Act. . . .

In *Chouinard* v. *Chouinard* (1969), 10 D.L.R. (3d) 263 at 264-65, 1 N.B.R. (2d) 941 (C.A.), Limerick J.A. speaking for the court discusses the meaning of cruelty:

> Cruelty which constitutes a ground for divorce under the *Divorce Act*, whether it be mental or physical in nature, is a question of fact. Determination of such a fact must depend on the evidence in the individual case being considered by the Court. No uniform standard can be laid down for guidance; behaviour which may constitute cruelty in one case may not be cruelty in another. There must be to a large extent a subjective as well as an objective aspect involved; one person may be able to tolerate conduct on the part of his or her spouse which would be intolerable to another. Separation is usually preceded by marital disputes and unpleasantness. The Court should not grant a decree of divorce on evidence of merely distastful [sic] or irritating conduct on the part of the offending spouse. The word cruelty denotes excessive suffering, severity of pain, mercilessness; not mere displeasure, irritation, anger or dissatisfaction; furthermore, the Act requires that cruelty must be of such a kind as to render intolerable continued cohabitation.

In *Bens* v. *Bens* (1983), 50 A.R. 197 at 198 (C.A.), Kerans J.A. states:

> Relief was denied on the ground that cruelty was not made out. Cruelty is conduct of a kind, in the words of the *Divorce Act*, "to render intolerable the continued co-habitation of the spouses". See *Feldman v. Feldman* (1970), 75 W.W.R. (N.S.) 715 . . . Judges have avoided any more precise definition, but the standard of tolerable behaviour should, in general terms, reflect the contemporary community standards and not the judge's personal views nor what may have been considered tolerable in the past.

On reviewing the petitioner's allegations, bearing in mind the judicial comments as to the standards in the cases cited, I note firstly that the petitioner does not anywhere in his affidavits nor in the petition state that his wife's conduct has caused him to suffer. One can infer that he has been displeased with her attitude and conduct but his displeasure appears to be based on their differing views. There are absolutely no particulars of the alleged cruelty in the petition for divorce other than the reference to "Sec. 8 subsection 2(b)(ii)". He does not indicate that his wife deliberately chose a course of conduct that he found so intolerable that he could not continue cohabitation with her.

In his affidavit of 12th November 1986, he complains that his wife threatened several times to leave him holding all debts. He further states that she demanded a family of her own. In his 26th November 1986 affidavit, he elaborated on his reasons for not wanting children and characterized his wife's desire for children as seeking a status symbol and her desire to be the centre of attention together with the child. In his view, the "glamour and hype" of a newborn baby would quickly wear off and their problems would worsen.

It is clear from the petitioner's material that his wife has a strong desire to have children and was taking fertility drugs whereas he appears very determined not to have children and refers to his wife's concern about his "seeing someone else due to our lack of sex". He does not deny his own alleged refusal to have sexual intercourse with his wife.

He alleges that his wife is jealous of material items that others have and lists some examples. From an examination of his income and expenses as well as their debts, none of which are in arrears, it is apparent that they have in fact been able to meet their financial obligations. The petitioner alludes to his wife's desires for material items but does not say that she has been irresponsible in her spending nor that her expressed wishes have caused him to suffer.

Upon reviewing all of the petitioner's allegations, I cannot find that the respondent has been guilty of conduct that has caused the petitioner to suffer. I am not persuaded that the petitioner has shown his wife to delight in or be indifferent to his suffering, if indeed such suffering existed. Nor am I persuaded that the respondent has been shown to have been cruel, merciless or hard-hearted toward her husband. On the contrary, it appears that her desire for a child is a normal expectation in a marriage unless there are good and valid reasons why the birth of a child should be denied. No such valid reasons were revealed, other than the concern of the loss of her income. The petitioner's preoccupation with the marital debts and his insistence that she continue to pay her share of those debts according to his apportionment appears to be the petitioner's principal reason for refusing to have a child and engage in marital sex.

Realizing that the test for cruelty is largely subjective, I am unable to find that the petitioner has established the respondent's cruelty toward him which could be characterized to be of such a kind as to render intolerable their continued cohabitation.

The petition for divorce is refused.

B. (Y.) v. B. (J.)

(1989), 20 R.F.L. (3d) 154 (Alta. Q.B.)

VEIT J.: — The petitioner has applied for a divorce on two grounds — adultery and mental cruelty. The petition is presented for judgment on affidavit evidence only without appearance in court, pursuant to the provisions of R. 568. The original affidavit presented by the petitioner stated merely:

5(b) The grounds for my divorce are the breakdown of our marriage.

In a supplementary affidavit, the petitioner swears:

4. That there has been a marriage breakdown which is evidenced by the following:

The respondent, since celebration of the marriage has treated me with mental cruelty of such a kind as to render continued cohabitation intolerable. Particulars of such mental cruelty are as follows:

(a) The Respondent has admitted to me and to my eldest daughter, S., that he is a practising homosexual.

There is no other evidence relating to the grounds for divorce. . . .

On being informed that additional submissions with respect to the adequacy of the grounds would be required, counsel for the petitioner cited *Countway* v. *Countway* (1968), 70 D.L.R. (2d) 73 (N.S.T.D.); *Spicer* v. *Spicer*, [1954] 1 W.L.R. 1051, [1954] 3 All E.R. 208 (P.D.A.); and *Gardner* v. *Gardner*, [1947] 1 All E.R. 630 (P.D.A.). In each of these cases, the petitioner was granted a divorce based on mental cruelty caused by a homosexual relationship of his or her spouse. However, in each of those cases, there is a recognition by the court that homosexual practices by a spouse "do not, as such, entitle the other spouse to a decree of divorce": *Countway* v. *Countway*, at p. 76. As to what additional conduct is required, in *Countway*, for example, the respondent refused to maintain a normal sexual relationship with his wife and told her that he did not love her. In *Spicer*, when the husband had asked his spouse to discontinue an association with a woman, "she persisted in it against his entreaties and against his best endeavours" [p. 209]; the wife was prepared to admit that her persistent friendship with the intervener had amounted to cruelty to the husband. In *Gardner*, the court referred to a course of conduct over a period of years including the repulsion of the wife to sexual relations with her husband to the degree that the marriage was not consummated during the first four years of its existence; that before the marriage, the wife had made arrangements to live after the ceremony with the woman with whom she had been living prior to the ceremony; and that she absented herself from the conjugal home for extensive periods, against the husband's wishes, and told the husband that during those periods she was living with another woman. It also relied in particular [p. 633] "on a letter which she wrote to her husband on the subject of her proposed change of sex".

In summary, in each of the cases cited by the petitioner something in addition to homosexual practices was submitted in evidence as constituting the grave conduct necessary to ground a divorce judgment. Moreover, as our Court of Appeal has held in *Anderson* v. *Anderson*, [1972] 6 W.W.R. 53, 8 R.F.L. 299, 29 D.L.R. (3d) 587, there is an element of wilfulness in mental cruelty; being a homosexual is not equivalent to treating your spouse with cruelty. Cruelty implies callousness or indifference as referred to in that judgment.

. . . The fact that Parliament has also authorized divorce judgments to be issued in the absence of appearances in court does not mean that the standards of cruelty have been relaxed. The fact that the husband does not contest his wife's petition does not relieve the wife from the test which Parliament has established.

In addition, the conduct relied upon to establish cruelty must be intolerable to the petitioner. There are no particulars in the supplementary affidavit of the subjective aspect of the grounds invoked. As the court remarked in *Chouinard* v. *Chouinard* (1969), 1 R.F.L. 101 at 103, 10 D.L.R. (3d) 263, 1 N.B.R. (2d) 941 (C.A.): "one person may be able to tolerate conduct on the part of his or her spouse which would be intolerable to another". The petitioner must provide some basis for a court's determination that the husband's conduct made continued cohabitation with him intolerable to her. In this case, there is not even an assertion by her to this effect.

In summary, this evidence does not meet the petitioner's burden of proving the grounds set out in s. 8(2)(*b*)(ii) of the Act. She has leave to reapply on additional affidavit evidence.

NOTES AND QUESTIONS

1. In *Thompson* v. *Thompson* (1982), 29 R.F.L. (2d) 321 (Ont. H.C.), Misener L.J.S.C. interpreted the test from *Knoll*, above, as follows (at 327): "Put in other terms, it is my obligation to decide . . . whether or not the conduct, viewed objectively, goes beyond what can be characterized as differences in temperament or differences of opinion over aims and desires, and what amounts to what can fairly be called serious misconduct."

2. As *Knoll* and *Gilbert* illustrate, the courts held that s. 3(d) of the *Divorce Act* of 1968 incorporated both a subjective and objective test. The objective test was considered necessary to ensure that mere incompatibility did not become a basis for divorce whereby the parties could avoid the three or five years waiting period under s. 4(1)(e). See also *Hiltz* v. *Hiltz* (1970), 2 R.F.L. 178, 2 N.S.R. (2d) 434

(T.D.), affirmed (1970), 11 R.F.L. 35, 4 N.S.R. (2d) 547 (C.A.); *Ifield* v. *Ifield*, 24 R.F.L. 237, [1976] W.W.D. 63 (Sask. Q.B.); *Luther* v. *Luther* (1978), 5 R.F.L. (2d) 285, 26 N.S.R. (2d) 232 (C.A.); *Fjermestad* v. *Fjermestad* (1980), 16 R.F.L. (2d) 137 (B.C. S.C.); and *Lake* v. *Lake* (1982), 30 R.F.L. (2d) 5 (B.C. S.C.). Nevertheless, the objective element of the test was downplayed in the years immediately preceding the repeal of the 1968 Act. Divorces were granted, especially in uncontested cases, on the basis of evidence that revealed little more than incompatibility. See, for example, *Mes* v. *Mes* (1981), 24 R.F.L. (2d) 257 (Ont. H.C.) and Professor McLeod's annotation to the case in those reports. Should a more rigorous application of the test for cruelty be used under the new Act in light of the fact that the requisite period for the separation ground is now only one year?

3. The courts have persistently refused to attempt an inclusive definition of cruelty and have not given great weight to previously decided cases dealing with similar conduct. As a result, similar conduct may satisfy the test in one case and not in another. For example, refusal of sexual intercourse constituted cruelty in *Delaney* and *Lewis* v. *Lewis* (1982), 44 N.B.R. (2d) 268 (Q.B.), but it did not in *Markus* v. *Markus*, 3 R.F.L. 306, [1971] 2 W.W.R. 35, 16 D.L.R. (3d) 520 (Sask. Q.B.); *Ebenal* v. *Ebenal*, 2 R.F.L. 180, [1971] 1 W.W.R. 473, 15 D.L.R. (3d) 242 (Sask. C.A.); and *Boivin* v. *Massicote* (1977), 4 R.F.L. (2d) 315 (Que. S.C.). What circumstances might convince the court that refusal of sexual intercourse is cruelty?

4. Could a divorce be granted on the basis of s. 8(2)(b)(ii) in the following situation? A husband suffers from premature ejaculation. He refuses to seek or accept medical help despite his wife's requests and despite his awareness of the obvious emotional and mental stress caused to the wife. See *Katopodis* v. *Katopodis* (1979), 27 O.R. (2d) 711 (C.A.). Compare *Rouleau* v. *Wells* (1980), 124 D.L.R. (3d) 766 (Que. S.C.).

5. The respondent need not intend to be unkind or cruel. Mental illness is no defence to a petition on the basis of cruelty: *Castillo* v. *Castillo* (1986), 3 R.F.L. (3d) 423 (N.B.Q.B.). How is intent to be hurtful, to embarrass, etc., if present, nevertheless relevant? See *Emmerson* v. *Emmerson* (1970), 2 R.F.L. 147 (B.C.S.C.); *Wittstock* v. *Wittstock*, 3 R.F.L. 326, [1971] 2 O.R. 472, 18 D.L.R. (3d) 264 (C.A.); and *Thordarson* v. *Thordarson* (1978), 5 R.F.L. (2d) 92 (Ont. C.A.).

6. In almost every case where a divorce is granted on the basis of cruelty the parties will be living separate and apart. Nevertheless, a woman may succeed in establishing cruelty even if she continues to cohabit with her husband. In *Horne* v. *Horne*, 5 R.F.L. 394, [1972] 3 W.W.R. 153 (B.C. S.C.), McIntyre J. stated (at 395):

> The presence of small children needing her care might influence a mother to "tolerate the intolerable". A woman without funds and without means of earning, living in a remote area far from help and friends, might also find herself in the same situation.

See also *MacDonald* v. *MacDonald* (1975), 23 R.F.L. 303 (Man. Q.B.); *Pongor* v. *Pongor* (1976), 27 R.F.L. 109 (Ont. C.A.); and *Boulos* v. *Boulos* (1980), 14 R.F.L. (2d) 206, 24 Nfld. & P.E.I.R. 370 (Nfld. T.D.).

7. Three reported cases in which the courts granted petitions under the 1985 *Divorce Act* on the basis of mental cruelty are *Desmarais* v. *Desmarais* (1988), 13 R.F.L. (3d) 64 (Alta. Q.B.); *Tramsek* v. *Tramsek* (1994), 6 R.F.L. (4th) 66 (B.C.S.C.); and *Clark* v. *Clark* (1995), 18 R.F.L. (4th) 234 (Sask. Q.B.). In *Desmarais*, the court held that the wife's "persistent complaining" and "continual verbal abuse" constituted cruelty. In *Tramsek*, the husband would periodically scream at his wife and then not speak to her for long periods of time. Rothery J. described (at 241-242) the husband's behaviour this way in *Clark*:

> . . .he took all of her [the wife's] pay cheques after he required her to sign them over to him, and locked them in a metal cabinet of which he only had the key. He also discouraged the family from visiting Carol's relatives and tried to forbid Carol from visiting her own friends. These are all indicia of one who exerts extreme control over another human being. That Carol may have allowed such behaviour earlier in their marriage does not make the behaviour any less appropriate. She eventually found it intolerable.

8. In *Bell-Ginsburg* v. *Ginsburg* (1993), 48 R.F.L. (3d) 208 (Ont. Gen. Div.), Rosenberg J. dismissed a motion to strike a wife's claim for general damages for breach of fiduciary duty, misrepresentation, fraud, endangerment, battery, and intentional infliction of emotional distress in circumstances somewhat similar to those in *B.(Y.)* v. *B.(J.)*. After four years of marriage, Mrs. Bell-Ginsberg discovered that her husband had had a number of affairs with men. Until that time, the wife had been unaware that her husband was bisexual. The wife was seriously concerned that she had been exposed to the human immunodeficiency virus.

9. Conduct after separation was considered in *Storr* v. *Storr* (1974), 14 R.F.L. 346 (N.S.C.A.); *MacRae* v. *MacRae* (1974), 15 R.F.L. 270 (P.E.I. S.C.); *Meikle* v. *Meikle*, [1974] 4 W.W.R. 670, 45 D.L.R. (3d) 765 (B.C. S.C.); *McMurdy* v. *McMurdy* (1975), 22 R.F.L. 312 (Ont. H.C.); *Ifield* v. *Ifield* (1976), 24 R.F.L. 237 (Sask. Q.B.); *Randell* v. *Randell* (1977), 1 R.F.L. (2d) 135 at 145 (Ont. H.C.); *Whetstone* v. *Whetstone* (1979), 9 R.F.L. (2d) 168, 17 A.R. 17 (T.D.); *Barbour* v. *Barbour* (1980), 18 R.F.L. (2d) 80 (Nfld. T.D.); *Johnson* v. *Johnson*, 24 R.F.L. (2d) 70, [1981] 6 W.W.R. 316 (B.C. S.C.); *Payritis* v. *Payritis* (1982), 26 R.F.L. (2d) 300 (B.C. S.C.); and *Greggain* v. *Hunter* (1984), 31 Sask. R. 311 (U.F.C.). Nevertheless, Morse J. refused to consider conduct after separation in *Saunders* v. *Saunders* (1975), 22 R.F.L. 210 (Man. Q.B.) and *Thibodeau* v. *Thibodeau* (1975), 27 R.F.L. 114 (Man. Q.B.).

4.   Bars to Proceedings

(1) INTRODUCTION

Section 11 of the *Divorce Act* resembles s. 9 of the 1968 Act. The wording of s. 11 indicates that it is the duty of the court to ascertain whether or not any of the relevant bars exist, even if neither party raises this issue. See *Schuett* v. *Schuett*, 2 R.F.L. 248, [1970] 3 O.R. 206 (C.A.); *MacIntosh* v. *MacIntosh* (1976), 28 R.F.L. 218 (P.E.I. S.C.); *Singh* v. *Singh* (1976), 25 R.F.L. 20 (B.C. S.C.); and *Money* v. *Money* (1987), 5 R.F.L. (3d) 375 (Man. C.A.). However, this duty may be of more theoretical than practical significance in an undefended divorce, especially one dealt with by means of affidavit evidence alone.

(2) COLLUSION

Section 11(1)(a) of the 1985 *Divorce Act* retains collusion as an absolute bar to an application for divorce. Section 11(4) defines the term in essentially the same manner as it was defined in the 1968 Act. The following article examined the extent to which the 1968 statutory definition altered the common law concept of collusion.

SOPINKA, "THE DIVORCE ACT, 1968: COLLUSION CONFINED"

(1969), 47 Can. Bar Rev. 31-39 (Footnotes Omitted)

. . . The bogey of collusion, which has ranged unchecked by statutory definition over the field of divorce law since the passage of the Imperial statute, The Divorce and Matrimonial Causes Act, 1857, probably has created more difficulty in the administration of divorce law than any other factor. It served as a convenient vehicle for the introduction of individual judicial views of public policy in divorce cases. These views, as the decided cases vividly attest, presented a varied and confusing tableau to the practising lawyer. If he erred in choosing one line of authority rather than another the consequences reflected not only on the client's cause but on the solicitor himself. The only safe course was to adopt a definition so strict that even the purist could find no fault. The safest course however was not to act in divorce cases at all.

The adoption of the safe course, however, was bewildering to the client. Either he was kept completely at arms length from his spouse or negotiations and agreements about matters of custody, maintenance and property settlement were carried on as if divorce were merely a side issue while to the client it was central to the whole business.

To remedy the evil the Committee on Divorce recommended a definition of collusion in the following terms:

> Collusion shall be a bar to divorce, being a corrupt agreement or conspiracy to which the petitioner or respondent is a party, to effect some illegal, wrongful or improper purpose such as the bribery of a respondent or co-respondent not to defend the action or to appear as a witness or to perform an illegal or improper act in order to furnish evidence, or to pretend to do so, to give false evidence thus deceiving the court or depriving it of an opportunity to learn the truth and an agreement for the reasonable support and maintenance of a husband or wife or children shall not be deemed to be collusive.

Parliament gave effect to this recommendation by defining collusion in section 2(c) of the Divorce Act, 1968. While couched in different terms, it is submitted that the meaning is the same. . . .

In the past, judicial definition of collusion exhibited three levels, ranging from the most restrictive to the more expanded definition:

Level one   The most restrictive "a corrupt agreement or conspiracy to which the petitioner is a party, to obtain a divorce by means of manufactured evidence, or some fraud or deceit practised on the court".

Level two   The restrictive definition was expanded by extending it to apply to any agreement to withhold or abandon a defence otherwise open to one of the respondents or to suppress evidence.

Level three Levels one and two were further expanded to include an agreement in which, in consideration of a promise to bring and conduct a divorce proceeding, on valid grounds, the plaintiff was provided with substantial benefits in the form of maintenance, costs, division of marital property and the like if the agreement could be characterized as a bribe to bring proceedings.

Courts have had no difficulty in classifying as collusive, agreements under level one because the presentation of a false case clearly perverted or tended to pervert the course of justice. Such agreements are manifestly included in the statutory definition in the Divorce Act.

Agreements coming under level two presented more difficulty. Here the grounds for a divorce exist but may be subject to defences open to one of the parties such as condonation, connivance, adultery by the plaintiff or petitioner, lack of domicile and the like. If a party agrees that these defences will be suppressed in whole or in part the court is prevented from getting at the truth and may grant a divorce which, but for the agreement, would not have been granted. The result is a subversion of the course of justice. *Prima facie*, therefore, such agreements were properly characterized as collusive in the past, and, it is submitted are collusive under the Divorce Act because they are entered into "for the purpose of subverting the administration of justice" and "to deceive the court".

Does it follow, then, that an agreement not to defend is *per se* collusive irrespective of the facts? There may not be a defence that has any chance of success.

[The author examines the case law dealing with such agreements and continues:]

These cases point the way to the proper interpretation of the statutory definition of collusion. The court cannot conclude that every agreement not to defend is collusive. It must determine on the evidence whether the agreement was entered into "for the purpose of subverting the administration of justice". In the face of such an agreement in the absence of any evidence as to the defences open to the respondents and the facts to support them a *prima facie* case of collusion exists. It is only a *prima facie* case, however, which may be rebutted by evidence that satisfies the court that the agreement did not suppress any defence having a reasonable chance of success and was entered into merely to save the parties the time and expense of protracted litigation or otherwise to "smooth the asperities of litigation". If a judge is satisfied that there has been such a full and frank disclosure of the facts that he is able to come to the conclusion that the decree would have been granted if defended, it seems highly unreasonable to refuse a decree simply on the basis of the existence of the agreement.

Agreements of the type classified under the third level referred to above which provide for the institution of divorce proceedings in return for financial benefits presented the greatest difficulty to the courts in the past. Much of the confusion, of which the Committee on Divorce complains, was caused by cases which deal with such agreements.

[After discussing some of the cases where agreements of the type classified under the third level were held to be collusive, Sopinka concludes:]

The rationale of these cases is that the court must be satisfied that the plaintiff has received a real injury and genuinely seeks relief. If the plaintiff is only nominally seeking relief which is actually desired by the defendant wrongdoer then the court will refuse to allow the wrongdoer to obtain the divorce.

This reasoning had some justification in administering a divorce law based exclusively on the matrimonial offence concept. A divorce was only to be granted to the innocent against the guilty. If the court found that the situation in substance as opposed to form was reversed then it refused the decree. The Divorce Act however has departed from the matrimonial offence concept. It introduces the marriage breakdown concept and enables the so-called guilty spouse to divorce the innocent. . . .

A departure from the matrimonial offence concept would therefore suggest the elimination altogether from the definition of collusion the type of agreement outlined under level three. It seems futile to analyze the motives of the petitioner to see whether it is the injured party who seeks relief when the injured party may be divorced against his or her will in certain circumstances and in others a divorce may be granted on grounds which involve no matrimonial offence at all.

While the change in the basic concept of divorce suggests the narrowing of collusion as to exclude agreements under level three it is submitted that an examination of the definition itself clearly leads to that conclusion. An agreement for financial benefits to the petitioner in consideration of the commencement of proceedings for divorce, where valid grounds exist, (especially if disclosed to the court) cannot, it is submitted be characterized as being "for the purpose of subverting the administration of justice." Such an agreement "in no way distorts the grounds upon which relief is sought, nor does it provide for the suppression of material facts". It is submitted that the saving clause of the definition was inserted to make it abundantly clear that such agreements were to be excluded. It cannot be interpreted to refer to the usual separation agreement *simpliciter*, which makes no mention of divorce. A statutory exclusion would hardly be necessary to cover such an agreement. No case has found such an agreement to be collusive. . . .

In summary, it appears that in order to eliminate the uncertainty in the law of collusion which kept the parties at arms length, hampered reconciliation and discouraged settlement of support, custody and property issues, Parliament has narrowed the definition of collusion. It is the author's conclusion that Parliament intended to remove the taint of collusion from those troublesome agreements by which divorce proceedings are agreed to be brought in return for financial benefits by way of support or for the division of marital property and costs. Such an agreement could not, of course, provide for the fabrication or manufacturing of evidence, the withholding of a just defence or the suppression of evidence.

NOTES AND QUESTIONS

1. In *Gillett* v. *Gillett* (1979), 9 R.F.L. (2d) 97, 9 Alta. L.R. 238 (T.D.), the court expressly adopted the views of Sopinka regarding agreements that he classified under level three. Miller J. also quoted with approval the following passage from the reasons of Begg J. in *Grose* v. *Grose*, [1965] N.S.W.R. 429 (S.C.):

> It seems to me that collusion would at least arise in the following types of cases. First, where a party undertakes to provide false evidence in the procuring of a divorce; obviously this would be collusion. Secondly, it might arise where the effect of the agreement, and indeed the intention of the agreement, was to suppress evidence in a court which would result in a different order being made by that court than the order contemplated. Thirdly, it would seem to me to arise in cases where a defence is abandoned for a consideration. That is in cases where parties agree not to urge a substantial and bona fide defence which would, by virtue of that agreement, deprive the court of an opportunity of fulfilling its statutory functions of determining the issues involved and which would lead to a decree or order being improperly obtained.

See also *Tannis* v. *Tannis*, [1970] O.R. 323, 8 D.L.R. (3d) 333 (H.C.), where the court expressly held that an agreement that made the settlement of a support claim conditional on divorce was not collusive.

2. Collusion does not arise if the petitioner or applicant is not, either directly or indirectly, involved in the improper arrangement or agreement: *Milne* v. *Milne*, [1970] 1 O.R. 381 (C.A.).

3. *Singh* v. *Singh* (1976), 25 R.F.L. 20 (B.C. S.C.) is a rare example of a case in which collusion was held to bar the granting of a divorce. The court found that the petitioner and the respondent had entered into an agreement whereby they would marry in order to give the petitioner immigration status, they would separate before the marriage was consummated, and the petitioner would petition for divorce after three years. See also *Johnson* v. *Ahmad* (1981), 22 R.F.L. (2d) 141 (Alta. Q.B.) where the court characterized a similar arrangement as a collusive "conspiracy to subvert the administration of justice". The wife then petitioned for divorce again, relying on s. 4(1)(c) of the 1968 *Divorce Act* which permitted a divorce if the respondent spouse was missing for three or more years. The Alberta Court of Queen's Bench held in *Ciresi (Ahmad)* v. *Ahmad* (1983), 31 R.F.L. (2d) 326 that this petition was not based on collusion since the parties had only agreed to live separate and apart for three years. There was no agreement that the husband would disappear in order to establish grounds for divorce under s. 4(1)(c). In an annotation to *Ciresi* (31 R.F.L. (2d) 326) Professor McLeod argued (at 327) that collusion did not exist in any of these cases:

> No evidence was suppressed or fabricated. The facts existed and were put before the divorce court. A decree nisi is not denied because the marriage is collusive, but because the divorce is.

Indeed, the courts in most divorce cases involving "immigration marriages" do not find collusion. In part, this result rests on the view that no social purpose is served by insisting on the maintenance of a marriage that was a mere travesty from the outset. See, e.g., *Fernandez (Alacrio)* v. *Fernandez* (1983), 34 R.F.L. (2d) 249 (Man. Q.B.).

(3) CONDONATION

The purpose of the bar of condonation is to prevent a spouse who agrees to resume or continue cohabitation with a partner who has committed a matrimonial offence from holding that offence over the other's head forever afterwards. However, if condonation is an absolute bar it may discourage attempts at reconciliation. The innocent spouse may fear losing the ground for immediate divorce as a result of a failed attempt at reconciliation. The 1968 *Divorce Act* retained condonation as a bar to petitions based on fault grounds but reduced it to a discretionary bar (s. 9(1)(c)). Furthermore, its application was suspended for up to 90 days during cohabitation for the purpose of reconciliation (s. 2). These provisions are now contained, with some modified wording, in ss. 11(1)(c) and 11(3) of the 1985 *Divorce Act*.

The doctrine of revival, which is discussed below, was abolished by s. 9(2) of the 1968 *Divorce Act* (see now s. 11(2) of the *Divorce Act*).

LEADERHOUSE v. LEADERHOUSE

4 R.F.L. 174, [1971] 2 W.W.R. 180 (Sask. Q.B.)

[The wife's petition was based on physical cruelty. The evidence disclosed that throughout the marriage the respondent frequently assaulted the petitioner. Nevertheless, the parties cohabited for a total of five and one half years. Disbery J. dealt with the issue of condonation as follows. A divorce was granted on the basis of an uncondoned assault which took place during the last month of cohabitation.]

DISBERY J.: — . . . Acts of cruelty can, of course, be condoned in the same manner as any other matrimonial offence. Prior to the coming into force of the Act all condonations by operation of law were expressly or impliedly conditional, the condition being that the spouse whose wrong had been condoned would not thenceforward commit any further matrimonial offence. If such spouse did commit a subsequent offence the condonation was lifted and the innocent spouse was free to bring an action in the court based on the offence which had been condoned, and also with respect to such subsequent offence. . . Thus the law did not recognize condonation as ever constituting an absolute and unconditional forgiveness.

Condonation has now been made absolute by s. 9(2) of the Act. . . .

The essential elements of condonation.

Condonation of a matrimonial offence requires three essential elements, namely:

(1) A knowledge by the innocent spouse of the matrimonial offence which has been committed by the other spouse.

(2) An intention by the innocent spouse to forgive and remit the offence — an *animus remittendi.*

(3) The reinstatement in his or her marital position of the guilty spouse by the innocent one — the *factum of reinstatement.*

There must be both forgiveness of the offence and reinstatement of the erring spouse: *Blyth* v. *Blyth*, [1966] 1 All E.R. 524 at p. 537.

The forgiveness

The nature of the forgiveness required is forgiveness in the legal sense as implying that the legal remedy for the wrong is waived by the injured spouse. . . . Robertson C.J.O., in *Wood* v. *Wood*, [1944] O.W.N. 9, [1944] 1 D.L.R. 493, said at p. 494: "To constitute condonation there must be an actual intention to forgive and to be reconciled." . . .

Reinstatement

The element of reinstatement is, in my opinion, best defined by Lord Chelmsford L.C. in *Keats* v. *Keats and Montezuma*, supra, where he said at p. 763:

> . . . it became necessary for the learned Judge to explain to them (the jury) in this case what amounted in law to condonation. This he did by stating that it meant 'a blotting out of the offence imputed, so as to restore the offending party to the same position which he or she occupied before the offence was committed.' . . . It must be such a blotting out of the offence as restores the wife to her former position. . . .

Mutual desire of the spouses for reinstatement

An innocent spouse who desires to condone the offence which has been committed by the guilty spouse and thus resume their married life together cannot bring such to pass unless the guilty spouse is willing that such be done. . . .

WATKINS v. WATKINS

(1980), 14 R.F.L. (2d) 97 (Nfld. T.D.)

[The husband petitioned on the basis of his wife's adultery. After the petition was issued, the couple had sexual intercourse. Goodridge J. dealt with the issue of condonation as follows.]

GOODRIDGE J.: — . . . It used to be considered that sexual intercourse between spouses taking place after a known act of adultery amounted to condonation of that act. This is no longer necessarily the case.

Under the present law of condonation there are three essential elements. These are: (a) knowledge of the matrimonial offence; (b) an intention to forgive; and (c) the restoration into the marriage of the guilty spouse. . . .

As to the questions of fact that arise out of the three points, my finding is as follows:

While there would appear to have been knowledge by the innocent spouse of the adultery of his wife, I am somewhat doubtful that he was aware of the extent of the adultery. Apart from admitted acts of intercourse, I imagine that he entertained suspicions only. This of course is not relevant in this case, as when the sexual intercourse took place between the spouses after the adultery the respondent was either clearly pregnant or had already given birth to a child of whom the petitioner was not the father.

On the evidence, there was clearly no intention on the part of the petitioner to forgive. The sexual intercourse took place evidently solely with a view to personal satisfaction. The respondent testified that while she participated in the intercourse she was not an instigator of the intimacy and it would appear was not an altogether enthusiastic participant.

Quite apart from the first two considerations, however, there was clearly no intention to restore the respondent into the marital relationship. Reconciliation was clearly the farthest thing from the minds of the spouses. She was about to have or had already had a child by an adulterous relationship. The parties were not living nor proposing to live as man and wife and in fact were formulating plans for a separate existence and discussing matters such as custody of the children.

On the facts of the case I find that the subsequent intercourse between the spouses did not amount to condonation of the adultery of the respondent and therefore I award the decree. . . .

In addition to that, even if there was condonation, I may still grant the decree if I am of the opinion that the public interest would be better served thereby.

In this case a child has been born of whom the petitioner was not the father. I cannot hold otherwise than that the public interest would not be served by my refusing the decree, for to do so would be to require that there be interjected into the marriage a foreign element, namely, a fourth child conceived in adultery, a situation that should not be imposed upon the petitioner without his consent, and there is no such consent. . . .

NOTES AND QUESTIONS

1. For other cases in which the courts did not find condonation despite the fact that the parties had engaged in sexual relations, see *Macdougall* v. *Macdougall*, 3 R.F.L. 175, [1970] 3 O.R. 680, 13 D.L.R. (3d) 696 (C.A.); *Nielsen* v. *Nielsen* (1971), 2 R.F.L. 109 (Ont. H.C.); *Grandy* v. *Grandy* (1972), 7 R.F.L. 69, 3 N.S.R. (2d) 750, 26 D.L.R. (3d) 359 (C.A.); *Aucoin* v. *Aucoin* (1976), 28 R.F.L. 43, 15 N.S.R. (2d) 399, 72 D.L.R. (3d) 674 (C.A.); *Douglas* v. *Douglas*, 27 R.F.L. 29, [1977] 1 W.W.R. 95 (Man. Q.B.); and *Pellegrini* v. *Pellegrini* (1976), 30 R.F.L. 293 (Ont. H.C.). See, however, *Blue* v. *Blue*, 5 R.F.L. 31, [1971] 2 W.W.R. 238, 17 D.L.R. (3d) 226 (Sask. Q.B.) where frequent acts of sexual intercourse were held to establish the wife's condonation of the husband's cruelty, even though the wife testified that she let him into her apartment and engaged in sexual intercourse out of fear of his causing a disturbance.

2. Continued or resumed cohabitation may not lead to a finding of condonation. First, s. 11(3) provides that condonation does not include the continuation or resumption of cohabitation for a period of, or periods totaling, not more than 90 days if such cohabitation is continued or resumed with reconciliation as its primary purpose. Second, continued or resumed cohabitation may not establish that an actual reconciliation has occurred. A wife may return to the matrimonial home simply because she has no other place to go: *Khader* v. *Khader* (1975), 20 R.F.L. 365 (Ont. C.A.). See also *Strachan* v. *Strachan* (1969), 72 W.W.R. 383, 10 D.L.R. (3d) 780 (B.C. S.C.); *Wellsby* v. *Wellsby*, [1975] W.W.R. 160, 53 D.L.R. (3d) 476 (B.C. S.C.); *Aucoin* v. *Aucoin* (1976), 72 D.L.R. (3d) 674 (N.S. C.A.); and *L'Hoir* v. *L'Hoir* (1978), 2 R.F.L. (2d) 23 (B.C. S.C.). Sometimes the courts appear to equate an actual reconciliation with a successful one. In *Einarson* v. *Einarson*, 4 R.F.L. 355, [1971] 5 W.W.R. 478, 20 D.L.R. (3d) 126 (B.C. S.C.), the wife returned to live with her husband after obtaining a *decree nisi*. Both spouses hoped that they would be able to salvage the marriage. Although they cohabited for over a year, the court found that the attempt had degenerated into a "loveless co-existence" after about two months. The court held that, as there had been no reconciliation, the wife had not condoned the husband's cruelty.

3. Notwithstanding condonation, s. 11(1)(c) empowers the court to grant the divorce if "the public interest would be better served by granting the divorce". A similar power existed under s. 9(1)(c) of the 1968 *Divorce Act*. Marriage breakdown alone was considered sufficient reason to conclude that the decree would be in the public interest in *Trites* v. *Trites* (1969), 1 R.F.L. 296 (N.S. T.D.); *Harasyn* v. *Harasyn* (1970), 2 R.F.L. 105 (Sask. Q.B.); *Jaworski* v. *Jaworski* (1973), 10 R.F.L. 190 (Ont. H.C.); *Mark* v. *Mark* (1973), 15 R.F.L. 73 (Ont. H.C.); and *Saunders* v. *Saunders* (1975), 22 R.F.L. 210 (Man. Q.B.). This factor was fortified by the need to bring stability to the lives of the children of the marriage in *Getson* v. *Getson* (1970), 2 R.F.L. 91 (N.S. T.D.). See also *Neilsen* v. *Neilsen*, [1971] 1 O.R. 393

(H.C.) and *Raney* v. *Raney* (1973), 13 R.F.L. 156 (Ont. H.C.). In *Allan* v. *Allan* (1971), 7 R.F.L. 96 (B.C. C.A.), Robertson J.A. stated (at 98):

> My view is that no benefit to the public can result from keeping the parties . . . bound together in marriage but that, on the contrary, the public interest requires their release from a marriage which, in its latter years, has brought the parties a great measure of unhappiness and, in addition, has at times called the situation between wife and husband to the attention of their neighbourhood in an unseemly way; a marriage, moreover, which has not the slightest chance of bringing benefit to anyone if it is forced to continue.

The liberal interpretation of the public interest adopted in the vast majority of reported cases means that condonation is rarely a bar to divorce. See, however, *Ifield* v. *Ifield* (1976), 24 R.F.L. 237 (Sask. Q.B.) and *Blue* v. *Blue* (1971), 5 R.F.L. 31 (Sask. Q.B.).

4. Under the doctrine of revival, condonation was always conditional upon the other spouse not committing a further matrimonial offence. If a matrimonial offence were committed after condonation, the earlier offence would be revived. The offence that revived the earlier offence did not necessarily have to be of the same nature or degree as the earlier offence, nor did it have to be of itself a ground for the matrimonial relief sought by the innocent spouse: *Beard* v. *Beard*, [1946] P. 8 (C.A.). Section 9(2) of the 1968 Act abolished the doctrine of revival. See now s. 11(2) of the *Divorce Act*. Can you think of any reasons why the legislature would abolish the doctrine?

5. Notwithstanding the abolition of the doctrine of revival, it appears settled that the court may examine the respondent's condoned conduct to determine if a subsequent course of conduct amounts to cruelty: *Croft* v. *Croft* (1970), 1 R.F.L. 136, 10 D.L.R. (3d) 267 at 271 (N.S. T.D.); *Olson* v. *Olson*, 4 R.F.L. 86, [1971] 3 W.W.R. 506 at 508 (Sask. Q.B.); *Crosby* v. *Crosby* (1971), 6 R.F.L. 8 at 9 (Ont. H.C.); *Jaworski* v. *Jaworski*, [1973] 2 O.R. 420 (H.C.); *Raney* v. *Raney* (1973), 1 O.R. (2d) 491 (H.C.); *Storey* v. *Storey* (1973), 10 R.F.L. 170, 4 Nfld. & P.E.I.R. 229 (P.E.I. S.C.); and *Ifield* v. *Ifield* (1976), 24 R.F.L. 237, 66 D.L.R. (3d) 311 at 319 (Sask. Q.B.).

6. In *Grant* v. *Grant* (1979), 9 B.C.L.R. 306 (S.C.), Wetmore L.J.S.C. suggested that the abolition of the doctrine of revival precluded a court from granting a divorce on the basis of the condoned behaviour even if it would be in the public interest to grant the divorce. Do you agree that there is a conflict between the abolition of the doctrine of revival and the reduction of condonation to a discretionary bar?

Generally, as indicated in Note 3, above, courts grant divorces notwithstanding condonation if it is perceived to be in the public interest to do so. The concern raised in *Grant* is not addressed.

(4) CONNIVANCE

Like condonation, connivance is only a bar if a divorce is sought in circumstances described in s. 8(2)(b). Connivance is not defined in the *Divorce Act* but it has a relatively well-established meaning at common law.

MADDOCK v. MADDOCK

[1958] O.R. 810 (C.A.)

[This was an appeal by the plaintiff from the dismissal of his action after a trial by King J. on May 13, 1958. The action was an action for divorce and the trial judge found that adultery had been proved but dismissed the action on the ground of connivance.

The facts taken from the judgment of Schroeder J.A. showed that the plaintiff and the defendant wife were married August 10, 1940, and resided at all times thereafter in a rented house on Gore St. The plaintiff and the co-defendant were both drivers for the Canada Bread and had known each other for two years prior to the events out of which this action arose. The men and their respective wives associated together during this period, going together to dances, picnics, theatres and other social activities. At some time, not specified, the plaintiff's wife suddenly told the plaintiff that the co-defendant had asked her to go away with him and that she intended to do so if she could not get along with him. Thereafter matrimonial relations deteriorated and while husband and wife continued to live together, marital intercourse ceased. The wife asked the plaintiff for a separation and he finally agreed. On October 10 a separation agreement was executed, and while that agreement was silent as to who should remain in occupation of the matrimonial home, apparently it was agreed that the husband should move out. He remained in the house until the following day, when he moved with the few belongings to which he was entitled under the agreement. As he was moving out, he met the co-defendant going into the house with his clothes. The plaintiff denied any knowledge of the co-defendant's intention to move in or of any arrangement between him and the co-defendant that he should do so.

The trial judge on these facts found connivance. In his reasons for judgment he said:

> Now, this would appear to me to be more than a coincidence. It seems to me to lead to the almost inescapable conclusion that there must have been some understanding between the plaintiff and the male defendant.
>
> It would be hard otherwise to believe that a male defendant, apart from some understanding with the husband, would have the temerity to move in his belongings while the husband was removing his from the matrimonial home.
>
> In the present case — if I understood the evidence correctly, and I believe I did, — the plaintiff and the male defendant were actually brushing past each other as one was taking his things from the house and the other was bringing his things into the house.
>
> The inference, it seems to me, is clear that the understanding between the plaintiff and the male defendant was that the plaintiff would move out of his home and that the male defendant would move in.
>
> Certainly, it appeared to me that the plaintiff recklessly permitted the adultery, which he has alleged, to take place between his wife and the male defendant; and, indeed, that he facilitated the commission of such adultery.]

SCHROEDER J.A.: — . . . I think it is clear from the learned trial Judge's reasons that he attached the most vital significance to the fact that the co-respondent was moving his personal belongings into the Gore St. house at the same time as the plaintiff was moving out, and despite the latter's emphatic denial, he refused to believe that this was a purely coincidental occurrence. . . .

With the greatest deference to the opinion of the learned trial Judge, I am unable to place a construction upon the evidence which would support his conclusion that the plaintiff was guilty of connivance which precluded his right to a decree dissolving the marriage.

It is of the very essence of connivance that the person complaining of the misconduct should have consented or wilfully contributed to the commission of the adultery or have promoted it in some other way, so that it would appear that he had what has been frequently described in the authorities as "a corrupt intention". . . .

It is well recognized, of course, that a petitioner may connive at adultery otherwise than by giving an express consent. If, with a corrupt intention, he stands by and permits the act to take place he may be guilty of connivance by acquiescence.

. . . It may be that the plaintiff was too easily prevailed upon to yield to his wife's desire for a separation, and perhaps his failure to protest when he saw the defendant moving into the home as he was leaving it, is open to criticism. It must be borne in mind, however, that he had entered into a formal separation agreement with his wife and that he was bound, by the covenant to which he had subscribed, to live separate and apart from her. Even if he had taken steps on that occasion to prevent the co-respondent from moving into his late home, what would have prevented this man from returning to it as soon as the plaintiff's back was turned? The circumstance which gave rise to the suspicion in the learned trial Judge's mind must be weighed against the positive statements of the plaintiff that he did not know that the co-respondent had arranged to move into his house. It is evident, however, that the defendant wife knew and that she acted with complete independence and in arrant and shameless disregard of her husband's wishes or his sensibilities. I should think that if there had been a guilty arrangement entered into between the plaintiff and the co-respondent as the learned Judge suggests, the plaintiff would have taken great pains to avoid even the slightest appearance of evil, and the fact that the co-respondent's act of moving into the premises coincided in the point of time with the plaintiff's moving out is equally, if not more, suggestive of his innocence in the matter. It is also noteworthy that he made no attempt to conceal this fact when testifying, although the action was unopposed. . . .

LAIDLAW J.A.: — It will be convenient and helpful to state certain propositions or principles of law respecting connivance. . . .

1. Connivance may consist of any act done with corrupt intention of a husband or wife to promote or encourage either the initiation or the continuance of adultery of his or her spouse, or it may consist of passive acquiescence in such adultery.

2. Corrupt intention of the husband or wife seeking a divorce is an essential ingredient of connivance, and the conduct of the husband or wife seeking the divorce must show that he or she, as the case may be, willingly consented to the adultery of the other spouse.

3. The issue is whether on the facts of the particular case, the husband or wife seeking the divorce was or was not guilty of the corrupt intention of promoting or encouraging either the initiation or the continuance of the adultery of the other spouse.

4. Acts done by a husband or wife seeking a divorce or by any person employed by him or her, as the case may be, to keep a watch on the other spouse to see whether or not his or her suspicions of adultery are well-founded or unfounded, do not necessarily constitute connivance and, likewise, if one spouse does nothing without lulling into a sense of security, the other spouse about whom he or she, as the case may be, is suspicious, but merely watches her, he is not necessarily guilty of passive acquiescence amounting to connivance.

5. "The Court should not allow its judgment to be affected by importing, as principles of universal application, pronouncements made with regard to wholly different circumstances and be led to a conclusion contrary to the justice of the case": *Churchman* v. *Churchman*, [1945] P. 44, at p. 52.

6. There is a presumption of law against the existence of connivance and the Court should not find a spouse guilty of connivance unless the evidence shows clearly that all the essential ingredients thereof exist in the particular facts under consideration. . . .

I am satisfied that in the particular circumstances of this case the plaintiff's conduct does not show that he had a "corrupt intention" to encourage or promote the adultery of his wife and therefore he was not guilty of connivance. . . .

[LEBEL J.A. dissented, holding that the inference of passive connivance drawn by the trial judge was correct. The appeal was, accordingly, allowed.]

FLEET v. FLEET

7 R.F.L. 355, [1972] 2 O.R. 530 (C.A.)

GALE C.J.O. (orally): — This is an appeal from a judgment dismissing a petition for divorce by reason of the petitioner's connivance.

The trial Judge held that the conduct of the petitioner in not making her presence known immediately upon arrival at the scene where her spouse was committing adultery was connivance. It is our unanimous view that he erred in that conclusion, particularly when regard is had to the evidence of both the petitioner and a corroborating witness. I refer to the petitioner's evidence as follows:

> MR. CLARK: Mrs. Fleet at the time you spotted the car, was this action in progress? [Sexual intercourse between the respondents.] A. Yes Sir.
>
> Q. And is it correct to inform this Court that you just witnessed the completion of it, and as they sat there talking? A. That is correct.

The petitioner's evidence was corroborated by a witness who had accompanied the petitioner to the scene of the misconduct. He stated that the said act had already commenced as he and the petitioner drove into the road overlooking the gravel pit where the car occupied by the respondents was located. On that evidence we are of the view that connivance was not proven and the petitioner ought to have been granted a decree *nisi*. We also point out that it would not be connivance even if the misconduct had not commenced at the time the petitioner and her witness arrived. The learned trial Judge appeared to be of the opinion that at any time a petitioner becomes aware that the adultery may take place it is incumbent upon the petitioner to stop it or become disentitled to any relief by reason of connivance. In our view, that is not the law and I refer to *Maddock v. Maddock*, [1958] O.R. 810, 16 D.L.R. (2d) 325. . . .

NOTES AND QUESTIONS

1. What is the basic difference between connivance and condonation?

2. Section 11(1)(c) of the *Divorce Act* authorizes the court to grant a divorce notwithstanding connivance if this serves the public interest. Should the courts adopt the same approach towards determining the public interest in this context as they have in relation to condonation?

(5) REASONABLE ARRANGEMENTS FOR THE SUPPORT OF CHILDREN

GEDDART v. GEDDART

(1993), 50 R.F.L. (3d) 102 (Man. C.A.)

[After extensive negotiations, the parties agreed to joint custody of their seven year old son, with the physical care being alternated on a monthly basis. They also agreed that the husband would pay $500 monthly as child support during those months when the child was with the wife. Bowman J. stayed the uncontested divorce application because she was not satisfied with the child support arrangements. The husband appealed.]

HUBAND J.A.: . . . The wife testified that she is endeavouring to make a career for herself as an opera singer, and is enjoying some success in a highly competitive field. She earned $22,378 in 1992, but her expenses for tax purposes were $14,286, so her net earnings were modest indeed. She maintains an apartment in Winnipeg which is sufficient for the needs of herself and of the child when he is living with her. She is frequently on the road, either to perform or to promote the furtherance of her career.

The wife has confidence that she will succeed as an opera singer, and says that the precise schedule of custody sharing is of great help because she can now schedule both performances and auditions with the certainty that she will be available during certain months of the year. With this confidence in her own earning power, she seeks no spousal maintenance and she is content with the contribution of $500 per month as child maintenance during the months the child is with her.

The husband is well employed as a carpenter, earning $32,800 per year gross, which translates into $25,800 net after taxes and other deductions.

Bowman J. expressed concern over the wife's modest income, in spite of the wife's optimism concerning future earnings. Obviously, the maintenance figure is based in part on that positive prognostication. If the wife's optimism proves misplaced, it would constitute changed circumstances and would entitle her to seek an upward variation of maintenance for her son while in her custody.

At the end of the day counsel for both parties requested that the divorce be granted and the custody arrangements approved. . . . But Bowman J. stayed the granting of the divorce decree because she was not satisfied that reasonable arrangements for the support of the child were in place.

. . .At the time of the hearing on June 28, 1993, this court allowed the [husband's] appeal and removed the stay, with reasons to follow.

There has been no suggestion that the child of this marriage will not be properly maintained. Before the court are two responsible, intelligent, mature people who care for their child. Both are represented by competent counsel. Both want the child to have a high standard of care. Both have suitable accommodation for him. The monthly maintenance of $500 while the child is in the wife's custody is far from a trifling sum. Moreover, as noted, the husband will have the full cost of maintenance during the six months of the year that the child is with him.

I do not foresee it, but even assuming that the wife encounters financial difficulties, there is every reason to believe that the husband would assure that the child's needs are fully met.

This is not a case of a party refusing to pay reasonable maintenance. Nor has there been any withholding of financial information upon which a rational decision on the quantum of maintenance might proceed. Full disclosure has been made as to the incomes and future prospects of the parties and of their plan to care for and provide accommodation for the child.

The discretion to stay a divorce decree is not to be exercised in order to make minor modifications to what the parents have agreed upon after fair and fully informed negotiations where the interests of the child were understood and recognized.

I am drawn to the conclusion that, in the circumstances of this particular case, the discretion to stay the divorce decree was wrongly exercised and, consequently, it was removed. It is unfortunate that it became necessary for the parties to proceed with an appeal, with the additional costs involved for both of them in that process. Under the circumstances, it is not a case where the costs of appeal should be awarded to either side.

BRIAND v. BRIAND

(1996), 153 N.S.R. (2d) 157 (N.S. S.C.)

GOODFELLOW J. [In Chambers]:— Sandra Jeanne Briand, now 30 and George William Edward Briand, now 28 were married August 1, 1986 and separated in December, 1993. Their marriage was blessed with two children, Julianne Marie Briand, born November 12, 1986 and Christopher Nathon Briand, born August 9, 1988.

The parties consented to an order in Family Court February 15, 1994 dealing with custody of the children to Mrs. Briand and providing access by the children to Mr. Briand. No order or provision was made with respect to child support. No written separation [agreement] was entered into by the parties; however, Mrs. Briand agrees to be responsible for outstanding debts to Shaw Cable and Nova Scotia Power and Mr. Briand to take responsibility for the telephone account of approximately $350.

Mrs. Briand filed a statement of financial information showing child tax credit, GST rebate and social assistance, all of which total $1,321 per month and Mr. Briand filed a statement of financial information indicating GST rebate of $11.50 and income of $1,008 for a total of $1,019.50, an annual income of $12,234.

Mrs. Briand filed her application for an undefended divorce and outlined the school position of the children and went on to state, "as my income is very limited, I cannot afford to have the children involved in organized sports, brownies, scouts, etc." and further "I believe at the present time that the respondent cannot afford to pay any amount of child support." The draft corollary relief judgment does place a duty upon Mr. Briand to notify Mrs. Briand and the Director of Maintenance in writing of any changes in his employment or income situation. . . .

Is the Court able to satisfy itself that proper arrangements have been made for the children where no child support is sought or provided for?. . .

In most circumstances, including this case, where some capacity, albeit very limited, exists for the non-custodial parent to share in the support of children, the failure to make some order of contribution would amount to failure to follow the statutory direction. Responsibility for children is a shared responsibility of *both* parents to be determined according to their relative abilities to contribute. The Court must recognize that responsibility even where the degree of contribution appears to be minimal in the overall basic financial requirements of the children.

This factual situation where the custodial parent obtains the majority of her "income" from Social Assistance highlights a problem that has been with us for a long time, namely, the reality that any child support paid by the non-custodial parent to the recipient of Social Assistance will not have a direct benefit to the children due to the Provincial Government policy of reducing Social Assistance dollar for dollar for the amount paid by the non-custodial parent. Matters of policy are for the Provincial Government, and it is not for the Court to differentiate between parents and effectively relieve a parent of her/his responsibility because all or a major source of "income" comes from the public through Social Assistance. To do so . . . will differentiate between those custodial parents who earn relatively low incomes, ie. $10,000 or $11,000 of a comparable amount to Mrs. Briand's Social Assistance. . . .In any event the Courts are bound by the direction of the *Divorce Act* to enforce the responsibility of parents for their children to the extent of their capacity. . . .

We now have available some general guidance in the Federal *Draft* Child Support Guidelines. They are at present of no legislative force or effect. [The Guidelines came into effect May 1, 1997.] Nevertheless, it is appropriate for a court to take into account all available guidance in determining what is reasonable under s. 15, and it seems to me that rarely will the Court be able to meet its duty, under s. 11(b) without careful consideration of the guidance provided by the child support guidelines. . . . Rarely can that duty be met without a consideration of the Draft Child Support Guidelines and in most cases an order depending on all the circumstances that is at least to the minimum level of *basic* support covered by the draft guidelines.

On any further application, the Court should be provided with as much information and documentation that is available as to the parties' income from all sources in the year to date of the application.

I have concluded that I am not satisfied proper arrangements have been made for the children and something substantially greater than nothing must be provided and accordingly the divorce application is stayed.

ORELLANA v. MERINO

(1998), 40 R.F.L. (4th) 129 (Ont. Gen. Div.)

CAMPBELL J.:—This is an application for divorce *simpliciter*. There are two children of this marriage. The parties separated in July 1990. The girls have lived with their mother since separation and, pursuant to an order of Webster Prov. J. of December 12, 1990, the applicant has custody of the children and the respondent is required to pay $50 per month per child.

The respondent left Canada in 1991 until he returned in August 1995. The respondent has exercised very little access to the girls since then. He has not exercised access at all since the summer of 1996. He is in arrears of child support and the order is filed with the Family Responsibility Office.

When the respondent attended at the applicant's lawyer's office for service of the divorce documentation, he declined to disclose his address. His attendance for service was arranged by the applicant who, although she is unaware of his present address, obviously has a means of communicating with him.

On the 1st of June, 1998, I stayed this divorce on the basis that I was not satisfied that s.11 of the *Divorce Act*, R.S.C. 1985 (2d Supp.), c.3, as am. by S.C. 1997, c.1 had been addressed. I decided that appropriate financial arrangements had not been made for the support of the children. Although the respondent appears to be gainfully employed, there is no current information as to his present ability to pay support.

Counsel for the applicant, by way of a letter directed to me (rather than an affidavit of the applicant) advises *inter alia* that

(a) she does not have sufficient information to bring a support motion before the court in an attempt to obtain child support in accordance with the current Guidelines;

(b) The Respondent has exercised very little access to the children. The Applicant is currently engaged to be married and her partner acts as a father to the children. The Applicant's partner is prepared to support the children. . . .

(c) The Applicant has built a life for herself and the children with the help of her current partner. She wishes this divorce so that she and her partner can marry and unite their family.

It would place an undue hardship on the Applicant to require her to determine the Respondent's current financial situation prior to granting her divorce. If she is unable to obtain this information she will remain indefinitely tied to a man who is no longer a part of her life or her children's.

Counsel seeks to have the court exercise its discretion and grant the divorce, despite the principles of the new *Child Support Guidelines*, SOR/97-175 and s.11 of the *Divorce Act*.

In the past, there has been much criticism of the courts with regard to inconsistent child support orders. The *Child Support Guidelines* clearly intend to offer consistency to Canadian children by requiring Canadian parents to meet their financial obligation to their children in a fair, consistent and predictable manner. What the applicant seeks would, in my view, represent a complete abrogation of the court's obligation and a direct contravention of the intent and principles of the *Child Support Guidelines*.

A support order of $100 per month for two children would be required of any non-custodial parent earning only $9,000 per year. There is no evidence whatsoever to indicate that Mr. Merino is only earning an income of that level. Minimum wages for a 40 hour work week offers a yearly income of over $14,000.

It is not for the applicant to choose not to bother to try to obtain reasonable support. The applicant offers no reason whatsoever why she has not sought to inform the Director of the Family Responsibility Office of this man's return and present employment or why she has not attempted to update an order that is seven-and-a-half years old.

Although the applicant's present partner has obviously treated the children as his own, and is apparently willing to "help", the primary financial obligation remains with the natural parents of these children.

Unless the applicant's partner intends to adopt the children (with or without Mr. Merino's consent), the respondent's obligation to his daughters continues.

The court is not persuaded to act on a letter from counsel to exercise its discretion to allow Mr. Merino to avoid his obligation to his daughters due to some reluctance by the applicant (the basis of which is as yet unknown) to ensure that her daughters obtain an appropriate level of support.

The divorce was stayed on the 1st of June, 1998. There is nothing properly before the court upon which the court could or is willing to exercise its "discretion" to change that status.

McLEOD, "ANNOTATION"

(1998), 40 R.F.L. (4th) 129

In *Orellana* v. *Merino*, Campbell J. refused to grant a wife's application for divorce because he was not satisfied that reasonable financial arrangements had been made for the support of the children. Although his decision not to grant the divorce is correct on the facts of the case, his comments on when a judge may decline to grant a divorce under s. 11(1)(b) of the *Divorce Act* are more problematic.

Pursuant to s. 11(1)(b) of the Act, a judge must stay the granting of a divorce unless he or she is satisfied that reasonable arrangements have been made for the children's support. The purpose behind s. 11(1)(b) of the *Divorce Act* is to force the parents to address the issue of child support before obtaining a divorce.

Granting a divorce does not affect a child's right to support. A parent can obtain child support after divorce under the *Divorce Act* and a child can obtain support under provincial child-support legislation. Although it makes sense to force a payor who seeks a divorce to prove that he or she has discharged his or her child-support obligation, different considerations apply where a custodial parent seeks a divorce.

Practically, a custodial parent has to support a child in his or her care. Although a non-custodial parent may be required to pay child support, a custodial parent must make up any shortfall from personal resources. If a custodial parent does not make adequate arrangements with the other parent for the support of a child, he or she makes sacrifices, the child does without or the State provides welfare assistance.

Section 11(1)(b) of the *Divorce Act* is intended to minimize the chance that either of the latter two contingencies will occur.

If a custodial parent is able to support the child and is prepared to do so, a court should grant the custodial parent's application for divorce regardless of whether the non-custodial parent is paying sufficient child support. The child's needs will be met and the State will not be called upon to support the family. No public interest justifies denying the custodial parent's application for a divorce.

A custodial parent may be prepared to maintain a child because it is not worth his or her time and money to seek support from the other parent or because the other parent is content to leave the parent and child alone if he or she is not required to pay child support. Either of these may be a good reason in a particular case not to pursue the issue of child support if a custodial parent has sufficient resources to maintain the child.

In *Orellana* v. *Merino*, the wife failed to explain her reason for not claiming increased child support from her husband or why the outstanding child-support order remained appropriate. This was an error in judgment. A lawyer drafting an affidavit in support of a divorce must address child support. Campbell J. was correct to stay the wife's application for divorce in the first instance to force her to explain her inaction.

The *Divorce Act* puts an onus on a petitioner to explain why a judge does not have to worry about the children's financial needs. There must be some evidence before a judge that the children's needs will be met. A petitioner's divorce affidavit or testimony must address child support. If the support paid is less than the Guidelines amount, a petitioner must explain why. If the explanation is reasonable, a court should grant the divorce. Judges are not charged with ensuring that every non-custodial parent pays Guidelines support before granting a divorce, just that reasonable arrangements for child support have been made. In deciding what is reasonable a court must consider the Guidelines.

In *Zarebski v. Zarebski* (1997), 29 R.F.L. (4th) 93 (Ont. Gen. Div.), Campbell J. granted a mother's application for a divorce notwithstanding the fact that she had no information about the father's whereabouts or his income. Rather than prolong the divorce proceedings, she was prepared to support the children herself. Campbell J. stated that the mother's solution was not "ideal" but "reasonable arrangements" do not have to be "ideal".

The wife's lawyer [in *Orellana*] responded to the stay by sending the judge a letter outlining her client's position. This is not an acceptable way to provide information to a judge in divorce proceedings. Campbell J. is correct to reject the lawyer's letter explaining why her client did not seek increased spousal support as sufficient evidence to discharge the onus under s. 11(1)(b) of the *Divorce Act*. A lawyer or party cannot send a letter to a judge and expect the judge to treat the letter as evidence. Evidence in divorce proceedings may be by viva voce testimony or an affidavit. It is a small matter for the lawyer to take the evidence in the letter and put it into an affidavit for the wife to swear.

Even then, it is questionable whether Campbell J. would have granted the divorce. Campbell J. appears to be of the view that pursuant to s. 11(1)(b), a petitioner must prove that the non-custodial parent pays Guidelines support or explain why not. The wife opted for "why not". She stated that she did not have sufficient information to justify an application to increase child support and that her new partner, whom she planned to marry, could and would support the children. Campbell J. was not convinced. With respect, it is submitted that the wife's explanation, if contained in an affidavit, should be sufficient to satisfy the onus under s. 11(1)(b) of the *Divorce Act*. The children's needs will be met and the State will not be called upon to contribute to child support.

The possibility that the husband is paying insufficient support should not be determinative of whether Campbell J. grants the divorce. If the husband wanted the divorce, Campbell J. could reasonably stay the divorce until the husband proved that he was honouring his child-support obligations. A person should not be allowed to seek relief if he or she is not honouring related legal obligations.

By denying the wife a divorce, Campbell J. prevents her and her new partner from regularizing their relationship and marrying. The wife does not have sufficient information to bring a support application and should not have to spend money needed to support herself and the child to pursue the husband for child support if she has a reasonable alternative.

The husband had been ordered to pay $100 monthly child support. As Campbell J. notes, this is minimal child support. The wife offered no evidence that the husband earned only about $9,000 annually to justify the order. In fact, her lawyer indicated that the mother did not know how much the husband earned. Campbell J. appears of the view that a custodial parent has an obligation to obtain financial disclosure or bring proceedings to determine reasonable child support before a court should grant a divorce. With respect, this is not realistic.

The husband refused to disclose his income and financial circumstances. He was in arrears of child support.

The wife's position is simple: he won't pay and I don't want to spend my money getting an order that he won't pay anyway. Campbell J. seems to ignore the fact that it costs money to bring a support claim. It takes time and uses judicial resources. A judge should not force a person to spend money that he or she may not have or add to the court lists if there is no need for the action or little likelihood that the recovery will justify the cost.

Campbell J. states that the wife's new partner has treated the children as his own and is willing to "help" with child support. In fact, the lawyer's letter stated that the step-father was willing to support the children, not just help with their support. This should have been sufficient to satisfy the onus under s. 11(1)(b) of the *Divorce Act*. Campbell J. states that the step-father's willingness to support the children is insufficient to satisfy the onus under s. 11(1)(b) because the primary financial obligation remains with the natural parents of the children. With respect, even if this were true, it is no reason to deny the divorce. Section 11(1)(b) does not direct a judge to deny a divorce unless everyone is paying his or her proper share of child support. A court should grant the divorce if proper arrangements for child support have been made. The fact that a person with a legal obligation will support the children should be sufficient.

The wife's new partner has assumed the role of a parent and has an obligation to support the children under the Family Law Act. A natural parent's child-support obligation does not have priority to a step-parent's obligation pursuant to the *Divorce Act* or the *Family Law Act*. It is submitted that as long as someone with a legal obligation to support a child will do so, a court should not delay a custodial parent's application for divorce: cf. *Zarebski* v. *Zarebski*, supra.

It is submitted that Campbell J. was correct in rejecting a lawyer's letter as information to satisfy s. 11(1)(b) of the *Divorce Act*. The Act requires a petitioner to adduce evidence that reasonable arrangements for child support have been made. A letter from counsel is not such evidence. However, the suggestion that the information contained in the letter would be insufficient evidence to justify a divorce if properly before the court should be approached with caution.

NINHAM v. NINHAM

(1997), 29 R.F.L. (4th) 41 (Ont. Gen. Div.)

ASTON J:— **The Facts:**

The parties began to live together in the spring of 1980 and, but for a brief separation in the early 1980's, continued to cohabit until Mrs. Ninham left the home on August 9, 1995. They were formally married November 27, 1993, after having first obtained a provincial marriage licence.

There are three children of the marriage: Janice Ninham, born March 19, 1980 (now 17 years of age); Candace Doxtator, born September 30, 1981 (now 15); and Harley Ninham, born September 21, 1985 (now 11).

Since the separation almost two years ago, Candace and Harley have resided with their father on the Oneida Reserve in what was formerly the family home. The oldest child, Janice, has resided with her mother in the city of London. The parties both have Native status. They resided together at the Oneida Reserve for the 15 years or so that they lived together as a family. The parties and their children remain closely connected to their culture and the values and beliefs of the Native community.

Mr. Ninham has worked for the Oneida Administration Roads Department for approximately 15 years. . . . His current rate of pay is $630 per week or $2,730 per month. In addition, he earns overtime. So far in 1997, he has earned a little more than $2,000 in overtime. I find as a fact that his employment income, including overtime, should be assessed at $35,000 per annum.

Mrs. Ninham is in her final term of a two year community college course that involves both academic terms and co-op terms. She will finish her present co-op placement in August or September this year and requires one more academic course to graduate. She could graduate as early as November this year or, if not, then next spring. She is in the Office Administration - Executive program and hopes to become an executive secretary.

There were three interim orders in this proceeding dealing with custody and access arrangements and with the issue of interim spousal support and interim child support. . . .

The interim orders . . . required Mr. Ninham to pay $400 per month in spousal and child support, commencing December 1, 1995. He has never paid anything whatsoever on account of those orders. Initially, he was evasive in his explanation as to why he had not paid anything on account of the support, but in the end he admitted that the real reason for his non-payment is that the order is contrary to his own beliefs in that under his understanding of "custom law", the fact that his wife decided to leave the family meant that she gave up responsibility for the home and children but that she also gave up any rights or benefits that might have been related to fulfilling her family responsibilities. Since the separation 22 months ago, he has paid off or paid down debts of approximately $7,000 plus whatever was owing at the time of separation on his truck but he has pointedly ignored a credit card debt with The Bay because he claims that he never signed for the card and never used it.

It is also worth noting that Mr. Ninham's financial statement is woefully inadequate and even misleading in its inaccuracies and omissions. . . .

. . .[H]e says, with respect, that he considers it his own responsibility to raise his children and disagrees that the court has the authority to tell him what his parental responsibilities are. . . .

Mrs. Ninham's present income consists of an education stipend of $1,045 monthly, a child tax credit and G.S.T. rebate, which all in all provide her with an income of $1,170 per month or approximately $14,000 per annum net of income tax.

Mrs. Ninham's attitude towards the authority of the court is not dissimilar to that of Mr. Ninham. . . . It is not difficult to understand her lack of effort in formal enforcement steps with respect to the interim order. It is abundantly clear from the evidence of the parties that they pay some lip service to the orders of the court but that they each truly consider their family problem to remain a problem that will be solved, if at all, outside of the judicial arena.

The Claim for Divorce:

Although "customary marriages" and even divorces have been recognized by courts in Canada, Indian marriages and divorces are nevertheless governed by the respective provincial and federal laws applicable to all other citizens. The parties in this matter chose to marry under a provincial licence and now choose to seek relief under the *Divorce Act*.

Section 11(1)(b) of the *Divorce Act* provides that it is the duty of the court "to satisfy itself that reasonable arrangements have been made for the support of any children of the marriage, having regard to the applicable guidelines, and, if such arrangements have not been made, to stay the granting of the divorce until such arrangements are made".

The amount of child support to be paid according to the Federal Child Support Guidelines can now be determined and ordered by the court but I am not satisfied that Mr. Ninham will honour such an order any more than he has honoured the interim orders in this proceeding. I am also not satisfied that Mrs. Ninham will necessarily take any steps to enforce any court ordered support.

The granting of the divorce is, therefore, stayed indefinitely to ascertain whether, in fact, support payments as ordered by this court are, in fact, being made for the support of the children. No judgment dissolving the marriage shall be granted until further evidence is provided that satisfies the court's obligation under s.11(1)(b) of the *Divorce Act*.

McLEOD, "ANNOTATION"

(1997), 29 R.F.L. (4th) 43

Lawyers and judges often state that hard cases make bad law. Justice Aston's reasons for judgment in *Ninham* v. *Ninham* may be the exception that proves the rule. The major issues in dispute were divorce, child support and custody/access. Apparently, neither party was impressed by the legal system or court orders. Aston J. strictly applies the relevant legal principles to promote societal expectations and values whether the parties like it or not.

. . . As Aston J. noted, the parties paid lip service to court orders but considered their family problems to be something to be solved outside of the judicial arena.

The obvious question is: why are two people who do not want or respect court orders before a judge? Should a court force parties to accept court orders if neither wants the orders? While Aston J. does not expressly address the issue, his attitude appears to be that he has no choice in the matter. No one forced the parties to invoke the litigation process. Spouses can settle their disputes between themselves and rearrange their rights to suit themselves, so long as children's interests are not compromised. However, once a person invokes the litigation process a judge must decide the dispute according to law. A judge has no power to dispense palm-tree justice. Parties cannot give a judge power by agreement that he or she does not otherwise have.

Pursuant to s. 11(1)(b) of the *Divorce Act*, a court must stay a divorce if it is not satisfied that reasonable arrangements for child support have been made. In the past, judges have stayed a divorce if the parties settled child support for an unreasonably low amount of money. As Aston J. points out, the amount of child support to be paid under the Act is established under the guidelines. In most cases a court has no discretion to depart from the guideline amount. If the parties have agreed to a different amount, a judge may approve and order the amount only if he or she is satisfied that any shortfall in formal child support is made up by other provisions of the agreement which benefit the child.

The problem in *Ninham* is that even if Aston J. orders the proper amount of support, the husband is unlikely to pay and the wife is unlikely to take steps to enforce any court-ordered support. Given the husband's income source, state enforcement would not likely succeed. Accordingly, Aston J. stayed the granting of the divorce to ascertain whether the husband would honour the child-support order. In this way, the husband controls whether he receives his divorce.

The effect of Aston J.'s decision is that in deciding whether reasonable arrangements for child support have been made, a court should take into account whether any support order will be paid. Ensuring reasonable arrangements for child support have been made means more than just deciding the correct amount of support.

Pursuant to s. 11(1)(b) of the *Divorce Act*, a court may stay the granting of a divorce to a payor who refuses to pay reasonable child support. However, a court should not deprive a payee of a divorce because a payor is unlikely to pay. A court should deprive a person of a right or privilege only to force the person to act in a legally acceptable manner. If the wife was prepared to co-operate in enforcing a support order, she should not be deprived of a divorce that she wanted because the husband would not pay. In *Ninham*, the husband was unlikely to pay and the wife was unlikely to force him to pay. Neither party would act as the legislation required and Aston J. withheld relief. . . .

Overall, Aston J. reaches a reasonable solution in a difficult case. None of his orders is likely to be honoured or enforced. The parties do not want or respect the judge's authority over them. Given time, they may well work things out by themselves or with the assistance of friends and relatives. Aston J. had no choice but to apply the law to encourage compliance with societal norms, even if the parties reject the norms. One is left to wonder if the litigation was conceived by the parties or by lawyers who failed to appreciate the parties' determination and convictions. If it all started over a divorce, did the wife care whether the husband got the divorce? If she did not and would not require welfare assistance to support the children, why should the state interfere in their lives?

NOTES AND QUESTIONS

1. For other cases dealing with s. 11(1)(b) of the *Divorce Act*, see *Harper* v. *Harper* (1991), 78 D.L.R. (4th) 548 (Ont. Gen. Div.); *Bailly* v. *Bailly* (1991), 36 R.F.L. (3d) 224 (Alta. Q.B.); *Archibald* v. *Archibald* (1991), 38 R.F.L. (3d) 310 (Ont. Gen. Div.); *Dumas* v. *Dumas* (1992), 43 R.F.L. (3d) 260 (Alta. Q.B.); *Malcolm* v. *Malcolm* (1995), 10 R.F.L. (4th) 242 (Ont. Gen. Div.); *Zarenski* v. *Zarebski* (1997), 29 R.F.L. (4th) 93 (Ont. Gen. Div.); *Kendall* v. *Kendall* (1997), 161 N.S.R. (2d) 157 (N.S. S.C.); *Arbeau* v. *Arbeau* (1997), 30 R.F.L. (4th) 192 (N.B.C.A.); and *Close* v. *Close* (1999), 50 R.F.L. (4th) 342 (N.B.Q.B.). In the last case, the wife sought a divorce and did not want any child support for her daughter. The wife was afraid of her husband who had had no contact with the child for about four years and had never paid support. Although the wife was on social assistance, she intended to remarry soon

after the divorce and move to the U.S. Justice Guerette granted the divorce without making a child support order, noting (at 344): "If the granting of a divorce order is bound to result in harassment . . . of the recipient spouse, surely the Court is entitled to take that into account."

2. What should be the court's response where the custodial parent receives social assistance and the other spouse can pay more than agreed, either formally or informally? In "Annotation" (1987), 8 R.F.L. (3d) 216 Professor McLeod argues (at 218):

> It is not the concern of the law of support to protect the public purse. . . . If welfare is providing for the child as well as the payor could, there is no family law reason for the court to interfere. It should not allow "Treasury"-related considerations to affect divorce proceedings to change marital status.

Do you agree with this latter position?

3. In *Marinovic* v. *Marinovic* (1989), 20 R.F.L. (3d) 404 (Ont. H.C.), Salhany L.J.S.C. held that s. 11(1)(b) does not preclude the granting of a motion for a divorce judgment in advance of the disposition of a claim for child support. In effect, he concluded that leaving child support for future judicial determination can constitute making reasonable arrangements for child support.

4. *Federal Child Support Guidelines* came into effect May 1, 1997. By virtue of s. 15.1(3), child support orders under the *Divorce Act* must be in accordance with the Guidelines. Regarding the Guidelines, see Chapter 8, **CHILD SUPPORT**. As illustrated in the cases reproduced above, for various reasons parties in a divorce proceeding may not seek a child support order. They may be content with informal arrangements of various types, an existing child support order, or child support provisions in a separation agreement. In these circumstances, the court's duty under s. 11(1)(b) comes into play and the amendments of 1997 stipulate that in exercising this duty the court must consider the Guidelines. In "An Update of Case Law under the Child Support Guidelines" (1998-1999), 16 C.F.L.Q. 261, Justice David Aston reports (at 266) that "uncontested applications for divorce are being refused in record numbers, with courts insisting that the necessary information be provided to ascertain what the guideline amount should be, and to explain any discrepancy between the proposed support for the children and the apparent guideline amount."

5. Under s. 9(1)(f) of the 1968 *Divorce Act* the court had a duty to refuse a decree based on the separation ground if "the granting of the decree would be unduly harsh or unjust to either spouse or would prejudicially affect the making of such reasonable arrangements for the maintenance of either spouse as are necessary in the circumstances". For rare examples of a court actually refusing to grant a decree on this basis, see *Williston* v. *Williston* (1972), 10 R.F.L. 357, 5 N.B.R. (2d) 136 (C.A.) and *Biggar* v. *Biggar* (1981), 25 R.F.L. (2d) 54 (P.E.I. S.C.). Compare *Bigelow* v. *Bigelow*, 4 R.F.L. 388, [1972] 1 W.W.R. 624 (Man. Q.B.). There is no similar provision in the 1985 *Divorce Act*.

5.   Reconciliation and Conciliation

(1) DUTY OF LAWYER

Examine s. 9(1) of the *Divorce Act*. The threefold duty imposed upon every legal advisor by this provision does not apply "where the circumstances of the case are of such a nature that it would clearly not be appropriate". What circumstances do you think were envisaged as falling within this exception? Can a lawyer who believes that it is too late in the day to discuss reconciliation with a spouse who seeks legal advice regarding the dissolution of the marriage establish compliance with s. 9(1) even though he or she never undertakes the threefold duty?

Section 9(1)(a) requires a lawyer acting on behalf of a spouse in a divorce proceeding to draw to the attention of the spouse "those provisions of this Act that have as their object the reconciliation of the spouses". Which provisions fulfill this description?

It is also the duty of every legal advisor to inform the spouse of the marriage counselling or guidance facilities known to the advisor that might be able to assist the spouses to achieve a reconciliation. Does s. 9(1)(b) impose any obligation on a lawyer to familiarize himself or herself with the "marriage counselling or guidance facilities" available in the area?

Finally, each legal advisor is required to discuss with the spouse "the possibility of the reconciliation of the spouses". Does this mean that a lawyer is to attempt to play the role of marriage counsellor?

Sections 9(1) and (3) are similar to s. 7 of the 1968 *Divorce Act*. It is generally believed that s. 7 produced few reconciliations. It may, however, have resulted in more frequent use of divorce counselling; that is, preparation for the consequences of divorce (see Mendes da Costa, "Divorce" in Mendes da Costa, ed., *Studies in Canadian Family Law*, Vol. 1 (Toronto: Butterworths, 1972) 359 at 377-378).

Section 9(2) of the *Divorce Act* was introduced in 1985 to encourage the use of mediation to resolve corollary matters. According to the Department of Justice in *Evaluation of the Divorce Act: Phase II: Monitoring and Evaluation* (Ottawa: Department of Justice, Bureau of Review, 1990) at 123, this provision "represents a compromise response to the much stronger request by the divorce mediation community for a mandatory visit to a divorce mediator where custody and access are in dispute". The Department of Justice concluded that most lawyers discussed the possibility of mediation with their clients, but that there was little evidence to suggest that it was encouraged. As a result, the Department found (at 124) that the "use of divorce mediation is still a rare alternative".

(2) DUTY OF THE COURT

Section 10(1) of the *Divorce Act* requires the court "before considering the evidence, to satisfy itself that there is no possibility of the reconciliation of the spouses, unless the circumstances of the case are of such a nature that it would clearly not be appropriate to do so". In cases where the evidence is presented entirely by affidavit, the court will presumably be content with the statement in the affidavit or affidavits that there is no possibility of reconciliation.

Where oral evidence is presented, the court itself can direct inquiries to the spouses in open court to determine if reconciliation is a possibility. If one spouse denies that there is a possibility of reconciliation, the court usually concludes that there is no possibility of its occurrence even if the other spouse expresses a fervent and sincere hope that there will be a reconciliation: *Paskiewich* v. *Paskiewich* (1968), 2 D.L.R. (3d) 622 (B.C. S.C.); *Khalifa* v. *Khalifa* (1971), 4 N.S.R. (2d) 576 (T.D.); *Geransky* v. *Geransky* (1979), 13 R.F.L. (2d) 202 (Sask. Q.B.); and *McDermid* v. *McDermid* (1989), 21 R.F.L. (3d) 47 (Sask. C.A.). See also *Roadburg* v. *Braut* (1994), 4 R.F.L. (4th) 96 (B.C.C.A.). But see *MacKay* v. *MacKay* (1975), 24 R.F.L. 216 (P.E.I. Fam. Div.), reversed on another point (1976), 10 Nfld. & P.E.I.R. 22 (P.E.I.C.A.).

If the possibility of reconciliation appears to exist, the court is obliged by s. 10(2) of the *Divorce Act* to adjourn the proceedings and may nominate a marriage counsellor to assist the parties to achieve a reconciliation. Where the proceedings are adjourned, either spouse may apply after 14 days for a resumption of the proceeding: s. 10(3). The Manitoba Court of Queen's Bench held in *Nash* v. *Nash* (1976), 28 R.F.L. 41 that (under a similar provision in the 1968 Act) the proceedings must then be resumed even if the other spouse insists this is premature.

By s. 10(4) of the *Divorce Act* a counsellor nominated by the court under s. 10 is not compellable or competent to disclose any admissions or communications made to him or her as nominee. Section 10(5) makes it explicit that evidence of anything said or any admission or communication made in the course of assisting spouses to achieve a reconciliation is not admissible in any legal proceedings. There was conflicting case law under the 1968 Act concerning whether or not the equivalent section applied only to counsellors nominated by the court. See *Robson* v. *Robson*, [1969] 2 O.R. 857, 7 D.L.R. (3d) 289 (H.C.); *Cronkwright* v. *Cronkwright*, 2 R.F.L. 241, [1970] 3 O.R. 784 (H.C.); *Shakotko* v. *Shakotko* (1976), 27 R.F.L. 1 (Ont. H.C.); *Geransky* v. *Geransky*, above; and *Ferguson* v. *Ferguson* (1980), 16 R.F.L. (2d) 207, 28 Nfld. & P.E.I.R. 498 (P.E.I. S.C.). In *R.* v. *Pabini* (1994), 17 O.R. (3d) 659, the Ontario Court of Appeal held that section 10(5) only applies to statements made to counsellors appointed under the *Divorce Act*.

Even if section 10(5) does not apply, a common law privilege may preclude the admission in matrimonial proceedings of statements made during counselling sessions or during reconciliation attempts. See *Robson*, *Cronkwright*, and *Pabini*. The Ontario Court of Appeal held in *Pabini* that the common law privilege did not apply in criminal proceedings instituted against the husband for the murder of his wife.

6.   Effective Date of Divorce

Under the 1968 *Divorce Act*, the court originally granted a decree *nisi* of divorce. One of the spouses then had to apply, generally after three months, for a decree absolute. The necessity to make application for a decree absolute does not exist under the 1985 *Divorce Act*. Generally, the divorce "takes effect" on the 31st day after the day on which the judgment granting the divorce is rendered: s. 12(1). If an appeal is launched the divorce takes effect when the appeal process is exhausted: s. 12(3)-(6).

Under s. 12(2) a court may order that the divorce is effective in less than 31 days. This power exists only if, *inter alia*, the court is "of the opinion that by reason of special circumstances the divorce should take effect earlier than the thirty-first day after the day on which the judgment is rendered".

NOTES AND QUESTIONS

1. Section 13(2) of the 1968 *Divorce Act* allowed the court to abridge the normal waiting period of three months for a decree absolute if it believed that "by reason of special circumstances it would be in the public interest." Most of the reported cases in which the time was abridged under s. 13(2) of the *Divorce Act* involved a cohabitation arrangement where children had been or were about to be born. See *Harding* v. *Harding* (1968), 67 D.L.R. (2d) 371 (N.S. Div. and Mat. Ct.); *Fleming* v. *Fleming* (1968), 1 R.F.L. 332, 66 W.W.R. 124, 69 D.L.R. (2d) 710 (N.W.T. Terr. Ct.); *Garrett* v. *Garrett* (1968), 1 R.F.L. 335, 1 D.L.R. (3d) 504 (N.S. T.D.); *Baia* v. *Baia*, 1 R.F.L. 348, [1970] 3 O.R. 165 (H.C.); *Barca* v. *Barca* (1972), 9 R.F.L. 78 (Alta. T.D.); *Longmuir* v. *Longmuir* (1974), 19 R.F.L. 117 (Ont. H.C.); *Flannigan* v. *Flannigan* (1976), 26 R.F.L. 331 (B.C. S.C.); and *Baker* v. *Baker* (1982), 17 Sask. R. 101 (Q.B.). In *Mascarenhas* v. *Mascarenhas* (1999), 44 R.F.L. (4th) 131 (Ont. Gen. Div.), the husband intended to marry his common law partner, who was pregnant, in Niagara Falls on the way back to their home in North Carolina. Without further explanation, the justice noted (at 134): "An immediate divorce was granted by this Court during the proceedings."

Should the desire to remarry as soon as possible be a "special circumstance"? It was held not to be in *Hansford* v. *Hansford*, 9 R.F.L. 233, [1973] 1 O.R. 116, 30 D.L.R. (3d) 392 (H.C.) and *Hughes* v.

Hughes (1975), 24 R.F.L. 265, 10 Nfld. & P.E.I.R. 170 (P.E.I. S.C.). But see *Bowler* v. *Bowler* (1977), 4 R.F.L. (2d) 27 (Ont. H.C.); and *Lester* v. *Lester* (1983), 26 Man. R. (2d) 249 (Q.B.).

2. The appeal referred to in s. 12(3)-(6) is an appeal from the granting of the divorce itself. Therefore, a decree can take effect even if an appeal relating to corrollary relief is taken. See *Fullerton* v. *Fullerton*, 5 R.F.L. 356, [1972] 1 O.R. 782 (C.A.) and *Chadderton* v. *Chadderton*, 8 R.F.L. 374, [1973] 1 O.R. 560 (C.A.).

3. In *Fraser* v. *Fraser* (1989), 23 R.F.L. (3d) 30 (Ont. H.C.), the court concluded that it had the power under s. 10 of the *Divorce Act* to order a stay of the judgment of divorce where the parties had reconciled after the judgment was granted but before it took effect. The 1968 Act expressly empowered the court to rescind the *decree nisi* in such circumstances, but this provision was dropped from the 1985 Act. See also *Alexa* v. *Alexa* (1995), 14 R.F.L. (4th) 93 (B.C.S.C.), where a divorce was set aside when the husband died before it took effect.

4

FAMILY PROPERTY

1. Introduction

The Ontario *Family Law Act* (the *FLA*), which came into force on March 1, 1986 fundamentally changed the law governing the property rights of spouses on marriage breakdown and on death. In order to understand the operation of this legislation, one must have a basic grasp of the historical background.

(1) HISTORICAL BACKGROUND

(a) The Law Prior to the *Family Law Reform Act, 1978*

The enactment of Part I of the *Family Law Reform Act, 1978* was an attempt to eliminate the inequities produced by the system of separate property. The norm of separate property was itself introduced in the 19th century by a series of *Married Women's Property Acts* as a response to the inequities flowing from the doctrine of unity of legal personality. According to this doctrine, the husband and wife became one legal personality upon marriage. In effect, the common law treated the husband as that legal personality. A wife did not have an independent right to contract, to sue or be sued, or to make a will. The husband acquired the right to manage and control all the wife's freehold lands and he was entitled to the rents and profits. A wife was unable to dispose of the land without his consent. If the husband predeceased her, all rights in the freeholds were resumed by her. If she predeceased him, the husband acquired rights as life tenant in all her freeholds of inheritance of which she died solely seised provided the husband had issue born alive by the wife capable of inheriting her freeholds. This was called curtesy and was abolished in Ontario by s. 48 of the *Succession Law Reform Act, 1977*. The wife's leaseholds belonged to the husband during coverture and he had absolute power to dispose of them during his lifetime. All other personalty held by the wife, except jewellery and clothing suitable to her rank, vested absolutely in the husband. He could dispose of it *inter vivos* or by will.

The common law compensated for the wife's loss of legal personality in some ways. A husband was liable for his wife's ante-nuptial debts, her torts, and for debts incurred by her after marriage to procure necessaries of life. On her husband's death, a wife was entitled by virtue of her dower (abolished by s. 70 of the *Family Law Reform Act, 1978*) to an estate for life in a third of all the freehold estates of inheritance of which he had been seised in possession at any time during the marriage.

To some extent, the law of equity made it possible for a wife to acquire and hold property independently through the concepts of a married woman's separate estate and restraint upon anticipation. These developments, which appear to have had little impact in Canada, enabled the propertied classes in England to keep the family property intact by preserving it from falling into a daughter's husband's hands.

The *Married Women's Property Acts* of the 19th century whittled away at the concept of unity of legal personality. In part, they gave wives the right to acquire and hold property. They established a separate property regime under which marriage created no property rights apart from the inchoate rights of dower and curtesy and the contingent rights created by the law of succession. In brief, a husband and wife were to be treated as strangers for the purposes of determining the ownership of property.

The system of separate property often resulted in hardship when the marriage ended. The traditional roles assumed by marriage partners ensured that the property was usually paid for by the husband and taken in his name. In such a situation, it belonged to him absolutely. This economic inequality meant that a wife frequently had no property on marriage breakdown.

Prior to the passage of family property law reforms, the courts had various tools available to mitigate the harshness of the separate property regime. One of these was an old rule called the presumption of advancement, whereby the law presumed that a husband who paid for property taken in his wife's name or who transferred property into his wife's name intended to make a gift to her of the property. This presumption could be rebutted: *Bible* v. *Bible* (1974), 15 R.F.L. 105 (Ont. C.A.). Nevertheless, it was a useful device whereby a wife could claim legal and equitable title to property in her name regardless of the financial contributions to its acquisition. See, for example, *Maysels* v. *Maysels* (1974), 14 R.F.L. 286, 3 O.R. (2d) 321 (C.A.), affirmed (1975), 19 R.F.L. 256, 17 N.R. 111 (S.C.C.). The presumption of advancement could also be used to buttress the presumption that the beneficial interests followed the legal estate in those situations where the property was taken in the names of both spouses and the husband provided the purchase price. See, for example, *Lindenblatt* v. *Lindenblatt* (1974), 18 R.F.L. 247, 4 O.R. (2d) 534 (H.C.). In any event, Canadian courts have generally given great weight to the paper title if title is held jointly. In *Kearney* v. *Kearney*, [1970] 2 O.R. 152, 10 D.L.R. (3d) 138 (C.A.), the wife was the sole contributor to the purchase price of a home held jointly by the spouses. The court found that the beneficial ownership was also held jointly, even though the presumption of advancement never applied when a wife made the financial contributions.

Neither the presumption of advancement nor the presumption that the beneficial interest follows the legal interest could be used to assist a wife where the title to the property was taken in the husband's name alone. It was in this situation that the concept of separate property worked the greatest hardship. For a short time, some judges attempted to find in s. 12 of the *Married Women's Property Act* (repealed S.O. 1978, c. 2, s. 82) a broad, discretionary power to adjust existing property rights between spouses. Development of this approach — frequently labeled "Palm-tree justice" — was effectively precluded by the Supreme Court of Canada in *Thompson* v. *Thompson*, [1961] S.C.R. 3, 26 D.L.R. (2d) 1. Thereafter, the chosen means of recognizing the contribution of a non-titled spouse to the acquisition of property was through the use of trust concepts — in particular, the resulting and constructive trusts.

The concept of resulting trust was sufficiently malleable to enable the courts to achieve equitable results in many marriage breakdown situations. Through a resulting trust analysis, a non-titled spouse could be declared to have an interest in the matrimonial home based on a direct contribution to the purchase price: *Re Whiteley* (1974), 4 O.R. (2d) 393, 48 D.L.R. (3d) 161 (C.A.). In this situation, it was well-established that a presumption of resulting trust arose. This presumption could be rebutted by evidence of a contrary intention on the part of the contributing spouse or displaced by a presumption of advancement (see above). In the decade before the legislative reforms, the courts extended the presumption of resulting trust to situations where the contribution of the non-titled spouse to the acquisition was an indirect one. Most often this involved paying for household expenses. See, for example, *Madisso* v. *Madisso* (1975), 21 R.F.L. 51, 11 O.R. (2d) 441 (C.A.), leave to appeal refused (1975), 11 O.R. (2d) 441n (S.C.C.). Even a contribution in the form of labour during construction of the home could be recognized through a resulting trust: *Trueman* v. *Trueman*, 5 R.F.L. 54, [1971] 2 W.W.R. 688 (Alta. C.A.).

Problems remained, however. Traditionally, the resulting trust arose where a person without legal title contributed to the purchase price. In this limited situation, equity presumed that the contributor did not intend a gift. The presumed intention of the contributor created a trust under which the beneficial interests were proportionate to the financial contributions of the parties. Once the presumption of resulting trust was extended to situations involving indirect financial or non-financial contributions, this "historical anchorage" was lost: Laskin J., dissenting, in *Murdoch* v. *Murdoch*, [1975] 1 S.C.R. 423 at 454. The courts became more and more concerned with the actual intentions of the parties in order to determine if the contribution to family life should be considered a contribution to the acquisition of property. Increasingly, judges suggested that the resulting trust depended on a common intention of the spouses to share the beneficial interest. Not only was this a departure from the traditional analysis, but a resulting trust analysis that emphasized the common intention of the spouses seemed very artificial in family situations. While the matrimonial relationship was harmonious, the parties did not usually address themselves to the issue of property ownership. After the relationship faltered, evidence regarding intention was often conflicting and self-serving. Where the contribution was indirect, it also became increasingly difficult to quantify the extent of the beneficial interest held by the non-titled spouse. Finally, it should be emphasized that contributions through household management and child-raising were not treated as relevant contributions giving rise to a presumption of resulting trust. The contribution to family life by a homemaker was left wholly out of account. A leading authority on the law of trusts concluded (Cullity, "The Matrimonial Home — A Return To Palm-Tree Justice: Trust Doctrines Based On (a) Intent And (b) Unjust Enrichment" (1979), 4 E. & T.Q. 277 at 286):

> It seems beyond dispute that the traditional principles of resulting trusts are inadequate to deal with problems concerning the ownership of matrimonial property. If they are applied strictly, the consequences may be quite fortuitous and manifestly unjust. If an attempt is made to extend the principles to indirect contributions, the inquiry quickly ceases to have much contact with reality and the principles themselves become distorted.

For many, the notorious case of *Murdoch* v. *Murdoch*, [1975] 1 S.C.R. 423 illustrated the inability or unwillingness of the courts to use equitable principles to achieve justice between spouses on marriage breakdown. For some four years after their marriage in November 1943, the Murdochs worked on ranches as a hired couple earning $100 per month plus room and board. In 1947, the husband and his father-in-law purchased a guest ranch for $6,000. The husband paid half of the purchase price. Mr. Justice Martland (Judson, Ritchie and Spence JJ. concurring) stated (at 427) that Mr. Murdoch paid his portion out of his own assets. Laskin J. pointed out (at 441) that an indeterminate part of the husband's share of the purchase price of this first property came from savings from the earnings of the couple, which were received by the husband.

The couple operated the guest ranch as a joint venture with the wife's father until 1951. During this time, the husband held an outside job that required him to be away from home during the day for some five months of the year. Therefore, the wife accompanied guests on park hikes and fishing and hunting trips. She also did other necessary chores around the ranch. This ranch was sold in 1951 and Mr. Murdoch received $3,500 from the proceeds of sale.

With this money and a loan from Mrs. Murdoch's mother, the husband, by a series of transactions involving ranches, acquired a valuable ranch registered in his name alone. Until separation in 1968, the wife continued to assist in the operation of the various ranches partly because the husband maintained his outside employment. At trial, the wife testified (at 443) that she was involved in "haying, raking, swathing, mowing, driving trucks and tractors and teams, quietening horses, taking cattle back and forth to the reserve, dehorning, vaccinating, branding, anything that was to be done".

After separation in 1968, Mrs. Murdoch claimed an interest in the ranch in her husband's name. The majority of the Supreme Court applied a resulting trust analysis. Accepting the trial judge's analysis of the facts, the majority held that Mrs. Murdoch could not establish a financial contribution. Insofar as the claim rested on a contribution through physical labour, the majority accepted the trial judge's finding that Mrs. Murdoch had not made a substantial contribution to the acquisition of the ranch in that "what the appellant had done, while living with the respondent, was the work done by any ranch wife." Because the wife's contribution could be characterized as the performance of the usual duties of matrimony, it could not by itself raise the presumption of resulting trust. In other words, she did what she did simply because she was married to Mr. Murdoch; not because she expected to gain an interest in any property in his name.

Laskin J. dissented. He clearly disagreed with the trial judge's assessment of the facts. He held that the wife had made a modest financial and a substantial physical contribution to the acquisition of the ranch. Although he indicated that the principles of resulting trust could be adapted to cover the situation, he urged the use of the constructive trust as a remedial device in property disputes on marriage breakdown. In particular, he identified the following weaknesses in a resulting trust analysis (at 454):

> What complicates the application of a presumption of a resulting trust, in its ordinary signification arising from the contribution of purchase money to the acquisition of property, is that in the case of husband and wife the contribution may relate only to a deposit on property which has to be carried on mortgage or instalment payments for many years; that where the spouses have lived together for some years after the acquisition, without any thought having been given to formalizing a division of interests claimed upon the breakdown or dissolution of the marriage, the presumption (as a mere inference from the fact of payment of money) is considerably weakened if not entirely dissipated; and that there is no historical anchorage for it where the contribution of money is indirect or the contribution consists of physical labour. Attribution of a common intention to the spouses in such circumstances (where evidence of the existence of such an intention at the material time is lacking) and resort to the resulting trust to give it sanction seem to me to be quite artificial.

The use of the constructive trust as a remedial or restitutionary device in property disputes was approved by three Supreme Court Justices in *Rathwell* v. *Rathwell*, 1 R.F.L. (2d) 1, [1978] 2 S.C.R. 436; adopted by a majority in *Pettkus* v. *Becker*, [1980] 2 S.C.R. 834, 8 E.T.R. 143; and finally used in a unanimous judgment in *Sorochan* v. *Sorochan*, 2 R.F.L. (3d) 225, [1986] 2 S.C.R. 38.

Although the constructive trust analysis might have effectively eliminated the harshness of the separate property regime on marriage breakdown, it developed too late to stem the tide of legislative reform. Eventually, all the legislatures in the common law provinces enacted comprehensive matrimonial property regimes. In Ontario, certain limited reforms were accomplished by the *Family Law Reform Act*,

S.O. 1975, c. 41 (repealed S.O. 1978, c. 2, s. 78). In addition to destroying the vestiges of unity of personality, this Act abolished the presumption of advancement between husband and wife. It also provided that where husband and wife took property as joint tenants, the presumption was that the beneficial interest was also held jointly. (See now s. 14 of the *FLA*.) A final provision of the Act was inserted to preclude the characterization of a spouse's contribution to the acquisition of property as that of a "reasonable spouse in the circumstances" when applying the concept of resulting trust.

(b) The *Family Law Reform Act, 1978*

The 1978 Act featured deferred sharing of some assets coupled with considerable judicial discretion. It provided for the general retention of separate property during the marriage coupled with the division of family assets and, in certain circumstances, non-family assets on marriage breakdown. The norm for the division of family assets was that of equal division, although there was authority to divide these assets unequally (s. 4(1) and s. 4(4)). Non-family assets were divided only in limited circumstances set out in s. 4(6) and s. 8 of the Act.

Family assets were defined in s. 3(b) to include the matrimonial home and all other assets "ordinarily used or enjoyed by both spouses or one or more of their children while the spouses are residing together for shelter or transportation or for household, educational, recreational, social or aesthetic purposes". The courts held that casual or occasional use for the purposes listed was not sufficient, but that the use had to be "in the course of the customary mode of life of the person concerned": *Taylor* v. *Taylor* (1978), 6 R.F.L. (2d) 341 at 353 (Ont. U.F.C.). Nor was an intention to use the asset for the purposes listed sufficient to render it a family asset. Thus, a pension or funds in an R.R.S.P. were not family assets: *Leatherdale* v. *Leatherdale*, 30 R.F.L. (2d) 225, [1982] 2 S.C.R. 743. This result was viewed as a major flaw in the scheme for property division in the Act (see *A Brief to the Attorney-General of Ontario Respecting the Family Law Reform Act* (Toronto: Ontario Status of Women Council, 1983) at 13).

On marriage breakdown a spouse could bring an application for a division of family assets (s. 4(1)). As noted earlier, this section specified that the spouses were then *prima facie* entitled to have the family assets divided equally. Under s. 4(4) a court could order an unequal division where an equal division was inequitable having regard to the factors listed.

A division of non-family assets could be made under s. 4(6) or s. 8 of the Act. An application could be made under s. 8 by a spouse or former spouse at any time except after the death of a spouse. A claim by one spouse or former spouse under s. 8 had to be based on a contribution of "work, money or money's worth in respect of the acquisition, management, maintenance, operation or improvement of property, other than family assets, in which the other has or had an interest." Initially, the courts took the view that the contribution required to trigger s. 8 had to be directly related to the property in issue and that such a contribution had to be substantial. See, for example, *Silverstein* v. *Silverstein* (1978), 1 R.F.L. (2d) 239, 20 O.R. (2d) 185 (H.C.); *Meszaros* v. *Meszaros* (1978), 22 O.R. (2d) 695 (H.C.); *McIntyre* v. *McIntyre* (1979), 9 R.F.L. (2d) 332 (Ont. H.C.); and *Boydell* v. *Boydell* (1978), 2 R.F.L. (2d) 121 (Ont. U.F.C.). However, in *Leatherdale*, above, the Supreme Court of Canada held that this approach was too restrictive. It held that Mrs. Leatherdale made a s. 8 contribution to her husband's R.R.S.P. and Bell Canada shares by using her income for family expenses thereby freeing up some of her husband's income.

The court also held, however, that the wife's work in the home did not qualify as a s. 8 contribution.

Section 4(6) required the court to make a division of non-family assets in two situations. The first involved the unreasonable impoverishment of family assets by the other spouse. The second was where the result of the division of the family assets was inequitable having regard to the factors set out in s. 4(4) and "the effect of the assumption by one spouse of any of the responsibilities set out in subsection 5 on the ability of the other spouse to acquire, manage, maintain, operate or improve property that is not a family asset." The responsibilities listed in s. 4(5) were "child care, household management and financial provision".

The second situation referred to in s. 4(6) caused the courts considerable difficulty. Some of the cases, such as *Bregman* v. *Bregman* (1978), 7 R.F.L. (2d) 201, 21 O.R. (2d) 722 (H.C.), indicated that there should be a division of non-family assets or an unequal division of family assets to rectify the inequity whenever there was a great disparity between the assets accumulated by the spouses and the non-owning spouse had contributed to the responsibilities listed in s. 4(5). See also *Colville-Reeves* v. *Colville-Reeves* (1982), 27 R.F.L. (2d) 337, 37 O.R. (2d) 568 (C.A.). Other cases such as *Young* v. *Young* (1981), 21 R.F.L. (2d) 388, 32 O.R. (2d) 19 (C.A.) seemed to reject this approach. In *Leatherdale* v. *Leatherdale*, above, the Supreme Court of Canada indicated that there should be a division of non-family assets where the non-owning spouse had assumed a greater share of the family responsibilities listed in s. 4(5). However, the court did not clarify whether a share of non-family assets should be awarded where there was a great disparity in the value of assets accumulated by the spouses and the division of family responsibilities could only be characterized as "normal" or "equal".

In addition to the property regime described above, the *Family Law Reform Act* of 1978 introduced substantial changes to the law governing possession of the matrimonial home, support, and domestic contracts. Parts II (Matrimonial Home), III (Support Obligations), and IV (Domestic Contracts) of the *FLA* are modeled on the corresponding provisions of the 1978 *FLRA*.

While the 1978 reforms relating to support, matrimonial homes, and domestic contracts thus proved to be generally acceptable, a number of problems relating to the division of assets under Part I of the *Family Law Reform Act* soon became apparent. First, entitlement varied depending on the nature of the assets accumulated by the spouses. As the concept of marriage as a partnership in which each spouse contributes in various ways to the financial gain of both spouses became increasingly accepted, it seemed odd that only assets used for family purposes were subject to the general rule of equal division. Second, the Act did not distinguish between property acquired before or after marriage. Again, this seemed to conflict with the partnership concept whereby only the property to which the non-owning spouse has contributed in some way should be shared. Third, the Act provided for considerable judicial discretion. Judges were authorized to divide family assets unequally and to divide non-family assets in accordance with their views of equity or fairness. The guidelines for the exercise of this discretion were vague. Fourth, the fact that there was no *prima facie* right to share equally the value of pensions built up during the marriage caused great concern since a pension is often the major asset held by an employed spouse. Finally, Part I did not apply when the marriage ended because of the death of a spouse. This meant that a spouse whose marriage broke down could be in a better position than a widower or widow.

(c) The *FLA*

By the mid 1980s there was general agreement that the property regime established under the 1978 Act was in need of reform. There was, however, disagreement over the nature of the reform required. Some individuals and groups favoured limited reforms, such as the inclusion of pensions in the pool of family assets and the extension of the regime to marriages ended by the death of a spouse. Others wanted more fundamental change. In the end, the latter view prevailed. On March 1, 1986 the *FLA* came into force. Part I of the Act introduced a modified version of the regime proposed by the Ontario Law Reform Commission in 1974. Deferred sharing of the economic gain achieved by both spouses during the cohabitation under the marriage is now the norm in Ontario. Briefly, a deferred sharing regime involves the retention of separate property while the marriage is an ongoing concern. Once the marriage has broken down, the profits of the marriage are divided equally between the two spouses.

Part I of the *FLA* is the subject of most of this chapter. However, the next section examines the continued development of the common law. At the same time as the legislative reform process was underway, the Supreme Court was developing the use of the principle of unjust enrichment and the remedy of constructive trust in property disputes involving spouses and unmarried cohabitees. The relationship between this judge-made law and the statutory scheme presents difficulties that will be explored in the later analysis of Part I of the *FLA*.

Unmarried couples, both opposite-sex and same-sex, are not presently covered by the statutory regime of the *FLA* because they are not spouses within the definition of s. 1(1). Unmarried cohabitees do have access to common law remedies that apply irrespective of their marital status. In its *Report on The Rights and Responsibilities of Cohabitants under the Family Law Act* (Toronto: 1993), the Ontario Law Reform Commission recommended that the definition of "spouse" in s. 1(1) of the *FLA* be amended to include unmarried, opposite-sex cohabitees who cohabit continuously for at least three years or who cohabit in a relationship of some permanence and are the parents of a child. It is also possible that the definition of spouse in s. 1(1) of the *FLA* will not withstand a *Charter* challenge. Recall *Miron* v. *Trudel* (1995), 13 R.F.L. (4th) 1 (where the Supreme Court of Canada held that insurance legislation that differentiated between unmarried and married opposite-sex couples violated the *Charter); Taylor* v. *Rossu* (reproduced in Chapter 1) and *Walsh* v. *Bona* (reproduced in Chapter 1).

FURTHER READING

1. For summaries of the common law treatment of married women's property, see Hardingham and Neave, *Australian Family Property Law* (Sydney: Law Book Co., 1984) c. 1; Hovius and Youdan, *The Law of Family Property* (Toronto: Carswell, 1991) c. 2; Holcombe, *Wives and Property: Reform of the Married Women's Property Law in Nineteenth-Century England* (Toronto: University of Toronto Press, 1983) c. 2; and McCaughan, *The Legal Status of Married Women in Canada* (Toronto: Carswell, 1977) at 5-10.

2. The focus of this chapter is on the legislative reforms that occurred in Ontario. For an analysis of the legislation in each province, see: McLeod & Mamo, eds., *Matrimonial Property Law in Canada* (Toronto: Carswell) (looseleaf service).

3. Unmarried cohabitees , including same-sex partners, can enter into "cohabitation agreements" dealing with their property rights. See s. 53(1) of the *FLA*. They can elect to opt into Part 1 of the *FLA* by providing for incorporation of its terms into their contract. See generally, Chapter 9, **DOMESTIC CONTRACTS**.

(2) THE USE OF TRUST DOCTRINES

RATHWELL v. RATHWELL

1 R.F.L. (2d) 1, [1978] 2 S.C.R. 436

[This case arose prior to the implementation of statutory matrimonial property regimes. After a lengthy marriage, Mrs. Rathwell commenced an action in the Saskatchewan courts for a declaration that she had an interest in one-half of all real and personal property owned by Mr. Rathwell. She had contributed to the acquisition of the property by pooling her money with her husband's in a joint bank account at the beginning of the marriage and by working extensively on the farm properties owned by the husband. The Supreme Court of Canada upheld the Saskatchewan Court of Appeal's decision declaring that Mrs. Rathwell had a one-half interest in the lands acquired by the husband before separation. In the course of his reasons for judgment, Dickson J. (Spence J. and Laskin C.J.C. concurring) explained the distinction between a resulting trust and a constructive trust and urged the use of the latter as a remedial device in matrimonial property disputes. Only that portion of the judgment is reproduced here.]

DICKSON J.: — . . . On the legal front, acceptance of the notion of restitution and unjust enrichment in Canadian jurisprudence (*Deglman* v. *Guaranty Trust Co.*, [1954] S.C.R. 725, [1954] 3 D.L.R. 785) has opened the way to recognition of the constructive trust as an available and useful remedial tool in resolving matrimonial property disputes. Lacking that, a court is reduced to searching for actual, inferred or, possibly, imputed agreement (common intent) when the plain fact is that there rarely is agreement because the parties do not turn their minds to the eventuality of separation and divorce. . . .

In broad terms matrimonial property disputes are much alike, differing only in detail. Matrimonial property, i.e., property acquired during matrimony (I avoid the term "family assets" with its doctrinal connotations) is ordinarily the subject matter of conflict. One or other or both of the spouses may have contributed financially to the purchase. One or other may have contributed freely given labour. The contribution may have been direct or indirect in the sense of permitting the acquisition of an asset which would otherwise not have been acquired. Such an indirect contribution may have been in money or it may have been in other forms as, for example, through caring for the home and family. The property is acquired during a period when there is marital accord. When this gives way to discord, problems arise in respect of property division. There is seldom prior express agreement. There is rarely implied agreement or common intention, apart from the general intention of building a life together. It is not in the nature of things for young married people to contemplate the break-up of their marriage and the division, in that event, of assets acquired by common effort during wedlock. . . .

The need for certainty in matrimonial property disputes is unquestionable, but it is a certainty of legal principle hedging in a judicial discretion capable of redressing injustice and relieving oppression.

One limit to the exercise of that discretion is clear. If the husband and wife have agreed from the time of acquisition to hold the property in distinct shares on the basis of their contribution to the purchase price or on some other basis, the plain duty of the court is to give effect to this agreement.

Another limit is equally clear. There is not, in the absence of legislative enactment, any such doctrine as "family assets" . . . The mere fact of marriage does not bring any pre-nuptial property into community ownership or give the courts a discretion to apportion it on marital breakdown.

A third limit: Although equity is said to favour equality, it is not every contribution which will entitle a spouse to a one-half interest in the matrimonial property. The extent of the interest will be proportionate to the contribution, direct or indirect, of the spouse. Where the contributions are unequal, the shares will be unequal. A spouse who fails to make a contribution has no claim in justice to assets acquired wholly by the efforts of the other spouse. . . .

Resulting trusts are as firmly grounded in the settlor's intent as are express trusts, but with this difference — the intent is inferred or is presumed as a matter of law from the circumstances of the case. That is very old doctrine, stated by Lord Hardwicke in *Hill* v. *Bishop of London* (1738), 1 Atk. 618, 26 E.R. 388. The law presumes that the holder of the legal title was not intended to take beneficially. There are certain situations — such as purchase in the name of another — where the law unfailingly raises the presumption of resulting trust: *Dyer* v. *Dyer* (1788), 2 Cox Eq. Cas. 92, 30 E.R. 42; *Barton* v. *Muir* (1874), 44 L.J.P.C. 19; *The Venture*, [1908] P. 218 (C.A.). The presumption has always been regarded as rebuttable: *Rider* v. *Kidder* (1805), 10 Ves. 360, 32 E.R. 884.

If at the dissolution of a marriage one spouse alone holds title to property, it is relevant for the court to ask whether or not there was a common intention or agreement that the other spouse was to take a beneficial interest in the property and, if so, what interest? Such agreements, as I have indicated, can rarely be evidenced concretely. It is relevant and necessary for the courts to look to the facts and circumstances surrounding the acquisition or improvement of the property. If the wife without title has contributed directly or indirectly in money or money's worth to acquisition or improvement, the doctrine of resulting trusts is engaged. An interest in the property is presumed to result to the one advancing the purchase moneys or part of the purchase moneys. . . .

The presumption of a resulting trust is sometimes explained as the fact of contribution evidencing an agreement; it has also been explained as a constructive agreement. . . . The courts are looking for a common intention manifested by acts or words that property is acquired as a trustee. . . .

The difficulty experienced in the cases is the situation where no agreement or common intention is evidenced and the contribution of the spouse without title can be characterized as performance of the usual duties growing out of matrimony. . . . Some of these situations may be analyzed as agreement or common intention situations. Such intention is generally presumed from a financial contribution. The doctrine of resulting trusts applies. In others a common intention is clearly lacking and cannot be presumed. The doctrine of the resulting trust then cannot apply. It is here that we must turn to the doctrine of constructive trust. . . .

The constructive trust encompasses a more uncertain amplitude than the resulting trust. English law has long treated it as an analogous institution to the express trust arising in certain definite situations such as the assumption of trustee duties by a stranger to a trust, the participation in the fraud of a trustee by a stranger, and reception and dealing with trust property by a stranger in ways inconsistent with the trust: *Barnes* v. *Addy* (1874), 9 Ch. App. 244; *Soar* v. *Ashwell*, [1893] 2 Q.B. 390 (C.A.). The hallmark of the constructive trust is that it is imposed irrespective of intention: indeed, it is imposed quite against the wishes of the constructive trustee.

The examples mentioned above are situations where a man against his will is brought within the express trusteeship institution, but in the United States the constructive trust has never been so limited. Its amplitude oversteps the substantive trust machinery. It is a remedial mechanism.

The constructive trust amounts to a third head of obligation, quite distinct from contract and tort, in which the court subjects "a person holding title to property . . . to an equitable duty to convey it to another on the ground that he would be unjustly enriched if he were permitted to retain it": *Murdoch* v. *Murdoch* at p. 383, per Laskin J., citing Scott, Laws of Trusts, 3rd ed. (1967), vol. 5, p. 3215. The constructive trust is an obligation of great elasticity and generality.

Where a common intention is clearly lacking and cannot be presumed but a spouse does contribute to family life, the court has the difficult task of deciding whether there is any causal connection between the contribution and the disputed asset. It has to assess whether the contribution was such as enabled the spouse with title to acquire the asset in dispute. That will be a question of fact to be found in the circumstances of the particular case. If the answer is affirmative, then the spouse with title becomes accountable as a constructive trustee. The court will assess the contributions made by each spouse and make a fair, equitable distribution having regard to the respective contributions. The relief is part of the equitable jurisdiction of the court and does not depend on evidence of intention. . . .

The constructive trust, as so envisaged, comprehends the imposition of trust machinery by the court in order to achieve a result consonant with good conscience. As a matter of principle, the court will not allow any man unjustly to appropriate to himself the value earned by the labours of another. That principle is not defeated by the existence of a matrimonial relationship between the parties; but, for the principle to succeed, the facts must display an enrichment, a corresponding deprivation and the absence of any juristic reason — such as a contract or disposition of law — for the enrichment. Thus, if the parties have agreed that the one holding legal title is to take beneficially, an action in restitution cannot succeed. . . .

It seems to me that Mrs. Rathwell must succeed whether one applies classical doctrine or constructive trust. Each is available to sustain her claim. The presumption of common intention from her contribution in money and money's worth entitles her to succeed in resulting trust. Her husband's unjust enrichment entitles her to succeed in constructive trust. . . .

PETTKUS v. BECKER

19 R.F.L. (2d) 165, [1980] 2 S.C.R. 834

DICKSON J. (LASKIN C.J.C., ESTEY, MCINTYRE, CHOUINARD and LAMER JJ. concurring): — The appellant Lother Pettkus, through toil and thrift, developed over the years a successful bee-keeping business. He now owns two rural Ontario properties, where the business is conducted, and he has the proceeds from the sale, in 1974, of a third property located in the province of Quebec. It is not to his efforts alone, however, that success can be attributed. The respondent Rosa Becker, through her labour and earnings, contributed substantially to the good fortune of the common enterprise. She lived with Mr. Pettkus from 1955 to 1974, save for a separation in 1972. They were never married. When the relationship sundered in late 1974 Miss Becker commenced this action, in which she sought a declaration of entitlement to a one-half interest in the lands and a share in the bee-keeping business.

I *The facts*

Mr. Pettkus and Miss Becker came to Canada from central Europe separately, as immigrants, in 1954. He had $17 upon arrival. They met in Montreal in 1955. Shortly thereafter, Mr. Pettkus moved in with Miss Becker, on her invitation. She was 30 years old and he was 25. He was earning $75 per week; she was earning $25-$28 per week, later increased to $67 per week.

A short time after they began living together, Miss Becker expressed the desire that they be married. Mr. Pettkus replied that he might consider marriage after they knew each other better. Thereafter, the question of marriage was not raised, though within a few years Mr. Pettkus began to introduce Miss Becker as his wife and to claim her as such for income tax purposes.

From 1955 to 1960 both parties worked for others. Mr. Pettkus supplemented his income by repairing and restoring motor vehicles. Throughout the period Miss Becker paid the rent. She bought the food and clothing and looked after other living expenses. This enabled Mr. Pettkus to save his entire income, which he regularly deposited in a bank in his name. There was no agreement at any time to share either moneys or property placed in his name. The parties lived frugally. Due to their husbandry and parsimonious life-style, $12,000 had been saved by 1960 and deposited in Mr. Pettkus' bank account.

The two traveled to western Canada in June 1960. Expenses were shared. One of the reasons for the trip was to locate a suitable farm at which to start a bee-keeping business. They spent some time working at a bee-keeper's farm.

They returned to Montreal, however, in the early autumn of 1960. Miss Becker continued to pay the apartment rent out of her income until October 1960. From then until May 1961 Mr. Pettkus paid rent and household expenses, Miss Becker being jobless. In April 1961 she fell sick and required hospitalization.

In April 1961 they decided to buy a farm at Franklin Centre, Quebec, for $5,000. The purchase money came out of the bank account of Mr. Pettkus. Title was taken in his name. The floor and roof of the farmhouse were in need of repair. Miss Becker used her money to purchase flooring materials and she assisted in laying the floor and installing a bathroom.

For about six months during 1961 Miss Becker received unemployment insurance cheques, the proceeds of which were used to defray household expenses. Through two successive winters she lived in Montreal and earned approximately $100 per month as a baby-sitter. These earnings also went toward household expenses.

After purchasing the farm at Franklin Centre the parties established a bee-keeping business. Both worked in the business, making frames for the hives, moving the bees to the orchards of neighbouring farmers in the spring, checking the hives during the summer, bringing in the frames for honey extraction during July and August and the bees for winter storage in autumn. Receipts from sales of honey were handled by Mr. Pettkus; payments for purchases of beehives and equipment were made from his bank account.

The physical participation by Miss Becker in the bee operation continued over a period of about 14 years. She ran the extracting process. She also, for a time, raised a few chickens, pheasants and geese. In 1968, and later, the parties hired others to assist in moving the bees and bringing in the honey. Most of the honey was sold to wholesalers, though Miss Becker sold some door to door.

In August 1971, with a view to expanding the business, a vacant property was purchased in East Hawkesbury, Ontario at a price of $1,300. The purchase moneys were derived from the Franklin Centre honey operation. Funds to complete the purchases were withdrawn from the bank account of Mr. Pettkus. Title to the newly acquired property was taken in his name.

In 1973 a further property was purchased, in West Hawkesbury, Ontario, in the name of Mr. Pettkus. The price was $5,500. The purchase moneys came from the Franklin Centre operation, together with a $1,900 contribution made by Miss Becker, to which I will again later refer. 1973 was a prosperous year, yielding some 65,000 pounds of honey, producing net revenue in excess of $30,000.

In the early 1970's the relationship between the parties began to deteriorate. In 1972 Miss Becker left Mr. Pettkus, allegedly because of mistreatment. She was away for three months. At her departure Mr. Pettkus threw $3,000 on the floor; he told her to take the money, a 1966 Volkswagen, 40 beehives containing bees, and "get lost". The beehives represented less than ten per cent of the total number of hives then in the business.

Soon thereafter Mr. Pettkus asked Miss Becker to return. In January 1973 she agreed, on condition he see a marriage counsellor, make a will in her favour and provide her with $500 per year so long as she stayed with him. It was also agreed that Mr. Pettkus would establish a joint bank account for household expenses, in which receipts from retail sales of honey would be deposited. Miss Becker returned; she brought back the car and $1,900 remaining out of the $3,000 she had earlier received. The $1,900 was deposited in Mr. Pettkus' account. She also brought the 40 beehives, but the bees had died in the interim.

In February 1974 the parties moved into a house on the West Hawkesbury property, built in part by them and in part by contractors. The money needed for construction came from the honey business, with minimal purchases of materials by Miss Becker.

The relationship continued to deteriorate and on 4th October 1974 Miss Becker again left, this time permanently, after an incident in which she alleged that she had been beaten and otherwise abused. She took the car and approximately $2,600 in cash, from honey sales. Shortly thereafter the present action was launched.

At trial Miss Becker was awarded 40 beehives, without bees, together with $1,500, representing earnings from those hives for 1973 and 1974.

The Ontario Court of Appeal varied the judgment at trial by awarding Miss Becker a one-half interest in the lands owned by Mr. Pettkus and in the bee-keeping business.

II *Resulting trust*

This appeal affords the court an opportunity to clarify the equivocal state in which the law of matrimonial property was left, following *Rathwell* v. *Rathwell*, [1978] 2 S.C.R. 436, 1 R.F.L. (2d) 1, [1978] 2 W.W.R. 101, 1 E.T.R. 307, 19 N.R. 91, 83 D.L.R. (3d) 289.

Broadly speaking, it may be said that the principles which have guided development of recent Canadian case law are to be found in two decisions of the House of Lords: *Pettitt* v. *Pettitt*, [1970] A.C. 777, [1969] 2 W.L.R. 966, [1969] 2 All E.R. 385; and *Gissing* v. *Gissing*, [1971] A.C. 886, [1970] 3 W.L.R. 255, [1970] 2 All E.R. 780. In neither judgment does a majority opinion emerge. Though it is not necessary to embark upon a detailed analysis of the two cases, the legacy of *Pettitt* and *Gissing* should be noted. First, the decisions upheld the judicial quest for that fugitive common intention which must be proved in order to establish beneficial entitlement to matrimonial property. Second, the Law Lords did not feel free to ascribe or impute an intention to the parties, not supported by evidence, in order to achieve "equity" in the division of assets of partners to a marriage. Third, in *Gissing* four of the Law Lords spoke of "implied, constructive or resulting trust" without distinction.

A majority of the court in *Murdoch* v. *Murdoch*, [1975] 1 S.C.R. 423, 13 R.F.L. 185, [1974] 1 W.W.R. 361, 41 D.L.R. (3d) 367, adopted the "common intention" concept of Lord Diplock in *Gissing* [at p. 438]:

> Difficult as they are to solve, these problems as to the amount of the share of a spouse in the beneficial interest in a matrimonial home where the legal estate is vested solely in the other spouse, only arise in cases where the court is satisfied by the words or conduct of the parties that it was their common intention that the beneficial interest was not to belong solely to the spouse in whom the legal estate was vested but was to be shared between them in some proportion or other.

In *Murdoch* it was held that there was no evidence of common intention. In *Rathwell*, supra, common intention was held to exist. Although the notion of common intention was endorsed in *Murdoch* and in *Rathwell*, many difficulties, chronicled in the cases and in the legal literature on the subject, inhered in the application of the doctrine in matrimonial property disputes. The sought-for "common intention" is rarely, if ever, express; the courts must glean "phantom intent" from the conduct of the parties. The most relevant conduct is that pertaining to the financial arrangements in the acquisition of property. Failing evidence of direct contribution by a spouse, there may be evidence of indirect benefits conferred: where, for example, one partner pays for the necessaries while the other retires the mortgage loan over a period of years, *Fibrance* v. *Fibrance*, [1957] 1 All E.R. 357.

The artificiality of the common intention approach has been stressed. Professor Donovan Waters in a comment in (1975) 53 Can. Bar Rev. 366 stated [at p. 368]:

> . . . In other words, this 'discovery' of an implied common intention prior to the acquisition is in many cases a mere vehicle or formula for giving the wife a just and equitable share in the disputed asset. It is in fact a constructive trust approach masquerading as a resulting trust approach.

. . .

In *Murdoch* v. *Murdoch* Laskin J. (as he then was) introduced in a matrimonial property dispute the concept of constructive trust to prevent unjust enrichment. It is imposed without reference to intention to create a trust, and its purpose is to remedy a result otherwise unjust. It is a broad and flexible equitable tool which permits courts to gauge all the circumstances of the case, including the respective contributions of the parties, and to determine beneficial entitlement. . . .

Although the resulting trust approach will often afford a wife the relief she seeks, the resulting trust is not available, as Professor Waters points out, at p. 374: "where the imputation of intention is impossible or unreasonable". One cannot imply an intention that the wife should have an interest if her conduct before or after the acquisition of the property is "wholly ambiguous", or its association with the alleged agreement "altogether tenuous". Where evidence is inconsistent with resulting trust, the court has the choice of denying a remedy or accepting the constructive trust.

Turning then to the present case and common intention, the evidence is clear that Mr. Pettkus and Miss Becker had no express arrangement for sharing economic gain. She conceded there was no specific arrangement with respect to the use of her money. She said: "No, we just saved together. It was meant to be together, it was ours". The arrangement "was without saying anything . . . there was nothing talked over . . ." She testified she was not interested in the amount Mr. Pettkus had in the bank. In response to the question "but he never told you that what he was saving was yours?" she replied: "I never asked".

It is apparent Mr. Pettkus took a negative view of Miss Becker's entitlement. His testimony makes it clear that he never regarded her as his wife. The finances of each were completely separate, except for the joint account opened for the retail sales of honey. Mr. Pettkus was asked in cross-examination: "you both saved together?" and replied: "I saved, she didn't". Uncommitted to marriage or to a permanent relationship it would be difficult to ascribe to Mr. Pettkus an intention, express or implied, to share his savings. Miss Becker said they were to "save together" but the truth is that Mr. Pettkus saved at the expense of Miss Becker.

With respect to the period from 1955 until the spring of 1961, the trial judge found:

> Now the plaintiff claims a share in the said farm on the ground that at the beginning of their relationship they had implicitly agreed to carry on a common enterprise, the plaintiff paying the living expenses and the defendant doing the saving. I am sure that the plaintiff would not have voiced such a proposition explicitly at the time, bent as she was on marriage, for fear of scaring away a prospective husband. *I find that her contribution to the household expenses during the first few years of their relationship was in the nature of risk capital invested in the hope of seducing a younger defendant into marriage.*

> Moreover, the evidence does not clearly show that from 1955 to May 1961 the plaintiff contributed more than the defendant to the overall expenses of the household, so that *I find that the $12,000 accumulated by the defendant was due to his superior salary, his frugal living and his off-job gains from repairs.* It is to be noted that the plaintiff made also some savings. (The italics are mine.)

Whatever the passage may lack in point of gallantry, the words italicized represent findings of fact by the trial judge, negating common intention. . . .

In the view of the Ontario Court of Appeal, speaking through Wilson J.A., the trial judge vastly underrated the contribution made by Miss Becker over the years. She had made possible the acquisition of the Franklin Centre property and she had worked side by side with him for 14 years, building up the bee-keeping operation.

The trial judge held there was no common intention, either express or implied. It is important to note that the Ontario Court of Appeal did not overrule that finding.

I am not prepared to infer, or presume, common intention when the trial judge has made an explicit finding to the contrary and the appellate court has not disturbed the finding. Accordingly, I am of the view that Miss Becker's claim grounded upon resulting trust must fail. If she is to succeed at all, constructive trust emerges as the sole juridical foundation for her claim.

III *Constructive trust*

The principle of unjust enrichment lies at the heart of the constructive trust. "Unjust enrichment" has played a role in Anglo-American legal writing for centuries. Lord Mansfield, in the case of *Moses* v. *MacFerlan* (1760), 2 Burr. 1005, 97 E.R. 676, put the matter in these words: "the gist of this kind of action is that the defendant, upon the circumstances of the case, is obliged by the ties of natural justice and equity to refund the money". It would be undesirable, and indeed impossible, to attempt to define all the circumstances in which an unjust enrichment might arise. . . . The great advantage of ancient principles of equity is their flexibility: the judiciary is thus able to shape these malleable principles so as to accommodate the changing needs and mores of society, in order to achieve justice. The constructive trust has proven to be a useful tool in the judicial armoury. . . .

How then does one approach the question of unjust enrichment in matrimonial causes? In *Rathwell* I ventured to suggest there are three requirements to be satisfied before an unjust enrichment can be said to exist: an enrichment, a corresponding deprivation and absence of any juristic reason for the enrichment. This approach, it seems to me, is supported by general principles of equity that have been fashioned by the courts for centuries, though, admittedly, not in the context of matrimonial property controversies.

The common law has never been willing to compensate a plaintiff on the sole basis that his actions have benefitted another. Lord Halsbury scotched this heresy in the case of *Ruabon SS. Co. Ltd.* v. *London Assce.*, [1900] A.C. 6 (H.L.) with these words, at p. 10: "I cannot understand how it can be asserted that it is part of the common law that where one person gets some advantage from the act of another a right of contribution towards the expense from that act arises on behalf of the person who has done it." Lord Macnaughten, in the same case, put it this way, at p. 15: "There is no principle of law that a person should contribute to an outlay merely because he has derived a benefit from it". It is not enough for the court simply to determine that one spouse has benefitted at the hands of another and then to require restitution. It must, in addition, be evident that the retention of the benefit would be "unjust" in the circumstances of the case.

Miss Becker supported Mr. Pettkus for five years. She then worked on the farm for about 14 years. The compelling inference from the facts is that she believed she had some interest in the farm and that that expectation was reasonable in the circumstances. Mr. Pettkus would seem to have recognized in Miss Becker some property interest, through the payment to her of compensation, however modest. There is no evidence to indicate that he ever informed her that all her work performed over the 19 years was being performed on a gratuitous basis. He freely accepted the benefits conferred upon him through her financial support and her labour.

On these facts, the first two requirements laid down in *Rathwell* have clearly been satisfied: Mr. Pettkus has had the benefit of 19 years of unpaid labour, while Miss Becker has received little or nothing in return. As for the third requirement, I hold that where one person in a relationship tantamount to spousal prejudices herself in the reasonable expectation of receiving an interest in property and the other person in the relationship freely accepts benefits conferred by the first person in circumstances where he knows or ought to have known of that reasonable expectation, it would be unjust to allow the recipient of the benefit to retain it.

I conclude, consonant with the judgment of the Court of Appeal, that this is a case for the application of constructive trust. As Wilson J.A. noted [at R.F.L. p. 348]: "The parties lived together as husband and wife although unmarried, for almost 20 years, during which period she not only made possible the acquisition of their first property in Franklin Centre by supporting them both exclusively from her income during 'the lean years', but worked side by side with him for 14 years building up the bee-keeping operation which was their main source of livelihood."

Wilson J.A. had no difficulty in finding that a constructive trust arose in favour of the respondent by virtue of "joint effort" and "team work", as a result of which Mr. Pettkus was able to acquire the Franklin Centre property, and subsequently the East Hawkesbury and West Hawkesbury properties. The Ontario Court of Appeal imposed the constructive trust in the interests of justice and, with respect, I would do the same.

IV *The "common law" relationship*

One question which must be addressed is whether a constructive trust can be established having regard to what is frequently, and euphemistically, referred to as a "common law" relationship. The purpose of constructive trust is to redress situations which would otherwise denote unjust enrichment. In principle, there is no reason not to apply the doctrine to common law relationships. It is worth noting that counsel for Mr. Pettkus, and I think correctly, did not, in this court, raise the common law relationship in defence of the claim of Miss Becker, otherwise than by reference to the Family Law Reform Act, 1978 (Ont.), c. 2. . . .

I see no basis for any distinction, in dividing property and assets, between marital relationships and those more informal relationships which subsist for a lengthy period. This was not an economic partnership, nor a mere business relationship, nor a casual encounter. Mr. Pettkus and Miss Becker lived as man and wife for almost 20 years. Their lives and their economic well-being were fully integrated. The equitable principle on which the remedy of constructive trust rests is broad and general; its purpose is to prevent unjust enrichment in whatever circumstances it occurs.

In recent years, there has been much statutory reform in the area of family law and matrimonial property. Counsel for Mr. Pettkus correctly points out that the Family Law Reform Act of Ontario, enacted after the present litigation was initiated, does not extend the presumption of equal sharing, which now applies between married persons, to common law spouses. The argument is made that the courts should not develop equitable remedies that are "contrary to current legislative intent". The rejoinder is that legislation was unnecessary to cover these facts, for a remedy was always available in equity for property division between unmarried individuals contributing to the acquisition of assets. The effect of the legislation is to divide "family assets" equally, regardless of contribution, as a matter of course. The court is not here creating a presumption of equal shares. There is a great difference between directing that there be equal shares for common law spouses and awarding Miss Becker a share equivalent to the money or money's worth she contributed over some 19 years. The fact there is no statutory rÉgime directing equal division of assets acquired by common law spouses is no bar to the availability of an equitable remedy in the present circumstances. . . .

VI *Causal connection*

The matter of "causal connection" was also raised in defence of Miss Becker's claim, but does not present any great difficulty. There is a clear link between the contribution and the disputed assets. The contribution of Miss Becker was such as enabled, or assisted in enabling, Mr. Pettkus to acquire the assets in contention. For the unjust enrichment principle to apply it is obvious that some connection must be shown between the acquisition of property and corresponding deprivation. On the facts of this case, that test was met. The indirect contribution of money and the direct contribution of labour is clearly linked to the acquisition of property, the beneficial ownership of which is in dispute. Miss Becker indirectly contributed to the acquisition of the Franklin Centre farm by making possible an accelerated rate of saving by Mr. Pettkus. The question is really an issue of fact: Was her contribution sufficiently substantial and direct as to entitle her to a portion of the profits realized upon sale of the Franklin Centre property and to an interest in the Hawkesbury properties and the bee-keeping business? The Ontario Court of Appeal answered this question in the affirmative, and I would agree.

VII *Respective proportions*

Although equity is said to favour equality, as stated in *Rathwell*, it is not every contribution which will entitle a spouse to a one-half interest in the property. The extent of the interest must be proportionate to the contribution, direct or indirect, of the claimant. Where the contributions are unequal, the shares will be unequal.

It could be argued that Mr. Pettkus contributed somewhat more to the material fortunes of the joint enterprise than Miss Becker but it must be recognized that each started with nothing; each worked continuously, unremittingly and sedulously in the joint effort. Physically, Miss Becker pulled her fair share of the load: weighing only 87 pounds, she assisted in moving hives weighing 80 pounds. Any difference in quality or quantum of contribution was small. The Ontario Court of Appeal in its discretion favoured an even division and I would not alter that disposition, other than to note that in any accounting regard should be had to the $2,600 and the car, which Miss Becker received on separation in 1974. . . .

I would dismiss the appeal with costs to the respondent.

[MR. JUSTICE RITCHIE agreed with this conclusion, but preferred a resulting trust analysis. He reasoned, in part:]

I should make it plain at the outset that in my opinion contributions made by one spouse and freely accepted by the other for use in the acquisition and operation of a common household give rise to a rebuttable presumption that, at the time when the contributions were made and accepted, the parties both intended that there would be a resulting trust in favour of the donor to be measured in terms of the value of the contributions so made. . . .

It will be seen that in the case of *Gissing* v. *Gissing, supra*, four of the Law Lords spoke of "implied constructive or resulting trusts" without any apparent distinction and this is to be found in other English authorities, but it is nevertheless noteworthy that when there is a conjugal relationship between the parties the presumption of a resulting trust arises for the benefit of the donor wherever there is evidence of a contribution of money or money's worth having been made by one spouse toward the acquisition of property by the other, and this presumption persists until the relationship is dissolved unless it is rebutted by "evidence showing some other intention".

It is contended on behalf of the appellant that the five-year difference in age between the parties constituted evidence justifying the learned trial judge in making the following finding:

> Now, the plaintiff claims a share in the said farm on the ground that at the beginning of their relationship they had implicitly agreed to carry on a common enterprise, the plaintiff paying the living expenses and the defendant doing the saving. I am sure that the plaintiff would not have voiced such a proposition explicitly at the time, bent as she was on marriage, for fear of scaring away a prospective husband. I find that her contribution to the household expenses during the first few years of their relationship was in the nature of risk capital invested in the hope of seducing a younger defendant into marriage.

With the greatest respect for those who take a different view, I cannot but find that this gratuitously insulting conclusion is based upon the trial judge's opinion that, whatever her motives may have been, the respondent's intention in making the contributions was to benefit the appellant and it is clear that they were acquiesced in and indeed freely accepted by him to be applied for and toward the maintenance and operation of a joint household. Accordingly, the last quoted comments of the trial judge in my view support the existence of a common intention giving rise to a presumption of a resulting trust and nothing said by him in this paragraph can be considered as evidence rebutting the presumption to which the contributions made by the respondent give rise.

[MARTLAND J., BEETZ J. concurring, expressed agreement with the reasons of RITCHIE J. However, he explained why he could not accept the application of a constructive trust in this situation. In particular, he noted:]

In my opinion, the adoption of this concept involves an extension of the law as so far determined in this court. Such an extension is, in my view, undesirable. It would clothe judges with a very wide power to apply what has been described as "palm tree justice" without the benefit of any guidelines. By what test is a judge to determine what constitutes unjust enrichment? The only test would be his individual perception of what he considered to be unjust.

As stated in the reasons of my brother Ritchie, the determination of this appeal in the respondent's favour can be made in accordance with existing authority and without recourse to the concepts of unjust enrichment and constructive trust.

SOROCHAN v. SOROCHAN

2 R.F.L. (3d) 225, [1986] 2 S.C.R. 38

DICKSON C.J.C.: — In this appeal, the court is called upon to consider whether the appellant, Mary Sorochan, is entitled to an interest in the farmland owned by the respondent. The central issue is whether a court can impose a constructive trust in a situation where a "common law" wife has contributed her labour for a number of years to preserving and maintaining a farm and doing all of the domestic labour, despite the fact that her spouse already owned the property prior to the date cohabitation commenced.

I FACTS

Mary and Alex Sorochan lived together for 42 years, between 1940 and 1982, on a farm in the Two Hills district of Alberta. During this time, they jointly worked a mixed farming operation and had six children. They never married. Mary Sorochan did all of the domestic labour associated with running the household and caring for the children. In addition, she worked long hours on the farm. The family lived in modest circumstances.

At the time the parties began living together, Alex Sorochan was the owner, along with his brother, of six one-quarter sections of farmland. In 1951, the land was divided between the two brothers and the respondent became the registered owner of three one-quarter sections. From 1942 to 1945, and from 1968 to 1982, the respondent worked as a travelling salesperson. During these periods, Mary Sorochan often assumed responsibility for doing all of the farm chores on her own. In 1982, due to the failing health of the appellant and the deteriorating relationship between the couple, Mary Sorochan moved to a senior citizen's home. She subsequently commenced this legal action for an interest in the farm upon which she had worked for 42 years.

II JUDGMENTS

Alberta Court of Queen's Bench

At trial, Purvis J. of the Alberta Court of Queen's Bench, relying on *Pettkus* v. *Becker*, [1980] 2 S.C.R. 834, 19 R.F.L. (2d) 165, 8 E.T.R. 143, 117 D.L.R. (3d) 257, 34 N.R. 384 [Ont.], held that "the law of constructive trust can be extended to cover situations such as the one disclosed in the evidence in these proceedings". He found that Alex Sorochan was enriched by his association with Mary Sorochan and that she had suffered a corresponding deprivation. Purvis J. also found that there was no juristic reason justifying the enrichment. Mary Sorochan had prejudiced herself with the reasonable expectation of receiving an interest in the property and Alex Sorochan knew of that expectation. Purvis J. noted, in particular, that in 1971 Mary Sorochan had asked the respondent to transfer land into her name.

Accordingly, Purvis J. ordered the transfer of one of the three quarter sections of land into the name of Mary Sorochan, upon her undertaking to transfer title forthwith to her six children. He also ordered Alex Sorochan to pay $8,000 in cash forthwith to Mary Sorochan and a further $12,000 within one year, the latter sum to be reduced to $7,000 if paid within six months.

Alberta Court of Appeal

The Court of Appeal reversed the trial judge's order and rejected the finding of a constructive trust in favour of Mary Sorochan. Lieberman J.A., for the court, held that the trial judge had erred in his interpretation of *Pettkus* v. *Becker*, stating [at p. 120]:

> Plaintiff's counsel argues that a constructive trust has been created here by reason of the unjust enrichment of the defendant as a result of the plaintiff's labours, but she has been unable to point out any accumulation of assets by the couple during the relevant period.

> In *Pettkus* Dickson J., as he then was, said at p. 183:

> 'For the unjust enrichment principle to apply it is obvious that some connection must be shown between the acquisition of property and corresponding deprivation. On the facts of this case, that test was met. The indirect contribution of money and the direct contribution of labour is clearly linked to the acquisition of property, the beneficial ownership of which is in dispute.'

> Unfortunately, the facts in the case at bar do not fall within that principle. There is no link between the acquisition of the property in question and the plaintiff's labour.

III UNJUST ENRICHMENT

. . .

Before a constructive trust can be imposed in this case, the court must find that there has been an unjust enrichment. In *Pettkus* and *Rathwell*, the court outlined three requirements that must be satisfied before it can be said that an unjust enrichment exists. These include:

(a) an enrichment;
(b) a corresponding deprivation; and
(c) the absence of any juristic reason for the enrichment.

In the present appeal, the appellant worked on the farm for 42 years, during which time she received no remuneration from the respondent. She did all of the household work, including the raising of their six children. In addition, she looked after the vegetable garden, milked the cows, raised chickens, did farmyard chores, worked in the fields, hayed, hauled bales, harvested grain and helped to clear the land of rocks. She also sold garden produce, milk and eggs to pay for food and clothing for the family and for the schooling of the youngest child. On numerous occasions when Alex Sorochan was engaged in his sales activities, Mary Sorochan was left with sole responsibility for the operation of the farm.

The trial judge held that there was "clear evidence of enrichment" to the respondent. The Court of Appeal found that Mary Sorochan "performed all the work of a diligent farm wife". In my view, it is clear that the respondent derived a benefit from the appellant's many years of labour in the home and on the farm. This benefit included valuable savings from having essential farm services and domestic work performed by the appellant without having to provide remuneration. Professor McLeod, in his annotation of *Herman* v. *Smith* (1984), 42 R.F.L. (2d) 154, 34 Alta. L.R. (2d) 90, 18 E.T.R. 169, 56 A.R. 74 (Q.B.), a case involving a contribution primarily in the form of housekeeping services, summarized the enrichment aspect of the judgment at p. 155:

> The initial point raised is: Has the man received a benefit? In the case, the benefit resulted from the claimant performing the normal 'spousal' services. No attempt was made to state the issue on any other basis. The rendering of spousal services amounts to a valuable service.

In addition, through the appellant's years of labour, the farm was maintained and preserved as valuable farm land. It did not deteriorate in value through neglect or disuse, as it no doubt would have in the absence of Mary Sorochan's faithful and long years of labour. The appellant's maintenance and preservation of the land, therefore, conferred a significant benefit on the respondent. . . .

On the other side of the coin, the labour done by Mary Sorochan during those 42 years constituted for her a corresponding deprivation. The trial judge concluded that this was the case. Moreover, the case law indicates that the full-time devotion of one's labour and earnings without compensation can readily be viewed as a deprivation. . . .

The third condition that must be satisfied before a finding of unjust enrichment can be made is also easily met on the facts of this case. There was no juristic reason for the enrichment. Mary Sorochan was under no obligation, contractual or otherwise, to perform the work and services in the home or on the land. In *Pettkus*, the court held that this third requirement would be met in situations where one party prejudices himself or herself with the reasonable expectation of receiving something in return and the other person freely accepts the benefits conferred by the first person in circumstances where he or she knows or ought to have known of that reasonable expectation.

Mary Sorochan came to live with Alex Sorochan on his farm. Together they worked the land, had six children and held themselves out to the community as married. In my view, Mary Sorochan had a reasonable expectation of receiving some benefit in return for her 42 years of domestic and farm labour. Indeed, it was reasonable for her to believe that this would take the form of an interest in the property. In 1951, when the two brothers split their joint ownership of the land, Mary Sorochan was asked to sign the conveyancing documents to bar any dower entitlement to the lands ceded to Alex Sorochan's brother. At the time of their first child in 1941, Mary Sorochan asked Alex Sorochan to get married. She testified at trial that he responded "later on". In 1971, she asked him to transfer part of the land into her name, which he refused to do. These incidents convince me that Alex Sorochan knew or ought to have known that Mary Sorochan had a reasonable expectation of obtaining some share in the land in return for her long-term commitment to working the farm and raising their six children.

In my view, to deny Mary Sorochan any form of relief would be unjust. I conclude, therefore, that the three preconditions for unjust enrichment have been satisfied in this case.

IV CONSTRUCTIVE TRUST

The constructive trust constitutes one important judicial means of remedying unjust enrichment. Other remedies, such as monetary damages, may also be available to rectify situations of unjust enrichment. We must, therefore, ask when and under what circumstances it is appropriate for a court to impose a constructive trust. . .

In this regard, the first issue to be considered is the causal connection requirement, upon which the Court of Appeal's decision turned. Relying on the decision in *Pettkus*, the Court of Appeal held, and the respondent now submits, that before a constructive trust can be imposed, some connection must be shown between the deprivation and the actual *acquisition* of the property in question. Alex Sorochan already owned the land at the time Mary Sorochan moved in with him; it is maintained, therefore, that she did not contribute in any way to the acquisition of the farm.

It is understandable that this issue could be a source of confusion. Since the early constructive trust cases involved situations where there was some acquisition of property, there was a tendency to treat a particular manifestation of a general principle as the rule itself. . . .

In my view, the constructive trust remedy should not be confined to cases involving property acquisition. While it is important to require that some nexus exist between the claimant's deprivation and the property in question, the link need not always take the form of a contribution to the actual acquisition of the property. A contribution relating to the preservation, maintenance or improvement of property may also suffice. What remains primary is whether or not the services rendered have a "clear proprietary relationship" [p. 156], to use Professor McLeod's phrase. When such a connection is present, proprietary relief may be appropriate. . . .

In the present case, Mary Sorochan worked on the farm for 42 years. Her labour directly and substantially contributed to the maintenance and preservation of the farm, preventing asset deterioration or divestment. There is, therefore, a "clear link" between the contribution and the disputed assets. . . .

In addition to the causal connection requirement, it is often suggested that the reasonable expectation of the claimant in obtaining an actual interest in the property as opposed to monetary relief constitutes another important consideration in determining if the constructive trust remedy is appropriate. . . . A reasonable expectation of benefit is part and parcel of the third precondition of unjust enrichment (the absence of a juristic reason for the enrichment). At this point, however, in assessing whether a constructive trust remedy is appropriate, we must direct our minds to the specific question of whether the claimant reasonably expected to receive an actual interest in property and whether the respondent was or reasonably ought to have been cognizant of that expectation. As concluded above, Mary Sorochan did have a reasonable expectation in obtaining an interest in the land and Alex Sorochan was aware of her expectation in this regard.

In assessing whether or not an in rem remedy is appropriate, a final consideration in this case is the longevity of the relationship. The appellant worked the farm for 42 years of her life. In my opinion, this constitutes a further compelling factor in favour of granting proprietary relief.

Under these circumstances, I conclude that it was appropriate for the trial judge to provide relief, at least in part, by way of constructive trust.

V THE APPROPRIATE REMEDY

There remains the question of the appropriateness of the trial judge's remedial orders. After considering the equities and the circumstances of the parties, he awarded Mary Sorochan title to one third of the farm property by way of constructive trust, on the condition that she transfer title forthwith to her six children. This portion of the farm had an assessed market value of $40,000 in 1983. The total value of the farm was approximately $138,000. It appears that the trial judge's order for proprietary relief was motivated by Mary Sorochan's desire to devise an interest in the lands she had worked for 42 years to her children. This further explains the condition stipulated by the trial judge that title be transferred forthwith to her children, a matter to which I shall return below. The trial judge allowed Alex Sorochan to retain full title to the other two-thirds of the farm, which included the home quarter. In so doing, Alex Sorochan could continue to live on the farm and derive his income from the land.

In addition to the constructive trust remedy, the trial judge made an order for monetary relief for $20,000 (to be reduced to $15,000 if paid within six months). In my opinion, it was open to the trial judge to make this type of lump sum award. The statement of claim of Mary Sorochan had requested not only proprietary relief, but as well "such further Order that this Honourable Court may deem just".

To remedy the unjust enrichment, therefore, the trial judge relied in part on the constructive trust device and in part on a straightforward monetary award.

The quantum of the trial judge's award has not been challenged by either party, except insofar as the respondent contends that no remedy whatsoever should have been granted. Under these circumstances, and bearing in mind that the trial judge is much better situated to assess what is fair and just in light of the particular facts of each case, I am inclined to defer to the trial judge's ruling in all but one respect.

In my view, the trial judge erred when he made Mary Sorochan's entitlement to the land contingent on her immediate transfer of title to her children. Mary Sorochan is the one who suffered the deprivation and it is she who is entitled to the remedy — not her children. She may well decide to transfer title to the land to her children, but this will be her decision alone to make. . . .

PETER v. BEBLOW

(1993), 44 R.F.L. (3d) 329 (S.C.C.)

CORY J. (concurring) (L'HEUREUX-DUBE and GONTHIER JJ. concurring): — The issue in this appeal is whether the provision of domestic services during 12 years of cohabitation in a common law relationship is sufficient to establish the proprietary link which is required before the remedy of constructive trust can be applied to redress the unjust enrichment of one of the partners in the relationship. Further, consideration must be given to the extent to which the remedy of constructive trust should be applied in terms of amount or proportion.

Factual Background

In April 1973, the respondent asked the appellant to come and live with him. That same month, the appellant, together with her 4 children, moved into the respondent's home in Sicamous, B.C. At the time, 2 children of the respondent were living in the home. The parties continued to live together in a common law relationship for over 12 years, separating in June 1985. During this entire time the appellant acted as the wife of the respondent. She was a stepmother to his children until 1977 while they remained in the home. As well, she cared for her own children, the last one leaving in 1980.

During the 12 years, the appellant cooked, cleaned, washed clothes, and looked after the garden. As well, she worked on the Sicamous property, undertaking such projects as painting the fence, planting a cedar hedge, buying flowers and shrubs for the property, and building a rock garden. She built a pig pen. She kept chickens for a few years, butchering and cooking them for the family. During the winters, the appellant shoveled snow, chopped wood, and made kindling. The respondent did not pay the appellant for any of her work. Both the appellant and the respondent contributed to the purchase of groceries and household supplies, although the respondent contributed a greater share.

In the first year of the relationship the appellant did not undertake outside work and spent 8 hours a day doing housework and work on the Sicamous property. In subsequent years, she took part-time work as a cook from June to October. During these months she worked some six hours a day at a rate of $4.50 per hour. Except for one winter when she worked at a bakery, the appellant received unemployment insurance benefits in the winter months.

Throughout the relationship, the respondent worked on a more or less full-time basis as a grader operator. His work frequently took him out of town to various locations in British Columbia.

Before he met the appellant, the respondent had lived in a common law relationship with another woman for 5 years. When she left his home he hired housekeepers. The last housekeeper he had before the appellant came to his home was paid at a rate of $350 per month.

The trial judge accepted the appellant's testimony that the respondent had asked her to live with him because he needed someone to care for his 2 children. This need arose when the welfare authorities expressed some concern that the respondent left the children alone when he was working away from home.

When the parties met, the appellant had savings of $100. In 1976, she purchased a property in Saskatchewan for $2,500. She sold this property in 1980 for $8,000 and purchased a property at 100 Mile House for $6,500. She used the remainder of the sale proceeds for a trip to Reno. At the time of trial, the appellant still owned the 100 Mile House property.

The respondent had purchased the Sicamous property in 1971 for $8,500. Some $900 was paid in cash and the balance of $7,600 was secured by a mortgage. The respondent was able to pay off the mortgage in 1975. The estimated market value of the Sicamous property as of 1987 was $17,800. The property's assessed value in that year was $23,200. In that same year, the respondent rented the property. The tenants were given an option to purchase it for $28,000. The option was not exercised.

With the passage of time, the respondent began to drink heavily and became verbally and physically abusive to the appellant. As a result, the appellant moved out of the Sicamous home on June 7, 1985. At the time of the trial, she was on welfare and lived in a trailer court in Sicamous. The respondent, by that time, had retired and was living on a houseboat in Enderby, B.C. The Sicamous house and property were vacant.

The appellant brought an action claiming that the respondent had been unjustly enriched over the years of the relationship as a result of the work which she performed in his home without payment of any kind. She sought to have a constructive trust imposed on her behalf in respect of the Sicamous property or, in the alternative, monetary damages as compensation for the labour and services she provided to the respondent.

Position of the Respondent

The respondent conceded that there was an unjust enrichment but contended that there was no corresponding deprivation suffered by the appellant. It was said that she was adequately compensated for her services by the respondent's provision of free shelter and a large portion of the groceries.

Second, it was argued that the domestic services provided by the appellant did not establish any causal link to or proprietary interest in the Sicamous property.

The Court of Appeal clearly agreed with the respondent on these issues. With respect, I believe they erred in reaching these conclusions.

Should the Remedy of Constructive Trust be Applied to the Case at Bar?

1. *Enrichment*

It should not be forgotten that the trial judge specifically found that there had been an enrichment to the respondent "since he obtained the services of the Plaintiff as a housekeeper, homemaker and in fact stepmother without compensation." Indeed, it was conceded before us that the respondent was enriched by the work and contributions of the appellant.

2. *A Corresponding Deprivation*

It is again important to first consider the finding of the trial judge on this issue. He stated:

> . . . the plaintiff was deprived of any compensation for her labour since she devoted the majority of her time and energy and some of the monies she earned towards the benefit of the Respondent, his children and his property.

That finding would seem sufficient in itself to warrant the conclusion that the appellant suffered a deprivation which corresponds to the enrichment of the respondent.

Indeed, I would have thought that if there is enrichment, that it would almost invariably follow that there is a corresponding deprivation suffered by the person who provided the enrichment. There is ample support for the proposition that once enrichment has been found, the conclusion that the plaintiff has suffered a corresponding deprivation is virtually automatic. . . . In *Everson* v. *Rich* (1988), 16 R.F.L. (3d) 337, the Saskatchewan Court of Appeal, applying *Sorochan*, stated, at p. 342:

> The spousal services provided by the appellant were valuable services and did constitute a benefit conferred upon the respondent. The provision of those services was a detriment to the claimant by virtue of the use of her time and energy.

I agree with this reasoning. As a general rule, if it is found that the defendant has been enriched by the efforts of the plaintiff, there will, almost as a matter of course, be deprivation suffered by the plaintiff. As Professor James McLeod pointed out ((1988) 16 R.F.L. (3d) 338) in his annotation of *Everson* v. *Rich, supra*, "the deprivation requirement is satisfied by showing the plaintiff expended effort or does not have what he/she had or might have had" [at p. 338]. Particularly in a matrimonial or long term common law relationship it should, in the absence of cogent evidence to the contrary, be taken that the enrichment of one party will result in a deprivation of the other.

Business relationships concerned with commercial affairs may, as a result of the conduct of one of the corporations involved, result in a court's granting a constructive trust remedy. The constructive trust has been appropriately used to redress a gain made through a breach of trust in a commercial or business relationship (See, for example, *Canadian Aero Service Ltd.* v. *O'Malley*, [1974] S.C.R. 592). Yet how much closer and trusting must be a long term common law relationship. In marriages or marriage-like relationships commercial matters and a great deal more will be involved. Clearly, parties to a family relationship will, in a commercial sense, share funds and financial goals. More importantly, couples, such as the parties to this case, will strive to make a home. By that I mean a place that provides safety, security, and love, and which is as well frequently the place where children may be cared for and nurtured. In a relationship that involves living and sleeping together, couples will share their worst fears and frustrations and their fondest dreams and aspirations. They will plan and work together to achieve their goals. Just as much as parties to a formal marriage, the partners in a long term common law relationship will base their actions on mutual love and trust. They too are entitled, in appropriate circumstances, to the relief provided by the remedy of constructive trust.

This remedy should be granted despite the fact that family will seldom keep the same careful financial records as business associates. Nonetheless, fairness requires that the constructive trust remedy be available to them and applied on an equitable basis without a minute scrutiny of their respective financial contributions. Indeed, in a situation such as the one presented in this case, it may be very difficult to assess the value of making a house a home and of sharing the struggle to raise children to become responsible adults.

In the present case, although there was no formal marriage, the couple lived and worked together in the most intimate of relationships. They shared work and the monies which they earned. The amount of the contributions may have been varied and unequal. Yet the very fact that, in addition to her household work, the appellant contributed something of the income from her outside employment indicates that there was a real sharing of income. As a result of the relationship, the Sicamous property was looked after and maintained. None of this could have been achieved without the efforts of the appellant.

Certainly, it cannot be said that the relationship was so short-lived that it should not give rise to mutual rights and obligations. Twelve years is not an insignificant period of time to live in a relationship based on mutual trust and confidence. In those circumstances, there is a strong presumption that the services provided by one party will not be used solely to enrich the other. Both the reasonable expectations of the parties and equity will require that upon the termination of the relationship, the parties will receive an appropriate compensation based on the contribution each has made to the relationship.

The respondent asserts that because the appellant loved him she could not have expected to receive compensation or an interest in the property in return for the contributions she made to the home and family. However, in today's society it is unreasonable to assume that the presence of love automatically implies a gift of one party's services to another. Nor is it unreasonable for the party providing the domestic labour required to create a home to expect to share in the property of the parties when the relationship is terminated. Women no longer are expected to work exclusively in the home. It must be recognized that when they do so, women forgo outside employment to provide domestic services and child care. The granting of relief in the form of a personal judgment or a property interest to the provider of domestic services should adequately reflect the fact that the income earning capacity and the ability to acquire assets by one party has been enhanced by the unpaid domestic services of the other. Marcia Neave in "Three Approaches to Family Property Disputes — Intention/Belief, Unjust Enrichment and Unconscionability", in T.G. Youdan, ed., *Equity, Fiduciaries and Trusts* (Scarborough, Ont.: Carswell, 1989), lucidly sets out the position in this way, at p. 254:

> The characterization of domestic services as gifts reflects a view of family relationships which is now out-dated and has a differential impact on women, since they are the main providers of such services. Women no longer work exclusively in the home. Those who do so sacrifice income that could otherwise be earned in paid work. Couples who decide that one partner, usually the woman, will forgo paid employment to provide domestic services and provide child care, presumably believe that this arrangement will maximize their economic resources. Grant of relief, whether personal or proprietary, to the provider of domestic services would recognize that the income-earning capacity of one partner and his ability to acquire assets have been enhanced by the unpaid services of the other and that those services were only provided free because it was believed that the relationship would continue.

This same reasoning has been recently applied in the context of divorce in *Moge* v. *Moge*, [1992] 3 S.C.R. 813. It is appropriate to recognize that the same principle should be applied to long term common law relationships.

In the present case it cannot be said, as the respondent suggests, that the contributions of the appellant were minor or that they were compensated by the provision of free accommodation. It is true that the appellant did not devote all of her energy to the home or family business as did Mary Sorochan. . . . However, the mere fact that the appellant was able to engage in part-time employment does not detract from the fact that she provided extensive and valuable services to the respondent for which she was not compensated.

It cannot be forgotten that the trial judge recognized that the appellant worked to create a "home" for the respondent. The nature and extent of her efforts were clear from the evidence, but one rather touching indication of her dedication is that she helped the children to make Christmas gifts. The value of the commitment of a homemaker, such as the appellant, should not be underestimated. The partner who provides domestic services often works far in excess of 40 hours per week in order to provide a "home". Women who work in the home may have given up a career or a type of work which would enable them to improve their earning capacity. These are matters which should be taken into account when considering both the benefits conferred and the deprivation suffered by a claimant who has been a partner in a long-term common law relationship.

The balancing of benefits conferred and received in a matrimonial or common law relationship cannot be accomplished with precision. Although it may well be essential in a commercial relationship to closely scrutinize the contributions made by each of the business partners to the acquisition of property, such an approach would be unrealistic and unfair in the context of a family relationship. Ordinarily, the trial judge will be in the best position to assess all the evidence presented and to estimate the contribution made by each of the parties. The nature of the relationship, its duration, and the contributions of the parties must be considered. Equity and fairness should form the basis for the assessment. There was ample evidence presented in this case to justify the finding of the trial judge that there had been a deprivation suffered by the appellant.

3. *Absence of Juristic Reason for the Enrichment*

In *Becker* v. *Pettkus*, supra, Dickson J. had this to say, at p. 849, with regard to juristic reasons for the enrichment:

> . . . I hold that where one person in a relationship tantamount to spousal prejudices herself in the reasonable expectation of receiving an interest in property and the other person in the relationship freely accepts benefits conferred by the first person in circumstances where he knows or ought to have known of that reasonable expectation, it would be unjust to allow the recipient of the benefit to retain it.

The test put forward is an objective one. The parties entering a marriage or a common law relationship will rarely have considered the question of compensation for benefits. If asked, they might say that because they loved their partner, each worked to achieve the common goal of creating a home and establishing a good life for themselves. It is just and reasonable that the situation be viewed objectively and that an inference be made that, in the absence of evidence establishing a contrary intention, the parties expected to share in the assets created in a matrimonial or quasi-matrimonial relationship, should it end.

Kshywieski v. *Kunka Estate* (1986), 50 R.F.L. (2d) 421, is a decision of the Manitoba Court of Appeal. It determined that, in the absence of evidence of a promise of marriage, a promise of compensation, or an expectation on the part of the plaintiff that she would be remunerated for her services, it was not unjust for the defendant or his estate to retain the benefit of the spousal service conferred upon him by the plaintiff. Professor McLeod in his annotation ((1986) 50 R.F.L. (2d) 421) summarized the conclusion in this case in these words, at p. 422:

> Without some prejudicial conduct such as request, inducement, acquiescence or the holding out of future benefit, no restitutionary relief could be awarded.

In the case at bar the British Columbia Court of Appeal relied on the *Kshywieski* decision. It concluded that because the respondent's promises to marry the appellant were made when he was drunk, she could not have taken them seriously. As a result, it was found that there was no prejudice occasioned by the appellant. In my view, the Court of Appeal was in error in this conclusion.

It is not necessary that there be evidence of promises to marry or to compensate the claimant for the services provided. Rather, where a person provides "spousal services" to another, those services should be taken as having been given with the expectation of compensation unless there is evidence to the contrary. This was the approach properly taken by the Saskatchewan Court of Appeal in *Everson* v. *Rich*, supra.

In the case at bar, the trial judge appropriately drew the inference that, in light of the duration of the relationship and the appellant's contribution to the home and property, she would reasonably have had an expectation of sharing the wealth she helped to create. He concluded that:

> . . . there is no juristic reason for the enrichment. She was under no obligation to perform the work and assist in the home without some reasonable expectation of receiving something in return other than the drunken physical abuse which she received at the hands of the Respondent.

When a claimant is under no obligation, contractual, statutory, or otherwise, to provide the work and services to the recipient, there will be an absence of juristic reasons for the enrichment. . . .

In summary, then, there was unjust enrichment of the respondent by the work of the appellant. The appellant suffered a corresponding deprivation. There was no juristic reason for the enrichment, that is to say, there was no obligation of any kind upon the appellant to provide the services to the respondent. It follows that the trial judge was correct in his finding that there had been an unjust enrichment, a corresponding deprivation, and no juristic reason for providing the enriching services. It remains to be considered what remedy should have been provided in the circumstances. Would a monetary judgment have been appropriate or should the remedy of constructive trust have been granted?

The Appropriate Remedy

In *Sorochan* v. *Sorochan*, it was noted that, although the constructive trust provides an important judicial means of remedying unjust enrichment, there are other remedies available, such as monetary damages. The first question to be resolved is which remedy is appropriate in the circumstances of this case? In *Sorochan* it was said that the court must consider whether there is a causal connection between the deprivation suffered by the plaintiff and the property in question, because in order to justify the imposition of a constructive trust a court must be satisfied that there is a "clear proprietary relationship" between the services rendered and the disputed assets. . . .

In addition to the causal connection requirement, Dickson C.J. stated that the claimant must have reasonably expected to receive an interest in the property and that the respondent ought to have been aware of that expectation. He also observed that, in considering whether a constructive trust is the appropriate remedy, the duration of the relationship should be taken into account.

The difficulty of establishing a causal connection between unjust enrichment arising from the provision of domestic services and the property has been the subject of scholarly debate (see, for example: Ralph E. Scane, "Relationships 'Tantamount to Spousal', Unjust Enrichment, and Constructive Trusts" (1991) 70 Can. Bar Rev. 260; Keith B. Farquhar, "Causal Connection in Constructive Trusts" (1986-88) 8 Est. & Tr. Q. 161; Berend Hovius and Timothy G. Youdan, *The Law of Family Property* (Scarborough, Ont.: Carswell, 1991); Ian Narev, "Unjust Enrichment and De Facto Relationships" (1991) 6 Auckland U.L. Rev. 504). As Professor Ralph Scane (supra, at p. 289) put it, the difficulty with looking for a causal connection in such cases is "that the unjust enrichment created by receipt of the benefit of [domestic] services . . . seeps throughout all of the assets of the defendant". Thus, the contributions which indirectly created accumulated family wealth for the parties cannot be traced to any one property. However, I do not think that the required link between the deprivation suffered and the property in question is as difficult to establish as it may seem.

This court has specifically recognized that indirect financial contributions to the maintenance of property will be sufficient to establish the requisite property connection for the imposition of a constructive trust. In *Becker* v. *Pettkus*, supra, the fact that Ms Becker paid the rent, purchased the food and clothing, and looked after other living expenses, enabled Mr. Pettkus to save his entire income, a goodly amount of money which he later used to purchase property. Even though Ms Becker's financial contributions did not directly finance the purchase of the property, it was

held that her indirect financial contribution was sufficient to entitle her to a proprietary interest in the property purchased by Mr. Pettkus upon the dissolution of the
relationship.

It seems to me that in a family relationship the work, services, and contributions
provided by one of the parties need not be clearly and directly linked to a specific
property. As long as there was no compensation paid for the work and services
provided by one party to the family relationship, then it can be inferred that their
provision permitted the other party to acquire lands or to improve them. In this case
the work of the appellant permitted the respondent to pay off the mortgage and, as
well, to purchase a houseboat and a cabin cruiser. In the circumstances, the trial
judge was justified in applying the constructive trust to the property which he felt
would best redress the unjust enrichment and would treat both parties in a just and
equitable manner. . . .

In *International Corona Resources Ltd.* v. *LAC Minerals Ltd.*, [1989] 2 S.C.R.
574, it was determined that the constructive trust is not reserved to situations where
a right of property is recognized. As a remedy, the constructive trust may be used to
create a right of property and this obviates the need to find a pre-existing property
right by means of equitable tracing rules. However, La Forest J. indicated that a
restitutionary proprietary remedy should not automatically be granted. He found
that, since proprietary rights give the plaintiff priority over the legitimate claims of
third party creditors, further guidance was needed for determining those situations
in which it would be appropriate to award a proprietary remedy. Thus, La Forest J.
concluded that the constructive trust should only be awarded when the personal
monetary award is insufficient; that is, when there is reason to grant to the plaintiff
the additional rights that flow from recognition of a right of property.

I agree with my colleague that there is a need to limit the use of the constructive
trust remedy in a commercial context. Yet I do not think the same proposition should
be rigorously applied in a family relationship. In a marital or quasi-marital relationship, the expectations the parties will have regarding their contributions and interest
in the assets acquired are, I expect, very different from the expectation of the parties
engaged in a commercial transaction. As I have said, it is unlikely that couples will
ever turn their minds to the issue of their expectations about their legal entitlements
at the outset of their marriage or common law relationship. If they were specifically
asked about their expectations, I would think that most couples would probably state
that they did not expect to be compensated for their contribution. Rather, they would
say, if the relationship were ever to be dissolved, then they would expect that both
parties would share in the assets or wealth that they had helped to create. Thus, rather
than expecting to receive a fee for their services based on their market value, they
would expect to receive, on a dissolution of their relationship, a fair share of the
property or wealth which their contributions had helped the parties to acquire,
improve, or to maintain. The remedy provided by the constructive trust seems to
best accord with the reasonable expectations of the parties in a marriage or quasi-
marital relationship. Nevertheless, in situations where the rights of bona fide third
parties would be affected as a result of granting the constructive trust remedy it may
well be inappropriate to do so. (See Berend Hovius and Timothy G. Youdan, *The
Law of Family Property*, at p. 146.)

It follows that in a quasi-marital relationship in those situations where the rights
of third parties are not involved, the choice between a monetary award and a constructive trust will be discretionary and should be exercised flexibly. Ordinarily both
partners will have an interest in the property acquired, improved, or maintained
during the course of the relationship. The decision as to which property, if there is

more than one, should be made the subject of a constructive trust is also a discretionary one. It too should be based on common sense and a desire to achieve a fair result for both parties.

There will, of course, be situations where an award for a monetary sum may be the most appropriate remedy. For example, where the relationship is of short duration or where there are no assets surviving its dissolution, a monetary award should be made. Professors Berend Hovius and Timothy G. Youdan (*Law of Family Property*, at p. 147) provide the following list of factors which I think are helpful in determining that a monetary distribution may be more appropriate than a constructive trust:

(a)   is the "plaintiff's entitlement . . . relatively small compared to the value of the whole property in question";

(b)   is the "defendant . . . able to satisfy the plaintiff's claim without a sale of the property" in question;

(c)   does "the plaintiff [have any] special attachment to the property in question";

(d)   what "hardship might be caused to the defendant if the plaintiff obtained the rights flowing from [the award] of an interest in the property."

In this case the appellant contributed to the maintenance and the preservation of the home. She painted the fence, planted the cedar hedge, installed the rock garden, and built the chicken coop. Nevertheless, her principal contribution was made through the provision of domestic services. Her work around the house and in caring for the children saved the respondent the expense of hiring a housekeeper and someone to care for the children. As a result, he was able to use the money which he had saved to purchase other property and to pay off the mortgage on the Sicamous property.

The trial judge found that since the respondent was now retired and living on a War Veteran's Allowance, a monetary award would be "impracticable, probably unrealistic and would not be reasonable under the circumstances" and imposed a constructive trust upon the Sicamous property. I think he was correct in doing so. It could reasonably be inferred that, given the work she had done, the appellant would expect to receive a share in the Sicamous property when the relationship ended. Further, although there was no specific evidence that the appellant had formed an emotional attachment to the property, it would not have been unreasonable for the trial judge to have inferred this in light of the work which she had done on the property. In addition, the property was vacant at the time of the trial and the respondent was retired and living on his veteran's pension in another community. Clearly, he has no particular attachment to the property. A monetary award would be meaningless. Therefore, it was both reasonable and appropriate to choose the Sicamous property as the object of the constructive trust. In the circumstances of this case, the application of the constructive trust remedy was eminently suitable.

Was the Amount of the Appellant's Interest Reasonably Determined?

There are, generally speaking, two methods of evaluating the contribution of a party in a matrimonial relationship. The first method is based upon the value received. This can be thought of as quantum meruit, that is, the amount the defendant would have had to pay for the services on a purely business basis to any other person doing the work that was provided by the claimant. Alternatively, it can be based upon what is termed "value surviving," which apportions the assets accumulated by the couple on the basis of the contributions made by each. Value surviving is the approach that has been traditionally employed in cases of constructive trust. However, there is no reason why quantum meruit or the value received approach could not be utilized to quantify the value of the constructive trust. The remedy should be flexible so that it can be readily adapted to the situation presented in any given case. In many cases the cost of retaining and presenting expert evidence as to the value of the property may be beyond the reach of the parties and at times clearly impractical. This in itself indicates the need for maintaining flexibility in the remedy.

Here, the trial judge undertook the same type of quantum meruit analysis employed in *Herman* v. *Smith* (1984), 42 R.F.L. (2d) 154 (Alta. Q.B.). That is, he calculated the appellant's contributions on the basis of what the respondent would have been required to pay a housekeeper. It has to be noted that his calculations were favourable to the respondent in that he used the amount paid prior to the commencement of the common law relationship as a basis for the calculation and then reduced it by 50 percent to allow for the value of the accommodation that the appellant received from the respondent. This was a fair means of calculating the amount due to the appellant.

Nonetheless, I would observe that the value surviving approach will often be the preferable method of determining the quantum of a claimant's share. This method will usually be more equitable and will more closely accord with the expectation of the parties as to how the assets which they have accumulated should be divided upon termination of the relationship. Further, the utilization of the value surviving method will avoid the difficult task of assigning a precise dollar value to the services provided by someone who has dedicated him- or her-self to raising children and caring for a home. Instead, the contributions of the parties can more accurately be expressed as a percentage of the accumulated wealth existing at the termination of the relationship. Thus, for pragmatic reasons, the value surviving method may be the preferable one in many cases. No matter which method is used, equity and fairness should guide the court in determining the value and contributions made by the parties. In this case awarding the Sicamous property to the appellant reflected a fair assessment of her contribution to the relationship. . . .

MCLACHLIN J. (LA FOREST, SOPINKA and IACOBUCCI JJ. concurring): — I have had the advantage of reading the reasons of Justice Cory. While I agree with his conclusion and with much of his analysis, my reasons differ in some respects on two matters critical to this appeal: the issues raised by the requirement of the absence of juristic reason for an enrichment and the nature and application of the remedy of constructive trust.

In recent decades, Canadian courts have adopted the equitable concept of unjust enrichment, *inter alia*, as the basis for remedying the injustice that occurs where one person makes a substantial contribution to the property of another person without compensation. The doctrine has been applied to a variety of situations, from claims for payments made under mistake to claims arising from conjugal relationships. While courts have not been adverse to applying the concept of unjust enrichment in new circumstances, they have insisted on adhering to the fundamental principles which have long underlain the equitable doctrine of unjust enrichment. . . .

The basic notions are simple enough. An action for unjust enrichment arises when three elements are satisfied: (1) an enrichment, (2) a corresponding deprivation, and (3) the absence of a juristic reason for the enrichment. These proven, the action is established and the right to claim relief made out. At this point, a second doctrinal concern arises: the nature of the remedy. "Unjust enrichment" in equity permitted a number of remedies, depending on the circumstances. One was a payment for services rendered on the basis of quantum *meruit* or quantum *valebat*. Another equitable remedy, available traditionally where one person was possessed of legal title to property in which another had an interest, was the constructive trust. While the first remedy to be considered was a monetary award, the Canadian jurisprudence recognized that in some cases it might be insufficient. This may occur, to quote Justice La Forest in *International Corona Resources Ltd.* v. *LAC Minerals Ltd.*, [1989] 2 S.C.R. 574, at p. 678, "if there is reason to grant to the plaintiff the additional rights that flow from recognition of a right of property." Or to quote Dickson J., as he then was, in *Becker* v. *Pettkus*, [1980] 2 S.C.R. 834, at p. 852, where there is a "contribution [to the property] sufficiently substantial and direct as to entitle [the plaintiff] to a portion of the profits realized upon sale of [the property]." In other words, the remedy of constructive trust arises where monetary damages are inadequate and where there is a link between the contribution that founds the action and the property in which the constructive trust is claimed.

Notwithstanding these rather straightforward doctrinal underpinnings, their application has sometimes given rise to difficulty. There is a tendency on the part of some to view the action for unjust enrichment as a device for doing whatever may seem fair between the parties. In the rush to substantive justice, the principles are sometimes forgotten. Policy issues often assume a large role, infusing such straightforward discussions as whether there was a "benefit" to the defendant or a "detriment" to the plaintiff. On the remedies side, the requirements of the special proprietary remedy of constructive trust are sometimes minimized. . . .

Such difficulties have to some degree complicated the case at bar. At the doctrinal level, the simple question of "benefit" and "detriment" became infused with moral and policy questions of when the provision of domestic services in a quasi-matrimonial situation can give rise to a legal obligation. At the stage of remedy, the trial judge proceeded as if he were making a monetary award, and then, without fully explaining how, awarded the appellant the entire interest in the matrimonial home on the basis of a constructive trust. It is only by a return to the fundamental principles laid out in cases like *Becker* v. *Pettkus* and *LAC Minerals* that one can cut through the conflicting findings and submissions on these issues and evaluate whether in fact the appellant has made out a claim for unjust enrichment, and if so what her remedy should be.

1. *Is the Appellant's Claim for Unjust Enrichment Made Out?*

I share the view of Cory J. that the three elements necessary to establish a claim for unjust enrichment — an enrichment, a corresponding deprivation, and the absence of any juristic reason for the enrichment — are made out in this case. The appellant's housekeeping and child-care services constituted a benefit to the respondent (1st element) in that he received household services without compensation, which, in turn, enhanced his ability to pay off his mortgage and other assets. These services also constituted a corresponding detriment to the appellant (2nd element) in that she provided services without compensation. Finally, since there was no obligation existing between the parties which would justify the unjust enrichment and no other arguments under this broad heading were met, there is no juristic reason for the enrichment (3rd element). Having met the three criteria, the plaintiff has established an unjust enrichment giving rise to restitution.

The main arguments on this appeal centred on whether the law should recognize the services which the appellant provided as being capable of founding an action for unjust enrichment. It was argued, for example, that the services cannot give rise to a remedy based on unjust enrichment because the appellant had voluntarily assumed the role of wife and stepmother. It was also said that the law of unjust enrichment should not recognize such services because they arise from natural love and affection. These arguments raise moral and policy questions and require the court to make value judgments.

The first question is: Where do these arguments belong? Are they part of the benefit-detriment analysis, or should they be considered under the third head — the absence of juristic reason for the unjust enrichment? The Court of Appeal, for example, held that there was no "detriment" on these grounds. I hold the view that these factors may most conveniently be considered under the third head of absence of juristic reason. This court has consistently taken a straightforward economic approach to the first two elements of the test for enrichment: *Becker* v. *Pettkus*, supra; *Sorochan* v. *Sorochan*, [1986] 2 S.C.R. 38; *Peel (Regional Municipality)* v. *Ontario*, [1992] 3 S.C.R. 762 (hereinafter *"Peel "*). It is in connection with the third element — absence of juristic reason for the enrichment — that such considerations may more properly find their place. It is at this stage that the court must consider whether the enrichment and detriment, morally neutral in themselves, are "unjust".

What matters should be considered in determining whether there is an absence of juristic reason for the enrichment? The test is flexible, and the factors to be considered may vary with the situation before the court. For example, different factors may be more relevant in a case like *Peel*, supra, at p. 803, a claim for unjust enrichment between different levels of government, than in a family case.

In every case, the fundamental concern is the legitimate expectation of the parties: *Becker* v. *Pettkus*, supra. In family cases, this concern may raise the following subsidiary questions:

(i) Did the plaintiff confer the benefit as a valid gift or in pursuance of a valid common law, equitable, or statutory obligation which he or she owed to the defendant?

(ii) Did the plaintiff submit to, or compromise, the defendant's honest claim?

(iii) Does public policy support the enrichment?

In the case at bar, the first and third of these factors were argued. It was argued first that the appellant's services were rendered pursuant to a common law or equitable obligation which she had assumed. Her services were part of the bargain she made when she came to live with the respondent, it was said. He would give her and her children a home and other husbandly services, and in turn she would look after the home and family.

This court has held that a common law spouse generally owes no duty at common law, in equity, or by statute to perform work or services for her partner. . . .

Nor, in the case at bar, was there any obligation arising from the circumstances of the parties. The trial judge held that the appellant was "under no obligation to perform the work and assist in the home without some reasonable expectation of receiving something in return other than the drunken physical abuse which she received at the hands of the Respondent." This puts an end to the argument that the services in question were performed pursuant to obligation. It also puts an end to the argument that the appellant's services to her partner were a "gift" from her to him. The central element of a gift at law — intentional giving to another without expectation of remuneration — is simply not present.

The third factor mentioned above raises directly the issue of public policy. While it may be stated in different ways, the argument at base is simply that some types of services in some types of relationships should not be recognized as supporting legal claims for policy reasons. More particularly, homemaking and childcare services should not, in a marital or quasi-marital relationship, be viewed as giving rise to equitable claims against the other spouse.

I concede at the outset that there is some judicial precedent for this argument. Professor Marcia Neave has observed generally that "analysis of the principles applied in English, Australian and Canadian courts sometimes fails to confront this question directly. . . . Courts which deny or grant remedies usually conceal their value judgments within statements relating to doctrinal requirements." (Marcia Neave, "Three Approaches to Family Property Disputes — Intention/Belief, Unjust Enrichment and Unconscionability," in T.G. Youdan, ed., *Equity, Fiduciaries and Trusts* (Scarborough, Ont.: Carswell, 1989), at p. 251). . . . On the judicial side, the view of the respondent is pointedly stated in *Grant* v. *Edwards*, [1986] 2 All E.R. 426, at p. 439, per Browne-Wilkinson V.-C.:

> Setting up house together, having a baby and making payments to general housekeeping expenses . . . may all be referable to the mutual love and affection of the parties and not specifically referable to the claimant's belief that she has an interest in the house.

Proponents of this view, Professor Neave, *supra*, at p. 253, argues, "regard it as distasteful to put a price upon services provided out of a sense of love and commitment to the relationship. They suggest it is unfair for a recipient of indirect or non-financial contributions to be forced to provide recompense for those contributions." To support this position, the respondent cites several cases: *Kshywieski* v. *Kunka Estate* (1986), 50 R.F.L. (2d) 421 (Man. C.A.); *Hougen* v. *Monnington* (1991), 37 R.F.L. (3d) 279 (B.C. C.A.); *Prentice* v. *Lang* (1987), 10 R.F.L. (3d) 364 (B.C. S.C.); *Hyette* v. *Pfenniger*, B.C. S.C., Dec. 19, 1991, unreported [reported at 39 R.F.L. (3d) 30].

It is my view that this argument is no longer tenable in Canada, either from the point of view of logic or authority. From the point of view of logic, I share the view of Professors Hovius and Youdan that "there is no logical reason to distinguish domestic services from other contributions" (*The Law of Family Property* (Scarborough, Ont.: Carswell, 1991), at p. 136). The notion that household and childcare services are not worthy of recognition by the court fails to recognize the fact that these services are of great value, not only to the family, but to the other spouse. As Lord Simon observed nearly thirty years ago: "The cock bird can feather his nest precisely because he is not required to spend most of his time sitting on it" ("With All My Worldly Goods," *Holdsworth Lecture* (University of Birmingham, 20th March 1964), at p. 32) [The Holdsworth Club, "With All My Worldly Goods. . . ." by Sir Jocelyn E. Simon, at pp. 14-15]. The notion, moreover, is a pernicious one that systematically devalues the contributions which women tend to make to the family economy. It has contributed to the phenomenon of the feminization of poverty which this court identified in *Moge* v. *Moge*, [1992] 3 S.C.R. 813, per L'Heureux-Dubé J., at pp. 853-54.

Moreover, the argument cannot stand with the jurisprudence which this and other courts have laid down. Today courts regularly recognize the value of domestic services. This became clear with the court's holding in *Sorochan*, leading one author to comment that "[t]he Canadian Supreme court has finally recognized that domestic contribution is of equal value as financial contribution in trusts of property in the familial context" (Mary Welstead, "Domestic Contribution and Constructive Trusts: The Canadian Perspective" [1987] Denning L.J. 151, at p. 161). If there could be any doubt about the need for the law to honestly recognize the value of domestic services, it must be considered to have been banished by *Moge* v. *Moge*, *supra*. While that case arose under the *Divorce Act*, R.S.C. 1985, c. 3 (2nd Supp.), the value of the services does not change with the legal remedy invoked.

I cannot give credence to the argument that legal recognition of the value of domestic services will do violence to the law and the social structure of our society. It has been recognized for some time that such services are entitled to recognition and compensation under the *Divorce Act* and the provincial Acts governing the distribution of matrimonial property. Yet society has not been visibly harmed. I do not think that similar recognition in the equitable doctrine of unjust enrichment will have any different effect.

Finally, I come to the argument that, because the legislature has chosen to exclude unmarried couples from the right to claim an interest in the matrimonial assets on the basis of contribution to the relationship, the court should not use the equitable doctrine of unjust enrichment to remedy the situation. Again, the argument seems flawed. It is precisely where an injustice arises without a legal remedy that equity finds a role. This case is much stronger than *Rawluk* v. *Rawluk*, [1990] 1 S.C.R. 70, where I dissented on the ground that the statute expressly pronounced on the very matter with respect to which equity was invoked.

Accordingly, I would agree with Cory J. that there are no juristic arguments which would justify the unjust enrichment, and the third element is made out. Like him, I conclude that the defendant was enriched, to the detriment of the plaintiff, and that no justification existed to vitiate the unjust enrichment claim. The claim for unjust enrichment is accordingly made out and it remains only to determine the appropriate remedy.

2. *Remedy — Monetary Judgment or Constructive Trust?*

The other difficult aspect of this case is the question of whether the remedy which the trial judge awarded — title to the matrimonial home — is justified on the principles governing the action for unjust enrichment. Two remedies are possible: an award of money on the basis of the value of the services rendered, i.e., quantum *meruit*; and the one the trial judge awarded, title to the house based on a constructive trust.

In Canada the concept of the constructive trust has been used as a vehicle for compensating for unjust enrichment in appropriate cases. The constructive trust, based on analogy to the formal trust of traditional equity, is a proprietary concept. The plaintiff is found to have an interest in the property. A finding that a plaintiff is entitled to a remedy for unjust enrichment does not imply that there is a constructive trust. As I wrote in *Rawluk*, *supra*, for a constructive trust to arise, the plaintiff must establish a direct link to the property which is the subject of the trust by reason of the plaintiff's contribution. This is the notion underlying the constructive trust in *Becker* v. *Pettkus*, supra, and *Sorochan* v. *Sorochan*, *supra*, as I understand those cases. It was also affirmed by La Forest J. in *LAC Minerals*, *supra*.

My colleague Cory J. suggests that, while a link between the contribution and the property is essential in commercial cases for a constructive trust to arise, it may not be required in family cases. . . .

I doubt the wisdom of dividing unjust enrichment cases into two categories — commercial and family — for the purpose of determining whether a constructive trust lies. A special rule for family cases finds no support in the jurisprudence. Neither *Pettkus*, nor *Rathwell* [*Rathwell* v. *Rathwell* (1978), 1 R.F.L. (2d) 1], nor *Sorochan* suggests such a departure. Moreover, the notion that one can dispense with a link between the services rendered and the property which is claimed to be subject to the trust is inconsistent with the proprietary nature of the notion of constructive trust. Finally, the creation of special rules for special situations might have an adverse effect on the development of this emerging area of equity. The same general principles should apply for all contexts, subject only the demonstrated need for alteration. . . .

Nor does the distinction between commercial cases and family cases on the remedy of constructive trust appear to be necessary. Where a monetary award is sufficient, there is no need for a constructive trust. Where a monetary award is insufficient in a family situation, this is usually related to the fact the claimant's efforts have given her a special link to the property, in which case a constructive trust arises.

For these reasons, I hold the view that in order for a constructive trust to be found, in a family case as in other cases, monetary compensation must be inadequate and there must be a link between the services rendered and the property in which the trust is claimed. Having said this, I echo the comments of Cory J. . . . that the courts should exercise flexibility and common sense when applying equitable principles to family law issues with due sensitivity to the special circumstances that can arise in such cases.

The next question is the extent of the contribution required to give rise to a constructive trust. A minor or indirect contribution is insufficient. The question, to quote Dickson J. in *Becker* v. *Pettkus*, *supra*, at p. 852, is whether "[the plaintiff's] contribution [was] sufficiently substantial and direct as to entitle her to a portion of the profits realized upon sale of the . . . property." Once this threshold is met, the amount of the contribution governs the extent of the constructive trust. . . . Cory J. advocates a flexible approach to determining whether a constructive trust is appropriate, an approach "based on common sense and a desire to achieve a fair result for both parties". . . . While agreeing that courts should avoid becoming overly technical on matters which may not be susceptible of precise monetary valuation, the principle remains that the extent of the trust must reflect the extent of the contribution.

Before leaving the principles governing the remedy of constructive trust, I turn to the manner in which the extent of the trust is determined. The debate centres on whether it is sufficient to look at the value of the services which the claimant has rendered (the "value received" approach), or whether regard should be had to the amount by which the property has been improved (the "value survived" approach). Cory J. expresses a preference for a "value survived" approach. However, he also suggests . . . that "there is no reason why quantum *meruit* or the value received approach could not be utilized to quantify the value of the constructive trust." With respect, I cannot agree. It seems to me that there are very good reasons, both doctrinal and practical, for referring to the "value survived" when assessing the value of a constructive trust.

From the point of view of doctrine, "[t]he extent of the interest must be proportionate to the contribution" to the property: *Becker* v. *Pettkus*, *supra*, at p. 852. How is the contribution to the property to be determined? One starts, of necessity, by defining the property. One goes on to determine what portion of that property is attributable to the claimant's efforts. This is the "value survived" approach. For a monetary award, the "value received" approach is appropriate; the value conferred on the property is irrelevant. But where the claim is for an interest in the property one must of necessity, it seems to me, determine what portion of the value of the property claimed is attributable to the claimant's services.

I note, as does my colleague, that there may also be practical reasons for favouring a "value survived" approach. Cory J. alludes to the practical problems with balancing benefits and detriments as required by the "value received" approach, leading some to question whether it is the least attractive approach in most family property cases (see *Davidson* v. *Worthing* (1986), 6 R.F.L. (3d) 113, McEachern C.J.S.C.; Hovius and Youdan, *supra*, at pp. 136ff). Moreover, a "value survived" approach arguably accords best with the expectations of most parties; it is more likely that a couple expects to share in the wealth generated from their partnership, rather than to receive compensation for the services performed during the relationship.

To summarize, it seems to me that the first step in determining the proper remedy for unjust enrichment is to determine whether a monetary award is insufficient and whether the nexus between the contribution and the property described in *Becker* v. *Pettkus* has been made out. If these questions are answered in the affirmative, the plaintiff is entitled to the proprietary remedy of constructive trust. In looking at whether a monetary award is insufficient, the court may take into account the probability of the award's being paid, as well as the special interest in the property acquired by the contributions: per La Forest J. in *LAC Minerals*. The value of that trust is to be determined on the basis of the actual value of the matrimonial property — the "value survived" approach. It reflects the court's best estimate of what is fair, having regard to the contribution which the claimant's services have made to the value surviving, bearing in mind the practical difficulty of calculating with mathematical precision the value of particular contributions to the family property.

I turn now to the application of these principles to the case at bar. The trial judge began by assessing the value received by the respondent (the quantum *meruit*). He went on to conclude that a monetary judgment would be inadequate. The respondent had few assets other than his houseboat and van, and no income save for a War Veteran's Allowance. The judge concluded, as I understand his reasons, that there was a sufficiently direct connection between the services rendered and the property to support a constructive trust, stating that "[the appellant] has shown that there was a positive proprietary benefit conferred by her upon the Sicamous property." Accordingly, he held that the remedy of constructive trust was made out. This approach accords with principles discussed above. In effect, the trial judge found the monetary award to be inadequate on the grounds that it would not be paid and on the ground of a special contribution to the property. These findings support the remedy of constructive trust in the property.

The remaining question is the quantification of the trust. The trial judge calculated the quantum *meruit* for the housekeeping for 12 years at $350 per month and reduced that figure by 50% "for the benefits she received." The final amount was $25,200. He then reasoned that, since the services rendered amounted to $25,200 after appropriate deductions, it follows that the appellant should receive title to the respondent's property, valued at $23,200. The missing step in this analysis is the failure to link the value received with the value surviving. As discussed above, a constructive trust cannot be quantified by simply adding up the services rendered; the court must determine the extent of the contribution which the services have made to the parties' property.

Notwithstanding the trial judge's failure to make this link, his conclusion that the appellant had established a constructive trust entitling her to title to the family home can be maintained if a trust of this magnitude is supported on the evidence. This brings me to a departure from the methods used below. The parties and the Court of Appeal appear to have treated the house as a single asset rather than as part of a family enterprise. This led to the argument that the appellant could not be entitled to full ownership in the house because the respondent had contributed to its value as well. The approach I would take — and the approach I believe the trial judge implicitly to have taken — is to consider the appellant's proper share of all the family assets. This joint family venture, in effect, was no different from the farm which was the subject of the trust in *Becker* v. *Pettkus*.

With this in mind, I turn to the evidence on the extent of the contribution. The appellant provided extensive household services over a period of 12 years, including care for the children, while they were living at the house and maintenance of the property. . . . The trial judge held that while the respondent worked in the construction business:

> . . . he would be away from home during the week and would return on the weekend whenever possible. While he was absent, the Plaintiff would care for the property in the home and care for the children while he was away.
>
> . . .
>
> In effect, the Plaintiff by moving into the Respondent's home became his housekeeper on a full-time basis without remuneration except for the food and shelter that she and the children received until the children left home.

The respondent also contributed to the value of the family enterprise surviving at the time of breakup; he generated most of the family income and helped with the maintenance of the property.

Clearly, the appellant's contribution — the "value received" by the respondent — was considerable. But what then of the "value surviving"? It seems clear that the maintenance of the family enterprise through work in cooking, cleaning, and landscaping helped preserve the property and saved the respondent large sums of money, which he was able to use to pay off his mortgage and to purchase a houseboat and a van. The appellant, for her part, had purchased a lot with her outside earnings. All these assets may be viewed as assets of the family enterprise to which the appellant contributed substantially.

The question is whether, taking the parties' respective contributions to the family assets and the value of the assets into account, the trial judge erred in awarding the appellant a full interest in the house. In my view, the evidence is capable of supporting the conclusion that the house reflects a fair approximation of the value of the appellant's efforts as reflected in the family assets. Accordingly, I would not disturb the award.

I would allow the appeal with costs.

NOWELL v. TOWN ESTATE

(1997), 30 R.F.L. (4th) 107 (Ont. C.A.)

[Nowell, the female plaintiff, and Town, a married man, had an affair for 24 years. Throughout the affair, the man's marriage and family responsibilities continued. Nowell and Town maintained separate residences and never cohabited. Thirteen years after the relationship began, Town, by then a prominent and successful artist, purchased a farm. Town and Nowell spent most weekends at the farm. Nowell contributed to life at the farm, including cooking, cleaning, gardening and organizing social events. She was not paid for those services. Nowell also assisted with Town's art exhibits, but third parties often paid her for this work.

Town often assured Nowell that he would look after her. During the relationship, he gave her many works of art. She subsequently sold most of them for over $120,000. After the relationship ended, Nowell was left essentially destitute and she demanded a settlement of $100,000. Town, who by then had assets worth at least $20 million, delivered certain works of art to Nowell. She subsequently sold many of those works for over $125,000.

Nowell brought an action after Town died for a declaration that he had been unjustly enriched as a result of the services she performed during their relationship. She sought the imposition of a constructive trust against his estate, or damages. The trial judge dismissed the action. He found that Nowell had contributed much to Town's life, but that Town, in turn, had enriched her life. In addition to receiving gifts of substantial value, Nowell benefitted personally and professionally from the opportunity to participate in Town's social and artistic life. Nowell appealed.]

BY THE COURT:— In our view, the trial judge misapprehended the evidence concerning the nature of the relationship between the appellant and Mr. Town. Theirs was not a "casual" relationship. The nature of that relationship as testified to by the appellant is amply corroborated by the testimony of the other witnesses. The relationship lasted for twenty-four years, and for the last thirteen years resembled a quasi-spousal relationship.

This error was material to the finding by the trial judge that there was no unjust enrichment, and that the appellant had been fully compensated over the years by Mr. Town and others. The appellant clearly made out a claim for unjust enrichment—an enrichment, a corresponding deprivation, and the absence of any juristic reason for the enrichment, see *Peter* v. *Beblow* (1993), 44 R.F.L. (3d) 329 at 337 (S.C.C.). The appellant made Mr. Town the focal point of her life and there was clear evidence of an enrichment to him and a corresponding financial deprivation to her. The many services performed by the appellant were capable of founding an action for unjust enrichment: *Peter* v. *Beblow, supra* at pp. 337-41.

The trial judge made no express finding that the transfer of $100,000 worth of paintings to the appellant at her request constituted a final settlement of any claim that the appellant may have had. In our view, this transfer did not constitute a final and binding settlement of her rights. At the time she wrote the letter relied upon by the respondent, the appellant was 52 years of age and had been left essentially destitute after a relationship of over twenty years. On the other hand, Mr. Town had assets of between $20 and $50 million. In this respect, we think that the trial judge also erred in failing to take into account the evidence of the many assurances over the years by Mr. Town that he would look after the appellant. Admittedly, as the trial judge said, these assurances did not "in themselves" create a legal relationship. These assurances were, however, cogent evidence of the nature of the relationship and had to be considered along with the other substantial body of evidence.

We have considered the appropriate order to be made in light of these errors. In our view, it would not be in anyone's interest to order a new trial. We are also not persuaded that the appellant's claim for 20% of the estate on the basis of a constructive trust was made out. The appellant is, however, entitled to a monetary award as compensation for unjust enrichment: see *Peter* v. *Beblow*, at p. 343. Although it is difficult to quantify what amount is appropriate in these circumstances, giving the matter our best consideration, we think that a proper disposition is to allow the appeal, set aside the order below and award the appellant the amount of $300,000. The appellant is entitled to her costs of the appeal and the trial before Justice Jarvis.

McLEOD, "ANNOTATION"

(1997), 30 R.F.L. (4th) 108

The reasons for judgement of the Ontario Court of Appeal in *Nowell* v. *Town Estate* are disappointing. The case provided the Ontario Court of Appeal with an opportunity to clarify a number of issues in the law of unjust enrichment, including:

1. whether the law of unjust enrichment applies differently between "spouses" than between strangers;
2. when a person has received fair value for benefits conferred;
3. whether the compensation for benefits conferred must come from the defendant;
4. how a court values personal services in unjust enrichment cases; and
5. the nature of the causal connection between benefits conferred and property necessary to impose a remedial constructive trust to redress unjust enrichment.

Unfortunately, the Court of Appeal did not expressly comment on any of these issues. Instead, the court substituted its opinion of what was reasonable compensation for Nowell's contributions for that of the trial judge. . . .

The trial judge and the Court of Appeal agreed that whether Nowell was entitled to relief depended on whether Town had a juristic right to retain the benefit of Nowell's services without further accounting. The trial judge held that there was no unjust enrichment, but the Court of Appeal disagreed.

Is there a rule for "family law" and another rule for everyone else?

The trial judge in *Nowell* v. *Town Estate* did not view Nowell and Town as "cohabiting" or involved in a "spousal" relationship. The Ontario Court of Appeal took exception with the trial judge's characterization of the parties' relationship. The court stated that the relationship was not "casual" but "quasi" spousal. Courts should not use "pretend legalese". "Quasi" is not a term of art, nor is it a word capable of easy definition. At best, it means "sort of" or "like" or "almost". If the relationship in *Nowell* v. *Town Estate* was "quasi" spousal, it was non-spousal.

Why then did the Court of Appeal go out of its way to institutionalize the couple's relationship by labeling it "quasi" spousal (whatever this means)? Presumably, the inference is that there are different unjust enrichment rules for "spouses" than for other people. A quasi spouse (like a common law spouse) is under no obligation to render services to a partner and there is a presumption that such services will be compensated. As a result, there is an almost automatic unjust enrichment following the breakdown of an informal family. Nowell's efforts to support Town's career and Town personally are a valuable benefit to Town. The issue is whether Nowell received fair value for the benefits she conferred.

In *Peter* v. *Beblow*. . . the Supreme Court of Canada held that a party to a "spousal" relationship does not receive fair value for benefits conferred if the other partner to the relationship retains most of the family property when the relationship ends. The trial judge held that the case was not like *Peter* v. *Beblow*. By this he meant that there was no merging of the parties' economic, social and emotional lives.

By labelling the relationship "quasi" spousal, the Court of Appeal is trying to take advantage of the bias in favour of providing relief to family partners when a relationship breaks down. Notwithstanding the Court of Appeal's repeated statements in other cases that it will not review a trial judge's determination of facts or exercise of discretion unless the conclusion reached is perverse, this is what the court did in *Nowell* v. *Town Estate*. The court relabeled the Town/Nowell relationship with a "non-label" which looked like a label that carried a presumptive right to relief.

The couple formed a symbiotic relationship which met each of their needs and interests. Nowell received an entry to a world and lifestyle that she might not have been able to achieve on her own. She also received valuable gifts throughout the relationship. The legislators created matrimonial property rights for married couples. The Supreme Court of Canada extended similar rights to unmarried couples. The reasons in *Nowell* v. *Town Estate* come close to asserting an almost automatic right to relief to long-time lovers.

Fair value for benefits conferred

In most cases, a defendant defends an unjust enrichment case by alleging that the plaintiff received fair value for benefits conferred. In *Peter* v. *Beblow* . . . the British Columbia Court of Appeal held that if a person got as much money as he or she gave and received corresponding "personal" services to those rendered, he or she received fair value for benefits rendered. The Supreme Court of Canada rejected this analysis and held that in deciding whether a spouse received fair value for services rendered, a court had to look at the totality of the parties' relationship. By pooling their resources and efforts, the parties contribute equally yet differently to the overall success of the relationship. Accordingly, they should each share in the financial resources of the relationship as well as the non-financial resources. The same policies that promote division of matrimonial property upon marriage breakdown, promote sharing family property upon breakdown of an informal family.

In a "family" or "spousal" context, the determination of whether a person received fair value for benefits conferred involves an analysis of what was acquired by the "family" unit and how it was distributed between the "spouses" when the relationship ended. Town amassed a substantial estate during the course of the parties' relationship and retained almost all of it when the relationship ended. If *Nowell* v. *Town Estate* is a "family" or "spousal" case, it is arguable that she did not receive a fair share of the family resources.

The trial judge adverted to the nature of Nowell's relationship with Town. There is no indication that he missed any aspect of the relationship. He appreciated that Town had benefitted from Nowell's efforts. He assessed Nowell's recovery under the relationship and held that she had received fair value for benefits conferred. He held that the cash and property Nowell received during the relationship, plus the additional $100,000 she received upon relationship breakdown, was adequate compensation for any benefits conferred. Accordingly, Town was not unjustly enriched by her efforts. The Court of Appeal held that the trial judge was wrong in his conclusion and awarded Nowell $300,000. Why? Why not $200,000, $400,000 or a round million dollars?

The Court of Appeal does not explain how the trial judge erred in finding that Nowell had received fair compensation for services rendered, aside from questioning his characterization of the relationship. The trial judge adverted to the same considerations as did the Court of Appeal but decided on a different amount of compensation. The only difference in the analysis was that the trial judge labelled the couple's relationship as "casual", while the Court of Appeal labelled it as "quasi-spousal".

A label is a shorthand method of describing a concept or, in this case, a relationship. That the courts chose different words to describe the same relationship should not make any difference if each appreciated the nature of the relationship. The only reason for working the word "spousal" into the label by the Court of Appeal was to increase the value of the services. The obvious question is whether Nowell and Town's relationship falls within the "family"/"spousal" unjust enrichment rules.

In most families, one spouse assumes greater responsibility for the economic needs of the family and the other spouse assumes greater responsibility for the non-economic needs of the family. During the time the family is intact, the members share the economic and non-economic benefits produced by the family. Upon breakdown, each should share in the economic benefits as well as the non-economic benefits. . . .

Having said this, just because the Court of Appeal labels the relationship "quasi" spousal does not bring it within the family analysis. It is submitted that when the trial judge stated that the case was unlike *Peter* v. *Beblow*, he meant that there was no sharing of family functions to promote the family. There was no family. There was a relationship which had some of the attributes of a spousal relationship but not many. The facts in *Nowell* v. *Town Estate* raise, more than any other constructive trust case to date, the nature of a family and how its members should be treated upon marriage breakdown.

The trial judge did not believe that the parties' relationship was a family or spousal relationship. If the Court of Appeal disagreed, it should have explained why. What is the dividing line that distinguishes "family" from other relationships? People have a right to know the legal consequences flowing from a relationship to decide whether they wish to enter or continue the relationship. Unfortunately, the Court of Appeal sidestepped the issue and as a result its conclusion may have limited effect outside the facts of the particular case.

Must compensation for benefits conferred come from the defendant?

In deciding whether Nowell received fair value for services rendered, should a court consider only the compensation from Town? During the course of the relationship, Nowell received valuable gifts from Town. She also received gifts and benefits from others with whom she was involved through Town. But for her relationship with Town, she would not have been in a position to obtain the various gifts and benefits. Accordingly, it is submitted that all of the benefits attributable to her relationship with Town should be taken into account and not only those benefits that flow from Town.

The trial judge took the totality of the benefits Nowell received into account in deciding whether there was an unjust enrichment. The Court of Appeal appears to agree with the trial judge on this point but did not expressly decide the point.

How should a court value personal services?

Judges have provided little concrete guidance how to value personal services in unjust enrichment cases. In *Peter* v. *Beblow*, the Supreme Court of Canada held that "spousal services" go beyond purely domestic services and it is unfair to link the value of a spouse's benefit to the family to the value of domestic services on the open market.

The same services may have a different value depending on whether they are rendered in the course of a business or family context. In a business context, home and child-care services will be valued on a market basis. In a family context, home and child-care services are valued by reference to the family wealth. In *Peter* v. *Beblow*, the Supreme Court of Canada decided that spouses can expect their services to be valued on a wealth-acquired/maintained basis, regardless of whether they have any direct proprietary effect. By contributing to the efficient operation of the family, a spouse indirectly contributes to the acquisition, maintenance and preservation of wealth. Therefore, the value of the services should be tied to the value of the family wealth.

In most cases, an unmarried spouse does not receive as much of the family wealth when a relationship ends as does a married spouse. Unfortunately, no one has explained why the entitlements should be different in light of McLachlin J.'s comments in *Peter* v. *Beblow* that the same policies that supported granting property rights to married spouses support granting relief to unmarried spouses. If the policies are the same, the results should be the same. Nor have any judges explained how they are quantifying the dollars necessary to compensate a spouse for services rendered. In *Nowell* v. *Town Estate*, the Court of Appeal admits that it does not know how to value Nowell's services. The justices apparently "put their heads together" to reach a consensual fair result. The assumption is that a community decision is more reliable than an individual decision. Individual differences are "evened out" through group decision-making. If this is the way the Court of Appeal intends to deal with unjust enrichment cases, it can count on a large number of appeals. . . .

On the current law, unjust enrichment cases are decided differently in a family/spousal setting than between strangers. The Supreme Court of Canada included married and unmarried spouses who cohabited within the family/spousal line of cases. If the Court of Appeal intends to extend the category of relationships justifying special treatment beyond cohabitees, it should identify which relationships should be singled out and why such a relationship is sufficiently important to society that it should be treated in a special way. Unfortunately, while the Court of Appeal seems to consider the Nowell/Town relationship "special", the court does not identify the characteristics justifying this conclusion nor what social function the relationship performs that justifies the law imposing rules on the parties to which they did not agree.

Even if *Nowell* v. *Town Estate* is a "family" case, this does not explain why the court awarded Nowell $300,000. If the couple had been married, she would have received half of the parties' net family property. In *Peter* v. *Beblow*, the Supreme Court of Canada held that the same policies that promote sharing family property promote sharing property between unmarried spouses. If so, Town should have received half the family property. However, courts rarely award an unmarried spouse the same amount as a married spouse would receive on a property division. To date, the judges have not explained why this is so or how they value personal services. The Court of Appeal added nothing to the discussion in *Nowell* v. *Town Estate*. If the justices could not explain how they reached their number, they cannot say the trial judge was wrong. There is no consistency in the cases to date, even when decided by the same courts. With respect, *Nowell* v. *Town Estate* was as good a case as any for the court to explain how to value personal services. . . .

The nature of the connection between property and benefits necessary to justify constructive trust

In *Peter* v. *Beblow*, a majority of the Supreme Court of Canada held that a court could not award a constructive trust to redress unjust enrichment unless there is a connection between the benefit conferred and the property against which the proprietary interest is asserted: see also *Reynolds* v. *Reynolds* (1995), 13 R.F.L. (4th) 179 (Ont. C.A.). . . .

The Court of Appeal did not explain why it did not impose a constructive trust in *Nowell* v. *Town Estate*. Was it because the necessary causal connection was lacking or because money was an adequate remedy?

The contract issue

Traditionally, courts have maintained that restitution stops where contract begins. Town gave Nowell paintings that she demanded when their relationship ended. Did Nowell demand and Town agree to give the paintings as compensation for any benefits conferred during their relationship?

The Court of Appeal dismisses the defence that Town had a juristic right to retain any benefits conferred as a result of an informal contract between him and Nowell. The court states simply that the trial judge did not find that a contract existed. On his analysis, the trial judge did not need to find a contract or settlement to deny relief. The trial judge was satisfied that, with or without a contract, Nowell received adequate compensation for benefits conferred.

Since the Court of Appeal did not agree with this conclusion, it should have decided whether Nowell and Town agreed to settle claims arising from their relationship in exchange for the paintings. If there was no deal, why did Town turn the paintings over after the relationship was ended? By waiting until Town died to pursue her claim, Nowell neutralized any evidence Town might have adduced about the parties' understanding when he turned over the paintings.

Conclusion

The result in *Nowell* v. *Town Estate* confirms that if an appeal court wants to intervene, it will. The task for lawyers is to figure out when a court will want to intervene. Does the result at trial seem shocking or unreasonable? If not, an appeal court is unlikely to intervene. If so, an appeal court will find a way to intervene. Most judges try to achieve what they feel is a fair result on the facts of a case. The Court of Appeal's job is not to substitute its opinion of what is "fair" for that of the trial judge but to establish principles for trial judges to follow. With respect, the Ontario Court of Appeal did not do this in *Nowell* v. *Town Estate*.

Family law in the 1990s is beginning to look like family law in the 1970s. The result in a particular case depends more on an exercise of judicial discretion than an application of legal rules. When a relationship ends, the spouse with the larger net worth can expect to transfer money or property to the spouse with the lesser net worth, regardless of legal niceties. In *Nowell* v. *Town Estate*, the Ontario Court of Appeal extends the class of relationships to which this philosophy applies to long-term committed affairs. Why? What is so important about this relationship that society should intervene to impose a bargain on the parties that they did not make for themselves?

NOTES AND QUESTIONS

1. Why did the Supreme Court in *Pettkus* v. *Becker* unanimously conclude that the shares should be equal? Didn't Pettkus make a greater contribution to the acquisition of the property? During the first five years of the relationship, while the initial capital was being accumulated, he earned considerably more than Becker did. Later she was unemployed and also ill for a period of time. Finally, Pettkus looked after the bee-keeping operation on his own during most of 1972. Should any of this have made a difference?

2. Would Becker have succeeded if Pettkus had explicitly told her, when the relationship began, that all property acquired as a result of their efforts would belong to him exclusively? See *Spence* v. *Mitchell* (1993), 1 R.F.L. (4th) 28 (Ont. Gen. Div.) and *Harper* v. *Harper* (1995), 166 A.R. 212 (Q.B.).

3. One of the arguments put forward by Pettkus was that the courts should not develop equitable remedies that in effect give "common law" spouses rights similar to those provided by the legislature for married persons. After all, the legislature deliberately did not extend the statutory property regime to unmarried cohabitees while it did make the support provisions of the *Family Law Reform Act* applicable to many unmarried cohabitees. Do you find Mr. Justice Dickson's response to this argument convincing? How did Madam Justice McLachlin deal with this point in *Peter* v. *Beblow*?

4. The *Pettkus* case had a sad and tragic postscript. Mr. Pettkus did everything he could to keep his property. When he was finally ordered to sell his bee farm to pay the settlement, he allowed the bees to starve to death to reduce the farm's value. In the end, he paid about $80,000 but much of this went to cover Ms. Becker's legal fees. Ms. Becker's bitterness and disillusionment led to her suicide. She left a note explaining that her action was a protest against the slowness and failure of the legal system.

5. The emphasis on "reasonable expectations" in *Pettkus* v. *Becker* and *Sorochan* v. *Sorochan* is problematic. Is it consistent with Dickson C.J.'s castigation of the role of intention in the context of resulting trust? Is it sufficient that the claimant had a reasonable expectation of receiving some benefit or must there be an expectation of payment or of receiving an interest in specific property? See Hovius and Youdan, *The Law of Family Property* (Toronto: Carswell, 1991) where the authors suggest (at 124):

> [A]ll that is necessary is the parties' reasonable expectations of benefitting from the property of each of them. Such an expectation will typically exist in spousal relationships, and in other relationships in which the lives and economic well-being of the parties are integrated; and it should be presumed to exist in such relationships except where the evidence establishes a contrary intention, for example, that a contribution was in fact made as a gift in the sense that it was made for the exclusive benefit of the other party.

How did Cory J. and McLachlin J. deal with the concept of reasonable expectation in *Peter* v. *Beblow*?

6. In "Unjust Enrichment — Special Relationship — Domestic Sevices — Remedial Constructive Trust: *Peter* v. *Beblow*" (1993), 72 Can. Bar Rev. 539, Professor Farquhar suggested (at 543) that the approach taken in *Peter* v. *Beblow* is "sufficiently different from that applicable in the general law of restitution to make it a point of significance whether the plaintiff and defendant can in any given case be said to have been in a 'relationship tantamount to spousal'". Is there any guidance provided by the Supreme Court of Canada regarding this point? Do the Ontario Court of Appeal's reasons in *Nowell* help?

7. Contributions by way of domestic services raise practical problems about the balancing of benefits and detriments. How is this issue dealt with in *Peter* v. *Beblow*?

8. In "Supreme Court should not be domestic bargaining agent" *The London Free Press*, October 2, 1993, at p. E5, Karen Selick argued that there was a juristic reason why Beblow should have been able to keep the property in his name:

> If Peter and Beblow traded household services against rent and groceries for 12 years, we can only conclude that each one valued what he or she was gaining from the deal more than they valued what they were giving up. Otherwise, why would they have done it? If Beblow had known

in advance that the price would include his house, there might have been no deal. . . . The juristic reason, on both sides, was that this couple had made a deal: they had a right to come before the court and have that deal enforced, not rewritten.

9. Out of a concern to maintain doctrinal integrity, Madame Justice McLachlin proceeded in *Peter* v. *Beblow* on the basis that unjust enrichment ought not be divided into commercial and family categories to determine whether a constructive trust lies. In the end, is there much difference between her position and that of Cory J.?

10. In *Pettkus* v. *Becker*, Mr. Justice Martland predicted that the acceptance of the remedial constructive trust would result in "palm tree justice". Has he been proved correct?

11. In Hovius and Youdan, *The Law of Family Property* (Toronto: Carswell, 1991), the authors state (at 106):

> Now that the general principle of unjust enrichment (along with its range of remedies, including constructive trust) is available to deal flexibly with non-financial and indirect financial contributions, the resulting trust should be restricted to direct financial contributions and voluntary transfers. In particular, contributions by way of labour or services and improvements to property (whether by money spent or by labour) should not be dealt with by resulting trusts. Even direct contributions to the payment of mortgage and similar indebtedness owed by the other party are, because of the need for flexibility, more suitably dealt with by the general principle of unjust enrichment.

Do you agree?

For two recent examples where resulting trusts were found based on contributions to the purchase price of property acquired within the context of a common law relationship, see *Billinghurst* v. *Reader* (1997), 151 D.L.R. (4th) 753 (Ont. Gen. Div.) and *Fancy* v. *Quilty* (1998), 37 R.F.L. (4th) 409 (Nfld. T.D.). See also *Spence* v. *Michell* (1997), 33 R.F.L. (4th) 147 (Ont. C.A.) where the presumption of resulting trust was rebutted and the court concluded that the man had gifted a home to his common law partner.

12. Former partners in same-sex relationships successfully brought claims based on unjust enrichment in *Anderson* v. *Luoma* (1986), 50 R.F.L. (2d) 127 (B.C. S.C.) and *Regnier* v. *O'Reilly* (1997), 31 R.F.L. (4th) 122 (B.C.S.C.).

13. For additional post-*Peter* v. *Beblow* cases involving claims by unmarried cohabitees based on unjust enrichment, see *Grant* v. *Moore* (1993), 48 R.F.L. (3d) 345 (B.C.S.C.) (monetary compensation); *Kainz* v. *Bleiler Estate* (1993), 1 R.F.L. (4th) 188 (B.C.S.C.) (claim failed); *Harrison* v. *Kalinocha* (1994), 1 R.F.L. (4th) 313 (B.C. C.A.) (constructive trust); *Kelly* v. *Russ* (1994), 1 R.F.L. (4th) 384 (Alta. Q.B.) (constructive trust and monetary compensation); *Warren* v. *Fell Estate* (1994), 2 R.F.L. (4th) 48 (B.C.S.C.) (claim failed); *Shephard* v. *Sonnenberg* (1994), 2 R.F.L. (4th) 67 (B.C.S.C.) (monetary compensation); *Dorflinger* v. *Melanson* (1994), 3 R.F.L. (4th) 261 (B.C.C.A.) (constructive trust); *Mariano* v. *Manchisi* (1994), 8 R.F.L. (4th) 7 (Ont. Gen. Div.) (constructive trust); *Hatfield* v. *Shubrook* (1984), 8 R.F.L. (4th) 366 (B.C.C.A.) (constructive trust); *Crick* v. *Ludwig* (1994), 9 R.F.L. (4th) 114, 117 D.L.R. (4th) 228 (B.C.C.A.) (monetary compensation); *Pelican* v. *Karpiel* (1994), 10 R.F.L. (4th) 113 (Ont. C.A.) (constructive trust); *Brouillon* v. *Mercel* (1995), 16 R.F.L. (4th) 371 (Ont. Gen. Div.) (claim failed); *Pickelein* v. *Gillmore* (1997), 27 R.F.L. (4th) 51 (B.C.C.A.) (monetary compensation); *Harvey* v. *Rogers* (1997), 27 R.F.L. (4th) 344 (Alta. Q.B.) (constructive trust translated into monetary compensation); *Clark* v. *Vanderhoeven* (1997), 28 R.F.L. (4th) 152 (Ont. Gen. Div.) (monetary compensation based on value of constructive trust); *Bebbington* v. *Carter* (1997), 28 R.F.L. (4th) 305 (B.C.S.C.) (constructive trust); *Strachan* v. *Brownridge* (1997), 31 R.F.L. (4th) 101 (B.C.S.C.) (monetary compensation); *Baird* v. *Iaci* (1997), 32 R.F.L. (4th) 109 (B.C.S.C.) (monetary compensation); *Hall* v. *Finnigan* (1997), 32 R.F.L. (4th) 134 (B.C.S.C.) (monetary compensation); *Billinghurst* v. *Reader* (1997), 151 D.L.R. (4th) 753 (Ont. Gen. Div.) (resulting and constructive trusts); *Lakusta* v. *Jones* (1997), 34 R.F.L. (4th) 431 (Alta. Q.B.) (monetary compensation); *Fodi* v. *Bartl* (1998), 35 R.F.L. (4th) 451 (B.C.S.C.) (claim failed); *Hamilton* v. *Begert* (1998), 36 R.F.L. (4th) 21 (Ont. Gen. Div.) (monetary compensation for direct financial contribution to construction of home only); *Halliday* v. *Halliday*

(1997), 37 R.F.L. (4th) 192 (Ont. C.A.) (claim failed); *Roering* v. *Nicholson* (1998), 38 R.F.L. (4th) 51 (B.C.S.C.) (claim failed); *Bell* v. *Michie* (1998), 38 R.F.L. (4th) 199 (Ont. Gen. Div.) (claim failed); *Leisner* v. *Russell* (1998), 39 R.F.L. (4th) 351 (B.C.S.C.) (monetary compensation based on value of constructive trust); *McManus* v. *Marchuk* (1998), 40 R.F.L. (4th) 105 (Alta. Q.B.) (claim failed); *Trotter* v. *Trotter* (1998), 42 R.F.L. (4th) 117 (Ont. C.A.) (constructive trust); *Pawluk* v. *Pawluk* (1999), 44 R.F.L. (4th) 289 (B.C.C.A.) (monetary compensation); *Wong* v. *Wong* (1999), 47 R.F.L. (4th) 396 (B.C.C.A.) (constructive trust); and *Shannon* v. *Gidden* (1999), 1 R.F.L. (5th) 105 (B.C.C.A.) (monetary compensation). In *Halliday* and *Trotter*, the parties had resumed cohabitation after their divorces.

As indicated above, in a number of these cases the courts awarded monetary compensation after determining the value of the constructive trust that might have been awarded. This was done to justify a monetary sum calculated on the basis of the "value survived" approach. Is this in keeping with the majority reasons in *Peter* v. *Beblow*? In *Pickelein* v. *Gillmore* and in *Shannon* v. *Gidden*, the B.C.C.A. concluded that it was open to a court to directly take the "value survived" approach in determining the extent of a monetary award. In *Pickelein*, the court noted that the "value received" approach would have resulted in the dismissal of both parties' claims since their contributions to the respective properties over the years were equal. The "value survived" approach allowed both parties to share in the increased value of the properties brought about by their joint contributions.

14. For further reading, see Litman, "The Emergence of Unjust Enrichment as a Cause of Action and the Remedy of Constructive Trust" (1988), 26 Alta. L. Rev. 407; Paciocco, "The Remedial Constructive Trust: A Principled Basis for Priorities over Creditors" (1989), 68 Can. Bar Rev. 315; Neave, "Three Approaches to Family Property Disputes" in Youdan, ed., *Equity, Fiduciaries and Trusts* (Toronto: Carswell, 1989) at 247; Bala and Cano, "Unmarried Cohabitation in Canada: Common Law and Civilian Approaches to Living Together" (1989), 4 C.F.L.Q. 147; Scane, "Relationships Tantamount to Spousal, Unjust Enrichment, and Constructive Trusts" (1991), 70 Can. Bar Rev. 260; McLeod, "Case Comment: *Peter* v. *Beblow*" (1993), 44 R.F.L. (3d) 396; Farquhar, "Unjust Enrichment — Special Relationship — Domestic Services — Remedial Constructive Trust: *Peter* v. *Beblow*" (1993), 72 Can. Bar Rev. 539; Schnurr, "Claims by Common Law Spouses and Same Sex Partners Against Estates" [1996] Spec. Lect. L.S.U.C. 35; and McInnes, "Unjust Enrichment and Constructive Trusts in the Supreme Court of Canada" (1998), 25 Man. L.J. 513.

2.   Part I of the *Family Law Act*

(1)   OVERVIEW

The key feature of the property regime established by Part I of the *FLA* is that spouses are entitled to an equal share of the total financial product of the marriage, determined by calculating the net family property (defined in s. 4(1)) of each spouse, when the relationship ends. The basic premise underlying the regime is that both spouses make a vital and essentially equal contribution to the economic viability of the family unit and hence to the acquisition of wealth by the unit. This premise is reflected in the Preamble and is clearly articulated in s. 5(7).

The regime only applies to those who qualify as spouses as that term is defined in s. 1(1). The good faith requirement in paragraph (b) of this definition has been interpreted to mean that the claimant must have intended to be validly married according to the applicable law: *Harris* v. *Godkewitsch* (1983), 41 O.R. (2d) 779 (U.F.C.); *Reaney* v. *Reaney* (1990), 28 R.F.L. (3d) 52 (Ont. H.C.); and *Debora* v. *Debora* (1998), 43 R.F.L. (4th) 179 (Ont. C.A.). In *Reaney*, the man knew that he was already married to another woman at the time he went through the marriage ceremony. He also realized that, according to Ontario law, he lacked the capacity to marry. Accordingly, he did not qualify as a "spouse" under s. 1(1). The Deboras were married only in a religious ceremony that did not comply with the *Marriage Act*, R.S.O. 1990, c. M.3. The man advised the woman that he wished to continue receiving a widower's pension and, therefore, their marriage should not be registered with the authorities for some time. Seven years later, the couple married in a civil ceremony. The Ontario Court of Appeal held that the woman only became a "spouse' for the purposes of Part I of the *FLA* after the second ceremony. It stated (at 184) that a person who participated in a marriage ceremony knowing that it did not comply with the provincial law could not claim to be acting "in good faith" even if he or she believed the ceremony created a marriage. For a critical comment, see McLeod, "Annotation" (1998), 43 R.F.L. (4th) 179.

The deferred sharing of financial gain during the relationship is superimposed on the separate property regime. Ownership of property between spouses is determined by the ordinary rules of property law, as modified to a minor extent by s. 14. Section 10 provides a procedure whereby ownership or possessory rights of the spouses may be determined at any time in accordance with these modified rules. The Ontario Court of Appeal confirmed in *Miller* v. *Miller* (1996), 20 R.F.L. (4th) 191 that s. 10 is procedural only, a vehicle for determining and enforcing substantive rights that have their origins elsewhere.

Until a court orders otherwise, spouses are generally free to deal with their separate property. However, where a spouse intentionally or recklessly depletes his or her net family property, the court may determine that equalization of the net family properties is unconscionable and may vary the equalization entitlement. See s. 5(6), analyzed later in this chapter. Part II of the *FLA* also places restrictions on dealings with a matrimonial home to protect the possessory rights of the non-owning spouse. These restrictions and the law governing possession of a matrimonial home are examined in Chapter 5, **THE MATRIMONIAL HOME**.

When certain events, as set out in s. 5(1) to (3), occur (often referred to as "triggering events"), the spouse whose net family property is less than that of the other spouse is entitled to one-half the difference between them. The triggering events set out in s. 5(1) occur when a divorce is granted, when a marriage is declared a nullity, or when the spouses are separated and there is no reasonable prospect of resumed cohabitation. Under s. 5(2), a surviving spouse is also entitled to one-half of the difference between his or her net family property and that of the deceased spouse. The estate cannot make an equalization claim even if the surviving spouse's net family property is greater than that of the deceased. Rules are established by s. 6 to govern the relationship among equalization claims, rights under the will, and rights on intestacy under the *Succession Law Reform Act*, R.S.O. 1990, c. S.26 on intestacy. Finally, s. 5(3) permits one spouse to apply to the court under s. 7 to "have the difference between the net family properties divided as if the spouses were separated and there were no reasonable prospect that they would resume cohabitation" if "there is a serious danger that one spouse may improvidently deplete his or her net family property."

Only s. 5(3) permits equalization claims during an ongoing marriage relationship. The apparent intention underlying this provision is to provide a remedy where one spouse by reason of disease, addiction to drugs or senility is not competent to make sensible day-to-day decisions regarding the management of his or her property. However, the subsection may also apply if one spouse is about to gamble away property on a speculative and unwise venture or if one spouse wants to make inordinate gifts to third parties. If a court makes an order for a sharing of economic gains based on s. 5(3), then neither spouse may make a further application under s. 7 in respect of the marriage: s. 5(4). This provision effectively precludes equalization claims, even if one of the other triggering events later occurs, unless a domestic contract between the spouses provides otherwise.

In many situations, but especially when an application for equalization of net family properties is based on s. 5(3), it may be prudent to apply for a preservation order under s. 12. As Granger J. explained in *Lasch* v. *Lasch* (1988), 13 R.F.L. (3d) 434 at 438 (Ont. H.C.), the purpose of an order under s. 12 is to ensure that there are sufficient assets held at trial by the spouse with the greater of the two net family properties to satisfy the equalization payment due to the other spouse. In the absence of orders under s. 12, the owning spouse remains free to deal with his or her property, other than a matrimonial home, after the valuation date. Section 5 does not confer proprietary rights upon the spouse who is owed an equalization sum once a triggering event has occurred. Nor can the debtor spouse obtain and register a certificate of pending litigation upon the commencement of a s. 7 application unless he or she is also claiming an interest in land held by the other spouse: *McMurdo* v. *McMurdo* (1988), 13 R.F.L. (3d) 317 (Ont. Master). Therefore, a spouse who is owed an equalization sum under s. 5 is in a vulnerable position. By the time a court order for payment is made under s. 9, there may be few assets held by the other spouse and it may be difficult to enforce the judgment. Orders under s. 12 are intended to prevent this situation. Accordingly, a s. 12 order should be made in equalization proceedings wherever there is a real risk that the ability of a spouse to satisfy an equalization payment is likely to be impaired by his or her dealings with property prior to trial. For an analysis of s. 12, see Hovius and Youdan, *The Law of Family Property* (Toronto: Carswell, 1991) at 235-240. See also *Gaudet (Litigation Guardian of)* v. *Young Estate* (1995), 11 R.F.L. (4th) 284 (Ont. Gen. Div.) and *Webster* v. *Webster* (1997), 37 R.F.L. (4th) 347 (Ont. Gen. Div.). In its *Working Paper on Property Rights on Marriage Breakdown* (Vancouver: Ministry of the Attorney General, 1989), the Law Reform Commission of British Columbia recommended that if a scheme similar to Part I of the *FLA* were adopted in British Columbia, the legislation should provide for the registration of a notice of application whenever a spouse applied for equalization of net family properties. Where a spouse registered such a notice and subsequently registered against the land a judgment entered in the same proceeding, the priority of the judgment would date from the registration of the notice of the application. See pp. 134-135 of the *Working Paper*.

Where a triggering event other than that specified in s. 5(3) occurs, entitlement to an equalization claim arises independent of court action. The wording of s. 5(1) suggests, for example, that as soon as the spouses separate without reasonable prospect of resumed cohabitation, the spouse with the lesser of the two net family properties is entitled to one-half the difference between the two. The occurrence of a triggering event, therefore, creates a statutory entitlement to the sum of money necessary to equalize the net family properties. To enforce this entitlement a spouse may bring an application for equalization under s. 7 and the court is then empowered by s. 9 to make various orders to ensure that this sum is realized in a fair and effective manner.

The statutory entitlement to equalization of net family properties is not, however, absolute. It is subject to the power of a court to award a greater or lesser amount under s. 5(6). Enforcement of the entitlement may also become statutorily-barred if a s. 7 application is not commenced within the limitation periods set by s. 7(3). Note, however, that a court may extend the period under s. 2(8). For an analysis of the limitation periods and the application of s. 2(8), see Hovius and Youdan, *The Law of Family Property* (Toronto: Carswell, 1991) at 228-232. See also *Olender* v. *Olender* (1993), 44 R.F.L. (3d) 195 (Ont. Div. Ct.); *Busch* v. *Amos* (1994), 9 R.F.L. (4th) 36 (Ont. Div. Ct.); *Nixon* v. *Nixon* (1994), 10 R.F.L. (4th) 122 (Ont. Gen. Div.); *Newton* v. *Newton* (1995), 11 R.F.L. (4th) 251 (Ont. U.F.C.); *Douthwaite* v. *Douth-*

waite (1997), 32 R.F.L. (4th) 90 (Ont. Gen. Div.); and *Novosel* v. *Novosel* (1999), 1 R.F.L. (5th) 233 (Ont. C.A.).

It is clear from the wording of s. 5 and s. 7(2) that the statutory entitlement under s. 5 does not create any interest by one spouse in the property of the other. See *Nevarc Holdings Ltd.* v. *Orchid Communications Inc.* (1990), 28 R.F.L. (3d) 330 (Ont. Gen. Div.). Nevertheless, a court can make certain orders affecting property once it has determined the sum to which a spouse is entitled on a s. 7 application. See s. 9(1)(b) and (d). For commentary on the question whether the creditors of a spouse or deceased spouse's estate have priority over a spouse who is owed an equalization sum, see Hovius and Youdan, *The Law of Family Property* (Toronto: Carswell, 1991) at 211-214.

Regarding the impact of bankruptcy on claims under Part I of the *FLA*, see Klotz, "Bankruptcy Issues in Family Law" (1992), 14 Adv. Q. 18; Merchant and Vogel, "The Bankruptcy Dodge" (1993), 9 C.F.L.Q. 161; Klotz, "Bankruptcy Problems in Family Law" in L.S.U.C., *Family Law: Rules, Fairness and Equality* (Special Lecture Series, 1993); Ontario Law Reform Commission, *Report on Family Property Law* (Toronto: 1993) at 16-18; Goldwater, "Bankruptcy and Family Law" (1997-98), 15 C.F.L.Q. 139; and Klotz, "Pitfalls and Pointers in High Debt Cases" (1997-1998), 15 C.F.L.Q. 187.

When the parties cannot settle the equalization entitlement, an application under s. 7 is required. Section 7(1) permits the court to "determine any matter respecting the spouse's entitlement under section 5". Where an application is made under s. 7, each party must serve on the other and file with the court a statement of property in accordance with s. 8. The practice relating to the form and delivery of the statement required is governed by Rule 13 of the *Family Law Rules*, O. Reg. 114/99 and Rules 61.14 and 70.04 of the *Rules of Civil Procedure*, R.R.O. 1990, Reg. 194. Because accurate determination of the equalization entitlement depends on accurate disclosure of the spouses' assets and liabilities, the courts have frowned on inadequate statements and have sometimes used costs as a penalty. See *Silverstein* v. *Silverstein* (1978), 1 R.F.L. (2d) 239 (Ont. H.C.); *Tylman* v. *Tylman* (1980), 30 O.R. (2d) 721 (H.C.); *Payne* v. *Payne* (1982), 31 R.F.L. (2d) 211 (Ont. H.C.); and *Skrlj* v. *Skrlj* (1986), 2 R.F.L. (3d) 305 (Ont. H.C.). See also *Beiser* v. *Beiser* (1999), 44 R.F.L. (4th) 192 (B.C.S.C.) regarding the spouses' obligations in filling out such statements. In *Burnett* v. *Burnett* (1999), 50 R.F.L. (4th) 223 (Ont. S.C.J.), the husband, who lived in Switzerland, avoided complete financial disclosure and ultimately did not appear at trial. The court attributed a value of $12 million to the husband's business assets largely on the basis of two letters to his brother regarding his will. The resulting equalization payment was over $6.5 million, with pre-judgment interest of $225,315.63.

The key to determining entitlement under s. 5 is obviously the calculation of each spouse's net family property so that one-half of their difference can be determined. The definition of "net family property" in s. 4(1) suggests the following analysis for calculating a spouse's net family property:

1. Determine the valuation date in accordance with its definition in s. 4(1). This date determines what property is to be included in the calculation and fixes the time for valuing the property.
2. List the property owned by the spouse on the valuation date.
3. Determine if any of the spouse's property is excluded by s. 4(2). To ensure that it is only the gain attributable to the joint efforts of both spouses during the marriage relationship that is shared, the definition of net family property

provides for certain excluded property and deductions from the value of included property.

4. Determine the value of property owned by the spouse on the valuation date which is not excluded.

5. Calculate the amount of the spouse's debts and liabilities on the valuation date. Since the net family properties of the spouses are intended to represent the net financial product of their marriage relationship, s. 4(1) permits a spouse to deduct debts and other liabilities on the valuation date from the value of included property.

6. Deduct the figure arrived at in step #5 from that determined under step #4.

7. Determine the value of the property, other than a matrimonial home, that the spouse owned on the date of the marriage. Since only the gain after the marriage is shared, the Act allows a pre-marital property deduction. However, for policy reasons, there are special rules governing the matrimonial home in the calculation of the net family property.

8. Calculate the value of the debts and other liabilities of the spouse on the date of the marriage.

9. Deduct the figure arrived at in step #8 from that determined under step #7.

10. Subtract the figure arrived at in step #9 from that determined under step #6. If the result is a negative number, it is deemed to be zero by s. 4(5).

Once the net family property is determined for both spouses, it is then possible to calculate entitlement under s. 5. The smaller of the two figures is deducted from the larger. This figure is then divided by one-half. This amount represents the entitlement of the spouse with the lesser of the two net family properties.

Under s. 5(6) the court may, however, award a spouse a greater or lesser amount "if the court is of the opinion that equalizing the net family properties would be unconscionable" having regard to the factors listed. Section 5(7) helps to emphasize that equalization is the norm.

As indicated above, the final result of the equalization of the net family properties is that one spouse is entitled to a monetary sum. Section 9 then empowers the court, in an application under s. 7, to make various orders to ensure that this sum is realized in a fair and effective manner.

It should be noted that spouses can opt out of Part I of the Act or modify the rules applicable to their relationship by entering into a domestic contract. Part IV of the Act provides a framework within which couples are allowed great freedom to determine the rights and obligations arising out of their relationships. Chapter 9, **DOMESTIC CONTRACTS** deals with the types of contracts recognized by the Act, the formal requirements that are imposed, and the effect of such contracts.

NOTES AND QUESTIONS

1. For judicial commentary on the framework provided by Part I of the *FLA*, see *Oliva* v. *Oliva* (1986), 2 R.F.L. (3d) 188 (Ont. H.C.); *Hamilton* v. *Hamilton* (1996), 92 O.A.C. 103 (C.A.); and *Fair* v. *Jones* (1999), 44 R.F.L. (4th) 399 (N.W.T.S.C.) (dealing with Part III of the *Family Law Act*, R.S.N.W.T. 1988, c. M-6 which is modeled on Part I of Ontario's *FLA*).

2. In *Weinstein* v. *Weinstein (Litigation Guardian of)* (1997), 30 R.F.L. (4th) 116 (Ont. Gen. Div.), a wife made a will leaving her estate to her grandchildren. Subsequently, she became mentally incapacitated due to Alzheimer's disease. The husband applied for an equalization of the spouses' net family property under s. 5(3) of the *FLA* and he was awarded $2.5 million. The husband made a will leaving the bulk of his estate to The University of Western Ontario. After his death, the grandchildren successfully argued that the original order equalizing the net family properties should be set aside because they had

not received notice of the proceedings. For a critical comment, see McLeod, "Annotation" (1997), 30 R.F.L. (4th) 117.

3. Courts awarded applicants interim equalization payments in *Walters* v. *Walters* (1997), 28 R.F.L. (4th) 95 (Ont. Gen. Div.) and *Kleinman* v. *Kleinman* (1998), 37 R.F.L. (4th) 1 (Ont. Gen. Div.).

4. In *Maljkovich* v. *Maljkovich Estate* (1995), 20 R.F.L. (4th) 222 (Ont. Gen. Div.), the husband murdered his wife following separation and while they were negotiating property matters. He filed an election under s. 6 of the *FLA*, but Jennings J. ruled (at 231) that "based on considerations of public policy, the applicant cannot be permitted to profit from his wrong by making an election under section 6". The judge suggested (at 231) that the husband's application would also have failed if he had launched it on the basis of s. 5(1) before the murder. Do you agree? See Professor McLeod's annotation to the case on p. 222.

5. For a critical examination of some of the technical defects in the Ontario property regime, see Raphael, "The Need to Reform the Division of Property Provisions in the Family Law Act" (1999), 21 Adv. Q. 380.

As noted earlier, the property regime created by Part I of the *FLA* is based on the concept of marriage as a partnership in which each spouse contributes equally to the financial product generated during the marriage relationship. Support for this concept is provided in the first excerpt that follows. However, the partnership concept has been criticized. Some see it as overcompensation for the homemaker spouse, others see it as appropriate for "traditional" marriages, but not for "modern" marriages in which both spouses work outside the home and accumulate wealth. Still others see it as a concept based on formal equality, which provides inadequately for the needs of many wives on marriage breakdown. These themes are also explored in the materials that follows.

LAW REFORM COMMISSION OF BRITISH COLUMBIA, *WORKING PAPER ON PROPERTY RIGHTS ON MARRIAGE BREAKDOWN*

(Vancouver: Ministry of the Attorney General, 1989) 59-60 and 62-65 (Footnotes Omitted)

[This Working Paper was superseded by a Final Report (No. 111), which was submitted to the Attorney General in March, 1990.]

It is a fairly straightforward exercise to identify reasons for dividing property between the spouses on marriage breakdown. Two commonly accepted (but inconsistent) rationales supporting entitlement are that it is an incident of marriage, and that entitlement flows from the contributions of the spouses.

If entitlement is regarded as an incident of marriage, the reason for dividing property between the spouses when their marriage ends is because they (presumably) intended to share their property equally. The fact of marriage in itself justifies an equal division of property on marriage breakdown.

If the intentions of the spouses do not control entitlement to family property, then shared rights must depend upon a theory of contribution. On marriage breakdown, property will be divided in accordance with the value of each spouse's contribution. . . .

A philosophy adopted in a number of other jurisdictions is that entitlement depends upon contribution to the well being of the family. Each spouse shares mutual obligations and responsibilities. These include child care, household management and financial provision. Each of these obligations is of equal worth to the family. Consequently, while entitlement to family property depends upon contribution, this is only a general principle. There is no direct correlation between the value of direct and indirect contributions and the interest to which a spouse is entitled. Courts, for the most part, may not consider the actual contributions of the parties when determining an appropriate division of family property. Contribution is the reason, but not the yardstick, for dividing family property.

Some may find it curious that a philosophy, which proclaims that rights to family property are based on spousal contribution to the acquisition of the property over the course of the marriage, does not determine entitlement by assessing the relative contributions of the parties. The approach adopted by such legislation can only be explained by acknowledging that it is a highly pragmatic response to the problems that must be resolved when dividing family property. Little is to be gained by a minute assessment of each party's contribution. Moreover, comparing the contributions of income earners and of homemakers is likely to be exceedingly difficult if not wholly impractical.

Ontario's legislation dividing family property is based on a theory of contribution. ... The Ontario legislation deems the contributions of the spouses to be equal. Dividing family property by reference to the actual contributions of the spouses is a position that has been rejected in most Canadian (and, for that matter, commonwealth) jurisdictions in favour of a position which is based on the view that each spouse contributes equally to the family unit.

Consider some examples:

1. Spouse A makes $30,000 a year. Spouse B is a homemaker.
2. Spouse A makes $300,000 a year. Spouse B is a homemaker.
3. Spouse A makes $50,000 a year. Spouse B makes $20,000 a year. Both spouses share household chores.
4. Spouse A makes $40,000 a year. Spouse B is a homemaker. There is one child of the marriage.
5. Spouse A makes $40,000 a year. Spouse B is a homemaker. There are four children of the marriage.

The question to be resolved in each case is whether the spouses have contributed equally and, if not, how to assess their contributions. Suppose it is decided that Spouse A and Spouse B in example 1 contribute equally. Should Spouse A in example 2 be entitled to more because of a much larger contribution of income each year?

Under the Ontario legislation, in each example, the spouses would be deemed to have contributed equally to the acquisition of family assets. No inquiry is made into the actual contributions of the spouses to determine their entitlement, save only in the most exceptional circumstances.

An approach based on the actual contribution of the spouses leads to either ludicrous results or impossible or inappropriate comparisons. Consider examples 4 and 5. If actual contributions are to be taken into account, should Spouse B in example 5 be entitled to more than Spouse B in example 4 because more children means, presumably, more work? Suppose Spouse B in example 5 has the assistance of a housekeeper. How should that be taken into account? If, looking to the actual contributions of the spouses, it is concluded that spouses A and B in example 5 do contribute equally, what result should follow in another case where spouse A makes $5000 a year less? Should one compare the value of contributions or should the comparison be based on quality (were the contributions to the best of each spouse's ability)? Should agreements respecting contribution have any significance (the spouses agree that Spouse A will cease outside employment and look after the children)?

Entitlement based upon the fact that spouses contribute to the acquisition of assets makes sense and provides a rationale or theoretical basis for devising legislation governing the division of family property. It seems clear, however, that dividing property by reference to the quantifiable contributions of the spouses is an undertaking which has little to commend it. The Australian Law Reform Commission offered the following comments on systems for dividing family property that depend upon quantifying the relative contributions of the spouses:

> The emphasis of the present law upon the assessment of the parties' respective contributions to the acquisition, conservation or improvement of property and to the welfare of the family is impractical and inappropriate. It involves invidious and value-laden assessments of each spouse's performance in the marriage and it engenders expense, delay and bitterness, while not influencing the outcome in the general run of cases.

The Australian Law Reform Commission commented on the subjective value judgments that must be made about the way in which priorities should be set for income-earning, homemaking and social pastimes. For example, should distinctions be drawn between a workaholic and a person who forgoes a higher income to spend more time with the family? Can a standard be identified for the assessment of a homemaker's contribution? The Commission observed:

> . . . Even if standards of performance in financial and non-financial contributions could be assessed, an attempt to compare performances in these dissimilar activities seems futile. To the extent that the comparison involves an assumption that each spouse is alone responsible for one form of contribution, it would be incorrect, in many marriages. It is unrealistic to make separate assessments of financial and non-financial contributions as if each could be severed from other aspects of the marriage relationship.

Basically, assessing actual contribution involves the comparison of apples and oranges. It cannot be done unless some common unit of comparison can be identified. No one has yet managed to do that.

FINEMAN, "IMPLEMENTING EQUALITY: IDEOLOGY, CONTRADICTION AND SOCIAL CHANGE: A STUDY OF RHETORIC AND RESULTS IN THE REGULATION OF THE CONSEQUENCES OF DIVORCE"

[1983] Wis. L. Rev. 789 (Footnotes Omitted) (Copyright © by the University of Wisconsin)

This article is an exploration of the tension between "instrumental" and "symbolic" law reform. It examines this phenomenon in the context of the feminist reform movement to revise the rules governing the economic incidents of divorce in Wisconsin. The tension in this particular reform movement arose from the potentially conflicting goals of result equality (which I will argue would have been "instrumental" reform), and rule equality (which I consider "symbolic" reform). Both of these concepts of equality incorporate and depend upon certain theoretical and factual assumptions about society, the role of women and the function of law. Yet there are important areas where these underlying assumptions, and reforms that might be based on them, diverge from each other. It is my argument that, given the socioeconomic factors that typically disadvantage women in the market while simultaneously favoring their assumption of the major domestic responsibilities, result equality must be the primary focus of any effective reform of the economics of divorce.

Symbolic divorce reform, in the form of rule equality, expresses the more traditional association of equality with sameness of treatment. Rule equality avoids the pitfalls of protective or paternalistic rules, which can be used to hurt women as well as to help them. Rule equality assumes that the groups subjected to the rules are fundamentally the same, a view that is compatible with the highly important symbolic task of defining the appropriate relationship between the sexes.

The different socioeconomic positions of women and men in our society, however, suggest that, at least for the foreseeable future, genuine reform can only be achieved through a rational, but potentially unequal, division of economic assets between husbands and wives at divorce. In such a reform these important allocation decisions would represent individualized attempts to achieve parity in position, or result equality, between the spouses. . . .

In a divorce, resources are often scarce or nonexistent. No set of rules can adequately address this problem, particularly since economic dislocation caused by divorce is treated, except in extreme cases, as a matter to be handled by private law. Within the context of the private model, however, there are both historical and practical reasons for concluding that distribution of even scarce resources should be made based on future need. The strongest arguments along this line can be made when there are children who must be cared for. The failure to give paramount consideration to future need in these cases is already contributing to the creation of an impoverished matriarchy, a new class of women made poor or marginally poor by divorce who virtually alone assume the important social task of caring for children.

The state may choose not to intervene directly to ensure that these women and their children are provided for at a level similar to the standard of living they enjoyed before divorce, but it should fashion better rules. These rules should not be designed to punish or disadvantage husbands, but should nonetheless recognize the functions that ex-wives perform in assuming major responsibility for the children. For instance, a rule requiring that the family home be allocated to the custodial parent could do much to aid such women. Current housing expenses would then remain stable and the children would not be forced to adjust to a new neighborhood, an apartment, and possibly a new school at the same time they are adjusting to their parents' divorce. In addition to the imputed income benefits of such an allocation, the equity in the house would provide some insurance to the custodial parent against a termination or decrease in child support caused by the death, illness, unemployment, or simple obstinacy of the non-custodial parent. The equity would also be available after the children reached adulthood to assist them with education or the establishment of their own families.

The imposition of a rule equality model in the divorce context would seem to be strikingly insensitive to these considerations.

[In "Shifting Perspectives on Marital Property Law" in Thorne, ed., *Rethinking the Family: Some Feminist Questions* (New York: Longman, 1982) at 115, Professor Prager notes that some feminists oppose any sharing of property by husbands and wives on marriage breakdown. She suggests that this position reflects the view that the traditional economic structure of marriage is a short-term concern. Once true economic and social equality of the sexes is achieved, each spouse will have property and the power that goes with it. Professor Prager also suggests that a separate property regime is favoured by some to send a signal to all women that dependency will not be rewarded. In this way, the marital property regime becomes a tool of social engineering designed to foster the economic and psychic independence of women. A separate property regime, by refusing to compensate a spouse who remains in the home, encourages each spouse to function as an income earner. Professor Prager concludes, however, that some form of property sharing should remain for several reasons. First, she doubts that the functionally gender-neutral world will ever materialize. Second, even if it does, spouses may continue to adopt a sharing mentality in marriage causing them to subordinate self-interest. Third, the individually-oriented separate property model works to undermine stability and co-operation in marital relationships. It rewards self-interested choices by spouses and punishes conduct of accommodation and compromise.]

(2) CALCULATING THE NET FAMILY PROPERTY

(a) Determining the valuation date

Section 4(1) defines "valuation date" as the earliest of five dates. In the context of a marriage breakdown, the earliest of these is almost certainly going to be the date on which the spouses separated and there was no reasonable prospect of resumed cohabitation. Pinpointing that date may be difficult because, as Killeen L.J.S.C. pointed out in *Czepa* v. *Czepa* (1988), 16 R.F.L. (3d) 191 at 196 (Ont. H.C.), the course of marital discord is rarely simple and each case has its own unique facts. In some circumstances, the date of separation may be an issue. More often, there will be legitimate dispute over when there was no longer a reasonable prospect of resumed cohabitation.

There is extensive case law examining the concept of "living separate and apart" in the context of divorce proceedings. The cases generally apply the concept of separation in the same way in determining the valuation date. See, for example, *Winegarden* v. *Winegarden* (1988), 15 R.F.L. (3d) 284 (Ont. Dist. Ct.); *Vogel* v. *Vogel* (1989), 18 R.F.L. (3d) 445 (Ont. H.C.); *Oswell* v. *Oswell* (1990), 28 R.F.L. (3d) 10 (Ont. H.C.); *Torosantucci* v. *Torosantucci* (1991), 32 R.F.L. (3d) 202 (Ont. U.F.C.); *Memisoglu* v. *Memiche* (1995), 170 N.B.R. (2d) 285 (C.A.) and *Raymond* v. *Raymond* (1997), 34 R.F.L. (4th) 234 (N.B.Q.B.). In all of these cases the judges accepted that spouses can be separated without a reasonable prospect that they will resume cohabitation, notwithstanding that they both live under one roof. See also *De Acetis* v. *De Acetis* (1991), 33 R.F.L. (3d) 372 (Ont. Gen. Div.); *Arvelin* v. *Arvelin* (1996), 20 R.F.L. (4th) 87 (Ont. Gen. Div.); and *Pelchat* v. *Pelchat* (1996), 13 O.T.C. (Gen. Div.).

In *Newton* v. *Newton* (1995), 11 R.F.L. (4th) 251 (Ont. U.F.C.), Czutrin J. expressed (at 261) "some reservation in using *Divorce Act* cases where the issue is 'living separate and apart'" and noted that the determination of the valuation date was of much greater practical significance than the decision regarding when the spouses first separated for the purposes of assessing grounds for divorce. He added (at 261):

> In the absence of undisputed evidence of an actual separation, whereby the parties no longer reside under the same roof and steps are taken to financially separate affairs and there is no indication that any further efforts are made to resume cohabitation, extreme caution should be exercised in fixing a valuation date.

See also *Ellis* v. *Ellis* (1996), 11 O.T.C. (Fam. Ct.). Can this concern be addressed without altering the concept of "living separate and apart"?

CARATUN v. CARATUN

(1987), 9 R.F.L. (3d) 337 (Ont. H.C.)

[Mrs. Caratun, the petitioner, moved out of the family home on July 18, 1981 and cohabitation never resumed. She argued, however, that the valuation date should be set at some point in 1984 because there was a reasonable possibility of reconciliation until that time.]

VAN CAMP J.: — . . .

VALUATION DATE

It is defined in s. 4(1) as "the date the spouses separate and there is no reasonable prospect that they will resume cohabitation". The parties separated on 18th July 1981 and have not reconciled. The problem arises as to whether there was then any reasonable prospect that they would resume cohabitation. The evidence shows that the respondent led the petitioner to believe that there was such a prospect of reconciliation until January 1984. As late as July 1984, the respondent was walking in and out of her home at will to see his child and was portraying himself to an outsider as the man of the house. Following the separation in 1981, in order to obtain an agreement with respect to custody, the respondent saw the petitioner frequently and had sexual relations with her. Persuaded by him, the petitioner withdrew her application for custody on the ground that there was an attempt to reconcile. In March 1982 the petitioner acknowledged that the respondent was a fit father and that there was a possible reconciliation. From the date of separation, however, the respondent had put off the resumption of cohabitation on the ground that he could not cohabit with her as long as she had an order for custody and, subsequently, he postponed it again until she had some weight off and, finally, until she would stop smoking. I find that there was never any intention on the respondent's part to reconcile and that there was no reasonable prospect that they would resume cohabitation after the separation in July 1981.

One reason for the postponement of the valuation date after separation until the date when there was no reasonable prospect of resumption of cohabitation would be that only on that latter date would each of the spouses make plans for their assets as a separated person. In this case the petitioner was showing the tendency that the psychologist referred to as "her tendency to believe that what she wants will come true and disregards the signs to the contrary". I find that there was no reasonable prospect that they would resume cohabitation after July 1981. The unfairness of his leading her to think to the contrary might be assessed in deciding whether equalization is unconscionable, but she suffered no monetary loss thereby. . . .

NOTES AND QUESTIONS

1. Why might Mrs. Caratun have argued in favour of the later valuation date? How does the date affect the equalization claim?

2. For other cases in which the prospect of resumed cohabitation was explored, see *Woeller* v. *Woeller* (1988), 15 R.F.L. (3d) 120 (Ont. Dist. Ct.); *Czepa* v. *Czepa* (1988), 16 R.F.L. (3d) 191 (Ont. H.C.); *Evans* v. *Evans* (1988), 16 R.F.L. (3d) 437 (Ont. H.C.); *Lessany* v. *Lessany* (1988), 17 R.F.L. (3d) 433 (Ont. Dist. Ct.); *Johnston* v. *Johnston* (1989), 21 R.F.L. (3d) 399 (Ont. H.C.); *Oswell* v. *Oswell* (1990), 28 R.F.L. (3d) 10 (Ont. H.C.); *DaCosta* v. *DaCosta* (1990), 29 R.F.L. (3d) 422 (Ont. Gen. Div.); *Golini* v. *Golini* (1991), 31 R.F.L. (3d) 289 (Ont. U.F.C.); *Torosantucci* v. *Torosantucci* (1991), 32 R.F.L. (3d) 202 (Ont. U.F.C.); *Bilas* v. *Bilas* (1994), 3 R.F.L. (4th) 354 (Ont. Gen. Div.); *Huisman* v. *Huisman* (1994), 8 R.F.L. (4th) 145 (Ont. U.F.C.); *Newton* v. *Newton* (1995), 11 R.F.L. (4th) 251 (Ont. U.F.C.); and *Cox* v. *Cox* (1997), 32 R.F.L. (4th) 70 (Ont. Gen. Div.). In *Torosantucci*, Beckett U.F.C.J.

put the issue this way (at 206): "The question is whether a reasonable person, knowing all the circumstances, would reasonably believe that the parties had a prospect or expectation of resuming cohabitation."

(b) The concepts of property, ownership and value

(i) Property

The calculation of a spouse's net family property under the *FLA* requires a determination of the value of all non-excluded property owned by a spouse on the valuation date. This determination may involve some complex issues. What is property? Note the definition in s. 4(1). What is meant by ownership? More particularly, does ownership for the purpose of Part I include beneficial ownership? If so, do the trust concepts continue to be relevant? Finally, what is meant by value? These issues are explored in the cases and materials that follow. Because pensions are very important practically and give rise to special difficulties, they will be the subject of a separate section.

HOVIUS AND YOUDAN, *THE LAW OF FAMILY PROPERTY*

(Toronto: Carswell, 1991) 241-242 (Footnotes Omitted)

There is no simple answer to the abstract question, what is property? The subject-matter of property is not, of course, restricted to tangible things such as land and chattels but extends to intangibles such as shares, money in a bank and goodwill of a business. There is, moreover, no closed list of the possible subjects of property. In addition, there is no comprehensive definition, in the sense of a set of "necessary and jointly sufficient conditions", that enables one to determine whether something is property. The law operates pragmatically in characterizing things as property so that something may be property in one context but not in another.

Certain characteristics are commonly associated with private property. The right to alienate provides an example. The presence or absence of such a characteristic is indicative whether or not something is property. But such characteristics are not conditions of property. Therefore, the absence of a common characteristic does not mean that something is necessarily not property.

Despite the indeterminacy in the term "property", it may be stated that property is a concept that is concerned with access to wealth and control over it. Moreover, assistance in determining its meaning in a particular context may, indeed must, be derived from that context. The *Family Law Act* gives some explicit direction by providing a definition of "property".

. . . More generally, the meaning of the term "property" in the context of Part I of the *Family Law Act* must be determined after taking account of the purposes of the *Family Law Act* generally and Part I in particular.

BRINKOS v. BRINKOS

(1989), 20 R.F.L. (3d) 445 (Ont. C.A.)

CARTHY J.A.: — In this proceeding for divorce and related relief, the husband appeals from the refusal of the trial judge to include in "net family property" the wife's entitlement to the income from a trust for her lifetime [4 R.F.L. (3d) 381, 25 E.T.R. 81]. The trial judge held that a future interest in income from property does not fall within the equalization scheme of the Family Law Act, S.O. 1986, c. 4.

When the wife was a small child her parents established a bank account for her and made gifts to that account through the years. At the date of marriage, June 1965, the value of that account was $224,475. Following the marriage but prior to 1972, the father made additional contributions of $71,750. On 1st January 1972 the wife settled a trust with her mother and brother as trustees. By the terms of the trust, the wife was granted an inalienable life interest in the net income from the trust property. In addition, a discretionary power was vested in the trustees to encroach upon the capital. At the time of the settlement the gifts from her parents with accumulated interest totalled $305,175 and were transferred into the trust. In January 1980 the father made a further gift, this time to the trust, in the amount of $100,000. On the date of separation, September 1982, the assets of the trust had a market value of $609,933. . . .

The parties agreed that the sum of $224,475 was property "owned on the date of marriage", and was thus a deduction from the calculation of net family property of the wife under s. 4(1). The disagreement arises as to the treatment of the interest of the wife in the future income stream as of the date of separation. The trial judge found that this interest is not "property" within the meaning of s. 4(1). He, therefore, did not have to consider the further question of whether those portions of the income stream attributable to the $71,750 contribution and the $100,000 contribution are "excluded property" under s. 4(2) of the Act. . . .

The basic position of the wife is that the scheme of the Act is to divide accumulated assets between the spouses but to leave future income as the basis for any support order. Thus, one should be restrictive in applying the definition of "property" to avoid it being divided twice, once for its capitalized value, and what remains for support. In furtherance of the same position, it is submitted that the legislature could not have contemplated creating a situation where the capitalized value of the income might exceed the ability of one spouse to pay the other within the ten-year period contemplated by s. 9 of the Act. The example is put of a middle-aged judge whose position and income is secure, subject to the contingency of being removed for misbehaviour, who could never afford to pay a spouse one half of the present value of that future income. The wife's contention is that neither the judge's salary nor the income from this trust should be considered as "property" because both are personal entitlements which cannot be alienated, the salary because of the dependence upon personal service, and the trust because of the provision against alienation. Alternatively, if it is property, there is no power in the wife to dispose of it, and it, therefore, has no market value to add to "net family property".

The trial judge found the language of s. 4(1) to be reasonably capable of two interpretations and adopted the construction contended for by the wife as more consistent with the intention of the legislature.

I cannot agree that the subsection raises interpretative doubt on its face. The opening language of s. 4(1) is plain, direct and broad, firmly embracing a present interest in future income from the trust corpus. The arguments put against that plain meaning relate to the consequences flowing from such an interpretation, but, on my analysis, the concerns expressed are either unreal or can be resolved within the general intent of the Act.

Taken from the beginning, the $224,475 was "property" as it came into the marriage, as admitted by the parties, and it never changed its character. It grew through gifts, capital gains, and some reinvestment of income by the wife, but it remained "property". When the trust was settled, the "property" was divided into two portions, the corpus and the income entitlement. The present value of the expectancy of the wife's heirs to the corpus is considerably less stripped of the income and that difference in the value did not disappear; it was retained by the wife as a presently vested entitlement in respect to personal property.

. . .[T]he life interest in this case is property in itself, and under the particular definition must certainly be a vested interest in the settled estate, which is clearly personal property. Thus, the life interest is itself property, as generally understood, and an interest in property under this definition.

In this case, the interest is a vested one. The word "contingent" raises the argument that if income streams are included, then other forms of income, such as that of a judge or that associated with a professional licence, which could never have been contemplated by the legislature, must also be included in the definition. This raises indirectly the apparent disagreement between the judgment of Van Camp J. in *Caratun* v. *Caratun* (1987), 61 O.R. (2d) 359, 9 R.F.L. (3d) 337, 28 E.T.R. 59, 43 D.L.R. (4th) 398 (H.C.), and that of Killeen L.J.S.C. in *Linton* v. *Linton* (1988), 64 O.R. (2d) 18, 11 R.F.L. (3d) 444, 29 E.T.R. 14, 49 D.L.R. (4th) 278 (H.C.), as to whether a professional licence is property within s. 4(1). The former reasons that it is property and the latter that it is not. Madam Justice Van Camp's reasoning was applied by Legg J. in *Berghofer* v. *Berghofer* (1988), 15 R.F.L. (3d) 199, 61 Alta. L.R. (2d) 186, 92 A.R. 42 (Q.B.).

These cases deal with whether a licence to practise a profession is property and no such issue is before this court. The arguments may merge, as they have, but it is one thing to look at a degree or licence earned by mutual efforts of the spouses, determine if it is property, and then seek to value it; it is quite another to look to the future income to be derived from a combination of that licence and the personal efforts of the licensee and determine if that is property and value it. I will confine my attention to the latter issue.

I cannot accept that the entitlement to earn income as a judge, or under a licence, is a contingent interest in the pool of money which may be earned in the future. There is no identifiable property, except perhaps the licence itself. If it is property, and if it has a value (and no opinion is here expressed), that value cannot be a capitalization of the future income stream. The licence will earn nothing without the services of the licensee and the earnings are based upon the value of the services provided, not upon the mere existence of a licence to perform.

The words "vested" and "contingent" should, in my view, be read in their legal sense as developed in the law of real property and estates. This legal meaning was succinctly put by MacKinnon L.J. in *Re Legh's Resettlement Trusts*, [1938] Ch. 39 at 52, [1937] 3 All E.R. 823 (C.A.):

> As I understand the rules of law upon such a problem, a future estate or interest is vested when there is a person who has an immediate right to that interest upon the cessation of the present or previous interest. But a future interest is contingent if the person to whom it is limited remains uncertain until the cessation of the previous interest.

This language has no application to income of an individual dependent upon personal service. The wife, here, has an interest in the corpus of the trust, being the income from time to time earned by it, and it would be a contingent interest if it did not arise until after the death of another. In the case of a professional practising under a licence, it cannot be said that there is a contingent entitlement to income in the future within the legal meaning of those words where personal service and effort, rather than an external event, are required to produce that income.

A related proposition put forward by the wife is that her interest in this trust cannot be property because, by its terms, it is incapable of being transferred. Jowitt's

Dictionary of English Law, 2nd ed. (1977), contains this definition of "property" at p. 1447:

> In its largest sense property signifies things and rights considered as having a money value, especially with reference to transfer or succession, and to their capacity of being injured. Property includes not only ownership, estates, and interests in corporeal things, but also rights such as trade marks, copyrights, patents, and rights *in personam* capable of transfer or transmission, such as debts.

Jowitt cannot have intended to exclude from property anything rendered inalienable by choice or agreement. The last three lines of this definition must be taken to mean that the item under consideration be intrinsically capable of transfer. This would exclude personal income because it is inseparable from the personal effort required to attract it; it does not exclude a vested entitlement to income even though it is not marketable. This remains property without a market value, but with a very real value to the owner.

In the present case, the fund of money and investments was originally capable of transfer and was transferred into the trust. Before transfer, it had a value within the marriage, and after transfer, despite the provision as to inalienability, the income entitlement had value within the marriage. Its character as property of a spouse did not change and, sensibly, fits as an item to be shared on dissolution under the philosophy of the Act.

Inalienability suggested the further argument that the legislature could not have contemplated dividing an asset that could not be sold or assigned to provide cash or consideration for the equalization. There could, it is said, be cases where the ten-year period for payment permitted by s. 9 would not be sufficient to enable the payment to be made. This issue has been addressed in *Marsham* v. *Marsham* (1987), 59 O.R. (2d) 609, 7 R.F.L. (3d) 1, 38 D.L.R. (4th) 481 (H.C.), where Walsh J. was dealing with a future pension entitlement which was the largest asset of either spouse and could not be expected to be divided until its receipt. The right to the pension was "property" under s. 4(1) "property" (c) of the definition and was properly included in "net family property" and given a present value. Mr. Justice Walsh analyzed the authorities dealing with the competing interests of resolving property issues as soon as possible after the marriage breakdown and being practical and fair to the parties. His solution in that case was to impose a trust upon the husband of a portion of the pension proceeds under s. 9(1)(d) of the Act.

This solution was intricate and more complicated than an order for a direct payment and was not as effective for the wife as an immediate payment. However, it made full use of the comprehensive powers in s. 9(1) to assure that the equalization entitlement was accomplished. The same could be done here, or in similar situations, as needed.

In passing, I note the similarity between the pension entitlement and the life interest in a trust and that the one might be considered *ejusdem generis* with the other.

The argument was put that the Act contemplates separating assets for immediate division from income for future support. It is said that any interpretation which puts the present value of income into the assets invites confusion and duplication of benefits. This argument again shows the danger of interpreting language which describes entitlement by looking to potential results. If this income is not part of net family property and remains with the wife, it presents a larger pool of assets for justifying future support payments to the husband, but if divided, it diminishes the justification for any such application. Any court analyzing such an application for support would see the whole picture and exercise its discretion in keeping with the philosophy of the Act — to be even-handed and fair in its treatment of the spouses. Double recovery would be obvious and difficult to justify.

Having decided that the present value of the future income from the trust is "net family property" of the wife (subject to the deduction of the capital value of the fund at the date of marriage), I must now consider whether any portion of that value should be excluded under s. 4(2). . . .

The sum of $71,750 was a gift made to the wife by her father after the date of marriage and prior to the settlement of the trust. It was transferred into the trust. Is this "property . . . acquired by gift . . . from a third person after the date of the marriage"? On the same reasoning as applied to s. 4(1), it is my view that the wife split this asset into two portions, retaining the income stream for herself. This portion of the property, being the value of the income, retained its character as property which had been acquired from a third party during marriage. Thus, the attributed value of the income stream from that sum on the date of the marriage breakdown should be excluded under s. 4(2)1.

It was argued that s. 4(2)2 applies and that the income should not be excluded because the donor did not expressly state that it was to be excluded from the spouse's net family property. A careful analysis of the language of item 2 indicates that the income referred to is income from property in item 1. In this case the property in item 1 is the entitlement to income and, thus, the reference in item 2 in the present context must be to income upon income. When the expert valuations are analyzed it is evident that it was assumed that the wife would be drawing down the income from year to year and there is no compounding within the valuation. Thus, income on income has not been included in any calculations and need not be excluded.

The father made a further gift directly to the trust in the amount of $100,000 and the same reasoning applies as to the earlier gift directly to the wife. In making the gift of the corpus to the trust, there was a coincident gift of the income to his daughter, which became property acquired after marriage from a third person. Accordingly, the value of the income stream attributed to that gift should be excluded under s. 4(2)1. . . .

[The present value of the wife's right to the trust income, after removing the income attributable to the post-marriage gifts of $71,750 and $100,000, was $263,154. Therefore, the wife had to pay an additional $131,577 over the equalization amount awarded by the trial judge.]

DaCOSTA v. DaCOSTA

(1992), 40 R.F.L. (3d) 216 (Ont. C.A.)

The judgment of the court was delivered by:

LABROSSE J.A.: — This is an appeal by the husband from the judgment of Granger J., dated October 18, 1990, awarding an equalization payment to the wife. The wife cross-appeals for prejudgment interest and costs.

The main issue in this appeal is the husband's interest in the capital of the estate of Henry W. Biddle (the "estate"). The trial judge valued the interest at $596,783. This accounted for a substantial part of the equalization payment of $533,440, which the trial judge arrived at as follows:

EQUALIZATION AT TRIAL

	HUSBAND	WIFE
Land — Oriole Parkway	615,000	
Less commission	36,900	
	578,100	
Cedar Dee	380,000	
Household Items	60,000✔	
Jewellery	8,500	8,500
Art		1,000
Vehicles	15,000	
Tractor Cattle Horse	4,700	
Savings	11,325	11,200
Pension	51,000	
Securities	30,550	77,250
Biddle Estate Income	141,649	
Capital	596,783	_____
Total Assets	1,877,607	97,950
Deductions		
4(1)(a) - Debts	12,414	
4(1)(b) - Pre-marriage		
Cottage	213,000	
Household	25,000	2,000
Savings	41,338	18,000
Securities		17,500
Insurance	13,000	6,000
Jewellery		1,600
Biddle Estate Income	148,581	
Capital	179,442	
	632,775	
Less debt	26,925	
	605,850	
4(2)	149,613	50,000
Total Deductions	767,877	95,100

[767,877 is in error. Debts of 12,414 have been added twice]

| Net Family Property | 1,109,730 | 2,850 |
| Equalization | −553,440 | +553,440 |

The amounts in dispute have been check-marked.

. . .

The parties were married on October 17, 1980, and they separated on March 27, 1987.

The husband is 64 years of age. He is the adopted great-grandson of the late Henry W. Biddle, who died in Pennsylvania in 1923, leaving a substantial estate. Until 1972 Pennsylvania did not recognize adopted children for the purpose of testamentary dispositions. The law was changed by the decision of the Supreme Court of Pennsylvania, as a result of which natural and adopted children were accorded equal treatment: *In re Tafel's Estate*, 449 Pa. 442, 296 A.2d 797 (Pa. 1972).

Before this decision the husband had been excluded from any payments from the estate. The change in the law led the trustees of the estate to make an application to include the husband as a beneficiary of the estate. This application was opposed by the husband's two brothers (the natural children). It was rejected at trial but was eventually successful on appeal to the Supreme Court of Pennsylvania: *In re Biddle's Estate*, 487 Pa. 616, 410 A.2d 782 (Pa. 1980), *certiorari* denied (*sub nom. DaCosta v. DaCosta*) 449 U.S. 824, 66 L.Ed.2d 27, 101 S.Ct. 84 (U.S.Pa. October 6, 1980).

As a result, the husband has been sharing in distributions of the estate's income since 1976.

On the death of Henry Biddle's sole surviving grandchild, Isabella Sage, now 87 years of age, the capital of the estate will be distributed among the surviving great-grandchildren.

Husband's Interest in the Capital of the Estate

The husband's position is that the Supreme Court of Pennsylvania dealt only with his right to share in the income of the estate and that the issue of whether he has an interest in the capital of the estate has never been adjudicated. If he should survive Isabella Sage, he will be required to litigate his right to share in the capital of the estate. At the present time he has, at best, a possible right to a contingent interest, that is to say, an interest contingent upon surviving Isabella Sage and upon successfully asserting his right in the Pennsylvania courts to a share of the capital of the estate. Whatever interest he may have is so uncertain that it cannot come within the definition of property. . .From the material before us, it is my understanding that on the death of Isabella Sage, the trustees of the estate will be obliged to file an accounting with the Pennsylvania courts setting out the status of the estate and make recommendations as to who should be entitled to share in the capital or remainder of the estate. Under the law in Pennsylvania, the trustees could not recommend persons other than those who have been sharing the income. Anyone objecting to the trustees' recommendation may file an objection, necessitating a court ruling.

However, if there are objections, it seems clear on the basis of the expert evidence that the husband will overcome them. His interest is not subject to the usual contingency of litigation. It has already been decided that he was a child for the purpose of sharing in the distribution of income. To reach a different conclusion for purposes of the distribution of capital, on the basis of *res judicata* or on the basis that the will expressly excluded an adopted child, would be illogical.

Is the Husband's Interest "Property" under s. 4(1) of the Act?

. . .

Although they can be factually distinguished from the present case, the following decisions are helpful in deciding the present case. The courts held that the particular interest involved in these decisions was "property" subject to valuation on the date of separation and subject to deduction of the value at the time of marriage.

Mittler v. *Mittler* (1988), 17 R.F.L. (3d) 113 (Ont. H.C.), involved a spouse's entitlement to reparation damages, resulting from incarceration in a German concentration camp, that were not paid until after marriage. McKinlay J. held that the spouse had, at the time of marriage, a contingent interest in personal property, analogous to a cause of action, in an amount to be determined at a later date, and that this interest came within the definition of "property." In *Black* v. *Black* (1988), 18 R.F.L. (3d) 303, 31 E.T.R. 188, 66 O.R. (2d) 643 (H.C.), Walsh J. concluded that shares held in trust for a spouse and not received until after marriage were "property." He stated, at p. 320 [R.F.L.]:

> "The definition of 'property' contained in s. 4 of the Act is all-encompassing. It specifically, and therefore intentionally, includes not only a vested, but also contingent, not only a present, but also a future interest in real or personal property."

And in a case which bears more similarity to the present one, Philp J. in *Nicol* v. *Nicol* (1989), 21 R.F.L. (3d) 236 (Ont. H.C.), held that an interest in real property, acquired under a will prior to marriage and subject to the contingency of surviving a life tenant who was still alive at the date of separation, came within the definition of "property." . . .

In my view, the trial judge's conclusion was correct. The husband's interest in the estate is a contingent interest and it is "property" within the definition of s. 4(1).

Lastly, on this issue the husband submits that if his interest in the capital of the estate is found to be "property," it should be substantially discounted. Since, it is contended, he will have to assert a claim to a capital interest in the Pennsylvania courts, whether he will be entitled to any interest, and the amount thereof, is unknown. The trial judge failed to allow any discount in this respect or, further, for the possibility that the husband may predecease Isabella Sage.

I have already dealt with the first part of this argument. The contingency that he will have to assert his claim has not been established, nor is it realistic to doubt that he will succeed if it should prove necessary for him to litigate this question. . . .

With respect to the last part of the argument, there was evidence as to the proper discount to apply to account for the possibility of the husband predeceasing Isabella Sage. The trial judge did not deal with this contingency in his reasons, or in his calculations, to arrive at the equalization payment. It is not in dispute that an adjustment must be made. The amounts used by the trial judge for the value of the husband's interest in the capital of the estate were $596,783 as of March 27, 1987 (valuation date), and $179,442 as of October 17, 1980 (date of marriage), for the purpose of deduction under s. 4(1)(b). The parties agree that these amounts should be reduced to $530,730 and $165,135 respectively.

No other discount is applicable. . . .

Additional Issue: Payment of Equalization

There is one further issue. Faced with an equalization payment of $442,374, based in large part on the contingent interest in the capital of the estate, the husband complains of unfairness. Why, he asks, should he pay now for something he may never receive? He submits that to deal with the matter equitably the wife's share of his contingent interest should be held in trust and should be payable only after he receives his interest. . . .

As to the merits of the husband's position, the unfairness complained of appears obvious. The equalization requires the husband to pay immediately the wife's share in a benefit he may never receive. Does the Act permit the relief being sought? . . . In my view, it was foreseen by the legislation in s. 9(1)(c) and (d) that in certain cases the equalization payment, or part thereof, be paid in the future.

In a case which bears some similarity to the present case, Walsh J. granted relief under s. 9(1)(c) and (d). In *Marsham* v. *Marsham* (1987), 7 R.F.L. (3d) 1, 59 O.R. (2d) 609, 38 D.L.R. (4th) 481 (H.C.), the matrimonial property included a spouse's vested pension rights. Walsh J. had to deal with a pension package with inherent uncertainties as to future income, future taxes, exemptions, and options. There were also problems in valuation and in determining the wife's proper share. He acknowledged that whenever reasonably possible, the matrimonial property should be divided once and for all, but he went on to consider whether that portion of the equalization payment representing the pension interest could and should be satisfied separately from the usual cash equalization payment. He also recognized that it might be unfair to make the husband pay now for something he may never receive.

Walsh J. reviewed the "if and when" approach which had been taken in cases of pensions in the western provinces and, on the basis of the provisions of the Act, concluded that it was appropriate to order a sharing of the pension benefits when the benefits became available and an immediate division of the remainder of the matrimonial property. To accomplish his purpose, he ordered that a trust be imposed on the pension to protect the wife's interest. . . .

It is open to us to require the husband to make the equalizing payment forthwith, but would it be appropriate when such a substantial portion of the payment represents the contingent interest? Moreover, is it fair to compel him to make a cash payment to the wife in respect of an interest which he is presently unable to enjoy, except for the income, and which he may never receive in his lifetime? I think not.

In these circumstances it is my view that it is appropriate, pursuant to s. 9(1)(d)(i), to direct the husband to hold his interest in the capital of the estate in trust for the wife to the extent of her interest therein. The asset, however, is located in a foreign jurisdiction, and to protect the wife the husband should be required to provide her with security, as foreseen under s. 9(1)(b), to ensure that she receives payment when the same is forthcoming to the husband from the estate. The security shall be by way of a bond or charge on property located in Ontario or by way of any other security satisfactory to the parties. If the parties cannot agree, the issue will be resolved by this court.

Since the wife will not receive payment until the husband is in receipt of the capital interest, it is also appropriate that she be paid interest on her share in the interim.

If the husband's capital interest is excluded from the equalization, the husband's assets are reduced from $1,766,254 (less $530,730) to $1,235,524, and the total deductions are also reduced from $878,656 (less $165,135) to $713,521. From the difference of $522,003 is deducted the wife's net family property of $2,850, for a balance of $519,153. One half of this amount, $259,576.50, represents the equalization payment.

The parties are in agreement that if payment is to be made upon receipt of the capital interest, the discount for the possibility of the husband predeceasing Isabella Sage no longer applies. The value of the husband's capital interest reverts to the amount of $596,783, used by the trial judge in his calculation of the equalization payment. The non-discounted value of the capital interest in the sum of $179,442 is deducted from this amount, leaving a difference of $417,341, representing the net growth in the capital interest during the marriage. On receipt of the capital interest, the husband is to pay to the wife one half of the difference, namely, $208,670.50.

Accordingly, the judgment herein shall provide that the husband shall be trustee for the wife of her share in the husband's contingent interest in the estate, that he shall not do or omit to do any act that would prejudice the wife's interest therein, and that he shall provide security for the wife's interest as aforesaid. Interest on the sum of $208,670.50 is to be based on the yearly average prime rate of the Royal Bank of Canada. Interest is to be payable from the date of the trial judgment and is to be paid annually on December 31. . . .

NOTES AND QUESTIONS

1. As *Brinkos* and *DaCosta* indicate, beneficial interests in express trusts are clearly property within the definition of s. 4(1). See also *Black* v. *Black* (1988), 18 R.F.L. (3d) 303 (Ont. H.C.). It is also implicit in the reasoning of the Supreme Court in *Rawluk* v. *Rawluk* (1990), 23 R.F.L. (3d) 337 that a beneficial interest under a resulting trust is property for the calculation of a spouse's net family property. The trustee, on the other hand, does not generally have a property interest that has value even though he or she has the legal interest in the property. In *Skrlj* v. *Skrlj* (1986), 2 R.F.L. (3d) 305 (Ont. H.C.), the wife held money in two bank accounts for her children. None of it was included in her net family property. See also *Kelly* v. *Kelly* (1986), 50 R.F.L. (2d) 360 (Ont. H.C.); *Porter* v. *Porter* (1986), 1 R.F.L. (3d) 12 (Ont. Dist. Ct.); and *Hodgins* v. *Hodgins* (1989), 23 R.F.L. (3d) 302 (Ont. H.C.).

2. For analysis of *Brinkos*, see Grant and Brent, "*Brinkos* v. *Brinkos*: Practical Guidance on Property and Valuation Issues from the Court of Appeal" (1990), 6 C.F.L.Q. 79 and Cole, "*Brinkos* v. *Brinkos* and the Concept of Value to Owner" (1990), 6 C.F.L.Q. 227.

3. In *Weicker* v. *Weicker* (1986), 4 R.F.L. (3d) 1, 72 A.R. 264 (Q.B.), the husband was entitled under his father's will to receive the income from a trust fund until age 65. If the husband lived to age 65, he would then be entitled to the trust fund itself. The court concluded that the husband's interest in the father's estate was not available for distribution on marriage breakdown. In its reasons, the court did not expressly deal with the issue of whether the right to income from the trust was property owned by the husband but it implicitly concluded that it was not. Regarding the husband's interest in the fund itself, McBain J. concluded (at 18):

> I am satisfied that he has only a contingent interest in these funds. He does not "own" them as contemplated by s. 7(1) of the Act. He has not acquired this property as yet, although there is now great likelihood that he will.

Would the result be different in Ontario? If so, how would the contingent interest be valued? See the annotation to the case by Professor McLeod (1986), 4 R.F.L. (3d) 1. See also *Black* v. *Black* (1989), 18 R.F.L. (3d) 303 (Ont. H.C.) and *Mittler* v. *Mittler* (1988), 17 R.F.L. (3d) 113 (Ont. H.C.).

4. Does a wife have a property interest in any of her father's property while he is still alive if she is listed as the sole beneficiary under his will? See *Dunning* v. *Dunning* (1987), 8 R.F.L. (3d) 289 (Ont. H.C.).

CARATUN v. CARATUN

(1992), 42 R.F.L. (3d) 113 (Ont. C.A.), leave to appeal refused (1993), 46 R.F.L. (3d) 314n (S.C.C.).

The judgment of the court was delivered by MCKINLAY J.A.: — This is an appeal in a matrimonial matter brought by the husband, Victor Caratun, respondent at trial, in an action commenced by his wife, asking that the court set aside awards made in favour of his wife, respondent on appeal, of lump sum spousal maintenance of $15,000; child support in the amount of $500 per month commencing November 30, 1986, and continuing as long as the respondent wife has access to the child of the marriage; and payment of an amount of $30,000 to reimburse her for her contribution towards the obtaining of the appellant's dental licence [reported at (1987), 9 R.F.L. (3d) 337, 61 O.R. (2d) 359, 28 E.T.R. 59, 43 D.L.R. (4th) 398 (H.C.)]. The respondent, Victoria Caratun, cross-appeals for a revaluation of the family assets.

The parties, both citizens of Romania at the time, met there in December of 1972 while the appellant was completing his internship in medicine. In June of 1973 the respondent moved from Romania to Israel with her family, where she obtained employment as a draftsperson. She earned the sum of £1800 Israeli per month in 1977.

The appellant had completed high school, attended technical school for a year, and then attended medical school, from which he ultimately graduated. To become a dentist in Romania, it was first necessary to be qualified as a medical doctor and then proceed to study dentistry. The appellant practised dentistry in Romania from 1973 to 1977.

From June 1973 to November 1976, the respondent travelled from Israel to Romania every six months to visit the appellant. The appellant and respondent petitioned the appropriate authorities on several occasions for permission to marry, as was then required by Romanian law. On six separate occasions their petitions were denied. The respondent kept up an untiring lobby for the purpose of obtaining the necessary permission, which ended in success in August of 1976. The parties were married in Bucharest on November 17, 1976, and two weeks later the respondent returned to her home in Israel. Four months later, having received permission to emigrate from Romania, the appellant joined the respondent in Israel under her sponsorship.

Within three months of the appellant's arrival in Israel in May of 1977, he unilaterally decided to leave that country. Had the appellant become a citizen of Israel, it would have been impossible for him to claim refugee status for the purpose of immigrating to a Western country. He learned that the only likely way of immigrating to the West was to become a voluntary intern in a refugee camp for an unspecified period of time. In August of 1977 the appellant left Israel for Greece without the respondent. The respondent remained in Israel for approximately one month, during which time she settled her financial affairs. She then resigned a tenured position, which she held at the University of the Negev, and joined the appellant in Greece. She became pregnant a few months later. The parties resided in a refugee camp in Greece for approximately nine months. Late in May of 1978, they arrived in Toronto, and on August 15, 1978, their son, Victor Daniel Caratun, was born.

Madam Justice Van Camp made two important findings of fact with respect to the period involved in the foregoing factual summary. First, she found that the appellant's marriage and subsequent relationship with the respondent was, on his part, for the purpose of obtaining permission to leave Romania and immigrate to North America to practise dentistry there. Secondly, she found that the appellant had ascertained that it was easier for a couple with children to immigrate to North America and, consequently, the petitioner became pregnant while the couple were interned in Greece.

After they arrived in Toronto, it was necessary for the appellant to become reasonably proficient in English in order to obtain a licence to practise dentistry. From July 1978 until January 1979, he attended a course at George Brown College, paid for by the Canadian government. In addition, he received a training allowance in the amount of $1,900 from Canada Manpower. From the time of their arrival in Canada until the appellant obtained his licence to practise dentistry in May of 1981, both parties worked very hard — the respondent at jobs on the assembly line in a factory, as a beautician in her home, and as a hairdresser. Shortly after their arrival the appellant worked on weekends and in the evenings as a dishwasher and a waiter. In 1979 he obtained employment at a dental lab, and in December of that year he was employed at the Toronto General Hospital Dental Clinic at a salary of $18,000 per annum. During this time he continued his efforts towards passing examinations to obtain his licence to practise dentistry in Ontario. After a number of attempts, he finally succeeded in obtaining his licence in May of 1981.

Two days after the appellant was notified that he had passed his final exam and was qualified to practise dentistry, he advised the respondent that he wished a divorce. The trial judge found July 18, 1981, to be the valuation date for purposes of the *Family Law Act, 1986*, S.O. 1986, c. 4 (the "F.L.A.")...

Contribution towards the Obtaining of Appellant's Dental Licence

The reasons of the trial judge make it quite clear that Dr. Caratun's primary objective in marrying Mrs. Caratun and fathering their child was to assist him in immigrating to North America to practise dentistry. Mrs. Caratun worked extremely hard over a number of years in Israel and in Canada to assist Dr. Caratun in attaining his ultimate objective. Two days after attaining that objective, he rejected Mrs. Caratun as his wife, at a time when family assets were next to non-existent but his future income-earning ability was substantial.

Facts such as these raise difficult legal questions, given the purpose of the F.L.A., on the one hand, and its specific provisions, on the other. The combining of spousal efforts over a number of years to provide for the education and professional qualification of one spouse is not unusual in our society. The inevitable result, if there is a separation on attaining the joint objective, is that one family member is left with no assets and often very little in the way of educational or professional qualifications with which to sustain herself or himself in the future. The extreme unfairness of the situation is patent, but the possibility of a legal remedy is far from settled law.

Dental Licence as "Property"

Mrs. Caratun's position at trial, which was accepted by the trial judge, was that Dr. Caratun's dental licence is property within the meaning of that word as defined in s. 4(1) of the F.L.A., of which the relevant portion reads: "'property' means any interest, present or future, vested or contingent, in real or personal property."

That definition is broadly framed, and includes all conceivable types of property in the traditional common law sense. However, it does not, by its terms, extend the meaning of property beyond those limits. The contrary argument is that in construing that definition one must keep in mind the F.L.A. policy of marriage partnership, which requires, on final separation, the equal division of wealth accumulated during the marriage; and that a licence to practise a particular profession constitutes wealth in the matrimonial context.

Two important cases at the trial level have reached opposite conclusions on this issue — the trial decision in this case and the decision of Killeen L.J.S.C. in *Linton* v. *Linton* (1988), 11 R.F.L. (3d) 444, 29 E.T.R. 14, 64 O.R. (2d) 18, 49 D.L.R. (4th) 278 (H.C.). Both decisions include detailed and thoughtful analyses of this issue, and substantial reference to authorities, both Canadian and American. The American decisions are so varied as to be of little assistance. Although all purport to be based on the wording of the particular statute involved, they reach varying results based on statutes with very similar wording.

In determining the issue of whether a professional licence constitutes "property," the cases and the numerous articles written on the subject concentrate primarily on two aspects of the problem: first, the nature or characterization of a licence, and, second, the difficulty of valuing a licence in the family property context.

(i)   *Characterization of Licence*

The broad definition of property in the F.L.A. clearly encompasses many forms of intangibles — a classification into which a licence must fall if it is to be considered property. The common law has never had any difficulty in dealing with property evidenced by pieces of paper representing bundles of rights — such as a share certificate with its attendant rights to dividends, voting privileges, and distribution of assets on corporate dissolution. If a licence to practise a profession is property, what are its attendant rights? Apart from possible benefits, such as the right to join professional groups and clubs — which are not relevant in this context — the only real right conferred on the holder of the licence is a right to work in a particular profession. That right, assuming it is held at the time of separation, is a present right to work in the future, and it will continue for as long as the holder of the right is professionally and personally able to perform the activity involved. It is the nature of the right given by the licence which, in my view, causes insurmountable difficulties in treating such a licence as property for matrimonial purposes. Those difficulties arise, first, because it is not a right which is transferable; second, because it requires the personal efforts of the holder in order to be of any value in the future; and, third, because the only difference between such a licence and any other right to work is in its exclusivity.

(a)   *Non-transferability*

One of the traditional indicia of property is its inherent transferability. That transferability may, of course, be precluded either by law or by contract. In contrast, the right or licence to practise a particular profession is, by its very nature, a right personal to the holder, incapable of transfer. It is very different in nature from the professional practice which may be built up by the licensee after attaining the licence. The practice itself is clearly capable of transfer for value, although the market is limited to other licensees. Where spouses separate before a practice has been built up, there is nothing available for transfer. . . .

It is clear that many rights or things which are restrained from transfer by law are, by agreement or otherwise, inherently transferable and are of value to their owners. Such rights or things fall within the normal legal definition of property, and would clearly fall within the statutory definition of property in the F.L.A. However, rights or things which are inherently non-transferable, such as the right to practise a profession, clearly do not constitute property in any traditional sense.

(b) *Requirement of Personal Efforts of the Licensee*

Under the F.L.A. the types of property included in the statutory definition are very broad-ranging. The definition is in the F.L.A. for the purpose of determining the value of the property to be included in arriving at "net family property" to be equalized under s. 5. I see no way in which that definition can be interpreted to include work to be performed by either spouse in the future. It goes without saying that without the personal efforts of the licensee, the licence will produce nothing. The only provisions in the F.L.A. that allow one spouse to share in the fruits of the other spouse's future labours are the support provisions, which do not form a part of the equalization payment under s. 5.

The policy of the F.L.A. emphasizes principles of partnership during marriage, and self-sufficiency following its termination. When the marriage ends, the partnership ends. Placing a value on future labours of either spouse for purposes of the equalization payment would frustrate those policy objectives.

(c) *Right To Work in General*

The only difference between a professional licence and the ability and right of any individual to perform a particular type of work is in the exclusive nature of a professional licence. Only those who have successfully survived the rigors of professional training have the right to practise their profession. Nonetheless, the difference between the right to practise a profession and the right to work at any job which requires special skill or knowledge is a right which differs only in scope, but not in substance. A plumber, carpenter, or an electrician spends a substantial period of time in apprenticeship before becoming proficient at his trade; a salesman spends a substantial period of time developing a clientele in order to enhance his income; a business executive may spend a substantial period of time in university and then working his way up the corporate ladder to attain his level of income. Should the law consider all of these attainments as property for the purposes of determining the equalization payment under the F.L.A.? Clearly not. I see no interpretation of the F.L.A., either specifically under s. 4, or generally, which would allow the court to treat such attainments as property.

(ii) *Valuation of Licence*

It is clear from the considerations referred to above that there are substantial difficulties, both practical and conceptual, in treating licences as "property." In addition, the valuation of such a right would be unfairly speculative in the matrimonial context. A myriad of contingencies, including inclination, probability of success in practice of the profession, length of physical and mental capability to perform the duties of the profession, competition within the profession, and many others, all render a fair valuation of the licence unusually difficult. But a further potential inequity arises: support orders may be varied if circumstances change, but no amendment of an equalization payment is possible regardless of changed circumstances.

The valuation approach approved by the trial judge in this case was to compare the appellant's actual professional income since attaining his dental licence up to

September 1986 with the average earnings of an honours university graduate of the same age during the same period. His future professional income from 1986 until his expected retirement age of 65 was determined, based on his actual income level adjusted by the rate of growth of income for dentists according to the American Dental Association. The difference between his projected future earnings and those of honours graduates was valued at an annual discount rate of 2.5 per cent according to the *Rules of Civil Procedure*. Based on this approach, a valuation of the dental licence as of valuation date, July 18, 1981 was found to be $379,965. This valuation did not take into account any of the contingencies of the type referred to above. Another method of valuation, which resulted in the figure of $219,346, was to compare the expected career earnings of the average dentist obtaining his licence in July 1981 and retiring in November 2013, to the average earnings of honours university graduates for the same period.

Either valuation approach is logical, if the licence is "property." However, it would be equally logical to treat a university degree as property, and then value that degree by comparing incomes of university graduates with those of high school graduates. In the matrimonial context, the fallacy lies in treating a licence as property on valuation date, when most of its value depends on the personal labour of the licensed spouse after the termination of the relationship. That future labour does not constitute anything earned or existing at the valuation date.

For all of the above reasons, it is my view that a professional licence does not constitute property within the meaning of s. 4 of the F.L.A.

Constructive Trust

The trial judge decided that the appellant's dental licence was property within the meaning of s. 4 of the F.L.A. However, she did not include the value of the licence in the appellant's net family property, but rather decided that the licence would be held by the appellant subject to a constructive trust in favour of the respondent in the amount of $30,000 — that amount representing the value of the respondent's contribution to the acquisition of the licence. Given a finding that the licence constituted property, it is my view that the court had no discretion as to whether or not to include its value in net family property under s. 5(1) of the Act.
. . .

The trial judge stated that she did not see "any reason in principle why a professional licence cannot be subject to a similar proprietary interest in the form of a constructive trust" [at p. 355 R.F.L.]. I agree that if the licence constituted "property," then there is no reason why, in a proper case, that property could not be subject to a constructive trust. However, if the licence does not constitute property, then there is nothing to which the constructive trust could attach. None of the cases relied on by the trial judge in this case assist in establishing that a licence is property to which a constructive trust can attach.

Unequal Division of Net Family Assets

The trial judge considered a possible method of compensating Mrs. Caratun would be to order an unequal division of net family assets pursuant to s. 5(6), treating the respondent's contribution to her husband's professional training as a "circumstance relating to the acquisition, disposition, preservation, maintenance or improvement of property." Since I am of the view that the licence does not constitute property within the F.L.A., an unequal division of net family property would not solve this dilemma, as the parties had accumulated next to nothing in the way of family assets at the date of separation.

Compensatory Support

The partnership theory of marriage espoused by the F.L.A. and any ordinary sense of fairness require that some form of compensation be afforded the respondent in this case for her substantial contribution towards the career aspirations of her husband. The need for a remedy is made even more pronounced in this case because Dr. Caratun separated from his wife immediately upon obtaining his licence. Nonetheless, any such remedy must be provided in accordance with the provisions of the relevant statutory provisions.

. . .[I]n this case the applicable legislation is the corollary relief provisions of s. 11(1) of the *Divorce Act*, S.C. 1967-68, c. 24, R.S.C. 1970, c. D-8 (the "old *Divorce Act* ") . . .[The section gave a board discretion to the courts to order spousal support if they thought it "fit and just to do so" in light of the "conduct . . .condition, means and other circumstances" of the spouses.] The wording in the old *Divorce Act* is somewhat different from the wording of the support provisions of the F.L.A. However, s. 11(1) is expressed in broad terms and encompasses all of the relevant factors outlined under the provisions of the F.L.A.

In this case it is clear from the facts found by the trial judge that the respondent made a significant contribution to the marriage relationship, and more particularly to the ability of the appellant to attain his dental licence. Although the evidence did not disclose the dollar terms of the economic consequences of the relationship to Mrs. Caratun, it is clear that she gave up the practice of her profession in Israel and came to this country, where she worked as a waitress and hairdresser, to assist her husband to attain his professional objective. Mrs. Caratun sacrificed, or at least delayed, her personal career advancement to assist her husband in furthering his. Both of their future lives were affected substantially as a result. His income-earning ability and future prospects have been enhanced significantly. While she is not destitute, her income-earning ability and future prospects have been diminished significantly.

I am of the view that a compensatory support order pursuant to s. 11(1) of the old *Divorce Act* is appropriate in this case. The trial judge took all of the relevant factors into consideration in arriving at the amount of $30,000, which she considered an appropriate amount to reflect the respondent's contribution to the obtaining of the appellant's dental licence, and awarded that amount in a lump sum. I see no reason to disturb that decision.

Cross-Appeal

The respondent argues in her cross-appeal that, given the trial judge's finding that the licence constituted property within the terms of the F.L.A., the full value of the licence should have been included in net family assets for the purpose of determining the equalization payment. I think that result logically follows. However, given the trial judge's reasons as a whole, had she proceeded in that manner, it would have been appropriate to then order an unequal distribution pursuant to s. 5(6) of the F.L.A., and the result would have been the same.

NOTES AND QUESTIONS

1. For other cases where one spouse was awarded support to compensate for a contribution to the education or career of the other, see *Keast* v. *Keast* (1986), 1 R.F.L. (3d) 401 (Ont. Dist. Ct.); *Magee* v. *Magee* (1987), 6 R.F.L. (3d) 453 (Ont. U.F.C.); *Emery* v. *Emery* (1987), 11 R.F.L. (3d) 194 (Ont. Dist. Ct.); *Gasparetto* v. *Gasparetto* (1988), 15 R.F.L. (3d) 401 (Ont. H.C.); and *Colletta* v. *Colletta* (1993), 50 R.F.L. (3d) 1 (Ont. C.A.). This type of support was once generally labeled "compensatory support". However, more recently it has also been referred to as "restitutionary support" because "compensatory support" has come to mean support awarded to compensate one spouse for the negative effect of the relationship on his or her earning capacity. In particular, see *Moge* v. *Moge* (1992), 43 R.F.L. (3d) 345 (S.C.C.), reproduced in Chapter 6, **SPOUSAL SUPPORT**.

2. For further reading, see Granger and Small, "Compensatory Support" (1987), 2 C.F.L.Q. 1; Welsh, "Apportioning Degrees Earned During Marriage: An Equitable Justification" (1987), 45 U. of T. Fac. L. Rev. 272; Bala, "Recognizing Spousal Contributions to the Acquisition of Degrees, Licences and Other Career Assets: Towards Compensatory Support" (1989), 8 Can. J. Fam. L. 23; Hovius and Youdan, *The Law of Family Property* (Toronto: Carswell, 1991) at 269-286; Hatch, "The Division of Professional Degrees and Licences upon Marital Breakdown" (1993), 2 Dal. J. Leg. Studies 245; and McCallum, "*Caratun* v. *Caratun*: It Seems That We Are Not All Realists Yet" (1994), 7 C.J.W.L. 197.

(ii) Ownership

RAWLUK v. RAWLUK

(1990), 23 R.F.L. (3d) 337 (S.C.C.)

CORY J. (DICKSON C.J.C., WILSON and L'HEUREUX-DUBE JJ. concurring): — At issue in this appeal is whether the doctrine of constructive trust can be applied to determine the ownership of assets of married spouses under the provisions of the *Family Law Act, 1986*, S.O. 1986, c. 4.

FACTUAL BACKGROUND

Jacqueline and Harry Rawluk were married in 1955 when Harry Rawluk was 24 years old and Jacqueline was 21. For the next 29 years, until they separated permanently in 1984, the Rawluks worked together in two business operations. The first was a farm machinery sales and service business. The second was a cash-crop and livestock farming operation carried on at different times and in different places throughout the marriage.

Two years prior to the marriage Mr. Rawluk had bought a New Holland Farm Equipment franchise for the region of Newmarket, north of Toronto. He also farmed a modest rented acreage on a cash-crop basis. Shortly after the marriage Mr. Rawluk's father died. The spouses then took over the farm that had been run by his parents.

For the first few years of the marriage Mrs. Rawluk devoted most of her time to raising the couple's three children and performing a wide range of farm chores. During the early 1960s, however, she began helping her husband in the farm machinery shop. In 1964 the Rawluks moved to a new family farm on a 23-acre parcel in Newmarket. Five years later, the farm machinery operation was moved to this farm when the building that had housed the business burned down. From that time on, Mrs. Rawluk played a large role in running the farm machinery business. She performed all the bookkeeping functions, did most of the invoicing and banking and operated the parts department. At the same time, she maintained her active involvement in all aspects of the farming operations. In addition to the usual daily farm chores, she took care of birthings, needling and feeding of the animals, did the employee payroll and bookkeeping, assisted with augering wheat and helped to transport employees and crops at harvest.

Throughout the late 1950s and 1960s the Rawluks acquired a number of parcels of land. In 1958 they purchased two lots on Faulkner Avenue, in the township of Whitchurch-Stouffville, adjoining a lot the husband had bought before the marriage. In 1963 they bought a cottage property in Haliburton. In the same year they acquired a nine-acre parcel in Newmarket that was used primarily as farmland but also to store equipment from the machinery business. In 1964 they acquired the matrimonial home farm, located adjacent to this nine-acre parcel. In 1966 they bought another ten-acre parcel near Sharon, Ontario. Title to all these properties was registered in Harry Rawluk's name except for the cottage which was originally in joint tenancy until Mr. Rawluk transferred it into his wife's name for tax purposes.

The money required to buy these properties and run the businesses came from a single bank account. Over the years the account was virtually always maintained in the husband's name. The sole exception was during a span of about one year when the husband converted it to a joint account, a period that coincided with Mrs. Rawluk's decision to put $7,000 of her inheritance from her mother's estate into the business operations.

Much of the cash generated by property rents and machinery sales never reached the bank account. For many years the spouses deposited and stored the cash in a teapot in a china cabinet in their home. Both husband and wife, as their cash requirement dictated, dipped into this teapot. Unfortunately this casual arrangement became a source of friction and discord. . . .

Spurred on by a desire to gain an independent income, Mrs. Rawluk went to night school in the early 1970s and qualified as a registered nursing assistant. In 1974 she worked full time at a Newmarket hospital. Mr. Rawluk complained about her absence from the business operations. As a result, from 1975 until just before the Rawluk's first separation, she worked only part time, mostly in the evenings, so that she could continue her previous work in the farming and farm machinery businesses.

The Rawluks first separated in early 1982 when Mr. Rawluk left the home. In the fall of that year they reconciled and Mr. Rawluk returned. During that year Mr. Rawluk gave up his farm machinery franchise and devoted much of his time to attending auction sales, particularly of antiques. Mrs. Rawluk continued her nursing at the hospital in Newmarket, but now on a full-time basis. By the late spring of 1984 the Rawluks' relationship had significantly deteriorated. On 1st June 1984 they agreed that they were, in fact, living separate and apart under the same roof. . . .

Under the *Family Law Act, 1986*, deferred sharing regime, equalization of matrimonial property is calculated according to the value of the property at valuation date. As of the valuation date of 1st June 1984, the Newmarket farm and machinery lot had been valued at $400,000 and the Sharon property at $139,000. In the Rawluks' case the value of the matrimonial property, particularly the Newmarket home farm and machinery lot, had increased dramatically by the time of the trial in 1986 and has continued to do so since then. In order to share in one half of the increase in value, Mrs. Rawluk claimed by way of a remedial constructive trust a beneficial one-half interest in the home farm and machinery lot and the Sharon property.

There can be no doubt that the industry and dedication of Mrs. Rawluk was such that they would, apart from the *Family Law Act, 1986*, entitle her to have her proprietary interest in the properties in issue recognized. Indeed it is conceded by the appellant that the facts of this case would support a declaration of constructive trust unless, as he contends, the remedy is abolished and superseded by the *Family*

Law Act, 1986. As an owner, Mrs. Rawluk would be entitled to a share in the property to the extent of its value as of the date of trial.

THE JUDGMENTS BELOW

Supreme Court of Ontario

(1986), 55 O.R. (2d) 704, 3 R.F.L. (3d) 113, 23 E.T.R. 199, 29 D.L.R. (4th) 754

At trial, Walsh J. held that a remedial constructive trust could be imposed by the court to determine the ownership of assets of married spouses under the *Family Law Act, 1986.* He determined that the *Family Law Act, 1986,* requires a court to decide issues of ownership prior to equalizing net family property. He held that in determining ownership a court must look to both legal and beneficial interests, including an interest arising by means of constructive trust. He observed that it was unlikely that the Ontario legislature would deny married spouses a remedy that they would have had if unmarried. Having decided that the constructive trust doctrine survived the enactment of the *Family Law Act, 1986,* he found that the facts supported a declaration of constructive trust with regard to the Newmarket home farm and machinery lot and awarded Mrs. Rawluk a one-half interest in the contested property.

Ontario Court of Appeal

(1987), 61 O.R. (2d) 637, 10 R.F.L. (3d) 113, 28 E.T.R. 158, 43 D.L.R. (4th) 764

The Court of Appeal affirmed Walsh J.'s decision. It decided that the provisions of the *Family Law Act, 1986,* far from superseding the constructive trust, appear to incorporate that doctrine into the process of determining ownership and equalizing net family property. The Act's provisions, it was said, clearly direct a court to determine ownership prior to ordering equalization. Accordingly, the constructive trust remedy should be applied as a part of the first step of ownership determination. The court reviewed several provisions of the Act in order to demonstrate that to deny the constructive trust remedy to married spouses in Ontario would create inconsistencies and inequalities. The court declined to decide whether a constructive trust can be forced upon a beneficiary to require that person to share in a decline in the value of property following valuation date. It simply noted that s. 5(6) of the Act might be used in such a situation to award an amount that differs from the standard equalization payment.

POSITION OF THE APPELLANT

The appellant contended, however, that the equalization provisions of the *Family Law Act, 1986,* supersede and implicitly abolish the remedy of constructive trust as it applies to the division of matrimonial property held by married persons in Ontario.

THE HISTORICAL BACKGROUND

The issue presented by this appeal arises from a unique convergence of common law and statutory provisions, both of which are of relatively recent origin. The Canadian law of trusts with regard to matrimonial property was only in its infancy when the Ontario Law Reform Commission first proposed a matrimonial property regime of deferred equal sharing in its 1974 Report on Family Law (Ontario Law Reform Commission, Report on Family Law, Pt. IV (1974), p. 55). The Ontario legislature used that report as a model for the provisions of the *Family Law Act, 1986*, but declined to expressly clarify the relationship between the provisions of the Act and the doctrine of constructive trust, as it evolved during the late 1970s and early 1980s.

(a) *The doctrine of constructive trust and its application in matrimonial cases*

[A discussion of the history of constructive trust and of the major Canadian cases is omitted.]

These cases show that in Canada the doctrine of remedial constructive trust has been accepted for almost a decade as an important remedial device whose prime function is to remedy situations of unjust enrichment. It is clear that at the time that the *Family Law Act, 1986*, was enacted, the constructive trust was widely recognized as the pre-eminent common law remedy for ensuring the equitable division of matrimonial property. The validity and importance of the remedy designed, as it is, to achieve a measure of fairness between married persons and those in a marital relationship, must have been well known to the framers of the legislation. It would seem unlikely that they would, without a precise and specific reference, deprive parties of access to such an equitable remedy.

(b) *The ensuing legislation*

(i) *The Family Law Reform Act*

. . . Although it appears that the majority of provincial courts, including Ontario, found that a spouse could claim an interest in property either by means of a constructive claim or pursuant to the pertinent legislation, the issue was . . . never resolved by this court.

(ii) The *Family Law Act, 1986*

In 1986, the *Family Law Reform Act* was replaced by the *Family Law Act, 1986*. In contrast to s. 8 of the *Family Law Reform Act*, the provisions of the *Family Law Act, 1986*, did not attempt to duplicate the constructive trust remedy. Instead, the statute provided that all property should be equalized upon separation through the transfer of money from the title-holding or owning to the non-owning spouse.

Prior to this case the trial courts in Ontario have followed one of two approaches in deciding whether these equalization provisions implicitly abolish the use of the constructive trust in the matrimonial property context. The majority of the decisions followed the reasoning of Walsh J. in the case at bar even before it was affirmed by the Ontario Court of Appeal: see *Seed* v. *Seed* (1986), 5 R.F.L. (3d) 120, 25 E.T.R. 315 (Ont. H.C.); *Leslie* v. *Leslie* (1987), 9 R.F.L. (3d) 82, 27 E.T.R. 247 (Ont. H.C.); *Cowan* v. *Cowan* (1987), 9 R.F.L. (3d) 401 (Ont. H.C.); and *Corless* v. *Corless* (1987), 58 O.R. (2d) 19, 5 R.F.L. (3d) 256, 34 D.L.R. (4th) 594 (U.F.C.). This approach was rejected, however, in two lower court decisions: *Benke* v. *Benke* (1986), 4 R.F.L. (3d) 58, 25 E.T.R. 124 (Ont. Dist. Ct.), and *Leonard* v. *Leonard*, [1987] O.J. 1488 (unreported).

The reasoning set forth in the *Benke* decision was adopted by the appellant. In that case, the wife had claimed an interest in her husband's farm on resulting or constructive trust principles. The trial judge denied her claim, holding that the constructive trust could not be applied in the context of the *Family Law Act, 1986*, and that the facts did not support a finding of resulting trust. In his opinion, the *Family Law Act, 1986*, fully addressed the question of unjust enrichment between spouses by providing for monetary equalization based on the value of property at the time of separation. As he stated at p. 78:

> What Laskin J. (in *Murdoch*) declared to be "the better way" is now in place. The less adequate way was the doctrine of constructive trusts, and that less adequate way should no longer be available to, in effect, change the date of valuation whenever, either because of deflation or inflation, it suits the interests of one of the spouses to seek to advance it. If, in the total scheme of things, some injustice continues, it will be an injustice that arises from the application of an act of the legislature, and it will be for the legislature to correct it.

This position has been criticized. As Professor James McLeod comments in his annotation to *Benke* v. *Benke*, at p. 60:

> In the end, cases such as *Benke* v. *Benke* . . . reflect an unwillingness on the part of the judiciary to investigate the realities of a relationship. It is easier to strictly apply an equal division in all cases than to determine whether such division is fair to the particular parties. It is easier, but is it fair?

I prefer the approach taken by Walsh J. and the Ontario Court of Appeal. In my view, far from abolishing the constructive trust doctrine, the *Family Law Act, 1986*, incorporates the constructive trust remedy as an integral part of the process of ownership determination and equalization established by that Act.

PROVISIONS OF THE *FAMILY LAW ACT, 1986*, WHICH INDICATE THAT THE CONSTRUCTIVE TRUST DOCTRINE SHOULD CONTINUE TO PLAY A ROLE IN DETERMINING THE ASSETS OF SPOUSES AND THEIR DIVISION

It is trite but true to state that as a general rule a legislature is presumed not to depart from prevailing law "without expressing its intentions to do so with irresistible clearness" (*Goodyear Tire & Rubber Co.* v. *T. Eaton Co.*, [1956] S.C.R. 610 at 614, 56 D.T.C. 1060, 4 D.L.R. (2d) 1). But even aside from this presumption, when the structure of the *Family Law Act, 1986*, is examined and the ramifications of a number of its provisions are studied, it becomes apparent that the Act recognizes and accommodates the remedial constructive trust.

At the outset, the Act's preamble recognizes not only the need for the "orderly and equitable settlement of the affairs of the spouses", but also "the equal position of spouses as individuals within marriage" and the fact that marriage is a "form of partnership". These fundamental objectives are furthered by the use of the constructive trust remedy in appropriate circumstances. It provides a measure of individualized justice and fairness which is essential for the protection of marriage as a partnership of equals. Thus the preamble itself is sufficient to warrant the retention and application of this remedy.

In addition, various provisions of the Act lead to the same conclusion.

(a)   Sections 4 and 5

Sections 4 and 5 of the *Family Law Act, 1986*, create a two-step property division process that emphasizes the distinction between the determination of legal and equitable ownership and the equalization of net family property. These sections require a court first to determine individual "ownership piles" and then to equalize the spouses' assets by ordering the spouse with the larger ownership pile to pay money to the spouse with the smaller pile.

Before property can be equalized under s. 5 of the *Family Law Act, 1986*, a court is required by s. 4 to determine the "net family property" of each spouse. Under s. 4(1) this is defined as "the value of all the property . . . that a spouse owns on the valuation date". "Property" is defined in the same subsection as "any interest, present or future, vested or contingent, in real or personal property". This all-encompassing definition is wide enough to include not only legal but beneficial ownership. The appellant has conceded that "property" as defined under s. 4(1) includes a beneficial interest arising from an express or resulting trust. I see no reason why the remedial constructive trust should not be included in the list of equitable principles or remedies that may be used to calculate the beneficial ownership of net family property.

It is important in this respect to keep in mind that a property interest arising under a constructive trust can be recognized as having come into existence not when the trust is judicially declared but from the time when the unjust enrichment first arose. As Professors Oosterhoff and Gillese state, "the date at which a constructive trust arises . . . is now generally accepted to be the date upon which a duty to make restitution occurs" (Oosterhoff and Gillese, A.H. Oosterhoff: Text, Commentary and Cases on Trusts, 3rd ed. (1987), at p. 579). Professor Scott has stated in Law of Trusts, op. cit., at pp. 323-24, that:

> The beneficial interest in the property is from the beginning in the person who has been wronged. The constructive trust arises from the situation in which he is entitled to the remedy of restitution, and it arises as soon as that situation is created . . . It would seem that there is no foundation whatever for the notion that a constructive trust does not arise until it is decreed by a court. It arises when the duty to make restitution arises, not when that duty is subsequently enforced.

I agree completely with the position taken on this issue by the authors of these helpful texts.

. . . As a result, even if it is declared by a court after the parties have already separated, a constructive trust can be deemed to have arisen when the duty to make restitution arose. It should therefore be considered as part of the property owned by the beneficiary at valuation date.

It must be emphasized that the constructive trust is remedial in nature. If the court is asked to grant such a remedy and determines that a declaration of constructive trust is warranted, then the proprietary interest awarded pursuant to that remedy will be deemed to have arisen at the time when the unjust enrichment first occurred. But, as Professor Scott makes clear, the fact that the proprietary interest is deemed to have arisen before the remedy was granted is not inconsistent with the remedial characteristics of the doctrine.

The distinction between a share in ownership and a share in property value through an equalizing transfer of money is more than an exercise in judicial formalism. This distinction not only follows the two-step structure of the Family Law Act, 1986, but reflects conceptual and practical differences between ownership and equalization. Ownership encompasses far more than a mere share in the value of property. It includes additional legal rights, elements of control and increased legal responsibilities. In addition, it may well provide psychological benefits derived from pride of ownership. Where the property at issue is one to which only one spouse has contributed, it is appropriate that the other spouse receive only an equalizing transfer of money. But where both spouses have contributed to the acquisition or maintenance of the property, the spouse who does not hold legal title should be able to claim an interest in that property by way of a constructive trust and realize the benefits that ownership may provide. The imposition of a constructive trust recognizes that the titled spouse is holding property that has been acquired, at least in part, through the money or effort of another. The non-titled spouse's constructive trust interest in this property is distinct from the right to an equalizing share of property value that is derived not from an independent property right but from the status as a married person.

(b) Section 5(6)

Section 5(6) of the *Family Law Act, 1986*, allows a court to "award a spouse an amount that is more or less than half the difference between the net family properties if the court is of the opinion that equalizing the net family properties would be unconscionable". The Court of Appeal observed that if a post-valuation date increase or decrease in property values is significant enough to render a simple equalization unconscionable, a court might utilize s. 5(6) to remedy the resultant inequities. I need not and do not express any opinion as to whether s. 5(6) could be used in that way or whether the Court of Appeal's observation is correct. I have assumed solely for the purposes of argument that s. 5(6) might be available in some cases as an alternative remedy for dealing with post-valuation date changes in value. Even so, the section does not have the effect of supplanting the constructive trust remedy. The constructive trust is used in the matrimonial property context to allocate proprietary interests, a function that is totally distinct from the process of determining how the value of matrimonial property should be distributed under the equalization process.

Under the Act a court is, as a first step, required to determine the ownership interests of the spouses. It is at that stage that the court must deal with and determine the constructive trust claims. The second step that must be taken is to perform the equalization calculations. Once this is done, a court must assess whether, given the facts of the particular case, equalization is unconscionable. The s. 5(6) analysis, even if it could be considered, would be a third step — a last avenue of judicial discretion which might be used in order to bring a measure of flexibility to the equalization process. This step in the process, if it could be used, would have to be kept distinct from the preliminary determinations of ownership.

(c) Section 10

Section 10 of the *Family Law Act, 1986*, reinforces the Act's emphasis on the importance of individual ownership, even within a regime of deferred sharing. This section allows a spouse to apply to a court to determine a question of ownership or possession prior to equalization, and thus to assert some degree of control over matrimonial property during cohabitation. . . .

The creation under s. 10 of a proprietary remedy that can be commenced during cohabitation provides further evidence that the Ontario legislature could not have intended the provisions of the *Family Law Act, 1986*, to completely supersede the remedial constructive trust. Section 10 enables non-titled spouses to assert control over matrimonial property during cohabitation to the extent that their beneficial interests entitle them to do so. Even if the appellant's argument that the *Family Law Act, 1986*, equalization provisions replace the constructive trust remedy were to be accepted, this would not prevent a deserving spouse from obtaining a declaration of constructive trust in his or her spouse's property during cohabitation pursuant to s.

10. Certainly such an application will not necessarily be followed by separation and equalization of property.

Since a spouse can thus obtain a constructive trust remedy prior to separation, it would be inconsistent to deny a spouse the same remedy when it is sought after a separation. To take such a position would encourage spouses to apply for a constructive trust interest early in a marriage, perhaps thereby creating unnecessary marital stress, fostering costly litigation and penalizing those spouses who waited until separation to enforce their common law rights. It is unlikely that the legislature intended a spouse's rights to depend on whether or not a constructive trust had been declared before or after the separation.

(d) Section 14

. . .The appellant argues that the provisions of s. 14 expressly preserve the doctrine of resulting trust and by implication abolish all other non-express trusts. I cannot accept that contention. Section 14 is, I believe, intended not to specifically preserve but rather to modify the resulting trust doctrine as it applies in the context of the *Family Law Act, 1986*. If anything, the combination of these modifying provisions and the legislature's silence on the subject of remedial constructive trust supports the view that the constructive trust is maintained in an unmodified form.

(e) Section 64(2)

. . . Although the necessary purpose of this section, as stated in subs. (3), is to equalize the legal rights of married men and married women, subs. (2) expressly declares that married persons shall have the same legal capacities as unmarried persons. Ever since this court's decision was rendered in *Pettkus* v. *Becker*. . ., it has been clear that the constructive trust remedy can be utilized by unmarried cohabitants. It would not only be inequitable, but would also contravene the provisions of s. 64(2), if married persons were precluded by the *Family Law Act, 1986*, from utilizing the doctrine of remedial constructive trust which is available to unmarried persons.

CONCLUSION

The review of the cases decided by this court from *Murdoch* v. *Murdoch* . . . to *Sorochan* v. *Sorochan* . . . demonstrates the importance that has been attached to the use of the remedy of constructive trust to achieve a division of property that is as just and equitable as possible. A marital relationship is founded on love and trust. It brings together two people who strive and sacrifice to attain common goals for the benefit of both partners. When it is terminated and acquired assets are to be divided, then in this of all relationships the concept of fairness should predominate in making decisions as to ownership. This was the fundamental equitable principle underlying the application of the constructive trust remedy to matrimonial cases. Where the application of the principle would achieve the goal of fairness it should not be discarded unless the pertinent legislation makes it clear that the principle is to be disregarded.

The *Family Law Act, 1986*, does not constitute an exclusive code for determining the ownership of matrimonial property. The legislators must have been aware of the existence and effect of the constructive trust remedy in matrimonial cases when the Act was proposed. Yet neither by direct reference nor by necessary implication does the Act prohibit the use of the constructive trust remedy. Indeed, the foregoing review of the provisions of the Act supports the view that the constructive trust remedy is to be maintained. The Act's two-step structure and its individual provisions indicate that the constructive trust remedy still has an important role to play in the determination of matrimonial property disputes in Ontario. The application of the remedy in the context of the *Family Law Act, 1986*, can achieve a fair and just result. It enables the courts to bring that treasured and essential measure of individualized justice and fairness to the more generalized process of equalization provided by the Act. That vital fairness is achieved by means of a constructive trust remedy and recognition of ownership.

In this case fairness requires that the dedication and hard work of Jacqueline Rawluk in acquiring and maintaining the properties in issue be recognized. The equitable remedy of constructive trust was properly applied.

I would therefore dismiss the appeal with costs.

MCLACHLIN J. (dissenting) (LA FOREST and SOPINKA JJ. concurring): — . . . It is not disputed that apart from the statute, this would be an appropriate case for the court to declare a constructive trust entitling the wife to a half interest in the property. This leaves the question of whether the *Family Law Act, 1986*, changes the situation.

The answer to this question depends on the answer to two sub-issues. The first concerns the nature of the doctrine of constructive trust. Is it a concept of substantive property law, automatically vesting in the wife a half interest in the property at the time of separation? Or is it a remedial device, to be applied only where other remedies for unjust enrichment are unavailable or inadequate?

If the doctrine of constructive trust is a remedial device, the further question arises of whether the doctrine should be applied where a statute already provides a remedy for the alleged unjust enrichment.

As I see the problem, the issue in this case is not whether the *Family Law Act, 1986*, ousts the remedy of constructive trust. I agree with Cory J. that it does not. In my view, the real question which must be answered is whether the doctrine of constructive trust, as it has been developed by this court, finds application where a statute already provides a remedy for the unjust enrichment complained of.

III. DECISION ON THE ISSUES

I would answer the questions posed above as follows:

1. The doctrine of constructive trust, as it has developed in Canada, is not a property right but a proprietary remedy for unjust enrichment; as such, the availability of other remedies for the unjust enrichment must be considered before declaring a constructive trust.

2. The doctrine of constructive trust should not be applied in this case because the *Family Law Act, 1986*, provides a remedy for the unjust enrichment of the husband to the detriment of the wife.

IV. DISCUSSION

(1) *The nature of the constructive trust in Canada: Substantive or remedial?*

An express trust is one which arises from the intention of the settlor or trustee. A constructive trust is one imposed apart from the wishes of the settlor, by operation of law. . . .

The traditional English view, which does not recognize the constructive trust as a general remedy for unjust enrichment, but sees it as an obligation attaching to property in certain specified circumstances, holds that a constructive trust is a property right, just like any other trust. . . .

In Canada, we have not followed the traditional English view of the constructive trust as a limited doctrine applying in limited, clearly defined cases. Rather, we have moved toward the American view of the constructive trust as a general equitable remedy for unjust enrichment. This development is of relatively recent standing. . . .

The new concept of constructive trust now prevailing in Canada differs from the traditional English concept in two respects. The first is its foundation in the concept of unjust enrichment. As Professor Waters, in Law of Trusts in Canada, 2nd ed. (1984), at p. 385, puts it:

> . . . though the constructive trust remains in common law Canada a collection of liability situations, it now has a theme. The constructive trust in the area of spousal or quasi-spousal property "arises . . . out of inequitable withholding resulting in an unjust enrichment," [quoting from Dickson J. in *Rathwell* v. *Rathwell*] and this is the theme, the basis of the defendant's liability.

The new concept eliminates the need to find recognizable categories in which the constructive trust can be applied, relying instead on the more general concept of unjust enrichment arising from a contribution by one to property held in the name of the other to the detriment of the contributing party.

The second main difference between the traditional English concept of trust and the doctrine now accepted in Canada is the remedial nature of the Canadian doctrine. The trust is not viewed as an institution but as a remedy, as a means of compelling a person to surrender an unjust enrichment: see Scott, The Law of Trusts, 3rd ed. (1967), vol. 5, p. 3416, para. 462.1; Waters, op. cit., at p. 388. . . .

Although the constructive trust is remedial, that is not to say that the remedial concept of constructive trust does not give rise to property interests. When the court declares a constructive trust, at that point the beneficiary obtains an interest in the property subject to the trust. That property interest, it appears, may be taken as extending back to the date when the trust was "earned" or perfected. . . .

The significance of the remedial nature of the constructive trust is not that it cannot confer a property interest, but that the conferring of such an interest is discretionary and dependent on the inadequacy of other remedies for the unjust enrichment in question. The doctrine of constructive trust may be used to confer a proprietary remedy, but does not automatically presuppose a possessory property right. Thus, even where the tests for constructive trust are met — unjust enrichment, corresponding deprivation, and no juridical justification for the enrichment and justification — the property interest does not automatically arise. Rather, the court must consider whether other remedies to remedy the injustice exist which make the declaration of a constructive trust unnecessary or inappropriate. . . .

This brings us to the issue raised in this case. Given that the doctrine of constructive trust, as it has developed in Canada, is remedial, what is the relationship of the remedy of constructive trust to other remedies for unjust enrichment? While Dickson C.J.C. alludes to this issue in *Sorochan* v. *Sorochan*, little Canadian jurisprudence exists on the question. In these circumstances, it may be useful to have regard to the American experience. . . .

The American law on constructive trusts, as set out in the Restatement of Restitution, recognizes the panoply of remedies for unjust enrichment and the need for the court, in considering a claim for constructive trust, to select among them. As a general rule, the remedies which operate in personam must be brought first, for example, actions for money had and received, quantum meruit and account. As Waters, op. cit., states at p. 391:

> *Only when these actions are inadequate* . . . are American courts willing to entertain the equitable proprietary remedies, the constructive trust and the equitable lien. [emphasis added]

And, at p. 393, Waters counsels caution in applying the remedy of constructive trust where other personal remedies lie:

> It is already clear from the English experience with the "new model" constructive trust that, if this remedy is employed where personal remedies would suffice, it threatens to upset the operation of other doctrines.

Waters goes on to point out the dangers associated with conferring possessory rights on a plaintiff and concludes:

> . . . let us reflect on the consequences of declaring a proprietary right to remedy the situation. It can produce unregistered and unregistrable interests capable of binding the land in the hands of immediate title holders, and successors taking with notice.

Thus I arrive at this point. Without denying the importance of the remedy of constructive trust, it must be remembered that it may be only one of several remedies for unjust enrichment. It must also be remembered that as a proprietary remedy, its imposition may interfere with the operation of other doctrines and the exercise by others, including third parties, of the rights attendant on their interests in the property made subject to the trust. For these reasons, it may be wise to insist that a plaintiff have exhausted his or her personal remedies before imposing the remedy of constructive trust.

Against this background, I return to the first of two questions I posed at the outset. Is the doctrine of constructive trust as it has developed in Canada a substantive doctrine of trust, automatically conferring a property interest where the basic criteria for the trust are made out? Or is it a remedy, to be applied where necessary to remedy unjust enrichment?

The answer must be that in Canada constructive trust, at least in the context of unjust enrichment, is not a doctrine of substantive property law, but a remedy. It follows that a constructive trust cannot be regarded as arising automatically when the three conditions set out in *Pettkus* v. *Becker* are established. Rather, the court must go on to consider what other remedies are available to remedy the unjust enrichment in question and whether the proprietary remedy of constructive trust is appropriate. . . .

2. *Whether the doctrine of constructive trust should be applied in the case at bar*

This case poses the question of whether the doctrine of constructive trust should be applied where there exists a comprehensive statutory scheme providing a remedy for the situation where one spouse holds exclusive title to property to which the other spouse has contributed.

The *Family Law Act, 1986*, sets up a comprehensive statutory scheme which recognizes the contributions of both spouses to the acquisition, preservation, maintenance or improvement of property during the marriage. It addresses the question of unjust enrichment between spouses by providing for a monetary equalization payment based on the value of the "net family property" at the valuation date, i.e., the time of separation (s. 5(1)). . . .

The question may be put thus: given that there was an unjust enrichment arising from the fact that the property to which the wife contributed was in the husband's name, does the Family Law Act, 1986, provide a remedy, which makes it unnecessary to resort to the doctrine of constructive trust? In my opinion, the answer to this question must be affirmative.

Both the statutory remedy and the remedy of constructive trust are, on the facts of this case, directed to the same end. The purpose of a constructive trust, as already discussed, is to permit a party without title to receive compensation for his or her contribution to the acquisition and maintenance of property standing in the other's name. The purpose of the *Family Law Act, 1986*, is the same: it sets up a scheme to equalize the property holdings of each party to a marriage, regardless of who holds legal title. The only difference for the purposes of this case is that the *Family Law Act, 1986*, provides for the equalization to be accomplished by a payment of money based on the value of the property at the time of separation (a remedy in personam), while the doctrine of constructive trust would give a beneficial interest in the land which persists to the date of trial (a proprietary remedy).

If the doctrine of unjust enrichment is to be applied in this case, it is not for the purpose of rewarding the wife for her contribution to the property held in the husband's name, but for the purpose of permitting her to share in the increase in value of the property after separation. But this cannot support a claim for a constructive trust for two reasons.

First, the Act contemplates the problem that assets may increase or diminish in value between the date of separation and trial; s. 5(6)(*h*) permits the trial judge to vary the equal division of property as at separation, on the basis of circumstances relating to the disposition or improvement of the property. I agree with Cory J. that this step of the process is distinct from the preliminary determinations of ownership.

Second, it would appear that the elements necessary to establish a constructive trust are not present where the enrichment occurs as a result of appreciation of the market value of the land after separation. Under the statute, the wife already receives a payment sufficient to give her 50 per cent of the family property, valued at the date of separation. There is no unjust enrichment there. What then of the fact that because of delays in obtaining judgment, the value of the property held in the hands of the husband increases pending trial? True, this is an enrichment of the husband. But there is no corresponding deprivation to the wife giving rise to an injustice. The husband is not being enriched at her expense or because of her efforts. In these circumstances, the first two requirements of a constructive trust posited in *Pettkus* v. *Becker* — unjust enrichment of one party and corresponding deprivation of the other — are absent.

In the final analysis, the *Family Law Act, 1986*, provides complete compensation for the wife's contribution to the date of separation. Any disproportionate enrichment must occur because of the increase in value due to changing market conditions after that date. But that does not constitute an unjust enrichment under the principles set forth in *Pettkus* v. *Becker*, given that the wife made no contribution after that date. As a matter of legal principle, the legislature having provided a remedy for the unjust enrichment which would otherwise have occurred in this case, it is not for this court to impose an additional equitable remedy aimed at correcting the same wrong.

I add that application of the remedy of constructive trust to the statutory scheme may pose practical problems. The scheme under the Act is relatively clear and simple; the basic rule is equality between the spouses, an equality effected by an equalization payment from one spouse to the other, based on the value of the property at the valuation date, usually the date of separation. In most cases the parties can ascertain without difficulty what payment must be made, thereby settling their affairs without lengthy litigation. Grafting the remedy of constructive trust on to this scheme would add uncertainty and promote litigation featuring detailed inquiries into how much each party contributed to the acquisition, preservation, maintenance and improvement of the property to the end of having the court declare a constructive trust in one of the parties. Moreover, property rights which third parties have acquired in the interval may be adversely affected. One returns to Professor Water's warning that to employ constructive trust where personal remedies suffice threatens to upset the operation of other doctrines.

One must also consider the converse situation to that of this case — the situation where instead of increasing in value after separation, the property loses value. Is the amount recoverable by the spouse lacking title to be diminished accordingly? One judge has said yes, imposing a beneficial constructive interest in the property on the wife as at separation, against her wishes and at the behest of the husband: *McDonald v. McDonald* (1988), 11 R.F.L. (3d) 321, 28 E.T.R. 81 (Ont. H.C.). So we arrive at the anomaly of the equitable remedy of constructive trust being applied against the wishes of the party found to have been unfairly treated, at the behest of the party who has been unjustly enriched. What does this leave of the maxim that he who seeks the aid of equity must come with clean hands? The fallacy at the root of such an approach is that of treating the *remedy* of constructive trust as though it were a *property interest*, which for the sake of consistency must be imposed regardless of the circumstances or of other remedies.

It is suggested that the position of the wife should not be worse than it would have been had the parties not married. The answer to this submission is that the legislature, acting within the proper scope of its authority, has chosen to confine the Act to married persons. Some Acts governing distribution of marital property apply to unmarried couples. While it may be a ground for criticism of the legislation, the fact that a person covered by legislation may be treated less generously than someone not under the statute cannot give rise to a claim for unjust enrichment; the doctrine of unjust enrichment does not go as far as that.

My colleague, Cory J., suggests that s. 10 of the *Family Law Act, 1986*, shows that the legislators did not intend to oust the remedy of constructive trust. In this regard, I reiterate that it is not my view that the doctrine of constructive trust is entirely ousted by the Act. The equalization provisions of the Act, providing as they do a remedy for unjust enrichment in the equalization process, may preclude establishment of the conditions necessary to found a constructive trust after separation. But in other circumstances, for example, before separation, the requirements for a constructive trust may be made out. It may be noted that s. 10 does not recognize automatic entitlement to property by way of trust or otherwise. It is necessary to apply to the court for a declaration of the property interest sought. At the time of that application, a court considering a request for a declaration of constructive trust would be required to consider whether, in view of the circumstances and the availability of other remedies, a constructive trust might appropriately be declared.

It may seem anomalous that a married person might be able to obtain a declaration of constructive trust before but not after separation. It must be remembered, however, that the equalization provisions of the Act provide an alternative remedy to which the spouse becomes entitled upon separation. The fact that that remedy may not be as advantageous in some cases as the remedy of constructive trust does not justify the court in altering the doctrine of constructive trust.

I cannot leave this question without alluding to the quite different provisions found in Acts regulating the division of marital property in provinces other than Ontario. As Cory J. points out, the relationship between the constructive trust doctrine and its "statutory equivalents" has been variously treated in different jurisdictions. While it is interesting to consider dispositions in other jurisdictions, it should be noted that the legislative provisions from province to province are not truly equivalent. In particular, none of the provincial statutes governing the division of marital property, save that of Ontario, appears to have a statutorily fixed and inflexible valuation date, the feature of the Act which gives rise to the wife's grievance in this case. There can be no simple or universally applicable answer to the question of whether the doctrine of constructive trust will apply in a statutory context: in each case, the circumstances of the case and the efficacy of alternative remedies conferred by the applicable legislation must be examined to ascertain whether, in that situation, a declaration of constructive trust should be declared.

In this case, I conclude that the remedy of constructive trust is neither necessary nor appropriate, given the remedies available under the *Family Law Act, 1986*.

V. CONCLUSION

I would set aside the judgments of the Court of Appeal and the trial judge, and refer the matter back to the trial judge to determine whether an adjustment should be made under s. 5(6)(*h*) of the *Family Law Act, 1986*, to reflect the increase in value of the land held in the husband's name since separation, and to adjust the amount of the equalization payment due to the wife, on the basis that she is not entitled to a constructive trust vesting her with a beneficial half interest in the property as at the date of separation.

NOTES AND QUESTIONS

1. Under the *FLA*, aside from extraordinary circumstances that might be brought within s. 5(6) (discussed later in this chapter), the quantity and quality of spousal contributions to the marriage partnership are non-issues. Does *Rawluk* v. *Rawluk* once again establish the importance of contributions — their quantity, quality, value, connection to property, etc. — even on marriage breakdown?

2. The statutory regime established by Part I of the *FLA* is designed to operate with only limited judicial discretion. The continued relevance of the constructive trust introduces flexibility, but it does so by increasing judicial discretion. Do you agree with Cory J.'s statement in *Rawluk* that "a measure of individualized justice and fairness . . . is essential for the protection of marriage as a partnership of equals"? Can this flexibility be provided by s. 5(6) in the Ontario scheme?

3. In cases such as *Sorochan* and *Peter* v. *Beblow*" (reproduced earlier in this chapter), the Supreme Court of Canada stressed that the constructive trust was a remedy and not a substantive property right. Professor Farquhar observes in "Unjust Enrichment — Special Relationship — Domestic Services — Remedial Constructive Trust: *Peter* v. *Beblow*" (1993), 72 Can. Bar Rev. 538, at 550-551:

> The chief implication of this position is that, because it is remedial, it cannot arise until a court has made the appropriate ruling. Thus, unless the court exercises a discretion to make the order retroactive, third-party dealings with the property in question, prior to the order, may place the plaintiff at risk. If, by contrast, the constructive trust is seen as substantive, it would arise at the moment of the unjust enrichment and the plaintiff would thereafter be protected by its proprietary nature. The truly remedial nature of the constructive trust following unjust enrichment seemed to be cemented by the decision in *LAC Minerals Ltd.* v. *International Corona Resources Ltd.* [[1989] 2 S.C.R. 574], and as a result the decision in *Rawluk* v. *Rawluk* came as a surprise.

See also Waters, "The Constructive Trust in Evaluation: Substantive and Remedial" (1990), 10 Est. and Tr. J. 334.

4. In *Rawluk*, the motive for the wife's claim to the benefit of a constructive trust over property in the name of her husband was to gain benefit from the increases in value of the property after the valuation date. More recently, a number of reported cases feature claims based on contributions made during cohabitation before marriage. See, e.g., *Bigelow* v. *Bigelow* (1995), 15 R.F.L. (4th) 12 (Ont. Div. Ct.) (successful); *M. (S.P.)* v. *(M.) (I.R.)* (1997), 28 R.F.L. (4th) 367 (Ont. Gen. Div.) (successful); *Rarie* v. *Rarie* (1997), 32 R.F.L. (4th) 232 (Ont. C.A.) (monetary sum awarded); *Franken* v. *Franken* (1997), 33 R.F.L. (4th) 264 (Ont. Gen. Div.) (unsuccessful); *Walmsley* v. *Walmsley* (1998), 41 R.F.L. (4th) 454 (Ont. Gen. Div.) (successful); and *Fair* v. *Jones* (1999), 44 R.F.L. (4th) 399 (N.W.T.S.C.)(successful). The latter case dealt with Part III of the *Family Law Act*, S.N.W.T. 1997, c. 18 modeled on Part I of the Ontario's *FLA*. Vertes J. stated (at 417): "The petitioner's contribution was the conferral of a benefit on the respondent resulting in a corresponding deprivation to the petitioner. There is no juristic reason why the respondent should have the sole benefit of the 'commencement date' value for this property without some recognition of the petitioner's contribution." See also *Campbell* v. *Campbell* (1998), 41 R.F.L. (4th) 53 (Alta. Q.B.). Can you think of other situations where it may be advantageous for a spouse to seek a declaration of constructive trust?

5. For other cases where the non-owning spouse asked the courts to impose a remedial constructive trust, see *Peper* v. *Peper* (1990), 38 E.T.R. 212 (Ont. H.C.), affirmed (1994), 3 R.F.L. (4th) 24 (Ont. C.A.) (successful); *Filipponi* v. *Filipponi* (1992), 40 R.F.L. (3d) 396 (Ont. Gen. Div.) (unsuccessful); *Docherty* v. *Docherty* (1992), 42 R.F.L. (3d) 87 (Ont. Gen. Div.) (unsuccessful); *Price* v. *Price* (1994), 3 R.F.L. (4th) 1 (Ont. Gen. Div.) (unsuccessful); *Reynolds* v. *Reynolds* (1995), 13 R.F.L. (4th) 179 (Ont. C.A.) (unsuccessful); *Wolfe* v. *Wolfe* (1995), 13 R.F.L. (4th) 415 (Alta. Q.B.) (successful); *Roach* v. *Roach* (1997), 33 R.F.L. (4th) 157 (Ont. C.A.)(successful); *Abraham-Sherman* v. *Sherman* (1998), 37 R.F.L. (4th) 26 (Ont. Gen. Div.)(unsuccessful); and *Tracey* v. *Tracey* (1998), 41 R.F.L. (4th) 278 (Ont. Gen. Div.)(successful).

6. Many of the cases after *Rawluk* appear to consider, at least implicitly, what the result would be under the relevant matrimonial property legislation before determining whether a married defendant has been unjustly enriched or which remedy is appropriate. Does this accord with the reasons of Cory J. in *Rawluk*? See Youdan, "Resulting and Constructive Trusts", *Special Lecture Series*, Law Society of Upper Canada (1993) at 187.

7. Do you agree with the result in the *McDonald* case discussed by Madame Justice McLachlin? See also *Amsterdam* v. *Amsterdam* (1991), 31 R.F.L. (3d) 153 (Ont. Gen. Div.). Compare *Arndt* v. *Arndt* (1991), 6 O.R. (3d) 97 (Gen. Div.), affirmed (1993), 15 O.R. (3d) 389, where the court refused to impose a "reverse constructive trust" partly because the owning spouse was somewhat responsible for the decline in value of the property. In confirming this result, the Ontario Court of Appeal appeared to implicitly accept the concept of a "reverse constructive trust."

8. One could infer from comments by the Ontario Court of Appeal in *Rawluk* v. *Rawluk* (1987), 10 R.F.L. (3d) 113 (at 116) that decreases in value can trigger s. 5(6). The dissenters in the Supreme Court (*Rawluk* v. *Rawluk* (1990), 23 R.F.L. (3d) 337) stated (at 378) that both decreases and increases could be considered. The majority (at 366) explicitly left the question open. In *Merklinger* v. *Merklinger* (1996), 26 R.F.L. (4th) 7, the Ontario Court of Appeal confirmed that post-valuation events (in that case the husband's conduct affecting the property) could trigger an unequal sharing of the net family properties. See also *Macedo* v. *Macedo* (1996), R.F.L. (4th) 65 (Ont. Div. Ct.) and *Brett* v. *Brett* (1996), 24 R.F.L. (4th) 224 (Ont. Gen. Div.), affirmed (1999), 46 R.F.L. (4th) 433 (Ont. C.A.).

9. In *Gallant* v. *Gallant* (1998), 42 R.F.L. (4th) 353, the Manitoba Court of Appeal held that there should be an unequal division of the marital property owned at separation because of a subsequent substantial decrease in the value of the husband's property. As a result there was no need to consider the constructive trust argument presented by the husband. Commenting on *Rawluk* and the resultant situation in Ontario, Huband J. stated (at 360-1):

It is not for me to say that the majority decision was wrong and the minority reasons were correct in the Rawluk case with respect to the Ontario legislation. I do observe, however, that the existence of parallel remedies, each of a completely different nature, creates uncertainty and promotes litigation. . . . Given the broader discretionary power given to the court under . . .The Marital Property Act in Manitoba, in my opinion we need not consider any alternative remedy, and the legal gymnastics of resort to an inappropriate parallel remedy can be avoided in this jurisdiction.

Compare *Martin* v. *Martin* (1998), 42 R.F.L. (4th) 251 (Nfld. C.A.).

10. The Law Reform Commission of British Columbia's draft legislation, modeled on the Ontario scheme, explicitly directed the courts to consider "a significant change in the value of assets between the valuation date and the date of trial other than changes caused by either of the spouses": *Working Paper on Property Rights on Marriage Breakdown* (Vancouver: Ministry of the Attorney General, 1989) at 126. Commenting on the developments in Ontario, the Commission observed (at 126, footnote 8): "It is a sign that the legislation is defective, at least in part, when the courts must resort to common law tools that were intended to be replaced by the legislation." In its *Report on Family Property Law* (Toronto: 1993), the O.L.R.C. recommended the following amendments to the *Family Law Act* to deal with fluctuations of value between the valuation date and the trial:

1) the addition of a separate provision empowering a court to vary an equalization payment if an asset has fluctuated in value, if necessary to prevent an inequitable result;

2) the adoption of a specific prohibition against the application by a spouse for a declaration of resulting trust with respect to property owned by his or her spouse, based on the common or presumed intention of the spouses regarding his or her contribution, either direct or indirect, to the acquisition, preservation, or enhancement of the property; and

3) the adoption of a specific prohibition against the application by a spouse for a declaration of a remedial constructive trust with respect to property owned by his or her spouse, as restitution for his or her contribution, either direct or indirect, to the acquisition, preservation, or enhancement of that property.

The *Family Law Act*, S.P.E.I. 1995, c. 12, specifically permits the court to award a spouse an amount that is more or less than half the difference between the net family properties "if the court is of the opinion that equalizing the net family properties would be inequitable because of a substantial change after the valuation date in the value of any property included in either spouse's net family property". The court used this provision in *Ballum* v. *Ballum* (1999), 49 R.F.L. (4th) 176 (P.E.I.T.D.).

11. For an analysis of the relationship between a remedial constructive trust and bankruptcy and tax law, see O.L.R.C., *Report on Family Property Law* (Toronto: 1993) at 46-50.

12. Where one spouse makes a direct contribution to the purchase price of property registered in the name of the other, a resulting trust may arise: *Hamilton* v. *Hamilton* (1996), 92 O.A.C. 103 (Ont. C.A.). See s. 14 of the *FLA*. For an example of a case where the presumption of a resulting trust was rebutted, see *Clark Drummie & Co.* v. *Ryan* (1999), 170 D.L.R. (4th) 266 (N.B.C.A.).

13. Ownership claims by one spouse based on adverse possession of the jointly owned matrimonial home failed in *Gorman* v. *Gorman* (1998), 36 R.F.L. (4th) 448 (Ont. C.A.) and *Wigmore* v. *Wigmore* (1998), 38 R.F.L. (4th) 133 (Ont. Gen. Div.).

(iii) Value

HOVIUS AND YOUDAN, *THE LAW OF FAMILY PROPERTY*

(Toronto: Carswell, 1991) 291-314 (Footnotes appear at the end of the excerpt.)

Valuation of Property

1. INTRODUCTION

. . .

Despite the importance of the valuation of property for the working of Part I of the Act, the Act does not define "value" nor prescribe any particular method of valuation. In fact, the Act gives very little guidance as to how property is to be valued. It simply refers to the "value" of property in the definition of "net family property" in section 4(1) and the "value" of excluded property in section 4(2).

The Act also gives no explicit guidance as to onus of proof with respect to property valuation.[4] . . . In *Menage* v. *Hedges*, Fleury U.F.C.J. dealt with the onus of proof as follows:

> The Act does not state on whose shoulders lies the burden of establishing the value of the net family property. The only reference to onus of proof can be found in s. 4(3) dealing with excluded property. The entire scheme of the Act and the new Rules of Civil Procedure (and by analogy of the amended Unified Family Court Rules) is to ensure full and fair disclosure so as to foster an early settlement of all the issues raised in the proceedings. Section 8 clearly imposes an obligation on each party to serve and file a sworn statement disclosing particulars of a party's property, debts and other liabilities. In many cases, the filing of a statement in compliance with this section may constitute the first notice to the other party of the existence of certain assets or debts. Because the property or debts being described are that of the deponent and presumably may have been or may still be under his control, the primary onus of establishing the values referred to in the statement should reside on the deponent. In the absence of any contest by the opposing party, it may not be necessary for the deponent to call further evidence to jusify the valuations arrived at, but where a real issue is raised as to the figures used the onus is on the deponent to establish on a balance of probabilities the accuracy of his sworn statement. Because of the nature of the claims made in proceedings of this type, it is only reasonable to consider each party as having to discharge the civil burden of proof concerning the value of his or her respective assets and debts.[6]

2. TIMES FOR VALUATION

The Act does deal expressly with the time as of which property is to be valued. The definition of "net family property" requires the valuation of property owned on the "valuation date", subject to the exclusion of the value of excluded property owned "on the valuation date" and the deduction of the value of property "calculated as of the date of the marriage". . . .

The inflexible tying of valuation to the dates of valuation prevents the use of hindsight in determining values as at those dates. In *Menage* v. *Hedges*[14] the valuation of the husband's loan portfolio could only take account of experience of recovery of loans up to the valuation date; evidence of payment performance after the valuation date was irrelevant. In *Harry* v. *Harry*[15] the appraisal by one valuator of company shares was flawed because it was "based in part on financial statements of the company after valuation date". In *Heon* v. *Heon*[16] the valuation of a nursing home business at the date of marriage on October 18, 1970 could take account only of the facts known at that date:

> Although the nursing home industry has recently experienced rapid growth, the fair market value on October 18th, 1970 cannot consider growth in subsequent years unless it was predictable at that time.[17]

As Granger J. recognized in *Heon* v. *Heon*, facts occurring after the valuation date should be taken into account to the extent that they were predictable at that date. Evidence of subsequent events may, therefore, be relevant in "assessing the fundamental assumptions underpinning the opinions"[18] given as to value. The position taken by Granger J. in *Heon* v. *Heon* with respect to methods of valuation may be questioned. He said that:

> [o]nly the methods of valuation available in 1970 must now be employed in determining fair market value in 1970. If a more accurate method of valuation has been developed since the date

of marriage I should disregard such method as it would not have been known to a prospective purchaser in 1970.[19]

Granger J.'s aim was to obtain the fair market value at the date in question and that aim, in his view, was achieved by determining what a purchaser would have paid at that date. However, the purpose of the valuation in the context of the *Family Law Act* is to determine the amount of spouses' net family property; to determine the economic product of the marriage. This context does not, surely, require such a literal application of the fair market value approach. It is unnecessarily artificial to require a valuator today to use less effective methods of valuation used in an earlier period.

3. METHODS OF VALUATION: GENERAL CONSIDERATIONS

Apart from the provisions dealing with valuation dates, the Act does not give any directions about the valuation of property for the purpose of the Act. In the absence of statutory prescription of any particular method of valuation, there is no one "right" method of valuing property. In general, choice of appropriate methods of valuation depends on the particular asset under consideration, the particular purpose for which valuation is sought, and the evidence relating to value available in a particular case.[20] Walsh J., in *Rawluk* v. *Rawluk*, expressed a flexible view of property valuation for the purpose of the *Family Law Act*:

> While the Act speaks of value, it contains no definition of that term nor, indeed, guidelines of any kind to assist in the determination of its meaning other than the provision contained in s. 4(4) that when value is required to be calculated as of a given date, it shall be calculated as of close of business on that date. Absent any statutory direction, "value" must then be determined on the peculiar facts and circumstances as they are found and developed on the evidence in each individual case. While this approach does not lead to uniformity and predictability of result, it does recognize the individuality inherent in each marriage and case and permit the flexibility so often necessary to ensure an equitable result.[21]

Each judge should not, however, feel completely free to determine the method of valuation that appears most suitable in the circumstances of the particular case. The interests of justice demand reasonable predictability and this requires a large measure of uniformity in the methods of valuation adopted. There should not be unalleviated rigidity, nor should there be unpredictable exercise of individual discretion.

Ordinarily, the appropriate measure of value is the fair market value of the asset in question: "the highest price obtainable in an open and unrestricted market between informed and prudent parties, acting at arm's length and under no compulsion."[22] The fair market value measure of value has indeed been used in numerous cases dealing with a variety of types of property.[23] Some cases[24] suggest fair market value is the only measure of value for the purpose of Part I of the *Family Law Act*. This view gives rise to difficulty in two distinct situations. The first is where the asset in question does not have a market value. The view that fair market value is the only measure of value has the result in this situation that no value can be attributed to the asset in question. In *Corless* v. *Corless*,[25] Steinberg U.F.C.J. held that the husband's LL.B. degree and membership in the Law Society of Upper Canada qualified "as property within the meaning of s. 4 of the *Family Law Act* "[26] but he then held that no value could be attributed to these assets:

> ... the term "value" referred to in s. 4 of the Family Law Act is the "exchange value" of the property eligible for inclusion in the "net family property" formula. It presumes that the property

in question can in law be exchanged. It follows that if a property is in law incapable of being exchanged, it cannot have any value within the meaning of the Act. It is only in those cases where an asset, although exchangeable, has no clear marketability, that a "value in use" approach *may* have some limited relevance as one indicator of the potential exchange or market value of the property in question.[27]

This view is wrong in principle. The fact that a particular item has no exchange value is relevant as a factor in determining whether that item is property but once it is decided that something is property, there is no reason why one particular measure of value should be taken to be the only way of valuing it. The view taken in *Corless* v. *Corless* has, moreover, been rejected by the Ontario Court of Appeal in *Brinkos* v. *Brinkos*[29] and by the myriad of cases in which value has been placed on pension rights, assets which are generally not transferable and for which no market exists.

The view that fair market value is the only measure of value also gives rise to difficulty where the asset in question has a market value but in the circumstances of the case that value is an inappropriate measure for the purpose of the *Family Law Act*. A variation on the facts of *Brinkos* v. *Brinkos*[31] provides a useful illustration. In the case itself, the wife's interest in income was subject to a provision which made it inalienable. Assume, however, that her interest had not been subject to such a provision and thus was, technically, transferable. The price that a purchaser would pay for her interest would be a very poor indicator of its value, particularly in the circumstance that the trustees had a discretionary power of encroachment over capital. The interest was in fact worth much more to her than it would have been worth to any purchaser.[32]

It may be concluded, therefore, that ordinarily fair market value is the appropriate measure of value. Another method of valuation should, however, be used both where the property has no fair market value and where fair market value is an inappropriate measure of value for the property in question. As Fleury U.F.C.J. said, in *Menage* v. *Hedges* in approving the view of a valuator, S.R. Cole:

> He recommends that fair market value be retained as an initial guide in assessing the value of property but that the court retain its freedom to depart from fair market value concepts where this would result in an inequitable valuation. The court could then use the concept of fair value to correct obvious inequities arising out of a servile application of the fair market value approach.[34]

. . .

5. VALUATION OF PARTICULAR TYPES OF PROPERTY

. . .

(b) Interests in Businesses

Where shares are held in a company that are traded on a stock exchange their value will ordinarily[89] be easily determined by their share price at the relevant time. In other cases, value is determined less easily. Even where fair market value is the appropriate measure of value, there are a number of different ways of determining value and the choice and application of the most suitable depends on the circumstances of the particular case. However, a balance sheet approach to valuation is ordinarily inappropriate since the generally accepted accounting principles reflected in a balance sheet "are not concerned with value. They are strictly concerned with the reporting of items on an historical cost basis."[90] Four cases — *Heon* v. *Heon*,[91]

Woeller v. *Woeller*,[92] *Lessany* v. *Lessany*[93] and *Black* v. *Black*[94] — may conveniently be used to illustrate the courts' approach to valuation of business interests.[95]

In *Heon* v. *Heon*[96] the husband's shares in a private company carrying on a nursing home business were required to be valued as at the date of the marriage. The valuation that was accepted was a "capitalized cash flow approach to value":

> In this approach, the after-tax cash flow that the business can be expected to sustain is capitalized, after allowing for the necessary annual capital reinvestment to sustain the existing operation.[97]

In *Woeller* v. *Woeller*[98] both valuators used the approach of capitalizing the earnings of a private company. . . .

Although the capitalization of earnings approach was appropriate in the circumstances in *Heon* v. *Heon* and *Woeller* v. *Woeller*, it may not be appropriate where the earnings of the business are dependent on the personal effort of a proprietor of the business. In *Lessany* v. *Lessany*[101] the husband owned shares in a private company "which he founded and which he [ran] almost singlehandedly".[102] The wife's valuator used the earnings approach in arriving at a fair market value but the Court rejected this approach and, in the circumstances, preferred the liquidation approach taken by the husband's valuator. The Court approved of the latter valuator's view that an analysis using "a capitalization of representative earnings is not workable for a company that is owner-managed, operates in a high tech, high risk environment and operates out of rented premises and has been given formal notice to vacate by the landlord". In the valuator's experience, "owner/manager dominated businesses are not worth much on a going-concern basis because the earnings are attributable to the uncompensated efforts of the owners".[103]

The husband in *Black* v. *Black*[104] owned shares in five private holding companies. These companies, either directly, or through the intermediary of other holding companies, owned substantial interests in a number of publicly traded companies. Although one of the holding companies in question had control over publicly quoted companies, the husband did not have control since he was an equal shareholder with his brother in the holding company. The valuations produced on behalf of each of the husband and of the wife were, again, markedly different. The valuation date was March 13, 1981. Subject to certain qualifications, the valuation done for the husband placed a value of $14,707,000 on the husband's business interests whereas that done for the wife valued them at $34,801,000. In this case, the valuators for the two parties used different approaches. The husband's valuator used a market value approach relying on the evidence of previous sales of comparable interests in the holding companies in question. On the basis of this evidence, he concluded "that the trading prices of the underlying public companies were reflective of the husband's business interests during the period 1978 through 1985 . . .".[105] The valuator for the wife used a "notional sale" approach:

> He considered the husband to be part of the control group and, thus, any valuation of his shares must be on an "en bloc" basis, that is to say, based entirely on the pro rata intrinsic value of their underlying business interests without regard to their public trading prices.[106]

Walsh J. rejected the approach taken by the wife's valuator and accepted that taken by the husband's. He accepted the valuation of $14,707,000 on the following basis:

> In weighing and assessing all of the evidence adduced and the merits of the opposing opinions advanced, I found the following facts to be the most determinative of the value of the husband's business interests: the highly-illiquid nature of those interests and the substantial third party debt to which they were subject; that a purchaser of them would not be buying control or a route to

control of their underlying public companies; and a comparison of the actual prices that were paid in arm's length transactions between shareholders.[107]

(c)   Interests in Professional Practices

The husband in *Dibbley* v. *Dibbley*[108] was a partner in a firm of chartered accountants. The value of his interest was composed of the amount of accounts receivable to which he was entitled, the amount of his capital account, and the value of his goodwill in the firm. If a partner left the firm with the freedom to continue to work for clients of the firm, he obtained nothing for goodwill. If he did not retain such freedom, he was entitled to payment in respect of goodwill which at the valuation date was fixed at $70,000. The value of the husband's goodwill in the firm was, accordingly, determined to be $70,000.

Corless v. *Corless* was concerned with valuation of the interest of a partner in a lawyer's practice. The value of this interest was held to consist of the amount of his capital account and the value of unbilled work done by him[109] as at the valuation date subject to a deduction for income tax liability at the rate of 35%. Nothing was included for goodwill. . . .

Both the husband and the wife in *Menage* v. *Hedges*[114] were medical practitioners. Although an interest in a medical practice could constitute property to which value could be attached, in the circumstances of this case no value was attached to the practices of either the husband or the wife. The husband did not work out of an office, he had no patients of his own and he worked mainly as a cardiovascular surgical assistant for other surgeons. The Court rejected the wife's argument that the value of his practice "could be computed by reviewing the past income generated by the medical practice and by capitalizing this so-called income stream":[115]

> Because of the unique character of the [husband's] practice, it is quite obvious that no goodwill attaches to it. His income from medicine is not attributable to anything but his skill and efforts. There is simply no "excess earning power" in his practice that can be translated into money terms.[116]

The wife did operate "out of an office where some goodwill might be generated".[117] However, at the valuation date her practice had only been established for three months and it was conceded "that there was simply no goodwill attaching to her practice".[118]

A doctor's practice was valued in *Katz* v. *Katz*.[119] Both valuators "agreed that the appropriate method of valuation was the capitalization of excess earnings generated by the practice". The excess earnings were determined by taking the "maintainable earnings" of the practice and deducting an appropriate salary for the doctor. The excess earnings were then discounted for income tax and then capitalized to produce a value for the goodwill of the practice. This value, along with the amount of working capital, constituted the total value of the practice.

Both *Menage* v. *Hedges*[120] and *Katz* v. *Katz*[121] bring out the point that a person's expectation of receiving an "income stream" from his or her skill and personal effort is not property. Similarly, the entitlement of a partner to a share in the future income attributable to his or her efforts should generally not be included in the value of the partnership interest.[122] Nor should the value of shares of a company generally be included to the extent that the value of those shares reflects the future income that is dependent on the efforts of a proprietor.[123] Where, on the other hand, an amount in respect of goodwill can be obtained on a sale of a practice or on a individual leaving a firm or in the sale of the assets of or shares in a company, then the value of that goodwill should be included in the determination of net family property and its value should be determined on the basis that the individual would cooperate in maximizing its value.[124]

---

4 *Cf.* s. 4(3). . . .

6 (1987), 8 R.F.L. (3d) 225 at 243-244 (Ont. U.F.C.). *Cf. Crutchfield* v. *Crutchfield* (1987), 10 R.F.L. (3d) 247 at 253 (Ont. H.C.), affirmed (4 April 1990), CA 768/87 (Ont. C.A.) where it was held that the husband was not entitled to any discount from the value of his dentist's practice with respect to tax liabilities: "The onus to adduce such evidence was on the husband, and he failed to meet it. Therefore, I make no allowance for any such potential tax." See also *Remus* v. *Remus* (1986), 5 R.F.L. (3d) 304 at 310-311 (Ont. H.C.). *Cf. Kelly* v. *Kelly* (1986), 2 R.F.L. (3d) 1 (Ont. H.C.). . . .

14 *Supra*, note 6.

15 (1987), 9 R.F.L. (3d) 121 (Ont. Dist. Ct.).

16 (1989), 69 O.R. (2d) 758 (H.C.).

17 *Ibid.* at 766. See also *Martin* v. *Martin* (1988), 17 R.F.L. (3d) 78 (Ont. H.C.). . . .

18 *Woeller* v. *Woeller* (1988), 15 R.F.L. (3d) 120 at 131 (Ont. Dist. Ct.).

19 *Supra*, note 16 at 767.

20 For example, where evidence of sales of comparable properties is available, fair market value may be proved by such evidence. Where such comparisons are not available, fair market value may need to be proved by other methods, such as by capitalization of earnings produced by the property.

21 (1986), 3 R.F.L. (3d) 113 at 122 (Ont H.C.), affirmed (1987), 10 R.F.L. (3d) 113 (Ont. C.A.), which was affirmed (1990), 23 R.F.L. (3d) 337 (S.C.C.).

22 *Heon* v. *Heon, supra,* note 16 at 766 per Granger J. For other definitions of fair market value see Cole, "Valuations of Property" in Bissett-Johnson and Holland, eds., *Matrimonial Property Law in Canada* at V-6, 7.

23 See e.g., *Dibbley* v. *Dibbley* (1986), 5 R.F.L. (3d) 381 (Ont. H.C.) (accountant's partnership interest); *Crutchfield* v. *Crutchfield, supra,* note 6 (dentist's practice); *Corless* v. *Corless* (1987), 5 R.F.L. (3d) 256 (Ont. U.F.C.) (lawyer's partnership interest); *Heon* v. *Heon, supra,* note 16; *Woeller* v. *Woeller, supra,* note 18; *Black* v. *Black* (1988), 18 R.F.L. (3d) 303; *Remus* v. *Remus, supra,* note 6; *Lessany* v. *Lessany* (1988), 17 R.F.L. (3d) 433 (Ont. Dist. Ct.) (all concerned with shares in private companies); *Crawford* v. *Crawford* (1987), 6 R.F.L. (3d) 308 (Ont. H.C.) and *Martin* v. *Martin, supra,* note 17 (both concerned with land).

24 See *Dibbley* v. *Dibbley, Corless* v. *Corless, Crawford* v. *Crawford, Martin* v. *Martin, Heon* v. *Heon, Crutchfield* v. *Crutchfield, ibid.*

25 *Supra*, note 23.

26 *Ibid.* at 274.

27 *Ibid.* at 277.

29 (1989), 69 O.R. (2d) 225 (C.A.).

31 *Supra*, note 29.

32 *Cf.* the example given by Fleury U.F.C.J. in *Menage* v. *Hedges, supra,* note 6 at 245:

> Obviously, there would have to be some evidence adduced to convince the presiding judge that inequity or unfairness would result from the strict application of the fair market value approach. Numerous examples come to mind to illustrate how fair value will frequently produce more

equitable results. One will suffice: in most marriage breakdowns one party retains the bulk of the furniture while the other party must refurnish his new quarters entirely. To insist on a pure fair market value approach to assess the value of the furniture and household contents of the party left in possession of the matrimonial furniture would produce grossly inequitable consequences because of the limited market for used furniture and because of the very substantial depreciation applied to such furniture.

34 *Supra*, note 6 at 245.

89 In special situations (such as where the shares carry control of the company or where they do not carry control but are a large block that could not be readily traded), the stock market price may be an imperfect guide as to value.

90 Cole, *supra*, note 22 at V-3. See also *Remus* v. *Remus, supra*, note 6. Contrast *Peer* v. *Peer* (1989), 19 R.F.L. (3d) 388 (Ont. H.C.) where, in a case in which there was "no professional evidence to assist the court in assessing the value of the business" (at 394), the court valued a business in which husband and wife were held to be partners, as follows (at 394):

> . . . take the financial statement for 1985 . . . and subtract the withdrawals made. This figure will give a fair and equitable value. This figure will then be divided in a pro rata manner in accordance with each party's money investment into the business up to 1985.

91 *Supra*, note 16.

92 *Supra*, note 18.

93 *Supra*, note 23.

94 *Supra*, note 23.

95 See also *Remus* v. *Remus, supra*, note 6; *Perrier* v. *Perrier* (1987), 12 R.F.L. (3d) 266 (Ont. H.C.).

96 *Supra*, note 16.

97 *Ibid.* at 768.

98 *Supra*, note 18.

101 *Supra*, note 23.

102 *Ibid.* at 436.

103 *Ibid.* at 438.

104 (1988), 31 E.T.R. 188 (Ont. H.C.).

105 *Ibid.* at 193.

106 *Ibid.* at 194.

107 *Ibid.* at 196.

108 *Supra*, note 23.

109 The lawyer spouse's entitlement in respect of unbilled work was determined by taking his hours worked but not billed, (multiplied it would seem by his normal hourly rate) subject to deduction for: (1) work not billable; (2) work which would be billed under the normal rate; (3) work referable to administration; (4) work to be billed in the far-off future and therefore discounted for inflation and the cost of financing; and (5) cost of collection.

114 *Supra*, note 6.

115 *Ibid.* at 259. The court relied both on the view in *Corless* v. *Corless, supra*, note 23, that property should not be valued by a "value in use" measure of value and the reasoning at first instance in *Brinkos* v. *Brinkos* (1986), 25 E.T.R. 81 (Ont. H.C.) that right to future income is not property. *Corless* v. *Corless*

is incorrect in suggesting that property must necessarily be valued according to exchange value and the reasoning and decision at first instance in *Brinkos* v. *Brinkos* were rejected by the Court of Appeal (see *supra*, pp. 257-260). Nevertheless, the view that a capitalized value should not be attributed to expected future income arising from personal skill and effort is well founded and was approved by the Court of Appeal in *Brinkos* v. *Brinkos, supra*, note 29.

116 *Supra*, note 6 at 264.

117 *Ibid.*

118 *Ibid.*

119 (1989), 21 R.F.L. (3d) 167 (Ont. H.C.)

120 *Supra*, note 6.

121 *Supra*, note 119.

122 *Cf.* McLeod, "Annotation" (1989), 20 R.F.L. (3d) 445 at 446; Cole, "*Brinkos* v. *Brinkos* and the Concept of Value to Owner" (1990), 6 C.F.L.Q. 227 at 235.

123 See *Lessany* v. *Lessany, supra*, note 23 (see *supra*, p. 310-311). *Cf. Peer* v. *Peer, supra*, note 90.

124 See *Dibbley* v. *Dibbley, supra*, note 23; *Crutchfield* v. *Crutchfield, supra*, note 6.

SENGMUELLER v. SENGMUELLER

(1994), 2 R.F.L. (4th) 232 (Ont. C.A.)

[In proceedings under the *FLA*, the husband was ordered to make an equalization payment of $368,556.06. The trial judge deducted $137,697.69 in calculating the husband's net family property to account for notional disposition costs. The wife appealed the decision to deduct the notional disposition costs.]

MCKINLAY J.A. (for the court): . . . At the time of trial Mr. Sengmueller had approximately $26,000 of non-taxable assets with which to satisfy the equalization payment of $368,556.06. The balance of his assets at that time consisted primarily of an R.R.S.P., two parcels of real estate (one of which included the matrimonial home), and Film Sound Services Ltd., the business from which he earned his livelihood. Their value as at valuation date, April 21, 1988, was found to be $85,272, $250,000, $375,000, and $161,854 respectively, less the trial judge's finding as to the tax cost of realization in amounts of $38,789, $36,911, $35,862, and $26,134 respectively. . . .

Notional Costs of Disposition

The trial judge, in valuing net family property, deducted as a debt or other liability under s. 4(1) of the Act amounts estimated as taxes (but not other types of costs of disposition, such as real estate commissions), which would be exigible if the assets involved were realized upon. Counsel for Mrs. Sengmueller argues that he was in error in so doing, relying on the decisions of this court in *McPherson* v. *McPherson* (1988), 63 O.R. (2d) 641, and in *Starkman* v. *Starkman* (1990), 75 O.R. (2d) 19. In deducting tax costs, the trial judge relied on *Heon* v. *Heon* (1989), 69 O.R. (2d) 758 (H.C.).

The *McPherson* case, decided under the *Family Law Reform Act*, R.S.O. 1980, c. 152, involved shares held by the husband in a private company. The husband and wife acted as true partners in the company, although their shareholdings did not reflect that fact. Evidence was adduced before the trial judge to show the tax implications to the husband of satisfying the award out of earnings and/or assets of the company. The trial judge, in arriving at the amount payable to the wife, ignored the tax consequences. On appeal to this court, a deduction for taxes was allowed.

In my view, it is equally appropriate to take such costs into account in determining net family property under the *Family Law Act* if there is satisfactory evidence of a likely disposition date and if it is clear that such costs will be inevitable when the owner disposes of the assets or is deemed to have disposed of them. In my view, for the purposes of determining net family property, any asset is worth (in money terms) only the amount which can be obtained on its realization, regardless of whether the accounting is done as a reduction in the value of the asset, or as a deduction of a liability: the result is the same. While these costs are not liabilities in the balance-sheet sense of the word, they are amounts which the owner will be obliged to satisfy at the time of disposition, and hence, are ultimate liabilities inextricably attached to the assets themselves. This is consistent with *McPherson* but goes beyond it.

If assets are transferred in specie or are realized upon to satisfy the equalization payment, the amount of tax and other disposition costs is easily proven, assuming the availability of a preliminary calculation of the equalization payment. The real problem arises when the equalization payment is satisfied with liquid assets not subject to disposition costs, and there are other assets to be valued for the purposes of s. 4(1) which will inevitably be subject to disposition costs at some time in the future. Two questions then arise: First, in what circumstances should disposition costs be deducted, and second, how should the amount of the deduction be calculated?

Counsel for Mrs. Sengmueller takes the position that both *McPherson* and *Starkman* stand for the following propositions, to quote from his factum: "In valuing an asset, an allowance for taxes should not be made where it is not clear if the asset will ever be disposed of, or where the payor does not have to dispose of an asset that would attract liability in order to make the equalization payment." I agree with the first proposition but not with the second.

Support for the first proposition is found in *McPherson*. Finlayson J.A. commenced his analysis with the following comment, at p. 645:

> It makes little sense, in my view, to visit the entire costs of the disposition on one spouse when dealing with a division of a non-family asset: they, like the benefits, are to be shared equally.

After discussing some of the cases which have grappled with this issue, he stated further, at p. 647:

> The cases appear to turn on their own facts and if I might hazard a broad distinction, an allowance should be made in the case where there is evidence that the disposition will involve a sale or transfer of property that attracts tax consequences, and it should not be made in the case where it is not clear when, if ever, a sale or transfer of property will be made and thus the tax consequences of such an occurrence are so speculative that they can safely be ignored.

The result in that appeal (decided, as I have said, under the *Family Law Reform Act*) was that income tax liability was deducted in calculating the value of the business involved. The reasons give us the following guidance: first, that as a basic principle the entire costs of disposition of assets should not be visited on one spouse and that those costs, like benefits, should be shared equally; and second, that this principle should be departed from only where the timing of disposition, and thus disposition costs, is "so speculative" that such costs "can safely be ignored." The basic principle is very easy to apply; unfortunately, the exception is not.

Counsel for Mrs. Sengmueller relies on both *McPherson* and *Starkman* for his second proposition, i.e., that allowance for taxes should only be allowed where the payor must dispose of an asset that would attract tax liability in order to make the equalization payment.

The evidence in *McPherson* indicated the necessity of withdrawing moneys from the company to pay to the wife her entitlement under the old *Family Law Reform Act* (thus attracting tax). However, in analyzing the principles involved, Finlayson J.A. did not suggest that *only* when realization of an asset is required to satisfy a payment from one spouse to the other should disposition costs be taken into consideration. Indeed, the portions of his reasons quoted above make it clear that that was not his view.

In *Heon* v. *Heon*, decided under the *Family Law Act, 1986*, Granger J. distinguished the objectives under the *Family Law Reform Act* from those under the *Family Law Act, 1986*, and concluded that the appropriate procedure was to value all assets as of valuation day as if there were an actual sale on that day with taxes and other disposition costs deducted. However, Catzman J.A., speaking for the court in *Starkman*, considered that a fairer method of arriving at the equalization payment than that applied in *Heon* v. *Heon* was to require clear evidence of the likely fact of disposition of an asset before allowing deduction of disposition costs.

The reasons in the *Starkman* case indicate that the appeal was argued on the basis that it was necessary to realize on the R.R.S.P. and on the company shares involved in order to meet the equalization payment. It was clear that the evidence adduced did not satisfy that position and there was no evidence of any other likely date of disposition. In my view, the decision went no further than that.

In general terms, this court in *Starkman* approved the application under the *Family Law Act, 1986* of the approach recommended by Finlayson J.A. in *McPherson*. If the evidence satisfies the trial judge, on a balance of probabilities, that the disposition of any item of family property will take place at a particular time in the future, then the tax consequences (and other properly proven costs of disposition) are not speculative, and should be allowed either as a reduction in value or as a deductible liability.

R.R.S.P.s, in particular, are taxable in full, regardless of the time of realization, whether they are cashed in total, or taken by way of annuity.

In dealing with a business, one should fairly consider the nature of the business, the possible requirement that the business could only operate if the owner spouse continued to be involved, any shareholder agreement which required sale of his or her shareholding in specified circumstances, and myriad other possible considerations in the individual case. Different considerations would be relevant in dealing with other types of assets.

By requiring evidence of the expected time of the disposition, and by making a present value calculation, courts could avoid inevitable unfair results flowing from the application of the approach used in *Heon* v. *Heon*, and from the approach suggested by the appellant.

A short unsophisticated example will point up the possibility for gross unfairness if paying spouses could only deduct disposition costs when disposition of the assets is necessary to satisfy the equalization payment. On separation, a husband's assets consist solely of liquid non-taxable bonds totalling $850,000. He has been paying tax annually on the interest, and accruing the balance. His wife's assets consist of an R.R.S.P. worth $500,000, a parcel of real property worth $500,000, for which she paid $100,000, and liquid non-taxable bonds in the amount of $150,000. The calculation of their assets and liabilities (without taking disposition costs into account) results in the wife being required to pay an equalization amount to the husband of $150,000. From a practical standpoint, she must satisfy the equalization payment to her husband from the bonds, because she cannot meet the test of needing to sell the real property or the R.R.S.P. to satisfy the equalization. A few years later she, being of retirement age and wishing to maintain her standard of living to the extent possible, needs to sell the real property and take the R.R.S.P. in the form of an annuity. In so doing, her ultimate tax liability will be substantially in excess of the amount *she was required to pay to her husband* as an equalization sum.

The decision in *Heon*, in my view, points up a different possibility of unfairness. For example, apply the *Heon* approach of a notional disposition on valuation day, and assume that the parties in the above example were both in their early forties. The wife could deduct the full amount of tax which would have been payable on disposition of her R.R.S.P. and realty *as if* she had disposed of them on valuation day, resulting in a deduction of tax of approximately $25,000. *Her husband would have to pay to her* an equalization payment of approximately $37,500 — a difference of $187,500 from the result applying the approach pressed by counsel for Mrs. Sengmueller. This result would obtain even if she had no intention of disposing of those assets for some substantial period of time.

It would be much fairer to require her to adduce evidence (see s. 4(3) of the Act) from which the trial judge could assess the likely time of disposition, the likely disposition costs at that time, and the present value of those costs as at the valuation date. The deduction allowed would be substantially less than would be the case if assets were valued *as if* disposed of on valuation day. It is true that such calculations are not exact, but courts have never refused to make assessments merely because the evidence available is less than precise.

From the *McPherson* case I glean three rules to apply in all cases:

(1) apply the overriding principle of fairness, i.e., that costs of disposition as well as benefits should be shared equally;

(2) deal with each case on its own facts, considering the nature of the assets involved, evidence as to the probable timing of their disposition, and the probable tax and other costs of disposition at that time, discounted as of valuation day; and

(3) deduct disposition costs before arriving at the equalization payment, except in the situation where 'it is not clear when, if ever,' there will be a realization of the property.

Under the *Family Law Act* it does not matter whether the third rule is applied as part of the valuation of the asset involved or whether the deduction is made as an inevitable liability which exists on valuation day, although it is not payable until some time in the future.

[The court affirmed the trial judge's decision.]

NOTES AND QUESTIONS

1. There is a general consensus that, in the absence of special circumstances, there should be a discount for the spouse's future tax liability in determining the value of a pension. Although some pre-*Sengmueller* decisions had refused to discount the value of an R.R.S.P. (see, e.g., *Fleet* v. *Fleet* (1992), 43 R.F.L. (3d) 24 (Ont. H.C.)), it is now generally accepted that R.R.S.P.s should be treated in the same way. See e.g., *James* v. *James* (1994), 3 R.F.L. (4th) 226 (Ont. Gen. Div.) and *Appleyard* v. *Appleyard* (1998), 41 R.F.L. (4th) 199 (Ont. C.A.).

2. In *Brosseau* v. *Shemilt* (1995), 16 R.F.L. (4th) 129 (Ont. Gen. Div.), a major portion of the equalization payment was to be satisfied by a transfer of the husband's R.R.S.P. to the wife. The effect of the rollover provisions in the *Income Tax Act* was that this transfer would have no immediate tax consequences and the wife would eventually have to pay tax on the proceeds of the R.R.S.P. As a result, the husband's R.R.S.P. was not discounted as of the date of valuation. See also *McClure* v. *McClure* (1995), 16 R.F.L. (4th) 457 (Ont. Gen. Div.) (no tax deduction in R.R.S.P. where husband given option of satisfying equal payment by transfer).

3. Should the cost of cleaning up hidden pollution be considered in valuing land when calculating net family property? See *Montague* v. *Montague* (1996), 23 R.F.L. (4th) 62 (Ont. C.A.).

4. What guidance did the Ontario Court of Appeal give in *Sengmueller* regarding the extent to which taxes payable some time in the future should be discounted? For commentary, see *Mannarelli* v. *Mannarelli* (1998), 41 R.F.L. (4th) 117, at 124 (Ont. Gen. Div.). Should there be any consideration of the costs of disposition including taxes if it is unclear when, if ever, a spouse will dispose of the property? See *Cassidy* v. *Cassidy* (1996), 17 R.F.L. (4th) 402 (Ont. Gen. Div.); *Balcerzak* v. *Belcerzak* (1998), 42 R.F.L. (4th) 297 (Ont. Gen. Div.) and *Ward* v. *Ward* (1999), 44 R.F.L. (4th) 340 (Ont. Gen. Div.).

5. For further reading, see Kary, "Farmland, Free Markets and Marital Breakdown" (1992), 11 Can. J. Fam. L. 41; Blom and Freedman, "Solutions to Difficult Financial Issues" (1996-7), 14 C.F.L.Q. 61; Wolfson, "*Sagl* v. *Sagl*: Valuation of an Interest in a Discretionary Trust under Ontario's *Family Law Act*" (1998-99), 16 C.F.L.Q. 521; Grant, "Business Interests and Family Law" (1999), 17 C.F.L.Q. 67; McLeod and Mamo, eds., *Matrimonial Property Law in Canada* (Toronto: Carswell) (looseleaf service) V-1 to V-25; and Cole and Freedman, *Property Valuation and Income Tax Implications of Marital Dissolution* (Toronto: Carswell) (looseleaf service).

(c) Deductions and Exclusions

FOLGA v. FOLGA

(1986), 2 R.F.L. (3d) 358 at 362-363 (Ont. H.C.)

[At the time of the marriage, the husband owned a house (referred to as "Frederick Street" in the reasons for judgment). The parties lived in this house for three years following the marriage. It was then sold and the husband purchased another house, which became the family home.]

GRAVELY L.J.S.C. (orally): — ... The respondent [the husband] claims a deduction for the equity in Frederick Street pursuant to s. 4(1)(*b*) of the Family Law Act. The petitioner says that there should be no deduction because Frederick Street was the matrimonial home. By the terms of s. 4(1)(*b*), the value of an interest in a matrimonial home may not be deducted. ...

The term "matrimonial home" also is defined in s. 4(1):

'matrimonial home' means a matrimonial home under section 18 and includes property that is a matrimonial home under that section at the valuation date.

Section 18 is in Pt. II of the Act, and that part of the Act deals with issues relating to the matrimonial home. Section 18(1) reads:

18. — (1) Every property in which a person has an interest and that is or, if the spouses have separated, was at the time of separation ordinarily occupied by the person and his or her spouse as their family residence is their matrimonial home.

Once spouses occupy a property as a matrimonial home they acquire all the rights set out in Pt. II. For a property to be treated as a matrimonial home as defined in s. 18, the spouses have to be either living in the property or to have been living in it at the time of separation. It appears also that to qualify for a deduction under s. 4(1), the matrimonial home must be as defined by s. 18 at the valuation date.

These definition sections then suggest the status of a matrimonial home is not immutable and a spouse may lose the protection given by the matrimonial home status and that a spousal owner may regain the right to deduct under s. 4(1)(*b*). Here it appears that although Frederick Street was once the matrimonial home it is no longer so under s. 4(1) or 18 since the parties were not ordinarily resident in it at the date of separation. Not being a matrimonial home, it now qualifies for deduction under s. 4(1)(*b*).

Counsel for the petitioner argues vigorously against this conclusion. He suggests the whole thrust of law reform in this area has been towards protection of the benefits of the matrimonial home for both spouses and that I should not be restricted to the definition of "matrimonial home" contained in the Act.

I do not think I can go beyond the definition in the statute. The words "matrimonial home" are technical words in the context of the statute and the definitions are very specific. Part II of the Act gives very extensive rights to spouses in relation to a matrimonial home, and I assume the legislature intended to substitute those specific rights for the more general concepts set out in the former legislation.

The respondent then will be able to deduct his former equity in Frederick Street of $12,000 for the purpose of determining his net family property.

DaCOSTA v. DaCOSTA

(1990), 29 R.F.L. (3d) 422, at 446-448 (Ont. Gen. Div.)

GRANGER J.: — . . . At the date of marriage Mr. DaCosta owned 291 Oriole Parkway, which was subject to a mortgage in the amount of $30,000. As they were residing in 291 Oriole Parkway at the time of separation, Mr. DaCosta is not entitled to include the value of the property in his net family property as of the date of marriage. The issue is whether he is required to include the mortgage in the value of his property on the date of marriage.

In *Menage* v. *Hedges* (1987), 8 R.F.L. (3d) 225 (Ont. U.F.C.), Fleury U.F.C.J. was faced with a somewhat similar situation and stated at pp. 255-56:

> *Debts on date of marriage*: The respondent in his latest financial statement deposes that, as of the date of marriage, he was indebted to his father in the sum of $43,574. The question as to how to deal with this indebtedness is a very difficult one indeed. Counsel for the respondent urges me to simply ignore the sum of $43,230 since it is related to the acquisition of the matrimonial home. It is misleading, however, to include the sum of $8,230 in this submission since this represents unpaid interest charges incurred before the marriage. These unpaid charges have nothing to do with the actual acquisition of the home. This expense is more in the nature of rent arrears and as such should definitely be considered as an independent debt at the date of marriage. The more difficult question concerns the inclusion or exclusion from this computation of the sum of $35,000 borrowed in order to purchase the matrimonial home. This difficulty highlights one more of the shortcomings of this hastily drafted piece of legislation. While s. 4(1)(*b*) clearly eliminates the matrimonial home from consideration when computing the value of property owned on the date of the marriage, it does not show the same discriminatory bent when addressing the quantum of debts. No debts are eliminated from the calculation, be they related to the acquisition of the matrimonial home or to one of the items of excluded property. I can find no statutory authority that would allow me to ignore this $35,000 in computing the net property owned by the respondent at the date of marriage. The Act clearly calls for "deducting . . . [from net property owned on valuation day] the value of property, other than a matrimonial home, that the spouse owned on the date of the marriage, after deducting the spouse's debts and other liabilities, calculated as of the date of the marriage." I am asked, in the name of fairness and equity, to disregard the clear language of the statute and to read into this section a refinement that would eliminate debts incurred for the acquisition of the matrimonial home or with respect to any of the excluded

properties. Such an argument was pressed on Mr. Justice Walsh with respect to s. 4(1)(*a*) in *Rawluk* v. *Rawluk*, supra, and his response was as follows at p. 123:

> "In my view, the wording of s. 4(1)(*a*) is not discretionary. A spouse's debts and other liabilities cannot be allowed or disallowed as a deduction from his or her net family property on the basis of fairness, equity or for any reason other than the spouse seeking their exclusion as a deduction, has failed to prove that they were, in fact, a bona fide debt or liability existing on the valuation date."

> In my opinion, these same comments apply to s. 4(1)(*b*). No useful analogies can be drawn from cases decided under the Family Law Reform Act because under that Act there were specific provisions for unequal division where inequities arose. Under the Family Law Act, the legislator has broadened the basis for redistribution of wealth but has specifically limited the exceptions to the general rule. I have no jurisdiction to substitute what I might have included in this legislation for what the legislator clearly stipulated. As a result, I can see no basis for ignoring the full amount of Dr. Hedges' debt of $43,574 as of the date of marriage. In the circumstances, I find that the net property on the date of marriage, before considering the specific exclusions in s. 4(2), is $52,208.

In *Menage* v. *Hedges* the debt was not secured against the land in the form of a mortgage and accordingly was required to be deducted from the husband's property as of the date of marriage. In this case the mortgage was secured against the land and reduced the value of the matrimonial home. The house could not be sold without discharging the mortgage or at least reducing the value of the house. In my opinion, to exempt the value of the matrimonial home from the value of Mr. DaCosta's property as of 6th October 1980 but require him to reduce the value of his other property by the amount of the mortgage would ignore that the mortgage was attached to the land. Such an interpretation would lead to an absurd result and would not be in keeping with the avowed intent of the F.L.A., which is to equalize the value of wealth accumulated during the period of cohabitation.

NOTES AND QUESTIONS

1. Do you agree with Gravely L.J.S.C.'s conclusion in *Folga* that only the property occupied as the family residence on the valuation date qualifies as a matrimonial home for the purpose of Part I of the *Family Law Act*? In his annotation to the case, Professor McLeod supports this conclusion but he acknowledges that it reveals "one of the glaring inconsistencies" in the Act. He concludes (at 360):

> The pre-marital home exclusion from deduction will likely only catch the unwary. If the home is sold and another (or the same) acquired the day after [marriage], the deduction remains for the cash brought in. If the home is kept and not occupied until years later, but is in fact the family residence on the valuation date, the deduction is lost. Perhaps the most startling scenario arises where a pre-marital home is sold and a new home acquired relying almost exclusively on financing without using the proceeds of the earlier sale. The cash is deductible and the net value of the home, after deducting debts (s. 4(1)) is likely to be negligible. If the purpose of the Act was fairness, it falls short. If it was to protect the largest asset for most families or somehow give the home a talismanic effect in law, its operation is erratic.

The case law generally favours the result reached in *Folga*. See *Leslie* v. *Leslie* (1987), 9 R.F.L. (3d) 82 (Ont. H.C.); *Robinson* v. *Robinson* (1989), 22 R.F.L. (3d) 10 (Ont. H.C.); *Flynn* v. *Flynn* (1989), 20 R.F.L. (3d) 173 (Ont. Dist. Ct.); *Zabiegalowski* v. *Zabiegalowski* (1992), 40 R.F.L. (3d) 321 (Ont. U.F.C.); *Smith* v. *Smith* (1995), 13 R.F.L. (4th) 379 (Ont. Gen. Div.); *Arvelin* v. *Arvelin* (1996), 20 R.F.L. (4th) 87 (Ont. Gen. Div.); and *West* v. *West* (1997), 33 R.F.L. (4th) 87 (Ont. Gen. Div.). The Ontario Court of Appeal affirmed this approach in *Nahatchewitz* v. *Nahatchewitz* (1999), 1 R.F.L. (5th) 395, where the court also held that the value of the deduction was not discounted because of real estate fees paid on its disposition approximately one year after marriage. The Ontario Court of Appeal specifically disapproved of *Miller* v. *Miller* (1987), 8 R.F.L. (3d) 113 (Ont. Dist. Ct.), where Misener D.C.J. was faced with a fact situation similar to that in *Folga* and ruled that Mr. Miller could not include the value of the home he brought into the marriage in the calculation of his pre-marital property deduction. See also *Gervasio* v. *Gervasio* (1999), 45 R.F.L. (4th) 345 (Ont. Gen. Div.).

2. *Menage* v. *Hedges* was followed in *Leeson* v. *Leeson* (1990), 26 R.F.L. (3d) 52 (Ont. Dist. Ct.), which involved a mortgage on the matrimonial home at marriage. However, mortgage debts relating to the matrimonial home have been ignored in the calculation of the pre-marital property deduction in *Miller* v. *Miller* (1987), 8 R.F.L. (3d) 113 (Ont. Dist. Ct.); *Murphy* v. *Murphy* (1987), 17 R.F.L. (3d) 422 (Ont. Dist. Ct.); *Hulme* v. *Hulme* (1989), 27 R.F.L. (3d) 403 (Ont. H.C.); *DaCosta* (reproduced above); and *Reeson* v. *Kowalik* (1991), 36 R.F.L. (3d) 396 (Ont. Gen. Div.). Which approach is supported by the wording of the Act? Which seems fairer and more in keeping with the policy behind the Act?

3. A possible objection to the approach in *Da Costa* is that the spouse who borrows money to purchase the matrimonial home before marriage will be in a more advantageous position than one who pays cash for the home and acquires other pre-marital property through borrowing. This may not seem fair in light of the fact that in both situations the spouse's net worth at marriage may be identical, but it merely reflects the fact that a spouse who acquires pre-marital property other than a matrimonial home is in a better position than one who owns the matrimonial home at marriage. The fundamental issue that must be confronted is whether the special treatment accorded the matrimonial home in the rules governing the pre-marital property deduction and the exclusion of property is justified. Is it fair or logical that a spouse who buys the matrimonial home before marriage should be treated differently from one who brings money into the marriage and then buys the matrimonial home? Is it reasonable that a spouse who inherits $200,000 after marriage and uses it to purchase stocks can exclude the stocks from the calculation of his or her net family property but if the money is used to purchase a matrimonial home then its value must be included?

4. The special rules relating to the matrimonial home appear to be based on the premise that both spouses usually contribute significantly to its preservation and maintenance. If so, there may have to be adjustments to the equalization payment where this is not the case. For example, one spouse may have inherited the home only months before the valuation date. In this situation, the initial effect of the inheritance has not been significantly eroded by spousal efforts affecting family and home. Section 5(6), particularly paragraph (h), might be invoked to justify granting the owning spouse a greater share of the net family properties. Similarly, where the matrimonial home is brought into a short marriage it seems unfair to allow the non-owning spouse to have equal benefit of the pre-marital value. Indeed, paragraph (e) of s. 5(6) appears to have been included specifically to deal with this situation. On the application of s. 5(6) in this situation, compare *Murphy* v. *Murphy* (1987), 17 R.F.L. (3d) 422 (Ont. Dist. Ct.); *Futia* v. *Futia* (1990), 27 R.F.L. (3d) 81 (Ont. H.C.); *Lendrum* v. *Lendrum* (1997), 33 R.F.L. (4th) 20 (Ont. Gen. Div.); and *Chambers* v. *Chambers* (1997), 34 R.F.L. (4th) 86 (Ont. Gen. Div.). See also McLeod, "Annotation" (1989), 17 R.F.L. (3d) 423. Where the spouses cohabit for more than five years, paragraph 5(6)(e) is not applicable and the court will be even more hesitant to adjust the equalization payment on the basis that one spouse brought the matrimonial home into the marriage: *Cassidy* v. *Cassidy* (1996), 17 R.F.L. (4th) 403 (Ont. Gen. Div.).

5. In its *Report on Family Property Law* (Toronto: 1993), the O.L.R.C. recommended that the legislature amend paragraph (b) of section 4(1) and section 4(2) to end the special treatment of the matrimonial home for the purposes of Part I of the *FLA*. When the North West Territories legislature adopted legislation modeled on Part I of Ontario's *FLA*, it did not provide for the exclusion of the value of the matrimonial home from the pre-marital property deduction. See Part III of the *Family Law Act*, S.N.W.T. 1997, c. 18.

6. *Folga* illustrates that the deduction in respect of pre-marital property can be taken even where the property no longer belongs to the spouse on the valuation date or cannot be traced into other property owned by the spouse. By way of contrast, exclusion of property under s. 4(2) is permitted only if the property described in paragraphs 1 to 4 still belongs to the spouse on the valuation date or can be traced into property, other than the matrimonial home, that belongs to the spouse on the valuation date. Other important consequences also flow from the distinction between exclusions and deductions. These are explored in the cases, notes and questions that follow.

MITTLER v. MITTLER

(1988), 17 R.F.L. (3d) 113 (Ont. H.C.)

MCKINLAY J.: — . . . As I understand the evidence, Mrs. Mittler was incarcerated during World War II in a German concentration camp, and became entitled as a result of that incarceration to damages from the German government in the form of a pension. No moneys were in fact paid to Mrs. Mittler until after her marriage to Mr. Mittler. The moneys to which Mrs. Mittler was entitled under that pension fall into three categories: first, $7,210 referable to a period prior to her marriage, but which was neither quantified nor paid until after the marriage; second, $30,369 which was paid to her during the marriage and prior to the date of separation; and, third, $18,198, being the commuted value as of the date of separation of the pension payable to Mrs. Mittler after separation.

All of these moneys have an identical source and character, and I consider that all fall within the definition of "property" in s. 4(1) of the F.L.A. . . .

What Mrs. Mittler had at the time of her marriage was a contingent interest in personal property, analogous to a cause of action. Any right which she had against the German government probably arose on her incarceration, but certainly arose not later than the time it was determined that reparations would be made. Her incarceration ended substantially before the date of marriage, and the facts also indicate that the determination to pay reparations was also made prior to the date of marriage. Although no payments were actually received until after the marriage, there can be no doubt that a right existed at the time of marriage to receive amounts to be determined at a later date. . . .

The first step in calculating net family property is to determine the value of all property owned on valuation date, and to deduct therefrom all debts and liabilities as of that date. The next step is to deduct the value of property, other than the matrimonial home, that the spouse owned on the date of the marriage, after deducting therefrom the spouse's debts and other liabilities, all calculated as of the date of marriage. Without going further, it would appear that the total value of all of the German moneys, valued as of the date of marriage, should be deducted pursuant to para. (b) of the definition of net family property. However, this ignores the first clause in the definition of net family property which reads:

"net family property" means the value of all the property, *except property described in subsection (2)*, that a spouse owns *on the valuation date* . . . [emphasis added]

The relevant portions of s. 4(2) read:

(2) The value of the following property that a spouse owns *on the valuation date* does not form part of the spouse's net family property. [emphasis added]

3. Damages or a right to damages for personal injuries, nervous shock, mental distress or loss of guidance, care and companionship, or the part of a settlement that represents those damages.

5. Property, other than a matrimonial home, into which property referred to in paragraphs 1 to 4 can be traced.

I have no doubt that the moneys to which Mrs. Mittler was and is entitled are all in the nature of damages as described in cl. 3 above.

Counsel for Mrs. Mittler argues that, since $7,210 of those moneys represented reparations to which she was entitled for a period prior to her marriage, that amount should be deducted from net family property as property owned on the date of marriage. It appears to me that he is correct in that claim, because her "interest in" those moneys was clearly owned on the date of marriage. However, she also owned an interest in the moneys received after marriage and before separation, and in the moneys to which she was entitled after separation. This causes a problem in calculating net family property. The statutory provisions seem to indicate that Mrs. Mittler could deduct from net family property the value *at marriage* of all three amounts of damages, and also exclude from net family property the value of any German moneys — or assets into which those moneys could be traced — owned *on valuation date*. That in effect would constitute a double deduction, and would not only be patently unfair, but would be contrary to the whole scheme of the F.L.A. That being the case, it is necessary to reconcile the apparent conflict between these provisions in their application to the facts of this case.

In considering s. 4(2), it is argued for Mrs. Mittler that the amount of $30,369 which was paid to her during her marriage and prior to separation, which was not retained in a separate and identifiable cash account, is nonetheless traceable into Canada Savings Bonds owned by her on the date of separation, and is therefore excluded from the calculation of net family property. She cannot accomplish this tracing by a clear following of specific funds into her bank accounts and thence out for the purchase of Canada Savings Bonds, as required by the "first in first out" principle established by the rule in *Clayton's Case* (1816), 1 Mer. 572, 35 E.R. 781. However, it is argued on her behalf that her only income during marriage was income received from her employment in Mr. Mittler's company, and that for a number of years all of those moneys went to pay family expenses, and after that practice ceased, all of her moneys went to increase the amount owing by the company to her in her loan account. She takes the position that since she had no source of funds other than the German moneys, those moneys must have been used for the purchase of Canada Savings Bonds. In effect, counsel for the respondent wishes me to decide that the onus of proving on a balance of probabilities a tracing of assets to satisfy s. 4(2)5 can be discharged by proving general rather than specific facts that would lead to that conclusion. I cannot accept that position. Had the legislature wished to modify for the purposes of the F.L.A. the well known principles of tracing as set out in *Clayton's Case*, it could have used language clearly indicating that intention. I therefore find that tracing is not possible on the facts of this case, and the $30,369 cannot be excluded from the calculation of net family property pursuant to s. 4(2)3 and 5.

The $18,198 valued as of valuation date, to which Mrs. Mittler would be entitled after the date of separation, is clearly property which she owned on valuation date and which constitutes damage within cl. 3. Consequently, no tracing is required with respect to that property to have it excluded from the calculation of net family property.

It remains to be considered whether the $7,210, referable to the period before marriage, and the $30,369 received during cohabitation may be deducted as property owned on the date of marriage. Under the definition of net family property in s. 4(1), the only property that is not included in the first calculation — i.e., the total value of all property owned on valuation date — is property described in s. 4(2). Since neither of these sums constitutes such property, because that property or property into which it could be traced was not owned on valuation day, I see no reason in logic or in policy why those amounts should not be deducted as property owned at the time of marriage. The amount to be deducted will of course reflect the value of the property at the date of marriage.

In reaching the conclusion that those two amounts may be deducted as property owned on the date of marriage, I have considered what appears to be the policy of the legislature in excluding damages or the right to damages from the calculation of net family property. The purpose can only be to permit spouses to retain for their own purposes property which is completely personal to them, and to which they are entitled for the purpose of replacing some aspect of their enjoyment of life which cannot be truly shared with any other individual, no matter how close the relationship. The legislature has seen fit to limit that exclusion to property received as damages which has been retained in its original form or property into which it can be traced. However, the legislature has also seen fit to allow a deduction for the purpose of calculating net family property of the value of property owned at the time of marriage, undoubtedly on the basis that such property was not acquired during the "partnership" and was not obtained as a result of any joint effort on the part of the spouses. Thus, I consider that property in the nature of damages as defined in s. 4(2)3, owned on the date of marriage, which property is not in existence in its original or in a traceable form at the valuation date, can be deducted pursuant to s. 4(1) in arriving at the value of net family property. This would result in the two sets of payments — the one for $7,210 and the other for $30,369 — being deducted at their value as of the date of marriage.

One problem in dealing with such a deduction in this case is that no evidence was adduced at trial as to the value of those amounts as of the date of marriage. It was undoubtedly assumed that the $7,210 was valued at the date of marriage, and no valuation issue was raised by counsel for Mr. Mittler. The second amount was not valued as of the date of marriage because counsel were relying upon or responding to the tracing argument. If counsel have difficulties in agreeing to the amount to be deducted, I may be spoken to on that point. . . .

Property and debts of Mr. Mittler on date of marriage

At the date of marriage Mr. Mittler owned property and owed one debt, valued by him as of that date as follows:

Mittler Bros. Agency	$20,000
Directa Trading Co. Ltd.	33,500
Stamp collection	25,000
Interest on Hungary apartment	6,500
Duplex at 4870 Melrose Ave., Montreal	33,000
Cash in bank	3,000
Furniture	12,000
Less:	
Mortgage on 4870 Melrose Ave.	18,000
Total	$115,000

Counsel for Mr. Mittler argues that, although those properties had a net value of $115,000 at the time of marriage, that amount, reflected in 1985 dollars by using the Consumer Price Index, would be equivalent to $367,270 on valuation date. It is this latter amount which Mr. Mittler claims should be deducted in calculating his net family property. It must be acknowledged that failing to account for inflationary increases in value raises possible inequities, such as inequities between the application of the definition of net family property under s. 4(1) and the application of s. 4(2), which excludes certain properties from the calculation of net family property. The problem can be best illustrated by a simple example. Assume that a painting was obtained by inheritance shortly before marriage in 1964, the value at marriage being $30,000, and the value at valuation date being $150,000. If one deducts the value in 1964 dollars for the purpose of determining net family property, then there is an amount of $120,000 at valuation date which must be shared between the spouses. Now assume that the same painting was obtained by inheritance by one of the spouses shortly after the marriage in 1964, the value at that time being $30,000 and the value at valuation date being $150,000. In that situation, the full value of the painting — $150,000 — would be excluded from the calculation of net family property by virtue of s. 4(2)1.

Of course, there are many types of assets which may be owned by a spouse on the date of marriage which either will have disappeared long before valuation date, or will have changed so substantially as to be unrecognizable as the original asset; for example, a young corporation operated at the time of marriage may grow significantly in size and complexity prior to valuation date. Such is the situation with Mr. Mittler's companies in this case. To deduct the valuation date value of such assets would be clearly inequitable to the non-owning spouse.

Counsel for Mr. Mittler, however, argues that the effect of inflation alone, and not the effect of other types of changes in the value of assets, should be taken into consideration, and there is some logic and fairness in such an approach. The legislature obviously intended that assets owned by a spouse at the time of marriage should be exempt, at some value, from the effect of the statutorily imposed "partnership". The question is, what is the "value" to be exempt? Growth in the value of assets in excess of that attributable to inflation alone must surely have been intended to form part of net family property. To hold otherwise would lead to importing impossibly complicated problems into an already complicated procedure, and would often lead to gross inequities. However, such considerations would not arise if only the purely inflationary element were considered.

But what does the statute say? Paragraph (b) of the definition of "net family property" in s. 4(1) of the F.L.A. requires the deduction of:

> "net family property"
>
> (b) the *value of property*, other than a matrimonial home, that the spouse owned on the date of marriage, after deducting the spouse's debts and other liabilities, *calculated as of the date of the marriage*. [emphasis added]

It is argued that the above definition only requires that the *calculation* (that is, the deducting of debts and other liabilities from property) be done as of the date of marriage, and that the calculation does not determine the *value* to be deducted. I have difficulty accepting that argument. On a grammatical reading of the definition, it is clear that what is being calculated is the "value of property", and that that value is calculated as of the date of marriage. There is no suggestion anywhere in s. 4(1) that the result of that calculation should be altered to reflect the effect of inflation.

I conclude with some reluctance that the legislature has directed the court, in deducting the value of property owned at the date of marriage, to deduct only the value based on date of marriage dollars. Although proceeding thus will often create apparent inequities, I consider that this practice is required by the text of s. 4(1). . . .

OLIVA v. OLIVA

(1988), 12 R.F.L. (3d) 334 (Ont. C.A.)

[Mr. Oliva's relatives, who were also his business partners, provided the down payment for several rental properties both before and after the marriage. The remainder of the purchase price was raised through mortgages on the properties and rental income was then used to pay off the mortgages. The trial judge held that the husband had an interest in the properties equal to that of each of his relatives and that he had acquired his initial interest in the properties by way of gift. Regarding the properties acquired before the marriage, he permitted the husband to deduct the value of his interest at marriage. Regarding the properties acquired after the marriage, the husband was allowed to exclude only the value of the original gift at the time it was made. McDermid L.J.S.C. reasoned ((1986), 2 R.F.L. (3d) 188 at 205-206):

> Tony Oliva is not entitled to have excluded his share of the value of the properties in excess of the down payment since that portion of their value was acquired with income from the properties, which income was not expressly excluded by the donors from his net family property.

The husband appealed.]

The decision of the court was as follows: — . . . While we might have found that none of the properties was a gift but all were part of the business and partnership activities among the partners, we are not disposed to interfere with any of [the] findings of fact. It follows that the deductions made by the local judge with respect to the properties acquired before marriage based upon s. 4(1) will stand. Under that section, the net family property is determined after deducting the value of the property owned on the date of marriage and that is the procedure the local judge followed. With respect to the two properties found to be gifts after the marriage, the position is different. There, s. 4(2) provides that, with respect to property acquired by gift after marriage, "the value of the . . . property that a spouse owns on the valuation date does not form part of the spouse's net family property". It follows that the whole value including any appreciation therein after the date of the gift cannot be included. The local judge excluded only the actual value of the gift at the time it was made.

We believe therefore that the judgment must be amended to determine the net family assets of the husband so as to exclude the value of those two properties as of the valuation date. Section 4(2)2 provides that income from the property, unless expressly otherwise stated in the gift, will be included. It follows that any income from those properties used to pay or reduce the interest or principal of the mortgages or used in any other way to increase the equity or value of those two properties should not be excluded. There is no evidence of income being used for any purpose other than reduction of the mortgage.

We are not aware of the precise figures that will result and if counsel cannot agree we refer the matter back to the local judge of the Supreme Court to make that determination. In all other respects the appeal including the appeal as to costs will be dismissed. . . .

HO v. HO

(1993), 1 R.F.L. (4th) 340 (Ont. Gen. Div.)

Ferrier J.: — . . . (b) *Exclusions*

During the course of the marriage, the husband's father and mother made substantial cash gifts to either the husband or the wife, or both.

The husband's evidence and position is that any funds advanced by his father to the wife were intended for him and that they were advanced to the wife solely for tax purposes — the explanation being that because the husband was employed and the wife was not, she was in a much lower tax bracket, and if the funds were transferred to her, the interest income thereon would attract much less tax than if the funds were transferred to him. Thus, there is no issue that the funds were gifts. The only issue is whether or not they were gifts to the husband or gifts to the wife. . . .

The effect of the wife's evidence is that her father-in-law simply gifted the funds to her. I accept the evidence of the husband that the funds were transferred to Mrs. Ho for tax purposes. That does not end the matter, however. Mr. Ho cannot have it both ways. The funds are either his wife's or his. If they are his, then there would be no basis upon which Mrs. Ho would have to pay tax on the interest derived from the funds. Clearly, if Mr. Ho had been asked by the Department of National Revenue, in 1989, whose funds they were, he most certainly would have answered "my wife's." That answer would have been true and he cannot now, in the face of the separation and the *Family Law Act*, reverse the facts.

Accordingly, I find that the gifts referred to in evidence and summarized at tab 36 of Exhibit 10 have been established by the wife.

From the $200,000 received by the wife in November and December 1988, she advanced approximately $146,000 to her husband, in April 1989, to permit the husband to invest in the property on Queen Street. An issue arises as to whether or not the advance to the husband was a loan or a gift. As I have above determined, these funds were the sole property of the wife. She readily advanced the funds to her husband and no loan documentation was undertaken. She was quite willing to assist her husband in his investment endeavours.

I note as well that the husband indicated that he had forgotten about the balance of the $200,000 which had been forwarded by his father to his wife. If he were truly the owner of those funds, I find it quite unlikely that he would forget about the approximately $50,000 still in his wife's bank account. His lack of attention to those funds tends to support the wife's contention that the $200,000 gift was a gift without any qualifying understandings or conditions.

I accept the evidence of the wife that she expected to be repaid the $146,000. The husband did not suggest that the $146,000 advanced to him by the wife was a gift. He could not do so because of his position in reference to the $200,000 gift from Mr. Ho, Sr. As well, because of this position, the husband gave no evidence concerning his alleged obligation to repay the money.

The wife's counsel indicated that, in any event, the situation in reference to the $146,000 is "a wash." In other words, the husband's net family property statement would show it as a liability and the wife's would show it as a receivable. To this extent, counsel for the wife is correct. However, because the funds were a gift from Mr. Ho, Sr., and because the wife is able to trace those funds to the receivable due from her husband, the value of the asset (the receivable) may be excluded under the *Family Law Act*. This is the correct treatment of the $146,000.

As to the balance of the exclusions sought by the wife, although to some extent there was a commingling of funds, I am satisfied, on the basis of the evidence of the wife and the copies of her bank account statements, that she has succeeded in tracing the $5,400 amount in reference to the Honda and the $10,000 Canada Savings Bond purchased November 1, 1989. Beyond those items and the $146,000 loan to the husband, the funds received from Mr. Ho, Sr. have been commingled with other funds to such an extent that it is not possible to trace the items claimed by the wife, as set out in Exhibit 20. Accordingly, the wife is entitled to exclusions totalling $161,400.

The husband seeks to exclude the sum of $20,000, which was in his bank account at the date of separation, having been received from his father two weeks previously. In my view, the husband's position in this respect is correct. The husband is unable to establish any other exclusions.

Accordingly, the net family property of each party is as follows:

ITEM	HUSBAND	WIFE
Land	$ 310,000	$ 340,000
Chattels	51,400	51,800
Savings	42,193	58,068
Securities	41,115	28,865
Accounts Receivable	—	146,000
Debts, etc.	274,881	61,717
	146,000	13,000
Exclusions	20,000	161,400
Net Family Property	—	401,616

Equalization Payment
Due — Wife to Husband   200,808

In the above calculation I have allowed $13,000 disposition costs in reference to the husband's interest in the Queen Street property. As well, I have allowed the $17,000 disposition costs in reference to the matrimonial home owned by the wife.

Against the equalization payment is to be set off the $146,000 owing by the husband to the wife, leaving a net of $54,808 owing by the wife to the husband.

SMITH v. SMITH

(1996), 22 R.F.L. (4th) 228 (Ont. Gen. Div.)

Leitch J.:— The petitioner moves for an order determining whether the Worker's Compensation Board pension received by the respondent is property within the meaning of s. 41 of the *Family Law Act*, R.S.O. 1990, c. F.3 and if the pension is determined to be property, whether it is to be included and calculated in the respondent's net family property. The petitioner and the respondent were married April 16, 1966 and separated February 1, 1994.

The respondent had three claims with the Worker's Compensation Board. On June 30, 1994 the Regional Medical Adviser for the Board recommended a total award of 10% for permanent impairment dating back to January 1, 1989. As a result she was paid $9,807.72 as compensation for the period January 1, 1989 to July 1, 1994 and awarded a monthly award of $150.81 from and after July 1, 1994. Subsequently, the respondent elected to receive a lump sum payment of the monthly award for her permanent disability and received $30,845.17.

The respondent's right to receive the disability benefits awarded by the Worker's Compensation Board is within the definition of property set out in s. 4(1) of the *Family Law Act* (*Yee* v. *Yee* (1990), 25 R.F.L. (3d) 366 (Ont. C.A.) leave to appeal to the Supreme Court of Canada refused (1991), 31 R.F.L. (3d) 206 (S.C.C.).

After reviewing the provisions of the *Worker's Compensation Act*, R.S.O. 1990 c. W.11 and specifically ss. 36, 37, 40, 41 and 43 thereof, I am satisfied that the payments pursuant to that *Act* on account of a worker's partial or total disability are based on net average earnings of the worker at the time of the injury. I note in particular that s. 43 provides that a worker who suffers injury resulting in permanent impairment or temporary disability for 12 continuous months is entitled to compensation for future loss of earnings up to age 65. The level of compensation is equal to 90% of the difference between the worker's net average earnings before the injury and the net average earnings that the worker is likely to be able to earn after the injury in suitable and available employment. I am of the view that an award pursuant to the *Worker's Compensation Act* is paid for loss of earnings and is not paid to reflect compensation for disability. I note that effective in 1989 the *Worker's Compensation Act* was amended (S.O. 1989, c.47, s. 13) to include s. 42 which provides that a worker that suffers permanent impairment as a result of an injury is entitled to receive compensation for non-economic loss in addition to other benefits under the *Act*. This section which was proclaimed into force January 2, 1990 does not apply to the respondent who was injured prior to that time.

Having reached the conclusion that the benefits paid to the respondent pursuant to the *Worker's Compensation Act* are compensation for loss of earnings and cannot be characterized as compensation for a disability, I am of the view that these benefits cannot be excluded from the respondent's net family property pursuant to s. 4(2) para. 3 of the *Family Law Act* in that they are not damages for personal injury. The facts of this case are distinct from those considered in *Fahner* v. *Fahner*, unreported, (January 28, 1994), Doc. Sudbury 10,315/91 (Ont. Gen. Div.) and *Vanderaa* v. *Vanderaa* (1995), 18 R.F.L. (4th) 393 (Ont. Gen. Div.).

An additional consideration is whether this compensation paid for loss of earnings is sharable property pursuant to the provisions of the *Family Law Act*. As I noted in *Vanderaa* v. *Vanderaa*, in my view compensation for wage loss which accrued during a period prior to the date of separation is sharable property as such compensation is, in essence, income replacement and should be sharable to the extent that it replaces income which would have been earned but for injuries sustained prior to the date of separation. On this motion the petitioner referred me to *Solomon* v. *Solomon* (1990), 100 N.S.R. (2d) 73 (N.S. T.D.), where the court held that an award of compensation under that Province's *Worker's Compensation Act* received by the wife prior to the date of separation is wholly a matrimonial asset because it was made and paid in respect of income which, if accumulated in an account, would be a matrimonial asset. The court, at p. 76, accepted the husband's submission that:

> . . . there is no reason why the wife should be excused from having to contribute her earnings, or her compensation for lost earnings, to the matrimonial pot, anymore than the husband could have set aside part of his earnings in a savings account and claimed that they were not matrimonial assets.

I concur with that reasoning and find the portion of the award which replaces wages prior to the date of separation is sharable which, but for the injury, would have been earned.

On this motion the petitioner submits relying on a decision of the Alberta Queens Bench in *Rohl* v. *Rohl* (1993), 48 R.F.L. (3d) 220, that once the respondent's right to the monthly benefits from Worker's Compensation Board was converted and received as a lump sum, those payments have the same character as matrimonial property as any other funds held by the spouses and do not differ from wages earned and saved or pensions or other income received and saved. In my view, however, the facts in *Rohl* v. *Rohl* are distinct from those considered on this motion because in *Rohl* v. *Rohl* the lump sum award was received prior to the date of separation. I am not inclined to the view that by electing to receive a lump sum payment from the Worker's Compensation Board, the respondent has changed her benefits from a future loss of income stream to a fully vested pension which must be included as part of her net family property. I came to a similar view in *Vanderaa* v. *Vanderaa* with respect to damages paid as compensation for a future wage loss. In my view compensation for a wage loss accruing after the date of separation which is paid as a lump sum after the date of separation is not sharable property.

Therefore, I find that the lump sum payment of $30,845.17 shall not be included in calculating the defendant's net family property. However, the sum of $9,053.67 representing compensation for income lost by the respondent during the period January 1, 1989 to the date of separation shall be included in her net family property for the purposes of equalization.

GOODYER v. GOODYER

(1999), 168 D.L.R. (4th) 453 (Ont. Gen. Div.)

[In 1994 the husband's father, Henry Barron, set up a joint investment account for himself and the husband. The funds were invested in various mutual funds from time to time. The father died in 1995 and the husband became entitled by the right to survivorship to the account. In June 1996 the husband and wife signed a joint account agreement which the court held was effective as a gift to the wife of a joint interest in the account. In July of that year the husband placed $150,000, raised through a mortgage, into the account. Throughout this period, the husband made significant withdrawals from the account mainly to pay the family's living expenses.]

Perkins J.: . . .**Tracing the funds in the account**

Importance of the issue

In light of my conclusion on the issue of an intended gift of an immediate joint interest to the wife in the investment account, it might be said that the tracing issue does not arise. However, counsel took some pains to present the evidence on this issue and in case this decision is reviewed by a higher court, I ought to proceed with my analysis of the facts and law. I am also told by counsel that the method of tracing in these circumstances has not been dealt with in a recent family law case, and indeed I have not found any.

Facts

It was conceded by the husband that he was unable to trace specific mutual fund sales and purchases all the way from the initial purchases when the account was opened down to the separation. The husband was able to provide a summary (exhibit 6) of the monthly statements from the brokerage showing transactions in the investment account and provided the statements themselves for some of the key months, namely: February, 1994, the month when the account was opened in the joint names of the husband and Henry Barron, the proceeds of Henry Barron's account at his previous brokerage were paid into the new account and the initial purchases of mutual funds were made; June, 1996, the month the husband and the wife signed the joint account agreement discussed above and the month ending just a few days before the husband deposited $150,000 (from a mortgage loan) into the account; and June, 1997, the month the spouses separated.

The account balance was generally declining from its opening until July, 1996, as the spouses (and Ashley [the husband's son]) were living off the income and, because the income was not sufficient, they were eating into the capital. Because of this, the husband took out a mortgage and placed the $150,000 mortgage proceeds in the investment account on July 3, 1996 in an effort to generate greater income.

The husband also provided a summary of the number of units of specific funds that he owned at particular times (exhibit 5). It tracked the number of units of four particular mutual funds over the three key months of February, 1994, June, 1996 and June, 1997.

Legal issues

At issue here is an attempt by the husband to exclude part of the investment account from the net family property equalization to be carried out under the *Family Law Act*. The initial contribution to the account was by way of gift. . . .

As the husband conceded that he could not trace individual purchases and sales of mutual fund units from the date the account was opened until the date of separation or the application of the different sources of funds to purchases, there is a need to consider how the tracing provisions of the *Family Law Act* apply to this case.

Tracing is a remedy invented by equity to deal with the wrongful disposition of trust property. Its application in this case results from the use of the word "traced" in par. 5 of subs. 4(2) of the *Family Law Act*, which has been interpreted by the cases, rightly in my respectful view, as a borrowing of as much of the equitable law of tracing as will comfortably fit in the context of an equalization of the spouses' net family properties.

Spouses are not usually trustees for each other in their dealings with property during the marriage (although in this case I have decided that the husband was a trustee of the legal title to the investment account for himself and his wife jointly). Their dispositions of property generally within a marriage, and the dispositions in this case in particular, are not wrongful appropriations of trust funds. Tracing is a fault based concept applied after the fact in family law to a series of transactions that were never wrongful and have not become so by reason of the separation of the spouses. The tracing concept was adopted because the *Family Law Act* property scheme has a bias in favour of sharing the value of assets in existence at the separation date and a bias against the exclusion of assets from the equalization calculation. Hence the onus on the spouse seeking to exclude assets, and hence the requirement that the spouse seeking to exclude a gift received during the marriage be able to trace it from its original form into assets in existence at the separation.

Counsel also put before me the cases of *Allgeier* v. *Allgeier* (1996), 26 R.F.L. (4th) 65 (Ont. Gen. Div.), and *Rosenthal* v. *Rosenthal* (1986), 3 R.F.L. (3d) 126 (Ont. H.C.) on the issue of whether tracing has to be done forward from the original gift (*Rosenthal*) or can be done backward from the separation to the date of the gift (*Allgeier*). The statutory language (subs. 4(2)) and the law of equity generally establish, as *Rosenthal* points out, that one must start at the original gift and follow the transactions forward from there.

I think the husband has discharged the onus on him to trace the gift from Henry Barron by showing the monthly transactions in the account from its opening to the date of separation. Fortunately for him, there were only two, readily identifiable, capital injections into the account: the original gift from Henry Barron together with the money borrowed when the account was set up; and the $150,000 mortgage proceeds added in July, 1996. The identification of securities bought and sold each month is possible through the statements, though specific shares or units are not identifiable by a certificate number. I do not think it is necessary to count the number of units of specific funds and demonstrate that the number never sank below a given level, as the husband's lawyer attempted to do. The account statements are a sufficient record of the continuity of the account itself and the transactions in it to satisfy the tracing requirements of subs. 4(2). The real issue is how the sources of funds translate into excluded and not excluded portions of the account as of the separation date, taking the issue of interest and dividends into account.

The wife's counsel sought to rely on the venerable rule in *Devaynes* v. *Noble* (1816), 1 Mer. 572, 35 E.R. 781 (Eng. Ch. Div.), which adopts the principle of first in, first out for tracing money deposited to and withdrawn from an account. In other words, the first money put into the investment account, the gift from Henry Barron, would be deemed to be the first money withdrawn and used up for the family's living expenses, payments on loans against the securities in the account and any other charges against the account. The net result would be no exclusion for the husband, as all of the original gift money would have been used up.

The husband's lawyer countered with an argument for a pro rata allocation of the withdrawals and charges as between the original gift and the subsequent deposits, most notably the $150,000 mortgage funds from July, 1996. He relied on *Ontario (Securities Commission)* v. *Greymac Credit Corp.* (1986), 55 O.R. (2d) 673, 30 D.L.R. (4th) 1 (Ont. C.A.); affirmed [1988] 2 S.C.R. 172, 52 D.L.R. (4th) 767 (S.C.C.). That case went to some lengths to confine the application of the old rule in *Clayton's Case*. The rule was strongly criticized by both the trial judge and the Court of Appeal as being a legal fiction that did not accord with people's sense of what is right or sensible, except possibly in a dispute between a bank and its customer, which was the fact situation at issue in *Clayton's Case. Ontario (Securities Commission)* v. *Greymac Credit Corp.* involved unauthorized withdrawals by a trustee from a mixed trust fund that belonged to two beneficiaries. In a very strong and carefully reasoned decision by Morden J.A., the Court of Appeal concluded that the rule in *Clayton's Case* was not to be applied in a contest between two equal beneficiaries of a trust fund and that a pro rata approach was to be adopted. The appeal from this decision to the Supreme Court was dismissed from the bench without calling on the respondent.

If *Ontario (Securities Commission)* v. *Greymac Credit Corp.* represents the law of tracing generally in trust cases, on the basis that a pro rata approach is more sensible and just, it must also be the law for family law cases where tracing is to be carried out under subs. 4(2) of the *Family Law Act*. There is no reason to resort to the old legal fiction in these circumstances, even though the *Family Law Act* has a bias against exclusions. Once an exclusion for gift property is established, the amount of the exclusion should be calculated in accordance with the new rule as set out in *Ontario (Securities Commission)* v. *Greymac Credit Corp.. Mittler* v. *Mittler* (1988), 17 R.F.L. (3d) 113 (Ont. H.C.) must be taken to have been overruled on this point.

Applying the pro rata method in this case

Immediately after the account was set up in March, 1994, the securities in it were valued at $210,635 but the net value after deducting the balance of the loan used to purchase the securities was $140,378. The net equity, all of which came from the Barron gift to the husband, represented 69.28% of the securities. The total value of the account declined steadily each month (with minor exceptions) to $132,867 at the end of June, 1996, of which the net equity was $68,440 or only 51.51%. The loan balance had also fluctuated from $70,257 in March, 1994, to a maximum of $97,299 in June, 1995, and then to a low of $64,427 in June, 1996. The loan balance declined overall by 9.04%. The net equity declined by 105.11%.

The account was credited with interest and dividends over the years, some of which were attributable to the original capital and some of which resulted notionally from the injection of loan funds, but none of the interest and dividends is entitled to be excluded from the equalization calculation under subs. 4(2) par. 2, because there was no express statement by Henry Barron that the income from his gift was to be excluded. In any event, the interest and dividend credits were in fact used up, as shown by the sharply declining net equity position with only a minimal decline in the loan. I realize that this is a last in, first out accounting of the dividends and interest, but this makes sense — the husband, the wife and their broker intended the capital to be maintained as much as possible in order to generate future income. A deliberate choice was made to spend the interest and dividends and not pay the loan off. I think that I should give effect to actual intent to allocate the interest for daily living expenses, rather than rely on a presumption or a legal fiction.

The husband's lawyer tried to persuade me that the pro rata approach means that, in this case, the husband's exclusion for the Barron gift is fixed at 69.28% of the securities in the account, as the original gift money represented 69.28% of the original account value. By his calculation, the husband would be entitled to an exclusion of $85,362 as of the separation date. However, the actual picture by June, 1996 was very different — the net asset was much less than that amount. I see no reason why I should not look at the reality in June, 1996, when the net value of the asset had declined to its lowest point. As the wife's lawyer said, the husband cannot exclude an amount greater than what he actually had at any given point. See also Fridman, G.H.L., *Restitution* (2d ed.), 433, and *James Roscoe (Bolton) Ltd.* v. *Winder*, [1915] 1 Ch. 62 (Eng. Ch. Div.). So the exclusion as of June 30, 1996 was $68,440.

In July, 1996, the account was increased by the mortgage loan proceeds of $150,000. The account records show the capital injection on July 3, so the June 30 statement (which is only two business days away from the mortgage loan date) should be used for calculation purposes. The account then consisted of a net position of $68,440 and the $150,000 in new mortgage funds was immediately used for a securities purchase in the same amount. On the investment account statements, the mortgage funds are shown as part of the owner's equity in the account. Thus of the total securities in the account of $282,867, the net equity of $68,440 apart from the mortgage funds represented 24.20% and the mortgage funds of $150,000 represented 53.02%, with the balance of 22.78% being the loan advances within the investment account. The ratio of net equity to mortgage funds was 24.20 : 53.02, or in other words the total "equity" portion of the account was 31.34% from the Barron gift and 68.66% from the mortgage loan.

By June 30, 1997, the total account had risen and then declined in value to $248,279; the total equity (including the mortgage loan proceeds) had declined to $131,148. The loan balance on the account had increased substantially, from $74,172 to $117,131, using up all the interest and dividend income on the securities and more. In my view the application of the pro rata principle from *Ontario* v. *Greymac* calls for the $131,148 account balance net of the loan to be apportioned between the Barron gift and the mortgage funds on the basis that 31.34% of it, or $41,101.78, is traceable from the Henry Barron gift. That is the amount of the exclusion to which the husband would be entitled, if the account were not jointly owned by the spouses.

A final note on the exclusion of the traced gift from Henry Barron. If the account was jointly owned, counsel were agreed that, on the authority of *Colletta* v. *Colletta* (1993), 50 R.F.L. (3d) 1 (Ont. C.A.), the husband's exclusion would be half the amount he would have been able to exclude if the account was his alone. In this case, the exclusion on the basis of my finding of joint ownership would be $20,550.89.

NOTES AND QUESTIONS

1. The differential treatment by the *FLA* of pre-marital property and excluded property is dramatically illustrated by *Black* v. *Black* (1988), 18 R.F.L. (3d) 303 (Ont. H.C.). Under the terms of the will of the husband's grandparents, one half of the residue of their estates was directed to be held in trust by the husband's father for the husband and his younger brother until the latter reached 25 years of age. At that time each brother would receive an equal share of the *corpus* of the trust. When the husband married in 1964, the value of his share in the *corpus* of the trust was $468,050. The husband received his share of the *corpus* in 1969 and its value on the valuation date was $6.2 million. The husband claimed that these assets were inherited after the marriage and that he was, therefore, entitled to exclude their entire value of $6.2 million in calculating his net family property. But the court concluded that the husband inherited the assets prior to the marriage and that he was only entitled to a pre-marital property deduction of $468,050.

2. For a critical comment on the way in which McKinlay J. handled the overlap between a deduction and an exclusion in *Mittler*, see McLeod, "Annotation" (1989), 17 R.F.L. (3d) 115 at 121.

3. Although McKinlay J. did not refer to it, the legislative history of the *FLA* reinforces her conclusion that the amount of the pre-marital property deduction is fixed at the time of the marriage, with no indexing or credit system for simple inflation. The presentation of the Canadian Bar Association — Ontario Branch to the Standing Committee on the Administration of Justice regarding the draft bill specifically alluded to the fact that inflation would drastically reduce the value of the pre-marital deduction in a long marriage. Although the Association suggested changes, including the possibility of adjusting the value of the deduction in accordance with the Consumer Price Index during the marriage, the Committee did not adopt them. See Ontario, Standing Committee on Administration of Justice, *Transcripts* (1st Session, 33rd Parl., Nov. 25, 1985) J-12, 5.

For other arguments that an increase in the value of pre-marital property solely due to inflationary pressures cannot be attributed to the joint efforts of the spouses and so should not be shared, see McLeod, "Annotation" (1984), 39 R.F.L. (2d) 2 at 2-3 and Law Reform Commission of British Columbia, *Working Paper on Property Rights on Marriage Breakdown* (Vancouver: Ministry of the Attorney General, 1989) at 77-83. See also Botsford, "Net Family Property and the Use of Constant Dollar Values" (2000), 17 C.F.L.Q. 327.

4. Another issue that has arisen regarding the pre-marital property deduction is whether it can ever be a negative figure. If it can, then there will, in effect, be an addition to the net family property to reflect the fact that the spouse entered the marriage with a negative balance. In *Jackson* v. *Jackson* (1986), 5 R.F.L. (3d) 8 (Ont. H.C.); *Menage* v. *Hedges* (1987), 8 R.F.L. (3d) 225 (Ont. U.F.C.); *Silverberg* v. *Silverberg* (1990), 25 R.F.L. (3d) 141 (Ont. H.C.); and *McDonald* v. *McDonald* (1995), 17 R.F.L. (4th) 258 (Ont. Gen. Div.) the courts included a negative figure for the pre-marital property deduction in the calculation of the net family property. Does this approach accord with the general policy underlying the Act?

5. The onus of proving a deduction or exclusion is on the person claiming it: s. 4(3) of the *FLA*. The onus of proof may be significant in many situations because evidence regarding the existence of pre-marital property or the acquisition of property by gift is often stale or uncertain. It has been especially important in cases involving alleged debts owed to relatives (see, for example, *Wasylyshyn* v. *Wasylyshyn* (1987), 8 R.F.L. (3d) 337 (Ont. Dist. Ct.); *Pinette* v. *Pinette* (1987), 6 R.F.L. (3d) 212 (Man. Q.B.); *De Acetis* v. *De Acetis* (1991), 33 R.F.L. (3d) 372 (Ont. Gen. Div.); *Amaral* v. *Amaral* (1993), 50 R.F.L. (3d) 364 (Ont. Gen. Div.); *Arvelin* v. *Arvelin* (1996), 20 R.F.L. (4th) 87 (Ont. Gen. Div.); and *Dimoff* v. *Dimoff* (1999), 47 R.F.L. (4th) 137 (Ont. Gen. Div.)) or where one spouse asserts that gifts or inheritances can be traced into property still owned on the valuation date (see, for example, *Humphreys* v. *Humphreys* (1987), 7 R.F.L. (3d) 113 (Ont. H.C.); *Menage* v. *Hedges* (1987), 8 R.F.L. (3d) 225 (Ont. U.F.C.); *Vogel* v. *Vogel* (1988), 18 R.F.L. (3d) 445 (Ont. H.C.); and *Flatters* v. *Brown* (1999), 48 R.F.L. (4th) 292 (Ont. S.C.J.)). In *Silverberg* v. *Silverberg* (1990), 25 R.F.L. (3d) 141 (Ont. H.C.), the wife's employer gave her jewellery at a time when they were having an affair. Mr. Justice Granger concluded (at 150):

> I am sure that part of the reason for Mr. Greenberg giving Mrs. Silverberg the jewellery resulted from their relationship and accordingly part of the value represents a gift. I am also sure that part

of the value of the jewellery represents a bonus or payment for Mrs. Silverberg's work within Mr. Greenberg's law practice. Accordingly, part of the value of the jewellery should be excluded property, but, as I am unable to determine on the evidence which part is represented by a gift and therefore excluded, the plaintiff [Mrs. Silverberg] has failed to satisfy the onus of determining the property to be excluded as required by s.4(3) of the F.L.A.

Doesn't this seem rather harsh in the circumstances?

6. The cases appear to accept that property may be partially acquired by gift and partially by purchase and that the portion of the value of the property attributable to the gift after marriage is excluded from net family property. See *Leslie* v. *Leslie* (1987), 9 R.F.L. (3d) 82 (Ont. H.C.); *McDonald* v. *McDonald* (1988), 11 R.F.L. (3d) 321 (Ont. H.C.); *Cotter* v. *Cotter* (1988), 12 R.F.L. (3d) 209 (Ont. H.C.); *Silverberg* v. *Silverberg* (1990), 25 R.F.L. (3d) 141 (Ont. H.C.); and *Andreoli* v. *Andreoli* (1990), 27 R.F.L. (3d) 142 (Ont. Dist. Ct.). Explain how the analysis of the Ontario Court of Appeal in *Oliva* supports the general proposition that property may be partially acquired by gift for the purpose of s. 4(2)1.

7. Several cases, in addition to *Ho*, hold that a spouse will not be permitted to assert that a transaction which was characterized in one way for tax purposes should be treated differently for family law purposes. See *Dashevsky* v. *Dashevsky* (1986), 49 R.F.L. (2d) 404 (Man. Q.B.); *Rosenthal* v. *Rosenthal* (1986), 3 R.F.L. (3d) 126 (Ont. H.C.); *McDonald* v. *McDonald* (1988), 11 R.F.L. (3d) 321 (Ont. H.C.); *Black* v. *Black* (1988), 18 R.F.L. (3d) 303 (Ont. H.C.); *Battye* v. *Battye* (1989), 22 R.F.L. (3d) 427 (Ont. H.C.); and *Karakatsanis* v. *Georgiou* (1991), 33 R.F.L. (3d) 263 (Ont. Gen. Div.). This view is not universally accepted, however. See *Nickerson* v. *Nickerson* (1990), 27 R.F.L. (3d) 321 (Alta. Q.B.) and *Pickelein* v. *Gilmore* (1994), 5 R.F.L. (4th) 245 (B.C.S.C.).

8. The increase in value of excluded property between the date of acquisition and the valuation date may be due to factors other than capital appreciation, such as efforts of the owning spouse or improvements funded by the owning spouse. Consider the following example. Five years after his marriage a husband inherits a rental property valued at $50,000. He immediately sells Canada Savings Bonds, which he acquired through a payroll deduction plan during the marriage, to finance renovations of the property costing $50,000. At separation, some five years later, the property is worth $150,000. Can the husband exclude the entire value of the property?

9. The special treatment in s. 4(2)2 of income from property received as a gift or inheritance from a third party after the marriage highlights the general rule that income from excluded property is included in net family property. However, in *Ormerod* v. *Ormerod* (1991), 34 R.F.L. (3d) 319 (Ont. U.F.C.), the court held that prejudgment interest on general damages received as a result of a motor vehicle accident fell within section 4(2)3. See also *Elliot* v. *Elliot* (1995), 10 R.F.L. (4th) 424 (Ont. Gen. Div.). Would income earned after the receipt of the damages, but before the valuation date, be accorded similar treatment?

10. In *Smith* v. *Smith*, Leitch J. concluded that workers' compensation for the loss of earnings were not damages for personal injury and could not be excluded under s. 4(2) paragraph 3. She then went on to include in net family property only the portion of the compensation relating to income lost before the valuation date. The portion relating to the loss of future income was not included because it was not "shareable property". Similarly, in *Vanderaa* v. *Vanderaa* (1995), 18 R.F.L. (4th) 393 (Ont. Gen. Div.), Madam Justice Leitch included the portion of a settlement following a motor vehicle accident relating to the loss of earnings prior to the valuation date, but excluded the portion relating to future lost earnings. Is this a reasonable approach? Is there a statutory basis for it?

For a review of the inconsistent case law dealing with (i) damage awards and settlements which include compensation for loss of earning capacity, (ii) workers' compensation payments , (iii) payments under employee disability plans, and (iv) disability benefits payable pursuant to the Canada Pension Plan; see the reasons of Quinn J. in *Iurincic* v. *Iurincic* (1998), 40 R.F.L. (4th) 258 (Ont. Gen. Div.).

11. Section 4(2)5 introduces the concept of tracing into matrimonial property disputes. The word "trace" is not defined in the Act and the question arises whether the term is to be taken as referring to the common law and equitable rules of tracing or whether it is being used in some special sense. The

cases generally assume the former. However, these tracing rules are designed to deal with situations that are hardly analogous to a claim for an exclusion under a matrimonial property regime. At the very least there are difficulties in adapting these rules to fit the general scheme of the Act. Ultimately the courts may decide that tracing is used in a special sense in the Act and develop quite different rules. In this regard, the Ontario cases should be compared with Alberta cases such as *Harrower* v. *Harrower* (1989), 21 R.F.L. (3d) 369 (Alta. C.A.); *Roenisch* v. *Roenisch* (1991), 32 R.F.L. (3d) 233 (Alta. C.A.); *Brokopp* v. *Brokopp* (1996), 19 R.F.L. (4th) 1 (Alta. C.A.); and *Timms* v. *Timms* (1997), 29 R.F.L. (4th) 392 (Alta. Q.B.). See, generally, Ziff, "Tracing of Matrimonial Property: A Preliminary Analysis" in Hughes and Pask, eds., *National Themes in Family Law* (Toronto: Carswell, 1988) 55 and Hovius and Youdan, *The Law of Family Property* (Toronto: Carswell, 1991) at 358-370.

A possible liberalization of the tracing rules in Ontario is suggested in *Bennett* v. *Bennett* (1997), 34 R.F.L. (4th) 290 (Ont. Gen. Div.). The husband inherited $40,000 and shortly afterwards purchased some farmland (Parcel "C") for $35,000. There was evidence of the inheritance and the later purchase, but there was no evidence of where the funds were in the interim. The husband admitted that they might have been intermingled with family funds in a joint bank account. Metivier J. reasoned (at 305):

> With respect to parcel "C" and the tracing of inherited funds which went to purchase it, I find the proximity of the two events (the inheritance and the purchase) to be such that, on a reasonable balance of probabilities, the inherited funds were used for this purchase. Strict tracing rules would not provide for this result but common sense and a reasonable view of how this couple could have found the amount of money required for the purchase of the land leads to a conclusion that the strict tracing rules should be relaxed. Professor McLeod, in an annotation to *Berdette* v. *Berdette* (1991), 33 R.F.L. (3d) 113 (Ont. C.A.), is of the view that such rules could be relaxed where there is no trustee-beneficiary equity and relationship. Equity and the facts of this case call for it.

> The tracing only leads to a particular asset, that being parcel "C". There is available therefore an exclusion for the value of that property as of the date of separation, s. 4(2)2, *Family Law Act*. That exclusion is valued at $27,750.

12. In its *Report on Family Property Law* (Toronto: 1993), the O.L.R.C. recommended (at 77):

> [S]ection 4 of the *Family Law Act* should be amended to provide that all gains or losses in the capital value of an asset listed in section 4(2) and income earned on such an asset must be included in the net family property of its owner. The Commission further recommends that gains or losses in the capital value of an excluded asset should be defined as the change in value occurring between the later of the date of marriage and the date of receipt, and the valuation date.

> In effect, the above recommendation will end the "exclusion" of assets from net family property. Rather, all assets will be included in the calculation, but a spouse will be able to deduct from her [sic] net family property the value of an asset of the type listed in section 4(2) at the later of the date of marriage or the date of receipt.

HOVIUS AND YOUDAN, *THE LAW OF FAMILY PROPERTY*

(Toronto: Carswell, 1991) 383-389 (Footnotes Omitted)

NEGATIVE NET FAMILY PROPERTY

In determining an equalization claim, a spouse's net family property cannot be a negative figure. If the computation of a spouse's net family property results in a negative figure, the spouse's net family property is deemed to be equal to zero by section 4(5).

The computation of a spouse's net family property will result in a negative figure whenever the total value of the deductions a spouse can claim exceeds the value of included property owned by the spouse on the valuation date. For example, a spouse may owe debts which exceed the value of property which must be included in the calculation of net family property. The general rule is that a debt may be deducted in determining a spouse's net family property. If, therefore, a spouse has sufficient included property, the debt will result in a reduced net family property regardless of the nature of the debt. In this situation the debt will, in effect, be shared by both spouses. Although the responsibility for payment of the entire debt will remain with the debtor spouse, its deduction from the net family property causes both spouses to share the financial burden equally. However, where the spouse who is liable for the debt has not acquired included property with sufficient value to offset the debt, the resulting negative net family property is deemed to equal zero. As a result, the portion of the debt which caused the negative net family property is ignored. [For a recent case explaining the general treatment of debts at the valuation date, see *DeFaveri* v. *Toronto Dominion Bank* (1999), 45 R.F.L. (4th) 141 (Ont. C.A.).]

In part, section 4(5) reflects the recommendations of the Ontario Law Reform Commission in its 1974 *Report*. In addressing the question whether a debt should be allowed to result in a negative residuary estate (this was the term used by the Commission to describe the concept called the net family property in the Act), the Commission acknowledged that the recognition of a negative residuary estate would be analogous to the usual law and economics of business and professional partnerships. Moreover, this would permit the sharing of losses as well as gains and so produce a symmetrical scheme. Nevertheless, the Commission recommended that, subject to one exception (analyzed below), a spouse's post-nuptial debts and liabilities should be taken into account only to the extent that they resulted in the reduction of the residuary estate of that spouse to zero. The Commission noted the possibility that "if a negative net or residuary estate were caused by the business or professional misfortunes of a husband, it was quite likely that a wife would have made no contribution to the situation. She may have been unaware of it and, even had she known, she may have had no means of preventing it." The Commission also felt that change to the existing law should not be any more drastic than necessary:

> Full participation in gains, as of right, will be a new concept in the law of Ontario, but it is a necessary step in view of the present imbalance in the economic positions of the partners in a marriage. Full sharing of losses may seem to follow as a matter of theoretical symmetry, but, unlike the sharing of gains, this would not necessarily be an advance towards the goal of minimizing economic disadvantages.

Nevertheless, the Commission would have allowed an exception to the rule that there be no negative net family property. It suggested that "there should be a sharing of debts unpaid at the termination of the matrimonial property regime that were assumed for the purpose of discharging either the obligation to support children of the marriage or for the purpose of contributing towards the mutual support of both spouses". It reasoned:

> In the normal course of events, financial provision to meet these obligations will be a matter of private arrangements between the spouses. Upon the termination of the matrimonial property regime, however, it may appear, as a matter of formal legal responsibility that one spouse must undertake to discharge a disproportionate share of these liabilities, notwithstanding that they were incurred pursuant to specific legal obligations that are essential for the maintenance and benefit of the family as a whole.

To ensure the sharing of family debts, the Commission recommended that "whenever the debts of one spouse exceed his or her assets, the spouse responsible for the payment of debts in these categories should be allowed to claim a negative residuary estate to the extent that the subtraction of the amount of such debts causes his or her residuary estate to become a negative figure".

Section 4(5) of the *Family Law Act* gives effect to the main recommendation of the Commission, but it does not implement the suggested exception. A spouse's net family property is deemed to be zero regardless of the nature of the debts which caused the negative figure. However, the suggested exception is partially recognized in section 5(6). Section 5(6)(f) specifies that one of the items that a court must consider in determining whether equalization of the net family properties would be unconscionable is "the fact that one spouse has incurred a disproportionately larger amount of debts or other liabilities than the other spouse for the support of the family". Consider the following situation:

> On the valuation date, a wife has included assets valued at $1,000. She owes her mother $5,000 as repayment of a loan used to pay for some of the living expenses of the family. Her N.F.P. would be -$4,000 but for section 4(5) which deems it to be $0. Her husband has acquired some assets during the marriage and has no debts related to the day-to-day living expenses of the family. His N.F.P. is $10,000.

Clearly, the wife has incurred a disproportionately larger amount of debt for the support of the family than the husband. A court might conclude, in light of section 5(6)(f), that it would be unconscionable simply to equalize the net family properties by ordering the husband to pay the wife $5,000. If the net family properties were merely equalized, the husband would be left with a net gain during the marriage of $5,000 and the wife's net gain would be only $1,000 after payment of the debt. An order requiring the husband to pay the wife $7,000 is possible (indeed, probable) under section 5(6). In this way, the husband and wife effectively share the debt.

However, the inclusion of paragraph (f) in section 5(6) is not the same as providing for the sharing of family debts in the manner recommended by the Commission. First, section 5(6) creates a discretionary power which may or may not be exercised. In some situations it may be difficult to convince a court that equalization of net family properties is "unconscionable" even though one spouse has incurred a family debt which resulted in a negative figure in the computation of net family property. Second, section 5(6)(f) only applies when one spouse has incurred a disproportionately larger amount of debt than the other spouse for the support of the family. If the above example is changed slightly, section 5(6)(f) might not apply even though the computation of the wife's net family property resulted in a negative figure due to the existence of a family debt. If the husband also incurred a family debt of $5,000, it is questionable whether one could conclude that the wife incurred a disproportionately larger amount of debt for the support of the family. Perhaps the court would resort to the "catch all" factor listed in section 5(6), namely, paragraph (h), to justify an unequal sharing of net family properties. However, this is problematic and would likely depend on all the circumstances of the case. Third, it is doubtful whether section 5(6) can be used to order one spouse to pay a sum that is greater than the spouse's net family property. If it cannot, then section 5(6) provides no remedy where the debt which resulted in a negative figure in the computation of the net family property of one spouse exceeds the value of the other spouse's net family property. Returning to the original example, if the husband's net family property is only $1,000, then it is likely that section 5(6) only permits the court to order the husband to pay $1,000 to the wife. She would still be responsible for the $5,000 debt and would leave the marriage with a loss of $3,000. The husband would have no gain or loss and would, in effect, only have contributed $1,000 to the repayment of the debt. . . .

It is not only the existence of debt which can result in a negative figure in the computation of a spouse's net family property. A negative figure also occurs where the pre-nuptial property deduction exceeds the value of included property. For example, a spouse may have suffered a capital loss in relation to his or her ante-nuptial property which is not offset by the value of other included property. Alternatively, a spouse may have sold ante-nuptial property to provide funds for the living expenses of the family. Theoretical symmetry would again suggest that if gains made during the marriage are shared, losses should be also. However, the Ontario Law Reform Commission rejected this approach as "inconsistent with the purpose of the matrimonial property regime" and concluded that capital losses to ante-nuptial property should always be borne by the spouse who owned that property. It, therefore, recommended that the deductible value of ante-nuptial property should never exceed the value of such property, or of property acquired in substitution therefor, at the date of the termination of the matrimonial property regime. The Ontario legislature adopted a compromise. If the spouse has sufficient included property, then any reduction in the value of the ante-nuptial property will be reflected in a reduced net family property and it will, in effect, be shared by the other spouse. However, to the extent that any such reduction results in a negative figure in the computation of net family property, it will be ignored since section 4(5) deems the net family property to be equal to zero.

This approach might be questioned on the basis that it is inconsistent with the concept of marriage as an economic partnership. If the net gain created during the partnership by either spouse is to be shared, it might be argued that any net loss should also be shared. Even if this general concept is rejected, there may be particular situations in which the refusal to allow a negative net family property is unfair. Consider the following example:

> A husband has an investment valued at $50,000 at the time of the marriage. During the marriage he gradually uses this investment to supplement the funds needed for family expenses. He has assets worth only $10,000 on the valuation date. His N.F.P. would be -$40,000 but for section 4(5) which deems it to be $0. Meanwhile, his wife has acquired assets using her income during the marriage valued at $50,000 on the valuation date. Her N.F.P. is $50,000.

If the net family properties were simply equalized, the husband would be left with a net loss during the marriage of $15,000 and the wife's net gain would be $25,000. In this situation a court might be convinced that it would be "unconscionable" to equalize the net family properties having regard to the disposition of the husband's property and the acquisition of property by the wife. The wife might be ordered to pay more than $25,000 to the husband.

Section 5(6) might, therefore, be available once again to redress gross inequity caused in some particular circumstances by section 4(5). However, as noted above, it is questionable whether section 5(6) can be used to order one spouse to pay a sum that is greater than that spouse's net family property. It is possible, therefore, to conceive of situations where section 5(6) would provide no remedy for a spouse who has used ante-nuptial property to provide for family expenses even though equalization of net family properties seems unfair. A modified version of the example given above serves to illustrate the point:

> A husband has an investment valued at $50,000 at the time of the marriage. During the marriage he gradually uses this investment to supplement the funds needed for family expenses. He has assets worth only $10,000 on the valuation date. His N.F.P. would be $-40,000 but for section 4(5) which deems it to be $0. Meanwhile, his wife has acquired assets by inheritance during the marriage valued at $50,000 on the valuation date. Her N.F.P. is $0.

Since the wife has no net family property, it is likely that section 5(6) does not permit the court to order her to pay any amount to the husband even though she leaves the marriage with a net gain of $50,000 and her husband has a net loss of $40,000.

In light of this example, a legislative amendment to Part I might be considered appropriate. Either section 5(6) could be modified to indicate clearly that a court can order payment of a sum that is greater than the spouse's net family property or section 4(5) could be altered to permit the court to recognize a negative net family property where it is equitable to do so.

(d) Sample Problems

Calculate the net family property for each spouse in the following fact situations.

1. A daughter, on the death of her mother, inherits her parents' home. Shortly thereafter she marries and she and her husband move into the home. They live in the home until separation. At the time of the marriage, this is the wife's only asset and she has no liabilities. The home is valued at $100,000 at the time of the marriage. The husband has assets valued at $150,000 at that time and liabilities of $50,000.

   Six years later the spouses separate with no reasonable prospect of resumed cohabitation. At that time the home is valued at $125,000. The wife still has no other assets and no liabilities. The husband now has assets valued at $250,000 and liabilities of $150,000. None of his property is excluded under s. 4(2).

2. The facts are identical to #1 above, except that the wife inherits the home valued at $100,000 after the marriage and the spouses begin to live in it after that date.

3. The facts are identical to #2 above, except that the spouses never move into the home. Instead the wife rents it out and uses the income to rent an apartment for herself and her husband.

4. The facts are identical to #1 above, except that the spouses only live in the home for one year and then move into a rented apartment. The home is then rented to a third party.

5. A wife has no assets or liabilities on marriage. However, she inherits her parents' home two years after the marriage. At that time it is valued at $100,000. The home is never used as the family residence. The wife mortgages the home immediately and spends the $50,000 raised by the mortgage renovating the home. It is valued at $180,000 when the wife and husband separate five years later without reasonable prospect of resumed cohabitation. At that time, the balance on the mortgage is $40,000. The wife has other assets valued at $50,000 on separation and no other liabilities. At the time of the marriage, the husband had no assets. He owed $3,000 on a student loan. On separation, the husband had assets valued at $130,000 and liabilities of $33,000. The student loan was paid off by the husband during the first two years of marriage.

6. At the time of the marriage, the husband owns a Volvo valued at $5,000 and the wife has a bank account with $5,000 in it. Two years later, the wife is given a BMW as a graduation gift by her father. She sells it and uses the

proceeds to buy a Chevrolet and some furniture. The husband inherits a home four years after the marriage. At that time it is valued at $200,000. Shortly after, the husband sells Bell Canada shares for $50,000 and uses the proceeds to renovate the house. The shares were purchased during the marriage by the husband through Bell Canada's employee-share plan. The house, which is never used as the family residence, is valued at $280,000 when the spouses separate without reasonable prospect of resumed cohabitation.

Other than the house, the husband has the following assets on separation: a Volvo station wagon valued at $21,000, a Canada Savings Bond valued at $11,000, and Bell Canada shares valued at $25,000. The wife's assets on separation are as follows: the Chevrolet valued at $10,000, furniture (purchased with the proceeds from the sale of the BMW) valued at $12,000, and a money purchase pension plan with $40,000 standing to her credit. The matrimonial home is jointly owned and is valued at $190,000. It has a mortgage with a balance of $52,000. Finally, the couple's joint bank account to which they both contribute has a balance of $12,500 on separation.

(3) VARIATION OF THE EQUALIZATION PAYMENT

FERGUSON v. KALUPNIEKS

(1997), 27 R.F.L. (4th) 437 (Ont. Gen. Div.)

[The wife's net family property was $127,995.51, while the husband's was zero. Although there is no express statement in the reasons that the husband's NFP was a negative figure which was deemed to be zero by s. 4(5) of the *FLA*, this can reasonably be inferred.]

Beckett J.:–. . .The main issue is whether there should be an unequal division of the net family property pursuant to s. 5(6) of the *Family Law Act*. The following are the relevant facts.

The parties married on the 14th of February 1985. At that time, Mr. Kalupnieks was 36 years of age, and she was 32. He had been previously married, and was supporting his child of that marriage. Mr. Kalupnieks was a dental surgeon practising near Toronto. The Applicant was employed as a nurse at Toronto Western Hospital, having obtained her registered nursing degree in 1977. Following marriage, the Applicant continued to work part-time. Furthermore, she completed her university training and obtained a Bachelor of Science degree in nursing in 1992. Except for periods following the birth of her three children, the Applicant worked part-time and for about a year prior to separation, she worked full-time in her profession. The parties have three children, Matejs, now age 10, Nikolajs, age eight, and Marissa, now age 6.

The parties enjoyed an excellent standard of living. Mr. Kalupnieks had an income of near $80,000 per annum and Mrs. Kalupnieks had her income from her employment as a nurse. Just prior to marriage, the parties entered into an agreement to purchase a home. The transaction closed in May 1985 and shortly thereafter, title was transferred from joint ownership into the name of the Applicant alone. They purchased a more expensive home in November of 1987 in Aurora, and again, title was taken in the name of the wife. Two other major assets, a Trimark RRSP and a

Mackenzie Fund Savings Plan were maintained in the name of the wife. The husband maintained an $11,000 RRSP in his name . . .acquired prior to the marriage. Both worked hard and enjoyed the fruits of their success. Sadly, all of this began to unravel following the death of a patient of the Respondent caused by his negligent administration of an anesthetic. As a result, in May of 1993, the Royal College of Dental Surgeons of Ontario revoked the Respondent's licence having found him guilty of professional misconduct. The husband appealed this licence revocation. The disciplinary process was expensive; he incurred approximately $80,000 in legal costs but he was unable to pay. On December the 8th, 1993, he made an assignment in bankruptcy. He appealed the decision of the College, but was unable to raise the funds to cover his legal costs. His wife, perhaps prudently, refused his request to consider refinancing the matrimonial home for this purpose. As a result, he abandoned his appeal in June of 1994, at which time the revocation of his licence to practice became effective. His ability to earn a good income was thereby lost.

Fortunately, because of the bankruptcy, very significant debts were eradicated, including for example, over $82,000 owing to Revenue Canada. On the other hand, assets, including the matrimonial home, were protected from the financial collapse of the Respondent as they had been long before registered in the Applicant's name and now comprise a major share of her net family property. I heard no evidence to suggest that the debt accumulated by the Respondent was in any way incurred improperly or recklessly, or even imprudently, save and except for the argument that the loss of his licence to practice was caused by his negligence.

The Applicant now argues that this case demands an unequal division of net family property pursuant to s. 5(6) of the *Family Law Act*. . .:

In this case, before an unequal division of net family property can be ordered, the section requires that the court must find that an equal division would be unconscionable especially having regard to s.5(6), (b), (d), or (h).

Discussion

The Applicant's submission was that the Respondent incurred heavy debt and thereby impoverished the family, and further, that his negligent behaviour, in which the Applicant seems to equate with recklessness, caused him to lose his licence to practice Dentistry, thereby, depleting the family assets and incurring further debt.

The fact that equal division creates hardship on a spouse does not constitute unconscionability justifying an unequal division. *Arndt* v. *Arndt* (1991), 37 R.F.L. (3d) 423 (Ont. Gen. Div.), aff'd (1993), 48 R.F.L. (3d) 353 (Ont. C.A.), leave to appeal to S.C.C. refused (1994), 1 R.F.L. (4th) 63. See also, *Skrlj* v. *Skrlj* [cited by Respondent] (1986), 2 R.F.L. (3d) 305 (Ont. H.C.). In *Fenn* v. *Fenn* (1987), 10 R.F.L. (3d) 408 (Ont. H.C.), the court held that the equalization payment to be paid by the wife was inequitable, but not unconscionable.

There is a clear trend in the case law requiring *mala fides*, improper intent, or at least reckless disregard for the economic effects of a spouse's conduct on family property. In *Berdette* v. *Berdette* (1988), 14 R.F.L. (3d) 398 (Ont. H.C.), Granger J. held that some kind of *mala fides* is required before an unequal division will be ordered. His decision was confirmed on appeal, although the Court of Appeal did not comment on Granger J.'s *mala fides* analysis.

In *Balloch* v. *Balloch* (1991), 35 R.F.L. (3d) 189 (Ont. Gen. Div.), Greer J. refers to and adopts a number of cases that have put a high threshold on unconscionability. These include: *Kelly* v. *Kelly* (1986), 50 R.F.L. (2d) 360 (Ont. H.C.), where Potts J. equated "unconscionable" with "shocking"; and *Magee* v. *Magee* (1987), 6 R.F.L. (3d) 453 (Ont. U.F.C.), where Goodearle J. stated that unconscionable referred to an imbalance which is "shockingly unfair".

In *Hapichuk* v. *Hapichuk*, [1988] O.J. 466 (H.C.), Clarke L.J.S.C. observed that s. 5(6) is a severely circumscribed exception to the rule of equal division and that there are public policy reasons why departures from it should be uncommon. He said that because the legislature chose "unconscionable" rather than "unreasonable" or "inequitable", it must have intended a rigorous test for the except [sic].

In her submissions, the Applicant's counsel acknowledged that the test for unconscionability is strict and that the conduct complained of must "shock the conscience of the court". One of the cases cited by the Applicant, *Peake* v. *Peake* (1989), 21 R.F.L. (2d) 364 (Ont. H.C.), specifically disagrees with the more liberal approach of some courts that equate "unconscionable" with "inequitable". In *Peake*, the wife saved money and made payments on the house, while the husband spent his income. Smith J. commented that the court generally looks for reckless dissipation of assets or extravagance. In *Braaksma* v. *Braaksma* (1992), 41 R.F.L. (3d) 304 (Ont. U.F.C.), cited by the Applicant, there are various definitions of "unconscionable" cited, all essentially referring to something that is "shockingly unfair".

With respect to the argument that the Respondent incurred heavy debt and thereby impoverished the family, the Respondent's counsel points out in his submissions that business investments, even highly speculative ones that go bad, are not enough to order an unequal division, as long as they are made toward valid business ends. *Moore* v. *Moore* (1987), 7 R.F.L. (3d) 390 (Ont. H.C.); *Cowan* v. *Cowan* (1987), 9 R.F.L. (3d) 401 (Ont. H.C.). See also *Jahnke* v. *Jahnke*, [1995] O.J. 3238 (Gen. Div.) and *Portigal* v. *Portigal* (1987), 12 R.F.L. (3d) 45 (Alta. C.A.).

Similarly, debts incurred for the benefit of the family do not justify unequal division. The Applicant refers to *Thompson* v. *Thompson* (1993), 43 A.C.W.S. (3d) 966 (Ont. Gen. Div.). In *Thompson*, the husband had a large debt load that was incurred for the benefit of the family. However, the court found that the debt was tainted with recklessness and bad faith; that the husband had dealt with his debts in a secretive way that deprived his wife of the opportunity to attempt to secure the rest of the family's finances. The court ordered an unequal division of property, requiring the husband to be responsible for all of his debts.

However, the *Thompson* case, in my view, is clearly distinguishable from the case at bar, in that there is no evidence of bad faith on the part of the Respondent. Indeed, it appears that he was always open about his situation with his family. Further, the Applicant was able to protect herself by refusing to encumber the matrimonial home to help defray the Respondent's legal bills. Another case considering debts is *Jukosky* v. *Jukosky* (1990), 31 R.F.L. (3d) 117 (Ont. Gen. Div.). The husband incurred debts, failed to make a reasonable effort to work, and was unable to account for monies and debts. An unequal division of property was made in that he was ordered to bear sole responsibility for his debts. Even after taking into account this unequal division, the wife still owed the husband an equalization payment. It was ordered that the wife could set off this amount against the lump sum child support ordered in light of the husband's non-compliance with an earlier order. Although this case has some similarities to the case before me, there appears to be a crucial attitudinal difference between Mr. Jukosky and the Respondent. The Respondent has at all times tried to work and does not have property or debts that are unaccounted for. In fact, the Respondent argues that there was no depletion of family assets, as the bankruptcy had the effect of wiping out the family's debts, while leaving other family assets unaffected.

The Applicant argued that the Respondent's negligent conduct, which resulted in the loss of his licence to practice Dentistry constituted reckless depletion of his net family property. This argument appears to be premised on the Applicant equating recklessness with negligence and referred to Black's Law Dictionary definition of recklessness, which includes negligence. However, the definition also includes stronger words such as wanton and willful.

In interpreting "reckless" in the context of s. 5(6)(d), one must consider the entire subsection as it refers to a "spouse's intentional or reckless depletion". In my view, the word "intentional" indicates the type of recklessness that is envisioned in this paragraph. It is not enough that the person was careless or made an honest mistake, there must be some culpability or *mala fides* behind the depletion. Absent such a state of mind, the depletion must be so excessive as to shock the conscience of the court. See, *Filipponi* v. *Filipponi* (1992), 40 R.F.L. (3d) 296 (Ont. Gen. Div.).

In conclusion, I am of the opinion that no evidence exists to support a finding of unconscionability in this case with the result that family property must be divided equally. I found no evidence of bad faith or secrecy in relation to the debts incurred, or the licence lost. The extent of the depletion is not so egregious as to shock the conscience of the court. Even if the facts of this case suggest an equal division would be unfair, which I do not believe to be the case, they fall far short [of] meeting the very high threshold required in the *Family Law Act*. It is clear that the legislature intended to virtually remove the discretion from the courts to award other than an equal division of family property. There was nothing that I heard in the evidence to suggest that the husband had deliberately placed himself in the unfortunate position which resulted in his licence cancellation; no doubt, this was the furthest thing from his intentions. While I accept that it was his professional negligence that caused the tragedy with respect to his patient, I cannot equate such negligence with the un-conscionability contemplated in s. 5(6). As a result, the Applicant shall pay the Respondent an equalization payment of $63,997.76 . . . .

MITTLER v. MITTLER

(1988), 17 R.F.L. (3d) 113, at 156-157 (Ont. H.C.)

[Mr. Mittler had given his son from a previous marriage substantial gifts throughout his second marriage. In particular, the son had received all of the shares in two companies established and built up by Mr. Mittler. The value of these shares was not clearly established, but it appears to have been around $.5 million. One half of these shares were transferred in 1970, and the rest in 1982, some three years before separation. Regarding these transfers, McKinlay J. stated (at 154):

> [T]he 1970 transfer of shares was part of an estate plan which Mr. Mittler had decided upon prior to that date. I have some doubt as to whether he intended during the 1970s to transfer all of the Directa shares to his son prior to his death, but I have no doubt that his intention throughout was that his son should own Directa at some stage. Marital problems probably precipitated the transfer in 1982.

In addition to the shares, the father gave his son gifts of money, including $82,500 to purchase a home. The husband's net family property still exceeded $1.2 million and the wife's, although not definitely established, was less than $100,000.]

MCKINLAY J.: — . . .

Application of s. 5(6)(d)

Counsel for Mrs. Mittler takes the position that there should be an award in favour of Mrs. Mittler of more than one half the difference between the net family properties of the parties, because of the intentional depletion of his net family property by numerous gifts to his son Ronald. It is true that over the years substantial amounts of money were paid to Ronald Mittler as salary from Directa, both at times when he worked for the company during vacation, and also at times when he performed no services whatsoever for the company. Mr. Mittler also gifted the $82,500 referred to above to Ronald Mittler at the time of his purchase of a home, and was the source of the funds with which Ronald Mittler purchased all of the Directa shares. However, given the amount of work expended by Mr. Mittler in the development of the Directa companies, and the fact that Ronald Mittler was his only child, I see nothing unconscionable in those acts. Although Mr. Mittler was not as generous towards Mrs. Mittler's two daughters as he was towards his son, he did provide for them in a reasonably generous manner while they lived with him, and also provided very substantially towards the funding of their education. Therefore, I do not consider it appropriate to make an order pursuant to the provisions of s. 5(6).

FUTIA v. FUTIA

(1990), 27 R.F.L. (3d) 81 (Ont. H.C.)

WEST L.J.S.C.: — The parties to these divorce proceedings were married 2nd August 1986. They separated 10th May 1988 and have lived separate since that date. The petitioner is entitled to judgment for divorce based on separation in excess of one year.

The petitioner wife alleged that the respondent husband had treated her with physical and mental cruelty of such a kind as to render intolerable their continued cohabitation. Such a finding is not necessary to support a judgment for divorce in this case. Counsel for the petitioner contended that such a finding was relevant to the issue of division of family property. The relevance of such evidence will be addressed later in these reasons. There is evidence which the court accepts that the respondent assaulted the petitioner on more than one occasion. The police were called twice but no charges were laid. On one occasion the petitioner sought medical assistance but the medical report filed on her behalf did not disclose any serious injury. . . .

The major asset of the parties is the matrimonial home. It is a house located at 7125 Madiera Road, Mississauga. It was purchased by the respondent in 1986 prior to but in contemplation of the marriage. It was purchased for $106,000 subject to a first mortgage of $78,000. All of the down payment for this property was contributed by the respondent. The parties are agreed that at the date of separation the value of the matrimonial home was $200,000 and that the first mortgage then stood at $76,000.

Before purchasing 7125 Madiera, the respondent resided in another house owned by him and a brother. They sold this other house and the respondent used the proceeds to purchase the matrimonial home. Additional funds were required and these were advanced to the respondent by his mother. It appears to be common ground that the respondent was indebted to his mother at the date of separation in the sum of $30,000. The total indebtedness against the matrimonial home was therefore $106,000 and the net equity in the home at the date of separation was

$94,000. After allowing notional costs of sale of 5 per cent or $10,000 the amount to be divided between the parties becomes $84,000.

The respondent is an autobody painter. He now has his own business. Before that he was regularly employed and enjoyed a good income. The petitioner has a limited education and is trained as a seamstress. She has worked for her parents in this capacity and has received some income from them. More recently she has worked in a pizza store and has a very limited income. The respondent has been responsible for almost all of the cost of maintaining the matrimonial home. This brings us to the key issue in dispute between the parties, that is, whether the petitioner is entitled to an equal division of the matrimonial home. Under the provisions of s. 5 of the *Family Law Act* each party is entitled to an equal division of family property. By virtue of subs. (6) the court may award a spouse an amount that is more or less than one half if it is of the opinion that equalizing of the net family properties would be unconscionable having regard to the factors enumerated therein. The only factor which has particular relevance to this case is contained in para. (*e*) which allows an unequal division if an equal division would be "disproportionately large in relation to a period of cohabitation that is less than five years." Counsel for the respondent contends that the petitioner should receive less than 50 per cent since the respondent paid all of the down payment for the matrimonial home as well as most of the expenses of its upkeep during cohabitation. Counsel for the petitioner contends that the cruelty of the respondent towards the petitioner is a factor which would neutralize the impact of s. 5(6)(*e*) since it explains the reason why the period of cohabitation was so short.

While conduct may in some limited circumstances be relevant to the division of family property I am not persuaded that it is relevant to the issue in this case and accordingly I reject that argument. I reject the argument that the court should consider conduct of the respondent and disregard the shortness of cohabitation. In my view it would indeed be unconscionable for the petitioner to receive an equal division when she had contributed virtually nothing to the acquisition of the matrimonial home whose value increased substantially between the date of purchase and the date of separation.

The question then becomes how much less than 50 per cent should the petitioner receive. The petitioner contends that if an amount less than 50 per cent is considered it should be not less than 40 per cent. The respondent proposes the division be fixed at 30 per cent.

Having regard to the length of cohabitation which was one year and nine months and relating that period to the contemplated norm of five years, I accept the submission of counsel for the petitioner and find that she is entitled to receive 40 per cent of the net equity of the matrimonial home or $33,600. . . .

WATERS v. WATERS

Ont. Dist. Ct., Doc. #1024/86, McNeely D.C.J., Dec. 29, 1986

[The husband and wife separated in 1985 after cohabiting for thirty years. They had no children and each worked in a factory. The wife's income in the last six or seven years before separation had been considerably greater than the husband's. Since the couple held all major assets jointly and were jointly liable for existing debts, the net family properties of the husband and wife were equal. The wife contended that the judge should use s. 5(6) to order that she was nonetheless entitled to an equalization payment. The husband had been an alcoholic for some years and a problem drinker for a longer period of time. He had been irresponsible with money to such an extent that his mother managed his finances before the marriage, his wife managed them during cohabitation and his sister did so after the separation. The wife had also done a greater share of the household duties.]

MCNEELY D.C.J.: — . . . Clearly, however difficult it may sometimes be to weigh and assess the emotional, financial, spiritual and other contributions to a marriage, anyone called upon to make such a decision respecting this marriage on the basis of the evidence called at trial would say that the greater contribution has been that of the plaintiff [the wife]. I would make that finding if the Family Law Act required me to make such a global assessment of the contribution of the parties to the marriage as a step in deciding whether the present equal division of assets and liabilities should be disturbed. In my view however the Act does not require such a global assessment to be made.

The preamble to the Act states that marriage is to be recognized as a form of partnership. Section 5(1) provides that on divorce or separation the combined net family property is to be divided equally. Section 5(6) provides that in severely limited circumstances a sharing other than equal may be ordered by the Court. The rationale of equal sharing is expressed in s. 5(7) of the Act. . . .

Section 5(7) does not say that inherent in the marital relationship there should be equal contribution. It says inherent in the marital relationship "there is equal contribution." The rationale is hardly self-evident. Spouses differ in earning capacity, education, intelligence, physical and emotional health, affection for children, interest or ability in child raising, spending habits and a host of other attributes. These attributes will determine to a large extent what contribution they make to the marital relationship. To say that it is inherent in the relationship that the contributions are equal is to say something that is patently untrue. Section 5(7), unless it is to be regarded as an affront to common sense, must mean that as a matter of public policy the contributions are deemed equal (even when they are not) and that this deemed equality of contribution is the rationale for the equal division of family property provided for in s. 5(1).

The evidence in the present case therefore that the actual contribution to the marital relationship of the plaintiff in terms of performance of household duties, financial contribution, responsible emotional commitment, and general responsibility exceeded that of the husband does not in itself justify a departure from equality. It would not justify departure even if, on a global assessment of their contributions, it could be said that the wife's contributions so greatly exceeded the husband's that an equal sharing of assets would be unconscionable.

The Court is authorized to order an unequal division of the family property only pursuant to s. 5(6) and only in those cases where an equal sharing would be unconscionable having regard to the specific factors named in clauses (a) to (h). . . .

The fact that these listed factors do not include factors such as child care, performance of household duties, and financial contribution which are important factors of family contribution in the normal case is a clear indication that s. 5(6) was not intended as a means of departing from the rule of equal sharing by an attack on the legal fiction of equal contribution embodied in s. 5(7). While s. 5(6)(h) is wide in its terminology it must receive an interpretation which is consistent with the scheme of the Act and with the legal presumption embodied in s. 5(7) rather than a wider interpretation which would subvert the scheme of the Act and make redundant and unnecessary most of the preceding clauses of s. 5(6).

There are compelling public policy reasons which support the view that departures from equality should be uncommon. Most spouses cannot afford costly adversarial litigation which under the guise of searching for an ideal of fairness and equity would often leave both spouses despoiled of their assets. Moreover s. 5(1), by making the death of a spouse the legal equivalent of divorce, nullity or separation as far as its consequences are concerned, has changed the law of succession. Any uncertainty created by s. 5(6) as to the wife or husband's proper share of net family property will now extend in many cases to the distribution of his or her estate and this in turn will make uncertain not only the share of the surviving spouse but the share of others interested in the deceased's estate. Unless s. 5(6) has a limited application, the Act will not only encourage a large volume of expensive and socially destructive litigation between spouses but will spawn a whole new class of posthumous litigation between the surviving spouse and the other interested beneficiaries of the deceased spouse's estate, commonly the children of one or both of the spouses. . . .

LeBLANC v. LeBLANC

(1988), 12 R.F.L. (3d) 225 (S.C.C.)

The judgment of the court was delivered by LA FOREST J.: — In this case, the appellant wife, Florence Theresa LeBlanc, brought an action for divorce against her husband, Jean-Marie LeBlanc, and an application for a division of property under the New Brunswick *Marital Property Act*, S.N.B. 1980, c. M-1.1. The divorce was granted and no appeal is taken from that decision. This appeal is concerned solely with the division of property under the *Marital Property Act*.

Facts

The parties were married in 1957 when the wife was pregnant with their first child. The husband was then 17 and the wife, 16. Seven children were born in the first eight years of the marriage. The husband worked fairly regularly for the first four or five years of the marriage. Subsequently, he worked only at occasional odd jobs. He was an alcoholic and drank heavily on a daily basis. He took virtually no part in the bringing up of the children.

The wife worked from time to time in the early years of the marriage, but the family lived largely on welfare until the youngest child was born in 1965. Shortly thereafter, the wife began working full time at a takeout restaurant, working a 3 p.m. to 3 a.m. shift. Eventually, she took out a loan for $12,000 and bought the restaurant. By dint of hard work and the help of the children, she was able to expand the business, which for some years has provided the major part of the family's income. The husband's participation in the business over the years consisted in occasionally running errands and aiding in contractual arrangements for the purchase of delivery vehicles and repairs.

In 1975 the wife bought a house for the family, which was and remains in her name. She and her husband contributed $1,000 each to the down payment. The rest of the purchase price was borrowed. The loan was paid in instalments out of income from the restaurant. Some time later, the wife purchased land upon which a cottage was built. The husband contributed to the building of the cottage by participating in the supervision and hiring of workers and seeing to the landscaping, fencing and planting of trees. The wife at some time purchased a new automobile which was and is registered in her name.

The courts below

The overall finding of the trial judge, Creaghan J., was that the husband "made no contribution to child care, that he made no contribution to household management, and in fact he made no financial contribution to the family in any way, shape or form": (1984), 54 N.B.R. (2d) 388 at 393, 140 A.P.R. 388. Consequently, he held that "adequate and sufficient grounds have been established for an unequal division of the family assets". He was "unable to find that the respondent is entitled to any percentage of the family assets". Later in his judgment, however, he recognized that the husband "did in fact contribute $1,000.00 towards the purchase price of the dwelling" and that "[i]n addition and since then he has been of assistance to the petitioner in the operation of her business . . . particularly when from time to time it was necessary to purchase vehicles and also when it was necessary to negotiate contracts for the repairs of the business premises". As "compensation", the trial judge ordered that the husband be paid the "arbitrary" sum of $6,000.

A majority of the New Brunswick Court of Appeal (Rice and Angers JJ.A., Hoyt J.A. dissenting) (1986), 1 R.F.L. (3d) 159, 25 D.L.R. (4th) 613, 68 N.B.R. (2d) 325 at 329, 175 A.P.R. 325, overturned the decision of the trial judge, finding that there was:

> . . . some type of communication between the spouses as seven children were born and raised . . . and during the last eight years of the marriage they vacationed in California and Florida together; the expense of one of those trips was paid partly by the husband. It is inconceivable that during this lengthy period there were no communications between the husband and his children so as to negate any fatherly advice, generosity, and love or aid and other useful deeds inherent to child care, household management and even financial provision.

The court went on to hold that "[a]ny contribution to the fulfillment of [the spouses'] joint responsibilities entitles each spouse to an equal share in the marital assets independent of the degree and quality of the contribution" (p. 330).

In brief, despite the testimony of the children regarding the husband's entire abdication of responsibility as a father, the majority in the Court of Appeal speculated that it was inconceivable that the husband had not performed "useful deeds". Whatever these were, however, one should not overlook the trial judge's findings that the husband contributed nearly nothing to the family over a period of 26 years. Most importantly, the majority in the Court of Appeal characterized the *Marital Property Act*, S.N.B. 1980, c. M-1.1, as instituting a regime that leaves the trial judge with virtually no discretion to divide the marital property on anything other than an equal basis in situations like this.

Analysis

In my view, neither the words of the Act nor the authorities cited by the Court of Appeal support the restricted interpretation of the trial judge's discretion adopted by the majority of the Court of Appeal. The words of the Act are not ambiguous. The relevant sections interact as follows. Section 2 is an interpretative provision in the nature of a preamble announcing the general framework and philosophy of the legislation. It reads:

> 2 Child care, household management and financial provision are joint responsibilities of spouses and are recognized to be of equal importance in assessing the contribution of the respective spouses to the acquisition, management, maintenance, operation or improvement of marital

property; and *subject to the equitable considerations recognized elsewhere in this Act the contri-*
bution of each spouse to the fulfillment of these responsibilities entitles each spouse to an equal
share of the marital property and imposes on each spouse, in relation to the other, the burden of
an equal share of the marital debts. [emphasis added]

The provisions of ss. 3 and 7, *inter alia*, work this framework out in detail. Section
3(1) states the practical effect of the principle set forth in s. 2: the marital property
is to be divided equally on the breakdown of the marriage. Section 7, *inter alia*,
spells out the circumstances in which the principle may be departed from or its
consequences attenuated.

In common with similar provisions in other jurisdictions, s. 2 establishes the
general principle that each spouse is entitled to an equal share of marital property.
The principle is put into effect on the dissolution, nullity or breakdown of a marriage
by s. 3(1). The principle must be respected. In applying that principle, courts are not
permitted to engage in measurements of the relative contributions of spouses to a
marriage. Nevertheless, it should not be overlooked that the principle is expressly
made subject to the equitable considerations recognized elsewhere in the Act. Among
these considerations are those spelled out in s. 7. That provision enables the court
hearing the matter, notwithstanding ss. 2 and 3, to award unequal shares where it is
of the opinion that an equal division would be inequitable having regard to a number
of factors therein spelled out, including the residual consideration in s. 7(*f*), namely:

(f) any other circumstances relating to the acquisition, disposition, preservation, maintenance,
improvement or use of property rendering it inequitable for the division of marital property to be
in equal shares.

While a court should, in the words of Galigan J. in *Silverstein* v. *Silverstein*
(1978), 20 O.R. (2d) 185 at 200, 1 R.F.L. (2d) 239, 87 D.L.R. (3d) 116 (H.C.), "be
loath to depart from [the] basic rule [of equal division]", it should nonetheless, as he
indicates, exercise its power to do so "in clear cases where inequity would result,
having regard to one or more of the statutory criteria set out in cls. (*a*) and (*f*)". This
does not, as previously indicated, mean that a court should put itself in the position
of making fine distinctions regarding the respective contributions of the spouses
during a marriage. Nonetheless, where the property has been acquired exclusively
or almost wholly through the efforts [of] one spouse and there has been no, or a
negligible, contribution to child care, household management or financial provision
by the other, then, in my view, there are circumstances relating to the acquisition,
maintenance and improvement of property that entitle a court to exercise its discretion under s. 7(*f*).

This is such a case. While the trial judge found that the husband did contribute
$1,000 as part of the down payment of the matrimonial home, and was from time to
time of some assistance in the operation of the wife's business, his overall findings
are sufficient to warrant the exercise of his discretion. Without entering into details,
he found the husband's drinking was "to say the least excessive, continuous and
persistent". All the assets were in the wife's name, and these had been "earned
entirely by her labour, with a great deal of assistance from her children when they
were old enough to enter the labor force"; "the husband made no contribution to
child care . . . to household management, and in fact he made no financial contribution to the family in any way, shape or form". . . .

I have no difficulty concluding that the wife in this case is entitled to the lion's
share of the marital property. Some problems, it is true, arise from the manner in
which the trial judge stated his reasons. He did not explicitly rely on s. 7(f) and there

is an apparent contradiction in his original statement that the husband had made absolutely no contribution to the family and his later holding that the husband should be "compensated" for the small contribution he did make. The judge also described the $6,000 awarded to respondent as "compensation".

But these irregularities should not blind us to the essentials of what the trial judge determined. He clearly found, as a matter of fact, that the acquisition, preservation and improvement of the marital property resulted almost exclusively from the wife's efforts and that there was no significant contribution by the husband in child care, household management or financial provision. This, in his view, constituted sufficient grounds for the exercise of his discretion to depart from the usual rule of equal division. Nor does the trial judge's general description of the payment of $6,000 to the husband as "compensation" make a difference. What the trial judge in fact did, correctly in my view, was to make a division of the marital property so as to avoid the inequity that would have resulted from an equal division, namely $6,000 to the husband and the remainder to the wife. Hoyt J.A. observed that this if anything appears to be generous to the respondent. It is sufficient for me to say that in the circumstances the trial judge was entitled to exercise his discretion under s. 7(f) and that he made no error in exercising it as he did. . . .

BERDETTE v. BERDETTE

(1988), 14 R.F.L. (3d) 398 (Ont. H.C.)

[The parties married in 1976 and separated in 1984. They had three children. Throughout the marriage the wife was the beneficiary of a substantial income from an estate. Shortly after marriage, the husband unilaterally decided to return to university and the wife funded his education and maintained the family. After graduation, the husband earned little from a consulting business he established. In addition to her financial contribution to the family, the wife had primary responsibility for child care and household maintenance.

Proceedings were instituted by Mrs. Berdette in an attempt to secure all the proceeds of sale of the matrimonial home and the cottage. Both had been purchased in joint names, but the wife had provided the funds. Granger J. concluded that, at the time title was taken in joint tenancy, Mrs. Berdette intended to make a gift of a one-half interest in each property to her husband. Accordingly, he held that the wife's claim that the husband held his interest in trust for her failed. Mr. Justice Granger then turned to s. 5(6).]

GRANGER J.: — . . . Mrs. Berdette submits that it would be unconscionable to award Mr. Berdette equalization of the net family property on the grounds that there was a gross disparity in contribution to the marriage. . . .

Mr. Berdette submits that in determining if equalization would be unconscionable I should only have regard to those factors set out in s. 5(6)(a) to (h) which would preclude consideration of the respective contributions of the parties to the marriage.

In *Waters* v. *Waters*, [1987] W.D.F.L. 324 (Ont. Dist. Ct.), 29th December 1986 (not yet reported), McNeely D.C.J. held that a departure from the rule of equal sharing could not be based on a gross disparity of contribution to the marriage even if such equal sharing would be unconscionable. . . .

The reasoning and conclusions of McNeely D.C.J. are extremely persuasive as they appear to implement the generally held view that the purpose of the *Family Law Act* was to remove conduct and contributions to the marriage as a consideration in dealing with property acquired during the period of cohabitation. . . .

If there was any doubt as to whether s. 5(7) could be considered in determining if equalization would be unconscionable, such doubt was removed by the Supreme Court of Canada in *LeBlanc* v. *LeBlanc*, [1988] 1 S.C.R. 217, 12 R.F.L. (3d) 225, 84 N.B.R. (2d) 33, 214 A.P.R. 33, 81 N.R. 299, which, although decided under the New Brunswick *Marital Property Act*, S.N.B. 1980, c. M-1.1, interpreted sections which virtually mirror s. 5(6) and (7) of the *Family Law Act*. Section 2 of the *Marital Property Act* states that the joint assumption of responsibilities inherent in a marital relationship entitles a spouse to an equal division of property on separation. Section 7 of the *Marital Property Act* allows the court to make an unequal division if an equal division would be inequitable given the considerations set out in s. 7(*a*)-(*f*). . . .

In his annotation of *LeBlanc* v. *LeBlanc*, Professor McLeod clearly sets out the purpose of Pt. I of the *Family Law Act* and the basis for equalization, stating at pp. 226-27:

> In general, however, the courts and the various legislation regimes have directed their efforts towards equalizing the value of spousal property that accrues during marriage. As indicated earlier, the equalization entitlement is based on the fact that the common spousal efforts have been focused on promoting, inter alia, the economic wellbeing of the family. The corollary to this should be that, if one of the parties had not focused his or her actions on the wellbeing of the unit, then an equalization may be inappropriate. Whether the lack of effort should result in an unequal distribution in the particular circumstances of a case will involve an assessment of all of the facts, including the extent of the failure to contribute, the length of the marriage and the knowledge by the other spouse of the lack of effort. For example, where the unequal contribution is less than a total abdication, is of relative short duration in a long-term marriage, and the other spouse acquiesced in the conduct, it would not be unreasonable to equalize the property. . . .

> The cases are consistent in holding that the courts will not enter into a fine balancing of the parties' respective contributions. Rather, in order for the difference in contribution to be operative there must be a gross disparity: *Sullivan* v. *Sullivan* (1986), 5 R.F.L. (3d) 28 (Ont. U.F.C.). Further, it is not simply contributions toward the acquisition, maintenance or preservation of property that are relevant. The philosophy of matrimonial property legislation is that each spouse contributes to the family unit in an agreed upon fashion and the unit acquires property and performs other functions that benefit both spouses. Thus, the entire contribution of each spouse should be considered in deciding whether there have been substantially disproportionate contributions . . . .

> In *LeBlanc* v. *LeBlanc* the Supreme Court of Canada appears to adopt the above analysis. The husband did not lose his entitlement to an equal division of property simply because the wife had made a substantially greater contribution to the acquisition of property. Indeed, matrimonial property legislation was enacted in Canada to redress the unfairness that resulted under the separate property system from the division between financial provision and home and child care in "traditional" families: . . . Rather in *LeBlanc*, the husband lost his entitlement to an equalization because he made no significant contribution to home care, child care or financial provision. . . .

> In *LeBlanc* the Supreme Court of Canada refused to make fine distinctions regarding the respective spousal contributions. The court seemed to be directing its attention to whether one spouse had abdicated (entirely or substantially) his responsibility to the family unit.

Therefore, applying *LeBlanc* v. *LeBlanc*, I am required to consider the contributions of the spouses as defined in s. 5(7) to determine if equalization would be unconscionable.

The gross disparity in contributions which I have already found to exist is only relevant if the failure to contribute is *mala fides*: *McCutcheon* v. *McCutcheon* (1986), 2 R.F.L. (3d) 327 (Ont. Dist. Ct.); and *Velikov* v. *Velikov*, [1988] W.D.F.L. 352 (Ont. H.C.).

Professor McLeod, at p. 227 of his annotation to *LeBlanc* v. *LeBlanc*, suggests that the reason for the gross disparity in contributions may not be relevant as a result of the language used by La Forest J.:

> Although a wilful or intentional refusal to contribute should justify an unequal division, what if the reason for the failure to contribute results from ill health or other disability? Had the court used language such as "abdicate", it would be easy to read in some requirement of "mens rea" or wilfulness or recklessness. However, the court spoke simply of a failure to contribute. This suggests that it is the objective fact of contribution/non-contribution that is relevant. In *LeBlanc* the husband's failure to contribute appeared to be a direct result of his alcohol problem. If alcoholism is regarded as a disease, then, similarly, a physical or mental inability should not excuse a failure to contribute. It is difficult, however, to ignore the nagging thought that alcoholism is regarded by many (including judges?) as different from diseases generally and still contains an element of fault or choice which is not associated with other diseases or disabilities.

To scrutinize the contribution of each spouse to the marriage without regard to intention or ability would be unduly harsh and unjust and not within the intent and spirit of the *Family Law Act*.

If one spouse is unable to contribute as a result of sickness or injury and his or her spouse acquiesces, then the gross disparity would not affect the property division. If, however, the disparity arises from a *mala fides* failure to contribute or an abdication which was not accepted by the other spouse, such disparity will affect the division of net family property.

If I am correct in my interpretation of s. 5 of the Act, it will be necessary for the court to scrutinize the internal family contributions and the conduct of each spouse to ascertain if an actionable disparity exists.

It was my impression based on all of the evidence that it was the intention of Mr. Berdette to abdicate his role within the marriage in order to promote his own career. Mr. Berdette did not allow Mrs. Berdette any input into his decisions and accordingly Mrs. Berdette did not acquiesce to Mr. Berdette's decision not to contribute to the marital partnership.

The sole remaining issue is whether the gross disparity of contribution by the spouses results in the equalization of the net family property being unconscionable within the meaning of s. 5 of the Act.

. . . In this case an equalization of the net family property would be shocking and unconscionable and would require redress through an unequal division in favour of Mrs. Berdette, if she had not made a gift to Mr. Berdette of an undivided one-half interest in the matrimonial home and cottage.

Mrs. Berdette cannot make a gift of property to her husband and then claim it would be unconscionable for him to retain the value of such gift. Accordingly Mr. Berdette is entitled to retain his share of the two properties. If Mrs. Berdette had other net family property I would find it unconscionable for Mr. Berdette to share in the value of such property. . . .

BERDETTE v. BERDETTE

(1991), 3 O.R. (3d) 513 (C.A.)

[The Ontario Court of Appeal dismissed the wife's appeal. The court concluded: (1) there was evidence to support the finding that the wife made gifts to the husband of a half-interest in each of the house and cottage at the times that they were purchased; (2) the gifts were not invalid as a result of undue influence or duress; and (3) the finding that the wife made valid gifts of the half-interests in the properties defeated any claim based on either a resulting or a constructive trust. Mr. Justice Galligan then turned to the argument that the trial judge should have applied s. 5(6) to allow the appellant a 100% interest in each property.]

GALLIGAN J.A.: — . . . Granger J. held that s. 5(6) of the *FLA* should not be applied because it was not unconscionable for the respondent to retain the value of property which had been given to him by gift. Counsel for the appellant argued that he erred in failing to apply it to allow her client a 100 per cent interest in the two properties, because it was unconscionable that the parties should have equal interests in them. In my opinion, Granger J. was correct when he declined to apply s. 5(6) in the circumstances of this case. The language which he used in doing so, however, might leave open the impression that s. 5(6) might have been applicable had the respondent's interests in the properties not been obtained by gift. In my opinion, for two reasons which I will develop, s. 5(6) was inapplicable to this case. . . .

The intent of this legislation is to establish partnership and equal sharing of property accumulated during marriage. That intent is not effected, however, by the sharing of the assets themselves as was done under the *Family Law Reform Act*, R.S.O. 1980, c. 152, which preceded the *FLA*. It is done by the sharing of the *value* of the assets. The distinction is crucial and is one that is not infrequently overlooked. . . . In my view, the definition of "net family property" contained in s. 4(1), the opening words of s. 4(2), s. 5(1) and s. 5(6) all show that the *FLA* does not provide for the distribution of property. Rather, it provides for the payment of money when the net family property of one spouse is less than that of the other.

[T]he court must take the following steps in determining spouses' rights under Part I of the *FLA*:

1. The court must establish the net family property of each spouse. It is only when that function has been performed that the court is in a position to apply s. 5(1) of the *FLA*, which is the next step. This first step must be undertaken in light of the provisions of s. 4. This means that the court must:

   (a) determine what "property" each spouse owned on valuation day, and

   (b) value that property after making deductions and allowing exemptions as provided in s. 4.

2. The court must determine whether one spouse's net family property is less than that of the other. If so, s. 5(1) provides for equalization, which is effected by ordering a payment of one-half of the difference between them. However, before making that order, the court must proceed to the third step.

3. The court must decide whether, because of the considerations contained in s. 5(6), it would be unconscionable to equalize the net family properties. If so, the court may make an award that is more or less than half the difference between the net family properties. If not, the net family properties are equalized as set out in step 2.

. . .

I think it must now be taken as settled that the considerations which could lead a court to find unconscionability under s. 5(6) can have no bearing upon the issue of ownership of property, which is fundamental to the determination of net family property under s. 4(1). Therefore, those considerations could have no bearing upon whether, on valuation day, the respondent was a joint owner of the two properties with the appellant. Thus the trial judge could not have applied those considerations to deprive the appellant of joint ownership in the properties, which had been given to him as a gift.

My second reason for holding that s. 5(6) does not apply in this case is that there is no difference between the net family properties of these parties. As mentioned earlier, no assets or properties other than the two at issue in this case were found by the trial judge to be included in the net family property of either spouse. Because he found each of them to have a half-interest in the properties, their net family properties were of equal value. Section 5(1) provides that the spouse whose net family property is the lesser of the two is entitled to one-half of the difference between them. The entitlement in s. 5(1) is a statutory one. In order for a spouse to benefit from it he or she must come within the statutory condition of entitlement. In this case there is no difference between the two net family properties. There is no "lesser of the two". Thus, by its terms, s. 5(1) does not apply in this case.

Because s. 5(1) is inapplicable, s. 5(6) can have no application either. The latter subsection authorizes an award of more or less than half the difference between the net family properties. Where, as here, there is no difference between the net family properties, s. 5(6) can have no operation. Because s. 5(6) by its terms is inapplicable to the issues to be decided in this case, the unconscionability considerations in paragraphs (a) to (h) were irrelevant. I conclude, therefore, that this ground of appeal must fail.

Before leaving this aspect of the case I wish to make reference to one of the conclusions reached by Granger J. He held that because of the decision of the Supreme Court of Canada in *Leblanc* v. *Leblanc*, [1988] 1 S.C.R. 217, 12 R.F.L. (3d) 225, a court, in determining unconscionability under s. 5(6), was required to take into account considerations set out in s. 5(7). Counsel for the respondent in this court argued that there was a significant difference between the language of the New Brunswick statute [*Marital Property Act*, S.N.B. 1980, c. M-1.1] which was under consideration in *Leblanc* and the relevant provisions of the *FLA*.

As I have found that s. 5(6) of the *FLA* is inapplicable to the facts of this case, it is unnecessary to decide that issue here. In fact, I think it is undesirable to make any comment upon it. I therefore leave that issue open until it is necessary to decide it. . . .

HEAL v. HEAL

(1998), 43 R.F.L. (4th) 88 (Ont. Gen. Div.)

MacKenzie J.:–. . . At the time of trial (October, 1998), the petitioner [the wife] was 54 years of age and the respondent was 55 years of age. The parties were married on January 20th, 1968. The final separation between them took place on or about the 31st of March, 1997. There is no separation agreement between the parties governing their relations. There were three children of the marriage, a son and two daughters but for purposes of this proceeding there are only two children of the marriage, Elizabeth, age 20 and Meredith, age 18.

Briefly, the parties met in high school some 7 years prior to their marriage. In the first year of their marriage (1969), they acquired their first home, aided by an inheritance received by the petitioner from her mother's estate. The first child arrived in 1973, and the daughters of the parties, Elizabeth and Meredith, arrived in 1978 and 1980, respectively. During the period from 1973 through to approximately 1980, the petitioner worked on a part-time or "fill-in" basis with the law firm in which she had worked full-time as a legal secretary prior to the arrival of the first child, as well as working at home on a contract basis preparing transcripts of court proceedings.

The petitioner has a Grade 12 business diploma and has taken miscellaneous computer courses; she has qualifications as a payroll administrator.

It is undisputed that throughout the period of the marriage the respondent has been fully employed, except for a period of six weeks when he entered a residential facility for treatment of alcoholism in or about December of 1981. For the last 21 years, commencing approximately in 1976, the respondent has been employed as a chemical waste processor. His educational status is Grade 10 completion, plus studies in radio/television at a provincial trade institute. [The husband earned approximately $52,500 per year.]. . .

It is also admitted that the respondent developed a severe drinking problem in the late 1970's which undoubtedly exacerbated the domestic pressures of a chronically ill child and financial concerns. It is further acknowledged that the effects of the drinking problem became acute in 1981, finally resulting in the acknowledgment by the respondent to the petitioner that he did have a severe drinking problem and in his admission to a residential treatment facility for a period of six weeks. As previously indicated, it is noteworthy that other than the six week absence from his employment, agreed to by his employer, the respondent did not lose such employment.

About 1980, the petitioner resumed her full-time employment, working as a payroll administrator for the Molson Group of corporations on a full-time basis until 1989. At that time, she was forced to leave her employment due to the health problems of Meredith which required full-time care and attention. She returned to full-time employment in 1993 or 1994 and has continued in full-time employment with various employers in different capacities to the present date. Her current employment dates from June of 1998. [The wife earned approximately $34,000 per year.]. . .

Equalization of Family Property

. . . Counsel for the petitioner contends that sub-clauses (c) and (h) of subsection 5(6) are engaged by the factual situation in the present case. It is argued that although there was no intention on the part of the respondent that could be characterized as bad faith or malicious, it is vastly unjust that the respondent should be able to walk away from the sale of the matrimonial home with half the net investment therein which was originally funded through the petitioner's inheritances [from her mother] and at the same time be able to walk away from the marriage with his savings ("thrift plan" in the approximate sum of $58,000.00). In addition, it is submitted that the funding by the petitioner from her inheritance monies [a subsequent inheritance of about $90,000 from an uncle] of the replacement van vehicle and the substantial cost of the improvements thereto are within the parameters referred to in sub-paragraph (c) and (h) of subsection 5(6). In sum, the petitioner contends that it is so manifestly inequitable to permit even or equal distribution of net family property in the present case as to meet the unconscionable standards stipulated in s.5(6).

The use of the term "unconscionable" has provoked different interpretations by the courts. The current state of the law on this point is that the word "unconscionable" can be equated with the word "shocking"; *Kelly* v. *Kelly* (1986), 50 R.F.L. (2d) 360, 2 R.F.L. (3d) 1 (Ont. H.C.); *MacDonald* v. *MacDonald* (1997), 33 R.F.L. (4th) 75 (Ont. C.A.). The term "shocking" indicates a situation or circumstances such as to shock the conscience in a situation where the party seeking relief has been put in a position so unfair as to cry out for redress. Accordingly, the word "unconscionable" must mean more than a mere consideration of "fairness" or "reasonableness". The use of the word creates a threshold where unequal division of family property may be ordered where to do otherwise would be patently unfair or inordinately inequitable; *Sullivan* v. *Sullivan* (1986), 5 R.F.L. (3d) 28 (Ont. U.F.C.); *Filipponi* v. *Filipponi* (1992), 40 R.F.L. (3d) 296 (Ont. Gen. Div.).

In determining unconscionability, the court must have regard to the factors set out under s.5(6) to determine whether there are any equities that favour one of the parties. If such factors exist, the court must then consider their magnitude to determine if an equalization of net family property would be unconscionable. The test of unconscionability must be applied having regard to all of the factors in clauses (a) to (h) in subsection (6), since the cumulative effect of the factors may result in a unconscionability even though no single factor considered in isolation would give rise to unconscionability; *Waters* v. *Waters* (December 29, 1986), Doc. 1024/86 (Ont. Dist. Ct.).

On the facts of this case presented in the evidence, the petitioner does not meet the burden of establishing unconscionability within the meaning of the case law. It might be legitimately found to be unfair or unreasonable that she is not entitled to an unequal distribution of the net family property having regard to her utilization of inheritance money for the common good of the parties and their family during cohabitation. The fact remains that there is no evidentiary basis to invoke any of the other factors in support of a finding of unconscionability in the present case; neither of the parties appear to have incurred debts or liabilities recklessly or in bad faith nor did either of the parties behave recklessly or intentionally in conduct that would deplete their respective net properties. The respondent, except for a six-week period of rehabilitation and non-employment previously described, worked throughout the marriage in accordance with his capabilities and appears to have worked substantial amounts of over-time. The benefits of that over-time accrued to the family's benefit, as did the efforts of the petitioner while she was attempting to carry on her secretarial service from the household. Although the petitioner's evidence if accepted indicates that the respondent did very little to assist her in household matters even while the petitioner herself was employed outside the house, I am not satisfied that this fact is of the type required to push what might be considered unfair or unreasonable by lay-standards over the legal threshold into unconscionability under s.5(6) of the *Divorce Act*. In the result, the equalization of net family properties of the parties shall be in accordance with s.5(1) of the *Act* on a 50/50 basis. . . .

NOTES AND QUESTIONS

1. For the women's rights groups that appeared before the legislative committee examining the draft legislation that eventually became the *FLA*, the most important issue was the extent of judicial discretion. They spoke strongly against any lessening of the threshold test in the proposed legislation for a variation of the equal sharing of net family properties, believing that any increase in discretion would be used to justify a lesser share for the spouse who had not acquired property during the marriage — traditionally, the wife. In particular, they opposed the recommendation of the Canadian Bar Association — Family Law Section that the word "inequitable" should replace "unconscionable". See Hovius and Youdan, *The Law of Family Property* (Toronto: Carswell, 1991) at 392.

2. Unlike the legislation in some provinces such as British Columbia, the *FLA* does not specify that the court should consider the needs and means of the spouses in determining if the equal sharing rule should be varied. This indicates that, in Ontario, the primary purpose of the deferred sharing of gains during the marriage is to recognize the past contributions of the spouses, not to provide the financial resources for an independent future life. In its *Working Paper on Property Rights on Marriage Breakdown* (Vancouver: Ministry of the Attorney General, 1989), the Law Reform Commission of British Columbia suggested (at 47) that the consideration of the needs of the spouses in determining property

rights was inappropriate and unnecessarily blurred the distinction between property rights and support obligations. Do you agree? See also Bissett-Johnson, "Annotation" (1990), 28 R.F.L. (3d) 373.

3. It should be noted that the power to award an unequal share of net family properties is not the only avenue available to the courts to ensure that equity is done in the overall circumstances of the case. Through the use of the constructive trust, for example, the courts have ensured that a non-titled spouse who has contributed to the acquisition or maintenance of a particular asset shares in the growth of the value of the asset following the valuation date. Recall *Rawluk*. A support order, especially one based on the concept of restitutionary support, can also ensure that a spouse leaves the relationship fairly rewarded for past contributions.

While the development of restitutionary support orders indicates that one of the purposes of a support order may now be to ensure that one spouse is not unjustly enriched by the contribution of the other spouse to his or her career potential, it is still inappropriate to award support simply because the equal sharing of net family properties seems unfair. For this reason, the result in *Hines* v. *Hines* (1988), 23 R.F.L. (3d) 261 (Ont. H.C.) is questionable. In that case, the wife owed her husband an equalization payment of $48,000, largely because she had brought the matrimonial home into the marriage. The only way in which she could satisfy this payment was by selling the home. To prevent this result, Walsh J. awarded her $38,000 as lump sum support, which was applied to her obligation under Part I of the Act. It is doubtful that this order can be explained on any basis other than an attempt to use support to offset an unfair result under Part I and so circumvent the requirement of an equal sharing of net family properties unless such sharing is unconscionable.

In *Jantzen* v. *Jantzen* (1998), 35 R.F.L. (4th) 282, the Manitoba Court of Appeal emphasized that support orders should not award lump sum support simply to redistribute property. In his critical annotation, Professor McLeod suggests (at 284): "Maintaining the formal distinction between support and property rights undermines a court's ability to ensure that an order maximizes each spouse's future prospects. A court should divide property according to the matrimonial property rules and then decide whether a support order is necessary to fully redress the economic consequences of the marriage on the spouses."

4. Several of the factors listed in s. 5(6) of the *FLA* were initially proposed by the Ontario Law Reform Commission in the *Report on Family Law: Part IV: Family Property Law* (Toronto: Ministry of the Attorney General, 1974). However, the scheme enacted by Part I of the *FLA* differs considerably from that proposed by the Commission. As a result, the relevance of some of the factors, for example, those listed in paragraphs (a) and (c), has become questionable. See Hovius and Youdan, *The Law of Family Property* (Toronto: Carswell, 1991) at 398-405.

5. In *Balogh* v. *Balogh* (1996), 24 R.F.L. (4th) 181, the Ontario Court of Appeal overturned an unequal division of net family properties awarded by the trial judge because the husband had secretly sent gifts worth about $10,000 to his family in Hungary.

6. An illustration of the kind of situation that was clearly intended to be encompassed by paragraph (d) of s. 5(6) is provided by *Harry* v. *Harry* (1987), 9 R.F.L. (3d) 121 (Ont. Dist. Ct.). Mr. Harry transferred shares valued at $170,800 to his daughter for no consideration a few days before separation. Mossop D.C.J. found (at 126) that "the true motivation for the timing of the gift . . . was to create another impediment to the legitimate claims of the wife" and concluded that equalization of the remaining net family property would be unconscionable. To remedy the situation, Mossop D.C.J. added $85,400 to the equalization payment due to the wife. See also *Burnett* v. *Burnett* (1997), 33 R.F.L. (4th) 356 (Ont. Gen. Div.).

It should be noted that the *FLA* does not empower the court to alter the calculation of a spouse's net family property by attributing to him or her property that no longer belongs to the spouse on the valuation date. If, for example, Mr. Harry's net family property had been reduced to zero by the gift, s. 5(6) would only have permitted the court to allow the wife to retain her net family property of $85,290.80. Nor does the *FLA* permit the court to declare gifts void or to order recovery of the gift from the recipient (compare *Marital Property Act*, R.S.M. 1987, c. M-45, s. 6(7), (8), (9) and (10)).

For an analysis of the adequacy of the safeguards in the *FLA* to protect a non-owning spouse against intentional depletion of net family property by the other spouse, see Hovius and Youdan, *The Law of Family Property* (Toronto: Carswell, 1991) at 409-420. These pages also explore the possible use of the *Fraudulent Conveyances Act*, R.S.O. 1990, c. F.29 in this situation. This issue is addressed in *Polsinelli* v. *Polsinelli* (1991), 33 R.F.L. (3d) 138 (Ont. Gen. Div.) and *Stone* v. *Stone* (1999), 46 O.R. (3d) 31 (Ont. S.C.J.). In the latter case, Justice Hockin stated (at 53) that Part I of the *FLA* "creates a creditor-debtor relationship which takes the form of an open or running account which becomes a settled account on separation or death". Having characterized the Act in this questionable fashion, he then used the *Fraudulent Conveyances Act* to declare "void" certain transfers that Mr. Stone made to his children a few weeks prior to his death. The transfers were intended to reduce his net family property and the children knew of this intention.

In its *Report on Family Property Law* (Toronto: 1993) at 86-100, the O.L.R.C. examined the existing anti-avoidance provisions in the *FLA* and concluded they were inadequate. It recommended that Part 1 be amended to provide as follows:

(a) where a spouse transfers an asset with the intent to defeat a claim that his or her spouse may have under the Act, the value of that asset should be included in his or her net family property;

(b) where a spouse has insufficient assets to satisfy an equalization claim calculated on the basis of the value of an asset transferred with the intent to defeat a claim that his or her spouse may have under the *Family Law Act*, and the transferee knew, or ought to have known, of his or her intent to defeat the claim, the following rules apply:

(i) the transaction is voidable as against his or her spouse;

(ii) where the transaction is avoided,

a. the property in the asset is revested in the spouse;

b. the transferee is entitled to restitution for the value given in consideration of the transfer, subject to a deduction for the value of any benefit received from the use or enjoyment of the property; and

c. the transferee is liable for any depreciation in the value of the asset from the date of the transfer;

(iii) where the transaction is avoided and, prior to avoidance, the asset has been further transferred:

a. to a *bona fide* purchaser for value without notice, the transferor is liable for the proceeds of the transfer, or, in the event that the transfer was undertaken in bad faith, for the market value of the asset, whichever is higher; and

b. to a subsequent transferee not acting in good faith, or to a donee, the subsequent transferee or donee is liable in the same manner as the first transferee;

(c) where a spouse transfers an asset within three months of initiating a separation, a rebuttable presumption arises that he or she intended to defeat a claim that his or her spouse may have under the Act; and

(d) where a spouse applies to have a transaction avoided under paragraph (b), the transferee should receive notice of this application and have the rights of a party to the application.

7. Do you agree with the reasoning in *Futia*? Should the reason for the short period of the cohabitation be considered? See also *Clayburn* v. *Clayburn* (1997), 29 R.F.L. (4th) 12 (Ont. Gen. Div.) In the result, the wife in *Futia* received almost an equal share of the net family properties. Was this too much?

8. In its *Working Paper on Property Rights on Marriage Breakdown* (Vancouver: Ministry of the Attorney General, 1989), the Law Reform Commission of British Columbia observed (at 101) that

paragraph (e) in s. 5(6) of the *FLA* was included because of the special treatment accorded the matrimonial home. Explain.

9. In *Murphy* v. *Murphy* (1987), 17 R.F.L. (3d) 422 (Ont. Dist. Ct.); *Andreoli* v. *Andreoli* (1990), 27 R.F.L. (3d) 142 (Ont. Dist. Ct.); and *Reeson* v. *Kowalik* (1991), 36 R.F.L. (3d) 396 (Ont. Gen. Div.), the net family properties were shared equally even though the husbands had owned the matrimonial homes prior to a short marriage. See also *Cassidy* v. *Cassidy* (1996), 17 R.F.L. (4th) 403 (Ont. Gen. Div.) where the marriage lasted six years. However, there was an unequal sharing in similar circumstances in *Stewart* v. *Stewart* (1991), 39 R.F.L. (3d) 88 (Ont. Gen. Div.); *Pratt* v. *Musselman* (1996), 24 R.F.L. (4th) 308 (Ont. Gen. Div.); *Lendrum* v. *Lendrum* (1997), 33 R.F.L. (4th) 20 (Ont. Gen. Div.); and *Chambers* v. *Chambers* (1997), 34 R.F.L. (4th) 86 (Ont. Gen. Div.).

10. After a series of conflicting lower court cases, the Ontario Court of Appeal held in *MacNeill* v. *Pope* (1999), 43 R.F.L. (4th) 209 that cohabitation by the spouses before their marriage must be considered in computing the period of cohabitation for the purposes of s. 5(6)(e). Do you agree?

11. The Ontario Court of Appeal has also settled the question whether post-valuation date events can be considered in the application of s. 5(6). In *Merklinger* v. *Merklinger* (1996), 26 R.F.L. (4th) 7, it interpreted s. 5(6) as permitting the courts to adjust the equalization payment in light of all circumstances existing at the time the case is decided. See also *McCutcheon* v. *McCutcheon* (1986), 2 R.F.L. (3d) 327 (Ont. Dist. Ct.); *Davies* v. *Davies* (1988), 13 R.F.L. (3d) 278 (Ont. H.C.); *Perrin* v. *Perrin* (1988), 17 R.F.L. (3d) 87 (Ont. Dist. Ct.); *Fletcher* v. *Fletcher* (1993), 1 R.F.L. (4th) 117 (Ont. U.F.C.); *Macedo* v. *Macedo* (1996), 19 R.F.L. (4th) 65 (Ont. Gen. Div.); *Brett* v. *Brett* (1996), 24 R.F.L. (4th) 224 (Ont. Gen. Div.); and *Gallant* v. *Gallant* (1998), 166 D.L.R. (4th) 79 (Man. C.A.).

The O.L.R.C. recommended in its *Report on Family Property Law* (Toronto: 1993) that the *FLA* be amended to state expressly that courts may consider post-separation conduct to the extent that it is relevant to the factors listed in s. 5(6). It also proposed that there be a separate provision granting the courts the power to vary an equalization payment to recognize a substantial post-valuation date change in the value of an asset if necessary to ensure an equitable result, having regard to the cause of the fluctuation. Such a provision appears in s. 6(6) of the *Family Law Act*, S.P.E.I. 1995, c. 12.

12. In *Crawford* v. *Crawford* (1997), 33 R.F.L. (4th) 381 (Ont. C.A.), the husband remortgaged the matrimonial home to consolidate his debt payments. His wife gave her consent only after he promised in writing that she would get $46,000 more from the proceeds when the home was eventually sold. The court held that this was an agreement falling within s. 5(6)(g), but that the net family properties (including the home's value) should nonetheless be shared equally. Equal sharing was not unconscionable given that the debts related to family expenses.

13. Unlike s. 5(7) of the *FLA*, the New Brunswick legislation considered in *LeBlanc* v. *LeBlanc* did not expressly state that equal contribution to the listed responsibilities is inherent in the marital relationship. It was this expression in s. 5(7) that heavily influenced McNeely D.C.J. in *Waters* v. *Waters*. Do you think this is a sufficient basis on which to distinguish *LeBlanc*? See also *Fair* v. *Jones* (1999), 44 R.F.L. (4th) 399 (N.W.T.S.C.), where the court noted the less onerous threshold in the New Brunswick legislation.

For a favourable comment on the approach adopted in *Waters*, see Higginson, "Unequal Sharing of Net Family Properties in Ontario: Will the Exception Swallow Up the Rule?" (1987), 2 C.F.L.Q. 283. For policy arguments in favour of the Supreme Court's approach in *LeBlanc*, see Saskatchewan Law Reform Commission, *Proposals Relating to Matrimonial Property Legislation: Report to the Minister of Justice* (Saskatoon: Saskatchewan Law Reform Commission, 1985) at 9 and Law Reform Commission of British Columbia, *Working Paper on Property Rights on Marriage Breakdown* (Vancouver: Ministry of the Attorney General, 1989) at 55, 64, 66-67.

In *Brett* v. *Brett* (1999), 46 R.F.L. (4th) 433, the Ontario Court of Appeal confirmed that s. 5(6) of the *FLA* constitutes the sole authority for an unequal sharing of net family properties. The court also stated (at 444-445):

> None of the factors set in s. 5(6) (a) to (h) require the court to examine the spouses' respective contributions to household management, child care, and financial provision. If this was to be an

area of specific inquiry to determine if the equalization of net family properties would be unconscionable, the factors listed in s. 5(6) would have been expanded. . . . In establishing the equalization of net family properties in the *Family Law Act*, the Legislature did not intend for the courts
to undertake a post-mortem examination of the sharing of responsibilities to determine if equalizing the spouses' net family properties would be "unconscionable".

Earlier in its reasons, the court noted that the trial judge had correctly concluded that the husband had
not abdicated his child care responsibilities following separation. As Professor McLeod points out in
his annotation to the case in the R.F.L.'s, this may indicate that an unequal sharing can still occur if
there is an abdication of family responsibilities. However, the case suggests that an unequal sharing will
not follow simply because there has been a disparity, perhaps even a gross disparity, in contributions to
family life.

14. In *Berdette* v. *Berdette*, the Ontario Court of Appeal held that s. 5(6) does not apply if the net
family properties are equal. Do you agree with this interpretation? At first glance, the Ontario Court of
Appeal's holding may seem insignificant. In virtually every situation, one spouse's net family property
will be somewhat larger than another's. Even if all major assets are held jointly, one spouse's wardrobe
or cash on hand is likely to be somewhat more valuable than the other's. If s. 5(6) is then available to
allow the court to grant the entire net family properties to one spouse, the holding in *Berdette* can always
be limited to the facts of that case. However, it is possible that the Ontario Court of Appeal in *Berdette*
intended to indicate that the power under s. 5(6) is limited to dealing only with the difference between
the net family properties. If so, a legislative amendment may be necessary to deal with situations such
as the following:

Three weeks before the valuation date, a husband gives his son shares valued at $50,000. This
reduces his net family property to $101,000. The wife's net family property is $100,000.

The O.L.R.C. recommended claw-back provisions to deal with this type of situation (see above,
note 6). It also recommended that s. 5(6) be amended "to empower courts to order an equalization
payment, calculated on the basis of each spouse's net family property, where the spouses have equal net
family properties, if the result would otherwise be unconscionable, having regard to the factors listed in
section 5(6)." See O.L.R.C., *Report on Family Property Law* (Toronto: 1993) at 68.

(4)   IMPLEMENTATION OF THE EQUALIZATION ENTITLEMENT

HOVIUS AND YOUDAN, *THE LAW OF FAMILY PROPERTY*

(Toronto: Carswell, 1991) 449-470 (Edited footnotes follow the excerpt.)

1.   INTRODUCTION

To determine a spouse's entitlement under section 5, the net family properties
of the spouses must be calculated. Once this is done, the spouse with the lesser of
the two net family properties is entitled to one-half the difference between them
unless the court awards a greater or lesser amount under section 5(6). The end result
is that one spouse owes the other a monetary sum (which will be referred to as the
equalization sum in this chapter). Section 9 then empowers the court to make various
orders to ensure that this sum is realized in a fair and effective manner.

Section 9 is, therefore, an implementation provision that only comes into play
after the court has determined the equalization sum under section 5. The section
cannot be used to short circuit the process by, for example, removing assets from
the net family properties and dividing them equally. Although section 9(1)(d) does
empower the court to order the transfer of property from one spouse to the other,
this can only be done after the equalization sum has been calculated based on all
included property owned by each spouse on the valuation date.[1]

The range of options available under section 9 is extensive:

> ... (1) the whole amount can be ordered paid forthwith; (2) if necessary, to avoid hardship, the whole amount can be paid in instalments not exceeding ten years; (3) security may be imposed for the whole or part of the amount; (4) to satisfy all or part of the amount, property may be transferred to the receiving spouse absolutely, for life, or a term of years; (5) to satisfy all or part of the amount, property can be placed in trust or vested in a spouse absolutely, for life, or a term of years; (6) to satisfy all or part of the amount, any property may be partitioned or sold.[2]

The section, therefore, provides the court with considerable flexibility enabling it to balance the interests of the debtor spouse and creditor spouse while choosing the most appropriate method of satisfying the equalization sum in a particular case.[3] In addition, section 11(2) empowers the court to make special orders regarding operating businesses or farms to avoid their sale or the serious impairment of their operations. . . .

2. PAYMENT FORTHWITH

Section 9(1)(a) establishes the court's power to order that one spouse pay to the other the amount to which the latter is entitled under Part I. Since the entitlement created by section 5 itself is to a sum of money, the inclusion of this power naturally follows. Indeed, it is the legislature's decision not to confine the court's power to orders for immediate payment that requires explanation.

The legislature clearly recognized that an order requiring immediate payment of the equalization sum could cause hardship for the debtor spouse in some circumstances. Hence, it empowered the court, if necessary to avoid hardship, to delay the payment for a period of up to ten years or to order payment by instalments during a period not exceeding ten years. This concern is reinforced by section 11(1) which forbids the court from making an order that would require or result in the sale of an operating business or farm or that would seriously impair its operation unless there is no reasonable alternative method of satisfying the award. While certain of the additional powers listed in section 9(1) can, therefore, be explained on the basis that the debtor spouse should not suffer undue hardship in the realization of the equalization sum, others are included for the benefit of the creditor spouse. If the court could only render a money judgment, the creditor spouse would in all cases have to rely for enforcement on the general debtor-creditor law. This could lead to future enforcement problems. In an attempt to avoid these potential problems, the legislature empowered the court to order that property be transferred from one spouse to the other or that it be sold to satisfy the order. The power to order that security be given for the performance of an obligation imposed by the implementation order can be explained on the same basis. In summary, the legislature enabled the courts to choose the most appropriate method of satisfying the equalization sum in each individual case in light of the interests of both the debtor spouse and the creditor spouse.

Many reported cases[10] indicate that the judges begin their assessment of the appropriate method of satisfying the equalization sum with a preference for orders for immediate payment of the entire equalization sum. Such a preference seems reasonable since section 5 itself creates an entitlement to a sum of money. Of course, judges should remain open to the possibility that additional or alternative orders may be necessary to ensure that the equalization sum is realized in a fair and effective manner.

3. SECURITY

Under section 9(1)(b) a court may order that security be given for the performance of an obligation imposed by the implementation order.[11] Such security may
include a charge on property, which can then be registered to ensure priority over
subsequently acquired interests of third parties.[12] The awarding of security pending
payment in full is particularly appropriate where a court orders deferred payment or
payment by instalments pursuant to section 9(1)(c) and there is some concern whether
the money will be paid.[13]

Where an order for security has been made, the court has authority under section
13 to vary or discharge the order on the application of either party. Variation or
discharge might be appropriate in a number of circumstances including situations
where the obligation has been satisfied or where a valid case is made for the disposition of property involved or the transfer of the charge to another piece of property.

Section 13 also empowers a court, on notice to all persons having an interest
in the property, to direct the sale of property for the purpose of realizing the security
or charge imposed.

4. DEFERRED PAYMENT OR INSTALMENT PAYMENTS

(a) When permitted

Section 9(1)(c) permits the court to order that the equalization sum be paid in
instalments during a period not exceeding ten years or that payment of all or part of
the sum be delayed for a period not exceeding ten years. This power can only be
exercised, however, "if necessary to avoid hardship". Thus, the creditor spouse is
entitled to immediate satisfaction of the equalization sum unless this would cause
hardship to the debtor spouse.

Where the equalization sum is created mainly by the inclusion of the value of
a pension in the debtor spouse's net family property, this spouse may not be able to
raise the money necessary to make the payment immediately since the value of the
pension will usually not be accessible. Even if the debtor spouse has sufficient other
liquid assets to permit immediate payment, any order resulting in the sale or transfer
of all or a substantial portion of these assets may be unduly harsh since it would
leave the debtor spouse with only the benefit of a pension which may not be realized
for many years. Some judges have, therefore, ordered deferred payment or payment
by instalments in this situation.[14]

Immediate satisfaction of the equalization sum may also cause hardship where
the debtor spouse's major assets comprise a business or farm which is the source of
this spouse's livelihood. In this context, section 11(1) must be considered. It prohibits
a court from making an order under section 9 that would require or result in the sale
of an operating business or farm or that would seriously impair its operation unless
there is no reasonable alternative method of satisfying the equalization sum. Where
immediate satisfaction of the equalization sum would have this effect, deferred
payment or payment by instalments may represent a reasonable alternative method
by which the sum could be realized. In *McDougall* v. *McDougall*,[16] the wife was
entitled to an equalization sum of $63,980.93. Almost all of the husband's assets
consisted of shares in a farming operation conducted by himself, his father and his
brother. Finding that the immediate payment of the equalization sum would probably
necessitate a sale of the husband's interest in the farm business and that the husband
had "no employment or other economic prospects outside that business",[17] Killeen
D.C.J. concluded that "the fair order is to direct that the defendant pay the equali-

zation sum in five yearly instalments".[18] He also ordered that post-judgment interest be paid on the equalization sum which was to be secured against the husband's shares.

In some situations the solution adopted in *McDougall* v. *McDougall* will not be economically feasible. This was the conclusion reached by Craig J. in *Leslie* v. *Leslie*.[19] . . .

The situations analyzed above represent perhaps the most obvious examples where immediate satisfaction of the equalization sum could cause hardship. However, such hardship could arise in other circumstances and for other reasons.[23] Deferral for a short period of time has, for example, been ordered in some cases[24] to allow the debtor spouse to liquidate assets in an orderly fashion or otherwise raise the necessary funds.

(b) Corollary orders

If the court orders deferred payment or payment by instalments, it may make certain corollary orders under section 9(2) either at the time the original order is made or, on motion, at a later time. It can order that the debtor spouse furnish the other spouse with specified financial information, which may include periodic financial statements. It can also require the debtor spouse to permit inspections of specified property by or on behalf of the other spouse.

(c) Variation

Section 9(3) permits the court to vary the order for deferred payment or payment by instalments where "there has been a material change in the circumstances of the spouse who has the obligation to make instalment or delayed payments". While it might be anticipated that most applications for variation will be made by the debtor spouse for additional deferment of the payment or a reduction in the instalments because of deteriorating financial circumstances, there might well be situations where a creditor spouse could successfully invoke the court's jurisdiction. For example, accelerated payment might be appropriate if the debtor's circumstances have improved. Also, in cases where deferred payment or payment by instalments was ordered to allow the debtor spouse to continue to operate a business or farm, the financial position of this spouse may be deteriorating to such an extent that there is a legitimate concern whether the order will ever be fulfilled. Section 9(3) appears to be broad enough to allow the court to order sale of the debtor's assets so that the equalization sum can be realized before the value of these assets declines even further. The financial statements and inspections of property contemplated by section 9(2) might serve to alert the creditor spouse to the need for a variation order on this basis.

Even if a material change in circumstances is established, section 9(3) explicitly prohibits the court from varying the amount of the equalization sum. Also, subsection (4) provides that the power to vary the order does not permit the court to postpone payment beyond the original ten year period.

(d) Interest

Section 9 does not specifically empower the court to order the payment of interest on deferred payments or payments by instalments. However, payment of interest has been ordered in several cases,[26] presumably pursuant to sections 139 and

140 of the *Courts of Justice Act, 1984*.[27] In other cases, the courts have not addressed the issue,[28] while in a third set of cases[29] the judges have specifically directed that no interest be paid without explaining the rationale for this decision.

As a general principle, interest should normally be payable from the date of the order providing for deferred payment or payment by instalments. Otherwise, the creditor spouse's payment will be diminished by the effect of inflation and there will be a *de facto* unequal sharing of net family properties. Moreover, delay in the realization of the equalization sum is obviously detrimental to the creditor spouse who is denied the use of the money in the interim. Unless there is good reason why this detriment should be borne solely by the creditor spouse,[31] compensation in the form of interest is appropriate.

5.   PROPERTY ORDERS

(a)   Introduction

Under section 9(1)(d) the court is empowered to make a number of orders dealing directly with the spouses' property where "appropriate to satisfy an obligation imposed by the order". . . .

(b)   Transfer of property

Section 9(1)(d)(i) has provided the basis for what has become known as an "if and when" order regarding the portion of the equalization sum attributable to a pension held by the debtor spouse to prevent the hardship that could result if immediate payment of the sum was required. Under such orders, the court directs that the debtor spouse hold a portion of the pension in trust for the other, with payments generally to commence once the pension is received.

Except for these special orders relating to pensions, orders requiring the transfer of property to satisfy the equalization sum have been infrequent. In several cases,[35] however, the courts have ordered a transfer of the debtor spouse's interest in a jointly owned matrimonial home to the creditor spouse. In *Oliva* v. *Oliva*[36] the husband owed the wife an equalization sum of $28,729.10. His most substantial asset was a partnership interest in a hairdressing business and McDermid L.J.S.C. found that it was most unlikely that his partners would consent to the sale of any partnership property to pay the equalization sum. Immediate satisfaction of the equalization sum could, therefore, only be achieved by looking to the husband's equity in the jointly owned matrimonial home. Rather than order the sale of that asset and payment out of the husband's share of the proceeds, McDermid L.J.S.C. acceded to the wife's request that the court order the husband to transfer his interest in the matrimonial home and its contents to the wife in satisfaction of $24,750.00 of the total sum owing. The balance was to be paid within one year with interest. In this way the equalization sum could be realized and the wife and children could continue to reside in the matrimonial home.

Corless v. *Corless*[41] is another case in which the power to transfer property was utilized partly to ensure that the wife and children would be able to continue living in the matrimonial home. In the proceedings for equalization of net family properties, Mrs. Corless applied for an exclusive possession order allowing her and the children to remain indefinitely in the jointly owned matrimonial home. Steinberg U.F.C.J. was reluctant to grant this order because it would tie up the husband's equity of $37,807.50 and this was the only resource that the husband could realistically tap to pay the equalization sum of $22,651. Also, the judge believed that the husband should purchase the wife's interest in a partnership which owned the offices in which the husband's law firm was located. This interest was valued at approximately $9,956. To resolve these matters, the Court made several unique orders. The wife's interest in the partnership was vested in the husband and the husband's interest in the home was vested in the wife. Since the value of the husband's interest in the home exceeded the combined value of the wife's interest in the partnership and the equalization sum due to her, the wife then owed the husband $5,200.50. This amount was secured by requiring the wife to grant the husband a mortgage on the matrimonial home.

The *Corless* v. *Corless* case is unique in two respects. First, the value of the property that the debtor spouse was required to transfer exceeded the equalization sum due to the other spouse. As a result, the latter owed the former a sum of money after the transfer. Second, the Court ordered the transfer of property from the spouse entitled to an equalization sum to the other spouse.

In both respects, Steinberg U.F.C.J. may have exceeded his powers and certainly interpreted section 9(1)(d)(i) more broadly than other judges have. Section 9(1)(d)(i) does not give the court a general authority to divide the spouses' property in a fair and equitable manner. Rather, it only permits the court to order property transfers where this is an appropriate means of realizing the equalization sum owing to one spouse. It is difficult to characterize an order requiring the creditor spouse to transfer property to the debtor spouse as a means of satisfying the debt.[46] Numerous cases[47] have, therefore, concluded that the court has no authority under Part I of the Act to rearrange assets between the parties and then compensate for any difference in value by requiring one spouse to pay a sum of money to the other. In effect, this is what occurred in *Corless* v. *Corless*. It is also doubtful whether a court can order the debtor spouse to transfer property valued at more than the equalization sum and then require the creditor spouse to pay the difference.[48] This may be characterized as using section 9(1)(d)(i) to create a new equalization entitlement rather than to satisfy an existing one.

While Steinberg U.F.C.J. probably interpreted the power granted by section 9(1)(d)(i) too broadly, some cases contain comments tending too far in the opposite direction. In *Heon* v. *Heon*, Granger J. stated categorically:

> Equalization is to be satisfied by a money judgment. The court can only order property transferred or sold if such order is required to satisfy a monetary equalization payment (see s. 9(1), F.L.A.). As long as a spouse can satisfy a monetary equalization payment, he or she is entitled to retain his or her property and a court should not transfer property or order the sale of jointly held property. . . .
>
> In my opinion, s. 9(1)(d)(i) of the F.L.A. should not be used to redistribute assets, where the paying spouse can satisfy the equalization payment by an immediate cash payment. Transfer or sale of assets under s. 9(1)(d) should only be resorted to in order to ensure the equalization payment is satisfied. In this case there are sufficient assets available which can be liquidated to satisfy the equalization payment and a transfer of the R.R.S.P. [from the husband to the wife] cannot be justified under s. 9(1)(d)(i).[50]

In other cases Granger J. has held that, even if his restrictive test for the application of section 9(1)(d) is met, a sale of jointly held property should be ordered under paragraph (ii) rather than a transfer of the debtor spouse's interest in that property to the creditor spouse. In *Wilson* v. *Wilson*, he said:

> If the parties are prepared to agree upon current value of the assets and the means of effecting the equalization payment, including transfer of property, the court can give effect to such an agree-

ment. Failing any such agreement, however, the court should order the sale of all jointly held property in order to ensure that fair market value is obtained.[51]

He elaborated on this point in a later case:

> In *Wilson* . . . I held that a court should not transfer property to satisfy an equalization payment or allow a joint owner to purchase his or her co-tenant's interest for a fixed price.
>
> A joint tenant is entitled to the highest price for his or her interest which may be more than the appraised value of the property. In today's real estate market, the appraised value of the property may not reflect the fair market value. The true test of the fair market value is to sell the property in an open market. Unless the parties agree to a transfer of the property at an agreed price, the property should be listed for sale and sold, to ensure that fair market value is obtained.[52]

Both Granger J.'s general approach to section 9(1)(d) and his virtual refusal to consider transfers of property as an appropriate means of satisfying an equalization claim are suspect. The language of section 9(1)(d) indicates that the powers granted in the two subparagraphs can be used to satisfy an equalization sum "if appropriate". In effect, Granger J. substitutes the word "required" for "appropriate", thereby robbing section 9(1) of some of its intended flexibility. He attempts to insert certainty and predictability into the application of section 9(1),[53] but the legislature's choice of words indicates that the court is to exercise discretion in determining how the equalization sum is to be realized. According to the test articulated by Granger J., the powers granted by section 9(1)(d) should only be exercised where the debtor spouse lacks sufficient liquid assets to satisfy the equalization sum. However, there may be other circumstances where an "orderly and equitable settlement of the affairs of the spouses"[54] requires the exercise of these powers. For example, an "if and when" order under subparagraph (i) regarding the portion of the equalization sum attributable to a pension held by the debtor spouse may be appropriate even if the debtor spouse could, by selling all other assets, satisfy the payment.[55] Again, an order under subparagraph (ii) requiring the sale of jointly held property and payment out of the debtor spouse's share of the proceeds may be an appropriate way to ensure payment without future enforcement problems even if the debtor spouse could make the payment by liquidating other assets.

Similarly, Granger J.'s assertion that a court should only order a transfer of the debtor spouse's interest in jointly held property to satisfy the equalization sum where both spouses favour such a transfer and agree on the present value of this interest seems unduly restrictive.[57] The legislature granted the courts the power to transfer the property not only where both parties consent, but whenever this is an appropriate method of satisfying an equalization sum. Where the creditor spouse wishes to remain in the jointly owned matrimonial home, for example, a transfer of the debtor spouse's interest in total or partial satisfaction of the equalization sum may be the best way to bring the parties' relationship to an end in an "orderly and equitable" manner. A forced sale of the matrimonial home could be very disruptive for the creditor spouse and any children involved. On the other hand, an order for exclusive possession would tie up the debtor spouse's equity in the home and would require the spouses to continue their economic relationship to some extent.

It must be acknowledged, however, that Mr. Justice Granger's concern that a transfer of property requires an accurate valuation of the property at the time of trial is a legitimate one. Certainly, the court cannot simply adopt the value that was used in calculating the net family properties because there may well have been a change in the property's value since the valuation date. While the requirement for yet another valuation introduces even more complexity and difficulty into the equalization process, a transfer of property to satisfy the equalization sum should remain an option as long as the court has sufficient evidence to allow it to assess the present value of the property in a realistic fashion.

One further complication that may be introduced by the transfer of property should be noted. A transfer of property may necessitate a reassessment of the treatment of notional sale costs and taxes payable on the disposition of the property in calculating the net family property of the transferor.[58] If property is transferred between the spouses, there will be no immediate sale and the transferor will not have to pay commission to a real estate agent. It would, therefore, be inappropriate to take these notional sales costs into account in the calculation of the transferor's net family property. Moreover, the "rollover" provisions in the *Income Tax Act*[59] may apply so that there are no immediate tax consequences for the transferor. Instead, there may be future tax consequences for the transferee who steps into the transferor's shoes for tax purposes. These consequences should be considered in determining how much of the equalization sum is satisfied by the transfer.

(c) Sale of Property

Subparagraph (ii) of section 9(1)(d) empowers the court to order the partition or sale of any property "if appropriate to satisfy an obligation imposed by the order". The most common order made under this subparagraph requires the sale of property held jointly by the spouses with payment of all or some of the equalization sum to be made out of the debtor spouse's share of the proceeds.[60] Since a sale of jointly held property will frequently be required in any event so that both spouses can realize their ownership interest,[61] ordering the sale under section 9(1)(d) and stipulating that the equalization sum be paid out of the proceeds interferes little with the property rights of the debtor spouse while it ensures payment without future enforcement problems. Orders for the sale of property owned exclusively by the debtor spouse with payment of the equalization sum out of the proceeds interfere more significantly with the proprietary interests of this spouse. However, they too may be appropriate in some cases[63] to avoid future enforcement problems which might be anticipated if the court simply imposed an obligation to pay a sum of money. . . .

6. SPECIAL POWERS RELATING TO OPERATING BUSINESSES OR FARMS

As previously noted, section 11(1) prohibits a court from making an order under section 9 that would require or result in the sale of an operating business or farm or that would seriously impair its operation unless there is no reasonable alternative method of satisfying the equalization sum. In some circumstances, deferred payment or payment by instalments may be a reasonable way in which the debtor spouse can satisfy the equalization sum while continuing to operate a business or farm. In *Leslie* v. *Leslie*,[70] the Court concluded that any form of deferred payment was not economically feasible and it carefully designed an order requiring the sale of some farm property to permit payment of the equalization sum without undue impairment of the farm operation.

Section 11(2) provides for additional orders whereby the equalization sum may be satisfied without a sale or serious impairment of a business or farm operation. Under paragraph (a), a court may order that the debtor spouse pay the other spouse a share of the profits from the business or farm. If the business or farm is incorporated, paragraph (b) empowers the court to order "that one spouse transfer or have the corporation issue to the other shares in the corporation".[71]

The prohibition created by section 11(1) is obviously not absolute. A court is prohibited from making an order under section 9 that would require or result in the sale of an operating business or farm or that would seriously impair its operation only if there is a reasonable alternative method of satisfying the equalization sum. The effect of section 11(2) is to expand the range of alternatives the court may consider. But if none of these is viewed as a reasonable way of satisfying the award, then the court may make an order for immediate satisfaction of the equalization sum even if this order would bring the business or farm operation to an end.

There are no reported cases in which the special powers granted by section 11(2) have been utilized. This may be explained partly by the fact that the courts have looked first to the various options provided by section 9(1) itself, including deferred payment or payment by instalments. Where one of these represents a reasonable way of satisfying the equalization sum without a forced sale of the farm or business, there is no need to examine the possible use of section 11(2). On the other hand, where none of these other options is economically feasible, it is unlikely that an order for the sharing of profits in some way will be either, particularly if the creditor spouse is to be compensated for the loss of the use of the capital represented by the equalization sum. Moreover, an order under section 11(2) would require the spouses to continue their economic relationship to some extent and thus provide fertile ground for future dispute.[74] This will be enough to make such orders unattractive to both parties in most circumstances. In conclusion, orders under section 11(2) are likely to remain rare.

7. PREJUDGMENT INTEREST

There is no provision in the *Family Law Act* regarding prejudgment interest. However, sections 137-140 of the *Courts of Justice Act, 1984*[75] apply. Pursuant to section 138(1), "a person who is entitled to an order for the payment of money is entitled to claim and have included in the order an award of interest thereon at the prejudgment interest rate,[76] calculated from the date the cause of action arose to the date of the order". Section 140(1) then empowers the court "where it considers it just to do so" to disallow such interest, allow it at a higher or lower rate, or allow it for a period other than that provided in section 138. Thus, a successful litigant has a *prima facie* right to prejudgment interest and the onus is upon the party to persuade the trial Judge to exercise his or her discretion to the contrary.

Prejudgment interest on the equalization payment ordered under Part I of the *Family Law Act* has been allowed in some cases[81] and denied in others.[82] To some extent the different results can be explained by the individual circumstances of each case, but it also appears that some judges allow prejudgment interest more readily than others. The cases do reveal that the following factors[83] have been influential:

1. whether the debtor spouse unreasonably refused payment or caused delays in the proceedings;[84]
2. whether the assets of the debtor spouse could have been liquidated easily so as to satisfy the equalization sum;[85]
3. whether the creditor spouse obtained an order restraining the sale of assets by the debtor spouse or in some way prevented liquidation of the assets;[86]
4. whether the assets of the debtor spouse produced income;[87]

5. whether the assets of the debtor spouse appreciated following the valuation date;[88]
6. whether the debtor spouse supported the creditor spouse following separation;[89]
7. whether the creditor spouse had the use of assets owned partly or exclusively by the debtor spouse following the valuation date;[90] and
8. the size of the equalization sum and the amount of interest that would be payable.[91]

---

1 *Marsham* v. *Marsham* (1987), 7 R.F.L. (3d) 1 (Ont. H.C.). See also *Skrlj* v. *Skrlj* (1986), 2 R.F.L. (3d) 305 (Ont. H.C.); *Humphreys* v. *Humphreys* (1987), 7 R.F.L. (3d) 113 (Ont. H.C.); *Wilson* v. *Wilson* (1988), 14 R.F.L. (3d) 98 (Ont. H.C.); *Batler* v. *Batler* (1988), 18 R.F.L. (3d) 211 at 213 (Ont. H.C.); *Alger* v. *Alger* (1989), 21 R.F.L. (3d) 211 (Ont. H.C.); and *Heon* v. *Heon* (1989), 22 R.F.L. (3d) 273 at 294 (Ont. H.C.). Cf. *Porter* v. *Porter* (1986), 1 R.F.L. (3d) 12 (Ont. Dist. Ct.); *Storms* v. *Storms* (1988), 14 R.F.L. (3d) 317 (Ont. Dist. Ct.); *Suchostawsky* v. *Suchostawsky* (16 October 1990), Kitchener 19292/89 (Ont. Gen. Div.), where the court ordered sharing of a pension without determining its value on the valuation date and including this value in the net family property calculation.

2 *Marsham* v. *Marsham, ibid.* at 20.

3 This point is stressed in *Kukolj* v. *Kukolj* (1986), 3 R.F.L. (3d) 359 at 371 (Ont. U.F.C.); *Marsham* v. *Marsham, supra,* note 1 at 20; and *Hilderley* v. *Hilderley* (1989), 21 R.F.L. (3d) 383 at 394-395 (Ont. H.C.).

10 See, e.g., *Skrlj* v. *Skrlj, supra,* note 1; *Humphreys* v. *Humphreys, supra,* note 1; *Cotter* v. *Cotter* (1988), 12 R.F.L. (3d) 209 (Ont. H.C.); *Wilson* v. *Wilson, supra,* note 1; *Batler* v. *Batler, supra,* note 1; *Heon* v. *Heon, supra,* note 1; *Baker* v. *Baker* (1989), 22 R.F.L. (3d) 346 (Ont. U.F.C.); *Butt* v. *Butt* (1989), 22 R.F.L. (3d) 415 (Ont. H.C.); and *Hodgins* v. *Hodgins* (1989), 23 R.F.L. (3d) 302 (Ont. H.C.).

11 The wording of paragraph (b) indicates clearly that the granting of security is meant to ensure compliance with other court orders implementing the equalization award. It is not by itself a method of implementing the award.

12 See s. 2(11).

13 See, e.g., *Kukolj* v. *Kukolj, supra,* note 3; *Rawluk* v. *Rawluk* (1986), 3 R.F.L. (3d) 113 (Ont. H.C.), affirmed (1987), 10 R.F.L. (3d) 113 (Ont. C.A.), which was affirmed (1990), 23 R.F.L. (3d) 337 (S.C.C.); *Corless* v. *Corless* (1987), 5 R.F.L. (3d) 256 (Ont. U.F.C.); and *McDougall* v. *McDougall* (1989), 23 R.F.L. (3d) 320 (Ont. Dist. Ct.).

14 See *Kukolj* v. *Kukolj, supra,* note 3; *Messier* v. *Messier* (1986), 5 R.F.L. (3d) 251 (Ont. Dist. Ct.); and *Smith* v. *Smith* (1987), 5 A.C.W.S. (3d) 353 (Ont. Dist. Ct.).

16 *Supra,* note 13.

17 *Ibid.* at 326.

18 *Ibid.*

19 (1987), 9 R.F.L. (3d) 82 (Ont. H.C.).

23 Where the creditor spouse is granted exclusive possession of the matrimonial home owned exclusively or partly by the debtor spouse, immediate satisfaction of the equalization sum may also cause hardship. See *Ward* v. *Ward* (1990), 26 R.F.L. (3d) 149 (Ont. C.A.).

24 This appears to have been the basis for the deferral of payment of part of the equalization sum in *Oliva* v. *Oliva* (1986), 2 R.F.L. (3d) 188 (Ont. H.C.), varied (1988), 12 R.F.L. (3d) 334 (Ont C.A.) and *Peake* v. *Peake* (1989), 21 R.F.L. (3d) 364 (Ont. H.C.). See also *Rawluk* v. *Rawluk, supra,* note 13.

26 See, e.g., *Oliva* v. *Oliva, supra*, note 24; *Woeller* v. *Woeller* (1988), 15 R.F.L. (3d) 120 (Ont. Dist. Ct.); and *McDougall* v. *McDougall, supra*, note 13.

27 S.O. 1984, c. 11. The *Courts of Justice Act, 1984* was explicitly referred to in *Oliva* v. *Oliva, supra*, note 24. The judges in *Woeller* v. *Woeller, supra*, note 26 and *McDougall* v. *McDougall, supra*, note 13 ordered payment of interest without alluding to the jurisdictional basis for such orders.

28 See, e.g., *Rawluk* v. *Rawluk, supra*, note 13 and *Kukolj* v. *Kukolj, supra*, note 3. Where the order for deferred payment or payment by instalments is silent regarding postjudgment interest, such interest may still be payable pursuant to s. 139(1) of the *Court of Justice Act, 1984* at the postjudgment interest rate established by the Act. See *Rickett* v. *Rickett* (1990), 25 R.F.L. (3d) 188 (Ont. H.C.) where Granger J. simply assumed postjudgment interest would be payable.

29 See, e.g., *Messier* v. *Messier, supra*, note 14; and *Peake* v. *Peake, supra*, note 24.

31 Where, for example, the creditor spouse is granted exclusive possession of a matrimonial home owned partly or wholly by the debtor spouse and the creditor spouse is not required to pay occupation rent, interest on the deferred payment of the equalization sum might not be appropriate. While the creditor spouse is denied the benefit of immediate payment, he or she has the use of an asset owned by the debtor spouse. This should be taken into account in determining whether any interest should be payable and, if so, the rate.

35 In addition to the cases discussed in the text, see *Peake* v. *Peake, supra*, note 24. See also *Hulme* v. *Hulme* (1989), 27 R.F.L. (3d) 403 (Ont. H.C.) where the wife was ordered to transfer ownership of a car to the husband in partial satisfaction of the equalization sum.

36 *Supra*, note 24.

41 *Supra*, note 13.

46 In *Alger* v. *Alger, supra*, note 1, the Court explicitly held that it had no authority under s. 9(1)(d)(i) to order that the creditor spouse transfer property to or hold property in trust for the debtor spouse.

47 See, in particular, *Skrlj* v. *Skrlj, supra*, note 1; *Humphreys* v. *Humphreys, supra*, note 1; *Cotter* v. *Cotter, supra*, note 10; *Wilson* v. *Wilson, supra*, note 1; and *Heon* v. *Heon, supra*, note 1. In *Humphreys* v. *Humphreys*, Mr. Justice Galligan went so far as to warn (at 126): ". . . if persons continue . . . to come to court with the expectation that the court will rearrange their assets and use the equalization provisions of the Act to make orders to compensate for different values of assets, . . . they will do so at a very serious risk of costs."

48 It can certainly be implied from the cases listed in note 47 that the court has no such power. See also McLeod, "Annotation" (1989), 22 R.F.L. (3d) 415.

50 *Supra*, note 1 at 297-298.

51 *Supra*, note 1 at 110-111.

52 *Batler* v. *Batler, supra*, note 1 at 213.

53 In *Heon* v *Heon, supra*, note 1, he explained (at 298): "In my opinion, a strict interpretation of the F.L.A. will provide separating spouses with rules that they know will be applied, and, however harsh, will reduce matrimonial litigation."

54 This is explicitly declared to be the purpose of the Act in the preamble. Walsh J. referred to these words in *Marsham* v. *Marsham, supra*, note 1 at 22 in determining that an order under s. 9(1)(d)(i) was appropriate.

55 See, e.g., *Marsham* v. *Marsham, supra*, note 1.

57 This assertion would presumably apply with equal force to a transfer of property held exclusively by the debtor spouse.

58. This was noted by Potts J. in *Kelly* v. *Kelly* (1986), 2 R.F.L. (3d) 1 at 9 (Ont. H.C.).

59 Section 73 and s. 146(16) of the *Income Tax Act*, R.S.C. 1952, c. 148, as amended by S.C. 1970-71-72, c. 63 and as subsequently amended. See generally, Interpretation Bulletin IT-325R; Suzuki, *Income Tax Consequences of Separation and Divorce* (1984); and *Canadian Master Tax Guide*, 43rd ed. (1988).

60 See, e.g., *Marsham* v. *Marsham, supra*, note 1; *Humphreys* v. *Humphreys, supra*, note 1; *Wilson* v. *Wilson, supra*, note 1; and *Dimitry* v. *Dimitry* (1990), 26 R.F.L. (3d) 418 (Ont. C.A.). See also *Rickett* v. *Rickett, supra*, note 28 where the Court found that the wife held one-half of the beneficial interest in the home for the husband. The Court ordered the sale of the home and the payment of the equalization sum out of the husband's share of the proceeds.

61 Theoretically, separated spouses could continue to hold property jointly even after their net family properties have been equalized. However, spouses whose personal relationship has ended are unlikely to wish to do so. If the court does not order the sale of jointly held property under s. 9(1)(d) as a method of realizing the equalization sum, a sale order under s. 10(1) of the Act or under the *Partition Act*, R.S.O. 1980, c. 369 may still be required. See, e.g., *Skrlj* v. *Skrlj, supra*, note 1; *Humphreys* v. *Humphreys, supra*, note 1; and *Cotter* v. *Cotter, supra*, note 10.

63 Such orders were made in *Folga* v. *Folga* (1986), 2 R.F.L. (3d) 358 (Ont. H.C.) and *Leslie* v. *Leslie, supra*, note 19.

70 *Supra*, note 19.

71 Regarding the use of such orders and the impact of a provision in the articles of incorporation providing that no shares may be transferred without the consent of the board of directors, see Mannering and Hainsworth, "Private Corporations — Keeping Control in the Wake of the Family Law Act, 1986 (Ontario)" (1990), 6 C.F.L.Q. 23.

74 Such disputes might involve the determination of the business' or farm's profits or allegations that the business or farm is not being operated efficiently. See, generally, McLeod, "Annotation" (1986), 2 R.F.L. (3d) 2 and Law Reform Commission of British Columbia, *Working Paper on Property Rights on Marriage Breakdown* (1989) at 132-133.

75 S.O. 1984, c. 11. The Ontario Court of Appeal confirmed the applicability of this statute's provisions regarding prejudgment interest in *Starkman* v. *Starkman* (1990), 28 R.F.L. (3d) 208 at 216.

76 Section 137(1)(d) of the *Courts of Justice Act, 1984* defines "prejudgment interest rate" as "the bank rate at the end of the first day of the last month of the quarter preceding the quarter in which the proceeding was commenced, rounded to the nearest tenth of a percentage point". This clause was enacted by S.O. 1989, c. 67, s. 5 and altered the previous definition. It applies only to causes of action arising after October 23, 1989.

81 See, e.g., *Skrlj* v. *Skrlj, supra*, note 1; *Evans* v. *Evans* (1988), 16 R.F.L. (3d) 437 (Ont. H.C.); *Mittler* v. *Mittler* (1988), 17 R.F.L. (3d) 113 (Ont. H.C.); *Fitzpatrick* v. *Fitzpatrick* (1988), 17 R.F.L. (3d) 278 (Ont. Dist. Ct.); *Heon* v. *Heon, supra*, note 1; *Hodgins* v. *Hodgins, supra*, note 10; *Sutherland* v. *Sutherland* (1990), 26 R.F.L. (3d) 49 (Ont. Dist. Ct.); *Andreoli* v. *Andreoli* (1990), 27 R.F.L. (3d) 142 (Ont. Dist. Ct.); *Starkman* v. *Starkman, supra* note 75; and *Balcombe* v. *Balcombe* (1990), 30 R.F.L. (3d) 177 (Ont. Div. Ct.). See also *Bauerfind* v. *Bauerfind* (1989), 19 R.F.L. (3d) 375 (Alta. Q.B.).

82 See, e.g., *Rawluk* v. *Rawluk, supra*, note 13; *Dibbley* v. *Dibbley* (1986), 5 R.F.L. (3d) 381 (Ont. H.C.); *Humphreys* v. *Humphreys, supra*, note 1; *Leslie* v. *Leslie, supra*, note 19; *Harry* v. *Harry* (1987), 9 R.F.L. (3d) 121 (Ont. Dist. Ct.); *Moore* v. *Moore* (1987), 7 R.F.L. (3d) 390 (Ont. H.C.); *Woeller* v. *Woeller, supra*, note 26; *Black* v. *Black* (1988), 18 R.F.L. (3d) 303 (Ont. H.C.); *Katz* v. *Katz* (1989), 21 R.F.L. (3d) 167 (Ont. U.F.C.); *Butt* v. *Butt, supra*, note 10; *Barbeau* v. *Barbeau* (1989), 26 R.F.L. (3d) 282 (Ont. H.C.) and *Dimitry* v. *Dimitry, supra*, note 60.

83 These are factors that have been considered in various cases. There is, however, no consensus in the cases that each of these factors is relevant. It should also be noted that many of these cases were decided before the amendments of 1989 which provide a longer list of factors to be considered than did the old legislation. Significantly, however, the new list of factors continues to include "the circumstances of the

case" and "any other relevant consideration". Therefore, the amendments do not bring to an end the debate over which factors are relevant.

84 In particular, see *Leslie* v. *Leslie, supra,* note 19, where Craig J. noted (at 102) that "the instant case cannot be compared with a case where money is wrongfully withheld by a defendant" and *Katz* v. *Katz, supra,* note 82 where Wallace U.F.C.J. stated (at 172): "[T]his is not an appropriate case for prejudgment interest to be awarded as the action proceeded expeditiously, and the material respecting valuation which needed to be accumulated was substantial and complex." This comment suggests that prejudgment interest should only be awarded if there has been an undue delay caused by the debtor spouse. This view has not been generally adopted.

85 See, e.g., *Humphreys* v. *Humphreys, supra,* note 1; *Heon* v. *Heon, supra,* note 1 at 302; and *Sutherland* v. *Sutherland, supra,* note 81. Obviously, this factor overlaps to some extent with the first one listed.

86 See *Heon* v. *Heon, supra,* note 1 at 302. Again, there is considerable overlap between this factor and the first two listed.

87 This was a determining factor in the award of interest in *Skrlj* v. *Skrlj, supra,* note 1 and *Andreoli* v. *Andreoli, supra,* note 81. Indeed, some cases seem to suggest that prejudgment interest should not be awarded if there is a *bona fide* dispute regarding the equalization sum unless the debtor spouse has earned income from his or her assets since the valuation date. See, e.g., *Harry* v. *Harry, supra,* note 82; *Woeller* v. *Woeller, supra,* note 26; and *Jukosky* v. *Jukosky* (1990), 31 R.F.L. (3d) 117 (Ont. Gen. Div.). See also McLeod, "Annotation" (1987), 4 R.F.L. (3d) 338; McLeod, "Annotation" (1987), 8 R.F.L. (3d) 338; McLeod, "Annotation" (1988), 15 R.F.L. (3d) 122; and McLeod, "Annotation" (1989), 21 R.F.L. (3d) 389. *Cf.,* however, *Mittler* v. *Mittler, supra,* note 81; *Fitzpatrick* v. *Fitzpatrick, supra,* note 81; and *Heon* v. *Heon, supra,* note 1 at 302.

88 See *Heon* v. *Heon, supra,* note 1 at 302. Of course, if this fact has resulted in an unequal sharing of the net family properties in favour of the creditor spouse, then an award of prejudgment interest would not be appropriate.

89 In *Dibbley* v. *Dibbley, supra,* note 82; *Harry* v. *Harry, supra,* note 82; *Moore* v. *Moore, supra,* note 82; *Black* v. *Black, supra,* note 82; and *Butt* v. *Butt, supra,* note 10, the courts refused to award prejudgment interest partly because the debtor spouse had supported the creditor spouse following separation. In his note on the *Black* v. *Black* case ((1988), 18 R.F.L. (3d) 303), Professor McLeod explains (at 304-305) the relevance of this factor:

> If the money were paid promptly, the income from capital could properly be taken into account in assessing the needs and means of the recipient. In *Black* if the money had been paid promptly, the wife would have had no need . . . and no support would have been awarded. By paying support as he did, the husband put the wife into the same position as to income that she would have been in had early payment been made, and any benefit to him and loss to her from delayed payment was redressed. Accordingly, the decision to refuse prejudgment interest seems reasonable. It should be a question in each case whether the support paid properly addressed the basis for awarding prejudgment interest.

In *Mittler* v. *Mittler, supra,* note 81, prejudgment interest was awarded to the wife but an amount equal to the interim support payments paid by the husband during the period covered by the interest payment was deducted.

90 In *Dibbley* v. *Dibbley, supra,* note 82; *Moore* v. *Moore, supra* note 82; *Dimitry* v. *Dimitry, supra,* note 60; and *Marsh* v. *Marsh, supra,* note 82, the courts refused to award prejudgment interest partly because the debtor spouse had exclusive possession of the matrimonial home.

91 See *Rawluk* v. *Rawluk, supra,* note 13; *Leslie* v. *Leslie, supra,* note 19; and *Black* v. *Black, supra,* note 82. However, in *Heon* v. *Heon, supra,* note 1, Granger J. stated (at 302): "The size of the equalization payment should not be a factor in determining if prejudgment interest should be awarded."

Section 140(2) now explicitly lists "the amount claimed and the amount recovered in the proceeding" (paragraph (e)) as a factor to be taken into account. However, this paragraph is unlikely to end the debate over whether the size of the equalization payment by itself should be a consideration. By referring to both the amount claimed and the amount recovered in the same paragraph, s. 140(2) may simply be indicating that the reasonableness of the amount originally claimed is a factor.

NOTES AND QUESTIONS

1. For more recent cases where one spouse was ordered to transfer property to another to satisfy all or part of the equalization payment, see *James* v. *James* (1994), 3 R.F.L. (4th) 226 (Ont. Gen. Div.); *McDonald* v. *McDonald* (1994), 5 R.F.L. (4th) 215 (Ont. Gen. Div.); *Brosseau* v. *Shemilt* (1995), 16 R.F.L. (4th) 129 (Ont. Gen. Div.); *Marjanovic* v. *Marjanovic* (1996), 24 R.F.L. (4th) 108 (Ont. Gen. Div.); *Burnett* v. *Burnett* (1997), 33 R.F.L. (4th) 356 (Ont. Gen. Div.); and *Best* v. *Best* (1997), 31 R.F.L. (4th) 1 (Ont. C.A.), reversed (1999), 49 R.F.L. (4th) 1 (S.C.C.). In *Best*, the S.C.C. commented (paragraph 109) that the choice of the appropriate implementation method was "highly contextual and fact-based".

2. Regarding the tax consequences of property transfers between spouses on marriage breakdown and the way in which such transfers may be used to minimize the tax consequences of the breakdown, see Arnold, Edgar, Li, and Sandler, *Materials on Canadian Income Tax, 11th ed.* (Toronto: Carswell, 1996); Beam and Laiken, *Introduction to Federal Taxation in Canada, 19th ed.* (North York: CCH Canadian Limited, 1998); and Cole and Freedman, *Property Valuation and Income Tax Implications of Marital Dissolution* (Toronto: Carswell) (looseleaf service).

3. Recall the use of an "if and when" order regarding the husband's contingent interest in the Biddle estate in *DaCosta* v. *DaCosta* (1992), 40 R.F.L. (3d) 216 (Ont. C.A.).

4. The cases reported after the Hovius and Youdan text was published continue to exhibit considerable divergence in the treatment of prejudgment interest. Prejudgment interest was awarded in *Verboom* v. *Verboom* (1991), 83 D.L.R. (4th) 434 (Ont. Gen. Div.); *Christian* v. *Christian* (1991), 37 R.F.L. (3d) 26 (Ont. Gen. Div.); *Salib* v. *Cross* (1993), 15 O.R. (3d) 521 (Gen. Div.); *Sengmueller* v. *Sengmueller* (1994), 17 O.R. (3d) 208, 2 R.F.L. (4th) 232 (C.A.); *Price* v. *Price* (1994), 3 R.F.L. (4th) 1 (Ont. Gen. Div.); *Saeglitz* v. *Saeglitz* (1994), 3 R.F.L. (4th) 244 (Ont. U.F.C.); *McDonald* v. *McDonald* (1994), 5 R.F.L. (4th) 215 (Ont. Gen. Div.); *Zander* v. *Zander* (1994), 8 R.F.L. (4th) 35 (Ont. Gen. Div.); *Purcell* v. *Purcell* (1995), 11 R.F.L. (4th) 181 (Ont. Gen. Div.); *Bascello* v. *Bascello* (1995), 18 R.F.L. (4th) 362 (Ont. Gen. Div.); *Calvert (Litigation Guardian of)* v. *Calvert* (1997), 32 O.R. (3d) 281 (Gen. Div.); *Brett* v. *Brett* (1999), 46 R.F.L. (4th) 433 (Ont. C.A.); and *Singh* v. *Singh* (1999), 1 R.F.L. (5th) 136 (Ont. S.C.J.). No prejudgment interest was awarded in *McQuay* v. *McQuay* (1992), 39 R.F.L. (3d) 184 (Ont. Div. Ct.); *Godinek* v. *Godinek* (1992), 40 R.F.L. (3d) 78 (Ont. Gen. Div.); *DaCosta* v. *DaCosta* (1992), 40 R.F.L. (3d) 216 (Ont. C.A.); *Lefevre* v. *Lefevre* (1992), 40 R.F.L. (3d) 372 (Ont. Gen. Div.); *Bigelow* v. *Bigelow* (1993), 48 R.F.L. (3d) 424 (Ont. Gen. Div.); *MacNeal* v. *MacNeal* (1993), 50 R.F.L. (3d) 235 (Ont. Gen. Div.); *Mollicone* v. *Mollicone* (1994), 9 R.F.L. (4th) 155 (Ont. C.A.); *Ward* v. *Ward* (1999), 44 R.F.L. (4th) 340 (Ont. Gen. Div.); and *Nahatchewitz* v. *Nahatchewitz* (1999), 1 R.F.L. (5th) 395 (Ont. C.A.).

The leading case on prejudgment interest is *Burgess* v. *Burgess* (1995), 24 O.R. (3d) 547 (C.A.). The court reviewed the case law and held that, as a general rule, a payor spouse is required to pay prejudgment interest on an equalization payment owing to a payee spouse in order to encourage timely settlement of equalization claims. The court also confirmed that, as indicated in *McQuay* v. *McQuay* (1992), 8 O.R. (3d) 111, 39 R.F.L. (3d) 184 (Div. Ct.), the principles for awarding prejudgment interest on equalization payments are not identical to those used in commercial cases. It approved a line of lower court decisions indicating that no prejudgment interest will be awarded "where, for various reasons, the payor spouse cannot realize on the asset giving rise to the equalization payment until after the trial, does not have the use of it prior to trial, the asset generates no income, and the payor spouse has not delayed the case being brought to trial."

5. For recent cases where the equalization payment was deferred or ordered to be paid by instalments, see *Best, supra*; *MacDonald* v. *MacDonald* (1997), 33 R.F.L. (4th) 75 (Ont. C.A.); and *Balcerzak* v. *Balcerzak* (1998), 41 R.F.L. (4th) 13 (Ont. Gen. Div.). In each of these cases post-judgment interest was ordered.

6. Reluctance to deal with property claims on separation by making one spouse a minority share-holder in a corporation controlled by the other is illustrated in *Faulkner* v. *Faulkner* (1998), 166 D.L.R. (4th) 378 (Alta. C.A.).

7. A court cannot, under provincial matrimonial property legislation, order transfers of property located on land reserved for Indians under the federal *Indian Act*. However, the value of that property can be included in the net family properties and a court can require a monetary payment to equalize the spouses' net family properties. See *George* v. *George* (1996), 24 R.F.L. (4th) 155 (B.C.C.A.) where a compensation order adjusted the division of family assets located on a reserve.

Under the recently enacted *First Nations Land Management Act*, S.C. 1999, c. 24, the fourteen First Nations who entered into a Framework Agreement on First Nation Land Management with the federal government are required by s. 17(1) to "establish general rules and procedures, in cases of breakdown of marriage, respecting the use, occupation and possession of first nation land and the division of interests in first nation land".

(5) PENSIONS

ONTARIO LAW REFORM COMMISSION, *REPORT ON PENSIONS AS FAMILY PROPERTY: VALUATION AND DIVISION*

(Toronto: 1995) 8-17, 25-29, 33-45, 51-52, 59-62, 84-87, and 260-267.

(Footnotes follow each chapter.)

CHAPTER 2   PENSIONS: BASIC CONCEPTS

1. INTRODUCTION

. . . A pension plan has been defined as "a plan organized by an employer, a union or a government, primarily to provide a monthly annuity for a participating member after retirement. It will frequently provide additional benefits payable on the premature death, disability or termination of employment of the member".[1] Although in the past pensions were considered to be "fringe benefits", they are now usually considered to be an integral part of the employee's compensation package.[2]

There are two components to every pension plan: first, the terms and conditions of the plan itself, including the basis on which benefits are paid to members; and second, the financial arrangements that must be made by the plan sponsor to ensure that the plan is able to meet its financial obligations to its members.[3] In Ontario, all aspects of creating and administering a provincial pension plan are governed by the *Pension Benefits Act*;[4] the Pension Commission of Ontario is the administrative body responsible for the regulation of pensions (with the exception of pensions for federally regulated employees).

2. TYPES OF PENSIONS

(a) PRIVATE PLANS

Pension plans can be divided into private and public sector plans. Private sector plans include company-sponsored plans, union-sponsored plans, and multi-employer or jointly trusted plans. In the case of company-sponsored plans, pensions are created by a document that describes the terms of the plan as approved by the board of directors. In unionized workplaces, the company pension plan is usually negotiated, and its terms are referenced in a collective agreement.[5] In some employment sectors, such as the construction and garment industries, multi-employer plans are more common. These plans are administered by a board of trustees consisting of representatives from labour and management or by union-appointed trustees.

Private plans can fall under provincial or federal jurisdiction.[6] Private plans falling under federal jurisdiction include those in the areas of interprovincial and international transportation and banking, and they are governed by the federal *Pension Benefits Standards Act, 1985*.[7] This Act applies to Air Canada, the Canadian Broadcasting Corporation, Canadian Airlines, Via Rail, and all banks.[8] All private provincial plans are regulated by the Ontario *Pension Benefits Act*. The provisions of this Act apply to "every pension plan that is provided for persons employed in Ontario".[9]

(b) PUBLIC PLANS

Public plans provide pensions to public sector employees. They are based on specific pieces of legislation and can fall under federal or provincial jurisdiction.[10] Federal public plans are regulated by the *Pension Benefits Division Act*.[11] This statute applies to federal government employees whose pension plans fall under the *Public Service Superannuation Act*,[12] the *Royal Canadian Mounted Police Superannuation Act*,[13] the *Royal Canadian Mounted Police Pension Continuation Act*,[14] the *Canadian Forces Superannuation Act*,[15] the *Members of Parliament Retiring Allowances Act*,[16] the *Defence Services Pension Continuation Act*,[17] the *Diplomatic Service (Special) Superannuation Act*,[18] the *Governor General's Act*,[19] and the *Special Retirement Arrangements Act*.[20]

There are also several provincial plans for public service employees.[21] In Ontario, these include plans established under the *Teachers' Pension Act*,[22] the *Ontario Municipal Employees Retirement System Act*,[23] the *Legislative Assembly Retirement Allowances Act*,[24] and the *Public Service Pension Act*.[25] These plans are subject to the *Pension Benefits Act*.

(c) GOVERNMENT-SPONSORED PLANS

Plans sponsored by the federal government include the *Canada Pension Plan* (CPP)[26] and *Old Age Security* (OAS)[27]. The OAS benefits are available to individuals in Canada who have reached the age of sixty-five and who meet the minimum residency requirements. A Guaranteed Income Supplement and Spouse's Pension Allowance are available in prescribed circumstances.[28]

3. TERMS AND CONDITIONS

(a) CONTRIBUTORY AND NON-CONTRIBUTORY PLANS

Pension plans may be contributory or non-contributory. "Contributory" plans require employee members to contribute to the cost of the plan; "non-contributory" plans do not. The employer is responsible for the funding of non-contributory plans. The funding of pension plans is subject to pension legislation governing the accumulation and investment of the contributions set aside each year; this legislation ensures that the funds are adequate to meet the obligation of providing benefits to members.

Most pension plans, including all public service pension plans, are contributory and require that some contribution to the plan be made by the participating members.

For example, private sector pension plans often require contributions of five percent of salary; public sector plans usually require between six and seven percent.[29] Under some plans, members are entitled to make additional voluntary contributions. This has the effect of increasing the pension benefit that the member ultimately receives.[30]

(b) PENSION FORMULA

An essential feature of any pension plan is the formula that sets out the basis on which the pension benefit is paid. In some pension plans, benefits are based on contributions by the member and the employer; in other plans, they are determined by a prescribed formula.

(i) Defined Benefit Plans

A defined benefit plan is a pension plan that "defines a distinct benefit that the participating member will receive at retirement".[31] The majority of plan members in Ontario belong to defined benefit plans. These plans may be contributory or non-contributory. Employer contributions in a defined benefit plan vary from year to year. The annual employer contribution represents an amount that is sufficient to fund current and projected future liabilities. The amount of such contributions depends on factors such as investment return on the fund, mortality rates of members, and rates of inflation.[32] There are three types of defined benefit plans: final earnings plans, career average earnings plans, and flat benefit plans.[33]

a. Final Earnings Plans

In final earnings plans (including final average and best average earnings plans), the employee's pension benefit is "based upon his or her length of service and average earnings for a stated period before retirement".[34] The typical final earnings pension provides between one and two percent of average earnings in the five years before retirement, multiplied by the number of years of service. The final earnings formula is commonly used in public sector plans and in large private plans. Most contributory final earnings plans integrate their benefits with CPP, and benefits are reduced to reflect the fact that the member will also be receiving CPP.[35]

b. Career Average Earnings Plans

In career average earnings plans, "the member's pension for each year of service is equal to a percentage of earnings for that particular year".[36] Career average earnings plans can be less advantageous for employees unless the plans are "updated" from time to time to produce a result that comes closer to a final average plan. The updating is effected by the employer altering the "base year" in the pension formula, for example, to a more recent year with a higher salary.[37]

c. Flat Benefit Plans

In flat benefit plans, pension benefits are based on a specified dollar amount per year of service; for example, twenty dollars per month for each year of service. The formula for flat benefit plans does not take into consideration differences in earnings, or inflation. To compensate for this factor, new agreements are negotiated through the collective bargaining process between employers and employees to increase the pension benefit payable.[38]

(ii) Defined Contribution Plans

In defined contribution plans, also referred to as "money purchase" plans, employees and employers each contribute a specified amount. The contributions are accumulated with interest in an account for the benefit of the employee. The account continues to grow until the employee retires, and the employee is then entitled to a pension that can be purchased, based on the account balance. The amount of the pension is not usually ascertainable until the member retires. Commonly, both employees and employers contribute five percent of income, an amount that may be reduced by contributions required for CPP.[39]

(iii) Hybrid and Combination Plans

Hybrid plans contain features of defined benefit and defined contribution plans. In hybrid plans, the pension benefit is based, in part, on the accumulation of a defined contribution and, in part, on a defined benefit formula. The pension will be the greater of two types of benefits, for example, "the greater of a defined benefit, of, say 1 3/4 per cent of salary for each year of service, and the pension that can be generated by defined contributions of say 5 per cent from the member matched by the employer".[40] Combination plans include characteristics of both defined benefit and defined contribution plans, and pension benefits are the sum of both benefits. The employer usually funds the defined benefit portion of the plan, and the employee contributes to the defined contribution component.[41]

(c) RETIREMENT COMMENCEMENT DATES

There are three possible retirement commencement dates: normal, early, and late or postponed. Each pension plan, in compliance with the provisions of the *Pension Benefits Act*, sets out the applicable retirement commencement ages. . . .

(d) DEATH AND SURVIVOR BENEFITS

(i) Pre-Retirement Benefits

In Ontario when a member dies prior to the commencement of pension payments, there are at least three types of death and survivor benefits. Effective January 1, 1987, in plans where the member is vested and dies before the pension comes into pay, a surviving spouse has the option of an immediate or deferred pension or a cash lump-sum payment.[48] The value of the death benefit must be equal to the commuted value of the member's post-1986 deferred pension.[49] With respect to employment prior to January 1, 1987, the beneficiary is entitled to a return of the member's contributions with interest.[50]

If the member has no spouse, or the spouse is living separate and apart from the deceased, or the spouse has signed a waiver, the member may designate a beneficiary to receive the same death benefit. If there is no designated beneficiary, the death benefit is paid to the member's estate.[51] Some pension plans also provide for spouses' pensions and children's pensions where the member dies prior to retirement.[52]

(ii) Post-Retirement Benefits

In Ontario, when a member dies after retirement, a survivor benefit in the form of a joint-and-survivor pension is available for a surviving spouse who is residing with the member at the date of retirement.[53] The joint-and-survivor pension is at least sixty percent of the total pension[54] and is payable until the death of the surviving spouse. . . .

(e) WITHDRAWAL OF BENEFITS

(i) Vesting and Locking-in

Before January 1, 1965, there were no vesting rules.[59] Currently, there are two sets of vesting rules in Ontario, depending on whether the pension benefit accruals occurred before January 1, 1987, or on or after that date. For benefits accruing prior to January 1, 1987, pensions are vested after the employee completes ten years of employment or membership and reaches age forty-five.[60] For benefits accruing after December 31, 1986, pensions are vested after twenty-four months of membership.[61] Vesting arrangements may be more generous in particular pension plans.[62]

Once a pension is vested, pension contributions are locked in—that is, they cannot be withdrawn or lost on termination of employment.[63] On termination, the member is entitled to have the commuted value transferred to a locked-in prescribed retirement savings arrangement under the *Pension Benefits Act*, to an insurance company for purchase of an annuity payable on the early retirement date, or to another pension plan if the new plan administrator agrees to such a transfer.[64] The amount cannot be received in cash. If employment is terminated where the pension is not vested and the plan is contributory, the member has the right only to a return of his or her contributions plus interest.[65]. . .

7. VALUATION OF PENSIONS

Pensions may be valued for a number of purposes, including determining portability rights on termination of employment, value of death benefits, transfer values on marriage breakdown, and valuation for family law purposes. The method of valuation employed will vary depending on whether the plan is a defined benefit plan or a defined contribution plan.

(a) CONTRIBUTIONS METHOD

In the contributions method of valuation, the value of the pension equals the contributions to the plan together with investment yield. The contributions method is used in a number of contexts. For example, in a defined contribution plan, the member may wish to transfer his or her interest in the pension asset out of the plan on termination of employment. Where the pension is vested, the member is entitled on termination to the accumulated value of the pension, including employer and employee contributions plus an interest factor.[108] Where a defined contribution plan is not vested, the amount paid to the member consists only of employee contributions plus interest.[109] Similarly, where a defined contribution plan is valued for family law valuation purposes, the value is equal to total employee and employer contributions plus an interest factor. In essence, the contributions method is similar to valuing a bank account. . . .

(b) ACTUARIAL METHODS

. . .

(ii) Computation of Capitalized Value of Pensions on Marriage Breakdown

Under the Ontario *Family Law Act*,[113] pension assets must be valued along with the other assets owned by spouses at the time of marriage breakdown. In performing these valuations, actuaries must conform to the current law regarding valuations for family law purposes and to the Canadian Institute of Actuaries' Standard of Practice.[114] This standard is applicable only to the valuation of defined benefit plans.

The purpose of the Standard of Practice and the assumptions and principles developed in the current law is to provide a "present value" of the future pension benefits accruing to the member spouse. Patterson defines "present value" in the following terms:[115]

> the funds that must be invested at the valuation date so that, after allowing for income in the form of interest on both the original fund and on investment of income, the total funds are just adequate to provide the annual pension benefits, including any indexing, taking into consideration the fact that the recipient of the pension must survive to receive any individual payment.

An actuary, in calculating the present value of a defined benefit plan, determines a sum that, "if set aside on the valuation date, would accumulate sufficient interest as of the retirement date to produce the level of pension accrued during the marriage".[116] According to Patterson, the actuary takes into consideration the following factors in determining the present value:[117]

(a) the probability that the member, and the member's spouse, if appropriate, will survive to enjoy the pension benefits to which the member is entitled in any particular year in the future;

(b) such pension benefits may be indexed over the years to fully or partially reflect inflation;

(c) the taxes that will be deducted from such income; and

(d) the value of a pension is determined assuming that such value will be invested and that the interest the investment earns will be reinvested.

A number of factors are taken into account in the calculation of present value, such as assumptions relating to mortality, interest rates, inflation rates, and retirement age. Two calculations are used to determine the present value. First, the value of the amount of the pension accrued to the valuation date is determined. The accrued pension is the amount of the pension payable in the form of a monthly annuity commencing on a set retirement date. Secondly, a series of discounts are made that reduce the value of the benefit, based on the member's age, prevailing interest rates, and income tax considerations.

The assumed retirement date has a significant impact on the value of the pension where the plan offers a subsidized early retirement. The retirement date may be the early retirement date, the actual retirement date, or the normal retirement date, or a date determined by a court as being the likely retirement date. Where a plan offers a subsidized early retirement, the early retirement date greatly increases the present value if it is taken into consideration. However, if the pension provided on early retirement is reduced actuarially, the present value is not affected by the early retirement provision.[118]

Once the present value of the pension is determined for each individual year, an inflation factor is applied to determine the inflated value of the pension in each future year, and then mortality tables are used to determine the number of years during which the member can expect to receive the pension. An interest factor is applied to the pension in each future year to determine the discounted present value at the valuation date. Finally, the values for each individual year are totalled to provide the required present value. Typically, the final value is discounted for future taxes. The manner in which this discount is to occur is the subject of considerable debate in Ontario.[119]

Under the provisions of the *Family Law Act*,[120] the actuary must reduce the value of the pension to reflect any pre-marriage accruals. This may be accomplished by doing two valuations—one as of the date of marriage and the other as of the date of valuation. In other cases, a pro-rating of the years of membership in the plan and the years of marriage is done to determine this value.[121]

The determination of present value can be made in two ways that have dramatically different impacts on the final value placed on the pension asset. The calculation can assume that the member will continue in employment with the plan sponsor until retirement or that the member will terminate employment at the date of the valuation. If it is assumed that the member will continue in employment until the retirement date, the actuary must take into consideration future increases in the value of the pension benefit due to the employee having attained a higher salary and increasing his or her years of service. This method of determining the present value is referred to as the retirement method. The retirement method assumes that the member's employment does not terminate on the valuation date. Rather, valuation is based on the member's projected salary, benefits, and service at the retirement date or at a date between the valuation and the normal retirement date.[122] The retirement method produces a higher value than the termination method,[123] particularly in the case of final average earnings plans where the member has many years of service and is close to retirement.[124]

If the assumption is made that the employee terminated employment on the valuation date, increases in the value of the pension benefit after the date of separation are not considered. This is referred to as the termination method. Using the termination method, the present value of the benefit is determined at the valuation date as if the plan member terminated employment on that date.[125] Under the termination method, future contingencies such as salary increases and the likelihood of the member remaining in employment until retirement age are not taken into account.[126]

---

1 Jack Patterson, *Pension Division and Valuation*[:] Family Lawyers' Guide (Aurora, Ont.: Canada Law Book, 1991), at 7.

2 Lawrence E. Coward, *Mercer Handbook of Canadian Pension and Benefit Plans*, 10th ed. (North York, Ont.: CCH, 1991), at 1 (hereinafter referred to as "*Mercer Handbook*").

3 *Ibid.*, at 4.

4 R.S.O. 1990, c. P.8.

5 Patterson, *supra*, note 1, at 9.

6 *Ibid.*, at 37-38.

7 R.S.C. 1985, c. 32 (2nd Supp.), s. 4(4).

8 E. Diane Pask and Cheryl A. Hass, "Division of Pensions: The Impact of Family Law on Pensions and Pension Plan Administrators" (1992), 9 Can. Fam. L.Q. 133, at 155.

9 *Supra*, note 4, s. 3.

10 Patterson, *supra*, note 1, at 7-8.

11 S.C. 1992, c. 46 (Schedule II).

12 R.S.C. 1985, c. P-36.

13 R.S.C. 1985, c. R-11.

14 R.S.C. 1970, c. R-10.

15 R.S.C. 1985, c. C-17.

16 R.S.C. 1985, c. M-5.

17 R.S.C. 1970, c. D-3.

18 R.S.C. 1985, c. D-2.

19 R.S.C. 1985, c. G-9.

20 S.C. 1992, c. 46 (Schedule I).

21 Patterson, *supra*, note 1, at 8.

22 R.S.O. 1990, c. T.1.

23 R.S.O. 1990, c. O.29.

24 R.S.O. 1990, c. L.11.

25 R.S.O. 1990, c. P.48.

26 *Canada Pension Plan*, R.S.C. 1985, c. C-8.

27 *Old Age Security Act*, R.S.C. 1985, c. O-9.

28 *Mercer Handbook*, *supra*, note 2, at 3.

29 *Ibid.*, at 33.

30 *Ibid.*, at 33-34.

31 Patterson, *supra*, note 1, at 12.

32 *Ibid.*

33 *Ibid.*

34 *Mercer Handbook*, *supra*, note 2, at 9.

35 *Ibid.*, at 10.

36 *Ibid.*

37 *Ibid.*, at 11.

38 Patterson, *supra*, note 1, at 14, and *Mercer Handbook*, *supra*, note 2, at 11-13.

39 *Mercer Handbook*, *ibid.*, at 13.

40 *Ibid.*, at 16.

41 *Ibid.*

48 *Pension Benefits Act*, *supra*, note 4, s. 48(1), (2).

49 *Ibid.*, s. 48(1), (2).

50 *Ibid.*, s. 36.

51 *Ibid.*, s. 48(6), (7), (14).

52 *Mercer Handbook, supra*, note 2, at 41-42.

53 *Pension Benefits Act, supra*, note 4, s. 44.

54 *Ibid.*, s. 44(3).

59 *Ibid.* ¶1305, at 1401.

60 *Pension Benefits Act, supra*, note 4, s. 36.

61 *Ibid.*, s. 37.

62 *Ibid.*, s. 64.

63 *Ibid.*, s. 63(1).

64 *Ibid.*, s. 42(1), and regulations to the *Pension Benefits Act*, R.R.O. 1990, Reg. 909, s. 21(1.1), as en. by O. Reg. 409/94, s. 3(1).

65 *Pension Benefits Act, supra*, note 4, s. 63(3), (4).

108 *Pension Benefits Act, supra*, note 4, s. 42(1).

109 *Ibid.*, s. 63(3).

113 R.S.O. 1990, c. F.3.

114 Canadian Institute of Actuaries, *Standard of Practice for the Computation of the Capitalized Value of Pension Entitlements on Marriage Breakdown for Purposes of Lump-Sum Equalization Payments* (September 1, 1993), reproduced *infra*, Appendix B.

115 *Supra*, note 1, at 123-24.

116 Dona L. Campbell and Miller Thomson, "Consideration of Retirement Benefits on Marital Breakdown", in *Pensions: Advising Clients in a Changing Environment* (Toronto: Law Society of Upper Canada, Department of Continuing Legal Education, 1991) (paper presented at program held in Toronto, October 30, 1991), at C-12.

117 *Supra*, note 1, at 123.

118 *Ibid.*, at 80.

119 *Ibid.*, at 301-02.

120 *Supra*, note 113.

121 Patterson, *supra*, note 1, at 159-60.

122 Sheryl Smolkin and Janet Downing, *Family Law: Voodoo Economics for Women* [:] *Pension Credit-Splitting Pitfalls* (January 29, 1993) (paper prepared for 1993 Institute of Continuing Legal Education, Canadian Bar Association — Ontario), at 13.

123 Campbell and Thomson, *supra*, note 116, at C-17.

124 Smolkin and Downing, *supra*, note 122, at 13.

125 Campbell and Thomson, *supra*, note 116, at C-16.

126 Smolkin and Downing, *supra*, note 122, at 11.

CURRENT LAW: PENSIONS AND THE *FAMILY LAW ACT*

CHAPTER 3

. . .

3. "IF AND WHEN" ARRANGEMENTS

(a) WHEN COURTS WILL MAKE "IF AND WHEN" ORDERS

Although the courts express a strong preference for a lump-sum settlement at the time of marriage breakdown,[20] such a settlement may be difficult for the member spouse where one of the assets is a large pension. For that reason, the courts have devised an "if and when" arrangement to permit the member spouse to satisfy any equalization claim with respect to a pension by undertaking to pay a share of the pension income to the non-member spouse "if and when" the pension becomes payable.

An "if and when" trust arrangement can be created by means of a domestic contract between the parties or by a court order.[21] The availability of "if and when" arrangements to settle pension property under the *Family Law Act* was first established in Ontario in *Marsham* v. *Marsham*.[22] An "if and when" order typically will not be made by the courts if the parties are young, the value of the pension is small, the equalization payment can be satisfied through available liquid assets, or the portion of the equalization payment relating to the pension benefits is relatively small.[23]

. . . The Court of Appeal in *Best* v. *Best*[25] sets out in greater detail the circumstances under which an "if and when" approach will be appropriate in Ontario. In this case, because the pension would likely not have become payable for another twenty years and the non-member spouse had a pressing need for funds, the Court held that an "if and when" arrangement would not be appropriate. The Court established a general rule that an "if and when" arrangement should not be ordered if the pension benefit will not be realized for ten or more years.[26]

(b) PENSION VALUATION AND "IF AND WHEN" ARRANGEMENTS

Because of the difficulties associated with valuing pensions, a number of early decisions avoided the problem simply by isolating the pension for separate treatment.[27] The pension was excluded from the calculation of net family property and divided separately "if and when" it was received. In *Porter* v. *Porter*,[28] for example, Kerr Dist. Ct. J. held that it was not possible for him to determine the value of the husband's pension as of the valuation date because no actuarial evidence was presented at trial. Instead, he took what was characterized as an "if and when" approach to valuation and divided the pension outside of the equalization process. . . .

The approach of excluding pensions from the *Family Law Act* equalization process, however, has been rejected. In *Marsham* v. *Marsham*,[31] Walsh J. stated as follows:

> While it may be permissible to use the 'if and when' approach as a method to both value and to settle the pension entitlement in other provinces, it clearly is not possible within the framework of the Ontario Act.

Part I of the Act requires that all property owned by a spouse on the valuation date be valued in order to determine his or her net family property so that the amount required to equalize the spouses' net family properties can be ascertained. While it may be possible to satisfy all or part of the equalization payment by an immediate transfer of the pension benefits in trust to the other spouse, nevertheless, in the first instance, the pension benefit must be valued for the purpose of determining the equalization payment.

In *Marsham*, the wife was entitled to an equalization payment of $80,000. While Walsh J. could have ordered that the husband make an immediate lump-sum payment, he held that it would be inappropriate to do so in the circumstances. Of the husband's net family property of $232,600, $107,400 consisted of his pension and severance pay, neither of which was available for an immediate payment. As a result, Walsh J. concluded that the portion of the equalization payment attributable to the husband's pension benefits ($48,500) should be satisfied by "directing that the husband holds his . . . pension plan in trust for the wife to the extent that she is entitled to a share or interest therein".[32] As a trustee, the husband was prohibited from dealing with the pension asset in a manner that would affect the wife's interest. Walsh J. adopted the pro-rated approach[33] approved by the British Columbia Court of Appeal in *Rutherford* v. *Rutherford*[34] and ordered as follows:[35]

> [T]he wife shall share in the husband's pension in the following proportion: one-half times the number of months of married cohabitation during which pension contributions were made, divided by the total number of months during which contributions were or will be made, times the pension benefits payable.

In addition to the approach adopted in *Marsham*, the courts have also ordered that a specific dollar amount will be payable on a periodic basis commencing on the normal retirement date. In this case, the pension is valued, and the monthly pension income available on retirement is determined. In *Kroone* v. *Kroone*,[36] for example, it was determined that the monthly pension income due under a defined benefit pension plan was $858.65 per month, payable at the age of sixty-five. The Court ordered an "if and when" agreement to satisfy the equalization payment under the *Family Law Act, 1986*,[37] in the following terms:[38]

> I believe that the plaintiff should be awarded her 50 per cent share of the accrued pension benefits of an 'if and when' basis in the monthly amount of $429.33 at the defendant's retirement.

The practice of using "if and when" arrangements to satisfy equalization payments has been less than satisfactory. The realization of the pension benefit occurs over the post-retirement life of the member, and the amount of the benefit paid depends on the life span of the member. As a result, an interest in the pension benefit to which a non-member spouse is entitled may never be realized if the member spouse dies prior to or soon after retirement. On the other hand, where the life span of the member spouse exceeds expectations, or the value of the pension benefit increases after separation, an overpayment to the non-member spouse may result.

4. "IF AND WHEN" ARRANGEMENTS INVOLVING PLAN ADMINISTRATOR

(a) INTRODUCTION

Spousal "if and when" arrangements, such as the one used in *Marsham* v. *Marsham*,[39] impose a trust obligation on the member spouse to comply with the order if and when the pension becomes payable. The administration of the trust is personal to the member. If the member leaves the jurisdiction or for some reason refuses to pay, the non-member spouse may find it difficult or impossible to enforce the terms of the trust.

To address this problem, amendments were made to the *Pension Benefits Act*[40] in 1988. It became possible to impose a trust on the administrator of the pension plan itself, in favour of the non-member spouse, requiring the plan administrator to pay a portion of the member spouse's pension directly to the non-member spouse after the commencement of the pension payments.[41]

Although the *Pension Benefits Act* generally prohibits the assignment of money payable under a pension plan,[42] section 51 gives the non-member spouse the right to a share of the periodic payments paid to the member on the member's retirement as long as the non-member spouse is entitled to an interest in the member's pension benefit under a domestic contract or an order under the property provisions of the *Family Law Act*.[43] Section 51 contemplates that one spouse may assign a "pension benefit" (that is, the monthly, annual, or periodic payments made under a pension)[44] to a non-member spouse by a domestic contract or may be ordered to do so by the court under Part I of the *Family Law Act*.

As a result of section 51, an "if and when" order can now be made under which the paying spouse is no longer a trustee of his or her pension entitlements for the non-member spouse. Instead, a portion of the member spouse's periodic pension payment is paid directly by the plan administrator to the non-member spouse on retirement.

Exceptions are made to the general prohibition against the assignment of a pension interest found in section 65 of the *Pension Benefits Act* for these purposes. Exceptions permit payment to be made to the non-member spouse if the member spouse terminates employment or dies or if the plan is terminated, where an order or domestic contract under the *Family Law Act* has been filed.[45]

The *Pension Benefits Act* permits the assignment of money payable under a pension plan, pursuant to the terms of a court order under the *Family Law Act* or a domestic contract, but only in circumstances where the money would otherwise be transferred out of the plan, namely: (1) on the date on which payment of the pension benefit commences; (2) on termination of employment; (3) to purchase a pension, deferred pension, or ancillary benefit from an insurance company on retirement;[46] (4) to provide a pre-retirement death benefit for the member's spouse, where the member dies before commencement of the pension benefits; or (5) on the wind-up of the plan.[47]

(b) OBLIGATIONS IMPOSED ON PLAN ADMINISTRATION IN EVENT OF TERMINATION OF EMPLOYMENT BY MEMBER SPOUSE

Various provisions in the *Pension Benefits Act*[48] and regulations[49] have been devised to provide some measure of security to the non-member spouse where there is a plan-administered "if and when" arrangement in place, and where the member spouse terminates employment. Section 51(5) of the Act provides that where a certified copy of a domestic contract or order under the *Family Law Act* is filed with the plan administrator, the non-member spouse has the same entitlements as the member on termination of employment. The options available to the member and the non-member on termination are as follows:[50]

(1) the right to transfer to another pension if the second plan agrees;

(2) the right to transfer the amount into a locked-in prescribed retirement savings arrangement under the *Pension Benefits Act*;[51]

(3) the right to use the funds to purchase a life annuity that will not commence before the early retirement date; and

(4) the right to elect a deferred pension in the same plan.

Section 46 of the regulations requires the plan administrator to notify the non-member spouse[52] of any termination of employment by the member, to provide the non-member spouse with a copy of the termination statement given to the member, and to advise the non-member of the options for transfer under section 42 of the *Pension Benefits Act*. The administrator must do this within thirty days of receiving notice of the member's termination of employment.

Section 20 of the regulations requires the non-member spouse to deliver a direction to the plan administrator within sixty days of receipt of the notice of termination of employment of the member. The direction must specify to the administrator the option being exercised by the non-member spouse. The plan administrator must then comply with the option selected within sixty days of receipt of the information from the non-member spouse.

(c) OBLIGATIONS IMPOSED ON PLAN ADMINISTRATOR IN EVENT OF MEMBER SPOUSE'S DEATH PRIOR TO RETIREMENT

Section 48(13) of the *Pension Benefits Act* provides for an assignment of a pre-retirement death benefit in a court order or in a domestic contract under the *Family Law Act*. This subsection appears to carry into effect a specified assignment under section 65(3). It provides that:

> 48. (13) An entitlement to a benefit under this section is subject to any right to or interest in the benefit set out in a domestic contract or an order referred to in section 51 (payment on marriage breakdown).

However, the ability of a member spouse to assign a portion of a pre-retirement death benefit where there is a surviving spouse is not clear. Although there is limited case law on this subsection, it is arguable that, where a domestic contract or a court order provides that any pre-retirement death benefit is payable to a non-member spouse, the non-member spouse is entitled to a portion of the pre-retirement death benefit even if a subsequent spouse might otherwise qualify for it by virtue of being a spouse of the member and living with the member at the time of the member's death. . . .

5. PROBLEMS WITH PLAN-ADMINISTERED "IF AND WHEN" ARRANGEMENTS

There are a number of deficiencies in the current regime under the *Pension Benefits Act* with respect to plan-administered "if and when" arrangements. These include timing problems, the likelihood that many "if and when" arrangements may violate the provisions of the Act that prohibit the assignment of more than fifty percent of the member spouse's pension benefits, and the definition of "spouse" in the *Pension Benefits Act*, which overlooks the inclusion of former spouses. . . .

20 See *Best v. Best* (1992), 9 O.R. (3d) 277, 41 R.F.L. (3d) 383 (C.A.) (subsequent references are to 9 O.R. (3d)).

21 *Family Law Act*, ss. 7, 54.

22 *Marsham* v. *Marsham* (1987), 59 O.R. (2d) 609, 7 R.F.L. (3d) 1 (H.C.J.) (subsequent references are to 59 O.R. (2d)).

23 Catherine D. Aitken, "Pensions Under Part I of the Family Law Act of Ontario", in Special Lectures of the Law Society of Upper Canada, 1993, *Family Law [:] Roles, Fairness and Equality* (Toronto: Carswell, 1994), at 231.

25 *Supra*, note 20.

26 *Ibid.*, at 282.

27 Alastair Bissett-Johnson and Winifred H. Holland (eds.), *Matrimonial Property Law in Canada* (Toronto: Carswell, looseleaf), at O-23.

28 (1986), 1 R.F.L. (3d) 12, at 26 (Ont. Dist. Ct.).

31 *Supra*, note 22, at 614. See, also, *Alger* v. *Alger* (1989), 21 R.F.L. (3d) 211, at 219 (Ont. H.C.J.).

32 *Marsham* v. *Marsham, supra*, note 22, at 624. The remaining $31,500 was ordered to be satisfied out of the proceeds of sale of the matrimonial home, which was directed to be listed for sale no later than June 30, 1990.

33 The pro-rated approach is only one of several formulae to effect a division by the "if and when" approach. See Jack Patterson, *Pension Division and Valuation [:] Family Lawyers' Guide* (Aurora, Ont.: Canada Law Book, 1991), at 221-28.

34 (1981), 30 B.C.L.R. 145 (C.A.).

35 *Marsham* v. *Marsham, supra*, note 22, at 624.

36 (1992), 41 R.F.L. (3d) 111 (Ont. Gen. Div.).

37 [R.S.O. 1990, c. F.3].

38 *Kroone* v. *Kroone, supra*, note 36, at 115.

39 *Supra*, note 22.

40 R.S.O. 1980, c. 373, rep. and replaced by the *Pension Benefits Act, 1987*, S.O. 1987, c. 35. See, now, the *Pension Benefits Act*, R.S.O. 1990, c. P.8 (subsequent references are to the 1990 Act).

41 The "if and when" option under the *Pension Benefits Act, ibid.*, is set out in s. 51.

42 *Pension Benefits Act, supra*, note 40, s. 65.

43 Part I (Family Property) and Part IV (Domestic Contracts).

44 *Pension Benefits Act, supra*, note 40, s. 1 "pension benefit".

45 Section 65(3).

46 The contract or order could provide for an assignment of moneys payable at retirement.

47 Dona L. Campbell and Miller Thomson, "Consideration of Retirement Benefits on Marital Break-down", in *Pensions: Advising Clients in a Changing Environment* (Toronto: Law Society of Upper Canada, Department of Continuing Legal Education, 1991) (paper presented at program held in Toronto, October 30, 1991), at C-38 to C-39.

48 *Supra*, note 40.

49 R.R.O. 1990, Reg. 909.

50 *Pension Benefits Act, supra,* note 40, ss. 37, 42.

51 See *Pension Benefits Act, ibid.,* s. 42(1)(b), and regulations, *supra,* note 49, s. 21(1.1), as en. by O. Reg. 409/94, s. 3(1).

52 The definition of "spouse" in s. 51(5) of the *Pension Benefits Act, supra,* note 40, does not appear to include a former spouse. This creates a problem, since in many cases the parties will be divorced by the time s. 46 of the regulations, *supra* 49, becomes applicable.

REFORMS AND PROPOSALS FOR REFORM IN CANADA

CHAPTER 4

1. INTRODUCTION

. . . There are two fundamental ways in which pension benefits can be distributed between spouses on marriage breakdown. The first method involves a private settlement between spouses and does not require any participation by the pension plan administrator. The second requires that the plan administrator facilitate the actual division of the pension benefit.

(a) PENSION DIVISION BY PRIVATE SETTLEMENT

A private settlement can take a number of different forms. For example, the member spouse can retain all of the rights to the pension benefit and simply compensate the non-member spouse for his or her share of it, either by a lump-sum payment of cash or the transfer of some other asset. Alternatively, the member spouse can simply agree to pay a share of the pension benefit directly to the non-member spouse once the pension comes into pay. This is known as a "spousal trust" or a "spousal 'if and when' arrangement".

(b) PENSION DIVISION INVOLVING PLAN ADMINISTRATOR

Pension division involving the plan administrator can be divided into the following two categories:

(1) Transfer: The plan administrator is responsible for calculating the value of the pension at a prescribed point in time, for example, at the time of marriage breakdown. The plan then transfers a portion of this amount into another pension vehicle for the non-member spouse, such as a locked-in registered retirement savings plan (RRSP), deferred annuity, or another pension plan with the permission of that plan.

(2) Benefit split: The plan administrator is responsible for paying two benefits out of the plan, one to the member spouse and the other to the non-member spouse. In some cases, an account is created for the benefit of the non-member spouse at the time of marriage breakdown. In other cases, the payment is divided between the spouses at the time of retirement.

Of the two options above, only the second option, a benefit split in the form of an "if and when" order, is currently available in Ontario. The pension division provisions in Ontario effectively prohibit the assignment of any money payable under a pension plan prior to the member's retirement, termination of employment, or death, or the winding-up of the plan.[5]

Four Canadian provinces—Manitoba,[6] Saskatchewan,[7] Quebec,[8] and New Brunswick[9]—have amended their pension legislation to permit a transfer out of the pension plan at the time of marriage breakdown. The federal government has also made this option available for pensions that fall under federal jurisdiction.[10]. . .

The federal *Pension Benefits Standards Act, 1985 (PBSA)* [54] provides for the division of pensions at source with respect to those pension plans covering employees in "included employment" as defined in the Act.[55] This applies to private sector plans in areas within federal jurisdiction, including banks and interprovincial and international transportation. Those provisions of the *PBSA* do not, however, apply to areas of "included employment" where "provincial property law" applies.[56] The *PBSA* provides that a "pension benefit, pension benefit credit or other benefit under a pension plan that is subject to provincial property law pursuant to this section is not subject to the provisions of this Act relating to the valuation or distribution of pension benefits, pension benefit credits or other benefits under a pension plan, as the case may be".[57]

Under the *PBSA*, a member or former member of a pension plan that falls under the Act may assign all or part of his or her pension benefit, pension benefit credit, or other benefit under the plan to his or her spouse on marriage breakdown or separation.[58] The division of the pension may be the result of an agreement or it may be ordered by the court.[59] The definition of spouse varies depending on whether the division is made pursuant to a court order or an agreement. Where the division is made pursuant to a court order, "spouse" has the same meaning it has in the applicable provincial property law. Where the division is made pursuant to an agreement, "spouse" includes persons of the opposite sex in a "conjugal" relationship who have cohabited for at least one year.[60]

The provisions of the *PBSA* provide that the plan administrator must divide and administer the pension benefit, pension benefit credit, or other benefit "in prescribed manner" in accordance with the court order or agreement once all appeals have been exhausted or time for appealing has expired.[61] For the purposes of the division, the non-member spouse is treated like a member who has terminated employment.[62] The non-member spouse has the option of transferring pension benefit credits into another pension plan with permission of the plan or into a locked-in RRSP, or the option of purchasing an immediate or deferred life annuity.[63] All transfers are subject to the solvency restrictions in the Act, and the Superintendent of Financial Institutions may require that a transfer be subject to certain terms and conditions.[64] The aggregate value of the pension benefit paid to the member and non-member spouses cannot exceed the value of the pension benefit that would have been payable to the member had the division not occurred.[65] The legislation gives both the member and the spouse a right to information about the plan.[66]

The non-member spouse also has the option of a deferred pension in the same plan. In this instance, the application of the *PBSA* results in a complete separation of the interests of the spouses as of the effective date of the division.[67] Where the non-member spouse elects a deferred pension, the non-member spouse is treated like a former member and is entitled to a pension, based on the member's period of employment and salary at the time of the division, once the non-member spouse reaches the pensionable age under the plan. The non-member spouse is also entitled to any other benefit or option that a former member would be entitled to under the plan with certain exceptions.[68]

The *PBSA* also provides for the division of a pension that is in pay.[69] The *PBSA* specifically permits the division of a joint-and-survivor pension benefit. The joint-and-survivor pension becomes payable as two separate pensions, one to the member and the other to the non-member spouse, but the aggregate value of the two separate pensions cannot be less than the actuarial value of the joint-and-survivor benefit.[70]

(f) PENSION BENEFITS DIVISION ACT

The *Pension Benefits Division Act (PBDA)* [71] provides for the division, on the breakdown of a marriage or common-law relationship, of pension benefits accrued under several federal public service pension plans.[72] The *PBDA* implements court orders or spousal agreements providing for the division of a member's pension benefits by allowing a plan member, his or her spouse, or a former spouse, to apply for a division of the member's pension benefits that accrued during the period of cohabitation.[73]

The non-member spouse does not have to wait for the plan member's retirement to receive a share of his or her former spouse's pension. Providing the terms of the *PBDA* can be met, the non-member spouse may apply for a division as soon as there is a court order or spousal agreement providing for the division. Spouses who have divorced, separated, or had their marriage annulled are eligible for division of pension benefits, providing there is a court order for the division.[74] Spouses who have separated are eligible for division as well if they have lived separate and apart for at least one year and there is a spousal agreement that provides for division of the member's pension benefits.[75] The transfer out of the plan is made as soon as the division is approved.

On approval from the Minister,[76] up to fifty percent of the value of the member's accrued pension benefits can be transferred to another pension plan if the plan so permits, to a locked-in retirement savings plan or fund of the prescribed kind, or to a financial institution for a purchase of an immediate or deferred life annuity.[77] This value is to be determined by generally accepted actuarial principles set out in the regulations.

---

5 *Pension Benefits Act*, R.S.O. 1990, c. P.8, s. 65(3).

6 *The Pension Benefits Act*, R.S.M. 1987, c. P32 (also C.C.S.M., c. P32).

7 *The Pension Benefits Act, 1992*, S.S. 1992, c. P-6.001.

8 *Supplemental Pension Plans Act*, R.S.Q., c. R-15.1.

9 *Pension Benefits Act*, S.N.B. 1987, c. P.5.1.

10 Both a benefit split and transfer are available for pensions governed by the *Pensions Benefits Standards Act, 1985*, R.S.C. 1985, c. 32 (2nd Supp.). Only a transfer is available for pensions governed by the *Pensions Benefits Act*, S.C. 1992, c. 46 (Schedule II).

54 *Supra*, note 10.

55 *Ibid.*, s. 4(4).

56 *Ibid.*, s. 25(2).

57 *Ibid.*, s. 25(3).

58 *Ibid.*, s. 25(4).

59 *Ibid.*, s. 25(5).

60 *Ibid.*, ss. 2(1), 25(1) "spouse".

61 *Ibid.*, s. 25(5).

62 *Ibid.*, s. 25(4), and *Pension Benefits Standards Regulations*, 1985, SOR./87-19, s. 18(4)(c), as am. by SOR/90-363, s. 4; SOR/94-0384, s. 4.

63 *PBSA, supra*, note 10, ss. 25(4), 26(1).

64 *Ibid.*, s. 26(4). The Superintendent of Financial Institutions is appointed under s. 5(1) of the *Office of the Superintendnet of Financial Institutions Act*, R.S.C. 1985, c. 18 (3rd Supp.), Part I, and is charged with the administration of the act: *PBSA, supra*, note 10, s. 2(1) "Superintendent", as am. by R.S.C. 1985, c. 18 (3rd Supp.), s. 38.

65 *PBSA, ibid.*, s. 25(8).

66 *Ibid.*, s. 28.

67 *Ibid.*, s. 25(4).

68 *Ibid.*, ss. 17(1)(a), (b), 21(2)-(6), 25(4).

69 *Ibid.*, ss. 2(1) "pension benefit", 25(4).

70 *Ibid.*, ss. 2(1) "joint and survivor benefit", 25(7).

71 *Supra*, note 10. Regulations calculating the value and division of the member's benefit have been promulgated: see *Pension Benefits Division Regulations*, SOR/94-612.

72 The public service pension plans subject to the *PBDA* include the *Public Service Superannuation Act*, R.S.C. 1985, c. P-36; the *Royal Canadian Mounted Police Pension Continuation Act*, R.S.C. 1970, c. R-10; the *Royal Canadian Mounted Police Superannuation Act*, R.S.C. 1985, c. R-11; the *Canadian Forces Superannuation Act*, R.S.C. 1985, c. C-17; the *Members of Parliament Retiring Allowances Act*, R.S.C. 1985, c. M-5, the *Defence Services Pension Continuation Act*, R.S.C. 1970, c. D-3; the *Diplomatic Service (Special) Superannuation Act*, R.S.C. 1985, c. D-2; the *Special Retirement Arrangements Act*, S.C. 1992, c. 46 (Schedule I); the *Lieutenant Governors Superannuation Act*, R.S.C. 1985, c. L-8; and the *Governor General's Act*, R.S.C. 1985, c. G-9; see *PBDA, supra*, note 10, s. 2 "pension plan", "spouse".

73 *PBDA, ibid.*, s. 4(1).

74 *Ibid.*, s. 4(2)(a).

75 *Ibid.*, s. 4(2)(b).

76 *Ibid.*, s. 7.

77 *Ibid.*, s. 8.

PENSION VALUATION UNDER THE *FAMILY LAW ACT*: DEFINED BENEFIT PLANS

CHAPTER 5

1. INTRODUCTION

The *Family Law Act*[1] requires that pensions be valued on marriage breakdown and that the value be settled through the equalization process. The *Family Law Act* does not, however, stipulate how that value is to be determined.[2] This has led to difficulties where the pension subject to valuation is a defined benefit plan. While the valuation of defined contribution plans is a relatively straightforward matter,[3] the valuation of defined benefit plans is considerably more complex.[4] It rests on certain assumptions concerning future events and contingencies. Because of the many factors involved in such calculations, valuations for the same plan can vary substantially, depending on the methods and assumptions on which they are based. Understandably, each party to a marriage breakdown seeks a valuation that will best serve his or her financial interests. Each spouse retains his or her lawyer to negotiate issues relating to pension valuation and, typically, each spouse engages his or her own actuary as well. When agreement cannot be reached, the result is often a lengthy and expensive judicial proceeding.[5] The effect of the current system of pension valuation has been characterized as "rough justice" at best.[6]

In this chapter, the Commission makes a series of recommendations that attempt to clarify the law regarding the appropriate actuarial methods, principles, and assumptions to be used in valuing defined benefit plans for the purposes of determining an equalization entitlement under the *Family Law Act*. The Commission believes that standards for the valuation of defined benefit plans valuation would reduce the expense, delay, and litigation arising from disputes concerning the proper valuation of pensions. . . .

The Commission therefore recommends that the *Family Law Act* should be amended to provide that the valuation of defined benefit plans for the purposes of determining an equalization entitlement under section 5 of the Act be made in accordance with "Pension Valuation Regulations" promulgated under that Act.

---

1 R.S.O. 1990, c. F.3, ss. 4, 5.

2 The *Pension Benefits Act*, R.S.O. 1990, c. P.8, does not prescribe a method to be used in the valuation of pensions for the purposes of determining a member's net family property under the *Family Law Act*, *supra*, note 1.

3 The value of a defined contribution plan is the accumulated value or the "actual accumulation of the fund": Jack Patterson, *Pension Division and Valuation [:] Family Lawyers' Guide* (Aurora, Ont.: Canada Law Book, 1991), at 61. An actuarial value of defined contribution plans is inappropriate (*ibid.*):

> You simply determine from the plan administrator the amount of the fund at the date of valuation and the amount of the fund at the date of marriage, and these values are used directly in the calculation of net family property.

4 Approximately sixty percent of public sector pension plans fall into the defined benefit plan category, as do approximately forty-two percent of private defined benefit plans. Ninety-one percent of all pension plan members in Canada belong to defined benefit plans. There are 8,284 defined benefit plans in Canada with 4,633,587 members. These represent 41.5 percent of all plans and 90.7 percent of all members of plans. There are 11,443 defined contribution plans (57.3 percent of all plans) with 430,561 members (8.4 percent of all members of plans). The percentage of plans and members do not add up to one hundred percent because certain plans not readily classified as either defined benefit or defined contribution plans are excluded: Statistics Canada, *Pension Plans in Canada—1990* (survey), Table 10, at 3.

5 Valuation costs vary from $400 to $1,000, but if actuaries must testify in court, the cost rises substantially and may be closer to the $2,500-$5,000 range: Law Reform Commission of British Columbia, *Working Paper on Division of Pensions on Marriage Breakdown* (Working Paper No. 65) (Vancouver: Ministry of Attorney General, December 1990), at 123 (hereinafter referred to as "B.C. Working Paper No. 65").

6 *Ibid.*, at 124, quoting E.M. Roche, "Treatment of Pensions upon Marriage Breakdown in Canada: A Comparative Study" (1986-87), 1 Can. Fam. L.Q. 189, at 215.

7 The Alberta Institute of Law Research and Reform (now Alberta Law Reform Institute), in *Matrimonial Property: Division of Pension Benefits upon Marriage Breakdown*, Report No. 48 (Edmonton: June 1986), at 57 (hereinafter referred to as "Alta. Report No. 48") argued the need for legislation in this area:

> Innocent bystanders must be protected against being prejudiced by lawsuits between spouses. Therefore, if there is to be a valuation and division, it must be on the basis of a valuation produced under a standardized procedure which will not involve pension plans and their administrators in litigation.

The Law Reform Commission of British Columbia recommended that a default method of valuation be provided for in regulations, but it was unwilling to recommend mandatory regulations for pension valuation: see *Report on the Division of Pensions on Marriage Breakdown*, Report No. 123 (Vancouver: Ministry of Attorney General, January 1992), at 106 (hereinafter referred to as "B.C. Report No. 123"). The proposed legislation set out in B.C. Report No. 123 is reproduced *infra*, Appendix D.

[An extensive description of the Ontario case law dealing with the valuation of pensions and the Commission's recommended regulations is omitted. See pp. 94-158 of the *Report*. The Commission also recommended reforms to "benefit splits" under the *Pension Benefits Act* and proposed that, in some circumstances, a non-member spouse could arrange for a transfer of a portion of the member spouse's pension into another pension vehicle. See pp. 159-259 of the *Report*. Finally, the Commission turned to the division of Canada Pension Plan Credits.]

DIVISION OF CANADA PENSION PLAN CREDITS

CHAPTER 8

1. INTRODUCTION

On January 1, 1987, the *Canada Pension Plan*[1] (the *CPP Act*) was amended to provide for mandatory division of pension credits or benefits between spouses on marriage breakdown. There has been some confusion and uncertainty concerning the splitting of CPP entitlements, particularly with respect to whether a spouse may waive entitlement to a share in the other spouse's CPP benefits. Although the plan itself does not provide for waiver, the legislation does permit provinces to enact legislation enabling spouses to agree that they will not divide CPP entitlements. No legislation on this point has been enacted in Ontario.[2] . . .

2. OPTING OUT OF CANADA PENSION PLAN

(a) INTRODUCTION

The *CPP Act* creates a contributory plan funded by the mandatory contributions of employers, employees, and the self-employed, as well as by the earnings generated by the investment of the funds in the plan.[6] A contributor to the CPP acquires certain entitlements, such as disability and retirement benefits; his or her spouse may also be eligible to receive those benefits.

In the case of marriage breakdown, the *CPP Act* provides for an equal division of the pension credits accumulated by both spouses during the marriage.[7] Once properly notified that a marriage has been dissolved by divorce or annulment, the Minister must divide equally the pension credits accumulated by both spouses while they were married and living together.[8] Spouses may also apply for such a division after they have been separated for more than one year.[9] The Act also provides for division of credits between qualifying common-law spouses.[10]

The CPP credit-splitting provisions respond to two concerns: first, the recognition that a homemaker makes an important contribution to the well-being of the family and should be compensated equally at retirement, and, second, the fact that income security is as important for non-contributors as it is for contributors. . . .

(c) RECOMMENDATIONS FOR REFORM

The Commission supports the reasoning behind the Alberta Institute's view that provincial legislation permitting spouses to waive or opt out of the federal CPP credit division scheme should not be enacted. More particularly, we believe that a high value must be placed on ensuring that individuals who have been earning wages for a substantial period should share CPP benefits with their spouses.

We appreciate that our support for the mandatory nature of CPP credit splitting may appear inconsistent with our more general view that the division of pension assets should not be mandatory. CPP benefits are distinguishable from other pensions at source, however, on two grounds. First, CPP benefits, together with other social programs, constitute a publicly funded social security scheme, entitlement to which should not be waivable. Secondly, the division of CPP credits, given the universal and centralized nature of the CPP scheme, is administratively straightforward and therefore relatively inexpensive.

The Commission recommends that the type of provincial legislation envisaged by section 55.2(3) of the *Canada Pension Plan*, permitting spouses to waive mandatory division at source of Canada Pension Plan credits, should not be enacted in Ontario.

3. CANADA PENSION PLAN CREDITS AND EQUALIZATION

Finally, we must consider whether the transfer or division of CPP credits ought to be taken into account in the equalization process under the *Family Law Act*.[22]

Entitlements under the CPP fall within the definition of "property" contained in the *Family Law Act*.[23] Accordingly, the value of entitlements earned during the marriage should be included in the calculation of net family property and accounted for in the calculation of the equalization claim. In practice, however, it appears that CPP credits are omitted from the calculation of net family property.[24]

It has been suggested that "[t]here is an unfortunate lack of coordination between the *Family Law Act* and the Canada Pension Plan".[25] Under the *Family Law Act*, CPP entitlements constitute "property", which must be included in "net family property" and accounted for in the calculation of an equalization claim. No provision is made for the separate treatment of such benefits. The *CPP Act*, however, mandates the division of pension credits on marriage breakdown if application is made to the Minister.

In the Ontario case of *Payne* v. *Payne*,[26] Misener L.J.S.C. held that CPP entitlements fall within the definition of "property" contained in the *Family Law Act, 1986*,[27] but for the following reasons should not be included in the calculation of net family property:[28]

> As I understand the provisions of the federal legislation that establishes this pension—the Canada Pension Plan . . . —a division of unadjusted pensionable earnings between former spouses is compelled in the case of all judgments for divorce granted after 1st January 1987 without the

necessity of an application by either of the former spouses. . . . The only right in the Minister of National Health and Welfare to refuse such a division is satisfaction that it would be detrimental to *both* of the former spouses to make it. . . . Moreover, absent provincial legislation authorizing the court to do so (and I am not aware of any such legislation in Ontario), any order of the court that purports to nullify any such division is not binding upon the minister and therefore—at least as I interpret the rights and duties of the minister—must be ignored by him. Section 53.5(4) and (5) imposes a duty upon the minister to notify each of the former spouses of the periods of unadjusted pensionable earnings to be divided, and to attribute the division so made to each of the former spouses. Therefore, it seems to me that, quite apart from constitutional considerations, absent provincial legislation specifically authorizing the inclusion of Canada Pension benefits in the calculation of the net family property, I ought not to do so on the simple ground that to do so would grant or likely grant to Mrs. Payne a greater entitlement than the Family Law Act gives her.

The solution adopted in *Payne* v. *Payne* has been said to have "substantial practical advantages".[29] It acknowledges the practical reality that, in most cases, a division of pension credits will occur under the *CPP Act*, either automatically or on application. It also avoids the necessity of having to calculate the value of CPP entitlements, as well as the risk of overcompensation that might occur if the full value of CPP credits is included in the calculation of the equalization obligation and, subsequently, a mandatory split is effected. On the other hand, it is not entirely clear that this approach rests on a correct interpretation of the *Family Law Act*. As some commentators have observed, "[t]he objection to this solution is simply that it is not permitted by the *Family Law Act*".[30]

In favour of inclusion, it can be argued that because CPP pensions constitute a form of wealth, they should be included in the calculation of the value of each spouse's assets for equalization purposes as required by the *Family Law Act*. Further, if CPP credits are split, it may appear unfair to the spouse who loses credits to ignore this fact in determining the quantum of any further equalization that the Act requires, at least in cases where the equalization is not based on an equal division of assets. We note that this was the conclusion reached by the Alberta Institute in its report.

On balance, we have concluded that the considerations in favour of excluding CPP pensions from net family property outweigh those against. In particular, the burden of valuation appears to be a very significant factor. For many parties, CPP pensions do not constitute a significant component of net family property. It would be inappropriate to require a complex valuation and then to require a mandatory division of CPP credits.

The Commission recommends that the definition of "net family property" in the *Family Law Act* should be amended to specifically exclude benefits payable to the spouse under *Canada Pension Plan*.

---

1 R.S.C. 1985, c. C-8, as am. by R.S.C. 1985, c. 30 (2nd Supp.).

2 It must be considered whether the general provisions of the *Family Law Act*, R.S.O. 1990, c. F.3, permitting spouses to enter into domestic contracts, would constitute enabling legislation of the requisite kind. A careful reading of s. 55.2(3) of the *CPP Act*, *supra*, note 1, as en. by R.S.C. 1985, c. 30 (2nd Supp.), s. 23, suggests that these *Family Law Act* provisions do not satisfy the requirements of the *CPP Act*. It appears that, to enable parties to contract out of the division of pension credits, the *Family Law Act* would have to contain an express reference to the *CPP Act*: see s. 55.2(3)(a). This seems to be the conclusion of the Ontario Court (General Division) in *Albrecht* v. *Albrecht* (1990), 31 R.F.L. (3d) 325 (Ont. Div. Ct.), rev'g (1989), 23 R.F.L. (3d) 8 (Ont. Dist. Ct.).

6 E. Diane Pask and Cheryl A. Hass, *Division of Pensions* (Calgary: Carswell, looseleaf), at XI-1.

7 *CPP Act, supra*, note 1, s. 55, as am. by R.S.C. 1985, c. 30 (2nd Supp.), s. 22; S.C. 1991, c. 44, s. 6, and s. 55.1, as en. by R.S.C. 1985, c. 30 (2nd Supp.), s. 23; am. by S.C. 1991, c. 44, s. 7.

8 *Ibid.*, s. 55.1(1)(a), as en. by R.S.C. 1985, c. 30 (2nd Supp.), s. 23; am. by S.C. 1991, c. 44, s. 7.

9 *Ibid.*, s. 55.1(1)(b), as en. by R.S.C. 1985, c. 30 (2nd Supp.), s. 23; am. by S.C. 1991, c. 44, s. 7.

10 *Ibid.*, s. 55.1(1)(c), as en. by R.S.C. 1985, c. 30 (2nd Supp.), s. 23; am. by S.C. 1991, c. 44, s. 7; s. 2(1) "spouse" as en. by R.S.C. 1985, c. 30 (2nd Supp.), s. 1(3).

22 *Supra*, note 2.

23 *Ibid.*, s. 4(1).

24 Catherine D. Aitken, "Pensions Under Part I of the Family Law Act of Ontario", in Special Lectures of the Law Society of Upper Canada 1993, *Family Law [:] Roles, Fairness and Equality* (Toronto: Carswell, 1994), at 8.

25 Berend Hovius and Timothy G. Youdan, *The Law of Family Property* (Toronto: Carswell, 1991), at 491.

26 (1988), 16 R.F.L. (3d) 8 (Ont. H.C.J.).

27 S.O. 1986, c. 4.

28 *Payne* v. *Payne, supra*, note 26, at 12.

29 *Ibid.*

30 *Ibid.*

BEST v. BEST

(1999), 49 R.F.L. (4th) 1 (S.C.C.)

MAJOR J. (Lamer C.J., Gonthier, Cory, McLachlin, Iacobucci, Bastarache and Binnie JJ. concurring): This appeal raised some of the contentious and confusing issues surrounding the treatment of pensions in the division of property when a marriage ends. A central issue here was the appropriate technique for determining the value of a defined benefit pension under Ontario's *Family Law Act*, R.S.O. 1990, c. F.3. The legal proceedings in this divorce action have been costly, and these reasons will hopefully end the parties' prolonged conflict.

I have concluded that, absent special circumstances, a *pro rata* method of pension valuation best achieves the purpose of the *Family Law Act*, namely, the equitable division of assets between spouses. It will be evident that, while the division of pensions can raise many complex questions, this Court can only address the limited issues involved in this particular appeal. It will be equally evident that legislative changes to the *Family Law Act* are required to provide further guidance for the equitable division of pension assets between spouses on the termination of marriage. In the absence of legislative action, couples undergoing divorces where pension benefits are an issue will have little choice in the absence of an agreement but to resort to expensive litigation.

The intent of the Ontario legislature, expressed in the *Family Law Act*, is to divide the value of all assets accumulated during the marriage equally among the separated spouses. To reach that result in the case at bar required determining the growth in value of the pension owned by the appellant husband during the marriage.

If it were not for the complexities of valuing defined benefit pensions, this would be relatively simple.

However, the Court was faced with two different actuarial methods for valuing the pension's growth during the marriage. The appellant [the husband] favoured the "termination *pro rata*" method, which required the pension benefit to be paid at retirement to be calculated as if the employee terminated employment on the date of separation. The pension's value on the date of separation is the present value of that income stream, using an assumed retirement age and accepted actuarial assumptions regarding rates of interest, inflation, and longevity. The value on the date of marriage is obtained by multiplying the value on the date of separation by a fraction equal to the number of years of pensionable service that occurred prior to the marriage over the total number of years of pensionable service prior to separation. The amount accrued during the marriage is the difference between the values on the date of separation and on the date of marriage; the non-employee spouse (in this case, the respondent wife) would be entitled to half that amount upon separation.

The respondent favoured the "termination value-added" method. This method uses the same process as the *pro rata* method to value the pension on the date of separation: the determination of the pension benefit earned followed by a calculation of the present value of that income stream on the date of separation. Under the value-added method, the value on the date of marriage is calculated in a similar way: the employee is assumed to have terminated employment on the date of marriage, the pension benefit earned to that point is calculated, and the present value for such an income stream, discounted back to the date of marriage, is determined. Once again, the amount accumulated during marriage is the difference between the two values, and the non-employee spouse is entitled to half of it.

The value-added method essentially treats the pension as an investment asset that grows with the employee's salary and increases with the compounding of amounts previously earned. Under the value-added method, each successive year is of increasingly higher value. As a result, in cases like this one where there is significant pensionable service prior to the marriage, the value-added method allocates more value to the later years of pension holding than to the earlier years. In this case, the marriage lasted for just over 12 (or approximately 37%) of the appellant's 32 years of pensionable service before separation, but the value-added method apportions about 88% of the pension's value to that period.

In contrast, the effect of the *pro rata* method is that all years of pensionable service are treated as equal; the growth of the pension is uniform over time, with no pension year more valuable than another. In this case, the *pro rata* method assigns approximately 37% of the pension's value to the marriage. Because this method assigns more value to the pre-marital years and less to the marital years than the value added method, it is obvious why the appellant submitted this method to be the more equitable.

I Facts

The appellant, Theodore Clifford Best, was born on April 14, 1935. He was employed as a school principal since 1960 and served as an elected trustee of the Ottawa Board of Education since 1972. He and the respondent, Marlene Shirley Best, were married on February 7, 1976, when Mr. Best was 40 years old. Both spouses had been married before, and this second marriage was turbulent.

The parties separated with no hope of reconciliation in February 1988, and a divorce judgment in 1989 ended their 12-year childless marriage. After the divorce, extensive litigation ensued over the division of property. The trial in 1993 lasted approximately 12 days. Many of the property disputes decided by the trial judge were not appealed. The important issue in dispute was the fair division of the appellant's pension rights as a member of the Teachers' Superannuation and Superannuation Adjustment Funds, in which he enrolled in September 1955, 20.52 years before the marriage.

The pension plan was a "defined benefit" pension, meaning that the annual pension benefit paid to retirees is calculated according to a benefit formula. In this case, upon retirement, the appellant was entitled to an annual benefit equal to 2% of the average of his five best annual salaries, multiplied by the total number of years of service prior to retirement. The appellant's pension also contained an early retirement provision, which allowed an employee to retire and obtain an unreduced pension without penalty as soon as the sum of the employee's age and years of service reached 90. The pension was indexed for inflation, both before and after retirement, according to the Consumer Price Index. The appellant's pension benefits vested prior to the date of marriage.

The Ontario Court (General Division) decided the action in the respondent's favour on October 15, 1993: see *Best* v. *Best* (1993), 50 R.F.L. (3d) 120 (Ont. Gen. Div.). At that time, the appellant was 58 years old and was still employed and accumulating pensionable service. The respondent was also 58 at the time, but was not employed, owing in part to poor health. The appellant retired on June 30, 1996, while the case was on appeal. The Ontario Court of Appeal dismissed the appellant's appeal on October 3, 1997: see *Best* v. *Best* (1997), 35 O.R. (3d) 577 (Ont. C.A.). At that time, both parties were 62 years old. . . .

III Judicial History

A. *Ontario Court (General Division) — Rutherford J. (1993), 50 R.F.L. (3d) 120 (Ont. Gen. Div.)*

In determining this appeal it is necessary to outline the careful and comprehensive reasoning of the trial judge. He first sought to determine the age at which the appellant was likely to retire, an important factor in the valuation of the appellant's pension. Had the appellant terminated employment on the date of separation, February 1988, he would have qualified for early retirement under the "rule of 90" by increase in age alone on September 9, 1992, at age 57.4. Rutherford J. concluded that, looking at it from the perspective of the date of separation, the evidence justified choosing that date as the most likely retirement date. Because he refused to use "hindsight", the assumption was that the appellant did not continue to earn pensionable service beyond February 1988. In choosing a probable retirement date of September 9, 1992, the trial judge had to ignore the fact that the appellant was still working on the date of judgment.

The trial judge then proceeded to the question of valuation methods. Because there was no significant dispute over the pension's value on the date of separation, the trial judge accepted the respondent's figure of $424,912.

The dispute over valuation methods arose when the parties' actuaries sought to determine the pension's value as of the date of *marriage*. The respondent's actuary, H. Wayne Woods, used the "termination value-added" method, which yielded a pension value of $52,871 on the date of marriage. Subtracting this from the pension's value at the date of separation ($424,912) yields $372,041, which the respondent argued was the proper value of the pension to be attributed to the appellant's net family property under the *Family Law Act.*

The appellant's actuary, Bernard Potvin, used what was called a "termination, prorated method." Under this method, because there had been significant pre-marital pensionable service, the pension contributed only $151,480 to the appellant's net family property.

. . . The trial judge accepted the respondent's valuation that the pension accumulated $372,041 in value over the course of the marriage. He discounted this amount by 28% for income tax, yielding a final value of $267,869. Rutherford J. then performed the equalization calculation under s. 5(1) of the *Family Law Act,* and, after an adjustment not relevant here, concluded that the appellant owed the respondent an equalization payment of $147,649.50.

Rutherford J. ordered the appellant to satisfy his equalization obligation first by transferring his interest in the matrimonial home, which he found to be worth $60,065, to the respondent. Given that the bulk of the equalization obligation was owing to the value of the pension, which would not produce income for the appellant until some point in the future, the court allowed the appellant to pay the remaining $87,584.50, with interest, in monthly installments over a 10-year period, similar to a mortgage repayment scheme. . . .

B. Court of Appeal for Ontario — Charron J.A. (Finlayson and Doherty JJ.A. concurring) (1997), 35 O.R. (3d) 577 (C.A.)

On October 3, 1997, the Court of Appeal dismissed the appellant's appeal. Charron J.A. agreed on all points with the trial judge's reasoning regarding pension valuation. She added that, since the trial judge's reasons had been released, the Court of Appeal had decided in *Kennedy* v. *Kennedy* (1996), 19 R.F.L. (4th) 454 (Ont. C.A.), that a retirement date must be chosen "on a case-by-case basis upon consideration of all the relevant evidence" (para. 12). Charron J.A. concluded that Rutherford J. had followed this rule by examining all the evidence before him in choosing a probable retirement date of September 9, 1992.

Charron J.A. also noted, at p. 585, that using "hindsight" in choosing a retirement date for valuation purposes would "introduce great uncertainty in the litigation process" and "may well militate against the early resolution of matrimonial disputes". Charron J.A., at p. 585, considered that post-separation evidence could be relevant to determine "the probable age of retirement *as contemplated* by the pension plan holder" on the date of separation (emphasis in original). Conduct contemplated as of the separation date, as well as the fact of separation itself, could also be relevant, but facts that were unknown to or not contemplated by the pension holder at separation could not.

Charron J.A. then addressed the appellant's argument that, instead of ordering monthly instalments, the trial judge should have ordered that the equalization payment be made on an "if and when" basis, such that the appellant would pay the respondent her share of the pension benefit if and when he received it. Charron J.A. adverted to the fact that many Ontario courts had made use of "if and when" orders, but that such orders are complicated and not always suitable. Charron J.A. concluded that Rutherford J. did not exceed his discretion by preferring an amortized payment scheme over an "if and when" arrangement.

Charron J.A. also rejected the appellant's argument that the spousal support order should terminate upon his retirement, and decided that Rutherford J. was within his discretion in his award of costs. She dismissed the appeal and awarded costs on appeal to the respondent. . . .

IV. Analysis

A. *Valuing the Defined Benefit Pension*

. . .

(2) *Valuation Methods*

Valuing a defined benefit pension prior to retirement is necessarily artificial. The true value of the appellant's pension benefit cannot be determined with finality until retirement, when the total number of years of service and the five best salaries are known with certainty. The actuarial profession has developed different valuation methods that reflect different assumptions, all of which are sound from an actuarial point of view. The problem is determining whether one method is preferable from a legal perspective under the *Family Law Act*.

The various methods of pension valuation upon marriage breakup can be generally classified according to two characteristics: (a) the way they determine the pension's value at separation, and (b) the way they describe the pension's growth in value during the period leading up to separation.

(a) *Termination Method v. Retirement Method*

The first methodological distinction concerns the way in which an actuary determines the pension's value on the date of separation. The two principal actuarial methods for this calculation are the "termination" method and the "retirement" method.

The "termination" method requires the actuary to determine the annual pension benefit by assuming that the employee spouse stopped working on the date of separation. The "retirement" method requires the actuary to consider possible post-separation increases in the pension's value in order to determine as closely as possible what the pension benefit will actually be when the employee retires in the future. The choice between termination and retirement methods raises many important questions, such as the use of post-separation evidence obtained in "hindsight" and speculation as to future salary increases owing to promotions and improvements in the terms of the pension plan. In this case, it suffices to note that the parties agreed to use a termination method.

Under the termination method, the pension's value on the date of separation is determined by calculating the benefit earned as of that date under the pension's benefit formula. This "pension benefit" is the annual amount that the employee would receive starting on the date of retirement. The actuary then determines the amount that, if invested on the date of separation, would provide the same income stream as the pension (the "lump-sum present value" or "capitalized value"). This calculation is also called "discounting": the pension benefit's value on the date of its payment is discounted back to yield its present value on the date of separation.

The discounting calculation requires the use of certain assumptions. First, the actuary must use an assumed date of retirement to determine the length of the discounting period. The later the retirement date, the longer the discounting period, the lower the pension's present value. The actuary also makes assumptions about the employee's longevity: the longer the employee lives, the longer the pension will be paid, the higher its value.

Finally, the actuary must choose a discounting rate to reflect the effects of inflation and investment return. Inflation is particularly important here in light of the fact that the appellant's pension is indexed, meaning that the value of the pension benefit increases to match the Consumer Price Index. Even if the appellant were assumed to terminate employment on the separation date, prior to the date he would actually retire and start receiving a pension benefit, the numerical value of the pension benefit would actually increase between termination and retirement in order to compensate for the dollar's loss of purchasing power over time. From my reading of the record, it appeared that the actuaries in this case accounted for indexing by using "net interest rates," meaning that the discounting rate used was lower than the usual risk-free rate of return. See Canadian Institute of Actuaries, *Standard of Practice for the Computation of the Capitalized Value of Pension Entitlements on Marriage Breakdown for Purposes of Lump-Sum Equalization Payments* (1993) (hereinafter CIA Standard of Practice), at pp. 10-11. This lower discounting rate reflects the fact that an indexed pension has a higher value than an unindexed one.

One member of the actuarial profession has noted that the term "termination method" is ambiguous and might suggest that post-separation increases in pension value owing to indexing should not be taken into account in determining the pension's value on the date of separation. See J.B. Patterson, "Confusion Created in Pension Valuation for Family Breakdown Case Law by the Use of the Expressions 'Termination Method' and 'Retirement Method'" (1998), 16 *C.F.L.Q.* 249, at pp. 249-56; J. Patterson, *Pension Division and Valuation: Family Lawyers' Guide* (2nd ed. 1995), at pp. 187-88. Accordingly, one case has adopted the term "real interest method" to describe a valuation method that adjusts the discounting rate to account for indexing. See *Bascello* v. *Bascello* (1995), 26 O.R. (3d) 342 (Ont. Gen. Div.), at pp. 354 and 360.

For present purposes, I will continue to refer to the method as a "termination" method, in accordance with the definition advanced by the Canadian Institute of Actuaries. See CIA Standard of Practice, *supra*, at p. 5. The reason is that the method used here still values the pension benefit on the assumption that the employee spouse terminated employment on the date of separation; it does not speculate as to post-separation salary increases owing to non-inflationary factors, such as promotions, plan improvements, and additional years of service. In those material respects, the method is still a "termination" method; it is simply a termination method whose discounting rate is a "net" or "real" interest rate to reflect the fact that the pension is indexed.

Under this termination method, taking account of indexing, the respondent's actuary determined the pension to have a present value of $424,912 on the date of separation. Apart from the appropriate retirement age, the appellant does not dispute the methodology used in this calculation. Although the appellant's actuary reached a slightly lower number ($421,983), probably because of different assumptions as to interest rates and longevity, the actuary did not consider the difference significant. I therefore accept the respondent's figure of $424,912 for the pension's value at separation.

(b) *Value-Added Method v. Pro Rata Method*

The controversy in this case arose because of the second characteristic that distinguishes pension valuation methods, that is the representation of the pension's increase in value over time. Different assumptions regarding how a pension increases in value over time result in different figures for the pension's value on the date of marriage. In the following example, the Canadian Institute of Actuaries describes the standard approaches to this issue:

> At valuation date # 1 (e.g., marriage), the plan member had 10 years pensionable service, had accrued $2,000 of annual pension entitlements, which at that date had a value of $5,000. At valuation date #2 (e.g., separation), the plan member had 25 years pensionable service, had accrued $30,000 of annual pension entitlements, which at that date had a value of $240,000.

> There are three possible approaches to addressing a member's pension entitlement acquired during marriage. One approach is sometimes referred to as "value added". Such approach develops the pension asset acquired during marriage as follows:

> $240,000 — $5,000 = $235,000

> [I omit the second method, referred to as the *pro-rata* (on benefits) method, which is not advanced by either party in this case.]

> A third approach is sometimes referred to as pro-rata (on service). Such approach develops the pension asset acquired during the marriage as follows:

> $(25 — 10)/25 \times \$240,000 = \$144,000$

See CIA Standard of Practice, *supra*, at p. 6. For brevity's sake, I refer to the *pro rata* (on service) method as the "*pro rata* method."

The different figures reached under the value-added and *pro rata* methods are the result of different theories about how a pension increases in value from the point where the employee enrols in the pension, where the pension has a value of zero, to the separation date. According to the *pro rata* method favoured by the appellant, the pension increases in value at a constant rate over time. The value-added method pressed by the respondent shows the pension increasing slowly at first and more quickly later, along a parabola or "growth curve."

The *pro rata* method will always assign the pension a higher value than the value-added method at any point in time prior to separation. This difference poses no problem if the employee spouse (here, the husband) only starts earning defined benefit pension rights *after* the date of marriage; the value at marriage is zero regardless of which method is used. But where the employee spouse was a member of the pension *prior* to the marriage, the values obtained for the date of marriage diverge widely, in this case in the amount of $220,561.

The evidence was, and the parties agreed, that both the value-added and *pro rata* methods are acceptable ways to value a defined benefit pension from an actuarial point of view. The legal question is whether any particular method is mandated or preferable under Ontario's *Family Law Act*.

(3) *Statutory Language*

In interpreting a statute, the courts should give effect to the intent of the legislature as expressed through the statute's text. Here the text of the *Family Law Act* does not prescribe how any particular asset's value is to be determined. The most guidance it gives is s. 4(1), which requires the court to calculate each spouse's "net family property", which is defined as the value of all assets owned by each spouse on the "valuation date" (here the date of separation, February 28, 1988) less the value of all assets owned on the date of marriage (here February 7, 1976). The statute's aim is then to divide equally the difference between the spouses' net family properties, such that neither spouse's share of the wealth accumulated during the marriage period exceeds the other's. There is room for judicial discretion to divide net family properties unequally (s. 5(6)), but it is not implicated in this case.

The respondent's position was that the value-added method fitted the statutory scheme as it calculated the pension's present value on both dates, enabling the court to plug both values into the net family property calculation, but that the *pro rata* method did *not* fit the scheme because it did not calculate the pension's present value on the date of marriage. The trial judge and the court of appeal agreed, preferring the value-added method because it was, in their view, "more consistent" with the calculation prescribed by s. 4(1).

I disagree as I am persuaded that the *pro rata* method in most cases and particularly in this one reaches a more equitable result, in conformity with the intent and language of the *Family Law Act*. The appellant's actuary, Bernard Potvin, testified that the *pro rata* method calculated the value at marriage by multiplying the present value on the date of separation by a fraction dividing the years of pensionable service prior to the marriage (approximately 20.52) by the years of pensionable service prior to separation (approximately 32.6). According to Mr. Potvin, this calculation yields a value of $270,503 for the appellant's pension as of the date of marriage. The appellant's net family property under s. 4(1) would be the separation value ($424,912) added to the value of the other assets owned by the appellant on the date of separation, less the marriage value ($270,503) added to the value of other assets owned by the appellant on the date of marriage. This calculation fits precisely within the mathematical operations described in s. 4(1).

The respondent submitted that the statute requires more. Specifically, she objected that the *pro rata* method used the value at separation to "construct an arbitrary figure" for the pension's value as of the date of marriage. The respondent read s. 4(1)'s provision that the value of the assets at marriage be "calculated as of the date of the marriage" to mean that the marriage value must be the *lump-sum present value* of the pension, meaning the amount that, if invested on the date of marriage, would produce the same return as the pension when the appellant retired. She argued that only a present value calculation produces a value "as of" the marriage date.

Although the respondent's theory of pension valuation is permissible under s. 4(1), it is not mandated. If the legislature had meant to prefer a present-value valuation method over any other method, it could easily have provided for it. I do not agree that s. 4(1)'s phrase "calculated as of the date of the marriage" reflects a legislative choice of one actuarial method of pension valuation over another. Instead it addresses the more basic issue that a spouse cannot exclude an asset from his or her net family property simply because the asset was owned before the marriage. If the phrase "calculated as of the date of the marriage" were left out of the statute so that it read: "'net family property' means the value of all the property . . . that a spouse owns on the valuation date, after deducting . . . the value of the property . . . that the spouse owned on the date of the marriage", it would mean a spouse could claim that assets owned before the marriage were not subject to equalization at all, even to the extent that they increased in value during the marriage.

By providing for a deduction of the value of property owned on the date of marriage *calculated as of the date of the marriage*, the statute ensures that increases in asset value during the marriage period are equalized between the spouses, regardless of whether the asset was owned by one of the spouses prior to the marriage. The language of the statute does not address the more challenging problem of what method should be used to determine the actual *amount* by which the assets' value increased.

The respondent submitted that the value at marriage calculated under the *pro rata* method is "artificial" because it varies depending on the date of separation, all other factors being equal. The respondent contrasted this with the value-added method, which produced a fixed pension value for the date of marriage irrespective of the value at the date of separation. Yet s. 4(1) does not provide that the value at marriage cannot be mathematically derived from the value at separation. As stated above, the statute does not address methods of valuation except to say that they must produce a value for the pension on the date of marriage and on the date of separation.

The respondent asserted that proponents of the *pro rata* method, such as the Ontario Law Reform Commission and the Canadian Institute of Actuaries, have "conceded that a legislative amendment would be required to introduce this method into the law of Ontario." This statement is inaccurate. It is true that the OLRC and the Canadian Institutes of Actuaries have recommended that the *pro rata* method be adopted in Ontario by means of legislation, but this recommendation results from their finding that the current law *fails to take a position* on the subject of pension valuation. Contrary to the respondent's argument, neither organization maintained that the *pro rata* method is foreclosed by the *Family Law Act*. . . .

The *Family Law Act* does not require that all property be stretched to fit one valuation method without regard to the fact that different types of assets may accumulate value in different ways. If proper consideration for the nature of a defined benefit pension suggests that a different method should be used to determine its value, the statute does not preclude it.

Because of the many contingencies involved in any effort to value a pension before it is "in pay", all valuation methods will involve some degree of artificiality. The expert witnesses in this case conceded as much during their testimony. The respondent's statement that the *pro rata* method "constructs" an "arbitrary" marriage value neglects the fact that all pre-retirement pension valuations rest on speculative assumptions. One such assumption is whether a lump-sum present value method provides an accurate model for the increase in a pension's value over time. The value-added method assumes it does, the *pro rata* method assumes it does not. Absent clear legislative direction, I am loath to conclude that the *pro rata* method, which enjoys the *imprimatur* of the actuarial profession, must be ruled out because it rests on a different assumption from another method. . . .

I am of the opinion that the *Family Law Act*, on its face, does not state any rule indicating a preference for the value-added method over the *pro rata* method or vice versa. This legislative silence means that the appellant's defined benefit pension must be valued according to the method that values the pension most equitably.

(4) *Equitable Concerns*

The Court's duty is to determine which valuation method most fairly apportions the pension's value to the pre-marital and marital periods. This fairness analysis should not be result-driven. The appellant argued the unfairness of the value added method by showing that it apportioned 88% of the pension's value to a period of marriage that constituted only 37% of the years of service. While this fact is relevant, it is not sufficient to carry the day. It is possible for an asset to increase slowly in value and then rise dramatically in a short period of time. It would be inequitable to deprive the respondent of her share of the good fortune that arose during the course of the marriage. The Court should decide which valuation method most nearly describes how the defined benefit pension's value varied over time, with proper regard for the nature of the asset itself.

At this point, it is worthwhile to recall the difference between a defined benefit pension and a defined contribution pension. The value of a defined *contribution* pension is directly related to the contributions made by the employer and, if applicable, the employee. Each contribution is used to purchase investment assets; the greater the contribution, the more investments are purchased, the greater the final pension benefit. It is obvious that a defined contribution pension increases in value more quickly when contributions are of greater value. Furthermore, because a defined contribution pension is essentially an investment account, the contents of which will be used to purchase a pension annuity at retirement, the value of that pension annuity necessarily tracks the value of the assets in the pension account, including increases owing to investment return. It stands to reason that growth of the pension's value can be represented in the same way as growth in the value of the investment assets. As a result, valuation of defined contribution pensions does not pose the problems encountered here. It is simply a matter of looking at the pension account statement for the date of marriage and the date of separation. See generally OLRC Report, *supra*, at p. 84, n. 3.

In contrast, an employee's interest in a defined benefit pension is not tied to specific pension assets or to the amount of contributions. The pension benefit formula in this case fixed the benefit with reference to years of service and the highest salaries earned. I therefore believe the trial judge confused the issue when (at pp. 140-41) he related the value of a year's membership in a defined benefit plan to the value of employee contributions during that year. Unlike an interest in a defined contribution plan, the ultimate annualized benefit paid to an employee under a defined benefit plan is unrelated to the size of contributions or rate of return on investment.

It is therefore far from self-evident that the increase in value of an interest in a defined benefit pension plan should be modelled after the increase in value of a defined contribution plan or an investment asset. This is a major weakness of the value-added method advocated by the respondent. The value-added method treats a defined benefit pension as a lump-sum investment that grows in value at an adjusted rate based on the prevailing risk-free rate of return. Because this produces a compounding effect, the value-added method assigns a greater portion of the pension's growth to the latter years before the valuation date. This assignment of value, however, is totally unrelated to any actual change in the value of the pension.

This is highlighted by an example. Suppose the appellant had actually terminated his employment on the date of *marriage*, and that, at that time, he had 20 years of service and the average of his five best-paid salaries was (hypothetically) $60,000. Under the benefit formula, he would have earned an annual pension benefit of $24,000 (2% x 20 x $60,000). Twelve years later, at the date of separation, since he had quit his job and not accumulated any more years of service or reached a higher salary level, his annualized pension benefit would still be $24,000. (The effect of pre-retirement indexing is ignored for purposes of simplicity.) Common sense would suggest that, since the interest in the pension has not changed over the course of the marriage, none of it should be considered "net family property" for equalization purposes.

Under the value-added method, however, the actuary would calculate (a) the lump sum that, if invested in risk-free assets on the date of separation, would produce an annual income of $24,000 at retirement. Assume the applicable discount rate and actuarial assumptions yielded a present value at separation of $100,000. Then the actuary would determine (b) the lump sum that, if invested in risk-free assets on the date of *marriage*, would produce the same stream of income ($24,000 annually) beginning on the date of retirement. Discounting $100,000 over the 12-year marriage period at a 3% interest rate yields a present value on the date of marriage of $70,138. Under the value-added method, the difference between the values of (a) and (b) — in the example, $100,000 minus $70,138, i.e. $29,862 — will be considered "net family property." This is so even though the annualized benefit to be paid — which is a defined benefit pension's only meaningful value — did not change at all after the marriage. The result is that the employee spouse (here, the appellant) must equalize a growth in assets that did not actually take place. I do not see any equity in that result. . . .

Another problem afflicting the value-added method as used in this case is the use of a different retirement age assumption in determining the value at marriage than is used for determining the value at separation. In valuing the pension at the date of separation, Rutherford J. chose an assumed retirement age of 57.4 years (the appellant challenged this decision, and it is dealt with in Section 5 below). However, in valuing the pension at the date of marriage, Rutherford J. adopted the respondent's actuary's use of a retirement age of 65. This different retirement age created a double reduction in the marriage value. First, it reduced the pension's present value at retirement because it contemplated that the pension would be paid out for 7.6 fewer years than if the appellant had retired at age 57.4. Second, it lengthened the discounting period for the date of marriage value: the first pension payment was discounted back from the year 2000 (when the appellant would be 65) instead of from 1992 (when he was 57.4).

The Court is at a disadvantage in evaluating the reason for choosing a retirement age of 65 in calculating the date of marriage value. The trial judge and the court of appeal did not address this, and neither did the respondent's submissions in this Court. Judging from the testimony of the respondent's actuary, the retirement age of 65 appeared to derive from the fact that, had the appellant terminated his employment on the date of marriage, he would not have satisfied the requirements of the "rule of 90" early retirement provision and could not have retired before the usual age of 65.

I do not believe that there was any reason to value the pension on the date of marriage in light of an assumption that the employee terminated employment on that date. That assumption ignored the actual economic facts that occurred during the marriage, namely that the appellant worked continuously and eventually brought himself within reach of early retirement.

It is true that there are compelling reasons not to take post-*separation* information into account when valuing the pension under a termination method — for instance, the notion that the non-employee spouse should not profit from the post-separation work of the employee spouse, and the concern that the employee spouse might behave strategically after the separation in order to decrease the value of the pension to be equalized. I consider the effect of these considerations in this particular case in Section 5 below. Regardless of the suitability of using post-separation evidence under a termination method, however, I do not believe there is any justification for refusing to use post-*marriage* evidence in calculating the date of marriage value. This is not "hindsight", since conduct occurring between marriage and separation necessarily occurred before the date of separation. I have difficulty imagining a situation in which an employee spouse would strategically seek to postpone the retirement date through conduct *prior* to separation in order to reduce the pension's present value. . . .

The respondent objected that the *pro rata* method is unfair because it does not reflect the impact of salary increases, which occur at fixed points in time and can significantly affect the pension's value. Instead, the *pro rata* method treats the factor of the "average of five best years' salary" as constant over the entire period of pensionable service. Because the highest-salaried years tend to be the later ones close to the separation date, the value assigned to earlier years under the *pro rata* method effectively credits earlier years with the value of higher salaries earned in later years. The respondent maintained that this is unfair, especially as applied in this case, where there is substantial pre-marital service. By attributing a significant portion of salary increases earned during the marriage to the pre-marital years, the *pro rata* method arguably undervalued net family property inequitably.

Although it is true that salary increases do occur at fixed points in time and can be clearly separated out as occurring before or during the marriage, the Court should consider the particular role that salary increases play in the appellant's defined benefit pension. In a defined *contribution* pension, a salary increase generally means an increase in contributions, which increases the assets held in the pension account. In a "career earnings" defined benefit plan, the salary earned in each individual year determines a portion of the final benefit, so changes in salary from year to year make a significant difference. In both cases, a year in which the employee's salary increased truly does make a higher contribution to the pension benefit than the foregoing years. But in a "best earnings" plan like the appellant's, a salary increase not only increases the value of the year in which it occurred, but also the value that was earned in all past years of service. As was stated above, each year of service adds 2% of the average of the five highest-salaried years, regardless of when those best-paid years occur. Thus, if an employee suffers a reduction in salary late in his or her career, for any reason, the pension benefit remains unaltered. The effect of a salary increase in a "best earnings" defined benefit pension is not limited to the particular year in which it occurred, but extends over the entire period of service.

The respondent's view of salary increases rests once again on the implicit premise that, in valuing the pension on the date of marriage, the Court should assume that the appellant terminated employment on that date. As noted above, there is no principled reason to ignore information that is definitively known at the time of separation in calculating the date of marriage value. Calculating the benefit accrued at marriage based on only the five best salaries earned up to the marriage date is turning a blind eye to the more accurate information available on the date of separation.

On a similar note, I think the *pro rata* method is preferable because it involves less speculation than the value-added method. Although any valuation of a pension before retirement will involve actuarial assumptions that can be proved wrong by future events, the *pro rata* method requires only one discounting calculation and also does not artificially ignore relevant information available at separation in determining the value on the date of marriage. The nature of a "best earnings" defined benefit pension makes this particularly important. I also note that the termination *pro rata* method appears to be the rule for valuation of defined benefit pensions in other Canadian provinces and in many American states. See Quebec *Regulation Respecting Supplemental Pensions Plans* (1990), 122 G.O. II, 2318, ss. 36, 37, 40; *Pension Benefits Act*, S.N.B. 1987, c. P-5.1, s. 44(8); *General Regulation - Pension Benefits Act*, N.B. Reg. 91-195, s. 28(2); *Corpus Juris Secundum* (1986), vol. 27C, § 558, at pp. 53-54; *Humble* v. *Humble*, 805 S.W.2d 558 (U.S. Tex. Civ. App. Beaumont 1991), at pp. 560-61.

It is possible that the value-added method may be reformed to address the concerns I have raised and that it might provide a fairer valuation if the pension were structured in a different way. Generally speaking, however, the *pro rata* method yields a valuation of a defined benefit pension that is fairer than the valuation produced by the value-added method. Since the *Family Law Act*'s primary goal is a division of assets that is fair to both spouses, I believe that the *pro rata* method is the preferable method of valuation under Ontario law.

One additional point deserves mention. While the parties here agreed to use a "termination" method of valuation, I do not wish to foreclose the possibility of future litigants' using a "retirement" method in a future case. My conclusion that all the information available at the time of separation should be used in calculating the pension's value at separation and at marriage ordinarily suggests that one should also consider post-*separation* information to the extent it bears upon the benefit formula. For instance, it is now known as a fact that the appellant retired at age 61 with 40.83 years of service. His best-salaried years could also be ascertained with precision. It is quite likely that such a calculation, which essentially corresponds to a "retirement" method, would have provided the fairest possible valuation of the defined benefit pension in this case.

I note that the use of a "retirement *pro rata*" method has found favour in other provinces. See *Family Relations Act*, R.S.B.C. 1996, c. 128, s. 74; B.C. Reg. 77/95, s. 6; *Hierlihy* v. *Hierlihy* (1984), 48 Nfld. & P.E.I.R. 142 (Nfld. C.A.), at p. 146. It also seems to be the rule among American "community property" states. See, e.g., Corpus Juris Secundum, supra, at p. 57; but see *Humble, supra* (rejecting the retirement *pro rata* method in favour of the termination *pro rata* method).

A retirement method could have much to recommend it, particularly given that a pension's true value might change drastically after the marriage due to changes in the benefit formula or substantial increases in salary. As I have suggested, there are compelling reasons to treat these changes as having an effect over the entire life of the defined benefit pension, not just at the time that they occur. The OLRC also favours a retirement method. See OLRC Report, *supra*, at pp. 104-106.

I am aware that a retirement *pro rata* method could take two possible forms. The Canadian Institute of Actuaries describes a "projected" retirement method, whereby the future accumulation of years of service, salary increases, and changes to the benefit formula would be estimated from an actuarial perspective. See CIA Standard of Practice, *supra*, at p. 5. This method could involve many speculative assumptions, but might be appropriate in a case where the employee spouse's final salaries and years of service were known with sufficient certainty prior to retirement. The OLRC recommends this type of method but suggests a discount for the possibility that the employee might terminate employment earlier. OLRC Report, *supra*, at p. 106; see also *Knippshild* v. *Knippshild* (1995), 11 R.F.L. (4th) 36 (Sask. Q.B.), at pp. 48-50.

Another possible retirement method is the one available in British Columbia, Newfoundland and certain American states, which could be called a "deferred" retirement method. Under this system, calculation of the ultimate amount due to the non-employee spouse is deferred until the actual retirement date, when the final years of service and best-salaried years are crystallized. *Cf. Rutherford* v. *Rutherford* (1979), 14 R.F.L. (2d) 41 (B.C. S.C.), at pp. 60-61, and *Hierlihy, supra*, at pp. 145-46. Decisions in other provinces — including some in Ontario — have employed this method or a similar one. See *Gilmour* v. *Gilmour*, [1995] 3 W.W.R. 137 (Sask. C.A.), at pp. 141-42; *Bourdeau* v. *Bourdeau* (July 27, 1993), Doc. 36779/90 (Ont. Gen. Div.), at pp. 65-66; *Rauf* v. *Rauf* (1992), 39 R.F.L. (3d) 63 (Ont. Div. Ct.), at pp. 65-66; *Porter* v. *Porter* (1986), 1 R.F.L. (3d) 12 (Ont. Dist. Ct.), at pp. 26-27; *Moravcik* v. *Moravcik* (1983), 37 R.F.L. (2d) 102 (Alta. C.A.), at p. 108; *George* v. *George* (1983), 35 R.F.L. (2d) 225 (Man. C.A.), at p. 243. A task force of the Canadian Institute of Actuaries has recommended the use of a "deferred settlement method" along these lines. See Canadian Institute of Actuaries Task Force on the Division of Pension Benefits upon Marriage Breakdown, Draft Paper, *The Division of Pension Benefits upon Marriage Breakdown* (1998), at p. 9. Because this valuation method necessarily defers division of the pension until retirement, it is usually used in conjunction with an "if and when" payment scheme, which is discussed below in Section C.

For present purposes, it is enough that the parties to this appeal have agreed to use a termination method. The possibility of using a retirement method remains open, and in view of its comportment with reality, desirable. I note that some sources have suggested that a deferred retirement method might be at odds with the present wording of the *Family Law Act*. This conclusion seems to be based on the view that the equalization payment should be calculated without regard to any change in asset value after separation. See OLRC Report, *supra*, at p. 105, and *Marsham* v. *Marsham* (1987), 59 O.R. (2d) 609 (Ont. H.C.), at p. 614. In addition, a deferred retirement method effectively equalizes the pension separately from other assets, which might appear at odds with s. 4 of the *Family Law Act*, which provides that each spouse's "net family property" is calculated by adding together the value of *all* the assets owned by the spouse. However, it may be that these statutory objections can be met and overcome. I leave them for another day.

For the foregoing reasons, I believe that the termination *pro rata* method produces a fairer valuation of defined benefit pensions for equalization purposes than the termination value-added method. The *pro rata* method is not without flaws, nor will it inevitably be preferable to the value-added method. Although cases may arise where other considerations will tilt the balance in favour of a different valuation method, the nature of defined benefit pension indicates that, as a general rule, the *pro rata* method is preferable.

(5) *Retirement Age Assumption*

The final struggle in the valuation debate is the assumption used by the trial judge that, on the balance of probabilities, the appellant would likely have retired at age 57.4, looking at the matter from the separation date. As stated, retirement age is crucial to valuation because it determines both the length of the discounting period and also the length of time that the pension will last. Both factors materially affect a pension's present value on the date of separation.

The presence of an early retirement provision such as the "rule of 90" will almost always be relevant to the choice of a likely retirement age. Before 1996, some Ontario courts applied a presumption that, unless the evidence clearly indicated otherwise, the employee spouse would retire as soon as an unreduced pension was available. See, e.g., *Weaver* v. *Weaver* (1991), 32 R.F.L. (3d) 447 (Ont. Gen. Div.), at p. 457; *Leeson* v. *Leeson* (1990), 26 R.F.L. (3d) 52 (Ont. Dist. Ct.), at p. 59; *Forster* v. *Forster* (1987), 11 R.F.L. (3d) 121 (Ont. H.C.), at p. 124; see also G.E. Burrows, *"Pension Considerations on Marriage Breakdown Retirement Age,"* (1995-96) 13 C.F.L.Q. 25, at p. 43; J.G. McLeod, Annotation to *Alger* v. *Alger* (1989), 21 R.F.L. (3d) 211 (Ont. H.C.). Although the Ontario Court of Appeal has rejected this presumption in favour of a decision based on all the evidence, the availability of early retirement without penalty continues to be an important factor, and a trial judge's finding of fact on the matter will not be disturbed lightly. See *Huisman* v. *Huisman* (1996), 21 R.F.L. (4th) 341 (Ont. C.A.), at p. 348; *Kennedy*, *supra*, at p. 460.

Determining when early retirement becomes available, if at all, has produced several different approaches in Ontario. The trial judge in this case assumed that the employee spouse terminated employment on the date of separation. That meant that the employee's years of service were frozen at that point, and the right to early retirement under the "rule of 90" could only be reached by virtue of the increase in the employee's age. Thus Rutherford J. concluded that, if the appellant here had truly stopped working on the date of separation, February 1988, he could only have collected an unreduced pension on September 9, 1992, at age 57.4.

Other decisions use a slightly different assumption, namely that the employee *continued to work* after the date of separation, such that eligibility for early retirement came more quickly as the employee aged and accumulated more years of service. See *Stevens* v. *Stevens* (1992), 41 R.F.L. (3d) 212 (Ont. U.F.C.), at pp. 214-15; *Alger* v. *Alger* (1989), 21 R.F.L. (3d) 211 (Ont. H.C.), at p. 215; *Deroo* v. *Deroo* (1990), 28 R.F.L. (3d) 86 (Ont. H.C.), at pp. 92-93; *Hilderley* v. *Hilderley* (1989), 21 R.F.L. (3d) 383 (Ont. H.C.), at pp. 388-89; *Miller, supra,* at pp. 121-22. Some sources refer to this method as a "hybrid termination/retirement method". See J.G. McLeod, Annotation to *Weaver* v. *Weaver* (1991), 32 R.F.L. (3d) 447 (Ont. Gen. Div.); see also Patterson, *Pension Division and Valuation, supra,* at p. 309; *Radcliff* v. *Radcliff* (November 25, 1994), Doc. Thunder Bay 3917-92 (Ont. Gen. Div.), at para. 23. Under this method, the appellant would have been eligible to take early retirement on June 7, 1990, at age 55.14.

Finally, a minority of decisions have chosen a retirement date based on actual evidence of when the employee spouse intended to retire, but concluded that, because the employee spouse must be taken to have terminated employment on the date of separation, the employee spouse would retire prior to satisfying the early retirement provision and therefore take a reduced pension. See *Salib* v. *Cross* (1993), 15 O.R. (3d) 521 (Ont. Gen. Div.), at pp. 532-34; *Rickett* v. *Rickett* (1990), 72 O.R. (2d) 321 (Ont. H.C.), at p. 333. This has been referred to as a "strict termination" method. See McLeod, *Annotation to Weaver, supra,* at p. 448.

Although it is important to distinguish these different approaches, I need not determine whether one of these approaches is preferable in this case. The parties do not challenge the decision to consider the increase in age alone, nor do they challenge the conclusion that, using that method, the appellant's earliest date for retirement with an unreduced pension was September 9, 1992.

The availability of early retirement, however, was only one piece of evidence that the trial judge considered in choosing the appellant's likely retirement date. The respondent had testified that the appellant was bored with his job and planned to retire as soon as he satisfied the rule of 90. At the time of separation, the terms of the pension plan provided a maximum pension benefit of 70% of the average of the best five annual salaries. The appellant was likely to reach that point in 1990. It was only in 1992, after the separation, that the pension plan was changed to allow accumulation of pension credits above 70%. On the other hand, the appellant had testified that he had never considered retirement except in a general sense, and that, in light of the new financial obligations that arose because of the breakup of the marriage, he could not afford to contemplate retirement. Based on this evidence, Rutherford J. chose a retirement date of September 9, 1992.

The appellant did not argue that this conclusion was unreasonable in light of the evidence available *prior* to separation. Instead, the appellant submitted that the trial judge should have considered evidence available *after* separation but before trial, in particular the fact that the appellant had continued to work past September 1992. According to the appellant, it was unfair to take the facts as frozen as of the date of separation. The appellant further invited this Court to consider the fact that he actually retired at age 61, while the case was before the Ontario Court of Appeal.

I believe the logic of a termination method demands exclusion of "hindsight" evidence. The termination method seeks to determine the value of a pension on the date of separation, assuming the pension holder terminated employment on that date. As I noted above, the termination method does not incorporate increases in the pension's value owing to events occurring after separation, such as post-separation years of service, plan improvements, and non-inflationary salary increases. This method has favoured the appellant in that it has excluded these important post-separation increases from his net family property. It would be unfair to the respondent to use hindsight in choosing a later retirement date but not in determining the number of years of service or the five best salaries. Just as the termination method prevents the respondent from benefiting from increases in the appellant's pension after separation, it protects her from reductions in its value owing to a later actual retirement date than was in contemplation at separation.

I therefore agree with the Ontario Court of Appeal that, under a termination method, post-separation evidence should not be used in determining a likely retirement date unless the evidence reflects facts that were within the employee spouse's contemplation at the time of separation. The result urged by the appellant would enable spouses with pensions to reduce the amount of their equalization payments and profit from the length of divorce proceedings by delaying their retirement until after the close of all proceedings. Although there is no evidence of strategic behaviour in this case, I do not support a rule that could encourage it.

I reach this conclusion because it is the most equitable in this case, notably in light of the parties' choice of a termination method. In a case involving, for example, a "projected retirement" method, it might be preferable to use all evidence available in order to reduce the speculative quality of the projections as to post-retirement improvements. In such a situation it might be fair to use hindsight evidence in choosing the retirement age as well.

B. Settlement of the Equalization Obligation

Having cleared the valuation hurdle, I am faced with a separate problem arising in the division of pensions: how the appellant is to settle his equalization obligation.

Once the pension and all other assets have been tallied to produce the appellant's "net family property", the appellant is required to pay the respondent an amount equal to one-half of the difference between his and her net family properties. Section 9 of the *Family Law Act* allows a court to choose among several methods for payment of the equalization amount, including an order of immediate payment, the granting of a security interest, an instalment scheme, postponement of payment, creation of a trust, and the transferral, partition or sale of property.

The appellant submitted that, because much of his equalization burden is owing to his pension, he should be allowed to satisfy his obligation under an "if and when" payment scheme, meaning that he would pay the respondent a share of the pension benefits "if and when" he received them. Ontario courts have enacted such arrangements by ordering the employee spouse to hold a fraction of the pension in trust for the non-employee spouse, pursuant to s. 9(1)(d)(i) of the *Family Law Act*. See *Hilderley, supra*, at p. 395, and *Marsham, supra*, at p. 624. Ontario's pension legislation also allows a court to order the pension plan administrator to pay over a portion of the pension benefit directly to the non-employee spouse. See *Pension Benefits Act*, R.S.O. 1990, c. P.8, s. 51.

The trial judge rejected the appellant's request but allowed him to settle his equalization obligation in instalments in the 10 years following the judgment. I believe this decision deserves deference. The choice of a method for settlement of the equalization obligation is highly contextual and fact-based. A payment method that is preferable in one case might be grossly unjust in another. . . .

An "if and when" payment scheme has clear advantages when a major part of the difference in net family properties is owing to the capitalized value of a pension. The spouse who bears the equalization burden cannot use the pension asset to satisfy it; one cannot sell an interest in one's pension or borrow money against it. If ordered to make an immediate payment, the spouse must sell or transfer other property. If the employee spouse's equalization burden is high owing to a valuable pension, an order for immediate payment of a lump sum could conceivably expose the employee spouse to severe hardship. An "if and when" scheme alleviates this danger by drawing the equalization payment from the pension asset itself. See OLRC Report, *supra*, at p. 46.

On the other hand, certain factors militate against the use of an "if and when" payment scheme. First and foremost, an "if and when" scheme also requires a continued financial association between the ex-spouses that obviates a "clean break" after the divorce. I note, however, that s. 9(1)(c) allows a court to delay an equalization payment for up to 10 years, suggesting that the Ontario legislature did not object to continued ties after divorce as long as they were only for a "limited" time. Thus an "if and when" scheme might be the appropriate option where retirement was clearly imminent. The Ontario Court of Appeal reached a similar conclusion in the homonymous but unrelated case of *Best* v. *Best* (1992), 41 R.F.L. (3d) 383 (Ont. C.A.), at p. 388.

However, a second complicating factor in the application of an "if and when" payment scheme is the determination of the appropriate "share" of each pension benefit to be paid over to the non-employee spouse. One might presume simply to multiply the pension benefit by the same *pro rata* fraction used in the valuation exercise: one-half of the years of service during marriage divided by the years of service to separation. But the appellant also suggests a second option using a different fraction: one-half of the years of service during marriage divided by the years of service to *retirement*, which is naturally a smaller fraction. Ontario courts appear to have recognized both options but employed the second one more frequently. See *Bourdeau, supra*, at para. 22; *Rauf, supra*, at para. 7; *Hilderley, supra*, at p. 395; *Marsham, supra*, at p. 624. In this case, the appellant offered us both possibilities without arguing which was legally preferable. I make no comment on the issue but simply point out that it complicates application of an "if and when" settlement.

A third and more serious difficulty with the scheme proposed by the appellant concerns the actual amount that is eventually paid. The parties have spent great energy litigating the proper method of valuation for a defined benefit pension in order that the appellant's "net family property" and equalization payment can be correctly determined as of the date of separation. But under an "if and when" scheme, it does not appear that payments end after the equalization amount has been paid, or that the non-employee spouse's interest is protected in the event that the pension is less valuable than expected. Instead, there is a risk that a pension holder who lives long, or whose pension benefit proves more valuable than expected, might end up overpaying the non-employee spouse. Similarly, if the employee spouse dies before the full equalization amount has been paid, underpayment will result. These risks prompted the following comments by the OLRC:

> The practice of using "if and when" arrangements to satisfy equalization payments has been less than satisfactory. The realization of the pension benefit occurs over the post-retirement life of the

> member. As a result, an interest in the pension benefit to which a non-member spouse is entitled may never be realized if the member spouse dies prior to or soon after retirement. On the other hand, where the life span of the member spouse exceeds expectations, or the value of the pension benefit increases after separation, an overpayment to the non-member spouse may result.

See OLRC Report, *supra*, at p. 37.

As an example, assume that the equalization amount on the separation date was $100,000 and that the court ordered that the appellant satisfy it by paying one-half of the pension benefit "if and when" it was received, but that the debt would grow at an interest rate of 5% to reflect the respondent's immediate entitlement to the money. If the appellant retired seven years after the separation date, his equalization debt would have grown to $140,710. Assume he began receiving $30,000 *per* year in pension benefits and paid over $15,000 to the respondent each year. Under this scheme, the appellant would have discharged the debt and interest thereon after approximately 11 years. However, the "if and when" scheme proposed here would require the appellant to continue to make payments after that point. See J. G. McLeod, Case Comment on *Monger* v. *Monger* (1994), 8 R.F.L (4th) 182, at pp. 188-89. In addition, if the appellant had died before that point, the respondent would have no claim against the appellant's estate for the outstanding portion of the debt.

These conclusions suggest that, if the Court were to employ the "if and when" payment scheme advocated by the appellant, there would have been no point in calculating the pension's capitalized value in the first place. The total amount paid under an "if and when" payment scheme seems to have no relation at all to the equalization payment calculated using the pension's capitalized value. It appears to me that the appellant's method not only defers the *payment* of the equalization amount, but also makes it impossible to calculate *the total equalization amount that will be paid*. Instead of being the vehicle for the payment of a fixed amount of money, the "if and when" method splits an indefinite stream of income.

I agree with the appellant that this is a reasonable and perhaps superior method of dividing pensions and that it deserves consideration when long overdue and much-needed legislative attention is turned to this area. However, it would seem to be inconsistent with the appellant's principal position in this case, namely that the equalization amount should be calculated by valuing the pension using the *termination pro rata* method. An "if and when" arrangement as advocated by the appellant makes the equalization amount contingent upon the actual amount of pension benefits that the employee spouse receives, essentially applying a "deferred" *retirement* method of valuation. The OLRC Report supports this conclusion when it notes that "if and when" arrangements "effectively take a retirement approach to pension division." See OLRC Report, *supra*, at p. 105. I find it somewhat inconsistent that the appellant espouses one valuation method for purposes of *calculating* his equalization obligation, but then requests that his actual *payment* be structured in a way suggesting that the pension's value is totally different.

Finally, the "if and when" method advanced by the appellant, in so far as it would employ a "deferred" retirement method of valuation raises the same potential conflict with the wording of the *Family Law Act* that was discussed at para. 93. While it might be possible to craft an "if and when" payment scheme that would clearly fit within the confines of the Ontario statute, it is unnecessary to decide this issue, because the instalment scheme ordered by the trial judge serves the principal purpose of saving the appellant from the hardship of making a large lump-sum payment before he begins to receive the pension. Furthermore, the recalculation of the equalization obligation using the termination *pro rata* method will reduce the appellant's payment burden. In light of the difficulties that seem to attend the crafting and administration of a fair "if and when" order in Ontario, I do not believe that Rutherford J. exceeded his discretion in choosing an instalment scheme for settlement of the appellant's equalization payment. . . .

[In his conclusion, Justice Major noted (at 63) that "duelling actuaries" were an "unfortunate consequence and a serious expense in divorce cases involving defined benefit pensions " and that this "regrettable situation will continue until legislation is enacted to provide guidance on the valuation" of such pensions in equalization calculations. The court remanded the case back to the trial judge to recalculate the equalization payment in accordance with the "termination *pro rata* method, using an assumed retirement date of September 9, 1992". L'Heureux-Dubé J. dissented, on the basis that only the value-added method of pension valuation captured the letter and spirit of the *FLA*.]

NOTES AND QUESTIONS

1. For commentary on *Best* v. *Best*, see McLeod, "Annotation" (1999), 49 R.F.L. (4th) 10 and Burrows and Hebert, " The Supreme Court of Canada and *Best* v. *Best*" (2000), 17 C.F.L.Q. 263. In the former, Professor McLeod asserts (at 10) that the case "is one of the more disappointing decisions of 1999" because it did not settle many hard issues. Mr. Burrows and Ms Herbert, who are pension valuators, conclude (at 275) that the "comments and decisions [regarding various issues] may have raised more questions and problems than they solved" and that the "discussion and decisions in this Supreme Court of Canada case certainly make it clear that valuing pensions for property equalization on marriage breakdown is complicated".

2. Does Justice Major endorse the "termination method" or the "retirement method" as the best way to value a defined benefit pension for equalization purposes? Professor McLeod in his annotation states (at 15):

[L]awyers and judges are left with no guidance as to how to decide the proper valuation method in a case. Given the time and money involved in an appeal to the Supreme Court of Canada and the frequency with which pension valuation cases arise, the Supreme Court of Canada's refusal or neglect to clarify the law is inexcusable.

Mr. Burrows and Ms Herbert worry (at 267) that the court's "comments in this area could raise new conflict and disagreement on the value of many pensions (not just those involving a pre-marriage period)".

3. Although he generally favoured the "termination *pro rata* method" over the "termination value-added method" for the determination of the value at marriage of a defined benefits pension, Justice Major left open the possibility that the latter method might be used in some cases. Is there any indication when this would be appropriate?

4. Why was the date of retirement important in valuing the pension in *Best*? Why was the pension valued for equalization purposes as if the husband retired in 1992 when he actually retired in 1996?

5

THE MATRIMONIAL HOME

1. Introduction

(1) SIGNIFICANCE OF THE MATRIMONIAL HOME

HOVIUS, "THE MATRIMONIAL HOME: AN ANALYSIS OF PART II OF THE FAMILY LAW ACT, 1986"

(1988), 16 R.F.L. (3d) 31 (Footnotes Omitted)

The matrimonial home occupies a special position in family property relations. It is usually the single item of property of greatest value owned by either or both spouses during their relationship. Moreover, it is the focal point of family life and so couples tend to view it as an asset belonging to both spouses, at least while the relationship is an ongoing one. In order to reflect this perception, the Ontario Law Reform Commission recommended the adoption of the basic principle of co-ownership in the matrimonial home, a principle that would entitle the husband and wife to equal shares secured by their joint control of the asset. While the Ontario legislature did not follow this recommendation, the *Family Law Act, 1986* does contain special provisions regarding the matrimonial home in determining the net family property of each spouse and alters the traditional property law governing ownership where one spouse dies owning an interest in the home as a joint tenant with a third person (s. 26(1)).

But the matrimonial home is more than a valuable asset. It is the shelter and focal point of the family. As a result, the spouses often develop deep emotional attachment to it. This may be especially true for a spouse who has functioned as a full-time homemaker during the relationship. Moreover, the right to occupy the matrimonial home satisfies one of the basic needs of individuals in our society, namely, the need for accommodation. It is, therefore, not enough to ensure that the spouses share the value of the matrimonial home when the relationship ends. In her critical analysis of American law dealing with the economic consequences of divorce, Lenore Weitzman notes that an equal division of marital property, however defined, frequently results in the forced sale of the couple's family residence. This compounds the financial dislocation and impoverishment of women and children generated by divorce. Where the spouses' only significant tangible asset is the matrimonial home and it is sold on the breakdown of the relationship so that the proceeds can be shared equally, often the custodial parent's share will be insufficient to acquire suitable accommodation. While this problem might be remedied by more generous support payments, the loss of the matrimonial home will invariably necessitate a move to a new accommodation. This may well disrupt a child's schooling or neighborhood and friendship ties, thereby creating additional stress and dislocation at the very time when the child most needs continuity and stability. For these reasons, Pt. II of the *Family Law Act, 1986* recognizes that the right to occupy the matrimonial home is important and that it cannot be governed by reference to ownership alone.

(2) HISTORICAL BACKGROUND

Even before the legislative reforms in the 1970s, the courts developed special rules governing the occupational rights in the family residence. Certain rights of occupation were vested by law in both spouses as a result of the rights and duties that flowed from the marital relationship itself. If the husband held both the legal and equitable title in the matrimonial home, his wife had a right to reside therein on two grounds. Her husband's duty to maintain her included the provision of accommodation. In addition, a married person had a duty to cohabit with his or her spouse. This duty conferred a corresponding right — namely, the right to consortium, which could be defined as the right of one spouse to the company, affection, co-operation and aid of the other. Where the wife owned the home, her husband had the right to reside in it based on his right to consortium: *Maskewycz* v. *Maskewycz* (1973), 13 R.F.L. 210 (Ont. C.A.). If the home was jointly owned then each spouse could use and occupy it on the basis of general ownership rights in addition to those rights of occupancy that flowed from the marriage relationship.

While the law recognized that a spouse had occupational rights in the matrimonial home, these rights were so limited, so uncertain, and so inadequately protected that legislative reform proved necessary. The right of the non-owning spouse to occupy the matrimonial home could be extinguished in several ways. The right ended when the marriage ended, whether by divorce or death. It also ceased to exist when the right to maintenance and the obligation of the spouses to live together ended. Accordingly, adultery or the commission of another matrimonial offence on the part of the non-owning spouse extinguished the right. *Richardson* v. *Richardson*, [1970] 3 O.R. 41, 12 D.L.R. (3d) 233 (H.C.) held that the right no longer existed once adequate alimony was being paid. This proposition was questionable, however, because the right was based not only on the duty to maintain but also on the conjugal obligation of spouses to live together. Finally, a court order under the *Married Women's Property Act*, R.S.O. 1970, c. 262 [repealed 1978, c. 2, s. 82] giving the owner exclusive possession would also end the other spouse's right to occupy the home. Such an order could be made where, for example, the husband who owned the home offered reasonably suitable alternative accommodation: *Beauchamp* v. *Beauchamp* (1970), 6 R.F.L. 43 (Ont. H.C.).

The court's authority to grant exclusive possession to one spouse by order under s. 12 of the *Married Women's Property Act* or by way of injunction could be exercised in favour of either spouse, regardless of which spouse owned the matrimonial home. As already noted, exclusive possession could be granted to the spouse who was the sole owner if it could be established that the other spouse had lost all occupation rights or that the owner offered reasonably suitable alternative accommodation. The courts also had discretionary power to grant exclusive possession to one spouse when both held the home jointly or to a non-owning spouse who had been deserted, whether actually or constructively. Few guidelines developed to determine when the courts should make orders and the cases were by no means consistent. Virtually all of the cases held, however, that before such an order could be made it had to be established that the spouse who was to be excluded had engaged in conduct that effectively destroyed the marriage relationship. Other factors, such as the financial position of both spouses, which spouse had custody of the children (if any), and the availability of alternative accommodation were also relevant in determining whether an order would be made.

While the position in Ontario prior to the reforms of 1978 was not free from uncertainty, it appears that the occupation right of the non-owning spouse was a purely personal right that was not enforceable against third parties who obtained title. A non-owning spouse's right might, therefore, be defeated by the unilateral dealings with the home by the owning spouse. In *Stevens v. Brown* (1969), 2 D.L.R. (3d) 687 (N.S. S.C.) the court held that a third party who purchased a matrimonial home from a married man who had deserted his wife was entitled to vacant possession free of any claim by the wife, even though the purchaser had notice of the vendor's marital status, his desertion, and the wife's continued occupancy. There was, however, some authority to suggest that a court could intervene by way of injunction restraining the owning spouse from entering into a contract for the sale of the matrimonial home and that the court had authority to set aside a sham transaction entered into by the owning spouse for the sole purpose of defeating the other spouse's occupation rights: *Lee v. Lee*, [1952] 2 Q.B. 489 (C.A.), noted in *Beauchamp, supra*.

Co-ownership of the matrimonial home by the spouses presented the courts with a special problem before the legislative reforms. In this situation, the spouses enjoyed possessory rights as owners as well as spouses. The issue that had to be confronted was whether a co-owner's *prima facie* right to partition or sale under the *Partition Act* was affected by the right of occupation that the other co-owner held as spouse and that could be enforced under s. 12 of the *Married Women's Property Act*. The relationship between these rights was examined in detail by the Ontario Court of Appeal in *Maskewcyz v. Maskewycz, supra*. Although some issues remained unresolved, it was established that an application by one spouse under the *Partition Act* for partition or sale of the jointly-held matrimonial home could only be granted after the court had considered the occupation rights of the other spouse. As a result, the courts viewed an application under the *Partition Act* as premature unless an application was also brought under s. 12 of the *Married Women's Property Act*. It became common practice for the spouse seeking partition or sale of the matrimonial home to bring applications under both the *Partition Act* and the *Married Women's Property Act* in the same proceeding.

The main problems regarding occupation rights in the matrimonial home prior to the legislative reforms can now be summarized. A non-owning spouse's right to occupy was dependent on good behaviour as a spouse. Even where the right clearly existed, it might be extinguished by unilateral dealings with the matrimonial home by the owning spouse. The courts had developed few guidelines to determine when a non-owning spouse should be given exclusive possession and they were slow to exclude the owning spouse even where the latter had committed a matrimonial offence. Finally, the relationship between a co-owner's *prima facie* right to partition or sale and the spousal right to occupation presented difficulties.

FURTHER READING

For further reading regarding the law prior to the legislative reforms, see Laskin, "The Deserted Wife's Equity in the Matrimonial Home: A Dissent" (1961), 14 U. of T. L.J. 67; Farley, "The Deserted Wife's Equity in the Matrimonial Home: Judicial Chivalry?" (1965), U. of T. Fac. L. Rev. 106; Silverman, "The Deserted Wife's Dilemma" (1971), 3 R.F.L. 235; Cullity, "Property Rights During the Subsistence of Marriage" in Mendes da Costa, ed., *Studies in Canadian Family Law* (Toronto: Butterworths, 1972) 179; and Ontario Law Reform Commission, *Report on Family Law: Part IV: Family Property Law* (Ottawa: Ministry of the Attorney General, 1974) at 35-38.

(3) OVERVIEW OF PART II OF THE FAMILY LAW ACT

Part II of the *Family Law Act* (the *FLA*) is modeled on Part III of the *Family Law Reform Act*, which was enacted in 1978 to replace the limited rights analyzed in the previous part of this book. Both spouses are given an equal right to possession of a matrimonial home, regardless of its ownership: s. 19(1). When only one of the spouses has an interest in the home, the other spouse's right of possession is a personal right that can only be asserted against the owning spouse: s. 19(2)(a). Adultery or the commission of another matrimonial offence by the non-owning spouse no longer ends that spouse's right to occupy the matrimonial home. However, this right terminates when the marriage ends unless a separation agreement or court order provides otherwise: s. 19(2)(b). Despite this general rule, a spouse who has no interest in a matrimonial home but is occupying it at the time of the other spouse's death, whether under a court order or otherwise, is entitled to retain possession against the spouse's estate, rent free, for 60 days after the spouse's death: s. 26(2).

Notwithstanding the spouses' equal right to possession, a court is authorized by s. 24 to grant exclusive possession to one spouse. Such an order can be made in favour of either spouse regardless of which spouse owns the matrimonial home. A court order for exclusive possession can provide that the non-owning spouse's possession will continue following the dissolution of the marriage. Orders made under Part II can be registered against land under the *Registry Act* and the *Land Titles Act*: s. 27. Registration would give third parties notice that they are dealing with a matrimonial home.

The significance of this fact will become apparent when the restrictions on the titled spouse's power to dispose of or encumber an interest in the matrimonial home are analyzed. These restrictions, which are important not only to the spouses themselves but to all third parties who acquire interests in property that could be a family residence, are imposed to protect a non-titled spouse's right to possession. As well, any spouse with a right to possession in a matrimonial home is granted a right of redemption and relief against forfeiture in certain proceedings by third parties: s. 22.

Section 26(1) provides that if a spouse dies owning an interest in a matrimonial home as a joint tenant and not with the other spouse, the joint tenancy is deemed to have been severed immediately before the time of death. As a result, the joint tenancy becomes a tenancy in common and the surviving joint tenant loses the benefit of the right of survivorship. The deceased's interest falls into his or her estate, rather than passing to the surviving tenant. The expropriatory nature of this provision was noted and confirmed by *Fulton* v. *Fulton* (1994), 17 O.R. (3d) 641 (C.A.). In its *Report on Family Property Law* (Toronto: 1993), the O.L.R.C. recommended (at 132) the repeal of s. 26(1).

Part II only applies to matrimonial homes that are situated in Ontario: s. 28(1). This is in keeping with the territorial limitation on provincial legislative power over property and civil rights imposed by the words "in the province" contained in s. 92(13) of the *Constitution Act, 1867*. As well, it is a general principle of private international law that only the jurisdiction where an immovable is situated has the power to determine the rights and interests in that property. Although Part II does not apply to a family residence situated outside the province, such a residence may still qualify as a matrimonial home for the purpose of calculating a spouse's net family property under Part I. That Part simply incorporates by reference the definition of matrimonial home contained in Part II. The definition does not itself exclude property situated outside of Ontario. Nor does s. 28(1) specify that property situated outside of Ontario is not a matrimonial home. It only states that Part II applies to matrimonial homes situated in Ontario. As a result, a cottage in Quebec was characterized as a matrimonial home in determining the spouses' net family properties under Part I in *Perrier* v. *Perrier* (1987), 12 R.F.L. (3d) 266 (Ont. H.C.).

(4) OCCUPATION RIGHTS OF UNMARRIED COHABITEES

HOVIUS AND YOUDAN, *THE LAW OF FAMILY PROPERTY*

(Toronto: Carswell, 1991) 580-585 (Edited footnotes appear at the end of the excerpt.)

Part II of the *Family Law Act* awards possessory rights to spouses and provides certain protection for those rights. The general definition of "spouse" in section 1(1) applies to determine who is covered by Part II. It stipulates that a spouse is "either of a man or woman who (a) are married to each other, or (b) have together entered into a marriage that is voidable or void, in good faith on the part of the person asserting a right under this Act". Therefore, persons who cohabit without going through any marriage ceremony are not covered by Part II.

The support obligations established by Part III of the *Family Law Act* do apply to certain cohabitees. Section 30 stipulates that every spouse has a duty to support the other spouse "in accordance with need, to the extent that he or she is capable of doing so". In Part III, a spouse includes "either of a man and woman who are not married to each other and have cohabited (a) continuously for a period of not less than three years, or (b) in a relationship of some permanence, if they are the natural or adoptive parents of a child".[36] Section 34(1) lists the types of orders that a court may make in an application for support. One of these is an order for exclusive possession of the matrimonial home.[37] In *Young-Foong* v. *Leong-Foong*[38] it was accepted that a cohabitee who fell within the extended definition of spouse could be granted an order for exclusive possession of the matrimonial home under this provision. However, a more recent Ontario District Court decision[39] held that, by definition, unmarried cohabitees cannot have a matrimonial home. Accordingly, the Court concluded that orders for exclusive possession of a matrimonial home could only be made if the dependant seeking exclusive possession as part of a support order was a spouse within the more restricted and traditional meaning of that term set out in section 1(1). This conclusion, based as it is on the definition of matrimonial home, appears to be the correct one.[40] In any event, the issue is of limited practical significance since a court can secure exclusive possession of the family residence for a cohabitee in a support application through the power granted by section 34(1)(c). It authorizes the court to require the respondent to transfer any property to the dependant absolutely, for life or for a term of years. A similar power is granted to a court under the *Succession Law Reform Act*[41] where a deceased, whether testate or intestate, has not made adequate provision for the proper support of a dependant who may, in some circumstances, be an unmarried cohabitee.[42] In addition, the court under that Act can order that a dependant be granted the possession or use of any specified property for life or a more limited period.[43]

In summary, the legislation in Ontario does not provide unmarried cohabitees with rights of occupation in the family residence corresponding to those of a spouse. Although the courts are authorized to make the exceptional orders referred to in the [previous] paragraph on an application for support by an unmarried cohabitee under the *Family Law Act* and the *Succession Law Reform Act*, the occupation rights of such cohabitees are generally determined by reference to the common law.

At common law, possessory rights of unmarried persons flow generally from proprietary rights. Where, for example, the legal ownership is in both parties, they both have an equal right to live in the home. Absent agreement, neither co-owner can exclude the other. Where domestic violence has occurred, however, it may be possible for the victim indirectly to obtain exclusive possession at least until an application for partition or sale is heard. Although there is no express authority in the Criminal Code for imposing exclusive possession as a condition on a peace bond, some judges have done so.[44] Also, an order restraining one spouse from molesting, annoying or harassing the other is available to unmarried cohabitees under section 46 of the *Family Law Act* if they satisfy the requirements of the extended definition of spouse contained in Part III of the Act. Such orders may have the effect of preventing a co-owner from exercising possessory rights.[45] Finally, it may be possible for one co-owner to be granted an interim injunction excluding the other pending partition or sale proceedings.[46]

In the absence of a legal or equitable interest in the property, the cohabitee's status will often be that of a bare licensee who must leave within a reasonable time once notice to quit is given.[47] In England, however, the courts have been developing the contractual licence as a method of conferring greater occupational rights on the non-owning cohabitee.[48] The seminal case is *Tanner* v. *Tanner*.[49] Mr. Tanner, a married man, was the father of twins born to a single woman who took his name. He provided a house for her and the children and she moved out of her rent-controlled flat. When the relationship broke down, Mr. Tanner sought possession of the house claiming that the woman was a bare licensee and that her licence to remain in the house had been revoked. Although the Court found that the woman had not acquired a proprietary interest in the house, it inferred[50] that she had a contractual licence to live in the house so long as the children were of school age and the accommodation was reasonably required for her and the children. As consideration for this agreement, the woman had given up her rent-controlled flat and looked after the children. Because the woman had, in fact, moved out following the adverse trial decision, the Court of Appeal did not issue an injunction to enforce the licence but awarded £2000 compensation for loss of the licence.

By way of contrast, the Court of Appeal refused to infer a contractual licence in *Horrocks* v. *Forray*.[51] Mr. Horrocks supported a woman, Mrs. Forray, for seventeen years before his death and they had a child. He bought a house for the mother and daughter to live in. Only on his death did his wife discover the existence of the house and the relationship. His executors gave Mrs. Forray notice to quit so that the house could be sold with vacant possession. Mrs. Forray claimed she had a right to stay there pursuant to a contractual licence. The Court of Appeal held that to establish such a contract, whether express or implied, it had to be proved that there was a meeting of the minds of the parties so that the contractual terms were reasonably clear, that the parties intended to create legal obligations, and that consideration flowed from each party. The Court found, perhaps surprisingly in light of *Tanner* v. *Tanner*,[52] that this test was not met.

Where a contractual licence is established, its duration is essentially a question of contractual interpretation. In *Tanner* v. *Tanner*, the Court inferred that the parties had agreed that the woman could occupy the home as long as the children were of school age and the accommodation was reasonably required for her and the children. In *Chandler* v. *Kerley*,[53] the Court of Appeal concluded that the contractual licence was terminable on reasonable notice. In that case, Mr. Chandler purchased a house from his fellow cohabitee, Mrs. Kerley, and her husband. At that time, the Kerleys were separated and Mrs. Kerley was living in the house with the two children of the marriage. Mr. Chandler bought the house so that he, Mrs. Kerley and the children could reside in it. He paid a reduced price for it because of his relationship with Mrs. Kerley. At the time of purchase, he indicated that if the relationship ended, he would not put Mrs. Kerley and the children out. In fact the relationship lasted only six weeks and Mr. Chandler sought possesssion. Mrs. Kerley claimed a contractual right to remain there for the rest of her life. The Court of Appeal held that she had a contractual licence, consideration for which was established by the reduced price. However, it also held that the licence was terminable on reasonable notice sufficient to enable her to find alternative accommodation. In the circumstances, the period was fixed at one year.

A contractual licence probably creates only personal rights in the licensee rather than proprietary rights. If that is correct, a purchaser of the home will not be bound by a contractual licence even if he or she has notice of the existence of the licence.[54] However, it has been held that it is enforceable against a trustee in bankruptcy[55] or the estate of a deceased owner.[56]

Even where the cohabitees are co-owners of the family residence, the existence of a contractual licence may be significant. If it can be established that one co-owner has agreed that the other is to have possession for a certain period of time, the court may decline to make an order for sale as requested by the first co-owner[57] or his or her personal representatives.[58]

There is a certain unreality and artificiality about the use of the contractual licence to secure occupation rights for unmarried cohabitees in some of the English cases. Often, one is forced to conclude that there was never any real agreement between the parties and that the courts are, in fact, imposing one in order to do justice. Rather than wait for the courts in Ontario to manipulate traditional legal concepts in a similarly creative fashion, the provincial legislature should enact laws to deal with the occupational rights of cohabitees, particularly where there are children of the relationship. Perhaps the time has come for the Ontario legislature to extend the occupational rights accorded to spouses and the protection of those rights established by Part II of the *Family Law Act* to, at least, unmarried cohabitees who satisfy the extended definition of spouse found in Part III of the Act.

---

36 Section 29.

37 Section 34(1)(d).

38 (1980), 1 F.L.R.A.C. 718 (Ont. Master), appeal dismissed (1980), 1 F.L.R.A.C. 721 (Ont. H.C.). In his short reasons, O'Leary J. stated, *obiter dictum*:

I am of the view that someone not a spouse for purposes outside Pt II [of the Family Law Reform Act, dealing with support], could be given exclusive possession of property owned by the one responsible for support if in the circumstances she could not reasonably be otherwise supported.

O'Leary J. did not specifically address the problem created by the definition of "matrimonial home".

39 *Czora* v. *Lonergan* (1987), 7 R.F.L. (3d) 458 (Ont. Dist. Ct.).

40 See, however, Bala and Cano, "Unmarried Cohabitation in Canada: Common Law and Civilian Approaches to Living Together" (1989), 4 C.F.L.Q. 147 where the authors express agreement (at 184-185) with the *obiter dicta* in *Young-Foong* v. *Leong-Foong*.

41 R.S.O. 1990, c. S.26, s. 63(2)(c).

42 See s. 57.

43 Section 63(2)(d). See, e.g., *Re Nalywayko* (1984), 17 E.T.R. 151 (Ont. Surr. Ct.) where an unmarried cohabitee was granted a one-half interest in a bungalow owned by the deceased cohabitee and the right to live in it for three years.

44 See Orlando, "Exclusive Possession of the Family Home: The Plight of Battered Cohabitees" (1987), 6 R.F.L. (3d) 83, fn. 47.

45 Such an order could, for example, specify that one of the cohabitees is not to have any contact with the other who brought the application. Even though both parties would continue to have equal right of possession, the one subject to the order would be unable to exercise the right without violating the order.

46 See, for example, *Hersog* v. *Hersog* (1975), 22 R.F.L. 380 (B.C. S.C.). Although the case involved married co-owners, there is no reason why an interim injunction pending partition or sale proceedings could not be granted in similar circumstances where the parties are not married to each other.

47 On licences generally, see Megarry and Wade, *The Law of Real Property*, 5th ed. (1984) ch. 14 and Cheshire and Burn, *Modern Law of Real Property*, 14th ed. (1988) ch. 18. See also Moriarty, "Licences and Land Law: Legal Principles and Public Policies" (1984), 100 L.Q.R. 376 and Dewar, "Licences and Land Law: An Alternative View" (1986), 49 M.L.R. 741.

48 For further analysis of the use of the contractual licence and the related doctrines of constructive trust and proprietary estoppel in recent English cases, see Chapter 8, "Developments in England and Australia". See also Holland, *Unmarried Couples: Legal Aspects of Cohabitation* (1982) at 75-82, and Bala and Cano, *supra*, note 40 at 181-183.

49 [1975] 3 All E.R. 776 (C.A.). For a comment, see Richards, "The Mistress and the Family Home" (1976), 40 Conv. 351.

50 Lord Denning M.R. would have gone further and would have been prepared to impose an agreement. See p. 780 of [1975] 3 All E.R. The other members of the Court of Appeal did not express a similar view. In *Hardwick* v. *Johnson*, [1978] 2 All E.R. 935 (C.A.), Lord Denning repeated his view that the licence can be imposed by the court in the absence of an agreement or contract.

51 [1976] 1 All E.R. 737 (C.A.).

52 Strict application of the test should have led to a finding in *Tanner* v. *Tanner* that a contractual licence did not exist in that case either. It has been suggested that the divergent results in the two cases reflect the fact that the court's sympathy lay with the widow in *Horrocks* v. *Forray*. Because of Mr. Horrock's extravagance during his lifetime, the estate would have been insolvent if his interest in the home could not be realized. See Holland, *supra*, note 48 at 77.

53 [1978] 2 All E.R. 942 (C.A.). For a comment, see Masson, "The Mistress's Limited Rights of Occupancy" (1979), 43 Conv. 184.

54 There have, however, been suggestions in the cases that the contractual licence is enforceable against a purchaser with notice of it. In *Tanner* v. *Tanner*, Lord Denning stated (at 780) that the Court would impose a constructive trust in favour of the licensee against a purchaser in this situation. See also *Binions* v. *Evans*, [1972] 2 All E.R. 70 (C.A.) and *Re Sharpe*, [1980] 1 All E.R. 198 (Ch. D.). In *Asburn Anstalt* v. *Arnold*, [1988] 2 W.L.R. 706 (C.A.), the Court reviewed these cases and concluded that a contractual licence does not create an interest in land and that it does not, therefore, necessarily bind a purchaser with notice. However, the Court accepted that a contractual licence may be part of the circumstances that would lead to the imposition of a constructive trust that would affect the purchaser.

55 See *Re Sharpe, ibid.*

56 *Hrynkiw* v. *Hrynkiw* (1979), 9 R.F.L. (2d) 374 (Ont. H.C.).

57 See *Forster* v. *Forster* (1980), 14 R.F.L. (2d) 236 (Alta. C.A.).

58 See *Hrynkiw* v. *Hrynkiw, supra*, note 56.

NOTES AND QUESTIONS

1. The conflicting case law regarding whether s. 34(1)(d) of the *FLA* permits a court to grant an exclusive possession order to an unmarried cohabitee as part of a support order was reviewed in *Williams*

v. *Hudson* (1997), 33 R.F.L. (4th) 111 (Ont. Gen. Div.). The court granted leave to appeal to the Divisional Court on the basis of the uncertainty.

2. Unmarried cohabitees, including those of the same sex, can apply for temporary exclusive possession of the family residence in British Columbia: *Family Relations Act*, R.S.B.C. 1996, c. 128, Pt. 10 (as amended). In Manitoba, exclusive possession orders can be made on the application of opposite-sex cohabitees: *The Family Maintenance Act*, R.S.M. 1987, c. F20, ss. 13 and 14. The recent legislation enacted in various provinces to provide emergency relief where there is domestic violence empowers the courts to grant temporary exclusive possession orders even if the parties are not married. See *Protection Against Family Violence Act*, S.A. 1998, c. P-19.2 (couple must be of opposite sexes); *The Domestic Violence and Stalking Prevention, Protection and Prevention Act*, S.M. 1998, c. 41; *Victims of Family Violence Act*, R.S.P.E.I. 1988, c. V-3.2 (in force 1996); and *The Victims of Domestic Violence Act*, R.S.S. 1994, c. V-6.02. For an analysis of this aspect of the Saskatchewan legislation, see Heinrichs, "Common Law Couples: Violence Yields Superior Property Rights in Saskatchewan" (1999),16 Can. J. Fam. L. 136.

3. In its *Report on the Rights and Responsibilities of Cohabitants under the Family Law Act* (Toronto: 1993), the O.L.R.C. recommended that the definition of "spouse" in s. 1(1) be amended to include unmarried persons of the opposite sex who have cohabited continuously for a period not less than three years or in a relationship of some permanence if they are the parents of a child. Part II of the Act would then be applicable to these couples. It also recommended the extension of the rights and obligations under the *FLA*, including Part II, to Registered Domestic Partnerships. Such partnerships could involve persons of the same sex. One of the consequential amendments suggested by the Commission was the replacement of the term "matrimonial home" with the term "family home".

4. Recall *M.* v. *H.* and *Walsh* v. *Bona* (reproduced in Chapter 1, **INTRODUCTION.**). Is there a constitutional obligation to extend Part II of the *FLA* to unmarried cohabitees, whether of the same or opposite sex?

2.   Identification of a Matrimonial Home

It is important to be able to identify a matrimonial home because this asset is accorded special treatment in the calculation of a spouse's net family property under Part I of the *FLA* and the rights granted in Part II apply only to matrimonial homes. The definition of matrimonial home is contained in s. 18. Note also the definition of "property" in s. 17.

Under s. 39(1) of the *Family Law Reform Act, 1978* any property occupied by the spouses as a family residence at any time during their marriage qualified as a matrimonial home. The Act also expressly provided in s. 39(2) that the definition of matrimonial home could be applied, notwithstanding that its application resulted in there being more than one matrimonial home. Where the couple occupied one property as a family residence and then moved to another, both properties were matrimonial homes so long as they were still owned by one or both spouses. The definition in s. 18(1) of the *FLA* makes it clear that this is no longer the situation.

Section 18(2) and (3) of the *FLA* are virtually identical to s. 39(3) and (4) of the 1978 Act. These latter two subsections were considered in the first case that follows.

HARTLING v. HARTLING

Ont. H.C., 1979 (unreported)

[Under the *Family Law Reform Act, 1978*, a matrimonial home was a family asset unless a domestic contract provided otherwise. In this case, the wife applied for an equal division of family assets and claimed that certain properties were matrimonial homes. Only the portion of the reasons dealing with the identification of the couple's matrimonial homes is reproduced here.]

MCDERMID L.J.S.C.: — . . . In this case, a separate appraisal was submitted for the value of the farmhouse and one acre of land. I have no hesitation in finding, in this case, that the farmhouse and one acre of land constituted the matrimonial home of Mr. and Mrs. Hartling since it was property in which Mr. Hartling had an interest and it was occupied by Mr. Hartling and Mrs. Hartling as their family residence from July 1974 until at least sometime in November 1974. Section 39(4) was designed specifically to deal with the situation present in this case, namely that where the residence is situate on a farm, in this case comprising approximately 200 acres, where only a small portion, in this case 1 acre, was "necessary to the use and enjoyment of the residence". I therefore find that the farm house and one acre constitute a family asset and that the remaining portion of the farm property is a non-family asset.

On the evidence, Mr. and Mrs. Hartling also occupied a two bedroom apartment in a building of 108 apartment units at 112 Baseline Road, London, Ontario, known, I believe, as the Valhalla Apartments. At the time Mr. and Mrs. Hartling lived in this building, it was owned by Comgord Limited, a corporation in which Mr. Hartling owned 50% of the common shares. From Mr. Hartling's evidence I would conclude that the fair market value of the two bedroom unit in which they resided was $16,000.00.

Mr. Ledroit, on behalf of Mrs. Hartling, urges that by virtue of Section 39(3) and section 3(b)(ii) the apartment unit is also a "family asset" and that she is entitled to one-half its fair market value, or $8,000.00.

There is no evidence in this case that the mere ownership of shares in Comgord Limited entitled Mr. Hartling, or any other shareholder, to occupy an apartment unit in the building in question. I infer from the evidence that he occupied it pursuant to a lease, in the normal way, there being no evidence to the contrary. Although Section 39(3) is not specifically so worded, it would appear to me to be more applicable to a condominium corporation.

There is no doubt then that within the provisions of Section 39(1), Mr. Hartling had a leasehold "interest" in the property, i.e., the apartment unit, and that it was occupied by him and Mrs. Hartling as their family residence. It therefore constitutes a matrimonial home. However, I emphasize that Mr. Hartling's interest in the unit arises not from his ownership of shares in the corporation but from his status as a lessee.

Although there was evidence adduced to establish the fair market value of the apartment unit as part of the apartment building, there was no evidence adduced to establish the value of the leasehold interest, if any. In my opinion, it would be that value, if any, in which the spouses are entitled to share and not the fair market value of the rental unit since, as I have indicated, Mr. Hartling was not entitled to occupy the apartment unit merely as a result of owning shares of the corporation which owned that unit. . . .

DaCOSTA v. DaCOSTA

(1990), 29 R.F.L. (3d) 422 (Ont. Gen. Div.)

[In August 1986 Mr. DaCosta used $149,613, which he had inherited after the marriage, together with other investments to purchase a hobby farm, the Cedar Dee Farm, for $380,000. Although the marriage was in difficulty after October 1986,

Granger J. concluded that the valuation date was March 27, 1987. When the Cedar Dee Farm was purchased, the spouses expected that Mr. DaCosta would operate the farm and that the family would use it as a weekend retreat.]

GRANGER J.: — ... There can be no doubt that at any given time spouses may have more than one matrimonial home, i.e., cottage, hobby farm or condominium. In this case it was the intention of the spouses to use Cedar Dee Farm as a weekend retreat. It had a beautiful house, swimming pool and stables for riding horses. The issue is whether it was ever "ordinarily occupied" by Mr. and Mrs. DaCosta as a matrimonial home. Again the evidence of Mrs. DaCosta is less than satisfactory. She claims to have cooked meals and moved furniture at Cedar Dee. I do not believe her on this aspect of the case. Prior to the closing of the purchase of Cedar Dee, Mrs. DaCosta attended at the farm on two occasions. After the closing she attended at the farm on no more than three occasions. They did not stay overnight at the farm nor did they do any cooking at the farm. Mrs. DaCosta did not attend at the farm after the end of October 1986. It was after this date that the furniture which would allow the farm to be used as a matrimonial home was delivered from the garage at 291 Oriole Parkway. After the furniture was delivered to the farm, Mr. DaCosta spent considerable time at the farm. I find it impossible to reconcile Mrs. DaCosta's position that Cedar Dee Farm was ordinarily used as a matrimonial home and her failure to attend at the farm between 1st November 1986 and 27th March 1987. Surely, if it was being used as a matrimonial home, she would have attended at the farm. In my view, because of the stress in the marriage, Mrs. DaCosta by her own choice never used Cedar Dee Farm as a matrimonial home. In order to be a matrimonial home, it must be ordinarily occupied by the spouses at the time of separation. In this case it was never occupied as a matrimonial home. They may have intended to occupy it as a matrimonial home but they never carried out their intention, notwithstanding that they had an opportunity to carry out such an intention. Accordingly, Mr. DaCosta is entitled to exclude from the value of Cedar Dee Farm as of valuation day the sum of $149,613 which he inherited from his mother, grandmother and great aunt after his marriage to Mrs. DaCosta: s. 4(2)1 and 5 of the F.L.A.

GOODYER v. GOODYER

(1999), 168 D.L.R. (4th) 453 (Ont. Gen. Div.)

PERKINS J.: - This case raises some interesting and difficult issues:

1. Is a housing unit occupied by the wife's mother within the spouses' matrimonial home a part of their matrimonial home as defined in subs. 18(1) of the Family Law Act? This has important implications in this case because the home was (or may have been) a gift or inheritance, and if this part of the home is not within the matrimonial home as intended by the act, the husband will be able to claim an exclusion from his net family property. [The other issues are omitted.]

Extent of the matrimonial home: is the "granny flat" included?

Facts

I have used a popular term to describe the wife's mother's accommodations within the house occupied by the spouses as their matrimonial home. In fact the unit was not sealed off from the rest of the house, although it did have an entrance at the rear of the house, which Mrs. Johnston used for her comings and goings. The area she occupied was on the ground floor of the house and included a bedroom, living room, bathroom and kitchen. It was an area of about 500 sq. ft. in a house of slightly less than 3000 sq. ft. (not including basement), or roughly 1/6 of the living area. (Numbers up to 800 sq. ft. were given for Mrs. Johnston's living area, but the diagram that was accepted as accurate by the parties shows an area of 500 sq. ft. at the very most.) The connection to the other rooms on the ground floor was through two doorways that had doors on them, but the doors could not be locked. The husband and wife (and Ashley [the husband's minor son from a previous marriage]) had their living room and kitchen on the ground floor as well and their bedrooms and bathroom upstairs. No renovations were done to accommodate Mrs. Johnston's needs. There was no rent charged for use of the area, though Mrs. Johnston did contribute to some household charges such as cable TV.

Mrs. Johnston's kitchen was actually the laundry room of the house and it was used by the wife (and I suppose other members of the family) when laundry had to be done. Mrs. Johnston's toaster oven sat on top of the dryer. This room also contained a freezer that was used for the whole family. The wife's evidence was that she often entered her mother's area to spend time with her in her living room and that the wife and family visitors also sometimes used the main floor bathroom for convenience rather than running upstairs. The husband corroborated this as he said that the wife's use of the main floor bathroom was a point of irritation - he didn't think it was right to impinge on Mrs. Johnston's space in this way. There was also evidence that the mother came occasionally into the main floor kitchen and dining room used by the spouses to eat and for socializing, though the wife admitted that there was not a lot of interaction between the husband and Mrs. Johnston. Nevertheless the husband acknowledged that they all gathered for cards on the main floor once or twice a week. Ashley sometimes went into Mrs. Johnston's area to use her VCR.

Law

The husband's first argument focuses on the words "ordinarily occupied by the person and his or her spouse as their family residence" in subs. 18(1). The husband says that the "granny flat", as I have called it, was not ordinarily occupied by the spouses and was not part of *their* family residence. Further, the argument goes that the granny flat was "normally used for a purpose other than residential", "residential" meaning residential for the spouses. In other words, quarters that were rented out to a tenant would not qualify as part of the spouses' matrimonial home and neither does this living area, submits the husband.

I have not been given any comparable cases and have not found any. My decision must be based entirely on an analysis of the statutory language.

Dealing first with subs. 18(1), I think the evidence shows here that the spouses did occupy the area in question as part of their ordinary mode of life. To occupy something ordinarily does not require constant or continual occupancy, nor does it require occupancy of every square metre. In this case, the evidence shows that Mrs. Johnston's bathroom, "kitchen" (really the family laundry room) and living room were all occupied from time to time on a free and easy basis by various members of the family, including the spouses and Ashley. Ashley's use of the area, while a dependent minor living with his father, is attributable to his father, in my view.

That leaves only the bedroom, about which there was no evidence of direct use by the wife, the husband or Ashley. However, I do not think that anything turns on that. The great majority of the area was used by various family members. The entire area was used by Mrs. Johnston as a resident of the family home and I do not see that subs. 18(1) was intended to exclude from the spouses' matrimonial home parts of the home used for residential purposes primarily or even exclusively by an extended family member who was not even paying rent. I think the word "family" in the phrase "ordinarily occupied by the person and his or her spouse as their family residence" is not meant as an exclusive word, leaving out parents, children or other close relations of either of the spouses. If Ashley were no longer a dependent minor, or if a niece or cousin were living in the home, should the provision be interpreted to subtract their exclusive use areas from the spouses' matrimonial home? "Family" is not defined in the *Family Law Act* for the purpose of s. 18 and nothing in the context of s. 18 requires that it be given a restrictive meaning as sought by the husband.

Nor does subs. 18(3) assist the husband, in my view. It talks about uses "other than residential", but does not qualify the word "residential" with a phrase such as "by the spouses". This area was used only for residential purposes, albeit primarily by Mrs. Johnston. Subs. 18(3) comes into play only if the area is "normally used for a purpose other than residential". There is no such use here.

I note that the only cases found by counsel that even come close to this one involve portions of the matrimonial home that were rented out to parties at arms' length from the spouses, and even they are in the majority against the husband: *Solonynko* v. *Solonynko* (1978), 1 F.L.R.A.C. 211 (Ont. H.C.); *C.* v. *C. (No. 1)* (1979), 11 R.F.L. (2d) 356 (Ont. Co. Ct.); *C.* v. *C. (No. 2)* (1979), 11 R.F.L. (2d) 364 (Ont. Co. Ct.). But see *Kozlowski* v. *Kozlowski* (1984), 39 R.F.L. (2d) 34 (Ont. H.C.) -- house used 75% for commercial boarding house operation is a matrimonial home only to the extent of 25%; and see the commentary in Mamo, Alfred P., *Matrimonial Property Law in Canada*, O-148 - O-150.

The husband's argument to exclude the "granny flat" from the spouses' matrimonial home must fail. He is not entitled to exclude any portion of the home from his net family property. . . .

NOTES AND QUESTIONS

1. A leasehold interest is a species of personal property, not realty. Why can a leasehold interest nevertheless qualify as a matrimonial home? Can a mobile home be a matrimonial home? See *Caldwell* v. *Caldwell* (1978), 1 F.L.R.A.C. 143 (Ont. Dist. Ct.). Can a sailboat be a matrimonial home? See *Clark* v. *Clark* (1984), 40 R.F.L. (2d) 92 (Ont. H.C.).

2. The term "family residence" connotes something more than simple occupation of a dwelling. It must be the residence around which the couple's normal family life revolves: *Taylor* v. *Taylor* (1978), 6 R.F.L. (2d) 341 at 350 (Ont. U.F.C.). A Florida condominium was held not to be a matrimonial home as it had only recently been purchased, and the family occupied it only to ready it for future use. See also: *Victoria and Grey Trust Co.* v. *Stewart* (1981), 22 R.F.L. (2d) 283 (Ont. Co. Ct.); *El-Sohemy* v. *El-Sohemy* (1980), 17 R.F.L. (2d) 1 (Ont. H.C.); and *Allgeier* v. *Allgeier* (1996), 26 R.F.L. (4th) 65 (Ont. Gen. Div.).

3. In *Mancini* v. *Mancini* (1982), 31 R.F.L. (2d) 418 (Ont. U.F.C.), Steinberg U.F.C.J. made the following comments (at 422-423) regarding s. 39(3) of the *Family Law Reform Act* (the predecessor provision to s. 18(2) of the *FLA*):

> Under this subsection, it would appear that there must be a connection between the owning of the shares and the right of residence in the housing unit. That connection is implied by the use of the word "entitling" in the legislation. By the use of this term, I conclude that the entitlement must be found:
>
> (a) in the fact that the owner of the share or shares has a controlling interest in the company to enable him to vote his shares so as to give him a right of residence in the housing unit; or
>
> (b) there must be a resolution or other company enactment or agreement by which the non-controlling ownership of shares entitled the shareholder to a residential unit.

Compare this view with *Jost* v. *Gomagan Gun Club Inc.* (1983), 54 N.B.R. (2d) 353 (Q.B.) where the court suggested (at 360) that the equivalent provision in the New Brunswick statute "only applies when such shares are issued by a corporation owning housing units or some type of co-operative housing entitling the owners of the shares to occupation of a unit as a dwelling house." For analysis of these cases, see Hovius and Youdan, *The Law of Family Property* (Toronto: Carswell, 1991) at 589-593.

4. For other cases where only the farm house and a small parcel of contiguous land constituted the matrimonial home, see *Youngblut* v. *Youngblut* (1979), 11 R.F.L. (2d) 249 (Ont. H.C.); *Badley* v. *Badley* (1980), 14 R.F.L. (2d) 345 (Ont. Co. Ct.); *Ling* v. *Ling* (1980), 17 R.F.L. (2d) 62, 29 O.R. 717 (C.A.); and *Dudley* v. *Dudley* (1981), 22 R.F.L. (2d) 337 (Ont. H.C.). See also *Meszaros* v. *Meszaros* (1978), 22 O.R. (2d) 695 (H.C.) and *Andreoli* v. *Andreoli* (1990), 27 R.F.L. (3d) 142 (Ont. Dist. Ct.).

5. A husband and wife live in two apartment units in a five-unit building owned by the husband. The other three units are rented out to third parties. Identify the couple's matrimonial home. See *Young* v. *Young* (1981), 21 R.F.L. (2d) 388 (Ont. C.A.) and *Kozlowski* v. *Kozlowski* (1984), 39 R.F.L. (2d) 34 (Ont. H.C.).

6. Cases in which there was a finding that a couple had more than one matrimonial home for the purposes of the *FLA* include *Perrier* v. *Perrier* (1987), 12 R.F.L. (3d) 266 (Ont. H.C.); *Reeson* v. *Kowalik* (1991), 36 R.F.L. (3d) 396 (Ont. Gen. Div.); and *Battye* v. *Battye* (1989), 22 R.F.L. (3d) 427 (Ont. H.C.), affirmed (1993), 48 R.F.L. (3d) 130 (Ont. C.A.). The latter case suggests that judges readily conclude that cottages are matrimonial homes. McKeown J. simply stated (at 431):

> The evidence was that Mr. and Mrs. Battye and their two sons attended regularly at the cottage in the early years of the marriage and, to a much lesser extent, in the last couple years of the marriage. It is clearly a matrimonial home.

Does this approach accord with the wording of the definition? Compare *Spinney* v. *Spinney* (1996), 4 O.T.C. 295 (Ont. Gen. Div.).

7. In *Ledrew* v. *Ledrew* (1993), 46 R.F.L. (3d) 11 (Ont. Gen. Div.), the wife owned a cottage which was used by the family on weekends and in the summers during the early 1980s. By 1985, some four years before separation, the husband and wife no longer spent any time together at the cottage. H.J. Smith J. concluded (at 17):

> . . . [T]here is no evidence forthcoming that the parties occupied the premises as a family residence after 1985. Even if, in the early 1980s, the White Cottage could have been categorized as the family's vacation residence, it had ceased to have that use or character for a number of years prior to separation. I find the White Cottage not to be a matrimonial home under s. 18(1) of the *Family Law Act*.

See also the *obiter dicta* of Feldman J. in *Reeson* v. *Kowalik* (1991), 36 R.F.L. (3d) 396, at 405 (Ont. Gen. Div.).

8. Where the spouses have more than one matrimonial home, they may designate one to be a matrimonial home in accordance with s. 20 of the *FLA*. If they register the designation of one home, is the other still a matrimonial home?

9. Can a couple effectively opt out of Part II of the *FLA* by designating their only residence as a matrimonial home under s. 20 and then canceling the designation? Can one spouse unilaterally defeat the other spouse's rights under Part II by designation and cancellation?

3. Orders for Exclusive Possession

Section 24 of the *FLA* allows the court to make exclusive possession orders regarding the matrimonial home and its contents. Such orders may be made on a temporary or interim basis (s. 24(2)). Final orders for exclusive possession for any period that the court directs are also possible. Such orders may continue even after the marriage relationship ends (s. 19(2)(b)). Section 24(1) confers upon the court ancillary powers respecting the following: contents of the home; release of other property that is also a matrimonial home from the application of Part II; payments in the nature of occupation rent; fixing the obligation to repair and maintain the home and to pay liabilities arising in respect of the property; and the authorization of dispositions or encumbrances of the home, subject to the right of the spouse who is granted exclusive possession. Any of the orders set out in s. 24(1) can be made regardless of the ownership of the matrimonial home and its contents and despite the provision in s. 19(1) that both spouses have an equal right to possession.

Section 24(3) sets out the factors that the court should consider in deciding whether to make an order for exclusive possession. Section 24(4) provides further guidance to the court by specifying criteria for the determination of the best interests of a child. The factors listed in s. 24(3) and (4) indicate that the court has considerable discretion in determining applications for exclusive possession.

Orders for exclusive possession can be registered against land under the *Registry Act* and the *Land Titles Act*. See s. 27 of the *FLA*.

Section 24(5) creates a new offence, the contravention of an order for exclusive possession. Section 24(6) provides the police with arrest powers in relation to this offence.

The first five cases that follow involve applications for exclusive possession on an interim or temporary basis. The last two deal with applications for such orders on a long-term basis. Is there a difference in the approach taken in the latter situation compared to the former?

PIFER v. PIFER

(1986), 3 R.F.L. (3d) 167 (Ont. Dist. Ct.)

SALHANY D.C.J.: — On 15th May 1986 the plaintiff obtained an order from the Honourable Judge E.G. McNeely granting her interim interim custody of the infant children and interim interim exclusive possession of the matrimonial home and contents. The defendant appeared on that application but was unrepresented by counsel and did not file any affidavit material. Because of the allegations contained in the affidavit of the plaintiff, the order was granted.

The matter was adjourned until 29th May 1986 when it was heard by the Honourable J.V. Scott. Counsel retained by the defendant appeared on his behalf but had not had the opportunity to file material. On consent, the order of Judge McNeeley was extended to 12th June 1986 in order to enable the defendant to file his material.

In the meantime, the defendant has launched his own application for interim interim custody and exclusive possession of the matrimonial home and contents. In his affidavit, he refutes most of the allegations made by the plaintiff against him. He says that he is better suited to look after the children, that the plaintiff should be required to leave the matrimonial home and that he should be entitled to return to the home and look after the children. Alternatively, he says that the material filed by both him and the plaintiff is so conflicting that it is impossible for this court to come down on the side of one or the other so as to determine whether an order of exclusive possession should be made under s. 24 of the Family Law Act, 1986, until, at least, cross-examinations have been conducted of the parties.

Counsel for the plaintiff argued that pending cross-examinations, the status quo should be maintained and that the plaintiff and children should be allowed to remain until the return of the motion. I have difficulty with that submission. The order made by Judge McNeeley granting the plaintiff exclusive possession has to be character-ized essentially as an ex parte order because there was only the affidavit material of the plaintiff and the babysitter, Linda Gregoire, before him for consideration. In my view, it would be unfortunate if one spouse could create a status quo by deciding to jump the gun and obtain an order ex parte on material that the other spouse does not have an opportunity to refute. What I must do at this stage is to assess all of the affidavit material before me and determine whether it supports a case for exclusive possession by either party or none at all. If it does not, then the existing order for exclusive possession should be dissolved and the defendant allowed to return to reside in the matrimonial home. . . .

Section 24(3) and (4) must be contrasted with s. 45(3) of the Family Law Reform Act, R.S.O. 1980, c. 152, the former legislation. It provided that:

> (3) An order under subsection (1) for exclusive possession may be made only if, in the opinion of the court, other provision for shelter is not adequate in the circumstances or it is in the best interests of a child to do so.

Under s. 45(3), the Ontario courts were generally reluctant to remove a spouse from the matrimonial home unless there was serious and weighty evidence of phys-ical or emotional harm to the children: *Campbell* v. *Campbell* (1978), 6 R.F.L. (2d) 392 (Ont. H.C.); *West* v. *West* (1982), 28 R.F.L. (2d) 375 (Ont. Master); and *Barrett* v. *Barrett* (1982), 29 R.F.L. (2d) 13 (Ont. H.C.). One of the reasons for this was probably due to the fact that s. 45(3) was framed negatively in that an order for exclusive possession could only be granted if the applicant could establish the two criteria, i.e., adequate provision for shelter or the best interests of the child: see *Re Janssen and Janssen* (1979), 25 O.R. (2d) 213, 11 R.F.L. (2d) 274, 1 F.L.R.A.C. 455 (Co. Ct.), and *Rondeau* v. *Rondeau* (1979), 12 R.F.L. (2d) 45 (Ont. Co. Ct.). Even where the preconditions have been met, the courts were generally reluctant to order eviction of one spouse if it was felt that the harm to the children could be prevented by other means such as a restraining order against the offending spouse: see *Metcalf* v. *Metcalf* (1984), 40 R.F.L. (2d) 332 (Ont. U.F.C.).

The new legislation not only expands the criteria, it also is framed differently. It is significant to note that the question of violence committed by one spouse against the other spouse or children is a separate factor from the question of "the best interests of the children affected". Nor do I think that what constitutes "the best interests of a child" in subs. (4) is to be restricted solely to the two questions in that subsection, i.e., the disruptive effects of a move to other accommodation or the child's views and preferences. In my view, what amounts to the best interests of the child may include many other factors such as the psychological stresses and strains to a child arising out of the daily friction between parents.

Turning now to the material before me, the parties were married on 11th December 1976 in Milwaukee, Wisconsin. They have two young daughters, Laura, aged 6, and Jennifer, aged 4. The plaintiff is a nurse and the defendant an accountant. Apparently, they enjoyed a relatively comfortable life-style until the defendant decided to go into business for himself and purchased a Go-Camping franchise which involved rental and sales of motor homes and travel trailers. Unfortunately, the business lasted only a few months and the defendant found himself unemployed. To assist in the family finances, the plaintiff decided to seek employment first in February 1984 in a doughnut shop and later in May 1984 as a nurse at the K-W Hospital where she remains today. The defendant sought and obtained work in the accounting department of a law office and later with a chartered accountant. Since February 1986 he has attempted to establish his own accounting business.

The material indicates that until the plaintiff began to work, she assumed most of the responsibility for looking after the children. After she began work, the parties shared that responsibility with the defendant taking an active role particularly when the plaintiff was working shift work at the hospital. In April it was decided to hire a babysitter, Linda Gregoire, so that the defendant could devote more time to his new business.

The main allegation of the plaintiff is that the defendant has, over the last four months, started to drink heavily at home starting in the afternoon around 4:00 p.m. until he passes out around 10:00 p.m. There is also an allegation that he smokes heavily, leaving live cigarettes in the ashtrays, and leaves on a propane heater after he has gone to bed. She also says that the arguments between them have increased in frequency since he began to drink heavily and this affects the children and frightens the babysitter. The allegations of excessive drinking are supported by the babysitter in her affidavit. Although the defendant concedes drinking alcohol, he denies that it is to excess and also denies that he is endangering his family by the use of cigarettes or the propane heater.

The balance of all of the material indicates to me that there is a great deal of stress and strain in this household which is obviously affecting the children. There is no doubt in my mind that it would be in the best interests of the children if they were relieved of that stress by the separation of their parents. If it were not for the serious allegations of drinking and bizarre conduct by the defendant, as supported by the affidavit of Linda Gregoire, I might have considered granting him interim interim exclusive possession and custody because of the fact that he has more time to devote to looking after the children. However, because of those allegations, I am of the view that it would be in the best interests of the children that the plaintiff have custody of them and exclusive possession of the matrimonial home. [The court awarded interim interim custody and exclusive possession to the wife.]

PERRIER v. PERRIER

(1989), 20 R.F.L. (3d) 388 (Ont. H.C.)

KOZAK L.J.S.C.: — On 18th May 1989 this court heard competing motions wherein both parents claimed interim custody of the children and interim exclusive possession of the matrimonial home.

The parties are husband and wife who reside at 421 Westbury Crescent in the city of Thunder Bay with their two children, a daughter, Aaren Nicolle, born 18th February 1978, and a son, Patrick Byron, born 1st March 1982. They have been married some 16 years. The husband is employed at the Thunder Bay Terminals, whereas the wife is enrolled at university as a full-time nursing student and in addition is employed on a part-time basis at the McKellar Hospital. Both parents, because of their careers, have shared in the raising of the children.

It is admitted that the marriage has deteriorated as a result of constant arguments, and that such arguments are having a detrimental effect upon the children because they have reached the stage of becoming volatile if allowed to go unchecked. Both feel that the other is to blame.

Matters came to a head as a result of an incident which occurred on 30th April 1989 and 1st May 1989 concerning the manner in which the mother disciplined the daughter for missing dancing classes. The husband responded by commencing a petition for divorce which was issued on 12th May 1989 and this was accompanied by a motion for an ex parte order for interim custody and exclusive possession of the matrimonial home on 15th May 1989, which was granted until the return date of these motions.

In seeking interim custody of the children and interim exclusive possession of the matrimonial home, the husband alleges that the wife has been extremely abusive towards the daughter and that she has exhibited some violence towards the daughter and himself. Counsel for the husband indicated that the party that was granted interim exclusive possession of the matrimonial home should also have interim custody of the children in that it is in the best interests of the children to remain in the matrimonial home. The wife states that the husband has grossly exaggerated the argument with the daughter and says that her disciplinary measures on that occasion were no more grievous than disciplinary measures imposed by the husband on previous occasions, none of which the wife classifies as child abuse.

The materials disclose that on 30th April 1989 the mother, feeling that Aaren had lied to her about attending dancing classes and feeling that the daughter was being insolent, attempted to hit her across the buttocks with a wooden dancing stick. Inadvertently the daughter was hit across the hand. The mother then held the daughter by the neck, but without pressure, so that she could speak to her. There is nothing to substantiate the husband's claim that the child's head was hit against the wall, causing a lump. The next afternoon the school called to say that Aaren was sick to her stomach and should be picked up.

The next day the daughter was again sick to her stomach, with the father stating the cause to be that the mother expressed a hatred for the child, whereas the mother states that the illness was caused because the husband countermanded her order and permitted the daughter to go to a soccer practice.

The material discloses certain other incidents between mother and daughter concerning the doing of homework, going skiing, and the use of strong language which I considered to be anything but supportive of extreme child abuse.

The parties' descriptions of the pushing and shoving as described in their supplementary affidavits do not contain that element of violence or volatility that would prompt a court to exclude either one from the matrimonial home. . . .

Section 19(1) of the Family Law Act provides that both spouses have an equal right to possession of a matrimonial home. In seeking interim exclusive possession of the home, there is an onus on the party claiming exclusive possession to satisfy the court that the criteria as set out in s. 24(3) of the Family Law Act exist so as to warrant the making of such an order. The husband relies upon his allegations of violence committed by the wife against himself and the daughter. I do not categorize the disciplinary measures which the wife employed against the daughter as being acts of violence of a type that should exclude a mother from a matrimonial home. Similarly, the confrontations between husband and wife which involved some pushing and shoving by both parties can hardly be classified as acts of violence. The husband also relies upon the best interests of the children. It may very well be in the best interests of the children to continue to reside in the matrimonial home but this factor only applies to exclusive possession of the home where the person claiming it has interim custody of the children.

With respect to the issue of interim custody, I find that both motions have some merit; however, it would not be in the best interests of the children to be under the custody, care and control of any one parent under the present circumstances at this stage of the proceedings. I do not consider the wife's disciplinary actions against the daughter to be abusive so as to deprive her of her right to custody of the children, by finding that the best interests of the children lie with the father. The parties have done a good job of sharing the task of raising the children and, in the absence of an interim custody order by this court, the parties will continue to have joint custody, care and control of the children pending the trial of this matter.

An interim custody order, along with interim exclusive possession of the matrimonial home, based on the materials filed, appears to be more calculated towards the gaining of a tactical legal advantage as opposed to determining what is in the best interests of the children. The court should not allow this to take place. Neither party should have to consider himself a failure at this point, nor should there be a winner-loser mentality at this early stage. In this case, neither party has persuaded the court as to the relative merits of their claims for interim custody and interim possession.

The mother should not be excluded from the matrimonial home or deprived of custody based on the materials filed by the husband.

Accordingly, there will be no order as to custody and both motions with respect to interim possession of the matrimonial home are hereby dismissed. The status quo which prevailed prior to the ex parte order of 15th May 1989 is therefore restored. Hopefully the parties, in sharing the matrimonial home and the custody of the children, will see fit to live in tranquility pending trial. In this regard there will be an order that the parties:

(1) not dissipate any assets;
(2) not molest, harass or annoy each other or the children;
(3) subject themselves to a psychological assessment.

There is no reason why the parties cannot get this matter ready for trial in short order. . . .

CHARRY v. CHARRY

(July 27, 1998), Doc. Thunder Bay 98-0633 (Ont. Gen. Div.)

KOZAK J.:–. . . The parties are husband and wife who were married on May 27, 1976 and separated on June 1, 1998. Although separated, in fact they both continue to occupy and reside in the matrimonial home with their daughter, Janelle, who will be ten years of age on September 19, 1998. . . .

The wife takes the position that she has always been the child's primary care giver and that until fairly recently the husband was always too busy and was never around. As a result she states that she was the one that was called upon to take the child to her figure skating, soccer and karate activities. The wife states that the husband owns and operates a business known as the J. C. School of Karate and that Janelle takes her karate classes at her father's place of business. The wife further states that the husband rarely attends family functions and is rarely seen on the home videos. As an example, she refers to his absence from Janelle's last birthday party, which was held at the Victoria Inn. The wife states that it is only during the last month that the husband has become a Disney dad by buying the child extravagant gifts and encouraging the child to go with him.

Because of his work at the hospital and E.C.S. [Environmental Control Systems], the husband readily admits that his long work hours resulted in his being absent from the home more than he would have liked. He states that he was driven to this rigorous work schedule because of the excessive spending habits of the wife, a situation which caused him severe stress and anxiety, for which he sought medical attention. Now that he has re-arranged matters at the hospital, and with his brother running E.C.S., the husband states that he is able to spend more time with Janelle. In particular, he says that he now plays baseball with his daughter; takes her to movies; goes kite flying, biking and swimming, and takes her to Ukrainian dance lessons. He also denies that he was absent from his daughter's last birthday party and states that he did, in fact, leave the hospital to attend Janelle's party. His presence at the party was confirmed by the wife's brother whose affidavit was filed subsequent to the wife's initial affidavit. The husband further states that the J. C. School of Karate is not a business and that he does not own it. It is simply a volunteer club where he teaches karate and where his daughter is actively involved in the sport. He refers to taking Janelle to Nova Scotia for a karate tournament. In paragraph 18 of his affidavit the husband describes the close relationship that he has with Janelle and his willingness to attend to her needs.

In seeking interim exclusive possession of the matrimonial home, the wife first of all states that she cannot afford to obtain suitable alternate accommodation at this time based on her present income. She also states that the home is close to Janelle's school but then indicates that Janelle takes the bus to school. The main thrust of the wife's claim for interim exclusive possession of the matrimonial home is her allegation that the husband has been emotionally abusive towards her. She states that the husband has badgered and harassed her to the point where she is having emotional difficulties. In this regard she refers to the husband waking her up to talk; calling her names in front of the child; listening to her telephone conversations; blocking doorways so that she must remain in the room; being denied her mail, and being threatened.

The husband denies intimidating the wife or employing any threats or violence. Furthermore, he denies intentionally listening to her phone calls or keeping her mail. He goes on to state that the marriage has failed because of the wife's excessive spending habits and that heated arguments ensued over finances during which times there was name calling on both sides. Affidavits by Primo Scalzo and James Glena, the brother of the wife were filed respectively on behalf of the husband and the wife, which touched upon the character of the parties. . . .

It has been stated that the matrimonial home is more than a valuable asset. It is the shelter and focal point of the family. Both spouses have an equal right to possession, regardless of ownership, subject to the court's discretion to order exclusive possession, by either spouse. Section 24(1) of the *Family Law Act* empowers the Court to make exclusive possession orders. Section 24(2) of the *Act* provides that the Court may, on motion, make a temporary or interim order under section 24(1) (a), (b), (c), (d) and (e). Section 24(3) outlines the criteria that the court shall consider in determining whether to make an order for exclusive possession. The factors set out in paragraphs (a) through to (f) are mandatory considerations.

Professor Nicholas Bala, in a paper entitled *Spousal Abuse in Custody and Access Disputes: A Differentiated Approach*, states as follows at page two:

Issues of spousal abuse may arise in some form in as many as half of all divorces and present complex challenging issues for judges, lawyers and other professionals involved in the justice system. There is a growing awareness of the nature and extent of spousal abuse, not only for the direct victims - most often women - but also of the potential harm for children who live in families where there is spousal abuse. Some situations involve a high potential for violence and a failure to take appropriate protective response may place children and adults at grave risk. But, in other situations where there has been a history of abuse, professionals may embark on an inappropriately aggressive response that can needlessly heighten tension and exacerbate relationships. Justice system professionals must have a sophisticated knowledge of issues related to domestic violence and an ability to respond in a differentiated fashion that recognizes the unique dynamics and concerns of each specific case.

This is a case where the parties have been married for 22 years and where there has been no long term history of abuse. Furthermore, the affidavit evidence does not present any cogent or compelling evidence that would involve a high potential for violence that would place the wife or the child at grave risk. The wife's allegations of spousal abuse, for the most part, consist of emotional upset due to the numerous arguments between the parties concerning household finances and the husband's determination to have such discussions at inopportune times, which the wife considered to be a harassment. Furthermore, she states that the husband has been staying home more and more in the evenings of late and that this is making her uncomfortable. The wife's fears of physical harm, should the parties continue to share residence in the matrimonial home, have not been substantiated. Nor can it be said that the evidence demonstrates that the well being of the child, Janelle, would be threatened from a continued sharing of the home by the spouses. In fact, the relationship between the father and the child has become even closer because of the additional meaningful time that is being spent with the child. The spouses have continued to occupy the matrimonial home and they have demonstrated that it is possible for them to live under the same roof. See *Rosenthal* v. *Rosenthal* (1986), 3 R.F.L. (3d) 126 (Ont. H.C.), where it was held that the wife's emotional condition, not being one of the enumerated factors, could not form the foundation of an exclusive possession order.

In addressing the other criteria under section 24(3), it is the finding of this Court that it would not be in the best interests of the child to evict either the wife or the husband from the matrimonial home. There would be a disruptive effect if there was to be a change in the status quo. Although the views and preferences of the child were not expressly ascertained, the evidence, as a whole, favours the status quo as representing the best interests of the child.

The financial position of each of the spouses is such that they would require the immediate sale of the $200,000.00 mortgage free home, with an equal splitting of the proceeds of the sale, before either party would be able to afford suitable alternate accommodation. This Court is reluctant to direct the pretrial sale of the matrimonial home in that there is a triable issue as to whether either party can obtain an exclusive possession order at trial where the evidence would be more complete. . . .

Neither the wife, nor the husband, have established, on a balance of probabilities, that they fall within the provisions of section 24(3) and, accordingly, their respective claims for interim exclusive possession of the matrimonial home are dismissed. . . .

This is a case where the mother has been the primary care giver and has proven herself to be a most fit parent with good parenting skills over an extended period of time. The father of late has become more involved in the child's life. He also is a fit parent with a willingness to meet the needs of the child. Taking into consideration the factors outlined in section 24(2) of the *Children's Law Reform Act*, it is the view of this Court that it would be in the best interests of the child, Janelle, that the mother have interim custody, care and control. This Court is not persuaded that the parties would be able to communicate and co-operate in the decision making process involving the incidents of custody, so as to warrant a joint custody order.

In refusing to make an order as to interim exclusive possession, it is not the intention of this court to promote a situation of discomfort and tension. I take it that given the separation status of the parties that two separate households have been established within the matrimonial home. . . .

VOLLMER v. VOLLMER

(April 3, 1998), Doc. 24608/98 (Ont. Gen. Div.)

AITKEN J.:— . . . The pivotal issue to be determined is whether Ms. Vollmer should be granted interim exclusive possession of the matrimonial home.

Background Facts:

The parties married on March 17th, 1990 in Poland. At the time Ms. Vollmer had a child, Agata Macierzynska born July 7th, 1980, and she was expecting Matthew Vollmer who was born on August 20th, 1990. Mr. Vollmer sponsored Ms. Vollmer and Agata as immigrants to Canada and they arrived in 1990.

Ms. Vollmer arrived in this country not knowing the language or the culture. Although Ms. Vollmer was a teacher in Poland, after her arrival in Canada she remained a homemaker. Mr. Vollmer has been the sole financial supporter of the family in Canada. Ms. Vollmer and the children returned to Poland for a few months in 1993 and 1994 and from October 1995 to May 1996. While she was in Poland for the 1995-1996 school year, Ms. Vollmer was employed as a teacher. At the present time, Ms. Vollmer is taking courses at St. Andrew's Adult High School in computer accounting in order to assist her in finding employment. She hopes to go to college after that.

There is some dispute as to when the parties separated. Ms. Vollmer alleges that the parties separated in 1994 and reconciled in May 1995 and that they have been living separate and apart under the same roof since 1996. Mr. Vollmer says the parties have been living separate and apart since October 23rd, 1994 when Ms. Vollmer moved into a separate bedroom and advised him that she was getting a divorce. He alleges that after that time the parties separated their financial lives, ceased to go out socially, stopped eating together and identified themselves to third parties as being separated. They both retained lawyers. Mr. Vollmer does not acknowledge any periods of reconciliation since 1994. In any event, both parties agree that the marriage has irrevocably broken down and that there is no possibility of a reconciliation.

Ms. Vollmer went to live in a shelter from March 6th, 1995 to late May 1995. In early June 1995, she took possession of a subsidized garden home in Kanata, but then changed her mind and did not move on moving day. . . .

Ms. Vollmer alleges that Mr. Vollmer has been verbally and emotionally abusive with herself and the children and physically abusive with Agata. Mr. Vollmer alleges that Ms. Vollmer is verbally abusive to him in the presence of the children and has been physically abusive with Agata. He also alleges that very recently she punched him on the jaw, poked him in the face, shoved him on his back, tried to block his escape from the house and threatened to kill him.

Each party denies the allegations of abuse made by the other party. There have been no cross-examinations and there are no affidavits from third parties. It is uncontested that the police have been called to the matrimonial home on at least two occasions during 1998-once by Mr. Vollmer and once by Ms. Vollmer. On the occasion when Ms. Vollmer called the police, they removed Mr. Vollmer from the home and escorted him to his parents' home. It is also common ground that the relationship between the parties is very strained in the household, with the majority of communications being hostile and critical. It is agreed that on one occasion Mr. Vollmer threatened to put a chain on a fridge in the basement where he keeps his food.

Issues Not in Dispute:

The parties are in agreement that Ms. Vollmer will have custody of both children and will provide their primary residence. They also agree that the matrimonial home should be listed for sale and sold as quickly as possible. These are very important factors which affect my determination of whether Ms. Vollmer should be given interim exclusive possession of the matrimonial home. . . .

Although the evidence regarding the parties' conduct is contradictory in terms of whose behaviour is more aggressive or abusive, both are alleging behaviour which if witnessed by the children would be harmful to their well-being. Children are entitled to live in an environment where they are not being constantly exposed to anger, hostility, lack of respect, stress and fear. There are enough allegations in the affidavits of both parties to suggest that this is the environment in which Matthew and Agata are now residing. Being exposed to such an environment is not in their best interests.

There is no suggestion that either Agata or Matthew want to reside with Mr. Vollmer. Both are in the middle of their school year and it would be disruptive for the children to move until the end of their school year.

Ms. Vollmer does not have any family in the Ottawa area with whom she can stay. Mr. Vollmer has his parents and two brothers in the area. Although he states he could not stay with either his parents or his brothers, I assume that they could offer some assistance on a very short-term basis. . . .

An order for interim exclusive possession of a matrimonial home should not be given lightly when it will have the effect of forcing one party out of the matrimonial home. The court must be concerned with giving one party an inappropriate advantage over the other party in terms of a claim for custody or access or in terms of a claim for exclusive possession or eventual ownership of a matrimonial home. The court must also be concerned with putting too great a financial burden on a family.

In this case, the parties agree that Ms. Vollmer will have custody of the two children. Mr. Vollmer is not seeking equal time sharing for either of the children. All he wants is reasonable, unsupervised access to Matthew and the right to be consulted on major decisions affecting Matthew. He acknowledges that Agata will have whatever contact with himself that she wishes. An order granting Ms. Vollmer interim exclusive possession of the matrimonial home would not prejudice the access rights he is seeking.

The parties agree that the matrimonial home is to be listed for sale and sold as quickly as possible. Therefore an interim order for exclusive possession of the matrimonial home would be a temporary measure in effect only until the home can be sold and would not give either party any advantage in terms of any claim for long-term exclusive possession of the matrimonial home or eventual ownership of the home.

In all of these circumstances, and for the primary purpose of protecting the children from living on a daily basis in an environment of anger, stress and possible violence, I order Mr. Vollmer to move out of the matrimonial home by May 1st, 1998. Thereafter, Ms. Vollmer will have interim exclusive possession of the matrimonial home until its sale. . . .

HILL v. HILL

(1987), 10 R.F.L. (3d) 225 (Ont. Dist. Ct.)

FITZGERALD D.C.J.: — The parties to this proceeding are the applicant wife and the respondent husband. Under the Family Law Act the wife, aged 69, seeks interim relief from her husband of the same age by way of exclusive possession of the matrimonial house, support and costs. There is no lack of money available in the short term to either party but it is apparent that the husband's business is the major asset and income producer in a marriage which lasted some 40 years. Within two years of marriage in August 1947, the wife gave up her employment as a clerk and has since devoted herself to running the matrimonial house and raising two sons born in 1951 and 1954.

The husband formed his own business firm in 1950. At first the wife assisted in that business but after the birth of the second child ceased to be active in the firm. The business has prospered. The parties enjoyed a generous lifestyle but their interests diverged. Mrs. Hill devoted her energies to the house while Mr. Hill devoted his to the business. Eventually Mrs. Hill indicated that she would seek a separation.

The response to this was delivery to Mrs. Hill by one of her sons of a handwritten statement of what would happen if she proceeded with her intention. These included:

> We will evict you from house and cottage
>
> You will have no money for 2 or 3 years until support awarded
>
> You will die penniless and be buried in an indigent grave. . .
>
> You will be up against . . . best lawyers — money no object — we are going to drag this out
>
> No more medical payments by G.O. Hill
>
> We will take the car away
>
> How are you going to pay litigation costs?

It is apparent that "we" refers to Mr. Hill and at least one of his sons. The effect of this document was intimidating in the extreme and constitutes harassment of a particularly invidious character.

In addition on this application two affidavits were sworn by friends of Mrs. Hill who, since the separation was contemplated, received anonymous notes identified by a handwriting expert as being written by Mr. Hill. These vindictive missives are of some relevance in support of Mrs. Hill's contention that her husband has undertaken a deliberate campaign of what I regard as psychological warfare against her and her friends in the hope of undermining her resolve to obtain a fair settlement on separation. . . .

Meanwhile the wife alleges that she continues to be harassed by the husband and that his conduct and attitude have driven her to seek psychiatric help. This harassment has been subtle. It consisted of changing the pattern of delivery of money for household and personal expenses as well as the delay in coming to grips with the legal proceedings.

On the other hand Mr. Hill did pay all the usual household expenses and did continue to supply Mrs. Hill with money. He spent only part of his time in the matrimonial home preferring to spend his time at the family cottage. He did use the home for his noon hour siesta and slept there some week nights. She reports that he frequently tells her such things as "the judge and the lawyers say you are crazy to leave me" and "The judge is going to send you to an asyilum [*sic*] where you will be locked up for several months and observed through a one-way mirror". As a result of such actions and his underhand communications with her friends, the wife has begun to fear what her husband may do next and has begun absenting herself from home when he is there. Now that winter is approaching he will probably spend more time at home.

The report of Dr. Sheppard indicates that anxiety over the domestic situation, while not a cause of her neck pain, is a contributing factor. He says: "I believe that the continued co-habitation of Mrs. Hill and her husband is having a detrimental effect on her psychological state" and "since her decision to separate . . . the symptoms have been worse". . . .

In the short term both parties have the financial resources to find alternate accommodation. I find it is *not* feasible for the two of them to occupy the same dwelling having regard to the psychological warfare being waged by the husband against the wife and its effect upon her. Which of them should give up the house?
. . .

As to para. (*c*) [of s. 24(3) of the *Family Law Act*], the husband is worth at least $2 3/4 million and has available cash exceeding $150,000. The wife is worth $275,000 including cash of $39,000. If she is to maintain her lifestyle and finance an action involving the valuations necessary to a successful prosecution of her claim she can least afford to move.

As to para. (*e*) there is no evidence whatever from either party except that the respondent husband's two sons have physical room for his accommodation.

Paragraph (*f*) refers to "violence". In my view the violence in this context must be such that it makes continuation of joint cohabitation in the matrimonial dwelling impractical. Violence in my view includes psychological assault upon the sensibilities of the other spouse to a degree which renders continued sharing of the matrimonial dwelling impractical. Where, as here, the conduct of the husband in written and spoken communication to the wife is calculated to produce and does in fact produce an anxiety state which puts the wife in fear of her husband's behaviour and impinges on her mental and physical health, violence has been done to her emotional equilibrium as surely as if she had been struck by a physical blow. . . .

In my view the sense and purpose of the Family Law Act, which is a remedial statute and hence to be liberally construed, must surely include in the meaning of violence that violence causing injury to a spouse which can be achieved by words and deeds and is not restricted to the violence which can be achieved solely by physical abuse. . . .

In my view it is the conduct of Mr. Hill which has rendered the matrimonial home incapable of being shared. His is the lesser emotional attachment to the home. His is the lesser continuous use of the home. He will be the least inconvenienced by finding alternate accommodation. His are the greater resources to do so. . . .

For all the foregoing reasons it is "an equitable settlement of the affairs of the spouses" (preamble to the Act) that Mrs. Hill have interim exclusive possession of the matrimonial home and contents and I so order. . . .

MCLEOD, "ANNOTATION"
(1988), 10 R.F.L. (3d) 225

In *Hill* v. *Hill* FitzGerald D.C.J. takes the unusual course of making an order for interim exclusive possession which has the effect of ordering the husband out of the home. Although there is no question that the court has power to make such orders, the power appears to be rarely exercised. In fact, the analysis adopted and conclusion reached probably accord with the expectations of most people.

In effect, FitzGerald D.C.J. held that it is appropriate to make an order for interim exclusive possession where, on the facts, continued cohabitation is intolerable. In such circumstances if no order is made the weaker party will be forced to leave. In deciding whether continued cohabitation is intolerable the cruelty jurisprudence under the *Divorce Act*, R.S.C. 1970, c. D-8, would seem to be relevant.

In deciding whether the requirements of s. 24 of the *Family Law Act*, S.O. 1986, c. 4, have been met, FitzGerald D.C.J. held that "violence" is not restricted to physical violence but includes emotional and psychological harm. It would seem that any deliberate conduct that makes home life impossible or threatens the security of the other spouse falls within the concept of "violence" and justifies an order for exclusive possession.

Having decided that continued cohabitation is physically impossible and that one of the parties is in an unequal position, the court must decide who should receive possession. The easy answer would be that the "innocent" party should remain and the guilty party should leave. Such a simple causal link may not, however, reflect the reality of the entire marriage. FitzGerald D.C.J. has adopted a more neutral analysis focusing on which of the parties has the greater need for the home and which party is better able to function without the home. To decide these questions the court must take into account the emotional and physical state of the parties, the financial situation of the parties and the roles adopted in marriage. . . .

CICERO v. CICERO
(1978), 1 F.L.R.A.C. 49 (Ont. U.F.C.)

GRAVELY U.F.C.J.: — . . .There is a very serious dispute about what is to happen to the matrimonial home. Mrs. Cicero wants to live there with the children without her husband being present and Mr. Cicero wants the place sold and the proceeds divided equally.

It seems clear on the evidence that the parties are unable to live together in the same place, at least at the present time. It is clear also that the property is a jointly owned home and is a family asset within the meaning of that term in the Family Law Reform Act. Prima facie, then the husband is entitled to realize on his interest in the home and have it sold unless an order is made under s. 45 of the Act [the predecessor section of s. 24 of the *Family Law Act*].

I have carefully considered all of the evidence that was presented and I am satisfied that in this case the only reasonable disposition is an order for exclusive possession under s. 45 of the Act. . . .

This house is a modest house, probably the most modest, I would think, that could accommodate this family. The three bedrooms are occupied, one of them by an older child who is unable to remove himself from the care of his mother because of his medical condition.

The family has its roots in this area of the city. This is an Italian community and the children have known no other area. The children are near the school and they come home for lunch. The wife's relatives are nearby and can provide assistance to the wife as she may need it and it may be that that assistance might eventually extend to babysitting if the wife is able to find employment in the future.

There is no suggestion that there is any suitable alternative accommodation.

I am satisfied that it would not be in the interests of the children for the present situation to be changed in the reasonably foreseeable future and that it would be to their benefit to remain in the matrimonial home.

In regard to the economics of the situation, this property has been paid for. The maintenance is low. Even insofar as Mr. Cicero is concerned, I am not satisfied that his interests would be helped substantially by any sale of the premises.

He should understand that the order I am going to make does not provide for any change of the title. His interest in the property is still there and at some future time he can realize on that interest, perhaps at a profit.

There will be an order under s. 45 for exclusive possession of the matrimonial home in Mrs. Cicero. I do not propose at this time to attach a time limit to the possession order. The section provides for such an order to extend for life, but circumstances could change at any time, and, if so, a variation or a discharge order may be made under s. 46 of the Act. . . .

ROSENTHAL v. ROSENTHAL

(1986), 3 R.F.L. (3d) 126 (Ont. H.C.)

MCMAHON L.J.S.C.: — . . .The matrimonial home is located as I have indicated at 1905 Labelle Street, in the city of Windsor. By agreement of counsel, its estimated value is $130,000 with a present mortgage of $85,000 to $86,000.

The three sons are residing with the petitioner [the wife] in this home. Michael is in attendance at St. Clair College, and pursuant to the minutes of settlement that were formulated into the decree nisi, the respondent is paying $300 a month toward the support and maintenance of Michael [aged 21]. Jeffrey and Mark [aged 21 and 23 respectively], although not working, are in receipt of income, one through Unemployment Insurance, and the other as a result of a work related injury. Both of these young men are paying to their mother the sum of $30 per week; however, in her financial statement, the petitioner has indicated that the cost of groceries is $175 per week. It is quite clear that the amount being paid for room and board does not even cover the individual cost of groceries to each of these young people.

They are accordingly being subsidized by their parents. The shelter costs, as indicated by the material filed, would include the monthly mortgage payment, the taxes, the utilities, the insurance, and annual repairs. On a monthly basis, this results in a cost of some $1,541.50. . . .

Certainly, Mark and Jeffrey cannot be considered to be children affected by this application. As I have indicated by agreement, the respondent is already paying the sum of $300 for the support of Michael so that he might continue his education.

Paragraphs (b), (d), (e) and (f) [of s. 24(3) of the *Family Law Act*] in my view have no application to support the claim for exclusive possession by the wife.

The respondent is presently residing in a one-bedroom apartment, paying rent in the amount of $600 per month.

There is no question that Mrs. Rosenthal finds herself to be the aggrieved party in this unfortunate situation. The evidence of her doctor, heard by the court as a result of an application for an adjournment, clearly identifies the emotional stress that the petitioner is suffering as a result of the marital breakdown. However, the court must be bound by the provisions of the statute.

Mrs. Rosenthal in her evidence stated quite clearly that in her view, her choice of living standards should not in any way be affected by her husband's situation. This, of course, is an entirely unrealistic view of the result of a marital breakdown.

It is axiomatic that two people can live cheaper together than they can apart and this is something that Mrs. Rosenthal unfortunately must face. Her attempts to maintain the standard at which she was living prior to the marital breakdown must be viewed in the light of the moneys that are available to maintain that standard. Even during cohabitation, it is apparent that these two parties were living beyond their means, despite the relatively large joint income enjoyed by them. When one considers the financial statements filed by both parties, it becomes readily apparent that there are not sufficient funds to continue the occupation of the marital home.

Pursuant to the provisions of the statute, each party is entitled to a one-half interest in the matrimonial home. In order to have the court set aside that statutory right of the respondent, Mrs. Rosenthal must establish on the balance of probabilities that she falls within the provisions of s. 24(3). On the totality of the evidence, she has failed to satisfy the court that she has met this requirement. Unfortunate as it may be, it is the view of the court that the present situation cannot continue and it is in the best interest of both parties that the matrimonial home be sold for the best available price and that the excess moneys would, in accordance with the statute, be divided between them and form a portion of each net family property.

This will, of course, require Mrs. Rosenthal to acquire other accommodations, be it an apartment or a less expensive dwelling, either by rental or ownership. It is, of course, laudable that Mrs. Rosenthal might wish to have the three sons continue to reside with her. If that is their choice, then of course the sons, who are in receipt of income, would be required to pay their fair share of maintaining such accommodation.

The court is cognizant of the adverse effect that this determination will have upon Mrs. Rosenthal; however, as I have indicated, the court is bound by the provisions of the statute. There is no legal obligation upon this respondent to maintain Mark and Jeffrey in a style to which they have been accustomed. It is, for example, noted that each of the three boys owns and operates their own motor vehicle, as does Mrs. Rosenthal. To require Mr. Rosenthal to pay for the continuing occupation of the family unit in the matrimonial home would in effect be requiring him to support and maintain both Mark and Jeffrey under the present circumstances. Even apart from that, I am satisfied after review of the financial statements filed by both parties, that Mr. Rosenthal is entirely incapable of paying the amount that would be required to continue their occupancy of the matrimonial home at the price that I have indicated.

NOTES AND QUESTIONS

1. In *Dalep* v. *Dalep* (1986), 2 R.F.L. (3d) 19, the British Columbia Court of Appeal suggested that there were essentially two questions to consider in interim applications for exclusive possession. First, is shared use of the home a practical impossibility in the circumstances of the case? Second, if shared use is not practical, which of the spouses is favoured by an analysis of the balance of convenience? Do the Ontario cases reproduced above take a similar approach?

2. How are the issues of custody and exclusive possession inter-related? Why might a court be reluctant to determine these issues on an interim basis when the couple is still living under the same roof?

3. In *Stefanyk* v. *Stefanyk* (1994), 1 R.F.L. (4th) 432 (N.S.S.C.), Sanders J. was faced with a situation where the parties were still living in the home with their two children. The justice pointed out (at 439):

Interim orders cover a short period of time between granting the order and trial. They are intended to provide a reasonably acceptable solution to difficult problems which the parties are unable, by themselves, to resolve. My exposure to Mr. and Mrs. Stefanyk has been limited. It is really confined to their affidavits and my observations during their lengthy cross-examination. Owing to the fact that their positions are materially different in several respects, it is necessary for me to assess credibility and make specific findings of fact. I am prepared to do that. But I want each side to recognize that at trial, after a full investigation of all the facts and merits of the case, the trial judge may well come to conclusions substantially different than mine.

Concluding that "their marriage has broken down to the extent that it would be intolerable to expect Mr. and Mrs. Stefanyk to continue living together", the court granted interim custody of two young children and interim exclusive possession of the matrimonial home to Mrs. Stefanyk.

4. Kozak J. adopted an interesting and unusual solution in *Squitti* v. *Squitti*, (March 6, 1995), Doc. # Thunder Bay 84-95 (Ont. Gen. Div.), digested at [1995] W.D.F.L. 869 (Ont. Gen. Div.). Each party claimed interim exclusive possession and interim custody at a time when they were living separate and apart within the matrimonial home. The judge awarded interim alternating custody on a three-month rotating basis. The children were to remain in the matrimonial home. During each custody period the party having care of the children would have exclusive possession of the matrimonial home and the other party would live in a rental property they owned. However, subsequent proceedings revealed that this arrangement was never implemented and that the children resided with the mother: *Squitti* v. *Squitti*, [1997] O.J. No. 4781 (Gen. Div.).

5. In *Preszcator* v. *Preszcator* (1997), 33 R.F.L. (4th) 141 (Ont. Gen. Div.), Vogelsang J. granted interim custody of a child to her mother because the mother had been the primary care-giver. Although he found (at 142) that "the continued proximity of the applicant and the respondent in the same property is leading to anger and jealousy" and (at 143) that each party had been "guilty of petulant and immature behaviour", he concluded (at 143) that to exclude one of them from the farm would only exacerbate their financial problems.

6. As noted earlier in considering the position of unmarried cohabitees, several provinces have recently enacted legislation to provide emergency relief for married and unmarried persons where there is domestic violence. One of the remedies provided is a temporary exclusive possession order of the family residence. Typically, such legislation permits short-term orders without notice to the other party (*ex parte* orders) where family violence has occurred and the circumstances are serious or urgent. Police officers may be specifically directed to remove the other party from the residence. See *Protection Against Family Violence Act*, S.A. 1998, c. P-19.2 ; *The Domestic Violence and Stalking Prevention, Protection and Prevention Act*, S.M. 1998, c. 41; *Victims of Family Violence Act*, R.S.P.E.I. 1988, c. V-3.2 (in force 1996); and *The Victims of Domestic Violence Act*, R.S.S. 1994, c. V-6.02. This legislation deals explicitly with a number of issues that are left to be worked out through procedural rules or creative judicial interpretation in Ontario. Recall that *ex parte* orders were granted in earlier proceedings in *Pifer* and *Perrier*. See also *Family Law Rules*, O. Reg. 114/99, r. 14(12) - (15).

Court-ordered eviction from one's home without an opportunity to present evidence or argument obviously raises concerns of procedural fairness. See *C.(A.L.G.)* v. *Prince Edward Island* (1998), 157 D.L.R. (4th) 523 (P.E.I.T.D.), where certain aspects of Prince Edward Island's legislation were found to infringe s. 7 of the *Charter*. See also *Dolgopol* v. *Dolgopol* (1995), 127 Sask. R. 237 (Q.B.) and *Bella* v. *Bella* (1995), 132 Sask. R. 17 (Q.B.) where the reviewing judges concluded that the justices of the peace had acted without the urgency needed for an *ex parte* order.

7. Where one spouse finds it necessary to seek an interim exclusive possession order, it may be prudent in some circumstances to also obtain an order under s. 46(1) of the *FLA* restraining the other spouse from molesting, annoying or harassing the applicant. Section 46(2) establishes the offence of contravening a restraining order and s. 46(3) deals with police powers to arrest a person suspected of this offence. Regarding restraining orders and their enforcement, see *Maurico* v. *Maurico* (1979), 9 R.F.L. (2d) 243 (Ont. Prov. Ct.); *Layton* v. *Layton* (1982), 37 O.R. (2d) 201 (H.C.); *Scono* v. *Scono* (1984), 41 R.F.L. (2d) 57 (Ont. H.C.); *Wilkins* v. *Wilkins* (1987), 7 R.F.L. (3d) 199 (Ont. Prov. Ct.); *Colley* v. *Colley* (1991), 31 R.F.L. (3d) 281 (Ont. U.F.C.); *Hamilton* v. *Hamilton* (1996), 92 O.A.C. 103

(Ont. C.A.); *Chau* v. *Jiang (Guardian of)*(1997), 34 R.F.L. (4th) 249 (Alta. Q.B.); and *Cole* v. *Cole* (1998), 40 R.F.L. (4th) 54 (Ont. Gen. Div.).

8. The financial position of the spouses is likely to be a key circumstance militating against a long-term order for exclusive possession. In addition to *Rosenthal*, see *Greenall* v. *Greenall* (1984), 39 R.F.L. (2d) 225 (Ont. H.C.); *Braithwaite* v. *Braithwaite* (1984), 40 R.F.L. (2d) 415 (Ont. H.C.); *Nicol* v. *Nicol* (1989), 21 R.F.L. (3d) 236 (Ont. H.C.); *Norlander* v. *Norlander* (1989), 21 R.F.L. (3d) 317 (Sask. Q.B.); *Venslovaitis* v. *Venslovaitis* (March 3, 1989), Doc. # ND-146110/87 (Ont. H.C.) (digested at [1989] W.D.F.L. 703); *Balogh* v. *Balogh* (1996), 24 R.F.L. (4th) 181 (Ont. C.A.); and *Dolman* v. *Dolman* (1998), 38 R.F.L. (4th) 362 (Ont. Gen. Div.). In *Venslovaitis*, Morrissey J. stated:

> It has not been established that a move from the matrimonial home would have disruptive effects. The evidence satisfies me that the two younger children are good students and suffer from no physical, emotional or learning disability. They will, in my opinion, be able to adapt to new surroundings. The respondent failed to prove that there was no other suitable and affordable accommodation available for the respondent and the two children in her care. The matrimonial home equity represents a substantial asset in which both parties have an interest. It would be unfair to the petitioner to withhold from him his interest in this major asset since the capital is required by him to set up another residence. The proceeds of the sale will likewise assist the respondent in setting up another residence.

On the other hand, where there is no need to sell the home to realize its capital value and the parties can afford the carrying charges, a court will more readily delay sale and make an exclusive possession order: *Tward* v. *Tward* (1982), 31 R.F.L. (2d) 251 (Ont. H.C.); *Gies* v. *Gies* (1982), 30 R.F.L. (2d) 122 (Ont. Co. Ct.); *Caines* v. *Caines* (1984), 42 R.F.L. (2d) 1 (Ont. Co. Ct.); *Hutton* v. *Hutton* (1985), 48 R.F.L. (2d) 451 (Ont. Co. Ct.); and *Elliot* v. *Elliot* (1995), 10 R.F.L. (4th) 424 (Ont. Gen. Div.).

9. The cases generally suggest that, before a court will order exclusive possession overriding ownership rights for any significant period based on the best interests of a child, there must be some evidence to indicate that a move will significantly disrupt the life of the particular child involved. An example is *Crane* v. *Crane* (1986), 3 R.F.L. (3d) 428 (Ont. H.C.). The husband had custody of two children. He sought an order for exclusive possession of the jointly owned matrimonial home for two years so that the youngest child could continue attending the local elementary school. Mossop L.J.S.C. ordered the home sold and the proceeds divided. He stated (at 433-434) that "[t]he evidence relating to the criteria to be considered by the court in the legislation is either non-existent or very sparse in the case at bar so I must assume that there will be no great negative effects to the parties or the children in refusing to grant exclusive possession to the husband as he requests". See also *Davie* v. *Davie* (1979), 1 F.L.R.A.C. 530 (Ont. H.C.); *Greenall* v. *Greenall* (1984), 39 R.F.L. (2d) 225 (Ont. H.C.); *Silver* v. *Silver* (1984), 41 R.F.L. (2d) 344 (Ont. H.C.), affirmed (1985), 49 R.F.L. (2d) 148 (Ont. C.A.); *Hart* v. *Hart* (1985), 46 R.F.L. (2d) 274 (Nfld. U.F.C.); *Nicol* v. *Nicol* (1989), 21 R.F.L. (3d) 236 (Ont. H.C.); and *Scanlan* v. *Scanlan* (1990), 25 R.F.L. (3d) 241 (Ont. H.C.).

In *James* v. *James* (1994), 3 R.F.L. (4th) 226 (Ont. Gen. Div.), Walsh J. granted indefinite exclusive possession of the matrimonial home to the wife who had custody of three children. He reasoned (at 230):

> As the children have all continuously resided in the home since 1987 and are now well settled into the neighbourhood with friends and schools close by, and given the difficulties disclosed in the official Guardian's report [the children were angry and needed counselling to help them re-establish a relationship with their father], the best interests of the children clearly require that they remain in the matrimonial home and be sheltered from the disruptive effects of a forced move to new surroundings, new schools, and new friends for as long a period as possible.

See also *Elliot* v. *Elliot* (1995), 10 R.F.L. (4th) 424 (Ont. Gen. Div.), where the court granted exclusive possession to a mother and two children until the oldest child graduated from elementary school mainly because this child had problems and would not adjust well to a move.

10. The courts are reluctant to grant long-term exclusive possession orders where an emotional attachment to the home appears to be the only factor favouring such an order. In *D.* v. *D.* (1979), 13 R.F.L. (2d) 279 (Man. C.A.), the husband sought partition and sale of a jointly-held matrimonial home that had been occupied by the wife since separation. The couple's children were now adults who lived on their own. The wife sought to retain possession on the basis that the home was a "symbol, a centre, a concourse for family gatherings" (at 281). The Manitoba Court of Appeal held that the trial judge had correctly ordered partition and sale. It stated (at 281):

> We have no doubt that this sentimental attachment is sincere and deeply felt. But ought it to prevail over the right of a joint tenant to obtain the benefit of an asset he owns, particularly when he has no other significant assets? To give effect to the wife's contention for keeping the home unsold could deny to the husband the fruits of this asset for years ahead, perhaps even for the span of the wife's lifetime.

See also *Cipens* v. *Cipens* (1979), 7 R.F.L. (2d) 236 (Ont. U.F.C.); *Balogh* v. *Balogh* (1996), 24 R.F.L. (4th) 181 (Ont. C.A.); and *Dolman* v. *Dolman* (1998), 38 R.F.L. (4th) 362 (Ont. Gen. Div.).

11. As acknowledged by the Supreme Court of Canada in *Lamb* v. *Lamb* (1985), 46 R.F.L. (2d) 1, an exclusive possession order may affect the quantum of support that should be ordered. If the dependent spouse is granted possession of a home, the financial needs of that spouse may be significantly reduced. Where the other spouse has an interest in the home, that spouse is already providing for one of the major living costs for the dependent spouse.

The relationship between the equalization claim under Part I of the *FLA* and an order for exclusive possession of a matrimonial home is perhaps less obvious, but often no less important. In particular, orders for possession in favour of a spouse who does not have an ownership interest in the home may affect the other spouse's ability to satisfy an equalization claim through the payment of a monetary sum. As a result, a court may use its power to delay payment of all or part of the equalization sum for a period up to ten years: *Porter* v. *Porter* (1986), 1 R.F.L. (3d) 12 (Ont. Dist. Ct.); *Nicol* v. *Nicol* (1989), 21 R.F.L. (3d) 236 (Ont. H.C.); and *Ward* v. *Ward* (1990), 26 R.F.L. (3d) 149 (Ont. C.A.). Some courts have used s. 9 to transfer the entire interest in the matrimonial home to one spouse as a means of satisfying part or all of the equalization sum. See *Oliva* v. *Oliva* (1986), 2 R.F.L. (3d) 188 (Ont. H.C.), varied (1988), 12 R.F.L. (3d) 334 (Ont. C.A.) and *McCutcheon* v. *McCutcheon* (1986), 2 R.F.L. (3d) 327 (Ont. Dist. Ct.). In this way, the spouse can secure possession following the termination of the marriage without the need for a court order for exclusive possession. However, such orders can only be made where the transfer of property is an appropriate means for satisfying the equalization payment. See *Hoar* v. *Hoar* (1993), 45 R.F.L. (3d) 105 (Ont. C.A.).

12. In *Derrickson* v. *Derrickson* (1986), 26 D.L.R. (4th) 175, the Supreme Court of Canada held that the provisions of the *Family Relations Act*, R.S.B.C. 1979, c. 121, relating to the ownership and possession of immovable property, could not apply to lands on an Indian reserve. In the companion case of *Paul* v. *Paul* (1986), 26 D.L.R. (4th) 196 (S.C.C.), the court also concluded that exclusive possession orders relating to family residences on such lands could not be made under the provincial legislation. For analysis of these decisions, see Bartlett, "Indian Self-Government, Equality of the Sexes, and the Application of Provincial Matrimonial Property Laws" (1986), 5 Can. J. Fam. L. 188; Mossman, "Developments in Property Law: The 1985-86 Term" (1987), 9 Supreme Court L.R. 419 at 430 ff. and Turpel, "Home/Land" (1991), 10 Can. J. Fam. L. 17.

In *Wynn* v. *Wynn* (February 2, 1989), Doc. # Thunder Bay 4705/89 (Ont. Dist. Ct.) [digested at 14 A.C.W.S. (3d) 107], the court purported to find a way to avoid the effect of these decisions. The spouses were both Indians, as defined in the *Indian Act*, R.S.C. 1970, c. I-6, and the wife sought exclusive possession of a home located on a reserve. Wright D.C.J. acknowledged that he could not make an order for exclusive possession, but he issued an *in personam* order restraining the husband from interfering with the wife's possession of the home.

Under the recently enacted *First Nations Land Management Act*, S.C. 1999, c. 24, fourteen First Nations that entered into a Framework Agreement on First Nation Land Management with the federal government are required by s. 17(1) to "establish general rules and procedures, in cases of breakdown of marriage, respecting the use, occupation and possession of first nation land and the division of interests in first nation land". Presumably, these rules will deal with possession of the matrimonial home.

13. A spouse's right to claim an exclusive possession order under the *Family Law Act* is lost upon divorce. Even if the claim is properly put forward by a spouse, the court's authority to grant an exclusive possession order may be lost if there is a divorce before the matter is dealt with. See *Miller* v. *Miller* (1996), 20 R.F.L. (4th) 191 (Ont. C.A.) and *Finnie* v. *Finnie* (December 21, 1998), Doc. Goderich 408/97 (Ont. Gen. Div.). These cases cast serious doubt on the suggestion in *Luyks* v. *Luyks* (1998), 38 R.F.L. (4th) 464, at 466 (Ont. Gen. Div.) that a court has the authority under s. 24 to grant possession to a non-owning widow beyond the period set in s. 26(2).

14. In many cases, one party will remain in the matrimonial home on separation without a court order. If the other spouse has an ownership interest in the home, he or she may later seek occupation rent. The cases dealing with such claims are reviewed in *Bourdeau* v. *Bourdeau* (1999), 47 R.F.L. (4th) 97 (Ont. Master). See also *Ballum* v. *Ballum* (1999), 49 R.F.L. (4th) 176 (P.E.I.T.D.).

15. Where both spouses hold title to the matrimonial home, one spouse may seek an order for exclusive possession not only to exclude the other, but to ensure that the other does not obtain an order for partition and sale of the home. An order for exclusive possession in favour of one joint tenant is, in effect, a deferral of partition and sale until the order expires or is discharged under s. 25. See *Cipens* v. *Cipens* (1978), 7 R.F.L. (2d) 236 (Ont. U.F.C.); *Porter* v. *Porter* (1986), 1 R.F.L. (3d) 12 (Ont. Dist. Ct.); and *Nicol* v. *Nicol* (1989), 21 R.F.L. (3d) 236 (Ont. H.C.). It follows that partition and sale of a jointly owned matrimonial home should not be ordered prior to trial unless it is clear that the claim for exclusive possession is without merit. For cases examining whether partition and sale of a jointly held matrimonial home prior to trial would prejudice a claim that one spouse intends to put forward, see *Binkley* v. *Binkley* (1988), 14 R.F.L. (3d) 336 (Ont. C.A.); *Batler* v. *Batler* (1988), 18 R.F.L. (3d) 211 (Ont. H.C.); *Smith* v. *Smith* (1989), 22 R.F.L. (3d) 173 (Ont. H.C.); *Genttner* v. *Genttner* (1989), 23 R.F.L. (3d) 25 (Ont. Dist. Ct.); *Arlow* v. *Arlow* (1990), 27 R.F.L. (3d) 348 (Ont. Dist. Ct.) varied (1991), 33 R.F.L. (3d) 44 (Ont. C.A.); *Ames* v. *Bond* (1992), 39 R.F.L. (3d) 375 (Ont. C.A.); and *Harewood* v. *Harewood* (1993), 45 R.F.L. (3d) 449 (Ont. C.A.).

16. The relationship between the *Partition Act*, R.S.O. 1990, c. P-4 and the *FLA* was explored in *Silva* v. *Silva* (1990), 1 O.R. (3d) 436 (C.A.) and *Martin* v. *Martin* (1992), 38 R.F.L. (3d) 217 (Ont. C.A.). The Ontario Court of Appeal concluded that the *Partition Act* could apply to a jointly held matrimonial home. Indeed, the court ruled in *Martin* v. *Martin* that partition and sale of jointly owned property could not be ordered under s. 10 of the *FLA* unless there was an application to determine a question of ownership or possession.

17. *Allesandro Building Corp.* v. *Rocca* (1987), 8 R.F.L. (3d) 366 (Ont. C.A.), although decided under the *Family Law Reform Act*, indicates that a court should not grant an application for partition or sale of a matrimonial home without consideration of a spouse's statutory occupation rights. In that case, the husband's interest in the home, held jointly with his wife, had been transferred by the husband's trustee in bankruptcy to a mortgagee. The mortgagee sought partition and sale under the *Partition Act*. The Ontario Court of Appeal held that the wife's interest in the home could only be disposed of with her consent or by a court order authorizing the disposition following a finding that she was unreasonably withholding her consent. This case, therefore, suggests that a court should not order partition and sale of a jointly held matrimonial home until it is determined, pursuant to s. 23(b) of the *FLA*, that the objecting spouse is "unreasonably withholding consent". While this point was not expressly addressed in the cases where the courts have ordered the sale of a jointly held matrimonial home prior to trial, there was presumably an implicit finding in these cases that the spouse who opposed the sale was unreasonably withholding consent. Where a couple has separated, a refusal to consent to the sale of a jointly held matrimonial home to allow both spouses to realize their interests in it is likely to be characterized as unreasonable unless the sale would prejudice the claims of the objecting spouse.

18. The Ontario Court of Appeal held in *Martin* v. *Martin* (1992), 38 R.F.L. (4th) 217 that neither spouse can be given a right of first refusal where the court orders sale of a jointly held matrimonial home under the *Partition Act*. See also *Amaral* v. *Amaral* (1993), 50 R.F.L. (3d) 364 (Ont. Gen. Div.). However, the Ontario Court of Appeal granted a wife an opportunity to purchase the matrimonial home

in *Willemze-Davidson* v. *Davidson* (1997), 98 O.A.C. 335 where there was agreement on the value of the home and it was in the best interests of a child to remain in the home with its mother. In *Pastway* v. *Pastway* (1999), 49 R.F.L. (4th) 375 (Ont. Gen. Div.), the court permitted the husband to buy his wife's interest in the jointly owned matrimonial home before trial against her will at a particular price. Professor McLeod's annotation to the case was very critical.

4.   Dealings with a Matrimonial Home

As indicated in the last chapter, Part I of the *FLA* continues the separate property regime between spouses, subject to a system of deferred sharing of gains. Until a court orders otherwise (for example, by transferring the property under s. 9(1) or by making a preservation order under s. 12), the owning spouse is able to dispose of his or her assets subject only to the possibility that the transaction will be set aside under the *Fraudulent Conveyances Act*, R.S.O. 1990, c. F. 29. The position with regard to the matrimonial home is different. While ownership between the spouses is unaltered, a spouse who disposes of or encumbers an interest in a matrimonial home must ensure that the transaction complies with s. 21.

The primary purpose of s. 21 is to provide some protection for the possessory rights of the non-owning spouse established by Part II of the Act. However, the section also applies where the spouses are co-owners of the matrimonial home. Thus, the section may serve to protect the proprietary interest of one spouse against the other. In *Kozub* v. *Timko* (1984), 45 O.R. (2d) 558, 39 R.F.L. (2d) 146, the Ontario Court of Appeal held that a similar provision in the *Family Law Reform Act* applied where the wife, who owned the matrimonial home in joint tenancy with her husband, conveyed her interest in the home to her son. The husband did not learn of this conveyance until after the death of the wife. The court set aside the conveyance and held that it did not sever the joint tenancy between the husband and wife. The court left for future determination the question of whether a conveyance by one joint tenant of the interest in a matrimonial home to himself or herself had to comply with s. 42(1) of the *Family Law Reform Act* (now s. 21(1) of the *FLA*). The sole purpose and effect of such a conveyance is to sever the joint tenancy. It, therefore, affects proprietary rights of the other spouse who loses the right of survivorship but does not have any impact on the possessory rights established by Part II of the *FLA*. After a series of conflicting lower court decisions, the Ontario Court of Appeal settled the issue in *Horne* v. *Evans* (1987), 8 R.F.L. (3d) 195. It held that s. 42(1) of the *Family Law Reform Act* (now s. 21 of the *FLA*) did not apply to a conveyance by one joint tenant of the matrimonial home to himself or herself.

Section 21(1) of the *FLA* prohibits a spouse from disposing of or encumbering an interest in the matrimonial home unless at least one of four statutory conditions is met. Does s. 21(1) apply where the owning spouse merely rents out a room in the matrimonial home for a two-month period? Does it apply where the owning spouse mortgages the matrimonial home?

Any attempt by a spouse to dispose of, or place a direct encumbrance on, his or her interest in the matrimonial home without the consent of the other spouse violates s. 21. However, transactions which might indirectly lead to an execution directed against a spouse's interest in a matrimonial home are not caught. In *Bank of Montreal* v. *Bray* (1997), 33 R.F.L. (4th) 335, the Ontario Court of Appeal held that the renewal of an unsecured guarantee, given by the husband without the wife's consent, did not amount to an encumbrance of an interest in the matrimonial home. The Bank of Montreal could, therefore, enforce the guarantee against the husband's interest in the jointly owned matrimonial home. See also *First City Trust Co.* v.

McDonough (1993), 50 R.F.L. (3d) 197, 15 O.R. (3d) 586 (Gen. Div.) and *Enterprise Newfoundland & Labrador Corp.* v. *Kawaja* (1997), 29 R.F.L. (4th) 116 (Nfld. T.D.).

Because s. 21 only applies to spouses, a party who agrees to sever the divorce from the corollary relief claims may be vulnerable to dealings with the matrimonial home before these claims are dealt with. See *Love* v. *Baker* (1997), 30 R.F.L. (4th) 370 (Ont. Gen. Div.).

A husband is the sole shareholder of a company which owns a home that is leased to him and occupied as the family residence. The corporation mortgages the home without the wife's consent. Does s. 21 apply? See *Manufacturers Life Ins. Co.* v. *Riviera Farm Holdings Ltd.* (1998), 39 R.F.L. (4th) 1 (Ont. C.A.).

Examine the statutory conditions set out in s. 21(1). Notice that s. 21(1)(b) only refers to a separation agreement. This is because a purported release of possessory rights in a matrimonial home in a marriage contract is unenforceable (s. 52(2)) and does not affect the restrictions on alienation contained in s. 21. By virtue of s. 21(1)(c), a spouse can dispose of or encumber an interest in a matrimonial home if a court order has authorized the transaction or has released the property from the application of Part II. Section 23(b) empowers a court, upon application by a spouse or person having an interest in the property, to "authorize the disposition or encumbrance of the matrimonial home if the court finds that the spouse whose consent is required, (i) cannot be found or is not available, (ii) is not capable of giving or withholding consent, or (iii) is unreasonably withholding consent". Regarding the circumstances in which a spouse will be considered to be unreasonably withholding consent, see *Mills* v. *Andrewes* (1982), 31 R.F.L. (2d) 47 (N.S. T.D.); *Robbins* v. *Robbins* (1983), 35 R.F.L. (2d) 108 (Ont. Master); *Clarkson* v. *Lukovich* (1986), 2 R.F.L. (3d) 392 (Ont. H.C.), varied (1988), 14 R.F.L. (3d) 436 (Ont. C.A.); *Allesandro Building Corp.* v. *Rocca (No. 2)* (1987), 9 R.F.L. (3d) 422 (Ont. H.C.); *Borsch* v. *Borsch* (1987), 9 R.F.L. (3d) 444 (Ont. H.C.); *Royal Bank* v. *King* (1991), 35 R.F.L. (3d) 325 (Ont. Gen. Div.); and *Proc* v. *Proc* (1992), 42 R.F.L. (3d) 418 (Ont. Gen. Div.).

An order releasing property from the application of Part II may be made under s. 24(1)(b). Where the court grants exclusive possession of a matrimonial home to one spouse, it may release another property that is a matrimonial home from the application of Part II. In this situation s. 21(1)(c) would allow the owning spouse to deal with the other property without the other's consent.

Why is s. 21(1)(d) superfluous? Examine s. 20(4).

See ss. 21(2), 23(d) and 24(1)(g) to identify the potential remedies available when s. 21(1) is violated. In light of the wording of s. 21(2), it would appear that a transaction that does not comply with s. 21(1) is valid unless set aside by a court. On the effect of such a transaction and the circumstances in which a court should set it aside, see *Van Dorp* v. *Van Dorp* (1980), 30 O.R. (2d) 623 (Co. Ct.); *Mills* v. *Andrewes, supra*; *Robbins* v. *Robbins, supra*; *Bank of Montreal* v. *Norton* (1986), 36 R.F.L. (2d) 268 (Ont. H.C.); *Kozub* v. *Timko, supra; Robinson* v. *Royal Bank of Canada* (1995), 26 O.R. (3d) 627 (Gen. Div.); *Maimets* v. *Williams* (1997), 29 R.F.L. (4th) 207 (Ont. C.A.); *Parker* v. *Parker* (1997), 32 R.F.L. (4th) 289 (Ont. Gen. Div.); and *Banton* v. *Banton* (1998), 164 D.L.R. (4th) 176 (Ont. Gen. Div.).

Section 21(2) provides protection for the person who acquires an interest in a matrimonial home for value, in good faith and without notice that the property was a matrimonial home. "Notice" for the purpose of this subsection includes both actual and constructive notice that the property is a matrimonial home: *Stoimenov* v. *Stoimenov* (1985), 44 R.F.L. (2d) 14 (Ont. C.A.). See also *767648 Ontario Ltd.* v. *Engel*

(1993), 46 R.F.L. (3d) 382 (Ont. Gen. Div.), affirmed (1994), 1 R.F.L. (4th) 144 (Ont. C.A.). In *Stoimenov*, the court distinguished between the two types of notice as follows (at 21): "Actual notice means knowledge of the very fact required to be established, whereas constructive notice means knowledge of other facts which put a person on inquiry to discover the fact required to be established."

To facilitate conveyancing, s. 21(3) specifies that a statement by the person making the disposition or encumbrance verifying certain facts is deemed to be sufficient proof that the property is not a matrimonial home in the absence of notice to the contrary. In *Stoimenov*, the court held that the notice referred to is notice of the falsehood of the facts set out in the statement rather than notice that the property is a matrimonial home. The analysis in *Stoimenov* suggests the following relationship between subsections (2) and (3). Where an affidavit is given, the onus is on the spouse seeking to set aside the transaction to establish that the third party had notice of the falsehood. Once this is done, the transaction can be set aside unless the third party proves that despite notice of the falsehood he or she was without notice of the fact that the property was a matrimonial home. As *Stoimenov* demonstrates, notice of the falsehood may in some circumstances amount to notice that the property is a matrimonial home.

Section 21(3) differs from its predecessor in the *Family Law Reform Act*. In that statute the person to whom the disposition or encumbrance was made could rely on the affidavit unless he or she had *actual* notice to the contrary. By deletion of the word "actual" in the new provision, either actual or constructive notice of the inaccuracy of the facts contained in the affidavit will now negate the effect of the affidavit. As a result of this changed wording, persons dealing with property that might be a matrimonial home are likely to approach the affidavit with more caution than was the case under the old Act. Under the *Family Law Reform Act* a person who suspected that the property was a matrimonial home could still rely on a affidavit even if it contained false statements, provided the person did not have actual knowledge of the falsehood. Now, however, the facts that lead the person to suspect that the property is a matrimonial home could very well also amount to constructive notice of the falsehood of the statement. As a result, a solicitor acting for a party who is acquiring an interest in or receiving the benefit of an encumbrance of property that could be a matrimonial home should investigate what that party knows regarding the use of the property and the marital status of the other party in order to assess whether the affidavit can be safely relied upon.

Where the court is precluded by s. 21(2) from setting aside the transaction, the wronged spouse may be able to obtain another remedy under s. 24(1)(g). That paragraph empowers the court to direct the person who made a false statement under s. 21(3) (or a "person who knew at the time he or she acquired an interest in the property that the statement was false and afterwards conveyed the interest") to substitute other real property for the matrimonial home. Alternatively, the court can direct such persons to set aside money or security to stand in the place of the matrimonial home. Why are these remedies unlikely to be effective?

5.   Right to Redemption and Relief Against Forfeiture

Section 22 of the *FLA* is intended to give a spouse who has a right to possession by virtue of s. 19 the same right of redemption or relief against forfeiture as the other spouse. In an action by a mortgagee for foreclosure, possession, and payment on the convenant, s. 22(1) gives a spouse, who has a right to possession by virtue of s. 19, a statutory right of redemption and a statutory right to seek relief against the acceleration clause equal to that of the spouse who is directly liable to the mortgagee. See *Maritime Life Assurance Co.* v. *Karapatakis* (1979), 9 R.F.L. (2d) 265, 7 R.P.R. 229 (Ont. H.C.), which dealt with the equivalent provision in the *Family Law Reform Act*. In order to exercise the rights given by s. 22 effectively, the spouse must comply with the Rules of Civil Procedure and statutory provisions governing the exercise of similar rights by the owning spouse.

To ensure that the non-owning spouse is in a position to exercise the substantive rights given by s. 22, s. 22(1) provides that any person proceeding to realize upon a lien, encumbrance or execution, or attempting to exercise a forfeiture against the matrimonial home, must give notice to both spouses. The proper procedure for giving such notice in an action for foreclosure, possession and payment on the covenant by a mortgagee is detailed in *Maritime Life Assurance Co.* v. *Karapatakis*, above.

6

SPOUSAL SUPPORT

1. Introduction

Provincial law, which governs support obligations during marriage, offered various avenues of support for wives in Ontario prior to 1978. The most common way in which a wife obtained support after the marriage was through summary proceedings in Provincial Court (Family Division) under the *Deserted Wives' and Children's Maintenance Act*, R.S.O. 1970, c. 128. Desertion coupled with a failure to maintain was the sole basis for an order under this Act, but a dependent wife was deemed deserted where she was living separate and apart by reason of the husband's cruelty or uncondoned adultery. Adultery by the wife, if not condoned, was an absolute defence. Any acts that made her a deserter would also preclude relief.

Wives of more wealthy husbands obtained support through the common law action for alimony in the High Court. A husband's liability was conditioned upon his misconduct in the form of adultery, cruelty, or desertion. Matrimonial misconduct on the part of the wife was a defence.

Provincial law, contained in the *Matrimonial Causes Act*, R.S.O. 1970, c. 265, also governed support in nullity actions. This legislation exhibited the same basic features as alimony and deserted wives' maintenance: only the woman could obtain support, there was no expectation that women would maintain themselves, and misconduct in the form of adultery by the woman provided a complete defence.

Prior to the passage of the *Divorce Act* in 1968, the *Matrimonial Causes Act* also applied to divorce actions in Ontario. The *Divorce Act* of 1968 altered this situation by giving the courts the authority to provide for interim and permanent orders of maintenance on divorce. The Act gave limited guidance to the courts in dealing with maintenance. It simply directed the court to make an order "if it thinks it fit and just to do so having regard to the conduct of the parties and the condition, means and other circumstances of each of them." Nevertheless, the Act introduced significant reforms. It permitted husbands to obtain maintenance in appropriate cases, although this rarely occurred. It no longer barred maintenance for a spouse who had been guilty of marital misconduct.

By the 1970s the existing law of support, particularly that within provincial jurisdiction, was being severely criticized (see, for example, Ryan, "Maintenance Obligations in a New Legal Concept of Marriage" (1975), 21 R.F.L. 1). In its *Report on Family Law, Part VI: Support Obligations* (Toronto: Ministry of the Attorney General, 1974), the Ontario Law Reform Commission suggested that the existing law was deficient in three important respects: first, by characterizing support as an inherent incident of a wife's marital status, it perpetuated the view that married women occupied exclusively domestic roles and were chronic dependants; second, the paramount importance assigned to matrimonial fault made the law resemble a scheme of punishment and reward for behaviour during marriage; third, there were real cases of need that the law did not meet either because the wife had committed a matrimonial offence or because she could not establish that the husband had committed one. The Commission suggested that a primary objective of any reform should be the elimination of the underlying assumption that a wife was inherently dependent on her husband for support.

In 1975, the Law Reform Commission of Canada also called for major reforms of the law dealing with maintenance on divorce. In particular, it noted that the *Divorce Act* failed to provide any philosophical basis for the continuing support obligation after divorce. Nor did the Act provide the courts with "a legislative statement of the governing principles to be considered in determining the nature and extent of the financial obligation, if any, owed by one spouse to the other": Law Reform Commission of Canada, *Maintenance on Divorce: Working Paper 12* (Ottawa: Law Reform Commission of Canada, 1975) at 13. In the excerpt from the working paper that follows, the Commission set out the philosophy of spousal support that it felt should be explicitly recognized by legislation.

LAW REFORM COMMISSION OF CANADA, *MAINTENANCE ON DIVORCE: WORKING PAPER 12*

(Ottawa: Law Reform Commission of Canada, 1975) 17-19, 23-27 and 35-36

Marriage should be characterized in law as a union of legal equals in which there may be a division of function or a "role specialization", according to the emotional, psychological and financial needs of the spouses and the needs of their children. Financial rights and obligations based upon marriage should be legal results that *follow* from the internal arrangements made by the spouses in line with their priorities, circumstances and interests rather than being *imposed* according to traditional legal preconceptions of the sexually determined roles of each spouse. The purpose of the maintenance obligations on divorce should be to enable a former spouse who has incurred a financial disability as a result of marriage to become self-sufficient again in the shortest possible time. This should be achieved through new rules for financial provision in the *Divorce Act* that would be based on need and that are neither punitive nor fault-oriented. . . .

We suggest the following principles:

1. Marriage *per se* does not create a right to maintenance or an obligation to maintain after divorce; a divorced person is responsible for his or her own maintenance.
2. A right to maintenance may be created by reasonable needs following from:
   (a) the division of function in the marriage;
   (b) the express or tacit understanding of the spouses that one will maintain the other;
   (c) custodial arrangements made with respect to the children of the marriage at the time of divorce;
   (d) the physical or mental disability of either spouse that affects his or her ability to maintain himself or herself; or
   (e) the inability of a spouse to obtain gainful employment.
3. The purpose of maintenance on divorce is to provide the maintained spouse with financial support required to meet those reasonable needs recognized by law as giving rise to a right to maintenance during the transition period between the end of the marriage and the time when the maintained spouse should reasonably be expected to assume responsibility for his or her own maintenance; maintenance on divorce is primarily rehabilitative in nature.

4. A right to maintenance shall continue for so long as the reasonable needs exist, and no longer; maintenance may be temporary or permanent.

5. A maintained spouse has an obligation to assume responsibility for his or her own maintenance within a reasonable period of time following divorce unless, considering the age of the spouses, the duration of the marriage, the nature of the needs of the maintained spouse and the origins of those needs, it would be unreasonable to require the maintained spouse ever to assume responsibility for his or her own maintenance, and it would not be unreasonable to require the other spouse to continue to bear this responsibility.

6. A right to maintenance is not adversely affected, forfeited or reduced because of conduct during the marriage; or because of conduct after the marriage except
   (a) conduct that results in a diminution of reasonable needs; or
   (b) conduct that artificially or unreasonably prolongs the needs upon which maintenance is based or that artificially or unreasonably prolongs the period of time during which the person maintained is obliged to prepare himself or herself to assume responsibility for his or her own maintenance.

7. The amount of maintenance should be determined by:
   (a) the reasonable needs of the spouse with a right to maintenance;
   (b) the reasonable needs of the spouse obliged to pay maintenance;
   (c) the property of each spouse after divorce;
   (d) the ability to pay of the spouse who is obliged to pay maintenance;
   (e) the ability of the spouse with the right to maintenance to contribute to his or her own maintenance; and
   (f) the obligations of each spouse towards the children of the marriage.

These principles will now be discussed. . . .

The way in which the functions characteristic to marriage have been divided, and economic needs that exist at the time of divorce following from what each spouse did during marriage should become the fundamental criteria for maintenance when a marriage ends. A consideration of what actually occurred during the marriage would fill the vacuum left in the divorce law by Parliament's repudiation of the old assumption that, as a matter of law, the wife would always be the housekeeper, the full-time parent and in a condition of economic dependency, and that a husband would always be the wage-earner.

A division of function between marriage partners, where one is a wage-earner and the other remains at home will almost invariably create an economic need in one spouse during marriage. The spouse who stops working in order to care for children and manage a household usually requires financial provision from the other. On divorce, the law should ascertain the extent to which the withdrawal from the labour force by the dependent spouse during marriage (including loss of skills, seniority, work experience, continuity and so on) has adversely affected that spouse's ability to maintain himself or herself. The need upon which the right to maintenance is based therefore follows from the loss incurred by the maintained spouse in contributing to the marriage partnership. . . .

If a financial need exists for one spouse at the time of divorce, and this need has been created by or has resulted from the way in which functions were shared between husband and wife, then the needy spouse would have a claim to maintenance that the law should recognize and enforce. This claim would be based on the facts

of the spouses' experience during the marriage and not on the sex of the claimant.
. . .

We propose that a right to maintenance may arise from "the express or tacit understanding of the spouses that one will maintain the other" so long as such an arrangement, made either before or during marriage, results in a reasonable need for financial provision for the maintained spouse at the time of divorce. In almost all cases, the division of function in the marriage will itself account for the need upon which a maintenance claim is based, and no question of any special understanding, express or tacit, will arise. It is not uncommon, however, for people to marry with the understanding, for example, that each will help the other, in succession, through university or professional training. To illustrate, a wife who works to put her husband through university on the understanding that he will thereafter do the same for her, could probably not be said to have a need for maintenance arising out of the division of function in the marriage. But she may very well have a need for financial assistance with her own university training that is reasonable in light of her expectation that her spouse would provide such assistance, even though the marriage breaks down before the arrangement intended by the parties is complete. Another example might be where a well-to-do man married and provided his wife with everything, including a housekeeper, while she did little or nothing. Such a woman would have to learn how to do things for herself at the time of a marriage breakdown, and would therefore have reasonable needs arising out of the arrangement that existed during her marriage. These needs should be respected by the law, regardless of her gratuitous enjoyment of what may appear to some as a rather idyllic married life. The range of possible situations is as broad as the range of understandings that may arise between married people with respect to how they should cooperate to ensure that the interests and needs of each are satisfied. . . .

Custodial arrangements to children at the time of divorce should also be recognized as situations that may create needs upon which claims for maintenance can be based. Whether a need does arise in a custodial parent is a question of fact, not of law, and would turn on such matters as the age and number of children involved, whether they need constant care or are partially or wholly emancipated, whether suitable alternatives to care by the custodial parent (such as public day-care facilities) are reasonably available and whether their use would be in the best interests of the child and the effect that custody has on the ability of the custodial parent to provide for his or her own maintenance. . . .

The physical or mental disability of a spouse is another matter that should be a ground for maintenance at the time of divorce. Although we do not support the idea that marriage *per se* should involve the right or duty of maintenance after divorce, we do suggest that the physical or mental disability of a spouse at the time of divorce is a reasonable criterion upon which to found an obligation to maintain. Again, however, we do not see this as a principle of unlimited application. We believe the primary responsibility for the provision of care of persons with a permanent or long-term disability rests with the state and not with any afflicted person's spouse or former spouse. We also think it possible, in any particular case, for a court to strike a balance between the time during which the fact of marriage should create a maintenance obligation because of misfortune, and the time when the state should assume the burden. We will pursue this point below, when we discuss the duration of the maintenance obligation.

The inability of a spouse to obtain gainful employment at the time of divorce is conceptually similar to the inability of a physically or mentally disabled spouse to provide for himself or herself. The inability may have no logical connection to the fact that the person claiming maintenance was married to the person upon whom the claim is made, and performed a certain role within the marriage partnership. We believe, however, that during marriage it would be reasonable for the law to expect that the first resort for financial provision by an unemployed married person would be to his or her spouse, if capable, rather than to public assistance (excluding assistance for which the unemployed spouse has paid, such as unemployment insurance). An obligation based on these grounds should, like an obligation founded on physical or mental disability, survive the dissolution of the partnership for a reasonable time. . . .

A key concept in the above principle[s] is that of "reasonable needs". This represents a shift in emphasis away from the traditional theory for determining the amount of maintenance. That theory can best be summed up by the expression that a divorced man who was liable to pay maintenance had to support his former wife according to "the style in which she was accustomed to be kept". We believe this test is objectionable on several grounds, and that it is inconsistent with the philosophy of the principles of maintenance we have proposed.

First, we reiterate that the financial expectations created by the divorce law should not, even inferentially, allow marriage to be seen as a substitute for individual achievement or as an alternative to seeking training and education for the station in life to which an individual aspires. . . .

Second, divorce in the great majority of cases will create greater economic burdens than existed during the marital relationship. It is simply not possible for the life style of the former spouses to remain unaffected. . . .

The essence of the change we propose lies in the shift in legal emphasis towards a philosophy of individual responsibility. The significant legal effect of marriage under such a philosophy would be to create a right to rehabilitory financial assistance in the event that the circumstances during marriage impaired the ability of a spouse to assume that responsibility after divorce. Ensuring financial re-establishment for the needy spouse rather than attempting to perpetuate the life style of the defunct marriage for the "innocent" spouse would, we believe, be a reasonable and realistic basis for courts to employ in determining both the eligibility for and the amount of maintenance.

The standard of living enjoyed by the spouses during marriage would not cease to be an operative factor on divorce, and should be taken into account to the extent that it is *relevant* to the reasonable needs of each spouse. "Reasonable needs" will vary from individual to individual according to the marital and life experience of every person. . . .

Part II of the *Family Law Reform Act, 1978* was the Ontario legislature's initial response to the need for reform. The Act abolished the action for alimony, and repealed the *Deserted Wives' and Children's Maintenance Act* and those parts of the *Matrimonial Causes Act* dealing with support. It created equal, mutual support obligations. The duty of a spouse to support himself or herself was also statutorily recognized. The concept of fault as the basis for spousal support was abolished, although in extreme circumstances fault could still be considered in determining quantum. In place of fault, the legislation substituted need as the basic determinant of entitlement and provided the courts with guidelines to consider in determining the amount. For the first time, unmarried cohabitees could claim support if their relationship met certain statutory criteria. In addition to altering the substantive law of support, Part II of the *Family Law Reform Act* also contained provisions to facilitate the enforcement of support orders.

Part III of the *Family Law Act* (the *FLA*) replaced Part II of the 1978 Act. Although there were some significant changes, the basic features of the support law introduced by the *Family Law Reform Act* were retained.

The 1985 *Divorce Act* made substantial alterations to the law of support on divorce. Section 15.2(6) (s.15(7) until the numbers were altered by S.C. 1997, c. 1) of the current *Divorce Act* sets out the objectives that the court is to keep in mind in determining spousal support. Section 15.2(4) (previously s. 15(5)) identifies factors that the court is to consider and s. 15.2(5) (previously s.15(6)) explicitly specifies that "any misconduct . . . in relation to the marriage" is not to be taken into account.

In the following article, Professor Rogerson sets out three possible models of support and explores the extent to which each has been recognized in the new provincial and federal legislation. She does so in the context of an evaluation of the "causal connection test", which featured prominently in the case law and literature on spousal support in the latter half of the 1980s. Her criticism of the way in which the concept was being used in many cases to limit the duration and amount of support was echoed by the S.C.C. in *Moge* v. *Moge* (1992), 43 R.F.L. (3d) 345 which is reproduced later in this chapter. The majority quoted extensively from Professor Rogerson's article.

ROGERSON, "THE CAUSAL CONNECTION TEST IN SPOUSAL SUP- PORT LAW"

(1989), 8 Can. J. Fam. L. 95, at 95-96 and 106-118 (Footnotes Omitted)

1. INTRODUCTION

Causal connection: the words are not expressly found in any existing support legislation but they have become the new discourse in claims for spousal support after marriage breakdown and are understood as encapsulating a distinct philosophy of spousal support to be adopted by judges in structuring the broad discretion given to them under existing support legislation. Put simply (although, as will be shown below, the issue is not, in reality, nearly so simple) the idea behind causal connection is that spousal support should redress those economic needs flowing from or *caused by* the marriage and the economic inter-relationship which developed between the spouses during the marriage; and conversely, that spousal support should not be expected to redress economic needs which do not flow from the marital relationship. Again, on a very simplistic analysis, the causal connection model of spousal support can be contrasted with a model of spousal support often referred to as the traditional model of spousal support, in which the support obligation is understood as springing from the fact of marriage per se, the status of being married and the promise of support included in the marriage vows, rather than from anything which went on during the marriage. Under this latter model, marriage is understood as involving a guarantee of economic security for spouses which survives marriage breakdown in all cases where spouses are unable to attain on their own a standard of living which approximates the marital standard, or at least a reasonable standard of living. . . .

B. The Modern Law of Support

Since the late 1960s academics, policy makers and legislators have been engaged in the project of reconceptualizing the role of spousal support. The traditional model of support, based on ideas of fault, the presumed economic dependency of wives and the promise of a life-long guarantee of the marital standard of living in all cases of marriage breakdown, was viewed as no longer acceptable in a new social and legal milieu in which spouses were regarded as equal in legal status; in which marriage was understood as a personal relationship in which spouses could determine their own internal arrangements, unconstrained by traditional gender roles; in which it was becoming socially acceptable and more common for wives to participate in the labour force; and finally, in which marriage was recognized as a terminable union which spouses were entitled to leave, allowing them to create new lives and enter into new relationships.

Not surprisingly, no clear consensus has yet been arrived at with respect to the role of modern spousal support. The difficulty is due, in part, to the recognition of the diversity of marital relationships which exist and the very different social understandings and expectations of those entering marriage twenty years ago from those entering marriage today. However, even today conflicting understandings of marriage continue to exist; even particular individuals hold both traditional and modern views of marriage simultaneously. Finally, one is faced in this area with the problems, in terms of hardship to individuals, which can be created by changing the economic obligations in one area of social life, such as the family, without a corresponding change in other areas, such as the labour force and the state.

The lack of consensus with respect to the purpose of spousal support is reflected in the current support legislation which has been produced as a result of law reform efforts to come up with a replacement for the traditional law of spousal support. The legislation tends to consist of lists, sometimes very extensive lists as in the Ontario *Family Law Act*, of various objectives and criteria for the awarding of support. In some cases the criteria reinforce each other; in other cases they pull in different directions. Legislatures have not committed themselves to a single view of spousal support and judges are faced with the difficult task of trying to establish priorities and relationships between the various objectives envisioned for spousal support. What follows is an attempt to distil from existing legislation three different models or ways of thinking about and justifying modern spousal support. While they will be separated out for analytical purposes, it must be remembered that they are not pure models, and that under existing support legislation all three models interact and modify each other. It is, however, useful to separate them out because ultimately a choice has to be made as to which model provides the conceptual foundation for the law of spousal support.

(i) "needs and means"; spousal support as an income security scheme

One idea basic to the reform of spousal support law, and the idea on which there is perhaps the greatest consensus, is that support law should be primarily an economic remedy, a response to economic need; hence the characterization of modern spousal support as an income security scheme. On this understanding of the purpose of spousal support, the criteria upon which the traditional law of support were based — gender, status and conduct — were irrational because not related to need, and hence had to be eliminated. Thus, modern support legislation is framed in economic terms — the language of needs and means — and factors of gender, conduct and marital status per se have been eliminated. Section 30 of the *F.L.A.*, which constitutes the basic articulation of the spousal support obligation, reads:

> Every spouse has an obligation to provide support for himself or herself and for the other spouse, in accordance with need, to the extent that he or she is capable of doing so.

Under this scheme need on the part of one spouse, combined with means on the part of the other, would appear to be the basis of entitlement. The criteria which follow in s. 33(8) for determining "the amount and duration, if any, of support in relation to need" are largely economic, including the assets of the parties, their income and income earning capacity, their other support obligations and their economic needs. Similarly, section 15(5) of the *Divorce Act, 1985* [now s. 15.2(4)] directs the courts to "take into consideration the means, needs and other circumstances of each spouse . . . for whom support is sought".

Taken at face value, and interpreted apart from other understandings of spousal support law, the needs and means/income security model of spousal support does not require an argument that the economic needs of the claimant spouse have been caused by the marital relationship. Although such cases will obviously be included, the model goes beyond them. It is the fact of being married, combined with the existence of an economic need, which gives one an entitlement to draw on the resources of the other spouse. The basic argument that must be made in order to claim support is that an economic need exists. Spousal support can thus be claimed in all instances where a spouse is unable to meet his or her own needs through illness, disability, unemployment or lack of job skills. In this respect, the needs and means model of spousal support closely resembles the traditional model of support law, and like it appears to draw upon what are still fairly prevalent social assumptions that it is the primary responsibility of the family to provide a cushion of income security to those citizens who are unable to meet their own needs and that this is one of the obligations which is undertaken in marriage.

It cannot be disputed that there are indications in the legislation that spousal support is intended to perform this traditional social function. The legislation appears to contemplate as one of the purposes of spousal support the relief of the economic hardship which results when the economic support formerly provided by a spouse is withdrawn and the other spouse left without adequate financial resources. Section 33(8)(d) of the *F.L.A.* states that one of the objectives of spousal support is "to relieve financial hardship" and s. 33(9)(e) requires courts to consider the spouse's "age and physical and mental health" in assessing quantum of support. Similarly, s. 15(7)(c) of the *Divorce Act, 1985* [now s. 15.2(6)(c)] provides that one of the objectives of an order for spousal support . . . is to "relieve any economic hardship of the spouses arising from the breakdown of the marriage". . . .

It is possible to offer a causal connection justification for these "hardship" provisions which will link the support obligation to what occurred during the marriage: if support is being provided to a dependent spouse at the point of marriage breakdown, the *marriage breakdown* (as distinguished from the marriage) can be viewed as causing economic hardship to the extent that it causes the loss of the support that was being provided during the marriage and a severe decline in standard of living. As will be discussed below, such a causal connection argument is quite plausible as a justification for limited-term, transitional support. In any case where support has been provided during the course of the marital relationship, there will have been reliance upon that source of support, and detrimental reliance in that other sources of support and other ways of organizing one's life were not pursued or even contemplated. Thus, spousal support must be provided to allow an adjustment period in which the dependent spouse can reorganize his or her own life. However, to the extent that the needs and means/income security framework creates long-term support obligations based simply on the assumption of such a support obligation in the past, in cases of economic need not created by the marital relationship, it must be recognized that the obligation ultimately rests upon traditional ideas of status and promise.

One other difficult issue which arises under the needs and means/income security model of spousal support is that of assessing the compensable "needs" of the claimant, an issue which essentially involves determining the appropriate standard of living to be guaranteed by the income security scheme assuming the "means" are available: is it the marital standard of living, a reasonable standard of living, a subsistence standard of living, or whatever standard of living the claimant can achieve on his or her own (a standard which essentially negates all claims upon the income-security scheme)? The answer to that question does not flow inevitably from the conceptualization of support as an income security scheme and is the most discretionary aspect of the needs and means model. The answer requires further articulation of the vision of marriage on which the scheme is based and it is here that the influence of other models of spousal support embedded in the legislation may have an influence. One interpretation, which would define needs with respect to the marital standard of living, would bring the needs and means model very close to the traditional model of support. An indication of this approach is found in s. 33(9)(f) of the Ontario *F.L.A.* which, after directing courts to take into account the dependent's needs, goes on to state "in determining which the court shall have regard to the accustomed standard of living, while the parties reside together". . . .

Again, within this framework, a very expansive version of the causal connection argument can be made to justify a support obligation based on the marital standard of living: the enjoyment of a particular standard of living in the past can be viewed as having created the needs associated with that standard of living. The needs are thus related to the facts of the particular marriage. However, the same argument as was made above in relationship to the objective of relieving economic hardship applies. To the extent that the needs and means framework justifies a long-term, as distinct from a transitional, limited-term obligation to maintain the marital standard of living *simply* because it was enjoyed in the past, it is in essence not operating on a causal connection philosophy but on a more traditional philosophy rooted in the idea that marriage inevitably involves a guarantee of economic security. . . .

The needs and means framework for spousal support which exists within current legislation can thus, on some interpretations, create a scheme of support which in many ways resembles traditional support law. There are, also, however, other modes of spousal support embedded in the legislation which can be used to provide guidance in interpreting the concepts of "needs" and which generate other arguments for spousal support different from the argument that spousal support is based on a promise given upon entry into marriage and the mere enjoyment of a particular standard of living during the marriage.

(ii) *"economic advantages and disadvantages of marriage": the compensatory/ loss of opportunity model of spousal support*

Another model of spousal support, also strongly suggested by existing legislation, is what might be generally termed the compensatory model of support. Under this model the basic purpose of spousal support is to compensate claimant spouses both for the economic disadvantages which they have suffered as a result of the marriage and the economic advantages which they have conferred on the other spouse during the course of the marriage. This model of support is expressly contemplated by s. 15(7)(a) of the *Divorce Act, 1985* [now s. 15.2(6)(a)] which requires, as one of the objectives of a support order, that it "recognize any economic advantages or disadvantages to the spouse arising from the marriage or its breakdown". The comparable provision in the *F.L.A.* is s. 33(8)(a) which directs that an order for spousal support "recognize the spouse's contribution to the relationship and the economic consequences of the relationship for the spouse". Under this model, marriage is not understood as entailing a general guarantee of economic security and spousal support is concerned only with redressing the economic consequences which flow from the particular relationship of the spouses. Spousal support does not redress all needs — it only redresses needs created as a result of the marriage. This model is thus rooted in a philosophy of what could be termed causal connection, although because of the terminological problems discussed above, it may be preferable to label this a compensatory model of support.

Within this framework, the argument most frequently used to justify spousal support is the "disadvantage"-based argument that support should compensate a spouse who has sacrificed labour force participation in order to perform family responsibilities for the loss of economic opportunity suffered. Indeed, the loss of opportunity model, which makes spousal support analogous to a tort claim rather than a contractual claim, is often understood as synonymous for what I am labelling the compensatory model of support. . . . Along these lines, s. 15(5)(b) of the *Divorce Act, 1985* [now s. 15.2(4)(b)] directs that consideration be given to "the functions performed by the spouse during cohabitation" and s. 33(9)(l)(ii) of the *F.L.A.* specifically makes relevant to the assessment of spousal support "the effect on the spouse's earning capacity of the responsibilities assumed during cohabitation".

The concept of loss of opportunity, or more generally economic disadvantage suffered as a result of having performed family obligations, can also be extended to take into account the costs, both direct and indirect, of having primary responsibility as custodial parent, for the care of the children after marriage breakdown. The indirect costs would involve the continuing constraints imposed upon the custodial parent's labour force participation; the direct costs most associated with the daily support of children. The criteria for assessing support in the *F.L.A.* include both s. 33(9)(i) which refers to "the desirability of [a spouse] remaining at home to care for a child" and s. 33(9)(1)(vi) which refers to "the effect on the spouse's earnings and career development of the responsibility of caring for a child". As well, both the *F.L.A.* and the *Divorce Act* specifically include in the list of the four objectives of an order for spousal support that of sharing the economic burden of the care and support of children between the parents. [See paragraph 15.2(6)(b) of the *Divorce Act* and paragraph 33(8)(b) of the *F.L.A.*] . . .

Although a compensatory model of support certainly includes compensation for loss of income-earning opportunities and other costs incurred due to the performance of family obligations, it need not be confined to that. The *F.L.A.* speaks more broadly of the economic consequences to the spouse of the relationship and the *Divorce Act* speaks of the economic advantages as well as disadvantages flowing from the marriage. The compensatory model of support would cover compensation to a spouse for contributions to the relationship and to the family which are not adequately compensated by the award of matrimonial property, including the enhancement of the other spouse's income earning capacity as a result of those contributions. Compensation for contributions appears to be contemplated in the legislative provisions setting out the objectives of spousal support. As noted above, s. 15(7)(a) [now s. 15.2(6)(a)] of the *Divorce Act* refers to recognizing the *economic advantages* to the spouses arising from the marriage and s. 33(8) of the *F.L.A.* refers to recognizing the spouse's contribution to the relationship. The *F.L.A.* also includes in the list of criteria relevant to the assessment of support several factors related to spousal contribution: s. 33(9)(j) specifically refers to "a contribution by the dependent to the realization of the respondent's career potential" and s. 33(9)(1)(v) refers to "any housekeeping, child care or other domestic service performed by the spouse for the family. . . .".

Finally, it could be argued that the compensatory model of support covers claims not involving the assumption by one spouse of particular family responsibilities and the economic disadvantages and advantages flowing from these domestic arrangements. One can contemplate cases in which a disadvantage or loss is incurred merely because of the fact of marriage, such as the loss of support or pension benefits flowing from a prior marriage or relocating and the giving up of a secure job in order to marry. As well, it would be possible to argue, as suggested above, that there may be detrimental reliance flowing from the mere fact that economic support was provided to a spouse in the past, apart from any issue of that spouse performing domestic responsibilities. As a result of reliance on the marital resources spouses may not have pursued other economic opportunities, either in terms of their own earnings or support from other sources, and not been required to accommodate their lifestyle to what they could have achieved on their own. Marriage breakdown will at the very least involve an economic dislocation of the economic pattern created by the relationship. Thus, with respect to spousal support, the compensatory model could at the very least justify a limited-term support obligation for adjustment purposes. . . .

Even in the case of a person who through illness or disability is incapable of earning an income and contributing to his or her own support, the marriage has precluded the formation of other social and emotional relationships which might have been a source of both emotional and economic security. Again, because of the prior reliance upon the marriage, some adjustment period is required. This analysis would suggest that even on the compensatory model, because of the element of detrimental reliance on the marriage as a source of economic support, there would likely be some support awarded (although in some cases only for a limited period of time) in every case in which the marriage breakdown will result in a drop in standard of living.

One factor which both the *F.L.A.* and the *Divorce Act, 1985* make relevant to the assessment of support is the length of the marriage, the assumption being that a long-term marriage generates a stronger entitlement to support, both in terms of quantum and duration. It can be argued that this factor is both compatible with and supportive of a compensatory model of support and hence also of a properly applied causal connection theory of support. Length of marriage is a very convenient proxy for the kinds of concerns [to which] the compensatory model is directed. It is likely that the longer the period of cohabitation, the greater the probability of economic integration between the spouses and the greater the degree of contribution to the relationship. Length of cohabitation can therefore be correlated with loss of opportunity and detrimental reliance based upon the expectation that the relationship would continue to provide economic security. Particularly in a long-term relationship it is extraordinarily difficult to perform the kind of strict tort analysis that is required by a strict application of one loss of opportunity model. When one marriage has lasted for a very long time it is almost impossible to quantify the [losses] and detriments and to determine the economic position the spouses would have been in but for the marriage. As well, it is conceptually illogical to ignore the relationship if one is interested in compensating for contributions made to the relationship as well as losses suffered because of it. For both of these reasons, the purposes of the compensatory model are best served, in case of long-term relationships, by using the marital standard of living as a proxy for the economic losses suffered and contributions made to the relationship.

In fact, the problems of quantification of advantages and disadvantages, and the enormous speculation involved in crystal-ball gazing into the past exist in all but the shortest, childless marriages. This suggests more generally the need for more easily applied proxies and rules of thumb under the compensatory model. In the typical cases where the marriage has involved an economic inter-relationship and where there is an absence of either exceptional talents or disabilities the most sensible approach would appear to be to eschew exact quantification and backward-looking speculation and to concentrate instead on the future and establishing a reasonable standard of living for the claimant through a combination of his or her own efforts and payments from the other spouse. Thus in the typical case, the compensatory model thus merges, in terms of implementation, with the needs and means approach to spousal support which concentrates on standard of living post-marriage breakdown. However, in some cases the compensatory model will depart from the results of a pure needs and means model, as outlined above, in that entitlement does ultimately spring from some connection between the claim for support and the economic inter-relationship established during the marriage. Thus, if it can be established that a claimant's inability to attain a reasonable standard of living flows *solely* from illness or disability or other personal limitation, unaffected by what went on during the marriage, and as well that the other spouse does not retain economic advantages conferred by the claimant spouse for which compensation has not been received, then the only compensation due is for the dislocation suffered by the claimant from having to re-organize his or her life in order to adjust to a lower standard of living. As well, in short and/or childless [marriages there is not] the same presumption of a prima facie entitlement to a reasonable standard of living after marriage breakdown.

(iii)   *self-sufficiency, spousal independence, and the "clean break" model of spousal support*

The third dominant theme in the law of spousal support . . ., apart from "needs and means" and "compensation for economic advantages and disadvantages flowing from the marriage" is the idea of promoting spousal self-sufficiency post marriage breakdown. The basic idea in forming this model is that, in contrast to the old law of spousal support which tied the parties together economically forever even after divorce, a modern law of support should give more recognition to the fact that the marriage has ended and should encourage the economic disengagement of the parties and their assumption of responsibility for their own maintenance. The idea of promoting self-sufficiency was a dominant theme in the reform movement, producing a vision of spouse support as a transitional measure which would allow an economically dependant spouse to "rehabilitate" and become responsible for his or her own support. . . .

The concept of self-sufficiency has been expressly included in existing legislation. Section 15(7)(d) of the *Divorce Act, 1985* [now s. 15.2(6)(d)] lists as one of the four objectives of a spousal support order that it:

... in so far as practicable, promote the economic self-sufficiency of each spouse within a reasonable period of time.

Similarly, s. 33(8)(c) of the Ontario *F.L.A.* states that one of the four objectives of spousal support is to:

... make fair provision to assist the spouse to become able to contribute to his or her own support.

A concern with promoting spousal self-sufficiency can shape the law of spousal support in a variety of ways. On some interpretations, self-sufficiency would be regarded as an adjunct principle to either of the other two models of support discussed above. It would thus simply require that a claimant spouse be encouraged to utilize and develop his or her own income-earning abilities to the extent realistically possible post marriage breakdown so as to make a contribution to meeting his or her own needs, and thus recover to some extent what was lost economically as a result of the marriage. However, under this approach, the governing principles would remain those of either guaranteeing an adequate standard of living and/or adequately compensating the spouse for the economic consequences of the marriage. As discussed above, for practical purposes, the principles often become synonymous. Spousal support would be reduced to take into account the claimant's own income-earning capacity, but would not be eliminated unless the over-arching objectives of income security and/or compensation were met. . . .

[T]he relevant *Divorce Act* provisions qualify the goal of self-sufficiency by addition of the phrase ''in so far as possible'', while the relevant *F.L.A.* provision contemplates a spouse *contributing* to his or her own support, and not necessarily being wholly responsible for his or her own support.

However, the concept of self-sufficiency may also give rise to a full-fledged philosophy of support which is sometimes referred to as the ''clean break'' theory. Under this philosophy of support, cutting the economic ties between the spouses as quickly as possible becomes, in its own right, the over-arching goal of the law of spousal support. Support is, as a matter of principle for only a limited duration. The passage of time after divorce becomes the most significant factor in determining support obligations. After the passage of a few years, spouses are deemed to be responsible for themselves and thus self-sufficient, regardless of the negative economic consequences which may continue to flow from the marriage and the absence of anything resembling actual financial autonomy on the part of the formerly dependent spouse. A passage from the Law Reform Commission of Canada's Working Paper emphasizes the time factor:

The purpose of the maintenance obligation should be to enable a former spouse who has incurred a financial disability as a result of marriage to become self-sufficient again *in the shortest possible time*. [Emphasis added]

Of the three models of spousal support that have been discussed, the clean break model as a full-fledged philosophy of support would appear to have the least legislative support, the objective of encouraging self-sufficiency being carefully qualified. However, in terms of actual judicial results, priority is often being given to the clean break philosophy above either the income security or compensatory models of spousal support.

NOTES AND QUESTIONS

1. As you examine the cases that follow, consider which of Professor Rogerson's three models of support is being applied.

2. A variety of studies link poverty and divorce. In its *Evaluation of the Divorce Act* (1990), the Department of Justice found that two-thirds of divorced women had total incomes that, for various family sizes, put them below the "low income cut-offs" frequently used as the basis for poverty levels. Only 10% of ex-husbands were in similar straits, although 42% of men with sole custody fell below the various cut-off lines. In *Women and Poverty Revisited* (Ottawa: Minister of Supply and Services, 1990), the National Council of Welfare provided further empirical data concerning the economic consequences of single parenthood. Married women, although they constituted the largest group of poor women, had the lowest poverty rates, ranging from 10 per cent for wives with children under 18 to 6 per cent for wives 65 and over. Never married single-parent mothers had the highest poverty rate: 75 per cent of them fell below the poverty line. Other single-parent mothers had a poverty rate of 52 per cent. Overall, single-parent families headed by women had the highest incidence of poverty of all family types. Due to limited support payments, little job experience and an inadequate supply of subsidized day care, many of these mothers resorted to welfare for at least a short period of time. In *Poverty Profile 1996* (Ottawa: Minister of Supply and Services, 1998), the National Council of Welfare again reported that families headed by single mothers with children under 18 had the highest poverty rate of any family type — 61.4 per cent.

3. The adverse economic effect of separation or divorce is typically greater for women than men. Focusing on married persons with children who separated between 1987 and 1993, a study entitled *Family Income After Separation* conducted by Diane Galarneau and Jim Sturrock for Statistics Canada (1997) found that one year after separation women experienced a 23% loss in family income, adjusted for the number of family members. This loss (32%) was greatest for women who had not formed new relationships. At the same time, men registered a 10% gain in adjusted income. Two factors were cited to explain the gap. First, married women generally earn less than married men and so lose a major source of financial support on separation. Second, women almost always have custody of the children. See also Finnie, "Women, Men, and the Economic Consequences of Divorce: Evidence from Canadian Longitudinal Data" (1993), 30 Can. Rev. of Sociology and Anthropology 205.

4. Spousal support awards have increased following the S.C.C. decision in *Moge* v. *Moge* (1992), 43 R.F.L. (3d) 345. See Bala, "Spousal Support Law Transformed — Fairer Treatment for Women" (1994), 11 C.F.L.Q. 13 and Rogerson, "Spousal Support After Moge" (1997), 14 C.F.L.Q. 281. However, Miriam Grassby asserts in "Spousal Support — Assumptions and Myths Versus Case Law" (1995), 12 C.F.L.Q. 187 that levels of spousal support ordered by the courts or negotiated by the parties are often lower than the principles of family law suggest they should be.

5. Even if support awards escalate, the impact on the poverty statistics may be quite limited. In "The Limits of Family Law Reform or, the Privatization of Female and Child Poverty" (1990-91), 7 C.F.L.Q. 59, Professor Eichler cautions that the capacity of private family law to remedy the "feminization of poverty" is limited. She argues that, even if there were an equitable division of family property on marriage breakdown which took into account the needs of mothers and children and a system of more realistic support awards which were always paid, the impact on the poverty of women and children would be limited. In large part, this is because the majority of poor women and children live in ongoing marriages and would be unaffected by changes to property and support laws which apply on marriage breakdown. Also, the amount of property and income available for redistribution on marriage breakdown in many families is modest. Professor Eichler concludes that further reform of family law would, at best, alleviate the poverty of a small proportion of poor women and children. She urges a comprehensive reform of the public income security system and the overall economic structure. For a more recent article with similar themes, see Mossman, "'Running Hard to Stand Still': The Paradox of Family Law Reform" (1994), 17 Dalhousie L.J. 5.

6. For further reading, see Rogerson, "Winning the Battle, Losing the War: The Plight of the Custodial Mother After Judgment" in Hughes and Pask, eds., *National Themes in Family Law* (Toronto: Carswell, 1988) 21; Pask and McCall, *How Much and Why? Economic Implications of Marriage Breakdown: Spousal and Child Support* (Calgary: Canadian Research Institute for Law and the Family, 1989); Sugarman, "Dividing Financial Interests on Divorce" in Sugarman and Kay, eds., *Divorce Reform at the Crossroads* (New Haven: Yale University Press, 1990) 130; Carbone and Brinig, "Re-

thinking Marriage: Feminist Ideology, Economic Change and Divorce Reform'' (1991), 65 Tulane L. Rev. 953; Rogerson, ''Judicial Interpretation of the Spousal and Child Support Provisions of the *Divorce Act, 1985* (Part I)'' (1990-1991), 7 C.F.L.Q. 155; Grassby, ''Women in Their Forties: The Extent of Their Rights to Alimentary Support'' (1991), 30 R.F.L. (3d) 369; Morgan, Kitson, and Kitson, ''The Economic Fallout from Divorce: Issues for the 1990's'' (1992), 13 J. of Family and Economic Issues 435; Stewart and McFadyen, ''Women and the Economic Consequences of Divorce in Manitoba: An Empirical Study'' (1992), 21 Man. L.J. 80; Ross, ''Time Out of the Labour Force: Diminished Future Earnings Potential'' (1992), 42 R.F.L. (3d) 50; Engel, ''Compensatory Support in *Moge* v. *Moge* and the Individual Model of Responsibility: Are We Headed in the Right Direction?'' (1993), 57 Sask. L. Rev. 397; Finnie, ''Women, Men, and the Economic Consequences of Divorce: Evidence from Canadian Longitudinal Data'' (1993), 20 Can. Rev. of Sociology and Anthropology 205; Pulkingham, ''Private Troubles, Private Solutions: Poverty Among Divorced Women and the Politics of Support Enforcement and Child Custody Determination'' (1994), 9 Can. J. Law and Society 73; and Grassby, ''Spousal Support — Assumptions and Myths Versus Case Law'' (1995), 12 C.F.L.Q. 187.

2.   Making an Application for Support: Who? When? Where?

(1) THE *FAMILY LAW ACT*

(a) Who can apply?

The heart of Part III of the *FLA* is s. 33. In order to determine who can be required to pay support to whom under s. 33, one must examine the definition of ''dependant'' in s. 29. This definition leads one to ss. 30, 31 and 32 in order to determine whether support obligations are imposed. Section 30, in turn, requires an examination of the general definition of ''spouse'' in s. 1(1) and the extended definition of ''spouse'' in s. 29. In 1999, the *FLA* was amended (S.O. 1999, c. 6) to include ''same-sex partner''as a dependant to whom a support obligation is owed under Part III. The definition of ''same-sex partner'' appears in s. 29.

The extended definition of ''spouse'' in s. 29 closely resembles that previously contained in s. 14(b)(i) of the *Family Law Reform Act*. Section 14(b)(i) of that Act was the focus of the following cases. It specified that ''spouse'', for the purpose of support, included ''either of a man and woman not being married to each other who have cohabited (a) continuously for a period of not less than five years, or (b) in a relationship of some permanence where there is a child born of whom they are the natural parents, and have so cohabited within the preceding year''. Note that under the *FLA* the period of continuous cohabitation is now three years as opposed to five and that part (b) of the extended definition refers to adoptive as well as natural parents. The requirement that the cohabitation be within the year preceding the application has also been dropped. However, note s. 50. Under s. 2(8) of the Act, this limitation period may be extended if the delay in commencing proceedings was incurred in good faith, there will be no substantial prejudice to the other party as a result of the delay, and there are *prima facie* grounds for relief.

SANDERSON v. RUSSELL

(1979), 9 R.F.L. (2d) 81, 24 O.R. (2d) 429 (C.A.)

MORDEN J.A.: — . . . It is submitted by Bessie Sanderson, the respondent in this appeal, that she and Milton Russell, the appellant, not being married to each other, lived together as husband and wife from July 1971 to May 1977, and that, therefore, they cohabited "continuously for a period of not less than five years" as required by s. 14(b)(i)1. It is Mr. Russell's position that, apart from a four or five-day separation in February 1976, there was such cohabitation, but because of this period of separation there was not the requisite period of continuous cohabitation required by the Act. This defines the first issue to be resolved. . . .

Was there continuous cohabitation for not less than five years?

The appellant submits that, because he had moved out of the home he was sharing with the respondent from a Friday to the following Tuesday in February 1976, he did not cohabit continuously with the respondent for a period of not less than five years. As indicated, there is no issue that, apart from this long weekend, the parties did not cohabit for the whole of the period from July 1971 to May 1977.

The evidence concerning the February 1976 interlude is sparse. The respondent said that they had had a fight because the appellant went to a dance at a singles club and stayed to the end of it. The appellant said that he moved out because they could not agree on anything. He moved out of the house they were living in, taking his clothes and a small bed. He made a deposit of $100 on an apartment. At the urging of her parents, the appellant said that he went back to speak to the respondent and they were reconciled.

Morton Prov. J. described this episode as "nothing more than a temporary lovers' quarrel" which did not constitute a break in the cohabitation. Couture Co. Ct. J. agreed with this conclusion.

Undoubtedly the meaning of "cohabited continuously" will be tested from different vantage points in a great variety of situations. "Cohabit" is defined in s. 1(b) of the Act as meaning "to live together in a conjugal relationship, whether within or outside marriage". Put into more everyday language this means to live together as husband and wife, or, as His Honour Judge Honey put it in *Feehan* v. *Attwells*, Ont., 19th February 1979 (not yet reported), to live together "in a 'marriage-like' relationship outside marriage". Without in any way attempting to be detailed or comprehensive, it could be said that such a relationship has come to an end when either party regards it as being at an end and, by his or her conduct, has demonstrated in a convincing manner that this particular state of mind is a settled one. While the physical separation of parties following "a fight" might, in some cases, appear to amount to an ending of cohabitation, the test should be realistic and flexible enough to recognize that a brief cooling-off period does not bring the relationship to an end. Such conduct does not convincingly demonstrate a settled state of mind that the relationship is at an end.

The question will often be largely one of fact. In this case I think the conclusion that there was no break in the cohabitation is the correct one. . . .

STOIKIEWICZ v. FILAS

(1978), 7 R.F.L. (2d) 366, 21 O.R. (2d) 717 (U.F.C.)

STEINBERG U.F.C.J.: — This is an application brought by Krystina Stoikiew-icz against Stanley Filas, pursuant to which she has claimed: (1) maintenance for herself; (2) maintenance for her child Gerry Filas, born 4th July 1972; and (3) custody of the said child.

Mr. Filas did not attend at the hearing, and there seems to be no issue in respect of the custody and maintenance of the child. However, Krystina Stoikiewicz and Stanley Filas were never married. Therefore, to qualify for maintenance as a dependant under the Family Law Reform Act, 178 (Ont.), c. 2, the applicant must fall within the definition of "spouse" contained in s. 14(*b*)(i) of the Act. . . .

The relevant facts of the case are as follows:

(1) On 2nd September 1972 the parties began to reside in the same apartment. The respondent owned the building in question and had been living in a separate apartment therein. Prior to the respondent moving in with the applicant, they had been engaging in sexual relations, and she became pregnant. According to the applicant, "when I was pregnant, we fix the room up in the back and share the apartment".

(2) The respondent never shared a bedroom with the applicant, but slept separately from her in a room in the same apartment.

(3) The respondent never paid the applicant any support or maintenance for herself or the child. His contribution to the household, according to the applicant, was that he bought all of the furniture.

(4) When the respondent found out that the applicant was pregnant, he gave her an engagement ring, which she still wears.

(5) While the parties shared the apartment, the applicant received Mother's Allowance, which is a provincial welfare benefit.

(6) The nature of their personal relationship was described by the applicant as follows:

Q. Mrs. Stoikiewicz, did you live with Mr. Filas as husband and wife? A. That's the way it was.

Q. Did you share the same bedroom? A. No.

Q. I see. Did you have sexual relations with each other? A. Yes.

Q. Was it frequent or just occasional? A. Occasional. From time to time.

Q. Did you cook his meals? A. I cooked for him.

Q. And did he treat your child Gerry as his son? A. Yes.

Q. And who bought the groceries? A. I did.

Q. Did he give you money to buy groceries? A. No.

Q. You used your own money, did you? A. Yes.

Q. Where did you get that money from? A. I took it from Mother's Allowance.

Q. Now, did you live with him for about five or six years, on Mother's Allowance? A. I paid him $100 a month rent, for which I have receipts; but because he really wanted $200 a month rent, for that reason I was also doing washing and ironing and other things.

The issue, therefore, is whether the relationship between the spouses was such so as to amount to a cohabitation within the meaning of s. 14(*b*)(i). There is much to support a positive finding in that regard. For example: (1) the respondent gave the applicant an engagement ring; (2) they lived in the same apartment and engaged in occasional sexual relations; and (3) the applicant cooked and washed for the respondent.

Indeed, if the parties had been married they would not have been considered to be living "separate and apart" within the meaning of s. 4(1)(e) of the Divorce Act, R.S.C. 1970, c. D-8. . . .

There are, however, other aspects of their relationship which could support a negative finding, i.e., that the parties were not cohabiting with each other within the meaning of the Family Law Reform Act. These are that: (1) the applicant paid the respondent rent each month; and (2) the applicant did not look to the respondent for her support, but rather to the provincial government.

There are today many men and women living together without (for the lack of a better phrase) the benefit of clergy. There are many reasons for this — but it is safe to say that many couples who do so, do so in order that they can retain their personal freedoms unencumbered by the obligations which both the law and traditional morality impose on married spouses. Section 14(b)(i) is an intrusion upon that liberty, and thus, in my view, it ought to be strictly construed.

The intent of the Family Law Reform Act is to view the marriage relationship, for its purposes, primarily in the nature of an economic partnership. . . .

Maintenance benefits under the Act flow from the intermeshing of the relative productivities [sic] of each of the spouses, together with their economic needs, resulting from the way they have divided up their respective duties and obligations in the marriage, as defined in s. 4(5) of the Act. [See now s. 5(7) of the *Family Law Act.*] All this is premised upon the fact that each spouse has a duty to support and provide for the other. . . .

It is my view that unmarried persons cannot be found to be cohabiting within the meaning of s. 14(b)(i) unless it can be determined that their relationship is such that they have each assumed an obligation to support and provide for the other in the same manner that married spouses are obliged to do. . . .

In my view, the applicant has never cohabited with the respondent within the meaning of s. 14(b)(i) of the Family Law Reform Act. The evidence is clear that, although from time to time the parties were intimate, their economic life was on an arms-length basis. Any household services that the applicant provided to the respondent were in satisfaction of a portion of the rent. Neither of the parties looked to the other for support or assistance outside of their unusual rental agreement.

Accordingly, the applicant's claim for spousal maintenance is dismissed. . . .

[Custody was awarded to the mother and child support of $75 per week was ordered.]

LABBE v. McCULLOUGH

(1979), 23 O.R. (2d) 536 (Prov. Ct.)

WEISMAN PROV. CT. J.: — The applicant, Darlene Labbe, seeks support from the respondent, Steve McCullough, pursuant to the *Family Law Reform Act, 1978* (Ont.), c. 2 (The Act).

The respondent is a musician who tours the country with a musical group. He met the applicant in January of 1976, while performing in Kirkland Lake, Ontario. In March of 1977, the applicant moved to Toronto, where the respondent resides with his parents, in order to be near him and to further her career as a model. She rented an apartment in her own name and resided there until May of that year. The respondent was performing in other parts of the country during this entire three-month period except for a four-week span which he spent with Miss Labbe in her apartment. He continued to leave all his worldly possessions at his parents' except for those personal effects that were needed for his daily use.

In May of 1977, Miss Labbe moved to North Bay. Mr. McCullough resided with her for two weeks in July of that year while he was recuperating from a broken hand. A child, Katrina, was conceived during that two-week period. When the applicant informed the respondent that she was pregnant in August, he terminated the relationship.

While there was no formal engagement, there was some talk of marriage some day.

[Judge Weisman set out the facts and reasoning of *Stoikiewicz* v. *Filas* and distinguished the case in one line: "There are no such peculiar economic arrangements in the matter before me." He continued:]

I find on the evidence that the parties, while not married to each other, cohabited for a four-week period between March and May of 1977, and again for a two-week period in July of 1977. In making this finding I adopt the common definition of "cohabit" found in the fifth edition of the Concise Oxford Dictionary, *i.e.*, "live together". I further find that Katrina was conceived in July of 1977, and that the applicant and respondent are the child's natural parents. Darlene Labbe filed her application on June 13, 1978, which is within one year of the date on which the parties last cohabited.

These findings satisfy four of the five conditions set out in s. 14(*b*)(i), para. 2. It now becomes important to decide whether the parties cohabited "in a relationship of some permanence".

The following evidence would lead to a conclusion that theirs was not a relationship of some permanence:

1. They cohabited for only six weeks out of a total period of 19 months;
2. The apartment in Toronto and all its contents belonged exclusively to Darlene Labbe;
3. The respondent at all times left all his possessions in his parents' home.

The following evidence would lead to a conclusion that theirs was a relationship of some permanence:

1. The parties knew each other's whereabouts at all times between January, 1976 and August of 1977.
2. The applicant moved to Toronto in part to be with the respondent;
3. The respondent went to North Bay to be with the applicant while he recovered from his broken hand;
4. There was some talk of marriage some day.

In deciding this matter, I place great weight on the fact that the parties discussed the possibility of marriage some day. In my view, this gives the relationship a touch of permanence. The Legislature has used the words "some permanence" and I cannot find that there was no permanence to the relationship between Miss Labbe and Mr. McCullough.

The length of time the applicant and respondent cohabited was very brief. This, however, goes to the quantum of support that the respondent must provide, and not to his liability to do so. . . .

In my opinion, notwithstanding the tender age of the child, Katrina, in view of the brief and sporadic nature of the parties' cohabitation, the respondent should not be required to support the applicant for a lengthy period.

Accordingly, after assessing the needs of the applicant, and the respondent's ability to meet those needs, I have decided to order the respondent to provide support for the dependant spouse in the amount of $150 per month in advance for a period of 12 months commencing on April 1, 1979.

NOTES AND QUESTIONS

1. Do you agree with the Court of Appeal's conclusion in *Sanderson* v. *Russell* that a "settled state of mind that the relationship is at an end" is required before the continuity of the period of cohabitation is interrupted? What other approaches are possible? See Cudmore, "Annotation" (1979), 9 R.F.L. (2d) 82. *Sanderson* v. *Russell* has been applied in *Dicks* v. *Zavitz* (1979), 13 R.F.L. (2d) 179 (Ont. Prov. Ct.) where a woman and man were held to have cohabited continuously despite numerous separations lasting from three days to six weeks. In awarding support to the woman, the court held that she had never initiated the separations with the intent of ending the relationship but was merely demonstrating that she would not comply with the man's sadistic demands.

In *Harris* v. *Godkewitsch* (1983), 41 O.R. (2d) 779 (Fam. Ct.) the applicant was denied support. The applicant had entered the relationship with the respondent on the basis that she could come and go as she pleased. The applicant would occasionally absent herself without notice or the respondent's blessing. On one occasion, she went to Paris, France, for four months. Prior to her departure she indicated to friends that she would be there at least a year and might never return. It was held that the applicant failed to prove that she did not intend to end the continuous relationship with the respondent when she left for Paris. As a result, the period of continuous cohabitation was interrupted by her action.

In *Feehan* v. *Attwells* (1979), 24 O.R. (2d) 248 (Co. Ct.) the applicant's separation from the respondent for a single period of somewhere between one to three weeks did not breach the continuity of cohabitation. The court held that the applicant did not intend to withdraw from the relationship or terminate it but moved out only to reflect on the relationship and assess its merits.

In *Sullivan* v. *Letnik* (1994), 5 R.F.L. (4th) 313 (Ont. U.F.C.), the couple resided on a boat most of the time. However, the woman returned to her home occasionally and stayed away from the ship from May to December 1990 because she feared the man's temper. Beckett J. found that their personal relationship continued during this time and that the couple cohabited continuously from 1985 to 1992. He stated (at 319): "Whether couples are separated is a question of intent, not geography; at least one of the parties must intend to permanently sever the relationship."

If there is an interruption in cohabitation, *Kossakowski* v. *Sierchio* (1983), 36 R.F.L. (2d) 395 (Ont. Co. Ct.) suggests that the applicant must prove that there was no intention that the separation be permanent.

2. Does *Sanderson* v. *Russell* mean that one party can unilaterally bring the period of continuous cohabitation to an end?

3. In *Armstrong* v. *Thompson* (1979), 23 O.R. (2d) 421 (Co. Ct.), Quinlan Co. Ct. J. dealt with *Stoikiewicz* v. *Filas* as follows (at 423):

> The economic dependence theory is not applicable to this situation. In this instance, although the defendant spouse did work outside the home, there is nothing in the material to indicate that this was anything but a traditional married couple, each employed and making a contribution to the functioning of the home. The only difference from the traditional married couple situation was that there was not a "legal marriage". To say that because the dependent spouse worked outside the home, maintained her own bank account and spent her own money, is reason to deny the rights under s. 14 of the *Family Law Reform Act, 1978*, is not, in my view, what is contemplated in the Act. This suggestion is an overextension of the peculiar facts set out in *Re Stoikiewicz and Filas*.

The New Brunswick legislature has explicitly adopted the economic dependency test to determine if unmarried persons who have cohabited continuously for a period of not less than three years should be obligated to support one another. Unless a child is born of whom the cohabitees are the natural parents, the *Family Services Act*, S.N.B. 1980, c. F-2.2 imposes an obligation to support one another on a man and a woman who have "cohabited continuously for a period of not less than three years in a relationship in which one person has been substantially dependent upon the other for support" (s. 112(3)). See also the *Family Maintenance Act*, R.S.M. 1987, c. F20, s. 4(3). Should either the courts or the legislature impose a similar requirement in Ontario? Even if the "economic dependence theory" is rejected as a guide to the application of the extended definition of "spouse", it may resurface as a key factor in determining the amount of support or the length of time for which it is to be ordered.

4. As noted above, in October 1999 the Ontario legislature amended the *FLA* in response to the S.C.C. decision in *M.* v. *H.* (1999), 46 R.F.L. (4th) 32 (reproduced in Chapter 1, **INTRODUCTION**) to ensure that same-sex partnerships were covered by Part III. Section 30 was amended to specify that same-sex partners, as well as spouses, owed a support obligation to one another. A definition of same-sex partner was added to s. 29. It should also be noted that the definition of "spouse" for the purposes of support in the *Family Relations Act*, R.S.B.C. 1996, c. 128 specifies that "'spouse' means a person who . . . lived with another person for a period of at least two years if the application under this Act is made within one year after they have ceased to live together and, for the purposes of this Act, the marriage-like relationship may be between persons of the same gender" (s. 1(1)).

5. Both parts of the extended definition of "spouse" and the definition of "same-sex partner" in the *FLA* require cohabitation. Section 1(1) [previously s. 1(b) of the *Family Law Reform Act*] specifies "'cohabit' means to live together in a conjugal relationship, whether within or outside marriage". In *Feehan* v. *Attwells* (1979), 24 O.R. (2d) 248 (Co. Ct.), Honey Co. Ct. J. noted (at 251):

> "Conjugal" is defined in the Shorter Oxford English Dictionary as: "Of or pertaining to marriage or to husband and wife in their relationship to each other; matrimonial". Transposing the definition of "conjugal" to the definition of "cohabit" in s. 1(b) of the Act, I read "cohabit" to include living together in a "marriage-like" relationship outside marriage. This is in accordance with the general intent of the Act to impose family obligations upon family units in certain circumstances, regardless of the presence or absence of a legally recognized marriage.

Kurisko D.C.J. examined in some detail the legal meanings of "cohabit" and "conjugal" in *Molodowich* v. *Penttinen* (1980), 17 R.F.L. (2d) 376 (Ont. Dist. Ct.). His review of the case law led him to formulate the following questions as a guide to determining if a couple had been cohabiting in a conjugal relationship (at 381-382):

1. *Shelter:*

(a) Did the parties live under the same roof?

(b) What were the sleeping arrangements?

(c) Did anyone else occupy or share the available accommodation?

2. *Sexual and Personal Behaviour:*

(a) Did the parties have sexual relations? If not, why not?

(b) Did they maintain an attitude of fidelity to each other?

(c) What were their feelings toward each other?

(d) Did they communicate on a personal level?

(e) Did they eat their meals together?

(f) What, if anything, did they do to assist each other with problems or during illness?

(g) Did they buy gifts for each other on special occasions?

3. *Services:*

What was the conduct and habit of the parties in relation to:

(a) preparation of meals;

(b) washing and mending clothes;

(c) shopping;

(d) household maintenance; and

(e) any other domestic services?

4. *Social:*

(a) Did they participate together or separately in neighbourhood and community activities?

(b) What was the relationship and conduct of each of them toward members of their respective families and how did such families behave towards the parties?

5. *Societal:*

What was the attitude and conduct of the community toward each of them and as a couple?

6. *Support (economic):*

(a) What were the financial arrangements between the parties regarding the provision of or contribution toward the necessaries of life (food, clothing, shelter, recreation, etc.)?

(b) What were the arrangements concerning the acquisition and ownership of property?

(c) Was there any special financial arrangement between them that both agreed would be determinant of their overall relationship?

7. *Children:*

What was the attitude and conduct of the parties concerning children?

6. In *Zegil* v. *Opie* (1994), 8 R.F.L. (4th) 91 (Ont. Gen. Div.), Kurisko J. held that the parties cohabited for approximately two years and then lived separate and apart under the same roof for another year and a half. As a result, they were not "spouses" within the meaning of s. 29 of the *FLA*.

7. Did Nowell and Town cohabit in *Nowell* v. *Town Estate* (1997), 30 R.F.L. (4th) 107 (Ont. C.A.) (reproduced in Chapter. 4, **FAMILY PROPERTY**)?

A number of cases have recently dealt with spousal support claims in situations where the individuals never married and never lived together in the same residence. However, they carried on long-term "affairs", spending nights together fairly often and engaging regularly in sexual intercourse. In *Lehner* v. *Grundl* , 1995 CarswellOnt. 2077 (Ont. Gen. Div.), affirmed on this point, 1999 CarswellOnt. 1318 (Ont. C.A.), a man and woman spent most weekends at a cottage they had purchased together. Wilson J. concluded that "consenting adults with separate residences who visit one another cannot be said to cohabit." However, cohabitation was found to exist in *Thauvette* v. *Malyon* (1996), 23 R.F.L. (4th) 217 (Ont. Gen. Div.) where a man and woman began an affair while still married to others. After the man separated from his wife he maintained his own residence largely to facilitate access to his children. He spent three or four nights a week at the woman's house and paid most of the expenses associated with it. The woman was unaware of the man's affairs with at least three other women. In *Baird* v. *Iaci* (1997), 32 R.F.L. (4th) 109 (B.C. S.C.), the man and woman entered into a sexual relationship when the woman needed money to finance her dream of owning a farm. The man started paying the woman's rent and expenses and bought a farm which the woman managed in exchange for living in the house rent-free. One or two nights a week the man stayed at the farm. Over the course of their eight year relationship, the parties took business trips together and attended numerous social events as a couple. During the relationship the woman had sexual relations over a three year period with one of the farm labourers. The judge concluded (at 117) that the parties never cohabited, but were "business partners who were also 'weekend lovers'". Finally, the court in *Mahoney* v. *King* (1998), 39 R.F.L. (4th) 361 (Ont. Gen. Div.) concluded that there should be a trial to determine if the parties were spouses under s. 29 of the *FLA*.

The parties had a six year relationship during which the man paid many of the woman's expenses. During this time the man continued to reside with his wife and the woman received support payments from a previous common law spouse under an agreement that stipulated that support was to end if the woman ever cohabited with another for a period over sixty days. In his annotation to the case in the R.F.L.'s, Professor McLeod states (at 362):

> With respect, the case is an example of just how far removed from reality family law may be headed. The suggestion that a woman who carried on an affair with a man who was married and living with his wife may be a "spouse" under the *Family Law Act* is astounding. It is one thing to say that her actions may justify compensation for unjust enrichment: cf. *Nowell* v. *Town Estate* (1997), 30 R.F.L. (4th) 107, 35 O.R. (3d) 415 (C.A.), but to suggest that she is a spouse for support purposes under the *Family Law Act* seems to ignore the preamble to the Act, the words of s. 29 of the Act and remove whatever meaning is in the word "spouse".

8. In *Davies* v. *Vriend* (1999), 48 R.F.L. (4th) 43 (Ont. Gen. Div.), a man kept his own apartment and spent most nights in a home purchased in his name where his partner lived. The woman paid 2/3 of the mortgage and paid for the cable, telephone and food. The man paid the remainder of the mortgage plus maintenance costs. The couple took business and pleasure trips together. Matheson J. found that they were cohabiting.

9. A man and woman divorce in 1983. They cohabit from 1994 - 1996. Their adult son also lives in the home. Although they discuss the possibility, they never remarry. Are they spouses under s. 29 of the *FLA*? See *Ferreira* v. *Ferreira* (1998), 41 R.F.L. (4th) 101 (Ont. Gen. Div.). See also *DeSouza* v. *DeSouza* (1999), 48 R.F.L. (4th) 63 (Ont. Prov. Div.).

10. In *Gostlin* v. *Kergin* (1986), 1 R.F.L. (3d) 448 the B.C. C.A. dealt with the *Family Relations Act*, R.S.B.C. 1979, c. 121. Under that statute, support could be ordered where a man and woman lived together "as husband and wife for a period of not less than two years" (s. 1(c)). Lambert J.A. stated (at 452-453):

> For the purpose of safeguarding family life, the legislature has enacted provisions governing the financial arrangements of married couples. Section 57 of the Family Relations Act sets out the obligations of one spouse to the other during the course of the relationship. And s. 61 sets out the obligations between them should the relationship come to an end.
>
> But marriage does not suit every couple who want to share their living accommodation. For religious, moral, sexual, financial or other reasons they may be unable to marry or may prefer not to marry. Some couples may behave towards each other and towards the outside world as if they were married. Their relationship may be one of permanence and of commitment. They may eagerly embrace the obligations of s. 57. Other couples may prefer quite a different relationship. They may want to retain their independence from each other. They may find long-term commitments stifling, and emotional interdependence cloying. They would shun the obligations of s. 57.
>
> Surely society can accommodate those who prefer to live together without commitment. If there are not children involved, there is no reason to force financial commitments on couples who do not want them. Independence should be a choice. But how can a couple exercise that choice except by not getting married to each other and not making any commitment to each other? If that is their wish, the expiry of two years from the start of their relationship should not force them into mutual commitments that they do not want. . . .
>
> In deciding whether a couple lived together as husband and wife, I would be guided by the scheme and intention of the Act itself. The purpose of the legislative scheme is to impose on a unmarried couple the same obligations under s. 57 as are voluntarily undertaken by a married couple. So I would ask whether the unmarried couple's relationship was like the relationship of the married couple in that the unmarried couple have shown that they have voluntarily embraced the permanent support obligations of s. 57. If each partner had been asked, at any time during the relevant period of more than two years, whether, if their partner were to be suddenly disabled for life, would they consider themselves committed to life-long financial and moral support of that partner, and the answer of both of them would have been "Yes", then they are living together as husband and

wife. If the answer would have been "No", then they may be living together, but not as husband and wife.

Of course, in the particular circumstances of any case, the answer to that question may prove elusive. If that is so, then other, more objective indicators may show the way. Did the couple refer to themselves, when talking to their friends, as husband and wife, or as spouses, or in some equivalent way that recognized a long-term commitment? Did they share the legal rights to their living accommodation? Did they share their property? Did they share their finances and their bank accounts? Did they share their vacations? In short, did they share their lives? And, perhaps most important of all, did one of them surrender financial independence and become economically dependent on the other, in accordance with a mutual arrangement?

All those questions, and no doubt others, may properly be considered as tending to show whether a couple who lived together for more than two years have done so with the permanent mutual support commitment that, in the relevant sense of the Family Relations legislation, constitutes living together as husband and wife.

In "Unmarried Cohabitation in Canada: Common Law and Civilian Approaches to Living Together" (1989), 4 C.F.L.Q. 147, Professors Bala and Cano argue (at 198-199):

[T]he one specific aspect of the verbal test which Lambert J.A. articulates for determining whether parties have lived together as "husband and wife" is neither helpful nor correct. Surely after a relationship is over there is no meaningful way of asking — what would happen if one partner were disabled for life? Further, even during cohabitation, it is not clear what answer many legally married persons in our society would honestly give to this question.

For examples of cases applying *Gostlin* v. *Kergin*, see *Hyette* v. *Pfenniger* (1991), 39 R.F.L. (3d) 30 (B.C. S.C.) and *Baird* v. *Iaci* (1997), 32 R.F.L. (4th) 109 (B.C. S.C.).

11. In "Cohabitation and Spousal Obligations in Common Law Jurisdictions in Canada" (1990), 8 C.J.F.L. 265, Professor Farquhar explores the case law and concludes (at 298-299) that the following factors have been crucial in determining that a relationship should be characterized as spousal: the sharing of accommodation, sexual intimacy and the presence of actual dependency or a commitment to support. He states (at 299): "What the legislation and the cases amount to is this: Where there has been a relationship of such significance that it has led either to the actual dependency of one party on another, or the expectation that one will support the other in the event of a financial crisis, then an entitlement to support arises in the case of need."

12. Paternity may be an issue not only in relation to child support but also regarding spousal support since paragraph (b) of the extended definition of "spouse" in s. 29 of the *FLA* only applies if the man and woman are the natural or adoptive parents of a child. For a case illustrating this interrelationship, see *Donheim* v. *Irwin* (1978), 6 R.F.L. (2d) 242 (Ont. Prov. Ct.).

13. In *Gostlin* v. *Kergin*, the British Columbia Court of Appeal affirmed that the non-marital status of an applicant should not be a factor in "discounting" the amount of a support award. However, Professors Bala and Cano suggest in "Unmarried Cohabitation in Canada: Common Law and Civilian Approaches to Living Together" (1989), 4 C.F.L.Q. 147 (at 191):

In deciding whether to award support, courts will consider the duration and nature of a relationship, the degree of dependency and the nature of the contributions to the relationship, the ability to become self-supporting, and the payor's ability to provide support. In most cases involving "unmarried spouses" these factors militate against the awarding of spousal support. . . . It is the typical circumstances of unmarried relationships which militate against the awarding of support rather than the fact that the parties are not married.

14. In the *FLA* only Part III applies to unmarried cohabitees. Why did the legislature not adopt the extended definition of "spouse" in other parts of the statute? Should it have? The O.L.R.C. recommended in its *Report on the Rights and Responsibilities of Cohabitants under the Family Law Act* (Toronto: 1993) that the extended definition of spouse be adopted for the entire *FLA*.

Would a *Charter* challenge to this aspect of the *FLA* succeed? Recall that the Alberta Court of Appeal held in *Taylor* v. *Rossu* (1998), 39 R.F.L. (4th) 242 (reproduced in Chapter 1, **INTRODUC-TION**) that Alberta's *Domestic Relations Act* violated the *Charter* because it did not extend spousal support obligations to unmarried cohabitees. Alberta responded by amending the definition of "spouse" for the purposes of support and spousal agreements dealing with support. The Act now stipulates that "spouse" includes "a party to a common law relationship" and defines "a common law relationship as "a relationship between two people of the opposite sex who although not legally married to each other (i) continuously cohabited together in a marriage-like relationship for at least three years, or (ii) if there is a child of the relationship by birth or adoption, cohabited in a marriage-like relationship of some permanence."

15. Until changes to the regulations of both the *Family Benefits Act* and the *General Welfare Assistance Act* in Ontario in 1995, an applicant or recipient (referred to here as a "beneficiary") could collect social assistance as a single person, or single parent, while living with someone of the opposite sex for three years before this person was presumed to be a spouse. The effect of the changes to the regulations is to make beneficiaries living with someone of the opposite sex "spouses", unless sufficient evidence is produced to show that the relationship is of the roommate variety only. In order to achieve this result, the definition of "spouse" has been changed to include a person of the opposite sex residing in the same dwelling as the beneficiary if: (1) the person provides financial support to the beneficiary, the beneficiary provides financial support to the person, or the person and the beneficiary have a "mutual agreement or arrangement" regarding their financial affairs, and (2) "the social and familial aspects of the relationship between the person and the applicant or recipient amount to cohabitation". A presumption is created that a person of the opposite sex residing in the same dwelling as the beneficiary is a spouse unless evidence to the contrary, sufficient to satisfy the welfare administrator, is provided. See *Family Benefits Act Regulations*, Reg. 366 of R.R.O. 1990, amended by O. Reg. 409/95 and *General Welfare Assistance Act Regulations*, Reg. 537 of R.R.O. 1990, amended by O. Reg. 410/95.

The constitutionality of a similar "spouse-in-the-house" rule found in the regulations of the Nova Scotia *Family Benefits Act* was successfully challenged in *R.* v. *Rehberg* (1993), 111 D.L.R. (4th) 336 (T.D.). Kelly J. held that the regulation in question was flawed by being overly broad and focusing on the issue of residence rather than on financial contribution by the cohabitee. The Ontario regulations specifically target financial contribution as one of two determinative factors. Nevertheless, the Ontario Superior Court of Justice held in *Falkiner* v. *Ontario (Ministry of Community & Social Services)*, [2000] O.J. No. 2433 that the Ontario regulations constituted discrimination contrary to the *Charter* on the basis of sex and the analogous gound of "sole support mothers on social assistance". Belleghem J. disagreed, concluding that the regulation, if properly interpreted, could withstand *Charter* challenge.

16. Examine s. 33(3) of the *FLA*. In what circumstances can public agencies directly apply for a support order? In practice, the public welfare authorities do not often directly apply for support orders on behalf of the recipients of public money. More frequently, they pressure the recipients to apply by making the recipients of welfare or family benefits (commonly called "mother's allowance") fully aware of the possibility that payments may be reduced or eliminated if reasonable efforts are not made to obtain support from anyone legally responsible for support (see *General Welfare Assistance Act Regulations*, R.R.O. 1990, Reg. 537, as amended by O. Reg. 383/96, s. 4(5), and *Family Benefits Act Regulations*, R.R.O. 1990, Reg. 366, s. 8, as amended by O. Reg. 419/94). When a support order is made, the recipient of welfare or family benefits is often asked to make an assignment of payments to the municipality or Ministry in order to continue receiving full benefits. For a critical examination of the Ministry's application of s. 8 of the *Family Benefits Act Regulations*, see Lawrence, "Systemic Discrimination: Regulation 8 — *Family Benefits Act*; Policy of Reasonable Effort to Obtain Financial Resources" (1990), 6 J. Law & Social Policy 57.

In *A.M.* v. *A.C.*, [1995] O.J. No. 3539 (Ont. Prov. Div.), two male respondents to child support applications were able to obtain costs against the Ministry when blood tests proved they had not fathered the children. Although the applications were brought by the mothers of the children, the court held that it could award costs against the "real litigant" even though the Ministry was not a party.

(b) Where and When?

A support application under Part III of the *FLA* can be brought in the Ontario Court of Justice, the Family Court or the Superior Court of Justice. It should be noted that the Ontario Court of Justice does not have the same powers in making support orders as the other courts mentioned (see s. 34(2)). These limitations on the court's power should be considered in determining where the application is brought. It should also be recalled that the Ontario Court of Justice has no jurisdiction to hear applications under Part I or II of the Act.

Section 33 does not specify that the spouses must be separated before a support application is made. In *Galea* v. *Galea* (1980), 15 R.F.L. (2d) 191 (Ont. Prov. Ct.) the wife applied for support under the *Family Law Reform Act* even though the parties were still cohabiting. The parties agreed on the quantum of support and that there should be an attachment of the husband's wages in order to ensure that it was paid. The court made the order as requested even though it observed (at 192): ". . . this order is not due to a separation of the parties and to make sure that some of the income of the respondent goes into the hands of the wife and children rather than the hands of the race track . . .". It might also be possible to bring a support application on the eve of separation to provide funds so that the applicant can move out and relocate. Do you think the courts would entertain support applications where the spouses are still cohabiting but one of them believes that the other is not providing sufficient funds for the needs of the household?

Section 50(1) specifies that, generally, applications for support must be brought within two years from the day the spouses or same-sex partners separate. However, this subsection does not apply if the spouses or same-sex partners provided for support in a domestic contract: s. 50(2). In that situation, the application must be brought within two years of a subsisting default under the contract. See s. 2(8) which allows the court to extend the time limits provided certain conditions are met.

An application for support must be brought under the *FLA* while the parties are still spouses. Therefore, an application cannot be made after divorce. Section 36(1) provides that where a divorce proceeding has been commenced an application for support under the Act that has not been adjudicated is stayed unless the court orders otherwise. If a marriage is terminated by divorce and the question of support is not adjudicated in the divorce proceeding, an order for support made under the *FLA* "continues in force according to its terms": s. 36(3). It should also be noted that the *Rules of Civil Procedure* and the *Family Law Rules* permit a spouse to claim support as alternative relief under the *FLA* in a divorce proceeding. In this way, if the divorce is not granted, the court can still deal with the alternative claim for relief.

NOTES AND QUESTIONS

1. Why did the legislature restrict the powers of the Ontario Court of Justice in support proceedings?

2. In *Lefebvre* v. *Lefebvre* (1982), 30 R.F.L. (2d) 184, 38 O.R. (2d) 683 (Co. Ct.) the court held that the constitutional doctrine of paramountcy did not dictate that an order for support under provincial legislation automatically lapsed on divorce. As long as the issue of support had not been determined in the divorce proceeding, the order under provincial legislation could continue to operate after divorce. Forget Co. Ct. J. concluded, *obiter*, that a provincial support order did cease to be operative if a support order was made under the federal *Divorce Act*. He suggested that an order that no support be granted under the federal legislation would have the same effect.

Examine s. 36(3) of the *FLA*. Is this an implicit acceptance that orders made under provincial legislation cannot continue if the question of support was judicially determined in divorce proceedings?

3. In what circumstances should the court use its authority under s. 36(1) of the *FLA* to permit non-adjudicated applications under the Act to proceed even though divorce proceedings have been commenced? See *Lakhani* v. *Lakhani* (1979), 10 R.F.L. (2d) 156, 23 O.R. (2d) 575 (H.C.); *Dufrat* v. *Dufrat* (1982), 27 R.F.L. (2d) 455 (Ont. H.C.); *Smith* v. *Smith* (1986), 1 R.F.L. (3d) 61 (Ont. Fam. Ct.); *Muslake* v. *Muslake* (1987), 6 R.F.L. (3d) 280, 58 O.R. (2d) 615 (U.F.C.); *Gow* v. *Gow (No.1)* (1989), 18 R.F.L. (3d) 14 at 19 (Ont. H.C.); *Gow* v. *Gow (No.2)* (1989), 19 R.F.L. (3d) 292 (Ont. Prov. Ct.); and *Iwan* v. *Iwan* (1989), 22 R.F.L. (3d) 306 (Ont. H.C.).

Final orders pronounced under the provincial legislation are not stayed by s. 36(1). See *Middaugh* v. *Middaugh* (1981), 22 R.F.L. (2d) 388, 32 O.R. (2d) 681 (C.A.). Interim orders granted under the Act before the divorce proceeding is commenced also survive the stay imposed by s. 36(1). Even if the main application for support becomes stayed, the interim order continues in effect until the order is vacated or superseded by an interim order or final order in the divorce proceeding. See *Lovett* v. *Lovett* (1982), 26 R.F.L. (2d) 194 (Ont. Co. Ct.) and *Mongrain* v. *Mongrain* (1986), 1 R.F.L. (3d) 330 (Ont. H.C.).

4. Note s. 36(2) of the *FLA*, which permits the court dealing with a divorce proceeding to determine the amount of arrears owing under an order for support made under Part III and to make an order respecting that amount at the same time as it makes an order under the *Divorce Act*.

5. The relationship between provincial legislation dealing with support and the *Divorce Act* is examined in detail in Hogg, *Constitutional Law of Canada* 3rd ed., (Toronto: Carswell, 1992), c. 26, reproduced in Chapter 1 of this book. For further reading see Colvin, "Federal Jurisdiction Over Support After Divorce" (1979), 11 Ottawa L. Rev. 541 and Colvin, "Family Maintenance: The Interaction of Federal and Provincial Law" (1979), 2 Can. J. Fam. L. 221.

6. Where an application for support or an application to vary support is made under the *FLA*, each party must serve on the other and file with the court a financial statement: s. 41. Rule 70.04 of the *Rules of Civil Procedure*, R.R.O. 1990, Reg. 194 and Rule 13 of the *Family Law Rules*, O. Reg. 114/99 govern the preparation and filing of these statements.

7. Section 34(1) of the *FLA* empowers the court to award interim support pending the determination of the application for support.

8. Section 33(5) of the *FLA* allows the court, on a respondent's motion, to add as a party another person who may have an obligation to provide support to the same dependant. In what circumstances might a respondent make such a motion? See, e.g., *Hart* v. *Hart* (1987), 6 R.F.L. (3d) 445 (Ont. Master); *Baddeley* v. *Baddeley* (1989), 71 O.R. (2d) 318 (H.C.); and *Bell* v. *Mellows* (1994), 6 R.F.L. (4th) 5 (Ont. Prov. Div.). Could a party add an adult child as a party. See s. 32 of the *FLA*. See also *Smeland* v. *Smeland* (1997), 29 R.F.L. (4th) 360 (B.C.S.C).

(2) THE *DIVORCE ACT*

Applications for support under the *Divorce Act* may be made in the divorce proceeding itself to the court that has jurisdiction to grant the divorce. Once such an application is made, the court has authority to grant interim support: s. 15.2(2). Final orders may be made at the trial of the divorce proceeding. See ss. 2 ("divorce proceeding") and 15.2(1). As the Parliament of Canada's jurisdiction over support is ancillary to its legislative jurisdiction over divorce, the power to order support under the *Divorce Act* ceases if the court refuses to grant the divorce: *Lietz* v. *Lietz* (1990), 30 R.F.L. (3d) 293 (N.B. Q.B.). See also *Ninham* v. *Ninham* (1997), 29 R.F.L. (4th) 41 (Ont. Gen. Div.), where the court stayed the divorce under s. 11(1)(b) of the *Divorce Act*. The wife advanced a spousal support claim under that Act or, alternatively, under the *FLA*. Aston J. concluded (at 53): "Regardless of which legislation is applicable, the considerations and the result are the same in this particular case."

Applications for support can also be made in a separate corollary relief proceeding following the divorce. See ss. 2 ("corollary relief proceeding") and 15.2(1).

Section 4 specifies when a court has jurisdiction to hear and determine a corollary relief proceeding. It should be noted that the courts had held under the *Divorce Act* of 1968 that they had jurisdiction to make a maintenance order after the granting of the divorce as well as at the time the decree was granted: *Zacks* v. *Zacks*, 10 R.F.L. 53, [1973] S.C.R. 891; *Ouellet* v. *Ouimet* (1975), 7 N.R. 1 (S.C.C.); and *Lapointe* v. *Klint*, [1975] 2 S.C.R. 539. However, they were quite reluctant to exercise this jurisdiction (see Steel, "The Award of Maintenance Subsequent to Decree Nisi: A Question of Jurisdiction or Discretion?" (1981), 19 R.F.L. (2d) 33). To some extent, this reluctance reflected a recognition of the limited nature of Parliament's constitutional authority over support. Since Parliament's jurisdiction is ancillary to its power over divorce, there should arguably be a connection between the divorce and the need for support: *Wark* v. *Wark* (1986), 2 R.F.L. (3d) 337 (Man. C.A.). See also *Murphy* v. *Murphy* (1994), 10 R.F.L. (4th) 102, at 105 (Man. C.A.). Such a connection may become tenuous if the application for support is not made until some time after the divorce.

In *Delaney* v. *Delaney* (1995), 11 R.F.L. (4th) 155 (B.C. C.A.), the parties separated in 1982 and a court awarded the wife periodic support under the B.C. *Family Relations Act*. The divorce judgment of 1988 was silent regarding support. In 1991, the husband obtained a "Final Order" under the Act specifying that all support would terminate later that year. In 1993, a court granted the wife periodic support under the *Divorce Act* in a corollary relief proceeding. This order was upheld on appeal. The B.C. C.A. confirmed that (i) a support order can be made under the *Divorce Act* after the divorce is granted even if no such support was awarded at the time of the divorce, and (ii) any order made under the *Family Relations Act* does not preclude a support order under the *Divorce Act*.

Under the 1968 *Divorce Act*, it was unclear whether either party could ask for a determination of support or whether only the spouse seeking support could apply: *Gergely* v. *Gergely* (1979), 11 R.F.L. (2d) 221 (Ont. H.C.) and *Gigantes* v. *Gigantes* (1979), 12 R.F.L. (2d) 171, 27 O.R. (2d) 186 (H.C.). The wording of s. 15.2(1) of the current Act suggests that either spouse can apply. See *Strong* v. *Strong* (1987), 5 R.F.L. (3d) 209 (Ont. H.C.); *Clayton* v. *Clayton* (1989), 19 R.F.L. (3d) 430 (Ont. Div. Ct.); and *Callison* v. *Callison* (1989), 22 R.F.L. (3d) 123 (B.C. C.A.). Compare *Rehn* v. *Rehn* (1988), 13 R.F.L. (3d) 440 (Ont. U.F.C.). There are several reasons why one spouse might apply for a support order in favour of the other spouse. There may be an existing order under provincial legislation that the payor spouse thinks is too high. If a new order is made under the *Divorce Act*, the previous order will cease to be operative. An order under the *Divorce Act* may also be sought to effectively override the support provisions of a domestic contract that the payor spouse considers too onerous (see Chapter 9, **DOMESTIC CONTRACTS**).

NOTES AND QUESTIONS

1. A previous and subsisting order for support under provincial legislation does not preclude the court from making a new order under the federal *Divorce Act*. In *Pantry* v. *Pantry* (1986), 50 R.F.L. (2d) 240, 53 O.R. (2d) 667 the Ontario Court of Appeal held that interim relief could be ordered under the *Divorce Act* notwithstanding that a final order for custody or support had been made under the *Family Law Reform Act* prior to the commencement of the divorce proceedings. The court indicated that the master hearing the application for interim relief had a discretion. He could make an interim order under the federal Act or he could decide that the order under provincial legislation should continue and decline to make an order under the *Divorce Act*. See also *Callison* v. *Callison* (1989), 22 R.F.L. (3d) 123 (B.C. C.A.); *Strickland* v. *Strickland* (1991), 32 R.F.L. (3d) 179 (N.S. C.A.); and *Delaney* v. *Delaney* (1995), 11 R.F.L. (4th) 155 (B.C. C.A.).

2. Rule 69.14 of the *Rules of Civil Procedure*, R.R.O. 1990, Reg. 194 and Rule 13 of the *Family Law Rules*, O. Reg. 114/99 stipulate that any claims for support in divorce proceedings must be accompanied by a financial statement.

3.   Determining the Support Application

(1) INTRODUCTION

The quantum of spousal support, if any, to be awarded under Part III of the *FLA* is determined in accordance with ss. 30, 33(8), 33(9) and 33(10). Note the statutory obligation of each spouse and same-sex partner to support himself or herself to the extent to which this is possible. How does the *FLA* deal with the significance of misconduct in determining the quantum of support?

Although s. 33 lists many specific criteria to be considered by the court in dealing with support applications, no attempt is made to create a mathematical formula that can be applied in all situations nor even to indicate which factors should be given greatest weight. In its *Report on Family Law, Part VI: Support Obligations* (Toronto: Ministry of the Attorney General, 1975), the Ontario Law Reform Commission explained that flexibility was vital and that the relative importance of individual factors had to be determined in each case in light of the evidence presented.

Section 11 of the 1968 *Divorce Act* simply conferred a general discretion on a court when ordering spousal support to do what was "fit and just . . . having regard to the conduct of the parties and the conditions, means and other circumstances of each of them". By way of contrast, s. 15.2 of the current *Divorce Act* provides a list of factors to be considered (sub. (4)), specifies that marital misconduct is not to be considered (sub. (5)), and lists a series of objectives to be fostered (sub. (6)).

Once the traditional approach to and rationale for spousal support was rejected in the late 1960's and the 1970's, the courts were confronted with a number of issues such as the following:

1. Must a person demonstrate need before a support order can be made? Can support be used to compensate one spouse for past contributions to the other spouse's career in the absence of objective need?
2. How relevant is the pre-separation standard of living? Is the dependant spouse entitled to enjoy the same standard of living as the other spouse?
3. Can support be ordered where need, however defined, exists but is not caused by the division of functions between the spouses during the relationship? Must there at least be a connection between the need and the relationship's breakdown?
4. What is the effect of the duty of each spouse to provide, if possible, for his or her own support? Are there situations where a dependant spouse cannot be expected to seek employment?
5. Should limited term orders be used as a mechanism to encourage dependant spouses to become self-supporting?
6. At what point, if ever, can a payor spouse say: "I have fulfilled my obligation?"
7. What is the effect of the creation of a second family by the dependant spouse or the payor spouse?

Over the years, the case law dealing with these issues has been far from consistent. In "Economic Adjustment on Marriage Breakdown: Support" (1981), 4 Fam. Law Rev. 1 at 1, Rosalie Abella wrote:

To try to find a comprehensive philosophy in the avalanche of jurisprudence which is triggered by the Divorce Act and the various provincial statutes is to recognize that the law in its present state is a Rubic's cube for which no one has yet written the Solution Book. The result is a patchwork of often conflicting theories and approaches.

Lawyers, clients and judges are victimized by the breadth of discretion sanguinely allocated to the bench. Even where the statute purports to circumscribe the discretion by defining some of the ingredients that should go into a support judgment, reported decisions reflect wide difference in how much of each ingredient goes into a decision.

Despite significant legislative reform and a new avalanche of case law, her observations were echoed almost a decade later by Professor Rogerson. In "Judicial Interpretation of the Spousal and Child Support Provisions of the *Divorce Act, 1985* (Part I)" (1990-1991), 7 C.F.L.Q. 155, Professor Rogerson began her summary of a systematic review of all reported cases up to 1989 by noting (at 161):

The review of the case law proved in the end to be a much more difficult and frustrating task than originally envisioned. One of the strongest impressions left by a reading of the reported cases was the diversity of judicial approaches to issues of support, both in terms of the principles applied and the quantums awarded. Cases involving very similar facts were resolved in very different ways. That diversity in the case law reflects, in part, the absence of clear normative standards in the legislation. The legislative objectives articulated in the support provisions of the *Divorce Act* are vague and, particularly with respect to spousal support, potentially irreconcilable, thus failing to offer sufficient guidance to judges and creating the conditions for a wide range of judicial approaches. . . .

The absence of clear norms in the support provisions of the *Divorce Act, 1985* is also symptomatic of a more fundamental problem — the absence of a strong social consensus on the appropriate principles of support after marriage breakdown. Principles of support are ultimately rooted in social understandings of the meaning of marriage and parenthood. Those understandings are currently in a state of confusion as a result of significant social changes during the past two decades, in particular the increasing acceptance of divorce and the changing social roles of women.

In the 1990's the S.C.C. had two significant opportunities in *Moge* v. *Moge* (1992), 43 R.F.L. (3d) 345 and *Bracklow* v. *Bracklow* (1999), 44 R.F.L. (4th) 1 (both reproduced below) to provide structured guidance for the exercise of discretion in this area. The extent to which these cases provide concrete answers to the difficult questions is debatable. See McLeod, "Case Comment: *Moge* v. *Moge* " (1993), 43 R.F.L. (3d) 455; Bala, "Spousal Support Transformed — Fairer Treatment for Women" (1994), 11 C.F.L.Q. 13; Rogerson, "Spousal Support After *Moge*" (1996-97), 14 C.F.L.Q. 281; Davies, "Spousal Support under the *Divorce Act*: From *Moge* to *Bracklow*" (1999), 44 R.F.L. (4th) 61; and Grant, "The New Realities of Support" (2000), 1 R.F.L. (5th) 205. However, it is clear that these cases provide the touchstone against which the earlier case law must be re-assessed and that they have been very influential.

It is generally agreed that courts should deal with property issues before determining whether a final spousal support order is warranted and, if so, its amount. A substantial property award may eliminate any support entitlement. See, e.g., *Mason* v. *Mason* (1995), 18 R.F.L. (4th) 134 (Man. C.A.) and *Miller* v. *Miller* (1996), 22 R.F.L. (4th) 103 (Sask. Q.B.). In *Hunt* v. *Hunt* (1997), 35 R.F.L. (4th) 1 (Nfld. C.A.), the court held that, in determining the quantum of spousal support, one should consider: i) the respondent's obligations to provide support for any children, including those from a previous relationship; and ii) the amount necessary to allow a single person to live at a subsistence level. In the court's view, only the remaining amount was available for spousal support. See also s. 15.3 of the *Divorce Act* and s. 38.1

and s. 33(9) of the *FLA*. In *Schmid* v. *Smith* (1999), 1 R.F.L. (5th) 447 (Ont. S.C.J.), Justice Lack noted (at 453) that it was clear from these provisions that the court had to assess the quantum of child support before tackling spousal support. However, the justice pointed out that the rules for determining special or extraordinary expenses under the *Child Support Guidelines* created a conundrum because the amount of spousal support affected the allocation of these expenses. The *Guidelines* are analyzed in Chapter 8, **CHILD SUPPORT**.

NOTES AND QUESTIONS

1. The cases reproduced in this chapter deal with final orders for support. As noted earlier, interim support can be obtained under s. 34 of the *FLA* or s. 15.2(2) of the *Divorce Act*. The statutes do not distinguish between the principles applicable to interim support applications and those applicable to applications for final orders. However, since interim support is determined by summary proceedings, a court has less information and is not able or willing to engage in an in-depth analysis of the merits of the claim. If a claimant establishes an arguable case for entitlement to support, the court will confine its determination of interim support to the needs and means of the parties and defer a full examination of the merits to trial. In many cases, the focus is on immediate needs and means and an order is made to allow the applicant to maintain, to the extent possible, the standard of living that existed during the relationship. For some recent, reported cases dealing with interim support, see *Sencza* v. *Donahue* (1995), 18 R.F.L. (4th) 115 (Ont. Gen. Div.); *Eder* v. *Eder* (1995), 18 R.F.L. (4th) 454 (N.W.T.S.C.); *Peel* v. *Griffin* (1996), 19 R.F.L. (4th) 94 (Ont. Gen. Div.); *Robertson* v. *Hotte* (1996), 21 R.F.L. (4th) 452 (Ont. Gen. Div.); *Short* v. *Short* (1996), 21 R.F.L. (4th) 429 (B.C. S.C.); *Brecknell* v. *Brecknell* (1996), 23 R.F.L. (4th) 142 (B.C. S.C.); *Walters* v. *Walters* (1997), 28 R.F.L. (4th) 95 (Ont. Gen. Div.); *Payne* v. *Poirier* (1997), 29 R.F.L. (4th) 426 (B.C. Master); *Kyung* v. *Bowman* (1998), 35 R.F.L. (4th) 48 (B.C. S.C.); *Jackson* v. *Jackson* (1997), 35 R.F.L. (4th) 194 (Ont. Gen. Div.); *W. (B.H.)* v. *W. (C.M.)* (1997), 36 R.F.L. (4th) 329 (N.S. Fam. Ct.); *Webster* v. *Webster* (1997), 37 R.F.L. (4th) 347 (Ont. Gen. Div.); and *Davidson* v. *Davidson* (1998), 42 R.F.L. (4th) 154 (Alta. Q.B.).

Regarding the jurisdiction to vary an interim support order, see *Stannard* v. *Stannard* (1991), 34 R.F.L. (3d) 249 (Alta. Q.B.); *French* v. *Woods* (1992), 42 R.F.L. (3d) 345 (Ont. Gen. Div.); *Lamparski* v. *Lamparski* (1997), 35 R.F.L. (4th) 52 (B.C. S.C.); *Tremblay* v. *Tremblay* (1997), 39 R.F.L. (4th) 324 (Ont. Gen. Div.); *Chambers* v. *Chambers* (1998), 40 R.F.L. (4th) 351 (N.W.T.S.C.); and *Carter* v. *Carter* (1998), 42 R.F.L. (4th) 314 (Ont. Gen. Div.).

2. Section 15.2 (3) of the *Divorce Act* and s. 34 of the *FLA* provide a broad range of orders that can be made. Note the limitations on the jurisdiction of the Ontario Court of Justice in s. 34(2) of the *FLA*.

3. For recent cases dealing with the appropriateness of lump sum orders, see *Elliot* v. *Elliot* (1993), 48 R.F.L. (3d) 237 (Ont. C.A.), leave to appeal refused (1994), 3 R.F.L. (4th) 290 (S.C.C.); *MacNeil* v. *MacNeil* (1994), 2 R.F.L. (4th) 432 (N.S. C.A.); *Hauff* v. *Hauff* (1994), 5 R.F.L. (4th) 419 (Man. C.A.); *Mosher* v. *Mosher* (1995), 13 R.F.L. (4th) 385 (N.S. C.A.); *Balogh* v. *Balogh* (1996), 24 R.F.L. (4th) 181 (Ont. C.A.); *Sharpe* v. *Sharpe* (1997), 27 R.F.L. (4th) 206 (Ont. Gen. Div.); *Lauderdale* v. *Lauderdale* (1997), 29 R.F.L. (4th) 34 (Alta. C.A.); *Sagl* v. *Sagl* (1997), 31 R.F.L. (4th) 405 (Ont. Gen. Div.); *Gray* v. *Gray* (1998), 35 R.F.L. (4th) 456 (Alta. C.A.); and *Vermeulen* v. *Vermeulen* (1999), 2 R.F.L (5th) 140 (N.S. C.A.) . In *Lauderdale*, the court suggested (at 37) that lump sums should only be granted if: i) factors militate in favour of a "clean break", ii) there is concern that periodic payments will not be paid, or iii) there is a specific need for a capital sum for retraining or housing. Cases such as *Jantzen* v. *Jantzen* (1998), 35 R.F.L. (4th) 282 (Man. C.A.) emphasize that lump sum support orders should be based on support considerations and should not be issued to try to alleviate hardship or unfairness caused by the application of provincial family property provisions. In his annotation to the case, Professor McLeod criticizes the general tendency in Canadian cases to keep support and property issues distinct.

4. A court has power under both the *Divorce Act* or the *FLA* to order periodic support for a limited term. Such an order may be appropriate if the court is confident that it will be possible for the dependant

to achieve reintegration into the work force within a definitely foreseeable time. See, e.g, *Kent* v. *Frolik* (1996), 19 R.F.L. (4th) 152 (Ont. Gen. Div.) However, appellate courts have increasingly frowned on speculation of any sort, suggesting that an indefinite order can always be reviewed if circumstances change. See, e.g., *Forler* v. *Forler* (1997), 28 R.F.L. (4th) 33 (Ont. C.A.), where the court also pointed out that support would likely be justified even if the wife began to work full-time because of the projected disparity in incomes and the continuing effect of her withdrawal from the workforce.

A limited term order may also be used to motivate a reluctant dependent spouse or same-sex partner to become self-sufficient by seeking employment. If the dependant then seeks an extension, the onus will be on him or her to establish that there has been a material change of circumstances because reasonable efforts unforeseeably failed to secure employment. See *St. Germaine* v. *St. Germaine* (1996), 21 R.F.L. (4th) 244 (Alta. C.A.); *Scott* v. *Scott* (1996), 21 R.F.L. (4th) 436 (Alta. Q.B.); *MacPhail* v. *MacPhail* (1996), 26 R.F.L. (4th) 55 (Ont. Gen. Div.); *Purcell* v. *Purcell* (1996), 26 R.F.L. (4th) 267 (Ont. C.A.); and *Bakker* v. *Bakker* (1997), 34 R.F.L. (4th) 55 (Ont. Gen. Div.). See also *Trewin* v. *Jones* (1997), 26 R.F.L. (4th) 418 (Ont. C.A.) where the court found that the failure of the wife to secure employment within the period set in the original order constituted a material change in circumstances. However, it has become more common to make a "review order" where the dependant is expected to secure employment in the near future. Under such an order, either party can request that the matter return to the court within a set period of time for a review even if there has been no material change in circumstances. If the review proceeding does not occur, the order continues. In *Bildy* v. *Bildy* (1999), 44 R.F.L. (4th) 81 (Ont. C.A.) and *Nataros* v. *Nataros* (2000), 4 R.F.L. (5th) 290 (B.C. C.A.), the appellate courts transformed limited term orders into review orders. See also *Kennedy* v. *Kennedy* (1996), 26 R.F.L. (4th) 383 (Ont. Gen. Div.); *Baggs* v. *Baggs* (1997), 28 R.F.L. (4th) 185 (Ont. Gen. Div.); *Strachan* v. *Brownridge* (1997), 31 R.F.L. (4th) 101 (B.C. S.C.); *Choquette* v. *Choquette* (1998), 39 R.F.L. (4th) 348 (Ont. C.A.) (where such order refused and indefinite one granted); *Coulter* v. *Coulter* (1998), 43 R.F.L. (4th) 168 (B.C. C.A.); *Rogers* v. *Rogers* (1999), 45 R.F.L. (4th) 65 (B.C. C.A.); *Andrews* v. *Andrews* (1999), 50 R.F.L. (4th) 1 (Ont. C.A.); *Bergeron* v. *Bergeron* (1999), 2 R.F.L. (4th) 57 (Ont. S.C.J.); and *Krill* v. *Krill* (2000), 4 R.F.L. (5th) 249 (Alta. Q.B.). The British Columbia Court of Appeal recently examined the differences between a review order and a limited-term order in *Schmidt* v. *Schmidt* (1999), 1 R.F.L. (5th) 197. In his annotation to this case, Professor McLeod questions the statutory basis for such orders.

There may be situations where the sacrifices and contributions to the relationship, particularly if the relationship did not last very long, merit only a limited term periodic order to allow for the transition to life without support or for retraining. See *Turcotte* v. *Turcotte* (1996), 22 R.F.L. (4th) 364 (Ont. Gen. Div.); *Ferron* v. *Ferron* (1997), 31 R.F.L. (4th) 26 (Ont. Prov. Div.); *Jeffries* v. *Jeffries* (1997), 32 R.F.L. (4th) 345 (Ont. Gen. Div.); and *Juretic* v. *Ruiz* (1999), 49 R.F.L. (4th) 299 (B.C. C.A.).

5. Under the *Divorce Act* of 1968, jurisdiction to vary a corollary relief order rested only with the court of the province that made the order: *Rodness* v. *Rodness*, 23 R.F.L. 266, [1976] 3 W.W.R. 414 (B.C. C.A.) and *Ramsay* v. *Ramsay* (1976), 23 R.F.L. 147, 13 O.R. (2d) 85 (C.A.). This requirement caused hardship where one or both spouses moved to another province after the original order was made. Which court has jurisdiction to vary an order under the 1985 *Divorce Act* in this situation? How does the Act attempt to deal with the situation where the former spouses reside in different provinces? See ss. 5, 17, 18 and 19.

6. Which courts have jurisdiction to vary orders made under Part III of the *FLA*? See ss. 37 and 1.

7. Examine s. 17(4.1) of the *Divorce Act* and s. 37(2) of the *FLA*. An application for variation can be brought under either statute if there has been a change in the circumstances of the parties. An additional ground of variation under the *FLA* is the availability of fresh evidence. In *Willick* v. *Willick* (1994), 6 R.F.L. (4th) 161 (S.C.C.), a majority suggested the following threshold test for determining a change of circumstances (at 179-80, per Sopinka J.):

> In deciding whether the conditions for variation exist, it is common ground that the change must be a material change of circumstances. This means a change, such that, if known at the time, would likely have resulted in different terms. The corollary to this is that if the matter which is

relied on as constituting a change was known at the relevant time, it cannot be relied on as the basis for variation.

Although formulated in the context of child support, this test was applied by all the justices in *B.(G.) v. G.(L.)* (1995), 15 R.F.L. (4th) 201 (S.C.C.), a case dealing with the variation of spousal support. There has been some disagreement in the cases regarding whether a foreseen change in circumstances can meet this test if it was not taken into consideration at the time of the original order. Compare *Levergood* v. *Levergood* (1995), 17 R.F.L. (4th) 423 (Ont. Gen. Div.) and *Rousseau* v. *Rousseau* (1995), 18 R.F.L. (4th) 292 (B.C. S.C.). Which view do you prefer?

For some other recent cases dealing with variation of spousal support orders, see *Gorman* v. *Gorman* (1996), 20 R.F.L. (4th) 325 (Ont. Gen. Div.); *Stroud* v. *Stroud* (1996), 20 R.F.L. (4th) 392 (B.C. C.A.); *Pollak* v. *Pollak* (1996), 23 R.F.L. (4th) 53 (Ont. C.A.); *Lemyre* v. *Chahor* (1996), 23 R.F.L. (4th) 72 (Ont. Fam. Ct.); *Parker* v. *Parker* (1996), 26 R.F.L. (4th) 16 (N.B. C.A.); *Bradley* v. *Bradley* (1997), 29 R.F.L. (4th) 151 (Ont. Gen. Div.); *MacDonald* v. *MacDonald* (1997), 30 R.F.L. (4th) 1 (Alta. C.A.); *Liang* v. *Liang* (1998), 35 R.F.L. (4th) 290 (B.C. C.A.); *Cramer* v. *Cramer* (1998), 43 R.F.L. (4th) 52 (B.C. S.C.); and *Desjardins* v. *Desjardins* (1999), 44 R.F.L. (4th) 93 (Man. C.A.).

8. If a recipient of a spousal support award waits until after the expiry of a limited term order before seeking support for an additional period under the *Divorce Act*, s. 17(10) applies. Cases such as *Poohkay* v. *Poohkay* (1997), 30 R.F.L. (4th) 9 (Alta. C.A.) and *Garrison* v. *Garrison* (1998), 38 R.F.L. (4th) 435 (Ont. Gen. Div.) suggest that the expiration of a limited-term support order is not a major impediment to variation of the order as the courts readily found that the requirements of s. 17(10) were met. Compare these cases with *Dyck* v. *Dyck* (1996), 23 R.F.L. (4th) 224 (Alta. C.A.); *Sywyk* v. *Sywyk* (1996), 26 R.F.L. (4th) 403 (Ont. Div. Ct.); and *Schroder* v. *Schroder* (1998), 38 R.F.L. (4th) 395 (Alta. Q.B.).

9. The establishment of a second family by the payor often leads to an application for a reduction in an existing support order. A number of questions arise. Should a second family obligation affect first family obligations? Should the existing obligations to the members of the first family effectively preclude the payor from forming another family? What obligations should the payor's new partner have? Although there is case law to support almost every point of view on these issues, most of the cases attempt to balance the interests of the first and second families. This is especially so if the payor has support obligations to children in both families. The *Child Support Guidelines* now deal explicitly with the effect of other support obligations on child support orders. See Chapter 8, **CHILD SUPPORT**. Despite Madam Justice L'Heureux-Dubé's comment in *Willick* v. *Willick* (1994), 6 R.F.L. (4th) 161, at 195 (S.C.C.) that a "spouse's obligation to a new family cannot sever any obligation to the first family . . .", courts have sometimes terminated spousal support orders where they threaten the economic viability of the payor's new relationship: *Wolfe* v. *Wolfe* (1995), 15 R.F.L. (4th) 86 (B.C. S.C.) and *Roller* v. *Roller* (1997), 35 R.F.L. (4th) 373 (Sask. Q.B.).

It is now well established that a recipient's remarriage or cohabitation with another is not a ground for disentitlement to support. In *Harris* v. *Gilbert* (1997), 26 R.F.L. (4th) 199 (Ont. C.A.), the court found that the ex-wife's remarriage was a material change in circumstances justifying a reduction in the amount of support in light of the economic benefits flowing from the second relationship. However, the court refused to sanction the termination of the support order, noting (at 206) that the effect of the economic disadvantage suffered by the ex-wife from the role she adopted in the first marriage remained. See also *Ewart* v. *Ewart* (1979), 10 R.F.L. (2d) 73 (Ont. C.A.); *Barnard* v. *Barnard* (1982), 30 R.F.L. (2d) 337 (Ont. C.A.); *Horlock* v. *Horlock* (1984), 42 R.F.L. (2d) 164 (Ont. C.A.); *Rosario* v. *Rosario* (1991), 37 R.F.L. (3d) 24 (Alta. C.A.); *Rideout* v. *Rideout* (1995), 13 R.F.L. (4th) 191 (B.C. S.C.); *B.(G.)* v. *G.(L.)* (1995), 15 R.F.L. (4th) 201 (S.C.C.); *Nantais* v. *Nantais* (1995), 15 R.F.L. (4th) 201 (Ont. Gen. Div.); *Lamey* v. *Lamey* (1996), 19 R.F.L. (4th) 172 (P.E.I. S.C.); *Lauderdale* v. *Lauderdale* (1996), 21 R.F.L. (4th) 17 (Alta. Q.B.), reversed (1997), 29 R.F.L. (4th) 34 (Alta. C.A.); *Franken* v. *Franken* (1997), 33 R.F.L. (4th) 264 (Ont. Gen. Div.); *Tabel* v. *Tabel* (1997), 35 R.F.L. (4th) 379 (Sask. Q.B.); *Boudreau* v. *Bradbury* (1998), 38 R.F.L. (4th) 1 (B.C. S.C.); *Kits* v. *Kits* (1998), 42 R.F.L. (4th) 167 (B.C. S.C.); *Bell* v. *Bell* (1998), 42 R.F.L. (4th) 301 (Nfld. U.F.C.); *Savoie* v. *Savoie* (1999), 49 R.F.L. (4th) 336 (Man. C.A.); and *Lauderdale* v. *Lauderdale* (1999), 50 R.F.L. (4th) 411 (Alta. Q.B.). In *Savoie*, the court affirmed that the ex-wife's remarriage to someone who would provide shelter, pay for household expenses, and meet her lifestyle needs did not end her entitlement. However, it cut the quantum of support by one-half. In his annotation to the case, Professor McLeod asserts (at 340) that there are no rules to determine either the quantum or the duration of support in these cases and "anything can happen".

In *Fancy* v. *Shepard* (1997), 35 R.F.L. (4th) 430 (N.S. S.C.), the court held that a provision in the Nova Scotia *Family Maintenance Act*, which stipulated that spousal support ended when the recipient married, remarried, or began to live common law, was unconstitutional because it conflicted with sections 7 and 15 of the *Charter*. Glube C.J.S.C. stated (at 446) that "it is archaic to assume one spouse will 'take care' of the other". Do you agree? If so, how do explain the general duty, created by legislation such as the *FLA*, of spouses to support one another?

10. At one time courts held that once a spousal support application in a divorce proceeding was dismissed, no order for spousal support could be made in the future: *Cotter* v. *Cotter* (1986), 2 R.F.L. (3d) 124 (Ont. C.A.). Accordingly, courts sometimes awarded nominal support of $1.00 annually so that a payee could apply for variation if circumstances changed. Many lawyers and judges believed that such orders were not necessary after the passage of the 1985 *Divorce Act*. In 1995 Professor McLeod reported that "many judges have refused to grant nominal orders because they believed that a dismissal of a support claim at one time did not extinguish the claim for all time." See "Annotation" (1995), 14 R.F.L. (4th) 326, at 328. In *Murphy* v. *Murphy* (1994), 10 R.F.L. (4th) 103 (Man. C.A.), a majority expressly adopted this view. In dismissing an appeal from an order terminating spousal support under the *Divorce Act*, Philp J.A. noted that the wife was concerned about her ability to support herself in the future. He stated (at 105):

> These are not fanciful concerns. They may arise; and if they do, they can be dealt with. By way of example, if the wife lost her job and was unable to secure new employment, the support issue could be re-examined under the corollary relief provisions of the Divorce Act. She would have to establish that her inability to maintain job security is an economic disadvantage resulting from the marriage, from her non-participation in the labour force during the years when she remained at home, taking care of the household, and raising children.

However, the Ontario Court of Appeal concluded in *obiter dicta* in *McCowan* v. *McCowan* (1995), 14 R.F.L. (4th) 325 that the reasoning in *Cotter* v. *Cotter* applied equally to the 1985 *Divorce Act*. For critical commentary, see McLeod, "Annotation" (1995), 14 R.F.L. (4th) 326. A nominal order was made in *Bosomworth* v. *Bosomworth* (1997), 34 R.F.L. (4th) 71 (B.C. S.C.) and Professor McLeod suggested in his annotation to the case that "a court should routinely make a nominal order to protect future support entitlement if a spouse is entitled to support according to the statutory objectives but the putative payor has no ability to pay". Such an order was recently made in *Davies* v. *Davies* (1999), 50 R.F.L. (4th) 353 (B.C. S.C.).

(2) THE RELEVANCE OF CONDUCT

Section 33(10) of the *FLA* replaced the identically worded s. 18(6) of the *Family Law Reform Act*. The following case dealt with s. 18(6) of the old Act.

MOREY v. MOREY

(1978), 8 R.F.L. (2d) 31 (Ont. Prov. Ct.)

NASMITH PROV. J.: — . . . It seems to me that the legislature had clearly settled on a system of support obligations in which the conduct of the spouses is to be less relevant than it has been in the past with the focus shifting to more practical considerations as listed in s. 18(5) of the Act [now s. 33(9) of the *FLA*].

The obligation for support now exists quite apart from conduct but there appears to be some discretion left with the court to measure conduct and arbitrate as to when conduct has *reached a level* where it can properly be included in the considerations surrounding the support award.

Although that discretion seems to be limited to adjustments to the *amount* of support, the award could be reduced by the court to a level where the obligation was virtually eliminated as counsel has submitted should be done in this case.

The momentous question then remains as to what type of conduct should be considered. Or to put it another way — what level of misconduct is relevant to the calculation of support awards.

The search for a test of conduct should no doubt begin with the words of s. 18(6): "a *course* of conduct that is so *unconscionable* as to constitute an *obvious* and *gross repudiation* of the relationship".

It is hard to imagine a separation occurring without an "obvious repudiation" of the marriage by at least one of the parties and more often by both parties and for that reason I do not get much assistance from those words.

It then becomes a matter of interest to look more closely at the words "unconscionable" and "gross". According to Black's Law Dictionary, "unconscionable conduct" is: "Conduct that is monstrously harsh and shocking to the conscience". The Concise Oxford Dictionary definition of "unconscionable" is: "wholly unreasonable, not guided or restrained by conscience, (law) [unconscionable] *bargain*, contract too grossly unfair to be enforced".

The definition of "gross" in Black's Law Dictionary is as follows: "Out of all measures; beyond allowance; not to be excused; flagrant; shameful; as a gross dereliction of duty; a gross injustice; gross carelessness". The Concise Oxford Dictionary definition of "gross" includes:

> Luxuriant, rank; overfed, bloated, repulsively fat; flagrant, glaring; total, without deductions, not net; dense, thick, solid; nor ethereal, transparent, or impalpable; (of food) coarse, greasy, uncleanly, repulsive . . . (of senses etc.) not delicate, dull; coarse in manners or moral, unrefined, indecent.

I think it is apparent that the test of relevant conduct is to be a strict one. The words of the section themselves make it clear that the type of conduct contemplated is exceptional conduct.

The structure of this section is such that *a rule* is created whereby conduct, generally, is *not* to be considered at all, in support matters. There *is* an allowance for exceptions but if the test of relevant conduct is too easy, there is no doubt that the exception will eat up the rule in no time.

Simply knowing that the test is to be strict of course, will do little to prevent a wide range of results as various courts apply their own subjective tests in attempting to draw the line for relevant conduct.

[Nasmith Prov. J. then reviewed a number of English decisions, including *Wachtel* v. *Wachtel*, [1953] 1 All E.R. 829 (C.A.), which is considered to be the source of the language used in s. 33(10) of the *FLA*. He continued:]

Those principles gleaned from the English cases which are relevant to the matter before me and which, I think, are consistent with the wording of s. 18(6) of the Family Law Reform Act would include the following:

(a) The conduct must be exceptionally bad.
(b) The conduct must be such as could reasonably be expected to destroy the marriage.
(c) The conduct must have persisted in the face of innocence and virtual blamelessness on the part of the other spouse. (The black and white test from *Harnett*.)

(d) The commission of a so-called matrimonial offence is not necessarily sufficient by any means.

(e) The party raising the issue of relevant conduct should be prepared to undertake that there is a bona fide belief that the test in s. 18(6) can be satisfied while acknowledging the risks of punitive costs if the court finds on the whole of the evidence that the issue is frivolous.

(f) The pleadings or subsequent written particulars should set out a summary of the conduct relied on to meet the test so that the court can make a preliminary ruling based on the likelihood of the test's being met. . . .

Section 15.2(5) of the *Divorce Act* specifies that the court "shall not take into consideration any misconduct of a spouse in relation to the marriage" in determining entitlement to or quantum of spousal support. See also s. 17(6). Thus, marital misconduct is no longer a factor to be considered. Indeed, the more recent cases under the 1968 *Divorce Act* had already begun to downplay the significance of matrimonial fault (see Payne, "Spousal Maintenance in Divorce Proceedings"(1984), 41 R.F.L. (2d) 376; see also *Aubin* v. *Aubin* (1985), 44 R.F.L. (2d) 37 (Ont. H.C.)).

Does s. 15.2(5) preclude the court from examining whether a spouse substantially abdicated marital responsibilities? Does it prevent consideration of a spouse's conduct which may have had an impact on the spouse's present ability to support himself or herself? See *Westworth* v. *Westworth* (1999), 1 R.F.L. (5th) 186 (Alta. C.A.), where the court denied support to a wife who dissipated assets and closed down her business. The courts have also considered husbands' cruel conduct if it affected their wives' ability to work: *Martin* v. *Martin* (1993), 50 R.F.L. (3d) 77 (Sask. C.A.); *Zajdenbeutal* v. *Zajdenbeutal* (1994), 94 Man. R. (2d) 13 (Q.B.); *Scullion* v. *Scullion* (1995), 12 R.F.L. (4th) 421 (N.B. Q.B.); *Bascello* v. *Bascello* (1995), 18 R.F.L. (4th) 362 (Ont. Gen. Div.); and *Oakley* v. *Oakley* (1999), 49 R.F.L. (4th) (B.C. S.C.).

In *Ungerer* v. *Ungerer* (1998), 37 R.F.L. (4th) 41 (B.C. C.A.), the ex-wife had denied her ex-husband access to their child for five years, despite a court order and despite serving a prison term for contempt of court. She coached the daughter to falsely accuse her father of molestation. Eventually, she had so turned the child against her father that she no longer wished to see him. The court found (at 50) that the ex-wife's conduct was "sufficiently egregious to disentitle her to continued [spousal] support". The court held that s.17(6) of the *Divorce Act* was no bar to the consideration of this misconduct because it "occurred outside the marriage and after its termination" and so was not "in relation to the marriage". Do you agree with this interpretation of the statute?

NOTES AND QUESTIONS

1. Why does s. 33(10) of the *FLA* refer to a "course of conduct"? Can a single act amount to a course of conduct?

2. Can the conduct of the respondent be considered under s. 33(10) of the *FLA*? Is it relevant where the applicant's conduct is not in issue? Is it relevant only to determine if the applicant's conduct meets the test set out in s. 33(10)? Although the *Divorce Act* of 1968 required the courts to consider the conduct of the parties in determining maintenance, the courts refused to increase a maintenance order as a means of punishing the payor: *Chequer* v. *Chequer* (1972), 9 R.F.L. 208 (B.C. S.C.); *Rathwell* v. *Rathwell* (1984), 16 R.F.L. 387 (Sask. Q.B.); *K.* v. *K.*, 20 R.F.L. 22, [1975] 3 W.W.R. 708 (Man. C.A.); *Firestone*

v. *Firestone (No. 1)* (1971), 11 R.F.L. (2d) 150 (Ont. H.C.); and *Tremblay* v. *Tremblay* (1980), 17 R.F.L. (2d) 175 (Ont. H.C.). However, in *Melanson* v. *Melanson* (1991), 34 R.F.L. (3d) 323 (Ont. Gen. Div.), Campbell J. appeared to assume that the respondent's conduct could be considered under s. 33(10).The judge concluded that the husband's abusive conduct and the "occasional real or perceived extra-marital incidents" did not amount to a gross and obvious repudiation of the relationship. See also *Verdun* v. *Verdun* (1994), 9 R.F.L. (4th) 54 (Ont. Gen. Div.).

3. In *Lawless* v. *Lawless* (1979), 26 O.R. (2d) 214 (Prov. Ct.), the wife began to live with another man after she and her husband mutually agreed to separate. Nasmith Prov. J. concluded (at 216) that the wife's conduct could not be characterized as repudiation of the relationship since "the marriage had already been mutually repudiated in a fashion that was admittedly not gross or unconscionable". Do you agree with the view that conduct after separation cannot be considered under s. 33(10) of the *FLA*?

4. The wife in *B. (S.)* v. *B. (L.)* (1999), 2 R.F.L. (5th) 32 (Ont. S.C.J.) had several affairs and twice got pregnant with children not fathered by her husband. Although the conduct "was exceptionally bad and . . . could reasonably be expected to destroy the marriage", Justice McLean concluded (at 35) that the wife's support claim was not affected by s. 33(10) of the *FLA*. The husband had been aware of his wife's conduct and had continued the relationship. In one incident, he had encouraged his wife to partake in group sex involving himself, his brother, and his wife's female friend.

5. Section 18(6) of the *Family Law Reform Act* and s. 33(10) of the *FLA* have rarely resulted in reduced support. For additional cases illustrating that these provisions have been given a restrictive application, see *C.* v. *C.* (No. 2) (1979), 11 R.F.L. (2d) 364 (Ont. Co. Ct.); *Nadon* v. *Nadon* (1979), 18 R.F.L. (2d) 293 (Ont. H.C.); *Phillips* v. *Phillips* (1981), 24 R.F.L. (2d) 139 (Ont. Co. Ct.); and *Melanson* v. *Melanson* (1991), 34 R.F.L. (3d) 323 (Ont. Gen. Div.). However, in *Freid* v. *Freid* (1982), 30 R.F.L. (2d) 342 (Ont. Co. Ct.) the court held that the wife's conduct precluded periodic support. There the wife had refused on several occasions to measure the diabetic husband's insulin dose as punishment for his refusal to comply with her wishes. The husband's sight had so deteriorated that he no longer felt confident in measuring the drug dosage and he had married the wife partly to obtain her assistance in this task. Similarly, Mr. Justice Flaningan found that the wife's conduct satisfied the test set out in s. 33(10) in *MacDonald* v. *MacDonald* (May, 1991), unreported (Ont. Gen. Div.). The parties' 24-year marriage was punctuated by various violent acts, generally instigated by the wife. The husband finally declared the relationship at an end when the wife stabbed him twice without warning while he was driving. She served three months in jail following a criminal conviction. The wife's course of conduct resulted in a reduction of the quantum and duration of the support order. Although the husband felt he should not have to pay any support, the order provided for $700 per month for five years.

E. Macdonald J. applied s. 33(10) in a unique way in *Krigstein* v. *Krigstein* (1992), 43 R.F.L. (3d) 334 (Ont. Gen. Div.). The judge concluded that the wife's refusal to be up-front and honest about her relationship with another man after separation qualified as a gross and obvious repudiation of her marriage (at 343):

> For the sake of clarity, it is emphasized that the conduct of the friendship in itself is not something that the court should be concerned about. However, the economic implications of the friendship and the history of the manner in which Mr. Lubetsky and Mrs. Krigstein have treated their obligation to be forthcoming with respect to financial arrangements are such that their conduct is a course of conduct that is unconscionable and constitutes a gross and obvious repudiation of the relationship between Mrs. Krigstein and her husband. A different view may have been taken had the spouse and her friend been forthcoming with respect to financial matters and if there had been compliance with court orders designed at [*sic*] procuring this financial information.

(3) SELF-SUFFICIENCY, THE CAUSAL CONNECTION TEST AND COMPENSATION FOR THE ECONOMIC CONSEQUENCES OF MARRIAGE AND ITS BREAKDOWN

The idea behind causal connection as a basic test for entitlement to spousal support is that such support should redress those economic needs flowing from the marriage and the economic inter-relationship during cohabitation. This philosophy underpinned much of the Law Reform Commission of Canada's *Working Paper 12, Maintenance on Divorce* (Ottawa: Law Reform Commission of Canada, 1975), parts of which are reproduced in the introduction to this chapter. The dissenting judgment of Lamer J. in the following case gave further impetus to this view. The case also shed some light on the duty to become self-supporting where possible.

MESSIER v. DELAGE

(1983), 35 R.F.L. (2d) 337 (S.C.C.)

[Michel Messier, the appellant in the Supreme Court, and Dame Jocelyn Delage, the respondent, were married in 1962 and separated in February 1974. In 1975 Delage petitioned for divorce. A decree nisi was granted on 10th September 1975. It awarded custody of the two children of the marriage to the petitioner who was granted maintenance of $1,600 per month for herself and the children. The decree was made absolute on 30th December 1975. At the time of the divorce Delage, who had not worked outside the home during the marriage, was enrolled in a program of studies leading to a Master's degree in translation.

Within a year of the issuance of the decree absolute, Messier applied to reduce the maintenance. This application was dismissed on the basis that it was premature. Denis Lévesque J. noted, however, that the situation of the parties could be expected to change once Delage obtained her Master's degree, as she would then be able to obtain employment, at least on a part-time basis.

On 5th April 1979 Messier applied for a variation of both the maintenance and custody orders. His request for an order granting him custody of the eldest child, who had in fact been living with him since December 1978, was granted. Regarding maintenance, Messier offered to pay $500 per month for the child in Delage's custody but asked that all other obligations be terminated. Acknowledging that he was capable of paying spousal maintenance out of his net professional income of $56,000, Messier argued that Delage was no longer entitled to look to him for financial provision even though she had been unable to find full-time employment. He stressed that Delage had had five years following separation in which to reorganize her life; that she now had a Master's degree in translation, and at the age of 38 and in good health was fully able to support herself; and that she was no longer required to stay home to look after the children since the only child in her custody was 15 years old. Finally, he pointed out that Delage had earned $5,000 in 1978 as a free-lance translator.

Bergeron J., at trial, ordered that the maintenance payable be reduced to $1,200 per month as of 1st May 1979 and that as of 1st January 1980, the husband's sole obligation would be to pay $500 per month as maintenance for the child. The Court of Appeal reversed the judgment of the Superior Court in part by striking that portion of the trial court's order setting aside the maintenance payable to Delage as of 1st January 1980. In the result, maintenance of $1,200 per month was payable indefinitely. Messier appealed to the Supreme Court of Canada. He argued that the decision of the Court of Appeal effectively meant that the support obligation between former spouses survived the divorce indefinitely, thereby ignoring "the evolution in the status of married women", "the equality of treatment between the sexes established by the Divorce Act", and the trend to emphasize the duty to support oneself after marriage breakdown apparent in recent judicial decisions as well as reformed provincial support legislation.]

CHOUINARD J. (RITCHIE, BEETZ and ESTEY concurring): — . . . In the case at bar the issue turned exclusively on s. 11 of the Divorce Act. Subsection (2) of that section is concerned with four factors:

(a) The conduct of the parties;
(b) Their respective conditions;
(c) Their means;
(d) The other circumstances of either of them.

Section 11(2) states that an order may be varied from time to time or rescinded in light of the foregoing factors, which the court must weigh against each other. In my opinion what is significant about this subsection is that an order is never final. It may be varied from time to time or rescinded if the court thinks it fit and just to do so, taking these factors into consideration. The case at bar is itself an illustration of this rule, which allows a party from time to time to come back to the court. In December 1976, barely 12 months after the decree absolute, the appellant came back to the court in an unsuccessful attempt to have the alimentary pension which he had been ordered to pay the respondent cancelled. . . .

The conclusion that emerges from . . .the many cases cited by the parties is that each case is sui generis and should be decided in accordance with the factors mentioned. . . .

The machinery provided by the Divorce Act to take account of the conduct of the parties and changes in the condition, means or other circumstances of either of them is their right to apply to the court each time a change which is regarded as fundamental occurs. This is not to assume, as in the case at bar, that in eight months the respondent will no longer need support or be entitled to it: it means that if the situation arises it can be dealt with.

. . .[T]here is no reason in the case at bar to cancel the respondent's alimentary pension eight months in advance on the assumption that she will no longer need or be entitled to it at that time.

That does not mean that the obligation of support between ex-spouses should continue indefinitely when the marriage bond is dissolved, or that one spouse can continue to be a drag on the other indefinitely or acquire a lifetime pension as a result of the marriage, or to luxuriate in idleness at the expense of the other, to use the expressions one finds in some discussions of the subject. It also does not mean that a divorced person cannot remarry, or that his new obligations or new advantages as the case may be will not be taken into consideration.

With respect, none of these questions arises in the case at bar.

After their marriage the parties lived together for 12 years. They had two children, whose education was the respondent's constant concern. She never worked outside the home. Immediately after the divorce, she began studies in translation and took her Master's degree. She has since then been able to obtain part-time employment, which in the year preceding the trial judgment brought her some $5,000. The appellant's means enable him to pay the pension awarded, which in fact was reduced by the Court of Appeal in the same proportion as it was by the Superior Court to take into account the respondent's earnings and the fact that one of the children is no longer dependent on her. If other changes occur, it will be for the appellant to apply to the court again.

In my opinion the Superior Court erred in disregarding the actual factors submitted for its consideration and hypothesizing as to the unknown and then unforeseeable future and the Court of Appeal properly intervened.

For these reasons, I would dismiss the appeal with costs.

LAMER J. (dissenting) (MCINTYRE and WILSON JJ. concurring): — This appeal raises a question of importance at the present time in view of the current economic situation, the difficulty in finding work and the resulting high rate of unemployment. Should a divorced spouse who is working always bear the consequences of all this and provide for the needs of his unemployed former spouse, or is it for the government, if it cannot remedy, at least to alleviate the effects, and to what extent? . . .

Purpose of maintenance awarded to one of the spouses following a divorce

In my opinion, the purpose of maintenance is to reduce in material terms the consequences resulting from breaking the marriage bond. Maintenance will be awarded to a spouse who cannot provide for her own needs. The division of functions in traditional society has meant that it is nearly always the wife who is in this position. It was almost impossible for her, without proper training after several years of not earning her living, to find employment and so be able to provide for her own needs.

The evolution of society and of the status of women both require us to re-examine what the nature of maintenance should be. Formerly the ex-wife would, more often than not, remain a burden to her former husband indefinitely.

The courts have for some years recognized this development. In *Harding* v. *Harding* (1972), 8 R.F.L. 236, Dryer J. of the British Columbia Supreme Court said the following:

> 6th April 1972, Dryer J. (orally):— The old rule was that once a woman married a man she then acquired a status, and from that she was entitled to live in the position in life which his position in life would bring to his wife, insofar as that could be done, when they were separated. I do not think that is the law today. My view is this: If a man and woman marry, and as a result of that marriage the woman quits her job or in some other way removes herself from the economic world and thereby loses her ability to work or any opportunity to maintain herself or her children, then I think there is an obligation that attaches to the husband which would carry on and, of course, whether that is likely to happen depends to some extent on the length of the marriage. We have so many marriages nowadays, even those that last for several years, where both parties are working — they get married, they both go on working. Quite often the woman is earning more that the man. When that marriage is brought to an end I see no reason why either party, just on those simple facts, should acquire any right to income at the expense of the other.

No alimony was granted. . . .

In my view, this new approach by the courts is desirable. Women cannot on the one hand claim equal status without at the same time accepting responsibility for their own upkeep.

Furthermore, quite apart from the fact that the woman rather than the man is the recipient of maintenance, the divorce itself is intended to dissolve the marriage bond, whereas separation only changes the living arrangements. If the divorce terminates the marriage, it is desirable that the Divorce Act should apply to ensure the termination of all relations, even those that are financial, provided this must be borne in mind — that such a thing is possible.

In a working paper ((No. 12), Maintenance on Divorce (1975)) the Canada Law Reform Commission suggested the following at p. 30:

> We suggest that the period following divorce should be characterized in law as a time of economic transition for both spouses from the arrangements that were suitable to the marriage when one spouse may have made financial provision for both, to the single state when each should be, as before marriage, financially self-reliant. The law should require the former spouse who does not

have an economic need created by the marriage to assist the one who has such a need to become financially rehabilitated. . . .

Although the principles endorsed by the commission are not law, I agree with them. Indeed, I am allowed to do so because the Divorce Act, in particular s. 11(2) of that Act, is not a bar to a judge wishing to draw inspiration from these guidelines. In addition, and apart from the commission's recommendations, the family divisions of several courts have already been using similar principles and are now applying them with increasing regularity.

[After reviewing the post-divorce events, Lamer J. continued:]

Are these changes sufficient for a petition to cancel the maintenance?

The respondent contended that the fact she had obtained a university degree is not in itself a guarantee of employment. She has made a definite effort to become self-supporting. This is in no way a case of a lazy person who refuses to work. However, the circumstances are such that, as she has no employment, she is still entitled to receive a pension from her former husband.

The question in the case at bar is whether the ability to work is in itself a determining factor which justifies canceling the maintenance or whether, in addition, the respondent must actually be working.

The courts have hitherto held that the ability to work is a significant factor in determining the quantum of maintenance. . . .

However, I would go further.

In my view the evolution of society requires that one more step be taken in favour of the final emancipation of former spouses. To me, aside from rare exceptions, the ability to work leads to "the end of the divorce" and the beginning of truly single status for each of the former spouses. I also consider that the "ability" to work should be determined intrinsically and should not in any way be determined in light of factors extrinsic to the individual, such as the labour market and the economic situation.

As maintenance is only granted for as long as it takes to acquire sufficient independence, once that independence has been acquired it follows that maintenance ceases to be necessary. A divorced spouse who is "employable" but unemployed is in the same position as other citizens, men or women, who are unemployed. The problem is a social one and it is therefore the responsibility of the government rather than the former husband. Once the spouse has been retrained, I do not see why the fact of having been married should give the now single individual any special status by comparison with any other unemployed single person. In my view, the duty of a former spouse is limited in the case of retrainable persons to the retraining period and the discretion conferred on the judge in s. 11(2) to determine what is fit and just is not a bar to this conclusion, which the evolution of society has now made necessary. The rule is not absolute and remedy under s. 11(2) is never completely excluded to compensate for the financial negative effects of the marriage, but I would only make an exception to it in, to use the words of Bergeron J., "very special circumstances". That is not the case here.

I would allow the appeal, reverse the judgment of the Court of Appeal and restore the judgment at trial.

Appeal dismissed.

NOTES AND QUESTIONS

1. Did the majority in *Messier* v. *Delage* ever explain why, in the circumstances of the case, it was fit and just for the appellant rather than the state to continue to bear the responsibility for maintaining the respondent? What explanation would you give?

2. Lamer J. concluded that successful retraining justified cancellation of maintenance even though the dependent former spouse was still unable to find full employment. Apparently, he assumed the wife's unemployment was no longer caused by the role she adopted during the marriage. Do you agree with this assumption? For critical commentary, see Hovius, "Case Comment: *Messier* v. *Delage*" (1984), 36 R.F.L. (2d) 339 and Rogerson, " The Causal Connection Test in Spousal Support Law" (1989), 8 Can. J. Fam. L. 95 at 123-124.

The concept of causal connection, articulated by Lamer J. in dissent in *Messier* v. *Delage*, appeared to be adopted by a majority in what has become known as the trilogy: *Pelech* v. *Pelech* (1987), 7 R.F.L. (3d) 225 (S.C.C.); *Richardson* v. *Richardson* (1987), 7 R.F.L. (3d) 304 (S.C.C.); and *Caron* v. *Caron* (1987), 7 R.F.L. (3d) 274 (S.C.C.). All three cases arose under the 1968 *Divorce Act* and dealt specifically with the question of when a court should exercise its power to order support at variance with a separation agreement. Although this specific issue is examined in a later chapter, the cases are included here because they contain philosophical comments about spousal support and they soon became the starting point for analysis of spousal support in many cases.

PELECH v. PELECH

(1987), 7 R.F.L. (3d) 225 (S.C.C.)

[The parties married in 1954 and had two children. The wife did not enter the labour force, but did assist her husband in his business by acting as receptionist and bookkeeper. When they divorced in 1969 they entered into a settlement agreement, having each received independent legal advice. The agreement was incorporated into the divorce decree and the husband paid the amount specified, a total of $28,760 over a period of thirteen months. Over the following years, the wife's physical and psychological problems increased to the extent that she was unable to work. By 1982, her settlement sum was gone and she was on welfare. The husband prospered and his net worth increased from about $128,000 in 1969 to $1,800,000 in 1984. The wife applied to vary the original support order. The trial judge allowed the application because there had been a gross change in circumstances and ordered ongoing support of $2,000 per month. The B.C. C.A. overturned this decision and the wife appealed.]

WILSON J. (DICKSON C.J.C., MCINTYRE, LAMER and LE DAIN JJ. concurring): — Section 11(2) of the *Divorce Act*, R.S.C. 1970, c. D-8, confers on the court the power to vary a previous order for maintenance "having regard to the conduct of the parties since the making of the order or any change in the condition, means or other circumstances of either of them". This appeal specifically addresses the extent of the constraints, if any, imposed on that power by the existence of a valid and enforceable maintenance agreement. Should the parties be held to the terms of their contract or should the court intervene to remedy the inequities now alleged by one of the parties to be flowing from the bargain previously entered into freely and on full knowledge and with the advice of counsel? . . .

V. PRELIMINARY OBSERVATIONS

The central issue in this case concerns the effect of a valid and enforceable antecedent settlement agreement on the court's discretionary power under s. 11(2) to vary maintenance orders. Some preliminary observations might be helpful.

The first observation concerns the principle that a maintenance agreement can never totally extinguish the jurisdiction of the court to impose its own terms on the parties. This principle derives from the House of Lords' decision in *Hyman* v. *Hyman*, [1929] A.C. 601. . . .

The view that a freely negotiated and informed waiver of legal rights cannot oust the jurisdiction of the court is supported by the language of s. 11(2) and by the case law. Although the recent decision of this Court in *Messier* v. *Delage*, [1983] 2 S.C.R. 410, 35 R.F.L. (2d) 337, 2 D.L.R. (4th) 1, 50 N.R. 16 [Que.], did not involve a maintenance agreement, the *Hyman* principle underlies the view expressed by Chouinard J., speaking for the majority of the court, that s. 11(1) orders can never be truly final. . . .

Hyman and *Messier* settle the narrow issue of the court's jurisdiction to intervene. However, they do not answer the broader question of when it is fit and just to exercise that jurisdiction having regard to the enumerated factors. Accordingly, the second observation I would make concerns the change in emphasis which has occurred since the enactment of the current legislation in 1968. The jurisprudence discloses a distinct movement away from the concept of moral blameworthiness or "fault" and towards a search for what is fair and reasonable having regard to all the circumstances of the parties including their means and needs. . . .

While the shift in focus away from moral blameworthiness is salutary, it renders the calculation of what is "fit and just" under s. 11 much more difficult and complex. The courts are required to analyze the pattern of financial interdependence generated by each particular relationship and devise a support order that minimizes as far as possible the economic consequences of the relationship's breakdown. In this sense, each case is *sui generis* as declared by this Court in *Messier*. However, the order made must meet a uniform standard of fairness and reasonableness. . . .

The third and final observation I want to make concerns the significance under s. 11 of the fact that the parties have themselves agreed on the issue of maintenance. It is clear from the case law that this has to be an important factor in the court's consideration under either subsection (1) or (2). It is clear also that it has a significant impact on the degree or nature of the change in circumstances required to trigger the s. 11(2) discretion. Unfortunately, the extent of this impact has eluded definition. . . .

An examination of the case law reveals that the spectrum of opinion ranges from an extremely restrictive approach, which would allow intervention only where children are at risk or where the agreement is unconscionable, to a very broad approach which gives the parties' agreement very little weight and affirms the position of the court as the arbiter of what is fair and reasonable.

These preliminary observations may be summed up as follows:

1) It is a well established principle that the court's supervisory jurisdiction over maintenance cannot be extinguished by contract.

2) The general trend of the case law in fashioning maintenance orders has been to move away from "fault" and achieve an arrangement that is fair and reasonable in light of all the circumstances of the parties including their means and needs.

3) While it is generally accepted that the existence of an antecedent settlement

agreement made by the parties is an important fact, there is a wide range of views as to how this affects the legal principles governing the exercise of the discretion conferred in s. 11.

VI. ALTERNATIVE VIEWS

Lambert J.A.'s decision in the Court of Appeal reflects the view that an antecedent settlement agreement effectively restricts the power of the court under s. 11 of the Divorce Act. The clearest expression of this view is to be found in the judgment of the Ontario Court of Appeal in *Farquar* v. *Farquar*, [(1983), 43 O.R. (2d) 423 (C.A.)], in which Zuber J.A. held that the courts should overturn a valid and enforceable maintenance agreement only in "a narrow range of cases".

A very different and arguably more paternalistic philosophy is manifest in judgments of the Manitoba Court of Appeal such as *Newman* v. *Newman* (1980), 19 R.F.L. (2d) 122, 114 D.L.R. (3d) 517, 4 Man. R. (2d) 50, which minimize the importance of freedom of contract and impose on the parties a judicial standard of reasonableness notwithstanding their agreement to the contrary.

A third "compromise" view emerges from *Webb* [(1984), 46 O.R. (2d) 457 (C.A.)], where Blair J.A. suggests that the change in circumstances which triggers the court's discretionary power in s. 11(2) must be a "gross" or "catastrophic" change.

Finally, a fourth possibility is suggested by recurrent references in the case-law to specific categories of change as a justification for judicial intervention rather than simply change of a certain magnitude.

A. *The "Private Choice" Approach*

In *Farquar* the respondent wife expressly waived her right to maintenance in the minutes of settlement which were incorporated in the divorce decree. A year later she applied for a s. 11(2) variation and was granted a lump sum order. The husband appealed. Zuber J.A., for a unanimous court, agreed that the maintenance provisions imposed by the trial judge were much more appropriate than those arrived at by the parties in the minutes of settlement. However, he found that that was not the issue before him; the issue before him was whether the settlement should be respected and precluded judicial intervention.

Zuber J.A. started with the proposition that it is preferable for parties to settle their own affairs. He gave a number of reasons for this including that (1) the parties are more likely to accept and live with an arrangement they have made themselves as opposed to one imposed upon them; (2) the administrative burden of the courts is relieved by respecting the parties' freedom of contract; and (3) treating the agreement reached by the parties as final allows them to plan their separate futures with relative peace of mind. . . . Zuber J.A. also observed that property issues and maintenance issues are nowadays frequently intertwined in the terms of a settlement. Thus, it might be quite unfair to alter the provisions for maintenance without also altering the division of property.

Zuber J.A. acknowledged that there were nevertheless two kinds of circumstance in which a settlement is not binding. The first is where the settlement is invalid according to traditional common law or equitable doctrines. The second is comprised of "that narrow range of cases where a court will relieve against a matrimonial settlement even though the contract is valid" (p. 252). Unfortunately, Zuber J.A. did not find it necessary to elaborate on this "narrow range of cases" other than to reject the notion that change by itself is a determining factor. . . . Zuber J.A. applied these principles to the case before him and concluded that the Court had no basis on which to intervene and that the settlement freely negotiated by the parties should be respected.

B. *The Court's Overriding Power*

The core values underlying the approach in *Farquar* are those of individual responsibility and freedom of contract. An opposing view is to be found in the judgments of the Manitoba Court of Appeal in *Newman* v. *Newman*, supra, *Katz* v. *Katz* [(1983), 33 R.F.L. (2d) 412], and *Ross* v. *Ross* (1984), 39 R.F.L. (2d) 51, 6 D.L.R. (4th) 385, 26 Man. R. (2d) 122. In this line of cases the court asserts its supervisory role and finds that it is not significantly constrained by the presence of a binding agreement. Although the Court often acknowledges that the existence of an agreement is an important circumstance to be considered and that finality in the ordering of post-marital obligations is a laudable objective, a finding that the agreement does not meet the court's standard of fairness or reasonableness justifies an exercise of the s. 11(2) power. . . .

In summary, the Manitoba decisions do not distinguish in any significant manner between applications for maintenance in the face of an antecedent agreement and applications in which there is no such agreement. The court exercises its discretion on the basis of what it considers fair and reasonable whether or not the parties have, in effect, settled their own financial affairs.

C. *The Compromise*

In some cases an attempt has been made by the courts to forge a middle ground between the *Farquar* and *Ross* approaches by holding that, when there is an antecedent agreement, the s. 11(2) criterion of change can only be satisfied by a change of considerable magnitude. The courts which apply this standard often attempt to rationalize judicial intervention in terms of contract principles by describing such a change as one which negates a fundamental assumption upon which the original agreement was premised.

Wong L.J.S.C.'s decision at trial is an illustration. He regarded Mrs. Pelech's current impoverishment as a ''gross'' change in circumstances. In addition, he seems to suggest that the contractual arrangements were predicated on Mrs. Pelech's employability and eventual self-sufficiency. Time did not bear out that prediction. Although Wong L.J.S.C. does not expressly find that this vitiates the agreement, it seems to be an important legitimating factor in his ultimate decision to intervene. . . .

The emphasis on the magnitude of the change is also at the root of the Ontario Court of Appeal's decision in *Webb*. The parties in *Webb* entered into an agreement in 1981 which made ample provision for the wife and which expressly stated that the periodic payments were not subject to variation. Shortly after the issuance in 1982 of a decree nisi incorporating the agreement (minus the non-variation clause), the husband experienced a catastrophic and unforeseeable financial loss. He applied to vary the maintenance award. His application was dismissed at trial.

Mr. Justice Arnup, with whom Weatherston J.A. concurred, allowed Mr. Webb's appeal. He maintained that Zuber J.A.'s statement in *Farquar* that change, even if it is substantial, is not a sufficient basis for avoiding the terms of a valid agreement, did not extend to all change regardless of magnitude. Rather, he interpreted Zuber J.A.'s proposition as simply imposing an extremely heavy onus on the party seeking the variation. He found, therefore, that there was no distinction in principle between the views of the Ontario Court of Appeal and those of the Manitoba Court of Appeal as expressed in *Ross*. In addition, like Wong L.J.S.C., Arnup J.A. reinforced his decision by alluding to the lack of a factual basis at the time of the application to support the assumptions implicit in the separation agreement. In the present appeal Wong L.J.S.C., before concluding that the maintenance provision should be varied, emphasized the expectation of the parties that Mrs. Pelech would be employable, something which had not happened. In *Webb* Arnup J.A. pointed to the belief that the husband would be in receipt of large amounts of capital in the future. Like Mrs. Pelech's employability the capital did not materialize and Arnup J.A. accordingly concluded that the contract should be varied.

Blair J.A., in separate reasons, concurred in Arnup J.A.'s disposition of the case. He reviewed the jurisprudence and agreed that *Farquar* does not preclude a court from exercising its power where there has been a "profound change". He added that even in the absence of such change the courts will intervene in a "narrow range of cases where public policy is offended if [the agreement] makes a spouse a public charge, deprives children or is unconscionable" (p. 145).

D. *Specific Categories of Change*

Blair J.A.'s enumeration of separate categories of change in *Webb* suggests a fourth approach. Indeed, in several cases the courts have justified upsetting the terms of a valid agreement because of the nature rather than the degree of change experienced by the applicant. As Blair J.A.'s comments suggest, the cases can be divided into at least three separate types: where the applicant has become a public charge, where the terms of the existing agreement cause deprivation to children, and where the agreement is unenforceable on other grounds. . . .

VII. CONCLUSIONS

The need to compensate for systemic gender-based inequality advanced by Matas J.A. in *Ross* forms a counterpoint to the need for finality identified by Anderson J. in *Dal Santo* [(1975), 21 R.F.L. 117 (B.C. S.C.)] and approved by Zuber J.A in *Farquar* and Lambert J.A. in the present appeal. The Alberta Court of Appeal in *Jull* [(1985), 42 R.F.L. (2d) 113] describes the tension in terms of the competing values of fairness and freedom. While I am in sympathy with Matas J.A.'s concern, I believe that the case by case approach and the continuing surveillance by the courts over the consensual arrangements of former spouses which he advocates will ultimately reinforce the very bias he seeks to counteract. In addition, I believe that every encouragement should be given to ex-spouses to settle their financial affairs in a final way so that they can put their mistakes behind them and get on with their lives. I would, with all due respect, reject the Manitoba Court of Appeal's broad and unrestricted interpretation of the court's jurisdiction in maintenance matters. It seems to me that it goes against the main stream of recent authority, both legislative and judicial, which emphasizes mediation, conciliation and negotiation as the appropriate means of settling the affairs of the spouses when the marriage relationship dissolves.

However, as I stated at the outset, the *Hyman* principle that parties cannot by contract oust the jurisdiction of the court in matters of spousal maintenance is an established tenet of Canadian law. The question thus becomes the nature and extent of the constraint imposed on the courts by the presence of an agreement which was intended by the parties to settle their affairs in a final and conclusive manner. . . .

It seems to me that where the parties have negotiated their own agreement, freely and on the advice of independent legal counsel, as to how their financial affairs should be settled on the breakdown of their marriage, and the agreement is not unconscionable in the substantive law sense, it should be respected. People should be encouraged to take responsibility for their own lives and their own decisions. This should be the overriding policy consideration.

The test of radical change in *Webb* is an attempt to carve a fairly narrow exception to the general policy of restraint. It fails, however, in my opinion in one important particular. It makes the mere magnitude of the change the justification for the Court's intervention and takes no account of whether or not the change is in any way related to the fact of the marriage. In order to impose responsibility for changed circumstances on a former spouse it seems to me essential that there be some relationship between the change and the marriage. Matas J.A. hinted at this in *Ross*. In the case of a wife who has devoted herself exclusively to home and children and has acquired no working skills outside the home, this relationship is readily established. The former spouse in these circumstances should have a responsibility for a radical change in his ex-wife's circumstances generated as a consequence of her total dependency during the period of the marriage. By way of contrast, a former spouse who simply falls upon hard times through unwise investment, business adversity, or a life style beyond his or her means should not be able to fall back on the former spouse, no matter how radical the change may be, simply because they once were husband and wife.

Absent some causal connection between the changed circumstances and the marriage, it seems to me that parties who have declared their relationship at an end should be taken at their word. They made the decision to marry and they made the decision to terminate their marriage. Their decisions should be respected. They should thereafter be free to make new lives for themselves without an ongoing contingent liability for future misfortunes which may befall the other. It is only, in my view, where the future misfortune has its genesis in the fact of the marriage that the court should be able to override the settlement of their affairs made by the parties themselves. Each marriage relationship creates its own economic pattern from which the self-sufficiency or dependency of the partners flows. The assessment of the extent of that pattern's post-marital impact is essentially a matter for the judge of first instance. The causal connection between the severe hardship being experienced by the former spouse and the marriage provides, in my view, the necessary legal criterion for determining when a case falls within the ''narrow range of cases'' referred to by Zuber J.A. in *Farquar*. It is this element which is missing in *Webb*. Accordingly, where an applicant seeking maintenance or an increase in the existing level of maintenance establishes that he or she has suffered a radical change in circumstances flowing from an economic pattern of dependency engendered by the marriage, the court may exercise its relieving power. Otherwise, the obligation to support the former spouse should be, as in the case of any other citizen, the communal responsibility of the state.

VIII. DISPOSITION OF THE APPEAL

The dependency of the appellant Mrs. Pelech on social assistance is evidence of the extremity of her need. In addition, there are the observations of Wong L.J.S.C. at trial that her impoverishment is dire and her future prospects limited if not non-existent. However, although I agree with him that her present state evidences "a gross change in circumstances" since the time of the original order incorporating the minutes of settlement in 1969, no link is found by the trial judge between the change of circumstances and her former marriage to Mr. Pelech. Indeed, quite the contrary. Wong L.J.S.C. found that the psychological problems which have resulted in her inability to care for herself pre-dated the marriage and contributed to its failure. He specifically rejected the submission that they stemmed from the marriage or from the behaviour of the respondent during it. Wong L.J.S.C. also rejected the submission that the agreement was improvident and unconscionable. He found that it was entered into freely by Mrs. Pelech on the advice of counsel and was perfectly fair at the time it was made. He found, however, that the basic premise on which it was entered into, namely that Mrs. Pelech would be able to work and support herself, had not materialized.

While I realize that Mrs. Pelech's present hardship is great, to burden the respondent with her care fifteen years after their marriage has ended for no other reason than that they were once husband and wife seems to me to create a fiction of marital responsibility at the expense of individual responsibility. I believe that the courts must recognize the right of the individual to end a relationship as well as to begin one and should not, when all other aspects of the relationship have long since ceased, treat the financial responsibility as continuing indefinitely into the future. Where parties, instead of resorting to litigation, have acted in a mature and responsible fashion to settle their financial affairs in a final way and their settlement is not vulnerable to attack on any other basis, it should not, in my view, be undermined by courts concluding with the benefit of hindsight that they should have done it differently.

For these reasons I would dismiss the appeal. I would make no award as to costs.

[LA FOREST J. gave separate, concurring reasons. He stressed that all aspects of the marital relationship should, as much as possible, come to an end on divorce and that financial ties should continue only if necessary to provide for a former spouse whose needs were related to the marriage relationship. Thus the trial judge had erred in taking into account changes that were not attributable to the marriage or the settlement. He concluded: "This is not a case, as in my view *Richardson* [reproduced below] is, where the poverty of the spouse results from the marriage."]

RICHARDSON v. RICHARDSON

(1987), 7 R.F.L. (3d) 304 (S.C.C.)

[The parties married in 1967 and separated in 1979. They had two children. The wife worked full-time until the birth of the second child in 1974. Apart from two jobs of very short duration in 1974 and 1976, the wife did not thereafter work outside the home. The husband was a sergeant in the police force. *Family Law Reform Act* proceedings were settled in 1981 with the assistance of legal advice by minutes of settlement. They provided that the spouses would share equally the repayment of a $20,000 debt to the wife's mother, that the husband would assume additional debts of about $10,000 accumulated during the marriage, and that the wife would release her interest, worth about $11,000, in the matrimonial home to the husband. The settlement also specified that the wife would have custody of one child and the husband the other and that the husband would pay spousal support of $175 per month for one year and child support of $300 per month. The written settlement stipulated that it was a final and conclusive settlement of all claims between the parties. Two years later, the wife commenced divorce proceedings. Now on welfare, she sought spousal support and increased child support. The trial judge did not increase the child support, but awarded spousal support of $500 per month and indexed the support to keep up with inflation. The Ontario Court of Appeal struck the spousal support award and the indexing clause, but increased child support to $500 per month. Justice Grange, speaking for a unanimous court, stated:

> The trial judge granted maintenance to the wife notwithstanding the minutes of settlement upon the grounds that there had been a change of circumstance entitling the wife to that allowance. We can see no change of circumstance in either the wife or the husband that would justify that allowance.
>
> It is possible that the parties contemplated when limiting the support for the wife to the one-year period that the wife would, during that period, not only seek, but obtain employment. Indeed there is some suggestion in the evidence of the husband that that was so. The difficulty with that assumption, however, is that when the solicitor for the wife was examined in the previous proceedings, he was not permitted to give the substance of his advice to the wife and consequently, we do not know whether or not that was her contemplation at the time.]

WILSON J. (DICKSON C.J.C., MCINTYRE, LAMER and LE DAIN JJ. concurring): — The issue in this case is when is it "fit and just" for a judge to make an order for spousal maintenance under s. 11(1) of the Divorce Act, R.S.C. 1970, c. D-8 in an amount different from that agreed upon by the parties in an antecedent settlement agreement. . . .

In approaching this case the court should have regard to the principles enunciated in *Pelech* v. *Pelech* . . . that a court should vary a settlement agreement only where there has been a radical change in the circumstances of a former spouse and that change is the result of a pattern of economic dependency generated by the marriage relationship. I appreciate that that principle was stated in the context of a s. 11(2) application and that this case involves s. 11(1). I appreciate also that the wording of the two subsections is different. Section 11(1) provides that the court may make the order it thinks fit and just having regard to the condition, means and other circumstances of the parties. Section 11(2) states that an order made under s. 11(1) may be varied if the court thinks it fit and just to do so having regard to any change in the conditions, means or other circumstances of the spouses. Nevertheless, in my view, despite the difference in the statutory language, when a court is confronted with a settlement agreement reached by the parties the same criteria should be applied under both sections. The underlying rationale is the same under both, namely 1) the importance of finality in the financial affairs of former spouses and 2) the principle of deference to the right and responsibility of individuals to make their own decisions. . . .

In my view, the only difference under the two subsections is that in a s. 11(1) application the change being considered will have occurred between the signing of the agreement and the application for the decree *nisi* whereas in the s. 11(2) application the change will have occurred between the granting of the decree *nisi* and the application for variation.

Given that the *Pelech* test is applicable in a s. 11(1) as well as a s. 11(2) application, the test is not met on the facts of this case. No event has occurred which the appellant is peculiarly unable to deal with because of a pattern of economic dependency generated by the marriage. At the time the separation agreement was concluded Mrs. Richardson was unemployed and Mr. Richardson was a sergeant in the Ottawa police force earning approximately $40,000 per annum. The same conditions existed when the divorce proceeding was heard. Not only had there been no change of circumstances, as the Ontario Court of Appeal found, but it was also questionable whether Mrs. Richardson's position at the time could be attributed to a pattern of economic dependency developed during the marriage. As has already been mentioned, Mrs. Richardson was married in 1967 and worked continuously as a clerk-typist until the birth of her second child in 1974. She worked for one month in 1974 and for three months in 1976. The couple separated in November 1979. In sum, she was employed more often than not during the marriage. Moreover, the period of time from her last employment until the date of separation was not that great. In this sense it cannot be said that the marriage atrophied her skills or impaired their marketability. . . .

Child maintenance, like access, is the right of the child: *Cartlidge* v. *Cartlidge*, [1973] 3 O.R. 801, 11 R.F.L. 384 (Prov. Ct.). For this reason, a spouse cannot barter away his or her child's right to support in a settlement agreement. The court is always free to intervene and determine the appropriate level of support for the child . . . Further, because it is the child's right, the fact that child support will indirectly benefit the spouse cannot decrease the quantum awarded to the child.

The obligation to provide spousal support arises from different bases and therefore has different characteristics. As discussed in *Pelech*, the courts in making an award of spousal maintenance are required to analyze the pattern of financial interdependence generated by each marriage relationship and devise a support order that minimizes as far as possible the economic consequences of the relationship's dissolution. Financial provision may be temporary or permanent. Spousal maintenance is the right of the spouse and a spouse can therefore contract as to the amount of maintenance he or she is to receive. Where this happens the court will be strongly inclined to enforce that contract: see *Pelech* v. *Pelech*.

Given these differences between spousal and child maintenance, if the court's concern is that the child is being inadequately provided for, then that concern should be addressed by varying the amount of child support. . . . Accordingly, in the circumstances of this case Mrs. Richardson's support payments should not be increased simply because she has custody of a child. The Court of Appeal adopted the proper route and increased the child support payments. This part of the order is not being contested.

Counsel for the appellant also relies on another ground of appeal. He argues that the parties in this case limited the period of spousal maintenance because it was their common expectation that Mrs. Richardson would be employed within that period of time. This expectation did not materialize and therefore the judge hearing the petition for divorce was free to make the order he considered "fit and just" without regard to the minutes of settlement entered into by the parties. Counsel argues, in effect, that the lost or failed expectation represents a change of circumstances from those anticipated by the parties justifying a departure from the settlement agreement under s. 11(1) of the Divorce Act. . . .

However, the evidence of the parties' expectation in this case is unclear. . . .

In the absence of evidence of a common expectation of the parties it seems to me that the minutes of settlement entered into by the parties freely and on the advice of independent legal counsel (which are not unconscionable in the substantive law sense) should be respected subject to the principle enunciated in *Pelech*. The possibility that Mrs. Richardson would not be employed at the end of the one-year period was not unforeseeable. Although she had clerk-typist skills she had not been recently employed. It is not as though Mrs. Richardson had been guaranteed a specific job and through a series of unexpected events that job fell through. . . .

Having regard to Mrs. Richardson's circumstances at the time of the agreement including her skills, her previous record of employment and the fact that no employment position had been guaranteed to her, it cannot be said that the possibility of her being unemployed was completely outside the reasonable contemplation of the parties. I do not believe therefore that Mrs. Richardson is entitled on that ground to be relieved from the clause in the minutes of settlement which provides for the cessation of her maintenance at the expiry of the one-year period.

[The appeal was dismissed, La Forest J. dissenting. In his dissent, La Forest J. held that the test enunciated in *Pelech* should not apply to s. 11(1) of the Divorce Act. Under s. 11(2) the judge was being asked to vary an order by which it had already been judicially determined that the agreement was fit and just. Therefore, the judge's authority was confined to considering circumstances that had since intervened. Under s. 11(1) the judge had to determine whether the support provision in the agreement was "fit and just". Although the existence of the agreement was an important fact to consider, the judge was not bound by it. La Forest J. stated (at 319): "To allow separation agreements the kind of compelling weight argued for in this case is effectively to rewrite the Act so as to provide that where such an agreement exists, the trial judge's discretion is solely to vary the agreement in those cases only where radical or . . . catastrophic changes have occurred since it was made." He pointed out that neither the *Divorce Act* nor the various provincial statutes adopted the proposition that separation agreements were to have binding force unless radical changes occurred.

Turning to the facts of the case, La Forest J. concluded (at 325) that Mrs. Richardson's present situation flowed directly from the division of functions during the marriage: "During the years she stayed home with the children, her skills would . . . not only have atrophied; she would not have been able to gain the new skills that are so necessary today in her field as well as in others. . . . Mrs. Richardson is now in her mid-forties and must find time and energy to care for a child, factors that are by no means negligible in assessing her competitive position as against younger people with recent training". These factors alone were sufficient to justify the trial judge's decision.]

NOTES AND QUESTIONS

1. The third case in the trilogy handed down on June 4, 1987 was *Caron* v. *Caron* (1987), 7 R.F.L. (3d) 274. In that case, the parties were married in 1964 and separated in 1978. Two years later, with the advice of independent legal counsel, they concluded a separation agreement that settled property matters and provided, in paragraph 3, for the payment of support to the wife until such time as she "shall remarry or cohabit as man and wife with any person for a continuous period of time in excess of ninety (90) days" (at 276). In paragraph 7, the agreement provided also that "[n]otwithstanding the terms of the preceding paragraphs . . . the quantum of monthly payments by the Husband to the Wife . . . may be varied" (at 277-278) by a court if the circumstances of the parties changed after the agreement was entered into. The essential parts of the agreement were incorporated into the decree *nisi* of divorce. After the divorce, the former wife cohabited with a man for more than three months and the former husband ceased the support payments. The former wife, who was forced to accept social assistance, applied for a variation of the decree *nisi* to provide for renewed support. The application was denied at trial and this judgment was affirmed by the appellate court. The Supreme Court of Canada unanimously dismissed the former wife's appeal. It concluded that paragraph 3 was valid and enforceable and had been properly invoked by the respondent. Despite the *non obstante* language in paragraph 7, this paragraph was viewed as limited to a power to vary quantum. It did not authorize reinstatement of support where the right to such support had been forfeited under paragraph 3.

The Supreme Court of Canada also held that the power to vary maintenance under s. 11(2) of the 1968 *Divorce Act* should not be exercised in this situation. Wilson J. (Dickson C.J.C., McIntyre, Lamer, and Le Dain JJ. concurring) stated (at 282):

> [T]he court's power to vary maintenance in a divorce decree is very limited where the provisions in the decree are the result of a negotiated settlement freely entered into by the parties on the advice of independent legal counsel. The approach of the courts is to respect such settlements wherever possible and to exercise their power of intervention under the Divorce Act only in the case of a radical change in circumstances related to a pattern of economic dependency of one party on the other generated by the marriage relationship: see *Pelech*. We have no evidence in this case of such a change in circumstances.

2. In *Richardson*, Wilson J. felt that it was questionable whether Mrs. Richardson's situation could be attributed to a pattern of economic dependency developed during the marriage. La Forest J. specifically disagreed. Which view is more convincing?

The trilogy caused a vigorous debate in the case law and the literature over whether these decisions dictated that a claimant for support had to prove, even in the absence of an agreement, that his or her present inability to achieve self-sufficiency was caused by a pattern of economic dependency generated by the relationship. See, generally, McLeod, "Annotation" (1987), 7 R.F.L. (3d) 226; Higginson, "Causal Connection: The Development of a Threshold Test for Entitlement to Spousal Support: A Commentary on *Willms* v. *Willms, Weppler* v. *Weppler* and *Brace* v. *Brace*" (1989), 4 C.F.L.Q. 107; Salhany, "Causal Connection — Is There a New Test for Spousal Support?" (1989), 5 C.F.L.Q. 151; McDermid, "The Causal Connection Conundrum" (1989), 5 C.F.L.Q. 107; and Rogerson, "The Causal Connection Test in Spousal Support Law" (1989), 8 Can. J. Fam. L. 95.

Professor McLeod's annotation to the trilogy, which is partially reproduced below, along with his other annotations in the Reports of Family Law, initially proved influential.

MCLEOD, "ANNOTATION"

(1987), 7 R.F.L. (3d) 226, at 232-233

. . . The reasons of Wilson J. in *Pelech*, *Richardson* and *Caron* confirm a basic support model. In order to obtain support, a claimant must prove:

(1) need;
(2) that the need arises for a legally acceptable reason; and
(3) that the need/inability is causally connected to the marriage. . . .

The reasons purport to spell out a support model which emphasizes the individualistic nature of the support obligation. People enter marriage as individuals and leave it as such. Following marriage breakdown, the parties should be free to make new lives for themselves without an ongoing contingent liability. Where a spouse is unable to relate his/her inability to achieve self-sufficiency to the marital relationship, there is no reason to burden the other spouse with the support obligation. Based on the support model postulated in *Pelech*, *Richardson* and *Caron*, support is not to be awarded to compensate for systemic gender-based inequality in the workplace or society. Rather, it is to be awarded to minimize the economic loss incurred by a spouse from the roles adopted in marriage. If a spouse cannot prove his/her income or job position has suffered as a result of the marital relationship, no support should be awarded. The mere fact that a spouse has become accustomed to a higher standard of living during marriage by access to income of the other spouse does not guarantee a continuation of such standard or ongoing access to such income following marriage breakdown. Where, through the roles adopted during marriage, one spouse has made a significant contribution to the career of the other which is not fully recognized by the distribution of marital property, the appropriate means of recognizing the contribution is by a compensatory allowance (*Magee* v. *Magee* (1987), 7 R.F.L. (3d) 453 (Ont. U.F.C.)), not the indefinite maintenance of the accustomed standard of living. The question in each case must be the effect of the economic dependence, if any, arising during marriage on a person's ability to fend for themselves [*sic*] following marriage breakdown. In a long-term marriage, where the wife has not worked outside the home, the dependency is likely to be total and indefinite support may be appropriate. Where, however, a spouse can, in spite of the role adopted in marriage, reasonably be expected to contribute to his/her reasonable needs, income should be attributed and the decision of whether he/she requires assistance be made on such income base.

The tenor of Wilson J.'s comments is that the fact of marriage, per se, should be a neutral factor. In itself it does not create a support entitlement. If the claimant has lost nothing from his/her income position because of the marriage, he/she should receive no support. Where the marriage has caused the claimant economic loss, the quantum of support should be fixed to minimize this loss. The starting point for quantum may well be the accustomed standard of living but, if the payor can show that the claimant would not likely have achieved such standard, the quantum should be adjusted.

"Causal connection" between the need for spousal support and the marriage became the focus in many cases. In the late 1980s, this approach often led to the limitation of spousal support. The trilogy was often used to justify a denial of support or a limitation on the amount of support or its duration. In *Winterle* v. *Winterle* (1987), 10 R.F.L. (3d) 129 (Ont. H.C.), Salhany L.J.S.C. denied support to a husband who suffered from severe depression and schizophrenia and was unable to maintain employment. The husband was unable to prove a causal connection between his need and the marriage. In *Bast* v. *Bast* (1988), 13 R.F.L. (3d) 98 (Ont. H.C.), the wife was awarded support for only a two-year period where she had managed to obtain a job paying $14,000 per year. Although Salhany L.J.S.C. explicitly found that "a period of 21 years outside the work force . . . created a causal connection between the marriage and her dependency" and that the wife would likely never achieve the standard of living she enjoyed during the marriage, he concluded that "an order for support in this case should attempt to promote self-sufficiency at the same time recognizing that Mrs. Bast will need some time to gear down from her former standard of living." In his annotation to the latter case, Professor McLeod stated ((1988), 13 R.F.L. (3d) 99, at 99):

> By acknowledging that absence from the work force to care for home and family can be a sufficient causal connection between an inability to find reasonable work and the marriage to justify support, Salhany L.J.S.C. should put to rest the fears that the notion of causal connection would deny relief to "traditional" spouses.

Professor Rogerson responded to this comment as follows in "The Causal Connection Test in Spousal Support Law" (1989), 8 Can. J. Fam. L. 95, at 126-127:

To the contrary, the decision raises fears about the application of the test because the causal link, while found, extends only to cover a two-year adjustment period. Long after the two years Mrs. Bast will continue to suffer the economic disadvantages of the marriage, absent an extraordinarily large property settlement.

In her article, Professor Rogerson concluded (at 104) that ''with respect to the underlying philosophy of modern support law, some version of the causal connection test makes sense.'' However, she continued (at 104):

> Given both our current legislation and the social context in which it operates, it makes sense to understand spousal support as a claim springing not from the fact of marriage per se but from the economic relationship which developed between spouses during a particular marriage. In a society which recognizes a right to divorce and to remarry and in which marriage is not a stable social institution we cannot impose, on the basis of marriage per se, a life-long obligation of providing for the economic security of former spouses. However, the version of the causal connection test that is currently being practised is being so seriously misapplied that the term causal connection is actually a misnomer, masking what the test is really about. Rather than recognizing and redressing the economic consequences which flow from marriage, the test is one which in practice effectively fails to see existing causal connections and which ignores the economic consequences which flow from the marriage. It arbitrarily severs the causal links which exist between the post-divorce economic hardship of former spouses and what went on during the marriage. In essence it has become a clean break or deemed self-sufficiency theory rather than a true causal connection theory. What is new about the causal connection test as it has emerged in the past two years is not the terminology or the idea — those have effectively been around for a long time — but the narrow restrictive understanding of what constitutes a causal connection.

In her review of the reported cases in ''Judicial Interpretations of the Spousal and Child Support Provisions of the Divorce Act, 1985 (Part I)'' (1991), 7 C.F.L.Q. 155, Professor Rogerson concluded (at 180) that courts were generally sympathetic toward older women leaving long, traditional marriages, applying the objective of self-sufficiency in a reasonable and realistic fashion. However, even in these cases, the support awards provided ''only a very modest standard of living, and in almost all cases one that is significantly below that enjoyed by their husbands'' (at 195). Professor Rogerson found (at 243) that the low-quantum of awards was also a problem in mid-length marriages where there were often still children at home. The focus in these cases was often on ''rehabilitative support'' and it was generally assumed that self-sufficiency would be achieved even though it might be only after a fairly lengthy period. Once full-time employment was achieved, the courts often concluded that self-sufficiency had been achieved and support was terminated. In these cases, the causal connection test was used to reinforce the theme of employment as self-sufficiency. Professor Rogerson stated (at 210) that ''courts use causal connection reasoning to conclude that a former wife's low income is attributable to causes outside of the marriage: either to the woman herself or to the labour market.''

Gradually, an increasing number of appellate cases began to reject the causal connection test as the sole basis for entitlement to support and also began to take a more sophisticated approach to the determination of economic disadvantages flowing from the marriage relationship. See, e.g., *Heinemann* v. *Heinemann* (1989), 20 R.F.L. (3d) 236 (N.S. C.A.); *Lynk* v. *Lynk* (1989), 21 R.F.L. (3d) 337 (N.S. C.A.); *Doncaster* v. *Doncaster* (1989), 21 R.F.L. (3d) 357 (Sask. C.A.); *Trainor* v. *Trainor* (1989), 23 R.F.L. (3d) 39 (Sask. C.A.); *Droit de la famille — 598*, [1989] R.D.F. 15 (Que. C.A.); *Linton* v. *Linton* (1990), 30 R.F.L. (3d) 1 (Ont. C.A.); and *Currie* v. *Currie* (1991), 32 R.F.L. (3d) 67 (P.E.I. C.A.). This trend was confirmed in the following significant Supreme Court of Canada decision.

MOGE v. MOGE

(1992), 43 R.F.L. (3d) 345 (S.C.C.)

[The parties were married in Poland in the mid-1950s and moved to Canada in 1960. They had three children. The wife had limited education and no special skills or training. She generally worked evenings, cleaning offices, to supplement her husband's income as a welder. On separation in 1973, the court awarded the wife custody and spousal and child support. In 1980, a court ordered the husband to continue paying $150 per month to support his wife and remaining dependent child. The wife was laid off from her job cleaning a hotel in 1987 and she failed to find new employment. On the wife's application, the court increased spousal support to $200 per month and child support to $200 per month. By then, the husband had remarried and was earning approximately $2,000 per month. The wife later resumed part-time work and in 1989 the husband, who was now earning about $2,200 per month obtained an order terminating the support. On appeal, the Manitoba Court of Appeal reinstated the spousal support at $150 per month. The husband appealed that decision. The wife did not appeal the quantum.]

L'HEUREUX-DUBE J. (LA FOREST, GONTHIER, CORY and IACOB-UCCI J.J. concurring): — At the heart of this appeal lies the question of spousal support [reported at (1990), 25 R.F.L. (3d) 396, 64 Man. R. (2d) 172, 70 D.L.R. (4th) 236 (C.A.), varying (1989), 60 Man. R. (2d) 281 (Q.B.)]. Specifically, the court is asked to determine the circumstances under which spousal support ought to be varied or terminated pursuant to s. 17 of the *Divorce Act*, R.S.C. 1985, c. 3 (2nd Supp.) (the "Act"). In a broader sense, however, this case turns upon the basic philosophy of support within the Act as a whole. . .

V. THE TRILOGY AND ITS JURISPRUDENCE

The position of Mr. Moge before this court is that his support obligation to his ex-wife should be terminated on the basis of the reasoning in the so-called "trilogy." He submits that though those cases specifically concerned situations in which the parties had set out their respective rights and obligations following the dissolution of the marriage by agreement, the court was advocating a model of support to be relied upon even in the absence of a final settlement.

That model, he says, is characterized by such notions as self-sufficiency and causal connection. Effectively, his position is that his ex-wife should have been self-sufficient by now and, if she is not, no link may be drawn between that lack of self-sufficiency and the marriage. In other words, her current financial position is no concern of his.

. . .

Early on, Professor J.G. McLeod expressed the view that the trilogy cases apply beyond their facts and espoused the model Mr. Moge asks this court to apply. . . .

With respect, I cannot agree. A careful reading of the trilogy in general, and *Pelech* in particular, indicates that the court has not espoused a new model of support under the Act. Rather, the court has shown respect for the wishes of persons who, in the presence of the statutory safeguards, decided to forgo litigation and settled their affairs by agreement under the 1970 *Divorce Act*. In other words, the court is paying deference to the freedom of individuals to contract. . . .

Professor Julien D. Payne, in my view, best identifies the flaws of the early interpretation of the trilogy in "Further Reflections on Spousal and Child Support After *Pelech, Caron* and *Richardson*" (1989) 20 R.G.D. 477, when he states, at p. 487:

> Professor McLeod's proposed extension of *Pelech, Caron* and *Richardson* to non-consensual situations and to provincial statutes as well as the new *Divorce Act, 1985*, virtually eliminates the significance of statutory criteria, whatever their form and substance, and at the same time closes the door to the wise exercise of judicial discretion that can accommodate a diverse range of economic variables on marriage breakdown or divorce.

> Notwithstanding the common law's recognition of a spousal agency of necessity, it must not be forgotten that current spousal support laws are of statutory origin. Furthermore, subject to over-riding constitutional doctrines, the sovereignty of Parliament . . . remains paramount. Judge-made law may explain, but cannot override, statute law.

In addition, there are diverse appellate rulings in Canada that endorse the view that the principles articulated in the trilogy should not be applied to non-consensual situations. . . .

In light of my reading of *Pelech*, I decline to accede to Mr. Moge's argument that this court has already determined the basis on which entitlement, or continuing entitlement, to spousal support rests in the absence of a settlement agreement intended by the parties to be final under the Act.

Since this case is not one which involves a final agreement entered into between the parties in order to settle the economic consequences of their divorce, I leave for another day the question of causal connection under the Act, which was discussed in the trilogy in the particular context of a final settlement under the 1970 *Divorce Act*.

The present appeal not only does not involve a final settlement agreement but deals specifically with a variation application following a support order at the time of divorce, a question to which I will now turn.

VI. SPOUSAL SUPPORT

(1) *The Act*

Although subss. (4) and (7) of s. 17 [now s. 17(4.1) and (7)] of the Act are the two subsections directly applicable to this appeal, s. 15(2), (4), (5), (6), and (7)[now s. 15.2(1), (3), (4), (5), and (6)], and s. 17(1), (3), (6), (8), and (10) [now s. 17(1), (3), (4.1), (6), and (10)] of the Act are also relevant to the analysis: . . .

(2) *Introduction*

Before dealing squarely with the main issue raised by this appeal, there are a number of preliminary observations that I wish to make.

The first has to do with the argument raised by Mr. Moge that, quite apart from the trilogy, the Act espouses a self-sufficiency model as the only basis of spousal support. . . . Mrs. Moge disagrees. She points out that self-sufficiency is only one of many objectives which the Act directs a court of competent jurisdiction to consider in exercising its discretion under ss. 17(4) and 17(7), and that even then, the objective of self-sufficiency in s. 17(7) is modified by such terminology as "in so far as practicable." She further submits that there is now appellate court jurisprudence which recognizes that in cases such as her own, self-sufficiency will not be practicable, largely due to the residual effects of being outside the labour market for a protracted period of time.

The self-sufficiency model advanced by Mr. Moge has generally been predicated on the dichotomy between "traditional" and "modern" marriages. Often, in order to draw the line after which no more support will be ordered, courts have distinguished between "traditional" marriages in which the wife remains at home and takes responsibility for the domestic aspects of marital life, and "modern" ones where employment outside the home is pursued. Perhaps in recognition that, as Judge Rosalie S. Abella (now J.A.) wrote in "Economic Adjustment On Marriage Breakdown: Support" (1981) 4 Fam. L. Rev. 1, at p. 4, "[i]t is hard to be an independent equal when one is not equally able to become independent," courts have frequently been more amenable to finding that "traditional" marriages survive the so-called "causal connection" test than "modern" ones.

The "traditional" versus "modern" dichotomy is apparent upon an examination of the current spate of decisions in the area and is perhaps best reflected in *Heinemann* v. *Heinemann* (1989), 20 R.F.L. (3d) 236 . . .(N.S. C.A.). Speaking for the court, Hart J.A. states, at pp. 272 and 274 [R.F.L.]:

> It would appear that the courts have recognized a substantial change in the nature of marriages and the roles played by the parties. At one end of the scale we have the traditional marriage where one spouse is the breadwinner and the other the child-rearer, often entitled to be supported for life. At the other end we have the type of marriage where both spouses participate in the economic advancement of the family unit and although one may be disadvantaged for a period of time during the marriage by deserting career opportunities, this can be balanced upon dissolution by provisions promoting the self-sufficiency of that spouse and thereafter both parties go their own ways. In between these two extremes we still find a variety of marital arrangements that must be fairly dealt with upon dissolution. . . .

> In my opinion, *a judge today in approaching a maintenance order should continue to recognize the distinction between the traditional and the modern marriage.* Upon dissolution of a modern marriage the goal should be the placing of both parties in a position of economic self-sufficiency at the earliest possible time. . . . Temporal limits on maintenance should be utilized to accomplish this end, and illness or other factors not related to the marriage should not be used to justify the continuation of maintenance which otherwise should cease. [Emphasis added.]

The case of *Messier* v. *Delage* . . . is also apposite here, as it demonstrates this court's recognition of the reasonable limitations in attaining self-sufficiency that may be encountered by a wife who has performed traditional roles in a marriage. . . .

As Proudfoot J.A. held in *Story* v. *Story* [(1989), 23 R.F.L. (3d) 225, at 245 (B.C. C.A.)]:

> There may be cases where self-sufficiency is never possible due to the age of the spouse at the marriage breakdown. It is often, in my opinion, totally unrealistic to expect that a 45- or 50-year-old spouse who has not been in the job market for many, many years to be retrained and to compete for employment in a job market where younger women have difficulty becoming employed. Employment and self-sufficiency are simply not achievable. In those cases, the obligation to support must surely be considered to be permanent. That obligation must flow from the marriage relationship and the expectations the parties had when they married.

. . .

The same philosophy, grounded on this dichotomy and causal connection, also inspires decisions to deny support. In *Oswell* v. *Oswell* (1990), 28 R.F.L. (3d) 10, 74 O.R. (2d) 15 (H.C.), Weiler J. (now J.A.) decided that, as the wife had already pursued academic opportunities and had attained economic self-sufficiency as a result, it could not be said that she was in a worse position because of the marriage.

See also *Grohmann* v. *Grohmann* (1991), 37 R.F.L. (3d) 73, 62 B.C.L.R. (2d) 264, 86 D.L.R. (4th) 741, 5 B.C.A.C. 277, 11 W.A.C. 277 (C.A.).

There are, however, many cases which do not fall easily into either category. These cases pose difficulties for courts which attempt to make assessments based on two clear stereotypes, especially when determining the question of self-sufficiency. Newbury J. of the British Columbia Supreme Court makes this point particularly well in *Patrick* v. *Patrick* (1991), 35 R.F.L. (3d) 382, 62 B.C.L.R. (2d) 188, at pp. 398-399 [R.F.L.]:

> One might conclude that the marriage in the case at bar is not a traditional one in that it lasted only 10 years, the parties are comparatively young and healthy and both are trained professionals. In applying the factors mandated by subs. 15(7) of the *Divorce Act*, however, it is clear that Mrs. Patrick will suffer an ongoing economic disadvantage as a result of the breakdown of the marriage, within the meaning of subpara. (*a*), and that the care of Vincent will entail financial consequences over and above those normally compensated by means of child support, within the meaning of subpara. (*b*). It is true that Mrs. Patrick has not, like the wives in *Brockie* and *Swift v. Swift*, supra, taken herself out of the job market for many years to devote herself to the marriage, or suffered some mental or physical illness that will seriously impede her independence. However, the evidence is clear that, as a result of the breakdown of the marriage and her continuing child-rearing role, she will be disadvantaged financially and professionally, both in comparison to her situation had the marriage continued and in comparison to her situation had no marriage occurred at all. In my view, it is a legitimate function of spousal support under subs. 15(7), and, indeed, it is expressly mandated by that provision, to compensate to some extent for that disadvantage and to require the non-custodial spouse to pay his fair share thereof.

> . . .

However, in other cases, support is denied or terminated because the dependent spouse is deemed to have an adequate income, despite substantial disparity in the standard of living enjoyed by the former spouses, or because the court is of the view that any financial problems suffered by a former spouse must be dealt with in the same manner as would a single person. (See *Seward* v. *Seward* (1988), 12 R.F.L. (3d) 54, 85 N.S.R. (2d) 30, 216 A.P.R. 30 (Fam. Ct.). . .). And, even in the event that the hurdle of entitlement, or continuing entitlement, is overcome, the level at which self-sufficiency is set often demonstrates unmitigated parsimony. In *Cymbalisty* v. *Cymbalisty* (1989), 56 Man. R. (2d) 28 (Q.B.), at p. 32, the court held as follows:

> The evidence indicates that the likelihood exists that Mrs. Cymbalisty will become employed with Statistics Canada on a full time basis at some point in the future. Full-time employment would provide the additional security of pension and other benefits. *Although I do not restrict any period of spousal support to the eventuality of full-time employment, or obtaining of a job which would yield roughly $20,000.00 per year gross income, however, achieving that level of self-sufficiency would seem to meet the requisite of the Divorce Act, 1985.* [Emphasis added.]

> . . .

Given the concerns I harbour about making a spouse's entitlement to support contingent upon the degree to which he or she is able to fit within a mythological stereotype . ., the distinction between "traditional" and "modern" marriages does not seem to me to be as useful as perhaps courts have indicated so far. While it may reflect flexibility on the part of courts and constitute an attempt to achieve fairness, I am of the view that there are much more sophisticated means which may be resorted to in order to achieve the objectives set out in the Act, a matter which I will deal with later in these reasons.

The second observation I wish to make is that, in determining spousal support, it is important not to lose sight of the fact that the support provisions of the Act are intended to deal with the *economic* consequences, for both parties, of the marriage or its breakdown. Marriage may unquestionably be a source of benefit to both parties that is not easily quantified in economic terms. Many believe that marriage and the family provide for the emotional, economic, and social well-being of its members. It may be the location of safety and comfort, and may be the place where its members have their most intimate human contact. Marriage and the family act as an emotional and economic support system as well as a forum of intimacy. In this regard, it serves vital personal interests, and may be linked to building a "comprehensive sense of personhood." Marriage and the family are a superb environment for raising and nurturing the young of our society by providing the initial environment for the development of social skills. These institutions also provide a means to pass on the values that we deem to be central to our sense of community.

Conversely, marriage and the family often require the sacrifice of personal priorities by both parties in the interests of shared goals. All of these elements are of undeniable importance in shaping the overall character of a marriage. Spousal support in the context of divorce, however, is not about the emotional and social benefits of marriage. Rather, the purpose of spousal support is to relieve *economic* hardship that results from "marriage or its breakdown." Whatever the respective advantages to the parties of a marriage in other areas, the focus of the enquiry when assessing spousal support after the marriage has ended must be the effect of the marriage in either impairing or improving each party's economic prospects.

This approach is consistent with both modern and traditional conceptions of marriage in as much as marriage is, among other things, an economic unit which generates financial benefits (see Mary Ann Glendon, *The New Family and the New Property* (Toronto: Butterworths, 1981)). The Act reflects the fact that in today's marital relationships, partners should expect and are entitled to share those financial benefits.

Equitable distribution can be achieved in many ways: by spousal and child support, by the division of property and assets, or by a combination of property and support entitlements. But in many, if not most, cases the absence of accumulated assets may require that one spouse pay support to the other in order to effect an equitable distribution of resources. This is precisely the case here, as the parties are not wealthy; for the most part, all they appear to possess are their respective incomes.

Fair distribution does not, however, mandate a minute, detailed accounting of time, energy, and dollars spent in the day-to-day life of the spouses, nor may it effect full compensation for the economic losses in every case. Rather, it involves the development of parameters with which to assess the respective advantages and disadvantages of the spouses as a result of their roles in the marriage, as the starting point in determining the degree of support to be awarded. This, in my view, is what the Act requires.

A third point worthy of emphasis is that this analysis applies equally to both spouses, depending on how the division of labour is exercised in a particular marriage. What the Act requires is a fair and equitable distribution of resources to alleviate the economic consequences of marriage or marriage breakdown for both spouses, regardless of gender. The reality, however, is that in many, if not most, marriages, the wife still remains the economically disadvantaged partner. There may be times where the reverse is true and the Act is equally able to accommodate this eventuality.

These caveats having been made, the question of spousal support which lies at the heart of this appeal must be dealt with first by examining the objectives of the Act.

(3) *The Objectives of the Act*

Parliament, subject always to overarching constitutional norms, may set down any principles it wishes to govern spousal support. The task, then, is to determine the principles embodied in ss. 15 and 17 of the Act, bearing in mind that those principles may in fact engage the courts in a different type of analysis than that required under the 1970 *Divorce Act* when considering the question of support.

The most significant change in the new Act, when compared to the 1970 *Divorce Act*, may be the shift away from the ''means and needs'' test as the exclusive criterion for support to a more encompassing set of factors and objectives which require courts to accommodate a much wider spectrum of considerations. This change, of course, does not signify that ''means and needs'' are to be ignored. Section 15(5) of the Act specifically states that ''the court shall take into consideration the condition, means, needs and other circumstances of each spouse.''

I fully agree with Professor Payne, who has commented on these objectives in *Payne on Divorce*, 2d ed. (Toronto: Butterworths, 1988), at p. 101, that:

> Judicial implementation of the newly defined policy objectives should, to some degree, result *in a shift from the narrow perspective of a 'needs' and 'capacity to pay' approach*, particularly in cases where one of the spouses has substantial means: see *Linton v. Linton* (1988), 11 R.F.L. (3d) 444 (Ont. S.C.) (Killeen L.J.S.C.) [now affirmed (1990), 1 O.R. (3d) 1 (C.A.)]. It may also have an impact on the types of orders that will be used to effectuate one or more of the applicable policy objectives. In this context, it should be observed that the four policy objectives defined in the *Divorce Act, 1985* are not necessarily independent of each other. They may overlap or they may operate independently, depending upon the circumstances of the particular case. *Legislative endorsement of four policy objectives manifests the realization that the economic variables of marriage breakdown and divorce do not lend themselves to the application of any single objective.* Long-term marriages that ultimately break down often leave in their wake a condition of financial dependence, because the wives have assumed the role of full-time homemakers. The legitimate objective(s) of spousal support in such a case will rarely coincide with the objective(s) that should be pursued with respect to short-term marriages. Childless marriages cannot be treated in the same way as marriages with dependent children. The two-income family cannot be equated with the one-income family. A 'clean break' accommodated by an order for a lump sum in lieu of periodic spousal support can often provide a workable and desirable solution for the wealthy, for the two-income family and for childless marriages of short duration. Rehabilitative support orders by way of periodic spousal support for a fixed term may be appropriate where there is a present incapacity to pay a lump sum and the dependent spouse can reasonably be expected to enter or re-enter the labour force within the foreseeable future. *Continuing periodic spousal support orders may provide the only practical solution for dependent spouses who cannot be reasonably expected to achieve economic self-sufficiency. There can be no fixed rules*, however, whereby particular types of orders are tied to the specific objective(s) sought to be achieved. In the final analysis, the court must determine the most appropriate kind(s) of order, having regard to the attendant circumstances of the case, including the present and prospective financial well-being of both the spouses and their dependent children. [Emphasis added.]

> . . .

All four of the objectives defined in the Act must be taken into account when spousal support is claimed or an order for spousal support is sought to be varied. No single objective is paramount. The fact that one of the objectives, such as economic self-sufficiency, has been attained does not necessarily dispose of the matter. . . .

Many proponents of the deemed self-sufficiency model effectively elevate it to the pre-eminent objective in determining the right to, quantum, and duration of spousal support. In my opinion, this approach is not consonant with proper principles of statutory interpretation. The objective of self-sufficiency is only one of several objectives enumerated in the section and, given the manner in which Parliament has set out those objectives, I see no indication that any one is to be given priority. Parliament, in my opinion, intended that support reflect the diverse dynamics of many unique marital relationships. . . .

It is also imperative to realize that the objective of self-sufficiency is tempered by the caveat that it is to be made a goal only "in so far as is practicable." This qualification militates against the kind of "sink or swim" stance upon which the deemed self-sufficiency model is premised. . . .

That Parliament could not have meant to institutionalize the ethos of deemed self-sufficiency is also apparent from an examination of the social context in which support orders are made. In Canada the feminization of poverty is an entrenched social phenomenon. Between 1971 and 1986 the percentage of poor women found among all women in this country more than doubled. During the same period the percentage of poor among all men climbed by 24 per cent. The results were such that by 1986, 16 per cent of all women in this country were considered poor . . .

Given the multiplicity of economic barriers women face in society, decline into poverty cannot be attributed entirely to the financial burdens arising from the dissolution of marriage . . . . However, there is no doubt that divorce and its economic effects are playing a role. . . .

In the federal Department of Justice (Bureau of Review), *Evaluation of the Divorce Act — Phase II: Monitoring and Evaluation* (Ottawa: 1990), it was found, based on client interviews, that, following divorce, 59 per cent of women and children surveyed fell below the poverty line, a figure that dropped to 46 per cent when support was included in the calculation of their incomes (see pp. 92-93). However, a more realistic picture, as it is not restricted to the more affluent segment of the divorcing public, is probably revealed by an analysis of court files, which determined that in 1988, overall two thirds of divorced women had total incomes which placed them below the poverty line. When support was excluded, 74 per cent of divorced women fell below the poverty line (see pp. 94-95). It is apparent that support payments, even assuming they are paid, are making only a marginal contribution to reducing economic hardship among women following divorce. In contrast, a previous study released in 1986, *Evaluation of the Divorce Act — Phase I: Monitoring and Evaluation*, found that only 10 per cent of men were below the poverty line after paying support, and the average income was $13,500 above the poverty line in such one-person households after the payment of support.

. . .

Findings in the Report of the Social Assistance Review Committee, *Transitions* (Toronto: Ministry of Community and Social Services, 1988), show that support can be a significant factor in alleviating some of these negative economic effects. The report notes that recipients of social assistance who receive support payments are more likely to leave the program than those who do not, and that the length of time a recipient receives social assistance is inversely proportional to the total amount of support received. At p. 44, the report states:

The nearly 50% of single parents receiving [family benefit allowance] who receive no support payments at all averaged between 3.5 and 4 years in the program. The 11% receiving between $10 and $100 per month averaged 2.5 to 3 years, while those receiving between $100 and $200 per month averaged 2 to 2.5 years. Finally, the mere 6% receiving in excess of $200 per month averaged less than 2 years in the program.

These socio-economic observations, in my view, support the objectives set out in the Act in as much as they provide background information useful in determining the intent of the legislators should that intent ever be in doubt. . . .

It would be perverse in the extreme to assume that Parliament's intention in enacting the Act was to financially penalize women in this country. And, while it would undeniably be simplistic to identify the deemed self-sufficiency model of spousal support as the sole cause of the female decline into poverty, based on the review of the jurisprudence and statistical data set out in these reasons, it is clear that the model has disenfranchised many women in the courtroom and countless others who may simply have decided not to request support in anticipation of their remote chances of success. The theory, therefore, at a minimum, is contributing to the problem. I am in agreement with Professor Bailey, [*"Pelech, Caron,* and *Rich-ardson"* (1989-90), 3 C.J.W.L. 615, at 633], that:

> The test is being applied to create a clean break between the spouses before the conditions of self-sufficiency for the dependent partner have been met, *and will undoubtedly cause an increase in the widespread poverty (at least relative poverty) of women and children of failed unions.* [Emphasis added.]

In the result, I am respectfully of the view that the support model of self-sufficiency which Mr. Moge urges the court to apply, cannot be supported as a matter of statutory interpretation, considering, in particular, the diversity of objectives set out in the Act.

(4) *Doctrine and Jurisprudence*

A burgeoning body of doctrine and, to some extent, jurisprudence is developing both abroad as well as in Canada which expresses dissatisfaction with the current norms along which entitlement to spousal support is assessed. This body of doctrine, in particular, proposes, instead, a scheme based on principles of compensation. . . .

In Canada a major proponent of compensatory spousal support has been Professor Rogerson (see "The Causal Connection Test in Spousal Support Law" (1989) 8 Can. J. Fam. L. 95, and "Judicial Interpretation of the Spousal and Child Support Provisions of the *Divorce Act, 1985* (Part I)"), but the principles of compensatory support and their underpinnings have found favour among such other scholars and practitioners as Davies, ["Judicial Interpretation of the Support Provisions of the *Divorce Act, 1985*" (1992), 8 C.F.L.Q. 265, at pp. 270ff.]; Miriam Grassby ("Women in Their Forties: The Extent of Their Rights to Alimentary Support" (1991) 30 R.F.L. (3d) 369); Pask and McCall; Payne ("Further Reflections on Spousal and Child Support After *Pelech, Caron* and *Richardson*," at pp. 493ff); and, Proudfoot and Jewell, ["Restricting Application of the Causal Connection Test: *Story* v. *Story*" (1990), 9 Can. J. Fam. L. 143, at 151].

The theory, however, is not new, as is evident from the Law Reform Commission Working Papers and Report, 1972-1976. Antecedents of the compensatory spousal support model may be found in portions of the Law Reform Commission of Canada's Working Paper 12, *Maintenance on Divorce* (Ottawa: Information Canada, 1975). The commission recommended, inter alia, that the mere fact of marriage not create a right of maintenance and that the economic disabilities incurred due to marriage and the eventuality of children be compensated. . . .

Legislative support for the principles of compensation may be found in ss. 15(7)(a)-(c) and 17(7)(a)-(c), which are extremely broad in scope and which direct the court, in making or varying a support order, to recognize any economic advantages or disadvantages arising from the marriage or its breakdown, to apportion between the spouses any financial consequences arising from the care of children over and above those consequences which have already been made the subject of child support, and to relieve economic hardships arising from the marriage. As a matter of statutory interpretation, it is precisely the manner in which compensatory spousal support is able to respond to the diversity of objectives the Act contains that makes it superior to the strict self-sufficiency model.

Although the promotion of self-sufficiency remains relevant under this view of spousal support, it does not deserve unwarranted pre-eminence. After divorce, spouses would still have an obligation to contribute to their own support in a manner commensurate with their abilities. (Rogerson, ''Judicial Interpretation of the Spousal and Child Support Provisions of the *Divorce Act, 1985* (Part I),'' at p. 171.) In cases where relatively few advantages have been conferred or disadvantages incurred, transitional support allowing for full and unimpaired reintegration back into the labour force might be all that is required to afford sufficient compensation. However, in many cases a former spouse will continue to suffer the economic disadvantages of the marriage and its dissolution while the other spouse reaps its economic advantages. In such cases, compensatory spousal support would require long-term support or an alternative settlement which provides an equivalent degree of assistance in light of all of the objectives of the Act . . .

Women have tended to suffer economic disadvantages and hardships from marriage or its breakdown because of the traditional division of labour within that institution. Historically, or at least in recent history, the contributions made by women to the marital partnership were non-monetary and came in the form of work at home, such as taking care of the household, raising children, and so on. Today, though more and more women are working outside the home, such employment continues to play a secondary role and sacrifices continue to be made for the sake of domestic considerations. These sacrifices often impair the ability of the partner who makes them (usually the wife) to maximize her earning potential because she may tend to forgo educational and career advancement opportunities. These same sacrifices may also enhance the earning potential of the other spouse (usually the husband), who, because his wife is tending to such matters, is free to pursue economic goals. This eventually may result in inequities. . . . Hence, while the union survives, such division of labour, at least from an economic perspective, may be unobjectionable if such an arrangement reflects the wishes of the parties. However, once the marriage dissolves, the kinds of non-monetary contributions made by the wife may result in significant market disabilities. The sacrifices she has made at home catch up with her and the balance shifts in favour of the husband who has remained in the workforce and focused his attention outside the home. In effect, she is left with a diminished earning capacity and may have conferred upon her husband an embellished one.

The curtailment of outside employment obviously has a significant impact on future earning capacity. According to some studies, the earning capacity of a woman who stays at home atrophies by 1.5 per cent for each year she is out of the labour force. . . . Richard Kerr's *An Economic Model to Assist in the Determination of Spousal Support* (Ottawa: Paper prepared for the Department of Justice and Status of Women Canada, 1992), came to a similar conclusion. He posits that ''[f]or women whose labour force interruptions have lasted for 10 years or longer, the cumulative present value of post re-entry earning losses will typically exceed $80,000,'' over and above any loss incurred during the interruption itself. The figure is relative to women who have not interrupted their careers in such a fashion. He adds that ''[e]ven labour force interruptions lasting as little as two years can have significant long-term costs in terms of lost earnings ($30,000 or more)'' (p. 1). Labour force inter-ruptions are common and this accentuates the need for compensation. One Statistics Canada report, *Family History Survey: Preliminary Findings* [by Thomas K. Burch] (Ottawa: Minister of Supply and Services Canada, 1985), notes that 64 per cent of Canadian women report suffering working interruptions because of parenting or domestic responsibilities. The figure for men was less than 1 per cent (p. 26). The studies, while remaining untested, do illustrate the problems faced by women who re-enter the labour force after a period during which they stay at home to care for the family.

Often difficulties are exacerbated by the enduring responsibility for children of the marriage. The spouse who has made economic sacrifices in the marriage also generally becomes the custodial parent, as custody is awarded to the wife 75 per cent of the time, to both parents jointly in 13 per cent of cases, and to the husband alone in less than 8 per cent of divorces (see *Evaluation of the Divorce Act — Phase II: Monitoring and Evaluation*, at p. 101). The diminished earning capacity with which an ex-wife enters the labour force after years of reduced or non-participation will be even more difficult to overcome when economic choice is reduced, unlike that of her ex-husband, due to the necessity of remaining within proximity of schools, not working late, remaining at home when the child is ill, etc. The other spouse encounters none of these impediments and is generally free to live virtually wherever he wants and work whenever he wants.

The doctrine of equitable sharing of the economic consequences of marriage or marriage breakdown upon its dissolution, which, in my view, the Act promotes, seeks to recognize and account for both the economic disadvantages incurred by the spouse who makes such sacrifices and the economic advantages conferred upon the other spouse. Significantly, it recognizes that work within the home has undeniable value and transforms the notion of equality from the rhetorical status to which it was relegated under a deemed self-sufficiency model, to a substantive imperative. Insofar as economic circumstances permit, the Act seeks to put the remainder of the family in as close a position as possible to the household before the marriage breakdown.
. . .

The equitable sharing of the economic consequences of marriage or marriage breakdown, however, is not a general tool of redistribution which is activated by the mere fact of marriage. Nor ought it to be. It is now uncontentious in our law and accepted by both the majority and the minority in *Messier* v. *Delage*, supra, at pp. 416-417 [S.C.R.], that marriage per se does not automatically entitle a spouse to support. Presumably, there will be the occasional marriage where both spouses maximize their earning potential by working outside the home, pursuing economic and educational opportunities in a similar manner, dividing up the domestic labour identically, and either making no economic sacrifices for the other or, more likely, making them equally. In such a utopian scenario there might be no apparent call for compensation. The spouses are able to make a clean break and continue on with their respective lives. Such cases would appear to be rare. In most marriages in which both partners make economic sacrifices and share domestic responsibilities, or where one spouse has suffered economic losses in order to enable the other spouse to further a career, their roles should be considered in the spousal support order.

The Act refers to economic advantages and disadvantages flowing from marriage or *its breakdown*. . . . Sections 15(7)(*a*) and 17(7)(*a*) of the Act are expressly compensatory in character while ss. 15(7)(*c*) and 17(7)(*c*) may not be characterized as exclusively compensatory. These latter paragraphs may embrace the notion that the primary burden of spousal support should fall on family members, *not* the state. In my view, an equitable sharing of the economic consequences of divorce does not exclude other considerations, particularly when dealing with sick or disabled spouses. While the losses or disadvantages flowing from the marriage in such cases may seem minimal in the view of some, the effect of its breakdown will not, and support will still be in order in most cases. We must recognize, however, . . . that family law can play only a limited role in alleviating the economic consequences of marriage breakdown. M.T. Meulders-Klein has eloquently stressed the necessity to understand the complex relationships between the family, work, and state which result in poverty and dependence in some of its members. She recognizes that the ultimate solutions will require adjustments in all of these areas (Meulders-Klein, "Famille, état et sécurité économique d'existence dans la tourmente," in M.T. Meulders-Klein and J. Eekelaar, eds., *Family, State and Individual Economic Security*, vol. II (Brussels: E. Story Scientia, 1988), at p. 1077).

As economic consequences have to be shared in an equitable manner by both partners, it is my view that the Act, while envisaging compensation for the economic advantages and disadvantages of marriage or marriage breakdown, does not necessarily put the entire burden of such compensation on the shoulders of only one party. I stress here that in the discussion of spousal support one must not lose sight of the fact that the real dilemma in most cases relates to the ability to pay of the debtor spouse and the limits of support orders in achieving fair compensation and alleviating the economic burdens of the disadvantaged spouse. While the disadvantages of the kind I mention hereunder are compensable, though not necessarily automatically or fully compensated in every case, the ultimate goal is to alleviate the disadvantaged spouse's economic losses as completely as possible, taking into account all the circumstances of the parties, including the advantages conferred on the other spouse during the marriage.

The four objectives set out in the Act can be viewed as an attempt to achieve an equitable sharing of the economic consequences of marriage or marriage breakdown. At the end of the day, however, courts have an overriding discretion and the exercise of such discretion will depend on the particular facts of each case, having regard to the factors and objectives designated in the Act.

(5) *The Exercise of Judicial Discretion*

The exercise of judicial discretion in ordering support requires an examination of all four objectives set out in the Act in order to achieve equitable sharing of the economic consequences of marriage or marriage breakdown. This implies a broad approach with a view to recognizing and incorporating any significant features of the marriage or its termination which adversely affect the economic prospects of the disadvantaged spouse. Not all such elements will be equally important, even if present, to the awarding of support in each case. However, it may be useful to canvass some of the most common compensable advantages and recognized disadvantages which the Act envisages. They are not to be taken as exhaustive but only as examples of some of the losses and gains one spouse, usually the wife, incurs and confers which may be useful for the courts to consider in the exercise of their discretion.

The financial consequences of the end of a marriage extend beyond the simple loss of future earning power or losses directly related to the care of children. They will often encompass loss of seniority, missed promotions, and lack of access to fringe benefits, such as pension plans, life, disability, dental, and health insurance (see Heather Joshi and Hugh Davies, "Pensions, Divorce and Wives' Double Burden" (1992) 6 Int'l J. L. & Fam. 289). As persons outside of the workforce cannot take advantage of job retraining and the upgrading of skills provided by employers, one serious economic consequence of remaining out of the workforce is that the value of education and job training often decreases with each year in comparison to those who remain active in the workforce and may even become redundant after several years of non-use. All of these factors contribute to the inability of a person not in the labour force to develop economic security for retirement in his or her later years.

The most significant economic consequence of marriage or marriage breakdown, however, usually arises from the birth of children. This generally requires that the wife cut back on her paid labour force participation in order to care for the children, an arrangement which jeopardizes her ability to ensure her own income security and independent economic well-being. In such situations, spousal support may be a way to compensate such economic disadvantage.

If child-care responsibilities continue past the dissolution of the marriage, the existing disadvantages continue, only to be exacerbated by the need to accommodate and integrate those demands with the requirements of paid employment. In that regard, I adopt without reservation the words of Bowman J. in *Brockie* v. *Brockie* (1987), 5 R.F.L. (3d) 440 [reproduced later in this chapter]. . . .

It is important to note that families need not fall strictly within a particular marriage model in order for one spouse to suffer disadvantages. For example, even in childless marriages, couples may also decide that one spouse will remain at home. Any economic disadvantage to that spouse flowing from that shared decision in the interest of the family should be regarded as compensable. Conversely, the parties may decide or circumstances may require that both spouses work full time. This in and of itself may not necessarily preclude compensation if, in the interest of the family or due to child-care responsibilities, one spouse declines a promotion, refuses a transfer, leaves a position to allow the other spouse to take advantage of an opportunity for advancement, or otherwise curtails employment opportunities and thereby incurs economic loss. Such a situation occurred in *Heinemann* v. *Heinemann*, supra, where the court recognized that, despite the fact that the wife had worked full time for nearly the entire duration of the marriage, she had forgone her own career aspirations in the interest of the family. The family had made three major moves occasioned by advancements in the husband's career. This caused a lack of continuity to the wife's career and, in the result, the wife had no seniority, had obtained no promotions in her original career, and would have returned to it "at the bottom of the pile," thus obviously disadvantaged in comparison to her husband.

A spouse may contribute to the operation of a business, typically through the provision of secretarial, entertainment, or book-keeping services, or may take on increased domestic and financial responsibilities that enable the other to pursue licences, degrees, or other training and education. (See Nicholas Bala, "Recognizing Spousal Contributions to the Acquisition of Degrees, Licences and Other Career Assets: Towards Compensatory Support" (1989) 8 Can. J. Fam. L. 23; Joan M.

Krauskopf, "Recompense for Financing Spouse's Education: Legal Protection for the Marital Investor in Human Capital" (1980) 28 Kan. L. Rev. 379; and Payne, "Management of a Family Law File with Particular Regard to Spousal Support on Divorce," at pp. 441-442). To the extent that these activities have not already been compensated for pursuant to the division of assets, they are factors that should be considered in granting spousal support.

Although the doctrine of spousal support which focuses on equitable sharing does not guarantee to either party the standard of living enjoyed during the marriage, this standard is far from irrelevant to support entitlement (see *Mullin* v. *Mullin* (1991), supra, and *Linton* v. *Linton*, supra). Furthermore, great disparities in the standard of living that would be experienced by spouses in the absence of support are often a revealing indication of the economic disadvantages inherent in the role assumed by one party. As marriage should be regarded as a joint endeavour, the longer the relationship endures, the closer the economic union, the greater will be the presumptive claim to equal standards of living upon its dissolution (see Rogerson, "Judicial Interpretation of the Spousal and Child Support Provisions of the *Divorce Act, 1985* (Part I)," at pp. 174-175).

In short, in the proper exercise of their discretion, courts must be alert to a wide variety of factors and decisions made in the family interest during the marriage which have the effect of disadvantaging one spouse or benefiting the other upon its dissolution. In my view, this is what the Act mandates, no more, no less.

Such determination demands a complex and, in many cases, a difficult analysis. The same, of course, might be said of the evaluation of damages in contract or in tort. However, this complexity does not excuse judges from hearing relevant evidence or from fully applying the law. There are no easy recipes, nor are there neat compartments on which to rely, as families and family relationships are not simple. But there are few matters more important before the courts, given the repercussions on the future of the parties themselves and, in particular, their children.

. . .

Given the principles outlined above, spousal support orders remain essentially a function of the evidence led in each particular case. In some cases such evidence might come in the form of highly specific expert evidence which enables parties to present an accurate picture of the economic consequences of marriage breakdown in their particular circumstances. (See *Ormerod* v. *Ormerod* (1990), 27 R.F.L. (3d) 225 (Ont. U.F.C.), and *Elliot* v. *Elliot* (August 4, 1992), Doc. Hamilton-Wentworth V-178/91 (Ont. U.F.C.), [1992] O.J. No. 1665 (QL Systems) [reported at 42 R.F.L. (3d) 7, 95 D.L.R. (4th) 614].) Although of great assistance in assessing the economic consequences of marriage breakdown in a particular marriage, such evidence will not be required, nor will it be possible, in most cases. For most divorcing couples, both the cost of obtaining such evidence and the amount of assets involved are practical considerations which would prohibit or at least discourage its use. Therefore, to require expert evidence as a sine qua non to the recovery of compensation would not be practical for many parties, not to mention the use of court time which might be involved. It would be my hope, therefore, that different alternatives be examined.

One proposal put forth by Professor Rogerson would be for Parliament to consider enacting a set of legislative guidelines. . . .

One possible disadvantage of such a solution lies in the risk that it may impose a strait-jacket which precludes the accommodation of the many economic variables susceptible to be encountered in spousal support litigation.

Another alternative might lie in the doctrine of judicial notice. The doctrine itself grew from a need to promote efficiency in the litigation process and may very well be applicable to spousal support. . . .

Based upon the studies which I have cited earlier in these reasons, the general economic impact of divorce on women is a phenomenon, the existence of which cannot reasonably be questioned and should be amenable to judicial notice. More extensive social science data are also appearing. Such studies are beginning to provide reasonable assessments of some of the disadvantages incurred and advantages conferred post-divorce (see, for example, the study by Kerr). While qualification will remain difficult and fact-related in each particular case, judicial notice should be taken of such studies, subject to other expert evidence which may bear on them, as background information at the very least. . . .

In all events, whether judicial notice of the circumstances generally encountered by spouses at the dissolution of a marriage is to be a formal part of the trial process or whether such circumstances merely provide the necessary background information, it is important that judges be aware of the social reality in which support decisions are experienced when engaging in the examination of the objectives of the Act. . . .

VII. APPLICATION TO THE CASE AT BAR

Since this appeal involves an application for a variation order, here an order for the termination of support by Mr. Moge to Mrs. Moge, s. 17(4) of the Act applies.

As a necessary preliminary condition to making such an order, s. 17(4) of the Act requires that the court be satisfied that "there has been a change in the condition, means, needs or other circumstances of either former spouse . . . for whom support is or was sought occurring since the making of the support order or the last variation order made in respect of that order."

That there has been a change in the circumstances of the parties since the last support order was not seriously contested and I agree with both the trial judge and the Court of Appeal that the threshold requirements of s. 17(4) of the Act are satisfied.

The sole remaining consideration is whether the application of Mr. Moge to terminate support ought to have been granted in this case. In my view, it should not have, and the majority of the Court of Appeal was right in finding an error of principle on the part of the trial judge. I agree with Twaddle J.A., supra, at p. 177 [Man. R., p. 403 R.F.L.]:

> [E]ven if some degree of economic self-sufficiency is practicable, the level at which the wife can become self-sufficient may be lower than the husband's level of self-sufficiency. This disadvantage will often be attributable to the marriage. In such a case, the court will best meet the objectives prescribed by Parliament by supplementing the wife's earning ability with some maintenance. It would be contrary to those objectives to foreclose a traditional wife from all maintenance.

> In the case at bar, the learned judge in Motions Court did just that. In the passage from his reasons which I have quoted, he makes it clear that, in his view, this wife should have achieved total financial independence. With the greatest of respect to him, I think that is an error in principle. He failed to consider the disparity between the earning ability of each former spouse: he failed to have regard to the fact that the wife, having married in a traditional arrangement, was disadvantaged by it.

The four objectives of spousal support orders under s. 17(7) of the Act, as explicated above and applied by the Court of Appeal, are met in this case. For this reason, the following specific findings are in order based on the evidence in the record:

1. Mrs. Moge has sustained a substantial economic disadvantage ''from the marriage or its breakdown'' within the meaning of s. 17(7)(*a*) of the Act.
2. Mrs. Moge's long-term responsibility for the upbringing of the children of the marriage after the spousal separation in 1973 had had an impact on her ability to earn an income so as to trigger the application of s. 17(7)(*b*) of the Act.
3. Mrs. Moge continues to suffer economic hardship as a result of the ''breakdown of the marriage'' within the meaning of s. 17(7)(*c*) of the Act.
4. Mrs. Moge has failed to become economically self-sufficient notwithstanding her conscientious efforts.

These findings are irrefutable even in the absence of expert evidence relating to the appropriate quantification of spousal support. It follows that in view of all of the objectives of spousal support orders set out in s. 17(7) of the Act, continuing support is in order in this case. Accordingly, there was no error in the Court of Appeal. . . .

MCLACHLIN J. (concurring) (GONTHIER J. concurring): — I have read the reasons of L'Heureux-Dubé J. and would dispose of the appeal as she proposes. I wish to add, however, the following comments.

It seems to me important to emphasize that this is, first and last, a case of statutory interpretation. It is interesting and useful to consider how different theories of support yield different answers to the question of how support should be determined. However, in the end the judge must return to what Parliament has said on the subject. Parliament has enacted that judges considering applications for variation of support consider four different factors [set out in s. 17(7)]. . . .

The first thing the judge must consider are ''economic advantages or disadvantages . . . arising from the marriage or its breakdown.'' This heading brings in many of the considerations which my colleague discusses. It clearly permits the judge to compensate one spouse for sacrifices and contributions made during the marriage and benefits which the other spouse has received.

The second factor which the judge must consider is the ''apportionment'' of the ''financial consequences'' of the care of children. This heading also raises compensatory considerations. If a spouse, either before or after separation, has or continues to incur financial disadvantage as a result of caring for a child of the marriage, he or she should be compensated.

The third thing which the judge's order should do is grant relief from any economic hardship arising from the breakdown of the marriage. The focus here, it seems to me, is not on compensation for what the spouses have contributed to or gained from the marriage. The focus is rather post-marital need; if the breakdown of the marriage has created economic hardship for one or the other, the judge must attempt to grant relief from that hardship.

Finally, the judge's order must ''in so far as practicable'' promote the economic self-sufficiency of each former spouse within a reasonable period of time. This subhead raises the question of the degree to which ex-spouses should be expected to become self-sufficient, a contested point on this appeal. Several things about this subhead should be noted. First, unlike the first three factors, this one is stated in qualified language, beginning with the conditional phrase ''in so far as practicable.'' Second, economic self-sufficiency is not to be required or assumed; the verb used is "promote." By this language Parliament recognizes that actual self-sufficiency, while desirable, may not be possible or "practicable."

Considering the factors together, the judge's task under s. 17(7) of the statute is to make an order which provides compensation for marital contributions and sacrifices, which takes into account financial consequences of looking after children of the marriage, which relieves against need induced by the separation, and, to the extent it may be "practicable," promotes the economic self-sufficiency of each spouse. Neither a "compensation model" nor a "self-sufficiency model" captures the full content of the section, though both may be relevant to the judge's decision. The judge must base her decision on a number of factors: compensation, child care, post-separation need, and the goal, insofar as practicable, of promoting self-sufficiency.

The need to consider all four factors set out in s. 17(7) rules out the strict self-sufficiency model which Mr. Moge urged upon this court. The trial judge erred, in my respectful opinion, in giving no weight to the first three factors of s. 17(7) and in imposing a categorical requirement of self-sufficiency.

The majority of the Court of Appeal correctly rejected the view that there is an absolute obligation for a spouse to become self-sufficient and that there is a time after which one spouse should no longer have to support another. They placed considerable emphasis on the need to compensate Mrs. Moge for her contributions as homemaker and mother during the course of the marriage, and the permanent economic disadvantage she suffered as a consequence. . . . Having concluded that Mrs. Moge's earning potential had been diminished in this way by her contribution to the marriage, the Court of Appeal found she was entitled to an order of maintenance to supplement her own income. This conclusion represented a proper application of s. 17(7) of the *Divorce Act*, and I would dismiss the appeal from its decision.

This is sufficient to dispose of the appeal. However, I would like to add certain comments on the subjects of causation and evidence in connection with s. 17(7) of the *Divorce Act*.

I turn first to causation. Two of the subheads of s. 17(7) raise the requirement of causation by the marriage or its breakdown. Section 17(7)(a) speaks of advantages and disadvantages "arising" from the marriage or its breakdown. Section 17(7)(c) speaks of economic hardship "arising" from the breakdown of the marriage.

Parties sometimes argue that the economic disadvantage of their spouse was not caused by the marriage or its breakdown, or that her economic hardship was not caused by the termination of the marriage. Shades of these arguments surfaced in this case. It was said that Mrs. Moge voluntarily elected to be the primary homemaker and caregiver, that it was her choice and not the marriage that caused the resultant economic disadvantage. Similarly, it was suggested that her present need and lack of self-sufficiency was not the product of the marriage but of her failure to choose to upgrade her education so she could earn more money.

A formalistic view of causation can work injustice in the context of s. 17(7), as elsewhere. The question under s. 17(7)(a) is whether a party was disadvantaged or gained advantages from the marriage, as a matter of fact; under s. 17(7)(c), whether the marriage breakdown in fact led to economic hardship for one of the spouses. Hypothetical arguments after the fact about different choices people could have made which might have produced different results are irrelevant, unless the parties acted unreasonably or unfairly. In this case, for example, Mrs. Moge, in keeping with the prevailing social expectation of the times, accepted primary responsibility for the home and the children and confined her extra activities to supplementing the family income rather than to getting a better education or to furthering her career.

That was the actual domestic arrangement which prevailed. What Mrs. Moge might have done in a different arrangement with different social and domestic expectations is irrelevant.

Similarly, in determining whether economic hardship of a spouse arises from the breakdown of the marriage, the starting point should be a comparison of the spouse's actual situation before and after the breakdown. If the economic hardship arose shortly after the marriage breakdown, that may be a strong indication that it is caused by the family breakdown. Arguments that an ex-spouse should be doing more for herself must be considered in light of her background and abilities, physical and psychological. It may be unreasonable to expect a middle-aged person who has devoted most of her life to domestic concerns within the marriage to compete for scarce jobs with youthful college graduates, for example. Even women who have worked outside the home during the marriage may find that their career advancement has been permanently reduced by the effort which they devoted to home and family instead of their jobs, whether the woman be a janitor like Mrs. Moge or a well-trained professional. Sometimes the breakdown of the marriage may have left the woman with feelings of inadequacy or depression, which make it difficult for her to do more. In short, the whole context of her conduct must be considered. It is not enough to say in the abstract that the ex-spouse should have done more or be doing more, and argue from this that it is her inaction rather than the breakup of the marriage which is the cause of her economic hardship. One must look at the actual society and personal reality of the situation in which she finds herself and judge the matter fairly from that perspective.

What is required under s. 17(7) of the *Divorce Act* is a common-sense, non-technical view of causation . .

This leaves the question of evidence. I agree with my colleague that evidence of the spouses' respective contributions and gains from the marriage is necessary under s. 17(7)(*a*). I do not think the evidence need be detailed, in the sense of a year-by-year chronology of sacrifices and gains. This is not an exercise in accounting, requiring an exact tally of debits and credits for each day of the marriage. It is beyond the means of most parties and our overburdened justice system to devote weeks of lawyers' and experts' time to providing such a tally. Nor do I think it necessary. It is clear that certain things must be done to maintain a family. Income must be earned. Food must be bought and prepared. Children must be cared for. And so on. In most cases it will suffice if the parties tell the judge in a general way what each did. That will allow the judge very quickly to get an accurate picture of the sacrifices, contributions, and advantages relevant to determining compensation under s. 17(7)(*a*), making detailed qualification and expert evidence unnecessary. Poverty is one of the main problems arising from marital breakdown; it should not be made worse by long and expensive legal proceedings.

I would dismiss the appeal and dispose of costs in the manner which my colleague has ordered.

Appeal dismissed.

BALA, "SPOUSAL SUPPORT LAW TRANSFORMED — FAIRER TREAT-MENT FOR WOMEN"

(1994), 11 C.F.L.Q. 13 (Edited footnotes follow.)

1.   INTRODUCTION

The December 1992 decision of the Supreme Court of Canada in *Moge* v. *Moge* has transformed the way that family law practitioners and judges think about spousal support. Although some of the previous jurisprudence and scholarly writings continue to have relevance, *Moge* is the touchstone against which all that has gone before must be reassessed. *Moge* is the decision that is guiding the present development of the law.

The majority judgment of L'Heureux-Dubé J. discussed the social and economic background to divorce, recognizing the plight of many women at the end of marriage, and frankly acknowledging that the law has too often contributed to the "feminization of poverty". She responded to these concerns by articulating a broad approach, one that requires a "fair and equitable distribution of resources to alleviate the economic consequences of marriage or marriage breakdown for both spouses, regardless of gender". She recognized that this approach inevitably requires courts to engage in an "exercise of judicial discretion", for there are no "neat compartments on which to rely, as families and family relationships are not simple". It is an approach that has, in general, resulted in larger spousal support awards of longer duration than before *Moge*. The decision in *Moge* clearly strives to ensure fairer treatment for those whose lives are economically disadvantaged by marriage and divorce, usually (but not exclusively) women.

One critic, Professor J. McLeod, has characterized *Moge* as a "deconstructionist opinion . . . a statement of philosophy or opinion" which did "little more than decide . . . the particular issue before the court".[5] I reject this view. I believe that the approach of *Moge* towards spousal support, like that for other family law issues, such as the "best interests of the child" test for custody and access disputes, is inevitably one that gives significant judicial discretion and requires individualized application. But like the best interests test, *Moge* also established an approach that is, through further judicial elaboration, capable of giving judges and lawyers significant guidance in how to resolve the cases they must deal with.

Although *Moge* emphasizes the importance of spousal support for compensating for the economic consequences of roles assumed during marriage, it also makes clear that there is no simple model or test for spousal support; the issue of spousal support cannot be fully analogized to other legal issues, for example, by trying to develop a contract, compensatory or restitutionary model of support or marriage. However, as in other areas of law, such as where courts are dealing with unconscionability of contracts or reasonable notice for wrongful dismissal, the courts are gradually providing a significant degree of structure to the application of a multifactoral analysis. As in these other areas, there are also situations that are controversial and will defy easy categorization. . . .

2.   SPOUSAL SUPPORT: THE BACKGROUND TO MOGE

. . .

It is now only of academic interest whether Madam Justice Wilson *really intended* to articulate a model of support applicable to all situations, or whether her remarks were misunderstood by some judges or commentators. It is clear that the initial *effect* of the Trilogy was to make it more difficult for applicant spouses, invariably women, to get spousal support, in particular on an indefinite basis. Those who were seeking spousal support developed two broad types of response to this initial ''chilling effect'' of the Trilogy.

One response that gradually developed to the causal connection approach was for counsel to adduce expert evidence from economists about the economic losses suffered by spouses who gave up a career for a period of time in order to stay at home and provide domestic services, in particular child care. This culminated in 1992 in the trial decision in *Elliot* v. *Elliot*,[18] where Steinberg J. awarded a woman who was at home for 7 years looking after two young children a lump sum spousal support of about $70,000, in addition to child support and an equalization of family property. The spousal support award essentially represented one half the discounted present value of future earnings loss that the woman incurred as a result of loss of seniority and job skills due to her time out of the labour force. In effect, the court was satisfied, based on expert evidence, that this was her husband's ''share'' of the loss ''caused by'' marriage. While *Elliot* has been reversed on appeal,[19] in a post-*Moge* appellate decision, the trial judgment may be regarded as a response by counsel and the judge to a view that there was a need to *prove* that the marriage *caused* the woman to suffer economic loss. After *Moge*, this approach is no longer needed.

Another, more direct judicial response to the narrowing effect of the ''causal connection'' test was an explicit rejection of this as the basis for the law of spousal support, and a restriction of the Trilogy to situations where spouses entered into a separation agreementt. This was the approach of several provincial Court of Appeal decisions and was ultimately reflected in the 1992 Supreme Court of Canada judgment in *Moge* v. *Moge*. . . .

4. APPLYING MOGE

It is interesting that L'Heureux-Dubé J. emphasized *both* the need for ''efficient and speedy disposition'' of family disputes, *and* for having a ''broad approach'' that confers significant ''judicial discretion'' in assessing spousal support. Inevitably there is tension between these two objectives, as a highly discretionary regime requiring individualized assessments is more likely to promote litigation than one based on clear rules. At least in part, the solution to this paradox lies in the many specific directions offered by the Supreme Court for assessing and classifying situations. While perhaps not as neatly organized as some critics might have wanted, *Moge* does give judges and lawyers a set of discretion structuring factors that can help resolve the overlapping issues of entitlement to support, and the quantum, duration and form of spousal support.

The balance of this article is a brief discussion of some of the most important factors for dealing with spousal support, together with a discussion of how *Moge* and subsequent decisions indicate these factors are to be taken into account.

5. ENTITLEMENT TO SUPPORT

(a) Roles Assumed in Marriage: Traditional, New Traditional and Modern

Since *Moge*, arguably the single most important factor in the spousal support determination is the roles assumed during marriage.[30] Spouses who sacrifice their future employment prospects for the family or who further their partners' careers will generally receive support, while those who do not may not receive any support.

(i) *Traditional Marriages*

While *Moge* points out that the distinction between "traditional" and "modern" is not "sophisticated" enough to capture the full range of marital arrangements, it is still a useful typology. Women, like Mrs. Moge, who remain out of the labour force for substantial time periods and engage in the "traditional" role of taking primary responsibility for child care and domestic affairs while their husbands pursue careers are now regarded as "almost presumptively disadvantaged" and entitled to long term spousal support. This is particularly the case in a "traditional marriage" where there are children, the husband's career is at least moderately successful, and the marriage lasts at least 10 years.

The fact that there has been a long term marriage does *not*, however, obviate the need for the wife to take *reasonable* steps towards self-sufficiency, nor does it guarantee an "equalizing of incomes". In all but the longest marriages and most wealthy families, there is an obligation of at least partial self-support. Further, the higher income spouse invariably lives at a higher standard of living after divorce, and there will be incentives for anyone seeking support to also obtain employment to prevent a decline in living standards.

In *Ross* v. *Ross*[33] the Ontario Court of Appeal cited *Moge* to remove a three year time limitation from a spousal support award to a woman following the breakdown of a 23 year traditional marriage. In its brief decision the Court of Appeal emphasized that this was a "traditional" marriage with a long absence from the labour force. The woman's educational efforts by taking training as a Shiatsu therapist to become self-sufficient had not yet resulted in her securing employment. However, the Court did remark that if she was not successful "within a reasonable time . . . she will have to make career changes", emphasizing her obligation to become self-sufficient. . . .

(ii) *New Traditional Marriages*

Probably the most common division of labour in most Canadian marriages today involves both spouses being in the labour force for most of the marriage, but one spouse, typically the woman, making career sacrifices for the family, such as stopping work when children are young, working part-time and moving in accordance with dictates of a spouse's career. The spouse making these sacrifices usually has a much lower income. In *Cosper* v. *Cosper*, Judge Gass of the Nova Scotia Family Court remarked:[37]

> This case, as do many cases, causes us to re-think and broaden the definition of a "traditional marriage". There has been evolving a new "traditional marriage" wherein both spouses have worked throughout most, if not all, of the marriage, although the mother spouse has out of necessity often taken time from work to bear and rear children, or has taken positions which enable some flexibility, in order to combine both parenting and the career.

In *Cosper*, both spouses had Ph.D.'s but after more than 20 years of marriage and three children, the husband had a tenured university position earning $75,000 a year, while the wife was making only $35,000 a year. As the judge noted, various career decisions were made by the woman with the "tacit approval and encouragement of her husband", and as a result she was in a position where she would never "catch up" to his income and security. The court ordered $400 a month as permanent support. . . . .

(iii) *Modern Marriages*

In *Moge*, L'Heureux-Dubé J. suggests that "modern" marriages, where both spouses maximize earning potential and divide domestic labour equally will be "rare" and even "utopian". This may be overstating the infrequency of relationships in which there is a *rough* equality of contributions, especially since a support application "is not an exercise in accounting, requiring an exact tally of debits and credits for each day of marriage". Many divorces involve childless couples married 10 years or less where both spouses worked throughout the marriage; spousal support will rarely be appropriate in such cases.

In a number of cases judges have found that there was no career sacrifice and hence no entitlement to support. For example in the British Columbia case of *Nijjar* v. *Nijjar*[42] there was a 15 year marriage with two children. While the woman was out of the labour force for a few years when the children were born, for the last decade of the marriage both were working at low skilled jobs and had roughly equal incomes, with the husband having a slightly higher income. The court felt that the woman was economically self-sufficient and not disadvantaged by the marriage, and denied accordingly spousal support even though she was experiencing financial difficulties because of her spending decisions.

In the Ontario case of *Shackleton* v. *Shackleton*,[43] Whalen J. denied spousal support to a woman after 9 years of cohabitation in a marriage to which two children were born. The woman was 35 years of age at the time of trial. She was out of the labour force for about 5 years early in the marriage, but worked for the last 4 years of marital cohabitation. Her income was about $23,600 a year, and the husband's about $41,000 a year. She received custody of the children and $1100 per month child support. While the court recognized that her responsibilities for the care of the children would limit her future social and economic opportunities:

> [T]here was no evidence that the wife was denied any career plans or opportunities through the marriage. The wife did not express any educational, vocational, or other opportunities missed by the fact of the marriage. She did not indicate any hopes or ambitions that she might have pursued had she not become involved in the marriage or were she not now (and in the future) bearing primary responsibility for child care. Nor was there much evidence of the wife's situation in this regard prior to the marriage.

> With respect to the husband, there is no evidence that his employment has either been achieved or enhanced by the fact of the marriage, and, indeed, he had been employed at Algoma Steel for about 15 years prior to the marriage. While I am certain that the husband's role as the primary breadwinner entrenched him in his shift-work routine, there was no evidence that this did not accord with his ambitions.

> Given all of these circumstances, I am not persuaded that there is any disadvantage to the wife flowing from the marriage that cannot be adequately addressed by a proper award of child support.

Shackleton may be taken as illustrative of the fact that, at least in lower middle class families where the pre-marital career opportunities of the individuals were limited, courts will not use spousal support to equalize income differences that appear due to pre-marital career and education choices or labour market discrimination. At the very least, counsel must adduce some evidence to establish the linkage between one spouse's income levels and roles assumed during the marriage. . . .

(c) Career Enhancement of a Spouse — Restitutionary Awards

[This factor is given separate coverage in a later section of this chapter and Professor Bala's views are noted there.]

(d) Career Sacrifice in a Modern Marriage

Consistent with the analysis in *Moge*, there will be "modern" marriages where career sacrifices are made, usually by the woman, that should be compensated on divorce. In these cases, both parties pursue their careers, perhaps without children being involved, but one person makes a clear career sacrifice.

Prototypical of this situation was the British Columbia decision in *Bollum* v. *Bollum*,[52] where Justice Blair awarded a woman $5,000 a month for 15 months ($75,000 in total) in spousal support after a marriage that involved only 16 months cohabitation, in addition to a property award. The woman had given up a lucrative career in the United States to move to Vancouver, where her husband was in the process of developing an extremely successful business. She made minor contributions to the business, but the main purpose of the award was to recognize that the husband's career was not "impeded" or disrupted in any way by the marriage, whereas the wife suffered significant economic disadvantage. She was not in "need" in an absolute sense, since she could obtain employment in the United States, with a salary of about $70,000, but she had permanently lost a lucrative job (paying over $100,000 a year) as a result of career decisions made to accommodate the man, while her former husband's business increased significantly in value during the marriage.

(e) Quantification of Career Sacrifice

In some pre-*Moge* cases applicants for spousal support presented expert evidence from economists quantifying the amount of "career loss" suffered from taking time out of the labour force for family responsibilities, and obtained a lump sum support award. This type of support is sometimes referred to as "compensatory support", as it is intended to compensate the woman for her losses due to the role assumed in marriage.

In the 1992 trial decision in *Elliot* v. *Elliot*[54] Justice Steinberg of the Ontario Unified Family Court awarded a woman one half the discounted present value of the future earnings loss, to compensate for loss of seniority, experience and career progress for the domestic role she assumed in marriage. In some senses the trial decision in *Elliot* may be viewed as a pre-*Moge* response to the problem of the "causal connection" test. In *Moge* the Supreme Court mentioned *Elliot*, but did not specifically endorse it.

In October 1993 the Ontario Court of Appeal overturned the trial decision in *Elliot*.[56] While the Court of Appeal recognized that the wife had suffered a career loss due to her role in the home and awarded $1,000 per month spousal support, it considered a lump sum inappropriate. In part, the Appeal Court was concerned about the unfairness of such an award to the man, in that focusing on the woman's loss the trial judge ignored his ability to pay. Also there was a recognition that in some ways the man also sacrificed his career for the family, in this case by giving up the possibility of a job transfer to Saudi Arabia because of concerns about the effect of the move on his family. Perhaps more fundamentally, the Ontario Court of Appeal expressed philosophical concern about this form of lump sum compensation, since it treated marriage like a "tort", and attempted to accurately quantify inherently speculative losses. Awarding a lump sum to "compensate" a spouse would require a court to deal speculatively with unpredictable future employment contingencies, and even with the possibility of the remarriage of the recipient.

There will, however, be cases in which judges will want to promote a "clean-break" and award some form of lump sum, at least notionally to compensate for career losses. This will not, however, represent a judicial attempt to "quantify" the career loss. For example, in the British Columbia decision in *Banks* v. *Banks*[57] Baker J. awarded a woman a $35,000 lump sum support award instead of periodic support, after a 23 year marriage. While the judge did not accept expert evidence that the present value of her career loss was over $300,000, he recognized the need to "compensate" the woman for the reduction in her earning potential due to her assumption of domestic and child responsibilities in the family. A "compensatory lump sum" allowed her to buy out her husband's share in the former matrimonial home, and permitted a clean break.

These decisions suggest that applicant spouses should not normally undertake the expense of adducing expert evidence from economists about the exact loss due to career sacrifice from roles assumed during marriage. *Moge* indicates that judges can take general judicial notice that such losses occur, and leave quantification to more general principles where a lump sum is sought.

(f) Career Sacrifice: Whose Decision Was It?

At least on one reading of *Moge*, it may be important for a woman seeking support based on career sacrifice to show that a *joint* decision was made that a woman sacrifice her career for the family. In some recent cases it seems that counsel for respondent spouses have attempted to argue that a career interruption was not a joint decision and therefore should not be "compensated" through a support award.

This type of argument has largely been rejected by the courts. It has not been necessary to show that there was a clear joint decision that a woman should "give up" her employment for family purposes in order to be eligible for support. The courts recognize that most family decisions are made in a nebulous fashion.

Where periodic spousal support is being sought for a spouse who was at home or not working full-time, courts are generally not interested in inquiring into whose decision it was for a woman (or man) to give up employment in the labour force.[60] A retrospective inquiry into this subject would inevitably be fraught with difficulty.

Spouses who wish to resist claims for periodic spousal support on the grounds that they did not agree to a career interruption are only likely to be successful if there is a marriage contract to make their positions clear. This would provide clarity and fair notice for both spouses. Failing this, courts are likely to treat a career interruption as implicitly a mutual decision, or caused by economic circumstances beyond anyone's control, and hence the basis of a spousal support claim.

While the distinction may not always be easy to make, situations of unemployment (or underemployment) at the end of cohabitation that appear linked to economic conditions are not as likely to be the basis of long-term support awards as those where career interruption was based on decisions about assuming family responsibilities. When a decision is made to leave the labour force to assume family responsibilities, there will be a career *sacrifice* that should be compensated. If it is a long-term absence from the labour force, this may be a significant loss. If a spouse loses a job and stays at home, there will not be a *sacrifice* and there will be no *losses* to be *compensated*, though there may be *needs* that may result in at least a short-term support order being made.

It is apparent that if some form of "compensatory support" is being sought, there must be a clear, definable career path, like that of a teacher or nurse, that was sacrificed for the family. Some career changes and interruptions in marriage may be viewed as not linked to marital roles and therefore not result in this sort of claim, though support may be awarded on other grounds.

In *Rosin* v. *Rosin*,[62] three years into the marriage the woman, who was a certified physiotherapist, gave up her career and returned to university. Later she stopped working for a while after she had children and then pursued various part-time jobs, such as being a riding instructor. Justice Mclean of the Alberta Court of Queen's Bench observed that she "had been disenchanted with her existing career which she found to be inflexible and lacking in challenge", and concluded that "her career was not interrupted by the marriage [or] . . . by the mutual informed decision to become a parent". The woman's claim for a lump sum "compensatory maintenance award" was rejected, but the woman received 13 months of spousal support to assist her in completing a degree program.

(g) Self-Sufficiency

Although *Moge* extended the rights of dependent spouses to obtain support from their former partners, there clearly continues to be an obligation to take reasonable steps to become self-supporting.

There was a tendency after the 1987 Trilogy for Supreme Court judges to make assumptions about how long it would take for a woman to resume employment and become self-sufficient at a reasonable standard of living, resulting in spousal support orders of fixed duration. Since *Moge*, courts have tended to be more realistic, particularly having regard to the current economic situation in Canada, and have been more prepared to order indefinite spousal support, but generally with the expectation that the formerly dependent spouse will take steps to become self-sufficient.

In *Ross* v. *Ross*[64] the Ontario Court of Appeal deleted a condition for fixed duration of spousal support for a woman absent from the labour force for 23 years who was making as yet unsuccessful efforts to become self-sufficient. The Court did, however, comment:

> She is, however, far from achieving that status. She should be given reasonable time to determine if she can earn a reasonable income in her work as a Shiatsu therapist. If the appellant's financial circumstances do not improve within a reasonable time, as the trial judge noted, she will have to make career changes. Nonetheless, we do not think that the trial judge should have assumed that the appellant would be self-sufficient within three years.

In cases where reasonable efforts to achieve self-sufficiency have not been made, support may be reduced or even terminated. . . .

The recent Ontario Court of Appeal decision in *Robinson* v. *Robinson*[67] emphasizes the obligation to take reasonable steps to become self-sufficient, or bear the costs for post-separation actions that reduce economic prospects. The spouses separated in 1986 after 13 years cohabitation, during which the woman spent 7 years out of the labour force and the last 3 years working part-time. After separation, with her husband's financial support, she went back to University with the hope of going to law school, but failed to gain admission. Although there were positions available in her field of previous employment where the family had lived, she then chose to move to Toronto to live with her sister; she was only able to obtain lower paying work as a clerk in Toronto. The Court of Appeal ordered that spousal support of

$1,500 per month should be reduced to $400 a month for a five year period and then terminated. Madam Justice McKinley wrote:

> [I]t is surprising that her original degree, her job experience, and the additional year at university did not provide her with the ability to obtain more lucrative employment than that of an unskilled clerk. . . .

> [T]he evidence is clear that although there were positions available in her field of expertise in London, Ontario (where, as previously mentioned, she had spent her university years and all the years of her marriage), she did not apply for that type of work, and indeed did not want to re-enter that area of employment. It was her decision to move to Toronto and to accept a position as an unskilled clerk at Ontario Hydro. The trial judge should have considered the disparity between what Mrs. Robinson might have earned had she obtained a position in her field of expertise after a substantial absence, and what she would have been earning had she remained employed in that field during the period of her marriage; instead, he considered only the disparity between what she earned as an unskilled clerk and what she would have been earning had she remained employed during her marriage.

> Mrs. Robinson was compensated in substantial degree by the equalization payment made by Mr. Robinson, which was not considered by the trial judge in determining the amount of the support order. Also, it is important to remember that in this case a large portion of the assets which formed the basis of the equalization payment would not have been available had it not been for the use Mr. Robinson made of inherited moneys. Nor did the trial judge consider the objective and desirability of the spouses becoming self-sufficient as soon as possible after the dissolution of the marriage partnership to allow both to plan for their future lives independent of one another.

While the woman's career sacrifice and lower standard of living warranted some support, it was not to be indefinite, nor was it to equalize her standard of living to her former husband's. *Robinson* clearly demonstrates that women whose marriages are ending now must take responsible steps to become self-supporting or suffer the consequences. . . .

6. QUANTUM, DURATION AND NATURE OF THE ORDER

Issues of entitlement overlap with the quantum, duration and nature of orders. However, some factors more clearly relate to issues of quantum and duration, while others to entitlement.

(a) Quantum: Marital Standard of Living — Not an Equalization Model

The starting spot for the determination of quantum of periodic support is usually the applicant's proposed budget, deducting any income being received by the applicant from other sources, such as employment, to determine the "net need". Courts will disregard any expenses that are viewed as "unreasonable", which as a starting point will be assessed "in the context of the marital standard of living." Of course in reality in most situations the standard of living of both spouses is likely to drop after separation.

Professor McLeod, in his Annotation to *Moge*, raised the spectre that judges following this decision would attempt to have "equalization as a starting point", so that a wife's earnings plus support equal her husband's income minus support. It is clear from judgments rendered since *Moge* that an equalization of spousal income has not occurred and is not the "objective" of the courts. Indeed, in most cases it seems that a woman and the couple's children have a total household income that is less than or equal to the man's. Since *Moge*, after long term traditional or "near traditional'' marriages, where children have left home, most women seem to be receiving a quantum of ''top up'' support that gives them a total income of 50% to 75% of the man's ''after support'' income.

The failure to equalize incomes reflects several, often unarticulated ideas. In part, judges recognize that there are living expenses related to earning income; more fundamentally judges do not want to give payors the feeling that it is not worth working. There are proprietary notions related to earnings. There may also be a reluctance to force individual men to fully compensate women for income differences that are due to discrimination in the labour market or that may be attributable to pre-marital employment or education decisions.

On the other hand, when determining the ''reasonable needs'' of an applicant that should be met by her own income plus support, *Moge clearly* states that the ''level of self-sufficiency'' should not be set at a level of ''unmitigated parsimony''. This is a clear signal that some judges were setting too low a level of spousal support before *Moge*. The effect of *Moge* should be to increase the average amounts of support ordered by Canadian courts.

(b) Payor's Ability to Pay

As Madam Justice L'Heureux-Dubé pointed out in *Moge*:

> [T]he real dilemma in most cases relates to the ability to pay of the debtor spouse and the limits of support orders in achieving fair compensation and alleviating the economic burdens of the disadvantaged spouse.

In most situations, ability to pay and the previous marital standard of living are highly correlated.

Very wealthy spouses will be expected to pay support, at least for a transitional period of time to allow relief from the consequences of separation, even if there is no loss due to roles assumed during marriage. Thus in *Carr* v. *Carr*,[103] the husband of a very wealthy woman received $2,400 a month interim support, some of which was to pay family debts, even though he did not make any career sacrifices for the marriage.

Conversely, if a potential payor has very limited income, or income that roughly equals his spouse's income, courts are very reluctant to order support, even if there has been significant sacrifice and contribution by his partner.[104]

(c) Taking Account of Property Settlements

Once the court has established a ''reasonable standard of living'' for the applicant, having regard to her budget and the former marital standard of living, it will assess her own ability to meet these needs. This will usually involve looking at actual income from employment (or imputed income if there has been a failure to take reasonable steps to become self-sufficient).

The court will also take account of the income from any property owned by the applicant, and will impute a reasonable income stream from that property. In some cases the property settlement will eliminate the right to spousal support. . . .

In *Newsome* v. *Newsome*,[106] a woman received a property settlement worth $800,000 after 14 years of cohabitation, during which she looked after the man's daughters from a prior relationship. The woman also had about $250,000 of her own assets. Spousal support was denied as the property settlement represented an ''equitable sharing of the economic consequences of marital separation''. . . .

(d) Decrease in Ability to Pay — Retirement & Double Dipping

It is accepted by the courts that a decrease in the payor's income may be a grounds for variation of a spousal support order. Thus if a husband's income falls because he has lost his job and become unemployed, or has been forced to assume more poorly paid work, this is grounds for downward variation.[109]

If a payor voluntarily quits his job, a court is unlikely to take this into account in reducing his support obligation.[110] More controversial is the issue of whether a payor's actual or impending retirement should be the basis for lowering or eliminating spousal support.

There are cases that indicate that the mere fact that a payor has retired and is in receipt of pension income (as opposed to earned income) should eliminate the support obligation, in particular in situations where the applicant spouse has already received her ''share'' of the pension income through a property settlement.[111]

The more common approach is to take retirement and a previous pension settlement into account, but not use this as a determinative factor.[112] In cases where there is some time between separation and retirement, ''double dipping'' does not seem to be a dispositive argument because a portion of the pension reflects post-separation earnings, to which the claimant spouse may have some notional claim based on marital sacrifices and contributions. Further, needs created during marriage continue, and perhaps increase, as the person in receipt of support also reaches retirement age. On the other hand, where separation occurs close to or even after retirement, a property division of the pension may more fully and fairly be said to have ''used up'' any claim to support from the pension.

. . .

(h) Duration of Marriage

The duration of a marriage (or more accurately of cohabitation) is an important factor in determining the quantum of spousal support, and perhaps equally important the duration of a periodic order. In *Moge*, L'Heureux-Dubé observed that ''the longer the relationship endures, the closer the economic union, the greater will be the presumptive claims to equal living standards upon its dissolution.''

In a very short marriage, there may be insufficient time to establish roles or suffer losses due to the relationship, and spousal support may be denied altogether.

It is, however, difficult to directly equate the length of the marriage to the length of time that spousal support will be payable. As *Moge* demonstrates, support may be payable for a longer term than the period of marriage (or cohabitation). As noted earlier, in *Morison v. Morison*, a woman received what may amount to life-long spousal support after only 5 years of cohabitation, albeit in a second traditional marriage. . . .

7. CONCLUSION — THE FUTURE OF SUPPORT LAW

Some critics of the discretionary model of spousal support advocate legislative reform, perhaps through articulation of clearer verbal directons. Given the human and financial costs of family law litigation, some American scholars have gone so far as to advocate presumptive legislative guidelines with mathematical formulas based on such factors as the length of marrige, and the difference in spousal incomes after marriage or the income change of each spouse during marriage.[130]

However, given the difficulty in Canada of achieving consensus about such *relatively simple* issues as child support guidelines, quick legislative action on spousal support seems unlikely. Further, the generally positive effect of *Moge* on female post-divorce poverty should lessen political pressure for reform.

It seems likely that for the foreseeable future lawyers and judges will have to continue to take their directions from *Moge* and later interpretative caselaw. While this body of jurisprudence does not provide detailed direction, I have argued that there is now sufficient guidance to allow for the resolution of many cases without having to resort to the expense and bitterness of a trial.

---

5 J.G. McLeod, "*Case Comment: Moge v. Moge*" (1993), 43 R.F.L. (3d) 455, at 455 and 457.

18 (1992), 42 R.F.L. (3d) 7 (Ont. U.F.C.), reversed (1993), 48 R.F.L. (3d) 237 (Ont. C.A.), leave to appeal to S.C.C. denied (June, 1994), Doc. No. 23896 (S.C.C.). See also e.g. Ross, "Time Out of the Labour Force: Diminished Earnings Potential" (1993), 42 R.F.L. (3d) 50; and R. Kerr, *An Economic Model to Assist in the Determination of Spousal Support* (Ottawa: Department of Justice, 1992).

19 (1993), 48 R.F.L. (3d) 237 (Ont. C.A.), *Elliot* is more fully discussed below.

30 A recently released study confirms how significant marriage, and by implication marital roles, are for women's earnings. In 1992, never married women in Canada earned 99% of their male counterparts, while married women working full time earned only 66.6% of what married men did. Widowed, separated and divorced women working full time earned 77% of what men in the same position made. See "Women Gaining on Men's Wages", *Globe & Mail*, January 18, 1994, at B4.

33 (1993), 45 R.F.L. (3d) 230 (Ont. C.A.). See similarly *Laurence v. Laurence* (1993), 50 R.F.L. (3d) 26 (B.C. C.A.).

37 (1993), 46 R.F.L. (3d) 194 (Fam. Ct.) at 201. For a similar Ontario case, see *Tuomi v. Tuomi*, [1993] O.J. 687, [1993] W.D.F.L. 745 (Gen. Div.) per Cosgrove J. where a woman moved and worked part-time to look after 3 children in 18 years of cohabitation. She received $400 per month spousal support out of her husband's $60,000 per year income.

42 [1993] B.C.W.L.D. 456, [1993] W.D.F.L. 254 (S.C.), per Blair J.

43 (1993), 46 R.F.L. (3d) 211 (Ont. Gen. Div.).

52 [1993] B.C.J. 1356, [1993] W.D.F.L. 431 (B.C. S.C.).

54 (1992), 42 R.F.L. (3d) 7 (Ont. U.F.C.).

56 (1993), 48 R.F.L. (3d) 237 (Ont. C.A.) [Leave to appeal to the S.C.C. refused.] Other decisions where courts refused to make lump sum compensatory support orders include *Petley-Jones* v. *Petley-Jones* (1993), 48 R.F.L. (3d) 166 (B.C. S.C.) and *Au* v. *Au* (1993), 47 R.F.L. (3d) 342 (Alta. Q.B.).

57 [1993] B.C.J. 2342 [1993] W.D.F.L. 1685 (S.C.).

60 See e.g. *Dick* v. *Dick* (1993), 46 R.F.L. (3d) 279 (Ont. Gen. Div.), additional reasons at (May 27, 1993), Doc. No. Ottawa 40021/90 (Ont. Gen. Div.).

62 (1993), 46 R.F.L. (3d) 242 (Alta. Q.B.).

64 (1993), 45 R.F.L. (3d) 230 (Ont. C.A.), per Blair, Krever, Osborne JJ.A.

67 (1993), 48 R.F.L. (3d) 265 (Ont. C.A.), per Lacourcière, McKinley, Carthy JJ.A.

103 (1993), 46 R.F.L. (3d) 326 (B.C. S.C.).

104 *Reddy* v. *Reddy*, [1993] N.J. 71 (Nfld. T.D.); *Tingley* v. *Tingley* (1993), 49 R.F.L. (3d) 87 (N.B. Q.B.); and *McTaggart* v. *McTaggart* (1993), 50 R.F.L. (3d) 110 (Ont. Gen. Div.). However, in *Inverarity* v. *Inverarity* (1993), 50 R.F.L. (3d) 251 (Alta. Q.B.), a wife received a $10,000 lump sum to compensate for career sacrifices, even though spousal incomes were roughly equal at the end of the marriage.

106 (1993), 45 R.F.L. (3d) 115 (B.C. C.A.) at 141.

109 See e.g. *Wood* v. *Wood*, [1993] O.J. 524 (Gen. Div.).

110 See e.g. *Zarzycki* v. *Zarzycki* (1993), 47 R.F.L. (3d) 200 (Ont. Gen. Div.).

111 *Butt* v. *Butt* (1989), 22 R.F.L. (3d) 415 (Ont. H.C.) per Granger J.: *Hashem* v. *Hashem* (1993), 46 R.F.L. (3d) 303 (Nfld. U.F.C.). See also T.J. Walker, "Double Dipping—Can a Pension Be Both Property and Income?" (1994), 10 C.F.L.Q. 315-323.

112 See e.g. *Rivers* v. *Rivers* (1993), 47 R.F.L. (3d) 40 (Ont. Gen. Div.) per McKay J.; and *Smyth* v. *Smyth* (1993), 48 R.F.L. (3d) 280 (Alta. Q.B.).

130 See e.g. T. Oldham, ''Proposed Guidelines for Post-Divorce Income Sharing'', International Society of Law & The Family Conference, June 1993, Jackson Hole, Wyoming and C. Starnes, ''Divorce and the Displaced Homemaker'' (1993), 60 Univ. Chic. L. Rev. 67-140.

ROGERSON, "SPOUSAL SUPPORT AFTER *MOGE*"

(1997), 14 C.F.L.Q. 280, at 283, 303-304, and 385-387.

Over three years of lower court decisions applying *Moge* have confirmed what was anticipated from the beginning: that *Moge* has transformed the legal landscape of spousal support, just as the *Pelech* Trilogy did five years earlier. The clearest message coming out of the judgment — that support awards in the past have been unfairly parsimonious — has signalled a shift toward more generous spousal support awards. Post-*Moge* spousal support awards are, in general, for higher amounts and for longer periods of time than in the past. Most noticeably there has been a significant decline in the use of time-limited orders, and an increasing prevalence of indefinite and permanent orders. As a result of *Moge*, spousal support, which many had viewed as an anachronism that would disappear within a few years, has been revived as a serious legal obligation.

Despite this remarkable accomplishment, it must be acknowledged that the Supreme Court of Canada has not, as many had hoped, resolved all of the thorny issues plaguing the law of spousal support. Despite its attempts to clarify the basic principles for determining spousal support, a great deal of confusion still remains with respect to the precise implications of the compensatory model of spousal support which the Court endorsed, and its relationship to more traditional understandings of spousal support as a response to post-divorce need. As well, in its focus on basic principles, the Court did not seriously address the issues of assessment, with the result that enormous variations still exist in the quantum of support awarded in cases involving relatively similar circumstances. . . .

There is little doubt that *Moge* is a remarkable decision. Our highest court is to be commended for the breadth of its vision, its sensitivity to the economic reality of women's lives both during marriage and after marriage breakdown, and its strong commitment to ensuring fairer outcomes for women in the family law system. The decision sends out a strong message that support awards have been too restrictive and that the clean break principle is clearly inappropriate as a principle of general application. This message has definitely been heard and acted upon by lower courts. The spousal support cases decided since *Moge* reveal a pattern of more generous support awards than in the past. In general, support awards are for higher amounts and for longer periods of time. Most noticeably, time-limited orders which establish arbitrary deadlines for the attainment of self-sufficiency have become much rarer. *Moge* has revived spousal support as a significant legal obligation.

However, it is also apparent that the decision has not resolved all of the thorny questions with respect to the basic principles for determining spousal support. The more one reads the decision — and the more one reads lower court judgments struggling to apply it — the more one realizes how many questions still remain unanswered. In part, the explanation for this lies with the difficulty and the complexity of the issues. The Court undoubtedly saw its role as the laying down of general principles and guidelines, leaving the details of application to be worked out through exercises of judicial discretion on facts revealing the broad diversity of family arrangements. However, the task has been made more difficult than it need have been by ambiguous, and in some cases contradictory, statements within the judgment that leave the basic principles in a state of confusion. . . .

The landscape of spousal support post-*Moge* is both radically transformed and strikingly familiar. *Moge* has clearly reversed the trend toward minimalist spousal support awards that took hold with the first wave of modern family law reform. Spousal support awards post-*Moge* are more generous than they were in the past: more spouses are entitled to support and awards are, in general, for longer periods of time and higher amounts. Women who have remained out of the labour force for significant periods of time during marriage can now expect judicial recognition of the long-term economic consequences they will carry with them after marriage breakdown.

Yet from another perspective the current landscape of spousal support is a familiar one. Despite the gloss of a compensatory analysis, the expanded role of spousal support post-*Moge* appears to be driven, in large part, by a concern with responding to post-divorce need and preventing post-divorce poverty, rather than by principles of providing fair compensation to women for their unpaid labour in the home and providing for the equitable sharing between the spouses of the economic consequences of the marriage. Although there are exceptions, many lawyers and judges continue to feel more comfortable with a traditional understanding of spousal support as a private scheme of income security rather than with a compensatory model, and continue to rely upon the conventional concept of need (and its corollary, self-sufficiency) to structure and give content to the compensatory principle. As a result, it is those spouses who demonstrate the greatest economic need and who will experience the greatest economic hardship after marriage breakdown — whether by reason of age, illness, lack of skills, or a poor economy — who are viewed as the most sympathetic candidates for spousal support, while those who have youth, good health, and employability in their favour are seen as self-sufficient economic actors, despite their past and on-going responsibilities for the care of children.

While there may be more spousal support post-*Moge* and somewhat less post-divorce poverty, I fear that in the course of things the radical message of *Moge* with respect to the value of women's work in the home and their entitlement to compensation from their husbands has been diluted. While *Moge* has undoubtedly wrought some very positive developments in terms of how we treat those members of our society — mainly women — who assume primary responsibility for the care of children, much remains to be done. The current political climate is, unfortunately, not one that will render that an easy task.

From a broad political perspective, it is no surprise that the compensatory message of *Moge* is being subtly reshaped into a message of the obligation of family members to provide for each other's economic needs. In a period of diminishing public resources and a recessionary economy, the family has re-emerged as a central economic institution and a locus of economic security for vulnerable citizens. Our political language of rights and entitlements is being replaced with the language of obligations and responsibilities, with particular emphasis on the obligations of family members to care for each other. The fact that many citizens in need have no family resources to draw upon is lost from sight, as is the fact that it is women who will assume responsibility for many of the caring functions being delegated to the family, but whose claims of entitlement to compensation for their work are being delegitimated.

NOTES AND QUESTIONS

1. In "Compensatory Support: New Beginnings or a Return to the Past?" (1994), 11 C.F.L.Q. 129, Professor Davies commented on *Moge* as follows (at 141):

> Have we not come a full circle? Prior to 1968, alimony / maintenance was seen as a periodic allowance made by a husband to a wife to keep her in the standard to which he had accustomed her during the marriage. We have had a brief flirtation with the concepts of "clean break" and "self-sufficiency". We have had a lengthy and learned analysis by the Supreme Court of Canada on the "raison d'être" of spousal support. In the end, however, have we not returned to the notion that, in general, maintenance is an allowance paid by a husband to a wife to maintain her in the same standard to which she has been accustomed during cohabitation?

In an annotation to *Davidson* v. *Davidson* (1998), 33 R.F.L. (4th) 154 (Alta. Q.B.), Professor McLeod suggested (at 151) that the post-*Moge* cases revealed ". . . the emerging principle that there are no legal rules to determine spousal support, except that the spouse with the most money pays."

2. In their *Annual Review of Family Law, 1995* (Toronto: Carswell, 1995), Professor McLeod and Alfred Mamo concluded (at 215) that *Moge* v. *Moge* has done little to settle the confusion in the law of support: "Judges and lawyers continue to disagree about the state of the law because of differing interpretations of *Moge v. Moge*, but we express our confusion in more socially acceptable language!" For further (and generally more favourable) analysis of *Moge* v. *Moge*, see Foster, "*Moge* v. *Moge*: What it means to Family Lawyers" (1993), 43 R.F.L. (3d) 465; Engel, "Compensatory Support in *Moge* v. *Moge* and the Individual Model of Responsibility: Are We Headed in the Right Direction?" (1993), 57 Sask. L. Rev. 397; Winder, "Toward an Equitable Distribution of Resources: Spousal Support after *Moge* v. *Moge*" (1994), 16 Advocates' Q. 452; Grassby, "Spousal Support — Assumptions and Myths Versus Case Law" (1995), 12 C.F.L.Q. 187; Payne, "Spousal and Child Support After *Moge, Willick* and *Levesque*" (1995), 12 C.F.L.Q. 261; Rogerson, "Spousal Support After *Moge*" (1997), 14 C.F.L.Q. 281: and Davies, "Spousal Support under the *Divorce Act*: From *Moge* to *Bracklow*" (1999), 44 R.F.L. (4th) 61.

3. For cases since *Moge* emphasizing the compensatory nature of spousal support, see *Comeau* v. *Comeau* (1993), 1 R.F.L. (4th) 175 (N.B. Q.B.) (support limited to a four-year transitory period where the wife earned less than the husband, but there was no evidence to indicate that the wife's earning capacity had been affected by the marriage); *Kessel* v. *Kessel* (1993), 1 R.F.L. (4th) 324 (Ont. Gen. Div.) (no support where the wife had obtained a job as a waitress after separation and could not establish any economic disadvantage flowing from a five-year marriage); *Ondik* v. *Ondik* (1994), 1 R.F.L. (4th) 376 (Sask. Q.B.) (indefinite support ordered in a long-term, traditional marriage); *MacNeil* v. *MacNeil* (1994), 2 R.F.L. (4th) 432 (N.S. C.A.) (no support for a wife who worked full-time as a nurse during most of the marriage earning approximately the same as the husband); *Wilson* v. *Wilson* (1994), 5 R.F.L. (4th) 75 (Man. C.A.) (indefinite support following a long, traditional marriage); *Koberlein* v. *Barral* (1994), 5 R.F.L. (4th) 94 (Man. Q.B.) (indefinite support where the wife left a tenured position at a university so that she could spend more time with her husband); *Andersen* v. *Carter* (1994), 6 R.F.L. (4th) 90 (B.C. S.C.) (support limited to a two-year transitory period where the wife's inability to support herself was not connected to the marriage but to ill-health and a history of low-paying, short-term jobs); *Harris* v. *Harris* (1994), 7 R.F.L. (4th) 91 (B.C. S.C.) (support limited to a three-year transitory period where the wife worked full-time during most of the marriage but earned about one-half the amount her husband earned); *Lasalle* v. *Lasalle* (1994), 7 R.F.L. (4th) 100 (Alta. C.A.) (indefinite support where the court concluded that it was "a reasonable inference to assume that [the wife] would have attempted to establish some career pattern for herself" if she had not married and looked after children, even though the wife had been a single mother on welfare at marriage and had developed a sewing and drapery business during the marriage which ultimately failed after separation); *Juvatopolos* v. *Juvatopolos* (1994), 8 R.F.L. (4th) 191 (Ont. U.F.C.) (indefinite support where the wife had achieved her goal of becoming a hairdresser but the court considered it reasonable "to infer that had Mrs. Juvatopolos commenced her career some time earlier in the marriage, she might have built up a clientele and thus improved her income"); *Murphy* v. *Murphy* (1994), 10 R.F.L. (4th) 102 (Man. C.A.) (support terminated where the ex-wife obtained a job paying approximately the same as her husband's); *McGrath* v. *Holmes* (1995), 10 R.F.L. (4th) 161 (N.W.T. C.A.) (no support where the drop in the husband's income was not

related to the marriage or its breakdown); *Mason* v. *Mason* (1995), 10 R.F.L. (4th) 249 (Man. Q.B.) (no support where the economic advantages from the marriage, including $800,000 in assets, outweighed the economic disadvantages to the wife); *Andrews* v. *Andrews* (1995), 11 R.F.L. (4th) 117 (B.C. S.C.) (support limited to a $10,000 lump sum to provide the husband with approximately one year in which to find full time employment where the judge concluded that the husband had quit his job as a draftsman mostly for personal rather than family reasons); *Purcell* v. *Purcell* (1995), 11 R.F.L. (4th) 181 (Ont. Gen. Div.) (support for husband limited to a two-year period where the court concluded that he had not been economically disadvantaged by the marriage even though he had left one job and lost another largely because of family commitments); *Fiacco* v. *Fiacco* (1995), 11 R.F.L. (4th) 240 (Sask. Q.B.) (support for the wife limited to a $2,000 lump sum after a two-year marriage which had no impact on her earning capacity); *Underwood* v. *Underwood* (1995), 11 R.F.L. (4th) 361 (Ont. Gen. Div.) ($800 per month awarded to a wife for four years because it would take her six years to return to the top of the pay scale in the nursing position she obtained following separation); *Pope* v. *Pope* (1994), 12 R.F.L. (4th) 391 (Nfld. U.F.C.) (no spousal support where the marriage had not affected the wife's earning capacity and the marriage breakdown had more economic impact on the husband than the wife); *Mullins* v. *Mullins* (1995), 12 R.F.L. (4th) 461 (Nfld. U.F.C.) (support limited to a short transitional period where the wife was expected to return to her career as a nurse after a short time out of the workforce); *Jorden* v. *Jorden* (1995), 14 R.F.L. (4th) 97 (N.B. Q.B.) (lump sum of $27,500 awarded to a wife whose career as a nurse had been interrupted several times during the marriage); *Cuzzocrea* v. *Swain* (1995), 15 R.F.L. (4th) 300 (Ont. Gen. Div.) (no interim support for an unemployed husband where he could not establish that he suffered diminished earning capacity because of the roles adopted during the marriage even though he had looked after the children during previous periods of unemployment); *Prince* v. *Prince* (1995), 16 R.F.L. (4th) 236 (N.S. S.C.) (no support where the wife's earning capacity unaffected and she earned over $50,000 per year); *Myers* v. *Myers* (1995), 17 R.F.L. (4th) 298 (B.C. C.A.) (where the court upheld an indefinite award of $750 per month to a wife who earned over $47,000 per year); *Roberts* v. *Shotton* (1996), 22 R.F.L. (4th) 342 (N.S. S.C.) (support of $900 per month where wife quit job as waitress to go with husband to Italy, marriage lasted less than a year and wife lost seniority on return to job); *Strachan* v. *Strachan* (1996), 23 R.F.L. (4th) 259 (Sask. Q.B.) (no support where wife able to return to teaching after withdrawal from workforce to raise children and economic advantages from marriage relationship outweighed disadvantages); *Thorvaldson* v. *Vanin* (1996), 25 R.F.L. (4th) 273 (Sask. Q.B.) ($1000 per month where woman's inability to find employment ''in large part attributable to her eight year relationship with the respondent where he required or encouraged her to remain on the farm and not work elsewhere''); *Huisman* v. *Huisman* (1996), 30 O.R. (3d) 155 (C.A.) (six years support to ''top up'' the wife's salary where the wife's career had been adversely affected when she stayed home to look after a child for three and a half years early in the marriage); *MacDonald* v. *Rasmussen* (1997), 29 R.F.L. (4th) 310 (Sask. Q.B.) (no spousal support where husband paying $40,000 per year child support and wife was a medical doctor who could earn substantial income if she wished); *Luce* v. *Luce* (1997), 30 R.F.L. (4th) 196 (N.B. Q.B.) (no support after three year, childless marriage and both spouses worked); *Stefanyk* v. *Clancy* (1996), 27 R.F.L. (4th) 256 (N.S. S.C.) (support of $1,500 per month to a husband who had given up his job as a fire fighter captain in Alberta to move to Nova Scotia with his wife who earned $100,000 per year); *Munro* v. *Munro* (1997), 33 R.F.L. (4th) 464 (Ont. C.A.) (economic disadvantage found and support ordered where wife's children and husband's child from first marriages lived with the couple, even though the couple never had children together and both spouses worked throughout the marriage); *Giraud* v. *Giraud* (1997), 34 R.F.L. (4th) 255 (B.C. C.A.) (indefinite support where wife left job at start of two-year marriage on husband's assurance of economic security) ; *Blair* v. *Blair* (1997), 34 R.F.L. (4th) 370 (Ont. Gen. Div.) (indefinite support ordered where wife able to regain position as teacher at end of long marriage, but court noted she might have become a principal like her husband and she had contributed to his career); *Horvath* v. *Fraess* (1997), 36 R.F.L. (4th) 32 (Sask. Q.B.) (support for 1½ years after 4-year marriage and wife at home with child for last 2½ years); *Weekes* v. *Weekes* (1998), 36 R.F.L. (4th) 323 (Man. Q.B.) (limited term support where wife left a job in New York to live with husband in Winnipeg and relationship lasted only two years); *Montgomery* v. *Montgomery* (1998), 37 R.F.L. (4th) 295 (Sask. Q.B.) (no support where husband helped raise wife's four children from previous marriage and wife able to work outside home at times); *Hunter* v. *Hunter* (1998), 37 R.F.L. (4th) 453 (Man. Q.B.) (support for three years after five year relationship during which wife refused job transfer because of husband's job); *Berikoff* v. *Berikoff* (1998), 41 R.F.L. (4th) 31 (B.C.

S.C.) (no support where both spouses worked during marriage and had no children, even though wife now earning considerably less than husband); *Chrintz* v. *Chrintz* (1998), 41 R.F.L. (4th) 219 (Ont. Gen. Div.) (support for ten years where wife left job as a nurse to live with husband in Denmark and look after two children); *Heal* v. *Heal* (1998), 43 R.F.L. (4th) 88 (Ont. Gen. Div.) (support to "top up" wife's income where she returned to less remunerative employment after staying home with child for 3 years); *Jensen* v. *Learo* (1998), 43 R.F.L. (4th) 99 (N.B. Q.B.) (no support despite income disparity where marriage relationship lasted only five months and both spouses worked during marriage); *Moura* v. *Moura* (1998), 43 R.F.L. (4th) 344 (Ont. Gen. Div.) (spousal support where court assumed disparity in income due to wife's role in raising two children, even though she worked full-time throughout); *Bell* v. *Bell* (1998), 44 R.F.L. (4th) 77 (N.S. C.A.) (indefinite support where wife chose to work for less pay as nurse in nursing home to get shifts more conducive to family life); *Munn* v. *Munn* (1999), 44 R.F.L. (4th) 179 (Ont. C.A.) (support for five years where wife's role as homemaker and parent left her "vulnerable and economically disadvantaged upon the breakup of the marriage"); *Ward* v. *Ward* (1999), 44 R.F.L. (4th) 340 (Ont. Gen. Div.)(no support where wife lost a good job by refusing transfer just before separation); *Bellman* v. *Bellman* (1999), 46 R.F.L. (4th) 414 (B.C. S.C.) (support for an additional three years where wife had been out of the work force to look after the home and children, but had retrained and acquired a job in the seven years after the separation); *Browning* v. *Browning* (1999), 47 R.F.L. (4th) 255 (N.S. S.C.) (support to end eight years after separation where wife never totally out of workforce and had teaching qualifications); *Erickson* v. *Erickson* (1999), 47 R.F.L. (4th) 326 (N.S. S.C.) (indefinite support with no expectation of self-sufficiency after 16-year traditional marriage where wife gave up career opportunities to look after the children and home after she helped put the husband through school); *Dorey* v. *Snyder* (1999), 48 R.F.L. (4th) 67 (Ont. Gen. Div.) (support for only three more years where husband earned about twice as much as wife who had taken four years out of the workforce to look after two children as judge concluded: "Given the ages, employment background and education of the parties, their employment prospects are similar in the long run."); *Savoie* v. *Savoie* (1999), 49 R.F.L. (4th) 336 (Man. C.A.) (indefinite support of $300 per month after long, traditional marriage, despite wife's remarriage to a man who would provide all her reasonable needs); and *Juretic* v. *Ruiz* (1999), 49 R.F.L. (4th) 299 (B.C. C.A.) (even though spouses separated five months after marriage, court awarded support to wife for three years as she came from Guatemala at husband's request and needed language training).

4. In some cases, the respondent spouses have successfully argued that career interruptions were not joint decisions and, therefore, should not be considered economic disadvantages flowing from the marriage. See *Reardigan* v. *Reardigan* (1993), 1 R.F.L. (4th) 261 (Nfld. U.F.C.); *Ho* v. *Ho* (1993), 1 R.F.L. (4th) 340 (Ont. Gen. Div.); *Andrews* v. *Andrews* (1995), 11 R.F.L. (4th) 117 (B.C. S.C.); *Cuzzocrea* v. *Swain* (1995), 15 R.F.L. (4th) 300 (Ont. Gen. Div.); and *Ward* v. *Ward* (1999), 44 R.F.L. (4th) 340 (Ont. Gen. Div.).

5. Even though an applicant's earning capacity may not have been affected by the marriage, the courts will usually award at least limited-term support where he or she earns substantially less than his or her partner. As a result of the marriage breakdown, the lower income earner suffers a significant reduction in lifestyle and limited-term support or a small lump sum may be necessary to ease the transition. See *Andrews* v. *Andrews* (1995), 11 R.F.L. (4th) 117 (B.C. S.C.); *Fiacco* v. *Fiacco* (1995), 11 R.F.L. (4th) 240 (Sask. Q.B.); *Purcell* v. *Purcell* (1995), 11 R.F.L. (4th) 181 (Ont. Gen. Div.); *Mullins* v. *Mullins* (1995), 12 R.F.L. (4th) 461 (Nfld. U.F.C.); *Shaw* v. *Shaw* (1995), 14 R.F.L. (4th) 340 (B.C. S.C.); *O'Hara* v. *O'Hara* (1995), 15 R.F.L. (4th) 408 (N.B. Q.B.); *Hough* v. *Hough* (1996), 25 R.F.L. (4th) 319 (Ont. Gen. Div.); *Purcell* v. *Purcell* (1996), 26 R.F.L. (4th) 267 (Ont. C.A.); *Hopkinson* v. *Hopkinson* (1997), 34 R.F.L. (4th) 137 (B.C. C.A.); and *Motyl* v. *Motyl* (1998), 36 R.F.L. (4th) 268 (Sask. Q.B.). See also *Abels* v. *Abels* (1995), 17 R.F.L. (4th) 154 (N.B. C.A.) and *Luke* v. *Luke* (1997), 29 R.F.L. (4th) 319 (Man. C.A.) where indefinite support was awarded largely on this basis. However, compare *Cuzzocrea* v. *Swain* (1995), 15 R.F.L. (4th) 300 (Ont. Gen. Div.).

6. For post-*Elliot* cases refusing to award a lump sum equivalent to the present value of a wife's decreased earning capacity due to career sacrifice, see *Bilas* v. *Bilas* (1994), 3 R.F.L. (4th) 354 (Ont. Gen. Div.) and *Zander* v. *Zander* (1994), 8 R.F.L. (4th) 35 (Ont. Gen. Div.). However, lump sums of $27,000 and $39,000 were awarded to the wives in *Jorden* v. *Jorden* (1995), 14 R.F.L. (4th) 97 (N.B.

Q.B.) and *DeFaveri* v. *Toronto Dominion Bank* (1999), 45 R.F.L. (4th) 141 (Ont. C.A.) respectively to compensate for career interruptions.

7. The *Bilas* decision buttresses Professor Bala's observation that support awards have tended upwards since *Moge* v. *Moge*. The judge apportioned the total family income so that the wife would have $64,000 per year for herself and three children while the husband would have $36,000 for himself. See also *Andrews* v. *Andrews* (1999), 50 R.F.L. (4th) 1 (Ont. C.A.), where the appellate court upheld a decision awarding child and spousal support to the wife leaving her with monthly disposable income of $5,482 per month and the husband with $3,419. This latter figure was based on the assumption that he would be able to obtain a bonus at his new job and would earn extra income through part-time self-employment. In *Balcom* v. *Balcom* (1999), 2 R.F.L. (5th) 39 (N.S. S.C.), the court reduced but refused to end spousal support for a wife who had been employed for much of the marriage and had obtained a new job paying about $37,000 a year. Her ex-husband was earning about $55,000. In his annotation to the case, Professor McLeod concludes (at 42):

> Increasingly in longer-term marriages where a wife has deferred her career or vocation in favour of her family and has allowed the husband to establish a long-term job/career, courts try to ensure that once child support is factored out, the spouses have similar incomes. Top-up support is routinely ordered where a wife with full-time employment earns less than her husband. This means that when child support is taken into account, a payee often will have more of the family income than the payor. Although this makes sense in the abstract, the change [in the law of spousal support] is likely to be difficult for many payors to accept.

Thomas Bastedo, in a paper presented at a B.C. Continuing Legal Education Program, reported that his review of hundreds of spousal support cases indicated that courts in recent cases put at least 50% of the spouses' net disposable incomes in the dependent spouse's new family unit. See Grant, "The New Realities of Support" (2000), 1 R.F.L. (5th) 205, at 206-7. Stephen Grant suggests (at 209) that equalizing the net disposable incomes may be appropriate if the relationship has led to economic disadvantage for one spouse, but he questions this result where support is awarded on a non-compensatory basis.

8. The Newfoundland Court of Appeal in *Waterman* v. *Waterman* (1995), 16 R.F.L. (4th) 10 suggested (at 34-35) that spousal support should not be seen as primarily compensatory:

> . . . [M]odern concepts of marriage admit to considering spousal support as a type of matrimonial asset. Regarding it as such appears more in keeping with modern progressive ideas of marital status in that its consequential sharing ensues to the claimant spouse as a matter of right. . . .

> On the other hand, compensation entails the notion of a transfer of monetary resources from the owner's rightful control to the injured party. . . .

> Moreover, compensation connotes damages for loss or harm to person or property. While purely from an analytical perspective of marriage as an economic unit spousal support may be looked upon as compensatory, it is unlikely that many homemakers would take such a dismal view of their life's work.

It is unclear whether this different perspective would have any practical significance. The court acknowledged that, even if a spousal support claim is viewed as an assertion of the right to an asset of the marriage, the claim is conditional on the exercise of judicial discretion in accordance with the statutory guidelines as interpreted in *Moge*. In *Waterman*, the court emphasized (at 30) that "the longer the dissolved marriage's duration, the stronger is the case for equalizing the standards of living of the divorcing couple". Even so, the incomes were not equalized in this 32-year marriage because the husband had higher personal expenses as the primary income earner and the wife was expected to earn some extra income.

9. Regarding the current approach to the duty to take reasonable steps to support oneself, see *Skoda* v. *Skoda* (1997), 32 R.F.L. (4th) 151 (B.C. S.C.); *Reid* v. *Reid* (1997), 33 R.F.L. (4th) 145 (N.B. C.A.); *Muhle* v. *Muhle* (1997), 35 R.F.L. (4th) 95 (Sask. Q.B.); *Petrocco* v. *Von Michalofski* (1998), 36 R.F.L. (4th) 278 (Ont. Gen. Div.); *Rogers* v. *Rogers* (1999), 45 R.F.L. (4th) 65 (B.C. C.A.); *Hollenbach* v.

Hollenbach (1999), 47 R.F.L. (4th) 39 (B.C. S.C.); and *Erickson* v. *Erickson* (1999), 47 R.F.L. (4th) 326 (N.S. S.C.).

10. Section 17(10) of the *Divorce Act* specifically preserves the causal connection test where a court is asked to order the resumption of support after an original order providing for support for a definite period or until the happening of a specified event expires. Cases such as *Poohkay* v. *Poohkay* (1997), 30 R.F.L. (4th) 9 (Alta. C.A.) and *Garrison* v. *Garrison* (1998), 38 R.F.L. (4th) 435 (Ont. Gen. Div.) suggest that the expiration of a limited-term support order is not a major impediment to variation of the order as the courts readily found that the requirements of s. 17(10) were met. Compare these cases with *Dyck* v. *Dyck* (1996), 23 R.F.L. (4th) 224 (Alta. C.A.); *Sywyk* v. *Sywyk* (1996), 26 R.F.L. (4th) 403 (Ont. Div. Ct.); and *Schroder* v. *Schroder* (1998), 38 R.F.L. (4th) 395 (Alta. Q.B.).

11. The conflicting case law on the effect of reconciliation on a continuing, periodic support order is reviewed in *Rodboard* v. *Rodboard* (1993), 45 R.F.L. (3d) 451 (Ont. Gen. Div.).

12. There is considerable divergence in the case law regarding the question whether claimants should be able to share in their spouses' pension income as support if the pension, or at least part of it, has already been valued and shared as property. "Double dipping" in this way is especially a problem in Ontario, where "in specie" pension division is much less common than in the other provinces. For responses to this issue, see *Veres* v. *Veres* (1987), 9 R.F.L. (3d) 447 (Ont. H.C.); *Butt* v. *Butt* (1989), 22 R.F.L. (3d) 415 (Ont. H.C.); *Linton* v. *Linton* (1990), 30 R.FL. (3d) 1 (Ont. C.A.); *Flett* v. *Flett* (1992), 43 R.F.L. (3d) 24 (Ont. U.F.C.); *Vennels* v. *Vennels* (1993), 45 R.F.L. (3d) 165 (B.C. S.C.); *Rivers* v. *Rivers* (1993), 47 R.F.L. (3d) 90 (Ont. Gen. Div.); *Barlett* v. *Barlett* (1994), 2 R.F.L. (4th) 202 (Nfld. U.F.C.); *Nantais* v. *Nantais* (1995), 16 R.F.L. (4th) 201 (Ont. Gen. Div.); *Crawford* v. *Crawford* (1996), 24 R.F.L. (4th) 146 (Ont. Gen. Div.); *Wolch* v. *Wolch* (1996), 25 R.F.L. (4th) 256 (Man. Q.B.); *Shadbolt* v. *Shadbolt* (1997), 32 R.F.L. (4th) 253 (Ont. Gen. Div.); *Schmidt* v. *Schmidt* (1998), 36 R.F.L. (4th) 1 (B.C. C.A.); *Dolman* v. *Dolman* (1998), 38 R.F.L. (4th) 362 (Ont. Gen. Div.); *Hutchison* v. *Hutchison* (1998), 38 R.F.L. (4th) 377 (Ont. Gen. Div.); *Campbell* v. *Campbell* (1998), 40 R.F.L. (4th) 462 (Ont. Gen. Div.); *Carter* v. *Carter* (1998), 42 R.F.L. (4th) 314 (Ont. Gen. Div.); *Donovan* v. *Donovan* (1999), 44 R.F.L. (4th) 111 (Ont. Gen. Div.); *Caldwell* v. *Caldwell* (1999), 46 R.F.L. (4th) 446 (Ont. Gen. Div.); *Gemmel* v. *Gemmel* (1999), 47 R.F.L. (4th) 149 (Ont. Gen. Div.); and *Carter* v. *Carter* (1999), 49 R.F.L. (4th) 357 (Ont. S.C.J.). The cases are extensively reviewed in *Dick* v. *Dick* (1999), 4 R.F.L. (5th) 54 (Ont. S.C.J.). In his annotation to *Carter*, Professor McLeod suggests (at 357) that the law in this area is in a "confused state", but that whether "a spouse will be allowed to double-dip depends on whether the presiding judge thinks that it is 'fair' to do so on the facts of the case." On March 30, 2000, The Lawyers Weekly reported that the Supreme Court of Canada had granted leave to appeal in *Boston* v. *Boston*, an Ontario case raising the issue. The hearing will likely occur in the fall of 2000.

(4) RESTITUTIONARY SUPPORT

In addition to career sacrifices by one spouse, Madam Justice L'Heureux-Dubé explicitly recognized in *Moge* that a support award may compensate one spouse for benefits conferred that enhance the other spouse's earning capacity. In particular, such support has been used to recognize the contribution of one spouse to the acquisition of a degree, licence or other career asset by a partner. Recall *Caratun* v. *Caratun* (1992), 42 R.F.L. (3d) 113 (Ont. C.A.) (reproduced in Chapter 4. **FAMILY PROPERTY**) where a wife received a $30,000 lump sum under the *Divorce Act* as "compensatory support" for supporting her husband while he obtained dental qual-ifications. Similarly, the court in *Keast* v. *Keast* (1986), 1 R.F.L. (3d) 401 (Ont. Dist. Ct.) awarded a wife, who had supported the family while her husband returned to school to qualify as a doctor, "quasi-restitutionary support or compensatory sup-port" totaling $120,000 payable over a ten-year period in addition to ordinary periodic spousal support. Sometimes the court considers contributions to a spouse's education or career as one of several factors in determining support entitlement and quantum: *Dick* v. *Dick* (1993), 46 R.F.L. (4th) 219 (Ont. Gen. Div.); *Colletta* v.

Colletta (1993), 50 R.F.L. (3d) 1 (Ont. C.A.); and *Erickson* v. *Erickson* (1999), 47 R.F.L. (4th) 326 (N.S. S.C.).

The term ''compensatory support'' has often been used to describe this type of award. However, this term is somewhat confusing, especially in light of *Moge* v. *Moge*. Professor Bala suggests in ''Spousal Support Law Transformed — Fairer Treatment for Women'' (1994), 11 C.F.L.Q. 13, (at 30) that ''this type of award might be better characterized as 'restitutionary', in that it focuses on some sharing of the respondent's gain, rather than the applicant's loss.''

In determining the amount of restitutionary support awarded, a key factor will be the length of time between the acquisition of the career asset and the separation. The longer the period of time, the greater will be the reimbursement already received by the other spouse in the form of a higher standard of living during cohabitation and a larger share of net family property on separation. See Bala, ''Recognizing Contributions to the Acquisition of Degrees, Licences and Other Career Assets: Towards Compensatory Support'' (1989), 8 Can. J. Fam. L. 23 and *Colletta* v. *Colletta*, at 7.

(5) ONGOING CHILDCARE RESPONSIBILITIES

BROCKIE v. BROCKIE

(1987), 5 R.F.L. (3d) 440 (Man. Q.B.)

[The parties married in 1980 and separated in 1985. At marriage, the wife was pregnant and had just completed high school. She remained at home during the marriage, had no job skills and no work experience. After separation, the wife began work as a clerk in a shoe store and earned $520 per month. She wished to go to university. The husband earned over $35,000 per year and lived with another woman who contributed to the costs of their common household.]

BOWMAN J.: — . . . In turning my mind to the factors set out in s. 15 [of the *Divorce Act*, 1985], it is obvious that the functions performed during the period of cohabitation by each spouse, the economic advantages and disadvantages arising from the marriage, the financial consequences arising from the care of the child, are all factors leading inescapably to a substantial increase in spousal support. These are reinforced by the consideration of the economic hardship arising from a breakdown of the marriage and the promotion of economic self-sufficiency for the wife within a reasonable period of time.

I am further admonished by s. 15(7)(b) as follows in respect of spousal support:

(*b*) apportion between the spouses any financial consequences arising from the care of any child of the marriage over and above the obligation apportioned between the spouses pursuant to subsection (8).

This is a new provision and I have given some thought as to what might be encompassed within that consideration. It must be recognized that there are numerous financial consequences accruing to a custodial parent, arising from the care of a child, which are not reflected in the direct costs of support of that child. To be a custodial parent involves adoption of a lifestyle which, in ensuring the welfare and development of the child, places many limitations and burdens upon that parent. A single person can live in any part of the city, can frequently share accommodation with relatives or friends, can live in a high-rise downtown or a house in the suburbs, can do shift work, can devote spare time as well as normal work days to the development of a career, can attend night school, and in general can live as and where he or she finds convenient. A custodial parent, on the other hand, seldom finds friends or relatives who are anxious to share accommodation, must search long and carefully for accommodation suited to the needs of the young child, including play space, closeness to daycare, schools and recreational facilities, if finances do not permit ownership of a motor vehicle, then closeness to public transportation and shopping facilities is important. A custodial parent is seldom free to accept shift work, is restricted in any overtime work by the daycare arrangements available, and must be prepared to give priority to the needs of a sick child over the demands of an employer. After a full day's work, the custodial parent faces a full range of home-making responsibilities including cooking, cleaning and laundry, as well as the demands of the child himself for the parent's attention. Few indeed are the custodial parents with strength and endurance to meet all of these demands and still find time for night courses, career improvement or even a modest social life. The financial consequences of all of these limitations and demands arising from the custody of the child are in addition to the direct costs of raising the child, and are, I believe, the factors to which the court is to give consideration under subs. (7)(b).

In the present case, the wife faces all of these limitations and obligations and is totally unable at this time to become self-sufficient without substantial further education. She is well qualified intellectually to take such training and the question is what amount of money will enable her to do that.

The information which was placed before me indicates that she requires, to meet her reasonable needs, $1,650 per month net of tax. This does not take into account university tuition, books and other direct costs of education. For the most part, the expenses claimed are reasonable, but I believe they could be somewhat reduced. In addition, her maintenance can be supplemented by summer earnings during the long university vacation, and she may have resort to the modest capital sum remaining from the property division. I have concluded that the minimum amount of maintenance which can be awarded and which will permit her to support her child and to attain her educational goal is $600 per month as spousal support and $600 per month as child support. From any part-time or summer income and from her capital resources, she will have to pay income tax, tuition, books and other costs arising from her university attendance, as well as to supplement her living expenses.

Can the husband afford to make a payment of this magnitude? Looking at his gross and net income and taking into account his present lifestyle and shared expenses, I am of the view that he can do so without impoverishment. It is notable that the wife and child have been living in very strained and reduced circumstances, as compared to the husband and father, and have so far borne the full brunt of the economic hardship occasioned by the marriage breakdown over the past year. The husband has been able to live in a very comfortable apartment at a good address, has acquired substantial furnishings and continues to live in a better style than that which he did during the course of cohabitation. The maintenance now ordered will have the effect, after application of current tax tables, of a net cost to the husband somewhere in the neighbourhood of $750 per month. It will be time limited so far as the wife is concerned.

The wife will be obliged to take reasonable steps to register for university entrance or other post-secondary education and to complete her courses within the normal time. The order for maintenance will commence 1st February 1987 and will continue until 1st September 1990, at which time the maintenance for the wife will cease.

This arrangement should enable the wife to have the opportunity, which the parties initially agreed upon, to obtain a university education and to commence a career. This will enable her not only to become financially self-sufficient, but will also enable her to contribute financially to the future support of her son. . . .

NOTES AND QUESTIONS

1. See also *Stunt* v. *Stunt* (1990), 30 R.F.L. (3d) 353 (Ont. Gen. Div.) (where s. 15(7)(b) [now s. 15.2(6)(b)] of the *Divorce Act* was considered and Hoilett J. suggested (at 366) that one group of women who will typically require spousal support are those "with custodial responsibility for children"); *Legun* v. *Legun* (1993), 48 R.F.L. (3d) 13 (B.C. C.A.) (where the court increased the quantum and duration of spousal support in recognition of the effect that post-separation child care responsibilities were having); *Patrick* v. *Patrick* (1993), 49 R.F.L. (4th) 453 (B.C. C.A.), affirming (1991), 35 R.F.L. (3d) 382 (B.C. S.C.) (where spousal support was awarded largely because the custodial parent's continuing childrearing role would have financial consequences over and above those covered by child support); and *Hussein* v. *Hussein* (1994), 3 R.F.L. (4th) 375 (N.B. Fam. Div.) (where the court noted (at 392) that Mrs. Hussein's "ability to earn an income will be impaired in the future because of her ongoing responsibility for the primary care of the children."). In "Spousal Support After *Moge*" (1997), 14 C.F.L.Q. 280, Professor Rogerson concluded (at 368) that these cases were exceptional: "While giving some recognition to the impact of post-divorce childcare responsibilities, the decisions typically revealed an unwillingness to acknowledge that even a relatively short marriage may carry with it significant long-term economic consequences for the spouses if children are involved."

2. In some circumstances, the custodial parent may not be expected to seek employment until the youngest child begins school. See *Thorsteinson* v. *Thorsteinson* (1988), 52 Man. R. (2d) 115 (Q.B.) and *McLean* v. *Goddard* (1994), 3 R.F.L. (4th) 117 (N.S. Fam. Ct.).

3. Note s. 33(8)(b) and s. 33(9)(i) and (1) of the *FLA*.

(6) SICK AND DISABLED SPOUSES

BRACKLOW v. BRACKLOW

(1999), 44 R.F.L. (4th) 1 (S.C.C.)

[The parties married in 1989 after living together for four years. It was a second marriage for both and the wife brought two children into the relationship. The husband knew that the wife had health problems when the relationship started. The wife provided two-thirds of the household expenses for the first two years of the relationship as she earned more money and her two children were living with them. The couple later split the expenses evenly. After the wife became unemployed, the husband provided for the family. The couple separated in 1992 and divorced in 1995.

At the start of the relationship the wife left a job with full health and disability benefits because she wanted to get a management position. The husband supported this decision. A year later the wife found new employment, but her health deteriorated and she found the overtime stressful. The husband told her to leave this job and she did so after about a year. She worked at temporary jobs until she secured a full-time position in late 1990. In October 1991, she had to give up that job because of psychiatric problems that led to her hospitalization. She was repeatedly re-admitted to hospital after that time and never worked again. The wife suffered from bipolar mood disorder, obsessive compulsive disorder and fibromyalgia, which was aggravated by the stress of the marriage breakup.

The husband's income at time of trial was $3,764 per month and his portion of his new household expenses was $2,284 per month. The wife was ill and without means of support when the couple separated. The wife lived in subsidized housing and received $787 monthly in disability benefits. It was unlikely that she would ever work again. The wife obtained an interim order for spousal support of $275 per month, which was increased to $400 per month. The wife's application for permanent support was dismissed and the interim support order was terminated. The trial judge reasoned that no economic hardship befell the wife as a result of the marriage or its breakdown since she was in no different circumstances than if she had never married. The B.C. C.A., characterizing the relationship as a non-traditional marriage in which each spouse paid his or her own way, upheld the decision. The wife appealed.]

McLachlin J.(for the court):

I. Introduction

What duty does a healthy spouse owe a sick one when the marriage collapses? It is now well-settled law that spouses must compensate each other for foregone careers and missed opportunities during the marriage upon the breakdown of their union. But what happens when a divorce — through no consequence of sacrifices, but simply through economic hardship — leaves one former spouse self-sufficient and the other, perhaps due to the onset of a debilitating illness, incapable of self-support? Must the healthy spouse continue to support the sick spouse? Or can he or she move on, free of obligation? That is the question posed by this appeal. It is a difficult issue. It is also an important issue, given the trend in our society toward shorter marriages and successive relationships. . . .

V. Issue

Is a sick or disabled spouse entitled to spousal support when a marriage ends, and if so, when and how much? More precisely, may a spouse have an obligation to support a former spouse over and above what is required to compensate the spouse for loss incurred as a result of the marriage and its breakdown (or to fulfill contractual support agreements)? I would answer this question in the affirmative. . . .

VI. Analysis

A. Entitlement to Support

The lower courts implicitly assumed that, absent a contractual agreement for post-marital assistance, entitlement to support could only be founded on compensatory principles, i.e., reimbursement of the spouse for opportunities foregone or hardships accrued as a result of the marriage. I conclude, however, that the law recognizes *three* conceptual grounds for entitlement to spousal support: (1) compensatory; (2) contractual; and (3) non-compensatory. These three bases of support flow from the controlling statutory provisions and the relevant case law, and are more broadly animated by differing philosophies and theories of marriage and marital breakdown.

(1) The Historical Perspective: . . .The new legislation [federally in 1968 and 1986], while changing much, did not entirely supplant the traditional obligations to support. Legal equality did not translate into actual or substantive equality, and in its absence,

one spouse might still be obliged to support the other. Accordingly, the *Divorce Acts* of 1968 and 1986 and provincial family support and property legislation recognized that in many circumstances one spouse might still be required to provide support for the other upon marriage breakup. The new philosophy of spousal equality brought to the fore the idea that parties' agreements on support should influence their rights and obligations during the marriage and upon its breakup, as well as the idea that compensatory support should be awarded where it would be just to compensate a spouse for his or her contributions to the marriage or for sacrifices made or hardships suffered as a result of the marriage. Contractual support obligations, while not new, were given new emphasis by statutory stipulations that the courts take into account support agreements, express or implied, between the parties. The propriety of compensatory support was recognized by this Court in *Moge* [[1992] 3 S.C.R. 813] as flowing from the 1986 *Divorce Act*. While a few cases prior to *Moge* had acknowledged that support criteria extended beyond needs and capacity to pay, the reasons of L'Heureux-Dubé J. in *Moge* offered the first comprehensive articulation of the view that when a marriage ends, spouses are entitled to be compensated for contributions to the marriage and for losses sustained as a consequence of the marriage. The same reasons, however, made it clear that compensatory considerations were not the only basis for support. Judges must exercise their discretion in light of the objectives of spousal orders as set out in s. 15.2(6), and after having considered all the factors set out in s. 15.2(4) of the *Divorce Act*. By directing that the judge consider factors like need and ability to pay (as explored below), the new *Divorce Act* left in place the possibility of non-compensatory, non-contractual support.

(2) Modern Marriages: Marriage and Marriage Breakdown: In analysing the respective obligations of husbands and wives, it is critical to distinguish between the roles of the spouses during marriage and the different roles that are assumed upon marriage breakdown.

   To begin, when two spouses are married, they owe each other a mutual duty of support: 1986 *Divorce Act*. Marriage, as this Court has said, is a joint endeavour: *Moge*, supra, at p. 870. The default presumption of this socio-economic partnership is mutuality and interdependence. This comports with the statutes and with the reasonable expectations of Canadian society. Thus the *Family Relations Act* [of British Columbia] states: "A spouse is responsible and liable for the support and maintenance of the other spouse. . ." (s. 89(1)). Parties, of course (subject to the Act), may alter this expectation, either through explicit contracting (usually before the union is made with a prenuptial agreement), or through the unequivocal structuring of their daily affairs, to show disavowal of financial interweaving. The starting presumption, however, is of mutual support. We need not elevate to contractual status the marital vows of support "in sickness and health, till death do us part" to conclude that, absent indications to the contrary, marriages are generally premised on obligations and expectations of mutual and co-equal support.

   When a marriage breaks down, however, the situation changes. The presumption of mutual support that existed during the marriage no longer applies. Such a presumption would be incompatible with the diverse post-marital scenarios that may arise in modern society and the liberty many claim to start their lives anew after marriage breakdown. This is reflected in the *Divorce Act* and the provincial support statutes, which require the court to determine issues of support by reference to a variety of objectives and factors.

   The reason that a general presumption of post-marital support would be inappropriate is the presence in the latter half of our century of two "competing" theories of marriage and post-marital obligation: Carol J. Rogerson, ''Spousal Support After *Moge*'' (1996-97), 14 C.F.L.Q. 289; Carol J. Rogerson, ''Judicial Interpretation of the Spousal and Child Support Provisions of the *Divorce Act, 1985* (Part I)'' (1991), 7 C.F.L.Q. 155.

The first theory of marriage and post-marital obligation is the ''basic social obligation'' model, in which primary responsibility falls on the former spouse to provide for his or her ex-partner, rather than on the government. This model is founded on the historical notion that marriage is a potentially permanent obligation (although it revises the archaic concept of the wife's loss of identity with the voluntary secession of autonomy of two, co-equal actors as the basis for the ongoing duty). The payment corollary of this theory has been referred to as the ''income replacement model'', because the primary purpose of alimony payments, under the basic social obligation model, is to replace lost income that the spouse used to enjoy as a partner to the marriage union. The advocates of this theory vary in degree of fidelity. For example, some espouse permanent and indefinite support under this model. Others argue that the goal should be not just to meet the dependent spouse's post-marital needs, but to elevate him or her as closely as possible to the standard of living enjoyed during the marriage. Yet others, like Rogerson, contend that the social obligation entitlement to spousal support need not translate into a permanent obligation.

At the other end of the spectrum lies what may be termed the ''independent'' model of marriage. This model sees each party to a marriage as an autonomous actor who retains his or her economic independence throughout marriage. The parties, while they ''formally'' commit to each other for life at the time of their vows, regard themselves as free agents in an enterprise that can terminate on the unilateral action of either party. The theory of spousal support that complements this model is the ''clean-break'' theory, in which a former spouse, having compensated in a restitutionary sense any economic costs of the marriage on the other spouse, moves on with his or her life, possibly to enter into more such relationships. Again, the proponents vary in their degree of allegiance. Some prefer to characterize the clean-break model as encompassing ''transitional support'', in addition to straight restitution, due to the general dislocation costs of unwinding the partnership.

The independent, clean-break model of marriage provides the theoretical basis for compensatory spousal support. The basic social obligation model equally undergirds what may be called ''non-compensatory'' support. Both models of marriage and their corresponding theories of spousal support permit individual variation by contract, and hence provide a third basis for a legal entitlement to support.

These two theories (and I recognize that I paint with broad strokes, creating these two anchors for sake of simplicity) represent markedly divergent philosophies, values, and legal principles.

The mutual obligation model of marriage stresses the interdependence that marriage creates. The clean-break model stresses the independence of each party to the union. The problem with applying either model exclusively and stringently is that marriages may fit neither model (or both models). Many modern marriages are a complex mix of interdependence and independence, and the myriad of legislative provisions and objectives discussed below speak varyingly to both models. As *Payne on Divorce* (4th ed. 1996), at pp. 269-70, puts it, ''The economic variables of marriage breakdown and divorce do not lend themselves to the application of any single objective''.

The independent, clean-break model of marriage and marriage breakdown reflects a number of important policies. First, it is based on the widely accepted modern value of the equality and independence of both spouses. Second, it encourages rehabilitation and self-maximization of dependent spouses. Third, through its acceptance of a clean break terminating support obligations, it recognizes the social reality of shorter marriages and successive relationships.

These values and policies support the compensatory theory of support (and, to some extent, the contractual theory as well). The basic premise of contractual and compensatory support is that the parties are equal. As such, when the relationship ends, the parties are entitled to what they would receive in the commercial world—what the individuals contracted for and what they have lost due to the marriage, and its breakdown. Insofar as marriage may have created dependencies, it is the duty of dependent spouses to strive to free themselves from their dependencies and to assume full self-sufficiency, thereby mitigating the need for continued compensation.

The mutual obligation theory of marriage and divorce, by contrast, posits marriage as a union that creates interdependencies that cannot be easily unraveled. These interdependencies in turn create expectations and obligations that the law recognizes and enforces. While historically rooted in a concept of marriage that saw one spouse as powerful and the other as dependent, in its modern version the mutual obligation theory of marriage acknowledges the theoretical and legal independence of each spouse, but equally the interdependence of two co-equals. It postulates each of the parties to the marriage agreeing, as independent individuals, to marriage and all that it entails — including the potential obligation of mutual support. The resultant loss of individual autonomy does not violate the premise of equality, because the autonomy is voluntarily ceded. At the same time, the mutual obligation model recognizes that actual independence may be a different thing from theoretical independence, and that a mutual obligation of support may arise and continue absent contractual or compensatory indicators.

The mutual obligation view of marriage also serves certain policy ends and social values. First, it recognizes the reality that when people cohabit over a period of time in a family relationship, their affairs may become intermingled and impossible to disentangle neatly. When this happens, it is not unfair to ask the partners to continue to support each other (although perhaps not indefinitely). Second, it recognizes the artificiality of assuming that all separating couples can move cleanly from the mutual support status of marriage to the absolute independence status of single life, indicating the potential necessity to continue support, even after the marital "break". Finally, it places the primary burden of support for a needy partner who cannot attain post-marital self-sufficiency on the partners to the relationship, rather than on the state, recognizing the potential injustice of foisting a helpless former partner onto the public assistance rolls.

Both the mutual obligation model and the independent, clean-break model represent important realities and address significant policy concerns and social values. The federal and provincial legislatures, through their respective statutes, have acknowledged both models. Neither theory alone is capable of achieving a just law of spousal support. The importance of the policy objectives served by both models is beyond dispute. It is critical to recognize and encourage the self-sufficiency and independence of each spouse. It is equally vital to recognize that divorced people may move on to other relationships and acquire new obligations which they may not be able to meet if they are obliged to maintain full financial burdens from previous relationships. On the other hand, it is also important to recognize that sometimes the goals of actual independence are impeded by patterns of marital dependence, that too often self-sufficiency at the time of marriage termination is an impossible aspiration, and that marriage is an economic partnership that is built upon a premise (albeit rebuttable) of mutual support. The real question in such cases is whether the state should automatically bear the costs of these realities, or whether the family, including former spouses, should be asked to contribute to the need, means permitting. Some suggest it would be better if the state automatically picked up the costs of such cases: Rogerson, "Judicial Interpretation of the Spousal and Child Support Provisions of the *Divorce Act, 1985* (Part I)", supra, at p. 234, n. 172. However, as will be seen, Parliament and the legislatures have decreed otherwise by requiring courts to consider not only compensatory factors, but the "needs" and "means" of the parties. It is not a question of *either* one model *or* the other. It is rather a matter of applying the relevant factors and striking the balance that best achieves justice in the particular case before the court.

With these theories and policy concerns of marriage and marriage breakdown in mind, I turn to the pertinent statutes. They reveal the joint operation, in different provisions, of both legal paradigms, and hence the compensatory, non-compensatory, and contractual foundations for an entitlement to post-marital spousal support.

(3) The Statutes: The *Divorce Act* and the provincial support statutes are intended to deal with the economic consequences of the marriage breakdown for both parties. See, e.g., *Family Law Act*, R.S.O. 1990, c. F.3, preamble, which characterizes its purpose as "to provide in law for the orderly and equitable settlement of the affairs of the spouses upon the breakdown of the partnership". The statutes require a fair and equitable distribution of resources to alleviate these consequences, regardless of gender. See C. Martin, "Unequal Shadows: Negotiation Theory and Spousal Support Under Canadian Divorce Law" (1998), 56 U.T. Fac. L. Rev. 135, at p. 139 (identifying increased equity in distribution as a "primary objective" of the new *Divorce Act*). As this Court pointed out in *Moge*, per L'Heureux-Dubé J., the *Divorce Act* is premised on the doctrine of the equitable sharing of the economic consequences of the marriage and its breakdown. It is not confined to one type of marriage or one type of support.

Moge, supra, sets out the method to be followed in determining a support dispute. The starting point is the objectives which the *Divorce Act* stipulates the support order should serve: (1) recognition of economic advantage or disadvantage arising from the marriage or its breakdown; (2) apportionment of the financial burden of child care; (3) relief of economic hardship arising from the breakdown of the marriage, and (4) promotion of the economic self-sufficiency of the spouses: s. 15.2(6). No single objective is paramount; all must be borne in mind. The objectives reflect the diverse dynamics of the many unique marital relationships.

Against the background of these objectives the court must consider the factors set out in s. 15.2(4) of the *Divorce Act*. Generally, the court must look at the "condition, means, needs and other circumstances of each spouse". This balancing includes, but is not limited to, the length of cohabitation, the functions each spouse performed, and any order, agreement or arrangement relating to support. Depending on the circumstances, some factors may loom larger than others. In cases where the extent of the economic loss can be determined, compensatory factors may be paramount. On the other hand, "in cases where it is not possible to determine the extent of the economic loss of a disadvantaged spouse . . . the court will consider need and standard of living as the primary criteria together with the ability to pay of the other party": *Ross v. Ross* (1995), 168 N.B.R. (2d) 147 (N.B. C.A.), at p. 156, *per* Bastarache J.A. (as he then was). There is no hard and fast rule. The judge must look at all the factors in the light of the stipulated objectives of support, and exercise his or her discretion in a manner that equitably alleviates the adverse consequences of the marriage breakdown.

The *Divorce Act* and *Family Relations Act*, through their various provisions, accommodate both models of marriage and marriage breakdown outlined above. While the law has evolved to accept compensation as an important basis of support and to encourage the self-sufficiency of each spouse when the marriage ends, where compensation is not indicated and self-sufficiency is not possible, a support obligation may nonetheless arise from the marriage relationship itself. Turning to the specific provisions, the factors judges must consider in resolving support issues reveal the three different conceptual bases for spousal support obligations — contractual, compensatory, and non-compensatory. The judge must consider them all, and any or all of them may figure in the ultimate order, as may be appropriate in the circumstances of the case.

. . .Under the *Divorce Act*, compensation arguments can be grounded in the need to consider the "condition" of the spouse; the "means, needs and other circumstances" of the spouse, which may encompass lack of ability to support oneself due to foregoing career opportunities during the marriage; and "the functions performed by each spouse during cohabitation", which may support the same argument. In sum, these compensatory statutory provisions can be seen to embrace the independent, clean-break model of marriage and marriage breakdown.

While the statutes contemplate an obligation of support based on the grounds of contract and compensation, they do not confine the obligation to these grounds. The "ability and capacity of, and the reasonable efforts made by, either or both spouses to support themselves" (*Family Relations Act*, s. 89(1)(d)), suggests a concern with need that transcends compensation or contract. Even if a spouse has foregone no career opportunities or has not otherwise been handicapped by the marriage, the court is required to consider that spouse's actual ability to fend for himself or herself and the effort that has been made to do so, including efforts after the marriage breakdown. Similarly, "economic circumstances" (s. 89(1)(e)) invites broad consideration of *all* factors relating to the parties' financial positions, not just those related to compensation. The same may be said for the broad injunction of the *Divorce Act* that the court consider the "condition, means, needs and other circumstances of each spouse". To be sure, these factors may support arguments based on compensation for what happened during the marriage and its breakdown. But they invite an inquiry that goes beyond compensation to the actual situation of the parties at the time of the application. Thus, the basic social obligation model may equally be seen to occupy the statutory provisions.

Section 15.2(6) of the *Divorce Act*, which sets out the objectives of support orders, also speaks to these non-compensatory factors. The first two objectives — to recognize the economic consequences of the marriage or its breakdown and to apportion between the spouses financial consequences of child care over and above child support payments — are primarily related to compensation. But the third and fourth objectives are difficult to confine to that goal. "[E]conomic hardship . . . arising from the breakdown of the marriage" is capable of encompassing not only health or career disadvantages arising from the marriage breakdown properly the subject of compensation (perhaps more directly covered in s. 15.2(6)(*a*): see *Payne on Divorce*, supra at pp. 251-53), but the mere fact that a person who formerly enjoyed intra-spousal entitlement to support now finds herself or himself without it. Looking only at compensation, one merely asks what loss the marriage or marriage breakup caused that would not have been suffered but for the marriage. But even where loss in this sense cannot be established, the breakup may cause economic hardship in a larger, non-compensatory sense. Such an interpretation supports the independent inclusion of s. 15.2(6)(*c*) as a separate consideration from s. 15.2(6)(*a*). Thus, Rogerson sees s. 15.2(6)(*c*), "the principle of compensation for the economic disadvantages of the *marriage breakdown* as distinct from the disadvantages of the marriage" as an explicit recognition of "non-compensatory" support ("Spousal Support After *Moge*", supra, at pp. 371-72 (emphasis in original)).

Similarly, the fourth objective of s. 15.2(6) of the *Divorce Act* — to promote economic self-sufficiency — may or may not be tied to compensation for disadvantages caused by the marriage or its breakup. A spouse's lack of self-sufficiency may be related to foregoing career and educational opportunities because of the marriage. But it may also arise from completely different sources, like the disappearance of the kind of work the spouse was trained to do (a career shift having nothing to do with the marriage or its breakdown) or, as in this case, ill-health.

In summary, nothing in the *Family Relations Act* or the *Divorce Act* suggests that the only foundations for spousal support are compensatory. Indeed, I find it difficult to confine the words of the statutes to this model. It is true that in 1986 the *Divorce Act* was amended to place greater emphasis on compensation. This represented a shift away "to some degree" from the "means and needs" approach of the 1968 Act: *Payne on Divorce*, supra, at p. 267. But while the focus of the Act may have shifted or broadened, it retains the older idea that spouses may have an obligation to meet or contribute to the needs of their former partners where they have the capacity to pay, even in the absence of a contractual or compensatory foundation for the obligation. Need alone *may* be enough. More broadly, the legislation can be seen as a sensitive compromise of the two competing philosophies of marriage, marriage breakdown, and spousal support.

(4) The Case Law: Turning to the jurisprudence, Mr. Bracklow cites L'Heureux-Dubé J.'s statement in *Moge*, supra, that "marriage *per se* does not automatically entitle a spouse to support" (p. 864). That is true. To hold otherwise would swing the pendulum too far back and completely ignore the independent, clean-break model of marriage. But, in certain circumstances, marriage *may* give rise to an obligation. It is not the bare fact of marriage, so much as the *relationship* that is established and the expectations that may reasonably flow from it that give rise to the obligation of support under the statutes. This Court in *Moge*, per L'Heureux-Dubé J., emphasized that the court must consider all the objectives of support and all the factors relating to its award. These include non-compensatory factors, like need and means. Indeed, L'Heureux-Dubé J. expressly alluded to the propriety of non-compensatory support in *Moge*. She held that although the 1986 *Divorce Act* shifted the focus of support toward self-sufficiency and compensation, it did not eliminate the traditional consideration of "means and needs". Although *Moge* was primarily concerned with a claim for compensatory support, L'Heureux-Dubé J. noted that in other cases, *like those of sick or disabled spouses*, a support obligation might well lie even in the absence of a compensatory underpinning. She pointed out that while some of the provisions of the *Divorce Act* are compensatory in character, "[they] may not be characterized as exclusively compensatory" (p. 865). . . .

Following *Moge*'s broad view of causation in compensatory support and the concomitant acceptance of the availability of non-compensatory support, courts have shown increasing willingness to order support for ill and disabled spouses. Sometimes they have done this as a "transition" to self-sufficiency: *Parish v. Parish* (1993), 46 R.F.L. (3d) 117 (Ont. Gen. Div.). But more often, they have frankly stated that the obligation flows from the marriage relationship itself. Collecting cases,

Rogerson explains in ''Spousal Support After *Moge*'', supra, at p. 378 (footnotes omitted):

> The [more dominant] approach, . . . particularly in cases of earning capacity permanently limited by age, illness or disability, and the one generally supported by the developing Court of Appeal jurisprudence, has been to award continuing support without regard to the source of the post-divorce need. On this approach, which I earlier referred to as the *''basic social obligation''* approach, causal connection arguments have been rejected not only in determining entitlement to support, but also in assessing the extent of the obligation. The message coming from the cases adopting this approach appears to be that one takes one's spouse as one finds him or her, subject to all his or her weaknesses and limitations with respect to income-earning capacity; and a spouse with higher earning capacity has a basic obligation to make continuing provision for a spouse who is unable to become self-sufficient at the end of the marriage. One is simply not allowed to abandon a spouse to destitution at the end of a marriage if one has financial resources which might assist in relieving the other spouse's financial circumstances. [Emphasis added.]

Rogerson concludes that ''the non-compensatory principle . . . has come to play . . . a large role in the subsequent case law, providing in many cases a very generous basis for support'' (p. 384): see, e.g., *Ashworth v. Ashworth* (1995), 15 R.F.L. (4th) 379 (Ont. Gen. Div.) (non-compensatory permanent support ordered for disabled spouse who, on the judge's findings of fact, *benefitted* from the marriage, as opposed to needing any compensation). ''The current approach is typically justified by reference, first, to *Moge*'s rejection of the applicability of the causal connection test, and second, to the fact that the spouse who is ill suffers disadvantage from the *breakdown* of the marriage and the loss of financial support from the other spouse'' (Rogerson, ''Spousal Support After *Moge*'', supra, at pp. 378-79 (emphasis in original)).

To permit the award of support to a spouse disabled by illness is but to acknowledge the goal of equitably dealing with the economic consequences of marital breakdown that this Court in *Moge*, supra, recognized as lying at the heart of the *Divorce Act*. It also may well accord, in my belief, with society's sense of what is just. The Report of the Scottish Law Commission, *Family Law: Report on Aliment and Financial Provision* (1981), at pp. 111-12, a thoughtful analysis of the rationale and policy considerations of spousal support and illness, states:

> Financial provision on divorce is not . . . simply a matter of abstract principle. It is essential that any system should be acceptable to public opinion and it is clear from the comments we have received that many people would find it hard to accept a system which cut off, say, an elderly or disabled spouse with no more than a three-year allowance after divorce, no matter how wealthy the other party might be.

Divorce ends the marriage. Yet in some circumstances the law may require that a healthy party continue to support a disabled party, absent contractual or compensatory entitlement. Justice and considerations of fairness may demand no less.

In summary, the statutes and the case law suggest three conceptual bases for entitlement to spousal support: (1) compensatory, (2) contractual, and (3) non-compensatory. Marriage, as this Court held in *Moge* (at p. 870), is a ''joint endeavour'', a socio-economic partnership. That is the starting position. Support agreements are important (although not necessarily decisive), and so is the idea that spouses should be compensated on marriage breakdown for losses and hardships caused by the marriage. Indeed, a review of cases suggests that in most circumstances compensation now serves as the main reason for support. However, contract and compensation are not the only sources of a support obligation. The obligation may alternatively arise out of the marriage relationship itself. Where a spouse achieves economic self-sufficiency on the basis of his or her own efforts, or on an award of compensatory support, the obligation founded on the marriage relationship itself lies dormant. But where need is established that is not met on a compensatory or contractual basis, the fundamental marital obligation *may* play a vital role. Absent negating factors, it is available, in appropriate circumstances, to provide just support.

B. *Quantum of the Award*

The parties segregate entitlement and quantum for purposes of analysis in their submissions on how the Court should exercise its discretion. While I am content to deal with the case in this manner, it must be emphasized that the same factors that go to entitlement have an impact on quantum. In terms of the underlying theories, there is no strong distinction. The real issue is what support, if any, should be awarded in the situation before the judge on the factors set out in the statutes. For practical purposes, however, it may be useful to proceed by establishing entitlement first and then effecting necessary adjustments through quantum. As Rogerson notes, "What is emerging as the dominant approach offers a very broad basis of entitlement, with quantum operating as the only obvious limitation" ("Spousal Support After *Moge*", supra, at p. 383 (footnotes omitted)), going on to note that "[i]n most of the cases, the amounts awarded to ill or disabled spouses provide only a very modest or basic standard of living, and do not result in anything approaching equalization of income or even the marital standard of living".

On quantum (which refers both to the amount of support payments and their duration), both parties advance different "rules" for calculation. Mrs. Bracklow segregates the amount of the monthly payments and their duration. She argues that since the basis of support is her "need", that "need" determines the (minimum) amount of the monthly support payment to which she is entitled. The only issue, in her submission, is of duration — how long should Mr. Bracklow continue to meet that need? Her answer is that he must continue as long as her need persists, on the ground there is no principled reason to terminate non-compensatory support while need persists.

Mr. Bracklow, for his part, identifies length of the marital relationship as the critical factor in determining the amount of support. He sees the length of the marital relationship as a proxy for interdependency (and hence the moral obligation of non-compensatory support), relying on the comment in *Moge* that "[a]s marriage should be regarded as a joint endeavour, the longer the relationship endures, the closer the economic union, the greater will be the presumptive claim to equal standards of living upon its dissolution" (p. 870).

Both these arguments miss the mark in that they fix on one factor to the exclusion of others. The short answer to Mrs. Bracklow's argument is that need is but one of a number of factors that the judge must consider. Similarly, the short answer to Mr. Bracklow's contention is that the length of the marital relationship is only one of a number of factors that may be relevant. While some factors may be more important than others in particular cases, the judge cannot proceed at the outset by fixing on only one variable. The quantum awarded, in the sense of both amount and duration, will vary with the circumstances and the practical and policy considerations affecting particular cases. Limited means of the supporting spouse may dictate a reduction. So may obligations arising from new relationships in so far as they have an impact on means. Factors within the marriage itself may affect the quantum of a non-compensatory support obligation. For example, it may be difficult to make a case for a full obligation and expectation of mutual support in a very short marriage. (Section 15.2(4)(*a*) of the *Divorce Act* requires the court to consider the length of time the parties cohabited.) Finally, subject to judicial discretion, the parties by contract or conduct may enhance, diminish or negate the obligation of mutual support. To repeat, it is not the act of saying "I do", but the marital relationship between the parties that may generate the obligation of non-compensatory support pursuant to the Act. It follows that diverse aspects of that marital relationship may be relevant to the quantum of such support. As stated in *Moge* , "At the end of the day . . ., courts have an overriding discretion and the exercise of such discretion will depend on the particular facts of each case, having regard to the factors and objectives designated in the Act" (p. 866).

Fixing on one factor to the exclusion of others leads Mrs. Bracklow to an artificial distinction between amount and duration. The two interrelate: a modest support order of indefinite duration could be collapsed into a more substantial lump-sum payment. It also leads her to the false premise that if need is the basis of the *entitlement* to the support award, then the *quantum* of the award must meet the total amount of the need. It does not follow from the fact that need serves as the predicate for support that the quantum of the support must always equal the amount of the need. Nothing in either the *Family Relations Act* or the *Divorce Act* forecloses an order for support of a *portion* of the claimant's need, whether viewed in terms of periodic amount or duration. Need is but one factor to be considered. This is consistent with the modern recognition, captured by the statutes, of the variety of marital relationships in modern society. A spouse who becomes disabled toward the end of a very short marriage may well be entitled to support by virtue of her need, but it may be unfair, under the circumstances, to order the full payment of that need by the supporting spouse for the indefinite future.

Mr. Bracklow's fixation on the length of the marital relationship leads to other difficulties. He elevates this Court's observation in *Moge* about general expectations in long-term marriages to an immutable rule constraining the factors applicable to determining quantum of support. And he introduces "morality" into the calculation of quantum. This is unnecessary, because the statutes already state what the judge should consider. It is also unhelpful, because it does not in the end explain why the length of the marital relationship should serve as the sole "moral" determinant of support, to the exclusion of need and other factors. The flexible mandate of the statutes belies such rigidity.

Mr. Bracklow makes a final policy argument. In an age of multiple marriages, he asserts, the law should permit closure on relationships so parties can move on. Why, he asks, should a young person whose marriage lasts less than a year be fixed with a lifelong obligation of support? When can a former spouse finally move on, knowing that he or she cannot be drawn back into the past by an unexpected application for support?

Again the answer is that under the statutes, the desirability of freedom to move on to new relationships is merely one of several objectives that might guide the judge. Since all the objectives must be balanced, it often will not be possible to satisfy one absolutely. The respondent in effect seeks a judicially created "statute of limitations" on marriage. The Court has no power to impose such a limitation, nor should it. It would inject a rigidity into the system that Parliament and the legislatures have rejected. Marriage, while it may not prove to be "till death do us part", is a serious commitment not to be undertaken lightly. It involves the *potential* for lifelong obligation. There are no magical cut-off dates.

VII. Application

. . . Refocusing the facts of this case through the correct juridical lens suggests that while the early years of the Bracklows' union might indicate the atypical partnership of strict independence (rebutting the presumption of intra-marital mutual interdependency), by the end the Bracklows had established a more interdependent relationship. In addition to adjusting their expenses to a more even ratio, it is evident that Mr. Bracklow covered Mrs. Bracklow's needs in the early stages of her illness. Accordingly, it follows that divorce *did* in fact render Mrs. Bracklow in a state of economic hardship, as contemplated by s. 15.2(6)(*c*) of the *Divorce Act*.

Bearing in mind the statutory objectives of support and balancing the relevant factors, I conclude that Mrs. Bracklow is eligible for support based on the length of cohabitation, the hardship marriage breakdown imposed on her, her palpable need, and Mr. Bracklow's financial ability to pay. While the combined cohabitation and marriage of seven years were not long, neither were they (by today's standards) very short. Mrs. Bracklow contributed, when possible, as a self-sufficient member of the family, at times shouldering the brunt of the financial obligations. These factors establish that it would be unjust and contrary to the objectives of the statutes for Mrs. Bracklow to be cast aside as ineligible for support, and for Mr. Bracklow to assume none of the state's burden to care for his ex-wife.

I leave the determination of the quantum of support to the trial judge, who is in a better position to address the facts of this case than our appellate tribunal. My only comment on the issue is to reiterate that all the relevant statutory factors, including the length of the marital relationship and the relative independence of the parties throughout that marital relationship, must be considered, together with the amount of support Mr. Bracklow has already paid to Mrs. Bracklow. I therefore do not exclude the possibility that no further support will be required, i.e., that Mr. Bracklow's contributions to date have discharged the just and appropriate quantum. Absent settlement between the parties, these issues are for the trial judge to resolve.

VIII. Disposition

I would allow the appeal, set aside the judgment of the Court of Appeal, and remit the matter to the trial judge for assessment in conformity with these reasons of the quantum of the award on the basis that Mrs. Bracklow is legally eligible for post-marital support.

[When the matter returned to the trial judge, the wife's disability payments had increased to $846.44 per month. Her rental housing was subsidized and she lived very modestly. However, she had debts totalling over $8,000. The husband's income had risen to about $71,000 per annum and he was prospering. However, he was now supporting his unemployed new wife. The ex-wife sought an award of $400 per month indefinitely, while the husband argued that he had satisfied any support obligation he might have had by the amount he had already paid. The judge, reasoning that a time limit was appropriate because the wife's support entitlement was based on non-compensatory grounds arising out of a relatively short marriage awarded $400 per month for five years, with the time beginning to run on March 15, 1995. The arrears under this order stood at $16,000 at the date of the judgment in *Bracklow* v. *Bracklow (No. 2)* (1999), 181 D.L.R. (4th) 522 (B.C. S.C.) and the court ordered them to be paid at the rate of $400 per month after March 15, 2000.]

DAVIES, "SPOUSAL SUPPORT UNDER THE *DIVORCE ACT*: FROM *MOGE* TO *BRACKLOW*"

(1999), 44 R.F.L. (4th) 61 (Edited footnotes follow.)

I. Introduction

. . . In *Moge*, the Supreme Court of Canada concentrated on explaining compensatory support. *Bracklow* v. *Bracklow* concentrates on needs-based support. The importance of *Bracklow* is primarily two-fold: (a) it broadens the boundaries of entitlement to support and shifts focus from entitlement to quantum; (b) it draws a clear distinction between compensatory support and needs-based support.

Compensatory and needs-based support have different philosophical bases and should be kept separate. The cases after *Moge* blurred the differences between needs- and compensation-based support (or, rather, focused on compensatory support at the expense of needs-based support). Now needs-based support has come into its own right (or, more properly, come *back* into its own right). Coincidentally, the Supreme Court's analysis of needs-based support has pushed away the portals to entitlement, focusing us rather on amount and duration. . . .

II. Compensatory Support

. . . In most marriages, one party tends to suffer economic disadvantage and hardship, either from the marriage itself or its breakdown. This party is most likely to be the wife. This is because of the traditional division of labour within the institution of marriage. The most significant economic disadvantage generally arises from child care. However, this is not the only vehicle by which a wife may be disadvantaged financially. The aim of compensatory support is to compensate the disadvantaged spouse from the effect that these sacrifices have had on his or her economic well-being.

If, as is suggested, compensatory support will be appropriate in most cases, what should be the measure of that support? Insofar as economic circumstances permit, the parties should be placed in a position as close as possible to that of the household before the breakdown. The longer the marriage, the greater will be the presumptive claim to equal standards of living after dissolution.

Does the foregoing imply income-splitting? There is clear support for income-splitting in the judgment of Madam Justice Claire L'Heureux-Dubé. Marriage is seen as an economic unit which generates financial benefits. One such benefit is the wage-earning capacity of one or both spouses. Spouses are entitled to share these financial benefits. Equitable distribution can be achieved by the payment of support, the distribution of assets or a combination of the two. In many, if not most, cases, the absence of accumulated assets may require the payment of support.

In *Waterman* v. *Waterman*,[13] Marshall J.A., speaking for the Newfoundland Court of Appeal, found clear support for income-splitting in *Moge*. He said:[14]

> [I]t is only just that the earning capacity of the couple be regarded as a current asset in which the economically disadvantaged party, whose own economic independence was impaired in the greater interest of the dissolved marriage, has a contingent proprietary interest in the earnings of the former partner. Support for this premise can be gained from . . . *Moge*.

Later he said:"[T]he regarding of spousal support as a contingent matrimonial asset in which the claimant spouse may share as of right is not inconsistent with or foreclosed by *Moge* but is in concert with it."[15] Indeed, the courts have, in several instances, split the parties' incomes between them. Where there are dependent children, the method adopted is generally to determine child support first[16] and then to equalize the remaining income.[17] The balance of opinion, however, appears to be against income-splitting as a matter of course or as a matter of right. It has been pointed out that *Moge* itself is authority for the proposition that marriage *per se* does not entitle one to support: "The equitable sharing of the economic consequences of marriage or marriage breakdown, however, is not a general tool of re-distribution which is activated by the mere fact of marriage."[18] Only where there has been a sacrifice by one who requires compensation will compensatory support be appropriate.

Moge refers to equalizing standards of living — not equalizing incomes. Even equalizing standards of living is not guaranteed. However, disparities in standards of living may be indicative of economic disadvantages inherent in the role assumed by one party and this will increase with the length of marriage.

When the parties spend all their available income on living, then equalizing income and equalizing standards of living amount to the same thing. As Dickson J. said in *Forbes* v. *Forbes*:[20]

> When all the combined resources of the parents are spent on living expenses a fair and equitable support order is determined, not by looking at their estimated expenses, but instead by looking at their total resources and dividing those resources fairly. A fair division of total resources should result in the parents having roughly an equal amount of money for their personal use after they have taken care of the reasonable needs of the children.

However, where the available incomes exceed the amount required to live at the pre-separation standard of living, then income-splitting is unlikely to be appropriate. As Bastarache J.A. (as he then was) said in *Ross* v. *Ross*: "Although a long relationship will create a stronger "presumptive claim to equal standards of living upon . . . dissolution [of the marriage]" . . . spousal support is not aimed at achieving equalization of incomes after divorce."[21] Thus, while equalizing the parties' standards of living may be appropriate, particularly in long relationships, equalizing incomes should never be a goal in and of itself. Equalizing incomes may be appropriate but only on the facts of a given case after a due consideration of the factors and objectives listed in the *Divorce Act*, s. 15.2(4) and (6).[22]

III. Needs-Based Support

Objective (c) of s. 15.2(6) is to relieve economic hardship arising from the breakdown of the marriage. "Hardship" is an absolute (as opposed to a relative) term. It was discussed by MacDonald J. in *Hough* v. *Hough*[23] as follows:

> *The Concise Oxford Dictionary of Current English*, (8th ed.) (Oxford: Clarendon Press, 1990) at 538 describes hardship as a noun with the following definition:
>
> 1. severe suffering or privation;
> 2. the circumstances surrounding this.
>
> There was absolutely no evidence that suggests economic hardship if ordinary meaning is given to "hardship".[24]

If one spouse suffers hardship as a result of the marriage breakdown, he or she is eligible for support, regardless of lack of sacrifice and loss as a result of the marriage. Unlike compensatory support, where there is hardship, the marriage itself justifies an award of support.

In *Bracklow*, the Supreme Court of Canada found that the breakdown of the marriage had rendered the wife "in a state of economic hardship, as contemplated by s. 15.2(6)(c) of the *Divorce Act*." . . . One justification given by the Supreme Court of Canada for holding that Mrs. Bracklow was entitled to support was this:

> [I]t [the mutual obligation theory of marriage] places the primary burden of support for a needy partner who cannot attain post-marital self-sufficiency on the partners to the relationship, rather than on the state, recognizing the potential injustice of foisting a helpless former partner onto the public assistance rolls.

This view echoes that expressed by L'Heureux-Dubé J. in *Moge* where she opined that objective (c) of s. 15.2(6) might embrace the notion that the primary burden of spousal support should fall on family members, *not* the state.

The view that the primary obligation to support a former spouse should fall on his or her ex-spouse rather than the state accords with the notion adopted in older cases . . . but is at odds with views expressed in the [S.C.C.] trilogy. It is certainly at odds with the view popular in the 1970s (the heyday of the "clean break") that the corollary to divorce is remarriage and the ties with the "old" must be severed so that the new can survive.

The word "need" or "needs" is a far wider term than the term "hardship". Further, it is a relative (as opposed to absolute) term.

> "Need" or "needs" are not absolute quantities. They may vary according to the circumstances of the parties and the family unit as a whole. "Need" does not end when the spouse seeking support achieves a subsistence level of income or any level of income above subsistence.[33]

Absent sacrifice or loss entitling one to compensatory support, absent, too, hardship justifying hardship-based support, can a court, under the *Divorce Act*, award needs-based support? The answer appears to be "yes".

> Need alone may be enough.

The justification for such an award appears to lie in objective (a) of s. 15.2: "the recognition of any economic . . . disadvantages arising from the . . . breakdown." Additionally, justification can be found in objective (d), "promotion of self-sufficiency".

When will a court award needs-based support when neither compensatory support nor hardship-based support is justified? In *Bracklow* we are told that in such cases:

> It is not the bare fact of marriage, so much as the relationship that is established and the expectations that may reasonably flow from it that give rise to the obligation of support.

Essentially, then, the entire marriage — length, interdependencies and expectations — must be explored. The factors listed in s. 15.2(4) are relevant to both entitlement and quantum.

> At the end of the day . . . courts have an over-riding discretion and the exercise of such discretion will depend on the particular facts of each case, having regard to the factors and objectives designated in the Act.

Compensatory support is now familiar. Hardship-based support is circumscribed and therefore readily comprehensible. Needs-based support, however, is difficult to grasp (or, at least, to hold). While the Supreme Court of Canada has consistently said that marriage *per se* does not entitle one to support, *need* and marriage do, and, as we have seen, "need" is a relative term. We are perilously close to the notion that any diminution in a spouse's standard of living resulting from marriage breakdown warrants a support order, a notion that has largely been resisted by the courts since the early 1970s.

The Supreme Court of Canada seems aware that it is eroding the barriers to support entitlement. In *Bracklow*, McLachlin J. approved a comment by Professor Carol Rogerson: "What is emerging as the dominant approach offers a very broad basis of entitlement, with quantum operating as the only obvious limitation."

IV. Compensatory and Needs-Based Support Contrasted

The essence of compensatory support is to compensate the disadvantaged spouse for those sacrifices and losses resulting from the marriage relationship that have diminished earnings and earning power. A spouse who has sacrificed his or her own career by reason of playing a supportive role to the career of the other spouse is entitled to share the fruits of their combined work ("equitable sharing of the economic consequences of marriage" to use the phraseology of L'Heureux-Dubé J.). He or she is presumptively entitled to a standard of living equal to that of his or her spouse on dissolution because disparities in their respective standards of living are indicative of his or her sacrifices.

Equitable sharing of economic consequences of marriage and equality of post-dissolution standards of living are, then, part and parcel of and consistent with compensation for sacrifices made and losses resulting from the marriage. Needs-based support is philosophically distinct from compensatory support. The focus here is on alleviation of the need.

Promotion of self-sufficiency plays a subtly different role in the two forms of support. In needs-based support it plays the role of alleviating the need. In compensatory support it plays the role of mitigating the loss.

Albeit the focus in needs-based support is alleviating need, this is not to say that the quantum of support must be satisfaction of that need (even if the payor spouse has the means to do so). The factors and objectives of the Act must all be considered in determining that which is reasonable. Thus, for example, total satisfaction of the payee's need may be reasonable where the payor has the means and there is a joint expectation because of the length of the marriage or for some other reason. Partial satisfaction may be appropriate where the marriage is shorter, the means less etc.

Nonetheless, need is the focus of the enquiry into quantum in needs-based support; compensation is the focus of the enquiry on quantum in compensation-based support — fundamental differences which will lead to different results.

The effect of the payee's remarriage or cohabitation may differ depending on whether the payee is receiving compensatory or needs-based support. If the maintenance is compensation-based, then the marriage of the payee may have little or no effect since the payor still has an obligation to compensate the payee for the losses suffered through their marriage.[48] However, that loss may have been entirely or partially mitigated by virtue of the new marriage or cohabitation, in which case the quantum or duration of the maintenance will be affected.[49]

Professor J. McLeod has argued that, where maintenance is compensation-based, then the remarriage or cohabitation of the recipient should leave unaffected the maintenance obligation of the first spouse. The new marriage should be viewed in the same manner as the lottery winnings of a victim of personal injury, having nothing to do with the payor's obligation to compensate for losses sustained because of his or her action. Logical though this argument may be, in fact, the courts *do* see the remarriage or cohabitation as a change of condition, means etc. sufficient to trigger a review under s. 17, whether the support was compensatory or needs-based[51] and have treated the remarriage or cohabitation as justification for reducing or eliminating support, whatever the basis of that support may have been.[52]

When the applicant for a variation has satisfied the court that the cohabitation or remarriage is a change of circumstances warranting review under s. 17, the onus is then said to shift onto the recipient spouse to demonstrate that continuation of support is still warranted.[53] In *May* v. *May*,[54] Cosgrove J. opined that shifting the onus to the recipient was not appropriate to compensatory (as opposed to needs-based) support. It would seem that the differential in onus will be extremely difficult to apply when the support award in question is partly compensation-based and partly needs-based.

Clearly, remarriage or cohabitation of the recipient will be highly relevant to a support order based on needs. The new relationship will, in most cases, affect the needs of the recipient spouse so as to reduce or eliminate the need for support.

Limited-term support may be ordered whether the obligation is needs-based or compensation-based. Since the ultimate goal of compensatory support is to alleviate the disadvantaged spouse's economic losses as completely as possible, support should continue until the losses have been compensated for (assuming the payor has the means to do so). Thus Mr. Moge was required to continue to pay spousal support on an indefinite basis, albeit the period of the parties' cohabitation was exceeded by the number of years he had already paid support to his ex-wife. It has been said that it is improper to award limited-term compensatory support unless the judge is satisfied, on a balance of probabilities, that the inability to be fully self-sufficient that was caused by the marriage will have been overcome by the cut-off date.

Needs-based support is somewhat different. Whether the obligation to satisfy the recipient's needs requires full or only partial satisfaction depends on all the facts of the case, including the payor's means, the length of marriage etc. . . . . Thus, in *Bracklow* v. *Bracklow*, McLachlin J. (who sent the matter back to the trial judge to determine quantum) did not exclude the possibility that no further support would be required — *i.e.*, that Mr. Bracklow's contributions to date had discharged the just and appropriate quantum. It seems, then, that in needs-based support, it is not improper for a court to order limited-term maintenance, albeit there is no reasonable likelihood that the payee will be self-sufficient by the cut-off date.

V. Conclusion

At the outset I opined that the importance of *Bracklow* lies in two areas: (a) it has broadened the basis of entitlement to support so that now the focus is on quantum (which term comprises both amount and duration); (b) it has drawn a clear distinction between needs- and compensation-based support. With respect to the first of these points, in a critical annotation to the Ontario Court of Appeal's decision in *Munro* v. *Munro*, Professor J. McLeod wrote:

> If the Court of Appeal is correct in its conclusion, entitlement to support is not an issue any longer. Every spouse who earns less than his or her partner for any reason is entitled to support. The only issues are form, duration and quantum.

It is difficult to be unsympathetic to this view. The Supreme Court of Canada has eroded the boundaries of entitlement to such an extent that now a diminution in the living standard of the less well-off spouse makes a good case for needs-based support.

With respect to the second point, it is important to keep the two bases of support clear in one's mind as the quantum (amount and duration) of support depends upon the basis upon which the award is made. Having said this, it is naive to suggest that it is always a simple matter to identify the exact nature of the claim. Claims to support often involve a mix of both compensation and need.

The economic realities of divorce are that in most cases both parties must suffer a reduction in standard of living. In many cases, too, the burden of child support makes spousal support academic. It is in this climate that the principles relating to spousal support, set out in the Supreme Court of Canada decisions, must be tested.

---

13 (1995), 16 R.F.L. (4th) 10, 133 Nfld. & P.E.I.R. 310, 413 A.P.R. 310 (Nfld. C.A.).

14 *Ibid.* at p. 27 R.F.L.

15 *Ibid.* at p. 36.

16 As is required by s. 15.3 of the *Divorce Act.*

17 *E.g., Zaleschuk* v. *Zaleschuk* (1993), 1 R.F.L. (4th) 403 (Sask. Q.B.); *Reid* v. *Reid* (1993), 99 D.L.R. (4th) 722 (Alta. Q.B.).

18 *Moge* v. *Moge* (1992), 43 R.F.L. (4th) 345, at p. 386 *per* L'Heureux-Dubé J.

20 (1994), 2 R.F.L. (4th) 121, 117 Sask. R. 299 (Q.B.) at p. 127 R.F.L.

21 (1995), 16 R.F.L. (4th) 1, 168 N.B.R. (2d) 147, 430 A.P.R. 147 (N.B. C.A.), at p. 6 (R.F.L.). See also *Rea* v. *Rea* (1998), 42 R.F.L. (4th) 92, 166 D.L.R. (4th) 443, 131 Man. R. (2d) 95, 187 W.A.C. 95 (Man. C.A.) at p. 95 (R.F.L.) and *Jantzen* v. *Jantzen* (1998), 35 R.F.L. (4th) 282, 155 D.L.R. (4th) 656, 126 Man. R. (2d) 71, 167 W.A.C. 71 (Man. C.A.).

22 *Chalmers* v. *Chalmers* (1994), 2 R.F.L. (4th) 446 (B.C. S.C.); *Bettles* v. *Bettles,* 7 R.F.L. (4th) 153, 122 Nfld. & P.E.I.R. 341, 379 A.P.R. 341, [1994] 2 P.E.I.R. 394 (T.D.).

23 (1996), 25 R.F.L. (4th) 319, 30 O.R. (3d) 725, 14 O.T.C. 243 (Ont. Gen. Div.).

24 *Ibid.* at p. 328 R.F.L. *per* MacDonald J. Compare *Giraud* v. *Giraud* (1997), 34 R.F.L. (4th) 255, 155 D.L.R. (4th) 112, 100 B.C.A.C. 27, 163 W.A.C. 27, 44 B.C.L.R. (3d) 98 (B.C. C.A.). It is submitted that the British Columbia Court of Appeal wrongly equated the word "hardship" with the word "need". However, the practical implications of the British Columbia Court of Appeal's interpretation of the word "hardship" to coincide with "need" are little or nothing. The Supreme Court of Canada's embrace of needs-based support in *Bracklow* has essentially eclipsed the narrower hardship-based support: see *infra.*

33 *Myers* v. *Myers* (1995), 17 R.F.L. (4th) 298, 65 B.C.A.C. 226, 106 W.A.C. 226 (C.A.) at p. 301 R.F.L. *per* Finch J.A.

48 *Rosario* v. *Rosario* (1991), 37 R.F.L. (3d) 24, 120 A.R. 331, 8 W.A.C. 331 (C.A.); *Bracewell* v. *Bracewell* (1994), 4 R.F.L. (4th) 183, 152 A.R. 379 (Q.B.); *May* v. *May* (1993), 48 R.F.L. (3d) 432 (Ont. Gen. Div.); *Harris* v. *Gilbert* (1997), 26 R.F.L. (4th) 199, 32 O.R. (3d) 139, (sub nom. *Harris* v. *Harris*) 97 O.A.C. 14 (Ont. C.A.).

49 *Wrobel* v. *Wrobel* (1994), 8 R.F.L. (4th) 403, 160 A.R. 241 (Q.B.); *Campbell* v. *Rooney* (1995), 10 R.F.L. (4th) 351, (sub nom. *Campbell* v. *Campbell*) 129 Nfld. & P.E.I.R. 294, 402 A.P.R. 294 (P.E.I. T.D.). Compare *Kits* v. *Kits* (1998), 42 R.F.L. (4th) 167 (B.C. S.C.). Here the wife was entitled to compensatory support because of her role during the marriage. Since the separation, the wife had entered into a new relationship with a man who had significant assets and earned in excess of $100,000 (U.S.) per annum. Allan J. found she did not need spousal support from Mr. Kits to maintain her standard of living. Nonetheless, he awarded her lump sum spousal support in the amount of $35,000 to compensate her for economic disadvantage as a result of the marriage.

51 Assuming that the recipient's new union was not anticipated at the time of the original order: *B. (G.)* c. *G. (L.),* 15 R.F.L. (4th) 201, (sub nom. *G. (L.)* c. *B. (G.)*) 127 D.L.R. (4th) 385, 186 N.R. 201, [1995] 3 S.C.R. 370, [1995] R.D.F. 611.

52 See cases cited *supra* note 48.

53 *Wrobel* v. *Wrobel, supra* note 48; *Rideout* v. *Rideout* (1995), 13 R.F.L. (4th) 191 (B.C. S.C.); *Range* v. *Range* (1995), 14 R.F.L. (4th) 11 (B.C. S.C.).

54 *Supra* note 48 at p. 437.

NOTES AND QUESTIONS

1. In several annotations to cases in the Reports of Family Law, Professor McLeod has concluded that: i) entitlement is now largely a non-issue in spousal support cases, and ii) there are no legal rules to determine entitlement, form, duration, or quantum, except that the spouse with the most money will always pay. See, for example, (1997), 33 R.F.L. (4th) 464, at 467; (1998), 42 R.F.L. (4th) 155, at 159; and (1999), 49 R.F.L. (4th) 336, at 340. In his "Rules and Rulelessness in Family Law: Recent Developments, Judicial and Legislative" (Prepared for the National Judicial Institute, April 19, 1999), Professor Thompson also states that *Bracklow* leaves the law of spousal support without rules:

> *Bracklow* is a deeply-disappointing decision on all fronts. First, the parties spent five years before the courts, only to be sent back to the trial judge, for further hearing and assessment of duration and amount. Second, the Court's reasons are almost impenetrable, full of buzzwords and factors and abstract language, but no concrete guidance. Third, *Bracklow* offers a prime example of "rulelessness", of what's wrong with case-by-case decision making. The Supreme Court has "exported" the costs of rulelessness to provincial appellate courts, trial judges, counsel, and the parties, leaving us all to guess for the next five or six years what the law of spousal support might be.

2. Can *Bracklow* be characterized as an illness case, simply establishing that the onset of an illness during cohabitation, where there are mutual obligations of support, gives rise to a post-marital entitlement to support? Or, does the case stand for the principle that one spouse is entitled to support whenever he or she has legitimate needs and the other has means? If so, how does one define need?

3. How helpful are McLachlin J.'s models of support? If, as in *Bracklow*, the 'basic social obligation' model applies, is there an implication that the award will be a very modest one? Does *Bracklow (No. 2)* reinforce this view? In "The New Realities of Support" (2000), 1 R.F.L. (5th) 205, Stephen Grant suggests (at 209) that equalizing the net disposable incomes of spouses following their separation may be appropriate if the relationship has led to economic disadvantage for one spouse, but he questions this result where support is awarded on a non-compensatory basis.

4. In "Spousal Support After *Moge*" (1997), 14 C.F.L.Q. 281, Professor Rogerson reviewed (at 378-84) the illness cases and concluded (at 384):

> This is an area of the law of spousal support that is currently developing with little guidance from the *Moge* judgment and where the crucial issues of public policy and social values are not being addressed directly. Given the confusion in this area of the law, a fuller and more open debate about the desirable extent of support obligations in cases involving the permanent illness and disability of a former spouse is clearly required. Should the support obligation be permanent, regardless of the length of the marriage and the spouses' roles during the marriage? Do we really believe that entry into the institution of marriage in and of itself involves the assumption of a basic social obligation to make continuing provision for one's spouse, even after the end of the relationship? Do we really believe it is appropriate for a 50 year old wife leaving a seven year marriage to receive the same award as a wife leaving a twenty-five year traditional marriage? Might it be preferable, as many of the academic commentators have suggested, to tie the extent of the obligation to the length of the marriage? Is the social obligation assumed in entering into marriage only the obligation to meet the basic needs of one's spouse, or is it a more extensive obligation to be assessed in the context of the marital standard of living and the payor spouse's resources? Can the idea of an assumption of basic social obligations through entry into a defined social institution be applied to unmarried cohabitants who have not so clearly chosen to enter into a defined social institution or status? Is the re-introduction of fault (or at least the factor of gross misconduct) not a logical corollary of the reintroduction of extensive support obligations rooted in status alone? Can a spouse who has violated some of the basic obligations of a spouse be allowed to turn around and claim support by virtue only of his or her status as a spouse? Is this a path down which we want to tread? *Moge* has clearly left much work to be done in thinking about the appropriate framework for determining non-compensatory spousal support.

To what extent, if any, has *Bracklow* provided guidance in answering these questions?

5. Prior to *Bracklow*, the cases decided after *Moge* generally awarded continuing support to spouses whose earning capacity was permanently limited at the time of separation by illness or disability. See *Colletta* v. *Colletta* (1993), 50 R.F.L. (3d) 1 (Ont. C.A.); *Roy* v. *Roy* (1993), 1 R.F.L. (4th) 170 (Ont. Gen. Div.); *Sand* v. *Sand* (1994), 2 R.F.L. (4th) 136 (B.C. S.C.); *Clifford* v. *Clifford* (1995), 13 R.F.L. (4th) 374 (Sask. Q.B.); *Ashworth* v. *Ashworth* (1995), 15 R.F.L. (4th) 379 (Ont. Gen. Div.); *Kloos* v. *Kloos* (1996), 20 R.F.L. (4th) 1 (Man. C.A.); *Parsons* v. *Parsons* (1996), 22 R.F.L. (4th) 444 (Man. Q.B.); *Dithurbide* v. *Dithurbide* (1996), 23 R.F.L. (4th) 127 (B.C. S.C.); *Van Blaricom* v. *Van Blaricom* (1996), 24 R.F.L. (4th) 410 (Ont. Div. Ct.); *Messer* v. *Messer* (1996), 26 R.F.L. (4th) 352 (Sask. Q.B.), reversed (1997), 33 R.F.L. (4th) 426 (Sask. C.A.); *Stuart* v. *Stuart* (1997), 30 R.F.L. (4th) 204 (N.B. Q.B.); *Winfield* v. *Winfield* (1998), 35 R.F.L. (4th) 393 (Ont. Gen. Div.); *Butler* v. *Butler* (1998), 37 R.F.L. (4th) 226 (N.B. C.A.); *Sitwell* v. *Sitwell* (1998), 38 R.F.L. (4th) 401 (B.C. C.A.); *Taylor* v. *Taylor* (1998), 38 R.F.L. (4th) 408 (B.C. C.A.); and *Epp* v. *Epp* (1998), 40 R.F.L. (4th) 137 (B.C. S.C.). In *Hainsworth*, Haines J. specifically indicated (at 387) that the marriage had been economically advantageous to the wife and that she would have received no support if she had not been ill. In some cases involving relatively short marriages, the courts awarded support only for a transition period: *Andersen* v. *Carter* (1994), 6 R.F.L. (4th) 90 (B.C. S.C.); *Houle* v. *Houle* (1994), 9 R.F.L. (4th) 408 (B.C. C.A.); *Callura* v. *Callura* (1996), 24 R.F.L. (4th) 419 (Ont. Gen. Div.); and *Clayburn* v. *Clayburn* (1997), 29 R.F.L. (4th) 12 (Ont. Gen. Div.). No support was awarded in *Ennis* v. *Latter* (1998), 38 R.F.L. (4th) 247 (N.S. Fam. Ct.) where the couple cohabited outside of marriage for ten years, but the woman was an alcoholic who contributed little to the relationship. See also *Sullivan* v. *Sullivan* (1999), 3 R.F.L. (5th) 166 (Ont. S.C.J.) where the court stressed that the alcoholic wife had not sought help in the four years since separation.

In many cases, the courts awarded support even where the disability did not arise until after separation. See *Mahoney* v. *Mahoney* (1994), 3 R.F.L. (4th) 235 (Ont. Gen. Div.); *Gerget* v. *Gerget* (1994), 7 R.F.L. (4th) 322 (Ont. Gen. Div.); *Plattig* v. *Robillard* (1995), 16 R.F.L. (4th) 222 (B.C. C.A.); *Sheldon* v. *Sheldon* (1996), 21 R.F.L. (4th) 422 (Alta. Q.B.); *Dillon* v. *Dillon* (1997), 27 R.F.L. (4th) 197 (N.B. Q.B.); and *Coupar* v. *Coupar* (1998), 43 R.F.L. (4th) 443 (B.C. C.A.). However, in *McMullen* v. *McMullen* (1994), 5 R.F.L. (4th) 444, the New Brunswick Court of Appeal allowed the husband's appeal of a support order where his ex-wife had been self-supporting until she was disabled by a car accident sixteen years after separation and twelve years after divorce. The court ruled that the trial judge had erred by not requiring Mrs. McMullen to demonstrate that her "need was caused by the marriage or its breakdown." See also *Noseworthy* v. *Noseworthy* (1995), 17 R.F.L. (4th) 21 (Nfld. U.F.C.) where no support was awarded to a husband who became disabled one month after separation.

In "Spousal Support After *Moge*"(1997), 14 C.F.L.Q. 281, Professor Rogerson noted (at 383-384):

> What is emerging as the dominant approach offers a very broad basis of entitlement, with quantum operating as the only obvious limitation. In most cases, the amounts awarded to ill or disabled spouses provide only a modest or basic standard of living, and do not result in anything approaching equalization of income or even the marital standard of living. This is true even in cases involving long traditional marriages. It is not surprising, given that these are support obligations essentially rooted in status, to see consideration of fault playing an indirect, unspoken role in some of the decisions. Deserving spouses, who have basically fulfilled their marital obligations, are able to claim against the relationship; undeserving spouses, who have violated the basic norms of the relationship, are not.

4.   Enforcement of Support Orders

TOBIN, "ENFORCEMENT OF SUPPORT ORDERS IN ONTARIO"

(1998), 15 C.F.L.Q. 317 (Edited footnotes follow.)

1.   Introduction

Although all of the usual debt-collection remedies are available to enforce support arrears, the law accords a special status to child and spousal support payments, because dependents under support orders are among the most vulnerable creditors in our society. In an effort to address the massive default rates (that prior to 1986 were estimated at 85% of all family support orders) and resulting child poverty, virtually every jurisdiction in North America has enacted specific legislation governing the collection and enforcement of family support payments. This paper will review some of the specialized remedies available in Ontario to enforce family support payments.

2.   Family Responsibility and Support Arrears Enforcement Act, 1996

(a)   New Act

The *Family Responsibility and Support Arrears Enforcement Act*, 1996 ("FRA") which was proclaimed in force on May 12, 1997 replaced the *Family Support Plan Act* ("FSPA"). The FSPA, which had come into effect on March 1, 1992, replaced and renamed the *Support and Custody Orders Enforcement Act* that had been in effect since March 1, 1986.

The FRA contains most of the provisions that were found in the FSPA. It does, however, contain some new enforcement remedies that, when proclaimed and implemented, should make the collection from recalcitrant payors a little easier. The FRA also reflects the current government's policy of reducing its role in certain areas of society: voluntary opting out continues to be allowed and the functions of the Director may be assigned to the private sector.

(b)   Role of Director

(i) Application of Act: The FRA is administered by the Director of the Family Responsibility Office ("the Director"). The mandate or duty of the Director is to enforce support orders and the related support deduction orders filed in his or her office, and to pay the amounts collected to the person to whom they are owed. All support orders or support deduction orders filed in the Director's office at the time the FRA came into force are deemed to be filed for the purposes of the FRA.

The Director is mandated to carry out his or her duties in a practical manner. When one deals with the Director's office in an attempt to resolve matters in a practical manner, it is important to remember that the Director does not have a statutory right to compromise the support recipient's entitlement to support monies. The Director may, however, exercise discretion in the manner and method of enforcement. Courts have held that where the Director has failed to enter into settlement discussions he or she has acted unreasonably.[10]

The Director may employ any enforcement mechanism necessary to enforce support orders or support deduction orders filed in his or her office, whether expressly provided for in the Act or not. The Director may commence and conduct proceedings and take steps for the enforcement of such orders in the Director's name for the benefit of recipients. The Director may enforce arrears that accrued prior to the date the support order was filed with the Director and prior to the date the FRA came into effect. When enforcing a support order or a support deduction order, the Director may use different means at different times or at the same time. The Director has exclusive power to enforce a support order if filed in his or her office, subject to an assignment of the Director's powers (dealt with below).

The Director may require any person or public body in Ontario to disclose the name of the employer, place of employment, wages, salary or other income, assets, or address or location of the person against whom an order is being enforced (called "the Payor"). This is an expansion of the powers formerly granted under s. 6 of the FSPA. The Director may also request the Federal Department of Justice to conduct a search of certain federal information banks to assist in locating defaulting Payors.[16]

(ii) Refusal to Enforce: Despite the duties prescribed by section 5 of the FRA, the Director may at any time refuse to enforce a support order or support deduction order filed in the Director's office if, in his or her opinion, certain enumerated circumstances exist. The Attorney General may establish policies and procedures respecting the Director's refusal to enforce a support order or a support deduction order. These policies and procedures have not been published. If the Director refuses to enforce an order, he or she will notify both the Payor and the Recipient; therefore, the support order and related support deduction order are deemed withdrawn as of the date set out in the notice.

(iii) Termination of Support Obligation: The Director will cease enforcement of a support obligation provided for in a support order or support deduction order filed if the support obligation has terminated. The termination of a support obligation shall be determined in one of three ways:

(1) if the parties agree in the manner prescribed by the Regulations;[21]
(2) if the support obligation is stated in the order to terminate on a set calendar date; or
(3) if the Court orders the obligation has terminated.

If the parties to an order do not agree that the support obligation has terminated, the Court that made the support order (or, if it is a Domestic Contract, the Provincial Court or the Family Court) shall, on motion of a party to the order, decide if the support obligation has terminated and shall make an order to that effect. The Director is not a party to this motion. The Court may order repayment in whole or in part from the person who receives support after the obligation was terminated, if the Court is of the opinion that the person ought to have notified the Director that the support obligation had terminated. Before doing so, the Court must consider the circumstances of each of the parties to the support order. The Director must continue to enforce the support obligation and pay money received to the support recipient until the Director receives a copy of the order terminating the support obligation. Despite the termination of the support obligation the Director shall continue to enforce support arrears that accrued prior to the date the support obligation terminated. This method of terminating support obligations is expedient when compared to an application to vary the support order.

(iv) Assignment of Director's Powers: The Attorney General may now assign any of the Director's powers under the FRA to another person, agency, or body. . . .

(c) Support Orders

A ''support order'' is broadly defined as a provision in an order made in or outside Ontario and enforceable in Ontario[35] for the payment of money as support or maintenance. The definition of the support order in the FRA includes many of the powers given to the Court under section 34(1) of the *Family Law Act;* it also includes support provisions in domestic contracts and paternity agreements that have been filed pursuant to section 35 of the *Family Law Act.* While Court orders are automatically filed with the Director by the Court, domestic contracts and paternity agreements are filed with the Director only if the Recipient chooses to file them. It was established that the FSPA (and now presumably the FRA) applied to support orders made under the *Divorce Act* notwithstanding that the FSPA was Provincial legislation.[38]

Every support order made by an Ontario Court (other than a provisional order) must state in its operative part that the Director shall enforce the order unless it is withdrawn from his or her office. However, if considered appropriate, the Court may require that the operative part of the order provide that the support order and the related support deduction order may not be withdrawn from the Director's office. The Director retains his or her discretion to decide whether to enforce the order notwithstanding section 9(2) of the FRA.

(d) Support Deduction Orders

(i) The Support Deduction Order: Every Ontario Court that makes a support order must also make a support deduction order (SDO). As well, an SDO can be deemed, at the Director's discretion, to have been made with respect to a support order made outside of Ontario and that is enforceable in Ontario. An SDO is an order that permits the Director to require the Payor's income source . . . to deduct support payments from the Payor's income. An income source is defined generally as one that owes or makes payments whether periodically or in a lump sum to or on behalf of a Payor. The FRA extends the types of income that must be paid under an SDO to include lump sum payments and up to 100% of income tax refunds or other lump sum payments that are attachable under the *Family Orders and Agreements and Enforcement Assistance Act, Canada.* Under the FRA, irregular earnings and lump sums such as real estate commissions, salary draws, advances and severance pay will be subject to attachment. An SDO binds the Provincial Crown. Welfare payments are not subject to an SDO. The support deduction system operates in a way similar to the enforcement remedy of garnishment except that it applies immediately, without waiting for default to occur. The form of the SDO is prescribed by the Regulations.[47]

At the time an application or motion is filed with the Court the parties are required to complete and then file a Support Deduction Order Information Form.[48] At the same time as the support award is pronounced by the Court an SDO will also be made. A support deduction order must be made even if the Court cannot identify the Payor's income source at the time the support order is made. Once the support deduction order is made, the Clerk of the Court will complete the information form, which contains the support payment information, and file the SDO and the information form promptly with the Director. The support order itself will subsequently be entered in the usual way, but the SDO will be filed promptly with the Director to allow support deductions by the Payor's income source to begin as soon as possible.

Section 5(1) of the Act provides the Director has a duty to enforce only where both the support order and the SDO are filed in his or her office.

(ii) Opting Out: . . . The FRA now allows Recipients and Payors to opt out of the enforcement of the support order or SDO by the Director. They may do so by filing with the Director a written notice signed by both the Payor and the Recipient withdrawing the support order or support deduction order. Recipients who have opted out will be able to enforce support orders themselves. The SDO, however, remains enforceable only by the Director and will be enforced only when the parties have not opted out. Recipients and Payors may now fully opt out by filing a Notice of Withdrawal. The parties, however, will not be allowed to opt out if the Court has made an order requiring enforcement by the Director pursuant to s. 9(2) of the FRA. The order will likely be made where there is evidence that the Recipient could be coerced to opt out in situations of unequal bargaining power. It remains to be seen whether the Courts will make an order precluding opting out on its [sic] own motion and perhaps against the wishes of a Recipient, or will only make the order on a party's request. . . .

Recipients who have opted out by withdrawing the support order or the support deduction order may opt back in by written notice signed by either the Payor or the Recipient.

(iii) Enforcement of SDO: The Director will enforce an SDO until the companion support order is terminated or withdrawn and there are no arrears outstanding or until the SDO and accompanying support order are withdrawn. . . .

When the Director receives the SDO from the Court, a notice of the SDO will be mailed to the income source with a copy also being sent to the Payor. Until the income source begins making the deductions, the Payor must make the required support payment to the Director. The maximum amount available for deduction by the income source is 50% of the ''net amount'' paid by the income source to the Payor. The ''net amount'' is calculated by deducting the following amounts from the total amount owed by the income source to the Payor: Income Tax, Canada Pension Plan, Unemployment Insurance, union dues, and such other deductions as may be prescribed by Regulations. The Regulations do not allow any other deductions at this time. After receiving notice of the SDO, the income source must make the first remittance to the Director within 14 days after the first ''pay day'' to the Payor. Another exemption from deductions under an SDO are amounts owing to the Payor as reimbursement for expenses covered by a medical, health, dental, or hospital insurance contract or plan. Failure by an income source to make the proper deductions and remittance constitutes an offence under the FRA. In addition, the income source may be liable to pay any amounts that ought to have been deducted from the Payor's income and remitted to the Director.

If the Payor is of the opinion that, because of a mistake of fact, more money is being deducted under the SDO than is required, the Payor may bring a motion to the Court that made the SDO, naming the Director as Respondent. The Court will determine the issue in a summary manner and make such order as it considers appropriate in the circumstances. A Payor may also bring a motion to reduce the amount that is being deducted on account of arrears. The determination of this issue by the Court will be in a summary manner. At such motions, the Payor is presumed to have the ability to pay the amount being deducted for arrears, and the Court may vary this amount only if it is satisfied that the Payor is unable to pay this amount for valid reasons. It has been held that this type of reverse onus in a support enforcement proceeding does not violate a Payor's rights under the *Charter of Rights and Free-*

doms.[73] If the Court makes an order reducing the amount deducted on account of arrears, the accruing of arrears is not affected. Such an order would merely restrict the amount that may be collected under the SDO in respect of the income source in question. The Director is entitled to enforce the arrears in any other manner available at law. Where the Court has reduced the amount being deducted for arrears pursuant to an SDO, the Director can apply to the Court to increase the amount deducted for arrears where there has been an improvement in the Payor's financial circumstances.

Where there has been an interruption or termination of payment by an income source to a Payor (eg. by reason of layoff, disability, leave of absence, or termination of employment), both the income source and the Payor are required to give written notice to the Director's office within 10 days. If the income source resumes making payments to the Payor, both the Payor and the income source must notify the Director's office within 10 days of the resumption.

Once the Payor begins employment with another income source or becomes entitled to receive payments from another income source, the Payor must give written notice to the Director's office, including the name and address of the new income source. Failure to comply with these notice requirements constitutes an offence.

Where a Payor's employment with an income source is terminated and the Payor has commenced employment with a new income source, the Director will send a notice of the SDO to the new income source, and it will be required to deduct support payments from the Payor's income. The portability of the support deduction mechanism is one of its prime advantages.

An SDO can be varied only by order of the Court. Any agreement or arrangement by the parties to vary an SDO, or to avoid or prevent enforcement of an SDO is of no effect. An SDO cannot be varied unless the support order to which it relates is varied. This provision ensures that a Payor who is seeking to reduce or rescind arrears, or vary the ongoing amount of support, will take the necessary step of applying to vary the support order, rather than to obtain relief indirectly by simply applying to vary the SDO. The SDO should always be consistent with the support order, and this cannot occur unless a new SDO is made each time the order is varied.

(iv) Suspension of SDO: Although an SDO must be made each time a support order for periodic payments is made, the Court has the discretion to suspend the operation of an SDO. A suspension order can be granted only if: (1) it would be unconscionable, having regard to all of the circumstances, to have the support obligation paid by way of support deduction; or (2) the parties to the support order agree that they do not want support deduction to apply, and the Court requires the Payor to post adequate security, which must amount to at least 4 months' support payments.

A suspension order operates only in respect of the support deduction order. It does not in any way affect the Payor's obligation to make support payments under the support order, nor does it restrict the enforcement of the support obligation by other means. While the SDO is suspended, the Payor is required to make all support payments to the Director (unless the parties have opted out). If the suspension order is made on consent and the required security is not posted within the time period set out in the suspension order, of if the Payor fails to comply with the support order, the suspension order is automatically terminated. Similarly, if the suspension order was made on the grounds of unconscionability and the Payor subsequently defaults under the support order, the suspension order is automatically terminated. When a suspension order is terminated, the SDO is immediately reinstated, and the Director may immediately realize on any security that was posted. Accordingly, when default under the support order occurs, the support funds that are owing under the order will be disbursed to the Recipient out of the security monies, and the Director will send a Notice of Support Deduction Order to the Payor's income source if and when an income source is identified and located.

If the SDO is withdrawn while a suspension order is in effect, the suspension order is terminated and the security held by the Director will be repaid.

(e) Application Of SDO To Support Orders Made Before March 1, 1992 And To Domestic Contracts

The Director is entitled to enforce support payments under a domestic contract or a paternity agreement or a pre-existing Ontario support order [as if] an SDO had been made if the Director considers it advisable to do so. Alternatively, if the support Recipient requests the Director to apply the support deduction remedy to his or her order or contract, the request shall be granted if the Director considers it practical to do so. Before the support provisions in a domestic contract or a paternity agreement can be enforced, they must be filed under s. 35(1) of the *Family Law Act*. . . .

3. OTHER ENFORCEMENT REMEDIES

(a) Garnishment

The *Family Rules of the Ontario Court* (Provincial Division), and the Ontario Court (General Division) *Family Court Rules* [see now *Family Law Rules,* O.Reg. 114/99, Rules 26 - 32] provide a procedure for garnishment of debts owing to a support Payor. Put simply, a garnishment directs a person who owes money to a Payor (called a "Garnishee") to pay the money to the Creditor (called the "Recipient") instead of to the Payor. Garnishments are used to seize wages, pensions, bank accounts, rents, sums owing to Payor by the Federal government,[113] lump sum and periodic payments under the *Workers Compensation Act* (which sums are also subject to SDO's), and other amounts owed to Payors by third parties. . . .

(b) Writ of Seizure and Sale

The *Family Rules of the Ontario Court* (Provincial Division) and the Ontario Court (General Division) *Family Court Rules* [see now *Family Law Rules,* O.Reg. 114/99, Rules 26 - 32] provide for the issuance and filing of a Writ of Seizure and Sale for support enforcement purposes. . . .

(c) Charge Against Land

In addition to the filing of a Writ of Seizure and Sale, it is possible to register the actual support order in the Land Registry Office against specific land owned by the Payor, and thereby create a charge on the property. The charge may be enforced by sale of the property in the same manner as a sale to realize on a mortgage. A Court may order the discharge, in whole or in part, or the postponement of the charge, on such terms as to security or other matters as the Court considers just.

(d) Default Hearing

A support Payor who owes arrears may be compelled to file a financial statement and attend before the Court and explain the default. If the Payor does not attend

Court as required, the Court may issue a bench warrant requiring that the Payor be arrested and brought before the Court. At a default hearing, the Payor is presumed to have the ability to pay the arrears and to make subsequent support payments. Accordingly, the Payor has the onus of establishing an inability to pay for valid reasons. A "valid reason" would be an event over which the Payor has no control, rendering him or her without assets or income with which to meet his or her obligations, such as a disabling illness or involuntary unemployment. It has been held that this reverse onus provision does not violate the *Charter of Rights and Freedoms*. Unless the Payor can satisfy the Court that he or she is unable to pay for valid reasons, the Court may make a variety of orders, including an order for imprisonment for up to 90 days. In an enforcement proceeding the Court does not have the power to vary or vacate the support order; that jurisdiction lies only in the Court that made the support order. Support is the only civil debt for which a willful refusal to pay can result in imprisonment. This power of imprisonment should be exercised as a last resort, not for the purpose of punishment but to coerce the Payor to meet his Court ordered obligations.

(e) Restraining Orders Against Assets

A Court including the Ontario Court (Provincial Division) may make an order restraining the disposing or wasting of assets that may hinder or defeat the enforcement of a support order or SDO.

(f) Arrest of Absconding Payor

If the Court is satisfied that a Payor is about to leave Ontario and there are reasonable grounds to believe that he or she intends to evade his or her support payment obligations, the Court may issue a warrant for the Payor's arrest. Once the Payor is arrested, he or she is brought before the Court and any order available at a default hearing may be made. Only a Judge of the Ontario Court (Provincial Division) or of the Family Court has jurisdiction under this section.

(g) Reporting to Consumer Reporting Agencies

The Director may disclose information concerning a support Payor who is in arrears of support to a credit reporting agency (eg. Credit Bureau). The rational for this remedy is that a Payor may be encouraged to keep support current or risk a bad credit rating.

4. Priorities

Support orders and SDOs have priority over all other judgment debts regardless of when an enforcement process is issued and served.[133] . . . A support debt is now (after September 30, 1997) a "claim provable" in bankruptcy, and support obligations are not released upon a discharge from bankruptcy.[135]

---

10 *Director of Support & Custody Enforcement (Ontario)* v. *Glover* (1987), 11 R.F.L. (3d) 58 (Ont. Fam. Ct.) and *Director of Support & Custody Enforcement (Ontario)* v. *McIntyre* (1987), 11 R.F.L. (3d) 89 (Ont. Fam. Ct.). In the later case costs were assessed against the Director. A contrary view was expressed by the Court in *Director of Support & Custody Enforcement (Ontario)* v. *Couling*

(1988), 17 R.F.L. (3d) 53 (Ont. Dist. Ct.); if the Director acts in good faith in the execution of duties and within the statutory mandate costs will not be awarded against it: *Costello* v. *Somers* (1989), 21 R.F.L. (3d) 411 (Ont. Div. Ct.).

16 *Family Orders and Agreements Enforcement Assistance Act*, S.C. 1986, c. 5 and section 55 of the FRA.

21 O.Reg. 167/97, s. 1 to 6.

35 A support order made outside of Ontario under the *Divorce Act* is enforceable in Ontario once it has been filed with the Director. There is no need to register the Order in the Ontario Court before the Director will enforce it; see s. 13(2). It may also be registered in the Ontario Court (General Division); *Divorce Act*, s. 20(3), *Rules of Civil Procedure,* Rule 70.25, Rule 58 of the Ontario Court (Provincial Division), and Rule 75 of the *Family Court Rules.* All other support orders made outside of Ontario are enforceable in Ontario upon registration in an Ontario Court; see *Reciprocal Enforcement of Support Orders Act*, s. 9(3). Only orders made in reciprocating states may be so registered. See appendix for list of reciprocating states.

38 *Montaque* v. *Montaque* (1987), 11 R.F.L. (3d) 281, 61 O.R. (2d) 781 (Ont. U.F.C.).

47 Subsection 11(1), O.Reg. 167/97 subsection 7(1) and Form 1.

48 O.Reg. 167/97 subsection 7(2) and Form 2; subsection 11(2) and (3) of the FRA.

73 *Mancuso* v. *Mancuso* (1991), 35 R.F.L. (3d) 265 (Ont. Prov. Div.).

113 Under the *Family Orders and Agreements Enforcement Assistance Act*, S.C. 1986, c. 5, and the Regulations enacted pursuant thereto, the following Federal monies owing to a Payor may be attached for support enforcement purposes: unemployment insurance benefits (50%); income tax refunds (100%); GST rebates (100%); interest on Canada Savings Bonds (100%); Canada Pension Plan payments (50%); Old Age Security payments (50%); and certain agricultural and dairy subsidy payments (100%).

133 *Creditors' Relief Act*, R.S.O. 1990, c. C.45, s. 4(1) and FRA s. 30(1).

135 *Kutschenreiter* v. *Kutschenreiter* (1983), 46 C.B.R. (N.S.) 1 (Ont. H.C.); *Bankruptcy and Insolvency Act*, R.S.C. 1985 B-3, ss. 121(4) and 178(1)(b) and (c).

[Several key provisions of the *Family Responsibility and Support Arrears Enforcement Act, 1996* were proclaimed shortly after Barry Tobin wrote this article. They include Part V: Suspension of Drivers' Licences, under which the Director may direct the Registrar of Motor Vehicles to suspend a payor's driver's licence if he or she owes arrears on a support order. Payors are first given notices and an opportunity to pay the arrears in full or enter into a payment arrangement with the Director. Also, under s. 41, in a default hearing, the court may order a person who is financially connected to the payor to file a financial statement and any other relevant documents with the court or to be a party to the hearing. If the court is satisfied that the third party who has been made a party to the hearing was involved in sheltering the payor's assets or income from the enforcement of the support order, the court may make any order against the person, except an order for imprisonment, that it can made against the payor, to the extent of the value of the sheltered assets or income. Under s. 45, the Director may garnishee up to 50 per cent of the money held in joint bank accounts where one of the account holders is a payor under a support order. Where the bank has notified the Director that the funds are in a joint bank account, the Director shall hold the funds for a period of 30 days. The Director may release the funds after 30 days, unless a dispute to the garnishment is filed by the co-holder of the account, who is not the payor. If a dispute is filed, the court will determine the ownership of the funds seized under the garnishment. At the hearing, there is a presumption that the money sent to the Director is owned by the support payor. Finally, s. 46 provides for the interception of lottery winnings where a support payor wins a lottery in excess of $1,000.00. The Ontario Lottery Corporation must deduct from the payor the lesser of the full amount of the arrears owing and the full amount of the prize.

For further reading, see Goldwater, "Bankruptcy and Family Law" (1998), 15 C.F.L.Q. 115 and Klotz, "Pitfalls and Pointers in High Debt Cases" (1998), 15 C.F.L.Q. 187.]

_____

7

CUSTODY AND ACCESS

1. Introduction

Used in its broadest sense, custody of a child denotes the totality of rights and duties in relation to the infant. Section 20(2) of the *Children's Law Reform Act* (the *CLRA*) specifies: "A person entitled to custody of a child has the rights and responsibilities of a parent in respect of the person of the child and must exercise those rights and responsibilities in the best interests of the child." Section 20(2) refers to "rights and responsibilities . . . in respect of the person of the child". The Act contains special rules relating to the property of the child and distinguishes between custody of the child and guardianship of the property of the child (see ss. 47-60).

While the parents of the child are cohabiting, both are entitled to custody (s. 20(1) of *CLRA*). Either of them, with or without the consent of the other, "may exercise the rights and accept the responsibilities of a parent on behalf of them in respect of the child" (s. 20(3)). The law assumes, therefore, that a mother and father will act with the necessary co-operation and trust. If a dispute does arise between cohabiting parents regarding the upbringing of the child, s. 21 of the *CLRA* appears broad enough to permit either of them to apply to a court for a resolution of the specific issue. Section 21 authorizes orders "determining any aspect of the incidents of custody of the child". In *Chauvin* v. *Chauvin* (1987), 6 R.F.L. (3d) 403 (Ont. Dist. Ct.), Judge Killeen relied on s. 21 to order that two boys, who were in their mother's custody, should attend a French language school. In that case, the mother had transferred the children to an English language school and the father objected. See also *Templeman* v. *Templeman* (1990), 29 R.F.L. (3d) 71 (Ont. Dist. Ct.).

When the family unit breaks down the parents may come to an understanding or agreement regarding custody of their child. Section 20(4) of the *CLRA* stipulates that "where the parents of a child live separate and apart and the child lives with one of them with the consent, implied consent or acquiescence of the other of them, the right of the other to exercise the entitlement to custody and the incidents of custody, but not the entitlement to access, is suspended until a separation agreement or order otherwise provides". Where the parents cannot agree on custody or access, either can apply for a court order under s. 21 of the *CLRA*. Such an application may be made even if there is initially an agreement between the parents. The court has authority to disregard the terms of the agreement if it is in the best interests of the child to do so (see s. 56(1) of the *FLA*).

Part III of the *CLRA* governs custody and access applications under provincial law in Ontario. One of the express purposes of Part III is to "ensure that applications to the courts in respect of custody of, incidents of custody of, access to and guardianship for children will be determined on the basis of the best interests of the children" (s. 19(a)). To aid in the achievement of this objective, s. 24(1) specifies that custody and access issues are to be determined on the basis of the best interests of the child. The factors to be considered are set out in s. 24(2) and (3). Section 22 of the Act governs the jurisdiction of the court to make a custody or access order (see also s. 27).

Custody and access orders can be made under the *Divorce Act* in divorce proceedings or in corollary relief proceedings after the divorce. Section 16(8) stipulates that in making custody or access orders, "the court shall take into consideration only the best interests of the child of the marriage as determined by reference to the condition, means, needs and other circumstances of the child". Subsections 16(9) and (10) provide further guidance for the courts. The jurisdiction to hear divorce proceedings is governed by s. 3, while s. 4 specifies when a court has jurisdiction over corollary relief proceedings. Under s. 6 the court may transfer the divorce proceeding or corollary relief proceeding to a court in another province if an application for custody or access is involved, the application is opposed and the child of the marriage in respect of whom the order is sought is most substantially connected with the other province. The courts have held that, even if the statutory conditions for transfer are met, the decision to transfer is discretionary and is determined by the best interests of the child: *Bell* v. *Nelson* (1997), 35 R.F.L. (4th) 8 (Sask. Q.B.) and *Johnson* v. *Lennert* (1998), 41 R.F.L. (4th) 442 (Nfld. C.A.).

Professor Mnookin argues in "Child Custody Adjudication: Judicial Functions in the Face of Indeterminacy" (1975), 39 Law and Contemporary Problems 226, that the best interests test in custody cases does little more than give broad discretion to the courts. What is best for a child is indeterminative, in his view, for two reasons. First, it is difficult and sometimes impossible to predict the effects of a particular alternative for the child with any certainty. Current psychological theories are generally incapable of yielding such predictions, primarily because this requires the prediction of the future behaviour of the persons involved and the effect of such behaviour. Second, even if reliable predictions could be made, the decision-maker must assign some measure of utility to each possible outcome:

> Deciding what is best for a child poses a question no less ultimate than the purposes and values of life itself. Should the judge be concerned with the economic "productivity" of the child when he grows up? Are the primary values of life in warm, interpersonal relationships, or in discipline and self-sacrifice? Is stability and security for a child more desirable than intellectual stimulation? These questions could be elaborated endlessly. And yet, where is a judge to look for a set of values that should inform the choice of what is best for the child? Normally, the custody statutes do not themselves give content or relative weights to the pertinent values. And if the judge looks to society at large, he finds neither a clear consensus as to the best child rearing strategies nor an appropriate hierarchy of ultimate values.

Other commentators have also argued that the best interests of the child test is inherently vague, and inevitably permits or even requires judges to decide cases based on their personal values, beliefs or ideology. See, e.g., Toope, "Riding the Fences: Courts, Charter of Rights and Family Law" (1991), 9 C.J.F.L. 55, at 67; Boyd, "Potentialities and Perils of the Primary Caregiver Presumption" (1991), 7 C.F.L.Q. 1; Munro, "The Inapplicability of Rights Analysis in Post-Divorce Child Custody Decision Making" (1992), 30 Alta. L. Rev. 852; and Bala and Miklas, *Rethinking Decisions About Children: Is the 'Best Interests of the Child' Approach Really in the Best Interest of Children?* (Toronto: Policy Research Centre on Children, Youth and Families, 1993) at 1-2. In *Young* v. *Young* (1993), 49 R.F.L. (3d) 117 (S.C.C.), Madam Justice L'Heureux-Dubé (dissenting) noted these concerns and responded (at 199 and 206):

> Custody and access decisions are pre-eminently exercises in discretion. Case-by-case consideration of the unique circumstances of each child is the hallmark of the process. . . . The wide latitude under the best interests test permits courts to respond to the spectrum of factors which can positively and negatively affect a child. Such discretion also permits the judge to focus on the

needs of the particular child before him or her, recognizing that what may constitute stressful or damaging circumstances for one child may not necessarily have the same effect on another. . . .

It should not be assumed that a grant of discretion is an invitation to exercise personal prejudice, as it is well established in the jurisprudence that discretion in every instance must be exercised judicially and in conformity with the objectives and standards of the legislation. The application of the best interests test, if done in an individual case according to irrelevant or improper criteria, remains subject to the normal process of review on appeal.

In the same case, Madam Justice McLachlin commented on the best interests of the child test as follows (at 149-150):

. . . The express wording of s. 16(8) of the *Divorce Act* requires the court to look *only* at the best interests of the child in making orders of custody and access. This means that parental preferences and "rights" play no role.

. . . Parliament has recognized that the variety of circumstances which may arise in disputes over custody and access is so diverse that predetermined rules, designed to resolve certain types of disputes in advance, may not be useful. Rather, it has been left to the judge to decide what is in the "best interests of the child", by reference to the "condition, means, needs and other circumstances" of the child. Nevertheless, the judicial task is not one of pure discretion. By embodying the "best interests" test in legislation and by setting out general factors to be considered, Parliament has established a legal test, albeit a flexible one. Like all legal tests, it is to be applied according to the evidence in the case, viewed objectively. There is no room for the judge's personal predilections and prejudices.

There are various ways in which judicial discretion in custody cases can be limited. The first is to direct judges to consider a non-exhaustive list of factors deemed relevant to a child's best interests. The second is to create prescriptive rules or legal presumptions in favour of or against defined classes of claimants, such as primary caregivers. A third method is to apply legal presumptions favouring specific custody arrangements, such as joint custody. Finally, the legislation can proscribe the consideration of a specific factor, such as marital misconduct, unless it is demonstrably relevant to the decision in a particular case. See generally, Ehrcke, "Limiting Judicial Discretion in Custody Proceedings on Divorce" (1987), 6 Can. J. Fam. L. 211. As you study the statutory provisions and the case law, consider the extent to which any of these methods have been utilized in Canada.

The traditional custody order entrusts sole custody to one parent after separation and allows access by the other. In *Kruger* v. *Kruger* (1979), 11 R.F.L. (2d) 52, 25 O.R. (2d) 673 (C.A.), Thorson J.A. indicated (at 78) that the effect of such an order "is to clothe that parent, for whatever period he or she is awarded custody, with full parental control over, and ultimate parental responsibility for, the care, upbringing and education of the child, generally to the exclusion of the right of the other parent to interfere in the decisions that are made in exercising that control or carrying out that responsibility". Thus, the non-custodial parent who has a right to access has been traditionally considered to have no voice in the upbringing of the child. In accordance with this view the non-custodial parent with access has the right only to visit the child or be visited by the child in accordance with the order. While the right to access includes the right to manage the child during a visit and to consent to emergency medical treatment, it does not allow the parent to influence the child's life style, education or religion (see *McCutcheon* v. *McCutcheon* (1982), 29 R.F.L. (2d) 11, 41 N.B.R. (2d) 263 (Q.B.). See also *Glasgow* v. *Glasgow (No. 2)* (1992), 51 N.S.R. (2d) 13 (Fam. Ct.) and *McLean* v. *Goddard* (1994), 3 R.F.L. (4th) 117 (N.S. Fam. Ct.).

This description of the traditional custody and access order has never been universally accepted and must be reassessed in light of recent developments. First, the *Chauvin* case, above, indicates that s. 21 of the *CLRA* provides a mechanism whereby the non-custodial parent can obtain judicial scrutiny of a decision made by the custodial parent. Although the wording of the *Divorce Act* is significantly different, a custody order under that Act may contain conditions that may restrict the decision making power or activities of the custodial parent. See *Gordon* v. *Goertz* (1996), 19 R.F.L. (4th) 177 (S.C.C.) (reproduced later in this chapter) and *S.(L.)* v. *S.(C.)* (1997), 37 R.F.L. (4th) 344 (S.C.C.). In the former case, the father sought unsuccessfully to vary the custody order to prevent the mother's move to Australia with the child. In the latter, the S.C.C. removed a clause in the custody order limiting the religious activity in which the mother as custodial parent could involve the child. Significantly, the S.C.C. indicated in both cases that such restrictions could be imposed if they were in the child's best interests. See also *Mummery* v. *Campbell* (1998), 38 R.F.L. (4th) 301 (B.C. S.C.), where the court concluded, over the objections of the father, that it was in an eight-year-old girl's best interests to be baptized as she and the custodial mother wished.

Second, both the *CLRA* and the *Divorce Act* provide that in the absence of a contrary court order the parent with access has the right to make inquiries and to be given information regarding the health, education and welfare of the child (see s. 20(5) of the *CLRA* and s. 16(5) of the *Divorce Act*). While these statutory provisions only expressly provide for a right to be given information, the Manitoba Court of Appeal stated in *Abbott* v. *Taylor*, 2 R.F.L. (3d) 163, [1986] 4 W.W.R. 751, that similarly worded Manitoba legislation impliedly gave the non-custodial parent with access a right to participate in the process of making important decisions regarding the child. While the custodial parent continued to have ultimate authority to make such decisions, the court suggested that the parent with access had a right to be consulted.

Finally, a majority of the British Columbia Court of Appeal held in *Young* v. *Young* (1990), 29 R.F.L. (3d) 113 at 209 that the custodial parent cannot unilaterally prevent the access parent "from sharing his or her religious views with the child, whether that sharing takes the form of discussions, observance or other activities related in some way to those views". See also *Hockey* v. *Hockey* (1989), 21 R.F.L. (3d) 105 (Ont. Div. Ct.).

In *Young* v. *Young* (1993), 49 R.F.L. (3d) 117 (reproduced below), the Supreme Court of Canada divided sharply regarding the appropriate role of the access parent following family breakdown. The case involved a custodial mother who wanted to limit the access rights of a father who was a Jehovah's Witness, and in particular to restrict the extent to which he could share his religious views and observances with his children. Madam Justice McLachlin and Mr. Justice Sopinka emphasized the importance of the continued involvement of non-custodial parents in the lives of their children, reflected in s. 16(10) of the *Divorce Act* which provides for a presumption of maximum contact. Justice McLachlin wrote (at 151):

> The custodial parent's wishes are not the ultimate criterion for limitations on access. . . . The only circumstance in which contact with either parent can be limited is where the contact is shown to conflict with the best interests of the child.
>
> . . . Given the interest of the child in coming to know his or her access parent as fully as possible, judges may well be reluctant to impose limits on what the access parent may say or do with the child in the absence of some evidence suggesting that the activity may harm the child.

In her view, although a custodial parent seeking to restrict access does not have to prove harm, it is an important factor. Moreover, she indicated (at 157) that generally expert evidence should be adduced in an application to restrict access.

Because he concluded that the restrictions sought affected the father's freedom of religion, Mr. Justice Sopinka went further (at 166-169):

> The policy favouring activities that promote a meaningful relationship is not displaced unless there is a substantial risk of harm to the child. . . . Harm . . . in this context, connotes . . . a substantial risk that the child's physical, psychological or moral well-being will be adversely affected.

The position of Justices McLachlin and Sopinka, emphasizing the importance of a meaningful relationship between the child and the access parent, contrasts with the views of Madam Justice L'Heureux-Dubé (LaForest J. and Gonthier J. concurring). In lengthy reasons reviewing various aspects of custody and access, she favoured an analysis that characterized the access parent (at 184) as "a passive bystander who is excluded from the decision-making process in matters relating to the child's welfare, growth and development". She specifically stated (at 184) that neither s. 16(5) nor any of the other provisions of the *Divorce Act* conferred any authority on the non-custodial parent to participate, even through consultation, in the major decisions of a child's life. While acknowledging (at 183) that an access parent could ask a court to review a custodial parent's decision on the basis that it was not in the best interests of the child, she stressed (at 187) that the courts should generally support those decisions since custodial parents were "uniquely situated to assess, understand, ensure, and promote the needs of the child".

Her willingness to respect the views of the custodial parent extended to requests for restrictions on the activities of the access parent. She began (at 184) by rejecting the proposition that the custodial parent could never forbid certain types of contact between the access parent and the child. "For example, a custodial parent, aware of sexual or other abuse by the non-custodial parent, would be remiss in his or her duty to the child not to cut off access by the abuser immediately, with or without a court order." She also indicated (at 212) that judges who are asked by a custodial parent to place restrictions on the access parent should recognize that the "custodial parent normally has the best vantage point from which to assess the interests of the child, and thus will often provide the most reliable and complete source of information to the judge on the needs and interests of that child." She questioned (at 213) the role of mental health experts in determining the child's best interests and concluded that the evidence of experts was generally unnecessary. Thus, Justice L'Heureux-Dubé would have judges determine whether any restrictions on access are appropriate by applying a best interests test, placing considerable reliance on the evidence of the custodial parent.

The two justices whose views were decisive to the outcome in *Young* v. *Young* and the companion case of *Droit de la famille — 1150* (1993), 49 R.F.L. (3d) 317 (S.C.C.) were Justices Cory and Iacobucci. They wrote very brief judgments indicating that in *Young* the proper application of the best interests of the child test did not support forbidding Mr. Young from discussing his religion with the children, while it did support restrictions on the father's religious activities in *Droit de la famille*.

The split in the Supreme Court was again evident in *Gordon* v. *Goertz*, where a majority rejected Justice L'Heureux-Dubé's view that the courts should presume that a custodial parent's decision to move with a child is in the child's best interests.

While orders for sole custody to one parent and access to the other continue to be used in most cases, the court has authority under both the *CLRA* and the *Divorce Act* to deviate from this model. Parents, obviously, can also agree on other forms of custody arrangements after separation. There are several variants under which both parents continue to be actively and meaningfully involved in the upbringing of the child. Often the term "joint custody" is used to describe all of these arrangements. However, the term is most appropriate to describe a situation where both parents continue to have, at all times, joint legal responsibility for the child's upbringing. Used in this sense, it can be contrasted with a "split custody order" or an "alternating custody order". The following excerpt explains the differences between these various types of orders. It should be noted that the terms are not always consistently used in the way suggested by Ms Fineberg. For example, in *McLean* v. *Goddard* (1994), 3 R.F.L. (4th) 117 (N.S. Fam. Ct.), Niedemeyer Fam. Ct. J. used (at 120) the term "split custody" to refer to the custody arrangement labelled "alternating custody" by Ms Fineberg. The court in *Broder* v. *Broder* (1998), 42 R.F.L. (4th) 143 (Alta. Q.B.) described this arrangement as "parallel parenting" and suggested that it might be suitable where there was a high level of conflict between the parents. In s. 8 of the *Child Support Guidelines*, "split custody" is used to describe a situation where each parent has custody of one or more of the couples' children. In *Hamlyn* v. *Hamlyn* (1999), 50 R.F.L. (4th) 398 (Nfld. U.F.C.), the court distinguished between "joint custody" and "shared custody", even though, as Ms Fineberg indicates, these terms are often used interchangeably. It suggested that "shared custody" should be used only to describe situations where the child resides with each parent for a substantial period of time.

FINEBERG, "JOINT CUSTODY OF INFANTS: BREAKTHROUGH OR FAD?"

(1979), 2 Can. J. Fam. L. 417 (Footnotes Omitted)

The split custody order . . . gives physical "care and control" of the child to one parent and "legal custody" to the other parent. Somewhat paradoxically, the custodial parent does *not* have actual *physical* custody of the child, but almost as a guardian, has the exclusive right to formulate the important decisions in the child's upbringing. Actual physical custody resides with the parent having "care and control". . . .[For a rare example of its use in Canada, see *Metzner* v. *Metzner*, [1993] B.C.J. No. 1839 (Q.L.) (B.C. S.C.) where the court concluded that the only way in which to ensure that the father had a meaningful role in the lives of the children was to award him custody even though the children would live with the mother. For a description of the ongoing litigation since the original order, see *Metzner* v. *Metzner* (1999), 175 D.L.R. (4th) 587 (B.C. C.A.).]

The alternating custody order entrusts to one parent *full* custody, including care and control for a specified time period and then to the other parent for another period of time. When the child resides with one parent, that parent is entirely responsible for the upbringing of the child, although the temporarily non-custodial parent generally has the right to access. This arrangement *divides*, rather than *shares*, between the parents the responsibility for the child's upbringing. This is the crucial distinction between alternating and joint custody. . . .

In contrast to the split or alternating order, joint custody (or shared custody, as it is often called) *preserves*, at all times, both parents' joint, legal responsibility for the child's upbringing upon their separation. The crux of the order is that the separated parents continue to act as parents, sharing as equal as possible the authority and responsibility for the decisions that significantly affect the life of their child. Physical "care and control" is not isolated from "legal custody" nor do the parents divide custody in its broadest sense in such a way that it alternates between them during various times of the year.

A precise definition of joint custody is not possible as no one model is adequate to describe the possibilities open to separated families by such arrangements. In practice, however, the joint order may assume one of two forms. One kind provides that both parents have custody in the broad sense of the term with only one parent having "care and control". The other has the same element of "legal custody", but the parents alternate periods of "care and control". It should be stressed that the flexibility of the arrangement requires that the ultimate decisions on the practical aspects of joint custody must rest with the individual family. The resolution of issues, such as those affecting the child's place of residence, the amount of time spent with each parent, the quality of the child's life, the financial responsibility that each parent owes to the child, is dependent upon the framework within which joint custody will best function to satisfy the particular individual's needs and resources. It is thus probably erroneous to speak of "joint custody" as if it were a single finite disposition; rather it should be viewed as a broad range of post-separation custodial arrangements, the details of which are, of necessity, best worked out by the families involved.

In *Evaluation of the Divorce Act: Phase II: Monitoring and Evaluation* (Ottawa: Minister of Supply and Services, 1990), the Department of Justice found that, in 1987-88, mothers obtained sole custody in 72% of all Canadian divorces. Fathers received sole custody in about 15% of the cases and joint custody was the result in 12% of the cases. It also concluded that joint custody was rarely ordered over the objection of one parent and that joint custody was twice as likely to result if the parties used mediation facilities. In the four research sites studied by the Department, only 35 of 1170 cases resulted in a trial of the custody issue. In 77% of those cases, the mothers received sole custody. Statistics Canada reported that, at the time of divorce in 1995, 11% of dependent children were in the custody of their fathers, 68% in the custody of their mothers, and 21% in some form of joint custody (Statistics Canada, *Divorces 1995*, p. 20). Similar statistics are reported in Statistics Canada, *Divorces 1996 and 1997* (Ottawa, 1999). The latest National Longitudinal Study on Children and Youth data from Statistics Canada in 1998 suggests that only 6% of children live approximately equal periods of time with each parent after divorce, while 85% live mainly with their mother. See Special Joint Committee on Child Custody and Access, *For the Sake of the Children* (December, 1998), at 4.

Some cases suggest that the courts should refrain from using the traditional terms to describe living and decision-making arrangements after separation. In *Abbott v. Taylor*, above, the trial judge avoided the use of the terms "custody" and "access", choosing instead to order that the child live with the mother at certain times and with the father at other times. Additionally, he conferred on the mother "the prime responsibility for making any major decisions as to the education or medical matters or religious matters". The Manitoba Court of Appeal concluded (at 172) that it was acceptable to use "ordinary language in expressing the responsibilities which each parent should exercise with respect to the child". Twaddle J.A. explained, for the court (at 171-172):

The language of custody orders has ordinarily followed the language of the statute. Custody has, however, several aspects. If effect can be given to the statutory intention by the use of language more easily understood by the parties to the proceedings and the child whose custody is in issue, there can be no objection to it provided all the responsibilities of custody are conferred on the parents between them. I do not prescribe this choice of language, but approve of it when required in the best interests of the child.

The mother's appeal was allowed only to the extent that the court substituted "ultimate responsibility" for "prime responsibility" in the order. See also *Davis* v. *Davis* (1986), 3 R.F.L. (3d) 30 (Man. Q.B.); *Harsant* v. *Portnoi* (1990), 27 R.F.L. (3d) 216 (Ont. H.C.); *Da Costa* v. *Da Costa* (1990), 29 R.F.L. (3d) 422 (Ont. Gen. Div.); *Rix* v. *Rix* (1993), 50 R.F.L. (3d) 22 (P.E.I. S.C.); *Smith* v. *Gale* (1999), 49 R.F.L. (4th) 400 (Nfld. U.F.C.); and *Hamlyn* v. *Hamlyn* (1999), 50 R.F.L. (4th) 398 (Nfld. U.F.C.).

A move away from the traditional terminology may be beneficial in several respects. Use of the term "custody" suggests that one parent has possession, almost akin to ownership. It also implies that there is a "winner" and a "loser". Finally, the development of new language to describe the residential and decision-making arrangements after breakdown may encourage the parents and the courts to focus on the wide range of possible options that could ensure continued involvement by both parents. See, generally, Payne, "The Dichotomy Between Family Law and Family Crises on Marriage Breakdown" (1989), 20 R.G.D. 109 at 118-126. The current uncertainty and debate over the legal effect of a traditional custody and access order provides another reason to abandon the old labels and focus directly on what role each parent should play in the child's life. At the very least, judges should spell out the intended effect of any order even if the traditional labels are used. This will ensure that an order is given its intended effect and perhaps minimize further litigation.

A move away from the traditional language was one of the chief recommendations of the Special Joint Committee on Child Custody and Access in its report, *For the Sake of the Children* (December, 1998). This committee had an interesting origin and existence, described in detail in Bala, "A Report From Canada's 'Gender War Zone': Reforming the Child-Related Provisions of the Divorce Act" (available at www.queens.ca/law/bala/papers). After the House of Commons passed the amendments to the *Divorce Act* providing for the adoption of the *Federal Child Support Guidelines* (discussed in Chapter 8: **CHILD SUPPORT**), fathers and various fathers' rights groups lobbied the Senate committee that was studying the package. Some of their criticisms focused on the *Guidelines*, but many related to custody and access. They were upset that resolution of child support issues which had been raised by mothers and women's rights groups was occurring while their concerns, particularly over access, were ignored. To get the support of the committee and secure passage of the *Guidelines* legislation, the Liberal government made concessions in the form of a few changes to the *Guidelines*, a statutory commitment to a review of the *Guidelines* by May, 2002, and the establishment of a joint committee of the House of Commons and the Senate to study the child related parts of the *Divorce Act*. The committee clearly sought to encourage the meaningful involvement of both parents in the upbringing of their children following divorce, but it resisted the creation of a presumption in favour of joint custody as many fathers urged. Instead, a central recommendation of the committee's report was the abandonment of the traditional terminology of "custody and access" and the adoption of the term "shared parenting" to encompass all the rights and responsibilities of parents currently embodied by those terms. It further recommended (at 32):

...[P]arents [should] be encouraged to develop, on their own or with the help of a trained mediator or through some form of alternative dispute resolution, a parenting plan setting out details about each parent's responsibilities for residence, care, decision making, and financial security for children, together with the dispute resolution process to be used by the parties. Parenting plans must also require the sharing between parents of health, educational and other information related to the child's development and social activities. All parenting orders should be in the form of parenting plans.

...[T]he Minister [should] seek to amend the *Divorce Act* to require that parties applying to a court for a parenting order must file a proposed parenting plan with the court.

The suggested new language and the concept of "parenting plans" draws on reforms in England, Australia, and Washington State, which were considered by the committee. For commentary on these reforms, see Bainhaim, "The Children's Act 1989: The State and the Family" (1990), 20 Fam. Law 231; Ellis, "Plans, Protections, and Professional Intervention: Innovations in Divorce Custody Reform and the Role of Legal Professionals" (1990), 24 Univ. of Mich. J. of L. Reform 65; Dewar, "The Family Law Reform Act 1995 (Cth) and the Children Act 1989 (UK) Compared - Twins or Distant Cousins?" (1996), 10 Aust. J.F.L. 18; Ingleby, "The Family Law Reform Act - A Practitioner's Perspective" (1996), 10 Aust. J.F.L. 48; Chisholm, "Assessing the Impact of the Family Law Reform Act 1995" (1996), 10 Aust. J.F.L. 177; and Rhodes *et al*, *The Family Law Reform Act 1995: Can changing legislation change legal culture, legal practice and community expectations?* (Family Court of Australia, 1999). See also Alberta Law Reform Institute, *Family Law Project: Child Guardianship, Custody and Access - Report for Discussion No. 18.4* (Edmonton, October 1998).

The Minister of Justice's response to the committee's report was cautiously supportive, perhaps recognizing that opinion polls indicate that Canadians overwhelmingly believe that fathers get too little attention in the divorce courts. See "Needs of children and fathers ignored: poll", Southam Newspapers, November 23, 1998. At the same time, the government realized it was dealing with controversial matters and it did not want to offend women's groups that were critical of the report. Its *Response to the Report of the Special Joint Committee on Child Custody and Access* (Ottawa: Department of Justice, May 10, 1999) was vague, non-committal and called for more study and consultation with the provinces. It suggested that any resultant reforms should be dovetailed with the review of the *Federal Child Support Guidelines*, slated for completion in 2002. The *Response* did indicate that the introduction of new terminology would be given high priority.

Some writers have cautioned that changing the terminology used to describe the relationships between parents and their children after separation and divorce may have limited impact. In "Reforming Child Custody and Access in Canada" (1998), 15 Can. J. Fam. L. 13, Professors Cossman and Mykitiuk write (at 22):

To the extent that the problems of custody and access are structural ones - that the problems are deeply rooted in the gendered allocation of child-care responsibility - changing the language is at best a cosmetic approach.

...There is, equally, reason to be concerned that the new language will become as loaded as the old, since it is not the language per se that is at issue, but rather, the restructuring of parent-child relationships. The allocation of "primary residence" and/or "decision responsibility" to one parent only may, under a revised scheme, also become the focus of an emotionally explosive conflict. There is nothing inherently in the language of custody and access on the one hand, or shared parenting (and its allocation of primary residence and decision making responsibility) on the other, that makes either more or less conflictual in nature.

See also, Boyd, ''W(h)ither Feminism? The Department of Justice Public Discussion Paper on Custody and Access'' (1995), 12 Can. J. Fam. L. 331. At the same time, these authors worry that the shift to the concept of parental responsibilities and the development of parenting plans will result in increased parental authority after separation and divorce for the parent with whom the child does not habitually reside, commonly the father. Professors Cossman and Mykitiuk state (at 34-35):

> It is possible (and quite likely) under this regime [the Australian or English one], that the residential parent will continue to have the burden of quotidian child care responsibilities while the non-residential parent will have increased decision making ''responsibility'' about the child's educational, religious, residential and medical needs and not only a right to be consulted about these matters. In addition, this parent will have responsibilities for the care of the child when they are together.

Some judges have referred to the Joint Committee's *For the Sake of the Children* to issue orders in custody and access disputes in the form of ''parenting plans''. See, for example, *Smith* v. *Gale* (1999), 49 R.F.L. (4th) 400 (Nfld. U.F.C.) and *Hamlyn* v. *Hamlyn* (1999), 50 R.F.L. (4th) 398 (Nfld. U.F.C.) where Cook J. spelled out in considerable detail the living arrangements and the decision-making process. The court stressed that it was generally in the best interests of children to have continuing contact with both parents, spelled out a joint decision-making process with mediation in the event of an impasse, and set as a target approximately equal periods of residence with each parent.

Abduction of children by their parents, enforcement of custody and access orders, and wrongful removal of children from one jurisdiction to another are important topics which are only dealt with in an interstitial way in this chapter. For a more comprehensive examination, see McLeod, ''Enforcement of Custody and Access Orders'' in McLeod, *Child Custody Law and Practice* (Toronto: Carswell, looseleaf service). See also J.G. Castel, *Canadian Conflict of Laws*, 4th ed. (Toronto: Butterworths, 1997); B. Graham, *International Child Abduction: Issues for Reform* (Ottawa: Public Works and Government Services, 1998); McLeod, ''Annotation'' (1999), 45 R.F.L. (4th) 405; Kelsey and Hartwell, ''International Custody: Two Approaches to the International Shuttling of Children'' (1999), 13 Am. J.F.L. 188; and Tuft and Downing, ''Determining Child Custody Across Jurisdictions'' (1999), 56 Bench & B. Minn. 34.

2. Institutional Framework

ABELLA, ''PROCEDURAL ASPECTS OF ARRANGEMENTS FOR CHILDREN UPON DIVORCE IN CANADA''

(1983), 61 Can. Bar Rev. 443 (Footnotes Omitted)

. . .

I. *The Adversary System.*

. . . The essence of the adversary process is the provision of an impartial decision-maker before whom competing litigants can present their claims in the expectation of a just determination. It is for the parties to adduce whatever information they feel will advance their respective claims. The assertions are presented in accordance with accepted evidentiary and procedural boundaries. The judge completes the procedural triad as a dispassionate listener who receives the information from the advocates and ensures that it is submitted within the established boundaries. Not only is the process intended to result in a decision, it is intended optimally to result in the emergence of the truth. The judge, having listened to the parties present their perceptions of the facts, is expected to extrapolate those facts that appear more likely to represent accurately the history of the matter under dispute. In addition to making this assessment of credibility, the judge is expected to funnel the true facts through the relevant law. The distillation of the truth and the law is intended to result in a fair decision and ''justice for the litigants''.

Opponents of the adversary system, in family law generally and custody in particular, argue that it is inappropriate for several reasons. First, there is little that can realistically be said to be absolutely ''true'' about marital histories or children's interests. Although there must of necessity be some exploration of the past relationships between the parties, the nature of spousal or parent-child relationships is so subjective as to be incapable of translation into relevant factual evidence. . . .

Second, the argument is made that even if the truth could be ascertained, there is no clear law with which to synthesize it in order to arrive at a fair decision. The ''best interests'' test is so amorphous a doctrine, that it defies accurate explication. As a legal doctrine, it lacks the precision that makes a law functional and credible. It is, in short, not a legal principle at all but rather the apotheosis of behavioural scientific research in the field of child development. This calls for an assessment of a scientific and social rather than of a legal nature. The judge's solitary role as an arbiter of fact and law is therefore inappropriate.

There is the additional imputed handicap for a judge inasmuch as he or she is presumed to have limited socio-cultural experience, which could result in the imposition of arbitrary values on the litigants. . . .

These arguments against the adversary system in family law inevitably conclude either with a plea for its replacement by arbitration, mediation, a panel of experts, an inquiry, or the relaxation of the adversarial process. They are grounded primarily in a concern for the tender sensibilities of litigants who bruise easily under the assault of civil litigation. The alternatives proposed provide cushions rather than slings and arrows.

But those who negate the validity of the adversary system perform an indirect disservice to its consumers. No less than any other area of dispute, family problems may be beyond the ability of the parties involved to resolve on their own. No less than in any other area of human interaction, some degree of predictability of performance expectations is useful. This points to the need for clear legislation that defines the respective rights and obligations of the persons who have chosen to embark on a family relationship. It points too to the need for an appropriate structure in which to have those rights and obligations clarified when the parties themselves are unable or unwilling to do so. . . .

If one does not accept the need for laws that regulate the human condition in its family form, if one argues rather for flexible private standards of behaviour to be assessed on dissolution by an appropriate non-legal expert, then the decision-making process is less complicated an issue. But if one accepts the need for a degree of lawmaking to regulate familial expectations both during and after the subsistence of the family, then one has to assess which process best lends itself to the realization of the rights created by the law.

The determination of respective rights and duties is traditionally undertaken in the adversary system because this system provides a number of safeguards. Allegations can be tested by cross-examination; hearings are conducted in conformity with predictable rules of procedure and evidence; decisions are made by impartial umpires. Without these safeguards, the process en route to a decision will be chaotic. If the process itself is chaotic, the decision resulting from the process becomes suspect. How can one know whether each party had full, fair and equal opportunity to present all relevant evidence supporting his or her position unless the procedure through which the evidence was presented is structured and well-defined? Procedural informality is not an alternative to the adversary system — it is an abuse of it.

If, in addition to the need for laws that define rights, one accepts the need for structured procedures through which they can be exercised, one must choose carefully the forum in which these structured hearings are to be held.

Arbitration provides a forum in which an increasingly formalized hearing takes place before a non-judicial decision-maker. Its obvious advantage is speed — one can easily obviate the court's backlog by appointing a trained arbitrator to hear the dispute. There is what many perceive to be the added advantage that the hearing takes place in a less redoubtable environment than a courtroom. But the essence of the procedure remains the existence of an impartial decision-maker who hears the evidence usually in accordance with at least some of the evidentiary rules. It is, in short, the adversarial system operating outside the courtroom with somewhat less formality and predictability, and without a judge. The length of the hearing is often the same as a judicial trial would be but may be more expensive since the arbitrator is paid for by the parties. It is the adversary process without the judicial atmosphere, and therefore not generally considered a real alternative to it.

Conciliation or mediation, on the other hand, is now becoming a widely used way of bringing the parties together to try to effect an agreeable solution. It is not an alternative to the adversary system; rather, it is a complementary system. The purpose of mediation is to elicit agreement from the parties, with or without the help of their counsel, by exploring their respective absolute and bargaining positions. The process, although optimally intended to arrive at a decision, is, unlike arbitration, intended to arrive at a decision that is not imposed on the parties but is agreeable to both or all of them. If no consensus is possible, the discussions that took place are generally deemed confidential and the parties are free to pursue judicially-sanctioned remedies. Mediation has the inestimable benefit of providing to the parties a cathartic, informal procedure in which to canvass the possibility of an agreement.

In those few cases where negotiable settlements are not possible despite the efforts of lawyers or mediators, someone must ultimately decide the distribution of powers between the parties. In the absence of a better system, one is drawn to the judicial forum as a paradigm of due process.

Because one of the most attractive attributes of the adversary process is the presence of a dispassionate umpire, the suggestion that the adversarial system be replaced by something akin to an inquiry process is not widely supported. In an inquisitorial procedure, the judge would be permitted and even expected to enter the arena from time to time to elicit or encourage the elucidation of evidence that he or she feels is beneficial to the hearing. This procedure is justified on the grounds that, particularly in cases involving the needs of children, a more aggressive judicial stance is required to ensure that evidentiary lacunae created by counsel for the parties are not permitted to interfere with the court's right to have all relevant information before it. This suggests an inverted approach to what rights are at stake. It is not the essence of a custody case that the court has the right to have all relevant information. Rather, it is the right of the parties to prove their entitlement to the remedy requested that is the essence of a case. It is hard to reconcile their rights to prove their case fairly with the right on the part of the court to act as a transparent third or fourth party to the proceedings. Once having participated in the proceedings, how can the judge then make the transformation back to impartial decision-maker? There are other methods such as the appointment of a counsel for the child or an *amicus curiae* that meet the problem without jeopardizing the parties' rights to a fair hearing, or the child's rights to have his or her best interests and rights intelligently determined. . . .

It is not generally the court or its officers who are necessarily responsible for the ennui of the parties. The circumstances of the drama in which they find themselves are much more likely to be the cause, if not the object, of their hostility. . . .

The other criticisms of the adversary system — the deficiencies of assessing character through oral testimony, the dangers of myopic judicial speculation, and the spectre of irresponsibly pugnacious counsel — are all present in some form in whatever alternatives one proposes for solving a family's legal disputes. Through refinements to the existing process such as the use of experts, pre-trials, mediation, or legal representation for children, many of the criticisms can be neutralized without compromising the purpose of the process; namely, the expeditious and fair resolution of legal disputes. Without commenting on the efficacy of existing substantive law or the problems inherent in judicial discretion, subjects relevant to, but beyond the scope of this article, the balance of the article will continue to assume that a refined adversarial process of judicial decision-making is necessary to avoid the erosion and dilution of the integrity of the law of the family.

[Ms Abella's discussion of pre-trials is omitted. The new *Family Law Rules*, O. Reg. 114/99, envision at least one and possibly two or three conferences before a trial. In every defended case there must be at least one case conference to explore the chances of settlement, identify the issues that are in dispute, provide disclosure, note admissions, and set the next steps in the case. In addition, there can also be a settlement conference and a trial management conference or a combination of both. These rules apply to the Superior Court of Justice (Family Court) and the Court of Justice. The *Rules of Procedure*, R.R.O. 1990, Reg. 194 (as amended), which continue to apply to family cases in the Superior Court of Justice in those parts of the province where a unified Family Court has not yet been established, deal with pre-trials in Rule 50.]

III. *Mediation.*

Whereas the judicial process results in the imposition of a decision upon the parties, mediation attempts to achieve a consensus. Mediation is a process whereby a third person attempts to resolve a dispute by creating an environment of empathy and openness in the hopes of assisting the parties to understand each other's position and effect an agreement between them. It has a persuasive rather than a coercive ambience.

The benefits of mediation are obvious. Notwithstanding any refinements to the adversarial process, the better solution to resolving disputes between family members lies in achieving consensus rather than imposing judgment. In the short term, the benefit of mediation, if properly performed, is that it provides the parties with a better understanding of themselves, the issues, and the position of the other party. It also gives to the parties the sense that their privacy and family autonomy has remained sacrosanct. In the long term, this awareness may assist the parties in resolving future disputes in a flexible manner. . . .

The benefits for children in such a process are equally obvious. If adults can appreciate the nuances in their own or the gestures of their former partners, and if

they are helped through conciliation to protect themselves from any negative incidents of the nuances, then they will be better able to set aside their own irrational
proclivities in the interests of furthering the well-being of their children. Since parents
are generally in the best position to know and accommodate their children's needs,
they, rather than a judge, are the best people to make decisions about them. Where
they are handicapped by emotional disabilities resulting from injuries sustained in
the fall from marriage, they may need some assistance in once again being able to
make these decisions. Mediation provides this assistance and avoids the need for
judicial intervention.

Mediation cannot however be perceived as anything other than a complementary parallel to the adversarial system. There are still those, particularly in custody
matters, who refuse to compromise. Their refusal may have nothing to do with
wounded sensibilities — there may be a genuine inability to accede to the demands
of the other parties because of an intense belief that their own position is best for the
child. In those circumstances, one reverts to providing access to the judicial process
where the dispute will be resolved by judicial fiat.

Based on the assumption that a good bargain is better than a good fiat, mediation
will continue to be increasingly relied upon in assisting parties to settle disputes. It
also guarantees that only those matters that are incapable of prior resolution will be
dealt with by the courts. By reducing the possibility of accumulated backlogs,
speedier access to the court is provided for those who cannot or will not bargain.

Despite the utility and desirability of mediation, it is not yet a compulsory
process. The reasons for this are clear; bargaining involves the voluntary subjugation
of a party to the possibility that he or she may be persuaded to reduce demands and
settle for less. Unless a party is willing to enter into discussions freely, it is difficult
to see how agreement is possible. . . .

IV. *Expert Assessments.*

Independent expert assessments are as much an admission on the part of the
judicial system that it lacks omniscience in custody matters as it is a recognition that
the adversarial system with its partisan emphases cannot always be relied upon to
present a full picture to the court. They are also acknowledgments that the adversarial
system, while adept at gleaning historical or antecedent facts, is less well able to
encourage the evocation of social or consequential facts. Since custody involves the
formulation of policies and prognoses about the mental and physical well-being of
the child, mere facts about the child's background may be insufficient information
upon which to base a decision about the child's future placement. What is required
in most of these cases is an analysis of emotional, factual, and psychological factors,
only some of which a judge is able to ascertain from the perceptions of the parties
or their supporters. It is for these reasons that the adversary process has entrenched
the use of impartial expert assessments that investigate skillfully those facts that are
not otherwise ascertainable. A recommendation is made to the court that is not
binding but provides a valuable contribution to the mosaic that is being pieced
together.

. . . The communications made during the assessment are not confidential and
in fact the purpose of the assessment is to disclose to the court as much information
as possible about what the assessor has learned from and about the parties. The goal
of the assessment is not only to explore the psychological and psychiatric aspects of
a given custody dispute, but also, where possible, to provide a recommendation to
the court on the basis of these findings. The assessment will therefore likely include

the reason for the referral, the sources upon which the report or assessment is based, the number and duration of meetings or interviews with various parties, the recommendations of the clinician and the reasons for these recommendations, as well as the degree to which these recommendations represent either consensus, compromise or disagreement between the various parties. . . .

Since the test in custody is "best interests" and since the evidence required must necessarily go beyond materially demonstrable perceptions, it is difficult to see how informed judgments can be made about the best interests of children without at least the assistance of a non-partisan expert who can better attempt to evaluate the competing emotional claims that underlie the pursuit of legal remedies. Since the jurisprudential mandate includes assessing a child's emotional needs, the courts should make this assessment on the basis of the most complete evidence available. This evidence is often not complete without authoritative exploration of these needs. This is not a usurpation of the judicial function — it is an indispensable contribution to its proper exercise.

. . . In addition to providing assessments, then, mental health professionals may be of great service to lawyers in being able to deal with the psychological needs of a client. By operating in tandem, a lawyer, with the assistance of this professional, can assist the client in accepting the legal, practical and social consequences of what has just happened to him or her. These mutually reliant professional relationships enhance rather than detract from the abilities of either profession to meet the needs of their clients. . . .

V. *Independent Legal Representation for Children.*

Children are not parties to a divorce or custody action. At the same time, they are no less affected by the outcome than are the actual parties. This is an aberration in the adversarial process whereby as a rule no one is bound by a decision unless he or she was a party to the proceedings upon which the decision was based. Except in custody and divorce actions, anyone who may be bound by a decision is entitled to make representations and participate fully in the process that may ultimately result in a change of status.

To fill the vacuum between the lack of party status on the part of children, and the inevitability of their being affected by the outcome, the practice has gradually arisen in Canada of having lawyers represent children. To preserve independence, these lawyers are either appointed anonymously by the court from a panel of lawyers selected and specially trained for this purpose, or are retained privately by the child through a legal aid plan. They may be requested by the court under the court's inherent and *parens patriae* jurisdiction, or under the rules of procedure in various provinces. Once appointed, they act for the child as if the child were a party with full rights to participate in the trial, including discovery and participation in pre-trial discussions, to call and cross-examine witnesses, and to make submissions.

It is acknowledged in Canada that the wishes of a child are relevant in a custody proceeding. There is no agreement, however, on how old a child should be before his or her wishes are solicited. Nor is there any agreement on how those wishes should be presented to the court. The existence of a lawyer for the child assists in resolving the dilemma for the court inasmuch as it then becomes to some extent the child's lawyer's responsibility.

The role of the lawyer for the child in representing those wishes is still the subject of some debate. Most studies on the subject indicate that the lawyer's role should be to represent what the child wants in the same way as the lawyer would represent the wishes of any adult party to a custody dispute. The premise on which this position is based is that it is not for the lawyer to represent the child's best interests since the lawyer is incapable of making that judgment. Such a judgment anticipates the function of the judge whose role it is to assess and determine best interests based on all of the evidence presented. It would be premature for counsel for a child to attempt to represent the best interests of the child prior to having had the benefit of hearing all of the evidence.

The wishes of the child are not determinative but are one of a number of factors that the court must consider in deciding what is best for a child. The lawyer therefore cannot be seen to be acting irresponsibly when putting forward wishes of the child that do not strike him or her as sensible in the circumstances. If the child is going to have full and effective participation in the proceedings, he or she should be entitled to the same vigorous advocacy of a position that the other parties have.

In the event that the child's wishes are ambiguous, that the child is too young to express them, or that counsel is unable for some other reason to obtain instructions from the child, it is open to the lawyer for the child to take no position on the child's behalf but merely to act as someone who can assist the court in ensuring that all relevant information is before the court so that an informed judgment can be made. This may involve requesting the use of mediation or an assessment where these have not hitherto been canvassed by the parties. In this capacity the lawyer is an *amicus curiae* acting as the court's, not the child's, counsel, and should be so designated.

The question still remains however of how best to express to the court what the wishes of a child are. This can either be done through the evidence of a social worker, psychologist or other expert who has interviewed the child, or, less desirably and depending on the age of the child, by asking the child to give evidence under oath.

One of the most contentious methods of eliciting the child's wishes is the judicial interview of a child. This procedure developed in the absence of legal representation for children because judges appreciated the relevance of children's wishes and had no other vehicle for independently determining and weighing those wishes. Although these interviews used to take place privately, the practice has developed that insofar as it is possible, the requirements of natural justice be maintained. This means that it is normally explained in advance to all parties, including the child, that any opinions expressed or information given will be communicated to the parties, that a transcript will be made of the interview, and that the child's counsel and all other counsel may be present during the proceedings. The parties are not present. The judge may request from the parties a recommended list of questions to be put to the child so that issues the parties feel are relevant will be canvassed by the judge who, except for the information learned at trial, is a stranger to the family dynamics. The interview usually takes place at the end of the trial after the judge has had an opportunity of learning whatever of the history of the family is ascertainable.

Once the interview has been completed, the judge will then resume the proceedings by indicating to counsel what information he or she has learned. The parties are then given an opportunity to challenge or reply to the information either by submissions or by the calling of additional evidence.

Critics of the practice of judicial interviews refer to the secrecy of the process and the lack of proper training on the part of the judge fully to appreciate a child's motivations and perceptions. They suggest that in the short time available for such an interview, it is impossible without expert assistance fully to comprehend the nature of the information received from the child, particularly in view of the fact that the information is being tendered in an authoritarian and intimidating environment.

The procedure as well invades the concept of impartiality upon which the adversarial system is based inasmuch as it entails the unilateral participation of the judge who temporarily combines a legal with a social work mantle. Where other more objective methods of ascertaining wishes are available, therefore, they are preferable to the judicial interview.

In addition to protecting the impartiality of the court, other methods relieve the child of the responsibility of answering blunt questions about his or her wishes that may be difficult for the child to answer in a direct way. With a skilful inquiry, these wishes may be ascertained in a more subtle manner.

No one suggests that appointing counsel for children is a guarantee that their best interests will be served. But if one perceives the essence of custody actions to be not the right of a parent to custody of the child, but rather the right of the child to have his or her needs met by the person best able to meet those needs, then the focus must be on the child. To ensure that this continues to be the focus, an advocate for the child is often helpful, and frequently indispensable. The existence of a child advocate allows full participation in decisions that affect the child, and enhances the child's perception that the process is a fair one. . . .

LINTON v. CLARKE

(1994), 10 R.F.L. (4th) 92 (Ont. Div. Ct.)

[The children's parents separated in 1989. The parents entered into a separation agreement that provided that the mother was to have custody. The mother issued a divorce petition in 1992 and the father claimed custody of the children. The mother brought a motion for an assessment, alleging that the children were suffering from emotional problems caused by the father. The children were being treated at the Children's Psychiatric Research Institute. Justice Jenkins denied the mother's motion, reasoning:

> Section 30(1) of the *Children's Law Reform Act*, R.S.O. 1990, c. C.12, provides that the court may appoint a person to report on the needs of the children and the ability of the parties to satisfy those needs. An order for an assessment may be made before or during the hearing of a claim for custody.
>
> The children have been clinically assessed by the professional staff at the Children's Psychiatric Research Institute and the petitioner participated in that assessment. Either party can call that evidence during the trial.
>
> If the respondent is to pursue his claim for custody on the basis that he is able to provide a fuller, richer family life, it will be necessary for him to have his own assessment carried out by an independent expert who is prepared to attend in Montreal. Indeed, his counsel indicated that he is contemplating such an assessment.
>
> I agree with the respondent's contention that the staff of the London Custody and Access Project will not travel to Montreal as part of a regular assessment. If they were directed to do so, it would result in an inordinate delay and mean that this case could not proceed in January 1994.
>
> It has become the practice to order assessments prior to trial in virtually every custody case. That is a practice that should be re-examined. The *Children's Law Reform Act* specifically provides that an assessment may be ordered by a trial judge at the time of the hearing, should that become necessary. An assessment that is ordered by a trial judge and is focused on a particular area of

concern would, in my view, be of greater assistance to the court than a wide-ranging report prepared without direction.

In this case the trial judge will no doubt have the evidence of the clinicians from Children's Psychiatric Research Institute available to him, together with any assessment ordered by the respondent. If he requires a further assessment, he will be free to order such a report.

The motion is therefore dismissed without prejudice to either party to apply to the trial judge for an assessment, should that become necessary.

The mother appealed. Justice Granger began by outlining the arguments presented by the mother's counsel.]

Mr. Ste. Marie, in his argument, suggests that Justice Jenkins fell in error when he restricted the entitlement to an assessment to cases where there is a clinical issue. Mr. Ste. Marie argues that an assessment of the needs of the children and the abilities of the parents to satisfy those needs should be ordered in almost all cases notwithstanding that there may not be clinical issues to be determined. He suggests that the best interests of the children will be served if the parties can reach an agreement on custody without the necessity of proceeding to trial, and if an assessment by a third party expert can assist in resolving the custody dispute, then the assessment is in the best interests of the children. Many lawyers seek an assessment hoping that the assessor will facilitate a settlement to the dispute or hoping that the assessment, if favourable, will convince his or her spouse to withdraw a claim for custody. In his article, "Family Assessments in Custody and Access Disputes Under the Children's Law Reform Act, 1977" His Honour Judge Stephen Borins (1982) 24 R.F.L. (2d) 90 stated at p. 96:

> The earlier an assessment is ordered, the better it is for all concerned, in the sense that the resolution of the dispute will be made earlier than it would be if an assessment is not ordered until the trial is commenced.

In his article "Assessing the Assessor: Legal Issues" (1990) 6 C.F.L.Q. 179 Nicholas Bala states at pp. 190-191:

> (d) When and Why an Assessment Order Should Be Made
> There are almost no reported cases which refused an order for an assessment. This suggests that judges will order an assessment if either party requests it, provided that there is a genuine dispute over custody or access, and arrangements can be made to pay for an assessment. . . .
> ". . . There must be some evidence that the dispute is so intense as to prevent all the relevant factors coming out, or that there appears to be a parent-child problem that requires expert analysis and/or explanation, or finally that the assessment is necessary to allow the parties to understand the needs of the child and the need for cooperation." [[James G. McLeod] "Annotation to *Chapman*" (1985), 49 R.F.L. (2d) 47 at 48.]
> While it is true that there is an onus on the moving party to justify the request, it is submitted that there will be few contested custody or access disputes in which an assessment by a competent independent assessor will not meet at least one of the criteria McLeod proposes, which would suggest that it will not be a difficult onus to meet. Thus, if there is a genuine dispute, it may be appropriate for a resisting party to bear a tactical onus for demonstrating why an assessment should not be ordered.

. . .

Mr. Ste. Marie suggests that if there is a genuine dispute concerning custody and/or access, the court should order an assessment in order to have a complete picture of the children's needs as mandated by the Children's Law Reform Act. I agree with Mr. Ste. Marie that in custody proceedings, the trial judge should be provided with as much relevant information as possible in order that he or she can determine the best interests of the children. On the other hand, the cost of an assessment and the length of time required to complete such an assessment must be taken into account by a motions judge when asked to order an assessment of the needs of the children and the abilities of each parent to satisfy such needs. Lengthy delays in determining custody issues can never be in the best interests of the children.

In his annotation to the report of this case (1993) 50 R.F.L. (3d), James G. McLeod stated:

> Jenkins J.'s reasons for judgment in *Linton v. Clarke* underscore the changing judicial attitude towards the use of custody and access assessments. In the past it was common practice for judges to order assessments without specifying the areas of concern or the methods to be used. What often resulted was an assessment that was little more than one social worker's opinion of who should have custody or what access would be appropriate. Assessments were ordered not because there were clinical issues to be decided but to discover whether outside input could resolve the problem. In the end, many lawyers sought assessments hoping that the assessor would act as a facilitator and settle the dispute, or intending to use them as a means of intimidating the other party into withdrawing his or her claim for custody or access. With increasing frequency, judges have been questioning whether assessments should be ordered as a matter of course.
>
> . . .
>
> In *Linton v. Clarke* Jenkins J. notes that the practice of routinely ordering assessments before trial in contested custody and access cases should be re-examined. If unresolved clinical issues remain at trial, the judge should then direct that they be reviewed. Although there is much to commend this point of view, problems may arise because of the time it takes to conduct the assessment. To give effect to Jenkins J.'s comments, a two-stage analysis may be in order.
>
> First, the court should order a full-scale assessment early in the proceedings if it appears that clinical issues require expert input. It should, however, ensure that the assessor appointed is a specialist in the field to be studied. (Obviously, all assessors are not equally competent, nor do they all share the same area of expertise.) In the same vein, it must be remembered that some assessors have distinct personal prejudices that could affect the outcome of the case. Therefore, because the assessment is part of the judicial process, the courts should be careful to prevent the appearance of bias.
>
> Second, if there is no apparent reason for an assessment on the facts, the court should not order one hoping that the dispute will somehow be resolved. The litigation or mediation process should be allowed to work. The law provides for agreement or a judicial determination. It does not provide for arbitration or non-judicial decision making unless the parties agree. If it is later discoverd that an assessment is needed and the cost and time can be justified, one may be ordered at that time. The later in the process that one is directed, the more precise the issue should be. This is the point emphasized by Jenkins J.

In this case, Justice Jenkins appreciated that expert evidence was available from the Children's Psychiatric Research Institute regarding any clinical issues. He also correctly stated that the trial justice had the jurisdiction to order an assessment pursuant to s. 30(2) of the Children's Law Reform Act at the conclusion of the trial if he or she felt such an assessment was required. In my view, the statement of Justice Jenkins that the practice of ordering an assessment prior to trial in virtually every custody case, should be re-examined, is in keeping with the tenor of the judgment of the Supreme Court of Canada in *Young v. Young* (1993), 49 R.F.L. (3d) 117. The majority of the court was of the view that expert evidence is not required in all cases to establish the best interests of the child. In her dissenting reasons, Madam Justice L'Heureux-Dubé stated at pp. 212-213:

> I agree with my colleague that expert evidence should not be routinely required to establish the best interests of the child. In my view, it is a modern-day myth that experts are always better

placed than parents to assess the needs of the child. Common sense requires us to acknowledge that the person involved in day-to-day care may observe changes in the behaviour, mood, attitude, and development of a child that could go unnoticed by anyone else. The custodial parent normally has the best vantage point from which to assess the interests of the child, and thus will often provide the most reliable and complete source of information to the judge on the needs and interests of that child.

Furthermore, it is important to emphasize the importance of the evidence of children in custody and access disputes, and I would not wish to suggest that their testimony alone might not be a sufficient evidentiary basis upon which to restrict access. Courts have increasingly come to accept and understand in the criminal context that children themselves can be a reliable source of evidence to the judge (*R. v. Khan*, [1990] 2 S.C.R. 531). To disregard their evidence when their own interests are directly at issue would, in my opinion, be at odds with this clear evolutionary trend in the law.

Many legal commentators have noted the degree to which custody and access disputes have become a contest between experts, involving increasing amounts of time and money (see: Nicholas Bala, "Assessing the Assessor: Legal Issues" (1990) 6 C.F.L.Q. 179; Paula J. Caplan and Jeffery Wilson, "Assessing the Child Custody Assessors" (1990) 27 R.F.L. (3d) 121; Louis Gélinas and Bartha Maria Knoppers, "Le rôle des experts en droit québécois en matière de garde, d'accès et de protection" (1993) 53 R. du B. 3; M. Fineman, *The Illusion of Equality*). In the absence of clear legal presumptions about the best interests of children, judges have increasingly come to rely on the recommendations of experts to determine custody and access issues, believing that such experts possess objective, scientific knowledge and can in fact "know" what is in the best interests of the child. However, expert testimony, while helpful in some and perhaps many circumstances, is often inconclusive and contradictory (Gélinas and Knoppers, at p. 17). That this should be so is not surprising, since such assessments are both speculative and may be affected by the professional values and biases of the assessors themselves.

Even where such expertise is valuable, there are impediments in such reliance. Assessments may occasion delays in resolving proceedings and may at times constitute a significant disruption in the lives of both parents and children. The cost involved in routinely hiring experts to establish the best interests of the child only increases the expense of custody and litigation and is far beyond the resources of most divorcing couples. Furthermore, as Professor Bala points out, at p. 224, "much of what assessors ultimately recommend may simply be a matter of 'common experience and common sense.' "

Assessments should not be ordered in all cases as a vehicle to promote settlement of custody disputes. If the legislature had intended that assessments were to be a vehicle to settle custody disputes, the legislation would have mandated assessments in all cases.

In my view, assessments should be limited to cases in which there are clinical issues to be determined, in order that such assessments can provide expert evidence on the appropriate manner to address the emotional and psychological stresses within the family unit in the final determination of custody. The decision of Justice Jenkins is in harmony with the principles I have enunciated. I agree with his decision to dismiss the motion for an assessment at this time.

AUSTIN AND JAFFE, "ANNOTATION"

(1995), 10 R.F.L. (4th) 92

The central issue that was before the court in *Linton* v. *Clarke* is what a judge should consider when only one parent wants an assessment in a custody or access dispute. The reasons for judgment imply that a judge needs to have a "clinical" reason to support the assessment and order this intervention contrary to the wishes of the other parent.

1. *Can judges agree on what a "clinical" reason may be?*

For some judges a clinical reason may imply serious mental health problems for one of the parties or well-defined allegations of child abuse. In reality, any two parents who are prepared to put themselves and their children through the financial and *emotional* cost of a custody trial have a clinical problem.

In *Linton* v. *Clarke* there are specific reasons for the assessment, including the fact that the children are being treated at a children's mental health centre and report behavioural and emotional adjustment problems, including nightmares and sleep terrors. The judgment may express Mr. Justice Granger's view of assessments highlighted by *The Lawyers Weekly* headline of January 27, 1995, "Ontario's Divisional Court put brakes on a burgeoning industry: Child custody assessments ordered too frequently?" The judgment may reflect this viewpoint, which is being expressed more frequently.

Assessments have some benefits beyond the court proceedings. Many assessments offer parents some feedback about their children's adjustments to the separation and ways in which access schedules can maximize the match between parental skills and children's needs. As well, assessors can act as brokers to other community services to ensure parents and children receive the counselling they require in response to the stress and conflict from the separation.

2. *Why not rely on clinical information that already exists such as the CPRI report in this matter?*

Proper custody assessments require access to all the parties in order to observe and understand the individual parties and their interactions. Guidelines such as those adopted from the College of Psychologists forbid professionals from offering opinions about custody and access arrangements unless they have full access to all the information and parties in the custody dispute.

While the Granger judgment signals the end of the honeymoon between the courts and custody assessments, it could be better interpreted as a time to re-evaluate the quality of these assessments. Judges and lawyers should become familiar with the guidelines available for effective custody assessments and demand the best services for families in crisis. We agree with Mr. Justice Granger's criticism of poor assessments, but would urge other judges not to throw out "the baby with the bath water". Poor legal representation of clients in divorce proceedings would not lead us to conclude that they are better off without lawyers. We would rather put our energy into standards and training.

3. *Are assessments too costly and do they add to delays in the justice system?*

Most parents are concerned about legal costs and the length of time required to resolve child custody matters before the court. It is the rare person who can actually afford a custody trial to settle matters through this final adversarial confrontation. Assessment costs (approximately $1,800 per parent or $900 by Legal Aid) are minor compared to the cost of a custody trial. Many assessment delays are in starting the process, as a result of counsel not completing minimal referral requirements or delays in obtaining Legal Aid approval.

At the London Custody & Access Project over the past 15 years, 96 per cent of these difficult cases are settled without a trial. Since the majority of parents cannot afford a trial, is that not a worthwhile goal? Why wait to order an assessment at the trial and add to the costs and delay at a time when the parties are most exhausted financially and emotionally?

The court system is not in a good position to criticize custody assessments as being too expensive and slow. Most lawyers and their clients have become extremely concerned about the costs and delays in the criminal and civil justice systems that put justice beyond the financial means of the average person. If one considers the added delays of appeals, many people face periods of five to seven years to have their final court resolution. Someone's "day in court" can feel as if it is lasting a life time.

It is to be hoped that the judgment in *Linton* v. *Clarke* can stimulate more discussion on the role of assessments and the interaction among legal and clinical professionals in these complex matters. Families adjusting to a separation need caring, responsive and well-coordinated services by legal and mental health professionals. The challenges that lie ahead require the court to find the most effective means of collaborating with mental health professionals in a non-adversarial manner.

NOTES AND QUESTIONS

1. The vast majority of custody and access disputes are resolved through negotiation, settlement conferences, and mediation. Only a small portion of parents, perhaps as low as 3%, rely on judges to resolve their disputes. See Bureau of Review, *Evaluation of the Divorce Act* (Ottawa: Department of Justice, 1990).

2. A number of Canadian jurisdictions have begun to experiment with education courses to facilitate more effective resolution of parenting disputes. For example, two hour voluntary courses have been available in Alberta since 1993. In 1996, a pilot project was introduced in Edmonton whereby any parent who wished to bring an application relating to child support, custody or access before the Court of Queen's Bench in a divorce action had to attend an educational seminar entitled "Parenting after Divorce". It was conducted two nights per week and covered six hours. Course evaluations were sufficiently positive that the program has been extended across the province. For discussion of such programs, see Arbuthnot *et al*, "Does Mandatory Divorce Education for Parents Work?" (1996), 34 Fam. and Conciliation Courts Rev. 60; Cossman and Mykitiuk, "Reforming Child Custody and Access Law in Canada: A Discussion Paper" (1998), 15 Can. J. Fam. L. 13, at 63-66; and Special Joint Committee on Child Custody and Access, *For the Sake of the Children* (Ottawa: Government of Canada, 1999) at 28-30. The Special Joint Committee recommended that "all parents seeking parenting orders, unless there is agreement between them on the terms of such an order, be required to participate in an education program to help them become aware of the post-separation reaction of parents and children, children's developmental needs at different ages, the benefits of co-operative parenting after divorce, parental rights and responsibilities, and the availability and benefits of mediation and other forms of dispute resolution, provided such programs are available."

3. Section 9(2) of the *Divorce Act* requires that the lawyer acting in the divorce proceeding discuss with his or her client "the advisability of negotiating the matters that may be the subject of . . . a custody order" and inform the client "of the mediation facilities . . . that might be able to assist the spouses in negotiating those matters". See also s. 9(3).

Section 31(1) of the *CLRA* authorizes the court, at the request of the parties, to appoint a person selected by the parties to mediate any aspect of a custody dispute. Mediation conducted pursuant to this section can be either "open" or "closed", at the option of the parties. See s. 31(4) and (7). In "open" mediation, what goes on and is said during mediation can be revealed if a settlement is not reached. In "closed" mediation, the opposite occurs and everything is confidential. The latter type is prevalent.

The Special Joint Committee reported in *For the Sake of the Children*, at 32, that Quebec legislation requires divorcing parents to attend at least one information session about the benefits of mediation. If the parents then decide to use mediation, they are entitled to up to six sessions at public expense. The legislation permits opting out of the process, including the information session, in cases of domestic violence. The committee recommended (at 33) that "divorcing parents be encouraged to attend at least one mediation session to help them develop a parenting plan for their children". It added: "Where there is a proven history of violence by one parent toward the other or toward the children, alternative forms of dispute resolution should be used only when the safety of the person who has been the victim of the violence is assured and where the risk of violence has passed. The resulting parental plan must focus on parental responsibilities for the children and contain measures to ensure safety and security for parents and children."

For further reading regarding mediation of custody and access disputes, see Bailey, "Unpacking the 'Rational Alternative': A Critical Review of Family Mediation Claims" (1988), 8 Can. J. Fam. L. 61; Austin, Jaffe, and Hurley, "Incorporating Children's Needs and Views in Alternative Dispute Resolution Approaches" (1992), 8 C.F.L.Q. 69; Emery, *Family Relationships: Divorce, Child Custody and Mediation* (N.Y.: The Guildford Press, 1994); Irving and Benjamin, *Family Mediation* (Toronto: Sage Pub., 1995); Phegan, "The Family Mediation System: An Art of Distributions" (1995), 40 McGill L.J. 365; Landau *et al, Family Mediation Handbook*, 2nd ed. (Toronto: Butterworths, 1997); Goundry *et al, Family Mediation in Canada: Implications for Women's Equality* (Ottawa: Status of Women Canada, 1998); Irving and Benjamin, "Child Custody Disputes, Family Mediation and Proposed Reform of the *Divorce Act*" (1999), 16 C.F.L.Q. 413; and Noble, *Family Mediation: A Guide for Lawyers* (Toronto: Canada Law Book, 1999).

4. Arbitration of custody and access disputes is a more recent and less used innovation than clinical assessments or mediation. In "Incorporating Children's Needs and Views in Alternative Dispute Resolution Approaches" (1992), 8 C.F.L.Q. 69, the authors suggest arbitration is particularly suitable to deal with specific issues relating to post-separation childcare arrangements. As examples, they mention (at 77-78) "access disputes that centre on whether or not to include mid-week overnight visits or what time the weekend begins." They list (at 78) the following advantages of arbitration:

1. a time limited and cost effective procedure that promises clients some movement towards a decision;

2. protecting parents from using an assessment or mediation to stall for time and maintain the status quo;

3. focusing on parents' strengths and specific plans rather than on wide-ranging allegations;

4. avoiding raising negative topics about early history of parents and marital conflict that are usually outlined in an assessment;

5. clients feel that they have been heard in an informal setting (relative to court) and by a mental health professional with experience in children's and parents' adjustment to separation and divorce; and

6. arbitration can take careful consideration of children's wishes without disclosing the exact nature of their wishes to their parents.

In *Hodge* v. *Legault* (1998), 36 R.F.L. (4th) 211 (Ont. Gen. Div.), the court held that, where the parents agree to arbitration and choose the arbitrator, an arbitration award should be enforced unless the parent contesting its validity clearly shows that the award is not in the child's best interest. See also *Lenney* v. *Lenney* (1996), 24 R.F.L. (4th) 381 (Alta. Q.B.) where the parents had agreed to joint custody and the mediation of any disputes. The court refused to deal with a mother's application for sole custody until mediation had been tried.

5. The Washington State *Parenting Act of 1987*, Wash. Laws C.460, requires that a parenting plan must include a dispute resolution provision. A study of the early experience under the Act found that 57% of parents chose mediation and 16% court intervention. See Cossman and Mykitiuk, "Reforming Child Custody and Access Law in Canada: A Discussion Paper" (1998), 15 Can. J. Fam. L. 13, at 70-71.

6. Section 30 of the *CLRA* deals expressly with court-ordered assessments in custody or access disputes. What remedy is there if one of the parents refuses to attend or to undergo the assessment? See s. 30(6).

There is no specific provision in the *Divorce Act* for assessments. However, some courts have held that s. 30 of the *CLRA* applies to divorce proceedings in Ontario. See, for example, *Booth* v. *Booth* (1983), 33 R.F.L. (2d) 330 (Ont. H.C.) and *Linton* v. *Clarke* (1994), 10 R.F.L. (4th) 92 (Ont. Div. Ct.). See also Borins, "Family Assessments in Custody and Access Disputes Under the Children's Law Reform Act, 1977" (1982), 24 R.F.L. (2d) 90, at 93, which supports this interpretation. Superior court judges have also invoked their "inherent jurisdiction" to act for the welfare of children to order assessments. The Rules of Court, particularly those relating to the appointment of experts, may also provide a jurisdictional basis for such orders. See, generally, Bala, "Assessing the Assessor: Legal Issues" (1990), 6 C.F.L.Q. 179. That article also explores some of the judicial attitudes and secondary literature concerning the value of assessments prepared by mental health professionals. See also Blumall, "Child Custody Determination: Issues for Psychological Evaluation" (1980), 12 R.F.L. (2d) 18; R. Gardner, *Family Evaluation in Child Custody Litigation* (Cresskill, N.J.: Creative Therapeutics, 1982); Chisholm, "Preparing Your Client For Assessment or Mediation" (1987), 1 C.F.L.Q. 385; Barbara A. Chisholm and H. Christina MacNaughton, *Custody/Access Assessments: A Practical Guide for Lawyers and Assessors* (Toronto: Carswell, 1990); *Custody/Access Assessments: A View from Both Sides of the Mirror* (Toronto: L.S.U.C., Dept. Cont. Ed., 1992); Austin, Jaffe, and Hurley, "Incorporating Children's Needs and Views in Alternative Dispute Resolution Approaches" (1992), 8 C.F.L.Q. 69; Mayers, "Effective Processes in Custody/Access Assessments" (1994), 11 C.F.L.Q. 147; and Bala, "Children, Psychiatrists and the Courts: Understanding the Ambivalence of the Legal Profession" (1995-6), 13 C.F.L.Q. 261.

7. For some other reported cases in which judges refused to order assessments, see *Staffin* v. *Staffin* (1991), 35 R.F.L. (3d) 250 (Alta. Q.B.); *Levine* v. *Levine* (1993), 50 R.F.L. (3d) 414 (Ont. Prov. Div.); *Fattali* v. *Fattali* (1996), 22 R.F.L. (4th) 159 (Ont. Gen. Div.); and *Farmakoulas* v. *McInnis* (1996), 23 R.F.L. (4th) 235 (N.S. S.C.). Assessments were ordered in *Marko-Laschowski* v. *Laschowski* (1999), 44 R.F.L. (4th) 433 (Alta. Q.B.) and *Pellerin* v. *Pellerin* (1999), 49 R.F.L. (4th) 136 (N.W.T. S.C.) where the courts were convinced that they would provide evidence relating to the welfare of the child that otherwise might not be available to the court. The court also ordered an assessment in *Jarjour* v. *Brooks* (1999), 3 R.F.L. (5th) 91 (Man. Q.B.) where the report would be "extremely useful to assist the court in determining whether a court ordered shared parenting arrangement would be in the child's best interest". In *Tucker* v. *Tucker* (1998), 41 R.F.L. (4th) 404 the Alberta Court of Appeal noted that the appointment of an expert to perform an assessment had to a considerable extent replaced the court appointment of an *amicus curiae* in Alberta. For many years Alberta courts often appointed an *amicus curiae*, usually at government expense, who obtained home study reports or psychological assessments for the court's use and called evidence on behalf of the child. When lack of funding made this practice largely unavailable, the courts turned more often to assessments for the objective establishment of facts.

8. Perras D.C.J. provided the following guidelines regarding the role and nature of assessments in *Boody* v. *Boody* (1983), 32 R.F.L. (2d) 396, at 399-400 (Ont. Dist. Ct.):

> Custody and access cases revolve around the sole issue of what is in the best interests of the child. While from the lawyer's point of view this is a legal issue, from the assessor's purview, his assessment must be directed always with a helping attitude consistent with his training. . . .

> Children involved in a separation or divorce are always disadvantaged parties. A social investigation of their needs and interests by a qualified person is an affirmative step to protect their welfare. The role of the assessor is not to make the final judgment in the case, but to provide expert assistance to the court in making its determination of where the child's best interests lie in a custody dispute.

> The following are general guidelines for the assessor:

> > (1) He must assist the child and the court by ensuring that in his report the important facts affecting the best interests of the child are set out.

(2) He must ensure that any recommendation that he sets forth in his report to the court has been presented to the parents, the children, and their counsel and has some chance of acceptance especially if it involves some more than usual activity or co-operation by them.

(3) The report must give to the court an insight into the needs of the children and the ability of each parent to best satisfy those needs.

The report to be submitted by the assessor should contain the following information:

(1) An outline of the assessor's professional qualifications.

(2) A list of the issues presented for assessment.

(3) A description of the assessment process including the number of interviews and their participants.

(4) A detailed summary of the facts developed in the course of the assessment.

(5) An insight into the needs of the children and the ability of each parent to best satisfy those needs.

(6) An assurance that the recommendations in the report have been presented to the parents, children and counsel and that ways in which these can be implemented have been determined and discussed with all of the parties.

(7) An outline of possible alternative solutions, with advantages and disadvantages, which have been presented to parents, children and counsel.

(8) The recommendation or favoured solution of the assessor together with reasons.

It is not intended that the assessment usurp the trial process where the parties do not agree with the assessor's assessment and recommendations. It is obvious that where the assessor's reports are consistent with the facts established at trial and the law pertaining to those facts, they will be given considerable weight. The courts, however, will not routinely accept them. They have been successfully challenged in the past.

9. Three American scholars suggest that reports by mental health professionals in custody disputes can serve four functions:

A. *The Discovery Function*

First and foremost, through interviews or psychological tests, mental health professionals might be able to discover, and then bring to the court's attention, feelings, attitudes, and personality traits in the child(ren) and in the contestants that are relevant to the custodial decision and not otherwise readily apparent to the court. . . .

B. *The Articulating Function*

In addition to "discovering" attitudes and feelings in the parties before the court that are relevant to the court's deliberations but otherwise camouflaged, a psychologist may also be able to assist by articulating for the court, emotions the parties may find difficult to express . . . even when they have no fear of expressing their feelings, children will often be able to articulate them only in the vaguest of ways, if at all. But a sensitive clinical interviewer, in addition to helping a child to express thoughts and feelings, may also be able to articulate those feelings for the court far more precisely than a child ever could under the stress of a courtroom setting. . . .

C. *The Highlighting Function*

The expert psychological witness may serve the function of simply focusing the court's attention upon factors and considerations that are relevant to the court's decision but which otherwise may be neglected or given too little weight by the court. To take perhaps the most obvious example, in custody disputes in which a biological parent is seeking to regain custody of a child from a foster parent who has become the child's "psychological parent", a psychological witness could explain to the court the concept of the psychological parent, and discuss why maintaining the continuity of stable, loving parent-child bonds is important to the healthy development of children and why disrupting such bonds is, at best a risky proposition.

D. *The Analytical Function*

In any event, a contribution the psychological witness can always make in custody disputes — in addition to adding to the court's fund of data regarding the contestants and the children at issue — is to apply psychological logic to aspects of the evidence before the court to help it discern the implications of that evidence. That is, expert psychological witnesses can articulate for the court the reasons why custody decisions are likely to have particular outcomes in the circumstances of the case at hand. In fact, the expert's logic — which, in many instances, may appear to be little more than the application of common experience and common sense — can often substitute for the admittedly lacking empirical studies of how adult behaviour affects children. . . .

The expert's logic may not be the exclusive province of behavioral scientists. But, by virtue of their training and experience, behavioral scientists are more likely to be able to articulate the relevant meanings of observed behavioral patterns than most laypersons. And while . . . it may be naive to expect that psychological experts can furnish courts with truly neutral expertise, they can provide professional viewpoints.

(Litwack *et al.*, "The Proper Role of Psychology in Child Custody Disputes" (1979-80), 18 J. Fam. L. 289).

In *Delisle* v. *Delisle* (1998), 43 R.F.L. (4th) 186 (Ont. Prov. Div.), the assessor attempted to mediate the dispute and the mother objected. The court ordered a new assessment.

10. Granger J. indicated in *Weaver* v. *Tate* (1989), 24 R.F.L. (3d) 266, at 269 (Ont. H.C.) that an assessor appointed under s. 30 of the *CLRA* should only "report on the needs of the children and the ability of each party to satisfy those needs." He added (at 269) that the "section does not authorize the assessor to recommend which parent is to have custody". On appeal ((1990), 28 R.F.L. (3d) 188) the Ontario Court of Appeal explicitly disagreed, stating (at 189): "Although s. 30 does not direct that such a recommendation be made, we are of the view that it should be open to an assessor to do so in cases where he or she considers it appropriate and where the court does not direct him or her to the contrary."

11. In addition to assessments prepared by independent experts selected jointly by the parties or by the court, it is possible for individual litigants to retain their own mental health experts to perform an assessment and testify on behalf of that party. However, judges tend to demonstrate considerable scepticism in weighing the assessment of such experts. See generally Bala, "Assessing the Assessor: Legal Issues" (1990), 6 C.F.L.Q. 179, at 199-202.

12. While the evidence and opinion of experts is accorded great weight in most cases, the ultimate decision must be made by the court. It is an error of law to effectively delegate the decision-making authority to a psychiatrist, psychologist or social worker: *McClean* v. *McClean* (1985), 49 R.F.L. (2d) 235, 66 N.B.R. (2d) 65 (C.A.) and *Strobridge* v. *Strobridge* (1994), 4 R.F.L. (4th) 169 (Ont. C.A.). If the judge is convinced that the best interests of a child require a disposition other than that favoured by the expert, he or she must make an order effectively overruling the expert. The weight given to the expert's testimony or report will be affected by a number of factors such as the following: What are the expert's qualifications? How thorough was the assessment of the parties and child? Did the expert have an opportunity to assess all parties? Did he or she understand the nature of the proceedings? Did any of the parties lie to the expert? How recent was the assessment? Was the expert aware of all relevant facts? See *Tooley* v. *Tooley* (1972), 7 R.F.L. 317 (Ont. C.A.); *More* v. *Primeau* (1978), 2 R.F.L. (2d) 254 (Ont. C.A.); *R.* v. *B.* (1984), 38 R.F.L. (2d) 113 (Sask C.A.); *Weaver* v. *Tate* (1989), 24 R.F.L. (3d) 266 (Ont. H.C.), affirmed (1990), 28 R.F.L. (3d) 188 (Ont. C.A.); *K. (M.M.)* v. *K. (U.)* (1990), 28 R.F.L. (3d) 189 (Alta. C.A.); *Hurdle* v. *Hurdle* (1991), 31 R.F.L. (3d) 349 (Ont. Gen. Div.); *Fasan* v. *Fasan* (1991), 32 R.F.L. (3d) 121 (Ont. Gen. Div.); *Carlson* v. *Carlson* (1991), 32 R.F.L. (3d) 383 (B.C. C.A.); *Rezansoff* v. *Rezansoff* (1991), 32 R.F.L. (3d) 443 (Man. Q.B.); *Brigante* v. *Brigante* (1991), 32 R.F.L. (3d) 299

(Ont. U.F.C.); *Oldfield* v. *Oldfield* (1991), 33 R.F.L. (3d) 235 (Ont. Gen. Div.); *Tobias* v. *Meadley* (1991), 33 R.F.L. (3d) 349 (B.C. C.A.); *Lapierre* v. *Lapierre* (1991), 34 R.F.L. (3d) 129 (Sask. Q.B.); *C. (D.H.) v. M. (J.A.)* (1991), 82 D.L.R. (4th) 353 (Ont. Gen. Div.); *Britton* v. *Britton* (1991), 37 R.F.L. (3d) 253 (Ont. Gen. Div.); *Beck* v. *Beck* (1993), 48 R.F.L. (3d) 303 (P.E.I. T.D.); *Tyabji* v. *Sandana* (1994), 2 R.F.L. (4th) 265 (B.C. S.C.); *Brown* v. *Brown* (1994), 3 R.F.L. (4th) 135 (Ont. Gen. Div.); *Taylor* v. *Taylor* (1994), 6 R.F.L. (4th) 423 (B.C. S.C.); *Gunn* v. *Gunn* (1994), 10 R.F.L. (4th) 197 (Man. C.A.); *Walsh* v. *Walsh* (1998), 39 R.F.L. (4th) 416 (Ont. C.A.); and *Appiah* v. *Appiah* (1999), 45 R.F.L. (4th) 172 (Ont. C.A.).

13. The skeptical comments of L'Heureux-Dubé J. about the evidence of mental health professionals in *Young* v. *Young* (quoted in *Linton* v. *Clarke*, above) are somewhat puzzling in light of the facts that (i) the court-appointed experts in the case supported her position; (ii) she relied heavily on the work of American health care professionals such as J. Goldstein, A. Freud, and A. Solnit and their controversial book, *Beyond the Best Interests of the Child* (New York: Free Press, 1979) to support the traditional decision making power of the custodial parent; and (iii) in *Catholic Children's Aid Society of Metropolitan Toronto* v. *M. (C.)*, [1994] 2 S.C.R. 165, she placed great weight on the evidence presented at trial by a psychiatrist and social worker retained by the child protection agency. See also Bala, "Developments in Family Law: The 1993-1994 Term" (1995), 6 Supreme Court Law Review 453, at 467-468. Justices Cory and Iacobucci were less critical in *Young*, simply indicating (at 168) that "expert evidence is, while admittedly helpful in some cases, not always necessary to establish the best interests of the child". Justice McLachlin made similar remarks (at 157).

14. In Ontario, the government funds the Office of the Children's Lawyer, which may be asked by the court to provide representation for a child in a custody or access dispute. This Office has social workers and lawyers on staff, but it often chooses a lawyer from a panel of specially trained private practitioners.

15. Should legal representation of a child in custody disputes be statutorily required? Is it sufficient that the court have power to direct legal representation of a child in custody disputes? Should the court, as a compromise between these two positions, be statutorily required to determine whether legal representation is desirable to protect the interests of the child?

In *Bonenfant* v. *Bonenfant* (1981), 21 R.F.L. (2d) 173 (Ont. H.C.), the Official Guardian applied to represent the children of the marriage in divorce proceedings. Fitzgerald L.J.S.C. concluded (at 177-178):

> I have found nothing in this material of a nature that is not encountered in one form or another in virtually every contested custody matter. There is nothing to indicate that the children are being pressured by either parent or that they are being abused by either parent or that they are afraid or reluctant to speak their minds. There is nothing in this case to indicate that the court could not discover from the children what their feelings are in the matter. There is nothing in this case that indicates that the children require the intervention of a champion to present their plight to the court in order to enable the court to decide what is in the best interest of the children. There is no reason to suppose that an independent solicitor will be better able than the court to discover either the true feelings of the children or to resolve, in his advocacy, the possible conflict between what the children may think they want and what may be in their best interests. Nor is there any indication that the solicitor would need to call witnesses who would not be called in any event.

> There may indeed be cases where such intervention and advocacy would be useful but the present case is, in my opinion, not one of them. In addition, as a practical matter, the cost of the intervention in this case outweighs the probability of the intervention being of any substantial assistance to the court or to the children.

> I am aware of the decision of the Divisional Court in *Re Reid* (1975), 11 O.R. (2d) 622, 25 R.F.L. 209. In that case the so-called intended "surrogate father" was not called as a witness even though the trial judge found each parent equally acceptable as a prospective custodian. The appeal court felt that the issue could be resolved only by a new trial and, to ensure the calling of appropriate evidence and proper cross-examination and argument, the court appointed the Official Guardian to represent the children's interests.

The result in *Re Reid* was obviously desirable. I note, however, that the court was careful to say, per Galligan J. at p. 628:

> This case underlines that there is need in *some* cases for independent representation of the children. (The italics are mine.)

The Ontario Law Reform Commission, as quoted at p. 628, paints with a broad brush. It seems to call for an intervenor in every child custody case whether wanted or not and whether needed or not. The Law Reform Commission of Canada is more cautious and, with respect, more realistic. In my view there will be many cases where the court will welcome the assistance of counsel for the children and where the need for such assistance is clearly indicated. It is my opinion, however, that unless and until the appropriate legislature enacts otherwise, the court should not as a routine matter impose upon the parties to a custody proceeding the complication, expense, and enlargement of trial proceedings which must almost inevitably result from the appointment of additional counsel. Such a step should not be taken unless it is made to appear that justice is otherwise unlikely to be achieved and that there is a substantial risk that the court will be unable to carry out its duty to make a decision in the best interests of the children if the appointment is not made. The purpose of the appointment should clearly be to assist the court and not to dilute or usurp its function.

No such likelihood or risk being apparent at the present time in the present case, particularly where there is already a comprehensive independent assessment before the court, the application is denied without prejudice to its renewal at any time should circumstances require it.

See also *Lavitch* v. *Lavitch* (1985), 49 R.F.L. (2d) 1 (Man. C.A.), where the court stated (at 3): "The general rule is that there should not be separate representation of the children in custody disputes as it is undesirable to have children choosing between parents." This approach is also evident in *Bazinet* v. *Bazinet* (1998), 42 R.F.L. (4th) 140 (Ont. Gen. Div.), where the court declined the father's request for involvement by the Children's Lawyer, commenting (at 141) that the court was at liberty to "deal directly with the children" if it later proved necessary to have the children's input.

In *Young* v. *Young* (1989), 22 R.F.L. (3d) 444 (Alta. Q.B.), the court refused to appoint counsel to represent three children in a custody dispute, preferring to appoint an *amicus curiae* who would function in a neutral and impartial way to assist the court by ensuring that all available information was before it. See also *H. (S.)* v. *H. (W.)* (1999), 48 R.F.L. (4th) 305 (Nfld. U.F.C.) where a lawyer was appointed as an *amicus curiae* in a case of alleged improper touching of a four-year-old girl by the father.

For a critique of the practice of allowing independent representation of children in custody disputes, see Fineman, "The Politics of Custody and Gender: Child Advocacy and the Transformation of Custody Decision Making" in Smart and Sevenhuijsen, eds., *Child Custody and the Politics of Gender* (New York: Routledge, 1989). Compare Nasmith, "The Inchoate Voice" (1992), 8 C.F.L.Q. 43 where the author (a judge of the Ontario Court (Provincial Division)) simply assumes that children in custody and access cases before the courts will have a lawyer.

16. Occasionally, one parent arranges legal representation for the child in a custody dispute. The courts disapprove of this practice and generally will not allow it. See *Rowe* v. *Rowe* (1976), 26 R.F.L. 91 (Ont. H.C.); *Thatcher* v. *Thatcher* (1980), 16 R.F.L. (2d) 263 (Sask. Q.B.); and *Fiorellino* v. *Fiorellino* (1995), 18 R.F.L. (4th) 301 (Ont. Gen. Div.).

17. What role should counsel of a child take in a custody dispute? Should counsel's goal be to achieve the result desired by the child or to achieve the result believed to be in the best interests of the child? In the context of child protection hearings, there have been conflicting judicial pronouncements about the child's lawyer's role. Contrast *Re W.* (1980), 13 R.F.L. (2d) 280 (Ont. Prov. Ct.); *Re C.* (1980), 14 R.F.L. (2d) 21 (Ont. Prov. Ct.); and *C.A.S. Metro Toronto* v. *Duke K. and Mary K.* (1989), 2 Ont. F.L.R. 111 (Prov. Ct.). See also Day, "Counsel for Christopher: Representing an Infant's Best Interests in the Supreme Court of Canada" (1983), 33 R.F.L. (2d) 16; Nasmith, "The Inchoate Voice" (1992), 8 C.F.L.Q. 43; and Huddart and Ensminger, "Hearing the Voice of Children" (1992), 8 C.F.L.Q. 95. The Office of the Children's Lawyer has issued a *Policy Statement* indicating that, provided the child is competent to instruct the lawyer, the role of the child's lawyer is generally to advance the position

consistent with the child's wishes and preferences. However, the *Policy Statement* suggests that, if the lawyer believes the child is being unduly influenced by one parent, the lawyer may decline to advocate the outcome sought by the child. Even then, counsel should ensure that the child's wishes and preferences are known to the decision-maker together with information about how one parent may be influencing the child. See McTavish, *Office of the Children's Lawyer - Policy Statement - Role of Children's Counsel* (Toronto, April 3, 1995).

18. Section 89(3) of the *Courts of Justice Act*, S.O. 1994, c. 12 permits the court to appoint a "Children's Lawyer" to act as "litigation guardian of a minor". This provision and its predecessor have been used to appoint lawyers to act on behalf of children in custody and access disputes: *Zysman* v. *Tarkington* (1992), 39 R.F.L. (3d) 315 (Ont. Prov. Ct.); *Strobridge* v. *Strobridge* (1994), 4 R.F.L. (4th) 169 (Ont. C.A.); and *Zelinka* v. *Zelinka*, [1995] O.J. No. 3275 (Gen. Div.). Commenting on the predecessor provision which referred to the appointment of the Official Guardian, the Ontario Court of Appeal stated (at 177) in *Strobridge*:

> Section 89(3) authorizes the appointment of the Official Guardian as the children's litigation guardian and, once appointed, the Official Guardian will represent the children in that capacity. In most cases the Official Guardian will retain counsel, as happened here. Counsel will be instructed by the Official Guardian, who will act in a manner consistent with the children's best interests. I do not think that the Official Guardian, appointed to represent children under s. 89(3) of the *Courts of Justice Act*, is an amicus curiae.

In *Strobridge*, the court also stressed (at 180) that the lawyer appointed pursuant to s. 89(3) to act on behalf of a child in a custody and access dispute cannot simply advise the court of the child's views and preferences unless the parties consent. In other words, the child's wishes constitute evidence which must be proved in the normal way. Mr. Justice Granger indicated in *Zelinka* v. *Zelinka* that the Children's Lawyer's Office responded to this decision by making its willingness to act on behalf of a child conditional upon the parents' consent to permit the Children's Lawyer to make submissions on the child's wishes and preferences. Mr. Justice Granger strongly disapproved of this practice.

3.   Factors Relevant to the Custody Decision

(1) INTRODUCTION

This section of the casebook focuses on some of the factors that have most frequently been singled out to determine the child's best interests in reported custody cases. The following extract serves as a reminder that the courts should always keep in mind the particular circumstances of each child.

WAKALUK v. WAKALUK

(1976), 25 R.F.L. 292 (Sask. C.A.)

BAYDA J.A. (dissenting): — ... The issue of custody is without doubt the most important one — and was so treated by counsel at the hearing of this appeal — and the most troublesome. While at the hearing of the appeal the parties concentrated their attention on this issue they were not so minded at the hearing of the petition, even though the issue was far from settled. From the standpoint of custody the hearing of the petition was, in my respectful view, quite unsatisfactory. Virtually no evidence was directed to this issue. The parties primarily concerned themselves with adducing evidence to show whether, on the basis of the many marital battles engaged in by them, one or the other of them should be favoured by the trial judge in his determination of the issue of cruelty.

No one bothered to bring forward much information in respect of the two individuals who of all the persons likely to be affected by these proceedings least deserve to be ignored — the children. We know their names, sex and ages, but little else. Of what intelligence are they? What are their likes? Dislikes? Do they have any special inclinations (for the arts, sports or the like) that should be nurtured? Any handicaps? Do they show signs of anxiety? What are their personalities? Characters? What is the health of each? (This list of questions is not intended as exhaustive or as one that is applicable to all contested cases but only as illustrative of those questions which may be relevant.) In short, no evidence was led to establish the intellectual, moral, emotional and physical needs of each child. Apart from the speculation that these children are ''ordinary'' (whatever that means) there is nothing on which to base a reasoned objective conclusion as to what must be done for *this* child and *that* child, as individuals and not as mere members of a general class, in order that the welfare and happiness of each may be assured and enhanced.

Nor was any direct evidence led to show which of the parents, by reason of training, disposition, character, personality, experience, identification with a child's pursuits, ability to cope with any special requirements of a child's health, religious observance and such other pertinent factors (again the list is intended as only illustrative of matters which may be relevant), is best equipped to meet the needs of each individual child. The evidence presented on behalf of each side was principally, if not exclusively, geared to do one thing: show how badly one spouse treated the other. Such evidence is hardly a proper basis upon which to make a determination — a crucial one indeed from the standpoint of the children — as to which parent is best suited to meet the needs of the children and upon which to found an order for custody. How inconsiderate one spouse is of the other, or how one spouse reacts towards the other in a marital battle and the ability of a spouse to come out of a marital battle a winner, either actual or moral, are not high-ranking factors, if factors they be at all, in determining where a child's happiness and welfare lie, particularly whether such happiness and welfare are better assured by placement with one parent or the other. . . .

NOTES AND QUESTIONS

1. Do s. 24 of the *CLRA* and s. 16 of the *Divorce Act* dictate the ''child oriented approach'' urged by Bayda J.A. in *Wakaluk*? Note that the provincial legislation has a longer list of factors to consider in determining a child's best interest than its federal counterpart. In its *For the Sake of the Children*, the Special Joint Committee recommended (at 45) that the *Divorce Act* be amended to list the criteria that a court had to consider and urged that the list include:

i) the relative strength, nature and stability of the relationship between the child and each person entitled to or claiming a parenting order in relation to the child;
ii) the relative strength, nature and stability of the relationship between the child and other members of the child's family who reside with the child, and persons involved in the care and upbringing of the child;
iii) the views of the child, where such views can reasonably be ascertained;
iv) the ability and willingness of each applicant to provide the child with guidance and education, the necessaries of life and any special needs of the child;
v) the child's cultural and religious affiliation;
vi) the importance and benefit to the child of shared parenting, ensuring both parents' active involvement in his or her life after separation;
vii) the importance of relationships between the child and the child's siblings, grandparents and other extended family members;
viii) the parenting plans proposed by the parents;

ix) the ability of the child to adjust to the proposed parenting plans;

x) the willingness and ability of each of the parents to facilitate and encourage a close and continuing relationship between the child and the other parent;

xi) any proven history of family violence perpetrated by any party applying for a parenting order;

xii) the willingness shown by each parent to attend the required education session; and

xiii) any other factor that was relevant to a shared parenting plan.

2. What should be the response of the trial judge if he or she does not believe that the parties are presenting the most helpful and relevant information? Is this a situation in which a court-ordered assessment of the child and the parties is especially useful? Would independent representation of the child solve the problem? Should the judge actively seek information from the parties?

In *Gordon* v. *Gordon* (1980), 23 R.F.L. (2d) 266 (Ont. C.A.), the court stated (at 271):

A custody case, where the best interest of the child is the only issue, is not the same as ordinary litigation and requires, in our view, that the person conducting the hearing take a more active role than he ordinarily would take in the conduct of a trial. Generally, he should do what he reasonably can to see to it that his decision will be based on the most relevant and helpful information available. It is not necessary for us to go into details. In some instances it may well be sufficient for him to put the suggestion to counsel that a particular witness be called or information produced and, if the response is a negative one, to draw the appropriate inference from the absence of the evidence, depending on his assessment of the explanation given for such absence in all the circumstances.

In *Cooney* v. *Cooney* (1982), 27 R.F.L. (2d) 136, 36 O.R. (2d) 137, the Ontario Court of Appeal considered an appeal of a custody order on the grounds that there was insufficient information before the trial judge upon which he could properly determine the issue of custody and that the trial judge unduly emphasized the wife's adulterous conduct. Mr. Justice Cory, for the majority, noted that the trial judge was in the best position to assess the parties. Therefore, an appellate court should not lightly disturb the result reached at trial. He continued (at 142):

It is true that the trial judge indicated that the majority of the evidence was concerned with which party was at fault for the failure of the marriage. On the other hand, he obviously considered that he had heard sufficient evidence and seen enough of the parties to enable him to render his decision. No doubt, from time to time there will be cases which will require the trial judge to seek additional evidence to assist him. This may be a particularly important step if, for example, the child has special gifts or handicaps, unique needs or attachments to one parent. However, there is no indication here that Andrew suffered from an emotional or physical handicap. Rather, he appears to be a bright youngster doing well at school who pursues with relish all the physical activities that one might expect a healthy nine-year-old to enjoy. Clearly, he gets along well with his father and can enjoy skating, skiing and boating with him. Obviously, the trial judge did not consider that additional evidence was required to reach a decision in this case.

In dissent, Madam Justice Wilson quoted at length from Bayda J.A.'s reasons in *Wakaluk*. She stated (at 146): "To make a determination of the custody issue in the absence of an adequate evidentiary foundation on which to apply the 'best interests' test must surely constitute palpable error."

The B.C. C.A. held in *Cundy* v. *Irving* (1998), 37 R.F.L. (4th) 401 that the trial judge's extensive questioning of witnesses in a custody and access dispute was appropriate (at 402):

The judge was . . .properly carrying out the kind of inquiry one is often driven to in custody cases, where the court is not concerned with which of two adversaries has the better case, but with the best interests of the child. In that context, a judge will be justified more than he or she otherwise would, in asking questions he or she feels are necessary to make the critical decision concerning which of two parents the child should be placed with.

3. In "Hearing the Voice of Children" (1992), 8 C.F.L.Q. 95, Madam Justice Huddart and Ms. Ensminger stress (at 96) the need for a "child centred approach":

It is obvious that the best chance of predicting what regime will be in a child's best interests will come if the entire decision-making process is centred on the child. If we learn as much as we can about the children of a relationship, their needs, their affective ties, their capacities, their interests, and as much as we can about the abilities of those adults willing to care for them, we will be able to make orders that will take best advantage of the adult abilities available to fulfill the children's needs.

In turn, this leads them to stress that the views of the child must be heard and considered. They suggest (at 99-100) that this may cause a significant shift in focus:

> ... [W]hat are the questions about which the child's views are needed? In some cases the child herself may identify the important questions. The question of choice of custodial parent may not be the important question or even one that should be posed.

> This approach requires an analysis of the issues. Usually the fundamental issue between the parents in a contested case is one of control. Who is to have the final say when there is disagreement? Who is to control the life of the child? These disputes over control seem to result most frequently from a parent wanting to exclude the other parent from the children's lives in the interest of a second family, or from deep differences in cultural values between the parents, or both.

> A child may have a view on who should have that power, but in many cases the child is more concerned with more ordinary issues — where will he sleep and be fed regularly; where and when can he take his friends to visit; who will help him fix his bike; who will take her to Tuesday soccer practice and Saturday game; can he call his mom if he's with his dad; can she sleep over with her friend when she's spending the weekend with mom; can she still spend Thanksgiving at her grandparents; camp with her cousins — and the myriad of other everyday important things like that.

> No one, least of all the child, expects a judge to order the child's life on a daily basis. But the child does want the judge to understand that her physical, emotional, and social needs are as important as her parents' wishes. Listening to a child talk about her life and her parents' role in it should assist the judge in assessing the parents or other willing adults and their plans. Knowing that the child is going to talk about her needs to the judge might also help the parents make those plans, taking into account the child's views as to her own needs. A child's talking about her needs will certainly ensure that the decision-making process centres on her.

(2) DE FACTO SITUATION

MARSHALL v. MARSHALL

(1998), 42 R.F.L. (4th) 180 (N.S. C.A.)

[In an application to vary an interim order, the father, who was unrepresented, agreed that the court should make a final order of custody. The appellate court found that the father's consent was misinformed because the chambers judge suggested that there was little, if any, difference between an interim and final custody order. In its reasons, the court set out the appropriate approach to interim orders.]

Roscoe J.A. (for the court): . . . The issues before the court at the commencement of the application and those for which the parties prepared were *interim* custody and *interim* child support. The test to apply on an interim custody application is as set out by Justice Kelly in the following passage from *Pye* v. *Pye* (1992), 112 N.S.R. (2d) 109 (N.S. T.D.) at paragraph 5:

> . . .[T]he test in such an application was properly set out in *Webber* v. *Webber* (1989), 90 N.S.R. (2d) 55; 230 A.P.R.. 55 (F.C.), by Daley, J.F.C. at p. 57:

Given the focus on the welfare of the child at this point, the test to be applied on an application for an interim custody order is: *what temporary living arrangements* are the least disruptive, most supportive and most protective for the child. In short, the *status quo* of the child, the living arrangements with which the child is most familiar, should be maintained as closely as possible. With this in mind, the following questions require consideration.

1. Where and with whom is the child residing at this time?

2. Where and with whom has the child been residing in the immediate past? If the residence of the child is different than in #1, why and what were the considerations for the change in residence.

3. The *short-term needs* of the child including:

    (a) age, educational and/or preschool needs;

    (b) basic needs and any special needs;

    (c) the relationship of the child with the competing parties;

    (d) the daily routine of the child.

4. Is the current residence of the child a suitable temporary residence for the child taking into consideration the short-term needs of the child and:

    (a) the person(s) with whom the child would be residing;

    (b) the physical surrounding including the type of living and sleeping arrangements, closeness to the immediate community and health;

    (c) proximity to the preschool or school facility at which the child usually attends;

    (d) availability of access to the child by the non-custodial parent and/or family members.

5. Is the child in danger of physical, emotional or psychological harm if the child were left temporarily in the care of the present custodian and in the present home? (emphasis added)

The focus is on the status quo and the short-term living arrangements for the child. Although in this case the parties had been separated for a few years, and had consented to the first order, the test that should have been applied was the same: if there is no reason to change the existing situation, that situation should continue until the trial. There is authority for variation of interim orders: see *Foley* v. *Foley* (1993), 124 N.S.R. (2d) 198 (N.S. S.C.).

LiSANTI v. LiSANTI

(1990), 24 R.F.L. (3d) 174 (Ont. Fam. Ct.)

VOGELSANG PROV. J.: — Because of the unusual history of this proceeding, I thought it best to give some brief written reasons. An ex parte motion came before me on 11th January 1990. Being satisfied that the requirements of R. 17 had been met, I granted an interim order that the father, the moving party, would have custody of the two children of the marriage, Andrew and Antonette, who are 4 years old and 9 months old, respectively. The order directed the London Police, among other peace officers, to locate the children and deliver them up to the father. Later that day, a motion to set aside my order was brought before Genest Prov. J. by the wife. Genest Prov. J. purported to "suspend" my order and direct that the issue of interim custody be heard before me at a later date. Thus, this is the third appearance required to resolve the issue.

The husband and wife have been married for about four years and maintained, almost throughout their cohabitation, a matrimonial home in London. The husband, a draughtsman employed by the Ontario government, arrived home from work on 2nd January 1990 to find that his wife and children had gone. Only a few articles of clothing had been taken with them. It appears that the husband called around to find his family's whereabouts. The best he could accomplish was that they might be at the Women's Community House, a "transition" residence for the protection of battered women. In fact, that was their location.

In the affidavit evidence before me there were many substantial disagreements between the parties as to events in the past. Without passing yet on the relevance of those events, it struck me that they could be characterized, in the main, as individually trivial. That was the assessment of the wife's attending physician in his report of 22nd January 1990 but I am not as confident as the physician that the wife's rather precipitous flight to the shelter was "appropriate" in all of the circumstances. . . .

As to the merits of the motion as it was argued before me, it is enough to say that the matter was hotly contested. Mr. Winninger pressed his position that the fact that the mother was the primary caretaker of the children in the past should determine the issue. He says that I should make an inference, from that fact, that there exists a closer emotional bond between her and the children. With great respect to Mr. Winninger, I am unable to do so. There is nothing in the affidavit material which would satisfy me that either the mother or the father is unable to look after these two children in a perfectly acceptable, loving and caring manner in the short time between now and trial; nor is there any undisputed and cogent evidence of a more substantial bond with either parent.

The family lived together in the former matrimonial home until the sudden departure of the mother with the children. She now lives in a transition state and her future accommodation is not assured. However one may characterize the vicious squabbles between the husband and the wife, there is no doubt that their substance is absolutely disputed by the parties. The wife alleges that she was "abused" and Mr. Winninger asserts that she must not be "forced back" to the matrimonial home. It follows, in his argument, that the children must therefore remain in the shelter to avoid a separation from their mother. He says that her position as their mother has created a status quo which should not now be upset.

This is a question of interim custody. There is no reason why, even with extensive discovery, the trial of this action cannot be heard within 12 or 14 weeks. It is not my place to decide the ultimate issue. That is for the trial judge. The only question before me is where the best interests of these children will be assured between now and the trial.

Mr. Mamo argues that the existing status quo for the children is their residence with the father in their accustomed home. The father says in his affidavit that his religious associates of the Jehovah's Witness faith have arranged to assist him with child care while he is at work. Although Mr. Winninger thought that arrangement less than desirable, there is not a tittle of evidence that the father, with this available assistance, could not look after the children completely adequately in their usual surroundings. I agree that the mother unilaterally deprived the children of their accustomed home and the life that they had by removing them when she took her dispute with their father into her own hands. There was no evidence before me of any attempt by the mother to reach an agreement about custody with the father, or to bring an application either for exclusive possession of the matrimonial home or for interim custody of the children prior to her abrupt departure.

Mr. Mamo stresses that the actions of the wife were in contravention of the legislated equal custodial rights of a mother and father set out in s. 20(1) of the Children's Law Reform Act. I agree that the departure of the wife and the taking of the children, on substantially disputed grounds, was a complete denial of the husband's custodial rights which cannot stand to her credit on this motion. The best interests of the children, were they ever first considered by her, would have militated against such a result.

I should make reference to some of the evidence of the mother's affliction with Lupus erythematosus. There is no professional evidence that the disease affects any aspect of her physical or mental abilities. Indeed, that is specifically denied by the physician who continues to attend her and monitors the progress of the disease. Her suffering from this condition has played no part in my decision on this interim motion.

In the result, there is no clear and cogent evidence which would justify the mother's removal of the children from their accustomed environment. Their best interests, it seems clear to me, can be safeguarded by their father in the former matrimonial home and an interim order will go granting him their custody. The mother should have generous access to the children.

MOORES v. FELDSTEIN

12 R.F.L. 280, [1973] 3 O.R. 921 (C.A.)

[The plaintiff, respondent, sought custody of her daughter. The daughter, within days of her birth, had been delivered by the mother into the care of the appellants, the Feldsteins. The mother hoped that this would lead to reconciliation with her husband, who was not the father of the child. Within months, the mother requested the return of the child but proceedings were not begun until almost two years after the birth of the child and the child was almost four years old when the matter came to trial. The trial judge, finding that the child had not been abandoned and that the mother was not unfit, awarded custody to the mother. The Feldsteins appealed. The Ontario Court of Appeal decision is most important for its application of the "best interests of the child" test in a custody dispute between a parent and non-parents. The excerpt below focuses on the effect of the child's established, stable position with the Feldsteins.]

DUBIN J.A.: — . . . I am mindful that a trial judge has the advantage, denied to an appellate tribunal, of seeing the parties and benefitting from his personal observation of them. In custody matters, in particular, his judgment ought not to be interfered with, unless the appellate court is satisfied that he has failed to apply the correct principles or disregarded material evidence. After the most anxious deliberation at my command I conclude that the learned trial Judge did fall into error in both such respects, and I would allow the appeal and hold that the child should be left with the Feldsteins. . . .

It must be observed that in this case the mother, who has given up a child to the care and custody of others, seeks its return. Under such circumstances it is important in my opinion that the Court consider and give adequate weight to the present position of the child. As Laidlaw J.A. put it in *Re Duffell*, [1950] O.R. 35, at 39 (C.A.), affirmed [1950] S.C.R. 737:

While the child will obtain great benefits I have mentioned if the plan of the appellant be carried out, I am deeply conscious of the fact that the child cannot be removed from the custody of the respondents, after the great care and devotion given to it for more than twenty months, without much hardship to the child by reason of the change and perhaps much disturbance to its affections. Such a change of custody should not be made lightly. I think that before it is made by order of the Court, the person who asks for the order should show to the satisfaction of the Court that the proposed removal will enure to the welfare of the child. . . .

This principle was also enunciated by Lord MacDermott in the case of *J. v. C.*, [1970] A.C. 668, at 715, [1969] 1 All E.R. 788:

Some of the authorities convey the impression that the upset caused to a child by a change of custody is transient and a matter of small importance. For all I know that may have been true in the cases containing dicta to that effect. But I think a growing experience has shown that it is not always so and that serious harm even to young children may, on occasion, be caused by such a change. . . .

In my opinion, this is an important consideration in this case which, along with others, was overlooked by the learned trial Judge. I cannot help but feel in the circumstances of this case that serious harm may be occasioned by removing this bright, alert little girl from her present surroundings and placing her in the custody and care of someone who would now likely be quite a stranger to her. Unless the result of such a change is shown to be in the interests of the child, I would hesitate to risk the effect of such a disturbance.

This little girl has been with the Feldsteins, as I have already mentioned, for almost four years. In the report of the Official Guardian the little girl is described as follows: this child ''is a fair, blue-eyed healthy little girl, appears lively and curious. She is bright and alert and enjoys watching television and reflecting on what she sees. . . . The child is very fond of singing, loves clothes, and has a strong independent streak . . . She has three pet cats and a live rabbit.'' She is taken to the nearby Church of England on Sundays.

Mrs. Feldstein is described also in the Official Guardian's report ''as a very warm-hearted person with a strong motherly instinct''. Mr. Feldstein is described to be ''a rather aesthetic young man with a sensitive personality who enjoys his home''.

The Official Guardian's report went on to say that there was a strong atmosphere of warmth and care in this home, and there could be little doubt that the child receives excellent physical and emotional care. There is a possibility that she might be strongly over-indulged, but the care that she receives would appear to be beyond reproach.
. . .

I do not feel that I am bound by precedent to return the child to its mother when I have grave concern about its future if I were to do so, merely because the mother now desires her return. In my opinion it would be unfair to the child and not in her interests to expose her to such a risk.

In my view, since the evidence does not show that the child will benefit by the mere fact of its blood relationship with its mother, it cannot be said that the welfare of the child in its broadest sense will best be served by its being returned to her. In its present surroundings it will have the loving care of a father and a mother who will be able to devote their full time to her in her formative years. There will be no risk of the uprooting of the child from its present happy surroundings having a serious effect on her. Without the benefit of omniscience the safest course, in my opinion, is to leave the little girl where she is and where, I have every reason to believe, she will be loved and well cared for.

SPENCER v. SPENCER

(1980), 20 R.F.L. (2d) 91 (B.C. C.A.)

[The parties separated in December, 1979 when the respondent mother left the matrimonial home. Two children, aged approximately six and eight, remained with the father. In April 1980 the trial judge awarded custody to the mother although the father had done an "admirable job" in looking after the children following separation. He concluded that both parties were partly responsible for the separation and that each could provide a suitable home. He decided that the children should reside with the mother because she had been the primary caregiver before separation and could provide "that 'something' that only mothers seem to be able to provide". The Court of Appeal held that the trial judge had erred in stating that "mothers have an edge over fathers" because they are able to spend more time with their children. The court noted (at 97) that the father's employment as a teacher allowed him "to spend a good deal more time with the children than the respondent". The court next addressed the effect of the fact that the children had been with the father since separation.]

TAGGART J.A.: — . . . The learned trial judge did not deal with what, in my opinion, is the most important issue in the whole case, namely, whether the lives of the children should be disrupted by taking them from a stable and secure environment to a new environment where they must, so to speak, begin life afresh. He appears to have wholly disregarded the evidence on this issue.

Without placing blame on anyone for the breakup of the marriage, it seems obvious to me and is borne out by the evidence that the departure of the respondent had a staggering effect on the children.

The children have just recovered from the trauma. They have strong roots in the rural community where they live. For years they have lived in the same house. All their friends are there. They are happy and contented.

In the absence of the appellant they are in the constant care of a Mrs. Lambert who lives only a short distance from their home. This is an important relationship and should not be lightly disturbed.

The respondent admits that the children are happy and does not dispute the fact that they live in a stable and secure setting.

In the light of this evidence is it safe to take these children out of this environment? While I have no doubt that the respondent is a good mother and loves her children deeply, I do not think that it is possible to say on the evidence before us that there is not a grave risk in causing the children to be moved out of the Salmon Arm area at this time.

I do not think that it is possible to over-emphasize the need of young children to feel secure in every way. This feeling of security, which they now enjoy, may well be impaired if they are taken away from all their friends and the physical setting with which they are familiar.

I have not overlooked the fact that the learned trial judge, who saw the parties and heard the witnesses, placed stress on the fact that the respondent has a "zest for life" and that the children will not have the advantage of receiving the love and affection that only a mother can give. These are important matters but, in the circumstances of the case at bar, it seems to me that on balance the need of the children not to be uprooted from their stable and secure environment where they are living happily outweighs the need to live with their mother.

To leave the children where they are is not a gamble. To change the status quo is a gamble which I am not prepared to take.

I would allow the appeal and give custody of the children to the appellant, with reasonable and generous access to the respondent. In this respect it is of extreme importance that the children have a strong and continuing relationship with the respondent. I assume that both parties will do everything within their power to achieve this result. This will require great sacrifices on the part of both parents, financially and otherwise, but I am certain that both parties will be willing to bear these burdens.

RENAUD v. RENAUD

(1989), 22 R.F.L. (3d) 366 (Ont. Dist. Ct.)

BOLAN D.C.J.: — The plaintiff's claim is for custody of the children of the marriage, namely, Melissa Anne Renaud, born 29th July 1985, and Nicole Lea Renaud, born 28th October 1987. The defendant counterclaims for the same relief.

The status of the parties immediately before the separation was that the plaintiff (hereinafter called the wife) had assumed the traditional role in the family of being the primary caregiver for the children and looking after the home. The defendant (hereinafter called the husband) was steadily employed and devoted much of his spare time to raising the children.

Since the separation, the husband has had de facto custody of the children and the wife has had regular access pursuant to the order of the Honourable Judge Perras dated 23rd November 1988. It is important to examine how it came about that the husband obtained de facto custody of the children. . . .

I find as a matter of fact that the wife was locked out of the matrimonial home on 14th September 1988 and had no alternative but to leave without the children. The only alternative would have been for her to accede to his consistent demands that she return to live with him in the matrimonial home and that they would "work things out". I accept her evidence that he had slapped her before on two separate occasions and abused her verbally by hurling vile names at her. She was afraid to return to live with him. . . .

Both parties are warm and loving parents and both are capable of giving fit and proper care to the children. I cannot say that one home is better for the children than the other or that the plan of one parent for the children is any better than that of the other parent. The issue boils down to which parent should be the primary caregiver.

I am satisfied that the wife has rehabilitated herself from the marriage and is now on firm footing. She sought out and obtained full-time employment. Her plan to raise the children is simplistic but not uncommon with that of many other single mothers who parent their children. She impresses me as an unsophisticated person who is deeply attached to her children and has their best interests at heart.

The husband impresses me as a devoted father who is quite capable of managing the best interests of his daughters. Since the separation, his mother, Solange Renaud, has looked after the children while he is at work. I was impressed with Solange Renaud. She is a 48-year-old widow and has a deep attachment to the children. However, my main concern is the character of the husband. Following the separation, he acted in a mean-spirited manner in not allowing the wife access to the children. The only access she had to the children up to 23rd November was on one occasion when the husband attended with the children at the residence of the wife's brother where she was living. The wife had tried on many occasions to contact the children by telephone but she was repeatedly denied this meagre access. His refusal to deliver to the wife her bicycle is an example of his vindictiveness.

I am also concerned about the husband's fits of anger. During the marriage he was abrasive towards the wife and has continued to be so since the separation. I accept the wife's evidence that he physically assaulted her on two previous occasions during the marriage. I also accept her evidence that he verbally abused her during the marriage and also since the separation. Although the husband during the past year has parented the children in a fit and proper manner, I am not satisfied that it is in their best interests that he continue as the custodial parent.

In my view what is in the "best interests" for these two girls of tender years is that they reside with their mother. She was their primary caregiver from birth up until her banishment from the home by the husband. The husband has proven himself as a good parent; however, in the final analysis the girls are better off with their mother. . . .

NOTES AND QUESTIONS

1. For other cases illustrating the courts' reluctance to alter the *status quo* in interim custody applications, see *Terrien* v. *Terrien* (1984), 40 R.F.L. (2d) 40 (Man. C.A.); *Wahl* v. *Pavle* (1985), 49 R.F.L. (2d) 372 (B.C. C.A.); *Prost* v. *Prost* (1990), 30 R.F.L. (3d) 80 (B.C. C.A.); *Brown* v. *Brown* (1994), 3 R.F.L. (4th) 135 (Ont. Gen. Div.); *McEachern* v. *McEachern* (1994), 5 R.F.L. (4th) 115 (Ont. Gen. Div.); *M.(S.R.)* v. *M. (J.K.)* (1996), 24 R.F.L. (4th) 286 (Man. C.A.); *Fattali* v. *Fattali* (1996), 22 R.F.L. (4th) 159 (Ont. Gen. Div.); and *Corrigan* v. *Corrigan* (1998), 43 R.F.L. (4th) 48 (Ont. Gen. Div.).

Maintaining the most stable, least disruptive environment pending trial may be complicated if one parent moves. In *Leung* v. *Leung* (1998), 44 R.F.L (4th) 121 (B.C. C.A.), the mother left the matrimonial home and moved from Richmond to a nearby community. The Master granted joint interim custody of two young children to both parents, but ordered that they reside primarily with the mother. The father appealed, arguing that the status quo involved residence in the matrimonial home in Richmond where the children attended school and where their friends and relatives lived. The B.C. C.A. upheld the decision, partly on the basis that, prior to separation, "the status quo involved the mother having day-to-day care of the children, and access to the father when he was not working"(at 123). Is this a redefinition of "status quo"? Can this case be best understood as illustrating a tendency to favour the primary caregiver?

Of course, other factors relating to the child's best interests may convince a court that preservation of the *status quo* which has existed since separation should not continue until trial. See, for example, *G. (D.)* v. *Z. (G.D.)* (1997), 30 R.F.L. (4th) 458 (B.C. Master) and *Flegal* v. *Mazoka* (1999), 48 R.F.L. (4th) 90 (Sask. Q.B.). In both cases there were concerns about the care given by the mother. In *Van de Perre* v. *Edwards* (2000), 184 D.L.R. (4th) 486, the B.C. C.A. granted custody of a boy to a father and his wife, even though the boy had lived with his mother since birth. Portions of the D.L.R. headnote read as follows:

A woman conceived a child during a brief affair with a married, professional basketball player who had numerous other extra-marital affairs. The father's wife was determined to hold their marriage together, partly for the sake of their twin daughters. The mother was a Caucasian Canadian, while the father and his wife were Afro-Americans who intended to return to the United States after the father retired. The child lived with the mother prior to the trial of the custody proceedings. She depended heavily on her mother and friends for help in caring for him. The father's attempts to exercise access were initially resisted. The mother, who had poor employment qualifications and a spotty employment record, had affairs with other professional basketball players and continued an active social life after the birth of the child.

The parents agreed to the selection of an experienced clinical psychologist to prepare a report for the court pursuant to s. 15 of the *Family Relations Act*, R.S.B.C 1996, c. 128. The psychologist concluded that the mother likely had a personality disorder in that she was narcissistic, histrionic, and needed constant attention and approval. She acknowledged that the mother had acquired appropriate parenting techniques, but suggested that it was difficult to predict the extent to which these techniques would stand up to the stress that accompanied child rearing. The psychologist described the father as fairly healthy in his psychological functioning, although he exhibited both "dependent and avoidant" personality features. His daughters had a strong, positive attachment to him. The father's wife impressed the psychologist as a devoted mother with excellent parenting skills. The psychologist observed that the child was probably primarily attached to the mother, although not as strongly as might be expected. She also noted that the child had developed an attachment to the father, the father's wife, and their daughters. She concluded that the father's family unit swung the balance in his favour. The mother's family doctor testified favourably about the mother's parenting skills and the bond between mother and child.

The trial judge awarded custody of the boy to his mother. He emphasized the evidence of the family doctor, who was in a better position to assess the mother's relationship with the child than the psychologist. Although he acknowledged the father's wife's positive attributes, he reasoned that he had to determine whether the father alone or the mother alone would be better able to raise the child. This approach reflected his conclusion that the father's affairs posed a serious threat to the stability of his marriage. The father appealed. By the time the appeal was heard, the legislature had amended the *Family Relations Act* to provide for custody orders to non-parents and the father's wife indicated that she wished to apply for joint custody with her husband.

Held, the appeal should be allowed and custody awarded to the father and his wife jointly.

Although there were strong reasons for deference to trial decisions in family law cases, appellate courts should do more than simply rubber stamp trial judgments. Appellate interference was warranted where the trial judge committed serious errors, ignored relevant evidence and drew incorrect conclusions from the evidence.

The trial judge failed to engage in the close and detailed analysis that was required in respect of the backgrounds, characters, personalities, family environments and parenting abilities of each of the parents. He essentially ignored the very real concerns about the mother's suitability to raise a child. He became diverted from the central question of the best interests of the child by the arguments concerning the father's extra-marital affairs and the parties' attitudes to each other. The trial judge also erred in concluding that the father's marriage would not last and then assessing the father's ability to parent in isolation from the rest of his family. Finally, he gave no weight to the fact that it would be in the child's interest to live with a parent and family who would nurture his identity as a person of colour and would appreciate the day-to-day realities of racism and discrimination that Afro-Americans faced in North America.

Another justice of the B.C. C.A. immediately granted a stay of the appellate court's order while the mother sought leave to appeal: *Van de Perre* v. *Edwards* (2000), 184 D.L.R. (4th) 515. The Supreme Court of Canada subsequently granted the leave in July, 2000.

2. As *LiSanti* indicates, the courts sometimes frown on one parent's attempt at self-help. See also *Sobanski* v. *Sobanski* (1973), 9 R.F.L. 318 (Ont. H.C.); *Moldowan* v. *Moldowan* (1979), 13 R.F.L. (2d) 1 (Sask. C.A.); *Curri* v. *Curri* (1981), 34 O.R. (2d) 429 (Master); and *Miller* v. *Miller* (1999), 1 R.F.L. (5th) 391 (Ont. C.A.). What should Ms LiSanti have done, in Judge Vogelsang's view? Do you agree with the result in *LiSanti*?

Notwithstanding cases such as *LiSanti*, Professor McLeod and Alfred Mamo write in *Annual Review of Family Law, 1995* (Toronto: Carswell, 1995) (at 29-30) that unilateral removal of a child from the home upon separation usually helps the acting parent obtain custody:

Many lawyers and judges seem to forget that unilateral removal of a child from a person exercising custody rights is a crime: s. 283, *Criminal Code*. . . .

Courts at all levels should discourage wrongful removal of children. There should be a heavy onus on a person who removes a child without the other parent's consent to show why the welfare of the child justified such actions without prior court approval. The main reasons a parent removes a child without the consent of the other parent are that the child is at risk from the other parent or the removing parent wants to leave and does not want to leave the child behind. The former justifies unilateral removal to protect the best interests of the child but the facts must be carefully reviewed to ensure there is merit to the claim. The latter should not be held a sufficient reason to support unilateral removal of a child. A lawyer can have an interim (interim) custody proceeding in front of a judge in a matter of days. There is rarely a need to leave before a judge can deal with the matter.

In most cases the parent in "possession" of the child receives interim interim custody pending cross-examinations on the affidavits. He or she then often receives interim custody because there is no good reason to change child care arrangements in the short-term and by the time the matter gets on for final hearing a status quo has been established that most judges are reluctant to change. The system as it stands encourages wrongful removal of children upon family breakdown. A parent faced with a wrongful removal must act quickly to minimize potentially adverse consequences.

In *Howard* v. *Howard* (1999), 1 R.F.L. (5th) 375 (Ont. S.C.J.), the mother surreptitiously moved to London, Ontario with three children. Her leaving was not in response to an emergency or for reasons of immediate safety. The father continued to live in the matrimonial home in the small village of Nairn some twenty kilometres from London. The children's school was located three doors down from the home. Both parents sought interim custody. The father was a long-distance truck driver who had to be away from home frequently. However, he proposed that his mother, who had looked after the children previously while both parents worked, could assist him. Justice Aston referred to *LiSanti* and stated (at 376):

I agree wholeheartedly that one of the principles that the court must sustain in these matters is to discourage self-help and, rather, encourage the parties to put the matter before a judge if they cannot resolve custody and access issues between themselves. The fact that the children have been in London with their mother for a little over a month is not to be considered a factor in her favour in the decision now to be made. The only "*status quo*" that counts for anything is the "*status quo*" that existed up to 7 July [the date of the move].

Later, he added (at 378):

The circumstances under which Ms. Howard established a new residence for the children should not give her an advantage in the decision to be made, but neither should she be punished for leaving as she did. The only consideration is the best interests of the children.

It is in the best interests of the children to remain in the day-to-day care of their mother but also in their best interests, for now, to return to the matrimonial home in Nairn. That is not Ms. Howard's first choice, but she does claim temporary exclusive possession of the matrimonial home as an alternative and expresses her willingness to return to Nairn if the court determines that to be in the children's best interests. The adjustment of the children to the parental separation may be facilitated if other changes in their lives are deferred and minimized. Mr. Howard is apparently able to live in the rental property he owns in Nairn where his mother now resides.

In the result, the court awarded interim exclusive possession of the matrimonial home and interim custody to the mother on condition that she return to the home.

3. Examine s. 20(4) of the *CLRA*. Where s. 20(4) applies, the parent with whom the child resides has legal custody until a separation agreement or order provides otherwise. In interim proceedings the court is likely to preserve that situation unless it poses some risk for the child.

In *Richer* v. *Thompson* (1985), 46 R.F.L. (2d) 240 (Ont. Dist. Ct.) the court held that s. 20(4) only applies if there is clear evidence that the parent with whom the child does not reside after separation consents or acquiesces in the arrangement. In that case, the mother took the child without the father's consent on separation. The father took no action for a month because he hoped that a reconciliation could occur. When it became apparent that this would not happen, he seized the child. The mother sought an interim custody order and argued that s. 20(4) applied to give her legal custody that should be maintained until trial. The court held that s. 20(4) was not triggered in these circumstances. Nevertheless, the mother was granted interim custody on the basis that this was in the best interests of the child.

Where s. 20(4) does apply the parent whose custody rights are suspended can only regain custody through a separation agreement or court order. "Self-help" in the form of a seizure of the child or a refusal to return him or her after a visit could be a criminal offence. Section 283(1) of the *Criminal Code* specifies: "Everyone who, being a parent . . . of a person under the age of fourteen years, takes, entices away, conceals, detains, receives or harbours that person, whether or not there is a custody order in relation to that person made by a court anywhere in Canada, with intent to deprive a parent . . . who has the lawful care or charge of that person, of the possession of that person, is guilty of (a) an indictable offence and is liable to imprisonment for a term not exceeding ten years, or (b) an offence punishable on summary conviction." Consent of the other parent is a defence (s. 284), but consent of the child is not (s. 286). If the action "was necessary to protect the young person from danger of imminent harm or if the person charged with the offence was escaping from danger of imminent harm", then no offence is committed (s. 285). It should also be noted that no proceedings may be commenced under s. 283(1) "without the consent of the Attorney General or counsel instructed by him for that purpose": s. 283(2). Regarding the interpretation and application of these provisions, see *Cook* v. *R.* (1984), 40 C.R. (3d) 270 (N.S. C.A.), leave to appeal refused (1984), 65 N.S.R. (2d) 90 (S.C.C.); *R.* v. *Adams* (1993), 19 C.R. (4th) 277 (Ont. C.A.); *R.* v. *Mendez* (1997), 32 O.R. (3d) 67 (Ont. C.A.); and *R.* v. *Dawson* (1996), 25 R.F.L. (4th) 181 (S.C.C.). See generally, Johnstone, "Parental Child Abduction Under the Criminal Code" (1987), 6 Can. J. Fam. L. 271. See also s. 36(2) of the *CLRA*.

4. Consider the following situation: A mother and father have two children, aged four and six. Their relationship is deteriorating and the mother concludes that it is at an end. Without the father's knowledge or consent she takes the children with her and moves into a friend's house. When the father discovers these facts he demands that the mother and children return to the matrimonial home. The mother refuses to comply and will not allow the father to take the children with him.

> (a) Has the mother committed a criminal offence?
> (b) Who has lawful custody of the children?
> (c) Could the father obtain a court order under s. 36(2) of the *CLRA*?
> (d) What alternative courses of action were available to the mother?

5. Recall that the judge in *Perrier* v. *Perrier* (reproduced in Chapter 5) declined to make interim custody and interim possession orders partly to avoid making decisions that could determine the final custody arrangements without more information. See also *Bailey* v. *Bailey* (1987), 5 R.F.L. (4th) 431 (Ont. Gen. Div.).

In *Stefanyk* v. *Stefanyk* (1994), 1 R.F.L. (4th) 432 (N.S. S.C.), both parents were still living in the home when the father petitioned for divorce and filed a motion for interim custody of the couple's two children. Saunders J. concluded that the family could no longer live together in the home. Acknowledging that there was limited and conflicting evidence, the judge stressed (at 439) that interim orders "are intended to provide a reasonably acceptable solution to difficult problems which the parties are unable, by themselves, to resolve" and that "the trial judge may well come to conclusions substantially different than mine". In the circumstances, the impact of the interim custody order favouring the mother was considerably lessened by providing that the unemployed father would return to the home each day to care for the children while the mother went to work.

In several other cases dealing with interim arrangements, the courts have attempted to ensure continued, meaningful involvement by both parents in the child's upbringing. In *Rix* v. *Rix* (1993), 50 R.F.L. (3d) 22 (P.E.I. S.C.), the judge explicitly declined (at 25) to make an interim custody order, but indicated that the children should remain in the day-to-day care and control of their father with very liberal access by the mother. Presumably such a "non-order" preserved joint custody until trial. See also *Woodside* v. *Woodside* (1994), 8 R.F.L. (4th) 430 (Alta. Q.B.) and *Waugh* v. *Waugh* (1998), 42 R.F.L. (4th) 415 (Ont. Dist. Ct.).

6. The longer the trial of a custody dispute is delayed, the less likely will there be an order altering the arrangement prior to trial. Section 26 of the *CLRA* implicitly recognizes this fact by attempting to ensure prompt judicial determination of custody applications under that Act. In *Hurdle* v. *Hurdle* (1991), 31 R.F.L. (3d) 349 (Ont. Gen. Div.), Granger J. stated (at 353):

Unfortunately, s. 26 has been ignored by the profession and the court administration. This section should be afforded the purpose for which it was intended, to ensure custody matters are given priority in the judicial process. Court service managers must ensure this section is complied with when applications are made under the C.L.R.A. and should also apply this procedure to custody issues under the *Divorce Act*.

7. In *Poole* v. *Poole* (1999), 45 R.F.L. (4th) 56 , the B.C. C.A. emphasized stability and the status quo in overturning a trial judge's decision to grant custody of a seven-year-old girl to her father so that she could rejoin her teenage brothers who lived with the father on the family farm. The court reasoned (at 61-62):

> Directly related to the health and emotional well-being of the child and almost always a consideration when looking at best interests, is an examination of those circumstances which will create the most stable, least disruptive environment for the child. In assessing stability, one must decide what the "status quo" is for a given child. To this end Justice Stromberg-Stein in *Mitchell*, *supra*, made some useful comments and I propose to quote some passages from her reasons:

> **Status quo**

> The "status quo" implies the relationships and way of life of the child in a particular location, not merely a geographic locale. In a decision dealing with the ability of one parent to move a child, *Tucker* v. *Tucker* (1994), 148 A.R. 306 at 313 (Q.B.), Moore J. discussed the importance of stability in a child's life:

> Status quo should not be defined as merely a geographic place, but rather, "a way of life". The home, neighbourhood, school, church, friends, lifestyle and recreational amenities need to be taken into account when assessing the status quo, and the degree of change being proposed by the moving parent ... If all else is equal, it could not be in any child's best interest to substitute an uncertain situation for a certain one ... The onus of adducing evidence that it is in the best interests of the child to alter the agreement or status quo rests with the person seeking the change.

> In *Vandher* v. *Vandher* (23 March 1995), Vancouver D087757 (B.C. S.C.), Lysyk J. preserved the status quo where the splitting of the children was originally by consent and one child lived with the mother and the other child lived with the father. The fact that both children were thriving in their respective environments was a very significant consideration.

> What is Samantha's status quo in this case? It is significant to note that the mother has been her primary caregiver since birth, and for the last, almost four years (since March 1995), Samantha has been in the sole care and custody of her mother. During those four years, Samantha has established herself in a home, neighbourhood and school. Samantha participates in recreational pursuits such as swimming and skating and she has established friendships. In reading the transcripts, there is no evidence to indicate that Samantha has not been well looked after by the mother. She is happy, healthy and doing well in various activities.

> Madam Justice Stromberg-Stein correctly suggests that the parties seeking to alter a child's status quo must present evidence to show that the status quo is unsatisfactory and not in the best interests of the child and should therefore be changed. Again, after a thorough reading of the transcripts, I was unable to find such evidence.

See also *Armstrong* v. *Armstrong* (1997), 34 R.F.L. (4th) 38 (Ont. Gen. Div.); *Haider* v. *Malach* (1999), 48 R.F.L. (4th) 314 (Sask. C.A.); and *Behrens* v. *Stoodley* (1999), 3 R.F.L. (5th) 8 (Ont. C.A.).

8. In "An Empirical Study of the Attitude of the Judges of the Supreme Court of Ontario Regarding the Workings of the Present Child Custody Adjudication Laws" (1971), 49 Can. Bar Rev. 557, Adrian Bradbrook noted that the parent with custody of a child after separation has a distinct advantage when the court determines the final custody application. Writing some 15 years later, Professor McLeod observed in "Annotation" (1986), 3 R.F.L. (3d) 30, at 30-31:

> Regardless of judicial pronouncements that interim orders in no way infringe on the power of the trial judge to deal with the issue afresh, untrammelled by earlier interim proceedings, there can

be no doubt that in the overwhelming majority of cases the interim order establishes the norm for the final determination. . . . The fact the child lives with [one parent] in a stable and satisfactory environment creates the status quo. The onus is effectively on the other parent to show how [the first] is not meeting the needs of the child or how he [or she] can better meet them. He [or she] must show why an arrangement that is working should be set aside. . . . [C]ourts are generally hesitant about disrupting at any stage in a custody dispute a stable living arrangement that meets the needs of the children.

The continued importance of *de facto* custody arrangements was again stressed by Professor McLeod and Alfred Mamo in their *Annual Review of Family Law, 1995* (Toronto: Carswell, 1995) (at 59):

Status quo is especially important in pre-trial proceedings. Prior to examinations, courts routinely leave a child where he or she is rather than risk "bouncing" the child between homes. Then, after examinations have been conducted, judges routinely leave a child where he or she is because the child is doing fine and why move the child unnecessarily in the short-term. Judges are only deluding themselves or attempting to mask the importance of their non-decision when they say that the interim order does not bind the Trial Judge. . . .

In fact, the interim arrangement usually becomes the final arrangement because of the importance judges attach to continuity of child care and the status quo.

As Professor McLeod indicates, there have been several cases in which judges have cautioned that interim custody arrangements, whether by court order or agreement, should not be given undue weight. In *R. v. R.* (1983), 34 R.F.L. (2d) 277 (Alta. C.A.), Kerans J.A. stated (at 284):

We should remind ourselves that interim custody is just that: a makeshift solution until the correct answer can be discovered. If a judge could tell what is best at the outset, there is no need for an interim order. Interim orders are designed to minimize conflict between parents and cause the least harm to the child pending determination of the cause.

The interim dispute here was resolved by agreement. The parties sensibly made a working arrangement until trial. It does not follow that, because it worked, that arrangement is the best for the child. And the parties cannot, at trial, be treated as having somehow waived the right to put a different proposal. Indeed, such a view would discourage future litigants from agreeing to workable interim arrangements. I would not encourage turmoil in this way. Also, courts should take care not to permit a new status quo (created by delay) to decide what was not decided by the interim disposition.

Nevertheless, even in *R. v. R.*, Kerans J.A. hastened to add (at 284): "[A]ll other things being equal, it is not in the best interest of a child to substitute an uncertain situation for a certain one." Of course, this is exactly what the parent who has not had interim custody asks the court to do. Other cases in which the courts expressly downplay the significance of the interim order for the final custody decision include *Harden* v. *Harden* (1987), 6 R.F.L. (3d) 147 (Sask. C.A.); *Stefanyk* v. *Clancy* (1996), 156 N.S.R. (2d) 161 (N.S. S.C.); *Marshall* v. *Marshall* (1998), 42 R.F.L. (4th) 180 (N.S. C.A.); *Smith* v. *Gale* (1999), 49 R.F.L (4th) 400 (Nfld. U.F.C.); and *Hamlyn* v. *Hamlyn* (1999), 50 R.F.L. (4th) 398 (Nfld. U.F.C.).

9. Clearly, the parent who does not have *de facto* or interim custody should be prepared to present the court with practical, concrete plans for the care of the child if there is to be a realistic possibility of convincing the court that the *de facto* situation should be altered. That parent should also maintain close contact with the child before trial and the trial should occur as soon as possible. If the court can be convinced that a change in custody will not be very disruptive and presents no significant risk, the status quo arrangement may carry less weight. See *R. v. R.*, 34 R.F.L. (2d) 277, [1983] 5 W.W.R. 385 (Alta. C.A.); *Bell* v. *Kirk* (1986), 3 R.F.L. (3d) 377 (B.C. C.A.); *Harris* v. *Lyons* (1987), 8 R.F.L. (3d) 59 (N.B. Q.B.); and *Britton* v. *Britton* (1991), 37 R.F.L. (3d) 253 (Ont. Gen. Div.).

10. In *Sherrett* v. *Sherrett* (1987), 6 R.F.L. (3d) 172, the Ontario Court of Appeal concluded that the trial judge had erred in awarding custody of two children to their father while allowing two older children to remain with the mother. However, seventeen months had passed since the trial decision and no motion was made to stay the judgment pending appeal. In the end the court dismissed the appeal

because "we are hesitant now to disturb an arrangement which on the surface appears to be working tolerably well without having evidence of what problems would be caused by a further uprooting of the two youngest children".

11. The principle of ensuring stability in children's lives also governs the judicial response to applications for variation of custody orders. The existing order will not be disturbed unless it is clearly demonstrated that a change in custody would be in the child's best interests. See *Talbot* v. *Henry* (1990), 25 R.F.L. (3d) 415 (Sask. C.A.) and *Williams* v. *Williams* (1989), 24 R.F.L. (3d) 86 (B.C. C.A.).

12. In *K. (K.)* v. *L. (G.); (King* v. *Low)*, 44 R.F.L. (2d) 113, [1985] 1.S.C.R. 87, the Supreme Court recognized the importance of stability and continuity in a child's life. An unwed mother gave up her son for adoption a few days after his birth to a couple carefully chosen by her. Less than three months later the mother requested the child's return. When the couple refused to comply, the mother revoked her consent to the proposed adoption and sought custody. The trial judge awarded custody to the prospective adoptive parents on the basis that the benefits to the child of maintaining his relationship with the biological mother were outweighed by those resulting from maintenance of his present home stability and the existing bond with the couple. This decision was upheld by the Supreme Court of Canada. In delivering the judgment of the court, McIntyre J. stated (at 126):

> I would therefore hold that in the case at bar the dominant consideration to which all other considerations must remain subordinate must be the welfare of the child. This is not to say that the question of custody will be determined by weighing the economic circumstances of the contending parties. The matter will not be determined solely on the basis of the physical comfort and material advantages that may be available in the home of one contender or the other. The welfare of the child must be decided on a consideration of these and all other relevant factors, including the general psychological, spiritual and emotional welfare of the child. It must be the aim of the court, when resolving disputes between rival claimants for the custody of a child, to choose the course which will best provide for the healthy growth, development and education of the child so that he will be equipped to face the problems of life as a mature adult. Parental claims must not be lightly set aside, and they are entitled to serious consideration in reaching any conclusion. Where it is clear that the welfare of the child requires it, however, they must be set aside.
>
> In considering the facts of this case, it should be observed at once that the trial judge found that the adoptive parents, on the one hand, and the mother, on the other, were both capable of providing a satisfactory home for the child. This clearly is not a case where the choice is made easy by clear failure, on one side or the other, to measure up to the required standard. I have read the entire record and it is notable in this case that there is a total absence of the mutual recrimination usually found in such cases. Each party has accepted the proposition that the other can perform the parental duties well, but each seeks custody: the mother because of her love for the child she bore and from whom she has been separated, and the adoptive parents because they have come to look on the child as their own, as a member of their family to whom they have become attached as to their own children.

Stressing the significance of the bond between the child and the prospective adoptive parents, McIntyre J. concluded (at 129) that "there was evidence upon which a finding in favour of the adoptive parents could properly be made".

In a case comment ((1985), 4 Can. J. Fam. L. 514) W.J. Wardell stated (at 516-517):

> Rutter's work in the area of maternal deprivation and infant bonding points to the probability that as long as the child's capability to form bonds has been established early in life, then multiple bonding can, and does, take place. The "chief bond" developed with the mother-figure is the strongest bond but basically similar in nature to other bonds the infant forms. It would appear that the critical issue in terms of the young infant's adjustment in later life is whether the infant has formed *any* bonds, not merely whether those bonds have been disrupted. The negative effects of disruption of bonds will depend on such variable factors as the infant's age and gender, the manner of the disruption, the number of times bonding has taken place and been disrupted, and so on. While this thesis lacks full empirical proof, the theory of psychological parenting which is

premised on extremely limited bond-forming capability and emphasizes one-caretaker continuity has come under increasing criticism as being overly rigid, restrictive and unrealistic in terms of actual family and kin-group structures.

It is the psychological parenting theory, however, which underlies the *King v. Low* judgments at all three court levels. The "existing parental bonds" which go beyond the mere day-to-day care of the baby are emphasized in the trial judgment. To sever these bonds "would impair its prospects of functioning as a healthy human being as it grows older". This is a reference to Bowlby's maternal deprivation theory and, as noted above, not any longer the last word in child development theory. Had the trial judge taken into account the infant's bonding with its birth mother in hospital, and the benefit to a child of not only knowing but also of actual continued contact with its genetic parentage, and considered these factors in light of the revised bonding theory, he might have come to a different conclusion and awarded the baby to the birth mother. By the time the case reached the Court of Appeal, and certainly by the Supreme Court hearing when the child was three years old, return to the birth mother would be untenable by any theory unless contact had been maintained between families and the transfer effected with the greatest care. Even so, few would argue that after such a passage of time with a child so young, any interests of the child would be served thereby. The best hope for return of the child in the fact situation presented by *King v. Low* is a speedy resolution in a trial court unhampered by overly rigid and possibly outdated child welfare theory. A decision dealing with placement where the child is very young at the onset of the dispute will inevitably result in the award of the child to the caretaker parents by a higher court due to the mere passage of time.

See also *R. (A.N.)* v. *W. (L.J.)*, 36 R.F.L. (2d) 1, [1983] 2 S.C.R. 173.

In *S. (R.)* v. *H. (C.)* (1989), 20 R.F.L. (3d) 456 (N.B. C.A.), a natural mother regained custody of a 15-month-old from prospective adoptive parents who had been providing an excellent home for the child since its birth. The judgment rested in significant part on the evidence of a child psychiatrist that the child would adapt to a change in custody without long-term harmful consequences. In his view, the younger the child and the more gentle and humane the actual means used to change custody, the smaller the possibility of harm from such a change.

The latter case should be contrasted with *Sawan* v. *Tearoe* (1993), 48 R.F.L. (3d) 392 (B.C. C.A.); leave to appeal refused (1994), 3 R.F.L. (4th) 196n (S.C.C.). In *Sawan*, an 18-year-old aboriginal mother approached the Alberta child welfare agency to care for her one-month-old child and signed a consent to adoption. Within the ten-day statutory period of revocation, she gave the agency oral notice that she had changed her mind. The agency ignored her oral notification since the statute required a written notice, and placed the child for adoption with a couple in British Columbia. The mother began litigation to regain custody and succeeded at trial. However, the trial order was stayed pending appeal. When the child was 20 months old, the British Columbia Court of Appeal held that "family bonds" had been forged between the boy and the prospective adoptive parents to such an extent that his best interests required that the adoption should go ahead.

In "Developments in Family Law: The 1993-94 Term" (1995), 6 Supreme Court Review (2d) 453, Professor Bala comments (at 472) that cases such as *Sawan* dealing with disputes between biological parents and psychological parents stand "in marked contrast with American jurisprudence . . . which is much richer in its analysis of social and legal context, more critical of the opinions of mental health experts, and stronger in its support of biological parents." He cites *Matter of Guardianship of J.C.*, 608 A.2d 1312 (N.J. 1992) and *Santosky* v. *Kramer*, 102 S. Ct. 1388 as illustrative American cases. For a case comment on *Sawan* which is critical of the "psychological parenting theory", see Mosikatsana, "*Sawan* v. *Tearoe* " (1993), 11 C.F.L.Q. 89. See also Carasco, "Race and Child Custody in Canada" (1999), 16 Can. J. Fam. L. 11. The critics have suggested that the concept of "psychological parent" is invariably used by middle class psychological parents to keep custody of children in litigation against disadvantaged, lower income biological parents, who are often members of a visible minority or aboriginal group.

Most recently, the B.C. C.A. in *Birth Registration No. 99-00733, Re* (2000), 182 D.L.R. (4th) 281 (B.C. C.A.) overturned a lower court decision awarding custody to the father of a child whom the mother had placed for adoption without the father's knowledge. The majority concluded that leaving the girl with the prospective adoptive parents with whom she had bonded accorded with her best interests.

13. *K. (K.)* v. *L. (G.)* is also significant because it affirmed that the welfare of the child must be the predominant factor in custody disputes between biological parents and others. In doing so, the S.C.C. implicitly overruled the "trilogy": *McNeilly* v. *Agar*, [1958] S.C.R. 52, 11 D.L.R. (2d) 721; *Hepton* v. *Maat*, [1957] S.C.R. 606, 10 D.L.R. (2d) 1; and *Martin* v. *Duffell*, [1950] S.C.R. 737, [1950] 4 D.L.R. 1 and endorsed *Moores* v. *Feldstein*. The trilogy emphasized the right of natural parents to retain or regain custody unless they are shown to be unfit or to have abandoned the child. On the other hand, *K. (K)* v. *L. (G.)* stressed the importance of the bonding of children with psychological parents.

This does not mean that the blood tie is totally irrelevant. Rather, it has become only one factor in determining the best interests of the child. In *Hardcastle* v. *Huculak* (1987), 11 R.F.L. (3d) 363 (Sask. C.A.), Wakeling J.A. stated (at 366):

> Now all things being comparatively equal the welfare of a child is best served in the custody of one or both of his natural parents; there is the advantage of natural parental and filial love, of extended natural family relationships, and of the sense of security which comes from knowing, and knowing of, one's family and one's roots.

Justice Beetz said in *C. (G.)* v. *V.-F. (T.)* (1987), 9 R.F.L. (3d) 263 (S.C.C.) (at 291):

> A third person who wished to obtain custody of a child must rebut the presumption to the effect that the parent is in a better position to ensure [the] child's wellbeing. He [or she] must establish on a balance of probabilities that the development of the child is likely to be compromised if he or she remains with the father or mother or returns to live with them. The third person must also show that, unlike the person having parental authority, he or she is able to provide the care and affection needed by the child.

See also s. 24 (2)(g) of the *CLRA*. For cases analyzing the importance of the blood tie, see *More* v. *Primeau* (1978), 2 R.F.L. (2d) 254 (Ont. C.A.); *Gray* v. *Director of Child Welfare* (1987), 10 R.F.L. (3d) 162 (Alta. Q.B.); *M. (T.L.)* v. *F. (G.E.)* (1988), 15 R.F.L. (3d) 57 (Alta. C.A.); *H. (C.)* v. *S. (R.)* (1989), 20 R.F.L. (3d) 456 (N.B. C.A.); *M. (C.G.)* v. *W. (C.)* (1989), 23 R.F.L. (3d) 1 (B.C. C.A.); *G. (D.A.)* v. *L. (T.)* (1990), 25 R.F.L. (3d) 408 (N.S. Co. Ct.); *Wagner* v. *Lerat* (1991), 36 R.F.L. (3d) 374 (Sask. Q.B.); *Clapp* v. *Morin* (1991), 82 D.L.R. (4th) 353 (Ont. Gen. Div.); *Crocker* v. *Sipus* (1992), 41 R.F.L. (3d) 5 (Ont. C.A.); *Dyck* v. *Ginter* (1992), 43 R.F.L. (3d) 207 (Man. C.A.); *Marriott* v. *Mullin* (1994), 5 R.F.L. (4th) 263 (N.B. Q.B.); *Burnett* v. *Toole* (1994), 156 A.R. 104 (Q.B.); *M. (A.)* v. *P. (L.R.)* (1995), 14 R.F.L. (4th) 267 (Sask. Q.B.); *T. (E.J.)* v. *V. (P.M.)* (1996), 24 R.F.L. (4th) 269 (Man. C.A.); and *H. (D.)* v. *M. (H.)* (1998), 45 R.F.L. (4th) 270 (S.C.C.). In some of these cases, the non-parents seeking custody were not of the same race, culture and ethnic origin as the child. On the significance of this factor, see generally Davies, "Racial and Cultural Issues in Custody Matters" (1993), 10 C.F.L.Q. 1; Van Praagh, "Religion, Custody and a Child's Identity" (1997), 35 Osgoode Hall L.J. 309; and Carasco, "Race and Child Custody in Canada: Its Relevance and Role" (1999), 16 Can. J. Fam. L. 11.

14. In *Floyd* v. *Bertrand* (1984), 41 R.F.L. (2d) 458 (Ont. H.C.) the child was living with its mother and the step-father until the mother's death. Master Cork granted interim custody to the biological father on the basis that he would be able to obtain custody at trial and that it was best to move the child sooner rather than later. He added (at 463): ". . . it is better for the child to be brought up by the biological father, even though it means being separated from the child's half-sisters at an early age." For one of the few reported cases in which a step-parent was awarded custody in circumstances similar to *Floyd* v. *Bertrand*, see *Fullerton* v. *Richman* (1983), 40 O.R. (2d) 395 (Fam. Ct.).

Section 61(1) of the *CLRA* allows a "person entitled to custody of a child" to "appoint by will one or more persons to have custody of the child after the death of the appointer". What is the effect of such an appointment? See s. 61(7). If a parent with sole custody of a child specifies in the will that the step-parent is to have custody, does this preclude the other biological parent from applying for custody? If not, how much weight should the court give to the appointment?

15. Section 21 of the *CLRA* permits any person to apply for custody or access. See *Smith* v. *Hunter (Sears)* (1979), 15 R.F.L. (2d) 203, 27 O.R. (2d) 683 (H.C.), and *Smith* v. *Children's Aid Society of Kent*

(County) (1980), 29 O.R. (2d) 502 (Co. Ct.). For cases dealing with similar legislation in other provinces, see *Nfld. (Dir. of Child Welfare)* v. *T. (B.)* (1993), 110 D.L.R. (4th) 160 (Nfld. C.A.); *H. (M.E.)* v. *F. (R.M.)* (1994), 10 R.F.L. (4th) 77 (Sask. C.A.); *Ochapowace First Nation* v. *A. (V.)* (1994), 10 R.F.L. (4th) 152 (Sask. C.A.), leave to appeal refused (1995), 12 R.F.L. (4th) 169n (S.C.C.); and *Williams* v. *Williams* (1995), 13 R.F.L. (4th) 152 (Alta. Q.B.). Section 16(1) of the *Divorce Act* allows a person other than a parent to apply for custody or access in divorce proceedings. However, where the person is not a spouse directly involved in the proceedings, the court must grant leave to apply: s. 16(3). In *M. (R.)* v. *B. (G.)* (1987), 6 R.F.L. (3d) 441 (Nfld. T.D.) and *Arnink* v. *Arnink* (1999), 2 R.F.L. (5th) 24 (B.C. S.C.) it was held that leave should be granted unless the application was clearly frivolous or vexatious.

(3) CONDUCT

FISHBACK v. FISHBACK

(1985), 46 R.F.L. (2d) 44 (Ont. Dist. Ct.)

[The wife had custody of two daughters aged approximately eight and four since the parties' separation. Misener D.C.J. indicated that he reached his decision to grant custody to the father "with some hesitation, and without the degree of certainty as to its rightness that I would have liked" because Mrs. Fishback was a fit parent and "a mother is more in tune with a child of tender years — especially a girl."]

MISENER D.C.J.: — . . . I am certainly satisfied that, from the date of the marriage until the date of the separation, Mr. Fishback did at least as much as Mrs. Fishback in the care of the matrimonial home and in the care of the children. He kept a horse for the children on a farm about one mile away and frequently took the children with him to do the chores and for buggy rides. He looked after the yard, very often with the children as his "helpers". He did a share of the housework and his full share of attending to the children, including the changing of diapers. He has been described by at least one witness as an exceptional father. I accept the validity of that description without any reservation.

According to Mrs. Fishback, matrimonial discord became significant following Heidi's birth for entirely new reasons. She said that Mr. Fishback did not help her enough about the house. Needless to say, I do not believe Mrs. Fishback's testimony as to that. She said that Mr. Fishback was not sympathetic to her migraine headaches. Mrs. Fishback may have suffered some migraine headaches, but I am not satisfied either that it was significant or that Mr. Fishback was not sufficiently sympathetic. She said that Mr. Fishback tried too hard to induce her to go to the Baptist Church. She did not wish to go there. So far as I can determine, she did not wish to go to any church. And finally she said that she found sexual relations with Mr. Fishback insufficiently exciting.

The truth of the matter is that Mrs. Fishback found Mr. Fishback insufficiently exciting. He certainly appeared to me to be a very serious man. He does not consume alcohol. He is totally dedicated to old-fashioned family values. I am sure that he has little interest in going out to the picture shows or to dances or to very much in the way of what is usually called entertainment. He believes he should go to church and that his children should go to Sunday School. He is obviously a religious man, although I am sure not one disposed to publicly proclaim his religious conviction. Having watched him in the courtroom for two days, I am sure that Mr. Fishback never has acquired a reputation for being the life of the party, assuming he has ever been disposed to attend a party. Whether I be right or wrong in that assessment, however, I am sure that the only thing that bothered Mrs. Fishback about her married life was that, in her view, it was just too dull.

She soon found a way to make it more lively. In 1982 Mrs. Fishback renewed acquaintanceship with Mr. Brian Yeoman, a former schoolmate. He was at that time married, separated, and living with one Kim Billson, a young lady who testified before me. He soon separated from Miss Billson and in the spring of 1983 purchased or rented the mobile home directly across the street from the Fishback residence. Mrs. Fishback developed the habit of spending a few hours now and then with Mr. Yeoman in his home alone. Needless to say, her visits soon became a matter of public knowledge. Mr. Fishback questioned their propriety. He was assured that the visits were completely innocent and accused of being mistrustful.

On 4th May 1984 it became clear that Mr. Fishback had been wrongly accused. He came home from his work at about 5:00 a.m. The children were asleep and alone in their home. His wife was not at home. He finally broke into the Yeoman residence and found Mr. Yeoman and his wife in bed together. He woke them up. There was considerable upset. Mrs. Fishback denied that she had had sexual relations with Mr. Yeoman even though they were found in a state of nakedness together in the same bed. Mr. Fishback appears to have been at least half persuaded that he was being told the truth. The marriage continued until the date of the separation on 3rd August. On that date, the confession of adultery was made. Even then Mr. Fishback did not wish his wife to leave. He wanted to have counselling in the hope that they could solve their problems. Mrs. Fishback by this time wanted to end the marriage. And so the separation became final. Mrs. Fishback took the children and on 1st September 1984 set up a household in Woodstock with Mr. Yeoman and the children. Mr. Fishback remained in the matrimonial home.

My concern in deciding who should have custody is confined entirely to the best interests of the children. One conclusion I draw from the facts that I have so far related is simply that Mrs. Fishback was quite prepared — and I think that she consciously thought about it — to deprive the children of the benefit of the constant presence of a good father, of at least a good husband, if not a totally satisfactory one, and of a reasonably harmonious family relationship for no other reason than to find more excitement in life. I am not suggesting that she does not now genuinely love Mr. Yeoman; perhaps she does. Perhaps she is totally dedicated to him. The fact remains that she deliberately sought that state of affairs, knowing full well that the children could never derive a benefit anything close to the loss that they would suffer from it. This factor is not of great significance in determining what is in the present and future best interests of the children, but it certainly is a factor that is entitled to some weight in determining custody because it indicates, at least to some degree, the importance that each parent attaches to the best interests of the children in determining their own future conduct.

The first conclusion at which I have arrived, then, is that Mr. Fishback had shown by his past conduct a total dedication, even to the point of apparently closing his eyes to the obvious, to keeping the family together and to providing a happy marriage for his children. Mrs. Fishback on the other hand has shown that her own desires really have priority to her children. That is of course her privilege, but it inevitably represents an impediment, however slight, to her claim that she is better able to provide for the children now.

I proceed next to the factors that I think are more important but which can be more briefly justified. Except for the last nine months or so, the children have throughout lived at the matrimonial home. Krista spent her first year of school at

Tillsonburg. Both children enjoyed a very nice life in a very nice home and acquired good friendships. I am satisfied, in the description given of their reluctance to return to their home in Woodstock at the end of the periods of access, that they have missed that home. Doubtless, Mrs. Fishback is right in saying that they have become more settled in the routine as time goes by. Nevertheless, they obviously had, for a significant period of that nine months, a preference to be with their father. Their preference in itself is of little importance. What is important, however, is that Mr. Fishback clearly commands their affection and respect as much, if not more, than does Mrs. Fishback.

Mr. Fishback is obviously greatly interested in their moral, intellectual and emotional development. He has always shown a greater interest in their education than has Mrs. Fishback. He regularly read to Krista. I accept his testimony that Mrs. Fishback was not much interest[ed] in helping Krista with her learning. He alone sees to their attendance at Sunday School — something they actually enjoy. I was greatly impressed with Mrs. Ella Smith. She is 75 years of age. She is a retired school teacher. She teaches the children Sunday School at the Baptist Church. She in fact owns the farm where Mr. Fishback "boards" his horse. She lives just a mile from the matrimonial home. She has had a lot to do with the children and she dearly loves them. She regularly took Krista to the library when Mr. and Mrs. Fishback were living together. One day she made the mistake of telling Mr. Fishback that Mrs. Fishback was out too much. When Mrs. Fishback heard about that she forbade Mrs. Smith the right to take Krista to the library. To say the least, the punishment inflicted upon Mrs. Smith was at the expense of Krista's welfare, and neither appropriate nor indicative of much concern for Krista. Mrs. Smith bears no malice towards Mrs. Fishback for that. Indeed, she was obviously uncomfortable in the partisan position that she was placed in in testifying — so much so that she apologized to Mrs. Fishback as she left the courtroom for having to choose sides. She testified that, in her view and for the precise reasons she gave, Mr. Fishback was clearly better able to give the children the spiritual, cultural and intellectual assistance and guidance that every child needs. I place considerable weight on Mrs. Smith's assessment because I am satisfied of her dedication to the best interests of the children, of her sense of fairness towards both parties and of her judgment.

I think that Mr. Fishback's proposal for the care of the children, should he receive custody, is somewhat better than the present arrangements that Mrs. Fishback supplies. Mr. Fishback has become acquainted with Lucinda Tye. She is a married woman, without children, and separated from her husband. Mrs. Tye and Mr. Fishback have been keeping company. There is at least the probability that in due course they will marry, and I hope they do. Mrs. Tye testified. I was most impressed with her. She has become well acquainted with the children. She has for some time helped Mr. Fishback almost continuously in their weekend care. The children like her. Mrs. Tye does not stay overnight. Doubtless, Mr. Fishback would consider that immoral and wrong in the absence of marriage, and I am not able to say that he is wrong in that judgment, or, for that matter, that he is right in that judgment. Regardless, he proposes to have Mrs. Tye look after the children in their home at all times when he is unable to be there because of his employment. Mrs. Tye has undertaken in her testimony to do so, even at the expense of foregoing other employment opportunities. I am satisfied that that arrangement will be put in place immediately.

That is not to say that Mrs. Fishback has not so far fully and properly cared for the children in the last nine months. She has, and I am sure that she has cared for them well. But that care has been built around her relationship with Mr. Yeoman. Mr. Yeoman testified. While I do not wish to be at all unfair, I am obliged to say that neither his past performance nor his demeanour as a witness left me fully confident that his present relationship with Mrs. Fishback will last. They both say that they intend to marry. Needless to say, I hope they do and that it remains a happy one throughout. But I am not confident of the stability of Mrs. Fishback's life from here on in as I am of the stability of Mr. Fishback's. And I think that Mrs. Tye has more to contribute to the total upbringing of the children in non-economic terms than does Mr. Yeoman.

Those are my conclusions that in my view compel me to award the custody of the children to Mr. Fishback.

YOUNG v. YOUNG

(1989), 19 R.F.L. (3d) 227 (Ont. H.C.)

[The parties separated in 1985 after about 15 years of marriage. Both worked outside the home during the marriage, but the wife assumed primary responsibility for child care. The children remained with the wife after separation. The son, aged 11, and daughter, aged 13, wished to live with their father. Bolan L.J.S.C. explained why the children should remain in their mother's custody.]

BOLAN L.J.S.C.: — . . . Mrs. Young alleges that she was emotionally, physically, verbally and sexually abused by Mr. Young. The emotional and verbal abuse started with small — and at the time — insignificant incidents shortly after marriage. She never knew when Mr. Young was coming home from work. At times, he became sullen and would not talk to her for long periods of time. He never discussed his work with her because he thought she was stupid and would not understand his work. He would make derogatory remarks about school teaching in general; she considered this as a threat to her self-esteem. He told her no one else could or would ever love her. He made derogatory remarks to her in the presence of her friends. There were times when he would not speak to her for days.

Mrs. Young alleges that she was physically abused by Mr. Young on two occasions after separation. She also says she was sexually abused on several occasions starting in 1983. . . .

Linda Butler is a doctor of psychology and an expert in the field of clinical psychology. She first saw Mrs. Young on 27th November 1985 and described her as being depressed, anxious and suffering from long-standing emotional and verbal abuse. She had decided to leave the marriage to save herself from the destructive path she was on. She had low self-esteem and she was confused in her thinking.

It was Dr. Butler's impression that Mrs. Young was socially isolated and that she was having difficulty asserting herself. She presented the characteristic symptoms of emotional abuse. She saw her on a weekly basis and made progress reports every two-three months. Over the course of the next year, Mrs. Young's functioning improved particularly at work and with the family. Dr. Butler feels she has made good use of the therapy and that she could continue to resolve whatever issues remain unresolved.

It is Dr. Butler's opinion — based on clinical literature — that if a person is an abuser and does not take therapy that person is likely to be an abuser in another relationship. This becomes relevant if the children should witness an abusive relationship. If children live under conditions where there is an abusive relationship, the children themselves could become abused victims.

Barbara Pressman is an accredited marital and family therapist and an expert on wife abuse and family violence. She saw Mrs. Young for assessment on three different occasions. It was quite clear to her that Mrs. Young had experienced abuse.

Ms. Pressman gave evidence of a "cyclical pattern (behaviour) of abuse." It was her opinion that a male person (a boy) who is abused or who observes abuse can become an abuser — that, in 80 per cent of the time, he will become an abuser. In the case of a girl who observes abuse, she has the potential to become compliant to an abuser.

Ms. Pressman is presently doing rehabilitative work with abusive men. She says there is potential for an abuser to reform provided the person acknowledges that he is an abuser.

Claire Lowry is a doctor of psychology and is an expert in the field of clinical child psychology. Heather and John were referred to her by Dr. Butler. She first saw Heather on 21st May 1987. She expressed the view that Heather had some problems in dealing with her mother (Mrs. Young). She devalued her because she was an abused person (wife) and because she was responsible for the family breaking up. She also looked upon Mrs. Young and cast her as the "bad guy" or the "heavy" — the parent who said "No" to whatever Heather wanted.

Dr. Lowry says the chances of a "rapproachment" between Heather and Mrs. Young are very good. Heather has a real connection with her mother and they can talk to each other.

Dr. Lowry also saw John. He is less sophisticated and has found ways to articulate his problems. He has many strengths and the prognosis is that he can resolve the issues.

Dr. Lowry expressed her concern about the ability of an abuser to parent children. In this particular case she is concerned about Mr. Young's capacity for attachment, his ability to assess the needs of the children and his capacity to "socialize" the children, i.e., social values. On the other hand, Dr. Lowry says that Mrs. Young has a good feel for the children and she has no concerns about her ability to "parent" the children.

This is a summary of the various factors which I must consider in arriving at a proper determination as to which parent is best able to look after the interests of the children.

I am of the view that it is in the best interests of the children that the status quo should prevail and that they remain in the custody of Mrs. Young. There is no compelling evidence to suggest otherwise. I am mindful of the fact that the stated preference of the children should be considered — and I have considered it — however, there are other factors I should look at, notably, the abuse. I accept the evidence of Mrs. Young that she was abused by Mr. Young and I find the abuse to be emotional, verbal, physical and sexual. I find that this emotional and verbal abuse took place during cohabitation and after the separation. Where her evidence of abuse differs with that of Mr. Young, I prefer and accept her evidence. I was impressed with her truthfulness and sincerity as a witness. I cannot say the same for Mr. Young. I found him to be glib and evasive. The relevancy of this finding of abuse is that it goes to Mr. Young's ability to parent the children on a full-time basis. I accept the expert evidence of Dr. Butler and Barbara Pressman that:

1. An abuser who goes without therapy will continue to abuse in another relationship;
2. Children who witness abuse can become abused even though the abuse is not intentionally directed at them;
3. Abused male children often become abusers and abused female children may become compliant to abusers.

I also find that since the separation, Mr. Young did not at times have the children's best interests at heart. Throughout the period of access he manipulated them into obtaining more access for himself by showering them with lavishness, i.e., an unreasonable and incessant bombardment of baseball outings and weekends of fun and games. Furthermore, an incident occurred during the trial which reflects Mr. Young's manipulation of the children. On the weekend following the first week of trial Mr. Young obtained from Mrs. Young's residence (without her knowledge and consent) personal papers with respect to the cottage. Mr. Young had access to John that weekend starting on Friday. Heather was not with Mr. Young that weekend. The only reasonable inference I can draw is that John took the cottage documents and gave them to his father.

I accept Mrs. Young's opinions that the children are too young at this point to give paramountcy to their stated desire — which is to live with Mr. Young. She says perhaps they would be more mature to make this decision when they reach 16.

Heather and John require stability and consistency in their lives. This can best be achieved under the guidance and custody of Mrs. Young. She is best able to provide for the children the nourishment required for their social and moral development.

NOTES AND QUESTIONS

1. Examine s. 24(3) of the *CLRA* and s. 16(9) of the *Divorce Act*. Obviously, the conduct of a parent in dealings with the child is relevant. See, for example, *Killeleagh* v. *Killeleagh* (1986), 50 R.F.L. (2d) 103 (Ont. Dist. Ct.) and *H.* v. *J.* (1991), 34 R.F.L. (3d) 361 (Sask. Q.B.). Preventing meaningful contact between the child and the other parent can also be considered: *Renaud*, above. See also s. 16(10) of the *Divorce Act* which is analyzed later in this chapter.

2. In *Fishback*, it was asserted that marital misconduct is relevant to a parent's ability to raise the child if it reveals a willingness to place selfish interests ahead of those of the child. See also *Bosch* v. *Bosch* (1985), 49 R.F.L. (2d) 157 (Sask. Q.B.); *Stephens* v. *Stephens* (1986), 4 R.F.L. (3d) 200 (B.C. S.C.); and *Dawe* v. *Dawe* (1987), 11 R.F.L. (3d) 265 (Nfld. T.D.). In *Tyabji* v. *Sandana* (1994), 2 R.F.L. (4th) 265 (B.C. S.C.), Spencer J. stated (at 269):

> Custody is not awarded in any sense to punish the parent who is deprived of it. There is no contest between parents to see who most deserves the children or who is most responsible for the breakup of the family unit. . . . Responsibility for breaking up the marriage, where it lies clearly on one side more than the other, is not necessarily a test for awarding custody. It is relevant only if it shows that one parent or the other pursued, and will probably continue to pursue, his or her self-interest to the detriment of the children, or if it shows that one or the other is less believable on oath, it may result in that parent's evidence bearing upon custody receiving less weight.

Do you agree that marital misconduct should still be considered in this indirect way?

In *Weaver* v. *Tate* (1989), 24 R.F.L. (3d) 266 (Ont. H.C.), Granger J. granted custody of two children, aged eight and six, to their mother despite a recommendation by a psychologist, following an assessment under s. 30 of the *CLRA*, favouring the father. He concluded (at 276): "I am confident that Tate will do what is in the best interests of the children in the future, whereas Weaver will do whatever is in his best interest regardless of the best interests of the children." He noted that Weaver had had an affair during the first year of marriage and added (at 272): "I mention this because of the effect which Weaver's self-centred behaviour may have on his parenting abilities." In addition, he referred to the following facts. Weaver unilaterally made various career moves without regard to the effect of such decisions on his wife's career. During the last few months of cohabitation he refused to allow the family to move into a house he had purchased. As a result, the couple and their children lived in a cottage that was "unsuitable for the children". The decision was affirmed on appeal ((1990), 28 R.F.L. (3d) 188 (Ont. C.A.)). The court stated (at 188):

While we do not accept that all of the examples of the appellant's past conduct recited in the reasons for judgment were relevant to his parental ability within the contemplation of s. 24(3) of the Act, nevertheless the trial judge was entitled to conclude that some of that conduct was, as he found, self-centered and manipulative and supported his conclusion that the appellant would put his own interests ahead of the best interests of the children.

Unfortunately, the appellate court did not explain which examples of past conduct were relevant and which were not. Which, if any, would you consider relevant?

3. Conduct after separation must affect a person's ability to parent to be relevant. In *Annual Review of Family Law, 1995* (Toronto: Carswell, 1995), Professor McLeod and Alfred Mamo suggest (at 47):

The determination of what type of conduct affects a person's ability to parent and provide a suitable environment for a child reflects social and moral values. . . . As such, counsel should be careful about relying on older cases which may be based in a different social reality. At the present time, adultery, homosexuality or cohabitation outside marriage have little effect on a custody/ access determination.

In *Taylor* v. *Taylor* (1994), 6 R.F.L. (4th) 423 (B.C. S.C.), it was alleged that the mother had had sexual intercourse with a 15-year-old boy whom she had briefly taken into her home after the separation. A.G. MacKinnon J. stated (at 426-427):

I do not find it necessary to make a finding as to whether or not after separation from the respondent, the petitioner had sexual relations with her 15-year-old friend Joshua or with another person. There is no evidence to suggest that such conduct, if it did occur, had, or is likely to have, any adverse effect on the children.

4. Should the fact that one parent smokes ever be determinative? In *Bourdon* v. *Casselman* (1988), 12 R.F.L. (3d) 395 (Ont. Prov. Ct.), a father's access was terminated where he continued to smoke in the presence of his severely asthmatic son. See also *Schaefer* v. *Goode*, [1994] W.D.F.L. 100 (Ont. Prov. Div.) and *De Corte* v. *Sheppard*, [1994] W.D.F.L. 1083 (B.C. S.C.). Generally, see Wendling, "Smoking and Parenting: Can They Be Adjudged Mutually Exclusive Activities?" (1992), 42 Case Western Reserve Law Review 1025.

5. Newfoundland's *Children's Law Act*, R.S.N. 1990, c. C-13 specifically lists domestic violence as a factor to be taken into account in assessing a person's ability to parent. For arguments in favour of such a provision, see Bala *et al*, *Spousal Violence in Custody and Access Disputes: Recommendations for Reform* (Ottawa: Status of Women Canada, 1998).

In "Wife Battery and Determinations of Custody and Access: A Comparison of United States and Canadian Findings" (1990), 22 Ottawa L. Rev. 691, Lorenne Clark concludes (at 708-709):

. . . [A]n analysis of recent Canadian case law involving these issues does not demonstrate that the Canadian judiciary is interpreting the "friendly parent" and "conduct" provisions [s. 16(9) and s. 16(10)] of the Divorce Act, 1985 or the provisions regulating custody and access deter- minations in any of the provincial and territorial custody regimes, in a way which appears prejudicial to the protection of the interests of the battered wife. They routinely allow evidence of wife abuse to be admitted . . ., solicit expert opinion . . ., appear to have no difficulty seeing wife battery as an issue relevant to the considerations of the welfare and best interests of children . . ., and give it the weight that it deserves in the sense that they most often award sole custody to the wife in such situations, with access structured to protect the safety of the wife and/or children.

See also Bala, "Spousal Abuse and Children of Divorce: A Differentiated Approach" (1996), 13 Can. J. Fam. L. 166 and Kerr and Jaffe, "Legal and Clinical Issues in Child Custody Disputes Involving Domestic Violence" (1999), 17 C.F.L.Q. 1. In the latter article, the authors conclude (at 10): "Canadian case law shows that judges are willing to hold. . .that domestic violence *is* relevant to custody and access determinations and to accord the existence of spousal abuse significant and appropriate weight in deciding these issues."

For two recent reported cases where spousal abuse played an important role in determining custody, see *G. (D.E.)* v. *G. (D.T.)* (1997), 30 R.F.L. (4th) 320 (Ont. Gen. Div.) and *Carton* v. *Watts* (1998), 42

R.F.L. (4th) 149 (Alta. Prov. Ct.). In *Abdo* v. *Abdo* (1993), 50 R.F.L. (3d) 171 (N.S. C.A.); *Costa* v. *Costa* (1994), 4 R.F.L. (4th) 209 (Man. Fam. Div.) and *Alexander* v. *Creary* (1995), 14 R.F.L. (4th) 311 (Ont. Prov. Div.), the fathers were denied any access because of their abusive treatment of the mothers. An order for supervised access by a father who had just served a jail term for battering the mother was upheld in *MacLeod* v. *Savidant* (1992), 40 R.F.L. (3d) 443 (P.E.I. C.A.).

In "Reforming Child Custody and Access Law in Canada: A Discussion Paper" (1998), 15 Can. J. Fam. L. 13, Professors Cossman and Mykitiuk propose (at 61-62) that there should be a legislative presumption in favour of a custody award to an abused spouse and that the presumption should also indicate that unsupervised access be severely limited or denied.

6. Allegations of child sexual abuse by a parent occur in a small but significant number of custody and access cases. In "Allegations of Sexual Abuse When Parents Have Separated" (1999), 17 C.F.L.Q. 191, Professor Bala and John Schuman estimate (at 199) that allegations of physical and sexual abuse occur in less than 10% of litigated cases, representing about 1 or 2 per cent of all cases. Where such an allegation is made, the focus of inquiry shifts away from a general analysis of the best interests of the child towards an investigation of whether the abuse actually occurred. A wrong decision by a court either way can have grave consequences for the child involved. For an analysis of the difficult evidentiary and procedural issues that arise in these cases, see Bala and Anweiler, "Allegations of Sexual Abuse in a Parental Custody Dispute: Smokescreen or Fire?" (1987), 2 C.F.L.Q. 343. See also Wilson, "The Ripple Effect of Sexual Abuse Allegation and Representation of the Protecting Parent" (1986-1987), 1 C.F.L.Q. 159.

In general there are few false allegations of child sexual abuse; much more common are false denials by adults. However, experts in the field are coming to recognize that there is a much greater likelihood of falsehood if an allegation of sexual abuse is made in the context of parental separation. Bala and Schuman state (at 199): "Within the group of litigated family law cases that involve abuse allegations, the rate of unproven and unfounded allegations is quite high, probably in the range of 25 to 75 per cent. However, even where the allegation is considered unfounded, the incidence of deliberate fabrication or lying is low, in the range of unfounded allegations." They go on to suggest that most unfounded allegations are the product of miscommunication or misunderstanding. See also Zarb, "Allegations of Childhood Sexual Abuse in Custody and Access Disputes: What Care is in the Best Interests of the Child?" (1994), 12 Can. J. Fam. L. 91.

In *Annual Review of Family Law, 1995* (Toronto: Carswell, 1995), Professor McLeod and Alfred Mamo conclude (at 40):

> Allegations of sexual abuse in particular are difficult to prove. An unsubstantiated allegation of sexual abuse may have one of two potential consequences: it may plant the seed of fear in the mind of a judge who consciously or unconsciously may err on the side of caution or it may lead to a picture of the complainant as spiteful and vindictive.

For an example of the first reaction, see *C. (R.M.)* v. *C. (J.R.)* (1995), 12 R.F.L. (4th) 440 (B.C. S.C.) and *T. (M.)* v. *T. (J.)* (1997), 33 R.F.L. (4th) 430 (Ont. Gen. Div.). For examples of cases where unsubstantiated allegations of wife or child abuse clearly hurt a mother's claim to custody, see *M. (H.B.)* v. *B. (J.E.)* (1991), 33 R.F.L. (3d) 310 (B.C. S.C.); *Lin* v. *Lin* (1992), 38 R.F.L. (3d) 246 (B.C. C.A.); and *T. (K.J.)* v. *T. (T.L.)*, [1994] W.D.F.L. 1435 (B.C. S.C.). For their 1999 article, Bala and Schuman reviewed all reported Canadian Family Law cases between 1990 and 1998 dealing with sexual and physical abuse allegations in the context of parental separation. In 89 of the 196 identified cases, the court concluded that the allegation was clearly unfounded. The accusing party lost custody in 18 cases, although this was sometimes for reasons not directly related to the unfounded allegation. In only one case was the accuser charged (and convicted) for false reporting (mischief) in connection with the false allegation, though in three cases the accuser was cited for contempt of court in connection with denial of access. In a majority of reported cases where the judge found the abuse allegation unfounded, the accusing parent continued to have custody. Of the 51 cases where abuse was proved on the civil standard, access was denied in 21 cases and supervised in 16. The abuser was criminally charged in only 3 cases.

Lise Helene Zarb points out in "Allegations of Childhood Sexual Abuse in Custody and Access Disputes; What Care is in the Best Interests of the Child?" (1994), 12 Can. J. Fam. L. 91, at 106, that there are several explanations other than malice for unsubstantiated allegations of sexual abuse. She argues that judges should consider these alternative explanations before concluding that one parent's allegations were motivated by spite and denying this parent custody. She fears that if parents face dire consequences for mistaken allegations of abuse, they will be silent and children who have been sexually abused will suffer.

In its *For the Sake of the Children*, the Special Joint Committee recommended (at 90) that "to deal with intentional false accusations of abuse or neglect, the federal government assess the adequacy of the *Criminal Code* in dealing with false statements in family law matters and develop policies to promote action on clear cases of mischief, obstruction of justice or perjury".

(4) PARENT'S RELATIONSHIP WITH A THIRD PARTY

REID v. REID

(1975), 25 R.F.L. 209, 11 O.R. (2d) 622 (Div. Ct.)

GALLIGAN J. (orally): — This is an appeal by Keith Victor Reid (appellant) from the order of Judge Honey in the Surrogate Court of the County of Hastings, dated 4th October 1974. By that order, the learned trial judge made a custody award of the following children: Evelyn Victoria Reid, born 28th May 1966; Bradley Herbert Reid, born 6th December 1969; and Gwendolyn Catherine Reid, born 2nd January 1972. He awarded custody to Catherine Reid (respondent).

The appellant is 34 years of age and is employed steadily as a maintenance mechanic at DuPont of Canada in Kingston. He earns a good income. The respondent is presently 33 years of age. They were married in 1962 and until their separation on 7th January 1974 the appellant and respondent lived together in a two-storey, three-bedroom home, jointly owned by them at Corbyville, Ontario.

The learned trial judge found that the marriage broke down over several years prior to 1973. The appellant was a hard worker and good provider. The respondent was a good mother to the children. The trial judge refused to fix fault for the breakdown and found that the parties would have separated eventually, even if the respondent had not made the acquaintance of one Donald Reid.

In November and December 1973 the respondent met Donald Reid, who is not a relative of the appellant or respondent. Donald Reid is a master corporal in the Canadian Air Force; he is married with a family of three children. There is a boy aged 18, whose name is James, who testified at the trial of this case. He also has a daughter aged 11 and another son aged 9.

On 7th January 1974, while the appellant was at work, the respondent moved out of the family home, took the children and most of the furniture and moved in to live with Donald Reid. She had advised her husband in mid-December 1973 that she was having an affair with Donald Reid and that she wished to live with him. The appellant implored her not to leave.

Also on 7th January 1974 Donald Reid, while his wife was at work, packed up and moved out of his home and began living with the respondent in a small two-bedroom home in Trenton. Donald Reid's wife had no inkling of the fact that he intended to leave her until the day that he in fact did go. . . .

What has given all members of this court cause for concern is the question of whether it is in the best interests of the children that Donald Reid become their surrogate father. . . .

In the opinion of us all, the trial judge is under a very high duty to weigh carefully the suitability of the person who, in a practical sense, will stand in the position of a parent to the children as a result of the custody order that he makes. It is a particularly important duty, in a case such as this, where he has found that the surrogate parent proposed by one parent is fit and suitable to determine that the surrogate parent proposed by the other is also fit and suitable. This duty is one that can be discharged only by the trial judge, because he is the person who must objectively determine the welfare of the children. This duty cannot be delegated to another. In many cases the determination of this issue might well be decisive of the case.

In this case, there was evidence that Donald Reid was harsh with his own children and that basically he did not like children. His wife, Constance Reid, testified for the appellant, as did his son James, and a friend of James, one David Dzwolak. I do not think it appropriate to go into the evidence in any detail, except to say that it has given each member of this court cause to wonder whether it is in the best interests of these children to be in the charge of Donald Reid. . . .

For some strange reason known only to the respondent and Donald Reid, Donald Reid did not testify at the trial. No explanation was given as to why he did not testify. In a situation like this, it was open to the trial judge to infer that the reason he did not testify was that if he did testify his evidence would not be helpful to the respondent. It is difficult to understand why the trial judge did not draw that inference, particularly in the light of the uncontradicted evidence of Donald Reid's wife and son.

After giving his reasons for not accepting the evidence of Donald Reid's wife, which reasons on their face are erroneous, the learned trial judge resolved the problem of the suitability of Donald Reid as a person to be a surrogate father to these three children in the following words:

> I am left in the situation that I would have preferred to have seen him [Donald Reid] but my concern on that point is overcome by my respect for the mother and the way she gave evidence, insofar as her concern for her children, and she said unequivocally that she would not permit or tolerate anyone, including Don Reid, to abuse her children and I think that she is that kind of a mother. I think she is an affectionate, warm person. She will be combative if there is any attempt to abuse her children, and I think on that point, I can be assured that she will protect them, and I don't say that with any inference that Don Reid would not conduct himself other than properly with the children, but if there is any suggestion of that, I think it is closed by the mother's protective attitude that I find she would have with respect to her children.

Notwithstanding the great respect that we all have for the trial judge and the appreciation we have for the humane and sympathetic way in which he dealt with this most difficult of problems, we are all of the opinion that he was in serious error in his disposition of this aspect of the case.

He had the duty to determine whether it was in the best interests of these children to live in a home situation in which, for all practical purposes, Donald Reid was their father.

It was his duty to determine whether Donald Reid was a fit and proper person to be their father. However, he did not see or hear Donald Reid testify and he therefore did not have the opportunity to assess for himself Donald Reid's suitability as a surrogate father to these children. In effect, he delegated his responsibility to make that determination to the respondent, who of course cannot be called a disinterested person.

In this case where the scales are so evenly balanced as between the parents, I think the vital inquiry was as to the relative fitness of the surrogate mother and the surrogate father proposed by each parent. That inquiry was not properly made and in my opinion the issue was not properly determined. Accordingly, the order appealed from cannot stand and must be set aside. . . .[A new trial was ordered.]

NOTES AND QUESTIONS

1. As *Reid* indicates, the character and parenting skills of the person with whom a parent resides or intends to reside are relevant. Under s. 30(5) of the *CLRA* the court could require this person to attend for assessment by a court-appointed professional. See *Daller* v. *Daller* (1988), 18 R.F.L. (3d) 53 (Ont. H.C.). The stability of the relationship between the parent and the third party can also be considered. See s. 24(2)(f) of the *CLRA*. See also *Bell* v. *Kirk* (1986), 3 R.F.L. (3d) 377 (B.C. C.A.). Where the new partner also has children, Holmes J. suggested in *Barnes-Everatt* v. *Everatt*, [1994] W.D.F.L. 1201 (B.C. S.C.) that the court can consider the problems inherent in "blended families".

2. Where one of the parents has entered into a stable relationship with a third party who has good parenting skills, this may be a factor indicating that it is in the best interests of the child to be placed in the custody of that parent. See, for example, *Law* v. *Maxwell* (1984), 40 R.F.L. (2d) 189 (B.C. C.A.); *Bosch* v. *Bosch* (1985), 49 R.F.L. (2d) 157 (Sask. Q.B.); *Bartesko* v. *Bartesko* (1990), 31 R.F.L. (3d) 213 (B.C. C.A.); *Richter* v. *Richter* (1991), 34 R.F.L. (3d) 387 (Sask. Q.B.); and *Flatfoot* v. *Richard* (1994), 94 Man. R. (2d) 143 (Q.B.).

3. In *Palmore* v. *Sidoti*, 104 S.Ct. 1879 (U.S. Fla., April 25, 1984) the United States Supreme Court overturned a lower court decision granting custody of a young girl to the father. At the time of the parents' divorce custody was granted to the mother. She then married a black man and lived with him and the child in a racially-mixed housing complex. The mother, father and child were Caucasians. The Florida court, on an application by the father, concluded that it was in the best interests of the child to vary the custody order. It stated: "This court feels that despite the strides that have been made in bettering relations between the races in this country, it is inevitable that Melanie will, if allowed to remain in her present situation and attains school age and thus more vulnerable to peer pressure, suffer from the social stigmatization that is sure to come." The United States Supreme Court held that it was unconstitutional for the Florida court to consider the impact of racial prejudice in determining the best interests of the child. It reasoned (at 1882):

> It would ignore reality to suggest that racial and ethnic prejudices do not exist or that all manifestations of those prejudices have been eliminated. There is a risk that a child living with a step-parent of a different race may be subject to a variety of pressures and stresses not present if the child were living with parents of the same racial or ethnic origin.

> The question, however, is whether the reality of private biases and the possible injury they might inflict are permissible considerations for removal of an infant child from the custody of its natural mother. We have little difficulty concluding that they are not. The Constitution cannot control such prejudices but neither can it tolerate them. Private biases may be outside the reach of the law, but the law cannot, directly or indirectly, give them effect. "Public officials sworn to uphold the Constitution may not avoid a constitutional duty by bowing to the hypothetical effects of private racial prejudice that they assume to be both widely and deeply held." *Palmer* v. *Thompson*, 403 U.S. 217, 260-261, 91 S. Ct. 1940, 1962-1963, 29 L.Ed.2d 438 (1971) (WHITE, J., dissenting). . . .

> The effects of racial prejudice, however real, cannot justify a racial classification removing an infant child from the custody of its natural mother found to be an appropriate person to have such custody.

(5) SEXUAL ORIENTATION OF PARENT

BARKLEY v. BARKLEY

(1980), 28 O.R. (2d) 136 (Prov. Ct.)

NASMITH FAM. CT. J.: — Lynn is a ten-year-old girl whose mother and father are each applying, under s. 35 of the Family Law Reform Act, 1978 (Ont.), c. 2, for sole custody of her. The mother is homosexual and much of the evidence has sprung from this fact.

There are serious differences between the parents and I have ruled out the possibility of an order extending the ''joint custody'' rights with which they both came into this action. It apparently must be determined whether it is in Lynn's best interests for me to order that the mother have sole custody or that the father have sole custody.

Mr. and Mrs. B. were married in 1962 and they adopted three children. They separated in May 1977, shortly after Mr. B. returned from a lengthy posting with the armed forces in Egypt. Upon separation, all three children resided with the father, but at the time of trial, only Robert, aged 13 and Douglas, aged 15, remained with their father. There is no dispute about the boys and no order is sought to cover them.

The mother had generous access to the children following the separation, and she often moved back into the house to look after them during extended absences by the father. The evidence is that Lynn became increasingly unhappy living with her father and developed a desire to be with her mother on a full-time basis. The turning point in this arrangement came when the mother was upset at the father for allegedly leaving the children unattended. In March 1979 she unilaterally decided to keep Lynn with her. That move gave rise to these proceedings to settle Lynn's custody.

There is no allegation by the father as to any deficiencies in the parenting performance of the mother during the period of their cohabitation. The unique feature of the case, I think, is that the father's sole concern arises out of Mrs. B.'s being a declared homosexual and his case is built on that. From his evidence, I am convinced that he sincerely believes it would be harmful to his daughter to be raised in what he sees as a homosexual environment.

During Mr. B.'s absence in Egypt, the evidence shows that Mrs. B. developed a homosexual relationship with a 21-year-old woman who was employed as a part-time babysitter. That woman now resides full-time with Mrs. B. and the relationship is not hidden, at least insofar as the two women sleep in the same bed. No doubt Lynn will soon be aware of sexual ramifications of this arrangement, if she is not already.

The questions which arose from the trial were: Does the mother's homosexual relationship represent any risk to the healthy development of Lynn? If there is any discernible risk, what weight should be given to it? How does that risk measure up against other factors in the test as to which placement is in Lynn's best interests?

The court made a referral of the family to the family court clinic for an assessment and report on the question of which of the two placements was more likely to serve the best interests of Lynn. Mr. Robert Gardner, M.S.W., has given evidence and has filed a nine-page opinion with a lengthy bibliography of the literature on homosexual parenting. The intimate clinical analysis apparently satisfied Mr. Gardner that both parents had a reasonably good relationship with Lynn. But he concluded that Lynn felt a much greater closeness with Mrs. B., and some distance between herself and her father. The evidence was that Lynn was doing very well, and it was Mr. Gardner's opinion that Lynn's needs could be more adequately met, given a decision to allow her to remain with her mother. It is clear that Lynn's own preference to reside with her mother was a significant part of Mr. Gardner's considerations.

The father, through his counsel, demonstrated concerns about the possibility of proselytizing on the part of the mother and the possibility of Lynn's becoming homosexual. The father's counsel questioned Mr. Gardner's qualifications to give the opinion that neither proselytizing nor becoming a homosexual are a danger in this situation. With the consent of counsel, I have read the literature referred to in Mr. Gardner's bibliography, and I have found nothing to contradict Mr. Gardner's conclusions. The fact remains that there is no evidence before this court to justify my putting any weight on the danger of proselytizing or copying of sexual patterns. Accordingly, I am relieved of the difficult task of weighing any disadvantages of being homosexual.

However, whatever its origins, what has been referred to as the present "homophobic" attitude of our society is a reality to be faced and dealt with. Sooner or later (if not already) Lynn will become aware of her mother's atypical arrangement, and it will no doubt take on some significance for her. In a sense, she will have to bear the stigma of her mother's homosexuality. Mr. Gardner compared the phenomenon of this stigma with the stigma arising from some inter-racial marriages. But his report contained impressive authority for his position that the extent to which a child is raised in a happy and stable home will govern the way the child is able to cope reasonably with such forms of prejudice.

The degree of risk in the entire area of the child's necessary adjustments to the situation will depend, no doubt, on the good sense of the mother in handling the issue and on the interplay with peers and the public at large. It is possible that the public will not be aware of the homosexual situation. It is difficult to know to what extent Lynn's peers will know. It is difficult to know how Lynn herself will react.

It is my view that there has been a certain amount of liberalization of the public attitude about homosexuality and such cases as *People* v. *Brown* (1973), 49 Mich. App. 358, may well have put to rest any presumptions that homosexuality in itself renders a home an unfit place for children.

Three Canadian cases have been cited by counsel and from my own research, these would seem to be the only Canadian cases reported.

In *Case* v. *Case* (1974), 18 R.F.L. 132 (Sask. Q.B.), MacPherson J. stipulated that homosexuality was *not a bar* to an award of custody and that it was simply a factor to be considered along with others. On the facts, as he found them, custody of a ten-year-old daughter and a four-year-old son were granted to the father as against the homosexual mother. The court was influenced by what it saw as unfair and exaggerated charges by the mother as to the father's conduct, and I think he was concerned about the fact that the mother slept in the same bed with her homosexual partner and that he had not had the benefit of having the partner as a witness. Reference was made to the mother's hiding her partner from the court. The extent to which the homosexuality weighed against the mother may have been given away by the closing comments at p. 138:

> . . . I greatly fear that if these children are raised by the mother they will be too much in contact with people of abnormal tastes and proclivities.

In the subsequent case of *K.* v. *K.*, 23 R.F.L. 58, [1976] 2 W.W.R. 462, Rowe Prov. J., of the Alberta Provincial Court, distinguished the *Case* decision. His Honour agreed with the Saskatchewan court as to homosexuality being one factor to be considered along with all the others. In awarding custody to a homosexual mother, who also slept in the same bed as her partner, and did not engage in any sexual contact in the presence of the children, the trial judge was supported by strong evidence from a psychologist who testified that the mother and the child had a close relationship which was one of the best mother-child interactions she had seen in her professional practice. The psychologist noted that the child was happy, well-adjusted and doing very well in school, and concluded that [p. 61]:

> . . . the manner in which one fulfills one's sexual needs does not relate to the abilities of being a good parent.

The trial judge also accepted the evidence of a psychiatrist as to the mother's being an alert, pleasant and healthy person with no major problems, who was vitally concerned for the welfare of her daughter. The psychiatrist testified that homosexuality ''could be a factor'' and it depends mostly on the manner in which it was handled. The trial judge noted that he was satisfied that the relationship would be discreet and would not be ''flaunted to the children or the community at large''. It was pointed out by the trial judge that, unlike the *Case* situation, the homosexual partner was called as a witness and was quite impressive. In the face of the overwhelming support of the mother in the evidence, it is difficult to know how much weight was attached to the mother's homosexuality.

In *D.* v. *D.* (1978), 20 O.R. (2d) 722, 3 R.F.L. (2d) 327, 88 D.L.R. (3d) 578 (Co. Ct.), Smith Co. Ct. J. dealt with an application to vary a decree nisi. The decree had been silent as to custody and the father later sought custody of 13 and 8-year-old children who had been in his de facto custody since the separation. It was clear that the father was bisexual but that he was involved in a continuing homosexual relationship. The trial judge treated his homosexuality as [p. 333]:

> . . . [a] problem which may damage the children's psychological, moral, intellectual or physical well-being, and their orderly development and adaptation to society . . . The court's concern ought to be the children's position in their peer group, the children's sexual orientation and the manner in which the relationship of children to parent is or can be affected by the deviation from the norm in the latter's sexual preferences.

In awarding custody of the children to the father, which confirmed the status quo, the trial judge's concerns about the ''problem'' of homosexuality were apparently modified by the following findings:

(a) The father was bisexual;
(b) The father was discreet;
(c) He was not an exhibitionist;
(d) The public did not know about his sexual orientations;
(e) He did not flaunt his homosexual activities;
(f) He was not a militant homosexual;
(g) The court felt that he could ''cope with'' the problems;
(h) There was no evidence that the children would become homosexual;
(i) The main homosexual partner made a favourable impression on him.

It would appear that the *net* result of the analysis of the homosexual question was the placing of very little weight on the homosexuality of the father.

In the present case, a focus on the quality of the parent-child relationship here produces a good case for the mother as the more appropriate person to have custody of Lynn.

As in *D.* v. *D.*, any possible ill effects for Lynn from the mother's sexual orientation have been minimized by the following circumstances:

(1) She is not militant;
(2) She does not flaunt her homosexuality;
(3) She does not seem to be biased about Lynn's orientation, and seems to assume that Lynn will be heterosexual;
(4) There is no overt sexual contact apart from sleeping in the same bed;
(5) The sexual partner has a reasonably good relationship with the child.

Whatever significant risks remain in the area of Lynn's necessary adjustments to our "homophobic" society, they are too esoteric and speculative for me to attach much weight to. I think they must give way here to the more concrete indicia of "best interests".

An order will go granting custody of the child to the respondent with reasonable access to the applicant. . . .

NOTES AND QUESTIONS

1. See also *Bezaire* v. *Bezaire* (1980), 20 R.F.L. (2d) 358 (Ont. C.A.); *Droit de la famille-31* (1983), 34 R.F.L. (2d) 127 (Que. S.C.); and *Daller* v. *Daller* (1988), 18 R.F.L. (3d) 53 (Ont. H.C.). Compare, however, *Worby* v. *Worby* (1985), 48 R.F.L. (2d) 369 (Sask. Q.B.) and *Saunders* v. *Saunders* (1989), 20 R.F.L. (3d) 368 (B.C. Co. Ct.) where the father in each case was denied overnight access for as long as he continued to live in a homosexual relationship. In the late 1990's, it is difficult to find reported cases that take an explicitly negative attitude towards sexual orientation *per se*.

2. In *Re K.* (1995), 23 O.R. (3d) 679 (Prov. Div.) (reproduced in Chapter 11), Nevins Prov. Div. J. concluded that a statutory provision preventing same-sex couples from applying to adopt a child conflicted with the Charter. In his reasons, the judge briefly reviewed the views of experts on the effects of gay and lesbian parenting.

3. In *For the Sake of the Children*, the Special Joint Committee recommended (at 99) "that sexual orientation not be considered a negative factor in the disposition of shared parenting decisions".

4. For further reading see Gross, "Judging The Best Interests of the Child: Child Custody and the Homosexual Parent" (1986), 2 C.J.W.L. 505; Ehrcke, "Limiting Judicial Discretion in Custody Proceedings on Divorce" (1987), 6 Can. J. Fam. L. 211; Arnup, " 'Mothers Just Like Others': Lesbians, Divorce, and Child Custody in Canada" (1989), 3 C.J.W.L. 18; Tasker and Golombok, "Children Raised by Lesbian Mothers: The Empirical Evidence" (1991), 21 F. L. 184; Rosenblum, "Custody Rights of Gay and Lesbian Parents" (1991), 36 Villanova L. Rev. 1665; Meyer, "Legal, Psychological and Medical Considerations in Lesbian Parenting" (1992), Law and Sexuality 237; Brophy, "New Families, Judicial Decision-Making, and Children's Welfare" (1992), 5 C.J.W.L. 484; Baggett, "Sexual Orientation: Should It Affect Child Custody Rulings?" (1992), 16 Law and Psychology Review 189; Palash, "Gay and HIV-infected Fathers" (1993), 15 Family Advocate 57; Thompson, "Are Two Moms Too Many?" (1993), 42 De Paul Law Rev. 1125; Becker, "Strength in Diversity: Feminist Theoretical Approaches to Child Custody and Same-Sex Relationships" (1994), 23 Stetson Law Review 701; Davies, "Two Moms and a Baby: Protecting the Non-Traditional Family Through Second-Parent Adoptions" (1995), 29 New Eng. L. Rev. 1055; Wardle, "The Potential Impact of Homosexual Parenting on Children" [1997] U. Illinois Law Rev. 833; and Boyd, "Lesbian (and Gay) Custody Claims: What Difference Does Difference Make?" (1998), 15 C.F.L.Q. 133. The social science literature is reviewed in Buxton, "The Best Interest of Children of Gay and Lesbian Parents" in Galatzer and Kraus, eds., *The Scientific Basis of Child Custody Decisions* (New York: John Wiley, 1999), 319-356.

(6) TENDER YEARS DOCTRINE AND PRIMARY CARE-GIVER
PRESUMPTION

R. v. R.

34 R.F.L. (2d) 277, [1983] 5 W.W.R. 385 (Alta. C.A.)

[The parents were married in 1974. In 1978 they adopted a baby girl. The
mother ceased work to look after the child. In 1981 the mother left the matrimonial
home with the child. An interim custody agreement gave custody to the mother. The
mother lived and worked in a city 80 kilometers from the family farm where the
father continued to live. The child, who was four and a half at the time of trial, was
placed in a government approved daycare centre at 8:30 each weekday morning and
picked up at the end of the work day. Every second Friday the father picked up the
child and took her to the farm until the following Tuesday.

The trial judge in divorce proceedings awarded custody to the father. He
concluded that both parents were ''more than capable of providing for the material,
emotional and spiritual upbringing of the child'', but that life with father on the
family farm offered the better choice for the child as long as the mother had ''very
liberal access''. He stressed that the father had much more time to devote to the care
of the child during the day. Also, the paternal grandparents lived on the farm and
could look after the child during ''peak farm work periods''.

The mother appealed. One of the grounds put forward was that the trial judge
had failed to give any weight to the ''tender years doctrine''. The essence of this
doctrine is captured in the mother's statement at trial: ''[F]athers don't make good
mothers, there are certain things that a little girl, in fact any little child, I think needs
from a mother.'' The Alberta Court of Appeal, McGillivray C.J.A. dissenting, upheld
the trial judge's decision.]

KERANS J.A. (LAYCRAFT J.A. concurring): — . . . The next ground offered
is that the learned trial judge refused to consider what the mother calls the ''tender
years principle''. He said:

There is no longer, in my view, any historic or traditional right that favours either mother or
father. This issue must be decided on the merits of this case.

It is acknowledged for the mother that the learned trial judge was not bound to
give the mother custody of a child of tender years just because the child was of
tender years; it is argued, however, that he was bound to consider such a disposition
for that reason and he refused to do so. In my view, his reasons are misperceived. I
understand him simply to reject the ''rights'' approach to the determination of a
custody case in lieu of the ''best interests'' approach. The classic statement of the
''rights'' approach was that of Mulock C.J.O. in *Re Orr*, [1933] O.R. 212, [1933] 2
D.L.R. 77 at 80-81 (C.A.):

. . . the general rule is that the mother . . . is *entitled* to the custody and care of a child during what
is called the period of nurture, namely, until it attains about 7 years of age, the time during which
it needs the care of the mother more than that of the father, and then the father as against the
mother becomes *entitled* to the custody and care of his child . . . (The italics are mine.)

In my view, the learned trial judge was bound to reject this approach: see *Talsky* v.
Talsky, [1976] 2 S.C.R. 292, 21 R.F.L. 27, 62 D.L.R. (3d) 267, 7 N.R. 246.

In an allied argument, the mother suggests that the learned trial judge erred in
not giving decisive weight to the tender years ''principle'' as a ''factor''. This

argument is powerfully close to repeating the error of Mulock C.J.O. If the extreme youth of the child *must be* the deciding factor, then that factor gives the mother an undeniable right.

Should a pre-school child be with the mother? Spence J. (dissenting) in *Talsky* describes the answer ''yes'' as ''common sense''. Often, when we invoke common sense, we intend to invoke unstated conventional assumptions. As Einstein rather provocatively said, ''common sense is the collection of prejudices acquired by age 18''. I suppose that there is no harm in this unless the unstated conventions come to be doubted. That the female human has some intrinsic capacity, not shared by the male, to deal effectively with infant children is an assumption that was once conventionally accepted but is now not only doubted but widely rejected.

As recently as 1955, this rhapsodic commentary by Roach J.A. in *Bell* v. *Bell*, [1955] O.W.N. 341 at 344 (C.A.), attracted no adverse comment:

> No father, no matter how well-intentioned or how solicitous for the welfare of such a child, can take the full place of the mother. Instinctively, a little child, particularly a little girl, turns to her mother in her troubles, her doubts, and her fears. In that respect, nature seems to assert itself. The feminine touch means so much to a little girl; the frills and flounces and the ribbons in the matter of dress; the whispered consultations and confidences on matters which to the child's mind should only be discussed with Mother; the tender care, the soothing voice; all these things have a tremendous effect on the emotions of the child. This is nothing new; it is as old as human nature.
> . . .

This view confuses cultural traditions with human nature; it also traps women in a social role not necessarily of their choosing, while at the same time freeing men: if only a mother can nurture a child of tender years, then it is the clear duty of the mother to do so; because the father *cannot* do it, he is neither obliged nor entitled even to try. Also, it is seen by some as self-perpetuating: by putting the female child in the custody of somebody who accepts the maternal role model so described, the rule ordains that she will have just such a role model at close hand during her most impressionable years. Thus, the ''tender years principle'', which at first glance seems only innocently sentimental, is seen by many as part of a subtle, systemic sexual subordination.

In my view, it is no part of the law of Canada that a judge is bound to say that human nature dictates that only females can perform that parental role labelled as ''maternal''. I do not agree with Roach J.A.; I do not agree with the appellant mother.

Judicial comments about the ''tender years'' issue must be considered in an historical context. The fact is that there have been substantial changes over the past century in the attitude in our society about the ideal family situation. Once, it was accepted that the husband and father was the decision-maker for the family, even about child-rearing questions and even after a marriage breakdown. The statement by Mulock C.J.O. in 1933, quoted above, was a sign of the emergence of a new attitude. Note, however, that he conceded the right of the father to custody after age seven. In its origins, the ''tender years'' concept was a way to undermine the traditional model and recognize a new model. The new, ''modern'' marriage model involved not only the idea of the nuclear family, but also of the marital partnership, where all major decision-making is shared. The partnership model has only just recently been accepted fully into the law by the enactment of the Matrimonial Property Act, R.S.A. 1980, c. M-9, and similar statutes. The modern marriage model does not concede any special status to the father and therefore requires a new standard to decide custody cases. The courts adopted the ''best interests'' approach.

Some divergence in the roles of male and female was accepted in this newer model however. The husband could continue to be the bread-winner and the wife could have a special responsibility as a professional homemaker. This was not to say that she alone was to carry the burden of child-rearing. But there were and are, in this model, a measure of acceptably different parental roles based upon gender. To those who prefer this model, the views of Roach J.A. are simply inadequate.

To others, however, his views are anathema. In what might be called the supra-modern marriage, strenuous efforts are made to avoid *any* role distinction based upon sex. The many tasks of homemaking and child-rearing — indeed, child-bearing — are shared as completely as possible, and not on any gender basis. It follows, of course, that both fathers and mothers must, if this model is to work, acquire the skills and make the commitment which is required for effective parenting.

Taken in this context, the remarks made by judges in the past about "tender years principle" do not come to much. All that can be said in this age of changing attitudes is that judges must decide each case on its own merits, with due regard to the capacities *and* attitudes of each parent. We should take care not to assign to this idea or that (all actually of recent origin and unique to our society) the august status of being the only one consistent with human nature or common sense. And we must continue to recognize that the attitude toward child-rearing of the parties to the marriage which the judge is being asked to dissolve could reflect traditional, modern or supra-modern ideals or, more likely, some confused and contradictory spot on the spectrum between these extremes. For example, there is no point giving a father the custody of a child of tender years if that father believes child-rearing to be "women's work". That would not be in the best interests of the child. And we must remember that our role is not to reform society; our role is to make the best of a bad deal for the child who comes before us for help.

I should not be taken as avoiding or minimising the difficulty for a judge who must decide between parties to a custody dispute, who offer diametrically conflicting opinions about the proper role for a female in our society, and therefore the proper role model for a child. But this is not such a case. The parents do not disagree on this. The only question was whether the exposure to a female role model in the father's proposal was adequate. The learned trial judge found that it was and there was no cogent evidence to the contrary.

On my reading of his judgment, the learned trial judge did not find the father here to be any sort of a radical; he did, however, find him to be, perhaps uniquely, willing to spend a great deal of time with his little daughter. I can see no error in that. . . .

The last ground offered by the appellant is that the learned trial judge erred in putting decisive emphasis on the fact that the father had more weekday time available to share with his little daughter than did the mother. There is an irony in this; usually such a complaint is made by the father! Three points are made for the mother:

(1) It is argued in the factum that the mother is being punished for having to work. This is not fair, as Mr. Babki conceded during argument. Both parents here agreed that both had to work. Maintenance was not an issue. It is mere happenstance that the father has more free weekday time than does the mother. To decide the case on that circumstance is, I concede, collaterally to make the mother a victim of that circumstance. But we must, as I have already said, do what is right for the child, not what is fair to the parents. The mother has no right to demand sympathetic consideration for her circumstances if to do so is not in the best interests of the child. There is no merit to this point.

(2) It is said that the learned trial judge failed to appreciate that the advantages offered by the father are short-lived: by September next the child will, in any event, be in kindergarten and thereafter in school during most daylight hours. The learned trial judge was, however, well aware of this point. . . .

But, in a case where all else is equal, there is no error in deciding on the basis of the best interest of the child in the short term. This argument has no merit. Further, I detect a certain contradiction in the position of the mother. She says that the judge was wrong to decide the case on the basis of what the situation will be during the brief period before the child goes to school; yet, in invoking the tender years factor, she relies on just that.

(3) It is said that the learned trial judge unfairly deprecates professional child care. To do so would be error. In the absence of cogent evidence on the point, it is surely not fair to criticize those who select a style of child-rearing which is widely accepted now in our society. What the learned trial judge does, however, is something entirely within his province to do: he weighs the quality and quantity of the mother's proposal against that of the father. In this, there is no error.

It is said that the key is not quantity but quality. The quality of time spent with children is obviously more important than quantity (recognizing that in the early bonding period simple quantity is also vitally important). But I understand the learned trial judge here to say that each of the two parents offers time of equal value and the father offers more. I can see no reversible error in relying upon this as a deciding factor.

[In dissent, MCGILLIVRAY C.J.A. stated:] From his reasons it appears to me that the one consideration that weighed with the judge was that the husband, as a farmer, would be able to spend more time with the youngster on a daily basis than the wife would because the wife is working and has the child in a daycare centre during the daytime.

But, in basing his judgment on time available, he has, in my opinion, given no consideration to the proposition that a girl of tender years is best with her mother, when this should be regarded as " . . . one of the more important factors which must be considered in the granting of custody" (Spence J. in *Talsky* at p. 40). . . .

In my opinion the difference in amount of time that one parent can at any given period spend with the child is not of itself a sound criterion on which to base a custody order, particularly when the effect is to overturn the arrangement that the parties themselves had made. Quality not quantity of parental care should be weighed. The judge has held as between the husband and wife that one is not to be preferred to the other. He should have recognized the wife's advantage as a mother in relation to a child of tender years.

I am further of the opinion that the amount of time that can be spent with the youngster by the farmer husband is not a satisfactory basis for overturning the working arrangements that the parties had had, which would be given effect to by giving the wife custody, with the husband to have access for four days in every two weeks. First of all, there must be tens of thousands of children doing very well in daycare centres across the country. Moreover, the child will soon be going to school. The advantage of time available every day to be with the youngster is short lived. Had the mother chosen to go on welfare rather than to work, so as to be able to devote her entire working day to the child, it would appear that the advantage that the husband was found to have possessed by the trial judge would have been more than balanced by the attention the mother could give the child. I cannot bring myself to conclude in this day that custody should be determined by whether the mother has to work or not.

In my respectful view, the learned trial judge has erred in two respects: he is changing what was a workable arrangement, whereby the mother had de facto custody, with the husband having the child for four days every two weeks, and he has overlooked that special bond between a daughter of four and a half and her mother, or has at least not given any or sufficient weight to that factor. . . .

HARDEN v. HARDEN

(1987), 6 R.F.L. (3d) 147 (Sask. C.A.)

[The parties were married in 1978 and separated in 1985 when the father forced the mother to leave. Two children, aged six and three, remained with the father in the home. Before the separation, the father farmed and the mother remained in the home, caring for the children. Following separation, the father and children lived with his parents and the children spent a substantial amount of time with the grandmother while the father worked.

The trial judge awarded custody to the mother, in part because of his view that the custody of young children should be awarded to a mother ''unless there is some compelling reason to the contrary''. The father appealed, alleging that the trial judge had improperly relied on the tender years doctrine.]

SHERSTOBITOFF J.A. (for the court): — . . . The appellant, in advancing his argument against the validity of the tender years doctrine relied on the judgment of Kerans J.A. of the Alberta Court of Appeal in *R. v. R.* . . . I agree in large part with what is there said. It is not a part of our law that a court must find that a female, by virtue of her sex alone, is inherently superior as a parent, in the case of a child of tender years, to her husband, and if that is what the trial judge found in this case, he erred. However, an analysis of the judgment and evidence indicates that that was not the governing factor in the case. The parties, after the marriage, presumably by the assent of each of them chose the following roles: the husband as the breadwinner, and the wife as a mother. She did not work during the marriage and one of her primary functions was to care for, raise and nurture the children. The trial judge recognized that this decision and course of action on the part of the parties put the mother into a closer relationship with the children than the father, and all other factors being equal, he properly decided that the mother should have custody of the children. Accordingly, in my view, he reached the right result on the evidence. In a case where the parental roles were reversed, the decision might well be the opposite. Each case must be decided on its own facts. . . .

McLEOD, "ANNOTATION"

(1987), 6 R.F.L. (3d) 147 at 148

In *Harden* Sherstobitoff J.A. expressly agrees with the Alberta Court of Appeal and holds that a parent's gender does not, in itself, create a presumption in custody matters. Rather, in all situations, the court is to look to the reality of the particular case in order to determine who has been caring for the child and who is best equipped to meet the child's needs in the future. In many cases, as in *Harden*, custody of young children will be awarded to the mother. However, this will be because on the facts the mother is best equipped to deal with the child's needs.

Although Sherstobitoff J.A. denied the existence of a tender years doctrine, it may also be correct to say that the doctrine has been reformulated. That is, the parent who has had the major input to a young child's development will likely receive custody so long as the task has been reasonably carried out. Whereas in the past this person was regularly the mother because of the nature of the family unit, the change in women's roles in society has created a situation where both parents may share child-rearing responsibilities relatively equally. As well, in some situations, the husband has remained in the home to care for the children. The thrust of the decisions in *R.* v. *R.* and *Harden* seems to be that, where a parent has had primary childcare responsibilities and has carried them out properly, it will rarely be in the child's best interests for the child to be uprooted and separated from that parent. . . .

K. (M.M.) v. K. (U.)

(1990), 28 R.F.L. (3d) 189 (Alta. C.A.)

[The parties were married in 1981 and separated in 1987. They had a four and a half-year-old daughter and a newborn son. The children resided with the mother after the separation. In divorce proceedings the trial judge awarded custody to the father, largely because the mother had had some psychological problems. The mother appealed and the appellate court concluded that the trial judge had erred by disregarding a psychologist's second report which was much more favourable to the mother than the first and by misconstruing some other evidence. The appellate court determined that the case could be decided from the record and it proceeded to grant custody to the mother.]

STRATTON J.A. (for the court): — The trial judge noted [p. 120] that Dr. K.'s position gave "him flexibility to schedule his work so that he would enjoy his children", but he does not take notice that the same flexibility is apparent to Mrs. K.'s schedule. Mrs. K. is self-employed and works four to five hours a day. Some of her work can be completed in the home and she has some control in scheduling her appointments. She would obviously be able to devote much of her time to the children. Her mother also lives with her and would be available for child care. Dr. K. "would consider hiring a nanny" [p. 120]. . . .

While one must always consider such tangible factors as the residence which a parent proposes for the children, and the ability of a parent to provide for a child's material well-being, such considerations must take a secondary position to the children's emotional, psychological and intellectual needs. In large part provision may be made for a child's material well-being by ordering an appropriate regime of maintenance payments. The same cannot be said for the more intangible types of support mentioned. Neither can it be said in regard to the direct, hands-on parenting skills which are necessary to child rearing. The trial judge held the petitioner has good parenting skills and I agree. Further, they are proven parenting skills, while Dr. K.'s care-giving skills are untested on a continuous day-to-day basis. Mrs. K. has always been the children's primary care-giver. She has been the one who has wiped their noses, bathed them, maintained their health, driven them to school, tutored K., taken them to church and arranged for their daycare. Dr. K. has had a role in these matters, but it has been much more limited in nature. Mrs. K. has not only proven that she can cope with the daily pressures of child rearing, but she has exhibited an active and extended concern for the children's condition, means and needs. Indeed, in all primary aspects it was Mrs. K. who was charged with child rearing before the marriage broke down and I see no reason why that role should be changed now that the marriage has been dissolved. As the trial judge found, Mrs. K.

is a "good parent" with "good parenting skills" and as a result "both children have done well when in the custody of their mother". I do not see that it would be in the children's best interests to alter that situation.

The trial judge was concerned that Dr. K. was the psychologically more healthy parent. Having in mind Dr. Kneier's comments, I do not think it appropriate to put excessive reliance on psychological assessment conducted during the traumatic time surrounding the breakdown of the marriage. On a consideration of all the expert evidence available to us, I believe Mrs. K. to have overcome earlier psychological problems and that the children are more psychologically bonded to Mrs. K. than they are to Dr. K. M. is currently three years of age and has never lived with his father on a full-time basis. K. is seven years old and has been under Mrs. K.'s sole residential care for the past three years. I wish to be explicit that I am not here invoking the "tender years doctrine" which this court rejected in *R. v. R.* . . . In that decision the court pointed out the error in determining custody entitlement for the children of tender years by the "rights approach" (i.e., the mother's *entitlement* because of the age of the children), rather than the "best interest of the children approach". I fully agree.

In determining the best interests of the children it is, in my view, essential to examine the circumstances of what is often called the "primary care" of those children. In modern society it is, of course, clear that the primary care-giver is, by no means, always the mother. But in the present case, even during the marriage, it was Mrs. K. who was primarily responsible for child rearing in that she took care of their basic day-to-day needs and spent time with them. It was Mrs. K. to whom the children primarily related. The evidence indicates that her efforts were successful in terms of the well-being of the children. Dr. Kneier testified as to the psychological bond that existed between the children and Mrs. K. as follows:

> The children were comfortable in their mother's care. They were very aligned with their mother, and I felt that it would be traumatic for them to remove them from their mother and put them in the care of Dr. [K.] . . .

In reference to Mrs. K., Dr. Kneier also stated:

> Her position is enhanced in the sense that she has had these children, they are used to her, she has been their source of security, and they are living with her.

. . .

DOE v. DOE

(1990), 28 R.F.L. (3d) 356 (Ont. Dist. Ct.)

[The parties began cohabiting in 1979 and separated in 1987. The child was born in 1985. After the separation the mother and child moved in with the maternal grandmother. From January 1988 to October 1988 the child was in the primary care of the mother. The parties then entered into a joint custody arrangement which provided that the child would spend two weeks with each parent. An assessor's report indicated that the father was far more willing and likely to promote access and that the child should be placed with the father. A second report reached the same conclusion. The father worked full-time and would require full-time child care assistance. The mother was available as a full-time parent and she lived with her family who would help out.

In 1989 the father was awarded sole custody under the *CLRA* largely because of his willingness to promote access. (This aspect of the case will be explored later in this chapter.) Regarding the tender years doctrine, the trial judge concluded that it was at most a common sense rule and could be displaced by the facts of any given case. The mother appealed and obtained a stay pending appeal. Corbett D.C.J. allowed the appeal.]

. . . The appellant submits that the learned trial judge erred in failing to give proper weight to the principle of common sense that children of tender years should be given to the custody of their mother . . .Whether the tender years doctrine is styled a rule of common sense or not, the factual reality is that the bulk of child care, particularly of pre-school age children, is performed by mothers. The reality has not changed with the statutory recognition in s. 20(1) of the Children's Law Reform Act that the father and mother of a child are equally entitled to custody of the child. The tender years doctrine reflects that a young child is more likely to be cared for by the child's mother and, if that is the case, it is in the best interests of the child to remain with the mother unless there are other compelling reasons to uproot the child in the child's best interests. I do not find that the learned trial judge erred in his consideration of the tender years doctrine. . . .

Counsel for the appellant submits the learned trial judge erred in failing to consider the instability which would result from the custody plan put forward by the respondent. It is submitted that the sum and substance of the respondent's evidence with respect to his custody plan for the child was that she would be cared for by a continuous flow of different nannies or babysitters, a fact which the learned judge failed to fully consider. . . . He also submitted the learned trial judge failed to give sufficient weight to the fact that Cathy could be cared for most of the time by her mother.

Counsel for the respondent submitted that the fact that a parent works and requires daycare or babysitting services is a common experience and is not significant. She referred to the learned judge's finding on the evidence given at trial that other caregivers do not detract from the main parent-child attachment, provided the parents are routinely a close part of the child's environment.

In my opinion, the learned trial judge erred in placing custody of a pre-school age child with a working parent requiring nannies, as opposed to that of a parent who works part time on an irregular basis and who lives in a household with other family members.

I agree with the submission of counsel for the appellant that the learned trial judge did not give sufficient weight to the fact that Jane lives on a farm with her mother and her sister. While the learned trial judge noted the child had normal loving relationships with her grandmother and aunt, he failed to refer to the fact that Cathy lived with them and that her grandmother was always available in the home. . . .

Without in any way concluding that a working parent cannot be a good parent with the assistance of other caregivers, in my opinion, that is not the issue. In this case, when faced with a choice for a pre-school child between a fit, loving mother who is virtually a full-time parent, and a busy, full-time, fit, loving father who requires full-time child care assistance, it is an error in principle not to award custody to the parent who can devote substantial time to the child, particularly when the mother lives in a household with accessible relatives.

In several of the cases reproduced above, one parent appears to have been favoured because he or she would not require paid assistance to care for the children. The following case is included in this section because it also addresses this factor. It does not deal directly with the tender years doctrine or the primary caregiver presumption.

KLACHEFSKY v. BROWN

(1988), 12 R.F.L. (3d) 280 (Man. C.A.)

O'SULLIVAN J.A. (HUBAND J.A. concurring): — In this appeal from a judgment of Goodman J. [9 R.F.L. (3d) 428] we begin with the admonitions given to appeal courts that we should not interfere with custody decisions unless we can see palpable error in the judgment under appeal.

The mother is appealing from a decision by Goodman J. directing that two children should reside in Winnipeg during the school term rather than in Vancouver whither the wife's work has taken her.

The two children, a girl of the age of 8 years and a boy of $5\frac{1}{2}$, have been in the joint custody of father and mother since a separation which occurred in May 1982, after more than four years of marriage. The parents entered into a somewhat unusual arrangement whereby each parent would spend almost exactly the same amount of time each year with the children. Each parent set up a household in which the children were nurtured. The children would be one day in the father's home and the next day at the mother's home.

On 18th April 1987 the father married Lesley Elizabeth Taylor with whom he had a relationship of almost two years' standing. The custody arrangement continued with the children developing a concept that they have two families both of which they love dearly. But recently the mother has had to move to Vancouver to pursue her livelihood. The judge has found expressly: "The move to Vancouver is in the best interests of herself and her children". He also found that the children are well adjusted, very normal, loving, caring children.

At the end of a long trial the judge decided that the children should stay with the father in Winnipeg during the school term with generous access to the mother during holiday seasons. . . .

Normally, a trial judge, having taken into account the evidence given, and also his assessment of the characters and qualities of the persons who appear before him, sets out his conclusion clearly that the best interests of the children require whatever order he decides to give. What is extraordinary in the case before us is that the judge has said [p. 431]: "On balance, if this were a contest between Mr. Klachefsky and Ms. Brown, I would choose Ms. Brown". Despite this finding, he went on to conclude that the children would be best served by living with the father rather than the mother.

In my opinion, there is ample material on the record to support the judge's conclusion that on balance Ms. Brown would be the better parent. My perusal of the record satisfies me that he was correct in that assessment. The judge justified departing from his assessment of the two parents by saying [p. 432]:

> With some reluctance, I have determined that it is in the best interests of the children to remain in Winnipeg. In particular, in Winnipeg, there is no need for the reliance on daycare or other hired child caretakers.

After noting that, "This is a very difficult decision for the court to make", and after finding that, "The move to Vancouver is in the best interests of herself and her children", the judge said:

> My decision relates particularly to the fact that the new Mrs. Klachefsky will be available to the children 24 hours a day and that there is a wealth of extended family support available here in Winnipeg which is not available in Vancouver.

In my opinion, the trial judge committed a palpable error in placing undue emphasis on the fact that the mother in Vancouver will require paid assistance to provide care for her children. The younger child is now enrolled in kindergarten where he spends part of the day. Another portion of the day will be spent in a daycare facility, until he graduates to Grade I in six months' time. Both children will be returning home from school around 3:30 p.m. but the mother does not arrive home from work until around 5:30 p.m. She has made arrangements for a competent person to be at the home from 3:00 o'clock on until the mother's arrival. Daycare and home care arrangements of this kind are a fact of life which many parents and children face, and there was no evidence before the judge that the children would suffer the least harm from being exposed to a few hours when they are neither at school nor with their mother. Whether an alternate caregiver is paid or unpaid cannot be decisive of what is in the best interests of the children.

Further, the judge appears to have overlooked the testimony that, in the future, the mother's parents will probably spend their winter holiday time in Vancouver rather than Florida, and the evidence that there is available to the mother extended family in Vancouver.

The learned judge also, in my opinion, committed error in this case by failing to take into account the relative stability of the parents' way of life. Since the separation, the mother has maintained a stable family unit consisting of herself and her two children, with help from her mother and other people with whom she has had good rapport. There is every indication that she could maintain that stable home in Vancouver.

On the other hand, the evidence shows that the home provided by the father, however excellent it has been as found by the learned trial judge, has not been a stable one. . . .

In my opinion, given the judge's conclusions that as between the parents he would prefer Ms. Brown, a preference with which I agree, the judge fell into error in failing to take account the father's record of instability in his home life compared with her stability, and in giving far too much weight to the fact that the mother might have to rely on paid daycare for two hours a day while she looks after the children in Vancouver. . . .

PHILP J.A. (dissenting): — There is one thing upon which my colleagues and I agree: this is one of the most difficult custody cases any of us have ever heard. That is the view we all expressed following the appeal hearing. It is so because of the unusual joint custody arrangements which have been in place for over five years, in reality joint care and control as well as joint custody; it is so because the children, now 8 and 5 years of age, have flourished under these arrangements; it is so because they appear to have survived the breakup of the family unit as intelligent, well adjusted, bright, friendly, quite remarkable youngsters and have adapted well to the divided family units; and it is so because both parents are extraordinary people, and intelligent, caring, loving and involved parents. The trial judge summed it up: "This is an extraordinary case involving extraordinary persons".

The mother has moved to Vancouver to further her business career. By that act joint care and control of the children has been killed, and joint custody has been mortally wounded. The trial judge faced a dilemma: Which parent should be given custody of the children; and from which parent should custody be taken away?

After six days of trial, after hearing the evidence of the parents, the father's new wife, the maternal grandmother, the parties' employers and friends, some with professional qualifications, the trial judge concluded [p. 432]:

> In any event, this is not a contest between the parties. *The court must make its determination on the basis of what is in the best interests of the children.* With some reluctance, I have determined that it is in the best interests of the children to remain in Winnipeg. In particular, in Winnipeg, there is no need for the reliance on daycare or other hired child caretakers . . .
>
> My decision relates particularly to the fact that the new Mrs. Klachefsky will be available to the children 24 hours a day and that there is a wealth of extended family support available here in Winnipeg which is not available in Vancouver. [emphasis added]

The reasons of the trial judge were delivered orally immediately following the completion of the evidence and the arguments of counsel. As is often the case in such circumstances, the reasons are not a study in clarity and felicity. They contain such confusing statements as [pp. 431 and 432]:

> On balance, if this were a contest between Mr. Klachefsky and Ms. Brown, I would choose Ms. Brown.
>
> The move to Vancouver is in the best interests of [Ms. Brown] and her children.

As well, the trial judge made particular references to the fact that daycare would be required in Vancouver, but not in Winnipeg.

At the end of the day, however, the trial judge said that his determination must be made "on the basis of what is in the best interests of the children". That is the proper test, and I cannot say that in applying that test he committed palpable error.

My colleagues have come to the opposite conclusion. They are of the view that the appeal should be allowed; that custody of the children should be given to the mother; that the children should be uprooted from their environment since birth in which they have flourished, their neighbourhood, their friends, their extended family, their special "Alternative Program" schooling, and their established sports and cultural activities; and that the children should be bundled off on a voyage in uncharted waters.

The trial judge found that the children are "fond" of the father's new wife. There is evidence to support a stronger finding — that a loving relationship has developed between them. My colleagues would destroy that bond, and, as well, significantly alter the special relationship that exists between the children and their father (and that is surely the practical effect of changing the order as to custody) in order to accommodate the mother who has chosen to put her career interests above all else.

My colleagues have concluded that appellate interference is justified because the trial judge has committed palpable error and has misapprehended the evidence. Three instances are singled out from the evidence of the six-day trial.

Firstly, they say that the trial judge placed undue emphasis on the fact that the mother will require paid assistance to provide care for the children. Her circumstances in Vancouver will require daycare services for the younger child each afternoon, and babysitting arrangements for both children each day after daycare and school closing until the mother returns to work. Those arrangements are not required in Winnipeg. It was the intention of the new wife, after the birth of her child expected a few months after the trial, to remain at home to care for her baby and the children. In determining the best interests of the children, the trial judge was entitled to prefer the care that the new wife was prepared and anxious to provide, and the loving

684   CUSTODY AND ACCESS

relationship that had developed between the new wife and the children over a period in excess of two years, to that of paid "caregivers". I do not read from the reasons of the trial judge that the decisive factor was whether an alternate caregiver is paid or unpaid. It is a reasonable inference to be drawn that the trial judge looked to the quality and reliability of the care available from the new wife who testified at the trial, and from a daycare facility and a babysitter then available in Vancouver according to the evidence of the mother.

My colleagues have concluded, as well, that the trial judge failed to take into account the relative stability of the parents' way of life. This is the second instance in which they say the trial judge erred, and it is related to the third instance, their conclusion that the trial judge misapprehended the evidence when he said that the new wife "has been for the past two years and will continue to be a good caretaker for the children". . . .

There is ample evidence to support the finding that the home provided by the husband and the new wife is a stable one. I do not think the trial judge committed error in failing to arrive at the opposite conclusion on the basis of snippets from the evidence on the father's relationship with two other women, some years ago and prior to this relationship with his new wife.

Nor can I conclude that the trial judge misapprehended the evidence on how long the new wife had filled the role of a "caretaker" for the children. In my view, on any reasonable interpretation of that word, the new wife had performed that role at the time of the trial for at least two years. . . .

In this case our duty is clear. The trial judge is an experienced and respected Family Division judge. The evidence was there to support his findings. Those findings, however inelegantly expressed in his oral reasons, are to be respected. . . .

NOTES AND QUESTIONS

1. In an annotation to *Bendle* v. *Bendle* (1985), 48 R.F.L. (2d) 120 (Ont. Prov. Ct.), Professor McLeod explores the practical significance of the new approach in *R.* v. *R.*:

> If the doctrine is a rule of common sense, particularly, the onus rests on the father to show that he has been involved in the family life to the extent that the doctrine has no factual basis. If the doctrine has no factual basis, it ought not to be continued in any sense. If the doctrine is not even a rule of common sense, then no one has a "leg up" and both must show how their involvement with the child reflects on their ability to satisfy the child's needs. If the father has had no involvement with the children [sic], he would be unable to show, based on past practice, that he could care for the child. The mother, with a proven "track record" of caring for the child, would clearly have an advantage if she remained in the home with the child.

For recent cases in which the "tender years doctrine" is still described as a useful rule of common sense, see *S. (B.A.)* v. *S. (M.S.)* (1991), 35 R.F.L. (3d) 400 (Ont. C.A.) and *Lancaster* v. *Lancaster* (1992), 38 R.F.L. (3d) 373 (N.S. C.A.).

2. Many witnesses before the Special Joint Committee in 1998 expressed the view that judges still operate on the assumption that mothers are better parents than fathers. See *For the Sake of the Children*, at 15-16. The committee recommended (at 45) that there should be a specific legislative prohibition against "a preference in favour of either parent solely on the basis of that parent's gender." Section 8 of *The Children's Law Reform Act*, S.S. 1990-91, c. C-8.1, specifies: "In making, varying or rescinding an order for custody of a child, the court shall: . . . (c) make no presumption and draw no inferences as between parents that one parent should be preferred over the other on the basis of the person's status as a father or mother." Most academic commentators argue that the fact that the vast majority of children end up living primarily with their mothers after divorce does not reflect any judicial bias, but rather the predominant pattern of caregiving within the Canadian family even when the parents live together.

3. In *Tyabji* v. *Sandana* (1994), 2 R.F.L. (4th) 265 (B.C. S.C.), Spencer J. stated (at 270):

> Stereotypical gender views have no place in an award of custody. . . . Custody will not be awarded on the basis of any preconceived idea about daughters being with mothers and sons with fathers, or about age-appropriate placements, or about the rights of working parents of either sex not to be deprived of custody simply because they have a particular career path. In each case the court must determine the best interests of the children and all else must give way to that. . . . However, I am alive to the common sense suggestion that, often, small children will have formed a stronger emotional and physical bond with the mother. That must be weighed against any evidence which shows otherwise in a particular case, and against any evidence which shows that in spite of that bond at one stage of the children's lives, as strong a bond has since formed with the other parent, or that the probable futures of the parents puts one, rather than the other, in a position better to serve the best interests of the children from the time of the trial onwards.

The judge awarded custody of three children under the age of 6 to the father even though the mother had interim custody and the court appointed experts' assessments favoured the continuation of this arrangement. The mother was a member of the B.C. legislature who once described her position as ''almost a 24-hour-a-day, seven-days-a-week job.'' The father had, therefore, been actively involved in day-to-day childrearing before the separation. The mother's career would also require her to be absent from home frequently in the future. The judge assessed (at 279) ''her as a person who has an intense interest in the advancement of her career, which will compete with the children's needs for her attention.''

4. In *Garska* v. *McCoy*, 278 S.E. 2d 357 (W. Va. S. Ct., 1981) the court decided that there should be a presumption that the parent who has been the primary caregiver in the past should obtain custody of children of tender years, unless proven unfit. The court gave a partial list of the caring and nurturing activities that should be explored to identify the primary caregiver:

> . . . [T]he preparing and planning of meals; bathing, grooming and dressing; purchasing, cleaning and care of clothes; medical care, including nursing and trips to physicians; arranging for social interaction among peers after school; arranging alternative care; putting the child to bed at night, attending to the child in the middle of the night, waking the child in the morning; disciplining, teaching general manners and toilet training; educating; and teaching elementary reading, writing and arithmetic skills.

The court gave three reasons for creating the primary caregiver preference. First, the court wanted to prevent custody from being used as a bargaining chip or weapon in the non-custody issues underlying the divorce proceedings, such as the level of support payments; second, choosing between parents based solely on their relative degrees of fitness required a precision of measurement that was not possible given the tools available to judges; and third, divorcing couples could rely on the presumption to reach out of court settlements.

To what extent do the cases reproduced above recognize that primary care before separation is a factor in making the custodial decision?

For discussion of the primary caregiver presumption, see Neely, ''The Primary Caretaker Parent Rule: Child Custody and the Dynamics of Greed'' (1984), 3 Yale L. & Policy Rev. 168; Chambers, ''Rethinking the Substantive Rules for Custody Disputes in Divorce'' (1984), 83 Mich. L. Rev. 477; Ziff, ''The Primary Caretaker Presumption: Canadian Perspectives on an American Development'' (1990), 4 International J. L. & Fam. 186; Boyd, ''Potentialities and Perils of the Primary Caregiver Presumption'' (1990-1991), 7 C.F.L.Q. 1; Pask and McCall, ''*K. (M.M.)* v. *K. (U.)* and the Primary Care-Giver'' (1991), 33 R.F.L. (3d) 418; and Bala and Miklas, *Rethinking Decisions about Children: Is the "Best Interests of the Child Test" Really in the Best Interest of Children?* (Toronto: Policy Research Centre on Children, Families and Youth, 1993).

5. It has been suggested that many judges assume that mothers and fathers who are both in the workforce share parenting more or less equally. See Boyd, ''Child Custody and Working Mothers'', in Martin and Mahoney, eds., *Equality and Judicial Neutrality* (Toronto: Carswell, 1987) 168 and Boyd, ''Child Custody, Ideologies and Employment'' (1989), 3 C.J.W.L. 111. Professor Boyd concludes that this assumption is refuted by empirical studies. See also the comments of L'Heureux-Dubé (dissenting)

in *Young* v. *Young* (1993), 49 R.F.L. (3d) 117, at 186 (S.C.C.). Statistics Canada reports in *Families in Canada* (Ottawa: 1996, cat. No 96-307E) that in families with children under five years of age where both parents are employed, the mother spends an average of 2.2 hours per day on primary child care and 2.4 hours on domestic work while the father spends 1.2 and 1.4 hours respectively on these activities.

6. Professor Boyd also indicates that judges frequently prefer the parent who can offer a family set-up that most closely resembles the traditional nuclear family, including "female care". She suggests that the father is the most likely parent to benefit from this preference. Do you agree?

7. In its *Evaluation of the Divorce Act; Phase II: Monitoring and Evaluation* (Ottawa: Minister of Supply and Services, 1990), the Department of Justice concluded (at 134):

> [T]he pattern of custody awards at the end of the 1980's does not suggest a shift away from mother as the preferred custodial parent. When men show interest in the custody of the children, they are less likely than in the 1970's to receive sole custody but there is a greater likelihood of joint or split custody. Typically, men are awarded sole custody of the children of the marriage because the wife is not contesting the matter and, in fact, has little interest in her children, a pattern statistically more common for men.

8. For commentary on *Klachefsky* v. *Brown*, see: Goszer, "The Variation of a Joint Custody Order under Section 17 of the Divorce Act, 1985" (1989), 4 C.F.L.Q. 39; Devine and Murray, "Some Implications of Equal Time-Sharing Arrangements: New Directions in Parenting" (1989), 4 C.F.L.Q. 47; and Pask and McCall, "*Klachefsky* v. *Brown*: A Case of Competing Values" (1989), 4 C.F.L.Q. 73.

(7) SEPARATION OF SIBLINGS

The courts have accepted the principle that it is generally undesirable to separate children of the same family. See also 24(2)(a)(ii) of the *CLRA*. For a case in which the "non-separation of siblings" principle was particularly influential, see *Wereley* v. *Wereley* (1979), 14 R.F.L. (2d) 193 (Ont. H.C.). More recent cases where the principle played a role include *Harris* v. *Lyons* (1987), 8 R.F.L. (3d) 59 (N.B. Q.B.); *Dawe* v. *Dawe* (1987), 11 R.F.L. (3d) 265 (Nfld. T.D.); *Stark* v. *Stark* (1988), 16 R.F.L. (3d) 257 (B.C. S.C.); *Akister* v. *Rasmussen* (1991), 30 R.F.L. (3d) 346 (Sask. Q.B.); *Hurdle* v. *Hurdle* (1991), 31 R.F.L. (3d) 349 (Ont. Gen. Div.); *White* v. *White* (1994), 7 R.F.L. (4th) 414 (N.B. Fam. Div.); *Brinston* v. *Welsh* (1994), 7 R.F.L. (4th) 436 (Nfld. S.C.); *Lynch* v. *Lynch* (1995), 12 R.F.L. (4th) 367 (Ont. Gen. Div.); and *Clark* v. *Clark* (1995), 18 R.F.L. (4th) 234 (Sask. Q.B.).

The importance of this factor in any given case will depend, of course, on the closeness of the bond between the particular children involved as well as any other relevant circumstances, such as the length of time they have lived apart and become accustomed to other surroundings. For some cases in which it was held that the best interests of the children required separation of siblings, see *Zinck* v. *Zinck* (1974), 14 R.F.L. 106 (N.S. C.A.); *McLean* v. *Barnfield* (1980), 23 A.R. 557 (Q.B.); *McCabe* v. *Ramsay* (1980), 19 R.F.L. (2d) 70, 31 Nfld. & P.E.I.R. 481 (P.E.I. S.C.); *Nanji* v. *Nanji* (1987), 8 R.F.L. (3d) 221 (Ont. Master); *MacKenzie* v. *MacKenzie* (1987), 9 R.F.L. (3d) 1 (Man. C.A.); *Rose* v. *Rose* (1989), 22 R.F.L. (3d) 72 (Alta. Q.B.); *White* v. *White* (1990), 28 R.F.L. (3d) 439 (B.C. S.C.); *Jones* v. *Jones* (1994), 4 R.F.L. (4th) 293 (Sask. Q.B.); and *Poole* v. *Poole* (1999), 45 R.F.L. (4th) 56 (B.C. C.A.).

(8) WISHES OF THE CHILD

Two basic issues must be considered. What significance should be attached to the wishes of the child? How are the child's wishes to be ascertained?

WAKALUK v. WAKALUK

(1976), 25 R.F.L. 292 (Sask. C.A.)

[The court upheld the trial judge's award of custody. In his dissenting reasons, Bayda J.A. expressed his views on both the significance of the child's wishes and the way in which these should be discerned.]

BAYDA J.A.: — . . . I now turn briefly to another ground of appeal stressed by the appellant: that the learned trial judge was wrong in refusing to hear the children testify as to their wishes and preferences. Whether to allow a child to express his own wishes in a custody proceeding is a matter for the discretion of the trial judge. The age and maturity of the child are two important factors to consider in making that decision. There are, of course, other factors. Each individual case will reveal those other relevant factors.

If the trial judge should decide to allow a child to express his wishes, the judge should then decide upon the procedure he should use in the particular instance for the expression of those wishes. A certain procedure may be appropriate for one case but not another. To call the child as a witness and ask direct questions to establish his preferences is a procedure that should be discouraged. It is generally, but not always, inappropriate. In the present case the learned trial judge was right, in my respectful view, to decline to hear the children as witnesses, even though they were represented by independent counsel.

The procedure involving a judge speaking to a child, informally, in his chambers, also is not a particularly satisfactory one. To expect a child in such a short period and abnormal atmosphere (from the child's point of view) to choose between parents, and to expect to obtain from that child an accurate insight into the reasons for the child's feelings and preferences is ordinarily to expect too much. (I refrain from commenting upon the desirability of this procedure for the purpose of finding out first-hand something about the child's character and personality as opposed to his opinions and preferences respecting the parent he wishes to live with.)

A procedure involving a trained and competent third party, independent of the parents, charged with the responsibility of ascertaining the child's opinions and preferences using such techniques as are most likely to yield genuine feelings and wishes, and be least harmful to the child, over such period of time as may be necessary, and thereafter reporting to the court, by giving testimony or otherwise, is the procedure to be looked upon with the most favour.

Even if the wishes of a child are obtained there remains to decide what significance should be attached to those wishes. It must be remembered that the purpose of obtaining those wishes is not to give effect to them but to put the judge in a better position to decide what is in the best interest of the child. . . .

Cross J. in *Re S.*, [1967] 1 W.L.R. 396, [1967] 1 All E.R. 202, made these observations at p. 210, which are good to keep in mind:

> There are occasions when the wishes expressed by a boy of thirteen and a half may count for very little. In many cases it is unfortunately plain that they are reflections of the wishes of one of the parents which have been assiduously instilled into the ward and are not anything which could be called an independent exercise of his own will. Sometimes again the ward's wishes, although genuinely his own, are so plainly contrary to his long term interest that the court may feel justified in disregarding them.

JANDRISCH v. JANDRISCH

(1980), 16 R.F.L. (2d) 239, 3 Man. R. (2d) 135 (C.A.)

[In June 1976 interim custody of four children, born between 1963 and 1968, was awarded to the father. On March 29, 1977, custody was granted under provincial legislation to the mother with access to the father. The Court of Appeal confirmed this order. In March 1978 the father petitioned for divorce and again claimed custody. Custody was awarded to the father. The mother appealed. The Court of Appeal allowed the appeal and awarded custody to the mother. Only that portion of the reasons that comment on the trial judge's interview of the children in chambers is reproduced here.]

MONNIN J.A.: — . . . At the outset of the protracted hearing before Hewak J. the question arose whether the court should or should not interview the children to find out their true desires. Hewak J. at the outset properly refused to decide and proceeded to hear the evidence leaving the matter open.

Later on, counsel for the mother strongly urged that if the children were to be interviewed it ought to be in the presence of counsel or someone, be it court reporter or court clerk. Hewak J. overruled these objections and decided to interview the four children in his private chambers with no one present. The interview lasted more than 1½ hours. This court, which has the duty to review the record, has nothing with respect to this long interview. Counsel do not know what happened and the parents are in the same situation.

After this interview at the conclusion of the mother's testimony, the learned trial judge conducted his own examination and cross-examination of her for some 22 pages, namely from pages 1337 to 1359 of the transcript. The questions asked of the mother were obviously prompted by what one or more children told the judge during the interview. Here again the judge was working from an advantageous position. This should not be.

I am not prepared to condemn all interviews in camera by a trial judge. I honestly do not think that it is a wise or sound practice and this case seems to prove it. Such conduct leaves the trier of fact with information, evidence or call it what you wish, that the parties, counsel and members of the appellate tribunal have no knowledge of and absolutely no possibility of finding out what happened. It may be of use in exceptional circumstances but not in a hotly contested matter such as this one. In this bitter dispute where the views of the children have taken such exaggerated prominence, it was, in my view, unwise to question them in camera and then to use this information to question fairly severely one of the spouses only. . . .

HUBAND J.A.: — . . . Toward the end of the trial (at the time that the wife was giving her testimony), the learned trial judge decided that it would be of benefit to the court to interview the children for the purpose of determining their wishes as to custody. The learned trial judge stipulated that he would meet with the children alone in his chambers. No court reporter was present (and no record of the meeting was maintained by way of a tape recording). No clerk of the court was present. Counsel for the parties were not permitted to attend, nor were the parties themselves.

Once again, if the purpose of such an interview is simply to ascertain the wishes of the children, that can be done in a private meeting with or without the consent of one or both counsel. There should always be a record of what is said in such a conference. A trial judge has a discretion to interview children in private, without counsel, but if the rights of the parties are subject to appeal it is important there be some record of what has been said in the interview. If it is not possible to have a verbatim transcript, it is possible at least to have a statement from the trial judge as to what was said.

It is not proper, however, to go beyond the ascertainment of the wishes of the children. In the instant case, it became evident later in the proceedings that the children were asked, and gave their comments, on a range of topics extending well beyond their individual wishes. In effect, the children became private witnesses giving evidence in the cause to which only the trial judge is privy. I know of no basis in law for allowing such testimony as admissible evidence in the cause.

If a judge feels it is necessary to go behind a child's expression of desire as to custody, and to determine why the child prefers one parent over the other, and into the subject of parental imperfections and frailties, the proper course is for the child to be called as a witness so that the evidence is in the open and is subject to testing through cross examination.

O'SULLIVAN J.A.: — . . . I agree with the reasons for judgment delivered by MONNIN J.A. and HUBAND J.A.

NOTES AND QUESTIONS

1. Section 24(2)(b) of the *CLRA* affirms that the ''views and preferences of the child'' are relevant. A child's expressed wishes are not, however, binding on the court. What factors determine how much weight is to be given to the child's wishes? See also *Jespersen* v. *Jespersen* (1985), 48 R.F.L. (2d) 193 (B.C. C.A.); *McCartney* v. *McCartney* (1985), 49 R.F.L. (2d) 69 (Man. Q.B.); *Burgmaier* v. *Burgmaier* (1986), 50 R.F.L. (2d) 1 (Sask. C.A.); *Alexander* v. *Alexander* (1986), 3 R.F.L. (3d) 408 (B.C. C.A.); *Nanji* v. *Nanji* (1987), 8 R.F.L. (3d) 221 (Ont. Master); *Mamchur* v. *Mamchur* (1987), 11 R.F.L. (3d) 66 (B.C. S.C.); *Dawe* v. *Dawe* (1987), 11 R.F.L. (3d) 265 (Nfld. T.D.); *Young* v. *Young* (1989), 19 R.F.L. (3d) 227 (Ont. H.C.) (reproduced earlier in this chapter); *Rose* v. *Rose* (1989), 22 R.F.L. (3d) 72 (Alta. Q.B.); *Hiscocks* v. *Marshman* (1991), 34 R.F.L. (3d) 12 (Ont. Gen. Div.); *Lapierre* v. *Lapierre* (1991), 34 R.F.L. (3d) 129 (Sask. Q.B.); *Metz* v. *Metz* (1991), 34 R.F.L. (3d) 255 (Sask. Q.B.); *House* v. *Tunney (House)* (1991), 35 R.F.L. (3d) 68 (Sask. Q.B.); *Reddin* v. *Reddin* (1992), 39 R.F.L. (3d) 151 (P.E.I. C.A.); *Kosokowsky* v. *Kosokowsky* (1992), 95 D.L.R. (4th) 309 (Ont. Gen. Div.); *Beck* v. *Beck* (1993), 48 R.F.L. (3d) 303 (P.E.I. C.A.); *Boukema* v. *Boukema* (1997), 31 R.F.L. (4th) 329 (Ont. Gen. Div.); and *Leblue* v. *Leblue* (1997), 33 R.F.L. (4th) 118 (Alta. C.A.). In *Alexander*, the 12-year-old boy had taken the unusual step of writing to the Chief Justice of the province to indicate that he was dissatisfied with the trial judge's decision to award custody to the father. Nevertheless, the decision was affirmed on appeal. Two years later, the mother applied for a variation and the boy once again affirmed his preference. In allowing an appeal of a refusal to vary the order, Locke J.A. stated ((1988), 15 R.F.L. (3d) 363, at 365 (B.C. C.A.)):

> What the child wishes is not necessarily the best for the child, but there does come a point when at near adult years a child capable of responsible thought must now be deemed to be able to settle his own future in this important matter. Concomitant with that he must take the responsibility for his own actions. I think that that point has now been reached.

In *O'Connell* v. *McIndoe* (1998), 42 R.F.L. (4th) 77 (B.C. C.A.), the trial judge had granted custody of a 13-year-old boy to his mother over the boy's objection. By the time the case reached the appellate court, the boy had run away from his mother's home five times. The B.C. C.A. reversed the trial judge, stating (at 81): ''In order for custody orders relating to children in their teens to be practical, they must reasonably conform with the wishes of the children.''

2. In ''Incorporating Children's Needs and Views in Alternative Dispute Resolution Approaches'' (1992), 8 C.F.L.Q. 69, Gary Austin, Peter Jaffe and Pamela Hurley state (at 71-72):

> . . . Legal, and thus also clinical criteria for determining the children's best interests include such areas as attachment, parenting ability, length of time in a stable home, plans for care, permanence

and stability of the family unit, relationship by blood, and the children's view and preferences if they can be reasonably ascertained. The child's wishes must therefore be weighed in the context of his needs as indicated by the other criteria. A request for a clinician to interview a child alone to determine the child's wishes for the court would today be considered inappropriate. The child's wishes alone may be misleading without a full appreciation of the other factors in the family system that either influence the child or bear directly on his needs.

A child who expresses a wish with respect to the parent she wants to live with or the amount of time to be spent with the other parent may be identifying a set of arrangements that could indeed be in her best interests. The wish may reflect the actual conditions (e.g., good parenting, strong attachment, etc.) in the family system that influenced the child to make the wish. Examples would include: a child who wants to live with a particular parent because that parent shows more interest and love, has resided consistently in one location, and is more available; or, a child who, several years after the separation, wants to have more access to a parent because that parent can provide activities which interest the child who is now older, the parent is more available now than before the separation, and the child feels a need for more of a connection with that parent. The more congruency between the wish and the evaluation of the child's needs, the more weight the wish would carry in the assessment recommendations.

The weighing of the child's wishes should be moderated by the chronological and emotional age of the child. The older and more mature the child, the more weight accorded the wishes. Adolescents 16 and over in Ontario are able to act on their wishes as long as the parent in question agrees to the conditions (e.g., is willing to have the child live in his home.) Recommending arrangements contrary to the wishes of a 12- to 15-year-old would require considerable justification on the other best interests criteria, such as risk of family violence or parental incompetence, since such adolescents can exert considerable pressure on the family system that may already be vulnerable and strained. Younger children are especially susceptible to other influences, as outlined below, and their wishes need to be carefully viewed in the context of an adult evaluation of the circumstances. More mature children, even some below 12, are able to describe the basis of their wish, weigh the various options, appreciate the effects of enacting their wish on themselves, their parents, other members of their families, and their friendships and can accept some responsibility for those effects. In the final analysis, there is no easy formula to combine age and maturity in weighing wishes but the broader context of needs must always be considered.

3. The materials reproduced above identify several potential problems with the private interview of the child in the judge's chambers. To what extent does s. 64 of the *CLRA* address these concerns?

4. In *Uldrian* v. *Uldrian* (1988), 14 R.F.L. (3d) 26 (Ont. C.A.), the court confirmed that, while the *CLRA* requires the judge to consider the views and preferences of a child, there is no duty on the judge to interview the child. Judge Nasmith in "The Inchoate Voice" (1991-1992), 8 C.F.L.Q. 43 reports (at 64):

> The once prevalent practice of judges conducting private interviews with a child in chambers has pretty much vanished. . . . Recently, at a conference of Ontario judges from the Family Division, of the 40 judges in attendance, only two admitted to any recent use of this practice and, in each case, it was not just with the consent of all parties but upon the urging of all parties.

Interviews in the judge's chambers occurred in *Lindsay* v. *Lindsay* (1995), 19 R.F.L. (4th) 99 (Ont. Gen. Div.) and *Demeter* v. *Demeter* (1996), 21 R.F.L. (4th) 54 (Ont. Gen. Div.). However, in *Boland* v. *Boland* (1996), 24 R.F.L. (4th) 301 (Ont. Gen. Div.), Marshman J. indicated, in response to the parents' lawyers' request that he interview the children, that he preferred that the parents retain a member of the children's lawyers panel to represent the children. With the consent of the parties, the children's lawyer then advised the court of the children's wishes.

5. Professor McLeod and Alfred Mamo report (at 65) in *Annual Review of Family Law, 1995* (Toronto: Carswell, 1995) that courts continue to discourage parties from calling children as witnesses in open court in custody proceedings. They add: "However, if a child is old enough to give evidence and wishes to participate in the proceedings, it is difficult to see how a judge could prevent it."

There are indications that judges are becoming more receptive to the idea that children can give testimony in custody cases. In *Beck* v. *Beck* (1993), 48 R.F.L. (3d) 303 (P.E.I. C.A.), the three children testified at trial while the parents were outside the courtroom. Bean Prov. J. stated in *Levine* v. *Levine* (1993), 50 R.F.L. (3d) 414, at 420 (Ont. Prov. Div.) that there was no need for an independent assessment to ascertain the views and preferences of an 11-year-old boy since "he can do that himself by giving evidence at the trial." In *Young* v. *Young* (1993), 49 R.F.L. (3d) 117, at 213 (S.C.C.), Justice L'Heureux-Dubé (dissenting) suggested: ". . . [I]t is important to emphasize the importance of the evidence of children . . . and . . . their testimony alone might . . . be a sufficient evidentiary basis upon which to restrict access."

For arguments in favour of hearing the direct testimony of children in custody and access disputes, see Nasmith, "The Inchoate Voice" (1992), 8 C.F.L.Q. 43, at 63-65, and Huddart and Ensminger, "Hearing the Voice of Children" (1992), 8 C.F.L.Q. 95, at 100-101. The latter authors write:

> The child's statement of her views to the judge directly will probably be the most reliable evidence for a court. The judge can observe the child and assess her competency, understanding of the situation, and possible influence, without the screen of a third person. If those views are expressed in the courtroom, the procedural rights of the parents can be respected. As a secondary benefit, the parents will be forced to listen to, if not hear, their child. The child will know that her views are being stated as clearly as she can formulate them, in language she chooses as appropriate to be heard by her parents, without any danger of their being misstated by a well-meaning adult.

> Many participants in the adversary process are loathe to permit children to testify in court. Others seem to assume such testimony is inappropriate and to be discouraged. It is said that such an experience is harmful to the child, particularly if she is required to state a preference between parents. Pressure from parents, the need to choose between parents, fear of hurting an adult one loves and on whom one is dependent and the potential for vengeful retribution from a parent are among the perils cited. As in so much that is written in this area, there are no systematic studies underpinning these conclusions. It may be that the fears are exaggerated. Children whose divorcing parents cannot communicate rationally will usually have seen much more damaging fights than those in a courtroom. But most judges prefer to protect the child from the presumed harm.

> It seems that judges' protective attitudes toward the innocent child involved in a dispute between adults is based on their personal views as to the efficacy and fairness of calling the child as a witness to communicate her needs and wishes. The fear of psychological harm to a child, when measured against the value of a child's evidence, causes a judge to exclude an otherwise competent witness. It may be that the availability of the judicial interview has encouraged this judicial policy.

> We suggest that a child who agrees to give evidence should be restrained from testifying only where it is established on a preliminary motion or voir dire that the potential for psychological harm to the child is such that another method of eliciting the child's views must be found. If the child's views are not relevant, or the child is not competent to give evidence, the question of exclusion on policy grounds will not arise.

6. Recall that the Ontario Court of Appeal held in *Strobridge* v. *Strobridge* (1994), 4 R.F.L. (4th) 169 that a lawyer acting on behalf of a child in custody and access disputes cannot simply advise the court of the child's views and preferences unless the parties consent. The child's wishes, therefore, constitute evidence which must be proved in the normal way. The method preferred by most commentators continues to be through an assessment by an independent expert. See, e.g., Huddart and Ensminger, "Hearing the Voice of Children" (1992), 8 C.F.L.Q. 95, at 110-113.

7. The Special Joint Committee in its *For the Sake of the Children* recommended (at 23) that children "have the opportunity to be heard when parenting decisions affecting them are being made" and "have the opportunity to express their views to a skilled professional, whose duty it would be to make those views known to any judge, assessor or mediator making or facilitating a shared parenting determination".

(9) THE "FRIENDLY PARENT" PRINCIPLE

DOE v. DOE

(1990), 28 R.F.L. (3d) 356 (Ont. Dist. Ct.)

[The facts of this case are set out earlier in this chapter.]

CORBETT D.C.J.: — . . . *Risk of harm to child's relation with access parent*
I will next deal with the ground which formed the basis of the learned trial judge's decision, namely, where two parents seeking custody compare closely, having regard to the statutory "best interests" criteria, custody should be given to the parent more likely to support and promote the relationship with the other parent. The appellant submits the learned trial judge erred in awarding custody to the respondent solely on the basis of the expert testimony that the respondent would be better able to promote the appellant's relationship with the child than the reverse. The respondent submits it is in the child's best interest to live with the parent who is prepared to co-operate with respect to access where both parents can equally care for the child.

In considering this matter, the learned trial judge had regard to flexibility respecting access. Although the question of supporting the other parental relation may be considered separately from the question of access, how access has been provided is one area to consider in determining whether the other parental relation is being undermined or is in danger of being undermined. The issue has devastating consequences in that a capable, loving mother has been deprived of custody and a capable, loving father has sought custody solely as a result of conclusions respecting the ability of the mother to support the child's relation with her father. In what circumstances is custody in peril through failure to provide or unwillingness to provide access?

Since lack of co-operation respecting access tends to indicate lack of support of the other parental relation, I will review some of the evidence respecting access. Significantly, the learned trial judge does not discuss access in detail, merely making the general finding that Jane felt unable to be flexible and accommodating to changes requested by John. [Corbett D.C.J. concluded that Jane had been willing to comply with existing court orders but no more.]

In my opinion, provision of reasonable access and compliance with all court orders and relevant agreements is a sufficient standard which should not put custody in peril in the absence of evidence of a detrimental effect on the child or the child's relation with the access parent. The evidence and the findings respecting access fall short of any conduct or standard necessary to deprive a custodial parent of custody as a result of the problems respecting access. . . .

There being no findings respecting access, save respecting flexibility, I now turn to the evidence on the positive side, that is, that John is more likely to foster a relationship with the other parent.

I agree with counsel for the appellant, who submits that, on the whole of the evidence at trial, there was insufficient evidence to substantiate the testimony of Drs. Cooper and Sutherland that the appellant would fail to promote a healthy relationship between the respondent and the child. First and foremost, there is no evidence that Jane's attitude or feelings have in fact resulted in any impairment whatsoever of the successful relation between Cathy and her father. There is no evidence of any deleterious effects on Cathy and the evidence is overwhelming that the child was healthy both physically and emotionally and had attained excellent bonds with both her parents.

Second, there is no evidence or finding that the respondent was denigrated by the appellant or her family in the presence of the child. The evidence substantiated hostility by Jane against John, but there is no evidence substantiating any harmful effect on the child. Further, the evidence, if any, respecting the likelihood of its potential effect on the child is too speculative to deprive a parent of custody.

Third, the evidence shows Jane is capable of controlling and does control her feelings against John in relation to Cathy. Evidence of this control is seen in the careful preparation of Cathy to foster pleasant visits with John. An indication of the degree to which Jane is willing and able to control her resentment is evidenced by her dealing with the daily phone calls by John to his daughter from the age of three years. . . .

Dr. Cooper's opinion at trial was that Jane still maintained a strongly negative and suspicious opinion of John.

Neither this opinion nor Jane's negative feelings is sufficient to deny custody. Jane's feelings toward John must be related to the actual or likely impact on the child's relationship and on the child herself. No doubt many parents who separate have similar feelings and these may be maintained thereafter. The significant aspect is not the existence of hatred or hostile feelings, but the effects of these feelings in relation to the child.

In my opinion, the learned trial judge erred in law and acted on a wrong principle in depriving a fitting custodial parent of custody on the grounds that the other parent (at this time also custodial) is more likely to support the child's relation with both parents when no findings are made and no evidence is adduced that such failure exists and has resulted or is likely to result in undesirable effects on the child or on the child's relationship with either parent. The existence of antipathy and speculation as to its potential negative effects is not sufficient of itself to deprive a parent of custody. For this reason the appeal should be allowed and custody awarded to the mother. . . .

NOTES AND QUESTIONS

1. In *Fason* v. *Fason* (1991), 32 R.F.L. (3d) 121 (Ont. Gen. Div.), Mr. Fason still blamed his wife for the breakup of their marriage and he discussed this with the child. Granger J. concluded (at 127) that if the father received custody the child would "not be allowed to maintain a good relationship with his mother, which is absolutely essential". On the other hand, the judge believed that the mother would always "allow the emotional attachment between son and father to flourish". This was considered an important factor in favour of an award of custody to the mother.

In *Mooney* v. *Mooney* (1988), 15 R.F.L. (3d) 347 (P.E.I. C.A.), the appellate court upheld the trial judge's decision granting custody of three young children to the father even though the children had been in the mother's care for the two years since the separation. Carruthers C.J.P.E.I. stated (at 350-351):

There were many factors involved in this case which the trial judge obviously considered when he decided that the respondent was the parent best able to assure a consistent pattern of care for the children in the future. He clearly states in his judgment that a determinative factor in this case was the question as to which parent would most likely best facilitate future visitation by the non-custodial parent which becomes an important factor in cases where the parents are found to be relatively equal in regard to parental ability. It is also important to note that the trial judge is required by s. 16(10) of the Divorce Act to consider this factor. He obviously considered the custodial situation then in existence but came to the conclusion on the whole of the evidence that it was in the best interests of the children to grant custody to the respondent. I do not see how it can be said that he acted on some wrong principle so as to disturb his decision.

See also *Smith* v. *Smith* (1987), 7 R.F.L. (3d) 206 (N.S. Fam. Ct.); *Tremblay* v. *Tremblay* (1987), 10 R.F.L. (3d) 166 (Alta. Q.B.); *Stark* v. *Stark* (1988), 16 R.F.L. (3d) 257 (B.C. S.C.); *Moseley* v. *Moseley* (1989), 20 R.F.L. (3d) 301 (Alta. Prov. Ct.); *Rose* v. *Rose* (1989), 22 R.F.L. (3d) 72 (Alta. Q.B.); *Renaud* v. *Renaud* (1989), 22 R.F.L. (3d) 366 (Ont. Dist. Ct.) (reproduced earlier in this chapter); *Lapierre* v. *Lapierre* (1991), 34 R.F.L. (3d) 129 (Sask. Q.B.); *Evanoff* v. *Evanoff* (1991), 37 R.F.L. (3d) 393 (Sask. C.A.); *Kosokowsky* v. *Kosokowsky* (1992), 95 D.L.R. (4th) 309 (Ont. Gen. Div.); *Boland* v. *Boland* (1996), 24 R.F.L. (4th) 301 (Ont. Gen. Div.); and *Cavanagh* v. *Cavanagh* (1999), 47 R.F.L. (4th) 271 (N.S. C.A.).

In *Jarrett* v. *Jarrett* (1994), 10 R.F.L. (4th) 24 (Ont. Gen. Div.), Eberhard J. wrote (at 29):

I have considered, as a serious blemish in Ms Jarret's parenting record, her inability to cheerfully support access. It is both the law as set out in s. 16(10) of the Divorce Act and my considered and passionate belief that, except in the rarest and most extreme circumstances, the one thing that children of separating parents need more than any other single factor in order to emerge healthy and undamaged by the disintegration of their family is the opportunity to know that they are still loved by both parents. . . .

[Ms Jarrett] acts as though access is a favour that she may dole out depending on her plans and convenience and on her judgments as to [the father's] worthiness.

Notwithstanding "this very serious flaw" in the mother's ability to parent, the judge granted custody to the mother and permitted her to move the two boys to British Columbia.

2. In *Dupont* v. *Dupont* (1993), 47 R.F.L. (3d) 273 (B.C. S.C.) the court considered that the exaggerated criticism of the father's parenting while he had interim custody reflected poorly on the mother's character and the court in *Stefanyk* v. *Stefanyk* (1994), 1 R.F.L. (4th) 432 (N.S. S.C.) concluded that the mother's more positive description of the father's parenting ability indicated that she was more likely to foster contact between the father and the children.

3. Judges confronted with custodial parents who refuse to comply with access orders often indicate that if interference with access continues, they may reverse custody on the basis that it is in the best interests of the child to know and have contact with both parents. Generally, such threats ring hollow. Indeed, the interference with the relationship between the access parent and the child may cause the child to refuse to visit that parent and ultimately lead to a termination of access. See *Strobridge* v. *Strobridge* (1994), 4 R.F.L. (4th) 169 (Ont. C.A.). However, in *Tremblay* v. *Tremblay* (1987), 10 R.F.L. (3d) 166 (Alta. Q.B.), a custody order granting custody of two children to the mother was varied a year later because the mother adamantly refused to let the father see the children.

4. At the National Symposium on Women, Law and the Administration of Justice, June 10-12, 1991 in Vancouver, the Workshop on Family Law recommended repeal of s. 16(10) of the *Divorce Act*. Why would it make such a recommendation? For additional criticism of the provision, see Boyd, "W(h)ither Feminism? The Department of Justice Public Discussion Paper on Custody and Access" (1995), 12 Can. J. Fam. L. 331 and Cossman and Mytiuk, "Reforming Child Custody and Access Law in Canada: A Discussion Paper" (1998), 15 Can. J. Fam. L. 13, at 49-53. In its *For the Sake of the Children*, the Special Joint Committee reported (at 52): "Advocates for women, particularly those working with women who have experienced violence, argued against the friendly parent rule, saying that the presumption in favour of maximum contact could put women and children at risk." It, nonetheless, recommended (at 45) that the "willingness and ability of each of the parties to facilitate and encourage a close and continuing relationship between the child and the other parent" be listed as a factor in determining the best interests of a child.

4.   Joint Custody

RYAN "JOINT CUSTODY IN CANADA: TIME FOR A SECOND LOOK"
(1986), 49 R.F.L. (2d) 119 (Footnotes Omitted)

1:   THE LAW AND JOINT CUSTODY

1:1   *Historical context*

. . .[T]imes are changing. Today there are a number of significant social trends that should cause us to re-examine the traditional practice of awarding sole custody to mothers. The women's movement, for one, with its emphasis on equality of the sexes, has meant that more women are pursuing careers outside the home, while men are participating to a far greater extent in child rearing and household mainte- nance functions. As one writer puts it:

> The sole custody concept is a product of a world that no longer exists. It is based on the premise that mother is the nurturer, father is the breadwinner, and schools, church and extended family are there to offer support . . . Sixty per-cent of women with children now work. Fathers nurture. Parenting has become more complicated and the social supporting infrastructure is not what it was.

Moreover, child development research which, in the past, focused almost exclusively on the role of the mother, has recently emphasized the importance of fathers in the healthy development of children.

At the same time as fathers are participating more and gaining more recognition for their role, families are splitting up at an unprecedented rate. . . .

Given the above trends, it is not surprising that increasing numbers of fathers desire to remain involved with their children in a significant way following marriage breakdown and that many of them are seeking custody of their children. . . .

1:3   *Joint custody in Canada*

In contrast to the United States, no Canadian province has yet enacted legis- lation specifically making joint custody a preference in child custody arrangements or authorizing joint custody in the face of opposition by one or both parents. The law in this area appears to be governed by two cases of the Ontario Court of Appeal which were decided early in the debate over joint custody (1979), and which have since been followed elsewhere in Canada: see *Baker* v. *Baker* (1979), 23 O.R. (2d) 391, 8 R.F.L. (2d) 236, 95 D.L.R. (3d) 529 (C.A.), and *Kruger* v. *Kruger* (1979), 25 O.R. (2d) 673, 11 R.F.L. (2d) 52, 104 D.L.R. (3d) 481, 2 Fam. L. Rev. 197 (C.A.).

The *Baker* case was the first decision of a Canadian superior court on joint custody. In her trial judgment, dated 25th April 1978, reported at 3 R.F.L. (2d) 193 at 197, 1 Fam. L. Rev. 226, Boland J. wrote:

> Courts must be responsive to the winds of change. In today's society, the breakdown of the traditional family is increasingly common, and new ways of defining post-divorce family struc- tures are desperately needed. It is apparent that the traditional award of custody to the mother and access to the father is the cause of many of the problems and most of the tensions between parents and children and between the parents themselves. Our courts see many cases in which the father has been deprived of access. Gradually he loses interest or finds he cannot afford to continue his court battles, and as a result the child is deprived of the love, influence and financial support of its father. Joint custody would seem to be the ideal solution to present challenges and past experiences.

Unfortunately, even the strongest advocates of joint custody would probably agree that *Baker* was not an appropriate case for joint custody. Neither party in this bitter court battle requested or wanted joint custody; both had demonstrated an inability to cooperate in matters concerning the child. On the facts, then, it is not surprising that the Court of Appeal overturned the trial judgment. One writer, however, says that the appellate court went far beyond this to condemn joint custody as an alternative to the "traditional concept of custody and access" and to create a presumption in favour of sole custody in contested custody proceedings.

In its judgment, the Court of Appeal criticized the trial judge for not making any reference to the "legal literature" in her reference to "experts in the field of child study": see p. 244. In *Baker*, Boland J., however, may have been slightly ahead of her time. . . .[A]lthough there was considerable popular interest in joint custody at this time, there was little, if any, actual published social science research to substantiate her claims for this novel approach. Moreover, the appellate judgment suffers from the same deficiencies as the trial judgment. It makes reference to only one article . . . . Not stopping here, the court went even further, at p. 246, to adopt the value-laden and highly subjective words of a colleague in *McCahill* v. *Robertson* (1974), 17 R.F.L. 23 at 23-24 (Ont. H.C.), speaking on "divided custody":

> 'My judgment here is based on the very strong feeling that divided custody is inherently a bad thing. A child must know where its home is and to whom it must look for guidance and admonition and the person having custody and having that responsibility must have the opportunity to exercise it without any feeling by the infant that it can look elsewhere. It may be an unfortunate thing for the spouse who does not have custody that he or she does lose a great deal of the authority and indeed to some extent the love and affection of the child that might otherwise be gained, but this is one of the things which is inherent in separation and divorce. The parents cannot have it both ways.'

This was hardly a firm foundation upon which to limit joint custody "to the exceptional circumstances which are rarely, if ever, present in cases of disputed custody"! [p. 246].

. . . In *Kruger* v. *Kruger*, the [Ontario Court of Appeal] once again declined to award joint custody in the absence of the agreement of both parties. In this case, however, unlike *Baker*, the parents had cooperated in a de facto shared parenting arrangement prior to trial and the father had requested an order for joint custody in appealing an award of sole custody to the mother. A majority of the court held that the fact there was no "agreement" between the parties on the subject of joint custody was a major consideration in deciding whether to order it. The majority stated:

> The fact remains that in this case there is no agreement between the parties on the issue of joint custody. That fact, in my opinion, *makes all the difference* to the approach which should be taken by this court to the question whether it should now seek to impose an order for joint custody . . .(The italics are mine.)

In this case, lack of agreement seemed to be equated with the contesting of legal proceedings, from which the court inferred an unwillingness or inability of the parents to cooperate in child rearing. In fact, the only evidence of the wife's views on joint custody came indirectly through her counsel, on the appeal. When asked whether the wife would agree to or accept an order for joint custody, her counsel replied merely that his instructions were to support the trial judgment. From this, the court assumed at p. 79 that, "she is not agreeable to such an order and is not prepared to accept it of her own will".

Moreover, the court refused to assume that the two parties, who had been able to get along together as parents under the interim custody arrangement in effect before the trial, would continue to do so in future. The majority concluded at p. 82 that:

> . . . any court that is considering the making of an award of joint custody, should be guided by the following precepts: if the court has before it the right combination of thoughtful and mature parents who understand what is involved in such an arrangement and are willing to try it, the court should feel encouraged to go ahead with it; but if they are not evidently willing, the court should not seek to impose it on them, because it is then not likely to work, and because the price to be paid if it does not work is likely to be altogether too high to warrant taking the risk that is then present of trying it.

. . . Clearly, the majority did not wish to encourage joint custody as a judicial option, except on the consent of the parties — the very circumstances in which such an order would be unnecessary!

In a strong dissent, Wilson J.A. urges at p. 69 that:

> It is perhaps timely for courts in Canada to shed their 'healthy cynicism' and reflect in their orders a greater appreciation of the hurt inflicted upon a child by the severance of its relationship with one of its parents. While purporting to award custody on the basis of the child's best interests, our courts have tended to overlook that in some circumstances it may be in the child's best interests not to choose between the parents but to do everything possible to maintain the child's relationship with both parents.

In support of her opinion, she quotes the Law Reform Commission of Canada, in its Report on Family Law:

> The law should be made more flexible, making custody less an all-or-nothing proposition; a judicial determination that one parent will assume primary responsibility for raising and caring for a child should not necessarily exclude the other from the legal right to participate as a parent in many other significant areas of the child's life.

In her view,

> . . . that participation should only be terminated if the state of the husband and wife relationship is such as to make it necessary or desirable to do so. It certainly should not be done without due consideration being given to the full range of options open to the court.

Wilson J.A. then canvasses the various options open to the court, including joint custody, and expresses the opinion that "the appropriate option in any given case will be the one which best serves the needs of the child or children". Showing a keen awareness of the impact of divorce on all members of the family, she then goes on to say at p. 73:

> These developments in the approach of the courts to custody matters all reflect a new awareness that in the mind of a child authority and love are inter-related and that the transformation of a mother or father into a 'visitor' is a traumatic experience for a child frequently attended by feelings of rejection and guilt. And in many cases it is wholly unnecessary. Most mature adults, after the initial trauma has worn off, are able to overcome the hostility attendant on the dissolution of their marriages or at the very least are capable of subserving it to the interests of their children. This is particularly so now that the social stigma attending divorce has all but disappeared and men and women are picking themselves up and putting their lives together again. Indeed, the so-called 'friendly divorce' is one of the phenomena of our time. It is in this social milieu that more imaginative and, if I may say so, more humane custody orders find their place.

> And what if occasional resort has to be made to the courts when the parents cannot agree on a major matter affecting the child? Is this to be the determinative consideration? It seems to me to be a modest price to pay in order to preserve a child's confidence in the love of his parents and with it his own sense of security and self-esteem.

In the instant case, Wilson J.A. (as she then was) would have awarded joint (legal) custody to both parents with care and control of the children to the mother and liberal access to the father.

The decisions in *Baker* and *Kruger* did not sound the death knell for joint custody in Canada. Most likely, however, they slowed the acceptance of this custody option, particularly among the legal profession. As a result the full range of custody options envisaged by Wilson J.A. may not have been considered in all custody disputes and some Canadian children (and their families) may thereby have been deprived of an arrangement which would best serve their short- and long-term interests.

[By the mid-nineties about one-quarter of Canadian divorces involving children resulted in some form of joint custody, usually joint legal custody with the child residing primarily with the mother. See Statistics Canada, *Divorces 1996 and 1997* (Ottawa, 1999). Most of these arrangements result from agreements between the parents, but the courts have reconsidered their approach also. The Ontario Court of Appeal endorsed decisions of trial judges imposing joint custody without the consent of both parents in *Daoust* c. *Leboeuf* (1998), 35 R.F.L. (4th) 143 and *Walsh* v. *Walsh* (1998), 39 R.F.L. (4th) 416 (Ont. C.A.), where there was evidence the parents could co-operate in raising the children.]

LEONOFF,* "JOINT CUSTODY AND BEYOND"

(1995), 29 The Law Society Gazette 29

(Edited footnotes appear at the end of the excerpt.)

Introduction

It was during the late 1970's, a few years after I had begun to practice clinical psychology, that I first encountered the concept of shared legal custody and joint care of children as an option in divorce. I gravitated to the notion as I had myself suspected that sole custody with its legacy of infrequent visitation led in many cases to stressful deprivation from the non-custodial parent (NCP) which, in turn, was unhealthy for the welfare of children. This conclusion was soundly replicated by Wallerstein and Kelly in their 1980 ground breaking study described in the book "Surviving the Breakup."[1] The children who were best off were those who had frequent, uncomplicated contact with the NCP. Sole custody, as it was practiced, appeared to inadequately serve the children whose welfare it was intended to protect.

Although the Wallerstein study had not intended to look at custody issues, it indirectly supported the thesis that co-parental access may well be a positive influence for children following divorce. Sole custody, it seemed in this light, imposed disenfranchising barriers between one parent and the children. The meager access most often awarded tended to alienate fathers, in particular, whose involvement in their offspring often diminished following separation. Sole custody arrangements did not encourage a strong bond between the NCP and the child while saddling the custodial mother with a surfeit of duties and unending responsibilities.

Defenders of joint custody stated that it would reduce the trauma and alienation of divorce, hopefully attenuating the severe adverse consequences that had been observed in children and adults who had undergone the divorce experience. Hidden in the movement that soon developed in support of joint custody was an implicit belief in the inherent worth of the nuclear family and the desirability of approximating this same structure in a post-divorce framework.

Supporters wrote elegantly of its many advantages and predicted that it would arise as the model of choice. Joint custodial care acknowledged the mutuality of parenting and often led to a more balanced distribution of the work load. The children might be spared the loyalty struggles of the past as neither parent could automatically claim a distinct advantage in terms of influence or authority. The sharing of custodial power would lead to a kinder, more humane divorce with quicker, healthier resolutions for children as well as parents. The extended families on both sides would more likely find a place in such an arrangement and, coupled with the continuing proof of their parents' love and commitment, would feel less abandoned and rejected.

The rise of joint custody, then, was at the heart of public and private anguish concerning the pernicious impact of divorce on children and the subsequent societal pay out over many years. The tendency for the NCP, usually the father, to be marginalized while the custodial parent, mainly the mother, seemed fated to years of unremitting burden, led many advocates to argue that families should continue in their original form even if marriages fail. Dismal statistics outlining the failure of 'bare bones' sole custody, further strengthened the joint custody argument. NCPs often withdrew following divorce or visited irregularly and this coupled with substantial incidence of non-payment of support added fuel to the momentum for change.

Less rigid assumptions about role and gender, especially among the more educated classes, also inspired shifts in thinking about how the post-divorce family should be structured. Logically, it made perfect sense to envision a shared distribution of labour with each parent shouldering a sizable part of the overall burden. This support for joint parenting held firm despite fears from some quarters that it could be used as a ploy by men to reduce child support and to exercise control over women.

Gradually, a consensus formed, that involved fathers were more likely to pay support and to shoulder child care responsibilities and that such involvement was stimulated by joint arrangements. From a child rearing perspective, it was noted that children are destined by virtue of their developmental needs to love both parents and to seek equal contact with them. Overall, then, the time seemed ripe to re-think the whole issue of custody and access in the light of these findings and in view of changes in how society viewed the obligation to parent.

Joint Custody in Perspective

With its praises being sung from many quarters, some of us tended to view joint custody as the "Prozac" of divorce and, perhaps, we asked too much of any custody option to offset the often severe familial consequences of separation and divorce. We hoped that warring parents, whose disputes expressed the enormity of the rupture triggered by divorce, would adapt more quickly if there was the mutual endorsement and empowerment intrinsic to joint custody awards.

There is a body of research that in varying degrees and circumstances has supported the virtues of joint custody when applied to families and individuals who can function within its limits and exploit it for its opportunities. Most often, these represent parents who have voluntarily chosen shared parenting rather than having it imposed on them by statute or judicial decree. When successful, mothers and fathers in joint custody relationships with their ex-spouses tend to be more satisfied than their peers in sole custody arrangements.[6]

Yet, Steinman in a respected study of cases in which joint custody was assigned by the court, noted that even with children who have been living in joint custodial arrangements for a considerable part of their childhood, one-third were unhappy with the regimen and revealed signs of maladjustment.[7] . . . Before blaming this one-third failure rate on this form of care and control, however, we should probably accept that the effects of divorce can often be far-reaching and might in fact resist the efforts of any post-divorce custody option to fully offset them. The shattering of family bonds even in so called bad marriages can have enduring negative effects that last for years. Wallerstein and Kelly were evidently surprised in their longitudinal study of divorce families to discover that even five years after separation, many families floundered under the high stress effects of divorce.[10] . . .

Taking a realistic perspective, though, the outright condemnation of sole custody was perhaps premature as was the over-zealous adoption of joint custody as a means of maintaining the effective relevance of two parents in the lives of their offspring. In the light of more recent findings, however, the consensus remains that for highly motivated parents who voluntarily choose joint legal custody with varying degrees of sharing and who meet certain fundamental personal criteria, that joint custody can be a wise and effective option. This is not to say that joint custody in its various forms is well received by all children but, then, perhaps this has more to do with children's sentiments regarding divorce in general as compared to specific attitudes to joint custody itself. Parents who gravitate to joint custody tend to be those people who, despite conflict, remain willing and able to communicate as regards the children even when this communication is strained by the severe disappointments they may endure from each other.

When custody can be considered as one variable along side other important predictors of post-divorce outcome, then it can be approached more rationally with better results for families who require assessment and court intervention. Other factors beside custody which are also relevant to predicting outcome include: degree of conflict and inter parental strife, the relationship of the children to each parent, the emotional adjustment and well being of the custodial parent(s), child rearing practices, gender of the children and, finally, remarriage.[11]

The initial challenge is to predict when joint custody will work and when it will not. The second is to be pragmatic about what any custody option can offer and not to restrict measures to 'soft signs' such as happiness or voiced satisfaction as the only index of success. Discontent may be endemic to all kinds of post-separation alternatives without being necessarily harmful or inadequate. It seems evident, though, that no single care and control option is generalizable to all families. Parenting formulas need to be tailor made to suit the individual characteristics of the family in question. At best, a well thought out custody and access formula will allow for a faster recovery from the turmoil of divorce, protect against re-litigation and incessant conflict, and permit the relatively smooth regrouping of families. It must be added, though, that ill will, mistrust exacerbated by legal conflict and personality limitations may restrict the capacity of some families to adjust to any post-separation regimen no matter how reasonable.

If wrongly applied, joint custody can amount to no custody at all. It can fuel inter parental conflict and significantly prolong the adjustment process or stymie it. At the same time, joint custody can be successfully implemented by parents who dislike each other and who may not easily be on relating terms. They will, however, converse when necessary concerning their children and inherently protect the other's parental space while valuing their own. It is not so simple, then, to say that joint custody is only for those parents whose communication and cooperation is optimal for this may instill an ideal that is beyond the grasp of any parental couple who deem it necessary to separate.

Perhaps the major positive side effect of the joint custody movement in family law and the behavioral sciences has been the gradual clarification and amplification of the role of the NCP. When I first offered to provide family assessments for custody, for example, I can recall incidents when the NCP would be barred from obtaining information [from] schools, and doctors. Now, this is provided by law and is a standard provision. Prior to this evolution, as well, the NCP was seen in essentially non-parental terms and their role was depicted as that of a visitor as compared to a parent. Other innovations include: (1) more extensive visitation schedules such as two weekends out of three or extended weekend visits, (2) a growing tendency even in sole custody orders to share holiday periods and special days rather than restricting the NCP to two summer weeks in July or August, (3) providing outlets to the NCP for arbitration in the case of a major disagreement.

Hence, the role and contribution of the NCP has enlarged within a sole custody framework without [there] being necessarily a reciprocal increase in awards of joint custody. I suspect that joint custody will be an option to families who find their own way to it but that it will never be, nor should it be, an option of choice for parents who litigate to determine custody. When cases are litigated and assessments offered, the chances that these same people are suitable for some type of shared custodial arrangement is, in my experience, low.

With increases in the non-custodial side of the equation, though, have come more opportunities for conflict. This harkens to an important book written in 1979 by psychologist/lawyer, Joseph Goldstein and psychoanalysts Albert Solnit and the late Anna Freud which concluded that attachment to one parent had to be decisive in order to meet the child's inherent need for security and continuity of care.[13] The three argued that frequent visitation when it created acrimony and opportunities for more conflict was of little use to a child who could only feel terribly exposed in the crossfire between the parents. The danger, as they saw it, was that the child could become placed in the middle of a battle and fail to develop a sufficient tie to either parent. The authors did not oppose visitation in principle but suggested that control of the frequency be placed in the hands of the custodial parent. . . .

Here, we confront the phenomenon whereby a change in one dimension has implications for another. The tendency for there to be more access even in sole custody awards is associated with increased opportunities for conflict between the divorced parents. This finding is especially relevant to litigated cases where non-custodial status is involuntarily imposed on a person described as ''the loser.'' This is also where one's sense of fair play often takes a beating. If a custodial parent takes issue with the worth of the NCP, then it may be adding stress to the children to impose frequent access in a situation where it is clearly unwelcome, at least from the viewpoint of the primary parent. . . .

These dilemmas are always multi-factorial and raise complicated practical and legal issues. Would a NCP or his lawyer readily accept a recommendation that he not see the child frequently because the custodian is too harshly opposed to their input? Lawyers as well as clients most often measure their success in litigation in terms of the extent to which they are accorded involvement. Ironically, this opposes what Goldstein, Freud and Solnit attest to be central to the best interest principle.[13] Solutions to such paradoxes, as we can see, remain elusive. The answer seems less to solve them than to be aware of the problems they raise in the overall process.

The Choice of Joint Custody

My experience in working with joint custody as an option in divorce is that it works well when one motive in particular dictates its choice — a deep underlying commitment to children and especially the nurturing of children. Those successful joint custody families have parents who uphold co-parenting as a key value. They will intrinsically and automatically show a respect for the worth and contribution of the other parent even if they disagree with certain aspects of their approach or personality. The right of each parent to parent in their allotted time will never be questioned no matter how hurt or upset they are with each other. Typically, examination of the family history will reveal close, genuine relationships to children before and after the separation.

We can conceive of a joint custody continuum beginning with joint legal custody with standard access provisions and ending with joint physical custody including 50/50 sharing. In the latter case, the utmost in co-parenting, parents should reveal the above characteristics to a maximum degree. They should gravitate to shared parenting for the right reason and they should reveal a conspicuous recognition of the other's parental value no matter what the specific fate of their own personal relationship. Communication will be a usual occurrence as compared to being just possible and the parents will reveal some history of problem solving even after the separation occurred.

At the entry level of the joint custody scale, parents should reveal some core aspects of the above but may have certain discordant factors such as lifestyle differences, financial limitations, or parenting conflicts that would not permit a more elaborate shared arrangement. They should still be able to communicate and problem solve when necessary and it should be a choice of the parents or a recommendation that is readily acceptable to both parties. . . .

As a rule of thumb, I would add that joint custody should always be a specific option in the parents' mind even if they are guided by others towards adopting it. It should not be a choice born of mediation to stave off the worst aspects of divorce or used as a bargaining chip to insure cooperation in settling other issues. We must also guard against promoting joint custody as a palliative against the pain of divorce or the injury of being the NCP. These represent erroneous reasons for selecting this option and they will likely put the family at greater risk of difficulties in the future.

Perhaps it may be helpful, at this juncture, to outline the major contra-indications to any form of shared care and control. The presence of any one of these should eliminate the prospect of recommending such an option:

1. When one of the parents, usually the one most likely designated as the primary caretaker, resists or rejects it out of hand;
2. When one or both of the ex-spouses employ to a major degree a psychology of blame; . . .
3. When the child rearing premises of both parents are so discordant that the children are unlikely to be able to integrate them; . . .
4. When one or both parents exhibit a sense of ownership over the children and negate the importance of the other parent; . . .
5. When parents tend to argue through their children and use child rearing as a field of combat; . . .
6. When neither adult is adequate enough as a parent to assume the custodial role on their own; . . .
7. When there is evidence of mental illness, personality disorder or severe addiction in one or both parents;

8. When there is hotly contested litigation over custody, shared parenting is most often not an option. Here, I am not referring to those unresolved cases where the parents, although reasonable, cannot determine what is truly best for their children. These are people who are aware of the complex interactions of their family and are prepared to work matters out with the assistance of a family assessment. When disputes assume an irrational and escalating bent, however, and allegations and attacks on links predominate, joint custody, in any form, will not likely work.

Does Joint Custody Work?

. . .Where parents are both child focused and espouse nurturing as a major parenting goal, and where there is a willingness to adapt, coordinate and communicate in the service of that goal, plus a core of healthy self esteem and flexibility in the parents, then joint custody may well be the preferred option. This is especially true when there is a mutual willingness to implement such a strategy or if they can be easily swayed to consider such an option. When criteria are applied accurately and rationally in generating the proposal for joint parenting, then it can and does work well. The problem seems to me that it is often assigned indiscriminately to parents who cannot make use of it, or worse, function more poorly as parents because of it.

Despite the ideal that joint custody parents must acknowledge the value to the child of the continuing presence of the other parent, this may receive lip service and may not be the primary reason joint custody is adopted. It seems to be a more likely occurrence, for example, in well off families where financial settlements may be weighed against the right of the wealthier parent to be fully recognized as a joint custodian. In other situations, an ex-spouse may prove so fanatic in their sense of ownership and narcissistic identification with their children that they may extract a joint custody arrangement from the other parent in order to be appeased.

Besides these reasons for executing joint custody agreements, others also come to mind: (1) a way of resolving work place and scheduling demand such as faced by people on shift work; (2) a way to deny the divorce and a defence against real separation with its threat of depression and loss; (3) a way for one parent to soften the blow to the other when it is a unilateral choice unwelcome by the other person; (4) a psychological collusion between two parents who are both ambivalent about the demands imposed by parenting and who seek to halve the commitment.

When successful, joint custody agreements tend to be applauded differently by men and women. Women, in general, celebrate the increased freedom the arrangement gives and feel liberated from the role of primary care giver. Men, on the other hand, will often speak of the close relationships with children that they would not have had otherwise. In this sense, joint custody reverses the usual gender distinction where men may be uncomfortable with intimacy while women seek more. Here, women can experience more freedom and autonomy from domestic demands while men can enjoy the fruits of closer bonding with their children than they may have had before the marriage ended.

. . .There is no empirical support for imposing joint custody by statute or judicial ruling when it is not a goal of the parents themselves.

The Vista of Custody and Access

It may come as a surprise to lawyers who routinely litigate family matters and pursue access and custodial rights, that patterns of care and control may not be as important to the outcome for children of divorce as they may think. Instead, the emotional status of the parents, their capacity for empathy and support, and the quality of the parent-child relationships are the most vital factors in determining outcome independent of custodial pattern. Parents who can support and focus on their children's needs are better able to protect their children from the adverse consequences of divorce even in the context of parental hostility and dispute. . . .

Here we confront the reality that the effectiveness of the family law system in protecting children of divorce cannot exceed the aptitudes and personal resources of the clientele. Although we can contest which parent should perform what role, we cannot fully shield children from the real impact of their parents. We can, I believe, add or reduce stress and tension, but we have much less control over outcome than do the parents themselves. . . .

Beyond Custody

. . . Some legal practitioners will maintain that custody itself is confounding and that parenting plans devised through mediated settlements will effect the same end.[20] Although I can agree in theory with such sentiments, I do not expect that custody determinations will disappear from the judicial landscape. In part, this is due to the nature of divorce itself which for the majority of people creates serious handicaps in trust and communication that are most acute during the time of break up but that can last for many years. Secondly, there is always a concern that failure to conclude these matters in their entirety will lead more people to return to the courts for a second round.

I suspect that one of the problems hampering resolution in divorce disputes is that non-custodial status is often perceived as a non-position defined in the negative as the term implies. Hence, as a NCP, one "visits" as compared to "parents." Such a threat of negation is often perceived as a major injury for the NCP especially because in the eyes of the children one is no less an authoritative parent than the custodian. Here we may have confused matters by not clarifying the relative roles and responsibilities that will befall both parents even within a sole custody model. I suspect that this may well impel many fathers, for instance, to pursue joint custody for fear of being dispatched to a non-status position. One might also argue that this inherent injustice towards the non-residential parent helped to spur the joint custody movement as much as it being based on social and psychological principles. We are reminded that although joint legal and physical custody is a useful option for mature and reasonable people, it is not an effective antidote for the ills of sole custody.

Many parents, it seems badly misunderstand the notion of custody and too many interpret it as an oligarchic licence to rule. Such parents perceive their position in terms of rights or privileges as in the right to make all decisions on one's own or the right to alter access or change its terms. Although the custodian is indeed ultimately accountable for the children's welfare, the NCP also bears serious responsibility for the well being of the children. Although the balance of authority rests with the custodian, the distribution of responsibility should always be more balanced. I believe that it would be clearer, in this regard, to identify the two parents as primary and secondary custodians as compared to custodian and NCP. Although one could argue that such a distinction might obscure the differential necessary in establishing control of a child after divorce, one could also assert that it is the equation of non-custodial with non-parent that is behind much of the tensions in these agreements.

The following represents the dichotomy of rights versus responsibilities in custodial, non-custodial and joint custody conditions. Below is a description of each position in terms of this dichotomy. The intent would be to communicate to divorcing parents what responsibilities they must bear as compared only to specifying their custodial rights or lack of them.

	custodial	non-custodial	joint custodial
rights	A	B	C
responsibility	D	E	F

A.   Rights/Custodial Parent
— the right to be the final authority and guardian as to decisions concerning the children's welfare;
— the right to plan and coordinate the activites of the children;
— the right to reside with the children for the majority of time as set out in the separation agreement.

B.   Rights/Non-Custodial Parent
— the right to be consulted by the custodial parent regarding major decisions concerning the children's health, education and welfare;
— the right to be supplied all relevant information and feedback concerning the children which is of natural interest;
— the right to provide care and control of the children for the duration of the access visit.

C.   Rights/Joint Custodial Parents
— the right to exercise care and control of the children during the time period in which the children reside with that parent;
— the right to contribute to the important decisions regarding health, education and welfare that are far reaching in their impact on the children;
— the right to be accorded equal respect and value as a parent and to have this sentiment communicated to the children.

D.   Responsibilities/Custodial Parent
— the responsibility of facilitating access and promoting the children's relationship to the non-custodial parent;
— the responsibility to provide the best possible environment for the children;
— the responsibility to consult and receive input on decisions of importance to the welfare of the children;
— the responsibility to coordinate and implement the health, educational and welfare needs of the children;
— the responsibility to appreciate the frustrations born by the non-custodial parent who must accept a lesser role than that played in a normal family setting.

E.   Responsibilities/Non-Custodial Parent
— the responsibility of sustaining a meaningful and facilitating relationship with children during the limits of the access and telephone schedule specified in the separation agreement;
— the responsibility to contribute to the welfare of the children through support payments;

— the responsibility to contribute to the lives of the children by taking part in decision making and by demonstrating interest, commitment and concern;
— the responsibility to respect the custodial parent's ultimate answerability for decisions made on behalf of the children and to support this parent in that obligation.

F.   Responsibilities/Joint Custodial Parent
— the responsibility to communicate and cooperate in the raising of the children in conjunction with the other parent;
— the responsibility to affirm and support the equal value and authority of the other parent in the eyes of the children;
— the responsibility to coordinate and cooperate in the formation of plans and schedules concerning the children;
— the responsibility to contribute financially to the welfare of the children on the basis of the formula established in the separation agreement.

. . .

Conclusion

. . . The descriptive research on divorce does stress how difficult an occurrence divorce is for children and their parents. Children can adapt and accommodate to its stresses, especially if they have understanding and supportive parents. Empathic parents can make a success of any custody and model where as rigid, projecting or blaming parents will often fail their children no matter what custody arrangement is in place. In those cases where negative factors predominate, the challenge becomes one of damage control as compared to the promotion of well being. A primary conclusion, then, is that custody is important but is less pervasive an influence on post-divorce adjustment than the parents themselves in their close encounters with their children.

As to joint custody, I remain faithful to its premises but realistic about its application. It has had a significant impact on custody decisions and no one, neither lawyer nor mental health professional, has not been influenced by its bold challenge to separate the roles of spouse and parent and to forge new alliances. Joint custody in the right parental hands can be a useful model for providing care to children after divorce. It is not the panacea for divorce, however, and should remain an option for parents who can meet specific criteria. Clinical experience as well as the research literature does not support the blanket imposition of joint custody when it is not truly indicated. On the other hand, it [should] not be blamed for every mishap or moment of bewilderment that might befall a child in a joint parenting situation. Disruption and strain is endemic to divorce for children, especially in early stages, and to blame joint custody, *per se*, is to pursue a false ideal of a painless divorce. It also asks joint custody to be measured by a different standard than its counterpart in sole custody arrangements.

Perhaps the major benefit of the joint custody movement has been the impact on how sole custody is conceptualized and implemented. The willingness to award the child to the "winner" at the expense of the NCP has given way to a more sensitive and sophisticated assessment of the relative capacities both parents possess and what access schedule would best if their potentials. . . .

*Arthur Leonoff, Ph.D., C. Psych. is a psychologist and psychoanalyst in private practice in Ottawa. This paper was prepared for presentation at the Family Law Institute held jointly by the Carleton County Law Association and the University of Ottawa.

1. Wallerstein J.S. and Kelly, J.B., 1980. Surviving the Breakup: How Children and Parents Cope with Divorce, New York: Basic Books.

6. Kelly, Joan B., 1993. "Current research on children's postdivorce adjustment: no simple answers," Family and Conciliation Court Reviews, 31: 29-49.

7. Steinman, Susan, 1984. "Joint custody, What we know, What we have yet to learn, and the judicial and legislative implications," in Jay Folberg (ed.), 1984, Joint Custody and Shared Parenting, Washington D.C. Bureau of National Affairs and Association of Family and Conciliation Courts.

10. Kelly, Joan B., 1988. Longer term adjustment in children of divorce: converging findings and implications for practice, Journal of Family Psychology, 2: 119-140.

11. Lowery, C.R. and Settle, S.A., 1985. Effects of divorce on children: differential impact of custody and visitation patterns, Family Relations Journal of Applied Family and Child Studies, 34: 455-463.

13. Goldstein, J., Freud, A., and Solnit, A., 1979. Beyond the Best Interests of the Child, New York: The Free Press.

20. Payne, Julian D. and Edwards, Brenda, 1991. Cooperative parenting after divorce: a Canadian legal perspective, in Jay Folberg, Joint Custody and Shared Parenting (second edition), New York: Guildford Press, 11-15.

SINGER AND REYNOLDS, "A DISSENT ON JOINT CUSTODY"

(1988), 47 Maryland Law Rev. 497 (Footnotes Omitted)

. . .We have serious reservations about joint custody, particularly if it is court-imposed. . . .

None of the arguments advanced by proponents of court-imposed or presumptive joint custody is persuasive. First, proponents of court-imposed joint custody use the term "joint custody" to cover several quite different types of custody arrangements. Most important, they fail to distinguish joint *physical* custody from joint *legal* custody, in which the child resides primarily (or exclusively) with one parent — usually the mother — while the nonresidential father retains joint decision-making authority over the child's upbringing. Most "joint custody" arrangements — and virtually all court-imposed joint custody decrees — fall into the latter category. This latter category closely resembles the traditional maternal-custody-with-liberal-paternal-visitation arrangement with one essential difference: it accords the nonresidential father almost all of the rights but few of the responsibilities that raising a child entails.

Second, joint custody proponents make an unjustified leap from the common sense proposition that children do better after divorce if they maintain frequent contact with both parents to the startling conclusion that joint custody is the only way to ensure such contact. Neither logic nor data support this leap.

Third, virtually all of the studies relied upon by joint custody proponents involve voluntary rather than court-imposed joint custody arrangements; the limited success of voluntary arrangements simply does not support the imposition of joint custody on parents who oppose it. Moreover, the studies indicate that even voluntary joint custody arrangements produce significant risks for children, and create serious problems for both divorced parents and the judicial system.

The possibility of court-imposed joint custody also introduces significant distortions into the judicial process. Awarding joint custody, particularly joint legal custody, affords judges an easy and fair-sounding "fix" for resolving difficult custody disputes. It creates the illusion of equality and Solomonic wisdom and improperly allows a judge to avoid making a difficult — but often necessary — choice between two seemingly fit parents.

Finally, proponents of joint custody presumptions fail to consider the detrimental effect of their proposals on the already lopsided process of divorce bargaining. Proponents ignore what studies increasingly confirm: divorcing husbands routinely and successfully use the threat of a custody fight to reduce or eliminate alimony and child support obligations. The success of such "custody blackmail" has been identified as a major cause of the impoverishment of divorced women and their children.
. . .

The effect of a joint custody preference on divorce negotiation is particularly pernicious when that preference is coupled with a "friendly parent" provision, such as the one found in the proposed Maryland joint custody bill. A friendly parent provision directs the court, in awarding sole custody as an alternative to joint custody, to consider which parent is more likely to allow the children "frequent and continuing contact with the non-custodial parent." When only one parent seeks joint custody, the court, pursuant to the "friendly parent" provision, is likely to favor that parent in a sole custody award. This reality further increases the risks of opposing joint custody; not only may the court impose such an arrangement over the opposing parent's objection, but the mere fact of opposition is likely to diminish her chances of receiving sole custody. An extraordinary situation is created. A parent who does not believe that joint custody would be in her child's best interests is put in the difficult negotiating position of either "accepting" her spouse's request for joint custody or risking the loss of custody altogether in a contested trial.

IV. JOINT CUSTODY: A SUMMARY

No doubt joint custody can work well. Motivated, caring, and wealthy parents can manage a true sharing of the children. That sharing, unaccompanied by strife, may even benefit the children. But those parents do not need a judicial order to achieve joint custody; such arrangements can be accommodated easily under the existing umbrella of sole custody *cum* liberal visitation rights.

But joint custody, for the overwhelming majority of families, is a snare and a delusion. It is wrong to think that joint custody can work without committed parents, that it is likely to be in the best interests of the child, or that it will likely result in true sharing of parenting. Rather, joint custody is all too likely to be another millstone around the neck of the real custodial parent, who will find she has to share rights (but not responsibilities) with a recalcitrant former spouse, yet who is likely to find lessened support payments the real payoff to her of the arrangement. The sincerity of many joint custody advocates cannot conceal the reality that joint custody creates many harmful effects, and that a court order cannot overcome the difficult problems presented by a disintegrating family. Presumptive joint custody is an idea whose time has come and gone. [The authors go on to endorse the "primary caretaker preference" discussed earlier in this chapter.]

NOTES AND QUESTIONS

1. The *Divorce Act* explicitly states that the court may grant "custody . . . to any one or more persons" (s. 16(4)). It also stipulates in s. 16(10) that "the court shall give effect to the principle that a child of the marriage should have as much contact with each spouse as is consistent with the best interest

of the child''. See also s. 28 of the *CLRA*, which specifies that the court ''may grant the custody of . . . the child to one or more persons''. In *Catholic Children's Aid Society of Metropolitan Toronto (Municipality)* v. *H. (K.)* (1987), 6 R.F.L. (3d) 1 (Ont. Fam. Ct.) it was held that this provision did not create a presumption in favour of joint custody but merely authorized joint custody orders. See also *MacDonald* v. *MacDonald* (1998), 36 R.F.L. (4th) 257 (Nfld. C.A.), dealing with the Newfoundland legislation. Should there be an express statutory provision stating that the court should order joint custody to both parents, unless the best interests of the child dictate otherwise? Although many witnesses before the Special Joint Committee proposed a presumption in favour of joint custody, the committee ultimately decided in *For the Sake of the Children* (at 42) that presumptions favouring any particular form of parenting arrangement could obscure the differences between families. It feared that such a presumption might result in the imposition of such arrangements in some families where they were clearly inappropriate such as ''those with a history of domestic violence or of very disparate parenting roles''.

2. The term ''joint custody'' is used to describe a variety of arrangements. It is sometimes used to encompass ''split custody'' orders whereby one parent is granted ''care and control'' of the child while the other retains the right to make all of the decisions having a major impact on the child's life and development. See *Huber* v. *Huber* (1975), 18 R.F.L. 378 (Sask. Q.B.) and *Donald* v. *Donald* (1980), 3 Sask. R. 202 (Q.B.). Used in its broadest sense it may also include ''alternating custody'' whereby one parent is granted sole custody for a specific period of time and the other has sole custody during another period. However, the term ''joint custody'' is most frequently reserved to describe a situation where both parents have joint legal responsibility for the child's upbringing at all times. Even this arrangement can take a variety of forms. The child may reside with one parent almost all the time or there may be alternating, equal periods of residence.

3. Those child psychologists who favour joint custody clearly envisage frequent, meaningful contact between the child and both parents. An arrangement whereby the child resides with one parent and only visits the other on alternate week-ends is unlikely to provide such contact even if labeled ''joint custody'' because both parents continue to have joint legal responsibility for the child's upbringing. Moreover, such an arrangement ''is all too likely to saddle the mother [who is usually granted care and control] with the day-to-day worries of childcare and give the father psychological power and control'': *Globe and Mail*, ''No Joy in Joint Custody'' (June 28, 1985). See also Bailey, ''Unpacking the 'Rational Alternative': A Critical Review of Family Mediation'' (1989), 8 Can. J. Fam. L. 61; Holmes, ''Imposed Joint Legal Custody: Children's Interests or Parental Rights?'' (1987), 45 U.T. Fac. L. Rev. 300; and Delorey, ''Joint Legal Custody: A Reversion to Patriarchal Power'' (1989), 3 C.J.W.L. 33.

4. In ''Shared Parenting in Canada: Questions, Answers and Implications'' (1986-87), 1 C.F.L.Q. 79, Irving and Benjamin report on their empirical study of 201 shared parenting arrangements and strongly endorse the concept. They conclude (at 98):

> [C]hild custody statutes should rest on a presumption of shared parenting. By comparison with sole custody, shared parenting promotes joint co-parental involvement and decision-making as well as fiscal responsibility, and encourages maximum contact between child(ren) and both parents as a function of their respective circumstances. The present study indicates that this need not be a 50/50 split, either in time or in money, to be satisfying for all parties to the arrangement.

Compare Kurtz and Derevensk, ''Child Custody and Public Policy — A Contemporary Debate Revisited'' (1994), 11 C.F.L.Q. 57, where the authors review the literature and conclude that further study is required before a presumption in favour of joint custody is adopted.

5. The *Kruger* case discussed by Ryan should be contrasted with *Parsons* v. *Parsons* (1985), 48 R.F.L. (2d) 83, 55 Nfld. & P.E.I.R. 226 (Nfld. T.D.). In the latter case the parents agreed to joint custody in a separation agreement. The children alternated residence between the mother's home and father's home. Three years later, each parent sought sole custody. Although there had been some problems between the parents after separation, the children expressed the view that the arrangement should continue. The court made a joint custody order despite the expressed reservations of the parents. See also *Faunt* v. *Faunt* (1988), 12 R.F.L. (3d) 331 (Alta. C.A.); *Heyman* v. *Heyman* (1990), 24 R.F.L. (3d) 402 (B.C. S.C.); *Woodington* v. *Woodington* (1994), 154 N.B.R. (2d) 117 (Q.B.); *Hussein* v. *Hussein* (1994), 3 R.F.L. (4th) 375 (N.B. Q.B.); *Taker* v. *Taker* (1997), 27 R.F.L. (4th) 86 (B.C. S.C.); *Simon* v.

Simon (1997), 29 R.F.L. (4th) 141 (B.C. S.C.); and *Tacit* v. *Drost* (1998), 43 R.F.L. (4th) 242 (Ont. Gen. Div.) for other cases where existing shared parenting arrangements were continued over the objection of one parent. Of course, if such arrangements are clearly not working, it will be in the best interests of the child to award sole custody to one parent: *Gorham* v. *Gorham* (1994), 3 R.F.L. (4th) 88 (N.S. C.A.); *Lucken* v. *Hopkins* (1994), 8 R.F.L. (4th) 226 (B.C. C.A.); and *Ducas* v. *Varkony* (1995), 16 R.F.L. (4th) 91 (Man. Q.B.).

6. In *Abbott* v. *Taylor*, 2 R.F.L. (3d) 163, [1986] 4 W.W.R. 751 (Man. C.A.) Twaddle J.A., for the majority, stated (at 170-171):

> No doubt a court should be guided by the precept that such an arrangement [joint custody] should be tried only when both parents are thoughtful and mature and understand what is involved in it and are willing to try it, as was stated by Thorson J.A. . . . in *Kruger*, but I regard this statement as a matter of common sense rather than of legal principle. I would add, also as a matter of common sense, that the mere expression by one or both parents of an unwillingness to share custody should not preclude an order of joint custody if the court considers such unwillingness to be the manifestation of temporary personal hostility engendered by the trauma of a recent separation. To say otherwise would encourage one parent to avoid the participation of the other in deciding questions as to their child's future by a mere statement that he or she was unwilling to share the responsibility.

7. After reviewing a number of cases where joint custody was ordered over the objection of one parent, Bielby J. concluded in *Colwell* v. *Colwell* (1992), 38 R.F.L. (3d) 345, at 353 (Alta. Q.B.) that "this should be done only where it is in the best interests of the child, i.e., only where the parents have displayed an ability to co-operate and communicate over child-rearing decisions, notwithstanding personal differences, and where each has maintained an ongoing and meaningful relationship with the children over the period of separation."

8. Some judges clearly begin with a presumption in favour of joint custody. For example, in *Alfoldi* v. *Bard* (1989), 20 R.F.L. (3d) 290 (Ont. Dist. Ct.), Salhany D.C.J. stated (at 294): "It is only where the evidence reveals that one of the parties is not a suitable custodial parent or the circumstances would render a joint order unworkable that one party should be appointed sole custodial parent." More recently, Trussler J. stated in *P. (T.M.A.)* v. *P. (F.A.)* (1995), 14 R.F.L. (4th) 290, at 294 (Alta. Q.B.):

> The common view is that joint custody should not be awarded where there is animosity or lack of co-operation between the parties. I have always been concerned with that view because I have seen many cases where the residential parent has quite deliberately thwarted joint custody by ensuring that the parties did not get along. In many of those cases, the residential parent clearly was the best parent to be the primary caregiver and thus it was not appropriate for the children to live with the other parent.

> It is time that divorcing parents realized that it is in the best interests of children to have parents co-operate in the on-going care and nurturing of their children. . . . Notwithstanding they have separated, they remain the parents of their children and have a moral and legal obligation to share and co-operate in the raising of the children. Differences have to be set aside for the sake of the children.

> Children suffer the least ill effects from divorce where parents put aside their differences and co-operate with respect to the children. True joint custody is best for children.

Both parents were granted custody of four sons, even though the mother had had sole custody since separation, was bitter about the marriage breakdown and had only permitted the father limited, supervised access. See also *Brushett* v. *Brushett* (1993), 109 Nfld. & P.E.I.R. 129 (Nfld. T.D.); *Surka* v. *Surka* (1992), 40 R.F.L. (3d) 208 (Man. Q.B.); *Ysebaert* v. *Ysebaert* (1993), 47 R.F.L. (3d) 69 (Ont. Gen. Div.); *Fry* v. *Silkalns* (1993), 47 R.F.L. (3d) 169 (B.C. S.C.); *Brinston* v. *Welsh* (1994), 7 R.F.L. (4th) 436 (Nfld. S.C.); *Mudie* v. *Post* (1998), 40 R.F.L. (4th) 151 (Ont. Gen. Div.); *Hildinger* v. *Carroll* (1998), 162 D.L.R. (4th) 764 (Ont. Gen. Div.); *B. (P.J.)* v. *B. (M.M.)* (1998), 163 D.L.R. (4th) 566 (B.C. S.C.); *Smith* v. *Gale* (1999), 49 R.F.L. (4th) 400 (Nfld. U.F.C.); and *Hamlyn* v. *Hamlyn* (1999), 50 R.F.L. (4th) 398 (Nfld. U.F.C.).

9. In cases such as *Mbaruk* v. *Mbaruk* (1997), 27 R.F.L (4th) 146 (B.C. S.C.); *Mudie* v. *Post* (1998), 40 R.F.L. (4th) 151 (Ont. Gen. Div.); *M. (S.A.J.)* v. *M. (D.D.)* (1998), 40 R.F.L. (4th) 95 (Man. Q.B.), reversed (1999), 45 R.F.L. (4th) 301 (Man. C.A.); and *Smith* v. *Gale* (1999), 49 R.F.L. (4th) 400 (Nfld. U.F.C.) there was considerable conflict between the parents relating to access and other matters. In ordering joint custody, the courts appeared to fear that a sole custody order would lead to the non-custodial parent being shut out of the child's life.

10. In *Tauber* v. *Tauber* (1999), 43 O.R. (3d) 42 (Gen. Div.), the judge concluded that joint custody was inappropriate because the parents of an 18-month old child lacked the necessary trust and mutual commitment to co-operate. Justice Jennings awarded custody to the mother but required her to "consult" the father "in a timely manner" prior to making major decisions about the child's health, education, religion or general welfare. The stated intention (at 45) was that "so far as it is possible to do so, all major decisions be consensual and be taken by the wife after consultation with the husband".

11. In *Brundrett* v. *Brundrett* (1998), 35 R.F.L. (4th) 131 (Alta. C.A.), the parents had joint custody under an interim order which gave care and control of the child to the mother. At trial, the parents agreed that there should be joint custody, but each sought care and control. The judge awarded the mother sole custody because of the parents' behaviour since separation. The appellate court upheld the decision.

12. In its *Evaluation of the Divorce Act; Phase II: Monitoring and Evaluation* (Ottawa: Ministry of Supply and Services, 1990) the Department of Justice found (at VII) that 13% of custody arrangements in the four cities it studied were for some form of joint custody. Just under half of these involved joint physical custody. It also concluded (at VII):

> There is no evidence from either the lawyers or clients consulted that courts are imposing joint custody. Nor, as has sometimes been alleged, are women agreeing to joint custody through fear that not to do so will mean loss of custody. Rather, for the minority who choose this option, it was generally their first choice: they respected the parenting abilities of their ex-spouse and believed the decision to be in the best interests of the children. In retrospect, men we interviewed, in both Phase I and II, are somewhat more satisfied with the joint custody decision than women. Dissatisfaction by women centres mainly around the failure of their ex-spouse to share equally parenting duties and obligations.

Of the 35 cases that went to court in the four cities during the period covered by Phase II, joint custody was imposed in only two cases and in both this was the recommendation of the assessor (at 104). Couples whose disputes were mediated were almost twice as likely to have chosen joint legal custody (at 105). The Department observed (at 108):

> [T]he fears of feminists about the unanticipated consequences of joint custody were not substantiated by these Canadian data. As in the recent study by Morris, commissioned by the Canadian Research Institute for the Advancement of Women, there is no evidence that women felt coerced into this arrangement or that their rights have been undermined.

13. Under the federal and provincial *Child Support Guidelines,* a judge has discretion to depart from the Table amount where a parent exercises a right of access to, or has physical custody of, a child for at least 40% of the time. In *Penner* v. *Penner* (1999), 44 R.F.L. (4th) 294 (Man. Q.B.) the parents had joint custody and the father believed that the mother had reduced his time with the children following the adoption of the *Guidelines*. The mother suggested that economic motives underpinned the father's request that the children stay with him more often. Justice Little noted (at 297): "The parties' inability to separate care and control issues from financial ones is exaggerated by section 9 [of the *Guidelines*], which invites minute and perhaps not always relevant comparisons of time." See also *Spanier* v. *Spanier* (1998), 40 R.F.L. (4th) 329 (B.C. S.C.). See generally Chapter 8, **CHILD SUPPORT**.

5.   Access

M. (B.P.) v. M. (B.L.D.E.)

(1992), 42 R.F.L. (3d) 349 (Ont. C.A.)

ABELLA J.A. (TARNOPOLSKY J.A. concurring): — After a trial lasting several days, the respondent B.L.D.E.M. was given custody of her daughter J., born on January 3, 1985. The child's father, B.P.M., the appellant in this appeal, was denied access. The parties had separated in May 1985 and were divorced on January 27, 1991. This proceeding was not part of the divorce but arose out of a contempt application brought by the appellant along with a request for expanded access.

A brief history of the parents' relationship to each other and to the child provides instructive background information. The father and mother met in 1982 in Calgary, Alberta, and married in December 1983 after living together for almost a year. The mother's son, J., had just turned five years old at the time of her marriage to B.P.M.

The father's behaviour began to be disruptive and disturbing during his wife's pregnancy. He was abusive towards J., undermined his wife's relationship with her family, and had "violent rages." The behaviour accelerated after J.'s birth, with the father becoming increasingly violent and often threatening to kill his wife. The mother finally left in 1985 because she was afraid for her and her children's — particularly J.'s — safety.

The harassment escalated after the mother left. The father put the furniture the mother had temporarily left in the house in storage, parked his car on her new street, stole the rim and two tires from her car, and broke into her home (for which he was convicted, fined, and spent a day in jail). When he had access to J., then a baby, he would sometimes threaten not to bring her back. On other occasions when he had access, he would remain in his car with the baby for much of the time (including the night) in front of his wife's house. He left notes on the mother's car letting her know that he knew where she had been, and with whom. He would bang on her door late at night until he was allowed in, then run through the house to see who was there. The police were called to remove him. He threw stones at her window after 2 A.M. one evening, resulting in her having to call the police. He waited in his car for her outside her work, causing her to exit through the back, followed her to day care, and followed her home. She was given phone numbers of women's shelters by professional advisers and she testified that she was afraid she would be killed.

During this period after their separation, the mother sought and obtained restraining orders against her husband, but did not try to prevent access until February 1986, when she brought an application to deny access or have it supervised. In April 1986 this request was denied by a court in Alberta, as was her most recent request for a restraining order. She was given custody and the father was granted overnight and unsupervised access.

In October of 1986, as a direct result of the father's harassment, the mother moved with her two children to live with her mother in Prescott, Ontario. She testified that she left "for my safety, my sanity and my children's safety."

The mother did not see the father, nor did she hear from him, until two years later, when he arrived in Prescott at her mother's house where she was living with her two children. The father had moved to Ottawa in 1988 and quickly sought — and obtained — access to his now three-year-old daughter. The mother, in turn, quickly sought and obtained a restraining order. Initially, in October 1988 the access was supervised and took place during the day in a neutral person's home. Gradually, the visits became unsupervised, longer, overnight starting in December 1988, and finally, in May 1989, lasting the whole weekend.

All visiting arrangements were pursuant to court orders granted largely on consent, and supplemented by the assistance provided by mediation and by the information provided by a report from the Official Guardian, as well as a psychiatric assessment of the father. The final order granting the father overnight access on alternating weekends was made by Cosgrove J., on December 4, 1989, based on documentary evidence and oral submissions from counsel.

Problems with access in Ontario appeared to become serious when overnight visits originated. The father would swear at and verbally abuse the mother in front of the child when he came to pick her up at the McDonald's restaurant in Brockville.

When the first overnight access visit was to take place, the child hid in the car, rolled up the windows, and begged her mother not to make her go. Her father banged on the car windows and yelled threats. On one occasion he yelled at J. that if she did not come with him, he would tell a judge, who would then put her mother in jail.

Because neither B.L.D.E.M.'s own mother nor brothers were prepared to see the father again, K.W., with whom she had by then started living, acted as an intermediary by driving J. to and from access drop-off locations. The beginning of overnight visits every two weeks also coincided with the beginning of J. having nightmares and wetting her bed. At first these took place for a few days before and after visits, but eventually the nightmares and bedwetting happened daily. Normally an outgoing child, J. became quiet before and after visits.

Despite the stress for mother and child surrounding the visits, the mother never denied, or attempted to deny, access to J.'s father. When visits were missed, whether because of J.'s illness or because of the difficult logistics inherent in the father living in Ottawa and the child living in Prescott, make-up visits were readily agreed to and arranged by the mother.

In July 1990 the mother notified her lawyer that she would be moving to Thunder Bay because, having completed a two-year course at a community college, Lakehead University was the only place in Ontario which would allow her to complete a university degree in one year. When informed of the move, the father also decided to move to Thunder Bay to attend Lakehead University.

After one of the access visits during the summer of 1990 and before the move to Thunder Bay, J. had bruises on her tail bone and on the inside of the thigh, and soreness, redness, and swelling in her genital area. The mother took her to a doctor, who was unable to draw any conclusion. But in Thunder Bay, after the first overnight access visit in Thunder Bay, and because she was increasingly anxious over J.'s bedwetting, nightmares, and changed behaviour, the mother again took J. to a doctor.

This doctor, in turn, referred her to Dr. Diana M. Johnson, a specialist in child and family psychiatry. Dr. Johnson, after examining J., advised the mother to stop access visits because, in her view, there was a possibility that J. had been sexually abused by her father.

Access was accordingly stopped, despite the outstanding court order. As a result, the father initiated these proceedings by applying for expanded access rights and for an order finding the mother in contempt of court for non-compliance with the order of Cosgrove J. of December 4, 1989. The mother cross-applied for a variation of the same order by denying further access to the father. Reports by doctors over the next several months did not conclude that sexual abuse had taken place. As a result, a series of orders reinstating access followed from October 1990 to May 1991, ordering that the December 4, 1989, order of Cosgrove J. granting overnight access be stayed, to be replaced by supervised access. Even with supervised visits, however, the child had stomach aches, continued to wet her bed, was always reluctant to go, and was uncharacteristically silent before and after visits.

Ultimately, a trial took place in June 1991, before Wright J., whose judgment is the subject of this appeal by the father.

The trial judge, after five and a half days of evidence, made several crucial observations about the father's personality and behaviour. While persuaded that sexual abuse had not taken place, he was convinced that the child had, as a result of the father's behaviour, suffered "undue emotional stress." Relying on personal observations, patterns of conduct, and the evidence and reports of doctors and social workers, the trial judge concluded that the father saw J. "as a thing" rather than as a person, "wants what is his," and "will not accept anyone saying no to him." It was this temperament that had led the father to make "his wife's life miserable" after their separation, a course of belligerent and harassing conduct he repeated with a girlfriend in Ottawa when she rejected him.

The trial judge found the father to be "obsessed with exercising his right of access to his child and this has overridden what would be the child's desires or in the child's interest on several occasions." In his view, "the father has no understanding of the emotional needs and rights of his daughter." Most importantly, Wright J. concluded that, while the father may not have "emotionally abused" the child, J. had nonetheless been "subjected to a great deal of stress . . . out of the claim to enforce access," stress which the trial judge found to be in no way due to the mother. Rather, he found that:

> The stress is engendered simply by the husband's conduct . . . by the father's personality, his dynamic thrusting, overwhelming nature, . . . by the father's refusal to accept anything but his full rights, by his lack of understanding of children and the needs of this particular child and his obsession with maintaining contact with his daughter at all costs . . .

> The child is now six years of age. *The child has been subjected to stress arising from access for four of those six years and there is no indication that the child will not be subjected to further stress if this situation continues. The child's health is suffering.* [Emphasis added.]

It was the father's submission that since the access had stopped because of allegations of sexual abuse, and since the court had concluded there was no such abuse, the access originally ordered by Cosgrove J. in December 1989 should be reinstated by virtue of the operation of s. 29 of the *Children's Law Reform Act*. . . .

The possibility of variation must be available because when courts order custody or access, they sift through histories of relationships to attempt, as well as possible, to prognosticate their futures. Relationships vary, particularly when the key relationship is to a child who is in a continual state of evolution en route to adulthood. What appeared to be in the child's best interests at the particular moment in his or her evolution when a court order was imposed, may no longer meet those needs at a later point on the evolutionary continuum. Hence, the legitimacy of the possibility of variation orders.

The requirement that the change which triggers a variation application be a material one, on the other hand, addresses the desire to protect the child from unnecessary and trivial adversarial weaponry. This does not mean that an order, once made, calcifies, defying re-examination in the face of a child's changed needs. As long as the state of childhood continues, the right to have a determinative "best interests" standard attaches to the child.

The meaning of "best interests" is as fluid as each child's circumstances. What is certain, however, is that the focus of the exercise is on the child. . . .

This by no means excludes the parental perspective. The needs of children and their parents are obviously inextricable, particularly between children and the parent on whom they depend for their day-to-day care, where only one parent has this primary responsibility. The structure of an environment that fits the child's interests would undoubtedly be reinforced if the economic and emotional needs, especially of custodial parents, were factored in, given the symbiosis of their sense of well-being.

But the central figure in the assessment is the dependent child. And that is why, despite the fact that s. 24(2)(*g*) refers to "the relationship by blood or through an adoption order between the child and each person who is a party to the application," the existence of such a relationship guarantees no rights to custody or access. The rights in custody and access are those of the child: see Bernard M. Dickens, "The Modern Function and Limits of Parents Rights" (1981) 97 Law Q. Rev. 462. Ideally, this will mean an ongoing and positive relationship with both parents.

But while the father submits that, as the father, he is automatically entitled not to be prevented from seeing his child, it is clear, as Wilson J. said in *R. (A.N.) v. W. (L.J.)* (1984), 36 R.F.L. (2d) 1, at 3, that "the law no longer treats children as the property of those who gave them birth but focuses on what is in their best interests." The child, though ambivalent, is not averse to seeing her father as long as access is infrequent and supervised. The mother, having attempted unsuccessfully almost from the child's birth, to accommodate the father's incessant and obsessive behaviour to avoid stress for the child, found that, in the end, nothing could attenuate his harassment. Eventually, on behalf of her child, she attempted through this court proceeding, and in response to the father's contempt application, to end the seemingly endless stress.

Wright J., having heard the evidence, was satisfied that the stress had only increased with time, both for the child and for the mother. He concluded that this stress was a material change from the circumstances before Cosgrove J. In addition, the trial judge observed that Cosgrove J. had heard no viva voce evidence, nor had he given any reasons for his access order.

I agree with his assessment. The stress was cumulative and unrelenting, and in its intensity constituted a material change. In these circumstances Wright J. was entitled to conclude that the stress had become intolerable and unnecessarily so.

There was no evidence of any bond whatsoever between this child and her father. On the contrary, there was evidence that she was hostile towards him during supervised access visits, withdrawn before and after visits, had nightmares, and some bedwetting. I do not believe, therefore, that Wright J. erred in concluding that it was not in the child's best interests to continue even supervised access by the father. Notwithstanding the fact that the actual supervised access visits seemed bearable to J., they clearly had a very negative effect on her before and after the visits.

The purpose of supervised access, far from being a permanent feature of a child's life, is to provide "a temporary and time-limited measure designed to resolve a parental impasse over access. It should not be used . . . as a long-term remedy": Norris Weisman, "On Access after Parental Separation" (1992) 36 R.F.L. (3d) 35, at p. 74. Yet no other form of access is even thinkable for this child. In the absence of any, let alone a significant demonstrable benefit to the child, and based on the solid evidence of four years of harassing, insensitive, disruptive, and harmful behaviour from the father, Wright J. made no error in terminating access by the father to the child based on the material change reflected in the child's stress.

It is not a question of what standard should be used to deprive a parent of access, it is a question of what standard should be used in deciding what form of access, if any, should be ordered. The answer is clear from the statute: the standard is the child's best interests. . . .

This child is in needless pain and has been in this stressful situation throughout her relationship with her father. Nor is there any countervailing benefit to her or any evidence of a subsiding trend. Wright J. rightly concluded that there was no reason for this ongoing, relentless, unhealthy, and unconstructive stress to continue. The biological link cannot be permitted to trump the child's welfare and best interests. . . .

[Finlayson J.A. dissented. His reasons reveal (at 362) that Wright J. declined to find the mother in contempt when she refused to grant the father access in accordance with Cosgrove J.'s order because the mother acted in good faith in relying on the opinion of a child psychiatrist that her child had been sexually abused. This ruling was not appealed. Justice Finlayson concluded (at 366) that Wright J. erred in varying the access provisions of Cosgrove J.'s order "by engaging in what was in effect a hearing de novo on the appellant's fitness to have access to his daughter, instead of concentrating on whether there had been a material change in circumstances from those considered at the hearing before Cosgrove J. that affected or was likely to have affected J." He pointed out that the allegations of sexual abuse which were the focus of the mother's assertion that there had been a change in circumstances were found to be totally unsubstantiated by Wright J. who also concluded that J. had not suffered emotional abuse during the access visits. He continued as follows.]

This brings me to a consideration of the applicable law. The guiding principle in access questions, as enunciated in ss. 19 and 24 of the Act, is the best interest of the child. In general, the courts grant access to the non-custodial parent so that the child will maintain contact with his or her natural parents. This principle is enunciated in the *Divorce Act, 1985*, S.C. 1986, c. 4, . . . in s. 16(10) . . . .

Access is refused when the non-custodial parent poses a threat of harm to the child. See, for example, *Bourdon* v. *Casselman* (1988), 12 R.F.L. (3d) 395 (Ont. Fam. Ct.), in which a father who smoked was denied access to a severely asthmatic child because of the possibility of harm to the child. In that case access was simply not in the child's best interest.

The question arising on these facts is whether the denial of access can be sustained in light of the finding that there was no danger to the child. The following analysis indicates that, in cases where there is no threat of harm to the child, the courts' approach has evolved from the absolute stance that access is always granted, to the position that there may be circumstances in which it is appropriate to deny access.

The earlier approach is seen in *Ader* v. *McLaughlin*, [1964] 2 O.R. 457, 46 D.L.R. (2d) 12 (H.C.), which contains a statement that access is invariably granted unless there is a threat of harm to the child. . . .

A similar statement is found in *Tremblay* v. *Tremblay*, 10 R.F.L. (3d) 166, 54 Alta. L.R. (2d) 283, [1987] 6 W.W.R. 742, 82 A.R. 24 (Q.B.), where the court considered the appropriate course of action after the custodial parent, the mother, had denied access to the father. The court stated, at p. 169 [R.F.L.]:

> *I start with the premise that a parent has the right to see his or her children and is only to be deprived of that right if he or she has abused or neglected the children.* Likewise, and more important, a child has a right to the love, care and guidance of a parent. To be denied that right by the other parent without sufficient justification, such as abuse or neglect, is, in itself, a form of child abuse. [Emphasis added.]

In the final result, custody was transferred from the mother to the father because of the mother's interference with the father's access.

In *Roy* v. *Roy* (1983), 32 R.F.L. (2d) 38, 19 Man. R. (2d) 278, the Manitoba Court of Appeal considered whether the natural mother of four children should be deprived of access. The mother had custody of the children following the separation; however, she suffered a mental breakdown, following which the father assumed care and custody of the children. The father was subsequently awarded custody, with reasonable access to the mother. Shortly after the visits began, the children began to refuse access. The court stated that [at p. 43 R.F.L.]:

> [A] strong case must be established before access is denied. As in questions of custody, the welfare of the child is paramount. *It is sometimes necessary for the protection of a child to deny access where visits of a parent are harmful and disturbing to the children.* [Emphasis added.]

While noting that the children's reaction to access was understandable given the mother's illness and the circumstances of the access visits, the court concluded that the trial judge had overemphasized the children's natural reaction to the trauma of the years preceding the divorce. The court concluded that harm to the children had not been established and made an order for reasonable access by the mother. The court cautioned the mother that reconciliation with the children would be a gradual process and that the father had an obligation to assist in this regard.

An erosion of the absolute statement in *Ader* v. *McLaughlin*, supra, is seen in *Boileau* v. *Boileau* (1979), 13 R.F.L. (2d) 275 (Ont. Div. Ct.), where the court denied access to an adoptive father in circumstances where there was no possibility of harm and yet no perceived benefit to the child. The trial judge had granted the adoptive father access to three children based on the principle that a denial of access should not occur unless there is a clear danger to the children or harm is apprehended. On appeal the Divisional Court examined the rationale underlying this principle, namely, that there is a presumption that a child will benefit from continued connection with each parent. The court noted that the only interest of the adoptive father in the children was as leverage in his relationship with the mother, and concluded that [at p. 278]:

> ... [I]t is my opinion that, in the circumstances of this case, the learned trial judge erred in principle in concluding that it was only if he was satisfied of apprehended harm that he could deny access to the children on the part of Mr. Boileau. With respect in the circumstances the case called for an examination of the circumstances in the light of the principle: What is the best interests of the children? I am satisfied that the evidence discloses that it is not in the best interests of the children that Mr. Boileau have access to them but, on the contrary, it is in the best interests of the children that he not have access to them. [Emphasis added.]

Rather than stating the absolute that access is to be granted in the absence of harm, the court found that, in the circumstances of the case, access was not in the child's best interest. This indicates that a case-by-case approach to access is appropriate. It may also reflect a subtle shift in focus in the way that the courts view the best interest of the child. In the *Ader* case any non-harmful parental contact was seen to be in the child's interest. This is in contrast to the *Boileau* approach, which stressed that the parental contact must be beneficial to the child.

[A brief reference to *Johnson* v. *Johnson* (1987), 12 R.F.L. (3d) 352 (B.C. S.C.) and *Weiss* v. *Kopel* (1980), 18 R.F.L. (2d) 289 (Ont. Prov. Ct.) is omitted.]

These cases demonstrate that, while the best interest of the child clearly contemplates that the child must be protected from harm, an absence of harm does not necessarily compel the conclusion that access is in the best interest of the child.

However, it appears that the circumstances in which access is denied remain quite narrow. What is required to deny access is a finding that there will be no benefit to the child, which requires an examination of the individual circumstances of each case. Given the statutory framework for access decisions, the child should be the exclusive focus of the courts' attention.

This review of the law presupposes an initial hearing to determine custody and access. This was the standard imposed upon Cosgrove J. and, on all of the evidence, his decision appears to have been in accordance with accepted principles of law. The problem in the case on appeal is that Wright J. embarked upon the same enquiry without being satisfied that there had been a change in circumstances which justified a change in the access ordered by Cosgrove J. In my opinion, there was no evidence of a material change in circumstances within the meaning of s. 29 of the Act. There was different evidence and more current evidence, but any evidence of a change in circumstances indicated that the situation had changed for the better by the intro-duction of supervised access.

I am mindful that Abella J.A. has stated that the cumulative effect of the unrelenting stress in the case on appeal does constitute a material change in circum-stances. I agree that it could, if there was any evidence to support a finding that the circumstances following the last order of Cosgrove J. had brought a long-simmering problem to a head. However, in my opinion, this is not such a case. As I have pointed out, the only new evidence that related to stress on the child was that supervised access seemed to have worked effectively to reduce stress to the point where access was working to the benefit of the child.

I am not alone in this view of the evidence. Counsel for the Official Guardian was most positive on the hearing of the appeal that supervised access had proven to be effective and urged that the appeal be allowed to the extent of permitting super-vised access to the father. Counsel gave an undertaking to the court that the Offical Guardian was prepared to take on the responsibility of supervising access and would review the situation after four to six months with a view to making recommendations to the parties as to appropriateness of enlarging access. With respect, I find it unusual that this court and the court below would ignore, without reasons, the recommen-dations made by the Official Guardian, which has been actively involved with the problems of this couple and their child since it was introduced into the matter in November of 1991 at the invitation of the court. The Official Guardian had a wealth of material to support its recommendations in the form of reports and testimony of social workers involved in supervising visitations by the respondent father.

This case has caused me a great deal of concern. Ordinarily, I am reluctant to interfere with the judge of first instance in cases involving the welfare of children of a marriage. On the other hand, I am reluctant to support an order which denies a parent the right to see his or her child under any circumstances unless I am persuaded otherwise by cogent evidence that relates to the welfare of the child.

There can be no doubt that the appellant has been an unremitting nuisance to the respondent and has caused a great deal of disruption to her life. However, almost all of this is in the past. Wright J. acknowledges that the appellant has changed and that he is no longer up to his old tricks of harassing his wife. . . .

With great respect, I think it is too early to give up on what has turned out to be a protracted mediation exercise, even though it has not been as successful as the court had hoped. Cosgrove J. put a lot of thought and effort into reconstructing this shattered relationship involving the two parents and their child, and, on the evidence, some success was achieved. Indeed, were it not for the unfounded charge of sexual abuse by Dr. Johnson, this matter might not have come back to the court. I understand

and sympathize with Wright J.'s impatience with the appellant after the court became involved in yet another hearing with respect to this child. However, under s. 29 of the Act, he was called upon to play a restricted role. It was a mistake on his part to take an enlarged view of his jurisdiction and decide to reach down and cut the Gordian knot. In doing so, he ignored the evidence which indicated that Cosgrove J.'s escalated reintegration of the family was working in the best interests of the child. Overseeing these matrimonial problems can be time-consuming and frustrating, but it is a task which the legislature has imposed upon us, and in this particular case, it is one that may be with us for some time. We must all work within the system and attempt as best we can to make the legislation effective. . . .

McLEOD, "ANNOTATION"
(1993), 42 R.F.L. (3d) 350

. . . The contempt finding was not appealed; the appeal was restricted to the cancellation of the access. The contempt finding may prove to be satisfying to parents who find themselves in the mother's position. Sexual abuse is very difficult to establish. Parents in the mother's position are "damned if they do and damned if they don't." If they cancel access, they are accused of frustrating access and of disobeying a court order. If they fail to act, they are accused of failing to protect the child. . . .

In *M. (B.P.)* the court found that the child had not been abused. One can infer from the court's dismissal of the contempt application that it was satisfied that the mother's belief was reasonably and honestly held. If courts intended to allow someone to ignore a court order to protect a child on that basis, they should also insist that an immediate application be brought to terminate or restrict the access. Unfortunately, the court in *M. (B.P.)* did not comment on the problem of one parent withholding access based upon a mistaken belief that the child was at risk. Is a parent entitled to withhold access if he or she suspects that the access plans pose a risk to the child? The right to ignore a court order should be restricted to clear cases of threatened danger and should be conditional upon immediate court action.

The application to terminate access in *M. (B.P.)* was for a variation. The reasons reveal substantial disagreement about the burden of proof on access variation applications. Although Abella J.A. formally supports casting a significant onus upon the parent applying to vary, in fact, she effectively removes any such burden. Notwithstanding her comments that custody and access orders should to some degree be final, she equates variation with the best interests of the child. The original order should be accepted as reflecting the best interests of the child at the time it was made. If it is no longer in the child's best interests to continue the arrangement, a material change in circumstances must have occurred. Finlayson J.A., on the other hand, states that there will be a material change in circumstances only if the facts are materially different. In the former case, the merits and variation threshold become one. In the latter, they are separate. Although Finlayson J.A.'s view reflects the traditional variation analysis, Abella J.A.'s view probably reflects the way most people and judges deal with the problem. As well, the general overriding policy of protecting and promoting the best interests of the child supports her analysis.

The judges also hold substantially different opinions about the parties' respective conduct. Abella J.A. feels that the access problems are the father's fault and finds the mother blameless in the conflict. Although conflict can be one-sided, often, it is not. In Finlayson J.A.'s reasons he notes that the mother continually tried to restrict the access, that her earlier affidavit in Ontario bordered on perjury, and that she violated a court order. Apparently, Abella J.A. views the mother as a victim, a perception that colours the judge's perspective. It is a short jump from Abella J.A.'s reasons to the position that an overbearing parent may quickly have his or her access terminated. It is a question of where to draw the line. How over-bearing must someone be before his or her conduct becomes oppressive? Does a parent's susceptibility to pressure make termination the more likely result? Abella J.A. seems to be troubled by the father's fixation on his right to have contact with the child. But how does one distinguish between sincere interest and fixation? Abella J.A. finds that the father had no appreciation of the effect that his conduct had on the child. Finlayson J.A. notes that the trial judge held that the child had not been sexually or emotionally abused. The problem may not be the conduct towards the child, but the effect of the interparental conflict. If "blame" for the conflict is to be apportioned, parental conduct returns as a factor to be considered.

It is difficult to read the reasons in *M. (B.P.)* without feeling that access, in particular, is at risk if you are a "bad" person or if you are not considerate of your partner. Earlier cases have suggested as much, but *M. (B.P.)* is the first case in recent years in which the Court of Appeal has made so strong a statement. The potential implications of the judgment are as interesting as the reasons themselves. One point that lurks below the surface is the effect of politicizing custody and access disputes. If a father is involved in a father's rights movement and a mother is sensitized to the broad nature of abuse and the creation of a negative environment, stress is inevitable. If the stress adversely affects the child, as seems likely, the easiest way to protect the child is to remove the stress; in other words, terminate the access. Access then becomes very much a non-judicial issue. If the custodial parent is in favour, access occurs. If the custodial parent is opposed, it does not. That may be the reality of access rights in any event. But should the courts promote this position? . . .

The reasons in *M. (B.P.)* highlight the changing or diverse views of many people. It is no longer correct to say that a person may be a bad spouse but a good parent. The two seem to be intimately intertwined. Spousal abuse that occurs in front of the children is in itself child abuse. Children who grow up with abusers are apt to become victims or abusers themselves: see Peter G. Jaffe, David A. Wolfe, and Susan Kaye Wilson, *Children of Battered Women* (Newbury Park: Sage Publications, 1990). Parental stress affects children and, if sufficiently severe, access must be terminated or custody changed. *M. (B.P.)*, provides some insight into how the courts may address parental roles and responsibilities in a conflict. On the facts of the case, the denial of access does not seem to be unreasonable. One is therefore left to ask: How far should the reasons be extended and how broadly should misconduct/abuse be defined?

NOTES AND QUESTIONS

1. Matheson J. stated in *Michel* v. *Hanley* (1988), 12 R.F.L. (3d) 372, at 374 (Sask. Q.B.):

Most judicial decisions suggest (*e.g. Stroud* v. *Stroud* (1974), 4 O.R. (2d) 567, 18 R.F.L. 237, 48 D.L.R. (3d) 527 (H.C.)) that the primary consideration, as with custody, is the welfare and best interests of the child. Merely determining that the granting of access will not pose a clear danger to the child, and thereby granting access because of a "right" to access, does not resolve the question as to whether the granting of access would be in the best interests of the child.

In *Family Law in Canada*, Christine Davies, it is suggested, at p. 542, that it is not because of a "right" possessed by a parent that access may be granted if there is no danger to the child in doing so, but because it is perceived that incalculable benefits will accrue to the child from contact with both parents. The benefits were generally described as having more than one parent available to influence the development of the child, and to provide affection, comfort, companionship, and emotional and material support. Viewed in this context, the "right" to access is not absolute, to be denied only when danger to the child is perceived, but to be granted only after assessing the presumed benefits which will accrue to the child upon the exercise of the "right".

2. Available research suggests generally children who have regular contact with the non-custodial parent (usually the father) do better than children who see the non-custodial parent infrequently or not at all. See Wallerstein and Blakeslee, *Second Chances: Men, Women and Children a Decade after Divorce* (New York: Tichnor and Fields, 1989) and Levanthal, "Divorce, Custody and Visitation in Mid-Childhood" in Galatzer and Kraus, eds., *The Scientific Basis of Child Custody Decisions* (New York: John Wiley, 1999).

3. A parent is almost always granted access. In *Evaluation of the Divorce Act; Phase II: Monitoring and Evaluation* (Ottawa: Ministry of Supply and Services, 1990), the Department of Justice found that the files of divorce cases in four Canadian cities revealed that access was denied in less than 3% of the cases. Reported cases where access is denied or ended mostly involve situations where there is a real risk of physical or emotional harm to the child as a result of access (*G. (R.A.)* v. *M. (T.L.)* (1988), 17 R.F.L. (3d) 180 (B.C. C.A.); *H. (E.)* v. *G. (H.)* (1995), 18 R.F.L. (4th) 21 (N.S. C.A.); *Neill* v. *Best* (1995), 18 R.F.L. (4th) 440 (N.S. Fam. Ct.); *A. (J.I.)* v. *K. (A.I.)* (1997), 33 R.F.L. (4th) 438 (Ont. Gen. Div.); and *R. (M.)* v. *S. (K.)* (1998), 35 R.F.L. (4th) 346 (N.B. Q.B.)) or where a parent has lost contact for a number of years (*T. (K.)* v. *C. (R.W.B.)* (1990), 25 R.F.L. (3d) 433 (Ont. Prov. Ct.)). There are also cases where the relationship between a child and the non-custodial parent has become so negative that access has become very stressful and the child resists visits. The child's negative attitudes may be due to the attitudes and actions of the custodial parent. In *Katz* v. *Katz* (1989), 21 R.F.L. (3d) 167 (Ont. U.F.C.), three teenaged children had become alienated from their father and did not wish to see him. Wallace U.F.C.J. concluded that, given the ages of the children, a forced access regime was not in their best interests and she ordered that the father be allowed reasonable access if the children wished to see him. See also *James* v. *James* (1994), 3 R.F.L. (4th) 226 (Ont. Gen. Div.); *Strobridge* v. *Strobridge* (1994), 4 R.F.L. (4th) 169 (Ont. C.A.); *Long* v. *Long* (1994), 8 R.F.L. (4th) 269 (Ont. Gen. Div.); *Rosenke* v. *Rosenke* (1998), 36 R.F.L. (4th) 288 (Alta. C.A.); *Bellman* v. *Bellman* (1999), 46 R.F.L. (4th) 414 (B.C. S.C.); and *Lidkea* v. *Jarrell* (1999), 49 R.F.L. (4th) 324 (Ont. C.A.). Compare these cases with *Roy* v. *Roy* (1983), 32 R.F.L. (2d) 38 (Man. C.A.) and *MacInnis* v. *MacInnis* (1992), 40 R.F.L. (3d) 345 (Ont. U.F.C.).

Richard A. Gardner coined the term "parental alienation syndrome" to describe the condition of children who have become totally alienated from one parent because of the actions of the other. See *The Parental Alienation Syndrome: A Guide for Mental Health and Legal Professionals* (Cresskill, N.J.: Creative Therapeutics, 1992). This concept and the suggestion that it is a clinically diagnosable condition has been controversial and Dr. Gardner has himself cautioned in *Addendum III: Recommendations for Dealing with Parents Who Induce a Parental Alienation Syndrome in their Children* (Cresskill, N.J.: Creative Therapeutics, 1996) that he is aware of American cases where mothers lost custody of their children because of pre-mature and incorrect diagnosis of the syndrome. For further reading on the subject, see Johnson and Roseby, *In the Name of the Child: A Developmental Approach to Understanding and Helping Children of Conflicted and Violent Divorce* (New York: Free Press, 1997) and Faller, "The Parental Alienation Syndrome: What is it and What Data Support It?" (1998), 3(2) Child Maltreatment 100.

4. For many children, the "access problem" is that the non-custodial parent visits too rarely or not at all. Can or should the courts do anything to force or encourage unwilling or reluctant non-custodial parents to visit? Would educational programs help?

5. In some cases the courts have concluded that renewed contact between the child and the non-custodial parent is in the child's best interest even if that parent has not visited the child or been visited by the child for years. See *Pike* v. *Pike* (1984), 38 R.F.L. (2d) 71 (Ont. H.C.); *Bedard* v. *Bedard* (1984), 43 R.F.L. (2d) 331 (Man. C.A.); *S. (E.A.)* v. *B. (K.M.)* (1989), 24 R.F.L. (3d) 220 (Ont. Dist. Ct.); and *Savidant* v. *MacLeod* (1991), 32 R.F.L. (3d) 266 (P.E.I. T.D.). Contrast these cases with *DeSilva* v. *Giggey* (1996), 21 R.F.L. (4th) 116 (N.B. Q.B.) and *F. (W.)* v. *R. (G.)* (1997), 32 R.F.L. (4th) 420 (N.B. Q.B.).

6. In "Allegations of Childhood Sexual Abuse in Custody and Access Disputes: What Care is in the Best Interests of the Child?" (1994), 12 Can. J. Fam. L. 91, Lise Helene Zarb concludes her examination of the case law involving allegations of sexual abuse as follows (at 104-105):

> Although each case will depend on its individual circumstances, it seems that where sexual abuse of a child by a parent is proven on the balance of probabilities, the courts tend to award supervised access or deny access completely. Judges do not award unsupervised access in this type of situation. Where the allegations are not proven, the accused is typically granted supervised or unsupervised access to the child. Supervised access is usually ordered unless it is clear that the allegations of sexual abuse are unfounded and the child is not at risk.

See also Kerr and Jaffe, "Legal and Clinical Issues in Child Custody Disputes Involving Domestic Violence" (1999), 17 C.F.L.Q. 1 and Bala and Schuman, "Allegations of Sexual Abuse When Parents Have Separated" (1999), 17 C.F.L.Q. 121.

In *Leveque* v. *Leveque* (1993), 54 B.C.L.R. 164, MacFarlane J.A. of the British Columbia Court of Appeal outlined (at 167) the test for awarding supervised, as opposed to unsupervised, access in these situations:

> When the welfare of children is concerned, the question is not whether specific allegations of misconduct with a third party have been proven, but whether on the whole of the evidence there arises a real risk to the children if access is given without protection against that risk. The degree of risk can only be determined by carefully weighing all the evidence and the judge's assessment of the character of the parties.

For an example of a reported case where a court chose to err on the side of caution and ordered supervised access even though the alleged abuse had not been proven, see *C. (R.M.)* v. *C. (J.R.)* (1995), 12 R.F.L. (4th) 440 (B.C. S.C.). Compare *P. (G.L.)* v. *P. (J.M.)* (1990), 27 R.F.L. (3d) 64 (B.C. S.C.) and *W. (K.M.)* v. *W. (D.D.)* (1993), 47 R.F.L. (3d) 378 (Ont. Prov. Div.) where the judges considered the allegations to be false and ordered unsupervised access.

In *D. (D.L.)* v. *W. (R.J.)* (1994), 10 R.F.L. (4th) 130 (Sask. Q.B.), Dickson J. concluded that the evidence relating to possible sexual abuse was inconclusive. However, the father's request for unsupervised access was denied because there had been some inappropriate behaviour involving the girls and he generally failed to control his sexual impulses. In an *obiter dictum*, Dickson J. indicated (at 133) that access might have been denied except that the mother did not oppose continued supervised access:

> I am very skeptical of supervised access. In most cases I fail to see any value in it for the children. In most cases in which the question comes up, I think no access is better for the children than an artificial supervised arrangement that may develop in the children a conviction that the supervised parent is a threatening presence in their lives. Surely they will almost certainly develop a resentment that they are required to associate with someone who could hurt them. If a parent is not fit to have unsupervised access to his children, if his behaviour is a risk to their safety, what value can his supervised presence have to them? Such access does not present a true picture to them. It may give them a distorted view of that parent and a false sense of security in his presence.

7. What should a custodial parent do if he or she suspects that the access parent has abused the child during a visit? Recall the refusal of Cosgrove J. to find the mother in contempt in *M. (B.P.)*. See also *M. (B.)* v. *W. (N.G.)* (1998), 36 R.F.L. (4th) 249 (Ont. Gen. Div.). In *Young* v. *Young* (1993), 49 R.F.L. (3d) 117 (S.C.C.), L'Heureux-Dubé J. (dissenting) suggested (at 184) that "a custodial parent, aware of sexual or other abuse by the non-custodial parent, would be remiss in his or her duty to the child not to cut off access by the abuser immediately, with or without a court order." The majority did not directly address this point, although L'Heureux-Dubé J. mentioned it to illustrate her disagreement with McLachlin J.'s statement (at 150-151) that the custodial parent did not have the right to forbid certain types of contact between the access parent and the child.

In "Canada: Struggling to Find a Balance on Gender Issues" (1994-1995), 33 University of Louisville Journal of Family Law 301, Professor Bala describes (at 305-306) the debate over the proper response of a family lawyer whose client claims that the other parent will abuse the child if a court order is followed:

> It was not only judges who were divided about how to resolve disputes about children, but also lawyers who were . . . debating their role in these cases, as was revealed in an important professional discipline decision. A prominent feminist lawyer was charged with professional misconduct as a result of her involvement in a case in which the mother of a three-year-old girl alleged sexual abuse. The trial judge rejected these allegations and ordered the child transferred to her father's custody within ten weeks. Following the order, but before the mother gave over custody, the mother reported further allegations of abuse, which were supported by a social worker. The lawyer in question was retained by the mother to attempt to have the order varied or appealed. The lawyer wrote in a letter that, pending an appeal hearing, the mother "should seriously consider" not allowing the child to be transferred as required by the original court order. The mother then "went underground" with the child, but ultimately contacted the father and eventually voluntarily gave him custody.
>
> In the meantime, the lawyer was charged with breach of her professional obligations, in particular for "subverting the law by counseling or assisting in activities which are in defiance of it." The Discipline Committee of Ontario's Law Society accepted the principle that a lawyer counseling disobedience of a court order ordinarily is in breach of professional obligations, but this conduct is acceptable if the lawyer:

>> [has a] reasonable and honest belief of . . . imminent risk or danger to a child, and that there [is] an immediate application to a court to have the issues determined forthwith. Once that application is made and the facts have been presented before a court of competent jurisdiction however briefly, if that court refuses to act to change an outstanding order, then the obligation of the client is to "trust in the efficacy of the legal system" and adhere to the court order, and then if so advised, to seek a full hearing for a permanent change.

> (*Law Society of Upper Canada v. Curtis*, LAWYERS WKLY. Sept. 29, 1993, at 1323-018 (full-text).)

This decision has not escaped criticism. See, e.g. "Lawyers Can Counsel Clients to Disobey Court Orders", *Lawyers Weekly*, October 15, 1993 at 1 & 10 where Alfred Mamo commented:

> Saying you have to have a reasonable and honest belief . . . means nothing. In matrimonial law, people have what they consider to be reasonable and honestly held beliefs about a lot of things.
>
> Many times clients are looking for a way out of an order that they don't like. Custody and access cases are very emotionally saturated—and I think that as a result counsel is always being asked to try and interpret this sort of thing so as to allow someone to avoid compliance with the order.

8. As *M. (B.P.)* v. *M. (B.L.D.E.)* illustrates, wife abuse, particularly if it has continued after separation, can affect the determination of access. See also *Abdo* v. *Abdo* (1993), 109 D.L.R. (4th) 78 (N.S. C.A.) (access terminated in part because it affected the abused mother negatively); *Cairns* v. *Cairns* (1994), 3 R.F.L. (4th) 397 (N.B. Fam. Div.) (supervised access only where the father had been abusive before and after separation and used extremely profane and degrading language in his dealings with the mother in front of the child); *Costa* v. *Costa* (1994), 4 R.F.L. (4th) 209 (Man. Fam. Div.) (no access until the abused mother was emotionally strong enough to handle the idea that the father would have a continuing role and the father received help to control his anger); and *Alexander* v. *Creary* (1995), 14 R.F.L. (4th) 311 (Ont. Prov. Div.) (no access in part because the father's abuse of the mother during their relationship showed that he was unable to control his temper). However, a decision to grant supervised access to a father who had just been released from jail for assaulting the mother was upheld in *Savidant* v. *MacLeod* (1992), 40 R.F.L. (3d) 443 (P.E.I. C.A.). In *Fullerton* v. *Fullerton* (1994), 7 R.F.L. (4th) 272 (N.B. Fam. Div.) the ongoing violence witnessed by the children when their mother came to pick them up after a visit constituted "a material change in circumstance". The judge concluded (at 275) that a "complete denial of access by the children to their father, however, is contrary to their right" and that the "ongoing risk of harm to the children can . . . be substantially eliminated if the

parties have no contact with each other''. The solicitors were to make arrangements for a third party acceptable to both parties to pick up and return the children.

9. Access is almost always granted to the non-custodial parent regardless of the wishes of the other parent. Where a non-parent seeks access, the courts have generally deferred to the wishes of the custodial parent or parents. The onus is clearly on the applicant in that situation to show that access would be in the child's best interest. Moreover, the courts place considerable weight on the extent to which access by the non-parent might undermine the child-parent relationship. See *Hofer* v. *Stewart* (1984), 41 R.F.L. (2d) 211 (Man. Q.B.), affirmed (1985), 34 Man. R. (2d) 158 (C.A.); *Laszlo* v. *Laszlo* (1984), 39 R.F.L. (2d) 383 (Man. Q.B.); *Mockford* v. *Mockford* (1985), 31 Man. R. (2d) 257 (Q.B.); *Milne* v. *Milne* (1985), 44 R.F.L. (2d) 241 (B.C. C.A.); *Lapp* v. *Dupuis* (1985), 45 R.F.L. (2d) 28 (Man. C.A.); *Cyrenne* v. *Moar* (1986), 2 R.F.L. (3d) 414 (Man. C.A.); *Tramble* v. *Hill* (1987), 7 R.F.L. (3d) 85 (Ont. U.F.C.); *Fishburne* v. *Eggleton* (1987), 12 R.F.L. (3d) 251 (B.C. S.C.); *Lusher* v. *Lusher* (1988), 13 R.F.L. (3d) 201 (Ont. Fam. Ct.); *Driaunevicius* v. *Wilson* (1990), 25 R.F.L. (3d) 85 (Man. Q.B.); *Salter* v. *Borden* (1991), 31 R.F.L. (3d) 48 (N.S. Fam. Ct.); *Rice* v. *Rice* (1992), 42 R.F.L. (3d) 281 (N.B. Q.B.); *G. (M.L.)* v. *G. (K.L.)* (1993), 49 R.F.L. (3d) 437 (B.C. C.A.); *Hooper* v. *Hooper* (1996), 23 R.F.L. (4th) 441 (N.B. Q.B.); *B. (M.)* v. *W. (C.)* (1997), 31 R.F.L. (4th) 351 (N.S. Fam. Ct.); *M. (B.)* v. *W. (N.G.)* (1998), 36 R.F.L. (4th) 249 (Ont. Gen. Div.); and *F. (N.)* v. *S. (H.L.)* (1999), 49 R.F.L. (4th) 250 (B.C. C.A.). However, in *Moreau* v. *Cody* (1995), 15 R.F.L. (4th) 174 (Ont. Prov. Div.), the court granted unsupervised access for one afternoon per month to the maternal grandparents. Their daughter had died eight months previously and their relationship with the father had soured. For a similar situation and result, see *McLellan* v. *Glidden* (1996), 23 R.F.L. (4th) 106 (N.B. Q.B.).

The Special Joint Committee "found the testimony of grandparents and their representatives extremely compelling" *(For the Sake of the Children*, at 56) and it recommended (at 57) that the provinces consider amending their family law "to provide that maintaining and fostering relationships with grandparents and other extended family members is in the best interests of children and that such relationships should not be disrupted without a significant reason related to the well-being of the child''. For further reading see Foster and Freed, "Grandparents' Visitation: Vagaries and Vicissitudes" (1979), 23 St. L.U.L.S. 643; Zaharoff, "Access to Children: Towards a Model Statute for Third Parties" (1981), 15 Fam.L.Q. 165; and Landau, "Visiting Rights of Grandparents: How to Balance the Best Interests of the Child and the Interests of Parents and Grandparents" (1986), 5 C.J.F.L.181.

10. In *K. (S.K.)* v. *K. (D.J.)* (1995), 15 R.F.L. (4th) 90 (B.C. S.C.), Melnick J. suggested (at 93-94) that the general approach taken to access claims by non-parents (see note 9) should also apply where access is sought by "a person who is not a natural parent of the child and whose relationship as a step-parent with the child was neither extensive or significant".

11. In *Low* v. *Low* (1994), 4 R.F.L. (4th) 103 (Ont. Gen. Div.), the husband told the wife before their marriage in 1989 that he was unable to father a child because of a low sperm count. They decided upon artificial insemination by anonymous donor. The husband participated throughout the process and signed all necessary documents. The child was born in April 1990 and the husband certified that he was the father when the birth was registered. By that time serious difficulties had arisen in the marital relationship and the parties separated within days of the birth. The husband had flexible access until December 1990, but problems arose. The parties unsuccessfully tried mediation to resolve the dispute. In February 1991 the mother terminated access. Thereafter, the husband had sporadic access pursuant to various orders and agreements. The mother was hostile towards the husband and stated that her anger would preclude successful access. The husband was very frustrated by the mother's attempts to thwart his access. He had vented his frustration both verbally and physically, but he had not threatened anyone with violence.

In divorce proceedings the mother agreed that the child was "a child of the marriage" under the *Divorce Act* since the husband stood "in the place of a parent" (see s. 2). However, she argued that there should be no access and that the husband could not be declared to be the father under the *CLRA*. Ferrier J. granted liberal, detailed access to the husband. The judge also granted a declaration under the *CLRA* that the husband was the father, noting (at 133) "Nowhere in s. 5 is there any suggestion that 'the relationship of father and child' must have a biological or genetic character." Ferrier J. adopted (at 114) the public policy arguments expressed by the Superior Court of New Jersey in *S.* v. *S.*, 440 A.2d 64, at

68 (1981): "[T]he best interests of the child, the mother, the family unit and society are served by recognizing that the law surrounding AID insemination deals with the creation of a family unit and more particularly with the creation of parent-child relationships.".

12. In *Johnson-Steeves* v. *Lee* (1997), 33 R.F.L. (4th) 278 (Alta. C.A.), the mother asked a man to help her conceive a child on the basis that he would provide support but otherwise she hoped to raise the child on her own. The father paid child support and visited the child for three one- week periods in the first year after the birth. The mother then asked the father to bow out of their lives. The appellate court upheld an order providing for access.

13. If it appears likely that the parents can work out the details of the access by the non-custodial parent, the court order may simply grant "reasonable access". Often, however, the order for access will spell out the details regarding the visitation rights of the non-custodial parent. The possible variations in the structure of access orders are limited only by the bounds of the judge's and counsels' creativity. For examples of access orders carefully tailored to meet the particular circumstances of the parties, see *Elbaz* v. *Elbaz* (1980), 16 R.F.L. (2d) 336, 29 O.R. (2d) 207 (H.C.); *Weiss* v. *Kopel* (1980), 18 R.F.L. (2d) 289 (Ont. Prov. Ct.); and *Ryan* v. *Ryan* (1986), 3 R.F.L. (3d) 141, 60 Nfld. & P.E.I.R. 162 (Nfld. T.D.). Regarding the court's authority to stipulate the terms and conditions of access, see ss. 28 and 34 of the *CLRA* and s. 16(6) of the *Divorce Act*.

14. Access orders are notoriously difficult to enforce effectively. In an annotation to *Rutherford* v. *Rutherford* (1986), 4 R.F.L. (3d) 457 (B.C. S.C.), Professor McLeod wrote (at 458-459):

> The reasons for judgment in *Rutherford* v. *Rutherford* highlight the frustration of an access parent who finds his or her access rights interfered with. Ultimately, there is very little one can do to force the custodial parent to provide meaningful access. In many cases, access is an immediate thing for the purposes of a vacation or a special family gathering. Once the custodial parent denies access at that time, the opportunity may not be available at a later date. A custodial spouse's willingness to cooperate in furthering the child's relationship with the access spouse may be affected by many factors including continuing animosity with the other parent or improper linkage of access and support.

> In reality, there is little the court can do to assist the access parent in the face of interference with access by the custodial parent. The judicial process, overall, is too slow and its tools too blunt.

> The denial of access is treated as contempt of court. The normal means of punishment are censure, fine or imprisonment. None of these directly provides access. Fines simply reduce the family income of the lower income family or become a licence to break the law for those that can afford it. Courts are extremely wary of putting a custodial parent in jail, having regard to the best interest of the child. In any event, jailing will only increase the animosity between the spouses and is likely to further erode the access parent's relationship with the child when the child finds out, which is likely to happen.

> In many cases, like *Rutherford*, the courts have indicated that if interference with access continues, they may reverse custody on the basis it is in the best interest of the child to know and have contact with both parents. If one parent will not provide such contact, the other should be given the opportunity. As well, to continue the parental conflict shows an inability to submerge personal desires to benefit the child. In fact, such threats by the courts ring hollow. The more likely scenario is that access will be terminated if it proves sufficiently unsettling to the child, even where the problem may be laid squarely at the feet of the custodial parent.

> Even more insidious to the position of the access parent is the subtle "poisoning" of the child's mind by the custodial parent. If the child receives enough negative information about the access parent, it is likely to affect him. The process may be so subtle and slow that it escapes notice until too late. . . .

> As appears clear, the courts are not equipped to respond to the problems involved. Ultimately, it must be questioned whether the problem is properly a legal and justiciable one or whether it should, in part, be turned over to the mental health profession. Where access problems are rooted

in parental animosity and are not a response to evidence of abuse or real concern for the child's welfare, which concerns can be objectively dealt with and responded to, it may well be that thought should be given by judges and legislators to a form of compulsory conciliation to see if the problem can be addressed at its real level: between the parents.

In *Yunyk* v. *Judd* (1986), 5 R.F.L. (3d) 206, the Manitoba Court of Queen's Bench suggested that there was a third option for dealing with repeated denials of access: to order additional access for the non-custodial parent.

See also Professor McLeod's annotation to *Wood* v. *Miller* (1993), 45 R.F.L. (3d) 244 (Ont. U.F.C.).

For a review of the principles that the court should apply in contempt proceedings based on a refusal to comply with an access order, see *Genua* v. *Genua* (1979), 12 R.F.L. (2d) 85 (Ont. Prov. Ct.); *O'Byrne* v. *Koresec* (1986), 2 R.F.L. (3d) 104 (B.C. S.C.); *Myke* v. *Myke* (1992), 42 R.F.L. (3d) 322 (Ont. U.F.C.); *Thomas* v. *Pearcy* (1993), 48 R.F.L. (3d) 407 (Ont. Gen. Div.); and *Paton* v. *Shymkiw* (1996), 26 R.F.L. (4th) 22 (Man. Q.B.). In the last case, the judge found the mother in contempt because she told her six-year old son that he did not have to see his father if he did not wish to. As penalties, the mother had to reimburse the father for reasonable expenses incurred as a result of wrongful denial of access and she had to attend an educational course.

Section 36 of the *CLRA* does provide a mechanism whereby the court can directly enforce access. Under s. 36(2) the court can order the sheriff or police to locate, apprehend and deliver the child to the person entitled to access where the custodial parent is unlawfully withholding the child. In *Allen* v. *Grenier* (1997), 145 D.L.R (4th) 286 (Ont. Gen. Div.), the court stated that orders under s. 36(2) should be made only after there had been a withholding of a child contrary to the access order. In *McMillan* v. *McMillan* (1999), 44 O.R. (3d) 139 (Gen. Div.), the father obtained, on consent, an amendment of the divorce judgment directing the Niagara Regional Police to assist the father in apprehending the children for the purpose of exercising his visitation rights. The police were reluctant to get involved and the father recognized that it would be upsetting to the children for the police to arrive at their home and take them to visit their father. The father brought a series of applications to have the mother found in contempt of court. Each time the judges threatened that the mother could be imprisoned if she continued her behaviour and each time the mother would co-operate for a short period of time. Finally, Justice Quinn found the mother in contempt and sentenced her to five days in jail, commenting (at 145-147):

> Access is the source of endless conflict in many matrimonial cases. This is not surprising since no matter how detailed and structured the access schedule may be there is still the need for the estranged spouses to achieve some degree of co-operation, consensus and compromise for the schedule to run smoothly. However, the fact that access orders produce so much conflict is a good reason not to treat their breach lightly.

> . . . Perhaps, had tougher sanctions been the norm in this area of the law from the outset, and had been known to be so, some of the last eight years of acrimony could have been avoided. In any event, it falls to this court to somehow impress upon Ms. McMillan, and upon the public in general, that court orders are to be obeyed; and, unless appropriate penalties are imposed for breaches thereof, orders are rendered meaningless.

> . . . Mr. Crowe, on behalf of Ms. McMillan, strenuously argued that incarceration would not be in the best interests of the children. I agree. But when would it *ever* be in the best interests of children to send the custodial parent to jail? To create, repair or enhance the relationship between the access parent and the children? I should think that imprisoning the custodial parent is a very high price to pay if this is the only result sought to be achieved. Of all the sentencing factors applicable in this case, I think the most important one is the need to preserve the integrity of the administration of justice; and that, as I see it, can only be achieved through a sentence of incarceration. It was also argued on behalf of Ms. McMillan that a jail sentence would deleteriously affect the relationship of the children with their father. This is troubling, but, again, could not the same thing be said in most cases of this nature? In my opinion, a court should be careful not to allow such arguments to declaw the court when it comes to sentencing for contempt in respect of access.

See also *B. (L.)* v. *D. (R.)* (1998), 40 R.F.L. (4th) 134 (Ont. Gen. Div.) where a jail term of nine days was imposed.

15. For a rare case in which a custodial parent's persistent refusal to allow the other parent to exercise access rights granted by court order led to a reversal of the custody decision, see *Tremblay* v. *Tremblay* (1987), 10 R.F.L. (3d) 166 (Alta. Q.B.). Recall the discussion of the "friendly parent" principle earlier in this chapter. In *Fergus* v. *Fergus* (1997), 33 R.F.L. (4th) 63 (Ont. C.A.), the police were often involved in the enforcement of the father's access to children who did not wish to see him. The trial judge found the mother in contempt of a court order and sentenced her to 30 days in jail. He also granted custody of the two youngest children, aged 13 and 11, to the father. Nine O.P.P. officers assisted in the transfer of custody. The mother appealed and obtained a stay of the trial judge's order within a matter of days. She was released from custody and the father agreed that the children should live with her. While in their father's custody, both children attempted to escape and the police were involved in relocating them.

16. In *Frame* v. *Smith* (1987), 9 R.F.L. (3d) 225 (S.C.C.), a majority of the court concluded that a father did not have a right of action either in tort or for breach of fiduciary duty against the mother and her husband for interfering with his access rights under a court order. The plaintiff claimed both out-of-pocket expenses estimated at $25,000 and damages for severe emotional and psychic distress. For commentary that generally supports Madam Justice Wilson's dissent, see Leon, "The Wisdom of Solomon: A Comment on *Frame* v. *Smith*" (1988), 3 C.F.L.Q. 397 and Diamond, "Enforcement of Custody and Access Orders" (1989), 4 C.F.L.Q. 303.

17. Separated or divorced parents frequently view child support and access as two parts of a bargain. Generally, the law does not. The following cases confirm the principles that denial of access by the custodial parent does not affect the obligation of the other parent to provide child support, nor does the failure to pay support affect the right to access: *Re Bockner* (1971), 6 R.F.L. 34 (Ont. H.C.); *Hill* v. *Humphrey* (1972), 7 R.F.L. 171 (Ont. C.A.); *Wright* v. *Wright* (1973), 12 R.F.L. 200 (Ont. C.A.); *Woodburn* v. *Woodburn* (1976), 21 R.F.L. 179 (N.S. T.D.); *Patton* v. *Patton* (1982), 27 R.F.L. (2d) 202 (N.S. T.D.); *Twaddle* v. *Twaddle* (1985), 46 R.F.L. (2d) 337 (N.S. C.A.); *Turecki* v. *Turecki* (1989), 19 R.F.L. (3d) 127 (B.C. C.A.); *Lee* v. *Lee* (1990), 29 R.F.L. (3d) 417 (B.C. C.A.); *Director of Maintenance Enforcement of P.E.I.* v. *Houston* (1992), 43 R.F.L. (3d) 153 (P.E.I. C.A.); *Campbell* v. *Campbell* (1993), 44 R.F.L. (3d) 229 (B.C. C.A.); *McGregor* v. *McGregor* (1993), 49 R.F.L. (3d) 17 (N.B. Q.B.); *Hyde* v. *Lang* (1996), 22 R.F.L. (4th) 317 (Ont. Gen. Div.); and *Martin* v. *Martin* (1998), 42 R.F.L. (4th) 251 (Nfld. C.A.). However, child support was suspended until access was granted in *Kett* v. *Kett* (1976), 28 R.F.L. 1 (Ont. H.C.); *Pickard (Coffin)* v. *Coffin* (1980), 16 R.F.L. (2d) 380 (P.E.I. S.C.); *Brownell* v. *Brownell* (1987), 9 R.F.L. (3d) 31 (N.B. Q.B.); *Casement* v. *Casement* (1987), 9 R.F.L. (3d) 169 (Alta. Q.B.); *Harrison* v. *Harrison* (1987), 10 R.F.L. (3d) 1 (Man. Q.B.); *Wilbur* v. *MacMurray* (1991), 122 N.B.R. (2d) 79 (Q.B.); and *Kuntz* v. *Kaytor* (1995), 10 R.F.L. (4th) 246 (Sask. Q.B.). Significantly, the New Brunswick Court of Appeal in *McGregor* v. *McGregor* (1994), 3 R.F.L. (4th) 343 suggested (at 349) that child support might be suspended or terminated in response to a failure to comply with an access order if this would not harm the child; in other words, if the custodial parent could afford adequate child care without the support. See also *Welstead* v. *Bainbridge* (1995), 10 R.F.L. (4th) 410 (Ont. Gen. Div.) and *Paynter* v. *Reynolds* (1997), 34 R.F.L. (4th) 272 (P.E.I. C.A.).

The adoption of *Child Support Guidelines* affects this issue. Generally the courts have little or no discretion regarding the child support award in the vast majority of cases. It is doubtful that a court can link access and child support under the *Guidelines*, except perhaps when deciding support for adult children or non-biological children under ss. 3(2) and 5. In *A. (J.A.)* v. *A. (S.R.)* (1999), 45 R.F.L. (4th) 165 (B.C. C.A.), Madam Justice Southin stated (at 171):

> . . . [T]he law is believed to be that, even if one parent deliberately and maliciously destroys the relationship between the other parent and the children of their marriage, which is what the respondent has done if the allegations [of child abuse] are false, that other parent must still pay the Guidelines amounts. If that is the law, then the law, on this point, lacks a moral basis.

Do you agree? Generally, see Chapter 8, **CHILD SUPPORT**.

18. In *Ungerer* v. *Ungerer* (1998), 37 R.F.L. (4th) 41 (B.C. C.A.), there were numerous access problems and the mother served a jail term for contempt. Problems continued and eventually the daughter refused to see her father. The court ended the husband's obligation to pay spousal support in part because of the wife's intransigent refusal to facilitate access, reasoning (at 50) that s. 17(6) of the *Divorce Act* was no bar to the consideration of this conduct because it was not "conduct in relation to the marriage".

19. In 1989 the Ontario legislature passed legislation intended to allow more effective enforcement of access orders. See *Children's Law Reform Amendment Act, 1988*, Bill 124. This legislation would, *inter alia*, allow for speedy access to the courts, empower the courts to order compensatory access when access is wrongfully withheld and permit court orders requiring the custodial parent to provide security that would be forfeited if access were wrongfully withheld. The Bill received Royal Assent on June 20, 1989 but has never been proclaimed into force. The main opposition to the Bill came from women's groups claiming that it would simply provide fathers with an institutional means of harassing mothers through motions over minor or imagined interference with access rights. See also *Family Law Statutes Amendment Act, 1999*, S.A. 1999, c. 22, adding a new Part 7.1, Enforcement of Access Orders, to Alberta's *Domestic Relations Act*, R.S.A. 1980, c. D-37.

20. For further reading, see Weisman, "On Access After Parental Separation" (1992), 36 R.F.L. (3d) 35. This article contains an extensive bibliography.

YOUNG v. YOUNG

(1993), 49 R.F.L. (3d) 117 (S.C.C.)

MCLACHLIN J.: — This case raises the question whether a divorced parent, who does not have custody, should be able to offer his children his religious views over the objection of the custodial parent. This issue raises, in turn, the question of the place of the "best interests of the child" standard in the Canadian constitutional system.

THE BACKGROUND

Mr. and Mrs. Young were married in 1974. They had three daughters. In 1987 the Youngs separated. Mrs. Young took custody of the children; Mr. Young had access, subject to court imposed restrictions following from Mrs. Young's objection to his religious activity with the children.

The separation was marked by a protracted series of court battles. It is unnecessary to detail the many disputes over which the parties joined issue before the case finally came on for trial. Suffice it to say that one of those issues was the disagreement between the parents over which religious activities Mr. Young might appropriately undertake with his daughters. Mrs. Young was brought up in the Anglican church. She expressed a wish that her children be brought up in the United Church, although the evidence suggests that religion, particularly organized religion, does not play an important role in the life of Mrs. Young. Mr. Young converted to the Jehovah's Witness faith two years prior to separation from his spouse. He wished, at the very least, to communicate his faith to his children. To this end, he read Bible stories and discussed his beliefs with his children during his periods of access. He also questioned them about religious matters during these periods.

The evidence shows that the older two daughters like their father but, as time went on, came to dislike his religious instruction. There was evidence that by exposing his older children to his religious beliefs, Mr. Young was damaging his relationship with his children and contributing to the stress the children were experiencing in adjusting to their parents' separation. On the other hand, the evidence also established that the children were functioning in an entirely normal fashion, suggesting that neither their mental nor physical health had been adversely affected by the dispute between their parents over Mr. Young's religious instruction, or by that instruction itself.

The trial judge granted custody of the children to Mrs. Young and access to Mr. Young. But Mr. Young's access was again restricted by court order. The order provided that Mr. Young not discuss the Jehovah's Witness religion with the children, not take them to any religious services, canvassing, or meetings, and not expose the children to religious discussions with third parties without the prior consent of Mrs. Young. Both parties were ordered not to make adverse remarks about the other's beliefs. Mr. Young was also enjoined from preventing blood transfusions for the children, should the need arise. The basis of the order was the trial judge's finding (1989), 24 R.F.L. (3d) 193, at p. 211, that "the religious conflict [between the parents] was causing a problem for the children." She wrote, at p. 215:

> There will be certain restrictions because that is necessary to protect the best interests of these children. That can only be done by putting an end to this religious conflict. The respondent has become so involved in enforcing his rights he has completely overlooked the welfare of the children. The respondent can have a meaningful relationship with his children without promoting his religious beliefs. . . . If the respondent is seriously interested in retaining a relationship with his children, he will have no difficulty abiding by the restrictions I propose to place on him when he has access.

. . . Mr. Young appealed. The Court of Appeal (1990), 50 B.C.L.R. (2d) 1, Southin J.A. dissenting in part, set aside the limitations on religious discussion and attendance, on the ground that it is in the best interests of children that they come to know their non-custodial parent fully, including his or her religious beliefs. The majority concluded, at p. 108, that restrictions should not be placed on the freedom of an access parent to discuss religion with his or her child, or to involve the child in religious activities, unless either "the existence of, or the potential for, real harm" to the child was established on the evidence, or the evidence established that the child did not consent to being subject to the access parent's views or practices. . . .

A. The Limitations on Mr. Young's Access

1. *The Constitutional Validity of the Best Interests of the Child Standard*

. . . Two questions arise. First, what does the "best interests of the child" test require? Second, does this test, properly understood, infringe upon the guarantees of freedom of religion, expression, association, and equality under the *Canadian Charter of Rights and Freedoms*?

. . .

The wording of the Act

Parliament has adopted the "best interests of the child" test as the basis upon which custody and access disputes are to be resolved. Three aspects of the way Parliament has done this merit comment.

First, the "best interests of the child" test is the *only* test. The express wording of s. 16(8) of the *Divorce Act* requires the court to look *only* at the best interests of the child in making orders of custody and access. This means that parental preferences and "rights" play no role.

Second, the test is broad. Parliament has recognized that the variety of circumstances which may arise in disputes over custody and access is so diverse that predetermined rules, designed to resolve certain types of disputes in advance, may not be useful. Rather, it has been left to the judge to decide what is in the "best interests of the child," by reference to the "condition, means, needs and other circumstances" of the child. Nevertheless, the judicial task is not one of pure discretion. By embodying the "best interests" test in legislation and by setting out general factors to be considered, Parliament has established a legal test, albeit a flexible one. Like all legal tests, it is to be applied according to the evidence in the case, viewed objectively. There is no room for the judge's personal predilections and prejudices. The judge's duty is to apply the law. He or she must not do what he or she wants to do but what he or she ought to do.

Third, s. 16(10) provides that in making an order, the court shall give effect "to the principle that a child of the marriage should have as much contact with each spouse as is consistent with the best interests of the child." This is significant. It stands as the only specific factor which Parliament has seen fit to single out as being something which the judge must consider. By mentioning this factor, Parliament has expressed its opinion that contact with each parent is valuable, and that the judge should ensure that this contact is maximized. The modifying phrase "as is consistent with the best interests of the child" means that the goal of maximum contact of each parent with the child is not absolute. To the extent that contact conflicts with the best interests of the child, it may be restricted. But *only* to that extent. Parliament's decision to maintain maximum contact between the child and both parents is amply supported by the literature, which suggests that children benefit from continued access: Michael Rutter, *Maternal Deprivation Reassessed*, 2d ed. (Harmondsworth: Penguin, 1981), Benians, "Preserving Parental Contact," in *Fostering Parental Contact: Arguments in Favour of Preserving Contact between Children in Care and Parents* (London: Family Rights Group, 1982).

Wood J.A., in the Court of Appeal, put the matter as follows, at p. 93:

> It seems to me that at the very least, by enacting this subsection [s. 16(10) of the *Divorce Act*], Parliament intended to facilitate a meaningful, as well as a continuing, post-divorce relationship between the children of the marriage and the access parent.
>
> Without limiting the generality of the adjective "meaningful", such a relationship would surely include the opportunity on the part of the child to know that parent well and to enjoy the benefit of those attributes of parenthood which such person has to share. In most cases that would clearly be in the best interests of the child, and the best interests of the child, not parental rights, are the focus of the whole of s. 16 of the Act.

I would summarize the effect of the provisions of the *Divorce Act* on matters of access as follows. The ultimate test in all cases is the best interest of the child. This is a positive test, encompassing a wide variety of factors. One of the factors which the judge seeking to determine what is in the best interests of the child must have regard to is the desirability of maximizing contact between the child and each parent. But in the final analysis, decisions on access must reflect what is in the best interests of the child.

It follows from this that the proposition, put to us in argument, that the custodial parent should have the right to forbid certain types of contact between the access parent and the child, must fail. The custodial parent's wishes are not the ultimate criterion for limitations on access: see *King* v. *Low*, [1985] 1 S.C.R. 87, at p. 101. The only circumstance in which contact with either parent can be limited is where the contact is shown to conflict with the best interests of the child.

Risk of harm to the child is not a condition precedent for limitations on access. The ultimate determinant in every case must be the best interests of the child. Many decisions on access may involve no reference to harm. For example, a judge might conclude that it is not in the best interest of a child that he or she see the access parent every day on the ground that this would result in undue disruption to the child's schedule of activities. Again, a judge might conclude that it is in the best interests of the child that he or she move with the custodial parent to a distant location, notwithstanding that this will limit the access of the other parent. Optimum access may simply not be in the best interests of the child for a variety of circumstances.

On the other hand, in some cases the risk of harm may be a factor to be considered in determining what is in the child's best interests. For example, where the limits on access relate to the quality of access — what the access parent may say or do with the child — the question of harm may become highly relevant. Given the interest of the child in coming to know his or her access parent as fully as possible, judges may well be reluctant to impose limits on what the access parent may say or do with the child in the absence of some evidence suggesting that the activity may harm the child. The legal test is not harm; the *Divorce Act* makes this clear. However, in some circumstances, the risk of harm to the child, or the absence thereof, may become an important factor to be considered. To this extent I agree with the Court of Appeal that, in determining whether religious discussions and activities between parent and child should be curtailed, it may well behoove the judge to enquire whether the proposed conduct poses a risk of harming the child. In doing so, the judge should bear in mind that conflict between parents over the access issue does not necessarily indicate harm, nor does the objection of the child necessarily impose that conclusion. In some circumstances they may; in some, they may not.

I conclude that the ultimate criterion for determining limits on access to a child is the best interests of the child. The custodial parent has no "right" to limit access. The judge must consider all factors relevant to determining what is in the child's best interests; a factor which must be considered in all cases is Parliament's view that contact with each parent is to be maximized to the extent that this is compatible with the best interests of the child. The risk of harm to the child, while not the ultimate legal test, may also be a factor to be considered. This is particularly so where the issue is the quality of access — what the access parent may say or do with the child. In such cases, it will generally be relevant to consider whether the conduct in question poses a risk of harm to the child which outweighs the benefits of a free and open relationship, which permits the child to know the access parent as he or she is. It goes without saying that, as for any other legal test, the judge, in determining what is in the best interests of the child, must act not on his or her personal views, but on the evidence.

B. *The Constitutionality of the Test*

The first question is whether the *Charter* applies. Because of my conclusion later in these reasons that valid orders under the "best interests of the child" standard cannot violate the *Charter*, I find it unnecessary to decide whether the *Charter* applies to an action for access under the *Divorce Act* between two parents. For the purposes of this section, I assume that it does.

The constitutional focus in this case centres on the guarantee of freedom of religion in s. 2(*a*) of the *Charter* and the guarantee of freedom of expression in s.

2(*b*) of the *Charter*. The guarantees of freedom of association and equality apply only tangentially, if at all, and were not emphasized in argument.

The respondent says that the legislative provision for the "best interests of the child" violates his religious and expressive freedom. The argument is that in some cases the "best interests of the child" will require a judge to make an order limiting expressive or religious freedom. Therefore, it is submitted, the test is unconstitutional, unless it can be saved under s. 1.

In my view, this argument cannot stand. The reason is that the guarantees of religious freedom and expressive freedom in the *Charter* do not protect conduct which violates the best interests of the child test. . . .

2.   *Whether the Order of the Trial Judge is Valid under the Divorce Act*

The question is whether the trial judge correctly applied the "best interests of the child" test set out in s. 16(8) and (10) of the *Divorce Act*.

The trial judge took a custody-oriented approach to the question of whether the father should be allowed to discuss and practice his religion with the children. For her the first question (at p. 205) was "who gets custody and guardianship of the children and what flows from that." She concluded that custody confers on the custodial parent the exclusive "right" to make all decisions with respect to the child's education, health care, and religion. It followed inevitably, at p. 205, from this that she saw the custodial parent as possessing the "sole responsibility for . . . the religious instruction of the child." This exclusive right in Mrs. Young to determine the child's religious instruction led directly to her conclusion that Mr. Young should be prevented from discussing his religious ideas with the children. Having concluded that the religious conflict "must stop," she ordered it stopped in the manner which the custodial parent desired, without further discussion of whether another alternative might better serve the interests of the children.

This reasoning departs from the best interest of the child test as outlined earlier in these reasons in three respects. First, it places undue emphasis on the wishes of the custodial parent. The custodial parent is viewed as having the "right" to determine limits on access. In my respectful opinion, this rights-based approach is erroneous. The only question to be considered where limitation of access is in issue is what is in the best interests of the child. While the custodial parent has the obligation to make certain basic decisions as to how the child is educated, which may extend to religious matters, this does not automatically mean that religious contacts with the access parent of a different faith are to be excluded. It is not the wishes of the custodial parent that govern terms of access, but the best interests of the child.

Second, the trial judge failed to consider the benefits which might enure to the children from coming to know their father as he was — that is, as a devoutly religious man devoted to the Jehovah's Witness faith. She made no reference to Parliament's instruction in s. 16(10) that the child shall have as much contact with both parents as is compatible with her best interests.

Thirdly, the trial judge failed to consider adequately whether there was any evidence of a risk of harm to the children which might offset the benefit of full access to their father's values, including those related to religion. While in some circumstances access may be limited on grounds unrelated to harm, in cases such as this, where the issue is whether entirely lawful discussions and activities between the access parent and the child should be curtailed, it behooves the judge to enquire whether the conduct poses a risk of harming the child. While the trial judge alluded to the possibility that if Mr. Young continued to share his religion with the children, he would damage his relationship with the older two, she failed to allude to any other suggestion of harm and failed to consider whether such harm might outweigh the benefit to be gained from a freer, fuller relationship with their father.

The trial judge's undue emphasis on the "rights" of the custodial parent, coupled with her failure to consider the benefits to be gained from unrestricted contact with the access parent or whether those benefits were offset by a greater risk of harm to the children, may have clouded her appreciation of what was in their best interests. It was therefore open to the Court of Appeal to reconsider the matter and seek to give further guidance as to the factors to be considered in determining what is in the child's best interest in cases such as these.

Southin J.A. in the Court of Appeal took a similar but less absolute view of the rights conferred by custody. The custodial parent, according to her, has the "final say" on all matters of religion, although the "right to know" the access parent and the problems with the enforceability of any order restricting the conversation of the access parent led her to conclude that the trial judge's restriction in respect of religious conversations could not stand.

The majority of the Court of Appeal, by contrast, saw the matter less in terms of the custodial parent's "right" to decide all religious matters affecting the children, and more in terms of the best interests of the children. Unfettered by notions of the custodial parent's rights, the majority of the Court of Appeal asked simply what was in the best interests of the child. . . .

Thus, for the majority in the Court of Appeal, the prime concern was the best interests of the child. An order for custody vests the custodial parent with the power to determine the child's religious upbringing, to the extent that this parent can require the child to observe a faith until the age of discretion; this is in the child's best interests where the parents cannot agree. A custody order does not, however, give the custodial parent the "right" to limit the access parent's ability to share his or her religious views with the child, unless that is shown on the evidence not to be in the child's best interests. Viewed thus, the notions of custody and access unite in a common purpose of promoting the child's best interests.

The majority held that an access parent's conduct with his child may be limited where the evidence shows the existence of, or potential for, real harm to the child, or where the child does not consent to the instruction. On the latter point, Wood J.A. noted that while it may be in the best interests of the child that the custodial parent be allowed to enforce religious practices against the child's wishes, that rationale did not extend to the access parent. Both limitations on the right to access found by the Court of Appeal are grounded in the best interests of the child. The majority also held that expert evidence, based on scientific criteria, is required to show harm. While, for the reasons discussed earlier, I would not agree as a general proposition that in every case the risk of harm to the child must be established to justify limitations on access, in the context of the dispute in this case, I do not think that the majority of the Court of Appeal erred in placing considerable emphasis on the absence on the evidence of a risk of harm to the child.

I do not share the view of the majority of the Court of Appeal that expert evidence is required in all cases. Nor am I convinced that the failure of the child to consent to instruction necessarily precludes the conclusion that such instruction by the access parent is in the best interests of the child. Apart from these caveats, I substantially subscribe to the views expressed by Wood J.A.

The majority of the Court of Appeal held that the evidence did not establish that harm was being caused to the children. On the issue of the children's consent, Wood J.A. concluded that no order was necessary because Mr. Young had confirmed under oath that he would respect his children's wishes with respect to the activities they objected to — attending services with him and accompanying him on his proselytizing missions. In the end, the majority did not find that it was in the best interests of the children, all factors considered, that even this limited form of religious activity by the access parent be restricted.

If one accepts, as did the majority of the Court of Appeal, that the issue of the children's accompanying Mr. Young to services and in his evangelical efforts is resolved by Mr. Young's undertakings — and I see no reason not to do so given his record of compliance to date — the only issue is whether the order forbidding Mr. Young to discuss religion with his children is valid. Apart from the value of getting to know their father and the difficulty of enforcement which led Southin J.A. to reject this restriction, it is questionable that a proper application of the "best interests of the child" test supports it. Conflict between the parents is, in and of itself, not a sufficient basis for assuming that the child's interests will not be served. There was, in this case, evidence that the children were functioning in an entirely normal fashion, and had not been adversely affected by the dispute between their parents or by their father's religious instruction. We are left, then, with the trial judge's concern that Mr. Young's relationship with his children would deteriorate if he persisted in his religious instruction during his periods of access.

With the greatest respect to the trial judge, this was not, on the record in this case, a sufficient reason for restricting access. Insofar as the possible deterioration of Mr. Young's relationship with his daughters can be considered unfortunate, the alternative — a relationship which prevents them from knowing him as he is — is also undesirable. In these circumstances, any perceived harm to the children cannot be said to outweigh the benefits of unrestricted access. In short, this is not a case where the evidence supports the view that the best interests of the children require further curtailment of the father's communication of religious views and practices than already had been agreed to.

I conclude that the trial judge's orders preventing Mr. Young from discussing religion with his children were not supportable on the evidence. In view of Mr. Young's undertakings, the orders relating to church attendance and proselytizing were unnecessary. The order enjoining the respondent from preventing blood transfusions was unnecessary from a practical point of view. Parents should, of course, not make disparaging comments about the other parent's religion, but the matter might, on the record here, best have been left to the parents' good sense.

L'HEUREUX—DUBE J. (dissenting): — I have had the advantage of reading the opinion of my colleague Justice McLachlin. With great deference, I disagree both with her reasons and the result she has reached. Since I do not characterize the issue quite as my colleague does, I will pursue my own analysis.

The main issue in this case, in my view, concerns access by a non-custodial parent to his children whose custody was granted to the other parent. More precisely, this court must determine whether curtailment of access is warranted in the circumstances of this case. The focus of the inquiry is the standard applicable to such a determination. According to the Court of Appeal, the test is one of harm to the children. I disagree. In my view, the only applicable test is the best interests of the children, assessed from a child-centred perspective, a test which is mandated by the *Divorce Act*, R.S.C. 1985, c. 3 (2nd Supp.) (the "Act"), as well as provincial legislation, and which is universally applied and constitutionally sound. While the respondent, the father in this case, raises the issues of freedom of religion and expression and the infringement of his guarantees under s. 2(*a*) and (*b*) of the

Canadian Charter of Rights and Freedoms (the "*Charter*") due to the trial judge's order restricting access to his children, these questions simply do not arise in the circumstances of this case. If they do, I agree with my colleague that there is no infringement of the *Charter*. . . .

CUSTODY . . .

Despite these changes over time with respect to who is regarded as the appropriate custodial parent, the nature and scope of custody itself have remained relatively constant. The chief feature of such orders was, and still is, the implied, if not explicit, conferral of parental authority on the person granted custody. The long-standing rule at common law is that an order of custody entails the right to exercise full parental authority. In the case of a sole custody order, that authority is vested in one parent to the exclusion of the other.

The power of the custodial parent is not a "right" with independent value which is granted by courts for the benefit of the parent, but is designed to enable that parent to discharge his or her responsibilities and obligations to the child. It is, in fact, the child's right to a parent who will look after its best interests. . . .

It has long been recognized that the custodial parent has a duty to ensure, protect, and promote the best interests of the child. That duty includes the sole and primary responsibility to oversee all aspects of day-to-day life and long-term well-being, as well as major decisions with respect to education, religion, health, and well-being. This is reflected in the decision of the Ontario Court of Appeal in *Kruger* v. *Kruger* (1979), 25 O.R. (2d) 673, at p. 677, in which Thorson J.A. stated:

> In my view, to award one parent the exclusive custody of a child is to clothe that parent, for whatever period he or she is awarded the custody, with full parental control over, and ultimate parental responsibility for, the care, upbringing and education of the child, generally to the exclusion of the right of the other parent to interfere in the decisions that are made in exercising that control or in carrying out that responsibility.

. . .

The non-custodial parent retains certain residual rights over the child as one of its two natural guardians, among which is the right to apply to the court for variation of custody and access terms. Various other entitlements have been recognized at common law, including, subject to the best interests of the child, the right to access, the right to contest the child's adoption, the right to claim guardianship of the person of the child upon the death of the custodial parent, and the right to succeed to the child's property, among others (see Maidment, at p. 34; *Dussault* c. *Ladouceur*, supra; Law Reform Commission of Canada, *Report on Family Law* (1976); Law Reform Commission of Canada, "Children of Divorcing Spouses: Proposals for Reform" (Ottawa: 1985)).

The traditional decision making power of the custodial parent recognized by law is intimately connected to the welfare of the child, as the need for a secure and constant source of parental responsibility in the life of the child is well understood among those who are knowledgeable in the psychology of children. Joseph Goldstein, Anna Freud, and Albert J. Solnit in *Beyond the Best Interests of the Child* (New York: Free Press, 1979), identified three imperatives that must govern child placement decisions such as custody arrangements. Such decisions should: safeguard the child's need for continuity of relationships; reflect the child's, not the adult's, sense of time; and take into account the law's inability to supervise interpersonal relationships and the limits of knowledge to make long-range predictions (at pp. 31,

40, and 49). The need for continuity generally requires that the custodial parent have the autonomy to raise the child as he or she sees fit without interference with that authority by the State or the non-custodial parent, as it is the inability of the custodial parent to sufficiently protect those interests which poses the real threat to the welfare of the child. A custody award can thus be regarded as a matter of *whose* decisions to prefer, as opposed to *which* decisions to prefer. In the words of Bernard M. Dickens, "The Modern Function and Limits of Parental Rights" (1981), 97 L.Q.R. 462, at p. 473, "the identification of who is allowed to decide is no less important in theory, and more important in practice, than how choice is to be exercised between options.". . .

As Goldstein, Freud, and Solnit stress, an important function of the law on divorce or separation is to reinforce the remainder of the family unit so that children may get on with their lives with as little disruption as possible. Courts are not in a position, nor do they presume to be able, to make the necessary day-to-day decisions which affect the best interests of the child. That task must rest with the custodial parent, as he or she is the person best placed to assess the needs of the child in all its dimensions. In my view, this was eloquently expressed by Weatherston J. (later J.A.) in *McCahill* v. *Robertson* (1974), 17 R.F.L. 23 (Ont. H.C.), at pp. 23-24:

> *A child must know where its home is and to whom it must look for guidance and admonition* and the person having custody and having that responsibility must have the opportunity to exercise it without any feeling by the infant that it can look elsewhere. It may be an unfortunate thing for the spouse who does not have custody that he or she does lose a great deal of the authority and indeed to some extent the love and affection of the child that might otherwise be gained, but this is one of the things which is inherent in separation and divorce. The parents cannot have it both ways. As I say, in my view, *it is vitally necessary that the child know where its home is, to whom it is responsible and that there be no doubt in the mind of the child as to that.* Within those limits, the parent who does not have custody should, of course, have access to the child under terms which are as reasonably generous as possible, but without interfering with that basic responsibility on the parent having custody. [Emphasis added.]

Once a court has determined who is the appropriate custodial parent, it must, indeed it can do no more than, presume that that parent will act in the best interests of the child. As the New Brunswick Court of Appeal stated in *Fougère* v. *Fougère* (1987), 6 R.F.L. (3d) 314, at p. 316:

> Once courts award custody they must, in our view, support the custodial parent in that parent's reasonable efforts to bring up the children, including the right of the custodial parent to decide questions relating to the religious upbringing of the children.

As has been widely observed by those studying the nature and sources of changes in family institutions, popular notions of parenthood and parenting roles have undergone a profound evolution both in Canada and elsewhere in the world in recent years (see, generally, Martha Albertson Fineman, *The Illusion of Equality: The Rhetoric and Reality of Divorce Reform* (Chicago: University of Chicago Press, 1991); Lenore J. Weitzman, *The Divorce Revolution: The Unexpected Social and Economic Consequences for Women & Children in America* (New York: Free Press, 1985); Janice Drakich, "In Whose Best Interests? The Politics of Joint Custody," in Bonnie Fox, ed., *Family Bonds and Gender Divisions: Readings in the Sociology of the Family* (Toronto: Canadian Scholars' Press, 1988); Carol Smart and Selma Sevenhuijsen, *Child Custody and the Politics of Gender* (London: Routledge, 1989); and Susan B. Boyd, "Women, Men and Relationships with Children: Is Equality Possible?", in Karen Busby, Lisa Fainstein, and Holly Penner, eds., *Equality Issues in Family Law: Considerations for Test Case Litigation* (Winnipeg: Legal Research

Institute of the University of Manitoba, 1990)). One of the central tenets of this new vision is that child care both is no longer and should no longer be exclusively or primarily the preserve of women. Society has largely moved away from the assumptions embodied in the tender years doctrine that women are inherently imbued with characteristics which render them better custodial parents (for a discussion, see David L. Chambers, "Rethinking the Substantive Rules for Custody Disputes in Divorce" (1984) 83 Mich. L. Rev. 477). Moreover, both economic necessity and the movement toward social and economic equality for women have resulted in an increase in the number of women in the paid workforce. Many people have tended to assume that a natural result of this change would be the concurrent sharing of household and child-care responsibilities with spouses, companions, and, of course, fathers. In addition, the increased emphasis on the participation of fathers in the raising of children and financial support after divorce gave rise to claims by fathers and fathers' rights groups for legislative changes that would entitle them to the benefit of neutral presumptions in custody decisions.

A corollary of the acceptance of neutral parenting roles is the notion that children, after divorce, need to maintain contact with both parents. It is now widely assumed to be self-evident in the child's best interests to ensure the non-custodial parent's involvement in the life of the child. One result of these changes has been the emergence of joint custody awards, which are predicated explicitly on equality of parental responsibilities and the belief that children's interests are served by maximizing the involvement of both parents in decisions concerning the child.

The custody provisions of the Act reflect, to some degree, this evolving view of parental roles. Under the best interests test, courts no longer automatically grant custody according to the tender years doctrine. Instead, decisions are made according to the best interests of the child without the benefit of a presumption in favour of the mother, or, for that matter, the father. Section 16(4) of the Act, for the first time, specifies that a court may make joint custody orders. Section 16(10) of the Act contains the "friendly parent" rule, which directs courts, when granting custody, to take into account the willingness of the parent seeking custody to maximize the contact of the other parent with the child of the marriage. It is clear, then, that the Act envisages contact between the child and each of its parents as a worthy goal which should be, all other things being equal, in the best interests of the child. This is a value which courts have always recognized in generally granting generous access to the non-custodial parent.

Wood J.A., however, has interpreted the Act as reflecting significant changes to the traditional law of custody and access. More specifically, he expressed the view that s. 16(10) of the Act indicates a desire on the part of Parliament to enlarge the concept of access beyond its traditional scope. Therefore, according to him, the traditional decision making power of custodial parents has been curtailed by s. 16, which, taken as a whole, requires a distribution of rights between the parents. . . .

Professor Payne, in *Payne on Divorce*, at p. 144, shares the view that the access provisions in the Act do not confer any authority on the non-custodial parent to participate in the major decisions of a child's life. Rather, s. 16(5) of the Act provides that "[u]nless the court orders otherwise, a spouse who is granted access to a child of the marriage has the right to make inquiries, and to be given information, as to the health, education and welfare of the child." It does not mandate that the custodial parent consult with the access spouse when making such decisions with respect to the child. . . . Custody, as defined in s. 2(1) of the Act, "includes care, upbringing and any other incident of custody." Payne states, at pp. 145-146:

> The provisions of the *Divorce Act, 1985*, and particularly the definitions of "custody" and "access" in subsection 2(1) of the Act, apparently preclude Canadian courts from reverting to a narrow definition of custody. The word "includes" in the definition of custody necessarily implies that the term embraces a wider range of powers tha[n] those specifically designated in subsection 2(1) . . . . The opinions expressed in *Kruger* v. *Kruger, supra,* have thus been statutorily endorsed by the *Divorce Act, 1985.* Consequently, in the absence of a successful application to vary an unqualified sole custody disposition with respect to all or any of the incidents of custody, *the non-custodial spouse with access privileges is a passive bystander who is excluded from the decision-making process in matters relating to the child's welfare, growth and development. This remains true notwithstanding that subsection 16(10) of the Divorce Act, 1985 provides that the court shall promote "maximum contact" between the child and the non-custodial parent to the extent that this is consistent with the best interests of the child.* [Emphasis added.]

I could not agree more, given the wording of the Act itself and the generally accepted view of custody both before and since its enactment. The Act neither suggests nor requires the division of parental responsibilities between the custodial and access parent. If Parliament had intended such a result, it would have used much clearer and less ambiguous language.

It goes without saying that I do not share the assertion of my colleague that "the proposition, put to us in argument, that the custodial parent should have the right to forbid certain types of contact between the access parent and the child, must fail" [at pp. 150-151]. The proposition is not one of "rights"; it is one of duty and obligation to the child's best interests. For example, a custodial parent, aware of sexual or other abuse by the non-custodial parent, would be remiss in his or her duty to the child not to cut off access by the abuser immediately, with or without a court order. One cannot stress enough that it is from the perspective of the child's interest that these powers and responsibilities must be assessed, as the "rights" of the parent are not a criterion.

The arguments in favour of increased authority over the child by the access parent are closely related to those which support a presumption in favour of joint custody . . . . They rest on the premise that the relationship of authority and obligation that existed between each of the parents and the child during the marriage should and can continue, despite the fact that the parents may no longer be willing or able to co-operate on its exercise. While joint custody may remain an ideal solution in proper cases, particularly when parents are willing and able to co-operate, such premises are often based on illusion rather than reality, and may, in the words of Thorston J.A., amount to "a triumph of optimism over prudence" (*Kruger* v. *Kruger,* supra, at p. 681).

Unlike in other jurisdictions, the Act contains no presumption in favour of joint custody. Nor have Canadian courts generally accepted the view that joint custody is to be preferred in judicial orders as to custody and access. . . .

When parents are willing and able to share parenting responsibilities, they usually do so by agreement, which courts generally uphold. . . . Courts are also reluctant to interfere with shared parenting arrangements that have survived for a period of time after parental separation or divorce. . . .

But the reality of divorce and the circumstances of the parties cannot easily be dismissed. When implementing the objectives of the Act, whether considering joint custody or fashioning access orders, courts, in my view, must be conscious of the gap between the ideals of shared parenting and the social reality of custody and child-care decisions. Despite the neutrality of the Act, forces such as wage rates, job ghettos, and socialization about care-giving still operate in a manner that cause many women to "chose" to take on the care-giving role both during marriage and after divorce. Hence, ''we remain a good distance away from the kind of equality which would make decisions between mothers and fathers as to who is going to leave the workforce to care for young children truly gender neutral'' (S. Boyd, ''Is Equality Possible?'', at p. 76; Susan B. Boyd, ''Child Custody Law and the Invisibility of Women's Work'' (1989) 96 Queen's Quarterly 831). Moreover, research uniformly shows that men as a group have not yet embraced responsibility for child care. The vast majority of such labour, both before and after divorce, is still performed by women, whether those women work outside the home or not, and women remain the sole custodial parent in the majority of cases by mutual consent of the parties (see *The Evaluation of the Divorce Act, Phase II: Monitoring and Evaluation* (Ottawa: Department of Justice, 1990), at p. 99; Janice Drakich, ''In Search of the Better Parent: The Social Construction of Ideologies of Fatherhood'' (1989) 3 C.J.W.L. 69). Nor does a joint custody order in most cases result in truly shared custody. Rather, in day-to-day practice, joint custody tends to resemble remarkably sole custody, as in many such orders care and control remain with one person (C. James Richardson, *Court-based Mediation in Four Canadian Cities: Overview of Research Results* (Ottawa: Department of Justice, 1988), at p. 35; S. Boyd, ''Is Equality Possible?'', at p. 72; Martha Fineman, ''Dominant Discourse, Professional Language and Legal Change in Child Custody Decisionmaking'' (1988) 101 Harv. L. Rev. 727). The person who has performed the primary care-giving role within the marriage, as a rule, retains that obligation upon separation and divorce. Thus, the lived experience of child care for both women and children after divorce has changed much less than we might support or wish. . . .

Support for the decisions of the custodial parent in the discharge of his or her responsibilities remains crucial if the child is to flourish. The conferral of decision making authority on the custodial parent acknowledges and reflects the actual day-to-day reality of this task. It is well documented that the single parent bearing primary responsibility for the care of children often labours under increased social, economic, and emotional burdens that far exceed those of the intact family. That burden is acutely felt by the children, who typically experience a myriad of hardships in this situation (see Miriam Grassby, ''Women in Their Forties: The Extent of Their Rights to Alimentary Support'' (1991) 30 R.F.L. (3d) 369). These may include a reduction in the standard of living, fewer resources for discretionary activities such as sports, artistic and leisure activities, frequent changes of residence, disruptions of friendships, and often less parental attention, as the custodial parent is commonly required to devise new ways of fulfilling continuing needs with diminished resources. In the face of the enduring tasks and obligations of the custodial parent, courts must be wary of any expansion of the traditional rights of the non-custodial parent. The clear risk is that such changes will simply reduce the decision making power of the custodial parent, without any parallel reduction in the responsibilities. This creates no benefit, and may amount to pure disturbance, both to the women who, as a rule, provide the primary care and to the children who must function within such a regime.

The perception that upholding the authority of the custodial parent emphasizes the rights of the parent at the expense of the interests of the child misconceives the problem. It is precisely to ensure the best interests of the child that the decision making power is granted to the custodial parent, as that person is uniquely situated to assess, understand, ensure, and promote the needs of the child. . . .

As I stated at the outset, the custodial parent remains the decision-maker in all aspects of the child's life. It is to avoid the spectre of the child as the field upon which the battle of competing parental rights is played out that the law confirms the authority of the custodial parent. This policy serves two functions: it precludes such contests entirely and it provides the necessary support to the parent who bears the responsibility for the child. The wisdom of this approach lies in recognizing the ease with which the interests of the child could be obscured or forgotten were courts to get into the business of parceling out jurisdiction over the emotional, spiritual, and physical welfare of the child between parents who no longer agree. This brings us to the heart of this case, a consideration of the nature of access.

ACCESS . . .

Access rights exist in recognition of the fact that it is normally in the interests of the child to continue and foster the relationship developed with both parents prior to the divorce or separation. This being said, the right to access and the circumstances in which it takes place must be perceived from the vantage point of the child. Wherever the relationship to the non-custodial parent conflicts with the best interests of the child, the furtherance and protection of the child's best interests must take priority over the desires and interests of the parent. . . .

I am in agreement with my colleague that s. 16(10) indicates that Parliament has expressed its opinion that contact with each parent is valuable. On the other hand, it must also be recognized that the goal of maximum contact is not absolute and that access may be restricted where there is evidence that such contact would otherwise conflict with the best interests of the child. This limitation on maximum contact is both abundantly clear on a straightforward reading of the section and consistent with the spirit of the Act and its focus on the best interests of the child. In my view, the analysis may and should stop at this point.

As the ultimate goal of access is the continuation of a relationship which is of significance and support to the child, access must be crafted to preserve and promote that which is healthy and helpful in that relationship so that it may survive to achieve its purpose. Accordingly, it is in the interests of the child, and arguably also in the interests of the access parent, to remove or mitigate the sources of ongoing conflict which threaten to damage or prevent the continuation of a meaningful relationship.

Wood J.A. expressed the general concern that access rights remain vulnerable to the caprices of a vengeful custodial parent. In my view, courts should not be too quick to presume that the access concerns of the custodial parent are unrelated to the best interests of the child. Although the myth is that the custodial parent typically attempts to obstruct access of the other parent, studies in Canada, England, and the United States indicate that the problem tends to be quite the reverse. . . .

Furthermore, when considering the role of access parents with respect to their children, courts should not be blind to the broader context in which custody and access are exercised. A vast number of non-custodial parents are in default of their most serious obligations to their children, as is the respondent in this appeal: the responsibility to provide economic support. . . . The most pressing issue in child custody and access is the burden borne by women and children as a consequence of the failure of men to accept their responsibilities to their children. . . . There is a certain irony in the claim to greater contact and control on the part of access parents in the face of such widespread neglect of children's basic needs.

Where there is a genuine problem with access, the non-custodial parent is not without recourse in any case. This stems from the statutory directive to facilitate access where it is in the child's best interests and the role of the judge as the arbiter of those interests in the case of a dispute between the parents. . . .

BEST INTERESTS OF THE CHILD . . .

1. Content of the Rule. . .

Custody and access decisions are pre-eminently exercises in discretion. Case-by-case consideration of the unique circumstances of each child is the hallmark of this process. . . . The wide latitude under the best interests test permits courts to respond to the spectrum of factors which can both positively and negatively affect a child. Such discretion also permits the judge to focus on the needs of the particular child before him or her, recognizing that what may constitute stressful or damaging circumstances for one child may not necessarily have the same effect on another.

While the best interests test provides the focus and perspective from which to assess custody and access decisions, the test has nonetheless been subject to evaluation and criticism from various sources. The most common concern is that it is essentially indeterminate and fails to provide the necessary direction and criteria with which to make custody and access decisions . . . .

. . . In the result, a number of presumptions have been suggested to govern the best interests test in custody decisions, the most common of which is the primary care-giver presumption. (See S. Boyd, ''Potentialities and Perils of the Primary Caregiver Presumption'' [(1991), 7 C.F.L.Q. 1]) This presumption has developed in response to the trend toward joint custody, and the resultant erosion in both the financial resources and the authority of the parent with day-to-day obligations for child rearing. Boyd expresses the concerns underlying this presumption as follows, at p. 6:

> . . . a misplaced application of ''equality'' is evident in legislative and judicial trends toward entrenching fathers' rights in child custody law, such as joint custody and access enforcement. The importance of ensuring ''equal'' fatherly input into children's lives after family breakdown even if they were not ''equally'' involved before, has been elevated to arguably too high a level in recent years. The form which this trend often takes — retaining an active and full role for both father and mother in making decisions concerning the child (joint legal custody) — potentially inhibits the autonomy and exercise of discretion by the parent with physical care of the child.

However, as she points out, one of the principal rationales for endorsing this presumption is not to supplant the best interests of the child as the ultimate objective but to ensure that those interests are protected. The presumption explicitly restores the values of commitment and demonstrated ability to nurture as well as continued psychological parenting to the child, factors which may be overshadowed by other considerations in custody disputes. The primary care-giver presumption thus recognizes the obligations and supports the authority of the parent engaged in day-to-day tasks of child rearing.

In assessing all the relevant considerations, courts must be careful that the ideals of parental sharing and equality do not overcome the lived reality of custody and access arrangements, and that the child's needs and concerns are accommodated and not obscured by abstract claims of parental rights. This is not to say that the parent's interests may not coincide with the child's interests or that a court may never validly take a parent's interests into consideration. However, to further the best interests of the child, a recognition of the close relationship between the needs of the child and the needs of the remaining family unit of which he or she is a part is essential. . . .

2. Constitutionality of the Best Interests Test

[In this section of her reasons, Justice L'Heureux-Dubé concluded that the best interests test was not unconstitutionally vague because it was not "so uncertain as to be incapable of guiding a consideration of the factors relevant to custody and access determinations". Later she held that the *Charter* could not be used to challenge the trial judge's order on the basis that it infringed the father's freedom of religion. In her view, judicial orders in custody and access disputes do not involve state action and the *Charter* has no application to them. She added that, even if the *Charter* did apply, there would be no infringement of either freedom of expression or freedom of religion where an order restricted parental religious instruction or observance on the basis of the best interests test. That is, she concluded that these freedoms never encompass activities which are not in the child's best interests.]

3. Evidence

One might have thought that the clear and unequivocal language of the Act makes the best interests of the child the only consideration in matters of custody and access, and that the only evidence required for an order limiting access would be evidence indicating that the exercise of access in a particular manner is in the best interests of the child. This is the test which was applied in this case by all of the judges, including those at the Court of Appeal, who were seized of the matter at the interim stage, as well as the trial judge. The Court of Appeal, however, relying, in particular, on the decision of the Ontario Supreme Court in *Hockey* v. *Hockey*, supra, would elevate the test to one of harm, which the custodial parent must show in order to restrict access to the children by the non-custodial parent. I say at the outset that, even under such a severe test, the appellant has established that restrictions are required. However, the question is whether harm is the test. My answer is a clear no, for the reasons that follow.

As I noted above, the Court of Appeal has equated the alleged absence of harm in this case with the best interests of the child. However, no rationale is proposed for so defining the best interests of the child. Moreover, nothing in the Act mandates or even suggests that "real danger of significant harm to the child" be the sole consideration in matters of custody and access. . . .

The harm test by which the Court of Appeal proposes to qualify the best interests test inverts the basic focus of the inquiry into custody and access. Under the best interests test, courts must consider how to best foster the child's overall development and protect the child from conflict and the disruptive effects of divorce at a vulnerable point in his or her life. In contrast, the harm test essentially requires a court to determine how much conflict and stress a child should be required to endure in order that the parent's wishes may prevail. Once the pendulum swings in that direction, it is difficult to control. If not this much stress, why not a little more? If one type of conflict, why not that? Moreover, it may be difficult, if not impossible, even for an expert, to determine with any degree of accuracy whether the child has been harmed or will be harmed in the long run. However, the most serious deficiency of the harm test is the following. While the effects of custody and access decisions always remain uncertain to some degree, the harm test places any risk of miscalculation in the degree of stress or conflict occasioned by such decisions squarely on the back of the child, depriving the child of any presumption in his or her favour. Obviously this cannot be correct from the perspective of the interests of the child. To wait until harm has occurred to correct the situation is not only to waive the benefit of prevention, but also to increase the possibility of error. Instead of minimizing the risks, the harm test would maximize them.

A discussion of the research data on the long-term effects of divorce as well as custody and access decisions on children is helpful at this point to assess the consequences of adopting the harm standard as regards the welfare of children and the importance of adhering to the best interests of the child as the overarching goal in custody and access determination. While this remains an area of social science that has yet to be comprehensively researched, studies of both the effects of divorce and the role of conflict in the subsequent family life indicate that children often suffer more extensively than is generally acknowledged on divorce, and that those who must endure continuing conflict after divorce stand at serious risk of harm down the road. The resounding message is that courts must pay more, not less, attention to the needs of children on divorce.

I acknowledge at the outset the limits in applying such research to the wider population, as the studies to date have tended to focus on groups within a particular social class or locale. . . .

Nonetheless, a number of conclusions about the effects of divorce on children emerge with remarkable consistency in all of the major studies and psychological literature on children after divorce. One of the most important of these is the role of conflict in the welfare of the child. Along with the quality of the relationship with the custodial parent and the ability to maintain contact with the non-custodial parent, there is substantial evidence that continuing conflict is the most important factor affecting the ability of children to readjust to the new family situation after divorce. It appears that, above and beyond the disruption caused by divorce or separation itself, it is the discord and disharmony within the family which are most damaging to children in the aftermath of divorce. . . .

I agree with my colleague that expert evidence should not be routinely required to establish the best interests of the child. In my view, it is a modern-day myth that experts are always better placed than parents to assess the needs of the child. Common sense requires us to acknowledge that the person involved in day-to-day care may observe changes in the behaviour, mood, attitude, and development of a child that could go unnoticed by anyone else. The custodial parent normally has the best vantage point from which to assess the interests of the child, and thus will often provide the most reliable and complete source of information to the judge on the needs and interests of that child.

Furthermore, it is important to emphasize the importance of the evidence of children in custody and access disputes, and I would not wish to suggest that their testimony alone might not be a sufficient evidentiary basis upon which to restrict access. Courts have increasingly come to accept and understand in the criminal context that children themselves can be a reliable source of evidence to the judge (*R. v. Khan*, [1990] 2 S.C.R. 531). To disregard their evidence when their own interests are directly at issue would, in my opinion, be at odds with this clear evolutionary trend in the law.

Many legal commentators have noted the degree to which custody and access disputes have become a contest between experts, involving increasing amounts of time and money (see: Nicholas Bala, "Assessing the Assessor: Legal Issues" (1990) 6 C.F.L.Q. 179; Paula J. Caplan and Jeffery Wilson, "Assessing the Child Custody Assessors" (1990) 27 R.F.L. (3d) 121; Louis Gélinas and Bartha Maria Knoppers, "Le role des experts en droit québécois en matière de garde, d'accès et de protection" (1993) 53 R. du B. 3; M. Fineman, *The Illusion of Equality*). In the absence of clear legal presumptions about the best interests of children, judges have increasingly come to rely on the recommendations of experts to determine custody and access issues, believing that such experts possess objective, scientific knowledge and can in fact "know" what is in the best interests of the child. However, expert testimony, while helpful in some and perhaps many circumstances, is often inconclusive and contradictory (Gélinas and Knoppers, at p. 17). That this should be so is not surprising, since such assessments are both speculative and may be affected by the professional values and biases of the assessors themselves.

Even where such expertise is valuable, there are impediments in such reliance. Assessments may occasion delays in resolving proceedings and may at times constitute a significant disruption in the lives of both parents and children. The cost involved in routinely hiring experts to establish the best interests of the child only increases the expense of custody litigation and is far beyond the resources of most divorcing couples. Furthermore, as Professor Bala points out, at p. 224, "much of what assessors ultimately recommend may simply be a matter of 'common experience and common sense.' "

Given these concerns, while the evidence of experts may form a valuable and necessary part of some custody and access decisions, most of the time they are unnecessary to an ordinary determination of the best interests of the child. Nor does the prospect of access restrictions inevitably require resort to expert opinion, as it may be apparent to the judge from the evidence of the parties and often the children themselves that access should only be granted subject to certain conditions. . . .

In summary, as a matter of statutory interpretation, the *Divorce Act* mandates that, in decisions of custody and access, the sole consideration be the best interests of the child. The focus must remain at all times on the child, not the needs or interests of the parents, and parental rights play no role in such decisions except insofar as they are necessary to ensure the best interests of the child.

The custodial parent is responsible for the care and upbringing of the child, including decisions concerning the education, religion, health, and well-being of the child. Parental authority rests with the custodial parent, not for his or her own benefit, but in order to enable that parent to discharge effectively the obligations and responsibilities owed to the child.

As set out in the Act, maximum contact between the child and the non-custodial parent is a worthwhile goal which should be pursued to the extent that it is in the best interests of the child. Generous and unrestricted access, which is the norm, should be favoured except when such access would not be in the best interests of the child. However, ongoing conflict between parents which adversely affects the child must be minimized or avoided, as it is the single factor which has consistently proven to be severely detrimental to children upon separation or divorce.

The best interests of the child must be approached from a child-centred perspective. It is not simply the right to be free of significant harm. It is the right of the particular child in question to the best possible arrangements in the circumstances of the parties, taking into consideration the wide spectrum of factors which may affect the child's physical, spiritual, moral, and emotional well-being, and the milieu in which the child lives.

Where the question of restrictions on access arises, the best interests of the child must be determined by considering the "condition, means, needs and other circumstances of the child" as required by the Act. The totality of these circumstances must be considered. Nothing in the Act suggests that harm should be the controlling factor. To adopt the harm standard would be to invert the focus of the best interests test and place the risk of error on the child, contrary to the objectives of the Act.

Expert evidence, while helpful in some cases, is not routinely required to establish the best interests of the child. That determination is normally possible from the evidence of the parties themselves and, in some cases, the testimony of the children involved.

Freedom of religion and expression are fundamental values protected by the *Charter*. However, the best interests of the child standard in the *Divorce Act* does not offend *Charter* values, but is completely consonant with the underlying objectives of the *Charter*. The *Charter* has no application to private disputes between parents in the family context, nor does it apply to court orders in the area of custody and access. While a child's exposure to different parental faiths or beliefs may be of value, when such exposure is a source of conflict and is not in the best interests of the child, such exposure may be curtailed.

This brings us to the evidence in this case which led to the trial judge's order restricting the respondent's access.

APPLICATION TO THE CASE . . .

The majority of the Court of Appeal found no evidence of harm which would support the order made at trial. Even if I were to agree that some measure of harm must be demonstrated before the trial judge is entitled to restrict the respondent's religious activities with the children, a view I do not share, the evidence amply demonstrates the harm such religious activity has brought about. While the rationale underlying the right of access and the objective of maximum contact is to permit the relationship to flourish, in this case the contrary result has occurred, as it has antagonized the children. . . .

Although the respondent characterizes this litigation as an attack on his religious freedom, those beliefs are not at risk, as the restrictions place no limits on the respondent's ability to engage in religious practices himself. It is the effect of his practices on the best interests of his three daughters that is in question here.

In reaching her decision about the impact of these practices on the children, the trial judge relied in large measure on the reports of the two witnesses for the court, Donna MacLean, the family court counsellor whom she found to be thorough and highly credible in both her reports and testimony, and Dr. Williams, a psychologist.

In his first report, dated November 28, 1988, Dr. Williams found that the major obstacle to smooth access was the matter of religion. He found that the children were not significantly distressed by the issue at that time, but regarded it as a potential problem in the future. He stated:

> I see Natalie as being particularly vulnerable to such issues in light of the dynamics of her personality as well as her age. As such, in my judgement some agreement and/or understanding will need to be arrived at as to the degree of religious dogma to which Mr. Young can expose the children, bearing in mind that such beliefs and related activities are anathema to Mrs. Young.

In his assessment the following year (September 22, 1989), he reported that, although they were continuing to deal with the separation adequately, the children were under increasing pressure regarding family issues. They expressed antagonism to their father, no longer trusted him, and generally did not view him in a positive light. They were firmly opposed to attending religious services or being schooled in the tenets of his beliefs. The expert found that they were under stress from the religious issue and ongoing litigation, and conveyed a need to get it settled in order to get on with their lives. Dr. Williams found, with respect to the children's emotional and social foundation, that:

... I am of the opinion that it is in the best interests of the children that the dispute over tangible and philosophic/religious issues be settled conclusively ... nothing has been broken and thus there is no apparent need for repair. If, however, the children are obliged to labor at length under the pressures they are presently experiencing a destabilizing influence — particularly in the case of Natalie — will likely be exerted.

Donna MacLean, in her report of January 30, 1989, essentially corroborated this finding. In the updated report of April 18, 1989, she noted that the children were unhappy with the access visits and that their relationship with their father was deteriorating because he was making the children feel guilty and uncomfortable by questioning them.

The trial judge also had access to the direct testimony of the two older children, who wrote letters to the judge which are most revealing of their state of mind. From the letters, it is evident that both are afraid to disclose their thoughts about the visits to their father for fear that he will make them feel guilty. Adrienne, the eldest, wrote that she did not want to visit him or sleep overnight because she thinks he will trick her into doing things and quiz her about the Jehovah's Witness religion. She expressed frustration regarding access, visitation, and the court proceedings, saying, "It's driving me crazy." Natalie, the middle child, evinced considerable distress about the family situation, stating that her father makes her feel guilty and makes her cry when she wants to go home from access visits, and that she is afraid to tell him. She repeated that she wanted the court proceedings to be over.

In my opinion, this evidence amply demonstrates the stress the children were under; much of it related to the children's resistance to becoming involved in their father's religious practices. The trial judge can in no way be said to have erred in finding that the best interests of these children were served by removing the source of conflict, particularly as the ultimate purpose of the restrictions was to preserve the relationship between the respondent and his children.

Moreover, there was evidence leading the trial judge to conclude that the respondent would not respect the wishes of the children without an order to do so.
...

As the trial judge observed, the respondent was quite unconcerned with the conflict and stress on the children caused by the pursuit of his own religious interests. At the same time as he found the resources to press his claims to religious rights, he apparently did not find the payment of maintenance a top priority. Upon reading the evidence, I cannot disagree with the trial judge that the respondent's concern with religious rights had clearly overtaken the practical realities of parenthood and overshadowed his larger responsibilities to his children in this case.

Since writing these reasons, I have had the opportunity to read the joint reasons of my colleagues Cory and Iacobucci JJ. They invite the following comments.

First, as to the first part of the trial judge's order, contrary to their affirmation, the issue is not moot. It is precisely because the trial judge found as a fact that the respondent could not be trusted for the reasons she outlined, that she issued that order. How can a court of appeal reverse those findings of fact, and yet, on the same facts, affirm that such an order is no longer necessary, particularly when the court of appeal has not indicated where the trial judge has erred in her assessment of those facts?

As to the second part of the order, my colleagues assert that the best interests test does not support an order preventing the respondent from discussing religion with his children, on the ground that it is "difficult to accept that any genuine and otherwise proper discussion between a parent and his or her child should be curtailed by court orders" [at p. 168]. Otherwise, they suggest, a non-custodial parent who espouses a theory of evolution would be ordered, under the best interests test, not to discuss or explain his or her views to a child in the custody of a parent who is a member of a fundamentalist religion.

However, this scenario has nothing to do with the facts of this case. With respect, to equate the two scenarios is to misapprehend fundamentally the focus of the best interests test. It is not the fact that the parents differ in their fundamental beliefs that warrants the restrictions in this case. It is the finding of fact made by the trial judge, on the basis of evidence she found credible, that continuing conflict over religion, including the respondent's repeated attempts to discuss religious matters with the children against their clearly expressed desires, profoundly disturbed the children and was contrary to their best interests. At the time of trial, the respondent was not engaging in other religious activities with the children, as they had already been curtailed by the interim order almost a year and a half earlier. Therefore, it is *precisely* these continuing "discussions" that were disturbing the children, causing the deterioration of their relationship with their father and which, therefore, had to be curtailed.

I wish to emphasize two points. As I thought I made clear earlier in my reasons, a child's exposure to different parental faiths or beliefs may generally be of value and even of great value; there is no presumption that such exposure is not in the best interests of the child. Rather, the contrary is true. Second, as I also emphasized earlier, generous and unrestricted access should be favoured except where it is not in the best interests of the child. Hence, restrictions such as the trial judge found to be required in the second part of her order will be rare indeed and there is no reason to suppose that, absent a threat to the best interests of the child, any question of such restrictions will arise. However, it is important to acknowledge that in those rare cases where parents cross the line and engage in conduct which constitutes, in the words of my colleagues, "indoctrination, enlistment, or harassment" [at p. 168], courts have a duty to intervene in the best interests of children. The evidence strongly suggests that this is just such a case and that is the finding of the trial judge. . . .

LA FOREST J. (GONTHIER J. concurring): (dissenting). . . I am in agreement with the reasons of Justice L'Heureux-Dubé that the issue of access should be determined on the basis of what is in the best interest of the child. I also agree with her on the constitutional issue. . . .

Accordingly, I would allow the appeal and restore the order of the trial judge on all matters except the monetary issues. . . .

SOPINKA J.: — I have read the reasons of my colleagues Justice L'Heureux-Dubé and Justice McLachlin and I find myself in agreement with McLachlin J. as to the disposition of the appeal and with most of her reasons. While I agree with McLachlin J. that the ultimate determination in deciding issues of custody and access is the "best interests of the child test," it must be reconciled with the *Canadian Charter of Rights and Freedoms*. General language in a statute which, in its breadth, potentially confers the power to override *Charter* values must be interpreted to respect those values: see *Slaight Communications Inc.* v. *Davidson*, [1989] 1 S.C.R. 1038. It cannot be done the other way around and allow the best interests test in its broadest interpretation to read down *Charter* rights so as to accommodate this interpretation.

In my view, the test in s. 16(10) of the *Divorce Act*, R.S.C. 1985, c. 3 (2nd Supp.), as amended, and the *Charter* right involved in this case, namely, freedom of religious expression, can best be reconciled by interpreting the best interests test to allow the right to be overridden only if its exercise would occasion consequences that involve more than inconvenience, upset, or disruption to the child and, incidentally, to the custodial parent. The long-term value to a child of a meaningful relationship with both parents is a policy that is affirmed in the *Divorce Act*. This means allowing each to engage in those activities which contribute to identify the parent for what he or she really is. The access parent is not expected to act out a part or assume a phony lifestyle during access periods. The policy favouring activities that promote a meaningful relationship is not displaced unless there is a substantial risk of harm to the child. . . .

"Harm" is a term which, in this context, connotes an adverse effect on the child's upbringing that is more than transitory. The impugned exercise by the access parent must be shown to create a substantial risk that the child's physical, psychological, or moral well-being will be adversely affected. Exposure to new experiences and ideas may upset children and cause them considerable discomfort. Anything from starting school to having to go to bed may evoke a strong emotional response. This does not mean that these experiences are not in the long-term best interests of the child. Similarly, conflict between parents on many matters, including religion, is not uncommon, but in itself cannot be assumed to be harmful unless it produces a prolonged acrimonious atmosphere.

I would, therefore, go a step further than my colleague McLachlin J. and conclude that what is in the best interests of the child is the generally applicable test, but in its application to restrict religious expression, risk of substantial harm is not only an important factor but also must be shown.

Interpreted in this way, the statutory test in s. 16(10) of the *Divorce Act* does not constitute a limitation on freedom of religious expression. As my colleague points out, this freedom does not extend to protect conduct which is harmful to others. I would not, however, adopt her expansion of the term "injure" as used in *R. v. Big M Drug Mart Ltd.*, [1985] 1 S.C.R. 295, to arrive at the conclusion that anything that is not in the best interests of the child (on the basis of her definition of this test) is subtracted from the *Charter* right involved.

I would dispose of the appeal and the constitutional questions as proposed by McLachlin J.

CORY and IACOBUCCI JJ.: — We have read with great interest the excellent reasons of Justice L'Heureux-Dubé and Justice McLachlin. We are in agreement with their conclusions that the best interests of the child standard provided in ss. 16(8) and 17(5) of the *Divorce Act*, R.S.C. 1985, c. 3 (2nd Supp.), does not violate s. 2(*a*), (*b*), and (*d*), and s. 15 of the *Canadian Charter of Rights and Freedoms* substantially for the reasons given by our colleagues. In this respect, however, we wish to refrain from expressing any opinion on McLachlin J.'s discussion of whether, if an infringement of the *Charter* were found, such an infringement would be so trivial as not to warrant *Charter* protection. We similarly wish to reserve our views on the question discussed by L'Heureux-Dubé J. of whether or not the *Charter* applies to judicial orders made in custody or access proceedings.

We agree, again for many of the reasons she advances, with L'Heureux-Dubé J. that the issue of access to children should be determined on the basis of what is in the best interests of the child. In that respect, we also agree with both our colleagues that expert evidence is, while admittedly helpful in some cases, not always necessary to establish the best interests of the child; that question can be determined normally from the evidence of parties themselves and the testimony, where appropriate, of the children concerned.

We note that the majority of the British Columbia Court of Appeal (1990), 50 B.C.L.R. (2d) 1, held that the matters of the children attending religious services with the respondent and accompanying him on his proselytizing activities were resolved by the respondent's undertaking to respect his children's wishes in this regard. This leaves as the only remaining issue, whether the order forbidding the respondent from discussing his religion is valid. On this point, we agree with McLachlin J. that a proper application of the best interests of the child test does not support such an order. We find it difficult to accept that any genuine and otherwise proper discussion between a parent and his or her child should be curtailed by court orders. Indeed, curtailment of explanatory or discursive conversations or exchanges between a parent and child should be rarely ordered, in our view. To take an example, suppose custodial parent A is a member of a fundamentalist religion and access parent B is a scientist who espouses the pure Darwinian theory of evolution. We find it unacceptable that parent B should be ordered, under the rubric of the best interests of the child test, not to discuss or explain his views to his child as opposed to being forbidden from indoctrinating or otherwise undermining the religious choice made by the custodial parent for the child or children involved. Surely the best interests of the child test embraces genuine discussion of religious belief, as opposed to indoctrination, enlistment, or harassment, having the aim or effect of undermining the religious decision made by the custodial parent. . . .

DROIT DE LA FAMILLE - 1150

(1993), 49 R.F.L. (3d) 317 (S.C.C.)

[Only the headnote from the R.F.L.'s is reproduced here.]

The parents separated in 1984, after cohabiting for three years, and agreed in writing that the mother would have custody of their daughter and that the father would have access. The agreement was incorporated into a court order. The relations between the parents deteriorated following the father's conversion to the Jehovah's Witness religion. The mother, a Roman Catholic, objected to the father indoctrinating their child during his access visits. In 1987 the father brought a motion to have the agreement set aside, and sought custody or increased access. The trial judge stated that the court may intervene when a parent's religious practices harm the child's best interests. He then found that the father's religious fanaticism distressed the child. Although the trial judge held that the father could give the child religious instruction, he concluded that the father could not indoctrinate or involve her in Jehovah's Witness services, conferences, or door-to-door preaching until she was able to decide which religion she preferred. The father appealed, arguing that the child had to suffer real harm for his access rights to be restricted. A majority of the Court of Appeal upheld the trial judgment.

The father appealed.

Held — The appeal was dismissed.

Per L'Heureux-Dubé J. (La Forest and Gonthier JJ. concurring): — The *Civil Code of Lower Canada* ("CCLC") governs disputes between unmarried parents. According to art. 30, the sole consideration in custody and access cases is the best interests of the child. The child, not the parents, is the focus of the determination. The best interests of the child criterion does not mean simply that the child should not suffer harm; the standard comprises many factors that a court must take into account in determining rights of access, and harm to the child is only one. The child is entitled to an order that will provide the best conditions within which he or she can develop, in accordance with the circumstances of the particular case. Subject to the child's best interests, the right of custody includes the right to make decisions about the child's religious education, until he or she is able to do so. The access parent is not, however, thereby deprived of his or her parental authority: he or she may exercise those parental rights that do not oppose the exercise of custody by the custodial parent. Therefore, the access parent may provide his or her child with a religious education within these limits.

The criterion of the child's best interests set out in art. 30 CCLC and the broad judicial discretion that it entails are not contrary to the Constitution. The court's ability to exercise a broad judicial discretion is closely linked to the promotion of the child's best interests. That criterion refers to all the considerations relating to a child and can be applied to the circumstances of any case. Consequently, it is not vague within the meaning of s. 1 or s. 7 of the *Canadian Charter of Rights and Freedoms*.

The *Charter* does not apply to private conflicts between parents within the context of a family. Nor does it pertain to court orders made to resolve such disputes. Even if the *Charter* were to apply, the access parent's rights to freedom of religion, expression, and association are not absolute, and a court may limit them if they interfere with what is in the best interests of the child. Therefore, the restrictions placed on the access order did not infringe the father's *Charter* rights. Because the trial judge did not err in principle or in his assessment of the evidence, the appeal should be dismissed.

Per Cory and Iacobucci JJ. (concurring): — The fundamental issue in custody and access cases is what is in the best interests of the child. Parental differences of opinion about religion and the discussion of these differences with the child will not necessarily harm him or her. These conversations may, in fact, be beneficial. In the case at bar, the trial judge found that the father's religious practices distressed the child and, as a result, he restricted the father's access. The trial judge was in the best position to make findings about the credibility of the witnesses, and to assess the evidence of what was in the best interests of the child. He applied the correct test and the conditions imposed were not so unreasonable as to require intervention.

Per McLachlin J. (dissenting) (Sopinka J. concurring in the result): — Articles 653 and 654 of the *Civil Code of Quebec* ("CCQ") and art. 30 of the *Civil Code of Lower Canada* affirm the best interests of the child test in custody and access cases. The analysis in *Young* v. *Young* of the constitutionality of the best interests criterion set out in ss. 16(8), 16(10), and 17(5) of the *Divorce Act* also applies to the aforementioned articles of the CCQ and the CCLC. Accordingly, the standard and articles are constitutional and do not violate any *Charter* rights.

When a court is deciding whether an access parent should be allowed to share his or her religious beliefs with his or her child, the risk of harm to the child is significant to the determination of what is in the best interests of the child. The trial and appellate court judges erred when they concluded that the child was being harmed by the religious dispute between the parents and that restrictions would be necessary in the best interests of the child. Nothing in the evidence suggested that the parents' religious conflict was creating problems for the child or that the father's teachings were having a detrimental effect on her. In the absence of evidence that suggested that the child was not benefitting from full and free access, the trial judge should not have prohibited the father from sharing his religious values with his daughter. Accordingly, the appeal should be allowed.

NOTES AND QUESTIONS

1. Commentators have pointed out that these two decisions provide little guidance, not only because the court was badly split, but also because there was no real effort to reconcile the different results in the cases. See McLeod, "Annotation" (1994), 49 R.F.L. (3d) 129; Bailey, "Custody, Access, and Religion: A Comment on *Young* v. *Young* and *D.P.* v. *C.S.* " (1994), 11 C.F.L.Q. 317; How, "*Young* v. *Young* and *D.P.* v. *C.S.*: Custody and Access — The Supreme Court Compounds Confusion" (1994), 11 C.F.L.Q. 109; and Bala, "Developments in Family Law: The 1993-94 Term" (1995), 6 The Supreme Court Review (2d) 453.

In their *Annual Review of Family Law, 1995* (Toronto: Carswell, 1995) Professor McLeod and Alf Mamo conclude (at 18) "that most [lower court] judges seem to have formed the view that the cases really have little effect on the prior law. There is authority for almost any position in the two cases and most judges seem to have carried on as before relying on different paragraphs from the cases if they feel the need to reconcile their decision with the cases."

2. The reasons in the cases do, however, confirm that all custody and access disputes are governed by the best interests of the child test. Can the apparently divergent outcomes in the two cases be explained using this test? Alternatively, was the different wording of the two orders important?

3. Do you agree with L'Heureux-Dubé J.'s argument against expanding the role of the access parent?

4. It should be noted hat Sopinka J.'s opinion is closest to the position of most American cases, which was summarized in *Hanson* v. *Hanson* (1987), 404 N.W. 2d 460 at 463 (N.D.):

> [M]ost courts that have considered the question have refused to restrain a noncustodial parent during visitation periods from exposing the minor child to his or her religious beliefs and practices, absent a clear, affirmative showing that these religious activities will be harmful to the child.

5. One of the concerns of the courts is to avoid evaluating the religious beliefs or practices of the access parent. Is such an evaluation avoidable if a court is asked by the custodial parent to impose restrictions on the basis that exposure to certain beliefs (e.g., that the husband is head of the house) is not in a child's best interests? See *Burris* v. *Borris* (1991), 37 R.F.L. (3d) 339 (Alta. Q.B.).

6. Both Justice McLachlin and Justice L'Heureux-Dubé indicated in *Young* that the freedom of religion of parents is inherently limited by the best interests of their child. In *B. (R.)* v. *C.A.S. of Metropolitan Toronto* (1995), 9 R.F.L.(4th) 157 (reproduced in Chapter 10), a majority adopted a broader definition of the freedom. La Forest J. stated (at 215): "[T]he right of parents to rear their children according to their religious belief, including that of choosing medical and other treatments, is [a] ... fundamental aspect of freedom of religion." He went on to conclude (at 216) that any state restrictions on this right had to be justified under s. 1 of the *Charter* even if the state sought to impose them in the interests of the child. Justices Gonthier, McLachlin, Sopinka, and L'Heureux-Dubé concurred with this analysis.

7. In *Hodgins* v. *Hodgins* (1993), 45 R.F.L. (3d) 75 (Ont. Gen. Div.), the father's access was conditional on his refraining from corporal punishment. Compare *Sherry* v. *Sherry* (1993), 1 R.F.L. (4th) 146 (P.E.I. T.D.). In *Arsenault* v. *Arsenau* (1998), 38 R.F.L. (4th) 175 (Ont. Gen. Div.), the youngest child was very allergic to the father's cat. The court suspended overnight access at the father's home until the cat was permanently removed. In *Fruitman* v. *Fruitman* (1998), 37 R.F.L. (4th) 416 (Ont. Gen. Div.) the mother attempted unsuccessfully to obtain restrictions on the father's access because she feared that he would not observe the religious practice of orthodox Judaism, even though he was also Jewish and promised to observe the practices to the best of his ability.

8. The religious beliefs of a parent may be a factor in the custody decision itself if they bear on the well-being of the child. In *Moseley* v. *Moseley* (1989), 20 R.F.L. (3d) 301 (Alta. Prov. Ct.), Cook-Stanhope Prov. J. reviewed a large number of cases dealing with custody disputes where opposing religious views had caused difficulties between parents. The trial judge found (at 320) that "in the practice of her religious beliefs Mrs. Moseley has neglected the needs of her children". Furthermore,

Mrs. Moseley's religious beliefs made it impossible for her to foster a meaningful relationship between the children and their father. The judge stated (at 319):

> To grant Mrs. Moseley custody of these children would be to recognize her right as custodial parent to continue to direct their religious education. In order to protect the rights of these children to develop a reasonable relationship with their father and to support the father's right to play an active and meaningful role in their lives, the solution would have to be to enjoin Mrs. Moseley from teaching that their father is a sinner and that he would die in a lake of fire, or that they should dissociate from those like him or face a similar fate. To restrict Mrs. Moseley in such a way would be antithetical to the basic tenets of her faith, and would place upon her an impossible burden. It is not, however, only the weight of such a burden which has caused me to reject such a disposition. I am, rather, satisfied by the whole of the evidence that Mrs. Moseley's beliefs are so inflexible and intolerant of others, she would not be willing to compromise in any way on matters of access.

Custody was granted to the father. While granting access to the mother, the court imposed certain conditions (at 321-322):

> It should be perfectly clear, however, that by delivering the responsibility of primary care of these children to Mr. Moseley, he will henceforth direct all aspects of their education, whether religious or secular, and that any attempts by Mrs. Moseley to undermine this authority will be grounds for a review of the access provisions. It is not possible for these children to adjust to parental religious opinions which are so diametrically opposite if they continue to live with Mrs. Moseley. Evidence reveals that this has in the past caused them confusion, emotional upset and frustration. It is therefore necessary, as there is no half-way with Mrs. Moseley, to prohibit her from providing any form of religious indoctrination whatsoever during periods of access with the children.

For further discussion of judicial approaches to cultural and religious diversity in child custody and access disputes, see: Zemans, "The Issue of Cultural Diversity in Custody Disputes" (1983), 32 R.F.L. (2d) 50; Mucci, "The Effect of Religious Disputes in Child Custody Disputes" (1986), 5 Can. J. Fam. L. 353; J. Syrtash, *Religion and Culture in Canadian Family Law* (Toronto: Butterworths, 1992); Davies, "Racial and Cultural Issues in Custody Matters" (1993), 0 C.F.L.Q. 1; Chipeur and Bailey, "Honey, I Proselytized the Kids: Religion as a Factor in Child Custody and Access Disputes" (1993), 4 N.J.C.L. 101; Wah, "Religion in Child Custody and Visitation Cases: Presenting the Advantage of Religious Participation" (1994), 28 Fam. L.Q. 269; Wah, "Religion as a Factor in Child Custody and Visitation Rights Cases: Myths and Assumptions" (1994), 8 Am. J. Fam. L. 73; Van Praagh, "Religion, Custody and a Child's Identity" (1997), 35 Osgoode Hall L.J. 309; and Drobac, "For the Sake of the Children: Court Consideration of Religion in Child Custody Cases" (1998), Stanford Law Rev. 1609.

9. Section 20(5) of the *CLRA* and s. 16(5) of the *Divorce Act* expressly provide that, in the absence of a contrary court order, the access parent has the right to make inquiries and be given information regarding the health, education and welfare of the child. Are these statutory provisions directed at the custodial parent or do they encompass also individuals such as the child's doctor and school principal?

10. In *Chauvin* v. *Chauvin* (1987), 6 R.F.L. (3d) 93 (Ont. Dist. Ct.), the mother, who had custody of two boys, transferred them from a French school to an English one. The father objected and obtained an order under s. 21 of the *CLRA* requiring the mother to enroll them in a specified French school. Killeen D.C.J. stated (at 411) that "there has to be a strong evidential showing to support a displacement of an educational decision made by a custodial parent, otherwise custody orders and their consequences will be bereft of meaning and effect", but he found such evidence in this case. The S.C.C. allowed an appeal in *S. (L.)* c. *S. (C.)* (1997), 37 R.F.L. (4e) 44 (S.C.C.) and removed restrictions on the custodial mother's religious activities involving her child. The lower courts had granted custody to the mother who was a Witness of Jehovah, but ordered her not to bring the child to religious ceremonies or on door-to-door proselytizing. The mother was also prohibited from indoctrinating the child. The S.C.C. simply stated: "In the circumstances of this case, given the evidence before us, we are not satisfied that the best interests of the child has been compromised by the practices of the custodial parent." In *Mummery* v. *Campbell* (1998), 38 R.F.L. (4th) 301 (B.C. S.C.), the court concluded, over the objections of the non-custodial father, that it was in the best interests of an eight-year-old girl to be baptized as she and her mother wished. In light of these cases, could an access parent challenge the custodial parent's decision

to require the child to attend a particular church? If so, how would the court make the decision? Would it evaluate the religious belief in question?

11. Sometimes a custodial parent wishes to change a child's name without the consent of the other parent. Under the *Change of Name Act*, R.S.O. 1990, c. C.7, a custodial parent does not need the consent of a non-custodial parent unless such consent is required by court order or separation agreement. However, the custodial parent must give notice of an application to change the name to "every person who is lawfully entitled to access" (s. 5(6)). In *Silverberg* v. *Silverberg* (1990), 25 R.F.L. (3d) 141 (Ont. H.C.) and *Herniman* v. *Woltz* (1996), 22 R.F.L. (4th) 232 (Ont. Gen. Div.), Justice Granger held that a court could restrain a parent from changing a child's surname as an incident of custody. He also held that the onus was on the custodial parent proposing the change to demonstrate that it was in the child's best interest because it would benefit the child. See also *Giggie* v. *Guidry* (1997), 29 R.F.L. (4th) 31 (N.B. Q.B.) and *Pappel* v. *Bergen* (1998), 37 R.F.L. (4th) 88 (Man. Q.B.).

CARTER v. BROOKS

(1990), 30 R.F.L. (3d) 53 (Ont. C.A.)

MORDEN A.C.J.O.: — This is an appeal by the mother of a 6-year-old son from an order directing that she not remove the child from the province of Ontario except for day trips or short vacations without the consent of the respondent, the child's father.

The background of the proceeding is as follows. The appellant and the respondent were married in 1982. The child, Joel, was born in February of 1984. The parties separated in October of 1984 when the appellant left the matrimonial home with the child. Both parties lived in Brantford before the separation and have continued to live there. The appellant began a common law relationship with her present husband in 1985. In March of 1987 the appellant and the respondent were divorced. The divorce judgment contained no provisions relating to support or to custody and access. In October of 1988, the appellant and her husband were married and in July of 1990 they had a child. The appellant has had de facto custody of the child since the separation and the respondent has had regular access throughout the period of separation, including, at one time, every weekend, and, for the last 3 years, alternating weekends, mid-week access, summer access, and ad hoc visits and telephone calls.

In February of 1990, the appellant informed the respondent that she and her husband were contemplating moving to British Columbia to enable her husband to pursue a business opportunity in that province that had been offered to him. She appreciated the impact that this move would have on the relationship between their son and the respondent. The respondent objected to the move and subsequently brought an application in which he sought various items of relief, including an order restraining the appellant from removing the child from the county of Brant and an order of joint custody. The appellant brought a cross-application for an order of custody. . . .

In his reasons, the Judge said that there was "no serious issue" that a custody order should not be made and he made one in favour of the appellant. His reasons respecting the move to British Columbia are as follows:

> The issue that arises in this litigation comes forward because Joel's mother wishes to move to the Province of British Columbia with her new spouse, Mr. Brooks, and their family unit. The family unit would, of course, include Joel. A new business opportunity awaits Mr. Brooks in British Columbia and, on the material, it would appear to be a sound, legitimate business opportunity with potential remuneration for him beyond that which he currently enjoys in what is as

secure as any employment can be, here, in the Brantford area. He, therefore, has what can only be described as a better opportunity in British Columbia than he has with his secure employment here. The issue, put squarely, is: should his mother be able to take Joel with her to British Columbia so that the Brooks family can enjoy the better opportunity?

The test that I am required by law to apply in these circumstances is: what is in Joel's best interests? This Court has the right to impose conditions and limit mobility of the parent to remove the child from the jurisdiction. The question for me is: should that be done in this case? Should I impose a condition on the mobility of Mrs. Brooks, Joel's mother?

There are many pieces of evidence and many factors in evidence from the material and from the submissions of counsel. In my view, it boils down to one principal point of uncertainty and two principal points of certainty. I do not know what the impact on the Brooks family unit would be if the opportunity in B.C. was not realized. It may be that there will be some indirect effect on Joel if that opportunity is not taken. And it may be that that indirect effect could be negative.

I do know, and I am satisfied on the material and the submissions of counsel, that there is a close relationship between Joel and his father, and that that relationship would, of necessity, be negatively affected if the move of Joel to B.C. were to take place. I do know that Joel has enjoyed frequent access by his father; that has been fostered by both parents. Again, that move to B.C. would have to negatively affect that frequent access that Joel has enjoyed.

Given all of the evidence here, and given the certainties and uncertainty outlined above, I have concluded that, although there may be some potential economic benefit to Joel out of the move to British Columbia, the proposed move cannot be seen in any way as socially beneficial to him as it would be to remain in his present situation.

I conclude, therefore, that the move with the Brooks family unit to British Columbia is not in the best interest of Joel. There should, therefore, be a provision in the custody order that restricts the mother from removing Joel from this jurisdiction.

The appellant's main submission before us is, essentially, that the trial Judge, in the circumstances, erred in failing to give effect to the right of the custodial parent to remove the child from the jurisdiction. Mr. Amey refers, in particular, to three previous decisions of this Court: *Wright* v. *Wright* (1973), 1 O.R. (2d) 337, 12 R.F.L. 200, 40 D.L.R. (3d) 321 (Ont. C.A.); *Wickham* v. *Wickham* (1983), 35 R.F.L. (2d) 448 (Ont. C.A.); and *Landry* v. *Lavers* (1985), 50 O.R. (2d) 415, 45 R.F.L. (2d) 235, 17 D.L.R. (4th) 190, 10 O.A.C. 244 (Ont. C.A.). [These cases suggested that orders precluding a custodial parent from moving with the child should be made only where the access parent could show exceptional, special circumstances.]

The governing rule is, of course, that decisions respecting custody and access are to be made on the basis of the best interests of the child. . . .

As far as the state of the law is concerned, the proper course now [is] to make it clear that the only principle that governs is that of the best interests of the child and that it does not assist in applying this principle to rely upon a mechanical proposition such as that quoted in *Landry* which includes the expression "*the right to remove*". (Emphasis added.) This is not to say that a parent who has custody may not have important interests bearing on the best interests of the child which are entitled to considerable respect in the resolution of issues related to asserted access rights of the other parent.

What guidance can be given for the application of the best interests of the child test? This area of the law is no different from many others where, in the application of a broad legal standard, what is desired is both predictability of result and justice to the parties based on the particular circumstances of the case. It is often difficult to ensure by "rules" that both objects are met. If the rules are too precise, it may be that important circumstances in some cases will be left out of account in applying the governing test, and justice will suffer. On the other hand, if there are not certain common understandings in how the issue is to be approached, the danger is one of undue subjectivity, with the consequence of reduced predictability of result.

Having regard to the foregoing, I am satisfied that the best interests test cannot be implemented by the devising of a code of substantive rules, even if this could be done within the confines of a single case. It may be thought that it could be satisfactorily carried out by procedural or evidential rules embodying presumptions and onuses. Reference in this respect may be made to the state of the law in different American jurisdictions as described in a recent article (Bertin, "Relocation: No Common Ground" (1989) 11 Fam. Advocate 7 at 8):

> If it is possible to group, and there is always a danger in doing so, there are generally three legal approaches.
>
> First, the approach *in favor of relocation*, represented by the Minnesota view, by statute and case law, holding that a custodial parent can move in all circumstances, unless the noncustodial parent can prove by a preponderance of evidence that the move would not be in the best interests of the child.
>
> Second, the approach *against relocation*, represented by the New York view, holding that relocation of the custodial parent and child is prohibited unless the custodial parent can demonstrate compelling, exceptional circumstances or a pressing concern for the welfare of the custodial parent and child.
>
> Third, the middle position, represented by Illinois, Nebraska, South Dakota, and Michigan, holding that a child shall accompany the custodial parent whenever the custodian has a legitimate reason and the move is consistent with the best interests of the child.

. . .

With respect, I find none of these approaches to be particularly satisfactory. I am skeptical that general rules that do not admit of frequent exceptions can evenly and fairly accommodate all of the varying circumstances that can present themselves. For example, I incline to the view that a reasonable measure of respect should, generally, be paid to the views of a custodial parent who has decided to relocate. I am not sure, however, that this view should be implemented in a rule that, in all cases, places the onus on the other parent to prove that the move is not in the best interests of the child. What if there is an existing agreement between the parents that the custodial parent will not move the child without the permission of the other parent? Is it not reasonable to think that the agreement, at least at the time it was made, reflects the parties' views of the best interests of the child? If this is so and it is felt that the broad test should be administered by the application of a burden of proof, should not the burden be on the custodial parent to show why the agreement no longer reflects the best interests of the child? See, for example, *Crawford* v. *Crawford* (1985), 46 R.F.L. (2d) 331 at p. 334 (P.E.I. S.C., Fam. Div.), and *Coulter* v. *Coulter* (7 March 1984), Doc. No. D104218/82, Weiler L.J.S.C. (Ont. H.C.), at p. 15. The foregoing, I think, shows the difficulty of laying down hard and fast rules even of a procedural or evidential nature.

I think that the preferable approach in the application of the standard is for the Court to weigh and balance the factors which are relevant in the particular circumstances of the case at hand, without any rigid preconceived notion as to what weight each factor should have. I do not think that the process should begin with a general rule that one of the parties will be unsuccessful unless he or she satisfies a specified burden of proof. This over-emphasizes the adversary nature of the proceedings and depreciates the Court's *parens patriae* responsibility. Both parents should bear an evidential burden. At the end of the process, the Court should arrive at a determinate conclusion on the result which better accords with the best interests of the child. If this is impossible, then the result must necessarily be in accordance with the legal status quo on the issue to be decided.

In most cases, I would think, it is an important factor to take into account, in favour of the custodial parent, that the existing custody decision (by order or agreement) shows that from a day-to-day point of view the best interests of the child lie with the child's being with the custodial parent. Added to this, it is reasonable to think that an incident of custody includes the determination by the custodial parent of where the parent and the child shall live. Further, if there is a new family unit as a result of the custodial parent having remarried, the well-being of that family unit bears on the best interests of the child. See, for example, *Korpesho* v. *Korpesho* (1982), 31 R.F.L. (2d) 449, 19 Man. R. 142 (C.A.).

The nature of the relationship between the child and the access parent will always be of importance. The closer the relationship and the more dependent the child is on it for his or her emotional well-being and development, the more likely an injury resulting from the proposed move will be.

The reason for the move is important. If the motive is simply to frustrate access, then it would not be expected that a court would decide in favour of it. On the other hand, if the move is necessary, for example, for the maintenance of employment, this would count in favour of the move.

The distance of the move is, of course, of basic concern. The greater the distance, the more severe the impact of the proposed move will be on the relationship with the access parent. The degree of severity is also likely to be affected rather directly by the financial resources of the access parent.

The child's views are relevant. This is recognized by s. 24(2)(b) . . . of the *Children's Law Reform Act.*

Also, with respect to express statutory factors, s. 16(10) of the *Divorce Act* provides that:

> (10) In making an order under this section, the court shall give effect to the principle that a child of the marriage should have as much contact with each spouse as is consistent with the best interests of the child and, for that purpose, shall take into consideration the willingness of the person for whom custody is sought to facilitate such contact.

There is no reason to believe that this very general principle would not be taken into account whether or not it is expressed in statutory form.

The foregoing factors, of course, are far from representing a complete list. They are, however, of relevance to the instant case.

. . . The Judge's decision is entitled to due respect and, I think, should not be set aside unless the appellant can show the Court that the Judge erred in his appreciation of the evidence, in the inferences he drew from the evidence, or in his application of the relevant legal considerations.

In my view, the appellant has not met this test. While the Judge's review of the materials before him is rather terse, I am far from persuaded that he in any way misapprehended the evidence or drew the wrong inferences from it in arriving at this conclusion, or that he gave inappropriate weight to the relevant factors.

There were facts and considerations to which he did not refer expressly which supported his conclusion. For example, while he, quite fairly, referred to the appellant's husband's business opportunity in British Columbia as a "sound, legitimate business opportunity with potential remuneration for him beyond that which he currently enjoys . . . with his secure employment here," he did not mention that there was no real need for the appellant's husband to move. I do not mean to suggest that the courts should be quick to criticize proposed moves from this point of view and second-guess the decision of the parties involved, but it is a relevant factor when the impact of the move on the relationship between the access parent and the child is being considered. Related to this is the sparseness of the evidence respecting the appellant's husband's attempts to better his financial position in the Brantford area before opting to make a move with such profound impact on the relationship between the respondent and his son.

The submission on behalf of the child by his counsel is important. He put a synopsis of his submission to the Judge into written form before the hearing. In his submission, he paid tribute to the fairness of the appellant and her husband, and said that there was no doubt in his mind that the child belonged with his mother. He then said:

> However, it appears to me that, at this time, there is no compelling social or economic reason for the move to be made. Unquestionably, the mental and psychological health of a custodial parent is crucial, as any discontent or unhappiness on the part of the custodial parent will impact upon the child. I do not sense in Mrs. Brooks a lack of fulfillment, or an unhappiness in her career which would compel her to set roots down elsewhere. It appears that the primary motive is to further Mr. Brooks' career, and he is to be admired for his entrepreneurial streak. However, I note that he is employed on a full-time basis in Brantford, that he is not in imminent danger of losing that employment and that, very much to his credit, he is able in Brantford to continue to provide a comfortable lifestyle for Joel. Again, I do not sense about this matter any strong social or economic reason for the move, particularly as the move would affect to a considerable extent, Joel's relationship with his father. Joel very much enjoys the time he spends with his father and, although the history of access does not seem to be perfect, my impression is that the access has been quite constant and enjoyed by Joel throughout the last few years.

The submission concluded:

> Lastly, Joel has instructed me that he wishes the present situation to continue, in that he wants to live with his mother and wants to see his father on the same basis as he always has. I feel there is a responsibility on my part to be more than simply a mouth-piece for a 6 year old child, though my recommendation on Joel's behalf based on his best interests, is consistent with his stated wishes to me.

Further, while there was evidence of reasonable suggestions made by the appellant to ease the financial burden of the respondent's traveling to British Columbia to visit his son (and, also, her statement that she would bring the child to Brantford each summer), it is clear that the respondent, while not poor, does not enjoy the financial means to travel to British Columbia with any degree of frequency. It would appear that the trial Judge may have understated the matter when he said that the move would negatively affect the close relationship between the respondent and his child.

Having considered the evidence, and taken into account the benefits of the proposed move to the appellant's new family, of which the child was a member, the Judge came to the determinate conclusion in favour of the respondent that the move "is not in the best interest of Joel." Having regard to the state of the evidence, I do not see how we can properly interfere with the Judge's conclusion.

In the result, I would dismiss the appeal with costs.

MacGYVER v. RICHARDS

(1995), 11 R.F.L. (4th) 432 (Ont. C.A.)

[The child was born in December 1989, after the relationship between the parents had ended. The mother and father attempted a reconciliation, but the father's addiction to alcohol and his abusive conduct caused the relationship to break down again. In 1991, the mother was granted custody and the father access pursuant to minutes of settlement. The mother became involved with a man in the armed forces and they planned to marry. The man was transferred to Washington State for a four year stint and the mother wished to join him there with the child. The father, who had access every other weekend and two hours in the middle of each week, applied for an order preventing any move of the child outside the jurisdiction of Nippissing.

Judge Duchesneau-McLachlan ordered that the mother retain sole custody of the 4-year-old girl, that the father have access every second weekend, and that the child "reside in the City of North Bay until further Order of the Court". Because of the mother's fears over the father's continued abusive and threatening behaviour, the transfer of the child for access periods was to occur at the Supervised Access Centre. The mother successfully appealed to the Ontario Court (General Division). The resulting order of Justice Bolan confirmed the mother's sole custody, stipulated that access was to be as agreed between the parties, and deleted the requirement that the child remain in North Bay. The father appealed, seeking to have the order of Judge Duchesneau-McLachlan restored.]

ABELLA J.A. (GRANGE J.A. concurring): — The issue in this appeal is whether a custodial parent can change where he or she lives when the effect of that change is to prevent the other parent from continuing an established pattern of access with a child. . . .

The father's abusive conduct towards the mother, and his fluctuating interest in the child prior to his intensive treatment for addiction in 1992, were taken into account in deciding that Vanessa's mother was the parent most likely to provide care consistent with her best interests. While that conduct is undoubtedly relevant, I think the question of whether Vanessa should be required to remain in North Bay should be analyzed based on the father's current warm relationship with his daughter, and on an assumption of the father's sincerity in declaring his commitment to sobriety. The issue in this appeal, therefore, is not the scope of the right to move when one parent is abusive, but the scope of that right even when he or she is not. . . .

The evidence in this case clearly supported the trial judge's conclusion that it was in the child's best interests that the mother have sole custody. It also supported her conclusion that the father had a warm relationship with his daughter and that both he and the child hoped it would continue.

But it is, in my view, a quantum leap from the observation that a child has a good relationship with a non-custodial parent to the conclusion that the preservation of this relationship is the determinative factor in deciding what is in the child's best interests. In a dispute over mobility, the certainty of a good relationship between the parent with access and the child is known. The decision to move, on the other hand, contains uncertainty. But this does not mean that it will not be best for the child.

Both judges in this case relied on "the best interests of the child" in coming to diametrically opposite conclusions about how to achieve that result. Both acknowledged the factors they were required by statute to consider, including the child's relationship and ties to each parent, each parent's plans for the child's care, the likely stability of the proposed family units, the child's views, and expert psychological assessment. Having acknowledged the relevance of each of these factors, and having applied them to the same, undisputed facts, the two judges disagreed about the potential impact of those factors and facts on the child.

Clearly, there is an inherent indeterminacy and elasticity to the "best interests" test which makes it more useful as legal aspiration than as legal analysis. It can be no more than an informed opinion made at a moment in the life of a child about what seems likely to prove to be in that child's best interests. Deciding what is in a child's best interests means deciding what, objectively, appears most likely in the circumstances to be conducive to the kind of environment in which a particular child has the best opportunity for receiving the needed care and attention. Because there are stages to childhood, what is in a child's best interests may vary from child to child, from year to year, and possibly from month to month. This unavoidable fluidity makes it important to attempt to minimize the prospects for stress and instability.

The ''best interests'' test has to be understood in its context: it never arises when two parents live together, or agree to a decision about the child's care. Absent the kind of neglect which triggers child welfare legislation, parents are largely free to make whatever decisions they feel are best for their children. Parents who separate but *can* agree as to the child's care, are subject to no outside scrutiny of what they determine to be in the child's best interests. We generally respect a family's right to make decisions about its own children, and acknowledge, moreover, that at any given moment, it is difficult to say that any one of those decisions will not prove ultimately to be in the child's best interests. In other words, the only time courts scrutinize whether parental conduct is conducive to a child's best interests is when the parents are involved in the kind of fractious situation that is probably, in the inevitability of its stress and pain and ambiguity, least conducive to the child's or anyone else's best interests.

Deciding what is best for a child is uniquely delicate. The judge in a custody case is called upon to prognosticate about a child's future, and to speculate about which parenting proposal will turn out to be best for a child. Judges are left to do their best with the evidence, on the understanding that deciding what is best for a child is a judgment the accuracy of which may be unknowable until later events prove — or disprove — its wisdom.

The speculative nature of the task clearly cannot absolve judges from responsibility for exercising their judgment about what, according to the evidence, augurs best at that point for the balance of the childhood. It can, however, and should, in deciding the incidents of custody, give pause about the extent to which judges interpose themselves between the child and the parent responsible for exercising, on a daily basis, the kind of judgment a judge is called upon to make only once. The parent, not the judge, will be left to live with the daily consequences of caring for the child within the limits of that one judicial pronouncement.

This argues, it seems to me, for particular sensitivity and a presumptive deference to the needs of the responsible custodial parent who, in the final analysis, lives the reality, not the speculation, of decisions dealing with the incidents of custody. The judicial perspective should acknowledge the overwhelmingly relentless nature of the custodial responsibility, and respect its day-to-day demands.

Custody is an enormous undertaking which ought to be preeminently recognized by the courts in deciding disputed issues incidental to that custody, including mobility. The right or wish to see a child every weekend or two may be of genuine benefit to a child; but it cannot begin to approach the benefit to a child of someone who takes care of him or her every day. The scales used to weigh a child's best interests are not evenly balanced between two parents when one is an occasional and the other a constant presence. They are both, usually, beneficial. But, prima facie, one is demonstrably more beneficial than the other. . . .

In deciding what restrictions, if any, should be placed on a parent with custody, courts should be wary about intefering with that parent's capacity to decide, daily, what is best for the child. That is the very responsibility a custody order imposes on a parent, and it obliges — and entitles — the parent to exercise judgments which range from the trivial to the dramatic. Those judgments may include whether to change neighbourhoods, or provinces, or partners, or jobs, or friends, or schools, or religions. Each of those significant judgments may affect the child in some way, but that does not mean that the court has the right to prevent the change.

The inevitable genesis of a court having to make a decision is because of some stress and instability. To minimize future stresses, as opposed to more utopian and less realistic objectives, the court should be overwhelmingly respectful of the decision-making capacity of the person in whom the court or the other parent has entrusted primary responsibility for the child. We cannot design a system which shields the non-custodial parent from any change in the custodial parent's life which may affect the exercise of access. The emphasis should be, rather, on deferring to the decision-making responsibilities of the custodial parent, unless there is substantial evidence that those decisions impair the child's, not the access parent's, long-term well-being.

We must also forcefully acknowledge that the custodial parent's best interests are inextricably tied to those of the child. The young child is almost totally dependent on that parent, not on the parent seen during visits. While it would always be preferable to attempt to find a solution which protects the child's relationship with both parents, this ideal is simply not always possible. It is practically inevitable, when two parents no longer live together, that the child's relationship with each will be different. This means that the child, and each of its parents, must adjust to the new realities. The adjustments may be painful, including the adjustment of a parent seeing a child less often than anticipated. However painful, that parent's desires cannot be paramount. . . .

When, therefore, a court has been asked to decide what is in the child's best interests, and a choice must be made between the responsible wishes and needs of the parent with custody and the parent with access, it seems to me manifestly unfair to treat these wishes and needs as being on an equal footing. When one adds to this the dimension that a court's decision ought to favour the possibility that the former partners can get on with their lives and their responsibilities, one reaches the admittedly difficult conclusion that a parent with custody, acting responsibly, should not be prevented from leaving a jurisdiction because the move would interfere with access by the other parent with the child, even if the relationship between the child and the access parent is a good one. . . .

In the case before us, the trial judge put the mother in the Solomonic position of having to choose between her child and her marriage. The mother made it clear that she would never leave North Bay without her child, and the trial judge made it clear that the mother should continue to have sole custody. By deciding that the child should remain in North Bay, the trial judge disregarded the recommendations of an expert assessment that this new family would be in the child's best interests, effectively denied the mother the opportunity to carry on with her life, and deprived the child of the opportunity to live in a new family unit. Instead, the trial judge tied the future prospects of the mother and child to the visiting parent's wishes and convenience.

Her analysis essentially was that Vanessa was in familiar surroundings and had a good relationship with her father. This, it seems to me, is the situation in most cases and is therefore not particularly helpful in deciding whether it is in this particular child's best interests that she be prevented from leaving North Bay. In suggesting that the move was not "necessary," the trial judge was imposing an idiosyncratic, inappropriate and arbitrary test. The test is not whether a judge feels subjectively that a move is "necessary," but whether there is any reason to conclude that the move would not be in the child's best interests.

The effect of the trial judge's interpretation is that a custodial parent without the financial resources to provide access can never, absent an overwhelming justification, move with a very young child if the effect of that move is to interfere with an access relationship. It is an analysis that allows mobility only to those parents who have the money or the maturity to cope with the post-separation realities.

I agree with Justice Bolan that Vanessa's long-term best interests are tied to those of the parent responsible for her day-to-day care. There is no reason why her father's visiting rights should be permitted to create an insurmountable wall around North Bay for her mother. Custodial parents are expected to conduct their lives in conformity with the needs of their children, not with those of the parent with access. Where, as here, the mother is chained to the anchor of access and she, unlike the father, is thereby prevented from choosing her future, an error has clearly been made about the parent to whom the child's best interests are predominantly attached. Without denying the mutual affection between Lee MacGyver and Vanessa, it cannot be said, based on the evidence, that the accommodation of his wish to see her every two weekends is more conducive to the child's best interests than her mother's right to get on with her life and establish a new home for the child.

[LABROSSE J.A., concurring, gave brief separate reasons indicating that the trial judge misapplied *Carter* v. *Brooks* by failing to give sufficient weight to the reason for the proposed move and the mother's sense of well-being and happiness and by over-emphasizing the relationship between the child and her father.]

GORDON v. GOERTZ

(1996), 19 R.F.L. (4th) 177 (S.C.C.)

The judgment of Lamer C.J. and McLachlin, Sopinka, Cory, Iacobucci and Major JJ. was delivered by

McLACHLIN J.: — When parents separate, one typically enjoys custody of the child, the other access. So long as both parents live in the same area, this arrangement protects the child's continuing relationship with both parents. However, if the custodial parent decides to move away and change the principal residence of the child, the situation may change. The access parent may be unable to see the child as often as before, if at all. He or she may seek a review of the custody order, contending that removing the child from its familiar surroundings and restricting or depriving the child of access to the other parent is not in that child's best interests. With the prevalence of separated families and the increasing mobility of modern society, such applications are more common. On this appeal, we are asked to establish the principles that should guide judges in making these difficult decisions.

I. The Proceedings to Date

A) The Initial Order

The family resided in Saskatoon until the events precipitating this case, and both parents enjoy a warm and loving relationship with their child. Upon separating from the child's father in November 1990, the mother petitioned for divorce under the *Divorce Act*, R.S.C., 1985, c. (2nd Supp.). She obtained an order for interim custody of the child. The order granted the father reasonable access on reasonable notice.

The father saw the child frequently following separation. A custody access study prepared before trial showed that the father had "consistently spent more time with the child" than the mother had in the post-separation period. In a mediated agreement pending trial and judgment, the mother and father agreed that the child would reside with both parents on a rotating basis, and that if one party moved, the child would continue to reside in Saskatoon with the other.

The matter of custody came on for trial before Carter J. of the Unified Family Court of the Saskatchewan Court of Queen's Bench in February 1993. She dissolved the marriage pending appeal and awarded the mother permanent custody of the child with generous access to the father: (1993), 111 Sask. R. 1. Following the trial, the father continued to spend more time with his daughter than allowed by the order. The mother did not usually object to the additional time; indeed, it helped her to maintain a busy working schedule that often took her out of Saskatoon.

When the father learned in the fall of 1994 that the mother intended to move to Adelaide, Australia in January 1995, to study orthodontics, he applied for custody of the child, or alternatively, an order restraining the mother from moving the child from Saskatoon. The mother cross-applied to vary the access provisions of the custody order to permit her to move the child's residence to Australia.

B) The Variation Order

Gagne J. concluded that he should permit the child to go to Australia with her mother. After citing various decisions considering similar situations and noting the diverse results, he stated:

> I relied heavily on Judge Carter's judgment and her finding of fact that the mother was the proper person to have custody of this child. There will be an order that the petitioner be allowed to move to Australia to study orthodontics and to take the child Samantha with her.
>
> Now, the respondent will have liberal and generous access to Samantha in Australia on one month's notice and not to remove the child from Australia. Samantha's school should be interfered with as little as possible during these visits.

The Saskatchewan Court of Appeal upheld the order, finding "no serious error of principle" in the decision, and citing *Willick* v. *Willick*, [1994] 3 S.C.R. 670, in support of a conservative standard of review: (1995), 128 Sask. R. 156. ... The father now appeals to this Court seeking a change of custody, or alternatively, an order permitting access on terms which would allow the child to leave Australia. ...

IV   Analysis

The principles which govern an application for a variation of an order relating to custody and access are set out in the *Divorce Act*. The Act directs a two-stage inquiry. First, the party seeking variation must show a material change in the situation of the child. If this is done, the judge must enter into a consideration of the merits and make the order that best reflects the interests of the child in the new circumstances. I propose to discuss each stage in turn.

A)   The Threshold Condition: Material Change

... What suffices to establish a material change in the circumstances of the child? Change alone is not enough; the change must have altered the child's needs or the ability of the parents to meet those needs in a fundamental way: *Watson* v. *Watson* (1991), 35 R.F.L. (3d) 169 (B.C. S.C.). The question is whether the previous order might have been different had the circumstances now existing prevailed earlier: *MacCallum* v. *MacCallum* (1976), 30 R.F.L. 32 (P.E.I. S.C.). . . .

It follows that before entering on the merits of an application to vary a custody order the judge must be satisfied of: (1) a change in the condition, means, needs or circumstances of the child and/or the ability of the parents to meet the needs of the child; (2) which materially affects the child; and (3) which was either not foreseen or could not have been reasonably contemplated by the judge who made the initial order.

These are the principles which determine whether a move by the custodial parent is a material change in the "condition, means, needs or other circumstances of the child". Relocation will always be a "change". Often, but not always, it will amount to a change which materially affects the circumstances of the child and the ability of the parent to meet them. A move to a neighbouring town might not affect the child or the parents' ability to meet its needs in any significant way. Similarly, if the child lacks a positive relationship with the access parent or extended family in the area, a move might not affect the child sufficiently to constitute a material change in its situation. Where, as here, the child enjoyed frequent and meaningful contact with the access parent, a move that would seriously curtail that contact suffices to establish the necessary connection between the change and the needs and circumstances of the child.

The third branch of the threshold requirement of material change requires that the relocation of the custodial parent not have been within the reasonable contemplation of the judge who issued the previous order: *Messier* v. *Delage*, [1983] 2 S.C.R. 401. If a future move by the custodial parent was considered and not disallowed by the order sought to be varied, the access parent may be barred from bringing an application for variation on that ground alone. The same reasoning applies to a court-sanctioned separation agreement which contemplates a future move. In such cases, the application for variation amounts to an appeal of the original order.

Conversely, an order which specifies precise terms of access may lead to an inference that a move which would "effectively destroy that right of access" constitutes a material change in circumstances justifying a variation application. . . . Where, as here, the custody order stipulates terms of access on the assumption that the child's principal residence will remain near the access parent, the third branch of the threshold requirement of a material change in circumstance is met.

B) The Best Interests of the Child

(1) The Test

The threshold condition of a material change in circumstance satisfied, the court should consider the matter afresh without defaulting to the existing arrangement: *Francis* v. *Francis* (1972), 8 R.F.L. 209 (Sask. C.A.), at p. 217. The earlier conclusion that the custodial parent was the best person to have custody is no longer determinative, since the existence of material change presupposes that the terms of the earlier order might have been different had the change been known at the time.

. . . In order to determine the child's best interest, the judge must consider how the change impacts on all aspects of the child's life. To put it another way, the material change places the original order in question; all factors relevant to that order fall to be considered in light of the new circumstances.

What principles should guide the judge on this fresh review of the situation? This inquiry takes us to the last clause of s. 17(5) of the *Divorce Act*: ". . . in making the variation order, the court shall take into consideration only the best interests of the child as determined by reference to that change". The amendments to the *Divorce Act* in 1986 (S.C. 1986, c. 4 (now R.S.C., 1985, c. 3 (2nd Supp.)) elevated the best interests of the child from a "paramount" consideration, to the "only" relevant issue.

The best interests of the child test has been characterized as "indeterminate" and "more useful as legal aspiration than as legal analysis": per Abella J.A. in *MacGyver* v. *Richards* (1995), 11 R.F.L. (4th) 432 (Ont. C.A.), at p. 443. Nevertheless, it stands as an eloquent expression of Parliament's view that the ultimate and only issue when it comes to custody and access is the welfare of the child whose future is at stake. The multitude of factors that may impinge on the child's best interest make a measure of indeterminacy inevitable. A more precise test would risk sacrificing the child's best interests to expediency and certainty. Moreover, Parliament has offered assistance by providing two specific directions — one relating to the conduct of the parents, the other to the ideal of maximizing beneficial contact between the child and both parents.

In s. 16(9), Parliament has stipulated that the judge "shall not take into consideration the past conduct of any person unless the conduct is relevant to the ability of that person to act as a parent of a child". This instruction is effectively incorporated into a variation proceeding by virtue of s. 17(6). Parental conduct, however meritorious or however reprehensible, does not enter the analysis unless it relates to the ability of the parent to meet the needs of the child.

This stipulation is important in applications for variation of custody based on relocation of the custodial parent. All too often, such applications have descended into inquiries into the custodial parent's reason or motive for moving (see *Carter* v. *Brooks* (1990), 30 R.F.L. (3d) 53 (Ont. C.A.); *Colley* v. *Colley* (1991), 31 R.F.L. (3d) 281 (Ont. U.F.C.); and J. G. McLeod, "Annotation to *Williams* v. *Williams*" (1992), 38 R.F.L. (3d) 100, at p. 103). If the move is considered "necessary," the decision is considered justified, entitling the parent to retain custody in the new location. If, on the other hand, it is made for a less noble reason, the custodial parent may be required to choose between losing custody or moving. The focus thus shifts from the best interests of the child to the conduct of the custodial parent.

Under the *Divorce Act*, the custodial parent's conduct can be considered only if relevant to his or her ability to act as parent of the child. Usually, the reasons or motives for moving will not be relevant to the custodial parent's parenting ability. Occasionally, however, the motive may reflect adversely on the parent's perception of the needs of the child or the parent's judgment about how they may best be fulfilled. For example, the decision of a custodial parent to move solely to thwart salutary contact between the child and access parent might be argued to show a lack of appreciation for the child's best interests: see *McGowan* v. *McGowan* (1979), 11 R.F.L. (2d) 281 (Ont. H.C.); *Wells* v. *Wells* (1984), 38 R.F.L. (2d) 405 (Sask. Q.B.), aff'd (1984), 42 R.F.L. (2d) 166 (Sask. C.A.). However, absent a connection to parenting ability, the custodial parent's reason for moving should not enter into the inquiry.

The second factor which Parliament specifically chose to mention in assessing the best interests of the child is maximum contact between the child and both parents. Both ss. 16(10) and 17(9) of the Act require that "the court shall give effect to the principle that a child of the marriage should have as much contact with each former spouse as is consistent with the best interests of the child". The sections go on to say that for this purpose, the court "shall take into consideration the willingness of [the applicant] to facilitate" the child's contact with the non-custodial parent. The "maximum contact" principle, as it has been called, is mandatory, but not absolute. The Act only obliges the judge to respect it to the extent that such contact is consistent with the child's best interests; if other factors show that it would not be in the child's best interests, the court can and should restrict contact: *Young* v. *Young*, [1993] 4 S.C.R. 3, at pp. 117-18, per McLachlin J.

The reduction of beneficial contact between the child and the access parent does not always dictate a change of custody or an order which restricts moving the child. If the child's needs are likely to be best served by remaining with the custodial parent, and this consideration offsets the loss or reduction in contact with the access parent, then the judge should not vary custody and permit the move. This said, the reviewing judge must bear in mind that Parliament has indicated that maximum contact with both parents is generally in the best interests of the child.

(2) The Argument for a Presumption in Favour of the Custodial Parent.

The child's mother argues that the inquiry into the best interests of the child should begin with a presumption in favour of the custodial parent. This would place the onus on the access parent to show why remaining with the custodial parent is not in the child's best interest. I have concluded that this submission must fail. . . .

The 1985 *Divorce Act* now instructs courts that the interests of the parents are no longer relevant in custody determinations. As noted previously, the child's best interests are not merely "paramount", they are the only consideration. The revised Act also introduced statutory recognition of the principle that children generally benefit from contact with both parents. In the wake of these amendments, some judges began to question whether a presumption in favour of the custodial spouse should apply, and suggested that the only issue was whether the interests of the child would be better served by permitting the child to move with the custodial parent than by maintaining the status quo, where the move is contingent on the retention of custody, or transferring custody to the remaining parent. . . .

The Ontario Court of Appeal weighed both views in *Carter* v. *Brooks*. Morden A.C.J.O., speaking for the court, rejected the idea of a presumption in favour of the custodial parent. . . .

Although some have read *MacGyver* as a departure from *Carter* v. *Brooks* (see *Lapointe* v. *Lapointe*, [1995] 10 W.W.R. 609 (Man. C.A.), at p. 614), the difference between the cases may not be as great as sometimes supposed. Both cases urge careful consideration of the views of the custodial parent: the court is directed to accord them "a reasonable measure of respect" in *Carter*, and an "overwhelming respect" or "presumptive deference" in *MacGyver*. Despite the stronger language of the majority in *MacGyver*, neither decision proposes a legal presumption in favour of the custodial parent. Most importantly, both cases emphasize that the only and ultimate standard against which to evaluate the evidence is the best interests of the child: see J.G. McLeod, "Annotation to *MacGyver* v. *Richards* " (1995), 11 R.F.L. (4th) 433, at p. 435.

Against this background, I turn to arguments for and against a presumption in favour of the custodial parent.

In support of a presumption in favour of the custodial parent, it is argued that determining the principal residence of the child is a normal incident of custody and the court should accordingly defer to the custodial parent. It is further argued that the personal freedom of the custodial parent requires that he or she be permitted to decide where to live. Yet another consideration is that the presumption would make the outcome of variation applications more predictable. Assuming that in most cases the decision of the custodial parent will be the best for the child, a presumption would ensure a certain uniformity of result that will accord with the best interests of most children. I will deal with each of these arguments in favour of a presumption in turn.

The first proposition is that the custodial parent should be able to choose the child's residence because he or she has the legal responsibility of making all decisions concerning the child. The general obligation and right of the custodial parent to decide where the child shall live is not in dispute. Barring a situation which amounts to a material change in circumstances, the custodial parent may take the child wherever he or she pleases. When, however, the proposed move amounts to a material change, Parliament has decreed that the access parent is entitled to ask a judge to review the matter. The custodial parent has the right to decide where the child shall live, but that right is subject to the right of the access parent to apply for a change in custody once a material change in circumstances is established. . . .

It is thus no answer to an inquiry into the best interests of the child triggered by the material change to argue that the custodial parent has the right and responsibility to decide where the child shall live. The demonstration of a material change places that right at issue. The judge will normally place great weight on the views of the custodial parent, who may be expected to have the most intimate and perceptive knowledge of what is in the child's interest. The judge's ultimate task, however, is to determine where, in light of the material change, the best interests of the child lie.

The wording of the *Divorce Act* belies the need to defer to the custodial parent; rather, the Act has expressly stipulated that the judge hearing the application should be concerned only with the best interests of the child. The rights and interests of the parents, except as they impact on the best interests of the child, are irrelevant. Material change established, the question is not whether the rights of custodial parents can be restricted; the only question is the best interests of the child. Nor does the great burden borne by custodial parents justify a presumption in their favour. Custodial responsibilities curb the personal freedom of parents in many ways. The Act is clear. Once a material change is established, the judge must review the matter anew to determine the best interests of the child.

The argument that a presumption would render the law more predictable in a way which would do justice in the majority of cases and reduce conflict damaging to the child between the former spouses also founders on the rock of the *Divorce Act*. The Act contemplates individual justice. The judge is obliged to consider the best interests of the particular child in the particular circumstances of the case. Had Parliament wished to impose general rules at the expense of individual justice, it could have done so. It did not. The manner in which Parliament has chosen to resolve situations which may not be in the child's best interests should not be lightly abjured. Even if it could be shown that a presumption in favour of the custodial parent would reduce litigation that would not imply a reduction in conflict. The short-term pain of litigation may be preferable to the long-term pain of unresolved conflict. Foreclosing an avenue of legal redress exacts a price; it may, in extreme cases, even impel desperate parents to desperate measures in contravention of the law. A presumption would do little to reduce the underlying conflict endemic in custody disputes. As Bailey remarks [in "Custody, Access and Religion: A Comment on *Young* v. *Young* and *D.P.* v. *C.S.*" (1994), 11 C.F.L.Q. 317] (at p. 339):

... under the existing law the access parent may challenge decisions taken by the custodial parent, regardless of whether the access parent has decision-making power or not. If this power to challenge were made less meaningful by presumptive deference to the custodial parent, the result would not be to minimize conflict, but to disallow or inhibit challenges to the custodial parent.

Having considered the arguments supporting a presumption in favour of the custodial parent, I turn to those raised against it. The first stumbling block is the wording of the *Divorce Act* itself. As noted, the Act makes no reference to such a presumption. Indeed, the logic of the Act negates it. Parliament has decreed that a two-stage procedure must be used to decide applications for variation of custody and access orders: the threshold condition of establishing a material change in the circumstances or needs of the child and the ability of the parents to meet them; followed, if met, by a fresh inquiry into the best interests of the child. In imposing the threshold requirement of demonstrating a material change of circumstances, Parliament has laid a special burden on the party seeking variation, often the access parent. If the access parent meets that burden, the judge must then enter into a fresh inquiry as to where the best interests of the child lie. If Parliament intended to place yet another special burden on the access parent at the second stage, one would have expected it to say so.

Until a material change in the circumstances of the child is demonstrated, the best interests of the child are rightly presumed to lie with the custodial parent. The finding of a material change effectively erases that presumption. The judge is then charged with the fresh responsibility of determining the child's best interests ''by reference to that change''. To reinstate the presumption in favour of the custodial parent at this stage would derogate from the finding that the child's interests may, by reason of the change, no longer be best protected or advanced by the earlier order. It would be to reinforce the earlier order when its continuing propriety is the very issue placed before the court. This in turn would depreciate potential adverse effects of the established material change. In short, the two-stage procedure required by the *Divorce Act* supports the view of Morden A.C.J.O. in *Carter* v. *Brooks*, *supra*, that once the applicant has discharged the burden of showing a material change in circumstances, ''[b]oth parents should bear an evidentiary burden'' of demonstrating where the best interests of the child lie (p. 63).

A second argument against a presumption in favour of the custodial parent is its potential effect. If the presumption is to be introduced in cases based on relocation, it would seem as a matter of principle that it should be introduced in all applications for variation of custody and access. Again, had Parliament so intended, why would it not have said so?

A third argument against a presumption has been touched on in discussing the arguments raised in support of a presumption in favour of the custodial parent. This is the fact that Parliament has placed the duty of ascertaining the best interests of the child on the judge, not the custodial parent. To the extent that the judge is required, as a matter of law, to defer to the opinion of the custodial parent, the judge is required to cede part of the responsibility that Parliament has placed upon the judge and the judge alone. . . .

A fourth argument militating against the adoption of a presumption in favour of the custodial parent is its tendency to render the inquiry more technical and adversarial than necessary. The effect of the presumption might be to deflect the inquiry from the facts relating to the child's needs and the parents' ability to meet them to legal issues relating to whether the requisite burden of proof has been met. Instead of both parties simply presenting evidence on what is best for the child, the focus might shift to who has proved what. In this sense, the process may be seen as more inquisitorial than adversarial, "over-emphasiz[ing] the adversary nature of the proceedings", to quote Morden A.C.J.O. in *Carter* v. *Brooks, supra,* at p. 63.

Fifthly and most importantly, a presumption in favour of the custodial parent has the potential to impair the inquiry into the best interests of the child. This inquiry should not be undertaken with a mindset that defaults in favour of a preordained outcome absent persuasion to the contrary. It may be that in most cases the opinion of the custodial parent will reflect the best interests of the child. In such cases, the presumption might do no harm. But Parliament did not entrust the court with the best interests of most children; it entrusted the court with the best interests of the particular child whose custody arrangements fall to be determined. Each child is unique, as is its relationship with parents, siblings, friends and community. Any rule of law which diminishes the capacity of the court to safeguard the best interests of each child is inconsistent with the requirement of the *Divorce Act* for a contextually sensitive inquiry into the needs, means, condition and other circumstances of "the child" whose best interests the court is charged with determining.

A presumption in favour of the custodial parent may also impair the inquiry into the best interests of the child by undervaluing changes in the respective relationships between the child and its parents between the time of the custody order and the application for variation. The *Divorce Act*'s provision for variation of custody and access orders recognizes that the child's needs and the parents' ability to meet them may change with time and circumstance, and may require corresponding changes in custody and access arrangements. Children grow and mature, articulating new priorities and placing new demands on their parents. To the extent that the proposed presumption would give added weight to the arrangement imposed by the original custody order, it may diminish the weight accorded to the child's new needs and the ability of each parent to meet them. Consequently, its operation might be dangerous in a case, for example, where in the period following trial the access parent has demonstrated the desire, aptitude and temperament to assume a greater role in meeting the needs of the child, and the custodial parent has evinced a corresponding inability to do so.

Finally, the proposed presumption in favour of the custodial parent may be criticized on the ground that it tends to shift the focus from the best interests of the child to the interests of the parents. As mentioned earlier, underlying much of the argument for the presumption is the suggestion that the custodial parent has the "right" to move where he or she pleases and should not be restricted in doing so by the desire of the access parent to maintain contact with the child. However, the *Divorce Act* does not speak of parental "rights": see *Young* v. *Young,* supra. The child's best interest must be found within the practical context of the reality of the parents' lives and circumstances, one aspect of which may involve relocation. But to begin from the premise that one parent has the *prima facie* right to take the child where he or she wishes may unduly deflect the focus from the child to its parents.

For these reasons, I would reject the submission that there should be a presumption in favour of the custodial parent in applications to vary custody and access resulting from relocation of the custodial parent. The parent seeking the change bears the initial burden of demonstrating a material change of circumstances. Once that burden has been discharged, the judge must embark on a fresh inquiry in light of the change and all other relevant factors to determine the best interests of the child. There is neither need nor place to begin this inquiry with a general rule that one of the parties will be unsuccessful if he or she fails to satisfy a specified burden of proof.

While a legal presumption in favour of the custodial parent must be rejected, the views of the custodial parent, who lives with the child and is charged with making decisions in its interests on a day-to-day basis, are entitled to great respect and the most serious consideration. The decision of the custodial parent to live and work where he or she chooses is likewise entitled to respect, barring an improper motive reflecting adversely on the custodial parent's parenting ability.

C. Summary

The law can be summarized as follows:

1. The parent applying for a change in the custody or access order must meet the threshold requirement of demonstrating a material change in the circumstances affecting the child.
2. If the threshold is met, the judge on the application must embark on a fresh inquiry into what is in the best interests of the child, having regard to all the relevant circumstances relating to the child's needs and the ability of the respective parents to satisfy them.
3. This inquiry is based on the findings of the judge who made the previous order and evidence of the new circumstances.
4. The inquiry does not begin with a legal presumption in favour of the custodial parent, although the custodial parent's views are entitled to great respect.
5. Each case turns on its own unique circumstances. The only issue is the best interest of the child in the particular circumstances of the case.
6. The focus is on the best interests of the child, not the interests and rights of the parents.
7. More particularly the judge should consider, *inter alia*:
    (a) the existing custody arrangement and relationship between the child and the custodial parent;
    (b) the existing access arrangement and the relationship between the child and the access parent;
    (c) the desirability of maximizing contact between the child and both parents;
    (d) the views of the child;
    (e) the custodial parent's reason for moving, only in the exceptional case where it is relevant to that parent's ability to meet the needs of the child;
    (f) disruption to the child of a change in custody;
    (g) disruption to the child consequent on removal from family, schools, and the community he or she has come to know.

In the end, the importance of the child remaining with the parent to whose custody it has become accustomed in the new location must be weighed against the continuance of full contact with the child's access parent, its extended family and its community. The ultimate question in every case is this: what is in the best interests of the child in all the circumstances, old as well as new?

V. Application of the Test to this Case

The threshold requirement of material change in the circumstances of the child and the parents' ability to meet them was established by the mother's intended move to Australia and the consequent disruption of the child's life and diminution of the father's contact with her. The terms of the order of Carter J. were premised on the child's residence remaining within a reasonable distance of the access parent. The move would clearly breach this provision. Accordingly, the trial judge was required to embark on a fresh appraisal of the best interests of the child.

The reasons of the trial judge fall short of demonstrating that he engaged in the full and sensitive inquiry into the best interests of the child required by s. 17 of the *Divorce Act.* . . . [I]t is therefore appropriate for this Court to review the decision and, should it find the conclusion unsupported on the evidence, vary the order accordingly.

This case requires the Court to balance the benefits derived from continuing custody with the mother against the desirability of maintaining generous contact between the child and her father, as well as her extended Canadian family and her Canadian community. The fact that the child has been in the custody of the mother for some years, that the reasons for initially granting the mother custody have not been shown to have substantially changed, and that a change of custody at this time would probably be highly disruptive to her, argue in favour of the mother retaining custody. On the other hand, the child's access to her father, with whom she enjoyed a close relationship, has been greatly diminished as a consequence of her mother's move, and the child has been removed from her extended family and community in Canada. These factors are somewhat attenuated, however, by the fact that the father has the means to travel to Australia and spend time with the child, and that she could return to Canada for periodic visits with her family and community in Saskatchewan if the terms of access were varied.

Taking all these factors into account, I am of the view that the trial judge did not err in continuing the mother's custody of the child, notwithstanding her intended move to Australia. I find no support in the evidence, however, for restricting the father's access to Australia. Access in Canada would have the advantage of making the father's limited time with the child more natural while it allows her to maintain contact with friends and extended family. Accordingly, I would uphold the custody order and vary the access order to provide for access to be exercisable in Canada. I would add that both parents should equally share the cost of sending her to Canada, in that both have ample means. If the parties cannot agree on the details of access on these terms, or the necessary financial arrangements, they may apply to the Saskatchewan Court of Queen's Bench for direction.

VI. Conclusion

I would affirm the order of the trial judge granting the respondent custody. I would allow the appeal in part, to permit the father to exercise access to the child in Canada on the terms set out above. The parties will bear their own costs throughout.

. . .

GONTHIER J.: — I have had the benefit of the reasons for judgment of Madame Justice L'Heureux-Dubé and Madam Justice McLachlin. I concur in the reasons of McLachlin J. I also agree with L'Heureux-Dubé J.'s explanations of factors pertinent to assessing the best interests of the child and that they are to be considered in doing so, though I do not share her views on onus of proof.

MADAM JUSTICE L'HEUREUX-DUBÉ (concurring in the result only, La Forest J. concurring):— [In her reasons, L'Heureux-Dubé J. revealed that the girl was seven-years-old and that the mother had moved with her to Australia following the lower courts' decisions.]

I. Variation

. . . [T]he question at issue here requires us to determine the proper analysis governing a change of residence by the custodial parent when courts have to rule on a variation application such as the one before us. The answer to this question rests mainly on the view one takes of the notion of custody, a notion no longer controversial in my opinion.

At the outset, however, there are fundamental and uncontroversial premises which must be recalled:

1. It is the right of children that custody and access adjudications under the Act be governed by their best interests (ss. 16(8) and 17(5); *Young* v. *Young*, [1993] 4 S.C.R. 3, at p. 63 (per L'Heureux-Dubé J.) and p. 117 (per McLachlin J.)).

2. The best interests of the child test under the Act is constitutional (*Young*, *supra*, at p. 71 (per L'Heureux-Dubé J.) and at p. 124 (per McLachlin J.)).

3. The Act provides that the best interests of the child must be ''determined by reference to the condition, means, needs and other circumstances of the child'' (s. 16(8)) or, where ''there has been a change in the condition, means, needs or other circumstances of the child, . . . by reference to that change'' (s. 17(5)). It is thus from the child's perspective, and not from the perspective of either parent, that his or her best interests must be assessed (J. D. Payne, *Payne on Divorce* (3rd ed. 1993), at p. 279; *Young*, *supra*, at p. 63 (per L'Heureux-Dubé J.)).

4. Custody and access confer entitlements only to the extent that they enable both parents to discharge their responsibilities and obligations to their children in order to ensure and promote their best interests (*Racine* v. *Woods*, [1983] 2 S.C.R. 173, at p. 185 (per Wilson J.); *Frame* v. *Smith*, [1987] 2 S.C.R. 99, at p. 132 (per Wilson J.); *Young*, *supra*, at p. 59 (per L'Heureux-Dubé J.)).

5. The Act provides that, in making an order regarding the child, ''the court shall give effect to the principle that a child . . . should have as much contact with each spouse as is consistent with the best interests of the child'' (ss. 16(10) and 17(9); . . . *Young*, supra, at p. 53 (per L'Heureux-Dubé J.) and at p. 118 (per McLachlin J.)).

6. Agreements between parents as to any right of the child, be it custody, access or child support, are not binding on courts and must be viewed in light of the best interests of the child (*Pelech* v. *Pelech*, [1987] 1 S.C.R. 801, at p. 845 (per Wilson J.); *Richardson* v. *Richardson*, [1987] 1 S.C.R. 857, at p. 869 (per Wilson J.); *Willick*, *supra*, at p. 686 (per Sopinka J.) and at p. 727 (per L'Heureux-Dubé J.); *G. (L.)* v. *B. (G.)*, [1995] 3 S.C.R. 370, at pp. 396-99 (per L'Heureux-Dubé J.)).

With these premises in mind, I now turn to the notion of custody which lies at the heart of this appeal.

II. Custody

The starting point of the analysis is: what does custody encompass? [A ''survey of custody at common law, under the Act and provincial statutes as well as under the Civil Code of Quebec and various international documents, together with a comparative analysis of the trend in other jurisdictions'' led the justice to conclude that "the custody of a child within the context of divorce is an all-encompassing concept which grants the custodial parent the exclusive right to decide where the child shall live, subject to restrictions which may be ordered where the best interests of the child so require . . . as well as the non-custodial parent's right to apply for 'an order varying . . . a custody order or any provision thereof' pursuant to s. 17(1)(b) of the Act".]

III.   Restrictions on the Rights of Custodial Parents

Section 16(6) of the Act empowers a court to impose terms, conditions or restrictions in connection with its orders for custody and access. The imposition of restrictions on the rights of custodial parents are and should remain the exception rather than the rule. . . .

Having regard to these statutory parameters [sections 16(8) and 17(5) of the *Divorce Act*], limitations on the rights of the custodial parent should not be imposed as a matter of routine. Only if they are found to be required in the best interests of the child, from the child's point of view, can such limitations be justified. Consequently, it is evident that restrictions to incidents of custody cannot be made for frivolous reasons, for the sole purpose of insuring the non-custodial parent's access, to frustrate the custodial parent's mobility, as a bargaining tool, etc. . . .

Accepting that perspective, restrictions on incidents of custody, such as the right to determine where the child should live, should not be inferred, for instance, from generous or specified access provisions without more. . . .

IV.   Onus

The custodial parent's right, as part of the incidents of custody, to decide the place of residence of the child has consequences for the allocation of the burden of proof.

At the outset, it must be noted that there is no clear legal obligation on the part of the custodial parent to notify the non-custodial parent of a change of residence of the child, absent a court order under s. 16(7) of the Act or a valid consensual covenant to that effect. Nevertheless, it would be appropriate for the custodial parent to notify the non-custodial parent of a proposed change of residence except, of course, where there is a threat or fear of violence to the custodial parent or the child, or some other circumstance where such notice would not be in the child's best interests or may not be possible.

This being said, it seems clear that, as in any other type of litigation, the onus of proof lies on the party seeking the variation of a previous court order (Payne, *supra*, at p. 306). This is particularly so in cases implying a change of residence, given the custodial parent's right to elect the place of residence of the children. . . .

The non-custodial parent must bear the onus of showing that the proposed change of residence will be detrimental to the best interests of the child to the extent that custody or access should be varied or, exceptionally, where there is cogent evidence that the child's best interests could not otherwise be accommodated in any reasonable way, that the child should remain in the jurisdiction. Where, however, there is a covenant or court order expressly restricting the child's change of residence, the onus should shift to the custodial parent to establish that the decision to relocate is not made in order to undermine the access rights of the non-custodial parent and that he or she is willing to make arrangements with the non-custodial parent to

restructure access, when appropriate, in light of the change of residence of the child.
. . .

The difficulty, of course, lies in determining what standard should be applied by courts when deciding relocation disputes upon an application for variation of custody, a matter I will now turn to.

V. Standard for Resolving Relocation Disputes

Although the Act makes clear that the best interests of the child is the only consideration to be taken into account in making orders concerning children (ss. 16(8) and 17(5)), in assessing those interests, a number of factors must be considered, not the least of which is the desirability of promoting maximum contact between the child and the non-custodial parent, as the Act also makes clear (ss. 16(10) and 17(9)).
. . .

Important as contact with the non-custodial parent may be, it should be noted that not all experts agree on the weight to be given to such contact in assessing the best interests of children. Several studies suggest that, after parental separation, "the visits by the non-custodial parent will [likely] gradually diminish or terminate". . . . Other concerns relate to access enforcement and the risk of tensions between the parents as regards access. . . .

The paramountcy of the best interests of the child and the objective of promoting maximum contact with the non-custodial parent consistent with such interests are thus the two fundamental premises which must inform the decision of the court in an application to vary custody linked to the change of residence of the custodial parent.

Changes of residence, which might imply a move to another province, territory or country for instance, are inevitable in light of the economic needs and the growing mobility of our society as well as the desirable objective that individuals rebuild their lives after divorce or separation. Faced with such a change of residence, parents generally come to an agreement and re-arrange access modalities in order to ensure that the contact with the non-custodial parent is maintained in a meaningful way, in spite of the relocation. . . .

Parental agreements should be the rule and must be encouraged since parents are generally in the best position to assess the best interests of the child. In addition, such agreements minimize ongoing parental conflict and litigation, which are clearly not in the best interests of children. Research on the emotional impact on children of such conflict, notwithstanding its limits, widely supports this common sense observation. . . .

In the few cases where agreement between the parents is not possible, courts will be called upon to decide. It is never an easy task and sometimes courts can only choose between the lesser of two evils. . . . In order to assist courts in making those difficult determinations, some guidelines may be useful.

In the absence of express restrictions relating to the incidents of custody, such as the child's place of residence, it must be assumed that an existing custody order or agreement reflects the best interests of the child and that such interests lie with the custodial parent. There is nothing revolutionary about this proposition, which flows from the Act which states that courts, in making orders under s. 16(8), "shall take into consideration only the best interests of the child". . . .

The attribution of custody to one parent carries with it the presumption that such parent is the most able to ensure the best interests of the child, for whatever reasons custody is decided. For that matter, both parents may be loving, concerned and caring, they may be equally fit and good parents, but assessing the material, moral and psychological needs of a child commands a much broader inquiry. If, after conducting such an inquiry, or by mutual consent of the parties, a child's custody is entrusted to one of them, it necessarily follows that such parent has been found to be best able to ensure the best interests of the child, taking into account all the circumstances of the parties and the child.

. . . It follows that where, as here, a decision of the custodial parent is challenged by the non-custodial parent on the basis that it is not in the child's best interests, "[t]he emphasis should be . . . on deferring to the decision-making responsibilities of the custodial parent, unless there is substantial evidence that those decisions impair the child's, not the access parent's, long-term well-being" (*MacGyver* v. *Richards*, *supra*, at p. 445 (per Abella J.A.); emphasis added). It must be remembered, as Twaddle J.A. points out in *Lapointe* v. *Lapointe*, [[1995] 10 W.W.R. 609 (Man. C.A.)] at p. 620:

> In all but unusual cases, the custodial parent is in a better position than a judge to decide what is in the child's best interests. A judge can scrutinize the decision, ensure that it is reasonable and even say, when clearly shown, that the custodial parent's decision is in fact not in the child's best interests, but initially it is the person entrusted with the responsibility of bringing up the child who probably knows best.

. . .

The change of residence of the child will generally imply restructuring access. In most cases, it will be possible to re-arrange access in such a way that, if less frequent, it will be for longer periods of time (J. D. Montgomery, "Long-Distance Visitation/Access in Family Law Cases: Some Creative Approaches" (1991), 5 Am. J. Fam. L. 1, at p. 4; Payne, *supra*, at p. 318). Indeed, studies reveal that the quality of the non-custodial parent's relationship with the child is not tied to the duration or frequency of visits (J. S. Wallerstein, "Children of Divorce: Report of a Ten-Year Follow-Up of Early Latency-Age Children" (1987), 57 Am. J. Orthopsychiatry 199, at p. 208). . . . Furthermore, there are a number of ways other than personal visits to maintain contact, such as telephone calls or other technological devices. These are encompassed by ss. 16(10) and 17(9) of the Act which provide for facilitating "contact" between the child and both parents.

By itself, the proposed move of the child does not affect his or her relationship with the non-custodial parent nor does it put at issue the ability of the custodial parent to look after the best interests of the child. In most cases, however, such a change of residence does entail a change to access. All other factors being equal and given that access is but one factor which was taken into account in entrusting custody of the child to the custodial parent, it seems logical that, in order for a change to access to outweigh all other considerations, substantial evidence of a net detriment accruing to the child as a result of such change must be adduced by the non-custodial parent.

While a change of residence does entail some amount of adaptation on the part of the child as well as both parents, a variation of custody is clearly a more violent disruption in the life of a child. It must be remembered that if a transfer of custody is ordered, another move is to take place, that of the child with the non-custodial parent, with all it implies in terms of future limitations on the child's relationship with his or her primary caretaker. Those considerations underlie the court's general reluctance to interfere with the custodial parent's decision to relocate by ordering a variation of custody. . . .

Generally, disrupting the relationship of the child with his or her primary caregiver will be more detrimental to the child than reduced contact with the non-custodial parent (J. G. McLeod, "Annotation to *MacGyver* v. *Richards* " (1995), 11 R.F.L. (4th) 433, at p. 435; B. Hovius, "The Changing Role of the Access Parent" (1994), 10 C.F.L.Q. 123, at p. 132; M. Richards, ["Divorcing Children: Roles For Parents and the State" in Eekelaar and Maclean, eds., *Family Law* (1994)] at p. 252). However, where the children are older and can manifest their preferences, a change of custody may be envisaged, particularly when the relationship with the non-custodial parent is of such a quality and benefit to the child as to make a change of custody the best alternative taking into account all the circumstances. . . .

In the majority of situations, the child's best interests will be easily ascertainable. Where, for instance, access is not regularly exercised, not in the child's best interests nor significant enough, the child is very young or has clearly expressed his or her preferences to remain with the custodial parent or the proposed relocation is for a limited period of time, it will be rare that such relocation will impact on the child's best interests to the extent that custody should be varied.

Where, however, both parents have a good relationship with the child and both are proven equally capable of acting as the custodial parent, determining what is in the best interests of the child may be more difficult, but the line, no matter how fine, must nevertheless be drawn. . . .

Contrary to my colleague, I am of the view that *Carter* v. *Brooks* and *MacGyver* v. *Richard* reveal significant differences of approach. While *Carter* v. *Brooks* essentially stands for the proposition that the determination of the best interests of the child is best left to the discretionary realm of questions of fact where each relevant factor is to be equally considered and where no party bears any specified burden of proof, *MacGyver* v. *Richards* recognizes that courts should grant a "presumptive deference to the needs of the responsible custodial parent who, in the final analysis, lives the reality, not the speculation, of decisions dealing with the incidents of custody" (p. 444). Given that the decision-making authority of the custodial parent entails the right to decide where the child shall live, the onus to adduce substantial evidence that such decision is contrary to the best interests of the child must be placed on the non-custodial parent.

There are many reasons why, in my view, this principled approach is preferable to a case-by-case determination on the evidence of each case.

At the outset, it must be stressed that I do not suggest that such a principled approach overrides or replaces the best interests of the child as the ultimate test. It is rather a reinforcement of the best interests test and not a contradiction to it. It may well be that, in some circumstances, the custodial parent's decision to relocate may not accord with the best interests of the child and, upon review of the impact of that decision on the child, a court may conclude that a variation of custody or access or, exceptionally, a restriction on the child's mobility is in order. Quite the opposite from shifting the focus from the best interests of children, a principled approach, in adopting the best interests test as the guiding principle, provides much needed clarity and certainty in this difficult area of the law and minimizes the need to resort to protracted acrimonious negotiations or, even worse, traumatic and costly litigation which, ultimately, cannot but injuriously affect the children. In passing, it is interesting to note that similar rules which recognize the custodial parent's *prima facie* right to move with the child have been judged consistent with the best interests of the child in other jurisdictions, such as the United States . . . and Australia . . . where, like in Canada, all decisions affecting children are to be governed solely by their best interests.

Under *Carter* v. *Brooks*, the fact-specific case-by-case approach to the best interests of the child test, the absence of guidelines and the inherent discretion it involves foster unpredictability and inconsistency in the application of the law which, in turn, encourages litigation. This uncertainty takes its toll on individual justice by favouring the party most willing to take the risks and best able to bear the financial and emotional costs of litigation rather than inducing reasonable settlements which are, in the final analysis, the most appropriate means of ensuring that the best interests of the child will be met. Contrary to my colleague, I believe that, by reducing the incentive for litigation, the incentive for settlement is increased, not conflict. . . .

This Court is asked to provide a clear answer to the question of the mobility of custodial parents in the context of custody, an answer which strikes a balance between the need for certainty in this area of the law and the right of children to have their interests dictate every decision which concerns them. This fine balance, in my view, finds expression in the rule reinstated in *MacGyver* v. *Richards, supra*, whose effect is simply to translate into practical terms the right of the custodial parent to determine the place of residence of the child by placing the burden of proving that the move is not in the child's best interests on the party challenging the legal status quo. I agree with my colleague McLachlin J. that "the question is not whether the rights of custodial parents can be restricted". Rather, as I stated at the outset, the best interests of the child will always govern any decision affecting that child. However, what I am suggesting here is how to assess that best interest.

Given that day-to-day decisions affecting the child are clearly left to the custodial parent, there is no reason not to defer to his or her ability and responsibility to act in the child's best interests when it comes to other decisions, such as the change of residence of the child which will necessarily take into account the impact of access to the non-custodial parent by the child. . . .

To conclude, in assessing the merits of an application for variation under s. 17(5) of the Act linked to the change of residence of the child by the custodial parent, the guidelines which must inform the courts may be summarized as follows:

1.   All decisions as to custody and access must be made in the best interests of children, assessed from a child-centred perspective.
2.   In the absence of explicit restrictions on the incidents of custody, such as the child's place of residence, it must be assumed that an existing custody order or agreement reflects the best interests of the child and that the appropriate decision-making authority lies with the custodial parent.
3.   In determining the best interests of the child, courts must focus on the impact of the change of residence on the existing custody order and the appropriate modifications to access as the case may be, and generally not proceed to a *de novo* appraisal of all the circumstances of the child and the parties.
4.   The non-custodial parent bears the onus of showing that the proposed change of residence will be detrimental to the best interests of the child to the extent that custody should be varied or, exceptionally, where there is cogent evidence that the child's best interests could not in any reasonable way be otherwise accommodated, that the child should remain in the jurisdiction.
5.   The proposed change of residence of the child by the custodial parent will not justify a variation in custody unless the non-custodial parent adduces cogent evidence that the child's relocation with the custodial parent will prejudice the child's best interests and, further, that the quality of the

non-custodial parent's relationship with the child is of such importance to the child's best interests that prohibiting the change of residence will not cause comparable or greater detriment to the child than an order to vary custody.

6. Where there is an agreement or court order explicitly restricting the child's change of residence, the onus should shift to the custodial parent to establish that the decision to relocate is not made in order to undermine the access rights of the non-custodial parent and that he or she is willing to make arrangements with the non-custodial parent to restructure access, when appropriate, in light of the change of residence of the child. . . .

VI. Application to the Facts

. . . Given that the evidence supports the trial judge's conclusion that the impact of the change of residence of the child was less detrimental to her than ordering a variation of custody, I conclude that he did not err in upholding the custody of the respondent. . . .

WOODHOUSE v. WOODHOUSE

(1996), 20 R.F.L. (4th) 337 (Ont. C.A.)

[The parties had two sons, born in June of 1988 and April of 1990. During their marriage, child care duties were shared by both parties, with the assistance of the maternal grandmother. Following the breakdown of the marriage, the father paid support regularly and exercised access consistently. In November 1992, the parties signed a separation agreement which gave the mother custody of the children, subject to reasonable access on reasonable notice by the father. The mother agreed to give the father 60 days' notice of any intended change in residence of the children. The father was willing to forego a mobility clause on the basis that the mother had represented that she had no intention of leaving the province at that time. The divorce judgment was granted on March 30, 1993, but the terms of the separation agreement were not incorporated into the judgment. In July 1993, the mother married M, a native of Scotland. A few months prior to the marriage, the mother notified the father that she intended to move to Scotland with the children. As a result, the father applied for custody and, in the alternative, asked the court to restrict the mother from removing the children from the jurisdiction. The mother cross-applied, requesting permission for the move and for increased child support. The mother believed that she would have greater economic security if she were to move to Scotland with the children. The mother's new husband had secured gainful employment there and the mother expected to become a full-time homemaker. She sold her dance studio in contemplation of the move and was receiving social assistance. The children's maternal grandmother had returned to live in Scotland and would be nearby. The mother proposed that the father could have five access visits a year with the children, four of which were to be at his expense. She was prepared to accept a reduction in child support. She proposed to return to Canada for four weeks in the summer. Weekly telephone access and video tapes of special occasions were also offered to the father.

While waiting for the applications to be heard, the father consented to an order allowing the mother to vacation in Scotland with the children for a specified period of time. The mother unilaterally decided to remain in Scotland with the children for a further period of time, during which she extended her relationship with M, met his relatives and explored appropriate schooling for the children. The father obtained court orders requiring the mother to return to Ontario and awarding interim custody to him. The mother returned to Canada on the father's undertaking that he would not enforce the order pending the outcome of the proceedings. The parties consented to an assessment report and the Unified Family Court directed that the report address the issue of whether it was in the children's best interests to emigrate to Scotland. The assessor found that the children had a loving relationship with both parties and that they had a good relationship with M. It was his opinion that it was in the best interests of the mother and M to live in Scotland. However, he was of the view that to allow the children to emigrate would render it impossible for the children to maintain a meaningful relationship with their father. The assessor recommended that the children reside in southern Ontario, that the children maintain their current association with their father, and that access be increased to include overnight visits.

The trial judge found the evidence of the assessor helpful as a neutral participant and the report a valuable addition to the material before the court. He ordered that the children remain in their mother's custody but restricted their residence geographically to certain regional municipalities in Southern Ontario. The father was entitled to increased access, including overnight access and was also to pay increased child support. The trial judge did not come to any firm conclusion as to the economic effect on the mother and the new family unit if they were to remain in Canada as opposed to moving to Scotland. Although he recognized the positive effect on the children of being with a happy custodial parent, he found that this did not outweigh the detriment that dislocation would cause. He concluded that it was in the best interests of the children to maintain their relationship with their father and community in Ontario. Moreover, the trial judge found that the mother's plan for access would have considerable financial consequences for the father and that it did not provide frequent access. In effect, he concluded that the mother's plan of access would not preserve the quality of the relationship that the children had with their father. It was that difficulty more than anything else that prompted the trial judge to make the order he did.

The mother appealed the part of the trial judge's order that restrained her from removing the children to Scotland. The mother argued that in applying the legal standard of the best interests of the children, the trial judge erred by not giving sufficient consideration or weight to her views as the custodial parent and in placing too much emphasis on the evidence of the assessor. The mother argued that the assessor's report was a biased, access-driven report in that the assessor had a preconceived opinion that regular and frequent contact with the access parent was the most important factor in determining the best interests of the children.]

Weiler J.A. (Houlden and McKinlay JJ.A. concurring): . . .

Interpretation of the Provisions of the Separation Agreement

Counsel for both the appellant and the respondent agree that, although the provisions of the separation agreement between the parties were not incorporated into the divorce judgment, the principles enunciated by McLachlin J. in *Gordon* [v. *Goertz* (1996), 19 R.F.L. (4th) 117 (S.C.C.)] should govern the analysis in the present case. This position is sensible and is reinforced by the fact that one of the provisions in the separation agreement governing access mirrors s. 16(7) of the *Divorce Act*. This provision requires a custodial parent who intends to change the place of residence of a child to notify the person granted access of the proposed change. As

McLachlin J. found, the purpose of this provision is to give the access parent an opportunity to object to the change and to let the court decide what is in the best interests of the child provided that the threshold test is met.

The parties also agree that the threshold test of a material change of circumstances as found by the trial judge has been met in this case.

The decision in *Gordon, supra* dealt with an application to vary a prior order. The inquiry as to whether the order should be varied, although a fresh inquiry, was based on the findings of the judge who made the previous order as well as on the evidence of the changed circumstances. Separation agreements are not binding on the court because it is the interests of the children rather than those of the parents which are at issue: *Willick* v. *Willick* [(1994), 6 R.F.L. (4th) 161 (S.C.C.)]; and *Droit de la famille—1150*, [(1993), 49 R.F.L. (3d) 317 (S.C.C.)] at p. 109. Nevertheless, it is reasonable to think that at the time the separation agreement was made it reflected the parties' views of the best interests of the children: *Carter* v. *Brooks* [(1990), 30 R.F.L. (3d) 53 (Ont. C.A.)] at p. 63; *Willick* v. *Willick, supra.* The trial judge should therefore consider the prior agreement as well as the evidence of the proposed or changed circumstances. Even though the parties are, strictly speaking, governed by the provisions of the *Children's Law Reform Act*, R.S.O. 1990, c. C.12, both it and the *Divorce Act* state that the governing test is the best interests of the child. It was agreed by counsel that despite the differences in wording, the considerations are the same. Specifically, while the maximum contact principle contained in ss.16(10) and 17(9) of the *Divorce Act* is not articulated in the *Children's Law Reform Act*, the parties agree that this principle is nevertheless applicable when considering whether the provisions of a separation agreement relating to custody and access should be varied. The legal status of the relationship between the child and the parent is not in itself determinative of the best interests of the child. In this regard it is the actual involvement of the parent not the label attached to custody which is important. Whether there is a court order or a separation agreement, the court will be engaged in determining what is in the best interests of the child in all the circumstances, old as well as new. Here, the benefits to the child of the new location must be weighed against the continuance of full contact with the child's access parent, its extended family, and its community . . . .

Consideration of Factors Regarding the Best Interests of the Child

. . . I propose to group consideration of various factors [from *Gordon*] together.

The existing custody arrangement, the existence of a new family unit, the position of the custodial parent, and the ability of the custodial parent to meet the needs of the child.

John Murray wants to return to Scotland. He has employment in Glasgow to which he could return and he expects he would earn the equivalent of $36,000 Canadian a year. The mother wants to move to Scotland with him and to take the children. She is of the view that if she were to move to Scotland she would not have to work outside the home and could become a full-time homemaker. The children's maternal grandmother would be nearby. The mother has a high opinion of the educational system in Scotland and feels that the entire social fabric of life there would benefit the children. Were John Murray to remain in Canada he could eventually obtain landed immigrant status. His employment prospects as a carpenter here, however, were described by the trial judge as "very grim at the moment." At the time of trial the mother was receiving some social assistance.

The trial judge found that the mother was not seeking to move to Scotland in order to frustrate an order of the court or for the purpose of denying access to the father. He did not, however, come to any firm conclusion as to the economic effect on the mother and the new family unit if they remained in the Hamilton area with the children as opposed to moving to Scotland.

The appellant submits that the trial judge did not give sufficient weight to the economic impact of his decision on the new family unit and to the mother's position in general.

The respondent submits that if the mother remains here with the children there will not be a negative impact on them financially. The mother sold her dance studio in June 1993 in contemplation of moving to Scotland. It appears that she earned approximately $20,000 a year from it. After the sale, the mother had employment available to her as a dance instructor, which she refused because she did not wish to be bound by a contract if she was permitted to take the children to Scotland. The mother deposed in her affidavit that if she were not permitted to take the children to Scotland she would have to return to working outside the home and would likely pursue employment as a dance teacher. Given the mother's experience in running a dance studio for some sixteen years, and having regard to the offer of employment which she turned down because she did not wish to commit herself in the event the court allowed her to move with the children, it appears likely that the mother could find work as a dance instructor. The respondent submits that the past history of the mother's income from this employment, coupled with the $13,000 a year in support which the father was ordered to pay, is approximately equivalent to the $36,000 John Murray would earn as a carpenter in Scotland. If the mother is permitted to move with the children to Scotland, it is common ground that the father will not be able to maintain his present child support payments because of the cost of exercising access. It is not clear to what extent such costs would require a reduction of his obligation to pay support. In his evidence at trial, the father estimated the costs of exercising access to be in excess of $7,500. Assuming the mother resumed her employment, even if John Murray did not work outside the home, the family income of the new family unit would likely be about the same, whether or not the mother moved to Scotland with the children. The respondent's position is that, by his decision, the trial judge implicitly rejected the appellant's position on this issue.

One of the factors a court should carefully assess before limiting a custodial parent's decision to move with the children is the economic effect of its decision on the children. The fact that the trial judge's reasons do not expressly disclose his conclusion on this particular factor does not mean, however, that he ignored the evidence on this issue. Although the trial judge did not advert to the evidence on this point in detail, he made specific mention of John Murray's financial position in Canada. As pointed out by the respondent, there is evidence that the best interests of the children would not be affected adversely by the economic consequences of remaining in Canada. Considering the trial judge's reasons as a whole, including his award of increased support, he considered the economic consequences of his decision that the mother and children remain in Canada in applying the standard of the child's best interests.

This is not, however, the end of the inquiry. The question whether the trial judge attributed sufficient weight to the mother's position can only be determined upon consideration of all of the factors the trial judge was required to consider and having regard to his reasons as a whole.

The proposed relocation and the effect of this disruption on the children, the relationship between the children and each of their parents, the views of the children, and the desirability of maximizing contact between the child and both parents.

The trial judge found the distance of the proposed move daunting. The probable effect of the move on the children was predictable. Having gone through the disruption of their parents' divorce and the adjustment of having their mother's new partner come to live with them, they would have to leave their father, paternal grandparents, neighbourhood friends, and, in the case of Michael, his school. The trial judge found that during the marriage both parents had been involved in caring for the children. Following the breakdown of the marriage, the father had paid support regularly and had exercised access consistently.

Evidence of the relationship between the children and their parents, as well as of the views of the children, was placed before the court by way of an assessor's report, which was ordered on the consent of the parties. The assessor found that the children had a loving relationship with their mother and that they also liked and had a good relationship with John Murray. The assessor indicated that, contrary to what he had been led to believe by the mother, the children's relationship with their father was a close, comfortable and loving one. Michael stated that he wanted to go to Scotland so that his mother would not have to work (outside the home). Michael also indicated that when he did not see his father he missed him, that he liked going to Burlington to visit his father and that he liked to see his dad all the time. . . .

The appellant submits that the report is a biased access-driven report, not based on clinical tests, and that the trial judge erred in adopting the assessor's conclusion that it was in the bests interests of the children not to vary the terms of access but to preserve and enlarge the children's contact with their father.

As I have indicated, the assessment report was ordered prior to trial with the consent of the parties. The report cannot be said, therefore, to have been obtained with the aim of maximizing the views of the party who had hired the assessor. The trial judge correctly observed that the assessor's evidence was not determinative of the issue before him but was merely one piece of evidence for his consideration. In addition, he noted that it was up to him, not the assessor, to determine the facts. . . .

The trial judge also considered the extent to which access had been fostered by the custodial parent as he would have been required to do if he had been acting pursuant to s. 17(9) of the *Divorce Act*. The father, after receiving notice from the mother that she intended to move to Scotland with the children in February 1993, applied for custody or to enjoin the mother from taking the children to Scotland. While waiting for the application to be heard, the parties entered into an agreement which resulted in a consent order allowing the mother to vacation in Scotland with the children from March 16 to April 11, 1993. Notwithstanding this agreement, the mother did not return to Ontario with the children by April 11. Instead, she unilaterally decided to remain in Scotland with the children for a further period of time. During this time, the mother extended her relationship with John Murray, met his relatives, and explored appropriate schooling for the children in Scotland. It will be recalled that by this time she had sold her business and had only a six-month lease on a townhouse in Ontario. On April 16, the father returned to court and, on consent, obtained an order requiring the mother to return to Ontario on April 19, 1993. The mother again failed to return to the jurisdiction. The father returned to court on April 20 and was awarded interim interim custody of the children. In the meantime, the mother retained counsel in Scotland and obtained an order of the Scottish courts granting her interim custody of the children on April 19, 1993. In those proceedings the mother made no disclosure of the Ontario court proceedings and represented to the Scottish court that the children were resident in Scotland. When the mother was made aware of the order granting the father interim interim custody, she agreed to return to Canada on the father's undertaking that he would not enforce the order pending the outcome of these proceedings. The mother returned to Ontario with the children on April 26, 1993.

Although the trial judge found that the mother's failure to return with the children on April 11 and her continued sojourn in Scotland for another two weeks was a foolish act, he stated that it had little to do with his decision. . . .

In determining the child's best interests, the child's relationship with the access parent is a factor to consider. It cannot be denied that frequency of access bears some correlation to the child's relationship with the access parent. While it is the quality of the child's relationship and not simply the frequency of access which is the consideration, in general, the more frequently access has been, and can be, exercised, the stronger that relationship will be: see Kelly, "Current Research On Children's Postdivorce Adjustment", *Family And Conciliation Courts Review* (1993), Vol. 31 (1), p. 29 at 39; Johnston, "Research Update: Children's Adjustment in Sole Custody Compared to Joint Custody Families and Principles for Custody Decision Making", *Family and Conciliation Courts Review* (1995), Vol. 33 (4) p. 415 at 419. In *Gordon, supra*, McLachlin J. implicitly recognized this at p. 28 of her reasons when she noted that the child's close relationship to her father had been greatly diminished as a consequence of her mother's move. McLachlin J. found, however, that the means and the ability of the father to bridge the distance created by the move would help to attenuate the impact on the child of the diminished relationship with him. It was not disputed that the father had the time, and both parents had the means, to enable the father to exercise access.

The parties in the instant case are in greatly different circumstances. Unlike the situation in *Gordon, supra*, the relationship between the children and their father has not been diminished for the past year. The trial judge found that the access plan proposed by the mother would have considerable financial consequences for the father. Even allowing for a reduction in support payments by the father, he has limited financial means and, not being self employed, limited holiday time within which to exercise access.

Through s. 17(9), Parliament intended to promote, where appropriate, a meaningful, continuing post-divorce relationship between the children of the marriage and the access parent. This legislative decision is amply supported by social science research and literature which suggests that children benefit from a continuing relationship with the access parent: *Young* v. *Young* [(1993), 49 R.F.L. (3d) 117 (S.C.C.)] at p. 118. The mother's actions in remaining in Scotland with the children beyond the agreed period and in obtaining an interim custody order from the Scottish courts, raised the question whether, if permitted to move, she would comply with any Ontario order concerning access. Against this background, the comments of the trial judge take on a different light. The trial judge was troubled by the attitude shown by the mother during her trip to Scotland towards the father's desire to continue to play a significant role as the children's father. He took from her evidence that she did not regard this to be in the best interests of the children. The trial judge made the finding that the mother did not place sufficient importance on the children's contact with their father.

Deference to the Findings of the Trial Judge

The trial judge's reasons indicate that he found that the mother's view as to the best interests of the children overlooked an important consideration. In effect, the reasons conclude that the mother's plan of access would not preserve the quality of the relationship that the children had with their father. Although the trial judge recognized the positive effect on the children of being with a happy custodial parent, he concluded that it did not outweigh the detriment that dislocation would cause. The trial judge concluded that it was in the best interests of the children to maintain their relationship with their father and community, in Ontario.

. . . [W]hen the reasons of the trial judge are considered as a whole, his findings do not indicate any error. The facts adduced in evidence support the conclusion the trial judge drew from them. I would accordingly dismiss the appeal.

Osborne J.A. (dissenting): . . . In *Gordon* v. *Goertz*, McLachlin J. made it clear that the reasons for the custodial parent's move, or proposed move, are not usually relevant to the best interests inquiry. . . . Although in light of *Gordon*, the reasons for the proposed move can no longer be cast as an important issue in the best interests inquiry, the reasons for the move are still relevant in the case of a spouse who is proposing to move solely to frustrate legitimate access arrangements.

I would add that I think in most cases the reasons for the proposed move will surface because there is a manifest connection between the expected effects of the move and the custodial parent's reasons for proposing the move in the first place. The effect of the proposed move (in this case greater economic security, among other things) will be admissible and will generally be before the court. Nonetheless, *Gordon* makes it clear that there is no burden, or onus, on a custodial parent who is proposing to move to justify the move against a standard of necessity, or any other less onerous standard. . . .

The Third Option

Although McLachlin J. approached the issue of mobility in custody terms (that is, custody with the mother in Australia, or custody with the father in Saskatoon), I share Weiler J.A.'s opinion that McLachlin J. did not intend to rule out consideration of what counsel in their submissions following the release of *Gordon* v. *Goertz* referred to as the "third option"—the option of the custodial parent keeping custody but not being allowed to move with the children. . . .

It seems to me that McLachlin J. accepts that, after all relevant factors are balanced, the best interests of a child may support the conclusion that the child should remain with the custodial parent in the community to which the child is accustomed and in close proximity to an access parent with whom the child has a meaningful relationship. In other cases, after all relevant factors are balanced, the best interests of the child may support the conclusion that the child should be permitted to move with the custodial parent.

In a case where what I have referred to as the third option is an open option, the foundation for the inquiry will not be which parent should have custody, but whether the parent who does have custody should be permitted to move with the children when both the benefits and detriments of the move are taken into account by balancing them against each other. For reasons which I hope will be made clear shortly, I do not think that the appropriate question in this inquiry is whether the custodial parent should be entitled to move, having in mind the effect of the move on existing access arrangements. The effect of the move on existing access arrangements is merely one factor in the required balancing exercise.

In practice, the decision of a custodial parent to move often will not constitute a material change in circumstances in respect of custody, because the custodial parent typically will not move without the children. Such a move or a proposed move will, however, constitute a material change in circumstances in respect of access in that the existing access arrangements may be materially affected by the children's move with their custodial parent.

It is a fact of family law practice that in mobility cases many applications for custody by the non-custodial parent following a proposed move are motivated by tactical considerations. In such cases, the non-custodial parent's substantive position is that the custodial parent should not be permitted to move with the children. Whether this position is asserted by way of an application by the non-custodial parent to prevent the custodial parent from moving with the children, or by the non-custodial parent opposing the custodial parent's application for permission to move with the children, is a matter of no legal or practical consequence. In my experience it is a rare case where the custodial parent's position will exclude the option of staying with the children rather than moving. It is important to determine the position of the parents at an early stage. If, as is frequently the case, the custodial parent's position is that she will not move unless the children go with her, and the non-custodial parent claims custody only because of the move, it would not make much sense in these circumstances to embark upon a full-blown custody hearing.

Analysis

Notwithstanding Mr. Woodhouse's claim for custody, the central issue . . . was not who should have custody of the children, it was whether the children should be permitted to move to Scotland with Mrs. Woodhouse. . . .

In this case, both parents advanced conditional positions. Mrs. Woodhouse's decision to move to Scotland was conditional upon her being able to move with her children. Her position was that if the children could not come with her, she would not go. Mr. Woodhouse's position was that if Mrs. Woodhouse were to move to Scotland, he should have custody of the children. I think the trial judge was right in concluding that the real issue that he had to decide was not who should have custody, but was whether Mrs. Woodhouse should be permitted to move to Scotland with her children. This view of the case is entirely consistent with the parenting alternatives proposed by Mr. and Mrs. Woodhouse before and at trial.

Having properly dismissed Mr. Woodhouse's claim for custody, the trial judge went on to conclude that the children should not be permitted to move to Scotland with their mother. It falls to be determined if the trial judge in coming to that conclusion conducted the necessary "full and sensitive inquiry" into the best interests of the children. . . .

In my view, the majority's reasons in *Gordon* support the general proposition that one should not proceed on the basis of *any* presumptions about what is in the children's best interests. The proper course is to consider the individual circumstances of the child whose best interests the court has been called upon to ascertain. In contrast with the approach that I think has now been established by the majority in *Gordon* v. *Goertz*, in my opinion both the assessor and the trial judge in the instant case proceeded on a general assumption that there is a positive correlation between the frequency of access and the best interest of the children in all cases.

An examination of the assessor's report and his trial evidence reveals that he was strongly biased in favour of preserving a non-custodial parent's ability to exercise frequent access, particularly in the case of young children. This bias was not case-specific.

Just as according a presumptive deference to the custodial parent's decision to move may be said to tilt the inquiry too much in favour of the custodial parent, similarly asking the singular question whether it is in the children's best interests that access be decreased tilts the inquiry too much in favour of the non-custodial parent. Framing the inquiry in that way tends to limit the required balancing of relevant factors. The better approach is to determine whether there is a valid reason to decrease access when *all* of the relevant factors (including the custodial parent's decision to move, which is entitled to "great respect") are taken into account. That is to say that both the benefits and detriments of the proposed move must be considered and balanced. That consideration and balancing was not undertaken in this case. The trial judge unduly emphasized one detriment of the proposed move — reduced access — and did not give sufficient consideration to the benefits of the proposed move.

Rather than according great respect to Mrs. Woodhouse's decision to move, the trial judge seems to have given very little weight to it. He accepted the assessor's evidence, which was that allowing the move would be in the best interests of Mrs. Woodhouse and Mr. Murray; the assessor also was of the opinion that the children would benefit from broadening their experience and from having contact with their relatives and friends in Scotland. The trial judge did not question these conclusions. In my opinion, he did not give them due weight in the balancing process that is required to determine the best interests of the children.

The custodial parent's decision to move should be given great respect because it is accepted that there is a real connection between the best interests of the children and the best interests of the custodial parent. Typically, the custodial parent will have primary caregiver responsibilities, either as a result of an agreement or by court order, or both. Either the children's parents or the court will have determined that it is in the best interests of the children that they be in the day-to-day care of one parent, with the other parent exercising access. The access-related corollary is that the parents, or the court, will have determined that it is in the best interests of the children to have contact with the non-custodial parent. . . .

NOTES AND QUESTIONS

1. There is some confusion in the cases as to whether the access parent or the custodial parent must commence proceedings for a variation of an existing custody/access order where there is a planned relocation. See Hovius, "Mobility of the Custodial Parent: Guidance from the Supreme Court" (1996), 19 R.F.L. (4th) 292; Davies, "Mobility Rights and Child Custody: A Contradiction in Terms" (1997), 15 C.F.L.Q. 115 ; and Hovius, "Case Comment: *Woodhouse* v. *Woodhouse* and *Luckhurst* v. *Luckhurst*" (1996), 20 R.F.L. (4th) 373 (Ont. C.A.), at 383-84.

Who has to apply in the following situations? Who has to prove what?

1) A custody/access order specifies that the mother has custody and that the father has access on Wednesday evenings and every other weekend. There is no non-removal clause in the order and the mother wishes to move with the child to Australia.

2) The parents have joint custody and the order stipulates that the child will live with the father. The mother has generous access. The father wishes to move with the child to a city 200 kilometres away and the mother objects.

3) A custody/access order stipulates that the mother has custody of the child on condition that the child live in the Metro-Toronto area. The mother wishes to move to Windsor with the child.

4) There is no custody/access order, but the child resides with the mother with the approval of the father who sees the child frequently. The mother wishes to move to Sweden with the child.

5) The situation is the same as in #3, but the terms of custody and access are set in a separation agreement.

Another way of looking at these issues is to ask whether the mothers in situations # 1, 3, 4, and 5 and the father in situation #2 are legally entitled to move with the child without either the consent of the other parent or the court. If they are, do they nonetheless have a legal obligation to inform the other parent of the move? If so, must there be advance notice?

In *Relocation of Custodial Parents: Final Report* (Ottawa: Status of Women Canada, 1998), Professors Bailey and Giroux recommend (at 8) that the rules governing which parent must commence proceedings should be clarified, especially where there is no non-removal clause in the existing order but the move would interfere with the terms of the access order. They also suggest (at 8-9):

> If there is no general requirement that the custodial parent obtain a variation of the terms of the access prior to moving, Canada's law should be amended to require custodial parents to give notice of a proposed move to the other parent or the court. As well, the custodial parent should be required to propose new arrangements for access. The notice requirement should provide for exceptions in cases where notice would create a risk of domestic violence.

See also *For the Sake of the Children* (Ottawa, 1998), where the Special Joint Committee recommends (at 70) an amendment to the *Divorce Act* to require (a) that a parent wishing to relocate with a child, where the distance would necessitate the modification of agreed or court-ordered parenting arrangements, seek judicial permission at least 90 days before the proposed move and (b) that the other parent be given notice at the same time.

2. In *Woodhouse*, the mother stayed in Scotland with the children longer than stipulated in the consent order. How did this affect her chances of getting judicial approval for the desired move? The following cases illustrate rather varied responses to situations where the custodial parent has engaged in some form of "self-help" by simply moving with the child: *Murphy* v. *Jordan* (1996), 26 R.F.L. (4th) 82 (B.C. S.C.); *K. (M.M.)* v. *M. (P.R.)* (1997), 27 R.F.L. (4th) 285 (Ont. Gen. Div.); *Brooks* v. *Brooks* (1998), 39 R.F.L. (4th) 187 (Ont. C.A.); *Hurst* v. *Hurst* (1998), 39 R.F.L. (4th) 406 (Alta. C.A.); and *M. (T.K.)* v. *M. (P.S.)* (1999), 48 R.F.L. (4th) 393 (Alta. Q.B.).

3. In the vast majority of mobility cases prior to *Gordon* v. *Goertz*, the courts were, in effect, determining whether the custodial parent should be permitted to move with the child or whether the custodial parent should be precluded from moving by making custody conditional on the child residing in a particular location. The proposed move was conditional upon a favourable court ruling. The options canvassed by the S.C.C. in *Gordon* v. *Goertz* were whether the child should move with the custodial parent or whether the child should remain behind with the other parent. Following her summary of the law in *Gordon* v. *Goertz*, Justice McLachlin indicated: "In the end, the importance of the child remaining with the parent to whose custody it has become accustomed in the new location must be weighed against the continuance of full contact with the child's access parent, its extended family and its community." Was the S.C.C. signaling that the courts should adopt a new approach in all mobility cases and focus only or principally on these two options? Alternatively, was the court's approach simply a reflection of the particular fact situation, thereby leaving open the possibility of maintaining the status quo in most cases? Subsequent cases have adopted the same approach to these questions as the Ontario Court of Appeal in *Woodhouse*.

How would the analysis in *Woodhouse* have changed if the mother had indicated that she and her new husband would reside in Scotland, with or without the two boys? What result would the court have reached? For a case which may provide some insight, see *Bruce* v. *Bruce* (1997), 26 R.F.L. (4th) 219 (B.C. S.C.). Is there a difference between indicating that one will stay if this is the only way to retain custody and indicating that one will stay if a court rules that this is in the best interests of the child? See *Johnson* v. *Johnson* (1997), 28 R.F.L. (4th) 25 (Alta. C.A.).

4. Should the same test and factors be used if the choice is between maintaining the status quo and allowing the custodial parent to move with the child rather than between allowing the child to accompany the custodial parent to a new location and altering the custody arrangement? Did the S.C.C. answer this question in *Gordon* v. *Goertz*?

5. Did the majority in *Gordon* v. *Goertz* generally endorse the approach taken by the Ont. C.A. in *Carter* v. *Brooks*? If so, how do you explain the dramatically different outcomes in the two cases?

6. Professor Thompson suggested in "'Beam Us Up Scotty': Parents and Children on the Trek" (1996), 13 C.F.L.Q. 219, at 226: "The detailed analysis of the 'reason for the move' in *Carter* suggests, not a multi-factorial test, but a straight two-way test, to be met by the custodial parent: does the benefit or 'necessity' of the move outweigh the impact upon the access relationship?" Do you agree? Do Justice McLachlin's comments regarding the reason for the move in *Gordon,* which was decided after Thompson's article was published, preclude this approach? What is the approach in *Woodhouse*?

In "Relocation and Relitigation: After *Gordon* v. *Goertz*" (1998-1999), 16 C.F.L.Q. 461, Professor Thompson examines the relocation cases decided in the first 32 months after the S.C.C. decision. He found (at 477) that there were 118 cases, "a remarkable number". Regarding the reason for the move, he reports (at 490):

> The non-workability of *Gordon* is evident here, as the reason for the move is central to the analysis in almost every single case, starting with *Woodhouse*. If anything, the lack of a sufficient reason lies at the root of most "no" cases, rather than any significance to the access relationship. The reason for the move is so important that there is a creeping tendency to cast upon the moving parent an evidential burden to explain the move, which can easily become a legal burden, whether consciously or unconsciously.

Professor Thompson found that moves were permitted in 73 cases and denied in 45 cases. This ratio closely resembled that which had prevailed in Ontario in the period between *Carter* and *MacGyver*. There had been a dramatic decrease after *MacGyver* in the proportion of cases in Ontario where courts precluded the custodial parent from moving with the child. Professor Thompson also concludes (at 490): "The actual analysis by most courts [in the post-*Gordon* cases] more closely approximates that found in *Carter* than that in *Gordon*."

7. For additional post-*Gordon* appellate level relocation cases, see *Luckhurst* v. *Luckhurst* (1996), 20 R.F.L. (4th) 373 (Ont. C.A.); *Chilton* v. *Chilton* (1996), 26 R.F.L. (4th) 124 (B.C. C.A.); *Johnson* v. *Johnson* (1997), 28 R.F.L. (4th) 25 (Alta. C.A.); *Ligate* v. *Richardson* (1997), 34 O.R. (3d) 423 (C.A.); *Pisko* v. *Pisko* (1997), 151 D.L.R. (4th) 189 (Alta. C.A.); *Rockwell* v. *Rockwell* (1998), 43 R.F.L. (4th) 450 (B.C. C.A.); *Burns* v. *Burns* (2000), 3 R.F.L. (5th) 189 (N.S. C.A.); *Doiron* v. *Mahoney* (2000), 3 R.F.L. (5th) 206 (N.S. C.A.); and *Zeaton* v. *Zeaton* (1999), 3 R.F.L. (5th) 320 (Man. C.A.).

8. As indicated in *Gordon*, in the cases pre-dating the adoption of *Child Support Guidelines* sometimes a court would require a moving custodial parent to help pay for the increased cost of exercising access either directly or indirectly (by reducing child support). See *Curtis* v. *Curtis* (1990), 29 R.F.L. (3d) 235 (Ont. Gen. Div.); *Fasan* v. *Fasan* (1991), 32 R.F.L. (3d) 121 (Ont. Gen. Div.); *Armstrong* v. *Armstrong* (1993), 49 R.F.L. (3d) 456 (Man. C.A.); and *Jarrett* v. *Jarrett* (1994), 10 R.F.L. (4th) 24 (Ont. Gen. Div.). See also *Jacques* v. *Martin* (1995), 11 R.F.L. (4th) 224 (Ont. U.F.C.). In *Daller* v. *Daller* (1989), 22 R.F.L. (3d) 96, at 97 (Ont. C.A.), the court reversed a trial judge's order requiring the custodial mother to pay access transportation costs because the child's welfare demanded that "his mother retain all of her meagre income for the support of herself and her son".

Under s. 10 of the *Child Support Guidelines*, a court can reduce the amount of child support in circumstances where the payor can establish undue hardship. One of the circumstances listed in s. 10(2) as possibly giving rise to undue hardship is "unusually high expenses in exercising access to a child". However, even if unusually high access costs exist, the application for a reduction in child support must be denied unless the access parent can establish under s. 10(3) that his or her household's standard of living is lower than the custodial parent's. This is usually fatal to the claim. See generally Chapter 8: **CHILD SUPPORT**.

It is uncertain whether a court still has jurisdiction to order the custodial parent to pay directly for access costs. Some judges have held that s. 10 of the *Guidelines* exhaustively covers the issue of access costs: *South* v. *South*, [1998] B.C.J. 962 (B.C. S.C.). Professor McLeod has argued in several annotations in the Reports of Family Law that a court should be able to order a custodial parent to assume some of the costs of transportation relating to access simply as a condition of custody and independently of any child support issues. See, for example, his annotation to *Holtskog* v. *Holtskog* (1999), 47 R.F.L. (4th) 162 (Sask. C.A.). See also "Reforming the Child Support Guidelines" in *Federal Child Support Guidelines Reference Manual* (Ottawa: Dept. of Justice, looseleaf) where Professor Bala states (at K-75):

> The better view is articulated by the recent mobility cases where judges, in appropriate cases, exercise a discretion to require the custodial parent to pay all or part of the increased access costs. Technically, the judge is not reducing the Guidelines' child support order, which continues to be fully enforceable as child support, but rather is invoking subsection 16(6) of the *Divorce Act* to impose a "condition" on custody that permits the custodial parent to move, but requires that parent to pay all or part of the increased access costs, if and when access is exercised.

9. For articles in addition to those already referred to in these notes and questions, see Irving and Benjamin, "Mobility Rights and Children's Interests: Empirically-Based First Principles as a Guide to Effective Parenting Plans" (1995-96), 13 C.F.L.Q. 249; Bruch and Bowermesiter, "The Relocation of Children and Custodial Parents: Public Policy, Past and Present" (1996), 30 Fam. L.Q. 245; Wallerstein and Tanke, "To Move or Not to Move: Psychological and Legal Considerations in the Relocation of Children Following Divorce" (1996), 30 Fam. L.Q. 305; Ford, "Untying the Relocation Knot: Recent Developments and a Model for Change" (1997), 7 Columbia J. Gender and Law 1; Driscoll, "In Search of a Standard: Resolving the Relocation Problem in New York" (1997), 26 Hofstra Law Rev. 175; Boyd, "Child Custody, Relocation, and the Post-Divorce Family Unit: *Gordon* v. *Goertz* at the Supreme Court of Canada" (1997), 9 C.J.W.L. 447; and Hovius, "Case Comment: *Ligate* v. *Richardson* and *Pisko* v. *Pisko*" (1998), 32 R.F.L. (4th) 9.

8

CHILD SUPPORT

1. Introduction

This chapter does not exhaustively cover all of the law relating to child support. The issues that are common to both spousal and child support, such as enforcement of support orders, the relationship between the support provisions in the *Divorce Act* and the *Family Law Act* (the *FLA*) and the types of orders available, will not be canvassed again. Instead this chapter focuses on the factual elements that must be established before an obligation to support a particular child exists (2. Establishing a Support Obligation) and examines the determination of support (3. Determining Quantum).

Section 32 of the *FLA*, as well as legislation in some of the other provinces, stipulates that adult children have an obligation to support their parents who have "cared for or provided support for" them. Although still quite rare, claims by adults for support from their children succeeded in *Godwin* v. *Bolcso* (1996), 20 R.F.L. (4th) 66 (Ont. C.A.) and *Dragulin* v. *Dragulin* (1998), 43 R.F.L. (4th) 55 (Ont. Gen. Div.). See also *Newson* v. *Newson* (1998), 43 R.F.L. (4th) 221 (B.C. C.A.) where interim support was ordered. The court denied the claim in *Leung* v. *Leung* (1996), 20 R.F.L. (4th) 48 (Alta. Q.B.).

The birth of a child is not always a welcome event for the parents. Sometimes the father will insist that he never would have engaged in sexual intercourse but for the belief that the mother had taken contraceptive measures. This chapter begins by reproducing one of the American cases in which a plaintiff has sought damages for "contraceptive fraud".

STEPHEN K. v. RONI L.

164 Cal. Rptr. 618 (Cal. App. 2 Dist., May 12, 1980)

BEACH, ASSOCIATE JUSTICE

BACKGROUND:

The minor child, its guardian ad litem, and its mother brought a paternity suit against Stephen K. (Stephen). After admitting paternity, Stephen filed a cross-complaint "for fraud, negligent misrepresentation and negligence." The cross-complaint alleged that Roni L. (Roni), the child's mother, had falsely represented that she was taking birth control pills and that in reliance upon such representation Stephen engaged in sexual intercourse with Roni which eventually resulted in the birth of a baby girl unwanted by Stephen. Stephen further alleged that as a "proximate result" of Roni's conduct he had become obligated to support the child financially, and had suffered "mental agony and distress" all to his general damage in the amount of $100,000. Stephen also sought punitive damages of $100,000 against Roni for having acted "with oppression, fraud, and malice" towards him.

Roni moved for a judgment on the pleadings claiming that (1) to allow Stephen to recover damages would be against public policy, and (2) Stephen had failed to establish damages. The trial court treated Roni's motion as a general demurrer to the cross-complaint and ordered the action dismissed. Stephen appeals.

ISSUE ON APPEAL:

The sole issue in this case is: As between two consenting sexual partners, may one partner hold the other liable in tort for the birth of a child conceived in an act of intercourse where the one partner relied on the other partner's false representation that contraceptive measures had been taken? We conclude that in this case Roni's conduct complained of by Stephen did not give rise to liability.

DISCUSSION:

The critical question before us is whether Roni's conduct towards Stephen is actionable at all. Stephen claims it is actionable as a tort. Neither statutory nor judicial recognition of such a claim in California or elsewhere in the United States has been brought to the attention of this court. Though the presentation of the matter as a legal issue is somewhat novel, the social conditions underlying it have existed since the advent of mankind.

Broadly speaking, the word "tort" means a civil wrong, other than a breach of contract, for which the law will provide a remedy in the form of an action for damages. It does not lie within the power of any judicial system, however, to remedy all human wrongs. There are many wrongs which in themselves are flagrant. For instance, such wrongs as betrayal, brutal words, and heartless disregard of the feelings of others are beyond any effective legal remedy and any practical administration of law. (Prosser, Torts (3d ed. 1964) ch. 1, § 1 and 4, pp. 1-2, 18, 21.) To attempt to correct such wrongs or give relief from their effects "may do more social damage than if the law leaves them alone." (Ploscowe, *An Action For "Wrongful Life"* (1963) 38 New York U.L. Rev. 1078, 1080.) The present case falls within that category.

We are in effect asked to attach tortious liability to the natural results of consensual sexual intercourse. Stephen's claim is one of an alleged wrong to him personally and alone. Procedurally and technically it is separate and apart from any issue of either parent's obligation to raise and support the child. Although actually requiring the mother to pay Stephen monetary damages may have the effect of reducing her financial ability to support the child, we need not get into this area of discussion or resolve such problems as may exist in that area. In the posture of the case as presented to us, the state has minimal if any interest in this otherwise entirely private matter. Claims such as those presented by plaintiff Stephen in this case arise from conduct so intensely private that the courts should not be asked to nor attempt to resolve such claims. Consequently, we need not and do not reach the question of whether Stephen has established or pleaded tort liability on the part of Roni under recognized principles of tort law. In summary, although Roni may have lied and betrayed the personal confidence reposed in her by Stephen, the circumstances and the highly intimate nature of the relationship wherein the false representations may have occurred, are such that a court should not define any standard of conduct therefor. . . .

The claim of Stephen is phrased in the language of the tort of misrepresentation. Despite its legalism, it is nothing more than asking the court to supervise the promises made between two consenting adults as to the circumstances of their private sexual conduct. To do so would encourage unwarranted governmental intrusion into matters affecting the individual's right to privacy. . . .

We reject Stephen's contention that tortious liability should be imposed against Roni, and conclude that as a matter of public policy the practice of birth control, if any, engaged in by two partners in a consensual sexual relationship is best left to the individuals involved, free from any governmental interference. As to Stephen's claim that he was tricked into fathering a child he did not want, no good reason appears why he himself could not have taken any precautionary measures. Even if Roni had regularly been taking birth control pills, that method, though considered to be the most reliable means of birth control, is not 100 percent effective. Although slight, there is some statistical probability of conception. Of those women who for a year use birth control pills containing both estrogen and progestin, less than 1 woman out of 100 will become pregnant. However, as to those women using birth control pills containing only progestin, 2 to 3 women out of 100 will become pregnant. (U.S. Dept. of Health, Ed. & Welfare, Public Health Service, and Food and Drug Admin., *Contraception*, HEW Publication No. FDA 78-3069.)

The judgment is affirmed.

NOTES AND QUESTIONS

1. In *L. Pamela P.* v. *Frank S.*, 449 N.E. 2d 713 (N.Y., May 3, 1983); *Scrubb* v. *Hackett* (1987), 6 R.F.L. (3d) 275 (Ont. Fam. Ct.); *Boca* v. *Mendel* (1989), 20 R.F.L. (3d) 421 (Ont. Fam. Ct.); *Parris* v. *Wright* (1990), 99 N.S.R. (2d) 11 (N.S. Fam. Ct.); *Buschow* v. *Jors* (1994), 3 R.F.L. (4th) 39 (Sask. Q.B.); and *New Brunswick (Minister of Income Assistance)* v. *H. (S.)* (1996), 20 R.F.L. (4th) 312 (N.B. C.A.), the courts held that a mother's alleged deception regarding contraceptive measures had no bearing on the father's support obligation. The court put it this way in *Boca* (at 425):

> I know of no operative legal principle that would suggest that where a mother decides to have a child and this runs contrary to the wishes of the biological father, it can or should affect the child's right to support from the father or the mother's right to claim child support. There are reasons of public policy to avoid extending the considerations for determining child support into the realm of opinions about abortion or into the realm of singling out responsibility for birth control in each situation or into the realm of measuring the father's enthusiasm about being a father. Very simply, conception is a joint responsibility.

However, in *Buschow*, Halvorson J. suggested (in *obiter dicta* at 42) that there might be some limited circumstances in which the courts would take a different approach:

> The father argues that this [the approach in *Boca*] is too simplistic an approach to a complicated social issue. He may be right. There may be some point where the commitment between the parties is such that the support obligation is limited or curtailed. For example, in these modern times, a woman may wish to be inseminated from a particular gene pool and therefore selects a male with the appropriate characteristics. There may even be a contractual arrangement. Other examples could be conceived where inflexible application of the statute might create an injustice. While these situations would be rare, they emphasize the point that support obligations are not always automatically triggered by the birth of a child.

2. For further reading, see Mann, ''Misrepresentation of Sterility or of the Use of Birth Control'' (1987-88), 26 J.F.L. 623.

2.   Establishing A Support Obligation

(1) PROVING PATERNITY

SILBER v. FENSKE

(1995), 11 R.F.L. (4th) 145 (Ont. Gen. Div.)

GREER J.: — The Plaintiff, Louise Lena Dora Silber (''Silber''), moved for an Order requiring the Defendant, Wayne Gordon Fenske (''Fenske''), to pay interim child support of $2,500 per month to her for the benefit of Stephanie Leah Silber, born March 23, 1994, and requiring him to pay prenatal expenses of $2,923, and has requested an Order pursuant to s. 10 of the *Children's Law Reform Act*, R.S.O. 1990, c. C.12 requiring the parties and child to submit to blood tests to determine the child's paternity.

Fenske takes the position that the Silber made false representations to him that she was using contraception during their relationship, that he is not the father of the child but if he is, that this paternity was criminally induced and therefore he should not be obliged to pay support. If he is required to pay support, Fenske takes the position that there has been a breach of s. 7 of the *Canadian Charter of Rights and Freedoms* given his involuntary paternity or that having sex with Silber was falsely induced. Lastly, Fenske says that any statutory requirement to provide blood to determine paternity under s. 10 of the Children's Law Reform Act or any adverse inference that the Court may draw from his refusal to supply blood is contrary to s. 8 of the *Canadian Charter of Rights and Freedoms*.

1. Background

The parties were involved in an intimate relationship from late 1991 or early 1992 until July, 1993. Silber alleges that she became pregnant by Fenske near the end of their relationship. The child was born on March 23, 1994 and Fenske on April 14, 1994 certified under the *Vital Statistics Act* that he was the child's father. Fenske has now denied paternity and has not voluntarily submitted to a paternity blood test. He takes the position that Silber falsely represented to him that she would not ask for child support if he signed the Vital Statistics form. He further maintains that he did not know that he was the father of the child. He claims that Silber is estopped from relying on the registration form to establish the child's paternity or to further her claim for child support. . . .

2. Blood tests

The Court may grant leave to obtain a blood test of a person named when paternity is an issue. If such person refuses to submit to the blood test, the Court may draw an adverse inference from such refusal. [See s. 10 of the *Children's Law Reform Act*.]

In *Panaccione* v. *McNabb* (1976), 28 R.F.L. 182 (Ont. Fam. Ct.), the Court held at pp. 185 and 186:

> It would, therefore, be my view that when a court is asked to decide the issue of paternity, it should have before it the best evidence available and that should include expert scientific evidence by means of a blood test. When one of the parties is prepared to submit to such a test, whereas

the other refuses to do so, then I am of the view that the court can, and indeed should, make the appropriate inferences from such refusal.

. . . In the case at bar, we have a set of circumstances which cries out for such blood tests to be done. Unlike the situation in *McCartney* v. *Amell* (1982), 35 O.R. (2d) 651 (Fam. Ct.), where the parties' relationship was of short duration and the application not made for 9 or 10 years after the conception of the child, Silber and Fenske were intimately involved in a relationship of some two years duration, Fenske voluntarily signed the Vital Statistics form regarding parentage (although he is now reneging on that), and acknowledged having had sexual relations with Silber in May of 1993.

There is no evidence that such a blood test would physically harm any of the parties, nor is there any question as to the bona fides of the application. The Court should therefore grant leave permitting such blood tests to be obtained. See: *H.* v. *H.* (1979), 9 R.F.L. (2d) 216 (Ont. H.C.).

3. Is s. 8 of the Charter offended?

Fenske takes the position that he should not be subject to an unreasonable search and seizure if the Court grants leave to permit such blood tests to be obtained. He relies on s. 8 of the *Canadian Charter of Rights and Freedoms* which states that everyone has the right to be secure against unreasonable search and seizure. . . .

In the case at bar, given the wording of s. 10 of the *Children's Law Reform Act*, no one can take blood for purposes of a paternity test without that person's consent. In the event the consent is not given, the Court may draw an adverse inference but no one is forced to give the blood sample.

A careful analysis of s. 10 of the Act was made by Judge Lesage, as he then was, in *Evans* v. *Hammond* (April 5, 1979, unreported, County Court of the Judicial District of York) at p. 4 of his reasons where he ruled that s. 10 is:

> procedural because what it does is permit a party, in a civil proceeding, to ask the court for permission to ask certain persons for samples of their blood and to submit those samples in evidence. The effect of the submission of this evidence would be to assist the court in establishing whether or not any of such persons was, in fact the father of the child. The section goes on to say, in s-s. (3), that refusal to submit to such request permits the court to draw such inferences as it considers appropriate. In my view, the section does little more (and perhaps less) than to give legislative sanction to what I understand to have been a fairly common practice in the courts. I say that because there are many cases where a party to an affiliation proceeding has been asked by the other side to provide blood samples and the unexplained refusal to comply with that request has resulted in the court drawing an inference adverse to the refuser. That, it seems to me, is only reasonable, since in a civil case as this is the refusal of one of the parties to produce materially relevant evidence in their possession would, absent a reasonable explanation, almost inevitably result in the trier of fact concluding that such evidence would be either (a) helpful for the opposite party, and/or (b) harmful to the one who refused to produce it.

Neither compulsion nor coercion is involved in a s. 10 Order. See: *N.* v. *D.* (1985), 49 O.R. (2d) 490 (Fam. Ct.). At pp. 500 and 501 of that decision, Felstiner Prov. J. considers s. 8 of the *Charter*:

> The results of blood-taking may constitute strong evidence against the defendant. Consequently, if blood tests lead to a finding of parentage being made, a respondent may be ordered to pay monetary support for a number of years for the child. This is certainly a serious impact upon a respondent. . . .

I conclude that an order made under s. 10 would not constitute or cause an unreasonable search or seizure. For s. 8 to be violated, the search or seizure must be unreasonable. In a s. 10 situation, the taking of blood would not constitute an unreasonable search or seizure.

I concur with these reasons. The child's right to financial support from her father and her need to know who her father is, in order for the Court to determine such financial support cannot be overlooked in these circumstances.

4. Does s. 10 violate s. 7 of the Charter?

Fenske further takes the position that s. 10 violates his s. 7 *Charter* rights. . . .
Our Courts have already dealt with that issue in *P. (K.) v. N. (P.)* (1988), 15 R.F.L. (3d) 110 (Ont. H.C.) (leave to appeal to Divisional Court denied by Justice Walsh on September 7, 1988). There the Court held that s. 10 of the Act did not violate s. 7 of the *Charter*. There Rutherford J. held at pp. 111-112:

> It is well established law that there is no prima facie infringement of s. 7 until the defendant establishes both a deprivation of life, liberty or security of the person, and that the deprivation is in a manner contrary to the principles of fundamental justice. No s. 7 Charter breach is made out, however, unless there is an interference with the physical or mental integrity of the individual or with the individual's control over such integrity.
>
> I do not find that the impugned provision interferes with the physical or mental integrity of the individual. It does not authorize the forcible taking of blood. . . .
>
> If there is no compulsion or coercion involved in an order made under s. 10 of the Act, the provision constitutes neither a denial nor an infringement of the rights guaranteed by s. 7 of the Charter.

See also: *N. v. D., supra,* and *Honsinger* v. *Kilmer* (1984), 12 C.R.R. 276 (Ont. Fam. Ct.) where the Court noted that it is open to any such person to explain any refusal and for the Court to accept such an explanation. In *H. (N.)* v. *R. (J.D.)* (1990), 104 N.B.R. (2d) 173, the New Brunswick Court of Queen's Bench examined its legislative equivalent to s. 10 in light of s. 7 of the *Charter* and allowed the application for blood tests.

The case at bar is not a criminal case where the liberty of an accused is at stake. We are dealing with a civil family law matter respecting child support. One has to be careful not to lose sight of the rights of the child to financial support from both parents and her right to be raised with a reasonable standard of living commensurate with that of both of her parents.

[Greer J. granted Silber leave to obtain and introduce the results of blood tests and ordered Fenske, who earned approximately $300,000 per year, to pay interim interim child support of $2,250 per month. The issue of prenatal expenses was deferred.]

NOTES AND QUESTIONS

1. It is now clearly established that any court having jurisdiction to order child support can make a determination of parentage as a necessary and material step in the establishment of the obligation of support: *Sayer* v. *Rollin* (1980), 16 R.F.L. (2d) 289 (Ont. C.A.).

What is the distinction between a finding of paternity on a support application and a declaration of paternity? Does a finding of paternity have any effect outside of the support proceedings? See s. 8(1)6 of the *Children's Law Reform Act* (the *CLRA*).

It has been held that a person against whom an order for child support has been made can apply under s. 4(1) of the *CLRA* for a declaration that he is not the father of the child: *Raft* v. *Shortt* (1986), 2

R.F.L. (3d) 243, 54 O.R. (2d) 768 (H.C.). However, contrast *C. (C.A.)* v. *H. (J.R.)* (1992), 41 R.F.L. (3d) 73 (B.C. C.A.). Would such a declaration terminate the person's obligation to support the child? See *Raft* v. *Shortt* (1988), 17 R.F.L. (3d) 170 (Ont. Prov. Ct.).

2. In *D.* v. *S.* (1980), 30 O.R. (3d) 225 (Div. Ct.) the court noted (at 226) that "to grant leave for taking of blood tests is to interfere with an individual's personal liberty" and held that such leave should only be granted after the presentation of some admissible evidence.

In *Rhan* v. *Pinsonneault* (1979), 27 O.R. (2d) 210 (Co. Ct.), Clements Co. Ct. J. refused to grant leave under s. 10 of the *CLRA* where the applicant alleged that she had become pregnant during a "one-night stand" and had only brought the application for support as a result of pressure from the welfare authorities. He suggested the following criteria for the exercise of discretion under s. 10:

> (1) Were the applicant and respondent married at the time the child or children were born? This is the situation in *H.* v. *H.* [(1979), 25 O.R. (2d) 219 (H.C.)], where the husband was seeking divorce on grounds of living separate and apart from his wife since 1958 and the wife alleged that five children of the marriage resulted from the husband's access during separation. Here, clearly, there is a presumption that the husband is the father of the children born during marriage and the order was granted.

> (2) Did the parties cohabit in a common law relationship of some duration during which time or shortly thereafter a child was born?

> (3) Did the respondent admit sexual intercourse with the applicant at or near the time calculated to be the point of conception but now denies that he is the actual father of the child but alleges another is?

> (4) Although there was not a common law union, did the respondent admit to an extramarital relationship with the applicant wherein sexual intercourse occurred from time to time thus making it possible that he is the putative father?

> (5) Was the applicant able, through affidavit and other evidence, to establish a *prima facie* case of putative fatherhood notwithstanding the denial of the respondent as to fatherhood and/or ever having sexual intercourse with the applicant?

Was the court justified in refusing to grant leave to obtain blood tests in *Rhan*? See also *McCartney* v. *Amell* (1982), 35 O.R. (2d) 651 (Prov. Ct.) where the court refused leave in light of the fact that the mother had waited 13 years before seeking support from the putative father.

In *Wilson* v. *Stewart* (1982), 45 O.R. (2d) 95 (Fam. Ct.), Dunn Prov. Ct. J. disagreed with the reasoning in both *Rhan* and *McCartney*. The court granted leave to obtain blood tests even though the facts were very similar to those in *Rhan*. Dunn Prov. Ct. J. indicated (at 103) that the criteria or standards set by Judge Clements, particularly criteria #5, were "too burdensome" for the applicant. He noted (at 104) that the approach taken in *Rhan* would "virtually prohibit every child born out of a 'one-night stand' from having the opportunity of establishing parentage through the use of blood tests".

In *F. (M.)* v. *S. (R.)* (1991), 83 D.L.R. (4th) 717 (Ont. Prov. Div.), Nevins Prov. J. explicitly stated (at 722) that he had wrongly decided *McCartney* v. *Amell*, above. He concluded (at 721):

> . . . a request for leave to obtain blood tests under s. 10 should be granted unless:

> (a) it can be shown that the actual process of conducting the blood tests might prejudicially affect the health of the child, or

> (b) the actual request for leave to obtain the blood test is made in bad faith.

Recent cases indicate that delay in alleging paternity and in claiming child support will not preclude court orders for blood testing and child support. See *H. (S.)* v. *A. (L.)* (1992), 92 D.L.R. (4th) 310 (Ont. U.F.C.) (blood tests, a finding of paternity and a support order involving a 21-year-old); *D. (J.S.)* v. *V. (W.L.)* (1995), 11 R.F.L. (4th) 409 (B.C. C.A.) (blood tests ordered where the mother had been married to a third party at the time of the birth some 16 years earlier); and *Phiroz* v. *Mottiar* (1995), 16 R.F.L. (4th) 353 (Ont. Prov. Div.) (the court awarded child support about 15 years after the birth of a child out of wedlock, ruling that there was no limitation period and that the doctrine of laches did not apply to a support claim).

See also Tweney, "Analyzing Section 10 of the *Children's Law Reform Act*" (1996-97), 14 C.F.L.Q. 49.

3. The court in *Rhan* placed some weight on the fact that the application for support was brought at the insistence of welfare authorities. In *Wilson*, the court held that this was irrelevant since a father has an obligation to support his child regardless of whether a mother is slow in bringing suit or does so because of pressure from welfare authorities. Dunn Prov. Ct. J. also pointed out that the regulations promulgated under the *Family Benefits Act* require the welfare recipient to make reasonable efforts to realize any financial resources.

4. Where a husband denies that he is the father of a child born to his wife during their marriage, the courts are generally reluctant to grant leave for blood testing unless there are clear grounds for his denial. See *C. (M.)* v. *C. (L.A.)* (1990), 24 R.F.L. (3d) 322 (B.C. C.A.); *J. (R.)* v. *M. (S.)* (1990), 25 R.F.L. (3d) 105 (B.C. S.C.); and *G. (F.)* v. *G. (F.)* (1991), 32 R.F.L. (3d) 252 (Ont. Div. Ct.) In the latter case, Conant J. held that the husband had to rebut the presumption of paternity created by s. 8 of the *CLRA* before leave could be granted. Do you agree with this view?

Without blood tests, it will often be difficult for the husband to rebut the presumption of paternity. However, the presumption was rebutted without such tests in *Abbott* v. *Squires* (1991), 34 R.F.L. (3d) 303 (N.S. Fam. Ct.) where the court found that the wife had had sexual relations with another man during the time when conception likely occurred and that the husband was sterile as a result of a vasectomy.

5. The Manitoba Court of Appeal held in *L. (F.A.)* v. *B. (A.B.)* (1995), 125 D.L.R. (4th) 640 (Man. C.A.) that a superior court has inherent jurisdiction to consent to the blood testing of a child. However, it concluded that it would not grant such consent in the case because the testing would not be in the best interests of the child and upheld the lower court's declaration that the respondent was the father. The petitioner simply wanted to know if he had fathered the child born to a married women who had since died. The respondent, who was married to the mother at the time of the conception and birth, had raised the five-year-old child as his daughter. In *C. (M.S.)* v. *L. (R.)* (1997), 28 R.F.L. (4th) 262 (B.C. Master), the plaintiff sought to establish that he was the father of a child born to a married woman and being raised by the mother and her husband. The mother refused to consent to DNA testing of the child. The Master concluded that the child should have separate legal representation to ensure that its best interests could be determined before the court granted consent on behalf of the child.

6. S. 10 can be used to obtain blood samples not only for more traditional testing such as HLA (Human Leukocyte Antigen Test), but also for DNA testing: *S. (C.)* v. *L. (V.)* (1992), 39 R.F.L. (3d) 294 (Ont. Prov. Ct.), affirmed (1992), 39 R.F.L. (3d) 298 (Ont. Gen. Div.).

In "DNA Testing To Investigate The Ties That Bind — A Discussion of DNA Testing in Issues of Paternity" (1994-1995), 12 C.F.L.Q. 301, Jennifer Clay states (at 302-303):

> In paternity cases, the lab compares the bands [when DNA fragments are exposed to X-ray film, dark bands appear on the film resulting in a unique DNA profile or "fingerprint"] of the child and alleged father. If there is a "non-match", the alleged father is excluded. If there is a "match", the lab determines, using a population data base, how often the match occurs in the general population. The odds of a match can then be converted into a probability. For example, in all paternity cases where there is a match, the probability of paternity will be greater than 99.8%.

7. In *Low* v. *Low* (1994), 4 R.F.L. (4th) 103 (Ont. Gen. Div.), the wife, with the husband's encouragement, gave birth to a child conceived through artificial insemination by an anonymous donor. Ferrier J. granted a declaration under the *CLRA* that the husband was the father, noting (at 113): "Nowhere in s. 5 is there any suggestion that the relationship of father and child must have a biological or genetic character." Ferrier J. adopted (at 114) the public policy arguments expressed by the Superior Court of New Jersey in *S.* v. *S.*, 440 A.2d 64, at 68 (1981): "[T]he best interests of the child, the mother, the family unit and society are served by recognizing that the law surrounding AID insemination deals with the creation of a family unit and more particularly with the creation of the parent-child relationship." *Low* v. *Low* was applied in *Zegota* v. *Zegota-Rzegocinski* (1995), 10 R.F.L. (4th) 384 (Ont. Gen. Div.).

8. In Ontario, the law no longer distinguishes between children born inside or outside marriage. See sections 1 and 2 of the *CLRA*.

In those provinces where the rights of illegitimate children differ from legitimate ones, *Charter* challenges based on s. 15 have succeeded: *W. (D.S.)* v. *H. (R.)*, [1989] 2 W.W.R. 481 (Sask. C.A.); *Surette* v. *Harris Estate* (1989), 91 N.S.R. (2d) 418 (N.S. T.D.); *Milne (Doherty)* v. *Alberta (Attorney General)*, [1990] 5 W.W.R. 650 (Alta. Q.B.); *Panko* v. *Vandesype* (1993), 45 R.F.L. (3d) 424 (Sask. Q.B.); *Tighe (Guardian ad litem of)* v. *McGillivray Estate* (1994), 127 N.S.R. (2d) 313 (C.A.); *M. (R.H.)* v. *H. (S.S.)* (1994), 2 R.F.L. (4th) 207 (Alta. Q.B.); and *Massingham-Pearce* v. *Konkolus* (1995), 13 R.F.L. (4th) 313 (Alta. Q.B.).

(2) EXTENDED DEFINITION OF THE PARENT-CHILD RELATIONSHIP

The jurisdiction of the court to make an order regarding support under s. 15.1 of the *Divorce Act* is limited to "children of the marriage" as defined in s. 2(1) and s. 2(2). In order to be a "child of the marriage" an individual must be "a child of two spouses or former spouses". Section 2(2) specifies that a "child of two spouses or former spouses" includes "any child for whom they both stand in the place of parents" and "any child of whom one is the parent and for whom the other stands in the place of a parent". The definition of "child of the marriage" in the *Divorce Act* is essentially the same as that which was provided in the 1968 *Divorce Act*, although the latter used the latin expression "*in loco parentis*" rather than "in the place of a parent".

The *FLA* also includes (s. 1(1)) an extended definition of the parent-child relationship for the purpose of determining who is obliged to support a child pursuant to s. 31(1). The definitions of "child" and "parent" are essentially unchanged from those that appeared in s. 1(a) and s. 1(e) of the *Family Law Reform Act*.

AKSUGYUK v. AKSUGYUK

17 R.F.L. 224, [1975] 3 W.W.R. 91 (N.W.T. S.C.)

[In divorce proceedings, Morrow J. found that the petitioning husband was not the father of Phillip, a child of the respondent wife. The husband, although he may have suspected that the boy was not his, treated him in exactly the same way as the couple's other children. The court's reasoning on the question of whether or not Phillip was a child of the husband and wife as defined in s. 2 of the *Divorce Act* is set out below.]

MORROW J.: — . . . A basic statement of what is meant by in loco parentis is to be found in the judgment of Cottenham L.C. where at p. 967 of the report of his judgment in *Powys* v. *Mansfield* (1837), 3 My. & Cr. 359, 40 E.R. 964, he quotes from Lord Eldon: ". . . it is a person 'meaning' to put himself in loco parentis; in the situation of the person described as the lawful father of the child". An excellent definition in a Canadian Court is to be found in *Shtitz* v. *C.N.R.*, 21 Sask. L.R. 345, [1927] 1 W.W.R. 193, [1927] 1 D.L.R. 951 (C.A.), where at pp. 201 and 959 respectively Turgeon J.A. states:

> A person *in loco parentis* to a child is one who has acted so as to evidence his intention of placing himself towards the child in the situation which is ordinarily occupied by the father for the provision of the child's pecuniary wants.

. . .

In the case before me the petitioner husband acted as father to this boy right up to the date of trial and while he expressed a suspicion of the boy's paternity it is quite clear from the evidence, particularly of the respondent wife, that she gave him to believe the boy was issue of the marriage. To come within the meaning of "child" as used in the Divorce Act the person must either be the actual issue of the parties or in the position where he is treated in loco parentis in the view I take of the definition. But here the person Phillip is neither. He is not the issue. To be in loco parentis it seems to me the husband must "intend" to place himself in the position towards the child ordinarily occupied by the father, which intention must be based on the knowledge that someone else is the father.

In the result there will be no order of maintenance against the petitioner in respect of the child Phillip. The respondent shall have custody of this child. . . .

CARSON v. CARSON

(1986), 49 R.F.L. (2d) 459 (Ont. Prov. Ct.)

EGENER PROV. J.: — This is an application for support of two children who are the children of the applicant. For simplicity I refer to the parties as Mary, the applicant, George, her husband, and Todd, a male adult. Mary had her first child, a girl named Christine but called by everyone Crissy, on 13th May 1978 before she knew in any romantic way either George or Todd. Mary became pregnant in late September or early October 1982 and in January 1983 she married George. George Jr. was born 8th June 1983. During these proceedings it has been determined that Todd is the natural father of the child George Jr. The prime question before the court is: who are responsible to financially support the children?

As to the relationship between Mary and Todd, both have said that they were going out together occasionally but that they had sexual relations on only one occasion, that being late September 1982. It has been established by serological tests that Todd is the natural (or biological) father of George Jr. and he has accepted as fact that the law of Ontario imposes upon him the duty of contributing to the support of that child, but he maintains that Mary and George also have a support obligation so that he wants an assessment of proportion of support he should contribute. That may be left for later consideration.

The responsibility of George to support the children born to his wife is dependent upon the applicability of s. 1(a) of the Family Law Reform Act . . .

After hearing and reviewing the evidence in this matter I am satisfied that George did not become a parent of Crissy within the meaning of this definition as it has been interpreted by the case law that has dealt with the situation of a child brought into a marriage by one of the adult parties. In the present case I find that George never acted toward Crissy as a parent and that she never accepted him as her parent. George did do domestic things for Crissy that even a baby-sitter would do, but he did nothing that would be interpreted as being what a loving, concerned parent would do toward a child he wanted to be his own. On her part, Crissy spent as much of her time as she could with her maternal grandparents and ignored George as much as she could. She did not accept him, and a parental relationship is a mutual affair. I am impressed with the judgment of Thomson Prov. J. given in *Ogden* v. *Anderson*, delivered 28th March 1983 but unreported [digested [1983] W.D.F.L. 842, Ont. Prov. Ct., York No. D1263/82]. I accept the fact that a man who marries a woman with children and treats such a child or children kindly and supports them does not automatically become a parent, because if this is interpreted as law it places a totally unacceptable barrier to relationships developing between a person having children to support and others who might otherwise be prospective partners. Thomson Prov. J. said in part:

> My opinion that the issue of rationale suggests a relatively narrow view of the definition is reinforced by two other factors. The first is the definition itself, which is quite tightly worded. We are not just talking about intention; we are talking about settled intention. We are not just talking about the intention to treat someone as one's own child, but actually treating the child as a child of the family. Secondly, if one reads the section too broadly it creates clear, practical problems for both the natural parent and the person entering into a relationship with him or her. The parent (at least one who knows the law) is essentially being put in the position of having to say, 'If you want to form a relationship with me, you take my children as well. You not only take my children while we're together, but if the relationship doesn't work out you may be potentially liable to support my children until they reach the age of majority. You accept this responsibility simply by moving in and functioning as a supportive member of the unit you are now becoming part of.' If one does not see this as a problem, I think one only needs to look at some of the research work that has been done which examines the position of the woman in receipt of public assistance who is basically in the same position of saying: If you want me, you take on the support of my children.
>
> On the other side, from the perspective of the person who has moved in, a very broad interpretation could dissuade him from forming a close bond, from providing the emotional and other supports that children need. It requires him to be almost constantly stating and demonstrating his unwillingness to accept these children. I think that inevitably the losers in that kind of environment would be the children themselves, unless it can be said that the desire to create a fresh avenue for support overrides the potential harm done by a law which invites persons to perform poorly the substitute parent role when taking up residence with another person and that person's children.
>
> This has been a lengthy exposition in order to help you understand the approach I have taken to the definition, why I have accepted the rationale which I have and believe that it supports a fairly narrow view of the definition. It seems to me that within this context the factors that one would potentially look at in an individual case are very numerous. I think the cases make it clear that one should look at the whole relationship between the two parties and not just at one or two factors. One should look at such things as whether financial support was provided; did the parties marry; how long were they together; what was the day-to-day care of the children; what was the role of this person, who is said to be a parent, in vital activities such as education and discipline; how did the child and this person acknowledge one another in their respective roles?

So I have determined that George is not a parent to Crissy, but what about George Jr.? . . .

To briefly review the relationship of Mary, George and George Jr., Mary was at a place called the Fox's Den and saw George apparently for the first time. George had had too much to drink but Mary invited him, indeed persuaded him, to dance; later she took him home to her apartment. They had sexual intercourse, though George says he was too drunk to remember whether this occurred or not. In any event, they soon had sexual relations regularly. Prior to meeting George, Mary had sexual intercourse with Todd and on one occasion close in time to her meeting with George. Mary suspected she was pregnant when she missed her next menstrual period and she told Todd he might be a father or George could be, according to both Mary and Todd. Mary also says she told George the same thing, but she told George she thought he would be the father of her child and she continued to tell him during the rest of that year that she believed he was the father of the child she carried.

It is my view of the evidence that George knew or ought to have known that another man might be responsible for Mary's pregnancy. Considering how rapidly their first relationship had developed there was no justification for George to assume Mary had not had or was not having sexual relations with another man or men.

George and Mary married on 8th January 1983 and George Jr. was born 8th June 1983. In April 1984 the parties separated. Prior to marriage and from then to well after the separation there is no evidence of any denial of parentage by George. Indeed, it is clear that he anticipated the birth of the child with pleasure, was present at the birth, was a proud father showing off his son to friends and relatives, and in every way accepting George Jr. as his own. This was so irrespective of some suggestion put to him that the child might not be his biologically.

George had married Mary knowing she was pregnant and knowing he had had sexual relations with her and that he might be the father of her child. He did not by any word or deed or by any conduct indicate that he would accept the child upon condition that later it could be proved irrefutably to be his natural offspring. Such a marriage is not that rare as to be even considered unusual. When the husband then confirms the relationship of the child as a child of the family, the community, too, accepts the trio as one family. Within a social organization the relationship between two adults and a child is just as sacred as a marriage between two adults and may not be set aside unilaterally. The Family Law Reform Act simply confirms it as law that such a child towards which the married couple have demonstrated a settled intention to treat as a child of their marriage is a child towards which both owe a duty of support.

I find support for my interpretation of the law in the case of *Blommaert* v. *Blommaert* (1985), 50 O.R. (2d) 699 (Dist. Ct.), a case decided by Carter D.C.J. in which he found that the husband of a woman whose child was born during marriage and after other children of the marriage had been born [per headnote] "had demonstrated a settled intention to treat the child as a child of his family and that intention continued, at least until the time he was told the child was not his, if not afterwards", was responsible to support the child.

I thus find that George has an obligation to financially support George Jr.

As to what is the financial need of the child George, I find that Mary is herself responsible for part of the total cost of the care of the child. The fact that two men are also responsible for support does not alter the proportion that she should bear. She is voluntarily out of work. Her plan to live on unemployment insurance until it runs out and then to become a student under various support plans is unrealistic and, if not unrealistic, contrary to her obligations. I do think that, until she can get adequate care for George Jr., she is justified in being off work, but that ought not to be as prolonged a search as she suggests.

Considering that the care of George Jr. during his mother's working hours and for reasonable relief at other times is likely to be expensive and that the costs for Crissy are less onerous because of her age and her independent actions, such as staying with her grandparents voluntarily, and until home care is available, I find that the total cost of supporting George Jr. is, at this time, $350 a month. It is not putting much financial value upon the hours of nurturing care given by a mother to order that Mary provide $100 of the actual financial cost.

Of this amount the balance of $250 should be paid by the two men. I see no reason that it should not be divided equally at this time. Todd's expectation of returning to full employment is realistic and in the past he has been able to find employment in more than one field. George is at the moment earning the most money of the three, but upon my assessment he has higher personal needs. I would assess support at $125 payable by each of Todd and George per month commencing 1st January 1986. . . .

CHARTIER v. CHARTIER

(1999), 43 R.F.L. (4th) 1 (S.C.C.)

BASTARACHE J. (for the court): In this appeal, the Court is asked to determine whether a person who stands in the place of a parent to a child within the meaning of the *Divorce Act*, R.S.C., 1985, c. 3 (2nd Supp.), can unilaterally give up that status and escape the obligation to provide support for that child after the breakdown of the marriage. The Court unanimously decided that a person cannot do so and allowed the appeal at the hearing held on November 12, 1998. The following are the reasons for allowing the appeal.

Facts

The parties began a common law relationship in November 1989 and married on June 1, 1991. Their child, Jeena, was born on August 29, 1990. The parties separated in May 1992, later reconciled for a month or two, then permanently separated in September 1992.

Jessica is the child of the wife from a previous relationship. While the parties lived together, the husband played an active role in caring for both children and was a father-figure for Jessica. The parties discussed, but did not proceed with, the husband's adoption of Jessica. The parties did amend Jessica's birth registration to indicate, falsely, that the husband was Jessica's natural father and to change her name to his.

On March 17, 1994, in a consent judgment in proceedings under *The Family Maintenance Act*, C.C.S.M., c. F20, the husband acknowledged both Jessica and Jeena as children of the marriage and was granted access to them. He agreed to pay maintenance for Jeena, but the judgment was silent as to maintenance for Jessica and for the wife. The wife commenced divorce proceedings in February 1995 and included in her claim the request for a declaration that the husband stands in the place of a parent to Jessica. The husband contested the claim. The interim order of April 19, 1995 ordered the husband to pay monthly support for Jessica and for the wife, suspended access of the husband until a further order of the court and ordered a report from Conciliation Services concerning access. That report of October 1995 recorded the husband's desire to sever his relationship with Jessica.

At trial, De Graves J. ordered spousal support, a reduction in the monthly support for Jeena, awarded costs to the wife and found that the husband had repudiated his parental relationship with Jessica. On appeal, the Court of Appeal did not find that the award of spousal support warranted appellate review and dismissed the husband's cross-appeal. The Court of Appeal allowed the wife's appeal on the issue of the reduction of monthly support for Jeena. The Court of Appeal dismissed the wife's appeal for support for Jessica, set aside the trial judge's order as to costs and directed that no costs be awarded at trial.

It should be noted that both parties agreed that their rights and obligations under *The Family Maintenance Act* and the *Divorce Act* were identical for the purposes of the action and appeal, and that the courts should proceed as though the *Divorce Act* were the applicable statute. The same position was adopted in pleadings before this Court. . . .

Judicial History

De Graves J. held that it was abundantly clear in Manitoba trust and family law that the spouse standing in the place of a parent, having voluntarily assumed that role, had the right to withdraw unilaterally from that role: see *Carignan* v. *Carignan* (1989), 61 Man. R. (2d) 66 (Man. C.A.). In response to the appellant's submission that the case be revisited, he analysed the case. Before *Carignan*, the authorities were not clear in delineating who was "a child of the marriage" in the context of parties bringing to a marriage children of other relationships or unions outside that marriage. In *Carignan*, the court interpreted the words "at the material time" in s. 2(1) and 2(2) of the *Divorce Act* as referring only to the age of the child. De Graves J. found that the spouse who stood in the place of a parent was entitled to withdraw from that status at any time. He found that the respondent was entitled to and did, in July 1995, repudiate his obligation towards Jessica "as a child of the marriage".

De Graves J. noted that the appellant had not pursued Jessica's natural father for support although he was not a person without resources. He declared that the respondent was not obligated to pay any support for Jessica from July 1995. He would not order repayment of the support payments made, but the respondent was entitled to a credit on the appellant's award of costs. He ordered spousal support and child support for Jeena. . . .

Philp J.A. [in the Manitoba Court of Appeal] noted that the right of a person to terminate a relationship in which he or she stands in the place of a parent was well settled in Manitoba: see *Carignan, supra*. The court had found that it was not a status that once acquired could never be shed. He noted that modern marriages and other forms of cohabitation were often fragile and time-limited relationships and wondered how many obligations divorced or separated parties must carry with them as they travel from relationship to relationship.

Philp J.A. found that the principle in *Carignan* has been applied in Manitoba, but had not been universally followed in courts of other provinces, including British Columbia, Saskatchewan and Alberta, where it was clearly rejected. He found that where *Carignan* had not been followed, no clear alternative has emerged. He was of the view that the *Carignan* case has the virtue of establishing an understandable and easily determined basis for imposing or excusing responsibility. He also noted that the decision has not been uniformly accepted by academics.

Issue

Under what circumstances, if any, can an adult who is or has been in the place of a parent pursuant to s. 2 of the *Divorce Act* withdraw from that position?

Analysis

There is one body of case law, exemplified by *Carignan, supra*, that states that a person standing in the place of a parent is entitled to make a unilateral withdrawal from the parental relationship. The other body of case law is typified by *Theriault* v. *Theriault* (1994), 149 A.R. 210 (Alta. C.A.); it states that a person cannot unilaterally withdraw from a relationship in which he or she stands in the place of a parent and that the court must look to the nature of the relationship to determine if a person in fact does stand in the place of a parent to a child.

Before considering these two lines of authority, I would note that in both cases the courts have engaged upon a historical review of the doctrine of *loco parentis* and taken the view that the words "in the place of a parent" used in the *Divorce Act* were intended to have the same meaning. The doctrine of *loco parentis* was developed in diverse contexts, trust law, tort law, master-apprentice relationships, school-master-pupil relationships, wills and gifts..., at another time. Alison Diduck, in "*Carignan* v. *Carignan:* When is a Father not a Father? Another Historical Perspective" (1990), 19 *Man. L.J.* 580, explains how this common law doctrine was applied in family matters, over the years, in various jurisdictions. She concludes, at pp. 601-602, by saying:

> The *in loco parentis* doctrine is a creature of 19th century patriarchy. It evolved during a time when it was a morally offensive notion for a man to be held responsible for another man's child. As Mendes de Costa U.F.J. stated in a 1987 decision, it has "its roots deep in history" and "carries with it connotations of times past" (*Re Spring and Spring* (1987), 61 O.R. (2d) 743 at 748). Notwithstanding Parliament's choice of similar wording in the *Divorce Act, 1985*, it is arguably open to counsel (or to courts) to suggest that Parliament deliberately chose to reject the common law notion of *in loco parentis*, and that the current statute should be interpreted "free from the shadow of earlier authorities" (*Ibid.*, at 749...).

I agree that the policies and values reflected in the *Divorce Act* must relate to contemporary Canadian society and that the general principles of statutory interpretation support a modern understanding of the words "stands in the place of a parent".
. . .

In my view, the common law meaning of *in loco parentis* is not helpful in determining the scope of the words "in the place of a parent" in the *Divorce Act*.

This being said, it is my opinion that the decision in *Theriault, supra*, provides the proper approach to this issue as it recognizes that the provisions of the *Divorce Act* dealing with children focus on what is in the best interests of the children of the marriage, not on biological parenthood or legal status of children.

In the present appeal, the Court of Appeal, although noting that the decision has not been universally followed, confirmed the judgment in *Carignan* for essentially two reasons. The first reason is that the decision displays a "certain logic and reasonableness" because the modern institution of marriage has substantially departed from its traditional roots. Philp J.A. noted, at p. 156, that modern marriages are "often fragile and time-limited relationships" and therefore, this raises the question of how many obligations persons must carry with them as they move from relationship to relationship. It would not be logical, in his view, for a step-parent who takes on obligations with respect to a spouse's children to be saddled with this obligation indefinitely while a step-parent who takes on no such obligation is entitled to walk away from the relationship scot-free. The finding in *Carignan* avoids this inconsistency. The second reason, at p. 157, relates to the fact that the decision in *Carignan* establishes "an understandable and easily determined basis for imposing or excusing responsibility".

The decision in *Carignan, supra*, has been highly criticized as seen in the decisions reviewed above and in academic commentary, in particular that of Keith B. Farquhar, "Termination of the *In Loco Parentis* Obligation of Child Support" (1990), 9 *Can. J. Fam. L.* 99, and Diduck, "*Carignan* v. *Carignan*: When is a Father not a Father? Another Historical Perspective", *supra*. The most obvious criticism is that it nullifies the effect of the relevant provisions of the *Divorce Act*. If one can unilaterally terminate a relationship where a person stands in the place of a parent to a child, why define such a relationship as giving rise to obligations under the *Divorce Act*? . . .

I do not agree with the reasoning in *Carignan, supra*. As noted above, the words "in the place of a parent" must be given a meaning that is independent of the common law concept and reflective of the purposive and contextual approach to statutory interpretation advocated by this Court. Once a person is found to stand in the place of a parent, that relationship cannot be unilaterally withdrawn by the adult. The interpretation of the provisions of the *Divorce Act* relating to "child[ren] of the marriage" should be "given such fair, large and liberal construction and interpretation as best ensures the attainment of its objects": see *Interpretation Act*, R.S.C., 1985, c. I-21, s. 12. The reasoning in *Carignan, supra*, ignores one of the fundamental objectives of the *Divorce Act* as it relates to children. The provisions of the *Divorce Act* that deal with children aim to ensure that a divorce will affect the children as little as possible. Spouses are entitled to divorce each other, but not the children who were part of the marriage. The interpretation that will best serve children is one that recognizes that when people act as parents toward them, the children can count on that relationship continuing and that these persons will continue to act as parents toward them.

What, therefore, is the proper time period for determining whether a person stands in the place of a parent? The term "at the material time" has been interpreted with reference to the parental status to mean "the time of the commencement of the proceedings" (see *H. (L.)* v. *H. (L.H.)*, [1971] 4 W.W.R. 262 (B.C. C.A.)); "the time of the hearing" (see *Harrington* v. *Harrington* (1981), 33 O.R. (2d) 150 (Ont. C.A.) at p. 159); and has also been held to mean "whatever date is appropriate".

In *Carignan, supra*, the Manitoba Court of Appeal held that the words "at the material time" have no reference to when the parental status occurred or existed, but only to whether the step-parent is "in the place of a parent" when the child is under 16 or over 16 but in a dependant state. Huband J.A. noted that there is no reference to material time in s. (2) where the expression "in the place of a parent" is used. He held that a proper interpretation of the two sections is that the court can make an order for maintenance against a person standing in the place of a parent only if the child is under 16, or over 16 and in a dependant state. . . .

It is clear that the Court must address the needs of the child as of the date of the hearing or order. The existence of the parental relationship under s. 2(2)(*b*) of the *Divorce Act* must however be determined as of the time the family functioned as a unit. See Julien D. Payne, *Payne on Divorce* (4th ed. 1996), at p. 148. If the "material time" was to be interpreted as in *H. (L.), supra*, it would be difficult to find a parental relationship in situations where the step-parent has little contact with the child between the separation and the divorce proceedings. This is inconsistent with the purpose of the *Divorce Act*.

The facts of the present case demonstrate why this interpretation is appropriate. Until Mr. Chartier's unilateral withdrawal from the relationship, Jessica saw the respondent as her father in every way. He was the only father she knew. To allow him to withdraw from that relationship, as long as he does it before the petition for divorce, is unacceptable. The breakdown of the parent/child relationship after separation is not a relevant factor in determining whether or not a person stands in the place of a parent for the purposes of the *Divorce Act*. Jessica was as much a part of the family unit as Jeena and should not be treated differently from her because the spouses separated. The "material time" factor does not affect the determination of the parental relationship. It simply applies to the age considerations that are a precondition to the determination of need.

What then is the proper test for determining whether a person stands in the place of a parent within the meaning of the *Divorce Act*? The appellant argued that the test for whether or not a person stands in the place of a parent should be determined exclusively from the perspective of the child. I cannot accept this test. In many cases, a child will be very young and it will be difficult to determine whether that child considers the person as a parental figure. Further, an older child may resent his or her step-parent and reject the authority of that person as a parent, even though, objectively, that person effectively provides for the child and stands in the place of a parent. The opinion of the child regarding the relationship with the step-parent is important, but it constitutes only one of many factors to be considered. In particular, attention must be given to the representations of the step-parent, independently of the child's response.

Whether a person stands in the place of a parent must take into account all factors relevant to that determination, viewed objectively. What must be determined is the nature of the relationship. The *Divorce Act* makes no mention of formal expressions of intent. The focus on voluntariness and intention in *Carignan, supra*, was dependent on the common law approach discussed earlier. It was wrong. The Court must determine the nature of the relationship by looking at a number of factors, among which is intention. Intention will not only be expressed formally. The court must also infer intention from actions, and take into consideration that even expressed intentions may sometimes change. The actual fact of forming a new family is a key factor in drawing an inference that the step-parent treats the child as a member of his or her family, i.e., a child of the marriage. The relevant factors in defining the parental relationship include, but are not limited to, whether the child participates in the extended family in the same way as would a biological child; whether the person provides financially for the child (depending on ability to pay); whether the person disciplines the child as a parent; whether the person represents to the child, the family, the world, either explicitly or implicitly, that he or she is responsible as a parent to the child; the nature or existence of the child's relationship with the absent biological parent. The manifestation of the intention of the step-parent cannot be qualified as to duration, or be otherwise made conditional or qualified, even if this intention is manifested expressly. Once it is shown that the child is to be considered, in fact, a "child of the marriage", the obligations of the step-parent towards him or her are the same as those relative to a child born of the marriage with regard to the application of the *Divorce Act*. The step-parent, at this point, does not only incur obligations. He or she also acquires certain rights, such as the right to apply eventually for custody or access under s. 16(1) of the *Divorce Act*.

Nevertheless, not every adult-child relationship will be determined to be one where the adult stands in the place of a parent. Every case must be determined on its own facts and it must be established from the evidence that the adult acted so as to stand in the place of a parent to the child.

Huband J.A., in *Carignan, supra*, expressed the concern that individuals may be reluctant to be generous toward children for fear that their generosity will give rise to parental obligations. I do not share those concerns. The nature of a parental relationship is complex and includes more than financial support. People do not enter into parental relationships with the view that they will be terminated. I share the view expressed by Beaulieu J. in *Siddall* [v. *Siddall* (1994), 11 R.F.L. (4th) 325 (Ont. Gen. Div.)] at p. 337:

> It is important to examine the motive behind a person's generosity towards the children of the person they wish to be involved with or are involved with in a relationship. In many cases children are used as pawns by men and, on occasion, women who desire the attention of the children's parent and once the relationship between the adults fail, the children are abandoned. This is not to be encouraged. If requiring men to continue their relationship, financially and emotionally with

the children is a discouragement of generosity then, perhaps such generosity should be discouraged. This type of generosity which leaves children feeling rejected and shattered once a relationship between the adults sours is not beneficial to society in general and the children, in particular. After all, it is the court's obligation to look out for the best interests of the children. In too many of these situations the ultimate result is that the child is a mere object used to accommodate a person's selfish and personal interests as long as the relationship is satisfying and gratifying. As soon as things sour and become less comfortable, the person can leave, abandoning both the parent and child, without any legal repercussions.... It is important to encourage the type of relationship that includes commitment, not superficial generosity. If relationships are more difficult for a person to extricate him- or herself from then, perhaps, more children will be spared the trauma of rejection, bruised self image and loss of financial support to which they have become accustomed.

Huband J.A., in *Carignan, supra*, also expressed the concern that a child might collect support from both the biological parent and the step-parent. I do not accept that this is a valid concern. The contribution to be paid by the biological parent should be assessed independently of the obligations of the step-parent. The obligation to support a child arises as soon as that child is determined to be "a child of the marriage". The obligations of parents for a child are all joint and several. The issue of contribution is one between all of the parents who have obligations towards the child, whether they are biological parents or step-parents; it should not affect the child. If a parent seeks contribution from another parent, he or she must, in the meantime, pay support for the child regardless of the obligations of the other parent. (See *Theriault, supra*, at p. 214; James G. McLeod, Annotation on *Primeau* v. *Primeau* (1986), 2 R.F.L. (3d) 113 (Ont. H.C.).)

Some concerns may also be raised with regard to the relevance of adoption proceedings where obligations regarding all "children of the marriage" are identical under the *Divorce Act* and *The Family Maintenance Act*. I recall that Mr. Chartier did not finalize his plans to adopt Jessica. The simple answer to that is that legal adoption will nevertheless have a significant impact in other areas of the law, most notably trusts and wills; it retains its importance.

Conclusion

The Court of Appeal, by relying on *Carignan, supra*, made a distinction between children born of both parents and stepchildren. As mentioned earlier, the Act does not make such a distinction. Once it is determined that a child is a "child of the marriage" within the meaning of the *Divorce Act*, he or she must be treated as if born of the marriage. . . .

Even if a relationship has broken down after a separation or divorce, the obligation of a person who stands in the place of a parent to support a child remains the same. Natural parents, even if they lose contact with their children, must continue to pay child support.

On the facts of this case, the respondent stood in the place of a parent toward Jessica. The respondent represented to Jessica and to the world that he assumed full parental responsibility for her. Mr. Chartier is the only father that Jessica has known owing to the fact that the parties led her to believe that the respondent was in fact Jessica's biological father. The respondent even considered adopting Jessica and the parties had Jessica's birth registration amended to change Jessica's name to correspond to the respondent's. This was done by falsely submitting an application stating that the respondent was Jessica's natural father. After the separation, the respondent continued to have visits with Jessica. Eventually access was terminated with regard to both Jessica and his biological child, Jeena.

The respondent's unilateral withdrawal from the relationship with Jessica does not change the fact that he acted, in all ways, as a father during the time the family lived together. Therefore, Jessica was a "child of the marriage" when the parties separated and later divorced, with all of the rights and responsibilities which that status entails under the *Divorce Act*. With respect to support from the respondent, Jessica is to be treated in the same way as Jeena.

Disposition

At the hearing on November 12, 1998, the following decision was read:

> We are all of the view that this appeal be allowed and the judgment of the Court of Appeal be set aside. We declare that the respondent stands in the place of a parent to Jessica Marlo Chartier, reasons to follow.

> This case is accordingly remanded to the Court of Queen's Bench of Manitoba (Family Division) for determination of the quantum of child support. This Court orders interim support of $200.00 per month for Jessica as of this date, subject to an application to the Court of Queen's Bench to recover support from the date of the trial judgment to this date.

NOTES AND QUESTIONS

1. The case law generally supports the proposition that a man can only stand in the place of a parent if he knows that he is not the biological father of the child. In addition to *Aksugyuk*, see *Downing* v. *Masunda* (1984), 38 R.F.L. (2d) 359 (B.C. Co. Ct.); *McGuire* v. *MacDonald* (1986), 5 R.F.L. (3d) 186 (B.C. S.C.); *Ketchum* v. *Ketchum* (1988), 13 R.F.L. (3d) 221 (N.B. Q.B.); and *A. (T.)* v. *A. (R.C.)* (1999), 48 R.F.L. (4th) 205 (B.C. S.C.). See also McLeod, "Annotation" (1997), 26 R.F.L. (4th) 180. However, *Carson* suggests that the wording in the *FLA* supports a different approach. See also *Blommaert* v. *Blommaert* (1985), 50 O.R. (2d) 699 (Dist. Ct.). Compare *Kristoff* v. *Kristoff* (1987), 7 R.F.L. (3d) 284 (Ont. Dist. Ct.) where Mossop D.C.J. stated (at 289), in a support application under the *FLA*, that "the period of time necessary to achieve a settled intention to treat the child as his own should begin to run from the time the true facts as to paternity are made known to the deceived person".

In *M. (B.B.)* v. *M. (W.W.)* (1994), 7 R.F.L. (4th) 255 (Alta. Q.B.), twins were conceived during a separation of the spouses at a time when the wife was having sexual relations with the husband and another man. Doubts about the paternity of the children were canvassed during the marriage, but the husband treated them as his children. Madam Justice Veit concluded that the husband would be a parent under the *Divorce Act* even if he were not the biological father.

2. Is it possible for a man to have a settled intention to treat a child as part of his family without ever cohabiting with the mother? See *Do Carmo* v. *Etzhorn* (1995), 16 R.F.L. (4th) 341 (Ont. Gen. Div.). In *Cheng* v. *Cheng* (1996), 21 R.F.L. (4th) 58, the Ontario Court of Appeal allowed a mother to add the father's parents to a claim for child support on the basis that the *FLA* "does not exclude grandparents as persons who may be responsible for support of children". See also *Mitchell* v. *Mitchell* (1998), 41 R.F.L. (4th) 181 (Sask. Q.B.) and the annotation to the case by Professor McLeod in the R.F.L.'s.

3. The Saskatchewan Court of Queen's Bench in *M. (D.E.)* v. *S. (H.J.)* (1996), 25 R.F.L. (4th) 264 ordered a woman to pay support for the niece of her same-sex partner where the partner had custody of the niece during their relationship.

4. Section 1(1) of the *Family Relations Act*, R.S.B.C. 1996, c. 128 (as amended), stipulates:

> "parent" includes . . . (*b*) a stepparent of a child if (i) the stepparent contributed to the support and maintenance of the child for at least one year, and (ii) the proceedings under this Act by or

against the stepparent is commenced within one year after the date the stepparent last contributed to the support and maintenance of the child.

Section 1(2) then indicates:

For the purpose of paragraph (b) of the definition of "parent" in subsection (1), a person is the stepparent of a child if the person and the parent of the child (a) are or were married, or (b) lived in a marriage-like relationship for a period of at least two years and for the purposes of this Act, the marriage-like relationship may be between persons of the same gender.

Do you prefer this approach to that of the *Divorce Act* or the *FLA*? For a review of the cases dealing with these definitions, see *Adler* v. *Jonas* (1998), 48 R.F.L. (4th) 218 (B.C. S.C.).

5. In *Chartier*, the Supreme Court of Canada put an end to the debate over whether a person who assumes a parental role to a partner's child can abandon that role later. In his Annotation to the case, Professor McLeod comments (at 6 in the RFL's):

In *Chartier*, the parties cohabited, married, separated, reconciled and separated again, all within three years. As a result, Mr. Chartier acquires a long-term child-support obligation. Whether that is reasonable is not the question. The Supreme Court of Canada has decided that it is the law. The task facing many lawyers will be to advise their clients on how to prevent that from happening to them. It appears that the only way to prevent a long-term child-support commitment is never to establish a parent-child relationship with a partner's child. Social scientists will have to decide whether that is a good way to force people to interact. . . .

Bastarache J.'s reasons are clear on the central issue. A person who assumes the role of a parent to a child cannot abandon that role. The only way out of the parent-child relationship is not to form the relationship in the first place. A person seeking to avoid a parental relationship to a partner's child should minimize the money he or she spends on the child, try not to treat the child in the same way as his or her own child and discourage any attempt by the child to refer to him or her other than by first name. Somehow, that behaviour does not seem to promote the child's best interests.

In *Cook* v. *Cook* (2000), 3 R.F.L. (5th) 373 (N.S. S.C.), Campbell J. suggested that a court should hesitate before finding that a step-parent stood in loco parentis, especially where the biological access parent still took an active role in the child's life.

6. Before the S.C.C.'s reasons in *Chartier* were released, the Sask. C.A. held in *Johb* v. *Johb* (1998), 40 R.F.L. (4th) 379 that a stepparent's status as a parent obligated to provide child support was terminated where the custodial parent cut off any relationship between the children and the stepparent. Is this result correct in light of *Chartier*? Could a court refuse to order any child support in this situation even if the stepparent still has the status of parent? See the notes below.

7. It is possible that a child has a number of parents on whom he or she could call for financial support. At one time s. 33(7)(b) of the *FLA* expressly placed primary responsibility for support on the biological parents. There was considerable divergence in the case law regarding how courts were to recognize this primary responsibility. The Ontario Court of Appeal held in *M. (C.)* v. *P. (R.)* (1997), 26 R.F.L. (4th) 1 (Ont. C.A.) that this did not necessarily mean that the biological parents had to pay for more than one-half of the cost of child rearing and that the courts retained an overriding discretion to determine the appropriate apportionment. The reasons suggested that the apportionment should reflect the extent and nature of each parent's involvement with the child. Some cases held that the secondary nature of a step-parent's support obligation should be recognized by imposing a time limit on the order: *Spring* v. *Spring* (1987), 61 O.R. (2d) 743 (U.F.C.); *Pender* v. *Pender* (1989), 23 R.F.L. (3d) 435 (Ont. Div. Ct.); *Brett* v. *Cooper* (1990), 26 R.F.L. (3d) 420 (Ont. Prov. Ct.); *Larter* v. *Larter* (1993), 50 R.F.L. (3d) 386 (N.W.T. S.C.); and *A. (D.R.)* v. *M. (R.M.)* (1997), 30 R.F.L. (4th) 269 (Ont. Gen. Div.). In the last case, Ferrier J. stated (at 274):

Courts in other provinces have gone further in giving the biological father primary responsibility. Courts in British Columbia, Saskatchewan and New Brunswick have held that where a child's natural father has been providing ongoing support for the child since the disposition of the wife's first marriage and continues to do so . . ., the applicant must prove (a) that the support is inadequate and (b) that nothing further can be expected from the natural parent before the court will order support against the non-biological parent. Further, in these provinces, the courts made these decisions even in the absence of legislative provisions similar to s. 33(7)(b).

Professor McLeod suggested in his Annotation to *M. (C.)* v. *P. (R.)* (1997), 26 R.F.L. (4th) 1 (Ont. C.A.), (at 3) that the "psychological parent should be responsible for any improved lifestyle he or she has created for the child and for any shortfall in funding the first family's lifestyle, subject to his or her ability to pay." The B.C. S.C. accepted this approach in *Reich* v. *Sager* (1995), 20 R.F.L. (4th) 24 (B.C. C.A.), but the B.C. C.A. overturned the decision not to order the stepparent to pay child support and remitted the matter back to the trial court to determine the amount: (1997), 33 R.F.L. (4th) 101 (B.C. C.A.).

The statutory recognition of the primary responsibility of biological or adoptive parents no longer appears in the *FLA*. It was repealed by the *Uniform Federal and Provincial Child Support Guidelines Act*, 1997, S.O. 1997, c. 20. However, ss. 33(5) and (6) of the *FLA* still permit third parties to be added in support applications under the Act. The *Divorce Act* does not contain any comparable provisions. However, it has been held that a husband who stands *in loco parentis* to his wife's child can, under the Rules of Court, add the biological father as a party defendant in divorce proceedings: *Pye* v. *Pye* (1995), 15 R.F.L. (4th) 76, at 81 (B.C. S.C.) and *French* v. *Stevenson* (1996), 23 R.F.L. (4th) 155 (B.C. Master). In *Kolada* v. *Kolada* (1999), 48 R.F.L. (4th) 370 (Alta. Q.B.), Veit J. concluded (at 375) that the S.C.C. in *Chartier*, "when referring with approval to actions by one custodial parent against another non-custodial parent in a three or more parent situation", indicated that courts might allow the addition of third parties in child support proceedings even if there is no explicit legislative directive. Regarding the question whether the biological parent can add stepparents in divorce proceedings, see *Robinson* v. *Domin* (1998), 39 R.F.L. (4th) 92 (B.C. S.C.) and Professor McLeod's annotation.

8. For most situations involving biological or adoptive parents, the new *Child Support Guidelines* (analyzed later in this chapter) set a child support figure in accordance with the payor's income. The court has no discretion to deviate from the *Guidelines* Table amount simply because the child has a stepparent who also has an obligation to support the child or actually supports the child. A biological or adoptive parent must pay at least the table amount, unless a court has discretion to reduce it on some other basis such as "undue hardship" under the *Guidelines*. See *Gordon* v. *Paquette* (1998), 36 R.F.L. (4th) 382 (B.C. Master); *K. (M.J.)* v. *M. (J.D.)* (1998), 167 D.L.R (4th) 334 (Alta. Q.B.); and *Adler* v. *Jonas* (1999), 48 R.F.L. (4th) 228 (B.C. S.C.). In several cases, however, judges have exercised a discretion of mysterious source to alter the amount payable by the biological father under the *Guidelines* simply on the basis that a stepfather was also contributing: *Boyle* v. *Boyle* (1998), 41 R.F.L. (4th) 388 (Ont. Gen. Div.) and *Holmedal* v. *Holmedal* (1997), 43 R.F.L. (4th) 434 (Alta. Q.B.).

9. In *Chartier*, Bastarache J. stated: "Once it is shown that the child is to be considered in fact, a 'child of the marriage', the obligations of the step-parent towards him or her are the same as those relative to a child born of the marriage with regard to the application of the *Divorce Act*." If this remark was intended to refer to the amount of child support payable by stepparents as well as the duration of their legal obligation, then the *Guidelines* suggest otherwise. For most situations involving biological or adoptive parents, the *Guidelines* set a child support figure in accordance with the payor's income. Only rarely does the court have a discretion to deviate from this figure. However, s. 5 of the *Guidelines* provides a general discretion to order "such amount as the court considers appropriate, having regard to these guidelines and any other parent's legal duty to support the child" where "the spouse against whom an order is sought stands in the place of a parent for a child or the parent is not a natural or adoptive parent of the child".

Where the non-custodial parent is not added as a party to a claim for child support against a stepparent and is not under an existing court order to pay such support, the courts, especially after *Chartier*, tend to simply order the stepparent to pay the *Guidelines* Table amount: *Kolada* v. *Kolada* (1999), 48 R.F.L (4th) 370 (Alta. Q.B.); *Stanton* v. *Solby* (1999), 49 R.F.L. (4th) 422 (B.C. Master); *B. (S.)* v. *B. (L.)* (1999), 2 R.F.L. (5th) 32 (Ont. S.C.J.). In *Gordon* v. *Paquette* (1998), 36 R.F.L. (4th) 382 (B.C. Master), Master Nitikman stated in *obiter* (at 386) that this approach should be adopted even if the three (or more) parents are all parties to the application. The Master added (at 386):

This may result in Matthew receiving child support in excess of what he would receive if there were one payor instead of two. . . . Such a result appears, however, to be consistent with the intent or policy behind the Guidelines, namely, that a child should benefit from the income of all of his 'parents' and is entitled to a standard of living commensurate with those incomes.

See also *MacArthur* v. *Demers* (1998), 166 D.L.R. (4th) 172 (Ont. Gen. Div.) (biological father obligated to pay $150 per month under a separation agreement; court ordered stepfather to pay full Table amount of $545 per month) and *Bell* v. *Michie* (1998), 38 R.F.L. (4th) 199 (Ont. Gen. Div.) (biological father never paid support, had hardly seen children, had remarried and fathered two more children, and had been on welfare for five years; court ordered stepparent to pay full Table amount of $300 per month for 4 1/2 years).

In *Adler* v. *Jonas* (1999), 48 R.F.L. (4th) 228 (B.C. S.C.), Hardinge J. noted (at 238) that there was a considerable divergence of opinion in the cases regarding the application of s. 5 of the *Guidelines*. The justice set the non-custodial biological parent's support at the *Guidelines* Table amount of $141 per month and calculated her share of the extraordinary expenses in accordance with s. 7. Justice Hardinge then suggested the following approach to determining the amount of the stepparent's obligation under s. 5:

> 1) determine the *Guidelines* Table amount, which represents the upper limit of the amount that can be ordered;

> 2) determine the legal duty of any other parent, generally the *Guidelines* Table amount; and

> 3) decide whether the total contribution of both biological parents will achieve a fair standard of support for the child. If it will, then the court may not require the stepparent to pay any support. If it will not, the stepparent will be required to top up available funds until a fair standard is reached.

In the end, the court ordered the stepfather to pay $125 per month on the basis that this amount plus the mother's payment of $141 and the custodial father's notional contribution of $466 per month would provide "a sum equal to that which would have been available to her had her natural parents' marriage not broken down".

While Justice Hardinge tried to establish a formula for the calculation of a stepparent's support obligation, the Saskatchewan Court of Queen's Bench indicated in *Campbell* v. *Campbell* (1998), 37 R.F.L. (4th) 228 (Sask. Q.B.) that s. 5 of the *Guidelines* created a general discretion to be exercised in light of all the circumstances in each case.

10. In *Chartier*, Bastarache J. described the support obligations of biological parents and stepparents as "joint and several". See also *Theriault* v. *Theriault* (1994), 2 R.F.L. (4th) 157, at 164 (Alta. C.A.) and *Reich* v. *Sager* (1997), 33 R.F.L. (4th) 101, at 108 (B.C. C.A.). What does that mean?

Justice Veit observed in *Kolada* v. *Kolada* (1999), 48 R.F.L. (4th) 370, at 375 (Alta. Q.B.):

> . . .[I]t is not obvious how the legal concept of joint and several liability could apply . . . to the common responsibility of child support. How can a parent who earns $37,000 a year be jointly responsible for the child support obligation of a non-custodial parent who earns $150,000 a year?

(3) AGE LIMITS

ZEDNER v. ZEDNER

(1989), 22 R.F.L. (3d) 207 (Ont. Prov. Ct.)

[Dana Zedner, aged 19, lived with her mother and her mother's husband, Mr. Jackson, in her grandmother's house following her mother's remarriage in 1986. The husband assumed total control over the family. Life in the home became tense and stressful, with constant fights. The husband interfered with Dana's relationship with her mother and sister, who moved out of the home. Further facts are revealed in the following excerpt from King Prov. J.'s reasons.]

This is an application by 19-year-old Dana Zedner for support from her mother Susan Jackson. Susan Jackson disputes Dana's claim stating that, although Dana is enrolled in a full-time program of education, she has withdrawn from Mrs. Jackson's control. . . .

Dana had terrible fights with Mr. Jackson. On one occasion, as she was going out with a friend, he called her a "tart" and physically kicked her out the door. She says her mother stood by and watched. More upsetting to her than Mr. Jackson's behaviour was her mother's passivity. She could not believe her mother would let Mr. Jackson do that to her, that her mother would never have stood for that sort of behaviour towards her before. Mr. Jackson often threatened to have the C.A.S. take Dana away. Eventually things in the household became so unbearable that Dana began preparing her own meals and eating them in her bedroom. She spent as much time as she could in her room or out of the house. She talked to neither Mr. nor Mrs. Jackson.

In November 1987 Mr. and Mrs. Jackson purchased a three-bedroom condominium and moved into it. Dana stayed on in her grandmother's home and has had no contact whatsoever with her mother. She says that she did not want to go with the Jacksons and that it was clear that they did not want her to.

Susan Jackson gave testimony and in it indicated that she had hoped Dana would move with the Jacksons into the condominium. She admits that the relationship between Dana and the Jacksons was extremely bad but that she hoped Dana would "come to her senses" and see what the real world was like. There was no evidence that she at any time actually asked Dana to join them in the condominium. . . .

I have not reviewed the evidence in such detail in order to assign fault but rather to determine if the defence [based on s. 31(2) of the *FLA*] given by Mrs. Jackson has, in fact, been established. The predecessor to the Family Law Act, 1986, namely, the Family Law Reform Act, had a similar section (s. 16(2)). . . . In the case of *Haskell* v. *Letourneau* (1980), 25 O.R. (2d) 139, 100 D.L.R. (3d) 329, 1 F.L.R.A.C. 306, Judge Clements of the County Court stated that in order for the "withdrawal" to be an established defence, it must be *voluntary*. The court stated at p. 151:

> It is his choice, freely made, to cut himself away from the family unit. Once this choice is freely made and the responsibility accepted by the child, the family unit has, in effect, been severed and the responsibility of the parents to support the child thus ceases.
>
> If the child is driven from parental control by the emotional or physical abuse in the home brought on due to the circumstances in the home, then surely he cannot be compelled to remain there . . . The choice of leaving was not voluntary but of necessity to ensure the physical and mental well-being of the child.

The court goes on to say at pp. 152-53:

> To force [the child] to return to that residence and endure the emotional and personal stress present there or as an alternative to deny him support would be unthinkable for his best interest. This is especially true by virtue of the fact that his present home surroundings are placid and supportive and provide him with the means to secure his legitimate aspirations.

In the case of *Dolabaille* v. *Carrington* (1981), 32 O.R. (2d) 442 at 445, 21 R.F.L. (2d) 207, Judge Weisman of the Ontario Provincial Court (Family Division) stated:

> In my view the Legislature intended that a very limited or narrow approach be taken to the defence contained in s. 16(2) of the Act. In my opinion it is only applicable in the clearest of cases of a free and voluntary withdrawal from reasonable parental control.

Judge Weisman gave a number of reasons for this interpretation, among others, that, "it recognizes that most normal, emancipated teenagers go through a period in which they become difficult for their parents to control, and excludes them from the operation of s. 16(2)".

Judge Ingram of the Ontario Provincial Court (Family Division) dealt with the new wording of the Family Law Act, 1986, as compared to the predecessor Act. In the case of *B. (S.)* v. *B. (R.)*, [1987] W.D.F.L. 2228, 18th September 1987 (unreported), he stated that the above interpretations still applied. I agree. The new Act has simply changed the parameters of parental obligation. Now a child must be enrolled in a full-time program of education, but a child who is 16 years of age or older must not have withdrawn from parental control.

I am satisfied that in this case Dana did not voluntarily withdraw from parental control. Circumstances simply made it impossible for her to continue to live with her mother. Although there was some faint evidence that Mrs. Jackson would indeed have Dana live with her, this is not a realistic proposal. Mrs. Jackson and Dana have not communicated for almost two years; there is no evidence that any professional help has been sought to improve this situation; there is no evidence that anything would be different should Dana move in with Mr. and Mrs. Jackson; Dana is doing well in her present setting.

Dana had net earnings of about $220 a month. In January 1989 she signed minutes of settlement with her father, Ralph Zedner, whereby he is to support her at the rate of $200 monthly. Since that time he has made one payment and Dana has taken the appropriate steps to have that order enforced. Even if that order is enforced, Dana still requires support from her mother. She has no money saved, no money for emergencies and requires ongoing money for food, clothing, accommodation, transit, school fees, books and entertainment. It is clear that Dana has the ability and the determination to go on to a higher level of education in order to eventually establish herself in the adult working world. Her expenses are reasonable and modest.

Mrs. Jackson has an income of approximately $27,000 and shares all expenses with Mr. Jackson whose income is "somewhat higher". I am satisfied that Mrs. Jackson has the means to support her daughter Dana. She has a secure monthly income, no debts other than a mortgage and no dependents other than Dana. I am satisfied that a reasonable figure for support would be the sum of $300 monthly. . . .

The definition of "child of the marriage" in the *Divorce Act* is essentially the same as that which was contained in the *Divorce Act* of 1968. The definition was considered in the first two cases reproduced here. The third case dealt mainly with the calculation of the quantum of support for a university student under the *Child Support Guidelines*. The presumptive rule for children under the age of majority is set out in s. 3(1) in the *Guidelines*, while s. 3(2) deals with children over the age of majority.

HARRINGTON v. HARRINGTON

(1981), 22 R.F.L. (2d) 40, 33 O.R. (2d) 150 (C.A.)

[The parties separated in 1973. Their daughter left high school in 1975 at age 18 and moved out of her mother's home. For some years she lived on her own and supported herself. She was then hospitalized, diagnosed as schizophrenic, and returned to live with her mother. She was unable to undertake any stressful activities. In divorce proceedings in 1979, the trial judge held that she was no longer a "child of the marriage" under the *Divorce Act* because she had been self-supporting. The mother appealed.]

MORDEN J.A.: — . . . I turn now to the wife's claim for maintenance for the 22-year-old daughter. . . .

Evidence was adduced through a director in the Ministry of Community and Social Services that the daughter was probably eligible, by reason of her disability, to receive an allowance covering her basic needs under the Family Benefits Act, R.S.O. 1970, c. 157 and there was also evidence that, in the course of the hearing, an application was made on her behalf for such an allowance. The maximum amount of such an allowance would be close to $300 a month. This amount would be reduced, by applying a formula, by any support order in her favour over $60 a month. However, at the time of the trial it was not the policy of the ministry to require an adult child to seek support from his or her parents. The director also said that while there are provisions in the Family Benefits Act under which the ministry could directly take action to obtain support, they "would not apply in this case".

Following the hearing of the appeal we were advised, at our request, by counsel for the appellant that the daughter, in fact, has been receiving benefits under the Family Benefits Act between March 1979 and now in varying monthly amounts of $218, $286, $315, $240 and $257. While counsel for the respondent was not in a position to confirm these amounts he had no reason to dispute them. . . .

In my respectful view the trial judge erred in holding that the daughter was not a "child of the marriage". In arriving at this conclusion, he imported a requirement that is not contained in the statutory definition — the requirement that the child (I use this word in its relationship sense) not have previously left the matrimonial home as an adult. It may be thought that this requirement is implicit in the words "unable . . . to withdraw himself from their charge" and that the definition is not applicable because the child had already, once, withdrawn from the parents' charge. However, this is not what the provision says. By its use of the words "at the material time" the definition is directed to the child's situation at the time of the hearing. If the child is at that time unable to withdraw from his or her parents' charge, and the other conditions of the provision are met, then he or she qualifies as a child of the marriage.

On the facts of this case, this conclusion would be equally supportable by the alternative part of the statutory definition: "unable . . . to provide [her] self with necessaries of life". I appreciate that it might be arguable that the daughter's social security position takes her out of this branch of the definition but, as I shall indicate, I think this feature of the case is more appropriately considered in relation to s. 11 of the Divorce Act [establishing the court's discretionary power to order support].
. . .

In approaching s. 11(1) it is important to keep in mind its constitutional basis. To be valid it must be legislation in relation to divorce: B.N.A. Act, 1867, s. 91(26). It must have "a rational, functional connection" with this subject of federal power: *Papp* v. *Papp*, [1970] 1 O.R. 331 at 335-36, 8 D.L.R. (3d) 389 (C.A.). The proper inquiry should, therefore, be into the effect of the dissolution of the marriage on the support of the particular child in question. The legislation should be interpreted as being restricted to the "direct consequences of marriage and its dissolution": *Papp* v. *Papp*, at p. 338. . . .

It may be observed that, practically, in many cases it is not the legal dissolution of the marriage as much as the physical separation of the parties which has the effect, by ending the existing family unit, of rendering it difficult if not impossible for a child to receive the support he or she would otherwise have received. In the present case I am prepared to assume that had the parties not been divorced or separated, they would have taken the daughter in when she became ill and looked after her.

If this had taken place the question is: What burden would this have imposed on them? In view of the evidence adduced at the trial with respect to the eligibility of the child for an allowance under the Family Benefits Act, as confirmed by the information subsequently furnished to us, I do not think this burden would have been significant. I think that this is a relevant and important consideration. . . .

In the present case I think that it is reasonable to take the daughter's receipt of payments under the Family Benefits Act into account. I consider it to be a relevant "circumstance" on the central issue of whether it is "fit and just" to order that the husband pay maintenance. Having regard to the absence of a general parental obligation to support adult children [Under the *Family Law Reform Act* no support could be ordered for any child over the age of majority. See now s. 31(1) of the FLA. Note also s. 33(9)(1)(iii) and (iv).] it can hardly be said, in the particular circumstances of this case, that a parental obligation should come first and the state's second. The illness which has befallen the daughter is one of those misfortunes of life for which, at the present time, it is reasonable to expect some sort of social security response. It is in accord with the evidence in this case that the welfare authorities do not pursue the parents of adult children who are welfare recipients for support. It is not unreasonable, depending on the parent's ability to pay, to consider his or her obligation to be of a residual nature. I think that the approach of the Law Reform Commission of Canada in its Report on Family Law (1976), at p. 59, is a reasonable one and one which reflects the attitude of most people:

> We also suggest that a child remain eligible for court-ordered parental support beyond age 18 for reasons of his or her illness or disability. At present, responsibility for most disabled persons over 18 years has been assumed by the state — a policy that is both humane and proper. We do not propose that this be altered in any way. We suggest, however, that there may be circumstances where a disabled or sick young person would not be eligible for assistance under a federal or provincial program and whose reliance upon parental support may be jeopardized by the dissolution of the marriage. It would therefore be desirable for federal law to provide for the possibility of extended parental support, as the *Divorce Act* now does, while placing on the court the obligation in each instance to decide whether this would be appropriate in view of the eligibility and need of the child for maintenance from public sources.

The same approach is recognized by the Ontario Law Reform Commission in its Report on Family Law, Pt. VI, Support Obligations (1975), at pp. 156, 159.

In the present case the respondent's means after looking after his own obligations (see the Family Law Reform Act, ss. 14(*b*) and 15) and making maintenance payments to the appellant are not adequate to provide any significant amount to her for the daughter (I do not suggest that these obligations would not normally take second place) and the daughter's means, through welfare, are such that the appellant should have no practical need for contribution from the respondent.

For these reasons, I would dismiss that part of the appeal which relates to the maintenance of the daughter. . . .

SMITH v. SMITH

(1987), 12 R.F.L. (3d) 50 (B.C. S.C.)

OPPAL J.: — The petitioner husband seeks to vary a maintenance order by a declaration that his 20-year-old daughter is no longer a "child of the marriage" within the definition of the Divorce Act, R.S.C. 1970, c. D-8.

The issue in this application is as follows:

> ... whether the applicant's twenty year old daughter, who is unemployed and living at home is a "child of the marriage".

The background of this matter is as follows. The parties were divorced on 19th June 1978. They had two children including a daughter, Michele, who is the focal point of this application. Pursuant to the terms of the decree nisi the respondent husband was to pay maintenance of $100 per month per child for "as long as the aforementioned remained children of the marriage within the meaning of the *Divorce Act*". The respondent quickly fell into arrears on his maintenance payments. The arrears were cancelled by court order on 20th October 1980. The respondent is again in arrears and seeks an order pursuant to s. 11(2) of the Act to vary the order by declaring that his daughter, Michele, is no longer a "child of the marriage" within the definition of the Act and that her name should be deleted from the order, thus rescinding the requirement for payment for her maintenance.

Michele is 20 years of age. The respondent submits that she is in good health, has no mental or physical disabilities and is capable of working to provide herself with the necessaries of life. She is, however, a Grade X high school dropout who lives at home with the petitioner on whom she is financially dependent because she is unemployed. In the 2 1/2 years since leaving high school, she has only worked three months on a part-time basis. She has been unable to find full-time employment. There are two apparent reasons for her state of unemployment. Firstly, she has no particular qualifications or specialized training in any field. Secondly, it is deposed that she has been prevented from working on a full-time basis because of the somewhat depressed economy. She has applied for jobs at various women's sports-wear stores, however, has had no success. It is the daughter's ambition to become a model. She wishes to enroll at a modelling agency.

... Generally, there are two lines of authority on whether s. 2(*b*) ought to be given a liberal or a restrictive interpretation. In *Bruehler* v. *Bruehler* (1985), 49 R.F.L. (2d) 44 at 46 (B.C. C.A.), Hutcheon J.A., in chambers, stated as follows:

> ... the words "other cause" may be sufficiently wide to include a state of depression in a province where young people of 18 or 19 years of age are unable to obtain employment to provide themselves with the necessaries of life.

In *Weir* v. *Weir* (1986), 1 R.F.L. (3d) 438 (B.C. S.C.), Errico L.J.S.C. held that the words "other cause" are extensive enough to encompass a state of depression in a province resulting in employment being difficult to obtain. In that case the parties had a son who was 20 years of age, who was unemployed and was receiving social assistance. He resided with the mother. He had left school in Grade IX and his prospects for employment were poor.

In *Gartner* v. *Gartner* (1978), 5 R.F.L. (2d) 270 at 274, 27 N.S.R. (2d) 482, 41 A.P.R. 482, the decision of the Nova Scotia Supreme Court, Trial Division, Cowan C.J.T.D. stated as follows:

It seems to me that it was not the intention of the Divorce Act that parents should be required to support a child who is not ill or disabled, and who can withdraw himself from the parents' charge and can provide himself with the necessities of life, except that he cannot, in the present state of the labour market, find suitable work.

It may be instructive to examine the comments on *Weir* by Professor J.G. McLeod wherein he expresses concern that where support for adult children is dependent upon the inability to obtain employment and not merely on an unwillingness to work it may create a difficulty for a father who may be compelled to monitor both the job market and the efforts of his children to obtain employment. It is suggested that that may seem to place an unreasonable burden on the supporting spouse. The author suggests that perhaps the court should conduct a broad inquiry in order to determine whether the claimant should be required to seek retraining or further employment.

Whether an adult qualifies as a "child of the marriage" will depend upon the circumstances of each case. In the case at bar there is no evidence to suggest that the daughter has made no diligent efforts to obtain employment. Her financial dependence on her mother due to her unemployment and inability to find a job qualifies her as a "child of the marriage" within the meaning of the Act. This is a valid and legitimate "other cause". She clearly is in need of maintenance. The Act obviously contemplates circumstances where a child . . . is over the age of 16 but is still in need of support for a valid reason. Hence the respondent's maintenance applications to support her are to continue. However, they should not continue on an indefinite basis. The daughter must continue to make realistic efforts in order to obtain employment or retraining. It may be that her goals of becoming a model are unrealistic. Therefore, there ought to be a limit imposed upon the period of time during which the respondent's obligations are to continue. An appropriate period in the circumstances would be six months. By that time the daughter ought to have secured full-time employment. . . .

WESEMANN v. WESEMANN

(1999), 49 R.F.L. (4th) 435 (B.C. S.C.)

MARTINSON J.:

Introduction

Wendy Lynn Rantz has applied to set the amount of child support payable under the *Federal Child Support Guidelines* SOR/97-175 for Darren Wesemann who turned 19 the day of the hearing. Darren is an excellent student who is presently attending the University of the Cariboo in Kamloops, enrolled in the Engineering Transfer Program. Darren has a conditional admission to the University of British Columbia's Bachelor of Applied Science program in the fall of 1999 and will enter the second year of a four year engineering program. He now lives with his mother and her husband in Kamloops but will require housing while at U.B.C.

Mr. Wesemann has been paying $300 per month as required by a Divorce Order dated November 25, 1986, though he has not seen Darren for six years. Mr. Wesemann agrees that his son remains a child of the marriage as defined in section 2 (1) of the *Divorce Act* . . . and that support should continue.

Mr. Wesemann agrees that his *Guidelines* income is $41,500 and that the amount payable based on that income (the Table amount) is $356 per month. He argues, however, that this amount is too high and is inappropriate within the meaning of section 3(2) of the *Guidelines*. He says that an appropriate amount is $250 per month.

Issues

I must decide these questions:

1. What amount of maintenance should be payable based on the *Guidelines*?
2. Should the payments by made directly to Darren? . . .

Discussion

1. What amount of maintenance should be payable based on the Guidelines?

A. The Law: . . . **The law with respect to support for children over the age of majority can be looked at as a four step procedure:**

Step One: Decide whether the child is a "child of the marriage" as defined in the *Divorce Act*? If s/he is not, that ends the matter.

Step Two: Determine whether the approach of applying the *Guidelines* as if the child were under the age of majority ("the usual *Guidelines* approach") is challenged. If that approach is not challenged, determine the amount payable based on the usual *Guidelines* approach.

Step Three: If the usual *Guidelines* approach is challenged, decide whether the challenger has proven that the usual *Guidelines* approach is inappropriate. If not, the usual *Guidelines* amount applies.

Step Four: If the usual *Guidelines* approach is inappropriate, decide what amount is appropriate, having regard to the condition, means, needs and other circumstances of the child and the financial ability of each spouse to contribute to the support of the child?

I will now consider each of the steps in more detail.

Step One - Child of the Marriage: The *Guidelines* consider quantum (the amount) of support only, not eligibility for support. The Divorce Act sets out when a child continues to be entitled to support. . . .

Master Joyce, in a very helpful pre *Guidelines* decision, considered factors to be taken into account in deciding when a child over the age of majority remains a child of the marriage for the purposes of the payment of maintenance: *Farden* v. *Farden* (1993), 48 R.F.L. (3d) 60 (B.C. Master), at 64-65. These factors were adopted by the British Columbia Court of Appeal in *Darlington* v. *Darlington* (1997), 32 R.F.L. (4th) 406 (B.C. C.A.) and have been followed in a number of post Guidelines cases: *St. Arnaud* v. *St. Arnaud* (November 5, 1998), Doc. Vancouver D094477 (B.C. S.C.), *Kovich* v. *Kreut* (November 5, 1998), Doc. Chilliwack 5904/5871 (B.C. S.C.), *Kembi* v. *Kembi* (January 29, 1999), Doc. Vancouver D47977 (B.C. S.C.).

These are the *Farden* factors:

1. whether the course of studies is part time or full time;
2. whether or not the child has applied for, or is eligible for, student loans or other financial assistance;
3. whether the career plans of the child are reasonable and appropriate;
4. the ability of the child to contribute to his/her own support through part-time employment;

5. the age of the child;
6. the child's past academic performance and whether the child is demonstrating success in the chosen course of studies;
7. what plans the parents made for the education of their children, particularly where those plans were made during co-habitation;
8. in the case of a mature child who has reached the age of majority, whether or not the child has unilaterally terminated a relationship from the parent from whom support is sought.

There does not have to be evidence on all of the factors in order to be successful: *Darlington.*

Step Two - The Guidelines Amount: If there is no challenge to the usual *Guidelines* approach the amount payable is determined under the *Guidelines* in the same way it is decided for a child under the age of majority. This can be the table amount, the table amount plus an amount for extraordinary expenses for post secondary education based on s. 7 of the *Guidelines* or an amount for post secondary education only based on s. 7 of the Guidelines: *Whitley* v. *Whitley* (October 9, 1997), Doc. Rossland 4741 (B.C. S.C. [In Chambers]).

Step Three - Is the usual Guidelines approach inappropriate?: The usual *Guidelines* approach applies unless the person claiming it is inappropriate proves that it is inappropriate. This requires a judicial determination of inappropriateness: *Glen* v. *Glen* (1997), 34 R.F.L. (4th) 13 (B.C. S.C.). Otherwise, it would be unnecessary to include s. 3(2) (a).

Section 3(2) does not say how a court is to decide whether or not the usual Guidelines approach is inappropriate. It should be noted, however, that the language of this section is different from that found in s. 4, which gives the court some discretion if the income of a paying spouse is over $150,000. In s. 4 the court can move away from the *Guidelines* amount if it considers that amount to be inappropriate: *Plester* v. *Plester* (1998), 56 B.C.L.R. (3d) 352 (B.C. S.C.). S. 3 on the other hand allows the court some discretion to move away from the Guidelines if it considers that approach (not the amount) to be inappropriate.

The usual *Guidelines* approach is based on certain factors that normally apply to a child under the age of majority. That is, the child resides with one or both parents. The child is generally not earning an income and is dependent on his or her parents. The usual *Guidelines* approach is, in most cases, based on the understanding that, though only the income of the person paying is used to calculate the amount payable, the other parent makes a significant contribution to the costs of that child's care because the child is residing with him or her. The closer the circumstances of the child are to those upon which the usual *Guidelines* approach is based, the less likely it is that the usual *Guidelines* calculation will be inappropriate. The opposite is also true. Children over the age of majority may reside away from home and/or earn a significant income. If a child is not residing at home, the nature of the contribution towards the child's expenses may be quite different.

Step Four - What amount is appropriate if the under age amount is not?: If the usual Guidelines approach is inappropriate, a court must determine the amount that is considered appropriate, having regard to the condition, means, needs and other circumstances of the child and the financial ability of each spouse to contribute to the support of the child. It is helpful to consider: 1) the reasonable needs of the child, 2) the ability and opportunity of the child to contribute to those needs, and 3) the ability of the parents to contribute to those needs.

1. The reasonable needs of the child: This has two aspects to it. First, the child's needs for accommodation, food, clothing, and other miscellaneous expenses. Second, the child's actual post secondary expenses.

2. The ability of and opportunity for the child to contribute to his education: Post secondary education is a privilege, not a right: *Whitley* (at para. 21). Children have an obligation to make a reasonable contribution to their education. However, just because a child is earning income, it does not follow that all of that income must be applied to the child's education. The desirability of allowing the child to experience some personal benefit from the fruits of his or her labours should also be considered: *Glen* v. *Glen* (at para. 14).

It is a notorious fact that post secondary education fees are high and well paid employment for students is scarce: *Darlington* (at para. 17).

It may well not be appropriate to require a child to work part-time during the school year in addition to summer employment as that might interfere with the child's studies and ability to pass: *Darlington* (at para. 17); *Palmer* v. *Palmer* (September 8, 1998), Doc. New Westminster E004302 (B.C. S.C. [In Chambers]) at para. 15.

Nor should the availability of student loan money automatically require the child to obtain the loan. To see a student loan as simply income available to a child is a fundamental misunderstanding of the nature, implications and financial obligations of a loan to that student. A student loan is not a bursary, grant or scholarship fund, designed to defray a student's expenses. Rather, a student loan delays payment of certain expenses, rather than defraying them: *Palmer* (at para. 16).

3. The ability of the parents to contribute to those needs: This involves a consideration of the ability to pay of both parents. The court may choose to apportion the amount payable on a proportionate basis as contemplated by s. 7 of the Guidelines: *Whitley* (at paras. 19 and 20).

B. Applying the Law to the Facts

Step One - Child of the Marriage: It is agreed that Darren is a ''child of the marriage''. There is no doubt that his career plans are reasonable and appropriate and he is demonstrating success in his chosen course of studies. Both parents agree that he should pursue a career in engineering and are understandably proud of his achievements to date.

Step Two - The Guidelines Amount: There is a challenge to the usual *Guidelines* approach. It should be noted that there was not a claim for s. 7 expenses in this case.

Step Three - Is the Usual Guidelines approach appropriate?: In this case, Darren will not be residing at home for some eight months of the year, and has the ability to earn income and otherwise contribute to his expenses. His mother will be relieved of some of the ordinary financial responsibilities of a person living in the household. Because of these differences from the situation upon which the usual *Guidelines* approach is based, the usual *Guidelines* approach is inappropriate.

Step Four - What amount is appropriate?

1. Darren's reasonable needs: The tuition costs at U.B.C. will be between $2,295 to $3,000 per year. Campus housing will be $6,400 to $7,600 per year. Darren's books will be approximately $1,000. Therefore the basic expenses will range from a high of $12,200 to a low of $9,695. In the circumstances and in the absence of more specific information, I assess his reasonable needs at $11,000 per year.

2. Darren's ability and opportunity to contribute to those needs: Darren works part-time at Little Caesar's Pizza for eight hours a week at minimum wage. He will try to increase his work hours over the summer break from May to August inclusive. Because of Darren's excellent scholastic record, he will have scholarships in the amount of $3,300. He should be able to earn enough over the summer to contribute $1,000 towards his education and still "experience some personal benefit from the fruits of his labours". With a course of studies such as his, he should not have to work part time during the year. He therefore needs $6,700 additional funding.

3. The financial ability of the parents to contribute to those needs: I have considered all of the circumstances of the parties though I will not refer to all of the information provided to me. Mr. Wesemann has been working at Key West Ford for three years. His 1997 income as reported on his tax return was $39,197.58 and the income shown on his 1998 T4's was $43,984.13. Taking into account his new wife's net monthly income of $859.73, Mr. Wesemann's net available monthly income is $2,580. Using their combined income, he shows a monthly deficit of $516.97. He lists as expenses $400 toward liquor and cigarettes, $150 to an RSP and $300 child support for Darren. He only recently began contributing to an RSP. Some time ago Mr. Wesemann decided to undertake a career change and work in the trucking business. This did not work out well and he ultimately declared bankruptcy. He has been discharged for about two years. Mr. Wesemann submits that he needs a chance to get ahead. He now has steady employment, but to earn the money he is earning, he works long hours and does not take vacations. He is "on a tread mill" and needs a chance to get off of it. Mr. Wesemann has provided extended medical and dental coverage for his son. He says he will do things for his son, especially while Darren is in the Lower Mainland. I am unable to agree with Mr. Wesemann that his financial circumstances prevent him from making a contribution greater than $250 per month to his son's education. He has, to his credit, managed to pay the $300 per month required under the previous order. He may be required to reduce some of his expenses.

An appropriate amount of support is $350 per month. It is noteworthy that this will still leave Darren $2,500 short of the amount he requires.

Mrs. Rantz remarried in 1994 and has not been employed outside the home since 1990. For tax purposes she and her husband have split their income and $10,974.12 per year is attributed to her. Though not relevant to this application, Mr. Rantz earns $50,636.61. Mrs. Rantz is not in a financial position to provide a significant cash contribution to Darren's education herself. However, she will no doubt continue to provide a home when he is in Kamloops and to provide whatever other support she and Mr. Rantz are able to.

2. Should the payments by made directly to Darren?

Mr. Wesemann points out that he has not seen his son for some six years. He wishes to remedy that and views the direct payment of child support as providing a psychological link. In addition, Mr. Wesemann does not want to continue the involvement of the Family Maintenance Enforcement Program in this matter. They have been used because Mrs. Rantz did not want contact with him, not because he was not paying. Mrs. Rantz wishes to have the payments made directly to her. I do not have the views of Darren in this respect.

In the particular circumstances of this case, it is appropriate that the payments be made directly to Darren. There is every reason to suggest that he will use the funds responsibly. However, there should not be personal contact without Darren's consent. . . .

NOTES AND QUESTIONS

1. For other cases dealing with s. 31(2) of the *FLA* and its predecessor in the *Family Law Reform Act*, see *Tromblay* v. *Tromblay* (1981), 35 O.R. (2d) 567 (Prov. Ct.); *H.* v. *C.* (1982), 27 R.F.L. (2d) 28 (Ont. Prov. Ct.); *Distefano* v. *Haroutinian* (1984), 41 R.F.L. (2d) 201 (Ont. Fam. Ct.); *Schneider* v. *Moscovitch* (1984), 44 R.F.L. (2d) 209 (Ont. Fam. Ct.); *G. (L.)* v. *G. (F.)* (1989), 20 R.F.L. (3d) 157 (Ont. Fam. Ct.); *Heon* v. *Heon* (1989), 22 R.F.L. (3d) 273 (Ont. H.C.); *Figueiredo* v. *Figueiredo* (1991), 33 R.F.L. (3d) 72 (Ont. Gen. Div.); *Soltys* v. *Soltys* (1991), 34 R.F.L. (3d) 441 (Ont. Prov. Div.); *Lyttle* v. *Lyttle* (1992), 41 R.F.L. (3d) 422 (Ont. Prov. Ct.); *Fitzpatrick* v. *Karlein* (1994), 5 R.F.L. (4th) 290 (Ont. Prov. Div.); *Judd* v. *Judd* (1995), 16 R.F.L. (4th) 430 (Ont. Prov. Div.); and *Lynch* v. *Lynch* (1999), 1 R.F.L. (5th) 309 (Ont. S.C.J.). See also *Bennett (Guardian ad litem of)* v. *Bennett* (1993), 47 R.F.L. (3d) 61 (B.C. Prov. Ct.).

In *Fitzpatrick* v. *Karlein*, Nasmith Prov. J. reviewed the case law and concluded (at 294-295):

> I am persuaded that it is time to ask whether there is a valid basis for the "narrow" approach to the legislation now that the wording in s. 31 of the *Family Law Act* leaves open-ended the parental obligation to support a child after age 16 so long as the child remains a full-time student.

> The correct approach to the new legislation, in my opinion, once the defence under subs. 31(2) has been raised and it has been established that the child is past 16 years and outside of the control of the former custodial parent, is to assign to the child, as the applicant, the onus of demonstrating that the withdrawal was involuntary whether by reason of eviction or a living situation with the parent that is viewed as unbearable or impossible. . . . It is not just a matter of showing that the choice to become independent was reasonable or understandable. Under s. 31 of the *Family Law Act*, for a youth past the age of 16, who has, ostensibly, withdrawn from parental control to succeed in obtaining court-ordered support, it must be demonstrated by her that the withdrawal was involuntary.

> While I have sympathy for Carolyn and I understand her preference for living with the Bowens, she has not demonstrated that the living situation with her mother and Mr. Karlein was unbearable or impossible. She has shown that she was unhappy there; that she felt unloved; that she was feeling cut off from other members of the family. Her choice to move out made good sense to her. But it was a relatively free choice as it has been presented. Carolyn has not satisfied me that her withdrawal from her mother's control was involuntary.

Section 31(2) applies to all children over the age of 16, even those away at university. How does one determine if a university or college student has "withdrawn from parental control"? In *Figueiredo*, FitzGerald J. stated (at 73):

> For the child, this privilege is available on certain conditions, namely, that the child has not withdrawn from parental control and that the child is in need of support. The key word is "control". If the child wants to get support, the child must be prepared to submit to control by the paying parent. In my view, it is implicit in this section that the control sought to be exercised must be reasonable. What is reasonable will, of course, depend upon all of the surrounding circumstances and will vary with each individual case.

> Foremost among the aspects of control to be considered is the requirement of the section that, if the applicant for support is over the age of 16, he or she must be enrolled in a full-time program of education. It is not sufficient that the student be merely enrolled. The stipulation that it be a full-time program implies that the student, if he or she is to receive support, must devote to that program, in priority to all other diversions, whatever effort within the capability of the student is required to achieve an acceptable level of performance. At a minimum, then, the degree of control to which the student must submit is that required to ensure that he or she attends the educational

classes punctually and consistently, and devotes sufficient time and effort outside of school to keep up with all home study requirements.

How this control is exercised will vary with each individual situation. If the child is living at home, one would expect to find reasonable curfew rules on week nights, a control over spending, and reasonable consideration for the parent whose support is sought, particularly as the behaviour of the child may affect the well-being and employment of the parent. One would also expect to find reasonable consideration on the part of the parent for the well-being of the child. If the child, without justification, rejects such control or fails to pursue the course of education with reasonable diligence, that child, whether living at home or not, forfeits the right to parental support.

2. Under the *Divorce Act*, the term "child of the marriage" indicates that a person under the age of majority must not have "withdrawn from [the parents'] charge". In *Bast* v. *Dyck* (1997), 28 R.F.L. (4th) 131 (Sask. Q.B.), a depressed and suicidal sixteen-year-old girl moved out of her mother's house to live with her boyfriend and his parents. The mother accepted the move on the advice of a counselor and continued to support the girl financially. The court dismissed the father's application to vary an existing support order on the basis that the girl was no longer a "child of the marriage". Justice McIntyre reasoned (at 137):

I am not prepared to find at this time that Chandelle has voluntarily withdrawn from the charge of her parents. It is clear . . . that she is a troubled child. There is no indication that the present arrangement has any degree of permanence to it. She is a full-time highschool student. She maintains a relationship with both parents. The evidence does not satisfy me that she has chosen to reject or withdraw from her parents and assume an independent lifestyle. Young people in their latter teens can go through personal and emotional difficulties. A parent cannot terminate their [sic] responsibility at the first sign of a bump in the road.

See also *James* v. *James* (1995), 18 R.F.L. (4th) 463 (B.C. S.C.) and *C. (J.J.D.)* v. *C. (S.L.)* (1996), 25 R.F.L. (4th) 288 (Ont. Gen. Div.).

A person over the age of majority must also be under his or her parents' "charge" to qualify as a "child of the marriage" under the *Divorce Act*. In cases involving students living away from home, the courts have frequently simply equated this phrase with economic dependency. See, for example, *Coakwell* v. *Baker* (1994), 4 R.F.L. (4th) 345 (Ont. Gen. Div.); *Couturier* c. *Couturier* (1995), 162 N.B.R. (2d) 321 (B.R. N.B.); and *McKenster* v. *McKenster* (1996), 24 R.F.L. (4th) 325 (N.S. C.A.). However, some cases such as *Chaban (Brault)* v. *Chaban* (1985), 49 R.F.L. (2d) 22 (Man. Q.B.); *Pritchard* v. *Pritchard (Zinck)* (1991), 38 R.F.L. (3d) 45 (N.S. Fam. Ct.); and *Wieland* v. *Wieland* (1994), 3 R.F.L. (4th) 56 (Ont. Gen. Div.) have held that the child must be under parental control to some extent. In "Support for Adult Children" (1999), 17 C.F.L.Q. 39, at 45, Terry Hainsworth supports the approach in cases like *Couturier*:

The adoption of a strict economic test has many benefits. First, it avoids the necessity of having to make moral or value judgments within the context of a family setting. Second, it avoids the anomaly of having to assess conduct in a child support application when such assessment is irrelevant in applications between spouses. Third, in respect of "adult children" it does not undermine the role of parental authority because, by this stage, the normal emancipation process will be well advanced. Finally, it avoids the necessity of having to assign blame in situations where complex family dynamics may be involved.

Do you find this convincing? Is this approach possible under the *FLA* which refers specifically to "parental control"?

3. In an annotation to *Saunders* v. *Saunders* (1988), 14 R.F.L. (3d) 225 (Sask. C.A.), E.F. Anthony Merchant criticized those cases that simply assume that a person at university is a "child of the marriage" for the purpose of the *Divorce Act*. He stated (at 227):

Saunders accepts the assumption which has developed in the past 20 years. Judges have been to university. They hope their children will go as well and most do. One wonders whether the same assumption would have crept into the law were the 75 per cent of parents without university degrees interpreting "necessaries" and "unable . . . to withdraw from [parental] charge".

This criticism is harder to maintain now that some provincial statutes such as the *FLA* stipulate that all parents have an obligation to support a child enrolled in a full time program of education (unless the child has withdrawn from parental control).

4. Age limits in provincial child support legislation have survived challenges based on s. 15 of the *Charter* in *Penner* v. *Danbrook* (1992), 39 R.F.L. (3d) 286 (Sask. C.A.) and *Massingham-Pearce* v. *Konkolus* (1995), 13 R.F.L. (4th) 313 (Alta. Q.B.).

5. Support obligations can vary significantly from one province to another and the obligation under the *Divorce Act* can differ from that set in the provincial legislation. In *Michie* v. *Michie* (1997), 36 R.F.L. (4th) 90, the Saskatchewan Court of Queen's Bench noted that there was no obligation to support adult children under the provincial legislation, while there might be when the parents divorced. It held that this amounted to discrimination based on marital status, but held that there was no *Charter* violation because the discrimination was justifiable under s. 1. See also *Souliere* v. *Leclair* (1998), 38 R.F.L. (4th) 68 (Ont. Gen. Div.).

6. At the time of the divorce the spouses' 21-year-old daughter is employed and self-supporting. Later, she becomes ill and is unable to support herself. Does either parent have an obligation to support her under the *FLA*? If the daughter is living with her mother following the illness, can the mother apply under the *Divorce Act* for an order requiring the father to provide support? See *King* v. *King (No. 2)* (1979), 13 R.F.L. (2d) 222 (B.C. S.C.).

7. In *Crook* v. *Crook* (1992), 42 R.F.L. (3d) 297 (N.S. T.D.), Goodfellow J. stated (at 306) that there "have been occasions where [child support] orders were issued for children 50 years of age or more because of illness or disability". How likely are such orders? Would not the presence of disability pensions or other forms of social security enable the individual to "obtain the necessaries of life"? Even if the person is still considered a "child of the marriage", will any amount of child support be considered appropriate under s. 3(2) of the *Guidelines*?

In *Burhoe* v. *Goff* (1999), 50 R.F.L. (4th) 218 (N.B. Q.B.) the court declined to order the father to pay the *Guidelines* Table amount of $553 per month for a 21-year-old son who had Down's Syndrome and was living with his mother. The son received $530 per month as a disability pension and the mother received $430 per month as a "respite allowance". The court ordered the father who earned about $71,000 per year to pay the mother $65 per week as child support. No support was ordered in *Buzon* v. *Buzon* (1999), 48 R.F.L. (4th) 263 (Alta. Q.B.) where a mentally handicapped adult was living with his mother and collecting the maximum amount (about $820 per month) from the provincial Assured Income for the Severely Handicapped program.

8. Are parents obligated under the *FLA* to support a 20-year-old son who is unable to support himself because he cannot find employment? Should they be? Should the son be considered a "child of the marriage" under the *Divorce Act*? In addition to *Smith* and the cases referred to therein, see *Baker* v. *Baker* (1994), 2 R.F.L. (4th) 147 (Alta. Q.B.) (where the conflicting cases up to that point were reviewed and where the court concluded that the words "other cause" could encompass unemployment) and *McAdam* v. *McAdam* (1994), 8 R.F.L. (4th) 252 (Man. Q.B.) (where the court came to the same conclusion). See also *Bragg* v. *Bragg* (2000), 2 R.F.L. (5th) 344 (Nfld. U.F.C.) (where a pregnant daughter was a "child of the marriage") and *Gervais* v. *Tongue* (2000), 4 R.F.L. (5th) 225 (Ont. S.C.J.) (daughter with a new baby was a "child of the marriage").

9. In *Sullivan* v. *Sullivan* (1999), 50 R.F.L. (4th) 326 (Ont. Div. Ct.), a 23-year-old was only able to take one or two university courses per year because of a serious illness. The court concluded, nonetheless, that this constituted a full-time program for this particular student for the purpose of s. 31(1) of the *FLA*. It ordered the father to pay $867 per month, which constituted the *Guidelines* Table amount minus the disability pension the girl received. In his annotation, Professor McLeod stated (at 327) that the court had "simply ignored the words of the legislation to reach a fair result". Do you agree?

10. Before the adoption of the *Child Support Guidelines*, the courts had a general discretion to determine the appropriate child support order. Under the *Divorce Act*, they could decide where to draw the line regarding support for a child who had reached the age of majority in determining whether he or

she still qualified as a "child of the marriage". They could also deny support despite the finding that a child was a "child of the marriage" on the basis that an order was "unreasonable". The *Guidelines* appear to have changed little in this regard. Before a court can order support, it must conclude that it is dealing with a "child of the marriage" and the old case law should remain relevant. Then, a court has considerable discretion under s. 3(2) of the *Guidelines* in determining the quantum. This subsection simply substitutes "appropriate" for "reasonable".

Under the *FLA*, the obligation to support a child over the age of majority arises once the conditions set in s. 31 are met. These conditions give less flexibility to the courts than the term "child of the marriage". For example, a court could not conclude that a support obligation no longer existed because a university student refused to see her father. However, this factor might be given weight in determining the appropriate amount under s. 3(2) of the *Guidelines* and a court could conclude that an order for no support was appropriate.

11. The Manitoba Court of Appeal suggested in *Newman* v. *Thompson* (1997), 118 Man. R. (2d) 177 (Man. C.A.), at para. 17: "An order of child support for an emancipated child can only be justified as a means of requiring one parent to share the responsibility of educating a child who, but for the divorce, would have continued to receive the support of both parents." In *Trottier* v. *Bradley* (1999), 49 R.F.L. (4th) 432, the same court used this "flexible test" to conclude that a father should not be required to support his 23-year-old daughter who was pursuing a doctorate degree. The court noted that the daughter had unilaterally terminated the relationship with her father.

Until the 1990s, it was commonly thought that child support would terminate with the first college diploma or university degree. However, more recently courts have indicated that students seeking additional education may still qualify as "children of the marriage" : *Martell* v. *Height* (1994), 3 R.F.L. (4th) 104 (N.S. C.A.); *Jamieson* v. *Jamieson* (1995), 14 R.F.L. (4th) 354 (N.B. C.A.); *Parsons* v. *Parsons* (1995), 17 R.F.L. (4th) 267 (Ont. Gen. Div.); *Newman, supra*; and *Jonasson* v. *Jonasson* (1998), 37 R.F.L. (4th) 266 (B.C. S.C.). The N.S. C.A. stated in *Martell* v. *Height*, at 106:

> There is no arbitrary cut-off point based either on age or scholastic attainment, although as these increase the onus of proving dependency grows heavier. As a general rule, parents of a *bona fide* student will remain responsible until the child has reached a level of education, commensurate with the abilities he or she has demonstrated, which fit the child for entry level employment in an appropriate field. In making this determination the trial judge cannot be blind to prevailing social and economic conditions: a bachelor's degree no longer assures self-sufficiency.

As suggested in *Wesemann* and *Tottier* v. *Bradley*, one factor that has been considered in determining whether a child over the age of majority remains a "child of the marriage" is whether the child unilaterally terminated the relationship with the payor parent without legitimate reason. See also *Anderson* v. *Anderson* (1997), 27 R.F.L. (4th) 323 (B.C. S.C.) and *Farden* v. *Farden* (1993), 48 R.F.L. (3d) 60 (B.C. Master). However, Terry Hainsworth reports in "Support for Adult Children" (1999), 17 C.F.L.Q. 39, at 63-64, that courts usually strain to find an excuse for the child's conduct. Also, courts sometimes first warn that the quantum may be reduced or the obligation ended if the child continues to refuse to communicate with the payor: *Whitton* v. *Whitton* (1989), 21 R.F.L. (3d) 261 (Ont. C.A.).

Some courts have conditioned ongoing support upon the student providing information with respect to grades, costs and resources: *Brown* v. *Brown* (1993), 45 R.F.L. (3d) 444 (B.C. S.C.) and *Ciardullo* v. *Ciardullo* (1995), 15 R.F.L (4th) 121 (B.C. S.C.).

It should be noted that the *Guidelines* generally preclude consideration of the child's attitude to and relationship with the payor where the child is under the age of majority. In that situation the presumptive rule of s. 3(1) prevails: *Pohlod* v. *Bielajew* (1998), 38 R.F.L. (4th) 35 (Ont. Gen. Div.).

12. A student may earn sufficient money through part-time or seasonal work to meet all of his or her needs. If so, he or she will not qualify as a "child of the marriage" under the *Divorce Act*: *Barry* v. *Barry* (1995), 136 Sask. R. 277 (Q.B.) and *Charko-Ruhl* v. *Charko* (1997), 35 R.F.L. (4th) 138 (Sask. Q.B.) . If the student's earnings are not sufficient to enable him or her to withdraw from parental charge, then the earnings will still be relevant in determining quantum.

13. Where a student is living at home while attending university, the courts will generally determine the appropriate quantum of support in accordance with s. 3(2)(a) of the *Guidelines*; that is, as if the student were under the age of majority. This involves determining the Table amount and then adding, under s. 7, a proportionate amount of the education costs such as tuition, book purchases, and transportation. Before apportionment of the education costs, the student's contribution is deducted in accordance with s. 7(2). See *Glen* v. *Glen* (1997), 34 R.F.L. (4th) 13 (B.C. S.C.); *Holizki* v. *Reeves* (1997), 34 R.F.L. (4th) 414 (Sask. Q.B.); *Carnall* v. *Carnall* (1998), 37 R.F.L. (4th) 392 (Sask. Q.B.); *Garrison* v. *Garrison* (1998), 38 R.F.L. (4th) 435 (Ont. Gen. Div.); *Barnsley* v. *Barnsley* (1998), 43 R.F.L. (4th) 290 (Ont. Gen. Div.); *Mascarenhas* v. *Mascarenhas* (1999), 44 R.F.L. (4th) 131 (Ont. Gen. Div.); *Erickson* v. *Erickson* (1999), 47 R.F.L. (4th) 326 (N.S. S.C.); and *Mills* v. *Mills* (1999), 48 R.F.L. (4th) 184 (Sask. Q.B.).

Where the student leaves home to go to school, the cases use a variety of methods to determine quantum. Some such as *Wesemann* rely on the discretionary language of s. 3(2)(b) of the *Guidelines* to determine a fair amount in light of the student's needs, the student's resources and the parents' means. Justice Wilkinson acknowledged in *Woods* v. *Woods* (1998), 42 R.F.L. (4th) 123 (Sask. Q.B.) that this was a common approach where the child attended university in another city, but refused to use it where the daughter could take the same program at a local institution. Instead, the justice awarded the Table amount and apportioned the university costs that were not related to living expenses. In *Brockman* v. *Ofukay* (1998), 41 R.F.L. (4th) 426 (Sask. Q.B.), the court apportioned the total costs between the parents, after deducting the student's contribution. The Nova Scotia Family Court in *Bellman* v. *Bellman* (1999), 46 R.F.L. (4th) 414 (B.C. S.C.) awarded the Table amount for the four months that the student would be at home and apportioned the university costs in accordance with s. 7 of the *Guidelines*. In *Blair* v. *Blair* (1997), 34 R.F.L. (4th) 370 (Ont. Gen. Div.), the court awarded the Table amount for a single child for the whole year (there was a younger child at home) and apportioned the university costs without taking into account the residence and meal fees.

14. Should a court take into account a student's ability to access government loans in determining eligibility for or quantum of support? Should it matter whether the parents would have expected the child to seek loans if the family had remained together? Should a loan only be considered if the student chooses to obtain one?

In *Mascarenhas*, above, Campbell J. stated (at 135) that the adoption of the *Guidelines* caused a shift in the judicial approach to student loans: "Due to the wording of section 7(2), the preponderance of the case law suggests that student loans must be considered a 'contribution' from the child and, therefore, must be deducted from the gross post-secondary educational expenses that are proven." However, the justice then went on to suggest in *obiter* that this should be done only where the student actually obtained a loan and that the student could choose not to do so. Loans were considered part of a student's resources in *Evans* v. *Evans* (1998), 35 R.F.L. (4th) 158 (Sask. Q.B.); *Michie* v. *Michie* (1997), 36 R.F.L. (4th) 90 (Sask. Q.B.); *Barbeau* v. *Barbeau* (1998), 41 R.F.L. (4th) 24 (Ont. Gen. Div.); *Klotz* v. *Klotz* (1999), 44 R.F.L. (4th) 236 (B.C. S.C.); and *Mills* v. *Mills* (1999), 48 R.F.L. (4th) 184 (Sask. Q.B.). However, in *Bellman* v. *Bellman* (1999), 46 R.F.L. (4th) 414 (B.C. S.C.), Beames J. stated (at 421): "In keeping with recent authority from this province, I do not consider the student loans which might be available to Karycia [she had not applied] to be benefits to her for the purpose of determining support payable." In *Woods* v. *Woods* (1998), 42 R.F.L. (4th) 123 (Sask. Q.B.), the court did not take into account the Canada Student Loan that the daughter had received because both parents acknowledged that it was never their expectation that their children would go into debt to fund their education.

15. In *Wesemann*, the court ordered payment directly to the son. See also *Adam* v. *Adam* (1993), 50 R.F.L. (3d) 216 (Man. Q.B.); *Lilley* v. *Lilley* (1993), 50 R.F.L. (3d) 329 (B.C. S.C.); and *Shiels* v. *De Carli* (1996), 23 R.F.L. (4th) 95 (Ont. Gen. Div.). The courts refused to order payment directly to the child in *Williams* v. *Berridge* (1996), 21 R.F.L. (4th) 157 (Ont. Gen. Div.) and *Sherlock* v. *Sherlock* (1998), 36 R.F.L. (4th) 301 (B.C. S.C.).

3. Determining the Amount

(1) INTRODUCTION

Canada undertook a massive rule-based reform of its child support system with the adoption of *Federal Child Support Guidelines,* SOR/97-175, effective May 1, 1997. The *Uniform Federal and Provincial Child Support Guidelines Act,* 1997, S.O. 1997, c. 20, amended the *FLA* to provide for provincial Guidelines and the *Child Support Guidelines (Ontario),* O.Reg. 391/97, which are virtually identical to their federal counterparts came into effect on December 1, 1997. Ontario also adopted the federal table amounts for computational purposes. To date, Ontario has not asked the Governor in Council to adopt the provincial guidelines as applicable to divorce proceedings (see *Divorce Act,* s. 2(1) "applicable guidelines" and s. 2(5)). Accordingly, the provincial guidelines apply to proceedings under the *FLA* and the federal ones apply to *Divorce Act* proceedings, but this has no real practical significance.

Prior to the reforms, courts determined child support on a case-by-case basis in light of proven expenses associated with the child and on the parents' ability to meet those expenses. Under the *Guidelines,* the starting point (and in many cases the ending point) in determining quantum is the Table amount. To establish this amount, one need know only (1) the relevant provincial table (there are different tables for different provinces to reflect differences in tax structure); (2) the number of children "to whom the order relates"; and (3) the annual income of the payor or non-custodial parent. Variations from this Table amount are permitted in limited circumstances set out in the *Guidelines.* The incredible number of reported cases interpreting the exceptions should not mislead. Most commentators suggest that the *Guidelines* have succeeded in achieving the objectives of the new system set out in s. 1: adequacy or fairness, objectivity, efficiency, and consistency. See Bala, "First Impressions of the Implementation of the Guidelines" in *Federal Child Support Guidelines Reference Manual* (Ottawa: Dept. of Justice, looseleaf) and Thompson and Rockman, "Practitioner's View of the Guidelines" in the same work.

The first reading that follows is the Canadian government's explanation of the move towards child support guidelines in 1996. The *Guidelines* that were eventually adopted differ slightly from those envisaged in this piece. There then follows this author's brief description of other aspects of the 1996 federal child support package. The third reading consists of part of an annotation by Professor McLeod in which he introduces the circumstances where a court may deviate from the Table amount. Those relating to stepchildren and children over the age of majority have already been dealt with earlier in the chapter. Others will be examined briefly in the remainder of this chapter. Finally, the ability to deviate from the *Guidelines* by agreement is explored in Chapter 9: **DOMESTIC CONTRACTS.**

For additional readings on the *Guidelines,* see *Federal Child Support Guidelines Reference Manual* (Ottawa: Dept. of Justice, looseleaf); Bala, "Ottawa's New Child Support Regime: A Guide to the Guidelines" (1996), 21 R.F.L. (4th) 301; Finnie, "The Government's Child Support Package" (1997-98), 15 C.F.L.Q. 79; Colman, "Child Support Guideline – New Laws, New Challenges" (1997-98), 15 C.F.L.Q. 229; Aston, "An Update of Case Law under the Child Support Guidelines" (1998-99), 16 C.F.L.Q. 261; Maisonneuve, "Child Support under the Federal and Quebec Guidelines: A Step Forward or Behind?" (1999), 16 Can. J. Fam. L. 284; and T.W. Hainsworth, *Child Support Guidelines Service* (Canada: Canada Law Books, looseleaf).

THE NEW CHILD SUPPORT PACKAGE

(Ottawa: Government of Canada, March 6, 1996) 11-17 and 30-31.

. . .

Federal Child Support Guidelines

The Family Law Committee found that the current method of determining child support awards is viewed as subjective, arbitrary and unfair. To help parents, lawyers and judges set fair and consistent child support awards, the government will introduce Child Support Guidelines (''the Guidelines'') in the *Divorce Act*. The federal Guidelines will apply when a child support order is made in a divorce proceeding. Although they will not apply in cases of separation or when parents were not married — these situations are governed by provincial or territorial family law — the federal government is working closely with the provinces to encourage them to adopt guidelines in their own jurisdictions. By making the system more predictable and offering a simpler means to update awards, the introduction of guidelines can lower legal costs for parents, as well as legal aid and court costs for governments.

The Guidelines are designed to:

- establish a fair standard of support for children that ensures that children continue to benefit from the financial means of both parents after divorce;

- reduce conflict and tension by making the calculation of child support simpler and more objective;

- improve the efficiency of the legal process by giving courts and parties guidance in setting awards and encouraging settlement; and

- assure more consistent treatment of support-paying parents, while providing sufficient flexibility to ensure that awards are fair in individual family circumstances.

The Federal Child Support Guidelines are a modified version of the model developed by the Family Law Committee. The Guidelines have three main elements:

- Child Support Payment Schedules;

- rules to adjust the award to reflect four types of special child-related expenses; and

- rules to adjust the award in cases of undue hardship.

Presumptive Application of the Guidelines

Courts will be required to award the amount set out in the Child Support Payment Schedule, plus allowable special expenses, unless the court makes a written finding that the award causes undue hardship to either parent or to the child.

The Guidelines will not be mandatory for support awards that are negotiated out-of-court. However, they will provide guidance to parents as well as the courts — which are responsible for assessing whether reasonable arrangements have been made for the children's support.

Child Support Payment Schedules [The Tables]

The Child Support Payment Schedules show the basic amount that the support-paying parent should pay according to his or her income and the number of children. "Income" will be defined broadly in the Guidelines, but the income of a new partner or spouse will be relevant only if the court is asked to make a determination of undue hardship.

The Schedule amounts are fixed by a formula that calculates the appropriate amount of support in light of economic data on average expenditures on children across different income levels. The formula reserves a basic amount of income for the payer's self-support, and adjusts for the impact of federal and provincial income taxes. There are separate tables for each province to take differences in provincial income tax rates into account. . . .

A New Approach to Setting Child Support

Guidelines which — like the Federal Child Support Guidelines — set support payments as a share of the support-paying parent's income are known as percentage-of-income guidelines. This style of guideline is used in many American states and in New Zealand. They are premised on a number of findings from economic research on the costs of raising children:

- spending on children is not fixed but changes as the income of either parent changes;

- the amount a family spends on their children is directly related to the means of both parents;

- spending on children increases as the number of children increases, but the incremental costs associated with each additional child are lower, as the family benefits from economies of scale;

- there is little regional variation in the proportion of family income devoted to children;

- because spending on children is not fixed, but varies with both parents' incomes, the contribution of the support-paying parent can be set independently of the income of the custodial parent. This allows the child to benefit from increases in the custodial parent's standard of living, and recognizes that the support-paying parent will not have a greater capacity to pay support if the custodial parent suffers a drop in income;

- the custodial parent will also contribute to the children in relation to his or her own means. The custodial parent is expected to contribute an amount similar to what a support-paying parent with a similar income would be required to pay.

This new approach to setting child support payments improves upon the existing system in three fundamental ways:

Awards Will be Based on Average Expenditures on Children

Because of the difficulties involved in calculating the *specific* costs of raising a child, the Guidelines are based on studies of *average* costs of raising children. Applying these Guidelines will result in more consistent child support awards across similar income levels and will ensure that more children will receive adequate amounts of child support.

Awards Will Recognize that Expenditures Vary With Income

The amounts set out in the Schedules are based on economic studies which show that spending on children is not fixed, but is directly related to the income level of both parents and to the number of children in the family. Families spend more on their children as family income increases, and spending on children changes with the income of either parent. As well, while overall spending on children increases with the number of children, incremental expenses for additional children are not as high because the family benefits from economies of scale.

Children Will Benefit From the Means of Both Parents

Under the Guidelines, the parents' financial obligations toward the child are treated independently. The support-paying parent's contribution is set according to his or her own income, without reference to the income of the custodial parent. The Schedule awards reflect the amount that a parent with a particular level of income is expected, on average, to spend on his or her children. The custodial parent is expected to contribute a similar share of his or her income to meet the costs of raising the child. In this way, the children will share in increases or decreases in either parent's income, just as they would if the two parents had continued to live together.

Adjustments to the Guideline Amount

Child support guidelines need to have a degree of flexibility, because not all children or families are alike. The federal Guidelines are designed to strike a balance between the need for more consistent and predictable awards, and the need to ensure that awards are equitable in individual situations. Support awards can be adjusted in two ways to recognize individual family circumstances.

Special Child-Related Expenses [See s. 7 of the Guidelines]

While the Child Support Payment Schedules reflect average expenditures on children, some kinds of expenses for children do not lend themselves to averages. To ensure that support awards are equitable when there are extraordinary expenses for a child, four categories of special child-related expenses can be added to the Schedule amount if they are reasonable and necessary in light of the needs of the children and the means of the parents:

- net child care expenses for children . . . ;

- medical and health-related expenses over [$100] per year per child that are not covered by provincial or territorial health insurance plans;

- educational expenses for primary, secondary or post-secondary education, or for an educational program that meets a child's particular needs; and

- extraordinary expenses for extracurricular activities that allow a child to pursue a special interest or talent, or attend a specialized program.

When appropriate, the support-paying parent's contribution to these special expenses will be added to the Schedule amount.

Undue Hardship [See s. 10 of Guidelines]

A court will be able to award more or less than the Schedule amount plus allowable special expenses if this total amount causes "undue hardship" to either parent or to the child. The party pleading undue hardship will . . . have to show that he or she has a lower standard of living than the other party. The situations which might justify a finding of undue hardship are not limited, but could include:

- an unusually high level of debt, reasonably incurred to support the family or earn a living;

- significant access expenses, such as travel or accommodation costs; and

- obligations for the support of other children, or spousal support obligations.

To help ensure consistency, the court will be required to give written reasons for ordering child support that is more or less than the amount set out in the Guidelines.

Adjustments for Special Custody Arrangements [See s. 8 and s. 9 of Guidelines]

The Guidelines will provide a method for adjusting the support amount in cases of split custody (when each parent has custody of one or more children of the marriage) and shared custody (when parents share custody of the child fully and equally).

Application to Existing Child Support Orders

The new Child Support Guidelines will apply to new orders for child support made under the *Divorce Act*, and orders that change existing child support orders, made after the date that the Guidelines come into force.

This means that the new Guidelines and income tax rules for child support will not automatically affect the operation of existing child support orders. If neither parent seeks a change to their existing support order, then the order will not be affected by either the Guidelines or the tax change. However, either parent will be able to apply to a court to have their child support award varied to reflect the Guidelines and the new tax rules. . . .

Four-Year Review of Guidelines

. . . The Guidelines will redefine the way child support awards are determined. To ensure that the Guidelines operate as fairly and effectively as possible, it is important to carefully review their impact. Justice Canada will monitor and evaluate their operation over the first four years after they come into force. All of those who will use the guidelines — parents, mediators, lawyers and judges — will be asked to provide input. Research will be conducted on the impact of the Guidelines. Experience with the Guidelines will provide guidance as to how to further refine them. . . .

As indicated in the above excerpt from the *New Child Support Package*, federal child support guidelines were only part of the reforms announced on March 6, 1996. The government also promised and eventually delivered new rules regarding the taxation of child support.

For over 50 years, a parent receiving child support had been required to include it as part of income for income tax purposes. The paying parent was able to deduct the payments from income. In the majority of cases, this system reduced the two parents' combined income tax by shifting the tax burden from the non-custodial parent, who typically had the higher income and the higher tax rate, to the custodial parent, who tended to have the lower income and lower tax rate. This joint advantage was then supposed to be shared so that more money would be available to the child. Lawyers and judges were to take the tax system into account by "grossing up" the amount of child support to reflect the additional tax burden to the custodial parent due to the income tax shifting.

However, opponents of this system questioned whether these joint tax benefits were actually shared between the two households and claimed that they were often retained by the non-custodial parent. This argument featured prominently in a challenge to the inclusion rule based on s. 15 of the *Charter*. In *Thibaudeau* v. *R.* (1995), 12 R.F.L. (4th) 1, a majority of the Supreme Court of Canada (McLachlin and L'Heureux-Dubé JJ. dissenting) rejected the challenge. For commentary, see Young, "It's All in the Family: Child Support, Tax, and *Thibaudeau*" (1995), 6 Constitutional Forum 107; Argento and St-Hilaire, "Case Comment: *Thibaudeau* v. *R.*" (1995), 5 Can. Current Tax 103; Finnie, "Case Comment: *Thibaudeau* v. *R.*" (1995), 12 R.F.L. (4th) 162; and Wolfson, "Reflections on *R.* v. *Thibaudeau*" (1995), 13 C.F.L.Q. 163. *Symes* v. *Canada*, [1993] 4 S.C.R. 695 involved a challenge to another aspect of the *Income Tax Act*. If both parents earned income, the parent with the lower income could deduct child care expenses up to a maximum of $4,000 per year. Symes, a prominent feminist lawyer, claimed that she should be able to deduct the full expense of hiring a nanny from her income as a business expense. She argued that to earn professional income as a lawyer, she had to incur child care expenses not normally borne by men and that disallowing this deduction as a business expense discriminated against women. The S.C.C. rejected the claim, although it split along gender lines. The seven male justices held that child care expenses were "personal expenses" and not "business expenses". While they accepted that women disproportionately bear the burden of child care, they concluded that it had not been proved that women disproportionately incur child care expenses. The female dissenters concluded that child care expenses were legitimate business expenses. To disallow such a claim would have a differential impact on women and hence would constitute discrimination on the basis of sex contrary to s. 15 of the *Charter*. For commentary, see Eansor and Wydrzynski, "Troubled Waters: Deductibility of Business Expenses under the *Income Tax Act*, Child Care Expenses and *Symes*" (1993), 11 Can. J. Fam. L. 247; McAllister, "The Supreme Court in *Symes*: Two Solitudes" (1994), 4 N.J.C.L. 248; Young, "Child Care: A Taxing Issue?" (1994), 39 McGill L.J. 539; and Young, "Child Care and the Charter: Privileging the Privileged" (1994), 2 Rev. Constit. Studies 20.

Although a minority of separated and divorced parents paid more taxes under the inclusion-deduction system, most did not and it resulted in a loss of tax revenue of approximately $400 million per year. See the *New Child Support Package* (Ottawa: Government of Canada, March 6, 1996) at 9. In other words, the scheme amounted to a state subsidy of $400 million per year to separated and divorced parents.

Child support guidelines could ensure that the tax benefits offered by a deduction/inclusion rule did in fact result in increased child support awards. The Family Law Committee noted in its *Report and Recommendations on Child Support* (Ottawa: 1995) (at 76):

> ... the current deduction/inclusion system offers a *potential* benefit to the majority of divorced families, while the [recommended formula] ensures that this *potential* advantage is — in contrast to the current system of setting child support awards — indeed shared between the two households. In short, by eliminating the deduction/inclusion system there is less money to go around for divorced families, and both sides suffer — while government revenues obviously rise.

Notwithstanding this comment, the Committee indicated it favoured the elimination of the deduction/inclusion system provided that the increased tax revenues were passed on to children.

The Government of Canada announced in the *New Child Support Package* that the inclusion/deduction system would be phased out for the following reasons (at 7):

> ... [I]n the minds of most Canadians — including many support-paying parents — these tax rules no longer make sense. Few Canadians think it is right to tax child support as if it is the custodial parent's own income, or to provide a special tax break to the support-paying parent for performing the ordinary obligations of a parent.
>
> Many of those who participated in the consultations stressed that the tax benefit offered by the existing tax rules to some separated parents is not targeted to reach the children who need it most. As well, complex tax calculations make it more difficult for parents to negotiate a realistic level of support that they both see as fair.
>
> Many payers and recipients of child support also complained that the existing tax rules require the payer to make high monthly payments throughout the year in anticipation of a tax refund at year end, while leaving the recipient to worry about how much of the monthly payments should be set aside to cover the tax owing on them.

Following the tax changes of 1997, child support paid under a written agreement or court order made on or after May 1, 1997 is not deductible to the payor or included in the income of the recipient. Award levels under the new *Federal Child Support Guidelines* are determined on the basis of these new rules.

The new tax rules do not apply to awards made before May 1, 1997 unless:

a)   a court order or agreement made on or after May 1, 1997 changes the amount of child support payable under an existing agreement or court order;

b)   the agreement or court order specifically provides that the new tax rules will apply to payments made after a specified date (which cannot be earlier than April 30, 1997); or

c)   the payer and the recipient both sign and file a form with Revenue Canada (Form T 1157) stating that the new tax rules will apply to payments made after a specified date.

The tax changes do not apply to spousal support, which remains a deduction for the payor and an inclusion for the payee. It is, therefore, necessary to distinguish between spousal and child support in orders made on or after May 1, 1997. Where an amount in a written agreement or court order is not identified as being solely for the support of a spouse, it is treated as child support for income tax purposes.

The new tax rules were anticipated to produce revenue gains of about $15 million in the first year, $65 million in the second year, and $120 million in the third year for the federal government (and similar ones for the provincial governments). In the *New Child Support Package*, the federal government pledged (at 10) that it would "reinvest its anticipated revenue gains from the new tax rules in measures to benefit children. Specifically, they will fund the implementation costs of the Federal Child Support Guidelines and the new enforcement measures as well as, eventually, help to fund the doubling of the Working Income Supplement (WIS) of the Federal Child Tax Benefit."

McLEOD "ANNOTATION"

(1999), 49 R.F.L. (4th) 163

. . . The *Divorce Act* amendments and the Guidelines provide limited opportunities for a court to decide what is "fair" child support. In most cases a court should determine a payor's income and then apply the child-support tables to decide child support. A court may "top up" the Table amount of support to take into account certain special expenses: s. 7 of the Guidelines. The list of special expenses in s. 7 is exhaustive. A court cannot "add on" support for any other activity costs, no matter how beneficial the activity. . . . Although a court has a discretion as to whether to include the cost of a listed expense as "add-on" support, a court cannot reduce the Table amount of support under s. 7 of the Guidelines. A court's only discretion is whether to increase support under s. 7.

Courts also have a discretion to decline to award Guidelines support for an adult child if Guidelines support would be "inappropriate": s. 3(2) of the Guidelines. If a court decides that Guidelines support is inappropriate in a case, it has an unfettered discretion to decide child support. In most cases, when a court decides that Guidelines support is "inappropriate" under s. 3(2) of the Guidelines, the court calculates the total child-care costs and apportions these costs between the parents proportionate to income after taking into account what a child reasonably can contribute. However, the courts have not been able to agree as to when awarding Guidelines support is "inappropriate" under s. 3(2) of the Guidelines. There is authority for departing from the Guidelines where a child attends post-secondary school away from home because awarding Table support plus add-on support for post-secondary education costs would lead to duplication of shelter and food costs. However, not all judges are prepared to accept this as a rule. . . . There seems to be a consensus that Guidelines support is "inappropriate" if a child has sufficient resources to pay his or her post-secondary education expenses and contribute to his or her general expenses.

A court has a discretion not to order the Table amount of support where a payor earns in excess of $150,000 annually: s. 4 of the Guidelines. . . . Although Supreme Court of Canada confirmed [in *Francis* v. *Baker* (1999), 50 R.F.L. (4th) 228] that a court may increase or decrease the table amount of support under s. 4 of the Guidelines, Bastarache J. emphasized that a court should not do so as a matter of course. A court should not routinely require child-care budgets or fine-tune the Table amount of support. A court should depart from the presumptive rule only in clear cases. Practically, if Mr. Baker, who is one of a small number of people in the country earning $1,000,000 annually, could not convince the court to reduce the Table amount of support for two healthy, non-special needs children, it is difficult to anticipate a successful application to reduce support under s. 4 of the Guidelines. Most courts want to keep open the option of departing from the Guidelines even if they do not often do so. Courts dislike absolute rules that prevent them from addressing the equities on a case-by-case basis in family law.

The two most obvious cases where a court has a discretion whether to order child support and how much are ss. 5 and 9 of the Guidelines. Pursuant to s. 5 of the Guidelines, a court may order a person who assumed the role of a parent to pay whatever amount of support a court thinks is reasonable. Many, if not most, spouses form new family relationships when a family relationship breaks down. It was unclear prior to the enactment of the Guidelines how a court should determine step-parent support—in particular, how should a court apportion child support between a natural parent and a step-parent? The courts had not developed a consistent analysis of the issue prior to the enactment of the Guidelines, and the Guidelines provide no assistance in this regard. Section 5 of the Guidelines simply provides that a court may order a step-parent to pay whatever support seems reasonable. So far, the courts have not been able to agree on how to decide step-parent support under the Guidelines or whether a step-parent can have his or her Table support reduced to reflect the natural parent's support obligation.

Section 9 of the Guidelines allows a court to order child support that differs from Guidelines support where a payor has the child with him or her 40 per cent of the time. Section 9 does not explain how a court is to award support in such cases. On balance, most courts have applied s. 9 by analogy to s. 8 of the Guidelines. A court determines what each parent should pay to the other based on his or her income, prorates the amounts of support to reflect the percentage of time with the other parent and sets the two amounts off against each other to determine child support. Most courts add an arbitrary increase of approximately 50 per cent to reflect the increased cost of maintaining two households: cf. *Hunter* v. *Hunter* (1998), 37 R.F.L. (4th) 260 (Ont. Gen. Div.). This makes sense as long as each parent is left with sufficient money to provide a reasonable lifestyle for the child while the child is with him or her. Where this approach does not leave each parent with sufficient money to provide for the child, a court may make whatever order seems fair to reflect the reality of the situation.

Pursuant to s. 10 of the Guidelines, a court may order an amount of support that is different from Guidelines support where awarding Guidelines support would cause "undue hardship" to a parent or the children. The courts have approached s. 10 of the Guidelines with caution. Most judges adopt a high "undue-hardship" threshold to maintain the integrity of the Guidelines. In theory, if the courts had adopted a low undue-hardship threshold, they could easily have circumvented the Guidelines. The courts have continued to maintain this analysis, notwithstanding the fact that they have developed many indirect ways to accomplish what s. 10 of the Guidelines was intended to address. For instance, courts do not often grant undue-hardship relief where a payor complains about high access costs. However, a court may accomplish the same end by making the parents share access costs or arrangements as a condition of custody, especially in mobility cases: *Thorne* v. *Battilana* (April 22, 1999), Doc. FDSJ-909-96 (N.B. Q.B.). By doing so, courts avoid the standard-of-living comparison, which is fatal to most undue-hardship claims. A court cannot grant undue-hardship relief under s. 10 of the Guidelines unless the person seeking relief has a lower household standard of living than the other parent.

NOTES AND QUESTIONS

1. In "Reflections on *R. v. Thibaudeau*" (1995), 13 C.F.L.Q. 163, Lorne Wolfson suggested (at 170): "As unsatisfying as it may be, good old-fashioned judicial discretion may be the most reliable

method of ensuring the provision of fair and reasonable child support." Do you agree? Do you think the *Guidelines* strike the appropriate balance between the need for more consistent and predictable awards and the need for flexibility to ensure that awards are equitable in individual circumstances?

2. Canada's and Ontario's *Guidelines* are examples of a guideline model labelled a "percentage of income" model. It assumes that the custodial parent is making contributions proportionate to his or her income in the same manner as would have occurred without separation or divorce. Quebec has adopted a version of the "income shares" model of child support guidelines, which is prevalent in the United States. Quebec's guidelines apply to all applications under the Civil Code of Quebec and to almost all divorce-related applications. They determine the appropriate amount of child support in accordance with the income of both parents. See Fortin, "Quebec Guidelines for the Determination of Child Support" in *Federal Child Support Guidelines: Reference Manual* (Ottawa: Queen's Printer, 1997) J-1 and Maisonneuve, " Child Support Under the Federal and Quebec Guidelines: A Step Forward or Behind?" (1999), 16 Can. J. Fam. L. 284.

3. As noted earlier, the determination of the payor's income is key to determining the *Guidelines* Table amount. Sections 15 to 20 of the *Guidelines* contain rules for calculating income and ss. 21 to 25 deal with the parties' obligations to provide relevant information.

Determining the income of farmers and small business operators can present special problems. For a sample of the cases, see *Seidlikoski* v. *Hall* (1998), 40 R.F.L (4th) 427 (Sask. Q.B.); *Tidball* v. *Tidball* (1999), 45 R.F.L. (4th) 437 (Ont. Gen. Div.); *Cornelius* v. *Andres* (1999), 45 R.F.L. (4th) 200 (Man. C.A.); and *Rudachyck* v. *Rudachyck* (1999), 47 R.F.L. (4th) 363 (Sask. C.A.).

Cases examining the imputation of income are reviewed in *Lobo* v. *Lobo* (1999), 45 R.F.L. (4th) 366 (Alta. Q.B.). See also McLeod, "Annotation" (1999), 45 R.F.L. (4th) 2, which examines this issue and the calculation of income generally. An interesting case in which the court imputed income is *Montgomery* v. *Montgomery* (2000), 181 D.L.R (4th) 415 (N.S. C.A.). Its DLR headnote reads as follows:

When a husband and wife divorced in 1997, the husband held a managerial position in a government department, earning about $60,000 per year. The court issued a consent order requiring the husband to pay $1,864.33 monthly as combined spousal and child support. In 1999, the husband received an LL.B. which he had been pursuing on a part-time basis since 1990. He obtained an articling position for one year with the provincial government at a salary of approximately $20,000 and applied under s. 17 of the *Divorce Act*, R.S.C. 1985, c. 3 (2nd Supp.) for a variation of the support order. The husband was willing to pay child support based on an income of $20,000 in accordance with the *Federal Child Support Guidelines*, SOR/97-175. Acknowledging that it might take as long as ten years for a beginning government lawyer to achieve a salary equivalent to that of his previous managerial position, the husband suggested that he might pursue private sector employment after his call to the bar. He maintained that his career change stemmed from a desire to secure more satisfying employment, which would, in the long run, result in an increased level of income for himself and his dependants.

The Chambers Judge dismissed the application, holding that income should be imputed to the husband under s. 19(1) (a) of the *Guidelines*. That paragraph allowed the court to impute income where a spouse was intentionally under-employed, but provided an exception if the spouse's action was required by reasonable educational needs. The judge concluded that the husband's actions were not reasonable. In the course of the proceedings, the Chambers Judge occasionally and inadvertently referred to the husband as "the defence" and "the accused". In his oral reasons, he also characterized the husband's argument that the career change would ultimately be financially beneficial as "fanciful".

The husband appealed, alleging that the Chambers Judge had erred in law in his interpretation of s. 19(1) (a) of the *Guidelines* and that the reasons disclosed a reasonable apprehension of bias.

Held, the appeal should be dismissed.

The Chambers Judge made no error of law and his conclusions were fully supported by the facts. A court could impute income under s. 19(1) of the *Guidelines* even if the spouse was not intentionally trying to evade child support obligations or recklessly disregarding the needs of his children. In assessing the reasonableness of the husband's educational needs, all the circumstances, including his children's financial needs, should be considered to ensure that the children received a fair standard of support. The record did not disclose a reasonable apprehension of bias.

See also *Hunt* v. *Smolis-Hunt* (1998), 39 R.F.L. (4th) 143 (Alta. Q.B.). Compare *Woloshyn* v. *Woloshyn* (1996), 22 R.F.L. (4th) 129 (Man. Q.B.). Should the courts in such cases consider whether the fathers can return to their previous employment? Should it make any difference if it is clear that the career change would have occurred even if the family had stayed together?

4. For some recent cases exploring whether child support should be awarded retroactively; that is, for periods preceding the date of judgment, see *Brett* v. *Brett* (1999), 46 R.F.L. (4th) 433 (Ont. C.A.); *S. (L.)* v. *P. (E.)* (1999), 50 R.F.L. (4th) 302 (B.C. C.A.) (where the extensive case law is reviewed); *Schmuck* v. *Reynolds-Schmuck* (1999), 50 R.F.L. (4th) 429 (Ont. S.C.J.); and *Hrabluik* v. *Hrabluik* (1999), 1 R.F.L. (5th) 294 (Man. Q.B.).

5. Where a court is determining applications for both child and spousal support, it must give priority to child support: s. 15.3 of the *Divorce Act* and s. 38.1 of the *FLA*. A court must, therefore, assess child support first and only order spousal support to the extent that there are sufficient funds remaining in the hands of the non-custodial parent after deducting child support. In assessing the non-custodial parent's income for the purpose of determining the Table amount, any spousal support is not deducted if this parent is a payor of spousal support nor included if this person is a recipient of such support: *Schmid* v. *Smith* (1999), 1 R.F.L. (5th) 447, at 453 (Ont. S.C.J.). In that case, Justice Lack indicated that the *Guidelines* create a conundrum in cases where there is a request for both spousal support and an order for apportionment of ''special or extraordinary expenses'' relating to a child under s. 7. The statutory provisions noted above indicate that child support must be determined before spousal support. But the apportionment of special or extraordinary expenses, which is one component of child support, cannot take place until spousal support is assessed. This result flows from the rules for determining income in Schedule III to the *Guidelines*. By virtue of s. 3(2) of this Schedule III, any spousal support paid by the non-custodial parent to the other parent is deducted to calculate that person's income for the apportionment under s. 7. Similarly, for the purposes of s. 7 a parent receiving spousal support from the other parent is required to include the spousal support in his or her income. This latter result occurs because s. 3(1) of Schedule III of the *Guidelines* is not applicable: *Schmid* v. *Smith*. A similar conundrum exists in determining whether undue hardship exists under s. 10 of the *Guidelines* if the court uses Schedule II to compare the living standards of the two households. Justice Lack dealt with these problems by considering the mother's claim for an amount of child support relating to extraordinary expenses and the father's claim for a reduction of child support on the basis of undue hardship at various potential levels of spousal support. He then determined the amount of spousal support that the husband could pay and used that figure in apportioning the extraordinary expenses and assessing the undue hardship claim.

6. As Professor McLeod states in the portion of his annotation reproduced above, the adoption of *Child Support Guidelines* has limited the courts' discretion in awarding child support. Generally, the courts must award the Table amount unless one of the exceptions spelled out applies. However, surprisingly there is now considerable authority for the view that a court still has discretion to determine whether to make a child support order at all. On this view, the *Guidelines* only come into play once the court has answered that threshold question in the affirmative and is determining quantum. In one of the first and most influential cases, the British Columbia Court of Appeal rejected a father's attempt to obtain a variation of a divorce order that existed before the *Guidelines*: *Wang* v. *Wang* (1998), 39 R.F.L. (4th) 426 (B.C. C.A.). The father relied on s. 14(c) of the *Guidelines* which specify that the enactment of the *Guidelines* constitutes a change of circumstances for the purposes of s. 17(4) of the *Divorce Act* where the original order was made before May 1, 1997. He argued that, once he established a change in circumstances, the court was required to vary the order and, by virtue of s. 17(6.1) of the Act, to apply the *Guidelines* unless s. 17(6.2) applied. The B.C. C.A. rejected this analysis on the basis that the court retains a discretionary power to dismiss an application to vary an existing order to make the amount comply with the *Guidelines* where the existing order makes reasonable provision for child support. See

also *Garard* v. *Garard* (1998), 41 R.F.L. (4th) 1 (B.C. C.A.); *Sherman* v. *Sherman* (1999), 45 R.F.L. (4th) 424 (Ont. C.A.); *Browning* v. *Browning* (1999), 47 R.F.L. (4th) 255 (N.S. S.C.); *Baker* v. *Baker* (1999), 49 R.F.L. (4th) 162 (B.C. C.A.); *Strand* v. *Strand* (1999), 50 R.F.L. (4th) 174 (Alta. Q.B.); *Parent* c. *Pelletier* (1999), 1 R.F.L. (5th) 66 (N.B. C.A.); and *Laird* v. *Laird* (2000), 3 R.F.L. (5th) 241 (Alta. C.A.). In *Sherman*, the Ontario Court of Appeal based its decision on its interpretation of s. 14(c) of the *Guidelines*: "This section merely provides a triggering mechanism to permit a review of the circumstances to see whether there is a sufficient change, under the jurisprudence on 'change in circumstances', that a variation should be made in the support payments." However, most of these cases reason that the word "may" in s. 17(1) of the *Divorce Act* gives the courts a discretion not to vary the existing order. This reasoning can then also apply to an application for an original order since s. 15.1(1) of the Act similarly specifies that the court "may" make a child support order. Indeed, in *Fullerton* v. *Fullerton* (1999), 49 R.F.L. (4th) 255 (B.C. C.A.), the B.C. C.A. refused to make a child support order, apparently an original order, under the *Divorce Act* in the face of a "sensible and intelligent bargain" in a separation agreement. See also *Close* v. *Close* (1999), 50 R.F.L. (4th) 342 (N.B. Q.B.), where the court asserts, in *obiter*, that there is a general discretion not to order child support. For critical commentary on these cases, see McLeod, "Annotation" (1999), 45 R.F.L. (4th) 424 and McLeod, "Annotation" (1999), 49 R.F.L. (4th) 163.

The Saskatchewan Court of Appeal, in *Dergousoff* v. *Dergousoff* (1999), 48 R.F.L. (4th) 1 (Sask. C.A.), rejected the approach described in the previous paragraph. The court explained (at 16-18) that the word "may" in ss. 15.1(1) and 17(1) of the *Divorce Act* was not intended to give the courts a discretionary power. Rather, these sections both empowered the courts to act and imposed a duty on them to do so once certain conditions of fact and law existed. See also *Addison* v. *Schneider* (1999), 49 R.F.L. (4th) 181 (Man. Q.B.) and *Vandal* v. *Droppo* (1999), 138 Man. R. (2d) 102 (Man. C.A).

Most recently, a majority of the Ontario Court of Appeal indicated that *Sherman* had been incorrectly decided but left its reconsideration for another day: *Bates* v. *Bates* (June 19, 2000).

7. As noted in the previous chapter, it is doubtful that a court can link access and child support under the *Guidelines*, except perhaps when deciding support for adult children or non-biological children under s. 3(2) and s. 5. In *A. (J.A.)* v. *A. (S.R.)* (1999), 45 R.F.L. (4th) 165 (B.C. C.A.), Madam Justice Southin stated (at 171):

> . . . [T]he law is believed to be that, even if one parent deliberately and maliciously destroys the relationship between the other parent and the children of their marriage, which is what the respondent has done if the allegations [of child abuse] are false, that other parent must still pay the Guidelines amounts. If that is the law, then the law, on this point, lacks a moral basis.

Do you agree?

(2) HIGH INCOME EARNERS

SIMON v. SIMON

(1999), 1 R.F.L. (5th) 119 (Ont. C.A.)

[The parents of a son executed a separation agreement providing that the father, a professional hockey player, would pay the mother $2,200 per month as child support. From this amount, the mother was to place $750 per month in a trust fund for the child's future needs and education. These terms were incorporated into a divorce judgment. The father's income then rose dramatically to over $1,000,000 per year and the mother applied under the *Divorce Act* for an increase in child support to accord with the Table amount of the *Guidelines*, that is, $9,215 per month. The trial judge increased the monthly child support, but only to $5,000. He stressed the uncertainty of the father's future income and suggested that it would not be in the child's best interest to have to adjust to a sudden and dramatic change after experiencing a luxurious lifestyle for a few years. He also increased the trust component of the monthly child support payment to $1,000 per month, even though neither parent asked for a variation of that part of the original order. The mother successfully appealed. MacPherson J.A. wrote the reasons for the Ontario Court of Appeal.]

Introduction

In *Francis* v. *Baker* (1999), 177 D.L.R. (4th) 1 (S.C.C.), the Supreme Court of Canada provided a definitive interpretation of section 4 of the Federal Child Support Guidelines (''the Guidelines''). This provision deals with the situation where the annual income of the spouse against whom a support order is sought is over $150,000. Speaking for a unanimous court, Bastarache J.A. stated at p. 18: ''I find that in all cases Parliament intended that there be a presumption in favour of the Table amounts''. In that case, Mr. Baker was unable to rebut this presumption. He had an income of $945,000 at the relevant time. The trial judge had applied the Table amount to this income and ordered Mr. Baker to pay $10,000 per month in child support for his two children. The Supreme Court of Canada upheld this decision.

The principal question raised by the present appeal is whether *Francis* v. *Baker* should be applied in a situation where the parent paying support earns a very high income (approximately $1,400,000), but is quite young, has not accumulated substantial assets, and is pursuing a career characterized by uncertainty and risk (professional hockey player). A secondary issue raised by the appeal is whether a portion of the support payments should be placed in a trust fund with a view to safeguarding the child's future financial situation in light of the uncertainty about the father's ability to maintain his high income for many years. . . .

B. Issues

The issues raised by this appeal are:

(1) Did Kealey J. err by not increasing the monthly child support payment for Mitchell Simon from $2,200 to $9,215, the Table amount in the Guidelines?

(2) Did Kealey J. err when he increased the trust component of the monthly child support payment for Mitchell Simon from $750 to $1,000?

C. Analysis

(1) The Monthly Child Support Issue

. . . Kealey J. applied s. 4(b) of the Guidelines. He found that the Table amount of $9,215 was inappropriate. In reaching this conclusion, Kealey J. was influenced by factors relating to Mitchell, his father and his mother.

With respect to Mitchell, the judge said (Reasons, at p. 4):

It seems to me in determining what is ''appropriate'' under the Guidelines, that I consider the question from a long-term perspective and avoid deciding the matter on immediate and short-term considerations only. Mitchell will likely require the support of his father financially for another twenty years and probably for most of that period Mitchell's dad will not be earning anywhere near $1,000,000 U.S. per annum. In my opinion, it would be unfair and clearly not in the best interests of any child to experience luxuries and a lifestyle that will be of relatively short duration and then suddenly reduced.

Concerning Mr. Simon, the judge said that he was influenced by three factors (Reasons, at p. 3):

1. The sudden, extreme increase in the father's income.
2. The certainty of such an increased income level for two years only (perhaps a third) [under his contract with the Washington Capitals].
3. The precariousness of the future income predictability.

With respect to Ms. Simon, the judge was critical of the budget she presented to the court (Reasons, at p. 4):

> The applicant mother has not provided a reasonable credible child support budget. No sensible basis is offered for the child's activities and expenses claimed at $10,000 a year, for his clothing of $6,000 and many other alleged increases to the child's cost of care.

The appellant contends that Kealey J.'s reasoning on all of these points was faulty in light of the decision of the Supreme Court of Canada in *Francis* v. *Baker*. In essence, I agree with this submission; however, it needs to be stated that Kealey J. did not have the benefit of the Supreme Court's reasons in *Francis* v. *Baker* when he made his decision in the present case.

Kealey J.'s crucial error, in my view, was the imposition of a heavy burden on Ms. Simon to justify her child care budget. This is inconsistent with *Francis* v. *Baker* which establishes that the burden is on the paying spouse to demonstrate that the Table amount is inappropriate. As expressed by Bastarache J., at pp. 20-21:

> In my opinion, a proper balance is struck by requiring paying parents to demonstrate that budgeted child expenses are so high as to "exceed the generous ambit within which reasonable disagreement is possible": *Bellenden* v. *Satterthwaite*, [1948] 1 All E.R. 343, at p. 345.

Moreover, Kealey J. was selectively critical of individual items in Ms. Simon's budget. He singled out the items relating to Mitchell's activities and expenses ($10,000) and his clothing ($6,000) for particular criticism. This, too, is inconsistent with *Francis* v. *Baker*. Dealing with child expense budgets, Bastarache J. said, at p. 20:

> [T]here is nothing objectionable *per se* about recognizing that trial judges have the discretion to require custodial parents to produce child expense budgets in cases in which s. 4 of the Guidelines is invoked. Along with other factors, these budgets speak to the reasonable needs of the children, a factor expressly included in s. 4(b)(ii). What is objectionable, however, is that in the pre-Guidelines jurisprudence, custodial parents often had the burden of proving the reasonableness of each budgeted expense on a balance of probabilities. As explained above, under the Guidelines, custodial parents are entitled to the Table amount unless that amount is shown to be inappropriate. It follows that, while child expense budgets may be required under s. 4 in order to allow for a proper assessment of the children's needs, *custodial parents need not justify each and every budgeted expense. Courts should be wary of discarding the figures included in their budgets too quickly.* [Emphasis added.]

I make one other observation about the judge's criticism of the child's activities and clothing items in Ms. Simon's budget. He said that there was "no sensible basis" offered for these items. That is true in relation to the clothing item; however, in the cross-examination of Ms. Simon on her affidavit, she was not asked any questions about this item. So she had no opportunity to explain the amount she attributed to Mitchell's clothing. With respect to Mitchell's activities, Ms. Simon explained this item in some detail in her cross-examination. It included attendance at summer camp, skating lessons, golf lessons, music lessons, Scouts and, in a slightly longer time frame, hockey expenses. In light of this explanation, it seems somewhat unfair to employ the phrase "no sensible basis" unless reasons for this harsh conclusion were offered.

Turning to Kealey J.'s assessment of Mr. Simon's situation, in my view the judge did not consider the factor explicitly set out in s. 4(b)(ii) of the Guidelines, namely "the financial ability of each spouse to contribute to the support of the child". Instead, the judge got sidetracked into irrelevant factors—the sudden increase in Mr. Simon's salary and the possible uncertainty of its continuation because of the precariousness of a professional hockey career.

There is no question that Mr. Simon has the financial ability to pay the Table amount of support for Mitchell. Mr. Simon's counsel candidly acknowledged as much in his oral argument. Mr. Simon's income in 1997 was over $100,000 Canadian *monthly*. It is obvious that a monthly support payment of $9,215 would impose no hardship on him.

The other factors relied on by the judge—sudden increase in salary, uncertainty about Mr. Simon's salary in the future—are, in my view, irrelevant. The Table amounts are determined by *the income* of the paying spouse. Mr. Simon's income in June 1997 was $1,000,000 U.S. If it changes in the future, he can apply to have the child support order varied. It should not be effectively varied in advance by a judge speculating about his future income.

As I said at the outset, I agree with the appellant's submission that the present appeal is governed by the reasoning and result in *Francis* v. *Baker*. The respondent contends otherwise. In his factum he seeks to distinguish *Francis* v. *Baker* in this fashion:

> It is respectfully submitted that unlike the lifestyle enjoyed by Mr. Baker, Ms. Francis and their children, the lifestyle of Chris Simon, Lauri Simon and Mitchell Simon is to say the least modest. There is no dispute, indeed it is conceded that the Respondent herein receives a substantial income from professional hockey. On the other hand, it is submitted that he lives a moderate lifestyle. He has engaged a financial advisor to plan for the future. Unlike the children of Ms. Francis and Mr. Baker, Mitchell Simon has not enjoyed "the lavish life."

I disagree with this submission. Its error is that it emphasizes the paying spouse's lifestyle, not his income. Mr. Simon has an exceptionally high income. It is this income that s. 4 of the Guidelines requires be considered in a child support context. The wording of s. 4 is clear — the touchstones are "the income of the spouse against whom a child support order is sought" and "the financial ability of each spouse". How Mr. Simon uses his very high income once he has met his child support obligations is his own business. If he decides, contrary to Mr. Baker, to live modestly and invest most of his income with a view to his post-hockey future, that is certainly a commendable decision. However, it does not diminish his obligation to his son. The son's needs, and Mr. Simon's income and ability to pay, are the only factors relevant in an analysis under s. 4 of the Guidelines. Mr. Simon's current lifestyle is irrelevant.

Ms. Simon and Mitchell have had a difficult time since Mr. Simon ended the marriage five years ago when Ms. Simon was pregnant. For a time, before Mr. Simon provided support, they were on welfare. For several years, Mr. Simon paid $2,200 per month in child support. Ms. Simon's application to vary this amount was made at a time when Mitchell would be about to embark on school, sports, clubs and other activities. Her budget is, in my view, a reasonable one. The best evidence of this is the fact that the most expensive item she seeks, namely the means to buy a $200,000 home in Ottawa, is a modest request.

Mr. Simon, on the other hand, is in wonderful financial shape. His monthly salary is more that $100,000. He has no other dependants. Moreover, it should be emphasized that Mr. and Ms. Simon were married for three years. Mitchell is a child of their union. The Simons were a family. Viewed from Mr. Simon's perspective, supporting his son to the tune of less than 10 percent of his income does not seem unreasonable.

Francis v. *Baker* establishes that "in all cases Parliament intended that there be a presumption in favour of the Table amounts" (at p. 18). Based on the record before Kealey J., Mr. Simon had not rebutted the presumption. Accordingly, the judge erred by setting child support for Mitchell at $5,000 per month rather than $9,215, the Table amount.

(2) The Trust Issue

When the parties separated in 1994, they agreed that Mr. Simon would make child support payments of $2,200 per month. They also agreed that $750 of this amount would be placed in a trust fund to be saved for Mitchell's care and education after Mr. Simon's career as a professional hockey player had ended. This provision of the separation agreement became part of the divorce judgment on June 22, 1995.

In his decision on October 17, 1997, Kealey J. increased the amount that would have to be paid into the trust account to $1,000 per month. In my view, this component of the judge's decision was incorrect, for two reasons.

First, neither party asked for a variation of this provision of the separation agreement and divorce judgment. Both Ms. Simon's application and Mr. Simon's counter-application were silent on this point. The judge should not have varied a divorce judgment in a way neither party sought.

Second, I do not think that the discretion of the custodial parent with respect to the expenditure of child support monies should be fettered unless the non-custodial parent can establish a valid reason for doing so.

Counsel for Mr. Simon brought to our attention several American authorities in which judges have placed substantial components of child support payments in trust accounts in cases where the paying spouse was a professional athlete earning a very high income: see *T.(J.)* v. *D.(K.)*, 16 Fam. L. Rep. (BNA) 1046 (N.Y. Fam. Ct. 1989); *Branch* v. *Jackson* (1993), 629 A.2d 170 (U.S. Pa. Super.); *O. (M.L.)* v. *B. (T.R.)* (1996), 544 N.W.2d 417 (U.S. Wis.).

It may be that in some cases a court imposed trust to secure funds for a child's future care and education would be appropriate. However, in my view, absent a good reason for imposing a trust, the court should not do so. The presumption should be that a custodial parent will do his or her best to provide for both the child's immediate needs and his or her future care and education. Unless there is strong evidence establishing the need for a trust (e.g. the misuse of support payments by the custodial parent), I see no reason to interfere with the way in which the parent balances the present and future needs of the child in his or her custody.

A recent decision of the Saskatchewan Court of Appeal provides a helpful analysis on the trust issue. In *Bachorick* v. *Verdejo* [(1999), 175 D.L.R. (4th) 633 (Sask. C.A.)], a chambers judge ordered a father to pay $650 per month for each of two children into an education trust fund to be used for post-secondary educational requirements. This amount was to be deducted from the Table amount of $3,233.28 which the judge ordered the father to pay. The mother appealed the trust component of the chambers judge's decision.

The Saskatchewan Court of Appeal allowed the appeal on the trust issue. After a careful analysis of the philosophy of child support pre- and post- Guidelines, Jackson J.A. said, at pp. 641 and 642:

If a court were to assume the authority to make an order that a portion of maintenance must be set aside for the education needs of the children, it would seriously erode the certainty which the Guidelines seek to achieve.

In order to make a deduction from maintenance for future needs, a court must be satisfied that the maintenance amount exceeds the daily needs of the children. To be satisfied of this, the court would have to assess the budget of the custodial parent to determine where funds will be used and weigh the appropriateness of the expenditures based on some scale. This introduces into the process the very level of complexity, subjectivity and controversy the Guidelines were intended to eliminate.

A direction of this nature also raises questions about the extent to which a court should control the spending priorities of the custodial spouse. Prior to the Guidelines, the custodial parent submitted a budget, but this was only for the purposes of establishing quantum. Once the level of the maintenance was established, the custodial parent was at liberty to spend the maintenance according to parental dictates. The court did not compel the custodial parent to account for how the funds would ultimately be used. It would have been a rare case where a court would find it necessary to find a mechanism to control that spending. The Guidelines have not changed this basic principle.

. . .

Having regard for the continuing obligation to support dependent children, the purpose of maintenance, the purpose and the objectives of the Guidelines and the courts reluctance to interfere with the spending priorities of the custodial parent, the authority to make an order as was made in this case, if it exists, should be rarely exercised. On the facts of the case on appeal, there was no basis upon which the chambers judge could make the order establishing the trust fund. Once he determined that the amount established by the Guidelines was not inappropriate, he could not order that a portion of the maintenance award be paid into a trust fund.

I agree with all of this excellent analysis. In the present appeal, the Table amount of $9,215 is not unreasonable. Nor is there any evidence that Ms. Simon is not a responsible, dedicated and unselfish custodial parent. Accordingly, there was no reason for the judge to interfere with the decision the parents made about a trust fund when they separated and subsequently divorced.

Disposition

The appeal is allowed. The respondent is to pay child support for his son, Mitchell Simon, in the amount of $9,215 per month.

. . .The provisions of the judgment varying the trust provisions of the separation agreement and subsequent divorce judgment are deleted, thereby restoring the original provisions of the separation agreement and divorce judgment.

McLEOD, "ANNOTATION"

(2000), 1 R.F.L. (5th) 121

MacPherson J.A.'s reasons for judgment in *Simon* v. *Simon* fit well with Bastarache J.'s reasons for judgment in *Francis* v. *Baker* (1999), 50 R.F.L. (4th) 228 (S.C.C.) to explain how s. 4 of the *Federal Child Support Guidelines* works. The upshot seems to be that although a high-income payor may apply to reduce the Table amount of support under s. 4 of the Guidelines, he or she is unlikely to succeed. The Ontario Court of Appeal's decision to order the father to pay the Table amount of child support in *Simon* is even more difficult to understand than was the Supreme Court of Canada's decision to do so in *Francis* v. *Baker*. . . .

The Ontario Court of Appeal held that Kealey J.'s decision did not reflect the Supreme Court of Canada's decision in *Francis* v. *Baker*. In particular, Kealey J. erred in imposing a burden on the mother to justify the amount of support and her alleged child-care budget. The onus is on a paying parent to convince a court that the Table amount of support is excessive, not on the receiving parent to prove that he or she needs the Table amount of support. With respect, it is unrealistic to put the entire burden of proving that Guidelines support is excessive on the payor. The payee has all of the information about the child's actual and proposed lifestyle. He or she is the one who will be spending the money when it is received and has the best evidence as to how he or she plans to do so.

Child support belongs to the child and is meant to provide for the child's lifestyle expenses. A payee parent is a trustee of the child support received and there is nothing unreasonable about expecting a payee to explain how he or she plans to use the money to maintain the child.

When a proposal does not correspond with common sense, the onus should be on the person asserting the position to explain why his or her position is reasonable or, at least, not unreasonable in the circumstances of the case. In a family setting, $9,200 monthly after tax seems like a lot of money to spend on a five-year-old child with no special needs. Indeed, $9,000 monthly after tax seems like a lot of money to spend on any person! This is the thrust of the father's argument that the sheer size of the award raises an inference that it is excessive. The amount exceeds what most people consider necessary to maintain a child. . . . At some point, the amount of money had no reference to a child's needs and did not reflect any of the objectives of a child-support order.

The Ontario Court of Appeal accepts that a trial judge has a discretion to require a payee parent to file a child-care budget to explain how he or she plans to apportion the child support. However, it appears that a payee does not have to justify the reasonableness of the expenses set out in the budget. MacPherson J.A. adopts Bastarache J.'s analysis in *Francis* v. *Baker* that a payee is entitled to receive the Table amount of support unless a payor can convince a judge that the budgeted expenses are unreasonable. With respect, this does not really address the substance of Kealey J.'s concern. He decided that some of the budgeted expenses were unreasonable, not just that the mother did not prove that her expenses were reasonable. As a matter of practice, a payee asserts budgeted expenses as part of a child's reasonable lifestyle and a payor attacks expenses as unreasonable in the circumstances. While the distinction as to who has the onus of proof in respect of maintaining or attacking a child-care budget is important in law, the distinction is blurred in practice. The important issues are whether the budget expenses are unreasonable and, if so, what effect that should have on the quantum of child support.

The Ontario Court of Appeal confirms that a payor who wants to reduce the Table amount of support has the onus of convincing a court that the amount is excessive. However, MacPherson J.A. does not explain how a payor is supposed to do this. In *Francis* v. *Baker*, the Supreme Court of Canada rejected the father's submission that a court may infer that the Table amount of support is excessive solely on the basis of the sheer size of the award. This means that a payor has to prove that the Table amount is excessive, given the reasonable needs and expectations of the particular child in the case. The only way to do this is to present what the payor thinks is a fair budget and compare this to the Table amount of support. Alternatively, a court may adopt the family law equivalent of "res ipsa loquitur" and require a payee to produce a proposed child-care budget where the Table amount of support exceeds the amount that experience suggests children in similarly placed families require. This type of analysis is a variation of the ''sheer size of the award'' argument unsuccessfully advanced by the payor father in *Francis* v. *Baker*, except that this time the payor is not asking a judge to reduce support on the basis of the sheer size of the award but only to require the payee to provide a budget that explains how the money will be spent. The payor must then prove that the proposed apportionment of funds is ''unsuitable'', ''inappropriate'' or ''excessive''.

MacPherson J.A. suggests at para. 24 that Kealey J. put the entire onus on the mother to justify her expenses. If this is correct, the Court of Appeal was right to intervene. However, it is unusual in practice for all of the budget evidence to come from a payee. Inevitably, payors devote large amounts of time to reviewing a proposed budget and trying to convince the presiding judge that the proposed budget is ''unreasonable''.

The more interesting question is whether the court would have agreed to reduce the Table amount of support even if it was satisfied that the mother did not ''need'' the Table amount of support to maintain the child. I suspect not. The Guidelines change the way courts decide child support. A court now transfers a share of a payor's income to a payee as ''the child's share'' of the payor's income. Child support is now a form of wealth transfer, not a means to provide sufficient money to meet a particular child's needs. Unfortunately, neither the Supreme Court of Canada nor the Ontario Court of Appeal was prepared to address what happens if the Table amount of support clearly exceeds a child's reasonable needs.

With respect, this oversight probably doesn't matter in practice. If Mr. Simon cannot convince the Court of Appeal that $9,200 is excessive support for a five-year-old child with no special needs or skills, no one will be able to convince a court that the Table amount of support is ''excessive''.

At para. 29, MacPherson J.A. states that the historical family lifestyle and the payor father's current lifestyle are irrelevant to determining child support under s. 4 of the Guidelines. That Mr. Simon decides to live modestly and to invest most of his income for his future, while commendable, does not alter his child-support obligation. This is not a case of a payor's changing his or her lifestyle after separation in order to limit his or her child-support obligation. The payor and the rest of the family had lived modestly. The parents jointly determined the family lifestyle while the family was intact. Following family breakdown, the payor apparently no longer has any input into a child's lifestyle. The payor pays the money and the payee can establish any lifestyle he or she can afford.

Having said that ''need'' and ''ability to pay'' are the only considerations under s. 4 of the Guidelines, MacPherson J.A. states simply that the mother's budget is reasonable. Her application to increase support from $2,200 monthly comes at a time when the child is about to embark on school, sports, clubs and other activities. With respect, the suggestion that these activities for a five-year-old cost $9,000 monthly is so far from most people's reality that MacPherson J.A. should have addressed the child's ''need'' in more detail. He goes on to note that the most expensive item the payee seeks is a $200,000 home in Ottawa, which is a modest request. It may be a modest request on the father's income, but how does it compare to the father's home? More importantly, if the mother acquires the house in her name, child support is being used to acquire a capital asset for a custodial parent. If the house is held in trust for the child, the money at least is being used for the child's needs, albeit still to acquire a capital asset. Historically, courts disapproved awarding child support to acquire capital assets. Although MacPherson J.A. does not come right out and say it, this objection probably is no longer available to defend a child-support claim.

The father clearly has the ability to pay $9,000 monthly child support. However, MacPherson J.A.'s suggestion that the amount the father is required to pay as child support is less than 10 per cent of his $100,000 U.S. monthly income is misleading. Child support is expressed in after-tax dollars, while the payor's income is expressed in pre-tax income. On current Canadian taxation rates, the father would have to earn almost $20,000 [per month] to pay $9,000 monthly. Even taking current exchange rates into account, this is still significantly more than 10 per cent of his income. . . .

The other point that is not addressed in *Simon* is that the payor's income-earning life span is condensed. Professional athletes have a limited time when they can earn large amounts of money. Mr. Simon is a specialty player. He cannot expect his huge income to continue for more than a few years. He is doing the responsible thing by setting money aside for the future. He did not change dramatically his historical lifestyle. If he spent his money as if there were no tomorrow and then applied to reduce support when the large income ended, he would be expected to explain why he did not employ responsible fiscal management. However, paradoxically, he is not allowed to claim a reduction in support at the present time to reflect that he employs responsible fiscal management.

The Court of Appeal also disapproved Kealey J.'s setting aside part of the child support for future use. MacPherson J.A. states that Kealey J. was incorrect to do so for two reasons. First, neither party asked for a variation of the trust provision of the separation agreement and a court should not vary a divorce judgment in a way neither party sought. With respect, the wife forfeited her right to rely on the agreement when she claimed support contrary to the terms of the agreement. She had a choice: she could try to maintain the agreement or she could ask a court to award Guidelines support contrary to the terms of the agreement. She opted for the latter. . . .

The second reason proposed for striking the trust provision has more merit. MacPherson J.A. states that a court should not fetter a custodial parent's discretion as to how to spend child support unless there is a valid reason to do so. MacPherson J.A. acknowledges that a court has the discretion to limit how a parent spends child support, but the onus is on a payor to convince a court that there is a valid reason to do so. In this case, presumably, the reason is that the large income will not continue indefinitely. It is not in the child's best interests to go from extreme luxury to a modest lifestyle. Just as Mr. Simon employs responsible fiscal management to provide for the future to reflect the transitory nature of his income, his son should employ responsible fiscal management to reflect the transitory nature of the high child support. As the child is too young to do this, someone must do it for him. If the custodial mother's budget does not show that she has made plans to set aside funds for the child's future, a court should be able to step in and do so. The main consideration should be the child's needs and interests over the long term, not the mother's freedom to spend child support as she sees fit.

Admittedly, courts should not routinely limit a payee's discretion as to how to apportion child support. In most cases, there is not enough money to meet current needs, let alone put money away for the future. However, *Simon* is not "most cases". The child does not need $9,200 monthly to maintain a comfortable lifestyle. The reality is that the mother will enjoy the benefit of the child support indirectly by sharing the child's lifestyle. She also has direct access to the child-support money that is not spent on the child's needs. With numbers this large, a judge may realistically be concerned that money not spent on the child's needs will just get spent, with nothing to show for it. This seems to have been the issue in *Simon*.

MacPherson J.A. all but removes a presiding judge's discretion to decide what form of order is in a child's best interests. He states that unless there is strong reason to believe the contrary, a court should assume that a custodial parent will do his or her best to provide for the child's short-term and long-term interests: para. 38. The inference is that a payor must prove that there is a real risk of the payee's misuse of child support to justify limiting the payee's discretion as to how to spend the money. This will not be possible in most cases. Apparently, the court rejects the alternative that a judge may impose a trust to provide for a child's future if this seems to be in a child's best interests in a case, without proof of fault. A custodial parent's freedom of choice outweighs a judge's view of a child's best interests.

The Ontario Court of Appeal's refusal to maintain the trust contribution reflects the courts' unwillingness to engage in an assessment of children's needs on a case-by-case basis. A court should not put money into trust that is needed as daily child support. Accordingly, as MacPherson J.A. notes at paras. 39-41, a court cannot transfer money into trust without first ensuring that the money is not needed at the present time. To do so may result in a return to the old needs-and-means support model, which is rejected under the Guidelines. There is merit to this position as a general proposition. However, when a court is dealing with large amounts of support as in *Simon*, the wording of s. 4 of the Guidelines anticipates that a judge will at least decide whether the Guidelines approach is "suitable" or whether a court should depart from the presumptive Guidelines support.

The Ontario Court of Appeal is unwilling to give any substance to the discretion under s. 4 of the Guidelines as to deciding either quantum of support or the form of a support order. This reflects Bastarache J.'s reasons in *Francis* v. *Baker*, supra. While there is no doubt that maintaining the presumptive amount of support and the Guidelines approach will promote consistency and reduce litigation, doing so also fundamentally alters the nature of child support. Support is now an automatic transfer of a share of a payor's income, regardless of need or ability to pay in most cases. What little discretion exists under the Guidelines may be exercised only in as yet undefined extraordinary circumstances.

It is as difficult to have any sympathy for Mr. Simon as it was for Mr. Baker. Both men earn huge amounts of money and can afford the child support ordered. The concern in *Simon* is for the child's future and the status of child-support law. When Mr. Simon's income decreases, he should be able to reduce his support. This means that the child's lifestyle will decline dramatically, unless the mother has employed responsible fiscal management. Maintaining the trust in the case would have removed this concern. More fundamentally, the Guidelines appear to change our concept of child support. Even where a court has a discretion, need does not appear to be a significant consideration. . . .

NOTES AND QUESTIONS

1. For other recent cases dealing with high income earners, see *Greenwood* v. *Greenwood* (1998), 37 R.F.L. (4th) 422 (B.C. S.C.); *Hollenbach* v. *Hollenbach* (1999), 47 R.F.L. (4th) 39 (B.C. S.C.); *Ferreira* v. *Ouellet* (1999), 48 R.F.L. (4th) 75 (B.C. S.C.); *Andrews* v. *Andrews* (1999), 50 R.F.L. (4th) 1 (Ont. C.A.); and *McCrea* v. *McCrea* (1999), 1 R.F.L. (5th) 320 (B.C. S.C.). The *Guidelines* table amount was ordered in all these cases except *Hollenbach*.

2. In *Bachorick* v. *Verdejo* (1999), 175 D.L.R. (4th) 633 (Sask. C.A.), the Saskatchewan Court of Appeal questioned, without deciding, the jurisdiction of the courts to make an order requiring the custodial parent to put some of the money received as child support into a trust fund. The Ontario Court of Appeal noted this in *Simon*, but "was content to proceed" on the parties' assumption that there was

such jurisdiction. Should the court only make such orders where the custodial parent is not "responsible" and "unselfish"? In *Hollenbach*, Smith J. suggested (at 55) that, in response to a claim that the Table amount was inappropriate for the purpose of s. 4 of the *Guidelines*, "a custodial parent might well propose that a percentage of savings be set aside from the table amount of child support in order to secure the future needs of the children where a payor's source of income is unpredictable or subject to ongoing fluctuations."

(3) SPECIAL OR EXTRAORDINARY EXPENSES

McLAUGHLIN v. McLAUGHLIN
(1998), 44 R.F.L. (4th) 148 (B.C. C.A.)

[The couple had three children: Dana (aged 16), Kimberly (aged 14), and Sean (aged 8). The mother earned $50,000 per year and the father's annual income was $70,000. The table amount was $1,722 per month. The chambers judge ordered the father to pay $509.88 per month as additional child support under s. 7 of the *Guidelines*. The father appealed. Justice Prowse gave the reasons for the court.]

. . .The "Notes" to Schedule 1 of the Guidelines state that there are separate tables for each province because of differences in provincial income tax rates. The "Notes" also attempt to explain the basis upon which the tables operate. Notes 5 and 6 provide:

> 5. The amounts in the tables are based on economic studies of average spending on children in families at different income levels in Canada. They are calculated on the basis that child support payments are no longer taxable in the hands of the receiving parent and no longer deductible by the paying parent. They are calculated using a mathematical formula and generated by a computer program.

> 6. The formula referred to in note 5 sets support amounts to reflect average expenditures on children by a spouse with a particular number of children and level of income. The calculation is based on the support payor's income. The formula uses the basic personal amount for non-refundable tax credits to recognize personal expenses, and takes other federal and provincial income taxes and credits into account. Federal Child Tax benefits and Goods and Services Tax credits for children are excluded from the calculation. At lower income levels, the formula sets the amounts to take into account the combined impact of taxes and child support payments on the support payer's limited disposable income.

I will refer to the nature of this "formula" later in my reasons.

(c) Section 7(1)(f) of the Guidelines
(i) Introduction

It is apparent from my perusal of many of the dozens of cases decided under s. 7(1)(f) across the country that judges in British Columbia and elsewhere have been struggling to find some principled basis for deciding what expenses can properly be added to the base table amounts as "extraordinary expenses" within the meaning of s. 7(1)(f). The inability of judges to ascertain what Parliament intended to be included as ordinary expenses for extracurricular activities under the tables has resulted in a variety of approaches to the interpretation of s. 7(1)(f) with an accompanying inconsistency in results.

I will begin my analysis by referring to a few of the authorities which discuss s. 7(1)(f) in order to illustrate the different approaches which courts have taken to the interpretation of the words "extraordinary expenses". I will then set forth my view of the preferred approach to the interpretation of s. 7(1)(f). Finally, I will examine the expenses claimed by Ms. McLaughlin to determine whether the chambers judge erred in allowing them in whole or in part.

(ii) The Authorities

In fairness to the chambers judge, I note that many of the authorities to which I will refer, including decisions of the Courts of Appeal of Manitoba, Nova Scotia, Saskatchewan and Alberta, were decided subsequent to his decision.

In *Middleton* v. *MacPherson* (1997), 150 D.L.R. (4th) 519, 29 R.F.L. (4th) 334 (Alta. Q.B.), Madam Justice Moreau dealt with several issues arising under the Guidelines, including the interpretation of s. 7(1)(f). One question involved the determination of what were "extraordinary expenses for education" under s. 7(1)(d). Although s. 7(1)(d) is not in issue in this appeal, this aspect of Moreau J.'s analysis is apposite insofar as it discusses the meaning to be given to the words "extraordinary expenses", which appear in s. 7(1)(f).

After observing that it would be easier to determine what constituted an extraordinary expense if there were some indication in the Guidelines of what expenses were taken into account in setting the basic table amounts, Moreau J. resorted to dictionary definitions of the word "extraordinary". These definitions included: "exceptional"; "surprising"; "unusually great"; and "going beyond what is usual, regular, or customary". Madam Justice Moreau then noted that an expense which was not extraordinary for a family with a joint income of $60,000 per year could well be regarded as extraordinary for a family with a joint income of only $25,000 per year. In other words, she treated the combined incomes of the parties as a relevant factor in assessing whether expenses were extraordinary. In the result, she concluded that no hard-and-fast rules could be applied in determining whether expenses under s. 7(1)(d) were extraordinary, but that each case should be decided on its facts.

On the evidence before her, Moreau J. took into account the joint incomes of the parties ($45,000 per year), and concluded that expenses for lunch supervision, field trips, skiing, swimming, viola rental and private music lessons which extended beyond the basic school program, should be categorized as "extraordinary".

The next issue before Moreau J. involved s. 7(1)(f) of the Guidelines, and was framed as follows:

> Can expenses be classified as "extraordinary expenses" if the activity is purely recreational or is it necessary that such expense be related to a special talent of the child?

Madam Justice Moreau concluded that the wording of the section did not warrant restricting the expenses under s. 7(1)(f) to those involving a child's special talent. She concluded an expense of $615 per year for ballet was not a negligible expense having regard to the joint incomes of the parents, and that it qualified as an extraordinary expense under s. 7(1)(f).

In my view, the significance of Madam Justice Moreau's decision is that she relied on the combined incomes of the parents as an important factor in determining whether an expense claimed under s. 7(1)(f) was "extraordinary".

In *Sanders* v. *Sanders* (1998), 42 R.F.L. (4th) 239 (Alta. C.A.), the Alberta Court of Appeal adopted Madam Justice Moreau's approach to s. 7 expenses. At para. 11 of the Sanders decision, the Court stated:

> There are further claims under s. 7 for basketball registration, school registration, school supplies, and camp expenses. Given the total income of the parties [approximately $96,000] and using the

approach followed in *Middleton* v. *MacPherson*, these items cannot be categorized as extraordinary expenses.

The Nova Scotia Court of Appeal addressed s. 7 of the Guidelines in *Raftus* v. *Raftus* (1998), 159 D.L.R. (4th) 264 (N.S. C.A.). In that case, the mother applied for an additional $175 per month in child support under s. 7(1)(f) for three children aged 14, 11 and 8. The expenses totalled $2,259 annually and included amounts for swimming ($230), soccer ($160.50), Tae Kwan Do ($399), school activities ($420), and birthdays, Christmas and special events ($1,050). The mother had remarried and was not employed outside the home; the father was employed as a longshoreman earning $78,000 per year. The basic amount which the father was required to pay under the Guideline tables was $1,321 per month.

The trial judge in *Raftus* found that these expenses did not fall under s. 7(1)(f) of the Guidelines. The Court of Appeal dismissed the mother's appeal. Flinn J.A. wrote for the majority; Bateman J.A. wrote separate concurring reasons. . . .

Madam Justice Bateman . . . preferred an approach which took into consideration the expense of the activity in relation to the parents' incomes in determining whether it was extraordinary.

In response to the mother's submission that the quantum of support stipulated under the basic table was inadequate to provide for extracurricular activities, Madam Justice Bateman made the following observations at pp. 272-73:

> The Table amounts are fixed by a formula that calculates the appropriate amount of support in light of economic data on average expenditures for children across different income levels. There is no suggestion in the explanatory material that preceded and accompanied the implementation of the *Guidelines*, nor in the *Guidelines* themselves, that the child support amounts were fixed in accordance with the average cost of only a child's food, shelter and clothing. The wording of s. 7 is consistent with an inference that the Table amount of support is intended to include the payor's reasonable contribution to expenses for extracurricular activities and school/education expenses that are not extraordinary. An "intact" family's ability to fund extracurricular activities logically correlates with income. At lower income levels there is less discretionary income to accommodate a child's extracurricular activities. The increase in the Table amounts as the payor's income rises, must be intended to address greater participation in extracurricular activities, in addition to increased clothing, food and shelter costs. If the Table amounts require adjustment to provide adequately in this regard, this is to be done by amendment to the *Regulations* and not by judicial intervention.

Madam Justice Bateman recognized that assessing an expense on purely objective criteria to determine whether it was extraordinary would reduce litigation, and, in that respect, would promote one goal of the Guidelines, namely, "to reduce conflict and tension between spouses by making the calculation of child support orders more objective." In her view, however, such an approach would not promote another objective of the Guidelines: "to establish a fair standard of support for children that ensures they continue to benefit from the financial means of both spouses after separation." In concluding that the parents' combined incomes should be taken into consideration in determining whether an expense is "extraordinary", she stated at pp. 273-74:

> The relevance of financial means to the payment of add ons is expressly stated in the opening words of s. 7. Indeed s. 26.1(2) of the *Divorce Act*, which underlies the *Guidelines*, provides:
>
> 26.1(2) The guidelines shall be based on the principle that spouses have a joint financial obligation to maintain the children of the marriage in accordance with their relative *abilities to contribute* to the performance of that obligation. [Emphasis added.]

It is thus, in my view, appropriate and necessary when determining whether the expense fits within the "extraordinary" requirement of s. 7(1)(f) to assess it, subjectively, in accordance with the parents' incomes, using "income" as defined in the *Guidelines*. The definition of "extraordinary" invites a comparison to what is usual. A relatively modest expense for a child's extra-curricular activity may be "extraordinary" for parents who are living at a very low income level, but trivial for those with generous incomes. In this regard, there is no "usual" that cuts across income levels. There must be some attempt by the court to measure "extraordinary" in accordance with a norm. An income based, presumptive, capacity to pay is the foundation of the *Guidelines*. The Table amounts are to this extent, subjective not objective. But all payors with equivalent nominal incomes do not necessarily have the same ability to pay support. The *Guidelines* through the Table amounts, establish an income based threshold level of child support, but by means of s. 7 expressly recognize that ability to pay is linked not just to income but to the broader concept of "financial means". It is most consistent with the structure of the *Guidelines*, in my view, to assess the "extraordinary" nature of the expense, subjectively. For this purpose I would use the parents' joint incomes. This is not to require that, at this stage, the judge go into a detailed investigation of the financial "means" of the parents. That analysis occurs when the Court, having determined that the expense is extraordinary, considers its reasonableness.

In the result, Madam Justice Bateman was of the view that it was "fundamentally fair" to take an expansive approach to the meaning of "extraordinary expenses" by viewing the expense or expenses claimed in the context of the parties' joint incomes. This approach is similar to that espoused by Madam Justice Moreau in *Middleton, supra*.

After discussing whether an expense was extraordinary within the meaning of s. 7(1)(f), Madam Justice Bateman then went on to discuss the other considerations under s. 7, namely, whether the expenses were both reasonable and necessary. The question of reasonableness involved examining the "means" of the parties, taking into account the reality of their separate status and such other factors as their "...capital, income distribution, debt load, third party resources which impact upon a parent's ability to pay, access costs, obligations to pay spousal or other child support orders, spousal support received and any other relevant factors". [p. 275] on the basis that with respect to "add on" expenses, the Guidelines do not presume an ability to pay.

In concluding her analysis of s. 7(1)(f), Madam Justice Bateman agreed (at pp. 275-76) with the following comments from *Child Support Guidelines in Divorce Proceedings: A Manual* (1997), 2nd ed.; (James C. MacDonald, Q.C. and Ann C. Wilton, Carswell), at p. 49:

> The provision for special or extraordinary expenses, obviously, is a departure from the policy of uniform treatment for all families in divorce situations. This section recognizes that some kinds of expenses do not lend themselves to averages. It is an attempt to balance the goals of an efficient and effective system and, at the same time, respond to limited individual circumstances so that equity can be achieved. Whether a special or extra-ordinary expense will be allowed is primarily a matter for [the] discretion of the court.

On the evidence before her, Madam Justice Bateman concluded the trial judge did not err in finding that the expenses claimed, taken individually or collectively, were not extraordinary. It was, therefore, unnecessary for the trial judge to go on to determine whether they were necessary or reasonable.

While agreeing in the result, Mr. Justice Flinn, speaking for himself and Mr. Justice Jones, did not agree that assessing the extraordinariness of an expense engaged a consideration of the parents' incomes. In his view, parental incomes were an irrelevant consideration, and the test of extraordinariness was purely objective.

Mr. Justice Flinn stated that the plain meaning of the word "extraordinary" imported a reference to expenses which are "not usual", "additional to what is usual" or "exceptional". He concluded that this must be determined, not in light of parental income, but in relation to the nature of the activities and the nature of the expenses. It was only if the expenses were found to be extraordinary that the court would go on to consider the income of the parents to determine what additional amount, if any, should be paid. Flinn J.A. held that, to do otherwise, would be inconsistent with the objectives of the Guidelines, particularly s. 1(b): "to reduce conflict and tension between spouses by making the calculation of child support orders more objective".

Madam Justice Bateman's analysis of s. 7(1)(f) was adopted by the Saskatchewan Court of Appeal in *Kofoed* v. *Fichter* (1998), 161 D.L.R. (4th) 189, 168 Sask. R. 149 (Sask. C.A.). In that case, the mother applied for additional child support in the amount of $195 per month under s. 7(1)(f) of the Guidelines. The extracurricular expenses to which the husband was asked to contribute as "extraordinary" expenses totalled $2,341 per year and included expenses for gymnastics, softball, bowling, soccer, cubs, art and art supplies, and some sports equipment for three children aged 12, 10, and nine. The combined incomes of the parents was $60,000.

The trial judge in *Kofoed* allowed the expenses, relying primarily on two earlier decisions in which such expenses had been allowed. In brief reasons dismissing the appeal, Gerwing J.A., speaking for the Court, stated that it was undesirable for the Court simply to produce a list stating that certain categories of expenses were or were not "extraordinary" or "extracurricular". Rather, the Court preferred a case-by-case approach, taking into account the combined incomes of the spouses.

This "subjective" approach was specifically rejected by the Manitoba Court of Appeal in *Andries* v. *Andries* (1998), 36 R.F.L. (4th) 175 (Man. C.A.). In that case, the trial judge allowed $500 per annum for travel to baseball games for the child and his mother, and $180 per annum for school sports, as extraordinary expenses under s. 7(1)(f) of the Guidelines.

The Court of Appeal allowed the appeal. Mr. Justice Twaddle, speaking for the Court, stated that because the table amounts were based on the average amount spent on children at different income levels, the support payable under the tables must be taken to include "all ordinary expenses of child-rearing". He then turned to the "more difficult question" of what the Governor General in Council meant by "extraordinary expenses" as those words are used in ss. 7(1)(d) and (f) of the Guidelines. In answering that question, he referred to the judgment of Bateman J.A. in *Raftus* and that of Madam Justice Pardu to similar effect in *Rains* v. *Rains* (June 16, 1997), Doc. Sault Ste. Marie 16655/97 (Ont. Gen. Div.). He rejected their approach for the reasons set forth in the following extract at para. 22 of his reasons:

> The *Rains* approach has three flaws. Firstly, it requires a judge to consider the means of the non-custodial parent twice, once in deciding whether the expense is extraordinary and once in deciding whether the extraordinary expense is reasonable, an unnecessary duplication. Secondly, because the table amounts include some allowance for extracurricular activities, the approach may result, albeit unintentionally, in a payor being required to pay twice for the same extracurricular expense. And thirdly, because an extracurricular expense is less likely to be disproportionately high in relation to a wealthier payor's income than to that of a poorer payor, the *Rains* approach favours the wealthier payor, making it less likely that such a payor will be required to pay anything more for any extracurricular expense. I do not think these results are what the Governor General in Council intended. The payor's means, in my view, are to be taken into account only in deciding whether an expense otherwise found to be extraordinary is reasonable.

Mr. Justice Twaddle went on to state that he preferred the approach of Mr. Justice Orsborn in *Moss* v. *Moss* (1997), 159 Nfld. & P.E.I.R. 1 (Nfld. T.D.). He cited with approval the following passage at para. 66 of *Moss* with respect to the question of whether an expense was extraordinary:

> ...the Court should look at the nature of the expenditure, in the context of the particular activity to determine whether or not, when assessed against expenditures that might reasonably be anticipated in connection with the activity, the expenditure in question is exceptional and represents a marked departure. This will focus the inquiry more on the nature of the expenditure in question, and not on its amount.

Mr. Justice Twaddle continued as follows, at paras. 27-28:

> Following the *Moss* approach, an expense for an extracurricular activity is extraordinary only where it is out of proportion to the usual costs associated with that particular activity. For example, if the average costs of downhill skis is $500, then $500 for downhill skis would not be an extraordinary expense, but $1000 would be. The judge would still be required to apply the tests of necessity and reasonableness before determining that the payor should contribute to the extraordinary portion of this expense, but the initial determination of the extraordinary character of the expense would not involve consideration of the payor's means.

> This approach is consistent with the language and structure of s. 7(1) of the Guidelines. The word "extraordinary" in paragraphs (d) and (f) of s. 7(1) qualifies expense rather than activity. Just as the expenses in the other paragraphs of s. 7(1) are determined without reference to the means of the parties, so are those under paragraphs (d) and (f). All of the enumerated expenses are then subjected to the same tests of necessity and reasonableness.

Mr. Justice Twaddle stated that this objective approach allowed for regional differences within a province. For example, if an expense would be higher for someone in rural Manitoba than for the average parent in the province, the expense would be considered extraordinary.

In the result, the Court of Appeal in *Andries* disallowed the expenses claimed. The $500 for travel for baseball was disallowed on the basis that the child was almost 13 years old and there was no evidence either that the mother had to accompany him to games, or that other reasonable arrangements could not be made to reduce the expense to an average expense through car-pooling. The fees charged for participation in school sports were disallowed as not being extraordinary either in nature or amount ($60 for each of basketball, badminton and volleyball). The court concluded that these fees were not a marked departure from those which might reasonably be anticipated for participation in the sports in question.

A notably different approach to the meaning of the words "extraordinary expenses" under s. 7(1)(f) of the Guidelines was adopted by Madam Justice Webber in two decisions: *Ellis* v. *Ellis* (1997), 158 Nfld. & P.E.I.R. 193 (P.E.I. T.D. [In Chambers]), and *Campbell* v. *Martijn* (1998), 163 Nfld. & P.E.I.R. 126 (P.E.I. T.D. [In Chambers]). In those cases, Webber J. concluded that the payee's income should be the focal point in determining whether an expense was extraordinary within the meaning of s. 7(1)(f). . . .

(iii) The Preferred Approach to s. 7(1)(f)

It is evident from the decisions to which I have referred, and others, that the interpretation and application of s. 7 of the Guidelines, and, in particular, the meaning to be given to the words "extraordinary expenses" in s. 7(1)(f) has been controversial. The controversy has been fuelled by the lack of direction in the Guidelines themselves as to the proper interpretation of this section and by a genuine disagreement as to whether the objectives of the Guidelines are best achieved by a subjective approach to whether expenses claimed pursuant to this section are extraordinary, which takes into consideration the joint incomes of the parties, or an objective approach, which does not.

There is no dispute in the case law as to the meaning of the word "extraordinary". All of the decisions utilize dictionary definitions, including such synonyms as "unusual", "out of the ordinary" and "exceptional". Nor is there any dispute amongst judges that the use of the word "extraordinary" in s. 7(1)(f) to describe the type of expenses which can be added on to the basic table amounts, implies that "ordinary" expenses are included within the table amounts. The problem has been the difficulty of ascertaining the nature and extent of the extracurricular activities (in the case of s. 7(1)(f)), which are "ordinary" and, thus, included in the basic table amounts. If this could be determined, one could simply define extraordinary expenses as being those which are not ordinary; that is, those which are not included in the basic table.

Unfortunately, the manner in which the Guidelines were constructed creates an almost insurmountable barrier to resolving this circular problem. As earlier noted, the Guidelines are based on economic studies of average spending on children in families at different income levels in Canada. They represent a modified version of a model developed by the Federal/Provincial/Territorial Family Law Committee in its 1995 report and recommendations to the Federal government on the form the Guidelines should take. The Family Law Committee's model, in turn, utilized the Statistics Canada equivalence scale for low income families (the "40/30 equivalence scale") and applied it, with some adjustments, across all levels of income to come up with a rough estimate of how income for families at different income levels is spent.

Equivalence scales are described by the authors of "An Overview of the Research Program to Develop A Canadian Child Support Formula", by Ross Finnie, Carolina Giliberti and Daniel Stripinis (Ottawa: Communications and Consultation Branch, Department of Justice Canada, 1995), prepared on behalf of the Federal/Provincial/Territorial Family Law Committee. At p. 9 of that overview, the authors state:

> Equivalence scales are used to adjust family incomes to provide better comparisons of standards of living between households of different sizes. For example, a family with children might have a higher income than a childless couple, but its needs are also greater. What income would the larger family need to be as "well off" (in the sense of "standard of living") as the childless couple? That is, what makes them equivalent?
>
> The difference in the two families' incomes that leaves them equally well off can be expressed as a ratio, and the series of such ratios for all different family sizes becomes a standardized equivalence scale. These scales are normally expressed in "adult equivalence units": a single-person household has a reference value of one, while larger households have values greater than one, with these values depending on the family's size and composition (i.e., whether there are one or two parents). The precise value depends on the amount of income required to leave the larger family as well off as a single adult. For example, with the equivalence scale represented by the Statistics Canada low income measures (discussed later), a couple is judged to require 1.4 times the income of a single adult to be as well off.
>
> Equivalence scales are derived from estimates of what it costs families of different sizes to be as well off as the reference single adult. For families with children, the equivalence scale therefore depends on the estimated child costs. That is, the scale is based on estimates of how much more

income is required to leave a family with children as well off as a family without children and, in turn, as well off as the reference single adult. The complete equivalence scale (or series of ratios) is then constructed from a full set of cost estimates for families of all sizes and compositions.

The Statistics Canada equivalence scale is expressed in terms of gross income requirements rather than on the amount of money actually spent on a child. It is not based on any notion of fixed costs of a child. For these reasons, it is of little assistance in deriving the meaning to be given to the words "extraordinary expenses" in s. 7(1)(f). This is particularly so since the scale does not provide for extraordinary expenses associated with raising children. In recognition of this, s. 7 was incorporated into the Guidelines to deal with "add on" expenses, such as those referred to in s. 7(1)(f).

In the absence of any clear guidance as to what is meant by the words "extraordinary expenses" in s. 7(1)(f) in the Guidelines themselves, I prefer Madam Justice Bateman's analysis of this issue in *Raftus* to that of the majority in that case, to that of Madam Justice Webber in *Ellis* and *Campbell*, and to that of the Manitoba Court of Appeal in *Andries*. As earlier noted, her approach has also been adopted by the Saskatchewan Court of Appeal in *Kofoed*, and a similar approach has been adopted by the Alberta Court of Appeal in *Sanders*, following Moreau J.'s decision in *Middleton*.

I agree with Madam Justice Bateman that it is appropriate to have recourse to the combined incomes of the parties as an aid in determining whether an expense is extraordinary under s. 7(1)(f). In that regard, I adopt her analysis set out at paras. 44-49 of these reasons.

In my view, it is apparent from the inclusion of s. 7 in the Guidelines that the legislators appreciated that a purely objective approach based on the "average" expenditures of a family would be unfair. In adopting an "add on" approach under s. 7, they recognized the importance of addressing the needs of a particular family with particular expenses. In this regard, it is noteworthy that s. 1(b) of the Guidelines provides only that the Guidelines are intended to make the determination of child support "more objective"; it was not contemplated that they would make that determination completely objective.

While I sympathize with the underlying concern of Webber J. in *Ellis* that custodial parents with incomes significantly lower than that of the payor will not be able to afford to pay for extracurricular activities unless it is the payee's income which dictates whether an expense is extraordinary, I agree with Bateman J.A. that both s. 26.1 of the Act and the wording of s. 7 of the Guidelines are consistent with the conclusion that determinations affecting both parties' obligation to support their child should be based on their joint income. In situations in which there are no "add ons" under s. 7 or hardship factors under s. 10, it is only the payor's income which is relevant. But where both parties are expected to share additional expenses, as under s. 7, it is reasonable to utilize their joint incomes in determining whether an expense is extraordinary. The potential hardship to the low income-earning payee of a significant discrepancy between the income of the payor and the payee will be offset by the proportionate sharing of the expense in the event that it is found to be both necessary and reasonable.

What of the approach taken to s. 7 by the Manitoba Court of Appeal in *Andries* and the majority of the Nova Scotia Court of Appeal in *Raftus*? According to this approach, the income of the parties is irrelevant in determining whether an expense is extraordinary. It is only if the expense is otherwise found to be extraordinary, in the sense of being unusual or exceptional according to an objective standard, that one looks to the incomes of the parties to determine whether the expense is reasonable and in accord with the spending patterns of the parties prior to separation.

At para. 55 of these reasons, I set forth an excerpt from the reasons of Twaddle J.A. in *Andries* in which he cites three principal reasons for rejecting the subjective approach to the question of whether an expense is extraordinary. In summary, he concludes that the subjective approach is flawed because: (1) it requires the court to look at the means of the payor twice—once, with respect to whether an expense is extraordinary and, secondly, with respect to whether it is reasonable; (2) it may result in the payor paying twice for the same expense; and (3) it favours wealthy payors. I will deal with each of these concerns.

In my view, there is nothing illogical or inherently fallacious in taking the payor's income into account twice under s. 7, firstly in determining whether an expense is extraordinary, and secondly in determining whether it is reasonable. These are two separate, albeit related, concepts. It does not follow that simply because the payor's *means* are taken into consideration with respect to the question of reasonableness, the payor's *income* should not be taken into consideration in determining whether an expense is extraordinary. In that regard, I agree with Madam Justice Bateman that the income of the parties is only one of the factors to be considered in assessing the reasonableness of an expense. At that stage, the full means of the parties must be considered, including those factors set forth in *Raftus* and quoted at para. 48 of these reasons.

I also note that utilizing the objective approach advocated in *Andries* may result in the means of the parties not being considered in relation to an expense at all, since, if the expense is found not to be extraordinary, according to objective criteria, the question of the reasonableness of the expense never arises.

With respect to Mr. Justice Twaddle's second concern that payors might be assessed twice for the same expense, I agree with him that since it is impossible to know what the legislators contemplated as being included under the basic tables as ordinary expenses for extracurricular activities, it is possible the court could inadvertently make an award under s. 7(1)(f) for an expense which is partially or wholly included under the basic table. But, the inability to know what is included as an ordinary expense under the basic table makes it equally likely that a payee will be inadvertently deprived of a contribution to an expense which was not included under the basic table if an unduly restrictive interpretation of the words "extraordinary expenses" is utilized. To the extent that there is a possibility of error, I am of the view it is preferable to err on the side of inclusion of the expense, rather than exclusion. Such an approach is consistent with the best interests of the children in obtaining adequate support, including support sufficient to cover extracurricular activities.

With respect to Mr. Justice Twaddle's third concern that wealthy payors may reap an unfair benefit, I agree it is possible that a wealthy payor may be less likely than a less wealthy payor to have amounts added to the basic table amount as an extraordinary expense if the parties' incomes are taken into account. However, I do not consider this a significant problem since the basic table amounts applicable to payors who fit into the wealthy category are high. For example, in *Francis v. Baker* (1998), 34 R.F.L. (4th) 317 (Ont. C.A.), affirmed (1999) 50 R.F.L. (4th) (S.C.C.), the Ontario Court of Appeal upheld an award of maintenance for two children in the amount of $10,034 per month and resisted efforts by the payor husband to have that amount reduced. In my view, it is unlikely that children of wealthy payors will suffer if the courts find that additional expenses claimed under s. 7 are not extraordinary. There are other sections of the Guidelines, notably s. 4, which apply to them. Further, the vast majority of cases dealt with in our courts do not involve the wealthy. In my view, the courts have more reason to be concerned that middle-class payees and their children will be ill-served by applying a more restrictive, objective test to the question of whether expenses claimed are extraordinary.

Apart from these considerations, a problem I find with the *Andries* approach is that it focuses on one activity and one expense at a time. According to Mr. Justice Twaddle's analysis, as set forth at para. 57 of these reasons, an expense for an extracurricular activity is only extraordinary where it is out of proportion to the usual costs associated with that particular activity. In many cases, there may be several children participating in numerous activities. In such cases, no one expense, in itself, may be extraordinary, but the combination of expenses for all of the children could result in a total expense which would be extraordinary. In my view, it should be open to the court to determine that total expenses for extracurricular activities are extraordinary, even if no one expense, in itself, meets that definition.

Mr. Justice Twaddle also preferred the objective approach since, in his view, it had the advantage of taking into account regional differences such that an expense which would be regarded as ordinary in Winnipeg, might be viewed as extraordinary in The Pas. While this may be true, the advantage of the subjective approach is that it enables the court to deal not only with regional differences, but with differences specific to a particular family.

Whether one takes an objective or a subjective approach to the determination of what constitutes "extraordinary expenses for extracurricular activities", it is apparent that the parties will be required to call evidence to support or dispute the claim for such expenses. Similarly, other expenses claimed under s. 7 will require evidence to be led to enable the court to determine if they are justified. Despite the loss of certainty of result which must necessarily accompany this exercise, I support this flexibility in s. 7 of the Guidelines since it permits justice to be done on an individual basis with respect to expenses which do not fall under the basic tables. In my view, certainty of result should not be elevated to the paramount objective of the Guidelines at the expense of the fundamental fairness referred to by Madam Justice Bateman in *Raftus*.

In the result, I conclude that, in deciding whether an expense, or the totality of expenses claimed on behalf of children under s. 7(1)(f) are extraordinary, the court should take into consideration the combined income of the parties, as well as the nature and amount of the individual expense, the nature and number of the activities, any special needs or talents of the children, and the overall cost of the activities. This list is not intended to be exhaustive, as considerations may arise in other cases which may also be relevant. I note that in the only other decision of this Court dealing with s. 7(1)(f), *Cochrane* v. *Zarins* (1998), 36 R.F.L. (4th) 434 (B.C. C.A.), the Court concluded that a particular child's talents are a relevant factor in determining whether an expense for an extracurricular activity is extraordinary.

As earlier stated, once an expense or expenses are found to be extraordinary it is necessary for the court to proceed to determine whether the expenses are necessary in relation to the children's best interests and reasonable, having regard to the means of the spouses and those of the child, and to the family's spending pattern prior to separation. There appears to be a consensus in the authorities dealing with s. 7(1)(f) that those questions do not need to be addressed until the expense or expenses in question have been found to be extraordinary. That would also be true of "extraordinary" educational expenses under s. 7(1)(d). With respect to the other expenses included under s. 7(1), which fit under the rubric of "special" expenses as that word is used in the heading of the section, the expenses need not be extraordinary, but they must meet the tests of necessity and reasonableness.

With those observations in mind, I turn to the s. 7(1) expenses allowed by the chambers judge in this case.

(iv) Expenses Claimed in this Case . . .

(a) Tutor

Mr. McLaughlin does not take exception to contributing $141.60 per month toward the cost of a tutor for Sean who has a reading disability. His only concern is to ensure that he is contributing to an expense which is actually being incurred. In that regard, I note that there are provisions under the Guidelines for the continuing exchange of financial information relating to child support. . . . It is open to Mr. McLaughlin to request the information relating to all s. 7(1) expenses to which he has been ordered to contribute in accordance with these provisions.

(b) Child Care for Sean

This is the largest single expense to which Mr. McLaughlin has been ordered to contribute pursuant to s. 7(1)(a) of the Guidelines. The total child care expense is $380 per month, of which Mr. McLaughlin's proportionate share was found to be $224.20.

The chambers judge was satisfied that the child care expenses claimed by Ms. McLaughlin were both necessary in the best interests of Sean and reasonable in the circumstances.

Mr. McLaughlin submits that child care is not necessary because Dana (16 years) and/or Kimberley (14 years) should be able to provide care for Sean before and after school while their mother is at work. He also submits that the chambers judge failed to take into account the tax benefit to Ms. McLaughlin with respect to this expense as required by s. 7(3) of the Guidelines (quoted at para. 28 of these reasons).

Ms. McLaughlin submits her work schedule necessitates daycare for Sean both before and after normal school hours, and for school professional days, spring break, Christmas and extended periods during the summer months. She says Mr. Mc-Laughlin's suggestion that the older two children care for Sean is not realistic and would not permit them to pursue their own activities, including sports, social and volunteer activities.

. . . In my view, the chambers judge was fully justified in requiring Mr. Mc-Laughlin to contribute to the child care costs for Sean. The provision of consistent, reliable child care on a regular basis is clearly in Sean's best interests and is reasonable given the joint income of the families and the fact that Ms. McLaughlin is working full-time. There may be cases in which families simply have no financial alternative but to call upon their other children to assist in providing child care to younger members of the family. This is not one of those cases.

I now turn to the question of whether the chambers judge erred in failing to take into account any tax benefits to Ms. McLaughlin relating to child care costs [of $380 per month] pursuant to s. 7(3) of the Guidelines. The short answer to this question is "yes". Section 7(3) is expressed in mandatory language. The court must take the relevant tax considerations into account in determining the amount of an expense under s. 7(1). [These were dealt with in supplemental reasons reported at *McLaughlin* v. *McLaughlin* (1999), 44 R.F.L. (4th) 176 (B.C. C.A.) where the court concluded that the after tax cost to the mother was $248.33 per month and the father's proportionate share was $146.51 per month and not $224.20.] . . .

(c) Medical/Dental Premiums

The total amount of these premiums is $101.69 per month, of which Mr. McLaughlin's proportionate share was determined by the chambers judge to be $60. In arriving at this amount, the chambers judge deducted what he considered to be an appropriate amount to reflect the fact that the total premium also covered Ms. McLaughlin.

Mr. McLaughlin submits that this amount also carries with it tax consequences that benefit Ms. McLaughlin such that his contribution for this item should be reduced. This argument was not raised below and there is no readily identifiable amount attached to the tax benefit, if any, Ms. McLaughlin may receive with respect to this expense. I am, therefore, not prepared to interfere with the amount ordered by the chambers judge.

For the same reasons, I am not prepared to interfere with the decision of the chambers judge with respect to the amount Mr. McLaughlin has been ordered to contribute to pharmaceuticals which, in any event, is only $14.75 per month.

(d) Extracurricular Activities

Mr. McLaughlin was ordered to pay a total of $69.33 per month toward these expenses, of which $47.20 was for the activities themselves and $22.13 was for the cost of equipment.

As a matter of convenience, I will set forth those expenses again:

[Particulars of expenses]	[Total expense]	[Mr. McLaughlin's share]
Extracurricular activities (i) Dana's soccer	$95 per year	
(ii) Kimberley's soccer	$95 per year	
(iii) Sean's soccer	$95 per year	
(iv) Dana's softball	$95 per year	
(v) Kimberley's field hockey	$95 per year	
(vi) Kimberley's outdoor school	$95 per year	
(vii) Kimberley's softball	$95 per year	
(viii) Sean's swimming	$225 per year	
(ix) Sean's hockey/skating	$75 per year	
	$965 per year	
	($80 per month)	$47.20 per month
Extracurricular equipment	$37.50 per month	$22.13 per month

In my view, none of these expenses, individually, can be viewed as extraordinary expenses. The activities are common extracurricular activities for children of these ages and there are not, as there are in some cases, additional fees for such things as camps, trips, or expensive equipment. Nor is the total monthly amount associated with these expenses high, either in absolute terms, or in relation to the joint incomes of the parties ($120,000). In my view, Mr. McLaughlin's proportionate share of these expenses ($70 per month) must be treated as being included within the amount of maintenance he is paying under the basic table.

In the result, I would allow this ground of appeal to the extent of reducing the amount of child support to be paid by Mr. McLaughlin to Ms. McLaughlin by $70 per month.

NOTES AND QUESTIONS

1. The extensive list in s. 7(1) is exhaustive: *Stanton* v. *Solby* (1999), 49 R.F.L. (4th) 422 (B.C. Master).

2. Only paragraphs (d) and (f) of s. 7(1) stipulate that the named expenses must be ''extraordinary''. If expenses fall within the other paragraphs, they must be shared proportionately in accordance with s. 7(2) provided they satisfy the requirements of necessity and reasonableness. Some of these expenses are not at all ''extraordinary'' and the Senate's Standing Committee on Social Affairs, Science and Technology suggested in its *The Federal Child Support Guidelines: Interim Report* (1998) that the heading to s. 7 be changed to ''Additional or extraordinary expenses'' to reflect this fact.

In ''Reforming the Child Support Guidelines'' in *Federal Child Support Guidelines Reference Manual* (Ottawa: Dept. of Justice, looseleaf) Professor Bala proposes (at K-69) that paragraphs (a) and (f) be eliminated from s. 7(1) and replaced by automatic increases in the Table amount for preschool children of 25% and for children age 12 and over of 20%.

3. In ''Rules and Rulelessness in Family Law'', a paper prepared for the National Judicial Institute's Appeal Court Seminar of April 19, 1999, Professor Thompson states (para. 34-35):

> The only real area of difficulty [in the application of s. 7] has been the interpretation of ''extraordinary'' extracurricular expenses. The architects of the Guidelines did it to themselves, thanks to the misleading little notes found in Schedule I preceding the provincial tables. . . . Note 5 is plainly incorrect, while note 6 must be understood as aspirational. After a long wait, the federal government released its so-called ''technical report'' on the construction of the table amounts [Department of Justice Canada, *Formula for the Table Amounts contained in the Federal Child Support Guidelines: A Technical Report* (Dec. 1997)]. The formula is based upon a series of assumptions, built around equivalence scales, not any ''economic studies of average spending'', as none of the latter produced reliable numbers. . . .

> Courts were left by the federal Guidelines to assume that the table amounts actually included average expenditures on children, so that some clear line could be drawn between ''ordinary'' extracurricular expenses and those described as ''extraordinary'' in s. 7(1)(f). It turned out, of course, that the courts had to draw that line, on their own, unassisted by any ''studies''.

4. The terms ''subjective' and ''objective'' were adopted to explain the two approaches to s. 7(1)(f) outlined in *McLaughlin*. Are these terms helpful? Is one more objective than the other?

5. The Senate committee's 1998 report (see note 2) recommended that a new definition should be added to s. 7(1) to specify that ''extraordinary expenses'' in paragraphs (d) and (f) mean ''expenditures that exceed what would be considered typical amounts for parents at comparable income levels to spend for those purposes''.

6. Paragraphs (d) and (f) of s. 7(1) of the *Guidelines* are likely to be of more concern to middle income parents than to either lower income or upper income parents. Explain.

7. Section 7(3) of the *Guidelines* indicates that it is the after tax cost of an expense listed in expense that is apportioned. Regarding the determination of the value of the personal deduction for daycare, see *Kelly* v. *Kelly* (1998), 38 R.F.L. (4th) 444 (Alta. Q.B.).

8. In *Bland* v. *Bland* (1999), 48 R.F.L. (4th) 250 (Alta. Q.B.), a 15-year-old boy played AAA bantam hockey at a cost of $4,600 per year. The mother's income was $15,000 per year and the father's about $45,000. The parents accepted that the costs relating to the boy's hockey were extraordinary, but the father refused to contribute. The mother and her parents had paid for the expenses in the past and the mother indicated that the boy would play at this level whether or not the father contributed. Justice Burrows stated (at 255) that "a reasonable way to approach the question is to ask whether, assuming the participants in this conflict . . .were living together as a family unit, with their existing financial situation, it would be reasonable for [the parents] to decide that despite the talents of their son and the opportunities his participation in elite hockey might create, their resources are insufficient to allow them to pay the significant cost". The justice concluded that by this test the father's conclusion was not unreasonable and he was not required to contribute.

(4) SHARED CUSTODY

HUNTER v. HUNTER

(1998), 37 R.F.L. (4th) 260 (Ont. Gen. Div.)

BROCHENSHIRE J: The issue before me was the calculation of a child support order under the Federal Guidelines where custody of the child is shared, each parent having the child 50 percent of the time, and where the income of the parents is unequal. . . .

[The court determined that the mother's income was $29,000 per year and that the father earned $60,000 annually.]

The real issue is how to now interpret and apply s. 9. . . . The only case law referred to me, relating to s. 9 of the Federal Guidelines Regulation, was *McCargar* v. *McCargar* (June 25, 1997), Doc. Edmonton 4803 101512 (Alta. Q.B.), *O' Quinn* v. *O' Quinn* (1997), 165 N.S.R. (2d) 330 (N.S. S.C.), a decision of Gruchy J. of the Nova Scotia Supreme Court delivered December 17, 1997 and *Middleton* v. *MacPherson* (1997), 150 D.L.R. (4th) 519 (Alta. Q.B.), a decision of Moreau J. delivered June 12, 1997.

In *McCargar*, Veit J. decided, with two parents with equal income sharing the care of 3 children, that neither should make any payment to the other.

In *O' Quinn*, Gruchy J. was dealing with a situation where the children were to be shared back and forth with each parent having the children more than 40 percent of the time so that s.9 applied. The father had an income of $32,000 a year, and the mother's income was too low for her to make any contribution to child support. The order of Gruchy J. was that the father would pay to the mother, while the children were with the mother, $606 per month.

In *Middleton* counsel put to Madam Justice Moreau the issues in the form of a series of questions, to which she provided answers. The applicable question (among many) was one asking direction as to how s.9 would be applied. Madam Justice Moreau concluded that, although earlier drafts of the Guidelines approached it differently, the final version gave the court, in s. 9(c), a broad discretion in determining a fit award, but that the determination of what each spouse would pay under the applicable table is a useful standard of comparison when going on to consider s. 9(b) and s. 9(c). In the case before her, she found that on the tables, the husband would owe the wife $278 a month, while the wife would owe the husband $120 a month, with the difference between them being $158 owed by the husband to the wife. She did not make any finding under s. 9(b) other than findings on a series of special expenses under s. 7 and did not find any undue hardship under s. 9(c). Her award, in the end, was the difference between the table amounts that each spouse would pay to other for a whole year plus the amounts determined under s. 7.

In the case before me, Mr. Howie for the husband urges that I follow the approach of Gruchy J. in *O'Quinn*, by treating the father as paying support to the mother for 6 months of a year at his rate, with the mother paying support to the father for the other 6 months at her rate, and then take the difference between the 2 totals and divide it by 12 to give a monthly amount which the father, as the higher income earner, would pay to the mother each month.

Ms. Stam for the mother, urges that I follow the approach of Moreau J. and calculate the Guideline amount for each parent for 12 months of the year, take the difference between those amounts, divide it by 12, and that would be the amount payable by the father to the mother, subject to making an addition thereto under s. 9(b) to account for the extra costs incurred by each because of the shared custody arrangement.

I accept that s. 9(a) requires me to take into account the amount set out in the applicable Tables for each of the spouses. The applicable monthly amount for a $29,000 income is $258, and for a $60,000 income is $507. Having taken it into account, I fail to see why each of those numbers should be multiplied by 12, when the custodial period for each of the parents is 6 months and not 12. The . . . . result of using 12 months on each side is of course to double the amount of net support payable by the father to the mother. With the greatest of respect, I feel that Moreau J. may have been misled by comparison with s. 8, where of course the court is looking at split custody, with one or more children in the custody of each of the parents for all of 12 months.

I have concluded that the common sense approach, and the proper interpretation of s. 9 is for one parent to pay support only for the time the other parent has the child, so that in this divided situation, each parent should be paying to the other for half of the year. I conclude that this approach is peculiar to a s. 9 situation and cannot be taken to have application outside of s. 9.

I then have to consider s. 9(b) which brings home the fact that in shared custody arrangements, because each parent is providing a home for the child, the total costs are higher than they would be if only one parent had custody.

I was not provided with detailed child care budgets. The submissions of counsel, in part supported by the evidence, was that each parent has provided a room for their son, complete with furniture, and other amenities. Each has clothing for the child at his/her home. Similarly each has toys for the child. Obviously, the cost of groceries is only applicable when the child is with one of the two parents. Less obviously, but certainly, there are other expenses which would travel with the child back and forth. Ms. Stam, in submissions, urged upon me the *"Colorado Method"*. As I understand the submission, in the state of Colorado, presumably on the basis of empirical evidence, a determination has been made that roughly 50 percent of the costs of a custodial parent relate to fixed costs, so that in shared custody situations, an increase of 50 percent in the adjusting payment from one parent to the other in a shared custody, situation is seen as appropriate.

I am required under s. 9(b) to take into account, *"the increased costs of shared custody arrangements"*. In the absence of direct evidence quantifying such amounts, and in a situation where the amounts in question are small in any event, it seems sensible and appropriate to take guidance from a jurisdiction where presumably some empirical data was gathered and analyzed. My conclusion is that a 50 percent increase in the differential between the two support figures, to take into account the increased costs of shared custody is in this case appropriate.

The arithmetic calculations in this case would be that on the father's income of $60,000, his monthly Guideline figure would be $507, which for 6 months would be $3,042. At the mother's $29,000 income level, her monthly Guideline amount would be $258, which for 6 months would be $1,548. The difference between the two is $1,494. Divided by 12, I arrive at $124.50 a month. Increased by 50 percent this becomes $186.75.

I am further required to consider, under s. 9(c) the conditions, means, needs and other circumstances of each spouse and of any child for whom support is sought. Here, the father has the ability to pay, the mother has the need of assistance, there are no special conditions or circumstances and the parents have agreed between themselves to share the s. 7 type expenses proportionately according to their incomes.

The result therefore is that an order will issue for payment by the father to the mother of $186.75 per month for the support of the child, Thomas Douglas Hunter, born October 19, 1990, commencing April 1, 1998.

NOTES AND QUESTIONS

1. Section 8 of the *Guidelines* deals with "split custody", that is, situations where one or more children live with each parent. Here the method of determining child support is quite straightforward. The two child support obligations are calculated in accordance with the Table and then set off against each other. The parent with the higher obligation pays the difference between the two amounts. There is no discretion to depart from this method of calculation under s. 8 itself, although the calculation of the two amounts can involve the exercise of discretion as provided in other sections of the *Guidelines* such as s. 7 involving special expenses. Also, once the amount has been determined under s. 8, departures from that amount are allowed on the basis of undue hardship under s. 10. See, for example, *Scharf* v. *Scharf* (1998), 40 R.F.L. (4th) 422 (Ont. Gen. Div.), where the mother successfully argued that the s. 8 result should be adjusted under s. 10 in light of the significantly lower standard of living that the child residing with her would have compared to the child living with the father. See generally Rogerson, "Child Support Under the Guidelines in Cases of Split and Shared Custody" (1998), 15 Can. J. Fam. L. 11.

2. Section 9 of the *Guidelines* comes into play if and only if the amount of time the child spends with the payor satisfies the threshold set. Does it always apply where the parents have joint legal custody? Can it apply even if there is no joint or shared custody order?

3. Does s. 9 apply in the following situation? The child spends considerable periods of time (though less than 40%) with the access parent who provides about half the meals, buys half the children's clothes and provides a suitable second home for the child during visits? Is this result fair? See the comments in *Hall* v. *Hall* (1997), 30 R.F.L. (4th) 333 (B.C. Master).

Quebec's *Guidelines* provide for a reduction from the Table amount any time there is increased access above a minimum of 20%. Where access is between 20% and 40%, there is a "sliding scale" providing for a percentage decrease from the Table amount for every corresponding percentage increase in access. Over the 40% threshold, the situation is treated as one of shared custody and different rules apply.

4. Section 9 has raised concerns about introducing financial incentives into custody and access decisions and encouraging conflict and litigation over access in ways not in accord with the child's best interests: *Hall* v. *Hall* (1997), 30 R.F.L. (4th) 333 (B.C. Master); *Crick* v. *Crick* (1997), 43 B.C.L.R. (3d) 251 (B.C. S.C.); *McKerracher* v. *McKerracher*, [1997] B.C.J. No. 2257 (B.C. S.C.); *Spanier* v. *Spanier* (1998), 40 R.F.L. (4th) 329 (B.C. S.C.); and *Gore-Hickman* v. *Gore-Hickman* (1999), 177 D.L.R. (4th) 222 (Sask. Q.B.).

5. Where there is extended access, it may be contentious whether the 40% threshold is crossed. The method of counting the time when a parent has access or physical custody may be crucial. In many cases payors have argued that the time to be assessed should include only the time that the child is in the direct care of a parent. Once time at school or daycare is excluded, it is much easier for access parents to reach the 40% threshold. The courts have rejected this approach. See, for example, *Meloche* v. *Kales* (1997), 35 R.F.L. (4th) 297 (Ont. Gen. Div.). In *Kolada* v. *Kolada*, [1999] A.J. No. 609 (Alta. Q.B.), Veit J. suggested that the courts should count the hours that a child spends with the parent or is within the parent's responsibility. See also *Gore-Hickman* v. *Gore-Hickman* (1999), 177 D.L.R. (4th) 222 (Sask Q.B.), where Laing J. referred to the number of meals the children ate with each parent and the number of nights spent with each. Ultimately, however, the justice concluded (at 228): "I accept that calculation of hours where the same can be ascertained is the best method of calculating the time a child spends with each parent during the course of a year." This approach is generally more advantageous to the primary custodial parent than the counting of days or overnights which has also been adopted in cases such as *Ellis* v. *Ellis* (1997), 158 Nfld. & P.E.I.R. 193 (P.E.I. T.D.). Finally, in *Dennett* v. *Dennett* (1998), 225 A.R. 50 (Q.B.), Romaine J. suggested a more purposive rather than formalistic approach "to take into account the quality of time spent by each parent with the children, both in determining whether the arrangement is in spirit a situation of shared custody and in determining whether in fact there are increased costs of care of the children for either or both parents that might make Regulation 9 appropriate to the circumstances." See also *Penner* v. *Penner* (1999), 44 R.F.L. (4th) 294 (Man. Q.B.) and *Ball* v. *Ball* (1998), 170 Sask. R. 192 (Sask. Q.B.).

6. Section 9 provides a good deal of discretion in assessing the quantum of child support in shared custody cases. In "Child Support Under the Guidelines in Cases of Split and Shared Custody" (1998), 15 Can. J. Fam. L. 11, Professor Rogerson suggests (at 59) that the cases exhibit two competing approaches: one, the dominant one, which gravitates toward some version of an offset formula modeled on the split custody provision and the other which stresses the need for the exercise of discretion on a case-by-case basis. Which approach is adopted in *Hunter*? Why did the court in *Hunter* not follow *Middleton* and simply setoff the two Table amounts? How would the court in *Hunter* have calculated the appropriate amount of support if the child had resided with the father for only 40% of the time rather than 50%? Why was the amount produced by the calculation in *Hunter* increased by 50%?

For recent cases on the calculation of the amount of child support amounts under s. 9, see *Mac-Naught* v. *MacNaught* (1998), 37 R.F.L. (4th) 79 (P.E.I. T.D.); *Burns* v. *Burns* (1998), 40 R.F.L. (4th) 32 (Ont. Gen. Div.); *Spanier* v. *Spanier* (1998), 40 R.F.L. (4th) 329 (B.C. S.C.); *Ryba* v. *Schoenroth* (1998), 42 R.F.L. (4th) 97 (Sask. Q.B.), reversed (1999), 47 R.F.L. (4th) 381 (Sask. C.A.); *Soderberg* v. *Soderberg* (1998), 42 R.F.L. (4th) 403 (N.W.T. S.C.); *Stanford* v. *Cole* (1998), 43 R.F.L. (4th) 237 (Nfld. U.F.C.); *Collin* v. *Doyle* (1999), 44 R.F.L. (4th) 198 (Alta. Q.B.); *Penner* v. *Penner* (1999), 44 R.F.L. (4th) 294 (Man. Q.B.); *Cuddy* v. *Cuddy* (1999), 45 R.F.L. (4th) 131 (Ont. S.C.J.); *Dilney* v. *Dilney* (1999), 47 R.F.L. (4th) 133 (Nfld. U.F.C.); and *Dorey* v. *Snyder* (1999), 48 R.F.L. (4th) 67 (Ont. Gen. Div.).

In *Green* v. *Green* (May 18, 2000), the B.C. C.A. reviewed the various approaches to s. 9 and expressed scepticism about the use of any formula to determine the amount of child support. It stressed (para. 34) that discretion was built into the section and that the court should examine the increased cost of the shared custody arrangements in the particular case as well as the means and needs of each parent.

(5) UNDUE HARDSHIP

DEAN v. FRIESEN

(1999), 50 R.F.L. (4th) 363 (Sask. Q.B.)

[A mother and father separated in 1982 after seven years of marriage during which they had two children. A separation agreement provided that the father would pay nominal child support, but stipulated that the mother could apply for an increase if circumstances changed. The father remarried in 1985 and had three more children.

The father earned about $45,000 as a farmer, but he stated that he was so poor that there were times in the past winter when the family had no groceries. As a low income family, they qualified for some dental and health-related benefits for the three children under the provincial Family Income Plan. The mother remarried, but this second marriage ended in the late 1980's. She raised cattle as a hobby farmer and earned about $28,000 as a bus driver. The parties' oldest child was no longer a child of the marriage as she had become independent.]

Wilkinson J.: . . . At this level of income, the existence of a second family with three children constitutes a ground for the determination of undue hardship under s. 10(2)(d) of the *Guidelines*, and the court has discretion to award an amount of child support that differs from the *Guideline* amount. . . .

Under s. 10 of the *Guidelines*, even if a determination of undue hardship is made, the court must deny the application unless it is satisfied that the party suffering undue hardship has a standard of living lower than that of the other spouse. In this case, the comparison of household standards of living shows the respondent [the father] has the lower standard of living. The respondent's income, adjusted for average tax of $279.84 over the three year period, results in a net of $44,646.04. His spouse's net income after tax (averaged over three years) is $5,746 for a total household income of $50,392.04. At an income of $44,925, the *Guideline* amount for one child is $363 per month or $4,356 annually. Deducting $4,356 from the total household income results in total household adjusted income of $46,036.04. The low income measure for a household comprised of two adults and three children is $23,879. Accordingly, the respondent's household income ratio is $46,036 over $23,879 or 1.92.

The applicant's total household income is $24,406 after tax. Adding child support payments of $4,356 annually gives the applicant total household adjusted income of $28,762. The low income measure for a household consisting of one adult and one child is $14,535. The applicant's household income ratio is $28,762 over $14,535 or 1.97.

In this case, I consider an appropriate order for child support to be the sum of $236 per month, an amount which will make the parties' household income ratios relatively comparable. It also represents the *Guideline* amount the respondent would pay for four children at an annual income of $44,925, apportioned equally between all four children.

NOTES AND QUESTIONS

1. Section 10 provides a narrow exception because it applies only if 1) there is undue hardship and 2) the person seeking the adjustment resides in a household with a lower standard of living than that of the other parent. Even then, the courts claim a general discretion not to adjust the amount: *Matthews* v. *Hancock* (1998), 42 R.F.L. (4th) 72 (Sask. Q.B.); *Crawley* v. *Tobin* (1998), 42 R.F.L. (4th) 327 (Nfld. U.F.C.); and *Van Gool* v. *Van Gool* (1998), 44 R.F.L. (4th) 314, at 327 (B.C. C.A.).

2. Adjustments under s. 10 have been rare. Even if one of the circumstances listed in s. 10(2) exists and the parent seeking the adjustment resides in a household with a lesser standard of living, the courts may conclude that there is no undue hardship: *Hansvall* v. *Hansvall* (1997), 160 Sask. R. 201 (Q.B.); *Van Gool*, above; and *Chong* v. *Chong* (1999), 47 R.F.L. (4th) 301 (B.C. S.C.). In *Van Gool*, Prowse J.A. stated (at 328-329):

> Since the basic table amounts were designed to be a "floor" for the amount payable, rather than a ceiling, it is not surprising that the authorities have held that the threshold for a finding of undue hardship is high. Hardship is not sufficient; the hardship must be "undue", that is "exceptional",

"excessive" or "disproportionate" in all the circumstances. The onus is on the party applying under s. 10 to establish undue hardship; it will not be presumed simply because the applicant has the legal responsibility for another child or children and/or because the standard of living of the applicant's household is lower than that of the other spouse. The applicant must lead cogent evidence to establish why the table amount would cause undue hardship.

Sometimes the courts will expressly conclude that there is hardship, but that it is not "undue". See, e.g., *Chong*, above; *Wislesky* v. *Wislesky* (1999), 47 R.F.L. (4th) 208 (Ont. Gen. Div.); and *St. Croix* v. *Maxwell* (1999), 3 R.F.L. (5th) 161 (Ont. S.C.J.).

3. Most of the reported cases in which someone has successfully invoked s. 10 involve payors with support obligations to second families. In addition to *Dean* v. *Friesen*, see *Reiter* v. *Reiter* (1997), 36 R.F.L. (4th) 102 (B.C. Master); *Aker* v. *Howard* (1998), 43 R.F.L. (4th) 159 (Ont. Gen. Div.); and *Hanmore* v. *Hanmore* (1999), 47 R.F.L. (4th) 157 (Alta. Q.B.). Claims on this basis failed in *Walkeden* v. *Zemlak* (1997), 33 R.F.L. (4th) 52 (Sask. Q.B.); *Nishnik* v. *Smith* (1998), 39 R.F.L. (4th) 105 (Sask. Q.B.); *Wislesky*, above; *Chong*, above; and *Van Gool*, above. In some of these cases, the claims failed even though the payor's new family had a lower standard of living than that of the payee's family.

4. The *Guidelines* only allow access costs to be taken into account in lowering the amount of child support if the paying parent can satisfy the two hurdles in s. 10. First, he or she must establish that undue hardship arises out of "unusually high expenses in relation to exercising access to a child". Second, the court must conclude that the payor has a lower household standard of living. In general, access parents have not had much success in invoking s. 10. Often, this results from the mandatory comparison of household living standards test. But judges have also been reluctant to find that the expenses are "unusually high". In *Beeler* v. *Beeler* (1997), 32 R.F.L. (4th) 397 (Sask. Q.B.), Noble J. concluded that the cost of driving a long distance to exercise access was "not strictly speaking a hardship cost in a province like Saskatchewan where travel distances between communities are a reasonably common fact of life." The court also noted "that the father could combine his travel costs with another resident of Nokomis who fathered a baby with the mother and who incurs the same travel costs as he does in accessing that child". See also *Williams* v. *Williams* (1997), 32 R.F.L. (4th) 23 (N.W.T. S.C.) (access costs not "unusually high" where children lived in the Northwest Territories and access parent had moved to Nova Scotia) and *Button* v. *Button* (1999), 48 R.F.L. (4th) 258 (Nfld. U.F.C.) (cost of three trips annually to Newfoundland to exercise access did not result in "unusually high" access costs).

The Senate's Standing Committee on Social Affairs, Science and Technology expressed concern in its *The Federal Child Support Guidelines: Interim Report* (1998) that it was unfair for an access parent to absorb all the costs of exercising access particularly if the decision to move was the custodial parent's. It recommended that the *Guidelines* should provide, through a provision modeled on s. 7, for the proportional sharing of the access costs that result when one parent lives a considerable distance from the child. Do you agree? Should it make a difference who moves away?

In the cases pre-dating the adoption of the *Guidelines* sometimes a court would require a moving custodial parent to help pay for the increased cost of exercising access either directly through reimbursement or indirectly through reduced child support. The reduction of child support is now covered by s. 10 and its stringent requirements. It is uncertain whether a court still has jurisdiction to order the custodial parent to pay directly for access costs. Some judges have held that s. 10 of the *Guidelines* exhaustively covers the issue of access costs: *South* v. *South*, [1998] B.C.J. 962 (B.C. S.C.). Professor McLeod has argued in several annotations in the Reports of Family Law that a court should be able to order a custodial parent to assume some of the costs of transportation relating to access simply as a condition of custody and independently of any child support issues. See, for example, his annotation to *Holtskog* v. *Holtskog* (1999), 47 R.F.L. (4th) 162 (Sask. C.A.). See also "Reforming the Child Support Guidelines" in *Federal Child Support Guidelines Reference Manual* (Ottawa: Dept. of Justice, looseleaf) where Professor Bala states (at K-75):

The better view is articulated by the recent mobility cases where judges, in appropriate cases, exercise a discretion to require the custodial parent to pay all or part of the increased access costs. Technically, the judge is not reducing the Guidelines' child support order, which continues to be fully enforceable as child support, but rather is invoking subsection 16(6) of the *Divorce Act* to impose a ''condition'' on custody that permits the custodial parent to move, but requires that parent to pay all or part of the increased access costs, if and when access is exercised.

5. The circumstances listed in s. 10(2) are not exhaustive. In *Petrocco* v. *von Michalofski* (1998), 36 R.F.L. (4th) 278 (Ont. Gen. Div.), the children lived with the father and his new wife. Their combined income was about $300,000 per year. The mother's annual income, including spousal support, was about $40,000. The court concluded that s. 10 applied and reduced the mother's child support obligation from $516 per month to $150 per month. It reasoned (at 285) that payment of child support at the *Guidelines* level would constitute undue hardship for the mother because her role as access parent would be ''detrimentally affected by an inability to offer the children a reasonable level of activity and comforts relative to that enjoyed in their primary residence''. See also *Scharf* v. *Scharf* (1998), 40 R.F.L. (4th) 422 (Ont. Gen. Div.).

6. To compare household standards, s.10(4) indicates that the court may, but need not, use the formula set out in Schedule II. This formula appears complex, but this may be inevitable. Any comparison of household living standards has to determine the net income of the adult members and adjust for household size. Also, computer programs are available to make the necessary calculations.

The *Federal Child Support Guidelines Consultation Paper* (Ottawa: Dept. of Justice, 1999) reports (at 13) that the formula is used in only about a quarter of the undue hardship cases. In the others, judges use their discretion to compare standards of living in other ways, leading to diverse results.

7. Justice Boland in *Souliere* v. *Leclair* (1998), 38 R.F.L. (4th) 68 (Ont. Gen. Div.) rejected a *Charter* challenge to the requirement that each member of the household reveal his or her income.

8. Payees have very infrequently invoked s. 10(2) to increase the amount of child support above the *Guidelines* amount. See Joseph P. Hornick *et al*, *The Survey of Child Support Awards: Final Analysis of Pilot Data and Recommendations for Continued Data Collection* (Ottawa: Minister of Justice, 1999) at 29. In ''An Update of case Law under the Child Support Guidelines'' (1998-99), 16 C.F.L.Q. 261, Justice Aston suggests (at 292) that the ''most likely scenario for increased child support, based on undue hardship, is the split custody or shared custody situation in which the court may consider maintaining a similar standard of living for siblings''.

Can a failure by the access parent to exercise access lead to undue hardship for the custodial parent for the purpose of s. 10? See *Scotcher* v. *Hampson* (1998), 41 R.F.L. (4th) 271 (Ont. Gen. Div.).

9

DOMESTIC CONTRACTS

1. Introduction

The common law attempted to encourage the marriage relationship and its continuation. Accordingly, a contract that involved cohabitation without marriage was considered contrary to public policy and invalid. In addition, the courts generally recognized and enforced contracts made in consideration of marriage or contracts made by married persons for other valuable consideration only if such contracts did not anticipate separation by dealing with the rights and obligations of the spouses in the event they ceased to cohabit. However, agreements made by spouses after separation were not considered contrary to public policy. Prior to the *Family Law Reform Act* of 1978, such separation agreements were the only domestic contracts commonly used in Ontario.

The *Family Law Reform Act* altered the common law by giving recognition to marriage contracts that dealt with the rights and obligations of spouses upon separation, annulment or divorce and to cohabitation agreements between a man and a woman who were unmarried but cohabited. It also provided a framework for the making of all types of domestic contracts recognized in the Act: marriage contracts, cohabitation agreements, and separation agreements.

Part IV of the *Family Law Act* (*FLA*) is clearly modeled on Part IV of the *Family Law Reform Act*. It specifically recognizes marriage contracts, separation agreements and cohabitation agreements as domestic contracts that can, to some extent, override or modify the statutory rights of the parties. The general rule established in s. 2(10) is that a "domestic contract dealing with a matter that is also dealt with in this Act prevails unless this Act provides otherwise".

The next section of this chapter briefly examines the types of domestic contracts dealt with in Part IV of the *FLA*. The formal requirements and rules governing capacity to contract set out in the Act are the focus of the chapter's third section, while the fourth deals with the extent to which couples are free to govern their relationship by domestic contract. The chapter concludes with a sampling of the grounds on which a court may ignore or set aside such a contract.

The last two sections, in particular, reveal that there is a continuing tension between several conflicting policy objectives. While private settlement of disputes or potential disputes is viewed as desirable, there is also a recognition of the need to ensure that one party is not unduly exploited by the other and that the interests of children or other matters of public interest are not ignored. Thus, while the law permits considerable freedom of contract, it also imposes certain safeguards and controls. This involves a delicate balancing act because the limits on private ordering may, in effect, discourage a couple from attempting to settle disputes.

The following article provides both reasons why the legal system should permit and indeed encourage divorcing couples to work out their own arrangements and justification for imposing some limits on private ordering.

MNOOKIN, "DIVORCE BARGAINING: THE LIMITS ON PRIVATE ORDERING"

Eekelar and Katz, eds., *The Resolution of Family Conflict: Comparative Legal Perspectives* (Toronto: Butterworths, 1984) 366-372 and 375-379
(Footnotes Omitted)

THE ADVANTAGES OF PRIVATE ORDERING

Let me begin with the arguments supporting the presumption in favor of private ordering. The core reason is rooted in notions of human liberty. Private ordering is supported by the liberal ideal that individuals have rights, and should largely be left free to make of their lives what they wish. In Charles Fried's words, a regime of law that "respects the dispositions individuals make of their rights, carries to its logical conclusion the liberal premise that individuals have rights." Professor Fried has elegantly defended on a non-utilitarian basis the principle that "persons may impose on themselves [through contracts] obligations where none existed before." He argues that "the capacity to form true and rational judgments and act on them is the heart of moral personality and the basis of a person's claim to respect as a moral being." Thus, as a general proposition, enforcement of agreements made at the time of divorce can be justified as giving expression to a "free man's rational decision about how to dispose of what is his, how to bind himself."

Private ordering can also be justified on grounds of efficiency. Ordinarily, the parties themselves are in the best position to evaluate the comparative advantages of alternative arrangements. Each spouse, in the words of John Stuart Mill, "is the person most interested in his own well-being: . . . with respect to his own feelings and circumstances, the most ordinary man or woman has means of knowledge immeasurably surpassing those that can be possessed by anyone else." Through negotiations, there are opportunities for making *both* parents better off than either would be if a court or some third party simply imposed a result. A consensual solution is, by definition, more likely to be consistent with the preferences of each spouse than would a result imposed by a court. Parental preferences often vary with regard to money and child-rearing responsibilities. Through negotiations, it is possible that the divorcing spouses can divide money and child-raising responsibilities to reflect their own individual preferences.

Finally, there are obvious and substantial savings when a couple can resolve the distributional consequences of divorce without resort to formal adjudication. The financial cost of litigation, both private and public, is minimized. The pain of the formal adversarial proceedings is avoided. A negotiated settlement allows the parties to avoid the risks and uncertainties of litigation, which may involve all-or-nothing consequences. Given the substantial delays that often characterize contested judicial proceedings, agreement can often save time and allow each spouse to proceed with his or her life. In short, against a backdrop of fair standards in the shadow of which a couple bargains, divorcing couples should have very broad powers to make their own arrangements. Significant limitations are inconsistent with the premises of no-fault divorce. Parties should be encouraged to settle the distributional consequences of divorce for themselves, and the state should provide an efficient and fair mechanism for enforcing such agreements and for settling disputes when the parties are unable to agree.

CAPACITY

On an abstract level, I find the general defense of private ordering both appealing and persuasive. But it is premised on the notion that divorce bargaining involves rational, self-interested individuals — that the average adult has the intelligence and experience to make a well-informed judgment concerning the desirability of entering into a particular divorce settlement. Given the tasks facing an individual at the time of divorce, and the characteristics of the relationship between divorcing spouses, there are reasons to fear that this may not always be the case.

Informed bargaining requires a divorcing spouse to assess his or her own preferences concerning alternative arrangements. Radical changes in life circumstances complicate such assessments. Within a short period of time, separation and divorce often subject spouses to the stresses of many changes: "[S]pouses need to adjust to new living arrangements, new jobs, financial burdens, new patterns of parenting, and new conditions of social and sexual life." It may be particularly difficult for a parent to assess custodial alternatives. The past will be a very incomplete guide to the future. Preferences may be based on past experiences in which child-rearing tasks were performed in an ongoing two-parent family, and dissolution or divorce inevitably alters this division of responsibilities. Child-rearing may now have new advantages or disadvantages for the parents' own needs. A parent interested in dating may find the child an intrusion in a way that the child never was during marriage. Because children and parents both change, and changes may be unpredictable, projecting parental preferences for custody into the future is a formidable task. Nevertheless, most parents have some self-awareness, however imperfect, and no third party (such as a judge) is likely to have better information about a parent's tastes, present or future.

Separation often brings in its wake psychological turmoil and substantial emotional distress that can make deliberative and well-informed judgments unlikely. It can arouse "feelings about the former spouse, such as love, hate, bitterness, guilt, anger, envy, concern, and attachment; feelings about the marriage, such as regret, disappointment, bitterness, sadness, and failure; and more general feelings such as failure, depression, euphoria, relief, guilt, lowered self-esteem, and lowered self-confidence." Isolini Ricci has suggested that for many individuals "the emotions of ending a marriage" characteristically go through five stages during a two or three year period. For the first three stages, if Ricci's characterizations are correct, an otherwise competent person may at times have seriously impaired judgment. She suggests that the pre-separation stage is often marked by "anxiety, depression, hostility, and recurring illness." The separation stage can bring with it three dangerous side effects: "poor judgment; accident and illness-proneness, poor reflex action; and depression." The third stage, which follows the separation, arouses strong emotions that are "both natural and nasty." "Emotional roller-coasters are common at this stage, causing many people to feel permanent emotional instability." According to Ricci, "this is the worst possible time to make any permanent decisions — especially legal ones. Thinking and believing the worst about each other is one of the chief hazards of this stage, and such thoughts, exaggerated and extended, can lead to serious complications."

Such emotional turmoil may prevent for a time any negotiated settlement. Or it may lead to a settlement that a party later regrets.

> Frequently, the partner who wishes to end the marriage feels guilt at abandoning the spouse. Once the initiator finally broaches the topic of divorce, continued guilt, combined with the equally strong desire to leave, may produce a virulent form of the "settlement at any cost" mentality. At

the same time, the spouse who wishes to keep the marriage may escalate demands, motivated by feelings of humiliation and anger, combined with prospects of a bleak and unchosen future. Unreasonable demands may also be a means to prolong the marriage and ultimately prevent the marital breakup.

An opposite pattern was also noted by several of our respondents: guilt in the initiator may be expressed as anger directed at the non-initiator, in whom feelings of diminished self-worth may inhibit the ability to bargain constructively, or produce an abject acceptance of almost any terms. A settlement may thus be quickly arrived at whose inequitable and unworkable nature may not be apparent until several years and several court fights later.

Some might think that the stresses and emotional turmoil of separation and divorce undermine the essential premise of private ordering — the idea that individuals are capable of deliberate judgments. I disagree. After all, for most persons the emotional upheaval is transitory, and the stresses are an inevitable consequence of having to make a new life. Temporary incapacity does not justify state paternalism for an extended period of time. Nonetheless, safeguards are necessary, and the wooden application of the traditional contract defense of "incompetence" may not provide sufficient protection. More recent contract scholarship suggests a theory that respects the ideal of individual autonomy and the efficiency of private ordering, and avoids the unfairness of bargains that exploit a temporarily diminished capacity.

Professor Eisenberg recently suggested a concept of "transactional incapacity" to capture the notion that "an individual may be of average intelligence and yet may lack the aptitude, experience, or judgmental ability to make a deliberative and well-informed judgment concerning the desirability of entering into a given complex transaction." Eisenberg's concern was with situations where one party exploits the other party's incapacity to deal with a complex transaction, "by inducing . . . a bargain that a person who had capacity to deal with the transaction probably would not make." In such circumstances, Eisenberg suggests that neither fairness nor efficiency support application of the principle that a bargain should be enforced to its full extent. It is unfair because it violates conventional moral standards "to make a bargain on unfair terms by exploiting . . . incapacity." Moreover, "the maxim that a promisor is the best judge of his own utility can have little application: by hypothesis, the promisor is not able to make a well-informed judgment concerning the transaction."

An analogous concept could be applied to divorce bargaining within a system that encourages private ordering at the time of divorce. When one spouse knows or has reason to know of the diminished capacity, and exploits this incapacity, a court should reopen the agreement. Proof of exploitation is essential, however. For this, I would require a showing that the terms of the agreement considered as a whole fall outside the range of settlement. By providing a remedy only if a party exploited the other side's incapacity by securing an unusually one-sided bargain, this test will not create uncertainty in most cases. Many divorced spouses may in retrospect think they were unwise in accepting some provision, and some might be able to show a lack of deliberative judgment, but few will be able to show that the settlement as a whole would have been unacceptable to a competent person. Any additional uncertainty created for parties making "out of the ordinary" deals may not be a bad thing. Moreover, I would create a presumption against the application of this diminished capacity doctrine in any cases where the party making the claim was represented by counsel. Indeed, as Eisenberg suggests, "If a party who has been urged, fairly and in good faith, to seek advice, fails to do so, the doctrine of transactional incapacity would normally not apply, because the element of exploitation would be lacking"

— at least where the party has sufficient capacity "to understand the importance of getting advice."

A second prophylactic to guard against transitory diminished capacity would involve a "cooling-off" period, during which either party would be free to rescind a settlement agreement. In a commercial context, this period is often very short — typically three days. In the divorce context, I would make it considerably longer — perhaps sixty or ninety days. Like any safeguard, this one has costs. Some agreements may come apart even though they involve no exploitation whatsoever, simply because of ambivalence or a change of heart. Moreover, this cooling-off period might be used strategically by a party — a tentative agreement may be reached, only to be later rescinded, in order to wear an opponent down. Nonetheless, it would seem appropriate to have a fixed, reasonable "boundary line" as a rough estimate of the time within which the "transitory state of acquiescence" induced by guilt or anxiety might be expected to lapse. In cases where both parties have assigned counsel, it might be possible to have a shorter period.

UNEQUAL BARGAINING POWER

Let me now turn to a second possible justification for imposing limits on private ordering — the basic idea is simple; in negotiation between two competent adults, if there are great disparities in bargaining power, some bargains may be reached that are unconscionably one-sided.

The notion of bargaining power has intuitive appeal, but turns out to be very difficult to define. Without a complete theory of negotiations, it is hard to give precise substantive content to the notion of bargaining power, much less define precisely the idea of "relative bargaining power." Nonetheless, by briefly analyzing the five elements of the bargaining model I described in an earlier article, it is possible to suggest why some divorcing spouses may be seen as having unequal bargaining power.

First, there are the legal endowments. The legal rules governing marital property, alimony, child support, and custody give each spouse certain claims based on what each would get if the case goes to trial. In other words, the outcome the law will impose if no agreement is reached gives each parent certain bargaining chips — an endowment of sorts. These endowments themselves can create unequal bargaining power. For example, other things being equal, in a state where there is a tender years presumption in favor of maternal custody, a mother has considerably more bargaining power (at least if she wants custody) than the father. A new law creating a presumption against spousal support, on the other hand, would reduce the bargaining endowment of women as a class. To the extent that negotiated settlements simply reflect differences in bargaining power based on the legal rules themselves, this would not justify a claim of unfairness in an individual case. Instead, the legal endowments should be changed.

Second, a party's bargaining power is very much influenced by his or her preferences — i.e., how that party subjectively evaluates alternative outcomes. These preferences are not simply matters of taste — they can depend upon a party's economic resources and life circumstances. The parties' relative bargaining power depends on how they both subjectively evaluate the outcome a court would impose.

A third element that affects bargaining power has to do with uncertainty, and the parties' attitudes towards risk. Often the outcome in court is far from certain, and the parties are negotiating against a backdrop clouded by substantial uncertainty.

Because the parties may have different risk preferences, this uncertainty can differentially affect the bargaining power of the two spouses. If there is substantial variance among the possible court-imposed outcomes, the relatively more risk averse party is comparatively disadvantaged.

A fourth element that can create differences in bargaining power relates to the differential ability to withstand the transaction costs — both emotional and economic — involved in negotiations. A party who is in no hurry, enjoys negotiations, and has plenty of resources to pay a lawyer, has an obvious advantage over an opponent who is impatient, hates negotiations, and cannot afford to wait.

A fifth element concerns the bargaining process itself, and strategic behaviour. In divorce bargaining, the spouses may not know each other's true preferences. Negotiations often involve the attempts by each side to discern the other side's true preferences, while making credible claims about their own, and what they intend to do if a particular proposal is not accepted. "Bargainers bluff, argue for their positions, attempt to deceive or manipulate each other, and make power plays to gain an advantage." Some people are more skilled negotiators than others. They are better at manipulating information and managing impressions. They have a more refined sense of tactical action. These differences can create inequalities in negotiations.

In short, the relative bargaining power of divorcing spouses depends upon how each evaluates the consequences of what will happen absent an agreement. This, in turn, depends not simply upon the legal endowments, but each party's subjective evaluation of the outcome absent a negotiated agreement, and the probable transaction costs of a court-imposed resolution. To the extent that a spouse sees himself as lacking alternatives, and is perceived as being dependent upon resources controlled by the other spouse, he lacks bargaining power. Bargaining power thus has both subjective and objective elements.

[Professor Mnookin then examines two examples of negotiated outcomes that seem very one-sided. In the second, a wife agrees to sell her own half interest in a jointly-held home to her husband for $40,000 even though the home is worth about $150,000. She does this because she is very short of funds and wishes to buy a condominium and start over. Court action to realize her interest in the home would take about a year.]

In cases like this, the problem is not that W did not know what she was doing. To the contrary, her consent to this agreement is real. As Professor Dawson pointed out in his seminal article many years ago, "the more unpleasant the alternative, the more real the consent to a course which would avoid it." The underlying issue concerns in part the question of what pressures can legitimately be brought to bear in bargaining, and how and whether it is possible to regulate the manner in which such pressures are exercised. This would be an easy case if W had shown that she accepted $40,000 because of physical threats by H. The doctrine of "duress" has traditionally permitted a defense to enforcement of a contract brought about by threats of illegal conduct. In this case, however, H's conduct is not illegal, but it is nonetheless plain that H is taking advantage of W's desire to sell quickly. One's appraisal of the morality of H's conduct might well be influenced by an evaluation of whether he was somehow responsible for W's urgent need. . . .

While I am reluctant to allow a court to evaluate the fairness of the price in divorce bargains, I am deeply troubled by this second case. It seems clear that various doctrines of contract law are sufficient to permit intervention in egregious cases where it is thought that inequality in bargaining power has brought about unjust enrichment. The underlying philosophical and jurisprudential issues are difficult ones, but they do not, in my view, undermine the general reasons to favor private ordering, any more than the doctrines of duress or unconscionability undermine all of contract law. There are a variety of legal mechanisms to change the results. The bargaining endowments can be changed, and *ex post* review can be permitted to prevent unjust enrichment brought about by conduct that is viewed as morally unacceptable.

EXTERNALITIES — THIRD PARTY EFFECTS

Third party effects provide the last set of reasons that justify limiting private ordering. A legal system that gives divorcing couples freedom to determine for themselves their post-dissolution rights and responsibilities may lead to settlements that reflect the spouses' interests. But negotiated agreements can also have important consequences for third parties, and affect social interests that are not adequately weighed in the private negotiations. The economists' idea of "externalities" — the notion that in some circumstances market prices that are affecting the behaviour of buyers and sellers will not adequately reflect the full range of social costs — has application here. In negotiating divorce settlements, the spouses may make decisions that have consequences for third parties, which, if taken into account, would suggest that some other settlement might be more socially desirable.

A divorce settlement may affect any number of interests not taken into account in the spouses' negotiations. The state's fiscal interests can be affected, for example. The economic terms of the bargain between the two spouses may substantially affect the odds that a custodial parent will later require public transfer payments. The most important third party effects concern the children, although there can be externalities with respect to other family members as well. At a conceptual level, it is easy to see how a negotiated settlement may reflect parental preferences but not the child's desires or needs. From the perspective of spouses who are negotiating their own settlements, marital property, alimony, and child support issues are all basically problems of money, and the distinctions among them become very blurred. Each can be translated into present dollar values. Moreover, custodial arrangements can often be divided in a wide variety of ways. From a bargaining perspective, the money and custody issues are inextricably linked together. Negotiated settlements will certainly reflect parental preferences with regard to these money and custody issues. These preferences, of course, will not generally be determined solely by self-interested judgments. One hopes that parental preferences reflect a desire for their children's happiness and well-being, quite apart from any parental advantage. Nevertheless, it is also certainly possible that some parents may engage in divorce bargaining on the basis of preferences that narrowly reflect their selfish interests, and ignore the children's needs. A father may threaten a custody fight over the child, not because he wants custody, but because he wants to push his wife into accepting less support, even though this will have a detrimental effect on the child. A custodial parent, eager to escape an unhappy marriage, may offer to settle for a small amount in order to sever relations soon. A custodial parent may negotiate to largely eliminate the child's contact with the other parent, not because of the child's wants or needs, but because he despises his *ex*-spouse and wants to have nothing more to do with her.

Concerns about the effects of the divorce on the children underlie many of the formal limitations on private ordering — e.g., the requirement of court review of private agreements relating to custody and child support; the legal rules prohibiting parents from making non-modifiable and binding agreements concerning these elements. In addition, the potential conflict of interest between divorcing parents, on the one hand, and the children, on the other, have led many to advocate the appointment of counsel for children, so that the children's interests can be directly represented in the divorce proceedings. . . .

I believe divorcing parents should be given considerable freedom to decide custody matters — subject only to the same minimum standards for protecting the child from neglect and abuse that the state imposes on *all* families. The actual determination of what is in fact in a child's best interests is ordinarily quite indeterminate. It requires predictions beyond the capacity of the behavioural sciences and involves imposition of values about which there is little consensus in our society. It is for this reason that I conclude that the basic question is who gets to decide on behalf of the child.

A negotiated resolution is desirable from the child's perspective for several reasons. First, a child's social and psychological relationships with both parents ordinarily continue after the divorce. A process that leads to agreement between the parents is preferable to one that necessarily has a winner and a loser. A child's future relationship with each of his parents is better ensured and his existing relationship less damaged by a negotiated settlement than by one imposed by a court after an adversary proceeding. Notions of child protection hardly justify general judicial suspicion of parental agreements; the state's interest in the child's well-being in fact implies a concomitant interest in facilitating parental agreement.

Second, the parents will know more about the child than will the judge, since they have better access to information about the child's circumstances and desires. Indeed, a custody decision privately negotiated by those who will be responsible for care after the divorce seems much more likely than a judicial decision to match the parents' capacities and desires with the child's needs.

If parents have the authority to decide custodial arrangements, there is no doubt that parents may make mistakes. But so may judges. More fundamentally, given the epistemological problems inherent in knowing what is best for a child, there is reason to doubt our capacity to know whether any given decision is a mistake. Therefore, the possibility that negotiated agreements may not be optimal for the child can hardly be a sufficient argument against a preference for private ordering. Moreover, because parents, not state officials, are primarily responsible for the day-to-day child-rearing decisions both before and after divorce, parents, not judges, should have primary authority to agree on custodial arrangements. This means that courts should not second-guess parental agreements unless judicial intervention is required by the narrow child-protection standard implicit in neglect laws. This is not to suggest that the state does not have an important responsibility to inform parents concerning the child's needs during and after the divorce; nor does it mean that the state does not have an important interest in facilitating parental agreement. Nevertheless, the law in action, which acknowledges substantial parental power, seems preferable to existing doctrine, which imposes substantial restrictions on the parents' power to decide for themselves. . . .

NOTES AND QUESTIONS

1. The current interest in mediation of family disputes reflects a recognition that a primary function of family law is to provide a framework within which the couples themselves determine the rights and responsibilities arising out of their relationships. Note s. 9(2) of the *Divorce Act*; s. 3 of the *FLA*; and s. 31 of the *Children's Law Reform Act*. Regarding the concept of mediation, see Chapter 1, **INTRODUCTION**.

2. As Professor Mnookin observes, the preference for private ordering is based, in part, on the liberal ideals of individual autonomy and freedom of choice. See also Trebilcock and Keshvani, "The Role of Private Ordering in Family Law" (1991), 47 U.T.L.J. 533.

The premise that negotiations leading to domestic contracts involve two rational, self-interested individuals has been vigorously challenged. In "A Matter of Difference: Domestic Contracts and Gender Equality" (1990), 28 O.H.L.J. 303, Professor Cossman argues that the liberal model of contract is based on a male sense of self which is not shared by many females whose approach to negotiation may well be more altruistic. Also, she points out (at 318) that the private choice approach ignores the unequal bargaining positions of husbands and wives on marriage breakdown. Professor Neave asserts in "Resolving the Dilemma of Difference: A Critique of 'The Role of Private Ordering in Family Law' " (1994), 44 U.T.L.J. 97 (at 99):

> . . . [The] preference for private ordering takes insufficient account of the fact that men and women who are negotiating pre-martial and separation agreements are differently situated. Far from enhancing women's individuality and autonomy, such agreements may simply privatize unequal outcomes of divorce for men and women and exacerbate gender inequality.

See also Wiegers, "Economic Analysis of Law and 'Private Ordering': A Feminist Critique" (1991), 47 U.T.L.J. 170; Majury, "Unconscionability in an Equality Context" (1991), 7 C.F.L.Q. 123; Rose, "Women and Property: Gaining and Losing Ground" (1992), 78 Va. L.R. 421; Bendoni, "Gender Differences in Negotiations and the Doctrine of Unconscionability in Domestic Contracts" (1994-5), 12 C.F.L.Q. 21; and Rose, "Bargaining and Gender" (1995), 18 Harv. J. of Law & Public Policy 547. The remedy suggested by many of these authors is a more liberal application in the family law context of the contract law doctrine of unconscionable bargain which is examined in the last section of this chapter.

3. Craig Martin uses negotiation theory to argue in "Unequal Shadows: Negotiation Theory and Spousal Support Under Canadian Divorce Law" (1998), 56 U.T.Fac. L. Rev. 135 that the legal framework governing spousal support systematically disadvantages the spousal support claimant in negotiations. The claimant is likely to be less loss-averse, less concession-averse and more risk-averse relative to the respondent. These characteristics by themselves are disadvantages in negotiations. Moreover, the greater risk-aversion makes the support claimant more vulnerable to strategic behaviour and reduces the subjective value of her best alternatives to a negotiated agreement. These tendencies are caused, in Martin's view, by the law's characterization of spousal support as a discretionary redistribution of the respondent's income where the claimant can establish entitlement and the vagueness of the statutory provisions and indeterminacy of the process.

2.   Types of Domestic Contracts

Section 51 of the *FLA* defines "marriage contract", "separation agreement" and "cohabitation agreement" and specifies that each is a domestic contract. Why is it necessary to distinguish between the various species of domestic contracts?

A marriage contract may be made by a man and a woman who are married to each other or who intend to marry: s. 52(1). Can you think of situations where it may be especially appropriate for a couple to enter into a contract prior to their marriage? See Wolfson, "Love Ain't Easier the Second Time Around: Family Law Concerns of the Remarrying Client" (1998-99), 16 C.F.L.Q. 239. Why may a couple want to make a marriage contract while cohabiting in a marriage relationship? A married couple who have separated may wish to enter into a contract as a precondition to the resumption of cohabitation. Would such a "reconciliation agreement" be a marriage contract or a separation agreement? What matters cannot be dealt with in a marriage contract?

In "Resolving the Dilemma of Difference: A Critique of 'The Role of Private Ordering in Family Law'" (1994), 44 U.T.L.J. 97, Professor Neave argues (at 120) that statutes such as the *FLA* inappropriately allow marriage contracts to override the statutory rules dealing with the rights and obligations of spouses:

> Pre-nuptial agreements are negotiated at a time when couples are more likely to have unrealistic expectations of each other, may be reluctant to consider the possibility of future separation, and may have considerable difficulty in predicting the changes likely to occur in the future patterns of their lives. At this stage of their relationship couples may treat procedural safeguards simply as formalities to be overcome.

> . . . Nor does independent legal advice or a cooling-off period address the difficulty of providing for contingencies which may not occur until many years later. Thus parties should be unable to contract out of family law rules by relying on pre-nuptial or nuptial agreements.

Do you agree?

In *Kaddoura* v. *Hammoud* (1998), 44 R.F.L. (4th) 228 (Ont. Gen. Div.), a couple, wishing to marry in accordance with the Muslim tradition, agreed before the marriage that the husband would pay to the wife "Mahr", a gift or contribution for her exclusive property, totaling $35,000. The Muslim marriage certificate referred specifically to the payment of $5,000 immediately and $30,000 on demand by the wife, divorce, or the husband's death. When the marriage ended and a dispute over the payment of "Mahr" arose, the court concluded that the dispute was not justiciable as it was purely a religious matter to be resolved according to religious doctrine and principle. Could the court have taken this approach if the agreement had satisfied the formalities set out in the *FLA* for domestic contracts?

Section 53 deals with cohabitation agreements. In 1999, the Ontario legislature amended subsection 1 of s. 53 by striking out the words "A man and a woman" in the first line and substituting "Two persons of the opposite sex or the same sex": *Amendments Because of the Supreme Court of Canada Decision in M. v. H. Act, 1999*, S.O. 1999, c. 6. Why may a couple want to make a cohabitation agreement? What matter can a couple deal with in a cohabitation agreement that cannot be governed by a marriage contract? What happens to a cohabitation agreement if the couple subsequently become husband and wife?

Section 54, as amended in 1999, specifies that two persons of the opposite sex or the same sex who cohabited and are living separate and apart can enter into a separation agreement. Why may two people who cohabited find such an agreement useful? Why may a husband and wife who already have a comprehensive marriage contract that makes provision for the rights and obligations of each party on separation nevertheless need a separation agreement? Consider ss. 52 and 54 of the *FLA*.

The statutory definitions of "marriage contract" and "separation agreement", when interpreted literally, suggest that married couples who wish to enter into agreements in anticipation of imminent separation can only make a marriage contract. What practical difficulties could this cause for separated couples? Is there any way to avoid this result?

Note s. 59 which deals with paternity agreements. Agreements entered into under s. 59(1) are not domestic contracts for the purposes of the *FLA*. What, then, is the purpose of s. 59?

3. Capacity and Formal Requirements

(1) CAPACITY

By virtue of s. 55(2) a minor has capacity to enter into a domestic contract subject to the approval of the court. Such approval may be given before or after the minor enters into the contract. Note also subsections (3) and (4) dealing with mentally incapable persons.

(2) FORMAL REQUIREMENTS

The following cases dealt with s. 54(1) of the *Family Law Reform Act.* The only difference between s. 54(1) of the old Act and s. 55(1) of the *FLA* is that the former specified that contracts that did not comply with the formal requirements were void while the latter stipulates that they are unenforceable.

SANDERSON v. SANDERSON

(1982), 31 R.F.L. (2d) 320, 40 O.R. (2d) 82 (Ont. H.C.)

WALSH J.: — Without the assistance of their solicitors, the husband and wife in these proceedings, some eight months after they ceased to cohabit, entered into what can only be described as a "home-made separation agreement". The first provision of it was "that Gerald shall pay the amount of $200 per month to Wilma for the maintenance, assistance and the upbringing of their son, Dale, while he is attending school commencing on October 15, 1980, and likewise every month thereafter". The following paragraphs dealt with the matrimonial home, joint assets, debts and other matters. This agreement was typewritten and, while in the form of a statutory declaration, was actually signed by both the husband and the wife. It was not, however, witnessed.

Some 18 months after the execution of this agreement the wife, by a specially endorsed writ, instituted these proceedings against the husband for his default in the payment of support for their son, Dale, as provided in the agreement, claiming arrears thereunder in the amount of $3,400. The husband filed an affidavit of merits in which he stated that he had been advised by his solicitor and verily believed that the agreement was a domestic contract . . . was therefore void by s. 54(1) of [the Family Law Reform Act, hereinafter the FLRA] as it was not witnessed.

It would seem that the solicitors acting for both the husband and the wife felt that the determination of the wife's claim somehow depended on whether this "home-made separation agreement" was rendered void by the provisions of s. 54(1). . . . On consent they brought an application before the District Court Judge to have this issue determined on a point of law. The learned District Court Judge held that that portion of the agreement relating to the maintenance of the child of the parties was not void . . . . From this decision the husband now appeals.

No claim is being made by the wife in these proceedings under any part or provision contained in the FLRA. The provisions of the FLRA relating to domestic contracts apply only to proceedings instituted pursuant to the provisions of that Act. Any agreement which may be rendered void by non-compliance with s. 54(1) of that Act is void only for the purposes of that Act and is not otherwise void unless also rendered so by operation of law entirely apart from that Act.

The wife's claim here is not based on the FLRA at all but, rather, on the husband's written promise to pay. Whether that promise is contained in an agreement which is rendered void by s. 54(1) of the FLRA can and does make no difference whatsoever to the validity of the wife's claim as advanced here nor can it afford the husband any defence to that claim.

The provisions of the FLRA are simply irrelevant to the matters at issue in this proceeding. What is relevant is whether the wife's claim is properly brought under R. 33 of the Rules of Practice and Procedure and whether the husband's affidavit of merits discloses any valid defence. On these issues I express no opinion. . . .

GEROPOULOS v. GEROPOULOS

(1982), 26 R.F.L. (2d) 225, 35 O.R. (2d) 763 (Ont. C.A.)

ROBINS J.A.: — The question to be decided in this appeal is whether, in the light of s. 54(1) of the Family Law Reform Act [FLRA], an agreement contained in an exchange of correspondence between solicitors settling the claims in an action brought pursuant to the Act is enforceable.

The facts are simple and undisputed. The appellant wife and respondent husband were married in 1977 and separated in 1978. In March 1979 the wife instituted this lawsuit claiming support and division of family and non-family assets under the provisions of the Act. On 30th August 1979 the husband's solicitor wrote to the wife's solicitor as follows:

> It is our understanding that our respective clients have agreed upon a settlement of this matter on the following basis:
>
> 1. Our client will pay your client a lump sum of $3,000.00. The sum of $1,500.00 will be paid immediately and the balance three months thereafter.
>
> 2. In consideration for payment of the said sum of $3,000.00 your client will release any interest that she now has in the matrimonial home, cottage, family and non-family assets of our client and will waive any claim for maintenance.
>
> 3. The contents of the house and cottage shall be divided as the parties shall agree.
>
> 4. Your client shall keep the 1970 LeSabre automobile.

The wife's solicitor replied on 15th October 1979 stating:

> I have now had the opportunity to review the contents of your letter of August 30, 1979 with my client. My client has instructed me to accept your client's offer and accordingly I would ask you to prepare the necessary Separation agreement and forward to the undersigned copies thereof.

Subsequently, for reasons which have not been disclosed, the wife refused to adhere to the settlement. The action proceeded with the husband pleading by way of defence:

> 6. The Defendant states that the parties have settled all issues of support and division of property pursuant to an agreement concluded between the solicitors on behalf of the respective parties which was confirmed by the Plaintiff's solicitor by letter dated the 15th of October, 1979, which agreement the Plaintiff now refuses to abide by. The Plaintiff is therefore estopped from bringing this action and asserting the within claims.

On 21st September 1981 the husband applied in the Family Law Motions Court for judgment in accordance with the settlement reached between the parties. The motion came on before Eberle J. who, after a careful consideration of the matter, granted judgment in terms of the settlement. . . . The appeal from that order is founded on s. 54(1) of the FLRA. . . .

The term "domestic contract", by s. 50, includes a separation agreement and "separation agreement" is defined in s. 53: . . .

Counsel for the appellant contends that the settlement agreement between the parties involves items covered by s. 53, namely, support and division of property, and is therefore a domestic contract within the meaning of the Act and, to be binding, must be signed by the husband and wife and witnessed; that an agreement between solicitors detailing the terms of settlement of an action, although clearly authorized and approved by the parties, is nonetheless unenforceable in the absence of the formal requirements of s. 54(1); in short, that the failure to comply with s. 54(1) constitutes an absolute bar to the enforcement of agreements compromising claims between separated spouses in litigation under the FLRA.

Prior to the advent of the FLRA in 1978 no particular formal requirements were necessary for agreements between husband and wife save for the provision respecting marriage contracts found in s.4 of the Statute of Frauds, R.S.O. 1970, c. 444. The effect to be given to an agreement negotiated by their solicitors or counsel compromising a pending action between them was a matter to be governed by the principles of substantive law applicable generally to the enforcement by way of judgment of settlement agreements. Those principles are enunciated in the often quoted statement of Evans J.A. in *Scherer* v. *Paletta*, [1966] 2 O.R. 524 at 527, where, speaking on behalf of this court, he said:

> A solicitor whose retainer is established in the particular proceedings may bind his client by a compromise of these proceedings unless his client has limited his authority and the opposing side has knowledge of the limitation, subject always to the discretionary power of the Court, if its intervention by the making of an order is required, to inquire into the circumstances and grant or withhold its intervention if it sees fit; and, subject also to the disability of the client. It follows accordingly, that while a solicitor or counsel may have apparent authority to bind and contract his client to a particular compromise, neither solicitor nor counsel have power to bind the Court to act in a particular way, so that, if the compromise is one that involves the Court in making an order, the want of authority may be brought to the notice of the Court at any time before the grant of its intervention is perfected and the Court may refuse to permit the order to be perfected. If, however, the parties are of full age and capacity, the Court, in practice, where there is no dispute as to the fact that a retainer exists, and no dispute as to the terms agreed upon between the solicitors, does not embark upon any inquiry as to the limitation of authority imposed by the client upon the solicitor.

Since the enactment of s. 54(1), the effect of a settlement agreement not signed by the spouses, covering matters included in s. 53, has arisen in a number of cases and it appears there is a difference of judicial opinion on the question. . . .

Returning to the present case, it is conceded that the agreement in question was complete, definite and intended to be binding; there is no suggestion of any lack of authority on the part of the solicitor or of any mistake, misrepresentation, duress or other circumstance which might impair the settlement or render it unenforceable; nor is it suggested that the agreement was tentative or contingent upon the execution of any further document, specifically, the separation agreement referred to in the letter of the wife's solicitor of 15th October 1979. The case was argued in this court, as it was in the court below, on the basis that a final agreement of settlement had been concluded but, by virtue of s. 54(1), and that section alone, it was not binding on the wife or enforceable in law against her. . . .

I share the view that settlement agreements concluded by solicitors or counsel resolving outstanding claims in pending litigations under the Act are beyond the reason and purview of s. 54(1). The formal requirements laid down by the section are intended to ensure that asserted domestic contracts, be they marriage contracts (s. 51), cohabitation agreements (s. 52), or separation agreements (s. 53), are reduced to writing and in fact agreed to by the parties as evidenced by their witnessed signatures; this in essence is a statute of frauds type provision made referable to domestic contracts by the FLRA.

In my opinion, the section plainly is not aimed at or intended to apply to authorized settlement agreements like the present, made with legal advice during the pendency of court proceedings which, to be effective, require the intervention of the court. Such agreements derive their effect from an act of the court; their authenticity is assured by the court's supervision and control over them; and ample protection is afforded the parties to these agreements, wholly independent of the section. The court's jurisdiction to enforce settlements or refuse to do so, notwithstanding any agreement between solicitors or counsel, is well established; whether they should be enforced or not, in the final analysis, is a matter for the discretion of the court and, in litigation under the FLRA, a matter that would be subject to the court's overriding jurisdiction with respect to domestic contracts: *Scherer* v. *Paletta*, supra; 3 Hals. (4th) 650-51, paras. 1182-83; and ss. 18(4) and 55 of the Act [ss. 33(4) and 56 of the FLA].

No purpose is to be served in compelling agreements of this kind to comply with the formalities of s. 54(1) and, if not, permitting parties to withdraw at will from compromises properly entered into by their legal representative before trial of their action or, if the appellant's position were to be accepted, compromises concluded even during the trial of the action. It may well be that, given the nature of matrimonial litigation, prudence would dictate that lawyers ensure that settlements are signed by the parties personally and witnessed. But I cannot construe the section as requiring that an otherwise valid compromise of an action must be rendered void and defeated on this ground alone, nor do I believe that the legislation could have contemplated or intended that result. Such a construction would be wholly inconsonant with the established policy of encouraging the settlement of disputed claims and recognizing and preserving the validity of settlements freely and properly entered into under advice.

For these reasons, I have concluded that the settlement agreement in the case before us is outside the area s. 54(1) was designed to cover and was correctly held to be binding on the appellant. I would accordingly dismiss the appeal, in the circumstances, without costs.

CAMPBELL v. CAMPBELL

(1985), 47 R.F.L. (2d) 392, 52 O.R. (2d) 206 (Ont. H.C.)

STEELE J.: — . . . In the spring of 1983, when the parties finally separated, they began negotiations relating to a settlement agreement. However, no proceedings were commenced in the court. The defendant chose not to obtain legal advice, although he was requested so to do by the plaintiff's lawyers. After a meeting between the plaintiff's solicitor and the defendant, the defendant wrote to the plaintiff's solicitor outlining an agreement with respect to spousal support. Subsequently, there were additional meetings between the plaintiff's lawyer and the defendant discussing the defendant's finances, and a draft letter of settlement was prepared. Certain final revisions were made to that letter and, on 15th August 1983, the plaintiff's solicitor delivered a letter to the defendant which is the agreement in question. Without going into the details of the itemized matters therein, the letter was addressed to both the plaintiff and the defendant and contained the following words:

Re: Separation Agreement

This letter is to record the basis of the agreement between you which is to be embodied in a formal Separation Agreement as soon as possible.

The second to last paragraph of the letter was as follows:

Kindly confirm your acceptance of this agreement by signing the original of this letter.

The letter was signed by the plaintiff's solicitor and, below that, both the plaintiff and the defendant personally signed the letter under the word "accepted". The defendant does not deny signing the letter. It is clear from his cross-examination that he knew and agreed to the exact contents of it. The letter included the identical support payments that had originally been set out in the defendant's letter in early June 1983.

A formal separation agreement was not prepared or presented to the defendant until January 1984, at which time he refused to execute it, in effect saying that he had changed his mind. The defendant takes the position that the opening words of the letter of 15th August contemplate a separation agreement to be made in the future, and that the letter itself was not itself an agreement.

There are no facts in dispute. Clearly, the letter was signed by both parties as accepted, and the only issue is the construction of the letter itself and whether it violates s. 54 of the Family Law Reform Act because the defendant's signature is not witnessed. The separation agreement that was forwarded in January 1984 contained all of the items in the letter, but with two additional clauses to which the defendant objects. There is no question that the defendant signed the agreement freely and that he understood the terms of the agreement at the time it was signed, as accepted. The application is properly brought. In my opinion, there is no merit to the defendant's position that it was only an agreement to enter into a future agreement. The agreement is unqualified. The parties intended to hold themselves bound until the execution of a formal agreement . . . .

The defendant relies upon s. 54(1) of the Family Law Reform Act to the effect that his signature was not witnessed and therefore the agreement is void. . . .

The letter agreement was a domestic contract. In my opinion, there is no argument as to the contents of the agreement and no question as to the conscious, knowing execution of that agreement by the parties. If a legal proceeding had been instituted, I would adopt the reasoning in *Geropoulos* v. *Geropoulos* (1982), 35 O.R. (2d) 763 at 769, 26 R.F.L. (2d) 225, 133 D.L.R. (3d) 121 (C.A.). . . .

That case related to an agreement of settlement entered into between the solicitors for the two parties after the issuance of the writ. In the present case, the defendant should not be able to avoid the clear agreement that he entered into to avoid an action in court purely on the grounds that he refused to retain a solicitor or that no writ had been issued. . . .

Unfortunately, I cannot find that the doctrine of part performance applies to make what might be an otherwise void contract enforceable because the plaintiff has merely accepted the benefits of the agreement and no more.

In my opinion, there is no question the agreement was clearly entered into and has been honoured by the parties, except for the payment of money and except that the defendant now wishes to escape his obligations thereunder. The requirement of the witnessing of an agreement under s. 54 is to ensure that the parties in fact signed it and that there was no duress or other grounds to refuse its enforcement. The words of s. 54 do not require that the signature of each party be expressly witnessed but only that the agreement be witnessed. In the present case, the agreement was prepared and signed by the plaintiff's solicitor. He was the witness to it. It is undisputed that the parties accepted the agreement and signed it. It would defeat the intent of the Act encouraging settlement of disputes to hold, in this case, that the absence of a specific witness to the defendant's signature would allow him to escape the very settlement that he made.

NOTES AND QUESTIONS

1. Was *Sanderson* rightly decided? Could the same result occur today in light of s. 55(1) of the *FLA*? The result is criticized in Hovius and Youdan, *The Law of Family Property* (Toronto: Carswell, 1991) at 653-654. For a contrary view, see McLeod, "Annotation" (1988), 14 R.F.L. (3d) 201.

2. The imposition of formal requirements for domestic contracts is legislative recognition of the special nature of such contracts. By requiring that the contracts be in writing, the legislation seeks to avoid disputes over exactly what was settled by oral negotiation. See also s. 5(6)(g) and s. 24(3)(d). The formal requirements also serve to alert the parties to the fact that they are engaged in a serious matter that can have significant legal consequences for them. They are, therefore, less likely to enter the contract lightly. This "warning function" is explicitly noted by Mendes da Costa U.F.C.J. in *Grant-Hose* v. *Grant-Hose* (1991), 32 R.F.L. (3d) 26 (Ont. U.F.C.) at 45. Regarding the functions generally served by formal requirements relating to domestic contracts, see Law Reform Commission of British Columbia, *Report on Spousal Agreements* (Victoria: Queen's Printer, 1986) at 31-32.

3. For other cases illustrating that the *Geropoulos* principle only applies to the settlement of issues in litigation commenced before the agreement is reached, see *Tanaszczuk* v. *Tanaszczuk* (1988), 25 R.F.L. (3d) 441 (Ont. U.F.C.); *Davis* v. *Gregory* (1990), 29 R.F.L. (3d) 62 (Ont. Gen. Div.); and *Tucker* v. *Tucker* (1993), 48 R.F.L. (3d) 5, (Nfld. C.A.).

4. In *Thornton* v. *Thornton* (1983), 33 R.F.L. (2d) 266, the Ontario Court of Appeal held that the trial judge had erred in granting a motion for judgment pursuant to minutes of settlement entered into by the counsel for the husband and wife. There was some dispute over the husband's instructions to his solicitor and he insisted that the solicitor had exceeded his authority. Also, the terms of the minutes had not been reduced to writing and signed by the solicitors. The Ontario Court of Appeal specifically referred to these facts in distinguishing *Geropoulos*.

See also *MacDonald* v. *MacDonald* (1986), 4 R.F.L. (3d) 463 (N.S. T.D.), where the court suggested that "although normally the court should enforce agreements made between counsel with their clients' authority, that rule should be somewhat relaxed in domestic actions where the parties are negotiating under the traumatic conditions which normally exist in a separation and a divorce action". The wife was not considered bound by an oral agreement governing corollary relief in divorce proceedings where she repudiated the agreement one day after it was negotiated by counsel. It was noted that the husband was not prejudiced by her conduct in any way. Compare *Manley* v. *Manley* (1990), 29 R.F.L. (3d) 283 (Ont. H.C.) where the husband's motion for judgment in accordance with a settlement agreement was granted even though the wife was under a great deal of stress and attempted to repudiate the settlement one day after it was made. For other cases dealing with the enforcement of settlements, see *Paradis* v. *Chamberlain* (1991), 35 R.F.L. (3d) 215 (Ont. Gen. Div.); *Lee-Chin* v. *Lee-Chin* (1993), 1 R.F.L. (4th) 351 (Ont. U.F.C.); *Allen* v. *Allen* (1994), 1 R.F.L. (4th) 406 (B.C. S.C.); *Nigris* v. *Nigris* (1999), 44 R.F.L. (4th) 269 (Ont. Gen. Div.); *Rotstein* v. *Rotstein* (1999), 44 R.F.L. (4th) 358 (Ont. Div. Ct.); and *Bogue* v. *Bogue* (1999), 1 R.F.L. (5th) 213 (Ont. C.A.).

5. Where a settlement is intended to be enforceable as a domestic contract and not simply the basis for consensual orders in pending or ongoing litigation, the formalities prescribed by s. 55(1) should be met.

6. In *Campbell*, Steele J. suggested that the principle in *Geropoulos* should apply whenever pending litigation is settled, whether or not the parties had legal representation. However, Langdon J. indicated in *Davis* v. *Gregory* (1990), 29 R.F.L. (3d) 62, at 67 (Ont. Gen. Div.) that the bar to enforcement imposed by s. 55(1) can only be ignored "in cases of settlement of pending litigation by counsel or ratified following the advice of counsel."

7. *Campbell* illustrates the general desire of the courts to hold parties to agreements and thus promote negotiated settlements. A similar approach is evident in *Hyldtoft* v. *Hyldtoft* (1991), 33 R.F.L. (3d) 99 (Ont. Gen. Div.). In that case the wife, Mrs. Wilcox, signed the document some time before the husband signed it. The witness, Mr. McCormick, watched the husband sign and simply assumed that the wife had also signed it while he was in the room. Haines J. concluded (at 107):

> Mrs. Wilcox raised no objection to the agreement in Mr. McCormick's presence, nor did she choose to absent herself from the room. In my view, she accepted Mr. McCormick as the witness for both signatures, thereby affirming her earlier execution of that document. I am, accordingly, satisfied that the formalities required by s. 55(1) of the *Family Law Act, 1986* were met.

See also *Lecot* v. *Lecot* (1995), 19 R.F.L. (4th) 14 (Ont. Gen. Div.) where the court held (at 23) that a "home-made" separation agreement which the parties signed in each other's presence without legal advice and without witnesses to their signatures was enforceable. However, in *Sagl* v. *Sagl* (1997), 31 R.F.L. (4th) 405 (Ont. Gen. Div.), the court held (at 418) that the cohabitation agreement "falls on a technicality as the law is clear that this witness [of the signatures] is to be someone other than the party".

8. It should be noted that s. 55(1) specifies that a domestic contract that fails to comply with the formal requirements is "unenforceable". An unenforceable contract is a valid contract, unless set aside for some reason, and may have legal and practical effect. For example, the case law dealing with an analogous provision in the *Statute of Frauds* suggests that a court will not unwind a transaction simply because it was completed pursuant to an unenforceable contract. See, generally, Fridman, *The Law of Contract in Canada*, 3rd ed. (Toronto: Carswell, 1994) at 224-227. Unenforceable contracts may also influence the court's exercise of discretion in determining support or property applications. For example, such contracts, if written, might be considered under s. 24(3)(d) and s. 5(6)(g) of the *FLA*. See, generally, Hovius and Youdan, *The Law of Family Property* (Toronto: Carswell, 1991) at 650-652. See also *Corbeil* v. *Bebris* (1993), 105 D.L.R. (4th) 759 (Alta. C.A.). However, any sections providing for direct enforcement of a domestic contract, such as s. 35, are inapplicable to such contracts. A domestic contract that is unenforceable by virtue of s. 55(1) should also not override the statutory provisions dealing with property and support. See *Davis* v. *Gregory* (1990), 29 R.F.L. (3d) 62 (Ont. Gen. Div.) where the court concluded that an unenforceable domestic contract did not bar an application for equalization of net family properties.

4.   Effect of a Domestic Contract

(1)   PROPERTY

Section 2(10) of the *FLA* stipulates that a domestic contract dealing with a matter that is also dealt with in the Act prevails unless the Act provides otherwise. There are no provisions limiting the ability of the spouses to contract out of Part I of the Act. Accordingly, the spouses can preclude the equalization of net family properties under Part I of the Act by entering into a domestic contract that establishes a comprehensive scheme for the regulation of their property rights. Appropriate release clauses can be used to indicate clearly that the contract is intended to prevail over the statutory right to equalization of net family properties. Alternatively, the contract can simply modify the general rule that net family properties are to be equalized on the happening of the events listed in s. 5. For example, a husband and wife could agree in a marriage contract that the wife will be entitled to 60 per cent of the net family properties on separation. The parties can also stipulate that a specified property is not to be included in a spouse's net family property. In that event Part I would still apply but the value of this property would not form part of the spouse's net family property. Finally, s. 5(5) allows the spouses to stipulate in a domestic contract that they are entitled to apply to the court under s. 7 for a determination of any matter respecting their entitlement under s. 5 even though the net family properties have already been equalized pursuant to s. 5(3).

Any domestic contract entered into after the *FLA* came into force, at least where the parties have legal advice, will likely specifically address the relationship between the contract and Part I of the Act. Problems may arise, however, in relation to contracts that fail to take into account Part I of the Act specifically and clearly. Contracts validly made before the new Act came into effect and home-made agreements, both pre and post-*FLA,* often fall into this category. By virtue of s. 60(1), contracts validly made before the new Act came into effect are deemed to be domestic contracts for the purposes of the Act. Because the parties to most pre-existing contracts did not direct their minds to the rights later granted by the *FLA*, difficult issues of contractual interpretation may arise.

NURMI v. NURMI

(1988), 16 R.F.L. (3d) 201 (Ont. U.F.C.)

WALLACE U.F.C.J.: — . . . The final issue in this matter requires a finding of whether there was an agreement between the parties that ought to interfere with the equalization of their net family properties.

Both parties testified that they discussed an agreement before marriage, although the applicant pleads some lack of understanding of that agreement and a lack of specificity; a document was signed, however, by the parties eleven days after marriage. . . .

Counsel for the applicant submits that, because of the somewhat unusual form of the document executed by the parties and marked Ex. 6, it does not meet the definition of a domestic contract. I included it here in its entirety:

Jan. 11 1983

> In the case of legal separation or divorse [sic], I *Pauline Nurmi (Wife of Paul Nurmi)* being of sound mind, do hereby release any claim I may have or hereafter have thereto to the said premises known as 49 Kingslea Dr. composed of the northerly four feet of lot # 340 and the whole of lot # 341 according to the plan of survey known as Huntington Park plan # 964 Hamilton Ont. Solely owned by Paul Nurmi. I also release all claims to Mr. Nurmi's R.R.S.P. and Likewise to $15,000.00 investment capital.
>
> In witness and in the presence of   Nicki Klausmann
> _____
>
>   Herman Klausmann
> _____
>
>   J. Nurmi
> _____

I have not been referred to any contract case law which requires particular placement of signatures or form of wording in order to validate a contract and I find that Ex. 6 in its present form constitutes a domestic contract, although obviously its form is not a preferred one.

[Wallace U.F.C.J. rejected the argument that the applicant wife received no consideration because "the promise of marriage was consideration for the oral agreement; the oral agreement was subsequently confirmed in a written document."]

The applicant further submits that, even if the agreement is valid, it is unenforceable because of s. 52(2) which states:

> (2) A provision in a marriage contract purporting to limit a spouse's rights under Part II (Matrimonial Home) is unenforceable.

He refers the court to the case of *Sinnett* v. *Sinnett* (1980), 15 R.F.L. (2d) 115 (Ont. Co. Ct.), and submits that case stands for the proposition that the court cannot distinguish between possessory and title issues respecting the matrimonial home. With respect I must disagree; Pt. II of the Family Law Act clearly and specifically limits a spouse's powers respecting alienation and possession of a matrimonial home; that Part does not address a spouse's right to enter into a contract respecting ownership or degree of ownership of a matrimonial home. Section 52(2) renders a contract unenforceable only to the extent of Pt. II of the Act. In that the contract between these parties did not address possession or alienation, the applicant's submissions on this point must fail.

The applicant goes on to claim that, although the applicant released her interest in specific assets, namely, the matrimonial home and the respondent's R.R.S.P.s, he submits that she released her interest in the property as it was valued at that time but not at its present value (which is significantly increased). Exhibit 6 clearly states that the applicant releases "any claim I may have or hereafter have" and so I must find that the present day value of the matrimonial home and the respondent's R.R.S.P.s are excluded from any net family property calculation; in addition, $15,000 of property owned on the date of marriage by the respondent is also excluded in accordance with the terms of the agreement. . . .

In computing, then, the equalization of net family property of the parties, the property referred to in Ex. 6 will be "excluded property" within the meaning of s. 4(2)6 of the Family Law Act and will include the following:

(a) The present day value of the matrimonial home;
(b) The present day value of the respondent's R.R.S.P.;
(c) $15,000, the respondent's pre-marriage holdings.

BOSCH v. BOSCH

(1991), 36 R.F.L. (3d) 302 (Ont. C.A.)

[The parties were married in The Netherlands in 1976. At that time the husband, who had lived in Ontario for some time, was the owner of a house located on a six-acre lot near Woodstock. Shortly before the marriage, at the husband's request, the parties entered into a marriage contract in The Netherlands in the presence of a notary. The wife acknowledged that the purpose of the contract was to ensure that the house remained in the name of the husband. She understood that "it was to remain his exclusive property, and that she could have nothing to do with that property at any time". Soon after the marriage the wife joined her husband and they lived in the house until separation. The issue on appeal was whether the trial judge had erred in including the value of the matrimonial home in the calculation of the husband's net family property. This was the main asset held by either spouse on separation.

The key clause in the contract provided:

PART A —

PROPERTY

1. That all property, money, and rights of every nature and kind held by the parties hereto, whether held at the time of the marriage or obtained afterwards, shall remain the property of the respective parties but each shall contribute equally to the upkeep and maintenance of the household (and children). If both parties contribute to the purchase of any property for purpose of the household it shall be deemed to be held jointly in equal shares, and not in proportion to their respective contributions.]

ARBOUR J.A. (CARTHY J.A. concurring): — . . . [T]he question here is whether the parties have, by their marriage contract, "[dealt] with the matter that is also dealt with in this Act" in a manner such as to exclude the matrimonial home, which was owned by the husband before the marriage, from the calculation of his net family property for the purpose of equalization. They have not done so explicitly in the sense that they have not inserted a clause into their marriage contract to deal with their respective entitlement to equalization or to deal with the exclusion of some property from the calculation of their respective net family properties. This, of course, is hardly surprising since the Family Law Act, 1986 had not been enacted at the time of the contract.

On the other hand, every effort must be made to give effect to the intention of the parties expressed in a domestic contract, and since a domestic contract validly made before the coming into force of the Act is deemed by s. 60 to have been made pursuant to the Act, its intent should not be defeated simply because its language did not accurately anticipate the Act. Section 2(9) of the Family Law Reform Act, R.S.O. 1980, c. 152, which is substantially identical to s. 2(10) of the Family Law Act, 1986, was used to give effect to the intent of the parties expressed in a clause in a marriage contract which had been entered into in 1976, before The Family Law Reform Act, 1978, S.O. 1978, c. 2, was enacted, and which, therefore, did not express that intention in the very language of the Act: see *Engel* v. *Engel* (1980), 20 R.F.L. (2d) 33, 30 O.R. (2d) 152, 116 D.L.R. (3d) 309 (H.C.), per Walsh J. Under the Family Law Act, 1986, Wallace U.F.C.J. found that a domestic contract in which the wife released any claims she may have, in the case of legal separation or divorce, to specified property owned by her husband, constituted an agreement to exclude such property from the equalization process. (*Nurmi* v. *Nurmi* (1988), 16 R.F.L. (3d) 201 (Ont. U.F.C.), at pp. 210 to 214). . . .

. . . Under the Family Law Act, 1986, neither ownership nor any interest in the property of the title-holding spouse need be interfered with, as it is only the *value* of assets that is equalized. Therefore, provisions in a marriage contract dealing with ownership of property during marriage or even after its dissolution may not be sufficient to prevail over the equalization provisions of the Family Law Act, 1986. For instance, a provision which merely said that a particular spouse would continue to own the car after separation, while the other would continue to own the boat, does not address, and may not be adequate to displace, the provisions of the Act which contemplated a valuation of all things owned by each spouse on valuation date in order to equalize, by the payment of money, their economic posture as they come out of the marriage.

The entitlement of spouses in Ontario to equalization under the Family Law Act, 1986 is a new substantive right, quite independent from any right of ownership, which can be ousted by a domestic contract, even one that pre-existed the Act.

However, in order for a pre-existing contract to have that effect, it must deal, explicitly or by necessary implication, with "a matter" akin to the equalization provisions of the Act. An agreement as to ownership of property, without more, is insufficient. For the marriage contract to prevail over the equalization provisions of the Act, the contract must contain provisions which address, in their intent if not in their explicit language, the relative economic position of the parties upon the dissolution of the marriage, through the distribution of assets between them on the basis of ownership or otherwise. This can be done either through an agreement that a given property be excluded from a spouse's net family property, under s. 4(2)6 of the Act, or through an agreement in a domestic contract which deals with equalization-type rights so as to bring s. 2(10) into effect. . . .

Ultimately, whether a domestic contract prevails over the equalization provisions of the Family Law Act, 1986 will depend, in each individual case, on whether the parties turned their minds to the division of their assets, or to some other form of economic redress, upon the dissolution of their marriage. . . .

The marriage contract of the parties here is silent not only as to their respective entitlements upon the dissolution of the marriage but also as to their matrimonial home. Parties are not precluded from agreeing to exempt the value of the matrimonial home from the equalization process or from agreeing that the spouse who owned the house prior to the marriage will deduct its pre-marital value in the equalization process. The marriage contract in this case cannot, in my view, be taken as doing either.

I am not persuaded by the argument that this marriage contract must be interpreted, as suggested by the husband, to avoid a redundancy. It does not follow, in my view, that since the law of Ontario in 1976, when the contract was entered into, provided for separation of property during marriage, the parties must have intended to do something more than recognize that fact in their marriage contract. The evidence clearly indicates that the parties entered into this marriage contract to ensure that the house owned by the husband prior to the marriage would continue to be owned by him afterwards. Beyond that, their intention in entering that contract is quite speculative. There is no evidence as to why the parties, or one of them, thought it necessary to ensure the protection of that right by contract. Even if the parties knew that the law at the time offered them the very protection that they sought to enshrine in the contract, it does not follow, in my view, that they must be taken to have entered the contract for some other, different purpose. They may have wanted to express their intention in a contract that could survive an eventual change in the law; they may have had some concern as to whether the law of the Netherlands could ever be said to apply since they were being married there. There is no evidence that the notary who advised them in the Netherlands informed them in any way as to the law of Ontario or the law of conflicts. Furthermore, their contractual agreement as to ownership might not have been completely redundant at the time and could certainly have had significant consequences in the future. For instance, and without pronouncing on the merits of such argument, a marriage contract such as the one here could be used to defeat a claim by the wife, under s. 10 of the Family Law Act, 1986, for a declaration that she is the beneficiary of a constructive trust in relation to the property in question. In any event, I find nothing in either the terms of the contract, or in the expressed or implied intention of the parties, that leads me to conclude that they intended to deprive the wife of any entitlement, present or future, to share in the financial worth of her husband, reflected in part by his ownership of the house that became the matrimonial home. Even if it could be construed as addressing the question of ownership of property after dissolution of the marriage, in my view, the marriage contract here would still fail to prevail over the equalization provisions of the Family Law Act, 1986, which deal with distribution of wealth between former marriage partners, on a basis other than in accordance with owner-ship.

For these reasons, I have concluded that the trial judge was correct in attributing the value of the matrimonial home to the husband in calculating his net family property. . . .

FINLAYSON J.A. (dissenting): — . . . The agreement is unlimited in duration. While it makes no provision for death, separation, or the breakup of the marriage, I can think of no reason why it should not be construed as establishing a separation of property for all purposes. The parties were separate as to property before the marriage, and this status did not change as a result of the marriage. Unlike other jurisdictions, there is no community of property arising from marriage in Ontario. The husband had legal title to the matrimonial home at the time of the marriage, and title remains with him to this date. The agreement, therefore, has no legal efficacy during the marriage because the parties were perfectly free, after the marriage, to make any arrangements between themselves as to how their money and property were to be utilized with or without a formal contract. Accordingly, what legal purpose could there be to such a document if it did not contemplate a breakup of the marriage from any cause? Clearly the parties, the husband in particular, intended that the property that each brought into the marriage was to remain the separate property of that spouse regardless of what might later transpire. . . .

Accordingly, I am of the opinion that the domestic contract in question is sufficient to exclude the house and 6 acres of land owned by the husband from the husband's net family property by reason of s. 4(2)6 of the F.L.A. It follows that the equalization payment ordered by Misener J. must be set aside.

NOTES AND QUESTIONS

1. Section 70(3) of the *FLA* specifies that a separation agreement or marriage contract validly made before March 1, 1986 that excludes a spouse's property from the application of ss. 4 and 8 of the *Family Law Reform Act* is deemed to exclude the property from the application of s. 5 of the *FLA*. Regarding the effect of s. 70(3), see *Emond* v. *Emond* (1987), 10 R.F.L. (3d) 107 (Ont. C.A.); *Keller* v. *Keller* (1988), 14 R.F.L. (3d) 150 (Ont. H.C.); *Smith* v. *Smith* (1990), 29 R.F.L. (3d) 90 (Ont. Dist. Ct.); *Best* v. *Best* (1990), 30 R.F.L. (3d) 279 (Ont. Gen. Div.); *Kajtar* v. *Kajtar* (1992), 95 D.L.R. (4th) 525 (Ont. Gen. Div.); and *Calvert (Litigation Guardian of)* v. *Calvert* (1998), 36 R.F.L. (4th) 169 (Ont. C.A.).

In *Lay* v. *Lay* (2000), 4 R.F.L. (5th) 264, the Ontario Court of Appeal recently applied s. 70(3) to a marriage contract entered into just before the couple's wedding in 1985. The contract stipulated that the wife would retain sole ownership and control of specified property. It also stated that the spouses' rights and obligations relating to this property would be governed by the contract and not the *Family Law Reform Act*. The court held that the specified property value of the specified property was excluded from the wife's net family property.

2. In *Ablaka* v. *Ablaka* (1991), 32 R.F.L. (3d) 369 (Ont. U.F.C.), affirmed (1994), 4 R.F.L. (4th) 167 (Ont. C.A.), the parties entered into a marriage contract in 1987 that specified that the husband and wife would continue to own the property that each had brought into the marriage. In addition, the contract stipulated that the wife was "entitled to the property set out in Schedule 'A' or where such property was reinvested, the amount in which the wife reinvested said property in another asset". Wallace U.F.C.J. concluded (at 380) that the contract did not preclude an equalization claim by the husband but that "the contract shall prevail with respect to any property which was itemized in Schedule 'A' ". The value of the property was not included in the wife's net family property. See also *Best* v. *Best* (1990), 30 R.F.L. (3d) 279 (Ont. Gen. Div.).

3. Another difficult problem of interpretation that can be avoided by clear drafting concerns the effect of resumption of cohabitation on the rights and obligations created by a separation agreement. As a general rule, the provisions of a separation agreement cease to have operative effect if the parties resume cohabitation. See *Bebenek* v. *Bebenek* (1979), 11 R.F.L. (2d) 137 (Ont. C.A.); *Bailey* v. *Bailey* (1982), 26 R.F.L. (2d) 209 (Ont. C.A.); *Smart* v. *Wiewior* (1990), 28 R.F.L. (3d) 225 (B.C. C.A.); *Baron* v. *Baron* (1990), 29 R.F.L. (3d) 37 (Man. Q.B.); *Hill* v. *Hill* (1990), 29 R.F.L. (3d) 386 (Sask. Q.B.); *Livermore* v. *Livermore* (1992), 43 R.F.L. (3d) 163 (Ont. Gen. Div.); *Hodgson* v. *Hodgson* (1997), 28 R.F.L. (4th) 205 (Sask. Q.B.); and *Hulleman* v. *Hulleman* (1999), 2 R.F.L. (5th) 406 (Alta. C.A.). In each case, however, this issue must be determined in accordance with the intention of the parties. Where property has been transferred pursuant to the agreement, the court may be willing to infer that the parties intended an absolute and permanent transfer of ownership: see *Bebenek, supra*. In some circumstances, such a transfer, coupled with a clause whereby the transferor releases any interest in the property, may preclude the inclusion of the value of the property in the transferee's net family property when the couple subsequently separates again: see *Avery* v. *Avery* (1991), 33 R.F.L. (3d) 288 (Ont. Gen. Div.).

4. Sections 52 and 53 of the *FLA* stipulate that the parties to a marriage contract or a cohabitation agreement may deal with ownership of property or division of property upon the death of one of the parties. While s. 54 does not expressly provide that a separation agreement may cover the rights and obligations of the parties on death, such terms have also been given effect. See, for example, *Cairns* v. *Cairns* (1990), 25 R.F.L. (3d) 373 (Ont. H.C.) where it was held that the wife was barred from claiming an equalization of net family properties on the death of her husband. It should be noted, however, that the courts have been reluctant to find that one spouse has agreed not to claim his or her preferential share under the *Succession Law Reform Act* in the absence of clear and cogent language to that effect. See *Dalton, Re* [1934] O.W.N. 691 (Ont. H.C.); *Knoll, Re* [1938] O.W.N. 282 (Ont. H.C); *Cliff* v. *Schop*, [1948] O.W.N. 338 (Ont. H.C.); *Winter, Re* [1954] O.W.N. 726 (Ont. H.C.); *Draper, Re* [1956] O.W.N. 106 (Ont. H.C.); *Saylor, Re* (1983), 36 R.F.L. (2d) 288 (Ont. H.C.); *Cairns* v. *Cairns* (1990), 25 R.F.L. (3d) 373 (Ont. H.C.); and *Brant* v. *Brant* (1997), 16 E.T.R. (2d) 134 (Ont. Gen. Div.).

5. In the separation agreement, the spouses can agree that one of them has the exclusive right to possess the matrimonial home. By virtue of s. 2(10) of the *FLA*, such an agreement ousts the courts' jurisdiction to make an exclusive possession order under Part II. Where the owning spouse is to have exclusive possession pursuant to a separation agreement, the other spouse can release all rights under Part II. The owner can then encumber or dispose of any interest in the home without the consent of the other spouse: s. 21(1)(b). By virtue of s. 52(2), a provision in a marriage contract purporting to limit a spouse's rights under Part II is unenforceable. Thus, a court has the power to make an order for exclusive possession in favour of either spouse notwithstanding any provision in a marriage contract. However, the contract, if written, is a factor that the court must consider: s. 24(3)(d).

6. Under ss. 55.1 and 55.2 of the *Canada Pension Plan Act*, R.S.C. 1985, c. C-8, a provision in a marriage contract or separation agreement cannot preclude a division of unadjusted pensionable earnings one year after separation or on divorce unless the agreement specifically mentions that Act and indicates that there be no division and such a provision is expressly permitted under the provincial law that governs the agreement. While some provinces such as British Columbia, Quebec and Saskatchewan have specifically authorized the waiver of spousal rights to a division of pensionable earnings under the Plan, others such as Manitoba and Ontario have not. See *Wiemer* v. *Canada (Minister of Employment & Immigration)* (1998), 42 R.F.L. (4th) 242 (Fed. C.A.) where a division occurred despite a Manitoba separation agreement intended to definitively settle all aspects of the couple's relationship.

7. Section 58 of the *FLA* specifies that the manner and formalities of making a domestic contract and its essential validity and effect are governed by the proper law of the contract except that a contract, the proper law of which is a jurisdiction other than Ontario, is also valid and enforceable if entered into in accordance with Ontario's internal law. A contract that is valid according to its proper foreign law is nonetheless subject to ss. 33(4) and 56 of the Act: s. 58(b). Regarding the proper law of a contract, see Castel, *Canadian Conflict of Laws*, 4th ed. (Toronto: Butterworths, 1997) at 501-502 and c. 33.

The combined effect of ss. 15 and 58 can best be illustrated by an example. Assume that a husband and wife marry in Quebec and enter into a marriage contract. They later move to Ontario and live there as a family for a number of years before separating. The property rights arising out of their marital relationship are governed by the law of Ontario, that is the *FLA*. The effect of the marriage contract is determined by a combination of Ontario law and the proper law of the contract (probably the law of Quebec in this example). Although the proper law of the contract will generally determine the contractual rights of the parties (s. 58), the effect of these contractual rights on the equalization of net family properties will be determined in accordance with Ontario law. Thus, the spouse with the lesser of the net family properties will be entitled to equalization of the net family properties in accordance with Part I of the *FLA* unless the marriage contract provides otherwise (s. 2(10)). Because the parties are unlikely to have contemplated Part I of the *FLA* when the contract was executed, difficult problems may arise in determining the extent to which they intended to preclude equalization of net family properties. See *Sinnett* v. *Sinnett* (1980), 15 R.F.L. (2d) 115 (Ont. Co. Ct); *Kerr* v. *Kerr* (1981), 32 O.R. (2d) 146 (H.C.), affirmed (1983), 41 O.R. (2d) 704 (C.A.); *Roome* v. *Roome* (1984), 42 R.F.L. (2d) 337 (P.E.I. S.C.); and *Mittler* v. *Mittler* (1988), 17 R.F.L. (3d) 113 (Ont. H.C.). For a critical analysis of these cases, see Black, "Quebec Marriage Contracts in Common Law Courts: Room for Improvement" (1985), 45 R.F.L. (2d) 93.

8. Section 65 of the *Family Relations Act*, R.S.B.C. 1996, c. 128 permits the court to reapportion the division of property provided for in an agreement whenever the court considers the agreement "unfair". For an analysis of the case law applying similar provisions in earlier legislation, see Law Reform Commission of British Columbia, *Report on Spousal Agreements* (Victoria: Queen's Printer, 1986). The Commission concluded (at 20):

> The law has proven to be uncertain. No person can predict the effect a separation agreement will have, nor what the courts will determine is an appropriate division of family property. The result has been an invitation to litigate.

Cases applying this provision include *Walker* v. *Walker* (1997), 31 R.F.L. (4th) 63 (B.C. S.C.) and *Pang* v. *Wong* (1999), 48 R.F.L. (4th) 431 (B.C. C.A.).

(2) SPOUSAL SUPPORT

(a) **General**

The *FLA* expressly indicates that the parties may agree on support obligations in a marriage contract, a cohabitation agreement, or a separation agreement. Part IV of the Act contains one explicit limitation on the freedom to contract regarding support. Section 56(2) stipulates that a provision in a domestic contract to take effect on separation whereby any right of a party is dependent upon remaining chaste is unenforceable. Accordingly, *dum casta* clauses that specify that support is to paid during separation only so long as the recipient does not engage in sexual relations with a third party are ineffective. Section 56(2), however, expressly recognizes the validity of provisions in a domestic contract that terminate upon remarriage or cohabitation with another. Although s. 56(2) is not binding on a court exercising jurisdiction under the *Divorce Act*, it has been held that it represents public policy for federal as well as provincial purposes: *Sleigh* v. *Sleigh* (1979), 23 O.R. (2d) 336 (H.C.).

To encourage parties to enter into domestic contracts rather than resort to litigation, the *FLA* establishes a special mechanism for judicial enforcement of contractual support obligations. It applies notwithstanding an agreement to the contrary: s. 35(4). Under s. 35(1), a party to a domestic contract may file the contract with the court together with an affidavit stating that the contract or agreement is in effect and has not been set aside or varied by a court or agreement. Once the contract is filed in this manner, any provision for support may be enforced as if it were an order of the court where it is filed: s. 35(2).

A provision for support in a domestic contract that is filed with the court may also be varied or made the subject of an indexing order as if it were an order of the court where it is filed: s. 35(2)(b). However, the parties can preclude the exercise of these judicial powers by agreement: *Wark* v. *Wark* (1988), 14 R.F.L. (3d) 137 (Ont. Fam. Ct.), affirmed (1989), 18 R.F.L. (3d) 75 (Ont. Dist. Ct.), affirmed (1990), 28 R.F.L. (3d) 410 (Ont. Div. Ct.) and *O'Connor* v. *O'Connor* (1990), 28 R.F.L. (3d) 99 (Ont. Fam. Ct.).

(b) Judicial Controls

(i) Under the *Divorce Act*

It is clearly established that the parties cannot oust the jurisdiction of the court to grant spousal support under the *Divorce Act*. In *Pelech* v. *Pelech* (1987), 7 R.F.L. (3d) 225 (S.C.C.), all the justices accepted that a court had jurisdiction to intervene in the face of a valid agreement dealing with support. Although *Pelech* was decided under the 1968 *Divorce Act*, there is nothing in the new Act that alters the conclusion on this issue.

The real question is: when should jurisdiction to act be exercised in the face of a valid and enforceable contract? In *Pelech, supra*; *Caron* v. *Caron* (1987), 7 R.F.L. (3d) 274 (S.C.C.); and *Richardson* v. *Richardson* (1987), 7 R.F.L. (3d) 304 (S.C.C.), the trilogy dealt with in Chapter 6: **SPOUSAL SUPPORT**, the court came down firmly in favour of a restrictive approach.

FYFFE v. FYFFE

(1988), 12 R.F.L. (3d) 196 (Ont. C.A.)

[The parties were married in 1964. The wife left her employment to devote herself to being a full-time homemaker, caring for the husband's two minor children from a previous marriage. The parties separated in 1981, at which time the wife began proceedings under the *Family Law Reform Act*. These proceedings were settled and a consent judgment issued. Under the settlement, the wife received $257,000 in full satisfaction of all claims. The husband petitioned for divorce in 1984. The trial judge awarded the wife $675 per month in maintenance on her counter-petition. She concluded that a very large decline in interest rates coupled with a large severance payment received by the husband constituted sufficient change to justify overriding the agreement. The husband appealed.]

LACOURCIERE, J.A.: — . . . The principle now to be applied on the basis of *Pelech* and *Richardson* is that the court will not override a valid settlement agreement unless there has been a radical change in circumstances between the time of the agreement and the application for support, and, in addition, the radical change in circumstances flows from an economic pattern of dependency engendered by the marriage . . . . The narrowness of the exception to the finality of settlement agreements is based on the policy of encouraging spouses to settle their affairs with confidence that the settlement will not be interfered with lightly. . . .

. . . In the present case, while the continuing dependency of the wife is related to the marriage and to her decision to terminate her employment after the marriage, the change in interest rates is totally unrelated to the marriage. It would have been inconceivable, had the interest rate increased radically, for the husband to have sought return of part of the settlement money on the sole basis of a higher yield of income to the wife than at the time of settlement.

There is another aspect of the present case that mitigates against variation of the settlement agreement. . . .

The fluctuation in interest rates was not an unforeseeable event. In his perceptive annotation to *Pelech*, at p. 229, Professor McLeod commented on the question of foreseeability of change in the following words:

> In *Webb* v. *Webb*, supra, the Ontario Court of Appeal suggested that in order for a change in circumstances to justify overriding a settlement agreement, the change must be unforeseen. The settlement agreement is to be taken as final and conclusive of spousal rights in all existent and foreseeable circumstances. In *Richardson*, the court adverted to the expectations of the parties at the time the contract was entered into. Wilson J. pointed out in this regard that the possibility of the wife failing to find employment was not unforeseeable (p. 314). It appears from the reasons that the onus is on the claimant to establish the expectations of the parties and the "unforeseen" nature of the change in question; see *Barrett* v. *Barrett* (1985), 43 R.F.L. (2d) 405 (Ont. H.C.). The question of "foreseeability" is likely to generate significant dispute as lawyers and courts try to reconcile the reasonable expectations of the parties with what is reasonably foreseeable; see *Fyffe* v. *Fyffe*, supra [a reference to the trial judgment herein, supra]. The tenor of *Richardson* is broad enough that, if the agreement is entered into under common expectations, the mere fact they fail to materialize will not justify variation if this contingency should reasonably have been anticipated. That is, to justify intervention the common expectation as to the future must have been unexpectedly defeated (pp. 314-15).

Even assuming, therefore, as the learned trial judge found, that both parties contemplated that the wife would continue to receive an income based on a higher interest rate than in fact existed and that this was their common expectation, the possibility of a reduction in the interest rate was reasonably foreseeable. In other words, the change in circumstances caused by the drop in interest rate cannot be said to have been completely outside the reasonable contemplation of the parties. I am satisfied, therefore, that the previous settlement precludes judicial intervention and that the order under appeal should not have been made.

Accordingly, I would allow the appeal.

SMITH v. SMITH

(1990), 27 R.F.L. (3d) 32 (Man. C.A.), leave to appeal to S.C.C. refused (1991), 32 R.F.L. (3d) 159n (S.C.C.)

[The parties married in 1949 and separated in 1971. They had four children. During the marriage the wife assumed responsibility for home and childcare and was not employed outside the home. Upon separation the parties entered into a separation agreement whereby the husband agreed to pay $700 monthly plus $1,500 yearly as spousal and child support. The agreement was expressed to be final and nothing in the agreement indicated that the parties contemplated variation should their circumstances change. In 1976 the support provisions were incorporated into a divorce judgment. The husband earned $71,000 in 1976 and complied with the order until 1979. Thereafter, arrears accumulated. Some arrears were collected between 1984 and 1986, but the husband suffered a stroke in 1986 and was severely disabled. He began to receive a disability pension in 1986 and was receiving almost as much income as he had earned in 1976. However, the disability pension would end in 1992 when he turned 65.

The wife applied for an order fixing the arrears and for enforcement. The husband countered with an application to vary the order. At trial, the arrears were fixed at $73,563. The trial judge remitted a total of $20,200 in arrears and dismissed the husband's application to vary. The husband appealed.]

TWADDLE J.A. (HUBAND J.A. concurring): — . . . The jurisdiction of the court to vary a previous order as to maintenance is found in s. 17 of the Divorce Act, 1985. Section 17(4) requires that there be a change in the condition, means or other circumstances of the parties since the last order was made and that, in making a variation, the court have regard to that change.

This case, however, is slightly different from one in which the amount of maintenance is fixed by the court itself. What we have in this case is an order which does no more than confirm the agreement of the parties. Is the degree of change required to justify the variation of a court-fixed amount the same as that required to justify the variation of an amount determined by agreement of the parties?

That question has sorely vexed — and continues to vex — courts which deal with it. The answer of this court to it . . . was to recognize the agreement as being a factor, but not one of much significance. This answer was rejected, however, in *Pelech* . . . .

The court in *Pelech* was concerned with a provision that terminated maintenance as distinct from one that fixed it. In that circumstance the Supreme Court was of the view that the change must also be connected causally to the marriage. Such a requirement can readily be understood where the question is whether an obligation which has been discharged by agreement can be recreated by a court. Indeed, the jurisdiction of Parliament to permit a court to do so is itself in doubt: see *Wark* v. *Wark*, 2 R.F.L. (3d) 337, [1986] 5 W.W.R. 336, 30 D.L.R. (4th) 90, 42 Man. R. (2d) 111 (C.A.).

The situation is entirely different where the obligation to pay maintenance is continued by the agreement. The very fact that the obligation was created by the marriage provides the causal connection. But, before a court can vary the agreed amount of maintenance, there must be a change of circumstances of the degree which was described by Wilson J. as catastrophic. . . .

In my opinion, the alleged improvement in the financial circumstances of the wife and her alleged failure to strive for financial self-sufficiency are not changes of a kind which would warrant judicial interference with even a court-confirmed agreement with respect to maintenance. As to the periodic changes in the husband's income, I am not satisfied that they were changes of the character required. That point is of only academic importance, however, as a supervening change of sufficient magnitude to justify varying even a contractually final agreement has certainly occurred. The learned judge's decision that the stroke did not bring about such a change is, at least to me, inexplicable.

The real issue in this case is not whether the maintenance provisions of the court-confirmed agreement should be varied, but the extent to which they should be varied. The stroke brought about such a truly catastrophic change that some variation is a matter of necessity if the law is to be humane.

In considering the husband's financial circumstances, the learned judge also fell into error when she failed to note the extremely limited duration of the husband's present income. Although a court should ordinarily base its decision as to the amount of maintenance to be paid on the circumstances as they exist at the time of the hearing, that rule has no application in circumstances such as these. We are not dealing here with a case in which it is known simply that the husband's present income is of limited duration, but with a case in which it is also known that a substantial part of it can never be replaced.

In determining what the husband should now pay, I find it impossible to distinguish between the obligation to pay arrears and the obligation to pay current maintenance. No matter what his previous fault might have been, the husband has no prospect of paying more than that which can be exacted from his temporarily ample income. Having regard to his physical condition and his psychological need, the most that can be exacted from him is less than the current amount he is required to pay monthly.

[Twaddle J.A. rescinded all arrears and reduced the amount of future support to $200 monthly until the disability pension ended. Helper J.A., dissenting in part, would have fixed the arrears at $42,118 but would have deferred payment until the husband's death except for $100 monthly.]

MASTERS v. MASTERS

(1991), 34 R.F.L. (3d) 34 (Sask. C.A.)

[The parties married in 1957 and separated in 1976. At the time of separation they entered into a separation agreement whereby the husband agreed to pay $700 per month as spousal support. The agreement specified that it was a "full, complete and final settlement" and that it was "binding and conclusive on the parties for all time". A divorce was granted in 1977 and the decree specified that the husband was to pay $700 per month to the wife until she remarried or died "or until further order".

The husband helped the wife establish a business in 1982. She repaid the money he advanced and by 1989 was earning $60,000 per year. The husband stopped making support payments in 1988 and applied, under the *Divorce Act, 1985*, for a cancellation of his obligation to make such payments. The trial judge concluded that the parties should be held to their agreement. The husband appealed.]

WAKELING J.A. (GERWING J.A. concurring): — . . . When dealing with an application to vary the terms of a separation agreement, we are now guided by the trilogy decisions of the Supreme Court of Canada. . . . Of these decisions, *Pelech* v. *Pelech* has the most direct application. *Pelech* has not been favoured with an enthusiastic reception by all sections of the judiciary or the authors of legal texts and articles. It has been the obvious intention of many to restrict its application to the greatest extent possible, and in some cases to a greater extent than possible.

I take it that *Pelech* is authority for the proposition that, subject to limited exception, parties are expected to abide by the terms of their separation agreement. . . .

Wilson J. further indicates that if the agreement is otherwise enforceable, the only exception that should be considered is when the changed circumstances have a causal connection to the marriage. . . .

No causal connection has been shown to exist in this case. The only causal connection possible arises from the financial help that the appellant gave after the separation, which assisted the respondent to obtain her training and establish a business. Such assistance does not constitute a sufficient reason to warrant an exception to the general principle on the basis of a "causal connection."

It has been suggested that *Pelech* only applies to the circumstances where a spouse suffering unforeseen hardship seeks support after the agreed period of payment has expired. Such comment is undoubtedly grounded on the fact that *Pelech* arose out of that kind of factual basis, and on more than one occasion Wilson J. makes reference to "future misfortunes." References of this nature were not only appropriate but unavoidable because that was the nature of the case under consideration. Isolating such comments does not constitute a sound reason for the conclusion that the principle being enunciated is only intended to relate to situations identical to those which arose in *Pelech*.

If the principle established by *Pelech*, that parties to an agreement should be held to their bargain, is a worthy one, as I am prepared to take it to be, it is diminished and almost abandoned if it is only applicable in a *Pelech* factual situation. It is unacceptable to me that the principle is to be taken as sound when applied to a spouse in greater than expected need, but it is not sound when applied to a spouse in less than expected need.

In some cases, it is apparent that the principal criteria for application of *Pelech* is the identification of an intent that the agreement should constitute a clean break and a final determination of the parties' rights. *Publicover* v. *Publicover* (1987), 9 R.F.L. (3d) 308, 81 N.S.R. (2d) 91, 203 A.P.R. 91 (Fam. Ct.), is an example of the application of that approach. I accept that this is an important first step, for the concept enshrined by *Pelech* is that, absent rather special factors, the parties should be left to the bargain they made. If there never was a finality of that bargain intended by the parties, then there is little of substance, or perhaps of duration, in that bargain to warrant giving it judicial support.

There is no doubt the trial Judge found this separation agreement was intended to be final. He includes in his judgment some of the testimony given by the appellant that supports this conclusion. This finding of fact by the trial Judge is supported both by the agreement itself and the evidence given by the appellant, and his finding should therefore be accepted by this Court.

I do not perceive that the portion of the decree nisi which states "or until further order" is of compelling consequence. Every order is subject to review, and it cannot be otherwise. Had it been deleted entirely, the rights of the parties would be precisely the same. Similarly, its inclusion neither enhances nor detracts from the rights enjoyed by the parties. It is a bit of legal verbiage which should not carry the day when assessing the intent of the parties.

There are those who suggest that *Pelech* should not apply where the original contract was made in an earlier day when the legal consequences were not so severe. This can hardly be a sound basis for avoiding its application. The *Pelech* agreement was one made in 1969, a time when it is said the parties did not recognize the finality its terms would create, but this did not deter the Supreme Court from unanimously affirming its continued application.

The general principle enunciated in *Pelech* is not one which seeks to overrule a legislated right of review given by s. 17 of the Divorce Act; it simply provides a guideline for the exercise of a judicial discretion. . . .

The trial Judge further indicated that, irrespective of the dictates of *Pelech*, he would have exercised his discretion to dismiss the appellant's application. No sufficient reason has been advanced which would warrant overturning this decision in the circumstances of this case.

VANCISE J.A. (dissenting): — . . . What *Pelech* did not decide was an application by a payor for a variation of a settlement agreement negotiated between the parties and incorporated into a decree nisi, and which did not settle, once and for all, the rights of the parties. It is necessary to decide whether the rules established by the Supreme Court of Canada in *Pelech* are applicable in the circumstances where the payor applies to vary the settlement agreement because of a change in circumstances pursuant to s. 17(4) of the Divorce Act, 1985. . . .

The same issue was considered in *Wark* v. *Wark* (1989), 18 R.F.L. (3d) 75 (Ont. Dist. Ct.). Gautreau D.C.J. found that the radical change in circumstances need not be causally connected to the marriage when the applicant is the payor. He stated, at p. 89:

> The *Pelech* trilogy enunciated the philosophy behind the current support law and then set out the particular rules applicable to a case where the dependant after divorce comes back to have the support terms reinstated or increased. These rules were intended to apply only to that type of case and not to every case where a litigant seeks to vary an agreement.
>
> The second part of the rule requiring that the change have a causal connection to the marriage is designed to buttress the concepts of the clean break, equality, independence and individual responsibility. Its rationale is that one spouse should not be forever contingently liable to the other merely because they went through a form of marriage. But this part of the rule has no place in an application by the payor to vary. There is no logical reason that it should. The application is to do away with maintenance. If it were a requirement it would have the converse effect of perpetuating the ties of the broken marriage and defeating the ideal of self-sufficiency and the clean break because it would be the exceptional case where there could be any connection between the change and the marriage. Material changes which suffice to vary will be either that the wife's circumstances have profoundly improved and she is now a millionaire or that the payor was fired and his situation is now one of dire straits. The causes will usually lie outside of the marriage.

I agree with the conclusion and approach in . . . *Wark*. . . .

Conclusion

. . . How, then, does one apply the rule in *Pelech* to an application by a payor in circumstances where the dependent payee has become economically self-sufficient? The support model developed in *Pelech* is based on the premise that there is a valid, contractual support obligation which settled once and for all the obligations of the parties, which the applicant seeks to vary long after the contract was entered into and the parties had gone their own ways. The rule for variation in the present circumstances, where there is an ongoing obligation which the payor spouse contends is no longer required by reason of the changed circumstances of the payee, should not be the same as in an application by a dependent spouse who seeks to alter the finality achieved by the settlement agreement or the order. What the applicant payor seeks to achieve is independence between the parties and an end to their relationship. The *Pelech* rule — causality — is designed to promote and continue the concept of finality and independence. In an application by a payor, the contention is that that state has already occurred, the payee is economically independent, and the payor seeks finality and an end to all elements of the previous relationship. To continue support in circumstances where it is not needed has the opposite effect of achieving the objectives set out in *Pelech*. The causal connection test has no place within the general analysis and policy in an application by the payor to vary a settlement agreement. Thus, a modified rule emerges. In an application by a payor to vary or reduce the amount of support contained in a settlement agreement, the applicant must show (a) a radical change in circumstances (b) which was unforeseen at the time the contract was entered into. . . .

[Vancise J.A. concluded that there had been a radical change in circumstances, which was unforeseen when the contract was made. The success of the wife's business and her self-sufficiency constituted a radical change. Such self-sufficiency was not anticipated when the contract was made since the wife had no marketable skills and had not succeeded in obtaining employment.]

MASTERS v. MASTERS

(1994), 4 R.F.L. (4th) 1 (S.C.C.)

MCLACHLIN J. [for the Court]: This is an appeal from an order of a trial judge declining to vary support agreed to under a separation agreement. The wife was successful in both courts below. She was not represented by counsel at the hearing in this court, and we did not have the benefit of a factum of submissions from her.

No error in the findings or reasoning of the trial judge has been established. The trial judge found that the separation agreement was final. No unforeseen or radical change in circumstances from those contemplated at the time of the separation agreement was demonstrated. It is therefore unnecessary to consider the issue of whether, had such change been demonstrated, that change need be causally connected to the circumstances of the marriage, or if so, was demonstrated on the evidence in this case to have been causally connected.

We would dismiss the appeal with costs.

McLEOD, "ANNOTATION"

(1994), 4 R.F.L. (4th) 2

With respect, the Supreme Court of Canada's reasons in *Masters* v. *Masters* are unsatisfactory. . . .

In *Masters* v. *Masters* a majority of the Saskatchewan Court of Appeal held that *Pelech, Richardson*, and *Caron* applied to cases being decided under the 1985 *Divorce Act*, that the test to override agreements applied to applications made by payers as well as payees, that an agreement was final if the parties intended to settle the issue of support once and for all, and that the causal connection prerequisite continued to be part of the trilogy test. Both the trial judge and the Court of Appeal dismissed the husband's claim on the basis that he had not established a causal connection between the change alleged (the wife had achieved self-sufficiency and was not suffering any ongoing economic disadvantage) and the marriage. The Court of Appeal did not discuss the radical unforeseen change issue. The Supreme Court of Canada, however, held that because Mr. Masters had not provided a radical unforeseen change, it need not deal with the causal connection prerequisite. . . .

Masters v. *Masters* presented the Supreme Court of Canada with an opportunity to explain its comments in *Moge* v. *Moge* and to review the emerging trend of defining support in terms of compensation for economic disadvantage. The opportunity was not seized. The legal profession has been eagerly awaiting these reasons because of the philosophical conflict between the trilogy cases and *Moge*. Rather than identifying and resolving the problems that arise when a spouse attempts to override the support provisions of an agreement, the court, in its reasons in *Masters*, did little more than confirm that the radical unforeseen test continues to apply in some form to cases being decided under the 1985 *Divorce Act*.

B. (G.) v. G. (L.)

(1995), 15 R.F.L. (4th) 201 (S.C.C.)

[The parties were married in 1960 and divorced in 1986. The divorce judgment incorporated the support provisions of a separation agreement whereby, *inter alia*, the husband agreed to pay $2,600 monthly as spousal support. This sum was subject to reduction when the wife earned more than $15,000 annually. At the time of the agreement, the wife was dating a man with whom she later began to cohabit. The wife, aged 53, was not in the workforce but her partner gave her between $1,000 and $1,300 monthly and lent her $45,000 to purchase a condominium. The couple shared common expenses.

The husband's application to cancel spousal support under s. 17 was refused by the Quebec Superior Court, but he successfully appealed to the Quebec Court of Appeal. The Supreme Court of Canada restored the trial judgment regarding spousal support. Sopinka J. (Cory, McLachlin and Iacobucci JJ. concurring) simply noted that there was no basis on which to reverse the trial judge's conclusion that the wife's cohabitation with her new partner was foreseeable at the time of the agreement. Therefore, there was no material change in circumstances which was sufficient to vary the prior support order. He observed (at 271) that the Supreme Court of Canada "will have to review the application of the trilogy . . . to the support provisions of the 1985 Divorce Act," but stated (at 271):

> [T]his is not the appropriate case. Apart from being unnecessary to this decision, the case was not presented on this basis.

Madam Justice L'Heureux-Dubé (LaForest and Gonthier JJ. concurring) agreed with the result reached by the majority, but went on to deal with the extent to which the trilogy is still good law. Only a portion of her reasons regarding that issue are reproduced.]

For its part, academic commentary has generally been very critical of the trilogy. The commentator T. Heeney objected to the broad interpretation given to it ("The Application of *Pelech* to the Variation of an Ongoing Support Order: Respecting the Intention of the Parties" (1989), 5 C.F.L.Q. 217, at p. 217) [footnotes omitted]:

> In the trilogy, the Supreme Court of Canada has more or less stated that what is done should not be undone. Finality is the pervasive judicial objective that runs through *Pelech*, *Caron* and *Richardson* . . . . Rarely, however, has a case been more misunderstood than *Pelech*, and rarely have courts been so willing to extract principles out of context, and apply them to fact situations where they simply do not fit. The quest for finality has led judges to cast in stone agreements that were never intended to be permanent and inflexible, and to impose constraints of finality on ongoing maintenance relationships, where finality is impossible.

Similarly, Prof. C. J. Rogerson criticized the effect of the causal connection as contemplated in *Pelech* ("The Causal Connection Test in Spousal Support Law" (1989), 8 Can. J. Fam. L. 95, at p. 122):

> The current causal connection test . . . is more aligned with the clean break model of spousal support. Just as the clean break theory arbitrarily deems self-sufficiency to exist, the causal link theory arbitrarily deemed the causal link to have been broken, with the result that the claimant spouse is deemed responsible for his or her own support. Instead of presuming, until strong evidence to the contrary is led, a causal connection between a spouse's inability to meet his or her needs and what went on during the marital relationship, the causal link test presumes the opposite.

Prof N. Bala, for his part, cautions (''Domestic Contracts in Ontario and the Supreme Court Trilogy: 'A Deal is a Deal' '' (1988), 13 Queen's L.J. 1, at p. 61) [emphasis added]:

> while the promotion of finality is desirable, *this should not be used as a justification for precluding the judicial overriding of unfair agreements*. Rather than discouraging the parties from entering into such agreements, knowledge that the courts may intervene to set aside unfair agreements should encourage the parties to initially enter into agreements which are fair.

See also inter alia D.G. Duff, ''The Supreme Court and the New Family Law: Working through the *Pelech* Trilogy'' (1988), 46 U.T. Fac. L. Rev. 542; J.D. Payne, ''Further Reflections on Spousal and Child Support After Pelech, Caron and Richardson'' (1989), 20 R.G.D. 477; M.J. Bailey, ''*Pelech, Caron*, and *Richardson*'' (1989-90), 3 C.J.W.L. 615; P. Proudfoot and K. Jewell, ''Restricting Application of the Causal Connection Test: *Story v. Story*'' (1990), 9 Can. J. Fam. L. 143; C.J. Rogerson, ''Judicial Interpretation of the Spousal and Child Support Provisions of the *Divorce Act*, 1985 (Part I)'' (1990-91), 7 C.F.L.Q. 155; M. Neave, ''Resolving the Dilemma of Difference: A Critique of 'The Role of Private Ordering in Family Law' '' (1994), 44 U.T.L.J. 97. . . .

The current Act . . . adopted as its underlying philosophy a partnership in marriage and, at the time of a divorce, an equitable division of its economic consequences between the spouses. It thus rejected the presumption of economic self-sufficiency and substituted for it a number of criteria that would take into account the advantages and disadvantages to spouses accruing from the marriage or its breakdown. It did not, however, completely depart from the objective of economic self-sufficiency, although it underlined that this objective can only be pursued ''in so far as practicable''.

Paradoxically, after the enactment of the current Act, courts continued to rely on the pattern established under the 1968 Act, namely, the clean break model of self-sufficiency as a primary objective, i.e., economic self-sufficiency of the recipient of alimony, generally the wife, as soon as possible after the divorce. This tendency, which actually became more marked after 1985, was attributed to the Supreme Court's judgments in *Messier* v. *Delage* and the trilogy, and, in particular, to the causal connection which it advocated, although these cases were decided under the 1968 Act.

Vigorous criticism from academic writers (see, for example, Rogerson, ''Judicial Interpretation of the Spousal and Child Support Provisions of the *Divorce Act*, 1985 (Part I)'', supra; Payne, ''Further Reflections on Spousal and Child Support after Pelech, Caron and Richardson'', supra; D. Goubau, ''Une nouvelle ère pour la pension alimentaire entre ex-conjoints au Canada'' (1993), 73 Can. Bar Rev. 279), and the reaction of certain courts, in particular the Quebec Court of Appeal (*Droit de la famille — 1688*, supra, per LeBel J.A.), were quick to challenge this trend, which they contended was at odds with the very language of the 1985 Act and its underlying philosophy. In *Moge* v. *Moge* [(1992), 43 R.F.L. (3d) 345], the Supreme Court sought to put an end to the uncertainty that prevailed by adopting an interpretation of the 1985 Act consistent with its language and underlying philosophy, especially as regards support obligations and their subsequent variation. . .

This is the background against which this appeal comes to the Court. The specific point at issue is whether the criteria set out in the trilogy should continue to be applied under the 1985 Act.

In my opinion, the answer must be no and, in this connection, I agree with the analysis of Prof. Payne in "Spousal and Child Support After *Moge*, *Willick* and *Levesque*" (1995), 12 C.F.L.Q. 261, at p. 271 [emphasis added; footnotes omitted]:

> In my opinion, *Moge v. Moge* clearly demonstrates that we must turn to the *Divorce Act* to ascertain its application *in all divorce cases where spousal support is sought, including those where a separation agreement has been negotiated to regulate spousal support.* Under subsection 15(5) of the *Divorce Act*, an agreement is only one of many factors that must be considered in determining the right to, amount and duration of spousal support. Furthermore, all four of the objectives of spousal support orders under subsection 15(7) must be considered; their application *is not excluded simply because a final agreement or settlement has been negotiated.* There is no requirement or causal connection built into subsection 15(5) of the *Divorce Act*, although the notion of causal connection is recognized in subsections 15(7) and 17(7) of the *Divorce Act*. It is doubtful whether the principles defined in *Pelech*, *Caron* and *Richardson*, which were enunciated in the context of the *Divorce Act, 1968*, can survive. Although the Supreme Court of Canada trilogy was intended to provide more definitive guidelines that legal practitioners could apply with respect to the right to, amount and duration of spousal support, it has generated more confusion than precision and for that reason, if no other, is unlikely to survive when the Supreme Court of Canada reviews the question.

. . .

The question here at issue must, therefore, be considered in light of the 1985 Act and the criteria which flow from it, as interpreted in *Moge*, supra. First, it must be determined whether a sufficient change has occurred between the parties to require the Court's intervention. Second, the Court must assess the effect of the agreement in light of the factors and objectives that govern spousal support under ss. 15(5), 15(7), 15(8), 17(4), 17(7) and 17(8) of the Act [now ss. 15.2(4) and (6) and ss. 17(4.1) and (7)].

C. Variation of support orders

Variation of support orders is governed by s. 17 of the current Act. Section 17(4) [see now s. 17(4.1) relating to spousal support] states that before it varies a support order "the court shall satisfy itself that there has been a change in the condition, means, needs or other circumstances of either former spouse or of any child of the marriage". This provision applies to any variation of a support order, whether in favour of a spouse or of the children. Consequently, the test developed in *Willick* v. *Willick*, [1994] 3 S.C.R. 670, in connection with support for children applies mutatis mutandis to the variation of spousal support. To begin with, the judge must determine whether there has been a change in the parties' situation since the last support order.

(1) *Change*

What sort of change is appropriate? *Willick*, supra, explained what is meant by "change". Sopinka J. said the following (at p. 688):

> In deciding whether the conditions for variation exist, it is common ground that the change must be a material change of circumstances. This means a change, such that, if known at the time, would likely have resulted in different terms. The corollary to this is that if the matter which is relied on as constituting a change was known at the relevant time it cannot be relied on as the basis for variation.

. . .

(2) *Agreement*

The analysis which the court must undertake to determine the extent of the variation, once the sufficiency of a change has been established, was discussed in *Willick*, supra, where I noted in this connection (at pp. 734-735):

> Once a sufficient change that will justify variation has been identified, the court must next determine the extent to which it will reconsider the circumstances underlying, and the basis for, the support order itself. For the reasons below, I believe that it is artificial for a court to restrict its analysis strictly to the change which has justified variation. Moreover, while a variation hearing is neither an appeal nor a trial *de novo*, where the alleged change or changes are of such a nature or magnitude as to make the original order irrelevant or no longer appropriate, then an assessment of the entirety of the present circumstances of the parties . . . is in order.

Section 15(5)(*c*) of the 1985 Act [see now s. 15.2(4)(c)], which governs the initial support order, specifically provides, with respect to agreements entered into between spouses in contemplation of their divorce, that "[i]n making an order under this section, the court shall take into consideration . . . any order, agreement or arrangement relating to support of the spouse or child". An agreement is only one of the factors listed in s. 15(5) that should be taken into account in assessing inter alia the duration and amount of spousal support (*Brockie* v. *Brockie* (1987), 8 R.F.L. (3d) 302 (Man. C.A.)). In addition, the four objectives mentioned in s. 15(7) [see now s. 15.2(6)]must also be considered.

In s. 15(5), no mention is made of a necessary causal connection: it differs in this respect from s. 17(10), which does not apply here. In so far as a duty of support results from marriage (or from cohabitation under certain provincial statutes), the notion of causality can only be dealt with in accordance with the various principles and objectives set out in the 1985 Act. . . .

Section 17, which governs variation orders, restates for its part the general provisions applicable to a support order without specifically mentioning the obligation to take into account agreements concluded between the parties. One should not conclude, however, that such agreement should be ignored when applications to vary support orders are made, especially when they were intended to be a final settlement, and were ratified by the original support order, an order which must be taken into account. As Wilson J. said in *Pelech* (at p. 850):

> People should be encouraged to take responsibility for their own lives and their own decisions. This should be the overriding policy consideration.

Having said that, while it is true that the parties should be encouraged to reach an agreement on the economic consequences resulting from their divorce rather than going to the courts, such agreements are only one factor, "albeit an important one", which must be considered in the exercise of the judge's discretionary power . . . . The weight to be given to agreements will depend, first, on the extent to which the agreement reflects the principles and objectives stated in s. 17 of the 1985 Act and, second, on the scope and nature of the change which has occurred, taking into account all the circumstances of the parties. The more the agreement or support order takes the overarching principle of the Act into account in promoting an equitable distribution of the economic consequences of the marriage and its breakdown, the more likely it will be to influence the outcome of the variation application. In drafting future agreements, counsel would be well advised to articulate the bases on which both spousal and child support covenants have been negotiated.

I should mention in passing that, in such an equitable distribution, the spouses may agree on various ways of dividing their assets depending on their financial situation at the time of divorce. Thus, spousal support for an unlimited time, such as that contemplated by the parties here, may well be compensatory in nature rather than simply needs based, especially when the parties do not have the resources to make a lump sum payment at the time of divorce, which may also, in some cases, confer some tax advantages. In the absence of any such mention in the agreement, the parties' intention in this regard cannot be presumed. However, it is clear here that nowhere in the agreement is there a mention of any attempt to dispose of the financial resources of the parties in accordance with the criteria laid down by the 1985 Act. No mention is made, for example, of the advantages and disadvantages resulting to the former spouses from the marriage or from its failure. It would thus be open to conclude that spousal support, unlimited as to time, could have been set taking these matters into account. Those are facts which the trial judge cannot ignore on an application to vary where an agreement has been entered into between the parties at the time of divorce or later. In this connection, as I noted earlier, it would clearly be useful for the parties to mention the various factors and objectives they took into account in their agreement to share the economic consequences of the marriage and its breakdown.

Having said that, the fact remains that, under the 1985 *Divorce Act*, courts retain a discretionary power the exercise of which will depend on the particular facts of each case and which will be exercised in accordance with the factors and objectives mentioned in the 1985 Act. The existence of an agreement, final or otherwise, should not have the effect of precluding such an analysis. . . .

SHAFFER & MELAMED "SEPARATION AGREEMENTS POST-*MOGE*, *WILLICK* AND *L.G.* v. *G.B.*: A NEW TRILOGY?"

(1999), 16 Can. J. Fam. L. 51 (Footnotes omitted)

The law concerning the variation of consensual spousal support provisions is in a state of flux. Recent decisions from the Supreme Court of Canada suggest that the court may be willing to revisit the high variation standard set down in the *Pelech* trilogy and a minority of the court has already indicated what it thinks a new variation test should be. At the lower court level, some courts are already treating the trilogy as defunct; others continue to pay lip service to the trilogy while permitting variation on a much less stringent standard. . . .

The effect of the *Pelech* trilogy was twofold. First, the trilogy was seen by many as endorsing a "clean break" model of spousal support in which the primary goal of support orders was to sever the ties between the ex-spouses as quickly as possible. Although this interpretation of the trilogy was subsequently repudiated by the Supreme Court in *Moge* v. *Moge*less had a profound impact on spousal support awards for some time.

Second, the high threshold for variation of separation agreements trilogy led to the predictable result that it became extremely difficult to vary agreements deemed to be final settlements of the entitlements arising from the marriage. Both aspects of the *Pelech* test contributed to this. The requirement that a change be "radical" or "unforseen" created an almost unsurmountable hurdle since almost any change or misfortune that might befall a person can be said to be foreseeable, even if the parties did not actually foresee it. The causal connection aspect also proved extremely difficult to satisfy for both payors of support and payees. Establishing a link between a changed circumstance and a pattern of dependency built up in the marriage was nearly impossible for payors, since the changes that would affect their ability to pay (retirement, illness, disability) could not be said to be causally connected to the marriage. This led some — but by no means all — courts to conclude that the causal connection part of the *Pelech* test should not apply to payors. In the case of those receiving support — most of whom were women — the causal connection requirement posed problems because of the narrow view of causation adopted by the courts. Instead of recognizing that long term absences from full time participation in the paid labour force will have long term (if not permanent) consequences in terms of a woman's ability to become economically self-sufficient courts were quick to attribute an inability to obtain employment to forces extrinsic to the marriage.

In short, the result of the high variation standard articulated in the trilogy was that people were often stuck with "bad" deals - bad in the sense that they left one of the former spouses in a precarious financial state. This was particularly pronounced for women who frequently agreed to short term support on the expectation that it would not take them long to become financially self-sufficient - an expectation that often failed to materialize. Men, as payors of support, could also be left in difficult financial straits, if they suffered a substantial decrease in income but were refused variation on the basis that their decreased earning capacity had no causal relationship to the marriage.

A Gradual Retreat from the Trilogy: *Moge* v. *Moge*, *Willick* v. *Willick* and *L.G.* v. *G.B.* (A New Trilogy?)

Although it has not overruled the trilogy, the Supreme Court has rendered three decisions which suggest a willingness to depart from the trilogy's rigid variation test. In *Moge* v. *Moge* the Supreme Court's influential pronouncement on spousal support, the court indicated explicitly that it was not considering the trilogy's variation standard. Nonetheless, L'Heureux-Dubé J.'s emphasis on the need for courts to consider all of the objectives of the 1985 *Divorce Act*, and her acknowledgment that marriage may create long term if not permanent support obligations, can be viewed as incompatible with Wilson J.'s emphasis in the trilogy on finality and clean break. . . .

Like *Moge*, the decision in *Willick* did not directly take on the trilogy standard. The issue in *Willick* was the standard under s. 17(4) of the 1985 *Divorce Act* for varying child support terms the spouses had negotiated in a settlement agreement. Sopinka J. for the majority of the court held that s. 17(4) requires an applicant to establish a "material" change in circumstances, and he defined material change as "a change, such that, if known at the time, would likely have resulted in different terms." The obvious corollary to this was, as Sopinka J. put it, "that if the matter which is relied on as constituting a material change was known at the relevant time, it cannot be relied upon as a basis for variation." Although Sopinka J. reiterated the frequently made observation that the principles which govern the variation of spousal support do not apply to child support, in *L.G.* v. *G.B.* a minority of the court endorsed Sopinka J.'s material change test as applicable to variation of spousal support provisions as well.

L.G. v. *G.B.* constitutes the Supreme Court's most direct challenge to the validity of the trilogy variation standard. . . .

Although the implications of L'Heureux-Dubé J.'s judgment on the standard for variation of final settlements are, perhaps, obvious they are sufficiently important to warrant being spelled out. First, L'Heureux-Dubé J. has abandoned the radical change in circumstances standard and has replaced it by the lower standard of a material change. Second, the trilogy's narrow causal connection test has been replaced with a broader inquiry into the sufficiency with which the agreement satisfies the objectives of the *Divorce Act* both at the time the agreement was negotiated and in light of the material change. . . .

Although the Supreme Court has not yet overruled the trilogy, one can read the decisions in *Moge, Willick,* and *L.G.* v. *G.B.* as indicative of a gradual erosion of the trilogy standard. The court's path away from the trilogy has not, however, been entirely consistent. In *Masters* v. *Masters* a decision rendered between *Moge* and *L.G.* v. *G.B.*, the Supreme Court appeared to indicate satisfaction with the trilogy test by upholding a decision of the Saskatchewan Court of Appeal which applied a strict trilogy test to a variation application brought by a payor. Nonetheless, there are strong indications that the trilogy's days are numbered and as we explore in more detail in the next section, the trilogy has been abandoned by many lower courts.

For this paper, we set ourselves the task of trying to chart the development of the law on applications to vary final settlements after *Moge*. . . . Our central observation is that the trilogy has been abandoned in an astonishing number of cases. The departure from the trilogy occurs in four related ways. The most striking of these is the explicit rejection of the trilogy as law in favour of some other variation standard. Since *L.G.* v. *G.B.* a few courts have tentatively adopted L'Heureux-Dubé J.'s minority reasons as the current state of the law. Other courts have refrained from wholeheartedly embracing L'Heureux-Dubé J.'s approach, but have held that the majority judgment in *L.G.* v. *G.B.* has replaced the trilogy's radical change requirement with a requirement that there merely be a material change as defined in *Willick*, or a substantial change. Even before *L.G.* v. *G.B.*, some courts had rejected the trilogy on the basis of the reasoning in *Moge* that the 1985 *Divorce Act* supplants the trilogy by requiring courts to consider a number of factors in addition to the presence of an agreement when deciding whether to award spousal support. Finally, most courts have rejected the causal connection aspect of *Pelech*, with the result that few courts continue to demand a causal relationship between the changed circumstances and the marriage.

It should be noted that these trends to depart from the trilogy are far more pronounced in some parts of the country than in others. In particular, the courts in British Columbia, Alberta and Saskatchewan have been far more willing than courts in the rest of the country to hold that *Moge, Willick, L.G.* v. *G.B.* or some combination of these cases have altered the trilogy standard. In Alberta and British Columbia many courts have abandoned the radical change standard in favour of a lower threshold of ''material'' or ''substantial'' change . . . A few judges have gone so far to as explicitly adopt L'Heureux-Dubé J.'s judgment in *L.G.* v. *G.B.* as the new variation standard . . .. This trend is also visible in Saskatchewan, although the courts are more qualified in their embrace of the *L.G.* v. *G.B.* approach. . . .

East of Saskatchewan, the departure from the trilogy is not as pronounced. Most courts in Ontario, New, Brunswick and Nova Scotia continue to assert that the trilogy is good law although many do not require payors to satisfy the causal connection part of the *Pelech* test. . . .

We have also observed an increased willingness among many courts to adopt an expansive approach to the definition of change. Many courts view thwarted expectations relating to the economically dependent spouse's ability to get a job as a change in circumstances. For example, many courts will perceive a material change where a contract appears to have been based on the assumption that the economically dependent spouse (in all of the cases we reviewed, this was the wife) will be able to upgrade her skills and obtain a job but where the wife remains unemployed, or underemployed, despite her best efforts. This trend is visible in courts across the country.

This approach to the notion of change contrasts with the somewhat stricter approach of the trilogy. In *Richardson*, for example, the majority refused to see Mrs. Richardson's failure to obtain employment as a change in circumstances, even though the husband's evidence suggested that the settlement agreement was signed under the impression that Mrs. Richardson would be able to get a job within the one year period for which support was provided. . . .

We do not wish to convey the impression that the trilogy has been entirely abandoned. Some courts do continue to adhere to the trilogy approach. Yet, even in some of the cases in which the courts profess to be invoking the trilogy standard, a less stringent variation standard is actually being applied. Perhaps the most dramatic example of this is the controversial Ontario case of *Santosuosso* v. *Santosuosso* [(1997), 27 R.F.L. (4th) 234] in which the Ontario Divisional Court departed from a separation agreement while ostensibly applying the trilogy standard. In that case, following the breakdown of a 23 year traditional marriage, the spouses entered into a final separation agreement in which the husband agreed to pay spousal support of $1,400.00 for 24 months. In 1991, after the support had been exhausted, the wife applied for support under s. 15 of the *Divorce Act*. She argued that when the spouses entered into the contract they believed that she would be able to attain economic self-sufficiency by upgrading her education and obtaining employment. Instead, at the time of the application, the wife had not managed to complete an ungrading course and was working almost 60 hours a week at low paying jobs to earn $1,700 per month.

The Divisional Court agreed that Mrs. Santosuosso had suffered a radical change in circumstances that was causally connected to the marriage. Even though Mrs. Santosuosso had managed to obtain employment, the court found that she had suffered a radical and unforeseen change in circumstances because her expectations of self-sufficiency through reasonable working conditions had not materialized. The Court held as follows:

> It was not within the contemplation or expectation or reasonable anticipation of both parties that the applicant would be working almost 60 hours a week at low-level wages to earn $1,700 a month in 1996. Further, an underpinning of the agreement was that the wife would achieve what can be fairly described as a modest and realistic goal for financial independence having regard to her circumstances.

The court came to this conclusion even in face of the following provision in the separation agreement:

> The husband shall pay to his wife the sum of $1,400.00 per month for her support commencing June 1, 1988 for a period of twenty-four months. Thereafter, regardless of her situation, the wife shall forever be responsible for her own support, regardless of any change in circumstances, no matter how catastrophic such change in circumstances might be and releases any and all claims which she might have for any further support in the future.

Based upon the length and traditional nature of the marriage, the court held "there is no question on the facts" that Mrs. Santosuosso's changed circumstances related to the pattern of dependency in the marriage.

It is hard to buy the court's conclusion that Mrs. Santosuosso's circumstances were truly a radical and unforeseen change as contemplated by the trilogy. One might argue that a more plausible interpretation of what was going on in the case was a refusal of the court to defer to the contract not because it fell within the exception carved out by the trilogy, but because it did not accord with the court's sense of fairness. As a result, some commentators have decried the decision in *Santosuosso* as heralding the end to the finality of separation agreements.

Although *Santosuosso* is not the norm, it is not the only post-*Moge* decision to have departed from the terms of a settlement agreement because they do not represent a fair deal on spousal support. In the recent New Brunswick case of *Laroque* v. *Laroque* [(1998), 36 R.F.L. (4th) 73], the New Brunswick Court of Queen's Bench also refused to follow the terms of a settlement agreement for reasons that may be said to be somewhat more honest than those in *Santosuosso*. In *Laroque*, the parties separated after 19 years of marriage and entered into a separation agreement in which they agreed that the husband would not pay any support for the wife or their four children. When the husband petitioned for divorce, his application was refused on two occasions, both times because the parties had failed to make adequate provision for child support. On the husband's third application, the wife sought both spousal and child support. Deschenes J. took the view that the trilogy analysis had been overtaken by the minority judgment in *L.G.* v. *G.B.* and that the Ontario Divisional Court had applied this analysis in *Santosuosso*. Deschenes J. agreed that *Santosuosso* should be followed with one exception - the judge took the view that there was no need to show that a radical change in circumstances had occurred since the agreement was signed. Instead, the court must simply look to see how well the agreement embodies the principles of the *Divorce Act* and if it does not, the court is entitled to give it little weight. On the facts, the court held that there had been no change in circumstances, but declined to follow the agreement simply because it did not even come close to meeting the objectives of spousal support. Deschenes J. was clear that this was not a case of frustrated expectations (since the parties never seriously contemplated that the wife would be self-sufficient), but rather a case in which the court perceived the agreement as unfair.

Neither *Santosuosso* nor *Laroque* represents the state of the law. Nonetheless, both cases are useful examples of the degree of uncertainty that currently exists in the law on contract variation such that it is possible to move so far from the trilogy.

Conclusion

We wish to conclude with some brief reflections on the state of the law and on the weakening of the trilogy standard. First, given the range of judicial views on the treatment of "final" settlement agreements, clarification is — obviously — desperately needed. Although the minority decision in *L.G.* v. *G.B.* goes some of the distance in this regard, even assuming that it is ultimately adopted by the majority of the Supreme Court, we are not sure that it provides lower courts with sufficient guidance. Second, we regard the retreat from the trilogy as a welcome development. In our view, the trilogy established an unrealistic standard in which people's projections as to their future lives became virtually cast in stone. Experience has shown that all too often these predictions were overly optimistic, with the result that women — as economically dependent spouses — who assumed they would have little difficulty becoming financially self-sufficient were punished for their optimism. The recognition in *Moge* that the roles adopted during marriage can have long term implications for economic self-sufficiency is also relevant here, since it casts doubt on the degree to which it is possible at the time of entering into a separation agreement to anticipate fully the impact of the marriage on the dependent spouse's ability to become self-sufficient. For these reasons, we regard the movement towards a less deferential approach to settlement agreements than that articulated in the trilogy as a positive step. To return to the competing objectives Wilson J. identified in the trilogy, this time around, we believe that the balance should tilt towards fairness rather than finality.

NOTES AND QUESTIONS

1. Does the principle enunciated by the Supreme Court of Canada in the *Pelech* trilogy take sufficient cognizance of the public interest? Should spouses be allowed to determine, in effect, that one of them will rely on public assistance for support even if there has been a relationship of economic dependency during the marriage? What is the view of the Ontario legislature on this issue? See s. 33(4)(b) of the *FLA*.

2. As was pointed out by La Forest J. in *Richardson*, the authority to interfere with contractual provisions regarding spousal support under the *FLA* appears much broader than the principle enunciated in the trilogy. Is there any policy justifying a more restricted approach upon and after divorce?

3. Although Madam Justice Wilson introduced the requirement of unforeseeability in *Richardson* in the context of failed expectations, it appears that she intended this to be a general requirement applying to all changes in circumstances. This requirement may be viewed as an additional element in the *Pelech* test or as a functional test to determine if the change is truly radical.

The case law subsequent to the trilogy is divided on whether the test for foreseeability should be essentially objective or subjective. In particular, *Fyffe* v. *Fyffe* (1988), 12 R.F.L. (3d) 196 (Ont. C.A.); *Crowe* v. *Crowe* (1988), 16 R.F.L. (3d) 420 (Ont. H.C.); and *Stutchbury* v. *Stutchbury* (1989), 23 R.F.L. (3d) 170 (Ont. H.C.) indicate that the change must not have been reasonably foreseeable, while *Ritchie* v. *Ritchie* (1988), 16 R.F.L. (3d) 163 (B.C. S.C.); *MacMillan* v. *MacMillan* (1988), 18 R.F.L. (3d) 149 (N.S. T.D.); *Hood* v. *Hood* (1990), 72 O.R. (2d) 1 (Fam. Ct.); and *Allen* v. *Allen* (1999), 2 R.F.L. (5th) 1 (Alta. Q.B.) suggest it is enough if the parties did not foresee the change. Justice Sopinka's reasons in *B. (G.)* v. *G. (L.)* support the former view since he concluded (at 271) that the trial judge had correctly decided that there had been no material change of circumstances on the basis that it was foreseeable that the wife would cohabit with her friend. In his annotation to *Bradley* v. *Bradley* (1997), 29 R.F.L. (4th) 151 (Ont. Gen. Div.) in the RFL's, Professor McLeod suggests that, in the context of variation of an earlier order, a change should be considered "material" if 1) it was not taken into account at the time of the original order and 2) it would have made a difference if it had been. Should the test for a radical change be more stringent where the court is asked to make a support order that overrides a term of a domestic contract?

4. In *Publicover* v. *Publicover* (1987), 9 R.F.L. (3d) 308 (N.S. Fam. Ct.), Williams Fam. Ct. J. held (at 311-312) that the policies underlying the Supreme Court trilogy are only relevant when the parties to the agreement have "made a clear attempt to achieve a 'clean break', a termination of any further monetary relationship between the parties or an attempt to terminate any future role for the court (by, for example, a provision that quantum of maintenance will not be varied or will be varied only in accordance with a specified fixed identifiable formula or will terminate upon the happening of a specific event)". In each case the agreement and surrounding circumstances must be examined to determine whether the parties intended the arrangements to be permanent or whether they intended them to be variable by a court. For examples, see *Barrington* v. *Barrington* (1991), 38 R.F.L. (3d) 77 (Sask. C.A.); *Winsor* v. *Winsor* (1992), 39 R.F.L. (3d) 8 (Ont. C.A.); *Harris* v. *Gilbert* (1992), 39 R.F.L. (3d) 458 (Ont. Gen. Div.); *Golp (Silmarie)* v. *Golp* (1994), 1 R.F.L. (4th) 161 (N.S. C.A.); and *MacDonald* v. *MacDonald* (1997), 30 R.F.L. (4th) 1 (Alta. C.A.).

5. As noted by L'Heureux-Dubé J. in *B. (G.)* v. *G. (L.)* the trilogy has been subjected to considerable criticism. In "*Pelech, Caron* and *Richardson*" (1989-90), 3 C.J.W.L. 615, Professor Bailey commented (at 616):

> The decisions are consistent with the global trend toward privatization, our traditional protection of the private sphere of the family from state intervention, the current push for settlement of family law cases, and the new family law's emphasis on self-sufficiency and a clean break, phenomena which are all problematic for the disadvantaged. The privatized family, long exposed by feminists as a state-sanctioned arena for male abuse of power, will not produce agreements consistent with the standards of fairness embodied in our family laws because of the inequality of bargaining power between men and women in a patriarchal society. The general inequality of bargaining power of women in our society is exacerbated in the family law context by the fact that women are almost always the needy claimants, they usually have fewer resources to mount

legal battles, and they are more likely to have strong ties with their children and to be willing to trade away monetary rights for the sake of the children.

The trilogy's atomistic view of the family is consistent with dominant liberal discourse, which represents the oppressive relationship between husband and wife as a freely chosen contract between rational, unencumbered, autonomous individuals. The trilogy's notion of subjectivity ignores any social construction of self, as well as the limits on choice created by gender inequality. The atomistic family model is problematic for conservatives who cherish the traditional family as the cornerstone of society. It is also problematic for feminists who, while criticizing the family as an oppressive institution, do not want women cut off from this social support system before an adequate alternative is available, and who recognize the limits of individual rights as the basis of social organization. Of the many discourses prevalent in our pluralistic society, the trilogy seems most to reflect libertarian liberalism, in its conception of self and the family and its view of contracts. Libertarian liberalism stands for the free operation of the market economy, protection of privacy rights, resistance to distributive justice claims, and the position that the state should guarantee only formal legal equality, not actual equality.

6. For commentary on *Santosuosso*, see Grant, "The End of Finality" (1997), 27 R.F.L. (4th) 252 and Himel, "Bargaining in the Shadow of the 'End of Finality' " (1998), 16 C.F.L.Q. 399.

7. In *Wilkinson* v. *Wilkinson* (1998), 43 R.F.L. (4th) 258 (Alta. Q.B.), Sullivan J. reviewed the S.C.C. cases dealing with domestic contacts and concluded (at 270 - 272):

To summarize, *Pelech* established that variation of a spousal support agreement was appropriate where there had been a radical change in circumstances causally connected to the marriage. In *Moge*, the Supreme Court specifically declined to review this test. In *Willick*, the test was relaxed in the context of child support agreements such that a material change in circumstances was sufficient to warrant the variation of a child support order. While a minority of the Supreme Court held that *Willick* should also apply to spousal support orders, the majority in *B. (G.) c. G. (L.)* did not review the issue. Therefore, the test for varying a spousal support order remains a radical change in circumstances that is causally connected to the marriage. . . .

The wide disparity between the approaches to the *Pelech* standard [in subsequent cases] indicates that the courts across Canada are not satisfied with the test as it currently stands. In essence, the courts are looking for ways to circumvent the strict standard imposed by *Pelech* in order to ensure a fair result. While the goal of attaining a fair result is always laudable, the goal must be achieved within the bounds of the case law and precedents. The Supreme Court of Canada has laid down the test for variation of spousal support agreements. The Supreme Court of Canada has had the opportunity to reconsider the issue and has specifically refrained from doing so. Until the Supreme Court of Canada indicates otherwise, the test remains the same and should be followed by this Court.

Other cases adopting this view include *Walker* v. *Walker* (1997), 31 R.F.L. (4th) 63 (B.C. S.C.); *Y.(D.)* v. *Y.(H.)* (1998), 43 R.F.L. (4th) 408 (P.E.I. T.D.); and *Allen* v. *Allen* (1999), 2 R.F.L. (5th) 1 (Alta. Q.B.). In *McArthur* v. *McArthur* (1998), 44 R.F.L. (4th) 241 (Alta. Q.B.), the court refused an application for spousal support where a settlement in 1993 had given the wife almost all the family property and she could not establish that there had been a radical change in circumstances that related to the marriage. However, compare *Lipschitz* v. *Lipschitz* (1998), 41 R.F.L. (4th) 108 (B.C. S.C.), where the court held that the *Pelech* trilogy no longer applied. The court reinstated spousal support under the *Divorce Act* after a limited term order based on a separation agreement had ended, holding that a substantial and unforeseen change had occurred. See also *M. (L.S.)* v. *M. (E.J.)* (1999), 3 R.F.L. (5th) 106 (Ont. S.C.J.).

8. Should the S.C.C. adopt Justice L'Heureux-Dube's approach as set out in *B. (G.)* v. *G. (L.)*? Does it give enough guidance for the exercise of the courts' supervisory power under the *Divorce Act*? If a court has authority to review the provisions of every agreement relating to spousal support to ensure that they meet the objectives of the *Divorce Act*, what purpose is served by entering into agreements in the first place?

9. Note s. 17(10) of the *Divorce Act* which dictates that in some applications to vary a prior order the change must relate to the marriage, whether or not the previous order was based on an agreement.

(ii) Under the *Family Law Act*

Section 33(4) gives a court jurisdiction to set aside a provision for support or a waiver of the rights to support in a domestic contract and determine and order support under the Act where the applicant can establish one of three statutory criteria. This authority exists even though the contract is valid and enforceable and notwithstanding an express provision in the contract purporting to exclude the application of the subsection.

NEWBY v. NEWBY

(1986), 56 O.R. (2d) 483 (Ont. H.C.)

BOLAN L.J.S.C.: — . . . The petitioner and respondent were married on August 23, 1956. Four children were born of the marriage — all within the space of four years. There are no children under the age of 18.

In 1957 the respondent became employed with the Toronto Star. His work required him to be away from home for long periods of time. He travelled extensively and it was not unusual for him to be away for months. This lasted until 1967 when the respondent became a zone manager for the Toronto area and was not required to do any extensive travelling. The family moved to Mississauga into a large back-split home where they resided until the parties separated in 1979. Following the separation, they entered into a separation agreement in October of that year: see ex. 5. The petitioner had worked approximately 18 months during the marriage and she intended to find work after the parties separated because she felt she was able to work. The respondent was earning some $40,000 a year and he was of the view that the petitioner was not able to work.

Paragraph 3 of the separation agreement provides for support and maintenance payments by the respondent to the petitioner. It starts off at $750 a month and there are various provisions for escalation and de-escalation of these payments. This gave to the petitioner a gross income for her support and maintenance of $9,000 a year and left the respondent with a net income after tax of $13,000 a year. The petitioner presently receives $1,106.44 a month from the respondent. Since the separation agreement was signed, the respondent has overpaid the petitioner by $6,000. . . .

The first step is to determine the time frame which the *Family Law Act* contemplates in s. 33(4) (*a*). Does the phrase "results in unconscionable circumstances" mean at the time of the signing of the agreement or some time in the future?

In my view, s. 33(4) (*a*) contemplates circumstances which may arise in the future and which are the *direct* result of the provision for support contained in the separation agreement. Had the Legislature intended otherwise, it would have set it out in the legislation.

The next step is to determine if the provision for support contained in the separation agreement has resulted in unconscionable circumstances for the petitioner. The word "unconscionable" is defined in the Canadian Law Dictionary as "that which is contrary to the conscience of the Court". It is defined in Webster's New Collegiate Dictionary as shockingly unfair or unjust. Whether "unconscionable" is used in a legal or non-legal sense, it can best be described as "something which is shocking, oppressive, not in keeping with a caring society".

Several factors should be considered to determine if the provisions for support in a domestic contract (in this case a separation agreement) result in unconscionable circumstances. Each factor should be considered and weighed separately, and the court should then look at the cumulative effect of these factors.

Factors to be considered

1. *Facts surrounding the signing of the separation agreement*

Both parties received independent legal advice and were represented by counsel throughout the negotiations. The petitioner admits that the respondent did not influence her to sign the agreement. She says she told the respondent she was not satisfied with the support negotiated on her behalf, yet she signed the agreement because things were very difficult. She further told her lawyer she was not happy with what she was getting under the agreement. . . .

I find that the respondent negotiated the support payments on the basis that the petitioner was unemployable; however, I am equally satisfied that the petitioner negotiated the support provisions in the agreement on the basis that she would be able to work and that her income would be supplemented accordingly.

I am satisfied that the separation agreement was negotiated in good faith between the parties and that they both had independent legal advice. This is a factor which weighs in favour of the respondent in determining whether the support provisions in the separation agreement have resulted in unconscionable circumstances.

2. *Results of the support provisions of the separation agreement*

The second factor to consider is the effect which the support provisions in the separation agreement had on the parties. Paragraph 3 of the separation agreement provides for monthly payments of $750 per month. This gave the petitioner a gross yearly income of $9,000 a year. In addition she received $350 per month to support the children for a total gross annual income of $13,200. The respondent was left with *after tax* income of $13,000. The respondent found it difficult to live on this "after tax income"; yet the petitioner had to support herself and her three children on a gross income of $13,200.

It can hardly be said that the support negotiated for the petitioner was favourable to her or even fair. The seeds of her eventual hardship were sown in the meagre amount of support negotiated on her own behalf. Although the respondent may have negotiated a good deal for himself, it was inevitable that the petitioner would eventually find herself in her present financial bind.

Much has been made by the respondent that the petitioner frittered away the moneys she received from her equity in the matrimonial home. She received $34,181 from the sale of the home. She paid off two loans totalling $4,000 and bought some furniture. This left her with approximately $25,000 which she spent over the next three years to four years. She did take some holidays but they were not extravagant. It is obvious how the balance of the moneys was spent: she used it to make up for the meagre support payments she was receiving from the respondent.

I do not accept the respondent's evidence that the petitioner is a "spendaholic" who does not know how to manage her money. Considering the meagre amount she had to support herself, I would say she has managed her money in a responsible manner.

I find that the support provisions in the separation agreement were woefully lacking and completely unrealistic and it was only a matter of time before the petitioner would find herself facing financial hardship. This is a factor which weighs in favour of the petitioner.

3. *The parties today*

The petitioner is 57 years of age and in poor health. She suffers from high blood pressure and is manic-depressive. The prognosis is poor and she remains unemployable. In the past she suffered a nervous breakdown for which she was hospitalized. Her daughter has noted a marked deterioration in her mental state. I observed her demeanour in the witness stand and she strikes me as a rather pathetic individual. Her income which consists of support from the respondent of $1,106.44 and from her daughter Lee Anne of $116.66, is hardly adequate to see her through the month. By the middle of the month she is without groceries and is assisted by her children. She lives in a less than adequate apartment in a dirty and unkempt apartment building. She has no recreational or entertainment activities because she cannot afford it. Although she is not a public charge on society, it is only a matter of time before she does become one.

The respondent is 55 years old, self-assured and very successful who — rightfully so — basks in the fruits of his hard labour. He is the circulation manager of a large daily national newspaper and earns in excess of $90,000 a year. In addition, he has substantial assets, including a one-half interest in a luxury condominium valued at $190,000, a one-half interest in a cottage, and stocks and bonds. He has no debts. He is healthy and takes exotic holidays.

There is an enormous disparity between the parties. The cumulative effect of these factors together with the disparity in financial circumstances has resulted in unconscionable circumstances for the petitioner. It is shocking to this court that a 57-year-old woman from a 23-year-old marriage who raised four children while the husband was away for months at a time now finds herself in such dire financial straits — through no fault of her own. This woman's life is a shambles. She is in poor mental and physical health; she often runs out of food by the middle of the month.

On the other hand, the respondent — through hard work and financial acumen — has wealth, good health, and financial security.

I have found as a matter of fact that the provisions for support in the separation agreement have resulted in unconscionable circumstances. Should the court intervene and exercise its discretion to set aside the support provisions of the separation agreement? In my view, s. 33(4) (*a*) is an exceptional remedy which should only be exercised in exceptional circumstances. To do otherwise would be to encourage spouses to negotiate in bad faith with the knowledge that if one of them is not satisfied at a later date with the terms for support, he or she can always come back to the court to have it changed.

In my view, there are exceptional circumstances which, when looked at cumulatively, compel me to set aside the support provisions in the separation agreement. They are as follows:

1.   The amount negotiated for support in the separation agreement.

2. The deteriorating mental and physical condition of the petitioner.
3. The fact that the petitioner cannot work and is therefore unemployable.
4. The fact that the petitioner's financial hardship was not her own doing.
5. The respective positions of the parties today.
6. The fact that the petitioner has demonstrated need.
7. The ability of the respondent to pay.

[The provisions for support in the separation agreement were set aside and the husband was ordered to pay $2,000 per month support to the wife. The wife's application for equalization of the net family properties was, however, dismissed in light of the separation agreement.]

SALONEN v. SALONEN

(1986), 2 R.F.L. (3d) 273 (Ont. U.F.C.)

[The parties were married in 1977 and separated in 1984. In December 1984 the wife instructed her solicitor to prepare a separation agreement that both parties signed after obtaining independent legal advice. The agreement provided for $300 per month child support for the three children of the marriage. It also specified that the husband would assume all of the family debts (totaling approximately $6,000 to $8,000) in return for exclusive title to the matrimonial home. The parties had very little equity in the home. The agreement made no provision for spousal support.

At the time that the agreement was signed the wife intended to live with another man who would provide shelter for her and the children and the wife earned approximately $100 per week working part-time. Later the wife's relationship with the man broke down and she became unemployed. The wife was in receipt of welfare payments when she applied for support under the *FLA*. At that time the husband was earning approximately $32,000 gross annually. Nevertheless, he insisted he had insufficient means to provide even child support and was described by the trial judge as a "financial disaster".

In her application for support for herself and increased support for the children, the wife argued that the agreement should be set aside because it was an unconscionable transaction and because the husband had exerted undue influence and had failed to disclose the existence of a newly created pension plan at his place of employment. The trial judge refused to set aside the agreement on these grounds, holding that it was a valid agreement. Nevertheless, using the power granted by s. 56(1) of the Act, Goodearle U.F.C.J. increased the child support to $200 per month for each child. Finally, Goodearle U.F.C.J. refused to use s. 33(4) to set aside the waiver of spousal support in the agreement. Only the reasons dealing with s. 33(4) are reproduced here.]

GOODEARLE U.F.C.J.: . . . This leaves the applicant clinging tenuously to the provisions of s. 33(4)(*b*). . . .

In *Parro* v. *Parro* (1985), 46 R.F.L. (2d) 155 (Ont. Prov. Ct.), Morrison Prov. J., in dealing with s. 18(4) of the Family Law Reform Act (identical in substance to s. 33(4)(*b*)) recognized that the wife was in need of support, on public welfare, but he refused to set aside the separation agreement in favour of the statutory provision for these reasons [at p. 160]:

> As a general principle, it is not for the court to remedy a bad bargain. The agreement was in accord with the objectives of the statute which encourages parties to enter into voluntary negotiations to

settle differences. In my opinion, I ought to give effect to the agreement unless compelled to do otherwise by a substantive or gross change of circumstances that demands that I do so.

Also, in *Pelech* v. *Pelech* (1985), 45 R.F.L. (2d) 1, 61 B.C.L.R. 217, 17 D.L.R. (4th) 147 (C.A.), Lambert J.A. held that receipt of welfare ought not, per se, to create a support obligation if none would otherwise exist. He said at p. 10:

> Mrs. Pelech and others in similar circumstances will remain a charge on the community at large. But against that must be weighed, among other financial consequences, the financial advantages to the community in having binding maintenance settlements made by the parties themselves, rather than by judges and other public officers in facilities provided and maintained at public expense.

I am concerned that to give effect to this section on a perfunctory basis might well result in great mischief. For example, if a wife found herself bound by the support terms of an otherwise binding separation agreement, she could simply desist from further toil for wages, apply for welfare and thereafter seek a support order under this section. Surely this section was only intended to apply to situations where:

(1) the marriage created a situation of economic dependency; or
(2) the marriage term resulted in an obvious economic loss or disadvantage to the party claiming.

I find no help in these preconditions in the case at bar.

Welfare benefits have their origins in the philosophy of social assistance; i.e., society must and should help its indigents in time of obvious need. It should not be seen as a basis to thwart or jeopardize the bona fide bargainings of separating spouses whose "best laid plans" go amiss. For if so seen by other parties contemplating a binding arrangement, surely such parties must be timid and even reluctant to enter upon a bargain in good faith which, of course, would be unfortunate in the overall perspective of family law.

I believe the application of this section should be used with caution, even sparingly, to impugn or strike down an otherwise bona fide bargain between separating spouses.

And it has long been the law that such agreements should not be easily disregarded.

I do not believe that the legislature, in enacting the Family Law Act, intended that s. 33(4)(*b*) should interfere easily with the wisdom of this long-standing principle.

To succeed under this section, I might, to the already stated preconditions, add the following:

(1) The bona fides of the parties when entering upon the agreement should be seriously and obviously in question;
(2) The means of the potentially paying spouse is such that if the recipient were left on welfare, the public should quite reasonably be outraged;
(3) Circumstances of both parties have drastically changed from the time of the signing whereby welfare is simply no longer a realistic alternative.

There may well be others.

For the foregoing reasons, I cannot in conscience apply s. 33(4)(*b*). Her application for spousal support is therefore dismissed.

NOTES AND QUESTIONS

1. Could Mrs. Newby have satisfied the test established by the *Pelech* trilogy to determine when a court should override an agreement where a spouse claims support under the *Divorce Act*?

For other cases dealing with s. 33(4)(a) and its predecessor in the *Family Law Reform Act*, see: *Weiss* v. *Kopel* (1980), 18 R.F.L. (2d) 289 (Ont. Prov. Ct.); *Mance* v. *Mance* (1981), 22 R.F.L. (2d) 445 (Ont. Co. Ct.), affirmed (1983), 21 A.C.W.S. (2d) 471 (Ont. C.A.); *Butler* v. *Butler* (1982), 28 R.F.L. (2d) 183 (Ont. Fam. Ct.); *Lecot* v. *Lecot* (1995), 19 R.F.L. (4th) 14 (Ont. Gen. Div.); *P.(E.L.)* v. *P.(K.B.)* (1986), 49 R.F.L. (2d) 315 (Ont. Fam. Ct.); and *Scheel* v. *Henkelman* (1999), 3 R.F.L. (5th) 286 (Ont. S.C.J.). In *Olivier* v. *Olivier* (1988), 17 R.F.L. (3d) 440 (Ont. H.C.), Steele J. suggested (at 443) that a court should not override a valid settlement agreement under s. 33(4) unless there has been a radical change in circumstances that flows from an economic pattern of dependency engendered by the marriage. Given the wording of s. 33(4), would this approach further the legislative intent?

2. In *Salonen*, Goodearle U.F.C.J. suggested that a court should decline to exercise its authority under s. 33(4)(b) unless there has been a drastic change in circumstances since the agreement. This approach is clearly in line with the *Pelech* trilogy. Is it in keeping with the intent of s. 33(4)(b)? By way of contrast, the Ontario Divisional Court in *Burton* v. *Burton* (1998), 42 R.F.L. (4th) 310 (Ont. Gen. Div.) indicated that, once it is established that the applicant is on welfare, the court should determine whether to order spousal support simply in accordance with ss. 33(8) and (9) of the Act. This would give little, if any effect the existence of the waiver of support.

In "Domestic Contracts in Ontario and the Supreme Court Trilogy: 'A Deal is a Deal'" (1988), 13 Queen's L.J. 3, Professor Bala suggested (at 42):

> It would seem that if the dependant is receiving public assistance, it is not necessary to demonstrate that there has been a 'catastrophic' or 'unforeseen' change in circumstances; the test of s. 33(4)(b) may not be as high as that imposed [in the *Pelech* trilogy] under the *Divorce Act*. It is, however, submitted that the courts should be reluctant to invoke s. 33(4)(b) to increase support levels above that which public assistance would provide. . . .
>
> It is also the author's view that s. 33(4)(b) should not be invoked in situations where a substantial period of time has elapsed since the separation and the dependant's need for public assistance cannot in some way be linked to the marriage.

3. It has been held that the court should not exercise its jurisdiction under s. 33(4)(c) simply because there has been a default or delay in payments due under a domestic contract. See *McClelland* v. *McClelland* (1979), 1 F.L.R.A.C. 517 (Ont. Prov. Ct.); *Stevenson* v. *Stevenson* (1979), 23 O.R. (2d) 539 (Prov. Ct.); and *Mance* v. *Mance* (1981), 22 R.F.L. (2d) 445 (Ont. Co. Ct.). In the last case, Robson Co. Ct. J. made the following comment (at 451) about s. 18(4)(c) of the *Family Law Reform Act* (which was identical to s. 33(4)(c) of the *FLA*):

> It appears to me that what the Legislature was trying to correct was a situation where a person has made an agreement to pay support and has fallen into arrears under that agreement to such an extent that it appears necessary to the court to make a variation of the separation agreement in order to secure the support payment under it.

Might the legislative intent have been broader than this?

4. If the threshold for judicial interference with support provisions in a domestic contract is lower under provincial legislation than under the *Divorce Act*, the payor spouse may be able to preclude the application of the provincial legislation. Either spouse can commence divorce proceedings immediately after separation and request a determination of the support issue under the *Divorce Act*: *Clayton* v. *Clayton* (1989), 19 R.F.L. (3d) 430 (Ont. Div. Ct.). The federal law should then apply to the issue of support pursuant to the constitutional doctrine of paramountcy. Professor Bala indicates, *supra*, at 40, that this will influence the courts' approach to s. 33(4):

> [E]ither spouse can require spousal support issues to be dealt with exclusively under the federal divorce legislation, simply by commencing a divorce petition. It is the author's view that to

prevent inconsistencies or the relitigation of issues under the *Divorce Act, 1985*, courts will tend to interpret s. 33(4) of the F.L.A. in a manner consistent with the *Divorce Act* jurisprudence.

Just as the *Pelech* trilogy encouraged a restrictive approach to s. 33(4) of the *FLA*, a Supreme Court of Canada decision holding that the trilogy should not govern the exercise of the courts' supervisory power under the *Divorce Act* would likely result in a more liberal use of the subsection in the provincial statute.

5. In *Porter* v. *Porter* (1979), 8 R.F.L. (2d) 349, 23 O.R. (2d) 492 (H.C.), the court held that s. 18(4) of the *Family Law Reform Act* could only be invoked in an application for support under the Act. It therefore afforded no remedy for the husband in *Porter*, as he was required to pay support under an agreement. He sought to have the amount of support payable reduced although the separation agreement did not contain a variation clause. The husband wanted a reduction in light of the following facts: he was now living with and supporting a widow and her two children and the wife was earning a substantial salary. Would s. 35 of the *FLA* indirectly provide a remedy for a husband in Mr. Porter's situation? See below.

Because s. 33(4) of the *FLA* can only be invoked in an application for support, the time limits of s. 50 apply: *Menard* v. *Menard* (1987), 6 R.F.L. (3d) 235 (Ont. Dist. Ct.).

6. Where a court has incorporated the provisions of a separation agreement or other domestic contract into a support order under the *FLA*, it is not necessary to resort to s. 33(4) to obtain a variation. In that situation, either party can apply for a variation of the court order under s. 37. See *Ott* v. *Ott* (1982), 30 R.F.L. (2d) 370 (Ont. C.A.) and *Forder* v. *Forder* (1984), 40 R.F.L. (2d) 159 (Ont. Co. Ct.). While the court has jurisdiction to vary such an order whenever there has been a material change of circumstances, the policy considerations enunciated in the *Pelech* trilogy dictate that the court should be reluctant to do so where the provisions on which the order was based were intended to be a final, binding settlement of all support issues. See below.

7. By virtue of s. 56(2), "a provision in a domestic contract to take effect on separation whereby any right of a party is dependent on remaining chaste is unenforceable". Accordingly, *dum casta* clauses, which commonly provided that support would continue only so long as a spouse remained chaste, are no longer enforceable. Section 56(2), however, specifically recognizes the validity of provisions in domestic contracts that terminate upon remarriage or cohabitation with another. *Dum casta* clauses in domestic contracts entered into before the Act came into force will be given effect as though they provided that the right involved terminated on remarriage or cohabitation with another: s. 56(3). For a review of the cases examining the meaning of the phrase "living as husband and wife" in this context, see *Cooper* v. *Cooper* (1998), 42 R.F.L. (4th) 317 (Nfld. U.F.C.).

8. Section 58(1) of the *Succession Law Reform Act*, R.S.O. 1990, c. S. 26 authorizes a court, upon application, to order that adequate provision be made out of the estate of a deceased person for the proper support of a dependant where the deceased, whether testate or intestate, has not made adequate provision for the proper support of the dependant. By virtue of s. 57, the spouse or same-sex partner of the deceased is a dependant provided the deceased was providing support or was under a legal obligation to provide support immediately before his or her death. Section 57 stipulates that a person whose marriage was terminated or declared a nullity is a spouse for the purpose of the Act. Therefore, court orders can be made in favour of spouses or former spouses who qualify as dependants of the deceased. In addition, s. 57 provides that unmarried cohabitees qualify as spouses for the purpose of Part V of the Act if: (i) they have cohabited continuously for a period not less than three years; or (ii) they have cohabited in a relationship of some permanence and they are the natural or adoptive parents of a child. Finally, that section, as amended by *Amendments Because of the Supreme Court of Canada's Decision in M.v. H. Act, 1999*, S.O. 1999, c. 6, stipulates that same-sex partners qualify as dependants in the same circumstances.

The existence of a domestic contract dealing with support may determine whether a spouse, former spouse, or same-sex partner qualifies as a dependant of the deceased. If the deceased, immediately prior to his or her death, is contractually obligated to support a spouse, former spouse, or same-sex partner, then the latter clearly falls within the statutory definition of dependant. Where, however, a spouse has expressly waived the right to support during the deceased's lifetime, a contrary result follows. See *Mealey* v. *Broadbent* (1984), 40 R.F.L. (2d) 225 (Ont. Div. Ct.); *Smith* v. *Smith Estate* (1985), 21 E.T.R.

299 (Ont. Surr. Ct.); and *Taylor* v. *Taylor Estate* (1985), 53 O.R. (2d) 174 (Surr. Ct.). Contrast the earlier case of *Re Pflanzner* (1983), 15 E.T.R. 144 (Ont. Surr. Ct.). Since this result flows from the statutory definition of "dependant" in Ontario, the position may differ in other provinces. See, for example, *Boulanger* v. *Singh* (1984), 16 D.L.R. (4th) 131 (B.C. C.A.).

In light of the fact that a spouse or former spouse may be precluded from applying under Part V of the *Succession Law Reform Act* by a valid contractual waiver of the right to be supported during the deceased's lifetime, it is perhaps surprising that an express waiver in a domestic contract of the right to claim support after the death of the deceased does not bar an application by a spouse, former spouse, or same-sex partner who does qualify as a dependant. Section 63(4) specifies that an order for support may be made notwithstanding any agreement or waiver to the contrary and s. 62(1)(m) simply lists an agreement between the deceased and the dependant as a factor to be considered among many others in dealing with the application. The case law indicates that the weight accorded to an agreement that expressly waives or limits the right to apply under Part V of the *Succession Law Reform Act* varies in accordance with the circumstances of the case. See *Goldhar* v. *Goldhar* (1985), 21 E.T.R. 189 (Ont. Div. Ct.), affirmed (1986), 37 A.C.W.S. (2d) 282 (Ont. C.A), leave to appeal to S.C.C. refused (1986), 70 N.R. 173n; *Swire* v. *Swire* (1986), 23 E.T.R. 246 (Ont. Surr. Ct.), affirmed (1987), 10 R.F.L. (3d) 399 (Ont. Div. Ct.); *Fune* v. *Hoy Estate* (1995), 10 R.F.L. (4th) 361 (Ont. Gen. Div.); *Boyko* v. *Boyko Estate* (1998), 64 O.T.C. 9 (Ont. Gen. Div.); and *Vanderven* v. *Vanderven Estate* (1998), 72 O.T.C. 68 (Ont. Gen. Div.). See also *Wagner* v. *Wagner Estate* (1991), 37 R.F.L. (3d) 1 (B.C. C.A.) dealing with the *Wills Variation Act,* R.S.B.C. 1979, c. 435. In *Wagner*, the B.C. C.A. suggested that the policy underlying the trilogy should not be extended to cases under the *Wills Variation Act*. For a comment see Farquhar, "Spousal Agreements and Statutory Succession Rights — Comment on *Wagner* v. *Wagner Estate*" (1992), 11 Can. J. Fam. L. 151.

The power to override the support provisions of a domestic contract granted by s. 33(4) should be contrasted with the power to vary those provisions where the contract is filed with a court pursuant to s. 35(1). A provision for support in a contract that is filed with the court may then be varied or made the subject of an indexing order as if it were an order of the court where it is filed: s. 35(2)(b). There are several significant differences between the power to override support provisions under s. 33(4) and the power to vary them under s. 35(2). First, s. 33(4) only applies where a claim for support is made. Therefore, the limitation periods established by s. 50 apply and only the dependant can invoke the court's jurisdiction. On the other hand, s. 50 does not apply to an application for variation and either spouse can bring the application if the contract is filed. Second, the power to vary only applies where the filed contract provides for support. Unlike s. 33(4), therefore, it has no application where there is a waiver of the right to support. Third, the parties can stipulate in a domestic contract that the support provisions are not subject to the court's power to vary them or index them. On the other hand, the parties cannot oust the court's jurisdiction under s. 33(4).

In *Wark* v. *Wark* (1989), 18 R.F.L. (3d) 75 (Ont. Dist. Ct.), Gautreau D.C.J. concluded his discussion of contracting out of s. 35(2)(b) as follows (at 91):

> In summary, if the agreement specifically contracts out of the statute by means of express terms then this of course is an agreement to the contrary. If the agreement provides its own comprehensive mechanism for variation . . . this will also be an agreement to the contrary and if on examining the agreement as a whole the court is satisfied that the parties intended the agreement to be a full and complete code of their rights and liabilities, then, of course, this will also be an agreement to the contrary.

See also *O'Connor* v. *O'Connor* (1990), 28 R.F.L. (3d) 99 (Ont. Fam. Ct.) and *Zegil* v. *Zegil* (1993), 50 R.F.L. (3d) 317 (Ont. Gen. Div.).

It has been suggested that the courts should exercise their jurisdiction under s. 35(2) to vary support provisions in a domestic contract in exceptional circumstances only: McLeod, ''Annotation'' (1987), 6 R.F.L. (3d) 236. Indeed, Gautreau D.C.J. held in *Wark* v. *Wark* that the principles established by the Supreme Court of Canada trilogy should govern in this context. He stated (at 87-88):

> "Material change" should be given a meaning similar to "radical change" as employed in *Pelech*. This is not a perversion of meaning but a selection of meaning for "material change" is a relative thing. . . .
>
> [T]he court is justified in varying a separation agreement under the Family Law Act if there has been a material change in circumstances, in the radical sense, provided that the court is satisfied that the parties did not contemplate the change when they made the agreement and did not have it in mind as a probable occurrence.

When the decision was affirmed, the court explicitly declined to rule on this point: (1990), 28 R.F.L. (3d) 410 (Ont. Gen. Div.). See also *Stutchbury* v. *Stutchbury* (1989), 23 R.F.L. (3d) 170 (Ont. H.C.) and *Zegil* v. *Zegil* (1993), 50 R.F.L. (3d) 317 (Ont. Gen. Div.). Contrast *Hood* v. *Hood* (1990), 72 O.R. (2d) 1 (Fam. Ct.), where Nasmith Prov. Ct. J. concluded that once a contract was filed, the support provisions could be varied upon proof of a material change in circumstances in the ordinary sense unless the parties had contracted out of s. 35(2)(b). Provided the courts take the broad approach to the question of contracting out exhibited in *Wark*, it is difficult to envisage policy reasons for not favouring *Hood*.

(3) CHILDREN

Section 56(1) of the *FLA* gives the court the authority to disregard any provision of a domestic contract pertaining to the education, moral training, or custody of or access to a child if it is in the best interest of the child to do so. Courts acting under the *Divorce Act* have been guided by the same general principle, overriding provisions of a separation agreement that deal with custody, access or child support if this is perceived to be in the child's interest.

Recall that the parties may not deal with the custody of or access to their children in either marriage contracts or cohabitation agreements: s. 52(1)(c) and s. 53 (1)(c) of the *FLA*. What is the purpose of this limitation?

The custody and access provisions in a separation agreement may establish a *status quo* arrangement that the court will be reluctant to alter in the absence of clear evidence that it is not in the child's best interests. The fact that the parents agreed to a particular arrangement is also a factor to be considered, as it indicates their perceptions of the child's best interests at the time of the agreement: *Liang* v. *Liang* (1978), 5 R.F.L. (2d) 103 (Ont. H.C.) and *Sabbagh* v. *Sabbagh* (1994), 2 R.F.L. (4th) 44 (Man. C.A.). This point was made in relation to child support in *Willick* v. *Willick* (1994), 6 R.F.L. (4th) 161 (S.C.C.). Agreements are particularly important on interim custody applications. See *Colter* v. *Colter* (1982), 38 O.R. (2d) 221 (Master) and *Cabott* v. *Binns* (1987), 9 R.F.L. (3d) 296 (B.C. S.C.), affirmed (1987), 9 R.F.L. (3d) 390 (B.C. C.A.).

The effect of child support provisions in a separation agreement prior to the adoption of the child support guidelines was reviewed by the Supreme Court of Canada in *Willick* v. *Willick* (1994), 6 R.F.L. (4th) 161. For the majority, Sopinka J. stated (paras. 15 - 19):

... Clearly, the court is not bound by the terms of a separation agreement in exercising its jurisdiction to award support under the Act. See Wilson J. in *Pelech v. Pelech*, [1987] 1 S.C.R. 801, at p. 849. As stated by Professor McLeod in his annotation on *S. (A.J.) v. S. (G.F.)* (1987), 7 R.F.L. (3d) 292 (N.S. C.A.), at pp. 293-294, the true question is the effect of the agreement in restricting the court's discretionary jurisdiction.

The reasoning which supports the restrictions with respect to interspousal support does not apply to child support. In *Richardson v. Richardson*, [1987] 1 S.C.R. 857, at pp. 869-870, Wilson J. explained the different nature of the two rights:

> This inter-relationship [between spousal maintenance and child support] should not, how-ever, lead us to exaggerate its extent or forget the different legal bases of the support rights. The legal basis of child maintenance is the parents' mutual obligation to support their children according to their need. That obligation should be borne by the parents in propor-tion to their respective incomes and ability to pay: *Paras v. Paras, supra.* ... Child maintenance, like access, is the right of the child: *Re Cartlidge and Cartlidge*, [1973] 3 O.R. 801 (Fam. Ct.). For this reason, a spouse cannot barter away his or her child's right to support in a settlement agreement. The court is always free to intervene and determine the appropriate level of support for the child .... Further, because it is the child's right, the fact that child support will indirectly benefit the spouse cannot decrease the quantum awarded to the child.

As against the parties, the agreement operates as strong evidence that at the time each accepted its terms as adequately providing for the needs of the children. The correct approach was adopted by Anderson J.A. in *Dickson v. Dickson* (1987), 11 R.F.L. (3d) 337 (B.C. C.A.), at p. 358, who regarded the agreement as affording strong evidence "that the agreement made adequate provision for the needs of the children at the date the agreement was made."

Where, as here, the agreement is embodied in the judgment of the court, it is necessary to consider what additional effect is to be accorded to this fact. Section 11(1)(*b*) of the Act provides that "it is the duty of the court ... to satisfy itself that reasonable arrangements have been made for the support of any children of the marriage and, if such arrangements have not been made, to stay the granting of the divorce until such arrangements are made." It must be assumed that as long as the provisions of the judgment of the court stand unreversed, this duty was carried out and that at the date of the judgment it provided reasonable arrangements for the support of the children. ...

Therefore, in a variation proceeding, it must be assumed that, at the time it was made, the original child support order or the previous variation order accurately assessed the needs of the children having regard to the means of the parents. As such, the correctness of the previous order must not be reviewed during the variation proceeding. The previous order will not be departed from lightly and will only be varied if the requirements under s. 17(4) of the *Divorce Act* are properly satisfied. I now turn to this issue.

With the adoption of the *Child Support Guidelines*, the Parliament of Canada amended the *Divorce Act* in 1997 to include specific provisions dealing with consent orders and the effect of domestic contracts. See s. 15.1(5), (6), (7), and (8) and s. 17(6.2), (6.3), (6.4), and (6.5). Sections 15.1(7) and 17(6.4) allow a court to order support according to a settlement agreement that does not comply with the applicable guidelines if the court is satisfied that reasonable arrangements have been made for the support of the child. See also s. 33(14) of the *FLA*, which adds that "where support for the child is payable out of public money", consent orders deviating from the *Guidelines* must "not provide for an amount less than the amount that would be determined in accordance with the child support guidelines". Professor McLeod suggests in "Annotation" (1998), 33 R.F.L. (4th) 453, at 454:

> ...[I]n reviewing an agreement, a court should consider the extent of the deviation and why the parties have agreed not to comply with the Guidelines. Practically, unless the parties can show offsetting benefits, it is difficult to see how a court can approve any agreement that does not

comply with the Guidelines. After a brief period of adjustment, most judges will probably accept a consent with minimal explanation; otherwise, the system will slowly grind to a halt.

Of course, the parents can simply agree to informal arrangements or child support provisions in a domestic contract without securing a court order of any kind. As long as they are both content, the matter is unlikely to reach a court. Recall, however, that once one or both of them seek a divorce, s. 11(1)(b) of the *Divorce Act* directs the court "to satisfy itself that reasonable arrangements have been made for the support of any children of the marriage, having regard to the applicable guidelines, and, if such arrangements have not been made, to stay the granting of the divorce until such arrangements are made". See Chapter 3: **DIVORCE**.

Sections 15.1(5) and 17(6.2) of the *Divorce Act* permit a court to order child support that is different from the *Guidelines* amount if it would be inequitable to order the *Guidelines* amount in light of special provisions in a written agreement respecting the financial obligations of the spouses or the division or transfer of their property that directly or indirectly benefit the child. The following cases deal with the application of these provisions.

MARTIN v. MARTIN

(1999), 44 R.F.L. (4th) 125 (Ont. Gen. Div.)

MÉTIVIER J.: In this application, the husband sought sole custody of two children who are the subject of a current joint custody agreement. He also sought an order for the support of these children, pursuant to the Federal Child Support Guidelines.

The wife resisted both claims, and, at the outset of the hearing, the husband's counsel advised he would not be pursuing the custody claim.

The parties had settled all matters between them by way of an agreement dated December of 1995. At that time, the parties were living separate and apart, but under the same roof. Subsequently, pursuant to the agreement, the wife transferred her joint interest in the matrimonial home to the husband and assumed responsibility for the payment of certain family debts. This was expressly stated to be in consideration of the husband's covenant never to seek periodic child support from her. The parties agreed to share joint custody of their two children, who are now 6 and 8 years old.

They further agreed that the wife would move from the home, located in a small town outside of Ottawa, while the husband remained there with the children and retained their day to day care. This agreement was arrived at in consideration of, among other things, the fact that the matrimonial home was not selling despite having been offered for sale for a considerable time, and at a reduced price. The husband could more easily commute to work from that town than could the wife, and he was financially able to manage the expenses of the house and its upkeep on his own.

The husband's application for an order which will alter the separation agreement is based on the fact that the wife declared bankruptcy two years after the separation and is therefore able to maintain "a very good lifestyle because she has not paid any ongoing support for the children. As a result, the standard of living of the children has suffered."

There was no evidence as to the children's needs. The husband earns $44,500 per year. He resides in the home with a new partner who is also employed. The wife earns $39,300 per year.

The wife responded firstly as to custody by setting out in detail evidence as to her extensive and continuing involvement with the children. With respect to the issue seriously pursued, that of child support, the wife submits she should not have to pay because,

1)   the parties entered into a separation agreement;
2)   she shares various expenses including for extracurricular activities and clothes for the children and spends approximately $350 per month for them;
3)   her bankruptcy is not a material change which affects either the validity of the agreement or the children's standard of living; and
4)   she sees the children so frequently and the distance to be travelled is such that her access costs are significant.

Analysis

The only change alleged by the husband is that the bankruptcy of the wife has alleviated her debt position.

It is trite law to say that no agreement between the parties can bar the Court's jurisdiction to see that children are appropriately supported. I have therefore reviewed the agreement in detail.

The value of the property transferred to the father includes the mother's half share of the equity in the matrimonial home, which I find to be approximately $25,000 (I do not accept the father's bald assertion that the house was worth $140,000), together with the benefit of being freed of all responsibility for family debts which totalled $14,129. The father was also spared the expenses of a move.

It would be fair to assign some interest to the amount transferred. There is no evidence before me as to any such amount. It is clear that the debt load involved would have carried significant interest costs during the year and a half the mother carried it. Therefore, the transfer also bestowed a corresponding benefit for at least half that amount to the father.

All of these benefits were directly or indirectly passed on to the children. They were able to stay in their familiar home and schools; their residential parent was free of debts and able to devote more of his income to their support.

As well:

1)   The mother spends approximately $350 per month on expenses for the children.
2)   The mother maintains medical and dental insurance for the children.
3)   She sees the children alternate weekends, and two evenings per week, has them for holidays, attends their games, parent-teacher interviews, school activities, shares their care when they are ill and takes them to medical and dental appointments.

The real basis of the father's claim is that the mother has freed herself of the debts which she assumed, and she should now pay support since she has more disposable income.

The agreement in question did not provide for support in the event of a raise in the mother's income, an increase in the value of the former matrimonial home or any other aspect of this agreement where the terms were negotiated and settled as an interconnected whole.

The agreement did concede that the agreement as to child support could not be considered final as a court could determine that a variation would be in the best interests of the children.

Should the agreement be set aside as to the waiver of child support? If so, should the Guidelines then apply to fix the amount? The agreement in question appears to come within s.15.1(5) of the *Divorce Act* . . . .

Where any "specific provision" resides in the transfer of the matrimonial home or of other property, or, as in this case, in the assumption of debts, a most important factor to consider is the monetary value of the asset being transferred or of the debt being assumed. Where the amount in question is very large, then the benefit provided may be substantial enough to stand in place of child support for a lengthy period of time, all other things being equal; that is, in that the needs of the children continue to be comfortably met in the circumstances. In this case, the family debts totalled approximately $14,000, and the wife's equity in the home had a value of approximately $25,000, for a total benefit transferred of $39,000.

The parties freely entered into this agreement intending it to benefit both parties. The wife has met all her obligations. The husband wishes to take back his warranty to waive child support.

I am loathe to unravel only one term of a comprehensive separation agreement. There is no evidence of any material change not anticipated by the parties. In other circumstances, I believe a court would have been reluctant to set aside the child support provision as soon as the wife had paid the last dollar owing on the debts in question. Similarly the agreement would likely stand even if the value of the house had risen dramatically. The fact that the debts have now been erased by the bankruptcy should be irrelevant, because what has *not* changed is that the husband's responsibility for those debts was eliminated.

Over the four years from January 1, 1995 to January 1, 1999, the wife effectively "prepaid" child support. If one uses the total of $39,000 as the benefit transferred, then using the guideline amount of $561 per month, the respondent has "prepaid", between January 1, 1995 to January 1, 1999, an amount equal to ($39,000 divided by [5 years=60 months] = $650 per month. Manipulation of these numbers does not give a final answer since income tax deductions and inclusions would have changed the net amount for each party up to May 1, 1997.

As mentioned earlier, some interest factor should enter into the equation. But, since no evidence was adduced on the point, there will not be any "interest rate" factored into the total benefit. Whatever numbers are used, I find that the respondent has not yet used up the "credit" for child support which she obtained with the transfer of the property and the assumption of debts. That being the case, the application should be rejected on the basis that it is premature.

It is important to note that, while the benefit received by the father is significant, it is not of such a magnitude that it should for all time bar the contribution of the mother for direct child support. It may be that in the future, a court would find that the "credits" for the waiver of child support have been used up and the wife should begin to pay child support. I do not believe that that moment has yet arrived.

I come to this conclusion not solely as a result of the manipulation of theoretical "credits", but because of the particular facts of this case, including the extensive involvement of the mother in the children's lives, with those attendant costs resulting from her residence at a considerable distance, and the sharing of costs and all other responsibilities which the mother already assumes.

The husband's position is that the intervening bankruptcy of the mother leaves her with more disposable income. Without more, the husband submits, this means that she can contribute more to the children. This is true, but ignores the many other benefits bargained for and agreed upon. I do not see that the intervening bankruptcy and the release of the wife from onerous obligations should, in the absence of evidence that the children are not having all of their needs comfortably met, and where these are largely contributed to by their mother there is any reason to interfere with the agreement and to change one of the terms because one of the parties has bettered her position.

Another most important factor is the financial situation of the father and thus of the children. No evidence of any kind suggests that the children are not living as comfortably as ever with every one of their financial needs being met by the joint contributions of their parents. If this were not so, the result herein would be quite different.

For completeness of this analysis, if I were to exercise my discretion on these facts with the mother's income at $39,376, I would order that $200 per month be paid by the mother for the support of the children.

I order that the agreement continue in full force and effect. The provision for sharing of certain expenses as set out in paragraph 20 of the separation agreement, will be followed by the parties, except as varied below.

Since the mother already pays for part of the children's clothing, I am of the view this obligation should be made more formal. . . .

FUNG-SUNTER v. FABIAN

(1999), 48 R.F.L. (4th) 95 (B.C. C.A.)

HOLLINRAKE J.A. (for the court) : This is an appeal from an order which essentially dismissed an application for child support pursuant to the *Federal Child Support Guidelines.* . . .

The notice of motion filed by the appellant [the mother] sought an order that ''the existing written agreement between the parties be amended in accordance with the new Federal Child Support Guidelines noting special expenses to include special educational expenses or extraordinary expense for extra curricular activities; expenses for post-secondary education; health care needs - to be divided in proportion to income.''

The parties were married on June 28, 1975, separated on July 25, 1985, entered into a separation agreement on December 30, 1986 and were divorced on September 21, 1992. There are two children of the marriage: Kent, born May 23, 1982, and Pierce, born August 11, 1984. Both parties have since remarried.

On March 22, 1994 the parties agreed to an amended separation agreement (the ''Agreement''). By that agreement the parties share joint custody and guardianship of the two children. The agreement stated the income of the petitioner/appellant at $60,502, and $76,500 for the respondent/respondent. Child support payments were $600 for each child and the total of $1,200 was to be income in the hands of the appellant for taxation purposes. What were termed ''extraordinary'' expenses for health care, education or recreation were to be shared equally.

It is significant in this case that the support terms of the Agreement were not included in the divorce order nor was the amended agreement of 1994 reduced to an order of the court. Both parties were represented by solicitors throughout and it is obvious from reading the agreement that a good deal of time and thought went into it. The material before us asserts (by the respondent) that the appellant took ''a further two years of continuing negotiations before the [appellant] would sign the agreement.''

Before the judge below, as he saw it, ''the matter was . . . argued on the basis of an originating application for child support.'' . . .[In the court below, the judge concluded that the father's earnings for 1997 were $88,000 and $65,800 for the mother. He noted that the mother did not argue that the child support provided in the agreement was inadequate and that the ''sole basis for the petitioner's application is the introduction of the Federal Child Support Guidelines and the income tax implications that the Guidelines have created.'' He held that s. 14(c) of the *Guidelines* was not applicable because the application was for an original order under the *Divorce Act* and not a variation of an existing order. He concluded that there had been ''no material change in the circumstances of the parties . . .such that I should exercise my discretion to order child support beyond that which was set in the 1994 agreement.'']

What this Court must decide in this case is whether the judge below fell into error in exercising his discretion against making an order pursuant to s. 15.1(1) of the *Divorce Act*. The judge below did not enunciate the issue before him as being whether he should exercise his discretion in favour of an order under this section but as I read his reasons for judgment this was the approach he took. I reach this conclusion by reason of the judge saying in paragraph [32] of his reasons referred to above ''I first consider this question . . . whether, given the terms of the agreement, an order should even be made'' together with his statement at the outset of his reasons ''The matter was subsequently argued . . . on the basis of an originating application for child support.'' Such an application falls under s. 15.1 of the *Divorce Act*.

As can be seen from the above references to the reasons, the judge approached this question by initially concluding, correctly in my view, that s. 14(c) of the *Guidelines* does not assist the appellant and then asking himself ''can it still be said that there has been a sufficient change in circumstances such that the support agreed upon in 1994 should be varied. . . .''

The issue before the Court in this case, as I see it, is to what extent, if at all, does an existing separation agreement insofar as it relates to child support reflect on the discretion in s. 15.1(1) which says that ''a court . . . may . . . make an order requiring a spouse to pay for the support of any or all children of the marriage.''

I remind the reader that the judge below found the child support in the agreement was ''adequate'' and that there was no change in the children's needs and expenses aside from extraordinary ones from the date of the agreement to the application before him.

It is apparent from the above that the judge below was of the opinion that unless the applicant, here the appellant, could show a change of circumstances as is required for a variation order under s. 17, the court, as a matter of discretion, should decline to make the order requested under s. 15.1 as was done in this case.

With respect, I cannot agree with this approach of the judge or with his conclusion. I say this because in my opinion Parliament has considered and dealt with the issue of the significance of a written agreement on an application for child support under 15.1 of the *Divorce Act*. This is seen from s. 15.1(5) . . . . It is clear from s. 15.1(5) of the Act that a court may take a separation agreement into account on an application for child support. The extent to which such an agreement is material is to be found within s. 15.1(5).

I can see no reason in principle why a party cannot successfully apply for an original child support order simply because there is a written separation agreement in force. Such an agreement may lead to an order not strictly in accordance with the *Guidelines* if the payor in this case can bring himself within s. 15.1(5) of the Act but in my opinion it cannot in principle be used as a bar to a s. 15.1 *Divorce Act* order on the facts of the case before us.

I think the approach of Madam Justice Loo in the Supreme Court of British Columbia to this issue in *Duffield* v. *Duffield* (1998), 36 R.F.L. (4th) 374 (B.C. S.C. [In Chambers]) is the correct one. In that case there was a separation agreement which was not incorporated into the divorce order. What was sought was an order pursuant to s. 15.1 of the Act and the *Guidelines*. As in the case before us there was a release clause in the agreement which the respondent asserted was a bar to the application to impose the *Guidelines*. The respondent relied on the discretionary power in s. 15.1 of the Act and the agreement in submitting no order should be made. The petitioner succeeded and an order was made pursuant to s. 15.1 of the Act and the *Guidelines* were applied. In rejecting the respondent's argument the judge said this in part at p. 377:

> As the petitioner points out, her application is pursuant to s. 15.1 of the *Divorce Act*. No change in circumstance is required simply because there has never been an order for child support. Nonetheless, if a change in circumstance is required, there is one. The respondent's income has increased from $37,000 to $53,647 since the separation agreement. It is an increase of 31 percent, and the children have not benefited from the increase.

The judge then referred to s. 15.1(5) of the Act and said this at p. 378:

> The respondent does not indicate any "special provisions" in the separation agreement that directly or indirectly benefit the children or how a change in amount would be inequitable. The basis of his argument is simply that the parties entered into an agreement, that he has complied with the agreement, and that it would be unfair to change that agreement. That is not sufficient to justify overriding the application of the *Guidelines* in favour of a pre-existing agreement. Applying the *Guidelines* would require the respondent to pay more child support than initially agreed. That does not make it inequitable. In this case, there is nothing out of the ordinary that replaces the need for ongoing child support.

I share the views expressed by Madam Justice Loo in *Duffield* and I say this without any reference to her finding that there was a change in circumstances. In the court below in the case now before us, *Duffield* was distinguished by the judge on the ground of the finding of a change in circumstances. While that is a distinguishing fact in the *Duffield* case from the case before us, I repeat that in my opinion without that distinguishing fact, I think the principle enunciated by Madam Justice Loo is the correct one as to the significance in this case of a separation agreement to an application for an originating order for child support under s. 15.1 of the Act.

One further comment. On the exercise of the discretion in s. 15.1 in this case I think a comparison must be made between the provisions of the agreement to what the case would be should the order be made and the *Guidelines* applied. Here, with the impact of the income tax amendments in 1997 the difference between the net proceeds of child support under the agreement and under a s. 15.1 order of the court are significant in terms of the best interests of the children. This comparison is a factor supporting the discretion being exercised in favour of granting the order.

That being so, in my opinion, the judge's approach to the agreement here and its significance to the outcome of what must be seen as an originating application for child support amounts to an error in principle.

In my opinion, the entire order must be set aside and the matter remitted to the Supreme Court to determine child support in accordance with the Act and the *Guidelines*. On this referral it will be open to the parties to raise any issue relating to child support available to them under the Act and the *Guidelines*, including special or extraordinary expenses.

NOTES AND QUESTIONS

1. As explained in the previous chapter, **CHILD SUPPORT**, there is authority for the view that, even after the adoption of the *Guidelines* and the resultant legislative changes, a court still has discretion to determine whether to make a child support order at all. On this view, the *Guidelines* only come into play once the court has answered that threshold question in the affirmative and is determining quantum. This controversial reasoning is significant in the context of domestic contracts, because it suggests that a court can refuse to make an order in the face of a contract even if the conditions of s. 15.1(5) are not met. Indeed, in *Fullerton* v. *Fullerton* (1999), 49 R.F.L. (4th) 255, the B.C. C.A. refused to make a child support order, apparently an original order, under the *Divorce Act* in the face of a "sensible and intelligent bargain" in a separation agreement. The court made no reference to s. 15.1(5). Does *Fung-Sunter* also adopt this position?

2. Where a domestic contract or prior court order provides for an amount of child support that is higher than the amount payable under the *Guidelines*, the courts readily conclude that there are special provisions making an order for the *Guidelines* amount inequitable. See *Blackburn* v. *Elmitt* (1997), 34 R.F.L. (4th) 183 (B.C. S.C.); *Finney* v. *Finney* (1998), 40 R.FL. (4th) 249 (B.C. S.C.); *Rollman* v. *Rollman* (1998), 41 R.F.L. (4th) 146 (Sask. Q.B.); and *Vaillancourt* v. *Vaillancourt* (1998), 43 R.F.L. (4th) 135 (P.E.I. T.D.) (dealing with the comparable provincial legislation). In *Finney*, Sigurdson J. speculated (at 257) that "an agreement made with the knowledge of the *Guidelines* to pay an amount of child support greater than called for in the *Guidelines* may well, in itself, be a 'special provision'".

3. For other cases dealing with the interpretation and application of ss. 15.1(5) and 17(6.2) of the *Divorce Act* where the custodial parent seeks an order for an amount of child support in excess of that originally agreed to, see *Duffield* v. *Duffield* (1998), 36 R.F.L. (4th) 374 (B.C. S.C.) (application granted); *Wallace* v. *Wallace* (1998), 36 R.F.L. (4th) 428 (B.C. S.C.) (application granted); *Young* v. *Young* (1998), 39 R.F.L. (4th) 110 (B.C. S.C.) (application granted); *Aker* v. *Howard* (1998), 43 R.F.L. (4th) 159 (Ont. Gen. Div.) (application granted); *Monney* v. *Monney* (1999), 44 R.F.L. (4th) 264 (Man. Q.B.) (application granted); *Duncan* v. *Duncan* (1999), 1 R.F.L. (5th) 46 (B.C. C.A.) (application denied); and *Gore-Hickman* v. *Gore-Hickman* (1999), 177 D.L.R. (4th) 222 (Sask. Q.B.) (application denied).

4. Section 56(1.1) of the *FLA* stipulates that a court may, in determining child support, disregard any child support provision of a domestic contract "where the provision is unreasonable having regard to the child support guidelines, as well as any other provision relating to the support of the child in the contract". Section 33(12) of the Act states that a court may award an amount different from that set out in the *Guidelines* if it would be inequitable to order the *Guidelines* amount in light of special provisions in a written agreement respecting the financial obligations of the spouses or the division or transfer of their property that directly or indirectly benefit the child. In *Spencer* v. *Irvine* (1999), 45 R.F.L. (4th) 434 (Ont. S.C.J.), Lack J. stated (at 436):

> The separation agreement purports to make financial provision in consideration of forfeiture of child support rights. The agreement is not in default. Ms. Spencer did not file the agreement under section 37. She brings her claim for child support as an original application under section 33 of the *Family Law Act*, in spite of the agreement. Yet the agreement exists. Section 2(10) of the *Family Law Act* provides that a domestic contract that deals with any matter that is also dealt with in the Act prevails.

> Section 56(1.1) of the *Family Law Act* provides that in determining child support the court may disregard any pertinent provision of a domestic contract where the court considers the provision unreasonable having regard to the child support guidelines as well as to any other provision in the agreement relating to the support of the child. This section makes a provision for child support in a domestic contract reviewable by the court. The review will entail a comparison of the provision in the agreement with both the child support guidelines and any other provision in the agreement relating to support of the child.

The applicant, rather than the respondent, bears the onus of proving that the provision in the domestic contract should be disregarded in the light of the child support guidelines, and notwithstanding any other provision in the agreement for the support of the child.

In my view it is not sufficient for the court to conclude that a provision is inadequate "on the face" on no other basis than the existence of the child support guidelines. There must be a consideration by the court of whether the support provision meets or fails to meet the needs of the child having regard to any other relevant provisions in the agreement. Where, as in this case, the agreement makes provision for a transfer of property or other financial benefit which purports to meet the needs of the child, in whole or in part, that provision must be considered and assessed before a determination to disregard should be made. It is only after a determination is made under section 56(1.1) that the provision falls short of meeting the needs of the child that section 33(11) and 33(12) come into play. Then the onus shifts to the respondent.

I am of the view that the learned judge erred in failing to adequately consider the support provision, or lack of one, in light of the other provision of the agreement for the transfer of property before he exercised his discretion to disregard it. For this reason I am compelled to set aside the order [for interim support] of August 28, 1998.

See also *Babcock* v. *Babcock* (1999), 45 R.F.L. (4th) 14 (Ont. Prov. Ct.) dealing with s. 37(3.2) of the *FLA*.

---

5. Setting Aside a Domestic Contract

Section 56(4) of the *FLA* creates a statutory power to set aside a domestic contract or a provision in it. Under paragraph (c), this may be done "in accordance with the law of contract". A domestic contract is, therefore, liable to be set aside on an application under s. 56(4) wherever it is void or voidable pursuant to the general law applicable to all contracts. Paragraph (c) does not, however, alter the substantive law. Cases decided under the *Family Law Reform Act* that did not contain a similar provision consistently held that a domestic contract that was invalid according to the ordinary principles of contract law could not prevail over the provisions of that Act. Similarly, such contracts were given little or no weight in corollary relief proceedings under the federal divorce legislation.

The general law of contract indicates that a contract may be, or may become, invalid for various reasons related to its formation. Sometimes the parties' attempt to enter into a valid, operative contract is unsuccessful because the agreed terms are uncertain. The contract may also be rendered a nullity by the presence of certain kinds of mistakes. In these situations the contract is void *ab initio* and of no legal effect according to the law of contract. Void domestic contracts cannot prevail over legislation relating to the rights of the parties even if they are never set aside. They should readily be set aside if an application is made under s. 56(4). On other occasions the contract may be voidable rather than void. Where one party has been guilty of fraud, material misrepresentation, duress, undue influence or some other form of unconscionable conduct, the other is given the privilege of avoiding the contract. If the party permitted to avoid the contract does not do so, the contract remains valid and fully effective. According to contract law, such a contract also continues to be effective where a court refuses to set it aside because a bar to rescission exists. A bar may arise by virtue of undue delay or other conduct on the part of the party seeking rescission or because full restitution is impossible. Because s. 56(4)(c) only authorizes the court to set aside a domestic contract in accordance with the law of contract, the established bars to rescission should apply when the court is asked to set aside a voidable contract under that paragraph. See, however, *B. (J.F.)* v. *B.*

(M.A.) (1999), 1 R.F.L. (5th) 339 (Ont. S.C.J.), where the court set aside a separation agreement even though restoration of the status quo was impossible. The court concluded that "practical justice" could still be done through a monetary adjustment. As Professor McLeod asserts in his annotation to the case, it is unclear from the reasons whether the court is suggesting that the usual bars to rescission do not apply to applications under s. 56(4) or that no bar to rescission arose on the facts.

Although basic principles of contract law apply when a court is asked to set aside a contract under s. 56(4)(c), these principles allow the courts to focus on the particular circumstances of each case. The courts, therefore, can and should take into account the special nature of the spousal relationship and the unique circumstances in which domestic contracts are made.

Because s. 56(4)(c) already permits a court to set aside a contract "in accordance with the law of contract", paragraphs (a) and (b) are intended to grant the court the power to act in some circumstances even if the contract is valid according to the general principles of the law of contract. If the contract is to be disregarded in those circumstances, an application should be made under s. 56.

TROTTIER v. ALTOBELLI

(1983), 36 R.F.L. (2d) 199 (Ont. C.A.)

BROOKE J.A. (orally): — The court is unanimously of the opinion that this appeal must succeed. The plaintiff's claim was to set aside a separation agreement and for an order of the sale and equal division of the net proceeds of the former family assets, in particular, the matrimonial home. In the alternative she claimed for $10,000 for breach of a contract. By the separation agreement the plaintiff had renounced any right that she had to alimony or maintenance and to any claim against any assets whatsoever. The agreement was executed in the presence of her husband's lawyer, but without any independent legal advice.

The parties had married in 1971 and separated in 1976, some five years later. They were divorced in 1979 and she now lives with her second husband.

The agreement in question was entered into in March 1978, a few days after their separation and while she was living with her sister. This was not the first separation. They had first separated in 1976 when she walked out of the marriage, saying that they were too incompatible to live together. She returned three months later and after two years of attempted reconciliation had failed, she left again and went to live with her sister. It was then that the agreement was entered into.

The plaintiff gave evidence that after their separation and while she was with her sister, her husband had abused her in the sense that he had threatened her and that he had promised her orally that he would pay her $10,000 if she entered into the separation agreement. The trial judge disbelieved her evidence and believed her husband's evidence on this issue. There is no reason to doubt that finding. There was, however, evidence that at this time she was depressed. Her sister said so in her evidence and she described in some detail the plaintiff's state. The trial judge, in dealing with this evidence, while not doubting it, seems to have found that it was not conclusive in the absence of some, perhaps, medical testimony. In this setting, then, her claim was dismissed.

The case has been very well and very carefully argued in this court by counsel for both the appellant and the respondent. In our view, this agreement on its face was clearly unconscionable. This woman had contributed to the acquisition of the property, to the maintenance of the property, to the payment of the mortgage, and it was admitted by her husband in evidence that when the property was acquired it was their intention that she should have a one-half interest in it. In our view, these facts, together with the evidence of her sister as to this woman's state at the time the agreement was entered into and the absence of any independent legal advice in making this agreement within two weeks of their separation, establishes to the degree required that this agreement was unconscionable and cannot stand. This is so even if her husband's evidence is accepted.

The appeal therefore succeeds, the agreement is set aside and her interest in the properties is unaffected by it. There will be a direction for the sale of the real property in question and the division of the net proceeds after the cost of the sale.

CROUSE v. CROUSE

(1988), 88 N.S.R. (2d) 199 (T.D.)

[The parties married in 1975. They separated for about two months in 1984 as the petitioner wife felt that the husband generally dominated her and refused to involve her in any of the financial affairs of the family. In February, 1986 the petitioner began an intimate relationship with another man and she left the matrimonial home in May. In August, the husband found out about the wife's affair and problems then developed regarding the wife's access to the parties' son, Ryan, who continued to live with the husband in the matrimonial home.

Following negotiations through their solicitors, and after several draft agreements had been considered, the parties signed a separation agreement on December 2, 1986. This agreement, referred to as the minutes of settlement in the reasons, was made one day before a scheduled interim custody hearing. Under the agreement, the husband would have sole custody but the wife obtained very liberal and specific access. The wife gave up any claim in the equity of the home, the only significant asset of both parties. The agreement provided for no spousal support or child support, although the wife was required to contribute to Ryan's sports activities, etc. Early in January 1987, the petitioner advised her solicitor that she wanted to contest the validity of the agreement. Hallett J. dealt with this issue as follows.]

THE LAW

Dominant to a consideration of the issue of whether or not minutes of settlement should be varied is the fundamental principle that parties should be bound by their agreements. This obvious principle was recognized by the Supreme Court of Canada in the oft-cited case of *Pelech* v. *Pelech*. . . . However, that principle assumes that the agreement was not made while one of the parties was acting under duress or undue influence or was induced by a fraudulent misrepresentation to sign the agreement or that a plea of non est factum could be raised or that the agreement was unconscionable. If both parties were represented by counsel, the burden on the party who seeks to have the agreement declared invalid or varied is very great.

The petitioner alleges that her concern to be assured that she would have access to her child so dominated her thinking, induced, in her mind at least, by the respondent's insistence to her that she would not likely succeed in seeing her child to the extent provided in the November 27 and December 2 agreements if the case went to court, that she signed the minutes of settlement. . . .

The first issue is whether or not the minutes of settlement should be set aside or varied. I will first deal with the issue of "unconscionability". The law with respect to this issue is both statutory and judge made. Pursuant to s. 29 of the *Matrimonial Property Act*, S.N.S. 1980, c. 9, the court has power to vary an agreement that is unconscionable. . . .

To succeed on the ground that the bargain was unconscionable, the petitioner must show that there was inequality in the position of the parties arising out of ignorance, need or distress which left her in the power of her husband and, secondly, that the bargain she reached was substantially unfair to her. I shall first direct my attention to whether or not she was in a weaker position than the respondent at the time the agreement was made because of her distress and whether the respondent took advantage of her to pry from her an agreement which resulted in a division of assets which, by my calculations, resulted in his obtaining assets (less liabilities) worth approximately $20,000.00 while she ended up in a negative (minus $3,300.00) position.

The petitioner testified that the respondent convinced her that because she had left the home and child, a court would be unsympathetic to her pleas for liberal access. Because of her guilt feelings, the respondent was able to persuade her that this would happen if the custody hearing went ahead on December 3, 1986. The petitioner also testified that he convinced her he would be the more impressive witness before the court. She believed him because of the experience he had had in the courts. I accept her evidence that she was distraught over the likelihood as she perceived it of not obtaining liberal access if the court hearing proceeded. I accept her evidence that the respondent was pressuring her to sign the agreement or face the court proceedings on December 3, 1986. A look at the November 27, 1986, agreement as compared to the August draft shows that specific access was now included as a term in the November 27 agreement but that the proposal that the equity in the house be divided equally had disappeared to be replaced by a term that required the petitioner to convey her interest in the home to the respondent.

She states in her evidence that she was in effect a "basket case" during the fall of 1986 when the agreement was negotiated. On the other hand, the respondent testified that when he spoke to her on several occasions on the telephone he did not observe such a condition and that they had had several calm meetings over the subject of custody and division of assets. Counsel for the respondent argued that this case is just an example of the normal emotional warfare that goes on between parties who are in the process of being divorced. I have concluded that the petitioner was in a weakened position and that the respondent did take advantage of her. She is normally an intelligent and I would say fairly aggressive person; this showed from time to time while she was on the witness stand. There is no question that the respondent, a former R.C.M.P. officer, is [a] very self-centered man who would be quite willing to dominate the petitioner for his own ends. This was exemplified by his calm and rational demeanour on the witness stand; he is a good performer but just that, a performer. As to the condition of the petitioner at the time the agreement was negotiated, the evidence of her solicitor at that time, Mr. Mark Knox, was persuasive. He had just been admitted to the Bar in August of 1986 and had taken over the file from the senior partner in the law firm where he was employed. He testified that the petitioner seemed quite confused most of the time and she could get hostile at times. He testified to her calling him at home in the evenings in tears and that he found it difficult to get instructions as she seemed unable to focus on an issue. He testified she came to his office in tears and that she was in tears in his office during the period while they were negotiating the agreement. He testified that she had signed the November 27, 1986, agreement on a Thursday in his presence and that her emotional state at that time seemed to be dominated by the fact that the interim custody hearing was coming on December 3rd and that the agreement had to be resolved before that date. He testified that she was in a tumultuous state of mind and her primary concern was to have as much contact as possible with her son. He testified that the petitioner told him that her husband had told her that she might not have any contact with her son if the matter went to court. Mr. Knox testified that the petitioner was not concerned about property or maintenance; she was concerned about seeing her son and also concerned that the respondent might leave the jurisdiction and that she wanted a clause that custody would revert to her if he left the area; she was worried that she could not get these assurances if the matter went to court. . . .

I found Mr. Knox's evidence credible and confirmed the evidence of the petitioner as to her state of mind at the time. I accept the petitioner's evidence of the influence her husband's actions had on her. I find she was concerned about her access to her son to the point that she did not deal rationally with the other issues such as division of property. I find that this state was induced by the respondent's insistence and persuasive dominance that he would succeed in court against her on the custody issue because she had left the home. The respondent had weakened her to the point where he was able to dictate the terms of the separation and he did. In summary, I am satisfied on the evidence that at the time the agreement was negotiated, the petitioner was much the weaker of the two parties and the respondent took advantage of this fact to negotiate the property settlement. . . .

Having concluded that the respondent was exerting power over the petitioner in an unconscionable way in that he obtained a favourable bargain respecting the division of property by preying on the petitioner's insecurity on the issue of access, it is necessary to determine if the minutes of settlement were substantially unfair.

As stated, the division of assets in accordance with the terms of the minutes of settlement of December 2, 1986, is unconscionable. However, it is not simply a matter of determining if the asset division was unconscionable. Agreements made by separating spouses must be looked at as a package. One cannot simply decide an agreement is unconscionable if the division of assets is substantially unfair; it may be that viewed in the light of the custodial parent giving up any claim for child support, the overall agreement is fair and reasonable. In this case, the respondent gave up a claim for support for Ryan. However, this fact is not in this case strong enough to offset the very inequitable bargain made. It is important to consider the fact that the petitioner had legal advice. However, it is obvious that the emotional condition of the petitioner was such that she did not have any concern for the financial arrangements and she might just as well not have had legal advice. This state of mind was induced by the respondent by exercising the power he knew he possessed to scare her into an improvident agreement out of fear of losing liberal access to her child. Her solicitor, who was inexperienced, either did not or could not persuade her that such would not likely happen if the case went to court. Ryan was her only child and she is not capable of having another. Corroboration of the weak emotional state she was in is evident by the very substantial unfairness of the division of the assets apart altogether from the evidence of Mr. Knox. The petitioner is apparently intelligent, fairly tough-minded and anything but naive. She would never have agreed to the property division made in the minutes of settlement if she were not distressed and in a weakened state because of concern that she would not have liberal access to her child if the matter went to court. The respondent was able to convince her he would win in court and that she had better sign or lose liberal access. It is unconscionable for a parent to use threats that access will be limited as a bargaining chip in negotiations relating to the division of property. Had the petitioner directed her mind to the bargain she was making with respect to the division of assets, she surely would not have signed if it were not for her concern over access to her child. . . .

I am satisfied that the petitioner has proven that the respondent was in a stronger bargaining position than herself by exploiting her concern to see her child; this was an unconscientious use of power. As a result, he obtained a bargain that was substantially unfair looked at in its entirety. The agreement is therefore unconscionable and should be varied notwithstanding that it is with reluctance that I find myself varying an agreement negotiated by the parties with the assistance of counsel.

[Hallett J. varied the agreement by ordering that the husband pay $7,000 to the wife. An equal division of assets was considered inappropriate because the husband had primary responsibility for the son's support and care.]

BEST v. BEST

(1990), 30 R.F.L. (3d) 279 (Ont. Gen. Div.)

[In 1979 the parties entered into a pre-nuptial agreement. Each wanted to preserve certain assets for the benefit of children from previous marriages. The parties jointly consulted a lawyer who was a friend of the husband. The lawyer drafted the contract as instructed by the parties, advised them of their entitlement to independent legal advice and supervised the execution of the agreement. The agreement created a scheme whereby all of the wife's assets were to remain her separate property and the husband was not entitled to share in the growth of these assets. The husband's pre-marital assets were also to continue to be owned by him, but the contract provided that the wife would share in the growth or income of some of them.

The parties separated in 1988 and each sought a preliminary determination of the validity of the agreement in property proceedings under the *FLA*. Zelinski J. concluded that the agreement was valid and effectively excluded claims under s. 5. However, he indicated that either party was entitled to apply under s. 56(4)(b) of the *FLA* to set aside the agreement.]

ZELINKSI J.: — . . . On behalf of Mrs. Best, it is argued that she went to Mr. Dunlop, who was previously the solicitor of Mr. Best. She did not obtain independent legal advice. Time was short. Except in relation to the matrimonial home, the rights to which she was entitled to rely upon under the *Family Law Reform Act* were not explained to her, hence, she was unable to understand consequences of the contract. She did not intend that one of the consequences of the contract would be that, in her perception, she would only have the rights of a housekeeper.

Conversely, Mr. Loucks [acting for Mr. Best] argues that it is clear that there is an overwhelming body of opinion that the courts should not lightly interfere with contractual rights created by the parties, even in domestic situations.

I am satisfied that Mrs. Best was aware of the "nature" of the contract in the sense that she fully understood she was entering into an agreement intended to be binding upon the parties to it, including herself. The "consequences" of the contract were also understood by her in this sense of what it was that the contract was intended to do, namely, to preserve the rights each of the intended spouses had to the property that they then owned. However, she did not understand the "consequences" in the sense that she was setting up a regime for distribution of property which differed from the provisions of the *Family Law Reform Act* (and now of the *Family Law Act, 1986*). To have understood those consequences, she would have to have had her rights under the *Family Law Reform Act* explained to her. I am of the view that this is sufficient to enable Mrs. Best to seek relief under the statute. A generous and broad interpretation of s. 56(4) is not inconsistent with its language. . . .

. . . I hasten to add that the reasons I have adopted for the application of s. 56(4) to Mrs. Best's situation seemingly also apply to Mr. Best. He, too, can justify an argument that he did not understand the consequences of the contract because the provisions of the *Family Law Reform Act* were not explained to him, in order to advance a claim against the assets of Mrs. Best.

In the result, either party may make an application under s. 56(4) of the *Family Law Act, 1986* to set aside the contract or a provision in it. I do not believe that it is appropriate for me to go further at this time or to determine whether I would exercise my discretion to grant the relief contemplated by that section as this, in my view, is a determination that can only be made by the trial Judge who will have all of the information, including particulars of the assets of the parties and their values, available to him.

GRANT-HOSE v. GRANT-HOSE

(1991), 32 R.F.L. (3d) 26 (Ont. U.F.C.)

[The parties were married in 1977 and separated in 1987. In 1988 they signed a separation agreement which provided, *inter alia*, that the husband would pay $1,200 child support per month for the two children in the wife's custody; that he would pay her $200 a month spousal support for 12 months; and that the wife would have exclusive possession of the matrimonial home until the earliest of certain specified events, at which time it would be sold and the proceeds divided equally. When the agreement was negotiated, the husband believed that he was seeing a lawyer, but, in reality, he was being advised by a law clerk. She advised him that the court would not order partition and sale of the matrimonial home in any event and that $600 per month was the "going rate" for child support. The divorce judgment in 1989 contained no corollary relief. In 1990 the husband applied to set aside the separation agreement and to reduce child support. He alleged that he had not read or understood the agreement.]

MENDES DA COSTA U.F.C.J.: — . . . Section 56(4) is designed to provide a check to the overriding effect afforded a domestic contract by s. 2(10) and embodies the curative philosophy of the Act. The balance between these two provisions seems discernible in the Preamble of the Act, which propounds the necessity of providing in law for the "orderly and equitable settlement of the affairs of the spouses upon the breakdown of the partnership." In proceedings to impugn a domestic contract, the burden of proof lies upon the applicant.

(i) Nature or Consequences

Section 56(4)(*b*) speaks in language reminiscent of the common law doctrine of non est factum. However, the subsection enables a court to grant relief where a party did not understand the nature "or" consequences of a domestic contract, that is, relief would appear to be available where a party understood the nature of the document but did not understand its consequences. Moreover, by empowering the court to set aside a "domestic contract" or "a provision in it", the legislation seems to draw no distinction between a lack of understanding as to the very nature or character of the document as a whole and a lack of understanding of its individual contents: compare *Marvco Color Research Ltd.* v. *Harris*, [1982] 2 S.C.R. 774, 26 R.P.R. 48, 20 B.L.R. 143, 141 D.L.R. (3d) 577, 45 N.R. 302. The word "nature" relates to the fundamental character of the document, its class or type. The word "consequences" would seem to reach the effect or impact of the document upon the spouses' affairs. The words "a provision" would seem broad enough to cover any such provision, whether it be one relating to support or property.

Did the applicant understand the "nature" or "consequences" of the agreement? The position of the applicant is that he thought he was dealing with Linda Carey, a lawyer, whereas, as he later discovered, the lady he saw was Elaine Smith, a law clerk. The applicant asserted that he did not receive proper legal advice as to the substantive law relating to the equalization of the spouses' net family properties and to the matrimonial home. The applicant took the position, also, that when he attended at the Hughson Law Centre to sign the separation agreement, he did not read the document, and that, in relation to the matrimonial home, the document did not correspond to his instructions.

The applicant knew that the document he signed was a separation agreement. He had been given an early draft by Mr. Williams, the respondent's counsel, during the second meeting after matters relating to the spouses' separation, exclusive possession of the matrimonial home, and support had been discussed. He was then advised to obtain independent legal advice. The applicant contacted the Hughson Law Centre. He was introduced to Elaine Smith and saw her on three or four occasions, the first meeting lasting about 1 hour. He telephoned the Hughson Law Centre and spoke to Elaine Smith several times. The separation agreement contains 20 amendments, each initialled by the applicant. He signed the document, and his signature was witnessed by "Elaine F. Smith". She, likewise, witnessed his signature to schedule "B" of the agreement. The account of the Hughson Law Centre, Exhibit 3, was signed by Elaine F. Smith, as I have reviewed earlier in these reasons. From this account, it appears that the applicant's contact with the Hughson Law Centre commenced on February 11, 1988, and continued until the separation agreement was signed on May 20, 1988. During his cross-examination by Mr. Greenhow, the applicant stated that he did not sign cheques, letters, house leases, or mortgages without reading them. He acknowledged that he knew that the separation agreement governed his obligation to provide support for the respondent and the children. When asked whether he knew that it governed his rights to the matrimonial home, the applicant replied that his lawyer told him that everything was okay. . . . [T]he applicant was not a credible witness, and I do not believe that I can rely upon his evidence as to the separation agreement. In my opinion, the applicant knew what he was doing when he signed the document, and I find, as stated in para 22(1)(c), that the applicant understood the nature and consequences of the agreement. He has not persuaded me that the separation agreement should be set aside under s. 56(4)(*b*) of the Act.

Even, however, had I accepted the applicant's testimony, my conclusion would have been no different. In *Marvco Color Research Ltd* v. *Harris*, the Supreme Court of Canada considered, anew, the issue whether a party who has signed a document might be precluded by carelessness from raising the defence of non est factum. The judgment of the Court was delivered by Estey J. Referring to the Court's prior decision of *Prudential Trust Co.* v. *Cugnet*, [1956] S.C.R. 915, 5 D.L.R. (2d) 1, Estey J., at [pp. 585-586, 141 D.L.R.; pp. 785-786, [1982] 2 S.C.R.; pp. 59-60, 26 R.P.R.; pp. 155-156, 20 B.L.R.], stated;

In my view, with all due respect to those who have expressed views to the contrary, the dissenting view of Cartwright J. (as he then was) in *Prudential*, supra, correctly enunciated the principles of the law of non est factum. In the result the defendants-respondents are barred by reason of their carelessness from pleading that their minds did not follow their hands when executing the mortgage so as to be able to plead that the mortgage is not binding upon them. . . .

The defendants, in executing the security without the simple precaution of ascertaining its nature in fact and in law, have nonetheless taken an intended and deliberate step in signing the document and have caused it to be legally binding upon themselves. In the words of *Foster* v. *Mackinnon* this negligence, even though it may have sprung from good intentions, precludes the defendants in this circumstance from disowning the document, that is to say, from pleading that their minds did not follow their respective hands when signing the document and hence that no document in law was executed by them.

. . . In my opinion, the Legislature did not contemplate or intend that s. 56(4)(*b*) should be interpreted in a manner inconsistent with the principle enunciated by the Supreme Court of Canada. I know of no reason why a domestic contract should be set aside, on this ground alone, in circumstances where an agreement of another kind would be upheld.

Each case must, of course, depend upon its own circumstances. The court should consider all relevant facts, including the magnitude and extent of the carelessness alleged, and the context in which the carelessness occurred. In the case before me, the applicant, in executing the separation agreement, took an intended and deliberate step. The separation agreement complied with the formalities required by the Act. In this way, the applicant was exposed to the "warning" function of s. 55(1). The respondent negotiated the separation agreement through the office of Mr. Williams, her solicitor. From her evidence, which I accept, it appears that the first time she heard that the applicant felt that the agreement should be set aside was in July 1989. Her evidence was that, up until that time, as far as she could tell, the applicant abided by the terms of the agreement and made no objection to any of its terms. In my opinion, even had I accepted the applicant's testimony, I would have found that the separation agreement was legally binding upon him, and that he would have been unable to assert that, in signing the document, his mind did not follow his hand. To hold otherwise, I believe, would be wholly inconsonant with the necessity, expressed in the Preamble, of providing in law for the "orderly and equitable settlement of the affairs" of the parties.

Nor do I believe that the applicant could have disowned the separation agreement on the basis that he did not receive proper legal advice. The respondent's solicitor, Mr. Williams, suggested to the applicant that he obtain independent legal advice, and the applicant attended at the Hughson Law Centre. It is clear that the applicant retained the Hughson Law Centre and that the separation agreement emerged as a result of negotiations between the Hughson Law Centre and Mr. Williams's office. The authority of a solicitor arises from his retainer. In *Scherer* v. *Paletta*, [1966] 2 O.R. 524, 57 D.L.R. (2d) 532, the Ontario Court of Appeal considered the law generally applicable to the settlement of litigation by counsel. The judgment of the Court was delivered by Evans J.A. In the course of his judgment, at [pp. 534-535 D.L.R., pp. 526-527 O.R.], Evans J.A. enunciated this principle:

A client, having retained a solicitor in a particular matter, holds that solicitor out as his agent to conduct the matter in which the solicitor is retained. In general, the solicitor is the client's authorized agent in all matters that may reasonably be expected to arise for decision in the particular proceedings for which he has been retained. Where a principal gives an agent general authority to conduct any business on his behalf, he is bound as regards third persons by every act done by the agent which is incidental to the ordinary course of such business or which falls within the apparent scope of the agent's authority. As between principal and agent, the authority may be limited by agreement or special instructions but as regards third parties the authority which the agent has is that which he is reasonably believed to have, having regard to all the circumstances, and which is reasonably to be gathered from the nature of his employment and duties.

In my opinion, this principle applies to the situation before me. The applicant held out the Hughson Law Centre as his agent to negotiate the separation agreement. The respondent, it seems to me, was entitled to rely upon the fact that the Hughson Law Centre was the applicant's authorized agent "in all matters that may reasonably be expected to arise for decision" in the negotiation process. It was not the responsibility of the respondent to inquire into the knowledge or qualifications of the individual who advised the applicant, or to probe the quality of advice given. To interpret s. 56(4)(b) in this fashion would have far-reaching and, I believe, destructive effects on the relationship of solicitor and client, and on the negotiation, between solicitors, of domestic contracts. Such a construction would attribute to the statutory words a meaning that they do not reasonably embrace.

[Although Mendes da Costa U.F.C.J. concluded that there was no basis to set aside or override the agreement, child support was significantly reduced. Pursuant to the agreement, the provisions for child support could be varied if there was a "material change in circumstances." This test was met because of a considerable drop in the husband's income.]

DOCHUK v. DOCHUK

(1999), 44 R.F.L. (4th) 97 (Ont. Gen. Div.)

LACK J.: The wife claims equalization of net family property under the *Family Law Act*, R.S.O. 1990, c. F.3, as amended. The issue to be determined is whether a separation agreement should be set aside either on the grounds of duress, or lack of financial disclosure.

Kathleen Dochuk and Robert Dochuk married on December 28, 1982 after cohabiting since June 1980. They have two children. On January 21, 1996 they signed a "homemade" separation agreement which divided their assets and debts. The husband retained the matrimonial home and assumed the mortgage and a loan. He kept a mortgage receivable and some company shares as his assets and the wife kept her registered retirement savings plans and a time-share interest. The husband was required to pay the wife $108,000.00. On February 15, 1996, the wife moved out of the home and the next day the husband made the payment to her. In March 1997, the wife started this divorce action. She sought to vary the child custody and child support arrangements in the agreement. These issues were resolved before trial. She also asked that the separation agreement be set aside. In her petition she pleaded that she had not had independent legal advice when she signed the agreement. She also pleaded that the husband had failed to disclose the nature of his pension plan and any shares he held in the company employing him.

. . . Section 56(7) [of the *FLA*] provides that section 56(4) applies despite any agreement to the contrary. Accordingly the parties cannot oust the Court's jurisdiction to set aside a separation agreement, in appropriate circumstances.

In *Rosen* v. *Rosen* (1994), 3 R.F.L. (4th) 267 the Ontario Court of Appeal considered an appeal from a judgment setting aside a separation agreement under

section 56(4)(c) on the grounds of unconscionability. The wife had not had independent legal advice before entering into the agreement. The Court confirmed that
all of the common law rules that govern the validity of contracts in general continue
to apply to domestic contracts. The Court wrote that to establish unconscionability
a person must prove that the parties to the agreement were in unequal bargaining
positions and that one preyed upon the other's weakness to extract an agreement that
was improvident on its face. Taking advantage of the ability to prey upon the other
party is what produces the unconscionability. In assessing the wife's allegation, the
Court looked for evidence of vulnerability as demonstrated by abuse, intimidation,
learning disability, anxiety, stress, nervous breakdown, drugs or alcohol indulgence.
The Court found no such evidence. It allowed the appeal and set aside the judgment.

In the present case, the wife testified that she signed the separation agreement
because she feared the husband's reaction if she did not accept what he offered. She
stated that the husband was controlling and bad tempered. She gave evidence of
occasional violence, first occurring in 1987. He once struck her on the head and
threw her purse across the room. Another time he raised his fist to her. He once hit
her and knocked off her earring. On another occasion he put his fist through a door.
She discussed her problems with two doctors. She consulted a woman's shelter. She
asked the husband to seek counselling, but he did not. In the spring of 1995, during
a quarrel, he tried to close a car door on her leg. She called the police. The husband
sought medical assistance, but did not continue and did not take his medication.
Toward the end of 1995, the wife decided to leave him.

The husband admitted that he has a bad temper. He denied ever striking the
wife. He testified that the wife was subject to violent mood swings for which she
obtained medical help and was prescribed medication. He said that there were times
when she scratched him and kicked him in the groin. He was forced to protect himself
from her outbursts. He said the wife told him not to take his medication because it
was not what he needed.

There is no evidence that either party ever suffered any significant injury. No
criminal charges were ever laid. At trial no medical reports were filed. No witnesses
were called to substantiate the allegations. I find that both the wife and the husband
exaggerated their evidence about the conduct of the other. I also find that "each
gave as good as they got".

The husband was shocked by the wife's demand for separation, and at first
resisted. At almost the same [time as the wife's announcement of her intention to
leave], the wife purchased a home with a closing date of February 16, 1996. This
became the target date for completion of their agreement. This was a constraint that
the wife put upon herself. The husband did not impose it.

I am satisfied that each party had considerable input into the agreement. The
husband prepared the first draft. The wife revised it. She added provisions including
one that she was to be removed from the covenant on the mortgage on the home.
She consulted a lawyer about the second draft. He told her not to sign it. She rejected
that advice. The lawyer was not called as a witness at the trial. Although he sent a
reporting letter and account, the wife could not recall his name. I doubt that. She
took the extraordinary step of telephoning the husband's lawyer to corroborate that
he had told the husband not to sign the agreement. She also asked the husband's
lawyer to confirm that the agreement would be legally binding. She then re-typed
the agreement into what was its final form. She deleted the requirement that "an
attorney" witness the agreement. She added a clause: "Each Kathleen and Robert
have been assured by legal counsel that this document is legal and binding under
the provisions of The Family Law Act".

The agreement was signed in the presence of the husband's sister. Mrs. Bjorn-dihl testified that before the parties signed she asked them if they were happy with the agreement. The husband responded that he was not happy and asked what he had done that was so bad. The wife responded that she was happy. Mrs. Bjorndihl then asked them if they were sure they didn't want a lawyer. After the agreement was signed the husband was upset and walked away. The wife showed no sign of upset and started a conversation with Mrs. Bjorndihl's husband. This evidence was not challenged.

The wife made no attempt to set aside the agreement for over one year. In March 1997 on the day that the petition was served on the husband, she went to his home. She must have known that the husband would be extremely upset. They had an acrimonious discussion. If the wife were ever fearful of the husband's reaction it should have been on that day, in particular. Yet she went to his home, and there was no pressing reason for her to have done that.

The evidence of the parties' relationship, the circumstances surrounding the preparation and execution of the separation agreement and the subsequent conduct of the wife, satisfy me that when she executed the agreement the wife was not vulnerable to being preyed upon by the husband. For these reasons, the wife has failed to satisfy me that the contract was unconscionable.

Even if the contract is valid according to general principles of the law of contract it may still be set aside under section 56(4)(a) if a party has failed to disclose significant assets or liabilities. . . .

The wife alleges that the husband failed to disclose two assets. First, there is no reference in the separation agreement to the husband's registered retirement savings plan. The husband now concedes it had a value of $35,744.00 at separation. The plan resulted from a rollover of the husband's pension contributions when his pension plan was terminated in 1990. The wife testified that during negotiations she asked the husband about his pension. He told her that he did not have one. The husband testified that he did not recall that conversation. He also testified that during their negotiations he simply forgot that he had a registered retirement savings plan. I reject that. Second, the wife, in her pleadings alleges that the husband failed to disclose any share he held in the company employing him. This is not correct. The agreement shows the husband's corporate shares. However the value is listed at $3,500.00. This reflects what the husband told the wife. The husband testified that his opinion of value was simply a guess. The husband now concedes the shares were worth $13,014.00 at separation.

In *Demchuk* v. *Demchuk* (1986), 1 R.F.L. (3d) 176 (Ont. H.C.); additional reasons at (May 16, 1986), Doc. D112330/83 (Ont. H.C.), Clarke L.J.S.C. was of the view that non-disclosure whether consensual or innocent, falls within the ambit of s. 56(4)(a). His Honour also expressed the opinion that the statutory duty to disclose created by s. 56(4)(a) encompasses not only the existence of significant assets but also their extent and value. The latter view was also taken in *Underwood* v. *Underwood* (1994), 3 R.F.L. (4th) 457 (Ont. Gen. Div.); affirmed (1995), 11 R.F.L. (4th) 361 (Ont. Div. Ct.). Accordingly, the husband's assertion that his error and his omission were inadvertent does not assist him. I find that the undisclosed assets, worth $45,258.00 were "significant" in relation to the parties' disclosed net assets of $304,500.00. Therefore I conclude that the husband breached his duty to disclose significant assets.

Section 56(4) offers no guidance on how the Court's discretion to set aside a domestic contract should be exercised, once a vitiating factor has been found. There has been little judicial guidance.

In *Demchuk* (supra), Clarke L.J.S.C. observed that how the Court will exercise its discretion whether to set aside a separation agreement pivots on the facts of each case. His Honour set out the factors that he took into account. These included:

(a) whether there had been concealment of the asset or material misrepresentation;
(b) whether there had been duress, or unconscionable circumstances;
(c) whether the petitioning party neglected to pursue full legal disclosures;
(d) whether he/she moved expeditiously to have the agreement set aside;
(e) whether he/she received substantial benefits under the agreement;
(f) whether the other party had fulfilled his/her obligations under the agreement.

In an annotation to *Underwood* (Ont. Div. Ct.) (supra) at page 363 Professor MacLeod suggests that a Court should consider whether the non-disclosure was a material inducement to the aggrieved party entering into the agreement; in other words; how important the non-disclosed information would have been to the negotiations. I adopt this as another factor.

In *Rosen* (supra), the Ontario Court of Appeal re-affirmed the approach that Courts should take, in general, toward the validity of separation agreements. It is desirable that parties should settle their own affairs if possible. In doing so parties should know that the terms of such settlement will be binding and will be recognized. The Court of Appeal was clear that this approach is not applicable to contracts that are unconscionable. I conclude that where there are vitiating factors and a Court is being asked to exercise its discretion, the approach must be taken into consideration.

In the present case, the husband did not disclose the registered retirement savings plan during negotiations and I find that he purposely did this. However the wife referred to the existence of a pension plan in her petition. There was no evidence that the wife discovered the existence of the plan after the agreement was executed. As a result, I conclude that the wife did know, during negotiations, that the husband had some kind of retirement plan. She could have called the husband's union to inquire. She visited the family's financial advisor to obtain details of her registered retirement savings plans. She could have asked the advisor if the husband had any plans, and their value. The husband did misrepresent the value of his shares. However the wife did know of their existence. She could easily have obtained a price quotation from a newspaper, from a broker, or from the financial advisor. She obtained four opinions of the value of the matrimonial home, but she made no inquiries about the retirement package or the shares. It is not true, as she pleaded that she did not have independent legal advice. She had it and disregarded it. She showed a lack of care in pursuing legal disclosure.

The wife wanted to meet her time line. She wanted to be free of the mortgage and pool loan liability. She wanted to complete her real estate transaction. She needed funds to do that. The only immediately available money was $108,000.00, which the husband had obtained from a pay-down on the $127,000.00 mortgage, which he held. Although the parties' calculations showed that the husband owed the wife $110,250.00 she agreed to accept $108,000.00. The wife received the couple's interest in a time-share as part of the settlement. According to her evidence in pretrial examinations (which she disputed at trial) the time-share was worth $13,000.00. That value was not taken into account in arriving at the figure of $110,250.00. Its inclusion would have resulted in the final payment to the wife being reduced by $6,500.00. I conclude that was precisely why it was not taken into consideration.

The wife had decided that she wanted and needed $108,000.00 for February 16, 1996 and she was prepared to compromise her claim on that basis.

Section 56(4) only addresses non-disclosure of significant assets or debt or other liabilities existing when the domestic contract was made. However, they are not the only components that are taken into account in calculating a party's net family property. It does not follow that because the husband had an additional $45,258.00 in assets on separation that the wife would have been entitled to an increase of $22,629.00 in the payment that she received. The evidence disclosed that the pension plan, which was the source of the registered retirement savings plan, was in existence at the date of marriage. The husband was unable to establish a value at trial due to the passage of time, because the union had discarded its records. However, I am satisfied that the pension plan did have a value that the husband could have deducted from the value of his assets on separation to arrive at his net family property. Fairness dictates that the Court consider that in assessing the overall impact of the non-disclosure.

The evidence also disclosed that if the impact of the parties' pre-marriage assets been taken into account in their negotiations, very difficult and complex valuation issues and legal issues would have arisen. It would have taken the parties time and expense to explore those issues, had they undertaken to do so. The result could have been an adjustment, up or down, to the payment to the wife. The parties chose not to embark on that enquiry.

The husband's non-disclosure was willful, but the wife was not completely misled. She could have made further inquiries. The parties chose to ignore the legal advice that they each received. I am certain that with that assistance they would have explored the impact of pre-marriage assets on their calculations, but negotiations would have taken more time. The wife's principal motivation was a quick resolution so that she could receive the available cash and buy her house. In my view, because of her primary motivation, the non-disclosure would not have been an important factor in the negotiations. The parties chose to settle their own affairs, in their own way. For these reasons, I decline to set aside the agreement. . . .

The wife's claim for equalization of net family property is dismissed.

NOTES AND QUESTIONS

1. Although the doctrines of undue influence, duress and unconscionability are conceptually distinct, they overlap to a considerable extent and the courts have sometimes subsumed them under the general rubric of unconscionability. The resultant confusion was noted in *Williams* v. *Downey-Waterbury* (1994), 11 R.F.L. (4th) 106 (Man. C.A.).

2. The presence or absence of independent legal advice will often be a key factor in determining whether an agreement was entered into because of duress or undue influence or whether it should be set aside as an unconscionable bargain. The presence of independent legal advice was a key factor leading to the conclusion that the domestic contract was valid in *Mirus* v. *Mirus* (1980), 15 R.F.L. (2d) 152 (B.C. S.C.); *Richie* v. *Richie* (1980), 19 R.F.L. (2d) 199 (Ont. H.C.); *Deforest* v. *Deforest* (1982), 26 R.F.L. (2d) 337 (Sask. C.A.); *McVeetors* v. *McVeetors* (1982), 31 R.F.L. (2d) 218 (Ont. H.C.), affirmed (1985), 43 R.F.L. (2d) 113 (Ont. C.A.), leave to appeal refused (1985), 49 O.R. (2d) 225n (S.C.C.); *McEachern* v. *McEachern* (1984), 39 R.F.L. (2d) 77 (Ont. H.C.); *Blanchette* v. *Blanchette* (1984), 40 R.F.L. (2d) 20 (Sask. Q.B.); *St. Amour* v. *St. Amour* (1986), 1 R.F.L. (3d) 45 (N.S. Fam. Ct.); *Puopolo* v. *Puopolo* (1986), 2 R.F.L. (3d) 73 (Ont. H.C.); *Skolney* v. *Litke Estate* (1988), 13 R.F.L. (3d) 292 (B.C. S.C.); *Woolridge* v. *Doiron* (1993), 109 D.L.R. (4th) 407 (P.E.I. S.C.); *Williams* v. *Downey-Waterbury* (1994), 11 R.F.L. (4th) 106 (Man. C.A.); and *Francis* v. *Baker* (1997), 28 R.F.L. (4th) 437 (Ont. Gen. Div.). The absence of such advice was stressed in *Trottier* v. *Altobelli*. See also *Grossman*

v. *Grossman* (1982), 29 R.F.L. (2d) 300 (Ont. H.C.); *Mason* v. *Mason* (1981), 23 R.F.L. (2d) 68 (N.S. C.A.); *Graham* v. *Graham* (1988), 12 R.F.L. (3d) 84 (N.S. C.A.); and *Chandra* v. *Chandra* (1999), 45 R.F.L. (4th) 181 (Nfld. C.A.).

However, the fact that one or both parties did not have independent legal advice will not by itself justify setting aside the contract according to general contractual principles. In addition to *Dochuk*, see *Mercer* v. *Mercer* (1978), 5 R.F.L. (2d) 224 (Ont. H.C.); *Obermeyer* v. *Obermeyer* (1984), 40 R.F.L. (2d) 195 (Ont. Co. Ct.); *Bragg* v. *Bragg* (1986), 4 R.F.L. (3d) 173 (Nfld. U.F.C.); *Mushrow* v. *Mushrow* (1986), 4 R.F.L. (3d) 82 (Nfld. C.A.); *Kristoff* v. *Kristoff* (1987), 7 R.F.L. (3d) 284 (Ont. Dist. Ct.); *Martiniak* v. *Riley* (1988), 14 R.F.L. (3d) 40 (B.C. S.C.); *Fanning* v. *Fanning* (1989), 24 R.F.L. (3d) 135 (N.S. T.D.); *Ablaka* v. *Ablaka* (1991), 32 R.F.L. (3d) 369 (Ont. U.F.C.), affirmed (1994), 4 R.F.L. (4th) 167 (Ont. C.A.); *Sartor* v. *Sartor* (1993), 45 R.F.L. (3d) 250 (N.W.T. S.C.); *Rosen* v. *Rosen* (1994), 3 R.F.L. (4th) 267 (Ont. C.A.); *Clayton* v. *Clayton* (1998), 38 R.F.L. (4th) 320 (Ont. Gen. Div.); and *Settle-Beyrouty* v. *Beyrouty* (1996), 24 R.F.L. (4th) 318 (Ont. Gen. Div.). The latter case illustrates that a claim of unconscionable bargain will be difficult to establish if the party who got the better deal urged the other to obtain independent legal advice before signing.

As *Crouse* illustrates, the presence of independent legal advice does not, as a matter of law, prevent a finding of fraud, material misrepresentation, duress, undue influence or unconscionable bargain. See also *Farmer* v. *Farmer* (1979), 10 R.F.L. (2d) 243 (B.C. S.C.); *Youngblut* v. *Youngblut* (1979), 11 R.F.L. (2d) 249 (Ont. H.C.); *Kilburn* v. *Kilburn* (1980), 16 R.F.L. (2d) 306 (B.C. S.C.); *Howlett* v. *Howlett* (1983), 34 R.F.L. (2d) 195 (N.B. Q.B.); *Foggo* v. *Foggo* (1984), 40 R.F.L. (2d) 129 (Ont. H.C.); *Davidson* v. *Davidson* (1986), 2 R.F.L. (3d) 442 (B.C. C.A.); *Currie* v. *Currie* (1986), 5 R.F.L. (3d) 192 (N.S. C.A.); *Schmidt* v. *Schmidt* (1987), 7 R.F.L. (3d) 97 (Sask. Q.B.); *Richard* v. *Richard* (1993), 48 R.F.L. (3d) 132 (N.B. C.A.); *Murphy* v. *Murphy* (1995), 18 R.F.L. (4th) 107 (Ont. Gen. Div.); *Deguire* v. *Deguire* (1997), 34 R.F.L. (4th) 164 (Ont. Gen. Div.); and *Bennett* v. *Bennett* (1997), 34 R.F.L. (4th) 290 (Ont. Gen. Div.). Despite the result in these cases, Professor Majury argues in "Unconscionability in an Equality Context" (1990-1991), 7 C.F.L.Q. 123, at 144-149, that the presence of independent legal advice has often been given too much weight or significance. She states (at 144) that "the advice provides little or no protection but makes it difficult to challenge a domestic contract on the ground of unconscionability".

3. In *Crouse* the court indicated that the onus is on the party challenging the contract on the basis that it is an unconscionable bargain to show that it was a substantially unfair bargain resulting from an inequality in bargaining power. See also *Williams* v. *Downey-Waterbury* (1994), 11 R.F.L. (4th) 106 (Man. C.A.) where unconscionable bargains were defined as "grossly uneven bargains which result out of ignorance, need, or distress." In cases such as *Ablaka* v. *Ablaka* (1991), 32 R.F.L. (3d) 369 (Ont. U.F.C.), affirmed (1994), 4 R.F.L. (4th) 167 (Ont. C.A.) and *Hyldtoft* v. *Hyldtoft* (1991), 33 R.F.L. (3d) 99 (Ont. Gen. Div.) the judges concluded that *Mundinger* v. *Mundinger*, [1969] 1 O.R. 606 (C.A.) established that whenever a contract is improvident on its face, the onus is on the party seeking to uphold it to prove that he or she did not take unfair advantage of inequality in the position of the parties arising out of ignorance, need or distress. In *Mundinger*, the court quoted approvingly the following extract of a commentary by Professor Crawford in (1996), 44 Can. Bar Rev. 142, at 143:

> If the bargain is fair the fact that the parties were not equally vigilant of their interest is immaterial. Likewise, if one was not preyed upon by the other, an improvident or even grossly inadequate consideration is no ground upon which to set aside a contract freely entered into. It is the combination of inequality and improvidence which alone may invoke this jurisdiction. Then the onus is placed upon the party seeking to uphold the contract to show that his conduct throughout was scrupulously considerate of the other's interests.

The Ontario Court of Appeal used this quote as the basis for its description of the issue in *Rosen* v. *Rosen* (1994), 3 R.F.L. (4th) 267: "The question then becomes, was there an inequality between the parties, a preying of one upon the other which, combined with improvidence, cast the onus on the husband of acting with scrupulous care for the welfare and interests of the wife?"

4. Separation agreements arise out of intimate social relationships involving emotional circumstances that range from guilt and shame to fear and anger. These emotional factors, especially when

coupled with extreme financial need, may create a situation in which a vulnerable party is effectively prevented from freely consenting or protecting himself or herself in the bargaining process. As *Trottier* v. *Altobelli* illustrates, the general principles of contract law, in particular, the concept of unconscionability, are sufficiently malleable to allow the courts to intervene in such circumstances. However, emotional distress, even if accompanied by need, will not necessarily lead to a setting aside of the contract. In addition to *Dochuk,* see, for example, *McVeetors* v. *McVeetors* (1982), 31 R.F.L. (2d) 218 (Ont. H.C.), affirmed (1985), 43 R.F.L. (2d) 113 (Ont. C.A.), leave to appeal refused (1985), 49 O.R. (2d) 225n (S.C.C.); *McEachern* v. *McEachern* (1984), 39 R.F.L. (2d) 77 (Ont. H.C.); *M. (I)* v. *M. (D.A.)* (1984), 43 R.F.L. (2d) 205 (Ont. H.C.); *Bragg* v. *Bragg* (1986), 4 R.F.L. (3d) 173 (Nfld. U.F.C.); *Cadieu* v. *Cadieu* (1987), 12 R.F.L. (3d) 24 (Sask. C.A.); and *Gedak* v. *Gedak* (1988), 18 R.F.L. (3d) 131 (B.C. S.C.). In each situation, the key determinations will be whether the consent was freely given and whether the party under stress was incapable of resisting a substantially unfair bargain.

5. According to the general principles applicable to all contracts, a failure to disclose certain facts can amount to a fraudulent misrepresentation if the failure renders what has been stated a misrepresentation. Instances of telling a half-truth or deliberately failing to correct a statement that has become untrue are examples. However, complete silence not affecting in any comparable way something that was previously or concurrently revealed will not amount to misrepresentation unless the contract involved falls within a limited category of contracts *uberrimae fidei* where the parties must show utmost good faith towards each other. There is some authority for the view that interspousal agreements are contracts *uberrimae fidei* giving rise to an obligation on each spouse to make full disclosure of all relevant facts. In particular, cases such as *Lamers* v. *Lamers* (1978), 6 R.F.L. (2d) 283 (Ont. H.C.); *Couzens* v. *Couzens* (1981), 24 R.F.L. (2d) 243 (Ont. C.A.); and *Swanson* v. *Swanson* (1983), 34 R.F.L. (2d) 155 (B.C. S.C.) indicate that a failure to make full disclosure of the existence and value of all assets renders a separation agreement voidable. However, the courts in *Farquar* v. *Farquar* (1983), 35 R.F.L. (2d) 287 (Ont. C.A.); *Talarico* v. *Talarico* (1984), 38 R.F.L. (2d) 375 (Ont. H.C.); *McEachern* v. *McEachern* (1984), 39 R.F.L. (2d) 77 (Ont. H.C.); *Obermeyer* v. *Obermeyer* (1984), 40 R.F.L. (2d) 195 (Ont. Co. Ct.); *Tutiah* v. *Tutiah* (1985), 48 R.F.L. (2d) 337 (Man. C.A.); *Fyffe* v. *Fyffe* (1986), 4 R.F.L. (3d) 215 (Ont. H.C.); and *Webster* v. *Webster* (1986), 4 R.F.L. (3d) 225 (B.C. S.C.) refused to rescind separation agreements on this basis where the party asking for relief did not actively pursue disclosure. Although the results in these cases are consistent with the view that the agreements were not contracts *uberrimae fidei*, they can also be explained on the basis that, although there is a general duty to disclose relevant information in negotiating a domestic contract, a spouse who does not actively pursue disclosure of the value of assets of which he or she is aware must not consider this information relevant to the decision to enter the contract. In other words, the non-disclosure is not operative or material in the particular case and so cannot be relied on to invalidate the contract. See McLeod, "Annotation" (1986), 4 R.F.L. (3d) 227 and Hovius and Youdan, *The Law of Family Property* (Toronto: Carswell, 1991) at 704-706.

In *Saul* v. *Himel* (1994), 9 R.F.L. (4th) 419 (Ont. Gen. Div.), the court held that a separation agreement was not a contract *uberrimae fidei* but suggested that a marriage contract might be. See also *Murray* v. *Murray* (1994), 119 D.L.R. (4th) 46 (Alta. C.A.). On the other hand, Brockenshire J. concluded in *Underwood* v. *Underwood* (1994), 3 R.F.L. (4th) 457, at 461 (Ont. Gen. Div.), affirmed (1995), 11 R.F.L. (4th) 361 (Ont. Div. Ct.) that the cases generally characterize domestic contracts "as contracts *uberrimae fidei* importing obligations to disclose material facts and material changes".

In Ontario, the duty to disclose significant assets is now governed by s. 56(4)(a) of the *FLA*.

6. In *Underwood*, it was held that "the stream of income" from the husband's employment was a "significant asset" for the purposes of s. 56(4)(a). The husband's failure to disclose an increase in salary following separation was the basis for setting aside the support provisions in a domestic contract. See also *Picavet* v. *Paul* (1998), 42 R.F.L. (4th) 85 (Ont. C.A.).

7. A court is authorized by s. 56(4)(a) to set aside a domestic contract for non-disclosure even if the party seeking relief failed to pursue disclosure or expressly waived the right to disclosure. See s. 56(7). One might, therefore, be tempted to conclude that s. 56(4)(a) has significantly modified the common law relating to non-disclosure described in note 5. However, the section only creates a discretionary power. Whether or not this power will be exercised is dependent on the facts of each case and

failure to seek disclosure or the existence of an express waiver of the right to disclosure may cause the court to decline to use this power. In addition to *Dochuk,* see: *Demchuk* v. *Demchuk* (1986), 1 R.F.L. (3d) 176 (Ont. H.C.); *Salonen* v. *Salonen* (1986), 2 R.F.L. (3d) 273 (Ont. U.F.C.); *Mittler* v. *Mittler* (1988), 17 R.F.L. (3d) 113 (Ont. H.C.); *Ablaka* v. *Ablaka* (1991), 32 R.F.L. (3d) 369 (Ont. U.F.C.), affirmed (1994), 4 R.F.L. (4th) 167 (Ont. C.A.); and *Clayton* v. *Clayton* (1998), 38 R.F.L. (4th) 320 (Ont. Gen. Div.).

8. Mossop D.C.J. concluded in *Kristoff* v. *Kristoff* (1987), 7 R.F.L. (3d) 284 (Ont. Dist. Ct.) that a provision in a separation agreement requiring the husband to pay child support should be set aside where the wife failed to disclose that the child was fathered by another man. However, Greer J. held in *Saul* v. *Himel* (1994), 9 R.F.L. (4th) 419 (Ont. Gen. Div.) that a man could not sue his former wife for failing to inform him that he was not the father of one of her children. In that case, the parties separated in 1982 and in 1989 they signed a separation agreement requiring Saul to pay child support. In 1992, when the child was approximately twenty years old, Saul learned that he was not the biological father. His action for damages was dismissed. See also *S. (F.)* v. *H. (C.)* (1996), 133 D.L.R. (4th) 767 (Ont. C.A.).

9. Section 56(4)(b) appears to be closely related to the common law doctrine of *non est factum* whereby a court will not hold a party to a contract where he or she so misunderstood its true nature and intent as to negate the apparent consent. To succeed at common law, the party must prove that the document signed was fundamentally different from that which he or she believed it to be. Where a party failed to understand the precise meaning and content of the document but did have a good idea as to its general nature and purpose, the plea of *non est factum* will not succeed. Moreover, it will fail unless the party can demonstrate an absence of carelessness in the circumstances. To what extent are the circumstances covered by s. 56(4)(b) broader than those encompassed by the concept of *non est factum*?

How does s. 56(4)(b) re-enforce the desirability of independent legal advice for both parties who desire a legally effective domestic contract?

If one party is informed of the desirability of independent legal advice but chooses not to seek it prior to signing a domestic contract, should the court still allow that party to use s. 56(4)(b) to challenge the contract later? In *Ablaka* v. *Ablaka* (1991), 32 R.F.L. (3d) 369 (Ont. U.F.C.), affirmed (1994), 4 R.F.L. (4th) 167 (Ont. C.A.) the husband apparently never read the domestic contract before signing it. Wallace U.F.C.J. rejected the husband's claim that he did not understand the nature or consequences of the contract. She concluded that the claim failed because the husband "acted negligently". She also concluded that the wife's lawyer had no duty to ensure that the husband was informed of the merits of obtaining independent legal advice. The husband's failure to obtain such advice was described as "a choice he made" and "an act of negligence" for which the wife should not suffer.

10. Do the comments of Mendes da Costa U.F.C.J. in *Grant-Hose* on the authority of solicitors mean that a person can never rely on s. 56(4)(b) where the domestic contract is the result of negotiations between lawyers?

11. Section 56(5) of the *FLA* specifies that a court may set aside all or part of a separation agreement or settlement if "removal by one spouse of barriers that would prevent the other spouse's remarriage within that spouse's faith was a consideration in the making of the agreement or settlement". This subsection was inserted into the Act because the legislative committee considering an earlier draft became aware of situations where husbands refused to grant a *gett* — divorce recognized by the Jewish law — unless their wives agreed to the terms of a separation agreement. Since Jewish law does not permit a wife to grant a *gett* (she only has authority to refuse to accept one), a wife who is anxious to remarry within the Jewish faith may be unduly pressured to agree to unfavourable terms in the agreement in exchange for a divorce recognized by her faith. Section 56(5) now permits a court to set aside the contract, in whole or in part, in such circumstances. See generally, "Solution Sought to Problems of Jewish Divorce", *Globe and Mail* (June 17, 1985) "Ontario Measure Should Remove Simmering Jewish Divorce Issue", *Globe and Mail* (December 14, 1985); and Syrtash, "Removing Barriers to Religious Remarriage in Ontario: Rights and Remedies" (1986-1987), 1 C.F.L.Q. 309.

10

CHILD IN NEED OF PROTECTION

1. Introduction

(1) GENERAL

BALA "AN INTRODUCTION TO CHILD PROTECTION PROBLEMS"

Bala, Hornick, and Vogl, eds., *Canadian Child Welfare Law: Children, Families and the State* (Toronto: Thompson Educational Publishing, Inc., 1990) (Footnotes Omitted) (Reprinted with the permission of the author and publisher.)

LEGAL CONTEXTS AND THE PROTECTION OF CHILDREN

There are a number of different legal contexts in which issues related to the protection of children from abuse, neglect or ill treatment can arise.

Historically, the criminal law was the only legal tool employed to protect children. It still has an important role. It is a criminal offence to sexually abuse or physically assault a child. However, with regard to physical assault, caretakers can raise the defence of "using force by way of correction . . . if the force used does not exceed what is reasonable under the circumstances" [s. 43 of Criminal Code]. It is also an offence for a parent or guardian to fail to provide a child with "necessaries of life" or to abandon a child under the age of 10 [ss. 215 and 218 of the Criminal Code]. While the *Criminal Code* can be used to prosecute those who harm children, it is a blunt tool which is often difficult to use.

Persons charged with criminal offences are guaranteed a broad set of rights under the *Charter*. There is an onus upon the prosecutor to prove guilt according to the highest legal standard, "proof beyond a reasonable doubt." Abuse cases are especially difficult to prove because it is often necessary to rely heavily on the evidence of the child who was the victim of abuse. The traditional rules of evidence and procedure governing criminal cases made it difficult for children to testify and discounted their evidence. Bill C-15, which came into effect in 1988, has made it easier for children to testify and there has recently been a significant increase in the number of prosecutions in Canada, especially for sexual abuse.

Criminal investigations are handled by the police, and the presentation of the case in court rests with the Crown attorney. There are sometimes disagreements between these authorities and child protection agencies about how cases should be handled. Child protection agencies may be concerned about the effect on a child of prosecuting a parent; alternatively, the agency may favour a prosecution, but the police may be unwilling to proceed. There has recently been an effort to improve liaison and coordination between child protection agencies and those responsible for criminal prosecutions. This has tended to result in more support for the prosecution of cases. Even now, criminal prosecutions for physical abuse are rare, except in cases involving serious physical injury or death.

It is generally easier to prove abuse or neglect in a civil proceeding than in a criminal case. The rules of evidence are somewhat more relaxed in a civil trial, and the standard of proof is lower, requiring only proof "on the balance of probabilities." The *Charter of Rights* has more limited applicability to civil proceedings.

Abuse and neglect are most commonly dealt with as a child protection case. This is a civil proceeding in which the state-mandated child protection agency seeks to intervene in the family, either by making the child the subject of court-ordered supervision, or by having the child removed from parental care, on either a temporary or permanent basis.

Sometimes abuse or neglect issues are raised in a civil case involving separated parents who are in a dispute over custody or access to their children. With growing awareness of the problem of child abuse, the number of cases involving this type of allegation has increased.

It is also possible for a child who has been the victim of abuse, or a guardian acting on behalf of the child, to bring a civil suit for monetary damages. However, abusers frequently lack the financial resources to satisfy a judgment and such suits have been rare. Further, children are often reluctant to sue their parents, even after they reach adulthood. However, victims may feel a sense of psychological vindication from recovering an award, and such civil suits are becoming more common. It is also becoming more common for victims of abuse to seek monetary awards from their provincial Criminal Injuries Compensation Board. It is not necessary for there actually to be a criminal conviction for compensation to be granted, though there must be proof an offence occurred. In theory, the Board may seek reimbursement from an abuser for compensation paid, but in practice the Boards do not pursue abusers if they are without assets or reasonable income.

THE ROLE OF THE CHILD PROTECTION AGENCY

In every Canadian jurisdiction there is an agency which has legal responsibility for investigating reports that a child may be in need of protection and taking appropriate steps to protect children from ill-treatment. This may involve providing services to the child and parents in their home, or removing the child from the home on a temporary or permanent wardship basis. The child protection agency may provide services on either a voluntary basis, or an involuntary basis, making use of the legal system to require families to receive services. Child protection agencies are also responsible for arranging adoptions, though private agencies may be involved as well. In some localities child protection agencies assume other responsibilities related to their principal mandates, such as organizing programs for the prevention of child abuse.

Child protection agencies are given very significant powers under legislation to search for children who may be in need of protection and, if necessary, to force parents to surrender custody. These agencies receive all or most of their funding from the state. From a conceptual perspective, child protection agencies are agents of the state, exercising the coercive power of the state. In most Canadian jurisdictions, child protection services are provided by provincial employees serving out of local offices, typically of the Ministry of Social Services.

In Manitoba, Nova Scotia and Ontario there are local child protection agencies, called Children's Aid Societies or Child and Family Service Agencies. These agencies typically serve a particular geographical area. In Ontario, a few Children's Aid

Societies are denominational, serving only Catholic or Jewish families and children in a particular region. Recently, child protection agencies have been established in Ontario and Manitoba to serve native children exclusively. Even in provinces with these local semi-autonomous child protection agencies, ultimate statutory and financial responsibility for the agencies rests with the provincial government, and their employees should be viewed in many respects as agents of the state.

The structure of each child protection agency or local office is unique but they do share certain common features. Agencies have two basic functions: child protection (or family services) and child care. In some agencies workers have both child protection and child care responsibilities. Other agencies, however, have two types of workers.

Child protection workers are responsible for investigating suspected cases of abuse or neglect, and working with children and parents in their homes. Some agencies have intake departments, with a special mandate to deal with initial investigations and crisis situations; in such agencies if ongoing service is required, the cases are usually transferred to a family service worker after the initial investigation is completed by the intake worker.

Child care workers have responsibility for children who have been taken into care on either a temporary or permanent basis. Typically, children are actually cared for in foster or group homes, and child care workers have a liaison function with foster parents and group home staff. In some agencies, adoption work is done as part of child care while in others it is the responsibility of a separate department.

In some agencies there are specialized workers who are responsible for dealing with specific problems, such as adolescents living on the streets or child sexual abuse; in others, workers have a more generalized protection caseload. In some localities, particularly smaller agencies, staff members are responsible for both child protection and child care work. . . .

Child protection agencies are involved with the court system and must have access to adequate legal services. In some localities, especially larger centres, there are staff lawyers who are exclusively involved in representing agencies in child protection cases. In other places, child protection agencies hire lawyers in private practice to provide representation, typically establishing a relationship with a specific law firm. Use may also be made of court workers; these are employees of child protection agencies who are not lawyers but who are familiar with the court system. They are engaged to handle certain cases in court, typically those which are less contentious.

Child protection agencies provide services in conjunction with other agencies and professionals in private practice. For example, initial reports of suspected abuse or neglect may come from doctors in hospital emergency departments, public health nurses or teachers. When determining how a case should be handled, a protection agency may refer a case to a psychologist, psychiatrist or mental health clinic for an assessment, sometimes as part of the court process. If a child is taken into the care of an agency, it may be necessary for agency staff to work with therapists or educators. If there is a criminal prosecution, child protection workers will have to maintain contact with the police and Crown attorney's office. To be effective, child protection agencies must have good working relationships with others in the community.

Working for a child protection agency can be a difficult, stressful job. There are high turnover rates in these agencies. While most workers in this field are well-educated, having a college diploma or university degree, often in social work, they are typically relatively young and inexperienced. Young professionals often start their careers in these agencies and, after gaining some experience, move to less stressful work elsewhere in the helping professions.

Much of the stress in the child protection field relates to both the nature of the cases and the nature of the work. There is an inevitable degree of tension, as the role of child protection workers has both supportive and investigative functions. Child protection workers generally try to be supportive to parents and to provide services on an informal, voluntary basis. Indeed, most families that a worker comes into contact with do not end up in court, and in these cases the role of the protection worker can be regarded as similar to that of a therapist or counsellor, or an educator in parenting skills. However, the role of a child protection worker can also in some ways be viewed as similar to that of a police officer. Protection workers have legal responsibility for investigating allegations of abuse or neglect. Even if their involvement with a family is voluntary, in the event of later difficulties, anything a parent or child has told a worker may be relevant and admissible in a subsequent protection hearing.

Through education and disposition, most child protection workers want to have a therapeutic role, helping children and parents. But, understandably, workers may be viewed with hostility and distrust by parents. This often makes the job frustrating and contributes to the high turnover rate.

Some would argue that legal constraints make child protection work even more demanding. The law sometimes makes it difficult for child protection staff to take effective measures to protect a child. It is not enough for a worker to feel or believe that a child is at risk and should be removed from parental care. Involuntary removal can only occur if legal requirements are satisfied and the need for this is documented in court. However, if a child is inappropriately left in parental care and suffers further abuse, the worker will inevitably feel a sense of guilt and moral responsibility, and may even face civil or criminal liability for the failure to protect a child.

THE LAW AND THE CHILD PROTECTION PROCESS

Child protection agencies are charged with the legal and moral obligation of promoting the welfare of children, by ensuring that they are not subject to abuse or neglect. Provincial and territorial legislation gives these agencies the authority to intervene in the lives of parents and children in order to provide protection. While the legislation varies from one jurisdiction to another, and different judges have conflicting views about how to interpret and apply the legislation, the law clearly presumes that parents are capable of raising their children without state interference. The law places a burden on child protection agencies to clearly establish the need for intervention. . . .

CHILD PROTECTION LEGISLATION

Every Canadian jurisdiction has legislation in place to regulate child protection. While all of the legislative regimes deal with the same fundamental issues, there are significant variations in philosophy and approach.

Each statute defines ''child in need of protection,'' a key legal concept, as only children within this definition are subject to involuntary state intervention. Also, child protection legislation in every jurisdiction grants agencies the authority to apprehend children, that is, to take them into care prior to a court hearing, and provides for some form of interim custody hearing, at which a decision will be made about the care of the child pending a full hearing. If after a full protection hearing the court makes a finding that a child is in need of protection, there are essentially three types of orders that can be made: supervision, temporary wardship or permanent wardship.

Under a supervision order the child remains at home under parental care, but the home is subject to supervisory visits by the protection agency and any other conditions the court may impose. Temporary wards are placed in the care of the protection agency, usually in a foster or group home. Reunification with parents is generally contemplated when a child is made a temporary ward, and parents typically have the right to visit children who are temporary wards. Children made permanent or Crown wards are generally expected to be wards of the protection agency until they reach adulthood, though they may be placed for adoption without parental consent and occasionally are eventually returned to parental care.

Child protection legislation in each jurisdiction also provides for court review of prior orders to terminate, extend or change the nature of a prior order. Generally speaking, once a permanent ward is placed for adoption, the parents forfeit the opportunity to seek review.

In some jurisdictions adoption is governed by the same piece of legislation as child protection, as part of a comprehensive child welfare scheme. In other jurisdictions adoption is dealt with in a separate statute, though even in these jurisdictions child protection authorities are involved in some, though not all, adoptions.

There are significant differences in the philosophies reflected in different jurisdictions. Most statutes can be characterized as having a social work oriented or interventionist approach. They tend to have relatively vague definitions of child in need of protection, a broad scope for pre-trial apprehension, limited concern for procedural issues, and a relatively unsupervised scope for agency decision-making once a child is in care. Running through these statutes is a policy in favour of flexible, individualized decision-making. Intervention by the agency is seemingly presumed to be beneficial, though courts remain responsible for supervising and sanctioning the process.

By contrast, other jurisdictions, most notably Ontario and Alberta, have enacted more legalistic schemes, which narrow the grounds for state intervention. These statutes place greater emphasis on due process for parents, and have been more heavily influenced by the permanency planning movement.

Just as legislation differs from one jurisdiction to another, judges within a single jurisdiction often have differing views and philosophies about the child protection process. Some judges view the process as adversarial in nature, with a high onus on the state agency, which is challenging the integrity of the family unit, to justify its position. Other judges tend to view the process as a less adversarial inquiry intended to promote the welfare of the child. The attitude of the presiding judge can have significant impact on the manner in which child protection legislation is interpreted and applied. . . .

WHO SPEAKS FOR THE CHILD?

A fundamental question in the child protection area is: "Who speaks for the child?" It is a question which defies an easy answer. Some would argue that the protection agency, with its concern about the child's welfare, is speaking on behalf of the child. Others would point out that agencies often have institutional and professional constraints which prevent them from truly advocating what is best for the child. There may also be disagreement between the agency and foster parents or within the agency about how a particular case should be handled. While the agency will have an administrative mechanism for establishing how such disagreements will be resolved, there may still be controversy over what is truly best for the child.

In Ontario and Alberta the government has established offices of child advocacy, separate from child protection agencies, with responsibility to act as advocates for children involved in the protection process or in the legal care of a protection agency. These offices are not intended to provide legal representation for children in court, but rather to act as advocates for them within the context of the child protection system. The establishment of these offices reflects a concern that the bureaucratic nature of child protection agencies may not always be in the best interests of children.

Parents involved in protection cases typically believe that they know and care for their children more than any of the professionals. Parents may thus claim that they speak for their children.

The children who are the subject of a protection case may also have their own views about what they want to have happen. Some children are too young to express their views and older children are sometimes reluctant or ambivalent about expressing their views. However, many children involved in the protection process have definite ideas about their futures. In a number of jurisdictions, legislation specifies that courts should consider the "child's views and wishes, if they can be reasonably ascertained". [See, for example, Ontario's *Child and Family Services Act*, the *CFSA*, s. 37(3).] In some jurisdictions children involved in child protection proceedings can have lawyers who represent them and claim to speak on their behalf. In some cases a psychologist or other mental health professional will interview or assess the child and report the child's views to the court, and in some situations the child may come to court and testify.

In some sense the judges who decide child protection cases may be considered to be speaking for the child. Although they have a responsibility for balancing the rights of the litigants and acting in accordance with the legislation, judges may be regarded as having ultimate responsibility for the protection of children and acting on their behalf.

BALA "REFORMING ONTARIO'S *CHILD AND FAMILY SERVICES ACT*: IS THE PENDULUM SWINGING BACK TOO FAR?"

(1999), 17 C.F.L.Q. 121 (excerpt only; footnotes omitted)

1. INTRODUCTION

The Canadian media has been filled with reports that the child welfare system is "in crisis," with stories of child abuse deaths and recently completed or on-going public inquiries in several provinces into child abuse and the child welfare system. Canadian politicians are promising swift action to deal with this "crisis" in child welfare. In early May of 1999 the Ontario Legislature responded with a virtually unprecedented display of unanimity, enacting a broad set of amendments to the *Child and Family Services Act* (Bill 6) [enacted as *Child and Family Services Amendment Act (Child Welfare Reform), 1999*, S.O. 1999, c. 2] without any public hearings. These amendments are intended to increase protection to children from parental abuse and neglect. While no date has been set for implementation, it is very likely that these amendments will come into force early in 2000. [Most of them were proclaimed into force on March 31, 2000.]

This article discusses the context of the present problems in Ontario's child welfare system, with a particular emphasis on analyzing the effect of legislation and the court system in dealing with child welfare problems. . .

I argue that in the understandable effort to increase the protection afforded to children, we must also keep in mind the costs of intrusion and the risks of over-intervention. The amendments were enacted without public hearings or real public debate. I worry that the politicians may be looking for a relatively simple legislative solution to a complex set of human problems. While there was undoubtedly a need to amend some provisions of the Act, it is regrettable that there was not more consideration of the implications of the changes. I am concerned that the Legislature may have overreacted to some problems, and that some provisions in Bill 6 may create new problems. I argue that given the broad language of some of the amendments, the courts should take an approach to their interpretation that ensures that the changes truly improve the welfare of children. The courts face the difficult challenge of protecting children from situations of abuse and neglect while minimizing the risks of over-intervention for children.

While taking a legal focus, I recognize that legislation and the legal system alone have only a limited impact on the child welfare field, and that the decisions made by child protection workers and agencies about apprehension and placement often affect children more than those decisions made in court. However, what happens in the family courts has a significant impact on what happens in the broader child welfare system. Improving the legal system and the decision-making that is its central function can only have a limited role in improving the child welfare system.

Ensuring that there are adequate resources for training and service provision in the child welfare field, and in the related parts of health, child care, education, and social service sectors, is crucial to ensuring the protection and nurture of Ontario's children. One has to hope that the present focus of the politicians on the relatively inexpensive process of legislative reform is not a short-sighted or cynical effort to distract the public from vitally important issues that will involve greater resource expenditures. While the Ontario government has announced an increase in spending in the child welfare field, resource issues remain of critical importance in the broad field of children's services. Changes in the funding formula for child welfare agencies in Ontario base most funding on child protection investigations and children in care. This may discourage the provision of preventative services to families with children in their care, and encourage apprehensions.

2. THE CONTEXT FOR THE PRESENT REFORMS

a) The Political Context

Unfortunately, while the heightened media attention and political interest in the child welfare field is a recent phenomenon, the documenting of fundamental problems is not new. Over the past quarter century there have been a number of major inquiries in Ontario into the inadequacies of the child welfare system. While some of the current proposals to increase the effectiveness of the child welfare system in responding to cases of abuse and neglect are sound, other proposals create a risk of having a system that is overly intrusive. Further, some of the most fundamental problems in the child welfare system will require more complex solutions than enacting new laws; these problems are receiving relatively little public attention.

If we are to truly improve how our society deals with children whose parents are unable to adequately care for them, it is important to understand the context of the present crisis and avoid systemic overreactions that may create as many problems as they solve. . . .

In Canada, the child welfare system has often lacked strong political support. In the present time of fiscal restraint, other child-related services such as education and child health have a broader constituency and have tended to have greater public support. At least in part, the traditional lack of public concern with child welfare issues reflects the reality that the child welfare system tends to deal with those with little or no political power: children, especially those from lower socio-economic groups, female headed families, and aboriginal and visible minority communities. Further, the child welfare system deals with problems that have a complex interrelationship to other seemingly intractable social issues such as child poverty. Politicians are often slow to react to child welfare problems, sensing that there are unlikely to be fast, easy or inexpensive solutions to problems in the child welfare field.

The present public attention to the inadequacies of the child welfare system is at least in part a result of media efforts to publicize tragic, sensational child abuse deaths. It may also reflect a collective sense of guilt at the failure to protect our most vulnerable citizens. The increased public attention to child welfare issues is welcome, but one can only hope that this interest will be sufficiently sustained and that it will bring the necessary resources and systemic change need within the system. One reason for cautious optimism is that there is a growing recognition that failing to deal adequately with problems of child abuse and neglect has enormous long-term social costs in terms of future costs for the welfare, correctional and social service systems. Children who are victims of abuse and neglect and who do not receive proper intervention in childhood will likely be a burden on the economy in the future.

There are steps that can be taken that will reduce the risks of child abuse and neglect and more effectively intervene with those children whose parents cannot care for them adequately. But there is no simple or certain way to prevent abuse and neglect of children. Intervention in families where parents are perceived to be caring inadequately for their children will always involve difficult balancing, as removal of children from parental care comes with its own risks and costs. Intervention also raises fundamental value and political questions about the relationship of children and families to the state. Present knowledge and research about the effects of different child care arrangements is limited, and decisions about a child's future care will always have elements of uncertainty due to their predictive nature.

b) The Origins of Ontario's Child Welfare System

Until the latter part of the nineteenth century, there was little social or legal recognition of the special needs and vulnerabilities of children. Child abuse and neglect were common, and at a young age children began work in factories, mines and farms. In Canada, religious orders established orphanages for infants without a family to care for them, but it was common for children whose parents and relatives were dead or unable to care for them to be "apprenticed out" to work on farms and in shops, often in exploitative conditions.

Towards the end of the nineteenth century there was a growing awareness of the psychological and social importance of "childhood" as a distinct and formative stage of life. Reformers began to advocate for compulsory school attendance for children and abolition of child labour, as well as for the establishment of juvenile courts and training schools to deal with older children who were neglected, orphaned or delinquent. In 1893 the first Canadian legislation was enacted to allow for the establishment of Children's Aid Societies; judges were given the authority to commit to Society guardianship young children who were "dependent and neglected," as well as older youths who were "immoral or depraved." These Societies were responding to children who were dislocated by industrialization and urbanization; the Societies were primarily involved with immigrant children, orphans, vagrant children and youth, and "illegitimate children." While there was at least nominal judicial control over the process of the placing of children in the custody of a Society, in practice the agencies had very broad discretion to assume guardianship and make decisions for the care of children. Many of the judges who dealt with these cases lacked legal training; most of the children had no parental figure involved in their lives when taken into care, or their parents were poor and lacked the educational, financial or social resources to challenge the agencies in court. There was at that time in Canada little or no government support for the poor, and the primary way that the government financially assisted in the care of children was through the Children's Aid Societies.

By the middle of the twentieth century, provincially regulated child protection agencies were operating throughout Canada. The welfare state was slowly developing. Unwed mothers, who in the past rarely had the option of keeping a child, began to be eligible for public financial support; while this support was limited, it gave these woman a choice about keeping their children. In the mid 1950's the Supreme Court of Canada considered a case [*Hepton* v. *Maat*, [1957] S.C.R. 606] where a single mother was seeking custody of her child and articulated [at 607] as guiding principle that:

> *prima facie* the natural parents are entitled to custody unless by reason of some act, condition or circumstance affecting them it is evident that the welfare of the child requires that fundamental relation be severed. . . . the welfare of the child can never be determined as an isolated fact . . . as if the child were free from the natural parent bonds entailing moral responsibility, as if for example, he were a homeless orphan wandering at large.

Until the middle of the twentieth century, child welfare agencies were rarely involved in removing children from the care of parents who were expressing an interest in caring for them or challenging agency action in the courts.

In the early 1960s physicians became aware of the "battered baby syndrome" and the problem of physical child abuse was "discovered." Doctors and agencies became aware that abusive parents would lie about the cause of injuries to young children, and that child protection workers had to carefully investigate parenting practices; this required agencies to take a more investigative and adversarial role with parents.

In response to the "discovery" of the child physical abuse problem, the first child abuse reporting legislation was enacted in the mid-1960s. At the same time, there was a growing recognition of the importance of civil rights and that individuals had the right to restrictions on state interference in their lives. The first legal aid programs were being established to represent low-income individuals facing intrusive state action, first in the criminal context and then in the child protection field. Child welfare legislation began to reflect concerns with protection of due process and parental rights.

c) 1970s & 80s: Judicialization of Child Welfare & Family Preservation

The 1970s and 80s saw a number of related legal and social work and judicial developments that changed the child welfare system throughout North America, supporting the concept of "family preservation" and placing greater emphasis on the legal rights of parents and children.

One important dimension of change in that period was the development of a more "legalized" and rights-based society. In Canada the trend of giving individuals greater rights in their relationship with the state was both reinforced by and reflected in the introduction of the *Canadian Charter of Rights and Freedoms* in 1982. In the context of the child welfare system, parents and children were afforded greater legal rights, while agencies and child protection workers had to devote greater attention and resources to satisfying the requirements of the court system and justifying involuntary intervention.

The child welfare regimes of the first half of this century gave agencies broad discretionary powers, and made little attempt to distinguish between the child in need of protection and the child having behavioural difficulties or engaging in delinquent behaviour. The growing recognition of legal rights for children involved in protection proceedings was one of the most obvious aspects of the legalization of the child protection process. While there was significant variation between North American jurisdictions, the trend in late 1970s was towards the establishment of programs for legal representation of children involved in protection proceedings, though there was controversy over the exact role that these lawyers were to play in court.

Reinforcing the trend towards legalization and the granting of rights to children and parents was a growing recognition that too many children were being taken into state care, often with harmful long term consequences. There was also a growing awareness that some children and adolescents in state care were victims of abuse, most obviously in the large child welfare institutions that were slowly being closed, but also in foster care. Many children removed from parental care and placed in the care of a state agency were not being placed in stable, supportive environments, but would often "drift" through a series of unsatisfactory placements in foster care or institutions.

In the early 1970s there was also a growing challenge to the practice of removing children from parental care based on arguments that the process of separating children from parents was often emotionally damaging to children who were "attached" to their parents, even if the parents were far from ideal. There is a still a lack of good empirical research on the long-term effects of supporting children in the care of parents who have been neglectful or abusive as opposed to removing them from parental care. However, arguments in favour of leaving children in parental care in all but the clearest cases of abuse or neglect were forcefully articulated in the 1970s by the influential American scholars Goldstein, Freud and Solnit who advocated preservation of "continuity of relationships." Their ideas came to be reflected in the "permanency planning" theory. Permanency planning advocates favoured "family preservation" - leaving a child with parents whenever supports could be provided to minimize risks - and making decisions as early as possible in life to remove children from inadequate parents and place the child in another "permanent" home. In practice, however, at least in the 1980s, the family preservation aspects of permanency planning were emphasized while the making of early removal decisions was not.

Reinforcing other trends was a growing recognition that too often the decisions of social workers and judges to remove children from parental care reflected biases of class or race. In an Ontario child protection case [*Re Warren* (1973), 13 R.F.L. 51, at 52-53 (Ont. Co. Ct.), Matheson, J.] commented:

In a hearing such as this there is danger in over-reliance upon any group of witnesses self-conscious respecting their professionalization. I resolved not to fall victim to the bias of the profession, the group psychology of the social workers. . . . It was manifest from the opening that this was a contest between the right of a subsocioeconomic family to subsist together and the right of the public, represented by the Children's Aid Society, to insist upon higher standards of parental care than the couple . . . were capable of offering. Many witnesses called for the Society were persons of superior education. . . . One could not listen to their testimony with all the sombre implications of this application without resolving that this Court must not be persuaded to impose unrealistic or unfair middle-class standards of child care upon a poor family. . . .

In Canada the issue of systemic bias was most apparent in regard to aboriginal children. As the aboriginal residential schools began to close in the 1960s, provincial child welfare agencies began to provide services on reserves, but often in a culturally insensitive fashion. This resulted in as many as one third of the children in some aboriginal communities being removed from their homes, and often placed in white foster homes or adoptive families. Removing large numbers of aboriginal children from their communities has been criticized as "cultural genocide" with concerns being raised about the difficulties and identity problems experienced in adolescence by aboriginal children who have been adopted by white families.

In the 1970s and 80s the concerns about the need to respect legal rights and the desirability of preserving families led to pressures on law makers to change the legal regimes that govern child welfare in Canada. The changes affected child welfare legislation, judicial decisions and issues related to the administration of justice such as requiring legal training for child welfare judges and giving parents and children access to legal aid. While the nature and pace of change varied across the country, and some jurisdictions moved further away from early interventionist approaches, the broad trend was to increase legal regulation of the child welfare system, emphasize family preservation, and have a greater sensitivity to the concerns of aboriginal communities. The move towards a "family autonomy" model was perhaps most clearly apparent in the Ontario *Child and Family Services Act* of 1984. This Act included statements of principle that favoured "support for the autonomy and integrity of the family" and the "least disruptive alternative" for agency intervention. The definition of "child in need of protection" was narrowed. Vague grounds for agency intervention, like "parental unfitness," were eliminated, and the basis for state intervention was restricted to situations where there was a clear risk of serious harm to the child. If a court sanctioned state intervention, there was an onus on the agency to justify removal of the child from the home rather than providing support in the home. There was encouragement for the involvement of aboriginal communities in child welfare decision-making and service provision; for aboriginal children removed from parental care there was a strong statutory preference for placement in aboriginal homes.

Accompanying this type of legislative reform were profound changes in the cases being dealt with by child welfare agencies and in the services being provided. For example over the past thirty years there has been a steady and dramatic decline in the extent to which single mothers look to these agencies to place their newborn infants for adoption; single mothers now typically keep custody of their children, perhaps with agency support.

Agencies also developed an expectation that in child abuse and neglect cases that were assessed as "low risk" the child would remain with the family. Cases were increasingly dealt with on an "informal" or voluntary basis, with court proceedings and removal from parental care seen as a "last resort." Thus, in Ontario from 1971 to 1988, while there was a 160 per cent *increase* in the number of families receiving child welfare services (reflecting population growth, more stress on families and identification of more child welfare problems in the community), the number of children in care was cut by almost half and the ratio of children in care to total caseload fell by 80%.

While the number of children coming into agency care was falling, those children who were taken into care tended to be older and often more troubled than in the past. Changes in family structure and increases in labour force participation by women made it harder to find foster homes. Because of the recognition of the problem of abuse of children in state care, supervision and regulation of out-of-home placements was increased, and children in care were given greater access to advocates.

A significant development of the 1970s and 80s was the "discovery" of child sexual abuse. While children have been victims of sexual abuse and exploitation throughout human history, it was only in the late 1970s that professionals and the public began to be aware of the extent and effects of sexual abuse. The growing awareness of the widespread extent of child sexual abuse can be attributed to work with adult survivors of sexual abuse, first by feminists in the community and then by therapists and other mental health professionals. It became clear that victims of childhood abuse were often too frightened or guilty to disclose their abuse during childhood, or if they did disclose they were too frequently dismissed as lying or fantasizing. With the release of the *Badgley Report* [*Report of the Committee on Sexual Offences Against Children and Youth* (Ottawa: Ministry of Supply and Services, 1984)], it became clear that child sexual abuse was drastically unreported in Canada. Increased professional and public awareness led to programs to help children to disclose and as a result there was a massive increase in the reporting of childhood sexual abuse during the 1980s and early 1990s, both from children and from adult survivors reporting "historic abuse." Although there is little reason to believe that there is more child sexual abuse now than in the past (and perhaps reason for some optimism that increased awareness and reporting are leading to a reduction in the actual incidence of sexual abuse), the rising number of sexual abuse cases has sometimes overwhelmed an already stretched child welfare system.

d) Trying to Achieve a Balance in the 'Nasty' 90's

The past decade has been a difficult period in the public sector in Canada, with budget cuts and consequent morale problems for child welfare agencies, as well as for a range of related services including health, social services, welfare, education, justice and legal aid. Some of the resource cuts have directly affected the ability of child welfare agencies to provide services. Other cuts, for example to welfare payments in provinces like Ontario and Alberta, have indirectly affected these agencies, by placing poor families under greater stress and making it even more difficult for them to care for their children, thereby increasing demands for agency help.

At least in part the "family preservation" policies of the 1970s and 1980s were premised on the expectation that it would be possible to provide a range of preventative and support services in the community for high-risk parents and children. All too often these are the first services to be cut in times of financial restraint, raising concerns about the viability of some "family preservation" policies in the 1990s. The family preservation policies of earlier decades were also premised on a set of political and social beliefs in the importance of social supports for "the family." The 1990s have been a conservative time, with more emphasis on individual responsibility and accountability, and less on societal support and responsibility. "Family values" remain important, but society may be prepared to be more judgmental of parents who are seen to be inadequate and more prepared to intervene in the lives of children and remove them from parental care.

The notion of "children's rights" remains important, but these rights are now more likely to be defined to include "the right to protection and safety," as opposed to strictly legal rights. In some provinces, reductions in funding have curtailed child representation programs, though in Ontario the provision of counsel for children in protection cases has remained a priority and has not been reduced. Counsel for children have important responsibilities, including to ensure that all the evidence is before the court, to attempt to reduce delay, and in appropriate cases to facilitate settlement. However, the courts have indicated that there are limits to that role. In its 1994 decision in *Strobridge* v. *Strobridge* [(1994)], 4 R.F.L. (4th) 169] the Ontario Court of Appeal ruled that a lawyer appointed for a child "is not entitled to express his or her personal preferences on any issue including the children's best interests. Nor is counsel entitled to become a witness and advise the court about what the children's . . . preferences are." Unless admitted with the consent of the parties, this type of evidence is to be introduced by the child's lawyer calling witnesses who can be subject to cross-examination.

The concept of "parents' rights" remains important in the era of the *Charter*, as the Supreme Court of Canada recognized in 1994 in *R.B.* v. *C.A.S of Metro Toronto* [reproduced below]. At least four judges of the Court accepted that the parent-child relationship is worthy of constitutional protection, as an important aspect of constitutionally protected rights of "liberty and security of the person."
. . .

In its recent decision in *New Brunswick (Minister of Health & Community Services)* v. *G. (J.)*[(1999), 177 D.L.R. (4th) 124 (S.C.C.)] , the Supreme Court of Canada held that the provincial government was under a constitutional obligation to provide an indigent mother with legal representation where a child welfare agency was threatening to remove her child from her custody. The Court recognized that removing a child from parental custody has a "serious and profound effect on a [parent's] psychological integrity" and hence is a restraint on "security of the person" under section 7 of the *Charter*. Given the "profound effect on the lives of both parents and children" the "principles of fundamental justice" will generally require that indigent parents should usually be provided with counsel in these proceedings.

The cuts to legal aid funding have affected the ability of poor parents (who are those most typically involved in protection cases) to obtain legal representation, though the situation is not as bad in Ontario as in some other Canadian provinces. Giving parents procedural rights does not prejudice a child's welfare, since this type of right is consistent with getting the fullest information before the courts and having the best decision made. There cannot be a complete hearing of all the relevant evidence in a complex case between parents and a state agency about an issue of such fundamental importance as the parents' relationship with their child if the parents do not have counsel.

While the procedural dimension to parental rights is being recognized, the courts have also been balancing this with increasing recognition of the importance of the emotional well being of children. In its 1994 decision in *Catholic Children's Aid Society of Metropolitan Toronto* v. *M.(C.)*[(1994), 2 R.F.L. (4th) 313] the Supreme Court [of Canada] emphasized the importance of the psychological bonding of a child with foster parents. After a child was in the care of foster parents for several years and came to view them as her sole psychological parents, the Court considered the psychological harm that would result from removing the child from the care of the foster parents to justify a finding that the child was "in need of protection." This decision makes it substantially more difficult for a biological parent who has lost custody of a child for a period of years due to the parent's mental or emotional problems to regain custody of her child (provided that the agency has placed the child in a stable foster family), even if the parent has undertaken a course of treatment and regained the capacity to adequately parent. Similar decisions have held that even if the child is aboriginal, the courts will give precedence to psychological bonding after more than a year in care.

A number of recent decisions reflect a similar trend to restrict the substantive custodial rights of parents who clearly pose a significant risk to their children. In its 1997 decision in *Catholic Children's Aid Society of Metropolitan Toronto* v. *O. (L.M.)* [(1997), 30 R.F.L. (4th) 16 (Ont. C.A.)] the Ontario Court of Appeal held that where parents had been convicted and jailed in criminal court for killing one of their children, a judge could dispense with an oral hearing of evidence and grant "summary judgement" to make their other children Crown wards with a plan for adoption. The children's interest in having a timely decision made about their futures took precedence to the parents' right to have a full trial where there were "extreme facts" and the outcome was certain.

In its 1998 decision in *New Brunswick Minister of Health & Community Services* v. *L.(M.)* [(1998) 41 R.F.L. (4th) 339 (S.C.C.)] the Supreme Court of Canada upheld a trial judge's decision to terminate access rights to the parents of a permanent ward, emphasizing that "access is a right that belongs to the child, and not to the parents." Justice Gonthier wrote that "preserving the family unit only plays an important role if it is in the best interests of the child" endorsing the view that "the parents must be worthy of being 'visitors in their child's life.'" While this rhetoric must be understood in the context of the facts of the particular case, where there was significant evidence that the children were disturbed by visits with parents who had a history of marital violence and the children's lawyer was advocating termination of access, this decision clearly emphasized children's welfare over parental rights.

There are, however, also recent examples of Canadian appellate courts continuing to recognize the dangers of over-intervention and the need to find the right balance in the amount of state intervention. The Prince Edward Island Court of Appeal in *W. (N)* v. *Prince Edward Island (Director of Child Welfare)* [(1997), 33 R.F.L. (4th) 323 (P.E.I. C.A.)] stated:

> Legislators and courts have long ago abandoned the notion that children may be found to be in need of protection because a court deems it to be in the best interests of the child. There is a presumption children are to be left with their parents, and the autonomy and integrity of the family unit is to be maintained until such time as it is demonstrated that they are in need of protection. . . . The autonomy and integrity of the family unit is to be maintained not because this is a right of parents, but because of a recognition that a child's . . . interests are most appropriately served when they are raised by their parents. . . . courts must be careful not to authorize state intervention only on the basis that it is believed that the state can do a better job of raising a child than the parent.

The appeal court suggested that the standard of proof in a wardship case is not the " 'ordinary' civil standard of proof" but rather there must be "clear and cogent evidence, establishing with a high degree of probability" that the child protection agency has established its case. While other courts have not adopted this standard of proof, the decision reflects important judicial concerns about respect for familial autonomy.

In the past decade child development research work has emphasized the importance of the first years of life in terms of social, psychological and neurological development. This has led to a questioning of some "family preservation" policies that leave children, especially very young children, in homes where parental care is clearly inadequate.

At the same time, research also indicates that child welfare agencies often fail to provide good care for children who are removed from parental care, especially older children and those who may be hard to place for adoption. A 1998 Ontario report [*Voices From Within: Youth in Care in Ontario Speak Out* (Toronto: Ontario Office of the Child and Family Service Advocacy, 1998)] based on interviews with adolescents in state care revealed a disturbing picture. Perhaps most troubling were the stories that staff and foster parents were being physically and verbally abusive, including making racist insults to children in their care. Many of the youths experienced frequent moves and placement changes. As these youths come from disrupted home backgrounds, the frequent placement breakdowns reinforce their negative self image often in turn producing aggressive or self abusive behaviours; over half of the youths in young offenders facilities were previously involved in the children's service system. While the increased access to advocates for youth and increased supervision of placements in the child welfare system has undoubtedly resulted in less abuse than a few decades ago, it is clear that the system must be improved if children in the care of the state are to grow into healthy productive adults.

e) The Gove Inquiry in British Columbia

One of most significant developments in the child welfare field in Canada in the late 1990s has been the public focus on child abuse deaths, often in situations where the children were known to the agencies but were not removed from parental care. While there is no clear evidence that the child welfare system is providing less protection than in the past, the public and politicians are now focussing on the failings of the system and demanding measures be implemented to reduce child abuse and neglect.

The concern that agencies were not doing enough to protect children resulted in investigations and inquiries in British Columbia, Quebec, Ontario, Manitoba and New Brunswick. The British Columbia public inquiry by Family Court Judge Tom Gove, responding initially to the tragic death of 5 year old Matthew Vaudreuil who was killed by his mother, provided the most comprehensive study. The 1995 *Gove Report* resulted in new legislation in British Columbia as well as a substantial change in the administration of child welfare services in that province, with a new Ministry for Children and Families being created.

NOTES AND QUESTIONS

1. Part I of the *CFSA* governs the operations of the Children's Aid Societies in Ontario. While they continue to have considerable administrative autonomy, the agencies have become increasingly subject to controls by the Ministry of Community and Social Services. Note the revocation and takeover powers in ss. 22-24; the system of review procedures set out in ss. 66 and 68; the possibility of review by a Residential Placement Advisory Committee under ss. 34-36; and the powers of the Director set out in s. 77. The *CFSA* also includes provisions that permit the Minister to provide services directly or purchase them for children and their families, allowing a more direct provincial government role in child care: ss. 7-10 and 30(2).

2. There are significant differences in the philosophies underlying the child welfare statutes in operation in Canada. Many provincial statutes dealing with child protection can be characterized as

having a social work orientation or interventionist approach. Professor Bala explains in "An Introduction to Child Protection Problems" in Bala, *et al*, eds., *Canadian Child Welfare Law: Children, Families and the State* (Toronto: Thompson Educational Publishing, Inc., 1990) (at 13):

> They tend to have relatively vague definitions of child in need of protection, a broad scope for pre-trial apprehension, limited concern for procedural issues, and a relatively unsupervised scope for agency decision-making once the child is in care. Running through these statutes is a policy in favour of flexible, individualized decision-making. Intervention by the agency is seemingly presumed to be beneficial, though courts remain responsible for supervising and sanctioning the process.

In the latter half of the seventies, a wave of revisionist thinking called into question the premises of existing child welfare legislation and practice. See Wald's two seminal articles: "State Intervention on Behalf of 'Neglected' Children: A Search for Realistic Standards" (1975), 27 Stan. L.R. 985 and "State Intervention on Behalf of 'Neglected' Children: Standards for the Removal of Children from Their Homes, Monitoring the Status of Children in Foster Care, and Termination of Parental Rights" (1976), 28 Stan. L.R. 623. In "The Charter and Child Protection: The Need for a Strategy" (1986), 5 Can. J. Fam. L. 55, Professor Thompson describes (at 60-61) the revisionist thinking:

> The revisionists give expression to an increasing disenchantment with the child welfare system, questioning its implicit assumption of beneficent state intervention. Their agenda for reform reflects increased respect for family autonomy and a healthy scepticism toward agency claims of the benefits of intervention. A summary of their major proposals for change includes: 1) narrowing the grounds for intervention to serious, specific harms to the child; 2) circumscribing the circumstances for removal from the home, to those where the child cannot otherwise be protected from the specific harm alleged; 3) replacing the best interests test on disposition with a test of whether the child can be protected from specific harm; 4) heightening standards of proof and clearly allocating the burden of proof to the agency when intervention is sought; 5) requiring that agencies state specific and detailed plans for placement and services, with strict periodic court review of both agency and parental performance; and 6) imposing stricter time limits, with limited exceptions, for termination of parental rights.

Much of the revisionist thinking found its way into Ontario's Ministry of Community and Social Services' *Children's Act: A Consultation Paper* (1982), which heavily influenced the *Child and Family Services Act, 1984*. As Professor Bala explains in his second article reproduced above, the reforms of 1999 represent the return swing of the pendulum. These reforms will be discussed throughout the chapter.

3. For readings regarding the abuse and neglect of children, see Bagley, "Child Abuse and the Legal System" in Martin and Mahoney, eds., *Equality and Judicial Neutrality* (Toronto: Carswell, 1987); Dawson "Child Sexual Abuse, Juvenile Prostitution and Child Pornography: The Federal Response" (1987), 3 J. Child Care 19; Bagley and Thurston, *Preventing Child Sexual Abuse: Reviews and Research* (1989); Bagley and King, *Child Sexual Abuse: The Search for Healing* (London, New York: Tavistock/Rautledge, 1990); Rogers, *Searching for Solutions: The Report of the Special Advisor to the Ministry of National Health and Welfare on Child Sexual Abuse in Canada* (1990); Raycroft, "Abuse and Neglect Allegations in Child Custody and Protection Cases" in Bala, Hornick, and Vogl, eds., *Canadian Child Welfare Law: Children, Families and the State* (Toronto: Thompson Educational Publishing Inc., 1991); Hallett, "Criminal Prosecution for Abuse and Neglect" in Bala, Hornick, and Vogl, eds., *Canadian Child Welfare Law: Children, Families and the State* (Toronto: Thompson Educational Publishing Inc., 1991); Harvey and Dauns, *Sexual Offences Against Children and the Criminal Process* (Markham: Butterworths, 1993); Bissett-Johnson, "Family Violence: Investigating Child Abuse and Learning from British Mistakes" (1993), 16 Dalhousie L.J. 5; Smith, *Manufacturing "Bad Mothers": A Critical Perspective on Child Neglect* (Toronto: University of Toronto Press, 1995); F. Harris, *Martensville: End of Innocence* (Toronto: Dundurn Press, 1997); Day, "Memories Are Made of This" (1998-99), 16 C.F.L.Q. 363; C. Crosson-Tower, *Understanding Child Abuse and Neglect*, 4th ed. (Boston: Allyn and Bacon, 1999); and H. Dubowitz, ed. *Neglected Children: Research, Practice, and Policy* (Thousand Oaks, Cal., 1999).

4. For discussion of child protection legislation in Canada, see Somerville, "Governing Professional Intervention in the Family: Achieving and Maintaining a Delicate Balance" (1984), 44 R. du B. 691; Bissett-Johnson, "Protecting Children in the North" (1985), 4 Can. J. Fam. L. 413; Delevry and Cloutier, "The Child, the Family and the State: Seeking to Identify the Best Interests of the Child" in Hughes and Pask, eds., *National Themes in Family Law* (Toronto: Carswell, 1988); Bala, Hornick, and Vogl, eds., *Canadian Child Welfare Law: Children, Families and the State* (Toronto: Thompson Educational Publishing Inc., 1991); Barnhorst and Johnson, *The State of the Child in Ontario* (Toronto: Oxford University Press, 1991); Steinhauer, *The Least Detrimental Alternative* (Toronto: University of Toronto Press, 1991); Sammon, "The *Ontario Child and Family Services Act, 1984*: Maintaining the Balance Between Competing Rights" (1991-92), 8 C.F.L.Q. 129; Zisman, "New Act Marks Major Shift in Child Protection Law", (June 19, 1999) Vol. 19 No. 6 *The Lawyer's Weekly*, 15; and Bernstein et al., *Child Protection Law in Canada* (Toronto: Carswell) (looseleaf). See also Moorehead, "Of Family Values and Child Welfare: What is in the 'Best' Interests of the Child" (1996), 79 Marquette L. Rev. 517.

5. Civil suits for monetary damages by the survivors of childhood sexual abuse are now common. Section 81 of the *CFSA* authorizes the Children's Lawyer to begin an action on behalf of the child where he or she has suffered abuse. In *Queen (Litigation Guardian of)* v. *Hodgins* (1991), 36 R.F.L. (3d) 159 (Ont. Gen. Div.), a 9-year-old child (through her guardian) and her parents received a $25,000 judgment against a family friend who had sexually abused the child. However, almost all the cases involve adults bringing actions for abuse suffered during childhood, often against family members. The S.C.C.'s decision in *M. (K.)* v. *M. (H.)* (1992), 96 D.L.R. (4th) 289 facilitated these claims. The court held: (1) the limitation period applicable to the tort of assault and battery does not begin to run in an incest case until the victim is reasonably capable of discovering the wrongful nature of the perpetrator's act and the extent of her injuries; (2) incest is a breach of a parent's fiduciary duty to protect the child's well-being and health; and (3) as it is an equitable claim, an action for breach of fiduciary duty is not governed by the Ontario *Limitations Act*. For an article that anticipated much of the analysis in this case, see Des Rosiers, "Limitation Periods and Civil Remedies for Childhood Sexual Abuse" (1993), 9 C.F.L.Q. 43. See generally, J. Neeb and S. Harper, *Civil Actions for Childhood Sexual Abuse* (Markham: Butterworths, 1994) and Bala, "Tort Remedies and the Family Law Practitioner" (1998-1999), 16 C.F.L.Q. 423.

In *B. (W.R.)* v. *Plint* (1998), 161 D.L.R. (4th) 538, the S.C.C. held that the Government of Canada and the United Church of Canada were vicariously liable for sexual assaults perpetrated by officials on aboriginal students in residential schools. This holding has significantly increased the volume of civil litigation initiated by victims of abuse outside the family setting, particularly in child welfare institutions and aboriginal residential schools. For analysis, see Feldthusen, "Vicarious Liability for Sexual Torts" in N. Mullany and A. Linden, eds. *Torts Tomorrow: A Tribute to John Fleming* (Sydney, LBC Information Services, 1998).

6. In *J. (L.A.)* v. *(J. (H.)* (1993), 13 O.R. (3d) 306 (Gen. Div.), a mother was held liable in tort and for breach of a fiduciary duty for failing to take reasonable steps to protect her daughter from sexual abuse by her common law husband. Justice Rutherford reasoned that s. 79(2) of the *CFSA* codified this common law duty. He stated (at 315): "In the circumstances of this case, recognizing that the defendant mother was of limited means and education, it was still well within her ability . . . to take her daughter away from the abusive situation which she was well aware of or report the situation to the authorities with the probable result of the abuser being removed from the situation." Instead, the mother turned a blind eye and once deflected an inquiry by the Children's Aid Society. For a critical commentary on this case, see Grace and Vella, "Vesting Mothers With Power They Do Not Have: The Non-Offending Parent In Civil Sexual Assault Cases" (1994), 7 C.J.W.L. 184.

In *T. (L.)* v. *T. (R.W.)* (1997), 36 C.C.L.T. (2d) 207 (B.C. S.C.), an adult woman recovered damages from her father for sexual assault during her childhood. However, the court dismissed the woman's claim against her mother. The judge observed that the mother had "limited education and imagination" and concluded (at 222):

> . . . [I]t is not at all clear that [the mother] had the ability, awareness or means to take effective action in the circumstances. She did not act out of a wish to preserve the relationship with the plaintiff's father. She certainly did not encourage or enable the abuse. She simply could not come

to grips with the situation which was, in fact, a confusing one for her. . . . In the result, I cannot find that [the mother] was in breach of her duty to protect her daughter from her father's abuse.

See also *M. (M.) v. F. (R.)* (1997), 52 B.C.L.R. (3d) 127 (B.C. C.A.), where the court dismissed a claim against a mother involving abuse perpetrated by her son on the plaintiff, her former foster daughter. The court took account of the woman's lack of sophistication about sex in concluding that she was not negligent in failing to spot the abuse. The court considered that "there is good reason to be cautious [in imposing liability] because there is a grave potential for injustice to bystander parents if the court commits itself to broad . . . definitions of the duty resting on such parents." Compare *D. (C.) v. Newfoundland (Minister of Social Services)* (1996), 137 Nfld. & P.E.I.R. 206 (Nfld. T.D.), where foster parents were held liable, along with the director of child welfare, for their negligence when the mother's brother sexually assaulted a child in their care.

Can a child be in need of protection from the non-offending parent who ignores recurring incidents of abuse by the other parent? See *H. (A.), Re* (1994), 6 R.F.L. (4th) 33 (B.C. Prov. Ct.). For a comment on a similar American case, see "Comment: Revictimized Battered Women: Termination of Parental Rights for Failure to Protect Children from Child Abuse" (1992), 38 Wayne State Law Rev. 1549. See also *G. (T.L.M.), Re* (1996), 26 R.F.L. (4th) 192 (Alta. Prov. Ct.), where the mother was unable to protect her daughter from the sexual assaults of the girl's brother. For further reading, see B. Carter, *Who's to Blame: Child Sexual Abuse and Non-offending Mothers* (Toronto: University of Toronto Press, 1999).

7. Neglect of a child may constitute the basis for prosecution under the *Criminal Code*. It is, for example, a criminal offence for a parent or guardian to fail to provide a child with "necessaries of life" (s. 215) or to abandon a child under the age of ten (s. 218). Recently, there was a highly publicized case in Toronto in which a mother was charged, along with a child protection worker, with criminal negligence causing death when the mother allowed her young infant to starve to death. She was discharged, as was the social worker, following a preliminary hearing that took seven months: *R. v. Heikamp* (December 3, 1999), Hogan J. (Ont. C.J.). Also, in 1999 a couple, Robert Shaw and Starlene Gibson, were charged with criminal negligence because of their alleged failure to provide adequate supervision for their 5-year-old child who was killed when his bike was hit by a van. The charges sparked off a national debate on the extent to which the criminal law should be used to regulate parenting. See Maclean's, Oct. 4, 1999, 14.

8. Physical abuse may constitute assault (ss. 265 and 266 of the *Criminal Code*) or, depending on the consequences, a range of more serious offences against the person up to and including murder (s. 229). The criminal justice system also has a very significant role in combating child sexual abuse (see ss. 150- 155). The criminal law is an important symbol in our society. Effective prosecution of offenders can have significant deterrent effect, as well as serving to vindicate victims. Further, most sexual abusers appear to be highly resistant to treatment without the involvement of the courts and their rehabilitation is only likely to be possible if they are judicially required to accept treatment. It must also be acknowledged that some sexual offenders are not amenable to treatment and incarceration may be required to protect society.

In the last 15 years, there have been a number of legislative changes to the law to facilitate the giving of evidence by children in criminal prosecutions and to reduce the trauma of testifying. See s. 16 of the *Canada Evidence Act* and ss. 274, 486(1.1)-(1.4), 486(2.1), 486(2.3), 659, and 715.1 of the *Criminal Code*. Both s. 486(2.1) and s. 715.1 have been found by the S.C.C. not to infringe either s. 7 or s. 11(d) of the *Charter*: *R. v. Levogiannis* (1993), 25 C.R. (4th) 325 and *R. v. L. (D.O.)* (1993), 25 C.R. (4th) 285. On the interpretation and application of s. 715.1, see *R. v. F. (C.C.)* (1997), 154 D.L.R. (4th) 13 (S.C.C.).

Canadian courts have also shown an increased willingness to facilitate the proof of child sexual abuse by admitting into evidence: prior out-of-court statements of children in some circumstances (see, for example, *R. v. Beliveau* (1986), 30 C.C.C. (3d) 193 (B.C. C.A.), *R. v. Owens* (1986), 33 C.C.C. (3d) 275 (Ont. C.A.); *R. v. Khan* (1990), 79 C.R. (3d) 1 (S.C.C.) ; *Khan* v. *College of Physicians and Surgeons of Ontario* (1992), 94 D.L.R. (4th) 193 (Ont. C.A.); and *R. v. Rockey* (1996), 140 D.L.R. (4th) 503 (S.C.C.), but see also *R. v. R. (D.)* (1996), 136 D.L.R. (4th) 525 (S.C.C.) where the majority concluded that the out-of-court statements were not sufficiently reliable to be admissible for the truth of their contents); expert testimony about the general behavioural and psychological characteristics of child victims of sexual abuse (see, for example, *R. v. Beliveau* (1986), 30 C.C.C. (3d) 193 (B.C. C.A.); *R. v. B.(G)* (1988), 65 Sask. R. 134 (C.A.); *R. v. J. (F.E.)* (1990), 74 C.R. (3d) 269 (Ont. C.A.); and *R. v. Marquard* (1993), 108 D.L.R. (4th) 47 (S.C.C.), but see also *R. v. Olscamp* (1994), 35 C.R. (4th) 37 (Ont. Gen. Div.) where the court ruled such expert evidence inadmissible as too uncertain and unreliable); and testimony regarding prior acts of abuse of the accused (see, for example, *R. v. G. (K.A.)* (1988), 40 C.C.C. (3d) 333 (S.C.C.) and *R. v. B. (C.R.)* (1990), 76 C.R. (3d) 1 (S.C.C.)).

For discussion of the legislative and judicial changes in the laws governing criminal prosecutions for child sexual abuse, see: Bala, "Double Victims: Child Sexual Abuse and the Canadian Criminal Justice System" (1990), 15 Queen's L.J. 3; Sheppard, "The SCC and Criminal Evidence Reform: Recent Cases on Sexual Abuse of Children and Spousal Murder" (1991), 9 Can. J.Fam.L. 11; Castel, "The Use of Screens and Closed Circuit Television in The Prosecution of Child Sexual Abuse Cases: Necessary Protection for Children or a Violation of the Rights of the Accused?" (1992), 10 Can. J.Fam.L. 283; Young, "Child Sexual Abuse and the Law of Evidence: Some Current Canadian Issues" (1992), 11 Can. J.Fam.L. 11; Bala, "Criminal Code Amendments to Increase Protection to Children and Women: Bills C-126 and C-128" (1993), 21 C.R. (4th) 365; Harvey and Dauns, *Sexual Offences Against Children and the Criminal Law Process* (Toronto: Butterworths, 1994); Bala, and McCormack, "Accommodating The Criminal Process to Child Witnesses: *L. (D.O.)* and *Levogiannis*" (1994), 25 C.R. (4th) 341; MacIntosh, "Protecting Children: The Constitutionality of Sections 715.1 and 486(2.1) of the Criminal Code" (1994), 4 N.J.C.L. 234; Weisman, "The Admissibility of Hearsay Evidence: Defining and Applying Necessity and Reliability since *R. v. Khan*" (1995), 13 C.F.L.Q. 67; Renaud, "A Thematic Review of 'Principled Hearsay' in Child Abuse Cases" (1995), 37 Crim. L.Q. 277; and Stuesser, "Admitting the Out-of-Court Statements of Children" (1996), 24 Man. L.J. 483. See also Vella, "Recovered Traumatic Memory in Historical Childhood Sexual Abuse Cases: Credibility on Trial" (1998), 32 U.B.C.L. Rev. 91 and Day, "Memories Are Made of This" (1998), 16 C.F.L.Q. 363.

(2) ABORIGINAL CHILDREN AND THE CHILD WELFARE SYSTEM

DAVIES, "NATIVE CHILDREN AND THE CHILD WELFARE SYSTEM IN CANADA"

(1992), 30 Alta. L. Rev. 1200 (Edited footnotes follow.)

I. INTRODUCTION

The native population of Canada can be divided roughly into four groups:

a) **Status Indians** are those registered or entitled to be registered under the *Indian Act*. Status Indians are given certain rights and benefits under the *Indian Act*. There are approximately 416,000 status Indians in Canada.
b) **Non-status Indians** are those who by choice, or by operation of the *Indian Act* have given up or lost their status so that they no longer obtain the rights and benefits given by the *Indian Act*. There are approximately 75,000 non-status Indians in Canada.
c) **Metis**. There are at least two different views about the meaning of the term "Metis." Some maintain that the term refers to those of aboriginal ancestry who are descended from the historic Metis community of Western Canada. Others say that Metis refers to anyone of mixed aboriginal ancestry who identifies him or herself as a Metis as distinct from Indian or Inuit. There are approximately 60,000 Metis in Canada.
d) **Inuit**. (Originally called Eskimo). These aboriginal people live mainly in Canada's North. There are appoximately 27,000 Inuit in Canada.

. . .

Indian parenthood and a native child's cultural identity have for years been treated in a cavalier fashion. Today, the merits of keeping a child within his or her family and within his or her community are recognized and fostered. Involvement of the Indian community in the Child Welfare system as it relates to Indian children has, for the most part, been a positive development. A number of thorny questions remain to be answered, however. They are these. When the child's relationship with his or her natural parents has been severed and that child has now bonded with a new family, one that does not share his or her native background and heritage, should the factor of cultural identity outweigh the factor of psychological bonding? How does the child's emotional bond with a psychological parent fare against his need to be brought up in a native community? What weight on the scales should be given to the needs of an Indian Band to preserve its own culture and heritage?

II. LEGISLATIVE FRAMEWORK

Under s. 91(24) of the *Constitution Act, 1867* the Federal Government has legislative jurisdiction over Indians and land reserved for Indians. In 1951, the *Indian Act* was amended to provide that laws of general application that are in force in a province are applicable to Indians except where such laws are inconsistent with the *Indian Act* itself or with a treaty between Indians and the Crown.[9] Pursuant to this provision, both provincial child protection legislation and provincial adoption legislation have generally been held to apply to Indians.[10] Thus, provincial adoption legislation applies to Indian children, but an Indian child adopted by non-Indians does not lose his Indian status. Provincial legislation that states: "For all purposes an adopted child becomes upon adoption the child of the adopting parent . . ." is applicable to Indians only in so far as it does not conflict with federal legislation. If it were to deprive a child of his Indian status, then there would be a conflict. Thus, the provision is construed so as to make the child that of the adopting parent, *save for depriving him of status and that which goes to his essential Indian character and identity.*[11]

III. APPLICATION OF THE LAW: CHILD PROTECTION

. . .

Teaching Indian children the "white man's way" and concurrently discouraging the traditional beliefs and way of life was the path followed by missionaries and settlers in the nineteenth century. Right up to the 1970s, aboriginal children were taken from their communities to residential schools where they were deprived of the influence of their communities and discouraged (often harshly) from speaking their own language and practising their own beliefs and customs. Until the latter part of the 1940s, it was rare for either provincial government or private child welfare services to be offered on reserves. In a severe case, the Indian Agent would place the child with another family on the reserve or, if the child were older, send him or her to a residential school.

When the *Indian Act* was amended in 1951 to provide that provincial laws of general application were usually applicable to Indians, concern was felt by both provincial child welfare authorities and by Indian leaders, but for very different reasons. The provincial child welfare authorities were reluctant to extend their services onto reserves unless the federal government provided funding which it seemed less than eager to do. The Indian leaders did not want white provincial social workers interfering in reserve life. Thus, despite the obvious applicability of provincial child welfare legislation, the child welfare authorities did little on reserves except in the most extreme cases.

In recent years the federal government has softened its attitude. It has begun to reimburse some of the provinces and has also funded some Indian Bands under child welfare agreements. The services today, however, are still inconsistent. The extent to which provincial child welfare services are provided on a reserve will depend on the government agreement in existence. . . .

Meanwhile, since the 1950s, the number of aboriginal children in care has grown at an alarming rate and is only now starting to decrease. For instance, in 1985-86, Indian children were placed into care on average 2.7 times as often as other children across the country. A study in 1977 showed that native children represented about half the children in care in the Western provinces and almost 20% of all children in care across Canada.

What is the reason for these disproportionate figures? Several possibilities have been advanced:

1. Apprehensions are frequently carried out by white social workers with little or no understanding of the cultural background of the child or the very different methods of child rearing in Indian communities.

2. It is a well documented fact that Indians in Canada experience a higher level of unemployment than non-natives. According to the 1981 Census, only half of the adult native population under age 65 was in the labour force compared to 2/3 of non-natives. High levels of unemployment translate into poverty, poor, overcrowded housing and welfare dependency. Studies have shown a correlation between chronic poverty and child neglect.

3. Native families tend to be larger than non-native families. A study in 1974 showed that 52% of Indian women had 4 or more children compared to 21% in the total population. A recent Alberta Report points out that the Indian birth rate is 2 to 3 times higher than the non-Indian birth rate.

   The 1986 Census shows that 46.8% of the native population is under the age of 19 years compared with 29.1% of the total population. Thus, there are almost as many children as adults in the native population.

   Native families are frequently headed by a single female parent. In 1981 single female headed families comprised 17% of all native families compared with 9% of all non-native families in Canada. Further, the 1981 Census showed native single parent families headed by mothers had incomes of only 58% of their non-native counterparts.

4. The residential school system with its attendant encouragement of young native people to devalue their native ancestry drove a wedge between generations. This wedge caused difficulties both for the parents of the school attendees and for the attendees themselves.

5. From the 1950s (when provincial child welfare services were held to be applicable to Indians on reserves) until the mid 1970s (when changes started to be implemented), the activities of the welfare authorities took a somewhat rigid form. Native children believed to be in need were apprehended and placed in foster homes off of the reserve. There was little if any attempt to develop family support services or child placement resources on the reserves themselves. The results of this policy were disastrous.

Hundreds of native children were taken from their homes and placed in foster homes that were culturally and racially different from the child's own background. Bands were decimated. The children were often lost to the Band and frequently lost their own feelings of identity and self-worth resulting in anti-social behaviour and suicide. A native child, once taken into care, is less likely to be returned to his family than is a non-native child. Further, a native child who has been taken into care is less likely to be adopted than his non-native counterpart. Hence, a continuous circle of foster care placements takes its disastrous toll.

IV. THE WINDS OF CHANGE

By the mid-1970s, it was apparent that the child welfare system, as it had been applied to native children, was catastrophic. The term, "cultural genocide" was employed to describe the decimation of Indian communities that resulted from taking the young people away and depriving them of exposure to traditional culture. Indian leaders were concerned not only about what was happening to their people, but what was also happening to their communities with so many of the youth being brought up virtually ignorant of their cultural heritage. The mid-1970s saw cooperation among federal and provincial governments and native leaders in an attempt to involve native communities in the provision of child welfare services both on and off reserves. This involvement has taken various forms. Perhaps the most dramatic form is seen in the Spallumcheen Indian Band Child Welfare By-law. The Spallumcheen Indian Band occupies a reserve in the Okanagan Valley in British Columbia. It comprises approximately 400 members, over a hundred of whom reside off the reserve in neighbouring communities. During the 1970s, the Band experienced significant social disruption, unemployment, welfare dependency, alcohol dependency and petty crime. During that decade, 80 children were apprehended and admitted to the care of the British Columbia Superintendent of Child Welfare. This decimation of the Band by the exodus of this high percentage of its youth jolted the Band into dramatic action. After consulting with the British Columbian Union of Indian Chiefs, the Band enacted a By-law "for the care of our Indian children" which gave the Band exclusive jurisdiction with respect to the custody of a Band child whether on or off the reserve. The Federal Minister of Indian Affairs chose not to exercise his powers of disallowance of the By-law, despite its uncertain constitutional validity. Thus, the By-law came into effect September 3, 1980. After a highly publicized march on the residence of the Provincial Minister of Human Resources, the Provincial Government agreed to respect the authority of the Band as conferred by the By-law. The Spallumcheen Band, therefore, now has exclusive jurisdiction over the custody of Band children. The Federal Department of Indian Affairs funds the Band's child welfare program.

The principle difference between the Spallumcheem Band By-law and a provincial child welfare law is that a child may be apprehended by the Chief and Band Council or by any person authorized by them and brought before a meeting of the Chief and Band Council. Thus, the persons apprehending and the persons making the disposition are one and the same. In making a disposition, the Chief and Band Council are to be guided by Indian custom and preferences and, in the case of an older child, the child's wishes. If a child cannot be immediately returned to the family, placement is to be made according to the following order of preferences:

a)   with a parent;
b)   with a member of the extended family living on the reserve;

c) with a member of the extended family living on another reserve;
d) with a member of the extended family living off the reserve;
e) with an Indian living on the reserve;
f) with an Indian living off a reserve;
g) as a last resort — with a non-Indian living off the reserve.

However, in making a placement decision, the Chief and Band Council are required to give paramount consideration to the best interests of the child in question.

The By-law clearly has some advantages. First amongst these must be the involvement of the Band in decisions relating to Band children and a clear attempt to halt the exodus of Band children from the Indian community. Facets of the By-law have, however, been criticized. Professor J.A. MacDonald has said that there is a real concern over the potential for arbitrary decision making when a Band Council is assigned interventative, judicial and child placement powers.[35] Further, he said, "[s]ome Indians may question the capacity of a Band Council, frequently dominated by men, to render fair and impartial decisions in such a sensitive area as child custody."[36] One might add that this is particularly worrying when the concern of the Band is as much for the preservation of its own culture and heritage as for the needs of the individual child in question.

The Spallumcheen Band By-law provides the greatest autonomy to native peoples in the running of a child welfare system. However, it serves only a small group of Indians and the Federal Government has recently indicated that it will disallow any more of these By-law arrangements.

Arrangements giving less autonomy but serving a far wider segment of the native population, are becoming increasingly common. These arrangements involve Indian Bands in the delivery of child welfare services and taking on administrative responsibilities vis-a-vis Indian children. These arrangements differ significantly from the Spallumcheen Band By-law in that the law to be applied is the provincial child welfare legislation and the courts that determine disposition are the Provincial Courts. Under these arrangements, the native communities are involved in service and administration, they do not make the laws nor are the courts native courts. To this extent the arrangements have been criticized. The fact that provincial child welfare laws are applied means that there is little or no recognition of customary laws and tradition. The use of the Provincial Courts has been unfavourably compared to the Tribal Courts which determine child welfare matters on reservations in the United States.

A closer look at these "arrangements" reveals five main types: (1) An Agreement between the Federal Government and the Band (bi-partite); (2) An Interlocking Bipartite Agreement; Federal-Band/Provincial-Band; (3) A Tripartite Agreement between the Federal Government, the Provincial Government and the Band; (4) A Provincial/Band Agreement; and (5) A Federal/Provincial Agreement.

All Bands are now covered under one type or another arrangement for the provision of child welfare services. Not only are there differences in the types of Agreement, there are also differences in the levels of transfer of responsibility and control. Some Bands are initially given only responsibility for the provision of prevention services (basically providing support for families "at risk"). As expertise and proficiency increase more responsibility is given to the extent that some Bands or group of Bands have control and responsibility for the provision of the full range of child welfare services mandated under the Provincial Act becoming, under the Service Agreement, an "Indian child and family services authority."

Further, child welfare legislation of some provinces reflects greater sensitivity to native concerns and a recognition of the role played by the Band. For example, s. 73 of the *Alberta Child Welfare Act* provides that if the Director of Child Welfare has reason to believe that the child is an Indian, then consultation with the Chief of the Council or the Council of the Band should be sought before entering into a permanent Guardianship Agreement or applying for a Supervision Order or a temporary or permanent Guardianship Order in respect to the child. Similar provisions apply with respect to adoption.

· · ·

The *Child and Family Services Act*, of Ontario provides that one of the purposes of the Act is to recognize that Indian and native people should be entitled to provide, wherever possible, their own child and family services, and that services to Indian and native children and families should be provided in a manner that recognizes their culture, heritage and traditions and the concept of the extended family. Pursuant to Part X of the Act the Minister of Community and Social Services may enter into arrangements with Bands or native communities for the provision of child welfare services by an Indian or Native Child and Family Services Authority. If services are being provided to native children by a non-native agency, then that agency shall regularly consult with the appropriate Bands or native communities with respect to the provision of services.

· · ·

V. REPATRIATION

In the post war years, Indians saw their youth being removed from their cultural roots and reared in white homes. Since the mid-1970s much has changed. Native people are more involved in decision making. Consequently, there are less apprehensions, more services supporting children within the family and, if removal of the child is necessary, then more likelihood of him being placed in a native foster or adoptive home. All this is to the good. However, what of children that were already established in white foster homes? These children were caught in the cross-currents of a changing philosophy. Alienated from their cultural heritage, it was too late for many of them to turn back. The press reported heart rending tales of "repatriation" — Indian children established in white homes suddenly uprooted and returned to a native culture that has become alien to them.

A particularly horrendous case was that of *Jane Doe* v. *Awasis Agency of Northern Manitoba*.[57] This case caught the headlines in papers across the country. Jane was a native girl who had been adopted at the age of one by white parents. When she was fourteen the child was removed against her will from the adoptive parents by the defendant (a native child welfare agency). The Adoption Order was set aside at the instance of the defendant and the girl was sent to the care and custody of her natural parents on an isolated reserve in Northern Manitoba. For the ensuing six months the child lived what could only be described as a nightmare existence. She did not speak the Dene language and many of the reserve inhabitants, including her parents, did not speak English. Life on the reserve was foreign to her and she was treated as an outcast. On many occasions she was forcibly confined, raped and sexually assaulted by a number of the male inhabitants of the reserve. She contracted a venereal disease as a result of the sexual assaults and rapes.

She wrote of her plight to her former foster parents who contacted the defendants and attempted to seek assistance for her. The defendants did not come to the aid of the child. Ultimately, she was removed from the reserve by a fly-in doctor. She was hospitalized suffering from depression, adjustment disorder and venereal disease. She attempted suicide twice. A settlement of $75,000 was reluctantly approved by the Court. The Court was of the view that the figure was too low, but that the child would be damaged by the further trauma of litigation.

. . .

VI. ADOPTION

We have seen that an adopted Indian child does not lose his or her status by virtue of the adoption. The Alberta *Child Welfare Act* specifically provides that a person who adopts an Indian shall take reasonable measures on behalf of the child that are necessary for the child to exercise any rights he may have as an Indian. Further, as soon as the child is capable of understanding his status as an Indian, the adoptive parent shall inform the child of his status.

Until the mid-1970s, Indian children who were available for adoption were classified by child welfare authorities as "difficult to place." Little effort was made to find a home close to their original communities and many were placed in the United States. Since the mid-1970s, we have seen a greater involvement of native communities in child welfare matters. Increasingly, native children are being placed in foster and adoptive homes within their own communities. What, however, of the native child who has been placed in a non-native adoptive home? What weight will the courts place on the child's ancestry in determining to grant or refuse an adoption?

The leading case on this issue is *A.N.R.* v. *L.J.W. (Racine* v. *Woods).*[62] At age 6 weeks, the child had been placed in the care of non-native foster parents. She remained in their care almost continuously for six years when they applied to adopt her. The child's natural mother contested the adoption. The Supreme Court granted the adoption. In discussing the question of the child's Indian race and heritage, Wilson J. (who gave the judgment of the Court) said:

> In my view, when the test to be met is the best interests of the child, the significance of cultural background and heritage as opposed to bonding abates over time. The closer the bond that develops with the prospective adoptive parents the less important the racial element becomes.[63]

This case has been criticized. One writer has called the case another "instance of the suppression and misinterpretation of first nations' culture."[64] However, it is submitted that such criticism is unfair. When the guiding principle is the best interest of the individual child, then race and culture must be weighed in the balance with all other factors. In another case, race and cultural identity might outweigh the fact of bonding.[65] Much will depend on the length of time the child has been away from the home community, how long he or she has been with the proposed adopters and whether the proposed adopters are willing to expose the child to his or her Indian heritage etc. As Wilson J. said: "A child is not a chattel."[66] A child should not be bestowed on an Indian parent because he or she is Indian any more than on a white parent because he or she is white. Rather, the sole consideration should be, "what is best for this particular child?"

VII. CONCLUSION

In the United States the federal *Indian Child Welfare Act* provides that a Tribal Court has exclusive jurisdiction over "child custody proceedings" (broadly defined to include pre-adoptive and adoptive placement) if a child is domiciled or resident within the reservation of the Tribe.[67] If the child is not so domiciled or resident a State Court shall transfer any proceeding to the Tribal Court in the absence of good cause to the contrary and absent objection by either parent. The Tribe has the right to intervene in any State Court proceedings regarding the child's custody. In either court the following rule applies:

> In any adoptive placement of an Indian child under State law, a preference shall be given, in the absence of good cause to the contrary, to a placement with (1) a member of the child's extended family; (2) other members of the Indian child's tribe; or (3) other Indian families.

The rationale of the Act is twofold:

1. To promote the stability and security of Indian tribes. The large number of Indian children adopted by non-Indians threatened the continued existence and integrity of Indian tribes.
2. To avoid the damaging social and psychological impact on individual Indian children which is brought about by placements outside their culture.[68]

In Canada, our laws are steadily moving away from the concept of "parental rights" and focusing more on the best interests of the child. A child is seen less as a chattel in which a party has a proprietary interest and more as a unique person whose individual needs and wants should be paramount. The *Indian Child Welfare Act* of the U.S. involves the recognition of another right, that of the tribe. Canadian legislatures must think long and hard before they accept that a child's destiny should be determined, at least in part, by the rights of a party — a party whose rights may or may not coincide with the individual child's best interests.

 9 R.S.C. 1985, c. 1-5, s. 88.
10 *Natural Parents* v. *Superintendent of Child Welfare* (1976), 60 D.L.R. (3d) 148 (S.C.C.); *Nelson* v. *C.A.S. of Eastern Manitoba*, [1975] 5 W.W.R. 45 (Man. C.A.).
11 *Natural Parents* v. *Superintendent of Child Welfare*, *ibid.*
35 MacDonald, "Child Welfare and the Native Indian Peoples of Canada" (1985), 5 Windsor Yearbook of Access to Justice 284, at 287-288.
36 *Ibid.*, at 95.
57 (1990), 67 Man. R. (2d) 260 (Q.B.).
62 (1983), 36 R.F.L. (2d) 1 (S.C.C.).
63 *Ibid.*, at 13.
64 Monture, "A Vicious Circle: Child Welfare and the First Nations" (1989), 3 C.J.W.L. 1, at 14.
65 Compare *N. (K.)* v. *M. (K.M.)* (1989), 71 Alta. L.R. (2d) 42 (C.A.) (affirming in part 97 A.R. 38 (Q.B.)) (leave to appeal to S.C.C. refused 30th of November 1989) where a two-year-old child who had been in the care of the proposed adoptive parents since birth was returned to her Vietnamese mother since genetic and cultural factors outweighed that of bonding.
66 *A.N.R.* v. *L.I.W.* (1983), 36 R.F.L. (2d) 1 at 11 (S.C.C.).
67 25 U.S.C. 1901-1963. Discussed in *S. (S.M.)* v. *A. (J.)* (1990), 65 D.L.R. (4th) 222 (B.C. S.C.), rev'd. 89 D.L.R. (4th) 204 (B.C. C.A.).
68 *Mississippi Band of Choctaw Indians* v. *Holyfield* 104 L. Ed. 29 (1989) (S.C. of U.S.). See also *S. (S.M.)* v. *A. (J.)* (1990), 65 D.L.R. (4th) 222 (B.C. S.C.), rev'd. 89 D.L.R. (4th) 204 (B.C. C.A.).

NOTES AND QUESTIONS

1. The determination of when the state is justified in interfering with the parent-child relationship and the choice of disposition after a child is found in need of protection is particularly difficult and controversial when Canada's native peoples are affected. See *Mooswa* v. *Saskatchewan (Minister of Social Services)* (1976), 30 R.F.L. 101 (Sask. Q.B.); *Re M. (E.C.D.)* (1980), 17 R.F.L. (2d) 274 (Sask. Prov. Ct.); *R. (A.N.)* v. *W. (L.J.)*, [1983] 2 S.C.R. 173, 36 R.F.L. (2d) 1; *Re R. (H.I.)* (1984), 37 R.F.L. (2d) 337, [1984] 3 W.W.R. 223 (Alta. C.A.); *Re C. (D.L.)* (1986), 50 R.F.L. (2d) 245 (Alta. Q.B.); *Director of Child & Family Services (Manitoba)* v. *B. (B.)* (1988), 14 R.F.L. (3d) 113 (Man. C.A.), varied (1989), 25 R.F.L. (3d) 337 (S.C.C.); and *C. (J.M.N.)* v. *Winnipeg Child & Family Services (Central)* (1998), 33 R.F.L. (4th) 175 (Man. Q.B.). In *Mooswa* and *Re M. (E.C.D.)*, the courts ruled that a different standard of care should be applied to parents in rural aboriginal communities than would be applied in non-aboriginal, middle-class communities. This important issue was also considered in *B. (B.)*. The trial judge held that the 18-month-old twins who had been in foster care were no longer in need of protection and were to be returned to their mother. The mother had never had custody of the children. She was living in a four-room house with another five-year-old child, her 65-year-old mother, her sister, and her sister's two young children. The three adults, who were non-status Indians living on the outskirts of a reservation, received social assistance. Alcohol abuse in the home was evident. In deciding that the twins were not in need of protection, Martin Prov. J. stated:

> I have carefully reviewed the evidence and while I find that the B. condition, and I refer to the extended family at Easterville, deplorable by standards which I take to be the norm for middle class white society, I cannot find proof, on balance, of the kind required that would allow me to say that B.B. should be denied the return of her children.
>
> I find that none of the incidents referred to or the living conditions reported are so far out of the ordinary, for Easterville, that I can say that the children would probably be at risk if returned to the mother.

The Manitoba Court of Appeal overturned this decision. Monnin C.J.M., Lyon J.A. concurring, stated (at 115-116):

> That there is poverty in the area is not denied but poverty and the customs of the inhabitants of Easterville are not the issue. The sole issue is what is in the best interests of the twins . . .
>
> I do not accept as sound the principle enunciated by the trial judge that there are certain standards or norms which are acceptable for Easterville but unacceptable for the rest of the province. Economic conditions may differ but there is only one standard of care to be considered and applied whether the infants reside or whether the household is situated in Easterville, The Pas, Churchill, Brandon, Crescentwood, Tuxedo, West Kildonan or the Core area. In my opinion, the type of household in the case before us cannot provide the simple and essential elements of life since all three adults have shown themselves to be irresponsible where the other children are concerned and regularly over-indulge in alcohol.

The Supreme Court of Canada disagreed with the test applied by the Manitoba Court of Appeal. Sopinka J., for the court, stated (at 337):

> Although we do not agree with the test applied by the majority of the Court of Appeal, we agree with their conclusion that the children are in need of protection . . . . We are of the opinion, however, that the Court of Appeal failed to adequately consider the alternatives in s. 38 of the Act, and in addition, we have been told of evidence that indicates a change of circumstances have [*sic*] occurred. Accordingly, we would refer the matter back to the trial judge to consider what order is now appropriate under s. 38. The children are to remain temporary wards pending further order.

2. The *CFSA* specifies that one of its purposes is "to recognize that Indian and native people should be entitled to provide, wherever possible, their own child and family services, and that all services to Indian and native children and their families should be provided in a manner that recognizes their culture, heritage and traditions and the concept of the extended family" (s. 1(2)). See also 13(3), 34(2)(d), 34(10)(f), 35(1)(e), 36(4)(c), 37(4), 39(1), 47(2)(c), 57(5), 58(2)(b), 61(2)(d), 64(4)(d), 64(6)(e), 69(1)(e)

and Part X. For analysis, see Carasco, "Canadian Native Children: Have Child Welfare Laws Broken the Circle?" (1986), 5 Can. J. Fam. L. 111.

In "The Ontario *Child and Family Services Act, 1984*: Maintaining the Balance Between Competing Rights" (1991-1992), 8 C.F.L.Q. 129, W.J. Sammon reports (at 133) that by 1990 there were three Children's Aid Societies in Ontario whereby native peoples provided their own child and family services: Weech-it-te-win in Fort Frances, Payukaytano in Moosonee, and Tikinagan in Sioux Lookout.

3. For further reading, see Johnson, *Native Children and the Child Welfare System* (Toronto: James Lorimer and Co., 1983); Morse, "Native Indian and Métis Children in Canada: Victims of the Child Welfare System" in Verma and Bagley, eds., *Race Relations and Cultural Differences* (London: Croom Helm, 1984); Manitoba Review Committee on Indian and Metis Adoptions and Placements, *Final Report: No Quiet Place* (Winnipeg: Manitoba Community Services, 1985 (the "Kimmelman Report")); Indian and Northern Affairs Canada, *Indian Child and Family Services in Canada* (1987); Monture, "A Vicious Circle: Child Welfare and the First Nations" (1989), 3 C.J.W.L. 1; Sinclair, Phillips and Bala, "Aboriginal Child Welfare in Canada" in Bala *et al.* eds. *Canadian Child Welfare Law* (Toronto: Thompson Educational Publishing Inc., 1991); Zylberberg, "Who Should Make Child Protection Decisions for the Native Community?" (1991), 11 Windsor Y.B. Access Justice 74; Kline, "Child Welfare Law, 'Best Interests of the Child' Ideology, and First Nations" (1992), 30 Osgoode Hall L.J. 375; and Downie, "A Choice for K'aila: Child Protection and First Nations Children" (1994), 2 Health L.J. 99.

4. Although not decided in the context of child protection hearings, the recent S.C.C. decision in *H. (D.)* v. *M. (H.)* (1999), 45 R.F.L. (4th) 270 serves to re-emphasize that preserving a child's aboriginal heritage is only one factor in determining a child's best interests. This was a dispute for custody of a child who was both native and African-American. In determining whether custody should be granted to his biological grandparents (native) or his adoptive grandparents (non-native), the trial judge stated ([1997] B.C.J. No. 2144 (S.C.) at paragraph 46):

> Of course, [I's] aboriginal heritage and the ability of his biological grandfather to preserve and enhance it are important considerations, but we must not overlook the obvious fact that [I] has an African-American background and American citizenship. That heritage is also of importance and it is equally deserving of preservation and nurturing. This is not a case of taking an aboriginal child and placing him with a non-aboriginal family in complete disregard for his culture and heritage.

And at paragraph 47: "The submission that Ishmael's aboriginal heritage is virtually a determining factor here, oversimplifies a very complex case." The court awarded custody to the adoptive grandparents. The British Columbia Court of Appeal [*(D.)* v. *M. (H.)* (1998), 40 R.F.L. (4th) 370 (B.C. C.A.)], held that the trial judge placed too much emphasis on economic matters and under-emphasized ties of blood and culture. The trial judge's decision was reversed and custody was granted to I's biological grandparents. The matter was further appealed to the Supreme Court of Canada, where, "there being no error committed by the trial judge", the decision of the trial judge was restored: *(D.)* v. *M. (H.)* (1999), 45 R.F.L. (4th) 270. The biological grandparent applied for a rehearing on the basis that the adoptive grandparents failed to serve the Sagkeeng First Nation with a copy of the application for leave to appeal and the notice of appeal. The S.C.C. refused the application: (1999), 45 R.F.L. (4th) 273.

(3) THE LEGISLATIVE FRAMEWORK

Section 1 of the *CFSA* stipulates that the paramount purpose of the Act is to promote the best interests, protection and well being of children. While the amendments that came into effect in 2000 did not significantly change the specific wording, they did alter the structure of the section. This alteration is discussed by Professor Bala.

Reforming Ontario's *Child and Family Services Act*: Is the Pendulum Swinging Too Far?

(1999), 17 C.F.L.Q. 121 (footnotes omitted)

3. THE 1999 REFORMS TO ONTARIO'S C.F.S.A. – BILL 6

Declaration of Principle — Focus on the Child as "*the* Paramount Purpose": s. 1

Section 1(1)(a) of the Ontario's 1984 C.F.S.A. already states that "as a paramount objective [the Act] is to promote the best interests, protection and well-being of children." The *Panel of Experts Report* recommended that *the* "paramount" purpose of the Ontario Act should be "to ensure each child's entitlement to *safety,* protection and well-being." [After a series of coroners' inquests, the Ontario government appointed a committee to recommend legislative reforms relating to child protection. In 1998, it released the *Report of the Panel of Experts on Child Protection: Protecting Vulnerable Children.*]

Bill 6 did not adopt this recommendation in the form proposed. Rather it stipulates that s. 1(1)(a) should be amended to provide that: "*The* paramount purpose of this Act is to promote the best interests, protection and well-being of the child." That is the word "a" is amended to "the." But more significantly, the recommendation that "best interests" be replaced by "safety" was rejected. Bill 6 also provides that all other purposes of the Act, set out in section 1(2), should be "additional purposes" that are to be pursued only "so long as they are consistent with the best interests, protection and well-being of children."

It is not clear that this change is very significant. Even under this new principle, decision makers (child protection workers and judges) will need to make difficult decisions balancing immediate concerns about "protection" (which might favour removal from parental care) with concerns about emotional and psychological "best interests and well-being" (which might favour a child not becoming a ward of the state but rather remaining with the family).

Bill 6 also amends what will be section 1(2)2 so that state action only needs to be "the least disruptive . . . to help a child" instead of the present section 1(c) which requires the "least restrictive or disruptive" to the "child or family". The removal of the term "restrictive" may not be significant, but under Bill 6 the exclusive focus is on the disruption to the child, and disruption to parents is not to be directly considered. The new principles articulated in s. 1 make clear that the central focus of the child welfare system is to be *the child.* Notions of parental rights, culture, or aboriginal status are to be "secondary" to the focus on the child. This, however, may not be a significant change, at least in terms of how the courts have interpreted the present section 1.

Already in 1994 in *M. (C.)* [(1994), 2 R.F.L. (4th) 313 (S.C.C.)] L'Heureux-Dubé J. emphasized that "the first and 'paramount' objective of the Act is to promote the 'best interests, protection and well-being of children.'" She recognized that the 1984 C.F.S.A. has "one of the least interventionist" child protection regimes in Canada and commented:

> This non-interventionist approach is premised not with a view to strengthen parental rights, but, rather in recognition of the importance of keeping a family unit together as a means of fostering the best interests of children . . . the value of maintaining a family unit intact is included [in the Declaration of Principle] in contemplation of what is best for the child, rather than the parent.

She also emphasized the importance of s. 1 for guiding the courts in the interpretation of the Act: "The procedural steps and safeguards which govern the entire process under the Act . . . must always be construed in light of the clear purposes of section 1."

I submit that Bill 6 has not fundamentally altered these principles, though it has reminded decision makers that the focus is on the welfare of children, not the rights of parents or the convenience of agencies. It is significant that the Legislature did not adopt the recommendation of the *Panel* and make concerns about "safety" into a "paramount" position, and does not explicitly use this term, though of course "safety" is a component of "protection". One can appreciate the importance of the safety and protection of children in defining the mission of child welfare agencies. But it is only with hindsight that one can be certain of the steps that are necessary to ensure the safety of a child, and possible concerns about parental care will need to be balanced against risks of intervention, so that the child's "best interests . . . and well-being" may be promoted.

The following case illustrates various elements of the *CFSA*, as well as the role of the Children's Aid Society in protecting children.

CHILDREN'S AID SOCIETY OF TORONTO v. L. (E.L.)

(2000), 2 R.F.L. (5th) 78 (Ont. C.J.)

JONES J.:—

1: INTRODUCTION

This is an original protection application brought by the Children's Aid Society of Toronto (hereinafter referred to as the "society") for a finding that the child B.L.L., born on 8 August 1997 is a child in need of protection pursuant to clause 37(2)(*b*) of the *Child and Family Services Act*, R.S.O. 1990, c. C-11 (hereinafter referred to as the "Act") and further, for an order that he be made a Crown ward without access for the purposes of adoption.

The mother, Ms. E.L.L. consents to a finding that B.L.L. is a child in need of protection pursuant to clause 37(2)(*b*). Further, she is prepared to consent to a Crown wardship order provided she is granted access to B.L.L.

The father, Mr. Ew.L. contests that B.L.L. is a child in need of protection. He seeks B.L.L.'s immediate return. He indicates that he is prepared to co-operate with the society on a voluntary basis, but is opposed to a supervisory order's being made.

2: NARRATIVE HISTORY AND FINDINGS OF FACT

Both parents have intellectual limitations, but are residing independently in the community. They married shortly before B.L.L. was born and were intending to parent B.L.L. jointly. B.L.L. is Mr. Ew.L.'s first child. B.L.L. is Ms. E.L.L.'s second child; her first child was voluntarily placed for adoption approximately nine years ago.

B.L.L. has never been cared for by his parents; he was apprehended from the hospital on 11 August 1997. The decision to apprehend B.L.L. was made by the society after a meeting at the hospital attended by representatives from the various social agencies that had been involved with the family prior to B.L.L.'s birth. I was advised that the following persons were present: namely, Jayne Carnwell from Surrey Place, Sandra Bricker and Linda Henry from Metropolitan Toronto Association for Community Living, Margaret Heulen from the Department of Public Health, and Trisha Horrigan from the Family Residence. The decision to apprehend B.L.L. at birth was based not only on concerns arising from the intellectual limitations of the parents, but also on concerns arising from the parents' lifestyle, and living conditions as described to the society by persons who had actually met with the couple and visited their home.

2.1: Description of Mr. Ew.L. and Ms. E.L.L.'s Life Skills

Serious concerns around personal hygiene, nutrition, financial management, life style and housing were raised at the time of the apprehension. These same concerns have, more or less, continued unabated to date. This is true, notwithstanding the considerable efforts made by various agencies to assist this couple in addressing these concerns.

On the issue of life skills, I heard evidence in a number of areas. Mr. Ew.L. and Ms. E.L.L. continue to experience problems with housing. Although I was advised that they generally manage to pay their rent, they are only able to do so by sharing their accommodations with roommates who have been described as untrustworthy or abusive. The condition of their residence has been variously described as dirty, cockroach-infested and, on one occasion, as having rotting food in the refrigerator. Although the housekeeping standards have shown some improvements at various times, Mr. Ew.L. and Ms. E.L.L. have been unable to maintain these improvements. Budgeting continues to be an on-going problem for this family. For example, I was advised that periodically the phone has been disconnected and the family is frequently without money for food. Notwithstanding their limited finances, Mr. Ew.L. has managed to purchase a Sega machine with video games and has maintained his cable television subscription.

Ms. E.L.L. has experienced significant difficulty caring for herself. I heard that she required counselling on hygiene and has to be reminded to shower and to wash her hair on a regular basis. She appears to eat poorly and presents as pale and thin. In this regard, I was advised that, even when she was three months pregnant, she weighed ninety pounds. She does not eat at regular times and I was advised that she frequently comes to visits hungry. She and her husband use food banks on a regular basis and frequently access community based meal programs.

Mr. Ew.L. confirmed in his evidence that he habitually stays up to 4 a.m. or later playing video games or watching television. He indicated that he would not change this behaviour even if B.L.L. were returned as it was his belief that he would be able to stay up all day and supervise B.L.L. without any change in his habits. Mr. Ew.L. appeared to live without any routines and, although he indicated he wished to obtain regular employment, it appeared that he has not been regularly employed for many years.

2.2: Description of Mr. Ew.L. and Ms. E.L.L.'s Parenting Skills

All efforts to teach Mr. Ew.L. and Ms. E.L.L. the skills necessary to parent B.L.L. successfully have failed. With respect to Ms. E.L.L., I am satisfied that her lack of success has occurred because of her inherent intellectual limitations and was not related to her desire to learn such skills or her willingness to co-operate with her teachers. All the witnesses have described her as gentle and co-operative.

The reason for Mr. Ew.L.'s lack of success in acquiring the necessary parenting skills appears to be more complicated. Mr. Ew.L.'s intellectual limitations are not as marked as Ms. E.L.L.'s and it is possible that he might have learned these skills if his oppositional nature had not interfered with his ability to form therapeutic alliances. He appeared unable to modify his behaviour if he felt his independence or his sense of control was being challenged.

This stubbornness I see as seriously compromising his plan to care for his son. A good example of this refusal to modify his behaviour or accept new ideas arose in the context of the Thistletown parenting assessment. Mr. Ew.L. and Ms. E.L.L. spent a number of days in the intensive family therapy unit. I was advised that one of the therapists had corrected Mr. Ew.L. when he placed an opened jar of mayonnaise in the cupboard rather than in the refrigerator. After a lengthy, often heated exchange and after receiving a detailed explanation of the health risks associated with leaving an opened mayonnaise jar unrefrigerated, Mr. Ew.L. placed the jar in the refrigerator, all the time muttering loudly to himself that he would place it back into the cupboard as soon as the worker left.

Mary Rella from Thistletown Regional Centre testified that Mr. Ew.L. had great difficulty accepting suggestions from workers and often expressed anger when challenged. His low frustration level and his resistance to authority, coupled with his intellectual limitations have translated into a lack of progress in acquiring needed parenting skills.

The Thistletown Regional Centre prepared a report after Mr. Ew.L., Ms. E.L.L. and B.L.L. were assessed in the Intensive Family Therapy Unit. On separate occasions, each parent was assessed on his or her ability to be the primary care-taker for B.L.L.

Ms. E.L.L. was observed to become easily frustrated with B.L.L. She was observed to become angry with him if he did not do what she thought he should do or if she was unable to understand what the child wanted. The report noted that, at such times, she would rock him roughly and yell at him. Even when Mr. Ew.L. was present, he did not come to his wife's assistance. When asked why he did not do so, he is quoted as saying that "[Ms. E.L.L.] should try it on her own." Quickly, the assessment team concluded that Ms. E.L.L. was not capable of being the child's primary care-taker and, in fact, should not be left alone with B.L.L. Further, the team observed that Mr. Ew.L. was not a good source of support to Ms. E.L.L. in caring for B.L.L. It was noted that Ms. E.L.L. was unable to solve problems and that, unless she received hands-on assistance with B.L.L., her frustration would quickly escalate to a level of panic.

When Mr. Ew.L. was assessed on his ability to act as the primary care-taker for B.L.L., it was noted that, with some assistance and with prompting from the team to follow through with routines, he appeared able to meet the child's instrumental needs. The child was reported to respond positively to his father and Mr. Ew.L. was able to soothe B.L.L. when he was distressed. However, the assessment noted serious concerns about the general level of the father's parenting skills, his difficulty in accepting advice and in problem solving. The report concluded that B.L.L. would be at risk in Mr. Ew.L.'s care, not only because of his lack of parenting skills but, most importantly, because he did not recognise that leaving B.L.L. alone with Ms. E.L.L. posed the greatest risk to his son's safety and well-being. I was advised that, notwithstanding lengthy discussions with Mr Ew.L. about Ms. E.L.L.'s lack of knowledge around safety issues and her behaviour with B.L.L., which placed the child at risk, he refused to acknowledge that B.L.L. should not be left alone with Ms. E.L.L. He continued to maintain that Ms. E.L.L. just needed to "try harder".

The parents have regularly attended supervised access visits. I noted that the observations made by the access supervisors as to the quality of the interaction between B.L.L. and his parents generally accorded with the opinions expressed by the assessment team at Thistletown Regional Centre.

3: FINDING IN NEED OF PROTECTION

The society is seeking a finding under clause 37(2)(*b*) of the Act, which reads as follows:

> 37. – (2) A child is in need of protection where, . . .
> (b) there is a substantial risk that the child will suffer physical harm inflicted or caused as described in clause (a);

Clause (a) reads as follows:

> (a) the child has suffered physical harm inflicted by the person having charge of the child or caused by that person's failure to care and provide for or supervise and protect the child adequately;

On the facts I have found, there is more than sufficient evidence on which to find that there is a substantial risk that B.L.L. would suffer physical harm if placed in the care of his parents. Their lifestyle, living environment and intellectual limitations all lead to this inevitable conclusion.

Accordingly, I make a finding that B.L.L. is a child in need of protection pursuant to clause 37(2)(*b*) of the Act.

4: ORDER OF DISPOSITION REQUEST FOR CROWN WARDSHIP ORDER

The society seeks a Crown wardship order with no access for the purposes of adoption. The mother is prepared to consent to a Crown wardship order, provided she is afforded on-going access. She is opposed [to] the society's request that B.L.L. be placed for adoption, even if the foster mother is the one seeking the adoption order. She expressed the wish that B.L.L. remain in long-term foster care at the home of his current foster parents as she feels that they are taking very good care of her son.

Mr. Ew.L. seeks immediate return of B.L.L. In his plan of care presented verbally, he indicated that he plans to continue to live with Ms. E.L.L., but he would be B.L.L.'s primary caretaker. He did express the wish to obtain employment and, in that event, he indicated that he would place B.L.L. in day care. He promised not to leave B.L.L. alone with his mother. When asked how he intended to ensure that B.L.L. was not left along with his mother, he went so far as to say that, if he felt the need to go to the washroom when he was alone in the apartment with B.L.L. and Ms. E.L.L., he would control the urge until someone came to visit them. However, in cross-examination, he expressed his intention to continue to teach Ms. E.L.L. more about how to care for B.L.L. and help her to understand more about his needs. When questioned further, he reversed his position and stated that he did not feel that constant supervision of B.L.L. with Ms. E.L.L. was necessary as she was the mother and, as such, she had the right to be with the baby. His frustration with social workers coming into his home was evident when he testified that he felt that he and Ms. E.L.L. were doing a pretty good job taking care of themselves and it was not the social worker's job to talk about his habits. He said, ''She's not my mother. It's rude and it's embarrassing to have a worker coming into my home.''

The father's plan of care is patently unrealistic and unworkable and it is not in B.L.L.'s best interests. It is obvious to me that his parents would be unable to meet the needs of a child given the significant difficulties they are experiencing meeting their own needs. I do not see any possibility that their personal circumstances will change in the future so as to allow them to parent B.L.L.

I see no alternative but to grant the society's request for a Crown wardship order.

5: THE ACCESS ISSUE

5.1: Statutory Provisions

With respect to the making of an access order, a clear demarcation is made between all dispositions short of a Crown wardship order and a Crown wardship order. The Act creates a presumption against court-ordered access if an order of Crown wardship is made, no doubt to facilitate permanency planning by way of adoption as only children who are Crown wards without access orders are eligible for adoption.

Subsection 59(2) deals with the relationship between Crown wardship orders and subsequent access orders. Subsection 59(2) states:

> Where a child is made a Crown ward under paragraph 3 of subsection 57(1), the court shall not make an order for access by the person who had charge of the child immediately before intervention under this Part unless the court is satisfied that,
>
> (a) permanent placement in a family setting has not been planned or is not possible, and the person's access will not impair the child's future opportunities for such placement;
>
> (b) the child is at least twelve years of age and wishes to maintain contact with the person;
>
> (c) the child has been or will be placed with a person who does not wish to adopt the child; or
>
> (d) some other special circumstances justifies making an order for access.

Subsection 58(1) of the Act mandates that all access orders be made in a child's best interests. . . .

5.2: Parents Position on Access

Mr. Ew.L. and Ms. E.L.L. are vehemently opposed to adoption for B.L.L. as they wish to maintain contact with him. As I understand the argument in favour of access it rests on two grounds, namely,

1. In the circumstances of this case, long-term foster care with access does not limit in any way a permanent placement in a family setting as it is the society's plan to leave B.L.L. with his current foster family either as a long-term ward with access or as a candidate for adoption.
2. The recommendation of the Thistletown Regional Centre, which advocates long-term access to the parents, constitutes ''some other special circumstance'' that justifies the making of an order for access within the meaning of clause 52(2)(d). I am urged to grant the parents access in recognition of

their love and commitment to their son and their motivation to follow through with recommendations made during the assessment process.

Counsel referred to the Thistletown Regional Centre's recommendations, which read as follows:

1. In the best interests of [B.L.L.], the CAS should begin to make long-term plans in seeking adoptive parents for [B.L.L.].

2. Given [E.L.'s] and [E.L.L.'s] ability to connect with supports and their motivation to follow through with recommendations of the IFTU team during this assessment period, and their stated desire to parent [B.L.L.], an ideal arrangement in addressing the needs of these parents is to co-ordinate a parenting plan between [E.L.] and [E.L.L.] and [B.L.L.'s] foster and/or adoptive parents. This plan would require a great deal of support from all helping systems involved as well as commitment from [E.L.] and [E.L.L.] to work co-operatively with such systems and parents. This plan could include [E.L.'s] and [E.L.L.'s] having supervised access visits with [B.L.L.] as he develops.

5.3: Permanency Planning Long-Term Foster Care versus Adoption

Counsel for the mother argued that the making of an access order would not affect permanency planning in a family setting as B.L.L. would continue in the same foster home as a long-term Crown ward with access. It was noted that the foster mother had agreed to continue to care for him on a long-term foster care basis but she had expressed a desire to adopt and terminate access. Counsel argued that permanent placement in a family setting does not always refer to adoption and, in this case, long-term foster care would be as permanent as adoption. Further, he argued that there was no evidence before me that long-term foster care does, in fact, result in placements that are less permanent than adoptive homes.

At the request of counsel, I adjourned the matter to permit further evidence and submissions to be made on this point. When the trial recommenced, the society called Mr. Richard Partridge as an expert witness to give evidence on the issue of permanency planning for Crown wards. Mr. Partridge is an employee of the Ministry of Community and Social Services. Between 1993-1998, he held the position of Co-ordinator of the Crown Ward Review and the Private/International adoption department.

He testified on a number of issues including the Ministry's statutory obligation under section 66 of the Act to review the status of every Crown ward on an annual basis to determine whether an adequate plan of care has been developed for each Crown ward and to stimulate improvement in the overall service delivery to such children. Mr. Partridge brought to court a memorandum dated 25 March 1999 prepared by the Ministry from the data collected under the mandatory section 66 annual review of Crown wards that compared the Children's Aid Society of Metropolitan Toronto with the provincial average in a number of areas, including placement length, placement change, worker change, access ordered or exercised, and adoption breakdown or disruption.

The 1998 provincial statistics reveal the following trends. The average length of a placement for a Crown ward lasted twenty-eight months. Since becoming a Crown ward, 41% of Crown wards have been in one placement, 21% have been in two placements and 38% have been in three or more homes. In 1998, the average Crown ward was assigned a new social worker every twenty-four months and, more specifically, since becoming a Crown ward, 17% have had one worker, 42% have had two workers and 41% have had three or more workers. With respect to access, the report noted that, in 1998, 75% of Crown wards had an access order and, in 53% of the cases, access in some form was being exercised.

The figures on adoption breakdown or disruption were not collected province-wide in 1998 but, in the case of Crown wards managed by the Children's Aid Society of Metropolitan Toronto, it was noted that, out of the 1190 files reviewed, two cases were identified as arising from adoption disruption, and fourteen cases were flagged as adoption breakdowns. No data were available whether the adoptions referred to were private adoption or were society adoptions. Nor was I advised of the total number of children who are adopted Metro wide or province wide so I was unable to assess the relevance of this number other than to note that it was an extremely small number when compared with the number of Crown wards identified.

The statistics, although not complete, are informative. In Ontario, a Crown ward can expect to change caretakers every 2.3 years. Further, he or she can expect to be assigned a new social worker every two years. These statistics would suggest that, the younger a child is at the time he or she becomes a Crown ward, the more likely he or she is to experience multiple placements and several primary workers.

From his experience as co-ordinator of the Crown ward review department and previously, from his role as Children's Services Co-ordinator, Mr. Partridge outlined some of the reasons why placement changes in foster care might occur. He prefaced his remarks by saying that foster parents are generally a very dedicated, hard-working group. However, he noted that foster parenting is a job, and as in other occupations, people retire, transfer out of the area, leave for health reasons or quit to take up other employment opportunities. He observed that fostering is a difficult job emotionally and some people simply suffer burn out. In the case of foster parents, he indicated that marital separation and divorce might impact on fostering. Other times, Crown wards are moved to other settings in order better to meet their special needs or because the foster parents are unable to manage the ward's disruptive behaviour.

He compared foster parenting to parenthood. He noted that, unlike fostering, parenting is a life-long commitment. People and families make provision for their children regardless of life's changes. He noted that, in his experience as Co-ordinator of Private/International Adoptions, there are few adoption breakdowns when children are placed at an early age. Adoption breakdowns, in his experience, occur more frequently when older or "special needs" children are involved in an adoption.

No contradictory evidence was called by the parents. On the evidence, I am satisfied that an adoption is most likely to result in a permanent placement in a family setting for an infant or young child.

5.4: Special Circumstances Justifying Access

It was argued that the Thistletown assessment report and its recommendation for access with or without adoption constitutes some other special circumstances justifying an access order within the meaning of clause 59(2)(d). As I am persuaded that any access order I make must be in B.L.L.'s best interest in accordance with subsection 58(1) of the Act, I have assessed the proposed access not from the parents' perspective but from the child's perspective. The recommendation by Thistletown for continued access is not particularly helpful to me as I am persuaded that this recommendation for access focuses on the best interests of Mr. Ew.L. and Ms. E.L.L.; the very wording of the recommendation makes no mention of the effect that such access might have on B.L.L. or on his caretakers, but rather speaks to the parents' wishes, the parents' efforts and the parents' needs to parent B.L.L.

In evaluating the effect that continued access to his parents might have on B.L.L. and his best interests, I have identified the following questions as relevant to such a determination.

1. What is the society's long-range plan for this Crown ward?
2. Does this plan satisfy the need for permanency planning in light of the child's age?
3. What effect has the current access regime had on the child?
4. What effect would a termination of access have on the child?
5. Would continued access to the biological parents support or undermine the child's placement?

After reviewing the evidence, I have answered the questions in the following way:

1. The long-term plan proffered by the society contemplates that B.L.L. will be adopted by his current foster parents. An access order would preclude the foster family from adopting B.L.L. B.L.L. has been with this family since he was four days old and, by all accounts, sees this family as his psychological family. The foster parents have been described as experienced, competent parents who are prepared to make a life-long commitment to B.L.L., notwithstanding the fact that B.L.L. may be a "special needs" child who is already showing signs of language delay.
2. An adoption will afford B.L.L. his best chance of being raised to his majority in one home with one set of parents.
3. Although B.L.L.'s biological parents love him and he enjoys visits, B.L.L.'s primary attachment is to his foster family.
4. B.L.L. is young enough that, if his access to his biological parents is terminated, he will not remember them.
5. I do not believe that Mr. Ew.L. would be able to accept a secondary role in parenting and I am concerned that, over time, he would undermine the relationship between B.L.L. and his current foster family, which might well lead to a breakdown in placement. B.L.L.'s foster mother has indicated her desire to have access terminated because she feared access might prove too disruptive to B.L.L. and to her family.

From this analysis, the answer is clear; continuing contact with his parents is not in B.L.L.'s best interests.

6: CONCLUSION

In all the circumstances, I find that the least intrusive order I can make consistent with the best interests of B.L.L. is an order for Crown wardship with no access for the purpose of adoption, and I so order.

2. How Children Come to the Attention of Children's Aid Societies and the Courts

EX PARTE D.

5 R.F.L. 119, [1971] 1 O.R. 311 (H.C.)

WRIGHT J.: — This is a painful and difficult matter which first came before me sitting in Chambers in Weekly Court at Toronto on Tuesday, 6th October last, when I was asked to grant an order that a writ of habeas corpus for the child of the applicant should issue, directed to the director of the Children's Aid Society of Metropolitan Toronto. Notice of that application was given to the Attorney General in accordance with The Habeas Corpus Act, R.S.O. 1960, c. 169, s. 1(2).

At that time there was before me an affidavit by the applicant father describing the adoption of the child who was born in January 1967. It appeared that the child had been in his parents' home from 6th May 1969, under the supervision of the respondent's society, was adopted by its parents in December 1969, and remained domiciled in that home and raised as a member of the family until 24th September 1970.

On that day, it appeared from the father's affidavit, two representatives of the Children's Aid Society of Metropolitan Toronto attended at the family home between the hours of 4:00 and 5:00 p.m., stating that they had allegations with regard to acts of violence upon the boy. The father's affidavit said that the respondent's representatives advised him and his wife that they had been instructed to remove the boy from the home for medical examination; that this examination would be completed within one week and ''presented us with a document which they told me I must sign as otherwise they would obtain a court order and there would be consequential unpleasantness''. The father therefore signed what he believed to be a consent to removal for a medical examination. When the parents next saw the boy on 1st October 1970 he had been placed in a foster home and referred to the woman with whom he was then residing as ''his new mommy''. The father's affidavit then refers to the possibility of a hearing in the Juvenile and Family Court of the County of York at the earliest possible date and that this date could not be before 2nd November 1970.

On this material I issued an order on Tuesday, 6th October 1970, and a writ of habeas corpus was directed to the director of the Children's Aid Society of Metropolitan Toronto, returnable before the presiding Judge in Chambers this afternoon, Thursday 8th October 1970. At this time, five affidavits sworn today were filed. Two are by social workers employed by the Children's Aid Society of Metropolitan Toronto, one is by the mother, and two are by close neighbours of the family.

It appears from the affidavits of the social workers that a Mrs. P., apparently at her instance, was interviewed by a social worker some time between 22nd and 24th September 1970, and reported incidents on 22nd September when she saw the child being chased by the mother and abused with what would appear to be heavy and unnecessary violent discipline. Mrs. P. also reported seeing bruises on the child's stomach in spring time, 1970, but, in general, her account deals largely with a number of statements she says were made by the mother with regard to the discipline that the child received in the home. I must say that, if in fact this was the kind of discipline to which the child was subject, it shocks me, but in view of Mrs. P.'s statement that both parents love the child dearly, and the burden of a good deal of evidence before me, it would seem to me that the remedy may not be the removal of the child but the education and restraint of the parents. The social workers also obtained information from two persons in Kitchener who had not observed mistreatment of the child, but who confirmed some of the incidents which Mrs. P. said had been told her by the mother and added one or two similar reported incidents which I find equally shocking. I quote particularly and as an example of other reports a statement attributed to one of the Kitchener witnesses that the mother had told her that the ''child's face was smeared with faeces and the child was locked in the bathroom as a method of toilet training''.

Nothing else appears in the material before a warrant dated 24th September 1970 was secured and the two social workers from the Children's Aid Society visited the family home on 24th September 1970. I find it disturbing that action should have been taken to secure a warrant without those who made the charges pledging their oaths to the facts or without any investigation being made at the home with the parents or by observation of the child. Instead, it would appear that a warrant under s. 21 of The Child Welfare Act, 1965 (Ont.), c. 14, was issued by a Justice of the Peace reciting that, on information laid before him on oath, it appeared to him that there was reasonable cause to suspect that the child in question was in need of protection and authorizing one of the social workers "to search for the child and to enter [the family home], and to take him to and detain him in a place of safety".

With this warrant it appears that the two social workers visited the home, read the complaints to the parents, examined the child, and listened to the parents' comments on the complaints by which some of the statements attributed to the mother were corroborated in some measure. The parents mentioned an adoption application they had made for a little girl so that the boy would not be spoiled, which was pending until they moved into a new home. The report of the social workers then goes on ". . . advised [the parents] of the necessity of readmitting [the child] to our care until an investigation of these serious complaints could be done". A social worker made reference to the warrant and offered initially consent forms which the father agreed to sign. He reported the mother was upset and weepy at this point, and he carried on to say that the parents were reassured that investigation would be done as quickly as possible in the interests of the child and themselves, and said "they were reassured that the child would be returned to their care if we found in our investigations that the child had received satisfactory care from them".

The child was then taken to a hospital where a medical report, dated 24th September 1970, was prepared as to his physical condition. It reads as follows:

> [The child] is a three year old boy who was brought in Emergency for assessment of bruising. The child, himself, is very friendly and playful and outgoing with no problem in terms of behaviour to communicate or to get along with. He seems very friendly and very agreeable.
>
> On physical examination he has no obvious pain. He is well nourished and well developed for his stated age. He talks reasonably well although he does not have clear diction. He has bruises on his skin and a bruise on his right cheek and a bruise on his left side which is slightly tender. On his right elbow area there is a small red bruised area again. He has several very small scratch marks on his back and old abrasion on his right back again. The only finding which is disturbing is the scar on both buttocks which extends in a straight line from right to left, more marked on his left side. This was earlier described as a second or third degree burn which has scarred in. There is no other evidence of burning in any other area including the feet, thighs and hands. It is very unusual to obtain such a bruise by sitting himself into the water. However the remainder of his physical examination is normal.

On 6th October 1970, the day of the habeas corpus application before me, a notice of hearing was signed by the respondent. It was served on the applicant father and his wife on 7th October and gives notice of a hearing to determine "whether or not the above named child is in need of protection" before Little Prov. Ct. J. of the Provincial Court (Family Division) of the County of York on Thursday, 15th October 1970 at the hour of 2:00 o'clock, one week hence.

One of the social workers swears that the child is being detained by the Children's Aid Society *pursuant to the aforesaid warrant* and the consent of the parents pending the hearing in the Family Court on 15th October 1970.

The mother's affidavit now filed deals in detail with and endeavours to explain away some of the charges and in general she supports her husband's previous testimony with regard to the taking of the child and says in part:

> Neither my husband nor I had any idea that we were signing the child over or that he would be placed in a foster home but we understood that we were merely co-operating in settling unfounded and malicious rumours and since we had nothing to fear from the outcome of the medical examination, we submitted to them removing the child from our home . . . Before my husband signed the form presented to us he attempted to reach his solicitor, who was not in his office at that time. Notwithstanding this, we were pressed to sign it under threat of having a court order obtained against us.

The parents in their excitement apparently then lost the form of consent and the only one that they now produce and have subsequently found is an agreement form to which I will refer later.

I am very much impressed by affidavits by the two immediate neighbours which are entirely friendly and favourable to the parents and praise the care and affection which they have shown for their boy. Although they live one next door and the other two doors, they have never seen any treatment of severity or cruelty and speak very highly of the family and the parents' care of their children. . . .

On the evidence before me, I find as a fact that the only legal authority for the actions of the social workers of the Children's Aid Society of Metropolitan Toronto in taking away the child and dealing with him as they did, was the warrant. Under s. 23(1) of The Child Welfare Act, 1965, . . . it is provided that a child detained under such a warrant shall be returned to his parent or brought before a Judge within ten days of his detention. This has not been done. The child has been unlawfully detained since 5th October 1970. I am therefore going to order the return of the child to its parents.

It was argued, and apparently intended, that subs. (1) of s. 23 should not apply because of the written consent. I find as a fact from the evidence before me that the parents did not in fact consent to the action which was taken with regard to the child. They obviously consented to the child leaving the house for the purposes of the medical investigation, but their consent, in my view, did not effectively go further. In any event, it was not a full consent and was secured not frankly and fairly, but by the threat of the execution of the warrant or the securing of a Court order.

I am sorry that this case has come up in the form in which it has because it seems to me to disclose that the procedure of the Children's Aid Society of Metropolitan Toronto, in the circumstances, was inappropriate to the occasion and unlawful. I say I am sorry because it is evident that the Children's Aid Society of Metropolitan Toronto and all the Children's Aid Societies in Ontario perform an essential, basic and widely-supported function in our society. These societies deserve the support of every citizen in their work. I regret that I am moved to be critical on this occasion and to issue an order which in effect undoes their work.

My criticisms are these:

(a) I do not think that it is proper to apply for a warrant, as was done here, on the unsworn testimony of one neighbour supported by some information which was not corroborative of the most important allegation. There are so many motives which can inspire false or inflated or malicious reports in our society that I think the least that can be done is to require that, in normal cases, information be on oath by those professing the truth, so that the power of the law may be exercised against gossip or scandal or malicious invention.

(b) I think that when children are living in clean, comfortable and settled family homes where the conditions are equal to or above the average in the

community, strong evidence is required before a child should be taken out
of such a home.

(c) I think that when charges are made of this kind they should be investigated
on the spot and with the parents before a warrant is secured and not
afterwards.

(d) I think that if a warrant is secured it should be exercised. It should not be
used as an instrument to extort consents or agreements.

(e) I think it very important that parents who have been living a family life
with the child should clearly understand exactly what is involved when
social workers of the Children's Aid Society visit them. It is apparent to
me that there was a serious misunderstanding with regard to the activities
of the social workers. I think the onus is on them to satisfy those who
examine their visit that what they were doing was made perfectly clear to
the persons who are affected by it in the most tender part of their lives.

There is one further matter I would like to deal with and that is the welfare of
the child. Here is a little boy, a little over three and one-half years of age, who has
gone through the process of adoption, who has already been in the hands of the
Children's Aid Society, who has now been removed from the home where I suspect
he was schooling himself to be a member and is now made to embark interim on the
same process again.

If the child were in desperate need, if there had been fresh bruises or serious
medical observations, then, of course, the child's interest is to be taken away from
conditions which produce serious injury and threaten new dangers. Here I do not
find such reasons. It seems to me that the greatest damage that has been done has
been to move the child from its home, and the greatest issue that is raised is not
really the legal rights of which I have spoken, but what is best for the child.

I am not prepared to rule, although I am favourable to the proposition, that the
welfare of the child should take precedence over a right to a favourable decision on
a writ of habeas corpus. In this case I have come to the conclusion that I should give
such a favourable decision even if the return of the child interim to its home is
involved. I have done this for several reasons. First, I do not want to be thought in
any way to approve of the particular procedure in this case. Secondly, it seems to
me to be clear that the legal rights of the parents have been infringed contrary to
law. Thirdly, I would not want the Provincial Court Judge to think that my views
were different from those that I have expressed. Fourthly, I do not at this moment
share the apprehension and fears that have led to these proceedings, although I am
ready to concede that they may well be justified when the full evidence is available
from witnesses under examination.

I am, however, concerned with the immediate future of the child within the
next week and I ask counsel for the applicant father to consider with the parents
whether, in the circumstances, it might not be best to leave the child in its present
custody. I have tried to declare the rights of the parents in this case, as forcefully as
I can, but I do commend to them and to the society the desirability of working out,
if it is possible, something that would avoid the child going backwards and forwards,
if that is to be the ultimate decision of the Provincial Court (Family Division).

. . . What moves me is the abuse of the super-normal powers entrusted to the
Children's Aid Societies solely for the protection of children in need. They are not
provided to make the task of the social worker easier, to be twisted to extort consent,
to enter law-abiding homes and spirit children away, or to cut the bonds of blood or
adoption, but only to protect children against abuse and to cope with the emergencies

and challenges which the sufferings of children present to society and which cannot properly be dealt with unless we sacrifice in particular cases our ancient liberties and much that makes the future of children in our society worthwhile.

I order that the respondent deliver the child to its parents forthwith. Costs of applicant fixed at $75 to be paid by respondent forthwith.

NOTES AND QUESTIONS

1. Sections 21 and 23 of the *Child Welfare Act*, S.O. 1965, c. 14 (referred to in *Ex Parte D.*) were the predecessors of ss. 40 and 46 of the *CFSA*. These sections attempt to address one of the problems identified by the judge in *Ex Parte D.*; namely, that the children's aid society should not apprehend a child without investigating the situation fully and without consideration of alternative means of protecting the child.

Where support services in the home on a voluntary basis have not worked or are not feasible, the Act indicates that the child protection worker should consider the least disruptive measure available to protect the child in the following progression. First, the society could simply apply under s. 40(1) of the *CFSA* for a hearing to determine whether the child is in need of protection. This approach could be used where the society believes that the child can safely be left in his or her home pending the hearing. Second, the child protection worker may be able to obtain a warrant under s. 40(2) to apprehend the child. This alternative is available where the child's need for protection dictates removal from the home, but where there is enough time to obtain a warrant. In order to obtain a warrant to apprehend a child the worker must swear an information before a justice of the peace setting out reasonable and probable grounds to believe that the child is in need of protection and that a less restrictive course of action is either not available or will not protect the child adequately. The most drastic step that a child protection worker could take is apprehension of the child without a warrant under s. 40(7). This procedure may be adopted only if the worker believes, on reasonable and probable grounds, that the child is in need of protection and that there would be a "substantial risk to the child's health or safety" during the time necessary to bring a hearing or obtain a warrant.

If the child is apprehended with or without a warrant the child must be brought before the court within five days unless the child is returned to the home or a temporary care agreement is executed (s. 46(1)). In the interim, the child must be taken to a "place of safety" defined in s. 37(1).

2. Section 40(6) of the *CFSA* permits a protection worker acting under a warrant to enter premises specified in the warrant, by force if necessary, to search for and remove the child. Section 40(11) authorizes similar action where the worker is lawfully apprehending a child without a warrant.

In *M. (H.)* v. *Director of Child Welfare (Prince Edward Island)* (1989), 22 R.F.L. (3d) 399 (P.E.I. T.D.), Campbell J. ruled that s. 15(1) of the *Family and Child Services Act*, R.S.P.E.I. 1974, c. F-2.01 conflicted with s. 8 of the *Charter*. That subsection authorized the Director or a peace officer to "apprehend without warrant and take to a place of safety any child who is believed to be a child in need of protection." In practice, this provision was relied upon by the Director as the authority to enter and search without warrant. Campbell J. suggested (at 407) that a warrantless search and subsequent seizure could only be considered "reasonable" within the meaning of s. 8 if the authorities had reasonable and probable grounds to believe that (a) the child was in need of protection, (b) it was not feasible to obtain prior authorization in the circumstances, and (c) the child would be found in the premises. Since none of these safeguards was present in s. 15(1), it violated s. 8 of the *Charter*. Does the Ontario legislation satisfy the requirements suggested by Campbell J.? See also Thompson, "A Family Law Hitchhiker's Guide to the Charter Galaxy" (1988), 3 C.F.L.Q. 315 and Thompson, "Annotation" (1989), 22 R.F.L. (3d) 400.

M. (H.) should be compared with *Winnipeg South Child and Family Services Agency* v. *P. (M.)* (1989), 20 R.F.L. (3d) 99 (Man. Q.B.) where the court held that provisions of the Manitoba *Child and Family Services Act* which permitted apprehension of a child without a warrant whenever there were reasonable and probable grounds to believe that a child was in need of protection did not conflict with the Charter. See also *Winnipeg Child & Family Services (Central Area)* v. *W. (K.L.)* (1998), 41 R.F.L.

(4th) 291 (Man. C.A.). There, the court held that Part III of the *Child and Family Services Act*, S.M. 1985-86, c. 8, did not conflict with the s. 7 of the *Charter*. It stated (at 293) that "legislation accords with the principles of fundamental justice, even though there is no prior notice or judicial review of the decision to apprehend, so long as the subsequent proceedings are fair."

3. Section 46 of the *CFSA* provides that, where a child is apprehended, one of three options must be selected by the children's aid society as soon as is practicable and, in any event, within five days of detention. What remedy is available to the parent where none of these options is exercised within five days? Would a judge still have jurisdiction to hold a child protection hearing after the five-day limit has elapsed? See and compare *Re G.* (1976), 30 R.F.L. 224 (N.B. C.A.); *Candlish* v. *Saskatchewan (Minister of Social Services)*, 5 R.F.L. (2d) 166, [1978] 3 W.W.R. 515 (Sask. Q.B.); *Warnock* v. *Garrigan* (1978), 6 R.F.L. (2d) 181, 8 B.C.L.R. 26 (C.A.); *Catholic Children's Aid Society of Metropolitan Toronto* v. *S. (I.)* (1987), 12 R.F.L. (3d) 40 (Ont. Dist. Ct.); and *Family & Children's Services of King's County* v. *D. (E.)* (1988), 12 R.F.L. (3d) 104 (N.S. C.A.).

4. Where a child is apprehended, none of the parties will be prepared at the first appearance in court to proceed with a formal hearing to determine whether the child is in need of protection. Indeed, it is quite likely that all concerned will agree to an adjournment of the interim care hearing necessary to deal with the temporary care and custody of the child pending the trial. Sections 51 and 52 of the *CFSA* govern adjournments and interim care arrangements.

In "The Ontario *Child and Family Services Act, 1984*: Maintaining the Balance Between Competing Rights" (1992), 8 C.F.L.Q. 129, W.J. Sammon comments (at 176):

> Because any adjournment of this interim hearing will result, in most cases, in the child remaining in care, it is extremely important for counsel not to adjourn for a long period of time, only long enough to meet with the worker, review the Children's Aid Society's file, speak with important witnesses and prepare affidavit material to be used in the care and custody hearing. Although the Act provides for a hearing within 5 days, it is not unusual for this preliminary hearing to be adjourned for at least [a] 2-to-3 week period during which time the apprehended child will remain in care. This is a serious infringement on both parental and the child's right but it is the price that one has to pay to keep the legal and adversarial model for determining child welfare cases.

Recently, in another context, the Nova Scotia Court of Appeal recognized the possible adverse effects of delay on the child in *D. (B.)* v. *Family & Children's Services of Kings (County)* (1999), 49 R.F.L. (4th) 230 (N.S. C.A.). Justice Cromwell stated (at 233) that the effect of delay in disposition of a case is to be included in determining a child's best interest. The court upheld the trial judge's decision not to permit further exploration at the protection hearing of the possibility of placing two children with their grandparents. This possibility was first raised on the final day of a three-day hearing. Quoting the trial judge, Cromwell J.A. agreed (at 234) that in order to justify the delay, there would have had to have been "some basis in fact to believe that the potential benefit of arresting the process to consider the evidence would outweigh the harm done to the children's best interests by the delay."

5. Before the amendments that came into effect in 2000, s. 51(3) of the *CFSA* (governing temporary custody during adjournments) directed the court to return the child to the care of the person who had charge of the child immediately before the society's intervention unless "the court is satisfied that there are reasonable and probable grounds to believe that there is a substantial risk to the child's health or safety". In *Catholic Children's Aid Society (Metropolitan Toronto)* v. *L. (P.)* (April 18, 1986), Doc. No. North York C1815/86 (Ont. Fam. Ct.), Felstiner Prov. Ct. J. felt compelled to order that the child be returned to the mother pending the protection hearing despite "very grave concerns" about the mother's attitude and parental skills. He commented:

> . . . [T]he burden upon all Children's Aid Societies . . . is almost massive now, in that the risk must be substantial. The government, in that section, has said, in effect, that it is willing to subject infant children, helpless children, to risks which are significant but not substantial. That is the policy of the Province of Ontario and I am bound by that policy.

The decision was upheld on appeal: (June 25, 1986), Hawkings D.C.J. (Ont. Dist. Ct.). See also *Children's Aid Society of Peel (Region)* v. *V. (C.)* (1987), 8 R.F.L. (3d) 15 (Ont. Prov. Ct.).

Judge Felstiner was so upset by this provision in the Act that he wrote to the Chief Judge requesting that he raise the matter with the Deputy Minister of Community and Children's Services: Schmitz, "Thousands of Children Harmed by Protection Statute's Wording?" 6:14 *The Lawyers Weekly* (1 August 1986) 1. However, a number of cases soon emerged indicating that Judge Felstiner had set the threshold too high. In *Family & Children's Services of London & Middlesex* v. *G. (D.)* (1989), 20 R.F.L. (3d) 429, at 431 (Ont. Prov. Ct.) Vogelsang Prov. J. accepted that a "substantial risk" is one that is "real and apparent on the evidence . . . not a risk that is without substance or which is fanciful or speculative". See also *Child & Family Services of Kenora-Patricia* v. *T. (K.)* (1989), 21 R.F.L. (3d) 165 (Ont. Fam. Ct.). Finally, in *C.C.A.S. of Metro. Toronto* v. *D. (A.)* (1994), 1 R.F.L. (4th) 268 (Ont. Gen. Div.) Wilson J. specifically disagreed with Felstiner Prov. J.'s narrow interpretation and concluded (at 277) that "the correct interpretation of 'substantial' in s. 51(3) means actual, real, not illusory or speculative. 'Risk' means a real chance of danger to the health or safety of a child."

As a result of recent amendments to the *CFSA*, s. 51(3) now refers to "reasonable grounds that there is a risk that the child is likely to suffer harm". Whether this test is less onerous depends largely on the interpretation one took of the old "substantial risk" test and the interpretation that will be adopted of the new words. The B.C. C.A. decision in *S. (B.)* v. *British Columbia (Director of Child, Family & Community Service)* (1998), 38 R.F.L. (4th) 138 applying a definition of child in need of protection that required the agency to show that a child "is likely to be physically harmed by the child's parent" may provide some guidance.

6. In *C.C.A.S. of Metro. Toronto* v. *D. (A.)*, above, the court also dealt with s. 51(7) of the *CFSA* which permits the court in temporary protection applications to "admit and act on evidence that the court considers credible and trustworthy". Justice Wilson noted that most of the evidence in a motion for a temporary protection order will necessarily be in affidavit form and accepted (at 278) that the court may act on evidence "which is such that there is about it some apparent real sense of believability and reliability arising from the subject matter of the evidence, the proximity of the witness or author of the document to that subject matter, the nature of the relationship between the witness or author of the document and the person whose statements are recorded or repeated in evidence and the degree to which the evidence is material to the paramount issues in the case."

7. Delay in child protection proceedings is a major concern and usually impacts negatively on the parents' position. See Sammon "The Ontario *Child and Family Services Act, 1984*: Maintaining the Balance Between Competing Rights" (1992), 8 C.F.L.Q. 129, at 172-177 and Thompson, "Case Comment: *C.C.A.S. of Metropolitan Toronto v. M. (C.)*" (1994-1995), 12 C.F.L.Q. 45, at 51-53. Section 52 of the *CFSA* addresses this concern. However, W.J. Sammon reports (at 176-177):

> This provision is more symbolic than real. Although designed to protect parents and families with regard to the timing problems, it does not work in practice. Given the crowded dockets of the Provincial Court (Family Division) and the complex nature of these cases, there are not enough blocks of time available to ensure that these cases are dealt with in a fast and efficient manner. Often many months will pass between the time of interim care and custody order and the final determination and, as indicated, time is the ally of the Children's Aid Society and a parent's enemy. Perhaps counsel will have to be more vocal in their use of this tool by bringing it to the judge's attention during the proceedings and, if necessary, to the government's attention if the purpose of this provision is defeated by the inertia of the system itself.

See also decisions from the Nova Scotia Court of Appeal which indicate that the legislative provisions relating to timing and delays are not mandatory and that time limits may be extended to accommodate the best interests of the child: *Children's Aid Society & Family Services of Colchester (County)* v. *W. (H.)* (1996), 25 R.F.L. (4th) 82, and *Family and Children's Services of Kings County* v. *T. (H.)* (1996), 26 R.F.L. (4th) 13.

8. There are a number of methods employed to avoid an adversarial confrontation in court and as a result only a small fraction of child protection cases are resolved through litigation. After an initial investigation the child welfare agency may conclude that the child can remain in the home and the agency can work with the family on a voluntary basis. Some parents genuinely welcome the support

provided by an agency in dealing with a difficult child. Some observers argue, however, that many parents "agree" to the involvement of a protection agency out of fear that a refusal may result in court action. There is another problem with the agency's role in this situation. After a period of consensual involvement the child protection agency may decide that a child protection hearing is required. Then all of the evidence discovered during the period of consensual involvement can be used in the hearing.

Where a temporary or even permanent alternative to parental care is required, individuals such as grandparents, aunts, uncles or family friends can often provide the short-term or long-term care needed by the child. A parent may voluntarily agree that the child should live with a known and trusted person for a period of time.

A Children's Aid Society may also enter into a formal written agreement with the parents and, in some cases, the child. Section 29 of the *CFSA* governs temporary care agreements while s. 30 deals with special needs agreements. In *Ex Parte D.*, the judge clearly believed that the parents had been pressured into signing the agreement by a society that had not adequately investigated the alleged mistreatment. Section 4 of the CFSA now attempts to ensure that these agreements are entered into voluntarily and with full knowledge of their implications. Note also that s. 29(4) specifies that a society shall not make a temporary care agreement unless the society "is satisfied that no less disruptive course of action, such as care in the child's own home, is appropriate for the child in the circumstances". Finally, there are provisions in s. 29 to ensure that the child does not simply "drift into care" on a permanent basis without judicial scrutiny. The 1999 amendments reduced the period for young children to 12 months and, in s. 29(6.2), imposed a cumulative period scheme.

Regarding the problems raised by voluntary agreements between the society and parents, see Cruikshank, "Court Avoidance in Child Neglect Cases" in Baxter and Eberts, eds., *The Child and the Courts* (1978).

9. In determining what options to pursue, society workers may rely in part on standard assessment tools. The Child Mortality Task Force, established jointly by the Office of the Coroner for the Province of Ontario and the Ontario Association of Children's Aid Societies to study the deaths of children while receiving child welfare services, recommended the development of a comprehensive risk assessment tool for all Children's Aid Societies in Ontario: *Final Report* (July, 1997). This led to the development of a new standardized Risk Assessment Protocol involving three elements: eligibility for child protection services, an assessment of the child's immediate safety, and an assessment of the risk of future harm. After extensive training sessions, the protocol went into effect in 1999.

Parent capacity assessments, as discussed in *Children's Aid Society of Toronto* v. *L. (E.L.)* (reproduced earlier in this chapter) are intended to identify the strengths, weaknesses, and potential of individuals as parents. See generally, Daley, "Parenting Capacity Assessments" (1999), 17 C.F.L.Q. 101.

10. If a child is inappropriately left in parental care by the child protection worker and suffers further abuse, the worker will inevitably feel a sense of guilt and moral responsibility and may even face civil or criminal liability for the failure to protect the child. However, such liability is unlikely to exist except in extreme circumstances. In *M. (M.)* v. *K. (K.)* (1989), 38 B.C.L.R. (2d) 273 (C.A.), the court held that workers or the agency would only be liable if it could be proved that their negligence caused the subsequent injury to the child. In rejecting the claim in this particular case, the court was sympathetic to the fact that workers had a "very onerous" caseload and had to set priorities. In *R.* v. *Leslie* (April 29, 1982), unreported (Ont. Co. Ct.) [digested at 7 W.C.P. 431], the court held that workers were criminally liable for the failure to protect a child who was injured by his mother only if their conduct was "so negligent as to constitute a reckless or callous disregard for the safety" of the child. The charges were dismissed. For a discussion of these cases and the tragic deaths of Vicki Ellis and Kim Ann Popen, see Daly, "In Whose Best Interests? The Child Welfare Agent Before the Court" (1992), 8 C.F.L.Q. 215.

More recently, there was a highly publicized case in Toronto in which a child protection worker was charged with criminal negligence causing death as a result of a mother on her caseload allowing her young infant to starve to death. She was discharged, as was the mother, following a preliminary hearing that took seven months: *R. v. Heikamp* (December 3, 1999), Hogan J. (Ont. C.J.). Justice Hogan indicated that a committal of the worker for trial required some evidence of three elements:

1) a marked and substantial departure from the standard of a reasonable CCAS intake worker in the circumstances;
2) a wanton or reckless disregard for the life and safety of [the child] in the manner in which she handled the case; and
3) that [the social worker's] acts or omissions were a contributing cause of [the child's] death by chronic starvation.

Although mistakes were made by the worker and others, there was no evidence on which a reasonable jury could conclude that the first two elements were established.

Professor Bala reports in "Reforming Ontario's *Child and Family Services Act*: Is the Pendulum Swinging Back Too Far?" (1999), 17 C.F.L.Q. 121, at 141, that there had been an increase in the number of children apprehended and taken into care in Ontario even before the legislative reforms of 1999. He suggests that this was a response to concerns raised by coroners' reports and the media and also to the laying of criminal charges in the Toronto case.

11. Of course, overly aggressive intervention may also lead to criticism and legal proceedings. In *G. (A.) v. Superintendent of Family & Child Services* (1989), 21 R.F.L. (3d) 425 (B.C. C.A.), the social worker made some serious errors in investigating suspected sexual abuse by a father and inappropriately concluded that there were reasonable and probable grounds to believe the children were in need of protection. Subsequent investigation resulted in the return of the children to the parents without court intervention. The parents launched a civil suit but the action was dismissed at trial and this decision was upheld on appeal. The British Columbia Court of Appeal concluded that the plaintiffs had to prove more than errors in judgment. The plaintiffs had to show that there had been a "failure to carry out a duty to consider the matter" or that "the conclusion reached [was] so unreasonable as to show a failure to carry out the duty" (at 437). Here, the worker and the agency had acted because they believed the children to be in need of protection, thereby precluding a finding of bad faith.

Despite s. 15(6) and s. 40(14) of the *CFSA*, civil liability may be imposed in Ontario in extreme cases. An example is *B. (D.) v. Children's Aid Society of Durham (Region)* (1996), 136 D.L.R. (4th) 297 (Ont. C.A.), where both a social worker and Children's Aid Society were found liable to a father for compensatory and punitive damages. During a custody dispute, a mother raised allegations of sexual abuse against her husband, the father. The social worker concluded that the allegations were well-founded and instituted protection proceedings which were consolidated with the custody proceedings. After a number of days of trial, the society decided that there had been a mistake and offered to drop the protection proceeding if the father agreed not to claim costs. He refused and the proceedings continued for many days. In the end, the judge awarded sole custody to the father and ordered costs against the society for the portion of the 51-day trial dealing with child welfare. The father then successfully sued the social worker and society in negligence. The trial judge concluded that the social worker had developed a closed and biased mind and had acted in bad faith. As a result she made numerous errors. The judge described the society's conduct in forging ahead with the proceedings even after it realized that the father was not a danger to the child as unconscionable and akin to malicious prosecution. The Ontario Court of Appeal upheld the finding of liability, although it varied the damage award.

―――――――――

As *Ex parte D.* illustrates, one of the ways in which a Children's Aid Society may become involved is through a third party's report of suspected child abuse or neglect. To encourage reporting, legislation requires those who are aware that a child may be in need of protection to inform the appropriate authorities. In general, prosecutions under reporting laws are rare. Reproduced below is an excerpt from

BALA, "REFORMING ONTARIO'S *CHILD AND FAMILY SERVICES ACT*: IS THE PENDULUM SWINGING BACK TOO FAR?"

(1999) 17 C.F.L.Q. 121, at 165 & 166 (Footnotes omitted.)

(i) Reporting Child Abuse and Neglect: Section 72 [of CFSA]

A number of the recent child abuse deaths in Ontario raised concerns about professionals and community members being slow or unwilling to report suspected abuse to Children's Aid Societies. Bill 6 [amendments enacted in 1999 and most sections proclaimed on March 31, 2000] attempts to address these concerns by increasing reporting requirements. However, the major problems related to under-reporting do not arise out of the legislation. Rather, such problems as poor communication and mistrust between the C.A.S. and other agencies and professionals in their communities, and lack of training and support for community professionals need to be addressed. Bill 6 consolidates the reporting provisions with the relevant definitions of child in need of protection. This is useful for the purposes of public and professional education. However, when the widened reporting provisions are combined with the expanded definitions of child in need of protection, there is the prospect for a substantial increase in the number of cases reported to the C.A.S. Already only about one quarter of cases of abuse and neglect that are reported to the C.A.S. in Ontario are substantiated by the agencies, with another third being suspected, and about 40 per cent of the reports being regarded as unfounded. The prospect is that only a small portion of any increase in reporting will be high-risk cases.

At present, it is only an offence for professionals to fail to report reasonable suspicions of "abuse." Bill 6 extends the mandatory reporting to require professionals to report in any situation where they have "reasonable grounds to suspect" any situation where a child may be in need of protection.

The new section [72(2)] will require a person who has reported abuse to again report if the person later discovers a new basis to suspect abuse or neglect.

The new section [72(3)] provides that a person who has a duty to report shall report directly to the C.A.S. and shall not delegate this duty. While this amendment was presumably made to ensure that the agencies receive the fullest possible information, it may make busy professionals, who often work in teams, feel less inclined to report or delay reporting.

The *Panel of Experts Report* recommended abrogation of solicitor-client privilege, imposing a requirement on lawyers to report based on communication with clients, other than in the context of child protection proceedings. This recommendation would have been very controversial, especially with criminal lawyers who represent those charged with abuse, and is not included in Bill 6. [The solicitor-client privilege is recognized in s. 72(8).]

One of the issues not addressed by Bill 6 is the extent to which the C.A.S. may share information with other agencies and professionals in the community. Some of the under-reporting from community professionals may reflect a sense that information tends to "flow in only one direction," undermining the establishment of co-operative relationships with professionals that might encourage reporting.

NOTES AND QUESTIONS

1. Can a doctor who fails to report abuse be held civilly liable to a child who suffers as a result? See *Landerose* v. *Flood*, 551 P. 2d 389 (Cal., June 30, 1976); *O'Keefe* v. *Osorio* (1984), 27 American

Trial Lawyers Assoc. L.R. 392 (Illinois); and *Brown (Next Friend of)* v. *University of Alberta Hospital* (1997), 145 D.L.R. (4th) 63 (Alta. Q.B.). See also Brown and Truitt, "Civil Liability in Child Abuse Cases" (1979), 54 Chi.-Kent L.R. 753 and Bala "Tort Remedies & The Family Law Practitioner" (1998-99), 16 C.F.L.Q. 423.

2. Can a person who mistakenly reports child abuse to the child welfare authorities be held civilly liable to the parent? See s. 72(7) of the *CFSA*. See also the article by Professor Bala listed in the previous note.

3. The reporting obligations under the *CFSA* apply to everyone. However, only the professionals covered by s. 72(5) who learn the relevant information in the course of their professional or official duties commit an offence by failing to report: s. 72(4). There have been few cases in which persons have been charged with failure to report and most of these have led to acquittals. The cases and other aspects of reporting legislation are reviewed in Bessner, "The Duty to Report Child Abuse" (2000), 17 C.F.L.Q. 277.

4. Section 72(7) and (8) of the *CFSA* differentiate between the solicitor-client relationship and relationships involving other professionals. Is this justifiable?

In "The Duty of Confidentiality and the Child Beating Client: An Ethical Conundrum" (1995), 13 C.F.L.Q. 49, Ken Armstrong argues (at 56) that, although a lawyer may not have a legal obligation to disclose privileged communications under the child protection legislation, "the lawyer has an ethical obligation to disclose any confidential information, privileged or not, that indicates a child might be beaten in the future. Considering the nature of child abuse, a confession of past abuse should qualify". However, Marvin Bernstein suggests in "Towards a New Approach to Child Representation: How Less is More in Child Welfare Proceedings" (1994), 10 C.F.L.Q. 187, at 222-223, that the Ontario Rules of Professional Conduct permit but do not obligate a lawyer to disclose privileged information to prevent a crime. He is commenting specifically on the following situation. A competent child informs his or her lawyer in the context of a protection hearing that he or she has suffered abuse in the home of the custodial parent. The child also instructs the lawyer not to disclose this information to other professionals or to the court. Bernstein writes:

> . . . Even if the communications can be characterized as privileged, in Ontario the Rules of Professional Conduct permit the disclosure of confidential information, provided such disclosure is made in order to prevent a crime, in which case the lawyer must have reasonable grounds for believing that a crime is likely to be committed. It should be noted that the lawyer is not required to divulge the information in such circumstances, and should be careful not to divulge more information than is required. For example, if a child communicates to his or her counsel that there is ongoing abuse in the home, as opposed to historical abuse, the lawyer may breach the privileged relationship in order to prevent the child from being further abused, although the lawyer is not ethically bound to do so. Because the practical effect of a lawyer's disclosure in such circumstances will be to seriously impair the trust relationship with the child/client, it is suggested that it is preferable that the lawyer advise the child to disclose the information relating to abuse directly to the child protection professionals.

For further reading, see Stuart, "Child Abuse Reporting: A Challenge to Attorney-Client Confidentiality" (1987), 1 Georgetown J. of Legal Ethics 243 and Moesteller, "Child Abuse Reporting Laws and Attorney-Client Confidences: The Reality and the Specter of Lawyer as Informant" (1992), 42 Duke L.J. 203.

Recently, the Supreme Court of Canada confirmed that the solicitor-client privilege is not absolute. In *Smith* v. *Jones* (1999), 169 D.L.R. (4th) 385, Cory J. stated that in some situations, the importance of public safety may allow a lawyer to disclose information received during the solicitor-client relationship. Three factors must be considered: (i) is there a clear risk to an identifiable person or group of persons? (ii) is there a risk of serious bodily harm or death? (iii) is the danger imminent?

5. Section 40(4) of the *CFSA* provides that a person who reports the suspected child abuse or neglect to the society may apply to the court in an attempt to initiate a child protection hearing where

the society refuses to apprehend the child or to initiate the hearing itself. What is the purpose of this provision?

6. A number of Canadian provinces have formal child abuse registers. In these jurisdictions, child protection agencies are required to report cases of abuse to the centralized register. In theory, these registers may serve a number of functions:

(i) Detection and Identification. Parents who abuse their children may attempt to avoid detection by taking children to different hospitals or different doctors for treatment each time the abuse results in the need for medical attention. A check of the centralized register may confirm a suspicion of abuse.

(ii) Research. A register may be a valuable research tool, both for academic research into the nature, causes and treatment of abuse and for authorities monitoring child abuse and programs in a particular jurisdiction.

(iii) Case Management. Information gleaned from the register may cause an agency to emphasize a particular type of case because more serious abuse in the future may be predicted.

(iv) Screening. A register might be used to screen foster and adoptive parents, employees with responsibility for children, and those who require a licence to operate a facility such as a day-care centre.

The Ontario Child Abuse Register (see s. 75 and 76 of the *CFSA*) was the subject of a thorough review by an interdisciplinary study group headed by Professor Bala in 1987. In *Review of the Ontario Child Abuse Register*, the group concluded (at VIII):

The Register has very limited utility for identification and its deterrent effect is questionable. It is not effectively used for research or case management. There is substantial variability in the application of criteria for registration and the entire process raises very serious civil liberties concerns. The current Register has insufficient safeguards to be used for screening. *The Register system, in its present form, should be discontinued.*

Disbandonment of any form of register may be considered a viable option by some, but a significantly restructured register can play an important role in combating child abuse without compromising the rights of individuals identified as abusers.

Section 27 (not proclaimed into effect at the time of writing) of the *Child and Family Services Amendment Act, 1999* repealed the provisions setting up the Ontario Child Abuse Registry. In its place, the Ontario government and the Ontario Association of Children's Aid Societies are developing and implementing, as recommended by the Ontario Child Mortality Task Force, a province-wide database which will be accessible to all CAS's in Ontario and their workers. The purpose is to facilitate better tracking of high risk families and alert the system to past CAS involvement. In theory, this system will be easier to access than the Child Abuse Registry and provide more information to child protection workers.

Manitoba's legislation, which allows employers whose employees will be responsible for the care of children to access the register to screen job applicants, was altered to provide significant safeguards for individuals identified as abusers following the decision in *S. (H.S.)* v. *Director of Child & Family Services (Manitoba)* (1987), 8 R.F.L. (3d) 430 (Man. Q.B.). In that case, the court held that the existing legislation, which did not provide for notice in all cases and did not contain any procedure for removal of a registrant's name, violated s. 7 of the *Charter*. The legislation now provides for notice and the possibility of review by a registry review committee. At the hearing before this committee "the agency has the burden of proof on a balance of probabilities". Its decision, which must be accompanied by written reasons, can be appealed to the courts. The reformed provisions have withstood constitutional challenge: *B. (K.)* v. *Winnipeg Child & Family Services* (1992), 90 D.L.R. (4th) 630 (Man. Q.B.).

3. The Protection Hearing

(1) NOTICE

Those affected by the court proceeding must be properly notified of the time, place and nature of the proceedings. Examine s. 39 of the *CFSA* to determine who is entitled to participate in and receive notice of the hearing. Note that where a child is an Indian or native person, a representative chosen by the child's band or native community is a party to the proceeding.

The legislative history of the definition of "parent" in s. 37(1) indicates that the Legislature clearly believed it was inappropriate to require notice to be given to all fathers. Under the *Child Welfare Act*, S.O. 1978, c. 85, the courts held that all fathers were entitled to notice. See, for example, *Children's Aid Society of Toronto (Municipality) v. C.* (1979), 11 R.F.L. (2d) 100, 25 O.R. (2d) 234 (Prov. Ct.) where the court held that a father who was unaware of the birth of his son some six years before the hearing was entitled to notice of the protection hearing. Weisman Prov. J. commented as follows (at 103):

> ... I come to this conclusion reluctantly but can see no alternative in view of the language used in the Act. . . .
>
> Fortunately, some of the problems that result can be overcome. The Act and the rules provide relief where difficulties are encountered in serving a parent with notice of a protection hearing, or with notice of an application to dispense with a consent to adoption.

The Legislature responded by amending the Act. A new definition of "parent" was enacted by S.O. 1979, c. 98, s. 2(2). In *Catholic Children's Aid Society of Essex (County) v. W. (K.)* (1983), 37 R.F.L. (2d) 322, 44 O.R. (2d) 283 (Co. Ct.) the court held that the new definition was exhaustive. The court found that the biological father of the child in that case was not a "parent" for the purpose of a child protection hearing and, therefore, was not entitled to notice. This new definition was retained in the *CFSA* in 1984.

An obvious question is whether this differential treatment of fathers and mothers violates s. 15 of the *Charter*. A similar issue arises in the context of adoption proceedings where a number of cases have considered the *Charter*. In *M. (N.) v. Superintendent of Family & Child Services (British Columbia)* (1986), 10 B.C.L.R. (2d) 234 (S.C.), the court held that a paragraph of British Columbia's *Adoption Act* was unconstitutional because it discriminated on the basis of sex and marital status. The paragraph provided that parental consent was generally required before the court could make an adoption order, but that where the child was born out of wedlock only the mother needed to consent. The court was not persuaded that this blanket exclusion of unmarried fathers was justified because it permitted timely adoption of unwanted children where the natural father was unknown or could not be found. The court noted that in some cases it might be as difficult to locate a natural father or natural mother whose marriage had been terminated by divorce and that the Act already provided mechanisms for dealing with situations where the natural father could not be located.

Contrast *S. (C.E.) v. Children's Aid Society of Metropolitan Toronto* (1988), 49 D.L.R. (4th) 469 (Ont. Prov. Ct.) where the Divisional Court overturned the decision of Nevins Prov. J. and rejected a s. 15 challenge to the Ontario adoption consent provisions. The court noted that s. 131(1) of the *CFSA* (now s. 137(1), which provides a definition of "parent" similar to that in s. 37(1)) cast a fairly wide net for consent purposes and that only a "casual fornicator" who impregnated a woman and demonstrated no sense of responsibility for the natural consequences was ex-cluded. The case suggests that serious legislative attempts to address the unmarried father's position may receive deferential treatment by the courts. Professor Thompson comments in "A Family Law Hitchhiker's Guide to the Charter Galaxy" (1988), 3 C.F.L.Q. 315 at 343-344: "Much as the Divisional Court may have been correct in their [*sic*] result, that does not excuse a judgment that reads like a guest editorial in the Toronto Sun, typified by the Court's labelling of the excluded fathers as 'casual fornicators'."

Regarding the method of giving notice and what constitutes reasonable attempts to serve notice of a protection hearing, see *Re Pearson*, 10 R.F.L. 234, [1973] 4 W.W.R. 274 (B.C. S.C.).

Where the court is satisfied that the time required to provide notice might endanger the child's health or safety, the court may dispense with notice to a person: s. 39(7) of the *CFSA*. If such a dispensation is granted, the court cannot make a Crown wardship order or a temporary wardship order exceeding thirty days: s. 57(7).

Dispensation with notice is most often used to deal with medical emergencies, especially where a parent refuses to consent to certain medical treatment. Even in this situation, although the hearing may take place with extremely short notice, some effort must be made to hold a hearing and permit the parents to attend and participate in whatever hearing is held. See *Forsyth* v. *Children's Aid Society of Kingston (City)*, [1963] 1 O.R. 49, 35 D.L.R. (2d) 690 (H.C.). Indeed, the *CFSA* indicates that the protecting agency can only authorize medical treatment after a hearing and court order. Although a child protection worker may authorize a medical examination of the child upon apprehension (s. 40(9)), s. 62 grants power to the child protection agency to consent to and authorize medical treatment for the child only after a court has found the child to be in need of protection and has made a wardship order. In *Re L. (C.P.)* (1988), 70 Nfld. & P.E.I.R. 287 (Nfld. U.F.C.), the court held that legislation that permitted a child protection agency to authorize medical treatment without a court order as soon as the child was apprehended violated s. 7 of the Charter. The procedures provided by the *CFSA* for dealing with a medical emergency withstood a Charter challenge in *B. (R.)* v. *C.A.S. of Metropolitan Toronto* (1995), 9 R.F.L. (4th) 157 (S.C.C.) (reproduced later in this chapter). Mr. Justice La Forest summarized the procedural rights of the parents as follows (at 214):

> In sum, the appellants were entitled to such notice, access to information, and rights of represen-tation as may be fair and reasonable having regard to the nature of the proceedings and the urgency with which they must be carried out.

(2) NATURE OF THE HEARING

In a child protection hearing there are essentially two basic issues. First, the court must determine whether the child is in need of protection as defined in s. 37(2) of the *CFSA* and whether a court order is necessary to protect the child in the future (see s. 57(1)). Essentially, the court is required to decide if any state intrusion into the life of the child and family is warranted. Second, where the court concludes that a court order is necessary, the court must choose which of the orders under s. 57 would be in the child's best interests. These two issues are conceptually distinct. Indeed, s. 50(2) of the Act provides that "evidence relating only to the disposition of the matter shall not be admitted before the court has determined that the child is in need of protection". It is only in resolving the second issue that the statute specifically mandates the use of the best interests of the child test. Section 37(3) provides a non-exhaustive list of factors that the court may consider at this stage (see also s. 37(4)).

In *D. v. Children's Aid Society of Kent (County)*, below, the court stressed the need to preserve the distinction between the two issues raised in a child protection hearing, even if the children's aid society is seeking an order that would transfer custody from one parent to the other subject to the supervision of the society. A brief excerpt from the reasons for judgment follows.

D. v. CHILDREN'S AID SOCIETY OF KENT (COUNTY)

(1980), 18 R.F.L. (2d) 223 (Ont. Co. Ct.)

CLEMENTS CO. CT. J. (orally): — . . . At this point I should interject, although it will be made clear from findings later on, that at the time of the apprehension of the children and until the present time the natural mother, the appellant herein, and the natural father have lived separate and apart. The power given to the children's aid society under the Act is to impose an agency of the government on behalf of the society into the home when necessary. The contest, it must be remembered, is between the society and the natural parents in most instances. This is not a custody dispute between the parents, although the child's welfare is every bit as important as it always is in dealing with children, but rather an issue as to whether the conditions, in the home with the parent or the person in whose charge the children were, are such as to warrant the intervention of the state for the protection of the child. In *Re Mugford*, [1970] S.C.R. 261 (sub nom. *Children's Aid Society of Ottawa v. Mugford*, [1970] 1 O.R. 610n, 9 D.L.R. (3d) 123n, affirming [1970] 1 O.R. 601 at 607, 9 D.L.R. (3d) 113 where Schroeder J.A. of the Ontario Court of Appeal said: "The child's welfare lies first in the security of the home of its natural parents, and it is only when that protection cannot be furnished, with or without fault of the parents, that the State is justified in assuming duties of parenthood to the exclusion of the natural parents."

There is a civil onus on the children's aid society on the application of this nature but not the usual onus as stated in *Re Chrysler* (1978), 5 R.F.L. (2d) 50 at 58 (Ont. Prov. Ct.): "The authorities are clear that although the onus is of a civil nature where the contest over custody is between the mother and a children's aid society the onus is still very demanding and it must be clearly demonstrated that the child's best interests are served by removing her from the natural parent and placing her into the custody of the state in the agency of the children's aid society."

Reference was made to *Children's Aid Society of Kingston v. Reeves* (1975), 23 R.F.L. 391 (Ont. Prov. Ct.), and *Caldwell v. Children's Aid Society of Metropolitan Toronto* (1976), 27 R.F.L. 259 (Ont. Prov. Ct.), as well as *Re Brown* (1975), 9 O.R. (2d) 185, 21 R.F.L. 315 (Co. Ct.).

The standard of proof, therefore, is not that of the balance of probabilities per se; nor is there a test akin to the onus in criminal matters. No magic formula need be devised other than the heavy onus on the director of the children's aid society to satisfy the court the allegations necessary to intervene are met and clearly met without reference or deference to the second issue after a finding is made, i.e., the finding that the child is in need of protection, as to the appropriate placement under s. 30 of the Act. As has been said by the court in *Re Brown*, supra [at p. 189]: "Society's interference in the natural family is only justified when the level of care of the child falls below that which no child in this country should be subjected to." And in fact the Divisional Court, speaking through Grange J. in *Hansen* v. *Children's Aid Society of Hamilton-Wentworth* (1976), 27 R.F.L. 289, stated [at p. 292]:

> The learned trial judge stated several times in the course of the hearing that his only concern was the welfare of the child and in all matters of custody and placement of children the courts have recognized that that is the paramount consideration. I am not sure that that is a proper test in matters of this nature (see *Re Sarty* (1974), 15 N.S.R. (2d) 93, 19 R.F.L. 315) because by that test more children than I care to contemplate would be taken from their parents and placed in foster homes.

The following case suggests that, under the Nova Scotia legislation at least, the best interests of the child are to be considered at every stage of the protection hearing. Is this desirable? Is there any danger in this approach? Is it perhaps inevitable? Compare the wording of s. 1(a) of the *CFSA* with that of s. 2(2) of the *Children and Family Services Act*, S.N.S. 1990, c. 5, considered in the Nova Scotia case.

The case also raises issues relating to the meaning of the statutory term "in need of protection", which is the focus of the next section of this chapter.

NOVA SCOTIA (MINISTER OF COMMUNITY SERVICES) v. M. (B.)

(1998), 42 R.F.L. (4th) 208 (N.S. C.A.)

PUGSLEY, J.A. (for the court): The Minister of Community Services (the Agency) appeals from a decision and order of Judge Robert White of the Family Court, dismissing the Agency's application for a finding that the six children of the respondents, BM and LM, were children in need of protective services as defined by s. 22(2)(a) and (b) of the *Children and Family Services Act* . . . .

The grounds of appeal may be summarized as follows: Judge White failed to properly determine, and apply, the burden imposed on the Agency under the *Act*, and made a palpable and overriding error in his assessment of the facts disregarding material evidence.

Background

The children, EM (male, DOB January 8, 1986), SM (female, DOB May 15, 1988), JM (male, DOB January 1, 1990), RM (female, DOB December 31, 1992), GM (female, DOB October 16, 1994), and YM (female, DOB May 22, 1996) are the biological children of the respondents.

The respondents and their six children live in rural Nova Scotia and occupy a mobile home (64' by 14') located on a large tract of land. BM is apparently in his late 30's and his wife, LM, was 34 at the time of the hearing in December, 1997.

In mid-September, 1997, a confidential informant contacted the RCMP alleging that the respondent BM:

> * Dominated his wife, and children, and had openly stated that he did not believe the law in regard to discipline of children and that he would discipline his children as he saw fit; and
> * Had been witnessed by the confidential informant spanking his children and hitting them with a stick, leaving observable bruises.

It was further alleged that SM disclosed that her father had given her the bruise observed. Finally, concerns were raised that the children were schooled at home, did not socialize with other children, and that their only outing "would be to church".

Acting upon the referral, protection workers employed by the Agency attended at the mobile home on September 16, 1997. As the respondents would not permit the children to be interviewed by the protection workers, an *ex parte* application was made on behalf of the Agency for an investigative order pursuant to s. 26(2) of the *Act*.

The order was granted on September 18 authorizing the Agency, among other things, to enter the respondents' mobile home, conduct a physical examination of the children, remove the children for a medical examination if one was deemed reasonably necessary, and further to remove the children and attend with them at the offices of the Agency, or the RCMP in Antigonish to interview them with respect to the allegations made against their parents. The order further provided for the interview to be video taped.

The children were accordingly taken to the RCMP detachment in Antigonish and the three oldest, EM (eleven years, nine months), SM (nine and a half), and JM (six years, nine months), all provided individual video-taped statements, collectively lasting approximately two hours.

As a result of the interviews, the Agency sought, and subsequently obtained, certain assurances from the respondents, who by then had obtained legal advice, that they would not use corporal punishment while the Agency brought the matter before the Court.

The Agency initiated an application on September 25 for an order that the children were in need of protection. The interim hearing was resolved by a "without prejudice" consent order entered into by counsel for both parties.

During the course of the protection hearing heard in mid-December, 1997, the video-taped interviews of EM, SM and JM were introduced as exhibits. *Viva voce* evidence, in addition, was called on behalf of the Agency and the respondents. SM was the only child who gave *viva voce* evidence at trial. Judge White reserved decision after submissions were advanced on December 15, and subsequently released a written decision on December 23 dismissing the Agency's application. He declined to award costs, noting that there was no *mala fides* exhibited in the conduct of the Agency, and further concluded that none of the agents of the Agency acted in an excessive, or officious, manner.

Scope of Inquiry at the Protection Hearing

The *Act* provides a three-stage process — a process that may involve an interim hearing, a protection hearing, and finally, a disposition hearing.

The first stage requires the Agency, within five days of an application being made to determine whether a child is in need of protective services, to bring the matter before the Court for an interim hearing (s.39(1)).

At the end of the interim hearing, the Court is given a wide discretion to take steps for the protection of the child if the child is found to be in need of protection. The Court is obliged to dismiss the Agency's application, however, if it finds that there are no reasonable and probable grounds to believe the child is in need of protective services (s.39(2)).

In this case, the only evidence tendered before Judge White at the interim hearing was by way of affidavit deposed by Cathy Cashen, a protection worker employed by the Agency. No *viva voce* evidence was called. A "without prejudice" order, consented to by counsel for the parties, was issued declaring that there were reasonable and probable grounds to believe the children were in need of protective services. The children were permitted to remain in the care and custody of the respondents, subject to the supervision of the Agency.

The *Act* then provides for a second hearing, the protection hearing, which must be held not later than 90 days after the date of the application. If, as was determined in this case, the Court finds after the protection hearing that a child is not in need of protective services, the Court is obliged to dismiss the application brought by the Agency (s.40(5)).

If the Court determines at the conclusion of the protection hearing that the child is in need of protective services, the Court must convene a disposition hearing within 90 days. At the conclusion of the disposition hearing the Court has a number of options under s.42, including the option to ''dismiss the matter''.

All of the options available under s. 42 are to be made, however, in ''a child's best interests''. This phrase does not appear in the sections of the *Act* relating to the interim hearing, or the protection hearing.

A preliminary question is whether the Court, at a protection hearing, should consider the best interests of the children or whether the inquiry should be limited to the narrow question of whether the Agency has established that the children were in need of protective services pursuant to s. 22.

Section 76 of the former *Children's Services Act*, c. 8, S.N.S. (1976), provided that: ''In an action under this Act, the court shall apply the principle that the welfare of the child is the paramount consideration.''

Commenting on this provision, Jones, J.A., on behalf of this Court, in *Children's Aid Society of Halifax (City)* v. *Lake* (1981), 45 N.S.R. (2d) 361 (N.S. C.A.) stated at 375:

> An order cannot be made under the *Children's Services Act* on the sole ground that it is in the best interests of the child to do so without making a determination that the child is in need of protection. If a judge cannot make a finding that the child is in need of protection, he must dismiss the case.

In place of s. 76 of the former *Children's Services Act*, s. 2 (2) of the *Act* provides: ''In all proceedings and matters pursuant to this Act, the paramount consideration is the best interests of the child.''

The change of the wording ensures that the best interests of the child is an issue to be considered at every proceeding, and matter, including the protection hearing.

While some of Judge White's observations arguably related to this issue, unfortunately he failed to review the evidence or make any findings, as required by the *Act*, respecting the critical issue before him - namely, whether the Agency established that the children were in need of protective services pursuant to s. 22.

The Respondents' Disciplinary Beliefs

The respondents were married in June of 1984. The respondent BM is a manufacturer's representative, as well as a self-employed woodsman. The respondent LM, in addition to caring for and looking after the education of all of the children, sells her own crafts and baking products. She teaches the children with texts approved by the local Board of Education. She believes the public schools: ''. . . teach a lot of humanism and come from an atheist situation, an evolutionist and I would rather teach them from a theistic point of view and I prefer a creationist point of view . . .''.

Both respondents accept the Bible as literal truth ''inspired by God''. The respondents are not members of any church, but have found fellowship in the Southeastern Mennonite Conference.

The respondents testified that their disciplinary methods respecting the children are determined from their understanding of the Bible. It is therefore relevant to consider these beliefs.

The respondent BM testified that he believes: "... in the depravity of man. That man was born in original sin. ... even for that matter that a little child is born in sin."

BM states that he is commanded by the Bible to follow its guidelines which instruct children to be obedient to their parents "as foolishness is bound up in the heart of a child".

He acknowledges that there are many methods of discipline, but if a child is wilfully disobedient to his parents, then it is appropriate for that child to be chastised.

He explained chastisement as: "... where you would use ... ah ... the rod on the child, you would basically take the rod in your hand ... it's a stick and you would ... strike the child with the rod on the, ah, basically on the buttock area."

The purpose of chastisement, BM explained, is: "... for the moral moulding the character of the child and also to relieve the child of the guilt that he would have developed by disobeying you."

The respondent BM testified that his method of chastisement was "fairly constant. I don't vary it ... it's a very relaxed thing"; that his objective was to use the rod "maybe three times" as there was "no reason to hit them more". BM employed two "rods" (i.e. birch sticks) for discipline - the larger for the older children was about 18 inches long, tapering in width from three-eighths of an inch to one-half inch. The smaller, approximately 12 inches long, three-eighths inches wide, was made of "much lighter wood" and was usually used for the younger children.

The evidence discloses that the rod was used only on a child who was clothed, and on the child's buttocks. In the case of an infant, the rod was applied to the diaper.

The respondent BM was responsible for approximately 90 per cent of the chastisement in the home; discipline carried out by the respondent LM occurred only when BM was absent.

While the respondent BM acknowledged that a child being chastised would cry because "it would hurt ... there shouldn't be any physical harm to the child".

The initial pain would last "maybe a minute or two minutes ... I can't imagine there being much more pain beyond that". He stressed he did not want to hurt the child and was "very conscious ... of how much pain I'd be causing".

The respondent LM stressed that chastisement was only a "very minor area of the discipline in our home".

The respondent BM admitted using the rod to hit YM when she was approximately 15 months old. He testified that he gave her "maybe two very, very light swats on the diaper ... possibly for biting".

Chastisement was carried out usually in private to preserve "the child's dignity".

Findings of the Trial Judge

Section 22(2) of the *Act* provides:

A child is in need of protective services where

(a) the child has suffered physical harm, inflicted by a parent or guardian of the child or caused by the failure of a parent or guardian to supervise and protect the child adequately;

(b) there is a substantial risk that the child will suffer physical harm inflicted or caused as described in clause (a);

The trial judge made some specific findings: . . .

* . . . it does appear that the frequency with which punishment is administered, the reasons for such punishment for trivial incidents such as some sibling rivalry and some sibling squabbling, seems excessive when other methods to command obedience would be equally as practical and finally, the age of some of the children being disciplined appears to offend common sense as to their ability to appreciate the reason for the corporal punishment.

Having said this, on the one hand, I share the concerns of the child protection authorities over not only the issues related to the corporal punishment, but also on issues related to the emotional or psychological and social development of the children. *Notwithstanding these concerns, based upon the balance of probabilities, I am not persuaded that there is sufficient evidence before the court to make an order directing protective services.* (emphasis added)

. . . Unfortunately, the trial judge did not analyze the evidence in light of the issue raised in s. 22, nor did he make any specific findings respecting that evidence. This failure constituted a failure to exercise jurisdiction amounting to an error of law (*Lowe* v. *Tramble* (1980), 42 N.S.R. (2d) 481 (T.D.)).

It is necessary, therefore, to review the evidence to determine whether the Agency, at the protection hearing, met the burden of proof imposed on it, namely to establish on the balance of probabilities that the children, or one or more of them, were in need of protective services.

It is helpful in conducting this review, to consider the evidence arising out of s. 22(2)(a) separately from that relevant to s. 22(2)(b).

Section 22(2)(a)

The term ''physical harm'' as it appears in the section is not defined in the *Act*.

Both counsel direct our attention, however, to Professor E. A. Rollie Thompson's comments (see *The Annotated Children and Family Services Act*, August, 1991), at p. 41:

(1) *Degree of harm* Clause (a) does not on its face distinguish between degrees of physical harm. It does not require ''serious'' or ''substantial and observable'' harm. Does this mean that any physical harm, however slight, can give rise to intervention? Faced with the potential scope of such a wide definition, some courts have drawn back and introduced some threshold notion of degree of harm. . . . . .

It is submitted that some guidance may be drawn from a definition of ''bodily harm'' found in s.267 of the *Criminal Code* which covers ''any hurt or injury to the complainant that interferes with the health or comfort of the complainant and that is more than merely transient or trifling in nature''. A test of this kind would serve to ensure the screening-out of trivial cases, *while maintaining a low enough threshold to capture cases where the child has experienced observable bruising.* (emphasis added)

The Agency submits that there are three specific examples disclosed in the evidence where the children of the respondents experienced ''observable bruising'' amounting to physical harm from the actions of their father — a bruise on SM's buttocks, a bruise on JM's lower back, and a bruise suffered by RM. [The court concluded that the agency failed to establish that the first two bruises were caused by ''chastisement''. The father acknowledged that RM had suffered a bruise as a result of a spanking in the winter of 1997, but that it had not affected her and had disappeared in two days.]

... I conclude that in these circumstances, one observable bruise on a child who is particularly susceptible to bruising, is not sufficient to satisfy the burden imposed under s. 22(2)(a) that the child has suffered physical harm.

I would not disturb the conclusion of the trial judge that there was not sufficient evidence before the Court to make an order directing protective services under s. 22(2)(a).

Section 22(2)(b)

The term "substantial risk" that appears in this section is defined in s. 22(1) as meaning:

> ... a real chance of danger that is apparent on the evidence.

The Agency submits that Judge White imposed a heavier burden on the Agency than that imposed under the *Act*, when he stated:

> As well, I am cognizant of the current status of the law with respect to the rights of parents to raise their children in accordance with their religious beliefs. This is subject however, to the obligation of the state to intervene when there is a *pressing and substantial risk* to the child or children. More especially in the case law related to the charges under s. 43 of the Criminal Code of Canada, courts have to be aware as to whether there is *real risk of danger* to the child, that the age and sex of the child should be considered, that the effects flowing from the punishment, and the force does not exceed what is reasonable in the circumstances. It does appear that there are cases which state that the child must be capable of appreciating the reason for the correction. The fact that there is some bruising which is not extensive is not a ground for a criminal conviction. (emphasis added)

Section 22(2)(b) of the *Act* does not require the Agency to establish a "*pressing and substantial risk*" that a child will suffer physical harm. Rather, the burden is to establish that there is a "substantial risk". I conclude that the trial judge erred in imposing on the Agency a burden of adducing evidence greater than that imposed under s. 22(2)(b).

I do not agree with the Agency's submission that there is a significant difference between the term "a real risk of danger" as used by the trial judge, and a "real chance of danger" as used in s. 22(1) of the *Act*.

I further conclude, however, that the trial judge erred to the extent that he considered s. 43 of the *Criminal Code*, and cases decided thereunder, to be relevant to the issues in this case.

Section 43 of the *Criminal Code* provides: "Every schoolteacher, parent or person standing in the place of a parent is justified in using force by way of correction toward a pupil or child, as the case may be, who is under his care, if the force does not exceed what is reasonable in the circumstances."

The "reasonable force" exception in s.43 does not appear in the *Act*. A parent may not be criminally responsible for using force against a child, yet the child nevertheless may be in need of protective services under s. 22. . . .

I do not consider that the failure of the Agency to establish that the children, or one or more of them, have suffered physical harm under s. 22(2)(a) of the *Act* is determinative of the issue raised under s.22(2)(b). (*Children's Aid Society of Halifax (City)* v. *Lake* (1981), 45 N.S.R. (2d) 361 (C.A.)).

The trial judge noted that: "There was no medical evidence upon which the court could make a finding requiring an order for protective services."

I do not take this comment as anything more than an observation on the evidence, or lack of evidence, that was before him. While medical evidence might well assist the Agency to establish a child is in need of protective services, it is not essential for the Agency to adduce evidence of this kind in order to satisfy the burden imposed under s. 22(2)(a) or (b).

In view of the failure of the trial judge to make any specific findings, or analysis, of the evidence on this issue, the questions for this Court are whether the trial judge has erred, and if so, whether the Agency has met the burden to establish that there is a real chance of danger that the children, or one or more of them, will suffer physical harm inflicted by the respondents.

I consider the evidence on the following issues to be of particular significance in this case:

- the reasons for chastisement;
- the frequency of chastisement;
- the number of strokes employed by the respondents;
- the age of the children when chastisement commenced;
- the granting of authority to SM to discipline her younger siblings;
- the respondents' belief that incidental bruising should not be a concern.

(1) Reasons for Chastisement

. . . I conclude that chastisement often resulted from fairly minor breaches of the rules of the household.

(2) Frequency of Chastisement

EM advised that he was receiving "much less spankings than I use to . . . like maybe, once or twice a month, you know."

SM, as well, confirmed that she:

. . . hardly ever [is spanked] anymore. Usually it's like - once every two (2) months. . . . I used to get spanked a lot because I would hit [JM] on the head or bang a lot on the back, but I don't do that any more. . . . Cause I've learned. . . . Because they spanked me consistently every time I did it.

SM noticed the bruise on her buttock in May of 1997.

The frequency of chastisement, particularly with respect to JM [about twice a week], is very troubling. . . .

(3) The Number of Strokes Employed by the Respondents

The respondent BM testified that his goal was to: "Use three strokes and three strokes is usually . . . usually enough to bring a child under control."

Although he testified he did not vary his practice, he admitted that EM would sometimes receive "maybe 10" strokes at one chastisement. . . .

[Although his interview evidence was contradictory, SM indicated that he had once counted 35 strokes. The court concluded:] If a child, according to the respondent BM, can usually be brought "under control" when he administers three strokes of the rod, what possible justification could there be for 10 or 15, or as many as 35 strokes as the children indicated?

(4) The Age of the Children When Chastisement Commenced

The respondent BM testified that JM, a "quiet boy" was first chastised when about two and a half; GM, age two and over; RM, age two years; and YM at 15 months.

BM attempted to justify the chastisement of YM, notwithstanding her age, for: ". . . something . . . very serious such as biting . . . if a child is born in sin, certainly some of that sin is going to come out and the child is going to require correction."
. . .

Both parents expressed the view that the younger children require more chastisement because they disobey more often.

(5) The Granting of Authority to SM to Discipline her Younger Siblings

SM advised that she used the stick to discipline her two younger sisters, GM and RM. This activity was carried out when her parents were not present to discipline themselves.

. . . The respondent LM agreed under cross-examination that she had no control over the amount of force used in that situation but she was not prepared to rule out similar action in the future.

(6) The Respondents' Belief that Incidental Bruising should not be a Concern:

The respondent BM was asked about the bruise that was observable on RM's buttocks two days after she was chastised with a rod. She was four years of age at the time.

Q. So despite your good intentions, you marked your child, you bruised your child with a rod, did you, Mr. [BM]?

A. I corrected my child, in a way I believe I was supposed to. Ah, and *she was, ah, very, ah, defiant. And, ah, and it took that . . .*

Q. Are you telling me that there is something in the Bible that you - say it's okay to mark your child with a rod?

A. Yes sir . . . (emphasis added)

. . . The evidence of the disciplinary methods exacted by the respondents is extremely disturbing. Children, at an increasingly younger age, and at more frequent intervals, are disciplined with a rod for minor misconduct which the respondents characterize as disobedience. Although both respondents testified that they take care to ensure the children are not harmed, incidental bruising, in the words of the respondent, BM, "should not be a concern" when the purpose is to bring a child under control to relieve him or her of a "guilty conscience of disobedience".

The use of the rod for discipline purposes seems to be all pervasive. It occurred frequently, both in and outside the house, when the children were taken to visit relatives, and also occurred both in, and outside, the van used for transportation.

The respondents were not prepared, at least at the time of the protection hearing in December, 1997, to moderate their disciplinary methods as they believe that they are carrying out God's will as revealed to them in the Bible.

I am mindful that the Agency employees testified the children: ''. . . seemed comfortable at home and happy . . . engaged in conversation very naturally . . . very forthcoming, pleasant . . . didn't seem fearful . . . seemed happy and content and interacted freely with their parents.''

I have also noted the evidence of Dr. Sadler who examined the children approximately three times a year for their physical needs. She testified that they always were lively, and bright children, who interacted normally with their parents as well as herself.

The trial judge, as well, remarked: ''From my brief observation of these children, they appear to be lovely, healthy, intelligent and sharing children, but there do appear to be some deficits that could be addressed.''

Notwithstanding these favourable observations, the weight of the evidence convinces me that there is good reason to be troubled about the frequency of the use of the rod, the force with which it is applied, the young age at which it is introduced and the delegation to SM of the authority to use it.

While the parents are recognized as having the responsibility and the right to discipline their children in a manner they deem appropriate, which could include reasonable use of a rod, that right is restricted by the duty to ensure that no action they take will result in a substantial risk the children will suffer physical harm.

The rod was used on children who could not possibly understand the use of force, and was being used on children at decreasing age thresholds. The respondent BM acknowledged that:

> It's not very possible to strike a child . . . without leaving a . . . a reddish mark where the child is struck,
>
> Q. How long do the marks last?
>
> A. I don't know. Maybe, maybe . . . a - a hour. . . .
>
> Q. . . . What's the longest?
>
> A. Ah, maybe two days.

While the evidence falls short of demonstrating that the children have suffered ''physical harm'' within the meaning of s. 22(2)(a), I conclude that the Agency has established, on a balance of probabilities, there is a substantial risk that the children will suffer physical harm as a consequence of the actions of the respondents. . . .

I would order that the children are in need of protective services as defined by s. 22(2)(b). I would further direct that a disposition hearing be held within 90 days from the date of the order of the Court. At that hearing the Court will have the freedom to consider the options available under s. 42 that should be exercised in the best interests of the children.

NOTES AND QUESTIONS

1. The courts in *P.E.I. (Director of Child Welfare)* v. *W. (N.)* (1994), 10 R.F.L. (4th) 203 (P.E.I. C.A.) and *Winnipeg Child and Family Services (East Area)* v. *D. (K.A.)* (1995), 13 R.F.L. (4th) 357 (Man. C.A.) emphasized the need to maintain a clear distinction between the ''need for protection'' and ''disposition'' phases of the child protection hearing. In the latter case, the access father wanted the court to place the children in his custody. Twaddle J.A. stressed that the court could make such an order as the appropriate disposition of a child protection hearing only if it were first determined that the

children would be in danger if they were returned to the care of their mother and step-father. Once that determination was made, the court could then decide if their best interests would be served by placing them in the care of their father.

2. In "Taking Children and Facts Seriously: Evidence Law in Child Protection Proceedings" (1988), 7 Can. J. Fam. L. 11 and (1989), 7 Can. J. Fam. L. 223, Professor Thompson thoroughly examines the principal evidence issues that arise in child protection proceedings. To draw out the underlying rationales for evidence rulings, he posits three adjective law models of the protection process: the full-scale adversary model, the summary administrative model and the inquiry model.

In the full-scale adversary model, judges emphasize formality in procedure and strict application of the rules of evidence as essential elements of a due process model of decision-making. Judges in child protection cases who take a stricter view of evidence law tend to make reference to the adversarial model and its concern for reliability and fairness. See, for example, *T. (T.)* v. *Catholic Children's Aid Society of Metropolitan Toronto (Municipality)* (1984), 42 R.F.L. (2d) 47 (Ont. Fam. Ct.); *Catholic Children's Aid Society of Hamilton-Wentworth (Regional Municipality)* v. *S. (J.C.)* (1986), 9 C.P.C. (2d) 265 (Ont. U.F.C.); and *M. (W.)* v. *Director of Child Welfare for Prince Edward Island* (1986), 3 R.F.L. (3d) 181 (P.E.I. C.A.). Thompson concludes (at 304): "Cases applying this model are unusual, but are over-reported in the law reports, on account of their 'legal flavour'."

At the other end of the spectrum is the inquiry model. This model has found its greatest expression in British Columbia Court of Appeal decisions. See *H. (D.R.)* v. *Superintendent of Family & Child Services (British Columbia)* (1984), 41 R.F.L. (2d) 337; *H. (G.)* v. *Superintendent of Family & Child Service* (1984), 44 R.F.L. (2d) 179; and *Superintendent of Family & Child Service* v. *G. (C.)* (1989), 22 R.F.L. (3d) 1. See also *C. (E.)* v. *Catholic Children's Aid Society of Metropolitan Toronto (Municipality)* (1982), 37 O.R. (2d) 82 (Co. Ct.) and *Children's Aid Society of Hamilton-Wentworth (Regional Municipality)* v. *M. (P.)* (1988), 17 R.F.L. (3d) 46 (Ont. H.C.). In an often quoted passage in *H. (D.R.)*, Hinckson J.A. stated (at 340):

> The Act is intended to deal with children who are in need of protection. While the inquiry provided for by the Act is to be conducted upon the basis that it is a judicial proceeding, unlike some judicial proceedings it is not an adversary proceeding and there is no *lis* before the court. It is an inquiry to determine whether a child is in need of protection and, as the statute directs, the safety and well-being of the child are the paramount considerations.

Thompson, who is quite critical of the untrammelled inquiry model, describes its effect on evidence rulings in child protection cases in Part II of this article (at 303):

> Judges espousing the inquiry model consistently let all the evidence in, with objections going to weight when the judge sifts through the evidence at the end of the day. Here it becomes hard to find even a "core" of evidence rules which are consistently applied. Hearsay, opinion, prejudice and privilege rules are largely ignored or discounted, typically with a heavy emphasis upon the need for all relevant evidence to make the dispositional decision concerning the child. In my experience, this model is more prevalent than would appear from reported cases, as evidence issues are left unidentified, submerged beneath the findings of fact.

Thompson concludes (at 304) that the majority of protection cases fall somewhere between these two ends of the spectrum exhibiting the elements of the summary administrative model whereby the adversary process is softened in an effort to accommodate the best interests of the child:

> The majority of protection cases fall comfortably within the summary model, which accepts the validity of a "core" of evidence rules. Unfortunately, within this school, one judge's core or fundamental rule is another judge's technicality. This lack of uniformity is most noticeable on hearsay and opinion issues . . . . . The precise balance between adversary and inquiry characteristics within the summary model will be fashioned by each judge and even by individual judges on particular issues.

Professor Thompson proposes in the article that the finding stage should be clearly separated from the disposition stage of the child protection proceeding. During the finding stage "the conventional rules of evidence should be carefully and intelligently applied, including hearsay, opinion and prejudice rules, subject to statutory and judicial exceptions" (at 307). Once the court moves to the disposition issue, the introduction of the "best interests" standard broadens the substantive issues and "the rules of evidence can be appropriately relaxed" (at 307).

Cases decided after Professor Thompson wrote his articles continue to show considerable divergence in determining the admissibility of evidence in child protection hearings. In *Winnipeg Child and Family Services* v. *L. (L.)* (1994), 4 R.F.L. (4th) 10, the Manitoba Court of Appeal approvingly quoted Hinkson's comments in *H. (D.R.)*. It concluded that hearsay statements by children should be more readily admitted in child protection hearings than in criminal proceedings. In particular, there was no need to establish necessity as suggested by *R.* v. *Khan*, [1990] 2 S.C.R. 531 and *R.* v. *Smith*, [1992] 2 S.C.R. 915 in a criminal law context.

However, the B.C. C.A. concluded in *G. (J.P.)* v. *Superintendent of Family and Child Services* (1993), 46 R.F.L. (3d) 4 that: (1) "regardless of the relaxed rules that apply to protection hearings, there is no reason why the ordinary rules governing both civil and criminal proceedings should not apply with respect to disclosure of pertinent evidence" (at 9); and (2) the trial judge had erred in admitting a crucial hearsay statement of a 13-year-old boy without exploring whether he should give direct testimony. Similarly, the New Brunswick Court of Appeal ordered a new trial in *New Brunswick (Department of Health & Community Services)* v. *H. (B.)* (1994), 8 R.F.L. (4th) 137 where the original hearing was "rampant with the unreined admission of hearsay evidence" (at 141). See also *B. (J.), Re* (1998), 40 R.F.L. (4th) 165, at 200-202 (Nfld. C.A.).

In *New Brunswick (Ministry of Health & Community Services)* v. *M. (R.-M)* (1993), 50 R.F.L. (3d) 191, the N.B. C.A. ordered a new trial where the judge interviewed an 8-year-old girl *in camera* and then used the conversation to question the mother during her cross-examination without disclosing precisely what the child had said. The appellate court found that, although the trial judge could "hear in camera what amounted to the evidence of the child" (at 195), it was wrong to use that evidence against the mother "without allowing her to know what the evidence was and allowing her an opportunity to respond to it" (at 195).

3. Note s. 49 of the *CFSA*. Does it suggest that the courts should generally adopt an inquisitorial or investigatory approach in child protection hearings?

4. One of the most significant developments in the law of evidence in child protection proceedings has been the willingness to admit out-of-court statements by a child victim of abuse. In *H. (D.R.)* v. *Superintendent of Family & Child Service* (1984), 41 R.F.L. (2d) 337 (B.C. C.A.), leave to appeal to S.C.C. refused (1984), 14 D.L.R. (4th) 105n (S.C.C.) a child psychiatrist testified at trial that a five-year-old girl had indicated, through the use of anatomically accurate dolls, that her father had sexually abused her. The girl did not testify, but the trial judge found, largely on the basis of the psychiatrist's evidence, that sexual abuse had been established. The parents appealed, arguing, *inter alia*, that the trial judge had erred "in treating as factual the hearsay evidence upon which the opinions of the psychiatrist were based". The British Columbia Court of Appeal ruled (at 341) that "in this type of inquiry there is no inflexible rule that hearsay evidence is not admissible". It noted (at 340-341), however, that "no judge should be satisfied to act upon it in a case where direct evidence could be produced" and that "hearsay evidence should be given no more than its proper weight". The trial judgment was upheld. See also *M. (W.)* v. *Director of Child Welfare for Prince Edward Island* (1986), 3 R.F.L. (3d) 181, 60 Nfld. & P.E.I.R. 32 (P.E.I. C.A.) where the court held that a trial judge should investigate if direct evidence was available and if the circumstances indicated that hearsay evidence was reliable before ruling that hearsay evidence was admissible. For a discussion of the competing sources for this exception to the hearsay rule, its application, and the need for a coherent definition of its parameters, see Thompson, *op. cit.*, at 54-75 and Thompson, "Children Should Be Heard but Not Seen: Children's Evidence in Protection Proceedings" (1991), 8 C.F.L.Q. 1. See also Renaud "Hearsay in Child Protection Litigation after *R.* v. *Khan*: An Overview" (1995) 53 Advocate 87; and Stuesser, "Admitting Out-of-Court Statements of Children" (1996), 24 Man. L.J. 483 (dealing with the criminal law context). Recent cases exploring the exception include *G. (J.P.)* v. *Superintendent of Family and Child Services*, noted above; *Winnipeg Child and Family Services* v. *L. (L.)*, noted above; *M. (J.J.), Re* (1995), 11 R.F.L. (4th) 166 (Alta. C.A.); and *B. (J.), Re* (1998), 40 R.F.L. (4th) 165 (Nfld. C.A.).

In the latter case, the court stated (at 200-202):

> Since the decisions . . . in *R.* v. *Khan*, [1990] 2 S.C.R. 531 and *R.* v. *Smith*, [1992] 2 S.C.R. 915, the approach to hearsay evidence has changed from a search to determine whether the circumstances fall within one of the exceptions that had been judicially developed over the years, to a determination, on a principled basis, of whether the reception of the evidence, notwithstanding the dangers of its use without an opportunity to cross-examine and to have had the information stated on oath, can be justified on the basis of necessity and reliability.
>
> . . . [W]e see no reason why the principled approach to admission of hearsay evidence enunciated in *Khan* and *Smith* ought not to be applicable in child protection cases. . . .The *Khan-Smith* approach provides both the justification for the reception of the evidence (necessity and reliability) and, by imposing an admissibility threshold, accords to the party against whom the evidence will be used, protection against being prejudiced by the reception of untrustworthy information.
>
> To adopt the seductively simple approach of allowing all hearsay evidence to be received without any threshold test of admissibility, and relegating it merely to a consideration of the weight to be accorded to it, is in effect to abandon any pretext at deciding evidentiary issues according to appropriate principle and to expose those who may be adversely affected by the reception and use of the evidence (parents facing the loss of their children as a result of allegations they are in need of protection) to considerable risk of having their interests determined or at least influenced by potentially untrustworthy evidence which they may find difficult to rebut.
>
> Furthermore, such an approach would, in the vast majority of cases, insulate the decision to receive and act on the evidence from the possibility of appellate review.

5. The Ontario legislation contains two specific provisions permitting the admission of hearsay evidence. Section 51(7) allows the court to ''admit and act on evidence that the court considers credible and trustworthy in the circumstances'' in determining the temporary care of a child while the hearing is adjourned. This language has been held to permit the use of hearsay evidence. See *Children's Aid Society of Kenora (District)* v. *Paishk* (1984), 48 O.R. (2d) 591 (H.C.).

Much more sweeping in its potential scope is s. 50(1)(b) of the *CFSA*. If read broadly, it could conceivably abolish the hearsay rule in protection cases. Generally, however, the courts did not give the equivalent previous provision this revolutionary impact but left open the possibility of its use to admit individual items of hearsay depending on the circumstances. See Thompson, ''Taking Children and Facts Seriously: Evidence Law in Child Protection Proceedings'' (1988), 7 Can. J. Fam. L. 11, at 51-54 and (1989), 7 Can. J. Fam. L. 223, at 267-273. See also *Children's Aid Society of London and Middlesex* v. *B. (B.)* (2000), 4 R.F.L. (5th) 183 (Ont. S.C.J.). In *T. (T.)* v. *Catholic Children's Aid Society of Metropolitan Toronto (Municipality)* (1984), 42 R.F.L. (2d) 47 (Ont. Fam. Ct.), Nasmith Prov. J. made the following comments (at 51-52) regarding similar language in the *Child Welfare Act*:

> It seems to me that the section at most confirms the discretion of the trial judge to avoid technical, borderline or otherwise unnecessary hearsay exclusions, if there are grounds of necessity and circumstances tending to guarantee reliability. . . .
>
> The section so read is not inconsistent with a trend toward a more liberal exercise of discretion to admit evidence in cases where a child's welfare is the central issue.
>
> But to attribute anything more revolutionary for the law of evidence to this strange little section is, in my opinion, unwarranted and unwise. The law of evidence has developed painstakingly over the years. There would be a degree of irony in suddenly invoking special children's issues as an excuse for sweeping away these laws. Ironic, because surely sound decision making based only on reliable evidence is at least as important in court cases involving children as in any other instances of dispute resolution and it is at least equally important to the parties in these cases, including the children, that they have the right to prevent the admission of unreliable evidence that could prejudice the outcome.

In ''Reforming Ontario's *Child and Family Services Act*: Is the Pendulum Swinging Back Too Far?'' (1999), 17 C.F.L.Q. 121, Professor Bala argues, at 161, that the new s. 50(1)(b) ''is intended only to deal with evidence of past conduct towards children, and to make clear that any evidence of this type of conduct '*is* admissible', including prior reasons for a decision in a civil or criminal proceeding''.

However, he acknowledges (at 162) that the provision may be interpreted more broadly and suggests (at 162) that the "unfortunate wording and punctuation of section 50(1)(b) . . . illustrates the dangers of enacting legislation without public hearings".

6. Section 50(1)(a) of the *CFSA*, enacted in 1999, expressly authorizes a court to consider evidence about a person's past conduct towards any child admissible at any stage of a protection hearing, including determining if the child is in need of protection. Such evidence may be especially important where a child protection agency acts in a preventive manner as soon as a child is born to parents with previous problems involving other children. See, for example, *Catholic Children's Aid Society of Ontario* v. *M.* (1982), 36 O.R. (2d) 451 (Prov. Ct.).

In *B. (J.), Re* (1998), 40 R.F.L. (4th) 165, the Newfoundland Court of Appeal noted (at 193-196):

> In child protection proceedings, the determination of whether a child is in need of protection does not necessarily depend upon whether the parent of the child did or did not do a particular act but often depends upon a more holistic assessment of that person's ability to parent and attitudes towards parenting which can then be used as a basis for predicting whether, if the child remains in the care of that parent, his or her physical or emotional interests will be at risk.
> . . . Whilst the proof of an individual act, such as sexual abuse, might in itself be sufficient to trigger the conclusion that a child is in need of protection, it is not always the case that the establishment of a specific event of abuse is the only way in which to establish that a child is at risk. Indeed, there may well be circumstances where proof of one instance of inappropriate behaviour by a parent towards a child, for example excessive punishment, might not lead to the conclusion that the parent is unfit to continue to care for the child when viewed in the context of the parent's overall personality and past behaviour. For instance, a previous exemplary parenting record with the child in question and with respect to other children together with an acknowledgment by the parent of the inappropriateness of his behaviour might lead to the conclusion that his or her actions were an aberration not likely to be repeated.
> There is, therefore, inherent in the type of inquiry which a judge in a child protection case is often required to undertake, the notion that a full and thorough examination of the person's ability to parent should be undertaken. To obtain a full picture of the parent, his or her attitudes and behaviours, as they impact on parenting ability generally, must surely be relevant . . . .

It is, therefore, a necessary incident of the child protection litigation system that past parenting practices, as they relate not only to the child in question, but also other children and family members, can and should be examined and be used as a basis for concluding that a particular child is or is not in need of protection, where the issue at stake involves the custodian's parenting ability as a ground for the claim that the child is in need of protection. One need only postulate the circumstance where parents have had a number of children removed from their home as a result of bad parenting practices and are facing the birth of another child. Can it be said that the child protection authorities may not apprehend the child at birth on the basis of a demonstrated lack of parenting ability with respect to the other children but must wait to see if that child is abused or neglected, thereby exposing that child to risk of harm? To ask the question is surely to answer it. Child protection legislation must be interpreted in a fair and liberal manner to carry out its fundamental purpose which is to ensure the protection of children.

We agree with the approach taken in *Children's Aid Society of Winnipeg (City)* v. *F.* (1978), 1 R.F.L. (2d) 46 (Man. Prov. Ct.) where Carr, P.J. stated at page 51:

> So often in wardship cases, counsel for the parents will object to the introduction of "past parenting" evidence . . . Evidence of this kind has sometimes been characterized as similar fact evidence and this label has often, in my respectful opinion, confused the issue of admissibility . . . This type of evidence may, however, have a "dual aspect". Whereas evidence is often tendered in a child abuse case where the origin of injuries is uncertain and there is an attempt to prove that an individual who has been guilty of abuse in the past has repeated his/her conduct, there is another dimension to the evidence which makes the decision on admissibility an easy one. The evidence is relevant in determining whether a child is in need of protective guardianship. In deciding whether a child's environment is injurious to himself, whether the parents are competent, whether a child's physical or

mental health is endangered, surely evidence of past experience is invaluable to the court in assessing the present situation.

To similar effect see *Nova Scotia (Minister of Community Services)* v. *D. (P.)* (1990), 95 N.S.R. (2d) 196 (N.S. Fam. Ct.); *B. (M.J.), Re* (1991), 34 R.F.L. (3d) 219 (Sask. Q.B.) and *Prince Edward Island (Director of Child Welfare)* v. *W. (N.)* (1994), 10 R.F.L. (4th) 203 (P.E.I. C.A.) per Carruthers, C.J.P.E.I. at para. 25.

We conclude, therefore, that evidence of past parenting practices in relation to other children and family members is relevant to a determination of the fitness and ability of a person to parent a child who is alleged to be in need of protection and does not offend, and should not be excluded by, the application of the similar fact rule where the issue before the court is the custodian's parenting ability as a ground for the claim that the child is in need of protection. The determination in such circumstances involves a prediction as to whether the child is at risk in the future. The making of that determination necessarily involves an assessment of overall parenting ability which, in turn, can only be demonstrated by past actions and attitudes. Since it is the whole person who is being assessed, it would be artificial to limit the consideration of such past acts and attitudes to those which relate only to the child in question.

We reach these conclusions notwithstanding the fact that the Newfoundland legislation, in contra-distinction to the legislation in other jurisdictions (see, e.g. *Child and Family Services Act*, R.S.O. 1990, c. C.11, s. 50) does not expressly authorize a court to consider a custodian's past conduct toward any other child. Where such legislation does exist, it merely confirms an approach that is inherent in the investigative process contemplated by the Newfoundland legislation in any event.

7. The evidence of experts is commonly relied on in most child protection hearings. In *Re Warren* (1973), 13 R.F.L. 51 (Ont. Co. Ct.), Matheson Co. Ct. J. cautioned (at 52-53):

> In a hearing such as this there is danger in over-reliance upon any group of witnesses selfconscious respecting their professionalization. I resolved not to fall victim to this specific bias of the profession, the group psychology of the social workers, and in particular determined not to allow experts to usurp the function of the jury. Unwittingly, several witnesses have trespassed upon the forbidden territory of opinionizing upon the ultimate question. The conclusions which follow have been reached painfully by me after a painstaking consideration of the evidence in its totality and after a conscientious attempt to weigh that evidence. This includes in particular all witnesses called by the respondent. These persons called by the Warrens appeared to me to be full of goodwill and short in information.
>
> It was manifest from the opening that this was a contest between the right of a subsocio-economic family to subsist together and the right of the public, represented by the Children's Aid Society, to insist upon higher standards of parental care than the couple in question were capable of offering. Many witnesses called for the Society were persons of superior education with post-graduate degrees in social work or some other related specialty. One could not listen to their testimony with all the sombre implications of this application without resolving that this Court must not be persuaded to impose unrealistic or unfair middle class standards of child care upon a poor family of extremely limited potential.

Note s. 54 of the *CFSA*. Why is the power to order an assessment only available after the child is found in need of protection? What sanction is imposed if a person ordered to attend for assessment refuses to do so? Would the concerns expressed by Matheson Co. Ct. J. apply equally to the expert's report after the court-ordered assessment?

On the nature and use of expert evidence in child protection hearings, see Daley, "Parenting Capacity Assessments" (1999), 17 C.F.L.Q. 101; Groves, "Lawyers, Psychologists, and Psychological Evidence in Child Protection Hearings" (1979), 5 Queen's L.J. 241; Thompson, "Rules of Evidence and Preparing for Court" in Bala, Hornick and Vogl, eds., *Canadian Child Welfare Law: Children, Families and the State* (Toronto: Thompson Educational Publishing Inc., 1991) at 263; Horner, Guyer, and Kalter, "Clinical Expertise and the Assessment of Child Sexual Abuse" (1993), 32 Journal of American Academy of Child & Adolescent Psychiatry 925; Wolfe, "The Right Expert — Qualifications,

Training and Education'' (1994), 11 C.F.L.Q. 1; Bala, "Children, Psychiatrists and the Courts: Understanding the Ambivalence of the Legal Profession'' (1994), 39 Can. J. Psychiatry 526; and Bala, "Mental Health Professionals in Child-Related Proceedings: Understanding the Ambivalence of the Judiciary'' (1996), 13 C.F.L.Q. 260. The latter article contains (at 297-304) a helpful discussion of the use of expert testimony concerning the validity of allegations of sexual abuse.

8. In *New Brunswick (Minister of Health and Community Services)* v. *G. (J.)* (1999), 177 D.L.R. (4th) 124, the Supreme Court of Canada held that the provincial government was under a constitutional obligation to provide an indigent mother with legal representation where a child welfare agency was threatening to remove her child from her custody. The Court recognized that removing a child from parental custody has a "serious and profound effect on a [parent's] psychological integrity'' and hence is a restraint on "security of the person'' under section 7 of the *Charter*. Given the "profound effect on the lives of both parents and children'' the "principles of fundamental justice'' will generally require that the government fund counsel for indigent parents in these proceedings.

9. The Nova Scotia Court of Appeal referred to s. 43 of the *Criminal Code* in *Nova Scotia (Minister of Community Services)* v. *M. (B.)*. It noted that the "reasonable force'' exception in s. 43 did not appear in the N.S. *Children and Family Services Act*. Was the court suggesting that any use of force to control a child's behaviour caused the child to be in need of protection? If so, do you agree?

In *C.A.S. of Hamilton-Wentworth* v. *W.(C.)* (1991), 35 R.F.L. (3d) 284 (Ont. U.F.C.), costs were awarded against the society where the society had unsuccessfully brought child protection proceedings against a mother who was a member of a fundamentalist sect that advocated the corporal punishment of children in certain circumstances. Apparently, the society pursued the matter as a test case, desiring a determination of whether the administration of corporal punishment was in and of itself abuse. Van Duzer U.F.C.J. held that corporal punishment can be an acceptable, lawful means of punishment. It only became abuse if it exceeded the bounds of reasonableness and posed a danger to the child. The judge suggested that the following factors were relevant:

1) control — the mother used a large plastic spoon to spank the children in a controlled fashion;

2) consistency — the mother used corporal punishment only when the children were openly defiant;

3) safety — the punishment usually caused no physical marks, although on one occasion the Grade III son turned and the blow to the shoulder left a slight bruise;

4) degree of trauma — the punishment caused only minor upset;

5) other factors — the mother acted with compassion rather than anger, the children understood why they were being punished, and the punishment was age-appropriate.

For some cases on the interpretation and application of s. 43 of the *Criminal Code*, see *R.* v. *Ogg-Moss*, [1984] 2 S.C.R. 173; *R.* v. *Baptiste* (1980), 61 C.C.C. (2d) 438 (Ont. Prov. Ct.); *R.* v. *Taylor* (1985), 44 C.R. (3d) 263 (Alta. C.A.); *R.* v. *Dupperon* (1985), 43 C.R. (3d) 70 (Sask. C.A.); *R.* v. *Peterson* (1995), 124 D.L.R. (4th) 758 (Ont. Prov. Ct.); *R.* v. *D.(R.S.)* (1995), 102 C.C.C. (3d) 319 (Ont. Prov. Div.); *R.* v. *L. (V.)*, [1995] O.J. No. 3346 (Prov. Div.); and *R.* v. *James*, [1998] O.J. No. 1438 (Ont. Prov. Div.). The *Peterson* case gained considerable notoriety. Intervention by a bystander who opposed corporal punishment led to assault charges against an Illinois father who was spanking his five-year-old daughter on the trunk of a car in a mall parking lot in London. The girl had slammed the car door defiantly after being told not to shut it because her two-year-old brother's hand would be caught. The father was acquitted.

A *Charter* challenge to s. 43 was recently rejected by the Ontario Superior Court of Justice in *Canadian Foundation for Children, Youth and the Law* v. *Canada (A.G.)*, [2000] O.J. No. 2535 (Q.L.). See *National Post*, Dec. 8, 1999, A8. For arguments that the provision violates sections 7, 12 and 15 of the *Charter*, see Greene, "The Unconstitutionality of Section 43 of the Criminal Code: Children's Right to Be Protected From Physical Assault'' (Part I) (1998), 41 Crim. L.Q. 288 and (Part II) (1999), 41 Crim. L.Q. 462.

(3) FINDING A CHILD IN NEED OF PROTECTION AND DISPOSITION

One of the more significant changes to the *CFSA* made by the *Child and Family Services Amendment Act (Child Welfare Reform), 1999* dealt with the definition of "child in need of protection". The following excerpt discusses these changes.

BALA, "REFORMING ONTARIO'S *CHILD AND FAMILY SERVICES ACT*: IS THE PENDULUM SWINGING TOO FAR?

(1999), 17 C.F.L.Q. 121 (Footnotes omitted.)

(c)   The Definition of Child in Need of Protection: Section 37(2)

A central theme of criticism of the 1984 C.F.S.A. has been that children have been endangered because the definition of "child in need of protection" is too narrow, and that the definition required agencies to leave children with parents who abused or even killed them. However, all of the child abuse deaths arose in cases that were within the present definitions of "substantial risk of physical harm." The problems arose because of difficulties that agency workers had with evidence gathering or (at least with hindsight) from the failure to exercise proper judgement. No definition of child in need of protection will eliminate the need for professional judgement and sometimes very difficult individualized decision making.

Neglect added: Bill 6 adds section 37(2)(a)(ii) so that a child who suffers "physical harm" as result of a parental "*pattern of neglect* in caring for, providing for, supervising or protecting the child" is a "child in need of protection." (Emphasis added.) Since section 37(2)(a) of the 1984 C.F.S.A. already included a child who suffers physical harm as a result of a parental failure to "care and provide or supervise and protect the child adequately," there would not appear to be significant change by adding neglect. There may be controversy over the meaning of the term "*pattern*" of neglect, which suggests that there must be several incidents.

To the extent that the new words simply clarify the old definition, it is useful for educative purposes for child protection workers and potential child abuse reporters, making clear to them that neglect is included in the concept of "harm".

Emotional abuse and neglect widened: Because of the vagueness of the concept of "emotional abuse", the definition in the present section 37(2)(f) is intentionally narrow. The 1984 C.F.S.A emotional abuse provision is not frequently invoked. It requires the agency to prove "*severe* (i) anxiety, (ii) depression, (iii) withdrawal, or (iv) self destructive or aggressive behaviour", (emphasis added) *and* that the parent is unable or unwilling to provide services or treatment that would alleviate that condition.

Bill 6 amends this definition by providing that:

> 1. the condition only needs to [be] "*serious*" not "*severe*" and by adding "delayed development" to the list; and

> 2. adding to parental unwillingness or inability to provide services [section 37(2)(f.1)], cases where "there are *reasonable grounds*" (emphasis added) to believe a child's emotional condition "results from [parental] actions, failure to act, or pattern of neglect" [section 37(2)(f)].

I submit that under the new provision judges should require expert evidence from qualified mental health professionals to establish that the child has one of the conditions listed.

It is often difficult to be certain why a child or adolescent (or an adult) suffers from a particular emotional, psychological or behavioural condition. There may be a number of genetic, environmental, life history and parenting factors that have contributed. Section 37(2)(f) will require the agency to establish at least "reasonable grounds" (i.e. less than proof on the balance of probabilities) that the condition "*results* from" parental conduct or neglect. Even at this lower standard of proof, the *causal link* may be difficult to establish. The statute does not make clear how the courts should deal with interacting factors; the wording ("results from") would appear to suggest that the parental action or neglect must at least be the dominant factor in the child's condition.

As many as one fifth of the child and adolescent population in Ontario at some point has emotional or psychological problems that might fit within the listed conditions. If a broad interpretation of the new provisions were to be adopted, very large numbers of children might be considered to be in "need of protection," rather that merely being in need of mental health services. However, it is submitted that the courts should not take an expansive interpretative approach, as Bill 6 requires that the conditions must be "*serious*" (though not necessarily "*severe.*").

Further, the definitions also require that there must be parental failure to consent to treatment, or responsibility for the condition. One of the biggest problems that Ontario children and adolescents with emotional and behavioural conditions face is not parental unwillingness to seek help, but the lack of access to mental health professionals. While those who are financially well off may seek private treatment, for families and children who have to rely on the public education and health systems to diagnose and treat emotional, psychological and behavioural problems, there are very long waiting lists for mental health services. Frequently in low income families mental health problems cannot be properly addressed due to a lack of resources. Judges should not penalize families because of their inability to access mental health services.

"Substantial risk" that a child will suffer harm replaced by "risk of likely harm": Bill 6 will change the verbal formula for establishing that a child is in need of protection in situations where there is a concern about future risk as opposed to past harm. While this change is intended to provide for greater consistency in approach by agencies and judges, it is not clear that this change is intended to alter the approach taken by the leading precedents to this issue.

Under the 1984 C.F.S.A. future risk of physical, sexual or emotional harm is a ground for intervention if there is a "substantial risk" that a child will suffer harm. The concept of "substantial risk" appears at different places in the 1984 C.F.S.A., including the risk of future harm and in the test for keeping a child in interim care under s. 51. The *Panel of Experts Report* noted that there have been differing interpretations of the term "substantial risk" by protection workers and judges. [See the earlier analysis of interim care.] The *Panel* recommended that there should be a "clearer" and "less onerous" test.

There were some decisions which interpreted the term "substantial risk" as placing a burden on agencies that is "almost massive . . . in that the risk must be substantial . . . risks which are significant [are] not [necessarily] substantial." Most decisions, however, interpreted the term "substantial risk" as indicating that the agency must establish, on the balance of probabilities, that there is an "actual, real and not illusory risk" or that the agency faces an evidentiary burden that is "more than a mere suspicion."

Bill 6 is intended to provide a clearer test for risk of future harm, though whether it is less onerous depends on the interpretation one took of the old "substantial risk" test. The words of Bill 6 are less ambiguous, though there is still a lack of clarity in the new words.

For the risk of future harm, the new test uses the phrase: "risk that the child is likely to be harmed." While the term "risk" is unmodified, it is grammatically linked to "likely." This new test is not unproblematic. The term "risk" on its own might suggest that a *low* probability of future harm would suffice to allow intervention. But the word "likely" connotes more probable than not, and some dictionary definitions suggest an even higher standard, including as synonyms for "likely" such as "probable" or "to be expected" and even "apparently destined."

The 1998 decision of the British Columbia Court of Appeal in *S. (B.)* v. *British Columbia (Director of Child, Family & Community Services* [(1998), 38 R.F.L. (4th) 138 (B.C. C.A.)] may be helpful for the interpretation of the new future risk provision. The Court in that case was applying a definition that requires the agency to show that a child "is likely to be physically harmed by the child's parent." Justice Lambert concluded that in the context of a child protection proceeding, that the word "'likely' was to be used in the sense of a 'real possibility, a possibility that cannot sensibly be ignored having regard to the nature and gravity of the feared harm.'" The judge also went on to emphasize the need for a balancing of concerns, and the need to consider both the nature and the likelihood of harm. He warned of the dangers of over-intervention:

> I remain concerned that interpreting the word "harm" too broadly may result in casting the protection net too widely, thus leading to the removal of children from the care of their parents in circumstances in which the appropriate course of action would be to offer the family support services.
>
> I cannot conceive that the Legislature intended . . . to authorize the removal of children from their parents' care on the basis of any harm to those children, no matter how trifling or transitory the harm might be. I am of the view, therefore, that s. 13 must be interpreted as justifying a finding that a child is in need of protection only if the harm established is significant harm. By "significant", I mean harm that is more than trifling or transitory in nature; that is substantial enough to warrant government intervention, rather than government assistance through the provision of support services. Inadequate diet or hygiene, for example, would not meet this threshold; the type of life-threatening harm found in this case, would.

While it will ultimately be for judges to interpret the definitions in Bill 6, the definitional words (inevitably) still give decision-makers significant interpretative discretion. The new definition of future risk is somewhat clearer, and reminds decision-makers that there does *not* need to be certainty of future harm. However, the new definition ("risk of likely harm") may not be less onerous for agencies than the commonly used approach to the old test ("substantial risk").

Two cases reproduced earlier, *Children's Aid Society of Toronto* v. *L. (E.L.)* and *Nova Scotia (Minister of Community and Social Services)* v. *M. (B.)*, examined whether children were in need of protection. In the first case, the concern was the parents' lack of parenting ability and in the second, the parents' disciplinary techniques resulted in a protection hearing. In the two cases that follow, the state wished to override the parents' decision regarding appropriate medical care for their children.

K. (L.D.), Re

(1985), 48 R.F.L. (2d) 164 (Ont. Fam. Ct.)

MAIN PROV. J. (orally): — In my view, the agency has failed to discharge the onus it has in law to prove that this child is in need of protection and I intend to endorse the record, "Application Dismissed." The child L.D.K. is to be returned to the custody, care and control of her parents. . . .

L.D.K. was born on 5th May 1973 and she has resided with her parents in Winnipeg since the date of her birth. She is suffering from a fatal disease known as acute myeloid leukemia. It was diagnosed in the spring of this year and, thereafter, L. and her parents have travelled almost the length and width of this continent to seek medical attention with a view to prolonging and saving her life.

After consulting with doctors at the Sick Children's Hospital in Winnipeg, the family was advised that the recommended treatment was chemotherapy, which would necessitate blood transfusions. Because L. and her parents are Jehovah's Witnesses, they could not consent to any treatment which would include the transfusion of blood or blood products. L. strongly objected to chemotherapy whether or not blood would be given.

The family then travelled to Mexico, where further efforts were made to obtain assistance. Certain substances were administered which provided a very brief period of stabilization. When L.'s condition began to deteriorate, the family left Mexico and returned to Winnipeg. Thereafter, efforts were made to obtain assistance in Thunder Bay. Again, the only option offered was chemotherapy and blood transfusions and again it was unacceptable to the family. In due course, they arrived in Toronto following a referral from a physician in Thunder Bay to the Hospital for Sick Children.

Before attending at the hospital, the family consulted one Doctor Ockley, and efforts were made to obtain assistance from a Doctor Murray in the state of Florida.

The treatment proposed by Doctor Murray was a rigorous mega-vitamin regimen. The recommended substances were purchased and the treatment was administered. This resulted in a further period of stabilization for the child, but shortly thereafter her condition once more began to deteriorate. At this juncture, L. was admitted to the Hospital for Sick Children where her parents were hopeful of obtaining some form of treatment which would enable her to live.

I find that the Metropolitan Toronto Children's Aid Society has failed to prove that this child is in need of protection as defined by the Child Welfare Act, R.S.O. 1980, c. 66. . . .

Subclause (ix) [of s. 19] reads as follows: a child in need of protection is:

> (ix) a child where the person in whose charge the child is neglects or refuses to provide or obtain *proper* medical, surgical or other recognized remedial care or treatment necessary for the child's health or well-being, or refuses to permit such care or treatment to be supplied to the child when it is recommended by a legally qualified medical practitioner, or otherwise fails to protect the child adequately. (The italics are mine.)

So much turns upon the word "proper".

The physicians who are responsible for the treatment of leukemia at the Toronto Sick Children's Hospital recommend one treatment and one treatment only. That treatment consists of the administration of two drugs, namely, daunomycin and cytosinearabinoside. These drugs, like all drugs, are toxic, but, unlike most other drugs, they are extremely toxic. As I understand the therapy, when these two substances are administered they invade, amongst other things, the bone marrow, and either reduce or terminate the production of blood platelets, white blood cells and red blood cells. There is no specificity. The reduction of the blood platelets can lead to bleeding. The reduction of the white blood cells can leave the patient exposed to any number of infections. The reduction of the red blood cells can lead to anemia.

To counteract this lack of specificity and to put back into the patient the blood cells and platelets which are no longer being produced, the hospital would administer blood and blood products. If this blood and blood products are not given to the patient, any remaining red blood cells, white blood cells and platelets simply live out the balance of their very short lives and die. The ultimate result for the patient is death from oxygen starvation and heart failure.

The treatment as described by the physicians who have testified before this court is both intensive and aggressive and could go on for a considerable period of time. It is anticipated that repeated blood transfusions would be required to maintain the patient. The numbers ranged, but they climbed as high as 15 for any 1 cycle of treatment.

I have heard much evidence with respect to the rate of cure as a result of the administration of these drugs. The doctors from the hospital, that is to say, Doctor Zipursky and Doctor Freedman, testified that in their experience the rate of cure is 30 per cent. That means that after 2½ years 30 per cent of the patients have had no relapse. Doctor Ockley testified that in her view a more accurate figure would be more in the range of 10 per cent. She explained that many of the studies supporting the higher figure were faulty in that some of the patients in the worst condition were omitted from the statistics. If this is correct, it would obviously increase the rate of success.

I cannot place Doctor Ockley on the same level as Doctors Freedman and Zipursky with respect to expertise. She is a general practitioner and, in addition to that, she lacks experience both in general practice and in this specific area of acute myeloid leukemia in children.

I have also heard considerable evidence concerning the side-effects of these two toxic agents. These side effects are many and they are extreme. They range from nausea, vomiting and pain, to the loss of hair, to sterility and to death from heart failure, amongst other things. What is clear to me from the evidence is that, although these drugs and ones like them have been in use for some time, we are only now beginning to learn of the degree and scope of their side effects. What we have learned is described in the literature as merely ''the tip of the iceberg''.

During this past week while she has been confined in this hospital with other leukemia patients, L. has seen children who are undergoing chemotherapy treatment and have lost their hair, are crying from the pain and are begging not to have any further treatment. L.'s position is now, and has been from the day she saw a documentary on this disease, that she does not want any part of chemotherapy and blood transfusions. She takes this position not only because it offends her religious beliefs, and I am satisfied that it does, but also because she does not want to experience the pain and anguish associated with the treatment process.

L. has told this court clearly and in a matter-of-fact way that, if an attempt is made to transfuse her with blood, she will fight that transfusion with all of the strength that she can muster. She has said, and I believe her, that she will scream and struggle and that she will pull the injecting device out of her arm and will attempt to destroy the blood in the bag over her bed. I refuse to make any order which would put this child through that ordeal.

I am satisfied from what I know about L. and from what I have heard and read, particularly from Doctor Ockley, that the emotional trauma which she would experience as a result of any attempt at transfusion could have nothing but a negative effect on any treatment being undertaken.

L. and her parents have a proposed treatment plan. The family would take the child from this hospital and place her in the home of relatives. With the assistance of Doctor Ockley and with the back-up of Doctor Hobart at the Georgetown Hospital, a mega-vitamin therapy would be initiated. During this treatment L. would be surrounded by her family and she would be free to communicate with her God. She would have peace of mind and could get on with attempting to overcome this dreadful disease with dignity. In my view, she must be given that opportunity.

With this patient, the treatment proposed by the hospital addresses the disease only in a physical sense. It fails to address her emotional needs and her religious beliefs. It fails to treat the whole person. I accept the evidence of Doctor Ockley that this concept is very important, not only for L. but for any patient.

I accept that there are no statistics as to the rate of success of the mega-vitamin treatment. I have given that deficiency much consideration and it does concern me. But in the balance between what would happen here and what would happen in the home of L.'s relatives, the balance tips in favour of the latter despite the lack of those statistics. . . .

Who is L.D.K. and who are the members of her family? L. has a brother, whose name I believe is C. He is 5 years of age. I am satisfied that this family is a warm and close-knit unit. L.'s parents are both loving and concerned individuals. L. is a beautiful, extremely intelligent, articulate, courteous, sensitive and, most importantly, a courageous person. She has wisdom and maturity well beyond her years and I think it would be safe to say that she has all of the positive attributes that any parent would want in a child. She has a well thought out, firm and clear religious belief. In my view, no amount of counselling from whatever source or pressure from her parents or anyone else, including an order of this court, would shake or alter her religious beliefs.

I believe that L.K. should be given the opportunity to fight this disease with dignity and peace of mind. That can only be achieved by acceptance of the plan put forward by her and her parents. . . .

B. (R.) v. C.A.S. OF METROPOLITAN TORONTO

(1995), 9 R.F.L. (4th) 157 (S.C.C.)

LA FOREST J. (GONTHIER and MCLACHLIN JJ. concurring): — This appeal raises the constitutionality of state interference with child-rearing decisions. The appellants are parents who argue that the Ontario *Child Welfare Act*, R.S.O. 1980, c. 66, infringes their right to choose medical treatment for their infant in accordance with the tenets of their faith. They claim that this right is protected under both ss. 7 and 2(*a*) of the *Canadian Charter of Rights and Freedoms*.

FACTS

S.B. was born four weeks prematurely, on June 25, 1983. Soon after, she was transferred to the Hospital for Sick Children in Toronto because of her physical condition. Within the first few weeks of her life she exhibited many physical ailments and received a number of medical treatments. Her parents, the appellants, consented to all the treatments provided during those initial weeks. At their request, the attending physicians avoided the use of a blood transfusion in the treatment of S. because, as Jehovah's Witnesses, the appellants objected to it for religious reasons; they also claimed it was unnecessary.

On July 30, the child's hemoglobin level had dropped to such an extent that the attending physicians believed her life was in danger and that she might require a blood transfusion to treat potentially life-threatening congestive heart failure. On July 31, following a hearing on short notice to the appellants, Judge Main of the Ontario Provincial Court (Family Division) granted the respondent Children's Aid Society a 72-hour wardship, on the basis of the evidence of Dr. Perlman that a transfusion might be necessary and that it would not be for experimental purposes. A status review was held on August 3, but was adjourned; it resumed on August 18 and 19. Dr. Pape and Dr. Swyer both testified that although the child's condition had improved, it was still marginal, and they wished to maintain the ability to transfuse in case of an emergency. Dr. Morin, head of ophthalmology at the Hospital for Sick Children, testified that he suspected S. had infantile glaucoma and needed to undergo exploratory surgery within the following week to confirm the diagnosis. This procedure had to be performed under general anesthetic, and Dr. Swyer testified that a blood transfusion would be necessary. Main Prov. J. extended the wardship order for a period of 21 days: *Re B. (S.)* (1983), 36 R.F.L. (2d) 70. On August 23, S. received a blood transfusion as part of the examination and operation for the suspected glaucoma.

A second Provincial Court order terminated the respondent's wardship on September 15, and the child was returned to her parents: *Re B. (S.)* (1983), (sub. nom. *B. (S.M.) v. Children's Aid Society of Metropolitan Toronto (Municipality)*) 36 R.F.L. (2d) 80. Both orders of the Provincial Court were appealed to the District Court by the appellants. The respondent Children's Aid Society countered with a motion to dismiss, which was allowed on the grounds that the transfusion had been administered and the wardship terminated, thereby leaving no lis between the parties, and that the *Child Welfare Act* had been repealed and replaced by the *Child and Family Services Act, 1984*, S.O. 1984, c. 55, thus rendering the whole issue moot: *Re B. (S.)*; *B. (R.) v. Children's Aid Society of Metropolitan Toronto* (1985), 32 A.C.W.S. (2d) 149 [(July 17, 1985), Docs. Toronto 9141 and 9246, Webb D.C.J. (Ont. Dist. Ct.). [1985] W.D.F.L. 1676].

On an appeal to the Court of Appeal, that court held that the District Court had erred in so holding as there remained the issues of interference with the rights of the parents in determining their child's medical treatment, and of the constitutionality of the *Child Welfare Act*. These issues were referred back to the District Court and a hearing of the appeal, including the constitutional questions, was ordered on the merits: *Re B. (S.)* (1988), (sub nom. *B. (R.) v. Children's Aid Society of Metropolitan Toronto)* 63 O.R. (2d) 385, 47 D.L.R. (4th) 388, 15 R.F.L. (3d) 388. The District Court dismissed the appellants' appeal from the Provincial Court on the merits: (1989), 14 A.C.W.S. (3d) 10 [(February 10, 1989), Docs. York 9141 and 9246, Whealy D.C.J. (Ont. Dist. Ct.), [1989] W.D.F.L. 643, additional reasons at (June 9, 1989), Docs. York 9141 and 9246, Whealy D.C.J. (Ont. Dist. Ct.), [1989] W.D.F.L. 1011]. The court awarded costs against the respondent Attorney General of Ontario, who had intervened in the proceedings. The appellants' appeal to the Court of Appeal was dismissed. The respondent Attorney General of Ontario's cross-appeal on the issue of costs was also dismissed, Houlden J.A. dissenting: (1992), 10 O.R. (3d) 321, 96 D.L.R. (4th) 45, 43 R.F.L. (3d) 36, (sub nom. *Re S.*) 58 O.A.C. 93.

. . .

ISSUES

The following constitutional questions were set by the chief justice:

1. Does the *Child Welfare Act*, R.S.O. 1980, c. 66, s. 19(1)(*b*)(ix), together with the powers in ss. 30(1)2 and 41 and the procedures in ss. 21, 27, 28(1), (10), and (12), deny parents a right to choose medical treatment for their infants, contrary to s. 7 of the *Canadian Charter of Rights and Freedoms*?
2. If the answer to question 1 is in the affirmative, is s. 19(1)(*b*)(ix), together with the powers in ss. 30(1)2 and 41 and the procedures in ss. 21, 27, 28(1), (10), and (12) of the *Child Welfare Act*, R.S.O. 1980, c. 66, justified as reasonable limits by s. 1 of the *Canadian Charter of Rights and Freedoms* and therefore not inconsistent with the *Constitution Act, 1982*?
3. Does the *Child Welfare Act*, R.S.O. 1980, c. 66, s. 19(1)(*b*)(ix), together with the powers in ss. 30(1)2 and 41 and the procedures in ss. 21, 27, 28(1), (10), and (12), infringe the appellants' freedom of religion as guaranteed under s. 2(*a*) of the *Canadian Charter of Rights and Freedoms*?
4. If the answer to question 3 is in the affirmative, is s. 19(1)(*b*)(ix), together with the powers in ss. 30(1)2 and 41 and the procedures in ss. 21, 27, 28(1), (10), and (12) of the *Child Welfare Act*, R.S.O. 1980, c. 66, justified as reasonable limits by s. 1 of the *Canadian Charter of Rights and Freedoms* and therefore not inconsistent with the *Constitution Act, 1982*?

The issue raised in the respondent's cross-appeal was whether the District Court erred in making its award of costs against the Attorney General of Ontario.

The court rendered judgment from the bench on March 17, 1994. It dismissed the appeal and answered the first constitutional question in the negative. Question 2 does not, therefore, arise. The court, however, reserved decision, reasons to follow, as regards whether it was under question 3 or question 4 that the legislation was constitutionally valid. Decision was also reserved on the cross-appeal.

ANALYSIS . . .

Section 7 of the Charter

Turning now to s. 7 of the *Charter*, the appellants argued that the right to choose medical treatment for their infant is a liberty interest protected under s. 7 of the *Charter* and that the infringement of that interest in the present case did not conform with the principles of fundamental justice. Whealy D.C.J., we saw, dismissed the contentions of the appellants and the Court of Appeal simply stated that even on the assumption that s. 7 of the *Charter* afforded some protection to the interest claimed by the appellants, any infringement of their liberty was done in accordance with the principles of fundamental justice.

Section 7 of the Charter and Parental Liberty

Although I am of the view that the principles of fundamental justice have been complied with in the present case, I nonetheless propose to comment on the scope of the protection afforded by the *Charter* as it relates to the right of parents to choose medical treatment for their infant. This court has, on many occasions, stated that the principles of fundamental justice vary according to the context: see *R. v. L. (T.P.)*, [1987] 2 S.C.R. 309; *Pearlman v. Law Society (Manitoba)*, (sub nom. *Pearlman v. Law Society Judicial Committee*) [1991] 2 S.C.R. 869. An examination of the scope of the liberty interest appears warranted, since its formulation may affect the determination of the principles of fundamental justice. I also note that while this case can be disposed of solely on the issue of the right of parents to choose medical treatment for their infant, it is not without consequence for child protection as a whole. Intervention may well be compelling here, but this appeal raises the more general question of the right of parents to rear their children without undue interference by the state.

The appellants claim that parents have the right to choose medical treatment for their infant, relying for this contention on s. 7 of the *Charter*, and, more precisely, on the liberty interest. They assert that the right enures in the family as an entity, basing this argument on statements made by American courts in the definition of liberty under their Constitution. While, as I will indicate, American experience may be useful in defining the scope of the liberty interest protected under our Constitution, I agree that s. 7 of the *Charter* does not afford protection to the integrity of the family unit as such. The Canadian *Charter*, and s. 7 in particular, protects individuals. It is the individual's right to liberty under the *Charter* with which we are here concerned. . . .

The term "liberty" has yet to be authoritatively defined in this court, although comments have been made on both ends of the spectrum. [A discussion of a number of S.C.C. cases on the meaning of "liberty" is omitted.]

The above-cited cases give us an important indication of the meaning of the concept of liberty. On the one hand, liberty does not mean unconstrained freedom: see *Reference re s. 94(2) of the Motor Vehicle Act (British Columbia)*, [1985] 2 S.C.R. 486 (per Wilson J., at p. 524); *R. v. Videoflicks Ltd.*, (sub nom. *R. v. Edwards Books & Art Ltd.*), [1986] 2 S.C.R. 713 (per Dickson C.J.C., at pp. 785-786). Freedom of the individual to do what he or she wishes must, in any organized society, be subjected to numerous constraints for the common good. The state undoubtedly has the right to impose many types of restraints on individual behaviour, and not all limitations will attract *Charter* scrutiny. On the other hand, liberty does not mean mere freedom from physical restraint. In a free and democratic society, the individual must be left room for personal autonomy to live his or her own life and to make decisions that are of fundamental personal importance.

. . . On this point, the American experience can give us valuable guidance as to the proper meaning and limits of liberty. The United States Supreme Court has given a liberal interpretation to the concept of liberty, as it relates to family matters. It has elevated both the notion of the integrity of the family unit and that of parental rights to the status of constitutional values, through its interpretation of the Fifth and Fourteenth Amendments. *Meyer v. Nebraska*, 262 U.S. 390 (S. Ct. 1923), and *Pierce v. Society of Sisters*, 268 U.S. 510 (S. Ct. 1925), are the two landmark cases most often cited. In the former, the Supreme Court invalidated a statute that purported to limit the teaching of foreign languages. Its decision was grounded, in part at least, on a finding that the statute interfered with the right of the parents to control the education of their children. In *Pierce v. Society of Sisters*, the Supreme Court declared unconstitutional a statute that required that children attend public schools. . . .

Those two cases have survived the *Lochner* era, a much criticized period in which the Supreme Court engaged in substantive review of many economic and social statutes. Despite the lack of unanimity on the formulation of liberty and the role of the courts in reviewing legislation, the dicta on liberty, insofar as family matters are concerned, have been consistently broad. . . .

Where to draw the line between interests and regulatory powers falling within the accepted ambit of state authority will often raise difficulty. But much on either side of the line is clear enough. On that basis, I would have thought it plain that the right to nurture a child, to care for its development, and to make decisions for it in fundamental matters, such as medical care, are part of the liberty interest of a parent. As observed by Dickson J. in *R. v. Big M Drug Mart Ltd.*, ([1985] 1 S.C.R. 295), the *Charter* was not enacted in a vacuum or absent an historical context. The common law has long recognized that parents are in the best position to take care of their children and make all the decisions necessary to ensure their well-being. . . . Although the philosophy underlying state intervention has changed over time, most contemporary statutes dealing with child protection matters, and in particular the Ontario Act, while focusing on the best interests of the child, favour minimal intervention. In recent years, courts have expressed some reluctance to interfere with parental rights, and state intervention has been tolerated only when necessity was demonstrated. This only serves to confirm that the parental interest in bringing up, nurturing, and caring for a child, including medical care and moral upbringing, is an individual interest of fundamental importance to our society.

The respondents have argued that the ''parental liberty'' asserted by the appellants is an obligation owed to the child which does not fall within the scope of s. 7 of the *Charter*. . . .

While acknowledging that parents bear responsibilities towards their children, it seems to me that they must enjoy correlative rights to exercise them. The contrary view would not recognize the fundamental importance of choice and personal autonomy in our society. As already stated, the common law has always, in the absence of demonstrated neglect or unsuitability, presumed that parents should make all significant choices affecting their children, and has afforded them a general liberty to do as they choose. This liberty interest is not a parental right tantamount to a right of property in children. (Fortunately, we have distanced ourselves from the ancient juridical conception of children as chattels of their parents.) The state is now actively involved in a number of areas traditionally conceived of as properly belonging to the private sphere. Nonetheless, our society is far from having repudiated the privileged role parents exercise in the upbringing of their children. This role translates into a protected sphere of parental decision making which is rooted in the presumption that parents should make important decisions affecting their children both because parents are more likely to appreciate the best interests of their children and because the state is ill-equipped to make such decisions itself. Moreover, individuals have a deep personal interest as parents in fostering the growth of their own children. This is not to say that the state cannot intervene when it considers it necessary to safeguard the child's autonomy or health. But such intervention must be justified. In other words, parental decision making must receive the protection of the *Charter* in order for state interference to be properly monitored by the courts, and be permitted only when it conforms to the values underlying the *Charter*.

The respondents also argued that the infant's rights were paramount to those of the appellants and, on that basis alone, state intervention was justified. This was the conclusion reached by Whealy D.C.J. Children undeniably benefit from the *Charter*, most notably in its protection of their rights to life and to the security of their person. As children are unable to assert these, our society presumes that parents will exercise their freedom of choice in a manner that does not offend the rights of their children. If one considers the multitude of decisions parents make daily, it is clear that in practice, state interference in order to balance the rights of parents and children will arise only in exceptional cases. In fact, we must accept that parents can, at times, make decisions contrary to their children's wishes — and rights — as long as they do not exceed the threshold dictated by public policy, in its broad conception. For instance, it would be difficult to deny that a parent can dictate to his or her child the place where he or she will live, or which school he or she will attend. However, the state can properly intervene in situations where parental conduct falls below the socially acceptable threshold. But in doing so, the state is limiting the constitutional rights of parents rather then vindicating the constitutional rights of children. . . .

Once it is decided that the parents have a liberty interest, further balancing of parents' and children's rights should be done in the course of determining whether state interference conforms to the principles of fundamental justice, rather than when defining the scope of the liberty interest. Even assuming that the rights of children can qualify the liberty interest of their parents, that interest exists nonetheless. In the case at bar, the application of the Act deprived the appellants of their right to decide which medical treatment should be administered to their infant. In so doing, the Act has infringed upon the parental "liberty" protected in s. 7 of the *Charter*. I now propose to determine whether this deprivation was made in accordance with the principles of fundamental justice.

Principles of Fundamental Justice

This court has on different occasions stated that the principles of fundamental justice are to be found in the basic tenets and principles of our judicial system, as well as in the other components of our legal system . . . The state's interest in legislating in matters affecting children has a long-standing history. In *R. v. Jones*, ([1986] 2 S.C.R. 284), for example, I acknowledged the compelling interest of the province in maintaining the quality of education. More particularly, the common law has long recognized the power of the state to intervene to protect children whose lives are in jeopardy and to promote their well-being, basing such intervention on its parens patriae jurisdiction: see, for example, *Hepton v. Maat*, supra; *Re Eve*, (sub nom. *E. v. Eve*) [1986] 2 S.C.R. 388. The protection of a child's right to life and to health, when it becomes necessary to do so, is a basic tenet of our legal system, and legislation to that end accords with the principles of fundamental justice, so long, of course, as it also meets the requirements of fair procedure. Section 19 of the Act is but one of the numerous legislative expressions of the parens patriae power. It contemplates different situations where state intervention is mandated in order to ensure the protection of children. Only one of those is of interest here. It appears in s. 19(1)(*b*)(ix), which reads:

19.—(1) In this Part and Part IV,

. . .

(*b*) "child in need of protection" means,

. . .

(ix) a child where the person in whose charge the child is neglects or refuses to provide or obtain proper medical, surgical or other recognized remedial care or treatment *necessary* for the child's health or well-being, or refuses to permit such care or treatment to be supplied to the child when it is recommended by a legally qualified practitioner, or otherwise fails to protect the child adequately. [Emphasis added.]

I note at the outset that this section is not limited to situations where the life of the child may be in jeopardy. It encompasses situations where treatments might be warranted to ensure his or her health or well-being. Although broad in scope, the section is compatible with a modern conception of life that embodies the notion of quality of life.

The appellants do not really contest the legitimacy of the principle that the state may intervene to protect children. Rather, they take issue with the procedure for intervention provided in the Act, and seek a declaratory judgment setting out guide-lines that should be read into the Act for overriding parental choices. In light of the disposition of this appeal, there is no need to address in detail the availability of the remedy or the merits of the guidelines. Suffice it to say that the appellants propose that in a true emergency situation, there would be no need for a court order, as the common law permits doctors to provide treatment despite parental refusal. In a non-emergency situation, doctors would need a court order to override parental refusal, which could only be granted if the treatment was found by the court to be necessary, there was no alternative medical management, no doctor to provide alternative medical care, and 48 hours' notice and full disclosure to the parents.

While the pleadings have been centred mostly around the constitutionality of s. 19(1)(*b*)(ix) of the Act, it is necessary to examine briefly the powers conferred on the courts in ss. 30(1) and 41, as well as the procedure established in ss. 21, 27 and 28. This will enable us to have a better understanding of the scheme devised by the legislature, and to address the appellants' arguments relating to the conformity of the deprivation of their rights to the principles of fundamental justice.

When the Children's Aid Society has reasonable and probable grounds to believe that a child is in need of protection within the meaning of s. 19(1)(*b*)(ix) of the Act, it can apprehend the child without a warrant and take or confine him or her to a designated place of safety (s. 21). Upon such apprehension, s. 27 requires that the matter be brought before a court within five days for a determination of whether the child is in need of protection. Section 28 governs the procedure to be followed at the court hearing, and allows a judge to summon and compel witnesses, and to hear evidence from parents and other interested parties. Section 28(6) requires that a parent or other person with custody of the child must be given "reasonable notice" of the hearing. Section 28(10) allows the court to dispense with notice when it cannot be served and "any delay might endanger the health or safety of the child." If, at the s. 28 hearing, the court determines that the child is in need of protection, then it may make an order under s. 30(1) that the child be returned to its parents subject to Society supervision, or that it be committed as a ward of the relevant Children's Aid Society. Only when the latter order is made is the Children's Aid Society, pursuant to s. 41 of the Act, vested with all rights and responsibilities of a legal guardian, including the right to consent to medical treatment. Finally, the Children's Aid Society must apply to the court to have the child's status reviewed before the expiry of the wardship order (s. 37).

The appellants attack the general procedure under the *Child Welfare Act*, and, in particular, the specific way in which it was carried out in the present case. As for the constitutionality of the procedure under the Act, there is no need to discuss it at length, since I am of the opinion that the scheme designed by the legislature accords with the principles of fundamental justice. The parents must receive reasonable notice of the hearing in which their rights might be affected. "Reasonable" is a flexible criterion that permits adjustments to different situations. While it is possible to hold a wardship hearing without notice in situations of emergency, s. 28(11) of the Act provides that the wardship order cannot, in the absence of another hearing with notice, exceed 30 days. In *Re B.C.G.E.U.*, (sub nom. *B.C.G.E.U. v. British Columbia (Attorney General)*), [1988] 2 S.C.R. 214, this court held that an injunction granted ex parte did not violate s. 7 of the *Charter*. That case differs from the present one, but its underlying proposition holds true: the procedural requirements of the principles of fundamental justice can be attenuated when urgent and unusual circumstances require expedited court action.

Further, the wardship order depriving the parents of the right to refuse medical treatment for their infant is granted by a judge following an adversarial process where conflicting evidence may be presented. The parents can act through counsel, present arguments, cross-examine witnesses, and so on. The onus of proof is on the Children's Aid Society, and it has been recognized by the courts, and by Main Prov. J. in this case, that the Children's Aid Society must present a strong case.

Finally, the initial order granting wardship to the Children's Aid Society must be reviewed before its expiry. . . .

I now propose to analyze the scheme as it has been applied to this case, and respond to the other concerns voiced by the appellants. I shall first deal with the initial wardship order of July 31, 1983. I shall then turn to the status review of August 18 and 19, 1983.

(i) *Wardship Order of July 31, 1983*

The doctors responsible for S.'s care informed the Children's Aid Society that her life was at risk, because her parents were refusing to consent to a blood transfusion, the need of which, in the doctors' view, was imminent. It is upon those facts that the Children's Aid Society founded its reasonable and probable grounds to engage the process contemplated by the Act. The evidence indicates that the Children's Aid Society had to proceed diligently. The parents received notice of the hearing the day it was held. In light of the circumstances, the notice was reasonable. Main Prov. J., who acknowledged the short notice, limited the initial wardship order to 72 hours so as to enable the parties to come back before him with further evidence. And although the appellants were not able to present conflicting medical evidence at the initial hearing, they were nonetheless represented by counsel, who cross-examined the witnesses summoned by the Children's Aid Society and presented submissions. . . .

(ii) *Status Review of August 18 and 19, 1983*

The hearing of August 18 and 19, 1983, held pursuant to s. 37 of the Act, was to review S.'s status and to determine if the wardship order should be prolonged. The appellants received notice of the hearing at the beginning of the month of August. Although they would have had time to adduce some medical evidence to counter that of the Children's Aid Society with respect to the congestive heart condition, the appellants chose not to do so. While the child's health had slightly improved, the Children's Aid Society demonstrated, to the satisfaction of Main Prov. J., that an eventual blood transfusion was still a reasonable course of action, due to the fragile state of the child. The Children's Aid Society wished to retain the authority to consent to a blood transfusion if an emergency were to arise.

The hearing also revolved around the testimony of Dr. Morin, who testified that the child needed to undergo exploratory surgery under general anesthetic to confirm a diagnosis of infantile glaucoma, which, if established, would require surgery to preserve the child's sight. Evidence that S. needed to receive a transfusion in order to sustain the anesthetic was also adduced. The appellants argued that the testimony of the ophthalmologist took them by surprise, as they were not informed of it in the notice. In reviewing the evidence, however, it appears that even if the appellants and their counsel were unaware that Dr. Morin would be called to testify, they had for some time been aware of this aspect of S.'s condition. Dr. Pape, the neonatologist responsible for S.'s care, testified on August 18 that the suspected glaucoma was diagnosed when S. was three to four weeks old, and that she had discussed with the appellants the desirability of exploratory surgery. Moreover, Main Prov. J., who was sensitive to the fact that the appellants did not have time to seek their own medical opinion, recommended that they be permitted to seek a second opinion before the exploratory surgery. In fact, the appellants did consult an ophthalmologist beforehand, who simply confirmed Dr. Morin's diagnosis. I do not think that the failure to notify the appellants that Dr. Morin would testify violated the principles of fundamental justice. . . .

An examination of the application of the impugned provisions to the facts of this case amply demonstrates that the legislative scheme, which deprives parents of their right to choose medical treatment for their infant under certain circumstances, is in accordance with the principles of fundamental justice. Section 7 requires that a deprivation of liberty be in conformity with the principles of fundamental justice, but it does not guarantee the most equitable process of all; it dictates a threshold below which state intervention will not be tolerated: see *R. v. L. (T.P.)*, supra. Therefore, while the guidelines proposed by the appellants are more stringent than those found in the legislative scheme, the process nonetheless respects the constitutional requirements. In fact, those guidelines were, in substance, contemplated by the legislative scheme. Section 19(1)(*b*) (ix) of the Act applies to treatments which are deemed necessary. The hearing is adversarial so that a debate on the medical questions can be presented. The Act requires that the Children's Aid Society notify the parents of a hearing that might affect their rights. The epithet "reasonable" ensures that the process will be adaptable to a myriad of situations. The wardship order is circumscribed and must be reviewed before its expiry.

In sum, the appellants were entitled to such notice, access to information, and rights of representation as may be fair and reasonable having regard to the nature of the proceedings and the urgency with which they must be carried out. Tarnopolsky J.A. carefully examined these issues and concluded, and I agree with him, that the procedure, having regard to all the circumstances, did not violate the principles of fundamental justice.

Section 2(a) of the Charter

Turning now to s. 2(*a*) of the *Charter*, the appellants argued that the Act, which deprives them of the right to refuse medical treatment for their infant on religious grounds, violates their freedom of religion guaranteed by s. 2(*a*) of the *Charter*. . . . I note at the outset that it is the freedom of religion of the appellants — S.'s parents — that is at stake in this appeal, not that of the child herself. While it may be conceivable to ground a claim on a child's own freedom of religion, the child must be old enough to entertain some religious beliefs in order to do so. S. was only a few weeks old at the time of the transfusion.

. . . In *Droit de la famille* — 1150, (sub nom. *P. (D.)* v. *S. (C.)*) [1993] 4 S.C.R. 141, a case involving a custody dispute in which one of the parents was a Jehovah's Witness, L'Heureux-Dubé J. stated that custody rights included the right to decide the child's religious education. It seems to me that the right of parents to rear their children according to their religious beliefs, including that of choosing medical and other treatments, is an equally fundamental aspect of freedom of religion.

It is evident that the purpose of the Act is not directed at limiting the freedom of Jehovah's Witnesses to choose medical treatment for their children, including the freedom to refuse a blood transfusion on religious grounds. It was not until 1945 that the Jehovah's Witnesses adhered to that precept, while the Act originates from a law first adopted in 1927, *The Children's Protection Act*, R.S.O. 1927, c. 279. I do not rely solely on this historical fact, however. It seems to me that a simple reading of the Act makes it clear that its purpose is nothing more or less than the protection of children. But if the purpose of the Act does not infringe on the freedom of religion of the appellants, the same cannot be said of its effects. The legislative scheme implemented by the Act, which culminates in a wardship order depriving the parents of the custody of their child, has denied them the right to choose medical treatment for their infant according to their religious beliefs.

However, as the Court of Appeal noted, freedom of religion is not absolute. While it is difficult to conceive of any limitations on religious beliefs, the same cannot be said of religious practices, notably when they impact on the fundamental rights and freedoms of others. . . .

A more difficult issue is whether the freedom of religion of the appellants is intrinsically limited by the very reasons underlying the state's intervention, namely, the protection of the health and well-being of S., or whether further analysis should be carried out under s. 1 of the *Charter*. In support of this thesis, the respondents have brought to this court's attention a number of American cases in which the scope of freedom of religion was limited. However, these cases are of little assistance as the American Constitution contains no balancing provision comparable to s. 1 of the *Charter*. . . .

In my view, it appears sounder to leave to the state the burden of justifying the restrictions it has chosen. Any ambiguity or hesitation should be resolved in favour of individual rights. Not only is this consistent with the broad and liberal interpretation of rights favoured by this court, but s. 1 is a much more flexible tool with which to balance competing rights than s. 2(*a*). . . .

This is not to say that an elaborate examination of the criteria established in *R. v. Oakes*, ([1986] 1 S.C.R. 103), will always be necessary. The effect on religious beliefs will often be so insubstantial, having regard to the nature of the legislation, that *Charter* concerns will obviously be overridden. But in this case, it cannot be maintained that the effect on the rights of the appellants was of a minor character. As I am of the view that the Act seriously infringed on the appellants' freedom to choose medical treatment for their child in accordance with the tenets of their faith, it remains to be determined whether this infringement was justified under s. 1 of the *Charter*.

Section 1 of the Charter

Turning now to s. 1 of the *Charter*, the appellants have argued that the state has not demonstrated, on a balance of probabilities, that S. was in need of protection within the meaning of the Act when she was apprehended by the Children's Aid Society. This argument fails to distinguish between the demonstration of the necessity of the treatment, as contemplated in the Act, and the demonstration of the reasonable nature of the legislative scheme, under s. 1 of the *Charter*. For the reasons already stated, one must take for granted the necessity of the medical treatment and, thus, the need for protection under the Act.

The appellants have conceded that the state interest in protecting children at risk is a pressing and substantial objective. The Act allows the state to assume parental rights when a judge has determined that a child is in need of treatment that his parents will not consent to. As already stated, when discussing the conformity of state intervention with the principles of fundamental justice, the process contemplated by the Act is carefully crafted, adaptable to a myriad of different situations, and far from arbitrary. The Act makes provision for notice to be given, for evidence to be called, for time limits to be imposed upon Crown wardship and other orders, as well as for procedural protections to be afforded to parents. The restrictions the Act imposes on parental rights are, in my view, amply justified.

ADDENDUM

Since writing the foregoing, I have read the reasons of my colleagues Justices Iacobucci and Major. I must confess to being somewhat mystified by the purport they attribute to my reasons. I agree, of course, that parents may not, in the exercise of their right to nurture their children, refuse them medical treatment that is necessary and for which there is no reasonable alternative. That, I thought, was the conclusion I came to. That conclusion is, of course, clearly contemplated by s. 1 of the *Charter*, which is the provision that "guarantees the rights and freedoms set out in it," but it does so "subject only to such reasonable limits prescribed by law as can be demonstrably justified in a free and democratic society" and, as far as s. 7 is concerned, by the requirements of fundamental justice.

If my colleagues are concerned with my mode of approach — the approach, I may say, traditionally employed by this court from the earliest stages of *Charter* adjudication — I have concerns with their method of limiting one constitutional right against another without relevance to context. Thus, some of their remarks may be understood as supporting a parent's rights being overturned simply because a professional thinks it is necessary to do so. I would be very much concerned if a medical professional were able to override the parent's views without demonstrating that necessity. On my approach to the issues so far as s. 7 is concerned, it would be necessary to show that such action would not be contrary to the principles of fundamental justice. More generally, s. 1 requires an interference with the right to be demonstrably justified. That, I think, is perfectly right. In a case like the present, where there is no immediate urgency, a procedure meeting the demands of fundamental justice, which I was at pains to note the Act fully provides for, would be required.

In an emergency, the demands of fundamental justice are more easily met. In *R. v. Dyment*, [1988] 2 S.C.R. 417, at p. 432, this court alluded to a medical doctor's powers to take reasonable steps in such circumstances. These powers conform to the practices and procedures followed in this area and are consistent with principles of fundamental justice. The state's powers to exercise its legitimate *parens patriae* jurisdiction would, in my view, similarly be justified under the principles of fundamental justice. As well, these actions "prescribed by law" seem to me quite clearly to be "reasonable limits prescribed by law [that] can de demonstrably justified in a free and democratic society."

My colleagues express concern that my reasons would create a situation in which a child's right to life or security is reduced to a limitation of the parent's constitutionally protected right. I should observe that my approach is dictated by the nature of the case presented to us. The sole issue before us was that raised by the parents, i.e., that *their* constitutional rights were infringed in the circumstances in which medical treatment was given to the child. In such a case, the parent's rights must, under s. 1, be balanced against the interests of others in a free and democratic society — in this particular case, the right of their child. In that situation, I, not surprisingly, found the parent's rights were clearly overridden. If a situation arose where it was alleged that the child's right was violated, other rights might be raised as reasonable limits, but if the right alleged was the security of the child, as in the present case, then the child's right would again prevail over a parent's rights. In short, the issue raised governs the form, but not the substance, of the analysis. . . .

I add, incidentally, that I do not (as my colleagues Iacobucci and Major JJ. appear to suggest) think that liberty is all-encompassing. I have been at pains to underline that it is limited to those essentially personal rights that are inherent to the individual, which, in my view, include (and on this I believe we agree) the right of parents to nurture their children. Even as so defined, an interference with liberty may be justified as being in conformity with the principles of "fundamental justice." At bottom, I think "liberty" means the ordinary liberty of free men and women in a democratic society to engage in those activities that are inherent to the individual. These may not be extensive, but where they exist, they must under the Constitution be protected from state intervention unless that intervention can be justified. Sometimes that justification is evident. In other cases, it will require close contextual analysis. Here the security of the child was clearly paramount. What was more difficult, and what in the end the appellants really directed their argument to, is whether the procedures to determine respect for the parents' rights under the Act were sufficient to satisfy ss. 1 and 7 of the *Charter*. That such procedures must have effect before, and not following, the action invasive of the parents' rights, seems to me to be essential and to be clearly required by ss. 1 and 7. . . .

[L'Heureux-Dubé J. concurred with Justice La Forest's reasons with respect to the appeal, but disagreed with his treatment of the cross-appeal. Unlike the other members of the court, she would not have upheld the award of costs against the Attorney General of Ontario.]

LAMER C.J.C. (concurring in the result): — I have had the benefit of reading the reasons of La Forest J. and the joint reasons of Iacobucci and Major JJ. I am in agreement with them with respect to the result of this appeal. For the reasons stated by my colleagues Iacobucci and Major JJ., I agree that the impugned provisions of the *Child Welfare Act*, R.S.O. 1980, c. 66, now repealed, do not violate the freedom of religion guaranteed by s. 2(*a*) of the *Canadian Charter of Rights and Freedoms*. With respect to the analysis under s. 7 of the *Charter*, however, I have arrived at this result for reasons that are different from those of my colleagues. More specifically, I am of the opinion that the liberty interest protected by s. 7 has not been infringed because it includes neither the right of parents to choose (or refuse) medical treatment for their children nor, more generally, the right to bring up or educate their children without undue interference by the state. While this type of liberty ("parental liberty") is important and fundamental within the more general concept of the autonomy or integrity of the family unit, it does not fall within the ambit of s. 7.

[The next 34 paragraphs of the Chief Justice's reasons are omitted.]

To summarize my opinion, I would simply say that extending the scope of the word "liberty" in s. 7 to include any type of freedom other than that which is connected with the physical dimension of the word "liberty" would not only be contrary to the structure of the *Charter* and of the provision itself, but would also be contrary to the scheme, the context, and the manifest purpose of s. 7. Furthermore, it would have the effect of conferring prima facie constitutional protection on all eccentricities expressed by members of our society under the rubric of "liberty," in addition to taking away all legitimacy or purpose from other provisions of the *Charter*, such as s. 2 or s. 6, for example, since they would be redundant. It seems apparent to me that this cannot be the purpose of s. 7, or of the *Charter* itself, which is a constitutional instrument. It must also be clearly understood that this approach would inevitably lead to a situation where we would have government by judges. This is not the case at present, but I would emphasize again that it must not become the case. . . .

Finally, but without stating an opinion on the question, I would note, with respect, that I would be much more receptive to the appellants' argument and my colleague's reasons concerning the constitutional protection of parental rights if it had been argued that this right, or the freedom to make choices for our children, was protected by the freedom of conscience guaranteed by s. 2(*a*) of the *Charter*. As Dickson J. stated so aptly, at p. 346 of *Big M Drug Mart Ltd.*, it is precisely the rights associated with freedom of individual conscience that are central "both to basic beliefs about human worth and dignity and to a free and democratic political system."

[Justice Sopinka also concurred with the result. He stated that it was unnecessary to determine if the parents' liberty interest had been affected because "the threshold requirement of a breach of the principles of fundamental justice was not met".]

IACOBUCCI AND MAJOR JJ. (CORY J. concurring): — We have read the reasons of Mr. Justice La Forest, and we agree with the result that there has been no unconstitutional violation of the appellants' rights, under either s. 7 or s. 2(*a*) of the *Canadian Charter of Rights and Freedoms*. However, we respectfully disagree with La Forest J.'s reliance on s. 1 of the *Charter* and the principles of fundamental justice in s. 7 in order to establish the constitutionality of the repealed *Child Welfare Act*, R.S.O. 1980, c. 66. Instead, we conclude that the class of parents caught by s. 19(1)(*b*)(ix) of the Act simply cannot benefit from the protection of the liberty interest in s. 7 or freedom of religion encapsulated in s. 2(*a*) of the *Charter*. We therefore find the appellants incapable of crossing the first threshold of *Charter* analysis. There is thus no initial constitutional infringement and, consequently, no need to uphold any such infringement either through its consonance with fundamental justice or its status as a reasonable limit in a free and democratic society. . . .

It is important to bear in mind that the impugned provisions of the *Child Welfare Act* are geared to the promotion of the health, safety, and personal integrity of the child. To this end, although this appeal raises issues related to the right of parents to rear their children without undue influence by the state, it also touches on the s. 7 right of the child to life and security of the person. It is this perspective that we find absent from the reasons of La Forest J. As such, we are concerned by the fact that our colleague's decision creates a situation in which the child's right to life or security of the person is reduced to a limitation on the parents' constitutionally protected ability to deny that child the necessities of life owing to parental liberty and freedom of religion.

1. Section 7

We find that the right to liberty embedded in s. 7 does not include a parent's right to deny a child medical treatment that has been adjudged necessary by a medical professional. . . .

This is clearly a case where S.'s right to liberty, security of the person, and potentially even to life is deprived. It is important to note that the abridgment of S.'s s. 7 rights operates independently from the question whether the parents honestly believe that their refusal to consent to the transfusion is in the best interests of the child, since such a refusal shall, according to the appellants, prevent her from being "defiled in the eyes of God." Whether or not her parents' motivations are well-intentioned, the physical effects upon S. of the refusal to transfuse blood are equally deleterious.

We note that La Forest J. holds that "liberty" encompasses the right of parents to have input into the education of their child. In fact, "liberty" may very well permit parents to choose among *equally effective* types of medical treatment for their children, but we do not find it necessary to determine this question in the instant case. We say this because, assuming without deciding that "liberty" has such a reach, it certainly does not extend to protect the appellants in the case at bar. There is simply no room within s. 7 for parents to override the child's right to life and security of the person.

In any event, there is an immense difference between sanctioning some input into a child's education and protecting a parent's right to refuse their children medical treatment that a professional adjudges to be necessary and for which there is no legitimate alternative. The child's right to life must not be so completely subsumed to the parental liberty to make decisions regarding that child: *Re K. (R.)* (1987), 79 A.R. 140 (Fam. Ct.), at p. 147. In our view, the best way to ensure this outcome is to view an exercise of parental liberty which seriously endangers the survival of the child as falling outside s. 7.

Our colleague's reasons open the door to the possibility that a violation of a guardian's s. 7 rights will be found should the state deny a guardian his or her right to refuse a child in his or her charge medical treatment *and* should that denial fail to conform with fundamental justice. In the case at bar, S.'s condition, although believed to be serious, was not sufficiently urgent to prevent the Children's Aid Society from seeking a court ordered wardship, thereby complying with procedural fundamental justice. But what if S. were injured in a car accident and required an immediate blood transfusion to save her life? Even if her parents would have been in agreement that the transfusion was necessary and urgently required, their personal convictions would still likely have compelled them to refuse their daughter the treatment. To this end, this exercise of parental liberty can engender the death of an infant.

We find it counter-intuitive that "parental liberty" would permit a parent to deny a child medical treatment felt to be necessary until some element of procedural fundamental justice is complied with. Although an individual may refuse any medical procedures upon her own person, it is quite another matter to speak for another separate individual, especially when that individual cannot speak for herself and, in S.'s case, has never spoken for herself. The rights enumerated in the *Charter* are individual rights to which children are clearly entitled in their relationships with the state and all persons — regardless of their status as strangers, friends, relatives, guardians, or parents.

The suggestion that parents have the ability to refuse their children medical procedures, such as blood transfusions, in situations where such a transfusion is necessary to sustain that child's health is consistent with the view, now long gone, that parents have some sort of "property interest" in their children. Indeed, in recent years, this court has emphasized that parental duties are to be discharged according to the "best interests" of the child: *Young* v. *Young*, [1993] 4 S.C.R. 3; *Droit de la famille* — 1150, (sub nom. *P. (D.)* v. *S. (C.)*) [1993] 4 S.C.R. 141. . . .

The exercise of parental beliefs that grossly invades the "best interests" of the child is not activity protected by the right to "liberty" in s. 7. To hold otherwise would be to risk undermining the ability of the state to exercise its legitimate parens patriae jurisdiction and jeopardize the *Charter's* goal of protecting the most vulnerable members of society. As society becomes increasingly cognizant of the fact that the family is often a very dangerous place for children, the parens patriae jurisdiction assumes greater importance. Although there are times when the family should be shielded from the intrusions of the state, S.'s situation is one in which the state should be readily able to intervene not only to protect the public interest, but also to preserve the security of infants who cannot yet speak for themselves.

It is clear that a purpose of the *Charter* is to protect the individual from governmental interference. For this reason, as noted by our colleague La Forest J., many *Charter* rights have been given broad interpretations. In the instant appeal, concern has been raised that whittling down the ambit of "parental liberty" could deny parents a constitutional remedy should the state, without due process or substantive merit, arbitrarily decide to remove a child from a home. In our estimation, a more appropriate way of mitigating such a possibility would be to view such a removal as an interference with the child's own liberty or security interest, not that of the parent. With respect, such an approach obliges the state's parens patriae jurisdiction to be fairly exercised, both procedurally and substantively, without necessitating that the "liberty" interest embedded in s. 7 be extended to include parents' endangering the lives of children or denying them required medical treatment.

In sum, since we find the parental decision to withhold medical care to be outside the scope of "liberty" it does not qualify for *Charter* protection in the first place.

We have also read the reasons of the chief justice. He would confine the right to liberty in s. 7 to the "judicial" context, specifically criminal matters. He would also limit its reach to the physical or corporeal component of liberty, thereby leaving psychological coercion and emotional trauma outside of the scope of "liberty." With respect, we do not find it necessary to pronounce on such an important matter in these reasons, particularly since this court has not had the benefit of full argument on the appropriate contours between the rights protected by s. 7 and the freedoms covered by s. 2. We would consequently leave this determination for another day, and a case in which such issues arise more directly.

2. Section 2(a)

The parents of S. are constitutionally entitled to manifest their beliefs and practise their religion, as is their daughter. That constitutional freedom includes the right to educate and rear their child in the tenets of their faith. In effect, until the child reaches an age where she can make an independent decision regarding her own religious beliefs, her parents may decide on her religion for her and raise her in accordance with that religion.

However, the freedom of religion is not absolute. Although La Forest J. considered that limitations on this right are best considered under a s. 1 analysis, we are of the view that the right itself must have a definition, and even if a broad and flexible definition is appropriate, there must be an outer boundary. Conduct which lies outside that boundary is not protected by the *Charter*. That boundary is reached in the circumstances of this case.

We are of the view that the constitutional question should be: To what extent can an infant's right to life and health be subordinated to conduct emanating from a parent's religious convictions? With this perspective as a starting point, we find that the appellants do not benefit from the protection of s. 2(a) of the *Charter* since a parent's freedom of religion does not include the imposition upon the child of religious practices which threaten the safety, health, or life of the child. . . .

We are also reinforced in our findings by the decisions of lower courts not to view parents' refusal to consent to a blood transfusion for their children as activity protected by s. 2(a) . . . .

THOMPSON, "CASE COMMENT: *B. (R.) v. CHILDREN'S AID SOCIETY OF METROPOLITAN TORONTO*"

(1995), 9 R.F.L. (4th) 345

The Supreme Court of Canada has finally spoken. The *Canadian Charter of Rights and Freedoms does* have a significant role to play in child protection, and in parent-child relationships more generally. In spite of the divisions in *B. (R.) v. Children's Aid Society of Metropolitan Toronto*, only Lamer C.J.C. forecloses any role for the *Charter* in family matters. The other judges accept the *Charter's* role, disagreeing only about its operation at the outer limits presented in this case.

The consensus comes as a surprise. Section 7 and 2 claims made by parents in protection cases have been thoroughly unsuccessful in lower courts: see D.A. Rollie Thompson, "Why Hasn't the Charter Mattered in Child Protection?" (1989) 8 Can. J. Fam. L. 133. In *B. (R.)* the constitutional issues were raised in the context of a blood transfusion, where the result is so clear-cut that the complexities can be easily overlooked. The dismissal of this Supreme Court appeal from the bench one year ago seemed to augur badly for any jurisprudence.

Yet the reasons of La Forest J., which attract a five-judge majority on s. 2(a) and a four-and-three-eighths majority on s. 7, are a landmark. Someday his reasons may prove to be as seminal as *Meyer v. Nebraska*, 262 U.S. 390, 67 L.Ed. 1042, 43 S.Ct. 625, 29 A.L.R. 1446 (S. Ct. 1923), or *Pierce v. Society of Sisters*, 268 U.S. 510, 69 L.Ed. 1070, 45 S.Ct. 571, 39 A.L.R. 468 (S. Ct. 1925), in the United States.

1. *The Reasons of La Forest J.*

What distinguishes the reasons of La Forest J. from those of Iacobucci and Major JJ. is his recognition of the broader consequences "for child protection as a whole" and "the more general question of the right of parents to rear their children without undue interference by the state," however compelling may be the intervention in *B. (R.)* (at p. 200). In the result, there is "a protected sphere of parental decision making" in accordance with s. 7, which means that state intervention must be justified under "the principles of fundamental justice" (at p. 207). Similarly, parents are found to have "the right . . . to rear their children according to their religious beliefs" within s. 2(a) at (at p. 215), subject to the limits of s. 1.

Even though La Forest J. acknowledges the difficulties in defining "liberty" under s. 7, he says, "I would have thought it plain that the right to nurture a child, to care for its development, and to make decisions for it in fundamental matters, such as medical care, are part of the liberty interest of a parent'' (at p. 206). Plain it may be, but this ''individual interest of fundamental importance to our society'' was lost for the first 13 years of the *Charter*. Lost, because most judges fallaciously applied private custody concepts (parents have obligations, children have rights) to state intervention (therefore, parents have no constitutional rights, only children do.). Not so La Forest J., who appreciates the critical link between parental responsibilities and ''correlative rights to exercise them'' (at p. 207), especially against the intrusion of the state into family relationships.

The existence of ''parental liberty'' under s. 7 ensures that state intervention will be subject to *Charter* scrutiny for compliance with the ''principles of fundamental justice.'' La Forest J.'s detailed review of Ontario's *Child Welfare Act*, R.S.O. 1980, c. 66, procedures also demonstrates what kind of serious scrutiny the court expects, given the interests at stake. To similar effect is the majority's s. 1 analysis after finding that the parents' freedom of religion under s. 2(*a*) had been ''seriously infringed'' (at p. 217).

It is important to appreciate that La Forest J. attracts the support of four other judges on s. 2(*a*), with Sopinka J. joining in. On s. 7 Sopinka J. avoids defining ''liberty'' by concluding that ''the threshold requirement of a breach of the principles of fundamental justice was not met'' (at p. 248). As suggested earlier, that determination amounts to a three-eighths concurrence, for two reasons. First, Sopinka J. did *not* join in with the minority (Iacobucci and Major JJ. (Cory J. concurring)) and its truncation of s. 7 rights. Second, through his s. 2(*a*) concurrence he accepts the same parental rights under a different heading, one where the state bears the s. 1 burden of justifying intervention.

2. *The Minority Judgment (Iacobucci, Major and Cory JJ.)*

The joint reasons of Iacobucci and Major JJ. are prisoners of the facts, seen as ''parental liberty'' versus ''death of an infant'' (at p. 251). Under both s. 2(*a*) and s. 7 of the *Charter*, the minority reads ''internal'' limits on the rights of parents to exclude this situation from any constitutional scrutiny, without needing to resort to ''the principles of fundamental justice'' or ''reasonable limits.''

A line must be drawn within the ''right'' itself, they say, accepting that ''there are times when the family should be shielded from the intrusions of the state'' (at p. 252). That line wanders, with each verbal formulation moving the line this way and that:

''. . . the class of parents caught by s. 19(1)(*b*)(ix) of the Act simply cannot benefit from . . . the *Charter*.'' (at p. 249)

''. . . the right to liberty embedded in s. 7 does not include a parent's right to deny a child medical treatment that has been adjudged necessary by a medical professional.'' (at p. 250)

''There is simply no room within s. 7 for parents to override the child's right to life and security of the person.'' (at p. 251)

. . . not protect ''a parent's right to refuse their children medical treatment that a professional adjudges to be necessary and for which there is no legitimate alternative.'' (at p. 251)

''. . . to view an exercise of parental liberty which seriously endangers the survival of the child as falling outside s. 7.'' (at p. 251)

''The exercise of parental beliefs that grossly invades the 'best interests' of the child is not activity protected by the right to 'liberty' in s. 7.'' (at p. 252)

Where this line is drawn is critical, because parental conduct on the wrong side of the line receives *no* protection, and state intrusion, *no* scrutiny under the *Charter*, an all-or-nothing proposition. The broad traditional approach to rights definition employed by La Forest J. allows for a more finely tuned balancing of the interests, through the "principles of fundamental justice" and s. 1, as he points out in his addendum.

There is much talk of "children's rights" in the minority reasons, but with little explanation of how decisions should be made for an infant, who cannot speak, especially if the Constitution does not demand fair procedures. Is the decision to be made by doctors alone? Or by child protection workers? By judges without hearing from the parents? As La Forest J. trenchantly observes, at p. 219, "[h]ere what is attempted is to limit a right by another, with no stated mechanism for judicially determining just when, on the facts, the first right is overridden" or, for that matter, just *who* decides to override the parents' decision.

In the end, the minority's approach works only after the facts have been determined, and even then, only in the clearest of cases. It is a conclusion, with little guidance for other cases.

3. *Some Implications of the Decision*

This decision has various implications. First and foremost, almost every s. 7 decision in the field of child protection will have to be reconsidered, especially those in which any possibility of "parental rights" was dismissed. La Forest J.'s reasons ought to provide a new starting point for such challenges.

Second, the procedural content of s. 7's guarantees in protection matters has been fleshed out by La Forest J.: notice, adversarial hearing before a judge, access to information, rights of representation, burden of proof upon agency, heightened standard of proof, circumscribed wardship order, and full status review. And, apart from emergencies, these procedures "must have effect before, and not following, the action invasive of the parents' rights" (at p. 220). The latter raises serious questions about warrantless apprehensions and the former may spawn challenges to unfair procedures, as legislated or applied. It is hoped that one of the "principles of fundamental justice" would be interpreted to be speedy hearings (not at issue in *B. (R.)*), especially at the interim stage, when no finding has yet been made and the child has been removed from the parental home.

Following the lead of La Forest J., courts should be prepared to read *Charter* rights broadly in family matters, recognizing that the protection of children is a sufficiently important public purpose to justify limiting parental rights. The painstaking analysis of those limits by La Forest J. should signal an end to the fast-and-dirty s. 1 analyses that have been too prevalent in family law cases. The clear message of the Supreme Court of Canada is that the parent-child relationship is one of "fundamental importance" and that it deserves serious constitutional analysis and protection.

NOTES AND QUESTIONS

1. In *New Brunswick (Minister of Health & Community Services)* v. *G. (J.)* (1999), 177 D.L.R. (4th) 124, the Supreme Court of Canada held that the provincial government was obliged by s. 7 of the *Charter* to provide an indigent mother with legal representation where a child welfare agency was threatening to remove her child from her custody. The court unanimously recognized that removing a child from parental custody had a serious and profound effect on a parent's psychological integrity and

hence affected security of the person. The court also concluded unanimously that the principles of fundamental justice required a fair hearing and that the mother would not have such a hearing without a lawyer. A minority concluded that the mother's liberty interest was also engaged because the proceeding might deprive her of the right to make decisions on behalf of her children and guide their upbringing. The majority decided not to address the mother's right to liberty since it was possible to dispose of the case by focusing on the mother's security of the person and since "there have been differing views expressed about the scope of the right to liberty in the Court's previous judgments" (at 146).

2. Do you agree with the result in *K. (L.D.)*? Do you think the judge would have reached the same conclusion if the child had been three years old? See also *Couture-Jacquet v. Montreal Children's Hospital*, [1986] R.J.Q. 1221 (C.A.).

Where a person is competent to consent to treatment, that person's consent is generally required before any medical treatment can be given. See, *e.g.*, s. 10 of the *Health Care Consent Act, 1996*, being Schedule A of S.O. 1996, c. 2, which governs health practitioners in Ontario. The test for determining competency under the common law and the *Health Care Consent Act, 1996* is essentially the same. Section 4(1) of the Ontario legislation stipulates that a person is capable of giving or refusing consent to a particular treatment where "the person is able to understand the information that is relevant to making a decision concerning the treatment ... and able to appreciate the reasonably foreseeable consequences of a decision or lack of decision". If a child is capable, then it is his or her consent alone that is relevant. The child's parents cannot then provide the necessary consent if the child refuses treatment, nor veto treatment sought by the child. Indeed, the process of seeking the parents' views may well constitute a breach of confidentiality in those circumstances. Similarly, the CAS's authority to authorize medical treatment for a child who is a Society or Crown ward only applies if the child is not competent to consent and a parent's consent would normally be required. Should L.D.K. have been considered capable of giving or refusing consent to the chemotherapy?

In *Walker v. Region 2 Hospital Corp.* (1994), 4 R.F.L. (4th) 321 (N.B. C.A.), a 15-year-old boy, who was a Jehovah's Witness, had acute myeloid leukemia. The prognosis was that he would likely require blood transfusions as part of his treatment. He signed a patient release form and a medical directive only after specifically stipulating that he refused to permit blood transfusions under any circumstances. The hospital applied for an order that the child be declared a mature minor, capable of giving or refusing consent to medical treatment. The trial judge, although informed that the boy's doctors considered him sufficiently mature to give or withhold consent, granted the Minister of Health parental rights in regard to the medical treatment of the boy for two months and specifically directed that he be given blood transfusions if the doctors believed them to be necessary to preserve his life. The boy successfully appealed. The N.B. C.A. held (at 333) that the common law recognized that a minor could consent to his or her own medical treatment whenever he or she was "capable of understanding the nature and consequences of the proposed treatment" and that the right to consent to medical treatment included the right to refuse such treatment. The *Medical Consent of Minors Act*, S.N.B. 1976, c. M-6.1, had essentially codified this position, but specified that, where the patient was under 16, two doctors had to be satisfied that he or she was capable of understanding the nature and consequences of a medical treatment.

See also *Re Y. (A.)* (1993), 111 Nfld. & P.E.I.R. 91 (Nfld. U.F.C.) where Wells J. declared that a 15-year-old boy had the capacity in accordance with the common law to refuse blood transfusions.

Recently, similar issues surfaced in a highly publicized case involving a 13-year old Saskatchewan boy, Tyrell Dueck. Tyrell was diagnosed with a potentially lethal form of cancer in his thighbone. Tyrell and his parents belonged to a Christian Fundamentalist group that believed in faith-healing. Rather than under-go traditional chemotherapy treatments, Tyrell and his parents opted to go to Tijuana Mexico for treatment built around large doses of vitamins and a special diet. Upon their return, the Saskatchewan Court of Queen's Bench found the boy to be a child in need of protection and gave the province's social services department authority over health-care decisions. Shortly after Tyrell began chemotherapy, he refused further treatment and the case went back to court to determine if he was competent to make his own decisions in these matters. Two experts testified that, although Tyrell had the mental capacity to decide his treatments, he lacked the necessary medical knowledge and was dominated by his father. The court ruled that the boy did not appreciate or understand the medical treatments he required, that he was still a child in need of protection, and that the granting of consent continued to lie with the Minister of Social Services: *D. (T.T.), Re* (1999), 176 Sask. R. 152 (Sask. Q.B.). The cancer spread, the treatments were stopped, and Tyrell died.

A somewhat similar case transpired in London, England in 1999 when a court issued an order that doctors could proceed with a heart transplant operation involving a 15-year old girl who insisted that she would rather die. See "Girl, 15, forced to undergo heart transplant", *National Post*, July 19, 1999. In this case, the child's mother urged her daughter to undergo the operation and so the only issue was whether the girl had the mental capacity to make an informed, independent decision. The judge reasoned that the girl was too ill, overwhelmed, and confused to make a clear decision.

3. Where a patient is not capable of giving or refusing consent, both the common law and legislation such as the *Health Care Consent Act, 1996* recognize that others may validly make the decision for the incompetent person. For example, s. 20(1) of the *Health Care Consent Act, 1996* specifies that the following may provide or withhold the necessary consent for a person who lacks capacity to consent:

> [paragraph] 5. A . . . parent of the incapable person, or a children's aid society or other person who is lawfully entitled to give or refuse consent to the treatment in the place of the parent. This paragraph does not include a parent who has only a right of access. If a children's aid society or other person is lawfully entitled to give or refuse consent to the treatment in the place of the parent, this paragraph does not include the parent.

> [paragraph] 6. A parent of the incapable person who has only a right of access.

Subsections (3) and (4) go on to stipulate that the access parent may give consent only if (1) the custodial parent is unavailable, incapable, or is unwilling to assume the responsibility; or (2) the access parent believes that the custodial parent would not object.

As *B. (R.)* v. *C.A.S. of Metropolitan Toronto* indicates, refusal to consent may lead to child protection proceedings. In some situations, these may be hurriedly convened and conducted. For example, in *C.C.A.S. of Metropolitan Toronto* v. *F. (R.)* (1988), 66 O.R. (2d) 528 (Prov. Ct.), an infant was apprehended by the society at the Toronto Hospital for Sick Children shortly after midnight when the parents refused to consent to blood transfusions. The child protection hearing was convened by 1:30 a.m. By 5:30 a.m. counsel for the society and the parents had presented an agreed statement of facts and made their submissions. Soon after, Main Prov. J. ruled that the society had failed to prove, as then required by s. 51(3) of the *CFSA*, that there was a "substantial risk" to the child's health if the child remained in the parents' custody. The medical staff feared that the child, who had had periodic bouts of post-operative bleeding for eight days, might suddenly have an uncontrollable bleed and that this would constitute a threat to the child's life if they could not give a blood transfusion. Noting that the probability of another bleed was in the 30-40% range and that pressure treatment and drugs had controlled previous bleeds, Main Prov. J. concluded (at 533) that there was a "real chance of danger" to the child's health but that the "degree of risk falls short of being substantial". He also noted that the hearing could resume at short notice in the event of a new crisis. Would the amendments of 1999 and the revised wording of s. 51(3) affect this result?

After the ruling, the doctors at the hearing asked the judge what they should do if a life-threatening emergency developed. He responded (at 533):

> [A]s physicians you have a choice, despite the parents' instructions, should there be a life-threatening emergency. In such circumstances it is open to you to administer whatever form of treatment you deem necessary to save the child's life. What, if any, civil liability may result is a question you should direct to your legal counsel to address.

Section 27 of the *Health Care Consent Act, 1996* now specifies that a health practitioner may treat a child who is incapable of consenting and whose parents refuse to consent where the health practitioner believes that: (1) there is an emergency (defined as a situation where the child "is apparently experiencing severe suffering or is at risk, if the treatment is not administered promptly, of suffering serious bodily harm"); and (2) the parents did not properly act in the best interests of the child. Section 25 deals with emergency treatment where consent cannot be obtained promptly and "the delay required to obtain a consent or refusal on the [child's] behalf will prolong the suffering that the [child] is apparently experiencing or will put the [child] at risk of sustaining serious bodily harm". Section 29(4) then specifies that a health practitioner who, in good faith, administers treatment in accordance with s. 25 or s. 27 is not liable for administering treatment without consent. Could these provisions withstand a Charter challenge in light of *B. (R.)* v. *C.A.S. of Metropolitan Toronto*?

4. In *Children's Aid Society of Peel (Region)* v. *S. (P.)* (1991), 34 R.F.L. (3d) 157 (Ont. Prov. Div.), the court granted an interim order of custody to the society so that it could grant consent for a 13-year-old to have an abortion. The girl wanted the abortion despite the objections of her parents.

5. Several cases have dealt with situations where parents have refused to consent to relatively minor, but potentially life-saving, procedures needed by severely handicapped or impaired children. In *Superintendent of Family & Child Service* v. *D. (R.)* (1983), 34 R.F.L. (2d) 34 (B.C. S.C.), the court ordered that "a severely retarded boy approaching seven years, who shortly after birth suffered profound brain damage through meningitis which inflamed the lining of his brain and left him with no control over his faculties, limbs or bodily functions" be placed in the interim custody of the Superintendent to permit replacement of a shunt that drained excess cerebra-spinal fluid from around the brain. The parents and some medical advisors believed that it would be in the child's best interests to die rather than face life with his disabilities. McKenzie J. responded (at 49):

> I cannot accept their view that S. would be better off dead. If it is to be decided that "it is in the best interests of S.D. that his existence cease", then it must be decided that, for him, non-existence is the better alternative. This would mean regarding the life of a handicapped as not only less valuable than the life of a normal child, but so much less valuable that it is not worth preserving. I tremble at contemplating the consequences if the lives of disabled persons are dependent upon such judgments.

Although this comment suggests a "sanctity of life" rather than a "quality of life" approach, the court did hear considerable evidence about the quality of life that the child could expect. It was also influenced by the possibility that failure to replace the shunt might not result in death but in a life of pain and progressive deterioration. For commentary on the case, see Benjamin, "The Stephen Dawson Case: Who Speaks for the Child?" (1985), 42 R.F.L. (2d) 167 and Dickens, "Medicine and the Law Withholding Paediatric Medical Care" (1984), 62 Can. Bar Rev. 196.

In *New Brunswick (Minister of Health and Community Services)* v. *B.* (1990), 70 D.L.R. (4th) 568 (N.B. Q.B.), the parents, supported by some medical personnel, refused to consent to the administration of antibiotics to treat an infection that threatened the life of their severely mentally retarded and neurologically handicapped 10-year-old daughter born with encephalocele. Justice McLelland, relying on the philosophy and values set out in the *Charter*, concluded forcefully that the girl had the right to live regardless of her disabilities and transferred custody to the Minister for six months. The judge categorically rejected the suggestion by Professor Keyserlingk in "Non-Treatment in the Best Interests of the Child" (1987), 32 McGill L.J. 413 (at 428) that a child could have "such extensive brain damage that it would not be reasonable to think of him as having interests at all".

For a detailed discussion of the legal aspects of treatment decisions for newborn children, see Magnet and Kluge, *Withholding Treatment from Defective Newborn Children* (Cowanville, Quebec: Brown Legal Publications, 1985).

6. Should parents of a mentally disabled child have the right to authorize sterilization of the child in order to avoid problems that might be caused by the sexual behaviour of the child, particularly pregnancy? The Supreme Court of Canada ruled unanimously in *E.* v. *Eve*, [1986] 2 S.C.R. 388, (*sub nom. Re Eve*) 61 Nfld. & P.E.I.R. 273, that a court should not authorize sterilization of a mentally disabled adult under the court's *parens patriae* jurisdiction unless a clearly therapeutic purpose was established. This case also suggests that parents cannot validly consent to medical treatment of a child unless that treatment actually furthers the child's physical or mental health. See also *Re. K.*, 63 B.C.L.R. 145, [1985] 4 W.W.R. 724 (C.A.), leave to appeal to S.C.C. refused, 62 B.C.L.R. xlin, [1985] 4 W.W.R. 757 (S.C.C.).

7. Can a fetus ever be considered a "child in need of protection"? This issue was canvassed in *Children's Aid Society of Kenora (District)* v. *L. (J.)* (1981), 134 D.L.R. (3d) 249 (Ont. Fam. Ct.) where a child was born suffering from fetal-alcohol syndrome and was apprehended four days after birth. The doctor who had diagnosed the pregnancy at about 19 weeks contacted the local Children's Aid Society at that stage expressing concerns about the health of the fetus but the society refused to act, believing it lacked jurisdiction until after the birth of the child. Bradley Prov. J. suggested in *obiter* that the child was in need of protection prior to birth. If Bradley Prov. J. is correct, presumably the only way the society could have acted to protect the child would have been by obtaining a supervisory order placing conditions upon the behaviour of the expectant mother. See s. 57(1) of the *Child and Family Services Act*.

In *Children's Aid Society (Belleville)* v. *T. (L.)* (1987), 7 R.F.L. (3d) 191 (Ont. Fam. Ct.), Kirkland Prov. J. held that an unborn child could be a child in need of protection. In her last stages of pregnancy, the mother refused to seek medical care despite abnormal vaginal discharge that suggested the unborn child might be at risk. She was also homeless, sleeping in underground parking garages. After finding that the unborn child was in need of protection, the court ordered temporary custody to the children's aid society. As well, the mother was ordered to be hospitalized for a mental assessment under s. 10 of the *Mental Health Act*. Ms T. gave birth to a healthy nine-pound boy while she was still being involuntarily held for psychiatric treatment in hospital. However, the courts in *Re Baby R.* (1988), 15 R.F.L. (3d) 225 (B.C. S.C.) and *Re A.* (1990), 28 R.F.L. (3d) 288 (Ont. U.F.C.) held that they had no jurisdiction under the relevant child protection legislation to require mothers to obtain proper prenatal care and proper medical care on delivery.

Although not dealing directly with a statutory definition of "child in need of protection", the S.C.C. decision in *Winnipeg Child & Family Services (Northwest Area)* v. *G. (D.F.)* (1997), 31 R.F.L. (4th) 165 appears to settle the issue in the absence of new legislation. The Winnipeg Child and Family Services applied for an order requiring a pregnant woman to stay in a place of safety and refrain from the use of intoxicants during her pregnancy. Two of the woman's three previous children had been severely harmed before they were born due to their mother's glue sniffing. All three were made permanent wards of the state as a result of her chronic addiction. Initially, the order sought by the agency was granted, but it was stayed two days later and reversed by the Manitoba Court of Appeal. Notwithstanding the staying of the order, the mother remained voluntarily in hospital for treatment. The agency appealed further. In the meantime, the mother delivered a healthy child. Although the case was now moot, the court decided (at 173) to continue with the appeal because "[w]hile the problem that gave rise to these proceedings has been resolved, the legal issues it raised have not". In delivering the majority judgment, McLachlin J. identified two legal issues (at 201):

> (1) Does tort law, as it exists or may properly be extended by the Court, permit an order detaining a pregnant woman against her will in order to protect her unborn child from conduct that may harm the child?

> (2) Alternatively, does the power of a court to make orders for the protection of children (its *parens patriae* jurisdiction), as it exists or may properly be extended by the Court, permit an order detaining a pregnant woman against her will in order to protect her unborn child from conduct that may harm the child?

The majority held that neither tort law nor the inherent *parens patriae* jurisdiction permitted an order detaining the woman for treatment against her wishes. While she recognized that a child born alive can bring a tort action for injuries sustained while *in utero*, Justice McLachlin ruled that the common law did not recognize the unborn child as a legal or juridical person. Similarly, the majority declined to extend the courts' *parens patriae* jurisdiction to the protection of the unborn. To do so would "require a major change to the law of *parens patriae*. The ramifications of the change would be significant and complex [and involve] conflicts of fundamental rights and interests and different policy issues" (at 187). In particular, "to make orders protecting foetuses would radically impinge on the fundamental liberties of the pregnant woman, both as to lifestyle choices and how and as to where she chooses to live and be" (at 190). Justice McLachlin concluded (at 190): "If anything is to be done, the legislature is in a much better position to weigh the competing interests and arrive at a solution that is principled and minimally intrusive to pregnant women."

In his dissent, Justice Major (Sopinka J. concurring) placed more emphasis on the risk to the unborn child if its mother was not compelled to refrain from continuing her addictive habits. He characterized (at 198-99) the *parens patriae* jurisdiction as one of "undefined and undefinable breadth . . . [that] resides in the provincial superior courts to act on behalf of those who cannot act to protect themselves." He concluded (at 199-200):

> [A] superior court, on a proper motion should be able to exercise its *parens patriae* jurisdiction to restrain a mother's conduct when there is a reasonable probability of that conduct causing serious and irreparable harm to the foetus within her. While the granting of this type of remedy may interfere with the mother's liberty interests, in my view, those interests must bend when faced with a situation where devastating harm and a life of suffering can so easily be prevented. In any event, this interference is always subject to the mother's right to end it by deciding to have an abortion. . . .
>
> Once the mother decides to bear the child, the state has an interest in trying to ensure the child's health. What circumstances permit state intervention? The 'slippery slope' was raised. . . . Questions were raised about women who smoked, who lived with a smoker, who ate unhealthy diets, etc. In response to the query of where a reasonable line can be drawn it is submitted that the pen should not even be lifted. This approach would entail the state to stand idly by while a reckless and/or addicted mother inflicts serious and permanent harm on a child she had decided to bring into the world.
>
> There can be no general formula and each case must be decided on its own facts. However, as a minimum to justify intervention the following thresholds have to be met:
>
> (1) The woman must have decided to carry the child to term.
>
> (2) Proof must be presented to a civil standard that the abusive activity will cause serious and irreparable harm to the foetus.
>
> (3) The remedy must be the least intrusive option.
>
> (4) The process must be procedurally fair.

For commentary, see Martin, "Case Comment: *Winnipeg Child and Family Services (Northwest Area) v. G.(D.F.)*" (1988), 32 R.F.L. (4th) 381; Bartlett, "A Comment on *Winnipeg Child and Family Services (Northwest Area) v. G. (D.F.)*" (1997), 31 UBC Law Rev. 179; Rodgers, "*Winnipeg Child and Family Services v. D.G.F.*: Juridical Interference with Pregnant Women in the Alleged Interest of the Fetus" (1998), 36 Alta. Law Rev. 711; DeCoste, "*Winnipeg Child and Family Services (Northwest Area) v. D.F.G.* (1998), 36 Alta. L. Rev. 725; Elman & Mason, "The Failure of Dialogue: *Winnipeg Child and Family Services (Northwest Area) v. G. (D.F.)*" (1998), 36 Alta. L. Rev. 768;

For further reading, see Robertson, "Procreative Liberty and the Control of Conception, Pregnancy and Childbirth" (1983), 69 Virginia Law Rev. 405; Gallagher, "Prenatal Invasions and Interventions: What's Wrong With Fetal Rights" (1987), 10 Harvard Women's L. J. 9; Tateishi, "Apprehending the Fetus En Ventre Sa Mere: A Study in Judicial Sleight of Hand" (1989), 53 Sask. Law Rev. 113; Dawson, "*Re Baby R.*: A Comment on Fetal Apprehension" (1990), 4 C.J.W.L. 265; Dickens, "Comparative Judicial Embryology: Judges' Approaches to Unborn Human Life" (1990), 9 Can. J. Fam. L. 180; Dorzak, "Unborn Child Abuse: Contemplating Legal Solution" (1991), 9 Can. J. Fam. L. 133; Dawson, "A Feminist Response to 'Unborn Child Abuse: Contemplating Legal Solution'" (1991), 9 Can. J. Fam. L. 157; McConnell, "Sui Generis: The Legal Nature of the Foetus in Canada" (1991), 70 Can. Bar Rev. 548; Leavine, "Court-Ordered Caesarian Sections: Can a Pregnant Woman Refuse?" (1992), 29 Houston Law Rev. 185; Stern, "Court-Ordered Caesarian Sections: In Whose Best Interests?" (1993), 56 Mod. Law Rev. 238; Kirman, "Four Dialogues on Fetal Protection" (1993), 2 Health L. Rev. 31; Oliver, "State Intervention During Pregnancy and Childbirth: The Newest Challenge to Women's Reproductive Freedom" (1993), 2 Health L. Rev. 3; Jackman, "The Canadian Charter as a Barrier to Unwanted Medical Treatment of Pregnant Women in the Interests of the Foetus" (1993), 14 Health L. Can. 49; Martin and Coleman, "Judicial Intervention in Pregnancy" (1995), 40 McGill L.J. 947; Bailey-Harris, "Pregnancy, Autonomy and Refusal of Medical Treatment" (1998), 114 L.Q.R. 550; and Burgess, "Protective Custody: Will it Eradicate Fetal Abuse and Lead to the Perfect Womb?" (1998), 35 Houston Law Rev. 227.

In Canada, there is currently no legal obstacle to a woman's access to an abortion. Does a pregnant woman's right to abort her fetus necessarily carry with it a right to intentionally or recklessly inflict harm upon it? Would recognition of any degree of legal personality in the fetus necessarily and logically circumscribe the legal right to an abortion? Was the majority in the *Winnipeg Child and Family Services (Northwest Area)* case influenced by this concern? How did Major J. handle this point? Is his answer logical and convincing?

The Supreme Court of Canada has consistently denied any legal personality to the unborn child. In addition to the *Winnipeg Child and Family Services* case, see *R. v. Morgentaler*, [1988] 1 S.C.R 30 (striking down *Criminal Code* restrictions on abortion); *Borowski* v. *Canada (Attorney General)*, [1989] 1 S.C.R. 342 (declining to determine whether unborn child has right to life under s. 7 of *Charter*); *Tremblay* v. *Daigle*, [1989] 2 S.C.R. 530 (ruling that unborn child is not a "human being" for purpose of right to life under the Quebec *Charter of Rights and Freedoms* and holding that courts have no jurisdiction under that *Charter*, the Quebec *Civil Code*, or the common law to issue injunctions to prevent abortions in individual cases); *R.* v. *Sullivan*, [1991] 1 S.C.R. 489 (baby boy killed during birthing process not a "person" for the *Criminal Code* offence of causing death by criminal negligence); and *Dobson (Litigation Guardian of)* v. *Dobson* (1999), 174 D.L.R. (4th) 1 (S.C.C.) (born alive child cannot bring civil suit for pre-natal injuries caused by mother's negligent driving). For critical commentary, see McCourt, "Foetus Status After *R.* v. *Sullivan and Lemay*" (1991), 29 Alta. L. Rev. 916 and McCourt, "Fetus Status and Supreme Injustice: *Dobson* v. *Dobson*" (1999), 17 C.F.L.Q. 175.

8. Regarding the options available to the court once it has found a child in need of protection, see s. 57 of the *CFSA*. In keeping with the philosophy that the least disruptive alternative is to be favoured, s. 57(3) directs the court to keep the child in its home if possible. If the child cannot be left in its home, even subject to the society's supervision, s. 57(4) requires the court to consider placing the child with a relative, neighbour or other member of the child's community or extended family subject to supervision by the society. For examples of such placements, see *Children's Aid Society of Oxford (County)* v. *C. (T.)* (1986), 5 R.F.L. (3d) 151 (Ont. C.A.) and *L. (R.)* v. *Children's Aid Society of Metropolitan Toronto* (1995), 21 O.R. (3d) 724 (C.A.).

At one time s. 57(6) prohibited an order for Crown or permanent wardship unless the court was satisfied that the circumstances justifying the order were unlikely to change within a reasonably foreseeable time, not exceeding 24 months, so that the child can be returned to its home. See *Re M. (F.)* (1979), 11 R.F.L. (2d) 120 (Ont. Prov. Ct.) for a case illustrating the difficult task of attempting to assess the potential for improvement in a child's family life. The amendments which came into effect in 2000 repealed s. 57(6). However, it is likely that courts considering whether to issue a Crown wardship order will still consider whether the parents can resume care within a reasonable period.

Where a permanent wardship order is made, the child is removed from the home and the legal tie between parent and child is seriously threatened. By s. 63, the Crown, represented by the local children's aid society, has "all the rights and responsibilities of a parent for the purpose of the child's care, custody and control". It must be remembered also that Crown wardship can lead to adoption and the complete severance of the parent-child tie. Section 140 stipulates that the children's aid society "shall make all reasonable efforts to secure the adoption of . . . a Crown ward". The children's aid society may not, however, place a Crown ward for adoption until any access order made under Part III of the Act has been terminated (s. 140(2)(a)). Once a Crown ward has been placed for adoption, the child may be adopted without notice to the parents and without their consent (ss. 151(4)(c) and 137(2)). Because the underlying objective of a Crown wardship order is frequently to permit the eventual adoption of the child, the courts will consider the likelihood of adoption of a particular child before deciding to make such an order: *C.* v. *Children's Aid Society of Metropolitan Toronto (Municipality)* (1980), 20 R.F.L. (2d) 259 (Ont. Co. Ct.); *Children's Aid Society of Winnipeg (City)* v. *Clark* (1980), 20 R.F.L. (2d) 314 (Man. C.A.); and *Winnipeg South Child & Family Services Agency* v. *S. (D.D.)* (1990), 24 R.F.L. (3d) 290 (Man. Q.B.).

Under a temporary wardship order the society has "the rights and responsibilities of a parent for the purpose of the child's care, custody and control" (s. 63(2)). However, the parent retains any right he or she may have under the *Marriage Act* to give or refuse consent to the child's marriage (s. 62(4)). The court may also order that the parent retain any right he or she may have to give or refuse consent to the medical treatment of the child. See s. 62(1)-(3). In Ontario, no single temporary wardship order can be for a period longer than 12 months (s. 57(1) para. 2) and a child must not be a society ward for a continuous period exceeding 12 months if the child is less than six or 24 months if the child is six or over (s. 70(1)). See also subsections (2), (2.1), (3), and (4) of s. 70. For an analysis of the new, shorter time periods, see Bala, "Reforming Ontario's Child and Family Services Act: Is the Pendulum Swinging Back Too Far?" (1999) 17 C.F.L.Q. 121, at 152-158.

See generally, Bernstein, "Disposition and Post Disposition Issues Under the Child and Family Services Act" (1986), 1 R.F.L. (3d) 301 and Sammon, "The Ontario *Child and Family Services Act, 1984*: Maintaining the Balance Between Competing Rights" (1992), 8 C.F.L.Q. 129, at 180-186.

9. Access to a child dealt with under Part III of the *CFSA* may be ordered under s. 58. See also s. 59. What factors did the court examine in *Children's Aid Society of Toronto* v. *L. (E.L.)*, reproduced earlier in this chapter, in determining that there should be no access? See also *Children's Aid Society of Haldimand* v. *B. (R.)* (1981), 25 R.F.L. (2d) 56 (Ont. C.A.); *Saskatchewan (Minister of Social Services)* v. *M. (W.)* (1983), 32 R.F.L. (2d) 337 (Sask. U.F.C.); *Children's Aid Society of Metropolitan Toronto (Municipality)* v. *L. (J.)* (1987), 7 R.F.L. (3d) 329 (Ont. Fam. Ct.); and *New Brunswick (Minister of Health and Community Services)* v. *L. (M.)* (1998), 41 R.F.L. (4th) 339 (S.C.C.).

A child cannot be placed for adoption until an access order made under s. 58(1) has been terminated: s. 140(2)(a). Nor can an access order be made after a Crown ward has been placed for adoption and while the child continues to reside in the home of the prospective adopting parents: s. 58(7). Nor can a court make an order for access under the *CFSA* once an adoption order is made: s. 160(1). However, the Ontario Court of Appeal has become more receptive to applications by birth relatives for access following adoption under the *CLRA*. See Chapter 11, **ADOPTION**.

10. Note that a Crown ward cannot be placed for adoption until the time for launching an appeal of the order of Crown wardship has passed or the appeal is disposed of (s. 140(2)).

11. In *Children's Aid Society of Ottawa-Carleton (Regional Municipality)* v. *L. (D.J.)* (1980), 15 R.F.L. (2d) 102 (Ont. Fam. Ct.), Walmsley Prov. J. concluded that a prior custody order made under the *Divorce Act* had "no standing in face of the Crown wardship order". See also *Children's Aid Society of Halifax (City)* v. *McIlveen* (1980), 20 R.F.L. (2d) 302 (N.S. Fam. Ct.) where this view is more fully developed; and *Z. (G.M.)* v. *B. (T.F.S.)*, 18 R.F.L. (2d) 47, [1981] 1 W.W.R. 152 (Man. C.A.) where the court held that an access order made under the *Divorce Act* was terminated by an adoption order under provincial legislation. How would you explain these results in light of the federal paramountcy rule that applies under Canada's Constitution?

12. If a child is committed to the care of a child protection authority, the state incurs considerable expense in caring for the child. Section 60 of the *CFSA* authorizes the court to order the parents to make support payments for the child in this situation.

13. Part V of the *CFSA* sets out a number of rights of a child in the care of the child protection agency. See ss. 103-108. Section 61 of the Act also restricts the agency's exercise of discretion in providing for the care and custody of a child who is a society or Crown ward. For a detailed description of the child care system provided for children in need of protection, see Hepworth, *Foster Care and Adoption in Canada* (Ottawa: Canadian Council on Social Development, 1980). See also Cruickshank, "The Child in Care" in Bala *et al*, eds., *Canadian Child Welfare Law* (Toronto: Thompson Educational Publishing Inc., 1991); and Sherott, "Foster Care for Abused Children: An Unacceptable Solution" (1993), 57 Sask. L. Rev. 479.

14. Regarding subsequent judicial review of orders made under s. 57 of the CFSA, see ss. 64 and 65. In *C.C.A.S. of Metropolitan Toronto* v. *M. (C.)* (1994), 2 R.F.L. (4th) 313 (S.C.C.), the court struggled with the appropriate approach to a status review. The litigants presented two clear alternative views. The appellant mother argued that the threshold issue was whether there was a continuing need for a court order pursuant to s. 57. Only after the court had made this determination could it consider the best interests of the child. The respondent society argued that on a status review the court did not have to make a new determination that the child was in need of protection and that the sole issue was to assess what disposition was in the best interests of the child. Justice L'Heureux-Dubé, for the court, attempted

to adopt a middle position. Although recognizing (at 342) that the state agency must justify continuing intervention in the family by establishing the continued need for protection by way of a court order, she ultimately adopted (at 343) a "flexible approach" which "seeks to balance the best interests of children with the need to prevent indeterminate State intervention, while at the same time recognizing that the best interests of the child must always prevail". In particular, intervention by the state might be justified even if the parent could now reasonably care for the child. "The determination of whether the child continues to be in need of protection cannot solely focus on the parent's parenting ability, . . . but must have a child-centred focus and must examine whether the child, in light of the interceding events, continues to require State protection" (at 346). Since this child had become bonded with the foster parents, a protection order could be based on the need to protect the child from the emotional harm that would result if she were to be removed from their home and returned to her mother's care.

For commentary on *C.C.A.S. of Metropolitan Toronto* v. *M. (C.)*, see Freedman, "Parents' Rights and Best Interests of Children Under the *Child and Family Services Act*" (1994), 11 C.F.L.Q. 216 and Thompson, "Case Comment: *C.C.A.S. of Metropolitan Toronto* v. *M. (C.)*" (1994-95), 12 C.F.L.Q. 45.

Section 64(9) precludes a status review where a Crown ward has been placed for adoption and continues to reside in the prospective adopting parents' home. A *Charter* challenge to the equivalent provision in Nova Scotia legislation failed in *C. (D.)* v. *Family & Children's Services of Cumberland (County)* (1988), 16 R.F.L. (3d) 222 (N.S. C.A.).

15. Section 66 of the *CFSA* provides for an annual administrative review of the care of each Crown ward.

(4) REPRESENTATION OF THE CHILD

Section 38 of the *CFSA* specifically recognizes that a child may be represented by counsel. It also requires the court, whenever a child does not have legal representation, to determine whether legal representation is desirable to protect the child's interests and to direct that legal representation be provided for the child if at any stage of the proceedings such representation is considered desirable. Section 38 is similar to s. 20 of the *Child Welfare Act*, which is discussed in the following case. The mother asked the court to rule that a representative from the Official Guardian's Office did not have any status before the court because the mother's counsel represented the interests of the child. Incidentally, the Official Guardian was renamed the Children's Lawyer by S.O. 1994, c. 27, s. 43.

T. (T.) v. CATHOLIC CHILDREN'S AID SOCIETY OF METROPOLITAN TORONTO (MUNICIPALITY)

(1984), 39 R.F.L. (2d) 279, 46 O.R. (2d) 347 (Fam. Ct.)

THOMSON PROV. J.: — . . . Both the Official Guardian's representative and counsel for the mother submitted that they represented the child. The Official Guardian's office became involved as a result of a referral made by the society on the day that the order to produce was obtained.

Counsel for the mother submits that he represents the child and he should be permitted to continue his dual role at least until an order is made finding T.T. in need of protection or until a conflict of interest should develop. There is obviously no dispute that this child, aged 11 months, lacks capacity to retain her own lawyer. Counsel bases his argument upon s. 20 [en. 1982, c. 20, s. 1] of the Children's Law Reform Act, R.S.O. 1980, c. 68, which sets out the general custodial rights of parents in relation to their children. So long as no finding has been made that the child is in need of protection from the parent, it is argued that one of the incidents of custody is that of deciding whether the child shall be legally represented and, if so, by whom. In this case the mother has decided that her lawyer may represent the child as well.

In my opinion counsel correctly states, as a basic proposition of law, supported by the Children's Law Reform Act, that decisions on behalf of the incapable child are to be made by her parents and that this includes deciding whether to seek expert help when that child's interests or well-being are at stake. Where lawyers and the legal process are involved, a decision to seek legal assistance from the lawyer who also represents the mother would seem consistent with this proposition.

It is perhaps worth noting that there are those commentators who would argue that, for reasons related to their view of the role of the law in cases of alleged child neglect or abuse, it is important that parents determine whether and how their children are represented prior to a finding that there are grounds for modifying or terminating the parent-child relationship: see, e.g., Goldstein, Freud and Solnit, Before the Best Interests of the Child, (1979), c. 7.

I find, however, that there are at least three reasons for holding that a parent does not have such absolute authority in proceedings under the Child Welfare Act:

1. The Child Welfare Act expressly recognizes that a child may have separate legal representation in child protection proceedings. Beyond that, the court is given the power to order that legal representation be provided for the unrepresented child when it is felt that this is necessary "to protect the interests of the child". . . .

    In my view, this clear statutory recognition that the child may have separate interests worthy of representation would be of little value if a parent's nomination of her lawyer as counsel for the child meant that s. 20(1) was satisfied and, therefore, an order under s. 20(2) was not possible.

2. Child protection matters proceed from an allegation that the child is at risk within the parent-child relationship. Obviously, one should be careful not to characterize such an allegation as valid simply because it has been made. It is equally true that, from the child's perspective, the issue to be decided is of major importance. As well, it seems to me that in these cases it is risky to make the assumption which I would argue lies beneath the general assignment of decision-making to the parent: that the interests of the parent and the child who lacks capacity are in large measure identical. One may see the need for a separate child's voice because high risk situations might otherwise escape the court's attention; alternatively the fear may be that state intervention will be authorized in cases where this is unnecessary. . . .

    The Canadian Charter of Rights and Freedoms helps to reinforce the view that a child may have separate interests worthy of special protection in proceedings such as these. The argument is obviously more easily made when dealing with a child with legal capacity. However, there is a growing recognition that, in certain situations, children may have separate security or liberty interests requiring the protection of the Charter . . .

3. Major practical problems could arise if a separate lawyer for the child is not appointed until the first stage of the child protection matter is completed. The child's interests are not necessarily represented at the negotiation, pre-trial and conciliation stages when most cases are and should be resolved. Delay harmful to the child seems inevitable while the newly added lawyer obtains a transcript of that which has already transpired. It might even be necessary for witnesses to be recalled to offer evidence already given in the proceedings. The fact that, under the present Child

Welfare Act, the adjudication and disposition stages of the proceedings can become extremely intertwined reinforces these practical difficulties.

As a result, I find that counsel for the mother in these proceedings represents only the mother. It may be that, in carrying out this task, he will be speaking for the child's interests as well. However, I do not feel that he should be seen to be that child's specific legal representative.

This leaves the question of whether the representative from the Official Guardian's office represents the child. . . .

Once an order has been made under s. 20(2), I see no reason why the court should inquire into the means by which the government has ensured that such orders are complied with, other than to note that the office of the Official Guardian has been used as the mechanism through which counsel for children are made available. Further, I see no reason why the children's aid society, or anyone else for that matter, may not notify the Official Guardian's office at the time proceedings are commenced that legal representation for the child would appear to be indicated. As well, one of the parties, a representative from the Official Guardian's office or anyone else with a concern for the child or an interest in the proceedings might appear before the court asking that an order under s. 20(2) be made.

After hearing argument on this motion I determined that the child's interests ought to receive separate representation and I made a s. 20(2) order. Accordingly, Ms. Powell does in my view possess the necessary authority to represent the child, T.T.

The difficulties facing a lawyer in deciding the appropriate role to adopt when representing children is discussed in the following article by the judge who decided the above case.

THOMSON, "ELIMINATING ROLE CONFUSION IN THE CHILD'S LAWYER: THE ONTARIO EXPERIENCE"

(1983), 4 Can. J. Fam. L. 125 (Footnotes omitted.)

2.1: Rationale as a Foundation for Role

The issue of rationale is of primary importance since it is necessary to be very clear about why the child is being given a lawyer if the role of counsel is to be understood. I have suggested elsewhere that the child is entitled to legal representation because of the basic right of each person to be heard and in order to advance the child's position in matters of great importance in which neither parent nor state can be assumed to be acting in the child's interests. This viewpoint, which supports the role of the lawyer as an advocate, is taken because of the relevance of the child's preferences to the issue to be decided and the adversarial nature of the process by which these matters are resolved. Conversely, if the lawyer is seen as a means of fully informing the judge and thus overcoming the perceived weaknesses of the adversary system, an *amicus curiae* role is indicated. If one's view is that decision-making is improved as a result of an independent search on behalf of the child for a position felt to further the child's best interests, then a form of guardianship becomes preferable.

A review of materials that support the introduction of separate legal representation in Ontario reveals an uncertainty as to rationale. The earliest reference is found in the 1973 report of the Ontario Law Reform Commission and it is by far the clearest. A separate Office of the Law Guardian was proposed. Its sole job would have been to assist the court in its decision-making by ensuring that all available information was presented and, most important, by engaging in a separate evaluation of the child's best interests. Strong adversarial techniques were frowned upon and presentation of the child's wishes was not mentioned as relevant to the Law Guardian's task. In addition, the report did not consider whether asking lawyers, even with expert assistance, to determine what was in the child's best interests was an appropriate use of their skills.

More recently, both reports of the Attorney General's Committee on the Representation of Children, which led directly to the legislation, failed to deal with this issue, although the Committee did call for high quality representation and proposed a delivery model, through the Office of the Official Guardian, which, as will be seen, *might* be taken as support for a particular set of objectives and hence, a particular role. The Consultation paper that proposed the legislation was, at best, vague on this issue. . . .

Two further points about rationale, which are related to the issue at hand, should be made:

(a) The first is that, as one decides whether or not to provide children with legal representation, there may be a tendency to lose sight of how the broader policy objectives of child protection legislation might have an impact upon one's decision. It is here that one is faced with the fact that so little is known about what happens when lawyers for children enter the process. If, for example, child protection legislation is intended to represent support for the view that the least intrusive alternative is to be chosen when state intervention is required, one might at least ask whether the addition of the child's representative furthers these objectives. If the introduction of the lawyer, particularly one whose role has not been defined in advance, actually functions as a means of supporting excessive interference in the family and early intervention by child welfare authorities, then one might question whether the cost of adding the lawyer outweighs the conceptual benefits of doing so. At least one set of authors relied upon what they felt should be the goals of child protection legislation to support the view that lawyers should not be introduced until the disposition stage of the proceedings.

(b) Second, it can be argued that providing children with lawyers *should* proceed, but rarely does, from a consideration of whether one is thereby achieving the best results given limited resources. . . .

2.2: Choosing the Lawyer

The vehicle chosen for the provision of legal representation will be of major importance in the determination of role. If, for example, one adopts the approach of placing the lawyer in the court and as part of a staff directed by the judge, quick reference to the literature which demonstrates how lawyers adapt their role to meet the expectations of judges should make it easy to predict the result. Full-time placement in the court, as a government employee, would seem most consistent with an *amicus curiae* role. At least it would appear to make the lawyer uncertain how his or her role differs from that of the child protection authority; it may also seem unfair to the parents that two government authorities seek removal of their child. Even when independent duty counsel is placed in the court at point of first contact, the child is apt to have great difficulty seeing him or her as a lawyer, separate from others before the court.

Going further, it should not be surprising to discover that use of the private bar increases the likelihood of an advocacy position being adopted, at least when lawyers first begin the task. Use of a specialized private organization established for the purpose of child representation is apt to produce a role that accords with the policy-political perspective held by that organization. Finally, use of a government body whose primary experience relates to performance as guardian *ad litem* in custody and some child protection matters will produce a stance that incorporates elements of the guardian role.

In Ontario, the model proposed by the committee considering the issue, and the one that was ultimately implemented, involves the use of full-time employees of the Office of the Official Guardian as well as the private bar. Cases are referred to the Official Guardian's office; a certain number are selected for representation by his employees or representatives, with the majority being referred to a panel of private lawyers who must complete a training program before qualifying for placement on the panel.

The Official Guardian's office immediately recognized that this hybrid delivery model raised questions regarding its authority to dictate a position on role. At a minimum, such a position needed to be developed to clarify the role to be adopted by staff lawyers when representing children; in addition the issue of role was an obvious topic for the training sessions that were to be held.

A role statement was developed which combined elements of advocacy ("where the child does have the capacity to formulate and convey wishes, then in almost all cases counsel should advocate those wishes"), guardianship (an exception exists "where a child consistently expresses a wish to return to a situation of peril") and the role of *amicus curiae* ("counsel ... must, in every case, ensure that *all* material and relevant information is before the court"). While some care was taken to present the guidelines solely as those formulated for use by the Official Guardian's office and the training materials included articles that embraced more than one position, it is clear that the method chosen for delivering these legal services in Ontario has had an effect on the type of representation provided to the child. To the extent that "internal" guidelines are perceived by the private bar as directive rather than suggestive, that effect may be even greater.

. . .

2.3: Seeking an Appropriate Role

One may introduce the child's lawyer to the court while failing to clarify the role issue, but this should be done with a clear understanding of the "rather serious condition of role ambiguity" the lawyer will therefore bring to the task. . . .

We know from those who have observed the lawyer in Juvenile Court, that the role adopted will depend, to a great extent, on the individual predisposition that the lawyer brings to the task; as well, there is a tendency to modify one's approach in a way that conforms to the philosophy of the court and the lawyer will be greatly affected by the expectations of those persons he or she encounters in the process. The most influential of these will be the judge.

The obvious difficulty that this creates is that the lawyer in search of an appropriate stance becomes subject to the varying views of judges. The confusion

of judges concerning role is probably equal to that of lawyers. Normally one discovers judges' varying expectations as a result of inferences drawn from exposure
to their decision-making over time. The Ontario experience is unique because individual judges were prepared to articulate competing positions in judgments from the
bench. In two decisions released over a two-month period, one finds in the first a
clear and compelling defence of the lawyer's role as advocate and, in the second, a
strong statement of the lawyer's role as guardian and *amicus curiae*. Decisions from
a third court suggested that the lawyer may be excluded if he or she fails to advocate
in the manner dictated by the judge.

At this point, one could only sympathize with the individual counsel, seeking
an appropriate role in the face of contradictory advice in the literature, differing
expectations from the bench, conflicting pressures from others involved with the
case and a set of guidelines of uncertain status from the office in charge of assigning
him or her to cases and paying the fee.

A fresh participant was invited to enter the debate — the Law Society's Professional Conduct Committee. The report of the Subcommittee on the Legal Representation of Children, adopted by the Law Society, essentially brings the issue full
circle because of their finding that, absent a specific legislative enactment to the
contrary, the traditional solicitor and client relationship exists between lawyer and
child.

NOTES AND QUESTIONS

1. In his article, Thomson refers to three Ontario decisions where judges were prepared to articulate
competing positions regarding the proper role for a child's lawyer in protection hearings. In *Re W.*
(1979), 13 R.F.L. (2d) 381, 27 O.R. (2d) 314 (Prov. Ct.), Abella Prov. J. explained (at 382-385) her
support for the "advocacy role":

> I am persuaded that essentially the role of the lawyer for the child is no different from the role of
> the lawyer for any party: He or she is there to represent a client by protecting the client's interests
> and carrying out the client's instructions. At the same time, the lawyer is an officer of the court
> and as such is obliged to represent these interests in accordance with well-defined standards of
> professional integrity.
>
> There is a tendency to assume that the quintessential legal representative for the child is, or
> should be, a paragon of legal, psychological and sociological expertise. This is unrealistic. Lawyers
> generally have only legal skills, the proper utilization of which may undoubtedly involve some
> direct or indirect familiarity with or reliance upon other disciplines. Lawyers are called upon, in
> short, to exercise informed legal judgment. Lawyers for children can therefore be expected to do
> no more and no less than any other party's lawyer in the adversarial process. This is not to endorse
> the adversarial process in matters of family disputes; it is, rather, to acknowledge that it is through
> this process at present that these disputes are resolved. So long as the forum is the courtroom, the
> child's lawyer should represent his or her young client in a way which reflects equal participation
> with the other parties in this forum.
>
> Representing a client in these cases usually involves executing a client's instructions and,
> without being misleading, attempting to show through the evidence that these instructions or
> wishes best match the child's needs. In other words, a mother who wishes custody of her child
> expects her lawyer to present her case in such a way that her wishes are shown to be in the best
> interests of the child. It is, in most cases, an articulation of the client's rather than the lawyer's
> subjective assessment. It should be no different when the client is a child. Where, therefore, the
> child has expressed definite views, these views, rather than those of the child's lawyer, should
> determine what is conveyed to the court. The child's advocate is the legal architect who constructs
> a case based on the client's views.
>
> In its purest form, that means that the child's lawyer should present and implement a client's
> instructions to the best of his or her ability. And this, in turn, involves indicating to the court the

child's concerns, wishes and opinions. It involves, further, presenting to the court accurate and complete evidence which is consistent with the child's position. And too, there is an obligation to ensure, insofar as this is possible given the age and circumstances of the child, that the opinions and wishes expressed by the child are freely given and without duress from any other party or person. . . .

In many cases it is almost impossible to unerringly assess what is best for a child. Given this epistemological gap, why should the lawyer substitute his or her own opinion for that of the child? Consider too that a lawyer who formulates an opinion of the child's best interests is often making this judgment before the trial and therefore without the benefit of hearing all of the available evidence. Not even the most Solomonic of judges would be expected to perform this feat.

In a trial it is for a judge to determine ultimately what is in a given child's best interests. The bases for this determination include, among other evidence, the child's wishes. These wishes should therefore, whenever possible, be articulated so that the court has the benefit of knowing all relevant factors and so that the child has an effective and meaningful role in the proceedings which affect him or her no less than any of the other parties.

There must undoubtedly be a degree of flexibility in a child's lawyer's role as articulator of his or her client's wishes. The child may be unable to instruct counsel. Or the child may be, as in this case, ambivalent about her wishes. Or the child may be too young. Although there should be no minimum age below which a child's wishes should be ignored — so long as the child is old enough to express them, they should be considered — I feel that where a child does not or cannot express wishes, the role of the child's lawyer should be to protect the client/child's interests. In the absence of clear instructions, protecting the client's interests can clearly involve presenting the lawyer's perception of what would best protect the child's interests. In this latter role of promulgating the infant client's best interests, the lawyer would attempt to guarantee that all the evidence the court needs to make a disposition which accommodates the child's best interests is before the court, is complete and is accurate. There could in this kind of role be no inconsistency between what is perceived by the lawyer to be the child's best interests and the child's instructions. Where there is such conflict, the wishes of the child should prevail in guiding the lawyer.

In the case of a child who is capable of coherent expression the lawyer's role in representing the child's wishes does not preclude the lawyer from exploring with the child the merits or realities of the case, evaluating the practicalities of the child's position and even offering, where appropriate, suggestions about possible reasonable resolutions to the case. Offering advice is part of the lawyer's obligation to protect the client's interests. Obviously, however, given the vulnerability of most children to authority in general and given the shattered sensibilities in family disputes in particular, great sensitivity should be exercised during these exploratory sessions. The lawyer should be constantly conscious of his or her posture being an honest but not an overwhelming one.

This case involves a seven-year-old girl who expresses ambivalence about where she wants to live. She has offered no clear instructions to her lawyer. Counsel's role in protecting her client's interests would include, therefore, articulating, exploring and attempting to explain this conflict to the court by evidentiary means. Then, having heard the evidence of all parties, Ms. Losee could further assist the court by offering in final submissions her assessment of what the evidence reveals to be in her client's ''best'' interests. . . .

However, in *Re C.* (1980), 14 R.F.L. (2d) 21 (Ont. Prov. Ct.) and again in *C. (J.)* v. *C. (S.)* (1980), 31 O.R. (2d) 53 (Prov. Ct.), Karswick Prov. Ct. J. made a strong statement suggesting that the child's lawyer should act as guardian and *amicus curiae*. The lawyer, in his view, should communicate the child's wishes to the court and conduct the appropriate examinations and cross-examinations of witnesses to establish the basis for those views. However, he also believed that where giving effect to the child's wishes would, in the lawyer's opinion, be contrary to the best interests of the child, the lawyer should bring this to the attention of the court. He stated (14 R.F.L. (2d) 21, at 26):

> When one considers the fundamental importance of this issue of custody for the family and the community I do not think that the court can, nor should it, direct the child's counsel to take a strict adversarial role and act as a ''mouth-piece'', blindly advocating a view, preference or instructions which confound or shock his professional opinion of what is in the best interest of the child. It makes eminently good sense to have counsel take an active, real and positive role in

the social context of the family court and, as officers of this court, assume the obligation to adduce all relevant and material evidence on this issue of what is in the best interest of the child and, when called upon, to express a professional and responsible view of what that disposition should be.

In *Re A.* (1989), 23 R.F.L. (3d) 121 (Alta. Prov. Ct.), the Calgary Regional Child Welfare Director applied for a review of a temporary guardianship order and sought a permanent guardianship order regarding three children, aged 12, 11, and 8. Fitch Prov. J. noted, without any sign of disapproval, at 123:

> Counsel appointed for the children supports the director's application, although all three children have expressed a desire to return to live with their mother. While s. 78 of the Child Welfare Act provides that the court appoints a lawyer to represent a child if the court is satisfied that the interests or views of the child would not be otherwise adequately represented, it is common practice for counsel appointed pursuant to s. 78 to form their own opinion as to what is in the best interests of the children, even though that position may differ from the views of the clients, the children.

2. In "The Ontario Child and Family Services Act, 1984: Maintaining the Balance Between Competing Rights" (1991), 8 C.F.L.Q. 129, W.J. Sammon asserted at (190) that some lawyers who represent children in child protection proceedings in Ontario "feel that they are entitled to advise the court not only what the child wants but also what the lawyer believes is in the child's best interests. Accordingly, a situation can arise where the lawyer will be advocating a position opposed to the expressed instructions of his child client". He urged legislative guidelines to preclude this.

Notwithstanding Sammon's comments, a consensus has developed in Ontario regarding the child's lawyer's role. As noted by Thompson in his article, in April, 1980 the Professional Conduct Committee of the Law Society of Upper Canada appointed a sub-committee to consider the role of the lawyer representing children. It reported in May 1981. The Report read in part:

> When the child does not have the capacity to fully understand the consequences of the proceedings he is involved in then the relationship with his or her lawyer is not the normal solicitor/client relationship. . . . If the child is mature and responsible enough to accept the consequences of his or her acts and decisions and understands fully the nature of the proceedings and can express a preference as to its resolution, the Committee tends to favour the traditional solicitor/client approach rather than the guardian-type of representation. Decisions as to the capacity of the child to properly instruct counsel must be determined by the individual lawyer in the particular circumstances. One of the factors that the lawyer would take into account in making this decision would be the ability of the child to accept rationally the advice he or she is receiving. If the child stubbornly, without reason, refuses to accept the advice of the counsel, it may be that the child lacks the maturity to properly instruct counsel. . . .
>
> The Sub-Committee especially rejects the suggestions that there is a duty on the solicitor to make any disclosure to the court, or to anyone, with respect to the information in his possession acquired in the course of the solicitor and client relationship, even when, in the opinion of the solicitor, it is in the best interests of the child to act contrary to the child's instructions. The solicitor is not the judge of the best interests of the child, and is not, under any circumstances, to be excused for a breach of the solicitor and client relationship. If the solicitor does not believe he can accept the instructions of the child, then he should withdraw from the matter. He should, in all events, conduct himself as if he was acting for an adult.
>
> The Sub-Committee rejects the suggestions that the solicitor has a duty to the court to advise the court, or to help or assist the court in coming to its deliberation, if such advice or assistance constitutes a disclosure of information which is otherwise privileged, or if it is to act contrary to the instructions of the client. No such duty exists upon a solicitor in law, and there are no special circumstances made out in the case of infants. . . .
>
> The Sub-Committee feels that if the legislature . . . is of the view that some special circumstances exist in the case of infants requiring some special form of representation, that the legislature should be explicit in the wording of such legislation, and there should be no ambiguity whatsoever

in such legislation. Particularly is this so where such legislation would, in the ordinary course, be entirely contrary to the traditional role of the solicitor and client.

The Sub-committee noted that The Rules of Professional Conduct of the Law Society of Upper Canada modified the solicitor-client privilege by specifying: "Disclosure of information [concerning a client acquired in the course of the professional relationship] necessary to prevent a crime will be justified if the lawyer has reasonable grounds for believing that a crime is likely to be committed." Does this permit a lawyer to reveal information confided by a child where future child abuse appears likely? Recall the earlier discussion in the context of the duty to report abuse.

More recently, the Office of the Children's Lawyer has issued a policy stating that the role of the child's lawyer, provided the child is competent to instruct the lawyer, is generally to advance the position consistent with the child's wishes and preferences. However, the policy suggests that, if the lawyer believes the child is being unduly influenced by one parent, the lawyer may decline to advocate the outcome sought by the child. Even then, counsel should ensure that the child's wishes and preferences are known to the decision-maker together with information about how one parent may be influencing the child. See McTavish, *Office of the Children's Lawyer - Policy Statement - Role of Children's Counsel* (Toronto, April 3, 1995).

3. In *Catholic Children's Aid Society of Metropolitan Toronto* v. *M. (C.)* (1991), 35 R.F.L. (3d) 1 (Ont. Prov. Div.), Bean Prov. J. noted (at 14) that s. 38(1) of the *CFSA* implicitly accepts that a child may retain and instruct counsel in the usual fashion; that is, by private retainer. More commonly, a child in child protection hearings will obtain legal representation as a result of a court "direction" under s. 38(3). In that situation, the lawyer will be selected through the child representation program operated by the Children's Lawyer. Nonetheless, Judge Bean concluded (at 16) that this lawyer's "relationship as solicitor and client is with the child and with the child alone". Regarding the lawyer's role where the child is capable of instructing counsel, Judge Bean stated, at 15:

> It is beyond doubt that the duty of the counsel for an instructing child is to follow the child's instructions. Some judges and writers have attempted to place a condition upon the duty, where following the client's instructions might cause the child harm. ... I disagree with that latter proposition.

Judge Bean's comments about the lawyer's role where the child is capable of instructing counsel were *obiter*. The case itself concerned a child who was too young to give instructions. Judge Bean ruled that in this situation the lawyer had to withdraw from the case unless appointed and instructed by someone acting as litigation guardian. On appeal, Sutherland J. ruled in *Official Guardian* v. *M. (S.)* (1991), 35 R.F.L. (3d) 297, at 302 (Ont. Div. Ct.) that there was no need for a litigation guardian where a lawyer was appointed under s. 38(3) of the *CFSA*:

> It is ... clearly implied in that subsection that a litigation guardian is not required and that the legal representative, once appointed, is expected to put forth his views and arguments as to the best interests of the child without the need for an instructing party to the litigation.

When the case resumed, Bean Prov. J. indicated that the child's lawyer would have a limited role. He would not be able to give evidence from the floor or even make submissions on the best interests of the child. See *C.C.A.S. of Metropolitan Toronto* v. *M. (C.)* (1991), 37 R.F.L. (3d) 202 (Ont. Prov. Div.). In the accompanying annotation in the R.F.L.s, Professor McLeod endorsed the first point and strongly questioned the latter. Recall that the Ontario Court of Appeal stressed in *Strobridge* v. *Strobridge* (1994), 4 R.F.L. (4th) 169 that a lawyer appointed as child's counsel in a custody and access dispute could not simply advise the court of the child's views and preferences unless the parties consented. In other words, the child's wishes constitute evidence that must be proved in the normal way.

4. In "Towards a New Approach to Child Representation: How Less is More in Child Welfare Proceedings" (1994), 10 C.F.L.Q. 187, Marvin Bernstein supports the view that there is now a general consensus, in Ontario at least, that the role of the child's counsel is to advocate vigorously on behalf of an instructing child/client, regardless of counsel's own views concerning the child's best interests. He suggests that the "early dilemma" in child representation concerning an instructing child/client has largely been resolved and has been replaced by the "current dilemma" involving non-instructing child/

clients. He describes this dilemma as follows (at 235): ". . . [F]irst, whether child representation is required for the non-instructing child/client and if so, then, secondly, what should counsel's role be in the representation of a non-instructing child/client?"

Dealing with the first issue, he writes (at 254):

. . . I support a presumption against child representation in the case of non-instructing children, which presumption can be rebutted where one or more of the following circumstances exist:

(a) where a parent does not appear before the court;

(b) where a parent is not represented by counsel;

(c) where any of the parties to the proceedings may not have sufficiently competent legal representation; or

(d) where a Children's Aid Society or state agency may not be acting with total impartiality.

What guidance does s. 38(3) of the *CFSA* give?

Whether a child's counsel should be acting as *amicus curiae* or guardian in the case of non-instructing children is not completely settled. The Children's Lawyer's guidelines emphasize the role of guardian. See Himel, "The Lawyer's Role: Representing Children" in Bala, Hornick, and Vogl, eds., *Canadian Child Welfare Law* (Toronto: Thompson Educational Publishing, 1991) 196, at 199. However, Bernstein concludes (at 240): "In my view, the *amicus curiae* option may be an attractive option, as it allows the lawyer to use his or her legal training and investigative abilities, while eliminating the temptations to be a second social worker or judge, as the case may be."

5. The possibility of independent legal representation is only one example of the separate standing accorded to the child under the *CFSA*. See also ss. 39(4), 39(5), 39(6), 58(2), 64(4) and 69.

6. In *Re. C.*, above, Karswick Prov. J. suggested (at 29)that counsel for the parents in child protection hearings also has a duty to "ensure that all relevant evidence is adduced, that no such evidence is suppressed and, further, to be prepared to give an honest and professional statement of what they feel is in the best interest of the child and the reason for that position". How is this position to be reconciled with the traditional doctrine of solicitor-client privilege? Would this move away from a strictly adversarial process be desirable? See the annotation to the case by Professor McLeod ((1980), 14 R.F.L. (2d) 21).

7. For further reading regarding legal representation of the child in child protection hearings and other proceedings, see Leon, "Recent Developments in Legal Representation of Children: A Growing Concern with the Concept of Capacity" (1978), 1 Can. J. Fam. L. 375; Maczko, "Some Problems with Acting For Children" (1979), 2 Can. J. Fam. L. 267; Leon, "Canadian Children: Prospects for Legal Rights and Representation" (1979), 2 Fam. Law Rev. 16; McHale, "The Proper Role of the Lawyer as Legal Representative of the Child" (1980), 18 Alta. L. Rev. 216; Ramsey, "Representation of the Child in Protection Proceedings: The Determination of Decision-Making Capacity" (1983), 17 Fam. L.Q. 287; Himel, "Representing Children" in Bala, Hornick and Vogl, eds., *Canadian Child Welfare Law* (Toronto: Thompson Educational Publishing Inc., 1991); Nasmith, "The Inchoate Voice" (1991), 8 C.F.L.Q. 43; Peterson-Badali and Abramovitch, "Children's Knowledge of the Legal System: Are they Competent to Instruct Counsel?" (1992), 34 Can. J. Crim. 139; Bernstein, "Towards a New Approach to Child Representation: How Less is More in Child Welfare Proceedings" (1994), 10 C.F.L.Q. 187; and Ward, Translator, "The Legal Representation of Children: A Consultation Paper Prepared by the Quebec Bar Committee" (1996), 13 Can. J. Fam. L. 49.

11

ADOPTION

1. Introduction

BALA AND WILDGOOSE, CANADIAN CHILDREN'S LAW:
A COURSEBOOK

(Vol. 1, 1985), 371-375

A. Introduction

Adoption is the creation, by court order, of the legal relationship of parent and child between persons who were not so related by blood and the simultaneous severing of legal ties between the child and the biological parents.

The concept of adoption has existed in different forms in various societies. North American natives had customs providing for the care of children whose parents could not do so, whether due to death or for other reasons; the legal validity of Inuit custom adoptions was recognized in *Re Deborah E4-789* (1972), 6 R.F.L. 299 (N.W.T. Terr. Ct.). Adoption was unknown to the English common law, partly as it was viewed as a threat to the continuity of family lines and estates.

The first Canadian legislation providing for adoption was enacted in New Brunswick in 1873; most provinces only enacted adoption statutes in the years following World War I, when changing social conditions resulted in unprecedented numbers of children being left homeless after illegitimate birth. Unlike the laws of ancient Rome, which were designed to deal with problems of lineage and succession, Canadian adoption legislation is designed to promote the welfare of children without parents. In most provinces the law governing adoption constitutes part of a comprehensive scheme for child care, such as that found in Ontario's *C.F.S.A.* [*Child and Family Services Act*] Pt. VII.

Since the enactment of most provincial adoption laws in the latter part of the last century and in the early part of the present one, the social environment in which adoptions take place has changed greatly. Today [some] adoptions are step-parent adoptions, where the consequences of adoption may be very different than in a non-relative adoption. The growth and acceptance of one-parent families, both socially and through legislation, has reduced much of the social stigma and legal disadvantages of illegitimacy. As a result, fewer children born out of wedlock are being placed for adoption. The children available for adoption tend to be older children or children who suffer from a handicap. As you read the materials in this chapter, consider whether our adoption laws continue to make sense in light of these social changes.

An adoption proceeding is civil in nature, but it is somewhat different from most court proceedings. Usually a court is faced with resolving a dispute between two parties, one of whom may be the State, as in the case of child-protection action. An adoption proceeding involves the status of a person, the child in question; it is an action *in rem*. In granting an adoption order, a judge is not simply acting as a

State-appointed arbiter resolving a dispute, but rather is acting as an agent of the state in the sense of giving official sanction to a change in status. In an adoption, a court has an independent duty to ensure that statutory requirements are satisfied and, unlike the situation in ordinary civil actions, the parties cannot agree to waive the provisions of applicable legislation.

Though each Canadian province has its own legislation governing adoption, the basic statutory framework is similar throughout the country. The legislation restricts who may adopt a child and who may be adopted. Throughout North America concern exists about the unscrupulous placement of babies for adoption by operators motivated by a desire for profit, and invariably acting with little regard for the welfare of the child. As a result, legislation restricts who may arrange adoptions and how they are to be arranged; in particular, there are restrictions about receiving payment for placing a child or doing work in connection with an adoption. In Ontario, any person, other than a parent, who places a child for adoption must be licensed by the government and is subject to governmental control. In all jurisdictions there are provisions for obtaining the consent of the natural parents, and sometimes other persons, to an adoption; if these consents are not given, the court may dispense with the requirements for consent under certain circumstances. The legislation governs the holding of an adoption hearing, who may participate in the hearing, and the type of orders that can be made. Generally, there are provisions for an independent assessment of the suitability of the proposed adoptive home, with a report being made to the court, and for a probationary period during which the child lives in the adoptive home prior to making of a final order. The statute will specify the effects of an adoption order; generally, all legal ties with the biological parents will be severed and replaced by ties with the adoptive parents, though as shall be seen there are some important exceptions to this rule.

The statutory scheme in each province constitutes a complete framework for adoption, as the courts have no common law concepts on which to rely when dealing with adoption. As the statutory framework marks a departure from the common law and an infringement of parental rights, adoption statutes have historically been construed quite strictly; courts have tended to uphold the position of the natural parents unless there is clearly a contrary legislative intent. In recent years, however, courts seem to have been more concerned with upholding the integrity of the adoption process and have tended to restrict the rights of natural parents.

One can broadly classify adoptions as occurring in three situations: (1) an adoption may be arranged and carried out by the State's child-welfare authority; (2) adoptions are also arranged by a variety of other intermediaries, including lawyers, who bring together the two sets of parents; and (3) adoptions may be carried out by the biological parents of a child without the involvement of an intermediary.

Child-welfare agencies may have a child made a permanent ward and then place the child for adoption; frequently, the wardship order is made on an unopposed or consent basis, especially when the child is a very young infant born out of wedlock. Statutory provisions like Ontario's *C.F.S.A.*, s. 131(2)(b) [now s. 137(2)(b)], allow permanent wards to be adopted without the consent of the natural parents being required. Having a child made a permanent ward tends to give an agency considerable flexibility in terms of the placement of a child and in situations of adoption break-down and it has advantages in terms of dispensing with parental consent, particularly by fathers. Agencies may also arrange adoptions through a voluntary process that does not include any judicial process prior to the making of an adoption order. In Ontario, the *C.F.S.A.*, s. 131(2)(a) [now s. 137(2)(a)], allows the parents of a child to consent to the adoption of a child and to transfer legal guardianship of the child to an "adoption agency", usually the Children's Aid Society, pending placement in an adoptive home. As shall be seen, for a child born out of wedlock, Ontario's *C.F.S.A.* offers relatively extensive rights to a biological father, though in some cases his consent to an adoption is not required.

Besides child-welfare agencies, there are a number of other intermediaries who may arrange adoptions. Various agencies, often operated by religious groups, assist unwed mothers in placing newborn infants for adoption, recruiting adoptive parents, and providing confidentiality for all concerned. Individuals can also arrange adoptions, and professionals such as lawyers and doctors sometimes play this role. Legislation regulates the activities of intermediaries who arrange adoptions, and in Ontario the *C.F.S.A.* provides licensing requirements for those who arrange adoptions. Adoptions arranged by intermediaries other than child-protection agencies are often referred to as "private placement" adoptions; statistics for Ontario indicate that roughly one adoption in ten is a private placement.

Parents may also place their own children for adoption, though they do not have an unlimited freedom to "give their children away". Legislation in all jurisdictions prohibits a parent from receiving payment for the adoption of a child; and adoption will only be ordered if a judge is satisfied that this is in the child's "best interests". By far the most common type of parent-placement adoption occurs after divorce when the new spouse of the custodial parent adopts the child . . . . In such situations one can ask whether a biological parent should be totally excluded from the child's life after adoption. If so, under what circumstances and why?

The vast majority of adoption applications are dealt with on an unopposed basis; provided the appropriate procedures have been followed the judge will usually make the order without detailed consideration of whether the adoption is in the child's best interests. In the case of a public adoption, the child-welfare authorities will invariably have obtained the necessary consents or had the child made a permanent ward. The agencies select adoptive homes with some care, and there is rarely much at issue for a court to decide. Only if the natural parents intervene and attempt to stop the process is litigation likely. In the case of step-parent adoptions, it is not uncommon for the biological parent who is being "replaced" by the new spouse to oppose the application, and a potentially bitter contest may ensue.

NOTES AND QUESTIONS

1. The cases and materials that follow focus on the legal issues that arise in adoptions. For a consideration of some of the social issues, see Goldstein, Freud and Solnit, *Beyond the Best Interests of the Child* (New York: Free Press, 1973) at 9-52; Hepworth, *Foster Care and Adoption in Canada* (Ottawa: Canadian Council on Social Development, 1980) cc. 10-12; and Bean, ed., *Adoption: Essays in Social Policy, Law and Sociology* (New York: Tavistock, 1984).

2. Regarding aboriginal customary adoption and its legal effects, see *Re Adoption of Katie E7-1807* (1962), 32 D.L.R. (2d) 686 (N.W.T. Terr. Ct.); *Re Beaulieu* (1969), 3 D.L.R. (3d) 479 (N.W.T. Terr. Ct.); *Re Deborah E4-789* (1972), 6 R.F.L. 299 (N.W.T. Terr. Ct.), affirmed (1972), 8 R.F.L. 202 (N.W.T. C.A.); *Re Tagornak* (1983), 50 A.R. 237 (N.W.T. S.C.); *Michell v. Dennis*, [1984] 2 W.W.R. 449 (B.C. S.C.); *Casimel v. Insurance Corp. of British Columbia* (1993), 106 D.L.R. (4th) 720 (B.C. C.A.); Zlotkin, "Judicial Recognition of Aboriginal Customary Law in Canada: Selected Marriage and Adoption Cases", [1984] 4 C.N.L.J. 1; Silk, "Adoption Among the Inuit" (1987), 15 Ethos 320; Manitoba Community Services, *No Quiet Place: Review Committee on Indian and Métis Adoptions and Placements* (1985); and Sinclair, Phillips, and Bala, "Aboriginal Child Welfare in Canada" in Bala,

Hornick and Vogl, eds., *Canadian Child Welfare Law: Children, Families and the State* (Toronto: Thompson Educational Publishing Inc., 1991). In *Casimel*, the B.C. C.A. concluded (at 731):

> . . .[T]here is a well-established body of authority in Canada for the proposition that the status conferred by aboriginal customary adoption will be recognized by the courts for the purposes of the application of the principles of the common law and the provisions of statute law to the persons whose status is established by the customary adoption.

3. For a brief history and review of the adoption laws in the various provinces, see Daly and Sobol, *Adoption in Canada: Final Report* (Guelph: University of Guelph, 1993) at 67-99.

2.   Eligibility

(1) WHO MAY BE ADOPTED?

Section 146(5) of the *Child and Family Services Act*, specifies that the person being adopted must be a resident of Ontario. This requirement was the subject of the following case decided under the *Child Welfare Act*.

RAI, RE

(1980), 27 O.R. (2d) 425 (C.A.)

WEATHERSTON J.A.: — The appellants, Roy Chandan Persaud and Satya-vatee Persaud came to Canada in 1968 and have been Canadian citizens since 1975. They have applied to adopt Chandra Muni Rai (the child). Their application was dismissed without hearing from the appellants or the child, by His Honour Judge Webb, who found on the authority of *Khan, Re* (1978), 21 O.R. (2d) 748, 92 D.L.R. (3d) 287, that the child was not resident in Ontario. It is that finding that is the sole issue now.

When the appeal first came on for hearing, we decided to invite submissions from the Attorney-General of Canada, the Director of Child Welfare and the Official Guardian. That was done and they have all been heard from personally or through their respective counsel, for which we are grateful.

The child is the niece of the male appellant. She was born in Guyana on December 7, 1962, and came to Canada on February 27, 1977. She was admitted as a non-immigrant, a visitor. By the Regulations under the Immigration Act, R.S.C. 1970, c. I-2 (since repealed by the Immigration Act, 1976-77 (Can.), c. 52), she was deemed to have been granted entry for a limited period of not more than three months. Within that period of time she reported to an immigration officer. The report that he made out contains the following remarks: "pending adoption". She has been allowed to stay pending the examination that is required to be made by an immigration officer. That examination has not been concluded but awaits the outcome of this adoption application. The child has lived with the appellants since her arrival in Canada and is a student in a junior high school. The immigration authorities consider her to be a person seeking admission to Canada as an immigrant and have agreed that if the adoption order is made before the child's 18th birthday, they will recommend that the necessary Regulations be passed to regularize her admission to Canada as a permanent resident. . . .

Kahn, Re, supra, was an application by a 28-year-old man and his wife to adopt the 18-year-old brother of the male applicant. In that case, at pp. 748-9 O.R., p. 288 D.L.R., this Court expressed three concerns:

(1) If an adoption order is granted in order to regularize the child's presence in this country and to satisfy the requirements of the immigration laws, it appears to us that such an order does not fall within the intent and the purpose of the provincial adoption legislation. (2) Section 71 of the Child Welfare Act, R.S.O. 1970, c. 64, requires the child to be "resident" in this Province for the purposes of an adoption order. We do not think that someone here on a visitor's permit fulfils that requirement of residence. (3) Finally, the adoption of one brother by another with a 10-year age difference (as pointed out by the Director of Child Welfare in this case), appears to us to be inconsistent with the intent of s. 83 [am 1975, c. 1, s. 34] of the Child Welfare Act. It has the appearance of an accommodation adoption to get around the stringencies or requirements of the Immigration Act, R.S.C. 1970, c. I-2, and the Court and the provincial legislation should not be used as a means to achieve that end.

In the present case, it has been acknowledged by all concerned that the application is *bona fide* and was not made merely to enable the child to regularize her presence here. It is not an "accommodation adoption". The Director of Child Welfare has recommended that an order for the adoption of the child be made. The only question is whether she complies with the condition in s. 71 of the Act that she be "resident in Ontario".

Legal adoptions in Ontario are wholly statutory and the Legislature has used the residence of the child and of the adopting parents as the basis for the exercise of jurisdiction. We are not concerned in the present case whether the proposed adoption order would be given foreign recognition. That problem was discussed by Professor Gilbert D. Kennedy in an article entitled "Adoption in the Conflict of Laws", 34 *Can. Bar Rev.* 507 (1956). Whether or not an adoption order would be recognized by a foreign jurisdiction might be a factor when considering the best interests of the child — for instance, if the natural parents, domiciled elsewhere, opposed the adoption, or if property or inheritance rights would be affected. That is not the case here.

The status of a child under the immigration laws does not affect the jurisdiction of the Court. It is undoubtedly a factor to be considered before an adoption order is made, for adoption would not be in the best interests of a child if that child were likely to be deported immediately afterwards. It is also relevant when considering whether the applicants really intend to create a new relationship of parent and child, or whether the statute is being used for a collateral purpose.

. . . Residence is not established by mere presence in the Province on a casual visit, or while passing through. Indeed, in such a case, our Courts would decline jurisdiction to change the status of a person belonging to another civilized country because of the respect we have for the laws of that country. But, apart from exceptional cases, the purpose of the statutory requirement of residence will have been met if there is a reasonable connection between the child and Ontario, and if the child has lived here for sufficient time to enable an effective investigation to be made into the suitability of the adopting parents and whether the proposed adoption order would be in the best interests of the child.

In the present case, the child is no longer a mere visitor, whatever may be her technical status under the Immigration Act. She has lived in Ontario with permanent residents since her arrival on February 27, 1977, in the hope of adoption, and she attends school as a regular student. I think she has met the jurisdictional requirement that she reside in Ontario and that the application for adoption ought to have been dealt with on its merits. . . .

NOTES AND QUESTIONS

1. The question of residence is most often raised where the proposed adoptee is a foreign national. In such cases, there is the danger that the application for adoption is brought merely as a "sham or ploy

for immigration purposes" (*per* Grossberg Co. Ct. J. in *Re Raghbeer* (1977), 3 R.F.L. (2d) 42, at 44 (Ont. Co. Ct.)). It is clearly established that such "accommodation adoptions" that are not really intended to create a parent-child relationship should not be permitted: *Re Raghbeer*, above; *Re Government of Punjab, India, Birth Registration No. 77* (1978), 9 B.C.L.R. 184 (S.C.); *Re K.* (1978), 8 R.F.L. (2d) 97, 21 O.R. (2d) 748 (C.A.); and *Re S. (A.)* (1985), 46 R.F.L. (2d) 401 (Ont. Fam. Ct.). However, as *Rai* illustrates, the status of the child under immigration laws does not affect the jurisdiction of the court. In *B. (J.)* v. *S. (C.W.)* (1996), 19 R.F.L. (4th) 49 (Ont. Gen. Div.), the child was an 8-year-old American citizen who had been placed in the custody of two persons residing in Ontario by a Maryland court. The child was in Canada on a temporary ministerial permit. In finding that the child resided in Ontario and granting the adoption order, Steinberg J. referred to s. 67(c) of the *FLA* and noted (at 53): "Where the residency of the child with a person other than his parent is of such a quality that it has created a fresh domicile for him, it should be sufficient to clothe the court with adoption jurisdiction under subsection 146(5) of the *Child and Family Services Act*."

In *Shewraj* v. *Shewraj* (1982), 37 O.R. (2d) 64 (Fam. Ct.) and *Re S. (M.S.)* (1983), 40 O.R. (2d) 257 (Co. Ct.) the courts dealt with applications by fathers to adopt their own children who had been born out of wedlock. The purpose of the applications was to enable the fathers to sponsor their children as immigrants. While adopted children could be sponsored by Canadian residents, the Immigration Regulations in existence at the time did not allow fathers to sponsor their children if they were born out of wedlock. In both cases, the courts responded sympathetically. They were particularly concerned that failure to grant the adoption orders could lead to deportation of the children who had been residing with their fathers in Canada.

2. Section 56(2) of the *Child Welfare Act*, S.A. 1984, c. C-8.1 permitted a court to waive the requirement that the proposed adoptee reside in Alberta where it was satisfied that this was in the child's best interests. In *Re L. (H.K.)* (1988), 17 R.F.L. (3d) 451 (Alta. Q.B.), Gallant J. concluded (at 463) that he had "grave concerns about the appropriateness of our court to grant an adoption of an alien child who is not, and never has been, in Canada". This concern was based, in part, on the fact that the law of the child's domicile might not recognize the new status. The court dismissed a petition by a married couple, residing in Alberta, to adopt the wife's niece who lived with her family in India. Gallant J. noted (at 463) that the parents could apply to adopt the child in India and then they would be entitled to sponsor her for the purposes of immigration. He also referred (at 462) to the Immigration Regulations, which generally permitted Canadian citizens or permanent residents to sponsor a child under the age of 13 whom they intended to adopt provided the child was (i) an orphan, (ii) an abandoned child whose parents could not be identified, (iii) a child born outside of marriage who had been placed with a child welfare authority for adoption, (iv) a child whose parents were separated and who had been placed with a child welfare authority for adoption, or (v) a child one of whose parents was deceased and who had been placed with a child welfare authority for adoption.

When Pt. 6 of the Alberta *Child Welfare Act* was revised by S.A. 1988, c. 15, s. 35, there was neither an express requirement that the child be resident in Alberta nor any equivalent to the old s. 56(2). However, Murray J. concluded in *Re S. (H.)* (1995), 13 R.F.L. (4th) 301 (Alta. Q.B.) that a residency requirement existed by necessary implication.

3. The number of transnational adoptions of children from third world countries by Canadian families has increased dramatically in the last few decades. Although only Quebec keeps accurate records of such adoptions, Professors Daly and Sobol estimate that between 2,000 and 5,000 foreign children per year are adopted by Canadians: *Adoption in Canada: Final Report* (Guelph: University of Guelph, 1993) at 7. They suggest (at 37) that foreign adoption is now the most utilized means of adopting an infant in Canada. This reflects the "supply" of homeless or needy children in the developing countries and the "demand" for adoptable children in Canada. The latter is largely due to a marked decrease in the number of healthy children available for adoption within Canada as a result of the availability of contraception, increased resort to abortion, elimination of some of the stigma associated with single parenthood, and extended social benefits for single parents. In "The Adoption Alternative for Pregnant Adolescents: Decision Making, Consequences, and Policy Implications" (1992), 48 Journal of Social Issues 143, Professors Daly and Sobol estimate that only about 3% of pregnant adolescents who carry their babies to term place them for adoption.

Cross-border adoption most commonly involves the completion of the adoption in the country where the child is originally resident. This usually, but not invariably, involves the adoptive parents travelling to the foreign country, locating a child, pursuing the adoption application there, and then bringing the child to Canada. Canada's liberal rules governing the recognition of foreign adoptions generally ensure that such adoptions are recognized. The Canadian law is summarized in Castel, *Canadian Conflict of Laws*, 4th ed. (Toronto: Butterworths, 1997) at 443-449. Some have suggested that adoptions completed abroad be redone in the country to which the child is brought to avoid any recognition problems. See Carlson, "Transnational Adoption of Children" (1988), 23 Tulsa L.J. 317, at 352; Ellis, "The Law and Procedure of International Adoption: An Overview" (1993), Suffolk Transnat'l L.J. 361, at 389; and *Application for Adoption of M.* (1992), 16 Fam. L.R. 165 (S.C., A.C.T.).

In "GATT for Kids: New Rules for Intercountry Adoption of Children" (1994), 11 C.F.L.Q. 253, Professor Black explores the legal and social problems associated with transnational adoptions. He notes (at 269) that provincial adoption statutes, with the exception of Quebec's, "feature scattered and often dated responses" to such adoptions.

The article also describes the *Hague Convention on Protection of Children and Co-operation in Respect of Intercountry Adoption* which Canada signed on April 12, 1994. This Convention provides for a mandatory regime for intercountry adoptions involving ratifying states. Before such adoptions can take place the authorities in both states must ensure certain things. Those in the receiving state are required to ensure that the adoptive parents are eligible and suitable to adopt and that they have been counselled as might be necessary. They are also required to ensure that the child will be able to enter and remain in the receiving state in accordance with its immigration laws. The authorities in the country of origin are required to establish that the child is adoptable, that the appropriate consents have been given, and that the adoption is in the child's best interest. Only after the authorities of both states have agreed that the adoption may take place and that the child will be free to reside permanently in the receiving state may the child be physically transferred to the adoptive parents. The Convention does not stipulate where or when the adoption must take place. It could happen before or after the child is physically entrusted to the adoptive parents. It could occur either in the state of origin or the receiving state, although states of origin can provide that the adoption must take place there.

At its 1993 meeting, the Uniform Law Conference recommended a model provincial statute to implement the Convention: Uniform Law Conference of Canada, *Proceedings of the Seventy-fifth Annual Meeting* (1993), at 35 and 141.

For a recent account of the problems relating to adoption of Guatemalan infants by American and Canadian couples, see "Baby snatchers who thrive on poverty" *National Post*, A14 (July 29, 1999). For further reading on intercountry adoptions, see Duncan, "Intercountry Adoption: Some Issues in Implementing and Supplementing the 1993 Hague Convention on Protection of Children and Co-operation in respect of Intercountry Adoption" in J. Doek, *et al*, ed., *Children on the Move: How to Implement Their Right to Family Life* (Boston: Martinus Nijhoff, 1996); *International Adoption and the Immigration Process* (Ottawa: Citizenship and Immigration Canada, 1997); and Selman, "Intercountry Adoption in Europe after the Hague Convention" in B. Sykes and P. Alcock, ed., *Developments in European Social Policy: Convergence and Diversity* (Bristol: Policy Press, 1998).

4. Prior to 1979, the *Child Welfare Act* expressly provided that an adult could only be adopted where the applicant had raised the proposed adoptee during infancy under a *de facto* adoption. Under the *Child Welfare Act*, which was proclaimed in force in June 1979, adoption of persons who were 18 years of age or older or who had been married was permitted only in "special circumstances". What is the position under the *CFSA*? See s. 146(3).

5. Where the proposed adoptee is at least 18 years of age, certain provisions of the *CFSA* do not apply. For example, no parental consents are required. See s. 137(2) and definition of "child" in s. 3(1).

(2) WHO MAY ADOPT?

As a general rule the adopting parent must be at least 18 years of age (s. 147 of the *CFSA*). However, an adoption order can be made on the application of a person who is less than 18 years of age if the "court is satisfied that special circumstances justify making the order" (s. 147).

Can an unmarried person adopt a child in Ontario? Can two unmarried cohabitees jointly adopt a child (see ss. 146(4) and 136(1))? Section 136(1) incorporates by reference the definition of "spouse" contained in s. 10(1) of the *Human Rights Code*, R.S.O. 1990, c. H.19. It specifies that "'spouse' means the person to whom a person of the opposite sex is married or with whom the person is living in a conjugal relationship outside marriage".

This definition was successfully challenged in the following case by four lesbian couples who had been living together for a long time. All of the children involved had been conceived through artificial insemination and had been born to one of the partners during the currency of their respective existing relationships as a result of a joint decision. In an unusual move, the Attorney General intervened to argue against the validity of the legislation, although she also presented contrary arguments to the court.

K., RE

(1995), 15 R.F.L. (4th) 129 (Ont. Prov. Div.)

(Footnotes omitted.)

NEVINS PROV. J.:. . From the outset, it is important to appreciate that the issue in these cases is not whether homosexual persons in general may apply to adopt children. At present, there is no legal prohibition either in the Act or any other statute against a lesbian or gay person from applying to adopt a child and obtaining an adoption order if it is seen to be in the best interest of the child. In fact, since 1984, except for some precautionary provisions regarding applicants under the age of eighteen, any person who is over the age of sixteen has the right to apply for the adoption of a child, with no restrictions as to sex or sexual orientation.

Rather, the question is whether there is a constitutionally valid reason why an application for adoption by a homosexual couple, living in a conjugal relationship, one of whom is the biological mother of the child, should not be accepted by the court and decided on the basis of what is in the best interest of the child. . . .

Of significance in examining the existing adoption legislation is the fact that there is no prohibition of an individual person's applying to adopt a child, regardless of the sex or sexual orientation of the applicant. While amendments to adoption legislation over the years since its first introduction in 1921 have, at times, required "special circumstances" before an individual unmarried person could adopt — a restriction that was removed in 1984 — at no time has there ever been an absolute bar to an individual person's applying for adoption because of sexual orientation.

Of equal significance is the evolution of adoption legislation in so far as it permitted joint applications by couples. At the outset, adoption law prohibited joint applications by anyone other than a husband and wife. By 1984 and the passage of the *Child and Family Services Act*, the expression "husband and wife" was replaced with the present term "spouse", as defined in the *Human Rights Code*. This implicit recognition of the legitimacy of relationships involving unmarried couples was consistent with changes in other legislation at the same time that created legal support obligations and rights between unmarried couples. And so, since 1984, adoption legislation has excluded any requirement that joint applicants for adoption must be married spouses.

4: ACCEPTABLE STANDARD OF CHILD CARE

An essential prerequisite to the resolution of the equality issue before me is an appreciation of the level of child care that our society, through its laws, demands of parents. To this end, I believe it is appropriate to examine the *Child and Family Services Act* further and to consider the standard of child care concept that is imposed by the law and the courts in child protection cases under Pt. III of that Act.

Generally, Pt. III of the Act establishes the acceptable standard for the level of care that children receive at the hands of their parents. The presumption in the statute and the case law is that the preferable environment for the child in which to be raised is a stable, caring home, with natural parents, free to raise their children in a manner that they see fit. It is only when the level of care provided the children in that home falls below that which is seen to be acceptable by the community that the children are seen to be "in need of protection" and the state is authorized, and in fact compelled, to intervene in the best interests of the children.

In these "protection" cases, the law is clear that the state should not, and has no authority to, require of all parents that they provide the best possible care for their children, failing which the state will encroach upon the autonomy of the family unit. Our society does not demand perfection of parents, nor does it demand that parents produce assembly-line children, all reaching their full potential, free of any imperfections or defects. The expectation, rather, is that parents provide an adequate level of care for their children. And so long as the parents are providing such care, then the family and the parent-child relationship should remain inviolable, free from state intervention or intrusion. It is only when the care given to children is at a level that is seen to be unacceptable by community standards that the state, fastidiously monitored by the courts, is permitted to intervene.

Because of this philosophy, the Act sets out in subs. 37(2) certain categories of child care that are in and of themselves deemed to be inadequate, unacceptable by our community standards and that, if proven to exist, justify the ultimate violation of civil rights, involuntary intervention by the state in the family.

I have adopted and modified the same general approach to the parenting ability issue in the present cases. What does the available research reveal as to the ability of homosexual people to parent children in a manner that is considered "adequate" or acceptable by community standards? What evidence is there to indicate that children raised in a family structure in which both parents are homosexual persons, and particularly lesbian couples, exhibit symptoms or indicia of inadequate care significantly more often than one would see in the general population? Is there evidence that the fact of being raised and cared for by homosexual parents would likely lead to physical, emotional, sexual, psychological or social problems in children to a significantly greater degree or frequency than is present in children in the general population, raised by heterosexual parents? The answer to these questions is, in my opinion, fundamental to the resolution of the issues raised in these cases, for if the evidence does indicate that the fact of having homosexual parents is likely, on a balance of probabilities, to produce any combination of the symptoms described above to a significantly greater degree or frequency than one would normally expect to see in the general population of children raised in "traditional" family structures, then the homosexuality of the parents might be seen, in and of itself, to be a level of care below that which is acceptable in our community.

5: EVIDENCE OF THE ADEQUACY AND EFFECTS OF HOMOSEXUAL PARENTING

In the course of the hearing on this constitutional issue, I have been presented with a considerable amount of evidence on the ability of homosexual persons to parent, individually or as couples, and the effects of homosexual parenting on children. This evidence was presented principally through the extensive affidavits from Dr. Margrit Eichler, Dr. Rosemary Barnes, and Dr. Susan Bradley. These documents and the research papers accompanying them as exhibits, reviewed in considerable detail the scientific literature and research that has accumulated in this area over the last fifty years, and in particular since the mid-1970's. In addition to this affidavit evidence, I had the benefit of hearing viva voce evidence from Dr. Bradley. . . .

Having considered the evidence received through these sources, I come to the following factual conclusions:

The traditional family model of two, middle class, heterosexual parents in which the woman is a full-time housewife and the man has full-time paid employment outside the home, which has long been assumed to be the structure most favourable to healthy child development, is now a minority and several varieties of non-traditional families appear in our society, including families in which gay fathers and lesbian mothers are the primary care-givers. The sexual orientation of the parents is considered along with race, ethnicity, household composition and maternal employment as one of a number of ways in which families vary from the traditional model.

During this century, families in highly industrialized countries have been undergoing drastic changes, not just in the nature of their composition but in gender roles within the family. These changes have precipitated research into the dimensions of family interactions and the result of this research indicates a wide variety in the nature and degree of interaction between family members. Moreover, studies by various researchers have convincingly demonstrated that the same internal variations exist between same-sex couples and opposite-sex couples and that both groups demonstrate the full range of dimensions indicative of family structure. As Dr. Eichler pointed out [emphasis added.]: "Overall, the differences among opposite-sex couples and among same-sex couples are greater than the differences *between* these two groups."

Recent studies on the effects of the non-traditional family structure on the development of children suggests that there is no reason to conclude that alteration of the family structure itself is detrimental to child development. The prevailing opinion of researchers in this area seems to be that the traditional family structure is no longer considered as the only framework within which adequate child care can be given. Rather child development researchers have "highlighted the multiplicity of pathways through which healthy psychological development can take place and the diversity of home environments which can support such development".

Progressively more rigorous empirical research in the area of child development has produced the notion that *the most important element in the healthy development of a child is a stable, consistent, warm, and responsive relationship between a child and his or her care-giver.* Factors that appear to have a significant effect on the healthy emotional and psychological development of a child are more related to conflicts in spousal relations than family type or structure. A parent's capacity to support and be emotionally available to a child is enhanced in the context of a supportive relationship, especially if there is good communication, effective problem solving, and sharing of family responsibilities.

Research on the effects of gay and lesbian parenting on child development has focussed on various stereotypical beliefs regarding homosexual persons and couples. The results of this research, as discussed in detail in the evidence referred to, may be summarized as follows:

1. **Mental Health of Gay or Lesbian Individuals:** Homosexual individuals do not exhibit higher levels of psychopathology than do heterosexual individuals, and there is no good evidence to suggest that homosexual individuals are less healthy psychologically and therefore less able to be emotionally available to their children. Studies supporting this have resulted in the exclusion of homosexuality from the nomenclature of the two major psychiatric diagnostic systems, the *Diagnostic and Statistical Manual of the American Psychiatric Association* (DSM) and the *International Classification of Diseases of the World Health Organization* (ICD).

2. **Stability of Gay or Lesbian Relationships:** Despite stereotypical beliefs to the contrary, there is no evidence to support the suggestion that most gay men and lesbians have unstable or dysfunctional relationships. Couple relationships are substantially similar, regardless of whether the partners are of the opposite sex or the same sex and it is no longer possible to reason that homosexual relationships will necessarily be less stable than a heterosexual union. Therefore, children raised by gay or lesbian parents will not necessarily be more frequently subjected to the loss of important relationships than will children raised by heterosexual parents.

3. **Gender Development, Sexual Orientation and General Psychological Adjustment of Children of Gay and Lesbian Parents:** The reports and affidavits of both Drs. Bradley and Barnes reviewed in great detail the literature and studies in this area, the report of Dr. Barnes being particularly exhaustive. Having considered the research on the psychosexual development of children raised by lesbian mothers specifically in terms of children's gender identity, gender role, sexual orientation, intellectual functioning and general psychological adjustment, her conclusion was as follows:

   The children of lesbian mothers, like the children of heterosexual mothers almost invariably develop a gender identity and gender role behaviour which is within normal range and consistent with what is conventionally expected of their biological sex. The great majority of these children are heterosexual in their adult sexual orientation. The children of lesbian mothers show normal psychological development in each of the numerous measures in which they have been compared to the children of heterosexual parents, including intellectual functioning, symptoms of emotional disturbance, behavioural problems, social adjustment, relationship with peers, age-appropriate development tasks, self-concept and moral development.

   . . . Based on this evidence, I conclude there is no reason to believe the sexual orientation of the parents will be an indicator of the sexual orientation of the children in their care. Nor is there any evidence that the homosexual orientation of the parents, especially lesbian mothers, will produce any significantly greater incidence of psychiatric disturbance, or emotional or behavioural problems, or intellectual impairment than is seen in the population of children raised by heterosexual parents.

4. **The Effect of Social Stigma on Children of Gay or Lesbian Parents:** Although there is little evidence available on this question, there is to date no indication that the possible stigma or harassment to which children of gay or lesbian parents

may be exposed is necessarily worse than other possible forms of racial or ethnic stigma, or the stigma of having mentally ill parents.

. . .

7. SUBSECTION 136(1) OF THE *CHILD AND FAMILY SERVICES ACT* AND THE *CHARTER*

7.1: The Questions

The constitutional questions to be asked in these cases may be framed as follows:

Question 1: Does the requirement in s. 136 of the *Child and Family Services Act*, which incorporates s. 10 of the *Human Rights Code*, that spouses be of the opposite sex before they may apply for the adoption of a child, infringe rights guaranteed by subs. 15(1) of the *Canadian Charter of Rights and Freedoms*?

Question 2: If the requirement in s. 136 of the *Child and Family Services Act*, which incorporates s. 10 of the *Human Rights Code*, that spouses be of the opposite sex before they may apply for the adoption of a child, infringes a right guaranteed by subs. 15(1) of the *Canadian Charter of Rights and Freedoms*, is it justified by s. 1 of the *Charter*?

. . .

7.2: The Three-Step Analysis under *Andrews* v. *Law Society (British Columbia)*

7.2(a): Step 1 — *Distinction or Unequal Treatment in the Context of subs. 15(1)?*

The threshold question that must be answered in this analysis is whether the provision in question operates to deny homosexual persons one of the protected equality rights set out in subs. 15(1) of the Charter.

The effect of the definition of "spouse" in subs. 136(1) of the *Child and Family Services Act* is to deny to gay or lesbian people the right to apply, as a couple, to adopt a child. . . .

The relationships between these applicants exhibit all the elements of a spousal relationship, including a sexual commitment to each other and they share a committed sexual relationship because their sexual orientation is homosexual. It is the fact of their homosexuality that gives their relationship the quality of a spousal relationship. It is, at the same time, the fact of this homosexuality, this sexual orientation, that distinguishes them from other spouses in s. 136 of the Act. And it is solely because of this personal characteristic that they are prohibited from applying for the adoption of a child. This is, in my view, a denial of one of the protected rights under subs. 15(1).

. . .

There is, therefore, a distinction or unequal treatment of a group under subs. 136(1) and that unequal treatment is based on grounds that are analogous to those enumerated in subs. 15(1) of the Charter and relate to the personal characteristics of the group, namely sexual orientation. Further, the unequal treatment results in a denial of at least one of the rights protected in s. 15, in particular, the benefit of the law.

7.2(b): Step 2 — *Discrimination*

The next question is whether the unequal treatment described above is discriminatory. Recalling the comments of Chief Justice Lamer in *R.* v. *Swain* and Justice McIntyre in *Andrews* v. *Law Society (British Columbia)*, I have little difficulty coming to the conclusion that the differential treatment under s. 136 "has the effect of imposing a . . . disadvantage not imposed upon others or of withholding or limiting access to opportunities, benefits and advantages available to others." In these particular cases before me, all of the applicants are, by operation of the section in question, denied those benefits, advantages and special privileges that are inherent in the concept of adoption. . . .

What is even more inimical is that the group that is being considered, namely, homosexual couples living in a conjugal relationship, are denied opportunities, benefits and advantages that are not only available to the rest of the population, but are available to individual homosexual persons that is, *the right to apply for adoption and have their application considered in the context of whether it would be in the best interests of the child.* Put in its simplest terms, because of s. 136 the applicants are denied their "day in court" for no other reason than the fact that they are homosexual. I cannot imagine a more blatant example of discrimination.

I conclude therefore that the denial of one of the protected rights does result in discrimination, in that it withholds from this particular group of society opportunities, benefits and advantages available to others.

. . .

7.2(c): *Step 3 — Is the Discrimination Justifiable?*

To determine whether the discrimination under s. 136 is justifiable under s. 1 of the *Charter*, the two-pronged inquiry in *R.* v. *Oakes*, supra, must be conducted into: (i) the importance of the legislative objective; and (ii) the proportional reasonableness of the means used to achieve that end. . . .

7.2(c)(i): *The Legislative Objective*

. . . The Act in general deals with the welfare of children, and the adoption provisions are concerned with the establishment of a parent-child relationship in a manner discussed earlier. This is, in my opinion, one of the most, if not the most, important objectives any legislation could have, and it clearly passes the first stage of this inquiry.

The second aspect of the justification inquiry, and the final question in this constitutional analysis is the relationship between the definition of "spouse" in s. 136 and the goals of the statute. How does the prohibition against same-sex adoptions further the objectives of the legislation? Or, put differently, would permitting same-sex adoptions frustrate these objectives?

7.2(c)(ii): *The Proportionality Test*

While all of the preceding constitutional analysis is of course essential, this final phase is, in my view, the most important, for it is at this stage that focus is centred on the crucial issue in these cases, namely, *the best interests of the children*. It is in the context of "best interests" that we must consider whether the goal of the legislation is met by the existing discriminatory denial of equality rights.

The three-step process that is to be taken at this stage, in determining whether the denial of rights that I have found to exist is justified under s. 1 of the *Charter* is set out clearly in *R.* v. *Oakes*, supra. . . .

1. *Rational Connection*

The paramount and overriding objective of the legislation is clear: to promote the best interests, protection and well-being of children. In particular, the objective of Pt. VII of the *Child and Family Services Act* is to promote the best interests and well-being of children by ensuring that they will be cared for, raised and nurtured in a stable, secure, loving and committed family environment, legalized by an adoption order.

. . . I believe it is no coincidence that the evidence that I have received indicates consistently that of all the factors affecting the healthy development of a child, the element of a secure and loving home life is the most significant.

And so, while it is correct to say that the *paramount* objective of the legislation is the promotion of the best interests of children, it is clear, especially from examining the enumerated purposes of the Act in s. 1, that the overall goal of the legislation is the promotion of the best interests of children *within the family*.

What may be questioned at this point is the nature of the ''family'' contemplated by the provisions and philosophy of the Act. Although there has been no clear judicial pronouncement on this topic, it is obvious that the Act recognizes the fact of non-traditional families and affords them the same rights and protections as the more traditional form. By removing the requirement of marriage in the definition of spouse, unmarried or ''common law'' partners are given the right to apply for adoption, and by analogy, are given financial, custodial and property rights in other statutes. As discussed earlier, single persons are permitted to apply for adoption, without any restriction other than the best interests of the child. And so, the legislation accepts and respects the fact of single-parent families. As well, the concept of ''parent'' is no longer restricted to the biological parent but now includes any person, married or unmarried, an obvious reflection in the Act of the fact that non-traditional families are a fact of life in our society. . . .

Now there are unquestionably societal concerns regarding the influence of homosexual adults on children, and I believe I can take judicial notice of that. There are, as well, possible concerns that the existing research is as yet incomplete and not comprehensive, as Dr. Bradley has pointed out, at least to the extent that it would allay these societal concerns. It may be that no amount of research would ever mollify these concerns. However, I am bound by law and common sense to decide this issue on the basis of the evidence that I have available to me now, and not on speculation, unfounded prejudice and fears or on a reaction to the vociferous comments of an isolated and uninformed segment of the community.

If I accept, as I must from the evidence before me, that a stable, secure and caring family environment is in a child's best interests and is, in fact, the most significant and beneficial component in the healthy development of a child, and further that the paramount objective of the legislation is to promote the best interests of children primarily within the context of the family, then I must also accept from the evidence before me that there is no rational connection whatsoever between the goals of this legislation and a provision in that legislation that contains an absolute prohibition against adoption by homosexual couples. For there to be a rational connection with a provision that says that homosexual couples may *never* apply to adopt, there would have to be evidence that homosexual couples could never provide a stable, secure and caring environment for a child. But there is no evidence at all to support such a proposition. On the contrary, *there is no cogent evidence that homosexual couples are unable to provide the very type of family environment that the legislation attempts to foster, protect and encourage,* at least to the same extent as "traditional" families, parented by heterosexual couples.

There is no evidence at all that families in which both parents are of the same sex are any more unstable or dysfunctional than families with heterosexual parents. There is no evidence that children raised by homosexual parents are any more likely to develop gender roles or identities inconsistent with their biological sex than children raised by heterosexual parents. There is no evidence at all that children raised by homosexual parents will be significantly any different than children raised by heterosexual parents in all areas of their psychological development.

There is also no evidence at all that children raised by homosexual parents will be exposed to any greater degree of social stigma than to which children of heterosexual parents are exposed because of race or any number of other characteristics. In a number of decisions in custody cases from various jurisdictions, including one in Ontario, all have taken the position that, if such stigmatization does occur, it is merely another factor to be taken into account when determining the best interests of the child and is not sufficient reason, in itself, to deny a claim for custody.

There is, in short, no evidence that families with heterosexual parents are better able to meet the physical, psychological, emotional or intellectual needs of children than families with homosexual parents. Nor is there any evidence that children of families in which the parents are homosexual would receive less than the "adequate" level of care demanded of heterosexual parents, as discussed earlier in Pt. IV. If an "adequate" level of child care is the yardstick by which the law determines whether the state will encroach upon the autonomy of the family, surely we cannot demand a higher level of child care from homosexual parents as an excuse to deny them their constitutional equality rights. . . .

In my view, the inherent inconsistencies in this legislation, in so far as it is directed to the relationship between the best interests of children and the nature of "family" or the sexual orientation of parents, call into question the precise nature of the legislative scheme.

. . . [T]here is no sexual-orientation restriction in any other Part or section of the Act. Sexual orientation does not preclude an adoption application by any individual person, whether a parent, relative or complete stranger, yet it does preclude an application by the spouse of the parent. If parenting by a homosexual couple is intended to be inconsistent with the "best interests" objective of the legislation and therefore prohibited, is parenting by a single lesbian or gay person somehow consistent with that objective? Is the concept of "family" recognized by the statute to be expanded to include single homosexual parents, but not homosexual couples living in a conjugal relationship?

In my opinion, the "line" drawn by the legislation in this provision is irrational, not based on any compelling social interest and is a completely unwarranted infringement of specifically protected *Charter* rights.

There is not only no rational connection between the absolute prohibition in s. 136 and the paramount objective of the Act, namely, the best interests of children, but there appears to be no rational connection between the absolute bar in s. 136 and other sections of the statute. The provision does not meet the first requirement of the justification test.

2. *Minimal Impairment of Charter Rights*

Even if the available evidence were not as conclusive and overwhelming as it is to support the conclusion to which I have come as to the absence of a rational connection between s. 136 and the objectives of the statute, the definition of spouse in s. 136 imposes a limit on the *Charter* rights of homosexual persons that is not only excessive, but, in my view, totally unnecessary.

In the circumstances of these cases, what possible concern could there be over the question of whether an adoption would be in the best interests of these children that could not be identified, investigated and determined in the course of an adoption hearing? . . .

Even if there were evidence to raise the presumption that parenting by homosexual persons might not be in a child's best interest because of the sexual orientation of the parents, any number of mechanisms are in place, or could easily be put in place that would provide an alternative to the absolute denial of *Charter* rights: sexual orientation of the parents could be an enumerated head in the factors to be considered in determining the best interests of the child in subs. 136(2) of the Act; counsel could be appointed to represent the interests of the children and present evidence that would indicate the child's best interests would not be served; "adoption homestudies", Director's statements, reports of the adjustment of the child, all of which are options available to the court presently, could be a required, as they are now in "non-family" adoptions.

All of these, and, with some thought, many other forms of monitoring procedures might be instituted to ensure that the proposed adoption would be in the best interests of the child without denying to an entire group of our society its equality rights under subs. 15(1).

Therefore, even if there is a rational connection between the objectives of the legislation and the restriction on applications to adopt by homosexual persons, which I do not believe there to be, the objectives of the legislation could still be achieved without any denial of *Charter* rights. In my opinion, the objectives of the legislation can be achieved now, with the process and safeguards that are already in place, without the need to deny or impair any rights or freedoms.

3. *Proportionality*

Finally, it is my opinion that the effects of the provision in question are, on the evidence I have, disproportionate to the objective of the legislation, namely the promotion of the best interests of children. . . .

8: THE REMEDY

. . . Therefore the definition of "spouse" as it appears in subs. 136(1) of the *Child and Family Services Act* should be read and applied as if enacted in the following form:

> "spouse" means the person to whom a person of the opposite sex is married or with whom a person of the same or opposite sex is living in a conjugal relationship outside marriage.

The applicants for adoption in all the cases before me qualify as spouses within that definition, and the adoption applications will now be considered individually on their merits.

NOTES AND QUESTIONS

1. This issue has now been addressed by the *Amendments Because of the Supreme Court of Canada Decision in M. v. H. Act*, 1999 S.O. 1999 c.6. Section 6 of this Act adds paragraph (c) to s. 146(4) of the *CFSA*. It states that an application for adoption may be made "by any other individuals that the court may allow, having regard to the best interests of the child."

2. In *"A", Re* (1999), 181 D.L.R. (4th) 300 (Alta. Q.B.), two women were each involved in an exclusive, long-term relationship with a female partner. Each petitioned to adopt her partner's biological son. At the time the petitions were first presented, the *Child Welfare Act*, S.A. 1984, c. C-8.1, only provided for private adoptions by "spouses". By the time the court heard the petitions, the legislature had replaced the term "spouse" with "step-parent". The latter term was not defined, but speeches in the legislature and a letter of the Government House Leader indicated that it was broad enough to encompass a same-sex partner. The petitions were granted, after the court concluded that a same-sex partner of the biological parent of a child could indeed be a step-parent to the child for the purpose of adoption under the Act. The court considered this interpretation reasonable and just and in keeping with the overall goal of adoption legislation, which was to permit adoption when it was in a child's best interests. Through adoption, children of same-sex couples could acquire additional rights and a significant emotional benefit.

3. For further reading regarding adoption by same-sex couples, see Ali, "Homosexual Parenting: Child Custody and Adoption" (1989), 22 U.C. Davis L. Rev. 1009; Golumbok and Tasker, "Children Raised by Lesbian Mothers; the Empirical Evidence" (1991), 21 Fam. L. 184; Delaney, "Statutory Protection of the Other Mother: Legally Recognizing the Relationship Between the Non-Biological Lesbian Parent and her Child" (1991), 43 Hastings L.J. 177; Davies, "Two Moms and a Baby: Protecting the Non-Traditional Family Through Second-Parent Adoptions" (1995), 29 New Eng. L. Rev. 1055; D. Casswell, *Lesbians, Gay Men, and Canadian Law* (Toronto: E. Montgomery Pub., 1996); Shanley, "Lesbian Families: Dilemmas in Grounding Legal Recognition of Parenthood" in J. E. Hanisberg and S. Ruddick, ed., *Mother Troubles: Rethinking Contemporary Maternal Dilemmas* (Boston: Beacon Press, 1999).

4. In *Korn* v. *Potter* (1996), 134 D.L.R. (4th) 437 (B.C. S.C.), a doctor refused to provide artificial insemination to a lesbian couple. The lesbian couple successfully argued that the doctor's refusal contravened paragraph 3(b) of the *Human Rights Act*, S.B.C. 1984, c.22. The doctor sought judicial review of the British Columbia Council of Human Rights' decision pursuant to the *Judicial Review Procedures Act*, R.S.B.C. 1979, c.209. The court dismissed his petition.

5. When the application is brought by a person who is a spouse as defined in s. 136(1), the applicant's spouse can either join in the application as a co-adopter (s. 146(4)(b)) or give written consent to the adoption (s. 137(10)). How do the legal consequences of these two acts differ? Can one spouse ever adopt a child without at least the consent of the other? (see ss. 137(10) and 138).

6. Is it generally in a child's best interests to be adopted by a couple? In what circumstances should a single person be permitted to adopt? See *M. (S.K.A.)* v. *A. (C.)* (1995), 11 R.F.L. (4th) 25 (Alta. C.A.) where the court granted an adoption order to a 42-year-old widow even though the four-year-old's mother refused to consent.

7. The adopter need not be of the same religious faith as the adoptee: *Re Lamb*, [1961] O.W.N. 356 (Co. Ct.) and *Re R. (P.A.)* (1970), 4 R.F.L. 32 (Ont. H.C.). However, religion may have been a factor in the original placement of a child for adoption. See s. 61(2)(b) of the *CFSA*.

8. Non-aboriginals may adopt an aboriginal child in accordance with the relevant provincial legislation: *Nelson* v. *Children's Aid Society of Eastern Manitoba*, 21 R.F.L. 222, [1975] 5 W.W.R. 45 (Man. C.A.) and *Natural Parents* v. *Superintendent of Child Welfare (British Columbia)*, [1976] 2 S.C.R. 751, [1976] 1 W.W.R. 699. By virtue of s. 88 of the *Indian Act*, R.S.C. 1985, c. I-5, laws of general application that are in force in a province apply to Indians except where they are inconsistent with the *Indian Act* or a treaty between a first nation and the Crown. Pursuant to this provision, the courts have

concluded that provincial adoption legislation applies to Indian children, but that an Indian child adopted by non-Indians does not lose his or her Indian status.

9. The child's cultural and social background may, of course, be a factor in the original placement of the child for the purpose of adoption (see below) and in determining whether an adoption order would be in the best interests of the child (see ss. 61(2), 136(3) and 140(3) of the *CFSA*).

3.   Placement for Adoption

(1) INTRODUCTION

The term "placement" is often used to refer simply to the actual physical placing of a child in the home of the prospective adopting parents. However, it can also be used to describe the entire process of selecting adopting parents, placing the child in their home, and monitoring the situation until the court order for adoption is made. It is the broader concept of placement that is the subject of this section.

Section 141(1) of the *CFSA* stipulates that only a children's aid society or the holder of a licence issued under Part IX may place a child with another person for adoption. This basic rule is subject to the exception created by s. 141(8), which permits anyone to place a child with the child's relative (as defined in s. 136(1)), the child's parent or a spouse of the child's parent. Where a child is placed for adoption by a person other than a society or licensee, s. 146(1) indicates that an adoption order should not be made until the child has resided with the prospective adoptee for at least two years. Any person who unlawfully places a child for adoption is guilty of an offence punishable by a fine of not more than $2,000 or by imprisonment for a term of not more than two years or both: s. 176(1).

A children's aid society is not required to obtain a licence before placing children for adoption: s. 193(2). The society is specifically directed to seek adoptive parents for Crown wards: s. 140(1), but no Crown ward is to be placed for adoption until any outstanding order of access made under s. 58(1) has been terminated and any appeal from the Crown wardship order or from any decision reviewing it has been disposed of or abandoned or the time for commencing such an appeal has expired: s. 140(2). In *Children's Aid Society of Metropolitan Toronto* v. *S. (T.)* (1989), 20 R.F.L. (3d) 337 (Ont. C.A.), the court indicated (at 350) that a placement in this context includes a "deemed placement". A "deemed placement" occurs when foster parents receive approval to adopt a child already in their home on a foster placement. Thus, a children's aid society should not grant such approval until the preconditions of s. 140(2) are met. The Crown wardship order remains in effect pending the final adoption order. So long as the child resides with his or her prospective adopters the Crown wardship order cannot be the subject of a status review by a court: s. 64(9). A *Charter* challenge to the equivalent provision in Nova Scotia legislation failed in *C. (D.)* v. *Family & Children's Services of Cumberland (County)* (1988), 16 R.F.L. (3d) 222 (N.S. C.A.).

A children's aid society may also be involved in the placement of non-wards for adoption. Here, however, the society does not have a monopoly. An individual or non-profit agency may obtain a licence under Part IX for the purpose of placing a child for adoption. Lawyers, doctors and other private intermediaries generally become involved in adoption placements when they come into contact with unwed mothers who want their children adopted but who do not want to be involved with the child welfare agency. Licensees can only receive payment, generally from the adopting parents, for "prescribed expenses" and "proper legal fees and disbursements": s. 175.

In *K., Re* (1998), 44 R.F.L. (4th) 211 (Alta. Q.B.), two Alberta couples retained the services of a California lawyer who introduced the couples to "birth mothers". The lawyer charged a fee, in addition to medical expenses and support for the biological mothers. The pregnant women traveled to Alberta, delivered the babies and placed them with the adoptive parents. The adoptions were then processed in accordance with Alberta law. Sections 68.1 of the *Child Welfare Act*, S.A. 1984, c. C-8.1 prohibited the payment or receipt of fees, other than fees for medical and legal services, for facilitating the placement of a child for the purposes of an adoption. The court held that charging a fee for facilitation services contravened Alberta law. Nevertheless, the court approved the adoptions in the best interests of the two children. In *obiter*, the court stated that the Director had the discretion to commence a prosecution of the California lawyer under section 69(1). However, the court conceded (at 226-227) that any penalties imposed might be ineffective in the case of a non-resident:

> The legislation in its present form has not and seems unlikely to curtail unlawful facilitation by people outside Canada who are not deterred by laws, but only by sanctions. A state can prevent people from entering its borders and can restrict the flow of goods. But facilitation services involve little more than providing information to put willing parties in touch with each other. It is notoriously difficult to erect stop signs on the information super-highway. Neither the vigilance of the Alberta regulators nor the strength of its legislation can be faulted for a failure to stop a flow of information whose supply is not criminalized in the jurisdiction from which it emanates. This issue is broader than the geographical boundaries of Alberta. It may require international cooperation and legal solutions.

The court indicated that s. 68.1 and related provisions were adopted following negative publicity, including a segment on the CBS News program *60 Minutes*, suggesting that Alberta had become a haven for private adoptions of American children whose unwed fathers had not given consent to the adoption. It also referred to *Kessel* v. *Leavitt* 1998 WL 407096 (W. Va. July 22, 1998); *cert. denied*, 118 S. Ct. 266 (W. Va. October 6, 1997), in which a jury awarded $2 million in compensatory damages and $5.85 million in punitive damages to a father whose son was born in the U.S., placed with an Alberta couple by the same lawyer involved in the *K.* case, and adopted under Alberta law. The biological father unsuccessfully challenged the adoption in Alberta before beginning the civil action.

Under the Ontario legislation, a "homestudy" will usually be conducted to determine if the prospective adoptive parents are suitable before the physical placement of a child in the home. Where the child is being placed by a licensee, the licensee is generally required to notify the Director of the proposed placement and to submit a homestudy: ss. 141 and 142. In these circumstances, the Director must approve the placement: s. 142(2). If the children's aid society is placing the child, the society itself will often conduct a homestudy in accordance with the regulations before the placement of the child.

Generally, a child placed by a children's aid society or licensee must reside in the home of the prospective adopting parents for a period of six months before an adoption order is made: s. 149(1). At the end of this period, the local children's aid society or "a person approved by the Director or local director" prepares a report on the adjustment of the child in the home of the prospective adopting parents: s. 149(5). On the basis of this report, the Director determines whether or not to recommend the proposed adoption and files a statement to this effect with the court: s. 149(1). If the child has been placed for adoption by a children's aid society, the local director may make this determination and file the statement with the court: s. 149(2). Where the Director determines that it is in the best interests of the child that the six-month probationary period be dispensed with, the Director may so recommend after obtaining a report on the adjustment of the child: s. 149(1).

As noted earlier, many of the statutory and regulatory provisions governing the placement of children do not apply when a child is placed for adoption with a relative or where a step-parent seeks to adopt. Such placements can be made without a licence, without a homestudy and without the prior approval of the Director: s. 141(8). Unless the court orders otherwise, pursuant to s. 149(6), there is no provision for a study to determine how the child is adjusting in the home and neither the Director nor the local director of a children's aid society needs to provide a statement for the court recommending in favour of or against the proposed adoption. In these situations, both the placement and the processing of the adoption application are done privately. Indeed, the only control imposed by the state in most cases is the requirement of a judicial proceeding before the adoption order is made.

NOTES AND QUESTIONS

1. The present controls on placements for adoptions by individuals and agencies other than the children's aid society are more stringent than those recommended by the Ontario Law Reform Commission, *Report on Family Law; Part III: Children* (1973) at 51-54. Do you think the controls placed on private adoptions in the *Child and Family Services Act* are too restrictive? Are they too lenient? What policy objectives underlie any restrictions on such adoptions?

See generally, Witner et al., *Independent Adoptions* (1963); Grove, "Independent Adoption: The Case for the Gray Market" (1967-8), 13 Vill. L. Rev. 116; Embick, "The 'In Blank' Consent and the Independent Adoption: A Defence" (1968), 5 Willamette L.J. 50; Prichard, "A Market for Babies?" (1984), 34 U.T.L.J. 341; and M. J. Radin, *Contested Commodities* (Cambridge, Mass. : Harvard University Press, 1996), chap. 10.

2. A majority of infant adoptions in Canada now result from private placements: Sobol and Daly, "Canadian Adoption Statistics: 1980-1990" (1994), 56 Journal of Marriage and the Family 493. For an exploration of the reasons underlying this trend, see Daly and Sobol, *Adoption in Canada: Final Report* (Guelph: University of Guelph, 1993) at 59; and Daly and Sobol, "Public and Private Adoption: A Comparison of Service and Accessibility" (1994), 54 Family Relations 86.

(2) CHOOSING PROSPECTIVE ADOPTIVE PARENTS

At the present time there are many more people who wish to adopt young children than there are young children available for adoption. As a result, the way in which the children's aid society screens and ranks prospective adoptive parents is very important. For a general examination of the selection criteria used in public and private adoptions, see Daly and Sobol, *Adoption in Canada: Final Report* (Guelph: University of Guelph, 1993) at 55-57. In 1985, the Ministry of Community and Social Services warned the children's aid societies that the traditional guidelines used by the societies might be subject to challenge under the *Human Rights Code* or the *Charter*. In particular, the directive stipulated that age and marital status should no longer be used as a quick method of screening applicants. Nevertheless, Daly and Sobol conclude (at 56-57): "Homosexuals, single parents, and those over 40 would have considerable difficulty adopting an infant in either a public or private adoption. While their chances of adopting a special needs child are better, they are still limited." See also Freedman, *et al*, "Criteria for Parenting in Canada: A Comparative Survey of Adoption and Artificial Insemination Practices" (1988), 3 C.F.L.Q. 35; Katarynych, "Adoption" in Hornick, Bala and Vogl, eds., *Canadian Child Welfare Law: Children, Families and the State* (Toronto: Thompson Educational Publishing Inc., 1991); and Daly and Sobol, "Public and Private Adoption: A Comparison of Service and Accessibility" (1994), 43 Family Relations 86.

Views on interracial placements and adoption have undergone considerable change in the last 50 years. Professor Black reports in "GATT for Kids: New Rules of Intercountry Adoption of Children" (1994), 11 C.F.L.Q. 253 (at 283-284):

> ... Views on the wisdom of interracial adoption have undergone a number of transformations. At one point racist views stood against it, but in the 1950s and 1960s these were replaced by a civil rights approach under which such adoptions were accepted and practiced. This reached a zenith in 1971 before receding in the face of a new wave of objection. Particularly vocal among the opponents of transracial adoption have been Black social workers in North America and Britain. Such objections ... have had considerable practical implementation. ...

In the following excerpt, Professor Davies reviews the literature on interracial adoption to determine the extent to which it supports the premise that children run the risk of harm if raised outside their own race and culture. She also examines the interests of the child welfare authorities and racial or cultural groups in this issue.

DAVIES "RACIAL AND CULTURAL MATTERS IN CUSTODY DISPUTES"

(1993), 10 C.F.L.Q. 1, at 8-13, 14-16, and 21-24.

(Edited footnotes follow.)

● *Premise #2: Children run the risk of harm if raised outside their own race and culture*

The reasons given for this premise are primarily twofold. It is said that cultural identity is essential to develop one's feeling of self worth. As one writer put it, "pride in one's cultural heritage is essential to reducing the crisis of adolescent identity and resolving role conflict."

Secondly, in the United States, the placing of Black children in white foster or adoptive homes has been opposed by many in the Black community on the basis that it prevents a child from developing "survival skills" necessary to live in contemporary American society. In one writer's opinion:

> My basic premise, in opposing placement of black children in white homes, is that being black in the United States is a special state of being. At a time of intense racial polarity, recognition of this fact is crucial to survival. I question the ability of white parents — no matter how deeply imbued with good will — to grasp the totality of the problem of being black in this society. I question their ability to create what I believe is crucial in these youngsters — a black identity.

The need for a black child to develop survival skills is a sad commentary on North American society. One would like to think it is applicable to life south of the border and not to that north of it. I may, however, be naive in my beliefs in this regard. Certainly, I believe that better race relations will not be fostered if our children are brought up in a climate of hate and distrust.

Let us turn to the other reasons given for preferring racial congruity in child placement: the need for racial identity and the importance of self-esteem. These two facets are usually seen as interlinked: racial identity is *necessary* for the development of self-esteem. Is it true that the two *are* interlinked, *i.e.*, that one cannot have a healthy self-esteem without positive racial identity? Is it true that a positive racial identity and healthy self-esteem can only result from being brought up by someone of one's own race and culture?

First, then, the linkage between self-esteem and racial identity. Some recent studies indicate that self-esteem and racial self-perception may operate independently in children of one race adopted by parents of another. A team from the University of Texas in Austin carried out a study involving 30 Black families who had adopted Black children and 30 white families who had adopted Black children.[29] They found that the children of both sets of families had almost identical levels of self-esteem. Furthermore, the level of self-esteem of the adoptees was as high as that reported among individuals in the general population. However, there appeared to be a difference between the transracial and in racial adoptees in their sense of racial identity. Some of the Black children adopted by white families seemed to have a problem with racial identity (*i.e.*, some devalued or did not acknowledge a Black identity). Whether the Black children adopted by whites had a positive racial identity depended on whether the adoptive family nurtured the Black child's identity, gave the child access to Black role models and peers in the community and in school, paid attention to the child's Black heritage, etc. Thus, the study seems to show that self-esteem may be generated as effectively among Black children in white adoptive homes as in Black adoptive homes. Positive racial identity may also be generated in white adoptive homes, but the white adoptive parents must make efforts to foster this.

The authors of this study would be the first to acknowledge that theirs is not the definitive word on the correlation between self-esteem and racial identity. They do point out, however, that their findings support the findings of others.

There have been several studies conducted with respect to the success of interracial adoptions. These studies have been consistent in their findings that by far the majority of transracial adoptions are successful. As one team of researchers put it, ''There is no evidence that any of the serious problems of adjustment suggested by the critics of transracial adoption are present in any meaningful proportion for non-white children who have been adopted by white parents.'' Initially, researchers expressed caution that, whilst showing good adaptation as young children, the transracial adoptees might show themselves as less well-adapted in adolescence. However, subsequent studies have shown these fears to have been groundless and most of the adoptees were well-integrated into their families, experiencing no more than typical adolescent problems. This research contrasts markedly with the views expressed by some courts with respect to the danger of transracial adoption, particularly in the adolescent years.[33] As one writer has commented, ''The puberty argument has instilled in it a life of its own.''

It would be simplistic to suggest that transracial adoption is without its problems. The researchers all agree that it is important for the adoptive parents to make an effort to foster the child's sense of racial identity by affirming her racial heritage and by giving the child appropriate racially congruent role models and peers. However, the empirical research does not support the view that transracial adoption is in itself harmful to the child. Many of the problems transracially-reared children display in adolescence may be attributed to factors other than adoption, factors such as institutional or foster care and discrimination that might well have occurred regardless of the adoption. The Cawsey Report[35] states:

> Most of the young aboriginals in young offender centres are the product of foster homes, aboriginal as well as non-aboriginal. Being raised in a foster home contributes to the lack of identity and lack of culture which are so important to aboriginal youth. We were told repeatedly of aboriginal youths being beaten and abused in foster homes. Many of the aboriginal youth have been in a series of foster homes. As products of foster homes, they frequently do not know who they are. They are rootless and they are sometimes subjected to alcoholic or abusive foster parents. One

case was brought to our attention of an Indian youth who had been in 17 different foster homes. When we met him, he was in a young offender's centre for the seventh time.

This commentary would seem to support the view that injury to youths such as that referred to in the passage is more likely to be caused by the type of care than to the fact that the care is provided by someone of a different race. Foster care is itself imperfect in that it lacks stability, and bad foster care is disastrous. The child will be damaged no matter the race of the provider. I would submit that the view that children will suffer harm if not reared within their own racial and cultural group has no proof and validity.

. . .

(a) The Child Welfare Authorities . . . A child welfare authority at any given time will generally have in effect a policy with respect to placement. The authority will make placement decisions on the basis of that policy. This policy will generally have been developed in light of prevailing political as well as child-related considerations. The implementation of this policy may or may not be in the interests of an individual child who becomes subject to it.

To give some examples, in the United States, the policy followed by child welfare workers with respect to the adoption of Black children by white parents has changed significantly over the past number of years. In 1958, the Standards for Adoption Services of the Child Welfare League of America (C.W.L.A.) stated that, "Children placed in adoptive families with similar racial characteristics such as colour, can become more easily integrated into the family group and community." It also stated that, "Physical resemblances should not be a determining factor in the selection of a home, *with the possible exception of such racial characteristics as colour.*" By 1968, the C.W.L.A. had changed its position. The Standards provided:

> It should not be assumed by the agency or staff members that difficulties will necessarily arise if adoptive parents and children are of different racial origin. . . . In most communities there are families who have the capacity to adopt a child whose racial background is different from their own. Such couples should be encouraged to consider such a child.

Further, the Standards stated that "physical resemblances of the adoptive parents, the child or his natural parents, should not be a determining factor in the selection of a home." The proviso emphasized above was now removed.

In 1972, the National Association of Black Social Workers condemned transracial adoption. In direct response to this, the C.W.L.A. standards changed again so that in 1972, the Standards provided:

> While we specifically affirm transracial adoptions as one means of achieving needed permanence for some children, we recognize that other things being equal in today's social climate, it is preferable to place a child in a family of his own racial background.

In the Canadian context, we see a similar fluctuating policy applied with respect to the placement of Native children.

For many years Native Indian children were placed, both for purposes of foster care and for purposes of adoption, with white families. In Manitoba, Native children were placed as a regular, ongoing practice out of province.[44] By the mid-1980s, the approach to the placement of Native children had changed dramatically. Not only were they being placed with Native foster and adoptive parents more frequently, and wherever possible kept within their communities, the child welfare departments of some provinces pursued a policy of "repatriation." Thus, Native children who had settled into white homes were uprooted and relocated to Native communities.[45]

The shifting policies of the child welfare authorities both in the United States and Canada may, in part, be attributed to growing sensitivity to the needs of Black and Native children. It is, perhaps, not overly cynical to suggest that the shifting policy is also a product of political awareness of the claims of the Black and Native population of the two countries. Whatever the motivation of the policy in question, it may or may not be in the interests of a particular child that he be subject to it. It is important that we be aware that beneath the platitude "best interests of the child," policies are at work. These policies may not *in fact* reflect the interests of this particular child.

. . .

(d) Racial or Cultural Groups . . .

We have seen that in the United States there have been shifts in attitude with respect to the placement of Black children in white homes. One particularly violent shift was led by the National Association of Black Social Workers in 1972. This Association condemned bi-racial adoptions in such strong terms that such adoptions fell by 39 per cent in a single year. A position paper of the National Association of Black Social Workers, dated April 1972, states:

> [W]e have taken the position that Black children should be placed only with Black families whether in foster care or for adoption. Black children belong, physically, psychologically and culturally in Black families in order that they receive the total sense of themselves and develop a sound projection of their future. Human beings are products of their environment and develop their sense of values, attitudes and self concept within their family structures. Black children in white homes are cut off from the healthy development of themselves as Black people.
>
> Our position is based on:
>
> 1. the necessity of self-determination from birth to death, of all Black people;
>
> 2. the need of our young ones to begin at birth to identify with all Black people in a Black community; and
>
> 3. the philosophy that we need our own to build a strong nation.
>
> The socialization process for every child begins at birth. Included in the socialization process is the child's cultural heritage which is an important segment of the total process. This must begin at the earliest moment. Otherwise our children will not have the background and knowledge which is necessary to survive in a racist society. This is impossible if the child is placed with white parents in a white environment. . . .
>
> We the participants of the workshop have committed ourselves to go back to our communities and work to end this particular form of genocide.

We can see that the view of this group that Black children should be placed in Black homes is based on factors some of which stem from a perception of the Black child's interest, but some of which do not. The statement that, "we need our own to build a strong nation," and the reference to placement in white homes being "a particular form of genocide," clearly relate to the interests of the Black community as a whole rather than to the interests of an individual child.

The idea that interracial placement constitutes a form of genocide has particular relevance in the context of Canada's Native people. It is trite knowledge that a people's heritage is its children. If the community does not rear its own children, then the values and culture of the community are lost. For many years a disproportionate number of Native children have been reared by non-Natives. There were the missionaries with their misguided zeal to teach Indian children the white man's ways. There were the residential schools to which Native children were sent in an attempt to ''wash out'' their Indianness. There were the white social workers with no understanding of Native customs and parenting practices who took Native children into care and placed them with white families. There was the appalling poverty on reserves that left Native parents few resources with which to help their children. These and other factors have been dealt with by this writer elsewhere.[63]

Since the mid-1970s, changes have been made. The residential schools are no more. There is greater sensitivity among social workers to cultural differences, and attempts are made to place Native children in care within their communities. The Native communities themselves are more involved with the child welfare system as it relates to Native children. By virtue of a number of agreements between the federal and provincial governments and Indian bands, bands are involved in the provision of child welfare services and take administrative responsibility with respect to Native children. The level of responsibility and control of an Indian band will depend on the type of agreement it has with the provincial and/or federal government.

The child welfare legislation of some provinces reflects greater sensitivity to Native concerns. For example, the *Child and Family Services Act* of Ontario provides that one of the purposes of the Act is to recognize that Indian and Native people should be entitled to provide, wherever possible, their own child and family services, and that services to Indian and Native children and families should be provided in a manner that recognizes their culture, heritage and traditions and the concept of the extended family.[64] Section 57 of this Act provides as follows:

(4) Where the court decides that it is necessary to remove the child from the care of the person who had charge of him or her immediately before intervention . . . the court shall, before making an order for society or Crown wardship . . ., consider whether it is possible to place the child with a relative, neighbour or other member of the child's community or extended family . . .

(5) Where the child referred to in subsection (4) is an Indian or a native person, unless there is a substantial reason for placing the child elsewhere, the court shall place the child with,
(a) a member of the child's extended family;
(b) a member of the child's band or native community; or
(c) another Indian or native family.

. . .

Are the changes that have been made since the mid-1970s sufficient to satisfy the Native community? The answer seems generally to be ''No.'' Albeit Native people have greater control over the operation of the child welfare system as it relates to their children, the laws generally applied to them are the provincial child welfare statutes and the courts making decisions are the provincial courts. Canadian Natives point across the border to the Federal *Indian Child Welfare Act* and the tribal courts.

In the United States, the Federal *Indian Child Welfare Act*[66] provides that a tribal court has exclusive jurisdiction over ''child custody proceeding'' (broadly defined to include pre-adoptive and adoptive placement) if a child is domiciled or resident within the reservation of the tribe. If the child is not so domiciled or resident, a state court shall transfer any proceeding to the tribal court in the absence of good cause to the contrary and absent objection by either parent. The tribe has the right to intervene in any state court proceedings regarding the child's custody. In either court, the following rule applies: In any adoptive placement of an Indian child under

State law, a preference shall be given, in the absence of good cause to the contrary, to a placement with (1) a member of the child's extended family; (2) other members of the Indian child's tribe; or (3) other Indian families.

The rationale of the Act has been said to be,

1. To promote the stability and security of Indian tribes. The large number of Indian children adopted by non-Indians threatened the continued existence and integrity of Indian tribes.
2. To avoid the damaging social and psychological impact on individual Indian children which is brought about by placements outside their culture.[67]

Thus, the American statute does not pretend that it caters only to the best interests of the child. It caters equally to the interests of the Native community.

---

29 R. McRoy, L. Zurcher, M. Lauderdale & R. Anderson, "Self-Esteem and Racial Identity in Transracial and Inracial Adoptees" (1982) Social Work 522.

33 See *N. (K.)* v. *M. (K.M.)* (1989), 97 A.R. 38 (Q.B.), varied (1989), 71 Alta. L.R. (2d) 42 (C.A.), leave to appeal to S.C.C. refused (1989), 102 A.R. 239 (note) (S.C.C.); *P. (L.)* v. *H. (D.J.)* (1986), 69 A.R. 327 (Q.B.), rev'd in part (1987), 55 Alta. L.R. (2d) 227 (C.A.). Compare *Winnipeg Child & Family Services* v. *B. (B.A.)* (1992), 99 D.L.R. (4th) 504 (Man. Q.B.).

35 *Justice on Trial: Report of the Task Force on the Criminal Justice System and Its Impact on the Indian and Metis People of Alberta*, vol. 1 (1991) at 8-57, 8-58.

44 See the report of Associate Chief Judge E.C. Kimelman, "No Quiet Place" *Review Committee on Indian and Metis Adoptions and Placements* (1985, Manitoba Community Service) at 329.

45 See generally, C. Davies, "Native Children and the Child Welfare System in Canada" (1992) 30 Alta. L. Rev. 1200.

63 *Ibid.*

64 Section 1(f).

66 25 U.S.C. 1901-1963. Discussed in *S. (S.M.)* v. *A. (J.P.)* (1990), 65 D.L.R. (4th) 222 (B.C. S.C.), rev'd (1992), 38 R.F.L. (3d) 113, 89 D.L.R. (4th) 204 (B.C. C.A.).

67 See *Mississippi Board of Choctaw Indians* v. *Holyfield*, 104 L.Ed. 29 (S.C. 1989). See also *S. (S.M.)* v. *A. (J.P.)*, above, note 66.

NOTES AND QUESTIONS

1. The voluminous literature on interracial adoption is assessed and summarized in Bagley, *International and Transracial Adoptions* (Aldershot, Eng.: Avenbury, 1993); Triseliotis, "Intercountry Adoption: In Whose Best Interest?" in Humphrey and Humphrey, eds., *Inter-Country Adoption: Practical Experiences* (London: Tavistock, 1993); and Simon et al., *The Case for Transracial Adoption* (Washington, D.C.: American University Press, 1994). Generally, these authors support the conclusion reached by Professor Davies; that is, interracial adoption poses no great risk to the mental or developmental health of the children. However, Professor Black states in "GATT for Kids: New Rules for Intercountry Adoption of Children" (1994), 11 C.F.L.Q. 253, at 290, that "in distinction to the situation regarding most transracial adoptions, there is convincing evidence that in many instances adoption of aboriginal children by white Canadian families has not furthered the best interests of the individual adoptees". He cites C. Bagley's book (above) at 214-239. See also Mosikatsana, "Case Comment: *Sawan* v. *Tearoe*" (1994), 11 C.F.L.Q. 89, where the author categorically states (at 97): "The marginalization of racial minorities in Canada does not allow for children of colour to adapt successfully in white homes."

2. J. Triseliotis reports (at 122 in the article noted above) that there was "a virtual embargo on own-country transracial placements by the 1980s" in Britain. In *Re P. (A Minor)*, [1990] F.C.R. 260,

the English Court of Appeal noted (at 263) that both national guidelines and the local authority's policy indicated "that the aim of their social services is that every child shall be brought up by a family of the same race and ethnic group. Only when it is not possible to achieve this without undue delay affecting the child's development will other substitute families be considered which satisfy the majority of the child's particular needs." The court upheld a local authority's decision rejecting a European foster mother's adoption application even though she had looked after the black child "admirably" during the first 16 months of his life.

3. Absolute legal bars to interracial adoptions have been held unconstitutional in the United States: *Drummond* v. *Fulton County Dep't of Family & Children's Services* (1977), 563 F.2d 1200 (5th Cir.), cert. denied, 437 U.S. 910 (1978). However, Professor Black reports (footnote 83 in the article noted above) that "practical bars to such adoptions may be imposed by social workers and adoption agencies". See also Matias, "Separate is Not Equal: Challenging State Sponsored Barriers to Interracial Adoptions" in R. J. Simon, ed., *From Data to Public Policy: Affirmative Action, Sexual Harassment, Domestic Violence and Social Welfare* (Lanham, Md.: University Press of America, 1996).

4. The *CFSA* indicates that the child's racial, cultural and social background may be a factor in the original placement of the child for the purpose of adoption and in determining whether an adoption order would be in the best interests of the child: see ss. 61(2), 136(3) and 140(3) of the *CFSA*.

5. In *R. (A.N.)* v. *W. (L.J.)*, 36 R.F.L. (2d) 1, [1983] 2 S.C.R. 173, the Supreme Court of Canada reinstated an adoption order allowing a Caucasian couple to adopt an Indian child despite the mother's refusal to consent. The court was heavily influenced by the fact that the child had developed a bond with the couple in whose home she had lived for a number of years and had not had contact with her mother for four years. Acknowledging that the child's aboriginal background was a factor to consider in determining the child's best interests, Madam Justice Wilson, in delivering judgment for the court, observed (at 14):

> Much was made in this case of the inter-racial aspect of the adoption. I believe that inter-racial adoption, like inter-racial marriage, is now an accepted phenomenon in our pluralist society. The implications of it may have been overly dramatized by the respondent in this case.

For criticism of this case, see Carasco, "Canadian Native Children: Have Child Welfare Laws Broken the Circle?" (1986), 5 Can. J. Fam. L. 111, at 124; Bull, "The Special Case of the Native Child" (1989), 47 Advocate 523, at 526; and Monture, "A Vicious Circle: Child Welfare and First Nations" (1989), 3 C.J.W.L. 1, at 14. Professor Davies supports the result in "Native Children and the Child Welfare System in Canada" (1992), 30 Alta. Law Rev. 1200, at 1214 (reproduced in Chapter 10, above). For a similar result, see *Sawan* v. *Tearoe* (1993), 48 R.F.L. (3d) 392 (B.C. C.A.) which is reproduced later in this chapter.

In *C. (J.M.N.)* v. *Winnipeg Child & Family Services (Central)* (1997), 33 R.F.L. (4th) 175 (Man. Q.B.), Goodman J. notes (at 185) that the adoption in *R. (A.N.)* v. *W. (L.J.)* broke down. Despite this failure, Goodman J. determined that the child's best interests in this case lay in staying with his Caucasian foster parents rather having guardianship transferred to the Awasis Agency of Northern Manitoba, a native organization. The case sets out the portions of the Program Standards Manual dealing with native child placements in Manitoba.

6. In *H. (R.)* v. *B. (T.)* (1991), 36 R.F.L. (3d) 208 (Ont. Prov. Div.), the mother and father separated shortly after the mother became pregnant. The mother wished to have the child adopted by strangers or, if this were impossible, to retain custody herself. The father wanted the child adopted by his sister and brother-in-law. All of this was known to the adoption licensee two months before the child was born. The licensee took no steps to investigate the father's plan, but placed the child with prospective adoptive parents shortly after its birth. The extensive litigation which followed was eventually settled by a consent order placing the child with the father's relatives.

The court allowed a claim for costs by the father and his relatives against the licensee. In the course of his reasons, Nevins Prov. J. reviewed the proper role of a licensee under the *CFSA*. He stated (at 217) that the Act indicated that an adoption by relatives should generally be given priority. He pointed to sections 1 and 130 [now 136]. Do you agree with this interpretation of the Act?

7. In "Adoption" in Hornick, Bala and Vogl, eds., *Canadian Child Welfare Law: Children, Families and the State* (Toronto: Thompson Educational Publishing Inc., 1991), Ms. Katarynych reports (at 153) that some child protection agencies in Canada give birth parents a role in selecting among suitable applicants, without providing identifying information. She also indicates (at 152) that some agencies permit meetings between the two sets of parents once the selection has been made, provided the adoptive parents are willing and no identifying information is disclosed:

> The Children's Aid Society of Metropolitan Toronto, for example, will arrange for a meeting between the birth parents who are relinquishing and the adoptive parents who are receiving the child, to allow them to convey to one another what is important to them in the adoption process. The birth parent may, for example, have prepared a letter to be given to the child and discussed later if the child raises questions about the birth parent's inability to care for the child. The prospective adoptive parents may agree to provide the birth parent with periodic photographs or updates on the child. Such meetings can be pivotal for adoptive parents in ensuring that the reality of the child and his history are kept firmly in mind, and give a measure of peace to a birth parent who wishes to be assured that the child goes into an adoption in which the parental wishes for the child will be conveyed directly to those who will raise the child.

Some private adoption agencies, especially in the United States, are experimenting with a more open process that involves, for example, the exchange of identifying information and permits occasional visits by the birth parents. See Caplan, "A Reporter at Large: An Open Adoption, Part I", *The New Yorker* (21 May 1990) 40 and "Part II", *The New Yorker* (28 May 1990) 73. In "Adoption with Access or 'Open Adoption'" (1991-1992), 8 C.F.L.Q. 2883, at 289, the Adoption with Access Sub-Committee of the Canadian Bar Association — Ontario reports:

> Some Children's Aid Societies have been involved in situations where without a court order, arrangements were made between the adoptive family and one or more natural relatives with the assistance of the Children's Aid Society, for some degree of contact to occur after the adoption order was granted. However, some judges being advised of these informal arrangements have frowned upon them as an attempt to circumvent the intent of the legislation.

See also **Effect of Adoption** later in this chapter.

8. In *L. (C.)* v. *F. (A.)* (1998), 43 R.F.L. (4th) 332 (Ont. Gen. Div.), a mother and father, without the assistance of a society or a licensee, placed their child in the home of close friends one day after its birth. Within days, they met with a lawyer and signed consents to the adoption by the couple. The child's maternal grandmother commenced an application for custody. The parents responded by asking the court to dismiss her application on the basis that the child had been placed for adoption. The court held that the grandmother's application should go forward as there had been no placement in accordance with the provisions of the *CFSA*. It was on this basis that the court distinguished *M. (R.)* v. *M. (S.)* (1994), 20 O.R. (3d) 621 (C.A.). There the grandparents of a child who had been placed for adoption by a licensed agency with the consent of his mother and father were not allowed to apply for custody under s. 21 of the *Children's Law Reform Act*. The court held that Part VII of the *CFSA* provides a comprehensive code for adoptions and that the adoption process must be allowed to proceed to its conclusion without interference in accordance with s. 143(2) of the *CFSA*. Accordingly, the grandparents could not apply for custody. This case was applied in *Family, Youth & Child Services of Muskoka* v. *R. (L.)* (1998), 37 R.F.L. (4th) 166 (Ont. Gen. Div.), where the parents of the child initially consented to the adoption, but the mother later supported her parents' attempt to derail the process after the society placed the child for adoption. They brought an action to set aside the consents and for custody of the child. The court concluded that it could not grant interim access to either the mother or the grandparents. Only if the placement was invalid because of a defect in the consents could the court deal with a custody or access claim.

9. Partly as a result of the shortage of infants available for adoption, some infertile couples are prepared to consider "surrogate motherhood". This term is used to describe an arrangement by which a fertile woman is usually artificially impregnated with the semen of a fertile man who is usually married

to an infertile woman with the understanding that after the birth of the child the mother will give the child to the couple for adoption.

Would a surrogate motherhood contract be contrary to s. 175 of the *CFSA*? Would it make any difference if the biological mother was paid only her expenses? In *Doe* v. *Kelley*, 307 N.W. 2d 438 (Mich. App., May 5, 1981) the court held that a similar state law did not directly prohibit surrogate motherhood but that it did prevent a married couple from offering money to the mother in exchange for a promise to consent to adoption. The court also concluded that the law was constitutionally valid.

In its *Report on Artificial Reproduction and Related Matters* (1985), the Ontario Law Reform Commission examined the effect of the present law on surrogate motherhood arrangements and concluded that the existing law did not adequately deal with such arrangements. A majority of the Commission endorsed the practice and recommended that legislation should be enacted to establish a regulatory scheme governing surrogate motherhood arrangements. A striking feature of the proposed scheme is the need for prior court approval of the arrangement. One Commissioner, in a strong dissent, rejected the practice of surrogacy and recommended that a provincial offence be created whereby any professional assisting in the establishment of a surrogate pregnancy would be acting unlawfully.

The Royal Commission on New Reproductive Technologies adopted the following position on surrogate motherhood:

> . . .Our review of the evidence shows that the potential benefits [of preconception agreements] to a few individuals are far outweighed by the harms to others and to society. Commissioners believe strongly that preconception arrangements are unacceptable and should not be encouraged. Preconception arrangements commodify reproduction and children, they have the potential to exploit women's vulnerability because of race, poverty, or powerlessness and leave women open to coercion. Thus they contravene the Commission's ethical principles.

> The most appropriate ways to discourage commercial preconception arrangements are by criminally prosecuting those who act as intermediaries, and by making payments for preconception arrangements illegal.

(The *Royal Commission on New Reproductive Technologies, Proceed With Care: Final Report of the Royal Commission on New Reproductive Technologies* (Ottawa: Minister of Government Services, 1993) at 19.)

On surrogate motherhood, see Chisick and Baccus, ''Not Just a Human Incubator: Statutory, Contractual, and Tortious Problems in Gestational Surrogate Motherhood'' (1997), 25 Man. L.J. 49.

Although federal legislation to deal with commercial surrogacy and other issues raised by the new reproductive technology has been promised several times since the Commission's report, none has yet been enacted. For an examination of some of the effects of new reproductive technologies on family law, see Baird, ''Reproductive Technologies and the Evolution of Family Law'' (1997-98), 15 C.F.L.Q. 103.

(3) REMOVAL OF THE CHILD FROM THE PROSPECTIVE ADOPTING PARENTS' HOME

Decisions by a child protection agency to remove the child from the home of the prospective adopting parents can have grave consequences for all concerned, as is illustrated in the following case.

B. (D.) v. NEWFOUNDLAND (DIRECTOR OF CHILD WELFARE)

30 R.F.L. (2d) 438, [1982] 2 S.C.R. 716

WILSON J.:—The issue on this appeal is not one which normally confronts us. It arises out of a rather sad saga which discloses how one small boy can be caught in a legislative and administrative net and have to come to the highest court in the land to extricate himself. The chronological history of the matter is a procedural nightmare.

The child C. was born on 21st May 1977 and immediately following his birth became a ward of the Director of Child Welfare in Newfoundland. In January 1979 the appellants, Mr. and Mrs. B., applied to adopt a child, and in July 1980 C. was placed by the director in their custody with a view to adoption. A social worker was assigned to monitor the adoption in the normal manner and his reports, made to the director on 21st August 1980 and 23rd October 1980, were very favourable. However, on 8th January 1981 Mrs. B. was advised that allegations of child abuse by her husband had come to the attention of the director. Mrs. B., naturally greatly upset at this, denied any such abuse as did also her husband. Mr. B. was asked to return the child, which he did under protest on 9th January 1981. Neither Mr. nor Mrs. B. were able to elicit from the director or his staff the source of the allegations. Nor were they given any opportunity to respond. In seven days following the removal of C. from the B. home the six-month period of residence required for an adoption would have been completed. C. was returned to the foster home in which he had resided prior to his placement with the B.'s.

Immediately after the return of C. the B.'s advised the director that they wished to appeal his decision to the Adoption Appeal Board. He told them that in his opinion there was no right of appeal in a case where a child was removed from a prospective adoptive home prior to the expiry of the six-month period. The B.'s filed an appeal nonetheless but the appeal board apparently shared the view of the director and refused to entertain the appeal. The B.'s thereupon commenced habeas corpus proceedings in the Supreme Court of Newfoundland to try to get the child back. At the hearing of this application on 28th May 1981 the allegations of abuse against Mr. B. were fully canvassed and Noel J. held that they were unfounded. However, he dismissed the habeas corpus application on the basis that the director had a discretion under the Adoption of Children Act, 1972 (Nfld.), No. 36, as amended, and that he should not substitute his views for the views of the director. He did, however, state that: "It would be in this child's interest for the director to sit down with the [B.'s] and come to an agreement, subject to supervision, to give this boy a chance to have this fine home". The director indicated to the B.'s that he would not follow this advice and they thereupon appealed the decision of Noel J. to the Newfoundland Court of Appeal.

The Court of Appeal dismissed the appeal on the ground that the Adoption of Children Act is a complete code with respect to adoption and that habeas corpus does not lie. It held, moreover, that the *parens patriae* jurisdiction of the court, which had been put forward in argument by counsel for the B.'s, could be resorted to only where the legislation afforded no remedy. In the court's view the legislation in this case did afford a remedy. The director's decision was appealable to the Adoption Appeal Board and a mandamus would have lain to compel the board to hear the appeal. Although the B.'s had been treated unfairly by the director and the manner in which he made his decision was "to say the least most unfortunate", there was nothing the court could do.

The B.'s applied for leave to appeal to this court and, during the hearing of the application on 22nd June 1982, the court asked counsel for the director where and with whom C. was currently residing. It was then disclosed that, unknown to the B.'s, and indeed to the Newfoundland Court of Appeal at the time it heard the B.s' appeal on the habeas corpus application, C. had been in a new adoptive home since January 1982. This information was subsequently corrected by counsel for the director and the court advised that C. had been placed with Mr. and Mrs. J. for adoption in November 1981.

The court gave leave to appeal, granted the subsequent application of Mr. and Mrs. J. to intervene in the appeal and appointed separate counsel to represent the child C. All counsel agreed that there should be the fullest evidence before the court on the hearing of the appeal so that the matter could be brought to a finality and that it would be appropriate to have it taken on commission in Newfoundland. It was agreed also that it was in the child's best interests that the appeal be heard as soon as possible. An order to expedite was accordingly made.

[MADAM JUSTICE WILSON reviewed the case law regarding the use of a court's *parens patriae* jurisdiction to act in the best interest of a child in the face of legislation entrusting the care and control of children to statutory authorities. She concluded that a court could use its *parens patriae* jurisdiction if there were "gaps" in the legislation or to engage in judicial review, based on administrative law principles, of the authority's decisions even in the absence of "gaps". On either basis, the trial judge could have acted in this case. There was a "gap" in the legislation because there was no right of appeal from the Director's decision in this situation. Furthermore, an application for judicial review might well have been successful on the ground that the Director had failed to act fairly. The allegations of abuse had come from a completely unreliable source and no effort had been made by the Director to substantiate them.]

The available relief

What recourse then is open to this court to settle the rights not only of the B.'s but also of Mr. and Mrs. J., the intervenors, who through no fault of their own are now caught up in what must be a most traumatic and painful experience? Mr. and Mrs J. had apparently no knowledge of the claim of the B.'s to the child who had been so enthusiastically welcomed into their family until the bombshell was dropped on them by the registrar of this court.

We have now had the benefit of very complete evidence taken on commission in Newfoundland before Goodridge J. This includes the evidence of a pediatrician, two psychologists, a child psychiatrist, two social workers, the Director of Child Welfare and Mr. and Mrs. B. We have also had the benefit of thorough argument from counsel for the appellants and for the intervenors, from counsel for the director and from Mr. Day, counsel appointed by the court to represent C. Having been advised by Dr. Boddie, the child psychiatrist retained by him that C. was neither capable of instructing counsel nor "of expressing his wishes as to his future custodians", Mr. Day assessed his role as being to advance his client's best interests as he saw them to the court. In order to satisfy himself as to where C.'s best interests lay, Mr. Day conducted a very thorough investigation of C.'s social, medical and legal antecedents and of his present circumstances. In the course of this investigation he reviewed the director's files on C. and interviewed all the people who had had C. under care including the appellants and the intervenors, former foster parents, child welfare workers, health care persons and his teacher. He also spent time with C. at his present residence.

Mr. Day's submissions to the court, based on his investigations and the assistance he received from the professionals he retained on C.'s behalf, are that C.'s best interests were being served when he was a member of the appellants' family and would likely have continued to be served by his being left there. However, given that he was removed from their care by the director, the court must decide whether his best interests would now be served by leaving him where he is, i.e., with the intervenors, or by returning him to the appellants. This in turn would depend, counsel submitted, on whether the quality of care he would receive from the appellants would outweigh any prejudice to him arising from yet another move.

As to the quality of care available to C. in the appellants' home, Mr. Day stated that "the quality of care which can be afforded by the appellants is superior to a significant degree to that which can be afforded by the intervenors". He hastened to point out that this was not to say that C. was not currently being materially and emotionally well cared for to the best of their ability by the intervenors. He simply needs a great deal of care and attention and requires, according to counsel, "the time, patience, vigilance and sensitivity of supportive and stimulating custodians". The appellants are more able to spend time with C. and have been and continue to be motivated to do so. They clearly love him very much as witness their pursuit of this matter through all the various levels of the court. They want him back as their son despite the fact that they now have a baby girl of their own.

Mrs. B. is at home all day and Mr. B. is a businessman with considerable latitude in his working hours. Their elder son, L., is devoted to C. Mrs. J., on the other hand, has a job and both she and her husband function on fairly stringent work schedules. C. has to be looked after by a neighbour until they return from work. They are simply not able to give the child the time and attention he needs. They have two children, a boy of 9 and a girl of 7. In the context of the longer term interests of C. the appellants are more able to handle financial family contingencies and to save for their children's post-secondary education and training, which is a high priority with them. While financial security is not by any means a determining factor, it is a relevant one. It is not surprising, counsel submitted, that on the basis of the evidence Noel J. was concerned that C. have the opportunity of this fine home.

Nevertheless, Mr. Day submitted, the court must be concerned about the effect of another move on a boy who has lived up to this time what he described as "a nomadic existence". The advice he had received from the child psychiatrist was encouraging in this respect. The child was extremely resilient (doubtless as a result of his background to date) and Dr. Boddie was of the opinion that he would adjust to the return of his former home since "proper care and love can prevent permanent impairment due to separation". The pediatrician and psychologists who assessed C. were less sanguine on this count.

Having reviewed all of the evidence and considered the submissions of counsel, and being particularly impressed by the totally impartial and objective submissions of C.'s counsel, I am of the view that it is in C.'s best interests that he now be returned to the appellants. In so saying I am certainly not unmindful of the upset this will unquestionably involve for the child and that the courts have cautioned against the disturbance of the status quo. I am also aware that it will cause anguish for the intervenors. Indeed, hurt all round is the tragic feature of this sorry situation.

What kind of relief then is it open to this court to grant? As I understand it, the exercise of the court's *parens patriae* jurisdiction has traditionally resulted in an order for custody, the jurisdiction being of ancient origin and pre-dating the concept of adoption. It would, however, in my view serve C. ill if the court made an order for custody in favour of the appellants. Counsel for the director advised that if this were done it would amount in his view to a new placement and, since Mr. and Mrs. J. have already had C. in excess of the six-month period, a certificate could be issued by the director in their favour at any time. It is quite clear that further litigation would ensue if this court made an order for custody only, and this could hardly be in C.'s best interests. Moreover, an order for custody only would deprive C. of the status of being the appellants' "child" in the fullest sense of the term. If ever a child needed the security of that status, this one does. Accordingly, having found that the Newfoundland Court of Appeal was in error in considering itself powerless to safeguard the interests of this child, I would allow the appeal and make the order which that court ought to have made, namely, an order under s. 12 of the Adoption of Children Act, for the adoption of C. by the appellants.

NOTES AND QUESTIONS

1. The Supreme Court decision in *B. (D.)* is remarkable for a number of reasons. It is highly unusual for the Supreme Court of Canada to receive new evidence. The court also appeared to grant relief, the adoption order, that was not requested by the appellants. See Day, "Counsel for Christopher: Representing an Infant's Best Interests in the Supreme Court of Canada" (1982), 33 R.F.L. (2d) 16 and Bissett-Johnson, "Case Comment" (1983), 35 R.F.L. (2d) 27.

2. What remedies are available under the *CFSA* where a society or licensee removes a child from the home of the prospective adopting parents? See ss. 144 and 145. Regarding the circumstances in which a court might interfere with the result of a Director's review, see *B.* v. *A.*(1988), 13 R.F.L. (3d) 209 (Ont. H.C.) and *Children's Aid Society of Metropolitan Toronto* v. *Ontario*(1990), 27 R.F.L. (3d) 311 (Ont. Div. Ct.). See also *D. (C.J.)* v. *Superintendent of Family & Child Service*(1989), 22 R.F.L. (3d) 235 (B.C. S.C.).

3. Who has legal custody of the child after it is placed in the home of the prospective adopting parents but before an adoption is made: (a) where the child is a Crown ward? (b) where the placement is made by a licensee?, and (c) where the child is placed in the home of a relative by a natural parent? See ss. 63(1) and 137(5) of the *CFSA*.

4.   Consents to Adoption

(1) CONSENT OF THE ADOPTEE

The number of consents required before an adoption order can be made varies considerably depending on the circumstances and the type of adoption involved (see s. 137 of the *CFSA*). Under s. 137(6) an order for the adoption of a person who is seven years of age or more is not to be made without the person's consent. Before such consent is given the person is to be accorded "an opportunity to obtain counselling and independent legal advice with respect to the consent": s. 137(7). Such consent can be withdrawn within 21 days: s. 137(8).

Section 69(6) of the *Child Welfare Act* also required the consent of a child seven years or older, but it authorized the court to dispense with this requirement if this was in the best interests of the child. A similar provision was considered in *Re R.* 7 R.F.L. (2d) 344, [1979] 1 W.W.R. 496 (B.C. S.C.) where the court dispensed with the consent of a 16-year-old boy in a step-parent adoption. The boy was not aware of his true parentage and it was felt that disclosure at that particular time would be upsetting to the entire family. In *Re A.* 1980), 3 F.L.R.R. 47 (Ont. Prov. Ct.), Nasmith Prov. J. used s. 69(6) to dispense with the need for the consent of a 13-year-old boy. He expressed "serious reservations about this entire exercise" but decided that the judicial discretion should be exercised where the mother and stepfather believed the boy would be devastated if he learned that the stepfather was not his biological father. See also *Re H. (V.)*(1984), 47 O.R. (2d) 272 (Fam. Ct.) where the court dispensed with the requirement of consent of a seven-year-old girl because of concern over the confusion that would be caused in her mind by seeking her consent to an adoption that merely formalized an existing arrangement.

Note that under s. 137(9) of the *CFSA* the court may only dispense with the requirement that a child of seven or over consent where it is satisfied that obtaining the consent would cause the child emotional harm or the child is not able to consent because of a developmental handicap. Would the results reached in the cases outlined above have been different if s. 137(9) had been applicable?

Section 152(2) of the *CFSA* requires the court to be satisfied that any consent given by a child was given with the understanding of the nature and effect of an adoption order. Note also s. 152(3) and (4).

(2) PARENTAL CONSENT

(a) Granting consent and revoking consent

In all Canadian jurisdictions there are legislative provisions generally requiring the consent of parents to the adoption of their children (see, for example, s. 137 of the *CFSA*). Such provisions are in recognition of the presumption that parents are the natural custodians and guardians of their children and the fact that adoption generally severs irrevocably the connection between parent and child. A consent is not required if a child is already a Crown ward: s. 137(2). There is also legislative provision for dispensing with the consent of a parent to an adoption (see s. 138). It is the subject of the next section of this chapter.

Certain provisions in the Act attempt to ensure that the parent's consent has been given knowingly and voluntarily (see ss. 137(4), 137(11), 137(12) and 152(2)). As s. 175 makes clear, consent may not be given in return for money or other consideration.

The following cases deal with the nature of parental consent required and the possibility of revoking the consent.

RE ADOPTION NO. 71-09-013131

(1972), 9 R.F.L. 197 (B.C. S.C.)

HARVEY L.J.S.C.:—The petitioners for an adoption order are the paternal grandparents of the infant. The petition is not ready for hearing as the report of the Superintendent of Child Welfare has not been received. The infant's mother signed a form of consent to the proposed adoption on 15th October 1971 and now seeks, by notice of motion, to set this aside on the ground that her consent was not voluntarily given. She does not seek to revoke a consent which she acknowledges having given but rather to have it declared that she has not in fact and in law given such consent.

She argues therefore that, regardless of the form of consent which she admits having signed, the provisions of subs. (5) of s. 8 of The Adoption Act, R.S.B.C. 1960, c. 4, do not apply. That subsection reads:

> (5) No person who has given his consent to adoption, other than the child to be adopted may revoke his consent unless it is shown to the Court's satisfaction that such revocation is in the best interests of the child.

In addition to the usual adoption process and the affidavit of the mother in support of her motion, I had the benefit of viva voce evidence from the child's great-grandfather, from the father and mother and from a solicitor. The facts, as I find them, are briefly as follows:

The mother, then 16, and the father, then 18 were married on 23rd February 1971. The child was born about nine weeks later on 3rd May 1971. About 4½ months thereafter, on 23rd September 1971, the mother and father separated, the mother leaving the matrimonial home in Houston to live with her sister in Terrace. The mother hoped and expected that the separation would be temporary. For the father the marriage was at an end. Both agreed that the child should be left with the father's parents, the present petitioners, who live in Prince George; the mother thought this to be a temporary arrangement pending the resumption of cohabitation.

Also living in Houston at the time of the separation was the father's maternal grandfather, the father of the female petitioner. Within a few days of the separation he consulted a solicitor with a view to the adoption of the child by his daughter and son-in-law and was provided with forms of consent and supporting affidavits for this purpose. He had one set completed by the father and took the other set to Terrace where he tried to persuade the mother to complete them. At a private interview with him she refused to do so. Nevertheless he had her accompany him to a solicitor's office but she persisted in her refusal and the solicitor was unwilling to intervene.

The grandfather, as I will call him, said that at that time he thought there was some possibility of reconciliation between the child's mother and father. I am satisfied that he discussed this with the mother and intimated that the child would be returned to her if she and her husband became reconciled and that the adoption proceedings were, in the meantime, in the best interests of all concerned.

The grandfather reported the failure of his mission to the father, who then took the papers from him and went himself to Terrace to try to persuade the mother to sign them. Again she refused, although it is clear that the father held out the hope of reconciliation if she would do so and said that, regardless of adoption, she could see the child any time she wanted.

A few days later the mother telephoned her mother-in-law in Prince George asking to have the child returned to her, as she now had a good place in Terrace where she and the child could stay. This brought about a second visit from the father, who wanted to persuade her against this course and to renew his efforts to obtain her consent to adoption. To what extent reconciliation was discussed at the second meeting is not clear, but there is no doubt that she believed, on the basis of the discussions with the grandfather and more particularly with her husband, that there was a real possibility of reconciliation, that signing the consent to adoption was a step towards this end, that, regardless of adoption, she and her husband would regain the child upon their reconciliation and that, in any event, she could see the child any time she wanted. There is also no doubt that eventually she signed the form of consent because of these beliefs and would not otherwise have done so. Equally it is clear, upon his own statement, that when the father held out the hope of reconciliation with the intimation that signing the consent would facilitate it, he had neither the desire nor the intention of bringing this about. He had instigated the separation in the first place because, after the birth of the child, he found married life distasteful and restrictive and he had no intention of resuming it. Falsely and callously he led his wife to think otherwise and, in this way, induced her to sign the form of consent.

The solicitor to whom her husband took her on 15th October 1971 had not previously been involved in the matter and had little recollection of the event. He did recall that it was late in the afternoon and thought he had followed his customary practice in such matters by fully explaining to the mother, as was his duty, "the effect of the consent and of adoption, before she affixed her signature to the consent". The mother says that he did not read the document to her but merely asked if she understood it, to which she said "yes". She says however that she had read the document carefully at least twice and that her initial refusal to the grandfather had been because of para. 3 of the affidavit in her name which read:

> That I fully understand the effect of my consent and of adoption and that all my privileges, rights, duties, obligations and responsibilities in respect of the said child . . . will be extinguished upon adoption.

I am satisfied that she did not "fully understand" and did not sign "freely and voluntarily" in the words of para. 4 of her affidavit but that she signed because of her belief in the false representations of her husband. She signed because she had been led to believe that in so doing she would regain not only her husband but her child.

While I am not prepared to find that the solicitor wholly failed in his duty I do find that he was mistaken in the opinions expressed in paras. 4 and 5 of his affidavit appended to the form of consent, that it "appeared to be signed freely and voluntarily", and that the mother "appeared to understand fully the effect of her consent and of adoption". Indeed the solicitor says that he would have been more careful had he known that the mother was only 16, and that he would not have completed the documents had he known that twice in the preceding three weeks she had refused to sign the form of consent. He was not told and did not learn from any inquiry that the child had been left with the husband's parents because of the separation of the husband and wife only three weeks earlier and that in the meantime an abortive effort had been made through another solicitor to have the documents completed. He says that he noted some emotional upset on the part of the mother but did not regard this as unusual or significant. The rather perfunctory nature of the transaction is perhaps revealed in the fact that the form of consent is shown as having been signed at Smithers (substituted for Houston) while both affidavits swear to the signing having been done at Houston, whereas the entire transaction took place at Terrace. . . .

A consent, induced as this one was by fraud and undue influence, is neither free nor voluntary and is not binding. It is no consent at all. Equally it is plain that the mother, in the induced belief that the adoption of the child would not hinder her right to see the child at will or to regain the child upon reconciliation with her husband, had little or no understanding of the effect of adoption and of her consent thereto. . . .

There having been no "consent to adoption" by the mother within the meaning of The Adoption Act, s. 8(5) does not apply, nor do the cases of *Re E.'s Adoption* 1961), 34 W.W.R. 433, 27 D.L.R. (2d) 723 (sub nom. *Re B.J.E.*) (B.C.), and *Re Wells' Adoption* 1962), 37 W.W.R. 564, 33 D.L.R. (2d) 243 (B.C. C.A.). . . .

The motion is acceded to and the form of consent signed by the mother on 15th October 1971 is set aside.

SAWAN v. TEAROE

(1993), 48 R.F.L. (3d) 392 (B.C. C.A.)

The judgment of the court was delivered by

PROUDFOOT J.: — This is an appeal from a judgment pronounced June 19th, 1993, dismissing the petition of James and Faye Tearoe for the adoption of a child, then eighteen months old, and ordering the child returned to the respondent mother, Cecilia Sawan. . . .

The appellants contend that the learned trial judge erred in concluding that it was in the best interest of the child to revoke the respondent's consent to adoption, when the evidence established that the child had become strongly bonded to them.

Background to Proceedings

The facts, which are substantially not in dispute, are these: the child, the centre of the dispute, was born to Cecilia Sawan on December 3rd, 1991, in the province of Alberta. The mother was 18 years of age and unmarried. The father of the child was not involved in these proceedings. After the birth, the child remained in the hospital until December 13th, 1991, and then was released into the care of the mother. The child remained with the mother until January 6th, 1992. At that time, the mother approached the Alberta Family and Social Services and signed a one-month custody agreement with the department. The department placed the child in a foster home.

The child remained in the care of the foster home until January 30, 1992. During that period, the evidence is that the mother visited the child from two to four times. Near the end of this period, about January 28th to 30th, 1992, the respondent, Cecilia Sawan, first contacted the appellants, James and Faye Tearoe, concerning their adoption of the child.

It is not clear what happened next but the child was moved from the foster home and returned to his mother on February 1st, 1992. The child was again placed in the foster home on February 4th. On February 4th, 1992, Ms Sawan contacted the Tearoes again and asked them to come to Alberta and pick up the child. The Tearoes live in Victoria, British Columbia.

On February 6th, 1992, the Tearoes arrived in Fairview, Alberta, and took the child into their care. On the same day, the mother signed two forms: (i) a "Consent by Guardian to Adoption Placement" pursuant to the requirements of the Child Welfare Act, S.A. 1984, c. C-8.1, of Alberta.

On February 12, 1992, the respondent called the Ministry of Family and Social Services in Peace River, Alberta, and asked for her child to be returned, that is, she verbally revoked her consent. The evidence is that the respondent was told that her revocation had to be in writing.

On February 13th, 1992, the mother called the department again. She was reminded abut the necessity of written notice of revocation being sent to the department within ten days of the consent she had given on February 6th, 1992. On this date an official of the department advised the Tearoes by telephone that the mother was attempting to revoke her consent to adoption. They were told not to return the child as a written revocation had not yet been received.

On February 14th, the mother called the Tearoes and asked that the child be returned to her. Relying on the advice they had received from the Ministry of Family and Social Services in Alberta, their response was non-committal.

On February 19th, 1992, Ms Sawan made another call to the department to ascertain if the letter of revocation, which she stated she had sent, had been received. Although other correspondence had been received by the department from Ms Sawan, the letter in question did not arrive. It appears from the evidence that no written notice was ever received by the department.

Next, on February 24th, 1992, the department wrote to the respondent to clarify the situation. The letter concluded by asking the respondent, "do you wish to proceed with the placement or will you be seeking legal advice?" There was no response to the department's letter of February 24th, but on April 22nd, 1992, the respondent was again in touch with the department asking for the return of her child. At that time she stated she had not received the department's letter of February 24th, and a copy was mailed to her.

On May 21st, 1992, she wrote to the Tearoes asking them to return the child to her care. A copy of this letter was not forwarded to the department.

On May 29th, 1992, the Tearoes, wishing to complete the adoption, had their solicitor forward to Ms Sawan documents to be executed by her to complete the adoption. These were never completed and returned to the solicitor.

No further action appears to have been taken by the mother until October 1992, when she sought assistance to obtain legal advice through the education co-ordinator at the Woodland Cree Indian Band.

On December 8th, 1992, a solicitor in High Prairie, Alberta, wrote to the Tearoes' solicitor advising him that the mother had revoked her consent to the adoption of her child.

A petition for adoption was filed by the Tearoes on December 22nd, 1992. On April 23rd, Ms Sawan filed a petition in which she sought habeas corpus directing the return of her child. Alternatively, she sought sole custody or a declaration that her consent had been revoked.

An expedited trial date was obtained and the proceedings came on for hearing on June 14th, 1993. Judgment was given orally on June 19th, 1993.

The Parties to the Proceedings

The appellants, James and Faye Tearoe, are 49 and 47 years of age respectively. They are married and have one adopted child, Heidi, approximately 8 years of age. She has been with the appellants since birth. James Tearoe is employed as a forester with the Ministry of Forests for British Columbia. Mrs. Tearoe is a homemaker. She cares for Heidi and, at times, provides day care for another child.

The trial judge stated the following when commenting on the Tearoes [at pp. 19-20 unreported]:

> Mr. and Mrs. Tearoe are competent, caring, loving proposed adoptive parents. I have been impressed by them. They have testified to a very caring and close relationship where a bonding having been developed with between [sic] them, or between the four members of their family and I say four because Mr. Tearoe and Mrs. Tearoe, their daughter, Heidi, an adopted daughter, and of course the child in question. I have no doubt as [to] their suitability as adopting parents and I note the report of the Superintendent of British Columbia, that is the Superintendent of Family and Child Services, to the same effect.

. . .

Cecilia Sawan, now 20 years of age, is unmarried and is attending school. There is evidence that she has had some problems in her life, including alcohol abuse. There is also evidence that she has sought help for this problem.

Ms Sawan's mother is native; her father, non-native. Ms Sawan stated that she wishes to raise her son in her native culture. Recently, she has gained status as a member of the Woodland Cree Indian Band. She has not lived on the reserve for approximately six years. There is evidence that she has an extended family living on the reserve and off the reserve. There is little, if any, evidence of any contact by her with members of her family. Ms Sawan testified that she planned to return to the band but was uncertain as to when. The Woodland Band members speak Cree. She concedes she would have difficulties living on the reserve because she does not know the language. However, her evidence is that there are facilities to assist her in learning Cree.

Ms Sawan's future plans are not settled. She wants to complete her education. At present, she is financially supported by social assistance and the band. Ms Sawan testified that she has a fiancé, who is not a native Indian, and that they plan to marry in July 1994. Ms Sawan anticipates that her fiancé, who works in the oil fields in

Northern Alberta, will live on the reserve with her and her child. Ms Sawan's fiancé was not called as a witness.

The trial judge said the following with respect to Ms Sawan [at pp. 20-22 unreported]:

> With reference to Miss Sawan, her history is less significant in the terms that I've just described Mr. and Mrs. Tearoe. She's had problems in her life, some including alcohol. She testifies however as to changes she has made in her life and plans to continue with her education, hopefully to the university level, if funding is available. Her current academic achievements indicate that the academic ability to attain that goal is there.
>
> In addition, she wishes her son to be raised in her culture and know his extended family. . . . Her ultimate hopes are to live in the Woodland Cree Reserve after her schooling is complete and assist the members of that reserve. The band on the reserve speaks Cree; she does not. She has not lived on a reserve for some years and she has limited connection with the Woodland Cree Reserve at the present time.
>
> Nevertheless, she is a status Indian and a member of the band and her son is on the waiting list to become a band member. . . . [T]here is no reason to expect that the child will not be accepted as a band member.
>
> Insofar as Miss Sawan is concerned, her background, naivety, her lack of sophistication, despite all of those, I am impressed with her evidence and impressed with her attitude toward her child.

The Child

At the time of the trial the child was eighteen months old. It can be readily concluded from all the evidence presented that he is a healthy, happy, well-cared for child. He is one quarter native Indian. As just noted, his mother has placed his name on the list to become a member of the Woodland Cree Native Indian Band.

From the time of the child's birth to February 6th, 1992, the child had been in his mother's care, in total, for twenty-two days. The child has been with the appellants continuously since February 6th, 1992.

Reasons for Judgment of the Trial Judge

The trial judge found that the consent was signed freely and voluntarily, and that Ms Sawan understood all of the ramifications of the consent, both legally and emotionally. He also found that the mother was aware that if she wished to revoke her consent, it was necessary to do so in writing within ten days of her signing the consent. . . .

The trial judge found that the Alberta consent was legally executed. He concluded that if the consent was valid in Alberta, the consent would be valid in British Columbia, by reason of s. 9 of the British Columbia *Adoption Act*, R.S.B.C. 1979, c. 4. . . .

Notwithstanding his conclusion that the consent had been validly executed in Alberta, the trial judge went on to hold that the court, on the basis of equitable principles, could vitiate the written consent by giving effect to the mother's oral revocation.

The trial judge stated that if he was wrong in that approach, s. 8(7) of the British Columbia Adoption Act governed the question of revocation of the consent. Applying s. 8(7), he concluded that revocation of the consent the mother had given was in the best interests of the child, with the result that he dismissed the Tearoes' adoption petition and ordered the child returned to the mother. . . .

Discussion

I will deal first with the question of jurisdiction. As the petition for adoption has been filed in British Columbia and the respondent has filed her petition in this province, seeking the return of her child by having her written consent to adoption revoked, the relevant legislation is the British Columbia *Adoption Act*. The fact that we are dealing with a consent that was executed in another province, specifically Alberta, does not alter that position.

In his judgment, the trial judge concluded that Ms Sawan had given a valid consent under the Alberta law. I agree with that conclusion. Section 9 of the *Adoption Act*, referred to above, deals with out-of-province consents. The trial judge was correct in concluding that if the consent was valid in Alberta, the consent was, by reason of s. 9, valid in British Columbia.

In this case, revocation of the mother's consent does not depend on Alberta legislation. The trial judge was in error when he took the approach that the orally communicated revocation vitiated the consent.

As B.C. law applies, the applicable section is s. 8(7) of the *Adoption Act*, which reads:

> 8(7) No person who has given his consent to adoption, other than the child to be adopted, may revoke his consent unless it is shown to the court's satisfaction that the revocation is in the best interests of the child.

The trial judge dealt with this section as an alternative position. He stated [at p. 19 unreported]:

> The issue under that section is what is in the best interests of the child. And what, in terms of the British Columbia statute is in the best interest of the child, when one looks at that, one looks at what is in existence as of this date and what the future may hold.

I agree with these comments. . . .

This test of the best interest of the child is most clearly enunciated in the often-cited passage from the case of *King* v. *Low*, [1985] 1 S.C.R. 87, 44 R.F.L. (2d) 113. . . . Mr. Justice McIntyre . . . said . . . (at p. 126 [R.F.L.]):

> I would therefore hold that in the case at bar the dominant consideration to which all other considerations must remain subordinate must be the welfare of the child. This is not to say that the question of custody will be determined by weighing the economic circumstances of the contending parties. The matter will not be determined solely on the basis of the physical comfort and material advantages that may be available in the home of one contender or the other. The welfare of the child must be decided on a consideration of these and all other relevant factors, including the general psychological, spiritual and emotional welfare of the child. *It must be the aim of the court, when resolving disputes between rival claimants for the custody of a child, to choose the course which will best provide for the healthy growth, development and education of the child so that he will be equipped to face the problems of life as a mature adult. Parental claims must not be lightly set aside, and they are entitled to serious consideration in reaching any conclusion. Where it is clear that the welfare of the child requires it, however, they must be set aside.* (my emphasis)

Earlier, Madam Justice Wilson, in *R. (A.N.)* v. *W. (L.J.)*, [1983] 2 S.C.R. 173, discussed the best interest test when dealing with an adoption which involved inter-racial considerations. After commenting that the child should not become "a battle-ground" she stated (at pp. 187-188):

> In my view, when the test to be met is the best interests of the child, the significance of cultural background and heritage as opposed to bonding abates over time. The closer the bond that develops with the prospective adoptive parents the less important the racial element becomes.

When dealing with the best interests, the trial judge discussed a number of factors, the most critical of which were his comments in the following passages [at pp. 27-29 unreported]:

> Bonding; that is the bonding that Mr. and Mrs. Tearoe have described and others have described in their relationship with the child. Compared of course to the mother's short interval with the child, nevertheless this is not a child that was taken from the delivery room and delivered to the Tearoes. She had the child in her care and custody for a considerable period of time. That issue of bonding also must take into consideration the time interval between February 6 and today.
>
> . . .
>
> In my opinion, the connection between the mother and the child has not been irretrievably broken as in [*R. (A.N.)* v. *W. (L.J.)*]. . . . She has sought, albeit ineffectively, to seek the return of her child and she did within a relatively short period of time after she executed the consent.

This child was with his mother, in total, for twenty-two days. The child had been with the Tearoes for over 16 months when this matter went to trial. On the evidence, the trial judge's conclusion that the child was with his mother for a "considerable period of time" is plainly in error.

The trial judge's conclusion that "the connection between the mother and the child has not been irretrievably broken" is not supported by the evidence. There is no evidence from which to conclude either that a bond between the mother and the child had ever been established in the period during which the child was with her, or that if any such bond had been established it was likely still remaining at the time of trial. Indeed, the evidence establishes beyond doubt that the only mother and father this child knows are Faye and James Tearoe.

The welfare of the child is the paramount concern. This child presently lives in a loving, stable, comfortable environment, with a family that has looked after all his needs for virtually all his life. By all accounts the child is thriving. To end that relationship would destroy the family bonds that have been established between the child and the adoptive parents.

Although she offered no specific plans for the future, it is quite possible that Ms Sawan could also provide a loving environment in which the child could thrive if he were returned to her. But in the absence of any evidence from which it could reasonably be inferred that there ever was or now remains any bond between natural mother and child, or that such a bond could now successfully be established, it is impossible to conclude that the best interests of the child require the consent to adoption to be set aside.

Furthermore, common sense dictates that to disrupt the child from his present environment, and to put him through the uncertainty associated with an attempt to establish a bond with his natural mother, would cause him considerable trauma. In the absence of evidence from which it could reasonably be inferred that such trauma would be both minimal and fleeting in nature, it is impossible to conclude that the best interests of the child would now be met by setting aside the consent to adoption.

The trial judge stated the Tearoes are "competent, caring, loving, proposed adoptive parents" and that a close relationship had developed. To return this child, as requested by the respondent, is to place him in an uncertain future that would take away from him the continuity and stability which he now has. As in the *R. (A.N.)* case, the cultural background and heritage must give way in the circumstances of this case. A difficult choice must be made. The child's best interests must come first. The respondent has not discharged the onus which s. 8(7) places on her. It is not in the best interests of this child to revoke Ms Sawan's consent to adoption.

The child will remain with James and Faye Tearoe. The appeal is allowed and the orders of the trial judge set aside. The petition for adoption will be granted. The child will assume the name David James Tearoe.

NOTES AND QUESTIONS

1. *Re Adoption No. 71-09-013131* illustrates that the parental consent required must be a true, informed consent. For other cases in which it was alleged that the parental consent was invalid, see *McKeever* v. *Children's Aid Society of Metropolitan Toronto* (1975), 22 R.F.L. 346 (Ont. Co. Ct.); *Re J.* (1979), 9 R.F.L. (2d) 281 (Ont. H.C.); *R. (A.M.)* v. *Children's Aid Society of Winnipeg* (1983), 35 R.F.L. (2d) 113 (Man. C.A.); *T. (N.P.)* v. *Superintendent of Family & Child Service* (1987), 8 R.F.L. (3d) 405 (B.C. S.C.); and *B. (S.L.)* v. *C. (J.M.)* (1987), 10 R.F.L. (3d) 96 (Alta. Q.B.).

2. There is a possibility that prospective adoptive parents can retain custody of the child even if the natural parent establishes that his or her consent to the adoption of the child was not valid. See *Re Irving* (November 5, 1980), unreported (Ont. H.C.) [digested at 6 A.C.W.S. (2d) 170], affirmed (December 12, 1980), unreported (Ont. C.A.) [digested at 6 A.C.W.S. (2d) 391]. In this case the mother's consent was not valid as it was not signed and was not given seven days after the child's birth. The child was nevertheless placed for adoption by a lawyer who had a licence to place the child for adoption. The lawyer sought to have a proper consent signed some two months later and the mother refused. By the time the matter came to court, the child was seven months old and the court ordered that the prospective adoptive parents have custody and denied the biological mother access.

In *B. (S.L.)* v. *C. (J.M.)* (1987), 10 R.F.L. (3d) 96 (Alta. Q.B.), the mother decided to place the child for private adoption with C. (J.M.) and C. (B.S.). She signed a consent to adoption in their favour and they were granted guardianship by court order in November 1985. The C.'s separated in 1986 and agreed that C. (J.M.) should have custody of the child. After a divorce in 1987, C. (J.M.) married C. (P.J.). The mother applied for custody. The court concluded that the mother's consent to the adoption had no legal effect since it was conditional upon the child being adopted by the persons described in the consent. Nevertheless, it concluded that the child's best interests dictated that he remain with C. (J.M.), whom he regarded as his father. Although the court was not asked to make an adoption order, it indicated that it would have been prepared to dispense with the mother's consent to the adoption of the child by C. (J.M.) and C. (P.J.)

In *B. (C.S.), Re* (1998), 167 Sask. R. 114 (Sask. Q.B.), affirmed (1999), 47 R.F.L. (4th) 226 (Sask. C.A.), the judge found that the biological mother had consented to the adoption of the child. However, in *obiter*, he stated that if the consent had been invalid, he would have dispensed with the consent in the best interests of the child.

3. Section 137(8) of the *CFSA* gives a parent 21 days to revoke a consent to adoption. It appears that the revocation can occur even if the child has been placed for adoption. Note that the section specifies that where the person who revokes the consent had custody of the child immediately before the consent, the child shall be returned to him or her as soon as the consent is withdrawn.

A court may permit a parent to revoke the consent after the 21 day period if it is in the child's best interest: s. 139(1). See *Re B. (T.M.)* (1981), 26 R.F.L. (2d) 60 (P.E.I. S.C.); *Re D. (I.)* (1982), 30 R.F.L. (2d) 297, 41 N.B.R. (2d) 71 (Q.B.); *T. (N.P.)* v. *Superintendent of Family & Child Services* (1987), 8 R.F.L. (3d) 405 (B.C. S.C.); and *British Columbia Birth Registration No. 030279, Re* (1990), 24 R.F.L. (3d) 437 (B.C. S.C.), where the courts examined the meaning of the child's best interest in this context. Section 139(1) does not apply where the child has been placed with a person for adoption and remains in that person's care: s. 139(2). However, the parent could still seek to convince the court that an adoption order under s. 146(1) of the *CFSA* was not in the child's best interests. In *C. (B.L.)* v. *W. (B.J.)* (1997), 29 R.F.L. (4th) 175 (Alta. Q.B.), the mother of the child consented to the adoption of the child by the petitioners. The petitioners were subsequently charged with fraud or theft. As a result, the mother changed her mind and appeared in court to oppose the petition for adoption. The court nonetheless granted the adoption order. It held that the presumption of innocence forbade the consideration of possible guilt of a criminal offence as an element of parental fitness or in determining the best interests of the child.

4. At one time, it was often possible for natural parents to regain custody of their children at any time prior to an adoption order even if they had been placed for adoption. See, for example, *Martin* v. *Duffell*, [1950] S.C.R. 737 and *Re Mugford*, [1970] 1 O.R. 601 (C.A.), affirmed (*sub nom. Children's Aid Society of Ottawa* v. *Mugford*), [1970] S.C.R. 261, [1970] 1 O.R. 610n. This situation has now changed. In part, this is due to legislative provisions such as ss. 137(8) and 139(2) of the *CFSA*. However, as *Sawan* v. *Tearoe* and the cases discussed in it illustrate, the courts have also moved away from parental rights towards the best interests of the child test. More significantly, in applying this rather open-ended test, the courts in these cases have downplayed the importance of the blood tie and have been heavily influenced by the ''psychological parent theory''. This theory stresses the child's need for continuity and stability. It postulates that there is a risk of harm if a bond between a psychological parent and the child is broken. For analysis of the ''psychological parent theory'', an explanation of its influence, and a review of the literature criticizing it, see Davies, ''Racial and Cultural Issues in Custody Matters'' (1993), 10 C.F.L.Q. 1.

As noted in *Sawan* v. *Tearoe*, the Supreme Court of Canada's decision in *King* v. *Low* was a seminal case. It involved an unwed mother who gave up her son for adoption a few days after his birth to a couple carefully chosen by her. Fifteen days after the birth the mother executed the consent to adoption required by the N.W.T. *Child Welfare Ordinance*. When the child was three months old the mother revoked the consent (as apparently permitted under the Ordinance) and sought an order restoring custody of the child to her. The trial judge refused to grant the order, stressing that the child's best interests lay in maintaining the stable relationship already established with the prospective adoptive parents. The North West Territories Court of Appeal and the Supreme Court of Canada dismissed the mother's appeal. In its judgment the Supreme Court of Canada reviewed a number of cases and affirmed the trend away from preference for the rights of natural parents. It stressed that the welfare of the child must be the predominant factor, even in disputes between biological parents and others. See also *R. (A.N.)* v. *W. (L.J.)* (1985), 36 R.F.L. (2d) 1 (S.C.C.); *British Columbia Birth Registration No. 030279, Re* (1990), 24 R.F.L. (3d) 437 (B.C. S.C.); *G. (D.A.)* v. *L. (T.)* (1990), 25 R.F.L. (3d) 408 (N.S. Co. Ct.); *L. (W.R.)* v. *G. (C.D.)* (1994), 3 R.F.L. (4th) 43 (Man. Q.B.); and *British Columbia Birth Registration No. 99-00733, Re* (2000), 182 D.L.R. (4th) 280 (B.C. C.A.).

These cases should be contrasted with *S. (R.)* v. *H. (C.)* (1989), 20 R.F.L. (3d) 456 (N.B. C.A.) where a biological mother regained custody of a 15-month-old child from prospective adoptive parents who had been providing an excellent home for the child since its birth. The mother had signed a consent to the private adoption shortly after the birth but revoked this consent some four-and-one-half months later. New Brunswick's adoption law permitted a parent to revoke consent at any time prior to the granting of the adoption order, unless the child was placed for adoption by the Minister. The prospective adoptive parents refused to return the child to the mother and applied for an order dispensing with the requirement that the mother consent to the adoption. The trial court dismissed this application and granted custody to the mother. The prospective adoptive parents appealed and obtained a stay of the court order. The New Brunswick Court of Appeal concluded that the child should have been returned to the mother as soon as she revoked her consent and that the prospective adoptive parents should not benefit from their refusal to do so. The judgment rested in significant part on the evidence that the child would adapt to a carefully handled change in custody without long-term harmful consequences. See also *M. (C.G.)* v. *W. (C.)* (1989), 23 R.F.L. (3d) 1 (B.C. C.A.).

5. In his annotation to the *Sawan* v. *Tearoe* case, Professor McLeod writes ((1993), 48 R.F.L. (3d) 393, at 393-394):

> ... [T]he swiftness with which the appeal was processed is a credit to counsel and the court. Within one week of the trial decision, an appeal had been launched and a stay obtained. ... In less than a month, the appeal was processed and argued, and the following month the appellate court released its reasons. In child-care cases speed is vital. The longer a child remains and flourishes in a particular environment, the more difficult it will be to change his or her living

arrangements, regardless of the personal hardship to the adult claiming custody or the return of the child.

6. For commentary on *Sawan* v. *Tearoe*, see Mosikatsana, "Case Comment: *Sawan* v. *Tearoe*" (1994), 11 C.F.L.Q. 89 and Westad, *The God-Sent Child: The Bitter Adoption of Baby David* (Toronto: Penguin Books, 1994).

7. In *Manitoba (Director of Child Welfare)* v. *Y.*, 22 R.F.L. (2d) 417, [1981] 1 S.C.R. 625, a mother gave her consent to adoption seven days after birth. Two days later she attempted to withdraw her consent. However, by this time the child had been placed for adoption. The relevant legislation allowed revocation of consent until one year after the original consent was given or the child was placed for adoption, whichever occurred first. By placing the child for adoption so quickly the Director had effectively precluded any revocation of consent. The Supreme Court of Canada upheld the action of the Director, concluded that the mother could not revoke the consent, and stated that the mother was no longer entitled to the return of the child.

8. Examine the definition of "parent" in s. 137(1) of the *CFSA*. Note that a natural father does not always qualify as a parent and so his consent to the adoption is not always required.

The British Columbia Supreme Court held in *M. (N.)* v. *British Columbia (Superintendent of Family & Child Services)*, [1987] 3 W.W.R. 176, 10 B.C.L.R. (2d) 234, that s. 8(1)(b) of British Columbia's *Adoption Act* was unconstitutional because it discriminated on the basis of sex and marital status. It, therefore, violated s. 15(1) of the *Charter*. Section 8(1)(b) provided that parental consent was generally required before the court could make an adoption order, but that where the child had been born out of wedlock only the mother needed to consent. The court was not persuaded by the argument that the legislation was justified because it permitted timely adoption of unwanted children where the natural father was unknown or could not be found. The court noted that in some cases it might be as difficult to locate a natural father or natural mother whose marriage had been terminated by divorce and that the Act already provided mechanisms for dealing with situations where the natural father could not be located.

In *S. (C.E.)* v. *Children's Aid Society of Metropolitan Toronto* (1988), 49 D.L.R. (4th) 469 the Divisional Court overturned the decision of Nevins Prov. J. and rejected a s. 15 challenge to the Ontario adoption consent provisions. The court reasoned (at 472-478):

> Adoption is a very important matter. It is clear that in establishing the legal framework for it the legislature has given careful study to the complex issues involved in it. It has obviously considered that the best interests of the child are the paramount concern and that all so-called rights of the biological parents are subsidiary to what is best for the child. Debate could go on forever as to whether or not the legislative scheme that is embodied in the law of Ontario is the best one that can be devised by human beings. But the legislature considered all of the competing positions and decided the issue as it saw it in the best interests of the child. The legislation before the court has been carefully thought out after experiments with other legislative schemes had been tried and found by the legislature not to be in the child's best interests.
>
> When a legislature has weighed a complex social issue and has determined what to it is the best solution, the courts should be cautious indeed before using provisions of the Charter to frustrate the solution. . . .
>
> [O]ur reading of the sections as a whole lead us to the view that the only natural father who is not by definition a "parent" whose consent is required by s. 131(1) [now s. 137(1)] of the Act, is a male person who by an act of casual sexual intercourse impregnates a woman and demonstrates no sense of responsibility for the natural consequences of the act of sexual intercourse. It is a man who shows no sense of responsibility to the woman he has made pregnant nor to the life that he has helped to procreate. . . .
>
> We think it is an erroneous oversimplification to say that the mother and a father who does not fall within the statutory definition of parent are similarly situated. The mother because of physical necessity has shown responsibility to the child. She carried and gave birth to it. The casual fornicator who has not demonstrated any interest in whether he did cause a pregnancy or demonstrate even the minimum responsibility to the child required by s. 131 cannot be said to be

similarly situated to the mother. The statute recognizes as a parent, a father who demonstrates the minimum interest in the consequences of his sexual activity. Most fathers are defined as parents. Only those who do not demonstrate some responsibility to the child are not. It is thus apparent to us that the different statutory treatment of the two persons is based upon their respective demonstrated responsibility to the child, not upon their different sexes.

We do not think that a statutory difference in treatment between a natural parent who is responsible to her child and one who has not shown even minimal interest in whether a child exists because of his sexual activity can be said to be irrational, insidious or unfair.

We are thus of the opinion that the provisions of s. 131 of the Act does [*sic*] not violate s. 15 of the Charter.

Even if it could be said in some way which we are unable to accept that there is a violation of s. 15 we are satisfied that the provisions of s. 131 of the Act are saved by s. 1 of the Charter.
. . .

It is our opinion that the obvious objective of this legislation is to ensure that children whose parents are unwilling or unable to care for them receive early placement in a permanent home where they will have the opportunity to be reared as members of a family. There was ample evidence before the legislature, and there is ample evidence before this court, that such placement should be made as early in the child's life as possible, and that there should be a maximum feeling of certainty on the part of the adoptive parents and the child that the placement is permanent.

The evidence in this case is overwhelming that delay in placement or in finalizing the adoption incur[s] serious risks of long-term behavioural, emotional or psychological harm for the child. Delay in finalization of an adoption can cause intolerable strains on the prospective adoptive parents. The legislature has on reasonable grounds concluded that it is in the best interests of the child and the families by whom he or she is to be adopted that the process be as quick and certain as is reasonably possible.

The objective of providing for the well-being of children such as A.H. can surely be categorized as one of the highest priorities of government in a civilized society. The legislative measure by which the consent of the irresponsible casual fornicator is dispensed with is obviously fair and cannot be said to be arbitrary.

This particular legislative scheme can also be looked at in the light of a previous one that the legislature found to be unsatisfactory. For sometime before the enactment of this Act there was a legislative scheme in place in which all natural fathers were within a definition of "parent". Those professionals who were involved in the adoption process found, and the legislature was convinced, that the delays which were often encountered in determining who the father was and then getting his consent, or having it dispensed with, led to serious frustration of the legislative object of expeditious adoptions to the prejudice of the best interests of children and adoptive families.

This legislation does not impair in the least the right of natural fathers who have demonstrated their responsibility to the child they have fathered to participate in the adoption process. If there is little realistic possibility that the right of the casual fornicator would be accepted and exercised by him, a court should be cautious indeed before letting the protection of that right obstruct the fulfillment of an important governmental objective. We are of the opinion that the remote chance that a casual fornicator might wish to acknowledge and assume responsibility for the child he casually fathered bears no realistic proportion at all to the important government objective of providing for an expeditious and final adoption.

While it is not conclusive to the validity of the impugned legislation, it is worth noting what has been very properly said in para. 60 of the factum filed on behalf of the Attorney-General. That paragraph reads as follows:

> Provincial Legislatures throughout Canada have recognized the priority of the best interests of the child in establishing adoption procedures. In accordance with this priority, almost no provincial legislation gives status in adoption proceedings to those natural fathers who have not acknowledged parentage nor taken any steps beyond the time of conception to indicate their interest in the child.

We think it significant that the legislation enacted by the Legislature of Ontario in respect of adoptions is in substantial conformity with the legislative views taken in most of the other provinces.

See also *T. (D.)* v. *Children's Aid Society and Family Services* (1992), 92 D.L.R. (4th) 289 (N.S. C.A.) where the court found (at 293) "no merit" in a father's argument that his exclusion from the definition of parent violated s. 15 of the *Charter*.

9. In *British Columbia Birth Registration No. 99-00733, Re* (2000), 182 D.L.R. (4th) 280 (B.C. C.A.), an unmarried mother consented, within a few weeks of her daughter's birth, to the girl's adoption by a couple whom she helped to select. The couple agreed to facilitate continuing contact between the mother and the child. When the father learned of the placement of the child about four months later, he sought custody. The father planned to have the child live with him, his parents and his brother. The couple with whom the girl was living responded with a petition for adoption, asking that the court dispense with the father's consent. The girl's mother then indicated that she had changed her mind and supported the father's position. She asked the court to grant her joint custody or, at least, access.

The girl was thriving in the prospective adoptive couple's care. A clinical psychologist's report stated that the couple offered an ideal parenting, social and economic environment. It also concluded that the father had significant support from his family, was thoughtful in his concerns about the girl, and had a family background espousing positive child-rearing attitudes and moral values. However, it noted that the father had fewer economic and social resources and that, partly because of his relative youth, his future was less certain. The psychologist testified at trial that the child had bonded to the adoptive couple. He indicated that there was limited empirical evidence relating to a change of primary caregivers for a child of this age. He suggested that a short-term adverse reaction was likely, but that there were unlikely to be long-term negative effects if the new caregivers provided good care. The trial judge awarded custody to the father, but the B.C. C.A. overturned the decision, dispensed with the father's consent and granted an adoption order.

10. Where someone's consent is required for the adoption, that person is generally entitled to notice of the proposed adoption. See s. 138 of the *CFSA*. However, note s. 151(4).

In some provinces the courts have ruled that the absence of a specific statutory provision similar to s. 151(4) of the *CFSA*, directing that notice need not be given, means that it must be given to parents who previously consented to the adoption or whose consent is not required because the child is a permanent ward of a child protection agency. The cases are reviewed in *Re H.* (1992), 40 R.F.L. (3d) 13 (Alta. C.A.) where the court concluded that such "common law" notice should be provided only where a natural parent maintains a relationship or contact with the child after the wardship order. See also *B. (B.)* v. *New Brunswick (Minister of Health and Community Services)* (1995), 13 R.F.L. (4th) 350 (N.B. C.A.).

11. In *M. (R.)* v. *M. (S.)* (1994), 20 O.R. (3d) 621 (C.A.), the grandparents of a child who had been placed for adoption by a licensed agency with the consent of his mother and father applied for custody under s. 21 of the *Children's Law Reform Act*. The court held that Part VII of the *CFSA* provides a comprehensive code for adoptions and that the adoption process must be allowed to proceed to its conclusion without interference in accordance with s. 143(2) of the *CFSA*. Accordingly, the grandparents could not apply for custody. This case was applied in *Family, Youth & Child Services of Muskoka* v. *R. (L.)* (1998), 37 R.F.L. (4th) 166 (Ont. Gen. Div.), where the parents of the child initially consented to the adoption, but the mother later supported her parents' attempt to derail the process after the society placed the child for adoption. They brought an action to set aside the consents and for custody of the child. The court concluded that it could not grant interim access to either the mother or the grandparents. Only if the placement was invalid because of a defect in the consents could the court deal with a custody or access claim.

M. (R.) v. *M. (S.)* was distinguished in *L. (C.)* v. *F. (A.)* (1998), 43 R.F.L. (4th) 332 (Ont. Gen. Div.), where a mother and father, without the assistance of a society or a licensee, placed their child in the home of close friends one day after its birth. Within days, they met with a lawyer and signed consents to the adoption by the couple. The child's maternal grandmother commenced an application for custody. The parents responded by asking the court to dismiss her application on the basis that the child had been placed for adoption. The court held that the grandmother's application should go forward as, in contrast to the situation in *M. (R.)* v. *M. (S.)*, there had been no placement in accordance with the provisions of the *CFSA*.

12. Does the biological parent have any remedy if he or she discovers, after the child has been adopted, that the consent to the adoption was not valid? Does a biological parent have any remedy if he or she was unaware of the adoption proceeding because the required notice was not given? Examine ss. 156 and 157 of the *CFSA*. See also *Children's Aid Society of Metropolitan Toronto (Municipality)* v. *Lyttle* (1973), 10 R.F.L. 131 (S.C.C.); *C. (F.E.)* v. *T. (D.)* (1984), 38 R.F.L. (2d) 304 (Man. Co. Ct.); *S.* v. *Saskatchewan (Minister of Social Services)*, [1983] 3 W.W.R. 373 (Sask. C.A.); *R. (J.)* v. *New Brunswick (Minister of Health & Community Services)* (1990), 26 R.F.L. (3d) 62 (N.B. C.A.); *K. (L.)* v. *Saskatchewan (Minister of Social Services)* (1996), 23 R.F.L. (4th) 423 (Sask. C.A,); and *M. (R.K.)* v. *K. (L.D.)* (1996), 25 R.F.L. (4th) 285 (Alta. C.A.). In the last case, the mother retained custody of the child after separation. The father paid support and exercised regular access. The mother eventually remarried and her new husband adopted the child. However, notice had not been given to the biological father. The appellate court upheld a lower court decision that set aside the adoption order.

(b) Dispensing with the requirement of parental consent

Some of the cases discussed in the previous section including *R. (A.N.)* v. *W. (L.J.)* (1985), 36 R.F.L. (2d) 1 (S.C.C.); *L. (W.R.)* v. *G. (C.D.)* (1994), 3 R.F.L. (4th) 43 (Man. Q.B.); and *British Columbia Birth Registration No. 99-00733, Re* (2000), 182 D.L.R. (4th) 280 (B.C. C.A.) involved orders dispensing with parental consent in situations other than a natural parent/step-parent adoption. The cases that follow deal with the dispensation of parental consent in step-parent adoptions.

STOODLEY v. BLUNDEN

(1980), 17 R.F.L. (2d) 280 (N.S. C.A.)

PACE J.A.: — ... This is an appeal from the decision of O'Hearn Co. Ct. J. wherein he dispensed with the consent of the divorced natural father of a nine-year-old boy and permitted the child's adoption by the natural mother and her present husband. The application for adoption was made pursuant to the Children's Services Act, 1976 (N.S.), c. 8. The relevant sections of the statute read as follows:

> 16(3) Where the person proposed to be adopted is under the age of majority and is not a child in care, no order for the child's adoption shall be made, except as herein provided, without the written consent to adoption of the child's parents.

And:

> 17 Where the county court is satisfied that a person whose consent is required under subsection (2) or subsection (3) of section 16 . . .
>
> (g) is a person whose consent in all circumstances of the case ought to be dispensed with the county court may order that his consent be dispensed with, if it is in the interest of the person to be adopted to do so.

The female respondent married the appellant in March 1971 and the child whom the respondents seek to adopt was born on 3rd December 1971. This was the only child of the marriage. The natural parents separated in 1974 and subsequently divorced on 21st January 1976.

At the time of this application, the natural father was 29 years old and the natural mother was 27. Both parents have now remarried and the child is presently in the custody of his natural mother.

The child knows his father and enjoys his contact with him. As well, the child has a good relationship with his paternal grandmother and cousins. It would appear that the contact between the natural father and the child is not frequent, however, and this is somewhat understandable as the father is a fisherman and spends lengthy periods at sea.

The male respondent is 25 years old and has known the child since the child was three years of age. He is very fond of the child and appears to have supplanted the natural father with no ill effects upon the child. . . .

In my opinion, the test and the only test to be applied in determining the issue before us is whether there would be a positive contribution to the welfare of the child by dispensing with the consent of the natural father to the adoption. Application of this test requires a review of the past, present, and future circumstances which have or may affect the welfare of the child and to then determine whether the child will benefit by permanently cutting the parental tie.

In rendering his decision, O'Hearn Co. Ct. J. stated:

> In the instant case, I am strongly of the opinion that the child will on balance gain a great deal by granting the dispensation and allowing the adoption to take place. His rights on intestacy, of course, as well as under the Testators' Family Maintenance Act, R.S.N.S. 1967, c. 303, will, as far as we can now tell, be in all likelihood much more substantial where Mr. Blunden is the parent rather than Mr. Stoodley. More important, he will become a lawful member of the family, which is, in fact, his family, and be entitled to a fully recognized legal and social status as such with respect to other children in the family and his peers in general. He will not lose the association with his grandmother and cousins, nor need he necessarily lose the existing association with his natural father. The court cannot, of course, command that access be given to the natural father and it would be perhaps unwise to order if the court could do so in this particular case, but he will certainly retain most of the benefits mentioned by Zalev Co. Ct. J. in *Re Kennette and Munro*, [1973] 3 O.R. 156, 11 R.F.L. 21 (sub nom. *Re Munro*) 36 D.L.R. (3d) 180, i.e., whatever love, understanding and guidance the natural father can provide in the relationship, the intimacy of the relationship will depend upon the friendship between natural father and child to a large extent. If the association is not a normal one, that is the unfortunate outcome of the divorce rather than of the adoption.
>
> This case is factually quite distinguishable from those cases in Nova Scotia and Ontario where dispensation has not been allowed.
>
> The male applicant, it should be noted, while quite a young man, is the manager of a local building firm. His own family has a similar business and he expects to become part of that in due course. He and his wife belong to the same religious denomination and this family attends church together. He testified that the child has benefited from the marriage and from the new relationship with him, and I accept this testimony. While Mr. Blunden stressed the material advantages that adoption would provide for the child, he felt that even more important would be the child's own feeling that this step would bring him closer to his mother and stepfather. The child, while very young, is of an age to appreciate the symbolic effect of this and some of its social effect.

It appears that the child is and has been a normal, healthy child who enjoys the contact with his natural father and his paternal relatives. He has adapted well to his present home with the respondents and I think that there can be no doubt that mutual love and affection flows from this relationship. The mother has legal custody of the child and thus a secure home environment prevails under the present circumstances. In weighing all the factors which must be taken into account is the very difficult duty of looking to the future which cannot, by its very nature, be foreseen with certainty. The question immediately arises in making this determination: what positive advantage will the child receive in future which could not be obtained by preserving the non-consenting natural parent status? I cannot see with any degree of certainty that any advantages could be obtained by the child which could not be obtained by alternative legal means.

The male respondent can provide for the economic security of the child, either by will or other means, without the necessity of depriving the child of his inheritance from his natural father. The love and affection between the respondents and the child should not in any way be affected and, in fact, if the present relationship continues, the bonds should become more enduring as time progresses.

In my opinion, and after weighing all the factors, I am not satisfied that this is a case where the consent of the parent to the adoption should be dispensed with under s. 17 of the Children's Services Act.

I am not unmindful of the fact that in a case such as this we should not disturb the decision of the County Court Judge unless he erred by applying wrong principles of law or by ignoring or misinterpreting or misconstruing material evidence of fact. With deference to the judge, it is my opinion that he applied the evidence to matters chiefly concerned with custody and not to that of whether the consent of the appellant to the adoption should be dispensed with and thus he fell into reversible error.

In the result, the appeal should be allowed with costs, the dispensation of consent refused and the application for adoption dismissed.

R. (N.J.) v. M. (R.J.)

(1994), 5 R.F.L. (4th) 375 (Ont. Prov. Div.)

[The mother and father were divorced in the United States in 1986 and the mother and three children moved to Canada. The mother remarried in 1989. In 1990, the parents agreed to share custody of their oldest son and he began to reside with his father. At the same time the father consented to the adoption of the youngest child, a son, by the mother and her new husband. The husband also wished to adopt the daughter, aged 10. She executed a consent to the adoption, but the father opposed the adoption. The father had little contact with the daughter, although he paid support.The mother and husband applied for an order to dispense with the consent of the father.]

Hardman Prov. J.: . . . In considering an application under section 138, it is clear that the statutory test is one of best interests: . . .

Application of the Law

While it is clear the test is a strict one, with the onus squarely on the applicant, it is the application of this test to the facts that often leads to different outcomes. The benefits to the child in this application from the adoption are those commonly raised:

1. similar family name,
2. security at home in family unit,
3. benefit of stability in inheritance situation or upon the death of a biological parent,
4. confirmation of the reality of who is doing the parenting.
5. reaffirmation of sibling relationships.

Many cases . . . make it clear that the advantages must be weighed against the disadvantages. In this case, the father has had little contact with the child as the result of perhaps some resistance by the mother but more so as the direct result of the distance between the parties.

It is clear from the original "stipulation and agreement" that both parents had anticipated being very involved in the decisions affecting the lives of the children. Although there has been no abandonment or misbehaviour to disentitle the father, it is the reality that little, if any, bond exists between the child and the father, although clearly the father wishes to strengthen any existing bond and be a part of the child's life in the future. . . . [T]his court sees little loss to the child by a permanent separation given the lack of contact in the past few years.

However, it is this court's opinion that the emphasis should be on what is to be gained. . . .

There are circumstances before the court that are relevant:

1.   The child has lived most of her life in Canada with her mother.
2.   Since 1987, she has known the co-applicant as a fully involved parent.
3.   One of her brothers, only 21 months younger, has been adopted by the co-applicant.
4.   The child has executed a consent, being almost ten years of age at the time, and there has been no indication of any change in that position despite the child now being eleven years of age.
5.   It is the wish of the child, expressed through the mother as well, that she be adopted by the co-applicant.
6.   The mother has indicated that the child may continue to visit the biological father if she so desires.

Many cases state that matters such as name change, inheritance, and so on can and should be dealt with through less intrusive types of orders. Also, there is academic opinion . . . that suggest caution in using the vehicle of adoption, originally designed to place unwanted children, to "shore-up" step relationship families. Given the fluidity of family relationships, a cautious approach is an appropriate one. The matter before the court must therefore be approached cautiously but determined on the particular situation before the court. And the issues "must be perceived through the eyes of the child" . . . . In the article "Hearing the Voice of Children" (1992) 8 C.F.L.Q. 95, the authors reviewed issues dealing with what they call the "amorphous" best interests test (at page 95) and how to hear the voice of children on the matter. In this case, the court did not hear from the child viva voce but only has indirect information and an executed consent concerning that issue. Nevertheless, the child's opinion is properly before the court. It is one which is required by law and cannot be dispensed with by a court even on a best interests basis. It is clear the Act recognizes that it is a permanent right being affected and therefore provides for an effective veto by any child over seven (except in the limited circumstances of section 137(9)). . . .

There is ample reason before the court for the child to choose adoption: the co-applicant is her parent in her experience and her brother has affirmed his status already with that co-applicant. . . . The gain from her perspective no doubt is the solidifying of that family unit and also from her perspective she has nothing to lose in terms of her very slight relationship with her biological father. While it is this court's hope that she may decide to maintain a relationship with her biological father, and hence enhance her relationship with her older brother, nevertheless this application should be allowed. Based on the factors before this court and the application of the law to the facts, this court is prepared to find on a best interests basis that the consent of the respondent father should be dispensed with in the adoption of the child C.M.M.

WEISS, "THE MISUSE OF ADOPTION BY THE CUSTODIAL PARENT"

(1979), 2 Can. J. Fam. L. 141 (Footnotes Omitted)

... Since, as a general rule, the adoption terminates the access rights of the non-custodial parent, one may well suspect that the adoption procedure is not infrequently being used for a purpose other than that for which adoption was originally intended. Family adoptions become a way of restructuring relationships instead of a method of placing homeless children into family units. If this is the case, then family adoptions do not serve any legitimate purpose which would provide a valid reason for permitting a custodial parent to adopt a child over the objections of the non-custodial natural parent. Case law, however, gives examples of several arguments advanced for permitting family adoptions. Yet one must surely question whether or not these arguments are valid reasons to permit such adoptions.

7: FAMILY ADOPTIONS — AN UNNECESSARY ACTION

In arguing that the court should permit a family adoption over the objections of the non-custodial spouse, the custodial parent and spouse present the court with various difficulties which the child and the new family must face. The most common of these are: the child's surname is different from the rest of the family (if the custodial parent is the mother); the child needs some sort of symbolic process to prove to him that he really belongs to the new family; because the child is not really the child of the new spouse, there may be difficulties with succession should the new spouse die intestate or leave a poorly drafted will; and the presence of the non-custodial parent causes difficulties for the child or the new family unit. It is suggested, however, that there exist other solutions to these problems, solutions which do not involve tampering with legal status. The practitioner involved in situations where a family adoption is desired or the court being requested to waive the consent of the non-custodial parent should certainly consider these other options before considering the extreme remedy of adoption.

When the custodial parent is the mother, and she remarries and takes the name of the new spouse, the child of the first marriage will bear a different surname from that shared by his mother, step-father, and any other children, either of the new union or of the step-father. This may not be desirable because it can brand the child as being different, as not belonging to the new family unit. The child may thereby feel very much an outsider. Adoption, of course, can change this situation because adoption statutes include provisions for giving the adopted child a new name. Provincial statutes vary on whether or not the child can be given a new first name, but all agree he can be given a new surname. However, if the change of name is all that is needed to make the child feel a part of the new unit, the parent and step-parent can apply to change the child's name under the various provincial statutes dealing with name changes. Even where name change statutes require the consent of the non-custodial parent, such consent can be waived by the court. This change of name will remove any stigma the child sees in having a different surname, and will telegraph to the child that he is now very much the child of the step-parent. For most children, this step would probably have the same emotional connotations that adoption would. Like adoption, in many cases, the chief value of the name change is symbolic. The process could be treated as a very formal one which would give the child some sense of solemnity such as would surround a change in his status. A simple name change, however, would not entail all the legal ramifications of adoption, and it would not interfere with the child's relationship with the non-custodial parent.

Where the problem is that the child does not participate in the process that creates a bond between the parent and step-parent, adoption may be sought as a means of forging new family bonds. Such a step may even be desired by the step-parent who is unsure of his or her own position and tends to feel more like a custodian of the child than like a parent. It is questionable, however, whether or not adoption is a valid solution to these types of psychological difficulties. Family bonds are not created by legal processes. They develop over time as a result of interaction as a family. If the child is experiencing the need to feel a part of the new family unit, it is possible that other acts can alleviate the problem. For example, the child could be given a large part to play in the wedding of the parent and step-parent, and both parent and step-parent should be careful to speak of the child as if he were their own. If the need to feel a part of the new family is one experienced by the step-parent, however, the use of adoption should be viewed with even greater suspicion. The use of a legal process to overcome feelings of mere custodianship stresses the concept of ''rights'' as means by which adults control and possess children. The step-parent may well be guilty of using the child as an instrument to alleviate his own fears.

The question of succession should not be solved by adoption. No parent should remain without a will, and a well-drafted will can make provision for a step-child. . . .

The problems caused by the child's name, the need to feel part of the new family, and succession do not seem serious enough to warrant the legal changes involved in an adoption. Indeed, they may be mere rationalisations on the part of the custodial parent and step-parent whose real motivation is a wish to do away with the presence of the non-custodial parent on the fringes of the new family unit. There may be cases where the access rights of the non-custodial parent do create difficulties for the child, either by upsetting him or by interfering substantially with the upbringing of the child. In such instances, if the access of the non-custodial parent is really detrimental to the welfare of the child, the custodial parent can apply to the same court that determined the custody and access matters on divorce, and the access order can be reviewed. A parent and step-parent should not be permitted to use the adoption provisions to deprive the non-custodial parent of the right to access in situations where the court has previously preserved these rights. If the custodial parent cannot show that there is a good reason to deny access, he or she should not be permitted to use adoption to achieve the same result.

Whereas a family adoption may seem desirable as a way of fostering stability for a child who has undergone the upheaval of divorce, this may not always be the best solution. For example, in his decision in *Re Adoption No. 64-09-925411*, Berger J., saw as a benefit of adoption the fact that the mother could never again obtain custody of the child, even if the natural father should die. This, plus the change in legal status, he felt, should lead to the stability that was lacking in the child's life. While in light of the facts of this particular case the decision might be supportable, it is questionable in principle. Although custody is technically an impermanent situation in the sense that it is always open to judicial scrutiny, there is little chance that it will be changed without good cause. In this particular case, the natural mother would have had to show that the child was not being correctly cared for and that it would be best for the child to be returned to his natural parent. The mere fact that custody can be changed, however, should not foster instability any more than the fact that a child can be removed from his natural parents if found to be in need of protection. In addition, the longer the child remains with the custodial parent, the less likely it becomes that a court will wish to change the child's status. One might also question the satisfaction of Berger J., with the result that the non-custodial mother could never regain custody even if the father died. If the custodial parent were to die, a child might really be better off with the other parent, particularly if the death came soon after the divorce and remarriage, before the child had a chance to feel comfortable with the step-parent. Permitting a family adoption to intervene would mean the court would not be able to consider all the options upon the death of the custodial parent. The adopting step-parent, as the legal parent, would naturally assume custody of the child. . . .

NOTES AND QUESTIONS

1. List reasons that may motivate a parent and step-parent to adopt the parent's child from a previous marriage. Which of these can be achieved within the existing legal framework without adoption?

2. Should there be an alternative means of formalizing step-parent and child relationships, giving the relationship a clear legal identity and psychological stability? See Bodenheimer, "New Trends and Requirements in Adoption Law and Proposals for Legislative Change" (1975), 49 S. Cal. L. Rev. 10 where the author suggests that courts should be willing to grant joint custody orders to the parent and step-parent, thereby giving legal recognition to the relationship without cutting off all ties between the child and his or her other natural parent.

3. Under the *Change of Name Act*, R.S.O. 1990, c. C.7, which originally came into effect on April 1, 1987, a person with lawful custody of a child can apply to the Registrar General of Vital Statistics to change the child's surname. Although a parent with access must be notified of the application (s. 5(6)), his or her consent is not required unless a separation agreement or court order so specifies. In *Vanbuskirk* v. *Osborne* (1989), 19 R.F.L. (3d) 214 (Ont. Fam. Ct.), it was noted (at 215) "that the registrar's office, obviously in an attempt to provide some fairness, has developed a policy whereby if a letter of objection is received, it will 'red flag' a file giving the parent an opportunity to bring an application to the appropriate court to prevent the change of name". In *Harris* v. *O'Grady* (1989), 23 R.F.L. (3d) 185 (Ont. Dist. Ct.), the father of a five-year-old child responded to the mother's application to the Registrar General of Vital Statistics for a change in the child's surname by applying to the court for a variation in the custody order to preclude a change without his consent. The father's application was denied on the basis that he had not established that the name change was not in the child's best interests. See also *Mitchell* v. *Huitema* (1993), 44 R.F.L. (3d) 218 (Ont. U.F.C.), where Steinberg J. dismissed a similar application and suggested (at 223) that the Registrar General's practice of delay was inappropriate. However, Zelinski J. granted a variation of a custody order under the *Divorce Act* to preclude the custodial mother from formally changing a child's name in *Belisle* v. *Poole* (1994), 2 R.F.L. (4th) 165 (Ont. Gen. Div.). The judge reviewed the case law and concluded that a court had jurisdiction to preclude a name change if this was in the child's best interest. For a similar result, see *Nykilchyk* v. *Nykilchyk* (1994), 5 R.F.L. (4th) 253 (Ont. Gen. Div.).

Granger J. in *Silverberg* v. *Silverberg* (1990), 25 R.F.L. (3d) 141 at 148 (Ont. H.C.), added a provision to the custody order prohibiting the mother from changing the child's surname until "a court of competent jurisdiction has reviewed the evidence and determined the best interests of the child". Although the mother had not yet applied for a name change, Granger J. suspected that she would in the near future. See also *Herniman* v. *Woltz* (1996), 22 R.F.L. (4th) 232 (Ont. Gen. Div.); *Giggie* v. *Guidry* (1997), 29 R.F.L. (4th) 31 (N.B. Q.B.); and *Pappel* v. *Bergen* (1998), 37 R.F.L. (4th) 88 (Man. Q.B.).

The *Change of Name Act* does not preclude a custodial parent from informally changing a child's surname without applying for a legal name change: *Longlade* v. *Moxam* (1989), 20 R.F.L. (3d) 32 (Ont. Fam. Ct.). However, the court suggested that it had the authority to prohibit even an informal change if necessary to protect the child's best interests. In the circumstances of the case, the court dismissed the father's application to vary a custody order to restrain the mother and step-father from informally altering the child's surname for purposes such as registration at school. In *Belisle* v. *Poole*, Zelinski J., although granting an order precluding a formal name change, stated (at 177) that "there does not appear to be any reason why [the child] cannot continue to be enrolled in school by his 'informal' name of Poole, thereby preserving a name at school which is consistent with that of his mother and siblings".

4. Weiss notes, in the article reproduced above, that adoption of a child by one birth parent and a step-parent generally terminates the access rights of the other parent. However, legislation in some provinces specifically provides for the possibility of access by a biological parent in a step-parent adoption. It also now appears that courts in other jurisdictions including Ontario can order post-adoption access, either under the general legislation dealing with custody or access or the courts' inherent *parens patriae* jurisdiction. See the next section of this chapter. How might the possibility of access for the biological parent affect applications to dispense with a parent's consent to a step-parent adoption?

5. For other cases dealing with applications to dispense with parental consent to a natural parent/ step-parent adoption, see *Goldstein* v. *Brownstone* (1970), 3 R.F.L. 4 (Man. C.A.); *Smith* v. *Harvey* (1974), 19 R.F.L. 367 (Ont. C.A.); *Gardiner, Re* (1977), 4 R.F.L. (2d) 394 (Ont. C.A.); *Anderson, Re* (1978), 6 R.F.L. (2d) 169 (Sask. Dist. Ct.); *Anderson* v. *Ross* (1979), 10 R.F.L. (2d) 286 (Sask. C.A.); *H.* v. *M.* (1980), 18 R.F.L. (2d) 138 (Ont. Fam. Ct.); *Vincent* v. *Wall* (1980), 19 R.F.L. (2d) 342 (Ont. Prov. Ct.); *K. (S.)* v. *D. (M.S.)* (1980), 21 R.F.L. (2d) 271 (Ont. U.F.C.); *M.* v. *B.* (1984), 41 R.F.L. (2d) 187 (Ont. Co. Ct.); *Queensland Birth Registration 81/05916-17, Re* (1987), 8 R.F.L. (3d) 28 (B.C. S.C.); *M. (B.A.)* v. *B. (C.G.)* (1987), 10 R.F.L. (3d) 85 (Nfld. U.F.C.); *British Columbia Birth Registration No. 82-09-032673, Re* (1988), 12 R.F.L. (3d) 167 (B.C. S.C.); *K. (J.R.G.), Re* (1989), 22 R.F.L. (3d) 450 (Alta. Q.B.); *C. (P.E.)* v. *A. (R.)* (1989), 23 R.F.L. (3d) 414 (Nfld. S.C.); *T. (K.)* v. *C. (R.W.B.)* (1990), 25 R.F.L. (3d) 433 (Ont. Prov. Ct.); *D. (R.)* v. *S. (W.B.)* (1991), 33 R.F.L. (3d) 1 (B.C. C.A.); *M. (J.L.)* v. *L. (S.D.)* (1992), 42 R.F.L. (3d) 400 (N.S. C.A.); *Birth Registration No. 1480, Re* (1994), 112 D.L.R. (4th) 53 (B.C. S.C.); *J. (S.E.)* v. *G. (M.)* (1994), 6 R.F.L. (4th) 41 (Ont. Prov. Div.); *D. (R.P.)* v. *A. (K.W.)* (1995), 14 R.F.L. (4th) 249 (Sask. C.A.); and *Proposed Adoption of the Child with Birth Registration Number 88-02-005712, Re* (1996), 21 R.F.L. (4th) 121 (N.S. S.C.).

6. For further reading see Bissett-Johnson, "Step-Parent Adoptions in English and Canadian Law", Baxter and Eberts, eds., *The Child and the Courts* (Toronto: Carswell, 1978) 335; Khan, "Adoption by Parent and Non-Parent" (1978), 8 Fam.L. 146; Oppell, "Step-Parent Adoptions in Nova Scotia and British Columbia" (1981), 6 Dal. L.J. 631; Williams, "Step-Parent Adoptions and the Best Interests of the Child in Ontario" (1982), 32 U.T.L.J. 214; and Katarynych, "Adoption" in Bala, Hornick and Vogl, eds., *Canadian Child Welfare Law: Children, Families and the State* (Toronto: Thompson Educational Publishing Inc., 1991).

5.   Effect of Adoption

(1) INTRODUCTION

As a general rule, adoption places an adopted child in the same position as he or she would have been if born to the adopted parents and terminates all of the legal ties between the child and the biological parents (see s. 158 of the *CFSA*). The historical origins of this provision and its impact were described as follows by McRuer C.J.H.C. in *Re Blackwell*, [1959] O.R. 377, at 401-402 (H.C.):

All legislation in Ontario prior to 1958 had dealt with rights or interests of adopted children. There was a progressive legislative development toward putting the adopted child in substantially the same legal position as a child born in lawful wedlock. There were, however, legislative limitations both with respect to the extinguishment of rights acquired by birth and the creation of rights by adoption . . . In the light of all this the legislative approach to the problem was changed in the 1958 Act. This Act did not purport to declare rights but created a legal relationship from which legal rights and legal responsibilities flowed and likewise it destroyed the legal relationship arising out of the natural birth of the child . . . The only exception that is made is for the purpose of laws relating to incest and consanguinity of marriage.

Adoption under the *CFSA* generally exhibits the characteristics of the traditional or closed model of adoption. Under this model, adoption is perceived as a total transfer of parenthood. The birth parents' relationship with the child ends. Indeed, the adoptive parents are substituted for the birth parents on the child's birth certificate and the adoption records are sealed, to be opened in limited circumstances only. Strict confidentiality is guaranteed to the birth mother (who can carry on life "as if she never had a child"), the adoptive parents (whose life will not be disturbed by the biological parents), and the child (whose personal history starts with a new birth certificate). To complete the break, placement for adoption terminates outstanding access orders and a court cannot grant access to a biological parent at the time of the adoption or after.

Increasingly, there has been pressure to move to a more open adoption process. Although the term "open adoption" is difficult to define, it may encompass any arrangement whereby there is some form of communication between the birth parents and adoptive parents. In "The Changing Face of Adoption: The Challenge of Open and Custom Adoption" (1996), 13 C.F.L.Q. 333, Jeannie House states (at 342): "The main features of an open adoption include access by the natural/birth family, information about the child's history (medical and social), involvement of the child's birthparent/s in the adoption process (particularly in the choice of adoptive home), involvement of the older child in his or her own adoption." In various degrees, the legislatures, the courts and the adoption agencies have moved towards a more open process. Ms House reports (at 349) that the following "openness procedures" have been used in Canada, particularly by private adoption agencies: "birth mothers choosing from pre-selected, non-identifying family profiles (54 per cent); regular exchange of letters and information through adoption agency (34 per cent); pre-placement meeting of birth and adoptive parents without identifying information (18 per cent); and exchange of names (13 per cent)". For further reading, see Demick and Wapner, "Open and Closed Adoption: A Developmental Conceptualization" (1988), 27 Family Process 229; Phillips, "Open Adoption: A New Look at Adoption Practice and Policy in Texas" (1991), 43 Baylor L. Rev. 407; L.R. Melina and S.K. Roszia, *The Open Adoption Experience* (New York: Harper Collins Pub., 1993); Bernstein, "Using Mediation as an Effective Technique to Achieve Success in Open Adoptions" (1998-1999), 16 C.F.L.Q. 1; and Senoff, "Open Adoptions in Ontario and the Need for Legislative Reform" (1998), 15 Can. J. Fam. L. 183.

The remainder of this chapter focuses on the possibility of the maintenance or re-establishment of links between the adopted child and the biological parents by examining the law relating to access by biological parents to the adopted child and the confidentiality of adoption records. The issue of access arises most often in the case of adoption by a step-parent or relative. Disclosure of information is generally sought by adults who have been adopted and wish to discover their biological parentage although biological parents also may have considerable curiosity about their children who have been adopted.

NOTES AND QUESTIONS

1. In *Re Podolsky* (1980), 3 Man. R. (2d) 251, 7 E.T.R. 62 (C.A.) it was held that an adopted child in Manitoba was still a "lawful lineal descendant" of his/her natural parents for the purposes of intestate succession. The relevant legislation specified that on adoption "all prior parental ties of the child cease to exist in law". For a comment on the case, see Harvey, "Intestate Succession Rights of Adopted

Children in Manitoba: The *Podolsky* Case" (1981), 11 Man. L.J. 201, and Bolton, "*Podolsky* v. *Podolsky* — A Further Comment" (1981), 11 Man. L.J. 207. The Manitoba legislature responded by enacting legislation that explicitly stated that "all rights of the adopted child to inherit as a lawful descendant of the deceased natural parent . . . cease to exist." See *Re Purpur* (1984), 43 R.F.L. (2d) 225, 17 E.T.R. 253 (Man. C.A.).

In *Mernickle* v. *Westaway*, 1 B.C.L.R. (2d) 267, [1986] 3 W.W.R. 665 (C.A.) the court held that an adopted child could not take on the intestacy of a natural parent. The British Columbia legislative provisions were similar to s. 158 of the *Child and Family Services Act*. A similar result was reached in *Co-operative Trust Co. of Canada* v. *Saskatchewan (Administrator of Estates)* (1984), 36 R.F.L. (2d) 391, (*sub nom. Re Kowbel*) 27 Sask. R. 65 (Q.B.).

(2) ACCESS

A number of complex issues arise when considering whether a biological parent should have access after an adoption order has been made. A preliminary issue is whether existing orders granting access are terminated by the adoption. One view is that any right of access, including one under an access order, is terminated by an adoption order that is silent regarding access. See *Alberta Birth Registration 78-08-022716, Re* (1986), 1 R.F.L. (3d) 1 (B.C. C.A.). However, the court also concluded that a judge granting an adoption order had the power to order that an outstanding access order continue in force or to make an access order. See also *H.* v. *Y.* (1989), 19 R.F.L. (3d) 216 (B.C. S.C.); *R. (J.)* v. *New Brunswick (Minister of Health & Community Services)* (1990), 26 R.F.L. (3d) 62 (N.B. C.A.); *C. (D.H.)* v. *S. (R.)* (1990), 26 R.F.L. (3d) 301 (Alta. Q.B.); *D. (R.)* v. *S. (W.B.)* (1991), 33 R.F.L. (3d) 1 (B.C. C.A.); *Birth Registration No. 1480, Re* (1994), 112 D.L.R. (4th) 53 (B.C. S.C.); and *C. (E.S.)* v. *P. (D.A.)* (1997), 32 R.F.L. (4th) 97 (Alta. C.A.). The position set out in *Re Alberta Birth Registration 78-08-022716* is given specific statutory recognition in s. 85(2)(a) of the *Family Services Act*, S.N.B. 1980, c. F-2.2 and s. 38(1) of the *Adoption Act*, S.B.C 1995, c. 48. Both provisions stipulate that adoption ends any order for access unless the court specifies otherwise.

In Ontario, s. 143(1) of the *CSFA* provides that any outstanding order of access with respect to a child, other than an order made under Part III (Child Protection) of the Act, is terminated as soon as the child is placed for adoption by a children's aid society or licensee. Similarly, s. 140(2) specifies that an access order made under Part III itself must be terminated before a Crown ward can be placed for adoption. Finally, s. 160 stipulates that no court shall make an order under Part VII for access to the adopted child by a birth parent or a member of the birth parent's family. These provisions would suggest that the Ontario Legislature did not anticipate continued access by a birth parent following the child's adoption, at least where the adoption involves a Crown ward or a child placed by a licensee.

The situation may be different where the adoption involves relatives or a step-parent. Cases such as *Z. (G.M.)* v. *B. (T.F.S.)*, 18 R.F.L. (2d) 47, [1981] 1 W.W.R. 152 (Man. C.A.); *W.* v. *H.*, 25 R.F.L. (2d) 337, [1982] 1 W.W.R. 397 (Alta. C.A.); and *Kunkel* v. *Kunkel*(1994), 2 R.F.L. (4th) 1 (Alta. C.A.) suggest that adoption ends a right of access or a duty of support, even if set out in an order under the federal *Divorce Act*. However, Walsmley A.C. Prov. J. stated in *R. (S.)* v. *R. (M.)* (1995), 14 R.F.L. (4th) 180, at 194 (Ont. Prov. Div.) that "access orders made before a *relative* adoption survive the adoption order" [emphasis added]. This statement received apparent approval from the Ontario Court of Appeal in later proceedings involving the same child: *R. (S.)* v. *R. (M.)* (1998), 43 R.F.L. (4th) 116 (Ont. C.A.)

(reproduced below). See also *K. (S.)* v. *D. (M.S.)* (1980), 21 R.F.L. (2d) 271 (Ont. U.F.C.).

Another issue is whether a court has jurisdiction to grant an access order to the biological parent, either at the time of the adoption or subsequently. In the following cases, the Ontario Court of Appeal dealt with this question.

W. (C.G.) v. J. (M.)

(1981), 24 R.F.L. (2d) 342, 34 O.R. (2d) 44 (C.A.)

[The issue on appeal was whether a court could make an order for access in favour of a birth parent under s. 35(1) of the *Family Law Reform Act* shortly after the child had been adopted as a Crown ward under the *Child Welfare Act*. Section 35(1) stated that "the court may order that either parent or any person have . . . access to a child". The *Child Welfare Act* did not contain any provision comparable to s. 160 of the *Child and Family Services Act*. The Provincial Court judge declined to hear the application on its merits. A County Court judge allowed the appeal so as to permit a hearing on the merits on the basis that s. 35(1) permitted a court to order access to *any* person. The adoptive parents, supported by the Children's Aid Society, successfully appealed to a High Court judge. The Ontario Court of Appeal dismissed the birth mother's appeal.]

MACKINNON A.C.J.O. (ZUBER J.A. concurring): . . .

It is clear from a reading of the legislation that the Legislature wished to ensure that serving and protecting the best interests of the child be the paramount concern of public and private agencies and the Courts and that those interests would have to be seen to be served in the steps taken towards the making of a final adoption order. Once the final order of adoption has been made, with the natural parents having every opportunity to oppose the making of such order if they so desire, s. 80 makes it equally clear that there shall be no disclosure of information about the child or the natural parents except in certain particular and limited circumstances listed in s. 81(6) which are not present here. . . .

The Ontario *Child Welfare Act, 1978* deals specifically by way of special provisions with the care and protection of neglected, abused and abandoned children. It establishes a comprehensive and exhaustive code for the supervision, custody, access, wardship and adoption of such children to ensure that their best interests and welfare are protected and forwarded. The very title of the Act defines its purpose. Such children are not to be "dealt with" by the general provisions of another statute which are not directly concerned with them, unless, of course, the provisions of that statute say so in specific terms . . . .

From a reading of the . . . *Child Welfare Act, 1978*, the purpose of the adoption provisions is, in my view, clear. Keeping always in mind the best interests of the Crown wards, the Society endeavours to secure their adoption. It is hoped that adoption will ensure a safe and secure environment for the child, the stability and continuation of which should not be immediately threatened by access granted to the natural parents. The new adoptive parents on their part are given security from such upset and interference by the secrecy provisions of the Act. Such application for access, if permitted, would set the secrecy provisions of adoption orders at naught and render them meaningless. The adoption order creates a new family; the natural parents cease to be parents of the child and the past history of that relationship is expunged. The adopted child becomes, in the opening words of s. 86(1) *"for all purposes"* (emphasis added) the child of the adopting parent "as if [the adopted child] had been born to the adopting parent". The exclusion of the history of the blood and physical relationship between the natural parents and the child from further consideration could not have been expressed in clearer legislative terms.

The *Child Welfare Act, 1978* deals with the question of access to a child falling within the provisions of that Act in specific terms. Sections 35, 36 and 38 provide for the granting and terminating of access to Crown wards in extensive detail. Section 69(14) prohibits any interference with a child placed for adoption by visit, letter or telephone. Section 69(1), already quoted, makes it clear that any order with respect to access to the child, other than an order for access made under the *Child Welfare Act, 1978* terminates on the placement of a child for adoption.

Presumably and in theory a complete stranger to a child and its parents could make an application for access under s. 35 of the *Family Law Reform Act, 1978* and set the whole Court procedures in motion. Under such circumstances it seems to me a strange concept of having "your day in court" to proceed to a hearing when the facts are acknowledged. I would think that a preliminary application would dispose of such a matter.

It is *a fortiori* when an adoption order has just been made. Such an approach does not render the applicant any less a "person" but rather gives effect to s. 86(1) and (2) of the *Child Welfare Act, 1978*. This is particularly so when one considers the detailed sections which provide for the procedures and protections to all parties concerned leading up to the making of the adoptive order. In addition, of course, to give such an applicant "her day in court", as I have already noted, destroys the secrecy provisions of the *Child Welfare Act, 1978* because if there is to be a "day in court", elementary justice requires notice to be given to the adopting parents and their presence at the Court. To give such an applicant "her day in court" ignores the rights and protections given to the child and the adoptive parents by the legislation creating the new family unit and, equally important, ignores the right of hearing that could have and may have been exercised by such applicant prior to the granting of an adoption order.

Although I do not feel that there is any substantial conflict between s. 35(1) of the *Family Law Reform Act, 1978* and the provisions of the *Child Welfare Act, 1978*, what conflict or apparent inconsistency there is must be resolved in favour of the specific terms of the adoption sections of the *Child Welfare Act, 1978* which are paramount to the general provisions of s. 35(1) of the *Family Law Reform Act, 1978*. If, as the *Child Welfare Act, 1978* states, the order of adoption is final and irrevocable, wiping out, in the terms of s. 86(1) and (2), everything that went before, then s. 35(1) of the *Family Law Reform Act, 1978* can be reconciled with the adoption provisions of the *Child Welfare Act, 1978*.

If, as sometimes happens, the natural parent establishes a relationship with the child *after* the adoption order is made then such parent is "any person" and might apply for custody or access to the child under s. 35(1) of the *Family Law Reform Act, 1978*. That application would be determined in the child's best interests based in part on the extent and nature of the established relationship. One can think of cases, by way of example only, where the natural mother is a girl of 16 or 17 and the child is adopted by the mother's parents, the grandparents of the child. As the child grows, he or she knows the natural mother as "aunt" or sister but a close and warm relationship may be established. Under certain circumstances such a relationship might well give rise to an application for access or custody as the adoptive parents age or an unhappy relationship develops between the child and its adoptive parents.

In the instant case at the time of the application for access there was no relationship in law and there had been no relationship in fact established after the making of the adoption order. The adoption order was a declaration that it was in the best interests of the child that a new family be established and old relationships completely severed. In the instant case there are no grounds for interfering with that new relationship by directing a hearing on the merits of the appellant's application for access, there being on the facts and the law no "merits" to be heard and thus the appellant fails at the threshold of her application.

The appeal is accordingly dismissed without costs.

JESSUP J.A. (dissenting): — In my very respectful opinion MacKinnon A.C.J.O.'s judgment is good legislation but bad law. . . .

I cannot imagine a Judge granting access on the facts of this case but the natural mother is entitled to her day in Court.

CATHOLIC CHILDREN'S AID SOCIETY OF METROPOLITAN TORONTO (MUNICIPALITY) v. S. (T.)

(1989), 20 R.F.L. (3d) 337, 69 O.R. (2d) 189 (Ont. C.A.)

TARNOPOLSKY J.A.:—

THE PARTIES AND THE APPEAL

This appeal concerns two children: a girl, who is now 9 years old, and her younger brother, who is now 7.

In December 1981 the children were apprehended by the Catholic Children's Aid Society of Metropolitan Toronto ("the society") following a scalding incident, caused by their mother, as a result of which the girl will be permanently scarred. On consent of all parties, the children were found to be in need of protection and the society was granted wardship for three months, which was continued thereafter. The children were placed in the care of the foster parents when the girl was 2 years old and her brother was 3 months old. They have resided with the same foster parents ever since. Following the apprehension of the children by the society, the birth parents, who have since separated, and latterly the birth mother continued to see the children approximately once a month up to 10th November 1987, the date of the judgment appealed from herein.

With the passage of time the foster parents indicated their preparedness to adopt the children, but also their opposition to such adoption if it were accompanied with an order in favour of the birth parents for continued access. In order to facilitate such adoption, the society sought permanent wardship of the children and termination of access rights of the birth parents. In October 1985, upon a status review hearing under the Child Welfare Act, R.S.O. 1980, c. 66 (since repealed and replaced by the Child and Family Services Act, S.O. 1984, c. 55), Nasmith Prov. J. ordered Crown wardship for both children, with access for each birth parent to continue at least four times yearly and beyond the adoption by the foster parents, unless terminated by a court of competent jurisdiction.

In November 1987 Lissaman D.C.J. allowed an appeal by the society from Judge Nasmith's order and made an order for Crown wardship with a view to adoption, and further ordered that the birth parents be denied access to the children.

The children's birth mother appealed to this court, seeking restoration of the order of Judge Nasmith or, in the alternative, an order of Crown wardship for long-term foster care, with access by the birth parents. Her appeal was resisted by counsel for the society, for the children and for the foster parents. Counsel for the Attorney General of Ontario intervened to respond to the constitutional issues raised by the appellant mother. The children's birth father did not participate in the appeal. . . .

(1) Is there ambiguity in the legislation so as to permit the ordering of continuing access by birth parents to the children adopted by foster parents?

[Although the review hearing had occurred under the *Child Welfare Act*, the Ontario Court of Appeal wished to indicate that the result would be the same under the successor *CFSA*. It used the following "Table of Concordance":]

C.W.A.	C.F.S.A.
s. 38(5)	s. 55 [now s. 59]
s. 38(7)	ss. 54(7), 60(9) [now ss. 58(7), 64(9)]
s. 38(8)(*d*)	s. 134(2)(*a*) [now s. 140(2)(a)]
s. 69(15)	s. 137(1) [now s. 143(1)]
s. 69(16)	ss. 145(4)(c), 155 [now ss. 151(4)(c), 161]
s. 83	s. 151 [now s. 157]
s. 86(1)	s. 152(1), (2) [now s. 158(1), (2)]

At the review hearing Nasmith Prov. J. summed up [(1985), 48 R.F.L. (2d) 371, at 383] the effect of s. 38(5), (7) and (8)(*d*) as carrying "a strong implication that there *is* a legislated Hobson's choice between adoption and continuing birth parent access." However, he found ambiguity because of s. 69(15). Although I agree with him that the relevant provisions in s. 38 require a choice to be made and that there appears to be some conflict between that section and s. 69(15), I also believe that the sense of s. 38 is paramount and . . . I do not think that in *this* particular case, the choice is difficult. It is not a Hobson's choice.

It has to be remembered that s. 38(7) is concerned with children who have been committed as wards of the Crown. That section provides that once the child is placed for adoption in the home of the person approved and is residing there, an order for access cannot be applied for or made. However, what of pre-existing access orders? Clearly, by either s. 38(8)(*d*) or s. 69(15) any such orders would have to be terminated by court order before placement for adoption. There may be other access orders which, by s. 69(15), terminate automatically upon placement, but, as a result of s. 69(15), those made under the C.W.A. would have to be terminated by court order when a decision is made that a Crown wardship is to be replaced by an adoption. The comparable provision in the C.F.S.A., s. 137(1), is more explicit in providing that the access order which does not terminate automatically is one which is made under the "Child Protection" Part of the Act. This is repeated in s. 134(2)(*a*) of the C.F.S.A.

One of the reasons that Nasmith Prov. J. gave in finding an ambiguity in the C.W.A. is that, in a case such as the present one, there is no need for a *physical* "placement", since the children are already placed with the prospective adopting parents [p. 384]: "The so-called adoption placement would be a mere formalization, if you will, or a *deemed* placement." But I do not see why a placement cannot include a deemed placement. The word "placement" is not defined in the Act and, in the context in which it is used, does not necessarily indicate the moment of first physically placing a child in a particular home. It is more an abstract concept. Placement occurs when there is a coinciding of the decision that a child will be adopted with the time when the child is residing with the prospective adopting parents.

Another factor considered by Nasmith Prov. J. in concluding that the C.W.A. did not preclude granting both an access for birth parents and an adoption was that secrecy was irrelevant in this case. He referred to the majority decision of MacKinnon A.C.J.O. in *W. (C.G.) v. J. (M.)* (1981), 34 O.R. (2d) 44, 24 R.F.L. (2d) 342 (C.A.), as indicating that the purpose of limiting access by the birth parents to the children is to maintain secrecy. However, in that case other reasons for denying access by birth parents were given. . . .

I agree with counsel for the respondent society that the primary purpose indicated in the passage quoted from the *W. (C.G.)* case is family stability. Moreover, the value of family stability is emphasized in s. 86(1) of the C.W.A. (s. 152(1), (2) and (3) of the C.F.S.A.). The subsection declares that the adopted child becomes the child of the adopting parent and, equally important, ceases to be the child of his or her birth parents; and the birth parents cease to be the parents of the adopted child. Any continuing access to that child given to birth parents would be given to someone who is no longer a legal parent of that child. The granting of an access order after adoption would hamper the relationship between an adopted child and the adopting parents. It would put that relationship on an unequal basis with that of natural child-parent relationships, because a judicial or administrative official would determine who had access to the children, rather than having that determination made within the family unit.

It follows, therefore, that the legislation (both the C.W.A. and the C.F.S.A.) requires, in cases like the present, that there be termination of access by the birth parents by the time the children are placed for adoption: the choice was between continued Crown wardship with access or adoption with no access for birth parents. . . .

[The court went on to hold that the statutory provisions requiring termination of access upon placement of a Crown ward for adoption did not contravene the *Charter*. In "Annotation" (1989), 20 R.F.L. (3d) 337, Professor Thompson interpreted the case as follows (at 337):

> The Court of Appeal has now spoken: there is not room under the Ontario legislation, either the old Child Welfare Act or the new Child and Family Services Act, for legal access by natural parents to survive adoption. Prior to this decision, there had been some debate amongst lower courts, largely inspired by the trial decision here and other decisions of Nasmith Prov. J.: for a useful review of the cases, see Roselyn Zisman, "Access on Adoption", L.S.U.C., Representing Parents in Child Protection Cases (Toronto: Dept. of Educ., 1989).]

R. (S.) v. R. (M.)

(1998), 43 R.F.L. (4th) 116 (Ont. C.A.)

[A.R. was born on October 28, 1992. His mother, S.R., was 31 years old when A. was born. About four months before the child's birth, S. moved to Guelph to live with her 50 year-old sister, M.R. and her sister's 56 year-old husband, P.J. The parties agreed that the child would be raised by M. and her husband. In February, 1993, the mother changed her mind and asked for the child's return. M. and her husband refused. After attempted negotiations failed, S. applied for custody of A. in

June, 1993. Her sister and brother-in-law cross-applied in July. In September 1993, an interim order was made giving custody to M. and her husband, with access to S. for three hours every other weekend. In July 1994, M. and her husband applied to adopt A. and to dispense with S.'s consent to the adoption. The custody and adoption proceedings were consolidated in November 1994. The trial did not take place until March 1995 at which time the child had bonded with his aunt and uncle. He regarded their home as his and was unaware that he was related to S.R.]

ABELLA J.A. (for the court):
    . . . Based on the evidence before him, including a court-ordered assessment by Samuel R. Luker, and a report by Dr. Nitza Perlman who was retained by the adoptive parents, Judge Walmsley concluded that it was in the best interests of the child to remain with his aunt and uncle. But he was also firmly of the view that notwithstanding the pending adoption of A. by M. and her husband, there should be access by S.R. He recited four reasons for giving her access:

> (a) The mother has a healthy and comfortable relationship with the child and this relationship poses no threat to A.'s development and well-being;

> (b) Mr. Luker was in favour of *continuing* and *broadening* access to the mother as set out in his recommendation #4. He found that the custody parents were not opposed to access provided it was supervised, as they had a concern that the mother might abscond with the child;

> (c) Dr. Perlman found that the custody parents were strongly in favour of [A.] knowing his birth mother but worried that if she had *free* access it might interfere with [A.]'s sense of a secure environment;

> (d) Finally, it must be borne in mind that this is a "relative" adoption. The adoption order may make [M.R.] and [P.J.] the legal parents of [A.]. But it will also make [S.R.] his aunt and they will all still be part of the same extended family. Further, the evidence showed that were it not for the extended family concept and a cultural tradition of informal adoption within the family, [S.R.] would not have felt able to turn to [M.] and her husband for the support and commitment involved in raising a child. Clearly, access in the context of a "relative" adoption is a very different matter from access in the context of a stranger adoption. My conclusion is that [A.] should continue to enjoy an access relationship with his soon-to-be aunt. [Emphasis in the original]

In making an order for access, Associate Chief Judge Walmsley was making an order he knew would survive the adoption order. It was an order he considered not only jurisprudentially available, but in fact desirable in the context of these three adults being related to one another. In his words: "I conclude that access orders made before a relative adoption survive the adoption order, and that there exists in Ontario no jurisprudence to the contrary." He referred to a number of authorities in support of his conclusion that access and guardianship need not be inconsistent: *K. (S.) v. D. (M.S.)* (1980), 21 R.F.L. (2d) 271 (Ont. U.F.C.), Steinburg U.F.C.J.; *Catholic Children's Aid Society of Metropolitan Toronto v. H. (K.)* (1987), 6 R.F.L. (3d) 1 (Ont. Fam. Ct.), Main, Provincial Judge; *H. (J.) v. G. (B.)* (March 9, 1993), Doc. Toronto D1711/86 (Ont. Prov. Div.); and *P. (M.A.R.) (Litigation Guardian of) v. Catholic Children's Aid Society of Metropolitan Toronto* (1994), 9 R.F.L. (4th) 385 (Ont. Prov. Div.).

If there remained any doubt about whether an access order could survive an order for adoption, *Nouveau-Brunswick (Ministre de la santé & des services communautaires) c. L. (M.)*, a judgment of the Supreme Court of Canada, delivered October 1, 1998 [reported at 165 D.L.R. (4th) 58 (S.C.C.)], definitively articulates the possibility that in exceptional circumstances, access and adoption orders can co-exist.

Judge Walmsley's decision was appealed both by S.R. and by the adoptive parents. Efforts at access arrangements were unsuccessful and a long period of time elapsed between visits for S.R. Eventually, however, in an effort to settle the appeal, S. agreed to abandon her appeal on the following bases: (1) S.R. would have access to A.; (2) M.R. and P.J. would adopt him. In addition, the parties agreed to mediation in order to assist access arrangements. Minutes of Settlement giving effect to these terms were signed on December 3, 1996.

The adoption order was made on January 21, 1997.

Although the access arrangements initially appeared to be adequate, problems emerged by the spring of 1997. Efforts at mediation were unsuccessful and an application was brought by S. seeking unsupervised access, police intervention to enforce access, and mediation. M. and her husband sought to have access terminated. The matter was heard by O'Connor J.

The expert evidence before Justice O'Connor persuaded him that access to A. by S.R. was in the child's best interests. The expert evidence available to this panel confirms this conclusion. There is no doubt that the child has a good relationship with S.R. and that it would be in his interest to continue a relationship with her. He ordered overnight access every three weekends, plus an additional day every second weekend, in accordance with the terms of an outstanding interim access order. He also ordered mediation and police intervention to assist in the enforcement of access.

As recently as October 27, 1998, a report from Dr. James Deutsch, who reviewed all the documents but did not have access to any of the parties directly, stated:

> The descriptions in Dr. Paulker's report suggest that birth mother demonstrated a sensitivity and talent for mothering and a good-enough relationship based on respect for the autonomy and separateness of [A.]. In contrast, there are psychological limitations described in the adoptive parents, along with observations consistent with [A.] representing to some extent adoptive parents' own aspirations or anxieties regarding themselves. *There is a clear indication that the birth mother is a significant relationship figure in the life of [A.], whether or not he fully understands that she is his birth mother. The descriptions of their interactions would indicate that the relationship demonstrated an ease that was absent from the custodial relationship and was likely quite positive and helpful to this boy.* [Emphasis added.]

With respect to access, Dr. Deutsch concluded:

> It remains important for [A.] to have continuing, predictable access to his birth mother. It would be detrimental if this access were to be cut off. This would be true in both the short term and the long term.

His report also stresses what he views as the obligation on the part of the adoptive mother to:

> . . . address her ambivalence and to provide, to the best of her ability, support for this clearly valued child to understand and cope with his complex and distressing situation. His relationship with his biological mother will not go away; it cannot be wished away. Should its significance be denied or should he be deprived of it, there is significant risk of later issues of trust due to a sense of betrayal and withholding of respect for his autonomy.

We agree, therefore, with Justice O'Connor's decision that a positive relationship exists between A. and his biological mother and that he should continue to enjoy access to her.

Justice O'Connor found M.R. and P.J. largely responsible for the frustration of access rights. In his words:

[The] dispute has been significantly contributed to by the respondents. It does not lie with them to seek a remedy for an alleged harm caused or contributing to by them.

There was ample evidence to support this conclusion. As Dr. Jerome Paulker indicated in his assessment, which was undertaken pending the appeal from the decision of Associate Chief Judge Walmsley, the adoptive parents were anxious to terminate access and were determined to prevent A. from having any contact with his biological mother. They offered no evidentiary foundation for their desire to prevent access, either of a physical, psychological, or practical nature.

There is no doubt that S.R. agreed to the Minutes of Settlement permitting the adoption of A. only on the condition that she be given access. Notwithstanding this settlement, difficulties with access quickly emerged and it was clear that the adopting parents had every intention of attempting to deprive S.R. of access. This intention cannot be given legal effect. There is overwhelming evidence that access to S. is in the child's best interests. What is clearly not in A.'s best interests is to have his adoptive parents continue their preoccupation with thwarting this access.

We do not, however, see any basis for an order of mediation. Mediation cannot be effective unless both sides are genuinely open to the process. In the past five years, M.R. and P.J. have given every indication that they are not prepared to cooperate with mediators. Accordingly, we think an imposed process of mediation would impose an undue burden on S.R. with no likelihood of constructive results.

As to the assistance of the police, this can be a traumatic intervention for a 6 year-old child. It was requested by S. because of the consistent intransigence of M.R. and P.J. in frustrating rather than facilitating access. We expect at this stage that it is clear to them that their obstructive conduct will not be judicially tolerated. To continue to behave in a way which would leave S. no alternative but to invoke outside intervention, would reflect an unwillingness on their part to act in the child's best interests, a reflection that would certainly be relevant in any subsequent proceedings.

The amount of access should be once every four weekends from Friday at 6:00 p.m. until Sunday at 6:00 p.m. The respondent indicated her willingness to pick up and return the child.

Accordingly, the order of O'Connor J. is to be varied by an order directing that access take place once every four weekends. The order for mediation and police intervention are set aside. The appeal is otherwise dismissed with costs.

McLEOD, "ANNOTATION"

(1998), 32 R.F.L. (4th) 98

The Ontario Court of Appeal's reasons for judgment in *R. (S.)* v. *R. (M.)* signal the court's willingness to extend access to first-family members that survives a child's adoption. The court's reasons also suggest that a birth parent may be granted access to an adopted child in a broader range of cases than had previously been believed.

Standing to claim access varies from province to province under local custody and adoption legislation. In Ontario, a court may not make an order for access under the *Child and Family Services Act* (adoption legislation) once an adoption order is made: s. 160(1) of the Act. Accordingly, any application for access following adoption must be made under the *Children's Law Reform Act* (the provincial custody legislation). A parent or other interested person may claim custody or access under the *Children's Law Reform Act*. A birth parent is no longer a parent once an adoption order is made: s. 158(2), *Child and Family Services Act*. The adoption order severs the parent-child relationship. However, a birth parent should be able to claim access or custody to an adopted child under the *Children's Law Reform Act* in the same way as any other non-parent.

Historically, judges were divided as to whether to allow a birth parent to claim access after adoption. While most judges accepted the view that any interested person could apply for access to a child, some judges insisted that a biological parent could not rely on a pre-adoption relationship with the child to support an access claim: contrast the views in *W. (C.G.)* v. *J. (M.)* (1981), 24 R.F.L. (2d) 342, 34 O.R. (2d) 44, 130 D.L.R. (3d) 418 (C.A.). Post-adoption access had to be based on a post-adoption relationship between the person and the child. Those judges who allowed a birth parent to apply for access usually took the view that access should be granted only in an exceptional case. Most judges were reluctant to grant access to a birth parent after adoption because of the fear that maintaining a first-family relationship might undermine the stability of the child's new family: cf. *Catholic Children's Aid Society of Metropolitan Toronto* v. *H. (K.)* (1989), 23 R.F.L. (3d) 300 (Ont. C.A.), leave to appeal refused (1990), 25 R.F.L. (3d) xxxviii, *(sub nom. H. (K.)* v. *H. (J.))* 39 O.A.C. 160 (note), *(sub nom. H. (K.)* v. *H. (J.))* 113 N.R. 318 (note) (S.C.C.).

Some courts, primarily in Western Canada, suggested that judges should apply a more relaxed rule to determine whether to grant access to a birth-family member following a step-parent adoption where the child knew the reality of its situation and had an established relationship with various members of its former family. Although Society adoptions usually are preceded by parental abandonment or misconduct, a step-parent adoption may be motivated only by a desire to formalize the child's second-family living arrangements.

In *R. (S.)* v. *R. (M.)*, the mother allowed her sister and brother-in-law to raise her child while she attended to family matters out of the country. When she returned, they refused to return the child to her. The mother applied for custody, and her sister and brother-in-law applied to adopt the child. For some reason, it took almost two years for the applications to get to trial. By that time, the child was attached to the sister and brother-in-law. The trial judge felt that he had no choice but to confirm the child's living arrangements by granting custody to the sister and brother-in-law while they processed the adoption. The mother finally consented to the adoption on condition that she be granted ongoing access. The sister and brother-in-law agreed, obtained the adoption order and then interfered with the birth mother's access. The trial judge held that the access order survived adoption and the adoptive parents should not be allowed to create a conflict around access and then take advantage of the tension to cancel access. The Court of Appeal agreed.

Section 143(1) of the *Child and Family Services Act*, which provides that access orders terminate when a child is placed for adoption, does not apply to family adoptions since a child is not "placed" in a family adoption: see, as to family adoption, s. 146(1), (2) of the Act. There is nothing in the *Child and Family Services Act* that provides that an access order ends upon a family adoption. However, some judges suggested that the extinguishment of the parent-child relationship necessarily extinguished a pre-adoption access order because the order was based on a status that no longer existed. The Ontario Court of Appeal rejected this argument in *R. (S.)* v. *R. (M.)* by approving the trial judge's statement that an access order made before a family adoption survives the adoption order. As indicated, the *Child and Family Services Act* mandates a different result in the case of non-family adoptions. Although the Ontario Court of Appeal's brief reasons suggest that the trial judge's conclusion and comments are commonly held, in fact the law on point was unclear prior to *R. (S.)* v. *R. (M.)*: Hovius, *Family Law* (4th ed.), pp. 1049-1064.

Since the court does not think that there is anything inherently inconsistent between granting an adoption order and maintaining a first-family member's right to access, a birth parent or member of a first family should be able to seek access following adoption. The issue in such cases is whether access should be granted on the merits, according to the best interests of the child, on a case-by-case basis. Prior authorities should be approached with caution, to the extent that they suggest otherwise.

The court did not have to decide whether a birth parent or first-family member may apply for custody or access after a Society adoption or adoption arising by placement. However, the tenor of the court's analysis is that such people have standing to claim custody or access as "other persons". The issue is whether custody/ access is in the best interests of the child in the circumstances, not whether a first-family member has standing to seek the relief.

It is surprising that the court was so willing to accept the view that it was in the child's best interests to have continued contact with the mother. It is unlikely that the tension between the mother and the adoptive parents will decrease over time. Most courts are reluctant to extend access to a non-parent if the custodial parent objects and if continued contact may threaten the custodial parent's relationship with the child. The possibility that the mother will tell the child the truth—that his friend is really his mother and his parents are his aunt and uncle—could upset the child and his relationship with the adoptive parents. The real reason for continuing access appears to be that the adoptive parents obtained the mother's consent to adoption by agreeing to access and the court was not willing to let them circumvent their agreement. Although the birth mother is not a parent, neither is she simply a stranger.

The court also relied on "expert evidence" to support the conclusion to continue access. The report in question was prepared by a doctor who did not see or interview any of the participants. Instead, his opinion was based solely on reviewing the material prepared and filed by others. With respect, courts should be cautious about relying on an expert witness's opinion of what is in a particular child's best interests if the witness never interviewed the child or any of the adults involved in the child's life: cf. *Ligate* v. *Richardson* (1997), 101 O.A.C. 161, 34 O.R. 423 (Ont. C.A.). The opinions are second-hand, based on another person's observations and conclusions that may or may not be accurate.

The court's decision that a biological parent has standing to claim or enforce access rights after adoption is correct in Ontario but may not be so elsewhere. Standing to claim custody/access depends on the local legislation. As long as a person has an interest in the child's well-being, he or she should be allowed to maintain custody and access proceedings. The question of whether to continue contact should be decided on the merits of the case, not on jurisdictional grounds. However, it is surprising that the Ontario Court of Appeal considered the issue so settled that it did not even address any cases that suggested a contrary result. It is also surprising that the court was so willing to accept the trial judge's conclusion that continued contact is in the child's best interests, given the conflict between the birth mother and adoptive parents and the potential confusion when the child learns the truth and is forced to realign his relationship with the significant adults in his life.

NOTES AND QUESTIONS

1. In *D. (I.S.)* v. *F. (C.M.)* (1982), 27 R.F.L. (2d) 75 (Ont. Dist. Ct.), Kurisko D.C.J. refused to apply *W. (C.G.)* to an application for access by paternal grandparents whose grandchild had been adopted some years earlier by the mother and her new husband.

2. In *G. (C.)* v. *H. (J.)* (1989), 23 R.F.L. (3d) 300 (Ont. C.A.), the foster parents had been the child's *de facto* parents since his infancy. Their application to adopt was opposed by the child's grandparents who also wished to adopt the child. The trial judge dismissed the application but the appeal judge reversed this decision because she felt adoption by the foster parents would provide better stability for the child and provide him with a more secure and certain future than an order granting the foster parents custody with access to the grandparents. In doing so, she relied on the foster parents' assurance of access to the grandparents. The Ontario Court of Appeal dismissed a further appeal by the grandparents. It noted (at 301) that if the adoptive order was affirmed "no order for access can be incorporated". It also expressed agreement (at 301) with the finding that "access in the present circumstances is desirable". The endorsement on the appeal record indicated that Tarnopolsky J.A. agreed with the result and the reasons "except as to this court expressing its opinion whether it is desirable that the foster parents should grant access to the biological grandparents".

Some four years later, Nevins Prov. J. dealt with an application by the grandparents and the birth parent for an access order to this child in *H. (J.)* v. *G. (B.)*, unreported, March 9, 1993, Doc. Toronto D1711/86; affirmed May 31, 1993, unreported (Ont. Div. Ct.). The applicants alleged that the adoptive parents had immediately reneged on their promise to permit access following the adoption. Nevins Prov. J. held that he had jurisdiction to deal with the access application. He reasoned that the Ontario Court of Appeal in *W. (C.G.)* left open the possibility for such applications by birth relatives after adoption in exceptional circumstances. These were exceptional circumstances because (at 17) the applicants were "no strangers to the child and adoptive parents" and the adoptive parents gave "clear and unequivocal assurances" that there would be continued contact.

3. In *P. (M.A.R.)* v. *C.C.A.S. of Metro. Toronto* (1994), 9 R.F.L. (4th) 385 (Ont. Prov. Div.); affirmed (1995), 11 R.F.L. (4th) 95 (Ont. Gen. Div.); affirmed (1995), 15 R.F.L. (4th) 330 (Ont. C.A.), a woman (V.) brought M., and his half-sister (G.) from an orphanage in Mexico to Toronto with a view to adopting them. The relationship between V. and M. soured and V. turned M. over to the Society in 1992. He became a Crown ward in 1993. As part of that order, the court provided that the boy would have access to G. if V. approved. In fact, V. never permitted access. After V. adopted C., M. applied for a court order varying the terms of access to C. pursuant to s. 58 of the *CFSA*. V. moved to have the application dismissed summarily on the ground that it was prohibited by s. 160 of that Act. All of the courts involved concluded that neither s. 160 nor any other provision in the Act barred the application. When the court dealt with the merits of the application, it concluded that C.'s interests dictated that there be no variation, even though this would likely mean that there would be no contact between the children: *P. (M.A.R.) (Litigation Guardian of)* v. *V. (A.)* (1997), 33 R.F.L. (4th) 124 (Ont. Prov. Div.), reversed (1998), 40 R.F.L. (4th) 411 (Ont. Gen. Div.).

4. Manitoba has enacted legislation to specifically empower a judge to grant access to a natural parent where a child is adopted by the other natural parent and his or her spouse (enacted by S.M. 1979, c. 22, s. 70). See now *Adoption Act*, S.M. 1997, c. 47, s. 92(1). In *Williams* v. *Hillier*, 26 R.F.L. (2d) 164, [1982] 2 W.W.R. 313 (Man. C.A.) the court rejected the proposition that access should be granted to a natural parent in a step-parent adoption in extraordinary cases only. Monnin J.A. (O'Sullivan J.A. concurring) stated (at 176):

> Simply because spouses have lost all love for one another and have requested severance of the matrimonial bonds, it does not follow that automatically the love and ties between parents and child must also necessarily be broken. If access or visitation rights are detrimental to the child, then they should be refused, but not granted only in exceptional cases.

In that case, the biological father had been attempting for a number of years to gain access to two children adopted by the mother, his former wife, and her new husband. After numerous proceedings, some of which related to his attempts to prevent the adoption, he finally succeeded in persuading a majority of the Manitoba Court of Appeal that he should have access.

Would you favour reform in Ontario modelled on the Manitoba legislation? Is a step-parent adoption ever in the best interests of a child if it is also in the best interests of the child to maintain contact with the non-custodial biological parent? See *D. (R.)* v. *S. (W.B.)* (1991), 33 R.F.L. (3d) 1 (B.C. C.A.).

Would it be preferable to adopt legislation stipulating that the court can grant access in any adoption, if this is in the child's best interest? Following *R. (S.)* v. *R. (M.)*, is this now the law in Ontario in any event?

5. In *C. (F.M.), Re* (1996), 21 R.F.L. (4th) 406 (Sask. Q.B.), the adoptive parents asked that the adoption order spell out the access terms that had been negotiated with the birth mother. Section 16(1) of *The Adoption Act*, R.S.S. 1989-90, c. A –5.1 stipulated that, subject to ss. (2) and (3), any existing right of access of a birth parent was terminated upon the placement of a child for adoption by the birth parent, an agency and the director and that no access order could be made. Subsection (2) stated that a birth parent could have access if each adoptive parent consented. Subsection (3) indicated that in step-parent adoptions an access order would continue to be effective unless the court ordered otherwise. There was also a provision permitting an application for an access order in step-parent adoptions. Saskatchewan Justice argued that the court only had jurisdiction under the Act to grant access in step-parent adoptions. The court reasoned, however, that s. 16 only dealt with the situation of the parties from the time the child was placed for adoption until the adoption order. Thus, it had nothing to do with the court's authority to deal with access at the time of the adoption order or thereafter under the general statute dealing with access orders.

6. In "Adoption with Access or 'Open Adoption' " (1991-1992), 8 C.F.L.Q. 283, the Adoption with Access Sub-Committee of the Canadian Bar Association—Ontario concluded:

1) an increasing tendency to order Crown wardship with access combined with the prohibition in s. 140(2) on adoption placement of a Crown ward while such an order is in place has resulted in more children remaining in foster care (at 288);

2) there has been increasing use of informal arrangements whereby a birth parent has some degree of contact with the child after adoption (at 289); and

3) there are some situations such as adoptions of older Crown wards and step-parent adoptions where continued contact between the adoptee and a birth relative may be in the best interest of the child (at 289).

The committee recommended amendments to the *CFSA* to permit court-ordered birth parent contact with adopted Crown wards and suggested that the *Children's Law Reform Act* might be amended to "provide a restricted right to a birth parent to apply for access after a family adoption" (at 296).

7. Although Abella J.A. states in *R. (S.)* v. *R. (M.)* that the S.C.C. "definitely articulates the possibility that in exceptional circumstances, access and adoption can co-exist" in *New Brunswick (Minister of Health and Community Services)* v. *L. (M.)* (1998), 165 D.L.R. (4th) 58 (S.C.C.), the case actually dealt only with a court's jurisdiction to issue an access order in conjunction with an order for permanent guardianship (Crown wardship in Ontario). The court simply mentioned (at 77) that a provision in the New Brunswick statute specifically allowed a court to preserve a right of access even after adoption.

8. In *R. (S.)* v. *R. (M.)*, Justice Abella states that it was now clear to the adoptive parents "that their obstructive conduct will not be judicially tolerated". What is the likely judicial response if the parents continue to frustrate the biological mother's attempts to exercise access?

(3) CONFIDENTIALITY OF ADOPTION RECORDS

The issue of the confidentiality of adoption records has been very topical in the last few decades. The following excerpt from a Manitoba Law Reform Commission Report identifies the various interests that must be considered in determining whether adoptees should have access to information about their biological origins.

MANITOBA LAW REFORM COMMISSION, *REPORT ON THE CONFIDENTIALITY OF ADOPTION RECORDS*

(1979) 8-11 (Footnotes Omitted)

THE INTERESTS OF THE PARTIES IN THE ADOPTION TRIANGLE

Adopting Parents

The rationale for confidentiality of adoption records is ostensibly to best protect the diverse interests of the parties in the "adoption triangle". As for the adoptive parents, confidentiality protects the status given to them under s. 96(1) of *"The Child Welfare Act"* (that is, the status of being the parent of the adoptee for all lawful purposes). They are shielded from the possible pryings of the biological parents who may interfere with the proper upbringing of the adoptee. Confidentiality assures the adopting parents ". . . that they may treat the child as their own in all respects and need not fear that the adoption records will be a means of hurting the child . . . or of harming themselves." Confidentiality protects the adoptive parents against the fear that if the biological parents meet with the adoptee, the adoptee will leave them, effectively rendering them babysitters for many long years.

Yet research shows that the adoptive parents' fears with respect to adult adoptees are largely unfounded. One set of experts have found in their research of these reunions that there was no proven harm to the adoptive parents when the reunion took place with an *adult* adoptee. Other writers have stated, and, we believe, correctly, that adoptive parents should not feel threatened by such a reunion, since the *adult* adoptee is often seeking only his identity, and is not searching for a new set of parents. The adoptee will still consider his adoptive parents to be his true parents.

Biological Parents

As to the position of the biological parents, the picture that immediately springs to one's mind is that of a young single mother who gives up her child, and then tries to build her life anew, trying to forget the regrettable experience. As one correspondent put it, disclosure of identifying information to the adoptee ". . . would be a very cruel and destructive action for many natural . . . mothers who have tried to rebuild their lives. In my case it would bring only shock and heartbreak to me and my family." The effect of the present legislation and practice is to give biological parents an assurance of anonymity, an assurance that their indiscretions will never be divulged, and disclosure of identifying information to the adoptee would be directly contrary to these assurances.

Though this may be the common picture, some biological parents may have had second thoughts about giving up their child, and subsequently may develop a psychological need to meet, or at least to know more about the child they gave up. In fact, an American survey has indicated that 76% of the biological parents surveyed felt that adoptees should have access to information identifying their biological parents, and 86% desired updated reports on the child they had given up.

In spite of some of these statistics, we are of the view that the privilege of the biological parents to retain their anonymity, if they desire it, must be safeguarded in any proposal to alter the cloak of confidentiality surrounding adoption records.

Adoptees

As to the position of the adoptee, he may not be aware of his adopted status or, being so aware, may have no desire to have any contact with his biological parents. Certainly in his adolescence, contact with his parents could prove emotionally traumatic and confusing. Clearly then there are instances where it would not be in the adoptee's interest to supply his biological parents with identifying information. But conversely, there may often be instances where it may very much be in the adoptee's interests to have contact with or at least know more about his biological parents. The deep psychological needs of some adoptees go far beyond mere curiosity. They may be "genealogically bewildered", this bewilderment being cured only by more knowledge of their background, or perhaps meetings with one or both of their biological parents. Others maintain they are being denied access to their birthright, that part of their identity is to know who they are. . . .

Ontario has gradually moved towards increased disclosure of information regarding adoption. In 1978 a voluntary disclosure registry was established. In *Ferguson* v. *Ontario (Director of Child Welfare)* (1983), 40 O.R. (2d) 294 (Co. Ct.), Killeen Co. Ct. J. described the mechanisms of the registry as follows (at 310):

> The adoption disclosure registry is maintained in Ministry facilities at Toronto. An adopted child who is 18 or more years of age and a birth parent of the child may apply to a local Children's Aid Society to be registered in the registry at Toronto. If the Director ascertains that both the adopted child and birth parent are registered, he must then contact any living adoptive parent and obtain a written consent to the disclosure of the identifying information. If the adoptive parent refuses, the Director can do nothing further. If the adoptive parent consents, the Director must then obtain a written confirmation of both the adoptee and the birth parent. At this point, a "matching" occurs which permits the Director to divulge identifying information from the documents used on the court adoption application, . . . and the forms filed by adoptee and birth parent in the registry.
>
> The outline of the registry scheme demonstrates its extreme passivity: first, there is always the possibility that an adoptee will never learn of his true status because the Act casts no duty on anyone to disclose to the adoptee that he was adopted; second, each member of the triangle may, by failing to register or consent, as the case may be, roadblock a matching; third, the Ministry is under no obligation to disclose the availability of the scheme to triangle members or to advertise it publicly. The materials before me show that between the inception of the registry on June 15, 1979, up to December 31, 1981, only 49 matchings occurred even though in the order of twelve hundred adoptions now take place each year in Ontario and the registry scheme may be utilized by the thousands of triangle members who arise from past adoptions granted in Ontario.

The voluntary register was of no help to someone like Mrs. Ferguson whose birth parent did not register. However, it had been possible for some time to obtain a court order opening adoption records. Mrs. Ferguson applied for such an order under s. 80(1) of the *Child Welfare Act*. She was unsuccessful. The trial judge concluded that in light of the statute's emphasis on secrecy in the adoption process, an order should be granted only in compelling or exception circumstances. As an example of such circumstances, the court referred to situations where the applicant's mental or physical health required disclosure. Accordingly, the order was refused where Mrs. Ferguson's application was based solely on a desire to know more about herself and her roots. The Ontario Court of Appeal affirmed the trial judgment: (1983), 36 R.F.L. (2d) 405, 44 O.R. (2d) 78. The court held (at (R.F.L.) 407) that "sufficient cause [for the purpose of s. 80(1)] must be a cause of such gravity and importance to displace the statutory rights of the other parties as well as the interests of the province in maintaining the integrity of the adoption system". It also concluded (at 408) that ss. 2(b), 2(d) and 7 of the *Charter* did not have "any bearing whatever on s. 80(1) of the Child Welfare Act." The Court of Appeal noted (at 408): "The real basis of Mr. Wilson's argument in this court was an attack on the wisdom of the secrecy provisions of the Child Welfare Act dealing with adoption. This is a kind of argument that may be addressed appropriately to the legislature but which has little place in this courtroom." See also *Tyler* v. *Ontario District Court* (1986), 1 R.F.L. (3d) 139 (Ont. Dist. Ct.).

In *Ferguson* it was revealed that the Director and his officers had established a practice of releasing "non-identifying" information about the natural parent to adoptees who requested it. Killeen Co. Ct. J. stated that this practice was not authorized under the *Child Welfare Act*. This comment caused the Director to discontinue the policy and to refuse to disclose such information except in medical emergencies. Nevertheless, it appears that some children's aid societies continued to give non-identifying information in their possession to adoptive parents, adult adoptees and birth parents.

The *Child and Family Services Act, 1984,* passed in December 1984, continued the restrictive approach to disclosure exhibited in the *Child Welfare Act*. It did, however, provide, in s. 157(2), for the disclosure of non-identifying information by the Director in limited circumstances. This section, which was more restrictive than the practice of the Ministry noted in *Ferguson*, was not proclaimed in force. Instead, the Minister of Community and Social Services appointed a Special Commissioner to report to him on the matter of access to non-identifying and identifying information. After the provincial election in the spring of 1985, the new Minister announced that s. 157 would not be proclaimed until the report had been received. The report, parts of which are reproduced below, was released in November 1985.

GARBER, *THE REPORT OF THE SPECIAL COMMISSIONER, DISCLOSURE OF ADOPTION INFORMATION*

(Queen's Printer, 1985) (Footnotes Omitted)

FINDINGS OF THE INQUIRY

The Terms of Reference were accepted as an implied mandate that change was required in both the manner in which adoption information could be disclosed and in who should be eligible to receive such information. Although I had not made my own position explicit in respect of adoption disclosure prior to my appointment, the Ministry had reason to believe that my approach and disposition were toward openness in governmental disclosure of information. The appointment appeared to be a confirmation of this approach.

A short response to each of the questions posed in the Terms of Reference is offered at this point, without explanation or rationale to justify the points of view taken. The following serves, however, as an overview of my recommendations, which are presented in greater detail in the chapters that follow.

A. Access to non-identifying information

1. Should there be greater access to non-identifying information than is possible under either the *Child Welfare Act* or the *Child and Family Services Act*?

Yes, there should be greater access for adoptive parents, adoptees, birth parents, and birth siblings and grandparents of the adoptee.

2. What should be considered as non-identifying information? Are there categories of information that should be excluded or are there circumstances under which types of information may be considered as identifying?

Non-identifying information is that which does not disclose the identity of the adoptee, birth parents, birth relatives, or adoptive parents or their respective locations, or any other institutional identification which might lead to identifying the individuals listed. All other information of a social, medical, genetic, cultural, recreational, vocational, or personal nature should be considered as non-identifying.

Information with respect to the reasons for relinquishment of the child or the surrender of the child when it was taken into care is also included in non-identifying information. Information relating to circumstances of rape, incest, physical or sexual assault, or violence associated with the birth or the relinquishment of the adoptee should be disclosed with sensitivity and discretion by a counsellor who has had appropriate training.

Even the above non-identifying information pertaining to Indian and Native children should be considered as identifying information when it is to be made available to the child's Indian band or Native community, because many such bands and communities have a small population. Consequently, special disclosure provisions are recommended where notification to bands and Native communities is required under the Act.

3. If non-identifying information were to be made available should there be criteria for disclosure? Should it be available upon request or should it be released only for health reasons for example?

The recommendation is that non-identifying information should be available upon request, but with interpretive counselling.

Medical, genetic, and social/cultural information pertaining to an adopted child should be made available to family physicians or attending physicians by the adoptive parents; if they fail to or are unable to do so, it may be provided by a Director appointed by the Minister.

4. Who should have access to non-identifying information? Adoptive parents, birth parents, minor adoptees with consent of adoptive parents, adult adoptees with or without the consent of adoptive parents, adult siblings of adoptees?

The recommendation is that adoptive parents, birth parents, minor adoptees with the consent of adoptive parents, emancipated adoptees over the age of 16 (without the consent of adoptive parents), adult adoptees (without the consent of adoptive parents), adult birth siblings of adoptees, birth grandparents of adoptees, and the physician of the minor adoptee as specified above, should all have access to non-identifying information.

5. Who should have authority to release non-identifying information? A Ministry Director, a children's aid society that arranged the adoption, a private licensee that arranged the adoption?

The recommendation is that each or any of the above should have the authority to release non-identifying information, prior to the adoption order and post-adoption.

6. Should there be grounds for refusal of access and if so, what should these be? If access could be denied, should there be an appeal mechanism?

The recommendation is that there should be no reasonable grounds for refusal of a request for non-identifying information except as qualified above

with respect to information to go to Indian bands and Native communities or in situations where the applicant for information shows evidence of intent to cause harm to him/herself or others.

B. Access to identifying information

1. Who should be eligible to have access to identifying information through the Register? Birth parents, adult adoptees, adult siblings of adoptees, adoptive parents?

The recommendation is that access should be provided to all of those named above as well as to birth grandparents of the adult adoptee. Access should also be provided to Indian bands or Native communities, through a designated Indian or Native child and family service agency or an approved agency serving the jurisdiction of the band or community.

2. Should there be conditions or limitations on access rights for any of the above? For example should the adoptive parents' consent be required in addition to the consent of an adoptee and birth parent?

The first recommendation is that the adoptive parents' consent should not be required to release identifying information provided that the adoptee is an adult.

It is further recommended that access to identifying information be subject to accompanying mandatory interpretive counselling and the following consents:

- **adult adoptees should have access, on request, to their original birth certificate (including the original statement of live birth) and to other identifying information in their adoption file; i.e., no consent required;**

- **birth parents, adult birth siblings, and grandparents of adult adoptees should have access to identifying information about the adult adoptee, subject to the adult adoptee's consent;**

- **adoptive parents and minor adoptees with their adoptive parents' consent should have access to information which identifies the birth parents or other birth relatives, subject to the consent of the person(s) to be identified.**

- **where contact or reunion is sought by an adult adoptee or by a birth parent, adult birth sibling, or birth grandparents of an adult adoptee, the consent of the person(s) to be contacted shall be required. Any of the above-named may indicate their consent for contact or reunion by registering with the Disclosure Register.**

3. What should be the mechanism for disclosure of information either identifying or non-identifying in serious medical situations? Who should have the authority to disclose and who should be given access?

The recommendation is that no distinction be made with respect to medical information that is part of the non-identifying information; i.e., it should be provided on request. It is also recommended that birth parents and adoptive parents be encouraged to update the health and medical/genetic information in the adoptee's file so that societies, licensees or the Ministry may inform the affected parties as appropriate.

When identifying information is requested in a serious medical situation, the consents required above (#2) should be sought by the Disclosure Register.

Where the consents cannot be obtained and the need for disclosure is documented, a Director appointed by the Minister should have discretion to disclose the information without the required consents. Near death or death-bed reunions would be considered serious medical situations. Organ, tissue, or blood needs could be included as evidence of need to receive identifying information.

Where the emergency concerns the health or safety of a minor adoptee and the adoptive parents fail to give consent, the adopted child could be taken into care for its protection if that were required.

Discretion in the provision of information

A further recommendation is that discretionary authority should be provided in Bill 77 to a society, licensee, or Ministry Director to withhold information in exceptional circumstances such as where there is an admission by the applicant of intent to inflict harm to others or to oneself. These circumstances would serve as grounds for delay in providing identifying or non-identifying information. It is also recommended that the refusal to provide information or to delay its provision should be appealable to a Director appointed by the Minister. The Director should appoint a hearing officer to determine the disposition of the complaint. If the complainant remains unsatisfied with the result of the hearing, the Ministry or agency may be taken to court.

The Terms of Reference asked the Commissioner to consider whether or not any of the recommendations should be implemented retroactively or should apply only to adoptions that take place after the recommendations might be implemented. I was also asked to consider the manner in which the recommendations should be implemented, including possible requirements for counselling where information is disclosed.

It is recommended that all of the recommendations on disclosure and access to records should be implemented retroactively, in that the changes in disclosure are meant to redress the wrongs or limitations imposed upon birth parents, adoptees and adoptive parents by previous legislation.

The recommendation with respect to the manner of disclosure is that the release of non-identifying or identifying information, by or through a children's aid society, a licensee, or the Disclosure Register, shall be accompanied by counselling. A pre- and post-adoption counselling service shall be formally required of all agencies involved in adoption. The service should be offered pre-adoption, immediately post-adoption, at crises in the life of the adoption process, and in all requests for information or for reunion. A corollary recommendation is that counselling shall be mandatory for the applicant for information.

With respect to requests for search or contact, it is recommended that the Disclosure Register, or by referral a children's aid society or other approved agency, provide discreet intermediation and search capability on behalf of an applicant to the Register. The search shall be to determine if the person sought wishes to register, thereby indicating his/her decision to consent to contact or reunion or to refuse contact or reunion.

The Terms of Reference did not refer specifically to a number of topics which I felt were too important not to be addressed in this report. These include the necessity for post-adoption counselling services, the collection and security of adoption information, the roles and responsibilities of children's aid societies, private adoption licensees, and the Voluntary Disclosure Registry.

With respect to the latter, the recommendation is that the Voluntary Disclosure Register be renamed the Adoption Disclosure Register and that its mandate be expanded to include public education and information as well as active but discreet search and intermediary counselling services. . . .

Parenting whether by adoption or by birth is the provision of long, continuing, and loving care to a child. If the adoptive parents are accorded both the expectation and respect that is due them in the accomplishment of that task, then the question of access to knowledge of the adoptee's original parent(s) may be seen not as a desire for other parents but rather as the provision of basic facts for the benefit of the adoptee.

[In the later chapters of the Report, the Commissioner gives reason for his recommendations and provides greater detail regarding the way in which they should be implemented. Only that portion of the Report setting out the Commissioner's response to current arguments against disclosure is reproduced here.]

Continuing arguments against disclosure

Despite these pressures for disclosure, some individuals may still believe that the release of sealed or confidential information about the facts of adoption could be harmful to them or others. In the material reviewed for this report, the *very few advocates of restrictive disclosure* claimed the following:

1. Adoptive parents would lose their children if adoptees learned of their origins, and sought or established reunion with birth parents.
2. Adoptive parents believe they had an agreement with the government to maintain secrecy of the adoption and that the agreement was irrevocable.
3. Some adoptive parents believe that adoptees are indeed *their* children, over whom they may continue to exercise full parental authority regardless of the age of the adoptee.
4. Adoptive parents, some social workers, and other individuals fear that the disclosure of facts about adoptees' birth and relinquishment would be painful and harmful to the adoptees who should be spared this trauma, forever if possible, but at least until they are more mature. The ages of 20 or 25 or 30 were suggested as evidence of maturity.
5. Adolescent adoptees, like many adolescents, have problems becoming adult and struggling with the authority of their adoptive parents. The opportunity to discover birth parents would precipitate more conflict and should be avoided until they have matured.
6. A few adoptive parents and birth parents expressed concerns that adoptees would become angry that they were relinquished for adoption and would seek to retaliate.
7. Some adoptive parents had failed to inform their adopted child or had chosen not to inform their adopted child about the fact of adoption. Giving the adoptee the opportunity or right to discover this fact would undermine their relationship with the adoptee.
8. Adoptees were considered to have been taken into the new family and had no need for their biological parents. They had been cared for (usually since infancy) and were in fact the child of their adoptive parents. There didn't seem to be any good or compelling reason for the adoptee to seek or receive information about his birth family.

9. Birth parents should be protected from having old and forgotten wounds opened or having their past exposed.

It is noteworthy that most of these claims reflect the concerns, and perhaps the insecurity, of some adoptive parents. It might have been expected that the strongest objections to disclosure would have come from birth parents, who presumably have the most to hide. Only one letter was received on behalf of birth parents upholding the need for continued secrecy.

These arguments against disclosure, can, I believe, be challenged by both recent research and experience in Canada and elsewhere. I shall try to answer each of the claims against disclosure in turn:

1. That adoptive parents would lose their children if adoptees learned of their origins and sought reunions:

    Research studies in Canada, the United States, Britain and Israel on reunions of adoptees with birth parents or siblings identify a high satisfaction rate with the reunion (90%) and an equally high expression of love and affection for their adoptive parents. When the adoptive relationship was not a good one as perceived by the adoptee, a reunion or information was sometimes a substitute; but the inaccessibility of information did not prevent the alienation from occurring.

2. That there was an irrevocable ''agreement'' with adoptive parents to maintain secrecy:

    Although in earlier times adoption workers may have assured their clients — both adoptive parents and birth parents — that secrecy would be maintained forever, in fact there never was any such contract or agreement in law between the government and the participants to adoption. The law since 1927 has required that adoption records be sealed up by the courts. But the law can be changed. Initially the sealed records could be opened up only by the courts; more recently sealed information can be disclosed through the Voluntary Disclosure Register. As new situations or understandings arise, governments are responsible for modifying, correcting, or abrogating the law if it is in the public's interest to do so. No new legislation could ever be written if this were not the case.

3. That adoptive parents may continue to exercise full parental authority even over the adult adoptee:

    Parental responsibility and affection for children can, and indeed often does, last a lifetime. Parental authority, whether of adoptive parents or of natural parents, is limited to the childhood years, and ceases when the child becomes an adult. In Ontario for most purposes adulthood is deemed to arrive when the individual attains 18 years of age. Young people who reach 16 years of age can move out of their natural parents' or adoptive parents' home and declare themselves to be independent and emancipated and no longer under the authority of their parents.

4. That disclosure of facts about birth and relinquishment may be painful or harmful to adoptees:

    The protection of children from unnecessary pain or disruption is a reasonable duty that parents should fulfill. When the child becomes an adult, however, parents no longer have the responsibility, authority, or capacity to prevent painful facts from being revealed. Parents may choose to inform their children about illness, death, disease, crime and other painful events in life from the time they are very young. Lack of information may prove to be as harmful or perhaps more so than the revelation of the truth.

5. That disclosure, particularly to adolescents, may encourage conflict with adoptive parents:

Adolescent children may have more questions about who they are and what they will become than they did at earlier periods in their lives. Facts about their adoption, even non-identifying ones, provide some background about their birth parents that could be relieving. Research studies in England on adoptees who seek birth certificates and other information express relief and satisfaction that the adoptees now know something, where previously their past was a mystery. Canadian studies have verified the English results.

6. That adoptees might seek retaliation on birth parents:

Adoptees, as any other group, may have among them some few who would have criminal intentions. The law cannot be prescriptive or presumptive about adult adoptees' behaviour without evidence that they do indeed behave in this way in significant numbers. *No such evidence exists.* While adoptees have been reported to be disproportionately represented in child guidance clinics in some American studies, the explanations are not definite as to cause. It is attributed in part to their adoptive status and the ''immunological'' problems encountered in ''transplanting'' a child from a biological to an adoptive home. Also, adoptees are usually children who were placed with middle-income families, who would be more likely to use child guidance clinics than other families, either poorer or wealthier.

7. That disclosure of adoption would undermine adoptive parents' relationship with their adopted child:

Practices have changed in the advice given adoptive parents in telling children about their adoption. Before the 1960's there were arguments made that the less said the better. Since then the advice has been strongly in favour of telling as much as is known from the very earliest years of the adopted child's life with the adoptive family. If families since 1960 have chosen not to tell their children very much, they are indeed facing the risk of their adult adoptees' questioning whether any truths were told about their past. Adoptees who were placed before 1960 are now at least 25 or 26 years old, and are entitled to know the truth about their origins. Their mature years may help them appreciate their adoptive parents' intent and not have that interfere with their relationship.

8. That there is no real ''need'' to know about the birth family:

Research in Scotland, Canada, and the United States supports the adoptee's need for kinship with biological families, for psychological well-being realized by knowing one's origins, for genetic information that will affect the adoptee's life, and for other medical information about birth parents and relatives that may influence the way adoptees live, marry, and have children.

Generally, however, the courts have not yet been persuaded that there are compelling psychological reasons why an adoptee should learn about his or her origins. Adoption laws have not specified or elected psychological or social needs as ''compelling'', and the courts have usually not seen fit to add their sympathies, thoughts, or perceptions to the law. Even in those cases in Ontario where the judges appreciated the problem of not knowing about one's past, they considered that they were not empowered to change the law.

Two states in Australia, 17 in the United States, 4 provinces in Canada, as well as England, Scotland, New Zealand, Finland, Sweden and Israel are among those political jurisdictions that have recognized in law the value of disclosure of origins, including identifying information, to adoptees and some birth relatives. Changes in judicial rulings on "good cause" or "compelling reasons to know" will be directly related to such legislative changes that instruct the judges and the law.

9.   That birth parents should be protected from disclosure:

Birth parents have revealed in studies in the United States, Canada, and Australia that their interest in renewing their relationship with their relinquished child is strong. The prevailing view expressed by birth parents is of loss which, though it diminishes in part over time, is never fully accepted. Many of the birth parents in the studies reflect on the coercion and the impossibility of their situation when the relinquishment occurred. They do not regret the work of the adoptive parents and are very appreciative of them; however, the time elapsed since the relinquishment offers them a renewed possibility of reunion.

In response to this report, the Ontario legislature enacted the *Adoption Disclosure Statute Law Amendment Act, 1987*, S.O. 1987, c. 4. This Act, which received royal assent on February 3, 1987, repealed ss. 155-158 of the *Child and Family Services Act, 1984* and substituted new provisions dealing with disclosure of adoption information. See now ss. 161-174 of the *CFSA*. The Act reflects some of the recommendations of the Special Commissioner. In particular, s. 166 makes non-identifying information fairly accessible. Note, however, s. 171. The consent of the adoptive parents is no longer required for the disclosure of identifying information where the adult adoptee and the birth family member are both registered in the Adoption Disclosure Register. However, disclosure of identifying information will still not generally occur unless both an adult adoptee and a birth parent (or a birth grandparent or sibling) register and consent in writing to the disclosure: 167. Where there is no "match", the Registrar may be asked to conduct a "discreet and reasonable search" to determine if the non-registered person wishes to be named in the register; s. 169. Media reports indicate that the lack of resources has resulted in waiting lists and long delays in the disclosure process.

British Columbia's *Adoption Act*, S.B.C. 1995, c. 48, reverses the presumption of closure and confidentiality that typifies adoption in other provinces. An adult, adopted person may apply for a copy of the original birth registration and the adoption order. The Director of Vital Statistics must give a copy of the requested records unless the birth parent registers a disclosure veto "prohibiting the disclosure of a birth registration or other record": s. 65. The Director may also refuse if a "no-contact declaration" has been filed under s. 66 and the applicant refuses to sign an undertaking that he or she will not attempt to contact the vetoing party. Breaches of he undertaking are punishable by a fine of up to $10,000, imprisonment for up to ix months or both: s. 87.

For further reading see O'Donnell, "The Four-Sided Triangle: A Comparative udy of the Confidentiality of Adoption Records" (1983), 21 U.W.O.L. Rev. 129; chdev, *Unlocking the Adoption Files* (Massachusetts/Toronto: Lexington Books, 89); Daly and Sobol, *Adoption in Canada* (Guelph: University of Guelph, 1993);

Chumney, ''Tennessee's New Adoption Contact Veto is Cold Comfort to Birth Parents'' (1997), 27 U. Memphis L. Rev. 843; K. Wegar, *Adoption, Identity, and Kinship: The Debate over Sealed Birth Records* (New Haven, Conn. : Yale University Press, 1997); Senoff, ''Open Adoptions in Ontario and the Need for Legislative Reform'' (1998), 15 Can. J. Fam. L. 183; and W. Carp, *Family Matters: Secrecy and Disclosure in the History of Adoption* (Cambridge, Mass.: Harvard University Press, 1998).